A

COMMENTARY

ON THE

NEW TESTAMENT

JOHN TRAPP

BAKER BOOK HOUSE
Grand Rapids, Michigan 49506

Reprinted 1981 by
Baker Book House
from the second edition
issued in 1865 by
Richard D. Dickinson

ISBN: 0-8010-8855-0

PHOTOLITHOPRINTED BY CUSHING - MALLOY, INC.
ANN ARBOR, MICHIGAN, UNITED STATES OF AMERICA

A

COMMENTARY OR EXPOSITION

UPON ALL THE BOOKS OF THE

NEW TESTAMENT

WHEREIN THE TEXT IS EXPLAINED, SOME CONTROVERSIES ARE DISCUSSED, DIVERS
COMMONPLACES ARE HANDLED, AND MANY REMARKABLE MATTERS HINTED,
THAT HAD BY FORMER INTERPRETERS BEEN PRETERMITTED.

BESIDES, DIVERS OTHER TEXTS OF SCRIPTURE, WHICH OCCASIONALLY OCCUR, ARE FULLY
OPENED, AND THE WHOLE SO INTERMIXED WITH PERTINENT HISTORIES, AS WILL
YIELD BOTH PLEASURE AND PROFIT TO THE JUDICIOUS READER

THE SECOND EDITION, VERY MUCH ENLARGED THROUGHOUT

BY

JOHN TRAPP, M.A.,

PASTOR OF WESTON UPON AVON IN GLOUCESTERSHIRE

EDITED

BY THE REV. W. WEBSTER, M.A.,

LATE FELLOW OF QUEEN'S COLLEGE, CAMBRIDGE; JOINT EDITOR OF
WEBSTER AND WILKINSON'S GREEK TESTAMENT

The Preacher sought to find out pleasant words, and an upright writing, even the words of truth. Eccl. xii. 10.
Paulum quotiescunque lego, non verba audire videor, sed Tonitrua. Jerome.

TO

THE WORSHIPFUL HIS MUCH-HONOURED FRIEND,

COLONEL JOHN BRIDGES,

GOVERNOR OF WARWICK CASTLE, JUSTICE OF PEACE FOR THE COUNTY OF WARWICK, AND
ONE OF THE HONOURABLE COMMITTEE FOR THE SAFETY OF THAT COUNTY.

WORTHY SIR,

This book of mine doth at once both crave and claim your patronage; for I cannot bethink me of any one that (all things considered) hath better right to it and me than yourself. I must never forget, how that being carried prisoner by the enemies, you soon set me off by exchange; and after that, being by them driven from house and home, you received me to harbour; yea, being driven out of one pulpit (where they thought to have surprised me) you presently put me into another, where I had a comfortable employment and a competent encouragement. What hours I could then well spare from that *pensum diurnum*, of praying and preaching, I gladly spent in these notes upon the New Testament; as hating with the Athenians, ἡσυχίαν ἀπράγμονα, a fruitless feriation (Thucyd.); and holding with Cato, that account must be given, not of our labour only, but of our leisure also. *Non solum negotii, sed et otii reddenda est ratio.* (Cic. de Sen.) For that two-years' space (well-nigh) that I lived in your garrison, I think I may truly say with Seneca, *Nullus mihi per otium exiit dies, partem etiam noctium studiis vindicavi,* that I laboured night and day (amidst many fears and tears for the labouring Church and bleeding State), *Ut ad vitam communem aliquem saltem fructum ferre possem;* that I might be some way serviceable to the public, and to you. (Cicero.) And albeit I was even sick at heart sometimes of the affliction of Joseph, Amos vi. 6; and even ready through faintness to let fall my pen, as it befell Jerome, when writing upon Ezekiel, he heard of the sacking of the city of Rome by the Goths; yet as God (who comforteth those that are cast down, 2 Cor. vii. 6) gave us any *lucida intervalla* (this last triumphant year especially) I took heart afresh to set closer to the work which now by God's grace is brought to some period; and because I have ever held ingratitude a monster in nature, a solecism in manners, a paradox in divinity, an ugly sin (yea, if there be any sin against the Holy Ghost, it is this, said Queen Elizabeth in a letter of hers to the king of France), therefore I could do no less than dedicate this piece of my pains unto you, to whom I owe so very much; it being penned (most of it) within your walls and under your wing, where I so long sat and sang,

O Melibœe, Deus nobis hæc otia fecit.—Virg. Eclog.

The stork is said to leave one of her young ones where she hatcheth them; the elephant to turn up the first sprig toward heaven when he comes to feed; both out of some instinct of gratitude. The Egyptians are renowned in histories for a thankful people (Diod. Sic. lib. 2); and the Israelites were charged not to abhor an Egyptian, because they were once strangers in his land, and had tasted of his courtesies, Deut. xxiii. 7. The unthankful and the evil are fitly set together by our Saviour, Luke vi. 35. And, *Ingratum dixeris, omnia dixeris,* said the ancients. All that I can do by way of retribution for your many free favours is, to make this public acknowledgment thereof under my hand; that if any shall reap benefit by what I have written, they may see to whom, in part, they are beholden. Now the good Lord that hath promised a prophet's reward to him "that receiveth a prophet in the name of a prophet," Matt. x. 41; he that ministereth seed to the sower, and hath said, "That whoso watereth shall be watered also himself," Prov. xi. 25 (*Ipse pluvia erit.* Kimchi); he that is able to make all grace to abound toward you, that you may abound to every good work; the same God all-sufficient multiply your seed, and increase the fruits of your righteousness, being enriched in everything to all bountifulness, which causeth, through us, thanksgiving to God, 2 Cor. ix. 8, 10, 11. This is, and shall be, Sir, the daily desire of

Your Worship's affectionately observant,

JOHN TRAPP.

THE PREFACE TO THE READER.

"The manifestation of the Spirit is given to every man to profit withal," saith St Paul, 1 Cor. xii. 7. And "as any man hath received the gift, so let him minister the same to others," saith St Peter, 1 Pet. iv. 10. "We therefore learn that we may teach," is a proverb among the Hebrews, *Lilmod lelammed.* Prov. Rabbinicum. And I do therefore lay in and lay up, saith the heathen, that I may draw forth again, and lay out for the good of many. *Condo et compono quæ mox depromere possum.* Synesius speaks of some, who having a treasure of rare abilities in them, would as soon part with their hearts as their conceptions; the canker of whose great skill shall be a swift witness against them. How much better Augustus and Augustine! Of the former, Suetonius tells us that, in reading all sorts of good authors, he skilfully picked out the prime precepts and patterns of valour and virtue, sending the same to such of his servants and under-officers for tokens, as he thought they might do most good unto. θᾶττον ἄν εἴδῃς τὴν καρδίαν ἢ τὰ ἐν τῇ καρδίᾳ. And for the latter, he accounted nothing his own that he did not communicate; and somewhere professeth himself in the number of those, *Qui scribunt proficiendo, et scribendo proficiunt,* that write what they have learned, and learn yet more by writing. His last works are observed to be his best; *Eaque ad verbum excerpta aut ad domesticos aut ad exercituum provinciarumque rectores mittebat, &c.* (Suet. l. ii. c. 88.) And the reason is given by Melancthon, *Quia docendo didicit,* because by much trading his talent he had much improved it. Of Melancthon himself, one of his countrymen gives this testimony: It appears (saith he) that Melancthon was on this wise busied abroad in the world, that seeing and hearing all he could, he made profit of everything; and stored his heart, as the bee doth her hive, out of all sorts of flowers, for the common benefit. Pismires labour like bees, but with this difference: *Quod illæ faciant cibos hæ condant,* that the bees make their meat, the pismires gather it: both have their proper praise and profit. If I may be esteemed by thee (courteous reader) either the one or the other, it is enough; and that I may, *Enitar sane* (saith Gerson, and I with him), I will endeavour out of other men's good meditations and collections, to frame to myself (but for thy use) some sweet honey-comb of truth, by mine own art and industry, in mine own words and method; and then Envy itself cannot (likely) say worse of me (it cannot, truly, say so bad) as one doth of Hugo de Sancto Victore; *Ivonis deflorator est* (saith he) *quem per omnia fere αὐτολέξει sequitur,* He hath picked the best out of Ivo, and transcribed him word for word almost. I never envied Zabarel that arrogant brag of his, *Hoc ego primus vidi,* I was the first that ever found out this; and yet I hate extremely to be held a plagiarist. Remigius and Haymo seem to be but two friars under one hood. Cedrenus' imperial history is read (a great part of it) under the name of Joannes Curopalates; that is a foul blur to one of them, but to which I know not. And that is no praise to Lactantius in Erasmus' judgment, that having read Aristotle and Pliny writing of the same subject that he did, and borrowing much out of them, he never so much as once mentioneth them; as he doth Tully, whom he nameth indeed but disparageth. *Atqui candidius erat nominare eos per quos profecit, quam eum quem notat,* saith Erasmus; I have not spared to profess by whom I have profited, to tell out of whom I have taken aught; and that I hope shall excuse me for that matter, with the more ingenious; what fault else soever they may find with me. Faults will escape a man betwixt his fingers, let him look to it never so narrowly, saith Bishop Jewel. Some plain solecisms and harsh expressions have been found even in Tully's own works, as Augustine noteth. And Erasmus addeth, *Qualia nonnunquam excidunt et horum temporum scriptoribus, et in his mihi quoque.* Our times are (as one well observeth) partly accurately judicious, partly uncharitably censorious. The one likes nothing not exquisite, not sublimated; the other, nothing at all. Let them please themselves for me, I am of Jerome's mind, *Si cui legere non placet, nemo compellit invitum,* If any think good to read what I have written, let him; if otherwise, let him do as he will; but let him know, that every man cannot be excellent, that yet may be useful, σπάνιον τὸ θεῖον ἄνδρα εἶναι. *Honestum est ei, qui in primis non potest, in secundis tertiisve consistere,* saith the orator (Cicero). An iron key may unlock the door of a golden treasure ; yea, *ferrum potest quod aurum non potest*, iron can do some things that gold cannot. A little boat may land a man into a large continent, and a little hand thread a needle, as well as a bigger. Philadelphia had but little strength, yet a great door opened, Rev. iii. 8. Quintilian saith, it is a virtue in a grammarian, *aliquid ignorare*, to be ignorant of some things; *Una est de Grammatici virtutibus.* But say a man knew never so much, yet, in Pliny's judgment, it no less becomes an orator sometimes to hold his tongue, than to speak his mind : *Non minus interdum est Oratoris tacere quam dicere.* Plin. Apelles was wont to say, that those painters were in fault *qui non sentirent quid esset satis*, that understood not when they had done enough. And he's a good huntsman, saith Nannius, *qui plures feras capit, non omnes,* that can catch some beasts, though he take not all. Lysippus, that famous carver, was wont to set forth his best pieces to public view with this underwritten, Λύσιππος ἐποίει, οὐκέτι ἐποίησε, Lysippus hath somewhat more to do at this work. *Nihil perfectum, aut a singulari consummatum industria*, saith Columella, Nothing can be perfected at first. Let it be a praise proper to our Lord Christ to be author and finisher all at once ; and "out of the mouths of babes and sucklings to perfect praise," Heb. xii. 2 ; Matt. xxi. 16. Our first actions are usually but essays and enterprises ; review may ripen things, and second thoughts mend that which former faulted in, Δεντέραι φροντίδες βέλτεραι. (Appian.) But I cease to say more by way of preface or apology, having (as Octavius said to Decius, a captain of Antony's) to the understanding spoken sufficient, but to the ignorant or ill-affected too much, had I said less. Do thou (good reader) but observe Epictetus' rule, to take me by that handle whereby I may best be held, and then all shall be well betwixt us, *Ea quemque ansa prehendas, qua commode teneri queat.* There is yet one thing more that I have to tell thee, before we part, that what thou here readest are *verba vivenda non legenda*, words that thou must live as well as read. Lest else some learned Linaker, observing such a vast difference betwixt our laws and our lives, break out again into this pathetical protestation, *Profecto aut hoc non est Evangelium, aut nos non sumus Evangelici ;* For certain, either this is not the gospel, or we are not right gospellers.

THE EPISTLE TO THE READER.

THE worth of the author of this book is already well known in the Church of Christ, by some former labours of his which are extant; and they which are well acquainted with him cannot but know and testify that he is a man of singular prudence and piety, of an acute wit, of a sound judgment, and of an indefatigable spirit, who hath wholly devoted and given up himself to the service of God's Church, and doth naturally care for the good thereof; witness his constant preaching, even whilst the burthen and care of a public school lay upon him; and now in these calamitous and bloody times, wherein he hath suffered deeply, being driven from his charge, and forced to shroud himself in a garrison of the Parliament's, yet notwithstanding his daily labours amongst the soldiers, and in the midst of the noises of guns and drums, he hath betaken himself to writing of commentaries upon the sacred Scriptures. And besides this present book, he hath prepared for the press some notes upon Genesis, and now by the good hand of God's providence completed a comment upon the whole New Testament; the first volume whereof presents itself unto thee in this book, and the latter part is hastening after it, which thou mayest expect with all expedition. I presume that it will be superfluous for me to tell thee how useful and advantageous his labours in this kind may be; for though we have many comments in Latin, yet but few in English; and for want thereof, and a right understanding of the Scripture, daily experience shows how woefully many persons are led aside into erroneous ways; for that which the Apostle Peter saith of St Paul's Epistles, is true of all the word of God, 2 Pet. iii. 16, "That therein some things are hard to be understood, which they that are unlearned and unstable pervert to their own destruction." Bless God therefore for stirring up the hearts of those who are pious and judicious, to lay forth their labours this way; and amongst others, make use of this comment, which by God's blessing will prove no less pleasing than profitable, in regard to the variety and excellency of the matter contained therein; as also it will give great satisfaction to the more judicious, in regard of his pains in noting all the criticisms through these his labours; which that it may do, his prayers shall not be wanting, who subscribes himself,

Thine in the Lord,

SAMUEL CLARK.

Εἰς τὸν Ἰωάννην τὸν ἐκδοθέντα πρὸ τῶν προτέρων Εὐαγγελιστῶν.

Μέγιστον ὧδε σφάλμα σφαλμάτων πέλει,
Τυπογράφων ἃ δεξία χέεν ποτὲ,
Καὶ ὑστέρων προτέρον τὸ χείριστον πάνυ,
Εὐαγγελιστῶν ὕστατον τῶν τεσσάρων
Ὁρᾶται πρῶτον οὕτως ἠμφιεσμένον.
Ὁμοίαν ἄλλοις καὶ πεποίηκε τρισί
Ἐσθῆτα λαμπρὰν ἀνὴρ πολυμαθέστατος,
Κηρύκων ἄνθος ἱερῶν ἢ κλεὶς γραμμάτων,
Ὁ Τράππος.   Καὶ τριπόθητος αὐτῶν ἔκδοσις.
Ἀνέκδοτοι οὖν πόθεν ; Χριστῷ κεχαρισμένος
Ἰωάννης μαθητῶν περὶ πάντων ἔην.
Ἀρ' οὖν Ματθαῖε, Μάρκε, Λουκᾶ, ὑμέων
Νῦν ἔφθασεν, ἔξοχος ἠδ' ἀντάξιος τριῶν ;
Αὖ μηδαμῶς.   ὑμᾶς ἐκώλυεν βάρος,
Καὶ μέγεθος, καὶ περισσὸς πωλοούντων φόβος.
Οἷς νῦν κακοῦντος τοῦ Ἄρεος Βρεταννίαν,
Φαγόντος ἄνδρας, καὶ πιόντος κέρματα,
Ἔγεντο μέγα κακὸν τὸ βιβλίον μέγα,
Καὶ μηδὲν εἰ μὴ τυτθὸν, πολλ' ἀρέσκεται.
Ἀπολλύοντα παγκακὸν Σωτὴρ Θεός.
Ἀπολέσκοι, πρὶν πάντας καὶ πάντ' ἀπόλλυσι,
Καὶ ἀστράτειαν δοίη· ἵνα πάλιν τύχῃ
Τῇ εὐλαβείᾳ, τεχναῖς καὶ τύποις τόπος·
Καὶ προδρόμῳ τούτῳ ἔπωνται λοιποὶ ταχύ.
Καὶ τοῖς ταχὺ Πράξεις, καὶ ἡ Διαθήκη ὅλη.
Εἰ δὲ ἐπέλθῃ παλαιὰ καινῇ ὕστερον,
(Ὅπερ ποθοῦμεν πάντες καὶ ἐλπίζομεν·)
Τὸ ὕστερον πρότερον ἀρέσει τοῦτο σφόδρα.
                              Θωμοῦ Δουγάρδου.

Ἔτει ἀπὸ τῆς θεογονίας.
α. χ. μ. ε. Ἑκατομβ. ιθ.

Ad venerandum Autorem, ut Opus hoc aureum, aliaque quæ habet plurima, ferrea licet tempestate in lucem properet.

TAMEN Librorum quicquid est patiens libræ,
Donetur luci suaserim, abjecta mora;
Ut ne furori prædæ sit Mavortio,
Et Cythereæ voracem pascat conjugem.
Exemplar unicum facile cadit hostia
Sicariorum direptrici dexteræ.
Quæ nec Tonantis formidato fulmine
Tonanti sacra, pietate procul, involat.
Inauspicatus iste sic Pyreneus
Castis Parnassi vim parabat incolis.
Se liberabant sumptis alis virgines:
Nescit se docta vindicare pagina,
Præsens pernices nisi Prelum alas commodet.
His sublevata ter mille latebras petat;
Se trans immensa his moliatur æquora.
Nec si librorum, quos parit Prelum ferax
(Ferax, ut ignis; una de lucernula
Lucernas infinitas est accendere).
Horum, illorum, discerpat rabies viscera,
Idcirco cunctis metuas. Spes est pauculos,
Vel unum saltem diras fugiturum manus,
Postea germanos qui restauret Martyres.
Fratres trucidat septies denos Nothus,
Te minus uno, Jotham: ipse nam te absconderas,
Et, concionatus, tibi prospexti fuga.
    Illorum quæ discupio fatis eripi
Superque cladi stare, non in ultimis
Nisus Minervæ sunt admirandi tuæ,
Hæc jam qui Scripta Prelo subdis aurea,
Novum queis Fœdus illustras ritu novo,
Utile miscere dulci rarus artifex.
O si illustrando Veteri, lucis indigo,
Canoni, festinus operam sic insumeres:
Et ad umbilicum quas jam perductas habes
Soboles fœcundi capitis quam scitissimas
Easque plurimas in apertum funderes!
Fundas si salvas cupias tempestas monet.
Satius est ipse capsulas evisceres,
Musarum quam flagella Martis pulluli.
Quem non doleret, quem non illud ureret,
Ardere Opera, quæ Lector omnis ardeat:
Eviscera, Vir Erudite, tempori.

THO. DUGARD, A.M., Cantabrig.

Polemopoli, Mense Maio, 1644.

To the Learned, Reverend AUTHOR of these
ANNOTATIONS.

No, fear it not; although our worthies nine
Have gone before you in that work divine
(Their Annotations on the Sacred Pages,
Which makes them famous to succeeding ages),
Yet they have not prevented you. What you
Do here present will find acceptance too.
Have you not gospel for it? Did not John,
Whom the last year you sent abroad, alone,
To search the land, as Joshua sent out spies,
Come quickly back, and thus evangelize:
I every corner of the land have seen,
I by most learned hands turn'd o'er have been:
Of my aloneness all men notice took,
And asked, Where are Matthew, Mark, and
    Luke?
Of me they were most glad; yet grieved to see
The eagle thus without all company.
You have example too. The Reverend Head [1]
Of Sion College, lately published,
To his great praise, and others' good content,
His lucubrations on th' Old Testament.
He doubted not (and you as little may)
But that a tenth would be received with joy.
The nine divide the Sacred Text; each man
Is like a tribe in th' Land of Canaan:
But were they all conjoyned in every line,
Or were there nine great volumes for the nine,
Each having done the whole, and done it so,
That each did seem his fellow to out-do:
Yet you, and twenty more, would welcome be,
Bringing such gifts into the treasury.
Such ships as, fraught with precious wares, do
    come,
After the rest, are no less welcome home:
Nor are those stars, which do not first appear,
Less look'd upon; they make the night more clear.
Store is no sore. The more such books as this,
The Church the richer and the merrier is;
And can no more of them spare any one,
Than he that hath a score can spare the son.
    Hark, now methinks a thousand tongues I hear,
Saying, Show Trapp. The price? It is a dear,
But golden book. Oh that this author would
What he hath done to the New, do to the Old!
Things new and old out of his treasury
A good scribe brings; and so we hope will he.
Long may he live! and part of's time be spent
In bringing light to the Old Testament.

THOMAS DUGARD.

[1] Mr Arthur Jackson.

THE REVEREND AND HIS MUCH-HONOURED FATHER,

MR JOHN LEY,

PASTOR AND PREACHER OF GOD'S WORD AT GREAT BUDWORTH IN CHESHIRE,
AND ONE OF THE VENERABLE ASSEMBLY.

REVEREND SIR,

Now, by a sweet providence, is that happiness put into my hands, that I have long wished and waited for, viz. a fit opportunity of telling the world how highly I honour you, and how deeply I stand engaged to you. A most able and absolute divine (in another sense than Erasmus termed some in his time) I ever took you for, since I first became acquainted with you.[1] And how little mistaken I am therein, let your many elaborate lucubrations say for me; those accurate annotations upon the Pentateuch especially; of which precious piece, and the thrice-worthy author, I am as soon ready to say, as one did once of Erasmus and his adages

—quis nosset Erasmum,
Chilias æternum si latuisset opus ?

Or as another did of Calvin's Institutions,

Præter Apostolicas, post Christi tempora, chartas
Huic peperere libro secula nulla parem.

Sure I am, and not a little sensible, that he that here comes after you, shall but *actum agere*, he shall but *facem soli*, (*soli, inquam, in Sion*) *accendere*, he shall but *in nobilissimo theatro seipsum traducere*. Well, he may pick up *Præterita* with Drusius, or *spicilegium post messem* with Capellus; he shall hardly ever get so near you as the Latin orator did the Greek, *Demosthenes Ciceroni præripuit, ne primus esset orator ; Cicero Demostheni, ne solus*. But whither (or ere I wist) hath the just admiration of your singular worth transported me ? my design was not to praise you (for that were, as an ancient said of Athanasius, to praise virtue itself), but to profess my deep indebtedness unto you for your many fatherly favours and real courtesies done me since my adoption, *Quibus effecisti, ut viverem et morerer ingratus*, as he said to Augustus, this being the only wrong that ever you did me, that I must live and die unthankful. (Sen. de Benef. ii. c. 12.) These brief notes, passable (I say not praisable) only for their brevity, do humbly beg your perusal, and (*si tanti sint*) your patronage ; and surely may they but obtain your much-desired countenance and comprobation, I shall soon say with the orator, κατὰ παντας ἔχω τὰ νικητήρια, I fear not any man's censure. Whatever else is wanting in them, a will, I am sure, is not wanting, of laying forth my small talent to the honour of my Master and the good of my fellow-servants; those of mine own particular charge especially, to whom most of these things have been delivered, and of whom I can truly say, as Reverend Mr Stock did of his people in Bread Street, London, that he had rather win one of them than twenty others. Now that I may be fit and able to "fulfil the ministry that I have received in the Lord, so as to save myself and them that hear me," Col. iii. 17 ; 1 Tim. iv. 16, let your fatherly benediction and instant intercession to "the Father of all the fatherhood in heaven and earth,"[2] be never wanting to

Your most affectionately obsequious son and servant,

JOHN TRAPP.

Welford, this 16th day of Nov., 1647.

---

[1] *Absolutæ eruditionis et pietatis viris. Sic scripsit Theologis Parisiensib. Voluit autem, alienis ab omni eruditione et pietate, interprete Melancthon.*

[2] Eph. iii. 15, πατριὰ. Parentela.

Ad Libellum chartaceum, venerando Autori, ante manum huic Annotationum parti admotam, dono missum, Affatio. Quæ vice Præfationis, de Autore Opereque, esse possit.

Dominum, Libelle, gratulor tibi novum,
Mihi negatam tu sortem felix habes;
Viro futurus eximio jugis comes,
Qui floribus, quos fundit, seu Britannia,
Seu Latium, seu Palestina, simul Græcia,
Te fragrantissimis ornabit, instruet;
Ut olim Acheloi cornu implerunt Najades.
Qui proprii venustos fœtus ingeni,
Quibus venustiores nullum parturit,
Magisve densos, credet servandos tibi.
Qui quicquid audit est divino pectore,
Lingua facunda, moribus suavissimis.
Contra quam Sacra jam profitentes plurimi,
Docere recta callidi, non vivere.
Quam vellem scitus esse nunc Libellulus!
Forem ut tuæ felicitatis particeps,
Ejus beandus, gestandus, manu, sinu.
Tene fidelis quicquid mandarit tibi.
Furacibus cave sedulus ab unguibus.
Tibi ne maculas aut fœdas labes contrahe;
Subire vultus ut queas libens meos.
Abi jam, et Dominum a me saluta millies.

THOMAS DUGARD,
Art. Mag., Rector Barfordiæ.

A

COMMENTARY

OR EXPOSITION UPON

THE GOSPEL ACCORDING TO ST MATTHEW,

WHEREIN THE TEXT IS EXPLAINED, SOME CONTROVERSIES ARE BRIEFLY DISCUSSED, DIVERS COMMONPLACES
HANDLED, AND MANY REMARKABLE MATTERS HINTED, THAT HAD BEEN BY FORMER
INTERPRETERS PRETERMITTED.

CHAPTER I.

Ver. 1. *The Book*] THAT is, a roll or register, catalogue or calendar, a ciphering and summing up. (Gen. v. 1, זֶה סֵפֶר תּוֹלְדֹת, αὕτη ἡ βίβλος γενέσεως.)

Of the generations] That is, of the genealogies, as touching his humanity (St Matthew's main drift), for as touching his divinity (St John's chief scope and subject), "who can declare his generation?" Isa. liii. 8. "What is his name? and what is his son's name, if thou canst tell?" Prov. xxx. 4. He is without descent or pedigree, as Melchisedec, Heb. vii. 3.

Of Jesus Christ] Jesus shows he was God (for "besides me there is no Saviour," Isa. xlv. 21). Christ, that he was man, the anointed; for in respect of his manhood chiefly is this anointing with gifts and graces attributed to Christ. The name of Jesuits, therefore, savoureth of blasphemous arrogancy. One of their own gives the reason;—because he hath communicated unto us the thing signified by the name Christ, but not by the name Jesus.[1] And yet it is notoriously known (saith Dr Fulke, out of another of their own writers) that the most honourable name of Christian is in Italy and at Rome a name of reproach, and usually abused to signify a fool or a dolt. (Fulke in Rhem. Testam. on Acts xi., sect. 4, out of Christoph. Franch. Col. Jesuit. *in fine*.)

The Son of David] God's darling,[2] one that observed all his wills, Acts xiii. 22, and faithfully served out his time, ver. 36.

The son of Abraham] The friend of God and father of the faithful, reckoned here for honour's sake) as the next immediate father of Christ, whose day indeed he saw and rejoiced, (John viii. 56 (ἠγαλλιάσατο); he laughed, yea, leapt for joy of this man-child to be born into the world. Whose children we are, so long as we walk in the steps of his faith; that Christ, being formed in us, may "see of the travail of his soul and be satisfied" Isa. liii. 10, 11; he may "see his seed, and prolong his days upon earth." Such honour have all his saints, Psal. cxlix. 9.

Ver. 2. *Abraham begat Isaac*] The fruit, not more of his flesh than of his faith,[3] whence he is said to be "born after the spirit," Gal. iv. 29.

Isaac begat Jacob] After twenty years' expectance, and many a hearty prayer put up therewhile, Gen. xxv. 21.[4] So Adam lived "an hundred and twenty years ere he begat Seth;" whom God set as another seed instead of Abel, Gen. v. 3, with Gen. iv. 25, when Cain's family flourished and grew great in the earth. God usually stays so long that he hardly finds faith, Luke xviii. 8, till men have done expecting, and then he doth things that they look not for, Isa. lxiv. 3. Wait therefore upon him who waits to be gracious; and know this, that he is a God of judgment, Isa. xxx. 18, that is, a wise God, one that chooseth his times, and knows best when to deal forth his favours. See Isa. xlix. 8, with Psal. lxix. 13. Everything is beautiful in its season, saith Solomon, Eccl. iii. 11.

---

[1] *Rem signatam nomine Christi nobis communicavit, non autem Jesu.* Lindwood.

[2] *David, amatus vel amabilis. Unde Dido Pænis. Hinc Solomon dictus est Jedidiah.*

[3] *Vere fuit Isaac beatæ senectutis et emeritæ fidei filius.* Bucholcer.

[4] The Hebrew word is, "to frequent and multiply prayer."

Jacob begat Judah and his brethren] Brethren in iniquity (the most of them), a part of their father's punishment, for that three-fold lie in a breath, Gen. xxvii. 19, 20. Reuben was the beginning of his strength, "excelling in dignity and power," Gen. xlix. 3, that is (saith the Chaldee Paraphrast), in the principality and the priesthood. Both which he forfeited by his foul offence; the former to Judah, the latter to Levi. Howbeit, upon his return to God (though disinherited of the birth-right, yet) he had this honour of an elder brother, that he was first provided for. But Judah was he "whom his brethren should praise" (saith Jacob), in allusion to his name and in reference to his privilege, Gen. xlix. 8; for it is evident that our Lord sprang out of Judah (ἀνατέταλκεν), Heb. vii. 14, that branch from on high (ἀνατολή), Luke i. 78, that Shiloh, which some interpret His son (R. David). Others (Tranquillator, Salvator), the Prosperer, Pacificator, Safe-maker, &c.[1] Others, the son of her secundines, which is the tunicle that wrappeth the child in the womb.

Ver. 3. *And Judah begat Phares and Zarah*] Jerome is deceived, that deriveth the pedigree of the Pharisees from this Phares. They took their name either of Pharash, to expound as interpreters of the law, Rom. ii. 18; or of Pharas, to separate with a—"Stand further off, for I am holier than thou." Josephus saith, that the Pharisees seemed to outstrip all others both in height of holiness and depth of learning: σύνταγμά τι Ἰουδαίων εὐσεβεστέρων τὸν βίον, καὶ δοκούντων ἀκριβέστερον τῶν ἄλλων τὸν νόμον ἐφηγεῖσθαι. B. J. i. 4. As for Phares, he was a breach-maker (whence also he had his name, Gen. xxxviii. 29). He violently took the first birth-right, and became both a father of the Messias and a type. For Christ by his strength broke the power of death and hell; he broke down also the partition-wall that was betwixt the Jews and Gentiles, who when they shall be fully born, then shall the Jews, typified by Zarah, who thrust forth the hand first, as those that, willing to be justified by their works, and thinking to regenerate themselves, had the scarlet thread of the law's condemnation bound upon their hands, which therefore they drew back and fell from God,—then shall they, I say, come forth again, Rom. xi. 11, 12, 25, 26.

Of Thamar] A Canaanitess, but probably a proselyte. The Jews say she was Melchisedec's daughter, the high-priest, and was therefore to be burned, Lev. xxi. 9. But this may well pass for a Jewish fable: howbeit, that Melchisedec was a Canaanite, but a most righteous king and priest of the most high God, and was therefore not molested or meddled with by Kedar-laomer and his accomplices, I judge not unlikely. This Thamar, out of desire, partly of revenge, and partly of issue, fell into the sin of incest. Rahab was a harlot, Bathsheba an adulteress: yet all these grandmothers to our Saviour; who as he

needed not to be ennobled by his stock, so neither was disparaged by his progenitors, but took flesh of these greatest sinners to show that we cannot commit more than he can remit; and that by his purity he washeth off all our spots, like as the sun wasteth and wipeth away all the ill vapours of the earth and air.

And Phares begat Esrom] When he was about fourteen years of age, the year before they went down to Egypt, say some: others assoil it otherwise. (Pareus in Gen.; Funccius in Chronol. Com., Anno 2273.) Let him that readeth understand as he can. Christ (the Arch-Prophet), when he comes again, shall teach us all things.

Esrom begat Aram] While they sojourned in the land of Egypt; a miserable home, where was nothing but bondage and tyranny. And yet in reference to it, Moses (who was likewise born there) calls his son Gershom, or a stranger there, because born in Midian. The sons of Ephraim, about the birth of Moses, sought to break prison before God's gaol delivery: but this proved a great mischief to themselves, and no small heart-break to their aged father, 1 Chron. vii. 21, 22; Psal. lxxviii. 9. Besides that, it gave occasion, likely, to that cruel edict of Pharaoh: "Let us deal wisely" (St Stephen saith sophistically, subtilly, κατασοφισάμενος, Acts vii. 19), "lest they multiply and join also to our enemies, and fight against us" (as now they have fought against the Gittites, their own enemies, who detained from them the promised land, till their sins were full), and "so get them up out of the land," as lately they had essayed to do. "Therefore they did set over them taskmasters to afflict them with their burdens," Exod. i. 11, and to keep them from spawning so fast, after the manner of fishes (as the word imports), which multiply beyond measure. But God turned their wisdom into folly; they took a wrong course. For who knows not that your labouring men have the most and the strongest children? And notwithstanding this new Pharaoh's craft and cruelty,

Ver. 4. *Aram begat Aminadab, and Aminadab begat Naasson*] Who was hanged up in the wilderness, among the rest of their rulers, for folly committed with the mistresses of Moab. Neither escaped the common sort scot-free, for they fell in one day "three and twenty thousand," saith St Paul, 1 Cor. x. 8. "Four and twenty thousand," saith Moses: whereof a thousand were the chief princes, the other were inferiors, provoked to sin by their example. But why doth the apostle insist in the special punishment of the people? To show, saith learned Junius, how frigid and slender their defence is, how short their covering, who plead and pretend for their sins the example of their superiors.

And Naasson begat Salmon] Called, 1 Chron. ii. 11, Salmah. There was also a mount of this name (as touching the sound, though with difference of one letter in the original) whither Abimelech and his host resorted, Judg. ix. 48; and whereof

---

[1] *Tranquillator, Salvator, à themate Salah, unde Shalvah, tranquillitas. Unde etiam Lat. Salvere, Salvus, Salvare. Amama.*

the Psalmist speaketh: "When the Almighty scattered kings, they shall be white as snow in Salmon." Now it is storied of Andronicus, the old Emperor of Constantinople, that all things going cross with him, he took a Psalter into his hand to resolve his doubtful mind; and opening the same, as if it were of that heavenly oracle to ask counsel, he lighted upon this verse, and was thereby comforted and directed what to do for his greatest safety. To be "white as snow in Salmon" (Psal. lxviii. 14) is to have joy in affliction, light in darkness. "Salmon" signifieth shady and dark: so this mount was with dens and glimness; but made lightsome by snow. *Hoc autem obiter.*

Ver. 5. *And Salmon begat Booz of Rachab*] This the Evangelist might have by tradition. Salmon's genealogy is set down, 1 Chron. ii., Ruth iv.; but whom he married, nothing is reported.

And Booz begat Obed of Ruth] While Orphah wants bread in her own country, Ruth is grown a great lady in Bethlehem, and advanced to be great grandmother to the king of kings. There is nothing lost by God's service. ἡ μυριομακαριότης ἐστιν ἐν τῃ εὐσεβείᾳ.

And Obed begat Jesse] A good old man, but not very famous. Retired it seems he was, and drawn much up into himself;[1] neither thinking great things of himself, nor seeking great things for himself; but living among his own people; much of his son David's disposition, who loves his book the better since he saw the court, and sings, *Beatus ille qui procul negotiis,* &c. (Horat.) *Non vixit malè, qui natus moriensque fefellit.* He is not the least happy that is least observed.

Ver. 6. *And Jesse begat David the king*] But that was not his chief title: he gloried more in styling himself the servant of the Lord, Psal. xxxvi. 1, *tit.* So Theodosius esteemed it a greater honour that he was *membrum Christi* than *Caput Imperii. Numa etiam* τοῦ Θεοῦ ὑπηρεσίαν βασιλεύειν *existimabat.* Numa held the service of God the highest honour. (Plut. *in Vit.*)

David the king begat Solomon] Whom Bellarmine reckoneth for a reprobate: but (besides that he was God's *corculum,* and by him called Jedediah) he calleth himself in his sacred retractations, *Coheleth;* which being interpreted the Preacher, is a word of the feminine termination, and by some rendered *aggregata,* where understanding the substantive *anima,* they conclude here hence that he was renewed by repentance and reunited to the Church.

Of her that had been the wife of Uriah] His best children he had by this wife: the fruit of humiliation doubtless. (*Peccatum tametsi non bonum, tamen in bonum.* Aug.) The barren women's children are observed to have been the best, as Isaac, Samuel, John Baptist, &c., for like reason.

Ver. 7. *And Solomon begat Roboam*] A child of forty years old, a soft-spirited man; the Scripture notes him a פֶּהִי, easily drawn away by evil counsel. Green wood will be warping. Of him

[1] Λάθε Βιώσας. *Vive tibi, quantumque potes, prælustria vita.*

it might be said, as once it was of a certain prince in Germany, *Esset alius, si esset apud alios* (Bucholcer). But a man would wonder, that by so many wives Solomon should have but one son, and him none of the wisest neither. *Herôum filii noxæ.* He might (likely) bewail his own unhappiness in Rehoboam, Eccl. ii. 18, 19, as he is thought to do in Jeroboam, Prov. xx. 21. His mother was an Ammonitess: the birth follows the belly: the conclusion follows the weaker proposition.

And Roboam begat Abia] A man not right, yet better than his father: and for this to be commended, that he held and pleaded the true worship and service of God as the beauty and bulwark of his kingdom: relying also upon God, he discomfited Jeroboam: *Deo confisi, nunquam confusi.*

And Abia begat Asa] A better son sprung of the seed of bad Abia, of the soil of worse Maachah, whom St Jerome makes to be a worshipper of that abominable idol Priapus, otherwise called Baal-peor, Num. xxv. 5. For thus he translates that, 1 Kings xv. 13: *Insuper et Maachan matrem suam amovit, ne esset princeps in sacris Priapi, et in luco ejus. Nos pudore pulso, stamus sub Jove, cœlis apertis,* said the worshippers of Priapus. The people that came thereto (the sacrifice being ended) all stepped into a thicket, which was always planted near the altar of this god (Hos. iv. 13); and there, like brute beasts, they promiscuously satisfied their lusts; thereby, as they conceived, best pleasing their god (Hackwell's Apolog.). This villany Maachah may seem to have been guilty of, and was therefore worthily removed by her son Asa from being queen. *Sedes prima, et vita ima,* suit not well together. *Dignitas in digno est ornamentum in luto,* saith Salvian. Honour in a dishonest man is as a jewel of gold in a swine's snout.

Ver. 8. *And Asa begat Josaphat*] A godly king, but late-witted, and therefore paid for his learning twice at least in holy history. One thing in the narration of his acts is very remarkable. He placed forces in all the fenced cities; yet is it not said thereupon, that the fear of the Lord fell on the neighbouring nations. But when he had established a preaching ministry in all the cities, then his enemies feared and made no war, 2 Chron. xvii. 10. *Solidissima regiæ politiæ basis* (saith Paradinus in Symbolis) *est verum Dei cultum ubivis stabilire: alias qui potest aut Deus Reges beare, à quibus negligitur; aut populus fideliter colere, qui de obsequio suo non rectè instituitur?* The ordinances of God are the beauty and bulwark of a place and people.

And Josaphat begat Joram] That lived undesired and died unlamented. While he lived there was no use of him, and when he died, no miss of him: no more than of the paring of the nails or sweeping of the house (περιψήματα). He lived wickedly, and died wishedly, as it is said of King Edwin (Daniel's Hist.).

And Joram begat Ozias] Here Ahaziah, Joash, and Amaziah are written in the earth, not once set down in the roll: perhaps it was because they were imped in the wicked family of Ahab. This Uzziah, though a king, yet he loved husbandry, 2 Chron. xxvi. Thrift is the fuel of magnificence. He was at length a leper, yet still remained a king. Infirmities may deform us, they cannot dethrone us. The English laws (saith Camden, Elizabeth) pronounce, that the crown once worn quite taketh away all defects whatsoever: sure it is that when God once crowns a man with his grace and favour, that man is out of harm's way for ever.

Ver. 9. *And Ozias begat Joatham*] A pious prince, but not very prosperous. Grace is not given to any as a target against outward affliction.

And Joatham begat Achaz] A sturdy stigmatic, a branded rebel. The more he was distressed, the more he trespassed. "This is that Ahaz," 2 Chron. xxviii. 22. How many (now-a-days) are humbled, yet not humble! low, but not lowly! *Humiliantur, et humiles non sunt* (Bern. in Cantic.). *Qui nec fractis cervicibus inclinantur*, as Jerome complaineth: *quos multo facilius fregeris, quam flexeris*, as another hath it. These are like the creature called Monoceros, who may be killed, but not caught. *Interimi potest, capi non potest* (Plin.). *Plectimur à Deo*, saith Salvian, *nec flectimur tamen: corripimur, sed non corrigimur*. But if men harden their hearts against correction, God will harden his hand, and hasten their destruction.

Achaz begat Ezekias] Who stands betwixt his father Ahaz and his son Manasseh, as a lily between two thorns, or as a fuller between two colliers; or as that wretched Cardinal of Toledo in his Preface before the Bible, printed at Complutum in Spain, said that he set the Vulgar Latin betwixt the Hebrew and Greek, as Christ was set betwixt two thieves. Here observe (by the way) that Judah had some interchange of good princes, Israel none; and that under religious princes the people were ever religious; as under wicked princes, wicked. Most people will be of the king's religion, be it that it will be, as the Melchites were of old (Nicephorus), and the Papists still, if Mr Rogers (our protomartyr in Queen Mary's days) may be believed. The Papists, saith he, apply themselves to the present state, yea, if the state should change ten times in the year, they would ever be ready at hand to change with it, and so follow the cry, and rather utterly forsake God, and be of no religion, than that they would forego lust or living for God or religion (Acts and Mon.).

Ver. 10. *And Ezekias begat Manasses*] Who degenerates into his grandfather Ahaz, as the kernel of a well-fruited plant doth sometimes into that crab or willow which gave the original to his stock. This man was (till converted) as very a nonesuch in Judah as Ahab was in Israel;

yet no king of either Judah or Israel reigned so long as he. It was well for him that he lived so long to grow better, as it had been better for Asa to have died sooner, when he was in his prime. But they are met in heaven, I doubt not; whither whether we come sooner or later, happy are we.

And Manasses begat Amon] Who followed his father in sin, but not in repentance. "And thou his son, O Belshazzar, hast not humbled thine heart, though thou knewest all this; but hast lifted up thyself against the Lord," &c. Dan. v. 22. It is a just presage and desert of ruin, not to be warned. This was a bloody prince, therefore lived not out half his days. Queen Mary's reign was the shortest of any since the Conquest, Richard III. only excepted; yet she was *non naturâ, sed pontificiorum arte ferox*, say some.

And Amon begat Josias] Of whom that is true that Jerome writes of another, *In brevi vitæ spatio tempora virtutum multa replevit*; or, as Mr Hooker speaketh of King Edward VI., He departed soon, but lived long; for life consists in action: "In all these is the life of my spirit," saith Hezekiah, Isa. xxxviii. 15, 16; but the wanton widow is "dead while she liveth," 1 Tim. v. 6. That good king lived apace and died betime, being *deliciæ Orbis*, as Titus was called; and *Mirabilia mundi*, as Otho; having at his death (as it is said of Titus) one thing only to repent of, and that was his rash engaging himself in a needless quarrel, to the loss of his life and the ruin of that state.[1] When Epaminondas was once slain, his countrymen were no longer famous for their valour and victories, but for their cowardice and calamities. (*Nec virtutibus Thebani, sed cladibus insignes.*) When Augustus departed this world, we feared, saith one, the world's ruin, and were ready to wish that either he had never been born, or never died. When God took away Theodosius, he took away with him almost all the peace of that church and state: so he did of this, with Josiah, that heavenly spark, that plant of renown, that precious prince,

Qui regum decus, et juvenum flos, spesque bonorum,
  Deliciæ sæcli, et gloria gentis erat:

as Cardanus sang of our English Josiah, King Edward VI.[2]

Ver. 11. *And Josias begat Jechonias*] Rob. Stephanus restoreth and rectifieth the text thus: "Josias begat Jakin and his brethren, and Jakin begat Jechonias." For otherwise the middle fourteen (whereby St Matthew reckoneth) would want a man. Jehoahaz, younger brother to Jakin, had, after his father's death, stepped into the throne, but was soon ejected. Usurpation prospers not. Abimelech's head had stolen the crown, and by a blow on his head he is slain at Shechem. What got most of the Cæsars by their hasty ad-

---

[1] *Titus moriens, se unius tantummodo rei pœnitere dixit. Id autem quid esset non aperuit, nec quisquam certò novit.* Dio. in Tito.

[2] *Orbis ruinam timueramus.* Paterculus. *Ludovico XII. defuncto, tam subita orta est mutatio, ut qui prius digito cælum attingere videbatur, nunc humi serpere; sideratos esse diceres.*

Budæus. [Some think that Pedaiah (whose natural son Zorobabel was, 1 Chron. iii. 19) should be here reckoned, though he be not named, because he was born and died obscurely in Babylon. Verseius. Funccius. Magdeburg. *Præfat. ad Centur. 5.*]

vancement, *nisi ut citius interficerentur?* as one hath it. *Notandum,* saith the chronologer, *quod nullus Pontificum, egregii aliquid à tempore Bonifacii tertii pro sedis Romanæ tyrannide constituens, diu supervixerit. Quod et huic Bonifacio accidit.* It is remarkable that no pope of any note for activity in his office was long of life.

Ver. 12. And after they were brought to Babylon] This the Evangelist inculcates, and rings often in the ears of his impious countrymen, as a notorious public judgment on a nation so incorrigibly flagitious, so unthankful for mercies, so impatient of remedies, so incapable of repentance, so obliged, so warned, so shamelessly, so lawlessly wicked, *quorum maxima beneficia, flagitia, supplicia,* as the Centurists set it forth. Abused mercy turns into fury.

Jechonias begat Salathiel] Neri begat him naturally, Jechonias, legally; adopting him for his child that was his nephew, 1 Chron. iii. 17.

And Salathiel begat Zorobabel] Who brought forth the head-stone of the second temple with shoutings, crying, "Grace, grace unto it," Zech. iv. 7. He was a chieftain in the first year of Cyrus, Ezra ii. 2, and he lived to see the building of the temple, about the sixth year of Darius Nothus, which is a matter of an hundred years between. So he had a longer life than ordinary, which God granteth to some, because he hath something to be done by them. A short life in some cases is a blessing, 1 Kings xiii. 4, as grapes gathered before they be ripe are freed from the violence of the wine-press; as lambs slain before they be grown escape many storms and sharp showers that others live to taste of. Some wicked live long, that they may aggravate their judgment; others die sooner, that they may hasten it. But they are blessed, that whether they live, they live unto the Lord, or whether they die, they die unto the Lord, and in the Lord, their works following them. Rom. xiv. 8; Rev. xiv. 13.

Ver. 13. And Zorobabel begat Abiud] St Luke saith, Rhesa: hence the diversity of number and names. Matthew descends by the posterity of Abiud; Luke, of Rhesa, down to Joseph.

And Abiud begat Eliakim, and Eliakim begat Azor, &c.] These lived in those calamitous times of the people of God after the Captivity, and were not kings and captains, as being held under by other nations; but law-givers they were, as Jacob prophesied, and principal men among that people, "till Shiloh came," Gen. xlix. 10.

Ver. 14. And Azor begat Sadoc, and Sadoc begat Achim] Of these and the rest, as the Scripture sets down nothing more than their bare names, so neither is there any Jewish record, at this day extant, of their acts. So many miseries they had, one in the neck of another, that little liberty was left them to write; though I doubt not but the posterity of David were then carefully observed by as many as looked for the consolation of Israel. But among the Jews, since our Saviour's time, after the sealing up of the Babylonish Talmud, that is, after the year of Christ 500 to the year 1000, there

was little or nothing written, by reason of the grievous calamities that seized upon them.

Ver. 15. And Eliud begat Eleazar, &c.] These might be private persons, some of them, as Joseph and Mary were; it being the care and the endeavour of the Herods, and those before, that held the Jews in subjection, to suppress as much as might be the posterity of David, at least to keep them in a low condition; forasmuch as it was a certain and received truth among that people, that "Messiah the Prince" (Dan. ix. 25) should shortly come of that family. And this was that that held up the fainting hearts of the good people of those sad times (when prophecy failed them, and prosperity too), they looked for the "Desire of all nations," for the consolation of Israel, having little else to relieve them, for the external means, unless it were that בַּת קֹיל, that echo heard in the temple, they tell us of, which served them for an oracle; and the miracle of the pool of Bethesda granted by God to strengthen them in the true worship of God, under the persecution of Antiochus and other tyrants, till the days of John Baptist and the Lord Christ.

Ver. 16. And Jacob begat Joseph] Whose genealogy is here recorded, and not Mary's, it being not the custom of that people then to set forth the genealogies of women. As at this day, the Jews have an over-base conceit of that sex; saying that they have not so divine a soul as men, but are of a lower creation, &c., and therefore they suffer them not to enter the synagogue, but appoint them a gallery without. (Blount's Voyage into the Levant.)

The husband of Mary, of whom was born Jesus] This is the sum of all the good news in the world, such as surpasseth the joy of conquest or of harvest, Isa. ix. 3, 5, 6, and should therefore swallow up all discontents whatsoever.

Who is called Christ] The name of Jesus is *mel in ore, melos in aure, jubilium in corde* (Bernard): as it was to St Paul, who therefore names it nine several times in the ten first verses of his First Epistle to the Corinthians, as loth to come off it. Yet is not the name Jesus alone half so sweet as when Christ is added to it, as here. For Jesus Christ betokeneth such a Saviour as is anointed and appointed thereunto by God, consecrated to the office according to his Godhead, and qualified for it according to his manhood. In both natures a Saviour, and that *ex professo* (as you would say) and by consent of all three persons: the Son being anointed by the Father, with the Holy Ghost: and as Samson when clothed with the spirit saved the people, so Christ much more.

Ver. 17. So all the generations, &c., *are fourteen generations*] For memory' sake Matthew summeth up the genealogy of our Saviour into three fourteens (tessaradecades): like as some of the Psalms are, for the same reason, set down in order of the alphabet. *Discere voluit Socrates, nihil aliud esse quam recordari,* saith Tully (Tusc. Quest.). *Magis autem Christi meminisse debemus quam respirare* (Chrysost.). The soul should be as the ark of God, the memory like the pot of manna, preserving holy truths touching him that is "the Way, the Truth, and the Life."

Ver. 18. *Now the birth of Jesus Christ*] A γενέσει ad γέννησιν transit. And being to relate a strange thing, and till then never heard of, he elegantly stirs up the hearers' mind with this preface.

When as his mother Mary was espoused] An ancient and commendable custom. Adam took his wife the first day of their creation (she was espoused to him), but knew her not till after the fall: Lot's daughters were espoused, yet had not known man, Gen. xix. 8, 14. See Deut. xxii. 22. Yea, the very heathens had their espousals, Judg. xiv. 1, &c. *Placuit, despondi: nuptiis hic dictus est dies*, saith he in Terence. We agreed, were contracted, and the wedding-day appointed.

To Joseph, before they came together] Espoused they were by a special providence. 1. That Mary might not be held a harlot. 2. That being big, and needing necessary help, she might be provided for. 3. That the mystery of Christ might be made known by degrees.

She was found with child of the Holy Ghost] This wonderful conception of our Saviour is a mystery, not much to be pried into,[1] and is therefore called an overshadowing, Luke i. 35. Where also, lest any should mistake this *of* in the text for the material cause: as if the Holy Ghost had begotten him of his own substance (as fathers do their children), the whole order and manner of this conception, so far as concerneth us to know, is declared by the angel.

Ver. 19. *Then Joseph her husband, being a just man*] And yet withal a merciful, tender man of the Virgin's credit. Hence that conflict and fear within himself lest he should not do right.

And not willing to make her a public example] That is, to wrong her, as the same word is used and expounded by the author to the Hebrews of the Son of God, as here of the mother of God, Heb. vi. 6 with Heb. x. 29: παραδειγματίσαι. *Noluit ipse eam nec pœnis, nec infamiæ, imo nec risui exponere* (Aret.).

Was minded to put her away privily] Which yet he could hardly have done, without blame to himself and blemish to her. So far out we are (the best of us) when destitute of Divine direction. How shamefully was that good Josiah miscarried by his passions to his cost, when he went up against Pharaoh-Necho, without once advising with Jeremiah, Zephaniah, Huldah, or any other prophet of God then living by him!

Ver. 20. *But while he thought on these things*] And was not so well advised upon his course, God, who reserveth his holy hand for a dead lift, expedites him. The Athenians had a conceit that Minerva (their goddess) drove all their ill counsels to a happy issue. The superstitious

Romans thought that an idol, which they called Vibilia, kept them from erring out of their way.[2] The Divine providence is our Vibilia, that will not suffer us to miscarry, so long as we have an eye to the pattern that was showed us in the mount, Exod. xxv. 40. In the mount will the Lord be seen,[3] Gen. xxii. 14; Prov. iii. 26.

Behold the angel of the Lord appeared unto him] As of old he had done to Daniel, being caused to fly swiftly, or with weariness of flight (as the Hebrew hath it), with so good a will he did it, as thinking he could never come soon enough. Dan. ix. 21; Rev. i. 9.

Joseph, thou son of David] Albeit a poor carpenter. A man may be as high in God's favour and as happy in russet as in tissue. "I know thy poverty" (saith Christ to that Church), but that is nothing, "thou art rich," Rev. ii. 9.

Fear not to take unto thee] viz. from the hands of her parents, who have, by all right, the disposal of their children as a chief part of their goods. Therefore when Satan obtained leave to vex Job and to touch him in his possession, he dealt with his children also, Job i. 11—19.

For that which is conceived in her] "That holy thing," Luke i. 35, that Holy of Holies wherein the "Godhead dwelleth bodily," that is, personally; and is called the Son of God, saith the angel there. Yet not in respect of his human nature, for then there should be in the person of Christ two sons, viz. one of the Father and another of the Holy Ghost. Besides, Heb. vii. 3, he is "without father," as man, and "without mother," as God. All that can be gathered out of that place in Luke is, that he that was so conceived of the Holy Ghost was the natural Son of God. The union of three persons into one nature, and of two natures into one person, these are the great mysteries of godliness. The well is deep, as she said, and we want wherewith to draw (ἄντλημα), John iv. 11.

Is of the Holy Ghost] As the efficient, not as the material cause. The *virtus formatrix*, the formative faculty which the Virgin had not, is ascribed to the power of the Holy Ghost, framing and fashioning Christ of the substance of the Virgin sanctified miraculously and without man's help. But if no mother knows the manner of her natural conception, what presumption shall it be for flesh and blood to search how the Son of God took flesh of his creature? It is enough for us to know that he was conceived of the Holy Ghost, not spermatically, but operatively, yet secretly and mystically; the Virgin herself knew not how. Fearfully and wonderfully he was made, and curiously wrought in the lowest parts of the earth. Psal. cxxxix. 14, 15; Eph. iv. 9.

Ver. 21. *And she shall bring forth a Son*] Shiloh, the son of her secundines: that Son, that Eve made account she had got when she

---

[1] *Mirari licet, rimari non licet.*

[2] Jun. Emblem. *Ab erroribus viarum Dea Vibilia liberat.* Arnob. adver. Gentes.

[3] *Becilleia in stultitia tua* (ait Rab. Solomon ex Talmud. Hieros.), i. e. *in rebus in quibus es stultus, aderit tamen tibi Dominus.*

had got Cain: for said she, "I have gotten a man from the Lord;" or, as others read it (and the original rather favours it), "I have gotten the man, the Lord." But how far she was deceived, the issue proved. *Fallitur augurio spes bona sæpe suo.* Hope comes halting home many times.

And thou shalt call his name Jesus] Not of ἰάομαι, to heal, as some Hellenists would have it: although it be true that he is (Exod. xv. 26) the Lord the Physician, " by whose stripes we are healed " Isa. liii. 5; but of Jashang, whence Jehoshuah, Jesus. Two in the Old Testament had this name. The first when he was sent as a spy into Canaan, Numb. xiii. 16, had his name changed from Oshea, " Let God save," to Jehoshuah, " God shall save." Under the Law (which brings us, as it were, into the wilderness of Sin) we may wish there were a Saviour, but under the Gospel we are sure of salvation, since our Jehoshuah hath bound himself to fulfil all righteousness, and had therefore this name imposed upon him at his circumcision. For he assumed it not to himself (though, knowing the end of his coming and the fulness of his sufficiency, he might have done it), nor received it from men, but from God, and that with great solemnity, by the ministry of an angel, who talked with a woman about our salvation as Satan sometime had done about our destruction.

For he shall save his people from their sins] This is the notation and etymon, or reason of his name, Jesus,— a name above all names, Phil. ii. 9. Σωτήρ, saith the heathen orator,[1] is a word so emphatical, that other tongues can hardly find a word fit to express it. Salvation properly notes the negative part of a Christian's happiness, viz. preservation from evil, chiefly from the evil of sin (which is the mother of all our misery); from the damning and domineering power . thereof, by his merit and Spirit, by his value and virtue. Jesus therefore is a short Gospel, and should work in us strongest affections and egressions of soul after Him who hath saved us from the wrath to come. 1 Thess. i. 10. The Grecians, being set free but from bodily servitude, called their deliverer a saviour to them; and rang it out, Saviour, Saviour,[2] so that the fowls in the air fell down dead with the cry. Yea, they so pressed to come near him and touch his hand, that if he had not timely withdrawn himself, he might have beseemed to have lost his life.[3] The Egyptians preserved by Joseph, called him Abrech, or tender-father. The daughters of Jerusalem met David returning from the slaughter of the Philistines with singing and dancing. When the Lord turned again the captivity of his people, they were like them that dream, Psal. cxxvi. 1. And Peter, enlarged, could scarce believe his own eyes, with such an ecstasy of admiration was he rapt upon that deliverance. Oh, then, how should our hearts rejoice and our tongues be glad, Acts ii. 26; and how should we be vexed at the vile dulness and

deadness of our naughty natures, that can be no more affected with these indelible ravishments! Jacob wept for joy at the good news that Joseph was yet alive. Joannes Mollius, whensoever he spake of the name of Jesus, his eyes dropped. And another reverend divine amongst us, being in a deep muse, after some discourse that passed of Jesus, and tears trickling abundantly from his eyes before he was aware, being urged for the cause thereof, confessed ingenuously, it was because he could not draw his dull heart to prize Christ aright. Mr Fox never denied beggar that asked in that name; and good Bucer never disregarded any (though different in opinion from him) in whom he could discern *aliquid Christi.* " None but Christ," said that blessed martyr at the stake. And another in the flames, when judged already dead, suddenly, as waked out of sleep, moved his tongue and jaws, and was heard to pronounce this word, Jesus. (John Lambert, Julius Palmer. Acts and Mon.)

Here also we have an excellent argument of our Saviour's Divinity and omnipotency; forasmuch as the angel ascribeth unto him that which the Psalmist affirmeth of Jehovah, that he shall " redeem Israel from all his iniquities," Psal. cxxx. 8, with Hos. xiii. 4. λυτρώσεται. *Christus autem, non Pater, factus est ἀπολύτρωσις.*

Ver. 22. *Now all this was done, that it might be fulfilled*] An angel's testimony is not to be taken, if it be beside or against the written word. I am of them that keep the sayings of this book, saith the angel to the apostle, Rev. xxii. 5. " For ever, O Lord, thy word is settled in heaven," Psal. cxix. 82.

Ver. 23. *Behold a Virgin, &c.*] הָעַלְמָה, that Virgin, κατ᾽ ἐξοχὴν, that famous Virgin foretold, Isa. vii. 14. That he should be the seed of the woman was made known to Adam; but not of what nation till Abraham, nor of what tribe till Jacob, nor of what sex till David, nor whether born of· a Virgin till Isaiah. Thus by degrees was that great mystery of godliness revealed to mankind. If any Jew object, saith Chrysostom, how could a Virgin bring forth? *Dic ei, quomodo peperit sterilis et vetula?* Ask him, how could Sarah, when old and barren, bear a child? The bees have young, yet know not marriage. The Phœnix, they say, hath no parents. This head-stone of the corner was cut out of the mountain without hands (Dan. ii. 34); this flower of the field, this rose of Sharon (Cant. ii. 1), hath Heaven for his father, and earth for his mother. Was it not as easy to frame this second Adam in the womb, as that first Adam out of the mire? Herein see a miracle of mercy, that the incomprehensible God, that circle (whose centre is everywhere, whose circumference nowhere) should be circled and cooped up for nine months together in the narrow womb of a pure Virgin.

And shall bring forth a Son] Who in the birth opened the womb, Luke ii. 41, and so put her

---

[1] Cicer. *in Verrem.* [2] σωτήρ, σωτήρ. Plut. *in Vita Flamin.* [3] Tindal in his Annotat.

to pain likely, as other women. He hid the glory of his eternal nativity under a mean and temporary birth to purchase for us a heavenly and eternal birth. Whether the blessed Virgin were Deipara, the Mother of God, raised great storms in the Council of Ephesus, and came to commotions in the secular part, and excommunications among the Bishops—insomuch as the Emperor declared both sides heretics,—but forasmuch as she brought forth a Son that was God, we doubt not to style her the Mother of God; not Moll, God's maid, as one hath lately slandered some of us in print. At Rome (it is said) was seen, at the same time, about the sun, the likeness of a woman carrying a child in her arms: and a voice heard, Pan, the great god, is now about to be born, &c.

And they shall call his name Immanuel, &c.] By a wonderful and unsearchable union: the manner whereof is to be believed, not discussed; admired, not pried into: personal it is, yet not of persons: of natures, and yet not natural. As a soul and body are one man; so God and man are one person, saith Athanasius. And as every believer that is born of God, saith another, remains the same entire person that he was before, receiving nevertheless into him a divine nature which before he had not: so Immanuel, continuing the same perfect person which he had been from eternity, assumeth nevertheless a human nature which before he had not, to be born within his person for ever. This is so much the more wonderful, because the very angels (which are far greater in glory than man) are not able to abide the presence of God, Isa. vi. 2. But this is our ladder of ascension to God, John iii. 13. Faith first lays hold upon Christ as a man; and thereby, as by a mean, makes way to God, and embraceth the Godhead, which is of itself a consuming fire. And whereas sin is a partition-wall of our own making, denying us access, Eph. ii. 14; God is now with us: and in Christ "we have boldness and access with confidence by the faith of him." Christ's humanity serves as a screen to save us from those everlasting burnings; and as a conduit to derive upon us from the Godhead all spiritual blessings in heavenly places, Eph. i. 3: if any Assyrian invade us, we may cry, as they of old, "The stretching out of his wings doth fill thy land, O Immanuel," Isa. viii. 8, and we shall have help.

Ver. 24. Then Joseph, being raised from sleep, did as the angel, &c.] As well assured that it was of God, whom he was ready pressed to obey without sciscitation. *Jussa sequi, tam velle mihi, quam posse, necesse est.* (Lucan). If some princes will not endure that subjects should scan their laws, but require absolute obedience: if generals excuse not in a soldier the neglect of their commands, but severely punish even prosperous disorders: if Jesuits exact blind obedience of their wretched novices (our Throgmorton durst not give up the ghost

till he had obtained leave of his superior[1]), should not we much more obey God in his commands, counsels, promises, prohibitions, comminations, all?

Ver. 25. And knew her not till she brought forth] We think hardly of him that taketh to wife the widow and relict of another, that is left great with child, before she hath laid down her burden; how much more in this case! Besides, this might be part of the angel's charge to him, that after she had brought forth her Son Jesus she continued still a Virgin, *pie credimus*, but it is neither article of our creed nor principle of our religion. But that she vowed virginity is both false and absurd. For how could she promise virginity to God and marriage to Joseph? Sure it is, the blemish will never be wiped off from some of the ancients, who, to establish their own idol, of I know not what virginity, have written most wickedly and most basely of marriage, which both Christ honoured with his first miracle and the Holy Ghost by overshadowing the betrothed Virgin. As for the Papists that disgrace it, they appear herein more like devils than divines. 1 Tim. iv. 1. If the same God had not been the author of virginity and marriage, he had never countenanced virginity by marriage, as he did in the Virgin Mary.

CHAPTER II.

Verse 1. Now when Jesus was born in Bethlehem.] THE house of bread, that bread of life that came down from heaven, John vi. 50, and dwelt amongst us in this city of David, otherwise called Ephrata, that is, fruit-bearing; and situate (they say) in the very navel and centre of the earth, because in him all nations should be blessed: here was Jesus born, by mere accident in regard of his parents (who were brought hither by a tyrannical edict of the emperor, forcing all, even great-bellied women, to repair to their own city to be taxed, though it were in the deep of winter), but by a sweet Providence of God, to fulfil the Scripture and to settle our faith.

In the days of Herod the king] When the sceptre was departed from Judah, and the times were grown deplored and desperately wicked, Joseph found his brethren in Dothan, i. e. in defection; so did Christ, when he came: scarce were there four, or fewer found, that waited for the consolation of Israel. Then, also, when among the poor Gentiles a plentiful harvest, a very great number of elect were ready ripe, Matt. ix. 37; Luke x. 2; John iv. 35. Then, when *cuncta atque continua totius generis humani aut pax fuit, aut pactio* (Flor.), then came the Prince of Peace into the world, when all was at peace throughout the world.

Behold there came wise men] Neither kings nor cunning men, but sages of the East, Θεωρητικοί, contemplative persons, philosophers, interpreters of the laws of God and men (μάγοι, מהגים).

[1] *In articulo mortis nolebat obire, non impetrata à superiore venià.*

The tale of the three kings of Cullen is long since exploded.

To Jerusalem] So misreckoning of a point they missed the haven, and had like to have run upon the rocks. Had they met with the shepherds of Bethlehem, they had received better intelligence than they could from the learned scribes of Jerusalem. God hath chosen the weak of the world to confound the wise, 1 Cor. i. 27, 28. *Surgunt indocti et rapiunt cœlum, et nos, cum doctrinis nostris, detrudimur in Gehennam* (August. *Confess.* viii. 8). None are so far from Christ, many times, as knowing men. Some of the scribes and Pharisees were very atheists, for they knew " neither the Father nor the Son." Ulpian the chief lawyer, Galen the chief physician, Porphyry the chief Aristotelian, Plotinus the chief Platonist, Libanius and Lucian the chief orators of that age, were all professed enemies to Christ. No Church was founded at Athens, Acts xvii. 16, which yet Demosthenes calls the soul, sun, and eye of Greece, Euripides the Greece of Greece, Thucydides and Diodorus the common school of all men, the mart of good learning, &c.: ψυχὴν, καὶ ἥλιον, καὶ ὄφθαλμον ἑλλάδος. ἑλλάδος ἑλλάδα. κοινὸν παιδευτήριον πάντων ἀνθρώπων. The greatest clerks are not always the wisest men in the affairs of God. Howbeit, learned Nathaniel, Joseph of Arimathea, and Nicodemus, masters in Israel, were disciples to our Saviour; lest if he had called simple men only, it might have been thought, *quod fuissent ex simplicitate decepti*, that they were deceived out of their simplicity, saith one.

Ver. 2. *Saying, Where is he that is born King of the Jews?*] As presupposing a common notice. But the " kingdom of God cometh not by observation," Luke xvii. 21, neither is it of this world. Christ is somewhat an obscure King here, as Melchisedec was; and his kingdom consists in righteousness, and peace, and joy in the Holy Ghost, which the stranger worldling meddles not with, Prov. xiv. 10; Rom. xiv. 17. The cock on the dunghill esteems not this jewel.

For we have seen his star in the East] Some rumour of the star of Jacob they had heard and received, likely, either from Balaam's prophecy, Numb. xxiv. 17, who was an East countryman; or from the Chaldean sibyl, or from the Jews in the Babylonish captivity; and now they make their use of it. (Hugo. *Postill.*) But the Scripture giveth more grace, James iv. 6. Only take heed that " ye receive not the grace of God in vain," 2 Cor. vi. 1.

And are come to worship him] With a religious worship; to kiss at his mouth, as the word signifieth; and as Pharaoh said to Joseph, they shall all kiss at thy mouth. Woe worth to us, if we kiss not the Son with a kiss of faith and love (προσκυνεῖν), sith he is now so clearly revealed unto us, not by the sight of one star only, as to these, but by a whole heaven bespangled with stars, though not in every part, yet in every zone and quarter of it, as one saith of our Church. We have a word of prophecy (how much more is this true of the holy Gospel?) more sure than the voice that came from heaven in the holy Mount (saith St Peter), whereunto we shall do well to take heed, as unto a light shining in a dark place, 2 Pet. i. 19. Besides the works of God, those *regii professores*, as one calleth them, those catholic preachers, Psal. xix. 2, 3, those real postills of the divinity, Christ is purposely compared to sensible objects, as to the sun, stars, rose, rock, &c., that through the creatures, as so many optic glasses, we might see him that is invisible, having the eyes of our mind turned toward Christ, as the faces of the cherubim were toward the mercy-seat.

Ver. 3. *When Herod the king heard these things he was troubled*] At that wherein the sages and shepherds rejoiced. It is fair weather with the saints when foulest with the wicked. Abraham stands upon the hill, and seeth the smoke of the cities ascend like a furnace. " Behold, my servants shall rejoice, but ye shall be ashamed: my servants shall sing for joy of heart, but ye shall cry for sorrow of heart, and ye shall leave your name for a curse unto my chosen," Isa. lxv. 14, 15. Ælian (*Histor. Animal.*) compareth tyrants to swine, which if a man but touch they begin to cry, as dreaming of nothing but death; forasmuch as they have neither fleece nor milk, nor anything else, but their flesh only to forfeit. But *si præsepe vagientis Herodem tantum terruit, quid tribunal judicantis?* saith one. If Christ in the cratch were so terrible, what will he be on the tribunal?

And all Jerusalem with him] Perhaps to comply and ingratiate with the tyrant (as the Arabians, if their king be sick or lame, they all feign themselves so); or, as *homines ad servitutem parati;* so Tiberius called the Romans, who gave public thanks for all, even the wicked acts of their emperors (Tacitus); or as fearing some new stirs in the state, as the burnt child dreads the fire.

Ver. 4. *And when he had gathered all the chief priests*] The true picture of Popish councils, who propound grave questions as this was, Where Christ should be born? and pretend to worship Christ, but intend to worry him: the Council of Trent was carried, against the simplicity of Christ, with such infinite guile and craft, as that themselves will even smile in the triumphs of their own wits (when they hear it but mentioned) as at a master stratagem. It passed in France in manner of a proverb, That the modern council had more authority than that of the apostles, because their own pleasure was a sufficient ground for the decrees, without admitting the Holy Ghost. (Hist. of Council of Trent.)

Ver. 5. *And they said unto him, In Bethlehem*] Lo, how readily and roundly, out of the Scriptures, they could answer to this capital question; giving such signs of the Messias as did evidently agree to Jesus Christ. Yet were they for their obstinacy so infatuated, that when God showed them the man to whom their own signs agree, they cannot allow of him. Unless the Lord give a mind as well as means; sight, as well as light, and irradiate the organ as well as the object, we grope as blind men in the dark, Isa. lix. 10; we err in heart, as not knowing God's ways, yet cannot wander so wide as to miss of hell; to original blindness we add actual stubbornness, Psal. xcv. 8, the devil holding his black hand (as it were) afore our eyes, that we may not see and be saved, Acts xxvi. 19.

Ver. 6. *And thou Bethlehem, in the land of Judah, art not the least*] "Thou art the least," saith Micah, v. 2, viz. in comparison of greater cities, yet "not the least," saith Matthew, because out of thee shall come a Governor, &c. In Scripture, the place of holy men's birth is remembered and registered: God loves the very ground his servants tread on. "The Lord shall count, when he numbereth up the people, that this man was born there" (Psal. lxvii. 6, 7): how much more the man Christ Jesus? Any interest or relation to him ennobleth whatsoever place or person, and may justly comfort us against whatsoever troubles. The prophet Micah, whose words are here cited, opposeth the birth of this babe of Bethlehem to all the troops and troubles of Assyria, Mic. v. 1, 2.

For out of thee shall come a Governor] No sooner is this Child born, this Son given to us, but the "government is laid upon his shoulder," Isa. ix. 6, as the key of the house of David was upon Eliakim's, Isa. xxii. 22. Send ye therefore a lamb to this ruler of the land, Isa. xvi. 1; do him all hearty homage and fealty.

That shall rule my people] Or feed them;[1] for the art of feeding and ruling are sisters. David was taken from following the ewes to feed God's people; so was Moses, in whose absence, how soon was Israel, as silly sheep, gone out of the way! Christ is the arch-Shepherd, that feeds his people daily, daintily, plentifully, pleasantly, among the lilies, Cant. ii. 16; yea, in his garden of spices, in green pastures of his word, and by the still waters of his sacraments, where we go in and out, and find pasture, John x. 9, such as breeds life, and life in more abundance, ver. 10. We lie down in peace, Jer. xxiii. 4, and need not fear the spiritual Assyrian, Mic. v. 5, whiles we keep us within the hedge and run to the foddering places; submitting to the ministers, those under-shepherds, Cant. i. 7, 8, who are charged to feed Christ's sheep, his sheep with golden fleeces; yea, to do it (יָל, as the Syriac hath it) for me, for my sake (saith our Saviour), to whom Peter cannot better seal up his love than by taking care of his cure. I know how Bellarmine glosseth that text (John xxi. 16), "Feed my sheep," that is, *Regio more impera*, Rule like an emperor: *Supremum in Ecclesia dominium tibi assere*, saith Baronius, Domineer over the church, because the word here used (ποιμαίνω,—and so in John) signifieth as well to govern as to feed.

But what will they say to βόσκω, the other word there twice used by our Saviour, which always signifieth to feed, and not at all to govern? But these men catch at government, let go feeding, although the Fathers took the text only of feeding by doctrine, and that they beat upon, and urged altogether.

Ver. 7. *Then Herod, when he had privily called the wise men, inquired of them diligently*][2] The children of this world are wise in their generation, but so are serpents, foxes, &c., to the which the Church's enemies are oft compared. He thought by this means to have made all sure, but in the thing wherein he dealt proudly and politically, God was above them, as old Jethro hath it, Exod. xviii. 11. There is neither power nor policy against the Lord; "who ever waxed fierce against him, and prospered?" Job ix. 4.

Ver. 8. *And he sent them to Bethlehem*] It was a wonder he went not himself, or sent not some assassin underhand, to despatch the child immediately. But God befooled him. The Germans have a proverb, "Where God intends to blind any man, he first closeth up his eyes."[3] So the apostle, 1 Cor. iii. 19, He taketh the wise (σοφούς), the finest and choicest wits of the world, the rare and picked pieces: *Mentemque habere queis bonam et esse corculis datum est:* These he taketh, he catcheth and keepeth as beasts in a gin (so the word signifieth), and that in their own craft;[4] when they have racked their wits, and racked their fortunes, to effect their fetches; when they have done their utmost (as the word imports) to bring about their devilish devices.

That I may come and worship him] When he meant to worry him. *Cogitabat Jesum non colere sed tollere, non adorare sed necare.* Oh base dissimulation! such was that of those incendiary fugitives of Rhemes, Giffard, Hodgson, and others, who at the same time when they had set up, and set on savage to kill Queen Elizabeth, they put forth a book, wherein they admonished the English Catholics not to attempt anything against their prince. (Camden's Elizabeth.) In like sort Robert Parsons (that arch-traitor), when he was hatching an horrible treason against his natural prince and native country, he set forth his book of Christian Resolution, as if he had been wholly made of devotion. So Garnet (a little before the Powder-plot was discovered) wrote to the Pope that he would lay his command upon our Papists to obey their king and keep themselves quiet. Herod here, when he was whetting his sword, yet promised devotion, saith Chrysostom.[5] A fair glove upon a foul hand. The panther's skin is fairest, but his friendship is fatal, and his breath infectious. The above-mentioned Garnet, upon a treatise of equivocation, plastered on this title, A Treatise against Lying and fraudulent Dissimulation.

---

[1] ποιμανεῖ. Psal. lxxviii. 71. Ἀγαμέμνονα ποιμένα λαῶν. Homer. 1 Pet. v. 4; Cant. viii. 14; Psal. xxiii. 2, 3.
[2] ἠκρίβωσε. *Accuravit, et omnibus nervis incubuit.*
[3] *Deus quem destruet dementat.*
[4] δρασσεσθαι *est manu capere, et firmiter tenere.* ἐν τῇ πανουργίᾳ, *in veteratoria versutia.* Erasmus.
[5] *Quando gladium acuebat, devotionem promittebat.*

Ver. 9. *And lo the star*] A star either new-created, or at leastwise strangely carried : for it stands one while, moves another, appears in the lower region, is not obscured by the beams of the sun : so that some have thought it was an angel.[1] It moved slowly, as might be best for the pace and purpose of these pilgrims.

Till it came and stood over where the young child was] They show still at Bethlehem a little hole over the place where our Saviour was born, through which the star fell down to the ground. But who will not conclude that there was a vertigo in his head who first made a star subject to the falling sickness ? Fuller's History of Holy War.

Ver. 10. *When they saw the star*] The sight whereof they seem to have lost when they turned out of the way ; it led them to Jerusalem. But this text is excellently paraphrased and applied by Bishop Hooper, martyr, in a letter of his, written to one Mrs Anne Warcup, in these words (Acts and Mon.) : "Such as travelled to find Christ, followed only the star, and as long as they saw it they were assured they were in the right way, and had great mirth in their journey. But when they entered into Jerusalem (whereas the star led them not thither, but unto Bethlehem) and there asked the citizens the thing that the star showed before ; as long as they tarried in Jerusalem, and would be instructed where Christ was born, they were not only ignorant of Bethlehem, but also lost the sight of the star that led them before. Whereof we learn in any case, whilst we be going to seek Christ which is above, to beware we lose not the star of God's word, that only is the mark that shows us where Christ is, and which way we may come unto him. But as Jerusalem stood in the way, and was an impediment to these wise men ; so doth the synagogue of Antichrist (that bears the name of Jerusalem, that is, the vision of peace, and among the people now is called the Catholic Church) stand in the way that pilgrims must go by through this world to Bethlehem, the house of saturity and plentifulness, and is an impediment to all Christian travellers ; yea, and except the more grace of God be, will keep the pilgrims still in her, that they shall not come where Christ is adored. And to stay them indeed, they take away the star of light, viz. the word of God, that it cannot be seen, as you may read that other star was hid from the wise men while they asked of the Pharisees at Jerusalem where Christ was born. You may see what great dangers happened to these wise men while they were a learning of liars, where was Christ ; first they were out of their way, and next they lost their guide," &c.

Ver. 11. *And when they were come into the house*] Not a palace prepared for the purpose, as the Porphyrogeniti in Constantinople had, but in an inn was Christ born, as ready to receive all that come unto him (πανδοχεῖον) ; and

in a hole of the earth, an underground den, as Justin Martyr, Epiphanius, Eusebius, and Origen witness. *In hoc terræ foramine* (saith St Jerome, ad Marcell. tom. 1) *cælorum conditor natus est, hic involutus pannis, hic visus à pastoribus, hic adoratus à Magis, hic circumcisus, &c.* In this cell or hole was the world's Creator born, swathed, visited, adored, circumcised.

They saw the young child] For this Ancient of days, by joining his majesty to our vileness, his power to our weakness, suspended and laid aside his own glory, wherewith he was glorified with the Father before the world began, and voluntarily abased himself to the shape and state of a poor, feeble, helpless infant, that we might come to the fulness of the age in Christ. Eph. iv. 13.

With Mary his mother] Without any other assistance or attendance. Joseph haply was at work, or otherwise absent, lest the wise men should mistake him for the true father of the child.

And when they had opened their treasure, they presented unto him gifts] No great matters to make him rich ; for then, what needed the holy Virgin, at her purification, to have offered two young pigeons, as a token of her penury, that could not reach to a lamb ? Yet something it was, gold, frankincense, and myrrh (sent them in by a special providence of God) to help to bear their charges into Egypt, whither they were now to fly.

Gold, frankincense, and myrrh] The best commodities of their country, doubtless ; thereby (as by a pepper-corn, in way of homage or chief-rent) they acknowledged Christ to be the true Proprietary and Lord of all. Of the elephant it is reported, that coming to feed, the first sprig he breaks he turns it toward heaven. Of the stork Pliny tells us, that she offers the first-fruits of her young ones to God, by casting one of them out of the nest.[2] God is content we have the benefit of his creatures, so he may have the glory of them : this is all the loan he looketh for, and for this, as he indents with us, Psal. l. 15, so the saints restipulate, Gen. xxviii. 22. But he cannot abide that we pay this rent to a wrong landlord, whether to ourselves, as Deut. viii. 17, or to our fellow-creatures as they to their sweethearts, Hos. ii. 5.

Gold, frankincense, and myrrh] Aurum, Thus, Myrrham, Regique, Hominique, Deoque. A little of each, as Gen. xliii. 11. Lycurgus made a law that no man should be over-costly or bountiful in his offering of sacrifice, lest at length he should grow weary of the charge, and give God over.[3] Ought we not (saith one) often in soul to go with the wise men to Bethlehem, being directed by the star of grace, and there fall down and worship the little King ; there offer the gold of charity, the frankincense of devotion, the myrrh of penitency, and then return, not by cruel Herod or troubled Jerusalem, but another way, brœis. Amasii Trem.

---

[1] *Angelus in specie sideris figuratus.* Per.

[2] *Hinc pietatis cultrix à Latinis dicitur, Hafida ab He-*

[3] ἵνα μήποτε τιμῶντες τὸ θεῖοιν καταλείπωσιν. Plut.

a better way, unto our long and happy home? (Sutton's *Disce Vivere*.)

Ver. 12. *And being warned of God in a dream, &c.*] Thus were they pulled by a sweet Providence out of the lion's mouth, as Paul was (2 Tim. iv. 17); as Athanasius and Basil often; as Luther also; and Queen Elizabeth of famous memory, for whose execution a warrant once came down under seal, Gardner being the chief engineer. And when through a sea of sorrows she had swum to the crown, treasons there were every year so many, that she said in parliament, "She rather marvelled that she was, than mused that she should not be." (Camden's *Elizabeth*.) But no man is master of his own life, much less of another's, as our Saviour told Pilate. See Job xxiv. 22. "My times are in thy hands," saith David; "deliver me from the hands of mine enemies, and from them that persecute me," Psalm xxxi. 15. So Queen Elizabeth at Woodstock, after a great deliverance, "Lord, look upon the wounds of thy hands," said she, "and despise not the work of thy hands. Thou hast written me down in thy book of preservation with thine own hand. Oh read thine own hand-writing and save me," &c. (Camden's *Elizabeth*.) And God heard her, and hid the silver thread of her precious life in the endless maze of his bottomless mercies. Mr Fox makes mention of one Laremouth, *alias* Williamson, Chaplain to Lady Anne of Cleeve, a Scotchman, to whom in prison it was said, as he thought, "Arise, and go thy ways," whereto when he gave no great heed at first, the second time it was so said; upon this, as he fell to his prayers, it was said the third time likewise to him, which was half an hour after. So he arising upon the same immediately a piece of the prison-wall fell down. And as the officers came in at the outer gate of the prison, he leaping over the ditch escaped; and in the way, meeting a certain beggar, changed his coat with him, and coming to the sea-shore, where he found a vessel ready to go over, was taken in and escaped the search, which was straitly laid for him all the country over. (Acts and Mon.)

Ver. 13. *Behold, the angel of the Lord appeareth to Joseph in a dream*] Angels cannot enlighten the mind or powerfully incline the will (that is proper to the Holy Ghost to do), but as spirits and instruments of the Holy Ghost they can insinuate themselves into the phantasy (as here to Joseph), stir up phantasms of good things, propound truth to the mind, advise and persuade to it, as counsellors, and inwardly instigate, as it were, by speaking and doing after a spiritual manner, suggesting good thoughts as the apostate angels do evil. How oft had we fallen had not these guardians hindered (as Michael opposed Satan, Jude 9) by removing occasions, or casting in good instincts into us, either asleep or awake.

Take the young child, and flee into Egypt]

Perhaps through that terrible and roaring wilderness of Arabia (Deut. viii. 15): however, this was a part of his passion; for, from his cratch to his cross, he suffered many a little death all his life long; and as it is said of that French king (Hen. IV.), that he acted more wars than others ever saw, so our Saviour suffered more miseries than we ever heard of. Banished he was betimes, to bring back his banished to paradise, that is, above, their proper country; towards the which we groan and aspire, as oft as we look towards heaven, waiting, as "with stretched-out necks, for the manifestation of the sons of God" (ἀποκαραδοκία, Rom. viii. 19), and saying with Sisera's mother, "Why is his chariot so long in coming? why tarry the wheels of his chariots?" Judg. v. 28. "Make haste, my beloved, and be like a roe or a young hart upon the mountains of spices," Cant. viii. 14.

For Herod will seek the young child to destroy him] The devil in Herod, Rev. xii. 4. So Rev. ii. 10, "The devil shall cast some of you into prison," &c. Is the devil become a justicer, to send men to prison? By his imps and instruments (such as Herod was, that abuse their authority) Satan exerciseth his malice against the saints, lending them his seven heads to plot, and his ten horns to push; but all in vain, Psalm ii. 5.

Ver. 14. *When he arose he took the young child, &c.*] Whither God leads, we must cheerfully follow, though he seem to lead us, as he did Israel in the wilderness, in and out, backwards and forwards, as if we were treading in a maze;[1] although we were to go with him into those places (Hor. I. 32):

> *Pigris ubi nulla campis*
> *Arbor æstivâ recreatur aurâ :*
> *Quod latus mundi nebulæ malusque*
> *Jupiter urget.*

And departed into Egypt] A country, for its fruitfulness and abundance, anciently called, *Publicum orbis horreum*, the world's great granary or barn: *Horreum, unde hauriatur.* (Plin. Mela.) And to this day, so far as the river waters, they do but throw in the seed, and have four rich harvests in less than four months, saith a late traveller.[2] Hither fleeth the Son of God, as to a sanctuary of safety. And some say, that at his coming thither all the idols fell to the ground. Sure it is, that when the love of Christ once cometh into the heart, all the idol-desires of the world and flesh fall to nothing, Hos. xiv. 8.

Ver. 15. *And was there till the death of Herod*] Which was a matter of two or three years at least.[3] For Christ was born in 32 of Herod's reign, fled when he was about two years old, or soon after his birth (as others are of opinion), and returned not till Herod was dead, after he had reigned seven and thirty years.

That it might be fulfilled that was spoken, &c.]

---

[1] *Magnus est animus qui se Deo tradidit.* Senec.
[2] Blount's Voyage into the Levant.

[3] *Epiphanius vult hæc biennio post natum Christum contigisse.*

When the Old Testament is cited in the New, it is not only by way of accommodation, but because it is the proper meaning of the places both in the type and in the truth.

Ver. 16. Then Herod, when he saw that he was mocked] He had mocked them, and yet takes it ill to be mocked of them, to have his own measure: he never takes notice of this, that God usually maketh fools of his enemies; lets them proceed, that they may be frustrated; and when they are gone to the utmost reach of their tether, pulls them back to their task with shame.

Was exceeding wroth, and sent forth and slew] "In their anger they slew a man," saith Jacob of his two sons; "cursed be their anger, for it was fierce," &c., Gen. xlix. 6, 7. It is indeed the fury of the unclean spirit, that old manslayer (Gen. iv. 23), a very beast within the heart of a man; a short madness, as we see in Saul, whom the devil possessed by this passion (Eph. iv. 27); in Lamech, who slew a man in his heat, and boasted of it; as Alexander Phereas consecrated the javelin wherewith he slew Poliphron (Plutarch); in David, who swore a great oath what he would do to Nabal by such a time (1 Chron. xv. 2): and when Uzziah was smitten for his carting the Ark, how untowardly spake he! (so did Jonas too), as if the fault were in God (dogs in a chase sometimes bark at their own masters). Lastly, in Theodosius at Thessalonica, where being enraged at the slaughter of certain judges, slain by sedition, he did to death at hand of seven thousand men. Anger begins in rashness, abounds in transgression (Prov. xxix. 22), ends in repentance.[1] Jonathan therefore rose from the table in fierce anger (1 Sam. xx. 34), and, to prevent further mischief, went into the field to shoot: and Ahasuerus, to slake the fire of his wrath conceived against Haman, walked into his garden, ere he pronounced anything against him, Esth. vii. 7.

All the children] His own son also; which Augustus Cæsar hearing of, said, "it were better be Herod's swine than his son."[2] So Philip, King of France, ventured his eldest son twice in the wars against those ancient Protestants, the Albigenses, at the siege of Toulouse. And Philip, King of Spain, suffered his eldest son Charles to be murdered by the cruel Inquisition, because he seemed to favour Lutherans: for which that mouth of blasphemy, the Pope, gave him this panegyric, *Non pepercit filio suo, sed dedit pro nobis*: he spared not his own son, but gave him up for us. (Beza.)

According to the time which he had diligently inquired] Some think the wise men came before the purification, but Epiphanius will have it well-nigh two years after. Herod was curious in the search, that he might make sure work; but God defeated him. I kept the ban-dogs at staves' end (saith Nichol. Shetterden, martyr), not as

thinking to escape them, but that I would see the foxes leap above-ground for my blood if they can reach it, &c. (Acts and Mon.)

Ver. 17. Then was fulfilled that which was spoken] Fulfilling of prophecies is a convincing argument of the divinity of the Scriptures. Moses had foretold that God should dwell between Benjamin's shoulders, Deut. xxxiii. 12. This was fulfilled 440 years after, when the temple was set up in the tribe of Benjamin: so the prophecies of the coming of Christ and of Antichrist, and others in the Revelation, which we see daily accomplished.

Ver. 18. Lamentation, weeping, and great mourning] How impatient was Jacob in the loss of Joseph; David of Absalom, &c. Grief for sin (than which none more deep and soaking) is set forth by this unparalleled lamentation (Zech. xii. 10; Matt. v. 4): "Blessed are they that mourn" (πενθοῦντες), as men do at the death of their dearest children. But let such say to God, as St Jerome (ad Julian.) adviseth a friend of his in like case, *Tulisti liberos, quos ipse dederas: non contristor quod recepisti: ago gratias quod dedisti*: thou hast taken away whom thou hadst given me: I grieve not that thou hast taken them, but praise the Lord, that was pleased to give them.

Rachel weeping] That is, Bethlehem, in the way whereto Rachel died in child-birth, and was buried. "Give me children, or else I die:" give her children, and yet she dies. Well might Bethlehem weep, if at this massacre there were (as some affirm it) 14,000 infants butchered.

For her children] Those dear pledges and pieces of ourselves; called *cari* by the Latins, and φίλτατα by the Greeks, darlings, in whom is all our delight, Ezek. xxiv. 25; yet are they certain cares, but uncertain comforts.[3]

And would not be comforted] This confutes him in Plautus, that said, *Mulier nulla dolet cordicitus ex animo*, these mourned beyond measure, utterly refusing to be comforted by any fair words of the murderers excusing the matter (likely) to the miserable mothers, and promising amends from the king by some other means, or by any other way. But immoderate sorrow for losses past hope of recovery is more sullen than useful: our stomach may be bewrayed by it, not our wisdom; and although something we may yield to nature in these cases, yet nothing to impatiency.

Because they were not] A just judgment of God upon them for their unnaturalness to the Son of God, whom they shut out into a stable. The dulness and dissoluteness of these Bethlehemites required thus to be raised and roused up as by the sound of a trumpet or report of a musket; happy for them, if they had hearts "to bear the rod, and who had appointed it," Mic. vi. 9. But we many times mistake the cause of our misery, groping in the dark as the Sodomites,

---

[1] *Qui non moderabitur iræ, infectum volet esse dolor quod suaserit, et mens.* Hor. Epist. i. 2, 60.

[2] *Melius est Herodis esse porcum quam filium.* Macrob. Saturn. *Bassianus Imp. Getam fratrem supra matris pectus*

multo undantem sanguine obtruncabat, cum quidem ille clamaret, Mater, fer opem, interficior.

[3] Lambin. in Menech. Plauti, Act 1, Scene 1. *Domi domitus fui usque cum charis meis. Filius dicitur à* φίλος.

crying out upon the instrument, seldom reflecting ; our minds being as ill set as our eyes, we turn neither of them inwards.

Ver. 19. *But when Herod was dead*] Not long after this butchery at Bethlehem he fell into a foul and loathsome disease, whereof he died : [1] so did Sylla, that bloody man before him ; [2] so did Maximinus, and others after him. John de Roma, a cruel monk and inquisitioner (who used to fill boots with boiling grease, and so putting them upon the legs of those whom he examined, to tie them backward to a form, with their legs hanging down over a small fire, &c.), was smitten by God with an incurable disease, so loathsome that none could come nigh him, so swarming with vermin and so rotten, that the flesh fell away from the bones by piece-meal, &c. Twiford (who was executioner of Frith, Bayfield, Bainham, Lambert, and other good men) died rotting aboveground, that none could abide him. (Acts and Mon.) So did Alexander the cruel keeper of Newgate, and John Peter his son-in-law, who commonly, when he would affirm anything, used to say, If it be not true, I pray God I rot ere I die. Stephen Gardner rejoicing upon the news of the bishops burnt at Oxford, was suddenly seized by the terrible hand of God as he sat at meat ; continuing for the space of fifteen days in such intolerable torment, that he could not void by ordure, or otherwise, anything that he received ; whereby his body being miserably inflamed (who had inflamed so many good martyrs before) was brought to a wretched end ; his tongue hanging out all black and swollen, as Archbishop Arundel's did before him. (Acts and Mon.) But to return to Herod ; when he saw he should die indeed, that there might not be no mourning at his funeral, he commanded the Jewish nobility (whom he had imprisoned for that purpose in the Castle of Hippodromus) to be all slain as soon as ever he was dead. (Josephus.) And being at point of death, he commanded his son Antipater to be executed in the prison, whom but a little afore he had declared heir of the kingdom. In November, 1572, appeared a new star in Cassiopeia, and continued sixteen months. Theodore Beza wittily applied it (saith Mr Camden, Elizabeth) to that star at Christ's birth, and to the infanticide there, and warned Charles IX. to beware in this verse,

Tu vero, Herodes sanguinolente, time.

The fifth month after the vanishing of this star, the said Charles, after long and grievous pains, died of exceeding bleeding. *Constans fama est illum, dum è variis corporis partibus sanguis emanaret, in lecto sæpè volutatum, inter horribilium blasphemiarum diras, tantam sanguinis vim projecisse, ut paucas post horas mortuus fuerit :* persecutors (as they say of the devil) go out with a stench. Arius (saith one) voiding out his guts, sent his soul, as a harbinger to hell, to provide

room for his body : he was brought to confusion by the prayers of Alexander, the good Bishop of Constantinople, and his death was *precationis opus, non morbi.* (Socrat.) So, likely, was Herod's.

Behold an angel] Glad of an office to serve the saints, Heb. i. 14. They rejoice more in their names of office than of honour : to be called angels, watchmen (Dan. iv. 23), &c., than principalities, powers, &c. It was long ere Joseph heard from heaven, but God's time he knew was the best. And although he leave his people, to their thinking, yet he forsakes not. No, that he doth not, saith the author to the Hebrews. οὐδ' οὐ μὴ σε ἐγκαταλίπω. Heb. xiii. 5.

Ver. 20. *For they are dead which sought the young child's life*] God hid him, as it were, " for a little moment, until the indignation was overpast," Isa. xxvi. 29. So he did Jeremy, Baruch, Athanasius, Luther in his Patmos (as he used to call the castle of Wartburg), where when the Pope had excommunicated him, and the Emperor proscribed him, the Lord put into the heart of the Duke of Saxony to hide him for ten months ; in which space the Pope died, the Emperor had his hands full of the French wars, and the Church thereby obtained a happy halcyon. At which time a pretty spectacle it was to behold Christ striving with Antichrist for mastery. For whatsoever the Pope and his champions could do to the contrary, all fell out rather, as at Philippi, unto the furtherance of the gospel, Phil. i. 12. So was it here in Queen Mary's time ; do what they could, the Christian congregations in London were sometimes forty, sometimes a hundred, sometimes two hundred. I have heard of one (saith Mr Fox) that being sent to them to take their names and to espy their doings, yet in being among them was converted, and cried them all mercy. Harpsfield hearing that the queen lay a dying, hasted home from London to burn those six that he had in his cruel custody. Those were the last that were burnt. Many others escaped by the queen's death.

Ver. 21. *And he arose, &c., and came into the land of Israel*] Glad they were got out of such a hell as Egypt (Ezek. xx. 7, 8), where the Israelites having been for a time, brought back with them a golden calf ; Jeroboam brought home two ; and these good souls could not but get and gather guilt or grief. Hence David's moans at Mesech (Psal. cxx. 5), Lot's vexation at Sodom, Jeremy's wish for a cottage in the wilderness, far enough off from those adulterers and assemblies of treacherous men, those sacrificing Sodomites (Jer. ix. 2), of whom it might be said, as Aaron of the people, that they were wholly set upon sin, Exod. xxxii. 22 ; 1 John v. 19. But some of the saints forsake all (said Marsh the martyr) and commit themselves to painful exile, that, if it please God, Christ may come again out of Egypt. (Acts and Mon.)

Ver. 22. *But when he heard that Archelaus*]

---

[1] *Lento calore torrebatur. Ipsa quoque verenda putrefacta scatebant vermiculis.* Joseph.

[2] *Sylla sævus ita ut φόνων οὔτ' ἀρίθμος οὐθ' ὅρος esset,*

Plutarch. *In rustico prædio pediculari morbo periit.* ἡ τε πρότερον εὐτυχία δοκοῦσα τοιοῦτο περιῆλθεν αὐτῷ τέλος.

Neither good egg nor good bird, as they say. *Caracalla* (saith Dio) *nihil cogitabat boni, quia id non didicerat, quod ipse fatebatur:* never thought of any good, for he had never learned it. No more had this Archelaus. Pope Paul III., when his son Farnesis had committed an unspeakable violence on the person of Cosmus Chærius, Bishop of Fanum, and then poisoned him, held himself excused that he could say, *Hæc vitia, me non commonstratore, didicit:* he never learned this of the father. But Archelaus, though he could never attain to his father's craft, yet he had learnt his cruelty. Fierce he was, but foolish; savage, but silly; a slug, a slow belly, an evil beast; wherefore the Jews soon rebelled against him; and Augustus (after ten years' abuse of his authority) banished him to Vienna, or, as others say, to Lyons in France; setting up in his stead his brother Herod, the same that derided and set at nought our Saviour at his passion, as St Jerome writeth.

Ver. 23. *And he came and dwelt in a city called Nazareth*] Hence an opinion among the people that he was born there (John vii. 42), and so could not be the Messias, as the Pharisees on that ground persuaded: "For can any good come out of Nazareth?" John i. 46. The devils also, though they confessed him "the Holy One of God" (Mark i. 24, 25), yet they cunningly call him "Jesus of Nazareth," to nourish the error of the multitude that thought he was born there, and so not the Christ. When one commended the Pope's legate at the Council of Basil, Sigismund the Emperor answered, *Tamen Romanus est.* So, let the devil speak true or false, fair or foul, yet he is a devil still, beware of him. *Satan aliquando verax, sæpius mendax, semper fallax.*

That it might be fulfilled which was spoken by the prophets] For the Book of Judges was written by sundry prophets, in several ages. And there be very grave authors of opinion that Ezra (that skilful scribe) either himself alone, or with the help of his colleagues, godly and learned men like himself, inspired by the Holy Ghost, compiled and composed those books of Joshua, Judges, Samuel, and Kings, out of divers annals preserved by the Churches of those ages wherein those things were acted.

He shall be called a Nazarene] That great votary whereof Samson and the rest of his order were but types and shadows. The very name signifieth one separate and set apart from others, as Joseph was "separate from his brethren," Gen. xlix. 26. And it is ascribed to three sorts of men, usually set above others (as divines have well observed): 1. To such as are set apart to singular sanctimony, as the high priest, whose crown is called Nezer, Exod. xxix. 6. 2. To such as in dignity and authority are set above others, as kings, whose diadem is called Nezer, 2 Sam. i. 10. 3. To such as were separated by some religious vow, as to the order of the Nazarites, whose hair increasing on their heads, as an external sign of their vow, was called

Nezer, Numb. vi. 1. As for our Saviour, it is not likely that he nourished his hair; because the apostle saith (in that age) it was uncomely for men to have long hair, 1 Cor. xi. 14. It was enough for him that he was a Nazarite in the truth and substance of that law; and a singular comfort it is to us, that although we have broken our vows and so deeply gashed our consciences, as Jacob did (Gen. xxviii. 20, xxxi. 13); yet so long as it is of infirmity and forgetfulness, not of obstinacy and maliciousness, this famous Nazarite, this arch-votary, hath expiated our defaults in this kind; and through him we are in God's sight, as Jerusalem's Nazarites (Lam. iv. 7), "Purer than the snow, and whiter than the milk." And therefore, sith God thinks not the worse of us, let us not think the worse of ourselves for the involuntary violation of our vows.

CHAPTER III.

Ver. 1. *In those days came John the Baptist*] WHOM Chrysologus fitly calleth *fibulam legis et gratiæ*, the bond or buckle of both Testaments. He standeth as that angel, with one foot on the sea (the law), and with the other foot on the land (the gospel), Rev. x. 1.

Preaching in the wilderness of Judea] A place wherein we find six cities with their villages, Josh. xv. 62, but called a wilderness, because more thinly inhabited. In which sense we may say of Germany, that Aceldama or field of blood, and many other once rich and fertile countries, that they are become a wilderness, war being a tragedy that alway destroyeth the stage whereon it is acted; but for the wickedness of them that dwell therein it is that a fruitful land is turned into a wilderness, saith David, Psal. cvii. 34. And the heathen historian, Herodotus, saith little less, when he tells us that the ruin and rubbish of Troy are set by God before the eyes of men, for an example of that rule, that great sins have great punishments. *Jam seges est ubi Troja fuit.* (Ovid.) Now *alterius perditio sit tua cautio*, saith an ancient: not to be warned by others is a sure presage of ruin. (Isidore soliloq.) Scipio beheld and bewailed the downfall of Rome in the destruction of Carthage. And when Hannibal was beleaguering Saguntum in Spain, the Romans were as sensible thereof as if he had been then beating upon the walls of their Capitol. (Livy.) A storm oft-times begins in one place and ends in another. When the sword rides circuit (as a judge) it is in commission, Ezek. xiv. 17; Jer. xlvii. 6, 7. And, "When I begin" (saith God) "I will make an end," 1 Sam. iii. 12. We cannot but foresee a storm, unless we be of those in Bernard, who seek straws to put out their eyes withal.[1] If we break not off our sins by repentance (that there may be a lengthening of our tranquillity, Dan. iv. 27), a removal of our candlestick may be as certainly foreseen and foretold as if visions and letters were sent us from

[1] *Qui festucam quærunt, unde oculos sibi eruant.*

heaven, as once to the Church of Ephesus. God may well say to us, as to them of old, "Have I been a wilderness unto Israel, a land of darkness?" Jer. ii. 31; or, as Themistocles to his Athenians, Are ye weary of receiving so many benefits by one man? *Bona à tergo formosissima.* Our sins have long since solicited an utter dissolution and desolation of all; and that we should be made a heap and a hissing, a waste and a wilderness. Jer. xxv. 9; xlix. 2. *Quod Deus avertat.*

Ver. 2. *And saying, Repent ye*] Change your minds now at the preaching of the gospel, as they changed their garments at the promulgation of the law.[1] "Rend your hearts, and not your garments," plough up the fallows of your hearts; grieve for your sins, even to a transmentation, as those Corinthians did, and as Simon Peter counselled Simon Magus, that snake that had cast his coat but kept his poison; for although he carried the matter so cleanly and cunningly, that Philip took him for a true convert and baptized him, yet Peter soon saw that he was "in the gall" or venom "of bitterness" (for the word used, Deut. xxix. 18, whereunto the apostle alludes, signifieth both), and therefore prescribes him an antidote, the very same that John doth here to this generation of vipers, "Repent, if perhaps the thoughts of thy heart may be forgiven thee," Acts viii. 22, 23. His wicked thought is called ἐπίνοια: the godly change of mind that the apostle persuadeth him unto is called μετάνοια, he that by some mischance hath drunk poison (ראש, χολή), must cast it up again as soon as he can, ere it get to the vitals. Repentance is the soul's vomit, which is the hardest kind of physic, but the wholesomest. Happy is he that by the dung-port (Neh. iii. 14) of his mouth (in a sorrowful confession) can disburthen himself of the sin that both clogs and hazards his soul to death eternal. We ran from God by sin to death, and have no other way to return but by death to sin, Heb. xii. 1.

For the kingdom of heaven is at hand] q. d. Ye have a price put into your hands, a fair opportunity of making yourselves for ever. Will ye (like the vine and olive in Jotham's parable, Judg. ix. 9) not leave your sweetness and fatness, your *dilecta delicta*, beloved sins, although it be to reign, yea, and that in God's kingdom? Knowest thou not, that the goodness of God should lead thee to repentance? Rom. ii. 4; Psal. cxxx. 4. Is there not mercy with God therefore that he may be feared? Should not men rend their hearts, because God is gracious, and turn to the Lord, because he will "multiply pardon"? Joel ii. 12; Isa. lv. 7. To argue from mercy to liberty is the devil's logic, and makes God repent him of his favours to such, as David did of his kindness to Nabal. Rather we should argue from mercy to duty, as Joseph did to his master in a temptation; from deliverance to obedience, with David, Psal. cxvi. 8, 9. And therefore return to our

father's house, with the prodigal, because there is bread enough; therefore repent, because his kingdom is at hand, and would be laid hold on. As John Baptist was Christ's forerunner into the world, so must repentance be his forerunner into our hearts.

Ver. 3. *For this is he which was spoken of*] Whether these be the words of the Baptist or the Evangelist, it appears not, skills not: the most say, of the Evangelist concerning the Baptist.

By the prophet Esaias] Thus one Testament infolds another, as those wheels in Ezekiel; and the law preacheth faith in Christ, as well as the gospel, Rom. x. 6, 7.

The voice of one crying] Loudly and lustily; lifting up his voice as a trumpet (βοῶντος, *boantis, vociferantis*), or as the sound of many waters. Semblably St Paul was ordained to be a crier, 1 Tim. i. 11 (κήρυξ), and so is every faithful preacher, 2 Tim. iv. 2. He must cry, and be instant, stand to the work, and stand over it (ἐπιστηθι). *Sta cum diligentia*, saith the Syriac there, *clangite, clamate*, Isa. lviii. 1; Jer. iv. 5. Ye have to do with deaf men, dead men, living carcases, walking sepulchres of themselves. *Clames etiam ut Stentora vincas.* Now, therefore, as our Saviour lifted up his voice when he said, "Lazarus, come forth," so must Christ's ministers (when they speak to such as lie rotting and stinking in the graves of their corruptions) cry aloud, "Awake, thou that sleepest, and stand up from the dead, that Christ may give thee light," Eph. v. 14. Ecclesia (the Church) is a word in use among the Athenians, and signifies an assembly of citizens, called out of the multitude (as it were) by name, or in their ranks, by the voice of the public crier (ἐκκαλεῖν), to hear some speech or sentence of the senate. The Church, in like sort, is a company called out of the kingdom of Satan by the voice of God's ministers, as it were criers, to hear the doctrine of the gospel revealed from heaven. There are that observe,[2] that John Baptist entered upon his calling in the year of Jubilee, which used to be proclaimed by a crier with the sound of a trumpet, and that in allusion thereunto he is called, "The voice of a crier."

Prepare ye the way of the Lord] Suffer the terrors of the Lord to seize upon your souls: take not up bucklers against the strokes of God's law, bring not your buckets to quench the motions of his Spirit, knocking at your hearts by the hammer of his word; make much of the least beginnings of grace, even those they call repressing, since they prepare the heart for conversion. "Open the everlasting doors, that the King of glory may come in," that "Christ may dwell in your hearts by faith." As Esther leaned upon her two maids when she came before the king, so let the soul lean upon the attrition of the law and contrition of the gospel; so shall the King of glory stretch out the golden sceptre of his grace, and we shall live. As John Baptist was Christ's fore-runner into the world, so must repentance be

[1] *Ad mentem redite.* Erasmus. As the prodigal came to himself, who, till converted, had been beside himself. See

a like phrase, 2 Chron. vi. 37.   [2] Rolloc. in John i. 15.

his fore-runner into our hearts; for he that repenteth not, the kingdom of God is far from him : he cannot see it for his lusts that hang in his light.

Make his paths straight] (ἑτοιμάσατε. Heb. פנו, Isa. xl. 3. *Viam apertam et oculis intuentium conspicuam facite. Obstant enim affectus mundani, &c.* Erasmus.) Walk exactly, precisely, accurately, by line and by rule (Eph. v. 15) ; walk as in a frame, make straight steps to your feet, or else there is no passing the strait gate; so strait, that as few can walk in it, so none can halt in it, but must needs go upright. Plain things will join in every point one with another; not so, round and rugged things. In like sort, plain spirits close with God's truths, not those that are swollen, &c. The old heart will never hold out the hardship of holiness.

Ver. 14. *And the same John had his raiment of camel's hair*] Suitable to Elias (in whose spirit and power he came), who was thus habited. So those worthies, of whom the world was not worthy, wandered about in sheep-skins and goat-skins (Heb. xi. 37) ; but they were like the ark, without, covered with goat's hair; within, all of pure gold. God clothed our first parents in leather, when there was means of better clothing, to humble them, doubtless, and to shame all such as are proud of their clothes, which are the ensigns of our shame, and came in with sin as its cognizance. *Sæpe sub attrita latitat sapientia veste. Vestes sunt peccati testes. Vestium curiositas deformitatis mentium et morum indicium est.* Bernard.

And a leathern girdle about his loins] So had Elias, and God takes notice of it, and records it, when the pomp and pride of many monarchs lie hid in obscurity, buried in oblivion. Such love beareth the Lord to his people, that everything in them is remarked and registered. He thinks the better of the very ground they go upon, Psal. lxxxvii. 2—6; their walls are ever in his sight, and he loveth to look upon the houses where they dwell, Isa. xlix. 16.

And his meat was locusts] These creatures have their name in Greek from the top of the ears of corn (ἀκρίδες) which, as they fled, they fed upon. That they were man's meat in those eastern countries appears Lev. xi. 22, and Pliny testifieth as much (lib. xi. cap. 29). Coarse meat they were, but nature is content with little, grace with less. *Cibus et potus sunt divitiæ Christianorum*, saith Jerome.[1] Bread and water with the gospel are good cheer, saith another. Our Saviour hath taught us to pray for bread, not for manchet or junkets, but downright household bread ; and himself gave thanks for barley-bread and broiled fishes. A little of the creature will serve turn to carry thee through thy pilgrimage. One told a philosopher, If you will be content to please Dionysius, you need not feed upon green herbs. He replied, And if you can feed upon green herbs, you need not please Dionysius; you

need not flatter, comply, be base, &c.[2] The ancients held green herbs to be good cheer, and accounted it wealth enough, μὴ διψᾶν καὶ μὴ ῥιγᾶν, not to be thirsty, nor cold, saith Galen. But what miscreants were those Jews, that for ἀκρίδες, locusts, read ἐγκρίδες, sweetmeats, as Epiphanius noteth against the Ebionites. The best, we see, are liable to be belied.

And wild honey] Such as naturally distilled out of trees : as did that which Jonathan tasted with the tip of his rod, called honey of the wood, 1 Sam. xiv. 27. God made Jeshurun suck honey out of the rock, and oil out of the flinty rock, Deut. xxxii. 13. Hence Judea was called *Sumen totius Orbis.* (Heidfeldius.) And Strabo, that spitefully affirmeth it to be a dry, barren country, had not so much ingenuity as that railing Rabshakeh, 2 Kings xviii. 32.

Ver. 5. *Then went out to him Jerusalem*] Hitherto the prosopography of the Baptist: follows now the resort that was made unto him ; for by his divine doctrine and austere life he had merited among many to be taken for the Messiah, John i. 20.

And all Judea] That is, very many, as the word " all " is many times elsewhere taken in the New Testament.

And all the region round about Jordan] Stirred up by the noise of that new preacher. So sundry amongst us will be content to hear, if there go a great report of the man; or if he deliver some new doctrine, or deal in deep points, as Herod, Luke xxiii. 8. But these grow weary and fall off as those Jews did from John, for the which they were justly taxed by our Saviour, John v. 35; Matt. xi. 7.

Ver. 6. *And were baptized of him in Jordan*] Baptizing of proselytes was in use among the Jews before the days of John Baptist. From this custom (saith Broughton, in Daniel ix.), though without commandment and of small authority, Christ authorizeth a seal of entering into his rest, using the Jews' weakness as an allurement thither. As from bread and wine, used with the paschal lamb, being without all commandment of Moses, but resting upon the common reason given by the Creator, he authorized a seal of his flesh and blood.

In Jordan] At Bethabara, John i. 28, that is, at that very place where the people of Israel passed over Jordan and possessed the land. Baptism then was there first administered, where it had been of old foreshadowed. Here also we see that the acts of Joshua and Jesus took their happy beginning at one and the same place. And like as the people, after they had passed over Jordan, were circumcised before they received the land by lot of inheritance : so after we have been baptized, and thereby enrolled among the citizens of the New Jerusalem, the remnants of sin and superfluity of naughtiness must be daily pared off by the practice of

---

[1]   *Liba recuso,*
Pane egeo, jam mellitis potiore placentis.
                    Hor. Epist. i. 10, 11.

[2] *Adulator est qui ollam sectatus.* Becman. *Holus ab ὅλον. Prisci nihil obsonii sibi de esse existimabant, modo ne deesset holus.*

mortification, ere we can come to the kingdom of heaven, James i. 21; ἡ περισσεία τῆς κακίας. In allusion to the garbage and excrements of the sacrificed beast.

Confessing their sins] In token of their true repentance. For as only the man that is wakened out of his dream can tell his dreams; so only he that is wakened out of his sins can clearly confess them.[1] And this confession of sin, joined with confusion of sin (without the which, confession is but wind, and the drops of contrition, water), is that which in baptism we restipulate. "Not the putting away of the filth of the flesh, but the confident answer of a good conscience toward God," 1 Pet. iii. 21:[2] a clearing, cheering conscience, a heart washed from wickedness in this laver of regeneration, the baptism of repentance, the washing of the new birth, the being baptized with the Holy Ghost and with fire, this saveth, saith St Peter. Not as the efficient cause of salvation, for that is Christ alone: nor yet as a necessary instrument, for that is faith alone: but only as a badge of the saved, and a pledge of their salvation; as, on the other side, God will not own a viperous brood, though baptized, that bring not forth fruits meet for repentance. To such, baptism is not the mark of God's child, but the brand of a fool that maketh a vow and then breaketh it, Eccles. v. 4. For the font is Beersheba, the well of an oath; and there we swear (as David did) "to keep God's righteous judgments," Psal. cxix. 106; Isa. x. Now, if Zedekiah and Shimei paid so dear for their perjury, for their fast and loose with men, how will God revenge the quarrel of his covenant? The Spanish converts in Mexico remember not anything of the promise and profession they made in baptism, save only their name, which many times also they forget. In the kingdom of Congo in Africa, the Portuguese, at their first arrival, finding the people to be heathens, without God, did induce them to a profession of Christ, and to be baptized in great abundance, allowing of the principles of religion; till such time as the priests pressed them to lead their lives according to their profession; which the most part of them in no case enduring, returned again to their Gentilism. Such renegadoes we have amongst us not a few, that give themselves up to Christ, *Quoad Sacramenti perceptionem*, by external profession (Augustine); but when it comes once *ad vitæ sanctificationem*, to holiness of life, there they leave him in the open field, forsaking their colours, renouncing their baptism, and running away to the enemy. Now for such there is but one law, and it is martial law, Heb. x. 39: If any withdraw (ὑποστείληται) or steal from his captain (as the military term there used importeth) he doth it to perdition,—he is even a son of perdition, as Judas; who was circumcised indeed, as well as Peter, but better he had not. As it had been better for him never to have been

born, Mark xiv. 21, so, being born, never to have been circumcised, and thereby bound to the law. Unregenerate Israel is as Ethiopia, Amos ix. 7. And it had been happy that font-water had never been spilt on that face that is afterwards hatched with impudent impiety, Jer. iii. 3—5.

Ver. 7. *But when he saw many of the Pharisees and Sadducees*] Two leading sects among the Jews, but notable hypocrites, yet pressing to the ordinances. (Joseph. B. J.; Ant. Jud. xiii. 17.) A Doeg may set his foot as far within the sanctuary as a David, and let him. He may be caught, as those catch-poles sent to apprehend our Saviour, as Saul's messengers coming to Naioth were turned from executioners to prophets. "Come" (saith Latimer) "to the holy assemblies, though thou comest to sleep; for God, perhaps, may take thee napping."

He said unto them, O generation of vipers] Or adders, which are outwardly specious, inwardly poisonous: so are all hypocrites a mere outside, but God will wash off their paint with rivers of brimstone. Of the viper it is said, that when he hath stung a man he makes haste to the water, and drinks or dies for it. So did these Pharisees to baptism, hoping by the work done to avoid the wrath to come. But a man may go to hell with font-water on his face, unless with the water of baptism he have grace to quench the fiery darts of the devil: as that holy virgin, whereof Luther reports, that she beat back Satan's temptations with this only argument, I am a Christian.[3] The enemy quickly understood (saith he) the virtue of baptism, and the value of that vow, and fled from her. There are that boast and bear themselves bold on their Christendom; but hath not many a ship, that hath been named Safeguard and Goodspeed, miscarried at sea, or fallen into the hands of pirates. This generation of vipers conceited themselves to be Abraham's seed: so do many of the serpent's seed now-a-days, because of their baptism; but all in vain, unless they walk in the steps of that faith of our father Abraham, Rom. iv. 12. The old serpent hath stung them, neither is there any antidote for such but the flesh (not of the biting viper, but) of the slain Messiah, foreshadowed by the brazen serpent. See Isa. xxvii. 1. God hath promised to break for us the serpent's head, who hath so deeply set his limbs in us, yea, with his sore and great and strong sword, to punish Leviathan, that piercing serpent, and to slay the dragon that is in the sea.

Who hath forewarned you] Who hath privily and under-hand, as it were, showed you (ὑπέδειξεν, *clanculum indicavit et admonuit*), and set you in a course of avoiding the danger that hangs over your heads, as by a twined thread? The wrath of God is revealed from heaven, and hell hath enlarged herself, and even gapes for you: who

---

[1] ἐξομολογεῖσθαι. *Est aperta et clara voce confiteri.*

[2] ἐπερώτημα.

[3] *Legitur de quadam sancta virgine quæ quoties tenta-* *batur, non nisi baptismo suo repugnabat, dicens brevissime, Christiana sum. Intellexit enim hostis statim virtutem baptismi et fidei, et fugit ab ea.*

gave an inkling thereof, and sent you hither for help? &c.

From the wrath to come] Called the damnation of hell, chap. xxiii. 33, which hath torments without end and past imagination. For, "who knoweth the power of thine anger?" saith David. "Even according to thy fear, so is thy wrath," Psal. xc. 1; that is, as I conceive it, let a man fear thy wrath never so much, he is sure to feel a fair deal more thereof than ever he could have feared. When but a drop of God's displeasure lights upon a poor soul in this present world, what intolerable pain is it put to! "The spirit of a man may sustain his infirmity," saith Solomon, Prov. xviii. 14, *q. d.* some sorry shift a man may make to rub through an outward affliction, and to bear it off by head and shoulders, "but a wounded spirit who can bear?" *q. d.* the stoutest cannot possibly stand under it: there is no proportion between the back and the burden; it is able to crush and crack the mightiest amongst us. Judas chose a halter rather than to endure it: and well he might, when as Job (with whom God was but in jest, in comparison) preferred strangling and any death before such a life, Job vii. 15. But all this, alas, is but present wrath, and nothing at all to the "wrath to come," a phrase of speech that involves and carries in it stings and horrors, woe, and, alas, flames of wrath and the worm that never dieth, trembling and gnashing of teeth, seas of vengeance, rivers of brimstone, unutterable and insufferable tortures and torments. We read of racking, roasting, hanging, stoning, putting men under harrows of iron and saws of iron, scratching off their flesh with thorns of the wilderness, pulling their skins over their ears, and other exquisite and unheard-of miseries that men have here been put unto (ἐτυμπανίσθησαν, Heb. xi. 35);—but what is all this to the wrath to come? not so much as a flea-biting, as a prick with a pin, or fillip with a finger; no, though a man should go through a thousand cruel deaths every hour his whole life throughout. Oh, bless and kiss that blessed Son of God that bore for us the brunt of this insupportable wrath, even "Jesus that delivered us from the wrath to come," 1 Thess. i. 10; and shun sin, that draws hell at the heels of it. Is it nothing to lose an immortal soul, to purchase an ever-living death?

Ver. 8. *Bring forth therefore fruits*] *q. d.* You cannot wash your hands in innocency, wash them therefore in tears: there is no way to quench hell-flames but by the tears of true repentance; to prevent the wrath to come, but by bearing those fruits of righteousness that are by Christ Jesus to the glory and praise of God, Phil. i. 11. *Optima et aptissima pœnitentia est nova vita*, saith Luther; which saying, though condemned by Pope Leo, is certainly an excellent saying.

Meet for repentance] That weigh just as much as repentance, that may parallel and prove it to be right, evince and evidence it to be a "repentance never to be repented of," 2 Cor. vii. 10. There is no grace but hath a counterfeit. See

therefore that your graces be of the right stamp, an effectual faith, laborious love, patient hope, &c., as the apostle hath it. See that your performances and whole course be such as becomes repentance, and may justify it; as may bear weight in the balance of the sanctuary, and amount to as much as repentance comes to, 1 Thess. i. 3 (ἄξιον παρὰ τοῦ ἄγειν). And albeit your righteousnesses be but as a menstruous clout, and your works at best (if tried by the fire of the word, Isa. lxiv. 6; 1 Cor. iii. 13) would burn (which made good Nehemiah, xiii. 12, to pray for pardon of his reformations), yet upon your true repentance for the evil that cleaves to your best works, your souls may be saved from the wrath to come; yea, they are such "as accompany salvation," and comprehend it, as the Greek Scholiast expounds that text, Heb. vi. 9 (ἐχόμενα, i. e. κατεχόμενα σωτηρίας). Labour, therefore, to have a "heart full of goodness," as those Romans, xv. 14, and a life "full of good works," as Tabitha, Acts ix. 36, such as may beseem amendment of life.

Ver. 9. *And think not to say within yourselves*] Hypocrites are never without their starting-holes, out of which they must be ferreted. There are infinite turnings and windings in the heart of man, studious of deceiving itself by some paralogism (παραλογιζόμενοι ἑαυτούς, James i. 22). Therefore the apostle so oft premiseth, "Be not deceived," when he reckons up reprobates, 1 Cor. vi. 9; Eph. v. 6, &c.

We have Abraham to our father] What of that? so had Ishmael, an outcast,—Esau, a castaway, &c. External privileges profit not where nothing better can be pleaded. Nabal, the fool, was of the line of faithful Caleb, *Qui implevit post me*, "followed me fully," saith God, Numb. xiv. 24. Virtue is not, as lands, inheritable. Why should these men brag they had Abraham to their father, when they might have observed that God had raised up of this stone a son to Caleb?

God is able] His power is, 1. Absolute, whereby he can do more than he doth. 2. Actual, whereby he doth that only that he willeth. Some things he can do, but will not, as here, and Matt. xxvi. 53; Rom. ix. 18. Some things he neither will nor can, as to lie, to die, to deny himself, 2 Tim. ii. 13; Tit. i. 2; Heb. vi. 18, for these things contradict his essence, and imply impotency. But whatsoever he willeth, without impediment he effecteth, Isa. xlvi. 10; Psal. cxv. 3.

Of these stones to raise up children to Abraham] This he could do, though he will not. And yet he doth as much as this, when he takes the stone out of the heart; when of carnal he makes us a people created again, Psal. cii. 18; when out of a hollow person (one as empty and void of heart as the hollow of a tree is of substance) is fetched out a heart of oak, and of a wild asscolt born, is made a man: see both these similitudes, Job xi. 12. It was a strange change that Satan mentioned and motioned to our Saviour of turning stones into bread. But nothing so strange as turning stony hearts into hearts of flesh. This is a work of God's almighty power, the same that he put forth in raising Christ from the dead, Eph. i. 19 (where the apostle, the better to set forth the matter, useth a six-fold gradation in the original), and in creating the world, Psal. li. 10; 2 Cor. v. 17. The prophet Isaiah tells us, " that he plants the heavens, and lays the foundation of the earth, that he may say to Zion, Thou art my people," Isa. li. 16. And although man's heart be an emptiness, as in the creation, as herbs in winter, or as a breathless clod of earth, yet that hinders not, saith the prophet.

Ver. 10. *And now also is the axe laid to the root of the tree*] q. d. God is now taking aim where to hit, and how to fell you, as a man layeth his axe at that very place that he intends to smite at : he seeth well enough that all his patience and pains in digging, in dunging, and in dressing you, is to no purpose. He comes "seeking fruit from time to time, but findeth none," Luke xiii. 7. Now therefore he hath laid down his basket, and taken up his axe, as resolved to ruin you, unless present course be taken. Neglect not the present "now," lest ye be cut off for ever.[1] God will not alway serve you for a sinning stock. Since ye have a preacher, repent or perish. Let this spring distinguish between dead and living trees.

Every tree that bringeth not forth good fruit] So God is graciously pleased to style our poor performances; in every of which there is something of his, as well as something of our own. (Jerome.) That which is his he accepts, that which is ours he pardons. But good it must be, *quoad fontem*, the Spirit of God : and *quoad finem*, the glory of God. Negative goodness serves no man's turn to save him from the axe. It is said of Ithacius, that the hatred of the Priscillian heresy was all the virtue that he had. (Hooker *ex Sulpitio*.) The evil servant did not riot out his talent; those reprobates (Matt. xxv.) robbed not the saints, but relieved them not. Moab and Ammon were bastardized and banished the sanctuary to the tenth generation, for a mere omission, because they met not God's Israel with bread and water in the wilderness (Deut. xxiii. 4); and Edom is forethreatened for not harbouring them when scattered by the Chaldeans. (Obadiah.) Take we heed that live in the last age of the world, lest God hasten the calling of the Jews, and cast us off for our unfruitfulness, Rom. xi.

Ver. 11. *I indeed baptize you with water to repentance*] There is a twofold baptism, Heb. vi. 2, the doctrine of baptisms (βαπτισμῶν), viz. *Fluminis et flaminis*, external and internal, the putting away of the pollution of the flesh, and the answer of a good conscience (purged from dead works) to God-ward. When these two meet, when men are baptized with water to repentance,

then baptism saveth (σώζει), 1 Pet. iii. 21 ; that is, it effectually assureth salvation, whensoever by the Spirit and faith the baptized comes to be united to Christ, and to feel the love of God shed abroad in his soul, whereby is wrought in him a spirit of repentance, a grief for sin, as it is an offence against God. And hereupon St Peter saith, " Baptism saveth," in the present tense, implying that it is of permanent and perpetual use; effectual to save and seal up the promises, whensoever we repent. From which happy time, baptism once received, remains a fountain always open for sin and for uncleanness, to those that mourn over him that bled over them; a laver of regeneration, a washing of the spirit, who poureth clean water upon them, ridding and rinsing them from all their sins, past, present, and future, Zech. xii. 10, xiii. 1; Ezek. xxxvi. 25. Provided that they stand to the covenant and order of baptism, in a continual renovation of faith and repentance, as occasion shall be offered. This doctrine of baptisms (now cleared by divines) divers of the ancient doctors understood not, which disheartened Piscator from spending much time upon them.[2]

He that cometh after me] Whose harbinger and herald I am, whose *prodromus* and *paranymph*, friend and forerunner I am, as the morning star foreruns the sun, with whose light it shineth.

Is mightier than I] And will easily outshine me : " he must increase, but I must decrease ;" and this is the complement of my joy, John iii. 29, 30. To rejoice in the good parts of others, though it eclipseth thy light, and that from the heart, this is indeed to be able to do more than others ; this is to excel others in any excellency whatsoever, if this be wanting.

Whose shoes I am not worthy to bear] Christ thought John worthy to lay his hand on his holy head in baptism, who thinks not himself worthy to lay his hand under Christ's feet. The more fit any man is for whatsoever vocation, the less he thinks himself. " Who am I ?" said Moses, when he was to be sent to Egypt ; whereas none in all the world was comparably fit for that embassage. Not only in innumerable other things am I utterly unskilful, saith St Augustine, but even in the Holy Scriptures themselves (my proper profession), the greatest part of my knowledge is the least part of mine ignorance.[3] I, in my little cell, saith Jerome, with the rest of the monks my fellow-sinners, dare not determine of great matters.[4] This is all I know, that I know nothing, said Socrates ; and Anaxarchus went further, and said, that he knew not that neither, that it was nothing that he knew.[5] This is the utmost of my wisdom, said David Chytræus, that I see myself to be without all wisdom. And if I would at any time delight myself in a fool, saith

[1] *Ultimæ desperationis indicium est, quoties securis admovetur radici.* Erasmus, Annot.
[2] *A patrum lectione, postquam nonnullos evolvisset D. Piscator, sibi temperavit : aususque fuit dicere, Vix ullum patrum usum et efficaciam baptismi recte intellexisse.*
[3] *Non solum in aliis innumerabilibus rebus multa me latent, &c.* Epist. 119.

[4] *Ego in parvo tuguriolo, cum monachis, i. e. cum compeccatoribus meis, de magnis statuere non audeo.* Epist. ad August. cxii. 5.
[5] *Anaxarchus prædicabat se ne id quidem nescire, quod nihil sciret.* Tusc. 3.

Seneca, I need not seek far: I have myself to turn to.[1] Thus the heaviest ears of corn stoop most toward the ground; boughs, the more laden they are, the more low they hang: and the more direct the sun is over us, the less is our shadow. So the more true worth is in any man, the less self-conceitedness; and the lower a man is in his own eyes, the higher he is in God's. Surely John Baptist lost nothing by his humility and modesty here, for our Saviour extols him to the multitude, Matt. xi.; and there are that doubt not to affirm (where they have it I know not) that for his humility on earth he is dignified with that place in heaven from whence Lucifer fell. Sure it is, that "he that humbleth himself shall be exalted." If men reckon us as we set ourselves (*Tanti eris aliis, quanti tibi fueris*), God values us according to our abasements. The Church was black in her own eyes, fair in Christ's, Cant. i. 5—15.

With the Holy Ghost, and with fire] That is, with that fiery Holy Ghost, ἐν διὰ δυοῖν, that spirit of judgment and of burning, wherewith the "filth of the daughters of Zion is washed away," Isa. iv. 4; that they may escape that unquenchable fire mentioned in the verse next following. This fire of the spirit must be fetched from heaven, *Lumen de lumine*, from the Father of lights who giveth his Spirit to them that ask it; *Hinc baptismus dicitur* φωτισμὸς. It must be a coal from his altar, which when you have once gotten, your heart must be the hearth to uphold it; your hands, the tongs to build it; God's ordinances, the fuel to feed it; the priest's lips, the bellows to blow it up into a flame: so shall we find it (according to the nature of fire): 1. To enlighten us, as the least spark of fire lightens itself at least, and may be seen in the greatest darkness. 2. To enliven and revive us; for "whatsoever is of the Spirit is spirit," John iii. 6, that is, nimble and active, full of life and motion. A bladder is a dull lumpish thing, so is a bullet: but put wind into the one, and fire to the other in a gun, and they will flee far. Fire is the most active of all other elements, as having much form, little matter; and therefore the Latins call a dull dronish man a fireless man, which God cannot away with.[2] "What thou doest, do quickly," said our Saviour to Judas; so odious to him is dullness in any business. Baruch, full of the spirit, repaired the wall of Jerusalem earnestly, Nehem. iii. 20. *Se accendit*, he burst out into heat, and so finished his part in shorter time. "I press toward the mark," saith Paul, διώκω, I persecute it, Phil. iii. 14. Never was he so mad in persecuting the saints, Acts xxvi. 11, as after his conversion he was judged to be the other way, 2 Cor. v. 13; as Lucan says of Cæsar:—

In omnia præceps,
Nil actum credens, dum quid superesset agendum.

3. To assimilate: as fire turns fuel into the same property with itself; so doth the Spirit inform the mind, conform the will, reform the life, transform the whole man more and more into the likeness of the heavenly Pattern; it spiritualizeth and transubstantializeth us, as it were, into the same image from glory to glory (2 Cor. iii. 18), as the sun (that fire of the world) by often beating with its beams upon the pearl makes it radiant and orient, bright and beautiful like itself. 4. To elevate and carry the heart heavenward, as fire naturally aspireth, Job v. 7; and the spark fleeth upwards, to kindle our sacrifices, and make us heavenly-minded; to break out at length, though for a while it lie under the weight of sin, that doth so easily beset us, Heb. xii. 1; as fire may lie puffing and blowing under green wood, as almost smothered.[3] 5. To purify us (as fire doth metals) from "our dross, and to take away all our tin," Isa. i. 25; 1 Cor. ix. 11. For he is "like a refiner's fire, and like fuller's soap," Mal. iii. 2, whereby we are purified by "obeying the truth, unto unfeigned love of the brethren," 1 Pet. i. 22. 6. And that is the last property of the Holy Ghost and of fire (that I now insist upon), *Congregat homogenea, segregat heterogenea*: it unites them to saints, and separates them from sinners, for "what communion hath light with darkness?" 2 Cor. vi. 14. It maketh division from those of a man's house, if not of his heart; and yet causeth union with Gentile, Barbarian, Scythian, if truly Christian, Col. iii. 2. Oh, get this fire from heaven: so shall you glorify God (Matt. v. 16), and be able to dwell with devouring fire (which hypocrites cannot do, Isa. xxxiii. 14), get warmth of life and comfort to yourselves, give light and heat to others, walk surely, as Israel did by the conduct of the pillar of fire, and safely, as walled with a defence of fire, Zech. ii. 5. And if any man shall hurt such "fire shall proceed out of their mouths to devour them," Rev. xi. 5. So that a man had better anger all the witches in the world than one of those that are "baptized with the Holy Ghost and with fire," &c., especially if they be much mortified Christians, such as in whom this fiery spirit hath done with the body of sin, as the king of Moab did with the king of Edom (Amos ii. 1), burnt his bones into lime.

Ver. 12. *Whose fan is in his hand*] Though the devil and wicked men mightily strive to wring it out of his hand; for what, say they, need this shedding and this shoaling? this distinguishing and differencing of men into saints and sinners? Are not all the Lord's people holy? Numb. xvi. 3. Is there any man lives and sinneth not? but yet there is as wide a difference between sinner and sinner as is betwixt the bosom of Abraham and the belly of hell, Luke xvi. 26. 1. The godly man projects not sin as the wicked doth; but is preoccupied by it, against his general purpose, προληφθῆ, Gal. vi. 1. 2. He arts not the sin that he acts: he sins not sinningly; οὐ ποιεῖ

---

[1] *Si quando fatuo delectari volo non longe mihi quærendum est, me video.* Seneca. *Quod si ex parte aliquid didicerim, tamen in comparatione latitudinis intellectus, profecto nihil me intellexisse intelligo.* Baldus.

[2] *Segnis quasi scignis, id est, frigidus, ignavus. Tardis mentibus virtus non facile committitus.* Cic.

[3] The least spark of fire will endeavour to rise above the air: so the Spirit.

ἁμαρτίαν, 1 John iii. 9. He is not transformed into sin's image, as the wicked are, Mic. i. 5. His scum rests not in him; he works that out by repentance that he committed with reluctance, Ezek. xxiv. 11. 3. He is the better for it afterwards. His very sin (when bewailed and disclaimed) maketh him more heedful of his ways, more thankful for a Saviour, more merciful to others, more desireful after the state of perfection, &c. Whence grew that paradox of Mr John Fox, "That his graces did him most hurt, and his sins most good."[1] Whereas wicked men grow worse and worse, deceiving and being deceived, till at length by long trading in sin, being hardened by the deceitfulness thereof, they are utterly deprived of all (even passive) power of recovering themselves out of the devil's snare, 2 Tim. ii. 23; iii. 13; Heb. iii. 13; which is a conformity to the devil's condition. This their covering therefore is too short. Christ's fan is in his hand to take out the precious from the vile, Jer. xv. 19; and the ministers of Christ must separate (as the priests of old did) the clean from the unclean, drive the chaff one way and the wheat another: "for what is the chaff to the wheat, saith the Lord?" Jer. xxiii. 28. See this enjoined them, Isa. iii. 10, 11. Zwinglius, as in his public lectures he would very sharply rebuke sin, so ever and anon he would come in with this proviso, *Probe vir, hæc nihil ad te*: this is nothing to thee, thou godly man. (Scultet. Annal.) He knew that he could not beat the dogs, but the children would be ready to cry, whom therefore he comforted.

And he will throughly purge his floor] That is, his Church, called God's threshing-floor, Isa. xxi. 10, because usually threshed by God with the flail of affliction. That is one way whereby the Lord Christ doth purge his people, and separate between the son that he loves and the sin that he hates. This he doth also by his word and Spirit: "sanctifying them by his truth, his word is truth," John xvii. 17. "And such were some of you, but ye are washed, but ye are justified, but ye are sanctified in the name of our Lord Jesus Christ, and by the Spirit of our God," 1 Cor. vi. 11. Thus Christ purgeth his floor, here inchoatively and in part, hereafter thoroughly and in all perfection. In all which we may observe (saith a divine) this difference between Christ and the tempter. Christ hath his fan in his hand, and he fanneth us; the devil hath a sieve in his hand, and he sifteth us.[2] Now a fan casteth out the worst and keepeth in the best: a sieve keepeth in the worst, and casteth out the best. Right so Christ (and his trials) purgeth chaff and corruption out of us, and nourisheth and increaseth his graces in us. Contrariwise, the devil, what evil soever is in us, he confirmeth it; what faith or other good thing soever, he weakeneth it. But Christ hath prayed for his (though never so hard laid at) that their faith fail not, and giveth them in time of fanning, to fall low at his feet, as wheat, when the wicked, as

light chaff, are ready to fly in his face, as murmuring at their hard measure, with those miscreants in the wilderness.

And gather his wheat into the garner] *Mali in area nobiscum esse possunt, in horreo non possunt.* (Augustine.) The wicked may be with us in the floor, they shall not in the garner: for there shall in no wise enter into the City of the Lamb anything that defileth, or that worketh abomination, Rev. xxi. 27, βδέλυγμα. Heaven spewed out the angels in the first act of their apostasy; and albeit the devil could screw himself into paradise, yet no unclean person shall ever enter into the kingdom of heaven. Without shall be dogs and evil-doers, Rev. xxi. 8; no dirty dog doth trample on that golden pavement, no dross is with that gold, no chaff with that wheat; but the spirits of "just men made perfect," amidst a panegyris of angels, and that glorious amphitheatre, Heb. xii. 22. In the mean while, *Dei frumentum ego sum* (may every good soul say, with Ignatius), I am God's wheat: and although the wheat be as yet but in the ear, or but in the blade, yet when the fruit is ripe, he will put in the sickle (because the harvest is come), and gather his wheat into his barn, into his garner. It doth the husbandman good at heart to see his corn come forward, though the harvest be not yet, Mark iv. 28, 29. *Spes alit agricolas, sed adhuc mea messis in herba est.*

But will burn up the chaff with unquenchable fire] In reference to the custom of those countries, which was to cast their chaff into the fire. But this, alas, is another manner of fire than that. A metaphorical fire doubtless, and differs from material fire: 1. In respect of the violence, for it is unspeakable. 2. Of the durance, for it is unquenchable. 3. Of illumination, for though it burn violently to their vexation, yet it shines not to their comfort. 4. Of operation, for it consumes not what it burneth; they ever fry, but never die; *vivere nolunt, mori nesciunt;* they "seek death, but find it not," as those Rev. ix. 6. A just hand of God upon them; that they that once might have had life and would not, now would have death, and cannot.

Ver. 13. *Then cometh Jesus from Galilee*] Our Saviour came far to seek his baptism. Let not us think much of any pains taken, that we may partake of the ordinances. The Shunammite went (ordinarily) every sabbath and new-moon, on horseback, to hear the prophet, 2 Kings iv. 23. The good people in David's time "passed through the valley of Baca," Psal. lxxxiv. 6, from strength to strength, to see the face of God in Sion, though but in that dark glass of the ceremonies. And in Daniel's time they ran to and fro "to increase knowledge," Dan. xii. 4. In Zechariah's days the inhabitants of one city went to another, saying, "Let us go speedily to pray before the Lord, and to seek the Lord of hosts: I will go also," Zech. viii. 21. Our Saviour took it ill that men came not as far to hear him as the queen of Sheba did to hear

[1] παράδοξον ἀλλ' οὐ παράλογον. Capell on Temptations.
[2] Luke xxii. 31. σινιάσαι, Concussionem notat vehe-

mentissimam, quæ manibus et genibus fit, nunc in altum efferendo, nunc ab uno latere ad alterum agitando.

Solomon, Matt. xii. 42. The eunuch came as far to worship in the temple, Acts viii. 25. And of our fore-fathers in King Henry VIII.'s time Mr Foxe saith thus : " To see their travels, earnest seeking, burning zeal, readings, watchings, sweet assemblies, love, concord, godly living, faithful marrying with the faithful, may make us now in these our days of free profession to blush for shame. George Eagles, martyr in Queen Mary's days, for his great pains in travelling from place to place to confirm the brethren, was surnamed, ' Trudge over the world.'" (Acts and Mon.)

To be baptized of him] Not for any need he had (for he was a Lamb without blemish of natural corruption, and without spot of actual transgression, 1 Pet. i. 19), but merely for our benefit, to sanctify baptism to us, and to grace his own ordinance for us.

Ver. 14. *But John forbade him*] Flatly forbade him, and kept him out of the water with both hands earnestly ;[1] not out of disobedience, but reverence, though faulty and erroneous. The very best have their blemishes. *Omnibus malis Punicis inest granum putre, dixit Crates :* and the fairest apple-tree may have a fit of barrenness. But for involuntary infirmities, and those of daily incursion, there is a pardon of course, if sued out. And although Satan stood at the right hand of Joshua the high priest, because (as some will have it) his accusation was as true as vehement, and so Satan seemed to have the upper hand of him ; yea, although he was so ill clothed, yet he stood before the angel. Christ did not abhor his presence, nor reject his service, Zech. iii. 2.

I have need to be baptized of thee] There can be no flesh without filthiness, as a grave divine noteth upon this text (Dr Hall). Neither the supernatural conception nor austere life of John could exempt him from need of baptism.

And comest thou to me ?] *Amica σύρραξις,* a friendly falling out, but quickly made up. Most of our jarrings grow from mistakes. " Be swift to hear, slow to wrath ;" easily satisfied. Not like glasses, which being once broken, cannot be pieced again.

Quæ modo pugnârant jungunt sua rostra columbæ. Ovid

Ver. 15. *Suffer it to be so now*] Or, let be now : for the Baptist seems to have laid hands upon Christ to keep him off.[2] Our Saviour assents to that John had said, but yet shows cause why he should suffer it so to be for the present.

To fulfil all righteousness] Not legal only, and of equality, but that of his present condition also, and of equity ; to the end that all kind of sinners might have all kind of comfort in Christ, an absolute and all-sufficient Saviour.

Then he suffered him] The wisdom from above is gentle, and easy to be persuaded, when better reason is alleged *εὐπειθὴς,* Jam. iii. 17 :

as in Peter, John xiii. 8, first peremptory, but after conviction pliable. An humble man will never be a heretic : show him his error, and he will soon retract it. Joannes Bugenhagius (a reverend Dutch divine) lighting upon Luther's book *de Captivitate Babylonicâ,* and reading some few pages of it as he sat at supper, rashly pronounced him the most pestilent and pernicious heretic that ever the Church had been troubled with since the times of Christ. But a few days after, having seriously read over the book, and well weighed the business, he returned to his collegioners, and recanted what he had said amongst them ; affirming and proving that Luther only was in the light, and all the world besides in gross darkness, so that many of them were converted by him to the truth. (*Scultet. Annal.*) Joannes Denckius (a learned Bavarian) held this heresy, that no man or devil should be damned eternally, because God willeth that all should be saved : and Christ saith, " There shall be one shepherd and one sheep-fold." But being an humble-minded man, he was convinced and converted by Œcolampadius, and died of the plague (but piously) at Basil, A.D. 1528. Of Swenckfeldius the heretic, because he prayed ardently, and lived unblameably, Bucholcerus the chronologer was wont to say that his heart was good, but his head not well regulated.[3] But how that could be, I see not, so long as he lived and died in his detestable opinions, and would not forego them. If the leprosy were gotten into the head, the priest was to pronounce such utterly unclean, Levit. xiii. 44. And the prophet pronounceth his soul that is lifted up with pride and pertinacy not to be upright in him, Habak. ii. 4.

Ver. 16. *And Jesus when he was baptized*] Many of the ancients held that the day of Epiphany was the day of our Saviour's baptism. But that, I think, is but a conjecture. The Habassines, a kind of mongrel Christians in Africa, baptize themselves every year on that day in lakes or ponds ; thereby to keep a memorial of our Saviour's baptism in Jordan. This is (as Tindal was wont to say of a like matter) to pass by the provision, and lick the sign-post.

Went up straightway out of the water] And stood upon the shore, apart from the company, that all might see and hear what was now to be done. St Luke addeth (iii. 21), that he fell there upon his knees and prayed ; thereby teaching us, with what deep devotion we are to receive the sacraments, which are given us of God to signify, as by sign ; to assure, as by seal ; and to convey, as by instrument, Jesus Christ and all his benefits. The Father, Son, and Holy Ghost are there one in covenanting and working thy salvation. Stir up thyself therefore to hope and faith at the sacrament : speak to thy faith, as Deborah did to herself, Judges v. 12, " Awake, awake, Deborah, utter a song :" give glory to

---

[1] *διεκώλυεν, obnixe prohibebat, ad vim præpositionis διὰ exprimendam.*

[2] *Consentaneum est, injectâ manu Joannem conatum vetare*

Jesum. Erasmus.   [3] *Non defuisse Swenckeldio cor bonum sed caput regulatum.*

God, lay claim to the covenant: lean on Christ's bosom at that supper, and bethink thyself, with Esther at the feast, what suit thou hast to commence, what Haman to hang up, what lust to subdue, what grace (chiefly) to get growth in, &c. But for most communicants, urge them to prayer afore, in, and after sacrament, and they must say (if they say truly), as David did of Saul's armour, I cannot go with these, for I have not been accustomed to them, 1 Sam. xvii. 39.

And, lo, the heavens were opened unto him] As he was praying; for prayer is the key of heaven, wherewith we may take out of God's treasury plentiful mercy for ourselves and others. He cannot possibly be poor that can pray, Rom. x. 12. One said of the Pope, that he could never want money so long as he could hold a pen in his hand; of the faithful Christian it may safely be affirmed, he cannot want any good thing while he can call to God for it. If he can find a praying heart, God will find a pitying heart and a supplying hand. Now he is worthily miserable that will not make himself happy by asking. The ark and the mercy-seat were never separated. God never said to Israel, "Seek ye me in vain," Isa. xlv. 19. The hand of faith never knocked at heaven's gates, but they were opened, and the Spirit descended, though not so visibly as here at the baptism of our Saviour, nor a voice heard so audibly from heaven as then, yet as truly and effectually to the support of the poor suppliant: who while he prayeth in the Holy Ghost, Jude 20, receiveth new supplies of the Spirit (ἐπιχορηγία, Phil. i. 19; Eph. iv. 16), and is sweetly, but secretly, sealed up thereby to the day of redemption.

And he saw the Spirit of God descending] From the Father (who spake from the most excellent glory, 2 Pet. i. 17) upon the Son, who stood upon the shore, so that here was *concilium augustissimum*, a most majestical meeting of the three persons in Trinity, about the work of man's redemption, as once about his creation: Gen. i. 26, "Let us make man." The Hebrews interpret it, "I and my judgment-hall;" by which phrase the Trinity of old was implied. For a judgment-hall in Israel consisted of three at least; which, in their close manner of speech, they applied to God, but their posterity understood it not. And as in the matter of man's creation and redemption, so likewise of his sanctification, remarkable is that of the apostle, 1 Cor. xii. 4—7, where the diversities of gifts are said to be of the Spirit: the diversities of ministries (whereby these gifts are administered) of the Lord, that is, of Christ; and the diversities of operations (effected by the gifts and ministries) to be of God the Father.

Like a dove, and lighting upon him] This was shadowed of old, by Noah's dove lighting upon the ark: and serveth to denote Christ's innocency, purity, love to his little ones. κύουσι γὰρ ἀλληλὰς, saith Aristotle;[1] and another thus:

Felle columba caret, rostro non cædit, et ungues Possidet innocuos puraque grana legit.

That was more than ridiculous, nay, it was blasphemous, that those pilgrims that went to Jerusalem to fight in the Holy War (as they called it) did carry a goose before them, pretending it to be the Holy Ghost. These were drunk with the wine of the whore of Babylon's abominations; and not filled with the Spirit, as St Stephen was, and Barnabas, and others of old; as of late, among many, that famous Beza, *de quo collegæ sæpe dicebant, eum sine felle vivere.* And himself reports of himself and his colleagues, in an epistle to Calvin, that, disputing with a Spanish Jesuit about the Eucharist, "the Jesuit" (saith he) "called us *vulpes, et simias, et serpentes* (foxes, apes, serpents). My answer was this, *Non magis nos credere, quam transubstantiationem.*" So that angel John Bradford (as one calleth him) when he reasoned with Alphonsus a Castro; the friar was in a wonderful rage, and spake so high that the whole house rang again, chafing with om and cho, saith Mr Fox. But Bradford answered him with meekness of wisdom, and, like the waters of Shiloah at the foot of Sion, ran softly, Isa. viii. 6. He had been baptized with that Holy Ghost that descended upon our Saviour, who received not the Spirit by measure, but had a fulness, not of abundance only, but also of redundancy, John i. 14.

Ver. 17. *And, lo, a voice from heaven*] Whereupon St Peter foundeth the certainty of Christian faith and doctrine, 2 Pet. i. 17, especially since we have a more sure word of prophecy; for that former might have been slandered, or suspected for an imposture.

Saying, This is my beloved] My darling, he on whom my love resteth;[2] so that I will seek no further. Zeph. iii. 17. When the earth was founded, Christ was with his Father as his daily delight, sporting or laughing, always before him, *risum captans ac consilium*, Prov. viii. 30. Jerome.

In whom I am well pleased] The beloved, in whom he hath made us accepted, Eph. i. 6. God's Hephsibah, so the Church is called, Isa. lxii. 4; the dearly beloved of his soul, Jer. xii. 7; or, as the Septuagint render it,[3] his beloved soul, over whom he rejoiceth as the bridegroom over his bride, Isa. lxii. 5. Yea, "he will rest in his love," as abundantly well pleased, "he will joy therein with singing," Zeph. iii. 17. So well thinketh God of his Son Christ, and of us through him, as some of the ancients rendered this word, εὐδόκησα, *In quo bene sensi.* So (after Irenæus) Tertullian, Cyprian, and Augustine interpret it.[4] And yet, as well as he thought of his only Son, he spared him not, but "delivered him up for us all," Rom. viii. 32, whereupon St Bernard thus

---

[1] περιστερὰ, παρὰ, τοῦ περισσῶς ἐρᾶν. Herdfield.
[2] ἀγαπᾶν, quasi ἄγαν παύειν, Ἀγαπητός.
[3] ἔδωκα τὴν ἠγαπημένην ψυχὴν μοῦ. Dedi dilectam animam meam.
[4] εὐδόκιμοι Græcis dicuntur celebres, et de quibus magnifica est opinio. Erasm.

cries out, *O quantum dilecte, præ quo filius ipse aut non dilectus, aut saltem neglectus?* God so loved his Son, that he gave him all the world for his possession, Psal. ii.; but he so loved the world, that he gave Son and all for its redemption. One calls this an hyperbole, an excess of love, a *sic* without a *sicut*. God so loved the loved, so infinitely, so incomparably, so incomprehensibly, as that there is no similitude in nature whereby to express it. John iii. 16; Eph. iii. 18, 19. Abraham (God's friend) showed his love to him in not withholding his only son Isaac: but what was Isaac to Christ? or what was Abraham's love to God's? He did that freely and voluntarily, that Abraham would never have done but upon a command: besides, Isaac was to be offered up after the manner of holy sacrifices, but Christ suffered after the manner of malefactors. And yet further, Isaac was in the hand of a tender and compassionate father; but Christ died by the wicked hands of barbarous and blood-thirsty enemies, that thereby he might slay the enmity and reconcile us to God, Eph. ii. 15, 16; so making peace,[1] and paving us "a new and living way," with his blood, to the throne of grace, "wherein he hath made us accepted in the beloved," Eph. i. 6. David saw the features of his friend Jonathan in lame Mephibosheth, and therefore loved him. He forgave Nabal at Abigail's intercession; and was pacified toward Absalom at Joab's. Pharaoh favoured Jacob's house for Joseph's sake. Shall not God do as much more for Jesus' sake? Joseph was well pleased with his brethren when they brought Benjamin; bring but the child Jesus in our arms (as Simeon did, and as Themistocles did the king of Persia's child) and he cannot but smile upon us. Were he never so much displeased before, yet upon the sight of this his well-beloved Son, in whom he is well pleased, all shall be calm and quiet, as the sea was when once Jonas was cast into it.

CHAPTER IV.

Verse 1. *Then was Jesus led up*] LEST haply the people, hearing that testimony from heaven, should come and take him by force to make him a king, as John vi. 15, to try their love also to him, who was thus overclouded as the sun in his first rising.

Led up of the Spirit] The better to fit him thereby for the ministry. Luther observed of himself, that when God was about to set him upon any special service, he either laid some fit of sickness upon him beforehand, or turned Satan loose upon him; who so buffeted him (*eftsoons*) by his temptations, *ut nec calor, nec sanguis, nec sensus, nec vox superesset*, that neither heat, nor blood, nor sense, nor voice remained: the very venom of the temptations drank up his spirit,

and his body seemed dead, as Justus Jonas, that was by and saw it, reported of him in his epistle to Melancthon.[2] Hence also it was that in his sermons God gave him such a grace, saith Mr Foxe, that when he preached, they that heard him thought, every one, his own temptations to be severally touched and noted. Whereof when signification was given unto him by his friends, and he demanded how that could be? "Mine own manifold temptations," saith he, "and experiences are the cause thereof:" for from his tender years he was much beaten and exercised with spiritual conflicts, as Melancthon in his Life testifieth. Also Hieronymus Wellerus, scholar to the said Mr Luther, recordeth, that he oftentimes heard Luther his master report of himself, that he had been assaulted and vexed with all kinds of temptations (saving only with that of covetousness), and was thereby fitted for the work of the Lord. Whence also he was wont to say that three things make a preacher,—meditation, prayer, and temptation.

Into the wilderness] Likely the wilderness of Sinai, where Moses and Elias had fasted before. These three great fasters met afterwards in Mount Tabor, Matt. xvii. 3. God promiseth to turn his people's fasting into feasting, Zech. viii. 19. The devil took advantage of the place here, to assault our Saviour in the desert, but was beaten on his own dunghill, that we might overcome through him that loved us, Rom. viii. 37, the fiend being already foiled by Christ.

To be tempted of the devil] No sooner was Christ out of the water of baptism than in the fire of temptation. So David, after his anointing, was hunted as a partridge upon the mountains. Israel is no sooner out of Egypt than Pharaoh pursues them. Hezekiah no sooner had kept that solemn passover, than Sennacherib comes up against him. St Paul is assaulted with vile temptations after the abundance of his revelations, 2 Cor. xii. 7. And Christ teacheth us, after forgiveness of sins obtained, to look for temptations and to pray against them, Matt. vi. 13. While Jacob would be Laban's drudge and packhorse, all was well; but when once he began to flee, he makes after him with all his might. All was jolly quiet at Ephesus before St Paul came thither; but then, "there arose no small stir about that way," Acts xix. 23. All the while our Saviour lay in his father's shop, and meddled only with carpenter's chips, the devil troubled him not. But now that he is to enter more publicly upon his office of mediatorship, the tempter pierceth his tender soul with many sorrows, by solicitation to sin. (πειράζω from πείρω, to pierce through.) And dealt he so with the green tree? what will he do with the dry? Temptations (besides those that come from God, which are only *probationis*, not *perditionis*, as the other) are of two sorts: for either they are of seducement, Jam. i. 14, or of buffeting and

---

[1] εἰρήνη ἀπὸ τοῦ εἰς ἓν εἴρειν.

[2] *Lutherus in oppidum Eisleben honorifice introductus est, valetudine admodum imbecillâ, et tantum non desperatâ : quod*

sibi accidere semper, cum magni quippiam aggrederetur, dixit. Melchior Adam.

grievance, 2 Cor. xii. 7; either of allurement or affrightment. (*Irritamenta, vel terriculamenta.*) In the former we are pressed with some darling corruption, whereto our appetites by nature are most propense: in the latter we are dogged with foulest lusts of atheism, idolatry, blasphemy, murder, &c., that nature startles at: in these the devil tempts alone, and that so grossly, that the very flesh is ashamed of it. But in the former, that come more immediately from the flesh, the devil only interposeth himself, and speaks his good word for them; whence they are called messengers of Satan, 2 Cor. xii. 7; and, Eph. iv. 27, we are said in anger to "give place to the devil;" and in resisting of lusts, we "resist the devil," Jam. iv. 7.

Ver. 2. *And when he had fasted forty days,* &c.] All Christ's actions are for our instruction, not all for our imitation. We may not imitate the works miraculous of Christ, and proper to him as mediator. The ignorance of this caused some to counterfeit themselves Christ's: as one Moor in King Edward VI.'s time, and one Hacket in Queen Elizabeth's time, David George, and sundry others, according to Matt. xxiv. 24. Neither need we seek to imitate him in his infirmities, which (though they were not sinful, but only natural, and therefore unblameable) yet import a weakness (as that he was hungry, weary, sleepy, &c.), and so, though they be in us, yet we need not strive the attainment of them. But we must imitate the Lord Christ in all his imitable graces and actions: showing forth the praises or virtues of him that hath called us out of darkness into his marvellous light. (τὰς ἀρετὰς ἐξαγγείλητε, 1 Pet. ii. 9.) The word signifies to preach them abroad; for we should practise those virtues so clearly, that our lives may be as so many sermons upon the life of Christ. It is a dishonour to a dear friend to hang his picture in a dark hole and not in a conspicuous place, that it may appear we rejoice in it as an ornament to us: think the same of Christ's image and graces, show them forth we must, and express them to the world; walking in Christ, Col. ii. 6, yea, as Christ, 1 John ii. 6, who therefore left us a copy that we might write after it, a sampler that we might work by it, a pattern that we should follow his steps, 1 Pet. ii. 21 (ὑπογραμμόν. *Exemplar quod oculo conspicitur*). And although we cannot follow him *passibus æquis*, yet we must show our good-wills, stretching and straining our utmost, as St Paul did (ἐπεκτεινόμενος, Phil. iii. 14); striving what we can to resemble him, not as a picture doth a man in outward lineaments only; but as a son doth his father (for he is the Father of eternity, Isa. ix. 6) in nature and disposition; and as servants, labouring to do as our Lord, John xiii. 15, who therefore washed his disciples' feet, to give us an example of humility; as he did likewise of meekness, Matt. xi. 29; patience, 1 Pet. ii. 21; obedience, Heb. xii. 2; diligence and fidelity in his function, Heb. iii. 1, 2; fewness of words, yet

boldness of speech, going about and doing all possible good; beneficence to the poor saints, 2 Cor. viii. 9; constancy in profession, 1 Tim. vi. 13; forgiveness of others and love to the brethren, Eph. v. 2. "Be ye therefore followers herein of Christ, as dear children, not fashioning yourselves according to the former lusts in your ignorance; but as he which hath called you is holy, so be ye holy in all manner of conversation," 1 Pet. i. 14, 15.

He was afterward an hungred] Our Saviour was tempted all that forty days' space, saith St Luke: but these three worst assaults were reserved to the last. So deals the devil with the Church (which is Christ mystical, 1 Cor. xii. 12). He never ceaseth tempting, though never so often repulsed; and is therefore called Beelzebub, as some will have it, the lord of flies, because the fly is noted for an impudent creature, that will soon return to the bait, though beaten away but erewhile. (κυνάμυια *ponitur apud Homerum pro valde impudente; quia muscæ pervicaces sunt, &c.*) Hence those many bickerings and buffetings we meet with all our life long: and hence those sharpest encounters and terrible conflicts many times at the hour of death. The Israelites met with many trials and troubles in the wilderness, Amalek and the Amorites, sore thirst, and fiery serpents, &c., but were never so put to it as when they came to take possession of the promised land; for then all the kings of Canaan combined to keep them out. So the devil, furious enough at all times, most of all bestirs him at last cast, because he knows his time is but short, Apoc. xii. 12, for death sets a saint out of his gunshot (*a* βέλους). Satan may compass the earth, but not enter the lists of heaven. He tempted Adam in the earthly Paradise; he cannot tempt in the heavenly: hence his malice, whiles he may. *Morientium nempe bestiarum violentiores sunt morsus* (*ut ille olim de semidiruta Carthagine*): beasts that have their death's-wound, bite cruelly, sprunt exceedingly.

Ver. 3. *Then came unto him the tempter*] ὁ πειράζων. So called, because he politicly feels our pulses which way they beat, and accordingly fits us a penny-worth. He sets a wedge of gold before covetous Achan, a courtesan Cozbi before a voluptuous Zimri, a fair preferment before an ambitious Absalom: and finds well that a fit object is half a victory. So dealt his agents with those ancient Christians, ἐπρίσθησαν, ἐπειράσθησαν, they "were sawn asunder, they were tempted," saith the apostle (Heb. xi. 37), to wit, with the proffers of preferment, would they but have renounced their religion and done sacrifice to an idol. So the Pope tempted Luther with wealth and honour. But all in vain; he turned him to God, *Et valde protestatus sum,* saith he, *me nolle sic satiari ab eo,* he said flat, that God should not put him off with these low things. (Melch. Adam.) Here was a man full of the spirit of Christ. The tempter came to Christ, but found nothing in him; that matter was not malleable. In vain shall the devil strike fire if we find not tinder:

in vain shall he knock at the door if we look not out to him at the window. Let us but divorce the flesh from the world, and the devil can do us no hurt. *Ita cave tibi, ut caveas teipsum.* From that naughty man myself, good Lord, deliver me, said one.

If thou be the Son of God] As the devil quarrelled and questioned the law given in Paradise as nought, or naught; so doth he hear the voice from heaven as a mere imposture. And this he did out of deep and desperate malice; for he could not be ignorant nor doubtful. Neither is his dealing otherwise with us (many times), who are too ready (at his instigation) to doubt of our spiritual sonship. We need not help the tempter, by holding it a duty to doubt; this is to light a candle before the devil, as we use to speak. Rather let us settle and secure this, that we are indeed the sons of God and heirs of heaven, by passing through the narrow womb of repentance, that we may be born again, and by getting an effectual faith, the property whereof is to adopt as well as to justify; viz. *ratione objecti*, by means of Christ the object upon whom faith layeth hold, and into whom it engrafts the believer after an unspeakable manner. Now ye are all the children of God by faith in Christ Jesus, Gal. iii. 26; John i. 12, who hath both laid down the price of this greatest privilege, Heb. ix. 15; Gal. iv. 5, and sealed it up to us by his Spirit, crying, "Abba, Father," in our hearts, whatever Satan or our own misgiving hearts object to the contrary, Gal. iv. 6; Rom. viii. 15; Eph. i. 13.

Command that these stones be made bread] And so distrust the providence of God for relieving thy body in this hunger; help thyself by working a preposterous miracle, in this point of God's providence for this present life. Satan troubled David and Jeremiah, and so he doth many good souls at this day, who can sooner trust God with their souls than with their bodies; and for a crown than for a crust, as those disciples, Matt. xvi. 8.

Ver. 4. *But he answered and said, It is written*] "With his sore and great and strong sword" of the Spirit doth the Lord here "punish leviathan, that crooked piercing serpent," Isa. xxvii. 7. With these shafts out of God's quiver, with these pebbles chosen out of the silver streams of the Scriptures, doth he prostrate the Goliah of hell. The word of God hath a power in it to quail and to quash Satan's temptations, far better than that wooden dagger, that leaden sword of the Papists, their holy water, crossings, grains, dirty relics, &c. It is not the sign of the cross, but the word of the cross that overthrows Satan. He can no more abide by it than an owl by the shining of the sun. Set therefore the word against the temptation, and the sin is laid. Say, I must not do it, I may not, I dare not; for it is forbidden in such a place, and again in such a place. And be sure to have places of Scripture ready at hand (as Saul had his spear and pitcher ready at his head even while he slept), that ye may "re-

sist the devil," "steadfast in the faith," grounded on the word. Joseph overcame him by remembering the seventh commandment: and David, by hiding this word in his heart, Psal. cxix. 11. Wicked therefore was that advice of Dr Bristow to his agents, to labour still to get heretics out of their weak and false castle of Holy Scriptures into the plain fields of councils and fathers. The Scriptures are our armoury (far beyond that of Solomon, Cant. iv. 4), whither we must resort and furnish ourselves. One savoury sentence thereof shall do us more service than all the pretty, witty sayings and sentences of fathers and philosophers, or constitutions of councils.

Man liveth not by bread alone] Though ordinarily, as having a nourishing property inherent in it for such a purpose; yet so, as that the operation and success is guided by God's power and goodness, whereon (as on a staff) this staff of life leaneth, Ezek. iv. 16. "A wise woman buildeth her house," Prov. xiv. 1. As the carpenter lays the plot of the house in his head first, and contrives it, so doth she forecast, and further the well-doing of her family: and yet "except the Lord also build the house, they labour in vain that build it," Psal. cxxvii. 1. So the diligent hand and the blessing of God (meeting) make rich, Prov. x. 4, 22.

But by every word, &c.] That is, by anything else besides bread, whatsoever God shall think good, whatsoever he shall appoint and give power unto to be nourishment. Therefore if bread fail, feed on faith, Psal. xxxvii. 3. *Pascere fide:* so Junius reads that text. Jehoshaphat found it sovereign when all other help failed him, 2 Chron. xx. 6. And the captive Jews lived by faith, when they had little else to live upon, and made a good living of it, Hab. ii. 4. To this text the Jews seem to allude in that fiction of theirs, that Habakkuk was carried by the hair of the head, by an angel, into Babylon, to carry a dinner to Daniel in the den. (History of Bel and the Dragon, ver. 33.) It was by faith that he "stopped the mouths of lions, and obtained promises," Heb. xi. 33; and by faith that she answered the persecutors, "If you take away my meat, I trust God will take away my stomach." (Eliz. Young, Acts and Monuments.) God made the ravens feed Elias, that were more likely (in that famine) to have fed upon his dead carcase; and another time caused him to go forty days in the strength of one meal, 1 Kings xix. 8. Merlyn was nourished a fortnight together with one egg a day, laid by a hen that came constantly to that haymow, where he lay hid during the massacre of Paris. (French Chronicle.) And who hath not read or heard how, by a miracle of his mercy, God relieved Rochelle in a strait siege by an innumerable company of fishes cast in upon them? *Carissima semper munera sunt, author quæ preciosa facit.* Faith fears no famine (*fides famem non formidat*); and although it be but small in substance and in show (as the manna was), yet is it great in virtue and operation. The rabbins say, that manna had all manner of good tastes in it:

so hath faith. It drinks to a man in a cup of nepenthe, and bids him be of good cheer, God will provide for him. The Bishop of Norwich kept Robert Samuel, martyr, without meat and drink, whereby he was unmercifully vexed, saving that he had every day allowed him two or three morsels of bread, and three spoonfuls of water, to the end he might be reserved to further torment. How oft would he have drunk his own water! But his body was so dried up with long emptiness, that he was not able to make one drop of water. After he had been famished with hunger two or three days together, he fell into a sleep, as it were one-half in a slumber; at which time one clothed in white seemed to stand before him, which ministered comfort unto him by these words, "Samuel, Samuel, be of good cheer, and take a good heart unto thee; for after this day thou shalt never be either hungry or thirsty;" for speedily after this he was burned, and from that time, till he should suffer, he felt neither hunger nor thirst. And this declared he, to the end, as he said, that all men might behold the wonderful work of God. (Acts and Monuments.) He likes not to be tied to the second ordinary causes, nor that (in defect of the means) we should doubt of his providence. It is true, he commonly worketh by them, when he could do without, that we may not neglect the means, as being ordained of him. (David shall have victory, but by an ambush, 2 Sam. v. 19—24. Men shall be nourished, but by their labour, Psal. cxxviii. 2.) But yet so, as that he doth all in all by those means (he made grass, corn, and trees, before he made the sun, moon, and stars, by the influence whereof they are and grow). Yea, to show himself chief, he can and doth work, other whiles, without means, 2 Chron. xiv. 11, and against means, suspending the power and operation of the natural causes; as, when the fire burnt not, the water drowned not, the sun went back ten degrees, the rock gave water, the iron swam, &c. And then, when he works by means, he can make them produce an effect diverse from their nature and disposition; or can hinder, change, or mitigate their proper effect; as when at the prayer of Elias it rained not for three years and a half. "And he prayed again, and the heaven gave rain, and the earth brought forth her fruit," James v. 17, 18. A man would have thought that after so long drought, the roots of trees and herbs should have been utterly dried up, and the land past recovery; but "God heard the heavens" (petitioning to him that they might exercise their influence for the fructifying of the earth), and the "heavens heard the earth, and the earth heard the corn, the wine, and the oil, and they heard Jezreel," Hos. ii. 21. Let all this keep us, as it did our Saviour here, from diffidence in God's providence, and make us "possess our souls in patience," Luke xxi., hang upon the promise, and account it as good as present pay, though we see not how it can be effected. God loves to go a way by himself. "He knows how to deliver his," saith St Peter, 2 Epist. ii. 9, and he might speak it by experience, Acts xii. 9, if ever any man might. "The king shall rejoice in God," saith David of himself when he was a poor exile in the wilderness of Judah, Psal. lxiii. 11. But he had God's word for the kingdom, and therefore he was confident, seemed the thing ever so improbable or impossible. We trust a skilful workman to go his own way to work; shall we not God? In the sixth year of the reign of Darius Nothus was the Temple fully finished. That sacred work which the husband and son of an Esther crossed shall be happily accomplished by a bastard. The Israelites thought that Moses should presently have delivered them, and he himself thought as much, and therefore began before his time to do justice upon the Egyptian whom he slew and hid in the sand. But we see, God went another way to work; he sent Moses into a far country, and the bondage was for forty years after exceedingly increased upon them; yet all this to humble and try them, and to do them good in their latter end, Deut. viii. 2, 3. He crosseth many times our likeliest project, and gives a blessing to those times and means whereof we despair. He breaks in pieces the ship that we think should bring us to shore, but casts us upon such boards as we did not expect. Lose we then any particular means? saith one; it is but the scattering of a beam, the breaking of a bucket, when the sun and the fountain is the same. But we for the most part do as Hagar did: when the bottle was spent, she falls a crying she was undone, she and her child should die; till the Lord opened her eyes to see the fountain. It was near her but she saw it not; when she saw it she was well enough. "If thou hadst been here," said Martha, "my brother Lazarus had not died." As if Christ could not have kept him alive, unless he had been present. So if Christ will come and lay his hands on Jairus' daughter, Mark v. 23, and Elisha stroke his hand over Naaman's leprosy, they shall be cured, 2 Kings v. 11. So the disciples believed that Christ could feed so many thousands in the wilderness, but then he must have two hundred pennyworth of bread, Mark vi. 37. But our Saviour gave them, soon after, an ocular demonstration of this truth, "That man liveth not by bread alone," &c. "They shall be holpen with a little help," Dan. xi. 34. Why a little? that through weaker means we may see God's greater strength.

Ver. 5. *Then the devil taketh him*] Not in vision only or imagination, but really and indeed, as he was afterwards apprehended, bound, and crucified by that cursed crew. Spiritual assaults may be beaten back by the shield of faith; bodily admit of no such repulse. A daughter of Abraham may be bound by Satan, Luke xiii. 16, a Mary Magdalene possessed, a Job vexed, a Paul boxed, &c. (κολαφίζη, 2 Cor. xii. 7.) As for the souls of the saints, they are set safe out of Satan's scrape; shake his chain at them he may, muster his forces, Rev. xii. 7, which may band themselves and bend their strength against

Michael and his angels, Christ and his members; but they are bounded by God, who hath set his on a rock that is higher than they, Psal. lxi. 2. So that the floods of temptation (that the serpent casts out of his mouth after them) cannot come so much as to their feet, Psal. xxxii. 6. Or if it touch their heel, Gen. iii. 15, yet it can come no higher. There is no sorcery against Jacob, because God was a unicorn, Numb. xxiii. 22, 23, to take away the venom (saith Balaam the sorcerer); as waters, when the unicorn's horn hath been in them, are no longer poisonable, but healthful.

Into the holy city] Things are called holy either by nature, as God, who is truly, alway, and only of himself holy; or by separation, or being set apart to a holy use or end; which Origen calleth (Homil. xi. Num.) *sancta sanctificata*, by accession of external holiness from without: so Jerusalem is here called holy, because the city of God, where he was daily worshipped. And for the same cause was the ground whereon Moses and Joshua trod, called holy ground, and Tabor, the Holy Mount, 2 Pet. i. 18. And when we stand in our churches, saith Chrysostom, we stand in a place of angels and archangels, in the kingdom of God and heaven itself (αὐτος οὐρανὸς, Homil. xxxvi., 1 Cor. xi. 10), which they that profane, may justly fear to be whipped like dogs out of the heavenly temple, and city too. And surely it were to be wished that such profane Esaus now-a-days, as dare prate, or sleep, or laugh, and play the parts of jesters, or do anything else unbeseeming the service of God, would keep themselves from God's sanctuary, or that we had such porters to keep them out as they had under the law, 2 Chron. xxiii. 19.

And setteth him upon a pinnacle of the temple] "Height of place giveth opportunity of temptation. The longest robe contracts the greatest soil: neither are any in so great danger as those that walk on the tops of pinnacles. Even height itself makes men's brains to swim: as in Diocletian, who not content to be emperor, would needs be adored as a god; and Caligula, of whom it was said that there was never any better servant than he nor worse lord. Vespasian is reported to have been the only man that ever became better by the empire conferred upon him. *Accepto imperio melior factus est.* It is both hard and happy not to be made worse by advancement. Τιμή signifies both honour and loss; *chabad*, heaviness and honour; *honoro* and *onero* show that honour goeth not without a burthen. *Fructus honos oneris, fructus honoris onus.* (Cornel. à Lapide in Numb. xi. 11.) Pope Pius Quintus said thus of himself, *Cum essem religiosus, sperabam bene de salute animæ meæ: Cardinalis factus extimui; Pontifex creatus, pene despero.* When I was first in orders, without any further ecclesiastical dignity, I had some good hopes of my salvation; when I became a cardinal, I had less; since I was made Pope, least of all. The same thoughts of himself had Clement VIII., his immediate successor, saith

the same author. (*Non insulse Autor ocul. moral.* cap. 12.) *Præpositioni quot accident? Unum. Quid? Casus tantum. Quot casus? Duo. Qui? Accusativus, et ablativus. Hæc enim Prælatum oportet timere, accusari à crimine, et auferri à regimine, et sic ignominiose cadere.*

Ver. 6. *And he saith unto him*] The devil usually tempteth by speech, inward or outward. Senarclæus (Epist. ad Bucerum) telleth of a plain countryman at Friburg in Germany, that lying on his death-bed, the devil came to him in the shape of a tall terrible man, and claimed his soul, saying, "Thou hast been a notorious sinner, and I am come to set down all thy sins;" and therewith he drew out paper and ink, and sat down at a table that stood by, and began to write. The sick man answered, "My soul is God's, and all my sins are nailed to the cross of Christ. But if thou desire to set down my sins, write thus, 'All our righteousnesses are as a filthy rag,'" &c. The devil set down that, and bid him say on. He did: "but thou, Lord, hast promised, for thine own sake, to blot out our iniquities, and to make our scarlet sins white as snow." The devil passed by those words, and was earnest with him to go on in his former argument. The sick man said with great cheerfulness, "The Son of God appeared to destroy the works of the devil." With that the devil vanished, and the sick man departed.

If thou be the Son of God cast thyself, &c.] This is the devil's logic, to argue from mercy to liberty, to do wickedly with both hands earnestly, Micah vii. 3. Whereas the heathen could say, *In maxima libertate, minima licentia.* And the father, *Ideo deteriores sumus, quia meliores esse debemus*: therefore are we worse, because we ought to be better. (Salvian.) Remember but this, that thou art son to a king (said one to Antigonus), and that will keep thee from base courses. Take thou those spoils to thyself, Ανελοῦ σαυτῳ (said Themistocles to his friend that followed him), σὺ γὰρ οὐκ εἰ Θεμιστοκλῆς, for thou art not Themistocles, as I am: they are poor things, far below me. Shall such a man as I flee? Neh. vi. 11. Shall I do anything to the dishonour of my heavenly Father? and therefore sin, because grace hath abounded? Rom. viii. 1; that is not the guise of any of God's children. They walk honestly, bravely, gallantly, worthy of God, who hath done so great things for them. καλῶς, εὐσχημόνως, ἀξίως τοῦ Θεοῦ. The more privileges, the more engagements. Scipio, when a harlot was offered unto him, said, *Vellem, si non essem imperator.* It was an aggravation of the fall of Solomon, that God had appeared unto him twice; and of Saul, that he fell as if he had not been anointed, 1 Kings xi. 9; 2 Sam. i. 21. So it is of any of God's saints to sin, as if they had not been adopted.

Cast thyself down] Here our Saviour is tempted to self-murder, by an old manslayer. And when Moses, Elias, Jonas, and others of the best sort of saints, were in a fit of discontent, and grew weary of their lives, wishing for death, divines doubt not but Satan gave a push at them with his ten horns, to despatch and ease themselves of the present trouble by cutting off their own days. A dangerous and hideous temptation; yet such as may befall the best, and few escape it that live out their time. But in all the book of God we read not of any of the generation of the just that ever did it, Psal. xxxvii. 28. That God who kept them, will (if we look up to him) do as much for us. Only we must set against this bloody temptation with God's arm and with God's armour. The word and prayer are the ordinances and power of God, and, by his might, do extinguish all the fiery darts of the devil. Oppose the commination to the temptation. Herein Eve faltered (in her lest ye die, though she held the precept), and so fell.

For it is written] A vile abuse of sacred Scripture, to persuade thereby to sin or plead for it; yet what more ordinary with men of corrupt minds and reprobate concerning the faith, 2 Tim. iii. 8. *Qui cædem Scripturarum faciunt ad materiam suam*, as Tertullian speaketh (*De Præscript. advers. Hæret.*), who murder the Scriptures to serve their own purposes? But of this more elsewhere.

He shall give his angels charge over thee] Hitherto the old liar speaketh truth. But, *Satan et si semel videatur verax, millies est mendax, et semper fallax*, saith Bucholcer: Satan, though he may sometimes seem a true speaker, yet he is a thousand times for it a liar, and always a deceiver. Because our Saviour had alleged Scripture, he also would do the like in a perverse, apish imitation, but mars the masculine sense by clipping off that clause, "they shall keep thee in all thy ways;" that is, in those courses that are appointed thee by God. *In viis nostris, non in præcipitiis.* (Bern.) But as the Israelites in the wilderness, when they went out of God's precincts were out of his protection, so are all others. "As a bird that wandereth from the nest, so is a man that wandereth from his own place," saith Solomon, Prov. xxvii. 8. God made a law that none should molest a bird upon her nest, Deut. xxii. 6. Doth God take care of birds? A king undertaketh the safety of his subjects whilst they travel within due hours and keep the king's highway; else not. So doth God. He hath given his angels charge over us whiles we hold his way, which is like Jacob's ladder, where the angels were ascending and descending. Oh the dignity and safety of a saint, in a guard so full of state and strength! Well might David (after he had said, "the angel of the Lord pitcheth his tent round about them that fear him") presently subjoin, Taste and see how gracious the Lord is, in allowing his children so glorious an attendance, Psal. xxxiv. 7, 8.

And with their hands they shall lift thee up, &c.] As parents use to lift their little ones over rough and foul ways; or as servants in a house love to get up into their arms their young master. ἐπὶ χείρων, *in manus: ducta ab iis, significationis origine, qui onus aliquod gestatui attollunt in humeros.* (Beza.) In Christ and for Christ, they count it their greatest glory to do us any good office for soul or body; they save us from the foul fiends that else would worry us. These walk about as lions to devour us while alive, and to hinder our passage to heaven when we die; the other, as guardians, to keep us here, and to convey and conduct us through the devil's territories (who is prince of the air) when we go hence to heaven, Luke xvi. 22, in despite of the evil angels that would intercept us, Dan. x. 21.

Lest thou dash thy foot against a stone] Oh the tender care of our heavenly Father; he is so kind, and, in the best sense, fond over his little ones, that he cannot abide the cold wind should blow upon them, as we say, and hath therefore commanded "that the sun shall not smite them by day, nor the moon by night," Psal. cxxi. 6; yea, which way soever the wind fit, it must blow good to his; "Arise, O north, and blow, O south, upon my beloved, that her spices may flow forth," Cant. iv. 16. What so contrary as north and south wind, cold and hot, moist and dry? &c. Yet both must blow good to God's beloved. Well might God exalt his love above that of natural parents, which yet is wondrous great, saith the Psalmist, Psal. ciii. 13.

Ver. 7. *Jesus answered and said, It is written again*] Christ rejects not the Holy Scriptures, although perversely alleged and abused by Satan, but openeth them, by laying one place to another. So did those holy Levites in Nehemiah viii. 7, and St Paul in Acts ix. 22. συμβιβάζων. *Collatis testimoniis demonstrans.* Parallel texts, like glasses set one against another, cast a mutual light. And, as the lapidary brighteneth his hard diamond with the dust shaved from itself: so must we clear hard scriptures by others that are more plain and perspicuous.

Thou shalt not tempt the Lord thy God] Trust him we must, tempt him we may not. Now God is tempted, either when men are too much addicted to the means, as Thomas; or when they reject them, as Ahaz, who refused a sign, and ran to unlawful means, hiding all under this, I will not tempt God, Isa. vii. 12. Heathens could say, *Admotâ manu invocanda est Minerva*, and they noted him for a foolish carter, that when his cart stuck fast, cried to his god, and moved his lips, but not his hands to help himself. "If thou callest for knowledge," saith Solomon, "and criest for understanding"—there is prayer to God; "if thou seekest her as silver, and searchest for her as for hid treasures"—there is man's endeavour in the diligent use of the means; "then shalt thou understand the fear of the Lord, and find the knowledge of God"—there is the happy success, Prov. ii. 3—5. *Ora et labora* was an Emperor's motto. (Reusneri Symb.) St Augustine sets it down as a vanity of his youth, that he prayed God to help him against some special sins whereunto he was strongly addicted, but should have been full sorry that God should have heard him, because he was loth to part with them. How much better was that prayer of Sir Thomas More, *Domine Deus, fac me in iis con-*

sequendis operam collocare, pro quibus obtinendis soleo ad te orare ; " Lord God, make me to bestow pains in getting those things, for obtaining whereof I use to pray unto thee."

Ver. 8. *Again the devil taketh him*] This master-fly Beelzebub, though beaten away once and again, yet returns to the same place. See how shameless he is in renewing his temptations after a flat repulse. He solicits and sets upon our Saviour again (as Potiphar's wife did upon Joseph, for all his many denials), and is not only importunate, but impudent. Stand we therefore still upon our guard, and look for no ease here. The Roman captains, when they had once triumphed, took their ease ever after. So did not Cato, and is therefore highly commended. So may not we if ever we will be approved as good soldiers of Jesus Christ, 2 Tim. ii. 3. Our whole life is a continual warfare, and we must look for the continual hail-shot, hell-shot of satanical assaults and suggestions. (*Hannibal victor vel victus nunquam quiescebat. Ita nec diabolus.*) When Xerxes fought against the Greeks, " the sea was full of ships," saith the orator, " the earth of soldiers, the air of arrows," πληρὴς ἦν ἡ μὲν θάλασσα νέων, ἡ δὲ γῆ πέζων, ὁ δὲ ἀὴρ βελῶν. So fares it with the saints under Satan's batteries: no truce, but continual conflict. Ever since these two strong men fought, there is no more peace. St Paul sounds the alarm, " Arm, arm! take the whole armour of God and be ever in your harness," πανοπλίαν, Eph. vi. 11. And St Peter gives the reason, " Because your adversary the devil, as a roaring lion, walketh, and watcheth, night and day, seeking whom he may devour." This he doth out of his contrariety to God who careth for us, 1 Pet. v. 7, 8. For our encouragement, as the devil is *Leo* ὠρυόμενος, a roaring lion, so is Christ *Leo de tribu Juda,* ὁ ῥυόμενος, the lion of the tribe of Judah, that delivereth us, and maketh us more than conquerors; holding the crown of glory over our heads (as we are fighting), with this inscription, *Vincenti dabo,* " To him that overcometh will I give," &c. (*Christus est* ἀγωνοθέτης, *idem et antagonista, qui immittit et dirigit tentationes nostras.* Pareus.) Fight therefore and faint not, your reward is sure, your armour is of proof. Get on both those pieces of defence (as the girdle of truth, breastplate of righteousness, shoes of peace and patience, shield of faith, helmet of hope) and those also of offence, as the sword of the Spirit and darts of prayer. And then resolve with that aged citizen of Exeter in King Edward VI.'s time, who when the town was besieged, said, " That he would feed on the one arm and fight with the other, before he would consent to yield the city to the seditions." (Hayward's Life of Edward VI.) It is said of Sceva at the siege of Dyrrachium, that he so long resisted Pompey's army that he had 220 darts sticking in his shield and lost one of his eyes, and yet gave not over till Cæsar came to his rescue (*Densamque ferebat pectore sylvam.* Lucan); and of Sir Thomas Challoner (who

died A.D. 1566), that he served in his younger time under Charles V. in the expedition of Algiers, where being shipwrecked, after he had swum till his strength and his arms failed him, at length catching hold of a cable with his teeth, he escaped, not without the loss of some of his teeth. The like (and somewhat more) is reported of Cynegirus the Athenian in the Persian wars. These did thus for a corruptible crown or temporary honour; what should not we do for an eternal ? 1 Cor. ix. 25. Hold out, and hold fast that thou hast, that no man take thy crown from thee, Rev. iii. 11. Be of Queen Elizabeth's disposition, who provided for war even when she had most perfect peace with all men. God's Spirit sets up a standard in the saints, Isa. lix. 19. " And stronger is he that is in you than he that is in the world." That old serpent hath his head so bruised and crushed by Christ that he cannot now so easily thrust in his mortal sting, though he assay it never so often, unless we dally with him and lay ourselves open, unless we tempt Satan to tempt us by inconsideration, security, or venturing on the occasion. *Vitanda est glacies, si nolis cadere.* He that tastes of the broth will have a mind to the meat. The Nazarites might not only not drink wine, but forbear to eat of the grape whether moist or dried, Numb. vi. 3.

Into an exceeding high mountain] Whether mountains were made at first or cast up by the flood, there are that dispute. I think, made at first, Psal. xc. 2. Yet is the earth round (as an apple is, notwithstanding some knots and bunches in it). And that being round, and so naturally apt for motion (as the heavens are), it stands firm and unmoveable, Eccl. i. 3; this is admirable. God hath hanged it upon nothing, saith Job (xxvi. 7), in the midst of the heaven; like Archimedes' pigeon, equally poised with its own weight. But why took he our Saviour into so high a mountain ? That he might thence have the fairer prospect. And perhaps in imitation of God taking up Moses into the mount. The devil delights to be God's ape, that he may by counterfeiting the like to God, bring his holy ordinances into disgrace. Thus the heathens had their sacrifices, washings, tithes, oracles, &c. Vitruvius and others tell us that the temple of Diana at Ephesus and her image therein were made of cedar. So for Christ bruising the serpent's head, Satan hath set up Hercules killing the Lernæan Hydra. Which fable who seeth not plainly to have been hatched in hell, and suggested to the poets, in an apish imitation of God, merely to elude his oracle ? The like may be said of the fable of Orpheus his wife, suddenly snatched from him, for looking back upon her: which was made out of the story of Lot's wife. So their Hercules with his ten labours was the Scripture Samson. And their Sethon, king of Egypt, and priest of Vulcan (who was helped from heaven by his god against Sennacherib, king of Assyria, that invaded him), who could it be else but Hezekiah, king of Judah ? *Ita dia-*

bolus (operum Dei Momus) per Egyptios hoc egit, ut divinum Miraculum in Judæa editum vilesceret, fidem et authoritatem amitteret, et tanti operis gloria ad turpissima idola rediret. (Bucholcer.) Thus the devil attempted by his Egyptians to transfer the glory of a divine miracle upon himself.

And showeth him all the kingdoms of the earth] In their beauty and bravery. A bewitching sight, doubtless, and would have moved much with a carnal heart. (This world at the last day shall be burnt for a witch.) But here the devil's fire fell upon wet tinder, and therefore took not. Gain and glory! rule and riches! *Quis nisi mentis inops, &c.* Set but a wedge of gold in sight, and Joshua (that could stay the course of the sun) cannot stay Achan from lusting and laying hold on it. Balaam's ass never gallops fast enough after preferment. And Zimri will have his Cozbi, though he die for it. These three enchantresses, "the lust of the flesh, the lust of the eyes, and the pride of life," 1 John ii. 15, 16,—pleasure, profit, and preferment (the worldly man's Trinity)—whom have they not bewitched, befooled, bebeasted? St John showeth that a man may be very mortified, a father, yet wondrous subject to dote on the world. Of the which, nevertheless, we may say (as Aaron of the people) it is wholly set upon wickedness, Exod. xxxii. 22; or, as another sometimes said of an historian, "Both the words and shows of it are full of fraud." (Δολερὰ μὲν τὰ σχήματα, δολερὰ δὲ τὰ ῥήματα. Plutarch de Herodot.) It promiseth (as the devil here) great matters, but payeth, *pro thesauro carbones,* instead of mines, coal-pits. Captain Frobisher, in his voyage to discover the Straits, being tossed up and down with foul weather, snows, and inconstant winds, returned home, having gathered a great quantity of stones, which he thought to be minerals: from which, when there could be drawn neither gold nor silver, nor any other metal, we have seen them cast forth (saith Mr Camden) to mend the highways. How oft do the devil and the world give men stones and serpents instead of fish and bread, even the bread of deceit, Prov. xx. 17, that proves gravel in the teeth! How oft are they disappointed that hunt after lying vanities, and so forsake their own mercies! as Jonah freely acknowledged (ii. 8), for it had like to have cost him a choking. What got Balaam by running after his wages of wickedness, but a sword in his ribs? Numb. xxxi. 8. Achan by his wedge, but the stones about his ears? Judas by his thirty pieces, but the halter about his neck? Cranmer by his subscription, but such a wretched condition, as that there was left him neither hope of better nor place of worse, as Cole could say in a sermon at his recantation? *Adeo ut neque spem meliori, nec locum pejori fortunæ reliquerit. Ut jam nec honeste mori, nec vivere inhoneste liceret.* (Melch. Adam.) Many of the Romish runagates, that run thither for preferment, what little respect have they oftentimes, and as little content in their change! Ros-

sensis had a cardinal's hat sent him, but his head was cut off before it came. Allin had a cardinal's hat, but with so thin lining (means, I mean, to support his state) that he was commonly called "the starving Cardinal." Stapleton was made professor of a petty university, scarce so good as one of our free schools in England. Saunders was starved. William Rainolds was nominated to a poor vicarage under value. On Harding His holiness bestowed a prebend of Gaunt, or, to speak more properly, a gaunt prebend. Many others get not anything, so that they wish themselves at home again; and sometimes return in the same discontent in which they went.

And the glory thereof] Wherewith he hoped to dazzle our Saviour's eyes (those windows of the soul), and so to imprison his affections. But he mistook himself. This heavenly eagle had *oculum irretortum:* nothing moved with these tempting objects. But how many are there, alas, that have died of the wound of the eye! that have fallen by the hand of this vile strumpet, the world; who by laying forth her two fair breasts of profit and pleasure, hath cast down many wounded, as Solomon's harlot, Prov. vii. 26; and by the glittering of her pomp and preferment hath misled millions; as the going fire leads men into hedges and ditches, or as the serpent Scytale, which when she cannot overtake the fleeing passengers, doth with her beautiful colours astonish and amaze them, so that they have no power to pass away till she have stung them to death. (Pliny.)

Ver. 9. *And he saith unto him, All these things will I give thee*] A great catch sure: even just nothing; for he showed our Saviour only shows and shadows, apparitions and resemblances of things. The word also used in the former verse for "glory" signifieth an opinion or imagination (Δόξα). So St Luke styles all Agrippa's pomp, but a phantasy, Acts xxv. 23, μετὰ πολλῆς φαντασίας. David tells us, that man walketh in a vain shadow, Psal. xxxix. 6. Now a shadow is something in appearance, nothing in substance. So the apostle calleth all these things that the devil proffers our Saviour, σχῆμα, an accidental mathematical figure, without solidity or substance; and further tells us that this figure passeth away, is ever *in transitu,* 1 Cor. vii. 31, παράγω, like the streams of a river, that passing by the sides of a city, no man can stop: or if we could retain the things of this life, yet not the world only passeth away, saith the apostle, but the lusts thereof, 1 John ii. 17. So that a man cannot make his heart delight in the same thing still. *Vota post usum fastidio sunt.* We loathe after a while what we lusted after (as Amnon did Tamar), and quickly find a satiety, yea, an unsatisfyingness in the creature. For he that loveth silver shall not be satisfied with silver, not though he could heap up his hoards to the stars, and ingross a monopoly of all the wealth in the world. ἀπάντων ἡ πλησμονὴ, Eccl. v. 10. *Non plus satiatur cor auro, quam corpus aurâ.* You may as soon fill a bag with wisdom, a chest with virtue, or a circle with a triangle, as the heart of man with anything here below. All that earth can afford is *fumus aut funus*, saith one; *nugæ et μορμολύκειν*, saith another; vanity and vexation, saith Solomon the wise: to whose impartial verdict (grounded upon so good experience) we shall do well to subscribe, without believing the devil's cracks, or trying any further conclusions. The Centurists interpret "all these things will I give thee," thus: I will make thee pope. And indeed many popes were advanced to that see immediately by the devil, as histories relate; who had they but observed what is usually done at their enthronization, would never have been so hasty. For before the pope is set in his chair, and puts on his triple crown, a piece of tow or wad of straw is set on fire before him, and one appointed to say, *Sic transit gloria mundi*, the glory of this world is but a blaze. This is only matter of form and ceremony; as is also that, that one day in the year the pope's almoner rideth before him, casting abroad to the poor certain pieces of brass and lead, saying, Silver and gold I have none, but such as I have I give you; whereas that scarlet whore holds a golden cup in her hand, and her merchants that trade with her are the grandees of the earth, Rev. xviii., and are made rich by her, ver. 15. (Pareus in Apoc.) The Cardinal of Toledo hath a hundred thousand pounds a year coming in; the archbishops of Germany are free princes, many of them, and have revenues accordingly. Petrarch reporteth that in the treasury of Pope John XXII. were found after his death 250 tuns of gold. And of Boniface VIII. it is storied, that when he was taken by Philip the Fair, King of France, and his palace rifled, there was more treasure found than all the kings of the earth were able to show again. Otto, one of the pope's mice-catchers (*muscipulatores*), as the story calleth them, sent hither by Gregory IX., after three years raking together of money by most detestable arts, at last departing hence, he left not so much money in the whole kingdom as he either carried with him or sent before him. Judge by this what they did throughout all Christendom. The pope, saith one, could never want money so long as he could hold a pen in his hand. It was truly and trimly said by Pope Innocent IV., *Vere hortus deliciarum Papis fuit tum Anglia, et puteus inexhaustus*. Thus it was then; but how now? Bellarmine complains that since the pope was cried down for antichrist, his kingdom hath not only not increased, but every day more and more decreased. *Non modo non crevit ejus imperium, sed semper magis ac magis decrevit.* And Cotton the Jesuit confesseth that the authority of the pope of Rome is incomparably less than it was; and that now the Christian church is but a diminutive. Hereupon also the cardinals (who were wont to meet oftener) meet but once a week, because the businesses of the court of Rome grow fewer. And albeit the pope's good, and his blood, his honours and manners, rose together; yet abates he as little of his former

pomp and pride as the devil doth since his fall (*Os Papæ et oculus Diaboli, in eodem sunt prædicamento.* Sphinx.), in taking upon him here to dispose of all the kingdoms of the earth as his, and requiring our Saviour (the true Lord of all) to fall down and worship him. The cardinals he still createth with these words, *Estote fratres nostri et principes mundi.* And as another Diocletian (who was the first that affected that honour), he holdeth forth his feet to be kissed, having the sign of the cross shining with pearls and precious stones upon his shoe, *Ut plenis faucibus crucem Christi derideat*, saith mine author. *Stratagema nunc est Pontificium, ditare multos, ut pii esse desinant.* In a word, with his pomp and primacy, gain and glory, rule and riches, fat bishoprics and cardinalships, as he sought to insnare Luther and gain him to his side, so he gets and binds not a few fast to that rotten religion. *Pauper Lutherus multos fecit divites*, said Erasmus; it being then the ready way to preferment to write and rail against Luther, as Eccius, Coccius, and others found it. But Christ will one day whip such money-merchants and their customers out of his house, as he did those in the Gospel, John ii. 15; chase them out of his presence, as Nehemiah did Sanballat's son-in-law; curse them with a curse that "run greedily after the error of Balaam for reward," Jude 11. Let the Romish Balak offer as large as the devil doth here, every one that hath anything of Christ in him will answer with that noble Italian convert (Galeaceus Caracciolus, Marquess of Vico in Naples), who being tempted by a Jesuit to revolt for money, cried out, "Let their money perish with them, who esteem all the gold in the world worth one day's society with Jesus Christ, and his Holy Spirit. And cursed be that religion for ever," &c. At Augsburg there is a known price of ten florins a year to all that will turn Papists. (Crashaw's Life of Sandys.)

If thou wilt fall down and worship me] Luke saith, "Worship before me." So that to worship before an idol is to worship the idol, whatever the Romanist pretend and plead to the contrary. And not only so, but to fall down, as the devil would have had our Saviour here (though it be not come to worshipping), is a grievous sin. St John had not yet worshipped the angel, but only fallen down, as desirous to worship, and is taken up by the angel for that idolatrous gesture, Rev. xix. 10. Woe then to those Rimmonites that plead for an upright soul in a prostrate body; and allege for their warrant that of Apocryphal Baruch, chap. vi., "Wherefore when ye see the multitude of people worshipping them behind and before, say ye in your hearts, O Lord, it is thou that oughtest only to be worshipped." Serve we God with our bodies also; and say with David and Christ, "Lord, a body hast thou given me; Lo, I come to do thy will therewith," Psal. xl. 8. But what a desperate and detestable boldness was it in the devil to move speech of such a sin as this to our Saviour Christ. It was extreme sauciness in Satan to adjure our Saviour (whom he there calls the Son of the most high God) not to torment him; it was horrible impudency; but nothing comparable to this in the text, to worship the devil in person: than which what can be imagined more odious? We see then to what execrable sins the best may be tempted. A man is to expect (saith Capel on Temptation), if he live out his days, to be urged to all sins, to the breach of every branch of the ten commandments; and to be put to it in respect of every article of our creed. Have you not been tempted, saith another, in this or that kind? it is because God in mercy would not lead you into temptation. (Bain's Letters.) Yea, this is, in some sort, more to be acknowledged than victory, when ye were tempted. For not to be tempted is more immediately from God, and less in man's power, than to prevail against temptation. For nothing doth overcome us without our will: but without our will doth God lead us into trial: for he knoweth we would taste little of these if we might be our own carvers. "Simon, Simon," saith our Saviour, "Satan hath desired to have you to winnow you," that is, to trouble and hurt you, Luke xxii. 31, ταράξαι καὶ βλάψαι, saith Theophylact, as a challenger desireth to have one of the other side to combat with: as Goliah called for a man to match him. Now either God denies him, or delivers us, so that evil one toucheth us not, 1 John v. 18, viz. *Tactu qualitavito*, with a mortal touch, as Cajetan glosseth that text. "I have prayed for thee," saith our Saviour, "that thy faith fail not." He prayed for all, but especially for Peter, because more violently tempted, as because more shamefully foiled; therefore, "Go tell my disciples and Peter, that I am risen; and that thereby he is justified," Mark xvi. 7; Rom. iv. 25. I have prayed; so that the remedy was ready made before the disease, the salve before the sore, or else it might have come too late; as those that are stung by a scorpion, if they be not presently anointed with oil of scorpions, die for it: and as those that have drunk poison, if they take not an antidote immediately ere it get to the vitals, perish infallibly. God in Christ hath all plaisters and pardons ready made and sealed. Else we might die in our sins while the pardon is providing.

Ver. 10. *Get thee hence, Satan*] Avaunt, avoid, be packing! This was an indignity not to be endured, as great, every way, as if the basest scoundrel upon earth should assault the chastity of the greatest empress. Our Saviour therefore will endure him no longer, but commands him out of his presence, with utmost indignation. And surely madness, in case of God's dishonour, is far better than meekness. Here, if "we be beside ourselves, it is to God," as Paul said, 2 Cor. v. 13; and as he did, when he dealt with Elymas, the first-born of the devil, when he saw him perverting the deputy; "he set his eyes upon him," saith the text, as if he would have run through him. After which lightning follows that terrible thunder-crack, "O full of all subtilty

and of all mischief," &c. *Agnosce te primogenitum diaboli. Sic Cerintho Joannes Apostolus.* Acts xiii. 9, 10. So the angel of Ephesus could not abide those counterfeits, Rev. ii. 2. Nor could David brook the workers of iniquity: he casteth down the gauntlet of defiance against them, as his utter enemies, he "hateth them with a perfect hatred," Psal. cxxxix. 21, 22. Hezekiah pulled down the brazen serpent (when the people idolized it), and called it a piece of brass. And Josiah would not let stand the horses of the sun and other monuments of idolatry, upon any entreaty. King Edward VI., being laboured by some of his best friends to permit the Lady Mary his sister to have mass in her house, answered, He would rather spend his life, and all he had, than agree and grant to that he knew certainly to be against the truth. (Acts and Mon.) And another time, in his message to the rebels of Devonshire: "Assure you most surely," said he, "that we of no earthly thing under heaven make such reputation as of this one, to have our law obeyed, and this cause of God which we have taken in hand to be thoroughly maintained; from the which we will never remove an hair's breadth, or give place to any creature living, much less to any subject; wherein we will spend our own royal person, our crown, treasure, realm, and all our state, whereof we assure you of our high honour." (Acts and Mon.) Now God's blessing be on that blessed heart that hath such a stomach against God's dishonour; and can entertain all wicked attempts and assaults, with this *Apage* of our Saviour. And woe to them that cry *Euge* to such. Whether we say to the tempter, as our Saviour did, "Get thee hence," and not rather, as the angel, "The Lord rebuke thee," Jude 9, is questioned by some; because it is only to command the devil. But that we may and must say to him, no man doubts, as our Saviour did to the Pharisees, "Why tempt ye me, ye hypocrites?" Matt. xxii. 18; as Naboth did to Ahab, "God forbid me any such wickedness," 1 Kings xxi. 3; as Solomon to his mother, "Ask the kingdom also;" as the witch of Endor to Saul, "Why seekest thou to take me in a snare, to cause me to die?" 1 Sam. xxviii. 9. Thus, "Resist," saith Peter, 1 Pet. v. 9; "Stand fast," saith Paul, Eph. vi. 14. νικᾶν παρὰ τὸ νὲ εἴκειν. Resist, and Satan will flee, he is but a coward. Stand, and then Satan will fall. Not to yield is to conquer: if he cast us not down, we are then accepted, as if we did cast him down. We do "over-overcome," saith that great apostle, ὑπερνικῶμεν, Rom. viii. 37, because in our head, Christ, we overcome before we fight, and are sure of victory, Rev. xii. 1. *Quare apage sis, diabole, et tela tua in hoc semen mulieris converte: hunc si viceris, me quoque viceris*, said one; Devil, do thy worst to Christ: conquer him, and take all. (Solomon Gonerus apud Melch. Adam.)

For it is written] This two-edged sword our Saviour had found to be metal of proof, and therefore holds him to it. Only the Scriptures scare the devil, as only faithful prayer can charm him. Isa. xxvi. 16, prayer is called לחש‎, a charm. Athanasius writeth that evil spirits may be put to flight by that Psalm (lxviii.): "Let the Lord arise, and his enemies be confounded." But this is true of the whole word of God, which is armour of proof against the devil.

Thou shalt worship the Lord thy God] "Thou shalt fear the Lord thy God," saith Moses. So Matt. xv. 9 with Isa. xxix. 13. See Psal. ii. 11; Josh. xxiv. 14; Heb. xii. 28. Solomon sets the fear of God as the basis and beginning of God's work and worship, in the beginning of his works, Prov. i. 7. And again in the end of them, makes it the end and upshot of all. For they "that fear the Lord will keep his covenant," Psal. ciii. 13—18. Yea, they will work hard at it, as afraid to be taken with their tasks undone, Acts x. 35. *Deum si quis parum metuit, valde contemnit; hujus qui non memorat beneficentiam, auget injuriam.* (Fulgent.) They will give him both the shell of outward adoration and the kernel of inward devotion; truly, without halting; and totally, without halving: truly, both for matter and manner; totally, both for subject and object; as David, who did all the wills of God, θελήματα, and with all his heart, all the days of his life, Acts xiii. 36. The Gentiles could say, that God must be worshipped ἤ ὅλως ἤ μὴ ὅλως, either to our utmost, or not at all. And Plutarch compares our duty to a certain fish, which eaten sparingly hurteth; but being eaten up all, is medicinal.

And him only shalt thou serve] With inward worship, as before with outward. And so God only is to be served; for it supposeth Omniscience, Omnipresence, and Omnipotence, which are in none else but God. *Sunt qui colendi verbum, ἀπὸ τοῦ κολακεύειν dictum volunt, eo quod plerunque Dei hominumque cultus, cum adulatione et hypocrisi est conjunctus. Sic* α λατρεύειν, *Gallicum et nostrate* flatter. *Sic adorare quidam dictum volunt ab ore, tametsi mente magis quam ore vera fiat adoratio. Quinetiam adorare antiquis idem fuit quod agere.*

Ver. 11. *Then the devil left him*] If Christ command him away, there is no abiding for him. Here he was foiled and quelled, and, as it were, cast down and killed by Christ our champion. (Stuchius *de sacrific. Gentilium.*) He came into the field like another Goliah, cracking and calling craven, but ere he went thence, was made to hop headless, as he first a terror, afterwards a scorn, as it was anciently said of those chariots armed with scythes and hooks. Charles VIII., in his expedition against Naples, came into the field like thunder and lightning, but went out like a snuff: more than a man at first, less than a woman at last. Henceforth therefore, though we are ever to expect temptations till such time as we have gotten that great gulf between the devil and us, Luke xvi. 26, yet "fear none of those things that ye shall suffer," *Nulla major tentatio quam nulla tentatione pulsari.* Behold, the devil shall (by his imps and instruments)

cast some of you (not all) into prison (not into hell), that ye may be tried (not destroyed), and ye shall have tribulation ten days (so long, and no longer). "Be thou faithful unto death, and I will give thee a crown of life," Rev. ii. 10. Satan can look for no crown, he is in perdition already. His aim and endeavour is, to draw us into the same condemnation. This we escape, if we resist, steadfast in the faith: for then he perceives Christ, "the chief Captain of our salvation," to be there; and therefore flees his presence, ever since he felt his prowess. Chrysostom saith, that by the sacrament of the Lord's supper we are so armed against Satan's temptations, that he fleeth from us no otherwise than if we were so many *leones ignem expuentes*, lions that spit fire. It is not silly people's defying the devil and spitting at his name, that avails anything: for they spit not low enough; they spit him not out of their hearts: yea, they admit him thereinto by yielding to his suggestions; and are miserably foolish, as if men should startle at the name of fire, and yet not fear to be scorched with the flame thereof. Our safest way is to run to Ithiel and Ucal, as Agur did, Prov. xxx. 1, 2, to Christ "the author and finisher of our faith," Heb. xii. 2; who here gave the devil such an inglorious foil, trampled him in the mire, triumphed over him, and hath promised to "tread him under our feet shortly," Rom. xvi. 20.

And, lo, the angels came and ministered unto him] Perhaps food to his body, as once to Elias, 1 Kings xix. 5, 6, but certainly comfort to his soul, as to Jacob, Hagar, Daniel, Zacharias, Joseph, Cornelius, Paul, &c. Dan. ix. 21; Luke i. 11; Acts x. 4, 27, 23. Socrates and Theodoret tell us of one Theodorus, a martyr, put to extreme torments by Julian the apostate, and dismissed again by him, when he saw him unconquerable. Ruffinus tells us that he met with this martyr, a long time after this trial, and asked him, "whether the pain he felt were not insufferable?" He answered, "that at first it was somewhat grievous: but after a while, there seemed to stand by him a young man in white, who with a soft and comfortable handkerchief wiped off the sweat of his body (which through extreme pain and anguish was little less than blood) and bade him be of good cheer. Insomuch as that it was rather a punishment than a pleasure to him to be taken off the rack, sith, when the tormentors had done, the angel was gone. And how many unspeakable comforts ministered the good angels to the modern martyrs in their prisons, at the stake, and in the fire! Christ indeed was not comforted by them till the temptation was over; but to us they minister, many times, in the hour of temptation. They have power over the devils to restrain them: and (though invisibly and insensibly) are as ready to help and comfort us as the evil angels to tempt and trouble us: else were not our protection equal to our danger, and we could neither stand nor rise. An angel stood at Zacharias' right hand, Luke i. 11 (as the devil did at Joshua's, Zech. iii. 1), to show how ready and handy they are to defend and support the saints. It was as he was burning incense. The angels are busiest about us when we are in God's work: which to set forth, the hangings of the tabernacle of old were full of cherubims within and without. He said unto him, " Fear not, Zacharias." The blessed spirits (though they do not often vocally express it) do pity our human frailties, and secretly suggest comfort to us, when we perceive it not. Alway they stand looking on the face of God to receive commandments, for the accomplishment of all designs for our good; which they have no sooner received than they readily despatch, even with weariness of flight, as Dan. ix. 21, with so much swiftness, as if they had wearied themselves with flying. I read of a friar that undertook to show to the people a feather of the wing of the angel Gabriel. A plume of whose feathers it might better have become the pope to send to Tyrone the Irish rebel, than that plume of phœnix-feathers he sent to honour and encourage him; had his Holiness such command over angels, as they say he hath, or did he not rather collude in one thing, as that friar did in another? (Carleton's Thankful Rem. of God's Mercies.)

Ver. 12. *Now when Jesus heard that John was cast into prison*] For Herodias' sake, though under pretexts of fear of sedition, because of the great multitudes that followed and admired him, as Josephus hath it. This hath ever been an ordinary accusation cast upon the most innocent, to be seedsmen of sedition, and troublers of the state. Jeremiah was held and called a traitor, Elijah a troubler of Israel, Paul a pest, εὑρήκαμεν τοῦτον τὸν λοιμὸν, Acts xxiv. 5. *Luther, tuba rebellionis*, the trumpet of rebellion, &c. *Invenies apud Tacitum frequentatas accusationes majestatis, unicum crimen eorum qui crimine vacabant*, saith Lipsius. There was some colour of right, yea, of piety laid upon the French massacre, and by edicts, a fair cloak sought, to cover the impious fraud, as if there had been some wicked conspiracy plotted by the Protestants against the king, the queen-mother, the king's brethren, the king of Navarre, and the princes of the blood. For there was coin stamped in memory of the matter, in the forepart whereof (together with the king's picture) was this inscription, *Virtus in rebelles*. And on the other side *Pietas excitavit justitiam*. Not many years before this, Francis, king of France, when he would excuse to the princes of Germany (whose friendship he then sought after) that cruelty he had exercised against the Protestants, he gave out that he punished Anabaptists only, that bragged of enthusiasm, and cried down magistracy, stirring up the people to sedition as they had done not long before in Germany. (Scultet. Annal.) This foul aspersion cast upon true religion gave occasion to Calvin (then a young man of 25 years of age) to set forth that incomparable work, called his Institutions of Christian Religion, concerning which, Paulus Melissus long since sang,

Præter Apostolicas post Christi tempora chartas,
    Huic peperere libro sæcula nulla parem.

Since Christ's and the apostles' time no such book hath been written.

He departed into Galilee] *Succenturiatus prodit Joanni*, saith a learned interpreter. He therefore went into Galilee (which was under Herod's government) to be, as it were, a supply and successor to John, whom Herod had imprisoned. How well might the tyrant say of the Church, as those Persians did of the Athenians, βάλλομεν, οὐ πίπτουσι · τιτρώσκομεν, οὐ φοβέονται. " We overturn them, and yet they fall not; we wound them, and yet they fear not." (Stobæus.) St Basil bade the persecuted Christians tell the tyrants with a bold and brave spirit, Ἐὰν γὰρ παλὶν ἰσχύητε, παλὶν ἡττηθήσεσθε. " If ye prevail again, yet surely ye shall be overcome again." (Enarr. in Isa. viii. 10.) For there is neither power nor policy against the Lord. Charles V. (than whom all Christendom had not a more prudent prince, nor the Church of Christ (almost) a sorer enemy), when he had in his hand Luther dead, and Melancthon and Pomeran, and certain other preachers of the gospel, alive, he not only determined not anything extremely against them, or violated their graves, but also entreating them gently, sent them away, not so much as once forbidding them to publish openly the doctrine that they professed. (Acts and Mon.) For it is the nature of Christ's Church, the more that persecutors spurn against it, the more it flourisheth and increaseth, as the palm-tree spreadeth and springeth the more it is oppressed; as the bottle or bladder, that may be dipped, not drowned; as the oak, that taketh heart to grace from the maims and wounds given it, and sprouts the thicker; as fenugreek, which the worse it is handled (saith Pliny) the better it proves. (*Duris ut ilex tonsa bipennibus, per damna, per cædes ab ipso ducit opes animumque ferro.* Horat.) This made Arrius Antoninus (a cruel persecutor in Asia) cry out to the Christians, who came by troops to his tribunal, and proclaimed themselves Christians (so offering themselves to death): *O miseri, si libet perire, num vobis rupes aut restes desunt?* (Tertul. ad Scapulam. Ω δειλοὶ, εἰ θέλετε ἀποθνήσκειν, κρημνοὺς, ἢ βρόχους ἔχετε.) " O wretched men, if ye be so desirous to die, have you neither rocks nor halters wherewith to despatch yourselves?" Diocletian, after he had in vain done his utmost to blot out Christ's name from under heaven, and could not effect it (such was the constancy of the primitive Christians, that no sufferings could affright or discourage them, but that they grew upon him daily, do what he could to the contrary), laid down the empire in great discontent, and betook himself (as Charles V. also did) to a private course of life. (Bucholcer, Chronol.) As lambs breed in winter, and quails came with the wind, Numb. xi. 31, so good preachers and people spring most in hard times. No fowl is more preyed upon by hawks, kites, &c., than the pigeon, yet are there more doves than hawks or kites for all that, saith Optatus. μικρὸν ποίμνιον, Luke xii. 32. So the sheep; and so the sheep of Christ: "A little little flock," he calleth it, but such as all the wolves on earth and devils in hell cannot possibly devour. The Christians of Calabria suffered great persecution, A.D. 1560; for being all thrust up in one house together, as in a sheep-fold, the executioner cometh in, and amongst them taketh one, and blindfoldeth him with a muffler about his eyes, and so leadeth him forth into a larger place, where he commandeth him to kneel down; which being done he cutteth his throat, and so leaving him half dead, and taking his butcher's knife and muffler all of gore blood, cometh again to the rest, and so leading them one after another, he despatcheth them all, to the number of 88. (Acts and Mon.) All the elder went to death more cheerfully, the younger were more timorous. I tremble and shake (saith a Roman Catholic, out of whose letter to his lord this is transcribed) even to remember how the executioner held his bloody knife between his teeth, with the bloody muffler in his hand, and his arms all in gore blood up to the elbows, going to the fold, and taking every of them one after another by the hand, and so despatching them all, no otherwise than doth a butcher kill his calves and sheep. Notwithstanding all which barbarous cruelty, the Waldenses or Protestants were so spread, not in France only, their chief seat, but in Germany also, many years before this, that they could travel from Collen to Milan in Italy, and every night lodge with hosts of their own profession. It is not yet a dozen years since Pope Urban VIII. (that now sitteth), upon the surrender of Rochelle into the French king's hands, sent his breve to the king, exasperating him against the Protestants in France, and eagerly urging, yea, enforcing the destruction of all the heretics stabling in the French vineyard, as his inurbanity is pleased to express it. *Reliquias omnes hæreticorum in Gallica vinea stabulantium propediem profligatum iri.* (Bp. Hall's Answer to Pope Urban.) But "what shall be given unto thee? or what shall be done unto thee, thou foul tongue? Sharp arrows of the mighty, with coals of juniper," Psal. cxx. 3, 4, which burn vehemently and smell sweetly. God shall shortly put into the hearts of the kings of the earth (and this king among the rest of the ten) to hate the whore, to eat her flesh, and to burn her with fire, Rev. xvii. 16. (*Babylon altera adhuc stat, cito itidem casura, si essetis viri.* Petrar.) There are not many ages past since one of his predecessors broke open the gates of Rome, mouldered the wall, dispersed the citizens, and condemned the pope to a dark dungeon, lading him with bitter scoffs and curses. There are not many years past since the realm of France was ready, upon the pope's refusal to re-bless King Henry IV., upon conversion to them, to withdraw utterly from the obedience of his see, and to erect a new patri-

arch over all the French Church. (Philip le Beausandys.) The then Archbishop of Bruges was ready to accept it: and but that the pope (in fear thereof) did hasten his benediction, it had been effected, to his utter disgrace and decay. (Powell on Toleration.) Before he would do it, he lashed the king in the person of his ambassador, after the singing of every verse of *miserere*, until the whole Psalm was sung out. *Sed exorto Evangelii jubare, sagaciores, ut spero, principes, ad nutum hujus Orbilii non solvent subligacula,* saith a great divine of ours (Dean Prideaux). King Henry VIII. and the French king (some half a year before their deaths) were at a point to have changed the mass in both their realms into a communion: also to have utterly extirpated the Bishop of Rome, &c. (Acts and Mon., *Ex testimon.* Cranmeri.) Yea, they were so thoroughly resolved in that behalf, that they meant also to exhort the emperor to do the like, or to break off from him. The same emperor, to be revenged upon Pope Clement, his enemy, abolished the pope's authority throughout all Spain, his native kingdom, declaring thereby (the Spaniards themselves, for example) that ecclesiastical discipline may be conserved without the papal authority. (A.D. 1526, Scultet. Annal.) The Eastern Churches have long since separated; the other four patriarchs dividing themselves from the Bishop of Rome, and at their parting using these or the like words: Thy greatness we know, thy covetousness we cannot satisfy, thy encroaching we can no longer abide; live to thyself. (*Odi fastum illius ecclesiæ.* Basil.) Neither are the Western much behind, especially since all was changed in that Church,—manners, doctrine, and the very rule of faith, in the Trent Council. Then (according to some expositors) did "the second angel pour out his vial upon the sea" (upon that conflux of all sorts at Trent), "and it became as the blood of a dead man" (those deadly decrees are written with the blood of heretics), "and every living soul died in that sea," as once the fish of Egypt. (Field of the Church, Rev. xvi. 3.) For none that worship the beast "have their names written in the book of life of the Lamb slain from the foundation of the world," Rev. xiii. 8. Slain, I say, as in his Father's decree and promise, as in the sacrifices of the law and faith of his people; so in his members and martyrs, beheaded, as John Baptist, or otherwise butchered for the witness of Jesus and for the word of God. But the blood of the martyrs was the feeding of the Church. (*Sanguis martyrum, semen ecclesiæ.* Tert. *Testes veritatis per Illyricum.*) God was never left without witnesses, as is seen in our catalogues; but although John was cast into prison, yea, beheaded in the prison, as if God had known nothing of him (quoth that martyr), yet there never wanted a Jesus to go into Galilee: and that guilty Edomite Herod was sensible of it, Matt. xiv. 2, when he said to his servants, "This is John Baptist, he is risen from the dead." In like sort the Romish Edomite, after he had done to death Christ's two ancienter witnesses, that (Baptist-like) came in the spirit and power of Elias, to confute and confound their Baal-worships, yet to his great grief and regret he hath seen them revive and stand upon their feet again, Rev. xi. 10, in that heroical Wicliff, who is said to have written more than two hundred volumes against him, in that goose of Bohemia, that swan of Saxony (those three famous angels, that flew in the midst of heaven, having the everlasting gospel to preach to them that dwell on the earth), together with those other noble reformers in all Christian churches. (Pareus in Apoc. xiv. 6. *Hus* in that language signifieth a "goose," *Luther* a "swan," and John Huss at his death prophesied it.) By whom, ever since the pope was declared to be antichrist, his authority (saith Bellarmine) hath not only not increased, but daily more and more decreased. The fourth beast hath lost a head, as Cusanus the cardinal hath prophesied, A.D. 1464, and after him Trithemius the abbot, A.D. 1508. A sect of religion, saith he, shall arise once within this thirteen years, to the great destruction of the old religions. It is to be feared that the fourth beast will lose one of her heads. (*Secta religionis consurget, magna veterum destructio religionum; timendum ne caput unum amittat bestia quarta. Lib. de Intelligentiis Cœlestib.* Bucholcer, Chron.) This he writeth in his book concerning angels and spirits: what kind of spirit it was (black or white) that dictated unto him this prophecy, which fell out accordingly, and was fulfilled in M. Luther, I cannot tell. But the godly learned suspect it was from that evil spirit, who is said to have sung before,

Roma, tibi subito motibus ibit amor.

As the Emperor Frederick is reported also to have foretold in this distich,—

Roma diu titubans, variis erroribus acta,
Corruet ; et mundi desinet esse caput.

Ver. 13. *And leaving Nazareth*] Where he had his conception and education; and did therefore in a special manner affect them, and seek their good, but they would not. For when he would have healed Israel, then the iniquity of Ephraim broke out, as the leprosy in their foreheads, Hos. vii. 1; they refused to be reformed, they hated to be healed. Some few sick folk he healed there, and that was all he could do for them, more than marvel at their unbelief. He "could do there no mighty work," saith St Mark (vi. 5, 6,) and therefore left them, saith St Matthew: than the which he could hardly have done them a greater displeasure, for "woe be unto you, if I depart from you," Hos. ix. 12. In Ezekiel ix., x., and xi., God makes divers removes; and still as he goes out, some judgment comes in, till at length he was quite gone out of the city, chap. xi. 23. And then followed the fatal calamity in the ruin thereof. Oh pray that the sun of that dismal day may never arise, wherein it shall be said, that our candlestick is removed, Rev. ii. 5, that our sun is eclipsed, that the glory is departed from our English Israel, that Christ hath turned his back upon this our Nazareth; *Mittamus preces et lacrymas, cordis legatos,* saith Cyprian. *Currat pœnitentia ne præcurrat sententia,* saith Chrysologus. Wish we for our Church, as Forus did for the Romish synagogue, that we had some Moses to take away the evils and abuses therein. *Nam non unum tantum vitulum, sed multos habemus.* And then sing as another did,

Ah, ne diem illum posteri
Vivant mei, quo pristinum
Vertantur in lutum aurea
Quæ nos beârunt sæcula!

He came and dwelt in Capernaum] Happy town in so sweet and precious an inhabitant! and is therefore said to be lifted up to heaven, Matt. xi. 23, as Rev. vii. Among those that were sealed of the several tribes, Judah is first reckoned of all Leah's children, because our Lord sprang out of Judah: and Nephthalim (of all those of Rachel's side) because at Capernaum, in that tribe, he dwelt, *Ut utrobique superemineat Christi prærogativa,* saith an interpreter, that Christ may be all and in all. (Mede in Apocalyps.; Aquinas, Jerome in Matt. viii.) Here he dwelt in a house, either let or lent him; for of his own he had not where to rest his head, Matt. viii. 20. Here he paid tribute as an inhabitant; and hither he resorted and retired himself, when he was tired at any time with preaching and journeying, and was willing to take rest; which yet hardly he could do through the continual concourse, but was glad to get into a ship or desert to pray, eat, or sleep.

Which is upon the sea coast] That is, hard by the lake of Gennesareth in Galilee of the Gentiles. Josephus calls it a town, κωμὴν, because it was without walls (belike). For Strabo writeth that Pompey had commanded the walls of all fenced cities in those parts to be pulled down. St Jerome also saith it was a town, and that it so continued till his times. But St Matthew and St Luke name it a city, wherein there was a synagogue of the Jews, and a garrison of Herod's soldiers, because it bordered upon Arabia. It had fifteen thousand inhabitants at least, there being no town in Galilee that had fewer, saith Josephus (B. J. iii. 2). The inhabitants might be of the same mind with those of the Hague in Holland, who will not wall their town, though it hath two thousand households in it, as desiring to have it counted rather the principal village of Europe than a lesser city.

In the borders of Zabulon and Nephthalim] In the former whereof is Galilee, in the latter this Galilee of the Gentiles, where stands the town of Capernaum, and near unto it is a well of the same name, and of apt signification; for Capernaum, saith St Jerome, is by interpretation "the town of consolation." It was situate on this side Jordan, over against Bethsaida, otherwise called Julias, not far from Tiberias, and Tarichæa, famous places lying likewise upon the lake.

Ver. 14. *That it might be fulfilled, &c.*] The two Testaments may be fitly resembled to the double doors of the temple, one whereof infolded another: the Old is the New infolded; the New is the Old explicated. (Jerome in nom. Hebraicis.) For there are above 260 places of the Old Testament cited in the New: so that almost in every needful point the harmony is expressed.

By the prophet Esaias] That evangelical prophet, that speaketh of Christ's nativity, preaching, persecution, apprehension, death, resurrection, ascension, and second coming to judgment, so lively as no evangelist goes beyond him. (Bulling in Isa., *præf.*)

Ver. 15. *The land of Zabulon, and the land of Nephthalim, &c.*] In Zabulon were Nazareth, Bethsaida, Tiberias, Cana (where our Saviour turned water into wine), and Nain, where he raised the widow's son; so that she was twice a mother, yet had but one child, 2 Sam. xx. 18. In Nephthalim were the city of Abel (where they asked counsel of old, and so they ended the matter); Harosheth the city of Sisera, Riblah, Cæsarea, Philippi, and Capernaum. This borough was the seat of the evangelical kingdom; and it was fitly chosen for such a purpose, as that which by reason of the wonderful wholesomeness of the air, fertility of the soil, nearness to the river Jordan and lake of Gennesareth, neighbourhood of many great towns and famous cities, promised a plentiful increase and income of the evangelical harvest. Here the corn was white unto the harvest (as at Samaria) and solicited labourers. It is a minister's wisdom to seat himself, as near as may be, where most need is, and greatest likelihood of doing good, as St Paul did often. ("Come over into Macedonia and help us," Acts xvi. 9. "Thou hast well done that thou art come," Acts x. 33.) No church was founded at Athens, no good to be done there among those wits of Greece. The apostle tarried at Ephesus, while a door was opened, and then departed to other places. If thou perceive thyself unfit to do more good in any place, though it be not any fault of thine, saith a grave author, away to another. If the commodity of the place prevail more with thee there to abide, than the promoting of Christ's kingdom, to use thy talent elsewhere, it is to be feared thou wilt either lose thy gifts, or fall into errors and heresies, or, at least, become a frigid and dry doctor among such a people as have once conceived an incurable prejudice against thee. (Rolloc. Com. in John iv. 44.)

Galilee of the Gentiles] So called, either because it bordered upon the Gentiles, or because it was given away by David to Hiram, king of Tyre, or because it was inhabited by the Assyrians, who carried the people captive, and dwelt in their room.

Ver. 16. *The people which sat in darkness saw a great light*] For the day-spring from on high visited them, the bright Sun of Righteousness

(which had all Palestine for his zodiac, the twelve tribes for his signs) stayed longest in Zabulon and Nephthalim: Luke i. 2; Mal. iv. 2; and (St Jerome observeth) as these two tribes were first carried into captivity, and seemed furthest from heaven, as bordering on the Gentiles, and in many things symbolizing with them, having learned their manners; so redemption was first preached in these countries. Physicians are of most use where diseases abound. The prophets in Elisha's days planted at Bethel. There was at once the golden-calf of Jeroboam and the school of God.

Sat in darkness, and in the region and shadow of death] Note here that a state of darkness is a state of death. This is condemnation, this is hell above-ground and afore-hand, that "light is come into the world, and men love darkness better than light," John iii. 36. *Ut liberius peccent libenter ignorant.* (Bernard.) Now surely they shall one day have enough of their so much-desired darkness, Prov. xiv. 14. They know not the light, saith Job (xxiv. 13). They hate it, saith our Saviour, John iii. 20. They spurn and scorn at it, saith Solomon, Prov. i. 22; therefore shall they be filled in their own ways, while they are cast into utter darkness, a darkness beyond a darkness (σκότος ἐξώτερον), as it were a dungeon beyond a prison, where they shall never see light again, till they be enlightened with that universal fire of the last day to their everlasting amazement, 2 Thess. i. 8.

Light is sprung up] He brought them "out of darkness into his marvellous light." So he did the Samaritans by Philip's preaching and miracles, whereupon there was great joy in that city, 1 Pet. ii. 9; Acts viii. 8. So by the ministry of Farel, Viret, Calvin, and others, he drew the Genevans out of the dark midnight of damned Popery; in a thankful remembrance whereof they coined new money, with this inscription on the one side, *Post tenebras lux*, After darkness light. (Their posie till then had been, *Post tenebras spero lucem*, taken out of Job.) And on the other side, *Deus noster pugnat pro nobis*, Our God fighteth for us. (Scultet. Annal.)

Ver. 17. *From that time Jesus began to preach*] So he had done before John was imprisoned, John ii. and iii., but now more freely, and frequently more manifestly, and all abroad, as when the day-star hath done his devoir, the sun shines out to the perfect day, Prov. iv. 18.

And to say, Repent] Both for sin by contrition, and from sin by conversion. Change your minds and manners, your constitution and conversation, from worse to better (μετανοεῖτε); recover your lost wits with the prodigal (who repenting is said to come to himself), and become wiser after your folly (*Ab ἄνοια, dementia, et μετὰ, post.* Luke xv. 17.) Pull down the very frame of the old man, unmake yourselves, as St Peter hath it, ταῖς ἁμαρτίαις, ἀπογενόμενοι, 1 Pet. ii. 24. Undo what you had done before, and be ye transmanted and metamorphosed "by the renewing of your minds," Rom. xii. 2; for, "except a man be born again," not *desuper* only, but *denuo*, from above, but a second time ('Ανωθεν, John iii. 3, as Nicodemus understood our Saviour), except he go over all again that is past, rejecting it as unprofitable and begin anew, he cannot see the kingdom of God; where old things are past, all things are become new, 2 Cor. v. 17, a whole new creation.

For the kingdom of heaven is at hand] See what is said to this whole verse, iii. 2. For this was the sum and substance of the Baptist's, our Saviour's, and his apostles' sermons; and had need to be daily pressed and preached, sith it is our *pensum diurnum*, the first and continual work of God's Spirit in the faithful, who because they cannot wash their hands in innocency, wash them in tears; and by renewing their repentance, work and wear out all brackish and sinful dispositions, as sweet water will do the salt sea coming into it; as wine or honey casteth out the scum, as fast as it ariseth. Christ biddeth us as oft to pray, "Forgive us our trespasses," as we pray, "Give us this day our daily bread." He not only waits for repentance from the wicked, 2 Pet. iii. 9, but would also have his dearest children daily meet him, condemning themselves, Luke xiii. 5. "If ye repent not" also more and more, when ye see the examples of God's wrath upon others, "ye shall likewise perish." Besides, some sins are past in time that are not past in deed, if we dwell not in the undoing and reversing of them, Ezra x. 11, 12, and ix. 15. They were to begin anew their repentance, because they had not considered their marrying of strange wives.

Ver. 18. *And Jesus walking by the sea of Galilee*] Not for recreation's sake, or to deceive the time (for he had a great multitude attending upon him to hear the Word of God, as St Luke noteth), but as laying hold on the opportunity of calling Peter and Andrew, and after that James and John, to the apostleship. Our Saviour knew that a well-chosen season is the greatest advantage of any action; which, as it is seldom found in haste, so is too often lost in delay. The men of Issachar were in great account with David, because they had understanding of the times, to know what Israel ought to do, and when to do it, 1 Chron. xii. 32. So are they in great account with the Son of David, who regard and improve (as he did here) the season of well-doing, which they that lose are the greatest losers and the wastefullest prodigals; for of all other possessions two may be had together. But two moments of time (how much less two opportunities of time!) cannot be possessed together. Some are *semper victuri* (as Seneca saith), ever about to do better; they stand futuring and whiling out the time so long, till they have trifled and fooled away their own salvation. Let us sit ready in the door of our hearts (as Abraham did in the door of his tent) to apprehend occasions of doing good, as he to entertain passengers, to set a word or work upon its wheels, that it may be as "apples of gold in

pictures of silver," Prov. xxv. 11, pleasant and profitable; for everything is beautiful in its season, and how forcible are right words! Eccl. iii. 1; Job vi. 25. As the bee (so soon as ever the sun breaks forth) flies abroad to gather honey and wax, so be thou ready to every good work, waiting the occasions thereof, Tit. iii. 1. Now, now, saith David, and after him Paul, because (for aught we know), it is now or never, to-day or not at all, Psal. xcv. 7; 2 Cor. vi. 2. Opportunities are headlong, and once past, irrecoverable; *Ex hoc momento pendet æternitas.* (August.) God hath hanged the heaviest weights upon the weakest wires. Be quick therefore and abrupt in thine obedience, thou knowest not what a great-bellied day may bring forth, Prov. xxvii. 1. *Nescis quid serus vesper vehat.* Yea, thou mayest the very next hour be cut off from all further time of repentance, acceptation, and grace for ever.

He saw two brethren] He knew them and admitted them into his friendship well nigh a year before, John i. 39, but now calleth them from being fishers to be fishers of men. Peter is famous for his first draught, Acts ii. 41, whereby he caught and brought to the Church three thousand souls.

Casting their nets into the sea] God calleth men when they are busy; Satan, when they are idle. For idleness is the hour of temptation, and an idle person the devil's tennis-ball, which he tosseth at pleasure, and sets to work as he liketh and listeth. (*Veteres Romani Agenoriam Stimulam et Strenam intra 'mœnia pro diis coluerunt. Quietem vero extra urbem constituerunt.* Senec.) God hath ordained that in the sweat of his brow man should eat his bread, Gen. iii. 19. The Hebrew hath it, In the sweat of his nose; for he must labour till the sweat run down his nose. Which if he do, God hath promised that *manus motans*, the diligent, nimblehanded man shall not stay long in a low place. He shall stand before princes, as these painful fishermen were to stand before the Prince of Peace, and to be of his constant retinue; as, till then, their busy attendance on their calling was no less pleasing to Christ than an immediate devotion. Happy is that servant whom his Lord when he comes shall find serving God and man with his fat and sweat, as the fig-tree and vine in Jotham's parable, Prov. x. 4; xxii. 29; Judg. ix. 9.

For they were fishers] *Asinos elegit Christus, et idiotas*, saith one, *sed oculavit in prudentes, simulque dona dedit et ministeria.* Christ sends forth none to preach but whom he gifteth: where the comfort is, that a small hand may thread a needle, and a little bark do better in a small river than a great ship.

Ver. 19. *He saith unto them, Follow me*] And together with his word there went forth a power inclining them to follow, whereby it appears that they were not only of the many that are called, but of those few that are chosen, Luke v. 17. "The Lord knoweth who are his," saith

St Paul. But this knowing of his is carried secret, as a river under-ground, till by effectual calling he separates them from the rest, till they can "call upon the name of the Lord and depart from evil," 2 Tim. ii. 19. This when they are once taught of Christ they must be acting; when he hath tuned and touched us, we must make music, and whilst the Spirit embreathes us, we must turn about as the mill, and follow the Lamb wheresoever he goeth, as these disciples did, Rev. iv. 4.

And I will make you fishers of men] Of live men, Luke v. 10, ἀνθρώπους ζωγρῶν, as fishers desire to catch fish alive, because they are more vendible: an apt metaphor, wherein, 1. The world is compared to the sea, for its unsettledness, tumultuousness, the oppression that is in it (the lesser fish being devoured of the greater), and the sway that Leviathan, the devil, bears there, Psal. civ. 26. 2. The Church is compared to a boat, because it is continually tossed with the waves of affliction, as Noah, Jonah, the disciples, Paul, and those sea-faring men, "that stagger like a drunken man," and all their cunning is gone, Psal. cvii. 27. 3. The fish to be caught out of this sea and to be brought into this ship are men, John i. 42; Matt. viii. 24. Nature hath, as it were, spawned us forth into this worldly sea; where we drink iniquity like water, wandering confusedly up and down, till caught and cast into the fish-pool for the Master's use and service. Unwittingly we are caught, and unwillingly we are kept, as fishes labour to get out of the net and would fain leap back out of the boat into the water. 4. Ministers are fishers. A busy profession, a toilsome calling, no idle man's occupation, as the vulgar conceit it, nor needless trade, taken up alate, to pick a living out of. Let God's fishermen busy themselves as they must, sometimes in preparing, sometimes in mending, sometimes in casting abroad, sometimes in drawing in the net, "that they may separate the precious from the vile," &c., Jer. xv. 19; Matt. xiii. 48, and no man shall have just cause to twit them with idleness, or to say they have an easy life, and that it is neither sin nor pity to defraud them.

Ver. 20. *And they straightway left their nets*] As the woman of Samaria did her pitcher, Matthew his toll-book, and blind Bartimeus his cloak when Christ called for him. Look we likewise to this "author and finisher of our faith;" and for love of him cast away every clog, and the sin that doth so easily beset or surround us (εὐπερίστατον, Heb. xii. 1, 2). Divorce the flesh from the world, and there is no great danger. Admire not overmuch, rest not in, dote not on, cleave not to, the things of this life (those nets and snares of Satan, whereby he entangleth and encumbereth us), that we may attend upon the Lord (or sit close to him) without being haled away or distracted by these lusts of life (εὐπρόσεδρον τῷ κυρίῳ ἀπερισπάστως, 1 Cor. vii. 35). The deeplier any man is drowned in the world, the more desperately is he divorced from God,

deadened to holy things, and disobedient to the heavenly call, as the recusant guests in the Gospel, Matt. xxii. 5.

And followed him] Immediately, and without sciscitation. When Christ calls, we must not reason, but run, as Paul, Gal. i. 16; not dispute, but despatch, with David, Psal. cxix. 60. Go we know not whither, with Abraham; do we know not what, with Gideon. "If ye will inquire, inquire," saith Isaiah; "return, come," Isa. xxi. 12. God loveth *curristas*, not *quæristas*, saith Luther. A quick passage, and full of quickening; like that of the orator, *Si dormis, expergiscere; si stas, ingredere; si ingrederis, curre; si curris, advola*. (Cicer.) Courts have their *citò, citò*, quick, quick; and courtiers used to observe and improve their *mollissima fandi tempora;* so must Christians. God is but a while with men in the opportunities of grace. He comes leaping on the mountains, and skipping on the hills: and, being come, he stands at the door and knocks by the sound of his Word and motions of his Spirit. He sits not, but stands: while a man is standing we say he is going, Cant. ii. 8; Rev. iii. 20. And woe be unto us if he depart from us, Hos. ix. 12. God hath his season, his harvest for judgment, Matt. xiii. 30, and is now more quick and peremptory in rejecting men than of old: for how shall we escape if we neglect so great salvation as is now preached? Heb. ii. 2. Our Saviour would not suffer the man that said he would follow him, to let so much time as to bury his father, Matt. viii. 22. Excuses he takes for refusals, delays for denials. As Saul lost his kingdom, so doth many a man his soul, by not discerning his time: and troops of them that forget God go down to hell, Psal. ix. 17. *Quare castigemus mores et moras nostras.* Let us up and be doing, that the Lord may be with us.

Ver. 21. *He saw other two brethren, James, &c.*] Three pair of brethren, at least, our Saviour called to the apostleship; to show what brotherly love should be found amongst ministers, what agreement in judgment and affection. There the Lord commands the blessing, and life for evermore, Psal. cxxxiii. 3. As where envying and strife is, there is confusion, and every evil work, James iii. 16. Hence the devil laboureth (all he can) to set ministers at variance, and to sow dissension amongst them (as betwixt Paul and Barnabas), that the work may be hindered. *Divide et impera*, make division, and so get dominion, was a maxim of Machiavel, which he learnt of the devil. What woeful tragedies hath he raised of late betwixt the Lutherans and Zwinglians! What comedies have the Papists composed out of the Church's tragedies! To foster the faction, they joined themselves to the Lutherans in that sacramentary quarrel. They commended them, made much of them, and almost pardoned them all that loss they had sustained by them. (*Eos excusabant, in pretio habebant, ac tantum non ignoscebant iis.* Scultet.) This, that holy man of God, Œcolampadius, bitterly bewaileth in a letter to the Lutherans of Suevia. The error, saith he, may be pardoned through faith in Christ, but the discord we cannot expiate with the dearest and warmest blood in our hearts. (*Error condonari potest, modo fides adsit in Christum; discordiam, neque si sanguinem fundamus, expiabimus.*) They, on the other side (in their syngram or answer), handled that most innocent man so coarsely, *ut non objurgatione, sed execratione dignum sit,* saith Zwinglius, that they deserved not to be confuted but to be abhorred of all men. This was as good sport to the Papists as the jars betwixt Abraham and Lot were to the Amorites. But that one consideration (that we are brethren) should conjure down all disagreements (as betwixt them) and make us unite against a common adversary. The Low-Countrymen, suspecting the English (A. D. 1587), stamped money with two earthen pots swimming in the sea (according to the old fable), and wittily inscribed, *Si collidimur, frangimur,* If we clash we are broken. The Thracians, had they been all of one mind, had been invincible, saith Herodotus. And Cornelius Tacitus (who had been here in Brittany with his father-in-law Agricola) reporteth of our forefathers that they fell into the hands of the Romans by nothing so much as by their dissensions amongst themselves. *Rarus duabus tribusve civitatibus conventus. Ita dum singuli pugnant, universi vincuntur.* (Tacitus.) Pliny telleth of the stone Thyrræus, that, though never so big, while it is whole, it floateth upon the waters; but being broken, it sinketh. And who hath not read of Silurus's bundle of arrows? To break unity is to cut asunder the very veins and sinews of the mystical body of Christ, as the apostle intimateth, 1 Cor. i. 10 (κατηρτισμένοι), to hinder all true growth in godliness, Eph. iv. 16, and inward comfort, Phil. ii. 1, to drive away God, who appeared not to Abraham till the difference was made up, Gen. xiii. 14, &c., and to undo ourselves (*Præsente Loto, et vigente contentione, Deus non apparuit.* Par. *in loc.*): as the dragon sucketh out the blood of the elephant, and the weight of the falling elephant oppresseth the dragon, and so both perish together. (Plin. lib. 8, c. 12.) To prevent all which, and to compose all quarrels in this Egypt of the world, let it be remembered, as Moses told the two striving Israelites, that we are brethren. And, oh how good and how pleasant it is for brethren (in the ministry especially) to dwell together in unity, Psal. cxxxiii. 1.

Ver. 22. *And they immediately left the ship and their father*] These were wise merchants that parted with all to purchase the pearl of price. So did many martyrs, and knew they made a saver's bargain. Nicholas Shetterden writeth thus in a letter to his mother (Acts and Mon.): "What state soever your fathers be in, leave that to God, and let us follow the counsel of his word. Dear mother, embrace it with hearty affection; read it with obedience; let it be your pastime, &c. So shall we meet in joy at the last day: or else I bid you farewell for evermore." So Nicholas of Jenvile (a young man newly come from Geneva) was condemned to die, and sat in the

cart. His father coming with a staff would have beaten him. But the officers, not suffering it, would have struck the old man. The son, crying to the officers, desired them to let his father alone, saying he had power over him to do in that kind what he would; but Christ was dearer to him than the dearest friend on earth, &c. That of St Jerome is well known to most, and often alleged: "If my father stood weeping on his knees before me, my mother hanging on my neck behind me, and all my brethren, sisters, children, kinsfolk, howling on every side, to retain me in a sinful life with them, I would fling my mother to the ground, despite all my kindred, run over my father, and tread him under my feet, thereby to run to Christ when he calleth me." Rebezies and Danvile, two French martyrs, having been sorely racked, at night rejoiced together. After that Rebezies cried twice or thrice, "Away from me, Satan." His fellow being in bed with him asked why he cried, and whether Satan would stop him of his course? Rebezies said that Satan set before him his parents, "but by the grace of God," said he, "he shall do nothing against me." (Acts and Mon.)

Ver. 23. *And Jesus went about all Galilee*] Not (as the Circumcelliones of old) to make show of their holiness; nor as the Jesuits (into whom the Pharisees have fled and hid themselves) to gain proselytes and passengers that go right on their ways, Prov. ix. 15, but "he went about doing good," saith St Peter, Acts x. 38. The chiefest goods are most active; the best good a mere act. And the more good we do, the more God-like we be, and the more we draw nigh to the heavenly pattern. Religion is not a name, goodness a word; but as the life of things stands in goodness, so the life of goodness in action. So much we live, as we do. "O Lord, by these things men live," saith Hezekiah, "and in all these things is the life of my spirit," Isa. xxxviii. 16. And he that keepeth my commandments shall live in them, as the lamp lives in the oil, the flower in the earth, the creature by food. *Nos non eloquimur magna, sed vivimus,* said the ancient Christians. And holy Bradford accounted that hour lost wherein he had not done some good with tongue, pen, or hand. God hath set us our time and our task, Job xiv. 5, 6. David is said to serve out his time; and John Baptist, to finish his course, Acts xiii. 25. Up, therefore, and be doing, that ye be not taken with your task undone. Fruitless trees shall be cut down: short shooting loseth many a game. The master is an austere man, and looketh for his own with usury. (*Dies brevis est, et opus multum et operarii pauci, et paterfamilias urget.* Rab. Simeon.) It is an easy thing when the candle is out, and all still without din, to fall a napping: which will prove to your cost when God shall send forth summons for sleepers.

Teaching in their synagogues] Houses dedicated to the worship of God, wherein it was lawful (and usual) to pray, preach, and dispute, but not to sacrifice, Acts xv. 21. The temple at Jerusalem was the cathedral church; the synagogues as petty parish churches belonging thereunto. There were 480 of them in Jerusalem, as Manahen the Jew reporteth.

And preaching] Which is a further matter than teaching, and is therefore set after it here as an addition. It signifieth to publish, and (as a herald, κηρυττειν) to deliver a matter in the hearing of a multitude with greatest majesty, constancy, fidelity, and liberty of speech; not budging or balking any part of the truth; not huckstering the word of God or handling it deceitfully, but as of sincerity, as of God, in the sight of God, speaking in Christ. (καπηλευοντες, 2 Cor. ii. 17; corrupting, as men do by their false wares, or mixed wines.)

And healing all manner of sickness and disease] Both acute and chronic. None came amiss to this Jehovah Rophe, the Lord that healeth, as he styleth himself; this "Sun of Righteousness, that hath healing under his wings." (μαλακία proprie significat ignaviam stomachi. Νόσος, morbum vehementiorem et intensiorem, Exod. xv. 26; Mal. iv. 2.) To an Almighty Physician, saith Isidore, no disease can seem incurable. (*Omnipotenti medico nullus insanabilis occurrit morbus.*) He healeth with a wet finger (as we say) such patients as all the physicians in the country cast their caps at, and could not tell what to say to.

Ver. 24. *And his fame went through all Syria*] Fame followeth desert, as a sweet scent the rose. This gave occasion to the poets to feign that Achilles' tomb was ever garnished with green amaranth. "A good name is better than great riches," saith Solomon, Prov. xxii. 1. And if I can keep my credit, I am rich enough, said the heathen. (*Ego si bonam famam servasso, sat dives ero.* Plaut.) Blessing and good report are expressed by one and the same word in the Old Testament, to show what a blessing of God it is. And it could not but be a great comfort to David, that whatsoever he did pleased the people, 2 Sam. iii. 36. Cicero saith that perfect glory consisteth in these three things: if the multitude love a man, if they will trust him, and if they hold him worthy of admiration, praise, and honour. (Offic. ii. 5.) Now none of these were wanting to our Saviour, as appeareth in his holy history, and as others have fully set forth. "Do worthily in Ephratah, and so be famous in Bethlehem," Ruth iv. 11.

And they brought unto him all sick people] All that were in ill case and taking: for, *Si vales, bene est*, saith one; and, *Vita non est vivere, sed valere*, saith another. The Latins call a sick man *æger*, which some derive of *ai, ai*, the voice of complaint and grief. And the Stoics when they affirmed that to live agreeable to nature is to live virtuously and valiantly, although the body be never so out of order, they perceived when their own turn came to be sick, saith Jerome, *se magnificentius locutos esse quam verius*, that they had spoken more trimly than truly.

That were taken with divers diseases and torments] That were besieged and hemmed in on every side, as by an enemy straitened and perplexed (συνεχομένους), so that they knew not whither to look, only their eyes were toward Christ.

Diseases and torments] As of those that are put upon the rack. Pharaoh was so when God extorted from him that confession, "I have sinned;" which (being gotten off) he soon bit in again. The word here used in the original (βάσανος), properly signifieth the test or touch-stone, wherewith gold is tried; and, by a borrowed kind of speech, is applied to all kind of examination, and (peculiarly) to inquisition by torture, to any pain or painful diseases, as of the palsy, lunacy, &c., in this text, and viii. 6. As also to the torments of hell, Luke xvi. 23, whereof sicknesses are but a beginning, a foretaste, a very typical hell to those that have not the fruits of their sickness. (*Morbos virtutum officinas vocat.* Ambrosius.) And this "is all the fruits, even the taking away of their sin," Isa. xxvii. 9. I blush not to confess, saith a great divine of Scotland, that I have gained more sound knowledge of God and of myself in this sickness than ever I had before. (*Non erubesco profiteri, &c.* Rolloc. apud Melch. Adam.) Happy sickness, that draws the sick matter out of the soul. Physicians hold that in every two years there is such store of ill humours and excrements engendered in the body, that a vessel of one hundred ounces will scarce contain them. Certain it is, there is a world of wickedness and superfluity of naughtiness (that bed of spiritual diseases) daily gathered and got together in the sin-sick soul: which therefore we must labour to purge out by the practice of mortification, lest God purge and whiten us to our sorrow by some sharp sickness (Dan. xi. 35; xii. 10), as he did Gehazi, whose white forehead had made him a white soul: his disease cured him, as some are of opinion, 2 Kings v. 37.

Possessed with devils] Such as whose minds and senses the devil perverted.

Those that were lunatic] Or such as had the falling-sickness, as appeareth by those symptoms of this disease set down by St Matthew (xvii. 15). (Scultet. Exerc. Evang. ii. 12.) This is otherwise called *Morbus Sacer*. For the priests of old (that they might thereby enrich themselves) feigned that the gods tormented men with this, among other sudden and fearful diseases. (Becman, Orig. Ling. Latinæ.)

Ver. 25. *And there followed him great multitudes*] A good house-keeper shall not (likely) want company. "O thou that hearest prayer" (and so solicitest suitors), "to thee shall all flesh come," Psal. lxv. 2. Christ's miracles drew multitudes after him, then; and should still affect us with admiration and strong affection for the gospel, as the author to the Hebrews showeth, Heb. ii. 3, 4.

CHAPTER V.

Ver. 1. *And seeing the multitudes*] As sheep without a shepherd, or as corn ripe and ready, falling, as it were, into the hands of the harvest-man. The "children cried for bread, and there was none to break it," Lam. iv. 4. His eye therefore affected his heart, and out of deep commiseration

He went up into a mountain] This mount was his pulpit, as the whole law was his text. It is said to be in the tribe of Naphtali, and called Christ's mount to this day. As Moses went up into a mount to receive the law, so did Messias to expound it, and so must we to contemplate it. *Sursum corda.* Wind we up our hearts, which naturally bear downward, as the poise of a clock.

And when he was set] Either as being weary, or as intending a longer sermon. This at his first onset upon his office, and that at his last (when he left the world and went to his Father, John xiv. 15—17), being the longest and liveliest that are recorded in the Gospel. He preached, no doubt, many times many hours together. But as his miracles, so his oracles are no more of them written than might suffice to make us believe, and live through his name, John xx. 31. As the prophets of old, after they had preached to the people, set down the sum of their sermons, the heads only, for the use of the Church in all ages, so did the apostles record in their day-books the chief things in our Saviour's sermons, out of which they afterwards (by the instinct and guidance of the Spirit of God) framed this holy history. (Scultet. Annal. epist. dedic.)

His disciples came unto him] To sit at his feet and hear his word. Among the Jews the Rabbi sat, termed יושב or the sitter; the scholar, מתאבק or one that lieth along in the dust, a token of the scholar's humility, subjecting himself even to the feet of his teacher. Thus Mary sat at Jesus' feet, and heard his word, Luke x. 39. Thus all God's saints are said to "sit at his feet, every one to receive his word," Deut. xxxiii. 3. Thus Paul was brought up at the feet of Gamaliel, a great doctor in Israel, Acts xxii. 3. And this custom it is thought St Paul laboured to bring into the Christian Church, 1 Cor. xiv.

Ver. 2. *And he opened his mouth*] This phrase is not superfluous (as some may conceit), but betokeneth free and full discourse, Eph. vi. 19, of some weighty and important matter, Psal. lxxviii. 2, uttered with great alacrity of spirit and vehemency of speech.

And taught them, saying] He taught them sometimes (saith Theodoret) when he opened not his mouth, *sc. διὰ τοῦ βίου καὶ θαυμάτων,* by his holy life and wondrous works. A mirror for ministers, who as they should open their mouths with wisdom (heaven never opened in the Revelation, but some great matter followed), so their lives should be consonant to the tenor of their teaching, a very visible comment on the audible word. Timothy must be a stamp, a standard, a pattern, a precedent to the believers, both in word and conversation (τύπος), 1 Tim. iv. 12. Aaron must have both bells and pomegranates on his vesture. And ministers should

(as Gideon's soldiers) carry trumpets of sound doctrine in one hand and lamps of good living in the other. There should be a happy harmony, a constant consent between their lips and their lives, ἵνα συνδράμοι ὁ βίος τῷ λόγῳ, that their doctrine and conversation may run parallel, as Isidore saith in one place; or (as he hath it more emphatically in another), ἵνα ὁ λόγος ᾖ ὑπὸ τῆς πραξεως ἐμψυχώμενος, that their preaching may have life put into it by their practice. *Nolite,* saith one, *magis eloqui magna, quam vivere. Vivite concionibus, concionamini moribus :* Ὀρθοτομειτε, ὀρθοποδεῖτε : λέγοντες πρακτικῶς πράττοντες λογικῶς: *Sic vocalissimi eritis praecones, etiam cum tacetis.* Speak not, but live sermons, preach by your practice: the life of teaching is the life of the teacher.

Ver. 3. *Blessed*] The word signifieth such as are set out of the reach of evil, in a most joyous condition, having just cause to be everlastingly merry, as being *beati re et spe,* blessed in hand and in hope, and such as shall shortly *transire a spe ad speciem,* " for theirs is the kingdom of heaven." They are already possessed of it, as by turf and twig. There were eighty opinions among heathens about man's blessedness. These did but beat the bush : God hath given us the bird in this golden sermon. μακάριοι, *quasi* μὴ κηρὶ ὑποκείμενοι; *vel* ἀπὸ τοῦ μαλιστα χαίρειν. (Aristot.)

Are the poor in spirit] Beggars in spirit (*Mendici spiritu.* Tertul. *Qui suarum virium agnoscunt* οὐδένειαν, *hi pauperes spiritu*): such as have nothing at all of their own to support them, but being nittily needy, and not having (as we say) a cross wherewith to bless themselves, get their living by begging, and subsist merely upon alms. Such beggars God hath always about him, Matt. xxvi. 11. And this the poets hammered at, when they feigned that *litae* or prayers were the daughters of Jupiter, and stood always in his presence. (Homer.) Lord, I am hell, but thou art heaven, said Hooper. I am a most hypocritical wretch, not worthy that the earth should bear me, said Bradford. I am the unmeetest man for this high office of suffering for Christ that ever was appointed to it, said sincere Saunders. Oh that my life, and a thousand such wretches' lives more (saith John Careless, martyr, in a letter to Mr Bradford), might go for yours! Oh! why doth God suffer me and such other caterpillars to live, that can do nothing but consume the alms of the Church, and take away you so worthy a workman and labourer in the Lord's vineyard? But woe be to our sins and great unthankfulness, &c. (Acts and Mon.) These were excellent patterns of this spiritual poverty, which our Saviour here maketh the first; and is indeed the first, second, and third of Christianity, as that which teacheth men to find out the best in God and the worst in themselves. This Christ lays as the foundation of all the following virtues. Christianity is a frame for eternity, and must therefore have a good foundation;

sith an error there can hardly be mended in the fabric.

For theirs is the kingdom of heaven] Heaven is that true Macaria, or the blessed kingdom. So the Island of Cyprus was anciently called for the abundance of commodities that it sendeth forth to other countries, of whom it craveth no help again. Marcellinus, to show the fertility thereof, saith, that Cyprus aboundeth with such plenty of all things, that, without the help of any other foreign country, it is of itself able to build a tall ship, from the keel to the top-sail, and so put it to sea, furnished of all things needful. And Sextus Rufus writing thereof, saith, *Cyprus famosa divitiis, paupertatem populi Rom. ut occuparetur, sollicitavit.* Cyprus, famous for riches, tempted the poor people of Rome to seize upon it. What marvel then if this kingdom of heaven solicit these poor in spirit to offer violence to it, and to take it by force, sith it is all made of gold? Rev. xxi. 21 ; yea, search is made there through all the bowels of the earth to find out all the precious treasures that could be had, gold, pearls, and precious stones of all sorts. And what can these serve to? only to shadow out the glory of the walls of the New Jerusalem, and the gates, and to pave the streets of that city.

Ver. 4. *Blessed are they that mourn*] For sin, with a funereal sorrow (as the word signifieth), such as is expressed by crying and weeping, Luke vi. 25, such as was that at Megiddo, for the loss of good Josiah ; or as when a man mourns for his only son, Zech. xii. 10. (πένθος, *luctus ex morte amicorum.* Steph. As the widow of Nain ; as Jacob for Joseph ; as David for his Absalom.) This is the work of the Spirit of grace and of supplication: for till the winds do blow these waters cannot flow, Psal. cxlvii. 18. He convinceth the heart of sin, and makes it to become a very Hadadrimmon for deep-soaking sorrow, upon the sight of him whom they have pierced, Zech. xii. 10. When a man shall look upon his sins as the weapons, and himself as the traitor, that put to death the Lord of life, this causeth that sorrow according to God, that worketh repentance never to be repented of, 2 Cor. vii. 10.

For they shall be comforted] Besides the comfort they find in their very sorrow (for it is a sweet sign of a sanctified soul, and seals a man up to the day of redemption, Ezek. ix. 4), they lay up for themselves thereby in store a good foundation of comfort "against the time to come, that they may lay hold on eternal life," as the apostle speaketh in another case, 1 Tim. vi. 19. These April showers bring on May flowers. They that here "sow in tears shall reap in joy ;" they that find Christ's feet a fountain to wash in, may expect his side a fountain to bathe in. Oh how sweet a thing is it to stand weeping at the wounded feet of Jesus, as that good woman did! to water them with tears, to dry them with sighs, and to kiss them with our mouths! None, but those that

have felt it, can tell the comfort of it. The stranger meddleth not with this joy. When our merry Greeks, that laugh themselves fat, and light a candle at the devil for lightsomeness of heart, hunting after it to hell, and haunting for it ale-houses, conventicles of good-fellowship, sinful and unseasonable sports, vain and waterish fooleries, &c., when these mirth-mongers, I say, that take pleasure in pleasure, and jeer when they should fear, with Lot's sons-in-law, shall be at a foul stand, and not have whither to turn them, Isa. xxiii. 14 ; God's mourners shall be able to "dwell with devouring fire, with everlasting burnings," to stand before the Son of man at his second coming. Yea, as the lower the ebb, the higher the tide ; so the lower any hath descended in humiliation, the higher shall he ascend then in his exaltation. Those that have helped to fill Christ's bottle with tears, Christ shall then fill their bottle (as once he did Hagar's) with the water of life. He looked back upon the weeping women, and comforted them, that would not vouchsafe a loving look or a word to Pilate or the priests. Not long before that, he told his disciples, "Ye shall indeed be sorrowful, but your sorrow shall be turned into joy," John xvi. 20, 21. And further addeth, "A woman when she is in travail hath sorrow," &c., comparing sorrow for sin to that of a travailing woman : 1. For bitterness and sharpness for the time, throes of the new birth. 2. For utility and benefit, it tendeth to the bringing a man-child forth into the world. 3. For the hope and expectation that is in it not only of an end, but also of fruit ; this makes joy in the midst of sorrows. 4. There is a certain time set for both, and a sure succession, as of day after night, and of fair weather after foul. Mourning lasteth but till morning, Psal. xxx. 5. Though "I fall, I shall arise ;" though "I sit in darkness, the Lord shall give me light," saith the Church, Micah vii. 8. Jabez was more honourable than his brethren, saith the text, for his mother bare him with sorrow, and called his name Jabez, that is, sorrowful. But when he called upon the God of Israel, and said, "Oh that thou wouldst bless me indeed, and enlarge my coast," &c., "God granted him that which he requested," 1 Chron. iv. 9, 10. And so he will all such Israelites indeed, as "ask the way to Zion, with their faces thitherward," going and weeping as they go, to seek the Lord their God, Jer. l. 4, 5 ; he shall wipe all tears from their eyes (as nurses do from their babes that cry after them), and enlarge, not their coasts (as Jabez) but their hearts (which is better) ; yea, he shall grant them their requests, as him. So that as Hannah, when she had prayed, and Eli for her, she looked no more sad, 1 Sam. i. 18 ; David, when he came before God in a "woe-case" many times, yet when he had poured forth his sorrowful complaint there, he rose up triumphing, as Psal. vi. &c., so shall it be with such. They go forth and weep, bearing precious seed, but shall surely return with rejoicing, and bring their sheaves with them, Psal. cxxvi. 6; grapes of gladness (said that martyr, Philpot) when Abraham the good householder shall fill his bosom with them, in the kingdom of heaven. Then as one hour changed Joseph's fetters into a chain of gold, his rags into robes, his stocks into a chariot, his prison into a palace, his brown bread and water into manchet and wine,—so shall God turn all his people's sadness into gladness, all their sighing into singing, all their musing into music, all their tears into triumphs. *Luctus in lætitiam convertetur, lachrymæ in risum, saccus in sericum, cineres in corollas et unguentum, jejunium in epulum, manuum retortio in applausum.* He that will rejoice with this joy unspeakable, must stir up sighs that are unutterable.

Ver. 5. *Blessed are the meek*] Meekness is the fruit of mourning for sin, and is therefore fitly set next after it. He that can kindly melt in God's presence, will be made thereby as meek as a lamb: and if God will forgive him his ten thousand talents, he will not think much to forgive his brother a few farthings. (Πρᾶος *quasi* ῥᾶος, *quod mites omnibus*, scil. *faciles ac placidos reddant.* Becman.) Hence the wisdom from above is, first, pure, and then "peaceable, gentle, easy to be entreated," &c., Jam. iii. 17. And love is said to proceed out of a pure heart, a good conscience, and faith unfeigned, 1 Tim. i. 5. And when our Saviour told his disciples they must forgive till seventy times seven times, "Lord, increase our faith," said they, Luke xvii. 4, 5. Give us such a measure of godly mourning, as that we may be bold to believe that thou hast freely forgiven us, and we shall soon forgive our enemies. David was never so rigid as when he had sinned by adultery and murder; and not yet mourned in good earnest for his sin. He put the Ammonites under saws and harrows of iron, and caused them to pass through the brick-kiln, &c., which was a strange execution, and fell out while he lay yet in sin. Afterward we find him in a better frame, and more meekened and mollified in his dealings with Shimei and others, when he had soundly soaked himself in godly sorrow. True it is, that he was then under the rod, and that is a main means to make men meek. The Hebrew words that signify afflicted and meek, grow both upon the same root, and are of so great affinity, that they are sometimes by the Septuagint rendered the one for the other, as Psal. xxxvii. 11. עָנָו עָנִי. *Adversa enim hominem mansuetum reddunt,* saith Chemnitius. And, however it go with the outward man, the meek shall find rest to their souls, Matt. xi. 29. Yea, the meek in the Lord shall increase their joy, Isa. xxix. 19. And for outward respects, meek Moses complains not of Miriam's murmurings, but God strikes in for him the more. And he that said, "I seek not mine own glory," adds, "But there is one that seeketh it, and judgeth," John viii. 50. God takes his part ever that

fights not for himself, and is champion to him that strives not, but, for peace' sake, parteth with his own right, otherwhiles.

For they shall inherit the earth] One would think that meek men, that bear and forbear, that put and forgive, committing their cause "to him that judgeth righteously," 1 Pet. ii. 23 (as Christ did), should be soon baffled, and outsworn out of their patrimony, with honest Naboth. But there is nothing lost by meekness and yieldance. Abraham yields over his right of choice: Lot taketh it; and behold, Lot is crossed in that which he chose, Abraham blessed in that which was left him. God never suffers any man to lose by an humble remission of right, in a desire of peace. "The heavens, even the heavens, are the Lord's; but the earth hath he given to the children of men," Psal. cxv. 16: yet with this proviso, that as heaven is taken by violence, so is earth by meekness; and God (the true Proprietary) loves no tenants better, nor grants longer leases to any, than to the meek. They shall inherit, that is, peaceably enjoy what they have, and transfer it to posterity, they shall give inheritance to their children's children, Prov. xiii. 22. As, on the other side, frowardness forfeits all into the Lord's hands, and he many times taketh the forfeiture, and outs such persons, comes upon them with a *firma ejectione*, as upon Amalek, Abimelech, and others. Αὐθαδείας σύνοικος ἐρημία, said Plato. The Lord Treasurer Burleigh was wont to say, that he overcame envy and ill-will more by patience than pertinacy. His private estate he managed with that integrity, that he never sued any man, no man ever sued him. He was in the number of those few (said Mr Camden) that lived and died with glory. For as lowliness of heart shall make you high with God; even so meekness of spirit and of speech shall make you sink into the hearts of men, said Mr Tindal in a letter of his to John Frith, afterwards his fellow-martyr. (Acts and Mon.)

Ver. 6. *Blessed are those that hunger and thirst after righteousness*] The righteousness of Christ both imputed and imparted (*Justitia imputata, impertita*). This is in Christ for us, being wrought by his value and merit, and is called the righteousness of justification. This is in us from Christ, being wrought by his virtue and spirit, and is called the righteousness of sanctification. Both these the blessed must hunger and thirst after, that is, earnestly, and *afflictim* desire, as Rachel did for children, she must prevail or perish; as David did after the water of the well of Bethlehem, to the jeopardy of the lives of his three mightiest, 1 Chron. xi. 18; as the hunted hart (or, as the Septuagint readeth it, ἡ ἔλαφος, hind) brayeth after the water-brooks. The philosophers observe of the hart or hind, that being a beast thirsty by nature, when she is pursued by dogs, by reason of heat and loss of breath, her thirst is increased. (Aristot. Lucret. Oppian., Psal. xlii. 1.) And in females the passions are stronger than in males; so that she breathes and brays after the brooks with utmost desire: so panteth the good soul after Christ, it panteth and fainteth, it breatheth and breaketh for the longing that it hath unto his righteousness at all times, Psal. cxix. 20. She fainteth with Jonathan, swooneth and is sick with the Spouse, yea, almost dead with that poor affamished Amalekite, 1 Sam. xxx. 12. And this spiritual appetite and affection ariseth from a deep and due sense and feeling of our want of Christ, whole Christ, and that there is an absolute necessity of every drop of his blood. There must be a sad and serious consideration of man's misery and God's mercy. Whence will arise (as in hunger and thirst), 1. A sense of pain in the stomach. 2. A want and emptiness. 3. An eager desire of supply from Christ, who is the true bread of life, and heavenly manna; the rock flowing with honey, and fountain of living water, that reviveth the fainting spirits of every true Jonathan and Samson, and makes them never to thirst again after the world's tasteless fooleries: like as his mouth will not water after homely provision that hath lately tasted of delicate sustenance.

They shall be satisfied] Because true desires are the breathings of a broken heart, which God will not despise, Psal. li. 17. He poureth not the oil of his grace but into broken vessels. For indeed, whole vessels are full vessels, and so this precious liquor would run over, and be spilt on the ground. There may be some faint desires (as of wishers and woulders) even in hell-mouth; as Balaam desired to die the death of the righteous, but liked not to live their life; Pilate desired to know what is truth, but stayed not to know it; that faint chapman in the Gospel, that cheapened heaven of our Saviour, but was loth to go to the price of it. "The desire of the slothful killeth him," Prov. xxi. 25; Matt. xix. 22. These were but fits and flashes, and they came to nothing. Carnal men care not to seek, whom yet they desire to find, saith Bernard (*Carnales non curant quærere, quem tamen desiderant invenire; cupientes consequi, sed non et sequi*); fain they would have Christ, but care not to make after him: as Herod had of a long time desired to see our Saviour, but never stirred out of doors to come where he was, Luke xxiii. 8. But now, the desire of the righteous, that shall be satisfied, as Solomon hath it, that shall be well filled, as beasts are after a good bait (as our Saviour's word here signifieth). χορτασθήσονται *hoc proprie dicitur de armentis. Nam* χόρτον *est gramen aut pabulum.* Desires, as they must be ardent and violent, such as will take no nay, or be set down with silence or sad answers (whence it is that desire and zeal go together, 2 Cor. vii. 11), so if they be right, they are ever seconded with endeavour after the thing desired. Hence the apostle contents not himself to say, "that if there be first a willing mind," God accepts, &c., 2 Cor. viii. 12, but presently adds, "Now perform the doing of it; that as there was a readiness to will, so

there may be a performance also;" that is, a sincere endeavour to perform: as a thirsty man will not long for drink only, but labour after it; or a covetous man wish for wealth, but strive to compass it. And thus to run is to attain; thus to will is to work; thus to desire is to do the will of our heavenly Father, who accepts of pence for pounds, of mites for millions, and accounts us as good as we wish to be. He hath also promised to fill the hungry with good things, to rain down righteousness on the dry and parched ground, to fulfil the desires of them that fear him. So that it is but our asking and his giving; our opening the mouth and he will fill it; our hungering and his feeding; our thirsting and his watering; our open hand and his open heart. The oil failed not till the vessels failed: neither are we straitened in God till in our own bowels, 2 Cor. vi. 12. "Dear wife" (saith Lawrence Saunders the martyr), "riches I have none to leave behind, wherewith to endow you after the worldly manner; but that treasure of tasting how sweet Christ is to hungry consciences (whereof, I thank my Christ, I do feel part, and would feel more), that I bequeath unto you, and to the rest of my beloved in Christ, to retain the same in sense of heart always. Pray, pray: I am merry, and I trust I shall be, maugre the teeth of all the devils in hell. I utterly refuse myself, and resign me to my Christ, in whom I know I shall be strong, as he seeth needful." (Acts and Mon.)

Ver. 7. *Blessed are the merciful,* ἐλεήμονες] They that from a compassionate heart (melting with sense of God's everlasting mercy to itself, and yearning over the miseries of others) extend and exercise spiritual and corporal mercy. The former, which teacheth a man to warn the unruly, comfort the feeble-minded, support the weak, be patient toward all men, &c., 1 Thess. v. 14. The schoolmen thus, *Consule, castiga, solare, remitte, fer, ora,* usually excel and exceed the latter, which stirs a man up to feed the hungry, clothe the naked, visit the sick, &c., Matt. xxv. 35, 36.

Visito, poto, cibo, redimo, tego, colligo, condo.

1. In the nature of the gift, which is more noble. 2. In the object (the soul), which is more illustrious. 3. In the manner, which is transcendent, as being spiritual. 4. In the kind, which is more heavenly, as that which aims at our brothers' endless salvation. And this way the poorest may be plentiful, and enrich the richest with spiritual alms. As also the other way, something must be done by all the candidates of true blessedness. They that labour with their hands must have something to give to him that needeth, Eph. iv. 28; be it but two mites, nay, a cup of cold water, it shall be graciously accepted from a sincere heart, and certainly rewarded. And here the poor Macedonians may shame (and many times do) the rich Corinthians, that have a price in their hands but not a heart to use it; for it is the

love, and not the lack of money that makes men churls and misers. (Money-hoarders have no quicksilver, no current coin. Ward.) And hence it is that the richer men are many times the harder, as Dives: being herein like children, who when they have their mouths full, and both hands full, yet will rather spoil all than give any away. But do men give to God's poor? or, do they not rather lend it to the Lord, who turns pay-master to such? Do they not lay it out for him, or rather lay it up for themselves? The safest chest is the poor man's box. Make you friends with the mammon of unrighteousness (God hath purposely branded riches with that infamous adjunct, that we might not over-love them), "that when ye fail, they may receive you into everlasting habitations," Luke xvi. 9, that is, either the angels, or the poor, or thy well-employed wealth, shall let thee into heaven. Only thou must draw forth not thy sheaf alone, but thy soul also to the hungry, Isa. xxxviii. 10: show bowels of mercy, as our Saviour did, σπλαγχνίζομαι, Matt. xv. 32, to bleed in other men's wounds, and be deeply and tenderly affected in other men's miseries. This is better than alms; for when one gives an alms, he gives something without himself; but by compassion we relieve another by somewhat within and from ourselves. And this is properly the mercy to which mercy is here promised, and blessedness to boot.

For they shall obtain mercy] *Misericordiam, non mercedem*, Mercy, not wages: it being a mercy (and not a duty) in God, to render unto every man according to his works, Psal. lxii. 12. How much more according to his own works in us! But mercy he shall be sure of, that showeth mercy to those in misery. His soul shall be like a watered garden. "The liberal soul shall be made fat," saith Solomon; "and he that watereth shall be watered also himself," Prov. xi. 25; or (as Kimchi expounds it), He shall be a sweet and seasonable shower to himself and others. (*Etiam ipse pluvia erit, juxta Kimchi. Insignis hyperbole.* Merc.) His body also shall be fat and fair-liking. Thy health shall spring forth speedily, and thy bones shall be made fat, Isa. lviii. 10, 11. Or if he be sick, the Lord will strengthen him upon the bed of languishing, Psal. xli. 3; he will make all his bed in his sickness; as he did for that faithful and painful preacher of God's word (while he lived) Master William Whately, Pastor of Banbury (whom for honour's sake I here name), the most bountiful minister to the poor, I think (saith a learned gentleman that knew him thoroughly), in England, of his means. He abounded in works of mercy (saith another grave divine, that wrote his life), he set apart, and expended, for the space of many years, for good uses, the tenth part of his yearly comings in, both out of his temporal and ecclesiastical means of maintenance. (Edw. Leigh, Hen. Scudder.) A rare example: and God was not behind-hand with him; for in his sickness he could comfort himself with that precious promise, Psal. xli. 1, 3. "Blessed is he that considereth the poor" (*Qui præoccupat vocem petituri,* saith Austin, in Psal. ciii.); that prevents the poor man's cry; as he did, for he devised liberal things, seeking out to find objects of his mercy, and not staying many times till they were offered. Therefore by liberal things he stood, as God had promised; his estate (as himself often testified) prospered the better after he took that course above-mentioned. For, in the next place, not getting, but giving is the way to wealth, as the Sareptan found it, whose barrel had no bottom; and as Solomon assureth it, Eccl. xi. 1. The mercy of God crowneth our beneficence with the blessing of store. Thine horn shall be exalted with honour, and thou shalt not want, Psal. cxii. 9; Prov. xxviii. 27. Say not then how shall our own do hereafter? Is not mercy as sure a gain as vanity? Is God like to break? Is not your Creator your creditor? Hath not he undertaken for you and yours? How sped Mephibosheth and Chimham for the kindness their fathers showed to distressed David? Were they not plentifully provided for? And did not the Kenites, that were born many ages after Jethro's death, receive life from his dust, and favour from his hospitality? 1 Sam. xv. 6.

Ver. 8. *Blessed are the pure in heart*] That wash their hearts from wickedness, that they may be saved, Jer. iv. 14. Not their hands only, with Pilate, but their inwards, as there; "How long shall thy vain thoughts lodge within thee?" בקרבך These, however the world censure them (for every fool hath a bolt to shoot at that purity, which yet they profess and pray for), are the Lord's darlings, that purify themselves (in some truth of resemblance) as God is pure.

Pura Deus mens est, purâ vult mente vocari:
Et puras jussit pondus habere preces.

He will take up in a poor, but it must be a pure heart; in a homely, but it must be a cleanly house; in a low, but not in a loathsome lodging. God's Spirit loves to lie clean. Now the heart of man is the most unclean and loathsome thing in the world, a den of dragons, a dungeon of darkness, a sty and stable of all foul lusts, a cage of unclean and ravenous birds. The ambassadors of the Council of Constance, being sent to Pope Benedict XI. (*In hist. Concil. Constant.*), when he, laying his hand upon his heart, said, *Hic est Arca Noæ*, Here is Noah's ark; they tartly and truly replied, In Noah's ark were few men, but many beasts; intimating, that there were seven abominations in that heart, wherein he would have them to believe, were lodged all the laws of right and religion. This is true of every mother's child of us. The natural heart is Satan's throne, he filleth it from corner to corner, Acts v. 3, he sits abroad upon it, and hatcheth all noisome and loathsome lusts, Eph. ii. 2. There (as in the sea) is that Leviathan, and there are creeping things innumerable, crawling bugs and baggage vermin, Psal. civ. 25, 26. Now as many as shall see God to their comfort, must cleanse themselves from all filthiness of flesh and spirit, and perfect holiness in the fear of God, 2 Cor. vii. 1. This is the mighty work of the Holy Spirit, which therefore we must pray and strive for: beseeching God to break the heavens and come down, Isa. lxiv. 1, yea, to break open the prison-doors of our hearts by his Spirit, and to cleanse this Augæan stable. He comes as a mighty rushing wind, and blows away those litters of lusts, as once the east wind of God did all the locusts of Egypt into the Red Sea. And this done, he blows upon God's garden, the heart, and causeth the spices thereof so to flow forth that Christ saith, "I am come into my garden, my sister, my spouse; I have gathered my myrrh with my spice," Cant. iv. 16; v. 1.

For they shall see God] Here in a measure, and as they are able; hereafter in all fulness and perfection: they shall see as they are seen. Here, as in a glass obscurely, or as an old man through spectacles, 1 Cor. xiii. 12, ἐν αἰνίγματι, but there face to face. Happier herein than Solomon's servants, for a greater than Solomon is here. A good man is like a good angel, ever beholding the face of God. He looketh upon them with singular complacency, and they upon him to their infinite comfort: He seeth no iniquity in them, they no indignation in him. He looketh upon them in the face of Christ; and although no man hath seen God at any time, John i. 18, yet God, "who commanded the light to shine out of darkness, hath shined in our hearts," saith the apostle, "to give the light of the knowledge of the glory of God in the face of Jesus Christ," 2 Cor. iv. 6. Pure glass or crystal hath light coming through: not so stone, iron, or other grosser bodies. In like sort, the pure in heart see God, he shines through them: and as the pearl by the beams of the sun becomes bright and radiant as the sun itself, so "we all, with open face beholding as in a glass the glory of the Lord, are transformed into the same image from glory to glory, as by the Spirit of the Lord," 2 Cor. iii. 18.

Ver. 9. *Blessed are the peacemakers*] There are that, like salamanders, live always in the fire, and, like trouts, love to swim against the stream; that, with Phocion, think it a goodly thing to dissent from others; and, like Samson's foxes, or Solomon's fool, carry about and cast abroad firebrands, as if the world were made of nothing but discords, as Democritus imagined. But as St John speaketh in another case, these are "not of the Father, but of the world," 1 John ii. 16. He maketh great reckoning of a meek and quiet mind, 1 Pet. iii. 4, because it is like to his own mind, which is never stirred nor moved, but remaineth still the same to all eternity. He loves those that keep the staff of binders unbroken, Zech. xi. 7, 14; that hold the "unity of the Spirit," and advance

the bond of peace among others as much as may be, Eph. iv. 3. The wicked are apt (as dogs) to intertear and worry one another: and although there be not a disagreement in hell (being but the place of retribution, and not of action), yet on earth there is no peace among the workers of iniquity, that are trotting apace towards hell by their contentions, Rom. ii. 8. But what pity is it that Abraham and Lot should fall out! that two Israelites should be at strife amid the Egyptians! that John's disciples should join with Pharisees against Jesus! Matt. ix. 14; that Corinthians (for their contentions) should "be as carnal, and walk as men!" 1 Cor. iii. 3; that Lutherans and Calvinists should be at such deadly feud! Still Satan is thus busy, and Christians are thus malicious, that, as if they wanted enemies, they fly in one another's faces. There was no noise heard in setting up the temple: in Lebanon there was, but not in Zion. Whatever tumults there are abroad, it is fit there should be all quietness and concord in the Church. Now therefore, although it be, for the most part, a thankless office (with men) to interpose, and seek to take up strife, to piece again those that are gone aside and asunder, and to sound an *irenicum;* yet do it for God's sake, and that ye may (as ye shall be after awhile) be called and counted not meddlers and busybodies, but the sons of God. Tell them that jar and jangle (upon mistakes for most part, or matters of no great moment) that it is the glory of a man to pass by an infirmity, and that in these ignoble quarrels every man should be a law to himself, as the Thracians were (αὐτόνομοι), and not brother to go to law with brother because he treads upon his grass, or some such poor business, *ubi et vincere inglorium est, et atteri sordidum.* (Tacit.) Now "therefore there is utterly a fault (ἥττημα) amongst you, because ye go to law one with another," saith the apostle, 1 Cor. vi. 7. Not but that the course is lawful, where the occasion is weighty and the mind not vindictive. But the apostle disgraceth (in that text) revenge of injuries, by a word that signifieth disgrace or loss of victory. And a little before, "I speak to your shame," saith he; "is it so, that there is not a wise man amongst you?" no, not one that shall be able to judge between his brethren and compromise the quarrel? Servius Sulpitius (that heathen lawyer) shall rise up in judgment against us, *Quippe qui ad facilitatem, æquitatemque omnia contulit, neque constituere litium actiones, quam controversias tollere maluit,* as Tully testifieth. (Cicer. Philip. pic. 9.) *Concedamus de jure,* saith one, *ut careamus lite:* and, *ut habeas quietum tempus, perde aliquid.* Lose something for a quiet life, was a common proverb, as now amongst us so of old among the Carthaginians, as St Austin showeth. It were happy surely, if now, as of old, the multitude of believers were ἡ καρδία, καὶ ἡ ψυχή μία, of one heart and of one soul, Acts iv. 32. And, as in one very ancient Greek copy it is added, that there was not one controversy or contention found amongst them, καὶ οὐκ ἦν ἐν αὐτοῖς διάκρισις οὐδεμία. (Beza ex Beda.)

For they shall be called the children of God] They shall both be, and be said to be, both counted and called, have both the name and the note, the comfort and the credit of the children of God. And if any atheist shall object : What so great honour is that ? " Behold," saith St John, " what manner of love the Father hath bestowed upon us, that we should be called the sons of God," 1 John iii. 1. It was something to be called the son of Pharaoh's daughter, Heb. xi. 24, to be son-in-law to the king, with David, to be heir to the crown, with Solomon : but far more, that God should say of him, " I will be his Father, and he shall be my son ; and I will establish his kingdom, 2 Sam. vii. 14. This is the happy effect of faith ; for to them that believe on his name, gave he power and privilege to become the sons of God (ἐξουσίαν), John i. 12. Now, faith ever works by love, and love covereth a multitude of sins, 1 Pet. iv. 8, not by any merit or expiation with God, but by seeking and settling peace among men. And this is as sure and as sweet a sign of a son of the God of peace, as the party-coloured coats were anciently of the king's children, 2 Sam. xiii. 18.

Ver. 10. *Blessed are they that are persecuted*] To be persecuted (as simply considered) is no blessed thing ; for then it were to be desired and prayed for. But let a man love a quiet life, and labour to see good days, said those two great champions, David and Peter, Psal. xxxiv. 12 ; 1 Pet. iii. 10, who themselves had endured a world of persecution, and paid for their learning. The like counsel gives St Paul and the author to the Hebrews, 1 Tim. ii. 2 ; 1 Thess. iv. 11 ; Heb. xii. 11 ; for they felt by experience how unable they were to bear crosses when they fell upon them. It was this Peter that denied his Master upon the sight of a silly wench that questioned him : and this David that changed his behaviour before Abimelech, and thereupon gave this advice to all that should come after him.

For righteousness' sake] This it is that makes the martyr a good cause and a good conscience. *Martyrem facit causa, non supplicium*, saith Augustine : not the suffering, but the cause makes a martyr. And *Multum inter est, et qualia quis, et qualis quisque patiatur*, saith Gregory : it greatly skilleth, both what it is a man suffereth, and what a one he is that suffereth. If he suffer as an evildoer, he hath his mends in his own hands, *Talia quisque luat, qualia quisque facit ;* but if for righteousness' sake, as here, and if men say and do all manner of evil against you (falsely and lyingly, ψευδόμενοι) for my sake, as in the next verse, and for the gospel's sake, as Mark hath it, this is no bar to blessedness : nay, it is a high preferment on earth, Phil. i. 20, and hath a crown abiding it in heaven, beyond the which mortal men's wishes cannot extend. *Ultra cujus excellentiam mortalium vota non extenduntur.* (Scult.) But let all that will have share in these comforts, see that they be able to say with the

Church, Psal. xliv. 21, 22," Thou knowest, Lord, the secrets of the hearts, that for thy sake we are slain continually." Upon which words excellently St Austin, *Quid est, inquit, novit occulta ? quæ occulta, &c.* What secrets of the heart, saith he, are those that God is here said to know ? Surely these, that for thy sake we are slain, &c.; slain thou mayest see a man, but wherefore or for whose sake he is slain, thou knowest not, God only knoweth. *Potes videre hominem morte affici ; quare mortificetur nescis. Res in occulto est. Sunt qui causâ humanæ gloriæ paterentur*, as that Father goeth on. There want not those that would suffer death (and seemingly for righteousness' sake) only for applause of the world and vain-glory : as Lucian telleth of Peregrinus the philosopher, that merely for the glory of it he would have been made a martyr. ὡς ἐπὶ τούτῳ δόξαν ἀπολίποι, *et propterea ab Asiæ proconsule dimissus est, tanquam eâ gloriâ indignus.* The Circumcelliones (a most pernicious branch of the heresy of the Donatists) were so desirous to obtain (by suffering) the praise of martyrdom, that they would seem to throw themselves down headlong from high places, or cast themselves into fire or water. Alexander the coppersmith was near martyrdom, Acts xix. 33, who yet afterward made shipwreck of the faith, and became a bitter enemy to the truth that he had professed, 1 Tim. i. 19, 20, and iv. 14, 15. Felix Mauzius, an Anabaptist of Helvetia, being put to death for his obstinacy and ill practices at Tigere, praised God that had called him to the sealing up of his truth with his blood, was animated to constancy by his mother and brother, and ended his life with these words, " Lord, into thy hands I commend my spirit." What could any hearty Hooper, trusty Taylor, or sincere Saunders have said or done more in such a case ? It is not then the suffering, but the suffering for righteousness' sake, that proveth a man blessed and entitleth him to heaven. The Philistines died by the fall of the house, as well as Samson ; *sed diverso fine, ac fato*, as Bucholcer saith. Christ and the thieves were in the same condemnation. *Similis pœna, sed dissimilis causa*, saith Austin : their punishment was all alike, but not their cause. Baltasar Gerardus the Burgundian that slew the Prince of Orange, June 30th, 1584, endured very grievous torments : but it was pertinacy in him rather than patience, stupidity of sense, not a solidity of faith, a reckless disposition, not a confident resolution. Therefore no heaven followed upon it, because he suffered not as a martyr, but as a malefactor.

For theirs is the kingdom of heaven] " Surely if there be any way to heaven on horseback, it is by the cross," said that martyr, Bradford, that was hasting thither in a fiery chariot. The Turks account all them whom the Christians kill in battle, Mahometan saints and martyrs ; assigning them a very high place in Paradise. In some parts of the West Indies there is an opinion in gross, that the soul is immortal, and that there is a life after this life, where beyond certain hills (they know not where) those that died in defence of their country should remain after death in much blessedness; which opinion made them very valiant in their fights. Should not the assurance of heaven make us valiant for the truth? Jer. ix. 3; should we not suffer with joy the spoiling of our goods, Heb. x. 34, yea, the loss of our lives for life eternal? should we not look up, to the recompense of reward? to Christ the author and finisher of our faith, who stands over us in the encounter, as once over Stephen, with a crown on his head, and another in his hand, and saith, *Vincenti dabo*, to him that overcometh will I give this, Acts vii. 56; Rev. iii. 11. Surely this Son of David will shortly remove us from the ashes of our forlorn Ziklag, to the Hebron of our peace and glory, 1 Sam. xxx. 26, 31. This Son of Jesse will give every one of us, not fields and vineyards, but crowns, sceptres, kingdoms, glories, beauties, &c. The expectation of this blessed day, this nightless day (as one calleth it, ἀνέσπερος ἡμέρα. Naz.), must (as it did with David's soldiers all the time of their banishment) digest all our sorrows, and make us in the midst of miseries for Christ to over-abound exceedingly with joy, as Paul did. ὑπερπερισσεύομαι τῇ χαρᾷ, 2 Cor. vii. 4. Queen Elizabeth's government was so much the more happy and welcome, because it ensued upon the stormy times of Queen Mary. She came as a fresh spring after a sharp winter; and brought the ship of England from a troublous and tempestuous sea to a safe and quiet harbour. So will the Lord Christ do for all his persecuted people. "Ye see" (said Bilney the martyr, and they were his last words, to one that exhorted him to be constant and take his death patiently)— "ye see," saith he, "when the mariner is entered his ship to sail on the troublous sea, how he, for a while, is tossed in the billows of the same; but yet in hope that he shall once come to the quiet haven, he beareth in better comfort the troubles that he feeleth. So am I now towards this failing; and whatsoever storms I shall feel, yet shortly after shall my ship be in the haven, as I doubt not thereof by the grace of God," &c. Lo, this was that that held the good man's head above water—the hope of heaven. And so it did many others, whom it were easy to instance. Elizabeth Cooper, martyr, being condemned, and at the stake with Simon Miller, when the fire came unto her, she a little shrank thereat, crying once, Ha. When Simon heard the same, he put his hand behind him toward her, and willed her to be strong and of good cheer. "For, good sister," said he, "we shall have a joyful and sweet supper." Whereat she being strengthened, stood as still and as quiet as one most glad to finish that good course. "Now I take my leave of you" (writeth William Tims, martyr, in a letter to a friend of his, a little before his death) "till we meet in heaven: and hie you after. I have tarried a great while for you; and seeing you be so long in making ready, I will tarry no longer for you. You shall find me merrily singing, 'Holy, holy,

holy, Lord God of Sabaoth,' at my journey's end," &c. (Acts and Mon.) And I cannot here let slip that golden paraclesis, wherewith those forty martyrs (mentioned by St Basil) comforted one another, when they were cast out naked all night in the winter and were to be burned the next morrow: "Sharp is the winter," said they, "but sweet is paradise; painful is the frost, but joyful the fruition that followeth it. Wait but a while, and the patriarch's bosom shall cherish us. After one night we shall lay hold upon eternal life. Let our feet feel the fire for a season, that we may for ever walk arm in arm with angels. Let our hands fall off, that they may for ever be lifted up to the praise of the Almighty," &c. Δριμὺς χειμὼν, ἀλλὰ γλυκὺς ὁ παράδεισος· ἀλγεινὴ ἡ πῆξις, ἀλλ' ἡδεῖα ἡ ἀπόλαυσις μικρὸν ἀναμένωμεν, καὶ ὁ κόλπος ἡμᾶς θάλψει τοῦ πατριάρχου μιᾶς νυκτὸς ὅλον τὸν αἰῶνα ἀνταλλαξώμεθα.

Ver. 11. *Blessed are ye when men shall revile you, and persecute you, and shall say all manner of evil against you, falsely, for my sake*] There are tongue-smiters, as well as hand-smiters; such as malign and molest God's dearest children, as well with their virulent tongues as violent hands: "Such as will revile you," saith our Saviour, twit and upbraid you with your profession, hit you in the teeth with your God (as they dealt by David, and that went as a murdering weapon to his soul), and lay your preciseness and conscientiousness in your dish. This is the force of the first word. (Basil εἰς τοὺς μάρτυρας ὀνειδίσωσιν, Psal. ii. 10.) Further, "they shall persecute you," eagerly pursue and follow you hot-foot, as the hunter doth his prey. (Διώκειν *est more venatorum persequi prædam.* Aretius.) The word betokeneth a keen and eager pursuit of any other, whether by law or by the sword, whether by word or deed. For scoffers also are persecutors, as Ishmael, Gal. iv. 29, and for such shall be arraigned, Jude 15. And cruel mockings and scourgings are set together by the author to the Hebrews, as much of a kind, chap. xi. 35; especially when (as it follows in the text) they "shall say all manner of evil against you," call you all to pieces, and think the worst word in their bellies too good for you. This is collateral blasphemy, blasphemy in the second table, and so it is often called in the New Testament. God, for the honour he beareth to his people, is pleased to afford the name of blasphemy to their reproaches, as importing that he taketh it as if himself were reproached, Eph. iv. 31; Tit. iii. 2; Col. iii. 8; 1 Pet. iv. 4; 2 Pet. ii. 10. Thus the Israelites were of old called by the profane heathens, Apellæ (*Credat Judæus Apella.* Hor.), and Asinarii, as if they worshipped a golden ass-head, and in derision of their circumcision; as afterward they called the primitive Christians, murderers, church-robbers, incestuous, traitors to the state, &c.; and if inundations, famine, or other public calamities fell out, they presently cried out, *Christianos ad leones.* (Tertul. Apolog. *Si Tiberis ascendit, si terra movit, si fames, si lues.*)

So, in after times, the Arians called the orthodox Christians, Ambrosians, Athanasians, Homousians, what not? The pseudo-catholics, "speaking evil of that they knew not," Jude 10, disgraced the professors of the truth by the names of Wicklevists, Waldenses, Huguenots, poor men of Lyons, &c. Thus of old, as of late, Heretics, New-Gospellers, Puritans, all manner of evil they speak against us, but "falsely," that is our comfort; not caring what they speak, nor whereof they affirm, so they may promote their catholic cause and the devil's kingdom, which as it began in a lie, so by lies do they maintain it. A friar a liar, was anciently a sound argument in any man's mouth (saith Thomas Walsingham), *tenens tam de forma, quam de materia. Hic est frater, ergo mendax; sicut et illud, Hoc est album, ergo coloratum.* But the Jesuits have won the whetstone from all that went before them, for frontals and prodigious lies and slanders. Eudæmon Joannes, that demoniac, blusheth not to affirm that these are our decrees and doctrines, that no God is to be worshipped, that we must shape our religion according to the times, that gain is godliness, that we may make the public cause a pretence to our private lusts, that a man may break his word whensoever he thinketh good, cover his hatred with fair flatteries, confirm tyranny by shedding innocent blood. Salmeron the Jesuit hath published to the world in his Comment upon the Gospels, that the Lutherans now make fornication to be no sin at all. And a little afore the massacre of Paris, the monks slanderously gave out that the Huguenots met together for no other purpose than that (after they had fed themselves to the full) they might put out the lights and go together promiscuously, as brute beasts. Cenalis, Bishop of Auranches, wrote against the congregations of Christians at Paris, defending impudently that their assemblies were to maintain whoredom. The lives of Calvin and Beza were (at the request of the popish side) written by Bolseeus, a runagate friar, their sworn enemy; and though so many lines, so many lies, yet are they in all their writings alleged as canonical. (Acts and Mon.) Wickliff disallowed the invocation of saints, whom he called servants, not gods. For the word knave, which he used, signified in those days a child or a servant; not as it doth in our days, a wicked varlet, as his enemies maliciously interpret it;—Bellarmine for one, a man utterly ignorant of the English tongue. (Genebrard basely reporteth that Luther and Bucer died of drunkenness.) Hereupon the people are taught to believe that the Protestants are blasphemers of God and all his saints; that in England churches are turned into stables, the people are grown barbarous, and eat young children; that they are as black as devils, ever since they were blasted and thunder-struck with the pope's excommunication (*contraxisse amorem diabolicum,* Prid.); that Geneva is a professed sanctuary of roguery, &c.; that the fall of Blackfriars (where besides a hundred of his hearers slain, Drury the priest had his sermon and brains

knocked out of his head together) was caused by the Puritans, who had secretly sawed in two the beams and other timber. With like honesty they would have fathered the Powder Plot upon the Puritans, by their proclamations, which they had ready to be sent abroad immediately, had Fawx but fired the powder. And a certain Spanish author hath taken the boldness, since, to aver that they were the authors of that hellish conspiracy. *Puritanos eosdem tradit conjurationis sulphurariæ authores fuisse.* (*Author quidam Hispanicus,* D. Prideaux.) There is a book lately published, and commonly sold in Italy and France, containing a relation of God's judgments shown on a sort of Protestant-heretics by the fall of a house in Blackfriars, London, in which they were assembled to hear a Geneva lecture, October 26, 1623. And Dr Weston doubted not to make his boasts to a nobleman of England, that at the late conference and disputation between Fisher and Featly (with certain others of both sides), our doctors were confounded, and theirs triumphed and had the day; insomuch that two earls and a hundred others were converted to the Roman Catholic faith. Whereas he, to whom this tale was told, was himself one of the two earls, continuing sound and orthodox, and knew full well that there were not a hundred Papists and Protestants (taken together) present at that disputation. But this was one of their *piæ fraudes,* doubtless; much like their legend of miracles of their saints, which the Jesuit confessed to myself, saith D. Prideaux, to be for most part false and foolish; but it was made for good intention; and that it was lawful and meritorious to lie and write such things, to the end the common people might with greater zeal serve God and his saints. (Spanish Pilg.) So long since, because freedom of speech was used by the Waldenses, in blaming and reproving the dissolute life and debauched manners of the popish clergy, *Plures nefariæ affingebantur iis opiniones, a quibus omnino fuerant alieni,* saith Girardus: they were cried out upon for odious heretics and apostates. Manichees they were said to be, and to make two first beginnings of things, viz. God and the devil. (Field of the Church.) And why? because they preached and maintained that the emperor depended not upon the pope. Moreover, they were Arians too, and denied Christ to be the Son of God, because, forsooth, they denied a crust to be transubstantiated into Christ, as one speaketh, *Crustam in Christum fuisse transubstantiatam.* But blessed be God, that although they have in all ages spoken all manner of evil against us, yet they have done it falsely, and for Christ's sake; wherefore we may take up their books written against us, and "wear them as a crown." "Do well and bear it, is written upon heaven's gates," said that martyr, Bradford. "Christ himself," saith father Latimer, "was misreported, and falsely accused, both as touching his words and meaning also." Count it not strange to be traduced, disgraced, scandalized. Austere John hath a devil; sociable Christ is a wine-bibber, and the scribes and Pharisees (whose words carry such credit) say as much. *Contra sycophantæ morsum non est remedium.* It is but a vain persuasion for any child of God to think, by any discretion, wholly to still the clamours and hates of wicked men, who when they think well, will learn to report well. In the mean time, let our lives give them the lie—confute them by a real apology.

Ver. 12. *Rejoice and be exceeding glad*] Leap and skip for joy, as wantonizing young cattle use to do in the spring, when everything is in its prime and pride. (σκιρτάω, *Heb.* רקד *et* Psal. cxliv. *Significat proprie saltum animalium præ luxu.* Lorin. *Dicuntur lascivientes pecudes* σκιρτᾶν. Beza. Neh. viii. 10.) Thus George Roper, at his coming to the stake, fet a great leap. So soon as the flame was about him, he put out both his arms from his body, like a rood, and so stood stedfast, "the joy of the Lord being his strength," not plucking his arms in till the fire had consumed and burnt them off. So Doctor Taylor going toward his death, and coming within a mile or two of Hadley (where he was to suffer), he leapt and fetched a frisk or twain, as men commonly do in dancing. "Why, Master Doctor," quoth the sheriff, "how do you now?" He answered, "Well, God be praised, good Master Sheriff, never better; for now I know I am almost at home. I lack not past two stiles to go over, and I am even at my Father's house." Likewise Rawlins White, going to the stake, whereas before he was wont to go stooping, or rather crooked, through infirmity of age, having a sad countenance, and a very feeble complexion, and withal very soft in speech and gesture,—now he went and stretched up himself bolt upright, and bare withal a most pleasant and comfortable countenance, not without great courage and audacity, both in speech and behaviour. (Acts and Mon.) It were easy to instance the exceeding great joy of the apostles, Acts v. 41, who went from the council rejoicing that they were so far honoured as to be dishonoured for the name of Jesus; which Casaubon calleth *Elegantissimum oxymoron.* So Bradford: "God forgive me," saith he, "mine unthankfulness for this exceeding great mercy, that, among so many thousands, he chooseth me to be one in whom he will suffer." And in a letter to his mother: "For Christ's sake I suffer," saith he, "and therefore should be merry and glad; and indeed, good mother, so I am, as ever I was; yea, never so merry and glad was I as now I should be, if I could get you to be merry with me, to thank God for me, and to pray on this sort: Ah, good Father, that dost vouchsafe that my son, being a grievous sinner in thy sight, should find this favour with thee, to be one of thy Son's captains and men of war, to fight and suffer for his Gospel's sake; I thank thee, and pray thee in Christ's name, that thou wouldst forgive him his sins and unthankfulness, and make him worthy to suffer, not only imprisonment, but even very death for thy truth,

religion, and gospel's sake," &c. Whether Bradford's mother did thus or no, I know not; but William Hunter's mother (that suffered under Bonner) told him that she was glad that ever she was so happy as to bear such a child, as could find in his heart to lose his life for Christ's name's sake. Then William said to his mother, "For my little pain which I shall suffer, which is but for a little braid, Christ hath promised me a crown of joy. May not you be glad of that, mother?" With that his mother kneeled down on her knees, saying, "I pray God strengthen thee, my son, to the end; yea, I think thee as well bestowed as any child that ever I bare." "For, indeed," as Mr Philpot the martyr said, "to die for Christ is the greatest promotion that God can bring any in this vale of misery unto; yea, so great an honour, as the greatest angel in heaven is not permitted to have." This made John Clerk's mother, of Melda in Germany (when she saw her son whipped and branded in the forehead for opposing the pope's indulgences, and calling him Antichrist), to hearten her son, and cried out, *Vivat Christus ejusque insignia :* "Blessed be Christ, and welcome be these marks of his." (Scultet. Annal.) Constantinus, a citizen of Rhone (with three other), being, for defence of the gospel, condemned to be burned, were put into a dungcart, who thereat rejoicing, said that they were reputed here the excrements of the world, but yet their death was a sweet odour to God. When the chain was put about Alice Driver's neck: "Oh," said she, "here is a goodly neckerchief, blessed be God for it." Algerius, Christ's prisoner, thus dated his letter, "from the Delectable Orchard of the Leonine prison." "And I am in prison till I be in prison," said Saunders. (Acts and Mon.) "And, indeed," said Bradford, "I thank God more of this prison than of any parlour, yea, than of any pleasure that ever I had, for in it I find God, my most sweet God always." "After I came into prison" (saith Robert Glover, martyr, in a letter to his wife), "and had reposed myself there awhile, I wept for joy and gladness, my belly full, musing much of the great mercies of God; and as it were, thus saying to myself, Lord, who am I, on whom thou shouldst bestow this great mercy, to be numbered among the saints that suffer for thy gospel-sake?" "And I was carried to the coal-house," saith Mr Philpot, "where I and my six fellows do rouse together in the straw as cheerfully, we thank God, as others do in their beds of down." And in another letter to the Lady Vane: "I am now in the coal-house, a dark and ugly prison as any is about London; but my dark body of sin hath well deserved the same, &c. And I thank the Lord, I am not alone, but have six other faithful companions, who, in our darkness, do cheerfully sing hymns and praises to God for his great goodness. We are so joyful, that I wish you part of my joy," &c. "Good brethren," saith William Tims, martyr, "I am kept alone, and yet I thank God he comforteth me past all the comfort of any man; for I was never merrier in Christ." "You shall be whipped and burned for this gear, I trow," said one Mr Foster to John Fortune, martyr. To whom he replied, "If you knew how these words rejoice mine heart, you would not have spoken them." "Why," quoth Foster, "thou fool, dost thou rejoice in whipping?" "Yea," said Fortune, "for it is written in the Scriptures, and Christ saith, 'Ye shall be whipped for my name's sake.' And since the time that the sword of tyranny came into your hand, I heard of none that was whipt: happy were I if I had the maiden-head of this persecution.'" William Walsey was so desirous to glorify God with his suffering, that being wonderful sore tormented in prison with tooth-ache, he feared nothing more than that he should depart before the day of his execution (which he called his glad day) were come. Anthony Person, with a cheerful countenance, embraced the stake whereat he was to be burned, and kissing it, said, "Now welcome, mine own sweet wife, for this day shalt thou and I be married together in the love and peace of God." Lawrence Saunders took the stake to which he should be chained in his arms, and kissed it, saying, "Welcome the cross of Christ; welcome everlasting life." Walter Mill, Scot, being put to the stake, ascended gladly, saying, "*Introibo altare Dei.*" John Noyes, martyr, took up a fagot at the fire, and kissed it, and said, "Blessed be the time that ever I was born to come to this." Denly sang in the fire at Uxbridge: so did George Carpenter, the Bavarian martyr: so did Wolfgangus Schuh, a German; when he entered into the place heaped up with fagots and wood, he sang, "*Lætatus sum in his quæ dicta sunt mihi, In domum Domini ibimus.*" (Scultet. Annal.) Two Austin monks at Bruxelles, A.D. 1523 (the first among the Lutherans that suffered for religion), being fastened to the stake to be burnt, sang *Te Deum* and the Creed. Others clapped their hands in the flames in token of triumph; as Hawks and Smith, and five martyrs burnt together by Bonner. Bainham at the stake, and in the midst of the flame (which had half consumed his arms and his legs), spake these words, "O ye Papists, behold, ye look for miracles: here you may see a miracle: for in this fire I feel no more pain than if I were in a bed of down; but it is to me as a bed of roses." (Acts and Mon.) Now what was it else whereby these worthies (of whom the world was not worthy) quenched the violence of the fire, and out of weakness were made strong? Was it not by their heroical and impregnable faith causing them to endure, as seeing him that is invisible, and having respect, as Moses, to the recompense of reward? Heb. xi. 26, 27.

For great is your reward in heaven] God is a liberal pay-master, and no small things can fall from so great a hand as his. "Oh that joy! O my God, when shall I be with thee?" said a dying peer of this realm (the Lord Harring-

ton). So great is that joy, that we are said to enter into it, it is too full to enter into us, Matt. xxv. 21. Elias, when he was to enter into it, feared not the fiery chariots that came to fetch him, but through desire of those heavenly happinesses, waxed bold against those terrible things, *Atque hoc in carne adhuc vivens* (it is St Basil's observation); and this he did while he was as yet in the flesh. *Contra horrenda audax fuit, et cum gaudio flammeos currus inscendit.* (Basil.) For he had *oculum in metam* (which was Ludovicus Vives his motto), his eye upon the mark; he pressed forward toward the high prize, with Paul, Phil. iii. 14; and looking through the terror of the fire, saw heaven beyond it; and this made him so valiant, so violent for the kingdom. A Dutch martyr, feeling the flame to come to his beard: "Ah," said he, "what a small pain is this to be compared to the glory to come." Hellen Stirk, a Scotch woman, to her husband at the place of execution spoke thus, "Husband, rejoice; for we have lived together many joyful days, but this day in which we must die ought to be most joyful to us both, because we must have joy for ever; therefore I will not bid you good night, for we shall suddenly meet within the kingdom of heaven." The subscription of Mistress Ann Askew to her confession was this, "Written by me, Ann Askew, that neither wisheth for death nor feareth his might, and as merry as one that is bound toward heaven." "Oh, how my heart leapeth for joy," said Mr Philpot, "that I am so near the apprehension of eternal life. God forgive me mine unthankfulness and unworthiness of so great glory. I have so much joy of the reward prepared for me, most wretched sinner, that though I be in place of darkness and mourning, yet I cannot lament; but both night and day am so joyful, as though under no cross at all; yea, in all the days of my life I was never so merry, the name of the Lord be praised therefore for ever and ever; and he pardon mine unthankfulness. The Lord wondereth," saith he in another place, "how we can be so merry in such extreme misery: but our God is omnipotent, which turneth misery into felicity. Believe me, there is no such joy in the world as the people of Christ have under the cross. I speak by experience, &c. To this joy all other being compared, are but mournings, all delight sorrows, all sweetness sour, all beauty filth, and, finally, all things counted pleasant are tediousness." Great then, we see, is their reward in earth that suffer for Christ: they have heaven aforehand, they rejoice in tribulation, with joy unspeakable and glorious, 1 Pet. i. 8; they have an exuberancy of joy, such as no good can match, no evil over-match. "For though I tell you," said Mr Philpot in a letter to the congregation, "that I am in hell, in the judgment of this world, yet assuredly I feel in the same the consolation of heaven. And this loathsome and horrible prison is as pleasant to me as the walks in the garden in the King's Bench." (Acts and Mon.) What will it be, then, when they shall have crowns on their heads and palms in their hands; when they shall come to that general assembly (πανήγυρις), Heb. xii. 23, and have all the court of heaven to meet and entertain them; when they shall "follow the Lamb whithersoever he goeth," Rev. xiv. 4, and have places given them to walk among those that stand by, Zech. iii. 7 (that is, among the seraphim, as the Chaldee paraphrast expoundeth it), among the angels of heaven? (Allusively, to the walks and galleries that were about the temple.) *Majora certamina, majora sequuntur præmia,* saith Tertullian. *Quisquis volens detrahit famæ meæ, nolens addit mercedi meæ,* saith Augustine. The more we suffer with and for Christ, the more glory we shall have with and from Christ. Luther was wont to say, when any man spake evil of him, This will be accounted to my reckoning at the last day. *Mihi maxime prosunt,* saith he, *qui mei pessime meminerunt.* They are my best friends who speak worst of me. (Luther, Epist. ad Spalatin.)

For so persecuted they the prophets which were before you] Your betters sped no better: strange not therefore at it, start not for it. *Optimum solatium sodalitium.* Persecution hath ever been the saints' portion. How early did martyrdom come into the world! The first man that died died for religion. And although Cain be gone to his place, Acts i. 25, yet I would he were not still alive in his sons and successors, who hate their brethren, because they are more righteous, *Et clavam ejus sanguine Abelis rubentem circumferunt,* as Bucholcer speaketh. But that is not to be wished; or, at least, it is *magis optabile quam opinabile,* that ever a prophet shall want a persecutor while there is a busy devil and a malicious world. The leopard is said so to hate man, that he flieth upon his very picture, and teareth it: so doth the devil and his imps, God and his image. The tiger is said to be enraged with the smell of sweet odours; so are the wicked of the world with the fragrancy of God's graces. Noah rose up and condemned them by his contrary courses, and therefore underwent a world of calamities. Puritan Lot was an eyesore to the sinful Sodomites, and is cast out, as it were, by an ostracism. His father Haran, the brother of Abraham, died before his father Terah in Ur of the Chaldees, Gen. xi. 28. The Hebrews tell us that he was cruelly burnt by the Chaldees, because he would not worship the fire which they had made their god. *Sicut Persæ suum Orimasdam.* How often was Moses made (as Cato among the Romans) to plead for his life! And although David's innocency triumphed in Saul's conscience, yet could he not be safe, but carried his life in his hand continually, as he complaineth in Psalm cxix. 109, which was made, as is thought, in the midst of those troubles, out of his own observations and experiments. As for the prophets that came after, which of them have not your fathers slain? saith our Saviour to the Pharisees, whom he bids (by an irony) to fill up the measure of their fathers,

Matt. xxiii. 32—34; and foretelling that they shall deal so by the apostles (whom he there calleth, according to the custom of that country, prophets, wise men, and scribes), he demandeth of those serpents and brood of vipers how they can escape those treasures and hoards of wrath they have been so long in heaping? They had a little before delivered up John Baptist to Herod, and did unto him whatsoever they would, Matt. xvii. 11, 12. Thereupon our Saviour departed out of Judea into Galilee, as John the Evangelist hath it, lest he should suffer the same things from them. For though Herod were tetrarch of Galilee, and therefore it might seem a safer way for our Saviour to keep from thence (after John was beheaded) and to continue in Judea; yet forasmuch as he was but their slaughter-slave (as Bonner was to the rest of the bishops of those days), Christ knew that if he did decline their fury, there was no such cause to fear Herod. Therefore when some of the Pharisees, pretending good-will to him, bade him pack thence, for else Herod would kill him, he replied, Go tell that fox, that I know both my time and my task, which he would be doing at to-day and to-morrow, that is, as long as he listed, without his leave, Luke xiii. 31—33. τελειοῦμαι: τελειωθέντες. *Absolute vocantur, qui pro Christo sanguinem fuderunt.* (Beza.) And the third day, when his hour was once come, he should be sacrificed; but it must be in Jerusalem, and by the Pharisees, for it befell not a prophet to perish out of Jerusalem. There it was that Stephen was stoned, James slain with the sword, Peter imprisoned and destined to destruction, Paul whipped and bound, many of the saints punished oft in every synagogue, and compelled by the high priest's authority either to blaspheme or flee to strange cities, as appeareth in many places of the Acts, or rather Passions, of the apostles: for none (out of hell) ever suffered harder and heavier things than they. See what St Paul witnesseth of himself, and think the like of the rest, 2 Cor. vi. 5.

Ver. 13. *Ye are the salt of the earth*] As salt keepeth flesh from putrefying, so do the saints the world: and are therefore sprinkled up and down (here one and there one) to keep the rest from rotting. *Suillo pecori anima pro sale data, quæ carnem servaret, ne putresceret,* saith Varro. Swine and swinish persons have their souls for salt only, to keep their bodies from stinking above ground. Christ and his people are somewhere called the soul of the world. The saints are called all things; the church, every creature, Mark xvi. 15. Tabor and Hermon are put for east and west, Psal. lxxxix. 12, for God accounts of the world by the Church, and upholds the world for the Church's sake. Look how he gave Zoar to Lot, and all the souls in the ship to Paul, Acts xxvii. 24; so he doth the rest of mankind to the righteous. Were it not for such Jehoshaphats, "I would not look toward thee, nor see thee," said Elijah to Jehoram, saith God to the wicked, 2 Kings iii. 14. The holy seed is *statumen terræ*, saith one prophet: the earth's substance or settlement, Isa. vi. 13. (Junius.) The righteous are *fundamentum mundi*, the world's foundation, saith another, Prov. x. 25. (*Quia propter probos stabilis est mundus.* Merc.) I bear up the pillars of it, saith David, Psal. lxxv. 3. And it became a common proverb in the primitive times, *Absque stationibus non stare mundus :* but for the piety and prayers of Christians, the world could not subsist. It is a good conclusion of Philo, therefore, *Oremus, ut tanquam columna in domo vir justus permaneat, ad calamitatum remedium.* Let us pray that the righteous may remain with us, for a preservative, as a pillar in the house, as the salt of the earth. But as all good people, so good ministers especially are here said, for their doctrine, to be the salt of the earth; and for their lives, the light of the world. (*Doctrina salis est; vita lucis.* Aret.) Ye are salt, not honey, which is bitter to wounds. Ye are light, which is also offensive to sore eyes. Salt hath two things in it, *Acorem et saporem*, sharpness and savouriness. Ministers must reprove men sharply, that they may be " found in the faith," Tit. i. 13, and a sweet savour to God; savoury meat, as that of Rebekah, a sweet meat-offering, meet for the master's tooth, that he may eat and bless them. Cast they must their cruses full of this holy salt into the unwholesome waters, and upon the barren grounds of men's hearts (as Elisha once of Jericho), so shall God say the word that all be whole, and it shall be done. No thought can pass between the receipt and the remedy.

But if the salt have lost his savour, &c.] A loose or lazy minister is the worst creature upon earth, so fit for no place as for hell,—as unsavoury salt is not fit for the dunghill, but makes the very ground barren whereupon it is cast. Who are now devils but they which once were angels of light? *Corruptio optimi pessima*, as the sweetest wine makes the sourest vinegar, and the finest flesh is resolved into the vilest earth. Woe to those *dehonestamenta cleri*, that, with Eli's sons, cover foul sins under a white ephod: that neither spin nor labour, Matt. vi. 28, with the lilies, unless it be in their own vineyards, little in God's; that want either art or heart, will or skill, to the work; being not able or not apt to teach, and so give occasion to those black-mouthed Campians to cry out, *Ministris eorum nihil vilius:* their ministers are the vilest fellows upon earth. (Campian *in Rationibus.*) God commonly casteth off such as incorrigible; for wherewithal shall it be salted? there is nothing in nature that can restore unsavoury salt to its former nature. He will not only lay such by, as broken vessels, boring out their right eyes and drying up their right arms, Zech. xi. 17; i. e. bereaving them of their former abilities; but also he will cast dung upon their faces, Mal. ii. 3; so that, as dung, men shall tread upon them (which is a thing not only calamitous, but extremely ignominious), as they did upon the popish clergy; and the devil shall thank them when he hath them in hell, for sending him so many souls: as Matthew Paris telleth us he did those in the days of Hildebrand. *Literas ex inferno missas commenti sunt quidam, in quibus Satanas omni Ecclesiastico cætui gratias emisit.* As for themselves, it grew into a proverb, *Pavimentum inferni rasis sacrificulorum verticibus, et magnatum galeis stratum esse :* that hell was paved with the shaven crowns of priests and great men's head-pieces. God threatens to feed such with gall and wormwood, Jer. xxiii. 15.

Ver. 14. *Ye are the light of the world*] And must therefore lead convincing lives, though ye incur never so much hatred of those Lucifugæ, those Tenebriones of the world, that are ill afraid so much light should be diffused. But be ye blameless and harmless, the sons of God, without rebuke in the midst of a crooked and perverse nation (as the Baptist was), among whom ye shine as lights in the world; as those great lights (φωστῆρες, *luminaria*, Phil. ii. 15), the sun and moon (so the word signifieth), so that they that speak evil of you may be judged as absurd, as those Atlantes that curse the rising sun because it scorcheth them. Be as the stars at least; which are said to affect these inferior bodies by their influence, motion, and light. (Pliny.) So good ministers (as fixed stars in the church's firmament) by the influence of their lips, feed; by the regular motion of their lives, confirm; and by the light of both, enlighten many. And with such orient stars this Church of ours, blessed be God, like a bright sky in a clear evening, sparkleth and is bespangled, though not in every part, yet in every zone and quarter of it.

A city that is set on a hill cannot be hid] As that city that is mounted on seven hills, Rev. xvii. 9 (*Roma Radix Omnium Malorum*), and cannot be hid, but is apparently discerned and descried to be that great city Babylon: so Augustine and other writers call it: so Bellarmine and Ribera the Jesuit yield it. (*Roma; nec inficiantur Jesuitæ*, Rev. xviii. 2.) Joannes de Columna in his Mare Historiarum telleth us that Otho the emperor was once in a mind to make Rome the seat of his empire, as of old it had been. And having built a stately palace there, where formerly had stood the palace of Julian the Apostate (the Romans being much against it), he gave over the work. Theophanes, Zonaras, and Cedrenus report the like of Constans, nephew to Heraclitus, 340 years before Otho. Now that these and the like attempts took not effect, Genebrard saith it was a special providence of God to the end that the kingdom of the church foretold by Daniel might have Rome for its seat. If he had said, the kingdom of antichrist foretold by St Paul and likewise by John the divine, he had divined aright. But to return from whence we are digressed :—a minister while he lived a private person, stood in the crowd, as it were: but no sooner entered into his office, than he is set up on the stage: all eyes are upon him, as they were upon Saul, who was higher by head and shoulders than the rest of the people. In him (as in a picture in a glass window) every little blemish will be soon seen: and, as in the celestial bodies, every small aberration will be quickly noted and noticed. Now therefore as the tree of life was sweet to the taste and fair to the eye; and as in Absalom there was no blemish, from head to foot; so should it be with God's ministers. Singular holiness is required of such; as those that quarter arms with the Lord Christ, whom they serve in the gospel. The priests of the law were to be neither deformed nor defective. And the ministers of the gospel (for the word priest is never used for such by the apostles, no, not by the most ancient Fathers, as Bellarmine himself confesseth) must be τύποι, stamps and patterns to the believers in word and conversation; everything in them is eminent and exemplary. The world (though unjustly) looks for angelical perfection in them: and as the least deviation in a star is soon noted, so is it in such. Thrice happy he that (with Samuel, Daniel, Paul, and others) can be acquitted and approved by himself in private, in public by others, in both by God; that can by his spotless conversation slaughter envy, stop an open mouth, and draw testimony, if not from the mouths yet from the consciences of the adversaries, of his integrity and uprightness. Mr Bradford the martyr was had in so great reverence and admiration with all good men, that a multitude, which never knew him but by fame, greatly lamented his death: yea, and a number also of Papists themselves wished heartily his life. (Acts and Mon.) And of Mr Bucer it is reported that he brought all men into such admiration of him, that neither his friends could sufficiently praise him, nor his enemies in any point find fault with his singular life and sincere doctrine. Bishop Hooper's life was so good, that no kind of slander (although divers went about to reprove it) could fasten any fault upon him. And the man's life, saith Erasmus concerning Luther, whom he greatly loved not, is approved of all men; neither is this any small prejudice to his enemies, that they can tax him for nothing. *Tantam esse morum integritatem, ut nec hostes reperiant quod calumnientur.* (Erasmus.)

Ver. 15. *Neither do men light a candle to put it under a bushel, &c.*] Nor doth God set up a minister, and so light a link or torch, as the word λύχνος here signifieth, amongst a people, but for the disusing of the light of the knowledge of the glory of God in the face of Jesus Christ, 2 Cor. iv. 6. The heavenly bodies enlighten not their own orbs only, but send forth their beams far and near. The grace of God (that is, the doctrine of grace) that bringeth salvation hath appeared, or shone forth, as a candle on a candlestick; or as a beacon on a hill, teaching us to deny ungodliness, &c. (ἐπεφάνη), Tit. ii. 11, 12. *Dicuntur ἐπιφαίνεσθαι quæ repente con spectaculos omnium in se convertunt.* (Chrysost. in 2 Tim.) The priest's lips must

not only preserve knowledge, but also present it to the people, who shall seek it at his mouth. And John Baptist (that burning and shining light) was to give the knowledge of salvation, not by way of infusion, for so God only, but by way of instruction, Luke i. 77. The same word, in the holy tongue, that signifieth to understand, signifieth also to instruct and to prosper, they that teach others what they know themselves (as Abraham did those of his familiarity and family) shall know more of God's mind, yea, they shall be, as Abraham was, both of his court and council, Gen. xviii. 19. But the Lord likes not such empty vines, as (with Ephraim) bear fruit to themselves, Hos. x. 1; such idle servants as thrust their hands into their bosoms, dig their talents into the earth, hide their candles under a bed or bushel; living and lording it as if their lips were their own; barrelling and hoarding up their gifts, as rich cormorants do their corn; refusing to give down their milk, as curst kine; or resolving to speak no more than what may breed applause and admiration of their worth and wisdom, as proud self-seekers. The manifestation of the spirit was given to profit withal; and the Philippians were all partakers, or compartners of St Paul's grace; which he elsewhere calleth the gift bestowed on us, for many, that we may serve one another in love; yea, make ourselves servants to all, that we may edify some, 1 Cor. xii. 7 (συγκοίνωνοι), Phil. i. 7; 2 Cor. i. 11; Gal. v. 13; 1 Cor. ix. 19. Certainly the gifts of such shall not perish in the use, or be the worse for wearing, but the better and brighter; as the torch by tapping; they shall grow in their hands, as the loaves in our Saviour's, as the widow's oil, as that great mountain of salt in Spain, *de quo quantum demas, tantum accrescit,* which the more you take from it, the more it increaseth; or, lastly, as the fountains or wells, which, by much drawing, are made better and sweeter, as St Basil observeth, and common experience confirmeth. καὶ γὰρ τὰ φρέατα φασίν, ἀντλούμενα, βελτίω γίνεσθαι. Epist. 81.

And it giveth light to all that are in the house] He that alloweth his servant a great candle, or two or three lesser lights, looks for more work. God sets up his ministers, as candles on the candlestick of his Church, to waste themselves, wax and wick, for the lighting of men into life eternal. Let them therefore see to it, that they work hard while the light lasteth, lest their candlestick be removed, lest the night surprise them on the sudden, when none can work, Rev. ii. 5; John ix. 4, 5; lest they pay dear for those precious graces of his Spirit, in his faithful ministers, spent, or rather spilt upon them: lest God cause the sun to go down at noon, and darken the earth in the clear day, Amos viii. 9.

Ver. 16. *Let your light so shine before men*] We use to hang the picture of a dear friend in a conspicuous place, that it may appear we rejoice in it, as an ornament to us: so should we the image of Christ and his graces. And as pearls, though formed and found in the water, are like the heavens in clearness, so should all, but especially ministers: their faces should shine, as Moses when he came from the mount; their feet should be beautiful, Rom. x. 15; their mouths (as heaven in the Revelation) should never open, but some great matter should follow; their lives should be, as one speaketh of Joseph's life, *cælum quoddam lucidissimis virtutum stellis exornatum*, a very heaven sparkling with variety of virtues, as with so many bright stars. (Bucholcer.) The high priest of the law came forth to the people in habit more like a god than a man. *Os humerosque Deo similis.* (Virgil.) And Alexander the Great took him for no less, but fell at his feet, meeting him upon his way to Jerusalem. There are that hold, that by his linen he was taught purity; by his girdle, discretion; by his embroidered coat, heavenly conversation; by his golden bells, sound doctrine; by his pomegranates, fruitfulness in good works; by his shoulder-pieces, patience in bearing other men's infirmities; by his breastplate, continual care of the Church; by his mitre, a right intention; and by the golden plate upon it, a bold and wise profession of "Holiness to the Lord." The apostle also is exact in forming a minister of the gospel, 1 Tim. iii. 2—4: for he must be, 1. "Blameless" (ἀνεπίληπτος), such as against whom no just exception can be laid. 2. "Vigilant" (νηφάλεος), pale and wan again with watching and working. 3. "Sober" (σώφρων), or temperate, one that can contain his passions, master his own heart and keep a mean. 4. "Modest" (κόσμιος), neat and comely in his bodily attire, neither curious nor careless thereof, but venerable in all his behaviour; and one that keepeth a fit decorum in all things. 5. "Hospitable" (φιλόξενος), and harbourous. *Quicquid habent Clerici, pauperum est,* saith Jerome. 6. "Able and apt to teach" (διδακτικὸς), as Bishop Ridley, Dr Taylor, and Mr Bradford, who preached every Sunday and holiday ordinarily; and as Chrysostom, Origen, and some others, who preached every day in the week. 7. "Not given to wine" (πάροινος), no ale-stake, as those drunken priests, the two sons of Aaron, who died by the fire of God, for coming before him with strange fire, Lev. x. 2—9. 8. "No striker" (πλήκτης), neither with hand nor tongue, to the just grief or disgrace of any. 9. "Not greedy of filthy lucre" (αἰσχροκερδὴς), so as to get gain by evil arts; but honest, plain-dealing; and (as it follows in the text) patient, or equanimous, easily parting with his right for peace' sake (ἐπιεικὴς, Arist. Ethic. 5. 10), and ever preferring equity before extremity of law. 10. "Not a brawler" (ἄμαχος), or common barrator, a wrangler, as Ishmael. 11. "Not covetous," not doting on his wealth, or trusting to his wedge. Not without money, but without the love of money. The apostle here distinguisheth, "greedy of filthy lucre" (ἀφιλάργυρος), which is in getting, from covetousness, which consists in pinching and saving. 12. "One that ruleth well in his own house," &c. For the children's faults reflect upon the parents, and the servant's sin is

the master's shame. Besides, every man is that in religion that he is relatively; and so much true goodness he hath as he showeth at home. 13. "Not a novice" (νεόφυτος), a young scholar, rude and ungrounded; or a tender young plant in Christianity, as the word signifieth, that may be bent any way, but a well-grown oak, stable and steady. 14. Lastly, "he must have a good report of them which are without;" which he cannot but have, if qualified as above-said, 1 Tim. iii. 7. The same God which did at first put an awe of man in the fiercest creatures, hath stamped in the cruelest hearts an awful respect to his faithful ministers: so as even they that hate them cannot choose but honour them, as Saul did Samuel, Darius Daniel, Nebuchadnezzar the three worthies. Natural conscience cannot but stoop and do homage to God's image fairly stamped upon the natures and works of his people. So that when men see in such that which is above the ordinary strain and their own expectation, their hearts ache within them many times; and they stand much amazed at the height of their spirits and the majesty that shines in their faces. Either they are convinced, as Nebuchadnezzar, Darius, and Diocletian, who laid down the empire out of a deep discontent and despair of ever conquering the constancy of Christians by any bloody persecution; or, which is better, they are converted, and seeing such good works, they glorify God our heavenly Father, as Justin Martyr, who confesseth of himself, that by beholding the Christians' piety in life and patience in death (ὁρῶν δὲ ἀφόβους πρὸς θάνατον), he gathered their doctrine to be the truth, and glorified God in the day of his visitation. For there is no Christian, saith Athenagoras in his Apology to the Heathens, that is not good, unless he be an hypocrite, and a pretender only to religion. (οὐδεὶς χριστίανος πονηρὸς, εἰ μὴ ὑποκρίνηται τὸν λόγον.) *Vere magnus est Deus Christianorum*, said one Calocerius, a heathen, beholding the sufferings of the primitive martyrs. And it is reported of one Cecilia, a virgin, that by her constancy and exhortations before and at her martyrdom, four hundred were converted. Chrysostom calls good works unanswerable syllogisms, invincible demonstrations to confute and convert pagans. Julian the Apostate could not but confess, *Quod Christiana religio propter Christianorum erga omnes beneficentiam propagata est:* Christian religion spread by the holiness of those who professed it. Bede mentioneth one Alban, who receiving a poor persecuted Christian into his house, and seeing his holy and devout carriage, was so much affected therewith, as that he became an earnest professor of the faith, and in the end a glorious martyr for the faith.

Ver. 17. *Think not that I am come to destroy the law*] As the Pharisees slandered him only to bring him into hatred with the people; and as to this day they maliciously traduce him in their writings. Rabbi Maimonides, in his Mishna, hath a whole chapter concerning the punishment of the false prophet, that teacheth that he came to destroy the law. *Calumniare audacter: aliquid saltem adhærebit*, said Machiavel. A depraver, saith Plato, is *mus nominis;* a devil, saith Paul, 2 Tim. iii. 3. It is the property of defamations to leave a kind of lower estimation, many times, even where they are not believed.

I am not come to destroy] Gr. to loose, dissolve, or untie the law (καταλῦσαι), as those rebels, Psal. ii. 3, sought to do, but with ill success. For it tieth and hampereth men with an *Aut faciendum, aut patiendum*, either you must have the direction of the law, or the correction; either do it, or die for it. Thus the "law is a school-master," Gal. iii. 24, and such a one as that that Livy and Florus speak of in Italy, that brought forth his scholars to Hannibal, who had he not been more merciful than otherwise, they had all perished. The comfort is, that it is a school-master to Christ, who became bond to the law to redeem us that were under the law, from the rigour, bondage, irritation, and condemnation thereof. So that the use that now we have of it is only to be as Paul's sister's son, to show us our danger, and to send us to the chief Captain of our salvation, who came not to destroy the law, but to fulfil it.

But to fulfil it] To complete and accomplish it (πληρῶσαι), for he fulfilled all righteousness, and finished the work that was given him to do, John xvii. 4. A new commandment also gave he unto us, that we love one another; which love is the complement of the law and the supplement of the gospel. Besides, "Christ is the end of the law to every one that believeth," and commandeth us no more than he causeth us to do, Rom. x. 4; Ezek. xviii. 31; yea, he doth all his works in us and for us, saith the Church, Isa. xxvi. 12. Thus Christ still fulfils the law in his people; into whose hearts he putteth a disposition answerable to the outward law in all things, as in the wax is the same impression that was upon the seal. This is called the "law of the mind," Rom. vii. 25, and answereth the law of God without, as lead answers the mould, as tally answereth tally, as indenture indenture, Heb. viii. 8—10, with 2 Cor. iii. 2, 3; Rom. vi. 17.

Ver. 18. *For verily I say unto you*] This is his ordinary asseveration, which he useth in matters of weight only. For a vain protestation comes to as much, for aught I know, saith a worthy divine, as a vain oath. (Capel on Temptation.)

Till heaven and earth pass] And pass they must. The visible heavens being defiled with our sins that are even glued unto them (ἐκολλήθησαν. *Quasi bitumine ferruminata*), as Babylon's sins are said to be, Rev. xviii. 5, shall be purged with the fire of the last day, as the vessels of the sanctuary were that held the sin-offering. "The earth also, and all the works that are therein, shall be burnt up," 2 Pet. iii. 10. And this the heathens had heard of, and hammered at, that the world should at length be consumed with fire, as Ovid hath it (*Esse quoque in fatis meminit, &c.* Metam., lib. i.), and Lucretius disputeth it according to the natural causes. But Ludolfus of the life of Christ doth better, when he tells

us that of those two destructions of the world, the former was by water, for the heat of their lust, and the latter shall be by fire, for the coldness of their love. *Aqua, propter ardorem libidinis; igni, propter teporem charitatis*, ii. 87.

One jot] Which is the least letter in the alphabet. Irenæus calls it a half-letter; and Luther rendereth this text, *Ne minima quidem litera*, not so much as the least letter. The Jews fain that *jod* was added to the beginning of a masculine name, as in Jacob, Israel, &c., because it was taken from the end of a feminine, Sarai; solicitous lest the law should lose one *iota*. (*Nescit Scripturæ vel breve iota sacræ.* Prov.) But what meant the popish glossator to say, that the writings of the Fathers are authentical, *et tenenda omnia usque ad ultimum iota?* Shall the Fathers be put in equal balance with the Holy Scriptures?

Or one tittle] Not a hair-stroke, an accent on the top of a Hebrew letter, the bending or bowing thereof, as a little bit on the top of a horn. The Masorites have summed up all the letters in the Bible, to show that one hair of that sacred head is not perished.

Shall in no wise pass from the law] The ceremonial law was "a shadow of good things to come," saith the apostle, Heb. x. 1. This good thing was Christ. When the sun is behind, the shadow is before; when the sun is before, the shadow is behind. So was it in Christ to them of old (saith one). This sun was behind, and therefore the law or shadow was before. To us under the gospel, the sun is before, and so now the ceremonies of the law (those shadows) are behind, yea, vanished away. Before the passion of Christ (wherein they all determined) the ceremonies of the law were neither dead nor deadly: *nec mortiferæ, nec mortuæ*, saith Aquinas. After the passion, till such time as the gospel was preached up and down by the apostles, though dead, yet (for the time) they were not deadly. *Non mortiferæ, utcunque mortuæ.* But since that they are not only dead, but deadly to them that use them, as the Jews to this day. *Et mortuæ, et mortiferæ.* As for the moral law, it is eternal, and abideth for ever in heaven, saith David, Psal. cxix. 89. And albeit some special duties of certain commandments shall cease when we come to heaven, yet the substance of every one remaineth. We live by the same law (in effect) as the saints above do; and do God's will on earth as they in heaven. God himself cannot dispense with the breach of those laws that be moral in themselves (because he hateth sin by nature, not by precept only); such are all the ten commandments but the fourth. The fourth commandment (say divines) is moral by precept, not by nature; and so, the Lord of the sabbath may dispense with the literal breach of the sabbath. Of all the moral law, it is the opinion of some of our best divines (Zanchius, Prideaux), that since the coming of Christ it bindeth us not, out of any foregoing institution, as delivered to Moses in the mount; but as it is agreeable to the law of nature, which is common to Jews and Gentiles; and as it was explained and confirmed by our Saviour Christ in the Gospel. To conclude, the ministerials of this law shall pass away together with this life; the substantials shall pass into our glorified natures and shine therein, as in a mirror for ever.

Ver. 19. *Whosoever therefore shall break one of these least commandments*] So the Pharisees called and counted these weightier things of the law in comparison of their tithings, Matt. xxiii. 23, and traditions, Matt. xv. 3. They deemed it as great a sin to eat with unwashen hands as to commit fornication. *Dicunt Jesuitæ quædam peccata adeo esse in se et per se levia, ut factores, nec sordidos, nec malos, nec impios, nec Deo exosos reddant.* (Chemnitius.) But albeit some commandments are greater than some, as those of the first table (in meet comparison) than those of the second; yet that pharisaical diminution of commandments, that idle distinction of sins into gnats and camels, venial and mortal, motes and mountains, is by no means to be admitted. The least sin is contrary to charity, as the least drop of water is to fire. The least missing of the mark is an error as well as the greatest; and both alike for kind though not for degrees. חטאה *ἁμαρτία*, a missing of the mark, or swerving from the rule. Hence lesser sins are reproached by the name of the greater; malice is called murder; lustful looks, adultery; sitting at idolatrous feasts (though without all intent of worship), idolatry, 1 Cor. x. 14. See Job xxxi. 27, 28. Disobedience in never so small a matter (as eating a forbidden apple, gathering a few sticks on the sabbath day, looking into or touching the ark) hath been severely punished. Though the matter seem small, yet thy malice and presumption is great, that wilt in so small a thing incur the Lord's so high displeasure. What could be a less commandment than to abstain from blood? Yet is their obedience herein urged with many words, and that with this reason, as ever they will have God to do anything for them or theirs, Deut. xii. 22. The whole law is (say the schoolmen) but one copulative. Any condition not observed forfeits the whole lease; and any commandment not obeyed subjects a man to the curse, Deut. xxvii. 26; Gal. iii. 10. And so some one good action hath blessedness ascribed and assured to it, as peacemaking, Matt. v. 9, so he that shall "keep the whole law and yet offend in one point, is guilty of all," Jam. ii. 10. When some of the Israelites had broken the fourth commandment, God challengeth them for all, Exod. xvi. 28. Where, then, will they appear that plead for this Zoar, for that Rimmon?—a merry lie, a petty oath, an idle errand on the Lord's day, &c. Sick bodies love to be gratified with some little bit that favoureth the disease. But meddle not with the murdering morsels of sin; there will be bitterness in the end. Jonathan had no sooner tasted of the honey with the tip of his rod only, but his head was forfeited. There is a deceitfulness in sin, a lie in these vanities, Heb. iii. 13; John

ii. 21; "give them an inch, they'll take an ell." Let the serpent but get in his head, he will shortly wind in his whole body. He plays no small game but meaneth us much hurt, how modest soever he seemeth to be. It is no less than the kingdom that he seeketh, by his maidenly insinuations, as Adonijah. As therefore we must submit to God, so we must resist the devil, without expostulation, 1 Pet. v. 7—9; throw water on the fire of temptation, though but to some smaller sin, and stamp on it too. "Behold how great a matter a little fire kindleth," saith St James (iii. 5). A little poison in a cup, a little leak in a ship, or breach in a wall, may ruin all. A little wound at the heart and a little sin in the soul may hide God's face from us, as a cloud, Lam. iii. 44. Therefore as the prophet, when a cloud as big as a man's hand only appeared, knew that the whole heaven would be over-covered, and willed the king to betake himself to his chariot; so let us to our shelter, for a company comes, as she said, when she bore her son Gad. After Jonathan and his armourbearer came the whole host; and when Delilah had prevailed, came the lords of the Philistines. He that is fallen from the top of a ladder cannot stop at the second round. Every sin hardeneth the heart, and gradually disposeth it to greater offences; as lesser wedges make way for bigger. After Ahaz had made his wicked altar and offered on it, he brought it into the temple; first setting it on the brazen altar, afterwards bringing it into the house, and then, lastly, setting it on the north side of God's altar, 2 Kings xvi. 12—14. Withstand sin therefore at first, and live by Solomon's rule, "Give not water passage, no, not a little." Silence sin as our Saviour did the devil, and suffer it not to solicit thee. If it be importunate, answer it not a word, as Hezekiah would not Rabshakeh; or give it a short and sharp answer, yea, the blue eye that St Paul did (*ὑπωπιάζω*), 1 Cor. ix. 27. *Lividum reddo corpus meum.* (Aug.) This shall be "no grief unto thee hereafter, nor offence of heart," as she told David; the contrary may, 1 Sam. xxv. 31. It repented St Austin of his very excuses made to his parents, being a child, and to his schoolmaster, being a boy. He retracts his ironies, because they had the appearance of a lie, because they looked ill-favouredly. (Confess. i. 19; Retract. i. 1.) Bishop Ridley repents of his playing at chess, as wasting too much time. Bradford bewaileth his dulness and unthankfulness. (Acts and Mon.) David's heart smote him for cutting the lap of Saul's coat only; and that for none other intent than to clear his own innocency; that in which Saul commended him for his moderation. There are some that would shrink up sin into a narrow scantling, and bring it to this, if they could, that none do evil but they that are in gaols. But David approves his sincerity by his respect to all God's commandments, and hath this commendation, that he did all the wills of God (*θελήματα*), Psal. xviii. 21, 22; Acts xiii. 36. Solomon also bids "count nothing little that

God commandeth, but keep God's precepts as the sight of the eye," Prov. vii. 2. Those venturous spirits, that dare live in any known sin, aspire not to immortality, Phil. ii. 12; they shall be least, that is, nothing at all, in the kingdom of heaven.

And teacheth men so] As the Pharisees did, and all the old and modern heresiarchs. In the year 1559 it was maintained by one David George (that arch-heretic) that good works were pernicious and destructory to the soul. *Prodiit paradoxon, quod bona opera sint perniciosa ad salutem.* (Bucholc. Ind. Chron.) The Anabaptists and Socinians have broached many doctrines of devils, not fit to be once named amongst Christians. The Pneumatomachi of old set forth a base book of the Trinity, under St Cyprian's name, and sold it at a very cheap rate, that the poorest might be able to reach it and read it, as Ruffinus complaineth. In those primitive times, those capital heresies (concerning the Trinity and Christ's incarnation) were so generally held, that it was a witty thing then to be a right believer, as Erasmus phraseth it, *Ingeniosa res fuit, esse Christianum.* All the world, in a manner, was turned Arian, as St Jerome hath it, *Ingemuit orbis, et miratus est se factum esse.* (Arianum.) Orosius telleth us that the Goths, being desirous to be instructed in the Christian religion, requested of Valens the emperor to send them some to preach the faith unto them. He being himself an Arian, sent them Arian doctors, who set up that heresy amongst them. By the just judgment of God, therefore, the same Valens being overthrown in the battle by the Goths, was also burnt by them in a poor cottage, whither he had fled for shelter. *Justo itaque Dei judicio Valens à Gothis crematus est, quorum ille animis pestiferum errorum virus infuderat.* (Tertullian.) Heretics have an art of Pythanology, whereby they cunningly insinuate into men's affections, and many times persuade before they teach, as it is said of the Valentinians. It was therefore well and wisely done of Placilla the empress, when her husband Theodosius, senior, desired to confer with Eunomius, she earnestly dissuaded him; lest being perverted by his speeches, he might fall into his heresy. (Sozom. vii. 6, 7.)

Shall be least in the kingdom of heaven] That is, nothing at all there; as Matt. xx. 16. Either of these two sins here mentioned exclude out of heaven; how much more both? If single sinners that break God's commandments, and no more, shall be damned, those that teach men so shall be double damned: if God will be avenged on the former seven-fold, surely he will on the latter seventy-fold seven-fold. When the beast and the kings of the earth and their armies shall be gathered together (toward the end of the world) to make war against Christ, the multitude shall be slain with the sword, the poor seduced people that were carried along,

many of them (as those two hundred that followed Absalom out of Jerusalem) in the simplicity of their hearts, and understood not the matter, shall have an easier judgment, 2 Sam. xv. 11. But the beast was taken, and the false prophet, and were both cast alive (not slain with the sword, and so cast to the infernal vultures to be devoured by them as a prey; but cast alive), that they may feel those most exquisite pains, into a lake of fire burning with brimstone, Rev. xix. 20, 21, wherewith they are encompassed, as fish cast into a pond are with water.[1]

But whosoever shall do, and teach them] First do, and thereby prove what that good, holy, and acceptable will of God is, Rom. xii. 23; and then teach others what himself hath felt and found good by experience. Come, and I will tell you what God hath done for my soul. "Come, children, hearken unto me, I will teach you the fear of the Lord. I will instruct thee and teach thee in the way which thou shalt go: I will guide thee with mine eye. I will teach transgressors thy ways, and sinners shall be converted unto thee," Psal. lxvi. 16; xxxiv. 11; li. 13. Charity is no churl, Psal. xxxii. 8; but cries, I would to God that all that hear me this day were as I am. Andrew calleth Simon; and Philip, Nathaniel; the Samaritaness, her neighbours; and those good souls, one another, Hos. vi. 1. The love of Christ constrained the apostles, 2 Cor. v. 11; they could not but speak the things they had heard and felt; as little as the holy Virgin could conceal the joy she had conceived upon the conception of God her Saviour. They could not but be as busy in building stair-cases for heaven as these Pharisees were in digging descents to hell. Blind guides they were of the blind, and both fell into the ditch, but the guides fell undermost. By corrupt teachers Satan catcheth men, as a cunning fisher by one fish catcheth another, that he may feed upon both. Here they corrupted the law by their false glosses, as our Saviour sets forth. But where they kept Moses' chair warm, sat close and said sooth; all that they bid you observe, that observe and do, saith he, Matt. xxiii. 2, 3; for a bad man may cry a good commodity, and a stinking breath sound a trumpet with great commendation. Balaam, Satan's spel-man, may be (for the time) Christ's spokes-man, and preach profitably to others, though himself be a cast-away, 1 Cor. ix. 27; as water, when it hath cleansed other things, is cast into the sink. Hear such therefore, saith our Saviour, but do not after their works, for they say and do not: they speak by the talent, but work by the ounce; their tongues are bigger than their hands; their lives give the lie to their lips;[2] they shun the way themselves (with that priest and Levite) which they showed to others, when mercy should be showed to the

---

[1] *Dirissimum exitii genus quo hiatu præ reliquis devovebuntur.* Pareus.

[2] *Odi homines ignavâ operâ, philosophâ sententiâ.* Ennius. Συναδόντων μὲν τοῖς ἔργοις ἀποδεκτέον, διαφωνούντων δὲ λόγους ὑποληπτέον. Arist.

wounded man. Out of their own mouths therefore will God condemn them; and it is a fearful thing to fall into the punishing hands of the living God. As for those burning and shining lights, that have Urim and Thummim, bells and pomegranates, trumpets of sound doctrine in one hand and lamps of good life in the other, as Gideon's soldiers; they shall be great in the kingdom of heaven. He that holdeth them in his right hand here, Rev. i. 20, shall set them at his right hand hereafter, and give them to hear, as Ezekiel did, the noise " of a great rushing, saying, Blessed be the glory of the Lord," Ezek. iii. 12.

Ver. 20. *Except your righteousness shall exceed the righteousness of the scribes and Pharisees*] And yet they went far: 1. In works of piety, for they made long prayers, &c. 2. In works of charity, for they gave much alms. 3. In works of equity, for they tithed mint, anise, and cummin. 4. In works of courtesy, for they invited Christ often, &c. They were the most exact and accurate sect of that religion, as St Paul (who once was one of them) beareth them witness;[1] and so carried away the heart of the people, that there was no holy man that was not termed a Pharisee: and therefore among the seven kinds of Pharisees in their Talmud (whereof one sort was Pharisæus: *Quid debeo facere, et faciam illud,* such a one was he, Luke xviii. 18); they make Abraham a Pharisee of love, Job a Pharisee of fear, &c. Yea, it was commonly conceited among the Jews, that if but two of all the world were to go to heaven, the one should be a scribe and the other a Pharisee. And what high opinions they nourished of themselves may be seen in that proud Pharisee, Luke xviii. Like unto whom, how many civil justiciaries are there amongst us? who if they can keep their church, give an alms, bow their knee, say their prayers, pay their tithes, and once a year receive the sacrament (it matters not how corrupt hearts, how filthy tongues, how false hands they bear), can thank God for their good estate to Godward, and take up their seats, as it were, in heaven aforehand. But our Saviour says nay to it in this text; yea, sets a double bolt upon heaven's gates to keep out such. And when they shall come knocking and bouncing, with " Lord, Lord, open unto us," he shall say, *Discedite,* Depart ye; or as once he did to their fellow-Pharisees, Ye are they which justified yourselves before men, but God knew your hearts. And you shall now know (to your small comfort) that that which is highly esteemed amongst men is abomination in the sight of God, Luke xvi. 15. Civility rested in, is but a beautiful abomination, a smooth way to hell. The world highly applauds it, because somewhat better than out-

rageous wickedness; as a cab of dove's dung was sold in Samaria's famine at a very dear rate, &c.

Ver. 21. *Ye have heard that it was said by them of old*] Antiquity is venerable: and of witnesses, Aristotle witnesseth, that the more ancient they are, the more to be credited, as less corrupt. New things are vain things, saith the Greek proverb. And the historian condemneth his countrymen, as despisers of old customs, and carried after new.[2] But as old age is a crown, if it be found in the way of righteousness, Prov. xvi. 31, and not otherwise: so may it be said of these Kadmônim or the old Rabbins, later than Ezra, whom our Saviour here confuteth. Much might have been attributed to their authority, had they not rested upon the bare letter of the law, and wrested it sometimes to another meaning. Antiquity disjoined from verity is but filthy hoariness; and deserveth no more reverence than an old lecher, which is so much the more odious, because old. And as manna, the longer it was kept against the command of God the more it stank; so do errors and enormities. Laban pretendeth antiquity for his God, in his oath to Jacob: The God of Abraham, saith he, and the God of Nahor, the God of their father, judge between us, Gen. xxxi. 53. But Jacob sware by the fear of his father Isaac. He riseth not higher than his father, and yet doubts not but he worshipped God aright. Εμοὶ ἀρχαῖα Ιησοῦ ὁ Χριστὸς. (Ignat.) It is no good rule to say, We'll be of the same religion with our forefathers, unless we can approve it right by the Holy Scriptures. *Plus valet malum inolitum quam bonum insolitum :* and that, *Tyrannus, trium literarum mos,* too often carries it against truth. The image that fell down from Jupiter (for which there was so much ado at Ephesus, τοῦ Διοπετοῦς, Acts xix. 35) is said by the town-clerk to be such as could not be spoken against with any reason. And why? because it was wonderful ancient (as Pliny telleth us). For whereas the temple of Diana had been seven several times re-edified, this image was never changed;[3] and thence grew the so great superstition, by the covetousness of the priests. As likewise the Ancilia among the Romans; and Pessinuntium among the Asians. But what saith a noble writer, Antiquity must have no more authority than what it can maintain. Did not our predecessors hold the torrid zone inhabitable? did they not confine the world in the ark of Europe, Asia, and Africa, till Noah's dove, Columbus, discovered land? &c.

Thou shalt not kill : and whosoever killeth shall be in danger of judgment] That is, it shall be questioned whether it be fit he be put to death or not. Thus as Eve dallied with the

---

[1] ἀκριβεστάτη αἵρεσις, Acts xxvi. 5. *In hac hæresi sum :* i. e. *sic sentio.*

[2] πιστότατι οἱ πάλαιοι; ἀδιάφθοροι γὰρ. Rhet. lib. i. τὰ καινὰ κενὰ. Thucydides. *Athenienses suos ὑπερόπτας τῶν εἰωθότων, non sine probro appellitat. Cor Priscorum fuit si-*

cut porta porticus templi, at cor posterorum sicut forameniacus. Talmud Erublin. Papists boast much of antiquity, as once the Gibeonites did of old shoes and mouldy bread.

[3] *Virgineum fuit simulachrum longe antiquissimum, nunquam mutatum, septies restituto templo.*

command, saying, Ye shall not eat thereof, lest ye die (when God had said, Ye shall surely die whensoever ye eat), and so fell into the devil's danger; in like sort, these Jew-doctors had corrupted the very letter of the law, and made that doubtful and questionable which God had plainly and peremptorily pronounced to be present death. Before the Flood, indeed, some do guess and gather out of Gen. ix. that the punishment of murder, and such-like heinous offences, was only excommunication from the holy assemblies, and exclusion out of their fathers' families, as Cain was cast out from the presence of the Lord; that is, from his father's house, where God was sincerely served. Sure it is, that no sooner was the world repaired, than this law was established, " Whoso sheddeth man's blood, by man shall his blood be shed; " and this reason is rendered, "for in the image of God made he him," Gen. ix. 6. That image (it is true) is by the Fall defaced and abolished; yet are there some relics thereof still abiding, which God will not have destroyed. If any object, Why then should the murderer be destroyed, sith he also is made in the image of God? the answer is easy, because the murderer hath destroyed the image of God in his neighbour, and turned himself into the image of the devil. Besides, God hath indispensably and peremptorily commanded it: He that sheddeth the blood of any person, hasteneth to the grave, let no man hinder him, Prov. xxviii. 17. Say he escape the stroke of human justice, yet the barbarians could say (as of Paul, whom they took for a murderer) that divine vengeance will not suffer him to live, Acts xxviii. 4. "Bloody and deceitful men shall not live out half their days," Psal. lv. 23. Usually either God executeth them with his own immediate hand, as it might be easy to instance in many bloody persecutors and others; or he maketh them their own deathsmen, as Pilate; or setteth some other a-work to do it for them. As (among other examples of God's dealings in this kind) A.D. 1586, Walsh, Bishop of Ossory, in Ireland, a man of honest life, with his two servants, were stabbed to death by one Dulland, an Irish old soldier, whilst he gravely admonished him of his foul adulteries; and the wicked murderer escaped away, who had now committed 45 murders with his own hand. At length, revenge pursuing him, he was by another bloody fellow, Donald Spaman, shortly after slain himself, and his head presented to the Lord Deputy. Neither can I here omit (that which I had almost forgotten) the just hand of God upon that villanous parricide, Alphonsus Diazius, the Spaniard, who (after he had, like another Cain, 1 John iii. 12, killed his own natural brother, John Diazius, merely because he had renounced Popery and became a professor of the reformed religion, and was not only not punished, but highly commended of the Romanists for his heroical achievements) desperately hanged himself at Trent, upon the neck of his own mule, being haunted and hunted by the furies of his own conscience. *Senarclæus de morte Joan. Diazii,* A.D. 1551. *Seipsum desperabundus Tridenti de collo mulæ suæ suspendit.*

Ver. 22. *But I say unto you*] This is his teaching with authority, and not as the scribes. To their false glosses he opposeth his own sole and single authority. He delivers himself like a lawgiver: " but I say unto you," and you shall take it on my bare word, without any further pawn or pledge. He that is αὐταυτὸς, is likewise αὐτοπιστὸς. The Pharisees' phylacteries were not so broad but their expositions of the law were as narrow; which therefore our Saviour letteth out and rectifieth, by taking away their viperine glosses that did eat out the bowels of the text: and here observe with me, that Christ taketh not upon him to be a new lawgiver, but to be an interpreter of the old law by Moses. He maketh not new commands or counsels (as Popish expositors dream), but throws away all that earth that the Philistines had tumbled into that spring.

That whosoever is angry with his brother without a cause] Rashly giving way to unruly passion, and not taking reason into counsel, as the word here signifieth.[1] This is a degree of murder that the Pharisees dreamt not of, and a mortal sin, though the Papists conclude it venial from this very text, because not threatened (as calling fool) with hell fire. But judgment, counsel, and Gehenna, note not here different punishments, but only divers degrees of the damnation of hell, which is the just hire of the least sin. There is a lawful anger, as that of our Saviour, Mark iii. 5; Matt. xvi. 22. And we are bid " be angry, and sin not," Eph. iv. 26; Dan. iii. 19. Now he that would be angry and not sin must (for the matter) be angry at nothing but at sin, and that not so much as it is an injury to us as an offence to God. Next, for the measure, he must not be so transported with anger, as to be unfitted and indisposed thereby either for prayer to God or pity to men. Moses was very angry at the sight of the golden calf, yet could pray, Exod. xxxii. 19, 31. Our Saviour was heartily angry at the Pharisees, but withal grieved at the hardness of their hearts (συλλυπούμενος), Mark iii. 5. Jonas on the other side, through anger, thought to have prayed, but fell into a brawl with God, quarrelled with him for his kindness; and had little pity on so many poor Ninevites; though afterwards he yielded to better reason, and showed his submission by laying his hand upon his mouth, and saying no more, Jonas iv. 1—11. Anger is a tender virtue (saith one), and such as, by reason of our unskilfulness, may be easily corrupted and made dangerous. The wrath of man (usually) worketh not the righteousness of God: nay, it lets in the devil, that old man-slayer, and is the murder of the heart (as here), making way to the murder of the tongue and hand,

---

[1] εἰκῆ ab εἴκω, cedo ; qui cedit affectibus, adeo ut rationem *in consilium non adhibeat.* Piscat. in Rom. xiii. 4.

Jam. i. 20; Eph. iv. 26. It is the match to receive the fire of contention, and the bellows to blow it up, Prov. xv. 18. Now where strife is, there is confusion and every evil work, not murder excepted, Jam. iii. 16.

And whosoever shall say unto his brother, Raca][1] Anger (as fire), if smothered, will languish; but let out, will flame into further mischief. Cease from anger, saith David, for else thou wilt fret thyself to do evil, Psal. xxxvii. 8; Prov. xx. 32, 33. (Mercer.) And if thou hast done evil (or played the fool, as others read it), saith Agur, in lifting up thyself, and puffing against thy brother, against whom in thine anger thou hast devised some mischief, if thou hast thought evil against him, yet lay thy hand upon thy mouth: say not so much as Raca, utter not any so much as an inarticulate voice, snuff not, snort not, spit not, as he, Deut. xxv. 9; stamp not with clapping of the hands, as Balak, Num. xxiv. 10; say not so much as fie to thine offending brother, saith Theophylact; Thou him not, saith Chrysostom; call him not silly or shallow, one that wants brains, saith Irenæus, *qui expuit cerebrum*, as the word signifieth, if it signify anything.[2] Surely (saith Agur, setting forth the reason of his former precept by a double similitude) the churning of milk bringeth forth butter, and the wringing of the nose bringeth forth blood: so the forcing of wrath (the giving it its forth and full scope, and not suppressing it when it first begins to boil in a man's breast) bringeth forth strife. Let therefore the first heat of passion settle, and that darkness pass that hath clouded the mind. *Ut fragilis glacies, occidat ira morâ.* Walk into the garden with Ahasuerus, into the field with Jonathan, 1 Sam. xx. 11, when his father had provoked him to wrath, Eph. vi. 4 (against the apostle's precept). Divert to some other company, place, business, about something thou canst be most earnest at. Give not place to wrath, no, not a little; set God before thy tumultuating passions, and so silence them, else worse will follow. Say not with the civilian, *De minutis non curat lex:* the law takes not notice of small faults. God's law is spiritual, and reacheth to a raca, to a sirrah, &c. Rom. vii.

But whosoever shall say, Thou fool, &c.] How much more, rogue, bastard, devil, and other such foul and opprobrious terms, not fit to be mentioned among saints, yet common with many such as would be counted so. What makest thou here, thou arch-devil, troubling our city? said the Bishop of Geneva to Farellus, seeking to set up the reformed religion.[3] And a Spanish Jesuit disputing with us about the Eucharist (saith Beza) called us *vulpes, serpentes, et simias*, foxes, serpents, and jackanapes. Contrarily, it is observed of Archbishop Cranmer, that he never raged so far with any of his household servants, as once to call the meanest of them

varlet or knave in anger, much less to reprove a stranger with any reproachful word; least of all did he deal blows among them, as Bishop Bonner: who in his visitation, because the bells rung not at his coming into Hadham, nor the church was dressed up as it should, called Dr Bricket knave and heretic; and therewithal, whether thrusting or striking at him, so it was, that he gave Sir Thomas Josselin, Knight (who then stood next to the Bishop), a good flewet upon the upper part of the neck, even under his ear; whereat he was somewhat astonied at the suddenness of the quarrel for that time. At last he spake and said, What meaneth your lordship? have you been trained up in Will. Sommers's school, to strike him who standeth next you? The Bishop, still in a rage, either heard not, or would not hear. When Mr Fecknam would have excused him by his long imprisonment in the Marshalsea, whereby he was grown testy, &c., he replied merrily, So it seems, Mr Fecknam; for now that he is come forth of the Marshalsea he is ready to go to Bedlam. Our Saviour here threateneth a worse place, tormenting Tophet, the Gehenna of fire, to that unruly evil, the tongue, that being set on fire of hell, fetcheth words as far as hell to set on fire the whole course of nature, Jam. iii. 6.

Shall be in danger of hell fire] Gehenna, or the valley of Hinnom, was reputed a contemptible place, without the city, in the which they burnt (by means of a fire continually kept there) the carcases, filth, and garbage of the city, so that by the fire of Gehenna here is intimated both the restless torments of hell (sc. by the bitter cries and ejaculations of poor infants there burnt to Moloch), and also the perpetuity and endlessness of them. The idol Moloch or Saturn was represented by a man-like brazen body, with the head of a calf. The children offered were inclosed within the arms of this idol; and as the fire increased about it, the sacrifice with the noise of drums and other instruments filled the air, that the pitiful cries of the children might not be heard.

Ver. 23. *Therefore if thou bring thy gift to the altar*] To anger our Saviour here opposeth charity, which suffereth long and is kind. Charity envieth not, nor is rash, &c.; but beareth all things, believeth all things, hopeth all things, endureth all things. Strangers we must love as ourselves, Luke x. 27, 28; but brethren, as Christ loved us, with a preventing constant love, John xv. 15, notwithstanding provocations to the contrary.

That thy brother hath aught against thee] As justly offended as thee: see the like phrase, Luke vii. 40; Rev. ii. 4. If either thou have given offence carelessly, or taken offence causelessly. And two flints may as soon smite together, and not fire come out, as people converse

---

[1] *Vox convitii levioris.*

[2] κατάπτυστος. Chrysost. vit. *Syros hoc nomine uti pro τό κενός.* Hesych.

[3] *Quid tu diabole nequissime, ad hanc civitatem perturbandam accessisti? dicit Episcopus Genevensis.*

together, and not offences fall out. Now if it be a great offence, a considerable injury, to the just grief or disgrace of another, satisfaction must be given, and reconciliation sought (at least), ere the service can be accepted. For how can we look our father in the face, or ask him blessing, when we know that he knows there is hatred or heart-burning between us and our brethren?

Ver. 24. *Leave there thy gift*] The fountain of love will not be laded at with uncharitable hands. God appeared not to Abraham till Lot and he were agreed. Jacob reconciled to his brother, first builds an altar, &c.

And go thy way, first be reconciled] Unless thou wilt lose thy labour, and worse, as Saul and Judas did. God prefers mercy before sacrifice, and is content his own immediate service should be intermitted, rather than reconciliation be omitted. Confess your trespasses (παραπτώματα) one to another, saith St James (v. 16), your lapses and offences one against another, and then pray one for another, that ye may be healed; as Abraham, after reconciliation, prayed for Abimelech, and the Lord healed him. St Peter would have husbands and wives live lovingly together; or, if some household words fall out between them at any time, to peace again that their prayers be not hindered, as else they will be, 1 Pet. iii. 7. Dissension and ill-will will lie at the well-head and stop the current. The spirit of grace and supplication will be grieved by bitterness, anger, clamour; yea, made thereby to stir with discontent, and to withdraw, as loathing his lodging, Eph. iv. 30, 31. *Si quis est qui neminem in gratiam putat redire posse, non nostram is perfidiam arguit, sed indicat suam.* (Cic. Epist. lib. 2. ep. 17.) *Menander tamen dicit, reconciliationes esse lupinas amicitias.*

First be reconciled to thy brother] And, as a bone once broken is stronger after well setting, so let love be after reconcilement; that if it be possible, as much as in us lieth, we may live peaceably with all men. Let it not stick on our part howsoever, but seek peace and ensue it. Though it flee from thee, follow after it, and account it an honour to be first in so good a matter. I do not see (saith one) the Levite's father-in-law make any means for reconciliation; but when remission come to his doors, no man entertaineth it more thankfully. The nature of many men is forward to accept and negligent to sue for; they can spend secret wishes upon that which shall cost them no endeavour. But why should men be so backward to a business of this nature? Almighty God beseecheth sinners to be reconciled unto him, 2 Cor. v. 20. And, as when a man goes from the sun, yet the sun-beams follow him, shine on him, warm him; so doth the mercy of God follow us all the days of our lives, Psal. xxiii. 6. Our Saviour first sent to Peter that had denied him, and went to the rest that had forsaken

him. Aristippus (though but a heathen) went of his own accord to Æschines, his enemy, and said, Shall we not be reconciled, till we become a table-talk to all the country? And when Æschines answered he would most gladly be at peace with him: Remember therefore, said Aristippus, that although I were the elder and better man, yet I sought first unto thee. Thou art indeed, said Æschines, a far better man than I, for I began the quarrel, but thou the reconcilement. (Laert. lib. 2.) Guiltiness is commonly clamorous and implacable, and none so averse to reconciliation as they that are most injurious; as he that wronged his brother, thrust away Moses, saying, "Who made thee a ruler?" &c. "Wilt thou kill me?" &c. Acts vii. 27, 28.

Ver. 25. *Agree with thine adversary quickly*] *Habent aulæ suum Cito, cito.* God's work also must be done with expedition; opportunities are headlong, delays dangerous. Let not therefore the sun go down upon your wrath, lest it grow inveterate, as it proves in many, who not only let the sun go down once or twice, but run his whole race, ere they can find hearts and means to be reconciled.[1] "Cursed be their wrath, for it is deadly. O my soul, come not thou into their secret," Gen. xlix. 6, 7. It were much to be wished, that, as Livy hath it, *Amicitiæ immortales, inimicitiæ mortales essent*, enmities were mortal amongst us, amities immortal.

Lest thine adversary deliver thee to the judge] By his groans and moans to God, who is gracious (though thou art stiff) and will pay thee for thy pertinacy, Exod. xxii. 26 (and him for his patience), with extremity of law. Compound, therefore, and take up the suit before it come to execution and judgment. Suffer it not, as ill husbands do, to run on, and charges to grow from term to term, lest we pay not only the main debt, but the arrearages too, the time of God's patience, &c.

Thou be cast into prison] Into hell, worse than any prison. Of Roger, Bishop of Salisbury, the second man from King Stephen, it is storied, that he was so tortured in prison with hunger and other calamities accompanying such men, *ut vivere noluerit, mori nescieret*, live he would not, die he could not. This and much worse is the case of those that are cast into hell; they seek death, but find it not, they desire it, but it fleeth from them, Rev. ix. 6.

Ver. 26. *Thou shalt by no means come out thence till,* &c.] *i. e.* Never come out. Let our merit-mongers first go to hell for their sins, and stay all eternity there; then afterward, if God will create another eternity, they may have liberty to relate their good works, and call for their wages. But the curse of the law will first be served of such, as, seeking to be saved by the works of the law, are fallen from Christ; these shall never come out till they have paid the utmost farthing. And when will that be? We read of a miserable malefactor (John Chambone

[1] *Si quid benefeceris, levius plumâ est : at si offenderis, plumbeas iras gerunt.* Plaut.

by name) who had lain in the dungeon at Lyons the space of seven or eight months. This thief, for pain and torment, cried out of God, and cursed his parents that begat him, being almost eaten up with lice, and ready to eat his own flesh for hunger; being fed with such bread as dogs and horses had refused to eat. So it pleased the goodness of Almighty God, that Petrus Bergerius, a French martyr, was cast into the same dungeon; through whose preaching and prayers he was brought to repentance, learning much comfort and patience by the word of the gospel preached unto him. Touching his conversion he wrote a very sweet letter out of his bonds, declaring therein, that the next day after that he had taken hold of the gospel, and framed himself to patience according to the same, his lice (which he could pluck out before by twenty at once betwixt his fingers) now were so gone from him that he had not one. Furthermore, so the alms of good people were extended towards him, that he was fed with white bread, and that which was very good. His imprisonment, at utmost, lasted but while life; death as a gaoler knocked off his shackles, and set him into the glorious liberty of the saints above. So the penitent thief in the Gospel; and so that Robert Samuel, martyr, above mentioned. But not so those that are clapt up in the dark dungeon of hell. Their misery is as endless as easeless. A river of brimstone is not consumed by burning; the smoke of that pit ascendeth for ever. A child with a spoon may sooner empty the sea than the damned in hell accomplish their misery. All that wicked men suffer here is but a paying the use-money required for that dreadful debt, that must be paid at last by all that make not timely composition.

Ver. 27. *Ye have heard that it was said by them of old, Thou shalt not commit adultery*] This they corruptly restrained to the gross act, and made nothing of contemplative filthiness, hearts full of harlotry, hot as an oven with scalding lusts, Hos. vii. 6, very stews and brothel-houses, cages of unclean birds; besides eyes full of adultery, hands defiled with dalliance, tongues taught to talk obscenities and ribaldries. *Spurcitias Veneris eliminantes.* But Seneca could say, *Incesta est, et sine stupro, quæ stuprum cupit :* she is a whore that would be so had she but opportunity; and the Romans put to death a vestal virgin for singing this verse only,

Fælices nuptæ! moriar ni nubere dulce est.

St Paul's virgin is holy, not in body only, but in spirit also, 1 Cor. vii. 34. *Quæ quia non licuit non facit, illa facit.*[1] And for the avoiding of fornications, διὰ τὰς πορνείας, 1 Cor. vii. 2 (in the plural number, inward burnings as well as outward pollutions), let every man have

his own wife, &c. *Fecit quisque quantum voluit,* saith Seneca. Every one doeth as he desireth to do. And Polybius attributeth the death of Antiochus to sacrilege only in his purpose and will. Josephus indeed derideth Polybius for so saying; but with as little reason, as his countryman Kimchi (soured with the leaven of the Pharisees) sets this strange sense upon Psal. lxvi. 18: If I regard iniquity *only* in my heart, so that it break not forth into outward act, the Lord will not hear me, that is (saith he) so as to impute it, or account it a sin.

Ver. 28. *But I say unto you, that whosoever looketh on a woman to lust after her*] Lusting is oft the fruit of looking; as in Joseph's mistress, who set her eyes upon Joseph ;[2] and David, who saw Bathsheba bathing. Lust is quicksighted. How much better Job, who would not look, lest he should think upon a maid! and Nazianzen, who had learned (and he glories in it) to keep in his eyes from roving to wanton prospects! τοὺς ὀφθαλμοὺς σωφρονίσαι. And the like is reported of that heavenly spark, the young Lord Harrington; whereas those that have eyes full of adultery cannot cease to sin, saith St Peter. (2 Pet. ii. 14, μοιχαλίδος, full of the whore, as if she sate in the adulterer's eye.) And *facti crimina lumen habet,* saith another. Samson's eyes were the first offenders that betrayed him to lust, therefore are they first pulled out, and he led a blind captive to Gaza where before he had lustfully gazed on his Delilah. It is true, the blindness of his body opened the eyes of his mind. But how many thousands are there that die of the wound in the eye! Physicians reckon 200 diseases that belong to it; but none like this. For, by these loop-holes of lust and windows of wickedness, the devil windeth himself into the soul. Death entereth in by these windows, as the fathers apply that text in Jeremiah. The eye is the light of the body, saith our Saviour, and yet by our abuse, this most lightsome part of the body draweth many times the whole soul into utter darkness. Nothing, I dare say, so much enricheth hell as beautiful faces; while a man's eye-beams, beating upon that beauty, reflect with a new heat upon himself. *Ut vidi, ut perii !* (Propert.) Looking and lusting differ (in Greek) but in one letter (ἐκ τοῦ ὁρᾶν γίνεται τὸ ἐρᾶν). When one seemed to pity a one-eyed man, he told him he had lost one of his enemies, a very thief, that would have stolen away his heart. Democritus (but in that no wise man) pulled out his eyes; and the Pharisee (little wiser) would shut his eyes when he walked abroad, to avoid the sight of women; insomuch that he often dashed his head against the walls, that the blood gushed out, and was therefore called *Pharisæus impingens.*[3] How much better, and

---

[1] *Has patitur pœnas peccandi sola voluntas.* Juv. Sat. 13.

[2] *Conjecit in eum oculos,* Gen. xxxix. *Non dicit Moses, vidit, aspexit : sed hic fuit aspectus impudicus.* Pareus.

[3] *Democritus oculos sibi eruit, quod mulieres sine concupiscentia adspicere non possit. Sed nihil aliud fecit quam quod fatuitatem suam urbi manifestam fecit.* Tertullian in Apologet. *Voluptatem vicisse voluptas est maxima, nec ulla major est victoria, quam ea quæ a cupiditatibus refertur.* Cypr. de bon. pud.

with greater commendation had these men taken our Saviour's counsel in the following verses!

Ver. 29. *And if thy right eye offend thee, pluck it out*] That is, if it be either so natural or habitual to thee to go after the sight of thine eyes (which Solomon assigneth for the source of all youthful outrages, Eccles. xi. 9) that thou hadst as lief lose thy right eye as not look at liberty; out with such an eye (though a right eye): pull it out, and rake in the hole where it grew, rather than that any filth should remain there. Pluck it out of the old Adam, and set it into the new man. Get that *oculum irretortum*, that may look forth-right upon the mark, without idle or curious prying into, or poring upon, forbidden beauties, Prov. iv. 25. A prætor (said the heathen) should have continent eyes as well as hands. And the Greek orator wittily and worthily upbraided a certain wanton, that he had not pupils but punks in his eyes.[1] And Archesilaus the philosopher, observing one to have wanton eyes, told him that the difference was not great, whether he played the naughty-pack with his upper parts or his nether. Lot might not look toward Sodom. And Peter Martyr observeth out of Nathan's parable, that lust, though it once prevailed over David, yet it was but a stranger to him; he had enough of that once, for it cost him hot water. His eye became a fountain, he washed his bed which he had defiled (yea, his pallet, or under-bed) with tears.[2] So did Mary Magdalen, once a strumpet; her hands were bands, her words were cords, her eyes as glasses whereinto while silly larks gazed they were taken as in a day-net. She therefore made those eyes a fountain to bathe Christ's feet in, and had his blood a fountain to bathe her soul in, Zech. xiii. 1. To conclude, the sight is a deceitful sense, therefore bind it to the good abearance; call it from its out-strays, check it, and lay God's charge upon it for the future. Chaste Joseph would not once look on his immodest mistress; she looked, and caught hold on him, and that when she was a-bed; but her temptation fell like fire upon wet tinder, and took not.[3] It must be our constant care that no sparkle of the eye flee out to consume the whole by a flame of lust: but upon offer of wanton glances from others beat them back as the north wind driveth away rain, Prov. xxv. 23. A king that sitteth in the throne of judgment (and so any other man that sets seriously upon this practice of mortification) scattereth away all evil with his eyes, Prov. xx. 8. And this is to pluck out and cast away the right eye that offendeth us, as being an occasion of offence unto us. He that shall see God to his comfort,

shuts his eyes from seeing of evil. For wanton and wandering eyes (like spiders) gather poison out of the fairest flowers: and (like Jacob's sheep) being too firmly fixed on beautiful objects, they make the affections oft-times bring forth spotted fruits, Isa. xxxiii. 14, 15.

For it is profitable for thee that one of thy members perish] An eye is better lost than a soul. For every (unmortified) one shall be salted with fire, pickled up, as it were, and preserved for eternal torment: and every sacrifice (acceptable to God) shall be salted with salt of mortification and self-denial, Mark ix. 49.

And not that thy whole body should be cast into hell] As otherwise it will be: "For if ye live after the flesh ye shall die," &c. Rom. viii. 13. In Barbary, it is present death for any man to see one of the Zeriff's concubines; and for them too, if when they see a man, though but through a casement, they do not suddenly screech out. So here, a loose and lewd eye hazards the whole to hell fire. And is it nothing to lose an immortal soul? to purchase an everliving death? A man would be loth to fetch gold out of a fiery crucible, because he knows it will burn him. Did we as truly believe the everlasting burning of that infernal fire we durst not offer to fetch either pleasures or profits out of those flames.[4] Bellarmine is of opinion that one glimpse of hell's horror were enough to make a man not only turn Christian and sober, but anchorite and monk, to live after the strictest rule that can be. And there is a story of one, that being vexed with fleshly lusts, laid his hands upon hot burning coals to mind himself of hell fire that followeth upon fleshly courses.

Ver. 30. *And if thy right hand offend thee, &c.*] By wanton touches, by unclean dalliance; a further degree of this sin, and a greater incentive to lust; as we see in Joseph's mistress; when she not only cast her eyes, but proceeded to lay hand upon him, she became much more inflamed towards him; and had not his heart been seasoned with the true fear of God, there was so much the greater danger of his being drawn thereby to commit, not that trick of youth, as the world excuseth it, but that great wickedness, as he there counts and calls it.[5] *Visus, colloquium, contactus, osculum, concubitus*, are the whore-monger's five descents into the chambers of death. Off therefore with such a hand by all means; cry out of it, as Cranmer did of his unworthy right hand wherewith he had subscribed; and as John Stubbes of Lincoln's Inn, having his right hand cut off in Queen Elizabeth's time with a cleaver driven through the wrist with the force of a beetle

---

[1] οὐ κόρας, ἀλλά πόρνας. Κόρη *puellam et pupillam oculi significat*. Plut.   [2] In 2 Sam. xii. 4, there came a traveller to the rich man, &c., עין signifies both an eye and a fountain; as it is the spring of sin, let it be of tears.
[3] *Iisdem quibus videmus oculis flemus*. Josephus saith that Potiphar and his servants were at a feast; she was at home as feigning herself sick.
[4] *Apuleius cum amicam dissuaviaretur, ab illa hoc modo*

monitus est: heus tu scholastice, dulce et amarum gustulum carpis: cave ne nimia mellis dulcedine diutinam bilis amaritudinem trahas. Lascivis contrectationibus animi adulterium sæpe contrahitur. The archers shot at Joseph, but his bow abode in strength, Gen. xlix. 24. *Castus erat, non solum continens, ut Bellerophon.*
[5] *Principium dulce est, at finis amoris amarus.*
 Læta venire Venus, tristis abire solet.

(for writing a book against the marriage with the Duke of Anjou, entitled, The gulf wherein England will be swallowed by the French match, &c.), he put off his hat with his left hand, and said with a loud voice, God save the Queen. So when God strikes a parting blow between us and our *dilecta delicta*, our right-hand sins, let us see a mercy in it, and be thankful: let us say to these idols, Get thee hence, what have I to do any more with idols? Isa. xxx. 22; that God may say, as there, "I have heard him, and observed him: I am like a green fir-tree. From me is thy fruit found," Hos. xiv. 8; when he shall see thee pollute those idols that thou wast wont to perfume, Isa. xxx. 22.

And not that thy whole body be cast into hell] Our Saviour is much in speaking of hell. And it were much to be wished (saith St Chrysostom) that men's thoughts and tongues would run much upon this subject, there being no likelier way of escaping hell than by taking ever anon a turn or two in hell by our meditations.[1] A certain hermit is said to have learned three leaves, a black, red, and white one; that is, he daily meditated upon the horror of hell, the passion of Christ, the happiness of heaven.

Mors tua, mors Christi, flos mundi, gloria cœli,
Et dolor inferni sunt meditanda tibi.

Ver. 31. *It hath been said, Whosoever shall put away his wife, &c.*] This Moses permitted, as a law-maker, not as a prophet; as a civil magistrate, not as a man of God, merely for the hardness of the men's hearts, and for the relief of the women, who else might have been misused and mischiefed by their unmannerly and unnatural husbands, Mal. ii. 13. Those hard-hearted Jews caused their wives, when they should have been cheerful in God's service, to cover the altar of the Lord with tears, with weeping, and with crying out, so that he regarded not the offering any more. A number of such Nabals there are now-a-days, that tyrannize over and trample upon their wives, as if they were not their fellows, but their foot-stools, not their companions and co-mates, but their slaves and vassals. "Husbands, love your wives, and be not bitter against them," Col. iii. 16. He saith not (as it might seem he should with respect to the former verse), Rule over them, and show your authority over those that are bound to submit unto you; but, love them, that their subjection may be free and ingenuous. Live not, as Lamech, like lions in your houses, quarrelsome, austere, discourteous, violent, with high words and hard blows, such are fitter to live in Bedlam than in a civil society. The apostle requires "that all bitterness be put away," all, and in all persons; how much more in married couples! The heathens, when they sacrificed at their marriage feasts, used to cast the gall of the beast sacrificed out of doors. τὴν χολὴν ἐξέλοντες ἐρρίψαν. (Plutarch.) *Vipera virus ob venerationem nuptiarum evomit; et tu duritiem animi, tu feritatem, tu crudelitatem*

ob unionis reverentiam non deponis? saith Basil. I confess it were better be married to a quartan ague than to a bad wife (so saith Simonides), for there be two good days for one bad with the one, not one with the other; *febris hectica uxor mala, et non nisi morte avellenda.* (Scalig.) But that should have been looked to aforehand. A hard adventure it is to yoke one's self with any untamed heifer, that beareth not the yoke of Christ. And as grace, so good nature, a courteous disposition, is a thing to be especially looked at in a wife, which Eleazar, Abraham's servant, understood, and therefore singled out as a token of a meet mate for his son. "Let her offer me drink, and my camels also," saith he, Gen. xxiv. 13. But what if it prove otherwise, and men by leaping unadvisedly into the marriage estate, have drawn much misery upon themselves? *Quid si pro conjugio conjurgium contraxerint?* Varro answereth, *Uxoris vitium aut tollendum aut tolerandum est.* A wife's faults must be either cured or covered; mended, if we can; made the best of, if we cannot. If the first, she is made better; if the second, we. *Qui tollit hanc sibi commodiorem præstat: qui tolerat, ipse se meliorem reddit.* (Gellius.) *Aurelii vox est, uxor admonenda persæpe, reprehendenda raro, verberanda nunquam.*

Conjugium humanæ divina Academia vitæ est.

And hence it cometh to pass, that,

Quæ modo pugnarant, jungant sua rostra columbæ:
Quarum blanditias verbaque, murmur habet.

As on the other side, where this meekness of wisdom is not made use of by married folk, they are together in the house no otherwise than as two poisons in the stomach, as live eels in the pot, as two spaniels in a chain; their houses are more like kennels of hounds than families of Christians; or as so many fencing-schools, wherein the two sexes seem to have met together for nothing but to play their prizes and to try masteries. Job was not more weary of his boils than they are of their bed-fellows, cursing their wedding-day as much as he did his birth-day; and thirsting after a divorce as he did after death; which, because it cannot be had, their lives prove like the sojourning of Israel in Marah, where almost nothing could be heard but murmuring, mourning, conjuring, and complaining. *Leo cassibus irretitus dixit, si præscivissem.*

Ver. 32. *Saving for the cause of fornication*] Taken in the largest sense for adultery also. *Adulterium est quasi ad alterum, aut alterius locum.* (Becman de Originibus.) This sin strikes at the very sinew, heart, and life of the marriage knot, and dissolves it. Further, it directly fights against human society, which the law mainly respects, and was therefore to be punished with death, as a most notorious theft. "Master," say they, "this woman was taken in adultery, in the very act." In the very theft, saith the original (ἐπ᾽ αὐτοφώρῳ, John viii. 4), to intimate, belike, the great theft that is in adultery, whilst the

[1] *Utinam ubique de gehenna dissereretur. Non enim sinit jam gehennam incidere gehennæ meminisse.* Chrysost.

child of a stranger carries away the goods or lands of the family. Neither may any conclude from our Saviour's words to that woman (ver. 11), "Neither do I condemn thee," that adultery is not to be punished; any more than he may, that inheritances are not to be divided, because Christ, who was no magistrate, would not divide them, Luke xii. 14. The marriage-bed is honourable, and should be kept inviolable: society and the purity of posterity cannot otherwise continue amongst men; which is well observed by divines to be the reason why adultery is named in the commandment, under it all uncleanness being forbidden; when yet other violations are more heinous, as sodomy and bestiality.

Causeth her to commit adultery] Because it is God that both maketh and keepeth the bonds of wedlock, which is therefore called, "the covenant of God," Prov. ii. 17. Covenants are either, 1. Religious, as when a man tieth himself by vow to God, to shun such a sin or do such a duty. 2. Civil, between man and man, as in our common contracts, bargains, and businesses. Or, 3. Mixed, that are made partly with God and partly with man. And of this sort is the marriage-covenant, the parties thereby tie themselves first to God and then to one another. Hence it is that the knot is indissoluble, and cannot be undone or recalled at the pleasure of the parties that make it, because there is a third person engaged in the business, and that is God, to whom the bond is made; and if afterward they break, he will take the forfeiture. This David understood, and therefore upon his adultery cried out, "Against thee, thee only" (that is, chiefly) "have I sinned, and done this evil in thy sight," Psal. li. 4. A sin it is against the Father, whose covenant is broken; against the Son, whose members are made the members of an harlot; and against the Holy Ghost, whose temple is defiled, 1 Cor. v.

Ver. 33. *Thou shalt not forswear thyself*] An oath is ὅρκος *quasi* ἕρκος, a hedge which a man may not break. It must not be taken without necessity. Hence the Hebrew נשבע *nishbang*, is a passive, and signifieth to be sworn, rather than to swear. For if the doubt or question may be assoiled, or ended by verily or truly, or such naked asseverations, we are, by the example of our Saviour, to forbear an oath. But having sworn, though to his hurt, a man must not change, Psal. xv. 4, upon pain of a curse, yea, a book full of curses, Zech. v. 3, 4. It is not for men to play with oaths as children do with nuts; to slip them at pleasure, as monkeys do their collars; to snap them asunder, as Samson did his cords. It was an impious and blasphemous speech of him that said, "My tongue hath sworn, but my mind is unsworn." ἡ γλῶσσ' ὀμώμοχ', ἡ δὲ φρὴν ἀνώμοτος. (Euripides.) And who can but detest that abominable doctrine of the Priscillianists of old, and their heirs the Jesuits of late:

Jura, perjura, secretum prodere noli.

God will be a swift witness against perjured

persons, Mal. iii., as those that villanously abuse his majesty, making him an accessory, yea, a partner in their sin, thinking him like themselves, and therefore calling him to justify their untruths. Had Shimei peace, that brake his oath to Solomon? Or Zedekiah, that kept not touch with the king of Babylon? Or Ananias and Sapphira, that but uttered an untruth, swore it not? God punisheth perjury with destruction, man with disgrace, saith a fragment of the Twelve Tables in Rome; *perjurii pœna divina exitium, humana dedecus.* The Egyptians and Scythians punished it with death. So did Philip Earl of Flanders, and others. But where men have not done it, God hath hanged up such with his own hands, as it were, as our Earl Godwin; Rodolphus, Duke of Suabia, that rebelled against his master Henry, Emperor of Germany, to whom he had sworn allegiance; Ladislaus, King of Bohemia, at the great battle of Varna, where the raging Turk, provoked by his perjury, appealed to Christ; Michael Paleologus, Emperor of Constantinople, who for his perjury, and other his foul and faithless dealings, lieth obscurely shrouded in the sheet of defame, saith the history. Richard Long, soldier at Calais, deposing falsely against William Smith, curate of Calais, shortly after, upon a displeasure of his wife, desperately drowned himself. And within the memory of man, Feb. 11, 1575, Ann Averies forswore herself at a shop in Wood Street, London, and praying God she might sink where she stood if she had not paid for the wares she took, fell down speechless, and with a horrible stink died soon after. Thus God hangeth up evil-doers in gibbets, as it were, that others may hear and fear, and do no more so. *Alterius perditio tua cautio.*

But shalt perform unto the Lord thine oaths] As David, "I have sworn, and I will perform," &c., Psal. cxix. 106. And yet David was not always as good as his oath, as in the case of Mephibosheth, &c. Nor did Jacob of a long time perform his vow, Gen. xxviii. 21, though once, at least, admonished, Gen. xxxi. 13, till he was frightfully aroused by the slaughter of the Shechemites, and his own apparent danger, to go up to Bethel and do as he had promised.[1] The font in baptism is Beersheba, the well of an oath, there we solemnly swear ourselves to God, which St Peter calleth the stipulation of a good conscience, 1 Pet. iii. 21. This oath we renew when we come to the other sacrament; and often besides, when the Lord layeth siege to us by some disease or other distress, what promises and protestations make we, as Pharaoh and those votaries! Psal. lxxviii. But *sciapato il morbo, fraudato il Dio,* as the Italian proverb hath it; the disease or danger once over, God is defrauded of his due. See it in those, Jer. xxxiv., who forfeited their fidelity, though they had cut the calf in twain, and passed through the parts thereof (a most solemn way of sealing up covenants), and are sorely threatened for it, that God would in like sort cut them in

---

[1] *Jacob pater votorum nuncupatur.* Pareus.

twain and destroy them, which was the import of that ceremony. Virgil viii.

Ver. 34. *Swear not at all*] Not at all by the creatures[1] (which the Pharisees held no fault), nor yet by the name of God in common talk, lightly, rashly, and irreverently; for such vain oaths the land mourneth. Oaths, alas, are become very interjections of speech to the vulgar, and phrases of gallantry to the braver. He that cannot swear with a grace, wanteth his tropes and his figures befitting a gentleman. Not to speak of those civilized complements of faith and troth (which are counted light matters), who hears not how ordinarily and openly ruffianly oaths and abhorred blasphemies are darted up with hellish mouths, against God and our Saviour, whom they can swear all over, and seldom name, but in an oath? How can these pray, "Hallowed be that Name," that they so daily dishallow?[2] Some cannot utter a sentence without an oath, yea, a fearful one, an oath of sound, if enraged especially. Oh the tragedies, the blusters, the terrible thunder-cracks or fierce and furious language, interlaced with oaths, enough to make the very stones crack under them! Yea, to such a height and habitual practice hereof are some grown, that they swear and foam out a great deal of filth, and perceive it not. Had these men such distemper of body as that their excrements came from them when they knew not of it, it would trouble them. So it would, I dare say, did they believe the Holy Scriptures, threatening so many woes to them, yea, telling them of a large roll, ten yards long and five yards broad, full of curses against the swearer, yea, resting upon his house, where he thinks himself most secure, Zech. v. 2, 3. "Brimstone is scattered upon the house of the wicked," saith Job (xviii. 15), as ready to take fire if God but lighten upon it. They walk, as it were, upon a mine of gunpowder, and it may be just in God they should be blown up, when their hearts are full of hell, and their mouths even big with hellish blasphemies. Surely their damnation sleepeth not; God hath vowed he will not hold them guiltless, sworn these swearers shall never enter into his rest, Exod. xx. 7; Psal. xcv. 11. And for men, those that have but any ingenuity abhor and shun their company. The very Turks have the Christians blaspheming of Christ in execration, and will punish their prisoners sorely, when as through impatience or desperateness they burst out into them. Yea, the Jews, as their conversion is much hindered by the blasphemies of the Italians (who blaspheme oftener than swear), so in their speculations of the causes of the strange success of the affairs of the world, they assign the reason of the Turks prevailing so against the Christians, to be their oaths and blasphemies, which wound the ears of the very heavens. They can tell that swearing is one of those sins for the which God hath a controversy with a land, Hos. iv. 2;

Jer. xxiii. 10. And I can tell what a great divine hath observed, that the stones in the wall of Aphek shall sooner turn executioners than a blasphemous Aramite shall escape unrevenged. So much doth a jealous God hate to be robbed of his glory, or wronged in his name, even by ignorant pagans (how much more by profest Christians!) whose tongues might seem no slander. Those that abuse earthly princes in their name and titles are imprisoned, banished, or hanged as traitors. And shall these go altogether unpunished? Hell gapes for such miscreants, &c.

Neither by heaven] As the Manichees and Pharisees did, and held it no sin. But God only is the proper object of an oath, Isa. lxv. 16; Jer. xii. 6. The name of the creature, say some, may be inferred, the attestation referred to God alone. But they say better that tell us that the form of an oath is not at all to be indirect or oblique, in the name of the creature. Albeit I doubt not but he that sweareth by heaven sweareth by him that dwelleth in heaven, &c. And forasmuch as God clotheth himself with the creatures, Psal. civ., is it fit for us to spit upon the king's royal robes, especially when they are upon his back? But forasmuch as we must shun and be shy of the very show and shadow of sin, they do best and safest that abstain from all oaths of this nature, 1 Thess. v. 22. They do very ill that swear by this light, bread, hand, fire (which they absurdly call God's angel), by St Ann, St George, by our Lady, &c., by the parts of Christ, which they substitute in the room of God. The barbarous soldiers would not break his bones, but these miscreants with their carrion mouths rend and tear (oh cause of tears!) his heart, hands, head, feet, and all his members asunder. Let all such consider, that, as light a matter as they make of it, this swearing by the creature is a "forsaking of God," Jer. v. 7, a provocation little less than unpardonable; an exposing God's honour to the spoil of the creatures, which was the heathens' sin, Rom. i. 23; and abasing themselves below the meanest creatures, "for men verily swear by the greater," Heb. vi. 16. And the viler the thing is they swear by, the greater is the oath, because they ascribe thereto omniscience, power to punish, justice, &c., Amos viii. 14; Zeph. i. 3—5. Besides a heavy doom of unavoidable destruction denounced against such, they that speak in favour of this sin allege 1 Cor. xv. 31. But that is not an oath, but an obtestation; *q. d.* my sorrows and sufferings for Christ would testify, if they could speak, that I die daily. And that, Cant. iii. 5, where Christ seemeth to swear "by the roes and hinds of the field." But that is not an oath neither, but an adjuration: for he chargeth them not to trouble his Church; or if they do, the roes and hinds shall testify against them, because they do what those would not, had they reason as they have. In like sort

---

[1] *De jurando per creaturas, contra Lyram, et de juramenti usu, contra Anabapt. videbis* Pareum in Jacob, v. 12.

[2] *Sunt qui altius linguas suas in Christi sanguine demergunt, quam illi olim manus.*

Moses attesteth heaven and earth, Deut. xxxii. 1; and so doth God himself, Isa. i. 2. And for those phrases, "As Pharaoh liveth," "As thy soul liveth," &c., they are rather earnest vouchings of things than oaths.[1] And yet that phrase of gallantry now so common, "As true as I live," is judged to be no better than an oath by the creature, Numb. xiv. 21, with Psalm xcv. 11. And we may not swear in jest, but in judgment, Jer. iv. 2.

For it is God's throne] We must not conceive that God is commensurable by a place, as if he were partly here and partly there, but he is everywhere all-present. The heavens have a large place, yet have they one part here and another there, but the Lord is totally present wheresoever present. Heaven therefore is said to be his throne, and he is said to inhabit it, Isa. lxvi. 1, not as if he were confined to it, as Aristotle and those atheists in Job conceited it;[2] but because there he is pleased to manifest the most glorious and visible signs of his presence, and there in a special manner he is enjoyed and worshipped by the crowned saints and glorious angels, &c. Here we see but as in a glass obscurely, his toe, train, back-parts, footstool. No man can see more and live; no man need see more here, that he may live for ever. But "there we shall see as we are seen, know as we are known," see him face to face, Isa. vi. 1; lx. 13; lxvi. 1; Exod. xxxiii. 23; 1 Cor. xiii. 12. Oh how should this fire up our dull hearts, with all earnestness and intention of endeared affection to long, lust, pant, faint after the beatifical vision! How should we daily lift up our hearts and hands to God in the heavens, that he would send from heaven and save us; send his mandamus, and command deliverance out of Sion; yea, that himself would break the heavens and come down, and fetch us home upon the clouds of heaven, as himself ascended, that when we awake we may be full of his image, and as we have borne the image of the earthly, so we may bear the image of the heavenly! St Paul, after he had once seen God in his throne, being rapt up into the third heaven (like the bird of Paradise), he never left groaning out, *Cupio dissolvi*, "I desire to be dissolved and to be with Christ, which is far far the better."[3] And Pareus, a little afore his death, uttered this swan-like song,

Discupio solvi, tecumque, o Christe, manere :
Portio fac regni sim quotacunque tui.

Oh that I were in heaven! Oh that I might
Be ever with the Lord! Oh blissful plight!

Thus must our broken spirits even spend and exhale themselves in continual sallies, as it were, and egressions of thoughts, wishings, and longings after God, affecting not only a union, but a unity

with him.[4] St Austin wished that he might have seen three things, *Romam in flore, Paulum in ore, et Christum in corpore* : Rome flourishing, Paul discoursing, and Christ living upon the earth. But I had rather wish, with venerable Bede, "My soul desireth to see Christ my King upon his throne, and in his majesty."[5]

Ver. 35. *Nor by the earth, for it is his footstool*] A fault so common among this people, that St James saw cause to warn the believing Jews of it, to whom he wrote. They had taken up such a custom of swearing by the creatures, that after conversion they could not easily leave it. It is a poor plea to say, "I have gotten a custom of swearing, and must therefore be borne with." For who is it but the devil that saith to such, as the Jews to Pilate, "Do as thou hast ever done?" Mark xv. 8. The Cretians, when they wished worst to any one, they wished that he might take delight in an evil custom.[6] Break off, therefore, this ill use by repentance; and though you cannot suddenly turn the stream, yet swim against it, bite in thine oaths, and with bitterness bewail them; swear to God, as David did, thou wilt swear no more, and by degrees outgrow this ill custom.

For it is his footstool] And should be ours. For he hath "put all things under our feet," Psal. viii. 6. He saith not, under our hands, but under our feet, that we might trample upon them in a holy contempt, as the Church is said to tread upon the moon, Rev. xii. 1; and the way of the righteous is said to be on high, to depart from hell below, Prov. xv. 24. It is a wonder, surely, that treading upon these minerals, gold, silver, precious stones, &c. (which are but the guts and garbage of the earth), we should so admire them. God hath hid them in the bowels of the earth, and in those parts that are farthest off from the Church. Where they grow, little else grows that is aught; no more doth grace in an earthly heart. But to return from whence we are digressed : earth is God's footstool. How ought we then to walk circumspectly, that we provoke not the eyes of his glory! there is an honour due even to the footstools of princes, when they are on the throne especially. Oh, "be thou in the fear of the Lord all day long," saith Solomon, walk in the sense of his presence and light of his countenance, Prov. xxiii. 17. "He is not very far from any one of us," saith the apostle, not so far as the bark from the tree, or the flesh from the bones, Acts xvii. 27. This one God and Father of all is not only above all, and from his throne beholdeth all that is done here below, but "also through all, and in you all," Eph. iv. 6. Therefore no corner can secrete us, no cranny of the heart can escape his eye; all things are (for the outside) naked and (for the

---

[1] *Non est forma juramenti, sed asseverationis seriæ, et obtestationis domesticæ ; q. d. quam vere vivit Pharao*, &c. Alsted.

[2] Job xxii. 14. *Docuit Aristoteles providentiam Dei ad cœlum lunæ usque protendi, non ultra.*

[3] πολλῷ μᾶλλον κρεῖσσον. A transcendant expression, like that 2 Cor. iv. 17.

[4] *Mi sine nocte diem, vitam sine morte quietam,*
    Dei sine fine dies, Vita, quiesque Deus.

[5] *Anima mea desiderat Christum regem meum videre in decore suo.* Beda.   [6] *Cretenses cum acerbissima execratione adversus eos quos oderunt uti volunt, ut mala consuetudine delectentur optant ; modestoque voti genere efficacissimum ultionis eventum reperiunt.* Val. Maximus.

inside) open, dissected, quartered, and, as it were, cleft through the back-bone, as the word signifieth, before the eyes of him with whom we deal (γυμνὰ, τετραχηλισμένα), Heb. iv. 13.

Neither by Jerusalem : for it is the city of the great King] The place of his rest, the seat of his empire, and they the people of his praise and of his purchase (λαός τῆς περίποιήσεως, Sept.), Exod. xix. 5. Glorious things are spoken of thee, thou city of God. There was " the adoption, and the glory, the covenants, and the giving of the law, the service of God, and the promises," &c., Rom. ix. 4. Constantinople was acknowledged by Tamerlane to be, for her situation, an imperial city, and such as was made to command the world. Strasburg in Germany is called by scme *compendium orbis*, an abridgment of the world. But Jerusalem, by a better author, is styled princess of provinces, the joy of the whole earth, the pleasant land, &c. Lam. i. 1; Psal. xlviii. 2; Dan. viii. 9. It must needs be pleasant where God himself was resiant. But how is the faithful city become an harlot ! It was full of judgment, righteousness lodged in it, but now murderers. Her silver is become dross, her wine mixt with water, Isa. i. 21, 22. Bethel is become Bethaven, and Jerusalem turned into Jerushkaker. It fell again into the power of the Turks and Infidels, A. D. 1234 (after that the most warlike soldiers of Europe had there, as it were, one common sepulchre, but an eternal monument of their misguided valour), and so remaineth still, a poor ruinous city, governed by one of the Turk's Sanzacks, and for nothing now more famous than for the sepulchre of our Saviour, again repaired and much visited by the Christians, and not unreverenced by the Turks themselves. There are not to be found there at this time 100 households of Jews, and yet there are ten or more churches of Christians there.

Of the great King] The Jews much admired the greatness of Herod, and especially of the Romans, whose tributaries they were at this time.[1] Our Saviour mindeth them of a greater than these, one that is greater, greatest, greatness itself. Nebuchadnezzar styleth himself the great king, and brags of his Babel. The rich miser thinks himself no small thing, because of his country of corn.[2] Ahasuerus taketh state upon him, because he reigned from India to Ethiopia. Darius's flatterers held it meet that no man should ask a petition of any god or man, for thirty days, save of him. Diocletian would needs be worshipped as a god, and was the first that held forth his feet to be kissed, after Caligula. Amurath III., Emperor of the Turks, styled himself god of the earth, governor of the whole world, the messenger of God, and faithful servant of the great prophet. And the great Cham of Tartary is called by the simple

vulgar, the shadow of spirits, and son of the immortal God ; and by himself he is reputed to be the monarch of the whole world. For which cause every day (if all is true that is reported of him) as soon as he hath dined, he causeth his trumpets to be sounded, by that sign giving leave to other kings and princes to go to dinner. These be the grandees of the earth, and think no mean things of themselves. But compare them with the great King here mentioned, and what becometh of all their supposed greatness ? " All nations before him are but as the dust of the balance or drop of a bucket." *Quantilla ergo es tu istius guttæ particula ?* saith a Father : if all nations are to God but as the drop of a bucket, oh, what a small pittance must thou needs be, how great soever, of that little drop ?[3] And as he is great, so he looketh to be praised and served according to his excellent greatness. We should, if it were possible, fill up that vast distance and disproportion that is betwixt him and us, by the greatness of our praises and sincerity, at least, of our services, in presenting him with the best. "For I am a great King," saith God, Mal. i. 14 ; and he stands upon his seniority : offer it now to thy prince, will he accept thy refuse breadstuff ? &c. It is verily a most sweet meditation of St Bernard, whensoever we come before God in any duty, we should conceive ourselves to be entering into the court of heaven wherein the King of kings sitteth in a stately throne, surrounded with an host of glorious angels and crowned saints. With how great humility, therefore, reverence, and godly fear, ought a poor worm crawling out of his hole, a vile frog creeping out of his mud, draw nigh to such a Majesty ![4] The seraphims clap their wings on their faces when they stand before God, Isa. vi., as men are wont to do their hands when the lightning flasheth in their faces ; the nearer any man draws to God, the more rottenness he findeth in his bones, Hab. iii. 16. Abraham is dust and ashes ; Job abhorreth himself in dust and ashes ; Isaiah cries, Woe is me, for I am undone ; Peter, Depart from me, I am a sinful man. All these had right conceptions of God's greatness, and this is that that is required so oft in Scripture under the term of magnifying God ; when we get him into our hearts in his own likeness, and enlarge his room there ; when we take him into our thoughts under the notion of a great King, when we get so far as to conceive of him above all creatures, far above all the glory that can be found in earthly princes and potentates. Think of God as one not to be thought of, and when you have thought your utmost, as Tully affirmeth concerning Socrates described by Plato, and desireth of his readers concerning Lucius Crassus, that they would imagine far greater things of them than they find written,[5] so assure

---

[1] *Si animalibus (dixit Xenophanes) pingere daretur Deum proculdubio sibi similem fingerent, quia scilicet nihil animal animali superius cogitat. Sic et homo animalis,* 1 Cor. ii. 14.
[2] Luke xii. 16. εὐφόρησεν ἡ χώρα, *regio, non* χωρίον, *ager.*
[3] *Sol reliqua sidera occultat, quibus lumen suum fœnerat.*

Plin. lib. ii. c. 6. So doth the God of glory. Acts vii. 2.
[4] *Quanta ergo cum humilitate accedere debet e palude sua procedens et repens vilis ranuncula ?* Bern.
[5] *Ut majus quiddam de iis, quam quæ scripta sunt, suspicarentur.* De Oratore.

yourselves, your highest apprehensions of God fall infinitely short of his incomparable and incomprehensible greatness. And if he could add, if any think me over-lavish in their commendation, it is because he never heard them, or cannot judge of them,[1] how much more may we say the same of this "blessed and only Potentate, the King of kings and Lord of lords; who only hath immortality, dwelling in the light which no man can approach unto; whom no man hath seen, nor can see: to whom be honour and power everlasting. Amen." 1 Tim. vi. 15, 16.

Ver. 36. Neither shalt thou swear by thy head] That is, by thy health, which is the life of our lives, say some: by thy life, say others, which is a sweet blessing;[2] for a living dog is better than a dead lion; yea, though full of crosses, yet why is living man sorrowful? *q. d.* it is a mercy that amidst all his crosses he is yet alive. "Joseph is yet alive, I have enough," saith Jacob. They told him of his honour, he speaks of his life. Life is better than honour, and is not therefore to be laid to pawn upon every light occasion, as they that so often use, As I live, and As true as I live: whereof something before.

Because thou canst not make one hair, &c.] God is great in great things, saith St Augustine, and not little in the smallest. (*Magnus in magnis, nec parvus in minimis.*) What less than a hair, yet in making a hair white or black, God's power appeareth. The devil can as little create a hair of the head as he could of old a louse in the land of Egypt, Exod. viii. 18. There are miracles enough in man's body to fill a volume. It is the image of God and a little world (μικρόκοσμος), an epitome of the visible world, as his soul is of the invisible. The idea or example of the great world, which was in God from all eternity, is, as it were, briefly and summarily exprest by God in man. Hence man is called every creature; "Go preach the gospel to every creature," Mark xvi. 15, as if there were none to him, none besides him. A philosopher could say, "there is nothing great in earth besides man." And an orator, "the greatest thing in the least room is a good soul in a man's body." Man, saith the poet, is the masterpiece of the wisest workman; he is, saith the historian, the fairest piece of the chiefest Architect; the very miracle of daring nature, saith Trismegist.[3] Galen, a profane physician, after he had described the nature and parts of man's body, was forced to sing a hymn to that God that he knew not. And St Augustine complaineth, that men can admire the height of the hills, the hugeness of the waves, the compass of the ocean, and the circumvolution of the stars, and yet not once mark nor admire the power

and goodness of God shining in their own souls and bodies, as in a mirror.[4] "Fearfully and wonderfully am I made," saith David; "yea, and curiously wrought in the lowest parts of the earth;" that is, in my mother's womb, Psal. cxxxix. 13—15. A council was called in heaven when man was to be formed: "Let us make man," Gen. i. 26. And were not the birth of a child so common, should it fall out but once in an age, people would run together to see it, as to a miracle. Pliny wondereth at the gnat, so small a creature, yet making so great a buzzing; and so also at the butterfly. He also maketh mention of one that spent 58 years in searching out the nature of the bee, and could not in all that space attain to the full of it. What a shame is it for us, not to see God in every creature, in ourselves especially, and every the least part of us! There is not a hair upon our heads, white or black, but hath God for the maker and God for the master too. Let those that pride themselves in their hair, think what a heavy account Absalom made to God for that sin. *Absolon Marte furens, pensilis arbore, obit.* Long hair in women is a token of modesty. But modesty grows short in men, as their hair grows long, saith one. And Seneca, speaking of the curled and crisped youths of his time, telleth us that they had more care of their locks than of their limbs, and had rather the commonwealth should be disturbed than their frizzled tresses disheveled.[5] Pompey was taxed for this neat nicety: *Unico digitulo caput scalpit.* And of Helen, too curious of her hair at her mother's funeral, the poet bringeth in one that saith, ἔστιν ἡ πάλαι γύνη: This is old Helen still, no changeling in all this space. The holy women of old durst not adorn themselves with plaited or braided hair, as St Peter testifieth, but trusted in God, and decked themselves with a meek and quiet spirit, 1 Pet. iii. 3—5. And "doth not nature itself teach us," saith St Paul, "that it is a shame to a man to wear long hair?" It is objected, that the apostle intends such hair as is as long as women's. But it is answered, that Homer useth the same word of the Greeks, calling them καρηκομοῶντας Αχαίους, and yet they did not wear their hair long as women's. But as it is a shame to wear it, so it is a sin to swear by it, whether long or short, white or black. Neither helps it to say, The matter is but small we swear by. For, first, it is a forsaking of God, and count you that a small matter? Compare Jer. v. 7 with Jer. ii. 12, 13. Secondly, the more base and vile the thing is a man sweareth by, the greater is the oath, because he ascribeth that to a vile creature which is proper to God only, *sc.* to know the heart, to be a discerner of secrets, and an

---

[1] *Intelligat se ex iis esse, qui aut illos non audierint, aut judicare non possint.* Ibid.

[2] *Vita non est vivere, sed valere,* Sen. *Felix dicitur ab* ἧλιξ ἡλικία. Becman.

[3] *Nihil in terra magnum præter hominem.* Favorinus. Μέγιστον ἐν ἐλαχίστῳ, &c. Isocr. Σοφοῦ τέκτονος καλὸν ποίκιλμα. Eurip. τέχνημα σοφοῦντος δημιουργοῦ. Xeno-

phon. Τολμηροτάτης τῆς φύσεως ἄγαλμα.

[4] *Eunt homines mirari alta montium, ingentes fluctus maris, oceani ambitum, et gyros syderum, et relinquunt seipsos, nec mirantur.* Aug.

[5] *Rempub. turbari malunt quam comam.*
Pulchra coma est pulchro digestæque ordine frondes.
Sed fructus nullos hæc coma pulchra gerit.

avenger of falsehood. And if a man may not swear by his hair, much less by his faith and troth, that are much more precious; and to swear by them so oft and ordinary, what doth it argue but that we are low brought and hardly driven? For who but a bankrupt will lay the best jewel in his house to pledge for every trifle? Besides, they are not ours to pledge; for we have plighted them already to God. Lastly, he that pawneth them so oft, will easily forfeit them at length, as the pitcher goeth not so often to the well but at last it comes broken home. A man may soon swear away his faith and troth; and it is marvel if he that oft sweareth doth not too oft forswear, and so forfeit all. Swear not therefore at all in this sort. These petty oaths (as they count them) are great faults, and to be refused in our talk as poison in our meat.[1] The dishonour of them redounds to God, though he be not named in them. But of this see more verse 35.

Ver. 37. *But let your communication be, Yea, yea; Nay, nay*] That is, as St Basil interpreteth it, yea in speech and yea in heart; nay in speech and nay in heart: or thus, let your common communication be plain, true, and sincere, that your bare word may be taken, without any further asseveration. Not but that asseverations may be lawfully used, as verily, truly, indeed, &c. *Sed, parcius ista tamen*, not frequently or slightly, but advisedly and seriously, as our Saviour.[2] If thou be a creditable person and hast made faith of thy fidelity, with *Quod dixi, dixi*, thy word will be taken. Or if it will not, that credit is dear bought that is got by sin. Christ must be obeyed, though no man will believe us. But a good man's oath is needless, a bad man's bootless; for he that feareth not an oath, neither will he scruple a lie, but credit will follow honesty.[3] Whiles therefore the communication is ours (as Christ here speaketh), that is, in our own power and of our own accord, "let our yea be yea, and nay, nay;" and let it appear that ordinarily and in common conversation our word is as soon to be taken as our oath. But when for the glory of God and clearing of the truth, an oath is required of us, then it is not our communication, but another's. And in this case, for the manifestation or confirmation of a needful but doubtful truth, an oath may be safely and boldly taken, for an end of controversies and satisfaction of neighbours, Heb. vi. 16; yea, we may lay it up among our best services, and expect a blessing upon it (if rightly taken, according to Jer. iv. 2) as well as upon hearing or reading, because it is an ordinance of God, Deut. x. 20; Isa. lxv. 16, &c. Some of the ancients, I confess, as Jerome, Theophylact, Chrysostom, were in the error, that

the Lord did only permit swearing in the Old Testament (as he did divorcement that he approved not), and that in this text our Saviour did quite take it away. But Christ came not to destroy the law, but to fulfil it. God's holy name is still to be sanctified by taking a religious oath, upon just occasion, *sc.* when either the magistrate imposeth it, or when some private person will not believe a necessary truth without an oath, and we cannot otherwise demonstrate it. Thus Jacob sware to Laban, Boaz to Ruth, Jonathan to David. And if it be lawful in private betwixt two or more to admit God as a judge, why may he not as well be called as a witness? provided ever, that this be done warily and sparingly, using it not as food, but as physic, to help the truth in necessity. Our King Henry VI. was never heard to swear an oath; his greatest asseveration being, Forsooth, forsooth, verily, verily. I myself have used, saith Latimer, in mine earnest matters, to say, Yea, St Mary, which indeed is naught. Among the very heathens, *Ex animi sui sententia*, In very deed, was instead of an oath.

For whatsoever is more, cometh of evil] That is, of the devil.[4] That which St Matthew calleth the wicked one, chap. xiii. 38 (the self-same word with that in this text), St Mark calleth Satan, and St Luke the devil. Now can any good come out of such a Nazareth? Swearing is the devil's drivel, and swearers the devil's drudges, acted and agitated by that foul fiend: and though they be not always drunk when they swear, yet are they not their own men. "For know ye not," saith that great apostle, "that his servants ye are to whom ye obey?" His work swearers do (as those Jews did in the Gospel, John viii. 34), and his wages they shall receive, for they fall hereby into hypocrisy, as some copies have it (μὴ εἰς ὑπόκρισιν), Jam. v. 12, whiles they daily pray, But deliver us from that evil one, and yet entertain him by this sin: or rather, as other copies in our translation have it, they fall into condemnation. And at the last day, when the Master of the harvest shall gather out of his kingdom all such botches and scandals (τὰ σκάνδαλα), Matt. xiii. 41, 50, he will say to the reapers, "Gather ye first the tares, and bind them in bundles" (swearers with swearers, drunkards with drunkards, &c., sinners of a kind with their fellow-sinners), "and cast them into the fire, there shall be weeping and gnashing of teeth." Good, therefore, is the counsel of St James, "Above all things, my brethren, swear not;" whatever ye do, look to that: it is a senseless sin, and that which maketh the tongue to become, not a city, not a country, but a world of iniquity, Jam. iii. 6. It is the devil's hook without a bait, as having neither profit nor pleasure (many times) to draw to it, and that is no

---

[1] *Leviter volant, non leviter vulnerant.*
[2] *Gemina potius affirmatione et negatione utamur, quam Dei nomen usurpemus.*
[3] *Non ideo negare volo, ne peream, sed ideo mentiri nolo,*

ne peccem; dixit fœmina quædam in equuleo, apud Jerome.
[4] Ὁ πονηρὸς, that troublesome one, the troubler of the saints: *qui negotium nobis facessit, a* πένομαι πόνος, πονηρὸς, *malignus.*

small aggravation. The devils fell without a tempter, and are therefore left without a Saviour. Other sinners usually kill not till provoked, steal not till forced, whore not till enticed. But what hath God done to these monstrous men, that they should thus fly in his face, chop (as much as they may) his heart in pieces, and upon every small occasion shoot such chain-shot, as if they would make the windows of heaven to shake and totter? When Naboth was said to have blasphemed, Jezebel proclaimed a fast. When our Saviour was accused of that sin, the high priest rent his garments. When Rabshakeh had done it indeed, Hezekiah fell to his prayers, and humbled himself before God. Did these do thus for others, and wilt not thou do as much for thyself? God hath against thee, and is coming out armed with plagues and power. Oh meet him upon the way, with entreaties of peace, as Abigail did David; as Jacob did Esau: quench his flames with floods of tears. Learn of Shimei (when he had reproached David, and knew himself obnoxious) to be with God with the first, as he was with the king, 2 Sam. xix. 18—20; and as Joseph's brethren supplicated him for grace, whom they had reviled and misused, Gen. l. 17, do you the like. This do or you are undone for ever. This do, and do it seriously, and God must either forswear himself, or forgive thee thy swearing, if thou forego it.

Ver. 38. *Ye have heard, that it hath been said, An eye for an eye*, &c.] This law of like for like (which also was in use among the ancient Romans) the scribes and Pharisees had abused and distorted from its proper sense of public justice to private revenge; teaching the people to render evil for evil, to pay their enemies in their own coin, and to give them as good as they brought.[1] This is a dictate of corrupt nature, and her chief secretary Aristotle proclaimeth it. To be avenged of our enemies is held better in point of honour than to be reconciled unto them.[2] Flesh and blood suggesteth that it is matter of good metal to be quick of touch, as forward in returning as others are in offering wrong. "For if a man find his enemy, will he let him go well away?" said Saul, 1 Sam. xxiv. 19. This is quite against the principles of nature and common policy. To turn again and revenge is counted courage; which yet the word of God calleth cowardliness, disgrace, and loss of victory ($\eta\tau\tau\eta\mu\alpha$), 1 Cor. vi. 7. It is not manliness, but foolishness, Eccl. vii. 9. It is brutishness. Anger a dog, and he will fly in your face: touch an ass, and he will kick and wince. It is baseness so to be led by our passions as to be able to bear nothing, as Simeon and Levi, brethren in iniquity, that in their anger slew a man, and in their self-will digged down a wall, Gen. xlix. 6. Their father Jacob heard that Dinah was defiled, and held

his peace, Gen. xxxiv. 5; he reined in his passions, by setting God before them; and so that divine proverb was made good in him, "He that is slow to anger is better than the mighty; and he that ruleth his spirit (as Jacob) than he that taketh a city" (as his sons), Prov. xvi. 32. It is a godly man's part, at some times and in some places, to be deaf and dumb, as if he understood not; or as men in whose mouths are no reproof.[3] Which as David could skill of at some times, Psal. xxxviii. 14, and in his carriage towards Shimei, so at other times (when the flesh prevailed) he could not, Psal. xxxix. 2, 3, and in his expedition against Nabal. But Peter must put up his sword, if he mean to be Christ's disciple. And Christians must not so much as grudge one against another, unless they will be condemned: for behold, the Judge standeth before the door, as ready to right us, Jam. v. 9. As, if we retaliate we leave him nothing to do, unless it be to turn his wrath from our enemy, on whom we have been avenged already, upon ourselves, for our sin of self-revenge, Prov. xxiv. 17, 18. We use to say, if the magistrate be not present, we may offend another, to defend ourselves: but if the magistrate be present, there is no excuse. Now here the Judge standeth before the door, and crieth out unto us with a loud voice: Dearly beloved, avenge not yourselves, but rather keep the king's peace, and so give place to wrath, Rom. xii. 19: that is, to the wrath of God ready to seize upon thine adversary, if thou prevent it not by an over-hasty revenge of the wrongs offered thee: for it is written, Vengeance is mine, mine office and royalty, Psal. xciv. 1, 2. Is it safe to invade his part? to jostle the chief justice out of his seat? or is it fit that the same party should be both accuser and judge? pope in his own cause? depose the magistrate? at least appeal from God to himself, as if he would not sufficiently do his office? "Shall not God avenge his own, that cry night and day unto him, though he bear long with them?' I tell you that he will avenge them speedily," saith our Saviour, Luke xviii. 7, 8. "I will repay it," saith the Lord; but upon this condition, that we wait his leisure, and pre-occupate not his executions, saith St Augustine. Joseph, accused by his lewd mistress, either pleads not, or is not heard. He knew that though he suffered for a season, God would find a time to clear his innocency, and he was not deceived. Moses complained not, but was silent, when wronged by Aaron and Miriam; God therefore struck in for him, and struck Miriam with leprosy: Aaron escaped by his repentance. God is their champion that strive not for themselves.[4] "I seek not mine own glory, but there is one that seeketh it," saith Christ, John viii. 10. "He, when he was reviled, reviled not again; when

---

[1] *Neminem læde, nisi lacessitus et injuria affectus.* Cicero.
[2] *Inimicos ulcisci, potius quam iis reconciliari honestum censetur.* Arist. Rhet.
[3] *Tu quidem nihil prætermittis ut ego te interfici jubeam:*
ἐγὼ δὲ κύνα ὑλακτεύοντα οὐ φονεύω. *Sic Demetrio Cynico Vespasianus apud Dionem.*
[4] *Convitium convitio regerere quid aliud est quam lutum luto purgare?*

he suffered, he threatened not; but committed himself to him that judgeth righteously," and giveth to every transgression and trespass a just recompense of reward, 1 Pet. ii. 23; Heb. ii. 2. St Paul could not have wished worse to Alexander the coppersmith than "the Lord reward him according to his works," 2 Tim. iv. 14. This was not (saith an ancient author) a cursing or a reviling of him, but a prediction befitting an apostle, that revenged not himself, but gave place to wrath, and delivered up his enemy to God,[1] as David did his adversaries, as Simon Peter did Simon Magus, and the primitive Church did Julian the Apostate. And surely it is a fearful thing, when the saints shall say to God, concerning those that malign or molest them, as David sometimes said to Solomon, Thou knowest what Joab and Shimei did unto me: "do therefore according to thy wisdom, and let not their hoar heads go down to the grave in peace," 1 Kings ii. 6. If any hurt God's zealous witnesses, there goeth a fire out of their mouths to devour them, as the fire from heaven did the first and second captain sent for Elisha, Rev. xi. 5; better anger all the witches in the world than such, because God is for them. Little thought the Gibeonites in David's time, that the Lord had so taken to heart their wrongs, that for their sakes all Israel should suffer. Even when we think not of it, is the righteous Judge avenging our unrighteous vexations.

Ver. 39. *But I say unto you, that ye resist not evil*] For here to resist is to be overcome, saith St Paul, Rom. xii. 21. And in a matter of strife or disagreement, he hath the worst that carries it, saith St Basil. Yea, Aristotle himself yieldeth, that of the twain it is better to suffer the greatest wrong than to do the least.[2] And it was a heavy challenge and charge upon those carnal Corinthians, that had strife, divisions, and lawsuits amongst them; "Why do ye not rather take wrong? why do ye not suffer yourselves to be defrauded? Nay, ye do wrong, and defraud, and that your brethren," 1 Cor. vi. 7, 8. But be not deceived, saith he, to wit, with vain hope of impunity, for God is the avenger of all such as, like the angry bee, care not to sting another, though it be to the loss of their own lives.[3] Besides that, in resisting evil, we give place to the devil, whom if by patience and forbearance we could resist, he would flee from us. "We wrestle not against flesh and blood" (as we think we do, when we conflict with men like ourselves, that have done us injury), "but against principalities and powers," Eph. vi. 12; *q. d.* whiles we are busy in breaking those darts that men shoot from afar against

us; we are oppressed by the devil near-hand us, Eph. iv. 26.[4] Here, by the way, magistrates must be admonished to take heed how they aggravate punishment upon a malefactor out of private grudge; parents also and masters, how they correct in a rage and fury. For although they be public persons, yet to give correction in a choleric mood is to ease their heart by way of revenge, it is a degree of resisting evil. The tyrant saith, ἔξεστι μοὶ, it is in my power to do it; the good governor saith, καθήκει μοὶ. It concerneth me to do it in point of duty, quoth a philosopher.

But whosoever shall smite thee on the right cheek] Socrates, a heathen, when he had received a box on the ear, answered, What an ill thing is it that men cannot foresee when they should put on a helmet, before they go abroad?[5] And when he was kicked by another, If an ass should kick me, said he, should I spurn him again? But we have those, that professing to be Christians, lest they should seem to be Anabaptists in taking two blows for one, will give two blows for one, yea, for none, sometimes: it is but a word and a blow with them, as it was with Cain, Lamech, Esau, who said, "The days of mourning for my father are at hand, then I will slay my brother Jacob," Gen. xxvii. 48. In which words he either threateneth his father (as Luther thinketh) for blessing his brother, *q. d.* I will be the death of my brother, and so cause my father to mourn: or else he threateneth his brother (as most interpreters sense it) after his father's head is once laid, without any respect at all to his mother, whom he not so much as mentioneth. He took no great care how she would take it; and his deferring till his father's death was more out of fear of a curse than conscience of a duty. There are that read the words by way of a wish, Let the days of mourning for my father draw nigh, &c. And then it is a double parricide. Sure we are, that as concerning his brother he comforted himself, purposing to kill him. He threatened him, saith the Septuagint (ἀπειλεῖ), Gen. xxvii. 42, *q. d.* I will sit upon his skirts, and be even with him. The nature of ungodly men is vindictive, and rejoicing in other men's hurt (which is the devil's disease), especially if provoked by any injury or indignity, as smiting on the cheek.[6] But God will smite them on the cheek-bone so hard, as that he will break the teeth of the ungodly; smite them in the hinder parts, where we use to whip froward children, and so put them to a perpetual reproach, Psal. iii. 7; lxxviii. 66. Neither only will he smite upon their loins, but through them, yea, he will crack their crowns, cleave their skulls, wound their hairy scalps, be their locks never so bushy,[7]

---

[1] οὐκ ἐστὶ κατάρα, ἡ λοιδορία ἀλλὰ πρόρρησις πρέπουσα ἀνδρὶ ἀποστόλῳ μὴ ἐκδικοῦντι ἑαυτὸν, ἀλλὰ διδόντι τόπον τῇ ὀργῇ.

[2] *In rixa, is inferior est qui victor est.* ἀδικεῖσθαι ἤ ἀδικεῖν ἄμεινον.

[3] *Non minus mali est referre injuriam, quam inferre.* Lactant.

[4] *Cur adeo laboramus ulciscendis infirmissimorum hominum*

injuriis? Dum hæc tela eminus projecta frangimus, a diabolo opprimimur. Roloc. in locum.

[5] *Quam molestum est nescire homines quando prodire debeant cum galea?*

[6] Κὰν μέ φαγῇς ἐπὶ ῥίζαν ὁμῶς ἔτι καρποφορήσω, ὅσχον ἐπισπεῖσαι σοί, τράγε, θυομένῳ. *Dixit vitis hirco cum ab eo roderetur.* Æsop.

[7] *Lacones comam nutriebant ad terrorem.*

their looks never so lofty and terrible, that count it courage to turn again and revenge, which every Turk and heathen, nay, every bull and boar can do. The Lamb of God gave his cheeks to the smiters: so did Michaiah the meek, Job the just, and Paul the patient, Isa. l. 6; John xviii. 23; 1 Kings xxii. 24; Job xvi. 10; Acts xxiii. 2, 3; yet not so patient, but he could set forth his privilege, when he was to be scourged, and clear his innocency with meekness of wisdom; and so may we, yea, we may safely decline a likely danger, in some cases especially, as our Saviour did. *Apud Mahometanos ferunt paucas brevesque lites esse, quod temere litigantes publice flagellis cædantur.*

Ver. 40. *And if any man sue thee at the law, and take away thy coat*] Rather remit of thy right, and sit down by the loss, than suffer the trouble of a vexatious lawsuit: quiet is to be sought above profit: therefore Isaac removed his dwelling so oft, when the spiteful Philistines strove with him about the wells he had digged. Not but that we may take the benefit of the law, and crave the help of the magistrate, for preventing or punishing of wrong done us: as Paul sent to the chief captain, and appealed to Cæsar, Acts xxiii. 17; xxv. 10.

> *Lis legem genuit, legum lis filia; vivi*
> *Nec sine lite solet, nec sine lege potest.*
>   (Owen, Epigr.)

But this must be done neither with a vindictive nor a covetous mind, as the manner is. Therefore after, " Who made me a judge ? " our Saviour presently addeth, "Take heed of covetousness." He that complaineth of another to the magistrate, must, 1. Love his enemies. 2. Prosecute with continual respect to God's glory and the public good. 3. Use the benefit of the law with charity and mercy, without cruelty and extremity. 4. Use it as an utmost remedy, when it cannot otherwise be; lest strangers be filled with thy wealth, and thy labours be in the house of a lawyer, and thou mourn at last (with Solomon's fool) when thine estate is consumed upon him: there being but few such as Servius Sulpitius, of whom Tully reports, that he was not more a lawyer than a justicer, referring all things to moderation and equity, and not stirring up suits, but composing them. *Sordida poscimus ; nummia quidam haud inepte quosdam jurisconsultos vocat ; latrocinia intra mœnia exercent.* Columella. *Legulatorum fæces præsertim decem drachmariæ.* Philip. ix.

Ver. 41. *And whosoever shall compel thee to go a mile*] Under colour of the magistrate's authority, which he abuseth; rather than by resisting thou shouldst revenge thyself, go with him two miles, yea, as far as the shoes of the preparation of the gospel of peace can carry thee. In the course of a man's life many wrongs are to be put up, which whoso cannot

frame to, let him make up his pack, and be gone out of the world; for here is no being for him.[1] Many pills are to be swallowed down whole, which if we should chew them would stick in our teeth and prove very bitter. Patience is of continual use to us at every turn; it is as bread or salt, which we cannot make one good meal without. It is a cloak, to keep off all storms; a helmet, to bear off all blows; a paring-knife, that cuts the cross less and less, till it comes to nothing. As there be two kinds of antidotes against poison, viz. hot and cold, so against tribulation and temptation, prayer and patience; the one, hot; the other, cold; the one, quenching; the other, quickening, Dan. vi. 20. The king cried unto Daniel with a lamentable voice, ver. 21. Then Daniel talked with the king, &c., with a voice not distressed, as that of the king was: for as by faith he stopped the mouths of the lions, Heb. xi. 33, so by patience he possessed his own soul, Luke xxi. 19; he became master of himself, which is the only true manhood. So patience had her perfect work in Joseph; therefore he became, as St James hath it, "perfect and entire, wanting nothing," Jam. i. 4. Julius Cæsar, beholding the picture of Alexander in Hercules' temple at Gades, lamented that he had done no worthy exploit at those years, wherein Alexander had conquered the whole world. Joseph at thirty showed more true virtue, valour, piety, patience, purity, policy, knowledge of secrets, skill in government, &c., than either of them. Giles of Brussels, a Dutch martyr, when the friars at any time did miscall him, he ever held his peace at such private injuries, insomuch that those blasphemers would say abroad that he had a dumb devil in him. And Cassianus reporteth, that when a Christian was held captive of infidels, and tormented with divers pains and ignominious taunts, being demanded by way of scorn, Tell us what miracle thy Christ hath done? he answered, He hath done what you see, that I am not moved at all the cruelties and contumelies you cast upon me. Godly people can bear wrongs best of any; and although corrupt nature in them bustles eftsoons, and bestirs itself, yet they soon club it down, they reason themselves patient, as David, and pray down their distempers, as Paul, Psal. xliii. 1; 2 Cor. xii. 9. And albeit, with those two sons of thunder, they could find in their hearts to call for fire from heaven upon their adversaries, yet they will do nothing without leave. As they came to Christ, and said, "Wilt thou that we command fire from heaven?" &c., which when Christ disliked and denied, they were soon satisfied, Luke ix. 54. We must take up our crosses, and when God bids us yoke, he is the wisest man that yields his neck most willingly. Our Saviour gave Judas his mouth to be kissed when he came to betray

---

[1] Ἄγγαροι, *Persis dicebantur quos hodie postas vocamus.* Eph. vi. 15. *Qui nescit dissimulare, nescit vivere ; ut Saul,* 1 Sam. x. 27. *Levius fit patientia quicquid corrigere est nefas.*

Cedamus, leve sit quod bene fertur onus.   Pondus ipsa jactatione incommodius fit. Sen.

him, leaving us a pattern of like equanimity and patience.

Ver. 42. *Give to him that asketh thee*] Yet with discretion and choice of a fit object.[1] Which having met with, be not weary of well-doing; for in due season ye shall reap, if ye faint not, Gal. vi. 9. Giving is compared to sowing, which, in good ground, is usually with increase. Therefore a worthy minister, upon occasion, asking his wife whether there were any money in the house, she answered, that she knew but of one three-pence; well, saith he, we must go sow, that is, give something to the poor, knowing that to be the way of bringing in, Prov. xi. 24, 25; Deut. xv. 10. The mercy of God crowns our beneficence with the blessing of store.[2] Happy was the Sareptan that she was no niggard of her last handful. The more we give, the more we have: it increaseth in the giving, as the loaves in our Saviour's hands did. Never did a charitable act go away without the retribution of a blessing. How improvident therefore are we, that will not offer a sacrifice of alms, when God sets up an altar before us! It were an excellent course, surely, if Christians now, as they of old at Corinth, would lay up weekly a part of their gettings for pious and charitable uses; and that men would abound in this work of the Lord, as knowing that their labour is not in vain in the Lord (I speak of them that are able, for we may not stretch beyond our staple, and so spoil all). We read of a bishop of Lincoln, that never thought he had that thing that he did not give; and of one bishop of Rome (though that is a rare thing) that was so liberal to the poor, that when he was asked by certain ambassadors whether he had any hunting-dogs to show them, he answered, Yes. And bringing them to a great sort of poor people, whom he daily relieved at his table, These are the dogs, saith he, wherewith I hunt after heaven.[3] Bishop Hooper, also, had his board of beggars. Twice I was (saith Mr Fox) in his house in Worcester: where in his common hall, I saw a table spread with good store of meat, and beset full of beggars and poor folk. And this was his daily custom. And when they were served and catechised, then he himself sat down to dinner, and not before. Queen Anna Boleyn carried ever about her a certain little purse, out of which she was wont daily to scatter some alms to the needy: thinking no day well spent wherein some man had not fared the better by some benefit at her hands. The Savoy, Bridewell, and another hospital, founded by King Edward VI., upon a sermon of Bp Ridley's, do speak and testify both his tender heart and his bountiful hand. Bonfinius re-

lateth of Stephen, King of Hungary (and the same thing is reported of Oswald, King of England), that his right hand rotted not for a long time after he was dead. And well it might be so (saith he) that that hand should be kept from corruption, that never suffered any to beg, to hunger, to lie in captivity, or any other misery.[4] But these, alas, are the last and worst days, wherein love is waxen cold: men's hearts are frozen, and their hands withered up. A great deal of mouth-mercy there is, as in St James's time, Go thy ways and be fed, clothed, and warmed: but with what? with a mess of words, a suit of words, a fire of words: these are good cheap: but a little handful were better than a great many such mouthfuls. We may now-a-days wait for some good Samaritan to come and prove himself a neighbour; and after all complain, There is no mercy in the land, Hos. iv. 1. "Merciful men are taken away, the liberal man faileth from among the children of men," Isa. lvii. 1; Psal. xii. 1. Elias lacketh his hostess of Sarepta, and Elisha the Shunammite. Paul cannot find the purpuriss, nor Peter the currier. Abraham we have not, and Job we find not. Captain Cornelius is a black swan in this generation, that gave to him that asked, and from him that would borrow of him, turned not away, &c.

And from him that would borrow of thee, turn not away] Some are ashamed to beg and take alms, who yet, being pressed with great necessity, could be glad to borrow. And a greater kindness it might be to lend them a bigger sum than to give them a lesser. Here therefore a good man is merciful and lendeth, he will lend, looking for nothing again, Psal. cxii. 5: not looking that a poor neighbour should earn it out, or do as much for him some other way. Nay, we ought not in this case so to look for our own again as that that be the chief thing we aim at, but to obey Christ, and to do a poor man a pleasure. And what if "the wicked borroweth, and payeth not again," Psal. xxxvii. 21: let not others fare the worse for their fault. The godly make great conscience of paying that they owe, as the son of the prophets that was so sorry for the loss of the axe, "Alas, master! it was but borrowed," 2 Kings vi. 5. And Elisha bade the widow first pay her debts with her oil, and then live of the rest. Now from such borrowers turn not away: plead not excuse, make not delays when it is in thy hand to help them presently. "He that hideth his eyes (in this case) shall have many a curse," Prov. xxviii. 27. Not to do good (in this kind) is to do hurt; not to save a life, or uphold a poor man's declining estate, is to destroy it, Luke vi. 6; Mark iii. 4. Carnal reason will here

---

[1] Give such before they ask, Psal. xli. 1. *Qui præoccupat vocem petituri.* Aug.

[2] *Pauperum manus Christi est gazophylacium. Jul. Cæsar dicere solitus est, se vel tum imprimis ditescere, cum bene merentes aliquo munere prosequeretur; quanto magis egenos?*
Nunquam deficiunt charitates, cum dantur, habentur;
Cumque absumuntur, multiplicantur opes.

[3] *Hi sunt canes quos alo quotidie, quibus spero me cœlestem gloriam venaturum. Jam vero longe aliter, pauperibus sua dat gratis, nec munera curat.*

[4] *Merito manus illa corruptionis expers esse debuit, quæ neminem mendicare, esurire, et in captivitate, aut quavis miseria jacere, perpessa est.*

stand up and plead, as Nabal did, Shall I take my bread and my flesh, that I have provided for my shearers, and give it to strangers? 1 Sam. xxv. 11. So, shall I take my money or my means, which I have provided for my children, and give it or lend it to such and such? Here then you must silence your reason and exalt your faith. Consider how great an honour it is to be an almoner to the King of heaven; that by laying out upon such, you lay hold upon eternal life; that the apostle, 2 Cor. viii. 2, setteth out liberality by a word that signifieth simplicity, ἁπλότης, in opposition to that crafty wiliness that is in the covetous, to defend themselves from the danger (as they think) of liberality: that the liberal man deviseth liberal things, and by liberal things he shall stand. When a man would think he should fall, rather he takes a right course to stand and thrive: he lays up for himself a sure foundation.

Ver. 43. *Thou shalt love thy neighbour, and hate thine enemy*] This latter they drew as an inference from the former, by the rule of contraries. But logic, being the rule of reason, which now is corrupt, is itself in some respects corrupt also. Sure we are, be it what logic it will, it is but carnal divinity. Suitable it is to our nature, but so much the more suspicious. The Pharisees taught it, and were applauded. The Papists also little better (for the Pharisees are fled and hid in the Papists, as one saith the ancient heretics are in the monks): they teach, that in two cases only we are bound to help our enemies—in the case of extremity and of scandal. For other things, to love them, to pray for them, or do them good in other cases, it is but a counsel our Saviour gives, and no commandment. If men can do it, it is well; but if they cannot, it is not required. Thus say they, but what saith Christ, the law-maker, and so the truest interpreter thereof?

Ver. 44. *But I say unto you, Love your enemies*] A hard task, I must needs say, but, hard or not hard, it must be done, be it never so contrary to our foul nature and former practice. "The spirit that is in us lusteth after envy, but the Scripture teacheth better things," Jam. iv. 5, 6. And what are those? To go no further than the present text: 1. "Love your enemies," for the inside, be tenderly affected toward them, as heartily wishing their good every way; being glad of their welfare, and grieved when it falls out otherwise. Thus David was a sorrowful man when his enemies were in affliction, and put on sackcloth (ἀγαπᾶτε, q. ἄγαν πένεσθε, Psal. xxxv. 13). 2. Seal up our love to them by all good expressions, which are here referred to these three heads. 1. Bless them (εὐλογεῖτε), that is, speak kindly to them, and of them, let them have your good word. 2. Do good, that is, be ready to help them and relieve them at all essays. 3. Pray for them, that God would pardon their sins and turn their hearts. This

is our Saviour's precept, and this was his practice. He melted over Jerusalem (the slaughter-house of his saints and himself), and was grieved at the hardness of their hearts, Mark vi. 3. Next (for words) he called Judas, friend, not devil; and prayed, "Father, forgive them." And (for deeds) he not only not called for fire from heaven, or legions of angels against them, but did them all good for bodies and souls; for he healed Malchus' ear, washed Judas' feet, &c.; like that good Samaritan, he was at pains and cost with them, instructing them with patience, and proving if at any time he might pull them out of the snare of the devil, by whom they were taken alive at his pleasure.[1] Which also he did. For he converted the thief on the cross, who at first had reviled him, and graciously received those three thousand souls that had imbrued their villanous hands in his innocent blood, Acts ii. Thus our Saviour, full of grace and truth. And of his fulness (of redundancy, of his over-measure) we have all received, and grace for grace, as the child receiveth from the father limb for limb, part for part, &c., John. i. 16. He is the father of eternity; and all his children, in all ages of the Church, have resembled him somewhat in this sweet property, Isa. ix. 6. Abraham rescueth his nephew Lot, that had dealt so discourteously with him. Isaac expostulates the wrong done him by Abimelech and his servants, and forgiveth and feasteth them. Absalom inviteth Amnon to a feast, and Alexander, Philotas, to kill them thereat; but good Isaac doth it, to show there was no grudge or purpose of revenge. Jacob was faithful to Laban, who changed his wages ten times, and ever for the worse. Joseph entertained his malicious brethren at his house. And whereas their guilty hearts misgave them, that he "rolled himself upon them thereby," he feasted them on purpose to be reconciled unto them. As the Romans had their χαρίσθια, to the which were invited none but kinsfolks to continue love and to seek reconciliation, if there had been any breach. (Val. Max. ii. 1.) But to speak forward. Moses stands up in the gap for them that had so soon forgotten him. Joshua marcheth all night and fighteth all day for the Gibeonites that had deceived him. Samuel prayeth (and God forbid he should do otherwise) for an ungrateful people that had rejected him. David put on sackcloth, he wept and fasted, when his enemies were afflicted; he spared Saul's life, and afterwards Shimei's, when Abishai's fingers even itched to be taking off their heads, Psal. vii. 5. Elisha set bread and water before the Syrians that came to surprise him; and provided a table for them that had provided a grave for him. The disciples were solicitous of the salvation of the Pharisees that had accused them at the same time to our Saviour, Matt. xv. 12.[2] Stephen prays heartily for his persecutors, and prevailed (as St Austin thinketh) for Paul's conversion.

---

[1] 2 Tim. ii. 25, 26. ἐζωγρημένοι, taken alive, and in hunting by that hellish Nimrod.

[2] *Charitatis hoc fuit. Suos vituperatores in veritate informari cupiunt, &c.* Cart.

And being reviled, saith he, we bless; being defamed, we pray, 1 Cor. iv. 12, 13. Do my lord of Canterbury a shrewd turn, and then you may be sure to have him your friend while he liveth. This was grown to a common proverb concerning Archbishop Cranmer. And Lawrence Saunders, the martyr, being sent to prison by Stephen Gardner, Bishop of Winchester (who bade Carry away this phrensy fool, &c.), praised God for a place of rest and quiet, where to pray for the bishop's conversion. In the year of grace 1541, Robert Holgat obtained a benefice in a place where one Sir Francis Askew, of Lincolnshire, dwelt, by whom he was much troubled and molested in law. Upon occasion of these suits, he was fain to repair to London, where being he found means to become the king's chaplain, and by him was made Archbishop of York and President of the King's Council for the North. The knight before-mentioned happened to have a suit before the council there, and doubted much of hard measure from the Archbishop, whose adversary he had been; but he, remembering this rule of our Saviour, "Do good to them that hate you," &c., yielded him all favour that with justice he might, saying afterward merrily to his friends, he was much beholden to Sir Francis Askew, &c. This bishop, in the beginning of Queen Mary, was committed to the Tower, where he lay a year and half, and was at last deprived.

Ver. 45. *That ye may be the children of your Father*] That ye may appear to be, and will approve yourselves to be, the sons of God without rebuke amidst a perverse and crooked nation, Phil. iii. 15. Whilst we resemble him, not in outward lineaments only, as an image doth a man, but in nature and disposition, as a child doth his father. Now God, to make known his power and patience, endureth with much long-suffering the vessels of wrath fitted to destruction, Rom. ix. 21: such incarnate devils as march up and down the earth, with heart and hands as full as hell with all manner of mischief, lewdness, and rebellion. Neither doth he bear with them only, but gives them the gospel to call them to repentance, and strives with them by his Spirit, which they desperately resist, yea, despite, hardening their hearts as the nether millstone, Job xli. 24, refusing to be reformed, hating to be healed; till at length they lose all passive power also of escaping the damnation of hell, which is a conformity to the very devils. This is his dealing with rebels and reprobates. Neither so only, but that he might make known the "riches of his glory on the vessels of mercy, which he had before prepared to glory," Rom. ix. 13. He loved his elect not yet existing, nay, resisting, and effectually called them, not only not deserving, but not so much as desiring it. " For when we were enemies, we were reconciled to God by the death of his Son," Rom. v. 10. God so loved the world, the wicked and wayward world, " that he sent his only begotten Son," &c. Now, *Qui misit unigenitum, immisit spiritum, promisit vultum; quid tandem tibi negaturus est?* He that sent thee his Son, imparted unto thee of his Spirit, promised thee his favour; what will he deny thee? how shall he not with his Son give thee all things also? Rom. viii. 32.[1] Oh let his patience be our pattern, his goodness our precedent, to love and show kindness to our greatest enemies. So shall we force a testimony, if not from the mouths, yet at least the consciences of all, even the worst, that we are born of God, and do love him better than ourselves, when to please him we can so much cross ourselves in the practice of this most difficult duty.

For he maketh his sun to arise on the evil] A sweet mercy, but not prized, because ordinary; as manna was counted a light meat, because lightly come by. But should we be left in palpable darkness, as were the Egyptians for three days together, so that no man stirred off the stool he sat on, this common benefit would be better set by. The sun is, as it were, a vessel whereinto the Lord gathered the light, which, till then, was scattered in the whole body of the heavens. This David beheld with admiration, Psal. viii., not with adoration, as those idolaters that worshipped the queen of heaven, Jer. xliv. 17 (not so Job, chap. xxxi. 16). Truly, saith Solomon, the light is sweet, and a pleasant thing it is for the eyes to behold the sun, Eccl. xi. 6; and St Chrysostom wondereth at this, that whereas all fire naturally ascendeth, God hath turned the beams of the sun toward the earth, made the light thereof to stream downwards.[2] It is for our sakes and service doubtless, whence also the sun hath his name in the Hebrew tongue (*shemesh*), a servant, as being the servant-general of mankind; while he shines indifferently upon the evil and the good, and to both imparteth light and heat.

And his rain to fall] Not only upon flowers and fruit-trees, but also upon the briars and brambles of the wilderness. Those bottles of rain, the clouds, are vessels (saith one) as thin as the liquor which is contained in them; there they hang and move, though weighty with their burthen; but how they are upheld, and why they fall here and now, we know not, and wonder. This we know (and may well wonder), that God maketh his sun to shine and his rain to fall on the evil and unjust also. What so great matter is it, then, if we light up our candle to such, or let down our pitcher that they may drink? This is our Saviour's inference here. The dew we see falleth as well upon the daisy and thistle as upon the rose and violet. *Ingens multitudo hominum et pecorum decidentibus subito nubibus, ac effusis consertim aquis, submersa est, &c.* Bartholin. *Idem in cataclysmo universali contigit.* Pareus.

[1] *Nihil tandem ei negasse credendum est qui ad vituli hortatur esum.* Jerome.
[2] Hom. vii. *ad Pop. Antioch.* So the earth is not covered with water, that man may inhabit it. Sailors observe that their ships flee faster to the shore than from it; whereof no reason can be given, but the height of the water above the land.

On the just, and on the unjust] Those whom St Matthew calleth unjust, St Luke calleth unthankful, Luke vi. 35. Ingratitude is a high degree of injustice. God is content we have the benefit of his creatures and comforts, so he may have the praise of them. This is all the rent he looks for, and this he stands upon; he indents with us for it, Psal. l. 15, and God's servants, knowing how he expects and accepts it, do usually oblige themselves to it, as that which pleaseth him better than "an ox that hath horns and hoofs," Psal. vi. 9, 31. And they have been careful to return it, as the solid bodies that reflect the heat they receive from the sun-beams upon the sun again. But most men are like the moon, which the fuller it is of light, the further it gets off the sun from whom it receiveth light: like springs of water, that are coldest when the sun shineth hottest upon them: like the Thracian flint, that burns with water, is quenched with oil; or the Dead Sea, that swalloweth the silver streams of sweet Jordan, and yet grows thereby neither greater nor sweeter. "Do ye thus requite the Lord, O ye foolish people and unwise?" Deut. xxxii. 6. Do ye thus rob him of his praise, and so run away with his rent? Is this the best return we make him for his many matchless mercies and miraculous deliverances? Out upon our unthankfulness and unrighteous dealing! that can devour God's blessings as beasts do their prey, swallow them as swine their swill, bury them as the barren earth the seed; use them as homely as Rachel did her fathers' gods, yea, abuse them to his dishonour, as if he had hired us to be wicked; and fight against him with his own weapons, as Jehu did against Jehoram with his own men, as David against Goliath with his own sword, as Benhadad against Ahab with that life that he had given him. The injurious usage at the hands of the sons of men was that that caused God to make a world and unmake it again, to promise them 120 years' respite, and to repent him, so that he cut them short 20 years of the former number; yea, to perform the promised mercy and to repent him of it when he hath done, as David did of the kindness he had showed unworthy Nabal, 1 Sam. xxv. 21. Will not God take his own from such, and be gone, Hos. iii. 9, turn their glory into shame, Hos. iv. 7, blast their blessings, Mal. ii. 2, destroy them after he hath done them good, Josh. xxiv. 20, cause them to serve their enemies in the want of all things, that would not serve so good a master in the abundance of all things? Deut. xxviii. 47. What should a prince do, but take a sword from a rebel? what should a mother do, but snatch away the meat from the child that mars it? And what can the wise and just Lord do less than cut off the meat from the mouths, and take away his corn and his wine, his wool and his flax, from such as not only not own him to it, but go after other sweethearts with it, paying their rents to a wrong landlord? (*Amasios suos.*

Hos. ii. 5.) Thus he dealt by his unfruitful vineyard, Isa. v. 5, by the unprofitable servant, Matt. xxv. 28, by the foolish philosophers (for, as the chronicler speaketh of Sir Thomas More "I know not whether to call them foolish wise-men, or wise foolish-men"), that imprisoned (κατέχοντες) the truth in unrighteousness; and made not the best of that little light they had: God not only made fools of them, but "delivered them up to a reprobate sense," Rom. i. 28, and only for their unthankfulness, which is robbing God of his due. O therefore what will become of us, that so ordinarily abuse to his daily dishonour our health, wealth, wit, prosperity, plenty, peace, friends, means, marriage, day, night, all comforts and creatures, our times, our talents; yea, the very Scriptures, the gospel of truth, the rich offers of grace, and our golden opportunities? Is not religion turned by many into a mere formality and policy? our ancient fervour and forwardness, into a general lukewarmness and unzealousness? and (besides the love of many waxen cold) doth not iniquity abound in every quarter and corner of the land? which therefore even groaneth under our burthen, and longeth for a vomit to spue us out, as the most unthankful and unworthy people that ever God's sun shone upon and God's rain fell upon (the sun of Christ's gospel especially, and the rain of his grace) so fair and so long together? If there be any unpardonable sin in the world, it is ingratitude, said that peerless Queen Elizabeth in a message to Henry IV., King of France. The very heathens judged it to be the epitome of all evil: call me unthankful, saith one, you call me all that naught is.[1] Lycurgus would make no law against it, because he thought no man would fall so far below reason as not thankfully to acknowledge a benefit.[2] Thus nature itself abhors ingratitude; which therefore carrieth so much the more detestation, as it is more odious even to them that have blotted out the image of God.[3] Some vices are such as nature smileth upon, though frowned at by divine justice: not so this. "Wherefore have ye rewarded evil for good?" Gen. xliv. 4.

Ver. 46. *For if ye love them that love you, what reward have you?*] The Greek and Latin word (say the Rhemists) signifieth very wages or hire due for work; and so presupposeth a meritorious deed. But what will they say to St Luke, who calleth that χάρις, or grace, which St Matthew here called μισθὸς, a reward? It is a reward, but of mere grace (see Rom. iv.), that God will give to them that love their enemies.[4] "If thine enemy be hungry, feed him, &c. For thou shalt heap coals of fire upon his head, and the Lord shall reward thee," saith Solomon, Prov. xxv. 21, 22. A double encouragement, and all little enough. 1. Thou shalt heap coals on his head; those coals are (as Austin interprets it) *urentes pœnitentiæ gemitus*, the scorching sighs of true repentance: *q. d.* thou shalt melt these

---

[1] *Ingratum dixeris, omnia dixeris.*
[2] *Quod prodigiosa res esset beneficium non agnoscere.*

[3] *Ingratitudine nihil fœdius etiam inter barbaros.* Pareus.
[4] *Præmium, sed gratuitum.* Beza in Matt. vi.

hardest metals (as many of the martyrs did their persecutors), thou shalt meeken their rancour, overcome their malice, cause them to turn short again upon themselves and upon sight of their sin, shame themselves, and justify thee, as Saul did David. 2. "The Lord shall reward thee" (and all his retributions are more than bountiful), yet not of merit (for what proportion betwixt the work and wages? but first of mercy;—reward and mercy are joined together in the second commandment and Psal. lxii. 12; secondly, of promise, for our encouragement), sith our labour is not in vain in the Lord. Briefly, it is called a reward, not properly, but by similitude, because it is given after the work done. Next, it is a reward, not legal, but evangelical; promised in mercy, and in like mercy performed. Whence it is also called the "reward of inheritance," Col. iii. 24. Now an inheritance is not merited, but freely descendeth on sons, because they are sons. Let no son say, with profane Esau, What is this birthright to me? or with the prodigal in the gospel, Give me here the portion that belongeth unto me (such are those that love their friends only, here they have love for love, and that is all they are to look for); but look up to the recompense of reward, with Moses; and answer as Naboth, God forbid that I should so far gratify the devil and mine own evil heart, as to part with my patrimony, my hope of reward, for a little revenge, or whatsoever coin bearing Satan's superscription.

Ver. 47. *What do ye more than others?*] Singular things are expected and required of such as have received singular grace and mercy. As to be eminent in good works, to get above others, to have our feet where other men's heads are.[1] The way of the righteous is on high, saith Solomon; he goes a higher way to work than ordinary, and walks ἀκριβῶς, accurately, exactly;[2] he gets even to the very top of godliness, as the word importeth. He knows that more than the common stint is required of him, and that he must do that that the world will never do: as to be hot in religion, Rev. iii. 16. The carnal gospeller saith, *Religiosum oportet esse, non religantem,* it is fit to be religious, but not so conscientious. So, to be zealous of good works, Tit. ii. 14, but with discretion, saith the worldling. The King of Navarre told Beza he would launch no further into the sea than he might be sure to return safe to the haven.[3] Though he showed some countenance to religion, yet he would be sure to save himself. So, to abound in God's work, to have a heart full of goodness, as those Romans, chap. xv. 14; a life full of good works, as Tabitha, Acts ix. 33. But this is to be wise over-much, saith the flesh, Eccles. vii. 16. *Philosophandum, sed paucis.* Cicero. What need this waste? said Judas. It is too much for you to go up to Jerusalem to worship, said Jeroboam to the people, take a shorter cut rather to the golden calves. "They are idle, they are idle,"

said Pharaoh of God's busiest servants. So, God would have his to walk precisely, Eph. v. 15. This the mad world mocks at: to pluck out their right eyes, this is a hard saying, saith the sensualist, Matt. v. 29. To offer violence to God's kingdom; "fair and softly goes far;" and it is good keeping on the warm side of the hedge, saith the politician: to keep God's commandment as the apple of thine eyes; but how few are there that will not break the hedge of any commandment, so they may shun a piece of foul way? Lastly, to love an enemy, do good to them that hate us, &c. But this seems to be the most unreasonable and impossible. What? love those that hate and hurt them, that daily rage and rail at them, with such bitterness, as if they had been as far as hell for every word that tumbleth out of their mouths against them? &c. Love this man? Nay, then, love the devil himself. They will rather die a thousand deaths than endure such a one: if they could love him, yet they would not. They are prime Christians in these men's opinions that ascend to Saul's measure, "I will do thee no hurt, my son David." If they pass him by when he is in their power, as the priest and the Levite did the wounded man; if they fall not foul upon him with recriminations, and retaliate injuries, they have gone far and done fair: and such a measure of charity they hold little less than angelical, hardly here attainable. This is the voice and guise of flesh and blood. "The spirit that is in us lusteth to envy," and prompteth us to requite taunt with taunt, suit with suit, blow with blow, and holds them fools that do not. But this is the wisdom from beneath, and is earthly, sensual, devilish (James iii. 15, expounded): whereas that "from above is first pure, and then peaceable," (well assured of pardon of sin and peace with God, and thence) gentle or equable to men (ἐπιεικὴς), and easily persuaded, full of mercy (to an offending brother) and good fruits (friendly expressions), without wrangling or lawing (ἀδιάκριτος), and without hypocrisy: such as can be heartily reconciled, and love again without dissimulation, "not in word and in tongue, but in deed and in truth," Rom. xii. 9; 1 John iii. 18; not covering a potsherd with silver dross, a wicked heart with burning lips. Seven abominations are in such a heart, and his wickedness shall be showed before the whole congregation, as Absalom's usage of Amnon, Prov. xiv. 20; xix. 7; xxvi. 23—26. A godly man carries neither cruel hatred, a desire to hurt whom he hates, as Esau, nor simple hatred, where there is no desire to hurt, but a disdain to help: he forgives not only, but forgets, as Joseph, Gen. l. 20. (For injuries remembered are hardly remitted.) And although he loves not his enemies' sins, yet he doth their persons: striving to seal up his love by all loving usage both in word and deed. And herein he doth more than others; that which is singular, and in the world's

---

[1] τῶν καλῶν ἔργων προΐστασθαι, Tit. iii. 14.
[2] Eph. v. 15, ἀκριβῶς τὸ εἰς ἄκρον βαίνειν. Gellius.

[3] *Pelago se non ita commissurus esset, quin quando liberet, pedem referre posset.*

account, seraphical : that which (in truth) is extraordinary and above vulgar possibility, it is a high point of Christian perfection : and let as many as are perfect be thus minded. Benaiah was honourable among thirty, but he attained not to the fisrt three. A natural man may be renowned for his patience and beneficence ; but the child of God must herein go before all the wicked men in the world, and strive to be conformed to the first three, the blessed Trinity.

Ver. 48. *Be ye therefore perfect, even as your Father*, &c.] The child (saith one) is the father multiplied, the father of a second edition. Of Constantine's sons Eusebius reporteth, that they " put on their father's fashions, and did exactly resemble him.[1] And of Irenæus, the same author telleth us that he expressed to the life the learning and virtues of his master Polycarp. It were happy for us (and we must labour it) if we could pass into the likeness of the heavenly pattern. Our *summum bonum* consists in communion with God and conformity to him ; in keeping inward peace with God, that he " abhor us not because of the provoking of his sons, and of his daughters," Deut. xxxii. 19 ; and in seeking and keeping (as much as may be) peace with all men, and holiness ; purifying ourselves as he is pure, 1 John iii. 3 (in quality, though we cannot in an equality), from the love of every lust (the ground of all our wranglings, James iv. 1), but especially from the passions and perturbations of the heart, possessing ourselves in patience. For if patience have her perfect work we shall be perfect and entire, wanting nothing, James i. 4. For " perfect " St Luke hath it, " Be merciful," &c., vi. 37.

CHAPTER VI.

Ver. 1. *Take heed that ye do not your alms*] YOUR justice, saith the Syriac. For first, we do the poor but right when we relieve them ; for they have an interest in our goods, by virtue of the communion of saints, whereupon Solomon, " Withhold not," saith he, " good from the owners thereof," i. e. thy poor brethren. God, the great author and owner of all, hath intrusted the rich (as his stewards, as his almoners) with the wealth of this world. He hath intrusted them, I say, not lent it them (to speak properly, for that which is lent is our own, at least for a time), but put it into their hands only, for this end, that their abundance may be a supply for others' wants, 2 Cor. viii. 9, that their full cups may overflow into others' lesser vessels, &c., which if it be not done, they can bring in no good bills of account.[2] It is but justice then that we do the poor, and it is rapine or robbery (saith St Chrysostom) not to relieve them.[3] Secondly, alms is called justice, to teach that alms should

be given of things well gotten. In the reign of King Henry VIII. there was no one accused (but very unjustly) of heresy for saying that alms should not be given until it did sweat in a man's hand. The Jews called their alms-box, *Kupha shel tsedacha*, the chest of justice (Buxtorf, Syn.) ; and upon it they wrote this abbreviate, מביא " A gift in secret pacifieth wrath," Prov. xxi. 14. Selymus the Great Turk, as he lay languishing (his incurable disease still increasing), leaning his head in the lap of Pyrrhus the Bassa, whom of all others he most loved, " I see," said he, " O Pyrrhus, I must shortly die without remedy." Whereupon the great Bassa took occasion to discourse with him of many matters ; and amongst others, that it would please him to give order for the wellbestowing of the great wealth taken from the Persian merchants in divers places of his empire, persuading him to bestow the same upon some notable hospital for relief of the poor. To whom Selymus replied : " Wouldst thou, Pyrrhus, that I should bestow other men's goods, wrongfully taken from them, upon works of charity and devotion, for mine own vainglory and praise ? Assuredly I will never do it. Nay, rather, see they be again restored to the right owners ;" which was forthwith done accordingly ; to the great shame of many Christians, who minding nothing less than restitution, but making *ex rapina holocaustum*, do out of a world of evil-gotten goods cull out some small fragments, to build some poor hospitals or mend some blind way : a slender testimony of their hot charity.

Before men to be seen of them] As those are that act their part on a stage, and would please the spectators, that they may be applauded. " He that giveth," saith St Paul, " let him do it with simplicity," with ingenuity, accounting it enough that he hath God the witness of his heart, Rom. xii. 8 ; not but that men may see our good works, and their praise be sought, *modo tibi non quæras, sed Christo*, saith Aretius, so that you seek not yourselves therein, but set up Christ. Let your end be, that the light may be seen, not yourselves seen, Matt. v. 16. A fool hath no delight in understanding, saith Solomon, but that his heart may discover itself, i. e. that he may have the credit of it : but he takes a wrong course.[4] For honour (as a shadow) followeth them that seek it not,[5] as the Hittites told Abraham, he was " a prince of God amongst them ;" when himself had said a little before, " I am a stranger and a sojourner with you," &c. Gen. xxiii. 4, 5.

Otherwise ye have no reward of your Father, &c.] Ye take up your wages all aforehand. Fruit by the way-side seldom resteth till it be ripe. The cackling hen loseth her eggs, so doth the vainglorious hypocrite his reward. He layeth up his treasure, his wages, in the eyes and ears of men ;

---

[1] ὅλον ἐνεδύσαντο τὸν Κωνσταντῖνον ἐμπρέποντες τοῖς τοῦ πατρὸς καλλωπίσμασιν. Eusebius.

[2] Prov. iii. 27. *Adeo si quid agimus, nostrum est : si quid habemus, alienum.* Beddingf.

[3] *Rapina est pauperibus non impertire.* Chrysostom.

[4] *Tantum ut vanam famam captet.* Mercer. *Duntaxat ad ostentationem.* Bain.

[5] *Cæsar scripta sua Commentarios inscripsit, non historias. Et hoc ipso laudem veram meruit, quod falsam contempsit.* Lipsius.

which is a chest that hath neither lock nor key to keep it.

Ver. 2. *Therefore when thou doest thine alms*] Unless thou set light by thy reward, as Esau did by his birthright; unless thou holdest heaven hardly worth having, and art of that carnal cardinal's mind (Card. Burbon), who preferred his part in Paris before his part in Paradise.

Do not sound a trumpet before thee] As the Pharisees did, under a show of assembling the poor to take dole, but indeed to notify their liberality. If they had been truly liberal, they had made no noise of it. Those vessels yield most sound that have least liquor. *Vasa quæ magis continent, minus sonant.* (Seneca.)

As the hypocrites do] From whom as the saints differ in nature so they should in practice. We should have nothing common with them, no more than a chaste matron desires to have with a base strumpet, Cant. ii. 7. The spouse desireth to know where Christ feedeth, that she may repair to him; for why should I be, saith she, as one that turneth aside (or, that is covered and veiled, which was the habit of harlots, Gen. xxxviii. 15, 16), why should I be reputed a light housewife, whilst I turn aside by the flocks of thy companions? She would shun, and be shy of all appearance of dishonesty; so should we of hypocrisy. Those Christians of Corinth are much condemned by the apostle that carried themselves so carnally that a man could hardly discern them from other men. Richard Redman, Bishop of Ely, 1501, was not much to be commended for looking so like a Pharisee in that practice of his, of causing a bell to be rung wherever he came, to give notice to the poor of the place that they should have sixpence a-piece, as many as came to him. And why are alms-houses commonly built by the highway sides? &c.

That they may have glory of men] As Jehu, Come, see what a zeal I have for the Lord of hosts. Is thine heart upright as mine? &c. A gracious heart is not a blab of his tongue, but rests and rejoiceth silently in the conscience of a secret goodness. Not so the hypocrite, the self-seeker, the stage-player, for so the word "hypocrite" properly signifieth, such as though little better than rogues, yet sometimes represent the persons of princes, and carry themselves with other faces than their own, that they may have glory of men, that they may get a plaudit.[1] And herewith agree all the former expressions; whatsoever these men do is merely theatrical (πρὸς τὸ θεαθῆναι), hypocritical, histrionical. They sound a trumpet, as is usual on stages: they do their devoir in the synagogues, public assemblies, and streets, as stage-players act in open places, and by drums and outcries get as much company together as they can. And as they can act to the life those whom they personate, yea, outstrip

them in outward actions, so do hypocrites the true Christian. Doth the publican fix his eyes on the ground? those hypocrites in Isaiah will hang down their heads like bulrushes. Doth Timothy weaken his constitution with abstinence? the false Pharisee will not only weaken his constitution, but wither his complexion with fasting. Doth Zaccheus give half of that he hath to the poor? the pretender to piety and charity will bestow all his goods to feed the poor, and, besides, give his body to be burned, 1 Cor. xiii. 3, as Servetus did at Geneva, A.D. 1555. And all for a name, for a little glory among men, which is but a breath, and yet not able to blow so much as one cold blast upon hypocrites, when they shall be cast into unquenchable flames, when God shall wash off their varnish with rivers of brimstone. No natural face hath so clear a white and red as the painted. No rush is so green and smooth as the bulrush. He is curious to a miracle that can find a knot in it; yet within is nothing but a useless and spongy pith.[2] Over-fair shows are a just argument of unsoundness.

Verily I say unto you] q. d. You would little think it, and themselves will hardly believe it: for they are an impudent kind of people, and will not soon be said. But I assever and assure you of it, in the word of Amen, the faithful and true witness, Rev. iii. 14, all the words of whose mouth are in righteousness, there is nothing froward or perverse in them, Prov. viii. 8, that this is the very truth, and time will prove it so. Asses that have fed on hemlock, are so stupefied thereby, that they lie for dead, and feel not till half their hides be hilded off: then they rise and run away with a foul noise.[3] So these.

They have their reward] Paid them down upon the nail in ready money, and have given their acquittance. They take up all their wages afore the year's end, they receive it now, and leave none till hereafter.[4] It is all they are ever likely to have, and let them make them merry with it. *Egregiam vero laudem, et spolia ampla refertis.* A poor reward, God wot; but it is that they would have. It is their own reward, not God's, saith St Jerome.[5] As Judas went to his own place, a place of his own providing, Acts i. 25, so these have their own reward, much good may it do them. Here they have their consolation with Dives: let them look for no further reward in the day of refreshing, if they do, they are like to be disappointed, saith the Judge. To themselves they bore fruit, Hos. x. 1, and shall therefore be turned off as empty vines; when the faithful spouse that lays up her fruit for Christ, Cant. vii. ult., shall hear, "Thou art like a green fir-tree; from me is thy fruit found," Hos. xiv. 8. And albeit in her works of charity in secret, and without hope of reward from men, she may seem to cast her bread upon the waters, down the

---

[1] *Hos Plautus vocat Holophantas, qui omnia ostentant et mentiantur. Sic Roscius Ulyssis, aut Æneæ repræsentat personam, cum Ulysses non sit, nec Æneas.* Aretius.
[2] *Nodum in scirpo quærit.* Isa. lviii. 5.

[3] *Dimidia pellis parte propendente, fædum ruderem edunt.* Mathiolus.
[4] ἀπέχουσι, They receive it as their full pay, whence ἀποχή, an acquittance. Luke vi. 23.
[5] *Mercedem suam, non Dei.* Jerome.

river (as we say), or on the sea to feed fishes; yet after many days she shall be sure to find it, Eccl. xi. 1. That labour of love cannot be lost that we resolve to cast away (as the world accounts it) upon Christ.

Ver. 3. *But thou when thou doest thine alms*] The godly Christian must walk in a diverse way to a world of wicked people, as Noah did,[1] really reproving their darkness by his light, their pride by his lowliness, their vainglory by his modesty, their ostentation by his secret devotion; not only (planet-like) keeping a constant counter-motion to the corrupt manners of the most, but also shining forth fair with a singularity of heavenly light, spiritual goodness, and God's sincere service, in the darkest midnight of damned impiety.

Let not thy left hand know, &c.] A proverbial speech, *q. d.* secrete thyself as much as may be, cast away the vain affectation of human applause. Let not thy left hand (if it had so much skill) understand what thou givest, and to whom, how much, how oft, at what time, &c. God sets down every circumstance in his book of remembrance, Mal. iii. 16, as our Saviour (that true Archdeacon, as well as Archshepherd, 1 Pet. v. 4) sat and viewed the estate, mind, and gift of every one that cast money into the treasury, Mark xii. 41; and as he took special observation of those that came to hear him, how far they had come, how long they had been there, how little opportunity they had of providing for themselves, and how soon they might faint if sent away empty, Matt. xv. 32. *In pugillaribus suis omnia notat.* "I know thy work and thy labour," Rev. ii. 2, saith Christ to that church: so to us,—I know thine alms, and thy privacy. Many give much, and are little noted or noticed. It matters not, saith our Saviour, though thy left hand should not know what thy right hand doth; there is no loss in that. Some talents are best improved by being laid up. A treasure that is hid is safer from thieves. Steal we therefore benefits upon men, as Joseph did the money into the sacks. And as he made a gain of the famine, and bought Egypt; so may we of the poor we relieve, and buy heaven, Luke xvi. 9, Rom. ii. 10. *Ex fame quæstum captabat Josephus, et benignitate sua emit Egyptum, nos cœlum.*

Ver. 4. *Thy Father that seeth in secret*] And best accepteth of secret service. Cant. ii. 14, "O thou that art in the clefts of the rocks, let me see thy face, let me hear thy voice," &c.[2] He is all eye (πανόφθαλμος), he searcheth the hearts and trieth the reins, those most abstruse and remotest parts of the body, seats of lust: and as he is himself a Spirit, so he loveth to be served like himself, "in spirit and in truth." He sets his eyes upon such, as the word here signifieth, he looketh wishedly, fixedly, steadily; he seeth through and through our secret services, not to find faults

in them (for so he may soon do not a few, but those he winks at, where the heart is upright), but to reward them, as a liberal pay-master, "rich to all that call upon him," or do him any other business.[3] "Who is there even among you that shut the door for nought; that kindleth fire upon mine altar for nought?" Mal. i. 10, that gives a cup of cold water, and hath not his reward? David would not serve God on free cost, but was he not paid for his pains, and had his cost in again with usury ere the sun went down? Let him but resolve to confess his sins, and God (or ere he can do it) forgiveth him the iniquity of his sin, that in it that did most gall and grieve him, Psal. xxxii. 5. Let him but purpose to build God a house, God promiseth thereupon (for his good intentions) to build David an house for ever. So little is there lost by anything that is done or suffered for God. He sends away his servants (that do his work many times, and the world never the wiser), as Boaz did Ruth, with their bosom full of blessings; as David did Mephibosheth, with a royal revenue; as Solomon did the Queen of Sheba, with all the desire of her heart; as Caleb did his daughter Achsa, with upper and nether springs; or as once he did Moses from the mount, with his face shining. He shone bright, but knew not of it; yea, he hides his glorified face with a veil, and had more glory by his veil than by his face. How far are those spirits from this, which care only to be seen! and slighting God's secret approbation, wish only to dazzle others' eyes with admiration, not caring for unknown riches! Our Saviour (besides the veil of his humanity) says, "See ye tell no man." It is enough for him that he can say to his Father, "I have glorified thee on earth: I have finished the work that thou gavest me to do," John xvii. 4. His work he accounts a gift; his wages he looks for in another world, ver. 5. He was content his "treasures of wisdom should be hid," Col. ii. 3. And shall we fret ourselves, when our pittances of piety and charity are not admired? Is it not enough for us that we shall appear with him in glory, and then be rewarded openly? Col. iii. 3.

Shall reward thee openly] Ay, but when? at the resurrection of the just, Luke xiv. 14; at that great assize and general assembly he will make honourable mention, in the hearing of angels and men, of all the good deeds of his children; how they have fed the hungry, clothed the naked, &c., that which they had utterly forgotten; not so much as once mentioning their misdoings, Matt. xxv. Yea, he shall take them to heaven with him, where the poor men's hands have built him a house aforehand, and they shall receive him into everlasting habitations. But what shall he do in the mean while? "feed on faith" (as some read that text, Psal. xxxvii. 3), live upon reversions.[4]

---

[1] *Solus ipse diversa ambulavit via.* Chrys. de Noa.
[2] *Deus theatrum suum habet in latebris.* Bucer.
[3] *Thales interrogatus, num lateret Deos homo injuste agens, respondit, Ne cogitans quidem.* Βλέπειν παρὰ τὸ βάλλειν ὦπας, *ab adjiciendo oculos.* Beza.

[4] *Non igitur est dispendium eleemosyna sub conscientia Dei data, sed maximum compendium et præclarissima negotiatio.* Musculus. *Domum in cœlis manus pauperum ædificat.* Chrysostom. *Pascere fide.* Junius.

Yea, but while the grass grows the steed starves. But so cannot a merciful man, for he shall have mercy, Matt. v. 7; such a mercy as rejoiceth against judgment. Yea, he that can tender mercy to God, may challenge it from God by virtue of his promise; as David doth, "Preserve me, O God, for I am merciful," Psal. lxxxvi. 2. Mercy he shall obtain, 1. In his soul, which shall be like a watered garden, fresh and flourishing. For "the liberal soul shall be made fat; and he that watereth shall be watered himself," Prov. xi. 35. The spirits of wealth distilled in good works comfort the conscience. 2. So they do the body, too, when sick and languishing, Psal. xli. 2, 3. Mercy is the best cordial, a pillow of repose, a present remedy, Prov. xi. 17. For if thou draw out thy soul to the hungry, thy health shall spring forth speedily, Isa. lviii. 8, 10. 3. For his name: the liberal are renowned in the earth, as Abraham that free-hearted housekeeper, no penny-father; and Obadiah, that hid and fed the prophets by fifty in a cave. Zaccheus and Cornelius, Gaius and Onesiphorus, how precious are their names! how sweet their remembrance! Who honours not the memorial of Mary for her spikenard, and of Dorcas for her coats and garments? Acts ix. 39. Whereas "the vile person shall no more be called liberal" (in Christ's kingdom), nor Nabal, Nadib, "the churl bountiful," Isa. xxxii. 5. 4. For his estate: the most gainful art is almsgiving, saith Chrysostom. The poor man's bosom and the orphan's mouth are the surest chest, saith another. Whatsoever we scatter to the poor, we gather for ourselves, saith a third.[1] What we give to the poor, we lend to the Lord, who accounts himself both gratified and engaged thereby, Prov. xix. 17. Neither will he fail to bless the liberal man's stock and store, Deut. xv. 10, so that his righteousness and his riches together shall endure for ever, Psal. cxii. 3. 5. Lastly, his seed shall be mighty upon earth, ver. 21. The son of such a tenant that paid his rent duly, shall not be put out of his farm, Psal. xxxvii. 26. And that proverb is proved false by common experience: "Happy is that son whose father goeth to the devil;" for ill-gotten goods usually come to nothing: the third heir seldom enjoyeth them,[2] unless it be here and there one, that by repentance breaketh off, and healeth his father's sin by mercifulness to the poor, that the property may be altered, and so his tranquillity lengthened. Oh, therefore, that rich men would be "rich in good works, ready to distribute, willing to communicate" (εὐμεταδότους), 1 Tim. vi. 18, 19 (which was a piece of praise used to be ascribed to the ancient kings of Egypt). This, this were the way to "lay up for themselves a sure foundation;" yea, to "lay fast hold on eternal life;" when those that withhold their very crumbs shall not obtain a drop with Dives, whom to vex and upbraid, Lazarus was laid in the bosom of liberal Abraham. *Artaxerxes Longimanus quod manum*

haberet alteram longiorem, addere, dictitabat, esse magis regium, quam detrahere. (Plutarch.)

Ver. 5. *And when thou prayest*] A duty of that necessity, that neither the immutability of God's decree, Dan. ix. 1, nor the infallibility of the promises, Ezek. xxxvi. 37, nor the effectual intercession of our Lord Christ (who taught his disciples to pray), can dispense with us for not doing it. The Jews accounted it an "abomination of desolation" when the daily sacrifice was intermitted and suspended, as under Antiochus. Our Saviour perfumed his whole course, nay, his cross with this incense, and thereby purchased us this privilege, paved us this "new and living way" to the throne of grace, John xvi. 24; a sure and safe way to get mercy, ver. 23. The ark was never separated from the mercy-seat, to show that God's mercy is near unto such as affect his presence. Some favours he hath reserved to this duty, that will not otherwise be yielded, Psal. cvi. 23; Ezek. xxii. 30. As when he is fully resolved to ruinate a people or person, he silenceth his servants, and forbids them to solicit him any further, as he did Samuel interceding for Saul, and Jeremiah for Jerusalem.

Be not as the hypocrites] Who pretend to pray much, but indeed can do nothing at it, because destitute of the "spirit of grace and of supplication;" without whose help we know neither what nor how to pray, Zech. xii. 10; Rom. viii. 26: nay, Peter, James, and John will be sleeping when they should be praying in the very hour of temptation, Matt. xxvi. 38. There may be good words and wishes found in a worldling's mouth, "Who will show us any good?" but none but a David can with faith, feeling, and fervency say, "Lord, lift up the light of thy countenance upon me," Psal. iv. 6. Balaam may break forth into wishes and woulds, "Oh, let me die the death of the righteous," &c.; but can he pray, as David in like case, Psal. xxvi. 9, "Oh, take not away my soul with sinners, nor my life with bloody men!" An hypocrite may tell a persuasive tale for himself in earthly regards, or howl upon his bed in the want of outward comforts; cry in extremity, as a prisoner at the bar, as a pig under the knife; or importune God for grace, as a bridge to lead him to heaven, not for any beauty he seeth or sweetness he finds in it. But will he pray always, will he delight himself in God? saith Job.[3] No, surely, he neither doth nor can do it. When God defers to help at a pinch, as Saul, 1 Sam. xiii. 8; when grief and vexations increase, he frets and meddles no more with calling upon God, but grunts against him because he handles him not after his own mind, and betaketh himself to some other course. If God will not come at his call and be at his beck, away to the witch of Endor, with Saul, 1 Sam. xxviii. 7; to the god of Ekron, as Ahaziah to Baalim and Ashteroth, with the revolted Israelites,

---

[1] *Eleemosyna ars omnium quæ studiosissima.* Chrysostom. *Manus pauperum gazophylacium Christi. Quicquid pauperibus spargimus nobis colligimus.*

[2] *De male quæ sitis vix gaudet tertius hæres.* Horace.

[3] Hos. vii. 14. When God is rending away his soul, he roars. Job xxvii. 9.

2 Kings i. 2.[1] Wherein he is like to those barbarous Chinois, that whip their gods when they answer them not; or that resolute Ruffus, that profanely painted God on the one side of his shield and the devil on the other, with this inscription, *Si tu me nolis, iste rogitat :* or that desperate king of Israel, "Behold," saith he, "this evil is from the Lord, and what should I wait for the Lord any longer?" 2 Kings vi. 33. Lo, this is the guise of a godless hypocrite. Either "he calleth not upon God" (which is the description David giveth of him, Psal. xiv. 4), but is possessed, as it were, with a dumb devil, both in church and chamber. Or if by reading or otherwise he have raked together some good petitions, and strive to set some life upon them in the utterance, that he may seem to be well-gifted; yet he doth it not to serve God, but merely to serve himself upon God: "he draweth not nigh with a true heart," Heb. x. 13, uprightly propounding God's service in prayer, and not only his own supply and satisfaction. He is not brought into God's presence with love and desire, as Psal. xl. 8. He labours not with strife of heart to worship him with his faith, trust, hope, humility, self-denial, being well content that God's will be done, however, and truly seeking his glory, though himself be not profited, acknowledging the kingdom, power, and glory to be his, Matt. vi. 13. Lastly, working not by a right rule, from a right principle, nor for a right end; he cannot undergo the strife of prayer, as Jacob, who wrestled by might and sleight (so much the Hebrew word importeth, ויאבק, Gen. xxxii. 24—26), much less can he continue long in it, as David, he is soon sated, soon tired, Psal. xxvii. 4; cxix. 81, 123. If men observe him not, applaud him not, he giveth over that course, as tedious and unsavoury, that wherein he finds no more good relish than in the white of an egg or a dry chip. And in any extraordinary trouble, instead of calling upon God, he runs from him, Isa. xxxiii. 14, as Saul did, 1 Sam. xxviii. 7.

For they love to pray standing, &c.] Stand they might; so did the publican. And when ye stand and pray, saith our Saviour, not disliking the gesture, Luke xviii. 13; Mark ix. 25. It was commonly used among the Jews in the temple, especially at the solemn feasts, what time there was such resort of people from all parts, that they could hardly stand one by another. The primitive Christians also stood praying in their public assemblies, betwixt Easter and Whitsuntide especially, in token of our Saviour's standing up from the dead. Whence came that proverb amongst them, "Were it not for standing in prayer, the world would not stand."[2] Other gestures and postures of the body in prayer we read of. David and Elijah sat and prayed, 1 Chron. xvii. 16; 1 Kings xix. 4. Peter and Paul kneeled and prayed, Acts

ix. 40; Eph. iv. 13. Moses and Aaron fell on their faces and prayed, Num. xvi. 22. In secret prayer there is more liberty to use that gesture that may most quicken us and help the duty: Elijah put his head between his knees in prayer (as one that would strain every vein in his heart). But in public our behaviour must be such as may witness our communion and desire of mutual edification; there must be uniformity, no rents or divisions, 1 Cor. xiv. 40; and special care taken that our inward affection answer our external devotion; that we stand not in the synagogues, as these, with desire to be seen of men (as Saul was higher than the rest by head and shoulders), for that is putrid hypocrisy, hateful even amongst heathens. Tully taxeth Gracchus for this, that he referred all his actions, not to the rule of virtue, but to the favour of the people, that he might have esteem and applause from them.

That they may be seen of men] This was the wind that set the windmill a-work, the poise that made the clock strike. Pliny telleth us that the nightingale singeth far longer and better when men be by than otherwise. If Jehonadab had not seen the zeal that Jehu had for the Lord of hosts, he had been nothing so hot nor (in his own conceit) so happy. But Christian modesty teacheth a wise man not to expose himself to the fairest show, but rather to seek to be good than seem to be so.[3] Not so every loose and ungirt Christian: these, like Jeroboam's wife, never put on demure apparel but when they are to speak with the prophets; are never so holy as at church, and in the presence of those whose holiness they reverence.

Ver. 6. *But when thou prayest, enter into thy closet, &c.*] The proper place for secret prayer (as the family is for private prayer, Acts x. 3, 9, and the church for public, Luke iv. 16), that being sequestered from company, we may more fully descend into our own hearts, and be the freer from ostentation and hypocrisy, and from discursation and wandering of mind (*Anima dispersa fit minor*): as also for the demonstration of our faith, whereby we believe the omnipresence of God, who seeth in secret and rewardeth openly. Daniel indeed opened his windows, and prayed in an upper room, not to be more secret (as Pintus mistaketh it) but to be more seen; and yet not of vain ostentation, but of zealous and constant profession. The king had forbidden it (so did Henry III., King of France, forbid householders to pray with their families), Daniel did it notwithstanding, as aforetime. God must be obeyed rather than men, as not Scripture only, but nature teacheth.[4] He kneeled upon his knees three times a day and prayed; that had been his custom, and should be. David also at morning, at evening, and at noon, called

---

[1] *Flectere si nequeo superos, Acheronta movebo. Ab Ekron ubi colebatur Beelzebub, factus videtur, Acheron.*

[2] *Absque stationibus non substiteret mundus.* Tertul.

[3] *Sed vox tu es, præterea nihil.* Laco ad Philan.

Falleris, esse aliquid si cupis, esque nihil.

[4] Acts v. 29. Sic Socrates in Apologia, respondens, ἐγὼ μὲν, ὦ Ἀθηναῖοι, ἀσπάζομαι ὑμᾶς καὶ φιλῶ. πείσομαι δὲ τῷ Θεῷ μᾶλλον ἢ ὑμῖν.

upon God, and had his set times for such devotions. But the devil, as it is probable, 2 Sam. xi. 2, had caused him to come from his trench, and then did presently wound him. He knows well enough that a Christian's strength lies in his prayer (as Samson's did in his hair), that it buckleth all our spiritual armour close to us, and makes it useful, that a Christian can never want help whiles he can pray, Eph. vi. 18; as they were wont to say, the pope can never want money so long as he can hold a pen in his hand to command and send for it: that secret prayer is a soul-fatting exercise, as secret meals, we say, feed the body. The old serpent feels himself charmed and disabled to do hurt by these kind of duties. They have "poured forth a charm (לחש) when thy chastening was upon them," Isa. xxvi. 16. Yea, he is deeply wounded and driven out of the field by those arrows of deliverance, as the king of Syria was, 2 Kings xiii. 17, which therefore he keeps (what he can) from being multiplied and enlarged. Fervent prayers are the pillars of smoke wherein the Church ascendeth to God out of the wilderness of this world, and by an humble familiarity converseth, yea, parleyeth with him,[1] as Abram and Moses did (especially when Satan, sin, and conscience accuse), and standeth, as it were, upon interrogatories; such as are those, Rom. viii. 33—35.

And when thou hast shut thy door] So to shut out distractions, which yet will grow upon us, do what we can. For though the spirit is willing to wait upon God all the while of the duty, yet the flesh is weak. It being but partly mortified, draws away our thoughts many times; and putteth us to St Paul's complaint, "When I would do good, evil is present with me," Rom. vii. 21. Satan also will be jogging and interrupting us; and will needs be talking to us when we are most busily speaking to God, as the Pythoness troubled St Paul as he went to prayer, Acts xvi. 16. Worldly things likewise are so natural to us, and so near our senses, heavenly things are so supernal and supernatural, that we cannot without watching our senses, and travail of soul, stay our spirits long upon them. For help herein, St Augustine telleth us that the ancient Christians of Egypt were wont to use only short and pithy prayers and ejaculations,[2] such as was that of Elijah when he contended with the priests of Baal, charging God (in two words) with the care of his covenant, of his truth, and of his glory. Many other helps there are for the curing and casting out (in a comfortable measure) these by-thoughts, these birds that would rob Abraham of his sacrifice; these swarms of Egypt, that our hearts may be as so many Goshens;

these creeping things innumerable, as David hath it. This among the rest, that our Saviour here prescribeth, to retire into a secret place, as Abraham did into his grove at Beersheba, planted for the purpose (though that was afterwards abused by the heathens, and therefore forbidden the Israelites, Deut. xii. 3). Isaac had his oratory in the fields, where he prayed with deep meditation or soliloquy, as the word there signifieth. Rebekah upon the struggling of the babes, "went to inquire of the Lord," Gen. xxv. 22, that is, she went to some secret place to pray, and receive some revelation from God, say Calvin, Musculus, Mercer, others. Jacob had visions of God when he was all alone upon the way; Elijah prayed under the juniper; our Saviour in the garden of Gethsemane, and many times in the mount; Cornelius in some corner of his house; Peter on the leads,[3] where also he fell into an ecstacy or trance, and saw heaven open, his soul was separated (after a sort) from his body for the time, whiles he was talking with God, he was so transported and carried out of himself, *ut caro esset pæne nescia carnis*, as St Jerome testifieth of certain devout women of his time. For the place we pray in, no matter how mean it be, so it be secret. Where there is a Jeremiah, a Daniel, a Jonas, a dungeon, a lions' den, a whale's belly, are goodly oratories.[4] Shut the door to thee, remembering the weakness of thy flesh, and the malice of the devil, watching how to distract thee. Covenant with thy senses, and bind them to the good abearance all the while: look God full in the face, as David did, Psal. lvii. 7, call in and concentre thy thoughts, as men do the sunbeams into a burning glass: serve God with thy spirit, as Paul did, Rom. i. 9, say, "All that is within me, praise his holy name." Have thy heart at thy right hand, with Solomon's wise man, lay God's charge upon it to attend upon him; when it roves and wanders, call it in and chide it; judge and shame thyself for thy distractions, and strive to do better, so shall they never be imputed unto thee, Psal. xiii. 2. To be wholly freed from them is a privilege proper to the estate of perfection. Some diseases will not be cured near home, but men must repair to the bath or city for help. This infirmity is not to be healed till we come to heaven. No shutting of the door will do it, nor anything else, till the everlasting doors be opened unto us, till we enter in by the gates into the city of the living God, Rev. xxi. 24.

Pray to thy Father which is in secret] There are no dumb children in God's house; the least he hath can ask him blessing. All are not alike gifted, but every godly man prayeth unto thee, saith David, Psal. xxxii. 6; St Paul was

---

[1] 1 Tim. ii. 1, ἐντευξεις, parleyings with God. So 1 Pet. iii. 21, ἐπερώτημα, sc. *in precibus, quæ sunt electorum cum Deo colloquia.* Pasor.

[2] *Fratres Ægyptiaci brevissimis et raptim ejaculatis orationibus uti voluissent, ne per moras evanesceret et hebetaretur intentio.*

[3] Acts ix. 4; x. 10, ἐκστασις, *Quasi semoto ad tempus a corpore animo, cum Deo colloquitur.* Beza.

[4] If ye will not hear me out, send me to my prison again among my toads and frogs, which will not interrupt me while I talk with my Lord God.

no sooner converted but he was praying presently, Acts ix. 11. The spirit of grace is the spirit of supplication, and teacheth to cry, "Abba, Father," or Father, Father, Gal. iv . 5. And this very naming of the name of God in prayer (though it be no more), so it be done in faith, entitles a man to heaven, 2 Tim. ii. 19, if withal he depart from iniquity; when such as have the gift of prophecy and of doing miracles shall miscarry, and be turned off at the last day, because workers of iniquity, Matt. vii. And albeit God's weaker children cannot utter their mind unto him in well-couched words and variety of expressions, yet, if their broken language come from a broken heart, it avails more than affectation of rhetoric, without affection of prayer. Men are better pleased with the stammering and lisping of their own little ones than with all the plain speech of all the children in the town besides. Yea, because the soul is sick, the service is twice welcome. As, if a sick child reach us up a thing, we count it more than to send another of a laborious errand. " I will spare them," saith he, " as a man spares his own son that serveth him," Mal. iii. 17. The business of prayer is more despatched by sighs than speeches, by desires and groans of the heart, to our Father which is in secret, whether we can express them in words or no. " The Spirit also helpeth our infirmities " (he lifteth with us and before us, as the word signifies, συναντιλαμβάνεται, Rom. viii. 26), and maketh intercession in us and for us with groans unutterable. And he that searcheth the hearts knoweth what is the mind of the spirit. As he heareth us without ears, so he understandeth us without our words. If we can but groan out, Ah, Father, it is an effectual prayer. The voice is not simply required, John iv. 24. There is a great dispute (saith one) among the schoolmen about the speech of angels; but this they agree in, that one angel speaketh thus to another, when any one hath a conceit in his mind of anything, with a will that another should understand it, and that God should understand it, that is enough for the expression of it. So is it with the spirit of man in speaking to God : for the spirit agreeth to the angels. Yet we must pray for fit words also, Hos. xiv. 2, and strive to be enriched in all utterance, and in all knowledge, 1 Cor. i. 5, get a habit of heavenly-mindedness, let the heart meditate a good matter,[1] and then the tongue will be as the pen of a ready writer, Psal. xlv. 1; first prepare the heart, and then stretch out the hands, Job xi. 13. The heart should be praying a good while before the tongue; as before the seven trumpets were sounded at the opening of the seventh seal, there was half-an-hour's silence in heaven, Rev. viii. 1, 2. And surely if there be an honest heart and a good intention, an ability of prayer usually is in us, though we know it not; as a man may have money about him, and not know

so much, till necessity make him willing to search and glad to find it. Remember, however, the promise of the Spirit's assistance and God's acceptance, and know, that as in singing, so in praying, the pleasing melody is in the heart, Col. iii. 16. The voice which is made in the mouth is nothing so sweet as that which comes from the depth of the breast. As the deeper or hollower the belly of the lute or viol is, the pleasanter is the sound; the fleeter, the more grating and harsh in our ears.

And thy Father which seeth in secret] And heareth too : as he did Moses when he cried to God, but said nothing (Exod. xiv. 15. *Moses egit vocis silentio ut corde clamaret.* Aug.); and Hannah, when she moved her lips, but uttered not herself in an audible voice, 1 Sam. i. 13; and Nehemiah, when he lift up his heart to God, as he spake to the king, Neh. ii. 4; and as he doth still his praying people. His ears are into their prayers, saith St Peter, after David (1 Pet. iii. 12, εἰς δέησιν αὐτῶν. Psal. xxxiv. 25), that though their prayers are so weak they cannot ascend to him, he will descend to them. He " hearkened and heard " those good souls in Malachi (iii. 16), as loth to lose any part of their precious language. Thus the eyes of the Lord are upon the righteous (when they are praying especially), and his ears are open to their prayers. He seeth his Church when she is in the clefts of the rocks, Cant. ii. 14; when she is gotten into a corner and praying, he looks upon her with singular delight, and with special intimations of his love (as Ahasuerus dealt with Esther), and saith unto her, as he, " What is thy petition, and it shall be given thee," Esth. v. 3. And oh that every faithful soul, whiles it is sitting and feasting with God by secret prayer and other holy duties, would bethink itself what special boon it hath to beg, what Haman to hang up, what corruption to be subdued, what grace to be increased, &c. How should they be gratified, and their request granted, even to the whole of God's kingdom! The truth is, they might have anything : and that which Zedekiah said to his courtiers flatteringly, God performeth to his people really, " The king is not he that can do anything against you," Jer. xxxviii. 5. Luther was wont to say that prayer was after a sort omnipotent: for whatsoever God can do, that prayer can do. Of Luther himself, for his wrestling with God and prevailing (as he was mighty and happy that way), it was said, That man can have anything at God's hands. *Iste vir potuit quod voluit. De Luthero* Justus Jonas.

Will reward you openly] Here in part, hereafter in all perfection. He never said to the house of Israel, Seek ye me in vain, Isa. xlv. 19. "This poor man (for instance) prayed," saith David, pointing to himself, " and the Lord heard him, and delivered him out of all his distresses," Psal. xxxiv. 6. God is known by hearing of prayers; it is one of his titles, Psal. lxv. 3, it is

---

[1] *Verbaque provisam rem   non invita sequuntur.* Horat.

his praise above all heathen gods, Isa. xlv. 19, 20. By this Manasseh knew him to be God, 2 Chron. xxxiii. 13, and all Israel, 1 Kings xviii. 37, 39, when it came to a matter of competition. "Verily, verily, I say unto you, whatsoever ye shall ask the Father in my name, he will give it you," John xvi. 23. If we can find a praying heart, he will find a pitying: if we open our mouths, God will fill them: and he is worthily miserable that will not make himself happy by asking. Of some heathen princes it is said that they never sent away their suitors sad or discontented: this is most true of God; let a man bring right petitions, a clear conscience, faith in the promises, and hope to wait the accomplishment, and he shall not fail of the thing he asketh, or a better: as when God denied David the life of the child, but assured him of his salvation, "I shall go to him," &c., 2 Sam. xii. 23. So he denied his mother her particular request for that time, John ii. 4: and when his disciples asked him a curious question, "Wilt thou at this time restore the kingdom to Israel?" &c., that is not for you to know, saith he; but a better thing I can tell: you shall receive power after that the Holy Ghost is come upon you, Acts i. 7, 8. But many times God is graciously pleased not only to grant a man's prayer, but also to fulfil his counsel, Psal. xx. 4; that is, in that very way and by that very means that his thoughts pitch on. But say he do neither of these; yet the very ability to pray in the Holy Ghost is a sweet and sure sign of salvation, Rom. x. 13. And a very grave divine writeth thus: I cannot but prefer faithful prayers for some temporal mercy far before that mercy for which I pray. Yea, I had rather God should give me the gift of prayer than (without that gift) the whole world besides.[1] As for those that are *ita congregabiles* (saith another divine of good note), so very good fellows that they cannot spare so much time out of company as to seek God apart and to serve him in secret, they sufficiently show themselves thereby to have little fellowship or friendship with God, whom they so seldom come at.

Ver. 7. *But when ye pray, use not vain repetitions*] Babble not, bubble not, saith the Syriac, as water out of a narrow-mouthed vessel. Do not iterate or inculcate the same things odiously *et ad nauseam*, as Solomon's fool, who is full of words (saith he); and this custom of his expressed μιμητικῶς, in his vain tautologies.[2] "A man cannot tell what shall be; and what shall be after him, who can tell?" Eccl. x. 14. Such a one also was that Battus (to whom the Evangelist here hath relation), an egregious babbler.[3] In common discourse it is a sign of weakness to lay on more words

upon a matter than needs must: how much more in prayer! Take we heed we offer not the sacrifice of fools; God hath no need of such, 1 Sam. xxi. 15 with Psal. v. 5. He "is in heaven, and thou upon earth: therefore let thy words be few," Eccl. v. 2. Prayers move God, not as an orator moves his hearers, but as a child his father ("your Father knoweth that ye have need of all these things," ver. 8). Now a child is not to chat to his father, but to deliver his mind, humbly, earnestly, in few, direct to the point. St Peter would have men to be sober in prayer, that is, to pray with due respect to God's dreadful Majesty, without trifling or vain babbling, 1 Pet. iv. 7. He that is fervent in spirit, prays much, though he speak little, as the publican, Luke xviii., and Elijah, 1 Kings xviii. 36. But as a body without a soul, much wood without a fire, a bullet in a gun without powder,—so are words in prayer without spirit. Now long prayers can hardly maintain their vigour, as in tall bodies the spirits are diffused. The strongest hand long extended will languish, as Moses' hand slacked against Amalek. It is a praise proper to God, to have "his hand stretched out still," Isa. ix. 12. Our infirmity suffers not any long intention of body or mind. Our devotion will soon lag and hang the wing: others also that join with us may be tired out, and made to sin by weariness and wanderings. In secret indeed, and in extraordinary prayer with solemn fasting, or so when the heart is extraordinarily enlarged, our prayers may and must be likewise. Solomon prayed long at the dedication of the Temple, so did those godly Levites, Neh. ix. Our Saviour prayed all night sometimes, "and rising up a great while before day, he went apart and prayed," Mark i. 35. Of Luther it is reported that he spent constantly three hours a day in prayer, and three of the best hours, and fittest for study.[4] It was the saying of a grave and godly divine, that he profited in the knowledge of the word, more by prayer in a short space than by study in a longer. That which our Saviour condemneth, is needless and heartless repetitions, unnecessary digressions, tedious prolixities, proceeding not from heat of affection or strength of desire (for so the repetition of the self-same petition is not only lawful, but useful, Dan. ix. 17, 18; Mark xiv. 39. See Psal. cxlii. 1, and cxxx. 6), but either out of ostentation of devotion, as Pharisees, or opinion of being heard the sooner, as heathens, when men's words exceed their matter, or both words and matter exceed their attention and affection. See that these be matches, and then pray and spare not.

For they think they shall be heard for their much speaking] As Orpheus in his hymns, and

[1] *Malo accipere a Deo serias preces quam sine precibus universum hunc mundum.* Rolloc. in John vi. 23.

[2] Μὴ βαττολογήσατε. Ἐν πολυλογίᾳ πολυμωρία, *In multiloquio stultiloquium.*

[3] ——*sub illis*

Montibus inquit erunt, et erant sub montibus illis.
Risit Atlantiades, et me mihi perfide prodis?
Me mihi perfide prodis? ait. Ovid, Met. 2. 203.

[4] *Nullus abit dies quin ut minimum tres horas, easque studiis aptissimas, in orationem ponat.*

other pagans; calling, as the mariners in Jonah, "every man upon his God;" and lest they should not hit the right, closing their petitions with that *Diique Deæque omnes.* And as this was the folly and fault of pagans, so is it also still of the Papists, whom the Holy Ghost calleth heathens, with whom they symbolize, as in many things else, so in their battologies or vain repetitions: which are so gross that the devil himself (had he any shame in him) might well be ashamed of them.[1] In their Jesus-Psalter (as they call it) there are fifteen of these prayers: "Jesu, Jesu, Jesu, have mercy on me. Jesu, Jesu, Jesu, help me. Jesu, Jesu, give me here my purgatory." Every of which petitions are to be ten several times at once said over for a task. So on their church and college doors, the English fugitives have written in great golden letters, *Jesu, Jesu, converte Angliam, Fiat, Fiat.* These be their weapons, they say, prayers and tears. But the truth is, the Jesuits (the pope's blood-hounds) trust more to the prey than to their prayers; like vultures, whose nests, as Aristotle saith, cannot be found, yet they will leave all games to follow an army, because they delight to feed upon carrion. Their faction is a most agile sharp sword, whose blade is sheathed at pleasure in the bowels of every commonwealth, but the handle reacheth to Rome and Spain. They strive under pretence of long prayers and dissembled sanctity, which is double iniquity (*simulata sanctitas duplex iniquitas*), to subdue all to the pope, and the pope to themselves. Satan, they say, sent Luther, and God sent them to withstand him. But that which Vegetius (i. 24) said of chariots armed with scythes and hooks, will be every day more and more applied to the Jesuits; "at first they were a terror, afterwards a scorn."

Ver. 8. Be not ye therefore like unto them] God would not have his Israel conform to the heathens' customs, nor so much as once name their idols, Exod. xxiii. 13; Psal. xvi. 4. No more should Christians (as some are of opinion).[2] That of Cardinal Bembus is somewhat gross concerning their St Francis, *quod in numerum Deorum ab Ecclesia Romana sit relatus.* But this is like the rest; for if we may believe Baronius, we may see their lustral water and sprinkling of sepulchres in Juvenal's sixth satire; lights in sepulchres, in Suetonius' Octavius; lamps lighted on Saturday, in Seneca's 96th Epistle; distribution of tapers among the people, in Macrob. Saturnals, &c.

For your heavenly Father knoweth what things ye need, &c.] And therefore answereth many times before we ask, Isa. lxv. 24; as he did David, Psal. xxxii. He prevents us with many mercies we never sought him for; that our praises may exceed our prayers. "I am found of them that sought me not," saith God; but yet in the same place it is said, "I am sought of

them that asked not for me," Isa. lxv. 1. Importing, that we never seek to him for grace till effectually called by his grace. Howbeit, no sooner is any truly called, but he presently prayeth. Say not then, if God know our needs, what need we open them to him? The truth is, we do it not to inform him of that he knows not,[3] or to stir up mercy in him, who is all bowels, and perfectly pitieth us. But, 1. Hereby we acknowledge him as a child doth his father when he runs to him for food, Luke xi. 13. 2. We run that course of getting good things that he hath prescribed us, Jer. xxix. 11, 12. Which Moses and Elijah knew, and therefore the former turned God's predictions, the latter his promises, into prayers, Exod. ix. 33; 1 Kings xviii. 37. 3. Hereby we prepare ourselves holily to enjoy the things we crave; for prayer both sanctifieth the creature and increaseth our love and thankfulness, Psal. cxvi. 1. 4. Prayer prepareth us, either to go without that we beg, if God see fit, as David when he prayed for the child's life, and was fitted thereby to bear the loss of it; or else to part with that we have got by prayer, for the glory of God the giver of it. Those that make their requests known to God with thanksgiving, shall have (at least) "the peace of God that passeth all understanding," to guard their hearts and minds in Christ Jesus. (φρουρήσει, Phil. iv. 6, 7.) They shall have strength in their souls, the joy of the Lord shall be their strength, the glory of the Lord shall be their rereward, Psal. cxxxviii. 3; Neh. viii. 10; Isa. lviii. 8. In their marching in the wilderness, at the fourth alarm, arose the standard of Dan, Asher, and Naphtali; these were there reward of the Lord's host; and to these were committed the care of gathering together the lame, feeble, and sick, and to look that nothing was left behind. Unto this the prophet Isaiah seems (in that text) to allude, and so doth David, Psal. xxvii. 10: "When my father and mother forsake me, the Lord will gather me;" and this comfortable assurance was the fruit of his prayer.

Ver. 9. After this manner therefore pray ye] Forms of wholesome words are profitable. A set form of prayer is held fittest for the public, and for such weak Christians as are not yet able to express their own desires in their own words. The utterance of wisdom is given to some Christians only, 1 Cor. xii. 8, yet are all to strive unto it, that the testimony of Christ may be confirmed in them, 1 Cor. i. 5, 6. God will take that at first that afterwards will not be accepted. If words be wanting, pray that God that commands thee to take words and come before him, to vouchsafe thee those words, wherewith thou mayest come before him, Hos. xiv. 2. Speak, as the poor man doth, supplications, Prov. xviii. 23: so did the prodigal: forecast also (with him) what thou wilt say; premeditate of the matter, disposing it in due order (as one would do that

---

[1] *Gentes sunt Antichristus cum suis asseclis.* Pareus. *Battologiæ Pontificiæ vel Satanam ipsum pudeat.* Beza.

[2] *Non male dixit Tertullianus, Philosophos esse Hæreti-* *corum Patriarchas.*   [3] *Non sane ut Deus instruatur, sed ut mens nostra construatur.*

is to speak to a prince; "God is a great King," Mal. i. 23). Some think we must never pray but upon the sudden and extraordinary instinct and motion of the spirit. This is a fancy, and those that practise it cannot but fall into idle repetitions, and be confused; going forward and backward, like hounds at a loss, saith a good divine (Parr's Abba, Father), and having unadvisedly begun to speak, they know not how wisely to make an end. This to prevent, premeditate and propound to thyself fit heads of prayer: gather catalogues of thy sins and duties by the decalogue; observe the daily straits of mortal condition, consider God's mercies, your own infirmities, troubles from Satan, pressures from the world, crosses on all hands, &c. And as you cannot want matter, so neither words of prayer. The Spirit will assist, and God will accept, if there be but an honest heart and lawful petitions. And albeit we cannot vary them as some can: our Saviour in his agony used the self-same words thrice together in prayer, and so may we when there is the same matter and occasion. He also had a set form of giving thanks at meat; which the two disciples at Emmaus hearing, knew him by it, Luke xxiv. 30, 31. A form then may be used, we see, when it is gathered out of the Holy Scriptures, and agreeable thereunto. Neither is the spirit limited hereby; for the largeness of the heart stands not so much in the multitude and variety of expressions as in the extent of the affection. Besides, if forms were unlawful, then neither might we sing psalms nor join in prayer with others, nor use the forms prescribed by God.

Our Father which art in heaven] Tertullian calls this prayer a breviary of the gospel, and compend of saving doctrine (*breviarium totius Evangelii, et salutaris doctrinæ compendium*). It is framed in form of the decalogue; the three former petitions respecting God, the three latter ourselves and others. Every word therein hath its weight. "Our," there is our charity; "Father," there is our faith; "in heaven," there is our hope. "Father" is taken sometimes personally, as in that of our Saviour, "My Father is greater than I;" sometimes essentially for the whole Deity, so here. Now that God is in heaven, is a notion that heathens also have by nature; and do therefore in distress lift up eyes and hands thitherward. And lest man should not look upward, God hath given to his eyes peculiar nerves, to pull them up towards his habitation, that he might "direct his prayer unto him, and look up," Psal. v. 3, that he might feelingly say with David, "Whom have I in heaven but thee?" "Unto thee I lift up mine eyes, O thou that dwellest in the heavens. Behold, as the eyes of servants look to the hand of their masters," &c., Psal. cxxiii. 1, 2. It is reported of Farellus, that he preached so powerfully, that he seemed to thunder, and prayed so

earnestly, that he seemed to carry his hearers with him up into heaven (*ut audientes in cœlum usque subveheret.* Melch. Adam. *in Vita.*) But how oft, alas, do graceless men approach God with their leaden lips; and indeed reproach him in their formal prayers with that appellation, "Our Father which art in heaven?" Those brain-sick disciples of Martin Steinbach of Selestad in Germany, who would needs mend magnificat (as they say), correct the Lord's prayer as not well composed, are not worth mentioning.

Hallowed be thy Name] i. e. "Honoured by thy Majesty." "According to thy name, O God, so is thy praise," Psal. xlviii. 10. Now God's name is "holy and reverend," Psal. cxi. 9; "great and terrible," Psal. xcix. 3; "wonderful and worthy," Psal. viii. 1; Jam. ii. 7; "high and honourable," Isa. xii. 4; "dreadful among the heathen," Mal. i. 14; and "exalted above all praise," Neh. ix. 5. His glory is as himself, eternally infinite, and so abideth, not capable of our addition or detraction. The sun would shine though all the world were blind, or did wilfully shut their eyes. Howbeit to try how we prize his glory, and how industrious we will be to promote it, God lets us know that he accounts himself, as it were, to receive a new being by those inward conceptions of his glory, and by those outward honours we do him; when we lift up his name as a standard, saying, "Jevovah Nissi, The Lord is my banner," Exod. xvii. 15; when we bear (נשא) it up aloft (as the word used in the third commandment, whereunto this petition answers, signifieth), as servants do their masters' badges upon their shoulders:[1] "Being confident" (with St Paul) "of this very thing, that in nothing we shall be ashamed" (whilst we hallow this holy God, Isa. v. 16), "but that with all boldness or freedom of speech, as always, so now, Christ shall be magnified in our bodies, whether it be by life or death," Phil. i. 20.

Ver. 10. *Thy kingdom come*] Thy kingdom of power and providence; but especially enlarge thy kingdom of grace, and hasten thy kingdom of glory. The Jews pray almost in every prayer, "Thy kingdom come," and that *Bimheroth, Bejamenu*, quickly, even in our days. But it is for an earthly kingdom; that which the apostles also so deeply dreamt of, that our Saviour had very much ado to dispossess them. For most absurdly and unseasonably many times they would ask him foolish questions that way, when he had been discoursing to them of the necessity of his own death, and of their bearing the cross. Yea, St John very wisely interrupts him, Mark ix. 34, 37, 38, one time among the rest, as weary of such sad matter, and laying hold on something our Saviour had said by the by, tells him a story of another business. They were besotted with an odd conceit of honours and offices to be distributed here among them, as once in David's and Solomon's reign. And what shall we think

---

[1] *Elevavit, evexit :* confer Isa. v. 26. *Elevabit vexillum ad gentes. Judæorum massam adhuc ita inficit fermentum Pharisæorum, ut Messiam, quem tantis hodie exposcunt ulula-* tibus, non ut redemptorem expectant a peccato, sed ex gentium temporali juo. D. Prid., Lect.

of their opinion, that not content to affirm that after the fall of Antichrist, the Jews shall have a glorious conversion, and the whole Church such a happy halcyon as never before; but also that the martyrs shall then have their first resurrection, and shall reign with Christ a thousand years? Rev. xx. 4. Piscator holdeth, they shall so reign in heaven. Alstedius not only saith they shall reign here on earth, but beginneth his millenary about the year of our Lord 1694. Let our hearts' desire and prayer to God for Israel be that they may be saved, Rom. x. 1. Let us also pity and pray for such poor souls in Asia and America as worship the devil; not inwardly only, for so too many do amongst us, but with an outward worship. And this we should the rather do, because divines think that when all Israel shall be called, and, as it were, "raised from the dead," Rom. xi. 15, 26, when those "two sticks shall be joined into one," Ezek. xxxvii. 16, then shall many of those deceived souls that never yet savingly heard of God have part and portion in the same resurrection.

Thy will be done] God's will must be done of thee, ere his kingdom can come to thee. If thou seek his kingdom, seek first his righteousness. If thou pray, "Thy kingdom come," pray also, "Thy will be done." Pray it and do it; for otherwise thou compassest God with lies, as Ephraim did, Hos. xi. 12. Now the will of God is two-fold, secret and revealed, whatever Siguardus blasphemeth to the contrary.[1] His revealed will again is four-fold: 1. His determining will concerning us, what shall become of us, Eph. i. 5; 2. His prescribing will, what he requires of us, Eph. i. 9; 3. His approving will, by the which he graciously accepts and tenderly regards those that come to him in faith and repentance, Matt. xviii. 14; 4. His disposing will, and this is the will of his providence, 1 Cor. i. 1; Rom. i. 10. Now we should resign ourselves over to his determining will, as the highest cause of all things; rest in his approving will, as our chiefest happiness; obey his prescribing will, as the absolutest and perfectest form of holiness; and be subject to his disposing will, being patient in all trials and troubles, because he did it, Psal. xxxix. 9. David hath this commendation, that he did all the wills of God (Θελήματα), Acts xiii. 22. And it is reported, saith Mr Bradford, that I shall be burned in Smithfield, and that very shortly. *Fiat voluntas Domini. Ecce ego, Domine, mitte me.* "The will, of the Lord be done," said those good souls in the Acts, when they saw that Paul was peremptory to go up, Acts xxi. 14. This third petition, "Thy will be done," &c., was the last text that ever Mr Beza handled, and thereupon died; and departed rather than deceased (*deficere potius quam desinere visus est.* Melch. Adam.), to do God's will more perfectly in heaven, as he had done to his power on earth. They that thus do and suffer the will of God, are his Hephzibah, Isa. lxii. 4.

And it should be our constant care so to apply ourselves thereunto, that God may take pleasure in us, as in men after his own heart, and say of us, as he did of Cyrus, He is the man of my will, that executeth all my counsel, Isa. xlvi. 11. This is to set the crown upon Christ's head, Cant. iii. 11. Yea, this is to set the crown upon our own heads, 2 Tim. iv. 8, 9.

In earth as it is in heaven] By those heavenly courtiers. The crowned saints have no rest (and yet no unrest), crying, "Holy, holy, holy," &c., Rev. iv. 8. They follow the Lamb wheresoever he goeth, with *Usquequo, Domine ?* "How long, Lord ?" &c., Rev. vi. 10. Which words also were Mr Calvin's *symbolum*, that he frequently sighed out, in the behalf of the distressed churches. As for the glorious angels, though they excel in strength, yet they do God's commandments, hearkening to the voice of his word, Psal. ciii. 20. They rejoice more in their names of service than of honour, and ever stand before the face of our heavenly Father, as waiting a command for our good, Matt. xviii. 10 ; and so willing of their way that Gabriel is said to have come to comfort Daniel with weariness of flight, Dan. ix. 21. They do the will of God: 1. Cheerfully; whence they are said to have wings, six wings a-piece, Isa. vi. 2. 2. Humbly; therefore with two they cover their faces. 3. Faithfully, without partiality; with two they covered or harnessed their feet. 4. Speedily and zealously; with two they fly abroad the world upon God's errand, and for the good of them that shall be saved, Heb. i. 14, burning, and being all on a light fire, with infinite love to God and his saints, their fellow-servants, Rev. xxii. 9, whence they are called seraphims or burning creatures. 5. Constantly; Jacob saw them ascending, to contemplate and praise God, and to minister unto him, Dan. vii. 10. He saw them also descending, to dispense God's benefits and to execute his judgments, Rev. xv. 6. This they do, 1. Justly; whence they are said (there) to be clothed in pure white linen. 2. Diligently and constantly; therefore they have their breast girded. 3. Purely, and with faith, in receiving God's commandments : therefore are they said to have golden girdles. Go ye now, and do likewise ; otherwise ye may be as angels, for gifts and good parts, and yet have your part with the devil and his black angels.

Ver. 11. *Give us this day*] We have not a bit of bread of our own earning, but must get our living by begging. Peter himself was to obtain his very bread by humble petition, how much more his salvation ? He that shall go to God, as the prodigal did, with, " Give me the portion that pertaineth to me," shall receive the wages of sin, which is eternal death, Rom. vi. 23. God " giveth meat in abundance," saith Elihu, Job xxxvi. 31. " That thou givest they gather," saith David, Psal. civ. 28. And again, " Thou givest them their meat in due season." Now what more free than gift ?

---

[1] *Sunt qui voluntatis divinæ distinctionem in revelatam et arcanam, quasi ipsius diaboli crepitum blasphemare audent.* Sic Siguardin, admon. Christ.

Beggars also pay no debts, but acknowledge their insufficiency, and speak supplications in a low language, as broken men (*non sum solvendo*) : so must we. Oh lie daily begging at the beautiful gate of heaven : look intently upon God, as he did, Acts iii., upon Peter and John, expecting to receive something. And because beggars must be no choosers, ask, as our Saviour here directs, (1.) for quality, bread only, not manchets or juncates, but downright household bread[1] (as the word imports), "the bread of carefulness or sorrows," Psal. cxxvii. 2, which the singing Psalms interpret "brown bread." Our Saviour gave thanks for barley bread ; and his disciples were glad to make a sabbath day's dinner of a few ears of corn rubbed between their fingers. A very philosopher could say, He that can feed upon green herbs need not please Dionysius, need not flatter any man. And Epicurus himself would not doubt to content himself as well as he that hath most, might he but have a morsel of coarse meat and a draught of cold water.[2] The Israelites had soon enough of their quails : they had quails with a vengeance, because manna would not content them. They died with the meat in their mouths: and by a hasty testament, bequeathed a new name to the place of their burial, Kibroth-hattaavah, the graves of lust : *Cibus et potus sunt divitiæ Christianorum*, saith Jerome : Meat and drink are the Christian man's riches. Bread and cheese (saith another) with the gospel is good cheer. Nature is content with a little, grace with less, saith a third. A godly man as he asketh but for bread, so (2) for the quantity, but for daily bread, the bread of the day for the day, enough to bring him home with Jacob, so much only as will bear his charges, till he return again to his father's house.[3] He passeth through the world, as Israel through the wilderness, content with his omer by the day, with his statute-measure, with his Father's allowance. As he journeyeth to the promised land, he bespeaks the world, as Israel did Edom through whose country they would have passed : "Let me pass through thy land : we will not turn aside into the fields nor vineyards ; neither will we drink of the water of thy wells ; we will go by the king's highway, until we be past thy country," Numb. xxi. 21, 22. And as a traveller when he cometh to his inn, if he can get a better room or lodging, he will ; but if not, he is content, for he considereth it is but for a night. So the Christian pilgrim, if God send him in a plentiful estate, he gladly makes use of it ; but if otherwise, he can live with a little : and if his means be not to his mind, he can bring his mind to his means, and live upon reversions.[4] Give him but necessaries, he stands not upon superfluities. Give him but daily bread, that is, bread for necessity, saith the Syriac, so much as will hold life and soul together, saith Brentius. Sufficient to uphold and sustain nature, saith Beza (with the Greek scholiast), that wherewith our nature and constitution may be content, and he is well apaid and satisfied :[5] he cries out with Jacob, "I have enough ;" and with David, "The lines are fallen unto me in a fair place." A little of the creature will serve turn to carry him through his pilgrimage ; in his Father's house he knows is bread enough, Luke xvi. And on the hope of that he goes on as merrily, and feeds as sweetly, as Samson did of his honey-comb, or Hunniades when he supped with the shepherds.

This day] Or, as St Luke hath it, by the day :[6] for who is sure of to-morrow ? May not his soul this night be taken from him ? We are ἐφημερόβιοι, as Diogenes was wont to say of himself :[7] and should (as Quintillian speaketh of the birds and beasts) *in diem vivere*, taking no further thought than for the present sustenance. The Turks never build anything sumptuously for their own private use, but contenting themselves with their simple cottages, how mean so ever, commonly say, that they be good enough for the time of their short pilgrimage.

Ver. 12. *And forgive us our debts*, &c.] Loose us (saith the original) and let us go free, (ἄφες) : for unpardoned sinners are in the bond of iniquity, as Simon Magus, Acts viii. 23 ; and remission is called a relaxation (πάρεσις), Rom. iii. 25. The guilt of sin is an obligation, binding us over to condign punishment. God hath against us, Matt. v. 23, even our handwriting which is contrary to us, Col. ii. 14. This David confessed against himself, Psal. xxxii. 5, and upon his prayer obtained pardon. He only acknowledged the debt, and God crossed the book. God crossed the black lines of his sins with the red lines of his Son's blood. Thou forgavest me, saith David, the iniquity of my sin ; the malignity of it, the worst thing that was in it. For this shall every one that is godly pray unto thee, by mine example, and obtain like favour. For our God is a sin-pardoning God, Neh. ix. 31, none like him, Micah vii. 18. He forgiveth sin naturally, Exod. xxxiv. 6; abundantly, Isa. lv. 7; constantly, Job i. 27. He doth take away the sins of the world. It is a perpetual act of his, as the sun doth shine, as the spring doth run, Zech. xiii. 1. The eye is not weary of seeing, nor the ear of hearing, Eccl. i. 8; no more is God of showing mercy. All sins, yea, and blasphemies, shall be forgiven to the sons of men, saith our Saviour, Matt. xii. 31. As the sea covers not only small sands but huge rocks, Christ is the propitiation

---

[1] Τροφὴν, καὶ οὐ τρυφήν. Horat. *Opponit panem libis et placentis*, 1 Ep. 10.

[2] *Epicurus dicebat se cum Jove etiam paratum esse de felicitate certare, si aquam haberet et offam.*

[3] *Ale me pane præscripti vel demensi mei*, Prov. xxx. 8.

[4] *Scite et breviter.* Clem. Alex. Ὀλιγοδεὴς ὁ σπουδαῖος, Socrates ab Archelao ad facultates ampliores accersitus, εἰ μὴ ἱκανα, inquit, τὰ ὄντα ἐμοὶ ἀλλ᾽ ἐγὼ τοιούτοις ἱκανὸς καὶ οὕτω κακεῖνα ἐμοί. Arian. *ap. Stobæum.*

[5] *Panem necessitatis.* Syr. *Vitæ conservativum.* Brent. *In Annotat. Eum quo contenta esse possit natura et constitutio nostra.* Camer.

[6] Ἐπιούσιον, τοῦτ᾽ ἐστὶν ἐπὶ τὴν οὐσίαν ἐπαρκοῦντα καὶ ἁρμαζονται. Suid. καθ᾽ ἡμέραν, Luke xi. 3 ; xii. 20.

[7] *Dioque erat* ἀνέστιος, ἄπολις, ἄπατρις, ἀχρήματος, ἄστατος, ἐφημερόβιος.

or covering for our sins, are they how many and how great soever, as was sweetly shadowed of old by the ark covering the law, the mercy-seat covering the ark, and the cherubims over them, both covering one another. In allusion whereunto, " Blessed," saith David, " is the man whose transgression is forgiven, whose sin is covered. Blessed is the man to whom the Lord imputeth not sin."[1] A metaphor from merchants, who when they will forgive a debt, do not put it into the reckoning, and so do not impute it. Sin casteth men deep into debt and arrearages with God. It is called a debt of ten thousand talents, Matt. xviii. 24; Luke vii. 47. It casteth a man into a comfortless condition, makes him hide his face for shame, as Adam, causeth a continual sound of fear in his ears; so that he thinks every bush a bailiff, every shrub a sergeant, &c. An evil conscience hunts him, follows him up and down so close, like a blood-hound, hot-foot, that he sometimes serves himself, as that Jesuit in Lancashire, followed by one that had found his glove, with a desire to restore it to him; but pursued inwardly with a guilty conscience, leaps over a hedge, plunges into a marl-pit behind it unseen and unthought of, wherein he was drowned. This and worse is the case of a poor bankrupt sinner, he is caught and clapt up in prison, laid fast in bonds and chains of darkness; and " what can he give in exchange for his soul ? " Matt. xvi. 26. There is no feeing the sergeant, nor shifting off the arrest: sooner or later conscience will serve him with a writ to appear and answer at the great assizes before God's tribunal. Neither doth ignorance excuse him : for debt is debt, whether a man know of it or not, and will light so much the more heavily, by how much the execution is done upon him more unexpectedly. Now there is no way in the world of discharging this debt, but by the satisfaction of Christ our surety, who hath paid the utmost farthing for his elect. This good Samaritan hath discharged all for us; and God for Christ's sake accounts of our sins as if they had never been committed. He binds them in a bundle, seals them up as in a bag, Dan. ix. 24, and casteth them behind him, as old evidences, into the bottom of the sea, and all because mercy pleaseth him, Micah vii. 19. This he doth at first conversion, when he justifieth a sinner, Rom. iii. And whereas in many things we sin all, Jam. iii. 2, we have a pardon of courses for those weaknesses that are of daily incursion, included in that general pardon, which we have upon our general repentance. Only he looketh we should sue out our pardon by daily prayer for it. Entreat we God to remit our debts; and sith he must be satisfied, to take it out of his Son's coffers who is become surety for us; and saith unto his Father, in effect, as Paul to Philemon : If this Onesimus of mine hath " wronged thee, or oweth thee ought, put that on mine account," Philem. 18, 19, so long as he prays in my name for daily pardon. But whether shall we think less excus-

able, those Anabaptists[2] in Germany that omit this petition, " Forgive us our trespasses " (as conceiving themselves to be pure, and to have no more need of remission of sins) ; or those Atheists in father Latimer's days, who being not willing to forgive their enemies, would not say their *Pater Noster* at all. See the Note on verse 15.

As we forgive our debtors] Not as if God should therefore forgive us, because we forgive others ; but this is the argument. We do and can, by God's grace, forgive them, therefore God can and will much more forgive us ; sith all our goodness is but a spark of his flame, a drop of his ocean. No article of our creed is so much opposed by Satan as that of the forgiveness of sin by Christ's merits, which is the very soul of a church and the life of a good soul. All the former articles of the creed are perfected in this, and all the following articles are effects of this. Now one main means of settling us in the sound assurance of the pardon of our own debts, is, if we can forgive our debtors. He that can put away all purpose of revenge, and freely forgive his brother, may with boldness ask and expect forgiveness at God's hands. For mercy rejoiceth against judgment, James ii. 13 ; and our love to others is but a reflex of God's love to us. It is a fruit of justifying faith, Luke xvii. 4, 5. It is also a sweet seal of our election, Col. iii. 12, 13, and an effectual expression of our thankfulness. For hereby our unrighteousness shall commend the righteousness of God, Rom. iii. 5, both in respect of his admirable goodness in pardoning so great sins, and our thankful acknowledging of that grace in walking worthy of it.

Now if any ask, why the petition for pardon of sin is set after that for daily bread ? It is answered,

1. In the four former petitions we pray for good things, in the two latter we pray against evil.

2. Our Saviour condescends herein to our infirmity, who can sooner trust God for pardon than provision, for a crown than a crust.

3. That by an argument from the less to the greater we may the more boldly beg spirituals.

Ver. 13. *And lead us not into temptation*] Here we beg sanctification, as in the former petition, justification ; and are taught after forgiveness of sins, to look for temptations, and to pray against them. Temptations are either of probation (and so God tempts men) or of perdition, and so the devil. Both Abraham's great temptations began with one strain, לֶךְ־לְךָ, Get thee gone, Gen. xii. 1; xxii. 2. Here God led Abraham into temptation, but he delivered him from evil; yea, he tempted him and proved him, to do him good in his latter end, Deut. viii. 6. His usual way is to bring us to heaven by hell-gates, to draw light out of darkness, good out of evil. As the skilful apothecary maketh of a poisonful viper, a wholesome treacle ; as the

---

[1] ἱλασμὸς, 1 John ii. 2. כֹּפֶר Exod. xxv. 17. ἐπίθεμα, Sept. *Tectorium, operculum,* Psal. xxxii. 1, 2.

[2] Bullinger, cont. Anabapt. lib. i. cap. 1.

cunning artificer with a crooked unsightly tool, frameth a straight and beautiful piece of work; as the Egyptian birds are said to pick wholesome food out of the serpent's eggs; or as the Athenian magistrates by giving to malefactors hemlock (a poisonous herb) preserved the commonwealth. The devil tempts either by way of seducement, James i. 15, or grievance, 2 Cor. xii. 7. In the former he excites our concupiscence, rubs the firebrand, and makes it send forth many sparkles, carries us away by some pleasing object, as the fish by the bait. Yet hath he only a persuading sleight, not an enforcing might : our own concupiscence carrieth the greatest stroke. In the latter (those temptations of buffeting or grievance, horrid and hideous thoughts of atheism, idolatry, blasphemy, self-murder, &c.) himself, for most part, is the sole doer, to trouble us in our Christian course, and make us run heavily toward heaven. The Russians are so malicious one toward another, that you shall have a man hide some of his own goods in his house whom he hateth, and then accuse him for the stealth of them. Such is the devil's dealing oft-times with God's dearest children. He darts into their hearts his detestable injections, and then would persuade them that they are accessory to the act. Here our victory is, not to give place to the devil, but to resist steadfast in the faith : which that we may, pray we always "with all prayer and supplication," Eph. vi. 18, pray as our Saviour did, " Father, keep them from the evil," or from wickedness, John xvii. 15. Pray as our Saviour bids, "Lead us not," &c., that is, either keep us from occasions of sin, or carry us over them. Either preserve us from falling into sin, or help us to rise out of sin by repentance : grant us to be either innocent or pertinent. Deliver us from those devoratory evils (as Tertullian calleth them), such sins as might frustrate perseverance, 2 Thess. iii. 3 ; and from that evil or wicked one, that he touch us not, 1 John v. 18, that is, *tactu qualitativo* (as Cajetan expounds it), with a deadly touch, so as to alter us from our gracious disposition. Howbeit, sin and temptation come both under one name in this petition, to warn us and teach us that we can no further shun sin than we do temptation thereunto.

For thine is the kingdom] That is, all sovereignty is originally and transcendently invested in thee. Other kings are but thy servants and feudatories, by thee they reign, Prov. viii. 15, and of thee they receive their power, Rom. xiii. 1. Where then will they appear, that say to the king, *Apostata*, Job xxxiv. 18, that send messages after him, saying, " We will not have this man to reign over us," Luke xix. 14 ; that bespeak him, as that Hebrew did Moses, " Who made thee a prince and a judge amongst us ?" Exod. ii. 14 ; should they not rather send a lamb to this ruler of the earth ? Isa. xvi. 1, and bring a present to fear ? Psal. lxxvi. 11 ; should they not submit to his sceptre and confess his sovereignty ?

And the power] Some have kingdoms, that yet want power to help their subjects : as that king of Israel that answered her that had sodden her child, in that sharp famine of Samaria, where an ass's head was worth four pounds : " If the Lord do not help, whence shall I help ? " 2 Kings vi. 27. But the King of heaven is never at such a nonplus : he can do whatsoever he will ; and he will do whatsoever is meet to be done, for the good of his servants and suppliants. Peter wanted power to deliver Christ, Pilate wanted will, but God wants neither : what a comfort is that ! Let us rest on his mighty arm, and cast the labouring Church into his everlasting arms, Deut. xxxiii. 27. He is " able to do more than we can ask or think," Eph. iii. 20, and will not fail to keep that which we have committed unto him against that day, 2 Tim. i. 14.

And the glory] To wit, of granting our requests. Praises will follow upon prayers obtained, Psal. l. 15 ; what a man wins by prayer he will wear with thankfulness. Now "whoso offereth praise, he glorifieth me," saith God, Psal. l. 23 : and the Gentiles did not glorify God, neither were thankful, Rom. i. 21, 28. But the 24 elders ascribe unto him glory and honour, Rev. iv. 11. And this is a most powerful argument in prayer, as are also the two former. And it pleaseth God well to hear his children reason it out with him lustily, as Jacob did, and the woman of Canaan, Gen. xxxii. 9—12 ; Matt. xv. 25, 28. Because by showing such reasons of their requests, as our Saviour here directs us, they show proof of their knowledge, faith, confidence, &c. And besides they do much confirm their own faith and stir up good affections in prayer.

Amen] This Hebrew word, that remaineth untranslated in most languages, is either prefixed or preposed to a sentence, and so it is a note of certain and earnest asseveration ; or else it is affixed, and opposed, and so it is a note either of assent or assurance.[1] Of assent ; and that either of the understanding to the truth of that that is uttered, as in the end of the Creed and four Gospels ; or of the will and affections, for the obtaining of our petitions, 1 Cor. xiv. 16, how shall he say Amen at thy giving of thanks ? Of assurance next, as in this place and many others. It is the voice of one that believeth and expecteth that he shall have his prayers granted. It is as much as so be it, yea, so it shall be.

Ver. 14. *For if ye forgive men their trespasses*] Our Saviour resumeth, and inculcateth the fifth petition with a repetition ; because upon charity (which is chiefly seen in giving and forgiving) hangeth, after a sort, the restful success of all our suits, 2 Tim. ii. 8. Malice is a leaven that swells the heart and sours the sacrifice, 1 Cor. v. 7, 8. Out with it, therefore, that we may keep the feast or holy-day (Ἑορτάζωμεν) ; that we may (as we ought to do)

---

[1] It is used in all languages to betoken unity of faith and spirit. Ainsworth. *Christus Amen utitur quinquagies*. Gerard.

keep a constant jubilee, *nexus solvendo, et noxus remittendo.* This flesh and blood will not easily yield to. But we are not debtors to the flesh, Rom. viii. 12; we owe it nothing, but the blue eye that St Paul gave it, 1 Cor. ix. 27, ὑπωπιάζω. When Peter heard that he might not recompense to any evil for evil, but must studiously seek his conversion and salvation, "Lord," saith he, "how oft shall my brother sin against me, and I forgive him? till seven times?" this he thought a mighty deal; a very high pitch of perfection. Our Saviour tells him, till seventy times seven times, that is, infinitely, and without stint: yet he alludes to Peter's seven, and, as it were, illudes it, and his rashness in setting bounds to this duty and prescribing how oft to him that was the wisdom of the Father.

This is when my brother returneth, and saith, It repents me. But what if he do not?

In forgiving an offender, say divines, there are three things: 1. The letting fall all wrath and desire of revenge. 2. A solemn profession of forgiveness. 3. Re-acceptance into former familiarity. The first must be done however. For the second, if he say, I repent, I must say, I remit, Luke xviii. To the third a man is bound till satisfaction be given.

Your heavenly Father will also forgive you] Yet is not our forgiving men the cause of his forgiving us, but a necessary antecedent. The cause is only the free mercy of God in Christ. He puts away our iniquities for his own sake, Isa. xliii. 25. Nevertheless, forasmuch as he hath made us this promise here, our forgiving others (saith learned Beza) seemeth to have the nature of an intervenient cause, a cause, *sine qua non*, of his forgiving us. (Annot. in Luke xi. 4.)

Ver. 15. *But if ye will not, &c.*] This is a matter much to be observed, therefore so often inculcated. Judgment without mercy shall be to them that show no mercy, Jam. ii. 13. There is but a hair's-breadth betwixt him and hell that hath not his sins pardoned in heaven. Such is the case of every one that doth not from his heart forgive his offending brother, Matt. xviii. 35, or that saith, I will forgive the fault, but not forget the matter, or affect the person. Men must forbear one another and forgive one another, as Christ forgave them; and that if any man have a quarrel (μομφὴν) against any, Col. iii. 13, for else what thanks is it? The glory of a man is to pass by an infirmity, Prov. xix. 11. It is more comfortable to love a friend, but more honourable to love an enemy. If thou reserve in thy mind any piece of the wrong, thou provokest and daily prayest God to reserve for thee a piece of his wrath; which burneth as low as the nethermost hell, Deut. xxxii. 22. Neither will it help any, to do as Latimer reporteth of some in his days, who being not willing to forgive their enemies, would not say their *Pater Noster* at all: but instead thereof, took our Lady's Psalter in hand;

because they were persuaded that by that they might obtain forgiveness of their sins of favour, without putting in of so hard a condition as the forgiveness of their enemies into the bargain.

Neither will your Father forgive your trespasses] And if he do not, who can give pardon or peace, saith he in Job? The Rhemists talk much of one that could remove mountains; God only can remove those mountains of guilt that lie upon the soul. Men may forgive the trespass; God only the transgression. "Against thee, thee only, have I sinned," saith David, Psal. li. 4: and, "to the Lord our God belongeth mercies and forgivenesses," saith Daniel, Dan. ix. 9. Ministers remit sins ministerially, as Nathan did; God only authoritatively, and by his own power. "If the Son set us free, we are free indeed. Who shall lay anything to the charge of God's pardoned ones? It is God that justifieth;" or, as St Austin readeth the words, interrogatively, "shall God that justifieth?" No, verily; that were to do and undo: he keepeth no back-reckonings. Fear not therefore, though the devil or his imps, or our own misgiving hearts, condemn us: as the prisoner careth not though the gaoler or his fellow-prisoners condemn him, so long as the judge acquitteth him.

Ver. 16. *Moreover, when ye fast*] Fast then they must, yea, even after the Lord's ascension, when God's grace and Spirit was poured upon them in all abundance, Luke v. 35. This exercise hath still the warrant and weight of a duty, as well from precepts as examples of both Testaments.[1] And he that blamed the Pharisees here for fasting amiss, will much more blame those that fast not at all. The Israelites (besides other occasional) had their annual fast appointed them by God, Lev. xxiii. 27. It was called a day of expiations or atonements, in the plural; because of their many and sundry sins they were then to bewail and get pardon for. God had appointed them sundry sacrifices for several sins. But forasmuch as it might not be safe to confess some sins to the priest (as those that might bring them, by the law, in danger of death), of his grace he vouchsafed them this yearly fast, for expiation of their secret sins, and making their peace with their Maker, by a general humiliation. Now, albeit the circumstance of time be abolished, the equity of the duty abideth, and tieth us no less (if not more) than it did the Jews. Heathen Nineveh practised it: so did, in their superstitious way, the Egyptian priests, the Persian magi, Indian wizards, Priamus in Homer, &c. The Turks at this day have their solemn fasts (as before the fatal assault of Constantinople), wherein they will not so much as taste a cup of water, or wash their mouths with water all the day long, before the stars appear in the sky: which maketh their fasts (especially in the summer, when the days be long and hot) to be unto them very tedious. In the year of grace 1030 there arose a sect of fasters, that affirmed that

---

[1] Joel ii. 12; Isa. xxii. 12; Matt. ix. 14, 15; Acts xiii. 3; 1 Cor. vii. 5.

to fast on Saturdays with bread and water (as they called it) would suffice to the remission of all sins; so that men bound themselves to it by oath.[1] And many French bishops voted with them. But Gerardus Episcopus Cameracensis withstood and abandoned them. So great ignorance was there, even then, of the merits of Christ among the governors of the Church. The papists slander us, that we count fasting no duty, but only a moral temperance, a fasting from sin, a matter of mere policy: and outbrave us, as much as the Pharisees did the disciples with their often fasting. But, as we cannot but find fault with their fasts, in that, first, they set and appoint certain fasting days howsoever, to be observed upon pain of damnation, be the times clear or cloudy, &c. Secondly, they fast from certain meats only, not all; which is a mere mock-fast, and a doctrine of devils, 1 Tim. iv. 3. Thirdly, they make it a service of God, yet consecrate it to the saints. Fourthly, they make shameful sale of it. Fifthly, they ascribe (as those older heretics) merit unto it, even to the mere outward abstinence, as these Pharisees did, and those hypocrites in Isaiah (lviii. 3).[2] Now as we cannot but condemn their superstition, so neither is our forlorn oscitancy and dullness to this duty to be excused. God hath given us, alate especially, many gracious opportunities of public humiliations, more, I think, than ever before, since the Reformation. But, alas, how do many fast, at such times, for fashion, fear of law, or of mere form; so that they had need to send, as the prophet speaketh, for mourning women, that by their cunning they may be taught to mourn, Jer. ix. 17. And for private fasting, whether domestical with a man's family, Zech. xii. 12; 1 Cor. vii. 5; Acts x. 30; or personal by himself, as here, Matt. vi. 17; we may seem to have dealt with it, as the Romans with the Tarquins; they banished all of that name for Superbus' sake. And as the Nicopolites are said so to have hated the braying of an ass, that for that cause they would not endure the sound of a trumpet: so many are departed so far from Popish fasts, that they fast not at all; and so open the mouths of the adversaries. But acquaint thyself with this duty, thou that wouldst be acquainted with God. It is a foretaste of eternal life, when in holy practices we taste the sweetness of that heavenly manna, this angels' food, those soul-fatting viands, that makes us for a time to forbear our appointed food. It is a help to the understanding of heavenly mysteries, as Daniel found it (ix. 20). It fits us for conversion, Joel ii. 12, and furthers it, Acts ix. 9. Hence it is called a day of humiliation, or of humbling the soul, Lev. xvi.

because God usually by that ordinance gives an humble heart, to the which he hath promised both grace, 1 Pet. v. 5, and glory, Prov. xv. 33. It ferrets out corruption, and is to the soul as washing to a room, which is more than sweeping; or as scouring to the vessel, which is more than ordinary washing. It subdues rebel-flesh, which with fulness of bread will wax wanton, as Sodom, Jeshurun, Ephraim.[3] It testifies true repentance, by this holy revenge, 2 Cor. vii. 11, whiles we thus amerce and punish ourselves, by a voluntary foregoing of the comforts and commodities of life, as altogether unworthy, Psal. xxxv. 13. What shall I say more? Hereby we are daily drawn to more obedience and love to God, faith in him, and communion with him; a more holy frame of soul and habit of heavenly-mindedness. Whence our Saviour, after this direction for fasting, immediately subjoins that of laying up for ourselves treasure in heaven, ver. 19, 20. And, lastly, our prayers shall be hereby edged, winged, and made to soar aloft, which before flagged, fainted, and, as it were, grovelled on the ground. Therefore our Saviour, here, next after matter of prayer, adds this of fasting, which is a necessary adjunct of prayer (that which is extraordinary especially), as that which very much fits the heart for prayer and the severe practice of repentance.[4] Hence it is that elsewhere these two, fasting and prayer, go coupled, for most part, as Luke ii. 37; Matt. xvii. 21; 1 Cor. vii. 5, &c. A full belly neither studies nor prays willingly. Fasting inflames prayer, and prayer sanctifies fasting; especially when we fast and weep, Joel ii. 13, fast and watch, watch and pray, and take heed to both, Mark xiii. 33.

Be not as the hypocrites] For they fast not to God, Zech. vii. 5, 11, 12, but to themselves; they pine the body, but pamper the flesh; they hang down their heads, Isa. lviii. 5, but their hearts stand bolt upright within them.[5] Their fasting is either superstitious or secure; whiles they rest in the work done, or with opinion of merit; whereas the kingdom of heaven is not in meat and drink, Rom. xiv. 17. And whether we eat or eat not, we are neither the more nor the less accepted of God, 1 Cor. viii. 8; they fast for strife and debate, and to make their voices to be heard on high, Isa. lviii. 4: whereas secrecy in this duty is the best argument of sincerity. They "loose not the bands of wickedness," nor break off their sins by repentance: therefore God regards not (which they repine at), but rejects their confidence, and answers them according to the idols of their hearts. "When they fast," saith he, "I will not hear their cry," Jer. xiv. 12, they are not a button the better for all they can do.

[1] *Ex illa Synodica conclusione, feriâ sextâ jejunare constituerat, secta illa jejunantium originem suam habuisse videatur.* Func.

[2] *Cave, ne si jejunare cœperis, te putes esse sanctum: hæc enim virtutis adjumentum est, non perfectio sanctitatis,* &c. Jerome ad Celant.

[3] 1 Cor. ix. 27; Ezek. xvi.; Deut. xxxii. 15; Isa. xxviii. 1, 2. *Saturitas parit ferociam.*

[4] *Jejunium orationem roborat: oratio jejunium sanctificat.* Bern. in Quadrages., ser., 4.

[5] *Quid prodest tenuari abstinentia corpus, si animus intumescat superbia?* Jerome.

Displeasing service proves a double dishonour (*simulata sanctitas duplex iniquitas*); their outsideness is an utter abomination: they present the great King with an empty cask, with a heartless sacrifice, with a bare carcase of religion, as the poets feign of Prometheus.

Of a sad countenance] Make not a sour face, look not grim and ghastly, as the word signifieth;[1] so that one would be afraid to look on them, they do so disfigure their faces, so wanze and wither their countenances, so deform and (as St Jerome rendereth it) demolish their natural complexions; pining themselves to make their faces pale and meagre, that they may be noted and noticed for great fasters.[2] Such a one was that none-such Ahab, and those spungy bulrushes, Isa. lviii. 5, those hollow hypocrites, Jer. xiv. 12, that proud patriarch of Constantinople, that first affected the style of universal bishop; and is therefore pointed at by Gregory the Great, as the forerunner of Antichrist: yet by his frequent fasting, this proud man merited to be surnamed Johannes Nesteutes, John the faster. Such pains men will put themselves to for a name, so far they will trouble themselves to go to hell with credit. The Jesuits had set forth a psalter, a little before the powder-plot should have been acted, for the good success of a wicked counter-parliament. And to increase the iniquity, with wicked Jezebel, they would colour it with a fast: yea, with blasphemous Rabshakeh, they would by their hypocritical practices bear the world in hand, that they came not up against us without the Lord.

That they may appear unto men to fast] There is a great deal of seemingness, and much counterfeit grace abroad. The sorcerers seemed to do as much as Moses, the Pharisees to do more, this way, than the disciples. But bodily exercise profiteth little. Somewhat it may get at God's hands, as Ahab, for a temporary repentance, had a temporal deliverance; such is God's munificence, he is rich in mercy to all that do him any duty. But if the leaves of this exercise be so medicinable, what is the fruit? If the shadow thereof be so sovereign, what the substance? If the shell so profitable, what the kernel? Oh, let us rather seek to be good than seem to be so:[3] lest the Lord say of our outward shows, as Jacob said of Joseph's coat, "The coat is the coat of my son, some evil beast hath devoured him," Gen. xxxvii. 33. So the outward form of their fasting, praying, practising, is the form of my sons and daughters, but some evil spirit hath devoured them, that use it in hypocrisy. Lest men also say unto such, as John Capocius did to Pope Innocent III.,

preaching peace and sowing discord; "You speak like a God, but do like a devil."[4] You are fair professors, but foul sinners. And when the filthy sinner goes damned to hell, what shall become of the seeming saint? As the clown said to the Bishop of Cullen praying in the church like a bishop, but as he was duke, going guarded like a tyrant, "Whither thinkest thou the bishop shall go, when the duke shall be damned?"

They have their reward] All they looked after, and all they are to look for. The eagle, though she fly high, yet hath an eye to the prey below all the while. So hath the hypocrite to profit, credit, or some other base respects, and let him take it, saith our Saviour. *Non equidem invideo, miror magis*: Breath they have for breath; much good do them with it.

Ver. 17. *But thou, when thou fastest, anoint thine head*, &c.] Not but that a man is bound at such a time to abridge himself of the comforts and delights of life, whence it is called a day of restraint, Joel ii. 15, and of afflicting the soul.[5] The Ninevites sat in sackcloth, as unworthy of any covering. Others put ashes on their heads, in token that they deserved to be as far under as now they were above ground. David lay on the earth, 2 Sam. xii. 16. Daniel laid aside all delights of sense, as music, mirth, perfumes, ointments, &c. Our Saviour fasted to the humbling of his soul, Psal. xxxv. 13, weakening of his knees, Psal. lxix. 10, macerating and enfeebling of his body, Psal. cix. 24. And when upon the cross they offered him wine mingled with myrrh, to stupefy him and make him less sensible of his pain, he received it not, Mark xv. 23. To teach us (saith a learned interpreter) in our extraordinary humiliations for our sins, to forbear all such refreshments as might hinder the course of our just griefs. "Let your laughter be turned into mourning, and your joy into heaviness," Jam. iv. 9, such a heaviness as may be seen in the countenance, as the word importeth.[6] But when our Saviour biddeth anoint the head, at such a time, and wash the face, it is, as he expounds himself, "that we may not appear to men to fast:" in a private fast, eschewing wholly the show: in a public, not performing to the show, or to this end, that we may be seen.

Ver. 18. *That thou appear not unto men to fast*, &c.] Hypocrites fitly resemble the glow-worm, which seems to have both light and heat; but touch it, and it hath neither indeed. In the history of the world encompassed by Sir Francis Drake, it is recorded that in a certain island to the southward of Celebes, among the trees, night

---

[1] σκύθρωποι. *Demissis oculis, et subductis superciliis tetrici.* Chemnit.

[2] ἀφανίζουσι. *Christus alludit ad larvas, quibus Mimi veluti in theatrum prodibant, ut cum alias essent intus festine ridiculi, repræsentarent vultum mœstum.* Chemnit.

[3] *Ne appetat quisquam ultra videri quam est, ut possit ultra esse quam videtur.* Greg.

[4] *Verba tua Dei plane sunt, facta vero diaboli videntur.*

[5] *Vox Hebraica* Tsom, *significat affligere : unde* Aben Ezra *ait, ubicunque in scripturis afflictio animæ invenitur, ibi intelligitur jejunium. Græci dicunt* νηστείαν *a* νὴ *particula privante, et* στένομαι *quod est validum et firmum esse.* Pet. Mart. *Alii a* νὴ *et* ἐσθίειν, *cibum non comedere.*

[6] κατήφεια. *Tristitia cum vultus demissione.* Budæus. Ἀπὸ τοῦ κάτω φάη βάλλειν. *Ne te quæsiveris extra.*

by night did show themselves an infinite swarm of fiery-seeming worms, flying in the air, whose bodies, no bigger than an ordinary fly, did make a show, and give such light, as if every twig on every tree had been a lighted candle, or as if that place had been the starry sphere. This was but a semblance, but an appearance: no more is that of hypocrites, but a flaunt, but a flourish. A sincere man is like a crystal-glass with a light in the midst, which appeareth through every part thereof, so as that truth within breaketh out in every parcel of his life. There is in his obedience to God, 1. A universality, he doth every as well as any part and point of God's revealed will, so far as he knows it. 2. A uniformity, without prejudice or partiality (κατὰ πρόσκλισιν), 1 Tim. v. 21, without tilting the balance on one side. Inequality of the legs causeth halting, and an unequal pulse argues bodily distemper; so doth an unsuitable carriage an unsound soul, Psal. cxix. 104, 128; Matt. xxiii. 23. 3. Ubiquity: he is the same at home as abroad; in the closet as in the congregation; and minds secret as well as open holiness. Joseph was one and the same in his master's house, in the prison, and at court; no changeling or chameleon, not like the planet Mercury, that is good in conjunction with good, and bad with bad. The godly man's faith is unfeigned, 1 Tim. i. 5; his love cordial, 1 John iii. 18; his wisdom undissembled (ἀνυπόκριτος), Jam. iii. 17; his repentance a rending of the heart, Joel ii. 12; his fasting, and afflicting of the soul with voluntary sorrows, till his heart be as sore within him as the Shechemites' bodies were the third day after circumcision, Lev. xvi. 31, and xxiii. 37. He truly aims at pleasing God, and not at by-respects. This is truth in the inwards, Psal. li. 6; this is that "sincerity and truth," 1 Cor. v. 8; that simplicity and godly sincerity, 2 Cor. i. 12. A dainty word: it is a metaphor, saith one, from such things as are tried by being held up against the beams of the sun (as chapmen do in the choice of their wares) to see what faults or flaws are in them. It is properly used, saith Bp Andrews, of uncounterfeit wares, such as we may κρίνειν ἐν εἴλῃ, bring forth, and show them in the sun. And as a godly man is sincere, without wax or gross matter, as he is unmingled and true of heart, so he doeth truth, John iii. 21; he will not lie, Isa. lxiii. 9; that great real lie especially.[1] Hypocrites in doing good, they do lies, by their delusion, as gross hypocrites; by their collusion, as close hypocrites. Thus Ephraim compassed God with lies, Hos. xi. 12. His knowledge was but a form, his godliness a figure, Rom. ii. 20; 2 Tim. iii. 5; his zeal a flash, all he did, a semblance: as these Pharisees only appeared to fast and do other duties. But every fowl that hath a seemly feather hath not the sweetest flesh; nor doth every tree that beareth a goodly leaf bring good fruit, Luke viii. 18. Glass giveth a clearer sound than silver, and many things glisten besides gold. A true Chris-

tian cares as well to approve his inside to God as his outside to the world, Hos. vi. 4; and it is a just question, whether the desire of being or dislike of seeming sincere, be greater in him. He shows his worst to men and best to God, as Moses did, when going to the mount he pulled off his veil; and shents himself oft before God for that which the world applauds in him. God, he knows, seeth in secret, there is no tempting him with Ananias and Sapphira, to try whether he trieth the hearts or not. His sharp nose easily discerneth, and is offended with the stinking breath of rotten lungs, though the words or outward actions be never so scented and perfumed with shows of holiness.

Thy Father, which seeth in secret, shall reward thee openly] He is the rewarder of all that diligently seek him, Heb. x. 6, in this soul-fatting exercise: which, as it was seen and allowed by the Lord Christ, Luke v. 33, so it was never rightly used without effect. It is called the day of reconciliation or atonement, and hath most rich and precious promises, Joel ii. 13—21. It is sure God will pardon our sins, and that carries meat in the mouth of it, Psal. xlii. 1, 2. It is probable that "he will leave a blessing behind him" (and the rather, that we may therewith cheerfully serve him), even a "meat-offering and a drink-offering to the Lord our God:" according to that of ʃthe Psalmist, "There is mercy with thee that thou mayest be feared," i. e. served. Fulness of bread was Sodom's sin, and in those sacrificing Sodomites, Isa. i. 10, it was noted for an inexpiable evil, Isa. xxii. 14. They that fast not on earth, when God calls to it, shall be fed with gall and wormwood in hell; they that weep not among men shall howl among devils; whereas those that "sow in tears shall reap in joy," Psal. cxxvi. 5; they that mourn in time of sinning shall be marked in time of punishing; and as they have sought the Lord with fasting, Ezek. ix. 4—6, so shall he yet again "be sought and found" of such with "holy feasting," Zech. viii. 19; as he hath promised and performed to his people in all ages of the Church, not an instance can be alleged to the contrary. Those three great fasters met gloriously upon Mount Tabor. The Israelites fasting (and not till then) were victorious, Judg. xx.; Jehoshaphat was delivered, Esther and her people reprieved, Daniel had visions from heaven, Ezra help from heaven.[2] And surely if with fasting and prayer we can wrestle with God, as Jacob, we need not fear Duke Esau with his 600 cut-throats coming against us. *Si Deus nobiscum, quis contra nos?* Numa being told that his enemies were coming upon him as he was offering sacrifices, thought it sufficient for his safety that he could say, *At ego rem divinam facio*, but I am about the service of my God. (Εγὼ δὲ θύω, Plutarch.) When Jehoshaphat had once established a preaching ministry in all the cities of Judah, then, and not till then, the "fear of the Lord fell upon the neighbour

---

[1] εἰλικρίνεια. Or, as the eagle tries her young against the sun. *Sincerum mel, i. e. sine cera.*

[2] Judg. xx. 23; Ezra viii. 23; 2 Chron. xx.; Esth. iv. 16; Dan. ix. 26; Acts x. 30.

nations, and they made no war," 2 Chron. xvii. 8—10; albeit he had before that placed forces in all the fenced cities. Leotine Prince of Wales, when he was moved by some about him to make war upon our Henry III., replied thus: "I am much more afraid of his alms than of his armies."[1] Frederic the elector of Saxony, intending war against the Archbishop of Magdeburg, sent a spy to search out his preparations and to hearken out his designs. But understanding that the Archbishop did nothing more than commit his cause to God and give himself to fasting and prayer, *Alius, inquit, insaniat ut bellum inferat ei qui confidit se Deum defensorem habiturum.* Bucholcer. Let him fight, said he, that hath a mind to it: I am not so mad as fight against him that trusts to have God his defender and deliverer. It is reported, that at the siege of Mountabone, the people of God, using daily humiliation as their service would permit, did sing a psalm after and immediately before their sallying forth; with which practice the enemy coming acquainted, ever upon the singing of the psalm (after which they expected a sally) they would so quake and tremble, crying, "They come, they come," as though the wrath of God had been breaking out upon them. The soldiers that went against the Angroginans (where God was sincerely served amidst a whole kingdom of Papists) told their captains they were astonished, they could not strike. Some others said that the ministers, with their fasting and prayer, conjured and bewitched them, that they could not fight. It was the custom of this poor people, so soon as they saw the enemy to approach, to cry altogether for aid and succour to the Lord, &c.; while the soldiers fought, the rest of the people with their ministers made their hearty prayer to God, with sighs and tears, and that from the morning to the evening. When night was come, they assembled again together. They which had fought rehearsed God's wonderful aid and succour, and so all together rendered thanks. Alway he turned their sorrow into joy. In the morning, trouble and affliction appeared before them, with great terror on all sides: but by the evening they were delivered, and had great cause of rejoicing and comfort.

Ver. 19. *Lay not up for yourselves treasures upon earth*] This is the fourth common-place handled here by our Saviour, of casting away the inordinate care of earthly things, which he presseth upon all, by nine several arguments, to the end of the chapter. By treasures here are meant worldly wealth in abundance, precious things stored up, as silver, gold, pearls, &c. All these are but earth, and it is but upon earth that they are laid up. What is silver and gold but white and yellow earth? And what are pearls and precious stones but the guts and garbage of the earth? חסדא כמסא. Dan. ii. 45. The stone brake in pieces the iron, the brass, the

clay, and silver, &c. The prophet breaks the native order of speech, for clay, iron, brass, silver, &c., to intimate (as some conceive) that silver is clay, by an elegant allusion in the Chaldee, Should we load ourselves with thick clay? surcharge our hearts with cares of this life? Luke xxi. 34. It is said, "Abraham was very rich in cattle, in silver, and in gold," Gen. xiii. 2. There is a Latin translation that hath it, "Abraham was very heavy," ככד. And the original indifferently beareth both; to show, saith one, that riches are a heavy burthen, and a hindrance many times to heaven and happiness. They that have this burthen upon their backs can as hardly get in at the strait gate as a camel or cable into a needle, Matt. xix. 23, and that because they trust in their riches (as our Saviour there expounds himself), and here plainly intimates when he speaketh of laying up treasures, providing thereby for hereafter, for to-morrow[2] (so the word signifieth), and thinking themselves simply the safer and the happier for their outward abundance, as the rich fool did. The rich man's wealth is his strong city, saith Solomon, Prov. x. 15; his wedge, his confidence, his gold, his god; therefore St Paul calleth him an idolater, Eph. v. 5; St James an adulterer, Jam. iv. 4; because he robs God of his flower, his trust, and goeth a whoring after lying vanities: he soweth the wind and reapeth the whirlwind, he treasureth up wealth but withal wrath, Jam. v. 3; and by counting all fish that cometh to net, he catcheth at length the devil and all. Hence it is that St James bids such (and not without cause) "weep and howl for the miseries that shall come upon them." He looks upon them as deplored persons, and such as the philosopher could call and count incurable and desperate.[3] For the heart that is first turned into earth and mud will afterwards freeze and congeal into steel and adamant. "The Pharisees that were covetous derided Christ," Luke vi. 14, and perished irrecoverably. And reprobates are said by St Peter to have their hearts "exercised with covetous practices," 2 Pet. ii. 14, which they constantly follow, as the artificer his trade, being bound apprentices to the devil, 2 Cor. ii. 11. "Lest Satan should get an advantage against us, or overreach us," as covetous wretches do silly novices.[4] These as they have served an ill master, so they shall receive the "reward of unrighteousness and perish in their corruptions," 2 Pet. ii. 12, 13. Their happiness hath been laid up in the earth, nearer hell than heaven, nearer the devil than God, whom they have forsaken, therefore shall they "be written in the earth," Jer. xvii. 13; that is, in hell, as it stands opposed to having their names written in heaven. Those that are earthly-minded have damnation for their end, Phil. iii. 19. God, to testify his displeasure, knocks his fists at them, Ezek. xxii. 13; as Balak did at Balaam. And lest they

---

[1] *Ego, inquit, formido ejus eleemosynas magis certe multo quam ejus copias.* Powell.

[2] Θησαυρὸς παρὰ τοῦ εἰς αὔριον θεῖναι.

[3] *Aristoteles hoc judicat* ἀνιάτους. Ethic. iv. 1.

[4] ἵνα μὴ πλεονεκτηθῶμεν. *Metaph. ab avaris illis sanguisugis viduarum domos devorantibus.*

should reply, Tush, these are but big words, devised on purpose to affright silly people: we shall do well enough with the Lord; he addeth, ver. 14, "Can thine heart endure, or can thine hands be strong, in the days that I shall deal with thee? I the Lord have spoken it, and will do it." Oh that our greedy muck-moles (that lie rooting and poring in the earth, as if they meant to dig themselves through it a nearer way to hell) would consider this before the cold grave holds their bodies and hot Tophet burns their souls! the one is as sure as the other, if timely course be not taken. *O sæculum nequam*, saith St Bernard; O most wretched and miserable world, how little are thy friends beholden to thee; seeing thy love and friendship exposeth them to the wrath and vengeance of God, which burneth as low as the nethermost hell![1] How fitly may it be said of thee, as Solinus of the river Hipanis: they that know it at first commend it; they that have experience of it at last, do not without cause condemn it![2] Those that will be rich are resolved to get *rem, rem, quocunque modo rem*, as he saith, these fall necessarily into many noisome lusts that drown men in destruction:[3] desperately drown them in remediless misery (as the word signifieth). "Christ must be prayed to be gone," saith that martyr, "lest all their pigs be drowned. The devil shall have his dwelling again in themselves rather than in their pigs. Therefore to the devil shall they go, and dwell with him," &c. They feed upon carrion, as Noah's raven; upon dust, as the serpent; upon the world's murdering-morsels, as those in Job (xx. 15): "They swallow down riches," and are insatiate, as the Pharisees, Luke xi. 41. But they shall vomit them up again, God shall cast them out of their bellies.[4] Their mouths that cry, Give, give, with the horse-leech, shall be filled ere long with a shovelful of mould, and a cup of fire and brimstone poured down their wide gullets. It shall be worse with them than it was once with the covetous Caliph of Babylon, who being taken, together with his city, by Haalon, brother to Mango the great Chan of Tartary, was set by him in the midst of the infinite treasure which he and his predecessors had most covetously heaped up together, and bidden of that gold, silver, and precious stones, take what it pleased him to eat, saying by way of derision, that so gainful a guest should be fed with the best, whereof he willed him to make no spare. The covetous caitiff, kept for certain days, miserably died for hunger in the midst of those things whereof he thought he should never have had enough, whereby he hoped to secure himself against whatsoever dearth or danger. God loveth to confute carnal men in their confidences. They shall pass on "hardly bestead and hungry; and it shall come to pass, that when they shall be hungry, they shall fret themselves, and curse

their king and their God, and look upward. And they shall look unto the earth" (where they have laid up their happiness, but now lost their hopes), "and behold trouble and darkness, dimness of anguish; and they shall be driven into darkness," Isa. viii. 21, 22, utter darkness, where their never enough shall be quitted with fire enough, but a black fire without the least glimpse of light or comfort.

Where moth and rust doth corrupt, and where thieves, &c.] A powerful dissuasive from earthly-mindedness, by the uncertainty of riches, ever subject to a double danger or waste. 1. Of vanity in themselves. 2. Of violence from others: rust or robbery may undo us. As the fairest flowers or fruit-trees breed a worm oftentimes that eats out the heart of them; as the ivy killeth the oak that beareth it; so of the matter of an earthly treasure grows moth or rust that rots it. All outward things are of a perishing nature, they perish in the use, they melt away betwixt our fingers. St Gregory upon those words in Job xxxviii. 22, *Qui ingreditur in thesauros nivis?* "Who hath entered into the treasures of the snow?"—showeth that earthly treasures are treasures of snow. We see little children what pains they take to rake and scrape snow together to make a snow-ball, which after a while dissolves and comes to nothing. Right so the treasures of this world, the hoards that wicked men have heaped, when God entereth into them, come to nothing. "He that trusteth to his riches shall fall," Prov. xi. 28, as he shall that standeth on a hillock of ice or heap of snow. David, when got upon his mountain, thought himself cock-sure, and began to crow that he should never be moved. But God (to confute him) had no sooner hid his face but he was troubled, Psal. xxx. 6, 7. What is the air without light? The Egyptians had no joy of it: no more can a Christian have of wealth without God's favour. Besides, what hold is there of these earthly things, more than there is of a flock of birds? I cannot say they are mine because they sit in my yard. "Riches have wings," saith Solomon, Prov. xxiii. 5; "great eagles' wings to fly from us," saith a father; but to follow after us, *Ne passerinas quidem*, not so much as small sparrows' wings. Whereupon Solomon rightly argues, "Wilt thou set thine eyes upon that which is not?" that hath no real subsistence, that is nothing, and of no more price than mere opinion sets upon it? The world calls wealth substance, but God gives that name to wisdom only. Heaven is said to have a foundation, earth to be hanged upon nothing, Job xvi. 7. So things are said to be in heaven, as in a mansion; but on earth, on the surface only, as ready to be shaken off.[5] Hence the world is called a sea of glass, frail and fickle, mingled with fire of temptations and tribulations, Rev. xv. 2. The very

---

[1] *Quod solos tuos sic solet beare amicos, ut Dei facias inimicos.* Bern.
[2] *Qui in principiis eum norunt prædicant: qui in fine experti sunt, non injuriâ execrantur.* Sol. c. 24.

[3] Βυθίζουσι. *In profundum exitium demergunt, ita ut in aquæ summitate rursus non ebulliant.*
[4] τὰ ἐνόντα. *Quia divitiæ insident avari animo.* Beza.
[5] Ἐν οὐρανοῖς, ἐπὶ τῆς γῆς.

firmament (that hath its name from its firmness) shall melt with fervent heat, and the whole visible fabric be dissolved by the fire of the last day, 2 Pet. iii. 10. Solomon sets forth the world by a word that betokeneth change, for its mutability.[1] And St Paul, when he telleth us "that the fashion of the world passeth away," useth a word of art that signifieth a bare external mathematical figure, *Cui veri aut solidi nihil subest*," saith an interpreter, that hath no truth or solidity in it at all. Gelimer, king of the Vandals, being conquered, and carried in triumph by Belisarius the Roman general, when he stood in the open field before the Emperor Justinian, and beheld him sitting in his throne of state, remembering withal what a high pitch himself was fallen from, he broke out into this speech, "Vanity of vanities, all is vanity." That was Solomon's verdict, long since delivered up, upon well-grounded experience. But men love to try conclusions; and when they have done, " What profit," saith he, "hath a man of all his pains ?" what residue and remaining fruit (as the word signifieth) to abide with him ? Eccl. i. 3. When all the account is subducted (his happiness resolved into its final issue and conclusion) there resteth nothing but ciphers. A spider eviscerateth himself and wasteth his own bowels to make a web to catch a fly ; so doth the worldling for that which profiteth not but perisheth in the use : or say that it abide, yet himself perisheth, when to possess the things he hath gotten might seem a happiness; as the rich fool, Alexander, Tamerlane, others. Most of the Cæsars got nothing by their adoption or designation, but *ut citius interficerentur*, that they might be the sooner slain. All, or most of them till Constantine, died unnatural deaths and in the best of their time. " He that getteth riches and not by right, shall leave them in the midst of his days, and at his end shall be a fool," Jer. xvii. 11. God will make a poor fool of him. As he came forth of his mother's womb, naked shall he return, to go as he came, and shall take nothing of his labour, which he may carry away in his hand, Eccl. v. 15. Say his treasure escape both rust and robber, death as a thief will break in, and leave him not worth a groat. Who would not then set light by this pelf, and put on that Persian resolution, Isa. xiii. 17, " Not to regard silver, nor be desirous of gold ? " (*Animo magno nihil magnum*, Senec.) Who would not tread in the steps of faithful Abraham, and answer the devil with his golden offers, as he did the king of Sodom, " God forbid that I should take of thee so much as a shoe-latchet ? " When great gifts were sent to Luther, he refused them with this brave speech, " *Valde protestatus sum me nolle sic satiari a Deo*, I deeply protested that God

should not put me off with such poor things as these. The heathenish Romans had, for a difference in their nobility, a little ornament in the form of a moon (to show that all worldly honours were mutable), and they did wear it upon their shoes, to show that they did tread it under their feet, as base and bootless.[2] This is check to many Christians, that have their hands elbow-deep in the world, and dote as much upon these earthly vanities as Xerxes once did upon his plane-tree, or Jonas upon his gourd. There is a sort of men that say of the world as Solomon's chapman, " It is naught, it is naught : " but when they are gone apart they boast and close with the world. St Paul was none of these ; for " neither at any time," saith he, " used we flattering words, as ye know ; nor a cloak of covetousness, God is my witness." No, he looked upon the world as a great dung-hill, and cared to " glory in nothing, save in the cross of Jesus Christ," whereby the world was crucified to him and he to the world, Gal. vi. 14. So David, " My soul," saith he, " is even as a weaned child," that cares not to suck though never so fair and full a breast. So Luther confesseth of himself, " that though he were a frail man, and subject to imperfections, yet the infection of covetousness never laid hold of him ; " now I would we were all Lutherans in this, saith one.

Ver. 20. *But lay up for yourselves treasures in heaven*] That which you may draw out a thousand years hence. For in a treasure there are three things, — a laying up, a lying hid, and a drawing out for present use. Riches reach not to eternity. Therefore while others lay hold upon riches, " Lay thou hold on eternal life," 1 Tim. vi. 12, and that " by following after righteousness, godliness, faith, love, patience, meekness." This, this is the true treasure; this is to be rich, as our Saviour speaketh, toward God, and is opposed to laying up treasure for himself, Luke xii. 21, as here " laying up treasure in heaven" is to that of laying up treasure in earth.[3] Both cannot be done, because the heart cannot be in two so different places at once. The saints have their commoration on earth, but their conversation is in heaven. Here are their bodies, but their hearts are where Christ their head is. *Sancti ibi sunt ubi nondum sunt, et non sunt ubi sunt*, saith Chrysostom. The saints are there, in their affections, whither as yet they are not come in their attainments. All their ploughing, sailing, building, planting, tends to that life that is supernal, supernatural; they run for the high prize, they strive for the crown of righteousness, they breathe after the beatifical vision, with, " Oh when shall I come and appear before God ?" And as the Athenians, when they were besieged by Sylla,[4] had their hearts with

---

[1] חלוף Prov. xxxi. 8 *hoc est,* עולם *mundi, sic dicti quod transeat, nec quicquam in eo stabile sit.* Kimchi.

[2] *Baytacen habitantes odio auri coemunt hoc genus metalli, et abjiciunt in terrarum profundo, ne polluti usu ejus, avaritia corrumpant æquitatem.* Sol. cap. 68.

[3] εἰς Θεὸν πλουτεῖν· *Hoc est, omnia prædia in Deo collocare, et ab ejus unica providentia pendere.* Beza *in loc.*

[4] *Animos extra mœnia, corpora necessitati servientes intra muros habuerunt.* Paterc. St Paul's body was at Rome, his spirit with the Colossians (ii. 5).

him without the walls, though their bodies were held within by force: so the saints, though detained here for a while in a far country, yet their hearts are at home. They go through the world as a man whose mind is in a deep study, or as one that hath special haste of some weighty business; they wonder much how men can awhile to pick up sticks and straws with so much delight and diligence. The time is short (or trussed up into a narrow scantling), the task is long, of keeping faith and a good conscience; hence they use the world as if they used it not, as having little leisure to trifle.[1] There is water little enough to run in the right channel, therefore they let none run beside; but carefully improve every opportunity, as wise merchants, Eph. v. 15, and care not to sell all, to purchase the pearl of price. In a witty sense (saith Broughton out of Rabbi Bochai) Cain and Abel contain in their names advertisements for matter of true continuance and corruption. Cain betokeneth possession in this world, and Abel betokeneth one humbled in mind, and holding such possession vain. Such was his offering, sheep-kind, the gentlest of all living beasts, and therefore the favour of God followed him. And the offering of Cain was of the fruit of the earth, as he loved the possession of this world and the service of the body (which yet can have no continuance), and followed after bodily lusts. Therefore the blessed God favoured him not. Cain's chief care was to build cities, that he "might call his land after his own name," Psal. xlix. 11, and make his son, Lord Enoch of Enoch. Not so the better sort, Abel, Enoch, Noah, Abraham, they were content to dwell in tents, as looking for a city "which hath foundations, whose maker and founder is God," Heb. xi. 10. Abraham bought a piece of ground, but for burial only. Ishmael shall beget twelve princes, but "with Isaac will I establish my covenant;" and although he grow not so great as his brother (that man of God's hand, that had his portion here), yet he shall make reckoning, that "the lines are fallen unto him in a fair place, that he hath a goodly heritage," Psal. xvi. 6. Esau had his dukes, and grows a great *magnifico*; but Jacob gets first the birthright for a mess of red, red, which the hungry hunter required to be fed with, as camels are fed by casting gobbets into their mouths (so the word signifies). And after this he gets the blessing by his mother's means. And when Esau threatened him, and had bolted out some suspicious words, she seeks not to reconcile the two brethren by making the younger yield up again what he had got from the elder; but prefers the blessing before Jacob's life, and sends him away. This was to lay up treasure in heaven for her son, who took herein after the mother too (*partus sequitur ventrem*). For if Esau will but suffer him to settle in the Land of Promise, a type of heaven, he will spare for no cost to make his peace. Silver and gold he hath none, but cattle good store; 550 head of them sends

[1] 1 Cor. vii. 29, συνεσταλμένος,

he for a present to make room for him, as Solomon hath it. Let heaven be a man's object, and earth will soon be his abject. David counts one good cast of God's countenance far better than all the corn and oil in the country. Solomon craves wisdom and not wealth. Paul counts all but dross, dung, and dog's meat (σκύβαλα), Phil. iii. 8, so he may win Christ and get home to him, 2 Cor. v. 6. Here we have but a glimpse of those gleams of glory, we see but as in a glass obscurely, 1 Cor. xiii. 12. "Our life is hid with Christ in God," as the pearl lies hid till the shell be broken, Colos. iii. 3. Compare the estate of Prince Charles in his Queenmother's womb, with his condition at full age, in all the glory of his father's court: there is not so broad a difference as betwixt our present enjoyments (albeit our joys here are unspeakably glorious, 1 Pet. i. 8) with those we shall have hereafter. *Sursum igitur cursum nostrum dirigamus.* Let therefore our affections and actions, our counsels and courses, be bent and bound for heaven: our earthly businesses despatch with heavenly minds, and in serving men let us serve the Lord Christ. The angels are sent about God's message to this earth, yet never out of their heaven, never without the vision of their Maker. These earthly things distract not, if we make them not our treasure, if we shoot not our hearts over-far into them. The end of a Christian's life is (not, as Anaxagoras dreamed of the life of man, to behold the heavens, but) to live in heaven. This he begins to do here by the life of faith, by walking with God, as Enoch and Elijah, those candidates of immortality (so the ancients called them), by walking before God, as Abraham and David by walking after God, as the Israelites were bidden to do, Gen. vi. 9; 1 Kings ix. 4; Deut. xiii. 4. With God, a man walks by an humble friendship and familiarity; before him, by uprightness and integrity; after him, by obedience and conformity, by doing his "will on earth, as it is in heaven." And this is to "lay up treasure in heaven;" this is, as the apostle expresseth and interpreteth it, "to lay up in store for ourselves a good foundation against the time to come, that we may lay hold on eternal life," 1 Tim. vi. 19. There shall be stability of thy times, strength, salvation, wisdom, and knowledge; "for the fear of the Lord shall be his treasure," Isa. xxxiii. 6.

Ver. 21. *For where your treasure is,* &c.] *i. e.* Where your chief happiness is, there your affections will be settled: where the carcase is, there will the eagles be also. Beetles delight in muck-hills; but Christ's eagles are never in their pride till farthest off from the earth: they are said (even here) to "be set together with Christ in heavenly places," Eph. ii. 6. The Church in the Canticles hath this given her for a high commendation, that she had a "nose like the tower of Lebanon," Cant. vii. 4. *Si verborum faciem spectemus,* saith an interpreter, *quid poterit magis dici ridiculum?* The words *terminus nauticus.*

at first sight seem somewhat strange; for what so great a praise is it to have a nose like a tower? But by this expression is notably set forth that spiritual sagacity and sharpness of smell, whereby the saints resent and favour the things above, being carried after Christ, the true carcase, with unspeakable desire and delight. The earthly-minded, that have their bellies filled with God's hid treasure, the trash of this world, and take it for their portion, Psal. xvii. 14; these have their heads so stuft and their eyes so stopt with the dust of covetousness, that they neither see nor savour heavenly things. As they are of the earth, so they speak of the earth, and the earth hears them, John iii. 31. As the grasshopper is bred, liveth, and dieth in the same ground, so these *terrigenæ fratres*, these muck-minded men, are wholly earth in their whole course; and as the grasshopper hath wings but flieth not, sometimes she hoppeth upwards a little, but falleth to the ground again; so these have some light and short motions to godliness, when they hear a piercing sermon, or feel a pressing affliction, or see others snatched away by sudden death before them; but this is not of any long continuance, they return to their former worldliness. The devil hath got full possession of them, as once of Judas by this sin; and could a man rip up their hearts he might find there fair written, "The god of this present world," 2 Cor. v. 4. He holds his black hand before their eyes, lest the light of the glorious gospel should shine upon them. We cry, "O earth, earth, earth, hear the word of the Lord:" but the devil hath made a path-way over their hearts, so that the seed cannot enter. Earth is cold and dry, so are earthly-minded men to any holy duty. Earth is heavy, and bears downward, so do earthly affections. Earth doth often keep down the hot exhalations that naturally would ascend; so do those, holy motions and meditations. Earth stands still, and hath the whole circumference carried about it; so are God's mercies and judgments about earthly-minded men, and they are no whit moved thereat. Grace, on the other side, as fire, is active and aspiring. And as Moses would not be put off with an angel to go before the people, he would have God himself, or none; so the true Christian must have Christ, or nothing will give him content. Christ is his treasure, and hath his heart; all his cry is, "None but Christ, none but Christ." As the sun draws up vapours, so doth the Sun of righteousness the affections of his people. And as the hop in its growing windeth itself about the pole, always following the course of the sun, from east to west, and can by no means be drawn to the contrary, choosing rather to break than yield; so the saints (as well militant as triumphant) do "follow the Lamb wheresoever he goeth;" and being risen with Christ, and spiritualized by him, they seek the things that are above; their thoughts feed upon the fairest objects (such as

are those set down by the apostle, Phil. iv. 8), and run with much content, upon that firmament and those stars, in Daniel; that inheritance undefiled and unfadable, in Peter; [1] those palms and white robes, in the Revelation. They take ever and anon a turn or two on Tabor, and are there transfigured with Christ; or on Mount Olivet, where he was taken up, and have thence continual ascensions in their hearts. And as our Saviour in the interim between his resurrection and ascension, whiles he walked here on the earth, spake "of the things pertaining to the kingdom of God," and waited for his exaltation into heaven, Acts i. 3; so the faithful Christian (that hath his part in the first resurrection) walks, in his measure, as Christ walked, talks as he talked, he speaks of the things concerning the King, and therein his tongue is as the pen of a ready writer, 1 John ii. 6; Psal. xlv. 1. Of Origen it is said that he was ever earnest, but never more than when he treats of Christ.[2] And of St Paul it is well observed, that when he speaketh of heaven he useth a transcendent, lofty kind of language, his speech riseth higher and higher, as 2 Cor. iv. 17, a degree above the superlative: so Phil. i. 23, to be with Christ is far, far the better: so 1 Thess. ii. 19.[3] See how the apostle's mouth is opened, his heart enlarged, he cannot satisfy himself, nor utter his conceptions. This a Christian can do, he can sigh out a *cupio dissolvi*, "I desire to be with Christ," whom as he more or less enjoyeth here, in the same measure he is merry; like as birds never sing so sweetly as when they are got in the air, or on the top of trees. As when Christ withdraws his gracious presence and influence, he is all *amort*, you may take him up for a dead man. He cries after Christ, as idolatrous Micah did after his lost gods, Judges xviii. 14; and as King Edward III., having the King of France prisoner here in England, and feasting him one time most sumptuously, pressed him to be merry. The French King answered, "How can we sing songs in a strange land?" So the good soul is in great heaviness while Christ absents himself, and never heartily merry till she get home to him, till she lay hold on him whom her soul loveth.

Ver. 22. *The light of the body is the eye,* &c.] Here our blessed Saviour illustrateth what he had said before, of laying up, not on earth, but in heaven, by a fit similitude. Like as the eye is the light of the whole body, so is the mind of the whole man. "If therefore thine eye be single," that is, if thy mind be sincere, if thou have that one eye of the Spouse in the Canticles, Cant. iv. 9, that one heart promised in the new covenant, Ezek. xi. 19, set upon God alone, and not divided, and, as it were, cloven asunder (which is to have a heart and a heart), but minding the one thing necessary, as the main, and be not double-minded, or corrupted from the simplicity of Christ, 2 Cor. xi. 3,—then shall thy whole body, that is, thy whole both constitution and conversation, be lightsome,

[1] Dan. xii. 3, ἀμίαντος καὶ ἀμάραντος. 1 Pet. i. 4.
[2] *Nusquam Origenes non ardet, sed nusquam est ardentior,* *quam ubi Christi sermones actusque tractat.* Erasmus.
[3] *Hic oratio altius assurgit, &c.* Rolloc.

diaphanous, transparent, as a lantern that hath a candle in it, or as a crystal glass with a light in the midst, which appeareth through every part thereof. There will be an uniformity, equability, ubiquity, and constancy of holiness running through thy whole course, as the warp doth through the woof; when a double-minded man (that hath not cleansed his heart, nor washed his hands of worldly lusts) is unstable and uneven in all his ways (δίψυχος), James iv. 8; i. 8. "Thou shalt love the Lord thy God with all thy mind," Luke x. 27. "And with my mind I serve the law of God," saith Paul, which he acknowledged to be spiritual, though he were carnal in part, sold under sin. The old man is still corrupt according to the deceitful lusts (which sometimes so bemist and beguile the judgment, that a man shall think there is some sense in sinning, and that he hath reason to be mad), but be ye renewed in the spirit of your minds, in the bosom and bottom of the soul, in the most inward and subtile parts of the soul, and, as it were, the quintessence of it, Eph. iv. 22, 23. Reserve these upper rooms for Christ, and be not ye conformed to the world (who mind earthly things, and have damnation for their end, Phil. iii. 19), but be ye transformed by the renewing of your minds, Rom. xii. 2, that ye may see and prove by good experience (not by a notional knowledge only) what that good, and holy, and acceptable will of God is. Concerning the east gate of that temple in Ezekiel, thus saith the Lord, "This gate shall be shut, and shall not be opened, and no man shall enter by it, because the Lord God of Israel hath entered by it," Ezek. xliv. 2; here-through signifying, saith a divine, that although the heart of a Christian, which is the temple of the Holy Ghost, may let many things enter into it at other gates, yet must it keep the east gate, the most illuminate and highest power and part of it, continually shut against all men; yea, against all the world, and opened only to one thing, I mean to God, who hath already entered into it, and enlightened it with his Spirit. That as at the windows of Noah's ark there entered in no mist nor water, nothing else but one thing only, which is light; so at the east gate, no mist of human errors, no water of worldly cares, may enter in, but only the light of heaven, and a sanctified desire to be fast knit and perfectly united by faith and love to God.

Ver. 23. *But if thine eye be evil, &c. If the light that is in thee be darkness, &c.*] An evil eye is here opposed to a single eye, that looks on God singly abstracted from all other things, and affects the heart with pure love to him for himself, more than for his love-tokens. These we may lawfully have, but they may not have us. "If any man love the world, the love of the Father is not in him. For all that is in the world, the lust of the flesh, the lust of the eyes, and the pride of life" 1 John ii. 16, that is, pleasure, profit, and preferment,—these three, like those three troops of

the Chaldeans, Job i. 17, fall upon the faculties of the soul, and carry them away from God the right owner. The mind is filled with greater darkness than can be expressed. How great is that darkness! "The prince that wanteth understanding is a great oppressor: but he that hateth covetousness," that hath not his eyes bleared and blinded with the dust of earthly-mindedness, "shall prolong his days," Prov. xxviii. 16. "His watchmen are blind:" and why? "they are greedy dogs, which can never have enough, and they are shepherds which cannot understand; they all look to their own way, every one for his gain from his quarter," Isa. lvi. 10, 11.[1] Of this sort were those covetous Pharisees, that devoured widows' houses; therefore blind, because covetous, Luke xvi. 14, the property of which sin is to besot and infatuate, as it did Judas, who, though he wanted for nothing in our Saviour's retinue, but was sufficiently provided for, yet for filthy lucre basely sold his Master, and that for thirty silverlings (the known and pitched price of the vilest slave), and had the face, after all, to ask, "Master, is it I?" when he knew Christ to be the true God, and to know all things. Blazing comets (though but comets) as long as they keep aloft, shine bright, but when they decline from their pitch, they fall to the earth. So, when men forsake the Lord and mind earthly things, they lose that light they had, and are dissipated, destroyed, and come to nothing. Good, therefore, is the counsel of Solomon, "Labour not to be rich: wilt thou set thine eyes upon that which is not?" Or as Mercerus otherwise reads that text, "Wilt thou darken thine eyes upon them?"[2] As those that walk long in the snow, or that sit in a smoky corner, can see little at length. "Whoredom and wine take away the heart," saith Hosea (iv. 11), as they did Solomon's; they drew out his spirits, and dissolved his reason; so doth covetousness. It makes a man that he cannot see the net that is spread before him, which every bird can do, Prov. i. 17:[3] but whiles he coveteth the bait, loseth his life, as Shimei did by looking for his servants; as Lot, who had like to have run the same hazard, by choosing the plain of Jordan; as Jonas, that suffered himself to be cast into the sea, that the ship with her lading might come safe to shore. How many carnal minds, like Noah's raven, fly out of the ark of God's Church, and embrace this present world: and like the mariners, when they found out Jonas, yet fain they would have saved him. So many will rather venture their own casting away, than cast their worldly lusts over-board. How much better Joseph, who let go his garment to save himself, as Elijah did his mantle to go to heaven, and Bartimeus his cloak to come to Christ! How much better Moses, who by faith seeing him that is invisible, and having an eye to the reward, when he was come to years, as the text noteth, and therefore well knew what he did, for he was

[1] *Avidus a non videndo dicitur; et Midas secundum Etymologiam Græcam cæcus est.*
[2] Prov. xxiii. 4, 5. *Num facies obtenebrescere oculos tuos in eas?* Job xi. 17; Amos iv. 13.   [3] *Aves quæ vident rete suspensum non capiuntur, sed videntes periculum cavent.* Bayn.

no baby, refused to be called the son of Pharaoh's daughter and the world's darling; and choosing rather the afflictions of God's poor people than the pleasures of sin for a season, he esteemed the reproach of Christ (the worst part of him) greater riches than the treasures of Egypt. And why all this? "for he had respect to the recompense of reward," Heb. xi. 24—26. He set his foot, as it were, upon the battlements of heaven, and there-hence looked upon these earthly happinesses as base and abject, slight and slender, waterish and worthless. The great cities of Campania seem but small cottages to them that stand on the top of the Alps:[1] the moon covereth herself with a pale veil and shines not at all in the presence of the sun: no more doth the beauty and bravery of the world (wherewith carnal minds are so bedazzled and bewitched) to a man that hath been in Paradise with Paul, that hath already laid hold on eternal life. The moles of the earth, that are blind and cannot see far off, that have *animam triticiam*, a wheaten soul, with that fool in the Gospel, and know no other happiness than to have and to hold; these have their eyes blinded by the god of this world, as Isaac had his wells stopped up with earth by the Philistines. And as a small dish being held near the eyes hideth from our sight a great mountain; and a little hill or cloud, the great body of the sun, though it be far bigger than the whole earth; so these earthly trifles being placed near men's sight, do so shadow and over-cloud those great and glorious excellencies that are above, that they can neither truly behold them, nor rightly judge of them.[2] When men travel so far into the south that the sight of the north pole is at length intercepted by the earth, it is a sign they are far from it: so is it, that men are far from heaven when the love of the earth comes in betwixt their souls and the sight thereof. Earth-damps quench the spirit's lamp. Much water of affliction cannot quench that love, that yet a little earth may soon do.

Ver. 24. *No man can serve two masters, &c.*] The mammonist's mind must needs be full of darkness, because utterly destituted of the Father of lights, the sun of the soul: for ye cannot serve two masters, God and mammon. By mammon is meant earthly treasure, worldly wealth, outward abundance, especially when, gotten by evil arts, it cometh to be the gain of ungodliness, the wages of wickedness, riches of unrighteousness, filthy lucre.[3] When Joseph was cast into the pit by his bloody brethren, "What gain," saith Judah, "will it be if we kill him?" Gen. xxxvii. 26. The Chaldee there hath it, what mammon shall it be? what can we make of it? what profit shall we reap or receive thereby? Now these two, God and mammon, as they are incompatible masters, so the variance

between them is irreconcileable. "Amity with the world is enmity with the Lord," James iv. 4. Enmity, I say, in a sense both active and passive, for it makes a man both to hate God and to be hated by God: so there is no love lost on either side. "If any man love the world, the love of the Father is not in him," that is flat. But the deeper any one is drowned in the world, the more desperately he is divorced from God, who requireth to be served truly, that there be no halting; and totally, that there be no halving. Camden reports of Redwald the first king of the East Saxons that was baptized, that he had in the same church one altar for Christian religion and another for sacrifice to devils.[4] And Callenucius telleth us of a nobleman of Naples, that was wont profanely to say that he had two souls in his body, one for God and another for whomsoever would have it. The Ebionites, saith Eusebius, would keep the sabbath with the Jews and the Lord's day with the Christians, as if they were of both religions, when, in truth, they were of neither. So Ezekiel's hearers sat devoutly before the Lord at his public ordinances, and with their mouth showed much love, but their heart, meanwhile, was on their half-penny, it went after their covetousness, Ezek. xxxiii. 31. So the Pharisees heard Christ's sermon against the service of mammon, and derided him, Luke xvi. 13; and while their lips seemed to pray, they were but chewing of that murdering-morsel, those widows' houses that their throats (as an open sepulchre) swallowed down soon after. Thus filled they up the measure of their fathers, those ancient idolaters in the wilderness, who set up a golden calf, and then caused it to be proclaimed, "To-morrow is a feast to Jehovah," Exod. xxxii. 5. And such is the dealing of every covetous Christian. St Paul calleth him an idolater, St James an adulterer, for he goeth a whoring after his gods of gold and silver; and although he bow not the knee to his mammon, yet with his heart he serveth it. Now "obedience is better than sacrifice;" and, "know ye not," saith the apostle, "that his servants ye are to whom ye obey?" &c., Rom. vi. 16. Inwardly he loves it, delights in it, trusts on it, secures himself by it from whatsoever calamities. Outwardly, he spends all his time upon this idol, in gathering, keeping, increasing, or honouring of it. Hence the jealous God hateth him, and smites his hands at him, Ezek. xxii. 13, and hath a special quarrel against those that bless the covetous, whom the Lord abhorreth, Psal. x. 3. As for his servants, he strictly chargeth them to have their conversation without covetousness, Heb. xiii. 5, yea, their communication, Eph. v. 3, yea, their cogitation, 2 Pet. ii. 14; branding them for cursed children that have so much as their thoughts exercised that way. He will not

---

[1] *Postquam in montium verticem ascenderimus parva nobis et urbes et mœnia etiam videntur : sit parva videbuntur otium gloria divitiæ cum cœlum respicias.*

[2] 2 Pet. i. 9, μυωπάζοντες. *Muris oculos habentes, subterranei scilicet muris, hoc est, talpæ.* Gen. xxvi. 15. The

poets feigned Plutus, the god of riches, to be blind. *Divites facultatibus suis alligati magis aurum suspiciunt, quam cœlum.* Minut. Octan.

[3] *Magna est cognatio divitiis et vitiis.*

[4] *Unam Deo dicatam, alteram unicuique qui illam vellet.*

have his hasten to be rich, or labour after super-fluities, no, nor anxiously after necessaries. For worldliness (I say not covetousness), when men oppress themselves with multiplicity of business, or suffer their thoughts and affections to be continually almost taken up with minding these things on earth, is a main hindrance from heaven; it fills the heart with cares, and so unfits and deads it to divine duties.[1] The thoughts as wings should carry us in worship even to the mansions of God, which being laden with thick clay, they so glue us to the earth that the load-stone of the word and ordinances cannot draw us one jot from it. The soul is also hereby made like a mill, where one cannot hear another, the noise is such as takes away all intercourse (ὅπου οὐδεὶς οὐδὲν οὐδενὸς ἀκούει). If conscience call to them to take heed of going out of God's way, they are at as little leisure to listen as he that runs in a race; who many times runs with so much violence, that he cannot hear what is said unto him, be it never so good counsel. And having thus set their hearts and anchored their hopes upon earthly things, if ever they lose them, as it often falleth out, they are filled almost with un-medicinable sorrows, so as they will praise the dead above the living, and wish they had never been born, Eccl. iv. 1—3. Lo, this is the guise and guerdon of those inhabitants of the earth, those *viri divitiarum*, as the Psalmist styles them, those miserable muck-worms that prefer mam-mon before Messiah, gold before God, money be-fore mercy, earth before heaven; as childish a weakness, as that of Honorius the emperor, that preferred a hen before the city of Rome. Mam-mon, saith one, is a monster, whose head is as sub-tle as the serpent, whose mouth is wide as hell, eyes sharp as a lizard, scent quick as the vulture, hands fast as harpies, belly insatiable as a wolf, feet swift to shed blood, as a lioness robbed of her whelps.[2] Ahab will have Naboth's vineyard, or he will have his blood. Judas was both covetous and a murderer, and therefore a mur-derer because covetous. He is called also a thief; and why a thief but because a mammonist? Covetousness draws a man from all the com-mandments, Psal. cxvi. 36. And there want not those that have drawn the covetous person through all the commandments, and proved him an atheist, a papist, a perjurer, a profaner of God's sabbath, an iron-bowelled wretch, a murderer, an adulterer, a thief, a false witness, or whatsoever else the devil will. And can this man ever serve God acceptably? can he possibly please two so contrary masters? No; he may sooner reconcile fire and water, look with the one eye upward and with the other eye downward, bring heaven and earth together, and gripe them both in a fist, as be habitually covetous and truly re-ligious. These two are as inconcurrent as two parallel lines, and as incompatible as light and darkness. They who bowed down on their

knees to drink of the waters were accounted unfit soldiers for Gideon; so are those for Christ, that stoop to the base love of the things of this life (Βιωτικὰ); they discredit both his work and his wages; which Abraham would not, that an-cient and valiant soldier and servant of the most high God. For when Melchisedeck from God had made him heir of all things, and brought him bread and wine, that is, an earnest, a little for the whole, &c., he refused the riches that the king of Sodom offered him, because God was his shield and his exceeding great reward, Gen. xiv. 18, 19, 23; xv. 1; his shield against any such enemies as Chedorlaomer and his complices had been unto him, and his exceeding great reward, for all his labour of love in that or any other ser-vice, though he received not of any man, from a thread to a shoe-latchet.

Ver. 25. *Therefore I say unto you, Take no careful thought*, &c.] This life is called in Isaiah "the life of our hands" because it is maintained by the labour of our hands, Isa. lvii. 10. Never-theless, let a man labour never so hard, and lay up never so much, his "life consisteth not in the abundance of the things that he possesseth," saith our Saviour, and therefore bids, "take heed and beware of covetousness," Luke xii. 15. There is in every mother's child of us a false presumption of self-sufficiency in our own courses, as if we by our own diligence could build the house. The devil's word is proved too true. He said we should be like gods, which as it is false in respect of divine qualities resembling God, so is it true in regard of our sinful usurpation; for we carry the matter, for most part, as if we were petty gods within ourselves, not needing any higher power. This self-confidence, the daughter of unbelief and mother of carking care and carnal thought-fulness, our Saviour here by many arguments dissuadeth and decrieth. "Take no thoughtful care for your life, what ye shall eat," &c. The word here used in the original (μέριμνα) signifieth sometimes a commendable and Christian care, as 1 Cor. vii. 33, 34, "He that is married careth how to please his wife: likewise she careth how to please her husband." It implieth a dividing of the mind into divers thoughts, casting this way and that way and every way how to give best content. And this should be all the strife that should be betwixt married couples. This is the care of the head, the care of diligence, called by the Greeks σπουδὴ, μελέτη, ἐπιμέλεια. But there is another sort of care here spoken against, as unwarrantable and damnable; the care of the heart, the care of diffidence, a doubtful and carking care, joined with a fear of future events, a sinful solicitude, a distracting and distempering care, properly called μέριμνα, because it tortures and tears asunder the mind with anxious impiety and fretting impatiency.[3] This maketh a man, when he had done his utmost endeavour, in the use of lawful means, for his own provision or

---

[1] τὸν πολλά τεχνώμενον παντὰ εὖ τεχνᾶσθαι ἀδύνα-τον.

[2] *Quorum charismata, numismata, scripturæ, sculpturæ,*

quibusque ὁ ἄργυρος τὸ αἷμα ἐστὶ καὶ ψυχή, ut vulgo dici solet.

[3] μέριμνα παρὰ τοῦ μερίζειν τὸν νοῦν.

preservation, to sit down, and with a perplexed heart sigh out,—Sure it will never be, sure I shall die a beggar, be utterly destitute, &c. Surely I shall one day perish by the hand of Saul; were it not better for me to shift for myself, and to escape speedily into the land of the Philistines? 1 Sam. xxvii. 1. A sinful consultation, for had not God promised him both life and kingdom after Saul? but he said (very wisely) in his hasty fear, All men are liars, prophets and all, Psal. cxvi. 11. And again, "I said in my sudden haste, I am cut off," Psal. xxxi. 22.

What ye shall eat, or what ye shall drink, &c.] I would have you without carefulness about these things, saith the apostle, that ye may sit close to the Lord without distraction.[1] And again, "in nothing be careful." How then? Why, make your requests known to God in prayer, as children make their needs known to their parents, whom if they can please, they know they shall be provided for, Phil. iv. 6, 7. Little thought do they take where to have the next meal or the next new suit, neither need they.

Oh, but we have prayed, and yet are to seek.

Add to your prayer, supplication, saith the apostle there, strong cries out of a deep sense of our pressing necessities, and then see what will come of it. Δέησις *est petitio opis, qua egemus, nam* Δεῖν *est egere.*

I have done so to my poor power; and yet it sticks.

To thy supplication add thanksgiving for mercies already received, saith he; thanksgiving is an artificial begging. See something in thy most careful condition wherefore to be thankful. Praise God for what you have had, have, and hope to have.

What will follow upon this?

What? "The peace of God which passeth all understanding shall keep" as with a guard (φρουρήσει) or garrison "your hearts" from cares, "and minds" from fears, "in Christ Jesus." This shall be the restful success of your prayers and praises. And is it not good that the heart be ballasted with grace (βεβαιοῦσθαι), Heb. xiii. 9, rather than the body farced with meats? What brave letters and how full of life were written by Luther to Melancthon, afflicting himself with continual cares, what would be the issue of the imperial diet held by Charles V. and other states of Germany at Augsburg, about the cause of Christ's gospel? *Ego certe oro pro te,* saith he, *et doleo te, pertinacissimam curarum hirudinem, meas preces sic irritas facere.* "I pray for thee, and am troubled at it, that thou, by troubling thyself with unnecessary cares, makest my prayers of none effect for thee." And after many sweet consolations, mixed with reprehensions, he concludes, "But I write these things in vain, because thou thinkest to rule these things by reason, and killest thyself with immoderate cares about them; not considering that the cause is Christ's, who as he needs not thy counsels, so he will bring about his own ends without thy care-

[1] εὐπάρεδρον ἀπερισπάστος,

fulness, thy vexing thoughts, and heart-eating fears, whereby thou disquietest thyself above measure." *Sed scribo hæc frustra: quia tu secundum Philosophiam vestram, has res ratione regere hoc est, cum ratione insanire pergis et occidis teipsum.*

Is not life more than meat? &c.] And shall he that hath given us that which is greater and better deny unto us that which is less and worse? Shall we believe God's promises in the main, but not God's providence in the means: as the disciples when they had forgotten to buy bread, and as Abraham in the case of promise of issue of his body? Gen. xvi. 2. Excellent is that of the apostle, "he that spared not his own Son, but delivered him up for us all, how shall he not with him also freely give us all things?" Rom. viii. 32. Whereupon St Bernard, *Qui misit unigenitum, immisit spiritum, promisit vultum, quid tandem tibi negaturus est?* And to like purpose St Jerome: "Never think," saith he, "that God will deny thee anything, whom he inviteth so freely to feed upon the fatted calf." *Nihil unquam et negasse credendum est quem ad vituli hortatur esum.*

Ver. 26. *Behold* (or *cast your eyes upon*) *the fowls of the air*] Look upon them intently (ἐμβλέψατε), consider them wisely, learn of them carefully, to cast away carnal carefulness, and to cast all your care upon God, who careth for them, how much more for you? "Ask now the fowls of the air, and they shall tell thee," saith Job (xii. 7), "that there is a reward for the righteous, and a God that judgeth in the earth." As he made them at first for his own glory (that we might admire his workmanship in their multitude and variety of colours, tunes, and taste, 1 Cor. xv. 39), and for our both use and delight; so he knows them all, Psal. l. 11, and maintaineth them, providing both for their use, Psal. cxlvii. 9, and delight, Psal. civ. 12, giving us wisdom beyond them, Job xxxvii. 11, and yet setting us to school to them, to learn dependence upon God, both for preservation from evil, Matt. x. 29, and for provision of good, as here and Job xxxix. 16. He taketh care of the ostrich's young ones, and of the young ravens that cry unto him, Psal. cxlvii. 9. They are fed of God when forsaken of their dams and left bare and destitute, for out of their dung and carrion, brought before to the nest, ariseth a worm, which creepeth to their mouth and feedeth them. (Aristot., Hist. Animal. ix. 31.)

They sow not, neither do they reap, &c.] They take no care, nor have any to care for them, as geese, hens, and other tame pullen: and yet they are provided for, we see. And, oh, that we would see as our Saviour here enjoins us, and behold not only the fowls of the air, but the clouds above them, and other heavenly bodies! When one asked Luther, where he could be safe and at quiet? *sub cœlo,* said he. And to Pontanus the Chancellor of Saxony, he propounds to be viewed and weighed by him that most beautiful arch-work of heaven, resting upon no posts nor pillars, and 1 Cor. vii. 32, 35.

yet standing fast for ever and ever, merely up-held by the mighty hand of God. The clouds also, as thin as the liquor contained in them; "Behold," saith he, "how they hang and move, though weighty with their burden; they salute us only, or rather threaten us, and vanish we know not whither."[1] These things would be thought on, that God may be the better rested on. "Be not ye of doubtful mind," saith our Saviour, "live not in careful suspense, hang not as meteors in the air betwixt heaven and earth, uncertain whether to keep your standing, or fall to the ground; to trust God, or otherwise, as you can, to make sure for yourselves. Meteors are matters that few men can tell what to make of; Aristotle himself confesseth that he knew little of many of them.[2] And as little can the distrustful person tell what to make of those infinite projects and discourses in the air that he incessantly frames for the com-passing of his desires. When he needs but either to look up to the birds or down to the lilies, and learn, that if God feed and clothe them with-out any their care and pains, surely he will much more provide for his people that rely upon him, and with their reasonable pains and moderate care do serve his providence. Shall the great housekeeper of the world water his flowers, prune his plants, fodder his cattle, and not feed and clothe his children? Never think it. God provided for the necessity and comfort of the un-reasonable creatures ere he made them; grass for the beasts, and light for all living and moving creatures, and all for man, for the man in Christ especially. Compare Psal. viii. 4, 5, with Heb. ii. 6, 7, &c., and it will appear that whatsoever is spoken there of a man is applied to Christ; and so is proper to the saints, by virtue of their union with Christ. In which respect, saith one, they are more glorious than heaven, angels, or any creature: and shall these want food and rai-ment?

Ver. 27. *Which of you by taking thought can add one cubit unto his stature?*] And as little able are we (though we take never so much care and pains) to add one mite to that dimension of our estate, which God by his wise and power-ful providence hath allotted unto us. Every man shall have his statute-measure ($\sigma\iota\tau o\mu\acute{\epsilon}\tau\rho\iota o\nu$, Luke xii. 42, with Gen. xlvii. 12), his stint and proportion in his estate, as well as in his stature, to the which he shall come and not exceed. All carking care therefore is bootless and unprofit-able. Men may eat up their hearts thereby, and trouble their houses, Prov. xv. 27 (what with labour, and what with passion, a covetous man and his household never live at heart's ease, all is continually on a tumult of haste and hurry), but cannot add anything to their stature or estate, much less to their spiritual growth, which is hereby exceedingly hindered and hide-

bound: as we see in the recusant guests, the rich young Pharisee, and those other, that being called to be Christ's disciples, were so taken up with the care of their worldly business, that they could find no present leisure to follow Christ.

Ver. 28. *Consider the lilies of the field*] Con-template them, saith Luther: understand them well, saith Erasmus: learn how they grow, saith Beza: hang upon these fair flowers, with the busy bee, till you have sucked some sweet meditation out of them. God is to be seen and admired in all his wondrous works. A skilful artificer takes it ill that he sets forth a curious piece, and no man looks at it. There is not a flower in the whole field (the word here rendered lilies signifieth all sorts of flow-ers) but sets forth God to us in lively colours.[3] Not to see him, is to incur the curse he hath denounced against such as regard not the work of the Lord, that is, the first making, neither consider the operation of his hands, Isa. v. 12; that is, the wise disposing of his creatures, for our behoof and benefit. A godly ancient being asked by a profane philosopher,[4] how he could contemplate high things, sith he had no books? wisely answered, that he had the whole world for his book, ready open at all times and in all places, and that therein he could read things divine and heavenly. A bee can suck honey out of a flower, that a fly cannot do. Our Saviour could have pointed us to our first parents clothed, and Elijah fed, the Israelites both fed and clothed extraordinarily by God in the wilderness. Never prince was so served in his greatest pomp, nor Solomon in all his royalty, as they. But because all men have not faith to believe that miracles shall be wrought for them, he sendeth us to these more ordinary and more easy instances of God's bountiful and provident care of birds and lilies, that in them (as in so many optic glasses) we may see God's infinite goodness and be confident.

They toil not, neither do they spin] *Neque laborant, neque nent.* This is the sluggard's posy. How much better that emperor (Severus) who took for his motto, *Laboremus:* let us be doing. God made not man to play, as he hath done Leviathan, but commandeth him to sweat out his living. This was at first God's ordinance in Paradise, that his store-house should be his work-house, his pleasure his task, Gen. ii. 15. After the fall, it was enjoined as a punishment, Gen. iii. 19. So that now man is born to travail, and must labour with his own hands, neither eating the bread of idleness nor drinking the wine of violence, Job v. 7; Eph. iv. 28. That monk that laboureth not with his hands is a thief, saith an ancient: is a body-louse, sucking the blood of others, saith a Neoterick: he shall

---

[1] *Non decidentes, sed velut torvo vultu nobis salutatis subito diffugiunt.* Luther.

[2] $\mu\grave{\eta}\ \mu\epsilon\tau\epsilon\omega\rho\acute{\iota}\zeta\epsilon\sigma\theta\epsilon$, Luke xii. 29. *Meteora dicta volunt, quod animos hominum suspensos, dubios, et quasi fluctuantes teneant. Aristoteles fatetur se de quibusdam eorum adhuc dubi-*

tare, quædam vero aliquo modo attigisse. Magir. Physiolog.

[3] *Contemplamini. Cognoscite lilia agri. Discite quomodo, &c. Generatim flores campi denotat.*

[4] Anton. Erem. apud August. de doct. Christ. lib. 1, et Nicop. lib. 8, c. 40.

die in his iniquity, saith God, because he hath not done good among his people, Ezek. xviii. 18. He buried himself alive, as that Vacia in Seneca; "he shall be buried with the burial of an ass" when he is dead, Jer. xxii. 19. He shall hear, "O thou wicked and slothful servant," when he riseth again at the last day, Matt. xxv. 26. God puts no difference between *nequam* and *nequaquam*, an idle and an evil servant. This made Mr Calvin answer his friends with some indignation, when they admonished him, for his health's sake, to forbear studying so hard, *Quid? Vultis ut Dominus veniens me otiosum inveniret?* "What! would you that Christ when he cometh should find me idle?"

Ver. 29. *And yet I say unto you, that even Solomon in all his glory*] In all his bravery, which doubtless was very great, in the day of his espousals, especially, when his mother crowned him, Cant. iii. 11. Herod's cloth of silver did so dazzle the people's eyes in a sunshiny day, that they deified him.[1] Alcisthenes the Sybarite's cloak was sold to the Carthaginians by Dionysius for 120 talents. And Demetrius, king of Macedon, had a robe royal so stately and costly, that none of his successors would wear it, for avoiding of envy. There is no doubt but Solomon's royal robes were very sumptuous, being so mighty and wealthy a monarch. Great ones may go arrayed according to their state; and they that are in kings' houses wear softs, Matt. xi. 8. Yet is it reckoned as a fault in the rich man, Luke xvi. 19, that he was often clothed in purple and fine linen,[2] and God threatened to punish even princes and kings' children, and all other such as are clothed with strange apparel, Zeph. i. 8. The Jews for affecting the Chaldæan habit were soon after carried captive into Chaldea, Ezek. xxiii. 15. And what heavy things are thundered against those curious dames of Jerusalem by the prophet Isaiah, who being himself a courtier, inveighs as punctually against that noble vanity as if he had lately viewed the ladies' wardrobes. Our Saviour finds fault with the scribes that loved to go in long clothing, Mark xii. 38; and St James with those Christians that would fawn upon a gold ring and a goodly suit, James ii. 2. In the year 1580, great ruffs, with huge wide sets, and cloaks reaching almost to the ancles, no less uncomely than of great expense, were restrained here by proclamation, saith Mr Camden.[3] And need we not the like law now, when so many prodigals turn rents into ruffs, and lands into laces, *Singulis auribus bina aut terna dependunt patrimonia*, as Seneca hath it, hang two or three patrimonies at their ears, a pretty grove upon their backs, a reasonable lordship or living about their necks. This is far from that humility wherewith St Peter would have young men clothe themselves, 1 Pet. v. 5; and

from that meek and quiet spirit, wherewith, saith he, the holy women of old adorned themselves, not with plaited hair, and golden habiliments, 1 Pet. iii. 3, 4. Cyprian and Austin say that superfluous apparel is worse than whoredom: because whoredom only corrupts chastity, but this corrupts nature.

Ver. 30. *The grass of the field, which to-day is, and to-morrow is cast into the oven*] A fit resemblance of all outward things, the subject of our carking cares, likened (when they are at best) to the flower of grass, Isa. xl. 6. "The sun is no sooner risen," saith St James (i. 10, 11), "with a burning heat, but it withereth the grass, and the flower thereof falleth, and the grace of the fashion of it perisheth: so also shall the rich man fade away in his ways," his riches cannot ransom him. But as grass, when ripe, withereth, and is carried away, either by the teeth of beasts or hands of men; so are all, by impartial death. And as the scythe with a few strokes mows down thousands of piles and forms of grass; so do God's judgments millions of men, Psal. ix. 17; Prov. xi. 21. And as grass is to-day a flourishing field, to-morrow cast into the oven; so are the greatest into their graves (if not into that burning fiery furnace) then when they are in their prime and pride, in their greatest flourish, in the ruff of all their jollity. As the rich fool, therefore a fool because he stuck his clothes with these flowers of the field, these fading felicities, and thought himself thereby become (as Simon Magus) some great one, Acts viii. 9; James i. 10. Contrarily St James makes it a sign of a convert, that though of high degree in the world, yet he is herein made low, that he hath low thoughts of these low things, which he seeth to be mutable and momentary, as the flower of the grass; and bids him rejoice in that he is exalted, in that he is now made a greater man ever since (*Animo magno nihil magnum*): being converted he is become too big for these petty businesses. As a man grown up delights to deal in lands and lays by his cherry-stones. But we pity that want of wit which maketh the mind run on baubles, but never think on aught substantial.

O ye of little faith] Ye petty-fidians, ye small-faiths. Unbelief is that root of bitterness whence carefulness springeth. Hence it was that the heathen so abounded in it. Strive we therefore to a full assurance of faith and hope; so shall we roll ourselves upon God for all things needful to life and godliness. Faith fears no famine (*Fides famem non formidat.* Jer. *ex* Tert.), it quelleth and killeth distrustful fear, but awful dread it breedeth, feedeth, fostereth, and cherisheth. When a man can say with Abraham, "God will provide," he will be out of fear and doubt; when he can believe

---

[1] Acts xii. 22. *Hunc homines decorant quem vestimenta decorant.*

[2] ἐνεδιδύσκετο, *Verbum est quasi frequentativum, quo luxus divitis illius epulonis arguitur.*

[3] *Vestium curiositas deformitatis mentium et morum indicium est.* Bern. *Fulgent monilibus, sordent moribus.* Salvian. *Cultus magna cura, magna virtutis est incuria.* Cato.

not only God's promise, but his providence, as David, 1 Sam. xxvi. 10, 11.

Ver. 31. *Therefore take no careful thought, &c.*] From the fore-named grounds. Our Saviour here resumeth and enforceth the former exhortation. *Sollicitudo est ægritudo cum cogitatione*, saith the orator (Cic. Tusc. 4). Carefulness is a tormentful plodding upon businesses. It is, say divines, an act of fear and distrust, taking up not only the head, but chiefly the heart, to the very dividing and disturbing thereof; causing a man inordinately and over-eagerly to pursue his desires, and to perplex himself likewise with doubtful and fearful thoughts about success. Now our Lord Christ would have none of his servants to care inordinately about anything, but that, when they have done what they can in obedience to him, they should leave the whole matter of good or evil success to his care. To care about the issue of our lawful endeavours is to usurp upon God, to trench far into his prerogative divine, to take upon us that which is proper to him. And it is no less a fault to invade God's part than to neglect our own. Add hereunto, that God out of his wise justice ceaseth caring for such an one, and because he will not be beholden to God to bear his burden, he shall bear it alone, to the breaking of his back, or, at least, till he is much bowed and crushed under it. If we discern such as will put no trust in us, but love to stand upon their own ground, we give them good leave; as contrarily, the more we see ourselves trusted to, the more our fidelity is careful for them that stay upon us. Thus it is with our heavenly Father.

Saying, What shall we eat? &c.] Our Saviour by these distrustful questions graphically expresseth the condition of covetous caitiffs, their endless projects and discourses in the air. They are full of words, and many questions, what they shall do, and how they and theirs shall be provided for? They have never done either moaning themselves, or consulting to no purpose, in things that either cannot be done at all or not otherwise. And so some understand that of our Saviour, Luke xii. 29, Hang not in doubtful suspenses; after he had brought in the rich fool, ver. 17, reasoning and saying, "What shall I do?" &c.[1] And Solomon brings in such another fool, full of words, and he recites his words, "A man cannot tell what shall be, and what shall be after him, who can tell?" Eccles. x. 15. And in the next chapter, ver. 1 and so forward, he makes answer to many of these men's frivolous queries and cavils, when moved to works of mercy. Old men specially are taxed of this weakness, who are apt to cark, because they fear, saith Plutarch, ὅτι οὐκ ἔξουσι θρέψοντας καὶ θάψοντας, that they shall not have enough to keep them and bring them well home, as they call it; whence some con-

ceive that covetousness is called "the root of all evil," 1 Tim. vi. 10, because as there is life in the root when no sap in the branches, so covetousness oft liveth when other vices die and decay. It groweth, as they say the crocodile, as long as he liveth.

Ver. 32. *For after all these things do the Gentiles seek*] With whom if you should symbolize in sins, or not exceed in virtue, it were a shame to you. They studiously seek these things, they seek them with all their might; as being without God in the world, and therefore left by him to shift for themselves.[2] When we observe a young man toiling and moiling, running and riding, and not missing a market, &c., we easily guess and gather that he is fatherless and friendless, and hath none other to take care for him. Surely this immoderate care is better beseeming infidels that know not God, but rest wholly upon themselves and their own means, than Christians, who acknowledge God most wise and all-sufficient to be their loving father.[3] As we differ from heathens in profession, so we should in practice; and a gross business it is, that Jerusalem should justify Sodom, and it should be said unto her, "Neither hath Samaria committed half of thy sins, but thou hast multiplied thine abominations more than they," Ezek. xvi. 51. Such as have hope in this life only, what marvel if they labour their utmost to make their best of it? Now many of the poor pagans believed not the immortality of the soul, and those few of them that dreamt of another life beyond this, yet affirmed of it very faintly, and scarce believed themselves. Socrates, the wisest of heathens, spake thus to his friends at his death: "The time is now come that I must die, and you survive; but whether is the better of these two, the gods only know, and not any man living, that is my opinion."[4] "But we have not so learned Christ;" neither must we do as heathens and aliens from the commonwealth of Israel; sith now in Christ Jesus, we who sometimes were far off are made nigh by his blood, and have an access through him by one Spirit to the Father, Eph. ii. 13, 18.

For your heavenly Father knoweth that ye have need of all these things] Not with a bare barren notional knowledge, but with a fatherly tender care to provide for his own in all their necessities: which whoso doeth not, he judgeth him worse than an infidel. We need not be careful of our maintenance here in our minority and non-age, nor yet for our eternal inheritance when we come to full age. We are cared for in everything that we need, and that can be good for us. Oh happy we, did we but know our happiness! How might we live in a very heaven upon earth, could we but live by faith and walk before God with a perfect heart? He made himself known to be our gracious and

---

[1] μὴ μετεωρίζεσθε. διελογίζετο. *Mire convenit verbum* λογίζεσθαι, *quoniam istius modi homines, &c.* Beza.

[2] ἐπιζητεῖ, *Summo studio efflagitant.*

[3] κερδαίνοντες οὐ κοπιῶμεν. Naz.

[4] *Utrum autem sit melius Dii immortales sciunt: hominem quidem arbitror scire neminem.* Plato and Cic.

provident Father before we were born. And did we but seriously consider who kept and fed us in our mother's womb, Psal. xxii. 9, 10, when neither we could shift for ourselves nor our parents do aught for us, how he filled us two bottles with milk against we came into the light, bore us in his arms as a nursing-father, Numb. xi. 13, fed us, clothed us, kept us from fire and water, charged his angels with us, commanded all winds to blow good to us, Cant. iv. 16, all creatures to serve us, Hos. ii. 21—23, and all occurrences to work together for our good, Rom. viii. 18, how could we but be confident? Why art thou so sad from day to day? and what is it thou ailest or needest? Art not thou the king's son? said Jonadab to Amnon, 2 Sam. xiii. 4,—say I to every godly Christian. Profane Esau could go to his father for a child's portion; so could the prodigal, because a child; and had it. Every child of God shall have a Benjamin's portion here, and at length power over all nations, Rev. ii. 26, and possession of that "new heaven and new earth, wherein dwelleth righteousness," 2 Pet. iii. 13. Either therefore disclaim God for your Father, or else rest confident of his fatherly provision.

Certa mihi spes est quod vitam qui dedit, idem
Et velit, et possit suppeditare cibum.

God that giveth mouths will not fail to give meat also.

Ver. 33. *But seek ye first the kingdom of God and his righteousness*] That as the end, this as the means; for grace is the way to glory, holiness to happiness. If men be not righteous, there is no heaven to be had; as if they be, they shall have heaven and earth too: for godliness hath the promise of both lives; and godly men, in Scripture (Abraham, Job, David, others), were richer than any: and so men might be now if they would be as godly. The good God had furnished Constantine the Great with so many outward blessings, as scarce any man durst ever have desired, saith St Austin.[1] He sought God's kingdom first, and therefore other things sought him: and so they would do us, did we but run the same method. Riches and honours, delights and pleasures, life and length of days, seed and posterity, are all entailed upon piety, Prov. iii. 16, 17; Deut. xxviii. 1—14; Psal. cxii. 2, 3. The wicked in the fulness of his sufficiency is in straits, Job xx. 22, when the godly in the fulness of their straits are in all-sufficiency. Oh, who would not then turn spiritual purchaser, and with all his gettings get godliness? "Seek ye first the kingdom of God," saith divinity (first, before anything else; and first, more than any other thing). Seek ye first the good things of the mind, saith philosophy,[2] *Cætera aut aderunt, aut certe non oberunt.* But our senseless over-valuing

of earthly things and under-prizing of heavenly is that that maketh us so carkingly careful in the one, and so recklessly affected in the other. The lean kine eat up the fat, and it is nothing seen by them. The strength of the ground is so spent in nourishing weeds, tares, or corn of little worth, that the good wheat is pulled down, choked, or starved. Earthly-mindedness sucketh the sap of grace from the heart, as the ivy doth from the oak, and maketh it unfruitful. Correct therefore this ill-humour, this choke-weed: cast away this clog, this thick clay, that makes us like that diseased woman in the Gospel, that being held of a spirit eighteen years, could not look up to heaven, Luke xiii. 11. And learn to covet spiritual things, labour for the meat that perisheth not. Lay hold upon eternal life, whatever you let go. Temporal things are, *nec vera, nec vestra,* mutable and momentary, mixed and infected with care in getting, fear in keeping, grief in losing. Besides, they are insufficient and unsatisfactory, and many times prove instruments of vice, and hindrances from heaven.[3] Spiritual things, on the other side, are solid and substantial, serving to a life that is supernatural and supernal. They are also certain and durable, *Nec prodi, nec perdi, nec eripi, nec surripi possunt.* They are sound and sincere, a continual feast, without cessation or the least intermission,[4] they serve to, and satisfy the soul; as being the gain of earth and heaven, and of him that filleth both. Seek ye therefore first, &c. Our Saviour, in his prayer, gives us but one petition for temporals, five for spirituals, to teach us this lesson. Scipio went first to the capitol, and then to the senate, &c. Aristotle saith, first take care of divine things: that is the best policy. πρῶτον περὶ θείων ἐπίμελε. (Polit. vii. 8.)

And all these things shall be added unto you] They shall be cast in as an over-plus, or as those small advantages to the main bargain; as pepper and pack-thread is given where we buy spice and fruit; as a handful is cast into the sack of grain, or an inch of measure to an ell of cloth. These follow God's kingdom, as the blackguard do the court, or as all the revenue and retinue doth some great lady that one hath wedded. The night of Popery shall shame such as think much of the time that is spent with and for God; for in their superstitious zeal they were wont to say, Mass and meat hinders no man's thrift. It would be a great stay of mind, if the king should say to us for ourselves, the same that David did to Mephibosheth, "Fear not, for I will surely show thee kindness," and "thou shalt surely eat bread at my table continually," 2 Sam. ix. 7. Or if he should say to us for our children, as David did to Barzillai the Gileadite concerning Chimham: "Chimham shall go over with me, and I will do to him that which shall seem good unto thee:

---

[1] *Bonus Deus Constant. mag. tantis terrenis implevit muneribus, quanta optare nullus auderet.* Aug. Civ. Dei, 5. 25.

[2] *Quærite primum bona animi.* Cicero.

[3] *Lucrum in arca facit damnum in conscientia.* Aug.

[4] Ἀνὴρ ἀγαθὸς πᾶσαν ἡμέραν ἑορτὴν ἡγεῖται. Diog. ap. Plut.

and whatsoever thou shalt require of me, that will I do for thee," 2 Sam. xix. 38; hath not God said as much here as all this, and shall we not trust and serve him, cleave to him, and rest on him without fear or distraction?

Ver. 34. *Take therefore no thought for the morrow*] The Lord Christ, well knowing which way our heart hangs and pulse beats, beats much upon this string, drives this nail home to the head. When things are over and over again repeated and inculcated, it imports, 1. the difficulty, 2. the necessity, of the duty, 3. our utter averseness, or, at least, dulness to the doing of it. How hardly we come off with God in this most necessary but much-neglected duty, who knows not, feels not, bewails not? The world is a most subtle, sly enemy: and by reason of her near neighbourhood, easily and insensibly insinuates into us, and insnares the best hearts. Our Saviour saw cause to warn his disciples of the cares of life: and where was Thomas, when Jesus appeared to the rest of the disciples, the doors being shut, but either lurking for fear of the Jews (in probability), or packing up, and providing for one, now that his master was slain, and taken from him? Whatever the cause was, the effect was woeful, John xx. 24, 25. And albeit in both Testaments (as Scultetus observeth) the saints of God have been noted to be subject to divers infirmities, yet not tainted with this enormity of covetousness. Yet St John saw cause to. say to those that were fathers also: "Love not the world, nor the things that are in the world," 1 John i. 5. And David prays heartily, "Incline my heart to thy testimonies, and not to covetousness," Psal. cxix. 36. Satan will be busy with the best this way, as he was with our Saviour himself: he knew it a most prevailing bait. And when this would not work, he fleeth from him, as if despairing of victory. "Be sober therefore" (in the pursuit and use of these earthly things) "and watch, for your adversary the devil" watcheth you a shrewd turn by them, 1 Pet. v. 7. They are so near and so natural to us, that, through Satan's policy and malice, when we think upon them (that we may the better learn to flee and slight them) they stick to our fingers when we should throw them away; they catch us when we should flee from them; they come over us with feigned words usually, 2 Pet. ii. 3; to hide our faults from the view of others, or subtle thoughts and evasions, to blindfold the conscience, with colour of Christ, necessary thrift, &c. Whence it is called, cloaked and coloured covetousness, 1 Thess. ii. 5. A Christian hath ever God for his chief end, and will not, deliberately, forego him upon any terms. He errs in the way, thinking he may mind earthly things and keep God too: so being insnared with these worldly lime-twigs (like the silly bird), before he is aware, the more he struggleth the more he is entangled and disabled. All this, and more than this, our Saviour well knew; and therefore reiterates his exhortation,

¹ Pemble on Zech. vii. 14.

and sets it on with so many arguments. "Care not for the morrow," &c. "I will be *careless*, according to my name," said that martyr John Careless; "for now my soul is turned to her old rest again, and hath taken a sweet nap in Christ's lap. I have cast my care upon the Lord, who careth for me," &c. And Bishop Hooper, in a letter to certain good people taken praying in Bow churchyard, and now in trouble, writeth thus: "Read the second chapter of Luke; there the shepherds that watched upon their sheep all night, as soon as they heard Christ was born at Bethlehem, by and by they went to seek him. They did not reason, nor debate with themselves, who should keep the wolf from the sheep in the mean time; but did as they were commanded, and committed their sheep to him, whose pleasure they obeyed; so let us do now we be called, commit all other things to him that calleth us. He will take heed that all things shall be well; he will help the husband, comfort the wife, guide the servants, keep the house, preserve the goods, yea, rather than it shall be undone, he will wash the dishes and rock the cradle. Cast therefore all your care upon God," &c. Judea (as one hath well observed ¹) lay utterly waste for 70 years. Insomuch that after the slaughter of Gedaliah, when all, man, woman, and child, fled into Egypt, there was not a Jew left in the country. Neither find we any colonists sent thither, or any displaced to make room at their return. A wonderful providence, that so pleasant a country, left destitute of inhabitants, and compassed about with such warlike nations, was not invaded nor replanted for 70 years' space; but the land kept her sabbaths, resting from tillage, &c., and God kept the room empty, till the return of the naturals. Jeremiah, immediately after he had foretold the captivity, and the Chaldeans were now besieging the city, was bidden to buy a field of his uncle's son; which also he did, weighing him the money, and sealing the evidences: for although it might seem an ill time to make a purchase, yet he took no further care than to trust God, who had said, Houses, and fields, and vineyards shall be possessed again in this land. Now God's promises, he knew, were the best freehold, Jer. xxxii. 15. So in every seventh years' rest, the people were taught to depend on God's providence by faith. For though the owner of the field might gather, even on that year, for the maintenance of himself and family, Lev. xxv. 6, yet he was neither to sow his field, thereby to greaten his harvest, nor to hedge his field, or lock up his vineyard.

For the morrow shall take thought for the things of itself] That is, the providence that brings the day shall also bring new events to comfort us over all the evils of the day. First, no man is sure of life till to-morrow,—thou knowest not what this great-bellied day may bring forth.² Petrarch tells of a good old man, that being invited to a feast the next day, answered, "If you would have anything with

² *Nescis quid serus vesper vehat.*

me now, here I am : what is to be done to-morrow, think on it, you that have time before you, *Ego enim, à multis annis, crastinum non habui :* For I have not had, for these many years, a morrow to dispose of." Young men, he knew, may die, old men must die. *Senibus mors in januis, adolescentibus in insidiis,* saith Bernard. Old men may say, as Job (xvii. 1), " My breath is corrupt, my days extinct, the graves are ready for me." The young man, as Job (xvi. 22), " When a few years (perhaps a few hours) are come, I shall go the way whence I shall not return." Secondly, grant a man had a lease of his life, as Hezekiah had, yet who seeth it not to be extreme folly to anticipate future cares and combats before they come, yea, even those of the next day ; seeing they will come time enough to our sorrow, though we send not for them by our distrustful fore-thoughts, and so re-double our vexation ? It is possible that we may never feel the evils we fear. God may repent upon our repentance, and be better to us than our fears. And therefore what a weakness is it, to undergo certain trouble and care about uncertainties ? Or if they shall happen, we may have wit to foresee them, but no power to prevent them : and therefore to vex ourselves before they come is to be miserable before the time. It is excellent counsel, doubtless, that Solomon giveth us in this case : " Consider the works of God, for who can make that straight that he hath made crooked ? In the day of prosperity be joyful," make the best of thy present comfort, " but in the day of adversity consider ; God also hath set one against the other, to the end that man should find nothing after him," to wit, of those things that may come upon him in the course of his life, and after-times, Eccles. vii. 14. He cannot by wit foresee, or by policy prevent, ensuing changes. Therefore it is a great part of his wisdom to let certain and inevitable evils sleep, and keep in their stings till the time appointed ; and not to make himself a thousand times miserable by one individual misery. Let us manage the affairs and master the miseries of the present day ; and not, by too much fore-thoughtfulness and painful pre-conceit, suffer feigned or future evils before they seize upon us. I grant that a moderate (Christian) provident care and forecast is both convenient and commanded, both for provision of necessaries and prevention of dangers. See 1 Tim. v. 8 ; 2 Cor. xii. 14. We read, Rev. vi. 6, " A measure of wheat for a penny," &c. The word signifieth properly, such a measure of corn ($\chi o \tilde{\imath} \nu \iota \xi$) as was usually allowed for a day to servants. Hence that speech of Pythagoras, *Super chœnice non sedendum,* Rest not in the provision that sufficeth for the day ; but take care for the morrow. But this lawful care of necessaries, both for ourselves and ours after us, Prov. xiii. 22 (such as was that of Jacob for his own house, Gen. xxx. 30, and that of the good housewife,

Prov. xxxi. 15, 21), is not distressful, but delightful, because enjoined by God, who sendeth us to the pismire, to learn this care of hereafter, Prov. vi. 6.

Sufficient to the day is the evil thereof] [1] The strongest mind and best composed is weak enough to sustain the brunt and encounter of every day's crosses, whereof he is sure to have his back-burthen. Troubles without and terrors within are the saints' portion here. And what day shines so fair over them, wherein they meet not with a sharp shower ere night ? Sith therefore every day brings forth sufficient sorrow, and the heartiest man shall have his hands full, what a base and unworthy weakness is it (saith a reverend divine) to unfit and disable our already too weak minds, for a comfortable despatch, and digesting of daily uncomfortable occurrences, by such needless, fruitless, senseless distractions, vagaries of vanity, and utopian peregrinations ? &c.

CHAPTER VII.

Ver. 1. *Judge not, that ye be not judged*] *Hoc verbum quandam indaginem involvit.* The word [2] imports a kind of curious inquiry into other men's faults, that we may the more severely censure and subject them to a sinister interpretation. It signifies sometimes no more, I grant, than to reprehend, as Rom. ii. 1. But this, so it were wisely done, our Saviour would never have reprehended. " Thou shalt not hate thy brother in thy heart : " but (for prevention of such a mischief) thou shalt plainly (not perfunctorily, or in jest, bravery, form, derision) rebuke thy neighbour, and not suffer sin upon him, as some read it ; lest thou suffer for his sin : or, as others, lift not up his sin over him as an ensign,[3] blaze it not abroad to his just grief and disgrace ; but clap a plaister on the sore, and then cover it with thy hand, as chirurgeons use to do, that the world may be never the wiser. This were charity, which hides with her mantle a multitude of sins ; yea, prepares. covers and cures for the infirmities of others as fast as they breed them, 1 Pet. iv. 8. And the neglect hereof, the not giving vent to our hearts, by a wise and plain reproof, causeth abalienation of affection, dwelling suspicions, blind censures, a very habit of misprision and misinterpretation of all things, till men grow rusty with rancour and malice, the poison whereof would be soon drawn out by a seasonable reproof : this, well and wisely done, were far better than judging and grudging one against another, sith it is, " judge not, that ye be not judged," and " grudge not, that ye be not condemned," James v. 9. The sins of others we should hear of with indignation, fearfully and unwillingly believe, acknowledge with grief, never speak of them but in an ordinance, rather

---

[1] κακία, id est κάκωσις, labor improbus.
[2] κρίνειν etiam significat interpretari, et plerunque de somniis dicitur. Novarin.

[3] Lev. xix. 17. *Ne ejus peccatum luas. Ne tamen super eum peccatum tollas tanquam vexillum.*

hide them, as much as may be, with honest excuses, and make apology; as, that there are infirmities in the best, though we know them not, that as good gold, they are haply of the lightest, may want a grain or two of their just weight: but give them their allowance, and they may pass for current, &c. Be not rash in rejecting or sour in censuring your fellow-servants.[1] That saying is true, Three things are not subject to our judgments, the counsels of God, the Holy Scriptures, and the persons of men, Rom. xiv. 10. It is a good rule of the schoolmen concerning the judging of our neighbour, *Ut bona ejus certa, meliora; certa mala, minora; dubia bona, certa; dubia mala nulla judicemus:* that we make the best of everything that we can with truth, and not aggravate small faults; exclaiming, with Momus, against the creaking of Venus's pantofle.

That ye be not judged] Judge we must ourselves, and God will not judge us. Step from the bar, where thou hast arraigned, accused, witnessed, and pleaded guilty against thyself, to the bench, and there pass sentence of condemnation, judging thyself worthy to be turned into hell torments. Thus judge yourselves and spare not. But judge not others; namely, rashly, sinisterly, finally, and peremptorily, "lest ye be judged;" both first of God, into whose chair ye leap, and whose children ye condemn, even the generation of the just; as David once did, and befooled himself well-favouredly for it, when he had done. And secondly of men: good men must suspect you, bad men scorn you, and all men shun you, and desire to be rid of you, as unfit to live in a civil society.[2] Therefore judge nothing before the time, behold the Judge standeth at the door. It is the office of angels to sever the sheep from the goats, the tares from the wheat, the elect from the reprobate. Those that undertake peremptorily to determine of men's final estate, they know not of what spirit they are, with those sons of Zebedee; they take too much upon them, with those sons of Levi; they understand neither what they say nor whereof they affirm, with those impostors in Timothy, Numb. xvi. 7; 1 Tim. i. 7. Neither may they escape here uncensured, that for particular acts or petty failings take upon them rashly and harshly to censure their betters many times. Job and Jeremiah met with such as watched for their halting, and made them offenders for a word. These pry into every particular more narrowly than Laban did into Jacob's stuff, waiting as a dog for a bone, for anything less beseeming the saints, that they may fasten upon with their fangs, that they may tear with their teeth, and swallow down with those open sepulchres, their throats, the good names of others; censuring them

deeply for human frailties, unchurching and unbrothering them for unavoidable infirmities.[3] It is hard measuring of a man by his state and behaviour in a pelt, in a passion, which are violent, and have made the holiest, in their heat, little less than bestial, 1 Sam. xxv. 22.; Psal. cxvi. 9. The like may be said of sins strengthened by ancient custom, or natural inclination, or hereditary, the sins of our parents, or furthered by a multitude of temptations and enticements. Handle these gently in the judgment of charity, and joint them again in the spirit of meekness, considering thyself, lest thou also be tempted.[4] It is not to be liked, when men leap from the cradle of profession into the chair of censure, blinder than beetles at home, sharper than eagles abroad. Charity and humility would teach them to wink at small faults, as God doth, and to pitch upon that in another that is praiseworthy. Our Saviour is said to have loved the rich young Pharisee, for that little good he found in him; and Bucer never rejected any, though different in opinion, in whom he discerned *aliquid Christi*, anything of Christ. St Paul bids us consider one another, to whet on to love, Heb. x. 24, to pitch upon such good parts and properties as may engender love and sway us to a good opinion of our brethren. The wisdom from above is full of mercy and good fruits, without judging, &c. But they shall have judgment without mercy that use no mercy in their judgings, Jam. iii. 17. God shall bring home their own dealings to their own doors. "For with what judgment ye judge," &c. Only our Saviour is to be understood here of private and corrupt judgment passed upon others, out of sinful curiosity and ill-will, for *Nemo curiosus quin malevolus*, either to set up ourselves above them, or by condemning them to countenance our own evil courses. Magistrates may and must judge between the righteous and the wicked. Ministers must take out the precious from the vile, and say to the wicked, "It shall be ill with them, the reward of their hands shall be given unto them," Isa. iii. 11. "Wilt thou judge them, son of man, wilt thou judge them? yea, thou shalt show them all their abominations," Ezek. xxii. 2. How often doth our Saviour call the Pharisees hypocrites, serpents, vipers, &c. And how roundly dealt St Paul with the sorcerer, Acts xiii. 10, and with the incestuous person, 1 Cor. v. 13. Lastly, though we may not be many masters, Jam. iii. 1, supercilious and censorious, &c., yet we may all judge the tree by the fruit, call a spade a spade, a drunkard a drunkard, &c., and, leaving his final doom to the searcher of all hearts, judge and censure him, for the present, to be God's enemy, and in a most wretched estate. We both may and must condemn all sin

---

[1] *Noli esse alienæ vitæ aut temerarius judex, aut curiosus explorator.* Bernard. The Hebrew word for prayer hath the first signification of judging, because therein we must judge ourselves.

[2] *Jupiter hunc cœli dignatus honore fuisset; Censorem linguæ sed timet ipse suæ.* Sic. in Laur.

Vallam, severum censorem scriptorum, quidam lusit. Trithem.

[3] *Sunt quidem in Ecclesia Catholica plurimi mali, sed ex hæreticis nullus est bonus.* Bellarm. de not. Eccles. iv. 13.

[4] καταρτίζετε, Gal. vi. 1. *Aut sumus, aut fuimus, aut possumus esse quod hic est.*

in ourselves and others. But it is a fault to be itchingly inquisitive after other men's misdemeanors, to be an eves-dropper, Eccles. vii. 21, or to censure them, when they come to our knowledge, unmercifully and above the royal law. Let your ἐπιείκεια, moderation of utmost right, be known to all men: the Lord is at hand, Phil. iv. 5.

Ver. 2. *For with what judgment ye judge, &c.*] Our Saviour sets forth what he had said before by these two proverbial sentences, as well known among them as those amongst us: " Ye shall sow as ye reap, drink as ye brew, be served with the same sauce," &c.[1] Compare herewith those divine proverbs, Isa. xxxiii. 1; Prov. xii. 14; xiii. 2, 21; xiv. 14, 22; xxii. 8; Job vi. 8; Mark vi. 24. God delights to give men their own, as good as they brought, to pay them home in their own coin, or as the text here and the Hebrew proverb hath it, to re-mete them their own measure,[2] Isa. iii. 10, 11; with the merciful to show himself merciful, and with the froward to wrestle. He will be as froward as they for the hearts of them, beat them with their own weapons, overshoot them in their own bows, shape their estates according to their own patterns, and cause others to write after their copies, as it fared with Pharaoh, Adonibezek, Agag, &c. Sodom sinned in fulness of bread, and it is expressly noted that their victuals were taken from them by the four kings, Gen. xiv. 11. Their eyes were full of uncleanness, and they were smitten with blindness; they burned with lust, and were burned with fire; they sinned against nature, and against the course of nature fire descends and consumes them. Eglon, stabbed into the guts, finds his bane the same way with his sin. Sisera annoys God's people with his iron chariots, and is slain by a nail of iron. Jezebel's brains, that devised mischief against the innocent, are strewed upon the stones; by a letter to Jezreel she shed the blood of Naboth, and by a letter from Jezreel the blood of her sons is shed. Nebuchadnezzar destroyed Solomon's temple (that seven years' work of so many thousands), therefore let him be turned a grazing, and seven seasons pass over him, saith the oracle, Dan. iv. 16. The blasphemers in the Revelation " gnaw their tongues " through pain, and Dives (for like cause) was tormented in that part chiefly.[3] Appian scoffing at religion, and especially at circumcision, had an ulcer at the same time and in the same place. Phocas, a wild, drunken, bloody, adulterous tyrant, was worthily slaughtered by Heraclius, who cut off his hands and feet, and then his genitals by piecemeal. The Donatists, that cast the holy elements in the Lord's supper to dogs, were themselves afterward devoured of dogs. John Martin of Briqueras, a mile from Angrogne, vaunted everywhere that he would slit the minister's nose of

Angrogne, but was himself assaulted by a wolf, which bit off his nose, whereof he died mad. Sir Ralph Elerker, Knight Marshal of Calais, in Queen Mary's reign, being present at the death of Adam Damlip, martyr, bid the executioner despatch, saying that he would not away till he saw the traitor's heart out. Shortly after this Sir Ralph was slain, amongst others, in a skirmish at Bullein, and his heart cut out of his body by the enemies,—a terrible example to all merciless and bloody men, &c.; for no cause was known why they should use such indignation against him more than the rest, but that it is written, " With what measure ye mete, it shall be measured to you again." Bishop Ridley told Stephen Winchester that it was the hand of God that he was now in prison, because he had so troubled others in his time. And as he had inflamed so many good martyrs, so he died miserably of an inflammation, that caused him to thrust out his tongue all swollen and black, as Archbishop Arundel had died before him. The Archbishop of Tours made suit for the erection of a court, called Chambre Ardent, wherein to condemn the Protestants to the fire. He was afterwards stricken with a disease called " the fire of God," which began at his feet, and so ascended upward, that he caused one member after another to be cut off, and so died miserably. And there is mention made of one Christopher, an unmerciful courtier, who suffering a poor lazar to die in a ditch by him, did afterwards perish himself in a ditch. To return to the present purpose: Laurentius Valla censured all that wrote before him; Erasmus comes after, and censures him as much; Beza finds as many faults with Erasmus, and not without cause, as appeareth by that one passage among many in his annotations on Rom. vii. 21: " I find then a law, that when I would do good, evil is present with me; " *Erasmus Originem secutus, scripsit Paulum hoc Sermone balbutire, quum ipse potius ineptiat.* Scaliger the hypercritic gives this absurd and unmannerly censure: *Gothi belluæ, Scoti non minus. Angli perfidi, inflati, feri, contemptores stolidi, amentes, inertes, inhospitales, immanes.* The Goths are beasts, so are the Scots. Englishmen are perfidious, proud, fierce, foolish, mad-men, slow-bellies, inhospitable, barbarous. Another comes after him, and saith, His bolt, you see, is soon shot, and so you may happily guess at the quality of the archer. Tacitus speaks reproachfully of both Jews and Christians; and is paid his own as well, both by Tertullian and Lipsius.[4] If men suffer in their good names, they may thank themselves, mostly. Contempt is a thing that man's nature is most impatient of. Those that are given to slight and censure others, are punished with the common hatred of all. Imitation and retaliation are in all men naturally, as we may see in every child. And that of Solomon is in this sense

---

[1] κρίματος μέτρον, ver. 2, *est rigor juris moderationi et mitigationi oppositus.* Aret.

[2] See also Rev. xiii. 10, xviii. 6. *Middah cenegedh middah.* Psal. xviii. 26.

[3] *Quia lingua plus peccaverat.*

[4] *Tacitum Lipsius immemorem, secumque pugnantem; Tertullianus mendaciorum loquacissimum appellat.*

found most true, "As in water face answereth to face; so doth the heart of a man to a man." None are so shunned and censured as those that are most censorious. The places they live in groan for a vomit to spew them out.

Ver. 3. *And why beholdest thou*] Here is the true method of preaching, by doctrine and use, explication and application. Ministers must (as our Saviour in his text) bring hammers with their nails, Jer. xxiii. 29, and drive them into the very head, yea, goad men to the quick, Eccles. xii. 11; that the people's hearts may either break, as theirs, Acts ii. 37, or burst, as theirs, Acts vii. 54. A general doctrine, not applied, is as a sword without an edge, not in itself, but to us, through our singular fencelessness: or, as a whole loaf set before children, that will do them no good; the bellows will be burnt in the fire, but the dross remains still. A garment fitted for all bodies is fit for no body; and that which is spoken to all, is taken as spoken to none.

The mote that is in thy brother's eye] The mote or straw: the word "beam" seems rather to have reference to a straw than to a mote:[1] and this is an evil disease that I have seen under the sun, that men (and those of the better sort sometimes) hear nothing, talk of nothing, so willingly, as they do of other men's faults; Psal. l. 20, "thou sittest and speakest against thy brother," &c.[2] There is no discourse that men will sit so long at and be so taken with as this. "The words of the tale-bearer are as flatteries, and they go down to the bowels of the belly," Prov. xviii. 8. Many are never well, longer than they are holding their fingers in other men's sores, amplifying and aggravating their faults and failings, not only most severely, but almost tragically; not once mentioning their good parts and practices. These are like crows, that fasten only upon carrion, or the horse-fly, that if he happen into a field that is never so full of sweet flowers, yet if there be but a little filthy dung in it his eye and scent is only to that, and upon that only will he light.[3] David compareth such as these to the asp, that is quick of hearing, but very ill-sighted (having his eyes not in his forehead, but in his temples), weak, but full of poison. Herein only is the difference. That poison that asps vent to the hurt of others, they keep within them, without hurt unto themselves.[4] But the malicious censurer is his own worst enemy; for as he "sets his mouth against heaven, and his tongue walketh through the earth," Psal. lxxiii. 9, so by mis-judging (out of an inward hatred of another) all his actions and intentions, he pulls upon himself the hatred both of heaven and earth, for his trampling upon God's jewels, because a little sullied. God doth unwillingly see the faults of his children, Numb. vi. 21, 23; yea, he passeth by their iniquity, transgression, and sin, Micah vii. 18; with one breath both

these are reported: "The high places were not removed, yet nevertheless Asa's heart was perfect," &c. So 1 Pet. iii. 6, compared with Gen. xviii. 12. Sarah's whole sentence was vile and profane; not one good word in it, but this, that she called her husband Lord. God of his goodness takes notice of that word, and records it, by St Peter, to her eternal commendation. He spieth out and severeth gold, though but a dram, from a mass of dross; good grain, though but a handful, from a heap of chaff; cuts out that which is perished (as men do out of a rotten apple) and preserves the rest. Be ye therefore followers herein of God, as dear children; and walk in love, &c., Eph. v. 1, 2. It thinketh not evil, but "believeth all things, hopeth all things," 1 Cor. xiii. 5; strains to hold a good opinion where it hath least probability to induce it; rashly rejects none in whom it seeth signs of grace; according to that of our Saviour, "See that ye despise not one of these little ones," neither for error in judgment, Rom. xiv. 3—10, nor for slips and infirmities in life and conversation, and that because God despiseth them not, but guards them by his angels, and saveth them by his Son, whom he sent for the purpose, Matt. xviii. 10, 11; and 1 Thess. i. 4. "Knowing, brethren beloved, your election of God," viz. by your effectual faith, laborious love, patient hope (ver. 3), although they were so compassed with infirmities, as he doubted lest the tempter had tempted them, and his labour had been in vain, 1 Thess. iii. 5, he feared their utter apostasy. So, Heb. v. 10, he could not but be persuaded of them "better things, and such as accompany salvation," though he had justly and sharply reproved them for their dulness of hearing and slowness of proceeding; yea, sets before their eyes that terror of the Lord upon apostates, to quicken their pace and excite them to proficiency. "I am black," saith the Church, "but comely as the tents of Kedar, as the curtains of Solomon," Cant. i. 5. The Kedarites dwelt in tents and open fields, where all was exposed to the parching sun in the desert; but in Arabia's deserts, and they were very rich and glorious (see Ezek. xxvii. 21; Jer. xlix. 28, 29; Isa. xxi. 13, 16, 17), full of precious gems, gold, and pleasant odours. Arabia looked rudely, yet by searching it regularly, there were to be found things of greatest price. So is it with many of God's people, especially in the scorching heat of temptation, desertion, or outward affliction, &c. He that follows his own conjecture, may condemn a dear child of God, and approve a detestable heretic, as Philip did Simon Magus. If his eyes be too fast fixed either on the saints' infirmities or the hypocrites' fair pretences, they may bring forth, as Jacob's sheep did, spotted fruits.

But considerest not the beam that is in thine own eye] Most men's minds are as ill set as their

---

[1] *Generaliter significat quod siccum et leve est. Tertullianus stipulam vertit.*

[2] *Vituperant homines quam commendant promptius.* Plaut.

[3] *Vultures ad male olentia feruntur.* Basil.

[4] *Aspidi hebetes oculi dati, eosque non in fronte sed in temporibus habet.* Pliny, 16. 14. *Non est huic similis malitia; hæc habentibus pessima est.* Seneca.

eyes; they can turn neither of them inwards. They tell us of a kind of witches, that stirring abroad would put on their eyes, but returning home, they boxed them up again.[1] The philosophers call upon us to look to the hinder part of the wallet. And St James saith, "Be not many masters" or teachers: and mark the reason, which he prescribeth as a remedy; "for in many things we sin all," Jam. iii. 1, 2. Now those that in the sense of their own sinfulness are poor in spirit, will soon be meek and merciful to their fellow-sinners; they that have proved their own works, and found all to be (not good and very good, as God did his, but) naught and stark naught, as the figs in Jeremiah (xxiv. 2), will be content to bear one another's burdens, and restore such as are overtaken in a fault with the spirit of meekness, considering themselves lest they also be tempted, Gal. vi. 1, 2, 4. They will be as willing to lend mercy now, as they may have need to borrow mercy another time.[2] And consciousness of their own corruptions will make them compassionate towards others in this kind. The Greek word that signifieth to censure, signifieth also, and in the first place, to be idle.[3] Whereunto agreeth that of St Paul (speaking of wanton widows), "they learn to be idle, wandering about from house to house: and not only idle, but tattlers also, and busy-bodies, speaking of things that they ought not," 1 Tim. v. 13. Those that travel not with their own hearts, have both leisure and list to be meddling with others.

Ver. 4. *Or how wilt thou say to thy brother,* &c.] How impudent are hypocritical find-faults, that can say such things to others, when themselves are most obnoxious! whence is this, but either from a secret desire of purchasing an opinion of freedom from the faults they so boldly censure in others, or that they may thereby the sooner insinuate and ingratiate with them they deal with? The vulgar translation reads here *Frater sine,* &c.[4] "Brother, let me pull out the mote that is in thine eye," &c. "Burning lips and a wicked heart are like a potsherd covered with silver dross. When he speaketh fair, believe him not; for there are seven abominations in his heart," Prov. xxvi. 23, 25; but there lies a great beam of hypocrisy between him and himself, that he cannot discern them. These are they that by good words and fair speeches deceive the hearts of the simple, as the serpent did Eve.[5] You would think by their smoothing, soothing honey-words, they were wholly set upon seeking your good; when they merely serve not the Lord Jesus Christ, but their own bellies, as those Popish flesh-flies. "Faithful are the wounds of a friend" (fair they are and pleasant, saith the Chaldee here), "but the kisses of an enemy are deceitful,"

Prov. xxvii. 6, as were those of Joab to Amasa, and Judas to Christ. Καταφιλεῖν non est φιλεῖν, saith Philo. Love is not always in a kiss; there are that kiss and kill. David would not taste of their dainties, nor endure that they should pour upon him the sweetest ointments (as at feasts it was the custom among that people, Luke vii. 46). Indeed, if the righteous smite him, he would take it for a singular courtesy. "Let him reprove me," saith he, "it shall be an excellent oil," and shall soak into me, as soft oil doth into wooden vessels, Prov. xxvi. 6; Psal. cxli. 4, 5. It shall not break my head; my heart it may; and so make way for the oil of God's grace which is not poured save only into broken vessels; for indeed whose vessels are full vessels, and so this precious liquor would run over and be spilt on the ground, as Bernard hath it.

Ver. 5. *Thou hypocrite*] This is a dull generation, and must be rebuked sharply or cuttingly, that they may be sound in the faith.[6] And ministers, by our Saviour's example here, must learn so to instruct as to sharpen and set an edge upon the word, so as it may gore the crusty consciences of their hearers with smarting pain, that they may hear and fear, and God may heal them, Matt. xiii. 15. Christ turns himself here to such, and bitterly inveighs against them, as elsewhere likewise he doth (Matt. xvii. 17, iii. 7, xxii. 18; Luke xiii. 15), but especially chap. xxiii. of this Gospel, dragging them down to hell by a chain of eight several woes, as so many links, and closing up all with that terrible thunderbolt, "Ye serpents, ye generation of vipers, how can ye escape the damnation of hell?" verse 33; and all to show us how such kind of persons should be handled. As for those that are so proud and passionate that none dare declare their way to their face, God will lay them in the slimy valleys, where are many already like them, and more shall come after them; where-hence also they shall be brought forth to the day of wrath, Job xxi. 30—33, and, will they nill they, hear *Ite, maledicti,* Go, ye cursed, &c.

Thou hypocrite, first cast out the beam, &c.] St James telleth us that the wisdom from above is first pure and then peaceable, without judging, without hypocrisy. And these two last are set together to teach us that the greatest censurers are commonly the greatest hypocrites,[7] and as any one is more wise he is more sparing of his censures. Hence also St Peter, after he had said, "Lay aside all malice, guile, hypocrisy, envy," addeth, "and evil speakings;" to note, that censuring and all other evils of the tongue are gendered of any of the fore-mentioned. For wicked men are apt to muse as they use; as the envious devil accused God to our first parents

---

[1] *Lamiæ apud Plinium.*

[2] *Erratis veniam poscenti reddere par est.* Hor.

[3] Αργέω, *arguo, proprie ferior, post, reprehendo.* Becman.

[4] *Frater, quasi fere alter.* Gellius xiii. 10.

[5] *Pertinax Imp. vulgo dictus est* χρηστόλογος, *quod blandus esset magis quam benignus.* Aurel. Victor.

[6] *Hypocritis nihil stupidius.* Tit. i. 13, ἀποτόμως. *Metaph. a chirurgis, quos misericordes esse non oportet.* Celsus.

[7] It was said of Antony, he hated a tyrant, not tyranny. It may as truly be said of the hypocrite, he hates sinners, not sins. These he nourisheth, those he censureth. Dike.

of envy; the covetous person thinks all the world to be made of covetousness. Caligula did not believe there was any chaste person upon earth. And Bonner said to Mr Hanks, the martyr, I dare say that Cranmer would recant if he might have his living again: so measuring him by himself. Those that have a blemish in their eye think the sky to be ever cloudy; and such as are troubled with the jaundice see all things yellow. So do those that are overgrown with malice and hypocrisy, think all like themselves. Contrarily, Mary Magdalen thought the gardener should have had as much good-will to Christ as she had. Little did Jacob suspect that Rachel had stole her father's idols; or the disciples that Judas had harboured such a traitor in his heart, as treason against his Master. They rather suspected every man himself than Judas. And when our Saviour bade him, "What thou doest, do quickly," they thought he had meant of making provision, or giving something to the poor, John xiii. 26. Also when the woman poured the precious ointment upon our Saviour, and Judas censured the fact as a waste, though he did it because he was a thief, and cared not a pin for the poor, yet all the disciples approved of what he said, and are therefore made authors of his speech by one of the evangelists; so little did they perceive his craft or his covetousness, Matt. xxvi. 8. True goodness is not suspicious, censorious, quarrellous. It is for an Esau to complain of his father's store,—Hast thou but one blessing? of his brother's subtlety,—Was he not rightly called Jacob? The godly man casts the first stone at himself, and with Jacob cries out, I am not worthy, Lord, the least of thy loving-kindnesses. "Lo, I have sinned, and I have done wickedly; but these sheep, what have they done? Let thine hand, I pray thee, be against me," &c. (2 Sam. xxiv. 17,) said David, when he was come to himself; who before this, when he had defiled his conscience with the stain and sting of sin, both censured the fact of the cruel rich man (complained of by Nathan) with too much severity, even above the law; and shortly after tortured the miserable Ammonites without all mercy, putting them under saws, harrows, and axes of iron, and making them pass through the brick-kiln, &c. This he did before his conscience was awakened out of that dead lethargy (whereinto Satan had cast him) by the trumpet of the law; before he was convinced of sin by the sanctifying Spirit, and purged thereby from those pollutions he had remorselessly wallowed in. But if God will but once more make him to hear of joy and gladness, that his broken bones may rejoice; if he will but restore unto him the joy of his salvation, and establish him with his free spirit, then, instead of censuring, and setting against others, he will teach transgressors God's ways, and sinners shall be converted unto him, Psal. li. 8, 12, 13. He will no longer insult, but

in meekness instruct those that oppose themselves, if God peradventure will give them (as he had done him) repentance to the acknowledging of the truth; and that they may awake out of the snare of the devil, who (as the Ammonites were by David) are taken captive by him at his pleasure, 2 Tim. ii. 26. "Put them in mind," saith Paul, "to speak evil of no man." And why? "For we ourselves also" (even I, Paul, and thou, Titus) "were sometimes foolish, disobedient, deceived," &c., Tit. iii. 2, 3, and have yet still a world of work within-doors about the discovering and opposing, the mortifying and mourning over our own unruly lusts and unchristian practices. A sincere heart is ever most censorious and severe against itself. But it is set here by our Saviour as a visible brand upon the face of the hypocrite, that as he is ever tampering and meddling with other men's motes, so he never hath either leisure or pleasure to look into his own rotten heart and rebellious courses. Galileo used perspective glasses to descry mountains in the moon; so do these to find faults in those that are far better than themselves; they can pierce beyond the moon and spy the least mote in the sun, the smallest infirmity in the most glorious saint; yea, some errors and exorbitancies that never had any existence but in their imagination, detesting those sins in others that they flatter in themselves. *Utimur perspicillis magis quam speculis*, saith Seneca. Men are more apt to use spectacles than looking-glasses; spectacles to behold other men's faults than looking-glasses to behold their own. But those that would approve themselves no hypocrites must do otherwise.

And then shalt thou see clearly, &c.] There is in every godly man a holy bashfulness, an ingenuous modesty, that he would be foully ashamed to charge others with those crimes which he should allow in himself. Not so every profligate professor, frontless Pharisee, censorious hypocrite. These think, belike, to bind up their own bleeding souls with a palliate cure, as they call it, by goring very bloodily into other men's consciences, whereas they never yet purged their own. Thus dealt the priests and elders with our Saviour, the false apostles with Paul, Porphyry (and others of the same brand) with the primitive Christians, and the Papists with the Waldenses; whose freedom of speech, in blaming and reproving the dissolute manners and actions of the clergy (*Effecit ut plures nefariæ affingerentur iis opiniones a quibus omnino fuerant alieni*, saith Girardus) was the cause that they were reported to be Manichees, Catharists, what not?[1] And yet a certain Dominican was forced to confess that they were good in their lives, true in their speeches, full of brotherly love one towards another, but their faith, saith he, is incorrigible, and as bad as may be.[2] And why? but because they maintained that the pope was

---

[1] *Ejusdem furfuris iisdem quibus Manichæi et Cathari commaculati credebantur erroribus.* Ussier.

[2] *In moribus et vita sunt boni veraces in sermone, in cari-*

tate fraterna unanimes: sed fides eorum est incorrigibilis et pessima. Jacob Liclensten.

Antichrist, that the court of Rome was intolerably corrupted, the clergy debauched, &c. *Novum crimen Caie Cæsar, &c.* St Paul was become the Galatians' enemy, because he told them the truth, and so were these, the pontificians. There was found a certain postiller, that meeting with this precious passage in St Augustine, "The whole life of unbelievers is sin; neither is there anything good without the chiefest good;" *Crudelis est illa sententia*, said he: this is a cruel sentence.[1] This was a sinful censure, say I, passed by a man that was never truly humbled with the sight and sense of his own wicked and wretched estate by nature and practice; a stranger to himself, and therefore so uncharitable to another. It is not evil to marry, saith one, but good to be wary. So, it is not amiss to reprove an offender, but let a man take heed he hear not,—" Physician, heal thyself. Hypocrite, first pull the beam out of thine own eye."[2] The apostle, after he had given rules for reproving, Eph. v. 11—13, subjoins, ver. 15, "See that ye walk circumspectly," or exactly, that none may justly blame or blemish you with any foul fault. Infirmities are found in the best, and will be, till they come to be "the spirits of just men made perfect," Heb. xii. 23. And this is a means to make them warn the unruly with more feeling experience and compassion, Heb. ii. 17. But say they be guilty of gross sins (as these Pharisees), though they should begin at home, and first cast out the beam of their own eye, yet if they speak according to God's word, and the thing be so indeed, hear them hardly, Matt. xxiii. 2, 3, and mend by them. An angel may speak in an ass, and God by Balaam, Deut. xiii. 14. The words do but pass through him (as when a man speaks through a trunk), they are not polluted by him, because not his.

Ver. 6. *Give not that which is holy to dogs, &c.*] Having showed how, here our Saviour shows whom[3] we should admonish. Give not holy things, wholesome counsels or rebukes (called elsewhere "reproofs of life," Prov. xv. 31, precious balms, excellent ointments, which may heal a wound, but make none, Psal. cxli. 1) to dogs, that will not be taken by the ears; or swine, that if they light upon such a pearl, will only grunt and go their ways. "Beware of dogs, beware of evil workers," Phil. iii. 2, such especially as have wrought so hard, walked so far and so fast, that now they are set down to rest in the seat of the scornful.[4] Beware of such botches; there is no good to be done upon them, or to be gotten by them, but a great deal of danger. The Cynics admonished all they met; if men would not hearken, they counted it an easy loss to cast away a few words upon them. But our Saviour prescribeth us prudence and caution. He will not have holy speeches spent and spilt upon despisers, his pearls trampled on by swinish epicures. Mourn we may, with Jeremiah (ix. 1), for such mad dogs as furiously fly in the face of them that fairly tell them of their faults. Pray we must and pity such sensual swine, such sottish and scurrilous wretches, as grunt against goodness, and feed insatiably upon the garbage of carnal contentments.[5] As dogs and swine were unclean creatures and unfit for sacrifice, so are those for admonition that would entertain it with cruelty or scurrility. "Speak not in the ears of a fool," saith Solomon, "for he will despise the wisdom of thy words," Prov. xxiii. 9. And again, "Reprove not a scorner, lest he hate thee; rebuke a wise man, and he will love thee," Prov. ix. 8. David prays for a friendly reprover, Psal. cxli. 5. Job cries (xiii. 23), "Make me to know my transgression and my sin." Hezekiah stormed not at that sharp and sad message, Isa. xxxix. 8. Jonah, though tetchy enough, lays his hand upon his mouth, and seals up his prophecy with silence after God's reprehension. *Tacuit virgo licet publice perstricta.* The Virgin Mary held her peace, John ii. 5, when her Son took her up so short for her forwardness, before all the company. So did St Peter, when St Paul took him up for halting at Antioch, Gal. ii. 14, and commendeth that epistle wherein St Paul had witnessed that reproof, among the rest, 2 Pet. iii. 16. The two disciples going to Emmaus constrained that stranger, that had chidden them for their unbelief, to abide and eat with them, Luke xxiv. 29. And lukewarm Laodicea, so roundly reproved and sorely threatened with shameful spewing out, repented, and was reformed; as some ground and gather from that title our Saviour assumes in the preface to the epistle, "the beginning of the creation of God." Eusebius also testifieth that there was a flourishing church there in his days.[6] Next to the not deserving of a reproof, is the well taking of it. No sugar can bereave a pill of its bitterness. None but the gracious can say, "Let the righteous smite me." Bees only pass by roses and violets, and sit upon thyme, which is hot and biting. Most men, when we seek to fetch them out of their sins, to awaken them out of the snare of the devil, they fret and snarl, as those that are wakened out of sleep are apt to do. They snuff and take scorn, are as horse and mule, untameable, untractable; the more you rub their galled backs the more they kick. These stray asses will not be brought home, Exod. xxiii. 4, 5. These old bottles will break with such new wine; the more you touch these toads, the more they swell; the more you meddle with these serpents, the more they gather poison to spit at you. Go about to cool them, you shall but add to their heat, as the smith's forge fries when cold water is cast upon it; and as hot water if stirred casteth up the more fume. Joseph is for his good will in this kind hated

---

[1] *Omnis vita infidelium peccatum est, et nihil bonum sine summo bono.* Aug. de Vera Innocen. 56.

[2] *Nihil turpius est, dixit non nemo, Peripatetico claudo, Carere debet omni vitio quantum fieri potest, qui in alterum paratus est dicere.*

[3] *Hinc illud monitum,* Pythag. σιτίον εἰς ἄμισθα μὴ ἐμβάλλειν. Plut.

[4] Psal. i. 1, ἐν καθέδρᾳ τῶν λοιμῶν. Sept.

[5] χοιρὸς, of χέρας, filth. So *porcus; quasi spurcus.*

[6] *Post tam gravem* ἐπιτιμίαν *haud dubie resipuit.* Parcus.

of his brethren; Jonathan of Saul, who cast a javelin at him; Micaiah of Ahab, Amos of Amaziah, Jeremiah of his flagitious countrymen, Christ of the Jews, Paul of the Galatians, John Baptist of Herod. If John touch his white sin (and who will stand still to have his eyes picked out?) John must to prison. In other things he will dance after John's pipe; but if his incest be meddled with, John must hop headless. Stay to wrest that string in tune, and it will snap and break upon you. Now for such scoffing Ishmaels and furious opposites, that refuse to be reformed, hate to be healed, let them read their doom, Psal. l. 21, 22, and see here their destiny. Every good man is bound in conscience to pass by them as incorrigible, irreformable, and not to afford them so much as a pull out of the fire, so much as a caveat to prevent those curses that are coming upon them. But he that is filthy must be filthy still; he must wallow as a swine, and perish in his own corruptions; he must rage as a mad dog, and run unto the pit of hell, nobody must offer to stop or stay him in his career.

Ver. 7. *Ask, and it shall be given you, &c.*] Whereas it might be objected,—These are hard lessons, neither know we how to quit ourselves in the discharge of them. Our Saviour answers, as Isaiah did before him, " Seek ye the Lord while he may be found, call ye upon him while he is near," Isa. lv. 6; and as St James adviseth after him (i. 5), " If any man want wisdom, let him ask it of God." "Ask," saith he, "and it shall be given you." Run to the great Doctor of the Church, as Agur did to Ithiel and Ucal, Prov. xxx. 1, and he will teach you; seek his face and favour, and ye shall surely find it; knock at the beautiful gate of heaven with the hand of faith, and it shall open unto you (as the iron gate did to Peter) of its own accord, Acts xii. 10. Elisha's staff was laid (by his appointment) upon the dead child's face, but there was neither voice nor hearing. He went therefore himself, and shut the door upon them twain, and prayed unto the Lord, 2 Kings iv. 31, 33. This staff he knew was long enough to reach up to heaven, to knock at those gates, yea, to wrench them open. " Ask, therefore, that your joy may be full." " Hitherto ye have asked me nothing," saith Christ, disliking our dulness to this duty. *Quid est cur nihil petis? pete ne privatus de me queraris*, said Severus the emperor to his courtiers : What meanest thou to ask nothing of me? Ask, that thou mayest have no cause of complaint against me. And Pope Nicholas V. (a great favourer of learning), when he was told of some in Rome that made good verses; " They cannot be good poets," said he, " and I not know them. Why come they not to me, if good, *qui poetis etiam malis pateo*, who am a friend to poets though not so good?" Christ soliciteth suitors, " and the Father seeketh such to worship him," John iv. 23; not for anything he gets by it, but merely for our benefit; as the sun draws up vapours from the earth not for itself, but to

moisten and fatten the earth therewith. And although he come not ever at first call, yet be not discouraged with silence or sad answers. He is nearest to such suitors as, with Mary, cannot see him for their tears and griefs; if, with her, they continue to seek him in humility; if they rest not rapping and bouncing at his gates, he will open unto them, for their importunity, Luke xviii. 5—7. The saints sometimes have present audience, as Eliezer, Gen. xxiv. 15; Daniel (ix. 23); the disciples, Acts iv. 31; and Luther, who came leaping out of his closet with *Vicimus, Vicimus* in his mouth. But what if they have not? far be it from them to think that God is asleep or gone a journey, as the prophet jeereth at Baal : or that he wanteth ears, as the image of Jupiter did at Crete. (*Cretæ Jovis est imago, auribus carens.*) Questionless he that bids us ask, meaneth to give; as when we bid our children say, " I pray you, father, give me such a thing," we do it not but when we mean to give it them. If he defer help let it humble us, as it did David, Psal. xxii., " I cry in the day-time, but thou hearest not," &c. " But thou art holy," &c. Others have prayed and sped : " Our fathers trusted in thee, they cried unto thee and were delivered : but I am a worm and no man, yet will I call upon him " (not only in my sinking, but) from the bottom of the deeps. Let it also quicken us to further fervency, as it did St Paul, 2 Cor. xii. 8, and the Church, Psal. lxxx. 3, 7—19; never giving over the suit (with the importunate widow, Luke xviii. 11) till we have obtained it. He that prayeth, moveth God, not as an orator moveth hearers, but as a child his father. The end of oratory is to speak persuasively, not always to persuade; but the end of prayer is to prevail and speed; ye which are God's remembrancers, give him no rest till ye have what ye beg.[1] Ask, seek, knock; use an unwearied importunity; slip not any opportunity, pray without ceasing, pray continually; set aside all for prayer, wait upon it (as the word signifieth), Col. iv. 2, with Acts x. 7.[2] But must we never leave praying, may some say, till we have our request granted? there are other things to be done. True, and you must give over the words of prayer for a season, but never the suit of prayer. A beggar, for example, comes to a rich man's gate, and cries for an alms, but none there answers him. He being a poor man hath something else to do than to beg; and therefore he sits him down and knits or knocks, or patcheth, &c., and betwixt whiles, begs and works, works and begs. So should we, follow our necessary business, and yet continue our suit for grace. And the rather because beggars hold out to ask, where yet they have no promise it shall be given them; nay, when (many times) they are frowned upon, threatened, punished for begging. And whereas beggars come no nearer the house than the porch or entry, and so know not whether the

---

[1] Isa. lxii. 7. It shows *instantissimam necessitatem.* Aug.

[2] τῇ προσευχῇ προσκαρτερεῖτε, Col. iv. 2; Rom. xii. 12.

master of the house be providing for them an alms or a cudgel. All God's petitioners, that call upon him in truth, are admitted into the parlour, as I may so say, into God's special presence. "An hypocrite shall not come before him," Job xiii. 16; "but the upright shall dwell in his presence," Psal. cxl. 13. "He hideth not his face from such, but when they cry he heareth," Psal. xxii. 24.

And it shall be given you] It is not said what shall be given, because the gift is above all name, saith Austin. Like as Amos iv. 12, "Thus will I do unto thee:" thus? how? *Non nominat mala, ut omnia timeant*, saith Ribera out of Jerome. No evil is named, that they may fear all.

Ver. 8. *For every one that asketh receiveth, &c.*] And he is worthily miserable that will not be happy for asking. "Prayer," saith Lambert the martyr, "is in Scripture much commended, and many great and unmeasurable benefits are showed to ensue thereupon, that men should the more lustily give themselves thereunto." Thus Jacob wrestling with God, both by might and slight (as the word אבק signifieth), both by the strength of his body and force of his faith, he grounded his prayer upon God's gracious promise, which he rolls as sugar in his mouth, and repeats it again and again, Gen. xxxii. 9, 12. See the same course taken, 2 Sam. vii. 25; 1 Kings viii. 25, &c.; Dan. ix. 2, 3; Psal. xii. 5—7; Acts iv. 25, &c. Cast anchor of hope in the darkest desertion, wait for day, and pray, as those in the shipwreck, Acts xxvii., pleading that precious promise, Isa. l. 10. This help if we use not, we shall either pray coldly, offer incense without fire; or as the Pharisees, proudly; or as the Thessalonians, as men without hope; which is to deny our own prayers. He cannot possibly be poor that can pray in faith, because God is rich to all such, Rom. x. 12, and giveth richly (πλουσίως) to such as so ask, Jam. i. 5. Never did the hand of faith knock in vain at God's gate. The Ædiles (or chamberlains) amongst the Romans had ever their doors standing open, for all that had occasion of request or complaint to have free access to them. God's mercy-doors are wide open to the prayers of his faithful people. The Persian kings held it a piece of their silly glory to deny an easy access to their greatest subjects. It was death to solicit them uncalled. Esther herself was afraid. But the King of heaven manifesteth himself to his people, John xiv. 21, calls to his spouse with, "Let me see thy face, let me hear thy voice," Cant. ii. 14; and assigneth her negligence herein as the cause of her soul-sickness. The door of the tabernacle was not of any hard or debarring matter, but a veil, which is easily penetrable. And whereas in the temple none came near to worship but only the high priests, others stood without in the outer court. God's people are now a kingdom of priests, and are said to worship in the temple and at the altar, Rev. xi. 1. "Let us therefore draw near with a true heart, in full assurance of faith;" "let us come boldly to the throne of grace, that we may obtain mercy, and find grace to help in time of need," Heb. x. 22; iv. 16.

Ver. 9, 10. *Or what man is there of you, whom if his son ask bread, &c.*] By an argument from the less to the greater. Our Saviour sweetly confirmeth what he had said, that we may "ask in faith, nothing wavering," or being at an uncertainty, or at variance with himself, doubting whether he should believe or not.[1] This is no less unpleasing to God than unprofitable to us. God is the Father of all mercies, and loveth his far more than any natural father doth his own child; than Abraham did Isaac, or David Absalom. And according to his affections such are his expressions; for as he knoweth their needs, so he gives them all things richly to enjoy, 1 Tim. vi. 18. He giveth them not as he doth the wicked, *panem lapidosum*, a stone for bread; he feeds them not (as we say) with a bit and a knock.[2] He puts not into their hands ἀντὶ πέρκης σκόρπιον (as the Greek proverb hath it, whereunto our Saviour here alludeth), for a fish a scorpion; no, he feedeth them with the finest wheat, Psal. lxxxi. 16, "and filleth them with fat things full of marrow," Isa. xxv. 6. He nourisheth them with the best, as Joseph did his father's household in Egypt, according to the mouth of the little ones, or as so many little ones (saith the original),[3] tenderly and lovingly, without their care or labour. And whereas some natural parents have (monstrously) proved unnatural, Psal. xxvii. 10; as Saul to Jonathan, and those ἄστοργοι, Rom. i. 31; not so God: as himself is an everlasting Father, Isa. ix. 6, so is his love, Isa. xlix. 14; John xiii. 1. Men may hate their children whom they loved, but he "rests in his love," Zeph. iii. 17; they may cast out their babes, but he gathers them. Father Abraham may forget us and Israel disown us, Isa. lxiii. 16, "but thou, O Lord, art our never-failing Father, our Redeemer," &c. The fathers and governors of the Church may (out of an overflow of their misguided zeal) cast us out, and for a pretence say, "Let the Lord be glorified. But then shall he appear to your joy, and they shall be ashamed," Isa. lxvi. 5. The fathers of our flesh chasten their children after their own pleasure, but "he for our profit, that we might be partakers of his holiness," Heb. xii. 10. He feeds his people sometimes with "the bread of adversity and the water of affliction," Jer. xxx. 20; or gives them (as it were) a thump on the back with a stone to drive them downwards, and makes them eat ashes for bread, as David, Psal. cii. 9; their bread with quaking, as Ezekiel did (xii. 18); holds them to hard meat (some of the martyrs were fed with bread made, most part, of sawdust, and Ezekiel with bread prepared with cow-dung, iv. 15). He chasteneth

---

[1] Jam. i. 6, διακρινόμενος. *Alternantibus sententiis secum disceptans.* Budæus.

[2] *Alterâ manu fert lapidem, alterâ panem ostentat.* Plaut.

[3] Gen. xlvii. 12. ἐσιτομέτρει, say the Septuagint; whereunto our Saviour seems to allude, Luke xii. 42.

them also otherwhiles, not only with the rods of men, but with the severe discipline of scorpions, and this " seemeth not for the present to be joyous, but grievous ; nevertheless, afterward it yieldeth the peaceable fruits of righteousness to them that are thereby exercised," Heb. xii. 11. They shall sit down with Abraham, yea, in Abraham's bosom (as they used to lean at feasts), in the kingdom of heaven, Matt. viii. 11 ; and shall have (not a Benjamin's mess only, but) a royal diet, as Jeconiah had, every day a portion, Jer. lii. 34. Then shall the Lord stand forth and say to those men of his hand, who had their portion here, and whose bellies he filled with his hid treasure (the innkeeper gives the best bits to his guests, but reserves the patrimony for his children), " Behold, my servants shall eat, but ye shall be hungry," &c., Isa. lxv. 13.

Ver. 11. *If ye then being evil*] Even ye my disciples also ; for by nature there is never a better of us. But as the historian said that there were many Marii in one Cæsar, so there are many Cains and Judases in the best of us all. *Homo est inversus decalogus*, saith one : whole evil is in man, and whole man in evil ; yea, in the devil, whose works (even in the best of his saints) Christ came to destroy, to dissolve the old frame, and to drive out the prince of darkness, who hath there entrenched himself. And although sin in the saints hath received its death's wound, yet are there still in the best continual stirrings and spruntings thereof (as in dying creatures it useth to be), which (without God's greater grace, and the counter-motion of the Holy Spirit within them) would certainly produce most shameful evils. This put St Paul to that pitiful outcry, Rom. vii. 24, and made him exhort Timothy (though he were a young man rarely mortified) to exhort the younger women with all pureness, or chastity ; intimating, that through the corruption of his nature, even whilst he was exhorting them to chastity, some unchaste motions might steal upon him unawares.[1] A tree may have withered branches by reason of some deadly blow given to the root, and yet there may remain some sap within, which will bud and blossom forth again. Or as of some wild fig-tree, saith a Father, that grows in the walls of a goodly building, and hides the beauty of it, the boughs and branches may be cut or broken off, but the root, which is wrapped into the stones of the building, cannot be taken away till the wall be thrown down and the stones cast one from another. So sin that dwelleth in us hath its roots so inwrapped and intertwined in our natures, that it can never be utterly extirpated ; but pride will bud, Ezek. vii. 10, and the fruits of the flesh will be manifest, Gal. v. 19, though we be daily lopping off the branches, and labouring also at the root. Sin is an inmate that will not out, do what we can, till the house fall upon the head of it ; an hereditary disease, and that which is bred in the bone, will never out of the flesh ; a pestilent hydra, somewhat akin to those beasts in Daniel, that had " their dominion taken away, yet were their lives prolonged for a time and a season," Dan. vii. 12.

How much more will your Father which is in heaven give good things] Give the Holy Spirit, saith St Luke (xi. 13) ; for *nihil bonum sine summo bono*, saith St Austin ; when God gives his Spirit, he gives all good things, and that which is more than all besides. For it is a spirit of judgment and of burning, of grace and of deprecation, of knowledge, and of the fear of the Lord, of strength and of might, enabling both to resist evil of sin, and to endure evil of sorrow, Isa. iv. 4 ; xi. 2 ; Zech. xii. 10. And for good things, temporal, to trample on them ; spiritual, to reach after them. It is a free spirit, setting a man at liberty from the tyranny of sin and terror of wrath, 2 Cor. iii. 17 ; and oiling his joints, that he may be active and abundant in the Lord's work. This Holy Spirit is signified by those two golden pipes, Zech. iv., through which the two olive branches, the ordinances, empty out of themselves the golden oils of all precious graces into the candlestick, the Church. And how great a favour it is to have the Holy Spirit our inhabitant, see Joel ii., where, after God had promised the former and latter rain, floors full of wheat, and vats full of wine and oil, a confidence of all outward comforts and contentments ; he adds this as more than all the rest, " I will also pour out my Spirit upon all flesh," Joel ii. 23, 28. He will pour out, not drop down only sparingly and pinchingly, as some penny-father, but pour out, like a liberal householder, as it were, by pails or bucketfuls. And what ? my Spirit, that noble Spirit, as David calleth it, the Comforter, Counsellor, conduct into the land of the living. And upon whom ? upon all flesh : spirit upon flesh, so brave a thing upon so base a subject.[2] Next to the love of Christ indwelling in our nature, we may well wonder at the love of the Holy Ghost that will dwell in our defiled souls ; that this Spirit of glory and of God, 1 Pet. iv. 14, will deign to rest upon us, as the cloud did upon the tabernacle. How glad was Lot of the angels, Micah of the Levite, Elisabeth of the mother of her Lord, Lydia of Paul, Zaccheus of Christ, Obed-Edom of the ark ! And shall not we be as joyful and thankful for the Holy Spirit, whereby we are sealed (as merchants set their seals upon their wares) unto the day of redemption ? Eph. iv. 30. If David for outward benefits brake out into, " What is man, that thou art mindful of him ? " Psal. viii. 4 ; and Job (vii. 17) for fatherly chastisements, " What is man, that thou shouldest magnify him ? " &c., how should this best gift of his Holy Spirit affect and ravish us ! sith thereby all mercies are seasoned and all crosses sanctified ; neither can any man say (experimentally and savingly),

[1] *ἐν πάσῃ ἁγνείᾳ*, 1 Tim. v. 2.
[2] Psal. li. 12, *Opponitur carni spiritus*, i. e. res præstan-

tissima rei plane fragili et caducæ : quam tamen Dominus dignetur excellenti spiritus sui munere. Beza.

"that Jesus is the Lord, but by the Holy Ghost," 1 Cor. xii. 3.

Give good things to them that ask him] *sc.* If they ask in faith, bring honest hearts, and lawful petitions, and can wait God's leisure. Let none say here, as the prophet in another case, "I have laboured in vain, and spent my strength for nought," Isa. xlix. 4; I have prayed and sped not, the more I pray the worse it is with me. "The manner of our usage here in prison doth change" (saith Bishop Ridley in a letter to Bradford) "as sour ale doth in summer;" and yet who doubts but they prayed earn and earnestly, when they were in Bocardo, that college of Quondams, when those bishops were there prisoners? God is neither unmindful nor unfaithful, but waits the fittest time to show mercy, and will surely "avenge his own elect, which cry day and night unto him, though he bear long with them," Luke xviii. 7. The seed must have a time to grow downward before it grows upward. And as that seed which is longest covered riseth the first, with most increase; so those prayers which seem lost, are laid up in heaven, and will prove the surest grain. The more we sow of them into God's bosom, the more fruit and comfort we shall reap and receive in our greatest need.

Ver. 12. *Therefore all things whatsoever ye would,* &c.] *q. d.* To wind up all in a word (for it would be too tedious to set down each particular duty), let this serve for a general rule of direction in common conversation, and mutual interdealings one with another: "whatsoever ye would that men should do to you, do ye even so to them." This is the royal law, the standard of all equity in this kind, a sealed weight and rule, according to which we must converse with all men. Severus the emperor had this sentence of our Saviour often in his mouth; and commanded it to be proclaimed by the crier, whensoever he punished such of his soldiers as had offered injury to others. For there is no doubt (saith Mr Calvin upon this text) but that perfect right should rule amongst us, were we but as faithful disciples of *active* charity (if we may so speak) as we are acute doctors of *passive;* did we but love our neighbour as ourself. Charity (it is true) begins at home in regard of order, but not in regard of time; for so soon as thou beginnest to love thyself, thou must love thy neighbour as thyself; neither may any man at any time hide his eyes from his own flesh, that is, from his neighbour of the same stock with himself, Isa. lviii. 3.

For this is the law and the prophets] *i. e.* This is as much as either of them have said touching love to our neighbour. Yea, this is the sum of all that Christ and the apostles have spoken of it; for love (that seeketh not her own things, 1 Cor. xiii. 5) is both the complement of the law and the supplement of the gospel, Rom. xiii. 8, 10; Gal. v. 14; John xv. 12; and ver. 14, Christ maketh love to our brethren the same with keeping the commandments. So Acts xv. 20. St James in that sacred synod gives this suffrage, to lay upon the believing Gentiles no greater burden than these necessary things; "that they abstain from pollutions of idols, and from fornication, from things strangled, and from blood;" and in certain ancient manuscripts, as also by Irenæus and Cyprian, it is added, And what thing soever ye would not that others should do to you, that ye do not the same to them.[1] Timothy naturally cared for the Philippians (γνησίως), which was rare, Phil. ii. 20, 22. So should all Christians one for another, Gal. v. 13; 1 Cor. x. 24; Rom. xv. 1, 2. Self-lovers begin the black bead-role, 2 Tim. iii. 2.

Ver. 13. *Enter ye in at the strait gate*] Our Saviour having hitherto pointed out the right way of well-doing, and showed how to steer a straight course to the haven of happiness; now gives warning of certain dangerous rocks (against the which divers have dashed, to their utter destruction, and are therefore) carefully to be declined. Of these, the first he nameth is, the following of a multitude to do evil, the joining hand in hand with the rude rabble that are running apace toward the pit of perdition, which is but a little before them; the doing as most men do, which is to be utterly undone for ever.[2] The wicked (though never so many of them) go down to hell, and whole nations that forget God, Psal. ix. 17. Hence the gate thereto is grown so wide, and the way so well-beaten. But none that go that way return again, neither take they hold of the paths of life. "Enter therefore in at the strait gate," saith our Saviour.[3] *Vive ut pauci,* &c. Live as those few live that enter into life eternal, saith Cassianus; for if you will needs imitate the multitude, saith Austin, ye shall not be numbered among the living in Jerusalem, Isa. iv. 3, 4. "Save yourselves from this untoward generation," saith St Peter; shine amidst them as lamps, saith St Paul, as Abraham's lamp that shone out in the smoky furnace; as the wise men's star, that showed itself in the midst of darkness; like the moon that holds on her course, though the dogs bark at her never so long, never so loud; like the sun that rejoiceth as a bridegroom to run his race, though the Atlantes (a certain people) curse him at his rising, because scorched with his heat; or rather like God himself, who then doth his best works when men are worst, overcoming our evil with his good, and not suffering men's perverseness to interrupt the course of his goodness. Swim not down the stream of the times as dead fishes do; neither be carried along by the swing and sway of the place you

---

[1] Καὶ ὅσα μὴ θέλωσιν αὐτοῖς γίνεσθαι, ἑτέροις μὴ ποιεῖν. Beza.

[2] *Infernus ab inferendo dicitur, quia ita inferuntur et præcipitantur, ut nunquam ascensuri sint.*

[3] *Per viam publicam ne ingredere.* Pythag. *Si turbam imitari volueritis, inter paucos angustam viam ambulantes non eritis.* Aug.

dwell in.[1] Let not your lips be polluted by living among a people of polluted lips, with Isaiah, swear not with Joseph, curse not with Peter, comply not with the common sort, learn not, the manners of the mad multitude.[2] The worse they are, the better be you; the more outrageous they, the more courageous you, violent for heaven, and valiant for the truth; therefore walking exactly, and therefore "redeeming the time, because the days are evil;" and most men walk at all adventures. To walk with God (saith Bishop Babington) is a precious praise, though none do it but myself; and to walk with man, with the world, with a town or parish, in wicked ways, is a deadly sin, though millions do it besides. And it matters not (said Nicholas, Bishop of Rome) how small the number be, if godly, nor how great, if ungodly.[3] Noah condemned a world of wicked people by his contrary courses, "and became heir of the righteousness which is by faith," Heb. xi. 7, whilst he continued righteous, even in his generation, and kept himself unspotted in so foul a season. The apostle telleth us that to live according to the common course of the world is no better than to be acted and agitated by the devil, Eph. ii. 2. But God hath promised to take this unclean spirit out of the land, Zech. xiii. 2. *Fiat, Fiat.* And when Christ bids us enter in at the strait gate, we must know that his words are operative, to cause us to enter, as when he said, "Lazarus, come forth," and in the creation, "Let there be light." His word and Spirit go together. He works all our works for us, Isa. xxvi.

For wide is the gate] It may fitly be called the dismal gate, as that *porta scelerata* in Rome, so named because 300 gentlemen going out thereby to fight with some neighbouring enemies, perished.

And broad is the way, &c.] A dolorous way, as that way is at this day called, whereby our Saviour went bearing his cross to Calvary.

Ver. 14. *Because strait is the gate, and narrow is the way*, &c.] "In Lollards' tower, passing through six or seven doors I came to my lodging" (saith Philpot, martyr) "through many straits; where I called to remembrance, that strait is the way to heaven." The old copies read, Oh, how strait is the gate! by way of admiration, *q. d.* It is wondrous strait.[4] Not of itself, for Christ's yoke is easy, and his burden light; but we make it so hard and heavy to ourselves, by our singular peevishness and perverseness. Besides, the prince of darkness and his black guard favour this way, that is called holy, as little as the Philistine princes did David, yea, they persecute it to the death, as Saul did, Acts ix. Hence the way to heaven

is an afflicted way, a perplexed, persecuted way, crushed close together with crosses (as the word importeth[5]), as was the Israelites' way in the wilderness, or that of Jonathan and his armour-bearer, that had a sharp rock on the one side and a sharp rock on the other. And, whilst they crept upon all fours, flinty stones were under them, briers and thorns on either hand of them, mountains, crags, and promontories over them, *sic petitur cœlum*, so heaven is caught, by pains, by patience, by violence, affliction being our inseparable companion. "The cross-way is the highway to heaven," said that martyr. And another, "If there be any way to heaven on horse-back, it is by the cross." Queen Elizabeth is said to have swum to the crown through a sea of sorrows. They that will to heaven must sail by hell-gates. They that will have knighthood, must kneel for it; and they that will get in at the strait gate, must crowd for it. "Strive to enter in at the strait gate," saith our Saviour. Strive and strain even to an agony (as the word signifieth). Heaven is compared to a hill, Psal. cxxi. 1; hell to a hole. To hell a man may go without a staff (as we say), the way thereto is easy, steep, strewed with roses.[6] It is but a yielding to Satan, a passing from sin to sin, from evil purposes to evil practices, from practice to custom, &c. *Sed revocare gradum*, but to turn short again, and make strait steps to our feet, that we may force through this strait gate (so strait, that as few can walk in it, so none can halt in it, but must needs go upright), *hic labor, hoc opus est, opus non pulvinaris sed pulveris*, this is a work of great pains, a duty of no small difficulty. "Many, I say unto you, shall seek to enter," but seeking serves not turn. Men must strive, and strive lawfully, run, and run lustily, tug and take pains till they sweat and faint, to get through this strait gate, this perplexed way; as unpleasant to nature as the way to Nineveh was to Jonah; as rough and rugged as that was to the Church, Hos. ii. 6; as little traced and trod as the highways to Sion-hill, which were overgrown with grass, because few or none came to the solemn feasts, Lam. i. 4.

And few there be that find it] So hard is it to hit, and as dangerous to miss. Many by-ways there are (these are so many highways to hell), besides false guides and back-biasses not a few, to divert us: the devil with his false directions leading men hood-winked to hell, as Elijah did the Syrians to Samaria. The world with its allurements and affrightments,—oh, how hardly scape we through the corruptions that are in the world through lust![7] Our own hearts, how heavy are they to be drawn this way! A bear comes not so unwillingly to the stake. It goes

---

[1] *Argumentum turpissimum est turba.* Seneca.
[2] Isa. vi. 5. Τὶ ὡς ζῶντες ἐν κόσμῳ, δογματίζεσθε, Col. ii. 20.
[3] *Numerus pusillus non obest, ubi abundat pietas, nec multiplex prodest, ubi abundat impietas.*

[4] Τὶ στενὴ, i. e. Βάβαι, saith Theophylact; לֹא saith the Syriac. *Non quia dura, sed quia molles patimur.*
[5] Τεθλιμμένη, *pressa : res enim compressione fiunt arctiores.* Beza. *Manibus pedibusque obnixe omnia facere.* Terent.
[6] ὀλίγη ὁδὸς, μάλα δ' ἐγγύθι ναίει. Hes.
[7] *Irritamenta, terriculamenta*, 2 Pet. i. 7.

hard with a man when he must peremptorily deny himself; when he must deny all ungodliness and worldly lusts, as dear unto him as himself, and be tied to live holily, righteously, and soberly in this present world, Tit. ii. 12; making conscience of those duties which the most men's hearts rise at, as to be hot in religion, fervent in spirit, precise in his whole course, conscientious and cautious of the least sin, &c. Heaven is a stately palace with a narrow portal, hence so few enter it. The proud man with his high looks cannot stoop to it. The ambitious with his aspiring thoughts cannot bend to it. The malicious is swollen too big for it. The covetous with his load of thick clay cannot get through it. The drunkard with his rotten lungs, the adulterer with his wasted loins, can have no admittance into it. There can in no wise enter anything filthy or loathsome, abominable or detestable, which a man would abhor for the ill-savour (as the word signifieth, Rev. xxi. 27),[1] such as for the baseness thereof cannot be well named, it is so noisome to the senses. As soon may these men find fishes swimming in a wood, fruit-trees growing in the sea, heaven in hell, as enter into the strait gate, not living strictly. Which because few can frame to, but deride those that do (counting and calling them, as the Spaniards are said to do the Portugals, *pocos y locos,* few and foolish), therefore few are saved. Our Saviour calleth his flock a "little little flock," two diminutives, Luke xii. 42, standing (as that small army of Israel in Ahab's time) "like two little flocks of kids," 1 Kings xx. 27, when the wicked (as those Syrians then) fill the country. Was it not so, when Jerome complained that the whole world was turned Arian,[2] and Basil cried out, *An Ecclesias suas prorsus dereliquit Dominus?* Hath God utterly forsaken his Church? &c. "The love of many shall wax cold, but he that endureth to the end," &c. It is but a "he," in the singular, that endureth to the end, the "many" fall away from their former stedfastness.

Ver. 15. *Beware of false prophets, which come to you,* &c.] This is another dangerous rock, that the less careful may easily split against. Take heed, therefore, lest while ye shun a shelf ye fall not into a whirlpool. By corrupt teachers Satan catcheth men, as a cunning fisher by one fish catcheth another, that he may feed upon both. He circuiteth the world, seeketh whom to devour, and usually beginneth with violence and cruelty. If this take not, then he puts off the frock of a wolf, and makes his next encounter in sheep's clothing. Now what havoc he hath made by this means of silly souls laden with lusts, who knows not? The old Church was pestered with false prophets,

Deut. xiii. 1; 2 Pet. ii. 1. There were false prophets among the people, and there shall be false teachers among you, who privily shall bring in damnable heresies, and many shall follow their pernicious ways. This was Peter's prophecy; and Paul saith the same, Acts xx. 30: Grievous wolves shall enter in amongst you (in sheep's clothing you must think), speaking perverse things (while they pervert the Scriptures to the defence of their own devices), to draw away (ἀποσπᾶν) disciples after them. The word signifieth to pull them limb-meal, as wolves use to do the sheep they seize upon. A like expression there is, Deut. xiii. 13, where these naughty men are said to thrust or drive away folk from the true God, as Jeroboam is said to have driven Israel from following the Lord, 2 Kings xvii. 21. This they do, not so much by cruelty as by craft, by force as by fraud; "deceitful workers," St Paul calls them, "transforming themselves into the apostles of Christ," and ministers of righteousness, "and by good words and fair speeches deceive the hearts of the simple" and over-credulous, 2 Cor. xi. 13; Rom. xvi. 18. This they have learned of the devil, that grand juggler, who can soon transform himself into an angel of light. St John in his First Epistle tells us of many petty antichrists, even then gone out, 1 John iv. 1, who professing Christ's name, did yet oppose his truth. And in his Revelation, that the beast, which is the great antichrist, hath two horns like the lamb's, but speaks like the dragon, Rev. xiii. 11. The locusts also, which are his limbs and agents, have faces like women, insinuative and flattering. Tertullian tells us that the Valentinian heretics had a trick to persuade before they taught, whereas the truth persuadeth by teaching, doth not teach by persuading. And how much hurt Julian the Apostate did by this art in the Church of God is better known than that I need here to relate it.[3] It was not therefore without good ground of reason that Placilla the empress, when Theodosius senior desired to confer with Eunomius the heretic, dissuaded her husband very earnestly; lest being perverted by his speeches, he might fall into heresy. She knew their cunning, and, as it were, cogging of a die, Eph. iv. 14, where the apostle compareth seducers to cheaters and false gamesters, who have a device, by cogging of a die, to deceive the unskilful; and further telleth us, that they are wittily wicked by methods and crafty conveyances, winding up and down, and turning every way, to get the greatest advantage.[4] Neither was that good empress ignorant how catching we are this way, and inclinable to the worse side. As the Israelites soon forgot their God, and called for a calf, as the ten tribes were easily prevailed with to go after the two golden calves,

---

[1] Βδέλυγμα quod, propter fœditatem, nemo non aversatur. Βδέω, pedo.

[2] *Ingemuit orbis, et miratus est se subito factum esse Arianum.* Jerome.

[3] *Abduxit a fide plures Juliani versutia, quam antecedentium omnium Ethnicorum præceps sævitia.*

[4] ἐν τῇ κυβείᾳ, Quod verbum ductum est a lusu tesserarum. Erasm. τὴν μεθοδείαν τῆς πλάνης, Ibid. *Ingeniosi sunt methodici.*

and as the whole world wondered and wandered after the beast. This to prevent, as much as may be, God in delivering the law is most large in the second and fourth commandments, which we are most apt to transgress; that by superstition, this by profaneness.

Ver. 16. *Ye shall know them by their fruits*] That is, chiefly by their doctrines, which tend either to the infecting of the judgment with error or tainting of the life with uncleanness, or both; and commonly both, as those ancient heretics, whose pernicious, or, as other copies read, lascivious, ways many followed; by reason of whom the way of truth was evil spoken of (ταῖς ἀσελγείαις), 2 Pet. ii. 2. St Austin observeth, that in the loose and lascivious heretics, many foul-mouthed men met with matter of blaspheming the name of Christ, because they also would needs be held Christians. And Epiphanius adds, that for their sakes many heathens would not so much as have any conversation with Christians, or hear them speak.[1] Who hath not heard what a stumbling-block and back-bias to the conversion of the Jews, is the idolatry of the Papists and the blasphemies of other Christians? By their fruits they know such persons not to be of God, as their predecessors argued of our Saviour: "This man is not of God, because he keepeth not the sabbath day," John ix. 16. The proposition here was sound, had they not mistook themselves in the assumption, "He that keepeth not the sabbath is not of God." We may also safely reason in like sort. Such and such deny or question principles, as the Anti-trinitarians, Arians, Eutychians, and others not a few in the primitive Church, so pestered with arch-heretics, that it was then, as Erasmus hath it, an ingenuous thing to be a Christian. Had these been of God, they would have hearkened to his word, John viii. 47, which is plain in principles, and commandeth to hate false heterodox opinions, Psal. cxix. 104, and those that broach them, buzzing doubts in men's heads, Rom. xvi. 17; John x. 5. That heretic confuted by Junius took an ungain course for his own satisfaction, who confessed that he had spent two-and-twenty years in trying religions. He had been with Jews, Arians, Mahometans, and such sects; that at length he might find truth among them, which is, as he saith, *Viam per avia quærere*, to seek truth by wandering through all sorts of errors.[2] But truth, 1. is divine, grounded upon the Scriptures; wherein we have a most sure word, as Peter hath it; and self-sufficient, saith Paul, for instruction in righteousness, to make the man of God perfect, thoroughly furnished unto all good works. So that it is impossible God's elect should be finally deceived, 2 Pet. i. 19; 2 Tim. iii. 16, 17; though for a time they may be fearfully miscarried, as the young prophet was by the old Bethelite, and Barnabas by Peter, because they are all taught of God, Isa. xxx. 21; they have an unction within them, Matt. xxiv. 24, the Holy Ghost that enlighteneth both the organ and the object, John vii. 17; ii. 20; Job xxii. 28; and so teacheth them all things, that they understand the Scriptures, and grow to a certainty, Psal. xix. 7; Prov. i. 4. All Christ's sheep are rational, and will not follow a stranger, John x. 5; though they are simple to evil, yet they are wise to that which is good. If they be of any standing, and worth their years, as we say, they have a full assurance of understanding, Col. ii. 2, and (ver. 7) they are rooted and stablished in the faith, and in the present truth, 2 Pet. i. 12. So that, though man or angel should object against it, yet they would not yield to him, Gal. i. 8, 9. For he that is spiritual discerneth all things, as having the mind of Christ, 1 Cor. ii. 16; a spirit of discerning, and senses exercised to difference good from evil, Heb. v. 14; being able to give a reason of that he believeth, 1 Pet. iii. 15, to perform a reasonable service, even the obedience of faith, Rom. xii. 1; xvi. 26; whence floweth and followeth rest to his soul, Jer. vi. 16, and abundant consolation, Col. ii. 2. Say he cannot answer all the cavils of an adversary, yet he can hold the conclusion; and though he cannot dispute, yet he can die, as that martyr said, in defence of the truth, whereof he is fully persuaded in his own mind, Rom. xiv. 5, bottomed upon Scriptures, and ballasted therewith, as St Ambrose saith the bee is with a little stone, that she be not blown away with the wind.[3] 2. Secondly, truth is single, one and the same, at agreement with itself. But error is manifold, dissonant, and contradictory to itself. How often doth Bellarmine deny that in one place that he had affirmed in another! That the Scripture is the very word of God, saith he, can by no means be assured out of Scripture. But in another discourse, forgetting what he had said, he affirmeth, that among other arguments of the divinity of the Scriptures, there is sufficient proof to be had out of the Scriptures themselves. So, he cannot bethink himself, if you will believe him, where in all holy writ there is any promise made of pardon of sins to such as confess them to God.[4] Again, he teacheth that the substance of the bread in the sacrament is not turned into the substance of Christ's body *productivè*, as one thing is made of another; but that the bread goes away, and Christ's body cometh into the room of it *adductivè*, as one thing succeeds into the place of another, the first being voided. And this, saith he, is the opinion of the Church of Rome, himself being reader of controversies at

---

[1] *Ne accedunt quidem nos ad communionem accipiendæ doctrinæ—nec aures admovent.* Epiphanius.

[2] *Mihi certe Auxentius nunquam aliud quam diabolus erit, quia Arianus, ait Hiliarius: qui etiam vocavit Constantium, Antichristum.*

[3] *Aeris motus suspectos habet et lapillis sæpe sublatis per inania se librat nubila; ne leve alarum remigium præcipitent flabra ventorum.* Ambr.

[4] *Præter argumenta alia, etiam habetur ex Scriptura ipsa. Promissio de remittendis peccatis eis qui confitentur Deo non videtur ulla extare in divinis literis.* Bellarm. de Justif.

Rome. But Suarez, reader at Salamanca in Spain, confutes Bellarmine's opinion, terming it translocation, not transubstantiation; and saith it is not the Church's opinion. So the greatest Popish clerks cannot determine how the saints know our hearts and prayers; whether by hearing, or seeing, or presence everywhere, or by God's relating or revealing men's prayers and needs unto them. All which ways some of them hold as possible or probable, and others deny them, and confute them as untrue. Thus these great master-builders are confounded in their language, and thus hard it is to know what the Church malignant holdeth; her own dearest and learnedest sons know not, God having delivered them up to the efficacy of error, which frets as a gangrene, and spreads as leaven, souring the whole lump, 2 Thess. ii. 11; 2 Tim. ii. 17. Look how the heathens were at a mere uncertainty in their opinions and devotions; as the mariners in Jonah prayed to their several gods, and bade him do likewise. Others of them usually closed up their prayers with *Diique, Deæque, omnes*, lest haply they might mistake in any one. So are heretics. Having once stepped over the pale of truth, they know not where or when they shall stop or stay, but run on from bad to worse, deceiving, and being deceived, 2 Tim. iii. 13. Bertius and Barret, of Arminians became professed Papists; which differ no more, saith a learned man, than the Stoics of old did from the Cynics, by the wearing of their cloaks only. If the Lutherans admit of universal grace, the Huberians will thereupon bring in universal election, the Puccians natural faith, the Naturalists (as that Cistercian monster lately imprisoned at London did) will explode Christ and the Scriptures. A pestilent sect there was not long since in Arragon, whose founders were a hypocritical crew of their priests, who affecting in themselves and their followers a certain angelical purity, fell suddenly to the very counterpoint of justifying bestiality. These called themselves *illuminati*, as if they only had been in the light, and all the world besides in darkness. So besides the Gnostics, who held themselves to be the only knowing men, the Manichees derived their name of manna, because that whatsoever they taught was to be taken as food from heaven. Irenæus tells us of some that counted their own writings to be gospels. And the family of love set out their *Evangelium regni*.[1] Anabaptists brag much of their enthusiasms; and the Jesuits vaunt that the Church is the soul of the world, the clergy of the Church, and they of clergy; and yet for their wickedness, though a man, saith one, should declaim against them, till all the sand of the sea had run through his hour-glass, he could not possibly want matter. Can there any grapes be gathered of these thorns, any figs of these thistles?[2] Our Saviour makes use of these common proverbs to prove that this is so plain a truth, that none can be ignorant of it, if he have but his eyes in his head, or do not wink wilfully, as those *qui ut liberius peccent, libenter ignorant*, who are willingly ignorant, that they may sin without control.

Ver. 17. *Even so every good tree bringeth forth good fruit*] i. e. All sound doctrine tends to good life, and rotten opinions to wretched practices. As, besides the old heretics, we see in the Papists (their priests especially), of whom the Lord Audely (Chancellor of England in King Henry VIII.'s time) said to thirteen Calais men, prisoners for religion whom he discharged: "For God's sake, sirs, beware how you deal with Popish priests; for I assure you, some of them be knaves all."[3] After the 1000th year of Christ, there was nowhere less piety than in those that dwelt nearest to Rome, as Machiavel himself observed, who yet was himself none of the best, as is well known; for he proposeth Cæsar Borgia (notwithstanding all his villanies) as the only example for a prince to imitate. The Romish Pharisees, like the devils, are then thought to do well, when they cease to do hurt, saith Joannes Sarisburiensis. In popes (saith Papirius Massonius, a Popish writer, speaking of those popes that lived in the time of the Trent Council) no man now-a-days requireth holiness. They are thought to be very good, if not extreme evil; or anything better than the worst use to be.[4] The see of Rome, saith another, hath not merited a-late to be ruled by any better than reprobates. Divers popes have been necromancers, atheists, epicures, monsters, as Benno Cardinalis describes Hildebrand,[5] and Luitprandus reports of John XII., that he ordained priests in a stable among his horses, that he went in to his father's concubines, that he drank a health to the devil, &c. Benedict XII. had this epitaph set over him,

Hic situs est Nero, laicis mors, vipera clero;
Devius à vero, turba repleta mero.

I am not ignorant what is the common put-off of Papists, when urged with these and the like histories; viz. *Luitprandi illud non est, sed Anonymi cujusdam, qui hoc historiæ ipsius appenderit.* Luitprandus never wrote any such thing, but some other nameless author, that hath pieced it to his history, saith Bellarmine and Baronius. But who this nameless author was, or when he lived, or how it may appear that it was so indeed, they say not a word. So if we cite Benno Cardinalis. *Imo potius Lutheranus*, saith Bellarmine and Florimund. How disdainfully they reject the Fathers when they make against them, I need not here recite.[6] I

---

[1] *Dixerunt in Anabaptistarum Ecclesia nullum impium inveniri, omnes sanctos esse.* Scultet. Annal.

[2] The French have a berry which they name *Uve de spine*, the grape of a thorn. But this was a rare commodity. Ber.

[3] ἑκουσίως καταπίνων τὸ πικρόν. Justin Martyr.

[4] *In pontificibus nemo hodie sanctitatem requirit. Optimi putantur, si vel leniter mali*, &c.

[5] *Fuisse homicidam, adulterum, necromanticum, schismaticum, hæreticum.*

[6] *Inde probo hoc illius esse, illud non esse, quia hoc pro me sonat, illud contra me.* Faust.

would sooner believe one pope than a thousand Augustines, saith a Jesuit. And yet, when they cannot be heard, they are ready straight to cry out, as that heretic Dioscorus did in the Council of Chalcedon, "I am cast out with the Fathers, I defend the doctrine of the Fathers, I transgress them not in any point." If we produce their own doctors and schoolmen as witnesses of the truth, these men, say they, are catholic authors, but they stand not *recti in curia*, they must be purged.[1] So witty are heretics rather to devise a thousand shifts to elude the truth than once to yield and acknowledge it. They will not receive the love of the truth (as the intemperate patient will not be ruled by the physician). And for this cause God delivers them up to strong delusions, vile affections, base and beastly practices; as committing and defending of sodomy, and such like abhorred filth, not once to be named amongst Christians. But some having put away a good conscience, as concerning faith have made shipwreck, saith the apostle. A good conscience is, as it were, a chest, wherein the doctrine of faith is to be kept safe; which will quickly be lost, if the chest be once broken. And they "that turn from the truth" will prove "abominable, disobedient, and unto every good work reprobate," Tit. i. 14, 16. Matthew Paris, speaking of the court of Rome, saith, *Hujus fœtor usque ad nubes fumum teterrimum exhalabat.*

Ver. 18. *A good tree cannot bring forth evil fruit, &c.*] Heretics, then, and heterodoxes are not good honest men, as the vulgar counts them, for all their pretended holiness and counterfeit humility, Col. ii. 18. Were they humble men indeed, they would soon yield to the truth discovered unto them, and relinquish their erroneous opinions. Swenckfeldius could not be a good man, as Bucholcerus judged him, so long as he held fast his heresies, though he were much in the commendation of a new life, and detestation of an evil; though himself prayed much, and lived soberly. He bewitched many with those magnificent words and stately terms that he had much in his mouth, of illumination, revelation, deification, the inward and spiritual man, &c., but in the mean while he denied the human nature of Christ to be a creature, and called those that thought otherwise creaturists. He affirmed the Scripture to be but a dead letter; which they that held not, he called them scripturists. Faith, he said, was nothing but God dwelling in us, as Osiander after him. In a word, he was a leper in his head, and is therefore pronounced utterly unclean, Lev. xiv. 44. An evil tree cannot bring forth good fruit. That Popish inquisitor was quite out that said the Waldensian heretics may be discerned by their manners and words; for they are modest, true, grave, and full of

brotherly love one towards another, but rank heretics.[2] This was somewhat like Pliny's description of the Christians in that province where he was governor. And here I cannot omit, that when the Bishop of Worcester exhorted M. Philpot the martyr (being brought to his answer), before he began to speak, to pray to God for grace: "Nay, my Lord of Worcester," said Bonner, "you do not well to exhort him to make any prayer; for this is the thing they have a singular pride in. For in this point they are much like to certain arrant heretics, of whom Pliny maketh mention, that they sang antelucanos, hymns, psalms of praise, to God before break of day." But had Bonner and his fellow-buzzards but observed the burning zeal, sweet assemblies, watchings, prayings, holiness of life, patience in death, &c., of those that served God after the way that they called heresy, they might well have seen and said as much as the centurion did of our Saviour, Matt. xxvii. 54, and they might have replied, as our Saviour did of himself, "I have not a devil; but I honour my Father, and ye do dishonour me." "If I honour myself, my honour is nothing: it is my Father that honoureth me, of whom ye say, that he is your God," John viii. 49, 54. Cenalis, Bishop of Auranches, wrote against the congregation of Paris, defending impudently that their assemblies were to maintain whoredom. How much better and with more ingenuity the Bishop of Aliff, who preaching at Trent in the time of that Council, A.D. 1563, spake of the faith and manners of the Catholics and heretics; and said, that as the faith of the Catholics was better, so the heretics exceeded them in good life; which gave much distaste, saith the historian. But Bellarmine (had he been then and there present) would not likely have been much offended: "For we," saith he, "although we believe that all the virtues are to be found in the Church, yet that any man may be absolutely said to be a member of the true Church described in the Scriptures, we do not think that any internal virtue is required of him; but only an external profession of the faith, and such a partaking of the sacraments, as is perceived by the outward senses."[3] A pretty description and picture of a Papist; amongst whom if any be virtuous, it is by accident, and not as they are members of that Church. As Cicero wittily said of the Epicures, that if any of that sect proved good, it was merely by the benefit of a better nature; for they taught all manner of looseness and libertinism. But for the most part, such as their doctrine is, such is also their practice. The friars (saith one that had seen it, and so could well avouch it) are a race of people always praying, but seldom with sign of devotion; vowing obedience, but still contentious; chastity, yet most luxurious; poverty,

[1] Bellarmine saith to Irenæus, Tertullian, Eusebius, and Luther. I answer, *Omnes manifesti hæretici sunt.*
[2] *Sunt in moribus compositi et modesti, superbiam in vestibus non habeat—sed fides eorum, est incorrigibilis et pessima.*
[3] *Nos etiamsi credimus—tamen ut aliquis absolute dici posset pars veræ ecclesiæ non putamus requiri ullam internam virtutem, sed tantum externam professionem fidei, et sacramentorum communionem, quæ sensu ipso percipitur.*

yet ever scraping and covetous. And generally the devotions of Papists, saith he, are prized more by tale than by weight of zeal; placed more in the massy materiality of the outward work, than purity of the heart, from which they proceed. They hold integrity for little better than silliness and abjectness about Italy, and abuse the most honourable name of Christian, usually, to signify a fool, or a dolt, as is before noted out of Doctor Fulke. Are not these the fruits of a rotten religion, of trees specious without, but purified and worm-eaten within (as the word our Saviour here useth properly signifieth), which appears at length by their rotten fruits?[1] The true Christian will not cease to bear good fruit, what weather soever come, Jer. xvii. 7. The hypocrite will either bear only leaves, as the cypress tree, or apples of Sodom, grapes of Gomorrah. Of such we may say, as of Mount Gilboa, no good fruit grows on them; or as Stratonicus saith of the hill Hæmus, that for eight months in the year it was very cold, and for the other four it was winter; or as the poet said of his country, that it was bad in winter, hard in summer, good at no time of the year.[2] Campian of St John's in Oxford, Proctor of the University, A.D. 1568, dissembled the Protestants' religion. So did Parsons in Baliol college, until he was for his dishonesty expelled with disgrace, and fled to the Papists; where *cælum mutavit non animum*, neither good egg, nor good bird, as they say.

Ver. 19. *Every tree that bringeth not forth good fruit*, &c.] Fruitless trees are cut down to the fire. Short shooting loseth many a game. The idle servant is delivered to the tormentors; and unsavoury salt is cast out to be trodden on, as Ecebolius was. The barren earth "is nigh to cursing, whose end is to be burned," Heb. vi. 8. Pure gold discovers deadly poison. For there will sparkle out of the cup certain rainbows, as it were, and there will be heard, saith one, a fiery hissing of the gold thrusting out the poison. Whereby is signified, saith he, that God threateneth judgment and hell-fire to those that corrupt and poison heavenly doctrine. See more of this above, chap. iii. 10. Let us study and strive to resemble the tree of Paradise, that was fair to the eye and good to eat; and that tree of life, Rev. xxii. 2, that bringeth forth every month, twelve manner of fruits, &c. And those trees, Psal. xcii. 13, that being planted in the house of the Lord, bring forth best fruit in their old age. "I am like a green olive tree," saith David. Our bed is of green cedar, saith the spouse. Ephraim was like a green fir-tree, fat and sappy, &c., Psal. lii. 8; Cant. i. 16, 17; Hosea xiv. 8. Barrenness is no less a fault than ill fruit.

Ver. 20. *Wherefore by their fruits ye shall know them*] See ver. 16, where the self-same words are used. Lest any, under pretence of danger in hearing false prophets, should refuse to hear any, though they come with never so much evidence of truth, our Saviour wills and commands here, that examination and discretion go before both rejection of errors and receiving of truths. "Try all things; hold fast that which is good," 1 Thess. v. 21. As the mouth tasteth meat, so the ear must try and taste words, Job xii. 11; xxxiv. 3. He is a fool that believeth everything, nay, anything that tends to the cherishing of corruption and carnal liberty, or the advancing of corrupt nature, which is nothing else but a piece of proud flesh, and must be abased to the utmost.[3] Christians should abound in knowledge, and in every sense; so as readily to discern things that differ, Rom. xiv. 5; and not to be wherried and whirled "about with every wind of doctrine," Eph. iv. 14, as children, nor to be carried away as they are led, as Gentiles, 1 Cor. xii. 2. He that will take for true and trusty whatsoever any impostor puts upon him, shall be as foully deceived as Jacob was by Laban. Search and see whereto they tend, and what they drive at. If they would drive us from God, as Moses expresseth it, and draw us from the doctrine of godliness, that is grounded upon the word, to the truth whereof we have found God's Spirit persuading our hearts, and yielding us comfort in it, John vi. 45; 1 John ii. 27; abstain (or stand off) from all appearance of any such evil. Shun the familiarity of seducers, that discredit the truth; hear them not, their mouths should be stopped, Tit. i. 11; iii. 10. See how exceeding earnest the apostle is in this argument, 2 Thess. ii. 1—3; he knew well the danger: so Rom. xvi. 17. The Pharisees and false apostles would only have brought in a Jewish rite or two; yet are said to subvert the gospel, Gal. i. 7, and the apostle wisheth they were even cut off for it. Hymeneus and Philetus denied not the resurrection, but affirmed it only to be past already, and yet they are said to overthrow the faith of some, 2 Tim. ii. 18. And although we are wont to wonder at the absurdities of a contrary religion, and think a simple man may easily answer them; yet it is certain, the grossest adversaries of the truth are able to urge such reasons, and use such persuasions, as have in them great probability of truth, and may deceive the simple: "Ye therefore, beloved, seeing ye know these things before, beware lest ye also, being led away with the error of the wicked, fall from your own stedfastness." Which to prevent, "Grow," saith the same apostle there, "in grace, and in the knowledge of our Lord Jesus Christ," 2 Pet. iii. 17, 18. Exact of yourselves a growth in every grace, in humility, howsoever growing downward at least, if ye cannot find so comfortable a growth upward. Humility is both a grace and a vessel to receive grace; for God will give grace to

---

[1] σαπρὸς, of σήπω, to putrify. Suidas. *Pulchra ac sublimis est, sed fructu caret.* Plutarch.

[2] Ἀσκρῇ χεῖμα κακή, θέρος ἀργαλέη, οὐδέποτ' ἐσθλή. Hesiod.

[3] *Sub laudibus naturæ latent inimici gratiæ.* Aug.

the humble, and teach the lowly-minded, 1 Pet. v. 5; Psal. xxv. 9. Grow also in the knowledge of our Lord Jesus Christ; proving by experience in yourselves, what that good, that holy, and acceptable will of God is. Let your knowledge and practice run parallel, and be of equal extent. Study to live rather than to dispute,[1] to act rather than to contemplate: learn and labour to feel in yourselves the sweetness and goodness, the life and power, of that you know. The devil confessed Christ as well as Peter, Mark v. 7; Matt. xvi. 16, 17,—but the devil with a common knowledge, swimming in the brain, Peter with a saving knowledge, soaking to the heart root, and working upon the affections, those immediate springs of action. This is that knowledge, not apprehensive only, but affective too, that makes the mind good, full of incitations to good, glad of all occasions to do good, free from the stain and reign of former lusts, inclinable to serve God and our brethren by love, fearing the gospel more than the law, and God's goodness more than his justice. Now to grow in these graces and in this knowledge, is the ready way to secure ourselves from seducers, to approve ourselves to have been conscionable hearers of a sound ministry, such as are founded upon a rock, and are therefore unmoveable, such as have gotten a knowledge so clean and certain as no heretic can draw from us. And lastly, to save ourselves from that untoward generation, Acts ii. 40, our Saviour speaketh next of, in the subsequent verses, that have no more to show or say for themselves than Lord, Lord, &c.

Ver. 21. *Not every one that saith unto me, Lord, Lord, shall enter, &c.*] Not every verbal professor or forward pretender to me and my truth, shall be saved. That son of perdition called Christ Lord, Lord, yet betrayed him with a kiss; and is gone to his place. How many Judases have we, that speak Christ fair, but by their loose and lawless lives deliver him up to the scoffs and buffetings of his enemies! that bow the knee to him, and bid "Hail, King of the Jews!" yet smite him on the face, and bid him prophesy who smote him; that put a reeden sceptre in his hand, and make him a titular Lord only; having no more than a form of knowledge, Rom. ii. 20, a pretence of piety, 2 Tim. iii. 5, and a semblance of sanctimony, Luke viii. 18, contenting themselves with the name of Christians; as if many a ship had not been called Safe-guard or Good-speed, and yet fallen into the hands of pirates. These are blots of goodness, botches of the Church, as Augustus was used to term his three untoward children, *tres vomicas*, *tria cariomata*, mattery imposthumes, ulcerous sores. Epictetus complained that there were many would-be philosophers, as far as a few good words would go;[2] but were nothing for practice. Socrates made no distinction between σοφία and σωφροσύνη, knowing and doing. So to know good as to practise it, and evil as to avoid it, this he esteemed the only wisdom. Such as say well and do well, are to be embraced, saith Aristotle:[3] but their very profession is to be suspected that second it not with a suitable practice. *Nesciunt insani nesciunt, τοῦ καλοῦ τὸ καλὸν, qui non vivunt honeste*, saith another. There are that speak like angels, live like devils; that have Jacob's smooth tongue, but Esau's rough hands. *Audi, nemo melius: specta, nemo pejus: Loquitur hic ut Piso, vivit ut Gallonius*. All men admire Tully's tongue, saith St Austin, not so his practice.[4] Seneca could give excellent counsel to others, which himself did not take.[5] He is much taxed for flattery, luxury, covetousness, &c., and something he confesseth hereof (though covertly) in that sentence of his, in his book *de Tranquillitate*, *Nec ægroto, nec valeo*, I am neither sick nor sound. Lilies are fair in show, but foul in scent. Coin is white in colour, but draws a black line after it. Glow-worms seem to have both light and heat; but touch them only, and it will appear they have neither. Livy saith that the Athenians waged war against Philip of Macedon with letters and words.[6] So do many against the devil; they defy him with their mouths, but deify him in their lives; they spit at his name, but admit of his suggestions; they call Christ Lord, Lord, but in truth, and upon the matter, the devil is their good lord; for his servants they are to whom they obey. They lean upon the Lord and say, "Is not the Lord amongst us? none evil can come unto us," Mic. iii. 11. But he shall shake them off with a *discedite*, depart ye. He likes not this court-holy-water as they call it, these fair professions and deep protestations of love, when men's hearts are not with him, when there is not the power of religion, the practice of godliness. The leaves of profession he dislikes not, for as they are of medicinable use, Ezek. xlvii. 12, so they are good inducements to force a necessity of more fruit. But he looks for more than leaves. He goes down to his garden to see how it comes forward, in righteousness, peace, joy in the Holy Ghost; in meekness, tender-heartedness, love; in patience, humility, contentedness; in mortification of sin, moderation of passion, holy guidance of the tongue; in works of mercy, truth, and justice; in self-denial, love of enemies, life of faith; in heavenly-mindedness, sweet communion with God, comfortable longing for the coming of Christ, &c. These be those fruits, and that doing of God's will, without the which our Saviour here averreth there is no heaven to be

---

[1] *Nos non eloquimur magna, sed vivimus.*
[2] ἄνευ τοῦ πράττειν μεχρὶ τοῦ λέγειν.
[3] Συναδόντων μὲν τοῖς ἔργοις ἀποδεκτέον, διαφωνούντων δὲ λόγους ὑποληπτέον. Ethic.
[4] *Ciceronis linguam omnes fere mirantur, pectus non ita.*

Confess. iii. 4.   [5] *In plerisque, contra facere visus est Seneca quam philosophabatur.* Dio.
[6] *Athenienses literis verbisque bellum adversus Philippum Persei patrem gesserunt.*

had, no, though men profess largely, preach frequently, pray ardently, eat and drink at his table, dispossess devils in his name, &c. Judas did all this and was damned.[1] Shalt thou to heaven that doest no more? no, nor so much? Woe to all careless professors and carnal gospellers! The Lord will make all the churches know that he searcheth the hearts, Rev. ii. 23, and will not be beguiled with the fig-leaves of formality. And for those that carry it more cleanly, as they conceive, and can walk undiscovered, let them know that God (that he may make the name of the wicked to rot) many times so detects their guile, that their wickedness is showed to the whole congregation, Prov. xxvi. 26. Or if not so, yet certainly he will do it at that general judgment, that great assize (as it follows in the next verse) when it shall be required of men, *non quid legerint, sed quid egerint ; non quid dixerint, sed quomodo vixerint,* not how much they have talked of heaven, but how well they have walked in the way to heaven ; not a proffering of words, but an offering of works, as Agapetus hath it.[2] The foolish virgins were found with their *sic dicentes,* but the good servants with their *sic facientes.*

Ver. 22. *Many will say to me in that day,* &c.] That day of judgment, by an appellative proper called "that day," or at the day of death ; for every man's death's day is his doom's day, Heb. ix. Then they shall come bouncing at heaven-gates with "Lord, Lord, open unto us," and make no other reckoning but to enter with the first, which shows that a hypocrite may live and die in self-delusion, and miss of heaven in the height of his hopes. He hanged them upon nothing (as God hath hanged the earth, Job xxvi. 7) ; they prove unto him, therefore, as the giving up of the ghost, which is but cold comfort, and serve him no better than Absalom's mule did her master in his greatest need. "What," saith Job, " is the hope of the hypocrite, though he hath gained much, when God shall take away his soul? will God hear his cry when trouble comes upon him?" Job xxvii. 8, 9. Will his crying, Lord, Lord, rescue him in the day of wrath? No, no. God will pour upon him, and not spare, "fire and brimstone, storm and tempest ; this shall be the portion of his cup." The just execution of that terrible commination, Rev. iii. 16, shall certainly crush his heart with everlasting horror, confusion, and woe. Oh that this truth were thoroughly thought on and believed! but men are wondrous apt to deceive themselves in point of salvation. Therefore doth the apostle so often premise, " Be not deceived," when he reckoneth up reprobates, 1 Cor. vi. 9 ; Eph. v. 6, &c. Themselves they may deceive, and others, but "God is not mocked." Balaam seems, by his words and wishes, a friend to Israel ; yet he is so far from inheriting with them, that he is destroyed by them. This will be the portion of hypocrites from the Lord. If their hearts be not upright with him, he will

never give them his hand, no, though they follow him as close as Jehonadab did Jehu, 2 Kings x. 15. Their hopes shall fail them when at highest ; as Esau's did, returning from his venison.

Have we not prophesied in thy name?] A man may preach profitably to others, and yet himself be a cast-away, 1 Cor. ix. ult. Pendleton confirmed Saunders, and afterward turned tippet himself. Harding, a little before King Edward VI. died, was heard openly in his sermons in London to exhort the people with great vehemency after this sort, That if trouble came, they should never shrink from the true doctrine of the gospel which they had received, but take it rather for a trial sent of God to prove them whether they would abide by it or no. All which to be true, saith Mr Fox, they can testify that heard him, and be yet alive ; who also foreseeing the plague to come, were then much confirmed by his words. In Queen Mary's days he turned apostate, and so continued, notwithstanding an excellent letter of the Lady Jane Dudley, written to him while he was prisoner ; wherein she stirs him up to " remember the horrible history of Julian of old, and the lamentable case of Spira a-late, and so to return to Christ, who now stretcheth out (saith she) his arms to receive you, ready to fall upon your neck and kiss you, and last of all to feast you with the dainties and delicacies of his own precious blood: which undoubtedly, if it might stand with his determinate purpose, he would not let to shed again rather than you should be lost." And so she goes on most sweetly : *sed surdo fabulam,* she lost her sweet words. As likewise did William Wolsey, the martyr, upon Denton the smith of Wells in Cambridgeshire ; and some others, upon Mr West, chaplain to Bishop Ridley, who refusing to die in Christ's cause with his master, said mass against his conscience. Bishop Latimer, in a sermon before King Edward, tells of one who fell away from the known truth, and became a scorner of it, yet was afterward touched in conscience for the same. Beware of this sin, saith he, for I have known no more but that repented. Joannes Speiserus, Doctor of Divinity, and preacher at Augsburg in Germany, A. D. 1523, began to teach the truth of the gospel, and did it so effectually, that divers common harlots were converted, and betook themselves to a better course of life. (Scultet. Annal. p. 118.) But he afterward revolted again to the Papists, and came to a miserable end. The like is reported of Brisonettus, Bishop of Melda, a town of France, 10 miles from Paris. And who doubts but Judas the traitor was a great preacher, a caster out of devils, and doer of many great works in Christ's name, as well as other of the disciples? Nicodemus was nothing to him. He (saith one) was a night-professor only, but Judas in the sight of all. He was a slow scholar, Judas a forward preacher. Yet at last, when Judas betrayed Christ in the night, Nicodemus faithfully professed him in the day. Therefore will Christ

---

[1] *Cainistæ sunt offerentes non personam, sed opus personæ.* Luther.

[2] οὐ ῥημάτων προφορὰν ἀλλὰ πραγμάτων προσφορὰν.

confess him before God, angels, and men, when Judas shall hear, Avaunt, thou worker of iniquity, I know thee not. *Neronis (Quantus artifex pereo ?) quadrabit in te peritum et periturum. Sedeat in labris suada, sed et fibris gratia; quæ sola vere flexanima suada, et medulla suadæ penetrantissima. Summopere cavendum divino præconi, ne dicta, factis deficientibus, erubescant.* Let not the preacher give himself the lie, by a life unsuitable to his sermons.

And in thy name have done many wonderful works] By a faith of miracles, whereby a man may remove mountains, and yet miscarry, 1 Cor. xiii. 2. And here such as work wonders may deceive themselves in the main point of their own salvation; how much more may they deceive others in this or that particular point of doctrine? The coming of Antichrist is after the "working of Satan, with all power, and signs, and lying wonders, and with all deceivableness of unrighteousness in them that perish," 2 Thess. ii. 9, 10. Lying wonders they are called in regard not only of the end, which is to deceive, but of the substance; for the devil cannot do a true miracle, which is ever beside and against nature and second causes; such as whereof there can be no natural reason possibly rendered, no, though it be hid from us. The devil, I say, cannot do a miracle. He may juggle and cast a mist. St Jerome writes, that a certain damsel was brought to Macarius by her father, who complained that his daughter was by witchcraft turned into a mare. Macarius answered, that he could see no such thing in her, nothing but human shape, and that their eyes, that thought and said so, were blinded by Satan, wherefore turning himself to prayer, he obtained, that the mist might be removed from the parents' eyes, and then they saw their mistake. The like is reported of Mr Tindal the martyr, that being at Antwerp among a company of merchants, he hindered, by his presence and prayers, a certain juggler, that he could not play his feats; so that he was compelled openly to confess that there was some man there at supper that disturbed and letted all his doings. So that a man even in the martyrs of these days (saith Mr Fox) cannot lack the miracles of true faith, if they were to be desired. O ye Papists (said Bainham, in the midst of the flame), behold, you look for miracles: here now you may see a miracle; for in this fire I feel no more pain than if I were in a bed of down; it is to me as a bed of roses. But the devil is ashamed (saith Gretser the Jesuit) to confirm Luther's doctrine with miracles.[1] We could tell him and his fellows, of Myconius recovered out of a desperate disease by Luther's prayers, which Myconius acknowledged for a miracle to his dying day. And of another young man of Wittenberg that had sold himself to the devil, body and soul, for money, and sealed the obligation with his own blood, but was delivered by Luther's prayers out of the danger of the devil, who was compelled (saith Mr Fox) at last to throw in the obligation at the window, and bade the young man take it unto him again. But he that now requireth miracles for the confirmation of his faith, is himself a great miracle, saith Austin.[2] Manna ceased when they came into Canaan; as if it would say, Ye need no miracles now you have means. The wonderful preservation of Luther, that man of God, amidst so many potent enemies, the publishing and carrying of his doctrine, in the space of a month, throughout all Germany and some foreign countries, as it were upon angels' wings,[3] the establishing of the Reformation to be done by so weak and simple means, yea, by casual and cross means, against the force of so puissant and public an adversary, this is that miracle which we are in these times to look for.

Ver. 23. *And then will I profess unto them, I never knew you*] No, not when you professed most love to me, and did me (to see to) greatest service. I knew you well enough for "black sheep," or rather for rebrobate goats; I knew you for hirelings and hypocrites, but I never knew you with a special knowledge of love, delight, and complacency. I never acknowledged, approved, and accepted of your persons and performances. See Psal. i. 6; Rom. xi. 2. God's sharp nose doth easily discern, and is offended with the stinking breath of the hypocrite's rotten lungs, though his words be never so scented and perfumed, though his deeds be never so mantled and masked with shows of holiness. God utterly disowns and disavows all such, for if "any man have not the Spirit of God," saith Paul, the same "is none of his," Rom. viii. 9; be he whose he will be. And whereas he naturally delights in mercy, yet he will by no means clear the guilty; yea, he will "mock at their destruction, and laugh when their fear cometh." He will "spew them out of his mouth." Ah, he will ease him of his adversaries; and be as well paid thereof, as a man is that hath rid his stomach of the surfeit or sick matter that clogged it, Prov. i. 16. *Quod Deus loquitur cum risu, tu legas cum fletu.* Aug. Rev. iii. 16; Isa. i. 24.

Depart from me] Oh direful and dreadful sentence! such as shall make their very heartstrings crack (not their ears tingle only), and their hearts fall asunder in their bosoms, like drops of water.[4] Surely if the gentle voice of God in "the cool of the day" (*in aura diei*), Gen. iii. 8, were so terrible to our first parents; and if his sweet voice in the preaching of the gospel of grace be so formidable to the wicked, that Felix trembled, and the stoutest are quailed, the edge of their fury is rebated, their hearts often ache and quake within them; what will they do when the Lion of the tribe of Judah shall roar out upon them this fearful *Discedite* that

---

[1] *Pudet diabolum Lutheri doctrinam miraculis confirmare.* Melch. Adam. in Vita Lutheri.
[2] *Qui adhuc prodigia ut credat, inquirit, magnum est ipse prodigium.* Aug.

[3] *Evangelium tam celeri volatu ferebatur et quidem spatio menstruo per universam Germaniam, et aliquot regiones exteras, ut ipsi angeli cursores, &c.* Melch. Adam. in Vita Myconii.
[4] *Dicetur reprobis, ite; venite probis.*

breathes out nothing but fire and brimstone, stings and horrors, woe and alas, seas of vengeance, and the worm that never dieth, torments without end, and past imagination? The desperate soldiers (that would not have dreaded to dare the devil to a duel) fell before him to the ground, when, in the state of his humility, he said but, " I am he ; " how will the wicked stand before him in his majesty? If Gideon's torches and trumpets so daunted the proud Midianites, how shall these abide the terror of the last day?

Ye workers of iniquity] Ye that make it your trade and task, that do " wickedly with both hands earnestly," that are wittily wicked, and can act out iniquity; that dig in the devil's mines, row in his galleys, grind in his mill, and are not wearied; that live by your sins, as the labourer doth by his trade ; and esteem it as the means of a happy life.[1] Ye that, although ye cannot be charged with any crying crime, but have Lord, Lord, in your mouths, and a show of holiness in your lives, yet regard iniquity in your hearts ; and when you seem most of all highflown, have a leering eye upon some beloved sin, as the eagle hath upon her prey below when she soareth highest. Your very preaching in Christ's name (if not for his name) is with God a work of iniquity, and shall have the " wages of sin," which is death, when Christ comes to judgment.[2] Then they that would not obey those sweet commands, " Repent, for the kingdom of heaven is at hand. Seek ye the Lord while he may be found. Believe in the Lord Jesus, and thou shalt be saved, thou and all thy household," &c., shall have no other commandment left them to obey, but this horrible " Depart ye ; " which imports an utter separation from the beatifical vision and fruition of God; and this is the very hell of hell, &c. Meanwhile, whereto serves the world's *Euge*, when they are sure of Christ's *Apage?*

Ver. 24. *Therefore whosoever heareth these sayings of mine*, &c.] Here we have the conclusion of this, if not first, yet certainly fullest, of our Saviour's sermons; for matter most heavenly, and for order more than methodical. Most men think, if they sit out a sermon, it is sufficient; when the preacher hath once done they have done to. Away they go, and (for any practice) they leave the word where they found it, or depart sorrowful, as he in the Gospel, that Christ requireth such things as they are not willing to perform. Our Saviour had four sorts of hearers, and but one good, that brought forth fruit with patience. When St Paul preached at Athens, some mocked, others doubted, a few believed, Acts xvii. 32, but no church was founded there as at other places, because " Christ crucified " was preached, " unto the Jews a stumbling-block, and to those Greeks foolishness ; " whilst the Jews required a sign, and the Greeks sought after wisdom, 1 Cor. i. 22, 23. But what saith the prophet? " Behold, they have rejected the word of the Lord, and what wisdom is in them ? " Jer.

viii. 9. He is a wise builder, a wise servant, a wise virgin, a wise merchant (if our Saviour may be judge), that heareth these sayings of his, and doeth them. "And behold" (saith Moses), " I have taught you statutes and judgments: keep therefore and do them ; for this is your wisdom," &c. " A good understanding have all they that do thereafter." Deut. iv. 6 ; Psal. cxi. 10. David hereby became wiser than his teachers, ancients, enemies ; and Paul counted it his chief policy to keep a good conscience void of offence toward God and men (πεπολίτευμαι), Acts xxiii. 1, which cannot be until it may be said of a man, as Shaphan said of Josiah's workmen, " All that was given in charge to thy servants, they do it," 2 Chron. xxxiv. 16. For not the hearers of the law, but the doers shall be justified, saith Paul, Rom. ii. 12 ; shall be blessed, saith our Saviour often, Luke xi. 28 ; John xiii. 17; shall be made thereby the friends of Christ, John xv. 14, the kindred of Christ, Matt. xii. 50 ; the glory of Christ, a royal diadem in the hand of Jehovah ; yea, such as have the honour to set the crown royal upon Christ's head in the day of his espousals, 2 Cor. viii. 23 ; Isa. lxii. 3 ; Cant. iii. 11. " Be ye therefore doers of the word," saith St James, " and not hearers only," deceiving, or putting paralogisms (παραλογιζόμενοι), James i. 22, tricks and fallacies (sophister-like) upon your own souls. They that place religion in hearing, and go no further, will prove egregious fools in the end. Which to prevent, look intently and accurately (παρακύψας), saith that apostle, stoop down, and pry heedfully into the " perfect law of liberty " (as the cherubims did into the propitiatory, as the angels do into the mystery of Christ, as the disciples did into the sepulchre of Christ, 1 Pet. i. 12 ; John xx. 5), " and continue therein," till ye be transformed thereinto ; " not being forgetful hearers, but doers of the work : " so shall ye " be blessed in the deed." It is not enough to hear, "but take heed how you hear." Bring with you the loan of your former hearing. " For to him that hath shall be given, and with what measure ye mete it shall be measured to you." As ye measure to God in preparation and practice, he will measure to you in success and blessing : and every time that you hear, God will come to you in " the fulness of the blessing of the gospel of " peace, Rom. xv. 29. See that ye shift not off (παραιτήσησθε) him that speaketh, Heb. xii. 25. *Veniat, veniat verbum Domini, et submittemus illi, sexcenta si nobis essent colla*, saith a notable Dutch divine: Let God speak, and we will yield, though it were to the loss of a thousand lives. The Macedonians delivered themselves up to God, and the Romans to the form of doctrine that was delivered unto them, 2 Cor. viii. 7 ; Rom. vi. 17; they took impression from it, as the metal doth from the mould, or as the wax doth from the seal. David lifted up his hands to God's commandments, Psal. cxix. 48, he did " all the wills of God," Acts xiii. 35, who had set him both his time and his task. He sets

[1] *Latini medicinam et argentariam facere dicunt.* Beza.
[2] Our works must be works of God, wrought from God,

for God, in God, according to God, else they are but shining sins. Mr Harris at Paul's Cross.

all his servants a-work, and requireth their pains. Hos. x. 11, Ephraim was an heifer used to dance and delight in the soft straw, and could not abide to plough, but the Lord will make him both bear and draw. Religion is not a name, saith one (Mr Harris at Paul's Cross), goodness a word; it is active like fire, communicative like light. As the life of things stand in goodness, so the life of goodness in action. The chiefest goods are most active, the best good a mere act. And the more good we do, the more God-like and excellent we be, and the better provided against a rainy day.

Which built his house upon a rock] This rock is Christ; and conscionable hearers are living stones built upon him, Ephes. ii. 20; 1 Pet. ii. 5. The conies are a people weak and wise, saith Solomon, Prov. xxx. 26; and their wisdom herein appears, they work themselves holes and burrows in the bosom of the earth, in the roots of the rocks. Learn we to do the like, and be sure to dig deep enough (as St Luke hath it); which while the stony-ground hearers did not, their blade was scorched up, and came to nothing, Luke vi. 48. (*Exoriuntur, sed exuruntur.*) Some flashing joy they had upon the hearing of the word, and many meltings (according to the nature of the doctrine delivered); but these sudden affections, being not well bottomed, nor having principles to maintain them, they were but like conduits running with wine at the coronation, or like a land flood, that seems to be a great sea, but is soon gone again.

Ver. 25. *And the rain descended, and the floods came,* &c.] Many are the troubles of the righteous; they come commonly thick and three-fold, one in the neck of another, as Job's messengers.[1] "The clouds return after the rain," Eccles. xii. 2. There is a continual succession of miseries and molestations from the devil, the world, and the flesh, to them that hear and do the words of Christ: like the weather in winter, when a shower or two do not clear the air, but though it rain much, yet the sky is still overcast with clouds, which are dissolved upon the saints, sometimes in lesser and lighter crosses, as the smaller rain, sometimes in pressing and piercing calamities, like storm and hail.[2] The rain falls, the floods rise, the wind blows, and many a sharp shower beats upon the Christian's building; but, like Noah's ark, it is pitched within and without; like Mount Sion, it abides for ever immovable, because founded upon the Rock of ages. *Si nos ruemus, ruet Christus una, ille regnator mundi,* said that noble Luther: If we fall, Christ shall fall too, that Ruler of the world: and let him fall; I had rather fall with Christ, than stand with Cæsar. The devil stirs up a tempest against God's children, saith Ambrose, *sed ipse naufragium facit,* but himself maketh shipwreck. The Church, according to that Venetian motto, *nec*

fluctu, nec flatu movetur : and yet Venice hath but one street (they say) that is not daily overflowed by the sea.

And it fell not] Saving grace is unleesable, though it may be impaired in the degrees, and may recoil to the root, as sap doth in winter. Christ lives in the hearts of all his saints, Gal. ii. 20, and can die no more, Rom. vi. 10. Die he may as well at the right hand of his Father, as in the heart of a Christian.

A weak brother, for whom Christ died, may perish, 1 Cor. viii. 11.

No thanks to us if he do not, who by scandalous courses offend and wound his conscience; but Christ will not lose him so. *Destrui potest, ex parte, per interveniens scandalum; quod et verbum ἀπολέω aliquo modo denotat, non distrahi penitus caulâ, &c.*

There are that deny the Lord that bought them, 2 Pet. ii. 1.

Bought they were by Christ in their own conceit, and in the esteem of others, but it proved otherwise. Or, they were bought, that is, delivered, in a general sense (so the word here used often signifieth), from their superstition to the knowledge of salvation (I say not to saving knowledge), whereby they might preach to others, themselves being cast-aways. God hath charged Christ, as Mediator, to see to the keeping of the bodies and souls of all true believers, John vi. 39, 40. And he faithfully performed it. "Those thou gavest me I have kept," saith he, " and none of them is lost," John xvii. 12.

Christ makes exception of one that was lost, *Ibid.*

That shows he was never of his body; for can he be a Saviour of a son of perdition?

Why is he then excepted?

1. Because he seemed to be one of Christ's, by reason of his office.

2. He speaketh there in particular of the twelve: and to be an apostle was, in itself, but an outward calling.

Christians may lose the things that they have wrought, 2 John 8.

1. Temporaries may, and do; and of them it may be understood, ver. 9.

2. True Christians may: 1. In respect of the praise of men; all their former honour may be laid in the dust. 2. In regard of the inward sense and comfort, as David, Psal. xxxii. and li. 3. In respect of the fulness of the reward in heaven, their glory may be much lessened by their falls.

A righteous man may turn from his righteousness, and die, Ezek. xviii. 24.

From his righteousness imparted, or that of sanctification, he may turn in part, and for a time, and die a temporal death for his offence, as Josiah: not so from his righteousness imputed, or that of justification, so as to die eternally. Or the Holy Ghost may so speak, as of a thing

---

[1] *Fluctus fluctum trudit.* Πόνος πόνῳ πόνον φέρει—*dolor et voluptas invicem cedunt, brevior voluptas.* Sen.

[2] *Calamitas est propriè calamorum comminutio à grandine seu tempestate. Sic clades dicebantur surculorum detritio :*

strages à stratis arboribus. Becman. Scaliger. *Et esto ruat : Malo ego cum Christo ruere, quam cum Cæsare stare.* Epist. ad Melch. Burton of Melancholy.

impossible ; as, If an angel from heaven should preach any other doctrine, &c., Gal. i. 8, which cannot possibly be. So that this text concludes not categorically. The Comforter shall abide with us for ever, John xiv. 16. It is called an earnest, not a pawn. A pawn is to be returned again ; but an earnest is part and pledge of the whole sum.

What need then so many exhortations to perseverance ?

1. True grace in itself is leesable, in respect of us, who should fall from it, as Adam ; but we are kept by the power and promise of God to salvation ; and we need Christ's left hand to be under us, and his right hand over us, to clasp and hold us up. He keepeth the feet of the saints, 1 Sam. ii. 9, and preserves us from all such evil, as may frustrate our perseverance, 2 Thess. iii. 3 ; 1 John v. 18.

2. By these exhortations, as means, God's grace is promoted, and preserved in us.

3. We are but in part renewed, and are apt to backslide ; if we row not hard, wind and tide will carry us back again. Heed therefore must be taken, that we look not back with Lot's wife ; that our Jacob's ladder may reach to heaven ; that our oil fail not, till the Bridegroom come ; that our coat reach down to our heels, as Joseph's and the high priest's did ; that we sacrifice the beast with the tail, Gen. xxxvii. 3 ; Exod. xxviii. 4, 42 ; xxix. 22 ; that we keep in this fire of the sanctuary ; or, if it slack, that we rake it out of the ashes, and blow it up again into a flame, ἀναζωπυρεῖν, 2 Tim. i. 6 ; that we turn not again, as we walk, with those living creatures, Ezek. i. 12 ; nor be like Nebuchadnezzar's image, that began in gold, and ended in clay, Dan. ii. 33 ; that " we begin not in the Spirit and end in the flesh," Gal. iii. 3 ; that we go not backward as Hezekiah's sun, nor stand at a stay, as Joshua's, but rejoice to run our race, as David's, Psal. xix. 4 ; and go on to the perfect day, as Solomon's, Prov. iv. 18.

Ver. 26. And every one that heareth these sayings of mine, and doeth them not, &c.] Which is the greater number of hearers, for most men hear to hear, and not to practise.[1] Some hear merely of form, or for fashion' sake, or to save the penalty of the statute, or to find some recipe to procure a sleep, or to still the clamours of their consciences, or to make amends and purchase dispensation for some beloved lust, as Herod ; or expecting from the preacher some choice novelty, as Matt. iii. 8, some deep point, Matt. xii. 37, or dainty expressions, as Ezek. xxxiii. 32. Or they hear and jeer, Acts xvii. 32 ; hear and carp, as Doeg ; hear and resist the Holy Ghost, Acts vii. Or at least are no whit wrought upon, whether we pipe or lament to them. Or if they hear and admire, as those, Matt. xxii. 22 ; yet they amend nothing, or but for a season, as the stony ground, Matt. xi. 17 ; they are hearers of forgetfulness (ἀκροαταὶ ἐπιλησμονῆς), James i. 25 ; like hourglasses, they are no sooner full, but running

out again ; like nets or sieves, they retain only the chaff or weeds, let go the pure water and good corn. The word runs through them, as water through a riven vessel (that is the apostle's metaphor, Heb. ii. 1, μήποτε παραρνῶμεν), or as that which is written upon moist paper, as others will have it. A general cause of our not practising what we hear is, that we put this spiritual treasure into broken bags, this precious liquor into leaking vessels. Whereas our souls should be as the ark, and our memories as the pot of manna, to retain what we have received, that we may have it ready for practice, as Saul had his cruse and his spear at his head, and David his scrip and stones ready by his side. A heavy ear is a singular judgment, Isa. vi. 10 ; but a slow heart and a heavy hand, to conceive and do what we hear, paves a way to remediless misery ; besides the fool to boot which the judge here putteth upon him.

Shall be likened unto a foolish man] And he is a fool indeed whom Christ calleth fool. Conscionable hearers are counted good men (God wot), but simple, silly, and of no parts. But " wisdom is justified of her children." To walk precisely, is to walk wisely, Eph. v. 15. And he that heareth and guideth his feet in the way, is wise, Prov. xxiii. 19. And, " Who is a wise man amongst you, and endued with knowledge ? Let him show out of a good conversation his works," &c., Jam. iii. 13. All others are fools, because they fail in the main point of their salvation : they are troubled about many things, but neglect the one thing necessary ; they trifle out their precious opportunities, and in hearing or other services they do worse than lose their labour, for they commit sin and heap up wrath. Their house will down, as the spider's house doth, and all their building, ploughing, planting, sailing, come to nothing.

Which built his house upon the sand] Wherefore it soon sinks and shatters, as having not the loose earth thrown up first, by the practice of mortification and self-denial. Men should first sit down, and cast what it would cost them to build the tower of godliness, or e'er they leap into profession. They should put their hearts often to those grand questions of abnegation. Can I (as all must that will be Christ's disciples) deny myself in all my selves (for a man hath many selves within himself, and must utterly and absolutely deny them all), take up my daily cross (for *omnis Christianus crucianus*, every Christian is a Crucian or cross-bearer, saith Luther ; the rain will fall, the floods flow, the winds blow, and beat upon his building, he shall have many trials and temptations, that looks towards heaven, troubles without, terrors within, his back-burden of both), and follow Christ through thick and thin, by doing and suffering his whole will ? Many will follow Christ in such duties as suit with their humours, and no further, as the rusty hand of a dial ; they will break the hedge of his law, to shun a piece of foul way : they follow Christ, as *magnitudine, ut omne corpus ex eis contegant.* Isidore xi. 3.

---

[1] *Panætios apud Scythiam esse ferunt tam diffusâ aurium*

the dog follows his master, till he come by a carrion, and then he turns him up. Orpah made a fair proffer of going along with Naomi, but when she had better considered it, she turned again. Lot's wife set fair out of Sodom, but looked back. So do many forward hearers set their hands to God's plough, but (loth to plough up the fallow ground of their hearts, and to lay a good foundation in humiliation) they start aside like broken bows, and steal away like cowardly soldiers (ὑποστείληται), Heb. x. 38, and so judge themselves unworthy of eternal life, and unfit for God's kingdom, Luke ix. 62. For the foolish shall not stand in his sight, he hateth all the workers of iniquity, Psal. v. 5. Caleb was not discouraged by the giants, therefore he had Hebron given him, the place of the giants, when the spies and murmurers were never suffered to enter; no more shall they that hold not out to the death obtain the crown of life.

Ver. 27. *And the rain descended, &c.*] The old heart cannot possibly hold out the hardship of holiness, nor bear the brunt of persecution for well-doing. Like a chestnut cast into the fire, if not broken first on the top, it leaps out again; or like a false jade in a team, which being put to a stress, turns tail and tramples. When the godly hearer holds on his way to heaven, through all disasters; as those two kine of the Philistines that bore home the ark, held on their way, though they had calves at home, that might have made them turn back.

And it fell] The wise man's and fool's house come under a double difference. 1. In the foundation; this to see to, and above-ground, is little discerned. The temple is said to be as low under-ground as it was high above. 2. In the building itself. The unprofitable hearer is not cemented to Christ by faith, but laid loose, as it were, upon a sandy foundation, and so slips beside the ground-work in foul weather. He is not set into the stock as a scion, but only stuck into the ground as a stake, and is therefore easily pulled up. Whereas the true Christian is knit fast to Christ the rock by the ligament of a lively faith; and as a lively stone, is built up in a spiritual house, 1 Pet. ii. 5, growing up in the mystical body with so much sweetness and evenness, as if the whole temple (like that of Solomon) were but one entire stone. "He that is joined to the Lord is one spirit," 1 Cor. vi. 17. So that although, 1. Shakings and waverings in the very purpose of holy walking may befall a saint by violent temptations, Psal. lxxiii. 2, 13; yea, 2. Intermissions of the exercise of grace, as of life in a palsy or epilepsy; 3. Particular falls we are not exempted from,—Peter himself, though a pillar, fell from his former steadfastness, in part;—yet from intercision, prolapsion, from utter and irrecoverable falling away, they are freed, because founded upon a Rock, which can never be removed. He is both the "author and finisher of their faith," Heb. xii. 2; He

hath prayed and procured that it utterly fail not, Luke xxii. 32.

And the fall thereof was great] Great and grievous, because irreparable, irre-edifiable, as Jericho and the temple at Jerusalem. God lays them aside like broken vessels, of which there is no further use; and sith they will needs wallow again, as swine, in the filth of their former pollutions, he pronounceth upon them that fearful sentence, "Let him that is filthy be filthy still;" that unclean spirit entereth him again, and his dispositions to evil are seven times more inflamed than ever. He hath despised and despited the Spirit of Grace, and is in the ready road to the unpardonable sin, Heb. x. 26. The apostate cannot lightly choose unto himself a worse condition, Heb. x. 26. He casts himself into hell-mouth, Heb. x. 39, where "the backslider in heart shall be filled with his own ways," Prov. xiv. 14, and have the greater torment by how much he fell from greater hopes and possibilities of better; as Nebuchadnezzar from his monarchy, and as Cranmer from his high preferment to so low a condition, as that there was left him neither hope of better nor place of worse.

Ver. 28. *And it came to pass, when Jesus had ended these sayings*] All this then was but one sermon, though twice preached at several times, as some collect out of Luke. A long sermon it was, and yet the people staid it out. So did not those Capernaites, John vi., and therefore fell away from Christ; so did not Judas, and therefore met the devil at the door, John xiii. 30. It is a lamentable thing that a winter's tale shall be heard with more patience and pleasure than a powerful sermon; that if a preacher exceed his glass sometimes people sit at as little ease as if they were in a fit of an ague; and others profanely turn their backs upon the propitiatory, and depart without the blessing, Ezek. xliv. 5. In the Council of Agathon it was decreed that none should presume to go out before the minister had blessed the congregation. And in the fourth Council of Carthage, Let him that goes out of the auditory when the minister is speaking to the congregation, be excommunicated. *Ita missa est,* Ἄφεσις λαοῦ, were the old forms of dismission. And although Zacharias was long ere he came forth, yet the people staid his coming, Luke i. 21. But the word of the Lord is to the wicked a burthen, Jer. xxvii. 33, cords and bonds, Psal. ii. 3, yokes and bonds, Jer. v. 5. Hence they are so soon sated, and their attentions tired out and jaded, as it were.

The people were astonished at his doctrine] They were strangely transported, and rapt with an ecstasy of admiration and amazement.[1] They were at such a pass that they could neither say nor do, but stood amazed with their eyes set in their heads, as the word importeth. And surely the word never worketh so kindly as when it is received with admiration; yet may we not rest in that, as too many do; but get it mingled with

---

[1] ἐξεπλήσσοντο. *Ubi animus quasi attonitus, nec loquitur,*   *nec quicquam agit, sed apertis oculis aliquantisper quietus manet.* Lyser.

faith in our hearts that works by love, "holding fast the faithful word," as Paul bids Timothy, that part of it especially that in hearing he is pleased to sweeten unto us by the taste of his special goodness.

Ver. 29. *For he taught them as one having authority.*] Never man spake as he spake, said those catch-poles that came to take him, but were taken by him. For matter, his doctrine was not his own, but his Father's that sent him, John vii. 16. For manner, this prince of preachers had the tongue of the learned, Isa. l. 4 ; yet without ostentation of learning he delivered himself so plainly that the simplest might conceive him, and so powerfully that his enemies could not but confess that he " was true, and taught the way of God truly," Matt. xxii. 14. And for end, he seriously sought his Father's glory in the salvation of men's souls. A fair precedent for preachers ; who should thus seek to get within the people, and to maintain the credit of their ministry, that their words may carry an authority and command attention.

And not as the Scribes] Who, 1. Stuck in the bark of the law, and pierced not into the heart and sense of it. 2. Delivered " for doctrines the commandments of men " about washings, tithings, &c. 3. They sought not the glory of God, but praise of men ; and were therefore mad at our Saviour, as one that bare away the bell from them for a powerful preacher. 4. They rejected publicans and sinners, though penitent : so did not Christ. 5. They taught coldly and carelessly ; but he zealously and imperiously, as the lawgiver, and not as an interpreter only ; as that " prophet like unto me," saith Moses ; yea, far beyond him, or any other that ever spake with a tongue. For he could and did speak to the hearts of his hearers ; together with his word "there went forth a power," as to heal the bodies of those, Luke v. 17, so the souls of his elect ; he was a minister of the spirit and not of the letter only.[1]

CHAPTER VIII.

Ver. 1. *Great multitudes followed him*] MANY thousands, as *Bodinius De Claritate Christi* proveth out of ancient writers. This drew upon our Saviour the envy of the Pharisees, those cankered carls who, Sejanus-like, thought all lost that fell beside their own lips : as Nero, they spited all those whom the people applauded ; and tiger-like, laid hold with their teeth on all the excellent spirits of their times, as it is said of Tiberius.[2]

Ver. 2. *And behold there came a leper.*] This leprosy was most rife in our Saviour's time ; God

so ordering that Judea was sickest when her Physician was nearest. The Jews are still a nasty people ; and this kind of leprosy seems to have been proper to them, as *Plica Polonica, Morbus Gallicus, Sudor Anglicus.* No stranger in England was touched with this disease, and yet the English were chased therewith, not in England only, but in other countries abroad ; which made them like tyrants, both feared and avoided wherever they came. So were these Jewish lepers. Hence that fable in Tacitus, that the Israelites were driven out of Egypt for that loathsome disease. This, said one malevolent heathen, is the cause why they rest every seventh day. Bodinus observes it for a special providence of God, that in Arabia (which bordereth upon Judea) there are no swine to be found, lest that most leprous creature, saith he, should more and more infest and infect that people, who are naturally subject to the leprosy.[3] And another good author is of opinion that God did therefore forbid the Jews to eat either swine's flesh or hare's flesh, *quod ista caro facilè in malè affectis corporibus putrescat,* because in diseased bodies it easily corrupts and turns to ill humours.

And worshipped him] Which he would hardly ever have done, haply, had he not been a leper. *Morbi sunt virtutum officina :* diseases, saith St Ambrose, are the shop of virtues. King Alfred found himself ever best when he was worst ; and therefore prayed God to send him always some sickness ; Gehazi's leprosy cured him, his white forehead made him a white soul.

If thou wilt, thou canst, &c.] So another came with, " If thou canst do anything, help us." We never doubt of Christ's will to do us good (saith a great divine), but, in some degree, we doubt also of his power. True faith doubts of neither, but believes against sense in things invisible, and against reason in things incredible. Sense corrects imagination, reason corrects sense, but faith corrects both.

Ver. 3. *And Jesus put forth his hand,* &c.] The law forbade *contactum contagionis, non sanationis.* The high priest might enter a leprous house, &c. " We have not an high priest that cannot be touched with the feeling of our infirmities," Heb. iv. 15. Better might he say, than St Cyprian, *Cum singulis pectus meum copulo, mæroris et funeris pondera luctuosa participo, cum plangentibus plango, cum deflentibus defleo,* &c. Than St Paul, " Who is weak, and I am not weak ? Who is afflicted, and I burn not ? " 2 Cor. xi. 29. It was held a great condescension in King Alphonsus to use his skill for the recovery of one of his sick subjects : what was it here in Christ, the King of kings and Lord of lords ?

---

[1] *Optimi ad vulgus hi sunt concionatores, dixit Lutherus, qui puerilitèr, trivialitèr, popularitèr, et simplicissimè docent.* Melch. Ad. *in Vita.* Γραμματεῖς ἦσαν δευτερωταὶ τοῦ νόμου ; γραμματικὴν τινὰ ἐπιστήμην ἐφηγούμενοι. Epiphan. lib. 1 *Panarii. Scribarum doctrina erat torpida, elumbis, frigida.* Heb. ii. 3.

[2] *Quicquid non acquiritur damnum est.* Sen. *de Sejano. Nero omnium æmulus.* Ammian.

[3] *Summâ Dei bonitate id factum est, ne populos ad lepram proclives, animal leprosissimum magis, ac magis infestaret.* Jo. Bodin.

Ver. 4. *See thou tell no man*] Christ despised popular applause, accounting it no other than a little stinking breath. Some do all for a name. But we have not so learned Christ. His treasures were hid, Col. ii. 3. He sought not himself, but to set up him that sent him, John viii. 50.

Show thyself to the priest] That they may see that I am He that should come, that Jehovah the physician, that "Son of righteousness with health under his wings," &c.; that I came not to destroy the law, as they slanderously give out, but to fulfil it, that God may be glorified and the mouth of malice stopped.

Offer the gift, &c.] This is that pepper-corn we pay to God, who is content that we have the benefit of his favours, so he may have the glory of them. Not lepers only, but all sorts, after sickness, were bound to offer to God the ransom of their lives, Exod. xxxi. Hezekiah made a song and left it to posterity, for a seal of his thankfulness. Heathens in this case would consecrate something to their gods, to their Teraphim. The very word in Greek that signifies to heal (framed from Teraphim) signifies first to worship and serve God (θεραπεύειν), so showing us what they were wont to do in case of cure. But now-a-days *sciopato il morbo, fraudato il santo*, as the Italian proverb hath it. Sick men recovered, deal as shipwrecked men escaped; they promise God, as he in Erasmus' Naufragium did the Virgin, a picture of wax as big as St Christopher, but when he came to shore would not give a tallow-candle. This is a cursed kind of couzenage, Mal. i. 14.

Ver. 5. *There came unto him a centurion*] *Rarior est virtus veniens e corpore raro.* Soldiers are commonly fierce and godless creatures. But this noble centurion might well have made a commander in that Thundering Legion, and might well have had his hand in that Victoria Halleluiatica (as it was called) obtained by the orthodox Britons against the Pelagian Picts and Saxons here, *Victoriâ fide obtentâ, non viribus*, as the story tells us; a victory got by faith, and not by force, Κεραυνοβόλος. D. Ussier, *de Britann. Eccles. primord.* p. 332.

Ver. 6. *Lord, my servant lieth at home*, &c.] Not thrown out of doors, not cast sick into a corner, to sink or swim, for any care his master would take of him; no, nor left to be cured at his own charges. The good centurion was not a better man than a master. So was that renowned Sir Thomas Lucy, late of Charlecott in Warwickshire, to whose singular commendation it was in mine hearing preached at his funeral, and is now since published, by my much honoured friend Mr Robert Harris, that (among many others that would dearly miss him) a housefull of servants had lost not a master, but a physician who made their sickness his, and his cost and physic theirs.

*Cui blanda in vultu gravitas, et mite serena
Fronte supercilium, sed pectus mitius ore.*

Or (as mine *Alter Ego*) mine entirely beloved kinsman, Mr Thomas Dugard, expresseth it in his elegant epitaph : His servants' sickness was his sympathy, and their recovery his cost. *In quo viro ingenium pietas, artemque modestia vincit.*

Ver. 7. *I will come and heal him*] *Stupenda dignatio;* a wonderful condescending that the Lord of lords should vouchsafe to visit a poor servant and restore him to health.[1] It was a great favour that Queen Elizabeth did Sir Christopher Hatton, Lord Chancellor (who died nevertheless of grief of mind), that, when she had broken his heart with a harsh word, she was pleased to visit and comfort him, though it were all too late. What was it then for the Lord Christ in the shape of a servant to come down to the sick servant's pallet! Hunniades, when he felt himself in danger of death, desired to receive the sacrament before his departure; and would in any case (sick as he was) be carried to the church to receive the same, saying that it was not fit that the Lord should come to the house of his servant, but the servant rather to go to the house of his Lord and Master.

Ver. 8. *Lord, I am not worthy*, &c.] *Fidei mendica manus ;* faith is an emptying grace, and makes a man cry out with Pomeran : *Etiamsi non sum dignus, nihilominus tamen sum indigens.* By faith we come to see him that is invisible. Now, the more a man seeth of God, the less he seeth by himself; the nearer he draweth to God, the more rottenness he feeleth in his bones. Lord, I am hell, but thou art heaven (said Mr Hooper, martyr, at his death); I am swill and a sink of sin, but thou art a gracious God, &c.

But speak the word only, &c.] The centurion's humility was not more low than his faith lofty; that reached up unto heaven, and in the face of human weakness descries omnipotency.

Ver. 9. *For I am a man*] But thou, Lord, art more than a man; for the centurion here makes comparison with our Saviour, both in respect of his person and of his power, as of the less with the greater. For his person, he saith not, *Nam et ego sum homo, ut tu*, "For I also am a man such as thou art" (as the vulgar here corruptly renders it); but, "I am a man," a mere man; thou art God also, very God. And for his power, though subject to another, have soldiers at my beck and check, how much more hast thou, who art over all, an absolute power over sickness and death? The palsy, or, as some say, the epilepsy, was anciently called *Morbus sacer*, or the holy disease; for the priests, to enrich themselves, persuaded the superstitious people that this disease, as being sudden, hidden, and for most part incurable, was an immediate hand of God, and could be cured by none but priests. The medicines they gave were much like that of the French mountebank, who was wont to give in writing to his patients, for curing all diseases, these following verses :

centurionis servulum visitare. Ambros.

---

[1] *Ut cœli Dominus nequaquam dedignaretur*

Si vis curari de morbo nescio quali,
Accipias herbam, sed qualem nescio, nec quam :
Ponas nescio quo, curabere nescio quando.

They are thus Englished by one :

Your pain, I know not what, do not fore-slow,
To cure with herbs, which whence I do not know.
Place them (well pounc't) I know not where,
    and then
You shall be perfect whole, I know not when.

And I say to this man, Go, and he goeth, &c.]
King Ferdinand's ambassadors, being con-
ducted into the camp of the Turks, wondered
at the perpetual and dumb silence of so great a
multitude ; the soldiers being so ready and
attentive, that they were no otherwise commanded than by the beckoning of the hand or
nod of their commanders. Tamerlane, that warlike Scythian, had his men at so great command
that no danger was to them more dreadful than
his displeasure.

And to my servant, Do this, and he doeth it]
Such a servant is every saint to his God; at
least in his desire and endeavour. Such a centurion also is he over his own heart, which he
hath at his right hand, as Solomon saith ; that
is, ready prest to obey God in all parts and
points of duty. There were seven sorts of
Pharisees; and one was *Pharisæus, Quid debeo
facere, et faciam illud :* so they would needs be
called. But the true Christian only is such a
one in good earnest as the Pharisee pretends to
be.

Ver. 10. He marvelled, and said, &c.] What
can be so great a marvel as that Christ mar-
velleth ? So he wondered at his own work in
Nathaniel, John i. 47, and at his own love to
miserable mankind, when he calls himself
" Wonderful, Counsellor," &c., Isa. ix. 6. He
wondereth not, as the disciples did, at the
magnificence of the temple ; he was not a whit
taken with all the beauty and bravery of the
world set before him by the devil, as it were in a
landscape ; but at the centurion's faith he much
marvelled, it being a work of his own almighty
power, which he puts not forth but for great
purposes, Eph. i. 19. Where is easy to observe
in the original a sixfold gradation.

Ver. 11. Many shall come from the east] They
shall " fly as a cloud," saith Isaiah (speaking of
the conversion of the Gentiles), and so flock to
the Church, as if a whole flight of doves, driven
by some hawk or tempest, should scour into the
columbary, and rush into the windows, Isa. lx. 8.
The Tyrians had a hand in building the temple.
The molten sea stood upon twelve oxen, which
looked towards east, west, north, and south. The
New Jerusalem hath twelve gates, to show that
there is every way access for all sorts to Christ,
who is also fitly called the second Adam, the
Greek letters of which name (as St Cyprian observeth) do severally signify all the quarters of

the earth.[1] He was born in an inn, to show that
he receives all comers (πανδοχεῖον) ; his garments
were divided into four parts, to show that out of
what part of the world soever we come, if we be
naked, Christ hath robes to clothe us, if we be
harbourless, Christ hath room to lodge us. Jether, an Ishmaelite, may become an Israelite,
1 Chron. vii. 17 with 2 Sam. xvii. 25, and Araunah the Jebusite may be made an exemplary
proselyte, 2 Sam. xxiv. 18 with Zech. ix. 7. *Vide
Junium in locum.*

Ver. 12. But the children of the kingdom]
Those that had made a covenant with God by
sacrifice, Psal. l. 5 ; and therefore held their
heads on high, as already destined to the diadem.
Lo, these, in the height of their hopes and expectancies, shall be excluded; a foul and fearful
disappointment. Surely the tears of hell cannot
sufficiently bewail the loss of heaven. John of
Valois was son, brother, uncle, father to a king,
yet himself never was a king ; so here.

Into outer darkness] Into a darkness beyond
a darkness ; into a dungeon beyond and beneath
the prison. *In tenebras ex tenebris, infeliciter
exclusi, infelicius excludendi,* saith Augustine.
God shall surely say to these unhappy children
of the kingdom, when he casts them into condemnation, as Aulus Fulvius said to his traitor-
ous son when he slew him with his own hands,
Non Catiline te genui sed patriæ. I called you
not but to glory and virtue, neither to glory, but
by virtue, 2 Pet. i. 3. As you liked not the latter, so never look for the former. Every man is
either a king or a caitiff ; and shall either reign
with Christ, or rue it for ever with the devil.[2]
Aut Cæsar aut nullus, as he said to his mother :
and as those in the Turk's court, that are born of
the blood royal, but come not to the kingdom ;
they must die either by the sword or halter ; so
here.

Ver. 13. And as thou hast believed, &c.] Faith
hath a happy hand ; and never but speeds in
one kind or other. It hath what it would, either
in money or money's worth. Apollonius, saith
Sozomen, never asked anything of God in all his
life, that he obtained not. This man, saith one
concerning Luther, could have of God whatsoever he listed.

Ver. 14. He saw his wife's mother laid, &c.]
A wife, then, Peter had, and if a good wife, she
might be a singular help to him in his ministry ;
as Nazianzen's mother was to her husband, not
a companion only, but in some respects a guide
to godliness.[3] St Ambrose saith that all the
apostles were married men, save John and Paul.
And those pope-holy hypocrites that will not
hear of priests' marriage, but hold it far better
for them to have and keep at home many harlots than one wife[4] (as that carnal Cardinal Campeius defended) ; they might hear the contrary
out of their own canon law, where it is written,
Distinct. 29, *Siquis discernit Presbyterum conju-*

---

[1] Α. Ανατολή. Δ. Δύσις. Α. Αρκτος. Μ. Μεσημβρία.
[2] *Omnis homo aut est cum Christo regnaturus, aut cum
diabolo cruciandus.* Aug.

[3] οὐ σύνεργος μόνον ἀλλὰ καὶ ἀρχηγός ἐγένετο. Naz.
[4] *Honestius est pluribus occulte implicari, quam aperte cum
una ligari.*

gatum, tanquam occasione nuptiarum offerre non debeat, anathema esto. And again, Distinct. 31, *Siquis vituperat nuptia, et dormientem cum viro suo fidelem et religiosam detestatur, aut culpabilem æstimat, velut quæ regnum Dei introire non possit, anathema esto.* They might hearken to Paphnutius, a famous primitive confessor; who, though himself an unmarried man, mightily persuaded and prevailed with the Nicene Council, that they should not decree anything against priests' marriage, alleging, that marriage was honourable in all, and that the bed undefiled was true chastity. They might hear Ignatius, scholar to St John the Evangelist, pronouncing all such as call marriage a defilement, to be inhabited by that old dragon the devil.[1] But there is a politic reason that makes these men deaf to whatsoever can be said to them by whomsoever; and you shall have it in the words of him that wrote the History of the Council of Trent (a Council carried by the pope, with such infinite guile and craft, that the Jesuits, those *connubisanctifugæ, commeritricitegæ,* will even smile in the triumphs of their own wits, when they hear it but mentioned, as a master-stratagem). The legates in Trent Council (saith he) were blamed for suffering the article of priests' marriage to be disputed, as dangerous; because it is plain that married priests will turn their affections and love to wife and children; and by consequence, to their house and country: so that the strict dependence which the clergy hath upon the apostolic see would cease; and to grant marriage to priests would destroy the ecclesiastical hierarchy, and make the Pope bishop of Rome only. (Hist. of Council of Trent.)

Ver. 15. *And he touched her hand*] A speedy and easy cure of the fever, such as Hippocrates or Galen could never skill of. They do it not but by many evacuations, long diet, &c.; besides that, much gold must be lavished out of the bag as it is, Isa. xlvi. 6, the poor patient crying oft out, *ai, ai,* whence Æger, as some think (Becman). Christ, by his word and touch only, doth the deed in an instant. As he can blow us to destruction, Job iv. 9, nod us to destruction, Psal. lxxx. 16; so, when Heman thinks himself " free among the dead," free of that company, and the " mourners begin to go about the streets," he can speak life unto us, and keep us that we go not down to the pit, Psal. lxxxviii. 5; Eccl. xii. 5; Psal. xxx. 3.

She arose, and ministered unto them] Thereby to evince the truth of the miracle, and to evidence the truth of her thankfulness.

Ver. 16. *When the even was come*] In the morning he sowed his seed, and in the evening he withheld not his hand, Eccl. xi. 6. It is good to be doing whilst it is day. Mr Bradford, martyr, held that hour not well spent wherein he did not some good, either with his tongue, pen, or hand.

Ver. 17. *Himself took our infirmities*] The

prophet speaketh of spiritual infirmities, the evangelist applieth it to corporal. And not unfitly; for these are the proper effects of those. We may thank our sins for our sicknesses, Rev. ii. 22. She had stretched herself upon a bed of security, she shall be cast, another while, upon a bed of sickness. Asa had laid the prophet by the heels; and now God lays him by the heels, diseasing him in his feet, 2 Chron. xvi. 12. Sin is an universal sickness, Isa. i. 5, 6; like those diseases which the physicians say are *corruptio totius substantiæ.* And our lives are fuller of sins than the firmament of stars or the furnace of sparks. Hence all our bodily distempers, which when we groan and labour under, let us reflect and revenge upon sin as the mother of all misery. And when we are made whole, " sin no more, lest a worse thing come upon us."

Ver. 18. *To depart unto the other side*] Either to retire or repose himself after much pains (for *quod caret, alterna requie,* &c., the very birds, when building their nests, fly abroad sometimes from their work, for recreation' sake);[2] or else the better to edge the people's desires after him, now withdrawn. Luther gave this rule to preachers, for moderating their discourses: When thou seest thine hearers most attentive, then conclude; for so they will come again more cheerfully the next time. *Cum vides attentissime audire populum, conclude : eo alacriores redibunt.* (Luther.)

Ver. 19. *Master, I will follow thee,* &c.] As Samson followed his parents, till he met with an honey-comb; or as a dog follows his master till he come by a carrion. *Vix diligitur Jesus, propter Jesum.* But, as Isaac loved Esau, for venison was his meat, Gen. xxv. 28, and as Judah's rulers " loved with shame, Give ye," Hos. iv. 18; so do hypocrites; they serve not the Lord Jesus Christ, but their own bellies, Rom. xvi. 18; they have his person in admiration only for advantage, Jude 16; they can bear the cross with Judas, so they may bear the bag and lick their own fingers. Ephraim is an heifer that loveth to tread out the corn, because while it treads it feeds, Hos. x. 11. But such delicate self-seekers are rejected, as here; when those that have honest aims and ends hear, " Come and see," John i. 46.

Ver. 20. *The foxes have holes,* &c.] q. d. *Exigua mihi sunt subsidia aut præsidia. Nudus opum, sed cui cœlum terraque paterent,* as Ennius said of Archimedes. The great Architect of the world had not a house to put his head in; but emptied himself of all, and became poor to make us rich, not in goods, but in grace, not in worldly wealth, but in the true treasure, ἐκένωσεν, Phil. ii. 7; 2 Cor. viii. 9. Say we with that Father, *Christi paupertas meum est patrimonium :* prefer the reproach of Christ before the treasures of Egypt, Heb. xi. 26; and if, besides and with Christ, we have food and raiment, let us therewith rest content, 1 Tim. vi. 8. Say we have no house on earth, we have one in heaven not made with hands. Those good

---

[1] *Siquis coinquinationem vocet commixtionem legitimam, habet inhabitatorem Draconem Apostatam.* Ign. Epist. ad Philadelph.

[2] *Levandi laboris sui causa volucres passim ac libere volitant.* Cicero. 2. de Orat.

souls dwelt in "dens and caves of the earth," yea, "wandered about in sheep-skins and goat-skins," Heb. xi. 37, 38, that might have rustled in their silks and velvets, that might (Nebuchad-nezzar-like) have vaunted themselves on their stately turrets and palaces, if they would have let go Christ. But that, they knew well, had been to make a fool's bargain.

But the Son of man, &c.] So he styles himself, either to note the truth of his humanity or the depth of his abasement, the Son of God became the son of man, which was, as one said in a like case, to fall from the court to the cart, from a palace to a gallows. Among all the prophets, Ezekiel is most frequently styled the son of man, and that purposely; to keep him low amidst his many rare raptures and revelations. The heathen, when they would set forth a man miserable indeed, they called him τρισάνθρωπον, thrice a man.

Hath not whereon to lay his head] That the Messiah when he cometh shall not have where-on to sit, where to rest his body, is affirmed by the Jewish Gemarists. Our Saviour may seem here to allude to such a tradition.

Ver. 21. *Lord, suffer me first to go and bury*] Old men's fear is (saith Plutarch, and that makes them so gripple) that they shall not have θρέψοντας καὶ θάψοντας, those that will be careful to nourish them whiles alive, and to bury them decently when they are dead.

Ver. 22. *Follow me*] Let go things less necessary, and mind the main. Thy task is long, thy time is short; opportunities are headlong, and must be quickly caught, as the echo catch-eth the voice. There is no use of after-wit.

Præcipitat tempus, mors atra impendet agenti.
(Sil. Italic.)

Let the dead bury their dead] The dead in sin, their dead in nature. Ungodly men are no better than breathing ghosts, walking sepulchres of themselves. Their bodies are but living coffins to carry a dead soul up and down in. The saints only are heirs of life, 1 Pet. iii. 7, and all others are dead, stark dead in sins and trespasses, as the wanton widow, 1 Tim. v. 6, as Terence saith the same: *Sane hercle homo voluptati obsequens fuit dum vixit.* And of such dead corpses (as once in Egypt, Ex. xii. 30) there is no house wherein there is not one, nay, many.

Ver. 23. *And when he was entered, &c.*] Him-self was first in the ship where they were to suffer. Like a good shepherd, he goes before his sheep, John x. Like a good captain, he goes before his soldiers; and as it was said of Hannibal,[1] that he first entered the field and last went out of the field, so is it with Christ the captain of our salvation. "Fear not," saith he, "for I am with thee: be not afraid, for I am thy God," Isa. xli. 10. *Tua causa erit mea causa,* as that emperor told Julius Pflugius, who had been much wronged by the Duke of Saxony, in the emperor's employment.

[1] *Princeps prælium inibat, ultimus*

Ver. 24. *And behold there arose a great tem-pest*] Stirred up, likely, by the devil, to drown Christ (that male child of the Church, Rev. xii. 5) and his disciples; as he brained Job's chil-dren with the fall of the house. This is still the endeavour of Satan and his instruments: but to such we may, as Pope Pius II. wrote to the great Turk,

Niteris incassum Christi submergere navem :
Fluctuat, at nunquam mergitur, illa ratis.

And as the poet said of Troy, so may we of the Church,

Victa tamen vinces, eversaque Troja resurges :
Obruit hostiles illa ruina domos. Ovid. Fast.

Ambrose hath a remarkable speech to this purpose : *Diabolus contra sanctos tempestatem movet : sed ipse naufragium facit.* The devil stirs up a tempest against the saints, but him-self is sure to suffer shipwreck. The Church, as a bottle, may be dipped, not drowned; as the diamond, it may be cast into the fire, not burnt by it; as the crystal, it may be fouled, but not stained by the venom of a toad; as the palm-tree in the emblem, which though it have many weights at top and snakes at the root, yet it saith still, *Nec premor, nec perimor.* Lastly, as the north pole, *semper versatur, nunquam mergitur,* as St Jerome observeth.

Ver. 25. *Master, save us, we perish*] Troubles drive us to God (as bugbears do children into their mother's bosom), who delighteth to help those that are forsaken of their hopes. In prosperity, either we pray not at all—*Raræ fu-mant felicibus aræ,* or but faintly, yawningly, &c. *Oratio sine malis, est ut avis sine alis.* But in a stress, as here, our prayers, like strong streams in narrow straits, run mightily upon God, and will not away without that they came for.

Ver. 26. *And he saith unto them*] Christ first chides them, and then chides the winds and waves. Men are most malleable in time of misery, Job xxxiii. 23. Strike whiles the iron is hot. How forcible are right words! Those that are melted in the furnace of affliction will easily receive impression. Hamper Manasses, and he will hearken to you.

O ye of little faith] Ye petty-fidians: He calleth them not nullifidians. Faith is faith, though never so little of it. *Credo languida fide, sed tamen fide,* said dying Cruciger. Our consolation lies much in the comparative de-gree; but our salvation is in the positive. Much faith will yield unto us here our heaven; and any faith, if true, will yield us heaven here-after. Now for fear; that which is distrustful, faith quelleth and killeth it; as that which is awful and filial, it breedeth, feedeth, fostereth, and cherisheth.

Ver. 27. *Even the winds and the sea obey him*] He lays laws upon all creatures, which *conferto prælio, excedebat.* Liv.

are his hosts. The winds and sea fought for us apparently in that

Octogesimus octavus mirabilis annus : (Beza) so that the blasphemous Spaniards said, Christ was turned Lutheran. The like was done by the winds for Theodosius, in that famous battle against Maximinus. The soldiers that were then present told us, saith St Augustine (*de Civ. Dei*, v. 6), that the winds took their darts, as soon as they were out of their hands, and drove them violently upon the enemy. As for those that were cast at us by the enemy, they were with like violence carried back upon their own bodies. Hence sang Claudian the heathen poet in this sort concerning Theodosius,

O nimium dilecte Deo, cui militat æther,
Et conjurati veniunt ad classica venti.

Ver. 28. *Coming out of the tombs*] There the devil kept them, the more to terrify them with the fear of death all their lives long, Heb. ii. 15. Appius Claudius (as Capella witnesseth) could not abide to hear the Greek Zῆτα pronounced, because it represented the gnashing of the teeth of dying men. Chrysostom gives another reason hereof, that the devil hereby sought to persuade silly people that dead men's souls were turned into devils, and walked (as they call it) especially about tombs and sepulchres. Thus he oft appeared to people, in times of Popery, in the shape of some of their dead kindred, and haunted them till he had made them sing a mass for such and such a soul. Melancthon tells a story of an aunt of his, that had her hand burnt to a coal by the devil, appearing to her in the likeness of her deceased husband. And Pareus relates an example (much like this poor demoniac in the text) of a baker's daughter in their country, possest and pent up in a cave she had digged, as in a grave, to her dying day.

Ver. 29. *What have we to do with thee*] Horrible impudence. As if Christ were not concerned when his members are vexed. David felt his own coat cut and his own cheeks shaven in the coats and cheeks of his servants; and shall not Christ be as sensible of the abuses done to his? The sovereign suffers in the subject. Neither is it other than just, that the arraignment of mean malefactors runs in the style of wrong to the king's crown and dignity.

Jesus, thou Son of God] The devil speaks Christ fair, but only to be rid of him. So deal many by Christ's ministers, that rip up their consciences, and so put them into a hell above ground. St Mark tells us that they worshipped our Saviour; St Luke, that they adjured him. Satan, saith one, doth not always appear in one and the same fashion. At Lystra he appeared like a comedian, at Athens like a philosopher, at Ephesus like an artificer, and here like an exorcist; as to Saul, he appeared like the old prophet, who could not have spoken more

gravely, severely, divinely, than the fiend did. But as, when one commended the pope's legate at the Council of Basil, Sigismund the emperor answered, *Tamen Romanus est :* so when the devil comes commended unto us under what name soever, let us cry out, Yet he is a devil; and remember still to resist him, steadfast in the faith, 1 Pet. v.

Art thou come hither to torment us] To dispossess us. Lo, it is another hell to the devil to be idle, or otherwise than evil-occupied. Should not we hold it our heaven to be well-doing?[1] Learn for shame of the devil, saith father Latimer, to be busy about the salvation of your own and other men's souls, which he so studiously seeks to destroy. Athanasius hath a conceit, that the devil may be driven out of a body by repeating the 68th Psalm. Origen saith of devils, no greater torment to them than to see men addicted to the Scriptures: *In hoc eorum omnis flamma est, in hoc uruntur incendio.* Chrysostom saith, we may lash and scourge the devil by fasting and prayer, which the prophet Isaiah calls a charm or enchantment, Isa. xxvi. 16 (לחש).

Before the time] For they are respited and reprieved, as it were, in respect of full torment, and suffered, as free prisoners, to flutter in the air, and to course about the earth till that great day; which they tremble to think on, and which they that mock at, 2 Pet. iii. 3, or make light of, are worse than devils.[2]

Ver. 30. *A herd of many swine feeding*] *Suillo pecori anima pro sale data*, saith Varro. Swinish epicures also have their souls but for salt to keep their bodies from putrifying. That was a rotten speech of Epicurus, that life eternal was nothing else but an eternal gormandizing, and swilling, and swallowing of nectar and ambrosia.[3] The kingdom of God is another manner of thing than meat and drink, Rom. xiv. The devil desired to enter into the swine, because of their greediness. Eat not greedily, for this is *os porci habere*, as that pope is said to have. Drink not to drunkenness; for this sin robs a man of himself, and lays a swine in his room. No creature, besides man, will be drunk, but swine: and not swine either, but as they are conversant about men; for wild swine will not, they say.

Ver. 31. *So the devils besought him*] For threaten him they durst not, as little as the Gadarenes, ver. 34, because they found themselves overpowered. Time was when they had set upon our Saviour with utmost might and malice in the wilderness. The matter is well amended now. The same power, when he pleases, can change the note of the tempter to us. He will tread Satan under our feet shortly, Rom. xvi. 20. That which Vegetius said of chariots armed with scythes and hooks will be applied to the devils; at first they were a terror, and after a scorn.

Suffer us to go into the herd of swine] *Pos-*

---

[1] *Ut jugulent homines, surgunt,* &c. Horace.
[2] *Epicuri de grege porci.* κραιπάλην καὶ μέθην αἰώνιον, ὥστε ἀπάντα χρόνον διάγειν μεθύοντας.
[3] *Tantum abest ut in oves Dei habeat potestatem.*

sumus dicere porcorum quoque setas fuisse apud Deum numeratas nedum sanctorum capillos. We may safely say, that the bristles of swine are numbered with God, saith Tertullian (*de Fuga*), much more the hairs of saints; not one of them falls to the ground without their heavenly Father. Satan desired to have forth Peter to winnow, as Goliath desired to have an Israelite to combat with; he could not command him. He could not make a louse, Exod. viii. 18, fire a house, Job i. 19, drown a pig, without divine permission. Now we are of more price than many pigs before God, as that martyr well inferred. And if a legion of devils had not power over a herd of hogs, much less have they over Christ's flock of sheep, saith Tertullian.

Ver. 32. And he said unto them, Go] 1. To show his sovereignty over the creatures. He is the great proprietary of all, and may do with his own as he listeth. 2. To punish their sensuality in feeding upon swine's flesh, against the express letter of the law. *Ex uno sue quinquaginta prope sapores excogitantur*, saith Pliny. And there was a jolly pope (some kin, belike, to Pope Sergius, surnamed *Os porci*) that being, for his gout, forbidden swine's flesh by his physician, cried out to his steward, Bring me my pork, *al dispto di dio*, in despite of God. 3. To try whether was dearer to these filthy Gergesites, their swine, or their souls. They showed themselves to be of Cardinal Bourbon's mind, who would not part with his part in Paris, for his part in Paradise.

They went into the herd of swine] That thereby Satan might win upon the souls of the citizens (wedded and wedged to their worldly substance), and he failed not of his purpose. A cunning fetch of an old quadruplator. Be not ignorant of his wiles. Divorce the world from the devil, and he can do us no hurt.

Ran violently down a steep place into the sea] Cornelius Agrippa, the magician, being at point of death, called unto him a dog (a familiar devil) that went about with him, and said, *Abi a me perdita bestia quæ me perdidisti*, Get thee gone, thou cursed creature, thou hast undone me. Whereupon the dog presently departed, and cast himself headlong into the water.

And perished in the waters] So will detestable drunkards in the bottomless pit; those that, as swine their bellies, so they break their heads with filthy quaffing. These shall have a cup of fire and brimstone poured down their throats, Psal. xi. 6, and not obtain one drop of water to cool their flaming tongues. For why? Drunkenness, saith one, is a vice so vile, so base, so beastly, as that it transforms the soul, deforms the body, bereaves the brain, betrays the strength, defiles the affection, and metamorphoseth the whole man; making the understanding ignorant, the strong staggering, the trusty trothless, the virtuous vicious, and the precisest person a panderer to the profanest sin. (Huge *de Sancto Vict.*)

Ver. 33. And they that kept them fled] So

do parasitical pastors leave their forlorn flocks to danger and destruction; letting the devils hurry them to hell, and not caring whether they sink or swim. They that go down into this pit, or suffer others to go down by their default, cannot hope for God's truth, Isa. xxxviii. 18.

Ver. 34. They besought him to depart] This was as great madness, as to wish, because they had been scorched by the sun, they might see no more of it. And yet how many, alas, are there at this day that cry out of this madness, and yet imitate it! How many that prefer *haram domesticam aræ dominicæ*, as one long since complained, a swine-sty before a sanctuary! (Petr. Blessensis.) We are now become Gergesites, said that martyr in Queen Mary's days, that would rather lose Christ than our porkets. Take up your cross is a hard saying; therefore Christ must be prayed to be gone, lest all our pigs be drowned. The devil shall have his dwelling again in many men's selves rather than in their pigs. Therefore to the devil shall they go and dwell with him, &c. Thus Mr Bradford. And oh how justly shall Christ regest one day upon all unworthy Gadarenes, Depart from me, ye wicked!

CHAPTER IX.

Verse 1. *And he entered into a ship*] HE called not for fire from heaven upon those brutish Gadarenes that were so glad to be rid of him. Some wicked ones Christ punisheth here, lest his providence, but not all, lest his patience and promise of coming again to judgment, should be called into question, saith Augustine.

Came into his own city] Capernaum, a colony of the Romans, where our Saviour hired a house, and wore a stole or long garment, as a citizen. Happy town in such an inhabitant, and in this respect lifted up to heaven, Matt. xi. 23. Indeed, heaven came down to Capernaum; for the Lord so delighteth in his servants (how much more, then, in his Son) that their walls are ever in his sight, and he loveth to look upon the houses where they dwell, Isa. xlix. 16.

Ver. 2. *They brought unto him a man sick, &c.*] Show we like mercy to our sin-sick friends, bring them to the ordinances, present them to that Sun of righteousness that hath healing under his wings. To an Almighty physician no disease can be incurable. He is as able and as ready still to heal those that are brought unto him. He hath lost nothing by heaven, be sure. But as Aaron, though he might not lament over his dead sons, because as high priest he entered into the holy place, yet he still retained the affections and bowels of a father; so the Lord Christ, though in heaven, is no less loving and large-hearted to his than when he was in the flesh. Bring therefore all your brethren for an offering to the Lord; and if they cannot or will not come otherwise, bring them as the prophet bids, "upon horses, and in chariots, and in litters," Isa. lxvi. 20: *q. d.* though sick, weakly, and unfit for travel, yet rather in litters than not at all.

Son, be of good cheer] And well he might, when his sins were forgiven. This mercy is enough to make a man everlastingly merry. Viscount Lisle, in Henry VIII.'s time, died for joy of an unexpected pardon from his prince. How great then is the comfort of pardon from God! Such are bid to be glad, rejoice, and shout for joy, Psal. xxxii. 1, 11. And all others flatly forbid to take any comfort, Hos. ix. 1. *Etiamsi tibi læta obveniant omnia, non est tamen quod læteris.* (Ribera.)

Thy sins are forgiven thee] And yet his disease remained upon him for some while after. Behold, "he whom thou lovest is sick," said they of Lazarus, John xi. We must make a new Bible, ere we can necessarily conclude that God is heavily offended because we are heavily afflicted. He that escapes affliction may suspect his adoption, Prov. iii. 12.

Ver. 3. *This man blasphemeth*] True, had he been but a man, and had taken upon him to forgive sins by his own authority, as Popish priests do, to the subverting of some men's souls. I have known one, saith a reverend divine, who neither by education nor affection was disposed to Popery; who having the ill hap, when his conscience was perplexed, to fall into the hands of a Popish priest, became a Papist upon this reason, because, as the priest suggested, that religion afforded more comfort for the conscience than ours; and therefore more comfort, because it had and exercised a power to pardon sin, which our ministers neither did nor durst assume unto themselves.

Ver. 4. *Wherefore think ye evil, &c.*] Christ confutes their calumny, and proves himself to be God, and to have power to pardon sin, by discerning and condemning their evil thoughts. "I the Lord search the heart," Jer. xvii. Satan may give a shrewd guess; and so may men too; as Bartollus writes of Doctor Gabriel Nele, that by the only motion of the lips, without any utterance, he understood all men, perceived and read in every man's countenance what he meant, &c. But none can certainly know the thoughts of man, but God alone. It is his royalty to "know what is in man," John ii. 25.

Ver. 5. *For whether is it easier, &c.*] *q. d.* It is a work of one and the same Almighty power to pardon sin, and with a bare word only to heal the sick, such as are counted past cure especially. Think the same of the soul's sicknesses, and say with that ancient, *Ego admisi, Domine, unde tu damnare potes me, sed tu non amisisti, unde tu salvare potes me.*

Ver. 6. *That the Son of man hath power, &c.*] And therefore is more than a man. The Rhemists tell us of one man that could remove mountains. But none but the man Christ Jesus could ever remit sins. He only it is that blots out the cloud, and the thick cloud too, enorm-

ities as well as infirmities, Isa. xliv. 22, for this is a true axiom, *Peccata non minuunt justificationem,* though sins be different, justification is not. Take heed ye interline not God's covenant.

Ver. 7. *And he arose and departed*] He did as he was bidden; for he was healed on both sides. *Mallem obedire quam miracula facere,* said Luther.

Ver. 8. *They marvelled and glorified God*] When the proud Pharisees blasphemed and were hardened; and so voided the counsel of God against themselves, Luke vii. 30, or to their own singular disadvantage, *Suo maximo damno.* (Beza.)

Ver. 9. *A man named Matthew*] The other evangelists call him Levi; so shrouding his shame under a name less known. He plainly and ingenuously sets down his own more common name, and the nature of his offence, like as David doth penance in a white sheet, as it were, Psal. li. 1, which is an evident argument, both of the Scripture's divinity, and of the evangelist's gracious simplicity. If any should upbraid him with his old evil courses, he could readily have answered, as Austin did in like case, *Quæ tu reprehendis ego damnavi;* or as Beza, *Hic homo invidet mihi gratiam Christi.*

Sitting at the receipt of custom] These publicans rented the revenue of the sea and rivers of the Romans, as now the Jews do of the Turks, at a certain rate. And that they might pay their rent, and pick a living out of it, they were great gripers, and exacted extremely upon the Jews; who therefore hated them, and held them furthest off from heaven of any men. A faithful publican was so rare at Rome itself, that one Sabinus, for his honest managing of that office, in an honourable remembrance thereof, had certain images erected with this superscription for the honest publican.[1] Of this sort of sinners was Matthew, whom Christ converted into an evangelist; as he did Paul the persecutor into an apostle; Justin the philosopher into a martyr; Cyprian the rhetorician, and, as some think, the magician, into a famous light of the Church. I was an obstinate Papist, saith Latimer, as any was in England; insomuch, that when I should be made bachelor of divinity, my whole oration went against Philip Melancthon, and his opinions, &c.

And he arose and followed him] Julian the Apostate cavils at this passage; as if either this were false, or Matthew a fool to follow a stranger at the first call. But this atheist knew not the work of faith, nor the power of Christ's voice when he calls effectually. If Maris the blind bishop of Bithynia had been by to have heard this dead dog thus barking, he would surely have shaped him such an answer as he did once. For when Julian said unto him, Behold, thou art blind; doth the Galilean thy God care for thee? He replied, *O tu impie apostata, gratias agó*

---

[1] καλῶς τελωνήσαντι.　Suet. in Vespas.

Deo qui me cæcum reddidit, ne vultum tuum videam, ita ad impietatem prolapsum, O thou wicked apostate, I give my God thanks that hath made me blind, that I might not see that wretched face of thine.

Ver. 10. *As Jesus sat at meat in the house*] Matthew feasted Christ, for joy of his conversion. Yea, he made a feast, a feast like a king, a very sumptuous feast, as St Luke's word importeth,[1] he kept open house, a table for all comers. As princes at their coronation straw the streets with coin, make the conduits run wine, release prisoners, &c.; so here. " Kill the fatted calf, and let us be merry," said he at his son's return, Luke xv. 23. When a sinner repents there are gaudies in heaven: instruments of music are put into the angels' hands, and songs into their mouths. How well paid was Zaccheus, when salvation was come home to his house! When God was once reconciled to the people in the wilderness, after their sin in setting up the golden calf, to testify their great joy and thankfulness, they brought stuff more than enough to the building of the tabernacle. The centurion, when he once became a proselyte, built the Jewish synagogues that had been thrown down by Antiochus, Luke vii. 5. And Tyrus converted finds another manner of merchandise than formerly, namely, to feed and clothe God's saints with durable clothing, Isa. xxiii. 18.

Ver. 11. *And when the Pharisees saw it*] As envy is quick-sighted. See Ovid's description of it. Βασκαίνειν παρὰ τοῦ φάεσι καίνειν. The wicked look round about the saints, seeking to pick a hole in their coats; they pore and pry more narrowly than Laban did into Jacob's stuff. " Walk circumspectly," Eph. v. 15.

They said unto his disciples] 1. Not to him ; where the hedge is lowest, there the devil leaps over soonest; as he began his temptation with Eve, apart from her husband. *Calumniare audacter, aliquid saltem adhærebit,* is a maxim in Machiavel. It is the property of defamations to leave a kind of lower estimation many times where they are not believed. 2. These hypocrites would seem to say this in pure pity to the seduced disciples, whom they saw to do the same with their Master. An ordinary trick among make-bates. St Austin had these two verses written on his table,

Quisquis amat dictis absentum rodere famam,
Hanc mensam indictam noverit esse sibi.

Here is no room for railers.

Ver. 12. *But when Jesus heard that, he said*] Hence we learn, that although it be a servile business, as Plato calleth it, and an endless piece of work, to make answer and apology to all slanders (πᾶσιν ἀπολογεῖσθαι θεραπευτικὸν) ; yet where God's glory is interested, and the salvation of other men's souls hazarded, we must endeavour the clearing of our names, and the righting of our injuries and indignities cast upon us. But

let this be done with meekness of wisdom, with weight of reason, not heat of passion, and rather in God's words than in our own, as here.

Ver. 13. *They that be whole*] There are none such, but in conceit only. The civil justiciary ails nothing, complains of nothing, is as sound as a rock ; but no such sound heart can come to heaven ; as, in another sense, none but sound can come there. Only sensible sinners are capable of cure and comfort, such as see themselves Christless creatures.

Need not the physician] And the physician needs them as little ; he came not, cares not for them, they have as much help from him as they seek. Presumption is as a chain to their neck, and they believe their interest in Christ, when it is no such thing. They make a bridge of their own shadow, and so fall into the brook ; they perish by catching at their own catch, hanging on their own fancy, which they falsely call and count faith.

Ver. 14. *But go ye, and learn what,* &c.] In the history of Jonas, Christ found the mystery of his death, burial, and resurrection. Rest not in the shell of the Scriptures, but break it, and get out the kernel,[2] as the sense is called, Judg. vii. 15 ; stick not in the bark, but pierce into the heart of God's word. Lawyers say, that *Apices juris non sunt jus.* The letter of the law is not the law, but the meaning of it. John never rested till the sealed book was opened. Pray for the spirit of revelation, plough with God's heifer, and we shall understand his riddles, provided that we wait in the use of all good means, till God irradiate both organ and object.

I will have mercy] Both that which God shows to us and that which we show to others, spiritual and corporal. Steep thy thoughts, saith one, in the mercies of God, and they will dye thine, as the dye-fat doth the cloth, Col. iii. 12.

I came not to call the righteous] Those that are good in their own eyes, and claim heaven as the portion that belongs unto them. Scribonius writes of the cedar, *Quod viventes res putrefacit et perdit ; putridas autem restituit et conservat.* So Christ came to kill the quick and to quicken the dead.

But sinners to repentance] Not to liberty, but duty. Tertullian speaketh of himself, that he was born to nothing but repentance. This is not the work of one, but of all our days, as they said, Ezra x. 13. Some report of Mary Magdalene, that after our Saviour's resurrection she spent thirty years in Gallia Narbonensi, in weeping for her sins ; and of St Peter that he always had his eyes full of tears, *adeo ut etiam lachrymæ cutem genarum exederint,* insomuch as his face was furrowed with continual weeping. Let not him that resolves upon Christianity dream of a delicacy.

Ver. 14. *Then came to him the disciples of John*] These sided with the Pharisees against

---

[1] Luke v. 29, Δοχήν, *acceptionem, splendidum epulum, ut annotat* Erasm. ex Athenæo.

[2] *Veshibro,* the breaking of the nut.

our Saviour out of emulation and self-love, the bane and break-neck of all true love ; yea, they were first in the quarrel. A doleful thing, when brethren shall set against brethren, Hebrews vex one another, Exod. ii. ; and Christians, as if they wanted enemies, fly in the faces of one another. St Basil was held an heretic, even of them that held the same things as he did, and whom he honoured as brethren ; all the fault was that he outshone them, and they envied him the praise he had for opposing Arianism, which was such, as that Philostorgius the Arian wrote that all the other orthodox divines were but babies to Basil. How hot was the contention betwixt Luther and Carolostadius, merely out of a self-seeking humour and desire of pre-eminency. How extreme violent are the Lutherans against the Calvinists. In the year 1567 they joined themselves at Antwerp with the Papists against the Calvinists. And Luther somewhere professeth that he will rather yield to transubstantiation than remit anything of consubstantiation.

Why do we and the Pharisees fast often] The Pharisees were parlous fasters, when they devoured widows' houses, and swallowed ill-gotten goods as gnats down their wide gullets, which therefore Christ calls ἔνοντα, the inwards. Their fasts were mere mock-fasts. So were those of John, Archbishop of Constantinople, surnamed the Faster, who yet was the first that affected the title of universal bishop, so much cried down by Gregory the Great. These Pharisees had sided with and set on John's disciples in their master's absence ; like the renegado Jesuits, to keep up that bitter contention that is between the Calvinists and Lutherans, have a practice of running over to the Lutheran Church, pretending to be converts, and to build with them.

Ver. 15. *And Jesus said unto them*] He makes apology for his accused disciples ; so doth he still at the right hand of his heavenly Father, nonsuiting all accusations brought against us, as our advocate,[1] 1 John ii. 1, appearing for us as the lawyer doth for his client, Heb. ix. 24, opening his case and pleading his cause. He helpeth us also to make apology for ourselves to God, 2 Cor. vii. 11, and expecteth, that as occasion requires, we should make apology one for another, when maligned and misreported of by the world.

Can the children of the bridechamber, &c.] Our Saviour seeing them to sin of infirmity, and by the instigation of the Pharisees, who with their leaven had somewhat soured and seduced them in their master's absence, deals gently with them ; to teach us what to do in like case. A Venice-glass must be otherwise handled than an earthen pitcher or goddard : some must be rebuked sharply, severely, cuttingly,[2] Titus i. 13 ; but of others we must have compassion, making a difference, Jude 22.

Mourn as long as the bridegroom, &c.] Mourn as at funerals (so the word signifieth). This were incongruous, unseasonable, and unseemly at

a feast. It was a peevishness in Samson's wife that she wept at the wedding ; sith that is the day of the rejoicing of a man's heart, as Solomon hath it, Cant. iii. 11. Now Christ is the Church's spouse. He hath the bride, and is the bridegroom, as their master the Baptist had taught them, John iii. 29, and rejoiceth over every good soul, as the bridegroom rejoiceth over the bride, Isa. lxii. 5. Should not the saints therefore reciprocate ?

But the days will come] Our Saviour suffered much, even many a little death, all his life long ; and yet, till his passion, he accounts himself to be, as it were, in the bridechamber. Then it was especially that he alone trod the wine-press, and was roasted alive in the fire of his Father's wrath, &c.

When the bridegroom shall be taken from them] As now your master the Baptist is from you ; a just argument and occasion of your grief and fasting, if possibly you may beg him of God out of the hands of Herod. When the Duke of Bourbon's captains had shut up Pope Clement VIII. in the castle St Angelo, Cardinal Wolsey being shortly after sent ambassador beyond seas to make means for his release ; as he came through Canterbury toward Dover, he commanded the monks and the choir to sing the litany after this sort, *Sancta Maria, ora pro papa nostro Clemente*. Himself also, being present, was seen to weep tenderly for the pope's calamity. Shall superstition do that religion cannot bring us to ? Shall we not turn again unto the Lord with fasting, weeping, and mourning, if for nothing else, yet that our poor brethren may find compassion ? which is Hezekiah's motive to the people, 2 Chron. xxx. 9.

And then shall they fast] Note here, 1. That fasting is not abolished with the ceremonial law, but still to be used as a duty of the gospel. 2. That times of heaviness are times of humiliation. 3. That our halcyons here are but as marriage-feasts, for continuance ; they last not long ; never look for it.

Ver. 16. *No man putteth a piece, &c.*] Austerities of religion are not to be pressed upon new beginners. God would not carry the people to Canaan through the Philistines' country (though it were the nearest way) for discouraging them at first setting out. Our Saviour spake as the disciples could hear, Mark iv. 33. Discretion is to be used, and Christ's lambs handled with all tenderness.

Ver. 17. *Neither do men put new wine*] In the year of grace 340 arose certain heretics called *Ascitæ* or *Utricularii*, bottle-bearers, because they bare a bottle on their backs, affirming that they were no true Christians that did not so ; and alleging this text for themselves, as if they were the only new bottles filled with new wine. So those *districtissimi monachi*, Puritan monks (as one Englisheth it), who made themselves wooden crosses, and carried them on their backs, continually pleaded Matt. xvi. 24 to make for them.

---

[1] παράκλητον, in full opposition to κατήγορος, the accuser of the brethren, Rev. xii. 10.

[2] ἀποτόμως. Tremel, *dure*. Beza, *præcise, rigide*. Erasm. *severe, et ad vivum*. πενθεῖν.

This was, as Mr Tindal saith in another case, to think to quench their thirst by sucking the ale-bowl.

Ver. 18. *Behold, there came a certain ruler*] Jairus, the ruler of the synagogue. Few such came to Christ; but this man was driven out of doors by the cross, as the wolf is out of the wood by hard hunger. It was his only daughter, of a dozen years old, that was now at point of death. This makes him seek out Christ the best Physician. Men must be fatherless (childless) ere they find mercy, Hos. xiv. 3, and a poor afflicted people ere they will be brought to trust in the name of the Lord, Zeph. iii. 12. The αἱμοῤῥοοῦσα came not to Christ while she had a half-penny to help herself, Luke viii. 43.

But come and lay thine hands upon her] He thought Christ could not otherwise cure her. This was weakness of faith, far short of that of the centurion, who yet was a Roman soldier; whereas Jairus was a learned Jew. Knowledge therefore is one thing, faith another; and the greatest scholars are not always the holiest men. Neither have all God's people a like measure of true faith. This should humble and excite the weak, but not discourage them in their course; since the tallest oak was once an acorn, and the deepest doctor was once in his horn-book.

Ver. 19. *And Jesus arose and followed him*] As tendering the ruler's infirmity, and not taking advantages, or turning him off, for presuming to prescribe. Be we also ready to every good office, not picking quarrels or pleading excuses.

Ver. 20. *And behold, a woman, &c.*] This history and occurrence comes in here by a parenthesis, and by a sweet providence, for the exercise and increase of Jairus's faith and patience. Jairus could have wished her far enough at that time, because she hindered our Saviour from making haste to his dying daughter. But she shall be dead outright, the woman cured, and he thereby confirmed, ere his desire shall be accomplished; that God in all may be glorified.

Which was diseased, &c.] And had lavished money out of the bag for help, but had had none, Isa. xlvi. 6. Nay, she had suffered many things of the physicians, who had well nigh officiously killed her, and had utterly exhausted her.[1] This made Chaucer take for his motto, Farewell, physic; and the Emperor Adrian cry out upon his death-bed, Many physicians have killed the king, πόλλοι ἰατροὶ κατέκτειναν τὸν βασιλέα. Dio.

Came behind him] Either as abashed of her blushful disease, or because she could not come before him for the crowd, &c.

Ver. 21. *If I may but touch his garment*] This was a glorious faith of hers, and not much inferior to that of the centurion. Let us in like sort, when we feel the bloody flux of natural filth issuing out at our eyes, mouths, hands, and other parts, repair to Christ, and touch him by faith; so shall we feel that there goes a virtue out from him, to heal the soul. As fishes, when they are hurt, heal themselves again by touching the tench,

finding the slime of his body to be a sovereign salve; so must we, when wounded with sin, have recourse to Christ, and our faith will make us whole every whit.

Ver. 22. *But Jesus turned him about*] To take notice of it himself, and to notify it to others. For these reasons, saith Chrysostom: 1. To free the woman from fear, lest her conscience should call her recreant, as one that had stole a cure. 2. To make up in her what was wanting to her faith, if she should have any such thought to do so. 3. To manifest her faith, for other men's imitation. 4. To make known his omnisciency, and so his divinity. 5. To confirm the ruler's faith, and so fit him for further mercy. 6. To teach her and us that not his garment, but himself, did the cure. This makes against that Popish foppery in worshipping relics, as the syndon wherein Christ's body was enwrapped, of the virtue whereof Paleottus, Archbishop of Bonony, set forth a great book, A. D. 1617.

And the woman was made whole, &c.] That fable recorded by Eusebius is scarce worth relating; that this woman should set up at her door in Cæsarea Philippi a statue of brass in honour of our Saviour; near whereto grew a certain herb good for all diseases. Irenæus (far ancienter than Eusebius) reproveth the heretics, called Gnostici, for that they carried about them the image of Christ made in Pilate's time, after his own proportion; using also for declaration of their affection towards it to set garlands upon the head of it. And in Epiphanius's time (who lived soon after Eusebius) images and statues of Christ or the saints were abhorred by Christians. The Turks will not endure any image, no not upon their coin, because of the second commandment; and the Papists, for their imagery, they call idolaters.

Ver. 23. *He saw the minstrels, &c.*] An heathenish custom crept in among the Jews, as many the like are now amongst the Papists, who are therefore called heathens, Rev. xi. 2.

Cantabat mœstis tibia funeribus. Ovid.

The maid is not dead, but sleepeth] Death is but a sleep to the saints;[2] and as the sleep of the labouring man is sweet unto him, so is death most welcome to such as have most suffered. See my notes on John xi. 11.

Ver. 24. *And they laughed him to scorn*] This is daily done by the mad world, quite beside itself in point of salvation. They hear and jeer. God will laugh at their destruction.

Ver. 25. *He took her by the hand*] As it were to awaken her out of a deep sleep. He could have raised her without either coming down or laying his hands upon her. But as Jairus desired him, so he did for him. Who now shall dare to despise the day of small things? Zech. iv. 10.

Ver. 26. *And the fame hereof went abroad*] Though Christ had straitly charged the contrary, Mark v. 43, lest, being known too soon,

---

[1] *Medici persæpe ægros officiose occidunt.*

[2] *Plato Mortem ait esse οἷον ὕπνον, in Apol. Socr.*

he should stand in the way of his own design. Howbeit, when he drew nigh to his end, he raised the young man of Nain, and his friend Lazarus, in the open view of the people.

Ver. 27. *Two blind men followed him*] Misery makes unity. These two could the better agree to go together, because their cases were alike. Hooper and Ridley left jarring when they both were in prison.

Thou Son of David] Thou that art a true man, as we are; and seemest to say unto us, as David did to the men of Judah, " Ye are my brethren, my bone and my flesh," 2 Sam. xix. 12. " Have mercy on us." So the Church in Isaiah, when invaded and infested by the Assyrian, cries out, " The stretching out of his wings doth fill thy land, O Immanuel :" *q. d.* O thou that art also a man, and hast the heart of a man in thee, see to our safety. Necessity makes men beg many times of mere strangers, yea, of deadly enemies; as the Israelites did of the Egyptians, as Benhadad did of Ahab, and as the poor Jews of the Assyrians, Lam. v. 6. How much more boldly should we beg of Christ, our near kinsman! &c.

Ver. 28. *And when he was come into the house*] For till then he seemed to slight them, that they might the more earnestly importune him. He knows how to commend his benefits to us. *Cito data cito vilescunt.* Things lightly come by are lightly set by.

Ver. 29. *According to your faith*] Questionless (saith a famous divine) justifying faith is not beneath miraculous, in the sphere of its own activity, and where it hath warrant of God's word.

Ver. 30. *Straitly charged them, saying, See that no man, &c.*] He threatened them terribly[1] (as the word here used importeth) should they but open their mouths to make it known to any man. Some do all for a name: Christ (besides the veil of his humanity) says, nay, thunders, " See ye tell no man." How far are those spirits from this which care only to be seen, and wish only to dazzle others' eyes with admiration, not caring for unknown riches!

Ver. 31. *Spread abroad his fame*] Wherein they sinned, no doubt, though of never so good an intention. God's commandments must be kept as the apple of our eye; for else we charge him with folly.

Ver. 32. *A dumb man possessed with a devil*] Satan still gags many to this day, that they cannot pray to God, profess his name, utter themselves to the good of others. The spirit of faith is no indweller, but sits in the door of the lips. " I believed, therefore have I spoken," 2 Cor. iv. 13. The Carthusian monks speak together but once a week. It is a shame to Christians that they speak not often one to another, Mal. iii. 16, that they come together, not for the better, but for the worse, 1 Cor. xi. 17. *Inveniar sane superbus, &c., modo impii silentii non arguar, dum Dominus patitur,* saith Luther

(*Epist. ad* Staup.). Better I be counted proud than be sinfully silent.

Ver. 33. *The multitudes marvelled, &c.*] Others censured, a third sort tempted, a fourth applauded. What can we do, to undergo one opinion? to avoid variety of constructions?

Ver. 34. *Through the prince of devils*] There is a principal devil, then, prince of this world: and there are princes and principal spirits in countries and nations under him, Dan. x. 13. We read of the Prince of Persia hindering the matters of the Church. See more of this, chap. xii. 24.

Ver. 35. *And Jesus went about, &c.*] He was not by any affronts or hard usages of the enemy disheartened from well-doing; but as the moon continues her course, though dogs bark and leap at her, *En peragit cursus surda Diana suos;* so did he, and so must we. " For consider him that endured such contradiction of sinners against himself, lest ye be wearied and faint in your minds," Heb. xii. 3. *Convitia spreta exolescunt.* (Tacitus.)

Ver. 36. *He was moved with compassion*] His eye so affected his heart, that it even yearned (ἐσπλαγχνίσθη) towards those silly souls. *Ingemuit miserans graviter dextramque tetendit.* (Virgil.)

As sheep without a shepherd] Their pastors were impostors, as Bernard complained of those in his time their Episcopi; Aposcopi, (as Espencæus hath it), their overseers, by-seers. That judgment was now befallen them that Moses of old deprecated, Numb. xxvii. 17. And this troubled our Saviour more than their bodily bondage to the Romans, which yet was very grievous.

Ver. 37. *But the labourers few*] Such as will labour to lassitude (ἐργάται) in preaching Christ crucified; few such.

Ver. 38. *Labourers into his harvest*] Harvestmen, of all others, have the hardest labour, a sore sweating labour. So have faithful ministers. " The householder hath somewhat to do," said Luther; " the magistrate more, but the minister most of all. He labours more in a day many times, than the husbandman doth in a month. The sweat of the brow is nothing to that of the brain; the former furthers health, the latter impairs it, wearying and wearing out the body, wasting the vitals, and hastening old age, and untimely death:" *Labores Ecclesiastici alterant corpus, et tanquam ex imis medullis succum exhauriunt, senium mortemque accelerant.*

CHAPTER X.

Verse 1. *And when he had called the twelve*] HE had set them to pray, ix. 38, and now he sets them to work. *Ora et labora,* is an old proverb, and *Admota manu invocanda est Minerva,* said the heathens. To pray to pray, is to mock God and lose one's labour. Solomon saith, we must as well dig as beg for knowledge, Prov. ii.

[1] ἐνεβριμήσατο, *cum vehementi et fremente comminatione interdixit.*

2, 4, else to beg is bootless. The talk of the lips only brings want, Prov. xiv. 23. Christ seemed here to say to his praying disciples, as once he did to Moses, "Why criest thou unto me? speak unto the children of Israel, that they go forward," Exod. xiv. 15; or as afterwards he did to Joshua (vii. 10), "Get thee up, wherefore liest thou thus upon thy face?"

Ver. 2. *Now the names of the twelve*, &c.] Their names are registered and had in honour; when the grandees of the earth, those men of renown in their generation, lie either buried in oblivion or wrapt up in the sheet of shame: their memory, haply, is preserved, but stinks in the keeping, as that rich glutton, Luke xvi., who is not so much as named, as poor Lazarus is.

Peter, and Andrew his brother, &c.] They go coupled two and two together. And this first for their own sakes. "Two are better than one," saith Solomon, Eccles. iv. 9—12. For, 1. if they fall, the one will lift up his fellow, as that which is stronger shoreth up that which is weaker. 2. If two lie together, then they have heat. When Silas came, Paul burned in spirit, Acts xviii. 5. Whiles Jehoiada lived Joash was free and forward for God; he was the first that complained of the negligence of his best officers in repairing the temple, 2 Chron. xxiv. 4—6. While Bradford was alive he kept up Ridley, and so did Latimer Cranmer, from thinking upon revolt. 3. If one prevail, two shall withstand him. The enemy is readiest to assault where none is by to assist; and much of our strength is lost in the loss of a faithful friend; whence Paul so rejoiced that Epaphroditus recovered, Phil. ii. 27. For their own mutual help and comfort was it therefore that they were sent out by pairs: σὺν τέ δύω ἐρχομένω, as the poet speaks of his Ulysses and Diomedes, sent to fetch in the Palladium. Secondly, for the sake of others, that the bad might be the sooner set down and convinced, the better confirmed and settled in the truth, sith "in the mouth of two or three witnesses," &c. For this it was that God set forth those noble pairs, Moses and Aaron, Zerubbabel and Joshua, Paul and Barnabas, the two faithful witnesses, Rev. xi. 3, Luther and Melancthon,[1] Zuinglius and Œcolampadius, &c.

Ver. 3. *Bartholomew*] This, say some, was that Nathaniel, John i. He is by Dionysius quoted to have said of divinity, *Et magnam esse et minimam* (καὶ πολλὴν, καὶ ἐλαχίστην), that it was large in a little room. Ambrose Chircher the Jesuit tells of a tradition they have in China, that one Olo Puen (or Bartholomew) was brought thither from Judea in the clouds, and preached Christianity amongst them; whereof he left twenty-seven tomes behind him. *Sed fides sit penes authorem.*

Matthew the publican] See here, as in a mirror, Christ's free grace in such a choice, and Matthew's true grace in not dissembling his old

trade, but shaming himself, that God might be glorified; and thankfully crying out, with Iphicrates, ἐξ οἵων εἰς οἷα, from how sinful and shameful to how high and honourable a calling and course of life am I advanced!

Ver. 4. *Simeon the Canaanite*] Or a man of Cana[2] in Galilee (as Judas Iscariot), that is, a man of Kerioth: see Josh. xv. 25. Simon the zelot, St Luke calls him. Christ, when he called him to the apostleship, either found him or made him zealous: *Tardis mentibus virtus non facile committitur*. Cic. 5. Tusc.

Mediocribus esse poetis
Non Dii, non homines, non concessere columnæ.
(Hor. de Art. Poet.)

Ver. 5. *These twelve Jesus sent forth*] Out of deep commiseration of those poor scattered sheep, that lay panting for life, and well nigh gasping their last (ἐσκυλμένοι), Matt. ix. 30. Saul, that ravening wolf of Benjamin, and his fellow Pharisees, not only breathed out threatenings, but worried Christ's sheep, that bore golden fleeces, Acts ix. 10. Now, because he could not go to them all himself in person he sends out the twelve. Thereby also to teach them and us that no minister is so "thoroughly furnished to all good works," 2 Tim. iii. 17, but that he may need the advice and help of his fellow-labourers. And this, I conceive, was at first the end of erecting colleges and cathedrals.

Ver. 6. *To the lost sheep*] This is the common condition of us all. "All we like sheep have gone astray," Isa. liii. 6. The prophet saith not, like dogs; for these, though lost, will find their way home again. Nor like swine; for these also, when lugged, or against a storm, will hie to their home. But like sheep, that silly creature, than the which as none is more apt to wander, so neither any more unable to return.

Ver. 7. *The kingdom of heaven is at hand*] Repent therefore. Men will do much for a kingdom. And nothing less than a kingdom, and that of heaven, can buy men out of their sweet sins. How many hear we daily making answer to the motion of this heavenly kingdom offered them by God, as the olive and vine did in Jotham's parable? Shall I leave my fat and sweet sins, to reign, though with God?[3] And yet every man must be either a king or a caitiff; reign in heaven, or roar for ever in hell. And this the apostles were bid, wherever they came, to preach; not to sing mass, which is the chief office of priest among the Papists. And for the people, they are taught to believe that the mass only is a work of duty; but the going to sermons a matter of conveniency, and such as is left free to men's leisures and opportunities, without imputation of sin.

Ver. 8. *Heal the sick*] God glorifies himself by the fruits of our sin and the effects of his own wrath. This great Alchemist knows how to extract good out of evil. He can make golden

---

[1] *Divisæ his operæ sed mens fuit unica, pavit*
   Ore Lutherus oves, flore Melancthon apes.

[2] קנא *significat zelum.*

[3] *At Paris, ut vivat regnetque beatus, cogi posse negat.*

afflictions, 1 Pet. i. 7, medicinal sicknesses, fetch his own honour out of the depths of our sufferings, as wine draws a nourishing virtue from the flesh of vipers, and as scarlet pulls out the viper's teeth.

Freely ye have received] And so have we in some sort, and in some sense; sith no pains we take, no cost we are at, can possibly countervail so great a treasure as is concredited unto us.

Ver. 9. *Provide neither gold, &c.*] To wit, for this present voyage (for at other times our Saviour had money, and he put it not in a penny pouch, but in a bag big as that it needed a bearer), but now Christ would teach them, by experience of his fatherly providence in feeding and securing them, to trust him for ever.

Ver. 10. *Neither two coats*] This may be a burthen to you.

Neither shoes] But sandals, a lighter kind of wearing.

Nor yet staves] Either for offence or defence; a dog shall not wag his tongue at you; or not a staff that may cumber you. But take a staff (as St Mark, vi. 8, 9, hath it), *sc.* that may ease and relieve you in your hard toil and travel. A staff they might have to speak them the travellers, not soldiers; one to walk with, not to war with; a wand, not a weapon.

The workman is worthy of his meat] " Of his wages," saith St Mark; of both as labourers in God's harvest; of double honour, saith St Paul, both countenance and maintenance.

Ver. 11. *Inquire who in it is worthy*] That is, faithful, as Lydia was, Acts xvi. 15, and Philip the Evangelist, Acts xxi. 8, and Mary the mother of Mark, Acts xii. 12. Lo here, whither ministers should resort, and where should be their rendezvous, Psal. xxvi. 4, and Psal. xvi. 3. In the excellent ones of the earth should be their delight. I forget lords and ladies, said good Mr Fox, to remember God's poor saints.

Ver. 12. *And when ye come into an house*] Into the synagogues and other places of public meeting, our Saviour sends them not as yet, because they were but young beginners and wanted boldness and other abilities; but bids them teach privately, catechise from house to house, and not stretch the wing beyond the nest till better fledged and fitted for flight.

Ver. 13. *If that house be worthy*] The saints are the only worthies, of whom the world is not worthy, Heb. xi. 38. These shall walk with Christ, for they are worthy, Rev. iii. 4. But the heart of the wicked is little worth, Prov. x. 20.

Let your peace come upon it] Christian salutations are effectual benedictions. " We bless you in the name of the Lord," Psal. cxxix. 8.

Let your peace return unto you] Something will come of your good wishes; if not to others, to yourselves; you shall be paid for your pains, as the physician is, though the patient dies; as the lawyer hath his fee, though his client's cause miscarry. God will reward his ministers, though Israel be not gathered, Isa. xlix. 4, 5, *secundum laborem, non secundum proventum*, as

Bernard hath it, κατὰ τὸν κόπον, οὐ κατὰ τὸν κάρπον.

Ver. 14. *And whosoever shall not receive you*] Two sure signs of reprobate goats: 1. Not to receive Christ's ministers to house and harbour, accounting themselves happy in such an entertainment. 2. Not to hear their words. The most good is done by God's ministers commonly at first coming. Then some receive the word with admiration, others are daily more and more hardened: as fish, though fearful, stir not at the great noise of the sea, whereunto they are accustomed; and as birds that build in a belfry startle not at the tolling of the bell.

Shake off the dust of your feet] In token that you sought not theirs but them, and that you will not carry away so much as any of their accursed dust; that you will not have any communion at all with them, wait no longer upon them; that the dust of those feet (that should have been beautiful) shall be fatal and feral to them; that God shall henceforward beat them here as small as dust with his heavy judgments, as with an iron mace, Psal. ii. 9; and that hereafter he shall shake them off as dust, when they come to him for salvation at the last judgment.

Ver. 15. *It shall be more tolerable*] God can better bear anything than the abuse of his free grace in the offers of mercy. Profligate professors and profane gospellers shall one day wish, " Oh that I had been a Sodomite, that I had never heard a sermon! " or, " Oh that I might hear but one sermon more! " &c. Should Solomon forsake that God that had appeared unto him twice? Good turns aggravate unkindness, and nothing more torments those in hell than to think that they might have been happy had they been worthy their years, as they say.

Ver. 16. *Behold, I send you forth, &c.*] This might seem incredible to the disciples, sith they were sent among the " lost sheep of Israel." But strange though it seem, it is not so strange as true. Look for it therefore. " Behold : " Christ was in no such danger from Herod, that fox, as from those wolves the Pharisees.

As sheep in the midst of wolves] Who would make it their work to worry the flock and suck their blood: as did Saul, that wolf of the tribe of Benjamin, and the primitive persecutors. Under Diocletian 17,000 Christians are said to have been slain in one month, amongst whom also was Serena the empress. Those ten persecutions were so cruel, that St Jerome writes in one of his epistles, that for every day in the year were murdered 5000, excepting only the first day of January. St Paul fell into the hands of that lion Nero, *qui orientem fidem primus Romæ cruentavit*, as Tertullian hath it, who therefore also calleth him, *Dedicatorem damnationis Christianorum.* All the rest of the apostles are reported to have died by the hands of tyrants, save only St John; who, in contempt of Christianity and of Christ (that is, by interpretation, God's anointed),[1] was cast by Domitian into a vessel of scalding oil, but came forth fresh and unhurt, by a miracle. After this the Arian heretics raged extremely, and made great havoc of the innocent lambs of Christ. Giezerichus, an Arian, king of Vandals, is said to have exceeded all that went afore him in cruelty towards the orthodox side, of both sexes. In that Laniena Parisiensis 30,000 Protestants were basely butchered in one month, 300,000 in one year. Stokesly, Bishop of London, boasted upon his death-bed that he had been the death of 50 heretics in his time. His successor, Bonner, was called the common cut-throat, and slaughter-slave general to all the bishops of England.[2] "And therefore" (said a good woman, that told him so in a letter) "it is wisdom for me, and all other simple sheep of the Lord, to keep us out of your butchery stall as long as we can. Especially, seeing you have such store already, that you are not able to drink all their blood, lest you should break your belly, and therefore let them lie still and die for hunger." Thus she. But that above all is most horrid and hateful, that is related of the Christians in Calabria, A.D. 1560. For being all thrust up in one house together (saith Mr Fox) as in a sheepfold, the executioner comes in, and among them takes one and blindfolds him with a muffler about his eyes, and so leadeth him forth to a larger place, where he commandeth him to kneel down. Which being so done, he cutteth his throat, and so leaveth him half dead. Then, taking his butcher's knife and muffler all of gore blood, he cometh again to the rest, and so leadeth them one after another and despatcheth them all, to the number of 88. All the aged went to death more cheerfully, the younger were more timorous. I tremble and shake (saith a Romanist, out of whose letter to his lord all this is transcribed) even to remember how the executioner held his bloody knife between his teeth, with the bloody muffler in his hand and his arms all in gore blood up to the elbows, going to the fold, and taking every one of them, one after another, by the hand, and so despatching them all, no otherwise than doth a butcher kill his calves and sheep. In fine, would any man take the Church's picture? saith Luther; then let him take a silly poor maid, sitting in a wood or wilderness, compassed about with hungry lions, wolves, boars, and bears, and with all manner of cruel and hurtful beasts; and in the midst of a great many furious men assaulting her every moment and minute; for this is her condition in the world.

Be ye therefore wise as serpents, &c.] Let meekness be mixed with wariness, saith Nazianzen, that it may be the "meekness of wisdom," James iii. 13.[3] We must be neither foxes, nor yet asses. Meekness many times brings on injuries: a crow will stand upon a sheep's back, pulling off wool from her side. Now, therefore, as we must labour for columbine simplicity, and be no horned beasts to pelt or gore others (as the word ἀκέραιος here signifies), so for serpentine subtlety too, that we cast not ourselves upon needless dangers. The Roman rule was, *nec fugere, nec sequi*, Christianity calleth us not to a weak simplicity; but allows us as much of the serpent as of the dove. The dove without the serpent is easily caught; the serpent without the dove stings deadly. Religion without policy is too simple to be safe; policy without religion is too subtle to be good. Their match makes themselves secure, and many happy. A serpent's eye is a singular ornament in a dove's head. For,

Sit licet in partes circumspectissimus omnes,
  Nemo tamen vulpes, nemo cavere potest.

Harmless as doves] That neither provoke the hawk nor project revenge, but when pursued they save themselves, if they can, by flight, not by fight.

Felle columba caret, rostro non cædit, et ungues
  Possidet innocuos, puraque grana legit.

Sometimes they sit in their dove-cotes, and see their nests destroyed, their young ones taken away and killed before their eyes; neither ever do they offer to rescue or revenge, which all other fowls do seem in some sort to do.

Ver. 17. *But beware of men*] Absurd and wicked men, saith Paul, 2 Thess. iii. 2; "brutish men, skilful to destroy," saith the prophet, Ezek. xxi. 31; "Men-eaters," saith the Psalmist, Psal. xiv. 4; cannibals, that make no more conscience to mischief God's people than to eat a meal's meat when they are hungry. These be those *lycanthropi*, those wolves mentioned in the former verse. These are those mankind men that St Paul met with at Ephesus, 1 Cor. xv. 32. He fought with beasts after the manner of men, that is (as some interpret it), men fought with him after the manner of beasts. Such a man was that monster of Milan, in Bodin. de Repub. Such were the primitive persecutors, and such are the pseudo-catholics of these times. A Dutch woman they buried alive for religion, with thorns under her. Another they shamefully defiled in the sight of her husband, and then forced her to draw a sword and give her husband a deadly wound, her hands being ordered by them. The town of Barre, in France, being taken by the Papists, all kind of cruelty was there used. Children were cut up, the guts and hearts of some of them pulled out, which in rage they gnawed with their teeth. The Italians which served the king, did for hatred of religion break forth into such fury, that they did rip up a living child, and took his liver, being as yet red hot, and eat it as meat. John Burgeolus, president of Turin, an old man, being suspected to be a Protestant, and having bought his life with

---

[1] *In dolum olei immissum ferunt ludibrii causa, quia Christiani à Christo, et Christus ἀπὸ τοῦ χρίεσθαι.*
[2] In less than four years they sacrificed the lives of 800 innocents here, to their idols in Queen Mary's days.
[3] χρηστότης συνέσει κεκραμμένη. Nazianzen.

a great sum of money, was notwithstanding taken and beaten cruelly with clubs and staves; and being stripped of his clothes, was brought to the bank of the river Liger, and hanged, his feet upward, and head downward in the water, up to his breast. Then, he being yet alive, they opened his belly, pulled out his guts, and threw them into the river. And taking his heart they put it upon a spear, carrying it with contumelious words about the city. (Thuanus.) Were these men? or rather devils in the shape of men? What should I instance further in those late Irish unheard-of cruelties, so well known, and so much written of? such as whereof the devil himself might be ashamed, had he any shame in him. Lithgow, a Scot, after he had with King James's letters travelled through the greatest part of the known world, was, as he returned through Spain, in the city of Maligo, surprised by nine sergeants and carried before the governor, by whose appointment they stripped him of his clothes, robbed him of his money, put him into a dark dungeon, shackled him, starved him, wounded him, &c. In 10 hours he received 70 several torments. At last, all the lords inquisitors commanded him to receive 11 strangling torments at midnight, and to be burnt body and bones to ashes, though they had nothing against him but suspicion of religion. And yet after this God wonderfully delivered him. He was brought on his bed to our king, wounded and broken, and made this relation to the face of Gundamor, the Spanish ambassador.

They will scourge you] John Fortune, a martyr in Queen Mary's days, was thus threatened by one Mr Foster: You shall be whipped and burned for this gear, I trow. His answer was, I should be full glad of that. For it is written, "They will scourge you in their synagogues." And since the time that the sword of tyranny came into your hand, I heard of none that were whipped. Happy were I if I had the maidenhead of that persecution.

Ver. 18. *And ye shall be brought before governors*] Yea, they offered themselves to them, crying *Christiani sumus*, and so tiring them thereby, that one of them[1] in a great chafe cried out, *O miseri, si libet perire, num vobis rupes aut restes desunt?* Can ye find no other way to despatch yourselves, but that I must be troubled with you?

And before kings, for my sake] As Paul before Agrippa, and afterwards Nero; Luther before Charles V.; Lambert before Henry VIII.

Ver. 19. *Take no thought how or what ye shall speak*] Be not anxious about either matter or manner of your apology for yourselves. Ye shall be supplied from on high both with invention and elocution. Demosthenes, that great orator, was many times out when he spake to King Philip, and sometimes so amated that he had not a word more to say. Moses, that great scholar, feared he should want words

[1] Artius Antoninus, *apud* Tertul.

when he was to stand before Pharaoh, and professeth, that since God had called him to that service, he found less freedom of speech than before. Latomus of Lovain, a very learned man, having prepared an eloquent oration to Charles V., emperor, was so confounded in the delivering of it, that he came off with great discredit, and fell into utter despair. No wonder therefore though the apostles, being ignorant and unlettered men, were somewhat troubled how to do when brought before kings and Cæsars. Our Saviour here cures them of that care by a promise of help from heaven. And they had it, Acts v. 41 : xiii. 52. And so had the confessors and martyrs in all ages of the Church. *Nescio unde veniunt istæ meditationes*, saith Luther of himself in a letter to his friend. And in his book of the Babylonish captivity he professeth, that whether he would or no, he became every day more learned than other.[2] How bravely did Ann Askew, Alice Driver, and other poor women, answer the doctors, and put them to a nonplus! Was not that the Spirit of the Father speaking in them?

Ver. 20. *But the Spirit of your Father*] Who borroweth your mouth for the present, to speak by. It is he that forms your speeches for you, dictates them to you, filleth you with matter, and furnisheth you with words. Fear not therefore your rudeness to reply. There is no mouth into which God cannot put words : and how oft doth he choose the weak and unlearned to confound the wise and mighty, as he did Balaam's ass to confute his master?

Ver. 21. *And the brother shall deliver up the brother*] As Alphonsus Diazius did his own brother John at Neoberg, in Germany. So, Doctor London made Filmer, the martyr's own brother, witness against him, cherishing him with meat and money, and telling him he should never lack as long as he lived, &c. So, one Woodman was delivered by his own brother into his enemy's hands. Of him and other martyrs burnt with him, White, Bishop of Winchester after Gardiner, falsely affirmed in a sermon, Good people, these men deny Christ to be God, and the Holy Ghost to be God, &c. In the civil wars of France, the sons fought against their fathers, and brothers against brothers, and even women took up arms on both sides for defence of their religion. This is the effect of the gospel of peace, but by accident.

And the father the child] As Philip, King of Spain, who said he had rather have no subjects than heretics, as he called them : and, out of a bloody zeal, suffered his eldest son Charles to be murdered by the cruel inquisition, because he seemed to favour the Protestant side.

Ver. 22. *And ye shall be hated*] *Haud perinde crimine incendii quam odio humani generis convicti sunt*, saith Tacitus of those poor Christians, that by Nero were haled to death for setting the city of Rome on fire, which was done by himself. Tertullian telleth us that their name, and

[2] *Profitetur se quotidie, velit, nolit, doctiorem fieri.*

not their crime, was punished in Christians. So Luther complaineth that there was in his days no crime comparable to that of professing the gospel. *Nullum flagitium hodie par est huic uni et summo sacrilegio, sc. Evangelion Dei confiteri.* Luther, Epist. ad Episc. Sambiensem. Melch. Adam, in Vit. Brent.

But he that endureth to the end] Apostasy loseth the things that it hath wrought, 2 John viii. *Non quæruntur in Christianis initia, sed finis,* saith Jerome. It is the evening that crowneth the day, and the last scene that commends the interlude.

Ver. 23. *Flee ye into another*] That is, make all the haste that may be, as Cant. viii. 14. *Fuge, fuge, Brenti, cito, citius, citissime,* so friendly did a senator of Hala advise Brentius. He did so, and thereby saved his life. There was one Laremouth, chaplain to Lady Ann of Cleve, a Scotchman, to whom in prison it was said, as he thought, "Arise, and go thy ways." Whereto when he gave no great heed at first, the second time it was so said. Upon this, as he fell to his prayers, it was said the third time likewise to him; which was half an hour after. So he, arising upon the same, immediately a piece of the prison wall fell down; and as the officers came in at the outer gate of the prison, he leaping over the ditch escaped. And in the way meeting a certain beggar, changed his coat with him, and coming to the sea-shore, where he found a vessel ready to go over, was taken in, and escaped the search which was straitly laid for him all the country over. Tertullian was too rigid in condemning all kind of flight in time of persecution (*Lib. de Fuga Persecutionis*).

Ye shall not have gone over the cities of Israel] This is another comfort to the apostles and their successors, that though forced to flee from city to city, yet they shall still find harbour, and places of employment. They shall not have finished, that is, taught and converted, all the cities of God's Israel, both according to the flesh and according to the faith, till the Son of man be come to judgment. See Matt. xxiv. 30; Luke xxi. 27.

Ver. 24. *The disciple is not above his master*] Sweeten we the tartness of all our sufferings with this sentence, as with so much sugar. Blandina the martyr being grievously racked and tortured, cried out ever and anon, *Christiana sum,* I am a Christian; and with that consideration was so relieved and refreshed, that all her torments seemed but a pastime to her. (*Sub Antonino Philosopho in Gallia,* &c., Bucholcer.)

Ver. 25. *It is sufficient for the disciple,* &c.] And a fair preferment too, John xxi. 18. Peter thinks much that himself should be destined to die a martyr, and not John. What shall he do? saith Peter; Follow thou me, saith our Saviour. I shall show thee the way to an ignominious suffering, whatever becomes of John; though he shall suffer his part too. For if the head be crowned with thorns, should not the members feel the pain of it?[1]

If they have called the master of the house Beelzebub] That is, master-fly, such as Pliny calleth Μυιαγρὸς. The men of Elis sacrificed to Jupiter Muscarius (Ἀπόμυιος). He is otherwise called Jupiter Stercorarius, this Beelzebub: as the Scripture calls all the vanities of the heathen Gelulim, excrements, dunghill deities: a name too good for them. David would not do them so much honour as once to name them. And *Absit* (saith Jerome) *ut de ore Christiano sonet Jupiter omnipotens, et Mehercule, et Mecastor, et cætera magis portenta quam numina.* Beelzebub was the god of Ekron, that is, the devil of hell (for of Ekron comes Acheron). How prodigiously blasphemous then were these miscreants that called Christ Beelzebub. Wonder it was, that at the hearing thereof the heaven sweat not, the earth shook not, the sea swelled not above all her banks.

How much more shall they call, &c.] So they called Athanasius Sathanasius, Cyprian Coprian, Calvin Cain, Farellus devil. When he came first to Geneva, and began the Reformation there, he was haled before the bishop, and set upon in this sort: *Quid tu diabole nequissime ad hanc civitatem perturbandam accessisti?* What a devil meanest thou to meddle with the Scriptures? (said Stephen Winchester to Marbeck); seeing thou art so stubborn and wilful, thou shalt go to the devil for me.

Ver. 26. *Fear them not therefore*] Be not reviled out of your religion, but say, If this be to be vile, I. will be yet more vile. *Contra sycophantæ morsum non est remedium,* saith Seneca. *Didicit ille maledicere, et ego contemnere,* said he in Tacitus. If I cannot be master of another man's tongue, yet I can be of mine own ears. Dion writes of Severus, that he was careful of what he should do, but careless of what he should hear.[2] Do well and hear ill, is written upon heaven-gates, said that martyr. Ill men's mouths are as open sepulchres, saith David, wherein good men's names are often buried: but the comfort is, there shall be a resurrection as well of names as of bodies, at the last day.

For there is nothing hid that shall not be known] *q. d.* Deal not unfaithfully in the ministry: conceal not the truth in unrighteousness, betray not the cause of God by a cowardly silence. For (whatsoever you may plausibly plead and pretend for your false play) all shall out at length: and well it shall appear to the world that you served not the Lord Christ, but your own turns upon Christ: and so yourselves might sleep in a whole skin, let what would become of his cause and kingdom. Fearful men are the first in that black bill, Rev. xxi. 8. And God equally hateth the timorous as the treacherous.

Ver. 27. *What I tell you in darkness,* &c.] *q. d.* See that ye be valiant and violent for the

---

[1] *Non decet ut sub capite spinis coronato vivant membra in deliciis.* Zanch. lib. 10, cap. 28.

[2] ἐμμελὴς ἦν τῶν πρακτέων, ἀμελὴς δὲ τῶν περὶ αὐτοῦ λογοποιουμένων.

truth: declare unto the world all the counsel of God, which you have therefore learned in private, that ye may teach in public, not fearing any colours, much less stealing from your colours, Heb. x. 38.[1] *Quas non oportet mortes præeligere, quod non supplicium potius ferre, immo in quam profundam inferni abyssum non intrare, quam contra conscientiam attestari?* saith Zuinglius (*Epist. tertia*). A man had better endure any misery than an enraged conscience.

Ver. 28. *And fear not them which kill the body*] That cruelly kill it, ἀποκτείνειν (as the word signifies), that wittily torture it, as those primitive persecutors, with all the most exquisite torments that the wit of malice could devise: that kill men so that they may feel themselves to be killed, as Tiberius bade. Odull Gemmet suffered a strange and cruel death in France for religion. For when they had bound him, they took a kind of creatures which live in horse-dung, called in French *escarbots*, and put them unto his navel, covering them with a dish, the which, within short space, pierced into his belly, and killed him. The tragical story of their cruel handling of William Gardner, martyr, in Portugal, may be read in Mr Foxe's Martyrology, fol. 1242. At the loss of Heidelberg, Monsieur Millius, an ancient minister and man of God, was taken by the bloody Spaniards, who having first abused his daughter before him, tied a small cord about his head, which with truncheons they wreathed about till they squeezed out his brains. So they rather roasted than burnt many of our martyrs, as Bishop Ridley, and others. Neither would they let the dead rest in their graves, as Paulus Phagius, whose bones they digged up and burnt: so they raged exceedingly upon the dead body of Zuinglius, after they had slain him in battle, &c.[2] Now these that cruelly kill the body we must not fear. Our Saviour saith not, that can kill the body at their pleasure, for that they cannot; but that do kill it, when God permits them to do it. And then, too, *occidere possunt, lædere non possunt*, as he told the tyrant:[3] they may kill the saints, but cannot hurt them, because their souls are out of gunshot. St Paul's sufferings reached no further than to his flesh, Col. i. 25; his soul was untouched, he possessed that in patience amidst all outward perturbations.

But are not able to kill the soul] As they would do fain, if it were in their power. David oft complains that they sought after his soul, that they satanically hated him, &c. Now we commit thy soul to the devil, said the persecutors to John Huss. The Popish priests persuaded the people here at the burning of the martyrs, that when the gunpowder (that was put under their armholes for a readier despatch of them) gave a burst, then the devil fetched away their

souls. When Cranmer often cried in the fire, "Lord Jesus, receive my spirit," a Spanish monk ran to a nobleman then present, and would have persuaded him that those were words of despair, and that he was now entering into hell.[4] Upon the patient and pious death of George Marsh, many of the people said he died a martyr, which caused the bishop shortly after to make a sermon in the cathedral, and therein he affirmed that the said Marsh was an heretic, burnt like an heretic, and a fire-brand in hell. Of Nicolas Burton, martyr in Spain, because he embraced death for Christ with all gladness and patience, the Papists gave out that the devil had his soul before he came to the fire, and therefore they said his senses of feeling were past already.

But rather fear him] As one fire, so one fear drives out another. Therefore, in the second commandment, lest the fear of men's punishment should keep us from worshipping of God, great punishment is threatened to them that worship him not. If I forsake my profession, I am sure of a worse death than Judge Hales had, said that martyr. There is a martial law for those that forsake their captain, or else (under a colour of discretion) fall back into the rereward. They that draw back, do it to perdition, Heb. x. 39. And is it nothing to lose an immortal soul? to purchase an everlasting death? Should servants fear their masters because they have power over the flesh? Col. iii. 23; and should not we fear him that can destroy both body and soul in hell? Biron, Marshal of France, derided the Earl of Essex's piety at his death as more befitting a silly minister than a stout warrior: as if the fear of hell were not a Christian man's fortitude; as if it were not valour but madness to fight with a flaming fire, that is out of our power to suppress. This Biron, within few months after, underwent the same death that Essex did, and then if he feared not hell, he was sure to feel it.

Ver. 29. *Are not two sparrows,*[5] &c.] Birds flying seem to be at liberty, yet are guided by an over-ruling hand: they fly freely, yet fall by Divine dispose, and not as the fowler will. But we are better than many sparrows. God's providence is punctual and particular, extending even to the least and lightest circumstances of all our occurrences; whatever Jerome thought to the contrary, and Pliny with his *Irridendum vero curam agere rerum humanarum illud quicquid est summum:* It is a ridiculous thing, saith he, to imagine that God takes care of our particular affairs. How much better St Augustine, *Deus sic curat universos quasi singulos, sic singulos, quasi solos.* God's providence extends to every particular, both person and occurrence.

Ver. 30. *But the very hairs of your head,* &c.] As things of price, and such as God sets

---

[1] ὑποστείληται, Steal from his captain.
[2] *In corpus Zuinglii exanime valde sævitum fuit, &c.* Scultet. Annal., p. 348.

[3] Ἀποκτεῖναι με δύναται ὁ Νέρων, βλάψαι δε οὐ. *Thraseas,* apud Dion. in Nerone.
[4] Melch. Adam. in Vit. Cranmer.
[5] στρουθία, *Magna est emphasis diminutivi.*

great store by. Hence he enjoined his Nazarites, when they had accomplished their vow, to shave their heads, and put the hair in the fire, under their peace-offering, for a sacrifice to the Lord, Numb. vi. 18. The Ammonites paid dear for the hair they shaved off the heads and beards of David's messengers. So hath Bonner, I believe, ere this, for the martyr's beard he pulled off part of it, causing the other part thereof to be shaved, lest his manly act should be seen to the world. The three worthies were taken out of the fiery furnace with their hairs in full number, not one of them singed, Dan. iii. 27.

Ver. 31. *Fear not therefore*] This is the third time, in six verses, that they and we are bid to banish this cowardly base passion, this causeless, fruitless, harmful, sinful fear of men. He that fears God needs fear none else. Moses feared not Pharaoh, nor Micaiah Ahab, when they had once seen God in his majesty. Micaiah will not budge or alter his tale; as the lion fiercely pursued, will not alter his gait, they say, though he die for it. Doctor Taylor, martyr, when being sent for by Stephen Gardiner, his friends persuaded him not to appear, but fly. "Fly you," said he, "and do as your conscience leads you, I am fully determined, with God's grace, to go to the bishop, and to his beard to tell him that he doth naught." This he resolved to do, and this he did accordingly. For at his first appearance, "Art thou come, thou villain?" said the bishop. "How darest thou look me in the face for shame? Knowest thou not who I am?" "Yes, I know who you are," said he again, "Doctor Gardiner, Bishop of Winchester and Lord Chancellor, yet but a mortal man, I trow. But if I should be afraid of your lordly looks, why fear you not God, the Lord of us all? How dare you for shame look any Christian man in the face, seeing you have forsaken the truth, denied your Master Christ and his word, and done contrary to your own oath and writing? With what countenance will you appear before the judgment-seat of Christ, and answer to your oath?" &c.

Ye are of more value than many sparrows] Yea, than many other men, as one pearl is more worth than many pebbles, one little lark than many carrion-kites. Noah found more favour with God than all the world besides. The saints are called all things, Col. i. 20. Tabor and Hermon are put for the east and west of the world, Psal. lxxxix. 12, as if there were no world but Judæa, that pleasant land, that land of delight, Dan. xi. 16, 41, so styled, because in Judah was God known, and there were those excellent ones in whom is all God's delight, Psal. xvi. 3. He reckons of men by their righteousness, and accounts such more excellent than their neighbours, whomsoever they dwell by, Prov. xii. 26.

Ver. 32. *Whosoever therefore shall confess me*] A bold and wise confession of Christ is required of all his, who are therefore said to be marked

in their foreheads, Rev. vii. 3, an open place: and they that will not profess him shall be sorted with such as through excess of pain, and defect of patience, gnaw their own tongues, Rev. xvi. 10. Antichrist takes it in as good part, if his bond-slaves receive his mark in their hand only; the which, as occasion serveth, they may cover or discover, Rev. xiii. 16. He lets his use what couzenage they will, so it may help to amplify his kingdom. It was a watch-word in Gregory XIII.'s time, in Queen Elizabeth's reign, "My son, give me thy heart." Dissemble, go to church, do what ye will, but *Da mihi cor* : be in heart a Papist, and go where you will. Christ will endure no such dealing. He will have heart and tongue too, Rom. x. 9, he will be worshipped truly, that there be no halting; and totally, that there be no halving. We may as well (saith Zuinglius) do worship at the altar of Jupiter or Venus, as hide our faith for fear of antichrist.[1] "He that is not with me is against me," saith our Saviour. He likes not these politic professors, these neuter-passive Christians, that have *fidem menstruam*, as Hilary said of some in his time, that have *religionem ephemeram*, as Beza saith of Balduinus the French apostate, that can turn with the times, comply with the company, be (as the planet Mercury) good in conjunction with good, and bad with bad. These are they that do *virtutis stragulam pudefacere*, put honesty to an open shame, as the philosopher could say, And shall these men's faith "be found to praise and honour and glory?" 1 Pet. i. 7. It is not likely.

Ver. 33. *But whosoever shall deny me*] Not only utterly to renounce Christ, but out of base respects to dissemble him, is to deny him. Peter denied his Master as well in saying, "I wot not what thou sayest," as in swearing he never knew the man. The people of Israel, 1 Kings xviii. 11, that held their peace only when the prophet had said, "If the Lord be God, follow him," are blamed, and worthily, for their detestable indifferency. Indeed, they spake not against the prophet, but they durst not speak with him. Many such cold friends religion hath now-a-days. This they will dearly repent and rue, when they come to give account, with the world all on a light flame about their ears, and the elements falling upon them, as scalding lead or running bell-metal.

Him will I also deny before my Father] And the Father will entertain none but such as come commended to him by his Son, Christ. He will surely cashier all others, as the Tirshatha did those proud priests, that grew ashamed of their profession, and could not find their register, Ezra ii. 62.

Ver. 34. *Think not that I came to send peace*] Peace is twofold, *temporis et pectoris*, of country and of conscience. This latter is Christ's legacy, and the saints are sure of it. But the former they seldom find here; "In the world ye shall have trouble," saith our Saviour. Should we look

[1] *Ad aras Jovis aut Veneris adorare ac sub antichristo fidem occultare.*

for fire to quench our thirst? saith a martyr: and as soon shall God's true servants find peace and favour under Christ's regiment. This world is to the saints as the sea called Pacific, than the which there is nothing more troublesome and tumultuous; or as the Straits of Magellan, where, which way soever a man bend his course, he shall be sure to have the wind against him.

Ver. 35. *For I am come to set a man at variance,* &c.] By accident it fell out so, through men's singular corruption, causing them as bats to fly against the light of the gospel, to hate it as thieves do a torch in the night; or as the panther, which so hates man, that he tears his picture wherever he finds it.

Ver. 36. *And a man's foes shall be they,* &c.] Nicholas of Jenvile, a young man newly come from Geneva, was condemned and set in the cart. His own father, coming with a staff, would have beaten him but that the officers kept him off. Julius Palmer, martyr, coming to his mother, and asking her blessing, "Thou shalt," said she, "have Christ's curse and mine wherever thou goest." John Fetty, martyr, was accused and complained of by his own wife, and she was thereupon struck mad. Another like example there is to be read of an unnatural husband witnessing against his own wife, and likewise of children against their own mother, &c. So this saying of our Saviour is fulfilled. And it was not for nothing that Antigonus prayed so hard to be delivered from his friends; that Queen Elizabeth complained that in trust she had found treason.

Ver. 37. *He that loveth father or mother*] Levi said unto his father and his mother, "I have not seen him;" neither did he acknowledge his brethren, in that cause of God, nor knew his own children, Deut. xxxiii. 9. "If the Lord Christ call me to him," saith Jerome, "although my father should lie in my way, my mother hang about my neck to hinder me, I would go over my father, shake off my mother," &c. Nazianzen was glad that he had something of value (to wit, his Athenian learning) to part with for Christ. Nicholas Shetterden, martyr, in a letter to his mother, wrote thus: "Dear mother, embrace the counsel of God's word with hearty affection, read it with obedience, &c. So shall we meet in joy at the last day; or else I bid you farewell for evermore." "Away from me, Satan," said Rebezies, a French martyr, when Satan set before him his parents, to stop him in his course. And I know not by what reason they so called them my friends (said Borthwick, a Scotch martyr), that so greatly laboured to convert (indeed to pervert) me, neither will I more esteem them than the Midianites, which in times past called the children of Israel to do sacrifice to their idols.

He that loveth son or daughter, &c.] As did Eli, who honoured his sons above God, 1 Sam. ii. 29. This the Lord took so heinously, that he swore that this iniquity of Eli's house should not be purged with sacrifice nor offering for ever, 1 Sam. iii. 14. Samuel, who brought the old priest this heavy tidings, was afterwards unhappy enough in his two sons; and succeeded Eli in his cross as well as his place. It can hardly be imagined that he succeeded him in his sin after so fair a warning. But good David was surely too fond a father, and therefore smarted in his children, whom he cockered. God will have us to hold him to be better to us than ten sons: and to bestow all our love upon him, as most worthy. What he gives us back again, we may bestow upon others; loving our friends in God, and our enemies for God. But the love of Christ must constrain us to part with all, though never so dear and near unto us, for his sake. Mr Bradford, while he was a prisoner, wrote earnestly to his mother to pray God to make him worthy to suffer, not only imprisonment, but even very death for his truth, religion, and gospel. Femella Amatriciana, a most godly woman, understanding that her son went heavily on to his death for Christ, met him and encouraged him, bidding him look up to heaven, and behold the sun in his glory. Which when he had done, "Knowest thou not, my son," said she, "thou shalt shortly be in that heavenly palace, and there outshine the sun itself!" William Hunter the martyr's mother, said unto him, standing at the stake, that she was glad that ever she was so happy as to bear such a child as could find in his heart to lose his life for Christ's name's sake. Then William said to his mother, "For my little pain which I shall suffer, which is but for a short braid, Christ hath promised me a crown of joy; may you not be glad of that, mother?" with that his mother kneeled down on her knees, saying, "I pray God strengthen thee, my son, to the end; yea, I think thee as well bestowed as any child that ever I bare." John Clark, of Melden in France, being, for Christ's sake, whipped three several days, and afterward having a mark set in his forehead as a note of infamy, his mother beholding it (though his father was an adversary) encouraged her son, crying with a loud voice, "Blessed be Christ, and welcome be these his prints and marks." *Vivat Christus, ejusque insignia.* (Scultet. Annal.)

Is not worthy of me] viz. Because he holdeth not me worthy of more love than his best friends. Eli, for seeking to please his sons, Moses his wife, had like to have lost a friend of God, who had much ado to forbear killing him, Exod. iv. 24.

Ver. 38. *And he that taketh not up his cross*] *Omnis Christianus crucianus,* saith Luther. Every Christian is sure of his cross; but, first, it must be "his" cross, such as God hath laid upon him, not such as he hath created to himself (as Baal's priests, who cut themselves with knives and lancets, 1 Kings xviii. 28, the Circumcelliones of old, and the monks at this day, with their voluntary penances, &c.). Next, he must take it, and not stay till it be laid upon him; or then bear it as an ass doth his burden, because he can neither will nor choose; but he must be active in suffering and take God's part against himself. Nay, he must (as he may) be cheerful under his cross, and thankful for it, as a favour, an honour, Acts v. 41, and xx. 24. The very beasts take blows from their keepers. Turks, when cruelly lashed by their officers, give them thanks and go their ways. Porters go singing under their burdens, &c. *Levius fit patientiâ quicquid corrigere est nefas.* (Horat.)

And followeth after me] Or cometh not behind me (ὀπίσω μοῦ); and this not aloof off, as Peter, Matt. xxvi. 58, but close at heels, as Caleb, Numb. xiv. 24; walking in Christ, Col. ii. 6; as Christ, 1 John ii. 6; putting him on in his virtues, as Constantine's sons did their father, and preaching forth his praises, 1 Pet. ii. 9. He is a Saviour to none but those to whom he is a sampler; neither have any his redemption but they that take his direction; his benediction, but those that submit to his jurisdiction.

Ver. 39. He that findeth his life shall lose it] This is a strange expression, a riddle to the world, a seeming contradiction,[1] such as natural reason can never reconcile. But if the paradoxes of the Stoics might be proved, much more may those of the gospel. He that findeth his life, that is, redeemeth it with the forfeiture of his faith, with the shipwreck of his conscience, makes a loser's bargain, makes more haste than good speed; whiles in running from death as far as he can he runs to it as fast as he can. Christ will kill him with death, Rev. ii. 23; and sentence him as an apostate, unto double damnation.

He that loseth his life for my sake, &c.] For else all is lost, sith it is not *pœna* but *causa* that makes a martyr. Christ and the thieves were in the same condemnation; Samson and the Philistines in the same destruction, by the downfall of the house: *Similis pœna, dissimilis causa,* saith Augustine. Martyrdom is a crown, as old age, if it be found in the way of righteousness. One martyr cried out, Blessed be God that ever I was born to this happy hour. To another, when it was said, Take heed; it is a hard matter to burn. Indeed, said he, it is for him that hath his soul linked to his body, as a thief's foot in a pair of fetters. Can I die but once for Christ? said a third.

Shall find it] For the line of his lost life shall be hid in the endless maze of God's surest mercies. The passion days of the martyrs were therefore anciently called, *Natalitia salutis,* the birth-days of salvation, the day-break of eternal brightness. Those poor seduced souls that lost their lives in the Holy Wars, as they called them, and were persuaded that thereby they made amends to Christ for his death, were much to be pitied.

Ver. 40. He that receiveth you, receiveth me] And who would not be glad to entertain the Lord Christ? Elizabeth held it a great matter that the mother of her Lord should come to her, Luke i. 43. Behold Christ comes to us in his servants, in his ministers especially. Receive them, therefore, as so many angels, yea, as Christ himself, Gal. iv. 14, accounting their very feet (how much more their faces!) beautiful. We know with what great respect Cornelius entertained Peter. *Non tantus sum, ut vos alloquar,* said Tertullian to certain martyrs. He tells us

also that it was a custom of some in those times, *reptare ad vincula martyrum,* to creep to the martyr's bonds in way of honour to them, which perhaps was more than was meet.

Receiveth him that sent me] The heathens held it a great honour to entertain their gods; and the poets tell us of much evil that befell those that refused to do so. "That which we have heard and seen," saith St John, "declare we unto you, that ye also may have fellowship with us," 1 John i. 3. But what so great matter is that? might some say. You and your fellows are but men of mean condition. True, saith the apostle, but as mean as we are, our "fellowship is with the Father, and with his Son Jesus Christ," who will also come in and sup with such as receive his servants. And may they not be glad of such guests?

Ver. 41. He that receiveth a prophet in the name, &c.] Though, haply, he be no prophet. This takes away the excuse of such as say, They would do good, if they knew to whom, as worthy.

Shall receive a prophet's reward] Both actively, that which the prophet shall give him, by teaching him the faith of the gospel, casting pearls before him, &c. And passively, that reward that God gives the prophet, the same shall he give his host. Gaius lost nothing by such guests as John; nor the Shunammite or Sareptan by the prophets. Of such Christ seems to say, as Paul did of Onesimus, "If he owe thee ought, put that in mine account: I will repay it," Philem. 18, 19: and he, I can tell you, is a liberal pay-master. Saul and his servant had but five pence in their purse to give the prophet, 1 Sam. ix. 8. The prophet, after much good cheer, gives him the kingdom. Such is God's dealing with us. Seek out therefore some of his receivers, some Mephibosheth to whom we may show kindness.

He that receiveth a righteous man] Though not a minister, if for that he is righteous, and for the truth's sake that dwelleth in him, 2 John 2. The Kenites in Saul's time, that were born many ages after Jethro's death, receive life from his dust and favour from his hospitality. Nay, the Egyptians, for harbouring (and at first dealing kindly with) the Israelites, though without any respect to their righteousness, were preserved by Joseph in that sore famine, and kindly dealt with ever after by God's special command.

Ver. 42. Unto one of these little ones] So the saints are called, either because but a little flock, or little in their own eyes, or little set by in the world, or dearly respected of God, as little ones are by their loving parents.

A cup of cold water] As having not fuel to heat it, saith Jerome, nor better to bestow than Adam's ale, a cup of water, yet desirous some way to seal up his love to poor Christ. Salvian saith, that Christ is *mendicorum maximus,* the greatest beggar in the world, as one that shareth in all his saints' necessities. Relieve him therefore in them; so shall you lay up in store for

---

[1] παράδοξον ἀλλ' οὐ παράλογον.

yourselves a good foundation against the time to come; yea, you shall lay hold on eternal life, 1 Tim. vi. 19. Of Midas it is fabled, that whatever he touched he turned into gold. Sure it is that whatsoever the hand of charity touch, be it but a cup of cold water, it turns the same, not into gold, but into heaven itself. He is a niggard then to himself that is niggardly to Christ's poor. If heaven may be had for a cup of cold water, what a bodkin at the churl's heart will this be one day! Surely the devil will keep holiday, as it were, in hell, in respect of such.

Verily, I say unto you, he shall in no wise, &c.] By this deep asseveration our Saviour tacitly taxeth the world's unbelief, whiles they deal by him, as by some patching companion or base bankrupt, trust him not at all, without either ready money or a sufficient pawn. But what saith a grave divine? Is not mercy as sure a grain as vanity? Is God like to break, or forget? Is there not a book of remembrance written before him, which he oftener peruseth than Ahasuerus did the Chronicles? The butler may forget Joseph, and Joseph his father's house; but God is not unrighteous to forget your work and labour of love, which ye have showed toward his name, in that you have ministered to the saints, and do minister, Heb. vi. 10.

CHAPTER XI.

Verse 1. *He departed thence to teach, &c.*] Never out of action: the end of one good work was with our Saviour the beginning of another. So must it be with ministers: let them never look to rest till they come to heaven; but (as St Paul, that *insatiabilis Dei cultor*, as Chrysostom called him) teach God's people publicly and from house to house, incessantly warning every one night and day with tears, Acts xx. 20, 31. Dr Taylor, martyr, preached not only every Sabbath-day and holy-day, but whensoever else he could get the people together. So did Bishop Ridley, Bishop Jewel, &c. So did not their successors, once a year was fair with many of them (like the high priest in the law), as if they had concurred in opinion with that Popish bishop, that said, It was too much for any man to preach every Sunday, and that bishops were not ordained to preach, but to sing mass sometimes, leaving all other offices to their suffragans. It is as rare a thing at Rome, said Dr Bassinet, to hear a bishop preach as to see an ass fly. Oh what will these slow-bellies do when Christ riseth up? and when he visiteth, how will they answer him? Job xxxi. 14.

To preach in their cities] That is, in the cities of his twelve disciples, in the coasts of Galilee, while they were doing the same in Jewry. Maldonate the Jesuit will not have this to be the sense of this text, and only *quia, inquit, est hereticorum*, because it is the sense that the heretics (as he calls the Protestants) set on it. A goodly thing he holds it to dissent from them, though in a manifest truth. So George, Duke of Saxony,

was heard to say, Though I am not ignorant that heresies and abuses are crept into the Church, yet I will never obey the gospel that Luther preacheth. For hatred to the man he would not hearken to the truth he taught. This is to have the faith of Christ "in respect of persons," James ii. 1.

Ver. 2. *Now when John had heard in the prison*] "Put this fellow in prison," said Ahab of Micaiah, 1 Kings xxii. 27; who is thought to have been he that told him so barely of letting go Benhadad. So Jeremiah, that *concionator admirabilis* (as Kerkerman calleth him), was for forty years' pains and patience cast into a deep and dirty dungeon.[1] The apostles were often imprisoned: so were the ancient bishops under the ten first persecutions. "From the delectable orchard of the Leonine prison:" so Algerius, the Italian martyr, dates his letter. Within a few days of Queen Mary's reign, almost all the prisons in England were become right Christian schools and churches. Bocardo, in Oxford, was called a college of quondams, Cranmer, Ridley, Latimer, and others, being there kept captive. This is *merces mundi*: look for no better dealing.

Ver. 3. *Art thou he that should come, &c.*] This question the Baptist moved not for his own sake (for he was well assured, and had sufficiently testified, John iii.), but for his disciples' better settlement and satisfaction. This, whiles Tertullian observed not, he hath done the Baptist palpable injury in three several places; as if himself had doubted of the person of Christ. Let not us be troubled to be in like manner mistaken and misjudged.

Ver. 4. *Jesus answered and said, &c.*] Our Saviour rated them not, chased them not away from his presence, though zealously affecting their master, but not well, John iii., and envying for his sake, Gal. iv. 17. The man of God must not strive, but be gentle, apt to teach, patient: in meekness instructing those that oppose themselves, &c. 2 Tim. ii. 24. Friar Alphonsus, a Spaniard, reasoning with Bradford, the martyr, was in a wonderful rage, and spake so high that the whole house rang again, chafing with *om et cho*, &c. So that if Bradford had been anything hot, one house could not have held them.

Go and show John what things, &c.] He gives them a real testimony, an ocular demonstration. This was the ready way to win upon them, who might have suspected a simple assertion, not seconded with such undeniable arguments. Let our lives as well as our lips witness for us: *Vivite concionibus, concionamini moribus*, saith one. *Nos non eloquimur magna, sed vivimus*, said the Church of old. This is the way to slaughter envy itself, and to reign in the hearts of the righteous.

Ver. 5. *The blind receive their sight*] Our Saviour seems to say the same to John, that she did to Judah, Gen. xxxviii. 25. Discern, I pray thee, whose works are these. The end of his miracles was the proof of his majesty.
λαμπρότατα πράξας ἀλγεινότατα ἔπαθεν.

---

[1] Kerk. Rhet. Ecclesiast. c. ult.

The poor have the gospel, &c.] Gr. are gospelized (εὐαγγελίζονται) : they not only receive it, but are changed by it, transformed into it.

Ver. 6. *And blessed is he, &c.*] This he adds, as correcting the preposterous emulation of John's disciples, who stumbled also at his meanness. Howbeit our Saviour saith not, Cursed be ye for being offended in me ; but, Blessed is he, &c. God's tender lambs must be gently handled. *Evangelizatum, non maledictum missus es,* said Œcolampadius to Farellus, who was a most excellent preacher, but over-carried perhaps sometimes by his zeal for God. *Laudo zelum, modo non desideretur mansuetudo, &c.* I commend thine earnestness (as he there goeth on), so thou mingle it with mildness. Wine and oil are in their several seasons to be poured into men's wounds. Show thyself to be a gentle evangelist, and not a tyrannical law-maker.

Ver. 7. *And as they departed*] Due praise is to be given to the good parts and practices of others ; but rather behind their backs than before their faces, lest we be suspected of flattery, than the which nothing is more odious. Aristobulus, the historian, wrote a flattering book of the brave acts of Alexander the Great, and presented it to him. He read it, and then cast it into the river Hydaspes, telling the author that he had deserved to be so served as his book was, *Tu dignior eras ut eodem præcipitareris, qui solus me sic pugnantem satias.*

A reed shaken with the wind] A thing of nothing : a worthless, poiseless person. So the Jews esteemed John Baptist after a while, whom at first they so much admired. But he soon grew stale to them, and then they shamefully slighted him, John v. 35. And did not the Galatians do the like by St Paul ? Once they could have pulled out their eyes for him ; afterwards they would have pulled out his eyes if they could have come at him. " Where is then the blessedness ye spake of ? " saith he ; *q. d.* Once you held and professed yourselves a people much blessed in me,[1] how comes it that I am now so fallen out of your hearts ? But people are over-soon sated with the heavenly manna, and their affections to godly ministers are as Joab's dagger, as soon in, and as soon out. *Principes favebant Luthero, sed jam iterum videtis ingratitudinem mundi erga ministros,* said Melancthon.

Ver. 8. *A man clothed in softs ?*] (εἵματα ἀνὴρ) Which most men gaze at, go after, fawn upon. *Hunc homines decorant, quem vestimenta decorant.* Herein they resemble those dogs that kept Vulcan's temple ; of which Hospinian tells us that if any came to the temple with brave clothes, they would fawn upon them ; but if in ragged, they would tear them in pieces. Such a vanity as this was crept into the Church, James ii. 2. *Fulgent fere- monilibus, sordent moribus.* Cato could say, *Cultus magnam curam, magnam virtutis esse incuriam.* The Baptist was not a man of that make. His heart and his habit were equally

plain, simple. Buchanan seldom cared for a better outside than a rug gown girt close about him.

Ver. 9. *And more than a prophet*] Because he pointed out Christ with the finger, whom they only saluted afar off (ἀσπασάμενοι, Heb. xi. 13). Chrysologus calleth him, *legis et gratiæ fibulam.* Another resembleth him to the angel, that had one foot in the sea and another on the land. The law he resembleth to the sea, which is rough and moveable. The gospel to the land, which is firm and stable, &c.

Ver. 10. *Behold, I send my messenger*] Gr. τὸν ἄγγελόν μου, mine angel. So Phinehas is called an angel, Judges ii. 1. The priest an angel, Eccl. v. 6. Ministers of the gospel angels, 1 Cor. ix. 10. Ministers and angels have exchanged names and offices ; for are they not all ministering spirits ? Heb. i. 14. Did not angels first preach the gospel, Luke ii., the ministration whereof is now committed to us ? so that if there be a messenger, an interpreter, one among a thousand, to show unto man his righteousness, then will God be gracious unto him, &c., Job xxxiii. 23.

Ver. 11. *There hath not risen a greater*] Because he was Christ's immediate forerunner, now the nearer to Christ, the more excellent ; as the elements, the higher, the purer. John was beyond all the ancient prophets, both in dignity and doctrine ; yet he came behind the evangelists and apostles, not in the dignity of his office, but in the clearness of his doctrine concerning the Messiah, whom he saw present, but neither saw nor heard of suffering, dying, rising again, as they did. Macarius writeth that the prophets knew indeed that Christ should be born into the world for the work of our redemption, but whether or no he should die and rise again, this they knew not. *Verum longe errat Macarius,* saith one. The prophet Isaiah writes of all these more like an evangelist than a prophet, and is therefore called by an ancient, the Evangelical Prophet. Now the Baptist knew more than any prophet ; being as the morning-star that precedes the sun-rising. But how Aristotle should be said to be Christ's forerunner in natural things, as John Baptist was in supernatural, and that he was certainly saved (all which the divines of Collen affirmed in print,[2] and showed their reasons), I cannot conceive. And yet Sleidan tells us that in the Council of Trent, the salvation of heathens, by the power of nature only without Christ, was cried up, and afterwards defended by Soto, Vega, and Victoria, as Valentia witnesseth.

Ver. 12. *And from the days of John, &c.*] The Baptist is further commended from the good success of his ministry ; a sweet seal, but no sure sign of a sanctified preacher ; sith many causes give that to others, that themselves have not. Thus the lifeless heaven gives life to divers creatures, the dull whetstone sharpens iron. A stinking breath may sound a trumpet with great commendation, &c. Howbeit the fruitfulness of the

---

[1] Gal. iv. 15, μακαρισμὸς, *Beatitudinis prædicatio.* Beza.

[2] *Colonienses edunt librum de salute Aristotelis asseruntque illum fuisse præcursorem Christi in naturalibus.*

people is the preacher's testimonial, 2 Cor. iii. 2; and God delights to honour those of most sincerity with most success, as 1 Cor. xv. 10.

The kingdom of heaven suffereth violence] Men are resolved to have it, whatever pains or peril they pass through. As God's Israel violently invaded and overran the promised land, so do his elect lay hold on the promised inheritance. This true treasure, hitherto hid, Rom. xvi. 26, is now discovered and exposed to all that have a mind to it. Now therefore they are carried with all strength of affection after Christ; him they must have, whatever else they go without; towards him they fly as a cloud; and as a flock of doves they scour into the columbary, and rush into the windows, Isa. lx. 8.

And the violent, &c.] The valiant, Isaiah calleth them, that break through all difficulties, as did David's worthies, and walk about the world as so many conquerors: yea, more than conquerors they are, Rom. viii. 37, and what can that be but triumphers? 2 Cor. ii. 14.

Take it by force] Make a prey or a prize of it. *Diripiunt*, as Hilary rendereth it, making it a metaphor, from a tower or town sacked and ransacked by the enemy. Cyprus is an island so fruitful and pleasant, that it was anciently called Macaria, that is, blessed. And of it Sextus Rufus writeth, that being famous for riches, it thereby solicited the poverty of the people of Rome to seize upon it.[1] This may be more fitly said of heaven, that habitation of the happy ones, so eagerly and earnestly sought for by the saints, that nothing else will satisfy them. *Valde protestatus sum me nolle sic a Deo satiari*, said Luther, when great gifts were sent unto him, and a cardinalship offered him by the pope: God, he said, should not put him off with those petty things, he breathed after better. Heaven is had by the violent, earth inherited by those that are meek, Matt. v. 6. Where, though God would have his servants content with the least mercies (as being less than the very least), yet not satisfied with the greatest things in the world for their portion, sith they are born to better. If they be, as most are, slothful in seeking to possess themselves of heaven, he chides them, as Joshua did the seven tribes for their negligence, Josh. xviii. 2.

Ver. 13. *For all the prophets and the law, &c.*] i. e. The ministry of the prophets and the shadows of the law determined in John's preaching. As for the substance of the law, Christ came not to destroy, but fulfil it, Matt. v. 17, 18. See the notes thereon.

Ver. 14. *This is Elias*] Not the Tishbite, but yet the same that Malachi foretold should come in the "spirit and power of Elias." And surely, if we observe it (as here, Christ saith to the Jews, If ye will receive it), there is a wonderful agreement between the times of Elias and John Baptist, between Ahab and Herod, between Jezebel and Herodias, &c. The Jews also have a saying amongst them at this day,

when they are puzzled in any point, *Elias cum venerit, solvet omnia*.

Ver. 15. *He that hath ears to hear, let him hear*] Let him attentively listen, not with that outward ear only, that gristle that grows upon his head: but let him draw up his heart to his ears, that one sound may pierce both at once. Thus hear, and your souls shall live, Isa. lv. 3. A heavy ear is a singular judgment, Isa. vi. 10. The good Hebrews are taxed for their dull hearing, Heb. v. 11. Such ears are likely to be forced open by correction, Job xxxiii. 16, and be made hear the rod, Micah vi. 9. So that if they did but see their danger they would do as the prophet requires, "cut their hair and cast it away," under the sense of the horror of God's heavy displeasure, Jer. vii. 24, 29.

Ver. 16. *But whereunto shall I liken this generation?*] So great was the contumacy and obstinacy of this perverse people, the Pharisees especially, that the wisdom of God seems to be at a want for a fit word to utter to them, for their better conviction. And do not some such sit before us at this day, as senseless every whit of what is said to them, as the seats they sit on, the pillars they lean to, the dead bodies they tread upon? We may speak to them, alas, till we spit out our lungs, and all to as little purpose as Bede did, when he preached to a heap of stones.

Ver. 17. *We have piped unto you, &c.*] It is probable that children in those days were wont to solace themselves with songs in this sort: and thence our Saviour seeks to repress the pride and set forth the sin of his untoward hearers. Fit similes do excellently illustrate: and he is the best preacher, saith Luther, that delivereth himself vulgarly, plainly, trivially: not speaking in a Roman, English, or other lofty language, that the hearers are nothing the wiser for; nor yet puzzling them with scholastical craggy disquisitions, that breed wind, and not nourishment. But so attempering their discourses to the hearers' capacities, that their desires and endeavours may answer his: as it was between St Paul and the elders of Ephesus, Acts xx. 31—37. He tells them of his tears, and they answer him with tears: O happy compliance! But most of our hearers are like these in the text, which whether piped to or mourned to, are nothing at all affected.

Ver. 18. *For John came neither eating, &c.*] So froward men are and frample, that no preacher can please them. If he preach plainly, it will seem careless slubbering: if elaborately, curious affectation. And for his life; austere John hath a devil, sociable Christ is a wine-bibber. And it was the worse, because from scribes and Pharisees, whose word must carry such credit with it, as alone to condemn Christ; and whose life must be a rule to others. Do any of the Pharisees believe in him? In this case duty must be done, however it be construed. Evil men, when they learn to think well, will learn to report well. Let our lives and labours in the Lord's

[1] *Cyprus famosa divitiis paupertatem populi Rom. ut occuparetur, sollicitavit.*

work confute them : and though they should by their reproaches bury our good names in their throats, those open sepulchres, yet at utmost, when Christ comes to judgment, there shall be a resurrection of names as well as of bodies. " Be patient therefore, brethren, unto the coming of the Lord," James v. 7.

And they say he hath a devil] So Staphylus and Surius said that Luther learned his divinity of the devil. The Jesuits affirm that he was stirred up by the devil, and they were sent out by God to resist him. Himself knew all this, and took it well aworth. *Prorsus Satan est Lutherus* (saith he in an epistle to Spalatinus), *sed Christus vivit et regnat : Amen.* He adds his Amen to it.

Ver. 19. *The Son of man came eating and drinking*] Teaching us thereby, in the use of things indifferent, to do what we can to preserve our good esteem with others, that we may the sooner prevail with them. This was St Paul's " all things to all men." He turned himself into all shapes and fashions both of speech and spirit, to win men to God. St Austin spake broken barbarous Latin to the Roman colonies in Africa, to the end that they might understand him.[1] " When I come to Rome," saith Ambrose to Monica, " I fast on the Saturday : when I am at Milan I fast not." So you, to what church soever you come, *ejus morem serva,* do as others do ; not giving offence carelessly, nor taking offence causelessly. Calvin was cast out of Geneva for refusing to administer the Lord's supper with wafer-cakes or unleavened bread. " *De quo postea restitutus nunquam contendendum putavit*" (saith Beza in his Life), of which being afterwards restored, he thought best to make no more words, but to yield : though he let them know that he had rather it were otherwise.[2] Christ sets us to learn of the unjust steward, by all lawful (though he did it by unlawful) means, to maintain our reputation with men. For this defect he noted in the best, when he said, " The children of this world are wiser in their generation than the children of light," Luke xvi. 8.

But wisdom is justified of her children] Who all having a right estimate of her worth, do meanly esteem of other courses and discourses, do stand to her, and stickle for her, though never so much slighted by the world. There are that read it thus, " But wisdom is judged of her children,"[3] viz. the perverse Jews, who preposterously pass sentence upon their mother, whom they should rather vail to, and vote for.

Ver. 20. *Then began he to upbraid*] Haply, because these cities, drawn by the authority of the Pharisees, made less account of our Saviour's doctrine or miracles, by them maliciously depraved and disparaged. The blind led the blind, but both fell into the ditch, though their leaders lay undermost.

Because they repented not] There is a heart that cannot repent ; that hath lost all passive power of coming out of the snare of the devil ; that is, become such through long trading in sin, as neither ministry, nor misery, nor miracle, nor mercy can possibly mollify, Rom. ii. 5. Upon such you may write, " Lord, have mercy upon them." " Oh !" said a reverend man, " if I must be put to my option, I had rather be in hell with a sensible heart than live on earth with a reprobate mind."

Ver. 21. *Woe unto thee, Chorazin*] These littorals, or those that dwell by the sea-coast, are noted to be *duri, horridi, immanes, omnium denique pessimi,* rough, harsh, thievish, peevish people, and as bad as those that are worst. But that which aggravated these men's sin, and made it out of measure sinful, was the contempt of the gospel : which, as it is *post naufragium tabula,* so " how shall they escape that neglect so great salvation ?" See that ye shift not off him that speaketh from heaven, &c., μὴ παραιτήσησθε, Heb. xii. 25. Jerome tells us that Chorazin was in his time turned into a desert, being two miles distant from Capernaum. As for Bethsaida, our Saviour had therehence taken three of his apostles at least, to be lights of the world, but the inhabitants of this town loved darkness rather than light ; the apostles, their countrymen, could do no good upon them. Our Saviour therefore would not suffer so much as the blind man whom he had cured to be their preacher, but led him to the town's end, and there restoring him to sight, sent him away.

They would have repented long ago] Blind heathens, when any misery was upon them, would to their sackcloth and sorrows, thinking thereby to pacify God, and so they rested. In like sort there are amongst us, that when they are afflicted, especially in conscience, set upon some duty, so to lick themselves whole again, Isa. lviii. 5. They do as crows, that when they are sick give themselves a vomit, by swallowing down some stone, and then they are well. They rest in their repentance : hence Austin saith, " Repentance damneth more than sin."

Ver. 22. *It shall be more tolerable*] Men are therefore the worse, because they ought to be better :[4] and shall be deeper in hell, because heaven was offered unto them, but they would not. *Ingentia beneficia, flagitia, supplicia,* say the Centurists. Good turns aggravate unkindnesses : and men's offences are increased by their obligations. If Turks and Tartars shall be damned, debauched Christians shall be double-damned : because, though they defy not, yet they deny the Lord that bought them ; whilst by their unchristian conversation they tell the world that either there is no such thing as Christ, or if there be, yet that he is but a weak Christ, and that there is no such power in his death, or efficacy in his resurrection, to sanctify those that belong unto him.

---

[1] As *Ossum* for *Os, dolus* for *dolor, floret* for *florebit.*
[2] *Minime tamen dissimulans quod alioqui esset probaturus.* Beza.
[3] *Judicatur, vel sententia pronunciatur.* Camerar. Scultet.
[4] *Ideo deteriores sumus quia meliores esse debemus.* Salvian.

Ver. 23. *Which art exalted unto heaven*] viz. In the abundance of the means of grace, many times called the kingdom of heaven: for as the harvest is potentially in the seed, so is eternal life potentially in the ordinances. God sends up and down the world to offer salvation. Hence that phrase, My salvation is gone forth; hence they that reject the word preached are said to judge themselves "unworthy of everlasting life," Acts xiii. 46; hence, while Israel was without a teaching priest, they are said to have been "without the true God," 2 Chron. xv. 3; hence the Psalmist makes the blessings that come out of Sion to be better than any other that come out of heaven and earth, Psal. cxxxiv. 3.

Shalt be brought down to hell] With a violence, with a vengeance. As Ahasuerus said of Haman, that so much abused his favour, Hang him on the gallows that is 50 cubits high: so shall God say of such, Plunge them into hell much deeper than others, that whiles they were on earth set so light by my grace, though it even kneeled unto them, wooing acceptance, 2 Cor. v. 20.

It would have remained until this day] But God rained down hell from heaven upon them, and turned them into ashes, saith Peter; yea, their fire burnt to hell, saith Jude. 2 Pet. ii. 6; Jude 7. Some footsteps of it are yet to be found in the place, as Josephus relateth (B. J. S.), and something also may be read of it in Tacitus and Solinus. Both St Peter and St Jude say, they were set forth for an example, *Alterius perditio tua sit cautio.* Let their destruction be our instruction; lest heathen Herodotus rise up in judgment against us, who said that the coals and ashes of Troy burnt by the Greeks were purposely set before the eyes of men for an example of this rule, that national and notorious sins bring down national and notorious plagues from a sin-revenging God, τῶν μεγαλων ἀδικημάτων μεγάλαι εἰσι καὶ αἱ τιμωρίαι παρὰ τῷ Θεῷ.

Ver. 24. *It shall be more tolerable*] Infidelity then is, in some respect, a worse sin than sodomy, and a heavier doom abides it. They that suffer least in hell, suffer more than they can either abide or avoid. All they suffer here is but typical of the wrath to come. Here the leaves only fall upon them, as it were, but there the whole trees too. Here they sip of the top of God's cup, there they must drink the dregs, though it be eternity to the bottom. Howbeit Sodom shall suffer less than Capernaum, *mitius punietur Cicero quam Catilina*, saith an ancient, *non quod bonus, sed quod minus malus.* The beast and the false prophet were cast alive into the burning lake (which imports a most direful and dreadful degree of torment[1]), when the rest of the antichristian rabble shall be first slain with the sword (not cast in alive) and then thrown to the infernal vultures, to be torn in pieces as a prey, Rev. xix. 20, 21.

[1] *Dirissimum exitii genus.* Pareus.

Ver. 25. *At that time Jesus answered*] Here to answer is to continue to speak. Albeit if we compare herewith Luke x. 21, it may seem to be spoken in answer to the seventy disciples now returning, and relating what they had said and done in their voyage.

Lætius est quoties magno sibi constat honestum.
(Lucan.)

Ver. 26. *Even so, Father, for so,* &c.] Christ being tired out, as it were, by the untractableness of his hearers, turns him to his Father, and comforts himself with the consideration of his most wise decree and counsel: so must we in like case, accounting that we are a sweet savour unto God howsoever, even in them that perish, and that God shall have his end upon them, though we have not ours, 2 Cor. ii. 15.

Ver. 27. *All things are delivered unto me*] This the world's wizards acknowledge not; hence they stand off. But Christ is the Father's plenipotentiary and privy-counsellor, "unto all that are called, both Jews and Greeks, Christ the power of God, and the wisdom of God," 1 Cor. i. 24, as light as the world makes of him. But the more men see into his worth, the more they will repair to him.

And he to whomsoever the Son will reveal him] *Qui non habet Christum in horoscopo, non habet Deum in medio cœli.*

Ver. 28. *Come unto me*] Why do ye go about, as Jeremiah (xxxi. 22) hath it, and fetch a compass? "Why labour ye for that which satisfieth not?" Isa. lv. 2. "Can the son of Jesse give you vineyards and olive-yards," &c.? as Saul said; so say I, Can the world or the devil do for you as I can? Why come ye not unto me, that ye may be saved? Can you mend yourselves anywhere? &c. But the poor soul is ready to hang her comforts on every hedge, shift and shark in every by-corner for comfort, and never come at Christ with the hemorrhoids, till all be spent, till she be forsaken of her hopes. Men will not desire Christ, till shaken, Hag. ii. 7.

All ye] All is a little word, but of large extent. The promises are indefinite, and exclude none. It is not for us to be interlining God's covenant, and excepting ourselves, how bad soever, if broken-hearted.

That labour] Even to lassitude (κοπιῶντας), but to no purpose, labour in the fire where you can make nothing of your labour.

And are heavy laden] Poised to an inch (πεφορτισμένοι), ready to be weighed down to hell with the turn of a scale, with the dust of a balance superadded. Others might have Christ if they would come to him; but till then none will come. Steep thy thoughts in this sweet sentence, thou burdened soul, and come away to the Master (as they said to blind Bartimeus), for, "behold, he calleth thee."

And I will give you rest] No rest to the weary soul but in Christ (as the dove found no rest till she returned to the ark). It flies from this thing to that, as the bee doth from flower to flower to get honey, as Saul sought his asses from place to place. But as he found them at home after all, so must we find rest and refreshing in Christ, or not at all. Let him that walketh in darkness, and hath no light, "trust in the name of the Lord, and stay upon his God." As for those that will kindle a strange fire, and compass themselves about with the sparks of their own tinderboxes, let them walk while they will in the light of their fire, and in the sparks that they have kindled, but this shall they have of Christ's hand, they shall lie down in sorrow, Isa. l. 10, 11.

Ver. 29. *Take my yoke upon you*] q. d. Though freed by me from the damning and domineering power of sin, you must not think to live as you list.[1] To argue from mercy to liberty is the devil's logic: from mercy to duty is the right reasoning, as Rom. xii. 1. Christians must not be yokeless, aweless, masterless, Belialists, that wander at will as wild asses, or canes, ἀδέσποτοι, but they must yield the obedience of faith, and be adding to their faith virtue, and to virtue knowledge, &c., linking the graces hand in hand as in a dance (so the word signifies, ἐπιχορηγήσατε), 2 Pet. i. 5, 11, so shall they have an entrance ministered unto them further and further into Christ's glorious kingdom.

And learn of me] The Arch-prophet, the Counsellor, that excellent speaker, as he is called in Dan. viii. 13, that came out of the Father's bosom, and hath his Father's will at his fingers' ends. Besides what he taught us by himself and his servants, he hath written for us those excellent things of his law, those lively oracles. He hath also left us, as here, his own practice for a pattern of the rule, and for a complete copy (as St Peter calleth it, ὑπογραμμὸν, 1 Pet. ii. 21), to write after. Pindarus saith of Hiero Syracusanus, that he had cropped off the tops of all virtues;[2] Melancthon, of Frederick the elector of Saxony, that he had picked out the flower of all noble abilities and endowments.[3] The same author proposeth George, Prince of Anhalt, for an example of unparalleled piety, worthy of all men's imitation. Machiavel sets forth Cæsar Borgia (a far worse man) as the only pattern for a prince to express. St Jerome, having read the religious life and death of Hilarion, folding up the book said, Well, Hilarion shall be the champion whom I will imitate. How much rather should we say so of Christ: every of whose actions, whether moral or mediatory, were for our imitation. In his moral actions we should learn of him by doing as he did, 1 Pet. ii. 23. In his mediatory, by translating that he did to our spiritual life, as to die to sin, live to righteousness, &c.

For I am meek and lowly in heart] Lo, here is a piece of Christ's yoke, which he therefore so calleth, because as the yoke maketh the heifer hang down her head and frame to hard labour, so doth humility (the mother of meekness) work in our hearts, Hos. x. 11.[4] Ephraim was a heifer used to dance and delight in soft straw, and could not abide to plough: but the Lord will make him (and all his) both bear and draw, and that from their youth up, Lam. iii. And whereas meekness and lowly-mindedness go coupled here together, we must know that they are *virtutes collectaneæ*, as Bernard calleth them, a pair of twin-sisters, never asunder. Remember, saith Mr Tindal to Mr Frith, that as lowliness of mind shall make you high with God, even so meekness of words shall make you sink into the hearts of men.

And ye shall find rest unto your souls] These Christian virtues have *virtutem pacativam*, they lodge a sweet calm in the heart, freeing it from perturbations and distempers. An humble man saith, Who am I but I may be despised, abused, injured? And that which will break a passionate man's heart, will not break a meek man's sleep.[5]

Ver. 30. *For my yoke is easy*][6] After a man is once used to it a little: he cannot fadge so well with it perhaps at first, because an untamed heifer: but after a while, his commandments will be nothing grievous, "I delight to do thy will, O God," saith David.

And my burden light] Such as you may as easily bear away as Samson did the gates of Gaza; such as you may well run under, as a horse doth without a load, or a hind upon the mountains. It is no more burden than the wings are to the bird, wherewith it flies aloft where it listeth.

CHAPTER XII.

Ver. 1. *Jesus went on the Sabbath day*] St Luke calleth it "the second Sabbath after the first," chap. vi. 1, that is, the second anniversary or solemn feast from the first (δευτερόπρωτον), to wit, from the passover Sabbath, and this was Pentecost.

And his disciples were an hungred] Hereby he hardened and inured them to further and future trials: teaching them also to depend upon God's good providence for their necessary maintenance. The martyrs had their bread made of meal half mixed with saw-dust.

To pluck the ears of corn and to eat] This was their best Sabbath-day's dinner: may not we be glad of mean fare on any day, when our betters fared no better on so high a day? See my common-place of abstinence.

Ver. 2. *Behold, thy disciples do that which is*

---

[1] *In maxima libertate minima licentia.* Salvian.
[2] δρέπων κορυφὰς ἀρετῶν ἀπὸ πασῶν.
[3] *Freder. selegit florem ex omnibus virtutibus.* Scultet. Annal.

[4] ταπεινὸς quasi ἐδαφεινὸς, ab ἔδαφος, terra. *Humilitas, ab humo.*
[5] *Socrates cum in comœdia taxaretur ridebat: Polyagrus vero seipsum strangulabat.* Ælian. 5.
[6] χρηστὸς, useful, opposed to πονηρὸς, painful, tedious.

not lawful] This was as the proverb is, *Sus Minervam*, when blind Pharisees will be teaching Christ how the Sabbath is to be sanctified. Not Hebrews only, but also Greeks and barbarians rested from work on the seventh day: witness Josephus, Clemens Alexander, and Eusebius. Howbeit, to the Hebrews at Mount Sinai, God, for a special favour, made known his holy Sabbath, Neh. ix. 14, commanding them to do no servile work therein, Lev. xxiii. 7, 8. This excludes not works of piety, charity, and necessity, such as was this of the disciples in the text. The Jews in their superstition would not fight on the Sabbath, and therefore lost their chief city to the Romans, under the command of Pompey, who took the advantage of the day to do his utmost then against them.[1] In aftertimes they grew more rigid in this point: for on the Sabbath they would not spit, ease nature, get out of a jakes, if by mishap they had fallen into it, as that Jew of Tewkesbury. This ever was and is the guise of hypocrites, to strain at gnats and swallow camels. Witness our modern Pharisees, the monks and Jesuits, who stumble at straws and leap over mountains. Their schoolmen determined that it was a less crime to kill a thousand men than for a poor man to mend his shoe on the Sabbath-day.[2]

Ver. 3. *But he said unto them*] They had not proved a breach of the Sabbath, neither could they. A breach it had been, had not the disciples been hungry, and he denies it not, but confutes their present cavils by clear syllogisms, one in the neck of another, such as they could not answer, nor abide,[3] and therefore sought to destroy him, ver. 14. See here the lawful use of logic in divinity, and mistake not St Jerome, *Qui syllogizandi artem, applicatam Theologiæ, comparat plagis Ægypti:* understand him of that false sophistry, which the apostle calleth vain philosophy, Col. ii.

David did when he was an hungred] Note here, that our Saviour excuseth David from his necessity, not from his dignity, which in point of sin God regards not; *Potentes potenter torquebuntur.* And yet how many are there who think, that when they have gotten an office, they may oppress at pleasure, swear by authority, drink and swill without control? But height of place ever adds two wings to sin, example and scandal. And ill accidents ever attend such great ones, as, being absolute in power, will be too resolute in will and dissolute in life. Queen Elizabeth said that princes owe a double duty to God. 1. As men. 2. As princes. *Sedes prima et vita ima*, is as unsuitable as for those that are clothed in scarlet to embrace the dunghill, Lam. iv. 5.

Ver. 4. *And did eat the showbread*] The bread of proposition,[4] as the Greek text hath it; the face-bread, as the Septuagint call it; or

that which was daily set before the Lord, to in-mind him, as it were, of the twelve tribes by those twelve loaves; and to teach us to labour every day in the week (and not on the Sabbath only) for the bread that endureth to everlasting life; which the Son of man will give to every hungry David, John vi. 27.

Ver. 5. *Profane the Sabbath*] As ye count profaning of it: or they profane it by divine dispensation, whiles they do servile works in slaying sacrifices, and other things tending to the service of God, such as is now the ringing of the sermon-bell amongst us, as amongst the Protestants in France the letting off of a harquebus or pistolet, whereby they congregate.

Ver. 6. *But I say unto you*] q. d. Whereas you will here object, that that was done in the temple; I tell you I am greater than the temple: for in me the Godhead dwelleth bodily, Col. i. 19; as in the temple was the ark, where the glory of God appeared, so that it filled the temple sometimes. Take notice here, by the way, how good it is to have some grave and godly man to be a beholder and judge of our actions, to whom we may approve them, whatever other ill-affected think of them—*Equitem mihi plaudere curo*, saith the heathen poet. And Libanius (though an atheist) could say, Βασιλείου μὲ ἐπαινήσαντος κατὰ πάντων ἔχω τὰ νικητήρια (*ad* Basil). If Basil commend me, I care not what all others say of me. Christ's white stone will comfort a Christian against the black coals of the world's censures. If Demetrius have a good report of the truth, and such an one as St John to bear record for him, he need not care though Diotrephes prate as fast against them both with malicious words, 3 John 10, 12, as the Pharisees did here against the disciples, when Christ defended them.

Ver. 7. *But if ye had known*] And it was a foul shame for them not to know. "Who is blind as my servant?" &c., Isa. xlii. 19. Varro justly upbraided the Roman priests, that there were many matters in their own rites and religions that they understand not.[5] What kind of men they were, Tully (2, *de Finib.*) gives us to know in these words of his, *Ut majores nostri Cincinnatum illum ab aratro abduxerunt, ut Dictator esset, sic vos de Pelasgis omnibus colligitis bonos illos quidem viros, sed certe non pereruditos,* good honest men, but not guilty of much learning.

I will have mercy, and not sacrifice] q. d. I prefer the marrow and pith of the second table before the ceremony and surface of the first. See the notes on chap. ix. 14.

Ye would not have condemned the guiltless] Ignorance is the mother of misprision: the wisdom from above is without judging, Jam. iii. 17. And as any man is more wise, he is more sparing of his censures. Zanchy wonders that Lutherans,

---

[1] *Romani quoties dies hujusmodi rediissent fortissime percutiebant.*

[2] *Levius esse crimen mille homines jugulare, quam semel die Dominico pauperi calceum consuere.* Pareus in loc.

[3] *Manifestis syllogismis adversarios redarguit.* Gualt.

[4] ἄρτους προθέσεως, ἐνωπίους προκειμένους.

[5] Aug. Civit. Dei, iv. 1.

who profess to eat Christ corporally, should censure so bitterly.[1]

Ver. 8. *The Son of man is Lord of the Sabbath*] q. d. Say they were not innocent, yet have you no cause to condemn them for Sabbath-breach; sith I am Lord of the Sabbath, and may do with mine own as to me seems best. True it is that Christ hates sin by nature, not by precept only; and therefore cannot dispense with the breach of his own laws, those that be moral in themselves, such as are all the ten, but the fourth. The fourth commandment is moral, not by nature, but by precept, saith one, and so the Lord of the Sabbath may dispense with the literal breach of the Sabbath.

Ver. 9. *He went into their synagogue*] These were chapels of ease to the temple, of ancient use, Acts xv. 21, and Divine authority, Psal. lxxiv. 8. This here is called the Pharisees' synagogue, because they did *Dominari in concionibus*, Rom. ii. 19, 20, and are for their skill called princes, 1 Cor. ii. 8.

Ver. 10. *Which had his hand withered*] So have all covetous caitiffs, who may well be said, amidst all their hoards, to have no current coin, no quick-silver. They sit abroad upon what they have got, as Euclio in the Comedian: and when, by laying out their money, they might " lay hold on eternal life," they will not be drawn to it. But as Alphonsus, king of Spain, when he stood to be king of the Romans, was prevented of his hopes, because he, being a great mathematician, was drawing lines (saith the chronicler) when he should have drawn out his purse; so here.

Ver. 11. *What man shall there be, &c.*] If a sheep slipped into a slough must be relieved, how much more Christ's reasonable sheep, all which bear golden fleeces, and everything about whom is good either *ad esum*, or *ad usum?*

Ver. 12. *It is lawful to do well*] Nay, it is needful, sith not to do well is to do ill, and not to save a life, or a soul, is to destroy it, Mark iii. 4. Not to do justice is injustice, and not to show mercy is no better than cruelty, *non faciendo nocens, sed patiendo fuit.* Aul. de Claud.

Ver. 13. *And he stretched it forth*] So would our hold-fasts stretch out their hands to the poor, would they but come to Christ, and hear his voice, as this man did. But till then they will as easily part with their blood as with their good. All their strife is, who (like the toad) shall fall asleep with most earth in his paws: as when they die, nothing grieves them more than that they must leave that which they have so dearly loved whilst alive. I read of one wretch, who being at point of death, clapped a piece of gold in his own mouth, and said, Some wiser than some, I mean to have this with me howsoever.

Ver. 14. *How they might destroy him*] All envy is bloody. Men wish him out of the world whom they cannot abide; and would rather the sun should be extinguished than their candle obscured. David durst never trust Saul's pro-

testations, because he knew him to be an envious person. Nero put Traseas to death for no other cause but for that it was not expedient for Nero that so worthy a man as he should live by him.

Ver. 15. *Great multitudes followed him*] Maugre the malice of earth and hell. They lose their labour that seek to quell Christ, and subvert his kingdom: "Yet have I set my king upon mine holy hill of Sion," Psal. ii. 6. "The kingdom of heaven suffereth violence," Matt. ii. 12. Or (as Melancthon rendereth that text), *Vi erumpit, procedit, enititur : vi scilicet spirituali, ut sol enititur per nubes : ergo irriti hostium conatus.* It bursts through all, βιάζεται.

Ver. 16. *That they should not make him known*] This, his ambitious kinsmen, who sought to get credit and glory among men by his worthy works, upbraid him with, John vii. 4; "If thou do these things, show thyself to the world," say they; and so proclaim that they believed not in him, John vii. 7, with v. 44, xii. 43.

Ver. 17. *That it might be fulfilled*] The Old Testament is the New foretold; the New Testament is the Old fulfilled. Ezekiel saw a wheel within a wheel. This is, saith Bonaventure, the one Testament in the other.

Ver. 18. *Behold my servant*] My servant the Messias, as the Chaldee Paraphrast renders and expounds it. The Septuagint somewhat obscure the text by adding to it, "Behold my servant Jacob, and mine elect Israel." They are said to have translated against their wills; no wonder then they deal not so faithfully. Sure it is, that they have perverted sundry clear prophecies concerning Christ; as this for instance; which therefore our evangelist and the rest of the apostles allege not out of their translation but out of the Hebrew verity. The Latins drink of the puddles, the Greeks of the rivers, but the Hebrews of the fountains, said Johan. Reuchlin.

Whom I have chosen, my beloved, &c.] *Ecce electum, dilectum.* The Latins have a proverb, *Deligas quem diligas.* Choose for thy love, and then love for thy choice. God hath also chosen us in the Beloved, Ephes. i. 6, that we should be the beloved of his soul, or as the Septuagint there emphatically render it, "his beloved soul," Jer. xii. 7; ἔδωκα τὴν ἠγαπημένην ψυχὴν μου, *Dilectam animam meam*, Vulg.

And he shall show judgment] That is the doctrine of the gospel (whereby is conveyed into the heart that spirit of judgment and of burning (Isa. iv. 4), or the sweet effect of it, true grace, which is called judgment, a little below, ver. 20.

Ver. 19. *He shall not strive*] To bear away the bell from others.

Nor cry] "Nor lift up his voice," saith the prophet, as loth to lie hid, and therefore making an "O yes," as desirous of vain-glory and popular applause. *Laudes nec curat, nec quærit humanas.* He despiseth it as a little stinking breath, or the slavering of men's lips which he disdains to suck in.

---

[1] *Mirabar qui fieret, ut hoc hominum genus qui corpus*

Christi tam mitis modesti atque humani oraliter comedunt, &c.

Ver. 20. *A bruised reed shall he not break*] A reed shaken with the wind is taken for a thing very contemptible at the best, how much more when bruised, Matt. xi. 7. The wick of a candle is little worth; and yet less when it smokes, as yielding neither light nor heat, but only stench and annoyance. This men bear not with, but tread out: so doth not Christ, who yet hath a sharp nose, a singular sagacity, and soon resents our provocations. He hath also feet like burning brass to tread down all them that wickedly depart from his statutes, Psal. cxix. 118. But so do not any of his, and therefore he receiveth and cherisheth with much sweetness, not the strong oaks only of his people, but the bruised reeds too; nor the bright torches only, but the smoking wick: he despiseth not the day of small things. Smoke is of the same nature with flame;[1] for what else is flame, but smoke set on fire? So, a little grace may be true grace, as the filings of gold are as good gold (though nothing so much of it) as the whole wedge. The least spark of fire, if cherished, will endeavour to rise above the air, as well as the greatest; so the least degree of grace will be aspiring to more. Now those very pantings, inquietations, and unsatisfiableness, cannot but spring from truth of grace, which Christ makes high account of. That is a sweet saying of Brentius, *Etiamsi fides tua, &c.* Albeit thy faith be so small that it neither yields light to others, nor heat to thine own heart, yet Christ will not reject thee, *Modo incrementum ores;* so be it thou pray for more faith.

Till he bring forth] Gr. Thrust forth with violence (ἕως ἂν ἐκβάλη, Heb. xii. 3), the devil and the world in vain opposing the work of grace (called here judgment), which shall surely be perfected. He that is author, the same will be finisher of our faith; he doth not use to do his work to the halves, *non est ejusdem invenire et perficere*, we say. But that rule holds not here.

Ver. 21. *Shall the Gentiles trust*] This trust is here put for the whole service of God, it being the least, and yet the best we can render to him. And the more we know of his name, the more we shall trust in him, Psal. ix. 10.

Ver. 22. *One possessed with a devil, blind and dumb*] A heavy case, and yet that may be any man's case.[2] *Cuivis potest contingere, quod cuiquam potest.* Every one that seeth another stricken, and himself spared, is to keep a passover for himself; and to say, " Thou hast punished me less than my sins have merited," Ezra ix. 13. The devil had shut up from this man all passages to faith, saith Theophylact, by bereaving him of the use of his eyes, ears, and tongue. See a mercy in the use of our senses, &c. *Multo plures sunt gratiæ privativæ quam positivæ*, saith Gerson.

Ver. 23. *And all the people were amazed*] Admiration bred philosophy, saith the heathen. It bred superstition, saith the Scripture, when the world went wondering after the beast.[3] We may say, too, that it bred piety in this people, and still we see the word never works kindly, till men hear and admire it. Let others censure with the Pharisees; let us wonder with the multitude.

Ver. 24. *This fellow doth not cast out devils, &c.*] The devil that was cast out of the demoniac's body seems to have got into these men's hearts. But he was not his crafts-master: for what a senseless slander hear we? He should have arted it a little better, to have been believed. *Tenue mendacium pellucet*, saith Tacitus. This was such a lie as might be easily looked through. But envy never regards how true, but how mischievous. Witness the Popish Pharisees, who tell the poor misled and muzzled people in their sermons that the Protestants are blasphemers of God and all his saints; that the English are grown barbarous, and eat young children; that ever since the pope excommunicated us we are as black as devils; that the powder-treason was plotted, and should have been acted, by the Puritans; that the fall of Blackfriars in London likewise was wrought by the Puritans, who had loosened the rafters, &c.[4] That these are the opinions we hold and teach: 1. To worship no God. 2. To frame our religion to the times. 3. To account gain godliness. 4. To pretend public liberty to our private lusts. 5. To break our oaths, when it makes for our advantage. 6. To cover hatred with flattery. 7. To confirm tyranny with bloodshed, &c. These and the like, that Cacodæmon Joannes, the black-mouthed Jesuit, tells the world in print are our tenets and practices. Now " the Lord rebuke thee, Satan." But what reward shall be given to thee, thou false tongue? Even sharp arrows, with hot burning coals; yea, those very coals of hell from whence thou wert enkindled.

Ver. 25. *And Jesus knew their thoughts*] That they blasphemed in this sort, out of the devilish venom of their hearts fully possessed by Satan, who drew them into this unpardonable sin, which himself every day, nay, every moment, committeth. As one that had fallen into that sin, wished that his wife and children and all the world might be damned together with him; so doth the devil, out of his deep and desperate malice to mankind, draw some into this sin, that he may drown them in the same destruction with himself.

And said unto them] He could, as he did oft no doubt, have answered them with silence or punished them with contempt, committing his cause to him that judgeth righteously. He could have turned them off, as one did his railing adversary, with *Tu linguæ, ego aurium Dominus.* (Tacitus, Seneca.) But, inasmuch as God's glory was highly concerned, and his cause might have suffered if this cursed calumny had not been confuted. Our Saviour makes a most grave apology in the behalf of his doctrine and mira-

---

[1] τυφόμενον. *Sep.* καπνιζόμενον. *Heb.* בהם *Caligans, obscure lucens.*

[2] πᾶν προσδοκᾳν δεῖ ἄνθρωπον ὄντα. *Xenophon.*

[3] *Admiratio peperit philosophiam.* Rev. xiii. 3.

[4] *Ex dissolutis per Puritanos contignationibus*, &c. D. Prid. *Lect.*

cles, which he maintains and makes good by many demonstrative arguments.

Every kingdom divided against itself] *Divide et impera*, saith Machiavel. Make division and get dominion. Every subdivision, saith another, is a strong weapon in the hand of the adverse party. " Where strife is " (saith James, iii. 16) "there is confusion ; " as Castor and Pollux, if they appear not together, it presageth a storm. *Si collidimur frangimur*, If we clash we cleave, said the two earthen pots in the fable, that were swimming down the stream together. The daughter of division is dissolution, saith Nazianzen.[1] This the Jesuits know, and therefore do what they can to keep up the contentions between the Lutherans and the Calvinists. This the Turks know, and therefore pray to God to keep the Christians at variance. Discord was the destruction of our ancestors, as Tacitus testifieth, who was here in this island with his father-in-law Agricola, and saw it. And the Lord Rich in his speech to the Justices of England, in Edward VI.'s reign, could say, Never foreign power could yet hurt, or in any part prevail in this realm, but by disobedience and disorder in themselves. That is the way wherewith God will plague us, if he mind to punish us. And so long as we do agree among ourselves and be obedient to our prince, and to his godly orders, we may be sure that God is with us, and that foreign power shall not prevail against us, nor hurt us.

Ver. 26. He is divided against himself] But so he is not. There is a marvellous accordance even betwixt evil spirits. *Squamæ Leviathan ita cohærent, ut earum opere textili densato quasi loricatus incedat Satan et cataphractus*, as Luther elegantly and truly phraseth it. The devils in the possessed person were many, yet they say, " My name " (not our name) "is Legion." Though many, they speak and act as one in the possession. That kingdom, we see, is not divided.

Ver. 27. By whom do your children, &c.] That is, your countrymen. Not the disciples (as Augustine, *Civ. Dei*, and other ancients would have it), but the Jewish exorcists, of whom see Mark ix. 38 ; Acts xix. 9. As if our Saviour should have said, Unless that be a blemish in me that you hold to be a beauty in others, why should you condemn me for a conjurer ? Why doth your malice thus wilfully cross your consciences ? Certain it is, saith Erasmus, that the selfsame things are condemned as heretical in Luther's books, that in Augustine and Bernard's works are read and regarded as pious and orthodox sentences.[2] So these passages were gathered as heresies out of Tindal's works. He is not a sinner in the sight of God that would be no sinner. He that would be delivered, hath his heart loose already. It is impossible that the word of the cross should be without affliction and persecution. The gospel is written for all

persons and estates, prince, duke, pope, emperor. We cannot be without motions of evil desires, but we must mortify them in resisting them. God made us his children and heirs while we were his enemies, and before we knew him. Men should see that their children come to church to hear the sermon, &c. Were not these perilous heresies ?[3] Saith not the Scripture the same in sundry places ? Is not this to have the glorious faith of our Lord Jesus Christ in respect of persons ? James ii. 1. So the greatest errors that Henry Voes and John Esch, martyrs, were accused of, were, that men ought to trust only in God ; forsomuch as men are liars, and deceitful in all their words and deeds ; and therefore there ought no trust or affiance to be put in them.

Ver. 28. Then the kingdom of God is come unto you] A certain sign of the setting up whereof among you, is this casting out of devils " by the Spirit of God ; " or as Luke hath it, " by the finger of God ; " for the Holy Ghost is the essential power of the Father and the Son.

Ver. 29. A strong man's house, &c.] The devil is strong, but overpowered by Christ. He hath forcibly delivered us from the power of darkness, snatched us out of the Devil's danger, (ἐῤῥύσατο, Col. i. 13) ; so that, though he shake his chain at us, he cannot fasten his fangs in us. Stronger is he that is in the saints, than he that is in the world. Through Christ we shall overcome him, Rom. viii. 37.

Ver. 30. He that is not with me, is against me] " But the devil is not with me," saith Christ, " for all I do or suffer is to destroy his works." Let this sentence also be noted against neuters and Nicodemites, who stand halting betwixt two, and will be sure to hold themselves on the warm side of the hedge howsoever. Such were of old the Samaritans, Nazarites, Ebionites, and those Corinthians that would neither " be of Paul, nor Apollos, nor Cephas, but of Christ," 1 Cor. i. 12 ; that is, as some neuters say now-a-days, they are neither Cavaliers nor Roundheads, but good Protestants ; others are neither Papists nor Protestants, but Christians, that is, just nothing, Atheists. Christ hates neutrality, and counts it enmity ; he loathes lukewarmness, accepts not of any excuse in that case, Judges v. 16, 17 ; Dan and Ephraim are passed by in the reckoning up of the tribes, Rev. vii., as if they were soldiers put out of pay, and cut out of the rolls. So are all testable indifferents, out of God's book of remembrance, Mal. iii. 17.

Ver. 31. All manner of sin and blasphemy, &c.] All without exception, yea, though it be blasphemy, Isa. xliv. 22. God blots out the thick cloud as well as the cloud, enormities as well as infirmities. Man cannot commit more than he can and will remit to the penitent. The sun by his force can scatter the greatest mist, as well as the least vapour ; and the sea by its vastness

[1] *Omne divisibile est corruptibile ait philosophus*, Camer. *Medit. Histor.* cent. 2. cap. 23.

[2] *Compertum est damnata ut hæretica in libris Lutheri, &c.*

Eras. *Epist. ad Cardinal. Moguntin.*

[3] *Novum crimen C. Cæsar, et antehoc tempus inauditum,* Cic. *pro Ligar.*

drown mountains as well as mole-hills. The grace of our Lord "abounds to flowing over," saith St Paul, ὑπερεπλεόνασε, 1 Tim. i. 24. "The blood of Jesus Christ cleanseth us from all sin," saith St John (i. 7). *Ego admisi, unde tu damnare potes me, sed non amisisti unde tu salvare potes me*, saith Augustine. And yet Novatus, the proud heretic, denied possibility of pardon to them that had any whit fallen off in times of persecution, though they rose again by repentance. But God's thoughts of mercy are not as man's, Isa. lv. 8, he can and will pardon such sins as no god or man can do besides, Micah vii. 18. "Who is a God like unto thee?" For what? "That pardoneth all sorts of sin," &c. This none can believe without supernatural grace. We are ready to measure God by our model.

But the blasphemy against the Holy Ghost, &c.] This is nothing else, saith John Diazius, to that butcher his brother, *quam agnitam veritatem flagitiose insectari*, a malicious persecuting of the known truth. A sin it is of malice after strong conviction, expressed in words by a tongue set on fire by hell, and in actions coming from a venomous spirit, and tending to opposition and bitter persecution, if their malice be not greater than their power. This was committed by Saul, Julian, Latomus of Lovain,[1] Rockwood, a chief persecutor at Calice in Henry VIII.'s days, who, to his last breath, staring and raging, cried that he was utterly damned, for that he had sought maliciously the deaths of a number of the honestest men in the town &c. Stephen Gardiner said as much also in effect to himself, when he lay on his death-bed, and so both stinkingly and unrepentantly died, saith Mr Fox.

Ver. 32. *And whosoever speaketh a word, &c.*] As Peter did through infirmity, Paul through ignorance; those poor souls whom he haled to prison, and for fear of death compelled them to blaspheme Christ, Acts xxvi. 11. Tertullian reports the like of Claudius Herminianus, a persecutor in Cappadocia, *quod tormentu quosdam a proposito suo excidere fecerat*, that for spite that his own wife was turned Christian, he forced many, by tormenting them, to reneague Christ. Pliny writes also to Trajan, the emperor, that where he was governor there came to his hands a book, containing the names of many that for fear of death professed themselves to be no Christians. And when, saith he, they had at my command called upon the gods, offered incense to the emperor's image, and cursed Christ (which those that are Christians indeed will never be drawn to do), I thought good to dismiss them.[2]

But whosoever speaketh against the Holy Ghost] Not his person or essence (for many Sabellian, Eunomian, Macedonian heretics did so of old, and repenting found mercy), but his grace and special operation, by the which God comes nearer to man than he is in nature or person. This sin is against the immediate effects, work, and office of the Holy Ghost, against that shining light kindled by God's Spirit in man's soul, and that sweetness and comfort felt in Christ, that taste of the good word of God, and of the powers of the world to come, Heb. vi. 4—6.

It shall not be forgiven him, &c.] And why? Not because it is greater than God's mercy, or Christ's merits; but first by a just judgment of God upon such sinners, for their hateful unthankfulness in despising his Spirit; whence follows an impossibility of repentance, Heb. vi. 6, and so of remission, Luke xiii. 3. Secondly, such a desperate fury invadeth these men, that they maliciously resist and repudiate the price of repentance, Acts v. 31, and the matter of remission, 1 John i. 7, viz. the precious blood of Jesus Christ, whereby if they might have mercy, yet they would not, but continue raving and raging against both physic and physician, to their unavoidable ruth and ruin. How bold therefore is Bellarmine, who interpreteth this text of the difficulty and rarity only of remission, and not of an utter impossibility.

Ver. 33. *Either make the tree good, &c.*] q. d. Your blasphemy is therefore irremissible, because it is the fruit of so base a root of bitterness, as the desperate malice of your hearts, wilfully crossing your consciences; a wretched despising and despiting of God, and the work of his Spirit, out of revenge, Heb. x. 29. Draw not therefore a fair glove over so foul a hand, but show yourselves in your own colours.

Ver. 34. *How can ye, being evil, &c.*] The stream riseth not above the fountain; the bell is known of what metal by the clapper; what is in the well will be in the bucket; what in the warehouse will be in the shop; so what is in the heart will be in the mouth.[3]

*Æra puto nosci tinnitu; pectora verbis :
Sic est ; namque id sunt utraque, quale sonant.*

Ver. 35. *Out of the good treasure, &c.*] Out of his habit of heavenly-mindedness, out of that law of grace in his heart, "his mouth speaketh wisdom, and his tongue talks of judgment," Psal. xxxvii. 30, 31. Works not done from a principle of life within are dead works, saith the author to the Hebrews, be they for the matter never so good and praiseworthy. This moved Luther to say that good works make not men good; but good we must be first ere good can be done by us.[4] This moved Austin to say that *Omnis vita infidelium peccatum est*, the whole life of an unbeliever is sin, though Spira, the popish postiller, censure that saying for a cruel sentence; *crudelis est illa sententia*.

An evil man out of the evil treasure, &c.] Carnal hearts are stews of unclean thoughts, shambles of cruel and bloody thoughts, exchanges

---

[1] *Latomus confessus est inter horrendos mugitus, se contra conscientiam adversatum esse veritati.* Melancth.

[2] *Cum, præeunte me, Deos appellarent et imagini tuæ, thure ac vino supplicarent, præterea maledicerent Christo, &c.*

[3] *Qualia sunt principia, talia et principiata.*

[4] *Bona opera non faciunt bonos, sed prius oportet bonos esse quam faciamus bona.* Luther.

and shops of vain thoughts, a very forge and mint of false, politic, undermining thoughts, yea, oft a little hell of confused and black imaginations, as one well describeth them.

Ver. 36. *That every idle word, &c.*] Idle and waste words are to be accounted for ; what then evil and wicked ? Therefore " let thine own words grieve thee," as David somewhere hath it, thy frivolous and fruitless speeches ; for among a thousand talents of common communication (saith Cassiodore), a man can scarce find a hundred pence of spiritual speeches, *imo nec decem quidem obolos*, nay, not ten half-pence truly. It may be observed, saith another, that when men get into idle company (which, perhaps, they like not), the very compliment of discoursing extracteth idle if not evil speaking, to fill up the time. Plato and Xenophon thought it fit and profitable that men's speeches at meals and such like meetings should be written. And if Christians should so do, what kind of books would they be ?

Ver. 37. *For by thy words thou shalt be justified*] Our Saviour insists upon this subject because by words they had sinned against the Holy Ghost. A man's most and worst sins be his words. St Paul, making the anatomy of a natural man, stands more on the organ of speech than all the other members, Rom. iii. St James saith, " that the tongue is " not a city or country, but "a world of iniquity," James iii. 6. It can run all the world over, and bite at everybody, when the devil fires it especially. Peraldus (tom. i. 264) reckons up four-and-twenty several sins of the tongue : he might have made them more. God hath set a double hedge before it, of teeth and lips, to keep it up ; he hath also placed it between the head and the heart that it might take counsel of both. Children he will not suffer to speak till they have understanding and wit ; and those that are deaf are also dumb, because they cannot hear instruction, nor learn wisdom, that they may speak advisedly.

Ver. 38. *Then certain of the scribes and Pharisees*] Had not these, as one said of Nero, *os ferreum, cor plumbeum*, an iron face, a leaden heart, that could call for a sign after so many signs ? But it is a sign from heaven they would have (as Moses called for manna from thence, Samuel for rain, Elijah for fire, &c.), and much the nearer they would have been about our Saviour have gratified them. But he never meant it. They were now so clearly convinced of their blasphemy that they had nothing to say for themselves, but fawningly to call him Master, whom before they had called Beelzebub ; and to pretend themselves to be willing to learn, if they might see a sign. They could not see wood for trees, as they say. And who so blind as he that will not see ? *Sic fit, ubi homines majorem vitæ partem in tenebris agunt, ut novissime solem quasi supervacuum fastidiant*, saith Seneca. Men that have lived long in the dark may think the sun superfluous.

Ver. 39. *An evil and adulterous generation,*

&c.] *Spuria soboles*, a bastardly brood. So he calleth them, because utterly degenerate from their forefathers' faith and holiness.

Seeking after a sign] ἐπιζητεῖ, *summo studio efflagitat*. Seeking with utmost earnestness, as if it were such a business as must be done or they were undone. It is the guise of hypocrites to be hot in a cold matter, to show great zeal in trifles, neglecting the main meanwhile.

But the sign of the prophet Jonas] Nor that neither, but for a further mischief to them ; as their fathers had quails to choke them, a king to vex them, &c., and as Ahaz had a sign, whether he would or no, to render him the more inexcusable. *Deus sæpe dat iratus, quod negat propitius.* God gives his enemies some giftless gifts (ἄδωρα δῶρα, Soph.), as Saul gave Michal to David, to be a snare to him ; or as Christ gave Judas the bag, to discover the rottenness of his heart.

Ver. 40. *For as Jonas was three days, &c.*] In the history of Jonas, Christ found the mystery of his death, burial, and resurrection ; teaching us thereby to search the Scriptures—to search them to the bottom ; as those that dig for gold content not themselves with the first or second ore that offers itself, but search on till they have all. This we should the rather do, because we need neither climb up to heaven with these Pharisees nor descend into the deep with Jonas, sith " the word is nigh thee, even in thy mouth, and in thine heart," &c. Rom. x. 7, 8.

So shall the Son of man be three days, &c.] Taking a part for the whole. So Esther fasted three days and three nights, chap. iv. 16, and yet on the third day she went to the king, chap. v. 1. So, then, the fast lasted not three whole days and nights, but two nights, one full day, and two pieces of days.

Ver. 41. *They repented at the preaching of Jonas*] At one single sermon of a mere stranger, who sang so doleful a ditty to them as the destruction of their town, and yet they repented. What will become of us ? *Væ torpori nostro.* If Mr Bradford so complained of his own unprofitableness under means, in those dim days, what cause have we now much more! Here in London, saith he, be such godly, goodly, and learned sermons, which these uncircumcised ears of mine do hear, at the least thrice a week, which were able to burst any man's heart to relent, to repent, to believe, to love and fear that omnipotent gracious Lord. But mine adamantine, obstinate, most unkind, unthankful heart, hearing my Lord so sweetly calling and crying unto me, now by his law, now by his gospel, now by all his creatures, to come, to come even to himself ; I hide me with Adam ; I play not only Samuel running to Eli, but I play Jonas running to the sea, and there I sleep upon the hatches until he please to raise up a tempest, to turn and look upon me as he did upon Peter, &c.

Ver. 42. *The queen of the south, &c.*] The Ethiopian chronicles call her Mackeda, and further tell us that she had a son by Solomon, whom she named David. Sure it is that she came from a far country to hear Solomon, and was so taken with his wisdom that she could have been content to have changed her throne for his footstool. Now our Saviour took it ill (and well he might) that men came not as far, and set not as high a price upon him and his doctrine as she did upon Solomon and his wisdom, how much more that these hard-hearted Jews esteemed it not though brought home to their doors!

Ver. 43. *When the unclean spirit*] Unclean the devil is called: 1. *Affectione* (saith Jacobus de Voragine), because he loveth uncleanness. 2. *Persuasione*, because he persuades men to it. 3. *Habitatione*, because he inhabits unclean hearts; he finds them foul, he makes them worse. Wheresoever the Great Turk sets his foot once, no grass grows, they say, ever after. Sure it is no grace grows where the devil dwells. *Pura Deus mens est*, saith one. And religion loves to lie clean, saith another. The Holy Spirit will be content to dwell in a poor but it must be a pure house. The devil, on the contrary, delights in spiritual sluttishness. Harpy-like, he defileth all he toucheth; and camel-like, drinks not of that water that he hath not first fouled with his feet.

Is gone out of a man] In regard of inward illumination and outward reformation, 2 Pet. ii. 20; such as was found in Bishop Bonner, that breathing devil, who at first seemed to be a good man, a favourer of Luther's doctrines, a hater of Popery, and was therefore advanced by the Lord Cromwell; to whom he thus wrote in a certain letter: "Stephen Gardiner, for malice and disdain, may be compared to the devil in hell, not giving place to him in pride at all. I mislike in him, that there is so great familiarity and acquaintance, yea, and such mutual confidence, between him and M., as naughty a fellow, and as very a Papist, as any that I know, where he dare express it." Who can deny but that the devil was gone out of this man, for a time at least?

He walketh through dry places] Here the proverb holds true, *Anima sicca sapientissima*, sensual hearts are the fennish grounds that breed filthy venomous creatures. Job xl. 21, Behemoth lieth in the fens. This, Gulielmus Parisiensis applieth to the devil in sensual hearts.[1] Contrariwise, the spirits of God's saints, which burn with faith, hope, and charity, and have all evil humours dried up in them by that spirit of judgment and of burning, these the devil likes not. The tempter findeth nothing in them, though he seek it diligently. He striketh fire, but this tinder takes not. Cupid complained he could never fasten upon the Muses, because he could never find them idle. So here. Or thus, "he walketh through dry places;" *i. e.* he is discontented and restless (see the like, Jer. xvii. 5, 6), for otherwise dry and wet is all one with him.

Ver. 44. *He findeth it empty*] That is, idle

and secure, swept of grace, garnished with vice, the devil's fairest furniture. *Otia dant vitia.*

Ver. 45. *And taketh seven other spirits*] As the jailor lays more load of irons on him that had escaped his hands, and is now recovered.

And they enter in and dwell there] So they never do in a heart once truly sanctified. Lust was but a stranger to David (no home-dweller), as Peter Martyr observes out of that passage in Nathan's parable, 2 Sam. xii. 4, "And there came a traveller to the rich man," &c. Faith leaves never a slut's corner, Acts xv. 9.

And the last state of that man is worse] An apostate cannot choose unto himself a worse condition. It is with such, as in that case, Lev. xiii. 18—20. If a man had a boil healed, and it afterwards broke out, it proved the plague of leprosy. These are called forsakers of the covenant, Dan. xi. 30, and wicked doers against the covenant, ver. 32. Renegade Christians prove the most desperate devotees to the devil. We see by experience, that none are worse than those that have been good and are naught; or those that might be good, and will be naught. Such as were these Jews in the text, to whom therefore our Saviour applies the parable in these words.

Even so shall it be also unto this wicked generation] Their sins were not common sins (but as those of Korah and his accomplices), therefore they died not common deaths. As they pleased not God, but were contrary to all men, so wrath came upon them to the uttermost, 1 Thess. ii. 16, as Josephus witnesseth. And Mr Fox relates of Bonner, that wicked apostate, that as he wretchedly died in his blind Popery (after he had been long time prisoner in the reign of Queen Elizabeth), so, as stinkingly and blindly at midnight was he brought out, and buried in the outside of all the city, among thieves and murderers. A place, saith he, right convenient, with confusion and derision both of men and children, who, trampling upon his grave, well declared how he was hated both of God and man.

Ver. 46. *Desiring to speak with him*] Either out of curiosity or ambition, as Ambrose thinks; certain it is, at a most unseasonable time. Now as fish and flesh, so everything else is naught out of season.

Ver. 47. *Behold, thy mother and thy brethren*] This was a weakness in his mother; though otherwise full of grace, yet not without original sin, as the Sorbonists contend, but had need of a Saviour, as well as others, Luke i. 47. Scipio permits not a wise man so to do amiss once in his whole life, as to say, *non putaram*. How much better Crates, the philosopher,[2] who said that in every pomegranate there is at least one rotten kernel to be found; intimating thereby, that the best have their blemishes, their faults and follies.

Ver. 48. *Who is my mother, and who*, &c.]

[1] *In locis dormit humentibus, hoc est, in omnibus deliciis madentibus.*

[2] *Omnibus malis punicis inest granum putre.*

This meekest lamb was stirred with a holy indignation at so absurd an interruption, and sharps him up that delivers the message. Great is the honour that is due to a mother. Solomon set Bathsheba at his right hand, and promised her anything with reason. *Nescitne Antipater unicam matris lacrimulam omnes istius criminationes posse delere?* Knows not Antipater that one tear of my mother's can easily blot out all his accusations against her? said Alexander the Great. Brethren also, or near allies (as these were to our Saviour), are dearly to be respected, and greatly gratified, as were Joseph's brethren by him in his greatness. But when these relations, or their requests, come in competition with God's work or glory, they must be neglected, nay, rejected and abominated. For is there any friend to God? or any foe like him? Men be they pleased or displeased, he must be obeyed, and his business despatched, be the contrary occasions never so urgent in show, the pretences never so specious and plausible.

Ver. 49. *Behold my mother and my brethren*] *Sanctior est copula cordis quam corporis.* Spiritual kindred is better than carnal: "there is a friend that sticketh closer than a brother," Prov. xviii. 24. Christ is endeared to his in all manner of nearest relations and engagements. Oh, then, the dignity and safety of a saint! and oh, the danger and disaster of such as either by hand or tongue malign or molest them! What! will they wrong Christ's mother to his face? Will they force the queen also in the house? Esth. vii. 8. If Jacob's sons were so avenged for the indignity done to their sister Dinah, if Absalom for Tamar, what will Christ do, or rather what will he not do, for his dearest relations? How will this greater than Solomon arise off his throne, at the last day, to meet his mother halfway, and to do her all the honour that may be in that great amphitheatre! 1 Kings ii. 1. How sweetly will he accost his brethren that have been long absent from him in the flesh, though present ever in spirit, with Δεῦτε, "Come, ye blessed," &c., *q. d.*, where have you been all this while? They also shall be bold to say to him, as Ruth did to Boaz, Ruth iii. 9, Spread thy skirt over us, for thou art our near kinsman, or, one that hath good right to redeem.

Ver. 50. *For whosoever shall do the will*] Lo, here is the right way of becoming akin to Christ; and can we better prefer ourselves? It was an honour to Mark, that he was Barnabas's sister's son. David durst not in modesty think of being son-in-law to a king. Elymas the sorcerer affected to be held allied to Christ, and therefore styled himself Barjesus: as Darius, in his proud embassy to Alexander, called himself king of kings, and cousin to the gods. But the right way to be ennobled indeed, and inrighted to Christ and his kingdom, is, to believe in his name, and obey his will. This, this is to become Christ's brother, and sister,

and mother. Sister is named, to show that no sex is excluded. And mother last mentioned, that the prerogative of the flesh may be set aside and disacknowledged.

CHAPTER XIII.

Ver. 1. *The same day*] WHEREIN Christ had had a sharp bout and bickering with the scribes and Pharisees in the forenoon, he sat and taught the people (as it may seem) in the afternoon. A precedent of preaching twice a day. Chrysostom's practice was to preach in the afternoon, and by candle-light; as appears by his note on 1 Thess. v. 17, where he fetcheth a similitude from the lamp he was preaching by.[1] Luther likewise preached twice a day; which because one Nicolas White commended him in, he was accused of heresy in the reign of Henry VIII. And this commendable course began to be disgraced and cried down in our days as puritanical and superfluous. A learned bishop (Andrews) was highly extolled in print, for saying that when he was a lecturer in London, he preached in the morning, but prated only in the afternoon. A fair commendation for him.

He sat by the sea-side] As waiting an opportunity of doing good to men's souls; which was no sooner offered, but he readily laid hold on. So St Paul took a text of one of the altars in Athens, and discoursed on it to the superstitious people. A minister must stand ever upon his watch-tower, prompt and present, ready and speedy to every good work (as the bee, so soon as ever the sun breaks forth, flies abroad to gather honey and wax), accounting employment a preferment, as our Saviour did, John xvii. 4.

Ver. 2. *He went into a ship and sat*] Thinking, perhaps, there to repose himself, after his hard conflict with the Pharisees. But the sight of a new audience incites him to a new pains of preaching to them. And as he held no time unseasonable, so no place unfit for such a purpose. We find him eftsoons teaching not in the temple only and synagogues on the Sabbath day (as he did constantly), but in the mountains, in cities, in private houses, by the sea-side, by the way-side, by the well's-side, anywhere, everywhere, no place came amiss to him, no pulpit displeased him.

Ver. 3. *And he spake many things to them in parables*] A parable, saith Suidas, is διήγημα καὶ ὁμοίωσις πραγμάτων, a setting forth of the matter by way of similitude from something else that differs in kind, and yet in some sort resembleth and illustrateth it. Christ, the prince of preachers, varieth his kind of teaching according to the nature and necessity of his audience, speaking as they could hear, as they could bear, saith St Mark. Ministers, in like sort, must turn themselves, as it were, into all shapes

[1] Quench not the Spirit, σβέννυσι   δὲ αὐτόβιος ἀκάθαρτος. Chrysostom.

and fashions both of spirit and speech, to win people to God.

Behold, a sower went forth] Our Saviour stirs them up to attention by a "Behold." Which, though it might seem not so needful to be said to such as came far, and now looked through him, as it were, for a sermon: yet he, well knowing how dull men are to conceive heavenly mysteries, how weak to remember, hard to believe, and slow to practise, calls for their uttermost attention to his divine doctrine, and gives them a just reason thereof in his ensuing discourse. It fares with the best, whiles they hear, as with little ones, when they are saying their lesson; if but a bird fly by, they must needs look after it: besides the devil's malice striving to distract, stupify, or steal away the good seed, that it may come to nothing.

Ver. 4. *And when he sowed, some seed, &c.*] The word is a seed of immortality. For, 1. As seeds are small things, yet produce great substances, as an acorn an oak, &c., so by the foolishness of preaching souls are saved, like as by blowing of rams' horns the walls of Jericho were subverted. 2. As the seed must be harrowed into the earth, so must the word be hid in the heart, ere it fructify. 3. As the seedsman cannot make a harvest without the influence of heaven; so, let us, to the wearing of our tongues to the stump (as that martyr expressed it), preach and pray never so much, men will on in their sins, unless God give the blessing: Paul may plant, &c.[1] 4. As good seed if not cast into good ground yields no harvest; so the word preached, if not received into good and honest hearts, proves ineffectual. The Pharisees were not a button the better for all those heart-piercing sermons of our Saviour, nay, much the worse. 5. As the harvest is potentially in the seed, so is eternal life in the word preached, Rom. i. 16. As the rain from heaven hath a fatness with it, and a special influence more than other standing waters, so there is not the like life in other ordinances as in preaching. None to that, as David said of Goliath's sword.

Ver. 5—8. *Some fell upon stony places, &c.*] Our Saviour, his own best interpreter, explains all this to his disciples, ver. 18, 19. The intent of these several parables seems to have been to confirm that which he had said in the former chapter, ver. 50, that they that do the will of his heavenly Father shall be owned and crowned by him as his dearest relations and alliances. As also to teach the people not to rest in hearing, sith three parts of four hear and perish. Which loss is yet sweetly repaired by the fruitfulness of the good hearers, some whereof bring forth an hundred fold, some sixty, some thirty the fertility of one grain making amends for the barrenness of many; so that the sower repents not of his pains. It is well worth while, if but one soul be gained to God by a whole life's labour.

Ver. 9. *Who hath ears to hear, &c.*] q. d. Some have ears to hear, some not. So he divideth his hearers into *auritos et surdos.* All men have not faith, saith St Paul. Men's ears must be bored, as David's, their hearts opened, as Lydia's, ere the word can enter. Pray we that Christ would say Ephphatha unto us, and that when he opens our ears, and by them our hearts, that he would make the bore big enough: sith with what measure we mete, it shall be measured to us, and unto us that hear shall more be given, Matt. iv. 24. The greater diligence we use in hearing, the more apparent shall be our profiting.

Ver. 10. *And his disciples came and said unto him*] They came to him for satisfaction. Note this against those captious and capricious hearers, that maliciously relate to others that which to them seems not so well or wisely said by the preacher, and come not to the preacher himself, who can best unfold his own mind (all cannot be said in an hour) and make his own apology. Some sit behind the pillar, as Eli dealt by Hannah, to watch and catch what they may carp and cavil at. They contend themselves to have exercised their critiques upon the preacher, and that is all they make of a sermon, though never so savoury and seasonable. These are Herodian hearers.

Ver. 11. *Because it is given to you*] Plutarch thinks that life is given to men merely for the getting of knowledge. And the Greeks call man Φῶτα, for the inbred desire of light and knowledge that is naturally in all.[2] But desire we never so much, none can attain to sound and saving knowledge, but those only to whom it is given from above, into whose hearts Christ lets in a ray of heavenly light. Hence Prov. xxx. 3, 4, to know heavenly things is to ascend into heaven. And Luke xii. 48, to know the Master's will, is the great talent of all other: there is a "much" set upon it.

But to them it is not given] By a secret but most just judgment of God, who hath mercy on whom he will, and whom he will he hardeneth. The reason of many things now hid from us we shall see at the last day. Have patience, and be content in the mean while with a learned ignorance.

Ver. 12. *For whosoever hath, to him shall be given*] sc. If he have it for practice, not else, Zech. xi. 17. Men, to the hearing of the word, must bring with them the loan and advantage of former doctrine communicated to them, if they mean to do any good of it. And then, as Manoah believed (before the angel vanished in the sacrifice) and sought no such sign to confirm him, yet had it; so God will heap favours upon them, and every former shall be a pledge of a future. God gives grace for grace, that is, say some, where he finds one grace he gives another.

From him shall be taken away even that he hath] That he seems to have, saith St Luke,

[1] Mr Bradford, Serm. of Rep. *Meum est docere, vestrum auscultare, Dei perficere.* Cyril.

[2] τὸν βίον εἰς γνῶσιν ἀπὸ Θεοῦ δοθῆναι.

for indeed all that he hath is but a seeming, a semblance, he walketh in a vain show, he hath only the varnish of virtue, which God shall wash off with rivers of brimstone. Albeit hypocrites are commonly detected even in this life : how else should their names rot, as every wicked man's must ?

Ver. 13. *Therefore speak I to them in parables*] Because their wilful blindness and stubbornness deserves I should do it. They are sinners against their own souls, let them rue it therefore.

And hearing they hear not] *Audientes corporis sensu, non audiunt cordis assensu*, saith Augustine.

Ver. 14. *In them is fulfilled*] Ἀναπληροῦται, is again fulfilled, *q. d.* It is even with those now, as it was with those then. The same fable is acted, the scene only changed. Men's hearts are as hard as ever they were, the grace of the gospel hath not mended them a whit, nor ever will do, till God strike the stroke.

And shall not understand] *Deus iis in lingua sua Barbarus, qui in Christo, suis Attiticus*, their wit serves them not in spirituals.

Seeing, ye shall see, and not perceive] As Hagar saw not the fountain that was before her, till her eyes were opened.[1]

Ver. 15. *For this people's heart, &c.*] A fat heart is a fearful plague. " Their heart is as fat as grease, but I delight in thy law," Psal. cxix. 70. None can delight in God's law that are fat-hearted. Feeding cattle, we know, are most brutish and blockish. And physiognomers observe, that a full and fat heart betokens a dull and doltish dispostiton. Eglon's fat paunch would not part with the poniard : and Pliny tells of bears so fat that they felt not the sharpest prickles.

Their ears are dull of hearing] So were the disbelieving Hebrews, for the which they are much taxed and tutored by the apostle.[2] *Surdaster erat M. Crassus ; sed illud pejus, quod male audiebat*, saith Tully. These here hear very ill, for their no better hearing.

Their eyes they have closed] Or they wink hard with their eyes : they shut the windows, lest the light should come in : *ut liberius peccent libenter ignorant*, they do not what they might, toward the work. (Bern.)

Lest at any time they should see] See we may here (in that which they should have seen and done) the right order of repentance to salvation never to be repented of. The blind eye is opened, the deaf ear unstopped, the dull heart affected, &c. God first puts his laws into men's minds, that they may know them, and then writes the same in their hearts, that they may have the comfort, feeling, and fruition of them. And then it is, " I will be to them a God, and they shall be to me a people," Heb. viii. 10.

Ver. 16. *But blessed are your eyes, &c.*] Demaratus of Corinth was wont to say, that those Grecians lost a great part of the comfort of their lives, that had not seen great Alexander sitting on Darius's throne. St Austin wished but to have seen three sights, *Romam in flore, Paulum in ore, Christum in corpore*, Rome in the flourish, Paul in the pulpit, Christ in the flesh.

And your ears, for they hear] The turtle's voice, the joyful sound, the lively oracles, the precious promises of the word, therefore called " the word " by a specialty, because our ears should listen after no other word but that. Origen chides his hearers for nothing so much as for this, that they came so seldom to hear God's word ; and that when they came, they heard it so carelessly, *recte judicans*, saith Erasmus, *hinc esse præcipuum pietatis profectum aut defectum*, as one that well knew that men's growth in grace is according to their heed in hearing.

Ver. 17. *Desired to see those things that ye see, &c.*] They saw them, and saluted them only afar off, and in the dark glass of the ceremonies. " But we all with open face," &c., 2 Cor. iii. 18. The sea about the altar was brazen, and what eyes could pierce through it ? Now our sea about the throne is glass, like to crystal, clearly conveying the light and sight of God to our eyes. 1 Kings vii. 23 ; Rev. iv. 6. All God's ordinances are now so clear, that you may see Christ's face in them. Yea, as the glass set full against the sun receives not only the beams, as other dark bodies do, but the image of the sun ; so the understanding with open face beholding Christ, is transformed into the image and similitude of Christ.

Ver. 18. *Hear ye therefore the parable, &c.*] The disciples had asked him concerning the multitude, ver. 10, " Why speakest thou to them in parables ? " They pretended that the multitude understood him not, and therefore he should do well to show them the meaning. They were ashamed, belike, to bewray their own ignorance, but our Saviour calls to them also to hear the parable explained. We are all willing to make the best of our own case, to hide our crooked legs with long garments, &c. Nature need not be taught to tell her own tale.

Ver. 19. *The word of the kingdom*] So called, because it points to and paints out the way to the kingdom, and is therefore also called " The word of life, the power of God to salvation : " heaven is potentially in it, as the harvest is in the seed, as above I noted.

And understandeth it not] Considereth it not, as the Syriac here hath it, using the same word that David doth, Psal. xli. 1, " Blessed is the man that wisely considereth the poor and needy." Consideration sets on the word when it hath been heard (which else lies loose, and is driven away as chaff before the wind), maketh it to become an ingrafted word (λόγος ἔμφυτος, James i. 21), as the scions grafted into the stock, or as a tree rooted by the river's side, that removes not.

Then cometh the wicked one] The troubler of Israel, the master of misrule (ὁ πονηρὸς) ; he is one at church, whosoever is the other. A Doeg, a

---

[1] οὐ μὴ, ἀπαγορευτικῶς. Beza.

[2] Νωθροὶ ταῖς ἀκοαῖς, Heb. v. 11.

devil may set his foot as far within the sanctuary as a David. The sons of God cannot present themselves before the Lord but Satan comes also amongst them to do ill offices, Job i. 6.

And catcheth away that which was sown in his heart] That is, upon his heart (ἐν τῇ καρδίᾳ, *pro* ἐπὶ τῇ καρδίᾳ) ; for into his heart the seed never came, because the devil had made a path-way over it. People are now so sermon-trodden many of them, that their hearts, like foot-paths, grow hard by the word, which takes no more impression than rain doth upon a rock : they have brawny breasts, horny heart-strings, dead and dedolent dispositions. Hence they become a prey to the devil, as Abraham's sacrifice would have been to the fowls of the air, had he not huffed them away, Gen. xv. 11.

Ver. 20. *And anon with joy receiveth it*] Anon, or immediately. Temporaries are too sudden : and, or e'er they be soundly humbled, will be catching at the comforts, as children do at sweetmeats, stuffing themselves pillows with the promises, that they may sin more securely : *Præsumendo sperant, et sperando pereunt*, as one saith. These are your leap-Christians, so hot at first that they can never hold out.

> "Swift at hand gives in ere night,
> When soft and fair goes far."

With joy receiveth it] Or with grief, if the nature of the doctrine require it. For by one affection we are to understand the rest also. There is no grace but hath a counterfeit : *faciunt et vespæ favos, et simiæ imitantur homines*. The sorcerers seemed to do as much as Moses. Many apostates have had many meltings, and much sudden strong joy, so, as they have professed, the joy they have found at the hearing of the word hath been so great, that if it had continued but awhile, they could not have lived, but their spirits would have expired. Many examples there are of such. Howbeit in these flashings the truths of God (saith Mr Burroughs) pass by them, as water through a conduit, and leave a dew ; but soak not, as water into the earth.

Ver. 21. *Yet hath he not root in himself*] These flashy affections have not principles to maintain them, and therefore come to nothing. They are enlightened only as by a flash of lightning, and not by the sun-beam ; they do no more than taste of the good word of God, as cooks do of their sauces, they let nothing down, they digest it not, Heb. vi. 4, 5. "A good man is satisfied from himself," saith Solomon, Prov. xiii. 14 ; hath a spring within his own breast. *Hic sat lucis*, said Œcolampadius, clapping his hand upon his heart. This the temporary cannot say ; he is moved by some external principle, as are clocks, windmills, and the like : "the root of the matter is not in him," Job xix. 28. He wants depth of earth. Οὐκ ἐβάθυνε, saith another evangelist, the plough hath not gone deep enough ; and therefore, though the earth be good, and the seed good, yet being un-

covered, unburied, it miscarries. *Exoriuntur, sed exuruntur*, "His roots are dried up beneath, and above is his bud cut off," Job xviii. 16.

For when tribulation or persecution ariseth] As it will, for *ecclesia hæres crucis*, saith one. And opposition is *evangelii genius*, saith Calvin. It is but a delicacy to go about to divide Christ and his cross.

By and by he is offended] *Vadat Christus cum suo evangelio*, saith he. Let Christ keep his heaven to himself, if it can be had upon no other terms : he is resolved to suffer nothing. When it comes to that once, he kicks up profession, and may possibly prove a spiteful adversary of the same ministry which he once admired, as Herod ; and a proud contemner of the same remorse with which himself was some time smitten, as Saul. Crystal seems a precious stone, till it come to the hammering.

Ver. 22. *He that received the seed among thorns*] So the love of money is called, because it chokes the word, pricks the conscience, harbours vermin lusts. *Magna cognatio, ut rei sic nominis divitiis et vitiis.* Let rich men look to it, saith Gregory, that they handle their thorns without pricking their fingers ; that whiles they load themselves with earth, they lose not heaven, as Shimei, seeking his servants, lost himself.[1] "Set not thy heart upon the asses" (said Samuel to Saul), sith "to thee is the desire of all Israel." Set not your hearts, say I, on this world's trash, sith better things abide you. Martha was troubled about many things, but neglected that one thing necessary, to sit, as her sister did, at Christ's feet, and hear his word. This Christ checks her for.

And the deceitfulness of riches] The world is a subtle, sly enemy, that doth easily insinuate and dangerously deceive. We may safely say of it, as he sometimes did of an historian, Both its words and shows are full of fraud.[2] As the panther hides his deformed head, till the sweet scent have drawn other beasts into his danger ; so deals the world, alluring men by the deceitfulness of riches, and masking the monstrous and deformed head, the end thereof, under the gilded show of good husbandry, or disguised shape of sin. In a word, these outward things, howsoever as hosts they welcome us into our inn with smiling countenance, yet, unless we look better to them, they will cut our throats in our beds.

And he becometh unfruitful] Because the thorns over-top the corn ; whereas the good ground, though it hath many thorns, yet the corn ascends above them : grace is superior to corruption, the fruit springs up and increaseth, as St Mark (iv. 8) hath it. These thorny-ground hearers, though they stood out persecution, and shrank not in the wetting, as the stony-ground did, yet, because the plough had not gone so low as to break up the roots, whereby their hearts were fastened to earthly contents, they proved also unfruitful. See how far a man may go, and yet be never the nearer after all. The stony and thorny ground

---

[1] *Dum peritura paras per male parta peris. Viderint divites quomodo spinas sine punctione contrectent.*

[2] Δολερὰ μὲν τὰ σχήματα, δολερὰ δὲ τὰ ῥήματα. Plut. de Herodot.

were nearer to the nature of the good ground, than that of the highway, and yet fell short of heaven.

Ver. 23. *But he that received seed, &c.*] Which is but a fourth part, if so much, of those that have the word purely and powerfully preached unto them. As at Ephesus, Acts xix. 31, so in our church assemblies, the more part know not wherefore they are come together. They will say, to serve God, and hear his word, but who this God is, or how his word is to be heard, they neither know nor care. If the belly may be filled, the back fitted, &c.,[1] they have as much as they look after. And of such dust-heaps as these all corners are full; our Church is as much pestered and even dark with these epicures and atheists, who yet will not miss a sermon, as Egypt was with the grasshoppers. These are those last and loosest times, wherein, by reason of the overflow of iniquity, "the love of many is waxen cold, but he that endureth to the end shall be saved," Matt. xxiv. 12, 13. Where note, that for many that lose their love to God's word, it is but a he in the singular number that holds out therein to the end.

Some an hundred fold] As Isaac's seed did, that he sowed in the land of Canaan. This is not every man's happiness: yet we must propound to ourselves the highest pitch. "And let as many as are perfect be thus minded." That man for heaven, and heaven for him, that sets up for his mark, "the resurrection of the dead," Phil. iii. 11, that is, that perfection of holiness that accompanieth the estate of the resurrection.

Some sixty, some thirty] It befalls not every man to excel, but it behoves every man to exact of himself such a growth in grace, that his profiting may appear to all, and that he is "neither barren, nor unfruitful in the knowledge of Jesus Christ," 2 Pet. i. 8. The vine is the weakest of plants, yet bears abundantly. Philadelphia had but a little strength, yet a great door opened, Rev. iii. 8. The Colossians were but quickened, and not born, yet preciously esteemed of God, Col. ii. 13. He accepteth according to that a man hath, be it more or less, he blesseth our buds, Isa. xliv. 3. Courage, therefore, though not so fruitful as thou wouldst be. Thine earnest pantings, inquietations, and desires of better cannot but commend thee much to God. *Prima sequentem honestum est in secundis tertiisque consistere*, saith one. And *Summum dulmen affectantes, satis honeste vel in secundo fastigio conspiciemur*, saith another.[2] Aspire to the highest pitch, but be not discouraged, though ye fall somewhat short of it. Every man cannot excel.

Ver. 24. *The kingdom of heaven.*] viz. here on earth. For we have eternal life already, 1. *In pretio*, 2. *Promisso*, 3. *Primitiis*, in the price, promise, first-fruits. As God prepared Paradise

for Adam, so he hath heaven for his. Howbeit, he reserves not all for hereafter; but gives a grape of Canaan in this wilderness, where by righteousness, and peace, and joy in the Holy Ghost, God's people do even eat, and drink, and sleep eternal life, as it was once said of a reverend divine of Scotland.

Which sowed good seed in his field] Among the Romans it was, *probrum censorium agrum male colere*, a fault punishable by the censors, to be an ill seedsman, Plin. lib. 18. And when they would highly commend any, they would say, "He is an honest man, and a good ploughman.[3]

Ver. 25. *But while men slept*] Christ, the Lord of the husbandry, neither slumbereth nor sleepeth; but the under-labourers and land-holders, to whom he lets out his vineyard, are frequently found to be supine and secure, Zech. iv. 1. It fared with the good prophet, as with a drowsy person; who, though awake and set to work, is ready to sleep at it. And albeit we watch against greater, yet lesser evils are ready to steal upon us at unawares, as Austin hath it.[4]

His enemy came] This is the minister's misery. Other men find their work as they left it; but when ministers have done their best on one sabbath day, the enemy comes ere the next, and mars all. They sleep and are fearless; he wakes for a mischief, and is restless. Learn for shame of the devil (said father Latimer to careless ministers) to watch over your flocks. God will shortly send out summons for sleepers; and the devil waketh and walketh, seeking whom to devour. His instruments also are wondrous active in evil. O pray (said a dying man in the beginning of the German Reformation) that God would preserve the gospel; for the pope of Rome and the Council of Trent to bestir themselves wonderfully! May not we say as much and more now-a-days?[5]

And sowed tares among the wheat] Better it were rendered blasted corn, that yields nothing better at harvest than dust and chaff;[6] though it be in all things like the good corn, and the contrary appeareth not till towards harvest, when the dust is driven away by the wind, the chaff cast into the fire. Hereby are meant hypocrites and heretics, *qui nobiscum in horreo esse possunt, in area non possunt*, who shall be sifted out one day.

And went his way] As if he had done no such thing. Satan hides his cloven feet as much as he can, and would seem no other than an angel of light. Or *abiit, id est, latuit*, saith one: he went away, that is, he lurked, as his imps use to do, under the fair pent-house of zeal and seeming devotion, under the broad leaves of formal profession.

Ver. 26. *Then appeared the tares also*] Hypocrites are sure sooner or later to be detected. All

---

[1] *Si ventri bene, si lateri, &c.* Hor. Epist. I. 12. 5.

[2] Cicer. de Orat. Columella, lib. 1, *in præfat.*

[3] *Majores nostri siquem laudabant, ita laudabant, virum bonum, bonumque colonum.* Varro.

[4] *Adversus majora vigilantibus, quædam incautis minutiora surrepunt.* Aug.

[5] *Ut jugulent homines surgunt de nocte latrones.*
  Ut teipsum serves non expergiscere?
  Pontifex enim Rom. et Concilium Tridentinum mira moliuntur.

[6] *Frumentum adustum, ζιζάνιον, quasi σιτοσίνιον, quod frugibus noceat.* Aug.

will out at length. *Saeco soluto apparuit argentum.* When God turns the bottom of the bag upwards, their secret sins will appear; "They shall find themselves in all evil, in the midst of the congregation and assembly," Prov. v. 14. They that turn aside unto their crooked ways, shall be led forth with the workers of iniquity, Psal. cxxv. 5.

Ver. 27. *So the servants of the householder, &c.*] Godly ministers are much vexed at hypocrites and fruitless hearers. So was our Saviour at the Pharisees, Mark iii. 5; he looked on them with anger, being grieved at the hardness of their hearts. So was Paul at Elymas the sorcerer; he set his eyes upon him, as if he would have looked through him; after which lightning followeth that terrible thunder-clap, "O full of all subtilty," &c. So was Peter at Simon Magus, Acts xiii. 9, 10; and St John at Diotrephes. "I would they were even cut off that trouble you," Gal. v. 12. *Mihi certè Auxentius nunquam aliud quam diabolus erit, quia Arianus*, saith Hilarius, who also called Constantius Antichrist.

Ver. 28. *Wilt thou then that we go, &c.*] This was zeal indeed, but rash and unseasonable, and is therefore to be moderated by prudence and patience. Those two sons of thunder had over-quick and hot spirits, Luke ix. 55. Luther confessed before the emperor at Worms, that in his books against private and particular persons he had been more vehement than his religion and profession required. And he that writes the history of the Trent Council tells us, if we may believe him, that in *Colloquio Possiaceno*, Beza, speaker for the Protestants, entering into the matter of the Eucharist, spake with such heat, that he gave but ill satisfaction to those of his own party; so that he was commanded to conclude. Zeal should eat us up, but not eat up our discretion, our moderation.

Ver. 29. *Lest whilst ye gather up the tares*] Those that are now tares, hypocrites, may become good corn, good Christians. Jethro, an Ishmaelite by nation, may prove an Israelite by religion. Simon Magus may perhaps have the thoughts of his heart forgiven him, Acts viii. 22. In the year 1553, a priest at Canterbury said mass on one day; and the next day after he came into the pulpit, and desired all the people to forgive him; for he said he had betrayed Christ, yet not as Judas did, but as Peter; and so made a long sermon against the mass. Bucer, of a Dominican, became a famous Protestant, being converted by Luther's sermon before the emperor at Worms.

Ver. 30. *Bind them in bundles, &c.*] This shall be the angels' office at the last day, to bundle up swearers with swearers, drunkards with drunkards, &c., that they may suffer together, as they have sinned together, and pledge one another in that cup of fire and brimstone that shall then be poured down their throats, Psal. xi. 6. As in the meantime, brimstone is here scattered upon their habitation, Job xviii. 15, every moment ready to take fire, if God but lighten upon it with the arrows of his indignation, Psal. xviii. 14.

Ver. 31. *Is like to a grain of mustard-seed*] "Which soon pierceth the nostrils and brain," as Pliny noteth,[1] and "hurteth the eyes," as the very name in Greek importeth.[2] But that which our Saviour here observeth and applieth in it, is the smallness of the seed, the greatness of the stalk or tree that comes of it, and the use of the branches for birds to build in. This grain of mustard-seed sowed, is the word preached: which though it seem small and contemptible, proves quick and powerful. Hitherto fly the birds of the air, God's elect, for shade in prosperity, for shelter in adversity. Yea, as the trees of America, but especially of Brazil, are so huge, that several families are reported to have lived in several arms of one tree, to such a number as are in some petty village or parish here: so is the growth of the gospel, it runs and is glorified, 2 Thess. iii. 1, as the Jerusalem-artichoke overruns the ground, wheresoever it is planted. It was a just wonder how it was carried, as on angels' wings,[3] over all the world by the preaching of the apostles at first, and now again, in the late Reformation, by Luther and some few other men of mean rank, but of rare success. These were those angels that came flying with the everlasting gospel (no new doctrine as the adversaries slander it) in the midst of heaven, or betwixt heaven and earth, Rev. xiv. 6, 7; because their doctrine at first was not so clearly confirmed to others, not so fully understood by themselves. Melancthon confesseth, *Quod fugiamus habemus, sc. Pontificios : quos sequamur, non intelligimus.* And Cardinal Wolsey (saith the same Melancthon), reading the Augsburg Confession, saith, "that our cause concerning the righteousness of faith was stronger in the confirmation than in the confutation of the contrary opinion. *Quod verum est,* as he there yieldeth, *quia facilius construere in sophisticis quam destruere : In physicis contra.* But our John Wickliff, long before Luther, wrote more than 200 volumes against the Pope.[4] The Lady Ann, wife to King Richard II., sister to Wenceslaus, King of Bohemia, by living here was made acquainted with the gospel. Whence also many Bohemians, coming hither, conveyed Wickliff's books into Bohemia; whereby a good foundation was laid for a future reformation. After this, were stirred up there by God, John Huss, and Jerome of Prague; who so propagated the truth in that kingdom, that in the year of Christ 1451 the Church of God at Constantinople congratulated to the University of Prague their happy begin-

---

[1] *Sublimis fertur, quando non aliud magis in nares et cerebrum penetrat.* Pliny, xx. 22.

[2] Σίνηπι παρὰ τὸ σίνεσθαι τοὺς ὦπὰς, Heb. iv.

[3] *Evangelium tam celeri volatu ferebatur, et quidem spatio menstruo per universam Germaniam, et aliquot regiones ex-* teras, ut ipsi Angeli cursores, et hujus doctrinæ præcones esse viderentur. Melch. Adam.

[4] *Scripsit plus quam 200 volum. contra Papam.* Pareus in Apoc. 146.

nings, and exhorted them to perseverance. For before, the Hussites, by the mediation of Queen Sophia, who favoured them, had obtained of the king the free exercise of their religion throughout Bohemia. Howbeit, soon after this, they suffered great persecution by the Popish party, who yet could say no worse of them than this: In their lives they are modest, in their speeches true, in their love one towards another fervent; but their religion is incorrigible, and stark naught, saith Jacobus Leilenstenius the Dominican. And why stark naught? Reinerius, another of their persecutors, shall tell you. Their doctrine, saith he, "is most pestilent, 1. Because of so long standing. 2. Because so far spread. 3. For their show of purity, &c."[1] This paved a way for the great work which Luther began in Germany, the last of October, 1517. And it was strangely carried on: 1. By diligent preaching. 2. Printing good books. 3. Translating the Holy Scriptures into vulgar tongues. 4. Catechising of youth. 5. Offering public disputation. 6. Martyrologies. Here in England was a great door opened at the same time, but many adversaries. The establishing of that Reformation, how unperfect soever; to be done by so weak and simple means, yea, by casual and cross means (saith one[2]), against the force of so puissant and politic an enemy, is that miracle, which we are in these times to look for. It is such a thing (saith another) as the former age had even despaired of, the present age admireth, and the future shall stand amazed at.[3] King Henry VIII., whom God used as an instrument in the work, had first written against Luther, and afterwards established those six sacrilegious articles. And sitting in parliament, he thus complained of the stirs that were made about religion. "There are many," saith he, "that are too busy with their new sumpsimus, and others that dote too much upon their old mumpsimus." The new religion, though true, he and they all, for most part, envied: the old, though their own, they despised. John Frith withstood the violence of three of the most obstinate amongst them, Rochester, More, and Rastal: whereof the one by the help of the doctors, the other by wresting the Scriptures, and the third by the help of natural philosophy, had conspired against him. "But he, as another Hercules," saith Mr Fox, "fighting with all three at once, did so overthrow and confound them, that he converted Rastal to his part: Rochester and More were afterwards both beheaded for denying the king's supremacy." Reformation hath ever met with opposition, and never more than now, men fighting for their lusts, which they love as their lives, and are loth to part with. But Christ shall reign when all is done: and those golden times are now at hand, that the new Jerusalem,

which signifies the state of the Church in this world, when it hath passed the furnace of affliction, presently upon it shall be all of fine gold. Let us contribute thereunto our earnest prayers and utmost pains, not abiding among the sheepfolds with Reuben, nor remaining in ships with Dan, &c., Judges v. 16, 17; not standing off, and casting perils, as the priests and Levites in Hezekiah's days, 2 Chron. xxix. 11; but beginning the reformation, as Gideon did, at our own hearts and houses, lest, with Uzziah, instead of making up the breach, we prove makers of breaches. Were our dangers greater, thy single reformation may do much to prevent them, Jer. v. 1. As, were our hopes greater, thy sin and security may unravel them, and undo all, Eccl. ix. 18. One sin destroyeth much good: be moving therefore in thine own orb, and bestir thee as Nehemiah did, trading every talent wherewith Divine Providence hath intrusted thee for Jerusalem's welfare; giving no rest either to thyself or to God, as his remembrancer, until he have established, and made her a praise in the whole earth, Isa. lxii. 6, 7.

Ver. 32. *Which indeed is the least of all seeds*] That is, one of the least (μικρότερον), for there is as little or less than it, as poppy-seed, &c. Cypress seeds are said to be so small, that they can hardly be seen asunder; and yet of them grows so great and tall a tree, *Nusquam magis tota natura quam in minimis*, saith Pliny.[4] Tremellius testifieth, that things almost incredible are related of the wonderful growth of the Jewish mustard-seed. Maldonate also telleth us, "that in Spain he had seen little woods of mustard-seed trees; and that the bakers therehence fetch fuel to heat their ovens, and do other offices." The word of God (a thing worth observation, saith a modern divine) is in the gospel compared to mustard-seed; which (as one gathereth out of Pythagoras) of all seeds is most in ascent, taketh deepest root, and being mixed with vinegar is sovereign against serpents. Right so the word of God worketh effectually in us, begets an ascent in our affections, lays in us a sure foundation, and though it touch us sharply as vinegar, yet is a most powerful preservative against that old serpent.

Ver. 33. *The kingdom of heaven is like unto leaven*] Which soon diffuseth itself into the whole lump. The word of God is not bound, though the preacher, haply, be in bonds, 2 Tim. ii. 9, but runs, and is glorified, 2 Thess. ii. 1. In the beginning of Queen Mary's reign, almost all the prisons in England, saith Mr Fox, "were become right Christian schools and churches." During the time of Mr Bradford's imprisonment in the King's Bench and Counter in the Poultry, he preached twice a day continually, unless sickness hindered him: where also the sacra-

---

[1] *In moribus et vita sunt boni, veraces in sermone, in caritate fraterna unanimes: sed fides eorum est incorrigibilis et pessima. Eorum doctrina maxime est noxia. 1. Quia diuturnior. 2. Generalior. 3 Ob speciem puritatis.*

[2] Sir Edw. Sands' Relat. of West. Relig.

[3] *Eccles. Angl. reformationem desperasset ætas præterita,* admiratur præsens, obstupescet futura. Scultet. Annal. dec. 2. ep. dedicat.

[4] *Cupressi semina adeo sunt minuta, ut quædam oculis cerni non possint, et tamen in iis tanta est arbor, tamque procera.* Plin. xi. 2.

ment was administered. And through his means (the keeper so well did bear with him) such resort of good people was daily at his lecture and ministration of the sacrament, that commonly his chamber was well nigh filled therewith. Concerning the Christian congregation, saith the same author, " in Queen Mary's time, there were sometimes 40, sometimes 100, sometimes 200 met together. I have heard of one, who being sent to them to take their names, and to espy their doing, yet in being among them was converted, and cried them all mercy."

Ver. 34. *And without a parable spake he not,* &c.] A singular judgment of God upon them for their contumacy and contempt of the gospel: so it is now upon many people, that God taketh sometimes from their most illuminate teachers, clearness and perspicuity of expression, for a punishment of their unthankfulness and rebellion against the light. Thieves and malefactors that affect darkness (because the light discovers their evil deeds) are worthily cast into a dark dungeon: so here, Ezekiel, by the just judgment of God upon them, was no more understood by his hearers than if he had spoken to them in a strange language. Heraclitus, for his obscurities, was called the Dark Doctor, and it seems he affected it; for he oft commanded his scholars to deliver themselves darkly.[1] A minister is studiously to shun obscurity in his doctrine. But if nevertheless he prove obscure and hard to be understood, let the people see a hand of God in it, and rather accuse their own impiety than the preacher's inability.

Ver. 35. *I will utter things,* &c.] I will freely and plentifully eventilate them,[2] as a fountain casteth out her waters constantly and without spare. Charity is no churl: true goodness is communicative, and accounts that it hath not that good thing that it doth not impart:[3] as that Bishop of Lincoln never thought he had that thing which he did not give. It is not pouring out, but want of pouring out, that dries up the streams of grace, as of that oil, 2 Kings iv. 6. " The liberal soul shall be made fat: and he that watereth shall be watered also himself," Prov. xi. 25.

Ver. 36. *Declare unto us the parable*] Private conference hath incredible profit. The minister cannot possibly say all in an hour: seek settlement from his lips, who both must preserve, and present knowledge to the people. Junius was converted by conference with a countryman of his not far from Florence, Galeacius Caracciolus, by a similitude of Peter Martyr's in his public lectures on 1 Corinth., seconded and set on by private discourse. David was more affected by Nathan's " Thou art the man," than by all the lectures of the law, for a twelvemonth before.

Ver. 37. *Is the Son of man*] i. e. Signifies the Son of man: as circumcision is the covenant; that is, the sign of the covenant. And as

Christ saith of the sacramental bread, " This is my body," which Luther interprets synecdochically, for in, or under, this is my body. Calvin, after Tertullian and Augustine, interpret it metonymically, for this is the sign or the figure of my body. Hence the Jesuits presently cry out, the Spirit of God disagreeth not with itself. But these interpretations do utterly disagree, therefore they are not of the Spirit. But let them first agree among themselves, before they quarrel our disagreements ; for their own doctors are exceedingly divided even about this very point of the Eucharist, and know not what their holy mother holdeth. Bellarmine teacheth, that the substance of the bread is not turned into the substance of Christ's body *productivè*, as one thing is made of another, but that the bread goes away, and Christ's body comes into the room of it *adductivè*, as one thing succeeds into the place of another, the first being voided. And this, saith he, is the opinion of the Church of Rome, himself being reader of Controversies at Rome. But Suarez, reader at Salamanca, in Spain, confutes Bellarmine's opinion, terming it translocation, not transubstantiation, and saith it is not the Church's opinion.

Ver. 38. *The field is the world*] The Christian world, the Church, not the Roman Catholic Church only, the Pope's territories, as he would have it. The Rogatian heretics would needs have made the world believe that they were the only Catholics. The Anabaptists have the same conceit of themselves. Munzer their chieftain, in his book written against Luther, and dedicated to Christ the most illustrious Prince (as he styleth him), inveigheth bitterly at him, as one that was merely carnal, and utterly void of the spirit of revelation. And Pareus upon this text tells us, that in a conference at Frankendale, the Anabaptists thus argued, The field is the world, therefore not the Church ; that by the same reason they might deny, that tares breed in the Church. But tares are and will be in the visible Church, as our Saviour purposely teacheth by this parable.

The tares are the children of that wicked one] So called partly in respect of their serpentine nature, those corrupt qualities, whereby they resemble the devil ; and partly because they creep into the Church by Satan's subtlety, being his agents and emissaries. *Agnosco te primogenitum diaboli,* saith St John of that heretic Cerinthus. And hypocrites are his sons and heirs, the very freeholders of hell, and other sinners but their tenants, which have their part or lot with hypocrites, Matt. xxiv. 29.

Ver. 39. *The enemy that sowed them,* &c.] As Esther said, " The adversary and enemy is this wicked Haman," so Satan. Why then have men so much to do with him ? The Jews, as often as they hear mention of Haman in their synagogues, they do with their fists and hammers

---

[1] *Ab obscuritate dictus est* σκοτεινὸς. *Ad hoc etiam discipulos erudiebat, cum illud sæpius ingereret,* Σκότισον, *obscurus esto.* Joh. Bodin.

[2] *Eructabo, vel palam proloquar.*

[3] *Paulum sepultæ distat inertiæ Celata virtus.* Horat.

beat upon the benches and boards, as if they did knock upon Haman's head. We have those also that can bid defiance to the devil, spit at his name, curse him, haply;[1] but in the mean space listen to his illusions, entertain him into their hearts by obeying his lusts. These are singularly foolish. For it is as if one should be afraid of the name of fire, and yet not fear to be burnt with the flame thereof.

Ver. 40. *So shall it be in the end of this world*] As till then there can be no perfect purgation of the Church. Nevertheless, magistrates and all good people must do their utmost within their bounds to further a reformation a little otherwise than the cardinals and prelates of Rome; whom Luther fitly compared to foxes, that came to sweep a dusty house with their tails, and instead of sweeping the dust out, sweep it all about the house, so making a great smoke for the time, but when they were gone the dust falls all down again.

Ver. 41. *All things that offend*] Gr. All scandals (σκάνδαλα), pests, botches, blocks to others in the way to heaven. *Scandalum est rei non bonæ sed malæ exemplum, ædificans ad delictum,* saith Tertullian. Such were those proud, contentious, covetous prelates in the primitive Church, that Ammianus Marcellinus stumbled and stormed at.[2] Such were those loose and ungirt Christians of whom Lactantius[3] complaineth in his time, that they dishonoured their profession, to the scandal of the weak and the scorn of the wicked. Such was Pope Clement V., who so ill governed the Church, that Frederick, King of Sicily, began to call the truth of Christian religion into question, and had fallen utterly off from it, had he not been settled and satisfied by Arnoldus de Villa Nova, a learned man of those times. Forasmuch as Christians (the Papists he meant) do eat the God whom they adore, *sit anima mea cum philosophis,* said Averroes the Mahometan, let my soul be with the philosophers rather. Nothing more stumbleth that poor people the Jews, and hindereth their conversion, than the idolatry of Papists, and blasphemies of Protestants. Oh that God would once cut off the names of those idols, and cause the unclean spirit to pass out of the land, according to his promise, Zech. xiii. 2. *Fiat. Fiat.*

Ver. 42. *And shall cast them into a furnace of fire*] Lo, the good angels are executioners of God's judgments. There cannot be a better and more noble act, than to do justice upon obstinate malefactors. Howbeit, at Rome they would not suffer the common executioner to dwell within the city, nay, not so much as once to be seen in it,[4] or draw breath in the air of it. This was very strict in them, and that was very

just in God, that Twiford, which was executioner of Frith, Bayfield, Bainham, Tewkesbury, Lambert, and other good men, died rotting aboveground, so that none could abide to come near him.

Ver. 43. *Then shall the righteous shine*] Those that have here lain among the pots, smucht and sullied, shall then outshine the sun in his strength. Shine they shall in their bodies, which shall be clarified and conformed to Christ's most glorious body, the standard, Phil. iii. In their souls, those spirits of men made perfectly holy and happy. And in their whole person, as the spouse of Christ. *Uxor fulget radiis mariti,* she shall shine with the beams of his beauty. Three glimpses of which glory were seen in Moses' face, in Christ's transfiguration, in Stephen's countenance.

Who hath ears to hear, let him hear] q. d. This is worth hearing. Lend both your ears to such a bargain as this is. "What shall we say to these things?" saith the apostle, after he had spoke of glorification, Rom. viii. 31. q. d. We can never satisfy ourselves in speaking, you should never show yourselves sated in hearing.

Ver. 44. *Like unto treasure hid, &c.*] A treasure is a heap of precious things laid up for future uses.[5] By the treasure in this text, we are to understand either Christ, or life eternal gotten for us by Christ, or the gospel that offereth unto us Christ, and with him eternal life. The field wherein this true treasure lies hid, is the Church. The spades and mattocks wherewith it is to be digged up and attained unto, are hands and eyes, not poring in the earth, but praying toward heaven.

He hideth it] *Ne quis eum antevertat,* that none remove it, ere he hath made himself master of it. Holding fast that he hath, that no man take his crown from him. This he insures to himself, and cannot rest till he hath done it. He likes not to have with the merchant an estate hanging upon ropes,[6] and depending upon uncertain winds, but makes sure work for his soul.

Selleth all that he hath] Ever when justifying faith is infused, there is a through sale of all sin; the pearl of price will never else be had. And for outward comforts and contentments, every true son of Israel will be glad to purchase the birthright with pottage, spiritual favours with earthly, as did Galeacius the Marquess of Vico, Martinengus Earl of Barcha, &c.

And buyeth that field] Accounting it an excellent penny-worth, whatever it stand him in. Other faint-hearted chapmen cheapen heaven only, being loth to go to the price of it. A price they have in their hands, but they, like fools, look upon their money, and have no mind to lay it out upon any such commodity. Oh

---

[1] *Martinus Papæ exactor ex Anglia pulsus, cum a Rege salvum conductum peteret, respondit, Rex, Diabolus te ad inferos ducat et perducat, ad mare tamen ei commeatum dedit.* Revius.

[2] *Marcell. Episcoporum furores, luxum regio majorem, astum in captandis matronarum oblationibus, &c., taxavit.*

[3] *Nunc male audiunt castiganturque Christiani, quod aliter*

quam sapientibus convenit vivant, et vitia sub obtentu nominis celent. Lactant. de Opific. Dei prooem. Jac. Revius Hist. Pontif. Rom.

[4] *Censoriæ leges et foro et cælo, et spiritu urbi carnificem interdicunt, et urbis domicilio carere volunt.* Cic. pro Rabirio.

[5] Θησαυρός, παρὰ τοῦ τιθέναι εἰς αὔριον.

[6] *Fortunam rudentibus aptam.*

what madmen are they that bereave themselves of a room in that city of pearl, for a few paltry shillings or dirty delights!

Ver. 45. *The kingdom of heaven, &c.*] The wise merchant, besides the pearl of price, seeks out other goodly pearls, common gifts, which also have their use and excellency; but he rests not in them, as philosophers, politicians, and temporaries. These, as alchymists, who though they miss of their end yet find many excellent things by the way, so though they failed of the glory of God, yet they have many commendable good parts and properties. The wise merchant so seeks after these, that he minds chiefly the main, the " one thing necessary," in comparison whereof he counts all things else, though never so specious, dung, and dogs-meat.

Ver. 46. *Who when he had found one pearl, &c.*] Of far greater price than that precious adamant that was found about Charles Duke of Burgundy, slain in battle by the Switzers at Nantes, A. D. 1476. This adamant was first sold by a soldier that found it to a priest for a crown; the priest sold it for two crowns; afterwards it was sold for 7000 florins, then for 12,000 ducats, and last of all for 20,000 ducats, and set into the pope's triple crown, where also it is to be seen at this day. Christ is a commodity far more precious; surely he " is better than rubies," saith Solomon, "and all the things that may be desired are not to be compared unto him," Prov. viii. 11. "No mention shall be made of coral or of pearls; for the price of wisdom " (this essential wisdom of God) "is above rubies," Job xxviii. 18. Pearls are bred in shell-fishes of a celestial humour or dew: so was Christ by heavenly influence in the Virgin's womb. *Tanti igitur vitreum? Quanti verum margaritum?* (Tertullian.) Christ is to be sought and bought with any pains, at any price. We cannot buy this gold too dear. Joseph, the jewel of the world, was far more precious, had the Ishmaelitish merchants known so much, than all the balms and myrrhs they transported. So is Christ, as all will yield that know him. The pearls usually cast out with the flood, and gathered at the ebb, drew Cæsar's affections for the conquest of Britain, as Suetonius tells us. Shall not that unconceivable worth that is in Christ attract our hearts? &c.

Ver. 47. *Again, the kingdom, &c.*] Christ is an incessant teacher: learn then, for shame, lest he turn us off for non-proficients. Let one sermon peg in another; and every second potion set the first a-work.

Is like unto a net, &c.] An elegant comparison, wherein the fishers are the ministers, the sea the world, the net the word, the ship the church, the fishes the hearers. Basil, comparing the gospel to a net, makes fear to be the lead that sinketh it, and keeps it steady; and hope to be the cork, which keepeth it always above water. Without the lead of fear, saith he, it would be carried hither and thither; as without the cork of hope, it would utterly sink down.

Ver. 48. *And cast the bad away*] Algam, silices, arenulas, sordes (σαπρὰ). Beza. Here was of both sorts, till the separation was made. The visible Church resembles the ark, which was full of creatures of divers kinds, but most unclean. Fair she is, but as the moon, which is not without her blemishes. Separatists that leave her, therefore, yea, deny her, and remain obstinate for trifles, are not unfitly by one compared to the hedge-hog; which, saith Pliny, being laden with nuts and fruit, if the least filbert fall off, will sling down all the rest in a pettish humour, and beat the ground for anger with his bristles. *Mulæ ablactatæ matrem calcibus petunt.*

Ver. 49. *The angels shall come forth and sever*] But how shall the angels know them asunder, may some say? By that *signum salutare* that God hath set upon them, that mark in their foreheads, Ezek. ix. 47. Besides, by the lightsomeness of their looks shall the elect be known, lifting up their heads, because their redemption then draweth nigh; when reprobates shall look ghastly and ugly, being almost "mad with the sight of their eyes that they shall see, and the fear of their hearts wherewith they shall fear," Deut. xxviii. 34, 67.

From amongst the just] Amidst whom they might haply hope to hide themselves, laying hold upon the skirt of a Jew inwardly. But it will not be; for then, even their best friends will disavow them for ever. " Moses in whom ye trust shall judge you," John v. 45.

Ver. 50. *And shall cast them into the furnace*] An exquisite torment is hereby deciphered. This our Saviour had said in the same words, but a little afore, ver. 42. He here repeats it, that men may the better observe it. And I would to God, saith Chrysostom, that men would every day and everywhere discourse of hell torments, that they would take a turn in hell ever and anon by their meditations. Certainly did men believe the torments of hell, that weeping for extremity of heat, and that gnashing of teeth that's there for extremity of cold, they durst not but be more innocent; they would never offer to fetch profits or pleasures out of those flames. It was a speech of Gregory Nyssen, He that doth but hear of hell is without any further labour or study taken off from sinful pleasures: thus he then. But, alas, men's hearts are grown harder now-a-days; they can hear of hell, and be no more moved than they are to handle a painted toad.

Ver. 51. *Have ye understood all these things?*] See here the ancient use of catechising in the Christian Church. So afterwards, *Credis? Credo. Abrenuncias? Abrenuncio,* were the primitive questions and answer. Origen and Cyril were catechists. In the Reformation, catechising of youth was one main means of propagating the gospel. And the Jesuits, observing as much, have taken the same course for the propagating of their superstition, and have set forth divers catechisms. I remember, saith Melancthon, that Eberhard, the good Duke of

Wittemburg, would constantly hear the young gentlemen about the Court once a week rehearsing their catechisms ; which if any did not well, he was well whipt in the presence of the Duke and his courtiers. Bishop Ridley, in a letter of his to the brethren ; "I hear," saith he, "that the catechism in English is now (after Queen Mary came in) condemned in every pulpit. O devilish malice, and most spitefully injurious to the salvation of mankind ! Indeed Satan could not long suffer that so great light should be spread abroad in the world. He saw well enough that nothing was able to overthrow his kingdom so much, as if children being godly instructed in religion should learn to know Christ, whilst they are yet young. Whereby, not only children, but the elder sort also and aged, that before were not taught in their childhood to know Christ, should now even with children and babes be forced to know him."

Ver. 52. *Therefore every scribe*] *i. e.* Every teacher of the Church must be both learned and apt to teach. He must give attendance to reading first, and then to exhortation and doctrine, 1 Tim. iv. 13. Bishop Latimer, notwithstanding both his years and other pains in preaching, was every morning ordinarily both winter and summer about two of the clock at his book most diligently. And as the Rabbins have a proverb, *Lilmod lelammed*, men must therefore learn that they may teach, so did he. The Hebrew word Shachal signifieth, 1. To understand ; 2. To teach ; 3. To prosper. They that therefore learn that they may teach others, shall find that the pleasure of the Lord shall prosper in their hands, Isa. liii. 10.

That bringeth forth out of his treasury] *Extrudit copiose et alacriter* (ἐκβάλλει). That throweth out his store without spare, and dealeth forth his soul to the hungry hearer, desirous to spend and be spent for him. That hath a treasury of his own, and steals not all out of others. *Non libro sacerdotis, sed labro conservatur scientia.* He lays up good things into his heart, that therewith after they have been well fried for a while, he may feed many ; according to that, Psal. xlv. 1, "My heart is inditing (or frying) a good matter, my tongue shall be the pen of a ready writer." They are empty vines that bear fruit to themselves, Hos. x. 1. A wholesome tongue is a tree of life, Prov. xv. 4. God hath purposely put honey and milk under their tongues, Cant. iv. 11 ; Prov. xxiv. 13, that they may bring forth, as occasion requires, their new and old, that they may look to lip-feeding, that they may be in company like full clouds or paps, that pain themselves with fulness till eased of their milk, or like aromatical trees that sweat out their sovereign oils.

Ver. 53. *He departed thence*] As wanting, and yet waiting, the next opportunity to glorify God, and edify others. Ministers may hence learn, after their hardest labour, not to be weary of well-doing, but to be instant (or to stand close to their work) in season and out of season, even then when that good word of God, that seasons all things, to some seems unseasonable.[1] *Si decimus quisque, si unus persuasus fuerit, ad consolationem abunde sufficit,* as Chrysostom hath it. Say but the tithe of our hearers be persuaded, say but some one of them, it is sufficient encouragement. But what if not one ? yet our labour is not in vain in the Lord. The physician is both thanked and paid, though the patient recover not. And "though Israel be not gathered (as here Christ's countrymen would not be reclaimed), yet I shall be glorious (saith he by his servant Isaiah) in the eyes of the Lord, and my God shall be my strength," Isa. xlix. 5.

Ver. 54. *And when he was come into his own country*] Which naturally draws our hearts to it by a kind of magnetic power and property.[2] Egypt was but a miserable home to Moses, and yet his heart hangs after it, whilst he lived in Midian ; and therefore, in reference to it, he calls his eldest son Gershom, or a stranger there, to wit, where he now was, Exod. ii. 22. *Patriam quisque amat, non quia pulchram, sed quia suam,* saith Seneca. Bishop Jewel, when he first began to preach, chose there first to break the bread of life where he first had breathed the breath of life.

Insomuch that they were astonished] It's a lamentable thing that men should hear, rejoice, and wonder at the word, and for matter of practice leave it where they found it. And yet what more ordinary ? Men look round about a minister ; and though they cannot but admire his doctrine, yet, if they can find ever a hole in his coat through which to slip out, as here, be it but the meanness of his birth, or the unsightliness of his person, or the letsomness of his delivery, &c., it is enough.

Ver. 55. *Is not this the carpenter's son ?*] Why, but was he not architect of the world ? St Mark hath it, "Is not this the carpenter ?" Why, yes ; it may be so. Justin Martyr, an ancient writer, testifieth, that our Saviour, ere he entered upon the ministry, made ploughs, yokes, &c.[3] But was not that an honest occupation ? And did not this carpenter make a coffin for Julian, that persecuting apostate, as a Christian schoolmaster fitly answered Libanius, sarcastically demanding what the carpenter's son was now a-doing ? Thus those three miscreants, Saul, Shimei, and Sheba, took occasion to despise David, as the son of Jesse, who was *vir bonus et honestus, minus tamen clarus,* as one saith of him, a good honest man, but there's little said of him.

Ver. 56. *Whence then hath this man, &c.*] Hath he not got his skill by ill arts ? yea, by the black art doth he work these wonders ? sure he

---

[1] (ἐπίστηθι) 2 Tim. 4. 2.   *Dic importunus, Tu vis errare, Tu vis perire, ego nolo.* Aug.

[2] *Nescio qua natale solum dulcedine cunctos Ducit, et immemores non sinit esse sui.* Ovid.

[3] *Pater Christi politicus, putativus. Fabrum fuisse lignarium, et aratra ac juga, cæteraque ejusmodi fabricasse.* Justin.

never came by all these things honestly, and in God's name. Think it not much to be miscensured.

Ver. 57. *A prophet is not without honour, &c.*] This was an ordinary saying of our Saviour's, recorded by all four evangelists, and is therefore much to be marked. How common is it for familiarity to breed contempt! for men to scorn their own things, because at hand, though never so excellent and useful, to admire foreign things, though nothing comparable. Our corrupt nature heeds nothing we enjoy, as the eye seeth nothing that lies on it. Copy of the best things breeds satiety. God therefore usually teacheth us the worth of them by the want. *Bona a tergo fere formosissima*, Good things are most beautiful on the back-side.

Ver. 58. *He did not many mighty works*] Mark saith he could not do much for them. Christ, that could do all things by his absolute power, could hardly do anything by his actual power (could not, because he would not) for unbelievers. Note here that this journey of his to Nazareth must be distinguished from that set down Luke iv., though the same things are said of both: his countrymen, we see, were no changelings, but continued as bad as before, not a jot the better for that former visit.

Because of their unbelief] A sin of that venomous nature, that it transfuseth, as it were, a dead palsy into the hands of omnipotency. This infectious sorceress can make things exceeding good to prove exceeding evil.

CHAPTER XIV.

Ver. 1. *At that time, &c.*] WHEN he was cast out by his countrymen, he was heard of at the court. The gospel, as the sea, what it loseth in one place, it getteth in another. But what? had not Herod heard of Christ till now? It is the misery of many good kings that they seldom hear the truth of things. Alphonsus king of Arragon bewailed it. And of M. Aurelius, one of the best Roman emperors, it is said, that he was even bought and sold by his court parasites. As for Herod, he may seem to have been of Gallio's religion, even a mere irreligion. He lay melting in filthy pleasures, and minded not the things above. Whoredom, wine, and new wine had taken away his heart, Hos. iv. 11. St Luke, ix. 9, adds that he desired to see Christ, but yet never stirred out of doors to go to him; good motions make but a thoroughfare of wicked men's hearts; they pass away as a flash of lightning, that dazzleth the eyes only, and leaves more darkness behind it.

Ver. 2. *And said unto his servants*] So seeking a diversion of his inward terrors and torments. Perplexed he was and could find no way out, as St Luke's word (ix. 7.) importeth. (Διηπόρει, *de iis dicitur qui ita perplexi, et impediti quasi in*

luto tenentur, ut πόρον μὴ εὑρίσκουσι, exitum non inveniant, Beza.) Conscience will hamper a guilty person, and fill him oft with unquestionable conviction and horror. As those that were condemned to be crucified, bare their cross, that should soon after bear them: so God hath laid upon evil-doers the cross of their own consciences, that thereon they may suffer afore they suffer; and their greatest enemies need not wish them a greater mischief. For assuredly, a body is not so torn with stripes, as a mind with the remembrance of wicked actions. And here Cain runs to building of cities, Saul to the delight of music, Belshazzar to quaffing and carousing, Herod to his minions and catamites;[1] so to put by, if possible, that melancholy dumps and heart-qualms, as they count and call inward terrors. But conscience will not be pacified by these sorry anodynes of the devil. Wicked men may skip and leap up and down for a while, as the wounded deer doth; *sed hæret lateri lethalis arundo*, the deadly dart sticks fast in their sides, and will do without true repentance, till it hath brought them, as it did Herod, to desperation and destruction, so that he laid violent hands upon himself at Lyons in France, whither he and his courtezan were banished by Augustus.[2]

This is John the Baptist] Herod had thought to have hugged his Herodias without control when once the Baptist was beheaded; but it proved somewhat otherwise. Indeed so long as he played alone, he was sure to win all. But now conscience came in to play her part, Herod is in a worse case than ever; for he imagined still that he saw and heard that holy head shouting and crying out against him, staring him also in the face at every turn; as that tyrant thought he saw the head of Symmachus, whom he had basely slain, in the mouth of the fish that was set before him on the table. And as Judge Morgan, who gave the sentence of condemnation against the Lady Jane Grey, shortly after he had condemned her, fell mad, and in his raving cried out continually to have the Lady Jane taken away from him, and so ended his life.

Ver. 3. *For Herod had laid hold on John*] If John touch Herod's white sin (and who will stand still to have his eyes picked out?) John must to prison, without bail or mainprise; and there not only be confined, but bound as a malefactor, as a stirrer-up of sedition (*Unicum crimen eorum qui crimine vacabant*, as Lipsius noteth upon Tacitus). Neither bound only, but beheaded without any law, right, or reason, as though God had known nothing at all of him, as that martyr expresseth it. All this befell the good Baptist, for telling the truth, *Veritas odium parit*. If conscience might but judge, how many of our hearers would be found to have a Herod's heart towards their faithful ministers? Were there but a sword (of authority) in their hand, as he said to his ass, they would surely slay them, Numb. xxii. 29. They would deal by them no better than Saul did by

---

[1] τοῖς παῖσιν αὐτοῦ, to his boys, which haply were his serious loves.

[2] *Nam non multo post hæc, secutum est tyranni exilium et exitium.* Joseph. lib. 18. cap. 9.

David, 1 Sam. xviii. 10, whilst he was playing upon his harp to ease Saul's distracted mind, he cast a spear at him. The most savoury salt (if they can do withal) must be cast out, and trodden under-foot; as Calvin and other faithful ministers were driven out of Geneva at the first; whereupon he uttered these gracious words: Truly, if I had served men, I had been ill rewarded,[1] but it is well for me that I have served Him who never faileth his, but will approve himself a liberal paymaster, a rich rewarder.

And put him in prison] Having first laid hold upon all the principles in his own head that might any way disturb his course in sin, and locked them up in restraint, according to that, Rom. i. 18, wicked men detain the truth, that is, the light of their own consciences (which is as another John Baptist, a prophet from God), this they imprison in unrighteousness, and become fugitives from their own hearts, as Austin hath it.[2]

For Herodias' sake, his brother] *Quam vulpinando fratri eripuerat*, as one phraseth it.[3] And he had her not only for his wife, but for his mistress; for she ruled him at her pleasure, as Jezebel did Ahab, of which wretched couple it is said, that *Regina erat Rex, Rex vero Regina*. But it never goes well when the hen crows. How many have we known, whose heads have been broken with their own rib? Satan hath found this bait to take so well, that he never changed it since he crept into Paradise. And it is remarkable, that in that first sentence against man, this cause is expressed, Because thou obeyedst the voice of thy wife, Gen. iii. 17.

Ver. 4. *For John had said unto him, It is not lawful*] Others knew it to be so, but none durst tell him so but John. In like sort Elijah told Ahab that he had troubled Israel (those times and these did very much suit; John was another Elias, Herod and Herodias answered to Ahab and Jezebel). So Latimer presented for a new-year's gift to King Henry VIII. a New Testament, with a napkin, having this posy about it, Whoremongers and adulterers God will judge. He also wrote a letter to the king, after the proclamation for abolishing English books; where we may see and marvel at his great boldness and stoutness, who as being yet no bishop, so freely and plainly durst to so mighty a prince, in such a dangerous case, against the king's proclamation, set out in such a terrible time, take upon him to write and to admonish that which no counsellor durst once speak unto him, in defence of Christ's gospel. King Asa, though a godly prince, imprisoned the prophet for dealing plainly with him. Archbishop Grindal lost Queen Elizabeth's favour, and was confined, for favouring prophecies, &c., as it was pretended; but in truth, for condemning an unlawful marriage of Julio an Italian physician with another man's wife, whilst Leicester in vain opposed against his proceedings therein. (Camd.

Elizab.) God's truth must be told, however it be taken, and not be betrayed (as it is too oft) by a cowardly silence.

It is not lawful for thee to have her] And yet the pope frequently dispenseth with such incestuous marriages. King Philip III. of Spain, were he now alive, might call the Arch-duke Albert both brother, cousin, nephew, and son: for all this were he unto him, either by blood or affinity: being uncle to himself, cousin-german to his father, husband to his sister, and father to his wife, and all by papal dispensation. Abhorred filth!

Ver. 5. *And when he would have put him to death*] Why, what had the good Baptist done, that he must die? The people must be made believe that he suffereth for practising against the king. But this was so thin a falsehood that it might be transparently seen through.[4] Therefore Herod durst not kill him, though he much desired to do it, lest the people should move mutiny. He knew himself hated by them already for his cruelty and other crimes. Now if he should exasperate them afresh by executing the Baptist, whom they highly honoured, who knew what they would do? Tyrants, how terrible soever, have their fears, that curb and keep them in, for a time at least, from many notorious outrages. In the beginning of Queen Mary's reign, after the tumult at Bourn's sermon at the Cross (where the people flung daggers, and were ready to pull him limb-meal out of the pulpit, for persuading them to Popery), the Lord Mayor and Aldermen were willed to call a common-council, and to signify to the said assembly the Queen's determination, *sc.* that albeit her Grace's conscience is staid in matter of religion, yet she graciously meant not to compel or strain other men's consciences, otherwise than God shall, as she trusted, put in their hearts a persuasion of the truth that she is in, through the opening of the word unto them by godly, virtuous, and learned preachers.

Ver. 6. *But when Herod's birth-day was kept*] All this was a mere plot, as St Mark also intimateth, in those words of his, chap. vi. 21, "And when a convenient day was come." This birth-day then was the day appointed long before by Herod and his harlot for the acting of this tragedy.[5] A great feast must be prepared, the states invited, the damosel must dance, the king swear, the Baptist thereupon be beheaded, that the Queen may be gratified. And this tragedy was new acted at Paris, A.D. 1572, when the French massacre was committed under pretence of a wedding royal. Cardinal Lorrain gave a great sum of money to him that brought the first news thereof to Rome, and the pope caused it to be painted in his palace.

The daughter of Herodias danced] *Tripudiabat* tripped on the toe in a most immodest manner, as they used to do in their bacchanals, as the

---

[1] *Certe si hominibus servivissem, mala mihi merces persolveretur, &c.* Beza in Vita Calv.

[2] *Facti sunt a corde suo fugitivi.*

[3] Pareus Eccles. Hist.

[4] *Tenue mendacium pellucet.* Seneca.

[5] *Res tota ex composito gesta est.* Par.

word signifieth.[1] This old fornicator seemed to be taken and tickled with the sight, that like a madman he swears to give her her request, to the half of the kingdom, which yet was more than he could do, the kingdom being not his, but the Emperor of Rome's, to dispose of. So as Robert, Duke of Normandy, passed through Falaise, he beheld among a company of young maids dancing, one Arlet, a skinner's daughter, whose nimbleness in her dance so enamoured the Duke, that he took her for his concubine, and on her begat our William the Conqueror. Such and no better commonly are the effects of mixed dancings, which made Chrysostom say, *Ubi est saltatio, ibi est diabolus*, Where dancing is, there the devil is. And another ancient calleth dancing a circle, whose centre is the devil, blowing up the fire of concupiscence in the hearts both of the actors and spectators. Augustine saith, *Omnis motus et saltus petulantiæ est saltus in profundum cloacæ*, Every caper in the dance is a leap into a deep jakes. No sober man doth dance, saith Cicero.

And pleased Herod] Who was now well heated with wine as an oven, Prov. xxiii. 31, 33, for then his eyes were apt to behold strange women, and his heart to utter perverse things. *Gula Veneris vestibulum: Et Venus in vinis ignis ut igne furit.* But what a monstrous thing it is to behold green apples on a tree in winter, to find youthful lusts in old decrepit goats?

Ver. 7. *He promised with an oath*] He not only swore rashly, but confessed himself bound thereby to perform his oath (as the Greek word ὡμολόγησεν signifieth), to give her whatsoever she would ask; as Judah did Tamar, and as wantons use to do to their sweethearts. "Ask me never so much dowry and gift," saith Shechem, "and I will give according as ye shall say unto me: but give me the damsel to wife," Gen. xxxiv. 12.

Ver. 8. *And she being before instructed, &c.*] *Partus sequitur ventrem*, the birth follows the belly. Here was like mother like daughter, neither good bird nor good egg, as they say. Κακοῦ κορακὸς κακὸν ὦον. The mother and daughter both had an aching tooth at the Baptist, and sought an opportunity to be meet with him (ἐνεῖχεν αὐτῷ, Mark vi. 19): which now having gotten, they pursued to the utmost. The damosel came with haste to the king, saith St Mark, vi. 25, when once she had her lesson, as fearing, belike, she should come too late. Such another hussy as this was dame Alice Pierce, a concubine to our Edward III. For when as at a parliament in the fiftieth year of that king's reign, it was petitioned that the Duke of Lancaster, the Lord Latimer, chamberlain, and this dame Alice might be amoved from court, and the petition was vehemently urged by their speaker, Sir Peter la Mare; this knight afterwards at the suit of that impudent woman (working upon the king's impotencies) was committed to perpetual imprisonment at Nottingham. And another such history we have of one Diana Valentina, mistress to Henry II., King of France, whom she had so subdued, that he gave her all the confiscations of goods made in the kingdom for cause of heresy. Whereupon many were burned in France for religion, as they said, but indeed to maintain the pride and satisfy the covetousness of that lewd woman. This was in the year 1554. And in the year 1559, Ann du Bourge, a counsellor of state, was burnt also for crime of heresy; not so much by the inclination of the judges as by the resolution of the queen, provoked against him: because, forsooth, the Lutherans gave out that the king had been slain, as he was running at tilt, by a wound in the eye, by the providence of God, for a punishment of his words used against Du Bourge, that he would see him burnt.

Ver. 9. *And the king was sorry*] John's innocency might haply so triumph in Herod's conscience, as to force some grief upon him at the thought of so foul a fact. But I rather think otherwise, that all was but in hypocrisy, Luke xiii. 31. For lasciviousness usually sears up the conscience (till the time of reckoning for all comes) and brings men to that dead and dedolent disposition, Eph. iv. 19. Only this fox feigns himself sorry for John, as his father feigned himself willing to worship the Lord Christ, Matt. ii.; as Tiberius (Herod's lord and master) would seem very sorry for those whom for his pleasure's sake only, he put to death, Gallius Germanicus, Drusus, &c.[2] And as Andronicus the Greek Emperor, that deep dissembler, would weep over those whom he had for no cause caused to be executed, as if he had been the most sorrowful man alive, *Dissimulat mentis suæ malitiam artifex homicida.* This cunning murderer craftily hides his malice, saith St Jerome, and seeming sad in the face is glad at heart to be rid of the importunate Baptist, that he may sin uncontrolled.

For the oath's sake, and them which sat] All this was but pretended to his villany, and that he might have somewhat to say to the people, whom he feared, in excuse for himself. As that he beheaded the Baptist indeed, but his guests would needs have it so, because he had promised the damosel her whole desire, and she would not otherwise be satisfied. Besides, it was his birthday, wherein it was not fit he should deny his nobles anything, who minded him of his oath, &c. But the oath was wicked, and therefore not obligatory.[3] He should have broken it, as David in like case did, 1 Sam. xxv. 33, when he swore a great oath what he would do to Nabal. But Herod, for the avoiding of the sands, rusheth upon the rocks, prevents perjury by murder, not considering the rule, that no man is held so perplexed between two vices, but

---

[1] ὠρχήσατο, ἀπὸ τῶν ὄρχων, a vinearum ordinibus.

[2] *Commiserabatur eos in quos graviter animadvertebat.* Dio.

[3] *Juramenta contra bonos mores facta non sunt obligatoria: est regula in utroque jure.*

that he may find an issue without falling into a third.[1]

And them which sat with him at meat] These he had more respect to than to God. An hypocrite's care is all for the world's approval and applause. They should have showed him his sin, and opposed his sentence. But that is not the guise of godless parasites, those *Aiones et Negones aulici, qui omnia loquuntur ad gratiam, nihil ad veritatem*. These court parasites and parrots know no other tune or tone, but what will please their masters, *quorum etiam sputum lingunt*, as one saith, soothing and smoothing, and smothering up many of their foul facts, that they thereby may the better ingratiate.[2] *Principibus ideo amicus deest quia nihil deest:* there is a wonderful sympathy between princes and parasites. But David would none of them, Psal. ci. 7, and Sigismond, the emperor, cussed them out of his presence. And surely if wishing were anything (said Henricus Stephanus), like as the Thessalians once utterly overthrew the city called Flattery, so I could desire, that above all other malefactors, court parasites were utterly rooted out, as the most pestilent persons in the world.

Ver. 10. *And he sent and beheaded John*] Put him to death in hugger-mugger, as the Papists did and do still (in the bloody Inquisition-house especially) many of the martyrs. Stokesby, bishop of London, caused Mr John Hunne to be thrust in at the nose with hot burning needles, whiles he was in the prison, and then to be hanged there; and said he had hanged himself. Another bishop having in his prison an innocent man, because he could not overcome him by Scripture, called him privily to be snarled, and his flesh to be torn and plucked away with pincers; and bringing him before the people, said the rats had eaten him. And I have heard of a certain bishop, saith Melancthon, that so starved ten good men whom he held in prison for religion, that before they died they devoured one another. *Quis unquam hoc audivit in Phalaridis historia?* saith he: who ever heard of such a cruelty? But it so pleaseth God, for excellent ends, to order that all things here come alike to all, yea, that none out of hell suffer more than the saints. This made Erasmus say, upon occasion of the burning of Berquin, a Dutch martyr, *Damnari, dissecari, suspendi, exuri, decollari piis cum impiis sunt communia. Damnare, dissecare, in crucem agere, exurere, decollare, bonis judicibus cum piratis ac tyrannis communia sunt. Varia sunt hominum judicia; ille fælix, qui judice Deo absolvitur.* The Athenians were much offended at the fall of their general Nicias, discomfited and slain in Sicily; as seeing so good a man to have no better fortune.[3] But they knew not God, and therefore raged at him. But we must lay our hands upon our mouths when God's hand is upon our backs or necks: and stand on tiptoes, with Paul, to see which way Christ may be most magnified in our bodies, whether by life or by death, Phil. i. 20.

Ver. 11. *And his head was brought, &c.*] This was *merces mundi*, the world's wages to John for all his pains in seeking to save their souls. Surely as Cæsar once said of Herod the Great (this man's father), it were better to be Herod's swine than his son; so (saith one) many ministers have, through the corruption of the time, cause to think, it were better to be Herod's minstrel than minister, player than preacher, dancer than doctor.

And given to the damsel] The Romans condemned it for a detestable cruelty in Quintus Flaminius, that to gratify his harlot Placentina he beheaded a certain prisoner in her presence at a feast. This Livy calleth *facinus sævum atque atrox*, a cursed and horrid act: and Cato the censor cast him out of the senate for it. Neither was it long ere this tyrant Herod had his payment from heaven. For Aretas, king of Arabia (offended with him for putting away his daughter, and taking to wife Herodias), came upon him with an army, and cut off all his forces. Which loss all men interpreted, saith Josephus, xviii. 7, as a just vengeance of God upon him, for his unjust usage of the Baptist. And within a while after, being accused at Rome by his brother Agrippa, and convicted that he had 70,000 arms in readiness against the emperor, he was banished into France (as is above said) together with his Herodias, where he became his own deathsman.

And she brought it to her mother] As a most welcome present, and pleasant dish at this Thyestean supper. Whether it was carried about the table for a merry sight (as Aretius thinks), or whether she pricked his tongue with needles, as Josephus saith (as they did Tully's, setting up his head in the pleading place, *ubi iis concionibus multorum capita servarat*, as Seneca hath it), I have nothing to affirm. But we want not examples of some tigers and tigresses, that have taken pleasure in such unrighteousness; witness Hannibal's *O formosum spectaculum!* O goodly bloody sight! when he saw a pit full of man's blood; Valesas, his *O rem regiam*, when he had slain 300; Stokesly, his glorying on his death-bed, that he had been the death of 50 herewigs, heretics he meant; Story, his vaunting that he tossed a faggot at Denly the martyr's face, as he was singing a psalm, and set a wine bush of thorns under his feet, a little to prick him, &c. This he spake in the parliament in Queen Elizabeth's days, whom he usually cursed in his grace before meat, and was therefore worthily hanged, drawn, and quartered. Whereunto we may add that queen (another

---

[1] *Nemo ita perplexus tenetur inter duo vitia, quin exitus pateat absque tertio.*

[2] *Apud principes ἡ ἥκιστα ἡ ἥδιστα, ut sensit quidam Cræsi conciliarius.*

[3] *Nec te tua plurima Pantheu Labentem texit pietas.* Ἀνδρα ὁρῶντες θεοφιλῆ οὐδενὸς ἐπιεικεστέρα τυχῇ χρῆσθαι τῶν κακίστων ἀποκαραδοκίᾳ.

Herodias) who, when she saw some of her Protestant subjects lying dead and stripped upon the earth, cried out, The goodliest tapestry that she ever beheld.

Ver. 12. *And his disciples came and took*] A pious and courteous office, such as Joseph of Arimathea boldly performed to Christ, and those devout men to Stephen, making great lamentation over him, Acts viii. 2. Good blood will not belie itself: fire will not long be hid. Sir Anthony Kingston came to Bishop Hooper a little before he was burnt, and said, I thank God that ever I knew you, &c. And another knight came to George Tankerfield when he was at the stake, and taking him by the hand, said, Good brother, be strong in Christ, &c. Oh, sir, said he, I thank you, I am so, I thank God. It is a high praise to Onesiphorus that he sought out Paul, the prisoner, and was not ashamed of his chain, 2 Tim. i. 16, 17. And to David's brethren, that they came down to him to the cave of Adullam, though to their great danger, 1 Sam. xxii. 1; to the good women in the Gospel, that they came to the sepulchre to embalm Christ's body, though it were guarded by a band of soldiers; and to those Christians in Chrysostom's time that could not be kept from visiting the confessors in prison, though it were straitly forbidden them, upon pain of many mulcts and dangers.[1]

And went and told Jesus] Whom should we tell of the sufferings of his servants and ourselves, but Jesus? Say to him of his labouring Church, as they did once of his friend Lazarus, Behold, she whom thou lovest is sick, or otherwise hardly dealt with. "Then will he soon be jealous for his land, and pity his people," Joel ii. 18: he will play Phineas's part, and thrust a spear through the loins of his enemies, that offer to force the queen also in the house. But it's worth the noting that John's disciples, who before had emulated Christ and joined with the Pharisees against him, now repair unto him, and inform him of their master's death; being henceforth willing to become his disciples. Misery makes unity, and drives them to Christ, who, till then, had no such mind to him.

Ver. 13. *When Jesus heard of it, &c.*] Dangers must be declined, where they may be with a safe conscience. David and Peter (who had both paid for their learning) say both, What man is he that loveth life, and would see good (or quiet) days? Psal. xxxiv. 12; 1 Pet. iii. 10.

They followed him on foot] Hot-foot as they say. So the people resorted to Bishop Ridley's sermons, swarming about him like bees, and coveting the sweet juice of his godly discourses. Whose diligence and devotion is check to our dulness and devotion: if Christ would set up a pulpit at the alehouse door, some would hear him oftener.

Ver. 14. *Was moved with compassion, and healed their sick*] Christ's mercy was not a mouth-mercy: such as was that of those in St James's time, that said to their necessitous neighbours, Depart in peace, be warmed: but with what? with a fire of words. Be filled: but with what? with a mess of words. For they gave them not those things that were needful to the body, Jam. iii. 15, 16. But our Saviour, out of deep commiseration, both pitied the people, and healed them on both sides, within and without. Oh, how well may he be called a Saviour, which in the original is a word so full of emphasis, that other tongues can hardly find a fit word to express it by.[2]

Ver. 15. *His disciples came to him*] Not the multitudes. They forgat their bodily necessities to attend upon Christ, to hang upon his honey lips, preferring his holy word before their necessary food, as did Job, chap. xxiii. 12. Not only before his dainties and superfluities, but his substantial food, without which he could not long live and subsist. These hearers of our Saviour came out of their cities, where they had everything at full, into the desert, where they thought nothing was to be had, to hear him. I had rather live in hell, with the word, said Luther, than in paradise without it. Our forefathers gave five marks, some of them (which is more money than ten pounds is now), for a good book: and some others of them gave a load of hay for a few chapters of St Paul or St James in English. To hear a sermon they would go as many weary steps as those good souls did, Psal. lxxxiv. 7, or as these in the text; and neglect or hazard their bodies, to save their souls. How far are they from this that will not put themselves to any pain or cost of heaven! and if held awhile beyond the hour at a sermon are as ill-settled as if they were in the stocks, or in a fit of an ague: they go out of the church as out of a gaol.

This is a desert place, &c.] Christ knew all this, better than they could tell him: and to take upon them to tell him, was as if the ostrich should bid the storks be kind to her young ones, *Ac si struthiocamelus ciconiam τῆς στοργῆς admoneret.* Cartuo.

Ver. 16. *They need not depart*] Whither should they go from the great house-keeper of the world, the all-sufficient God? *Habet certè omnia, qui habet habentem omnia.* Augustine. Christ hath a cornucopia, a horn of salvation, plenteous redemption, &c. And if he give us a crown, will he deny us a crust? "The earth is the Lord's, and the fulness thereof." He feeds the ravens, and clothes the lilies. If meat be denied, he can take away our stomachs. He can feed us by a miracle, as he did Elias of old, and the Rochellers of late.

Ver. 17. *And they say unto him, We have here*] And were therefore ready to say with Nicodemus, "How can this be?" Christ had said, "Give ye them to eat," to try them only, as St John (vi. 6) hath it. And upon trial, he found them full of

---

[1] *Tametsi multis terroribus, minis, et periculis interdictum esset.* Chrysost. Orat. de duob. Martyr.

[2] *Sotera inscriptum vidi Syracusis. Hoc quantum est? Ita magnum, ut Latine uno verbo exprimi non possit.* Cicero.

dross, as appears by their answer. But the comfort is, he hath promised to try his people indeed, but not as silver, Isa. xlviii. 10; lest they should not bear any so exact a trial, as having more dross in them than good ore. And where he finds any the least grain of true grace, he cherisheth and enhanceth it, by a further partaking of his holiness. The disciples here were as yet very carnal, and spake as men, 1 Cor. iii. 3. They were ready to limit the Holy One, and say with those of old, " Can he prepare a table in the wilderness ? " They measured him by their model, and looked, as Naaman did, upon Jordan with Syrian eyes. This was their fault, and must be our warning; that when we think of God, we shut out Hagar and set up Sarah, silence our reason and exalt our faith; which killeth and quelleth distrustful fear, and believes against sense in things invisible, and against reason in things incredible.

But five loaves and two fishes] Tyrabosco was hardly driven, when from these five loaves and two fishes he concluded seven sacraments: two, belike, of God's making, and five of the baker's. So Cenalis, Bishop of Auranches, would prove the Church of Rome the true Church, because it had bells by which their assemblies be ordinarily called together : but the Church of the Lutherans was reported to be congregated by claps of harquebuses and pistolets; and so makes a long antithesis, by the which he would make good, the bells are the makers of the true Church. As that bells do sound, the other crack : bells open heaven, the other hell, &c.

Ver. 18. *Bring them hither to me*] Bring we all we have and are to Christ, that he may take off the curse and add the blessing. What the apostle saith of meat and marriage, is true of the rest, " all things are sanctified by the word and prayer," 1 Tim. iv. 3. To teach the people this it was, that the fruit of the trees was not to be eaten till the trees were circumcised, Lev. xix. 23.

Ver. 19. *And looking up to heaven, he blessed*] Heathens consecrated their cates before they tasted them, as appears by many passages in Homer and Virgil. Some say that the elephant, ere he eats his meat, turns up with his trunk the first sprig towards heaven. The Scripture, we are sure, says, that "men eat to God when they give thanks," Rom. xiv. 6. To whom then do they eat that give none ?

And the disciples, to the multitude] They grudged not of their little to give others some, and it grew in their hands, as the widow's oil did in the cruse. Not getting, but giving, is the way to thrive. Nothing was ever lost by liberality.

Ver. 20. *And were filled*] So David's cup overflowed, Psal. xxiii. 5; he had not only a sufficience but an affluence. So, at the marriage of Cana, Christ gave them wine enough for 150 guests, John ii. 10. Howbeit he hath not promised us superfluities. Having food and raiment, let us be content, 1 Tim. vi. 8. A little

of the creature will serve to carry us through our pilgrimage.

And they took up of the fragments] Thrift is a great revenue (*ingens vectigal parsimonia*), and good husbandry well-pleasing to God, Prov. xxvii. 26, 27, so it degenerate not into niggardise.

Twelve baskets full] If we consider what they are, we may wonder they left anything, as if, what they left, that they ate anything.

Ver. 21. *Were about five thousand*] Pythias is famous for that he was able, at his own charge, to entertain Xerxes' whole army, consisting of ten hundred thousand men. But he grew so poor upon it, that he wanted bread ere he died. Our Saviour fed five thousand, and his store not a jot diminished : but as it is said of a great mountain of salt in Spain, *de quo quantum demas tantum accrescit ;* so is it here.

Besides women and children] Which did very much add to the number, and so to the miracle. But they are not reckoned of here, (not out of any base esteem of them, as the Jews at this day hold women to be of a lower creation than men, and made only for the propagation and pleasure of men, but) because they eat little in comparison of men.

Ver. 22. *Jesus constrained his disciples*] Who seem to have been full loth to leave his sweet company. The presence of friends (how much more of such a friend!) is so sweet, that death itself is called but a departure. Christ compelled them, which is no more than commanded them (say some), to get into a ship : 1. Lest they should take part with the rash many-headed multitude, who would have made him a King, John vi. Thus he many times prevents sin in his by removing occasions. 2. To inure them to the cross, and to teach them, as good soldiers, to suffer hardship, which the flesh takes heavily. 3. To give them proof of his power, now perfected in their weakness, when they were ready to be shipwrecked, and to teach them to pray to him absent, whom present they had not prized to the worth, as appears, ver. 17. When we cast our precious things at our heels, as children, our heavenly Father lays them out of the way another while, that we may know the worth by the want, and so grow wiser.

He sent the multitudes away] That he might shun even the suspicion of sedition. We must not only look to our consciences, but to our credits. " Why should I be as one that turneth aside ? " Cant. i. 7, saith the Church, or as one that is veiled and covered, which was the habit of a harlot ? Why should I seem to be so, though I be none such ? We must shun appearances of evil, whatsoever is but evil-favoured. *Quicquid fecerit male coloratum.* Bern.

Ver. 23. *He went up into a mountain apart to pray*] Secret prayer fats the soul, as secret morsels feed the body : therefore is it said to be the banquet of grace, where the soul may solace herself with God, as Esther did with Ahasuerus at the banquet of wine, and have whatsoever heart can wish or need require. Only (because *anima dispersa sit minor*) get into such a corner, as where we may be most free to call upon God without distraction, remembering our own fickleness, and Satan's restlessness.

When the evening was come, he was there alone] Retire we must sometimes, and into fit places, to meet God, as Balaam did, Numb. xxiii. 15, but to better purpose; solacing ourselves and entertaining soliloquies with him, as Isaac did in the fields, Jacob upon the way, Ezekiel by the river Chebar, Peter upon the leads, Christ here upon the mountain. Whilst the disciples were perilling, and well-nigh perishing, Christ was praying for them: so he is still for us, at the right hand of the Majesty on high.

Ver. 24. *Tossed with waves*] So is the Church oft, therefore styled, " O thou afflicted and tossed with tempest, that hast no comfort," Isa. liv. 11. Jesus was absent all the while: so he seemeth to be from his darlings in their desertions; he leaveth them, as it were, in the suburbs of hell, and (which is worst of all) himself will not come at them. Howbeit as the eagle when she flieth highest of all from the nest, doth evermore cast a jealous eye upon her young; so doth this heavenly eagle.

For the wind was contrary] So it is ever lightly to the Church: this world being like the Straits of Magellan, wherein which way soever a man bends his course, he is sure to have the wind sit cross to him. But the comfort is, that whether north or south blow, they both blow good to a Christian, Cant. iv. 16.

Ver. 25. *And in the fourth watch, &c.*] Then, and not till then. His time is best, whatever we think of it: his help most sweet, because most seasonable: his hand commonly kept for a dead-lift.

Ver. 26. *They were troubled*] Ere they were helped: things oft go backward, ere they come forward with us. *Deus plagam sanaturus, graviorem infligit*: he knows how to commend his mercies to us.

And they cried out for fear] For fear of him, in whom was laid up all their comfort. But *pessimus in dubiis augur, timor.*—How oft are we mistaken, and befooled by our fears!

Ver. 27. *But straightway Jesus spake, &c.*] He waits to be gracious, Isa. xxx. 18. Our extremity is his opportunity. *Cum duplicantur lateres venit Moses.* God brings his people to the mount with Abraham, yea, to the very brow of the hill, till their feet slip, and then delivers them: when all is given up for lost, then comes he in, as out of an engine, ἐκ μηχανῆς.

It is I, fear not] *Quid timet homo in sinu Dei positus?* A child that is in his father's bosom fears no bugbears.

Ver. 28. *If it be thou, bid me come unto thee, &c.*] This fact of Peter some extol as an argument of his strong faith and love to Christ. But others of better judgment censure it as an effect of unbelief and rashness in him, requiring to be confirmed by a miracle; to the which, though our

¹ διὰ τί ἐδίστασας; *Sic dubito non inepte*

Saviour assented, yet we cannot say that he approved it. The other disciples believed Christ upon his bare word, but Peter must have a sign. He had it, but with a check, ver. 31.

Ver. 29. *And he said, Come*] Had the Pharisees asked a sign, they should have gone without, and have heard, Wicked and bastardly brood, as Matt. xii. 39. But a Peter shall have it, rather than he shall halt betwixt two, as the word is, ver. 31.¹ Christ condescends to his infirmity, and bids him come. And the like was his dealing with that virtuous gentlewoman, Mistress Honywood; who, doubting much of her salvation, was often counselled by a worthy minister to take heed of inquiries further than God's word, &c. Yet still did the temptation grow upon her, insomuch that having a Venice glass in her hand, and the same minister sitting by her; " You have often told me," said she to him, " that I must seek no further than God's word. But I have been long without comfort, and can endure no longer; therefore if I must be saved let this glass be kept from breaking; " and so she threw it against the walls. The glass rebounds again and comes safe to the ground; which the minister having gotten into his hands, saith, " Oh, repent of this sin, bless God for his mercy, and never distrust him more of his promise; for now you have his voice from heaven in a miracle, telling you plainly of your estate." " This was curiosity," saith my author, " and might have brought despair; yet it was the Lord's mercy to remit the fault and grant an extraordinary confirmation of her faith."

Ver. 30. *But when he saw the wind boisterous*] Every bird can sing in a sun-shine day; and it is easy to swim in a warm bath; but to believe in an angry God, as David; in a killing God, as Job; to stick to him in deepest desertion, as the Church, Psal. xliv. 17, 18; to trust in his name, and stay upon his word, where there is darkness and no light, as Isa. l. 10; to cast anchor even in the darkest night of temptation, when neither sun nor stars appear, as Paul and his company, Acts xxvii. 20, praying still for day, and waiting till it dawn, *O quam hoc non est omnium!* this is not in the power of every Peter, who yet shall be graciously supported that they faint not, neither sink under the heaviest burthen of their light afflictions. It was not so much the strength of the wind, as the weakness of his faith, that put Peter into this fit of fear. Be we faithful in weakness, though weak in faith, and it shall go well with us. Be as a ship at anchor, which, though it move much, yet removes not at all.

Ver. 31. *O thou of little faith, &c.*] Thou pettyfidian, small-faith; Christ chides Peter, and yet helps him. Involuntary failings, unavoidable infirmities, discard us not; as robberies done by pirates of either nation break not the league between princes; as lesser failings dissolve not the marriage-knot. Christ knew us well before he took us, yet took us for better for worse. 2. He " hates putting away," Mal. ii. 16, and herein, as he is above law, so his mercy is matchless, Jer. *explanari possit quasi sit a duo et ito.* Becm.

iii. 1. Joshua the high priest, though he was ill-clothed, yet he stood before the angel, Zech. iii. 3. Much will be so borne with, where the fault is of passion merely, or of incogitancy and inadvertency, as here.

Ver. 32. *The wind ceased*] As if it had been weary of blowing so big, and now desired rest after hard labour ; as the word here used importeth. Herodotus useth the same word in the same sense, where he speaks of a tempest layed by the magicians.[1] Rupertus calleth the winds the world's besoms, which are used by God to sweep his great house and purge the air.[2] If the prince of the air make use of them to sweep God's children, as he did Job's children, out of the world, it cannot be said, as 1 Kings xix. 11, that God is not in that wind ; for he numbereth their hairs, and counts their flittings ; and being the great Æolus, lays laws upon the winds and waves, which instantly obey him. No sooner was Christ in the ship but they were all at land.

Ver. 33. *Of a truth thou art the Son of God*] Not by creation, as Adam and the angels, Luke iii. 38 ; Job i. 6. Nor by adoption, as all believers, John i. 12. But, 1. By eternal generation, Prov. viii. 22 ; 2. By personal union, Psal. ii. 7.

Ver. 34. *They came into the land of Gennesaret*] Where he presently found some that observed him. When God sets up a light in any place, a burning and a shining light, there is some work to be done. A husbandman would not send his servant with his sickle to reap thistles and nettles only. The ministry sent to a place, is an argument of some elect there, 2 Thess. i. 5.

Ver. 35. *They sent out into all that country*] See their charity. The Philistines were not so ambitious of sending the plague, together with the ark, one to another, as these were of helping their neighbours to health, to heaven. We are born for the benefit of many, as Bucer's physicians told him, *Non sibi se, sed multorum utilitati esse natum.* (Melch. Adam.) Public persons especially must have public spirits. Kings have in Greek their names from healing ;[3] and rulers are called healers or binders-up of wounds, Isa. iii. 7.

Ver. 36. *And as many as touched, &c.*] Oh the matchless might and mercy of Christ our Saviour ! He condescends to their infirmity, and heals them promiscuously, not once questioning their deserts. He giveth to all men liberally, and hitteth no man in the teeth with his former failings or present infirmities, James i. 5. Be we also, by his example, ready to distribute, willing to communicate. This was the philosophical friendship of the Pythagoreans, the legal of the Essenes (a sect among the Jews, that had their names of healing),[4] and should be most of all the evangelical friendship of us Christians. " Thou shalt be called the repairer of the breach, the restorer," &c., Isa. lviii. 12 : a gallant title, better than a thousand escutcheons.

CHAPTER XV.

Ver. 1. *Then came to Jesus*] THEN, when the men of Gennesaret favoured and observed him. Satan stomacheth the prosperity of God's kingdom in any place, and stirreth up his to oppose it. Esau began with Jacob in the womb, that no time might be lost. As soon as ever the Church's child was born the devil sought to drown him, Rev. xii.

Scribes and Pharisees] Learned and lewd; these are Christ's greatest enemies, hypocrites especially, those night birds that cannot bear the light of true religion, but, as bats, beat against it.

Which were of Jerusalem] That faithful city was now become an harlot, her silver was degenerate into dross, her wine mixed with water, Isa. i. 22. The sweetest wine turns into the sourest vinegar, the whitest ivory burned, into the blackest coal. So about the year 1414, Theodoricus Urias, in Germany, an Augustine friar, complained, not without cause, *Ecclesiam Romanam ex aureâ factam argenteam, ex argenteâ ferream, ex ferreâ terream, superesse ut in stercus abiret.* Machiavel observed that there was nowhere less piety than in those that dwelt nearest to Rome.[5]

Ver. 2. *Transgress the tradition of the elders*] They cried up aloud traditions and the authority of antiquity. *Similem hodie dicam Papistæ nobis scribunt.* For as the philosophers fled and hid themselves in the heretics, as one saith, so did the Scribes and Pharisees in the Popish doctors. *Non tam ovum ovo simile* ; one egg or apple is not so like another as Pharisees and Papists. The Pharisees deemed it as great a sin to eat with unwashen hands as to commit fornication. Semblably, the Papists count it worse to deface an idol than to kill a man, to eat flesh or eggs on a fasting day than to commit incest, and for a priest to have one wife than ten harlots. Παράδοσις, say some, is the number of the Beast, 666. Pareus *in loc.*

Ver. 3. *He answered and said unto them*] He shapes them an answer by way of recrimination (ἀντέγκλημα) ; which is a singular means of conviction to the adversary, but hard to be done by us without some mixture of bitterness, such as was that in David to Michal, 2 Sam. vi. 21.

Transgress the commandment of God by your tradition] God's commands should be kept as the apple of the eye, Prov. vii. 2. They are broken by omissions, commissions, and failings in the manner ; like as a man may miss the mark by shooting short, or beyond, or wide. These Pharisees, as those Athenians of old (whereas they had most excellent laws, but most lawless natures), chose rather to live by their lusts than by their laws.[6] They had many traditions and unwritten verities, pretended to be invented and prescribed

---

[1] ἐκόπασεν. *Pacatus fuit, quasi vir stando delassatus.* Herod. *in Polymnia.* [2] *Scopus mundi.* Rupert. Virgil, Æneid, i. 65. [3] Αναξ *ab* ἄκος, Medela. *Chirurgis et reip. Medicus rex.* [4] Essenes from the Syriac אסא to heal; for besides the

Bible they studied physic. Godw. Antiq. Hebr.
[5] Machiavel. *Disput. de rep.* lib. 1. cap. 12.
[6] *Athenienses cum haberent æquissima jura, sed iniquissima ingenia, moribus suis quam legibus, uti malunt.* Valer. Max.

them by their elders, that by the observation thereof they might be the better enabled to keep God's commandments. These traditions they styled Mashlamnathoth, completions or perfections; because thereby they conceited that the written law was made more complete and perfect. And say not the Papists as much of their traditions? Buxtorf. Tiber.

Ver. 4. *For God commanded, saying*] This is called the first commandment with promise, viz. the first affirmative commandment, or the first in the second table; or the first of all the ten with promise.[1] For that in the second commandment is rather a declaration of God's justice and mercy, and that to the observers of the whole law; but here is a particular promise made to them that keep this particular commandment.

Honour thy father and mother] Among other good offices, nourish and cherish them, as Joseph did Jacob and his family, *Chepi tappam*, as a man nourisheth his little ones, lovingly and tenderly, Gen. xlvii. 12; be unto them as Obed was to Naomi, "a restorer of her life, and a nourisher of her old age," Ruth iv. 15. This the apostle commends to us, as a thing not only good before men, but acceptable before God, 1 Tim. v. 4. This the stork and the mouse teach us, by their singular love to their aged sires, Plin. x. 23. Cornelius was the staff of his father's age, and thereby merited the honourable name of Scipio among the Romans. Epaminondas rejoiced in nothing more, than that he had lived to cheer up the hearts of his aged parents by the reports of his victories. Our parents are our household gods, said Hierocles.[2] Æneas is surnamed Pius, for his love to his father, whom he bore upon his back out of the fire of Troy. And Aristotle tells how that when from the hill Ætna there ran down a torrent of fire that consumed all the houses thereabouts, in the midst of those fearful flames God's special care of the godly shined most brightly. For the river of fire parted itself, and made a kind of lane for those who ventured to rescue their aged parents, and pluck them out of the jaws of death.[3]

He that curseth father or mother] That giveth them an ill word (κακολογῶν), or but an ill look; for *vultu sæpe læditur pietas*. "The eye that mocketh at his father, and despiseth to obey his mother, the ravens of the valley shall pick it out, and the young eagles shall eat it."[4] Now they are cursed with a witness, whom the Holy Ghost thus curseth in such emphatical manner, in such exquisite terms.

Ver. 5. *But ye say, Whosoever, &c.*] The intolerable covetousness of the priests bred this abominable corruption of this commandment, as it did many other like.[5] See my notes on John ii. 14, 15. By the same arts at this day the Lady of

Loretto, as they call her, hath her churches so stuffed with vowed presents and memories, as they are fain to hang their cloisters and churchyards with them. The rood of grace in this kingdom had a man within it, enclosed with a hundred wires to make the image goggle with the eyes, nod with the head, hang the lip, move and shake his jaws, according as the value was of the gift that was offered. If it were a small piece of silver, he would hang a frowning lip; if a piece of gold, then should his jaws go merrily. The like was done by the blood of Hales, brought afterwards by the Lord Cromwell to Paul's Cross, and there proved to be the blood of a duck. In the year 1505, Pope Alexander sent a bull of pardons for money into England, dispensing thereby with such as kept away, or by any fraud had gotten, the goods of other men, which they should now retain still without scruple of conscience, so as they paid a ratable portion thereof to his Holiness' receivers. This was pure Pharisaism.

It is a gift by whatsoever, &c.] Some read it thus, by "Corban, or by this gift, if thou receive any profit by me;" understand, then let God do thus and much more to me, *q. d.* by Corban thou shalt receive no profit by me. Others thus, Corban, *anathema sit*, be it a devoted thing whatsoever I may profit thee by:[6] *q. d.* Being consecrated to God, it shall be beneficial to us both, and not here only in this life, but hereafter in that to come, whereas cost bestowed upon parents soon vanisheth, and reacheth no further than the life present.

Ver. 6. *And honour not his father and his mother*] Supple, *insons erit*. Our Saviour contents himself to relate the first words only of the tradition, as lawyers use to do the first words of the statute or canon they quote or argue upon.

Thus have you made the commandment of none effect][7] Ye have sought to shoulder God out of his throne, to divest and spoil him of his rule and authority, to ungod him, as it were, by making his commandment void and invalid. And do not Papists as much as all this, whiles they teach that a monk may not leave his cloister to relieve his father, but must rather see and suffer him to die for hunger in the streets. Lyra hath these very words, *Filius per professionem factam in religione, excusatur a subveniendo parentibus*. This Lyra was a famous English Jew, but an arrant Papist, as for most part all were then, for he flourished A.D. 1320.

Ver. 7. *Well did Esaias prophesy of you*] Of such as you, and so of you too. The prophets and apostles then spake not of them only with whom they lived, and to whom they wrote (as the Jesuits blaspheme), but their oracles and doctrines do extend still to men of the same

---

[1] Ephes. vi. 2: ἐντολὴ properly signifieth an affirmative commandment. See Dr Gouge on Dom. Duties.

[2] Οἱ γονεῖς ἡμῶν Θεοὶ ἐφέστιοι.

[3] πλησίον γὰρ αὐτῶν γενόμενος πυρὸς ποταμὸς ἐξεσχίθη. Arist. de Mundo, cap. 6.

[4] Prov. xxx. 17. *Effossos oculos voret atro gutture corvus.* Catul.

[5] ἡ φιλοχρηματία μητὴρ κακότητος ἁπάσης.

[6] ὁ ἐαν, *si quicquam, ut* Matt. x. 14, and xxiii. 18. Scultet.

[7] ἠκυρώσατε, of ἀ *et* κῦρος, rule, authority.

stamp and making. "In the volume of thy book it is written of me," saith David, Psal. xl. 7; he found his own name in God's book. And where he spake with Jacob at Bethel, there he spake with us, saith Hosea (xii. 4); and, "Whatsoever was written, was written for our learning, saith Paul, Rom. xiv. 4.

Ver. 8. *This people draweth nigh unto me, &c.*] And they are no changelings, for at this day, although they know better, and can write upon the walls of their synagogues this sentence, *Tephillah belo cauvannah cheguph belo neshamah*, that is, Prayer without the intention of the mind, is but as a body without a soul, yet shall not a man anywhere see less intention than in their orisons. "The reverence they show" (saith Sir Edwin Sands, who saw it) "is in standing up at times, and the gesture of adoration in the bowing forward of their bodies. For kneeling they use none (no more do the Grecians), neither stir they their bonnets in their synagogues to any man, but remain still covered. They come to it with washen hands, and in it they burn lamps to the honour of God,[1] but for any show of devotion or elevation of spirit, that yet in Jews could I never discern, but they are as reverent in their synagogues as grammar-boys are at school, when their master is absent. In sum, their holiness is the very outward work itself, being a brainless head and soulless body." Thus he.

And honoureth me with their lips] But prayer is not the labour of the lips, but the travail of the heart; the power of a petition is not in the roof of the mouth, but root of the heart. To give way to wilful distractions, is to commit spiritual whoredom in God's presence. Is it fit to present the king with an empty cask? or to tell him a tale with our backs towards him? Behold, "I am a great King," saith God; and they that stand before him, "must look to their feet," saith Solomon, that they stand upright, and that they offer not a heartless sacrifice, for that is the "sacrifice of fools," Eccles. v. 1, and ever held ominous.

But their heart is far from me] And so all they do is putrid hypocrisy. God loves "truth in the inward parts," Psal. xli. 6, and calls for the heart in all services, as Joseph did for Benjamin, as David did for Michal, "Thou shalt not see my face, unless thou bring it." In all spiritual sacrifices we must bring him the fat and the inwards. The deeper and hollower the belly of the lute or viol is, the pleasanter is the sound; the fleeter, the more grating and harsh in our ears. The voice which is made in the mouth is nothing so sweet as that which cometh from the depth of the breast. Eph. vi. 6, "Do the will of God from the heart." But woe be to all careless professors, to all loose and ungirt Christians! the Lord will make all the churches to know "that he searcheth the hearts and reins," and that "he will kill with death" all such as had rather seem to be good than seek to be so, Rev. ii. 23.

Ver. 9. *But in vain do they worship me*] For they lose their labour, and, which is worse, they commit sin. Displeasing service is double dishonour, as dissembled sanctity is double iniquity.

Teaching for doctrines the commandments of men] So do Papists. The pope can do all things that Christ can do, saith Hostiensis. He can of wickedness make righteousness, saith Bellarmine; of virtue, vice; of nothing, something. His determinations are *ipsissimum Dei verbum*, the very word of God, saith Hosius. Murders, treasons, thefts, &c.—there is no command of the moral law, but they can dispense with it; but none of their ceremonial law. Let God, say they, look to the breach of his own law, we will look to ours. Heathen Socrates and Cicero shall rise up against these pseudo-Christians, and condemn them. God, said Socrates, will be worshipped with that kind of worship only which himself hath commanded. He will not be worshipped, said Cicero, with superstition, but with piety: *Deus non superstitione coli vult sed pietate*.

Ver. 10. *And he called the multitude*] The Pharisees, those deaf adders, sith they would not be charmed, Christ will lose no more sweet words upon them; but turns them up as desperate, with this inscription on their foreheads: *Noluerunt incantari;* I would have healed these hypocrites, but they would not be healed. Yea, "When I would have healed Ephraim, then" (to cross me) "their iniquity was discovered," as the leprosy in their foreheads, Hos. vii. 1. And from such uncounselable and incorrigible hearers, if a minister depart, he doth but his duty; the desertion is on their part, and not on his. "The manifestation of the Spirit is given to every man to profit withal," 1 Cor. xii. 7.

Ver. 11. *Not that which goeth into the man, &c.*] Whether with clean or foul hands, taken meat makes not the man guilty of God's wrath. What! not if abused to surfeiting and drunkenness? saith Bellarmine, who is angry with Christ for this doctrine (as making against theirs directly), and therefore seeks to disprove him. We answer for and with Christ: that he speaks here of the moderate use of meats, which is indifferent. As for the abuse of it to surfeiting and excess, this is an evil that cometh out of the heart, and defileth the man, as being a flat breach of the law of God, who everywhere condemns it.

But that which cometh out of the mouth] That is, out of the heart, that muck-hill, through the mouth, as through a dung-port, that defileth a man worse than any jakes can do. Hence sin is called filthiness, abomination, the vomit of a dog, the devil's excrements, &c. The very visible heavens are defiled by it, and must therefore be purged by fire, as those vessels were that held the sin-offering. As for the soul, sin sets such ingrained stains upon it, as nothing can fetch out but the blood of Christ, that spotless Lamb.

Ver. 12. *Knowest thou that the Pharisees, &c.*] q. d. Why dost thou then thus call the people to

---

[1] *Sic ut posset quivis animo advertere quod servet illam pro consuetudine potius quam pro religione reverentiam.* De Theo-

dorico, Sidonius, Epist. i. 1.

thee, and exclude them ? It was a commendable charity in the disciples, to desire the better information of those that had causelessly accused them, verse 2, and to tender their salvation. " Be not overcome of evil, but overcome evil with good." *Speciosiùs aliquanto injuriæ beneficiis vincuntur quam mutui odii pertinaciâ pensantur,* saith a heathen, Val. Max. iv. 2.

Ver. 13. *Every plant which my heavenly Father hath not planted*] viz. By election, and watered by vocation. These Pharisees were reprobates, designed to detection here, and to destruction hereafter. Therefore as it is no wonder, so it is no matter, though they " stumble at the word, being disobedient, sith hereunto they were appointed," 1 Pet. ii. 8. Let them " stumble, and fall, and be broken, and snared, and taken," Isa. viii. 15. Christ is to reprobates a " rock of offence ; " but such a rock as that, Judg. vi. 21, out of which goeth fire and consumeth them.

Ver. 14. *Let them alone*] A dreadful doom ; like that, Hos. iv. 14, " I will not punish your daughters when they commit whoredom," &c. No so great punishment as not to be punished. And verse 17, of that same chapter, " Ephraim is joined to idols, let him alone : " *q. d.* he hath made a match with mischief, he shall have his belly-full of it. Never was Jerusalem's condition so desperate, as when God said unto her, " My fury shall depart from thee, I will be quiet, and no more angry," Ezek. xvi. 42. A man is ever and anon meddling with his fruit trees, paring and pruning, &c. ; but for his oaks, and other trees of the forest, he lets them alone, till he comes, once for all, with his axe to fell them.

Both shall fall into the ditch] Though the blind guides fall undermost, and have the worst of it.

Ver. 15. *Declare unto us this parable*] It was no parable, but a plain discourse, and easy to be understood, had not they been dull of hearing, and somewhat soured with the pharisaical leaven of the necessity of washing hands afore meat : though for that time, by a singular providence of God, they neglected ; which both gave occasion to the Pharisees' quarrel, and to this question, whereto our Saviour maketh a most plain and plenary answer.

Ver. 16. *Do not ye yet understand ?*] What ! not at these years, and after so long standing ? Will ye stand till ye wax sour again, and not give yourselves wholly to these things, that your profiting may appear to all ? [1] Is it not a shame to have no more wit at 60 years old than at six ? to be " always learning, yet never come to the knowledge of the truth ? " God expects a proportion of skill and holiness according to the time and means men have had, Heb. v. 12.

Ver. 17. *Whatsoever entereth in at the mouth*] In nature, *Animantis cujusque vita est fuga.* Life, were it not for the repair by daily nourishment, would be soon extinguished. Hence it is

called, " The life of our hand," because maintained by the labour of our hands, Isa. v. 7, 10. But that which our Saviour here driveth at is, to set forth the ridiculous madness of the Pharisees, while they placed a kind of holiness in those things that were evacuated and thrown into the draught. And do not Papists the very same ? *Qui gustavit ovum trahitur in carcerem, cogiturque de hæresi causam dicere,* saith Erasmus. To eat flesh, or but an egg, in Lent, is punished with death. Whereas in the year of Christ 330, Spiridion, a godly bishop in Cyprus, having not what else ready to set before a guest that came to him in Lent, set him a piece of pork to feed on. And when the stranger made scruple of eating flesh in Lent, saying, I am a Christian, and may not do it : Nay, therefore thou mayest do it, said he, because " to the pure all things are pure," and the kingdom of God consisteth not in meats and drinks, &c., Rom. xiv. 20.

Ver. 18. *Come forth from the heart*] That forth of sin and fountain of folly ; for " as a fountain casteth forth her waters, so doth the heart of man cast out its wickedness," Jer. vi. 7 ; and if the tongue be " a world of wickedness," Jam. ii., what is the heart, that seminary of sin, wherein is a πάνσπερμια, as Empedocles saith in Aristotle.[2] In this sea are not only that leviathan the devil (who there sets up his forts and strongholds, 2 Cor. x. 4, and doth intrench and incage himself), but creeping things innumerable, Psal. civ. 26, making that which should be the temple of God a den of thieves, a palace of pride, a slaughter-house of malice, a brothel-house of uncleanness, a raging sea of sin, Isa. lvii. 20, a little hell of black and blasphemous imaginations. The natural man lies rotting in the grave of corruption, wrapt up in the winding-sheet of hardness of heart and blindness of mind, and (as a carcase crawleth with worms) swarming with those noisome lusts, that were able to poison up an honest heart.

Ver. 19. *For out of the heart proceed evil thoughts*] These are the first and immediate issue of the sinful soul ; words and deeds, borborology and enormity, follow in their order. " And I dare be bold to say," saith a reverend divine,[3] " that though the act contract the guilt, because the lust is then grown up to a height, so that it is come to an absolute will in execution, yet the act of adultery and murder is not so abominable in God's eyes, as the filthiness of the spirit ; for it is the spirit that he mainly looks to," &c. Think not then that thought is free, for as inward bleeding will kill, so will concupiscence, whatever the Papists say in favour of it, as a condition of nature : and hence flow most of their most dangerous opinions, as justification by works, state of perfection, merit, supererogation, &c.

Ver. 20. *These are the things which defile a man*] Make him a loathsome leper in God's

---

[1] 1 Tim. iv. 15. Ἀκμὴν adhuc pro κατὰ ἀκμὴν, at these years ; now that you are at full stature, and in your full vigour ?

[2] As in that chaos, Gen. i., were the seeds of all creatures ; so in the heart, of all sins.

[3] D. Preston, of God's attributes.

sight, his heart being a filthy dunghill of all abominable vices, his life a long chain of sinful actions, a very continued web of wickedness. And whereas repentance is the soul's vomit, and confession the spunge that wipes out all the blots and blurs of our lives, that cunning man-slayer holds the lips close that the heart may not disburden itself by so wholesome evacuation, and doth what he can to hinder the birth of re-pentance, that fair and happy daughter of an ugly and odious mother, sin.[1]

Ver. 21. *Into the coasts of Tyre and Sidon*] That royal exchange of the world, as one calleth it. Hither retired our Saviour, as tired out with the Jews' perverseness. And here it's like he did much good, according to that was prophesied, Isa. xxiii. 18. Sure it is, that whereas here he would have hid himself, he could not, for the woman of Canaan came and fell at his feet as a suppliant for her daughter.

Ver. 22. *And cried unto him*] One copy hath it, "And cried behind him,"[2] which implies either that Christ had turned his back upon her, seeing her now coming towards him; or else that she was abashed to come into his presence, as being of an accursed kindred, de-voted to destruction.

Have mercy upon me, O Lord] She acknow-ledged her own sin in her daughter's sufferings. So did that other good woman, 1 Kings xvii. 18. Her son was dead, her sin was called to remembrance. And so must we see ourselves beaten on our sick children's backs, as David did, 2 Sam. xii. 16, and be humbled, labouring to mend by education what we have marred by propagation.

Thou Son of David] Thou that wast thyself born of a woman, pity a woman; thou that hast the bowels of a man in thee, hide not thine eyes from thine own flesh.

My daughter is grievously vexed with a devil] The devil doth his worst to her, therefore help. Misery makes men eloquent, beyond truth many times: but surely this woman's case was very doleful. It was her daughter, dear to her as her own soul,—*Filia, quasi φίλη*. The Greeks call children φίλτατα, the Latins *cara*.[3] And those at Rome that prayed and sacrificed whole days that their children might be *superstites*, long-lived, these were first called superstitious persons. *Quod nomen patuit postea latius*, saith Cicero (De Nat. Deor.). The word afterwards came to be of larger signification. This (perhaps only) daugh-ter was vexed and "grievously vexed," and that "of a devil;" who ever busy enough to do mischief, yet then chiefly bestirred him to set up his king-dom, when Christ came to pull it down: and as he once strove with Michael about a dead man's body, but it was that he might thereby set up himself in living men's souls; so he still seeks to possess himself of our bodies, that thereby he may the better wind and work himself into our hearts.

Ver. 23. *But he answered her not*] *Tacet ore, sed loquitur ei spiritu, ut fortius clamet*, saith an interpreter. Christ answereth her not with his mouth, but speaketh unto her by that sweet and secret voice of his Spirit, to cry louder. No man prays heartily but he hath so much comfort, at least, that he will come again to God, who secretly supports his suppliants, and by that peace incon-ceivable guards their hearts and minds that they pray and faint not (φρουρήσει), Phil. iv. 7.

Send her away, for she cries] Men may be tired out with incessant suits, as the unjust judge was, and as these disciples were weary to hear the poor woman's outcries, repeating the same re-quest over and over. Give her, therefore, say they, either an alms or an answer, that she may be silenced, and we eased. But it is otherwise with God, the oftener we come to him the better welcome; the louder we cry, the sooner we are heard; and the often repetition of the self-same petition, till we put the Lord out of countenance, put him (as you would say) to the blush, and even leave a blot in his face, as the Greek word signifies, Luke xviii. 5 (ὑπωπιάζῃ), this is the best melody we can make him. He looks out of the casements of heaven on purpose to hear it.

Ver. 24. *But unto the lost sheep*, &c.] He was properly the apostle of the circumcision, Rom. xv. 8; Heb. iii. 1, till the wall of partition was broken down by his resurrection. Then the veil rent, and it was open-tide. Then he became a light to lighten the Gentiles, as well as he was the glory of his people Israel.

Ver. 25. *Then came she and worshipped him*] She will not be said nay, or set down either with silence or sad answers; but, like another Gor-gonia, she threatens heaven, and is (as her brother speaks of her) modestly impudent and invincible. She will believe, as a man may say with reverence, whether Christ will or no. And to bring her to this it was that he so long held her off, for, *De-sideria dilata crescunt; at cito data vilescunt.* (Nazianzen.) Manna, that light meat, was but lightly set by, because lightly come by. But they that earn it before they eat it, and that know how they come by that they have, will set a high price upon it, and know how and why they part with it.

Lord, help me] Few words, but very forcible. When thou comest before God, "let thy words be few," saith Solomon, Eccles. v. 1. This St Peter calls "to be sober in prayer," 1 Pet. iv. 7, without trifling, or vain babbling, which the wise man calls "the sacrifice of fools." The Baalites' prayer was not more tedious than Elijah's short, and yet more pithy than short, charging God with the care of his covenant, truth, glory, &c.[4] It was Elijah that prayed loud and long, though in few words, yet very effectual. *Fratres Egypti-aci brevissimis et raptim jaculatis orationibus uti voluerunt* (saith Augustine), *ne per moras evanes-ceret et hebetaretur intentio.* Those ancient

---

[1] ἐχθροῦ πατρὸς φίλτατον τέκνον.
[2] Mark vii. 24, ἔκραξεν ὀπίσω αὐτοῦ, *a tergo ejus.*

[3] Lambin. in Menech. Plauti, Act. i. Scen. 1. *Domi domi-tus fui usque cum charis meis.*
[4] *Orationis brevitas pathos habet.* Aretius in loc.

Christians of Egypt were very brief in their prayers.

Help me] The word properly signifieth to run at one's cry that calls for help,[1] as the tender mother doth to her hungry child, when he sets up his note, and cries lustily.

Ver. 26. *And to cast it to dogs*] To whelps, saith St Mark.[2] So he calls her bitch, her daughter whelp. This might have easily damped and discouraged her. But she was that well-resolved Christian, whose part Luther saith it is to believe things invisible,[3] to hope for things deferred, and to love God when he shows himself most angry with him, and most opposite to him. Our Saviour was no sooner gone from this Canaanitess, but he heals the deaf and dumb man (though far weaker in faith than her) at first word, Mark vii. 33; and ver. 30 of this chapter, the Galileans no sooner laid their sick and lame friends at his feet, but he cured them without any more ado. He is "a God of judgment," Isa. xxx. 18, and knows how and when to deal forth his favours. He lays heaviest burdens on the strongest backs and proportions our afflictions to our abilities, holding us off for deliverance till he finds us fit for it, and giving us hearts to wait and want it till his time is come.

Ver. 27. *Truth, Lord*] Ναί Κύριε. This is *particula assentientis et obsecrantis*. How strangely doth God enable and enlarge his weak people many times in prayer! they are carried beyond themselves in a wonderful manner, and though otherwise rude in speech, and unlettered, yet then they have words at will, far above natural apprehension, and such as they are not able to repeat again; being, for the time, lost in the endless maze of spiritual ravishments, and ascending, with the Church, in those pillars of incense, out of this wilderness of the world, Cant. v. 6.

Yet the dogs eat of the crumbs] Lo, she locks herself within Christ's denial, and picks an argument of speeding out of a repulse; she gathereth one contrary out of another by the force of her faith. See the like, Deut. xxxii. 36; 2 Kings xiv. 26. Going into captivity was a sign of the Israelites returning out of captivity. Be it that I am a dog, saith this brave woman, yet some crumbs of comfort, Lord. Dogs, though they may not eat the children's meat (if they offer to do it, they are shut out of doors), yet, if children full-fed crumble their meat and make waste of it, as they will, and as the Jews now do, may not the Gentile dogs lick up those leavings? Thus she reasons it, and thus she makes use of anything she can lay hold of, whereby she may hope the better to prevail. Those that are hunger-starved are glad to feed upon hedge-fruit, and will make hard shift rather than perish. So, faithful hearers are not delicate, but can "suffer an exhortation," Heb. xiii. 22, bear a reproof, yea, suck honey, with the bee, out of bitter thyme.

Ver. 28. *O woman, great is thy faith*] Our Saviour had both reproached and repulsed her. Now he both graceth and gratifieth her; grants her request, and more, together with a high commendation of her heroical faith, which is here found aforehand to "praise and honour and glory," 1 Pet. i. 7.

Ver. 29. *And came nigh to the sea of Galilee*] Where, though he had lately been tired out, yet he will try again. Ministers must have patience with a perverse people, not resolving, as Jeremiah once in a pet, to speak no more to them in the name of the Lord, but proving if at any time God will give them repentance to the acknowledging of the truth, &c., 2 Tim. ii. 25. I beseech you (said Mr Bradford to one with whom he had taken great pains, but to no great purpose), I pray you, I desire you, I crave at your hands with all my very heart; I ask of you with hand, pen, tongue, and mind, in Christ, for Christ, through Christ, for his name, blood, mercy, power and truth's sake, my most entirely beloved, that you admit no doubting of God's final mercies toward you, howsoever you feel yourself, &c. Of this good martyr it is said, that in travailing with his own heart he would never give over till he had made somewhat of it; as in confession, till his heart melted; in seeking pardon, till quieted; in begging grace, till warmed and quickened: so in dealing with others he practised that which St Austin persuadeth every preacher to do, so long to beat upon and repeat the same point, till by the countenance, but especially by the conversation, of his hearers, he perceive that they resent and relish it. "Knowing the terror of the Lord," saith Paul, "we persuade men," 2 Cor. v. 11; we give them not over till we have prevailed with them and subdued them, though never so knotty and knorly.

And went up into a mountain] Either to pray, or to preach, or to rest and repose himself; but that would not be, for great multitudes resorted to him. The sun set on high cannot be hid, no more can Christ in the mount.

Ver. 30. *Having with them those that were lame, blind, &c.*] All these infirmities are fruits of sin (which hath made the world an œcumenical hospital) and accidents of life; for that which befalleth any man, may befall every man.[4] The privative favours that God shows us here (saith Gerson) are more than the positive: meaning by privative, God's preserving us from manifold mischiefs and miseries by his manutension.[5] They that are got to heaven are out of the gun-shot; for there is no more sickness, nor sorrow, nor crying, nor pain, for the former things are passed, Rev. xxi. 4. All corruptions, temptations, affliction, which stand, some above us, some about us (as the insulting Philistines about blind Samson), shall end with the same blow, fall with the same clap with ourselves. At Stratford-le-Bow were

---

[1] Βοηθεῖν, *quasi ἐπὶ βοὴν θεῖν, ad clamorem alicujus accurrere auxilii ferendi causa.* Beza.

[2] κυναρίοις, *catellis, ut majore contemptu loqui videretur.* Beza.

[3] *Credere invisibilia, sperare dilata, et amare Deum se ostendentem contrarium.* Luth.

[4] *Cuivis potest contingere quod cuiquam contigit.* Mimus.

[5] *Multo plures sunt gratiæ privativæ quam positivæ.* Gerson.

two martyrs burned at one stake (in the days of Queen Mary), Hugh Laverock, an old lame man, and John A. Price, a blind man. At their death, Hugh, after he was chained, casting away his crutch, and comforting the other, he said to him, Be of good comfort, my brother, for my Lord of London is our good physician: he will heal us shortly, thee of thy blindness, and me of my lameness. And so patiently they suffered.

Ver. 31. *They glorified the God of Israel*] They saw God in those miraculous cures and gave him his due praise. He is content that we should have the comfort of his benefits, so he may have the glory of them; that's all the rent and return he looks for. All the fee Christ required for his cures was, "Go and tell what God hath done for thee; go show thyself to the priest, and offer," &c. But we, instead of being temples of God's praise, become many times graves of his benefits. This made good David so oft to put the thorn to his breast, Psal. ciii. 1—3; and King Alphonsus not so much to wonder at his courtiers' ingratitude to him, as at his own to God.

Ver. 32. *I have compassion on the multitude*] My bowels yearn towards them. Neither is he less loving, now that he is in heaven, towards his poor penniless, necessitous people on earth; but when they are hardest put to it, and haply have not a cross to bless themselves with, as the proverb is, he so graciously provides, that though the young lions (or the strong ones, as the Septuagint have it) do lack and suffer hunger, yet they that seek the Lord want nothing that's good for them, Psal. xxxiv. 10. Aaron, though he might not bewail the death of his two sons, Lev. x., because he was high priest, yet his bowels of fatherly affection towards them could not be restrained. Christ retaineth still compassion, Heb. iv. 5, though free from personal passion; and, though freed from feeling, hath still yet a fellow-feeling, Acts ix. 5; Matt. xxv. 35. "*Manet compassio etiam cum impassibilitate*," saith Bernard.

Because they continue with me now three days] The Lord takes punctual and particular notice of all circumstances, how far they came, how long they had been there, how little able they were to hold out fasting to their own homes, &c. And so he doth still recount how many years, days, hours we have spent with him; what straits, losses, heats, colds, dangers, difficulties we have encountered with and passed through; all is exactly registered in his book of remembrance; "I know thy work, and thy labour," saith he, Rev. ii. 19. Men take much pains many times, and none regard it, reward it. But Christ takes notice, not of his people's works only, but of their labour in doing them, that he may fully recompense their labour of love, their loss of goods, &c. The godly shall know in themselves, not only in others, in books, &c., that they have "a better and an enduring substance," Heb. x. 34.

Ver. 33. *Whence should we have*, &c.] See their stupidity and diffidence, yet still budging

and breaking out upon all occasions.[1] What a life hath Christ with the best of us, ere he can bring us to anything? Corruption will have some flurts, some out-bursts. Nothing cleaves to us more pertinaciously than this evil heart of unbelief; like a fretting leprosy in our cottages of clay, though the walls be well scraped, yet it will never utterly out, till the house be demolished.

Ver. 34. *Seven, and a few little fishes*] Before, he had fed five thousand with fewer loaves. God can as easily maintain us with a little as with more; witness Daniel's pulse, and Elijah's cake on the coals and cruse of water, 1 Kings xix. 6; Luther's herring, and Junius's one egg a day, when means was short with him, by reason of the civil wars in France, so that he could not hear from his friends. It is not by bread only that man liveth, but by the word of God's blessing that maketh it nourishable. As if he break the staff of bread, that is, his own blessing, which is the staff whereon bread (that staff of life) leaneth, it can neither feed nor fill, make men neither fuller nor fatter.

Ver. 35. *To sit down on the ground*] He intended them not only a running banquet, a slight come-off, but a full feast, a good meal, and therefore bade them sit down and feed their fill. It was indeed on the bare ground that they sat; but so do the greatest lords in Turkey at this day; they sit at meat, with their legs gathered under them, flat upon the ground; and their cheer, when they feast most sumptuously, is only rice and mutton, with fair water out of the river.

Ver. 36. *And gave to his disciples*] So confuting their unbelief, and confirming their faith for the future. And the like he doth for us every time we receive the sacrament of his Supper. He bespeaks us there, as he did peremptory Thomas, John xx. 27.

And the disciples to the multitude] This is Christ's course to this day; by the hands of his faithful ministers to deal forth his favours, to give his Holy Spirit, which is, to give all good things, Matt. vii. 11, with Luke xi. 13, by the preaching of faith. This manna comes down from heaven in the dews of the ministry, Num. xi. 9; 1 Pet. i. 22. If our eyes see not our teachers, we cannot expect to hear the voice behind us, Isa. xxx. 20.

Ver. 37. *They did all eat and were filled*] They did eat to satiety, as men use to do at feasts, where the tables seem to sweat with variety. The Greek word here is, in its proper signification, used of fatting cattle, that have grass up to the eyes, such as is that in some parts of Ireland, where they are forced to drive out their cattle sometimes from the pastures into the commons, lest they should surfeit and spoil themselves.[2]

Seven baskets full] These baskets were bigger and of larger capacity than those coffins, Matt. xiv. 20. We read of Paul let down by the wall in

[1] *Discipuli ut homines nimis homines, &c.* Aret. in loc.
[2] ἐχορτάσθησαν. *Hoc proprie dicitur de armentis. Nam* χόρτον *Græci vocant gramen aut pabulum.* Beza.

a basket, Acts ix. 20.[1] It was such a vessel then that a man might sit in it: as the former may seem to have been no larger then a pie or pasty, the outside whereof, from the Greeks, we call a coffin.

Ver. 38. *And they that did eat*] See the notes on chap. xiv. 21. Herein was the majesty of the miracle, that there was no proportion between the men and the meat.

Ver. 39. *And he sent away the multitude*] Not without a blessing, and a great deal of good counsel. "Labour not for the meat which perisheth," &c. Amend your lives, for the kingdom of heaven is come home to you. Now that you have eaten and are full, beware that you forget not the Lord your God, &c., Deut. viii. 10, 11. Be not as children, with whom eaten bread is soon forgotten. This was wholesome counsel, and far better than their good cheer; for this would stick by them. Deal we so by our guests.

And came into the coasts of Magdala] This is held to be Mary Magdalen's country, better known by her than she was by it, as the island of Co was by Hippocrates, and Hippo by Austin.

CHAPTER XVI.

Ver. 1. *The Pharisees also with the Sadducees came*] Came forth, saith St Mark, to wit out of the coasts of Magdala, so soon as ever our Saviour arrived there, to quarrel him, and keep him from doing good. So active are the devil's instruments to hinder the kingdom of God and the good of souls. Truth never wants an adversary; she goes seldom without a scratched face, as the proverb is. The Pharisees and Sadducees, though at deadly difference betwixt themselves, yet can easily combine against Christ. So at this day, the priests disparage the Jesuits, the Jesuits the priests, the priests again the monks, the monks the friars, but they can all conspire against Protestants, whom they jointly persecute. Dogs, though they fight never so fierce, and mutually intertear one another, yet if a hare run by they give over, and run after her. Martial makes mention of a hare on the Sicilian shore, that having hardly escaped the hounds that hunted her, was devoured by a sea-dog; whereupon he brings her in thus complaining:

In me omnis terræque aviumque marisque
　　rapina est:
Forsitan et cœli, si canis astra tenet.

Tempting desired him] Or questioned him to and fro, sifted him by interrogatories, pretending to be his friends, and to seek satisfaction only.[2] All this savours strongly of putrid hypocrisy, *quæ ipsis domestica erat virtus*, as Aretius. Socinus did in like sort set upon Zanchius. "He was," saith Zanchius, "a learned man, and of unblameable conversation, but full of heresies, which yet he never propounded to me otherwise than by way of question, as seeming desirous to be better informed.[3] By this subtle means he drew away many, and sought to work upon Zanchius, as did also Matthæus Gribaldus, and some such others. But when they could not prevail, they brake friendship with him, and he with them, for the which he praiseth God from the bottom of his heart.

Show them a sign] Them,[4] by all means, as more worshipful men than the multitude, such as might merit an extraordinary sign. See here their Satanical arrogance. So Herod would see our Saviour, that he might see a sign from him. He looked upon him no otherwise than upon some common juggler, that would sure show him his best tricks. Thus these hypocrites here would gladly be gratified, but they were deceived.

Ver. 2. *When it is evening, ye say, It will be fair, &c.*] q. d. Are you so weatherwise (which yet is not your profession)? are ye so skilful in nature, and yet so ignorant of Scripture, as not to know that now is the time for the Messiah to come, and that I am he? Surely you are either notorious sots, or deep dissemblers, or both, in seeming so curiously to search after the truth, which yet you neither care to know, nor obey.

Ver. 3. *Can ye not discern the sign of the times?*] The men of Issachar were in great account with David, because "they had understanding of the times, to know what Israel ought to do," 1 Chron. xii. 32. "A prudent man foreseeth an evil, and hideth himself," Prov. xxii. 3. He foreseeth it; not by divination, or star-gazing, but by a judicious collection and connection of causes and consequences: as, if God be the same that ever, as holy, just, powerful, &c.; if sin be the same that ever, as foul, loathsome, pernicious, &c.; then such and such events will follow upon such and such courses. As God hath given us signs and fore-tokens of a tempest, so he hath also of an ensuing judgment, and blames those that take not notice thereof; sending them to school to the stork and swallow, Jer. viii. 7. If Elias see but a cloud as a hand arising from Carmel, he can tell that great store of rain will follow, that the whole heaven will anon be covered. Finer tempers are sooner sensible of change of weather. Moses, as more acquainted with God, spies his wrath at first setting out: so might we have done ere it came to this, and have redeemed a great part of our present sorrows, had we had our eyes in our heads, Eccl. ii. 14, had we not been of those wilful ones, who seek straws to put out their eyes withal, as Bernard hath it, or that wink for the nonce, saith Justin Martyr, that they

---

[1] κόφινος, σπυρίς, *sporta.*
[2] ἐπηρώτησαν, *vicissim interrogabant.*
[3] *Homo fuit plenus diversarum hæreseon, quas tamen mihi*

nunquam proponebat nisi disputandi causa, et semper interrogans quasi cuperet doceri. Zanch.
[4] αὐτοῖς, *ipsis,* i. q. *solis.*

may not see, when some unsavoury potion is ministered unto them.[1]

Ver. 4. *A wicked and adulterous generation*] See the notes on chap. xii. 39. The same wedge serves the same knot. They shall have no new answer from Christ, till they have made better use of the old. Let them return to thee, not thou to them, Jer. xv. 19.

And he left them, and departed] Because he saw his sweet words were even spilt upon them. *Frustra lavantur Æthiopes, et certatur cum hypocritis:* none are more obstinate and obdurate.

Ver. 5. *They had forgotten to take bread*] As wholly transported with fervour in following Christ, the bread of life. This is the fault of but a few now-a-days: worldly cares eat up heavenly desires, as the lean kine in Pharaoh's dream did the fat.

Ver. 6. *Take heed and beware of the leaven*] Or take knowledge of, and then take heed of, false doctrine;[2] which is fitly called leaven, because it soureth, swelleth, spreadeth, corrupteth the whole lump, and all this secretly, slily, easily, suddenly; neither can our eyes discern it from dough by the colour, but only our palate by the taste. Now the ear trieth words, as the mouth trieth meat, Job xxxiv. 3. Try all things before you trust anything. Those that sow false doctrine are somewhere in the Acts called λοιμοὶ, pests, botches, for their danger of infection, Acts xxiv. 5: some can carry their collusion so cleanly, that if possible the very elect might be deceived; like serpents, they can sting without hissing; like cur-dogs, suck your blood without biting. *Nota est Arrii κυβεία*, saith one, *qua Constantini de fide Nicæna elusit examen*, by the cogging of a dye, by the adding of one iota, they corrupted the sense of the whole synod.[3] The Valentinians had a trick to persuade before they taught.[4] The ancient Antitrinitarians set forth a base book of their doctrines under Cyprian's name, and sold it dog-cheap, that men might the sooner buy it, and be led by it, as Ruffinus complains. Take heed and beware of such: ye are not ignorant of their wiles.

Of the Pharisees and of the Sadducees] Κακοὶ μὲν θρίπες, κακοὶ ἠδὲ καὶ ἰπές. Never a barrel better herring. (Erasm. Adag.) Howbeit, the Sadducees affected, by their very name, to be held the only just men; haply because they held that all the reward that righteous men are to look for is here in this world. (Josephus.) The occasion of this heresy is said to be this: When Antigonus taught that we must not serve God for wages, his scholars understood him as if he had utterly denied all future rewards or recompense attending a godly life: and thence framed their heresy, denying the

resurrection, world to come, angels, devils, and lived as epicures and libertines.

Ver. 7. *It is because we have taken no bread*] Oh the dulness that is in the best to receive or retain heavenly mysteries! Surely, as owls see best by night, and are blind by day: so in deeds of darkness we are sharp-sighted, wise to do evil; but in spirituals we are blinder than beetles, our wits serve us not, we are singularly stupid and stubborn.

Ver. 8. *O ye of little faith*] *Fides famem non formidat.* It was want of faith that made them fear they should perish in the wilderness for lack of bread: God was better to them than their fears. He makes the best living of it that lives by faith. Feed on faith; so Tremellius reads that, Psal. xxxvii. 3.

Why reason ye amongst yourselves][5] They likely laid the fault of forgetfulness one upon another: but none found fault with himself for his unbelief and carnal reasoning.

Ver. 9. *Neither remember*] *Tantum didicimus, quantum meminimus.* So much we learn as we remember.[6] Our memories are naturally like hour-glasses, no sooner filled with good instructions and experiments than running out again. It must be our prayer to God that he would put his finger upon the hole, and so make our memories like the pot of manna, preserving holy truths in the ark of the soul.

Ver. 10. *Neither the seven loaves*] Learn to lay up experiences. If we were well read in the story of our own lives (saith a reverend man, Dr Sibbs) we might have a divinity of our own. The philosopher saith, that experience is *multiplex memoria*, because of the memory of the same thing often done ariseth experience, which should be the nurse of confidence.

Ver. 11. *How is it that ye understand not*] Ignorance under means is a blushful sin. The Scripture calls such, horses, asses, mules, and sends them to school to unreasonable creatures.

Ver. 12. *Then understood they how, &c.*] This chiding then was well bestowed. So was that, Luke xxiv. 29, upon the two disciples going to Emmaus, and that upon the Virgin Mary, John ii. 5; she laid her hand upon her mouth and replied not. And that upon the Corinthians for conniving at the incestuous person; and that upon the Laodiceans, Rev. iii. 14, for Eusebius telleth us that in his time it continued to be a flourishing church. It is said of Gerson, that he took not content in anything so much as in a plain and faithful reproof from his friend. It is a commendation to suffer the words of exhortation, Heb. xiii.

Ver. 13. *Whom do men say that I, &c.*] This question Christ asked, not as tickled with ambition to hear his own commendation (which

---

[1] *Qui festucam quærunt unde oculos sibi eruant.* Bern ἑκουσίως καταπίνοντες τὸ πικρόν.

[2] Ὁρᾶν, *cognitionis est,* προσέχειν, *autem cautelæ.*

[3] ὁμοιούσιον *ponentes pro* ὁμοούσιον.

[4] *Habuerunt artificium quo prius persuaderent quam doce-*

rent. Tertull. [5] τί διελογίζεσθε, *Disserere significat, ac verbis inter se disceptare.*

[6] *Discere voluit Socrates nihil aliud esse quam recordari.* Cic. Tusc. Quæst.

yet is held and said to be the only sweet hear-ing),[1] but as taking occasion to make way for their Christian confession, and likewise for their further information.

The Son of man am] So he was called: 1. Because a true man. 2. Because he passed for no more than an ordinary man. "How can this man give us his flesh to eat?" John vi. 52. 3. Because as man born of a woman, he was of few days and full of trouble: yea, he was the man that had seen affliction by the rod of God's wrath.

Ver. 14. *Some say that thou art John, &c.*] His body they saw was not John's, but they held then (and the Jews at this day hold) the Pythagorean transanimation, or passing of souls out of one body into another. So because they received not the love of the truth, God gave them up to the efficacy of error, even the better sort of them, 2 Thess. ii. 11: for there were that held Christ neither the Baptist, nor Elias, but a drunkard, a demoniac, &c. Who now can think to escape variety of censures? And why should any stumble at the diversity of opinions touching Christ and his kingdom?

Ver. 15. *But whom say ye that I am*] q. d. It behoveth you to say something that is better to the purpose, than the vulgar saith and cen-sureth. God will take that of some that he will not of others. Christ would not have his to stand doubtful, and to adhere to nothing certainly; to be in religion as idle beggars are in their way, ready to go which way soever the staff falleth; but to strive to a plerophory, a full assurance of knowledge, a certainty, as Luke hath it (i. 4), and to be fully per-suaded, ver. 1. A conjectural confidence, a general faith, the colliers' faith, as they call it, sufficeth not, to believe as the Church believes, &c. And yet Thomas Aquinas, that great schoolman, had no better a faith to support him at the last hour of his life: nor could he have any rest within, till he had taken up the Bible, and clipping it in his arms, said, Lord, I believe all that is written in this holy book.

Ver. 16. *Simon Peter answered, &c.*] As the mouth of the company, and one that being, haply, elder, and surely bolder than the rest, spake thus for them. But what a foul mouth of blasphemy opened those two popes (Peter's pretended successors), Leo I. and Nicholas III., that boasted that Peter was taken into fellow-ship of the individual Trinity?[2] Neither can that be excused that Jerome commenteth on the former verses ("Whom do men say that I am?" "But whom say ye that I am?") that our Saviour there purposely opposeth his dis-ciples to men, to intimate that they were some-thing more than men. This is something like that note of a Latin postiller upon Exod. xxx. 31, where, because it is said, ver. 32, "Upon man's flesh the holy ointment shall not be

poured, thou shalt anoint Aaron and his sons therewith," thence infers that priests are angels, and have not human flesh. These were human glosses, and savoured as little of God's meaning as that unsavoury speech of Peter, ver. 22 of this chapter, for the which he heareth, "Get thee behind me, Satan; thou savourest not," &c.

Thou art Christ, the Son of the living God][3] A short confession, but such as in few contain-eth whatsoever we believe concerning the per-son and office of Christ, *Brevis et longa planeque aurea est hæc confessio.* Well may we say of it, as St Bartholomew (quoted by Dionysius) did of the doctrine of Divinity, that it is Καὶ πολλὴ καὶ ἐλαχίστη, little and yet large.

Ver. 17. *Blessed art thou, Simon*] These and the following words of our Saviour to Peter were meant to all the apostles also, John xx. 22, 23. Christ took his beginning of one, to teach unity in his Church, in the confes-sion of faith. Note this against the Papists, who miserably wrest and deprave this text, to the proving of the papal monarchy. Gregory the Great, though he styled himself a servant of God's servants, and detested the pope of Con-stantinople for arrogating the title of Universal Bishop, during the reign of Mauritius; yet when he was slain, and succeeded by the traitor Phocas, he ceased not to flatter the same Phocas, to commend unto him the care of the Church of Rome, and to exhort him to remember this say-ing of our Saviour, "Thou art Peter," &c., and for no other end, than that he might extend his power by the favour of the parricide.

Ver. 18. *Thou art Peter*] i. e. Thou art a living stone in the spiritual temple, like as Peter saith all other Christians are, 1 Pet. ii. 5. And here Christ tells Peter why at first he gave him that name.

Upon this rock] That is, upon this thy rocky, thy solid and substantial confession of me. Austin saith, the rock is Christ, not Peter. But this, saith Stapleton, is *humanus lapsus in Augustino.* So the schoolmen say that St Austin stood so much for grace, that he yielded too little to free-will. But it was a true saying of learned Dr Whitaker's, in his answer to Campian, *Patres in maximis sunt nostri, in multis varii, in minimis vestri.* Not Peter, but Phocas, is the right craggy rock upon which the Popish su-premacy is founded.

I will build my Church] Christ calls not the Church βουλὴν, or σύγκλητον, which is properly a convention of lords and statesmen, but ἐκκλησίαν, which is an assembly of the common people, even those of the lower rank and condition;[4] according to that 1 Cor. i. 26, and Luke i. 48, "he hath regarded the low estate of his hand-maiden."

And the gates of hell, &c.] That is, all the power and policy of hell combined. The devil lendeth his instruments, the Church's enemies,

[1] ἥδιστον ἄκουσμα ἔπαινος. Xenophon.
[2] *Petrum in consortium individuæ Trinitatis assumptum jactarunt.* Revius.
[3] ὁ Υἱὸς τοῦ Θεοῦ τοῦ ζῶντος. *Singulæ dictiones suos habent articulos ἐμφατικῶς adjectos.* Aret.
[4] ἐκκλησιάζειν, *est concionari, cum populo agere.* Cameron.

his seven heads to plot, and his ten horns to push. Craft and cruelty go together in them, as the asp never wanders alone; and as the Scripture speaks of those birds of prey, Isa. xxxiv. 16, "none of them wants his mate." But yet all this shall not prevail: the devil may shake his chain at the saints, not set his fangs in them. For why? they stand upon a Rock that is higher than they, so that the floods of temptations and oppositions cannot come so much as at their feet; or if they reach to the heel, yet they come not at the head; or if they should dash higher upon them, yet they break themselves.

Shall not prevail against it] No, though the devil should discharge at the Church his greatest ordnance; say they were as big as those two cast by Alphonsus, Duke of Ferrara, the one whereof he called the Earthquake, and the other Grandiabolo, or the great devil.

Whether may the Catholic Church err in fundamentals?

It is answered, that though the universal Church of Christ, taken for his mystical body upon earth, and complete number of his elect, cannot err in matters fundamental, yet the external visible part of the Church may err, because the truth of God may be locked up within the hearts of such a company, as in competition of suffrages, cannot make a greater part in a general council; so that the sentence decreed therein may be a fundamental error.

Ver. 19. *And I will give unto thee the keys*] i. e. I will make thee and all my ministers stewards in my house, 1 Cor. iv. 1, such as Obadiah was in Ahab's house, as Eliakim in Hezekiah's, upon whose shoulder God laid the key of the house of David, so that he opened and none shut, and shut and none opened, Isa. xxii. 22. Now let a man so think of us ministers, how mean soever, and we shall not want for respect.

Ver. 20. *That they should tell no man*] viz. Till the due time. Everything is beautiful in its season, saith Solomon, Eccl. iii. 11. Taciturnity in some cases is a virtue, as here. The disciples might preach that Christ the Son of David was come to save the world; though they might not particularly point him out as the Son of the living God: which when Pilate himself heard he was afraid, saith the text, and sought to deliver him.

Ver. 21. *How that he must go to Jerusalem*] He must, *necessitate non simplici, sed ex supposito.* It being supposed that God had decreed this way (and no other) to glorify himself in man's salvation by the death of his dear Son (wherein the naked bowels of his love were laid open to us, as in an anatomy), it was necessary that Christ should be killed and raised again at the third day. *Voluntas Dei, necessitas rei.*

And be killed and raised again] That we might live and reign with him for ever, who else had been killed with death, as the phrase

is, Rev. ii. 23; that is, had come under the power of the second death. David wished he might have died for Absalom, such was his love to him. Arsinoe interposed herself between the murderer's weapons, sent by Ptolemy, her brother, to kill her children. The pelican not only feeds her young with her own blood, but with invincible constancy abides the flames of fire for their preservation. Christ is that good shepherd, who gave his life for his sheep: he is that true pelican, who saw the wrath of God burning about his young ones, and cast himself into the midst thereof, that he might quench it. He was delivered for our offences, and was raised again for our justification, which began in his death, but was perfected by his resurrection, Rom. iv. 25.

Ver. 22. *Then Peter took him*] Took him by the hand, and led him apart, as we do those we are most intimate with, in great courtesy and secrecy, to impart to them things of greatest importance. Peter was strongly possest with a fond conceit of an earthly kingdom; and as Joseph dreamt of his preferment, but not at all of his imprisonment, so neither could Peter think or hear of Christ's being killed, whom he had even now confessed to be the Christ, the Son of the living God. See here how easily we slide, by the deceitfulness of our hearts, from the mean to the extreme. Peter having made a notable profession of his faith, and being therefore much commended by Christ, presently takes occasion to fall from the true holiness of faith to the sauciness of presumption, in advising his Master to decline the cross.

And began to rebuke him, saying] No, he did not rebuke him, saith Maldonatus the Jesuit, but friendly counselled him only, as if ἐπιτιμᾶν were not to chide and charge, as masters do their servants, even with threatenings and menaces.[1] But these patrons of Peter (as they pretend) will not abide that he should be blamed for anything. Baronius blusheth not to say (and so to put the lie upon the Holy Ghost himself) that Paul was out in reproving Peter, Gal. ii. 14, and that it had been better manners for him to have held his tongue. Others of them have blasphemously censured St Paul in their sermons as a hot-headed person, of whose assertions no great reckoning was to be made by the sober-minded; and that he was not secure of his preaching, but by conference with St Peter, neither durst he publish his Epistles till St Peter had allowed them.

Ver. 23. *Get thee behind me, Satan*] Come behind me as a disciple, go not before me as a teacher; understand thy distance, and hold thee to thy duty, by moving in thine own sphere; that thou be not thus odiously eccentric, another Satan, who sets thee a-work thus to tempt me, as he once did Eve to seduce Adam: here Maldonatus is hard put to it to save Peter blameless, and saith that "Get thee behind me" is a Hebrew phrase, and imports no more than "Follow me." But

[1] *Non tantum significat reprehendere et increpare, sed etiam interminari et interdicere.* Gerh.

when he comes to consider that Christ calls him Satan, and that it would not be seemly that Christ should bid Satan follow him, he is forced to confess that it is the speech of one that bids another be packing out of his presence with indignation, like that of Christ to the tempter, Matt. iv., " Get thee hence, Satan." *Prosit tibi sternutatio tua.* (Maldonatus.) When the executioner wished Polycarp to be merciful to himself, he bade him hold his peace; he was his tormentor, not his counsellor.

Thou art an offence unto me] Thou doest thy good-will to hinder me in the course of my calling, as Mediator, wherein, say some, he sinned more grievously than afterwards he did in denying his Master, and was therefore so sharply rebuked. So when Socrates was solicited by Criton to break prison, and save his life by flight; Friend Criton, said he, thine earnestness herein were much worth, if it were consistent with uprightness; but being not so, the greater it is, the more troublesome.[1] I know not (said that Scotch martyr) by what reason they so called them my friends, which so greatly laboured to convert (pervert) me. Neither will I more esteem them than the Midianites, which in times past called the children of Israel to do sacrifice to their idols.

But the things that be of men] Erewhile it was of Satan, now of men. How easy is it to descry a devil in our best friends sometimes, as Rebezies the French martyr did in his parents! Satan suborns such as may do much with us, and works in them effectually for our hurt, as a smith doth in his forge, Eph. ii. 2. "They were tempted," and thereby "tormented," saith the apostle of those worthies ($\epsilon\pi\epsilon\iota\rho\acute{a}\sigma\theta\eta\sigma\alpha\nu$), Heb. xi. 37. Satan speaks to us sometimes by our friends, as through trunks and canes.

Ver. 24. *If any man will come after me*] Not step before me, prescribe to me, as Peter attempted to do, whose fault herein is purposely recorded, that he might not be (as by the Papists, for politic respects, he is) over-much magnified, nay, deified, as is above observed, and made collateral, a very copesmate, to Christ himself.

Let him deny himself] *Abdicet seipsum* ($\dot{a}\pi\alpha\rho$-$\nu\eta\sigma\acute{a}\sigma\theta\omega$), let him abrenounce himself flatly, peremptorily, again and again (as the word importeth), with a stout and stiff denial to so unreasonable a request, as self will be sure to make to a man his whole life throughout. Every one hath many a self within himself to say nay to, though never so dear to him. Levi said unto his father and to his mother, "I have not seen him, neither did he acknowledge his brethren, nor know his own children, that he might observe God's word, and keep his covenant," Deut. xxxiii. 9. This was much; but he that will be Christ's disciple must do more than this, he must deny himself, his own reason, will, affections, appetite, aims, ends, acts, righteousness, &c., he must utterly renounce himself, as much

as if he had nothing at all to do with himself. Yea, he must condemn and cast away himself, as God doth those reprobates whom he denieth, disowneth, and disavoweth for ever. *Horreo quicquid de meo est ut sim meus*, saith Bernard. *Ita cave tibi ut caveas teipsum*, saith another. So take heed to yourself, that you take heed of yourself. Oh misery! saith a third, we could not suffer a Lord, and yet we sustain to serve our fellow-servant, self.[2] Valentinian the emperor dying, affirmed, that he was proud of one of his victories only, viz., that he had overcome his own flesh, that worst of enemies. Of all slaveries, none so grievous to a good heart as to be a slave to himself. And this yoke of slavery, it is an easy matter to shake off, saith Seneca, but he is foully deceived; for a man will sooner say nay to all the world than to himself. This made Robert Smith the martyr write thus to his wife, "Be always an enemy to the devil and the world, but specially to your own flesh." There are some diseases that will not be cured, till we be let blood *ad deliquium animæ*, till the patient swoon: and such is sin; it is *corruptio totius substantiæ*, the sinner must be unmade, taken all asunder, ere the new creature can be made up in him; he must be stark dead to sin, ere he can live to righteousness, as St Peter hath it ($\dot{a}\pi o\gamma\epsilon$-$\nu\acute{o}\mu\epsilon\nu o\iota$), 1 Pet. ii. 24; and the word he useth there implieth, that the old frame must be utterly dissolved, and the whole man done to death, and offered for a whole burnt-offering. Instead of a ram, saith Origen, we must kill our ireful passions : instead of a goat, our unclean affections; instead of flying fowls, our idle thoughts and evil imaginations. Lo, this is that evangelical sacrifice, that rational service so much commended and called for, Rom. xii. 1. "Do this, and thou shalt live;" leave it undone, and thou art undone for ever. Pray therefore with him, *Domine, libera me a malo homine, meipso*, Lord, free me from an ill man, myself.

And take up his cross] Where self is renounced, the cross is easily borne. It is self (saith one) makes the cross pinch. Things puffed up with wind break when they come to the fire; so those that are puffed up, and filled with self, will suffer nothing. Privation is one of the principles of natural generation, so is self-denial of holy conversation. Fain would this flesh make strange of that which the Spirit doth embrace (said M. Saunders, martyr, in a letter written to his wife out of the prison). O Lord, how loth is this loitering sluggard to pass forth in God's path! It fancieth, forsooth, much fear of the fray-bugs, &c. Take up the cross and follow me through thick and thin, through fire and water. Oh, this is a hard saying, saith another martyr. But if there be any way on horse-back to heaven, surely this is the way. Only we must take up our cross, be active in it, and not stay till it be laid upon us whether we will or no. And then bear it patiently, not grin under the burden of it, as an-

---

[1] $\dot{\eta}$ $\pi\rho o\theta\upsilon\mu\acute{\iota}\alpha$ $\sigma o\hat{\upsilon}$ $\pi o\lambda\lambda o\hat{\upsilon}$ $\dot{a}\xi\acute{\iota}\alpha$ $\epsilon\dot{\iota}$ $\mu\epsilon\tau\grave{a}$ $\tau\iota\nu\grave{o}\varsigma$ $\dot{o}\rho\theta\acute{o}\tau\eta\tau o\varsigma$ $\epsilon\ddot{\iota}\eta$ $\epsilon\dot{\iota}$ $\delta\grave{\epsilon}$ $\mu\grave{\eta}$, $\ddot{o}\sigma\omega$ $\mu\epsilon\acute{\iota}\zeta\omega\nu$, $\tau o\sigma o\acute{\upsilon}\tau\omega$ $\chi\alpha\lambda\epsilon\pi\omega\tau\acute{\epsilon}\rho\alpha$.

[2] *O rem miseram! Dominum ferre non potuimus, conservo servimus.*

tic pictures seem to do under the weight of the house-side whereunto they are fastened. Drink off God's cup willingly, and at the first (said Mr Bradford), and when it is full; lest peradventure, if we linger, we drink at length of the dregs with the wicked, if at the beginning we drink not with his children. We must take up our crosses (saith another), and when God bids us yoke, he is the wisest man that yields his neck most willingly.

And follow me] Without sciscitation; let him go blind-fold whither I lead him, as Abraham did.[1] Neither may he leap over the hedge of the command, for avoiding the foul way of affliction, *Sed eundum quocunque Christus vocarit, etiamsi in ea loca migrandum esset.*

> *Pigris ubi nulla campis*
> *Arbor æstiva recreatur aura;*
> *Quod latus mundi nebulæ, malusque*
> *Jupiter urget.*   Horat. i. 22.

God hath predestinated us to be conformed to the image of his Son, in sufferings also, Rom. viii. 29. *Crux pendentis, cathedra docentis.* Plato was crook-backed, and his scholars counted it an ornament to go crooked like him. Aristotle lisped, and his scholars thought it an honour to lisp. Shall not we hold ourselves honoured that may suffer with Christ, and then be glorified also with him?

Ver. 25. *For whosoever will save his life*] That is parsimonious of it, when Christ calls him to be prodigal of it. Man is naturally a "life-loving creature."[2] What man is he that desireth life? I do, and I, and I, as Augustine brings men in, making ready answer. *Quis vitam non vult?* Life is sweet, we say, and every creature makes much of it, from the highest angel to the lowest worm, as that Father observeth. But life in God's displeasure is worse than death, as death in his true favour is true life, said Bradford to Gardiner; for such a death lays hold upon eternal life, as St Paul hath it, 1 Tim. vi. 19, or (as other copies read it) upon life indeed (τῆς ὄντως ζωῆς). For, *æterna vita vera vita,* saith Augustine. "None to that," as David said of Goliath's sword. "None but Christ, none but Christ," as that martyr cried in the flames. This love of Christ made them sacrifice their dearest lives to his name, yea, profess, as John Ardely did to Bonner, That if every hair of his head were a man, he would suffer death in them all for his sweet Christ's sake. My wife and my children are so dearly beloved unto me, that they cannot be bought from me for all the riches and possessions of the Duke of Bavaria; but for the love of my Lord God I will willingly forsake them, said George Carpenter, who was burnt at München in Bavaria.

Ver. 26. *For what is a man profited*] Francis Xanerius counselled John the Third, King of Portugal, to meditate every day a quarter of an hour on this divine sentence. If there could, saith a reverend divine, be such a bargain made,

that he might have the whole world for the sale of his soul, he should, for all that, be a loser by it.[3] For he might, notwithstanding, be a bankrupt, a beggar, begging in vain, though but for a drop of cold water to cool his tongue. Is it nothing then to lose an immortal soul, to purchase an ever-living death? The loss of the soul is in this verse set forth to be: 1. incomparable; 2. irreparable. If, therefore, to lose the life for money be a madness, what then the soul? What wise man could fetch gold out of a fiery crucible? hazard himself to endless woes for a few waterish pleasures? give his soul to the devil, as some popes did for the short enjoyment of the Papal dignity? What was this but to win Venice, and then to be hanged at the gates thereof, as the proverb is.[4] In great fires men look first to their jewels, then to their lumber; so should these see first to their souls, to secure them, and then take care of the outward man. The soldier cares not how his buckler speeds, so his body be kept thereby from deadly thrusts. The pope persuading Maximilian (king of Bohemia, afterwards emperor) to be a good Catholic, with many promises of profits and preferments, was answered by the king that he thanked his Holiness; but that his soul's health was more dear to him than all the things in the world. Which answer they said in Rome was a Lutheran form of speech, and signified an alienation from the obedience of that see; and they began to discourse what would happen after the old emperor's death.

Or what shall a man give in exchange] He would give anything in the world, yea, 10,000 worlds if he had them, to be delivered. But out of hell there is no redemption. Hath the extortioner pilled, or the robber spoiled thy goods? By labour and leisure thou mayest recover thyself again. But the soul once lost is irrecoverable. Which when the guilty soul at death thinks of, oh, what a dreadful shriek gives it, to see itself launching into an infinite ocean of scalding lead, and must swim naked in it for ever! How doth it, trembling, warble out that doleful ditty of dying Adrian the emperor:

> *Animula, vagula, blandula,*
> *Hospes comesque corporis,*
> *Quæ nunc abibis in loca*
> *Horridula, sordida, tristia,*
> *Nec, ut soles, dabis jocos?*

Ver. 27. *In the glory of his Father with his angels*] Great will be the glory of the man Christ Jesus at his second coming. He shall come riding on the clouds (not that he needs them, but to show his sovereignty), environed with flaming fire, mounted on a stately throne, attended by an innumerable company of angels (for they shall all come with him, not one of them left in heaven, 2 Thess. i. 7; Matt. xxv. 31), who shall minister unto him in this great work

---

[1] *Semper memento illud Pythagoricum,* "Επου Θεῷ. Boetius.
[2] ζῶον φιλόζωον. Æsop in Fab.
[3] Mr Ley's Monitor of Mortality.

[4] *Non magis juvabitur, quam qui acquirat Venetias, ipse vero suspendatur ad Portam ut est in proverbio.* Par. in loc.

irresistibly, justly, speedily, Rev. xv. 6, Christ himself shining in the midst of them, with such an exuberancy and excess of glory, as that the sun shall seem but a snuff to him. This glory, howsoever it is here called "The glory of the Father," because he is the fountain, as of the Deity, so of the divine glory wherewith Christ is crowned, Phil. ii. 9; 1 Tim. iii. 16; yet is it his own glory (as he is one with the Father and the Holy Ghost), and so it is called, Matt. xxv. 31; John xvii. 5. Now if Israel so shouted for joy of Solomon's coronation, and in the day of his espousals, that the earth rang again, 1 Kings i. 40; Cant. iii. 11; if the Grecians so cried out "Soter, soter," to Flaminius the Roman general, when he had set them at liberty, that the very birds, astonished at the noise, fell down to the earth: oh, how great shall be the saints' joy to see Christ the King in his beauty and bravery at the last judgment!

Ver. 28. *Which shall not taste of death*] The saints do but taste of death only, they do no more but sip of that bitter cup, which for tasting of that forbidden fruit in the garden, they should have been swilling and swallowing down for ever.

Till they see the Son of man, &c.] This verse is to be referred to the transfiguration recorded in the next chapter, where some of them had the happiness to see Christ in his kingdom; that is, in his heavenly glory, whereof they had a glimpse.

CHAPTER XVII.

Ver. 1. *And after six days*] Luke saith (ix. 28) about eight days after. It comes all to one. For Matthew puts exclusively those days only that went between, and were finished; but Luke puts the two utmost days also into the reckoning.

Jesus taketh Peter, James, and John] So, Mark v. 37, when he raised the damsel he took with him these three only; haply as best beloved, because bold; Boanergeses, more zealous than the rest; or the better to fit them for further trial: great feelings oft precede great afflictions. Howsoever, it is no small favour of God to make us witnesses of his great works, and so let us take it. As all Israel might see Moses go toward the rock of Rephidim, none but the elders might see him strike it. That God crucifies his Son before us, that he fetcheth the true water of life out of the rock in our sight, is a high prerogative. And no less surely that we are eftsoons transported in prayer, carried out of the body in divine meditation, and lost in the endless maze of spiritual ravishments; that we return from the public ordinances, as Moses did from the Mount, with our faces shining; that we are transfigured and transformed into the same image from glory to glory, and that the angel of the covenant doth wondrously, during the time of the sacrifice, while Manoah and his wife look on, &c. These are special privileges communicated to none but the communion of saints.

And bringeth them up into an high mountain] The name of this mountain no evangelist expresseth; but by common consent it was Mount Tabor (which Josephus calleth Itabirion), whereof Jerome writeth copiously and elegantly in his commentary upon the fifth of Hosea. Our Saviour, when he had some special work to do, went usually up into a mountain; to teach us to soar aloft in great performances especially, and to be heavenly-minded, taking a turn or two, ever and anon, with Christ in Mount Tabor, treading upon the moon, with the Church, Rev. xii. 1; having our feet at least where other men's heads are, on things on earth (Prov. xv. 24, "The way of life is above to the wise"); delighting ourselves in high flying, as eagles; never merry till gotten into the air or on the top of trees, with the lesser birds. Zaccheus could not see Christ till he had climbed the fig-tree. Nor can we see the consolation of Israel till elevated in divine contemplation, till gotten up into God's holy hill. The people tasted not manna till they had left the leaven of Egypt.

And was transfigured before them] This was while he was praying, as St Luke noteth. Prayer, rightly performed, is a parleying with God, ἔντευξις, *interpellatio*, 1 Tim. ii. 1, a standing upon interrogatories with him, ἐπερώτημα, 1 Pet. iii. 21, a pouring out of the heart unto him, Psal. lxii. 8, a familiar conference with him; wherein the soul is so carried beyond itself otherwhiles, *ut caro est pene nescia carnis*, as St Jerome speaks of certain holy women in his time, that they seemed in place only remote, but in affection to join with that holy company of heaven. So Dr Preston, on his death-bed, said he should change his place, but not his company. Peter praying fell into a trance. Cornelius praying saw heavenly visions. Mr Bradford, a little before he went out of the Counter, prayed with such plenty of tears and abundant spirit of prayer, that it ravished the minds of the hearers. Also when he shifted himself in a clean shirt made for his burning, he made such a prayer of the wedding garment, that the eyes of those present were as truly occupied in looking on him, as their ears gave place to hear his prayer. Giles of Brussels, martyr, was so ardent in his prayers, kneeling by himself in some secret place of the prison, that he seemed to forget himself. Being called many times to meat, he neither heard nor saw them that stood by him, till he was lift up by the arms; and then gently he would speak unto them, as one awaked out of a deep sleep. *Amor Dei est ecstaticus—sui nec se sinit esse juris.*

Ver. 3. *Moses and Elias appeared*] Those *immortalitatis candidati*, as the ancients called them. God had buried Moses, but brought him forth afterwards glorious; the same body which was hid in the valley of Moab appeareth here in the hill of Tabor. Christ by rotting refines our bodies also; and we know that when "he, who is our life, shall appear, then shall we also appear with him in glory," Col. iii. 4. As in the mean space, be not we conformed to this world, but rather transformed by the renewing of our minds, Rom. xii. 2; and in whatsoever trans-figuration or ravishment we cannot find Moses, and Elias, and Christ to meet (as here they did in this sacred synod), that is, if what we find in us be not agreeable to the Scriptures, we may well suspect it as an illusion.

Ver. 4. *Lord, it is good for us to be here*] *Hic plura absurda quam verba.* But he knew not what he should say, he was so amused, or rather amazed, at that blissful sight. So Paul, whether in the body or out of the body, when rapt into the third heaven, he cannot tell, God knoweth; and again, he cannot tell, God knoweth, 2 Cor. xii. 2, 3. Only this he can tell, that he heard ἄῤῥητα ῥήματα, wordless words, such things as words are too weak to utter, and at the thought whereof,

Claudicat ingenium, delirat linguaque, mensque.

It is as impossible to comprehend heaven joys, as to compass the heaven with a span or contain the ocean in a nut-shell. No wonder then though Peter cry out, It is good being here; or, it is better being here than at Jerusalem (so St Chry-sostom senseth it), whither our Saviour had said he must go, and suffer many things of the elders and be killed, &c. That St Peter liked not; but would build here rather. All men would have heaven, but not the rough way that leads to it; they would enter into Paradise, but not through that narrow portal of afflictions; they would sit in the seat of honour with Zebedee's children, but not drink of Christ's cup, much less be baptized with his baptism; that is, be doused over head and ears in the waters of miseries. They would feed on manchet, tread on roses, and come to heaven, as passengers at sea do many times to the haven, while they are sleeping, or before they are aware. But this is no less a folly than a delicacy, thus to think to divide between Christ and his cross, to pull a rose without pricks, to have heaven without hardship.

One for thee, one for Moses, one for Elias] He never thought of one for himself, he was so trans-ported; but he had provided ill for himself and us, if Christ had taken his counsel: for so he should have declined death, whereby life and im-mortality was brought to light to the saints, 2 Tim. i. 12. And this unadvised advice was so much the worse in Peter, because but six days before he had been sharply shent by our Sa-viour, and called Satan for such carnal counsel; and besides that, even then he heard Moses and Elias conferring with Christ about his de-parture, confirming him against it, Luke ix. 31. It is hard to say how oft we shall fall into the same fault (though foul) if left to our-selves.

Ver. 5. *While he yet spake*] But had no an-swer (because he deserved it not) to so foolish a proposition. Only the Father answereth for the Son, by the oracle out of the cloud, according to that, "I bear not witness to myself, but the Father

that sent me, he it is that beareth witness of me," John viii. 18.

A bright cloud overshadowed them] As a curtain drawn betwixt them and the heavenly glory; to the contemplation whereof they were not yet sufficient. Hereby also their senses were drawn off from beholding Christ's glory, to hear the voice from heaven, which by the cloud, as by a chariot, was carried into their ears with greater sound and solemnity. *Non loquendum de Deo sine lu-mine,* was a saying of Pythagoras; God may not be mentioned without a light.

This is my beloved Son, in whom] Here God maketh use of three diverse passages and places of his own Book, Psal. ii. 7; Isa. xlii. 1; Deut. xviii. 18, to teach us when we speak, to speak as the oracles of God, inure ourselves to Scripture lan-guage, 1 Pet. iv. 11. The voice also which Christ heard from heaven at his baptism, in his first in-auguration, is here repeated *totidem verbis,* in his transfiguration, which was no small confirmation to him, doubtless; as it was also to Peter and the rest, that this voice was the same in effect with his and their confession of Christ in the former chapter, ver. 16, "Thou art Christ, the Son of the living God."

In whom I am well pleased] ἐν ᾧ εὐδόκησα, In whom I do acquiesce, and have perfect and full complacency, singular contentment. And as in him, so in us through him, Zeph. iii. 17, he rests in his love to his, he will seek no further; *effecit nos sibi dilectos in illo Dilecto,* he hath made us accepted in that beloved One. Here we have God's acquittance for our better security.

Hear ye him] As the arch-prophet of the Church, Deut. xviii. 15, that Palmoni-hammedab-ber, as Daniel (viii. 13) calleth him, that excellent speaker, that master of speech that came out of the bosom of his Father, and hath his whole mind at his fingers' ends, as we say, "Hear ye him;" hear none but him, and such as come in his name and word. *Hæc vox* [*hunc audite*] *summam authori-tatem arrogat Christo* (saith Erasmus). *At nunc videmus passim dormitari ad Christi doctrinam seu crassam ac rudem, et concionis auribus inculcari quid dixerit Scotus, quid Thomas, quid Durandus,* &c. But what said St Augustine? when Mani-cheus, contesting with him for audience, said, Hear me, hear me: Nay, said that Father, *Nec ego tu, nec tu me, sed ambo audiamus apostolum, &c.* Neither hear thou me, nor I thee, but let us both hear Christ. Cyril saith, "that in a synod at Ephesus, upon a high throne in the temple, there lay *sanctum Evangelium* to show that Christ was both present and President there. He is *Rabbenu Doctor irrefragabilis Padre Cerephino, &c.* And if Popish votaries so observe their govern-ors, that if they command them a voyage to China or Peru, they presently set forward, to argue or debate upon their superior mandates they hold presumption, to disobey them, sacrilege; how much more should we give this honour, audience, and obedience to Christ, the wisdom and word of God?

Ver. 6. *They fell on their faces*] As amazed

and amated with that stupendous voice that came from the excellent glory, as St Peter phraseth it, 2 Pet. i. 17. So Moses and Elias hid their faces when God spake unto them, as not able to bear his brightness; rottenness entered into their bones. The very angels cover their faces before him with two of their wings, as with a double scarf, or as one claps his hands upon his face when it lighteneth and flasheth suddenly upon him. What a mercy is it then to us, that we are taught by men like ourselves; that we have this treasure in earthen vessels, this pearl of price in a leathern purse. Here lay the three disciples; and, had not Christ mercifully touched them and raised them, there they had lain for dead.

Ver. 7. *Jesus came and touched them*] Christ therefore kills his, that he may quicken them; casts them down that he may revive and raise them in the opportunity of time (ἐν τῷ καιρῷ), Hos. vi. 1, 2; 1 Pet. v. 6): not so the devil, that destroyer, that hath not his names for nought, Apollyon and Abaddon.

Ver. 8. *Save Jesus alone*] To teach them that Moses and Elias, the law and prophets, vail bonnet to Christ; that there is but one mediator, even the man Christ Jesus; that there is sufficient in him to satisfy the soul, to comfort the conscience.

Ver. 9. *Tell the vision to no man*] Tacitus, we say, is a good historian. Taciturnity, we are sure, is in some cases a great virtue, a high commendation. Consus, the god of counsel, had his temple in Rome, under coverture, saith Servius, *ut ostenderet consilium debere esse tectum.* There is "a time to be silent," saith Solomon, Eccl. iii. 7. Queen Elizabeth's motto was *Video, Taceo,* I see, and say nothing. A fit motto for a maid, in earth the first, in heaven the second maid, as one poet calleth her. Ministers should know when and to whom and in what order to set forth God's truths; to time a word with a learned tongue, as Isaiah hath it; to set a word upon its wheels, as Solomon; to circumstantiate it so as the people can hear, can bear, as our Saviour did. This is surely a high point of heavenly husbandry. As it is also in all sorts of Christians to be sober in prayer, 1 Pet. iv. 7, that is, as Bifield saith, to keep God's counsel, not to be proud, or boast of success, or speak of the secret sweetness of God's love, without calling; it is to conceal the familiarity of God in secret.

Ver. 10. *Why then say the scribes, &c.*] Christ had answered them this question once before; but they were unsatisfied by anything he could say, because strongly possest with the conceit of an earthly kingdom. But the occasion of the question might be this. Our Saviour had forbidden them to tell any man the vision; hence they might thus debate it. Forasmuch as Elias must first come (so the scribes teach, and they have a text for it, Mal. iv. 5), and now he is come, as we have seen in the mount, why shouldest thou, Lord, forbid us to tell it abroad, sith this might be an effectual argument with the Jews to move

¹ Antoninus *apud* Ussierium, *de*

them to acknowledge thee for the true Messias? To this our Saviour answereth.

Ver. 11. *And restore all things*] viz. In Malachi's sense, i. e. not simply, absolutely, perfectly, for the royalty of restoring all things so was reserved for Christ alone, Acts iii. 21, but comparatively, to the state of the old Church. So those renowned reformers, Luther, Farellus,&c.,abroad, Cranmer, Cromwell, &c., here at home, freed the churches from many burdens and bondages, did (for their time) worthily in Ephrata, and are therefore famous in Bethlehem. But as *ejusdem non est invenire et perficere* (it is a praise proper to Christ only, to be Alpha and Omega, author and finisher of that he sets about, Rev. i. 8; Heb. xii. 2), those brave men left many abuses and disorders in the Church unrectified, unreformed, which either they did not see or could not help. But now as more light is diffused, so great thoughts of heart, yea, and great hopes are conceived, that God will finish the work, and cut it short in righteousness, Rom. ix. 28; that he will cut off the names of the idols out of the land, and they shall be no more remembered, Zech. xiii. 2, yea, that he will cause the false prophets, and with them the unclean spirit, to pass out of the land. We read Neh. viii. 17, 18, of a feast of tabernacles so well kept by the Jews newly come out of captivity, with dwelling in booths and reading every day out of the law, &c., as had not been done in many hundred years before, no, not in the reign of David and Solomon.

Ver. 12. *But I say unto you, that Elias is come*] All that is likely to come, however the Papist Bellarmine (as it were to thwart Christ), by depraving that prophecy in the Revelation touching the two witnesses, which they say are Enoch and Elias, will needs persuade themselves and others, that Elias the Tishbite must come ere Antichrist be revealed. Their arguments I recite not; their author is Papias, who first devised and divulged this fable. Now Papias that ancient millenary, scholar to St John, was a man much respected for opinion of his holiness and learning, but yet *homo ingenii pertenuis*, saith Eusebius, not much oppressed with wit. But had he been never so absolute otherwise, he was surely out in this. And herein we may truly say of him as the Papists falsely said of another, *Berengarius cum esset multum peritus, multum erravit.*[1] But if Papias or any other ancient or modern writer should have said so much against the Popish dotages as this man hath done for them, Bellarmine, likely, would have answered, as in like case he did to Irenæus, Tertullian, Eusebius, and Luther, I answer, "they are all arrant heretics." *Omnes manifesti hæretici sunt.*

And they knew him not] As neither did they the Lord of glory, because God had hid him under the carpenter's son. Christians are all "glorious within," like the tabernacle, which was gold within and goat's-hair without: like Brutus' staff, which, as Plutarch reporteth, was gold within, horn without. They are princes

Christ. Eccles. success. et statu.

in all lands, but as princes in foreign lands, they are unkent and therefore unkist, as the northern proverb hath it. But as, had they known, they would never have crucified the Lord of glory: so, did the world know the worth of a saint, of such a one as was the Baptist especially,[1] they would have given him but too much honour, as Cornelius did Peter, as Chrysostom did Babylas, and as Tertullian did some other martyrs, to whom writing he says, *Non tantus sum ut vos alloquar,* I am not worthy once to speak unto you.

Ver. 13. *Then the disciples understood*] Different measures of light and grace are given at several times, as God pleaseth to dispense, John xii. 16; John ii. 22; John x. 41, 42. Joseph understood not his own dreams, nor the eunuch what he read, till afterwards. Wait at wisdom's gates, wear out her threshold : then shall we " know if we follow on to know the Lord," Hos. vi. 3. Beg and dig for understanding, and thou shalt be sure of it, Prov. ii. 3—5.

Ver. 14. *And when they were come to the multitude*] That was the next day after the transfiguration, Luke ix. 37, and in that nick of time, when the disciples could neither cure the lunatic nor answer their adversaries, Mark ix. 15, who had now sport enough to see them brought into the briers, and therefore jeered them before the people to some purpose. Most opportunely therefore, if ever, comes Christ to their succour, as it were out of an engine, and both cures the child and confounds the Pharisees. His late honour hindered him not from doing his office : his incomparable felicity made him not forget poor Joseph's misery. He knew he was much wished and waited for, and therefore makes haste from the mount to the multitude.

Kneeling down to him] Some understand the word of such an humble gesture of catching the party petitioned by the knees or feet, as the Shunammite used to the prophet, the Shulamite to her spouse, and Thetis to Jupiter, when she sued to him in her sons' behalf.[2]

Ver. 15. *For he is lunatic*] Or, he hath the falling sickness, as the symptoms show. A common disease, but (besides that) the devil was in it.[3] The soul manslayer makes advantage of our natural humours (which are therefore the bath of the devil, and the bed of diseases) to exercise his cruelty upon the poor creature by Divine permission ; seeking by the infirmities of the body to bring sin upon the soul.

For ofttimes he falls into the fire, &c.] The devil pushing him in, as it were, to destroy him, but could not. He is limited, and cannot do as he would, else he would soon end us. If God chastise us with his own bare hand, or by men like ourselves, whip us, as it were, privately and at home, let us thank him, and think ourselves far better dealt with than if he should deliver us up

to the public officer, to his tormentor, to be scourged with scorpions at his pleasure. The wicked he oft casts into the fire of lust and water of drunkenness, and they complain not : like a sleepy man (fire burning in his bed-straw), he cries not out, when others haply lament his case that see afar off, but cannot help him. It hath " set him on fire round about, yet he knew it not : and it burned him, yet he laid it not to heart," Isa. xlii. 25. See Prov. xxiii. 34, 35.

And oft into the water] Urbanus Regius, in a sermon of his at Wittenberg, made mention of a certain maid possessed by the devil; and when she should have been prayed for in the congregation, the devil made as if he had been departed out of her. But before the next public meeting, Satan returned, and drove the maid into a deep water, where she presently perished.

Ver. 16. *And they could not cure him*] The prayer of faith would have healed the sick, James v. 15, as Luther's prayer recovered a godly divine (that was far gone in a consumption, and given up for a dead man by the physicians) beyond all expectation. *Iste vir potuit quod voluit,* saith one of him. That man by the force of his faith could do whatsoever he would with God. *Fiat mea voluntas,* " Let my will be done," said one in his prayer; and then sweetly falls off, " my will, Lord, because thy will," and he had his request. But let not the unbeliever " think that he shall receive anything of the Lord," James i. 7, sith he shuts heaven-gates against his own prayers ; and by the evil operation of a misgiving heart, denies them before he presents them.

Ver. 17. *O faithless and perverse generation*] He reproves the nine disciples, but rejects them not. Christ in the very dunghill of unbelief and sinfulness can find out his own part of faith and holiness, as we see in Sarah, Gen. xviii. 12. That whole speech of hers was vile and profane (besides that for want of faith she laughed at the unlikelihood, and was therefore checked by the angel). One thing only was praiseworthy in that sinful sentence, that she called her husband Lord : this God hath taken notice of, and recorded to her eternal commendation and others' imitation, 1 Pet. iii. 6.

And perverse generation] Depraved, distorted, dislocated, Διεστραμμένη. *Homo est inversus decalogus.* Man now stands across to all goodness, is born with his back towards heaven, a perverse and crooked creature, Deut. xxxii. 5, having his upper-lip standing where his nether-lip should, Prov. xix. 1, and all parts else out of frame and joint, Rom. iii.

How long shall I suffer you ?] As they do, that willingly bear a burden and are content to continue under it. Christ bears with our evil manners, Acts xiii. 18, as a loving husband bears with a froward wife :[4] but yet he is sufficiently sensible, and therefore complains of the pressure,

---

[1] *Magnus atque admirabilis vir, si modo viri nomine designari illum fas est.* Chrysost. Orat. contra Gentiles.

[2] Γουνοῦμαι σε ἔγωγε, Iliad. α.

[3] *Lunaticus speculum miseriæ humanæ, et malitiæ Satanæ.* Pareus.

[4] *Ut qui volentes onus subeunt, et sub eo perdurant.* Beza. ἐτροποφόρησεν.

Amos ii. 13, and once cried out under the importable weight of it, "My God, my God, why hast thou forsaken me?" The earth could not bear Korah and his company, but clave under and swallowed them up: as it soon after spewed out the Canaanites, who had filled it with filthiness from corner to corner, Ezra ix. 11. Consider, how oft thou hast straggled over the mouth of the bottomless pit, and art not yet fallen into the boiling caldron, that fiery furnace. Oh stand and wonder at God's patience, and be abrupt in thy repentance, lest abused mercy turn into fury.

Ver. 18. *And he departed out of him*] Though with a very ill will, for he tore the child and well-nigh killed him. So when we do, by the prayer of faith, conjure and charm the devil out of our hearts (prayer is called a "charm," Isa. xxvi. 16), he will make all the hurly-burly he can, but out he must, though never so ill-willing.

And the child was cured] By his father's faith. What wonder, then, that the parents' faith be beneficial to the baptized infant?

Ver. 19. *Why could not we cast him out?*] They had heard why before, but either heeded it not or were not willing to hear on that ear. Loth they were to yield that it was any fault of theirs, that the cure was not effected by them, but by some other occasion (the father's faithlessness, the people's perverseness, &c.), which what it was, here they make inquiry. How unwilling are we that our penny should be held other than good silver! How ready to shift off him that speaks from heaven (παραιτήσησθε, Heb. xii. 25), and to mistake ourselves in the causes of our miscarriages!

Ver. 20. *Because of your unbelief*] q. d. That is the naked truth of it, never deceive yourselves: there is no shuffling will serve turn: be content (hard though it be) to hear your own. *Veritas aspera est, verum amaritudo ejus utilior, et integris sensibus gratior, quam meretricantis linguæ distillans favus.* A smart truth takes better with an honest heart than a smooth supparasitation.

If ye have faith as a grain of, &c.] The disciples might object, if no faith but that which is entire and perfect can do such cures as this, then we may despair of ever doing any. Our Saviour answers, that the least measure of true faith (fitly compared to mustard seed, for its acrimony and vivacity), if exerted and exercised, will work wonders. Neither is justifying faith beneath miraculous in the sphere of its own activity, and where it hath warrant of God's word, to remove mountains of guilt and grief. A weak faith is a joint possessor, though no faith can be a joint purchaser of sin's remission. And a man may have faith enough to bring him to heaven, though he want this or that faith, as to rely upon God without failing, Luke xviii. 1, 8, without feeling, Psal. xxii. 1, &c., as resolved, that God nevertheless will hear him in that very thing he prays for.

Ver. 21. *This kind goeth not out*] Some devils then are not so potent, politic, vile, villanous, as others: so neither are wicked men all alike wicked; some stigmatical Belialists face the heavens, burden the earth, please not God, and are contrary to all men, 1 Thess. ii. 15. Others are more tame and tractable, as the young man on whom Christ looked and loved him. Yet, as when one commended the pope's legate at the Council of Basil, Sigismund the emperor answered, *Tamen Romanus est:* so though the devil or his slaves seem never so fair-conditioned, they are neither to be liked nor trusted. He is a devil still, and will do his kind: they are wicked still, and "wickedness proceedeth from the wicked," as saith the proverb of the ancients, 1 Sam. xxiv. 13. I have read of one that would haunt the taverns, theatres, and whore-houses in London all day, but he durst not go forth without private prayer in the morning, and then would say at his departure, Now, devil, do thy worst; and so used his prayers as charms and spells against the weak, cowardly devil. This was not that prayer and fasting our Saviour here speaks of; men must not go forth to this spiritual fight, δορπὸν ἔλοντες, with their breakfast, as the Grecians in Homer, but praying and fasting from sin especially: for otherwise they do but light a candle before the devil, as the proverb hath it.

Ver. 22. *The Son of man shall be betrayed*] This our Saviour often inculcates, to drive them out of their golden dream of an earthly kingdom; which pleased them so well, that they could hardly forego it. It is no easy matter to be disabused, undeceived. Error once admitted is not expelled without much ado. It sticks to our fingers like pitch: take heed how we meddle.

Ver. 23. *And they were exceeding sorry*] Out of love to their Lord, saith Jerome; out of ignorance and stupidity, saith St Mark (ix. 32) and St Luke (ix. 45): so they grieve where no cause was, as we do oft upon like grounds and causes. How well might our Saviour have said to them, as afterwards he did to the women, "Grieve not for me, but grieve for yourselves." They knew well that if Christ suffered, they should not escape scot-free, *Hinc illæ lachrymæ.* We shrink in the shoulder when called to carry the cross, and pretend this and that for excuse, as Moses did the conscience of his own insufficiency, Exod. iv. 10, when the very truth was, he feared Pharaoh, lest he would have revenged the Egyptian's quarrel against him, whom he had slain, and hid in the sand: and as Peter pretended his dear love to his Master, Matt. xvi. 22, when it appears, ver. 26, he aimed indeed at the safeguard of his own life more than his Master's safety. Let care be taken that (whatever we make believe) we be not self-lovers (which begins that black bead-roll, 2 Tim. iii. 2), and "lovers of pleasures," profits, preferments, "more than lovers of God" (which ends it).

Ver. 24. *They that received tribute money*]

This didrachmum or half-shekel was formerly paid by the Israelites every year, after they were twenty years old, toward the temple, Exod. xxx. 13. Cæsar, by taking it from the temple and turning it to a tribute, did indeed take away from God that which was God's. This very tribute was paid afterwards by the Jews toward the Roman capitol, by virtue of a decree made by Vespasian. How just is it in God, that the spoiler should be spoiled, Isa. xxx. 1, that the Roman emperors, that so robbed and wronged God, should be robbed of their rights, as they are by the pope's usurpations.

Doth not your master pay tribute] Is he either born or bought free? See Acts xxii. 28. But if neither, they might (had they had any goodness in them) have spared him, so public, so profitable a person, that had so well deserved of the whole nation, so well merited an immunity, an indemnity. But all is lost that is laid out upon ungrateful persons or people. Covetousness hath no respect to anything but to its own profit, and knows no other language than the horse-leech's, Give, give, *Rem, Rem, quocunque modo rem,* without any respect of persons, how well deserving soever.

Ver. 25. *He saith, Yes*] Christ submitted himself "to every ordinance of man for the Lord's sake," 1 Pet. ii. 13; and hath bidden us, Give unto Cæsar those things that are Cæsar's, tribute to whom tribute is due, custom to whom custom, &c., Matt. xxii. 21; Rom. xii. 7. So doth not the great Heteroclite of Rome; he not only detains, but demands Peter-pence and other undue payments from kings and states. One pope said that he could never want money so long as he could hold a pen in his hand. This kingdom was of old called the pope's ass, for bearing his burdens and exactions. Innocent IV. said, that England was the pope's Paradise, and a pit that could never be drawn dry, *Hortus deliciarum et puteus inexhaustus.* What vast sums drained they hence in King John's days! Otto (one of the pope's muscipulatores, mice-catchers, as the story calleth them), sent hither by Gregory IX., after three years' raking together of money, left not so much in the whole kingdom as he either carried with him or sent to Rome before him. But I hope ere long the kings of the earth, awakened by their gross abuses put upon them, will fleece that withered whore, and burn her flesh with fire, a punishment fore-prophesied, and well befitting so foul an harlot.

Ver. 26. *Then are the children free*] q. d. And much more I (who am the natural, the only begotten Son of that King everlasting, the heir of all) am privileged from payments. Yet because few knew what Peter did, that he was the Christ, the Son of the living God, the Son also of David, according to the flesh, lest by his example he should occasion and encourage either the Jews to deny payment, or the Romans to defy the gospel as contrary to monarchy, he would not make use of his immunity, but sent to sea for money to make payment.

Ver. 27. *Lest we should offend them*] Better it is that a man part with his right than give just offence to any. This was St Paul's great care, 1 Cor. ix., and his constant counsel to others, Rom. xiv. 13—15. Let no man put a stumbling-block, much less a scandal, in his brother's way, that is, neither a lighter nor greater offence, but rather abridge himself of his lawful liberty. This is to express Christ to the world, to be made like unto him. Πρόσκομμα *notat leviorem offensam, qua aliquis non corruat;* σκάνδαλον *graviorem, ex qua quis prolapsus claudicet.*

Go thou to the sea] Here Jerome cries out, *Quid primum mirer in hoc loco nescio,* I know not what chiefly here to wonder at, whether Christ's prescience or greatness. His prescience, that he knew that the fish had money in his mouth, and that that fish should come first to hand. His greatness and power, that could create such a piece of money by his bare word, and cause it so to be, by commanding it so to be. Who would not fear this Lord of hosts? Who would not trust him for necessaries, who can and will cause all creatures to cater for his? But what a wonderful work of God was it, and a fair warning to us before these doleful days of war, had we been so wise as to have made good use of it, that God should send John Frith's Preparation to the Cross, in the fish-belly, to the University of Cambridge, a little before the commencement, some few years since. That such a book (saith the reverend man; Jer. Dyke, that relateth it) should be brought in such a manner, and to such a place, and at such a time, when by reason of people's confluence out of all parts, notice might be given to all places of the land; in my apprehension it can be construed for no less than a divine warning, and to have this voice with it, "England, prepare for the cross."

Take up the fish] Earthly men (saith one wittily) are like the fish here mentioned: either dumb, or nothing but gold in their mouths.

Give it unto them for me and thee] Upon this place, Papists would foolishly found their pope's primacy and clergy's privilege of immunity from payments to civil princes and magistrates: because Christ and Peter are set together. But in what trow? In paying of homage, not in receiving of honour. Christ paid tribute, to free us from the servitude of Satan, that rigid tax-master. Peter paid, because he had here a house and family, chap. viii. 5, and further to let his successors know that they paid tribute in Peter, and should learn in all due humility to submit to magistracy; and not to withdraw from public impositions and taxations, further than of favour they shall be exempted and privileged.

CHAPTER XVIII.

Ver. 1. *At the same time*] When he by paying tribute had been teaching them humility
and modesty, they most unseasonably discover
their folly and ambition: so another time, after
he had been washing their feet, and giving them
the sacrament, Luke xxii. See in them the
pravity, the canker of our natures, and what
cause God had to complain, Hos. vii. 1, " When
I would have healed Israel, then the iniquity
of Ephraim was discovered," as if it had been
on purpose to spite me, and spit venom in my
face.

Came the disciples] Peter also with the rest,
ver. 21, though Bellarmine will needs have it
otherwise (as if he were now at sea), because he
shall bear no part of the blame: take heed of
that that were sin, Hos. xii. 8.

Who is the greatest] *Quærunt non quærenda*,
saith Aretius: they should rather have inquired how to get into heaven than who should
be highest in heaven. *Ridiculum illud est, initia
ignorare, et ultima rimari*. But they dreamt of
a distribution of honours and offices (as once
in the days of David and Solomon), a worldly
monarchy, like the kingdoms of the earth; as
afterwards the Church was, and still is, transformed by antichrist into the image of the
beast, that is, of the Roman Empire: yet they
call it the kingdom of heaven, because they had
heard Christ many times call it so.

In the kingdom of heaven] i. e. In the state
and condition of the Church Christian. So to
this day among the Jews the kingdom of the
Messiah is called Malcuth hashamajim, the
kingdom of heaven; and rightly so: for, 1. The
King is heavenly. 2. He hath heaven for his
throne, whence he puts forth his power. 3. His
subjects are heavenly-minded, and trade for
heavenly commodities. 4. Their country is
heaven though their commoration be awhile upon earth, where they are pilgrims and strangers.
5. The government of this kingdom is wholly
heavenly and spiritual. (Cameron.)

Ver. 2. *And Jesus called a little child*] Nicephorus saith this was Ignatius, who was afterwards Bishop of Antioch; but I am not bound
to believe him. It is well known that he is full
of fictions. Christ calling for a little child, who
neither thinks great things of himself nor seeks
great things for himself, rightly and really confutes their preposterous ambition and affectation of primacy, and gives them such a dumb
answer as Tarquin did his son, when walking in
the garden he struck off the heads of the pop-
pies in the sight of the messenger: and as
Periander the Corinthian did Thrasybulus the
tyrant of Athens, when pulling off the upper
ears, he made all the standing corn equal, intimating thereby what a tyrant must do that
would live safe and quiet.

Ver. 3. *Except ye be converted*] i. e. Except

ye turn over a new leaf, and cast away these
fond conceits and crotchets, these golden dreams
of an earthly kingdom, and your high preferments therein, which like bullets of lead fastened
to the eye-lids of your minds, make you that
you cannot look upwards.

And become as little children] In simplicity,
humility, innocency, ignoscency, &c., not in
childishness, peevishness, pragmaticalness, talk-
ativeness, open-heartedness, &c. *Non præcipitur
Apostolis ut habeant ætatem parvulorum, sed ut in-
nocentiam*, &c. (Jerome.) How absurd was that
Anabaptist Aurifaber, who understanding this
text Nicodemically, as one saith, stirreth up
people wherever he came to carry themselves
childishly, if ever they would have heaven.
(Scultet. Annal.) Upon whose persuasion you
might have seen ridiculous imitations of boys
and girls; women especially, skipping up and
down, clapping their hands together, sitting
naked on the ground, tickling, toying, apishly
imitating one while Christ, another while antichrist, &c., pretending this text for their authority. So did Massæus the Franciscan, who is
famous amongst his fellow-friars, for that, at
the command of his superior, St Francis, he
wallowed on the ground as a little one, and
showed all, in obedience to this text, as Sedulius
testifieth. *Ridiculum caput!* Many such like
examples may be met with in the legends of the
Fathers, of such as were voluntaries in humility
(as the apostle styles them), or rather in hypocrisy, Col. ii. 18, θέλων ἐν ταπεινοφροσύνη.
For, *hujus virtutis postea homines Christiani adeo
studiosi et æmuli fuere, ut tota in hypocrisin vere
abierit*, saith Aretius, here. Humility in many
of the ancients degenerated into hypocrisy.

Ye shall not enter into the kingdom of heaven]
One sin allowed excludes out of the kingdom,
be it but ambition or some such inward evil,
such as the world takes no notice of, makes no
matter of. Inward bleeding killeth many times,
and God by killing Jezebel's children with
death (i. e. throwing them to hell) will make all
the Churches know that he searcheth the inwards, Rev. ii. 23.

Ver. 4. *Whosoever therefore shall humble*, &c.]
Children are not lifted up with pride, for the
great things they are born to, neither mind
they high places: but the child of a prince will
play with the poorest, and make him his mate.
Christians should not mind high things, but
condescend to the meanest, and be carried by
them, as the word signifieth (συναπαγόμενοι),
Rom. xii. 16; especially since we are all born
again by the same seed, there is no difference
at all in our birth or inheritance. Why then
look we so big one upon another? Why do we
slight or brow-beat any? Have we not all one
Father?

The same is greatest in the kingdom] He that
can most vilify and nullify himself, shall be
highest in heaven. When had David the kingdom given him in possession, but when he was
as a weaned child? When was Mephibosheth

advanced to David's table, but when he made himself a dog, and therefore fit only to lie under the table, yea, a dead dog, and therefore fit only for the ditch? He that is in the low pits and caves of the earth, sees the stars in the firmament; when they who are on the tops of the mountains discern them not. He that is most humble seeth most of heaven, and shall have most of it: for the lower the ebb, the higher the tide, and the lower the foundation of virtue is laid, the higher shall the roof of glory be over-laid.

Ver. 5. *And whoso shall receive one such, &c.*] St Luke (ix. 48) hath it, "whosoever shall receive this child in my name." Meaneth our Saviour the child, or those that were humble as that child? Both surely. See here how highly Christ regards and rewards humility, even the picture of it in little ones. Now, if the shadow of this grace have such a healing virtue, what then hath the body? If the leaves be so sovereign, what then the fruit?

Ver. 6. *But whoso shall offend, &c.*] By false doctrine, or loose life, or making a prey of their simplicity and humility, which many times draws on injury. A crow will stand upon a sheep's back, pulling off wool from her side. She durst not do so to a wolf or a mastiff.

That a millstone were hanged, &c.] The nether millstone, called in Greek the ass, either because it is the bigger and thicker of the two; or because the millstone was drawn about by the help of the ass, μύλος ὀνικὸς. This kind of punishment the greatest malefactors among the Jews were in those days put to, as saith St Jerome. And hereby is set forth the heaviest of hell-torments. Thus the beast of Rome (that grand offender of Christ's little ones, whom he worrieth and maketh havoc of) is threatened (by a like kind of punishment) to be cast alive into the burning lake, Rev. xix. 20. And for his city Babylon, a mighty angel is seen to take up a stone like a great millstone, and cast it into the sea, saying, "Thus with violence shall that great city Babylon be thrown down, and shall be found no more at all." This, by an elegant and emphatical gradation, notably sets forth the remediless ruin of Rome; in that an angel, a strong angel, taketh a stone, and a great stone, even a millstone, which he letteth not barely fall, but casteth, and with impetuous force thrusteth, into the bottom of the sea, whence nothing ordinarily is recovered, much less a millstone, thrust from such a hand with such a force.

Drowned in the depth of the sea] In that part of the sea that is farthest off from the shore: *q. d.* he is a brat of fathomless perdition, he shall be desperately drowned in destruction, *ita ut in aquæ summitate rursus non ebulliat.* So the Romans served their parricides, and the Grecians other grievous malefactors: they wrapped them up in lead, and cast them into the deep.

Ver. 7. *Woe to the world, because of offences*] Σκάνδαλον, *proprie tendicula, hoc est, lignum illud*

curvum, quo moto decipula clauditur. The world, besides the offences they give to the saints, they give and take much hurt one from another, and so heap up wrath; whiles, besides their own, they bring upon themselves their other men's sins to answer for. I have read of a woman, who living in professed doubt of the Godhead, after better illumination and repentance, did often protest that the vicious life of a great scholar in that town did conjure up those damnable doubts in her soul. When therefore corruption boils, and thou art ready to run into some reproachful evil, think the name of Christ and thy poor brother's soul lie prostrate before thee. And wilt thou trample upon that and throttle this?

It must needs be that offences come] By God's permission, Satan's malice, and man's wickedness: *Venenum aliquando pro remedio fuit* (Senec. *de Benef.*). God oft draws good out of evil, as wine draws a nourishing virtue from the flesh of serpents: as the skilful apothecary, of the poisonful viper, maketh an wholesome triacle, 1 Cor. xi. 10.

Ver. 8. *If thy hand or foot offend thee, &c.*] Chap. v. 29, 30, our Saviour forbids all his to defile themselves with the filth of sin; here, to offend others thereby. See the notes there.

Ver. 9. *Pluck it out*] This is the circumcision of the heart, the mortification of earthly members, which is no less hard to be done than for a man with one hand to cut off the other, or to pull out his own eyes, and then rake in the holes where they grew. And yet, hard or not hard, it must be done; for otherwise we are utterly undone for ever. Hypocrites, as artificial jugglers, seem to wound themselves, but do not: as stage-players, they seem to thrust themselves through their bodies, whereas the sword passeth only through their clothes. But the truly religious lets out the life-blood of his beloved lusts, lays them all dead at his feet, and burns their bones to lime, as the king of Moab did the king of Edom, Amos ii. 1. As Joshua put down all the Canaanites, so doth grace all corruptions. As Asa deposed his own mother, so doth this, the mother of sin. It destroys them not by halves, as Saul, but hews them in pieces before the Lord, as Samuel.

Ver. 10. *Take heed that ye despise not, &c.*] Gr. Look to it if you do, a foul mischief is towards you.[1] Look to it as you tender your own safety here or salvation hereafter. Cast not the least contempt upon Christ's little ones. As little as they are, they have a great Champion, Isa. xxxvii. 22, 23, and so many angels to right them and fight for them, that a man had better anger all the witches in the world than one of these little ones. I tell you, some great ones have been fain to humble themselves, and to lick the very dust of their feet sometimes, that they might be reconciled to them, Isa. lx. 14. If Cain do but lower upon Abel, God will ar-

---

[1] ὁρᾶτε, *Districte præcipientis verbum.*

raign him for it, Gen. iv. 6. Why is thy countenance cast down? Why dost look so doggedly? If Miriam do but mutter against Moses, God will spit in her face, Numb. xii. 14: and if Aaron had not made the more haste to make his peace by repentance, he also had tasted of the same sauce.

Their angels do always behold the face] Angels in the Syriac are named אפנים of the face, because it is their office and honour to look always on God's face. They are sent about God's messages to this earth, yet are never out of their heaven, never out of the vision of their Maker. No more are godly men, when busied in their callings. And howsoever slighted in the world, yet angels are sent forth for their safeguard and service, Heb. i. 14, yea, for the accomplishment of all designs for the saints' good, they stand alway looking God full in the face, to receive commandments.

Ver. 11. *For the Son of man came, &c.*] Therefore angels are so active and officious about them. This the reprobate angels could not bring their hearts to yield to, and therefore fell through envy from their first estate: and whereas the society of angels was much maimed by their fall, their room, say some, is supplied by the saints, whom therefore they take such care of and content in.

Ver. 12. *Doth he not leave the ninety and nine*] I am not, saith a divine, of their fond opinion that think the angels are here meant by the ninety-nine sheep, as if they were so infinite in number beyond the number of mankind:[1] yet, without question, they are exceeding many, and that number cannot be known of us in this world, Dan. vii. 10. Psal. lxviii. 17, "The chariots of God are 20,000, even thousands of angels: the Lord is among them as in Sinai," &c., that is, those myriads of angels make Sion as dreadful to all her enemies as those angels made Sinai at the delivery of the law. But the application of this parable makes it plain, that the hundred sheep are God's elect little ones; all which are set safe by Christ upon the everlasting mountains, and not one of them lost, John. x.; Matt. xxiv.

Ver. 13. *And if so be that he find it*] As he will most surely, for none can take them out of his hands; nor can he discharge his trust, should he suffer any one of them to wander and perish, as they will do, undoubtedly, if left to themselves, such is their sheepish simplicity, Isa. liii. 6. God hath charged Christ to see to the safe-keeping of every true sheep, John vi. 39, 40, and he performed it to the full, John xvii. 12. As for that son of perdition there excepted, he was never of Christ's body, yet is excepted, because he seemed to be, by reason of his office.

Ver. 14. *It is not the will of your Father*] Happy for us, that we are kept by the power of God to salvation, 1 Pet. i. 5, for else it were possible for us to fall away and perish: an in-

tercision there might be, nay, an utter excision from Christ, were not his left hand under us, and his right hand over us, Cant. ii. 6, and both his hands about us, to clasp and hold us fast to himself. But his right hand is our Jachin, and his left hand our Boaz, 1 Kings vii. 21. Both which pillars in the porch of Solomon's temple did show, not only by the matter whereof they were made, but also by the names whereby they were called, what stedfastness the elect stand in before God, both for present and future. For present they have strength in themselves; for future, God will so establish them with his grace, that they shall never wholly depart from him. As for reprobates, God saith of them, that that will die, let it die; they shall die in their sins, as the Lord threateneth the Jews; which is a thousand times worse than to die in a ditch or in a dungeon.

Ver. 15. *If thy brother shall trespass*] As trespass he will, "for it must needs be that offences come," ver. 7, such is human frailty. Two flints may as soon smite together, and not fire come out, as two or more men converse together and not trespasses in one kind or other fall out. A heathen could say, *Non amo quenquam nisi offendam:* for so, I shall know whether he love me or no, by his forbearing of me. And Augustine saith, *Qui desinit sustinere, desinit amare,* He that ceaseth to bear with me, ceaseth to love me. Here therefore our Saviour, after he had deterred his from doing wrong, instructeth them how to suffer wrong. If it be not considerable, it must be dissembled. As if it be, *Go and tell him*] ὕπαγε, Get thee gone to him presently, lest else the sore rankle, and thou hate him in thy heart, Lev. xix. 17: say not, he should come to me, &c., but get thee to him with speed. *Lech lecha,* as God said to Abraham, up and be packing; stand not to strain courtesy with him when both have haste; but seek peace and ensue it; it is best to be first in a good matter. Remember, said Aristippus to Æschines (with whom he was fallen out), that though I were the elder man, yet I first sought to thee. Verily, said Æschines, thou art not only an elder, but a better man than I; for I was first in the quarrel; but thou art first in seeking reconciliation. *Næ tu profecto vir me longe melior es, &c.* Plutarch.

Tell him his fault] God's little ones are so to be loved, as not to be let alone in their trespasses; but freely and friendly admonished, that they may see their sin and amend their way, as Denkius did when admonished by Œcolampadius.[2] He being a learned man held this heresy, that no man or devil should be damned eternally, but all saved at last, &c. But being withal an humble man, he repented; being converted by Œcolampadius, in whose presence he died at Basil of the plague, but piously, A. D. 1528.

Thou hast gained thy brother] To God and

---

[1] *Theophrastus, 99 oves vult esse angelos qui non erraverunt, unam perditum, genus humanum.*

[2] *Vir fuit doctus, demissi animi, Hebraicæ linguæ peritus, &c. Resipuit tandem conversus ab Œcolamp.* Scultet. Annal.

thyself, and if to God, to thyself surely for ever, as Philemon (how much more Onesimus!) to Paul, to whom they therefore owed themselves also. Sir Anthony Kingston thus spake to Mr Hooper a little before his martyrdom: I thank God that ever I knew you, for God did appoint you to call me, being a lost child. For by your good admonitions and wholesome reproofs, whereas I was before both an adulterer and fornicator, God hath brought me to forsake and detest the same.

Ver. 16. *Then take with thee one or two more*] Such as are faithful, and able both to keep counsel and to give counsel; that so, if we cannot lead him by the hand to Christ, we may bear him in his bed, as they did the palsyman, and so bring him to Christ by the help of friends.

That in the mouth of two or three] To blame then are they that proceed upon every idle supposition, suspicion, report, or rumour. Three manner of persons (said Father Latimer) can make no credible information. 1. Adversaries, for evil will doth never speak well. 2. Ignorant men, and . those without judgment. 3. Whisperers and blowers in men's ears, which will spew out in hugger-mugger more than they dare avow openly. To all such we must turn the deaf ear: the tale-bearer and tale-hearer are both of them abominable, and shut out of heaven, Psal. xv. 3.

Ver. 17. *Tell it unto the church*] That is, unto the church governors, the church representatives, as some think. Not the pope, whom Papists make the church virtual, and who, like a wasp, is no sooner angry but out comes a sting; which being out, is like a fool's dagger, rattling and snapping without an edge. Hence in the year 833, when Pope Gregory IV. offered to excommunicate Ludovicus Pius, the emperor, with his followers, the bishops that stood for the emperor affirmed, that they would by no means yield to the pope's pleasure therein, *sed si excommunicaturus veniret, excommunicatus abiret cum aliter se habeat antiquorum canonum authoritas.*[1] And in the year 1260, Leonard, an English doctor, answered the pope's legate, who pleaded that all churches were the pope's; that they were his indeed (so it went then for current, but) *tuitione non fruitione, defensione non dissipatione.* If he should cast out Jonas and keep Ham in the ark, they would decline and disclaim his censures. Jac. Revius. *Hist. Pontif.*

Let him be unto thee as an heathen and a publican] i. e. Neither meddle nor make with him; have thou neither sacred nor civil society with him. The Jews hated the presence, the fire, the fashion, the books of a heathen: as now a Papist may not join with a Protestant in any holy action, no, not in saying over the Lord's prayer, or saying grace at table. Howbeit of old a Jew might eat at the same table with a heathen, Lev. viii., and come to the same temple with publicans, so they were proselytes, Luke xviii. But they might do neither of these to an obstinate excommunicate, no more may we. Rebellion is as witchcraft, and obstinacy as bad as idolatry, 1 Sam. xv. 23.

Ver. 18. *Whatsoever ye shall bind*] Let no man despise your censure, for I will ratify it. Whatever you bind, i. e. forbid, prohibit, &c. As whatever ye loose, that is, command, permit, shall be seconded and settled by me in heaven, so that your word shall surely stand. Further, to bind, saith Cameron, is to pronounce a thing profane; to loose is to pronounce it lawful; as when the Jews say that David and Ezekiel bound nothing that was not bound in the law.

Ver. 19. *If two of you shall agree*] How much more then a whole church full of you! Great is the power of joint prayer, Acts xii. 12; Dan. ii. 18. Those in the Revelation whose prayers went up as a pillar of incense, and came before the Lord as the sound of many waters; the thundering legion, the Christians in Tertullian's time, that came, an army of them, not more to beseech than to besiege God by their prayers. This made Henry III., King of France, forbid the Protestant householders in his dominions to pray with their families. And a great queen said, that she feared more the prayers of John Knox and his complices than an army of 30,000 men. The house shook where the disciples were praying, Acts iv. The devil was forced to throw in the obligation to Luther and some others that were praying for a young man that had yielded himself body and soul to the devil for money, and had written the bond with his own blood. The Popish soldiers that went against the Angrognians in France, said that the ministers of that town with their prayers conjured and bewitched them, that they could not fight. Whiles Moses, Aaron, and Hur, lift up their hands and minds together in the mount, Joshua beats Amalek in the valley. He prevailed *precando*, more than he did *prӕliando*. Now for the fruit of prayer, said those brave spirits at Edgehill battle, where there was never less seen of man and more of God, as the noble general thankfully acknowledged.

Ver. 20. *There am I in the midst*] As to eye their behaviour, so to hear their suits. All that he requireth is, that they bring lawful petitions and honest hearts; and then they shall be sure to receive whatsoever heart can wish or need require. A courtier that is a favourite, gets more of his prince by one suit many times than a tradesman or husbandman haply doth with 20 years' labour: so doth a praying Christian get much goods at God's hands, as having the royalty of his ear and the command of whatsoever God can do for him. Isa. xlv. 11, "Concerning the work of my hands, command ye me." Hence that transcendent rapture of Luther in a certain prayer of his, *Fiat voluntas mea, Domine.* And hence that request of St Bernard to a certain friend of his

[1] Ussier, de Christianæ Eccl. statu et successione.

to whom he had given divers directions for strictness and purity, *Et cum talis fueris*, saith he, *memento mei:* when thou art become such a one, think on me in thy prayers.

Ver. 21. *And I forgive him? till seven times*] How many good people even at this day think if they forgive an offending brother some few times, that they have supererogated, and deserved to be chronicled, yea, canonized! It was a fault in Peter to presume to prescribe to Christ how oft he should enjoin him to forgive. Peter is still the same; ever too forwardly and forth-putting.

Ver. 22. *Until seventy times seven*] i. e. Infinities, *toties quoties*. God multiplieth pardons, Isa. lv. 7; so should we. "Love covereth all sins," Prov. x. 12, so large is the skirt of love's mantle. Betwixt God and us the distance is infinite, and if it were possible, our love to him, and to our friends in him, our foes for him, should fill up that distance, and extend itself to infiniteness. We may without sin be sensible of injuries (a sheep is as sensible of a bite as a swine), but it must be with the silence of a sheep, or at utmost the mourning of a dove, not the roaring of a bear, or bellowing of a bull, when baited. All desire of revenge must be carefully cast out; and if the wrong-doer say, I repent, you must say, I remit, and that from the heart; being herein like that king of England, of whom it is said that he never forgot anything but injuries. Every Christian should keep a continual jubilee, *nexus solvendo et noxas remittendo*, by loosing bonds and remitting wrongs, ἑορτάζωμεν, 1 Cor. v. 8.

Ver. 23. *Which would take account of his servants*] This God doth daily. 1. In the preaching of the law with its direction or correction, which he that trembleth not in hearing, saith that martyr, shall be crushed to pieces in feeling. 2. In trouble of conscience, which when open, tells us all we have done, and writes bitter things against us, though they be legible only (as things written with the juice of lemons) when held to the light fire of God's fierce wrath. 3. In the hour of death; for every man's death's day is his particular doom's day. 4. At the day of judgment, when we shall appear to give an account, 2 Cor. v. 10. Good therefore is the counsel of Cicero, 4 *in Verr.*, *Ita vivamus ut rationem nobis reddendam arbitremur*, Let us so live, as that we forget not our last reckoning. *Rationem cum domino crebro putet Villicus*, Let the steward oft reckon with his master, saith Cato.

Ver. 24. *Which owed him ten thousand talents*] A talent is said to be 600 crowns; 10,000 talents are well nigh 12 tons of gold. As oft therefore as thy brother offends thee, think with thyself what a price is put into thy hands, what an opportunity is offered thee of gaining so great a prize, of gathering in so rich a harvest.

Ver. 25. *His lord commanded him to be sold*] Those that sell themselves to do wickedly with Ahab, will sure repent them sore of their bargain, when God shall sell them off to the devil; who when he hath well fed them (as they do their slaves in some countries for like purpose) will broach them and eat them, saith Mr Bradford, chaw them and champ them, world without end in eternal woe and misery. One reason why the wicked are eternally tormented, is, because being worthless, they cannot satisfy God's justice in any time; and he will be no loser by them.

Ver. 26. *The servant therefore fell down*] This was the ready way to disarm his master's indignation, and procure his own peace, viz., to submit to justice and implore mercy. Thus Abigail pacified David; the prodigal, his father; nay, Benhadad, Ahab, that none-such, as the Scripture describes him. The very Turks at this day, though remorseless to those that bear up, yet receive humiliation with much sweetness. Humble yourselves under God's great hand, saith St James, and he will lift you up, Jam. iv. 10. The Lion of Judah rends not the prostrate prey.

Ver. 27. *Loosed him and forgave him the debt*] Every sin is a debt; and the breach of the ten commandments set us in debt to God ten thousand talents. He requires no more but to acknowledge the debt, and to come before him with a *Non sum solvendo*, tendering him his Son our all-sufficient surety, and he will presently cancel the handwriting that was against us: he will cross the black lines of our sins with the red lines of Christ's blood, and we shall be acquitted for ever.

Ver. 28. *And he laid hands on him, and took him, &c.*] Had he truly apprehended the pardon of his own sins, he would not have been so cruel to others. Had he thoroughly dyed his thoughts in the rich mercies of God, he would have showed more mercy to men. Therefore the apostles (when our Saviour had bidden them forgive, though it were oft in the same day) said unto the Lord, "Increase our faith." As who should say, The more we can believe thy love and mercy to us, the readier shall we be to do all good offices to men. But how rigid and cruel was David to the Ammonites, while he lay in his sin, and before he had renewed his faith, 2 Sam. xii. 30, 31.

Ver. 29. *And his fellow-servant fell down*] This had been sufficient to have broken the heart of a better man than he was any. The more manly and valiant any are, the more gentle and mild to the submissive, as was Alexander and Julius Cæsar; and on the contrary, the more base and cowardly, the more hard-hearted and bloody, as Minerius, the pope's champion, who at the destruction of Mernidol, in France, being entreated for a few poor souls that had escaped his all-devouring sword, although they had no more but their shirts to cover their nakedness, he sternly answered, I know what I have to do; not one of them shall escape my hands, I will send them to dwell in hell among the devils. But what came of it? his raging fury ceased not to proceed, till the Lord shortly after brought him, by an horrible disease (his guts by little and little rotting within him) to the torments of death and terrors of hell.

Ver. 30. *And he would not, but went, &c.*] The true portraiture of an ungrateful and cruel man, that plucketh up the bridge before others, whereby himself had passed over. He that will lend no mercy, how doth he think to borrow any ?

Ver. 31. *So when his fellow-servants*] The angels, say some, who when they see us backward to business of this nature, are sorry, and say our errand to their and our common Lord, *Angeli vident, dolent, et Domino omnia referunt* (Aret.). Or the saints on earth groan out their discontents, against the unmerciful, to God, who soon hears them, for he is gracious, Exod. xxii. 27 ; yea, the cries of the poor oppressed do even " enter into the ears of the Lord of sabaoth," Jam. v. 3.

Ver. 32. *O thou wicked servant*] Wicked with a witness, as that wicked Haman, so Esther called him, Est. ii. 6, who never till then had heard his true title. God will have a time to tell every man his own ; and for those that are now so haughty and passionate, that none dare declare their way to their face, God will lay them low enough in the slimy valley, where are many already like them, and more shall come after them, Job xxi. 31, 32.

Ver. 33. *Shouldst not thou also, &c.*] Which because he did not, his patent was called in again into the pardon-office, and he deservedly turned over to the tormentor. God will set off his own and all hearts else, from a merciless man, from a griping oppressor, as he did from Haman ; not a man opened his mouth to intercede for him, when he fell before that Jewess, the queen. " For he shall have judgment without mercy," saith St James, " that hath showed no mercy ; " whenas " mercy rejoiceth against judgment," as a man doth against his adversary, whom he hath subdued, James ii. 13.

Ver. 34. *And his lord was wroth*] So God is said to be, when he chides and smites for sin, as men used to do in their anger ; but somewhat worse than they, for his anger " burneth to the lowest hell," Deut. xxxii. 22.

Ver. 35. *If ye from your hearts forgive not*] Forget as well as forgive, which some protest they will never do, neither think they that any do. But what saith the heathen orator to this unchristian censure ? If any think that we, that have been once out, can never heartily forgive, and love one another again, he proveth not our false-heartedness, but showeth his own. *Siquis est qui neminem in gratiam putat redire posse, non nostram is perfidiam arguit, sed indicat suam.* Cicer. Ep. 37, lib. 2.

CHAPTER XIX.

Ver. 1. *And came into the coasts of Judea*] Upon the news of Lazarus his friend's sickness,

[1] *τό πρόσωπον αὐτοῦ ἐστήριξε,*

John xi. 8, with the hazard of his life, he came far on foot to the help of his friend. Much water cannot quench love. And this was our Saviour's last journey toward Jerusalem, to the which he steeled his face with fortitude, and was even straitened, or pained, till it were accomplished.[1] So was that martyr, who (because he seemed at his lodging to be somewhat troubled, and was therefore asked by one how he did ?) answered, In very deed I am in prison till I be in prison.

Ver. 2. *And great multitudes followed him*] Though he were then to die. For all that follows from this chap. xix.—xxvi., seems to be a relation of the acts of the last three months of his life. Follow God, was a moral precept of the heathen sages, *τοῖς θεοῖς ἔπου,* who therein placed the safety and happiness of a man. *Magnus est animus qui se Deo tradidit,* saith Seneca. He is a brave man that follows God through thick and thin, through whatsoever hardship.

Ver. 3. *Is it lawful for a man, &c.*] A captious question, purposely to put him to shame or peril afore the people. For if he liked divorce, the better sort would be offended and displeased ; if he disliked it, the common sort (those that followed him), for denying them that liberty that Moses had allowed them. One thing that created Jeremy so much trouble among the people of his time, was, that he persuaded them to the yielding up of the city to the Chaldeans, which Isaiah had so earnestly dissuaded them, not long before, in the days of King Hezekiah.

Ver. 4. *And he answered and said unto them*] Our Saviour would not divide the inheritance, when required to it, Luke xii. 13, but he would decide controversies touching divorces ; for in marriage matters many cases of conscience fall out fit to be determined by the minister, whose lips should both preserve and present knowledge to the people, whose house for this cause should be always open, as the Ediles' house in Rome was to all comers.

Ver. 5. *And said, For this cause, &c.*] *Dixit, duxit, benedixit,* these three things are said by Moses to have been done by God in the institution, and for the honour of marriage ; to the which still (saith Bifield on 1 Pet. iii. 2) God beareth so great respect, as that he is pleased to bear with, cover, and not impute the many frailties, follies, vanities, weaknesses, and wickednesses that are found betwixt man and wife.

For this cause shall a man leave father] viz., In regard of cohabitation, not of sustentation ; *Relinquet cubile patris et matris,* as the Chaldee rightly interprets it, Gen. ii. 24. And this was the first prophecy that was ever uttered in the world (saith Tertullian and Beda), venerable therefore for its antiquity ; like as is also that first hexameter, made by Phemonoe, in the year of the world 2580.

Συμφέρετε πτέρατ' οἰωνοὶ κηρόν τε μέλισσαι.

And shall cleave to his wife] Gr. Be glued to Luke ix. 51 ; xii. 50, *συνέχομαι.*

her, προσκολληθήσεται. A table will often cleave in the whole wood, before it will part asunder where it is glued. A husband ought to be as firm to his wife as to himself. See my notes on Gen. ii. 24.

And they twain shall be one flesh] This is point-blank against polygamy, which yet Anabaptists would bring in again, and Turks allow of. They learned it of Lamech, *qui primus unam costam in duas divisit*, saith Jerome, but had soon enough of it. So had Jacob, Elkanah, and other holy men of old, who lived and died in this sin of polygamy, and merely through mistake, as it is thought, of that text, Lev. xviii. 16, "Thou shalt not take a wife to her sister, to vex her," *i. e.* Thou shalt not superinduce one wife to another. Now the fathers took the word (sister) for one so by blood, which was spoken of a sister by nation, as those clauses (to vex her) and (during her life) do evince.

Ver. 6. *They are no more twain*] A man's wife is himself, ἑαυτὸν, Eph. v. 28 (as is likewise a man's country, Luke iv. 23, to cure his country is to cure himself), and they twain, saith our Saviour in the former verse, shall be εἰς σάρκα μίαν, into one flesh. The man misseth his rib, and the woman would be in her old place again, under the man's arm or wing; hence no rest till they be re-united and concorporated. "My daughter," said Naomi to Ruth, "should I not seek rest for thee, that it may be well with thee?" Ruth iii. 1. Why, then, should there be divorces for light matters? why should there be beating of wives, and laying upon them (as some) with their unmanly fists? Did ever any man "hate his own flesh," Ephes. v. 29, or but hide his eyes from it? Isa. lviii. 7, how much less tear it with his teeth, and pull it away piece-meal, unless it were mad demoniacs and rash divorcers? Christ, the best husband, hates putting away, Mal. ii. 16; yea, though never so much provoked to it, Jer. iii. 1; Job xiii. 1, he will not do it.

Ver. 7. *Why did Moses then command, &c.*] Sophister-like they oppose Moses to God, scripture to scripture, as if God were against himself. This is still the guise of graceless heretics; as also to mingle and jumble together truths with falsehoods, that falsehoods may pass the more current. See it in these Pharisees. It was true that Moses commanded (for the honour of the woman, and disgrace of the man) that he should give her an abscessionale, a bill of divorcement. But it was not true that Moses commanded to put her away. He permitted such a thing indeed as a civil magistrate by divine dispensation (better an inconvenience than a mischief), but that makes little for its lawfulness.

Ver. 8. *Moses, because of the hardness of your hearts*] *Ob duricordiam vestram*, saith Tertullian. For the relief of the wife, questionless, was this permitted by Moses, not as a prophet, but as a law-giver; so he suffered them to exercise usury upon strangers. And, at this day, they are, by the states where they live, permitted to strain up their usury to eighteen in the hundred upon the

Christians. And so they are used, as the friars, to suck from the meanest, and to be sucked by the greatest. But what saith our statute? Forasmuch as all usury, being forbidden by the law of God, is a sin and detestable, &c. And what saith our homily-book? Verily so many as increase themselves by usury—they have their goods of the devil's gift, &c. And what saith blind nature? Aristotle in one page condemneth both τοκιστὴν and κυβευτὴν, the usurer and the dicer. And Agis, the Athenian general, set fire upon all the usurer's books and bonds in the market-place; than which fire Agesilaus was wont to say, he never saw a fairer. But to return to the text: Moses noteth the hatred of a man's wife to be the cause of much mischief, Deut. xxii. 13, 14. Hence a divorce was suffered in that case, chap. xxiv. 3, lest the husband's hatred should work the wife's ruth or ruin, in case he should be compelled to keep her. He might put her away, therefore, but not without a double blur to himself. 1. By his writing of divorce, he should give testimony to her honesty, and that she was put away merely for his hard-heartedness toward her. 2. If she were again put away by a second husband, the first might not take her to wife again, as having once for ever judged himself unworthy of her further fellowship. Husbands should be gentle to their wives, because of their weakness: glasses are not hardly handled; a small knock soon breaks them. But there are a number of Nabals, a brood of Chaldeans, a bitter and furious nation, that have little growing in their furrows but wormwood; they have a true gall of bitterness in them, Col. iii. 20, whereas the very heathens, at their weddings, pulled the gall out of all their good cheer, and cast it away; teaching thereby the married couples what to do (τὴν χολὴν ἐξέλοντες, ἐρρὶψαν. Plut.). And God Almighty professeth that he hates putting away; threatening also to cut off such unkind husbands as by their harshness caused their wives, when they should have been cheerful in God's services, to cover the altar of the Lord with tears, with weeping and with crying out, so that he regarded not the offering any more, Mal. ii. 13. *Picus est imago ingrati mariti*, saith Melancthon. The pyanit is an emblem of an unkind husband; for in autumn he casts off his mate, lest he should be forced to keep her in winter: afterwards, in the spring, he allures her to him again, and makes much of her. The Athenians were wont to put away their wives upon discontent, or hope of greater portions. Solon, their law-giver (who permitted it), being asked whether he had given the best laws to the Athenians? answered, The best that they could suffer.

Ver. 9. *Except it be for fornication*] This sin dissolves the marriage-knot, and directly fights against human society. See the notes on Matt. xv. 32, and on John viii. 5. The apostle adds the case of wilful desertion, 1 Cor. vii. 15. The civil laws of the empire permitted divorce for divers other causes. In Turkey the woman may sue a divorce only then, when her husband would abuse her against nature, which she doth, by taking off her shoe before the judges, and holding it the sole upward, but speaking nothing for the foulness of the fact. (Blount's Voyage into the Levant.)

Ver. 10. *If the case of a man be so with his wife*] viz. That he may not rid his hands of her when he will; better be married to a quartan ague than to a bad wife, said Simonides.

It is not good to marry] It is not evil to marry, but good to be wary; to look ere one leap. *Alioqui saliens antequam videat, casurus est antequam debeat,* as Bernard hath it. Most men, as these disciples, look not to the commodities but discommodities of wedlock, and other things, and are discontented. But as there be two kinds of antidotes against poison, viz. hot and cold; so against the troubles of life, whether single or married, viz. prayer and patience, the one hot, the other cold, the one quenching, the other quickening.

Ver. 11. *All men cannot receive this saying*] Nor may we simply pray for the gift of continency, but with submission, sith it is not simply necessary to salvation, but only of expediency: inasmuch as he that can keep himself unmarried, hath little else to care for but how he may please the Lord, and attend upon his work without distraction, sitting close at it (as the Greek word signifies) and not taken off by other business.[1] An instance whereof was clearly to be seen in George Prince of Anhault, whose family is said to have been *ecclesia, academia, curia,* a church, an university, and a court; whose sanctity and chastity in the single estate to his dying day was such, that Melancthon publicly delivered it of him, that he was the man, that of any then alive, might most certainly expect the promised reward of eternal life.[2] But this is not every man's happiness; and where it is, the pride of virginity is no less foul a sin than impurity, saith Augustine. And Paphnutius, a single man, and a confessor in the primitive Church, said that the marriage-bed undefiled was true chastity.[3] Those Popish votaries, that boasted so much of the gift of continency in themselves, and exacted it of others, have (for a punishment of their arrogance and violence) been oft given up to notorious filthiness, as the Cardinal of Cremona, after his stout replying in the Council of London against priests' marriage, was shamefully taken, the night following, with a notable whore. Lanfrancus, Archbishop of Canterbury, a great enemy to priests' marriage, for all his gay show of monkish virginity and single life, had a son called Paulus Monachus Cadonensis, whom he so gladly preferred to be Abbot of St Alban's. Dr Weston (Prolocutor in the Disputation at Oxford against Cranmer, Latimer, and Ridley, who also passed sentence upon them, inveighing against Cranmer, for that he had been sometimes a married man), was not long after taken in adultery, and for the same was by Cardinal Pole put from his spiritual livings.

Save they to whom it is given] Maldonatus the Jesuit saith, it is given to any one that is but willing to have it, and asketh it of God; and that, because marriage is given to all that are willing to it. But this is, 1. False, for our Saviour excepts eunuchs. 2. Inconsequent, because the gift of marriage proceeds from a principle of nature, but continency from a special indulgence, 1 Cor. vii. 7; which they that have not are required to marry for a remedy. And yet Papists most injuriously forbid some to marry at any time, as their clergy, all at some times; and that, not as a precept of conveniency, but necessity and holiness.

Ver. 12. *Which were so born*] Of a frigid constitution of body, and unapt for generation. This is not continency, but impotency, effeminacy, a defect in nature.

Which were made eunuchs of men] *Evirati,* bereft of manhood, as in the court of Persia of old, and of Turkey at this day, where Christians' children are not gelded only, but deprived of all their genitals, supplying the uses of nature with a silver quill; which inhuman custom was brought in among them by Selymus II. out of jealousy lest his eunuchs were not so chaste as they should have been in keeping their ladies' beds. For though made eunuchs by men, yet are they not without their fleshly concupiscences, yea, they are *magni amatores mulierum,* as she in Terence saith.

Which have made themselves eunuchs] Not gelded themselves, as Origen and some others in the primitive times, by mistake of this text. (So Tertullian tells of Democritus, that he pulled out his own eyes, because he could not look upon women and not lust after them; wherein he did but publish his extreme folly to the whole city, saith he.) Nor yet tied themselves by vow to perpetual continency, out of a superstitious opinion of meriting heaven thereby, as the Essenes of old (Joseph. B. J. ii. 6), and the Popish clergy now; but live single, that they may serve God with more freedom, fighting against fleshly lusts (that fight against the soul) with those spiritual weapons, meditation, prayer, abstinence, &c., which are mighty through God to the pulling down of Satan's strongholds set up in the heart. Hence the Hebrew, Syriac, Chaldee, and Arabic render this text, *Qui castrarunt animam suam,* which have gelded their souls. And the truth is, there they must begin, that will do anything in this kind to purpose. *Incesta est, et sine stupro, quæ stuprum cupit,* saith Seneca. And St Paul's virgin must "be holy both in body and in spirit," 1 Cor. vii. 34.

Ver. 13. *Then were there brought unto him little ones*] By their parents, careful of their greatest good. We must also present ours, as we can, to Christ. And, 1. By praying for them before, at, and after their birth. 2. By timely bringing them to the ordinance of baptism with faith, and much joy in such a privilege. 3. By training

---

[1] 1 Cor. vii. 35. ἐυπάρεδρον, ἀπερισπάστως.
[2] *Ex Bucholcero Melancthonis auditore hoc habeo.* Scultet.

[3] *Congressum cum legitima uxore castitatem esse dicebat.* Hist. lib. i. cap. 11.

them up in God's holy fear; beseeching God to persuade their hearts, as Noah did for his son Japheth. We may speak persuasively, but God only persuades; as Rebekah might cook the venison, but it was Isaac only that gave the blessing.

And the disciples rebuked them] They held it a business below their Lord to look upon little ones. But it is not with our God, as with their idol, that had no leisure to attend smaller matters:

Non vacat exiguis rebus ad esse Jovi.

Christian children are the Church's nursery; the devil seeks to destroy them, as he did the babes of Bethlehem; but Christ hath a gracious respect unto them, and sets them on a rock that is higher than they.

Ver. 14. *For of such is the kingdom*] That is, all the blessings of heaven and earth comprised in the covenant belong both to these and such as these, Matt. xviii. 3. Let them, therefore, have free recourse to me, who will both own them and crown them with life eternal.

Ver. 15. *And he laid his hands on them*] So putting upon them his father's blessing, as Jacob did upon Joseph's sons, whom by this symbol he adopted for his own. And albeit our Saviour baptized not these infants (as neither did he those that were bigger), yet forasmuch as they were confessedly capable of Christ's gifts, they were doubtless capable of the signs and seals of those gifts; if capable of imposition of Christ's hands, of his benediction and kingdom, then capable also of baptism, which saveth us, saith St Peter, in the time present, because the use thereof is permanent (though the act transient) so long as one liveth, 1 Pet. iii. 21. Whensoever a sinner repents and believes on the promises, baptism (the seal thereof) is as powerful and effectual as as if it were then presently administered. The Decrees and Book of Sentences say that confirmation is of more value than baptism, and gives the Holy Ghost more plentifully and effectually. And the Papists generally abuse this text, to establish their sacrament of confirmation, or bishoping of children. But, 1. These were little infants, not led, but brought in their mothers' arms. 2. Confirmation, as they use it, was never commanded to Christ's ministers, nor practised by his apostles.

Ver. 16. *And behold one came*] One of good rank, a ruler, Luke xviii. 18, of good estate, for he was rich, and had great revenue (χρήματα, saith Luke, κτήματα, saith Matthew, xix. 22, he had a good title to that he had, and he lived not beside it). He was also a young man, in the prime and pride of his age, and had been well bred; both for point of civility, he came congeeing to our Saviour, Mark x. 1.[1] And for matter of piety, he was no Sadducee, for he inquires after eternal life, which they denied. And although but young, he hearkens after heaven: and though he were rich, he comes running to Christ

through desire of information; whereas great men use not to run, but to walk leisurely, so to maintain their authority. Lastly, he knew much of God's law, and had done much; so that he seemed to himself to want work, to be aforehand with God. Christ also looked upon him and loved him, as he was a tame creature, a moral man, and fit to live in a commonwealth.

What good thing shall I do?] A most needful and difficult question, rarely moved, by rich men especially, whose hearts are usually upon their half-penny, as they say, whose mouths utter no other language but the horse-leech's, Give, give; Who will show us any good? &c.; A good purchase, a good penny-worth? &c. Howbeit, by the manner of his expressing himself, this gallant seems to have been a Pharisee, and of that sort of Pharisees (for there were seven sorts of them, saith the Talmud) which was named, *Quid debeo facere, et faciam illud*, Tell me what I should do, and I will do it. They that know not Christ, would go to heaven by their good meanings and good doings; this is a piece of natural popery, that must be utterly abandoned ere eternal life can be obtained.

That I may have eternal life] He had a good mind to heaven, and cheapens it, but was not willing to go to the price of it, that thorough sale of all. Good desires may be found in hellmouth, as in Balaam some short-winded wishes at least. The spies praised the land as pleasant and plenteous, but they held the conquest impossible, and thereby discouraged the people. Many like well of Abraham's bosom, but not so well of Dives' door. They seek to Christ, but when he saith, "Take up the cross and follow me," they stumble at the cross, and fall backward. Their desires after heaven are lazy and sluggish, like the door that turns upon the hinges, but yet hangs still on them: so these wishers and woulders, for all their faint and weak desires after heaven, still hang fast on the hinges of their sins; they will not be wrought off from the things of this world, they will not part with their fatness and sweetness, though it be to reign for ever, Judg. ix. 11. Theotimus in St Ambrose would rather lose his sight than his sin of intemperance (*Vale lumen amicum*), so many, their souls.

Ver. 17. *Why callest thou me good?*] And if I be not good, much less art thou, what good conceits soever thou hast of thyself. Here, then, our Saviour learns this younker humility and self-annihilation. Phocion was surnamed Bonus, but what was his goodness more than a silver sin? *Laones neminem bonum fieri publicis literis columna incisis sanxerunt.* Plut. *in Quest. Græcis.*

There is none good but one, that is God] He both is good original (others are good by participation only), and doth good abundantly, freely, constantly: "For thou, Lord, art good, and ready to forgive," saith David, Psal. lxxxvi. 5; cxix. 68. "And let the power of my Lord be great," saith Moses, "in pardoning this rebellious people." In the original there is a letter greater

---

[1] γονυπετήσας, *genibus reverenter inflexis salutavit.*

than ordinary in the word *jigdal* (be great), to show, say the Hebrew doctors, that though the people should have tempted God, or murmured against him, ten times more than they did, yet their perverseness should not interrupt the course of his ever-flowing, over-flowing goodness, Num. xiv. 17. יִנְדַּל *Magnum jod quod valet decem, &c.* Buxtorf.

If thou wilt enter into life, keep the commandments] That is, saith Luther, *Morere*, die out of hand; for there is no man lives that sins not. It is storied of Charles IV., King of France, that being one time affected with the sense of his many and great sins, he fetched a deep sigh, and said to his wife, Now, by the help of God, I will so carry myself all my life long, that I will never offend him more; which word he had no sooner uttered, but he presently fell down and died. It is not our Saviour's intent here to teach that heaven may be had or earned by keeping the law; for Adam in his innocency, if he had so continued, could not have merited heaven, neither do the angels, nor could Christ himself, had he been no more than a man. None but a proud Luciferian would have said, as Vega, the Popish perfectionary, did, *Cœlum gratis non accipiam,* I will not go to heaven for nought, or on free cost. But our Saviour here shapes this young Pharisee an answer according to his question. He would needs be saved by doing, Christ sets him that to do which no man living can do, and so shows him his error. He sets him to school to the law, that hard school-master, that sets us such lessons as we are never able to learn (unless Christ our elder brother teach us, and do our exercise for us), yea, bring us forth to God, as that school-master in Livy did all his scholars (the flower of the Roman nobility) to Hannibal; who, if he had not been more merciful then otherwise, they had all perished.

Ver. 18. *Thou shalt do no murder*] Our Saviour instanceth the commandments of the second table only, as presupposing those of the first, for the second table must be kept in the first;[1] and the whole law, say the schools, is but one copulative. The two tables of the law (saith a reverend divine)[2] are, in their object, answerable to the two natures of Christ, for God is the object of one man or the other. And as they meet together in the person of Christ, so must they be united in the affections and endeavours of a Christian.

Ver. 19. *Thou shalt love thy neighbour*, &c.] Which because thou doest not (as appears, because thou wilt not part with thy possessions to relieve the poor), therefore much less doest thou love God, and therefore art not the man thou takest thyself for. Civil men overween themselves, and boast of their moral righteousness; yet make no conscience of the lesser breaches of the second table, nor yet of contemplative wickedness, which yet angereth God, Gen. vi. 6, and lets in the

devil, 2 Cor. x. And these are the world's very honest men, for lack of better, as a cab of doves' dung was dear meat in the famine of Samaria, where better could not be come by.

Ver. 20. *All these things have I kept*] Lie and all; as now the Popish Pharisees dream and brag that they can keep the law, and spare.[3] They can do more than any that ever went before them, Psal. cxliii. 3; Job xv. 14; Jam. iii. 2. Œcolampadius saith that none of the patriarchs lived out a full thousand years (which is a number of perfection), to teach us that here is no perfection of piety. David's heart smote him for doing that which Saul highly commended him for.

What lack I yet?] Gr. "Wherein am I yet behind with God?" (τὶ ἔτι ὑστερῶ). He thought himself somewhat aforehand, and that God, belike, was in his debt. Truly, many now-a-days grow crooked and aged with over-good opinions of themselves, and can hardly ever be set right again. They stand upon their comparisons—I am as good as thou; nay, upon their disparisons, "I am not as this publican." No, for thou art worse; yea, for this, because thou thinkest thyself better. This arrogant youth makes good that of Aristotle, who, differencing between age and youth, makes it a property of young men to think they know all things, and to affirm lustily their own placits.[4] He secretly insults over our Saviour as a trivial teacher, and calls for a lecture beyond the law, worthy, therefore, to have been sent to Anticyra; surely, as when Drusius in his defence against a nimble Jesuit, that called him heretic, alleged that heresy must be *in fundamentis fidei*, the Jesuit replied that even that assertion was heresy. So when this young man affirmed that he had ever kept the commandments, and asked, "What lack I yet?" Christ might well have said, "Thou art therefore guilty of the breach of all the commandments, because thou takest thyself to be keeper of all, and thou therefore lackest everything, because thou thinkest thou lackest nothing."

Ver. 21. *If thou wilt be perfect*] As thou boastest and aimest, and which never yet any man was, nor can be here. The misunderstanding of this text made some of the ancients count and call it *consilium perfectionis,* a counsel of perfection; such as whosoever did observe, should do something more than the law required, and so merit for themselves a higher degree of glory in heaven than others had. Hence Bernard writeth that this sentence of our Saviour filled the monasteries with monks and the deserts with anchorites.

Go sell all, &c.] A personal command (for trial and discovery), as was that of God to Abraham, "Go kill thy son Isaac." Christians may possess, but yet as if they possessed not; they must hang loose to all outward things, and be ready to forego them when called to lose them for Christ.

---

[1] *Primo præcepto reliquorum omniun observatio præcipitur.* Luther.
[2] Mr Ley's Pattern of Piety, p. 99.
[3] *Arrogantius mendacium nemo hominum de se dixit.* Pareus. *Insignem hypocritam se gloriatur.* Ib.
[4] πάντα εἰδέναι οἴεσθαι καὶ διοσχυρίζεσθαι. *Ethic.* 1.

And give to the poor][1] So shalt thou clear thyself from all suspicion of covetousness, which properly consists in pinching and saving; and so is distinguished by the apostle from extortion, which stands in immoderate getting, 1 Cor. vi. 10 ; 1 Tim. iii. 3.

And thou shalt have treasure in heaven] Far beyond the treasures of Egypt, which yet is called Rahab, Psal. lxxxix. 10, because of the riches, power, and pride thereof. Oh! get a patriarch's eye to see the wealth and worth of heaven, and then we shall soon make Moses's choice. In the year of grace 759, certain Persian magicians[2] fell into that madness, that they persuaded themselves and sundry others that if they sold all they had and gave it to the poor, and then afterwards threw themselves naked from off the walls into the river, they should presently be admitted into heaven. *Perierunt hac insaniâ permulti*, saith mine author. Many were cast away by this mad enterprise. How much better (if without superstition and opinion of merit) Amadeus, Duke of Savoy, who being asked by certain ambassadors that came to his court, what hounds he had, for they desired to see them, showed them the next day a pack of poor people feeding at his table, and said, These are the hounds wherewith I hunt after heaven. *Hi sunt canes mei quos alo quotidiè, quibus spero me cælestem gloriam venaturum. Funccius.*

Ver. 22. *He went away sorrowful*] That Christ should require that which he was not willing to perform. If heaven be to be had upon no other terms, Christ may keep his heaven to himself; he will have none. How many have we now-a-days that must be gainers by their religion, which must be another Diana to the craftsmasters? They are resolved, howsoever, to lose nothing, suffer nothing, but rather kick up all: *Jeroboamo gravior jactura regionis quam religionis.* The King of Navarre told Beza that in the cause of religion he would launch no further into the sea, than he might be sure to return safe to the haven. A number of such politic professors we have that come to Christ (as this young man did) hastily, but depart heavily, when once it comes to a wholesale of all for Christ, which yet is the first lesson, the *removens prohibens.*

Ver. 23. *A rich man shall hardly enter*] With that burthen of thick clay, that camel's bunch on his back. Heaven is a stately palace, with a narrow portal ; there must be both stripping and straining ere one can get through this strait gate. The greatest wealth is ordinarily tumoured up with the greatest swelth of rebellion against God.

Ardua res hæc est opibus non tradere mores ;
Et cum tot Cræsos viceris, esse Numam. Martial.

Vermis divitiarum est superbia, saith Augustine. Pride breeds in wealth as the worm doth in the apple, and he is a great rich man indeed, and greater than his riches, that doth not think himself great because he is rich. " Charge those

that are rich, that they be not high-minded " (for the devil will soon blow up such a blab in them, if they watch not), "and that they trust not in uncertain riches," 1 Tim. vi. 17, so as to make their gold their God, as all worldlings do, and worse, for could we but rip up such men's hearts, we should find written in them, " The God of this present world." They that mind earthly things have destruction for their end, Phil. iii. 19. Have them we may, and use them too, but mind them we may not, nor love them, 1 John ii. 15 ; that is spiritual harlotry, such as God's soul hateth, and he " smiteth his hands at," Ezek. xxii. 13.

Ver. 24. *It is easier for a camel, &c.*] Or cable rope, as some render it, κάμηλον, κάμιλον *funem nauticum.* Either serves, for it is a proverbial speech, setting forth the difficulty of the thing. *Difficile est*, saith St Jerome, *ut præsentibus bonis quis fruatur et futuris, ut hic ventrem istic mentem reficiat, ut de deliciis transeat, ut in cælo et in terra gloriosus appareat.* Pope Adrian VI. said that nothing befell him more unhappy in all his life than that he had been head of the Church and monarch of the Christian commonwealth. " When I first entered into orders," saith another pope (Pius Quintus), " I had some good hopes of my salvation ; when I became a cardinal, I doubted it ; but since I came to be a pope I do even almost despair." And well he might, as long as he sat in that chair of pestilence, being that man of sin, that son of perdition, 2 Thes. ii. 3. *Ad hunc statum venit Romana Ecclesia*, said Petrus Aliacus, long since, *ut non esset digna regi nisi per reprobos* (Cornel. a Lapide, Com. in Num. xi. 11). The popes, like the devils, are then thought to do well when they cease to do hurt, saith Johan. Sarisburiensis. They have had so much grace left, we see (some of them, howsoever), as to acknowledge that their good and their blood rose together, that honours changed their manners, and that they were the worse men for their great wealth ; and that as Shimei, seeking his servants, lost himself, so they, by reaching after riches and honours, lost their souls. Let rich men often ruminate this terrible text, and take heed. Let them untwist their cables, that is, their heart, by humiliation, James v. 1 and i. 10, till it be made like small threads, as it must be, before they can enter into the eye of a needle, that is, eternal life.

Ver. 25. *They were exceedingly amazed*] Because they knew that all men either are or would be rich ; and that of rich men, scarce any but trusted in their riches. Therefore, though our Saviour told them, Mark x. 24, that he meant it of those only that relied upon their riches, yet they remained as much unsatisfied as before, and held it a hard case that so many should miss of heaven. We have much ado to make men believe that the way is half so hard as ministers make it.

---

[1] πτωχοῖς, ἀπὸ τοῦ πτώσσειν, *quod ad pedes divitum accidant.* Such as beg from door to door.

[2] *Magi quidam ex Maurophoris Persis.*

Ver. 26. *With men this is impossible*] Because rich men's hearts are ordinarily so wedded and wedged to the world that they will not be loosened but by a powerful touch from the hand of Heaven. Think not, therefore, as many do, that there is no other hell but poverty, no better heaven than abundance.[1] Of rich men they say, What should such a man ail? The Irish ask, What they mean to die, &c. The gold ring and gay clothing carried it in St James's time, ii. 2. But he utterly disliked such partiality, and tells us that " God hath chosen the poor in this world, rich in faith, to be heirs of his kingdom." In which respect he bids the brother of low degree rejoice in that he is exalted in Christ.

But with God all things are possible] He can quickly root out confidence in the creature, and rivet rich men to himself. He can do more than he will; but whatsoever he willeth, that he doth, without stop or hindrance. Men may want of their will for want of power. Nature may be interrupted in her course, as it was when the fire burnt not the three worthies, the water drowned not Peter walking upon it, &c. Satan may be crossed and chained up; but who hath resisted the Almighty? who ever waxed fierce against God and prospered? Job ix. 4. Nature could say, all things are easy to God, and nothing impossible, Ῥάδια πάντα Θεῷ τελέσαι καὶ ἀνήνυτον οὐδέν (Linus Poeta). Howbeit for a finite creature to believe the infinite attributes of God, he is not able to do it thoroughly without supernatural grace.

Ver. 27. *Behold, we have forsaken all, &c.*] A great all, sure, a few broken boats, nets, household stuff (*Retia, navigia, reculas*, Pareus). And Christ maintained them too; and yet they ask, what shall we have? Neither is it without an emphasis, that they begin with a Behold. " Behold, we have forsaken all," as if Christ were therefore greatly beholden to them, and if the young man were promised treasure in heaven, doing so-and-so, then they might challenge it; they might say with the prodigal, " Give me the portion that pertains unto me."

Ver. 28. *Ye which have followed me in the regeneration*] As if our Saviour should have said, to forsake all is not enough, unless ye be regenerate; so some sense it. Others by regeneration understand the estate of the gospel, called elsewhere a new heaven and a new earth, 2 Pet. iii. 13; the world to come, Heb. ii. 5; for God plants the heavens, and lays the foundation of the earth, that he may say to Zion, Thou art my people. There are that understand by regeneration, the general resurrection (of which also some think Plato had heard, and therefore held, that in the revolution of so many years men should be just in the same estate wherein they were before). These that follow this latter sense, read the text thus, by an alteration of points, " Ye which have followed me, shall, in the regeneration (when the Son of man shall sit in his glory) sit upon twelve thrones," &c.

Ye shall also sit upon twelve thrones] And so many kings. Kings they are here, but somewhat obscure ones, as Melchisedech was; but shall then appear with Christ in glory, far outshining the sun in his strength, higher than all the kings of the earth, Colos. iii. 4; Psal. lxxxix. 27. When Daniel had described the greatness and glory of all the four monarchies of the world, at last he comes to speak of a kingdom, which is the greatest and mightiest under the whole heaven, and that is " the kingdom of the saints of the most high," Dan. vii. 18. So glorious is their estate even here, what shall it be, then, at that great day? And if the saints (every one of them) shall judge the angels, what shall the apostles do? Surely as they absolved or condemned men in this world, so shall it fare with them at the general judgment.

Ver. 29. *Shall receive an hundred-fold*] In reference to Isaac's hundred-fold increase of his seed, Gen. xxvi. 12, or that best of grounds, Matt. xiii. Those that do pillage us, they do but husband us, sow for us, when they make long furrows on our backs, Psal. cxxvi., and ride over our heads, Psal. lxvi. 12. Gordius the martyr said, it is to my loss, if you bate me anything in my sufferings. *Crudelitas vestra, nostra gloria*, said they in Tertullian, your cruelty is our glory; and the harder we are put to it, the greater shall be our reward in heaven. Nay, on earth too : the saints shall have their losses for Christ recompensed, either in money or money's-worth, either in the same or a better thing, *Majora certamina majora sequuntur præmia* (Tertullian). Job had all doubled to him; Valentinian, for his tribuneship, the empire cast upon him, after Julian the apostate, who had put him out of office for his religion.[2] Queen Elizabeth (whose life for a long while had been like a ship in the midst of an Irish sea) after long restraint was exalted from misery to majesty, from a prisoner to a princess. *Optanda nimirum est jactura quæ lucro majore pensatur*, saith Agricola. It is doubtless a lovely loss that is made up with so great gain. Had Queen Elizabeth foreknown, whiles she was in prison, what a glorious reign she should have had for 44 years, she would never have wished herself a milk-maid. So, did but the saints understand what great things abide them both here and hereafter, they would bear anything cheerfully. An hundred-fold here, and eternal life hereafter : oh, who would not then turn spiritual purchaser? Well might St Paul say, " Godliness is profitable to all things." Well might the Psalmist say, " In doing (in suffering) thy will, there is a great reward." Not for doing it only, but in doing it; for righteousness is its own reward. St Mark hath it thus : He that leaveth house, brethren, sisters, father, &c., shall receive the same in kind, house, brethren, sisters, father, &c. That is, 1. He shall have communion with God and his consolations, which are better than them all; as Caleacius, that Italian marquis that

---

[1] Luke ii. 41. *Divitiæ vocantur τὰ ἔνοντα, quia avari animo quasi insident.* Beza.

[2] *Qui pro Christi nomine amiserat tribunatum, retribuente Christo accepit imperium.* Oros.

left all for Christ, avowed them ; and as Paulinus Nolanus, when his city was taken by the barbarians, prayed thus to God, Lord, let me not be troubled at the loss of my gold and silver, for thou art all in all unto me. *Ne excrucier ob aurum et argentum ; tu enim es mihi omnia.* (Aug. C. D. i. 1.) Communion with Jesus Christ is *præmium ante præmium,* heaven aforehand, the anticipation of glory. 2. He many times gives his suffering servants here such supplies of their outward losses, in raising them up other friends and means, as do abundantly countervail what they have parted with. Thus, though David was driven from his wife, and she was given to another, God gave him a friend, Jonathan, whose love was beyond the love of women, 2 Sam. i. 26. So though Naomi lost her husband and children, Boaz, Ruth, and Obed became to her instead of all. The apostles left their houses and household stuff to follow Christ, but then they had the houses of all godly people open to them, and free for them, and happy was that Lydia that could entertain them ; so that having nothing, they yet possessed all things, 2 Cor. vi. 10. They left a few friends, but they found far more wherever they came. Wherefore it was a senseless sarcasm of Julian the apostate, when reading this text, he jeeringly demanded, whether they should have a hundred wives also, for that one they had parted with? 3. God commonly exalts his people to the contrary good to that evil they suffer for him ; as Joseph, of a slave, became a ruler ; as Christ that was judged by men, is Judge of all men. The first thing that Caius did, after he came to the empire, was to prefer Agrippa, who had been imprisoned for wishing him emperor. Constantine embraced Paphnutius, and kissed his lost eye. The King of Poland sent Zelislaus, his general, who had lost his hand in his wars, a golden hand instead thereof. God is far more liberal to those that serve him, suffer for him. Can any son of Jesse do for us as he can ?

Ver. 30. *But many that are first,* &c.] Because Peter and the rest had called for their pay (almost before they had been at any pains for Christ), he therefore quickeneth them in these words ; bidding them bestir themselves better, lest others, that are now hindermost, should get beyond them, and carry the crown. " Lay hold on eternal life," saith Paul, 1 Tim. vi. 19 ; intimating that it is hanged on high, as a garland, so that we must reach after it, strain to it. So run that ye may obtain ; look you to your work, God will take care of your wages ; you need never trouble yourselves about the matter.

CHAPTER XX.

Ver. 1. *For the kingdom of heaven,* &c.] That last sentence Christ further illustrateth and enforceth by this following parable. Peter and the rest were in danger to be puffed up with the pre-conceit of their abundant reward promised,

chap. xix. 28, 29. This to prevent, and that they might not stand upon their terms and tip-toes, they are again and again given to know, that "many that are first shall be last, and last first."

Which went out early in the morning] "God is found of them that seek him not," Isa. lxiii. 1. "Yea, the Father seeketh such to worship him," John iv. 23 ; he soliciteth suitors and servants. A wonderful condescension it is, that he looketh out of himself upon the saints and angels in heaven, Psal. cxiii. 6. How much more upon us poor earth-worms !

Labourers into his vineyard] Not loiterers. Jacob saw the angels, some ascending, others descending, none standing still. God hath made Behemoth to play in the waters, not so men ; they must be doing, that will keep in with God.

Ver. 2. *For a penny a day*] Not for eternal life (for this those murmuring merit-mongers never had, who yet had their penny), but something (whatever it were) that gave the labourers good content ; that it was for which each of them followed Christ, whether for meat perishing, or enduring, John vi. 27.

Ver. 3. *Others standing idle*] For any good they did, or could do, till sent into the vineyard, and set awork by God. Till then we are mere excrements of human society. *Nos numerus sumus,* &c.

Ver. 4. *Go ye also into the vineyard*] God hath his times to call men in ; only let them stand in God's way, wait at the posts of wisdom's gates, at the pool of Bethesda, &c. *Gratuita et inopinata est ad gratiam vocatio,* Ephes. i. 11. The separation of the saints is wonderful, Exod. xxxiii. 16.

Ver. 5. *About the sixth and ninth hour*] God hath his servants of all sexes and sizes, calling when and whom he pleaseth. And they have the comfort and credit of it that are first called, so they walk worthy of their time, and that vocation wherewith they are called, Ephes. iii. 1. Thus it was an honour to Mnason that he was an "old disciple," Acts xxi. 16 ; and to Andronicus and Junia, that Paul should say of them, "who also were in Christ before," Rom. xvi. 7.

Ver. 6. *And about the eleventh hour*] About five o'clock in the afternoon ; when it was well nigh time to leave work. *Nunquam sero si serio.* Howbeit delays are dangerous, opportunities are abrupt and headlong, and, if once past, irrecoverable. If, therefore, ye will inquire, inquire ; return, come, Isa. xxi. 12. They that say men may repent hereafter, say truly, but not safely. They that allege these here that came in at the eleventh hour, must consider that these were never called till then. But now God calleth, yea, "commandeth all men everywhere to repent," Acts xvii. 30. And now he is more peremptory, sure, than ever heretofore. See Heb. ii. 3. How many are daily taken away in their offers and essays, before they have prepared their hearts to cleave to God !

Ver. 7. *Go ye also into the vineyard*] At this hour the penitent thief was sent in, and he bestirred him; for he justifies Christ, condemns himself, chides his fellow for railing, prays for a part in Paradise, &c.; he lived much in a little time. Howbeit, this is a singular example, one of the miracles wherewith Christ would honour the ignominy of his cross. Neither is it often seen or read of, that old men are converted. They are usually so set in sin, that they are hardly removed; such an hoof they have over their hearts, that scarce anything will affect them. Abraham in the Old Testament, and Nicodemus in the New, were called in their old age. Name a third he that can. Conversion (as divines observe) usually falls out between 18 years of age and 28, when men have less of the world, which afterward steals away affection.

Ver. 8. *Saith unto his steward*] That is, to his Son Christ, whom he hath made judge of all, to give unto every man according to his works. This he will do with demonstration of his singular both justice (so that none shall receive less than was promised him) and mercy (so that all shall receive more than they deserved). For although their penny be here called their hire, and elsewhere their reward, yea, their wages, yet all is of grace.

Ver. 9. *And when they came*] These last labourers were first paid, because they trusted not to the worth of their own works, but to God's free grace and goodness; when the other are turned off in displeasure, with *Tolle quod tuum est, et vade:* Take thy penny, and be packing.

Ver. 10. *They supposed that they, &c.*] Good works are *mercatura regni cœlestis,* saith Bellarmine. But God is no such merchant. *Cœlum gratis non accipiam,* I will not have heaven for nothing, saith Vega. Thou shalt never have it therefore; I will give thee that gift.

Ver. 11. *They murmured, &c.*] They had that they agreed for, some temporal blessings, which is all that carnal men commonly care for. Or if any seek after spiritual things, it is not for any beauty he seeth or taste he findeth in them, but only as a bridge to bring them to heaven; as Spira confessed of himself. It is not good therefore to indent and bargain with God how much he shall give us, either of temporals or spirituals; for so you may have your penny, and yet be discontented that it is but a penny, and no more. Profits, pleasures, honours, appear to be but empty things, when men are to go into another world.

Ver. 12. *Thou hast made them equal*] Lo, this is the guise of graceless hypocrites, to be quarrelling and contending with God and man, as unworthily dealt withal. Thus those Jewish justiciaries, Isa. lviii. 3, hit God in the teeth with their good services and small thanks. So the proud Pharisee sets forth, not his wants, but his worth. Contrariwise, Jacob cries out in a low language, *Domine, non sum dignus,* Gen. xxx. 10. So doth Paul, 1 Cor. xv. 9; the centurion, Matt. viii. 6; the Baptist, Matt. iii. 11.

St Augustine, *Non sum dignus, quem tu diligas, Domine,* Lord, I am not worthy of thy love.

Ver. 13. *Friend, I do thee no wrong*] Friend he is called, not reprobate, though he were a murmurer, a merit-monger. In arguing the case with others, use hard arguments, but in a soft language. This will soonest work; for man is a cross, crabbed creature, and if roughly dealt with, will sooner slight you for your passion than regard your reason, though never so convincing, because not well managed. There are a generation whose words are swords, whose tongues are rapiers to run men through with, upon every small occasion, and their throats as a gaping grave to bury them in, Rom. iii. 12, 13.

Ver. 14. *Take that thine is, and go*] A fearful sentence. David blesseth himself from those men of God's hand, which have their portion here, and that is all they are to look for, Psal. xvii. 14. *Valde protestatus sum,* said Luther, when great gifts were offered him, *me nolle sic a Deo satiari.* A gracious spirit cannot rest satisfied with low things. The Turkish empire, as big as it is, saith the same Luther, is nothing else but a crust of bread, which the goodman of the house casteth to his dogs: *Turc. Imp. quantum quantum est, nihil est nisi panis mica, quam dives paterfamilias projicit canibus.* Luther.

Ver. 15. *Is it not lawful for me, &c.*] This is God's speech (who is the great Proprietary of all); it may not be ours, who have nothing of our own, but all in trust: so that when we present anything to God, we must say as David did, 1 Chron. xxix. 14, and afterwards Justinian the emperor, τὰ σὰ ἐκ τῶν σῶν σοὶ προσφέρομεν οἱ δοῦλοί σου. Of thine own we give thee; for all that is in the heaven and the earth is thine. St Bernard reports of Pope Eugenius, that meeting with a poor but honest bishop, he secretly gave him certain jewels wherewith he might present him. If God did not first furnish us, we should have nothing wherewith to honour him, or do good to others.

Is thine eye evil, because I am good] It is commonly observed that witches, and those that are in league with the devil to do mischief, are never given over so to do, till they come to have an evil eye. (Βασκαίνω quasi φάεσι καίνω.) Hence that, *nescio quis teneros, &c.,* and those that are bewitched are said to be overseen, that is, to be looked upon with an envious eye. Envy is a quick-sighted and sharp-fanged malignity, Prov. xxvii. 4, and doth *de aliena mente tam prompte quam prave conjicere,* as one saith, nimbly and naughtily guess at another man's meaning.

Ver. 16. *So the last shall be first, &c.*] This is the purport of the preceding parable. Application is the life of preaching.

Few are chosen] It is a strange speech of Chrysostom, in his fourth sermon to the people of Antioch, where he was much beloved and did much good. How many, think you, shall be saved in this city? It will be a hard speech to you, but I will speak it: though there be so many thousand of you, yet there cannot be found an hundred that shall be saved, and I doubt of them too; for what villany is there in youth! what sloth in old men! and so he goes on. *Non arbitror inter sacerdotes multos esse qui salvi fiant.* Chrysost. hom. 3. *in Act.* See the notes on Matt. vii. 14.

Ver. 17. *Took the twelve disciples*] To rouse them and raise them out of their carnal fears and dejections. Jerusalem was the saints' slaughter-house, Luke xiii. 33 (as Rome is now, which therefore is spiritually called Jerusalem, Egypt, Sodom, &c., Rev. xi. 8). Hither our Saviour bent his course; hereupon they were amazed and afraid, Mark x. 32, and gave him counsel to go back rather into Galilee for his own and their safety, John xi. 8. He takes them therefore apart, and tells them as followeth, what they must trust to; and that though he be brought to the dust of death, he will rise again gloriously, to their great comfort.

Ver. 18. *Behold, we go up to Jerusalem*] Behold, as it requires attention (and this was no more than need; for St Luke, xviii. 34, tells us that they understood none of these things, &c.), so it sets forth our Saviour's forwardness to go this dangerous voyage.

Ver. 19. *To mock, and to scourge, and to crucify him*] What are all our sufferings to his? and yet we think ourselves undone, if but touched; and in setting forth our calamities, we add, we multiply, we rise in our discourse, like him in the poet, τρὶς κακοδαίμων καὶ τετράκις, καὶ πεντάκις, καὶ δωδεκάκις, καὶ μυριάκις (Aristoph.). I am thrice miserable, nay, ten, twenty, an hundred, a thousand times unhappy. And yet all our sufferings are but as the slivers and chips of that cross, upon which Christ, nay, many Christians, have suffered. In the time of Adrian the emperor, 10,000 martyrs are said to have been crucified in the Mount of Ararat, crowned with thorns, and thrust into the sides with sharp darts, after the example of the Lord's passion. The chief of whom were Achaicus, Heliades, Theodorus, Carcerius, &c. (Acts and Mon.)

Ver. 20. *Then came to him, &c.*] Then, most unseasonably, when Christ had by the parable been teaching them humility, and now was discoursing of his death and passion, then came these sons of Zebedee to beg a principality in Christ's imaginary earthly monarchy. And this is not the first time of their so foul mistake, so unseasonable a suit to him, or strife among themselves. The leprosy was cured at once in Naaman; so is not corruption in the saints, but by degrees, and at times.

The mother of Zebedee's children] Set on by her two sons, who were ashamed to make the motion themselves (but as good they might, for Christ knew all, and therefore directs his answer to them, Mark x. 35), and she also was not well assured of the fitness of her request, and therefore came courtesying and craving a certain thing; not telling him what at first, as going somewhat against her conscience. And surely

her request had been impudent, but that she presumed upon her near alliance to Christ; for she is thought to have been sister to Joseph, who was *Pater Christi politicus;* and thence her boldness, by reason of her right of kindred by the father's side. And this is some kind of carnal excuse; yet not for her and her sons' folly and vanity, in dreaming of an earthly kingdom, and therein a distribution of honours and offices, as in David and Solomon's days.

Ver. 21. *What wilt thou?*] We may not over-hastily engage ourselves by promise of this or that to our best friends, but hold off and deliberate. *Alioqui saliens antequam videat, casurus est ante quam debeat.* Bernard.

The one on thy right hand]

Quid voveat dulci nutricula majus alumno? Horat.

Our Saviour had promised in the former chapter that the twelve should sit upon twelve thrones, &c. These men's suit was for the first and second seat. Self-love makes men ambitious, and teacheth them to turn the glass, to see themselves bigger, others lesser than they are; Paul, on the contrary, was least of saints, last of apostles.

Ver. 22. *Ye know not what ye ask*] Ye ask and miss, "because ye ask amiss," James iv. 1. A prayer for things not lawful begs nothing but a denial, as Moses did, in praying to enter into the land, Deut. iii. 25; as Job did in that peevish request of his, that God would "let loose his hand, and cut him off," Job vi. 8, 9; as the disciples did in that over-curious inquiry, "Lord, wilt thou at this time restore the kingdom of Israel?" Acts i. 6—8. Our Saviour answers that that is not fit for them to know. But a better thing he could tell them, that they should shortly after be clothed with the Holy Ghost. God sometimes in much mercy crosseth the prayers of his people, as he did David's, for the child's life, who, if he had lived, would have been but a standing monument of David's shame. Was it not better for him to have a Solomon? The saints have their prayers out, either in money or money's-worth, provided they bring lawful petitions and honest hearts.

Are ye able to drink of the cup, &c.] Afflictions are frequently set forth by this metaphor of a cup; taken, say some, from an ancient custom that the father of the family should give to each under his charge a cup fit for his use, according to his bigness; or, as others think, from the manner of feasts, whereat the symposiarch, or "ruler of the feast," as he is called, John ii., prescribed what and how much every man should drink.

And to be baptized with the baptism] Or plunged over head and ears in the deep waters of affliction. Of these we may say, as one doth of the Spa waters, that they are more wholesome than pleasant. Ever since Christ cast his cross into them, as Moses did that tree, Exod. xv. 25, the property of them is altered, the waters healed.

They say unto him, We are able] In your own conceit, at least, not else. For these two disciples, as they knew not what they asked, so they knew not what they answered. And yet Maldonatus hath the face to defend them in it, as if they here testified their alacrity, rather than betrayed their precipitancy: *Sed exitus acta probavit;* they showed their valour at Christ's apprehension.

Ver. 23. *Ye shall drink indeed of my cup*] *Illud solum quod suavius et limpidius.* The saints sip of the top of God's cup; as for the dregs, the wicked shall wring them out, and drink them up.

And be baptized, &c.] Or ducked, washed (not drowned), as St Paul was in the shipwreck; or as the baptized child, which shakes off the water, or is dried after baptism. Afflictions, saith one, are called baptism, because they set God's mark upon us (as baptism doth) that we belong to God; this for outward afflictions. And for desertion, it is called Christ's cup, because we are sure to pledge him in that too, and be conformed unto him, as was Job, David, Heman, Psal. lxxxviii. &c. Grace is no target against affliction; but the best shall have terrors within and troubles without, as sure as the coat is on their back or the heart in their belly.

Is not mine to give] i. e. It is no part of my present office; or, I have no such commission from my Father to give precedencies to all that affect them. Christ hereby seeks to raise up the low grovelling spirits of his apostles to things supernatural, supernal.

Ver. 24. *They were moved*] They were angry at that ambition in their fellows, that themselves were deeply guilty of. So Diogenes trampled Plato's pride, but with greater pride. So Crassus earnestly inveighed against covetousness in others, when there was not a more covetous caitiff than he upon the earth. So Gregory the Great stomached the title of universal bishop to the patriarch of Constantinople, which yet himself affected, and his successor, Boniface, arrogated and usurped.

Ver. 25. *Jesus called them to him, and said*] We must (by Christ's example) advance, cherish concord all we can, amongst ministers especially, by casting out those make-bates, emulation and ambition. Pareus was wont to say, that the only cause of all Church dissensions was, ministers reaching after rule and preëminence, as did Diotrephes.[1] And that if this evil humour could possibly be purged out, there would be a sweet symmetry, a happy harmony of all hearts.

And they that are great] The grandees of the earth. There is, saith one, a greatness belluine and genuine. In that, a beast may and doth exceed us; in this we exceed ourselves and others. "Great men are not always wise," saith Elihu, Job xxxii. 9. And *Nemo me major nisi qui justior,* said Agesilaus, when the king of

Persia styled himself the great king. *Calamitas nostra magnus est,* said Mimus concerning Pompey, the people applauding so handsome a solecism. *Privilegium unius conceditur in beneficium alterius,* saith a learned doctor; *et si vis esse vere magnus, ne sis instar utris folle tumidi, sed instar uteri prole gravidi; nec attollas inane supercilium, sed exhibeas utile ministerium.* Goodness is the only greatness.

Ver. 26. *But it shall not be so amongst you*] How express is that against Papal primacy and lordly prelacy. When the duke shall be damned, what will become of the bishop, said the clown to the Bishop of Cullen? Mr Whitehead refused a bishopric, because he liked not to be lorded. And Mr Coverdale being deprived of his bishopric in Queen Mary's days, would not (for the same cause) be reinvested in Queen Elizabeth's, but taught a school. Mr Knox would not have a bishopric, because it had *aliquid commune cum antichristo.*

Ver. 27. *Let him be your servant*] This is the ready way to rise. Neither may any think himself too good to serve the saints, to wash their feet, to minister to their necessities. Christ came out of the bosom of his Father to fetch them to heaven. The Holy Ghost disdains not to dwell in their hearts. Angels are desirous to do them any good office. Prophets think not much to minister to them, 1 Pet. i. 12. Paul, and Apollos, and Cephas are theirs, public servants to the Church; accounting it a far greater matter *prodesse quam præesse,* to seek men's salvation than to exercise dominion.

Ver. 28. *And to give his life a ransom*] A redemptory, a valuable rate, λύτρον, for it was the blood of God wherewith the Church was purchased, Acts xx. 28; silver and gold could not do it, 1 Pet. i. 18, 19; nor anything else but that counter-price given by Christ, ἀντίλυτρον, 1 Tim. ii. 6.

Ver. 29. *And as they departed from Jericho*] Christ cured one blind man as he went into Jericho, Luke xviii., and two as he went out; for all the haste he had to go to Jerusalem.[2] Hence such multitudes followed him, to make up his ensuing triumph.

Ver. 30. *When they heard that Jesus passed by*] Happy it was for them that, though blind, yet they were not deaf. For as death came in by the ear, so doth life. "Hear, and your soul shall live," Isa. lv. 3; a heavy ear is a singular judgment, Isa. vi. 11; a hearing ear a special favour, Prov. xx. 12. When God struck Zacharias, Luke i., he made him dumb, but not deaf. When God struck Saul, he made him blind but not deaf. When God struck Mephibosheth, he made him lame, but not deaf. There is a deaf devil, Mark ix. 25, and a deaf adder, Psal. lviii. 4, and a deaf man, that yet want for no ears, Isa. xliii. 8. But "he that heareth instruction is in the way of life," saith Solomon. These two blind beggars had heard of Christ by the hearing of the ear,

---

[1] *Infelicium ecclesiæ concertationem causam dixit ecclesiasticorum* φιλαρχίαν. In vita Parei.

[2] *Tres in his locis ita curatos esse crediderim.* Aretius.

but that satisfied them not, unless their eyes also might see him, Job xlii. 5. They way-lay therefore the Lord of light, who gives them upon their suit, both sight and light, irradiates both organ and object, cures them of their both outward and inward ophthalmies at once.

Thou Son of David] They knew and acknowledged Christ to be the true Messias. Few such knowing blind beggars now-a-days. They are commonly more blind in mind than body, loose and lawless vagrants; such as are neither of any church nor common-wealth; but as the baser sort of people in Swethland, who do always break the sabbath, saying, that it is only for gentlemen to sanctify it; or rather as the poor Brazilians, who are said to be *sine rege, lege, fide*, without any government, law, or religion.

Ver. 31. *And the multitude rebuked them*] In prayer, we must look to meet with many rubs and discouragements; but God's Spirit is heroic, and gets over them all. The devil will interrupt us, as the Pythoness did Paul, Acts xvi. 16; as the birds did Abraham, Gen. xv. 11; as those Samaritans did the Jews in building the temple, Neh. vi. Hence are we bid strive in prayer, Colos. iv. 2, and watch in prayer; for Satan will be at our right hand, as at Joshua's, Zech. iii. 1, watching his time to cast in, if not a profane, yet an impertinent thought, thereby to bereave us of the benefit of our prayers; besides our own natural in-devotion through hardness of heart, heaviness of body, multiplicity of worldly distractions and disturbances. All which we must break through, and cry the more earnestly, as Bartimeus here did, though checked by the multitude, " Have mercy on us, O Lord," &c. Daniel would not be kept from his God for any danger of death, Dan. vi., nor the French Protestants restrain prayer, though King Henry III. made a law to forbid them to pray with their families. The sun shall sooner stand still than the trade of godliness, and that continual intercourse that is betwixt God and the Christian soul.

Ver. 32. *And Jesus stood still*] See the admirable power of fervent prayer. *Preces Christum licet festinantem remorantur*, Christ stands and stays (for all the haste of his journey to Jerusalem, which till he had finished, oh how was he straitened, Luke xii. 50) to hear the blind beggars'. petition. So the sun once stood still in Gibeon, and the moon in the valley of Ajalon, upon the prayer of worthy Joshua, who set the trophies of his victory in the very orbs of heaven.

Ver. 33. *Lord, that our eyes might be opened*] " Truly the light is sweet, and a pleasant thing it is for the eyes to behold ‚the sun," Eccl. xi. 7, and yet how little is this mercy prized, because common. Our corrupt natures heed nothing that we enjoy, as the eye seeth nothing that lies on it, but things at a distance it discerns clearly. *Bona a tergo formosissima*. Copy of good things breeds satiety, and makes them no dainties, till God for our folly many times makes us see the

worth of them by the want of them, and so commends and endears his favours to us. But what a blindness is this, worse than that of Bartimeus, never to see the face but the back only of benefits.

Ver. 34. *And Jesus had compassion on them*] He made their case his own. *Misericordia* sounds as much as misery laid to heart. Christ's bowels sounded upon the sight and suit of these blind beggars, Isa. lxiii. 15, and this was beyond all alms, should he have done no more for them. For when one gives an alms, he gives somewhat without himself, but by compassion we relieve another by somewhat within and from ourselves, whiles we draw out our soul (not our sheaf only) to the hungry, Isa. lviii. 10.

And immediately their eyes received sight] This is not every blind man's happiness, that yet prays for sight. But there is a better eye-sight than that of the body, which if God vouchsafe to any in bodily blindness (as he did to that blind boy of Gloucester that had suffered imprisonment there for confessing the truth) it may be said to such surely, as Bishop Hooper the martyr did to him, Ah, poor boy, God hath taken from thee thy outward sight, but hath given thee another much more precious, &c. (Acts and Mon.) The like favour God showed to Didimus Alexandrinus, who though blind from his childhood, yet was not only an excellent artist, but an able divine; and wrote certain commentaries on the Psalms, and likewise on the Gospels; being now (saith Jerome, who relates it) above 83 years of age. Trithemius and Bozius report the like things concerning one Nicasius de Voarda, a Dutchman, who being struck blind at three years old, became nevertheless an excellent scholar, and skilful in the laws, which he publicly professed at Collen. Afterwards he proceeded Master of Arts at Lovain, Licentiate in Divinity at the same University, and lastly Doctor of the Laws at Cullen; where, after he had printed his public lectures, he died, and was buried in the Cathedral Church, A. D. 1491, 17 Calend. Septem.

CHAPTER XXI.

Ver. 1. *And when they drew nigh to Jerusalem*] IN this one verse, our Evangelist closely compriseth all that St John sets down of our Saviour's oracles and miracles from his 7th chap. to chap. xii. 12, viz. the history of five months and ten days; for Christ rode not into the city till the fifth day before his last passover, John xii. 12, having the day before been anointed by Mary at Bethany, John xii. 1, called here Bethphage, or the Conduit-house (*Bethphage à* בת *et* πηγή).

Ver. 2. *An ass tied, and a colt with her*] There are that by the ass understand the Jews laden with the law,[1] and by her foal, the Gentiles that wandered whither they would. That canon-

---

[1] *Oneramus asinum et non curat quia asinus est.* Bern.

ist made the most of it, that said that children are therefore to be baptized, because the apostles brought to Christ not only the ass, but the colt too.

Ver. 3. *The Lord hath need of them*] The Lord of all, both beasts and hearts ; for else how could he so soon have obtained the ass of her master ? Some read the text thus : " The Lord hath need of them, and will presently send them back again ; " to teach us to be no further burdensome or beholden to others than needs must.

Ver. 4. *All this was done that, &c.*] Here is the mystery of the history ; which would otherwise seem to some ridiculous and to little purpose. He hereby declared himself that King of his Church fore-promised by the prophets, how poor and despicable soever, as the world accounts it.

Ver. 5. *Tell ye the daughter of Sion*] Here was that also of the Psalmist fulfilled, " God is my King of old, working salvation in the midst of the earth," Psal. lxxiv. 12. For Jerusalem is by the Fathers observed to stand in the very centre and navel of the habitable earth, as if it were fatally founded to be the city of the great King.

Thy King cometh unto thee] All in Christ is for our behoof and benefit, 1 Cor. i. 30, and Mich. iv. 8, 9 : " Unto thee shall it come, O daughter of Zion, even the first dominion ; the kingdom shall come to the daughter of Jerusalem. Why then dost thou cry out aloud ? Is there no King in thee ? Is thy counsellor perished ? " A mandamus from this King will do it at any time, Psal. xl. 4.

Meek, and sitting upon an ass] Not upon a stately palfrey, as Alexander, Julius Cæsar, &c. ; no such state here. Christ's kingdom was of another world ; " He came riding meek ; " and his word (the law of his kingdom) is both to be taught and received with meekness, 2 Tim. ii. 25 ; James i. 21. At Genoa in Italy they show the tail of the ass our Saviour rode on for an holy relic ; and bow before it with great devotion. On Palm-Sunday, their priests bring forth an ass in state, and bow before him and worship him, as if Christ himself were there present ; which when the Turkish ambassadors once beheld at Craconia in Poland, they blessed themselves, and cried out, *O tetram impietatem ! Siccine asinum brutam bestiam adorari ?* O detestable impiety ! should an ass be so adored ? Neither will these dull dizards be reclaimed from such fond fopperies ; being herein like those Italian asses, which feeding upon the weed henbane, are so stupified, that they lie for dead, neither can they be wakened till half-hilded.

Ver. 6. *And the disciples went*] With a certain blind obedience they went on Christ's errand, though not very likely to speed. Their Master's sole authority carried them on against all difficulties and absurdities. When God commands us anything, we may not dispute, but dispatch ; argue, but agree to it, captivate our reason, exalt our faith.

Ver. 7. *And put on them their clothes*] Teaching us to honour God with the best of our substance, and to dedicate ourselves wholly to the Lord our God. Jonathan stripped himself, for his friend David, of the robe that was upon him, and his garments, even to his sword and his girdle, 1 Sam. xviii. 4. Christ suspended his glory for a season, laid aside his rich and royal robes, borrowed a cast-suit of us, that he might clothe us with his righteousness. And shall we think much to clothe him in his naked members, to part with anything for his sake and service ?

And they set him thereon] They that make religion dance attendance to policy (saith one) these set the ass upon Christ, not Christ upon the ass. Thus did Jehu, and before him Jeroboam, *cui gravior jactura regionis, quam religionis.* Thus do all our Machiavellians and the world's wizards, whose rule is, *Philosophandum sed paucis ; Religiosum oportet esse, sed non religentem, &c.* But what saith a father ? *Deum siquis parum metuit, valde contemnit.* And one thing, said Luther, that will be the ruin of religion is worldly policy, that would have all well however, and seeks to procure the public peace, by impious and unlawful counsels and courses, *Quæ vult omnia redigere in ordinem, et publicæ tranquillitati impiis consiliis mederi.*

Ver. 8. *And a very great multitude*] Bondinius saith, he was met at this time by 300,000 Jews, some whereof went before Christ, some followed after, according to the solemn rites and reverence used to be given to earthly kings in their most pompous triumphs. This was the Lord's own work.

Ver. 9. *Hosanna to the Son of David.*] So they acknowledge Christ to be the true Messiah, and congratulate him his kingdom over the Church ; and yet a few days after, these same, at the instigation of the priests and Pharisees, cry, Crucify : dealing by Christ as Xerxes did by his steersman, whom he crowned in the morning, and then took off his head in the afternoon of the same day : or as the fickle Israelites dealt by David, 2 Sam. xx., where we shall find the same hands that erewhile fought for David to be all theirs, do now fight against him under the son of Bichri, to be none of theirs.

Ver. 10. *Who is this ?*] Why ? could not they tell after so many miracles done among them ? Were they such strangers at Jerusalem ? Many live and die very sots, even in those places where they had " line upon line, precept upon precept," &c., and yet they are no wiser than the child new weaned from the breast, Isa. xxviii. 9 ; their wits serve them not in spirituals, though otherwise shrewd enough.

Ver. 11. *The prophet of Nazareth, &c.*] The archprophet they acknowledge him ; but of Nazareth of Galilee. They had not profited so much, or made so far progress in the mystery of Christ, as to know him to have been born a Bethlehemite. And to nourish this error in the people it was, that the devil, that old impostor, Mark i. 24, though he confessed Christ to be the " holy one of God," yet he calleth him " Jesus of Nazareth." *Satan etsi semel videatur verax, millies est mendax et semper fallax*, Satan never speaks truth, but with a mind to deceive.

Ver. 12. *And cast out all them that sold*] The zeal of God's house did ever eat him up. And (as revenge follows zeal, 2 Cor. vii. 11) he mars their markets, and drives them out of the temple with *Procul o procul este profani*.[1] And this deed of our Saviour's was altogether divine ; whiles as another Samson, he lays " heaps upon heaps " (yet without bloodshed) with the jaw-bone of an ass. St Jerome extolleth this miracle above the raising of Lazarus, restoring the blind to their sight, the lame to their limbs, &c., and adds this mystical sense of the text, *Quotidie Jesus ingreditur templum Patris, et ejicit omnes tam episcopos et presbyteros, quam laicos et universam turbam de ecclesia sua, et unius criminis habet, vendentes pariter et ementes.* Christ is every day casting out of his Church all these money-merchants, these sacrilegious simonists, both ministers and others, that make sale of holy things, which the very heathens abhorred, and others long since complained that benefices were bestowed *non ubi optime, sed ubi quæstuosissime*, as if a man should bestow so much bread on his ass because he is to ride on him.

The tables of the money-changers] This he did also at his first entrance into the ministry, John ii. 14, 15. See my notes on that text. The reformation of religion was Christ's chief care, and so it should be ours. And although little was done by his first attempt, John ii., yet he tries again : so should we, contributing what we can to the work continually, by our prayers and utmost endeavours ; wishing at least, as Ferus did, that we had some Moses to take away the evils in Church and State. *Non enim unum tantum vitulum, sed multos habemus*, saith he, for we abound with idols and evils, Exod. xxxii. 20.

Ver. 13. *Shall be called the house of prayer*] A principal piece of God's public worship, and here put for the whole. Christ himself never came into this house but he preached as well as prayed. In the sanctuary was the incense altar in the middle, a type of prayer ; the table of shewbread on the one side, betokening the twelve tribes, and the candlestick, a type of the word, on the other : to teach us that there is a necessity of both ordinances to all God's people.

But ye have made it a den of thieves] So Christ calleth not the money-merchants only, but the priests also that set them a-work. And whereas they cried, " the temple of the Lord, the temple of the Lord " (for to those was this speech first addressed, Jer. vii. 11), as if they could not do amiss because they served in the temple, the prophet tells them there, and our Saviour these here, that it is so much the worse. What should an angel of darkness do in heaven ? Who required these things at your hands, to tread the courts of my temple ? This is the gate of the Lord, into which the righteous only should enter, Psal. cxviii. 20. The Papists in like sort cry out at this day, *Ecclesia, Ecclesia, Nos sumus Ecclesia ;* and herewith think to shroud their base huckstering of holy things. For *omnia Romæ venalia*, all things are saleable and soluble at Rome. But this covering is too short, and their gross thieveries are now made apparent to all the world, as their rood of grace and the blood of Hales were at Paul's cross by that noble Cromwell ; and as their cheating trade of indulgencies and pope's pardons was by Luther, who by dint of argument overthrew those Romish money-changers, and drove the country of those χριστοκαπήλοι and χριστέμποροι, as Nazianzen fitly calleth them.

Ver. 14. *Came to him in the temple, and he healed them*] So true was that testimony given of our Saviour, Luke xxiv. 19, that he was a prophet mighty in deed, as well as in word, before God and all the people. *Nos non eloquimur magna, sed vivimus*, said the primitive Christians. Our lives as well as our lips should speak us right and real in religion ; as Christ here, by his cures, gave a real answer to that question, ver. 10, Who is this ? Let us learn to lead convincing lives ; these are the best apologies when all is done.

Ver. 15. *And the children crying, &c.*] To the great grief and regret of those cankered carls the priests and scribes ; but to the singular commendation of their parents who had so well taught and tutored them. So the children of Merindol answered the popish bishop of Cavaillon with such grace and gravity as was admirable. So, when John Lawrence was burnt at Colchester, the young children came about him, and cried in the audience of the persecutors, " Lord, strengthen thy servant, and keep thy promise."

Ver. 16. *Thou hast perfected praise*] Κατηρτίσω, thou hast given it all its parts and proportions,[2] thou hast completed and accomplished it. The Hebrew saith, *fundasti*, thou hast founded praise, and well bottomed it. *Quæ enim perfecta, sunt firmissima.* Now there is no mouth so weak into which God cannot put words of praise. And how oft doth he choose the silly-simples of the world to confound the wise and learned ? See my notes on Psal. viii. 2. And here it is observable that our Saviour answers warily to the captious question ; so as he may neither offend Cæsar, by taking upon him to be a king, nor stumble the people, who took him for no less, and he was well pleased therewith. Let our columbine simplicity be mixed with serpentine subtilty, that we run not ourselves heedlessly into unnecessary dangers.

Ver. 17. *And he left them*] As not willing to lose his labour, to cast away his cost upon men so unthankful, untractable.

Ludit, qui sterili semina mandat humo. (Ovid.)

---

[1] *In Græcorum sacris sacerdos exclamabat* τίς τῆδε, quis hic *? Respondebant qui aderant,* πόλλοι τ' ἄγαθοί τε πάρεισι.

Eras. præfat. in Adag.
[2] Αρτιον *est quod constat omnibus membris.*

Went out of the city into Bethany] Haply for safety' sake: undoubtedly for his delight and to refresh himself with his friend Lazarus, after his hard labour and little success.

Ver. 18. *As he returned into the city*] There his work lay chiefly; thither therefore he repairs betimes, and forgat, for haste, to take his breakfast, as it may seem, for ere he came to the city he was hungry, though it were but a step thither. A good man's heart is where his calling is: such a one, when he is visiting friends or so, is like a fish in the air; whereunto if it leap for recreation or necessity, yet it soon returns to its own element.

Ver. 19. *He came to it and found nothing*] He thought then to have found something; there was some kind of ignorance, we see, in Christ as man (but not that that was sinful). His soul desired the first ripe fruits, Micah vii. 1; yea, though they had not been ripe and ready, hard hunger would have made them sweet and savoury, as the shepherd's bread and onions were to Hunniades, when he was put to flight by the Turks; so well can hunger season homely cates, saith the historian. Of this promising fig-tree our Saviour might say, as Alciat of the cypress,

Pulchra coma est, pulchro digestæque ordine frondes,
Sed fructus nullos hæc coma pulchra gerit.

Ver. 20. *They marvelled, saying, &c.*] And well they might, for no conjurer, with all his skill, could have caused this fig-tree so suddenly to wither, with a word speaking. For the fig-tree is the most juiceful of any tree, and bears the brunt of winter blasts. Yea, Plutarch tells us that there issueth from the fig-tree such a strong and most vehement virtue, as that if a bull be tied unto it for some while he becomes tame and tractable, though he were never so fierce and fell before. No wonder therefore though the disciples wondered at so sudden an alteration.

Ver. 21. *If ye have faith and doubt not*] Or dispute not the matter as probable only and somewhat uncertain, but not altogether undoubted.[1] He that doubteth debateth it, as it were, with himself, puts the case to and fro, sometimes being of one mind, sometimes of another. Now "let not such a man think that he shall receive anything of the Lord," James i. 7. "If ye will not believe, surely ye shall not be established," Isa. vii. 9.

Ver. 22. *Whatsoever ye shall ask in prayer, believing*] Faith is the foundation of prayer, and prayer is the fervency of faith. "Cast thy burden upon the Lord," or thy request, thy gift upon the Lord, Psal. lv. 22, that is, whatsoever thou desirest that God should give thee in prayer, cast it upon him by faith, and it shall be effected. *Fidei mendica manus.* Faith and prayer are the soul's two hands, whereby she begs and receives of God all good things both for this and a better life. Hence of old when the saints prayed they spread out the palms of their hands, as to receive a blessing from God, 1 Kings viii. 22; Exod. ix. 29; Psal. cxliii. 6.

Ver. 23. *And when he was come into the temple*] Not into the inn or victualling house, though he had been so hungry by the way. He forgot that; the zeal of God's house had eaten him up; it was his meat and drink to do the will of his heavenly Father; this he preferred before his necessary food. And truly a man would wonder what a deal of work he did up in these three days' space, before his apprehension. All those sermons and discourses set down by Matthew from this place to chap. xxvi., by Mark from chaps. xi.—xiv., by Luke from chaps. xx.—xxii., and by John from chaps. xii.—xviii., were delivered by him in these three last days of his liberty. He dispatched them with speed, as if he had been loth to have been taken with his task undone. To teach us to get up our work, and to work out our salvation; not work at it only. Lazy spirits aspire not to immortality. The twelve tribes served God instantly day and night, and found all they could do little enough, Acts xxvi. 7.

Came unto him as he was teaching] *Otiosum vel tacitum facile tulissent,* saith an interpreter. If he would have been quiet or silent, they would never have questioned him. A wolf flies not upon a painted sheep; we can look upon a painted toad with delight. It is your active Christian that is most spited and persecuted. Luther was offered to be made a cardinal, if he would be quiet. He answered, No, not if I might be pope; and defends himself thus against those that thought him (haply) a proud fool for his refusal, *Inveniar sane superbus, &c. modo impii silentii non arguar.* (Epis. ad Staunc.) Let me be counted fool or anything, said he, so I be not found guilty of cowardly silence. The Papists, when they could not rule him, railed at him, and called him an apostate. *Confitetur se esse apostatam, sed beatum et sanctum, qui fidem diabolo datam non servavit.* (Epis. ad Spalatinum.) He confesseth the action, and saith, I am indeed an apostate, but a blessed and holy apostate, one that had fallen off from the devil. They called him devil, but what said he? *Prorsus Satan est Lutherus, sed Christus vivit et regnat. Amen.* Luther is a devil; be it so, but Christ liveth and reigneth, that is enough for Luther. So be it.

By what authority doest thou these things?] They saw that their kingdom would down, their trade decay, if Christ should be suffered thus to teach and take upon him in the temple as a reformer. When Erasmus was asked by the elector of Saxony, why the pope and his clergy could so little abide Luther, he answered, for two great offences, viz. *Ventres et culinas appeti, arcas exhauriri. Attigisse coronam papæ, et monachorum ventres* (Scult.), he had meddled with the pope's triple crown, and with the monk's fat paunches. *Hinc illæ lachrimæ,* hence all that hatred; and hence now-a-days those Popish questions to the professors of the truth: By what authority do ye these things? where had you your calling, your ordination? where was your religion before Luther? Whereunto it was well answer-

---

[1] Διακρίνεσθαι, *est alternantibus sententiis secum disceptare.* Budæus.

ed by one once, In the Bible, where yours never was.

Ver. 24. *I also will ask you one thing*] Our Saviour could have answered them roundly, that what he did he did by the will and appointment of his heavenly Father. But because he had avouched that so oft, and they believed him not, therefore he took another course. We must be ready to render a reason of our faith; but then it must be when we see it will be to some good purpose; as if otherwise, forbear, or untie one knot with another, as Christ here doth, *nodum nodo dissipat.* (Aret.)

Ver. 25. *The baptism of John, whence was it?*] That is, the whole ministry of John. As if our Saviour should have said, Know ye not by what authority I do these things? have ye not heard John's testimony for me? and can ye deny that he had his authority for what he spake from God? How is it, then, that ye ask me any such idle question as this; do ye not go cross to your consciences herein?

Ver. 26. *We fear the people*] Lest they should be stoned; and the people feared them, lest they should be excommunicated. Thus they were mutual executioners one to another; for all fear hath torment, 1 John iv. 18.

Ver. 27. *We cannot tell*] Lie and all: they could tell, and would not. Their reasonings within themselves, ver. 25, testify that they knew the truth, but would not acknowledge it;[1] they profess their ignorance rather: and such dealing we have from many learned Papists. Thus Bellarmine affirmeth that he never read in all the Bible a promise of pardon made to those that confess their sins to Almighty God. (*Bell. de Justif.*, lib. 1, cap. 21.) Baronius cannot see that Peter was in fault at Antioch, but Paul a great deal more, for taking him up for halting, Gal. ii. The wit of heretics will better serve them to devise a thousand shifts to delude the truth, than their pride will suffer them once to yield and subscribe to it.

Ver. 28. *But what think you?*] Christ reporteth himself to their own consciences, whiles he proveth John Baptist's ministry to be from heaven, by the happy success he had in converting the vilest sinners. See Jer. xxiii. 22; 1 Cor. ix. 2. The people's fruitfulness is the minister's testimonial, 2 Cor. iii. 2. If but one of a city, or two of a family be gained to God, it is a sign that the pastors are according to God's own heart, Jer. iii. 14, 15.

Ver. 29. *I will not*] This is the language of most men's hearts, when pressed to duty: and, as occasion serves, they discover an headstrong wilfulness in wickedness, that is, uncouncilable. As Pharaoh sat not down under the miracle, but sent for magicians; so do these, when the word comes close to their consciences, send for carnal arguments. And though the word doth eat up all they can say, as Moses' rod did, yet they harden their hearts, with Pharaoh, they brazen their brows, with him in the text, that said, "I

[1] *Mendacio nodum secant quem solvere sine impietate*

will not." "Nay," said the Israelites, "but we will have a king." And as for the word that thou hast spoken unto us in the name of the Lord, "we will not hearken unto thee," said those, Jer. xliv. 16.

But afterward he repented] So do but few. Men will be as big as their words, though they die for it, lest they should be accounted inconstant. These are niggardly of their reputation, but prodigal of their souls.

Ver. 30. *I go, sir*] I, but when, sir? *Stultus semper incipit vivere.* (Seneca.) Hypocrites purpose oft, and promise fair to do better, but drive off and fail in the performance; their morning cloud is soon dispersed, their earthly dew is quickly dried up, Hos. vi. 4, their heartless essays come to nothing, *Modo et modo non habent modum.* The philosopher liked not such as are *semper victuri*, always about to live better, but never begin. A divine complains that the goodness of many is like the softness of a plumb, soon crushed; but their wickedness is like the stone in the plumb, hard and inflexible.

Ver. 31. *Go into the kingdom of heaven before you*] And it were an arrant shame to be left behind by such; as that is a very jade, we say, that will not follow, though she will not lead the way. But these proud Pharisees hated to be in the same heaven with penitent publicans. And, as Quintilian said of some in his time, that they might have proved excellent scholars had they not been so persuaded of their own scholarship already. In like sort these over-weeners of themselves might have had place in heaven, had they not taken up their seats in heaven aforehand.

Ver. 32. *John came unto you in a way of right*] Which he both preached and lived. *Nos non eloquimur magna, sed vivimus.* John's practice was a transcript of what he preached; he burned within himself, he shone forth to others, John v. 35.

Ye repented not afterwards] No, not after his death, though ye saw me succenturiated to him, and preaching and pressing the same things upon you that John did. An hypocrite comes hardlier to heaven than a gross sinner, and hath far more obstacles. As he that must be stripped is not so soon clothed as one that is naked, and as he climbs not a tree so soon that must first come down from the top of another tree where he is perked, so is it here.

Ver. 33. *Planted a vineyard, and hedged it*] Of all possessions, saith Cato, *Nulla majorem operam requirit*, none requires more pains than that of a vineyard. Corn comes up and grows alone, Mark iv. 28. *Injussa virescunt gramina*, saith the poet; but vines must be dressed, supported, pruned, sheltered every day almost, John xv. 2. The Church is God's continual care, αἴρει, καθαίρει, *Amputat, putat*, &c., Isa. xxvii. 3, and he looks for an answerable return of fruits, Acts xii. 48. *Regnum Angliæ, regnum Dei*, said Polydore Virgil long since. The kingdom of England vel periculo non possunt. Pareus, *in loc.*

is the kingdom of God. It may well be said so, since the Reformation especially; neither is there anything more threateneth us than our hateful unfruitfulness. The cypress tree, the more it is watered, the less fruitful; so many of us, the more taught, the more untoward.

And went into a far country] As the impious husbandmen imagined, who put far away the evil day. But God shall shoot at such " with an arrow, suddenly shall they be wounded," Psal. lxiv. 7; as a bird is stricken with the bolt, whiles he gazeth at the bow. *Moræ dispendium fœneris duplo pensatur*, God pays men at length for the new and the old. (Jerome.)

Ver. 34. *He sent his servants*] scil. His prophets and ministers, whom the Lord sendeth to his people continually, not to teach them only, but to take account of their fruitfulness, to urge and exact of them growth in grace according to the means, "that they receive not the grace of God in vain," 2 Cor. vi. 1.

Ver. 35. *Beat one, and killed another*] This is the world's wages; this is the measure God's ministers meet with from the sons of men; never have any, out of hell, suffered more than such. Persecution is, *Evangelii genius*, saith Calvin, the evil angel that dogs the Gospel at the heels. And, *Prædicare nihil aliud est, quam derivare in se furorem*, &c., saith Luther. To preach faithfully is to get the ill will of all the world, and to subject a man's self to all kind of deaths and dangers.

Ver. 36. *Again he sent other servants*] Oh the infinite goodness and long-suffering of Almighty God! Jonas upbraided him with it most unworthily, in that brawl of his, chap. iv. 2. Paul admires it, Rom. ix. 22, teaching us to improve it to the practice of repentance, Rom. ii. 4. Ezekiel (iv. 4, 5) describes it by God's lying on one side for three hundred and ninety years together, which must needs be very troublesome. We cannot lay for a few hours on one side, but we must turn us. David, for the abuse of his ambassadors, fell very foul on the Ammonites. Rehoboam, for one servant of his slain by the ten tribes, raised a mighty army to chastise them. But God bears with men's evil manners, though he have power enough in his hand to deal with them at his pleasure.

Ver. 37. *They will reverence my son*] They will look another way for shame (so the word ἐντραπήσονται imports): they will never be able to look him in the face, they will be so abashed of their former villanies. But it fell out far otherwise, for these frontless fellows, past grace, as we say, had faces hatcht all over with impudency, and that could blush no more than a sackbut. Sin had woaded shamelessness in their foreheads, and they were as good at resisting the Holy Ghost as ever their fathers were.

Ver. 38. *This is the heir; come, &c.*] So that these husbandmen the Pharisees knew, and yet crucified the Lord of glory; and all this out of desperate malice, which had debauched their

¹ κακοὺς κακῶς ἀπολέσει αὐτούς.

reason, and even satanized or transformed them into so many breathing devils; they fell into that unpardonable sin, Matt. xii. 31.

Let us seize on his inheritance] Covetousness is bloody, Ezek. xxii. 13; Prov. i. 11, 13; 1 Kings xxi. 10. Ahab longed for a salad out of Naboth's vineyard, and must have it, though Naboth die for it, *Quid non mortalia pectora cogis, auri sacra fames!* Judas selleth his Master for thirty pence.

Ver. 39. *Cast him out of the vineyard, and slew him*] By wicked hands, Acts ii. 23, and are therefore abhorred of God and men, and exiled out of the world, as it were, by a common consent of nations for their inexpiable guilt. And in Constantinople and Thessalonica (where are many thousand Jews at this day), if they but stir out of doors at any Easter time between Maundy Thursday at noon and Easter-eve at night, the Christians, among whom they dwell, will stone them, because at that time they derided, buffeted, and crucified our blessed Saviour.

Ver. 40. *What will he do, &c.*] Nay, what will he not do? God will run upon them, even on their neck, upon the "thick bosses of their bucklers," Job xv. 26. They that would kill their enemy, strike not where he can defend himself. But so doth God, he strikes through all, yea, through the loins, Deut. xxxiii. 11, even to the very soul, Jer. iv. 10. This made Moses cry out, "Who knoweth the power of thine anger?" Psal. xc. 11. Surely it is such, as none can either avoid or abide.

Ver. 41. *They say unto him, he will miserably,*[1] &c.] Here they unwittingly read their own destiny, as David likewise did his, 2 Sam. xii. 5, 6. The wicked are presently self-condemned, Tit. iii. 11, and shall at last day stand speechless, Matt. xxi. 12, out of the conviction of their own consciences.

Ver. 42. *Did ye never read in the Scriptures*] Yes, full oft, but never applied such a place as this to themselves. A godly man reads the Scriptures as he doth the statute-book: he holds himself concerned in all that he reads; he finds his own name written in every passage, and lays it to heart, as spoken to him. The wicked, on the other side, put off all they like not, and dispose of it to others, as if themselves were none such. God forbid, said these to our Saviour, Luke xx. 16. But he convinceth them out of their own reading, to be the men he meant. Men may make some sorry shift, and shuffle for a while from side to side, as Balaam's ass did, but there is no averting or avoiding the dint of God's displeasure, otherwise than by falling down, as the ass did, and afterwards her master, being rebuked for his iniquity, "The dumb ass speaking with man's voice, forbad the madness of the prophet," 2 Pet. ii. 16.

Ver. 43. *The kingdom of God shall be taken from you*] A heavy sentence. We had better, saith one, be without meat, drink, light, air, earth, all the elements, yea, life itself, than that

Videtur paronomasia hæc in proverbium abiisse.

one sweet saying of our Saviour, " Come unto me, all ye that are weary and heavy laden, and I will refresh you."[1] The gospel is that inheritance we received from our godly forefathers, the martyrs; and it must be our care to transmit the same to our posterity, earnestly contending for the faith which was once delivered, Jude 3, once for all; for if lost, or any way corrupted, it will hardly be ever given again. Look to it, therefore, unfruitfulness forfeits all, as the merchant's non-payment of the custom forfeits all his goods. It is to be feared, saith one, lest Mr Herbert be a true prophet; and the gospel be, in its solar motion, travelling for the West, for the American parts, and quitting its present place of residence, and unworthy professors and possessors; and then farewell England.

Ver. 44. *And whosoever shall fall on this stone*] Christ is a stone of stumbling to his enemies, who stumble at his meanness, and a rock of offence, 1 Pet. ii. 8; but like that rock, Judg. vi. 21, out of which fire went and consumed them, *Nemo me impune lacessit*, saith he. The Corinthians abused certain Roman ambassadors, and were therefore burnt to the ground by L. Mummius. For *irasci populo Rom. nemo sapienter possit*, saith Livy thereupon. Christ is wise in heart and mighty in strength. Who ever hardened himself against him and prospered? Job ix. 4. Who ever bragged of the last blow? If his wrath be kindled, yea, but a little, woe be to his opposites; but if he fall upon them with his whole weight, he will crush them to pieces, yea, grind them to powder. They can no more stand before him than can a glass bottle before a cannon shot.

Ver. 45. *They perceived that he spake of them*] Who told them so, but their own guilty consciences? Every man hath a domestical chaplain within his own bosom, that preacheth over the sermon to him again, and comes over him with, "Thou art the man." Conscience is said to accuse or excuse in the meanwhile, μεταξὺ ἀλλήλων, Rom. ii. 15. In the interim betwixt sermon and sermon, conviction and conviction. So that personal and nominal application is therefore needless, because every man hath a discursive faculty within him, applying several truths to every man's particular uses. And, *ubi generalis de vitiis disputatio est, ibi nullius personæ est injuria*, saith Jerome: Where the discourse against vice is general, no man can justly complain of a personal injury. By preaching, Christ many times smites the earth, Isa. xi. 4, that is, the consciences of carnal men glued to the earth. God's words hit them full in the teeth, and make them spit blood. Now if they rage, as tigers, tear themselves at the noise of a drum, if they fly in the faces of their teachers, and seek revenge upon them, they are commonly cast into a reprobate sense, and seldom escape the visible vengeance of God.

Ver. 46. *But when they sought to lay hands on him*] And so showed themselves to be the same

our Saviour spake of, ver. 39, 42. As the pope and his emissaries do well approve themselves to be that false prophet, and his locusts, set forth in the Revelation. Their daily practice is a clear commentary upon that obscure prophecy, which the ancient Fathers, that lived not to see it fulfilled, could not tell what to say to. Future things are best understood by their events.

CHAPTER XXII.

Ver. 1. *Spake unto them again*] THAT by one discourse he might peg in another. He had but a while to be with men, and see how he bestirs him! Natural motion is more swift and violent toward the end of it. It was as pleasant to Christ to seek men's salvation as it is to the devil to seek their destruction; who therefore doth his utmost, because he knoweth that he hath but a short time, Rev. xii. 12, his malevolence is motive to his diligence.

Ver. 2. *Like unto a certain king*] God is a great King, and he stands upon his seniority, Mal. i. 8, will be served of the best, and curseth that cozener that doth otherwise, ver. 14. He scorneth to drink the devil's snuffs, to take his leavings.

Ver. 3. *They would not come*] They proved recusants, and this rendered them unworthy of eternal life, Acts xiii. 46. God's ministers sent to call them, must turn them over to him, with a *Non convertentur*, and let him deal with them.

Ver. 4. *Behold I have prepared my dinner*] Luke calleth it a supper. The kingdom of heaven is compared to both, to show that the saints do both dine and sup with Christ; they eat at his table continually, as Mephibosheth did at David's, yea, they have, as Jeconiah had, a continual portion from the king every day, a certain, all the days of their lives.

My oxen and my fatlings are killed] Gr. Are sacrificed, τεθυμένα, but here it is translated to common use, because even heathen princes began their solemn feasts with sacrifices (which was craving a blessing on their food in their way), and for that men should come to a feast as to a sacrifice. *Adeo ut gulæ mactetur appetitus*, as Novarinus here noteth.

Ver. 5. *But they made light of it*] God's rich offers are still slighted and vilipended; and most men turn their backs upon those blessed and bleeding embracements of his, as if heaven were not worth hearkening after;

———*Paris ut vivat regnetque beatus*
Cogi posse negat.—Horat. ep. 2. 10.

One to his farm, another to his merchandise] *Licitis perimus omnes*, More die by meat than poison. Worldliness is a great let to faith, though men cannot be charged with any great covetousness. See that ye shift not off him that speaketh to you from heaven, Heb. xii. 25.

Ver. 6. *Entreated them spitefully and slew them*] elementis, &c. Sel. *Pædag. Christ.*

[2] *Mallemus carere cœlo, terra, omnibus*

This is that sin which brings ruin without remedy, 2 Chron. xxxvi. 16. Josiah's humiliation could not expiate Manasseh's bloodshed. Our Popish prelates in less than four years sacrificed the lives of eight hundred innocents to their idols here in Queen Mary's days. That precious blood doth yet cry to heaven for vengeance against us. And it was a pious motion that one made in a sermon to this present parliament, that there might be a day of public humiliation, purposely set apart, and solemnly kept throughout the kingdom, for the innocent bloodshed here in those Marian days of most abhorred memory.

Ver. 7. *But when the king heard thereof*] And kings have long ears, this King of heaven especially. *Cui etiam muta clamant cadavera.—Ut taceant homines jumenta loquentur.* In case of the abuse of God's servants, a bird of the air shall carry the voice, and that which hath wings shall tell the matter, Eccl. x. 20. John Baptist was beheaded in the prison, as if God had known nothing of the matter, said that martyr. But when he maketh inquisition for bloods (which he oft doth with great secrecy and severity) he remembereth such to purpose, Psal. ix. 12, as he did Herod, Maximinius, Charles IX. of France, Felix of Wartenburg, and sundry other bloody persecutors. The king is said to hear of what was done, for blood crieth.

Sent forth his armies] The Roman spoilers, who were the rod in God's hand, and revenged the quarrel of his covenant. Howbeit they thought not so, Isa. x. 7. As in letting blood by leeches the physician seeks the health of his patient, the leech only filling of his gorge; so when God turns the wicked upon his people, he hath excellent ends, howbeit they think not so, but to destroy and cut off nations not a few, Isa. x. 7.

Ver. 8. *They which were bidden were not worthy*] Who were then? Such as came from the highways and hedges, ver. 9, that is, such as fit and show their sores to God, as the cripple and others do by the highway side to every passenger, to move pity. Such sensible sinners shall walk with Christ in white, for they are worthy.

Ver. 9. *Go ye therefore to the highways*] Those sinners of the Gentiles, Gal. ii. 15, who wandered in their own ways, Acts xiv. 16, and were, till now, without God in the world, Eph. iv. 18. These are those other husbandmen, to whom the householder would let out his vineyard, chap. xxi. 41—43, which truth to illustrate, this parable is purposely uttered, and principally, as it may seem intended.

Ver. 10. *Both bad and good, &c.*] Such a mixture there ever hath been, and will be here in the Church. Doeg sets his foot as far within the sanctuary as David. There are sacrificing Sodomites, Isa. i. 10, sinners in Sion, Isa. xxxiii. 14. We cannot avoid the company of those from whom we shall be sure to carry guilt or grief.

Ver. 11. *And when the king came in to see*] He is in the assemblies of his saints to observe their carriage, and to admeasure unto them in blessing as they do to him in preparation; he goes down into his garden to see whether the vine flourish, and the pomegranates bud, Cant. vi. 11; he walketh in the midst of the seven golden candlesticks, Rev. ii. 1. Now therefore we are all here present before God, said Cornelius, Acts x. 33.

Which had not on a wedding garment] i. e. Christ apprehended by faith, and expressed in his virtues by holy life. Justification and sanctification are the righteousnesses of the saints (δικαιώματα τῶν ἁγίων, Rev. xix. 8), wherewith arrayed they are beautiful even to admiration; as without the which, Satan stood at the right hand of Joshua the high priest, Zech. iii. 1, because (as some will have it) his accusation was as true as vehement, so that Satan had the upper hand of him, till such time as Christ bade, Take away the filthy garments from him; there he pardoned his sin in heaven; and unto him he said, Behold I have caused thine iniquity to pass from thee, and I will clothe thee with change of raiment; there he pardoned it in his own conscience also.

Ver. 12. *Friend, how camest? &c.*] Not wretch, rebel, reprobate. Hard reproofs administered in soft language break the bones. See the notes above on chap. xx. 13.

Not having a wedding garment] Is it fit to come to such a feast in thy worst? in the leathern coats, in the tattered rags and menstruous clouts of wretched old Adam?

And he was speechless] He was muzzled or haltered up,[1] that is, he held his peace, as though he had had a bridle or a halter in his mouth. This is the import of the Greek word here used. He was αὐτοκατάκριτος, self-condemned, Tit. iii. 11, and could not ἀνταποκρίνεσθαι, chat at God, Rom. ix. 30, as he used to do; he was gagged, as it were.

Ver. 13. *Bind him hand and foot*] He that comes into Christ's table without a wedding garment on his back shall not go out without fetters on his feet. Neither shall it help him, that he hath eat and drunk in Christ's presence; for his meat is sauced, and his drink spiced with that bitter wrath of God, Job xx. 23. He shall be taken as here, from the table to the tormentor. Look to it therefore, and come not hand overhead. The very heathens saw, and could say, that God was not to be served slightly or slubberingly, but with all possible preparation aforehand, οὐκ ἐν παρόδῳ προσκυνεῖν, αλλ' οἴκοθεν παρασκευασμένοι. Plut.

Ver. 14. *For many are called, &c.*] With an outward calling; but outward privileges profit not, where the hidden man of the heart is not right, where the power and practice of godliness is wanting. Many a ship hath been called Safeguard and Goodspeed, which yet hath split upon the rocks, or fallen into the hands of pirates.

Ver. 15. *Then went the Pharisees*] They were, as one saith, *Puncti et repuncti, minime si brutum animal fuisset, ratione prorsus viduum.* Novarin.

[1] ἐφιμώθη. *Occlusum est illi os quasi capistro et fræno ac*

tamen ad resipiscentium compuncti. They were stung with the former parables, and grew more enraged. It is a vain persuasion for any godly man to think by any discretion wholly to still and escape the clamours and hates of wicked persons; Christ himself could not do it.

How they might entangle him in his talk] As beasts are in the hunter's toil, or birds in the fowler's net.[1] Every man hunteth his brother with a net, was an old complaint, Mic. vii. 2. And, "They make a man an offender for a word, and lay a snare for him that reproveth in the gate," &c., Isa. xxix. 21. Doctor Story's rule to know an heretic was, They will say, The Lord, and, We praise God, and, The living God. So, The Lord, and not to say, Our Lord, is called by Steven Gardiner, *Symbolum hæreticorum,* the heretic's badge. But God will take these wizards in their own craft, 1 Cor. iii. 19, he will catch them in their own cunning, he will over-shoot them in their own bow, he will take his handful of them, so that they shall not make escape, as the word there signifies, ὁ δρασσόμενος, *comprehendens et quasi manum complens.* Aret.

Ver. 16. *With the Herodians*] i. e. Such as were of Herod's religion, as the Melchites, a kind of mongrel Christians in the East: so called of Melech, as one would say, of the king's religion, because they followed the decrees and examples of the emperors. Some think these Herodians were the same with the publicans, or toll-takers (so Origen and Cyril), whom the Pharisees took with them to our Saviour, as if the one exacted tribute, the other refused to pay, and both came to our Saviour, as to an impartial judge, to end the quarrel, and decide the controversy.

Master, we know that thou art true, &c.] Here is a fair glove, drawn upon a foul hand. "Burning lips and a wicked heart are like a potsherd covered with silver dross," Prov. xxvi. 23. There are those that will smile in your face, and at the same time cut your throat. Squier, sent out of Spain to poison Queen Elizabeth, anointed the pummel of the queen's saddle with poison covertly, and, as it were, doing something else, praying with a loud voice, God save the queen.

That thou art true, and teachest the way of God] These all are high commendations and necessary qualifications of a teacher and instructor of others. These cony-catchers tell the truth of Christ (for he was all this that they say of him and more), and yet they tell a lie, because they thought him not so, but spoke against their consciences. They thought, belike, to have tickled and taken our Saviour with their flatteries (as every wind will blow up a bubble), and so to have had what they would of him; but Christ was not for their turn. He was inadulabilis, unflatterable, and might better say than Politian did, *Assentatiunculis quorundam, aut etiam obtrectationibus non magis attollor aut deprimor, quam umbra mei corporis.* I am no more lifted up, nor

cast down with men's flatteries or slanders than with the shadow of mine own body. For I think not myself either longer or shorter at morning or at noon, because my shadow is so.

Ver. 17. *Is it lawful*] They make it a case of conscience. Dissembled sanctity is double iniquity. Covetousness goes cloaked or coloured, 1 Thess. ii. 5. So doth malice most times; but God will wash off its varnish with rivers of brimstone.

To give tribute] Κῆνσον, a kind of coin proper to this purpose. The Jews paid then to the Romans, as now they do to the pope, and other princes of Italy, a yearly rent for the very heads they wear. And yet how they brave it to our Saviour, and say, John viii. 33, "We were never in bondage to any man." And there is not a more vain-glorious people this day under heaven than the Jews, saith Alsted.

Ver. 18. *Why tempt ye me, ye hypocrites*] Hypocrites pretend Nathaniel in the skin of a Nicodemus, saith one; of a Demas rather, who made fair weather for a while, but at length forsook Paul, and became an idolatrous priest at Thessalonica, if Dorotheus may be believed. Jesus perceived these men's wickedness, and detected it. So dealt Peter by Simon Magus, whom Philip took for a very honest man, and baptized him. All will out at length; *Quod sis esse velis, nihilque malis.* Martial.

Ver. 19. *They brought unto him a penny*] *Monachi pecunias attingere pro piaculo ducunt.* No Capuchin among the Papists may take or touch silver. This metal is as very anathema to these, as the wedge of gold to Achan; at the offer whereof he starts back, as Moses from the serpent. Yet he carries a boy with him that takes and carries it, and never complains of either metal or measure.

Ver. 20. *Whose is this image,* &c.] Not that he knew not whose it was, but that he might refell them by their own answers, judge them out of their own mouth; and that the people (into whose hatred they thought by this captious question to draw him) might see that this was not more his than the Pharisees' own sentence.

They said unto him, Cæsar's] Julius Cæsar was the first that had his own face stamped in the Roman coin.

Ver. 21. *Render therefore unto Cæsar*] Not give, but render; as who should say, Ye give him but what belongs to him; ye do him but right, ye help him but to his own, and that which he may justly require of you, *In reddendo hostimentum patrocinii et defensionis,* in lieu of his care toward you.

And unto God the things that are God's] The Greek article is twice repeated, when he speaks of God more than when of Cæsar; to show, saith one, that our special care should be, τὰ τοῦ Θεοῦ τῷ Θεῷ, to give God his due. For if Cæsar will take to himself God's part, by commanding that which is sinful, to pay him such a tribute,

---

[1] παγιδεύσωσι, *Metaph. a venatione ferarum.* Piscator. | *Metaph. a feris quibus tenduntur laquei et retia.* Par.

Non est tributum Cæsaris, sed servitium diaboli, saith Chrysostom, it is not a paying of tribute to Cæsar, but a doing service to the devil. *Cur non et animam nostram Dei imaginem soli Deo consignemus*, saith one. Let God only have our soul, sith it bears his image. That was a witless and wicked speech of him, that said, that he had two souls in one body, the one for God, if he pleased, the other for any one else that would. But that was a gallant speech of the Prince of Condee, who being taken prisoner by Charles IX. of France, and put to his choice whether he would go to mass or be put to death, or suffer perpetual imprisonment? *Ut eligeret ex his tribus unum vel missam, vel mortem, vel perpetuum carcerem*, &c. (Hist. Gall.) The former, said he, by God's grace, I will never do. And for the two latter, let the king do with me what he pleaseth. God, I hope, will turn all to the best.

Ver. 22. *They marvelled and left him, and went their way*] With a flea in their ear, as we say.

Demitto auriculas ut iniquæ mentis asellus. Hor.

Confounded they were that they were so disappointed. Christ shaped them such an answer, as they could neither dislike nor digest. "The wise man's eyes are in his head, but the fool walketh in darkness," Eccl. ii. 14. *Ad pœnitentiam properat, cito qui judicat*. He that precipitates a censure shall soon see cause to repent him. How oft doth an open mouth prove a man's purgatory? We had great need therefore carry a pair of balances betwixt our lips, lest we be entangled in our talk. For,

Sic licet in partes circumspectissimus omnes,
Nemo tamen vulpes, nemo cavere potest.

Ver. 23. *The same day came to him the Sadducees*] *Vulpium capita possunt esse aversa, quorum tamen caudæ in face eadem coeunt.* Heretics may differ as much from one another, as they all do from the truth. Both Pharisees and Sadducees can conspire against Christ, though they cannot consent among themselves. These Sadducees were a brutish sect and sort of Jews, that held many monstrous opinions. Some of them are set down, Acts xxiii. 8. Divers other more gross may be read of in Josephus, who also tells us that they were but few of them, yet of the chief among the people. (Ant. 18, 2; B. J. 2, 7.) And no wonder, for even at this day atheists and epicures are rife; and among the great ones especially, who either think or could wish at least, there would be no resurrection, &c.

Ver. 24. *Master, Moses said*] They pretend Scripture, so did the devil, Matt. iv. So do heretics all; *Sed sensum afferunt, non auferunt*, but they fetch not the meaning from the Scripture, but fasten a sense (even that of their own devising) on the Scripture: *Cædem Scripturarum faciunt ad materiam suam*, saith Tertullian. They taw the text, as shoemakers do their over-leathers, saith Polydore Virgil, that they may

bring them to serve their turns; they lay the dead child of their own corrupt glosses in the bosom of holy Scripture, and then cry out, It is hers, and not theirs.

If a man die, having no children] This law these Sadducees seem to approve, when indeed they jeer it, as the mother of much monstrous confusion, if there ever be a resurrection. So deals the devil and his janizaries (Jesuits, I should say) at this day, by both Scriptures and fathers, whom they either elude or deride, further than they serve their turn, to confirm their falsehoods.

Raise up seed unto his brother] Our children are a principal part of ourselves, even the seed; as though now there were nothing left in us but the chaff.

Ver. 25. *When he had married a wife, deceased*] Thus they that will marry shall have trouble, aye, and that in the flesh, wherein they haply promised themselves most comfort and contentment. How many are there that seek an happiness here; and when to enjoy it might seem an happiness indeed, they die, and then all their thoughts perish. Instances we have in Alexander the Great, Julius Cæsar, Tamerlane, who making great preparation for the conquest of the Turkish Empire, died of an ague in the midst of his great hope and greatest power. The like might be showed of many learned men, that died, when they might have been most useful, as Keckerman, Perkins, Preston, Pemble, young Drusius, &c. All our learning is soon refuted with one black Theta, which, understanding us not, snappeth us unrespectively without distinction, and putteth at once a period to our writing and to our being.

Ver. 26. *And the third unto the seventh*] Happy it was, if seeing their brethren fall so fast, themselves were warned to number their own days and provide for death's coming. But this is not easily done; for we naturally dream of an immortality, Psal. xlix. 11; and it is death to us to think of death, though we see so many daily die before us. It fareth with us for the most part as with fatting cattle. The butcher comes to-day, and fetcheth away one, to-morrow and fetcheth away another, &c. The rest that are left behind do neither miss their fellows nor dread their own destiny. So here, this is brutish stupidity, shake it off.

Ver. 27. *And last of all the woman*, &c.] It is scarce credible that one woman should outlive seven husbands. But grant she did, yet impartial death, that had so oft-times cut off her head, hit her heart at last. Death, as an archer, aiming at us, misseth us eftsoons, and hitteth haply some beyond us, some short of us, some on either hand of us; now our superiors, now our inferiors, now our equals, till at length we also are wounded; and the longer death's hand is exercised, the more skilful it grows. Joannes de Temporibus, who is said to have lived in France above 300 years, died at length; so did the old, old, the very old man, A. D. 1635.

Ver. 29. *Ye do err, not knowing*] Ignorance is a breeder. All sins are seminally in ignorance. St Paul thanks it for all his persecutions, 1 Tim. i. 13. Aristotle makes it the mother of all the misrule in the world. (Ethic. 3.) All heresies, saith Chemnitius, are known to have proceeded, *Vel ex supercilio Samosateni fastu, vel ex Arrii dialectica, vel ex Ætii* ὀλιγομαθεία, from pride, sophistry, or ignorance.

Nor the power of God] Who can as easily raise the dead as he did at first create them. This the Athenians, with all their learning, understood not; and therefore counted all that St Paul could say to it, bibble babble (σπερμολόγος), because he preached Jesus, and *Anastasis*, or the resurrection, which they took to be some strange goddess, Acts xvii. 18, 19. They saw not how there could possibly be a regress from a privation to an habit. Neither can any of us see it, unless God by his Spirit of revelation give us to know what is the exceeding greatness of his power, according to the working of his mighty power, which he wrought in raising Christ, and us by him, Eph. i. 19, 20, where it is easy to observe a six-fold gradation in the original, and all to set forth the power of God, in Christ's and our resurrection.

Ver. 30. *For in the resurrection they neither marry*] Therefore our condition then shall be better than that of Adam's in Paradise, where he had need of a meet help, *Chenegdo*, such another as himself, a second self. St Luke adds the reason why men shall not marry in the resurrection, viz., they can die no more; and therefore need not marry for propagation of their kind and immortalizing of their name. Mahomet, as he professed that himself had a special licence given him by God to know what women he would, and to put them away when he would; so he promised to all his votaries and adherents the like carnal pleasures at the resurrection. Sensualists cast God and the things of God into a dishonourable mould; they rise not above their spring.

But are as the angels of God] ἰσάγγελοι. Are, that is, certainly shall be; yea, in their Head, Christ, they are so already. For God hath even here "raised us up together, and made us sit together in heavenly places in Christ Jesus," Eph. ii. 6. And at the resurrection, the just shall shine as the sun in heaven, nay, as the Son of God himself, with whom they shall appear in glory, as his spouse. *Uxor fulget radiis mariti*, is a maxim in law. Their vile bodies shall be conformed to his most glorious body, Phil. iii. 21, the standard in beauty, brightness, agility, immortality, &c., and other like unspeakable angelical qualities and perfections. Their souls shall be freed from all evil, fraught with all fulness both of grace and of glory.

Ver. 31. *Have ye not read*] In Moses, whose writings only they received, rejecting the rest. And the superstitious Jews at this day are said in their liturgy to read two lessons, one out of the law, which is read by some chief person,

another out of the prophets, which is read by some boy or mean companion. For savouring somewhat of these old Sadducees, they will in no sort do honour, neither attribute they that authority to any part of the Bible that they do to their law, which they do usually carry about their synagogue at the end of the service in procession, with many ornaments of crowns and sceptres; the children kissing it as it passeth by them.

Spoken unto you by God] It is God that speaketh in the holy Scriptures; it is the express mind of God that is there set forth unto us. See my True Treasure, p. 10, &c.

Ver 32. *God is not the God of the dead*] That is, in the Sadducees' sense, utterly dead and extinct for ever, but in St Paul's sense, Rom. xiv. 9. He is the God of the dead. For the dead bodies also of the faithful, whiles they lie rotting in the grave, and resolved into dust, are united to Christ; by means whereof a substance is preserved, sin only is rotted with its concomitant infirmities. But the rotting of the body is but to refine it; it is but as the rotting of corn under the earth, 1 Cor. xv. 36, that it may arise more glorious. Once, death to the saints is neither total, but of the body only; nor yet perpetual, but for a time only. See both these together, Rom. viii. 10, 11. Further, from this verse we may learn, that there is a two-fold knowledge to be gotten from holy Scriptures: 1. Express, "I am the God of Abraham," &c. 2. By due deduction and firm inference, God is the God of the living.

Ver. 33. *They were astonished at his doctrine*] This was well; but St Luke (xx. 39, 40) adds, that which was more strange: 1. That certain of the scribes said, Master, thou hast well said. No Jesuit had ever so much ingenuity. 2. That the Sadducees were thenceforth silent, and said no more.

Præstat herbam dare, quam turpiter pugnare.

Those Romish frogs, the Jesuits, will never have done, though never so much set down, but be still up with their hateful Brekekekex-coax-coax. (Aristoph. in Ranis.)

Ver. 34. *But when the Pharisees*] *Nunquam bella bonis, nunquam certamina desunt.* Truth never wants an adversary. Christ had many conflicts all his life long, but most and sharpest at last cast. At death, Satan will muster up all his forces against a Christian; that last encounter is like to be the sharpest; as Israel in the wilderness met with much hardship; but when they entered the land, all the kings of Canaan combined against them.

Ver. 35. *Then one of them which was a lawyer*] Pareus gathereth out of Mark, chap. xii. 28, that this lawyer was one of them that had applauded Christ for his conquest over the Sadducees in the last conflict, Luke xx. 39, and that for a penance he was enjoined by his fellow Pharisees to undertake this following disputation with Christ: *Ad liberandum igitur se suspicione, partes disputandi adversus eum nunc sibi imponi a collegio patitur.*

Tempting him, and saying] Saint Peter saith, "They found no guile in his mouth," which implies that they sought it, 1 Pet. ii. 23. There are that hear us merely to catch, cavil, and quarrel.

Ver. 36. *Which is the great commandment*] The Rabbins reckoned up 613 commandments of the law; and distinguished them into the greater and the lesser. These later they thought might be neglected or violated with little or no guilt. The Romish Pharisee have also their venial sins, their peccadillos, as we know; but the Scripture makes all sin mortal and destructory. A little strange fire might seem a small matter, yet it was such a sin as made all Israel guilty, as appears by the sacrifices offered for that sin, Lev. xvi.

Ver. 37. *Thou shalt love the Lord*] God must be loved and honoured by us, ἤ ὅλος ἤ μὴ ὅλως, saith one; truly, that there be no halting, and totally, that there be no halving; he will not divide with the devil, as the Circassians are said to divide their whole life between rapine and religion. God's service must be the *totum hominis*, Eccl. xii. 13; and the *bonum hominis*, Mic. vi. 8. We should love him infinitely; which, because we cannot, we must love him unfeignedly; but how far short we come of loving him with all our heart, soul, strength, &c. (which yet the Papists affirm feasible), appears by our lives, which, do what we can, are fuller of sins than the firmament is of stars or the furnace of sparks.

Ver. 38. *This is the first and great commandment*] In respect of order, quantity, and dignity. The second table is fulfilled in the first, and Luther is bold to say, *Primo præcepto reliquorum omnium observantia præcipitur;* in the first commandment is commanded the keeping of all the rest. We rightly love our very selves no further than we love God. And for others, we are bound to love our friends in him, our foes for him.

Ver. 39. *And the second is like unto it*] For it hath, 1. The same author, God "spake all these words." 2. The same tie. 3. The same sanction and punishment of the violation. 4. It requires the same kind of love and service; for the love of our neighbour is the service of God.

Love thy neighbour as thyself] Now, thou lovest thyself truly, really, fervently, freely, constantly, hiding thine own defects and deformities as much as may be. Thou wouldst have others rejoice with thee and condole with thee as occasion serves. Go thou now and do likewise to others. Howbeit our Saviour strains us up a peg higher, John xiii. 34. His new commandment of the gospel is, that we love one another not only as we love ourselves, but as he loved us. This form hath something in it that is more express (in which respect partly it is called a new commandment), and for the incomparable sufficiency of the precedent is matchless, and more full of incitation to fire affection.

Ver. 40. *Hang all the law and prophets*] Yea, and the gospel too; for love is both the complement of the law and the supplement of the gospel, Rom. xiii. 10; John xiii. 34. It is the filling up of the law (as the word πλήρωμα signifieth), for that it clotheth the duties of the law with the glory of a due manner, and seateth them upon their due subjects, with unwearied labours of constant well-doing. The prophets also hang (κρέμανται) upon the same nail of love with the law, so some frame the metaphor here used. As some others rather think that our Saviour in this expression alludeth to the Jewish phylacteries, Heb. *Totaphoth*, which were scrolls of parchment having the commandments written in them, which the Pharisees wear about their heads and arms to mind them of obedience to the law.

Ver. 41. *While the Pharisees were gathered*] *i. e.* Before the former meeting was dissolved. We should watch for and catch at all opportunities of working upon the worst. Dr Taylor preached every time he could get his people together, holyday or else.

Ver. 42. *What think ye of Christ?*] *Christus utramque paginam impleret.* All our search should be with those wise men for the babe of Bethlehem, who is wrapped up, as it were, in the swathing-bands of both the Testaments.

Whose son is he?] They were curious in genealogies. A shame therefore it was for them to be ignorant of Christ's descent and pedigree.

They say unto him, The Son of David] Herein they said well, but not all; for they conceived no otherwise of Christ than as of a mere man. Our Saviour therefore takes a text out of Psal. cx., and thereby convinceth them of his divinity. We must be well versed in the mystery of Christ, and neglect nothing needful to be known by us.

Ver. 43. *How then doth David in spirit*] The Spirit possessed David after a sort, and by his mouth uttered what he would publish to the Church concerning the Godhead of Christ. "Holy men spake of old as they were acted by the Holy Ghost," as they were forcibly moved, or borne away, and, as it were, carried out of themselves by the Holy Ghost (φερόμενοι), 2 Pet. i. 21.

Ver. 44. *The Lord said unto my Lord*] God the Father to God the Son; these two differ no otherwise than that the one is the Father, and not the Son, the other is the Son, and not the Father.

Sit thou on my right hand] As my fellow and co-equal, Zech. xiii. 7; Phil. ii. 6. And as Christ is at the right hand of his Father, so is the Church at the right hand of Christ, Psal. xlv. 9, which is a place both of greatest dignity and safety.

Ver. 45. *Lord, how is he his Son?*] This is that great mystery of godliness, which angels intently look into, 1 Pet. i. 12, as the cherubims did of old into the mercy-seat. That Christ should be David's Lord and David's Son, God and man in one person, this is that wonder of wonders. Well might his name be Wonderful, Isa. ix. 6.

Ver. 46. And no man was able to answer]
Though they were subtle sophisters, and mighty
in the Scriptures, yet they had nothing to oppose.
Magna est veritas, et valebit. Great is the truth,
and shall prevail.

Neither durst any man, &c.] How easily can
God button up the mouths of our busiest adversaries, yea, and plead for us in their consciences,
as he did for Mr Bradford and many more of the
martyrs, whom as they could not out-reason, so
neither could they but conceive well of the
martyrs' innocency, triumphing in their persecutors' consciences.

CHAPTER XXIII.

Ver. 1. Then spake Jesus to the multitude, &c.]
CHRIST having confuted and confounded the
Scribes and Pharisees, turns him to the people and
to his disciples; and that he might do nothing
to the detriment of the truth, he here cautioneth
that they despise not the doctrine of the Pharisees
so far as it was sound and sincere without leaven;
but try all things, holding fast that which was
good. Be advised, and remember to search into
the truth of what you hear, was the counsel of
Epicharmus. Νῆφε καὶ μέμνησο ἀπιστεῖν, *Videas
cui fidas. Deligas quem diligas.*

Ver. 2. Sit in Moses' chair] i. e. Have the ordinary office of teaching the people, but *quo jure,*
he questioneth not. The priests and Levites
should have done it, but the Scribes and Pharisees had for present taken it upon them, stept
into the chair, and there set themselves,[1] Rom.
ii. 20. So Hildebrand and his successors have
invaded Peter's chair, as they call the see of Rome;
but what said an ancient? *Non habent Petri
hæreditatem, qui Petri fidem non habent.* They
have no right to Peter's chair that have not
Peter's faith. The Index Expurgatorius commands (*sublatâ fide*) instead of *Fidem Petri,* to
print it *Sedem Petri. Perfrica frontem,* said
Calvus to Vatinius, *et digniorem te dic qui Prætor
fieres quam Catonem,* Put on a good face, and say
that thou art fitter for the office than Cato himself. (Quintil. lib. ix. cap. 2.) But what a bold
face had Barcæna the Jesuit, who, *Diabolo adve-
nienti occurrit obviam petiitque ut cathedram ejus
occuparet, quia erat dignior,* meeting the devil,
required his chair of him, as one that better deserved it. He had his desire, I doubt not. But
if Scribes and Pharisees sat in Moses' chair, it is
no news than for bad men to succeed better; as
Timotheus Herulus did Proterius the good Bishop
of Alexandria, and as Arminius did Junius in
the professor's place at Leyden.

Ver. 3. All therefore whatsoever] Not their
traditions, superstitions, and corrupt glosses upon
the law, but whatsoever they teach that is agreeable to truth; so long as they sit close to Moses'
chair, and keep it warm, as it were, hearken to

them. God's good gifts are to be acknowledged
and improved even in the worst, as David made
Saul's epitaph, 2 Sam. i., though the devil preached
his funeral, 1 Sam. xxviii. 19.

But do not ye after their works] Saith Chrysostom, *Si pastores bene vivunt, eorum lucrum est,
si bene dicunt, tuum. Accipe quod tuum est, omitte
alienum.* If ministers do well, it is their own gain;
if they say well, it is thine. Take thou what
thine own is, and let alone what is another man's.
Sylla and King Richard III. commanded others,
under great penalties, to be virtuous and modest,
when themselves walked the clean contrary way.
A deformed painter may draw a goodly picture;
a stinking breath sound a mighty blast; and he
that hath but a bad voice, show cunning in de-
scant. A blind man may bear a torch in a dark
night, and a harp make music to others, which
itself is not sensible of. Posts set for direction
of passengers by the highway side do point out
the way which themselves go not: and sign-
posts tell the traveller there is wholesome diet
or warm lodging within, when themselves remain
in the storms without. Leud preachers are like
spire-steeples, or high pinnacles, which point up
to heaven, but press down to the centre.

For they say, and do not] They had tongues
which spake by the talent, but their hands scarce
wrought by the ounce; like that ridiculous actor
at Smyrna, who pronouncing *O cœlum,* O heaven,
pointed with his finger toward the ground:[2] so
these Pharisees had the heaven commonly at
their tongues' end, but the earth continually at
their fingers' end. In a certain battle against
the Turks, there was a bishop that thus encouraged the army: Play the men, fellow-soldiers,
to-day: and I dare promise you, that if ye die
fighting, ye shall sup to-night with God in heaven. Now after the battle was begun the bishop
withdrew himself; and when some of the soldiers
inquired among themselves what was become of
the bishop, and why he would not take a supper
with them that night in heaven, others answered, *Hodie sibi jejunium indixit, ideoque non
vult nobiscum in cœlo cœnare.* This is fasting-day
with him, and therefore he will eat no supper,
no, not in heaven. Epictetus was wont to say
that there were many philosophers (we may say
divines) ἄνευ τοῦ πράττειν, μεχρὶ τοῦ λέγειν, as far
as a few words would go. But ὦ τλήμων, ἀρετὴ
λόγος ἀρ᾽ ἦσθα, &c., is religion now become a word?
goodness a name? as Brutus once cried out. Should
it be said of holiness, as it was once in another
place, *audivimus famam;* we have heard the fame
thereof with our ears, and that is all? Job xxviii.
22. The foolish virgins were found with their *sic
dicentes,* but the good servants shall be found with
their *sic facientes.* Christ was full of grace as well
as truth. John Baptist was both a burning and
shining light. Origen's teaching and living were
said to be both one.[3] That is the best sermon
surely, that is digged out of a man's own breast,

---

[1] καθίζω, *Sedeo. colloco.*
[2] Of this actor, Polemo, chaffing, said, οὗτος τῇ χειρὶ σο-
λοικίζει.

[3] *Spectemur agendo.* John i. 16. Καὶ ἔδειξε καὶ ἐδίδαξε.
Basil. *Quod jussit et gessit.* Bern. Ep. 41.

when he practiseth what he preacheth, *non verbis solum prædicans sed exemplis*, as Eusebius testifieth of Origen, and Mr Gataker of Mr Stock. As the want hereof occasioned Campian to write *ministris eorum nihil vilius*, their ministers are most base.

Ver. 4. *For they bind heavy burdens, &c.*] Their human traditions : so do the Popish doctors (heirs herein to the Pharisees, of whom this sermon is not more historical than of the other it is prophetical). The inferior clergy they make preach every day in Lent without intermission, throughout all Italy in the greater cities ; so as six days in the week they preach on the Gospel of the days, and on the Saturday in honour and praise of our Lady. Whereas the pope and bishops preach not at all. So for the laity ; they must fast with bread and water ; when the priests have their suckets and other sweet-meats three or four times on their mock-fast-days. What should we speak of their pilgrimages to Peru, Jerusalem, &c. ; penances, satisfactions, &c. ? And no man must question, but obey without sciscitation. Walter Mapes, sometime Archdeacon of Oxford, relating the pope's gross simony, concludes, *Sit tamen Domina materque nostra Roma baculus in aqua fractus, et absit credere quæ vidimus.* In things that make against our Lady-mother Rome, we may not believe our own eyes.

Ver. 5. *To be seen of men*] Theatrically, thrasonically, and for ostentation, as stage-players, or painted faces. See notes on chap. vi. ver. 2, 5. Saints more seek to be good than seem to be so.

They make broad their phylacteries] That is, conservatories, so called. 1. Because by the use of them the law was kept in remembrance. 2. Because the superstitious Pharisees conceited, that by the wearing of them about their necks, themselves might be kept from danger, as by so many spells : what they were, see the notes above, on Matt. xxii. 40.

Enlarge the borders of their garments] God had charged the Pharisees to bind the law to their hand, and before their eyes, Deut. vi. 8, wherein (as Jerome and Theophylact well interpret it) he meant the meditation and practice of his law. They (saith a learned author) like unto the foolish patient, which when the physician bids him take the prescript, eats up the paper ;[1] if they could but get a list of parchment upon their left arm and next their heart, and another scroll to tie upon their forehead, and four corners of fringe, or (if these be denied) a red thread in their hand, thought they might say, " Blessed be thou of the Lord, I have done the commandment of the Lord," 1 Sam. xvi. 13. What was this but, as Mr Tindal said in another case, to think to quench their thirst by sucking the ale-bowl ?

Ver. 6. *And love the uppermost rooms*] Which is a singular vanity, and yet hath bred greatest contestation in the Church ; as between the bishops of Rome and Constantinople, the archbishops of Canterbury and York justling in parliament for precedency, even unto blows and bloodshed : what doleful effects followed upon the contention between the Lord Protector and his brother in King Edward VI.'s days, raised by their ambitious wives, who could not agree about place ! The apostle's rule is, " in honour to prefer one another," Rom. xii. 10. And true humility is like true balm, that still in water sinks to the bottom ; like the violet, the sweetest but lowest of flowers, which hangs the head downwards, and hides itself with its own leaves.

Ver. 7. *And to be called of men Rabbi*] They were tickled with high titles, and thought it a goodly thing to be held and styled magnificos, to be fly-blown with flatteries. There is not a more vain-glorious people under heaven than the Jews. Hence that rabble of titles amongst them in this order (brought in a little before the nativity of our Saviour), Rabbi Rabban, Rab, Rabbi, Gaon, Moreh, Morenu and Moreh tsedek. So the friars proceed in their vain-glorious titles, from Padre benedicto to Padre Angelo, then Archangelo, Cherubino, and lastly Cerephino, which is the top of perfection. Are not these those ὑπέρογκα ματαιότητος the apostle inveighs against, those great " swelling titles of vanity ?" 2 Pet. ii. 18 ; Jude 16.

Ver. 8. *Be not ye called Rabbi*] Do not ambitiously affect such a title, as if you were the only ones, and others not worthy to be named in the same day with you. Swelling in the body is an ill symptom, but worse in the soul.

For one is your Master] καθηγητὴς. Your guide to godliness and happiness, your doctor and dictator, your oracle, your *ipse dixit*, whose bare word you are to take, without further proof or pawn.

And all ye are brethren] Not as the pope calls his cardinals brethren, when in creating them he useth this form, *Estote fratres nostri, et principes mundi. Odi fastum illius ecclesiæ*, saith Basil, which caused the lamentable separation of the Eastern or Greek Church from communion with the Latin, the other four patriarchs dividing themselves from the Bishop of Rome, for his encroaching upon them.

Ver. 9. *Call no man your father*] *i. e.* Give no man absolute power over you ; be not the servants of men, or slaves to their opinions or mandates, as friars are to their superiors, to argue or debate on whose commands is held high presumption ; to search their reasons, proud curiosity ; to detract or disobey them, breach of vow equal to sacrilege.

Ver. 10. *One is your Master*] Where then are *magistri nostri parisienses ?* our *doctores resolutissimi ?* our masters of opinions, whose word must stand for a law, whose tenets must pass for oracles ?[2] By the canon law, *Omnes sanctiones apo-*

---

[1] *Ac si puellus audito patris pii vestigiis insistendum, patris iter facientis singula vestigia observaret, et in iisdem pedes suos poneret.*

[2] *Quibus nihil placet nisi quod e capitis sui liripipio ipsi protulerint.* Muchesius.

stolicæ sedis irrefragabiliter sunt observandæ. The pope may not be disobeyed.

Ver. 11. *Shall be your servant*] The word signifies one that is ready pressed to raise dust, to do his utmost endeavour with all possible expedition in any business that he is set about. *Præbestinans, expeditus, paratus, promptus.*

Ver. 12. *And whosoever shall exalt himself,* &c.] Lo here a great miracle, saith Augustine,[1] God is on high, and yet the higher thou liftest up thyself, the farther thou art from him; the lower thou humblest thyself, the nearer he draweth to thee. Low things he looketh close upon, that he may raise them: proud things he knows afar off, that he may depress them. The proud Pharisee pressed as near God as he could: the poor publican, not daring to do so, stood aloof off; yet was God far from the Pharisee, near to the publican.

Ver. 13. *Woe unto you, Scribes,* &c.] By these eight dreadful woes, as by so many links of an adamantine chain, our Saviour draws these hypocrites down to hell, their place, and there leaves them to be reserved unto judgment. St Jerome was called *Fulmen Ecclesiasticum,* the Church's thunderbolt. How much more might this be attributed to Christ? How terribly doth he here thunderstrike these stupid Pharisees, though he saw well (saith Father Latimer) that whosoever will be busy with *væ vobis* shall shortly after come *coram nobis.*

Ye shut up the kingdom of heaven] By hiding heavenly truths, teaching damnable errors, excommunicating the well-affected, or corrupting them by evil counsel and example; and all this, ἔμπροσθεν *coram et in os,* before men, and to their faces, making fools of them, even while they look on, casting a mist before their eyes, as those Egyptian jugglers did, Exod. vii., and keeping from them that collyrium that should cure and clear up their eye-sight, Rev. iii. 18. Thus did Arundel, Archbishop of Canterbury, who bound up the word of God that it might not be preached in his time (as the historian's words are[2]), and was therefore (according to this woe here denounced) so smitten in his tongue that he could neither swallow nor speak for certain days before he died. Steven Gardiner was plagued in like manner, for like reason. And generally the Popish clergy are vexed with that grievous and noisome sore of devilish spite against the Reformation, Rev. xvi. 2, which they therefore oppose with might and main till wrath come upon them to the utmost. And albeit many of them escape the visible vengeance of God, yet this terrible woe, as a moth, doth secretly eat them up like a garment, and as a worm, eateth them up like wood, Isa. li. 8, as it did these Pharisees; on whose outside nothing could be discerned, all was as before, but their souls were blasted, seared, and sealed up to destruction. He that hath drunk poison falls not down dead presently in the place, but he hath his death about

him, as we say. Saul lived and reigned long after he was cast off by God; and the very devils are respited in regard of their full torment, but the more is behind.

Ver. 14. *Ye devour widows' houses*] Though they pretended to be great fasters, Luke xviii. 12, yet their bellies prepared deceit, as Eliphaz hath it, Job xv. 35, and their throats (those open sepulchres) swallowed up whole houses (such was their covetousness), and that of widows (such was their cruelty), and that under a pretence of long prayers, which was their hypocrisy; for while their lips seemed to pray, they were but chewing that morsel, that murdering morsel that made them receive the greater damnation. *Multi in terris manducant, quod apud inferos digerant,* saith Augustine. Many devour that on earth that they must digest in hell, where the never-dying worm will feed greedily upon all such covetous caitiffs as have the greedy worm under their tongues, and their ill-gotten goods gotten already into their bowels, as these Pharisees had; which therefore God shall fetch thence again with a vengeance, τὰ ἔνοντα, Luke xi. 41; Job xx. 15.

Make long prayers] God takes not men's prayers by tale, but by weight. He respecteth not the arithmetic of our prayers, how many they are, nor the rhetoric of our prayers, how eloquent they are; nor the geometry of our prayers, how long they are; nor the music of our prayers, the sweetness of our voice, nor the logic of our prayers, or the method of them, but the divinity of our prayers is that which he so much esteemeth. He looketh not for any James with horny knees through assiduity in prayer; nor for any Bartholomew with a century of prayers for the morning and as many for the evening; but St Paul, his frequency of praying with fervency of spirit, without all tedious prolixities and vain-babblings, this is it that God maketh most account of. It is not a servant's going to and fro, but the despatch of his business that pleaseth his master. It is not the loudness of a preacher's voice, but the holiness of the matter and the spirit of the preacher, that moveth a wise and intelligent hearer. So here, not gifts, but graces in prayer move the Lord. But these long prayers of the Pharisees were so much the worse, because thereby they sought to entitle God to their sin, yea, they merely mocked him, fleering in his face.

Ver. 15. *Ye compass sea and land*] They walked the round, as the devil doth, to gain proselytes; they spared for no pains to pervert men (as now the Jesuits those *Circulatores et Agyrtæ*). Should not we be as diligent and indefatigable to convert them to God? Shall we not be as busy in building stair-cases for heaven as seducers are in digging descents to hell? If Saul seeking asses found a kingdom, shall not we, by seeking others, find heaven?

Ye make him two-fold more the child of hell]

[1] *Videte magnum miraculum : altus est Deus, &c.*

[2] *Quod verbum Dei alligasset, ne tempore suo prædicaretur.* Tho. Gascon, in Dictionary of Theology.

Either because they relapse to Gentilism, as finding you so vile and vicious in your lives; or because ye teach them only ceremonies and superstitions; or, because you keep them ignorant of Christ, and plant in them an hatred of the truth, as the Jesuits do in their proselytes. So that of them we may say, as Ambrose did of Polemo, who of a drunkard, by hearing Xenocrates, became a philosopher, *Si resipuit a vino, fuit semper tamen temulentus sacrilegio.* Though he be now no drunkard, yet he remains drunk still with superstition.

Ver. 16. *Ye blind guides which say*] His watchmen are blind, was an old complaint, Isa. lvi. 10. Which that it is a foul fault, the Rabbins have there noted from one letter (in the original)[1] of the word rendered watchmen, bigger than his fellows. How many are there that thrust into the ministry, wanting both heart and art to teach the people? These lead their flocks to the pit's brink, wherein if they perish, themselves lie lowermost.

Whosoever shall swear by the gold of the temple] So by the gift on the altar, ver. 18, these, they taught, were tied; the other might for a sum be dispensed with, that swore by the temple or the altar. Not so those that swore by the gold of the temple, that is, dedicated to the temple, or by the gift on the altar; for these oaths brought these blind guides in commodity, which the swearer was forced presently to pay down. The people also were hereby made more free and forward to offer gold for the temple, sacrifices for the altar; because they were made believe that those presents were more precious than either temple or altar. Pretty devices these were to get money; and are they not still practised by Papists? Philip Brasier was abjured in Henry VIII.'s time for saying, that when any cure is done the priests do anoint the images, and make men believe the images do sweat in labouring for them. The rood of grace and blood of Hales is notorious. Our Lady of Loretto hath her churches so stuffed with vowed presents and memories, that they are fain to hang their cloisters and churchyards with them. They teach the people that as they may sooner go to Christ by St Dominick than by St Paul, so to swear by holy relics, and in swearing, to lay hand on them, is a more binding oath than to swear by God, laying hand on the Bible.

Ver. 17. *Whether is greater, the gold,* &c.] The cause must needs be more noble than the effect. But the dust of covetousness had put out the eyes of these buzzards, and expectorated their understandings. It is a besotting sin, and bereaves a man of right reason. *Avidus à non videndo.* Papists, our modern Pharisees, are most corrupt in those things where their honour, ease, or profit is engaged. In the doctrine of the Trinity that toucheth not upon these, they are sound enough.

Or the temple that sanctifieth the gold?] Solomon's temple was stone without and gold within,

[1] מֵם *Uli Tsaddi est majusculum.* Buxtorf. Tiber.

to show, saith one, the resplendent glory of Divine Majesty lurking within a human and humbled body. *Quid est templi illius aurum sive aurea claritas, nisi ad dextram patris sedentis immortalitas atque impassibilitas?* saith Rupertus, what is the gold of the temple but the glory of Christ at God's right hand?

Ver. 18. *But whosoever sweareth by the gift,* &c.] *Ubi utilitas, ibi pietas,* saith Epictetus, where there is gain there is godliness, ὅπου τὸ συμφέρον ἔκει τὸ εὐσεβὲς. And, *Deos quisque sibi utiles cudit,* saith another. All the worldling's ploughing, sailing, building, buying, buts upon commodity, he knows no other deity. These Pharisees strove to reduce all offerings to their own purses and paunches, though they rendered men thereby not only irreligious, but unnatural, Matt. xv. 5, 6. See the notes there.

Ver. 19. *Ye fools and blind*] The second time so, for behold they have rejected the word of the Lord (yea, the Word, the Lord Christ), and what wisdom was in them? Jer. viii. 9. True it is, they were accounted the only wise men. "Where is the wise? where is the scribe?" saith St Paul, 1 Cor. i. 20. As if wise and scribe were terms convertible. And for the Pharisees, they did so carry away the hearts of the people that there was no holy man that was not termed a Pharisee, as we find in their Talmud. And "after the most straitest sect of our religion I lived a Pharisee," saith Paul, Acts xxvi. 5. They were *omnium districtissimi,* and did utterly out-shine and obscure those other sects of Sadducees and Essenes, the latter whereof are not so much as mentioned in the gospel. And yet we see what esteem Christ had of them, and what titles he here bestows upon them. To teach us not to rest in man's applause, nor to think it sufficient that others think well of us. "But let every man prove his own work," Gal. vi. 4, and know that not he that commends himself, or is commended by others, is approved, but he whom the Lord commendeth, 2 Cor. x. 18.

Ver. 20. *Whoso therefore shall swear*] It was not lawful to swear by the altar, or by any creature whatsoever, Jer. v. 7 (much less by idols, Amos viii. 14. "I myself," saith Latimer, "have used in mine earnest matters to say, Yea by St Mary, which indeed is naught"). But though these oaths be formally naught, yet they are finally binding, and being broken, they are plain perjury, because they are all reduced to God himself, no otherwise than if they had been taken expressly by the name of God. Hence it is that the oaths of Papists, Turks, heathens (though superstitious), are obligatory, ὅρκος, *quasi* ἕρκος, An oath is a hedge, which a man may not break.

Ver. 21. *And by him that dwelleth therein*] By his grace in his ordinances, yea, by his glory, which sometimes filled the temple. This temple at Jerusalem, together with that of Diana at Ephesus (which was also built of cedar, in an apish imitation of God's temple, as Vitruvius and others witness) were destroyed much about one and the same time: "Believe me," saith Christ, "the hour cometh, when ye shall neither in this mountain, nor yet at Jerusalem, worship the Father," John iv. 21. Demosthenes saith, "That man's heart is God's best temple, where he dwells with delight, so it be beautified with modesty, piety, justice," &c. "And this is the end of our creation," saith another, "that man should be the temple of God, and God the altar of man."

Ver. 22. *By the throne of God*] Heaven is his throne and earth his footstool; yet may we not conceive that God is commensurable by the place, as if he were partly here and partly elsewhere; but he is everywhere all present. See more in the notes on Matt. v. 34.

Ver. 23. *Ye pay tithe of mint*] The Chaldee word for mint signifies also a book of histories, נבעא; because in that one poor herb large stories of God's wisdom, might, and love are described unto us. In tithing this and other pot-herbs the Pharisees were over and above solicitous, and even superstitious, and all for a name. So in the year of grace 1435, Capistranus the Minorite, being sent into Germany and other countries by Pope Nicholas, to preach obedience to the see of Rome, got a great deal of credit and respect to his doctrine by putting down dicing, carding, dancing, feasting, mask-interludes, &c., although he taught not one syllable of sound doctrine, touching Christ and his merits, obedience of faith, patience of hope, &c. There are both *magnalia et minutula legis*, the great and the lesser things of the law; both must be looked to. Hypocrites are nice in the one, but negligent of the other.

Judgment, mercy, and faith] So of old, to those bodily exercises and external rites, so stood upon by the hypocrites in their times, Isaiah opposeth judgment and justice, chap. i.; Hosea opposeth mercy and kindness, chap. iv.; Zechariah opposeth truth and fidelity, chap. viii., as more to be looked after and laboured for.

Ver. 24. *Which strain at a gnat*, &c.] A proverbial speech, warranting the lawful use of such expressions for illustration of a truth. The Greeks have a like proverb, Ανδρίαντα γαργαλίζειν, to gargle down an image, statue, or coloss; that is, to make no bones of a foul fault when matters of less moment are much scrupled. Saul kept a great stir about eating the flesh with the blood, when he made nothing of shedding innocent blood, 1 Sam. xiv. 33. Doeg was detained before the Lord by some voluntary vow belike, 1 Sam. xxi. 7. But better he had been further off, for any good he did there. The priests made conscience of putting the price of blood into the treasury, Matt. xxvii. 6, who yet made no conscience of imbruing their hands in the innocent blood of the Lamb of God. The Begardi and Beginnæ, a certain kind of heretics, A. D. 1322, held this mad opinion, that a man might here attain to

perfection, and that having attained to it, he might do whatsoever his nature led him to; that *fornicari peccatum non esse reputabant: at mulieri osculum figere mortale facinus arbitrabantur*, fornication was no sin, but to kiss a woman was a mortal wickedness, &c.[1] Archbishop Bancroft fell foul upon Master Paul Bayn, for a little black-work-edging about his cuffs, threatening to lay him by the heels for it, when far greater faults in others were winked at.

Ver. 25. *Ye make clean the outside*] True Ephraimites, or rather Canaanites, so they are called, Hos. xii. 7, 8, that is, mere natural men, Ezek. xvi. 4; the balances of deceit were in their hands, they loved to oppress, yet so long as thereby they grew rich, they flattered themselves, and said, "In all my labours they shall find none iniquity in me, that were sin." Hypocrites if they can but make fair to the world-ward it is enough. But as the fish sepia is bewrayed by the black colour which she casteth out to cover her; so the hypocrite is convinced by the very show of godliness under which he hoped to have lurked. God so discovers his deceitful courses, as that his wickedness is showed before the whole congregation, Prov. xxvi. 26.

Ver. 26. *Cleanse first that which is within*] God loveth truth in the inwards, Psal. li. 6. "O Jerusalem, wash thy heart," Jer. iv. 14 (not thy hands only, as Pilate did); this breeds constancy and evenness in all our outward behaviours, Jam. iv. 8. Grace and nature both begin at the heart, at the centre, and from thence goes to the circumference. Art and hypocrisy begin with the face and outward lineaments.

Ver. 27. *Ye are like unto whited sepulchres*] The Jews had their vaults or caves for burial. These the wealthier sort would paint, garnish, beautify at the mouth or entrance of them. And hereunto our Saviour alludeth, *Intus Nero, foris Cato: loquitur hic ut Piso, vivit ut Gallomus*, &c. It was said of the Sarmatians, that all their virtue was outward; and of Sejanus, that he had only a semblance of honesty, *Intus summa adipiscendi libido*, within he was full of extortion and excess.[2] Hypocrites seem as glow-worms, to have both light and heat; but touch them, and they have neither. The Egyptian temples were beautiful on the outside, when within ye should find nothing but some serpent or crocodile. Apothecaries' boxes oft have goodly titles, when yet they hold not one dram of any good drug. A certain stranger coming on embassage unto the senators of Rome, and colouring his hoary hair and pale cheeks with vermilion hue, a grave senator espying the deceit, stood up, and said, "What sincerity are we to expect from this man's hands, whose locks, and looks, and lips do lie?" Think the same of all painted hypocrites. These we may compare (as Lucian doth his Grecians) to a fair gilt bossed book; look within it, and there is the tragedy of Thyestes; or perhaps Arrius' Thalya; the

---

[1] Funcc. Chron. *ex Massei*, xviii.

[2] *Omnis Sarmatarum virtus extra ipsos.* Tac. i. 10. *Palam compositus pudor*, &c. Tac.

name of a muse, the matter heresy : or Conradus Vorstius' book-monster, that hath *De Deo* in the front, but atheism and blasphemy in the text.

Ver. 28. *But within ye are full*, &c.] Fair professors they were, but foul sinners, not close, but gross hypocrites, such as knew themselves to be so ; like as Jeroboam's wife knew herself to be disguised, when she went to the prophet ; and as the whore that offered sacrifice to cover her whoredom, Prov. vii. 14. This hypocrisy goes worthily coupled here with iniquity. It ariseth from secret atheism, as in Ananias and Sapphira, that noble pair of hypocrites, and paveth a way to the unpardonable sin, as in these Pharisees.

Ver. 29. *Ye build the tombs*, &c.] And lost their cost, because they received not their doctrine. So do the Papists at this day in their pretended honouring the ancient saints and martyrs, whose religion and practices they persecute in the true professors.[1] How much better Rabus Crispen, the French chronicler, Knox, Fox, and others, who have raised the martyrs, as so many Phœnixes, out of their ashes again, by recording their holy lives and Christian deaths ! And how shall Cope and Kemp stink for ever in the nostrils of all good people! The former for fouling so much fair paper in railing at, and casting reproach upon, the holy martyrs of the Protestant religion, in his sixth dialogue especially : the latter for disgracing them some few years since, excusing the powder traitors at the same time, in a sermon at St Mary's in Cambridge.

Ver. 30. *If we had been in the days*] Either these men grossly dissembled, or their hearts greatly deceived them ; for certainly a Herod and Herodias to John Baptist would have been an Ahab and Jezebel to Elias. But as it was said of Demosthenes, that he was excellent at praising the worthy acts of ancestors, not so at imitating of them.[2] In like sort may we say of the Pharisees, they could well declaim against their forefathers' cruelties, but not so well disclaim them. They were *adversus sua ipsorum vitia facundi satis*, as one speaketh in a like case. Shrill accusers of themselves.

Ver. 31. *Wherefore ye be witnesses*, &c.] Here our Saviour casts all their cost in their teeth, as if thereby they had meant to commend their fathers' cruelty in killing the prophets, sith they abetted it by persecuting him and his to the death. Malice is commonly hereditary, and runs in the blood ; and (as we use to say of runnet) the older it is, the stronger ; as in the deadly feud of Scotland taken away by King James.

Ver. 32. *Fill ye up then the measure*] *Ironice dictum.* It gives us to understand that sinners are stinted, and cannot do what mischief they would. If at any time they exceed their commission (as they are apt) and help forward the affliction, as

out of their innate malice they will, God will soon grow jealous for Jerusalem, and take them off, Zech. i. 14, 15. When wickedness hath filled her ephah, God will soon transport it into the land of Shinar, Zech. v. 8—11. When it is once ripe in the field, God will not suffer it to shed, to grow again, but cuts it up by a just and seasonable vengeance.

Ver. 33. *Ye serpents*] *Serpentum tot sunt venena, quot genera*, saith Isidore, *tot pernicies, quot species, tot dolores, quot colores.* See how our Saviour sharps up these heresiarchs, that, if possible, they might be made sound in the faith. So deals Peter by Simon Magus, Paul by Elymas, many of our champions by their Popish antagonists. Before God you are deceivers of the people (said Mr Philpot, martyr, to his persecutors), before God there is no truth in you. And to mocking Morgan he said, I must tell thee, thou painted wall and hypocrite, in the name of the living Lord, that God shall rain fire and brimstone upon such scorners of his word and blasphemers of his people as thou art. And afterwards, Thou art but an ass in the things of God, in that thou kickest against the truth, and art void of all godly understanding. Thou hast seduced others (said Bonner to Philpot), and madest them rejoice and sing with thee. Yea, my Lord, quoth he, we shall sing when you shall cry, Woe, woe, except ye repent. What an arrogant fool is this (said the bishop), I will handle thee like a heretic, and that shortly. I fear nothing, I thank God (said the other), that you can do unto me. But God shall destroy such as thou art, and that shortly, as I trust. Likewise to the Bishop of Chichester he spake thus : I perceive you are blind guides, and leaders of the blind, and therefore, as I am bound to tell you, very hypocrites, tyrannously persecuting the truth, which you are not able to disprove. Thus Hilary called Constantius Antichrist, and Auxentius devil, because they were Arians, *Mihi certe Auxentius nihil aliud erit quam diabolus, quia Arrianus.*

Ye generation of vipers] *Quarum morsus insanabilis. Sic contra sycophantarum morsum non est remedium.* See my notes on Matt. iii. 7. Vipers' teeth are buried in their gums, that one would think they could not bite : so hypocrites.

Ver. 34. *Wherefore, behold, I send you*] O the infinite goodness of God, in striving by his Spirit with refractory sinners in the use of the means, waiting their return !

Sed pensare solet vi graviore moram.

Prophets, wise men, and scribes] That is, apostles, pastors, and teachers, Ephes. iv. 11, whom he here calleth by the customary names of that country. Scribe was an honourable name, till Pharisees dishonested it by their hypocrisy.

Ye shall kill and crucify] If therefore we have not yet resisted unto blood, be content with

---

[1] *Vetus est morbus quo mortui sancti coluntur, vivi contemnuntur.*

[2] ἐπαινέσαι μὲν ἱκανώτατος ἦν τὰ τῶν προγόνων καλὰ μιμήσασθαι δὲ οὐκ ὁμοίως. Plutarch.

lighter crosses, and look for heavier. *Omnis Christianus crucianus.* (Luther.) It is but a delicacy to divide betwixt Christ and his cross.

Ver. 35. *From the blood of righteous Abel*] God reckons of men by their righteousness, Rom. x. The righteous (let him dwell where he will and by whom) is better than his neighbour, saith Solomon. This was Cain's grief, who was of that wicked one, and slew his brother; and wherefore slew he him, but because his own works were evil and his brother's righteous? So Alphonsus Diazius, that Cain the second, slew his brother John, because he could not win him to Popery, 1 John iii. 12. And I would this patriarch of the devil (as one calls Cain) did not still live in his sons and successors, who carry about his club that is red with Abel's blood, *Imo ut rem sacram adorant et venerantur*, think they do a goodly act in killing up the poor lambs of Christ. Cæsar is said to have slain Grecinus Julius, for this reason alone, for that he was a better man than that it was for the tyrant's behoof to suffer him to live, *Quod melior vir erat quam esse quenquam tyranno expediret.* (Senec. 2, de Benefic.)

Unto the blood of Zacharias] Most unworthily slain by his pupil Joas (as Linus likewise was by his scholar Hercules for a few sharp words that he gave him as he was teaching him).[1] Our Saviour instanceth in this Zacharias as the last prophet mentioned in the Scripture to have been slain by them, 2 Chron. xxiv., though they slew many more, not elsewhere mentioned, unless it be in that little Book of Martyrs, as one fitly calleth the eleventh to the Hebrews.

Ver. 36. *Shall come upon this generation*] In that last desolation of Jerusalem, whereof more in the next chap. God will not fail to punish persecutors. (See Acts and Mon. of the Church, fol. 1902 to 1950.) Good for them therefore is the counsel that Tertullian gave Scapula, a bloody persecutor, If thou wilt not spare us, yet spare thyself; if not thyself, yet thy city Carthage. *Si nobis non parcis, tibi parce; si non tibi, Carthagini.*

Ver. 37. *How often would I, &c.*] How then could they perish whom God would have saved? It is answered, *Voluntas Dei alia est præcepti, revelata antecedens, alia beneplaciti, arcana consequens.* By the former God willed their conversion, but not by the latter. A king wills the welfare of all his subjects; yet he will not acquit those that are laid up for treason, murder, and the like foul crimes. A father is willing to give his son the inheritance; yet if he prove an unthrift, he will put him beside it, and take another. "How oft would I have gathered?" that is (say some), by the external ministry of the prophets, sent unto thee, ver. 34, 35. Not by internal regenerating operation of the Spirit.

Even as a hen gathereth her chickens] Columbarum masculus ipse ovis incubat, sicut Christus ipse ecclesiam suam fovet.* (Chytræus in Levit. xii.) Of unreasonable creatures, birds, and of

birds, the hen excels in kindness to her young; so that she doubts not, in their defence, to encounter a kite, a dog, &c., *Iniquo et impari prælio*, though with greatest disadvantage.

And ye would not] Men may nill their conversion, then, though called by God, *Quo nihil est verius, sed et nihil turpius*, saith one. Men are not damned, because they cannot do better, but because they will do no better. *Cesset voluntas propria et non erit infernus*, If there were no will, there would be no hell, John xii. 39. Therefore they could not believe; they could not, that is, they would not, saith Theophylact out of Chrysostom, who yet usually extolleth man's free-will more than is meet.

Ver. 38. *Behold, your house is left, &c.*] City and temple both. God will not alway stand men for a sinning-stock. They that will not hear his word, shall hear his rod, and feel his sword too. Elisha hath his sword as well as Jehu and Hazael, 1 Kings xix. 17, and the one usually precedes the other. They therefore that say, Following of sermons will make men beggars, forget that to take away the gospel from Jerusalem was to leave their houses as well as God's house desolate.

Ver. 39. *Till ye shall say, Blessed, &c.*] That is, ye shall never see me, or not till the general judgment; when as you that would not obey that sweet voice of mine, "Come unto me, ye that are weary," &c., shall have no other command of mine to obey, but that dreadful *Discedite*, "Go, ye cursed, into everlasting fire," &c.

CHAPTER XXIV.

Ver. 1. *Departed from the temple*] NEVER to return more to it. In the 9th, 10th, and 11th chaps. of Ezekiel, God makes divers removes, and still as he goes out, some judgment comes in; and when he was quite gone, then followed the fatal calamity in the utter ruin of the city and temple. So it was then, and so it was now, according to that Hos. ix. 12, "Woe also to them when I depart from them." So Jer. vi. 8, "Be instructed, O Jerusalem, lest my soul be disjointed from thee, lest I make thee desolate, a land not inhabited." Whatever therefore we do, let us retain Christ with us; lay hold on him, as Magdalene did, take him by the feet as the Shunamite did the prophet, as the Shulamite held her spouse; constrain him to stay with us, as the two disciples going to Emmaus; cry

Vespera jam venit, nobiscum Christe maneto :
Extingui lucem ne patiare tuam.

To show him the buildings of the temple] As thinking by that goodly sight, haply, he might be moved to moderate the severity of that former sentence of leaving their house desolate unto them, chap. xxiii. 38. True it is, that Herod (to get the people's good will, which yet he could never do) had been at a wonderful charge in building

---

[1] *Cum ille Herculem verbulo asperiore inter erudiendum affatus esset, &c.* Bucholcer.

and beautifying the temple. Josephus the Jew (Antiq. xv. 14) tells us that for eight whole years together, he kept 10,000 men a-work about it; and that for magnificence and stateliness, it exceeded Solomon's temple, if his words exceed not the truth of the matter. This the disciples fondly thought would work upon our Saviour to reverse his former sentence, as above-said; but his thoughts were not as their thoughts. *Animo magno nihil magnum*, saith Seneca. The bramble reckoned it a great matter to reign over the trees; not so the vine and olive, Judges ix. 15.

Ver. 2. *There shall not be left here, &c.*] This was afterwards fulfilled, when the temple was so set on fire by Titus' soldiers, that it could not be quenched by the industry of man. Titus (it is said) would have preserved the temple, as one of the world's wonders, from being burnt, but could not; such was the fury of the soldiers, set a-work by God doubtless. And when, upon the taking of the city and temple, the army saluted him emperor, and many others by way of congratulation sent him crowns and garlands, he, by a memorable example of modesty, refused them, saying, that he had done nothing more than lent his hands and help to God, who declared his fierce wrath against that sinful people. *Non sese illa fecisse, sed Deo iram suam declaranti manus suas commodasse.* (Pareus.) And when Julian the apostate, to spite the Christians, permitted and encouraged the Jews to re-edify their temple at his charge, and they attempted it accordingly, they were hindered from heaven by a mighty earthquake, together with balls of fire issuing out of the ground works, and consuming the builders. There are that say, that at the same time the temple at Delphi was utterly overthrown by earthquakes and thunderbolts, and could never since be repaired. When Phocas the murderer sought to secure himself by building high walls, he heard a voice from heaven telling him that though he built his bulwarks never so high, yet sin within would soon undermine all.[1] We may say the same to the Jesuits, telling us so oft in their writings *de magnitudine Ecclesiæ Romanæ*, that be they never so high set, God, for their abominations, will abase them. It is observed of Rome, that since it became the pope's seat, it was never besieged by any, but it was sacked and ransacked. See its destiny elegantly and emphatically set forth, Rev. xviii. 21.

Ver. 3. *Came unto him privately, saying*] Because it was dangerous to speak publicly of the destruction of the temple, as the examples of Jeremiah and Stephen show. Howbeit, Micah the Morashite prophecied in the days of Hezekiah, saying, "Zion shall be ploughed, &c., and the mountain of this house shall be as the high places of a forest," Jer. xxvi. 18. And God stirred up many faithful witnesses to cry out against Rome in her ruff, and to foretell her ruin. In the year 1159 lived Johannes Sarisburiensis, who reproved the pope to his face, and wrote his Polycraticon, wherein he freely taxeth all the Romish hierarchy. Bernard also told the bishops of his time, that they were not teachers, but seducers, not pastors but impostors, not prelates, but Pilates, &c. And a certain painter, blamed by a cardinal for colouring the visages of Peter and Paul too red, tartly but fitly replied, that he painted them so, as blushing at the lives of their successors.

The sign of thy coming] viz. To destroy the temple.

And of the end of the world] Which they thought could not possibly outlast the temple. As they were wont to say in the primitive Church, *Absque stationibus non staret mundus* (Tertul.), the world could not stand if God's people did not stand before him in prayer. *Semen sanctum statumen terræ*, as Tremellius reads Isa. vi. 13.

Ver. 4. *Take heed that no man deceive you*] Try the spirits, and turn from false doctrines, as you would do from a serpent in your way, or from poison in your meats. Deceivers are sly and subtle, and that old serpent, more subtle than them all, catcheth the deceived by the deceiver, as the fisher doth one fish by another, that he may make a prey of them both. These, as harpies, have virgins' faces, vultures' talons; they are ravening wolves in sheep's clothing, &c. Shun them therefore, for they will increase to more ungodliness, and their word will eat as doth a gangrene, 2 Tim. ii. 16, 17. Theodosius tore the writings of the Arians that were presented to him;[2] and when he desired to confer with Eunomius, his empress Placilla dissuaded him very earnestly lest being perverted by his speeches he might fall into heresy.

Ver. 5. *Shall come in my name*] Or, under my name, saying, I am Christ, as Theudas the Egyptian, Judas the Galilean, Acts v. 36, 37. Barhocab, and others of old, who were miserably slain by the Romans. (Joseph. Antiq. xvii. 12, xviii. 20; B. J. ii. 12.) So one Moor in King Edward VI.'s time, took upon him to be Christ. So did Hacket in Queen Elizabeth's time; David George likewise and others in Germany. Here in England, at the Convocation held at Oseney under Steven Langton, 1206, a certain young man professed himself to be Jesus Christ; showing marks of wounds in his hands, feet, and sides. He brought also too women with him, whereof one took upon her to be our Lady, and the other Mary Magdalene. This counterfeit Christ for his labour was worthily crucified. That I say nothing here of Papists, who desperately deny the Lord that bought them, and wickedly set up Antichrist in his stead (as were easy to prove), who opposeth him not so much in his nature or person, as in his unction and function, and thence also hath his name, Ἀντίχριστος, non Ἀθεος, non Ἀντίθεος.

Ver. 6. *See that you be not troubled*] μὴ θροεῖσθε, or frighted, as soldiers are by sudden alarm.

---

[1] Ἐὰν ὑψοῖς τὰ τείχη ἕως οὐρανοῦ ἔνδον τὸ κακὸν εὐάλωτος ἡ πόλις. Cur.

[2] *Theod. Imp. laceravit scripta Arianorum pugnantia cum testimoniis divinis.* Selnec., Sozom. vii. 7.

Quid timet hominem homo in sinu dei positus?
David was undaunted, Psal. iii. 6 ; xxvii. 3. He
looked not downward on the rushing and roaring
streams of dangers that run so swiftly under him,
for that would have made him giddy : but stead-
fastly fastened on the power and promise of God
all-sufficient, and was safe. So at the sack of
Ziglag, 1 Sam. xxx. 6.

Ver. 7. *For nation shall rise, &c.*] See here the
woeful effects of refusing God's free offers of
grace. They that would have none of the gospel
of peace shall have the miseries of war. They
that loathed the heavenly manna shall be hunger-
starved. They that despised the only medicine
of their souls shall be visited with the pestilence.
They that would not suffer heart-quake, shall suffer
earthquake. Or as Bradford the martyr expresseth
it, they that trembled not in hearing, shall be
crushed to pieces in feeling. As they heap up
sin, so they treasure up wrath ; as there hath
been a conjuncture of offences, so there shall be of
their miseries. The black horse is at the heels of
the red, and the pale of the black, Rev. vi. 4.
God left not Pharaoh, that sturdy rebel, till he
had beaten the breath out of his body, nor will he
cease pursuing men with his plagues, one in the
neck of another, till they throw the traitor's head
over the wall.

Ver. 8. *All these are the beginning, &c.*] *q. d.*
There yet remain far worse matters than war,—
famine, pestilence, earthquakes. *Adhuc restant
gravissimi partus cruciatus.* And yet war is as a
fire that feeds upon the people, Isa. ix. 19, 20.
Famine is far worse than that, Lam. iv. 9. Pestilence is God's evil angel, Psal. lxxviii. 49, 50.
Earthquakes are wondrous terrible, and destructive to whole cities, as to Antioch of old, and to
Pleurs in Italy of late, where fifteen hundred men
perished together. A conflux of all these abides
the contemners of Christ's gospel. The holy
martyrs, as Saunders, Bradford, Philpot, &c ; the
confessors also that fled for religion in Queen
Mary's days acknowledged (as Ursinus relates)
that that great inundation of misery came justly
upon them, for their unprofitableness under the
means of grace which they had enjoyed in King
Edward's days. "When I first came to be pastor
at Clavenne," saith Zanchy, "there fell out a
grievous pestilence, that in seven months' space
consumed 1200 persons." Their former pastor,
Mainardus, that man of God, had often foretold
such a calamity for their popery and profaneness : but he could never be believed, till the
plague had proved him a true prophet ; and
then they remembered his words, and wished
they had been warned by him. When the Protestants of France began to grow wanton of
their peace and prosperity, to jangle among
themselves about discipline, and to affect a vain
frothy way of preaching, then came the cruel
massacre upon them. (Melch. Adam. in Vita
Bulling.)

Ver. 9. *And shall kill you*] Besides the butcheries at Jerusalem, that slaughter-house of the
saints, *Nero orientem fidem primus Romæ cruen-*

tavit, "Nero was the first Roman persecutor,"
saith Tertullian, who therefore calleth him
Dedicator damnationis Christianorum, the dedicator of the condemnation of Christians. He is
said to have made such a bloody decree as this,
*Quisquis Christianum se esse confitetur, is tanquam
generis humani convictus hostis, sine ulteriori sui
defensione capite plectitor,* Whoso confesseth
himself a Christian, let him be put to death
without any more ado, as a convicted enemy of
mankind.

Ver. 10. *And then shall many be offended*] As
not willing to suffer. How many revolted for
fear in the primitive times, were abjured here in
Queen Mary's reign, fell to Popery in the Palatinate, and other places in Germany, since the
troubles there, as fast as leaves fall in autumn !
Somewhat men will do for Christ, but suffer
nothing.

Ver. 11. *And shall deceive many*] Witness the
Eastern and Western Antichrist, those deceitful
workers, that have drawn millions of souls into
hell by their grand impostures. The world went
wondering after those two beasts, which, as the
panther, hid their horrid heads, that they might
take men with their flesh-pleasing superstitions.
And (as the serpent scytale) when they cannot
otherwise overtake the flying passenger, they so
bewitch him with their beauty and bravery, that
he hath no power to pass away.

Ver. 12. *And because iniquity shall abound*] In
these last and worst times, as Bernard yoketh
them, and as the Scripture oft describeth them.
There was never but one Noah, that with two
faces saw both before and behind him. But, lo,
that ancient of days, to whom all times are present, hath told us that the last shall be the
loosest, the dregs of time, the sink of sins of all
former ages.

The love of many shall wax cold] Conversation
with cold ones will cast a damp, and will make
one cold, as our Saviour here intimates ; there is
no small danger of defection, if not of infection by
such ; they are notable quench-coals. This both
David and Isaiah found, and therefore cried out
each for himself, "Woe is me," Psal. cxx. 5 ; Isa.
vi. 5. There is a compulsive power in company
to do as they do, Gal. ii. 14. "Why compellest
thou," &c. It behoveth us therefore to beware
upon whom the ends of the world are come, lest
we suffer a decay, lest leaving our first love, and
led away with the error of the wicked, we fall from
our former steadfastness, Rev. ii. 5 ; 2 Pet. iii. 17.
The world, saith Ludolfus (*De Vita Christi,* ii.
87), hath been once destroyed with water for the
heat of lust, and shall be again with fire for the
coldness of love. Latimer saw so much lack of
love to God and goodness in his time, that he
thought verily doomsday was then just at hand.
What would he have thought had he lived in
our age, wherein it were far easier to write a
book of apostates than a book of martyrs ?

Ver. 13. *But he that endureth*] It is but a he,
a single man, that holdeth out ; when many lose
their love, and therewith their reward, 2 John

viii. Ecebolus, Æneas, Sylvius, Baldwin, Pendleton, Shaxton, and many others, set forth gallantly, but tired ere they came to their journey's end. Of them that verse was verified, *Principium fervet, medium tepet, exitus alget*. Like the Galli Insubres, they showed all their valour in the first encounter. Like Charles VIII. of France, of whom Guicciarden noteth, that in his expedition to Naples he came into the field like thunder and lightning, but went out like a snuff. Like Mandrobulus in Lucian, who the first year offered gold to his gods, the second year silver, the third nothing. Or, lastly, like the lions of Syria, which, as Aristotle reporteth, bring forth first five whelps, next time four, next three, and so on, till at length they become barren. So apostates come at last to nothing, and therefore must look for nothing better than to be cast off for ever; when they that hold out and hold on their way, passing from strength to strength, from faith to faith, &c., shall be as the sun when he goeth forth in his strength; yea, they shall shine forth as the sun in the kingdom of their Father, Matt. xiii. 43. Caleb was not discouraged by the giants, and therefore had Hebron, the place of the giants; so those that hold out in the way of heaven shall be sure to have heaven. Thomas San Paulins, at Paris, a young man of eighteen years, being in the fire, was plucked up again upon the gibbet, and asked whether he would turn. To whom he said, That he was in his way toward God, and therefore desired them to let him go. That merchant of Paris, his case was nothing so comfortable, who, for jesting at the friars, was by them condemned to be hanged; but he, to save his life, was content to recant, and so he did. The friars, hearing of his recantation, commended him, saying, If he continued so he should be saved; and so, calling upon the officers, caused them to make haste to the gallows to hang him up, while he was yet in a good way, said they, lest he fall again.

Ver. 14. *For a witness unto all nations*] Whilst, with Moses, it slayeth the Egyptian, saveth the Israelite, is a savour of life to some, of death to others, who shall be left without excuse by the Gospel preached to them, as those that by their obstinacy have wilfully cut the throats of their own poor souls, refusing to be reformed, hating to be healed. Sure it is that the last sentence shall be but a more manifest declaration of that judgment which the Lord in this life, most an end, by his word hath passed upon people.

Ver. 15. *The abomination of desolation*] That is, antichrist, say some interpreters; and hitherto may fitly be referred that of Baronius, who in his annals of the year 964, reckoning up some popes monstrously wicked, he calleth them " the abomination of desolation standing in God's temple." Others understand it of the

Roman eagles or ensigns. Others of the Emperor Caius' statue, said by some to be set up in the sanctuary. As others again of Titus' picture placed there, which haply was that one great sin that so troubled him upon his death-bed.[1] But they do best that understand the text of those abominable authors of desolation, the Roman armies, who laid waste that pleasant land, and destroyed the nation; as besides what Daniel foretold is set forth by Josephus at large in his sixth and seventh book, *De bello Judaico*.

Spoken of by Daniel] Porphyry, that mad dog, running furiously at God and Christ, *Amanuenses Spiritus sancti, Danielem et Matthæum nefarie calumniatus est scripsisse falsa*, blasphemed these two secretaries of the Holy Ghost, Daniel and Matthew, as writer of false things. This was *contra solem mingere*.

Whoso readeth, let him understand] Let him strive to do so by reading with utmost attention, diligence, and devotion, weeping as John did, till the sealed book was opened; digging deep in the mine of the Scriptures for the mind of God, 1 Cor. ii. 15, and holding it fast when he hath it, lest at any time he should let it slip, Heb. ii. 1. Admirable is that, and applicable to this purpose, which Philostratus relateth of the precious stone Pantarbe, of so orient, bright, and sweet a colour, that it both dazzleth and refresheth the eyes at once, drawing together heaps of other stones by its secret force (though far distant), as hives of bees, &c. But lest so costly a gift should grow cheap, nature hath not only hid it in the innermost bowels of the earth, but also hath put a faculty into it, of slipping out of the hands of those that hold it, unless they be very careful to prevent it.[2]

Ver. 16. *Flee into the mountains*] As Lot at length did, for Zoar was too hot to hold him; so should Judea be for these, who were therefore to repair to Pella, beyond Jordan, where they were hid till the indignation was overpast, as Eusebius hath it, in the third book and fifth chapter of his history. Such a receptacle of religious people was Geneva in the Marian persecution. And such (blessed be God our strength for his unspeakable favour) is at this present Warwick Castle, to myself writing these things, and to many others in these troublous times. So Bucer and many godly people were entertained and safe-guarded by that noble Franciscus à Sickengen in the German wars.

Ver. 17. *Not come down to take any thing*] See here the miseries of war, which now, alas, we feel, and can seal to: being glad to flee for our lives with the loss of all, lest with Shimei, seeking to save our goods we lose life and all; glad if we may escape with the skin of our teeth. And how like are our present convulsions to end in a deadly consumption? War is called evil by

---

[1] *Titus moriens se unius tantum modo rei pœnitere dixit. Id autem quid esset non aperuit, nec quisquam certo novit, aliud aliis conjicientibus.* Dio. *in Vita* Titi.

[2] *In Vita Apollonii,* l. iii. c. 4. *Acervos lapidum non*

aliter ac apum examina pertrahit. Non modo occultis terræ visceribus abdidit, sed et facultatem indidit, qua ex captantium manibus effluerit, nisi provida ratione teneretur.

a specialty, Isa. xlv. 7. Sin, Satan, and war have all one name: evil is the best of them. The best of sin is deformity, of Satan enmity, of war misery. God yet offereth us mercy, as Alexander did those he warred against, whiles the lamp burned. Oh let us break off our sins by repentance, and be abrupt in it, lest we should seem to come short, Heb. iv. 1.

Ver. 18. *Return back to take his clothes*] The body is better than raiment; and although there is great use of clothes, in flight especially, to save us from the injury of wind and weather (for we carry the lamps of our lives in paper lanthorns, as it were), yet life for a prey (though we have nothing else) in a common calamity is a singular mercy. " A living dog is better than a dead lion," saith Solomon. The Gibeonites, to save their lives, submitted to the meanest offices, of being hewers of wood, &c. "Skin for skin," &c., Job ii. 4. We should be content to sacrifice all to the service of our lives.

Ver. 19. *Woe to them that are with child,* &c.] By the laws of nations women with child, babes and sucklings, maids and old folk, should be spared. But the bloody sword oft knows no difference, as Hos. x. 14, the mother was dashed in pieces upon her children, Hos. xiii. 16; their infants were dashed in pieces, and their women with child ripped up. So at the sack of Magdeburg by Charles V., and of Merindol in France by Minerius, where the paps of many women were cut off, and their children, looking for suck at their mother's breast, being dead before, died also for hunger. Many such barbarous butcheries have been acted lately in Ireland, and begin to be also now in England (poor England, now an Ireland!), as at Bolton in Lancashire lately. Help, Lord, or thy servant perisheth.

Ver. 20. *But pray ye*] Christ saith not, Fight ye, but Pray ye. To fight it boots not; for God hath resolved the land's ruin: but prayers are *bombardæ et instrumenta bellica Christianorum*, as Luther hath it, the great guns and artillery of Christians, whereby they may batter heaven, and make a breach upon God himself. *Flectitur iratus voce rogante Deus.* Something God will yield to the prayers of his people, even when he seems most bitterly bent, and unchangeably resolved against them. Christ here bids them pray, that their flight fall not out " in the winter," when the days are short, ways foul, and all less fit for such a purpose.[1] "Nor on the Sabbath;" when though it were lawful enough, yet it would be so much the more uncomfortable. This they were bid to pray above thirty years before the city was besieged. And they had what they prayed for. Their flight was not in winter, for the siege began about Easter, and the city was taken in September. Neither was it on the Sabbath-day, as we have cause to believe; for when Christ bids us pray for anything, it is sure he means to bestow it. As when we bid our children ask us this or that, it is because we mean to give it them.

Ver. 21. *Tribulation, such as was not,* &c.] Those very days "shall be affliction;" so Mark hath it, chap. xiii. 19, ἔσονται αἱ ἡμέραι ἐκεῖναι θλίψις. As if the very time were nothing else but affliction itself. He that can read the history of it without tears, hath hardly the heart of a man in him. Besides those many that perished within the walls, Josephus tells us of 1,000,000 of them slain by the Romans, and 97,000 carried captive. Oh, see the severity of God and tremble! Rom. xi. 22. *Alterius perditio tua sit cautio.* Scipio wept when he saw Carthage on fire. And when Saguntum was taken, the Romans were as much affected as if Hannibal *fuisset ad portas*, the enemy had been beating upon the walls of the Capitol.

Ver. 22. *There should no flesh be saved*] That is, no Jew left alive; the Roman soldiers had been so often beaten by them, that they desired nothing more than to rid the world of them. But God, for his covenant' sake, preserved a remnant of them, as he ever softeneth the sword of his justice in the oil of his mercy, as Nicephorus hath it.[2] Josephus attributeth it to Titus' clemency: but our Saviour here better, to God's infinite mercy to his elect. These are the salt of the earth, that sprinkled here and there, preserve it from putrefying and perishing. God gave all the souls that were in the ship to Paul, and all that were in Zoar to Lot. If it were not for his elect in the world, he would make a "short work in the earth," Rom. ix. 28.

Ver. 23. *Then, if any man shall say*] Here again our Saviour returns to the description of the last times, containing the rise, reign, and ruin of Antichrist, whose chief engine shall be to persuade Christ's corporal presence here and there in certain places, and to tie his worship and service to such or such a city, country, temple, &c., where he may be seen, touched, eaten, &c., as they feign in the eucharist.

Ver. 24. *If it were possible,* &c.] Fundamentally and finally the elect cannot possibly be deceived; because both "the deceived and the deceiver are with the Lord," Job xii. 13, 16. In the Primitive Church, those capital heresies concerning the Trinity and the incarnation of our Saviour did so prevail, *Ut ingeniosa res fuerit esse Christianum*, saith Erasmus, that it was a witty thing to be a true Christian. Arianism had so overspread the world, that Athanasius seemed to be alone, as did Elias before him, and Luther after him. But God in worst times reserved a remnant, and at all times will not see nor suffer any of his to miscarry; but will reduce them from their out-strays, as he did Latimer, who was (as himself confesseth) as obstinate a Papist as any was in England, till converted by Bilney; and as he did Denckius, a learned Dutchman, but a pestilent heretic, till converted by Œcolampadius; and as he did Francis Junius, a desperate atheist, till converted by conference with a country-man of his not far from Florence.

[1] χεῖμα παρὰ τὸ χέειν. Hyems, παρὰ τὸ ὕειν. Bruma, q. βραχὺ ἦμα, i. e. ἦμαρ. Becman.

[2] *Deus vindictæ gladium oleo miserationis semper emollit.*

Ver. 25. *Behold, I have told you before*] See, therefore, that ye stand alway upon your watch; for, for this end have I warned you: prevision is the best means of prevention. *Leo cassibus irretitus ait si præscivissem.* To sin after warning, is to fall with open eyes, which deserves no pity. Not to be warned, is both a just presage and desert of a downfall.

Ver. 26. *Behold, he is in the desert*] In such a hermitage, or blind chapel, built in a by-place to the honour of such a saint, as our Lady of Loretto, Hall, or Sichem (Lipsius' last dotages). " Behold, he is in the secret chambers," or conclaves, ἐν τοῖς ταμείοις (*scil.* of cardinals, &c.), or cupboards, as the breaden-god borne up and down in a box, or on an altar, and worshipped by the common people. The rebels of Norfolk in Edward VI.'s time, brought with them into the battle the pyx under his canopy, as the Israelites brought the ark, 1 Sam. iv. 3, and said it should save them. But as then the ark, so now the consecrated god, with all the trumpery about him, was taken in a cart, which was then instead of an altar, and there lay all in the dust. Believe them not therefore in any of these their fopperies and forgeries. " The simple believeth every word: but the prudent man looketh well to his going."[1] He is a slave to good reason, but not easily swayed by every new opinion.

Ver. 27. *So shall also the coming of the Son of man be*] Clear and conspicuous, as the lightning cannot be hid or hindered from being seen all the whole heaven over. Then shall all secret sins be made visible, as things written with the juice of lemons are legible when held to the fire; as visible shall they be, and legible too, as if written with the brightest lightning upon a wall of crystal.

Ver. 28. *For wheresoever the carcase is*, &c.] That is, saith M. Lambert, martyr, wheresoever is declared by the course of the Scriptures, the benefits granted to us by Christ's death, thither will men seek and fly, to know how they may enjoy the same. The sacrificed body of Christ (saith another) hath a most fragrant smell, inviting the saints (like birds of prey) to fly from far with marvellous swiftness to this dead but all-quickening carcase. Some interpret it thus: Where the carcase is, that is, the body of the Jews, that had forsaken God and his truth, and so was a dead carcase (confer Hos. xiii. 1), there will the Roman eagles and enemies be.

There will the eagles be gathered] The vulturine eagles especially, whereof read Job xxxix. 29, 30: they follow armies, and feed on carcases. Eagles the saints are called, 1. For their delight in high flying. 2. For their sharp-sightedness, and steadfast looking into the Sun of righteousness. 3. For their singular sagacity, in smelling out Christ, and resenting things above, for the which they are said to have " a nose like the tower of Lebanon," Cant. vii. 4. 4. For their feeding upon the bloody sacrifice of Christ, the true carcase. Briefly, this proverbial speech may be well understood, either

[1] *Fatuus*, אויל, *fatuellus*. Lips. Prov. xiv. 15.

of the conflux of the godly to the light and liberty of the gospel, or else of their indissoluble union with Christ to be perfectly enjoyed at the resurrection. For the sense of it is, that let the devil use what means soever he can by his emissaries, the false prophets, to divide betwixt Christ and his people, by telling them, There he is, or here he is, it will not be; for they will fly to him as a cloud, or as the doves to their windows, Isa. lx. 8. Nay, as the eagles to their carcase, with incredible swiftness; so forcible is the tie that is betwixt them, that they will not be kept asunder. The Israelites removed their tents from Mithcah, which signifies sweetness, to Hashmonah, which signifies swiftness, Numb. xxxiii. 29. To teach us, saith a divine, that no sooner have the saints tasted Christ's sweetness but presently they are carried after him with swiftness; they cannot rest till they are joined unto him whom their soul loveth. In reference to whom, Christ's last supper is called by the ancients, *Festum aquilarum, non graculorum*, a feast for eagles, not for daws.

Ver. 29. *Immediately after the tribulation of those days*] After that the mystery of iniquity hath wrought effectually, and is come to an upshot: after that Antichrist hath had his full forth, as they say, and hath completed his sin, Christ shall suddenly come, as it were out of an engine.

Shall the sun be darkened, &c.] Stupendous eclipses shall precede the Lord's coming, and other strange events both in heaven, earth, and sea, as Luke hath it. The frame of this whole universe shall shake, as houses give great cracks when ready to fall. See 2 Pet. iii. 10, and seek no further.

Ver. 30. *The sign of the Son of man*] That is, either Christ himself (by an Hebraism), or the dreadful dissolution of the world's fabric, or that cloud of heaven that was of old the sign of the Son of man in the wilderness, Exod· xiii. 21, or the scars of his wounds, or his cross, or something else that we cannot describe, and need not search into. Look how a king, when he would gather his forces into one, sets up his standard, or appoints his rendezvous; so, such shall be the brightness of Christ's coming, that all his shall be gathered unto him by that token, not to fight; but to triumph with him and divide the spoil, as it were, being more than conquerors; and what is that but triumphers? The expectation of this day must (as that did with David's soldiers at Ziklag) digest all our sorrows.

And then shall all the tribes of the earth mourn] This to prevent, we must judge ourselves, 1 Cor. xi. 31, and take unto us words against our sins, if we would not have Christ take unto him words against our souls, Hosea xiv. 3. Good men have been exceedingly affected at the hearing of God's judgments against others, as Hab. iii. 16.

Ver. 31. *And he shall send his angels*] As his apparitors and executioners. David went otherwise attended when he went against Nabal than when against Goliath; so Christ shall come, when he shall come again with his troops and trumpets.

With a great sound of a trumpet] Christ shall put forth his own mighty voice, Job v. 28, and 1 Thess. iv. 16, ministered by his angels, as in the text, and set forth by the sound of a trumpet, in allusion, belike, to Numb. x., where the people were congregated and called together by the sound of a trumpet to the door of the tabernacle. "The lion of the tribe of Judah shall roar from above, and thrust out his voice from his holy habitation, when he entereth into judgment with all flesh," Jer. xxv. 30, 31. As the lion roareth over his whelps, brought forth dead at first, and raiseth them from death to life, as Pliny reporteth.

And they shall gather together his elect] How shall they know them from reprobates? By God's saving mark set fairly in their foreheads, Ezek. ix. 9.[1] And by their blithe and merry countenances, cleared and cheered in the apprehension and approach of their full redemption, now drawing nigh. Besides, as servants know their master's harvest from another's, and can easily discern the corn from the cockle, so can the good angels soon single out the elect, about whom they have been familiarly conversant here on earth, as ministering spirits sent forth to minister to the heirs of salvation, ready pressed to any good office about them, Heb. i. 14.

Ver. 32. *Ye know that summer is nigh*] Which is so much the sweeter, because brought in and led out by winter: so will eternal life be to the saints, here tossed and turmoiled with variety of sufferings. Many sharp showers they must here pass through; "Light is sown for the righteous," &c., sown only; and seed-time we know is usually wet and showery. Howbeit, it is fair weather ofttimes with God's children when it is foulest with the wicked; as the sun rose upon Zoar when the fire fell upon Sodom. But if they should have never a good day in this world, yet heaven will make amends for all. And what is it for one to have a rainy day, who is going to take possession of a kingdom?

Ver. 33. *Know that it is near, &c.*] Some space then there shall be, it seems, between the foregoing signs and the coming of Christ. But though space be granted, yet grace is uncertain. Make sure work therefore betimes, lest ye come late, and be left without doors for your lingering.

Ver. 34. *This generation shall not pass*] viz. That generation that immediately precedes the end of the world. That this is the sense, appears by the antithesis, ver. 36: "But of that day and hour knoweth no man," *q. d.* the generation and age wherein Christ shall come ye may know by the signs that fore-show it, but the day and hour ye must not look to know, be you never so intelligent.

Ver. 35. *Heaven and earth shall pass, &c.*] What God hath written, he hath written. His word is established in heaven, saith David, Psal. cxix. 89; it endureth for ever, saith Peter, 1

Pet. i. 25; it remaineth firm as Mount Sion, and shall stand inviolable when heaven shall pass away with a great noise, and the earth with its works shall be burnt up, 2 Pet. iii. 10, to the terror and confusion of those profane scoffers who deridingly demand, "Where is the promise of his coming?" &c. ver. 4; that say, "Let him make speed and hasten his work, that we may see it," Isa. v. 19. "Woe to you that thus desire the day of the Lord. To what end is it for you? The day of the Lord is darkness, and not light," Amos v. 18. The great day of the Lord is near, it is near and hasteth greatly. It is a day of wrath, a day of trouble and distress, a day of wasteness and desolation, a day of darkness and gloominess, a day of clouds and thick darkness, to them "that are settled on their lees, and that say in their heart, The Lord will not do good, neither will he do evil," Zeph. i. 12—15.

Ver. 36. *But of that day and hour knoweth no man*] That the Lord will come it is *certo certius*, not more sure, than what time he will come is to us most uncertain. Sundry guesses have been given at it by both ancient and modern writers; most of which time hath already refuted. In the year of grace 1533 there was one that foolishly foretold that the day of judgment should fall out in October next ensuing. And this he gathered out of these words, *Jesus Nazarenus Rex Judæorum.* Likewise out of these, *Videbunt in quem transfixerunt;* the numerals of the former point to the year 1532, of the latter to 1533. Others there are that place the end of the world upon the year 1657. And for proof they make use of this chronogram, *MVnDI Conf Lagrat Io;* and further allege that the general deluge fell out in the year of the world's creation, 1657. The end of the world, saith another, will be in the year of Christ 1688, three jubilees and a half (or thereabouts) after the reformation of religion by Luther, &c. Joachimus Abbas had long since set the year 1258; Arnoldus de Villa Nova, the year 1345; Michael Stiphelius, St Luke's day in the year 1533; Cyprianus Leonitius, the year 1583; Joannes Regiomontanus, the year 1588; Adelbertus Thermopedius, the year 1599, April 3; Nicolaus Cusanus, the year 1700; Cardanus, 1800; Picus Mirandula, 1905, &c. So great hath been the folly and sin of many learned men, who have thus childishly set their wits to play in so serious a business, as one well censureth it.

But my Father only] *Ordine videlicet sciendi à se, non ab alio.* The Son knoweth it not but from his Father; like as he neither subsisteth nor worketh but from the Father. The set time of the general judgment God hath hid from us: 1. For his own glory, Prov. xxv. 2; Rom. xi. 36. 2. For our good, that we may watch always, and not wax secure as we would do with the evil servant, ver. 48, till the very day and hour, if we knew it.[2] The harlot in the Proverbs grew bold upon this, that her husband was gone forth for such a time, Prov. vii. 20.

---

[1] *Signo salutari.* Tremel.

[2] *Ideo latet unus dies ut observentur omnes.*

Ver. 37. *So shall the coming of the Son of man be*] Sudden and unexpected. Luther observeth, that it was in the spring that the flood came, when everything was in its prime and pride, and nothing less looked for than a flood; men sinned securely, as if they had lived out of the reach of God's rod, but he found them out. Security is the certain usher of destruction; as at Laish, Ziklag. Before an earthquake the air will be most quiet, and when the wind lies the great rain falls. *Frequentissimum initium calamitatis securitas*, saith the historian, Paterculus.

Ver. 38. *They were eating and drinking*] Wine, likely; because our Saviour hereupon bids his apostles take heed to themselves lest their hearts at any time should be overcharged with surfeiting and drunkenness, &c., Luke xxi. 34. Like as some do not improbably conjecture, that Nadab and Abihu were in their drink when they offered strange fire, because after they were devoured by fire from the Lord. Aaron and the priests are charged to drink no wine nor strong drink when they go into the tabernacle of the congregation, lest they die, Lev. x. 12, 8, 9. St Luke delivers the matter more roundly by an elegant asyndeton, "They ate, they drank, they married," &c., *q. d.* they passed without intermission from eating to drinking, from drinking to marrying, &c.; they followed it close, as if it had been their work, and they born for no other end. Of Ninius, second king of Assyrians, nephew haply to these antediluvian belly-gods, it is said, that he was old excellent at eating and drinking.[1] And of Sardanapalus, one of the same line, Tully tells us that his gut was his god. *Summum bonum in ventre, aut sub ventre posuit;* and Plutarch, that he hired men to devise new pleasures for him. See my Commonplace of Abstinence.

Until the day] They were set upon it, and would lose no time. Their destruction was foretold them to a day; they were nothing bettered by it; no more would wicked men, should they foreknow the very instant of Christ's coming to judgment. Joseph had foretold the famine of Egypt and the time when it should come; but fulness bred forgetfulness, saturity, security; none observed or provided for it. *Quod vel inviti norant, non agnoverant.*

Ver. 39. *And knew not*] *i. e.* They took no knowledge of Noah's predictions, or their own peril. Their wits they had buried in their guts, their brains in their bellies (as of the ass-fish it is said (*Arist. de Anim.*) that contrary to all other living creatures, he hath his heart in his belly); "whoredom, wine, and new wine take away the heart," Hosea iv. 11. Carnal sins disable nature, and so set men in a greater distance from grace, which is seated in the powers of nature. I read of some desperate wretches that drinking together, when one of them had drunk himself stark dead, the other, no wit warned

by that fearful example of God's wrath, poured his part of drink into the dead man's belly, *in quodam episcopatu potaverunt aliqui, &c.* (John Manl.)

And took them all away] Men are never less safe than when they are most secure. Babylon bore itself bold upon the twenty years' provision laid up aforehand, to stand out at siege. When it was nevertheless taken by Cyrus, some part of the city would not know or believe of three days after, that there was any such matter. (Herodot. lib. 1; Arist. Polit. lib. 3.)

Ver. 40. *The one shall be taken, the other left*] The Flood took all away in a manner; but at Christ's coming there shall be found a considerable company of such as shall be saved. He shall separate his saints with a wonderful separation, and make himself to be "admired in all them that believe," 2 Thess. i. 10. How carefully, then, should we work out our salvation, and ensure to ourselves our election by good works.

Ver. 41. *Two women shall be grinding at the mill*] A poor trade, a hard task. God would have every man in his honest occupation to humble himself by just labour, and so to accept of the punishment of their iniquity, Levit. xxvi. 41. But one of these two poor grinders at the mill is left by Christ for her pride and profaneness. Many are humbled, but not humble; low, but not lowly. To these Christ will say, *Perdidistis utilitatem calamitatis, miserimi facti estis, et pessimi permansistis,* Misery hath no wit mended you; woe be to you. (Aug. C. D. i. 33.)

Ver. 42. *Watch therefore,* &c.] *Læti simus, non securi* (Bernard). Whilst Ishbosheth slept upon his bed at noon, Baanah and Rechab took away his head. "Hold fast that thou hast, that no man take thy crown from thee," Rev. iii. 11. Whilst the crocodile sleepeth with open mouth, the Indian rat gets into him and eateth his entrails. Satan works strongest on the fancy when the soul is drowsy. The spouse therefore promiseth to get up early, Cant. vii. 12, to shake off security, and not to be found henceforth supine and sluggish, but to stand upon her watch; as of Scanderbeg it is said, that from his first coming to Epirus, he never slept above two hours in a night, but with restless labour prosecuted his affairs. Aristotle and some others would not sleep but with brazen balls in their hands, which falling on vessels purposely set on their bedsides, the noise did dissuade immoderate sleep. Our Saviour pronounceth them three times happy that watch, Luke xii. 37, 38, 43.[2] The blessed angels are called watchers, ἐγρηγόροι, Dan. iv. 10.

For ye know not what hour your Lord, &c.] He may haply come upon you, as Epaminondas did upon his sentinel, whom finding asleep, he thrust through with his sword, and being chid for so severe a fact, he replied, I left him but as I found him, *Talem eum reliqui, qualem inveni.*

---

[1] ἄριστος ἦν ἐσθίειν καὶ πίνειν. Athenæ Dipnosoph. ii.

[2] *Terque quaterque beati.* Virg. *Fælices ter et amplius.* Horat.

Ver. 43. *He would not have suffered his house,* &c.] And shall the children of this world be wiser for their houses than we for our souls? what are these earthly tabernacles, these clayey cottages, to our houses from heaven? All things here are terrene and abject, *nec vera, nec vestra,* subject to vanity and violence. Heaven only hath a foundation, Heb. xi. 10. Earth hath none, Job xxvi. 7. And things are said to be in heaven, but on earth, as ready with the least shake to fall off, Colos. i. 20. There is nothing of any stability or solid consistency in the creature. It is but a surface, an outside, all the felicity of it is but skin deep. Seek, therefore, first God's kingdom, &c.

Ver. 44. *Therefore be ye also ready*] Suetonius tells us that it was a piece of Julius Cæsar's policy never to fore-acquaint his soldiers of any set time of removal or onset, that he might ever have them in readiness to draw forth whithersoever he would.[1] Christ, in like manner, who is called the "Captain of our salvation," Heb. ii. 10. Our enemy is always ready to annoy us, should we not therefore look to our stand, and be vigilant? Solomon's wisdom, Lot's integrity, and Noah's sobriety, felt the smart of the serpent's sting. The first was seduced, the second stumbled, and the third fell, while the eye of watchfulness was fallen asleep.

For in such an hour, &c.] Christ will soonest seize upon the secure, 1 Thess. v. 3; such shall sleep as Sisera, who ere he awaked had his head fastened to the ground, as if it had been now listening what was become of the soul. See the notes on verse 42.

Ver. 45. *Who then is a faithful and wise servant*] So every man ought to be, but ministers especially, who should so far surpass others in these good qualities, as Saul did the people, than whom he was higher by head and shoulders. They should be faithful in all God's house as servants, as stewards and dispensers of the mysteries of God, to give to every man his demesne, his due measure of meat (σιτομέτριον, Luke xii. 42), and that which is fit for him, not (as he in the emblem did) straw to the dog, and a bone to the ass, &c., but to every one his portion, 1 Cor. iv. 1.

Ver. 46. *Blessed is that servant*] It was Augustine's wish, that Christ when he came might find him *aut precantem, aut prædicantem,* either praying or preaching. It was Latimer's wish (and he had it) that he might shed his heart-blood for Christ. It was Jewel's wish that he might die preaching, and he did so, for presently after his last sermon at Lacock in Wiltshire, he was, by reason of sickness, forced to his bed, from whence he never came off till his translation to glory.[2] I have heard the like of Mr Lancaster, a precious man of God, some time pastor of Bloxham in Oxfordshire, a man very famous for his living by faith. Cushamerus, a Dutch divine, and one of

the first preachers of the Gospel at Erfurt in Germany, had his pulpit poisoned by the malicious Papists there, and so took his death in God's work.[3] What, would you that the Lord when he comes should find me idle? said Calvin to his friends, who wished him to forbear studying awhile, for his health' sake.[4] And such a like answer made Doctor Reynolds to his physician upon the like occasion. Elijah was going on and talking with Elisha (about heavenly things, no doubt) when the chariot of heaven came to fetch him. There can be no better posture or state for the messenger of our dissolution to find us in than in a diligent prosecution of our general or particular calling.

Ver. 47. *Verily I say unto you,* &c.] A deep asseveration for our better assurance and encouragement. Christ is a liberal pay-master, and his retributions are more than bountiful. Abraham thought much that the steward of his house should be heir of his goods, Gen. xv. 2, 3. Not so the Lord Christ.

Ver. 48. *But and if that evil servant*] All places are full of such evil servants (and so is hell too), as future their repentance, and so fool away their salvation. Of such dust-heaps we may find in every corner : this is a depth of the devil, brimfull with the blood of many souls, to persuade them that they have yet long to live, and many fair summers to see; that there is no such haste, but that hereafter may be time enough. In space comes grace, and a few good words at last will waft them to heaven.

Ver. 49. *To eat and drink with the drunken*] Though he neither be drunk himself, not make others drunk, yet to be among wine-bibbers and flesh-mongers, as Solomon hath it, Prov. xxiii. 20, to company with such as a frequent and immoderate bibber, as Peter's word (ἐν πότοις) importeth, 1 Pet. iv. 3; to drink *ad numerum,* as Bullinger expresseth it, though there follow not an utter alienation of mind, this is here threatened. Excessive drinking is drunkenness (Ephes. v. 18), though men be strong to bear it, Isa. v. 22.

Ver. 50. *In a day when he looketh not,* &c.] As he did to that rich fool (*Stultitiam patiuntur opes,* Martial), who made account he had much good laid up in store for many years; but heard ere morning, *Stulte, hac nocte,* "Thou fool, this night," Luke xii. 19, 20. Then when like a jay he was pruning himself in the boughs, and thought least of death, he came tumbling down with the arrow in his side; his glass was run when he hoped it had been but new turned. *Sic subito tollitur qui diu toleratur.* God shall shoot at such with an arrow suddenly, Psal. lxiv. 7.

Ver. 51. *And shall cut him asunder*] Gr. διχοτομήσει, shall cut him in twain, that is, tear his soul from his body by main force, Job xxvii. 8, throw him out of the world, as it were, by a *firma ejectione,* and hurl him into hell, there to

---

[1] *Scilicet ut paratum et intentum momentis omnibus, quo vellet subito educeret.*

[2] Bishop Jewel's Life by D. Humphrey.

[3] *In suggestu veneno illito extinctus est.* Scult. Annal. 80.

[4] *Beza in Vita, An propter vitam vivendi perdere finem.*

undergo most exquisite torments, such as they did here that were sawn asunder, Heb. xi.; hewn in pieces, as Agag, 1 Sam. xv. 33; torn limb-meal, as Dan. iii. 29; 2 Sam. xii. 31.

And appoint him his portion with hypocrites] Hypocrites then are the free-holders of hell; other sinners are but as tenants and inmates to them, μέρος, *id quod in divisione obtigit*. Lorin.

CHAPTER XXV.

Ver. 1. *Then shall the kingdom of heaven*] Our Saviour here continueth his former discourse, and sets it on by a second parable to the same purpose; not so much for the difficulty of the matter, as for our dulness and backwardness to believe and improve it. Moses would have men whet good things upon their children's minds and memories, by going often over them, as the knife doth over the whetstone.[1] Solomon saith good counsel should be fastened as nails driven home to the head, Eccles. xii. 11. Paul holds it profitable to write the same things, though not in the same words, to his Philippians, chap. iv. 1. Peter slacks not to rouse up (διεγείρειν) those to whom he writes, by remembering them of those points wherein they were ready and well-rooted, 2 Pet. i. 12, 13. And Austin adviseth preachers so long to press the same truths, till they read in their hearers' very visage that they resent and relish them.

Unto ten virgins] Virgins without number, Cant. vi. 8. Professors at large, good and bad, one with another.

Which took their lamps] The solemnities of marriage were anciently performed and celebrated by night, Luke xii. 35 (Plutarch, Problem.), and the bridegroom brought to his lodging by the virgins bearing burning lamps before him.

Ver. 2. *Five were foolish*] That is, some were wise, and some others foolish, and these last usually the most imprudent, improvident, after-witted, *oculos habentes in occipitio*, that foresee not a following mischief, but come in with their fools' Had I wist, with their *Si præscivissem*, as the lion in the fable (μωραὶ quasi μὴ ὁρῶσαι). The Spaniards say of the Portuguese that they are *pocos y focos*, few and foolish. But of foolish virgins, that is, of profligate professors, that have no more than an outside, there are not a few, but more than a good many in all places, Cant. vi. 8, 9.

Ver. 3. *Took their lamps, and took no oil*] Empty casks, barren fig-trees, pretenders only to the power of godliness; of whom it may be said, as Livy saith of the Athenians, that they waged war against Philip the father of Persius, king of Macedonia (so these against the devil, the world, and the flesh); *literis verbisque, quibus solis valent*. These carry Uriah's letters about them destructory to themselves. For if religion be not good, why do they profess it? If it be, why do they

not practise it? To such it may fitly be said, as Archidamus to his son, rashly conflicting with the enemy without sufficient strength, *Aut viribus adde, aut animis adime*, so either add practise, or leave profession: and as Alexander having a soldier of his own name, and this soldier being a coward, he came to him and said, Either leave off the name of Alexander, or be valiant; so let these nominals either lay by their lamps or take oil with them.

Ver. 4. *But the wise took oil*] That is, true faith in their hearts, which, as oil, is spreading, softening, suppling, soaking. Christ putteth not upon his a washy colour of profession (a block-wood blue), but he dyeth them in grain, with true grace and holiness.

Ver. 5. *While the bridegroom tarried*] Tarry he doth. 1. To exercise our patience. 2. To eneager our desires. 3. That his elect may be all gathered. 4. That the mystery of iniquity may be fulfilled. 5. That the prophecies may be accomplished, &c.

They all slumbered] The wise ones also slept, but their hearts waked, Cant. v. 2; they slept but half-sleep, they napped and nodded (ἐνύσταξαν), they slept with open eyes as the lion doth; the spirit was willing to wake, but the flesh was weak and overweighed it. They slumbered, but it was by candle-light, they had their lamps burning by them, which the foolish had not.

Ver. 6. *There was a cry made*] By the trumpet of the archangel,[2] and the voice of God, say some interpreters; and Jerome reports it for an apostolical tradition that Christ shall come at midnight. But of that hour no man knoweth, saith the Judge himself. Others there are that expound this cry of the preaching of the gospel, according to that voice of the crier, " Prepare ye the way of the Lord," &c., Matt. iii. And here—*clames ut stentora vincas*, Cry aloud, spare not, &c.

Ver. 7. *And trimmed their lamps*] The foolish also made a fair flourish, and held themselves, haply, in case good enough for heaven; deceiving their own hearts, or rather deceived by them, whiles they use fallacious and specious sophisms, James i. 26, to make themselves believe their penny to be good silver, when as it is nothing better than a slip.

Ver. 8. *Our lamps are gone out*] They were not lighted lamps, but sparks of their own tinder-boxes; phantastical fire, an *ignis fatuus*, a painted flame, which neither heats nor lights. The glow-worm seems to have both heat and light, but touch it, and it hath neither. Alchemy gold may seem brighter and better than true gold, but it can neither pass the seventh fire, nor comfort the heart as a cordial: so here. A man may live by a form, but he cannot die by it. They that kindle a fire, but not of God's sanctuary, and compass themselves about with specious sparks, they may walk here for a while

---

[1] Deut. vi. 7. *Repetere sicut in acuendo. Shanan et Shanab sunt cognata.*

[2] *Recte ad Archangeli vocem referetur.* Arct.

in the light of their fire, and in the sparks that they have kindled. But when all is done, this is all they shall have of God's hand, they shall lie down to sorrow, Isa. l. 11.

Ver. 9. *Lest there be not enough, &c.*] The best have nought to spare, whatever Papists fancy of the church-treasury. The righteous is scarcely saved; at death he finds all he could do little enough; though he began betime, and bestirred himself to his utmost, hard and scarce gets he to heaven, though he hath instantly served God day and night, Acts xxvi. 7, with a kind of extension and vehemency (ἐν ἐκτενείᾳ).

But go ye rather to them that sell] *Salsa est derisio non cohortatio*, like that, Isa. xlvii. 13. As if God should say to Papists, Go to your indulgencers, pardon-mongers, annealers; or to carnal gospellers, Go to your parasitical preachers, that have soothed you up in your sins (and ye loved to have it so), or at the best, have shot off a few pop-guns only against gross sins, and licked you whole again presently with, I hope better things of you.

Ver. 10. *And they that were ready, went in, &c.*] The bridegroom waits no man's leisure: love is impatient of delays, leaps over all impediments, those mountains of Bether, or division, Cant. ii. 17, that it may have not a union only, but a unity with the beloved.

And the door was shut] Opportunity is headlong, and once lost, irrecoverable. It behoves us, therefore, to be abrupt in the work of repentance, Dan. iv. 27, as a work of greatest haste; lest we cry out, as he once, All too late, all too late; or as a great lady of this land did lately upon her death-bed, Time, time! a world of wealth for an inch of time. We want not time so much as waste it. Remember that upon this moment depends eternity. God hath hanged the heaviest weights upon the weakest wires.

Ver. 11. *Afterward came also the other virgins*] The greater number by odds that stand trifling and baffling with Christ, and their souls futuring their repentance, Epimetheus' post-masters, *semper victuri* in Seneca's sense. Jehoshaphat in temporals was ever wise too late, 2 Chron. xviii. 31, and xx. 36, 37, and paid for his after-wit; howbeit, in spirituals he was a wise virgin, made sure work for his soul, which was an high point of heavenly prudence.

Lord, Lord, open unto us] The self-soother (with Sisera) is dreaming of a kingdom, when Jael's nail is nearer to his temples than a crown; unless it be such a crown as Walter Earl of Athol (that Scotch traitor) had, a crown of red-hot iron clapped upon his head; being one of those tortures wherewith he ended at once his wicked days and desires of the kingdom.

Ver. 12. *Verily I say unto you, I know you not*] i. e. With a knowledge of approbation or delight. *Verba notitiæ, apud Hebræos secum trahunt affectum.* See more above in the note upon chap. vii. 23.

Ver. 13. *Watch therefore*] Lest ye smart for it, when God shall send out summons for sleepers. This is an exhortation answerable to that chap. xxiv. 42, and the upshot of that, this, and the ensuing parable. See the notes there.

Ver. 14. *And delivered unto them his goods*] There is scarce any man but hath some one thing or other in him, that is excellent and extraordinary; some special talent to trade with, some honey to bring to the common hive, have he but an heart to it. *Sua cuique dos est.* Let every man, according to his several abilities, improve what he hath to the common benefit. Freely he hath received, freely let him give; ability he hath none but from God; who yet, for our encouragement, is pleased to call that ours that is his own work in us.

Ver. 15. *According to his several ability*] Usurers use not to lend to those that cannot give pledge or security. Howbeit, we have nothing of our own, but according to the measure of our gifts and faith, Ephes. iv., the measure of the rule distributed to us, 2 Cor. x. 13, the measure of grace concredited, Rom. xii.

Ver. 16. *Went and traded*] Grace grows by exercise, and decays by disuse; as that side of the teeth which is least used in chewing is apt to have more rheum to settle upon it. Though both arms grow, yet that which a man useth is the stronger and bigger; so is it in both gifts and graces. In birds, their wings which have been used most are sweetest. Among trees, that which is planted and plashed against a wall, the more it is spread and laid forth in the branches, even to the least twig, the more warmth and vigour it gets from the sunbeams, and the more fruit it beareth. So here.

Ver. 17. *He also gained other two*] The Lord, as he hath a fatherly respect to our weakness so as not to over-lay us, so he takes well aworth what we are able, and exacts no more than he gives. Despise not therefore the day of small things, sith God doth not, Zech. iv. 10.[1] Neither cast away your confidence, because not good to such a degree; but be faithful in weakness, though weak in faith. A palsy-hand may receive an alms; he that had but half an eye might look upon the brazen serpent, and be healed.

Ver. 18. *Digged it in the earth*] Through sloth and pride; as many now-a-days will do no more service to God than may breed admiration amongst men. Some preachers (saith one) to win applause, set forth at first with such a strife to seem eloquent and learned, that they quickly spend their store; and then, rather than they would be observed to want, they will give over preaching, or else preach once a quarter, to air their learning, and keep it from moulding. Such another is the miser, like the Cornish chough, which will steal a piece of money, and hiding it in some hole, will never help herself or others with it afterward.

Ver. 19. *And reckoneth with them*] This is that we must also come to, 2 Cor. v. 10. Christ

[1] *Honestum est ei qui in primis nequit, in secundis tertiisve consistere.* Cic.

will one day say, *Redde rationem*, Give an account of thy stewardship. Cicero could say, Let us so frame our course, as that we reckon upon our last reckoning, and make account we must all come to an account. And because often-reckonings keep long friends, *Villicus rationem cum Domino crebro putet*, saith Cato, Let us be oft dealing with ourselves, and setting things to rights betwixt God and our own souls ; so shall we have the less to do at last cast. Sparing a little pains at first, doubleth it in the end ; as he who will not cast up his books, his books will cast up him at length.

Ver. 20. *He that had received five*] He was first called to an account, and if four, or but one of his five talents had lain dead and unoccupied he had been doomed for his ill-husbandry. See that ye receive not any grace of God in vain ; neither envy those that have much ; a proportion is expected, *Non tantum otiosi, sed cunctatores plectentur*. Thou idle, and therefore evil servant, ver. 26.

Ver. 21. *Thou hast been faithful over a few things*] So the Lord calleth the greatest measure of grace here attainable, in comparison of heaven's holiness and happiness, *Ne donis vel bonis nostris efferamur*. What is a spark to the sun, a drop to the ocean ?

Enter thou into the joy of thy Lord] A joy too big to enter into us, we must enter into it. A joy more meet for the Lord than the servant. Yet such a Lord do we serve, as will honour his servants with such a joy. Amongst men it is otherwise, Luke xvii. 7 ; Gen. xv. 2, 3 ; 1 Kings xi. 28, 40.

Ver. 22. *Lord, thou deliveredst unto me two talents*] It is with Christians as with planets. The moon goes her course in a month, the sun in a year, the rest not but in many years, yet at length they finish. Let us be doing as we can, and our reward is sure with God. Covet rather graces than gifts ; as to pray more fervently, though less notionally or eloquently. Stammering Moses must pray, rather than well-spoken Aaron. The Corinthians came behind in no gift, 1 Cor. i. 7, yet were babes and carnal, chap. iii. 2, 3.

Ver. 23. *Well done, good and faithful servant*] Though this second had the same good acceptance as the former, yet it follows not that they were both alike rewarded ; but had a different degree, as of grace, so of glory.

Ver. 24. *Lord, I knew that thou wert*, &c.] *Invalidum omne natura querulum*. A sorry senseless excuse it is that this man makes for himself ; and such as is both false and frivolous. It shows an utter emptiness of the oil of God's grace, when men's lips, like doors on rusty hinges, move not without murmuring and mal-contentedness.

Ver. 25. *I was afraid, and went and hid*, &c.] So God must bear the blame of his unfaithfulness. "The foolishness of man perverteth his way," and (then to mend the matter) his heart fretteth against the Lord, or at least he digests

his choler, as horses do, by champing on the bridle-bit, Prov. xix. 3.

Ver. 26. *Thou wicked and slothful servant*] God puts no difference betwixt *Nequaquam et nequam*, an idle and an evil servant. Had idleness been a calling, this servant had been both a good husband and a good fellow too. But what saith the heathen ? *Næ illi falsi sunt, qui diversissimas res expectant, ignaviæ voluptatem, et præmia virtutis.* (Sallust. in Jug.)

Ver. 27. *Received the same with usury*] Our Saviour doth no more patronize usury here than he doth injustice, Luke xvi. 1 ; theft, 1 Thess. v. 2 ; dancing, Matt. xi. 17 ; Olympic games, 1 Cor. ix. 24.

Ver. 28. *Take therefore the talent from him*] God will take his own, and be gone from an unworthy people or person, Hos. ii. 9. The idol shepherd's "arm shall be clean dried up, and his right eye utterly darkened," Zech. xi. 17. It is no hard matter to observe a wane and decay of God's gifts in them that use them not ; till at last, Zedekiah like, they may say, "When did the Spirit depart from me ? " 1 Kings xxii. 24. And as many of Ishbosheth's friends shrank together with Abner, so do men's abilities fail amain, when once they begin to fail, till at last God lays them aside, as so many broken vessels, and cause them to be forgotten, as dead men out of mind, Psal. xxxi. 21.

Ver. 29. *But from him that hath not, shall be*, &c.] See the notes on chap. xiii. 12 ; where the like is spoken, but with this difference. There our Saviour speaketh of proud men, such as arrogate to themselves that they have not ; here of the idle and evil persons, such as improve and employ not that they have ; the rust of whose worth shall rise up against them, James v. 3.

Ver. 30. *And cast ye the unprofitable servant*] Ἀχρεῖος, useless. That had his soul for salt only, to keep his body from putrifying, that worthless, sapless, useless man, that is no more missed when gone than the parings of one's nails, that never did good among his people, Ezek. xviii. 18, but lived wickedly, and therefore died wickedly. Away with such a fellow, saith Christ, from off the earth, which he hath burdened, ἐτώσιον ἄχθος ἀρούρης. Hom.

Ver. 31. *And all the holy angels with him*] He shall not leave one behind him in heaven. Oh ! what a brave bright day must that needs be, when so many glorious suns shall shine in the firmament, and among and above them all the Sun of righteousness, in whom our nature is advanced above the brightest cherub.

Upon the throne of his glory] Perhaps upon his angels, who are called thrones, Col. i. 16, and possibly may bear him aloft by their natural strength, as on their shoulders.

Ver. 32. *And before him shall be gathered all*] Then shall Adam see all his nephews at once ; none shall be excused for absence at this general assizes, none shall appear by a proxy, all shall be compelled to come in and hear their sentence ;

which may be, as some conceive, a long while a-doing. It may be made evident (saith one) from Scripture and reason, that this day of Christ's kingly office in judging all men shall last haply longer than his private administration now (wherein he is less glorious) in governing the world. Things shall not be suddenly shuffled up at last day, as some imagine. (Mr Shepeard's *Sincere Convert,* p. 87.)

And he shall separate them] Before he hears their causes; which is an argument of singular skill in the Judge; it being the course of other judges to proceed, *Secundum allegata et probata.* But he shall set men's sins in order before their eyes, Psal. l. 21, with items of the particulars.

Ver. 33. *The sheep on the right hand,* &c.] A place of dignity and safety. Our Saviour seems here to allude to that of Moses' dividing the tribes on Gerizim and Ebal. Those six tribes that came of the free-women are set to bless the people; as the other five, that came of the bond-women (whereunto is adjoined Reuben for his incest) are set to say Amen to the curses, Deut. xxvii. 11—13.

Ver. 34. *Come, ye blessed of my Father*] *Paterne alloquitur.* As who should say, Where have ye been, my darlings, all this while of my long absence? Come, come, now into my bosom, which is now wide open to receive you, as the welcomest guests that ever accosted me, &c. And surely if Jacob's and Joseph's meetings were so unspeakably comfortable: if Mary and Elisabeth did so greet and congratulate, oh what shall be the joy of that last day!

Inherit the kingdom prepared] Here (as in the Turk's court) every man is *aut Cæsar aut nullus,* as he said, either a king or a caitiff; as the sultan's children, if they reign not, they die without mercy, either by the sword or halter.

From the foundation of the world] Their heads were destinated long since to the diadem, as Tertullian hath it. King James was crowned in his cradle; Sapores, king of Persia, before he was born (for his father dying, the nobles set the crown on his mother's belly); but the saints were crowned in God's eternal counsel, before the world was founded.

Ver. 35. *For I was an hungred*] "For" in this place denoteth not the cause, but the evidence. It is all one as if I should say, This man liveth, for behold he moveth. Where it will easily be yielded, that motion is not the cause of life, but the evidence and effect of it. So here. Merit is a mere fiction, sith there can be no proportion betwixt the work and the wages.

Ver. 36. *Naked, and ye clothed me*] Darius, before he came to the kingdom, received a garment for a gift of one Syloson. And when he became king, he rewarded him with the command of his country Samus. (Ælian.) Who now will say that Syloson merited such a boon for so small a courtesy? A gardener, offering a rape-root (being the best present the poor man had) to the Duke of Burgundy, was bountifully rewarded by the duke, which his steward observing, thought

to make use of his bounty, presenting him with a very fair horse. The duke (*ut perspicaci erat ingenio,* saith mine author) being a very wise man, perceived the project, received the horse, and gave him nothing for it. Right so will God deal with our merit-mongers, that by building monasteries, &c., think to purchase heaven.

I was sick, and ye visited me] Our King Henry III., the same day that he set sail for France, himself did in person visit the poor and feeble, and dealt large alms; not refusing to kiss the sick and leprous. (Speed. 603.) This was well done, if without opinion of merit; and with the like mind that Dr Taylor, martyr, usually visited the alms-houses and hospitals, there to see what the poor and sick lacked, to procure them supplies, and to give them good counsel.

I was in prison, and ye came to me] Many Papists have hence concluded that there are only six works of mercy, *Visito, poto, cibo,* &c., whereas indeed there are many more. But it is remarkable out of this text, that the last definitive sentence shall pass upon men, according to their frowardness and freeness in showing mercy to the family of faith. And that the sentence of absolution shall contain a manifestation of all their good works, and that with such fervency of affection in Christ, that he will see and remember nothing in them but the good they have done. See my Common-place of Alms.

Ver. 37—39. *Then shall the righteous,* &c.] Not that there shall be then any such dialogism (say divines) at the last day: but Christ would hereby give us to understand that the saints rising again, and returning to themselves, can never sufficiently set forth such a bounty in Christ, whereby he taketh all they do to their poor necessitous brethren, in as good part as done to his sacred self.

Ver. 40. *One of the least of these my brethren*] What a comfort is this, that our own Brother shall judge us, who is much more compassionate than any Joseph. What an honour, that Christ calls us his brethren. What an obligation is such a dignity to all possible duty, that we stain not our kindred. Antigonus being invited to a place where a notable harlot was to be present, asked counsel of Menedemus what he should do. He bade him only remember that he was a king's son. Remember we that we are Christ the King's brethren, and it may prove a singular preservative. *Vellem si non essem Imperator,* said Scipio, when a harlot was offered unto him, I would, if I were not general. Take thou the pillage of the field, said Themistocles to his friend: Ανελοῦ σεαυτῷ, σὺ γὰρ οὐκ εἶ Θημιστο-κλὴς, for thou art not Themistocles.

Ye have done it unto me] Christ, saith Salvian, is, *Mendicorum maximus,* as one that shareth in all the saints' necessities; and who would but relieve necessitous Christ? Look out some Mephibosheth, in whom we may seal up love to deceased Jonathan. My goodness extendeth not to thee, saith David, but to the saints, Christ's receivers, Psal. xvi. 2, 3. Mr Fox never denied beggar that asked in Jesus' name. And being once asked whether he knew a certain poor man who had received succour from him in time of trouble, he answered, I remember him well: I tell you, I forget lords and ladies to remember such.

Ver. 41. *Then shall he say also, &c.*] Then: judgment as it begins here at God's house, so shall it at the last day. The elect shall be crowned, and then the reprobates doomed and damned.

Depart from me, ye cursed, &c.] A sentence that breathes out nothing but fire and brimstone, stings and horrors, woe, and, alas, torments without end and past imagination. Mercy, Lord, saith the merciless miser. No, saith Christ, Depart, be packing.

Yet bless me before I go.

"Depart, ye cursed."

To some good place then.

To hell-fire, not material fire, but worse in many respects.

But let me then come out again.

It is everlasting fire, eternity of extremity. This is the hell of hell; this puts the damned to their οὐαὶ οὐαὶ, as much as if they should say, οὐκ ἀεὶ, οὐκ ἀεὶ, Not ever, Lord, torment us thus. But they have a will to sin ever; and being worthless they cannot satisfy God's justice in any time; therefore is their fire everlasting.

But let me have some good company in my misery.

"The devil and his angels."

But who appointed me this hard condition?

It was prepared of old. The all-powerful wisdom did, as it were, sit down and devise most tormenting temper for that most formidable fire. And here it is hard to say, whether be more woeful, "Depart from me, ye cursed," or that which followeth, "into everlasting fire;" pain of loss, or pain of sense. Sure it is, that the tears of hell are not sufficient to bewail the loss of heaven; the worm of grief gnaws as painful as the fire burns. If those good souls, Acts xx., wept because they should see Paul's face no more, how deplorable is the eternal deprivation of the beatifical vision!

Ver. 42. *For I was an hungred, &c.*] Ill works are the just causes of damnation, as being perfectly evil. But good works can be no such causes of salvation, because due debts to God, and at the best imperfect.

Ver. 43. *I was a stranger, &c.*] These fools of the people had a price in their hands to get heaven (as Joseph by his bounty bought the land of Egypt), but they had no heart to it, Prov. xvii. 16. Richard son to Henry III. of England was elected king of Romans, being preferred therein before Alphonsus king of Spain, his competitor. The Spaniard pretended and complained to have been first elected. But being, it seems, a great mathematician, he was drawing lines when he should have drawn out his purse, and so came

prevented of his hopes.[1] And is not this many an Englishman's fault and folly?

Ver. 44. *Lord, when saw we thee, &c.*] They were sand-blind, and could not see Christ in poor Christians (μυωπάζοντες, 2 Pet. i. 9), whom they should have looked upon as the only earthly angels, the dearly beloved of Christ's soul, Jer. xii. 7; the house of his glory, Isa. lx. 7; an ornament of God, Ezek. vii. 20; a royal diadem in the hand of Jehovah, Isa. lxii. 3.

Ver. 45. *Inasmuch as ye did it not to one, &c.*] Omissions then are damnable sins. Ammonites and Moabites were bastardized and banished the beauty of holiness, the tabernacle of God, to the tenth generation, because they met not God's Israel with bread and water in the wilderness, Deut. xxiii. 3, 4. Not to do justice is injustice; not to show mercy is cruelty. Where then will oppressors appear, that grind the faces of the poor, that quaff their tears, and make music of their shrieks? "Go to now, ye rich men, weep and howl," &c., Jam. v. 1—3. If not relieving of the poor damns men, what shall robbing do, but double damn?

Ver. 46. *And these shall go away, &c.*] The sentence began with the godly, the execution with the wicked: both that the godly may see their desire upon their enemies, Psal. lviii. 10; lxxix. 10; and also, that in the others' misery they may behold, by the difference, their own felicity; and thereby be moved to lift up many an humble, joyful, and thankful heart to God.

CHAPTER XXVI.

Ver. 1. *And it came to pass when, &c.*] This is our evangelist's transition from the ministry of Christ's doctrine to the mystery of his passion. He had hitherto taught salvation, and now is declared how he wrought it. He had done the office of a doctor, now of a redeemer: of a prophet, now of a priest.

Ver. 2. *Is the feast of the passover*] At which feast, Christ our passover was sacrificed for us, 1 Cor. v. 7, and we were purchased by his blood, as Israel was typically out of the world by the blood of the paschal lamb; our hearts being sprinkled therewith by the hyssop bunch of faith, from an evil conscience, and our bodies washed with pure water, Heb. x. 22.

Ver. 3. *Then assembled together, &c.*] Here was met a whole council of caitiffs to crucify Christ. General councils may err then in necessary and fundamental points: as the Council of Ariminum and Seleucia (held in two cities, because no one was able to contain them for multitude, yet) decreed for Arius against the deity of Christ. The truth of God may be locked up within the hearts of such a company, as in competition of suffrages cannot make a greater part in a general council.

Ver. 4. *Take Jesus by subtilty, and kill him*] Craft and cruelty go commonly coupled in the Church's adversaries. Neither of them "wants

---

[1] Daniel's Hist. of England, 174.

their mate," as the Scripture speaks of those birds of prey and desolation, Isa. xxxiv. 16. These priests and elders were so bitterly bent against Christ, that nothing would satisfy them but his blood. All plants and other creatures have their growth and increase to a period, and then their declination and decay, except only the crocodile, who grows bigger and bigger, even till death. So have all passions and perturbations in man's mind their intentions and remissions, except only malicious revenge. This dies not, many times, but with the man (if that), as nothing can quench the combustible slime in Samosaris, nor the burning flame of the hill Chimæra, but only earth, 1 Pet. ii. 23. Saint Peter tells us, that our Saviour being reviled, did not only commit his cause to God, but himself to God: as expecting the increase of his enemies' opposition, till they had put him to death.

Ver. 5. *Not on the feast day, lest, &c.*] But God would have it on that feast day, and no other, Acts iv. 27. And here these wicked ones fulfil the divine decree: but no thank to them: more than to Haman for Mordecai's advancement, whereunto Haman held the stirrup only. *Divinum consilium dum devitatur impletur*, saith a Father.

Ver. 6. *Now when Jesus was in Bethany*] This history of a thing acted before Christ came to Jerusalem, comes in here somewhat out of place: to show the ground and occasion of Judas' treason, which was discontent at the loss of such a prize, and our Saviour's sharping him up for showing his dislike.

In the house of Simon the leper] A leper he had been, but was now healed, and haply by Christ: whom therefore he entertaineth in way of thankfulness, as Matthew also did.

Ver. 7. *An alabaster box of very precious, &c.*] Pliny telleth us that they were wont to keep the most costly ointments in boxes of alabaster. And Herodotus reckoneth μύρου ἀλάβαστρον, an alabaster box of ointment, among the precious things that Cambyses the Persian sent for a present to the king of Ethiopia. Mary thought nothing too costly for Christ. See the notes on John xii. 3.

Ver. 8. *They had indignation*] Not all, but one of them was displeased, viz. Judas (as John explains Matthew), who yet was of such esteem and authority amongst the disciples, that what he did they are all said to do, and possibly they might, some of them, be drawn to do the same by his example, and upon so specious a pretence of charity to the poor.

To what purpose is this waste?] All seems to be lost to flesh and blood that is laid out upon Christ, his servants and services. "The people is idle," said Pharaoh, when they would needs go worship in the wilderness. And Seneca jeers the Jews for wasting a seventh part of their lives on a weekly Sabbath. (Aug. de Civ. Dei.)

Ver. 9. *For this ointment might have been sold*] True, and better it had been sold, had it been a superfluous and idle expence; such as is now-a-days ordinary in fine clothes, sumptuous feasts, over stately buildings, &c. Back, belly, and building, these three B B B, like the daughters of the horse-leech, suck out the blood of men's substance. But here it is a senseless sentence that Judas uttereth, out of discontent only, that he missed of so fat a morsel. Avarice made Judas, as it did Sejanus, think all which he acquired not, to be lost, *Quicquid non acquiritur, damnum est.*

Ver. 10. *Why trouble ye the woman?*] Christ will patronize his well-doers, and stick to them, though all forsake them, 2 Tim. iv. 16, 17. He many times pleads for them in the consciences of their greatest enemies, who spend more thoughts about such than the world is aware of: and are "afraid of the name of God, whereby they are called," Deut. xxviii. 9, 10.

Ver. 11. *The poor ye have always with you*] To try and to exercise your liberality, yea, your justice, Matt. vi. 1, as the Syriac calleth it, Prov. iii. 27. Withhold not thy goods from these owners thereof.

But me ye have not always] Christ dwelt in the flesh, as in a tent or booth, John i. 14. He sojourned here for awhile only; his abode with us was but temporary, as the Greek word there importeth (ἐσκήνωσεν, *ex quo intelligitur Christi moram apud nos temporariam fuisse.* Beza.)

Ver. 12. *She did it for my burial*] This Mary perhaps understood not. So things that we think come to pass by hap-hazard are preordained, and sweetly ordered by Almighty God in his secret counsel, and by his fatherly providence, to excellent ends many times, such as we never thought on.

Ver. 13. *Be told for a memorial of her*] Though now she be sharply censured by the traitor for a waste-good. "Do well and hear ill is written upon heaven gates," said that martyr. But God will both right his wronged and honour his disparaged. Mary's name now smells as sweet in all God's house as ever her ointment did; when Judas' name rots, and shall do to all posterity. Yea, in the next world, Mary and such, we shall look upon, likely, with thoughts of extraordinary love and sweetness throughout all eternity: as Judas and such, with execrable and everlasting detestation.

Ver. 14. *Then one of the twelve, &c.*] sc. When he heard of the chief priests and elders meeting about such a matter, Satan sets him on, being now malcontent, to make one amongst them. That spirit of darkness loves to dwell in a soul that is clouded by passion: as in Saul when he was envious at David; and here in Judas, when defeated of his design, and fretted at his Master's reprehension.

Ver. 15. *What will ye give me*] Take heed and beware of covetousness, saith our Saviour, Luke xii. 15; for it is "the root of all evil," saith Paul, 1 Tim. vi. 10: a breach of the whole decalogue, as some divines have demonstrated and universal experience hath confirmed. These *sordida poscinummia,* as one calleth them, are still found everywhere:[1] such as will sell their souls to the devil with Ahab, not for seven years' enjoyment of the Popedom, as some have done, but for a few paltry shillings, as Judas here did, or some other pidling profit. This our Saviour calleth the "mammon of iniquity," which is the next odious name to the devil himself. Δεινὸς καὶ πάντολμος τῆς φιλοχρηματίας ἔρως. Isid. Pelus. Luke xvi. 9.

For thirty pieces of silver] "A goodly price," as the prophet in scorn and detestation calleth it. It was a known set price for the basest slave, Exod. xxi. 31; Joel iii. 3, 6. For so small a sum sold this traitor so sweet a Master, as had not only admitted him into his company, but committed the bag to him, and let him want for nothing. *Quid non mortalia pectora cogis, Auri sacra fames?* (Virgil.) Look well to it. For as there were many Marys in one Cæsar, so are there many Judases in the best. Let patrons especially look to it: for many of them are worse than Judas. He sold the head, they the members: he the sheep, they the shepherd: he but the body, they the souls, as that scarlet strumpet, Rev. xviii. 13.

Ver. 16. *And from that time he sought*] So it was no sudden, but a prepensed wickedness, done in cold blood, and upon mature deliberation. God's people when they sin, they are pre-occupated, and taken before they are aware, Gal. vi. 1. There is no way of wickedness in them, ordinarily, Psal. cxxxix. 24. It is of incogitancy: put them in mind, and they mend all. Or, it is of passion: and passions last not long. They deny not Christ that bought them: they can do nothing against the truth, they will not forego God upon any terms, they never sin with deliberation about this chief end: if they err, it is only in the way, as thinking that they may fulfil such a lust, and keep God too.

Ver. 17. *Now the first day*] That is, on the fourteenth day of the first month, according to the law. The priests, for politic respects, had adjourned this feast to the sixteenth day, being the Sabbath, against the letter of the law, that the celebrity might be the greater; and the people were ruled by them. Our Saviour followeth not a multitude, nor observeth man's tradition herein, but God's prescription: no more must we. This St Luke plainly intimateth in his ἔδει, Luke xxii. 7. Then came the day of unleavened bread when the Passover ought to be killed; though the custom were otherwise.

Ver. 18. *Go into the city to such a man*] Meaning some man of his special acquaintance, for so the Greek (ὁ δεῖνα) imports, though he named him not. So *Palmoni hammedabber,* "such an one the speaker," Dan. viii. 13.

Ver. 19. *Did as Jesus had appointed them*] With a kind of blind obedience; such as we must yield to God, notwithstanding all unlikelihoods or scruples whatsoever, cast in by carnal reason. This the Scripture calls the "obedience

[1] See Mr Dike's Caveat for the Covetous.

of faith," and commends it to us, in the examples of Abraham, Moses, others, Heb. xi.

Ver. 20. *He sat down with the twelve*] With Judas among the rest; though Hilary hold otherwise, for what reason I know not. Christ sat at the sacrament, when yet the gesture imported in the law was standing; and this sitting at the Passover was nowhere commanded, yet by the godly Jews was generally used. Let this "heap of wheat" (the Lord's supper, as some interpret it) be "set about with lilies," Cant. vii. 2, that is, with Christians, white, and of holy life; that is the main matter to be looked to.

Ver. 21. *And as they did eat, he said*] With a great deal of detestation of so horrid a fact; to see the frontless traitor bear himself so bold amongst them, having now hatched so prodigious a villany.

One of you shall betray me] But shall any therefore condemn the whole twelve, as if there were never a better? This were to "offend against the generation of the righteous," Psal. lxxiii. 15. This were to match in immanity that cruel prince of Wallachia, whose custom was, together with the offender, to execute the whole family, yea, sometimes the whole kindred. And yet this justice is done God's people many times by the Church malignant.

Ver. 22. *And they were exceeding sorrowful*] Not joyful (as some would have been) to find out other men's faults, and to exagitate them. Not only those that make, but that love lies, yea, or unseasonable truths in this kind, are shut out of heaven among dogs and devils, Rev. xxii. 15.

Lord, is it I?] He puts them all to a search, afore the sacrament. Let "a man therefore examine himself," &c., 1 Cor. xi. 28; who knows the error of his life? saith David, Psal. xix. 12. In our hearts are volumes of corruptions, in our lives infinite erratas. Socrates would say, when he saw one drunk, or otherwise disordered, *Num ego talis?* So would Mr Bradford, when he looked into the lewd lives of any others.

Ver. 23. *He that dippeth his hand, &c.*] My fellow-commoner, my familiar friend, Psal. xli. 10. This greatly aggravateth the indignity of the matter. He was *ex societate Jesu* that betrayed him. So do the pretended Jesuits, Jebusites, at this day. Julius Cæsar was slain in the Senate-house by more of his friends than of his enemies, *quorum non expleverat spes inexplebiles,* saith Seneca. But the wound that went nearest his heart was that he received from his son Brutus. Καὶ σὺ τέκνον Βροῦτε, this pierced him worse than any poniard. Queen Elizabeth's grief and complaint was, that in trust she had found treason.

Ver. 24. *The Son of man goeth*] That is, dieth, suffereth. Death was to him but an ἔξοδος, as it is called Luke ix. 31; that is, an out-going, or a departure. It was no more betwixt God and Moses, but "Go up and die," as it was said to another prophet, "Up and eat." He that hath conversed with God here, cannot fear to go to him; cannot hold death either uncouth or unwelcome.

But wee unto that man by whom, &c.] He bewails not himself, but Judas. So should we do those by whom we are traduced and injured. They, poor wretches, have the worst of it. Let us pity them, and pray for them, as the holy martyrs dealt by their persecutors. Ah! I lament the infidelity of England, said Mr Philpot. Ah! great be the plagues that hang over England, yea, though the gospel should be restored again. Happy shall that person be whom the Lord shall take out of the world not to see them.

Ver. 25. *Master, is it I?*] Desperate impudency! debauched hypocrisy! Had he the face to ask such a question? He could not but know that Christ knew all; yet hoped he, perhaps, that of his wonted gentleness, he would conceal him still, as he had done for certain days before. But incorrigible and incurable persons are no longer to be borne with. He heareth, therefore, "Thou hast said it," that is, Thou art the man I mean. Thus Christ pulls off his vizor, washeth off his varnish, and maketh him to appear in his own colours, a covetous caitiff, an impudent dog, a breathing devil, as Chrysostom hath it, a mischievous monkey; which creature hath the gravest countenance of any other, but is incessantly doing mischief. *Talis res est avaritia, amentes, stolidos, impudentes, canes pro hominibus, et dæmones ex canibus facit.* (Chrys.)

Ver. 26. *Jesus took bread*] From bread and wine used by the Jews at the eating of the paschal lamb, without all command of Moses, but resting upon the common reason given by the Creator, Christ authorizeth a seal of his very flesh and blood. And as the householder, at the end of that solemn supper, blessed God, first, taking bread, and again, taking wine; so that we should not turn his seal into superstition, he followeth that plainness: *ne miseri mortales, in istorum mysteriorum usu, in rebus terrestribus hæreant et obstupescant*, as Beza gives the reason. For which cause also, saith he, even in the old Liturgy they used to cry out to the people at the Lord's table, *Sursum corda*, Lift up your hearts; that is, Look not so much to the outward signs in the sacraments, but use them as ladders to mount you up to Christ in heaven. *Ut in cœlum usque ad Christum penetrarent.* (Beza.)

This is my body] "This is" referred to bread by an anomaly of the gender (the like whereof we find, Eph. v. 6), and so the apostle interpreteth it, 1 Cor. x. 16, and xi. 26. The sense then is, This bread is my true essential body, which is given for you: that is, by an ordinary metonymy.[1] This bread is the sign of my body, as circumcision is called "the covenant," that is, the sign of the covenant, and seal of the righteousness of faith, Rom. iv. 11. And as Homer calls the sacrifices, covenants;[2] because thereby the covenants were confirmed. Virgil calleth it *fallere dextras*, to deceive the right hands, for to break the oath that was taken, by the taking of right hands, &c. Transubstantiation is a mere fiction; and the learnedest Papists are not yet agreed whether the substance of the bread in this sacrament be turned into the substance of Christ's body *productive*, as one thing is made of another; or whether the bread goes away, and Christ's body comes into the room of it *adductive*, as one thing succeeds into the place of another, the first being voided. Suarez is for the first, Bellarmine for the latter sense. And yet because Luther and Calvin agree not upon the meaning of these words, "This is my body," the Jesuits cry out, *Spiritus sanctus a seipso non discordat, Hæ interpretationes discordant, Ergo:* for Luther interpreteth the words synecdochically, Calvin metonymically, after Tertullian and Augustine; "This is my body," for this is a sign or figure of my body, a seal also to every faithful receiver, that Christ is his, with all his benefits.

Ver. 27. *And he took the cup*] Anciently of glass, afterwards of wood, and lastly of silver or gold. Whence that saying of a father, Once there were wooden cups, golden priests; now there are golden cups, but wooden priests.

Drink ye all of it] This is express against that Antichristian sacrilege of robbing the people of the cup. Eckius[3] saith the people ought to content themselves with the bread only, because, *Equi donati non sunt inspiciendi dentes*, "A gift-horse is not to be looked in the mouth." He thought, belike, that laymen could not claim any right to the bread neither. Bellarmine, a little wiser, grants they have a right to the bread, but adds, that in eating the bread transubstantiated by the priest into the body of Christ, they drink his blood also. But Lombard (his master) denies this: saying, that the bread is not turned, but into Christ's flesh; nor the wine, but into his blood. And thus these Babel-builders are confounded in their language, and hard it is to know what the Church of Rome holdeth. The Council of Constance speaketh out, and saith, That albeit Christ instituted, and accordingly administered this sacrament in both kinds, *tamen hoc non-obstante*, all this notwithstanding, the authority of the holy canons and the approved custom of the Church hath and doth deny the cup to the laity. And Nicolas Shetterden, martyr, in his answer compelled the commissary to grant that Christ's testament was broken, and his institution changed from that he left it. But he said, they had power so to do. Christ's redemption is both precious and plenteous. He makes his people a full feast. Bread and wine comprehend entire food; for *humidum et siccum*, moist and dry, are all that is required unto food, Isa. xxv. 6. Therefore as he gave them in the wilderness the bread of angels, so he set the rock abroach for them, and so fed them with sacraments. They did "all eat the same spiritual bread, and they did all drink the same spiritual drink," 1 Cor. x. 3, 4, that the ancient Church might give no warrant of a dry communion. The Russians, a kind of mongrel Christians, com-

---

[1] Τοῦτο *refertur ad* ἄρτος *anomalia generis.* Pasor.

[2] αὐτὰρ κήρυκες ἄγανοι ὅρκια πιστὰ Θιῶν σύναγον.

[3] Apud Manlium in loc. com.

municate in both kinds; but mingling both together in a chalice, they distribute it both together in a spoon. (Breerwood's Inquiries.)

Ver. 28. *For this is my blood*] This cup is my blood, viz. in a sacramental sense; as before the bread is said to be Christ's body. If the words of Christ when he said, "this is my body," did change the substance, then, belike, when Christ said, "this cup is my blood," the substance of the cup was likewise changed into his blood, said Shetterden the martyr to Archdeacon Harpfield. And you can no more enforce of necessity (said another martyr) from the words of Christ the changing of the bread and wine into his body and blood, than the wife's flesh to be the natural and real flesh of her husband, because it is written, "they are not two but one flesh." Besides, whereas it is forbidden that any should eat or drink blood, the apostles notwithstanding took and drank of the cup, &c. And when the sacrament was administered, none of them all crouched down, and took it for his god. *Quandoquidem Christiani manducant Deum quem adorant*, said Averroes the Arabian, *sit anima mea cum Philosophis.* Sith Christians eat their God, I'll have none.

Which is shed] That is, shall shortly be shed. But all is delivered and set down in the present tense, here and elsewhere in this business: because to faith (which at this sacrament we should chiefly actuate and exercise) all things are made present, whether they be things to come (as to these disciples) or things past, as now to us. A communicant must call up his faith, and bespeak it as Deborah did herself, Judg. v. 12. Awake, awake, Deborah, utter a song. Ascend up to heaven in the act of receiving, and fetch down Christ: lean by faith upon his blessed bosom, cleave to his cross, suck honey out of this rock, and oil out of the flinty rock, Deut. xxxii. 13, *et intra ipsa redemptoris vulnera figite linguam*, as Cyprian expresseth it. Let faith have her perfect work, sith she is both the hand, mouth, and stomach of the soul.

For remission of sins] This includes all the benefits of the New Covenant, all the purchase of Christ's passion, sweetly sealed up to every faithful receiver. Christ instituted his holy supper, *tanquam καθαρτήριον ἀλεξίκακον*, a sovereign preservative or purgative, saith Ignatius. And by this sacrament we are fenced and strengthened against the devil and all his assaults, saith Chrysostom, *Ita ut nos fugiat tanquam si leones ignem exspuentes essemus*, so that he shunneth us, as if we were so many lions spitting fire at him.

Ver. 29. *I will not drink henceforth*] So he takes his farewell of his disciples: alluding, likely, to that custom among them of drinking no more till the next day after they had drunk each his part of the parting-cup. *Poculum ἀπολυτικόν.*

Drink it new with you in my Father's kingdom] Understand it either of the kingdom of grace (Peter saith that he and others did eat and drink

---

with Christ after he rose from the dead, Acts x. 41; we also feast with him daily by faith, at his table especially, where he is both feast-maker and feast-master), or of his kingdom of glory, frequently and fitly set forth by the similitude of a sumptuous supper, Matt. viii., Luke xiv. &c., such as to which all other feasts are but hunger.

Ver. 30. *And when they had sung an hymn*] The Jews at the Passover sang the great hallelujah, that is, the 113th Psalm with the five following Psalms. This they began to sing after that dismissory cup afore-mentioned. At all times we should sing hallelujahs, with grace in our hearts to the Lord; but at the sacrament the great hallelujah, the hosannah Rabbah. We should credit the feast by our spiritual jollity, shouting as a giant after his wine, singing and making melody to the Lord in our hearts. Chrysostom maketh mention of an hymn of thanksgiving, wont to be used by the monks of his time after they had supped : [1] and he calleth them angels for their holy and heavenly life and conversation. We should come from the Lord's table, as Moses did from the mount, with our faces shining, as the good women did from the sepulchre, "with fear and great joy," as the people went to their tents from Solomon's feast, "joyful and glad of heart," 1 Kings viii. 66. If those in the wilderness were so cheered and cherished by their idolatrous feast before the golden calf, that they "eat and drink, and rise up to play," 1 Cor. x. 7, how much more should we by this blessed banquet? To whet our stomachs, let faith feed upon some promise before the sacrament. A moderate breakfast gets a man the better stomach to his dinner, &c.

Ver. 31. *All ye shall be offended because of me*] Why? what had that righteous one done? Nothing but that his cross lay in their way, whereat they stumbled shamefully, and left him to wonder that he was "left alone," Isa. lxiii. 5. Adversity is friendless (ἄφιλον τὸ δυστυχὲς), saith one heathen (Ovid); *Et cum fortuna statque caditque fides*, saith another. Job found his friends like the brooks of Tema, which in a moisture swell, in a drought fail. *Tempora si fuerint nubila, solus eris.*

For it is written, I will smite] This our Saviour purposely subjoineth, for their support under the sense of their base deserting him. A foul sin it was, but yet such as was long since set down of them; not without a sweet promise of their recollection, "I will turn my hand upon the little ones," Zech. xiii. 7; or, I will bring back my hand to the little ones (*At reducam manum meam ad parvulos*), as Tremellius readeth it.

Ver. 32. *But after I am risen again, &c.*] Infirmities bewailed, break no square. *Peccata nobis non nocent, si non placent* (Aug.): our sins hurt us not, if they please us not. The Church stands as right with Christ when penitent, as while innocent, Cant. vii. 12, with chap. iv. 1, 2, &c. Her hair, teeth, temples, all as fair and well-featured as ever.

Ver. 33. *Though all men should be offended*]

---

[1] ὕμνος εὐχαριστήριος. Hom. 55 in Matt.

Peter spake as he meant, but his heart deceived him, as did likewise David's, Psal. xxxix. 1—3, and Orpah's, Ruth i. 10, and those Israelites in the wilderness, that were turned aside " like deceitful bows," Psal. lxxviii. 57. They levelled both eyes and arrows (that is, both purposes and promises) to the mark of amendment, and thought verily to hit; but their deceitful hearts, as naughty bows, carried their arrows a clean contrary way. So did Peter's here, so will the best of ours, if we watch them not.

Ver. 34. *Before the cock crow, &c.*] Christ mentioneth the cock, *quia tam strenuum pugnatorem decebat tale præconium,* saith one. The presumption of proud flesh never but miscarries; when humble self-suspicion holds out, and hath favour. The story of Pendleton and Saunders is better known than that it needs here to be related. (Acts and Mon.)

Ver. 35. *Though I should die with thee*] *Quot verba tot absurda,* as one saith of Peter's proposition of three tabernacles, &c. Sure it is he knew as little what he said here as there: how much more considerately those martyrs, who both said it and did it? "The heavens shall as soon fall, as I will forsake my faith," said William Flower. And "if every hair of my head were a man, I would suffer death in the opinion and faith that I am now in," said John Ardely.

Likewise also said all the disciples] Misled, as Barnabas afterward was (Gal. ii.), by Peter's example. " The leaders of this people cause them to err," Isa. ix. 16. Our Saviour (to teach us what to do in like case) striveth not with them for the last word; but lets them enjoy their own over-good conceits of themselves, till time should confute them.

Ver. 36. *Unto a place called Gethsemane*] By Mount Olivet stood this garden; and there he began his passion, as well to expiate that first sin committed in a garden, as to sanctify unto us our repasts and recreations. Here, after our Saviour had prayed himself " into an agony," Αγωνιζόμενος (to teach us to "strive also in prayer" as for life, and to struggle "even to agony," as the word signifieth, Colos. iv. 12), he was taken *quasi ex condicto,* and led into the city through the sheep-gate (so called of the multitude of sheep driven in by it to be offered in the temple) to be sacrificed, as a lamb undefiled and without spot.

Sit ye here, while I go and pray yonder] It may be lawful therefore in some cases to pray secretly, in the presence or with the privity of others, so there be some good use of them.

Ver. 37. *And he took with him Peter, &c.*] He took the same that had seen his glory in the mount, to see his agony in the garden, that they might the better stick to him. Let no man envy others their better parts or places; sith they have them on no other condition but to be put upon greater temptations, hotter services. If we could wish another man's honour, when we feel the weight of his cares, as David once did of Saul's armour, we should be glad to be in our own coat.

And very heavy] To faint, or fall away in his soul, to be out of the world, as we say ; " He sitteth alone, and keepeth silence, because he hath borne it upon him," Lam. iii. 28. Αδημονεῖν,—*hominum vestigia vitat.*

Ver. 38. *My soul is exceeding sorrowful*] He had a true human soul then, neither was his deity to him for a soul, as some heretics fancied; for then our bodies only had been redeemed by him, and not our souls (τὸ γὰρ ἀπρόσληπτον ἀθεράπευτον, as that Father hath it), if he had not in soul also suffered, and so descended into hell. The sufferings of his body were but the body of his sufferings; the soul of his sufferings were the sufferings of his soul, which was now *undequaque tristis,* beset with sorrows, and heavy as heart could hold, περίλυπος. The "sorrows of death compassed him, the cords of hell surrounded him," Psal. xviii. 4, 5, the pain whereof he certainly suffered, *non specie et loco sed* ἀνάλογον τι καὶ ἀνεκλάλητον, something answerable to hell, and altogether unspeakable. Hence the Greek Litany, " By thine unknown sufferings (δι' ἀγνώστων σοῦ παθημάτων), good Lord, deliver us." Faninus, an Italian martyr, being asked by one why he was so merry at his death, sith Christ himself was so sorrowful? Christ, said he, sustained in his soul all the sorrows and conflicts with hell and death due to us; by whose sufferings we are delivered from sorrow and fear of them all.

Tarry ye here, and watch with me] Yet not for my sake so much as for your own, that ye enter not into temptation, Luke xxii. 40.

Ver. 39. *And he went a little farther*] *Amat secessum ardens oratio.* St Luke saith he was violently withdrawn from them, about a stone's cast, and there he kneeled down and prayed, for farther he could not go, through earnest desire of praying to his heavenly Father, Luke xxii. 41. ἀπεσπάσθη. *Illud desiderium precandi eum incessit, ut illum quodam modo truderet.*

And fell on his face] He putteth his mouth in the dust, if so be there may be hope, Lam. iii. 29. This and the like humble gestures in God's service do at once testify, and excite inward devotion.

Let this cup pass] In the time of execution, they gave the malefactor a cup of wine, mingled with myrrh, Mark. xv. 23, to stupify his senses, and so to mitigate his pains. Hence the word calix or cup is put here and elsewhere for death itself, which, being terrible to nature, is therefore here with strong crying and tears deprecated by our Saviour, Heb. v. 7. This was natural in him, and not sinful in us, so it do not degenerate into that which is carnal fear of death.

Nevertheless not as I will, but, &c.] Here Christ doth not correct his former request (for then there should have been some kind of fault in it), but explicateth only on what condition he desired deliverance, and becometh " obedient unto death, even the death of the cross," Philip. ii. 8, crying out, " not as I will, but as thou wilt," which shows that he had a distinct human will from the will of his Father, and so was very man as well as God. And here Aristotle, that great philosopher, is clearly confuted. For he denies that a magnanimous man can be exceeding sorrowful for anything that befalls him.[1] Our Saviour (his Church's stoutest champion) was exceeding sorrowful even to the death; and yet of so great a spirit, that he yields up himself wholly to God. *Magnus est animus, qui se Deo tradidit; pusillus et degener, qui obluctatur*, saith Seneca. He is a brave man that trusts God with all.

Ver. 40. *And he cometh unto the disciples*] They were his care in the midst of his agony. So was Peter, upon whom he found time to look back when he stood to answer for his life. So was the penitent thief, whose prayer Christ answered, even when he hung upon the tree, and was paying dear for his redemption. Our High Priest bears the names of all his people on his shoulders and on his breast, so that he cannot be unmindful of them. Behold he hath graven them upon the palms of his hands, their walls are continually before him, Isa. xlix. 16, he loveth to look upon the houses where they dwell.

And findeth them asleep] When he should have found them at prayer for him. Prayer is the creature of the Holy Ghost; and unless he hold up men's eyes therewhile, even Peter, James, and John will fall asleep in prayer, and put up yawning petitions to God.

And saith unto Peter] Who had promised so much forwardness, and stood in so great a danger above the rest, Luke xxii. 31. For Satan earnestly desired to deal with him (ἐξῃτήσατο); he challenged Peter forth, as Goliath called for one to combat with. And was it for them to sleep then; or, with Agrippa's dormouse, not to awake till boiled in lead?

What? could ye not watch with me, &c.] How then will ye do to die with me, as erst ye promised me? If the footman have wearied you, "how will ye contend with horses?" Jer. xii. 5. If you cannot endure words, how will you endure wounds? If ye cannot strive against sin, how will you resist unto blood? Heb. xii. 4. If ye cannot burn your finger with Bilney, your right hand with Cranmer, how will you bear the burning of your whole body? Alice Coberly, being piteously burnt in the hand by the keeper's wife, with a hot key which she cunningly sent her to fetch, revoked.

Ver. 41. *Watch and pray*] Yea, watch, whiles ye are praying, against corruption within, temptations without. Satan will be interrupting as the Pythoness did Paul praying, Acts xvi. 16; as the fowls did Abraham sacrificing, Gen. xv. 11; as the enemies did Nehemiah with his Jews, building, who therefore prayed and watched, watched and prayed. Amongst all actions, Satan is ever busiest in the best; and most in the best part of the best, as in the end of prayer, when the heart should close up itself with most comfort. Watch therefore unto prayer, προσκαρτερεῖτε, Set all aside for it, and wait on it, as the

word imports, Col. iv. 2. While prayer stands still, the trade of godliness stands still; let this therefore be done, whatever is left undone. Take heed the devil take you not out of your trenches, as he did David, likely, 2 Sam. xi. 2; out of your stronghold, as Joshua did the men of Ai. "Little children," saith St John, "abide in God," 1 John ii. 28; keep home, keep close to your Father, if you mean to be safe, if that evil one shall not touch you, 1 John v. 18, nor thrust his deadly sting into you, &c.

The spirit indeed is willing] *q. d.* Though the spirit purpose otherwise, yet the flesh will falter, and ye will be foiled else. Or, our Saviour speaks this by way of excuse of their infirmity, *q. d.* I see you are willing, so far as you are spiritual and regenerate; but the flesh is treacherous and tyrannical. It rebels ever and anon, and would gladly reign. It hangs off, when called to suffer, and makes shy of the business. So Peter was carried whither he would not, John xxi. 18. So Hilarion chides out his soul (which plaid loth to depart) with *Egredere ô anima*, &c. So Mr Sanders, martyr, in a letter to his wife, a little before his death, Fain would his flesh, said he, make strange of that which the spirit doth embrace. O Lord, how loth is this loitering sluggard to pass forth in God's path, &c. So Mr Bradford going to his death. Now I am climbing up the hill, said he, it will cause me to puff and blow before I come to the cliff. The hill is steep and high, my breath is short, and my strength is feeble. Pray therefore to the Lord for me, pray for me, pray for me, for God's sake, pray for me. See more in the notes on John xxi. 18.

Ver. 42. *The second time, and prayed*] Prayer is that arrow of deliverance that would be multiplied, 2 Kings xiii. 17. God holds off on purpose that he may hear oft of us, that we may ply the throne of grace, and give him no rest. The Church, Psal. lxxx., commenceth thrice the same suit, but riseth every time in her earnestness, ver. 3, 7, 19. If thy petition be not lawful, never prefer it, as if it be, never give it over. God suspends thee, to eneager thee.

If this cup may not pass, except I drink] It passeth then, even while we are drinking of it. Τὸ πικρὸν μικρὸν, hold out faith and patience. It is but a storm, and will soon be over. It is but a death, and that is but the daybreak of eternal brightness. It is but winking (as that martyr said), and thou shalt be in heaven presently.

Ver. 43. *He came and found them asleep again*] After so sweet an admonition, so sovereign a reproof; who knows how oft an infirmity may recur, even after repentance? See it in Samson, in Jonah, in these apostles, for their contention "who should be greatest," &c.

For their eyes were heavy] For sorrow (saith St Luke, xxvi. 45), which, exhausting the spirits, renders a man more sluggish; and hindering concoction, sends up vapours to the brain, and so causeth sleep. This was somewhat, but not sufficient to excuse them. Christ took them with

[1] Μεγαλόψυχος οὐκ ἐστὶ περίλυπος. Arist. Eth.

him into the garden for their society and prayers. But they not only not help him, but wound him by their dulness unto duty, and instead of wiping off his bloody sweat, they draw more out of him. Judas had somewhat else to do now than to sleep, when Peter was fast, and could not hold up. Zechariah the prophet lay under such a like drowsy distemper, chap. iv. 1, for though awaked and set to work, he was even ready to fall asleep at it.

Ver. 44. *And he left them, and went away again*] A most memorable and imitable pattern of patience toward those that condole not, or that keep not touch with us, we must neither startle nor storm, but pass it by as a frailty.

And prayed the third time] A number of perfection. And, *Si ter pulsanti*, &c. Paul prayed thrice, and gave over, 2 Cor. xii., because he saw it was God's will it should be otherwise: pardoning grace he had, but not prevailing, ver. 9. So our Saviour here had an angel sent from heaven to strengthen him, that he might the better drink that cup which he had so heartily deprecated, Luke xxii. 43. Hence the apostle doubts not to say that he "was heard in that he feared," Heb. v. 7 : he was, and he was not ; there is no praying against that which God's providence hath disposed of by an infallible order. And when we see how God will have it, we must sit down and be satisfied. That which he will have done, we may be sure is best to be done.

Saying the same words] And they were no whit the worse for being the same. Let this comfort those that complain they cannot vary in prayer ; though that be a desirable ability. The Corinthians were enriched by God in all utterance and knowledge, 1 Cor. i. 5. But the business of prayer is more despatched by inward groanings than outward garnishes.

Ver. 45. *Sleep on now, and take your rest*] q. d. Do so, if you can, at least.[1] But now the hour is come, wherein you shall have small either leisure or list to sleep, though never so drowsy spirited, for "the Son of man is betrayed," &c. Luther readeth the words indicatively, and by way of question, thus, Ah! do ye now sleep and take your rest ? Will ye, with Solomon's drunkard, sleep upon a mast-pole ? take a nap upon a weather-cock ? Thus this heavenly eagle, though he love his young ones dearly, yet he pricketh and beateth them out of the nest. The best (as bees) are killed with the honey of flattery, but quickened with the vinegar of reproof.

Ver. 46. *Rise, let us be going*] To meet that death which till he had prayed he greatly feared. So it was with Esther, chap. iv. 16, and with David, Psal. cxvi. 3, 4. See the power of faithful prayer to disarm death, and to alter the countenance of greatest danger. *Quoties me oratio, quem pæne desperantem susceperat, reddidit exultantem,* &c. ? How oft hath prayer recruited me ? (Bern. Serm. 33 in Cant.)

Behold, he is at hand] Behold, for the miracle of the matter, yet now no miracle.

Tuta frequensque via est per amici fallere nomen :
Tuta frequensque licet sit, via crimen habet.

Ver. 47. *Lo, Judas, one of the twelve*] Lo, for the reason next afore-mentioned. The truth hath no such pestilent persecutors as apostates. *Corruptio optimi pessima,* sweetest wine maketh sourest vinegar.

With swords and staves] What need all this ado? But that the hornet haunted them, an ill conscience abused them, Exod. xxiii. 28. When he put forth but one beam of his Deity, these armed men fell all to the ground : nor could they rise again till he had done indenting with them, John xviii. 6.

Ver. 48. *Whomsoever I shall kiss*] Ah, lewd losel ! betrayest thou the Son of man with a kiss ?[2] Givest thou thy Lord such rank poison in such a golden cup ? Consignest thou thy treachery with so sweet a symbol of peace and love ?[3] But this is still usual with those of his tribe. *Caveatur osculum Iscarioticum.* Jesuits at this day kiss and kill familiarly ; *officiose occidunt,* as one saith of false physicians. When those Rhemish incendiaries, Giffard, Hodgson, and others, had set Savage a-work to kill Queen Elizabeth, they first set forth a book to persuade the English Catholics to attempt nothing against her. So when they had sent Squire out of Spain to poison the queen, they taught him to anoint the pummel of her saddle with poison covertly, and then to pray with a loud voice, God save the Queen. Lopez, another of their agents, affirmed at Tyburn, that he had loved the queen as he had loved Jesus Christ : which, from a Jew, was heard not without laughter. So Parsons, when he had hatched that nameless villany the powder-plot, set forth his book of resolution ; as if he had been wholly made up of devotion, *E societate Jesu fuit qui Jesum tradidit.*

Ver. 49. *Hail, Master, and kissed him*] But love is not always in a kiss, saith Philo the Jew ; nor in crying Rabbi, Rabbi, as the traitor here did, Mark xiv. 45, out of a seeming pity of his Master's misery. There are that think that he would have carried this his treachery so cunningly, as if he had had no hand in it ; and therefore kissed him as a friend, and so would still have been taken. (Aretius.)

Ver. 50. *Friend*] Sith thou wilt needs be so esteemed, though most unfriendly.

Wherefore art thou come ?] As a friend, or as a foe ? If as a friend, what mean these swords ? If as a foe, what means this kiss ? Christ knew well enough wherefore he came ; but thinks good to sting his conscience by this cutting question.

Laid hands on Jesus and took him] By his own consent, and ἡσυχάζοντος λόγου, as Irenæus hath it, while the Deity rested, and refused to put forth itself.

Ver. 51. *One of them which were with Jesus*] This was Peter, who asked leave to strike, but stayed not till he had it, out of a preposterous zeal to his Master, and because he would be a

---

[1] *Sarcasmus quo egebat discipulorum torpor.* Beza.
[2] κεταφιλεῖν οὐκ ἐστὶ φιλεῖν. Philo.
[3] *Sacramento pacis tradidit sacrificium pacis.* Jerome.

man of his word. A wonderful work of God it was surely, that hereupon he was not hewn in an hundred pieces by the barbarous soldiers. Well might the Psalmist say, " He that is our God is the God of salvation ; and unto God the Lord belong the issues from death," Psal. lxviii. 20. " My times are in thine hands," Psal. xxxi. 15. But this stout swords-man could not be found, when his Master was, after this, apprehended and arraigned. Plato hath observed, *Peritissimi lanistæ in ludo, sunt inertissimi in bello*, the most skilful fencers are the most cowardly soldiers.

Ver. 52. *Put up again thy sword*] See the notes on John xviii. 11.

For all they that take the sword] Without a just calling, as those sworn swords-men of the devil, the Jesuits, whose faction (as one saith of them) is a most agile sharp sword ; the blade whereof is sheathed at pleasure, in the bowels of every commonwealth, but the handle reacheth to Rome and Spain. Their design is to subdue all to the pope, and the pope to themselves.

Ver. 53. *Thinkest thou that I cannot pray*] *q. d.* Need I be beholden to thee for help ? Luther very boldly told his patron and protector, the elector of Saxony, that he, by his prayers, gained him more help and safeguard than he received from him ; and that this cause of Christ needeth not the help of man to carry it on, but the power of God, set a-work by the prayer of faith.[1] And this way, saith he, I will undertake to secure your highness's soul, body, and estate, engaged in the cause of the gospel, from whatsoever danger or disaster, *Sive id credat C. V. sive non credat*, whether your highness believe me herein or not.

More than twelve legions] A legion is judged to be six thousand foot and seven hundred horse. And this great army of angels is by prayer despatched from heaven in an instant. Are we then in any imminent danger ? send up to heaven for help by prayer, and God will send from heaven and help us. We need not help ourselves by seeking private revenge, as Peter here, or using sinister shifts, as David, Psal. xxxiv. 1, for in the same Psalm men are exhorted to ensue peace and pass by private wrongs ; because the " angels of the Lord encamp round about them that fear him, and deliver them."

Ver. 54. *But how then shall the Scriptures, &c.*] Why dost thou not then pray (might they object) for an army of angels, to rescue thee out of these wicked hands, that now hold thee prisoner, and will let out thy life-blood ? How then should " the Scriptures be fulfilled," saith he, " that have foretold my death ? " This was his constant care, even when he hung upon the cross, to fulfil the Scriptures ; and so to assure us that he was the very Christ.

That thus it must be] Why must ? but because it was, 1. So decreed by God. 2. Foretold by the prophets ; every particular of Christ's suffer-

ings, even to their very spitting in his face. 3. Prefigured in the daily morning and evening sacrifice ; this Lamb of God was sacrificed from the beginning of the world. A necessity then there was of our Saviour's suffering. Not a necessity of coaction (for he died freely and voluntarily), but of immutability and infallibility, for the former reasons and respects.

Ver. 55. *Are ye come out as against a thief ?*] Secretly, and by night, with all this clatter of people and clashing of arms, so to make the world believe strange matters of me ? whereas, had your cause and conscience been good, you would have taken a fitter time, and I should have had fairer dealing.

And ye laid no hand on me] Ye wanted no will, but ye could never find cause : and which of you now accuseth me of sin ? It is doubtless very lawful, and in some cases needful for Christians to defend their own innocency, and vindicate their wronged credit, as did Moses, Samuel, Paul, Melancthon : " I never have sought profits, pleasures, nor preferments," saith he, " neither was I ever moved with emulation or envy against any man," *Hanc conscientiam aufero, quocunque discedo*. This conscience I carry with me withersoever I go. Christ of all that ever lived, might best challenge his adversaries of injury : for of him it might be truly affirmed, what Xenophon doth of Socrates, what Paterculus doth of Scipio, *Quod nihil in vita nisi laudandum aut fecit, aut dixit, aut sensit*, that he did all things well, as the people testified of him, and never said or thought anything amiss.

Ver. 56. *That the Scriptures, &c.*] Which yet were no more the cause of the Jews' cruelty than Joseph was of the famine, than the astrologer is of the eclipse, or Tenterton steeple of the ebbing and flowing of the sea.

Then all the disciples forsook him and fled] Then, when there was no such need or danger to enforce them, Christ having capitulated with the enemy for their safety. They had leave to go free before ; what stayed they for then ? or why flee they now ? This was the fruit and punishment of their former sleeping, verse 43. Had they watched and prayed then, they had not now thus entered into temptation.

Ver. 57. *Where the scribes and the elders were*] A full council there may err. See the notes on chap. ii. 4, and on chap. xxvi. 3.

Ver. 58. *But Peter followed*] First, he fled with the rest, and then, remembering his promise, followed afar off ; but better he had kept him away, for he sat with the servants, so venturing upon the occasion of sin, which he should have studiously shunned ; and merely out of curiosity to see the end and issue of Christ's captivity. We many times tempt Satan to tempt us by our imprudence. Evil company is contagious, and sin more catching than the plague. Israel going down to Egypt brought a golden calf from thence ; Jeroboam brought two. A man may pass through

---

[1] *Judico Celsitud. Vest. plus a me præsidii et tutelæ habi-* *turam esse, quam mihi præstare. Huic causæ nullus gladius consulere aut opem ferre potest, &c.* Luth. epist.

Ethiopia unchanged ; but he cannot reside there, and not be discoloured.

Ver. 59. *Sought false witness*] Here Christ is convented and examined in the spiritual court with a great deal of injustice and subordination. They first sought false witness, as if they had obeyed our Saviour, who bade them ask those that heard him what he had said unto them, John xviii. 21.

Ver. 60. *Yea, though many false witnesses came*] So adultery was objected to Athanasius, heresy and treason to Cranmer. Also I lay to thy charge, said Bonner to Philpot, martyr, that thou killest thy father, and wast accursed of thy mother on her death-bed, &c. Queen Elizabeth wrote these lines in a window at Woodstock,—

> Much alleged against me,
> Nothing proved can be.

Freedom of speech used by the Waldenses against the sins of those times, caused, *Ut plures nefariæ eis affingerentur opiniones, a quibus omnino fuerant alieni,* saith Gerard, That many false opinions were fathered upon them, such as they never favoured.[1] So deal the Papists by us at this day ; they tell the seduced people that we worship no God, count gain godliness, keep no promises, eat young children, make nothing of adultery, murder, &c.[2] Good people, these men deny Christ to be God, and the Holy Ghost to be God, &c., said White, Bishop of Winchester, concerning Woodman and other holy martyrs, in a sermon.

Yet found they none] The enemies' likeliest projects oft fail. These false witnesses, as those Babel-builders of old, disagreed in their language, which God confounded, and so he doth to this day.

Ver. 61. *I am able to destroy the temple*] *Novum crimen Caie Cæsar.* For, what if Christ had said so ? Could not he as easily have reared a temple as raised the dead, restored the blind, &c. ? But the truth is, he never said so, but was misreported and falsely accused (saith Father Latimer), both as touching his words and meaning also. He said *Destruite,* Destroy ye ; they made it *Possum destruere,* I am able to destroy. He said *Templum hoc,* this temple, meaning his own body ; they added *manufactum,* made with hands, to bring it to a contrary sense, &c. Thus *mutilando vel mutando,* by chopping or changing, ill-minded men do usually deprave and wrest to a wrong meaning the most innocent passages and practises. So true is that of the comedian,

Nihil est quin male narrando possit depravarier :
Tu id quod boni est excerpis, dicis quod mali est.

Ver. 62. *Answerest thou nothing ?*] No, nothing, unless it had been to better purpose ; for σιγᾶν χρὴ, ἢ κρείσσονα σιγῆς λέγειν, saith the wise heathen. Either hold thy peace or say something that is worth hearing. And, πᾶσιν ἀπολο-

γεῖσθαι θεραπευτικόν. (Plato.) To answer every slight accusation is servile. Some are so thin they may be seen through, others so gross that they need no refutation.[3] These hypocrites were not worthy of an answer from our Saviour, who knew also that now was the time not of apologizing, but of suffering ; therefore "as a sheep before her shearers is dumb, so he opened not his mouth," Isa. liii. 7. Besides, he saw that his enemies were resolved to have his blood, and therefore held it more glorious, τῇ σιωπῇ τὸ ὄνειδος πνίγειν, as Basil hath it, to choke their spite with silence, *et injuriam tacendo fugere, potius quam respondendo superare,* as another saith, to set them down by saying nothing.

Ver. 63. *I adjure thee by the living God*] So had the devil done once before, *horrendo impudentiæ exemplo,* Mark iii. 7. *Sed os Caiaphæ et culens Satanæ in eodem sunt prædicamento.* It is nothing with the devil and his to pollute and dishallow that *nomen majestativum,* as Tertullian styleth it, that "glorious and fearful name of God," as Moses calleth it, Deut. xxviii. 58 ; and to call him in, at all turns, as an author or abettor, at least, of their abominable plots and practises. How much better that holy man that said, My heart, head, and tongue trembleth as oft as I speak of God ?[4] Yea, the very heathen sages had the same thoughts, that men ought to be better advised than to toss God's reverend name upon their tongues as a tennis-ball, or to wear his image for an ornament.[5] And surely, as St Mark relateth this history, one would think Caiaphas a very conscientious person. For he brings him in saying to our Saviour, "Art thou the son of that blessed one ?" Mark xiv. 61. So he calls God by a periphrasis, as if he were afraid once to name God, εὐλογητοῦ. *Baruch hu, quasi ipsum Dei nomen exprimere vereatur ;* when as yet presently after, he profanely adjureth our blessed Saviour "by the living God, that thou tell us whether thou be the Christ," &c. And this he doth, not out of any desire to know the truth ; but as seeking an occasion from his bold and free confession of the truth, to put him to death ; so going about to entitle God himself to his villanous enterprizes. See here the hateful nature of damned hypocrisy, and abandon it.

Ver. 64. *Thou hast said*] That is, as St Mark expresseth the Hebraism in plainer terms, "I am," *q. d.* Thou hast said it, and I must second it, I am indeed the promised Messias, and the only begotten Son of God. This was the naked truth without equivocation ; a device that the Jesuits have lately fetched from hell, for the consolation of afflicted Catholics, and for the instruction of all the godly, as Blackwel and Garnet blush not to profess in print. Let us learn here of our Saviour to make a bold and wise confession of the truth when called thereunto ; although we create ourselves thereby never so much danger

---

[1] See Alex. Cook's preface to his Abatement of Popular Brags.
[2] *Eudæmon. Johan. contra Casaub.*
[3] *Tenue mendacium pellucet.* Sen.

[4] *Linguâ, mente, et cogitatione horresco quoties de Deo sermonem habeo.* Nazianzen.
[5] ἐν δακτυλίῳ εἰκόνα Θεοῦ μὴ περιφέρειν. *Præcept.* Pyth.

from the enemy, who shall so be either converted, or at least convinced, and left inexcusable.

Hereafter shall ye see, &c.] *q. d.* Now I am in a state of abasement, God having hid his Son under the carpenter's son, whom ye have now bound, and shall shortly crucify. But not long hence ye shall see me in a state of advancement, sitting on the right hand of power, pouring out my Spirit upon all flesh, Acts ii. 33 ; and, after that, coming in the clouds of heaven, as in a chariot of state, to judge you that are now my judges, &c.

Ver. 65. *Then the high priest rent his clothes*] Which the high priest ought not by the law to have done, howsoever, Levit. x. 6 and xxi. 10, and here had no colour of cause at all to do ; no, not so much as Joab had, when for company, and at his Lord's command, he rent his clothes at Abner's funeral, whom he had basely murdered, 2 Sam. iii. 31.

Ver. 66. *He is guilty of death*] Servile souls ! they durst do no otherwise than concur with Caiaphas. So in Popish councils and conclaves the bishops and others (those *aiones et negones aulici*) have no more to do, but simply *inclinato capite* to say *Placet* to that which in the pope's name is proposed unto them. The legates in the Council of Trent were blamed for suffering the article of priests' marriage to be disputed. And in *Colloquio Possiaceno*, after that Beza had spoken much of the eucharist before the young king of France, the queen-mother and the princess of the blood, a Spanish Jesuit, having reproached the Protestants, did reprehend the queen-mother for meddling in matters that belonged not to her, but to the pope, cardinals, and bishops.

Ver. 67. *Then did they spit in his face*] Condemned prisoners are sacred things ; and by the law of nations, should not be misused and trampled on, but rather pitied and prepared for death. But these barbarous miscreants (not without the good liking of their lords the priests and elders) spare for no kind of cruelty toward Christ, who was content to be spit upon, to cleanse our faces from the filth of sin, to be buffeted with fists, and beaten with staves,[1] to free us from that mighty hand of God, 1 Pet. v. 6, and from those scourges and scorpions of infernal fiends.

Ver. 68. *Saying, Prophesy unto us, thou Christ*] This is daily done to Christ by the children of darkness, which sin securely, and say, Who seeth us ? they put it to the trial, as Ananias and Sapphira did, whether they shall be detected.

Ver. 69. *And a damsel came unto him*] A silly wench daunteth and dispiriteth this stout champion. *Sic et Elias ille fulminator ad mulierculæ (Jesabelis) minas trepidat, factus seipso imbecillior.* (Bucholcer.) What poor things the best of us are, when left a little to ourselves, when our faith is in the wane! *Regulus erat cum audebat omnium audacissimus : cum timebat, omnium timidissimus ; sic et Petrus.*

[1] ἐρράπισαν, *bacillis ceciderunt.* Beza.

Thou also wast with Jesus] She was just of her master's mind and making. We had need take heed where we set our children to service ; for, like water on a table, they will be led any way with a wet finger ; and as any liquid matter, they will conform to the vessel whereinto they are poured. Be sure to teach them God's fear, and to pray, and then wherever they come to live, they shall do good, and find favour, as the captive children did in the court of Babylon, Dan. i., and as the Hebrew girl did in Naaman's family ; that great lord lighted his candle at his handmaid's coal ; so good a thing is it to acquaint our children with the works of God, with the praises of his prophets.

Ver. 70. *I know not what thou sayest*] He makes as if he understood not either her words or her meaning. And this false dissembling was a true denying. St Mark saith, that now the cock crew, chap. xiv. 68. A fair warning to so foul a sinner ; but he took no notice of it, till Christ looked back upon him ; to teach us, that without the help of divine grace, no means can convert a sinner from the error of his way. God himself preached a sermon of repentance to Cain, but it prevailed not. Whereas Christ no sooner looked back upon this fallen apostle, but he went out and wept bitterly. Christ cured him with less ado than he did Malchus' ear,—that was healed by a touch, this by a look only.

Ver. 71. *And when he was gone out, &c.*] The orifice of his wound was not yet closed, and therefore bled afresh so soon again. Thus Lot committed incest two nights together, &c. See the note on ver. 43.

Ver. 72. *And again he denied with an oath*] This was fearful ; and the worse, because his Master, whom he forswore, was now (even as Peter's faith was) upon his trial, and might say, with wounded Cæsar, What, thou, my son Brutus ! Is this thy kindness to thy friend ? Scipio had rather that Hannibal should eat his heart with salt than that Lelius do him the least discourtesy.

Ver. 73. *For thy speech bewrayeth thee*] Jacob must name himself Esau, with the voice of Jacob. The Ephraimite must lisp out his Shibboleth in despite of his heart or habit. Each countryman is known by his idiom or dialect. The fool saith to every one, that he is a fool, Eccles. x. 3, when the wise man's tongue "talketh of judgment," Psal. xxxvii. 30.

Ver. 74. *Then began he to curse and swear*] This he had learned belike of the ruffianly soldiers, with whom, usually, execrations are but expletives, and horrible oaths interjections of speech. But though Israel play the harlot, yet why should Judah offend ? come not ye to Gilgal, neither go ye up to Bethaven, nor swear "The Lord liveth," Hosea iv. 15. David swore once such an oath, and it was enough of that once, 1 Sam. xxv. 22. But Peter swears and forswears again and again, and that after warning ; as Aaron went down and did that in the valley which he heard forbidden in the Mount, and then excuseth it by his fear of the people. That cowardly passion is the mother of many sins, of lying especially, Zeph. iii. 13, and swearing too, to save the life. But better die than lie: and better bear than swear. We may not break the hedge of any commandment to avoid any piece of foul way, but go in a right line to God. *Quas non oportet mortes præeligere, quod non supplicium potius ferre, imo in quam profundam inferni abyssum non intrare, quam contra conscientiam attestari?* saith holy Zuinglius in his third Epistle. What should not a man suffer, rather than sin? Peter sinned to some purpose, if it were, as some have thought, that he not only cursed himself, if he knew Christ, but also cursed Jesus Christ, that so he might appear to be none of his disciples.

And immediately the cock crew] *Gallicinium complevit Christi vaticinium.* The cock proved a preacher to Peter. Despise not the minister though never so mean; it is the foolishness of preaching that must bring men to heaven. Cocks call men out of their beds, and therehence have their name in the Greek tongue.[1] They constantly keep the law of crowing at those set times that nature hath enjoined them; they cry loud and thick against a storm. So do faithful ministers, when gotten upon their battlements; they clap their own sides first, and then constantly call up others. They cry aloud, and spare not, but lift up their voice like a trumpet, to tell Judah of their sins, &c. The roaring lion of hell trembleth at their note: and the world's Sybarites cannot bear their disturbances, and therefore wish them banished. But wisdom is justified of her children, and though fierce before, and untameable, yet now "a little child shall lead them," Isa. xi. 6.

Ver. 75. *And Peter remembered the word of Jesus*] Here began his repentance. If we remember not what is preached unto us, all is lost, saith the apostle, 1 Cor. xv. 2. If we leak and let slip, saith another, how shall we escape? Μήποτε παραρρυῶμεν, Heb. ii. 1, 3. The Spirit shall be the saints' remembrancer; and as the sea casts up her dead, so shall that come seasonably to mind, that was long before delivered, when God's good time is come to work upon the dead heart. God will be found of his that seek him not. Surely, mercy and truth shall follow them all the days of their lives, as the sunbeams follow the traveller that turns his back on them. He will bring back his banished, he will reduce his runagates, he will not suffer any of his to be utterly drowned, though haply they have been drenched in the waves of sin, lain some while in them, yea, and have also sunk twice or thrice, as Peter, to the very bottom. Now then how can any either presume of not sinning, or despair for sin, when they read of Peter thus fallen, and now thus remembering, thus rising again by repentance, and received to mercy? The like instances we have not a few, of Origen and other

primitive Christians, who, recanting for a season through fear of death, were therefore utterly excluded by Novatus from all hope of mercy; but not so by Christ. "Be not thou a terror unto me, O Lord," saith Jeremiah, and then I care not, though all the world condemn and cast me out. Bilney, Bainham, Benbridge, Abbes, Whittle, Sharp, and many other martyrs, having denied their Lord God, as they called it, for fear of the faggot, could have no rest till they had repented, and publicly revoked their much-bewailed recantations. Steven Gardiner, indeed, like another Ecebolius, cried out that he had denied with Peter, but never repented with Peter, and so both stinkingly and unrepentantly died, saith Mr Fox. It was a saying of the same Mr Fox, that his graces did him most hurt, and his sins most good. A paradox; but by our temptations, we know his meaning. As pain easeth a Christian, death revives him, dissolution unites him, so corruption clarifies him. I dare be bold to say (saith Augustine) that it is good for proud persons to fall into some foul sin, *unde sibi displiceant, qui jam sibi placendo ceciderunt. Salubrius enim Petrus sibi displicuit quando flevit, quam sibi placuit quando præsumpsit*, that they may be humbled, as Peter was, and so saved. (Aug. C. D. 14, 13.)

He wept bitterly] That one sweet look from Christ melted him; as God's kindness did the hard-hearted Israelites at the meet of Mizpeh. In this troubled pool Peter washed himself, in this Red Sea the army of his iniquities was drowned. As once his faith was so great that he leapt into a sea of waters to come to Christ, so now his repentance was so great, that he leapt, as it were, into a sea of tears for that he had gone from Christ. There are that say (and it may very well be) that henceforth he was ever and anon weeping; and that his face was even furrowed with continual tears.[2] He began soon after his sin, Mark xiv. 72, *cum se proripuisset*, when he had thrown himself out, as Beza renders ἐπιβαλὼν. He had no sooner took in poison, but he vomited it up again ere it got to the vitals. He had no sooner handled his serpent, but he turned it into a rod to scourge his soul with remorse. *Peccatum tristitiam peperit, et tristitia peccatum contrivit, ut vermis is ligno natus, sed ipsum comminuit.*

CHAPTER XXVII.

Ver. 1. *When the morning was come*] They had broken their sleep the night before, and yet were up and at it early the next morning, so soon as the day peeped (ὡς ἐγένετο ἡμέρα), Luke xxii. 66. So sedulous are the devil's servants. Esau began to bustle with Jacob even in the very womb, that no time might be lost.

Ver. 2. *And when they had bound him*] Bound he had been before this (to loose the cords of our

[1] ἀλέκτωρ, *quod nos excitet e lecto.*

[2] *Semper lachrymis suffusos habuisse oculos adeo ut etiam lachrymæ cutem genarum exederint.* Chrysost.

iniquities) : but belike they had loosed him again,' to try if by fair means they could make him belie himself.· So those martyrs were tempted, Heb. xi. 37. (ἐπρίσθησαν, ἐπειράσθησαν.) And this was Julian's way of persecuting the primitive Christians, as Nazianzen testifieth : *persecutioni suæ miscuit persuasionem ; ideoque fuit superioribus nocentior, et perniciosior.* So Bonner, after he had allowed William Hunter, martyr, an halfpenny a day in bread and drink in prison, persuaded with him, saying, If thou wilt recant, I will make thee a freeman in the city, and give thee forty pounds in good money, to set up thine occupation withal ; or I will make thee steward of mine house, and set thee in office. So, to reduce Dr Taylor, martyr, they promised him not only his pardon, but a bishopric.

Ver. 3. Then Judas, which had betrayed him] Might not Judas have sang care away, now that he had both the bag and the price of blood, but he must come and betray himself. Whiles he played alone, he won all ; but soon after, his own " wickedness corrected him, and his backslidings reproved him," Jer. ii. 19. Sin will surely prove evil and bitter, when the bottom of the bag is once turned upward. A man may have the stone, who feels no fit of it. Conscience will work once ; though for the time, one may feel no fit of accusation : Laban showed himself at parting. " Knowest thou not that there will be bitterness in the latter end ? " 2 Sam. xiii. 15. But the devil deals with men as the panther does with the beasts : he hides his deformed head, till his sweet scent have drawn them into his danger. Till we have sinned, Satan is a parasite ; when we have sinned he is a tyrant. But it is good to consider that of Bernard. At the day of judgment a pure conscience shall better bestead one than a full purse. *In die judicii plus valebit conscientia pura quam marsupia plena.*

When he saw that he was condemned] He hoped, belike, that Christ would, as at other times he did, have delivered himself by a miracle. Let no man flatter himself, as if there were no such hurt in sin ; for like dirty dogs, it doth but defile us in fawning : and like a treacherous host, though it welcome us into the inn with smiling countenance, yet it will cut our throats in our beds. Judas was first nibbling upon the silver bait, after which the hook of conscience troubled him.

He repented] That is, he changed his mind (μεταμεληθείς), from thinking well of his former actions. So those miscreants in Malachi are said to " return and discern," &c., Mal. iii. 18. So Rodolphus, Duke of Suabia, when, at the pope's instigation, taking up arms against Henry the emperor, he had lost his right hand in the battle, he sent for his bishops and other his confederates, and said unto them : Lo, this is that hand wherewith I swore that allegiance to my sovereign, which by your means and motion I have violated. *Videte an recta via me duxeritis,* &c. Consider whether you have led me on in a right way or not. (Func. Chronol.)

[1] Melancth. in Chronic.

Hic fuit ille cui Papa coronam misit cum ista inscriptione,
Petra dedit Petro, Petrus diadema Rodulpho.

And brought again the thirty pieces] So did James Abbes bring to the Bishop of Norwich his forty pence fastened upon him by the bishop ; which when he had received (saith Mr Fox) and was gone from the bishop, who had prevailed with him to recant, his conscience began to throb, and inwardly to accuse this fact, how he had displeased the Lord by consenting to their beastly illusions. In which combat with himself, being piteously vexed, he went to the bishop again, and there threw him his money, and said, it repented him that he ever consented to their wicked persuasions in taking of his money. Hereupon the bishop with his chaplains laboured afresh to win him again, but he was better resolved, and crying out to God for pardon of his sin (which Judas did not) he obtained mercy, and suffered martyrdom.

Ver. 4. I have sinned, &c.] Here was contrition, confession, restitution (most men go not so far, that yet profess large hopes of heaven) ; there was wanting that transmentation, conversion, obedience of faith that should have completed his repentance. He died in the birth, as that foolish child Ephraim. He confessed to men, and not to God ; and by his confession he sought no more than to ease his heart, as drunkards by vomiting rid their stomachs. So Latomus of Louvain confessed, *inter horrendos mugitus, se contra conscientiam adversatum esse veritati,* roaring and crying out, that against his conscience he had persecuted the truth of God.[1] In trouble of mind, all will out. Conscience, like Samson's wife, conceals not the riddle : like Fulvia, a whorish woman, who declared all the secrets of her foolish lover Cneius, a noble Roman. Sallust. in Bel. Catil.

What is that to us ? See thou to that] Miserable comforters, physicians of no value. " To him that is afflicted pity should be showed from his friend : but he forsaketh the fear of the Almighty," Job vi. 14. The devil and his imps love to bring men into the briers, and there leave them ; as familiar devils forsake their witches, when they have brought them once into fetters. Thus the old Bethelite, that had been at pains to fetch back the prophet, would not go back with him. Thus the Papists burnt Cranmer recanting, and the present prelates cast off their great anti-Sabbatarian, White, when they had served their turns on him. David, when he was hunted from Samuel the prophet, fled to Abimelech the priest, as one that knew that justice and compassion should dwell in those breasts that are consecrated to God. But Judas met with no such matter in the priests of his time. Those mischievous men left him, when they had led him to his bane.

Ver. 5. And he cast down the pieces of silver] That wages of wickedness burnt in his purse, in his conscience ; neither could it secure him in the day of wrath. See Zeph. i. 18 ; Ezek. vii. 19 ; Obad. 4 ; James iv. 1, 2. *Omnia fui, et nihil mihi profuit,* said Severus the emperor, when he lay a-dying. Most of the emperors gat nothing by their advancement to the empire, whereof they were so ambitious, but this, *Ut citius inter-ficerentur*, that they were slain the sooner. All, or most of them, till Constantine, died unnatural deaths. Achan's wedge of gold served but to cleave asunder his soul from his body; and the Babylonish garment but for a shroud.

And went and hanged himself] If you confess yourself to a priest, and not to God, said that martyr, you shall have the reward that Judas had. For he confessed himself to a priest, and yet went and hanged himself by and by. So did Pavier, town-clerk of London in Henry VIII.'s time, who had before sworn a great oath, that if the king's highness would set forth the Scripture in English, and let it be read of the people by his authority, rather than he would so long live, he would cut his own throat. But he brake promise; for shortly after he hanged himself. And about the same time, Foxford, chancellor to the bishop of London, a cruel persecutor and butcher of the saints, died suddenly in his chair, his belly being burst, and his guts falling out before him; as likewise Judas' did, *Cum quodam singulari crepitus fragore*, as the word ἐλάκησε imports, Acts i. 18. Selneccerus makes mention of a covetous bishop of Misna in Germany, who had the devil for his death's-man. And Dr Morton, late bishop of Durham, reports a story of his own knowledge, of one Sir Booth, a Bachelor of Arts in St John's College in Cambridge, who, being popishly affected, took the consecrated bread at the time of the communion; and forbearing to eat it, conveyed and kept it closely for a time, and afterwards threw it over the college wall. But, a short time after, not enduring the torment of his guilty conscience, he threw himself headlong over the battlements of the chapel, and some few hours after ended his life. "The spirit of a man may sustain his infirmity:" some shift or other a man may make to suffer whatsoever other calamities," but a wounded spirit who can bear?" Prov. xviii. 14: there is no fighting with a mighty fire, no bearing up sail against a storm. Job, when once wet to the skin, curseth the day of his birth, and thinketh it better to be strangled or hanged than longer to endure it, Job vii. 15. And yet God was but in jest, as it were, with Job, in comparison of Judas.

Ver. 6. *It is not lawful*, &c.] They would not suffer the price of blood to lie in a chest; but the blood itself they could well enough suffer to lie in their consciences. So our modern Pharisees (the Popish prelates) will not be present when the martyrs are condemned to death, but have a hypocritical form of interceding for them to the ˌsecular powers, whenas they themselves have delivered them up to the judges to be executed, *Quos suis præjudiciis damnarunt*, as one speaketh, having first degraded, excommunicated, and adjudged them worthy of death.

Ver. 7. *To bury strangers in*] Romans and others, with whom they would have nothing common, no not so much as a burial place, Isa. lxv. 4, 5. God complains of a people that "remain among the graves, and lodge in the monu-ments; which say, Stand by thyself, come not near to me, for I am holier than thou," &c.; sick they were of a *Noli me tangere*, strict in trifles, senseless of foul sins. There are that tell us, that the nature of this potter's field is such, as, if a stranger's body be laid in it, it consumes it to the bone in four-and-twenty hours; which it doth not to the body of any Jew. This, if it be true, saith one, it seems God would have the earth thus marked to preserve the memory of the bloody money by which it was purchased; and therefore he gave it a virtue to consume strangers' bodies ere they could corrupt, refusing the Jews; to show how they had lost their privilege to their own land, by crucifying their Lord, and strangers began to be possessed of it. Also, to teach us, that his hope is nearest incorruption, who is the greatest stranger from the sin of the Jews, that is, crucifying Christ.

Ver. 8. *Was called the field of blood*] Not the burial-place for strangers, as they would have had it called (thinking thereby to have gotten themselves an eternal commendation, for their love and liberality to strangers), but "the field of blood" (so the vulgar would needs call it, much against these masters' minds), for a lasting monument of their detestable villany, which they thought to have carried so cleanly, that the world should have been never the wiser; and therefore they would not kill Christ themselves, as they did Stephen; but, to decline the envy, delivered him up to Pilate to be put to death. It is hard if hypocrites be not, by one means or other, detected; how else should their names rot?

Ver. 9. *Then was fulfilled*] Those blind Pharisees not only observed not the sayings of the prophets which they daily read, but unwittingly also fulfilled them.

By Jeremiah the prophet] Indeed by Zechariah the prophet; but either Jeremiah had two several names (as was ordinary among that people), or else what Jeremiah had preached Zechariah long after committed to writing, as did likewise Obadiah, &c.

The price of him that was valued] A goodly price set there upon God, for all his pastoral pains with that perverse people; and hereupon Christ (who is hereby proved to be God), for all his inestimable worth, and incomparable love to lost mankind. If we be at any time undervalued, as we are sure to be (for the world knows us not, 1 John iii. 2), what so great a matter is it? Was not the Lord Christ infinitely underrated?

Ver. 10. *And gave them for the potter's field*] To the potter (saith Zechariah), in the house of the Lord. What the prophet sets down in short, and more obscurely, the evangelist expounds, and applies to Christ the antitype. So true is that observation of divines, that the Old Testament is both explained and fulfilled in the New, by a happy harmony.

Ver. 11. *And Jesus stood before the governor*] The best therefore and most innocent may be brought before magistrates, and accused of high treason, which ever was, as Lipsius observeth out of Tacitus, *Unicum crimen eorum qui crimine vacabant.* Elijah was held the king's enemy. Jeremiah laid by the heels for a traitor to the State. Paul styled a pest. Luther a trumpet of rebellion. Beza a seedsman of sedition, &c. Christ's accusers here shamelessly appeal him of matters that were evidently untrue. This Pilate saw, and therefore sought so many ways to deliver him.

Ver. 12. *He answered nothing*] Here the nimble lawyer would have presently argued, as the pope's legate did at the meeting of the princes at Smalcaldia in Germany. He brought letters from the pope to the elector of Saxony; and because the elector gave him not a present answer, he inferred, *Qui tacet consentire videtur.* Melancthon being by, made answer, *Hoc est sophisticum; est regula juris, sed non valet inconjecturalibus. Nam dicit, videtur, et argumentum videtur; solvitur per non videtur.*[1] Christ therefore answered nothing, because they alleged nothing but notorious lies, and such as he saw well the governor himself saw through, and therefore tried so many policies to set him free.

Ver. 13. *Hearest thou not, &c.*] Yes, well enough; but there is a time when a man should be as a "deaf man that heareth not, and as a dumb man that openeth not his mouth," Psal. xxxviii. 13. *Ego aurium Dominus, ut tu linguæ,* said he in Tacitus to his obstreperous adversary. If I cannot command thy tongue, yet I can command mine own ears. And the "prudent will keep silence in an evil time," saith Amos, v. 13. See the note above, on chap. xxvi. 62. Patience and silence were Isaac's apology to Ishmael. *Sile, et funestam dedisti plagam,* saith Chrysostom.

Ver. 14. *The governor marvelled*] That Christ should so betray his own cause, by an obstinate silence. But why marvelled he not as much at the impudency of the priests, pressing such palpable untruths against him? He did, no doubt; and yet against all equity yielded to their importunity. But should not magistrates be men of courage, *cœur-de-lions?* Solomon's throne was supported by lions; to show what manner of men such should be as sit in places of judicature.

Ver. 15. *The governor was wont*] In remembrance, say some, of their deliverance from the Egyptian bondage. A custom it was, and therefore obtained; but an evil custom, and therefore should better have been abrogated. Custom without truth is but hoariness or mouldiness of error, saith one. And custom without righteousness is but antiquity of iniquity, saith another. A custom they have in Rome at this day, that if a cardinal meet a condemned person going to execution, and put his hat on the malefactor's head, he is thereby set free. I see no sense for such a pardon. But the inhabitants of Berne in Germany gave a general pardon to most of their prisoners, and called home their banished that same day wherein the Reformation was received and established amongst them.[2] And they gave this reason for it.[3] Should some confederate prince pass through our coasts, we should for his sake pardon our offenders, upon promise of amendment. Now shall the King of kings, the Son of God, and our dear Brother, who hath done and suffered so much for us, come graciously unto us, and we not honour him this way also? Saul, for joy of his victory over the Ammonites, would not suffer such to be put to death as had spoken treason against him; for "to-day," said he, "the Lord hath wrought salvation in Israel," 1 Sam. xi. 13.

Ver. 16. *A notable prisoner, called Barabbas*] That is, by interpretation, his father's son, his white son, his darling, his tidling, whom he had cockered and not crossed from his youth. Such children are oft undone, as Absalom, Amnon, and Adonijah were by their parents' indulgence. How many a Barabbas, brought to the gallows, blameth his fond father, and haply curseth him in hell!

Ver. 17. *Whom will ye that I release?*] Pilate hoped they would never be so grossly wicked as to prefer such a stigmatical varlet. But why did he give them the liberty of such a choice? Why did he not rather (as Job) "break the jaws of the wicked, and pluck the spoil out of their teeth?" Job xxx. 17. Should not the standard be made of hardest metals? the chief post of the house be heart of oak? Was it not pusillanimity and popularity that misled Pilate, and so muzzled him, that he could not contradict the many-headed multitude?

Ver. 18. *For he knew that for envy*] His sin was the greater for his knowledge, Jam. iv. 17. *Omne peccatum contra conscientiam ædificat ad gehennam,* saith Gerson. When men imprison their light (that prophet from God), Rom. i. 18, and after conviction run away with the bit in their mouths, as it were, they run, without God's greater mercy, upon their utter ruin and destruction. Tostatus truly observeth, that Solomon's idolatry was a sin far more sinful than that of his wives, because against knowledge.

Ver. 19. *His wife sent unto him*] There are that think that this woman's dream was of the devil; thereby to have hindered the work of redemption by this composition. Satan and his agents, when they cannot conquer, would fain compound. Others will have it to be a divine dream, because it was sent, say they, for the better clearing of Christ's innocency, even while he stood at the bar; yea, for the salvation of this woman's soul, as Theophylact is of opinion. *Opus providentiæ Dei; non ut solveretur Christus, sed ut servaretur uxor.*

Ver. 20. *The chief priests and elders persuaded*] And prevailed. See then how needful it is that we pray for good governors; Jeroboam made Israel to sin; Peter compelled the

[1] Joh. Manl. *loc. com.* p. 406.   [2] Heidfeld.

[3] *Gravissimo hoc argumento usi.* Scult. Annal.

Gentiles to Judaize, Gal. ii. 14. As the corruption of a fish begins at the head, and as in a beast the whole body follows the head, so are the people over-ruled by their rulers.

Ver. 21. *They said, Barabbas*] This mad choice is every day made, while men prefer the lusts of their flesh before the lives of their souls. In the present instance we may see, as in a mirror, the inconstancy of the common sort (who erst cried Christ up for a prophet, and would have crowned him for a king) and the desperate madness of the priests, *Qui citius diabolum ex inferno petivissent quam Jesum*, as Pareus hath it, who would have desired the devil of hell, rather than Jesus. *Sic neutrum modo mas modo vulgus.*

Ver. 22. *Let him be crucified*] He whom erewhile they had little less than deified. See how soon evil company and counsel had altered them, like as walnut-tree roots embitter the roots of all the trees about them. *Si quis obsequatur Calliæ, statim reddet eum temulentum Callias; si Alcibiadi, jactatorem; si Crobylo, coquum, &c.*, saith Ælian. A man easily conformeth to his company.

Ver. 23. *Why? What evil hath he done?*] Why? but if he have done no evil, wherefore doth not Pilate pronounce him innocent, *contra gentes*, and quit him by proclamation? which because he did not, but the contrary, was he not therefore by a just judgment of God upon him, kicked off the bench by the Emperor Tiberius? Judge Hales came to an evil end for crossing his conscience. And Judge Morgan, who gave the sentence of that peerless Lady Jane Grey's death, presently fell mad; and in all his distracted fits, cried out continually, Take away the Lady Jane, take away the Lady Jane from me. It is reported of Nevessan, a better lawyer than an honest man, that he should say, He that will not venture his body, shall never be valiant; he that will not venture his soul, never rich.

Ver. 24. *He took water*] Too weak an element to wash off guilt; which is not purged but by the blood of Christ, or fire of hell.

And washed his hands] An old ceremony, used in this case, both by Jews (Deut. xxi. 6, 7; Acts xviii. 6) and Gentiles, as the scholiast upon Sophocles testifieth. And it was as much as to say, the guilt of innocent blood doth no more stick to my conscience than the filth now washed off doth to my fingers.[1] *Sed quid hoc est*, saith one: *Manus abluit Pilatus, et cor polluit.* "O Jerusalem, wash thy heart from wickedness," saith the prophet, Jer. iv. 14. God and nature begin at the heart. And cleanse your hands, ye sinners, but withal, "Purify your hearts, ye doubleminded," saith the apostle, Jam. iv. 8. The very Turks before prayer wash both face and hands, sometimes the head and privates. But bodily exercise only profiteth little.

See ye to it] See thou to that, said they to Judas, ver. 4. See ye to it, saith Pilate to them. "With what measure ye mete it shall be measured to you again," Matt. vii. 2. They are paid in their own coin: their own very words, by a just judgment of God, are regested upon them.

Ver. 25. *His blood be on us, and on, &c.*] God said Amen to this woeful curse, which cleaves close to them and their posterity, as a girdle to their loins, soaking as oil into their bones to this very day, Psal. cix. 18, 19. Thirty-eight years after this fearful imprecation, in the same place, and close by the same tribunal where they thus cried out, His blood be on us, &c., historians tell us, that Herod, wanting money, demanded of the Jews so much out of their treasury as would pay for the making of a water-course. But the Jews, supposing it a needless work, not only denied him, but gave many outrageous and spiteful speeches, tumultuously flocked about him, and with great clamours pressed upon him, even as he was in his seat. Whereupon to prevent mischief, he sent to his soldiers to apparel themselves like citizens, and under their gowns to bring with them a dagger or poniard, and mingle themselves amongst the multitude; which they did, observing who they were that made the greatest uproar. And when Herod gave the sign, they fell upon them, and slew a great multitude. Many also, for fear of loss or danger, killed themselves; besides others, which seeing this massacre, suspecting treason among themselves, fell one upon another. What a dispersed and despised people they are ever since! exiled, as it were, out of the world, by the common consent of all nations, for their inexpiable guilt. And beware by their example of wishing evil to ourselves or others, as our desperate God-damn-me's do at every third word almost, and God will undoubtedly take them at their words, as he did those wretches that wished they might die in the wilderness, Numb. xiv. 28. As he did John Peters, the cruel keeper of Newgate in Queen Mary's days; who commonly, when he would affirm anything, were it true or false, used to say, If it be not true, I pray God I rot ere I die; and he had his desire. So had Sir Gervase Ellowais, Lieutenant of the Tower, hanged in our remembrance on Tower-hill, for being accessory to the poisoning of Sir Thomas Overbury; who being upon the gallows, confessed it was just upon him, for that he had oft in his playing of cards and dice wished that he might be hanged if it were not so and so. In the year 1551, the devil in a visible shape lifted up a cursing woman into the air in Germany; and therehence threw her down in the view of many people, and brake her neck. Another brought her daughter to Luther, entreating his prayers for her, for that she was possessed by the devil, upon her cursing of her. For when she had said in a rage against her daughter, *Involet in te diabolus*, The devil take thee, he took possession of her accordingly. The same author relateth a like sad story of a stubborn son, cursed by his father, who wished he might never stir alive from the place he stood in, and he stirred not for three years. Cursing

---

[1] Εθος ἦν τοῖς παλαιοῖς οἴτε ἢ φόνον ἀνθρώπου ἢ ἄλλας σφαγὰς ἐποίουν, ὕδατι ἀπονίπτειν τὰς χεῖρας εἰς κάθαρσιν τοῦ μιάσματος.

men are cursed men. *Alterius perditio tua fit cautio.* Seest thou another suffer shipwreck, look to thy tackling.

Ver. 26. *And when he had scourged Jesus*] So to satisfy their cruelty, and move them, if it might be, to pity. But though they relented not at the sight, it's fit we should. Would it not grieve us at the heart, if we should see the king's son basely whipped by our adversaries, only for our affairs? Christ was scourged when we had offended, that he might free us from the sting of conscience, and those scourges and scorpions of eternal torments, that he might make us a plaister of his own blessed blood,[1] for by his stripes we are healed, by the bloody weals made upon his back we are delivered. We hold it a thing almost beyond belief, that the applying of medicines to the sword that wounded a man shall make the wounds heal in a man. But here is a mystery that only Christian religion can tell of, and of which there never was precedent in nature, that the scourging and wounding of one man should cure another. See the note on John xix. 1.

Ver. 27. *Then the soldiers of the governor*] " Barbarous and brutish men, skilful to destroy," Ezek. xxi. 31. " Let the young men arise and play before us," said Abner, 2 Sam. ii. 14. It is but a sport to soldiers to kill and put men to tormentful ends. At the taking of Tripolis in Barbary, the Turkish soldiers having in their hands one John de Chabos, a Frenchman born in Dauphine, they brought him into the town; and when they had cut off his hands and nose, they put him quick into the ground to the waist, and there, for their pleasure, shot at him with their arrows, and afterwards cut his throat. What insolencies and cruelties they exercised upon our Saviour for our sakes, even the whole band of them, we should read with regret for our sins, the weapons and instruments of all his sufferings; and see through his wounds the naked bowels, as it were, of his love to our poor souls.

Ver. 28. *And they stripped him*] That we might be clothed with the rich and royal raiment of his righteousness, that fleece of the Lamb of God, who taketh away, &c.

And put on him a scarlet robe] O'erworn and threadbare, no doubt; so to set him forth as an histrionical king, in contempt of him; but the kingdom of Christ came not by observation. He is an obscure king, as Melchisedec was, but yet a king, as he told Pilate; and this was that good confession witnessed by him, and celebrated by St Paul, 1 Tim. vi. 13.

Ver. 29. *And when they had platted a crown, &c.*] Christ, by wearing this crown of thorns, the first-fruits of the curse, took away the sin and curse of all his people; who must therefore, by their obedience, set a crown of gold on his head, Cant. iii. 11, as Canutus in his superstitious way set his crown upon the crucifix. See the note on John xix. 2.

And a reed in his right hand] So do all those still, that submit not to the sceptre of his king-

[1] *Sanguis medici factus est medicina phrenetici.*

dom,—that give him not full sovereignty over their souls.

Bowed the knee before him] With ludibrious devotion. So do hypocrites to this day. King Richard II., when he was to be deposed, was brought forth in royal array, whereof he was presently despoiled. Never was prince so gorgeous with less glory and more grief.

Ver. 30. *And they spit upon him*] So doth profaneness still cast dirt and drivel into Christ's face. See the note on chap. xxvi. 67. Robert Smith, martyr, in his examination before Bonner, made one of his doctors to say, that his breaden god must needs enter into the belly, and so fall into the draught. To which he answered: What derogation was it to Christ, when the Jews spit in his face? Smith presently replied, If the Jews, being his enemies, did but spit in his face, and we, being his friends, throw him into the draught, which of us deserveth the greatest damnation?

And smote him on the head] Or, into the head, εἰς κεφαλὴν: drove the thorns into his holy head with bats and blows, as Basiliades, the Duke of Russia, nailed an ambassador's hat to his head, upon some displeasure conceived against him. At the taking of Heidelberg, the Spaniards took Monsieur Mylius, an ancient minister and man of God, and having abused his daughter before his face, they tied a small cord about his head, which with truncheons they wreathed about, till they squeezed out his brains. The monks of Pignerol roasted the minister of St Germain, till his eyes dropped out. And the Spaniards suppose they show the innocent Indians great favour, when they do not, for their pleasure, whip them with cords, scratch them with thorns, and day by day drop their naked bodies with burning bacon. So very a devil is one man to another.

Ver. 31. *Put his own raiment on him*] God's hand was in this, that all men seeing him to suffer in his own habit, might acknowledge that it was very he, and not another that suffered in his stead. Mahomet in his Alcoran speaks very honourably of Christ, except only in two things. 1. He took up the Arian heresy, to deny his Deity. 2. He denied that he was crucified, but that some one was crucified for him. But what saith St Peter? " He his own self bare our sins in his own body on the tree," &c., 1 Pet. ii. 24.

They led him away] Quite out of the city, *Ut vera piacularis victima et* κάθαρμα *pro nobis fieret,* Heb. xiii. 12, 13. This was a mystery hardly understood by any of the faithful afore Christ; neither could we well have told what to make of it, but that the apostle hath there opened it to us, by the instinct of the Holy Ghost. " Let us therefore " (as he adviseth) " go forth unto him without the camp, bearing his reproach," accounting it our crown, as those apostles did that rejoiced in their new dignity of suffering shame for Christ's name, Acts v. 41. " It was their grace to be so disgraced." *Est et confusionis gloria, et gloriosa confusio.* (Ambr.)

Ver. 32. *They found a man of Cyrene*] A

stranger, coming out of the field towards Jerusalem, meets with an unexpected cross, and follows Christ, which occasioned him to inquire into the cause, and got him renown among the saints. In like sort, the faithful Christian (a stranger upon earth) comes out of the field of this world, with his face set toward Sion, and meets with many crosses by the way. But all while he follows Christ, let him inquire into the cause, and the issue shall be glorious.

Him they compelled to bear his cross] Not so much to ease Christ, who fainted under the burden, as to hasten the execution, and to keep him alive till he came to it. See the note on John xix. 17.

Ver. 33. *A place of a skull*] Here our thrice noble Conqueror would erect his trophies, to encourage us to suffer for him, if God call us thereto, in the most vile and loathsome places, as also to assure us that his death is life to the dead.

Ver. 34. *They gave him vinegar, &c.*] Cold comfort to a dying man; but they did it in derision, *q. d.* Thou art a King, and must have generous wines. Here's for thee therefore. See the note on John xix. 29. It were happy if this vinegar given our Saviour might melt our adamantine hearts into sorrow.

Ver. 35. *Parted his garments*] Let us likewise suffer with joy the spoiling of our goods, &c., Heb. x. 34; yea, the spoiling of our persons, to have our clothes also taken and torn from off our backs: Christ will say, "Bring forth the best robe, ring," &c. If a heathen could say, when he saw a sudden shipwreck of all his wealth, Well, fortune, I see thy intent, thou wouldst have me be a philosopher: should not a Christian conclude, Surely Christ would have me look after heavenly, that thus strips me of all earthly comforts?

Ver. 36. *They watched him there*] Lest haply he should get away thence by a miracle. But his time of getting out of their hands was not yet come. Here hung for a while that golden censer, Christ's body; which through the holes that were made in it, as through chinks or holes, fumed forth a sweet savour in the nostrils of his heavenly Father, Eph. v. 2, such as draweth all men to him, that have their "senses exercised to discern good and evil," John xii. 32; Heb. v. 14.

Ver. 37. *This is Jesus, the King of the Jews*] Pilate (by a special providence of God), intending nothing less, gives Christ a testimonial, and would not alter it, though solicited thereto. He did it to be revenged on the Jews for their senseless importunity to have him condemn an innocent, and withal, to put Christ to an open shame, as a crucified King. Like as that atheist Lucian blasphemously calls our Saviour the crucified cozener, Ἀνεσκολοπισμένον σοφιστὴν, the modern Jews contemptuously call him (in reference to his cross), "The Woof and the Warp."[1] And, at the sack of Constantinople, the image of the crucifix was set up by the insolent Turks, and shot at with their arrows; and afterwards in great

derision carried about the camp, as it had been in procession, those dead dogs railing and spitting at it, and calling it "The god of the Christians." Ten thousand martyrs were crucified on the Mount of Ararat under Adrian the emperor, crowned with thorns, and thrust into the sides with sharp darts, in contempt of Christ.

Ver. 38. *Then were there two thieves*] So he "was reckoned among the transgressors," Isa. liii. 12; a sinner, not by imputation only, for "he bare the sin of many" (*ib.*), but by reputation also, and therefore crucified in the midst (as the worst of the three, "chief of sinners," *Quasi maleficiorum rex esset*), that we might have place in the midst of heavenly angels, in those walks of paradise, Zech. iii. 7. The one of those two thieves went railing to hell (his crucifixion being but a typical hell to him, a trap-door to eternal torment), the other went repenting forthright to heaven, living long in a little time, and by prayer making his cross a Jacob's ladder, whereby angels descended to fetch up his soul. It is remarkable, and to our purpose suitable, that Rabus reporteth, that when Leonard Cæsar suffered martyrdom at Rappa, a little town in Bavaria, a certain priest, that had by the law for some villanous act deserved death, being led forth with him towards the place of execution, cried out often, *Ego ne quidem dignus sum, qui tibi in hac pœna associer, justo injustus,* I am not worthy to suffer with thee, the just with the unjust. At the death of George Eagles, martyr, in Queen Mary's days, two thieves being to be executed with him, he exhorted them to embrace the truth, and to persevere therein. Whereupon one of them scoffingly said, Why should we doubt of going to heaven, seeing this holy man shall go before us, as our captain in the way? we shall certainly fly thither straight, as soon as he hath made us the entry. But the other thief reproved him for it, and gave good heed to George Eagles' exhortation, earnestly bewailing his own wickedness, and crying unto Christ for mercy. This penitent thief exhorted the people upon the ladder, to beware of sin by his example: and so commending his soul to Christ, ended his life quietly, and in a godly manner. The mocker when he came upon the ladder would have said something, but could not; his tongue did so fumble and falter in his head, that he could not repeat the Lord's prayer, but became a singular instance of God's just judgment upon so profane a person.

Ver. 39. *Reviled him, wagging their heads*] God took notice of Cain's frowns, Gen. iv. 6, Miriam's mutterings, Numb. xii. 2, these men's noddings, Rabshakeh's lofty looks, Isa. xxxvii. 23, Laban's lourings, Gen. xxxi. 2, and sets them upon record. He is jealous for Jerusalem with a great jealousy, Zech. i. 14 (and jealousy is very wakeful, hardly shall the sly paramour avoid the husband's eye), if he see any indignity offered to his beloved spouse, he will arise and play Phineas' part, as that martyr said. The virgin daughter of Zion, though she be but a virgin, hath a champ-

---

[1] *Judæi perpetuo obganniunt nihil esse stolidius Christianis, quod salutem ex homine crucifixo sibi polliceantur.* Bucholcer.

pion that will not see nor suffer her to be abused, Isa. xxxvii. 22. See how he revileth her revilers, Isa. lvii. 3, 4. " But draw near hither, ye sons of the sorceress, the seed of the adulterer and the whore. Against whom do ye sport yourselves ? against whom make ye a wide mouth, and draw out the tongue ? are ye not children of transgression, a seed of falsehood ? " Yea, he giveth encouragement to his spouse, in a holy scorn to despise and deride her deriders, shaking her head at them, as they do at her, and saying, " Whom hast thou reproached and blasphemed ? " &c. *q. d.* Dost thou know what thou hast done ? &c. At Brightwell in Berkshire, one Lener said that he saw that evil-favoured knave Latimer, when he was burned at Oxford ; and that he had teeth like a horse. But the Lord suffered not this scorn and contempt of his servant to go unpunished. For that very day, and about the same hour that Lener spake those words, his son wickedly hanged himself.

Ver. 40. *And saying, Thou that,* &c.] Dogs will be barking at the moon (as these dead dogs do here at the Sun of righteousness), *At peragit cursus surda Diana suos.* Christ goes on with the work, nothing retarded by their jeers and buffooneries. *Didicit ille maledicere et ego contemnere,* said he in Tacitus, *Non tantum habemus otii, P. C.,* said Augustus to the senate, when they informed him of what such and such had said against him, We are not at leisure to listen to every slight slander raised of us. And of Severus the emperor it is recorded, that his care was, what was to be done by him, not what was said or censured of him.[1] " Do well and hear ill," is written upon heaven-gates, said that martyr. Railers are to be reckoned kill-Christs : words may more afflict than blows, Psal. xlii. 3, 10. As " with a murdering weapon in my bones," &c.

Ver. 41. *Likewise also the chief priests*] Sick of an ἐπιχαιρεκακία, the devil's disease, they petulantly insult over our dying Saviour with their satanical sarcasms ; which he answereth with silence, and by a brave composedness sets himself above the flight of the injurious claw. *Facile est in me dicere, cum non sim responsurus,* saith one. It is as impossible to avoid, as necessary to contemn the lash of lewd tongues, bitter terms, and scurrilous invectives. Those ears that were wont to hear nothing but angelical hymns are here filled with them, and he replies not. Princes use not to chide when ambassadors offer them indecencies, but deny them audience.

Ver. 42. *We will believe him*] They would not ; but rather have said, he had done it by the devil's help ; or have searched the devil's skull to find out some other trick to elude the truth.

Ver. 43. *He trusted in God*] These were cruel mockings, as those were called, Heb. xi. 36. Nothing troubled David more than to be hit in the teeth with his God, to have his religion laid in his dish, Psal. xlii., xliii. And it went to Job's heart to hear his friend Eliphaz (a

godly man otherwise) scoff him for his religion, Job iv. 6. Is not thy fear (or thy religion) become thy folly ? Zedekiah feared more to be mocked of the Jews than the Chaldees, Jer. xxxviii. 9.

Let him deliver him now] But what if he do not deliver him now, is he therefore no Son ? So they would seem to argue; and so Satan would fain persuade the saints when held awhile under the cross. But the apostle assures us otherwise, Heb. xii. 6—8.

Ver. 44. *The thieves also*] Both of them railed at first, till one of them was converted by a miracle (for it was one of those seven miracles wherewith Christ would honour the ignominy of his cross). Then till either they both reviled our Saviour, or the better of them seemed, at least by his silence, for a season to consent to the other. In whose example we see that every fool hath a bolt to shoot at afflicted godliness. Every cur is ready to fall upon the dog that he seeth worried ; and every passenger to pull a branch from a tree that is felled. But there is no small cruelty in composing comedies out of the tragedies of the church, and so to draw blood from that back which is yet blue from the hand of the Almighty. God threateneth Edom for but looking upon Jacob's affliction in the day of their calamity, Obadiah 13.

Ver. 45. *Darkness over all the land*] The sun hid his head in a mantle of black, as ashamed to behold those base indignities done to the Son of righteousness by the sons of men.[2] This darkness some think was universal ; not only over all the land of Judea, but over the whole earth (and so the text, ἐπὶ πᾶσαν τὴν γῆν, may be rendered). Tiberius, say they, was sensible of it at Rome ; Dionysius writes to Polycarpus that they had it in Egypt. And another great astronomer, Ptolomy (if I mistake not), was so amazed at it that he pronounced either nature now determineth, or the God of nature suffereth.

Unto the ninth hour] In this three hours' darkness he was set upon by all the powers of darkness with utmost might and malice. But he foiled and spoiled them all, and made an open show of them (as the Roman conquerors used to do), triumphing over them on his cross, as on his chariot of state, Colos. ii. 15, attended by his vanquished enemies with their hands bound behind them, Eph. iv. 8.

Ver. 46. *Jesus cried with a loud voice*] Therefore he laid down his life at his own pleasure ; for by his loud outcry it appears that he could have lived longer if he had listed, for any decay of nature under those exquisite torments that he suffered in his body, but much greater in his soul. That which for the present seems to have expressed from him this doleful complaint, was the sense of his Father's wrath in the darkening of the body of the sun over him ; which though God causeth to shine upon the just and unjust

---

[1] Ἐπιμελὴς ἦν τῶν πρακτέων, ἀμελὴς τῶν περὶ αυτοῦ λεγομένων· Dio.

[2] *Sol non fert aspectum illum miserandum, quem sine rubore et fronte Judæi irrident.* Aretius.

for their comfort, yet was not suffered to shine upon him for those three sorrowful hours together. When Theodorus, the martyr, was racked and tortured by the command of Julian the Apostate, an angel, in the form of a young man, stood by him and comforted him, wiping off his sweat with a fine linen cloth, and pouring cold water on his vexed limbs. When Mr Saunders, martyr, was examined before Stephen Winchester, he felt a most pleasant refreshing issuing from every part of his body to his heart, and from thence ebbing and flowing to each part again. William Hunter, martyr, cried out at the stake, Son of God, shine upon me, and immediately the sun shone out of a dark cloud so full in his face that he was constrained to look another way; whereat the people mused, because it was so dark a little before. And I myself was an eye-witness of a like answer returned from heaven, to a like prayer made by a penitent malefactor executed at Evesham in Worcestershire, many years since. But our Lord Christ was forsaken of all these creature comforts; and (which was worse than all) of his Father's favour, to his present apprehension; left forlorn and destitute for a time, that we might be received for ever.[1] Howbeit, perplexed though he were, yet not in despair; persecuted, yet not forsaken; cast down, yet not destroyed.[2] He could say My God, in the midst of all, by the force of his faith, which individuateth God (as a father saith) and appropriateth him to a man's self.[3] And Hilary hath a good note, which here comes in not out of place. *Habes conquerentem relictum se esse, quia homo est; habes eundem profitentem latroni in paradiso regnaturum, quia Deus est.* As man, he cries out My God, my God, &c., when, as God, he promiseth paradise to the penitent thief.

Ver. 47. *This man calleth for Elias*] A malicious mistake, a devilish sarcasm. While darkness was upon them they were over-awed and hushed; their mouths were haltered (as horses must be, saith the psalmist, Psal. xxxii. 9, as the sea was by our Saviour, Mark iv. 39, πεφίμωσο), and held in with bit and bridle lest they come near unto thee. But no sooner was it light again but they are at their old trade again, deriding our Saviour and depraving his words, as if, forsaken of his hope in God, he had fled to Elias for help. So when Cranmer, standing at the stake, cried out often, Lord Jesu, receive my spirit, a Spanish monk that heard him ran to a nobleman there present, and tells him that those were the words of one that died in great despair.

Ver. 48. *And filled it with vinegar*] Sorrow is dry, we say. This man of sorrows, more to fulfil the Scriptures than for his own satisfaction, though extreme dry no doubt (for now was the Paschal Lamb a-roasting in the fire of his Father's wrath), he saith, I thirst, and had vinegar to drink, that we might drink of the water of life, and be sweetly inebriated in that torrent of pleasure that runs at God's right hand for evermore, Psal. xvi. 11. See the note on John xix. 29.

Ver. 49. *Let us see whether Elias, &c.*] This mocking is the murder of the tongue, which therefore our Saviour suffered, *ut nos illusori Satanæ insultaremus*, saith one. It is reported of Aretine, that by a long custom of libellous and contumelious speaking against men, he had got such a habit that at last he came to diminish and disesteem God himself. May not the same be made good of these malicious miscreants?

Ver. 50. *Yielded up the ghost*] Or, let go his spirit, viz. to God that gave it, to whom also he recommended it, Luke xxiii. 46, teaching us what to do in like case. Our care herein may make even a centurion, a graceless person, to glorify God, saying, " Certainly this was a righteous man," ver. 47. When so great a clerk as Erasmus, dying with no better words in his mouth than *Domine, fac finem, fac finem*, is but hardly thought of. How much more that English Hubertus, a covetous oppressor, who dying made this wretched will-parole: " I yield my goods to the king, my body to the grave, my soul to the devil."

Ver. 51. *The veil of the temple was rent*] To show that there was an end to the Levitical liturgy, and that now there was free and open access for all saints to the throne of God's grace, for the veil was a figure of the spiritual covering which was before the eyes of the Church till Christ's coming.

And the earth did quake] To work a heartquake in the obstinate Jews, as in some it did; others of them had contracted such an habitual hardness, such a hoof upon their hearts, as neither ministry, nor misery, nor miracle, nor mercy could possibly mollify.

And the rocks rent] So they do wherever Christ makes forcible entrance into any heart. " I will shake all nations, and then the desire of all nations shall come," Hag. ii. 7. A man will never truly desire Christ till soundly shaken. God's shaking ends in settling; he rends us, not to ruin, but to refine us.

Ver. 52. *And the graves were opened*] To show that death was now swallowed up in victory by life essential; like as the fire swallows up the fuel, and as Moses' serpent swallowed up the enchanted serpents.

And many bodies of the saints] To show that the heart-strings of death, which before bound them in their sepulchres, were now broken, and they enlarged to attend our Saviour's resurrection.

Ver. 53. *And appeared unto many*] Not to converse again, as heretofore, with men, but to accompany Christ, that raised them, into heaven; and to be as so many ocular demonstrations of Christ's quickening power, whereby he shall also raise our vile bodies, and conform them to his glorious body, the standard, Phil. iii. 21.

---

[1] ἐγκατέλιπες *est plus quam* κατέλιπες, *ut deserere quam derelinquere.*

[2] 2 Cor. iv. 8, 9.

[3] ἡ πιστίς ἰδιοποιεῖται τὸν Θεόν.

Ver. 54. *Truly this was the Son of God*] i. e. A divine man, a demi-god, as these heathens reputed those in whom they beheld and admired anything above the ordinary nature of men, and their expectation.[1] Natural conscience cannot but stoop and do homage to the image of God stamped upon his people ; as being "afraid of that name of God whereby they are called," Deut. xxviii. 10. There are that think that these soldiers, our Saviour's executioners, were truly converted by the miracles they had seen, according to what Christ had prayed for them, Luke xxiii. 34. And it may very well be ; like as Paul was converted upon St Stephen's prayer ; as Justin Martyr and others were, by beholding the piety and patience of the primitive Christians, and as James Silvester, executioner at the martyrdom of Simon Laloe, at Dijon. He seeing the great faith and constancy of that heavenly martyr, was so compuncted with repentance (saith Mr Fox), and fell into such despair of himself, that they had much ado to fasten any comfort on him, with all the promises of the Gospel ; till at length he recovered, repented, and with all his family removed to the Church of Geneva. Christians have showed as glorious power (and have as good success) in the faith of martyrdom, as in the faith of miracles ; working wonders thereby upon those that have sought and sucked their blood.

Ver. 55. *And many women were there*] More hardy than the disciples, who all, save John, were fled and hid. Oh stand (saith Dr Sutton), and behold a little, with those devout women, the body of thy Saviour, hanging upon the cross. See him afflicted from top to toe. See him wounded in the head, to heal our vain imaginations. See him wounded in the hands, to heal our evil actions. See him wounded in the heart, to cure our vain thoughts. See his eyes shut up, that did enlighten the world ; see them shut, that thine might be turned from seeing of vanity. See that countenance so goodly to behold, spitted upon and buffeted, that thy face might shine glorious as the angels in heaven, &c. See the note on John xix. 25.

Beholding afar off] Either out of womanly modesty, or weakness of faith ; which, when it is in heart, is able by its native puissance to pull the very heart as it were out of hell, and with confidence and conquest to look even death and the devil in the face ; as we see in Anne Askew, Alice Driver, and other brave women, that suffered stoutly for Christ.

Ver. 56. *Among which was Mary Magdalen*] Love is strong as death ; good blood will never belie itself. Mary also the mother of Jesus was there, sitting with the sword through her heart, that old Simeon had foresight her. See John xix. 26, 27, with the note upon that text.

Ver. 57. *A rich man of Arimathea*] Not many such ; 'tis well there are any. Joseph was a counsellor, a senator, one of the Sanhedrim or

Seventy Seniors. Christ finds friends in the most tempestuous times and unlikely places ; as in Ahab's and Nero's court. Some good Obadiah, or Onesiphorus, to seek out Paul the prisoner, and refresh his bowels. Serena the Empress, wife to Dioclesian, that bloody persecutor, was a Christian, and a great friend to the true religion. So was the Lady Anne (wife to our King Richard II.), a disciple of Wickliff ; whose books also she conveyed over into Bohemia her country, whereby a good foundation was laid for the ensuing Reformation. John of Gaunt showed himself a great favourer of Wickliff. The like did the Elector of Saxony for Luther. George Marquis of Brandenburg, in a meeting of the Emperor and States at Augsburg, zealously professed that he would rather kneel down presently in the presence of them all, and yield his head to be struck off by the executioner, than deny Christ and his gospel. Scultet. Annal.

Ver. 58. *He went to Pilate*] It was time for him now or never to show himself, and to wax bold, Mark xv. 43. The Spaniards, they say, abhor dangers, never adventuring upon hard enterprises, but aiming to proceed securely. "Christ's disciples must speak and do boldly in the Lord," Acts xiv. 3, whatever come of it. *Audendo Græci pervenere Trojam.* Alexander never attempted anything, but he conceived it might be done, and he did it. Historians ascribe most of his success to his courage ; and tell us, that having a soldier of his own name in his army whom he knew to be a coward, he commanded him either to change his name, or show his valour. So saith Christ to all his Josephs and Nicodemuses, Either play the men, or pretend not to me.

Ver. 59. *He wrapped it in a clean linen cloth*] "Which he had bought new for the purpose," saith St Mark, xv. 46, to his no small cost ; for linen in those days was precious, so that a handkerchief among even the Roman rioters was a rich token, as appears out of the poet.[2] Neither did this rich man lose his cost ; for he is and shall be famous for it to the world's end ; though everybody be not at leisure to do as Paleottus, Archbishop of Bonony, did, who wrote a great book of the shadow of Christ's body in Joseph's new syndon ; which was also commented upon by the Professor of Divinity there.

Ver. 60. *And laid it in his own new tomb*] His own, which was now well warmed, sweetened, and sanctified by our Saviour's body, against himself should be laid there ; as afterwards he might and probably was, too. A new tomb it was, and fit it should be for that virgin body, or maidencorpse, as one calls it, untouched and untainted. Besides, else it might have been suspected, that not Christ but another arose ; or if he, yet not by his own, but by another's virtue: like him who revived at the touching of the bones of dead Elisha, 2 Kings xiii. Buried our Saviour was : 1. That none might doubt his death. 2.

---

[1] *υιος sine articulo, id est justus heros.* Beza.

[2] *Nam sudaria setaba ex Iberis miserunt mihi muneri Fabulus et Veranius.* Catul.

That our sins might be buried with him. 3. That our graves might be prepared and perfumed for us, as so many beds of roses, or delicious dormitories, Isa. lvii. 2. He was buried in Calvary, to note that he died for the condemned; and in a garden, to expiate that first sin committed in the garden; and in another man's sepulchre, to note that he died for other men's sins, as some will have it. Helena, mother of Constantine the Great, bestowed great cost in repairing this sepulchre of our Saviour, which the heathens out of hatred to Christ had thrown down, and built a temple of Venus on the same ground. And Jerusalem, that poor ruinous city, being governed by one of the Turks, Sanzacks, is for nothing now more famous than for the sepulchre of our Saviour, again repaired, and much visited by the superstitious sort of Christians, and not unreverenced by the Turks themselves.

Which he had hewn out in the rock] For his own use. See the like, 1 Kings xiii. 30. The Thebans had a law, that no man should make a house for himself to dwell in, but he should make first his grave. Charles V., emperor, five years before he died, even when he was employed in his greatest affairs, caused a sepulchre to be made, with all things appertaining to it, necessary for his burial, and that secretly, lest it might be taken for ostentation or hypocrisy: which things he had closely carried with him whithersoever he went five years together; some thinking there had been some great treasure in it; some other that there had been books of old stories: some thought one thing, some another. But the emperor smiling, said, that he carried it about him to mind him of his death.

And he rolled a great stone] Either for an inscription to the sepulchre, or for more safety to the body, or that the glory of the resurrection might be the greater, or all these together.

Ver. 61. *And there was Mary Magdalene*] Carefully watching where they laid the Lord's body, that they might not leave off their kindness to him living or dead, as she said of Boaz, Ruth ii. 20. Heavy they were as heart could hold: yet not hindered thereby from doing their duty to Christ. So Daniel, though sick, yet did the king's business. Even sorrow for sin, if it so exceed as to disable us for duty, is a sinful sorrow, and must be sorrowed for.

Ver. 62. *Now the next day that followed*] That is, on that high-day, that double sabbath, they that had so oft quarrelled with Christ for curing on the sabbath request a servile work to be done, of securing and sealing up the sepulchre. It is a common proverb, *Mortui non mordent*, Dead men bite not. But here Christ, though dead and buried, bites and beats hard upon these evil men's consciences. They could not rest the whole night before, for fear he should get out of the grave some way, and so create them further trouble. Scipio appointed his sepulchre to be so placed, as his image standing upon it might look directly towards Africa, that being dead, he might still be a terror to the Carthaginians.

And Cadwallo, an ancient king of this island, commanded his dead body to be embalmed, and put into a brazen image, and so set upon a brazen horse over Ludgate, for a terror to the Saxons. It is well known that Zisca, that brave Bohemian, charged his Taborites to flay his corpse, and head a drum with his skin; the sound whereof as oft as the enemies heard, they should be appalled and put to flight. And our Edward I. adjured his son and nobles, that if he died in his journey into Scotland, they should carry his corpse about with them, and not suffer it to be interred till they had vanquished the usurper and subdued the country. Something like to this the prophet Isaiah foretelleth of our Saviour (and we see it here accomplished), when he saith, "In that day the root of Jesse shall stand up for an ensign to the people, and even his rest" (or, as some read it, his sepulchre) "shall be glorious," Isa. xi. 10. There are that think that these words, "The day that followed the day of the preparation," are put ironically, or rather by way of a facetious jesting, asteismos, against the hypocritical sabbatism of the high priests, who would so workday-like, beg the body, seal the sepulchre, and set the watch on that sabbath, for the which they seemed to prepare so devoutly before it came.

Ver. 63. *Sir, we remember, &c.*] They that had forgotten so many sweet and savoury sayings of our blessed Saviour, and written them all in the sand, could remember (but for no good purpose) that which his disciples could not so readily call to mind for their good and comfort; no, nor understand it when plainly told them, Mark ix. 32. The soul should be as an holy ark, the memory as the pot of manna, preserving holy truths for holy uses. But most men have memories like nets, that let go the clear water, catch nothing but sticks and refuse stuff; or like sieves, that retain the chaff, let go the good corn; like the creature Cervarius, that if he but look back, forgets the meat he was eating, though never so hungry, and seeks for new; or Sabinus in Seneca, who never in all his life could get by heart those three names, of Homer, Ulysses, and Achilles. Old songs, old wrongs, &c., they can retain sufficiently; but in matters of God, their memories serve them not.

This deceiver said] "Men muse as they use." *Quis tulerit Gracchos?* who can endure to hear the devil taxing God of envy, as he did to our first parents? or these deceitful workers calling "the faithful and true witness," πλάνος, a deceiver, a cheater, one who doth profess an art of cozening men to their faces? for so the Greek word signifieth. We must look to hear all that nought is, either while alive, or when dead. *Melancthon mortuus, tantum non ut blasphemus in Deum, cruci affigitur*, saith Zanchy; and all because he pleased not, in all points, the peevish Lutherans. In like manner many lewd opinions were fathered upon John Wickliff, after he was dead; yea, some that were monstrous and diabolical, as that men ought, yea, that God himself ought to obey the devil. (Speed.) And this famous doctor dying of a palsy, hath this charitable eulogy or epitaph bestowed upon him by a monk, The devil's instrument, church's enemy, people's confusion, heretic's idol, hypocrite's mirror, schism's broacher, hatred's sower, lie's forger, flattery's sink; who at his death despaired like Cain, and, stricken by the horrible judgment of God, breathed forth his wicked soul to the dark mansions of the black devil (Tho. Walsingham). The servant is not greater than his master. Him they called Beelzebub, Samaritan (that is, conjuror), traitor, and here deceiver. But what a mouth of blasphemy opened that pseudo-Christian, Emperor Frederick the Second, who was heard oft to say that there had been three notorious impostors who had cheated the world, viz., Moses, Christ, and Mahomet! Oh base!

Ver. 64. *Command therefore*] How fain would the devil by his agents have kept Christ still in the grave, when there they had him. But all in vain; for his resurrection was to be the demonstration of his deity, Rom. i. 4, and the groundwork of our safety, 1 Cor. xv. 14. He turned therefore their counsel into foolishness, and in the sight of so many armed witnesses, rose the third day, in despite of them, breaking the bonds of death as easily as Samson did the green withs, Judges xvi. 7.

Lest his disciples come by night] A most vain and yet a most vexing fear, such as was that of Herod after he had beheaded John Baptist: he thought he heard that holy head ever shouting and crying out against him, for his cruelty. "This is John Baptist," said he (when he heard the fame of Jesus), "whom I have beheaded." "I will send the hornet," saith God, "before thee," Ex. xxiii. 28. What was that hornet, but the misgiving fear of the Canaanites' self-condemning consciences, that haunted them perpetually? So here.

Ver. 65. *Pilate said unto them*] He was willing to please both sides; and therefore condescends both to Joseph of Arimathea for his burial, and to the priests for securing the sepulchre. Κοινοφιλὴς, *erat utpote qui ab omnibus gratiam inire cupiebat; quales quidam per jocum placentas dixit.* But if I yet please men, saith Paul, as once I did when I was a Pharisee, "I am no more the servant of Christ," Gal. i. 10. He scorns that such base counterfaisance should be found in his followers, Colos. ii. 8. Mordecai will not crouch or curry favour, to die for it. Micaiah will not budge, though sure to kiss the stocks for his stiffness.

Ye have a watch] Appointed for the use and service of the temple, a band of garrison soldiers who had their captain, Acts iv. 1, and are here set to watch that true temple, wherein "the Godhead dwelt bodily," i. e. personally.

Ver. 66. *So they went and made the sepulchre sure*] And now they seemed to dance upon Christ's grave, as thinking themselves cock-sure of him. So did those bloody tyrants of the primitive times (who proudly engraved upon pillars of marble, *Nomine Christianorum deleto, qui Remp. evertebant*) make no other reckoning, but to raze out the name of Christ from under heaven. Therefore also they did not only constitute laws and proclamations against Christians, but did engrave the same laws in tables of brass, meaning to make all things firm for ever and a day. But he that sat in heaven, and said, "Yet have I set my king upon my holy hill of Sion," laughed at them; Jehovah had them in derision, Psal. ii. 4, 6. Look how Daniel was innocently condemned, cast into the lions' den, had the door sealed upon him, and, to see to, no hope or means of life was left him; and yet, by God's good providence, he came forth untouched, and was made a greater man than ever. So our blessed Saviour was innocently condemned, cast into the grave, sealed up among the dead, and to common judgment left as out of mind; yet early in the morning, at the time appointed by the power of his Deity, he raised himself from death, and gloriously triumphed over it and hell. Now "thanks be unto God which also causeth us to triumph in Christ," 2 Cor. ii. 14, having as prisoners of hope, brought us "out of the pit by the blood of the covenant," Zech. ix. 11, 12.

CHAPTER XXVIII.

Ver. 1. *The first day of the week*] Greek, of the sabbaths, εἰς μίαν σαββάτων. One day of seven is due to God of necessity. This the Scripture calls by an excellency the sabbath day, without a difference; as if it were the eldest brother to all the days of the week, which is called here and elsewhere sabbaths, in the plural, Psalm xxiv., title, "A psalm of David." To this the Greek addeth, "of the first day of the week," which now is the Christian sabbath, called "the Lord's day," Rev. i. 10, in honour of Christ, and in a thankful remembrance of his resurrection. See the note on John xx. 1.

To see the sepulchre] To see what the Pharisees had done with the Lord's body the day before (for they knew they had been tampering, and feared the worst, as love is suspicious) and to bring the spices, which by an easy error they had prepared, Luke xxiv. 1. They knew not, belike, that Joseph and Nicodemus had been at that cost and pains before them; neither did any of them consider that what they did herein was superfluous, for that it was "impossible for God's holy one to see corruption," Acts ii. 27. But he is pleased to pass by our well-meant weaknesses, where the heart is upright.

Ver. 2. *And behold*, &c.] The Holy Ghost here calls for as great attention as if we had been present and seen it. Remember (saith St Paul) "that Jesus Christ, of the seed of David, was raised from the dead, according to my gospel," 2 Tim. ii. 8. All the four evangelists have therefore punctually recorded it, that we may remember and ruminate it, as amain remarkable.

There was a great earthquake] Pythagoras

said the reason of earthquakes was, the meeting of the dead: an odd conceit.[1] But the true reason of this earthquake was our Saviour's rising from the dead, in despite of infernal spirits, who therefore quaked as much as the earth did, as Hilary hath it.[2] The earth shook both at Christ's passion and at his resurrection; Then, to show that it could not bear his suffering; now, to show that it could not hinder his rising.

Rolled back the stone] As an officer sent to let Christ out of prison, without the keeper's consent.

And sat upon it] In contempt of all their weapons, which fell out of their hands for woe, at the sight of the angel. And as a mighty man when he sits down shakes the bench under him, so do these the earth.

Ver. 3. *His countenance was like lightning*] So that though he appeared in a human shape, yet it might easily appear that he was more than a man; his visage showed his power, his habit of innocency, to the terror of the keepers, and comfort of the women.

Ver. 4. *The keepers did shake*] And well they might, as coming to see they had borne arms against God, and were therefore obnoxious to his wrath. It is a fearful thing to fall into the punishing hands of the living God here: how then will wicked men bear the horror of the last day, when they shall have an angry God over them, hell gaping beneath them, an accusing conscience within them, the world all on alight fire about them, the elements melting like scalding lead upon them, the good angels testifying against them, Job xx. 27, the evil angels waiting to worry them, and hurry them to hell? Oh the unspeakable achings and quakings of heart, the terrible apprehensions, the convulsions of spirit, that shall seize and surprise them at that dreadful day!

Ver. 5. *Fear not ye*] As the wicked are forbidden to rejoice for joy as other people, Hos. ix. 1, so the godly to fear, so long as they have Christ by the hand; no, though the earth be removed, and the mountains cast into the midst of the sea, Psal. xlvi. 2. David would not fear the shadow of death, the darkest side of death, death in its most hideous and horrid representations, because God was with him, Psal. xxiii. 4; when Manasseh, that faced the heavens in his prosperity, in trouble basely hides his head among the bushes, and is there-hence set, and bound with fetters, 2 Chron. xxxiii. 11. These desperate soldiers run away as dastards, when the women stand it out, and as true daughters of faithful Sarah they are not afraid with any amazement, 1 Pet. iii. 6.

I know that ye seek Jesus] God and his angels know our goodness, why then should we hunt after men's applause? *Cæsar hoc ipso veram laudem meruit, quod falsam contemsit,* saith Lipsius: It should suffice us to know that our faith, how little soever seen or set by the world, shall be found to praise, and honour, and glory at the appearing of Jesus Christ, 1 Pet. i. 7. The eclipsed moon shall by degrees wade out of the shadow.

Ver. 6. *He is not here*] *q. d.* You are much mistaken, and deserve to be chidden for your not crediting, or at least your not remembering, that he foretold you of his resurrection. All which notwithstanding, come see the place, &c., *q. d.* believe your own eyes at least. *Hilaris est hæc et plena gaudio invitatio,* saith an interpreter. What marvel then though they departed with fear for their faithlessness, and joy for the good news the angels had told, and showed them?

For he is risen] *Consentaneum est Phœnicem ante postremum annum Neronis, significâsse resurrectionem Christi et omnium credentium ex morte receptâ divinitùs vitâ.* The Phœnix is a fit emblem of the resurrection. (Dio *in Nerone.*)

Ver. 7. *And go quickly*] Angels are called seraphims for their burning zeal; and are said to be winged creatures for their speediness in serving God and his people. Gabriel wearied himself, as it were, with swift flight, to certify Daniel of his good acceptance in heaven, Dan. ix. 21. And this angel bids these women go quickly and carry the good news of the resurrection. Neither God nor angels can abide oscitancy and dulness in any. *Tardis mentibus virtus non facile committitur,* could the heathen say. (Cicero.)

Tell his disciples] And Peter with the first, Mark xvi. 7, because he is most dejected (and it is God that comforteth those that are cast down, 2 Cor. vii. 6; the Lion of the tribe of Judah spareth the prostrate prey[3]). The rest are in their dumps, as well they may, for deserting Christ; but Peter especially, for denying him. Now, therefore, that he is in a wilderness of ploddings and perplexities, Christ speaks to his heart, Hos. ii. 14. He loves to comfort those that are forsaken of their hopes.

Lo, I have told you] *q. d.* Begone now about your business; you have your full errand, and this is all I have at present to say to you. These good women, at first afraid of the angel, are now hardly persuaded to depart from him. They could have been content to have heard him further. How unspeakably delicious unto us shall be that innumerable company of angels, Heb. xii. 22, that world of angels, as the Hebrew doctors call it, that panegyris or congregation-house of the first-born, enrolled in heaven as free denizens! *O præclarum illum diem cum ad illud animorum concilium cœtumque proficiscar,* said the heathen orator. (Cic. *de Senect.*)

Ver. 8. *And they departed quickly*] According as they were bidden. A ready heart makes riddance of God's work, and does it up quickly, as afraid to be taken with its task undone. Baruch repaired earnestly, and had done quickly, Neh. iii. 30. Alexander being asked how he had so soon overrun so many countries, answered roundly, By making quick work, by despatching,

---

[1] *Nullam aliam causam dicebat terræ-motus quam conventum mortuorum.* Ælian.

[2] *Resurgente virtutum cœlestium domino infernorum trepidatio commovetur.*

[3] *Satis est prostrasse leoni.*

and not lingering long in a place. Μηδὲν ἀνα-βαλλόμενος. Plut.

With fear and great joy] A strange composition of two contrary passions; but frequently found in the best hearts, Psal. ii. 11. God loves at once familiarity and fear.

Ver. 9. *Jesus met them*] *En obedientiæ præmium, timoris remedium,* saith Pareus. God still meets his people in the use of his ordinances, showing them great and mighty things that they knew not before, Jer. xxxiii. 3.

Held him by the feet] As those that would lose him no more: the saints do still the same by faith; clasping about Christ and cleaving unto him, as it were by corporal contact.

Ver. 10. *Go tell my brethren*] Brethren still, though foully fallen, Jer. iii. 1. Infirmities discard us not, if bewailed, disclaimed, set against.

Ver. 11. *Some of the watch came into the city*] God would have the point of the resurrection well proved, for our better settlement, in so weighty a matter. The priests were unworthy to hear of it by an angel; they shall hear of it therefore by the profane soldiers, who came in to them much affrighted, and thunder-struck, as it were, and told them all. Now the confession of an adversary is held in law to be the most certain demonstration of the truth that can be.

Ver. 12. *They gave large money*] *q. d.* We know that you soldiers are good fellows, and both love and lack money. Now if you will but say thus and thus, you shall have a round sum paid you down in ready cash, &c. And what will not such men say or do for money? *Pecunia avidos fecit, forma mendacii industrios, jam illa promissio temerarios,* saith Aretius.

Ver. 13. *Stole him away while we slept*] If it were so, 1. Ye kept a good watch the while; and wanted some Epaminondas to slay you for sleeping. 2. If all asleep, who told you his disciples stole him? did you sleep waking, as lions do? or did they make so little noise that you never heard them about it? as Sir Francis Drake, at Trurapasa in the West Indies, found a Spaniard sleeping securely upon the shore; and by him 13 wedges of silver, which he commanded to be carried away, not so much as once waking the man. Surely here it was neither so, nor so; but the devil, who began at first his kingdom by lying, and by lying still upholds it, set these fellows a-work, to say, as they were taught, anything for money, though never so absurd and false. But money got on this manner will prove *aurum Tolosanum,* burn in thy purse, and bring God's curse upon all thy substance.

Ver. 14. *We will persuade him, and secure you*] Hypocrites have enough, if they can collogue with men, and escape the lash of the law. "God is not in all their thoughts," Psal. xiv. 3, or they think they can persuade him, and secure themselves. Hence that overflow of sin, through hope of impunity, and abundance of atheism.

Ver. 15. *So they took the money*] So sequacious are such men to sin, where anything is to be got by it. Balaam will venture hard for the wages of wickedness. Set but a wedge of gold in sight, and Joshua, that could stop the sun in his course, cannot stay Achan from fingering it.

And this saying is commonly reported] They were given up to believe this lie, "because they received not the love of the truth, that they might be saved," 2 Thess. ii. 10. There are that sense it otherwise. This saying is commonly reported; that is, this vile imposture of the priests and soldiers, wretchedly conspiring to cozen the world with such a base lie, is sufficiently known for a piece of knavery, and is so resented to this day. Think the same of the Trent conventicle carried by the pope and his agents with so much finesse, &c., but so as now all is come out, to their eternal infamy.

Ver. 16. *Went away into Galilee*] They had seen him twice or thrice before at Jerusalem; yet took a long journey here into Galilee to see him again. "Whom having not seen ye love," 1 Pet. i. 8. Austin's wish was to see *Christum in carne.* But if we had known Christ after the flesh, yet, saith St Paul, "henceforth should we know him so no more," 2 Cor. v. 16, sith the comfortable presence of his Spirit is better than his corporal presence, and more to our benefit, John xvi. 7. By this it is, that "though now we see him not, yet believing, we rejoice with unspeakable and glorious joy," 1 Pet. i. 8, and must not think much of a journey, yea, though it be not to a mountain in Galilee, but to the heavenly hills, from whence comes our help, to see the King in his beauty, *Christum regem videre in decore suo,* which was Bede's wish. Isa. xxxiii. 17.

Ver. 17. *They worshipped him, but some doubted*] Even whiles they worshipped, they doubted; yet was not their worship rejected. The Lord knoweth his still, 2 Tim. ii. 19. But they know not him still, as here in this text; howbeit they are "known of him," Gal. iv. 9, and their whole way both known and approved, Psal. i. 6.

Ver. 18. *All power is given to me*] Christ premiseth his power, and promiseth his presence, the better to persuade them to set upon his work, his great work, of subduing the world to the obedience of the faith. Better may this King of kings say, than that king of Spain, *Sol mihi semper lucet :* for he is Catholic Monarch; "the kingdoms of this world" (and of the other too) "are become the kingdoms of our Lord, and of his Christ, and he shall reign for ever and ever," Rev. xi. 15. As for the saints, how can they be but in an all-sufficiency, sith all is theirs, they being Christ's, and Christ being God's? What boldness may they take to go to Christ, as Jacob did to Joseph, when he understood that the sway of the whole land was in his hand, &c. See the note on Matt. xi. 27.

Ver. 19. *Go ye therefore*] In this my strength, as Gideon did against the Midianites, Judg. vii. 13; and though but a barley-cake, coarse and contemptible, yet shall ye overthrow the world's tents, yea, the strongholds of Satan; though you have but lamps and pitchers in your hands, yet shall ye achieve great matters. The apostles were those white horses whereupon the Lord Christ sitting, went forth conquering and to conquer. *Britannorum inaccessa Romanis loca, Christo patuerunt*, saith Tertullian. The Burgundians, much afflicted by the Hunnes, fled to Christ the God of the Christians ; whom after a long dispute, they determined to be a great God, and a great King above all gods. Sir Francis Drake tells us of twelve martyrs burnt for religion at Lima in Mexico, not two months before his coming thither. And he that set forth New England's first-fruits, assures us of some of those natives, that being converted to the faith, lived Christianly, and died comfortably.

Ver. 19. *And teach all nations*] Gr. disciple them, μαθητεύσατε, *Discipulate,* make them Christians first, and then teach them to observe, &c., ver. 20, as in baptism they have promised ; for otherwise it was pity that font-water was ever spilt upon their faces. In the kingdom of Congo, in Africa, divers of those heathens, by the persuasion of the Portugals, arriving there, were content to become Christians, and to be baptized ; allowing of the principles of religion, and professing Christ, till the priests pressed them to lead their lives according to their profession ; which the most part of them in no case enduring, they returned back again to their Gentilism. As for the Spanish converts in Mexico, they so little remember their covenant made with Christ in baptism, that many times they forget their very names soon after they have been baptized.

Baptizing them into the name of, &c.] That is, consecrating them unto the sincere service of the sacred Trinity, and confirming them by this holy Sacrament, in the faith of the forgiveness of their sins, and in the hope of life eternal. This

¹ Melancth. apud Manl.

is the end, use, and efficacy of baptism ; which, Piscator saith, few of the Fathers rightly understood ; those Popish asses certainly did not, who moved this foolish question, *An asinus bibens ex baptismo bibat aquam baptismi, et sic asinus dicendus sic baptisatus.*¹ Pity but these questionites had been present, when the young scholar reading publicly the fifth of the first of Corinthians for probation-sake, at the college of Bamberg, when he came to that passage, *Expurgate vetus fermentum,* &c. *Sicut estis Azymi.* He not understanding the word *Azymi,* read, *Sicut estis asini.* The wiser sort of prebendaries there present said among themselves, *Cum a sapientioribus nolumus hujusmodi audire, a pueris audire cogimur.* Children and fools usually tell the truth.

Ver. 20. *To observe all things*] Our obedience must be entire ; as for subject, the whole man ; so for object, the whole law, that perfect law of liberty. The gospel requireth, that in our judgments we approve, and in our practices prove, what that good and holy and acceptable will of God is. Those be good Catholics, saith Austin, *qui et fidem integram sequuntur, et bonos mores.* But let carnal gospellers either add practice, or leave their profession ; renounce the devil and all his works, or else renounce their baptism. As Alexander the Great bade one Alexander, a coward in his army, change his name, or be a soldier.

I am with you alway] viz. To preserve you from your enemies, prosper you in your enterprises, and to do for you whatsoever heart can wish or need require. When Christ saith, " I will be with you," you may add what you will ; to protect you, to direct you, to comfort you, to carry on the work of grace in you, and in the end to crown you with immortality and glory. All this and more is included in this precious promise.

A

COMMENTARY OR EXPOSITION

UPON

THE GOSPEL ACCORDING TO ST MARK,

WHEREIN THE TEXT IS EXPLAINED, SOME CONTROVERSIES ARE BRIEFLY DISCUSSED, DIVERS COMMONPLACES
HANDLED, AND MANY REMARKABLE MATTERS HINTED, THAT HAD BEEN BY FORMER
INTERPRETERS PRETERMITTED.

CHAPTER I.

Verse 1. *The beginning of the Gospel, &c.*]
THE history of our Saviour's life and death, St
Mark is recorded to have written at the request
of the Romans.[1] In the Latin tongue, say some
(who pretend to have seen the original copy at
Venice), but it is more likely in Greek, a tongue
(then) very well known to the Romans also. He
begins with John's ministry, passing over Christ's
birth and private life for brevity' sake (as it may
seem) though Papists feign many idle relations
thereof, and so expose us to the jeers of Jewish
and Turkish miscreants. There are that make
Mark an epitomator of Matthew. But forasmuch as he neither begins like Matthew, nor
keeps the same order, but relateth some things
that Matthew hath not, and other things much
larger than Matthew hath them ; judicious
Calvin thinks that he had not seen St Matthew's
Gospel when he wrote his (as neither had St
Luke seen either of them) : but that being acted
by the same Spirit, they agree so harmoniously
and happily ; an undoubted argument of the
Divinity of the Scripture, which therefore a
Greek Father calls παναρμονιωτάτην, every way
suitable to itself. (Nazianzen.)

Ver. 2. *As it is written in the prophets*] Isaiah
and Malachi ; so that there was no cause why
that dead dog Porphyry should here bark and
blaspheme, as if this testimony should be falsely
fathered on all the prophets, when Isaiah only was
the author of it.

Behold, I send my Messenger before thy face]
Malachi saith, " Before my face," in the person
of Christ ; to show that He and the Father are
one.

Ver. 3. *The voice of one crying*] Here Mark
begins the Gospel, at the preaching of the Baptist,
which the author to the Hebrews begins at the
preaching of Christ, Heb. ii. 3. But that is only
to prove that so great was our Saviour's glory in
his miracles, that it matcheth, yea, surpasseth
that of the angels, those ministers of the law.

[1] Euseb. Hist. Eccles. ii. 15, ex Clemente.

The ridiculous parallel of Apollonius Tyaneus
with our Saviour by Hierocles, and the malicious
exceptions of R. Nizachon against his doings and
miracles, are fully answered by Eusebius and
Munster. *Annot. in Mat. Hebraice.* As for John
Baptist, he professeth himself to be no more than
a voice. And so indeed he was *totus vox*, all
voice. His apparel, his diet, his conversation
did preach holiness as well as his doctrine, Mark
vi. 20 ; John v. 25.

Ver. 4. *John did baptize in the wilderness*]
Like as at the promulgation of the law, the
people were commanded to wash their garments,
and sanctify themselves ; so at the first publication of the Gospel, to wash their hands, and
cleanse their hearts ; and in testimony or profession thereof, to believe and be baptized for remission of sins.

Ver. 5. *All the land of Judea*] That is, a
great sort of them ; but John quickly grew stale
to them, John v. 35. *Principium fervet, medium
tepet, exitus alget.* Weak Christians easily fall
off, as leaves in autumn, or untimely figs, Rev.
vi. 13.

Ver. 6. *And John was clothed, &c.*] Elias also
was a rough hairy man. Those worthies, of
" whom the world was not worthy, wandered about
in sheep's skins and goat's skins," Heb. xi. 37 :
but they were like the ark, goat's hair without,
but pure gold within ; or like Brutus' staff, *Cujus
intus solidum aurum corneo velabatur cortice.*
(Plutarch.) Buchanan seldom cared for a better
outside than a rug-gown girt close about him,
yet his inside was most rich.

He did eat locusts] Good meat (to those there
at least) though coarse, and easily come by.
Tartarians eat the carrion carcases of horses,
camels, asses, cats, dogs, yea, when they stink,
and are full of magots, and hold them as dainty
as we do venison.

Ver. 7. *I am not worthy*] So Jacob cried out
of old. So the centurion, Matt. viii. So the
prodigal, Luke xv. So Peter, Luke v. 8. So Augustine, *Domine, non sum dignus quem tu diligas,*
I am not worthy of thy love, Lord.

Ver. 8. *With the Holy Ghost*] By whom your

iniquity is taken away, Isa. vi. 6, 7. See the note on Matt. iii. 11.

Ver. 9. *In those days*] When the people flocked so fast to John, that they might not mistake him for the Messias, and that his baptism might be the more famous.

Ver. 10. *He saw the heavens opened*] The visible heavens, so that the Baptist saw something above the stars : so did Stephen ; so could Christ when he was upon the earth. It is a just wonder that we can look up to so admirable a height of the starry sky, and that the eye is not tired in the way; some say it is 500 years' journey to it.[1] Other mathematicians tell us, that if a stone should fall from the eighth sphere, and should pass every day 100 miles, it would be 65 years or more before it would come to the ground.

Ver. 11. *In whom I am well pleased*] And in him with us, whom he hath made gracious or favourites in him, the beloved One, Ephes. i. 6. ἐχαρίτωσεν, *gratificavit.*

Ver. 12. *The Spirit driveth him*] That is, suddenly carrieth him (who was most willing to go) as that legal scape-goat, Numb. xvi., into the wilderness, and there permitted him to be tempted, but supported him under the temptation, that he came safe off again. *Sancti etiam nequaquam sui juris sunt, sed toti spiritus cedunt imperio.* The saints are at God's beck and check.

Ver. 13. *And was with the wild beasts*] Unhurt by them, as Adam was in the state of integrity. These fell creatures saw in Christ the perfect image of God ; and therefore reverenced him as their Lord, as they did Adam before his fall, see Job v. 21, 22.

Ver. 14. *Jesus came into Galilee*] To decline Herod's rage. And whereas it may seem that our Saviour herein took a wrong course, sith Herod was governor of Galilee ; we must know that the Pharisees were the men that delivered up John to Herod, Matt. xvii. 11, 12 ; and that but for them there was no great fear of Herod.

Ver. 15. *And saying, The time is fulfilled*] These were four of our Saviour's sermon-heads. The prophets of old were wont to set down some short notes of their larger discourses to the people, and to fasten them to the doors of the temple till the people had read them.[2] And then they were taken down by the priests, and laid up for the use of posterity.

Repent ye and believe, &c.] Repentance, then, is a gospel-duty, and (as some argue from this text) before faith ; the proper purchase of Christ's blood, Acts v. 31. Indeed, faith and repentance keep up a Christian's life (saith a learned man), as the natural heat and radical moisture do the natural life. Faith is like the innate heat ; repentance like the natural moisture. And, as the philosopher saith, if the innate heat devour too much the radical moisture, or on the contrary, there breed presently diseases ; so, if believing make a man repent less, or repenting make a man believe less, this turneth to a distemper. Lord,

cast me down (said a holy man upon his death-bed) as low as hell in repentance ; and lift me up by faith into the highest heavens, in confidence of thy salvation.

Ver. 16, 17, 18, 19, 20.] See the notes on Matt. iv. 18, &c.

Ver. 21. *He entered into the synagogue, and taught*] This is noted as remarkable in St Mark, that he often inculcateth that our Saviour taught.

Ver. 22. *And they were astonished*] If it could be said of Dr Whitaker, that no man ever saw him without reverence, or heard him without wonder, how much more of Christ, sith grace was "poured into his lips"? Psal. xlv. 2.

As one that had authority] Seest thou a preacher deliver the word with singular authority (as Paul, "We believe, therefore we speak "), esteem him very highly for the work's sake. The Corinthians are checked, for that they were unruly, and would reign without Paul, 1 Cor. iv. Zedekiah is blamed, 2 Chron. xxxvi. 12, because he humbled not himself before Jeremiah, a poor prophet, speaking to him from the Lord.

And not as the Scribes] Frigidly and jejunely. Didst thou believe thyself, thou wouldst never plead thy client's cause so coldly and carelessly, said Cicero to his adversary.

Ver. 23. *With an unclean spirit*] Gr. ἐν πνεύματι ἀκαθάρτῳ. In an unclean spirit. An unregenerate man is *in maligno positus*, as St John saith of the world, 1 John v. 19. He is *inversus decalogus* ; whole evil is in man, and whole man in evil, till at last (without grace) he be satanized and transformed into a breathing devil. By reason of the inhabitation of unclean spirits, our spirits have in them trenches, cages, forts, and strongholds of Satan, 2 Cor. x. 4.

Ver. 24. *What have we to do with thee?*] Not to do with Christ, and yet vex a servant of Christ? Could the devil so mistake him, whom he confessed? It is an idle misprision, to sever the sense of an injury done to any of the members, from the head.

Thou Jesus of Nazareth] Though the devils confessed Christ to be the Holy One of God, yet they call him Jesus of Nazareth ; to nourish the error of the multitude that thought he was born there, and so not the Messias. Neither did the devil's cunning fail him herein, as appears, John vii. 44.

Art thou come to destroy us?] Before the time : such is the infinite goodness of God that he respites even wicked men and spirits the utmost of their torments.

I know thee who thou art] This he spake, not to honour Christ, but to denigrate him, as commended by so lying a spirit. *Laudari ab illaudato, non est laus*, saith Seneca.

The Holy One of God] Some rest in praising the sermon, and speaking fair to the preacher. The devil here did as much to Christ, to be rid of him. So did Herod, Mark vi. 20.

Ver. 25. *Hold thy peace*] φιμώθητι, *capistrator*, be thou haltered up, or muzzled. Christ would

---

[1] Burton on Melancholy.   [2] Calvin in Esaiam.

not hear good words from an evil mouth. High words become not a fool, saith Solomon. The leper's lips should be covered, according to the law.

Ver. 26. And when the unclean spirit had torn him] So he will serve all that he is now at one with, as Bradford hath it. You are the devil's birds (saith he to all wicked ones), whom, when he hath well fed, he will broach you, and eat you, chew you, and champ you, world without end, in eternal woe and misery.

And cried with a loud voice] But said nothing, according to verse 25.

He came out of him] With as ill a will goes the worldling's soul out of his body. God tears it out, as Job somewhere hath it; death makes forcible entry, Job xxvii. 8.

Ver. 27. For with authority] As he taught, so he wrought with authority, ἐξουσία. The same word is used verse 22.

Ver. 28. His fame spread] Those that do worthily in Ephratah shall be famous in Bethlehem, Ruth iv. 11. Cicero worthily preferreth Cato before Socrates, *quoniam hujus dicta, illius facta laudantur.* But our Lord Christ was mighty both "in deed and word," Luke xxiv. 19.

Ver. 29. They entered into the house] Happy house in such a guest. If Elisabeth held it so great a matter, that the mother of her Lord should come unto her, Luke i. 43, what may Peter think, sith the Lord himself comes to give him a visit!

Ver. 30. Sick of a fever] πυρετὸς, which the Greeks denominate of the heat that is in it; the Germans of the cold. See the note on Matt. viii. 14.

Ver. 31. The fever left her] For Christ (the great Centurion that hath the command of all diseases, Matt. viii. 9) had rebuked it, Luke iv. 39, as once he did the Red Sea, Psal. cvi. 9, which therefore fled, Psal. cxiv. 3.

Ver. 32. When the sun did set] And the Sabbath was ended; for till then many held it not lawful.

Ver. 33. All the city] *i. e.* The sick folk in the city by a synecdoche. As all that were in debt or distress came to David, and he received them; so all that were diseased came to this Son of David, and he relieved them.

Ver. 34. Suffered not the devils to speak] For what calling had they to preach the gospel?

Ver. 35. And in the morning, &c.] The fittest time for prayer, or any serious business. Therefore not only David, Psal. v. 3, and other saints, but also heathens chose the morning chiefly for sacrifice; as Nestor in Homer, the Argonauts in Apollonius. The Persian magi sang hymns to their gods at break of day, and worshipped the rising sun. The Pinarii and Potitii sacrificed every morning and evening to Hercules, upon the great altar at Rome, &c. Men should rise betimes, on the Sabbath-day especially, both the better to prepare for the public, as also to consecrate as much time as they can, Psal. xcii. 2; Exod. xix. Shall Philistines be up betimes to go to see Dagon, Papists to matins, Israel to dance before their golden calf, Exod. xxxii. 5, 6; young men may go a-Maying, ringing, &c.; worldlings to their markets, fairs, by peep of day; and shall Christians lie bathing in their beds on their Lord's day?

Ver. 36. Followed after him] Gr. "Followed hard after him," as David's soul did after God, Psal. lxiii. 8, and as God's grace did after David, Psal. xxiii. 6.

Ver. 37. All men seek for thee] But few seek Christ seriously, seasonably, sincerely. Hence so many miss of him : *Vix quæritur Jesus propter Jesum.* All men seek themselves, and not the things of Jesus Christ, Phil. ii. 21.

Ver. 38. Let us go into the next towns] The neighbouring boroughs, κωμωπόλεις, such as were between a city and a town. Though secret prayer were sweet to our Saviour, yet he left it to preach and profit many.

Ver. 39. In their synagogues] Which were as chapels of ease, or petty parish churches, belonging to the temple, as the cathedral. In these it was lawful to pray, preach, and dispute, but not to sacrifice, Acts xv. 21.

Ver. 40. Beseeching him, &c.] *Morbi virtutum officina,* saith Ambrose. We are best when we are worst, saith another. Therefore King Alured prayed God to send him always some sickness.

Ver. 41. Touched him] *Immensæ gratiæ et bonitatis signum et tessera,* saith Calvin. And so it is of his infinite goodness, that he will touch our menstruous clouts, take at our hands our polluted performances.

Ver. 42, 43, 44.] See notes on Matt. viii. 3, 4.

Ver. 45. Could no more openly enter] For press of people, he was so frequented that he was forced to withdraw.

CHAPTER II.

Ver. 1. And it was noised] The Son of righteousness could as little lie hid as the sun in heaven.

Ver. 2. Many were gathered together] Erasmus observeth that Origen, in his sermons to the people, chideth them for nothing more than for their thin assemblies to hear the Word, and for their careless hearing of that, which they ought to attend to with utmost diligence; *recte judicans,* saith he, *hinc esse præcipuum pietatis profectum aut defectum.*

Ver. 3. Which was borne of four] *Apprehensis quatuor lecti extremitatibus, vivo cadaveri persimilis.* Wicked men are living ghosts, walking sepulchres of themselves. Bring them to Christ that they may be cured.

Ver. 4. They uncovered the roof] Which in those countries was flat, so that they might walk upon it, Deut. xxii. 8, preach upon it, Matt. x. 27, &c.

Ver. 5. When he saw their faith] By their works; as the goodness of the promised land was known by the grapes and fruits brought back by the spies. In all our good works, Christ's eye is upon our faith, without which "it is impossible to please God."

Ver. 6. *But there were certain of the scribes*] Little do preachers know when they preach, what hearers sit before them. *Araneo fel est, quod api mel.* Some of our hearers carry *fel in aure*, as it is said of some creatures, they carry their gall in their ears.

Ver. 7. *Who can forgive sins, &c.*] Man may remit the trespass, God only the transgression.

Ver. 8. *Perceived in his spirit*] That is, by his Deity, as 1 Tim. iii. 16; Heb. ix. 14. Or, by his own spirit, as 1 Pet. iii. 8, not by inspiration, as 2 Pet. i. 21.

Ver. 9.] See the note on Matt. ix. 5.

Ver. 10. *Hath power on earth*] *Christus jure divino omnia faciebat, non injusta aliqua virtute ac tyrannica.* Christ did all in his Father's right, and not perforce.

Ver. 11. *I say unto thee, Arise*] See here our Saviour's letters testimonial, whereby he approves his authority and power to be authentic. "Ye are our epistle," saith the apostle, 1 Cor. iii. 2.

Ver. 12. *We never saw it on this fashion*] Or thus, οὔτως: Bullinger observeth of this evangelist, *quod fucum sæcularis sapientiæ et eloquentiæ, rei per se alioqui splendidissimæ, nusquam allevit,* that he cares not to gild gold, or muddle over a topaz, but sets down things plainly without welt or guard of worldly wisdom or eloquence. Truth is like our first parents, most beautiful when naked.

Ver. 13. *And he taught them*] To teach us, that nothing can be better and more useful to the Church than wholesome teaching; which therefore our Saviour never neglected. It was grown to a proverb at Constantinople, Better the sun should not shine than Chrysostom not preach.

Ver. 14. *And as he passed by he saw Levi*] Our calling is of free grace, Ezek. xvi. 6; Isa. lxv. 1. The scribes and Pharisees are let alone, and this publican called to the work.

And he arose and followed him] Leaving his gainful trade, and following his own ignominy, ruin, death. *Nihil hic disputat unde vivere debeat:* faith fears no famine: Christ is an universal good, an "All in all."

Ver. 15. *Many publicans and sinners sat also*] All at Matthew's charge, and he thought it well bestowed, to bring them to Christ. So Paul, being himself assured of salvation, could do or suffer anything for the salvation of his poor countrymen. Rom. viii. 38, 39, with Rom. ix. 1, 2.

Ver. 16. *They said unto his disciples*] They durst not say it to him, where the hedge is lowest the beast breaks over. The devil, as the poet ——— *quæ desperat renitescere posse, relinquit.* What he hopes not to effect, he never attempts. (Horat. de Arte Poet.)

Ver. 17. *He saith unto them*] Though not for their sakes (for he knew it was to no purpose) yet for his other hearers' sakes, he makes apology, Jer. iii. 14, 15. God oft gives a pastor after his own heart, for a few that are to be converted.

Ver. 18. *The disciples of John and of the Pharisees*] Beza notes, that only here, and Matt. xxii. 16, Luke v. 24, is mention made in the gospel of the Pharisees' disciples, unhappy doubtless in such perverse tutors, somewhat akin to Protagoras, of whom Plato writeth (in Menone.) that he bragged of this, that whereas he had lived threescore years, he had spent 40 of them in corrupting of youth.

Ver. 19. *While the bridegroom is with them?*] Christ is *mel in ore, melos in aure, jubilum in corde.* There cannot be but music in his temple.

Ver. 20. *Then shall they fast*] Novices are not to be tied to the austerities of religion. The Pharisees are revived in the Anabaptists, *qui initiatis Christo ne risum quidem mediocrem admittunt,* saith Calvin, in Matt. ix. 15. Capistranus the minorite, sent by the Pope into Germany and other countries, A. D. 1453, to preach obedience to the see of Rome, gat a great deal of credit to his corrupt doctrine, by such a Pharisaical severity. *Sed tales Doctores meretur mundus suo fastidio veritatis,* saith one, they that will not receive the truth in love, are left to the efficacy of error. (Funccius in Chronolog.)

Ver. 21. *No man soweth*] See the notes on Matt. ix. 16, 17.

Ver. 22.] See the note on Matt. ix. 17.

Ver. 23, 24.] See Matt. xii. 1, 2, &c.

Ver. 25. *Have ye never read?*] *Satis salse, q. d. Ignoratis adhuc, quod adeo notum et tritum. Miror ego vestram vel inscitiam, vel ignaviam.* It is a shame for you, that you are yet so stupid or so stubborn.

Ver. 26. *And to them that, &c.*] Though meaner men than David.

Ver. 27. *The sabbath was made for man*] That is, for man's safety and advantage. As he would be undone without it, he would grow wild, and forget God; so, if it stand in the way of his safety, it is not to be observed, as if an enemy then assault us, we may fight with him. Pompey could never have taken Jerusalem, but that the superstitious Jews refused to defend themselves on the sabbath; which when he observed, he then on that day most fiercely assaulted them, and took their city. (Dio Cassius.)

Ver. 28. *Therefore the Son of man*] This Lordship taking beginning in Christ, seems to be, from him, derived to all that are in Christ. As Psal. viii. 4, 5, compared with Heb. ii. 6, 7. Whatever David speaks of man, is applied to Christ, and so is proper to the saints, by virtue of their union with Christ.

Is Lord also of the sabbath] And can dispense with it. The schoolmen say that God can dispense with the materiality of any precept in the decalogue, the three first excepted.

CHAPTER III.

Ver. 1. *There was a man there*, &c.] A FIT object inciteth and should elicit our bounty. Where God sets us up an altar, we should be ready with our sacrifices, with such sacrifice " God is well pleased," Heb. xiii. 16.

Ver. 2. *And they watched him*] So carnal men do still watch and pry into professors and their conversation, ἐποπτεύοντες, 1 Pet. iii. 2, curiously observing what they may catch and carp at. But it is a brave thing to throttle envy, to stop an evil mouth, to deny them occasion to blaspheme, as Christ did; to lead convincing lives, as Bradford and Bucer did, whom neither their friends could sufficiently praise, nor their foes find anything to fasten on. (Acts and Mon.)

Ver. 3. *Stand forth*] That the miracle might be notified, and God the more glorified. It is a dishonour to a parent to hang his picture in a dark corner : so here, we should show forth the virtues of him who hath called us, 1 Pet. ii. 9.

Ver. 4. *To do good or to do evil*] Not to do good then, as there is opportunity, is to do evil. *Qui non, cum potest, servat, occidit. Non faciendo nocens, sed patiendo fuit*, it is said of the Emperor Claudius. Not robbing only, but the not relieving of the poor, was the rich man's ruin, Luke xvi.; passive wickedness is taxed in some of the churches, Rev. ii., iii.

To save life] Gr. ψυχὴν, soul, for man, and man for the body of man. So Psal. xvi., " Thou wilt not leave my soul in the grave," that is, my body, as Piscator senseth it.

Ver. 5. *With anger, being grieved*] A sweet mixture of sinless passions, συλλυπούμενος, *simul dolens*. It is difficult to kindle, and keep quick the fire of zeal without all smoke of sin.

Ver. 6. *With the Herodians*] Whom yet they hated in their hearts; but they can easily comport and comply to do Christ a mischief, as conceiving that Christ pertained to Herod's jurisdiction.

Ver. 7. *But Jesus withdrew himself*] Tertullian condemneth flight in any case :[1] but *Patres legendi cum venia*. His scholar Cyprian was of another and better judgment. *Magister non tenetur in omnibus*.

Ver. 8. *From beyond Jordan*] πέραν τοῦ ἰορδάνου. This country by Josephus is called Peræa, as Ultrajectum in Germany.

Ver. 9. *Lest they should throng him*] Gr. θλίβωσιν, afflict him, press, or pinch him, as they did a piece of his passion, ver. 10.

Ver. 10. *As many as had plagues*] Gr. μαστίγας, stripes, scourgings. Whom the Lord loveth he chasteneth with lesser and lighter afflictions, and scourgeth every son, &c., with hard and heavy judgments, as plagues, banishments, persecutions. Oh the bloody wales that God hath left on the back of his best children ! Heb. xii. 6. *Non vulgares morbi sed sæviores, et inustulati, qui quasi clamitant de ira et pœna divina.*

[1] *Lib. de fuga persecut.*

Ver. 11. *Thou art the Son*, &c.] The matter is well amended since Satan's first onset upon Christ. Then it was, If thou be the Son of God. The same power, when he listeth, can change the note of the tempter to us.

Ver. 12.] See the note on Matt. xii. 16.

Ver. 13. *And calleth unto him whom he would*] *Nec volentis, nec volantis, sed Dei miserentis*, as a nobleman, after Paul gave it for his motto. It is not in him that willeth, nor in him that runneth, though he run as fast as a bird can fly; but in God that showeth mercy.

Ver. 14. *That they should be with him*] As his household servants, more happy herein than those of Solomon. Christ hath many retainers, few fast and faithful servants that follow him in the regeneration. There are those that will wear his livery, but serve themselves.

Ver. 15.] See the note on Matt. x. 8. *Mallem obedire quam miracula facere*, saith Luther. A man may do miracles in Christ's name, and yet perish. But whoso calleth upon the name of the Lord shall be saved.

Ver. 16. *And Simon he surnamed Peter*] Not now, but after that famous confession of his, Matt. xvi.

Ver. 17. *Boanerges*] Syr. *Benai-regeschi, filii fragoris*. Nazianzen saith they were so called, διὰ τὸ μεγαλόφωνον, for the bigness of their voice. Farellus was famous for his loud speaking, when the envious monks rang the bells to drown his voice as he was preaching at Metis, *ille contra ad ravim usque vocem intendit, nec vinci se a strepitu ullo passus est*. (Melch. Adam.) But there may be a great deal of force in a low language. Basil was said to thunder in his preaching, lighten in his life. Jerome was called *Fulmen Ecclesiasticum*, Athanasius *Magnes et Adamas*, A loadstone for his sweetness, and an adamant for his stoutness. The apostles had fiery tongues, but yet cloven. Barnabas and Boanerges, " the son of consolation and of thunder," make a good mixture. The good Samaritan pours in wine to search the sores and oil to supple them. Discretion must hold zeal by the heel, as Jacob did his brother; these two must be as the two lions that supported Solomon's throne. He that hath them, may be a Moses for his meekness and a Phineas for his fervour. It was a good caution that Œcolampadius gave Farellus, *Evangelizatum, non maledictum missus, et laudo zelum, modo non desideretur mansuetudo*. Thou art sent, not to rail, but to reveal holy truths in meekness of wisdom.

Ver. 18. *And Bartholomew*] See the note on Matt. x. 3.

Ver. 19. *And they went into the house*] But could not rest in the house; for a demoniac was brought home to him, and the multitude met to hear; and Christ gratified them, with the neglect of himself, Matt. xii. 22. Now to all his he saith, as Abimelech did to his soldiers, " What ye have seen me do, make haste and do as I have done," Judg. ix. 48.

Ver. 20. *They could not so much as eat bread*]

For when he was in the house to repose and re-fresh himself, they brought unto him a possessed person.

Ver. 21. *They went out to lay hold on him*] Some read, to lay hold on the multitude, as mad, because so eager and earnest, that they left not our Lord liberty for his necessary repose and repast. But if it be meant of Christ, his mother also may seem to have been in the common error, ver. 31. She was not then without original sin (as the Franciscans would have it, and do there-fore name Joachim and Anna kissing, by which kiss Anna conceived, say they, with the Virgin Mary), neither yet without actual sin, as here, John ii. 4. *Sed si peccatrix, non deprecatrix : quæ egebat, non agebat advocatum,* saith an ancient.

Ver. 22. *By the prince of devils,* &c.] A devil-ish blasphemy, occasioned perhaps by the former calumny of his kinsmen. What advantages make our adversaries of our smaller differences! Every subdivision is a strong weapon in the hand of the contrary party.

Ver. 23, 24, 25, &c.] See the notes on Matt. xii. 25, 26.

Ver. 29. *Hath never forgiveness*] And yet Bel-larmine teacheth that the sin against the Holy Ghost may be forgiven (lib. 2, *de Pœnitentia*, cap. 16). But it may be he was of their opinion that taught here in England in the reign of Henry III., that to question the pope's sanctions was the sin against the Holy Ghost. (Daniel's Hist. of England, p. 163.)

Ver. 30. *Because they said*] That sin unto death begins in apostasy, goes on in persecution, and ends in blasphemy.

Ver. 31. *Then came his brethren*] Here the Evangelist returneth to the history he had begun to set forth ver. 21.

Ver. 32. See the notes on Matt. xii. 47, 48.

Ver. 33. *Who is my mother,* &c.] Bishop Ridley is likewise said to have been very kind to his kinsfolks, yet not bearing with them any other-wise than right would require. (Acts and Mon.)

CHAPTER IV.

Ver. 1. *And he began again,* &c.] *sc.* The self-same day wherein he had had that busy bout with the blasphemous Pharisees. See the note on Matt. xiii. 1.

Ver. 2. *He taught them many things by para-bles*] Ministers must likewise fetch comparisons from things most familiar and best known to their hearers, as the prophets from fishes when they have to deal with the Egyptians ; from flocks and herds, when with the Arabians ; from merchandise and navigation, when with the Tyrians and Si-donians, &c. ; and as our Saviour from fishing, when he dealeth with fishers ; from sowing, when with seedsmen, &c.

Ver. 3. *Hearken, behold*] Christ well knew the fickleness of men's spirits, and how every small matter calls them off, when most earnestly set to hear. See the note on Matt. xiii. 3.

Ver. 4, 5, &c.] See the notes on Matt. xiii. 3 —5, &c.

Ver. 8. *Fruit that sprang up and increased*] This is spoken in opposition to the thorny ground, where the thorns grow up together with the corn, and overtop it ; whereas the good ground brings forth fruit increasing, and ascending : ἀναβαίνοντα καὶ αὐξάνοντα, and although it have many thorns, yet grace is superior to corruption, and keeps it under.

Ver. 9. *He that hath ears,* &c.] A form of speech to stir up attention ; like the Athenian, Ἀκούσατε ἄνδρες ; and our Oyez, from the French. Our Saviour cried and said so, saith St Luke.

Ver. 10. *And when he was alone*] Or solitary. A well-chosen season is a very great advantage.

Ver. 11. *Unto them that are without*] That are in the Church, but not of the Church. She hath her hang-byes, that are as wens or botches to the body.

Ver. 12.] See the note on Matt. xiii. 14, &c.

Ver. 13. *Know ye not this parable ?*] What a shame is that ! Gross ignorance, under excellent means of knowledge, is a blushful sin.

And how then will ye know all parables ?] Anaxagoras the philosopher found himself be-nighted, and complained, *omnia esse circumfusa tenebris,* that there was a general darkness upon men's understandings. *Empedocles angustas esse sensuum semitas dixit :* Empedocles said that the pathways of the senses were too narrow. And Democritus, that the truth lay hid in a pit that had no bottom. Melancthon was heard to say, that he did not believe that there was any one man to be found in all Germany that could rightly understand one whole page in Aristotle's Organon. How much less can any one under-stand gospel-mysteries, but by a supernatural light ! The Romans thought they had victory tied to them ; we have not the knowledge of divine truths tied to us, &c. But as the Romans dedicated a lake (the depth whereof was unknown) to Vic-tory, so must we be wise to sobriety ; and what we cannot comprehend of God's revealed will, run to Christ, and he will teach us, but still cry, " O the depth ! " Rom. xi. 33.

Ver. 16. *Immediately they receive it with glad-ness*] As children run away with sweetmeats. But the new birth is seldom without pain, and without a flux of mortification. Leap-Christians prove apostates.

Ver. 17. *Immediately they are offended*] They stumble at the cross, and fall backwards. These are prosperity-proselytes, holy-day servants, po-litic professors, neuter passive Christians.

Ver. 21. *Is a candle brought*] Or lighted. *q. d.* Take the benefit of the light of the gospel, suffer it not to stand under a bed or bushel ; for " there is nothing hid," viz. in our hearts, " but it shall be opened," viz. by the power of the word most plainly. *Lex, lux,* the word is a curious critique, Heb. iv. 12.

Ver. 22. *There is nothing hid,* &c.] *i. e.* The prophets have delivered nothing darkly of me, which you must not make more manifest, and for that end you are enlightened, Rom. xvi. 15. See Matt. x. 26.

Ver. 23.] See ver. 9.

Ver. 24. *Take heed what you hear*] As the husbandman is very curious in the choice of his seed.

With what measure you mete] *i. e.* As you mete to God in duty, so will God mete to you in mercy, Cant. i. 3.

Ver. *ibid. Shall more be given*] *sc.* If you bring with you a loan of your former hearings. He that hears as he ought, every time he hears he grows something more rich : he picks up the gospel's pearls, and presents them to God the next time, that he may have more. The good soul cannot be without some daily comings-in from Christ.

Ver. 25. *For he that hath, to him shall be given*] Grace grows by exercise, and impairs by idleness; as that side of the teeth which is least used in chewing, is apt to have more rheum settle upon it. Though both arms grow, yet that which a man useth is the stronger and bigger: so is it in grace. God giveth " grace for grace," and his righteousness is revealed from faith to faith ; that is, from a less measure to a greater, John i. 16 ; Rom. i. 17. Whereas it is easy to observe an eclipse and decay of God's gifts in them that use them not, till at last they may say with Zedekiah, "When went the Spirit of God from me ?"

Ver. 26. *So is the kingdom of God*] God sows and reaps in the Church, though none observes it, and hath his fruit in due season.

Ver. 27. *And should sleep*] Ministers must rest secure of the success of their endeavours, having diligently done their duties. The word may work many a year after ; as they say of the elephant, that she brings not forth till 13 years after she hath conceived.

Ver. 28. *First the blade, then the ear*] And the husbandman looks upon it with delight, in the hope of a harvest ; so doth God take in good part our weak beginnings, whiles we strive to be better : his blessing is upon our very buds, Isa. xliv. 3. The first springs in the womb of grace are precious to him, Eph. ii. 1.

Ver. 29. *Because the harvest is come*] After long looking for, James v. 7. (See the note there.) " When will it once be ?" saith God, Jer. xiii. 27.

Ver. 30. *Whereunto shall we liken, &c.*] The wisdom of God, the great Counsellor, seems to be at a fault for a fit expression low enough for our slow apprehension.

Ver. 31, 32] See the notes on Matt. xiii. 31, 32.

Ver. 33. *As they were able to hear*] Not as he was able to have spoken : a minister must masticate his matter as nurses do their children's meat, and speak to his hearers' shallow capacities ; or else he shall be a barbarian to them, and they to him. He is the best preacher, saith Luther, that preacheth vulgarly, trivially.

Ver. 34. *He expounded*] He read them the riddles, as it were, or untied the knots, ἐπέλυε.

So, Judges vii. 15, we read of a dream, and the interpretation, or breaking of it. A metaphor from the breaking of a nut to get the kernel.

Ver. 35.] See Matt. xiii. 53.

Ver. 36. *They took him*] viz. Out of that part of the ship where he had taught, into another part more convenient, where he might rest. For he had preached all that day, till the evening, without taking either repast or repose, verse 1.

Ver. 37] See the notes on Matt. viii. 24, 25, &c.

Ver. 38. *Asleep on a pillow*] Neither did the noise of the sea, nor the hurry of the seamen labouring for life, awake Christ, till his own time was come. Despair not, if help be not at hand at first, as we desire : but awake Christ, as here, and Isa. li. 9. God hath a mighty arm, but it may be asleep ; the Church therefore cries three times in a verse, " Awake."

Ver. 39. *Peace, be still*] That is, have done quickly : so much the ingemination imports, Gen. xli. 32.

Ver. 40. *Why are ye so fearful?*] *Increpatio cum admiratione :* as their " Master, carest thou not," &c., was *interrogatio conquerentis et reprehendentis.* But if Cæsar in a tempest could bid the bargeman be of good cheer, for he carried over the fortune of Cæsar, which could not miscarry ;[1] how much more might those that were upon the same bottom with Christ, have been confident of a safe arrival !

How is it that ye have no faith?] A little they had, Matt. viii. 26. But this unexercised was, to comfort, as good as no faith.

Ver. 41.] See Matt. viii. 27.

CHAPTER V.

Ver. 1.] See Matt. viii. 28.

Ver. 2. *A man with an unclean spirit*] Græce, ἐν πνεύματι ἀκαθάρτῳ. In an unclean spirit, *quod eum spiritus quasi inclusum teneret.* (Beza.) So the flesh is called " the old man," as if it were the whole of a natural man ; and the devil is said to " work effectually " in such, Eph. ii. 2. See the note on Mark i. 23.

Ver. 3. *Who had his dwelling among the tombs*] The burial-places of the saints were anciently thought to have a kind of holiness in them. Hence grew that superstition of meeting and praying together at the saints' sepulchres ; and afterwards of praying for them, and to them. Which to foment, the devil usually haunted such places, there to play his pranks.

Ver. 4, 5, 6.] See the notes on Matt. viii. 28.

Ver. 7. *I adjure thee by God*] *Exemplum horrendum impudentiæ sceleratorum spirituum,* saith Beza. To adjure one is to take an oath of him for our own security. An oath is not rashly to be undertaken, but by a kind of necessity, when it is exacted. Hence the Hebrew *Nishbang* is a passive, and signifieth to be sworn, rather than to swear.

[1] *Perge contra tempestatem : Cæsarem fers, et fortunam Cæsaris.* Plut.

Ver. 8. *For he said*] Or, For he had said : and so had put him into a new hell, as it were,

Qui si non aliqua nocuisset mortuus esset.

Ver. 9. *My name is Legion*] That is, a multitude. A legion was commonly among the Romans, saith Isidore, 6000 armed soldiers : 6666, saith Hesychius. So many devils were gotten in one poor man. Let us in him see what the best of us have deserved ; and, sith we have escaped, offer a passover each for himself.

Ver. 10. *He would not send them away, &c.*] Because, saith Cajetan, they have several regions where they most haunt, and do hurt ; and are therefore loth to be put out of their old quarters.

Ver. 11. *Nigh unto the mountains*] All this country was full of hills (*intercursantibus montibus Galaad*) and mountains of Gilead.

Ver. 12.] See Matt. viii. 20.

Ver. 13. *Jesus gave them leave*] If Christ condescended to the devils, though to the loss of others, will he not hear us ?

Into the sea] So that standing pool in Gadaris is called, which, Strabo saith, is of such a naughty nature, that if beasts taste of it, they shed their hair, nails, hoofs, or horns.

Ver. 14, 15.] See Matt. viii. 33.

Ver. 15. *They come to Jesus*] And, amazed with the miracle, they expostulate not an injury ; but, acknowledging him Lord of all, they beg him to be gone, lest they should sustain further loss by him. The devil shall have his dwelling again in themselves rather than in their pigs (as the martyr Bradford phrased it) : they will rather lose Christ than their porkets.

And in his right mind] *Sanguis medici factus est medicina phrenetici.* The chirurgeon's blood was the sick man's salve.

Ver. 17. *And they began, &c.*] See the note on Matt. viii. 34.

Ver. 18. *Prayed him that he might be with him*] This poor man had tasted how good the Lord is, and desired therefore to abide with him ; when his countrymen of Gadara had only seen his power, and were therefore glad to be rid of him.

Ver. 19. *Tell how great things, &c.*] This was all the fee Christ looked for for his cures. Words seem to be a slender and slight recompense ; but Christ (saith Nazianzen) calleth h mself the Word.

Ver. 20. *Began to publish in Decapolis*] A great mercy to them to have such a preacher sent amongst them. Bethsaida was denied this favour, Mark viii. 26.

Ver. 21. *He was nigh unto the sea*] Here, and now, it was that Levi made him a great feast ; whereof see chap. ii. 15, 16.

Ver. 22, 23, 24.] See the notes on Matt. ix. 18, &c.

Ver. 25. *And a certain woman*] This history fell out fitly, that Jairus might be confirmed, and the different degrees of faith in several saints the better discerned.

Ver. 26. *And had spent all that she had*]

Physicians are many of them *crumenimulgæ, et sordida poscinummia.* (Plaut.) They call their drugs δόσεις, gifts ; yet we pay dear for them, besides that they sometimes give their patient a "decipe" for a "recipe," which made Chaucer say, Farewell, physic.

Jurisconsultorum idem status et Medicorum :
  Damna quibus licito sunt aliena lucro,
Hi morbis ægrorum, agrorum litibus illi
  Dant patienter opem, dum potiantur opum.
            (Owen Epigr.)

Howbeit their greedy desire of money seldom prospereth with them.

Dicis te medicum, nos te plus esse fatemur ;
  Una tibi plus est littera quam medico.
            (Mendico sc.)

Ver. 28. *If I may but touch*] See the note on Matt. ix. 21.

Ver. 30. *That virtue had gone out of him*] As heat goeth out of the sun into the air, water, earth, earthly bodies, and yet remains in the sun ; so here. *Salienti aquarum fonti undas si tollas, nec exhauritur, nec extenuatur, sed dulcescit ; scientia, etiam docendi officio, dulcedinem sentiat, non sentiat minutias.* A fountain is not drawn dry, but cleared ; so skill is not lost by communicating it to others, but increased.

Ver. 32. *And he looked round about*] He confuted the rashness of his disciples, not with words, but looks. We may more fitly sometimes signify our dislike of sin by frowns than by speeches. As the north wind drives away rain, &c.

Ver. 33. *Came and fell down*] *sc.* Upon her knees, and at his knees, as suppliants used also to do among the heathens ; who therefore consecrated the knees to mercy. *Genua miseriæ consignavit antiquitas.* Γουνοῦμαι σ᾽ ἔγωγε. Hom.

Ver. 34. *Daughter, thy faith, &c.*] They that can shame themselves to honour Christ, shall receive much settlement and inward satisfaction.

Ver. 35. *Thy daughter is dead*] Christ commonly reserves his holy hand for a dead-lift.

Ver. 36. *Be not afraid, only believe*] Faith quelleth and killeth distrustful fear ; but awful dread it breedeth, feedeth, fostereth, and cherisheth.

Ver. 37. *Save Peter, and James, and John*] Still Andrew is excluded, though Peter's brother, an apostle of equal standing, and a good man : yet he is not offended, but content to be accounted a loyal subject for the general, though he was no favourite in these particulars.

Ver. 38, 39.] See Matt. ix. 23, 24.

Ver. 40.] See the note on Matt. ix. 24, &c.

Ver. 41. *Talitha cumi*] The Syriac was then the vernacular or vulgar tongue ; for the Jews had lost their ancient language, in that seventy years' continuance in Babylon.

Ver. 42. *They were astonished with a great astonishment*] Gr. ἐξέστησαν ἐκστάσει μεγάλῃ. With an ecstasy of admiration : they were even carried out of themselves, *vix sui compotes.*

Ver. 43. *That no man should know it*] Lest

he should be too soon known and acknowledged by the people. But when he knew that he was shortly to die, he openly restored to life Lazarus, and the widow's son. Everything is beautiful in its season.

CHAPTER VI.

Ver. 1, 2.] See Matt. xiii. 54.

Ver. 3. *Is not this the carpenter?*] τεκτὼν. Not the smith, as Hilary and Ambrose render it. Christ made yokes and ploughs, saith Justin Martyr. And hence in his preaching he drew similitudes from the yoke, Matt. xi. 29, and Luke ix. 62, saith à Lapide. See the note on Matt. xiii. 55.

Ver. 4.] See Matt. xiii. 57; John iv. 44.

Ver. 5. *He could do there no mighty work*] He could not, because he would not. Note here the venomous nature of infidelity, that transfuseth, as it were, a dead palsy into the hands of omnipotency, disabling Christ, in a sort, to do such a man good. Christ by his absolute power can do all things: by his actual power he can do no more than he will do.

Ver. 6. *And he marvelled*] Unbelief must needs be a monstrous sin, that puts Christ to the marvel.

Ver. 7. *By two and two*] Both for more authority, and for mutual comfort. Two are better than one, Eccl. iv. 9. See the note there, and on Matt. x. 1, 2.

Ver. 8. *Save a staff*] Such a one as may ease and relieve you, not such as may cumber and hinder you, Matt. x. 10. So that seeming contradiction is assoiled.

No money in your purses] Gr. No brass, χαλκὸν, in your girdles. The most usual material of money among the Roman princes was seldom gold or silver, most times brass, sometimes leather. *Corium formâ publicâ percussum*, as Seneca hath it. The like is said to have been used here in England, in the times of the Barons' Wars. And why not? sith opinion sets the price upon these outward good things; and anno 1574, the Hollanders, then being in their extremities, made money of paste-board.

Ver. 9—11.] See notes on Matt. x. 9, 10, 11.

Ver. 12. *That they should repent*] This must be done; or men are utterly undone, *Aut pœnitendum aut pereundum*. Hence repentance is so pressed and preached in both Testaments, Exod. xxiii. 20; with xxxiii. 2—4. Immediately after God had given the Law by the rules of threats whereof God the Father was to proceed (saith one), and after they had transgressed it, he could not go along with them, for he should destroy them: but his Angel, that is, Christ, he would send with them; who also would destroy them, if they turned not and repented according to the rules of his Law, the Gospel.

Ver. 13. *And anointed with oil many, &c.*] By the misunderstanding of this text, and that Jam. v. 14, *Pro pastoribus habuit Ecclesia unguen-*

tarios, et pigmentarios; qui hoc prætextu miseras oviculas non tantum ungerent, sed etiam emungerent.[1] This oil in the text was used, not as a medicine, but as a sign and symbol of that power of miraculous healing.

Ver. 14. *For his name was spread*] By miracles, as by wings the gospel quickly spread far and near. Eusebius saith that the gospel spread at first through the world like a sunbeam.[2] When Luther first stirred, it was carried through the Christian world as on angels' wings. This was that miracle, which we, in these last times, are to look for.

Ver. 15. *Or as one of the prophets*] Luke hath it, "One of the old prophets is risen again." Some great changes they looked for, now that the Messias was expected, according to Hag. ii. 7.

Ver. 16.] See the notes on Matt. xiv. 2, 3, &c.

Ver. 19. *Herodias had a quarrel against him*] Gr. ἐνεῖχεν αὐτῷ, hung over him, as highly displeased at him, and waiting an occasion to be even with him. *Veritas odium parit*, they that follow truth close at heels, may have their teeth struck out, though she be a good mistress. *Tange montes et fumigabunt*. As wild beasts cannot endure fire, so neither can carnal hearts fervency and plain dealing. Poor Zegedine suffered many years' captivity in misery and irons by the Turk, for one word in a sermon, which distasted a woman, without the least cause. Melch. Adam. *in Vita*.

Ver. 20. *For Herod feared John*] Holiness is majestical. "Holy and reverend is God's name," Psal. cxi. 9; therefore reverend, because holy. He honoureth his saints in the consciences of their greatest enemies.

He did many things] Or, as some copies have it, πολλὰ ἠπόρει, *multum hæsitabat*, "He doubted in many things;" he was often set at a stand, and knew not how to ward off the dry blows of the word, nor which way to look, it came so close to him.

Ver. 21. *Made a supper*] The ancients took a light dinner usually, and therefore called it *prandium quasi perendium*: at supper they feasted more freely, and therefore called it, Δεῖπνον παρὰ τὸ δεῖν παύειν, because then their day's work was done.

Ver. 22. *Came in and danced*] With immodest gesticulations and trippings on the toe, wherewith the old fornicator was so inflamed, that he swore she should have anything of him. ὠρχήσατο, *tripudiabat, Baccharum more*.

Ver. 23. *To the half of my kingdom*] What was his whole kingdom to the life of that precious man, of whom the world was not worthy? Shortly after he was turned out of his kingdom, and (it is to be feared) out of God's too.

Ver. 24. *And she went forth*] The men and women dined not together. In Barbary, 'tis death for any man to see one of the Zeriff's concubines.

Ver. 25.] See Matt. xiv. 8.

Ver. 26. *And for their sakes that sat with him*] *Sic plerique, malum iter ingressi, post cum se er-*

rare resciscant, non desciscunt tamen, ne leves vide-antur : sui dicti domini, ut dicunt, esse volunt. (Cartwright). Some, rather than be worse than their words, will violate their consciences.

Ver. 27—29.] See Matt. xiv. 10—12.

Ver. 30. *And the apostles gathered themselves to Jesus*] As the chickens frighted by the kite, hover and cover under the hen's wing, that had before lain dusting themselves in the sun-shine. So the disciples terrified, perhaps with the tidings of John's death, run to Christ for shelter, συνάγονται, under the shadow of the Almighty, Psal. xc. 1. *Fides est quæ te pullastrum, Christum gallinam facit, ut sub pennis ejus speres ; nam salus in pennis ejus,* saith Luther. It is faith that maketh thee the chicken, Christ the hen, that thou mayest hope for help under his wings.

Ver. 31. *Rest a while*] God would not have the strength of his people to be exhausted in his service, but that respect be had to the health of their bodies, as well as to the welfare of their souls. Therefore the priests of the law took their turns of serving in the order of their course, as Zacharias, Luke i. 8. And the ministers of the gospel are allowed to drink a little wine for their health's sake, as Timothy. Those that neglect their bodies must reckon for it. Col. ii. 23.

Ver. 32.] See Matt. xiv. 13.

Ver. 33. *Ran a foot thither*] That is, they came thither by land, not by sea. Κατὰ θάλασσαν καὶ πεζῇ *ubique opponuntur.* (Scultet.) Whether on foot or on horseback, for many of them were not able to foot it, as being weak, lame, maimed, &c.

Ver. 34. *They were as sheep, &c.*] They were all slaves to the Romans, and many of them lame and diseased, but nothing troubled Christ so much as this, that they wanted pastors and teachers. They that are without a teaching priest are said to be without God in the world, 2 Chron. xv. 3.

Ver. 35. *And when the day was now far spent*] Beza renders it, *Cum jam multus dies esset.* Our forefathers had a saying,

> The summer's day is never so long,
> But at length 'twill ring to even-song.

Ver. 36.] See Matt. xv. 15.

Ver. 37. *Shall we go and buy, &c.*] *q. d.* Yes, a likely matter surely ; where's your money ? have we 200 pence to cater for such a company ? It is *interrogatio cum admiratione, atque adeo cum ironia quadam conjuncta,* saith Beza. A question not without a jeer.

Ver. 38, 39.] See Matt. xiv. 17, and John vi. 8, 9.

Ver. 40. *Sat down in ranks*] *Gr.* ranks, ranks, that is, rank by rank,[1] as rows or borders of beds in a garden. *Ordinatim res in Ecclesia faciendæ.* Church-work is to be done decently, and in order.

Ver. 41, 42, &c.] See Matt. xiv. 20, and John vi. 12—14.

Ver. 46. *And when they had sent them away*] viz. the people, verse 45, and that with tokens of

singular good will, as the Greek word ἀποταξάμε-νος signifies, and so is used Luke ix. 61, Acts xviii. 21.

Ver. 47.] See Matt. xiv. 23, and John vi. 18, 19.

Ver. 48. *Would have passed by them*] Either the more to try them, or rather to spare them, because he foresaw they would be further frighted else.

Ver. 49. *A spirit*] Gr. a phantasm, or apparition, φάντασμα.

Ver. 50. *It is I*] I with an emphasis; *q. d.* It is I ; not a spirit. A concise kind of speech, importing his haste to comfort them. He comes " leaping over the mountains of Bether," all lets and impediments, Cant. ii. 17.

CHAPTER VII.

Ver. 1.] See the note on Matt. xv. 1.

Ver. 2. *With defiled*] *Gr.* with common hands, κοιναῖς χερσὶ. Common and defiled is one and the same in Greek and other languages; to show that those that come to holy things with common affections and carriages, profane them.

They found fault] ἐμέμψαντο. They mumped at it, as we say ; they dispraised, accused, complained. *Vituperant homines quam collaudant promptius,* saith one : another being demanded, what was the easiest thing in the world ? answered, to find fault with another. Μωμεῖσθαι ῥᾷον ἢ μιμεῖσθαι, saith a third ; it is easier to find a fault, than to mend it.

Ver. 3. *Except they wash their hands oft*] Or up to the elbow, or with utmost diligence, *sedulo et accurate.* (Syr.) The Pharisees deemed it as great a sin to eat with unwashen hands, as to commit fornication.[2] Do not our modern Pharisees the Papists as much ? Fornication is a money matter with them ; but to eat an egg in Lent, or the like, a deadly sin. You may see them sometimes in Italy go along the streets with a great rope about their necks, as if they were dropped down from the gallows. And sometimes they wear a sausage or a swines-pudding in place of a silver or gold chain. Is not this sufficient to deserve heaven by ?

Ver. 4. *Washing of cups*] βαπτισμοὺς, baptisms. The Pharisees were great washers of the outside. Whence Justin Martyr calls them Baptists, by a peculiar epithet.

Ver. 5, 6.] See the note on Matt. xv. 2, 3.

Ver. 7. *In vain do they worship me*] Sith they do lose their labour, and worse ; for they commit sin. Displeasing service is double dishonour.

Ver. 8. *Ye hold the tradition of men*] κρατεῖτε, With tooth and nail ye hold it, *Mordicus retinetis,* as if on that hinge hung all your happiness.

Ver. 9. *Full well ye reject*] *q. d.* It is finely done of you, is it not ? καλῶς. *Sane Bene. Ironice ;* ye are wise men therewhile. This was check to their masterships. *Sapientes sapienter in infernum descendent,* saith a father. The

---

[1] πρασιαὶ πρασιαὶ, *Hebraismus, ut* Exod. viii. 14.

[2] Godwin's Antiq. Heb.

world's wizards have not wit enough to escape hell.

Ver. 10. *Moses said*] Matthew hath it, God commanded, saying. Holy men spake of old as they were acted by the Holy Ghost, 2 Pet. i. 21.

Ver. 11. *It is Corban*] *i. e.* Consecrated, and cast into the treasury; therefore look for no duty from me. This is the Jews' solemn oath, in this case.

Ver. 12. *Ye suffer him*] *i. e.* Ye license him to deny his parents any further succour.

Ver. 13.] See Matt. xv. 6.

Ver. 14. *Called all the people*] For he saw there was no good to be done upon the Pharisees, and that he did but wash a tilestone, or a black-amoor; he turns him therefore to the common sort. Pearls must not be cast to pigs.

Ver. 15, 16, &c.] See the note on Matt. xv. 11.

Ver. 17. *His disciples asked him*] St Matthew saith, "Peter asked him;" but then it was in the name of all the rest, and therefore they are all blamed for their ignorance.

Ver. 18. *Are ye so without understanding also?*] What, no wiser at 17 years of age than ye were at seven? as rude and unskilful in the sixth year of your apprenticeship, as at the first onset? God requireth and expecteth a proportion of knowledge according to the means we have had, the time we have enjoyed them, the capacities and natural abilities that he had given us, and according to the places and stations wherein he hath set us to do him service. If the leaders of God's people cause them to err, how should those that are led by them do otherwise then be destroyed? Hence this sharp reprehension.

Ver. 19. *And goeth out into the draught*] Or into the long and lowermost gut, as physicians use the word, ἀφεδρὼν: and as it is, 1 Sam. v. 9, 12. Robert Smith, martyr, made one of Bonner's doctors that examined him, say, that his God must needs enter into the belly, and so fall into the draught. To which he answered, What derogation was it to Christ, when the Jews spit in his face? If the Jews (said Smith) being his enemies did but spit in his face, and we being his friends throw him into the draught, which of us deserveth the greater damnation? (Acts and Mon.)

Purging all meats] That is, leaving (by this separation) the nourishment of the body clear from the dregs.

Ver. 20. *That defileth the man*] Far worse than any jakes. Sin is the devil's excrement.

Ver. 21. *Evil thoughts, adulteries, &c.*] Even all sorts of sins against both the tables of the law, as is well observed by Grotius *in loc.* Here's pride and folly against the first commandment; blasphemy against the second and third; of sins against the fifth commandment he had spoken before; and here are murders against the sixth; adultery and fornication against the seventh; thefts and covetousness against the eighth; guilt against the ninth; evil thoughts against the tenth. See what a foul fountain, what a seminary of sin, man's heart is. If his

tongue be not a city, or a country, but a world of wickedness, Jam. iii. 6, what then is the heart!

Ver. 22. *An evil eye*] Envious, and rejoicing at the miseries of others, which is the property of Edomites, abjects, witches, and devils. Those that are bewitched are said to be over-looked, *sc.* with an evil and malicious eye. *Nescio quis teneros, &c.* Βασκαίνω, *fascino,* i. q. φάεσι, καίνω.

Ver. 23. *All these evil things*] Should God but break open that sink of sin that is within us, we should never endure the stench, but rid ourselves out of the world, as Judas, Ahitophel, &c.

Ver. 24. *Would have no man know, &c.*] There were therefore two wills in Christ: the one whereof rightly willed that which the other justly and wisely nilled.

But he could not be hid] He is a God that hides himself, Isa. viii. 17; we must fetch him out of his retiring-room by our fervent prayers.

Ver. 25. *For a certain woman*] Of an heroical faith, felt her want of Christ, and laid out for him.

Ver. 26. *A Greek*] *i. e.* a Gentile, as Rom. ii. 9, profane by profession; a Canaanite, St Matthew saith she was: confer Zech. xiv. 21.

Ver. 27. *To cast it unto dogs*] τοῖς κυναρίοις, unto whelps, for more contempt' sake, as Beza noteth. The pope made Dandalus, the Venetian ambassador, to come before him, tied in iron chains, and to wallow under his table with dogs, whilst his Holiness sat at supper. *Unde ei canis cognomentum apud suos,* saith Revius. He was ever after called the dog-ambassador.

Ver. 28. *Yes, Lord*] See the note on Matt. xv. 27.

Ver. 31. *Of Decapolis*] A little country consisting of ten cities. See Plin. lib. iii. cap. 18.

Ver. 32. *One that was deaf*] None of the evangelists have this story, but only Saint Mark.

Ver. 33. *And he took him aside, &c.*] Though these men's faith was but weak, yet he yieldeth unto them at the first word, who held off the Syrophenician before, to the third petition; he knew the strength of her faith. The skilful armourer trieth not an ordinary piece of arms with musket shot. The wise lapidist brings not his softer stones to the stithy. The good husbandman turns not the wheel upon his cumin, nor his flail upon his vetches. For his God doth better instruct him, Isa. xxviii. 26, 29.

Ver. 34. *He sighed*] As if himself had felt and fainted under the same burden; so the word ἐστέναξε signifieth. And he was so much the more sensible, as well weighing the cause.

Ver. 35. *His ears were opened*] So are the ears of all that belong to Christ, and their tongues loosed to his praise, which before were bound by Satan. O pray that God would make the bore of our ears as wide as may be, and teach us that "pure language," Zeph. iii. 9, that our tongues may run "as the pen of a ready writer," Psal. xlv. 1.

Ver. 36. *So much the more*] *Eò magis præfulgebat utique quia non visebatur,* as Tacitus saith of Brutus; the more he sought to secrete himself, the more he was noticed.

Ver. 37. *He hath done all things well*] Praise we him much more for his spiritual cures, of like kind, upon ourselves and others.

CHAPTER VIII.

Ver. 1. *The multitude being very great*] Yet not so great as the five thousand before fed with fewer loaves and more leavings. To teach us, that God's blessing, and not the muchness of meat, feeds and satisfies.

Ver. 2. *I have compassion, &c.*] See the notes on Matt. xv. 32—34, &c.

Ver. 3. *They will faint*] ἐκλυθήσονται, "their sinews will be loosened," as it useth to fare with men in fainting fits. Physicians sometimes let blood *usque ad deliquium animæ;* so doth God, as he did David often. See the note on Matt. xv. 32.

Ver. 4. *With bread*] That is, with the coarsest fare. *Horatius opponit panem libis et placentis,* lib. i. ep. 10. Bread is used for homely provision.

Ver. 5—7, &c.] See the notes on Matt. xv. 34—36.

Ver. 12. *And he sighed deeply*] His heart was straitened (as the word ἀναστενάξας signifies) and would have burst, but for a vent.

Expletur lachrymis egeriturque dolor.

So those marked mourners sighed and cried for others, who were altogether insensible of their own miseries, Ezek. ix. 4. So Habakkuk trembled and quivered for the Chaldeans' calamities, cap. iii. 16.

Ver. 13. *And he left them*] See the notes on Matt. xvi. 1, 2.

Ver. 15. *Of the leaven of Herod*] Of the Sadducees, saith Matthew; to the which sect some conceive that Herod had now joined himself, the better to still the noise of his conscience by making himself believe there was no judgment to come.

Ver. 16.] See Matt. xvi. 7.

Ver. 17. *Perceive ye not yet*] Christ reckons upon our time, and looks for improvement of our talents.

Ver. 18. *Do ye not remember*] All's lost that is not well laid up in this pot of manna, the sanctified memory, 1 Cor. xv. 2.

Ver. 19, 20.] See the note on Matt. xvi. 10, 11, &c.

Ver. 21. *How is it that ye do not understand?*] It is very ill taken when we improve not experiments. Of all things God can least abide to be forgotten.

Ver. 22. *And they bring a blind man unto him*] This is another of those miracles mentioned by St Mark only. See chap. vii. 32.

Ver. 23. *He took the blind man by the hand*] He could have delivered him to his friends, to lead him; but he did it himself, as holding it an honour, a pleasure, to do men in misery any office of courtesy.

And led him out of the town] Either that the miracle he wrought might be the less noticed, or as holding the inhabitants unworthy to behold it. All Israel might see Moses go towards the rock of Rephidim; none but the elders might see him strike it. Their unbelief made them unworthy this privilege; so might their unthankfulness the men of Bethsaida. Woe to thee, Bethsaida! It is no small favour of God to make us witnesses of his great works.

Ver. 24. *I see men as trees, walking*] This was done, saith an expositor, to the end that Christ's power might be the more distinctly known; as also to instruct men in their degrees and progresses of spiritual illumination, to give God the glory wholly, both for the beginning and for the accomplishment. He is author and finisher of our faith, Heb. xii. 2.

Ver. 25. *He saw every man clearly*] τηλαυγῶς, *Procul et dilucidè, longè latèque.* When we come to heaven, we shall see as we are seen, who now see but as in a glass obscurely, as old men do through spectacles, 1 Cor. xiii.

Ver. 26. *Neither go into the town*] Christ would not vouchsafe such an ungrateful people the benefit of one more preacher, though never so mean. This was a greater judgment upon them than if he had turned some other way that arm of the sea that brought so much wealth into their town.

Ver. 27, 28.] See the note on Matt. xvi. 13.

Ver. 29. *Thou art the Christ*] This was much in few. Here is not Thou art Peter, and upon this rock, &c. Which if either St Mark or St Peter had esteemed (as Papists now do) the foundation of the Christian Church, it had not been here omitted (as Beza well observeth), sith it goes for current among the ancients, that St Mark wrote this Gospel at St Peter's mouth.

Ver. 30.] See Matt. xvi. 20.

Ver. 31. *And after three days*] That is, within three days, or on the third day.

Ver. 32, 33.] See Matt. xvi. 22, 23.

Ver. 34. *Whosoever will come after me*] See the notes on Matt. x. 38, and Matt. xvi. 24.

Let him deny himself] Christianity (saith one) is *perpetua naturæ violentia,* a continual crossing of corrupt nature.

Take up his cross] It is but a delicacy that men dream of to divide Christ and his cross. Every Christian must be a Crucian, said Luther, and do somewhat more than those monks that made themselves wooden crosses, and carried them on their backs continually, making all the world laugh at them.

Ver. 35. *For whosoever will save his life*] As that revolting priest, host to Philbert Hamlin, martyr, slain by his enemy upon a private quarrel. As those Angrognians that yielded to the Papists that came against them, and were more cruelly handled by them than their neighbours that continued constant in the truth. As Denton, the smith of Wells, in Cambridgeshire, that could not burn for Christ, and was afterwards burned in his own house. As West, that was chaplain to Bishop Ridley, who, refusing to die for Christ's cause with his master, said mass against his conscience, and soon after pined away for sorrow. If I shrink from God's truth (said Doctor Taylor, martyr), I am sure of another manner of death than had Judge Hales, who being drawn, for fear of death, to do things against his conscience, did afterwards drown himself. (Acts and Mon.)

Ver. 36. *For what shall it profit a man*] And yet many do as Shimei, that, to seek his servants, lost himself. And as Jonas, that was content to be cast into the sea, that the ship with her lading might come safe to shore.

Ver. 37. *Or, what shall a man give?*] See the notes on Matt. xvi. 26.

Ver. 38. *In this adulterous and sinful, &c.*] The worse the times are the better we should be. Stars are most needed in a dark night. We may as well, saith Zuinglius, *Ad aram Jovis aut Veneris adorare, ac sub Antichristo fidem occultare.* Antichrist's limbs have their mark in their hand, which they may show or hide at pleasure; but Christ's members have their marks in their foreheads only. David's parents and brethren came down to him to the cave of Adullam, though to their great danger, 1 Sam. xxii. 1. Onesiphorus was not ashamed of Paul's chain at Rome, 2 Tim. i.

When he cometh in the glory] David going against Goliath, took only his sling, and a few stones; but when against Nabal, he marched better appointed. So Christ came at first in a mean condition; but when he comes again to judgment, he shall march furiously, attended with troops of saints and angels.

CHAPTER IX.

Ver. 1. *Shall not taste of death*] SAINTS only taste of death; sinners are swallowed up of it, they are "killed with death," Rev. ii. 23. Whereas the righteous do *mori vitaliter;* death is to them neither total nor perpetual, Rom. viii. 10, 11.

Ver. 2.] See the notes on Matt. xvii. 1.

Ver. 3. *Became shining*] στίλβοντα, glistering and sparkling as stars, which twinkle and beckon to us as it were to remember their and our Creator.

Ver. 4, 5, 6.] See notes on Matt. xvii. 3, 4, &c.

Ver. 7. *They were sore afraid*] ἔκφοβοι. And even ready to run away, as unworthy, Deut. ix. 19.

Ver. 8, 9, &c.] See *ubi suprà.*

Ver. 10. *And they kept that saying*] With much ado they kept it (as the word ἐκράτησαν imports), for the rest of the disciples were very inquisitive, likely, what was said and done in the mount. A friend that can both keep counsel and give counsel is worth his weight in gold.

Ver. 12. *Set at nought*] Vilified and nullified as an οὐτιδανὸς, or one that had nothing in him,

ἐξουθενωθῇ. *Vermis sum et non homo,* I am a worm, and no man, saith the Psalmist in the person of Christ.

Ver. 13, 14] See Matt. xvii. 14, 15, &c.

And the scribes questioning with them] Purposely to put them to shame in their Master's absence: Marcian the heretic, for his arroding the good names of others, was called *Mus Ponticus.* (Tertull.) And Epiphanius fitly resembleth heretics to moles, who do all their mischief by working under-ground. But if once they be above-ground, they are weak and contemptible creatures.

Ver. 15. *Were greatly amazed*] To see him come in so opportunely, in the very nick, which is his usual time. See the note on Matt. xvii. 14.

Ver. 18. *Teareth him*] "Teareth him as dogs do:" so the Greek word ῥήσσει signifieth, Matt. vii. 6.

Ver. 19. *Bring him unto me*] Thus man's perverseness doth not interrupt the course of Christ's goodness.

Ver. 20. *The spirit tare him*] Thus things oft go backward ere they come forward; as the corn grows downward before it comes upward. *Duplicantur lateres, venit Moses.* This child had never such a sore fit, as now that he was to be cured. See ver. 26.

Ver. 21. *Of a child*] παιδιόθεν. Neither yet is there any injustice with God, that little ones thus suffer: they are not innocents, but "estranged from the womb, they go astray as soon as they be born," Psal. lviii. 3; the first sheet or blanket wherein they are covered is woven of sin, shame, blood, and filth, Ezek. xvi. 4, 6. Infants have sin, though unable to act it; as Paul's viper, stiff with cold, might be handled without harm, yet was no less venomous. But no sooner can they do anything, but they are evil-doing, *Ut urtica statim urit, et cancri retrocedunt, et echinus asper est,* as young nettles will sting, young crab-fish go backward, and as the young urchin is rough, &c.

Ver. 22. *It hath cast him into the fire, &c.*] So doth blind zeal deal by them in whom it is.

Ver. 23. *All things are possible, &c.*] Questionless (saith a reverend man, Mr S. Ward) justifying faith is not beneath miraculous in the sphere of its own activity, and where it hath warrant of God's word. The prayer of faith is after a sort omnipotent, saith Luther.

But if thou canst do anything] This woeful father had no further patience to parley; but through weakness of faith, and strength of affection to his distressed child, breaks off his tale, and begs present help. "He that believeth, maketh not haste," Isa. xxviii. 16.

Ver. 24. *I believe*] This act of his in putting forth his faith to believe as he could, was the way to believe as he would.

Help thou mine unbelief] That is, my weak faith, which he counteth no better than unbelief; howbeit, God counts the preparation of the heart to believe, faith, as in those Samaritans, John iv. Dr Cruger cried out on his death-bed, *Credo languida fide, sed tamen fide.* Much faith will yield unto us here our heaven; and any faith, if true, will yield us heaven hereafter. Selnever Pædagog.

Ver. 25. *I charge thee*] *Cum emphasi dictum et magna authoritate*, saith one, when the Lion of the tribe of Judah roar on this wise, devils run and wriggle into their holes, as worms use to do in time of thunder.

Ver. 26. *And rent him sore*] The nearer any is to help and comfort, the more Satan roareth and rageth.

Ver. 27. *But Jesus took him by the hand*] Christ ever reserveth his holy hand for a dead-lift.

Ver. 28.] See Matt. xvii. 19, 20, 21. The history of the dispossession of the devil out of many persons together in a room in Lancashire, at the prayer of some godly ministers, is very famous. Read the book and judge. These ministers (being Nonconformists) were questioned for it in the High-commission Court, as if it had been a device to strenghen the credit of their cause. Saint's Everl. Rest.

Ver. 29. *But by prayer and fasting*] The cause why they could not cure the child, was unbelief; the cure of unbelief is sought and wrought by fasting and prayer.

Ver. 30. *And they departed thence*] *Clam et celeriter*, privily and hastily, as the Greek παρεπορεύοντο imports; and why they did so, see Luke ix. 53.

Ver. 31. *For he taught his disciples and said*] *i. e.* He said it often, that they might remember it once; which they had no mind to do, Luke ix. 43.

Ver. 32. *They understood not that saying*] They could not conceive that the Saviour of the world should suffer as a malefactor.

Ver. 33. *And being in the house*] *sc.* That he had hired there, Matt. viii. See Matt. xviii. 1.

Ver. 34. *Who should be the greatest*] viz. In Christ's earthly kingdom, in the which they vainly dreamt of a distribution of honours and offices, as once in the days of David and Solomon.

Ver. 35. *He sat down*] *Tanquam serii quicquam traditurus :* the teacher sat, the learners lay at his feet. See the note on Matt. v. 2.

Ver. 36.] See Matt. xviii. 2, 3.

Ver. 37. *Receiveth not me*] *Non removet sed corrigit*, saith Erasmus. He receiveth not me only, but him that sent me.

Ver. 38. *And John answered him*] John was soon sated with that sad discourse of our Saviour, and begins a relation of another business, little to the purpose.

Ver. 39. *Forbid him not*] It is probable that this man would not forbear, unless Christ himself should forbid him; which here he refuseth to do, and shows reason for it.

Ver. 40. *Is on our part*] Is to be esteemed among such as favour me in this furious age.

Ver. 41. *For whosoever shall give*, &c.] Much more he that shall cast out devils in my name, and out of love to me.

Ver. 42.] See Matt. xviii. 6.

He shall not lose his reward] For his cup of cold water he shall have a torrent of pleasure. If therefore ye will be wise merchants, happy usurers, part with that which ye cannot keep, that ye may gain that which ye cannot lose.

Ver. 43. *It is better for thee to enter*] The Trojans, after long debate, concluded it better to part with Helen, though a lady of incomparable beauty, than by retaining her longer, to venture their utter wreck and ruin.

Ἀλλὰ καὶ ὣς τοίηπερ ἐοῦσ᾽ ἐν νηῦσι νεέσθω, say they. (Hom. Iliad.) Did we but forethink what sin will cost us, we durst not but be innocent.

Ver. 44. *Where their worm*] As out of the corruption of our bodies worms breed, which consume the flesh; so out of the corruption of our souls this never-dying worm. This worm (say divines) is only a continual remorse and furious reflection of the soul upon its own wilful folly, and now woeful misery. Oh consider this before thy friends be scrambling for thy goods, worms for thy body, devils for thy soul. Go not dancing to hell in thy bolts, rejoice not in thy bondage, as many do; to whom the preaching of hell is but as the painting of a toad, which men can look on and handle without affrightment.

Never dieth, and the fire is not quenched] O *quam diuturna et immensa est eternitas !* said the devil once.[1] A child with a spoon may sooner empty the sea than the damned accomplish their misery. A river of brimstone is not consumed by burning.

Ver. 45. *It it better for thee*] καλόν ἐστι. It is a goodly thing to go, though maimed, to heaven.

To be cast into hell, where the fire] About the year 1152, King Louis of France cast the pope's bulls (whereby he required all fruits of vacancies of all cathedral churches in France) into the fire; saying, he had rather the pope's bulls should rest in the fire, than his own soul should fry in hell. (Speed's Hist.)

Ver. 46. *Where their worm dieth not*] *i. e.* Where there is eternity of extremity. Of all outward torments none more insufferable than that by fire; as of all inward, none like that of having worms ever grubbing and gnawing upon the entrails. Add hereunto, that worms and fire use to make an end of other things; not so here. The fire fails not, as did that fire in the valley of Hinnom, wherein the dead carcases were burnt without Jerusalem, Jer. xix. The worm dies not, as do those worms that swarm in sepulchres. Oh the terrors and torments, the fathomless perdition, the remediless misery into which the damned are plunged, without the least hope of ever either mending or ending ! Plato travelling into Egypt together with Euripides the tragedian, got much Hebrew learning ; he calleth hell πυριφλεγέθων, a fiery lake, and saith that there their worm dieth not, their fire is not quenched. (Phæd. p. 400.) This he might have from Isa. lvi. 24, though it be his practice, *lacte gypsum miscere*, as Irenæus spake, to stain the pure streams of divine truths with fabulous narrations.

Ver. 47. *And if thine eye offend thee, pluck it*

[1] Manlii loc. com.

out] Out with it, away with that earthly idol, that image of jealousy, Ezek. viii. 3, though it be to thee as a hand for profit, or an eye for pleasure.

Ver. 48. *Where the worm never dies*] This is three several times repeated, that it may the better be observed. *Utinam de Gehenna ubique dissereretur*, saith a father. Oh that word *never* (said a poor despairing creature on his death-bed) breaks my heart. This worm of conscience is worse than the fire, if worse may be : it is the very hell of hell, as being the furious reflection of the soul upon itself for all its neglected opportunities and flagitious practices. This will be a bodkin at thy heart one day (saith a reverend man), I might have been delivered.

Ver. 49. *For every one shall be salted with fire*] The spirit, as salt, must dry up those bad humours in us that breed the never-dying worm ; and as fire, must waste our corruptions, which else will carry us on to the unquenchable fire.

Ver. 50. *Salt is good*] Nature hath prudently mingled salt with all things, that they may not easily putrefy. *Greges enim pecorum urinam salsissimam effundere videmus, et in omnes stirpes salem infusum.* John Bodin. *Theat. Naturæ.*

Have salt in yourselves] *Habete in vobis sal. A cujus admonemur tribus literis* (*ut curiose observat quidam*), *Sapere, Agere, Loqui.* The conjuring of salt among the Papists is intolerably blasphemous ; it is thus : I conjure thee, O salt, by the living God, &c., that thou mayest be made a conjured salt to the salvation of them that believe. And that unto all such as receive thee, thou mayest be health of soul and body ; and that from out of the place wherein thou shalt be sprinkled, may fly away and depart all phantasy, wickedness, or craftiness of the devil's subtlety, and every foul spirit. By salt here we may understand mortification and holy discretion, or sincerity of doctrine and discipline, whereby the saints are seasoned and preserved from the putrefaction of sin and error ; from the plague of emulation and dissension, as those good souls (Miconius and his colleagues) who could say with comfort, *Cucurrimus, certavimus, laboravimus, pugnavimus, vicimus, et viximus semper conjunctissime, &c.* We have run together, striven, laboured, fought, overcome, and lived always together in much peace and concord.

And have peace one with another] By mortification, season, tame, and purge your own hearts of those lusts that war in your members, James iv. 1, and prove offensive to others, Mark ix. 43, so shall you be at peace one with another. Stomach-worms are killed with salt.

CHAPTER X.

Ver. 1. *And as he was wont, he taught*] *Prædicationis officium suscipit quisquis ad sacerdotium accedit.* (Greg. in Pastoral.) It was death for the high priest to enter the holy place, or to come abroad, without his bells and pomegranates.

St Mark is much in setting forth Christ's forwardness to teach.

Ver. 2, 3, &c.] See Matt. xix. 1—3, &c. The Athenians and Romans had their divorces also. Their bill was only this, *Res tuas tibi habeto*, Take what is thine own, and be packing.

Ver. 4. *Moses suffered to write*] Not commanded. There is a difference between a permission and a precept, properly so called. See the note on Matt. xix. 7. *Non statim probat Deus quod permittit*, God approves not presently whatsoever he permits.

Ver. 10. *And in the house*] This is one of those passages related by St Mark only.

Ver. 11. *Whosoever shall put away his wife*] *Annon columnæ Germanæ, atque imprimis Lutherus putidissime errarunt et turpissime se dederunt, cum illud sanctissimum scilicet consilium dederunt fortissimo illi et optimo Principi Philippo Landgravio, ut vivente adhuc priore legitima nimirum uxore, duceret alteram, hoc est adulteram?* saith Zanchy : Luther and his fellow-divines were shamefully out in licensing the Landgrave to put away his lawful wife, and marry another.

Ver. 12. *And if a woman have put away*] No such thing was permitted by Moses, but usurped by the women of those licentious times. Among Turks the woman may sue a divorce ; but only then when her husband would abuse her against nature. (Blount's Voyage.)

Ver. 13.] See Matt. xix. 13—15.

Ver. 14. *For of such is the kingdom of God*] As oft, therefore, as we see an infant, let us think that a teacher is given us of God, Psal. cxxxi. 1, 2.

Ver. 15—18.] See Matt. xix. 17, &c.

Ver. 19. *Defraud not*] Do no man injury either by force or fraud. This seems to be an abstract of all the other fore-mentioned commandments.

Ver. 20.] See Matt. xix. 20.

Ver. 21. *Loved him*] As a tame man, and fit to live in a civil society. Or he loved him, that is, he pitied him, as a self-deceiver : like as we pity moderate Papists. Common gifts should cause some union : for they are of a middle nature between nature and grace : as the spirits of a man are of a middle nature between his soul and body, and serve to unite both.

Ver. 22. *Went away grieved*] Which he would have not done, if he had loved God and his neighbour, as he professed to do. The Greek word λυπούμενος signifies, that he went away pouting and louring, *fronte nubila*, with a cloudy forehead, betokening his great discontent : he came hastily, but went away heavily.

Ver. 23. *That have riches*] Or rather, are had of riches. Have them we may, love them we may not, 1 John ii. 15.

Ver. 24. *For them that trust in riches*] As most rich men do, thinking themselves simply the better and the safer for them. This blab is soon blown up.

Ver. 25, 26.] See Matt. xix. 24—26.

Ver. 27. *With God all things are possible*]

This place is much pleaded by the Papists for their fiction of transubstantiation. I tell thee (said Bonner to Philpot) that God, by his omnipotency, may make himself to be this carpet, if he will. (Acts and Mon.)

Ver. 28, 29.] See Matt. xix. 27.

Ver. 30. *Brethren, and sisters, and mothers*] Mothers he cannot receive in kind, when once dead; but God will be to him better than ten mothers: communion with him shall yield more comfort than all outward comforts can. He can also make Jonathan more loving to David than any wife, and the kings of Moab and Ammon to be his foster-parents. This made Hermannus, Archbishop of Cullen, to reform his church, using therein the aid and advice of Martin Bucer: wherefore he was deposed by the Emperor, which he patiently suffered. Zech. x. 6, "They shall be as if I had not cast them off, and I will hear them." God will one way or other make up his people's losses; they shall have it again either in money, or money's-worth. *Ne excrucier ob aurum et argentum: tu enim es mihi omnia*, said Paulinus Nolanus, when the town was taken by the Barbarians. Let not my losses trouble me, Lord; for thou art mine exceeding great reward. (Aug. C. D. i. 1.)

Ver. 31.] See Matt. xix. 30.

Ver. 32. *Jesus went before them*] As most willing of his way, though he went now to suffer. Show we like forwardness, and say, "I am in prison till I am in prison."

Ver. 33, 34.] See Matt. xx. 17—19.

Ver. 35. *Whatsoever we shall desire*] One said he could have what he would of God; and why? but because he would ask nothing but what was agreeable to the will of God. *Fiat voluntas mea*, said Luther in a certain prayer; but then falls off sweetly, *Mea voluntas, Domine, quia tua*. One saith of Luther, *Vir iste potuit quod voluit apud Deum:* that man can do what he will with God. (Melch. Adam.)

Ver. 36, 37, &c.] See Matt. xx. 21, &c.

Ver. 39. *Ye shall indeed drink of the cup*] But not of that bitter cup of his Father's wrath, which he drank off in his passion. Only the saints fill up that which is behind of the sufferings of Christ, Col. i. 24, ὑστερήματα, *non* προτερήματα.

Ye shall be baptized] And come out of the waters of affliction with as little hurt as a babe doth out of the water in baptism, by the help of divine grace.

Ver. 42. *They which are accounted to rule*] All earthly ruledoms are but shows and shadows to that of God. Οἱ δοκοῦντες, *Qui videntur imperare.* They do but seem to rule.

Ver. 46. *Blind Bartimeus*] Named and celebrated in the Gospel, when many mighty monarchs are utterly forgotten, or else lie shrouded in the sheet of shame.

Ver. 47.] See Matt. xx. 29, &c.

Ver. 48. *The more a great deal*] True faith works its way through many obstacles, as the clouded sun doth.

Ver. 49. *Jesus stood*] The Sun of righteousness stood still to hear a poor beggar. I have seen the King of Persia many times (saith a late traveller) to alight from his horse to do justice to a poor body.

Be of good comfort] It seems by this that he was troubled in mind.

Rise, he calleth thee] So he doth every poor penitent, who therefore ought to come boldly to the throne of grace, sith the golden sceptre is thus held forth, Heb. iv. 16.

Ver. 50. *And he casting away his garment*] Though a beggar, he stood not upon the loss of his coat; but for joy of his calling, cast it from him. So John iv. 28; Heb. xii. 1.

Ver. 51. *What wilt thou, &c.*] Christ, though he know our thoughts and suits long before (for he is *intimo nostro intimior nobis*), yet he will have us utter our own wants in our own words, and make our requests known unto him with thanksgiving, Phil. iv. 6; this is as sweetest music in his ears.

Ver. 52. *Followed Jesus in the way*] Followed him now without a guide; or followed him, though going up to Jerusalem to suffer death. *Love is strong as death.*

CHAPTER XI.

Ver. 1.] See Matt. xxi. 1.

Ver. 2. *Whereon never man sat*] As if it had been done on set purpose. Here was a wheel within a wheel, Ezek. i., the better to convince the stubborn Jews of his kingly office.

Ver. 3. *Say ye that the Lord hath need of him*] See here six several arguments of our Saviour's Deity: 1. That he knew there was such an asscolt. 2. That he sent for it. 3. Foresaw that the masters of the colt would question them that set it. 4. That he professeth himself the Lord of all. 5. That he could tell they would send the colt. 6. That accordingly they did so. (Piscator.)

Ver. 4—6, &c.] See Matt. xxi. 9; Luke xix. 32.

Ver. 11.] See Matt. xxi. 12.

Ver. 12. *He was hungry*] This, and that he knew not but that there were figs on the tree, declare him to be the true man.

Ver. 13. *The time of figs was not yet*] viz. Of ripe figs; but if he could have found but green figs only, he would at that time have been glad of them. He looked for somewhat from that great show of leaves. But the old proverb became true, *Great bruit, little fruit.*

Ver. 14.] See Matt. xxi. 19.

Ver. 15. *Began to cast out*] As he had done before, John ii. 15. See the note there. Hath not the Lord done the like also a-late amongst us, casting out many church-choppers, that have been money-changers rather than ministers in the temple?

Ver. 16. *And would not suffer*] This is one of those things recorded by St Mark only.

Ver. 17. *My house shall be called, &c.*] He inveighs against the same fault with the same arguments as before, John ii.

Ver. 18. *Astonished at his doctrine*] While they hung upon his holy lips, Luke xix. ult.

Ver. 19. *He went out of the city*] Having first cried, and said, " He that believeth on me," &c., John xii. 42, to the end of that chapter.

Ver. 20.] See Matt. xxi. 20, and learn to stand in fear of Christ's curse: he can blow men to destruction, smite the earth with the rod of his mouth, Isa. xi. 4 ; Job iv. 9.

Ver. 21. *And Peter calling to remembrance*] So the fig-tree bare far better fruit now that it was dried, than when it was green and flourishing. *Instruunt nos Patres, tum docentes, tum labentes ;* the saints teach us, as by their instructions, so by their infirmities. (Aug.)

Ver. 22, 23.] See Matt. xxi. 21.

Ver. 24. *What things soever ye desire, &c.*] To an effectual prayer two things are here required : 1. An earnest desire after the thing prayed for ; " the desire of the righteous shall be satisfied," Prov. x. 24 ; but a cold suitor begs a denial. 2. A confident expectation of a gracious answer. He that prayeth and doubteth shutteth heaven's gates against his own prayers, James i. 7.

Believe that ye receive them] Even as soon as you ask, as the word λαμβάνετε signifies. See Dan. ix. 20, 21, 24.

Ver. 15. *And when ye stand, praying*] Several gestures in prayer are described, not prescribed, in God's book. The word στήκητε, here rendered stand, importeth a presenting one's self before the Lord, whether he stand, sit, or kneel, &c.

Ver. 26.] See Matt. vi. 14, with notes there.

Ver. 27—29, &c.] See Matt. xxi. 23—25, &c.

Ver. 30. *From heaven, or of men, answer me*] So when the enemies of reformation demand what we mean by so doing, ask them what they think of that we do ? Is it from heaven or of men ? if from heaven, why do not they approve it ? if of men, why do not they disprove it by the Scriptures ? Bucer and Melancthon framed a form of reformation according to the truth of the gospel, with the approbation of the peers and states of Cullen ; but the clergy, though not able to contradict it by good reason, yet rejected it with slander, and said that they had rather choose to live under the Turkish government than under a magistrate that embraced that reformation. (Melch. Ad. *in Vita Bucer.*)

Ver. 31—33.] See Matt. xxi. 25—27.

CHAPTER XII.

Ver. 1. *A certain man planted, &c.*] SEE the notes on Matt. xxi. 33.

Ver. 3. *And beat him*] Properly, they hilded him ; but by a metonymy, they beat him. *Sic percutimus vulpem, ut pellis ei detrahatur ;* so men beat a fox that they may the better hild him. (Δέρω *proprie excorio, pellem detraho.* Gerhard.)

Ver. 4. *Wounded him in the head*] Caput comminuerunt, they brake his head. Theophylact

interpreteth it, They completed their villany, and spent all their spite upon him (συνετέλεσαν καὶ ἐκορύφωσαν τὴν ὕβριν).

Ver. 6. *They will reverence my son*] They will surely be ashamed to look him in the face. This is the proper signification of the word ἐντραπήσονται. But sin had woaded an impudency in their faces, that they could blush no more than a sackbut.

Ver. 13. *To catch him in his words*] As hunters catch the beast in a toil, ἀγρεύσωσι, as fowlers catch the bird in a snare, as St Matthew's word here signifies (παγιδεύσωσι).

Fistula dulce canit, volucrem dum decipit auceps.

Ver. 14. *To give tribute*] This tribute the Jews then paid to the Romans as now they do to the Turks, for the very heads they wear. And yet they had the face to say to our Saviour, " We never were in bondage to any man," John viii. 33. But perhaps these Jews were of the sect of Judas Gaulonites, who would not be drawn by any torments to acknowledge any lord upon earth ; believing that God only was to be held their Lord and King. (Joseph. Ant. xviii. c. 2.)

Ver. 15—17, &c.] See Matt. xxii. 19—22.

Ver. 24. *Not knowing the Scriptures*] And yet they alleged and argued out of Scripture, but upon a false ground ; viz. that the state of men should continue in the other world such as it is here ; as to eat, drink, marry, generate, &c.

Ver. 25.] See Matt. xxii. 29—31, &c.

Ver. 26. *I am the God of Abraham*] Therefore thy God also, if thou walk in the footsteps of faithful Abraham, Rom. iv. 23, 24.

Ver. 28. *Asked him, which is the first*] All Christ's disciples must be Ζητητικοὶ, *Questionists*, and do the same to learn, that this scribe here doth for a worse purpose.

Ver. 29. *Is one Lord*] This the wiser heathens, as Pythagoras, Socrates, Plato, and Aristotle with his *Ens Entium miserere mei* (if that were his), acknowledged, Exod. xxxiv. 14. (εἷς Θεὸς ἐστὶ μόνος, Pythag. Buxtorf. Tib.) " Thou shalt worship none other God." Where the word אחר rendered *other* hath ר greater than ordinary, to show the greatness of the sin of serving other gods, and to set forth a difference between *acher*, other, and *echad*, one God ; one in three, and three in one.

Ver. 34. *Answered discreetly*] That he was better than the Pharisees used to be. He was *Egregie cordatus homo*, and began to lift up his head out of the mud towards heaven.

Ver. 35. *How say the scribes*] They were great genealogists ; how was it then that they were no better versed in the genealogy of Christ ? that they could give no better an account of his twofold nature ? of other things one may be ignorant, and yet be saved : not so here.

Ver. 36. *Said by the Holy Ghost*] The Psalms then are a part of Holy Writ by Christ's own testimony, who also, Luke xxiv. 44, divideth the Old Testament into the law of Moses, the prophets, and the Psalms. Yea, *Psalmorum liber quæcunque utilia sunt ex omnibus continet*, saith Augustine after Basil; the Psalms are a treasury of all holy truths.

Ver. 37. *The common people*] The lesser fishes commonly bite best.

Ver. 38. *Love to go in long clothing*] Down to the heels, as senators, or counsellors. A garment that Christ himself wore, as being a citizen or free denizen of Capernaum. But he loved not to go in it, as these Pharisees, these glorious masters of the Jews ;[1] he affected not this habit more than another out of pride and vain-glory, to be looked at, and admired by the vulgar. This they thought a goodly business.

Ver. 39.] See Matt. xxiii. 5, with the note.

Ver. 40.] See Matt. xxiii. 14, with the note.

Ver. 41. *And beheld*] He still sits and seeth the condition, gift, and mind of every almsgiver; and weighs all, not by the worth of the gift, but by the will of the giver. Lycurgus enjoined the Lacedæmonians to offer small sacrifices. For God, said he, respecteth more the internal devotion than the external oblation.

How the people cast money] χαλκὸν, brass; the worst was thought good enough for God and his poor. Something men will do, but as little as they can.

Ver. 42. *Two mites*] A mite is valued of our money to be three parts of one c. (Godw. Ant.) Her mite could weigh but little, but her heart weighed heavy; and so her heart, being put to her mite, gave it weight above the greater (but far more heartless) largesses of the Pharisees.

Ver. 43. *This poor widow*] Women are noted in the parable of the lost groat to be fond of money; widows especially, and poor widows, make much of that little they have, as their life; so it is called here, ver. 44, even all her life (ὅλον τὸν βίον), that is, her livelihood. All this she cast in, it being rather to and for the service of God than to the poor. She resolves, as a widow indeed, to trust wholly in God.

CHAPTER XIII.

Ver. 1. *What manner of stones, &c.*] HUGE stones, and so cunningly cemented, as it were inoculated, the one into the other, that a man would have thought and sworn almost, that they had been all but one entire stone.[2] Josephus writeth of these stones, that they were fifteen cubits long, twelve high, and eight broad.

Ver. 2. *There shall not be left one stone, &c.*] There is no trusting, therefore, to forts and strongholds; no, though they be munitions of rocks, as Isaiah speaketh. The Jebusites that jeered David and his forces were thrown out of their Sion. Babylon, that bore herself bold upon her twenty years' provision laid in for a siege, and upon her high towers and thick walls, was surprised by Cyrus. So was this goodly temple by Titus, who left only three towers of this stately edifice un-

razed, to declare unto posterity the strength of the place and valour of the vanquisher. But sixty-five years after, Elius Adrianus inflicting on the rebelling Jews a wonderful slaughter, subverted those remainders, and sprinkled salt upon the foundation.

Ver. 3.] See Matt. xxiv. 1—3, &c.

Ver. 4. *Shall be fulfilled*] or, have an end, συντελεῖσθαι, that is, be destroyed, as verse 2. Which yet these apostles held not destroyable till the world's destruction, as appears Matt. xxiv.

Ver. 5. *And Jesus answering them, &c.*] Not directly to their question, but far better to their edification. This was ordinary with our Saviour.

Ver. 7. *The end shall not be yet*] Neither of the world, nor of the temple.

Ver. 8. *The beginning of sorrows*] The sorrows and throes of child-birth, ὠδίνων, which are nothing so bad at first, as in the birth.

Ver. 9.] See Matt. x. 17, and xxiv. 9, with the notes.

Ver. 10. *Among all nations*] i. e. Among other nations than the Jews.

Ver. 11. *Neither do ye premeditate*] Con not your answers, as boys use to do their orations and school-exercises, which the Greeks call μελέτας, whereunto Beza thinks our Saviour here alludeth.

Ver. 12.] See Matt. x. 21.

Ver. 13. *And ye shall be hated of all men*] *Odio generis humani*, as Tacitus (lib. 15), speaking of the Christians under Nero. St Luke adds, " But there shall not an hair of your heads perish," for " the very hairs of your head are numbered," saith St Matthew (x. 30).

Ver. 14. *The abomination of desolation*] The Roman forces, therefore most abominable to God and his angels, because they desolated the pleasant land and abolished the true worship of God. See Rev. xvii. 4, 5.

Where it ought not] viz. In respect of the Romans, who did it only out of ambition and covetousness. See Isa. x. 7.

Ver. 15, 16, &c.] See Matt. xxiv. 15—17, &c.

Ver. 19. *For in those days shall be affliction*] Gr. "Those days shall be affliction," as if the very time were nothing else but affliction in itself. See the notes on Matt. xxiv. 21.

Ver. 20. *Except the Lord had shortened*] *Mutilaverat, truncaverat*, ἐκολόβωσε. Not in respect of the divine decree, but, 1. of the long miseries that the people had deserved. 2. Of the enemies' rage, that would have exceeded, See Zech. i. 13.

Ver. 24, 25, &c.] See Matt. xxiv. 29, &c.

Ver. 28. *Now learn a parable of the fig-tree*] We should not rest content with a natural use of the creatures, as brutes do, but pick some spiritual matter out of every sensible object. Thus Reverend Master Deering, when the sun shined on his face now lying on his death-bed, fell into a sweet meditation of the glory of God and his 'approaching joy. (Dr Hall's Art of Divine Meditation.)

---

[1] οἱ θέλοντες, *voluerunt cum summâ cupiditate.*

[2] *Quasi tota moles ex unico ingenti lapide in tantam magnitudinem consurgeret.*

Ver. 30. *Till all these things be done*] Begun they were in the destruction of Jerusalem, carried on by the enemies' rage against the Church, and to be ended with the last age of the Church, which begins at the coming of Christ in the flesh.

Ver. 34. *The porter to watch*] That the rest did their work.

Ver. 35. *When the master cometh*] But come he will to judgment, as sure as that he hath destroyed Jerusalem; this is a pledge of the other.

Ver. 37. *Watch*] What Cerbidius Scevola was wont to say of the civil law, holds more true of the divine law: *Jus civile scriptum est vigilantibus, non dormitantibus.* The law was written for those that observe to obey it. And that very good counsel that Bucer gives upon this text, *Merito semper sonare auribus nostris debet hæc vox, vigilate.* This word watch should be ever sounding in our ears, running in our minds. Let it be our constant care, that death do not surprise us suddenly. No guest comes unawares to him that keeps a constant table.

CHAPTER XIV.

Ver. 1. *After two days*] Two days after the former discourse. This Sun of righteousness shone most amiably toward his going down.

Ver. 2. *Not on the feast-day*] And yet they did it on the feast-day, as loth to lose the opportunity then offered them by Judas the traitor. But God had a special hand in it, that by the circumstance of time Christ might appear to be the true passover. He was crucified on the very true day of that feast.

Ver. 3. *Of spikenard very precious*] Or pure, right, sincere, ἄδολον, not sophisticate, or adulterate; so Theophylact interprets it. But Scultetus saith it was spikenard of Opis, a town not far from Babylon, whence the most precious odours and ointments were transported into other parts (πιστικῆς, melius ὀπιστικῆς).

Ver. 4.] See Matt. xxvi. 8.

Ver. 5. *Three hundred pence*] That is, 52 French pounds and more, as Budæus computes it. She spared for no cost.

They murmured against her][1] But Judas began; so dangerous a thing it is to converse with hypocrites. One rotten sheep may rot the rest. *Uvaque conspectâ livorem ducit ab una.* Great danger there is, if not of infection, yet of defection. Peter by his halting compelled others to do so too, Gal. ii. 13, ἐνεβριμῶντο.

Ver. 6—8, &c.] See Matt. xxvi. 10, 11, &c.

Ver. 14. *The guest-chamber*] In a private house, for the whole city was then turned into a great inn, for the receipt of strangers that came up to the feast.

Ver. 15, 16.] See Matt. xx. 18, 19, &c.

Ver. 17—19, &c.] See Matt. xxvi. 20, 21, &c.

---

[1] *Murmur et fremitus indignantium significatur.* Beza.

Ver. 21. *Good were it for that man*] For his own particular: for otherwise, in respect of the glory of God's justice, in that man's righteous condemnation, good it was that he was born.

Ver. 22, 23, &c.] Matt. xxvi. 26, &c. The Lord's supper is (as Justin Martyr saith) τροφὴ εὐχαριστηθεῖσα, food made up all of thanksgiving.

Ver. 25. *I will drink no more*] οὐκέτι οὐ μὴ, "I will not, not, not drink;" so Heb. xiii. 5, "I will not, not, not forsake thee." Our Saviour here seemeth to allude to that grace-cup (as they call it), after which they might not eat anything more till the day following.

Ver. 31. *1 will not deny thee*] The Syriac addeth Mari, that is, *Domine mi.* And this he affirmed, *magis ex abundanti.* So did Pendleton the apostate, when he said to Sanders the martyr, with greatest vehemency, I will see the uttermost drop of this grease of mine molten away, and the last gobbet of this flesh consumed to ashes, before I will forsake God and his truth. (Acts and Mon.)

Ver. 32, &c.] Matt. xxvi. 36.

Ver. 33. *Began to be sore amazed*] *Animo et corpore per horrescere, horripilari,* ὀρθοτριχεῖν. Now it was, that he took that terrible cup at his Father's hands, and drunk it off all at once, which we must else have been sipping and sucking at throughout all eternity.

Ver. 36. *Abba, Father*] Father, Father, with greatest earnestness. This was an effectual prayer, had he said no more. God can feel breath in prayer, Lam. iii. 56.

Not what I will, but, &c.] *Aposiopesis emphatica,* saith Beza.

Ver. 37. *Couldst thou not watch*] How, then, wilt thou die with me? So how will they endure wounds for Christ, that cannot endure words? See Jer. xii. 5.

Ver. 40. *Neither wist they what to answer*] They were ashamed to excuse it, yet fell again into it.

Ver. 41. *Sleep on now, take your rest*] If you can, at least, or have any mind to it, with so many swords and halberds about your ears. They were in heaviness, and yet are sharply reproved for relapsing so oft into the same sin. Let not us be more mild than Christ was, but deal freely and faithfully with all.

Ver. 42. *Rise up, let us go*] To meet the enemy in the face. See how courageous he grew upon his prayer.

Ver. 43.] See Matt. xxvi. 47.

Ver. 44. *Had given them a token*] σύσσημον. *Signum consignans, vel commune signum de composito datum;* a watchword, or as soldiers call it, the word.

Ver. 47. *And one of them*] Beza gathered from this text that Mark received not this Gospel from Peter, because Peter would no less have confessed this rashness in himself than he had done his denial of his Master.

And cut off his ear] This was his indiscreet zeal, proceeding *ab affectu carnis, non ab afflatu*

Spiritus sancti, from the flesh, not spirit. (Piscator.)

Ver. 51, 52. *And there followed him a certain young man*] That this was St John, Calvin counts a fancy. He might be one well affected to Christ, who, hearing the noise, came to see the news, and hardly escaped with the skin of his teeth; such is the rudeness and rage of persecutors.

Ver. 53.] See Matt. xxvi. 57, &c.

Ver. 54. *At the fire*] πρὸς τὸ φῶς. At the light, or by the light, that is (say some), by the candle-light (for that discovered him), referring *ad lumen* to *sedens.*

Ver. 55.] See Matt. xxvi. 59, &c.

Ver. 56. *Agreed not*] ἴσαι οὐκ ἦσαν. Were not matches, or amounted not to an accusation of death.

Ver. 61. *The Son of the Blessed?*] So God is called, because to be everlastingly blessed and praised of men and angels. Hence God is frequently set forth in the commentaries of the Hebrew doctors by Baruch-hu, He that is blessed. So Zacharias begins his canticle with, "Blessed is the Lord God," &c. Luke i. 68.

Ver. 62.] See Matt. xxiv. 30; Luke xxii. 70.

Ver. 63. *Rent his clothes*] So they used to do in case of blasphemy, to signify that their very hearts were rent with grief at so sad a hearing.

Ver. 64. *They all condemned him*] As a blasphemer, because he made himself the Son of God. This may comfortably assure us that we are freed by Christ from that crime of blasphemy we stand guilty of, for affecting a deity in our first parents.

Ver. 65. *Prophesy*] *Est hic sarcasmus amarulentissimus.* (Piscator.) This is a most bitter taunt.

Ver. 66.] See Matt. xxvi. 69, &c.

Ver. 68. *He went out*] Thinking to steal away, and here he heard the cock, but recanted not.

Ver. 71. *To curse and to swear*] Let him that stands, take heed, &c. *Cavebis autem si pavebis.* God had a sweet providence in all this, that Peter might be an eye-witness of our Saviour's sufferings.

Ver. 72. *And when he thought thereon*] Or adding to his grief, proportioning his sorrow to his sin;[1] or, throwing his garment over his head (which was the garb of deep mourners, 2 Sam. xvi. 30; Esth. vi. 12), so Theophylact expounds it. Or, *prorupit in fletum,* he burst out and wept. That is an impudent fable, that, long after this, he solicited the blessed virgin, after her assumption, to intercede to Christ for pardon of his thrice denying him, and that Christ thereupon made him and his successors his vicars here, &c. As Xaverius reporteth in Peter's life, written by him in the Persian language.

CHAPTER XV.

Ver. 1. *And straightway in the morning*] They thought once to have deferred his execution till

[1] *Augens, id est, abunde flevit,* ἐπιβαλὼν.

after the feast, chap. xiv. 2. But their malice was restless, as his was that said he would not away till he saw the martyr's (the traitor's he called him) heart out.

Ver. 2.] See Matt. xxvii. 1—3, &c.

Ver. 6. *Now at the feast*] Or, at each great feast, καθ' ἑορτὴν, viz. at the passover, pentecost, and tabernacles. The reason of this custom see in notes on Matt. xxvii. 15.

Ver. 15. *When he had scourged him*] Purposely to move the people to pity him, and therefore brought him forth so misused, with, "Behold the man." But this was ill done of Pilate nevertheless, as was also his comparing with Barabbas, though with intent so to have delivered him. For we may not do evil that good may come thereof.

Ver. 21. *And they compel one Simon*] ἀγγαρεύουσι, *cogunt invitum.* We all come off heavily, and shrink in the shoulder when called to carry the cross, as Peter did, John xxi. 18.

The father of Alexander and Rufus] Men famously known in the Church, and therefore here but named only. God will recompense even involuntary services.

Ver. 22.] St Mark very diligently describeth what fell out at Calvary; what Christ did and said on the cross, what was done and said to him there, how he gave up the ghost, &c., that we might have these things as ready, and at our fingers' ends, as he had who wrote the whole history of our Saviour's passion upon the nails of his hands.

Ver. 23. *Wine mingled with myrrh*] This was not the same potion with that in verse 36 and Matt. xxvii. 48, but another.

Ver. 25. *They crucified him*] i. e. they began to crucify him, but nailed him not to the tree till the sixth hour, John xix. 14.

Ver. 26, &c.] See Matt. xxvii. 35, 36, &c.

Ver. 33. *Darkness over the whole land*] Portending doubtless those dreadful calamities that were coming upon this perverse people, according to Isa. v. 30; viii. 22; Lam. iii. 1, 2; but clearly showing God's heavy displeasure against his Son, our surety, which made him also cry out with a loud voice in the next verse, as one so far forsaken, as not afforded the common benefit of sunlight.

Ver. 34. *Eloi, Eloi, lama sabachthani*] Psal. xxii. 1. It is thought by some that he repeated the whole two-and-twentieth Psalm, which is an admirable narration of the passion, and might well help him the better to bear it.

Ver. 35, 36.] See Matt. xxvii. 46, &c.

Ver. 37. *He gave up the ghost*] After which he went not to Limbus Patrum to preach there, as Papists dote, and would draw from 1 Pet. iii. 19.

Ver. 38.] See Matt. xxvii. 51.

Ver. 39.] See Matt. xxvii. 54, 55.

Ver. 40. *James the less*] viz. In stature, note, or age.

Ver. 41. *Followed him and ministered*] See Luke viii. 3.

Ver. 42. *The day before the sabbath*] Their

preparation to the sabbath began at three o'clock in the afternoon. The Jews of Tiberias began their sabbath sooner than others; those at Tsepphore continued it longer; adding *de profano ad sacrum*. (Buxtorf.) Among our forefathers, at the ringing of the bell to prayer on Saturday evening, the husbandman would give over his labour in the field, and the tradesman his work in the shop, and set themselves to prepare for the sabbath. Among the Jews at this day in many cities, there is one goes about and proclaims the approaching of the sabbath, about half an hour before it begins, that they may prepare.

Ver. 43. *Went in boldly unto Pilate*] It was boldly done indeed, thus to oppose, not the Jews only, but Pilate in that which he had done to Christ. Good blood will not belie itself.

Ver. 44, 45, &c.] See Matt. xxvii. 57, 58, &c.

CHAPTER XVI.

Ver. 1, 2. *And when the sabbath was past*] As God on the first day of the week drew the world out of that abhorred estate of nothing, and brought light out of darkness, so did Christ, on that day, draw his people out of an estate worse than nothing, and "brought life and immortality to light by the gospel," 2 Tim. i. 10.

The first day of the week] τῆς μιᾶς σαββάτων, one of the sabbaths. So the first day of the world is called, *Jom echad*, one day; that is, the first day, Gen. i. 5. For as that day was initial to the world, so the day of our Lord's resurrection is the beginning of our glorification; as in that day light was produced, so Christ rising, the light of righteousness and joy is risen to us. (Gerb. in Harm. Evang.)

Ver. 3.] See Matt. xxviii. 5, 6, &c.

Ver. 4. *And when they looked*] Or, as some read it, when they looked up; for till now they may seem either to have gone plodding on with their eyes downward, or else to have looked on one another, as people used to do when they are conferring.

Ver. 7. *Tell his disciples, and Peter*] q. d. Tell him howsoever, for he is in great heaviness; and this will be very good news to him. Tell him that Christ is risen again for his justification, Rom. iv. Or, tell his disciples and Peter, *quia ille se præ aliis incredulum ostenderat*, as Tolet hath it, because he hath expressed so much unbelief above the rest, and is, therefore, it may be, set here behind all the disciples, as inferior to them.

Ver. 8. *Anything to any man*] Whom they met with, but hastened to the disciples.

Ver. 9. *He appeared first*] This honour done to Mary Magdalene, Mark relateth more at large than the rest, though otherwise mostly he be more brief than the rest.

Ver. 10, 11, &c.] See Matt. xxviii. 9, 10.

Ver. 14.] See Luke xxiv. 36; John xx. 19.

Ver. 15. *Preach the gospel*] Eckius hence blasphemously inferreth that Christ did never command his apostles to write, but to preach only.

To every creature] That is, 1. To man, who is a little world, an epitome of every creature. 2. To the Gentiles also, who had been denied this favour of the gospel, as if they had been none of God's creatures.

Ver. 16. *He that believeth*] That which you preach.

And is baptized] As content to give up himself to Christ, and to receive his mark, making a public profession of the faith.

He that believeth not] He saith not, or Is not baptized; for it is not the want, but the contempt of baptism that damneth. Unbelief is a bloody sin, Heb. x. 26; a heavy sin, John iii. 19; a most ungrateful, inexcusable sin, such as shuts a man up close prisoner in the dark dungeon of the law, unto unavoidable destruction, Gal. iii. 23.

Shall be damned] Here is quick work. God will not stay so long now with people as he did of old, when there was not so much mercy offered. See the note on Heb. ii. 3.

Ver. 17. *In my name they shall, &c.*] This promise was peculiar to the primitive Christians and to such as lived immediately after Christ's ascension. That was an extraordinary providence, that when Squier, that traitor, A. D. 1597, had poisoned the pummel of Queen Elizabeth's saddle when she was to take horse; albeit the season were hot, and the veins open to receive any malignant tainture, yet her body thereupon felt no distemperature, her hand felt no more hurt than Paul's did when he shook off the viper into the fire. (Speed's Hist.)

Ver. 18. *It shall not hurt them*] No more shall the deadly poison of sin hurt those that have drunk it, if they belong to God, provided that they cast it up again quickly by confession, and meddle no more with such a mischief.

Ver. 19. *He was received up, &c.*] This St Luke more fully sets forth, Luke xxiv. 50, 51; Acts i. 9.

Ver. 20. *And they went forth*] viz. From Jerusalem, according to Isa. ii. 3; Psal. cx. 2.

COMMENTARY OR EXPOSITION

THE GOSPEL ACCORDING TO ST LUKE,

WHEREIN THE TEXT IS EXPLAINED, SOME CONTROVERSIES ARE BRIEFLY DISCUSSED, DIVERS COMMONPLACES
HANDLED, AND MANY REMARKABLE MATTERS HINTED, THAT HAD BEEN BY FORMER
INTERPRETERS PRETERMITTED.

CHAPTER I.

Verse 1. *Many have taken in hand*] Or, have attempted, ἐπεχείρησαν, but not effected. Hence some have concluded, that Luke wrote first of the four evangelists. Howbeit the common opinion is (and the most ancient copies say as much) that Matthew wrote his Gospel eight years after Christ, Mark ten, Luke fifteen, and John forty-two.

Ver. 2. *Which from the beginning were eye-witnesses*] Therefore it may seem his Gospel was not dictated to him by Paul (who was no eye-witness), as some ancients have affirmed. But if we can believe Tacitus or Suetonius in things that fell out long before they were born, because we are confident of their diligence in inquiring, how much more should we believe St Luke upon such doubted assurance? &c.

Ver. 3. *Having had perfect understanding*] Or, following them close at heels, and (as we say) hot-foot, παρηκολουθηκότι.

From the very first] Or, from above, ἄνωθεν, as inspired from heaven.

To write unto thee in order] καθεξῆς, distinctly, and yet coherently. A singular praise in an historian, for the which Ambrose much admireth this our evangelist above all the other.

Ver. 4. *Wherein thou hast been instructed*] Which thou hast received by hearsay, or by word of mouth; and wherein thou hast been catechised, receiving the mysteries of the faith by the ministry of the voice, κατηχήθης. And surely when we see men caring and casting how to find out this certainty here spoken of, and not be led by conjectural suppositions, but be fully persuaded as St Luke was, and would have his Theophilus to be, then there will be some hopes that the Lord's party will increase.

Ver. 5. *In the days of Herod*] Herod a stranger, upon the death of Antigonus, last of the Maccabeans, by Augustus' favour, was made King of Judea, and reigned 34 years. After his and his son's death, Judea was again reduced into a Ro-

man province, and the government thereof committed unto Pontius Pilate, then to Petronius, after him to Felix, Festus, Albinus, and Florus, whose cruelty provoked the Jews to rebellion and war, to their utter overthrow.

Of the course of Abia] According to their weekly waitings at the altar, 1 Chron. xxiv. God would not have his ministers over-wrought, though he require them to labour according to their strength, even unto lassitude. But how thankless is their labour that do wilfully over-spend themselves!

Ver. 6. *In all the commandments and ordinances*] That is, in all the duties of both the moral and ceremonial law.

Blameless] Ἄμεμπτοι, *sine querela*, saith the Vulgate, "without complaint." They neither complained of others, nor were complained of by others. As it is reported of Burleigh, Lord Treasurer in Queen Elizabeth's reign, that he never sued any man, nor did any man ever sue him, and was therefore in the number of those few that both lived and died with glory.

Ver. 7. *And they had no child*] Which was then held a heavy judgment, as that which rendered them suspected of impiety, sith godliness had the promise of increase both within doors and without.

Ver. 8. *In the order of his course*] He took but his turn, and served but his time. God never purposed to burden any of his creatures with devotion.

Ver. 9. *To burn incense*] In the incense of prayer, how many sweet spices are burned together, by the fire of faith, as humility, love, &c.

Ver. 10. *Praying without, at the time of incense*] Cant. iii. 6, the Church is said to ascend out of the wilderness of this world with pillars of smoke, *elationibus fumi*, that is, with affections, thoughts, desires toward heaven. And although she be black as smoke, in regard of infirmities, yet hath she a principle to carry her upwards.

Ver. 11. *Standing on the right side of the altar*] As Satan stood at the right hand of Joshua to molest him, Zech. iii. 1, so stand the angels at our right hand, in the public assemblies especially, to withstand him. And to signify this, the curtains of the tabernacle were wrought full of cherubims within and without.

Ver. 12. *He was troubled*] But without cause; he should have been comforted rather, for his sins were covered. How will wicked men stand before Christ?

Ver. 13. *For thy prayer is heard*] Both for a son, and for a Saviour.

Ver. 14. *Thou shalt have joy*] This is not every father's happiness. Many fathers are forced through grief for their untoward children to wish to die, as Elias did when he sat under the juniper, and as Moses did when wearied out by the people, Numb. xi. 15.

Ver. 15. *Great in the sight of the Lord*] *Significatur singularis quædam præstantia, ut* Gen. x. 9. He shall be singularly qualified.

Ver. 16. *Shall he turn to the Lord*] A high honour to have any hand in the conversion of souls. They that wise others shall shine in heaven, Dan. xii. 2.

Ver. 17. *In the spirit and power of Elias*] There is a great agreement between the times of Elias and John Baptist. Herod answereth to Ahab, Herodias to Jezebel, &c.

The disobedient to the wisdom of the just] i. e. By his preaching he shall turn the hearts of the Gentiles to the Jews, and by his baptism tie them up, as it were, together. He made them (according to the phrase that Josephus useth of him) to convent or knit together in baptism, ἐν βαπτισμῷ συνίεναι. (Joseph. Antiq., xviii. 7.)

Ver. 18. *For I am an old man*] Thus reason will be encroaching upon the bounds of faith, till she be taken captive by infidelity. Drive, therefore, Hagar out of doors.

Ver. 19. *That stand in the presence of God*] *Ut apparitor, ab apparendo*, ready pressed to any service.

Ver. 20. *And behold thou shalt be dumb*] His tongue that so lately moved through unbelief is now tied up. God will not pass by the well-meant weaknesses of his own, without a sensible check. He was also deaf as well as dumb: hence they made signs to him, ver. 62.

Ver. 21. *The people waited for Zacharias*] They would not away without the blessing prescribed to the priests, Numb. vi. In the council of Agathon it was decreed that people should not presume to go out of the temples before the ministers had blessed the congregation. (Canon 32.)

Ver. 22. *He could not speak unto them*] Hereupon a divine thus descants: *Tacuit pater vocis, et cessit in miraculum : Vox si sileat, cedit in contradictionem. Numquid æque obmutescit pater et filius? Johannes et Zacharias? Numquid et præco mutus est?* Let us leave to the Papists (saith another) *ministrorum muta officia, populi cæca obsequia,* their ministers' dumb offices; their people's blind obedience.

Ver. 23. *As soon as the days, &c.*] Zacharias, though he ceased to speak, yet he ceased not to minister. Though he were dumb, yet he was not lame, but could do sacrifice, and did it. We may not straight take occasions of withdrawing ourselves from the public services.

Ver. 24. *And hid herself*] *Obscurum qua id fecerit ex causa.* It is hard to say wherefore she did this, saith a learned interpreter, but likely out of modesty; and that she may make no show till she was sure, as also that the miracle might appear the greater.

Ver. 25. *Thus hath the Lord*] She saw that all her prayers that she had haply forgot, were not lost, but laid up with God, who now sends in the blessing that she had despaired of. The Lord oft doth things for his people that they look not for, Isa. lxiv., and stays so long that when he comes he finds not faith, Luke xviii. 8.

To take away my reproach among men] Barrenness was counted a dishonour, Gen. xxx. 23. "Their virgins were not praised," Psal. lxxviii. 63, that is, married, and commended for their fruitfulness. See the note on ver. 7.

Ver. 26. *Unto a city of Galilee*] God and his angels can find out his hidden ones, Psal. lxxxiii. 3, in what corner of the country soever.

Ver. 27. *Espoused to a man*] 1. The better to free her from suspicion of fornication. 2. That she might have one to provide for her when she was with child. 3. That the mystery of God manifested in the flesh might come to light by little and little, *Sensim sine sensu.*

Ver. 28. *Hail thou that art highly favoured*] κεχαριτωμένη. A salutation and not a prayer, as Papists pervert and abuse it. And when the Ave-Maria bell rings, which is at sun-rising, noon, and sun-setting, all men in what place soever, house, field, street, or market, do presently kneel down, and send up their united devotions to heaven by an Ave-Maria. Also, where one fasteth on Friday, which they count our Lord's day, many fast on Saturday, which they count our Lady's day. (Sand's Survey.)

Ver. 29. *She was troubled at his saying*] Affect not the vain praises of men, saith one. The blessed Virgin was troubled when truly praised of an angel. They shall be praised of angels in heaven, who have eschewed the praises of men on earth.

What manner of salutation] *Cujus esset* (saith one interpreter) *voluit enim probare spiritum. Qualis et quanta,* saith another; *Id est, quam honorifica et magnifica, ac proinde supra sortem suam posita.* What an honourable salutation it was, and more than she could acknowledge.

Ver. 30. *Fear not, Mary*] We are not fit to hear till quit of carnal affections and passions. The ear which tastes words as the mouth doth meat, when filled with choler or other ill-humours, can relish no comfort.

Ver. 31. *Shalt call his name Jesus*] See the note on Matt. i. 21. If it were such a mercy to Israel that God raised up of their sons for prophets, and of their young men for Nazarites, Amos ii. 11, what was it to Mary, and in her to all mankind, that she should be mother to the arch-prophet, to that famous Nazarite?

Ver. 32. *Son of the Highest*] Answerable to the Hebrew Elion, whence ἥλιος for the sun, *cujus antiquissima veneratio*, saith Beza, whom the ancients deify.

Ver. 33. *And of his kingdom there shall be no end*] St Paul saith indeed that he shall at the end of the world deliver up the kingdom to God the Father; not that his kingdom shall then cease, but that form of administration only, that he now useth in the collecting and conserving of his Church.

Ver. 34. *How shall this be?*] This is a speech not of unbelief, but of wonderment, as desiring also to be better informed.

Ver. 35. *The power of the Highest shall overshadow thee*] As once he did the confused chaos in the creation. This very expression was a great confirmation to the Virgin's faith, and may well serve for a caution to us not to be over-curious in searching into this secret.

Ver. 36. *Who was called barren*] It is observed that the barren women (so called in both Testaments) had the best children, as Sarah, Rebecca, Rachel, Elisabeth, &c., because long held off, and much humbled. Some also have observed that the New Testament affords more store of good women than the Old. (Dr Hall's Contemplation on the New Testament.)

Ver. 37. *For with God, &c.*] We never doubt of God's will, but we do in some measure doubt of his power. See them both running parallel, Job xlii. 2.

Ver. 38. *Behold the handmaid of the Lord*] Not Mall God's maid, as a black-mouthed Blatero hath blasphemed in print, that the Puritans rudely called her. (Stafford's Female Glory.)

Ver. 39. *Into the hill country*] Of Judea, southward of Jerusalem, into the city of Hebron, Josh. xxi. 9.

Ver. 40. *Saluted Elisabeth*] To whom she could not rest till she had imparted the good news, and both given and received some spiritual gift for mutual confirmation and comfort, Rom. i. 11, 12. Grief grows greater by concealing, joy by expression. Only the meeting of saints in heaven can parallel the meeting of these two cousins.

Ver. 41. *The babe leaped in her womb*] Such comfort there is in the presence of Christ (though but in the womb) as it made John to spring. What then shall it be in heaven think we?

Ver. 42. *Blessed art thou among women*] So is Jael, the wife of Heber, said to be, Judges v. 24. Who yet perhaps was hardly so good a woman as Deborah, that called her so. But it was no small confirmation to the blessed Virgin, to hear the same words from Elisabeth that she heard before from the angel.

And blessed is the fruit, &c.] Or, because blessed is the fruit of thy womb, therefore blessed art thou, &c. Yet more blessed (as

Austin saith) in receiving the faith than in conceiving the flesh of Christ. She conceived Christ when she yielded her assent to the angel, and said, Be it as thou hast said, let it even be so. We also conceive Christ in our hearts when we assent to the promises of pardon, of salvation by Christ: hoping perfectly for the grace that is to be brought unto us at the revelation of Jesus Christ, 1 Peter i. 13. It is with us all, as it was with that captive woman, Deut. xxi. If she consented to marry, she saved her life by it.

Ver. 43. *That the mother of my Lord, &c.*] That the Lord himself should come amongst us, as he did in the flesh, and doth still by his Spirit. Oh, what a mercy!

Ver. 44. *Leaped in my womb*] More like a suckling at the breast (as the word signifieth) than an embryo in the womb (βρέφος, *puer recens natus*, 1 Peter ii. 2). The Spirit then worketh, even in unborn babes that are elect, some kind of saving knowledge of Christ, answerable to faith in those that are grown up. The babe's motion here was not natural, but spiritual (saith one). Therefore John was sanctified in the womb, and did really rejoice at the presence of Christ in the Virgin. Now sanctification presupposeth justification, and that, faith. Yea, this joy was a true effect of faith in the Messiah; therefore infants are capable of faith: thus he. Seminal faith we cannot deny them.

Ver. 45. *Blessed is she, &c.*] Mary believed, so did not Zacharias, though a man, a priest, aged, learned, eminent, and the message to him of more appearing possibility. This, Elisabeth here seems to have an eye to.

Believed that there shall be, &c.] The same may be said of every believer. It is true also in cases ordinary. A persuasion that God will help and keep us, will indeed help and keep us, Mark ix. 23.

Ver. 46. *And Mary said*] See the benefit of good society, and how one Christian kindleth another. "As iron sharpeneth iron, so doth the face of a man his friend," Prov. xxvii. 17.

Doth magnify the Lord] Μεγαλύνει. Makes room for him, enlargeth her thoughts of him, throws wide open the everlasting doors, that the King of Glory may come in, in state.

My spirit rejoiceth] *Tripudiat*, danceth a galliard (which seemeth to come from the Greek word here used, ἠγαλλίασε ἐπὶ τῷ Θεῷ, *super Deo*), danceth Levaltoes in God, or for God my Saviour, as the matter and ground of my joy.

Ver. 48. *The low estate*] *Vilitatem*, the vile and abject condition. *Contra Mariæ merita, quæ prædicant Papicolæ.* Here is no mention of merit. See Beza Annot. in loc.

All generations shall call me blessed] How much more should we with one mind and one mouth bless God the Father of our Lord Jesus Christ! This is an honour that he much standeth upon, Rom. xv. 6.

Ver. 49. *He that is mighty*] האל The mighty strong God, ὁ δυνατός.

Hath done great things for me] No small things can fall from so great a hand. He gives like himself.

And holy is his name] God that is holy, is to be sanctified in holiness, Isa. v. 16, when men see their children especially (as here) the work of God's hands, Isa. xxix. 23.

Ver. 50. *From generation to generation*] Personal goodness is profitable to posterity.

Ver. 51. *He hath showed strength, &c.*] It appears by the whole frame of this holy song, that the blessed Virgin was well versed in the Scripture, which she here makes so much use of in sundry passages. She was *eruditionis pietatis et modestiæ delicium*, as one speaketh of the Lady Jane Grey. She had by much reading made her bosom *Bibliothecam Christi*, Christ's library, as a Father saith ; and may seem to have been exercised in the good word of God from her infancy, as 2 Tim. iii. 15, and as that sweet young gentlewoman, Mrs Elizabeth Wheatenhall, daughter of Mr Anthony Wheatenhall, of Tenterden, in Kent, deceased, who not yet being ten years old when she died, yea, before she was nine years old (not much above eight), could say all the New Testament by heart, and being asked where any words were, she would presently name book, chapter, and verse. One Mr Stoughton, a minister, writeth this upon his own knowledge and examination of her.

He hath scattered the proud] He by his strong arm hath so splitted them, that they shiver into pieces, διεσκόρπισε ; or hath made them as darts, which being among the enemies, are lost ; or hath hurled them hither and thither, as the wind doth the dust of the mountains.

Ver. 52. *He hath put down the mighty*] As he did Bajazet, the proud Turk, and set up Tamerlane, a Scythian shepherd ; who said that he was sent from heaven to punish Bajazet's rashness, and to teach him that the proud are hated of God, whose promise is to pluck down the mighty, and raise up the lowly.

Ver. 53. *He hath filled the hungry*] See the note on Matt. v. 6.

Ver. 54. *He hath holpen his servant*] He hath put under his hand, and raised him prostrate, taken him up at his feet, ἀντελάβετο. This he will not do for an evil-doer : he taketh not the ungodly by the hand, Job viii. 20.

Ver. 55. *As he spake to our fathers*] Who lived upon reversions, and died upon the promises, accounting them good freehold. God keeps promise with nights and days, Jer. xxxiii. 20, 25. How much more will he with Abraham, and his seed for ever !

Ver. 56. *And returned to her own house*] An honest heart is where its calling is. Such a one, when he is abroad, is like a fish in the air ; whereinto if it leap for recreation or necessity, yet it soon returns to its own element.

Ver. 57. *And she brought forth a son*] The voice of the Lord maketh the hinds to calve, Psal. xxix. 9, though of all other brute creatures they bring forth with greatest trouble, bowing themselves,

bruising their young, and casting out their sorrows, Job xxxix. 4, 6. How much more will he help his dear handmaids !

Ver. 58. *The Lord had showed great mercy*] And the greater, because in her old age. Births, with those that are ancienter, are with greater danger ; so is the new birth in old sinners.

Ver. 59. *To circumcise the child*] Infants are no innocents, they are conceived in sin, and the first sheet or blanket wherewith they are covered is woven of sin, shame, blood, and filth, Ezek. xvi. 4, 6. They were circumcised, to signify that we had better be flayed, and have our skin quite stript off, than to have it as a skin-bottle hanging in the smoke of filthy desires, and blown full of unclean motions with the breath of Satan.

Ver. 60. *He shall be called John*] Bucer here observeth that he that was high priest when Solomon built the temple was called John, and that there was herein a sweet suitableness. *Pulchre vero convenit*, saith he, *ut quo nomine sacerdos Salomonis typici, hoc et veri vocaretur ;* that the type and truth might accord in the very name.

Ver. 61. *There is none of thy kindred*] There is an inbred desire in us all of immortality ; we would eternize our names, and do therefore call our children, cities, lands, &c., after them, Psal. xlix. 11. But they do best that get assurance that their names are written in heaven. They that depart from God shall be written in the earth, Jer. xvii. 13, as Cain's son, Lord Enoch of Enoch, Gen. iv., and those men of renown, Gen. xi. 4, were.

Ver. 62. *And they made signs to his father*] Who, therefore, seems to have been deaf (as well as dumb) because he had not hearkened to the angel's speech, but gainsaid it.

Ver. 63. *And he asked for a writing-table*] *Tabellam, sc. ceratam, in qua olim stilo scribebatur*, saith Sa. He had an excellent faculty of whom Martial reporteth,

Currant verba licet, manus est velocior illis ;
Et vix lingua suum, dextra peregit opus.

Ver. 64. *And he spake and praised God*] And had he had as many tongues as he had hairs upon his head, he could never have sufficiently praised God for his son, but especially for his Saviour. See 1 Tim. i. 15—17. Zacharias believeth and therefore speaks, Psal. cxvi. 10. The tongue of the dumb sings, Isa. xxxv. 6.

Ver. 65. *And fear came on all*] This was either the fear of admiration at the many strange accidents about the birth of the Baptist ; or the fear of punishment, seeing so good a man as Zacharias so long to have suffered for his unbelief. (Ludolf. *de Vitâ Christi.*)

Ver. 66. *And the hand of the Lord*] That is, his grace and blessing. He had the honour to be *Legis et gratiæ fibula*, as Chrysologus hath it ; the buckle and boundary of the law and gospel.

Ver. 67. *Was filled with the Holy Ghost, and prophesied*] This was a plentiful amends for the late loss of his speech. See here the goodness of

God to all his. *Quibus non solum ablata resti-*
tuit, sed insperata concedit (saith Ambrose).
Ille dudum mutus prophetat. God is better to
his than their hopes.

Ver. 68. *Blessed be the Lord God of Israel*]
This is *Hymnus Evangelicissimus*, say both Bucer
and Pellican. A most evangelical canticle.

Redeemed his people] From the wrath of God
over them; the guilt and power of sin within
them; from Satan and the punishment of sin
without them.

Ver. 69. *An horn of salvation*] A cornucopia,
or a mighty Saviour, *qui instar bovis cornupetæ*
inimicos populi Dei prosternat atque dejiciat (Piscator), that can bestir him much better than that
he-goat, Alexander the Great, who had a notable
horn between his eyes, wherewith he cast down
the ram to the ground, and stamped upon him,
&c., Dan. viii. 7. *Macedones tunc temporis Ægea-*
des, id est caprini dicti sunt. Occasionem vide.
(Justin. *lib.* 7.) The Macedons were at that time
called Goat-sprung.

Ver. 70. *By the mouth*] There were many prophets, yet they had all but one mouth, so sweet
is their harmony.

Ver. 71. *That we should be saved*] Gr. Salvation from our enemies. This properly importeth
the privative part of man's happiness, but includes the positive too.

Ver. 72. *To perform the mercy*] God's love
moves him to promise, his truth binds him to
perform. See both these, 2 Sam. vii. 18, 21.
" For thy word's sake, and according to thine own
heart (that is, *ex mero motu*), hast thou done all
these things."

Ver. 73. *The oath which he sware*] ὅρκος *quasi*
ἕρκος, a hedge, which a man may not break; much
less will God.

Ver. 74. *Might serve him*] *Servati sumus ut*
serviamus. Christ hath therefore broke the
devil's yoke from off our necks, that we may
take upon us this sweet yoke, and not carry ourselves as sons of Belial. Serve we must still,
but after another manner, as the Israelites did,
when brought out of the Egyptian bondage; yet
thou shalt keep this service, saith Moses, Exod.
xii. 25.

In holiness and righteousness] These two make
up one perfect pair of compasses, which can take
the true latitude of a Christian heart.

Ver. 75. *Before him*] The sense of God's presence makes men conscientiously obedient to both
tables of the law. *Cave spectat Cato*, was a watch-
word among the Romans. *Noli peccare, Deus*
videt, Angeli astant, &c. Take heed what thou
doest, God beholds thee, angels observe thee, &c.

Ver. 76. *And thou, child*] scil. *qui nunc tantil-*
lus es, in virum magnum evades: Though little,
thou shalt prove great.

Thou shalt go before the face of the Lord] Any
relation to whom ennobleth, and advanceth all
worth.

Ver. 77. *To give knowledge*] Not by infusion,
Dan. i. 17, but by instruction. See the dignity
and duty of ministers.

Ver. 78. *Whereby the day-spring*] Or as Beza
rendereth it, the branch (ἀνατολὴ) from on high,
not from beneath, as other plants or branches.
So the anchor of hope entereth not into the
deep, but into that within the veil, Heb. vi. 19.

Ver. 79. *That sit in darkness*] This imports, 1.
continuance; 2. content.

To guide our feet] The superstitious pagans
thought that their goddess Vibilia kept them in
their right way when they travelled: but we
have a better guide to God. Arnob. *advers.*
Gent. lib. 4.

Ver. 80. *And the child grew*] Though his
meat was but coarse, and not so nourishing.
The blessing of God is the staff of bread: bread
would no more nourish without it, than a piece
of earth.

CHAPTER II.

Ver. 1. *A decree from Cæsar Augustus*] By a
sweet providence of God, that Christ might be
born at Bethlehem, according to the Scriptures.
Howbeit Augustus thought not so (as it is said
in another case of Nebuchadnezzar, Isa. x.),
but ambitiously sought the setting forth of his
own greatness, and large command, and carried
it without punishment; whenas David smarted
sore for a like offence. But God will take that
from others, that he will not bear with in his
own, Amos iii. 2.

That all the world] That is, the Roman
world; but such was their ambition, that though
they had but a part, yet they styled themselves
lords of all the world. So the Pope (the image
of that beast) will needs be styled universal
bishop. The great Turk (that Eastern antichrist) calls himself God on earth, sole monarch
of the world, commander of all that can be commanded, &c., and by many other such like
swelling titles.

Ver. 2. *When Cyrenius*, &c.] Quirinus, the
Latin writers call him. Now that the sceptre
was departed, Shiloh came.

Ver. 3. *And all went to be taxed*] To pay a
certain small sum of money in token of fealty. I
was once at a court-sermon (saith Melancthon)
on the Nativity day, and this was the text: but
the preacher, instead of discoursing on Christ's
incarnation, spent the whole hour, on a very cold
day, in persuading the people to obey magistrates,
and to give them as much money as they call
for. This is the guise of court-parasites, princes,
trencher-flies.

Ver. 4. *And Joseph also went up*] By a special
providence of God, as is above noted, ver. 1, and
not only so, but that the holy virgin might still
have with her the keeper and cover of her virginity; that the devil might not have occasion to
raise up false reports about her great belly.

Ver. 5. *Being great with child*] Yet could not
be excused. This was a cruelty in Augustus
(not to spare great-bellied women), but a mercy
of God to mankind; for what the better had it

been for us, if Joseph had gone to Bethlehem, and not Mary also?

Ver. 6. *The days were accomplished*] Her delivery might well be hastened, or at least facilitated, by her long journey; for it was no less than four days' journey from Nazareth to Bethlehem. Some say she was *gravida*, but not *gravata;* great-bellied, but not unwieldy: *Lumen enim quod in se habebat, pondus habere non poterat,* saith Augustine; but I am not bound to believe him.

Ver. 7. *And she brought forth her first-born*] Whether she were Deipara, the mother of God, was a great controversy, and raised a great storm in the Council of Ephesus; insomuch as the emperor declared both sides heretics. But forasmuch as she was the mother of Christ, Matt. i. 23, and Christ is God; in bringing forth Christ, she was the mother of God. Θεοτόκος *non* Θεοδόχος, *ut voluit Nestorius.* Whether she continued after this a virgin, *piè credimus sed nihil affirmamus.* But that she vowed virginity, as Papists say, we deny: for how could she promise virginity to God, and marriage to Joseph? There is a story, that when the old Romans had founded *Templum pacis,* they sent to ask Apollo how long it should stand? he answered, Until a virgin brought forth: this they took to be perpetual. But therein they were as much mistaken as those Africans, who having an oracle, that when the Romans sent an army into Africa, *Mundus cum tota sua prole periret,* thought that then the world should be at an end. But afterwards the Romans sent an army thither under the conduct of one Mundus, who in battle was slain, together with his sons, by the Africans; and discovered the illusion of the devil.

Wrapped him in swaddling-clothes] This pains she was at (such was her love), though newly delivered, and much weakened thereby. His swaddling-clothes were poor and ragged, as may be gathered out of the Greek word here used. Σπαργανόω, of Σπαράσσω, to rend.

Laid him in a manger] *Non in aureo reclinatorio,* saith Ludolphus, not in a stately room, as the *Porphyrogeniti* in Constantinople; not in the best but basest place of the inn, which is counted the meanest house of a city. Oh humble Saviour, whither wilt thou descend?

Ver. 8. *Keeping watch over their flock*] At the tower of Edar, say some, between Jerusalem and Bethlehem, where Jacob, returning from Mesopotamia, staid with his flock, after he had buried Rachel, Gen. xxxv. 21; Mic. iv. 8.

By night] Hence some gather that our Saviour was not born in the winter, because in winter they housed their cattle, and fed them not without-doors, Prov. xxvii. 25.

Ver. 9. *And, lo, the angel of the Lord*] Gabriel, likely, was sent, not to Zacharias or Simeon, &c., but to certain shepherds. God goes a way by himself. Had the sages of the East met with these shepherds, they had received better intelligence than they did from the learned scribes.

And the glory of the Lord] As when a king's son is born, bonfires are made, &c.

Ver. 10. *I bring you good tidings*] The first preacher of the gospel was an angel. God hath now taken this honour from the angels, and put it upon the ministers, who are in Scripture called angels, Rev. ii. 1, and angels ministers, Heb. i. 14. The old church had ἐπαγγελίαν, the promise, we have εὐαγγελίαν, the joyful tidings.

Ver. 11. *A Saviour*] The Greek word is so emphatical (as Tully witnesseth) that other tongues can hardly find a fit word to express it. The Grecians delivered by Flaminius, rang out Σωτὴρ, Σωτὴρ, with such a courage, that the birds, astonished, fell to the earth.

Ver. 12. *Wrapped in swaddling-clothes*] *In vilibus et veteribus indumentis,* saith Ludolphus. See the note on ver. 7.

Ver. 13. *Praising God*] Angels who have neither so much interest in Christ nor benefit by him as we, sing him into the world. And shall we be dumb? They sang when the world was created, Job xxxviii. 7. So now, that it was repaired by Christ.

Ver. 14. *Glory be to God on high*] Let God have all the glory, so we may have the peace and grace or good will (for of these angels, Saint Paul learned to salute with grace and peace). *Mihi placet distributio angelica,* saith Bernard, *gratanter accipio quod relinquis, relinquo quod retines: abjuro gloriam, ne amitterem pacem.* I am well content with the angels' distribution, I thankfully accept (Lord) what thou leavest; I meddle not with that which thou retainest. I forego the glory, so I may not miss of the peace. Thus he. It was the last speech of dying Chrysostom, Glory be to God from all creatures. Let the Jesuits (saith one) at the end of their books subscribe *Laus Deo et Beatæ Virgini.* Let this be the badge of the beast: cry we, *Soli Deo gloria,* glory be to God alone.

In earth peace] *Pax, quasi pactio conditionum.* Εἰρήνη παρὰ τὸ εἰς ἕν εἴρειν, a connectendo in unum. Christ is the great peace-maker; but only to the elect, called here the men of God's good will. When he was born, *Cuncta atque continua totius generis humani aut pax fuit aut pactio.* Flor. Hist. l. 4.

Ver. 15. *Let us now go even unto Bethlehem*] They did not reason nor debate with themselves (saith Bishop Hooper, martyr, in a letter to certain good people taken praying in Bow church-yard, and now in trouble) who should keep the wolf from the sheep in the mean time; but committed the sheep to him whose pleasure they obeyed. So let us do now that we be called; commit all other things to him that called us. He will take heed that all shall be well. He will help the husband, comfort the wife, guide the servants, keep the house, preserve the goods; yea, rather than it should be undone, he will wash the dishes, rock the cradle, &c.

Ver. 16. *Found Mary and Joseph, &c.*] They, though of the blood-royal, yet lay obscured, not thrusting themselves into observation, but well content with a low condition. *Beata Virgo in vili stabulo sedet, et jacet ; sed quod homines negligunt, cœlestes cives honorant et inquirunt,* saith Stella. The humble person is like the violet, which grows low, hangs the head downwards, and hides itself with its own leaves. And were it not that the fragrant smell of his many virtues betrays him to the world, he would choose to live and die in his self-contenting secrecy. Bernard.

Ver. 17. *They made known abroad*] True goodness is communicative ; there is no envy in spiritual things ; because they may be divided *in solidum :* one may have as much as another, and all alike. These shepherds, as those lepers, 2 Kings vii. 7, 9, said one to another, " We do not well ; this day is a day of good tidings, and we hold our peace," &c.

Ver. 18. *Wondered at those things*] Yet made little benefit of what they heard. " All the world wondered after the beast," Rev. xiii. 3. And it was a wonder there was no more wondering at the birth of our Saviour ; if that were true especially, that (besides the wise men's star, Matt. ii., and the angelical music in the air, &c.) among the Gentiles a voice was heard, The great God is now about to be born ; and that at Rome, the likeness of a woman carrying a child in her arms was seen about the sun, &c. These things are storied. Polydore Virgil reports out of Orosius, that on the very day of Christ's nativity, Augustus Cæsar caused proclamation that no man should style him Lord any longer, *Manifesto præsagio majoris Dominatus, qui tum in terris ortus esset ;* as presaging a greater than himself then born.

Ver. 19. *Mary kept all those things*] Her soul was a holy ark ; her memory like the pot of manna, preserving holy truths and remarkable occurrences.

Ver. 20. *As it was told unto them*] God, to show that he respected not persons, revealed this grand mystery to shepherds and wise men ; the one poor, the other rich ; the one learned, the other unlearned ; the one Jews, the other Gentiles ; the one near, the other far off.

Ver. 21. *For the circumcising of the child*] Christ would be circumcised, and so become bound to fulfil the law, that he might free us that were under the law, Gal. iv. 5. He shed his blood for us when he was but eight days old ; he took us into his family by baptism when we hung on our mother's breasts. Should we not then serve him betimes, remember him from our infancy ?

Ver. 22. *And when the days of her purification*] She was rather sanctified than polluted by bearing Christ, yet wrangleth not with the law, nor claimeth an immunity. Now if she were so officious in ceremonies, what in the main duties of morality ?

According to the law] This law of purification proclaims our uncleanness, whose very birth infects the mother that bare us. She might not till the seventh day converse with men, nor till the 40th day appear before God in the sanctuary,

nor then without a burnt-offering for thanksgiving, and a sin-offering for expiation of a double sin, viz. of the mother that conceived, and of the son that was conceived.

Ver. 23. *That openeth the womb*] This proves that Mary brought forth Christ in a natural way, and not *utero clauso,* by a miracle, as Papists would have it, to prove the fiction of transubstantiation.

Shall be called holy to the Lord] God requireth the first-born, as usually best-beloved ; that, together with our children, he might draw to himself the best of our affections.

Ver. 24. *A pair of turtle-doves*] Christ's mother was not rich enough to bring a lamb. Let this comfort poor Christians. I know thy poverty, saith Christ, but that is nothing, thou art rich, Rev. ii. 9. Smyrna, the poorest Church, hath the highest commendation.

Ver. 25. *Just and devout*] Or wary and cautious, εὐλαβὴς ; one that takes heed and is fearful of being deceived in that which he takes for right and current.

Waiting for the consolation of Israel] That is, for Christ's coming. This was the sugar wherewith they sweetened all their crosses : this was the dittany, by tasting whereof (as harts do) they shook off all the piercing shafts of their afflictions. Some Jews conclude the Messiah when he comes shall be called Menahem, the Comforter, from Lam. i. 6.

Ver. 26. *It was revealed unto him*] By an immediate oracle, κεχρηματισμένον. The idolatrous heathen made use of this word to signify their impious and diabolical oracles. The abuse of a word taketh not away the use of it.

Ver. 27. *And he came by the spirit, &c.*] So still, " the steps of a good man are ordered by the Lord," Psal. xxxvii. 23. He sets his Spirit as a tutor, to direct and convince us into all truth. Simeon, likely, had done as Daniel did, chap. ix. 2, found out by diligent search, that the fulness of time was come, and is therefore thus answered from heaven.

Ver. 28. *Then took he him up in his arms*] The blessedest armful that ever the old man had in his life. The patriarchs saluted him ἀσπασάμενοι, but afar off, Heb. xi. 13.

Ver. 29. *Lord now lettest thou thy servant*] In the Syriac it is, " Now thou openest the prison door ; " the prisoner must not, till then, go out ; nor we out of life till fairly dismissed. Simeon having laid in his heart (saith one) what he lapt in his arms, sung, *Nunc dimittis ;* I fear no sin, I dread no death ; I have lived long enough, I have my life ; I have longed enough, I have my love ; I have seen enough, I have my light ; I have served enough, I have my saint ; I have sorrowed enough, I have my joy : sweet babe, let this psalm serve for a lullaby to thee, and for a funeral for me. Oh sleep in my arms, and let me sleep in thy peace. Dying Velcurio broke out into these words, " *Pater est Amator, Filius Redemptor, Spiritus Sanctus Consolator ; quomodo itaque tristitiâ affici possim ?* " Dying Deering said, "*Ego omnium sanctorum minimus, credo et intueor in Christum, salutem meam.*"

Ver. 30. *For mine eyes have seen, &c.*] A great satisfaction. So it was to Job, chap. xlii. 5, when he could say, "I have heard of thee by the hearing of the ear, but now mine eye seeth thee." What shall it be to us when we shall see God face to face, &c. 1 Cor. xiii. 12. *Colamus hic Deum reverenter donec a spe ad speciem transeamus.* Worship we God with reverence till we come to see him face to face. Bucholcer.

Ver. 31. *Before the face of all the people*] As a banner displayed, as a beacon on a hill, or as the sun in heaven, to be beheld of all; as the brasen serpent was lifted up in the wilderness, &c., John iii. 15, ἐφάνη, Tit. ii. 11.

Ver. 32. *The glory of thy people Israel*] Oh! pity their perverseness, and pray their conversion, that the Jews may call God Abba, the Gentiles Father, Dan. xii. 11. There is a prophecy of the Jew's final restoration (saith Mr Case, God's waiting to be gracious), and the time is expressed, which is 1290 years after the ceasing of the daily sacrifice, and the setting up of the abomination of desolation; which is conceived to be about Julian's time, who assayed to re-build the temple of the Jews, but was hindered from heaven. This was *anno Dom.* 360, to which if you add 1290 years, it will pitch the calculation upon the year 1650.

Ver. 33. *Marvelled at those things*] Saints, the more they see into the mystery of Christ, the more are they transported with admiration. But most of all at the last day, 2 Thess. i. 10.

Ver. 34. *For the fall, &c.*] Being *reorum scopulus, piorum rupes.*

And for a sign, &c.] For a butt-mark, against whom his enemies shall shoot the shafts of their gainsayings; like as at the sack of Constantinople, the image of the crucifix was taken down by the Turks, and a Turk's cap put upon the head thereof, and so set up, and shot at with their arrows, calling it the God of the Christians.

Ver. 35. *Yea, a sword shall pierce, &c.*] This confutes that of Plautus: *Mulier nulla cordicitis dolet ex animo.* The word here rendered sword, properly signifies a long Thracian dart, entering into her soul. So that she was, I doubt not (as other mothers are), *ante partum onerosa, in partu dolorosa, post partum laborosa;* yet so, as that she made misery itself amiable by her gracious deportment, as one saith of the Lady Jane Grey.

That the thoughts of many hearts] As they are also now in these discriminating, shedding times. Affliction trieth men who are crocodiles, spunges, cameleons, &c. Before these days came (said Master Bradford, martyr) how many thought of themselves, that they had been in God's bosom, and so were taken, and would be taken in the world? But now we see whose they are; for to whom we obey, his servants we are, &c. In the Palatinate scarce one man in twenty stood out; but fell to Popery, as fast as leaves in autumn.

Ver. 36. *From her virginity*] i. e. She was a pure virgin when married to her husband. All are not virgins that pass for such; some have their secret conveyances; They can eat stolen bread, and afterwards so wipe their lips that not the least crumb shall be seen, Prov. xxx. 19, 20.

Ver. 37. *A widow of about eighty-four years*] She was now ripe, and ready, even of her own accord, to fall into God's hand, as ripe fruits do into the hand of the gatherer. And the thoughts of death had long since forbade the banns of a second marriage. *Cogita te quotidie moriturum, et de secundis nuptiis nunquam cogitabis.* Think of death, and the thoughts of marrying again will die within thee.

Ver. 38. *Gave thanks likewise*] *Succinuit Simeoni,* seconded Simeon, and sang the same song. This was somewhat extraordinary, as being against that, 1 Tim. ii. 12, and therefore fell out only in troublesome and confused times of the Church; as likewise Huldah the prophetess. Our *Prædicantissæ* have here no patronage.

Ver. 39. *According to the law of the Lord*] This is often recorded of them in this chapter, that they observed the law exactly, to their singular commendation. The law is to be kept as the apple of one's eye, Prov. vii. 2. Count nothing little that God commands. It is as much treason to coin pence as twenty-shilling-pieces. And they were commanded not to eat of the blood, as ever they looked for God's blessing.

They returned into Galilee] After they had first fled down into Egypt, Matt. ii.

Ver. 40. *And the grace of God was upon him*] Without measure: so that of his overflow we have all received "grace for grace," John i. 16. He had a fulness, not repletive only, but diffusive too; not of plenty only, but of bounty also; not only of abundance, but of redundancy. He was anointed with the oil of gladness, not only above, but for his fellows.

Ver. 41. *Now his parents went, &c.*] Every male was to appear thrice a year before the Lord. In the females it was a free-will offering, and well accepted.

Ver. 42. *And when he was twelve years old*] What he did from his infancy hitherto, the Scripture is silent; Papists feign many idle relations, and thereby expose us to the jeers of Jewish and Turkish miscreants. Where the Scripture hath no tongue, we must have no ears.

Ver. 43. *Joseph and his mother knew not*] One would wonder they should be so careless of so peerless a pearl; they might well think there were enough at Jerusalem, among the Herodians especially, that would have been glad to have despatched any that should take upon them to be Messias the Prince, as Daniel calleth him, chap. ix. 25. When they fled into Egypt for fear of Herod, they lost not the child Jesus; as neither there, nor in their return from thence; but at the feast they did, and in that greatest solemnity. Hence Stella observeth, that there is far greater danger of losing Christ in time of prosperity, and worldly affluence, than in days of persecution and tribulation. *In mundi fælicitate et affluentia, potius quam in persecutionibus et tribulationibus Christum amitti.*

Ver. 44. *Sought him among their kinsfolk*] They knew him to be of a disposition not strange and stoical, but sweet and sociable. Let not us stye up ourselves in a stern austerity, but run into the company of those now, that must be our everlasting companions in heaven.

Ver. 45. *And when they found him not*] The best are sometimes at a loss, and hard put to it for three days, or so. And this, mostly, for their security, as the Church in the Canticles.

Ver. 46. *Sitting in the midst of the doctors*] *Christus prius sedet in medio doctorum (ut recté distin.* 36, *Gratian) quam publice cœpit munus Mediatoris obire.*

Hearing them, and posing them] In this very year the temple was profaned, even at the passover. For the priests having opened the temple doors by night, as the manner was, found a great company of dead men's bones in the morning thrown here and there through the whole house. This, saith Josephus, was thought to have been done by the Samaritans, in spite to the Jews. But others think God had a special hand in it, to signify that the temple services were shortly to die and determine, now that the Lord of heaven and earth had taught therein with his own lively voice.

Ver. 47. *At his understanding*] Which was so large, even as man, that some have affirmed it to be infinite, and uncreated; but of this, his manhood being a creature, was incapable. Howbeit here our Saviour put forth a beam of his Deity, which yet he soon drew in again, and lay long after obscured.

Ver. 48. *Have sought thee sorrowing*] *Animo tristissimo, et afflictissimo.* God often cures a lethargy of security, by a fever of perplexity.

Ver. 49. *Wist ye not*] Men, be they pleased or displeased, God must be obeyed.

Ver. 50. *They understood not*] Yet were well versed in the Scriptures. If God give us not sight as well as light, we are still to seek.

Ver. 51. *And was subject unto them*] Labouring with his hands, &c., Mark vi. 5.

Ver. 52. *Increased in wisdom*] Being παιδαριο-γέρων, as Macarius was called, whilst a child, for his extraordinary grace and gravity. The exercise of his wisdom, as it was more enlarged, became more lovely in the sight of God and man.

CHAPTER III.

Ver. 1. *Pontius Pilate being governor*] Tacitus calleth him procurator only of Judea. But St Luke here makes little difference betwixt his office and the imperial honour of his master Tiberius; for he useth the same word to express both, ἡγεμονεύοντος· ἡγεμονία. The Earl of Flanders counts it a great prerogative, that he writes himself *Comes Dei gratia.* Others only *Dei clementiá.* The Duke of Milan, that he is the prime duke of Europe. The deputy of Ireland, that there cometh no vicegerent in Europe more near the majesty and prerogative of a king than he, &c.

Ver. 2. *Annas and Caiaphas being high priests*] By turns, John xi. 44; Acts iv. 6, contrary to the old order. Throughout the whole Turkish territories, there is but one Mufta, or high priest, and he is the supreme judge and rectifier of all actions, as well civil as ecclesiastical.

Ver. 3. *Preaching the baptism of repentance*] John's note was still repentance. Christ comes not where this herald hath not been before him. Yet now it is come to that pass, that many men scorn to hear a sermon of repentance. It is a sign, say some, that the minister hath been idle that week, or that his stock is spent when he comes to preach of such a common theme as repentance. If God be not merciful, we shall quickly dispute away all our repentance, as a famous preacher justly complaineth.

Ver. 4. *In the book of the words of Esaias*] Called a great roll, Isa. viii. 1 (because it treats of great things, *maxima in minimo*), and said to be written with the pen of a man, that is, clearly that the simplest of men may understand it, Deut. xxx. 11.

Ver. 5. *Every valley shall be filled*] Every hole, or hollow, φάραγξ, (Barathrum.) Fainting of heart unfits the way for Christ, as well as the swelling hills of pride. Plain things will join in every point one with another; not so, rough and hollow things: so plain spirits close with God's truths; not so, those that are swollen, and uneven.

Ver. 6. *All flesh shall see*] viz. All that order their conversation aright, Psal. l. 23, which is the life of thankfulness, ibid.

Ver. 7—9. See the notes on Matt. iii. 7—10.

Ver. 10. *What shall we do?*] q. d. What are those fruits worthy of repentance, that we in our places must bring forth? That we may find in ourselves that confident answer, stipulation, or interrogation, ἐπερώτημα, rather of a good conscience toward God, mentioned by St Peter, 1 Pet. iii. 21, in allusion (I suppose) to this text.

Ver. 11. *He that hath two coats*] Thus Tyre evidenced her repentance, Isa. xxiii. 18, by feeding and clothing God's saints with her merchandise. Thus Zaccheus, Dorcas, &c. This is all the lesson that for the present he sets them, being but young scholars in the school of Christ.

Ver. 12. *Then came also publicans*] These were toll-takers, custom-gatherers for the Romans, and most of them greedy gripers. Publicans they were called, because they took up *publica*, the goods of the empire. See the note on Matt. ix. 9.

Ver. 13. *Exact no more*] πράσσετε, make no more of your places, than ye may with a good conscience. Shun that mystery of iniquity that is crept into most callings. A great part of the

Turk's civil justice at this day is grounded upon Christ's words, "Thou shalt not do what thou wouldest not have done to thee."

Ver. 14. Do violence to no man] Διασείσητε, shake no man by the shoulders, toss no man to and fro to put him into a fright, smite no man with the fist of wickedness. Tamerlane took such order with his soldiers that none were injured by them: if any soldier of his had but taken an apple or the like from any man, he died for it. One of his soldiers having taken a little milk from a country-woman, and she thereof complaining, he caused the said soldier to be presently killed, and his stomach to be ript, where the milk that he had of late drunk being found, he contented the woman, and so sent her away, who had otherwise undoubtedly died for her false accusation, had it not so appeared.

Neither accuse any falsely] Get nothing by sycophancy, Μηδὲ συκοφαντήσητε. Oppress no man either by force or fraud, and forged cavillation, as it is rendered, Luke xix. 8.

Ver. 15. Whether he were the Christ] Yet John did no miracle, but he was a burning and a shining light, he thundered in his doctrine and lightened in his life. Hence was he so much admired.

Ver. 16. The latchet of whose shoes, &c.] By this expression the Baptist acknowledgeth Christ's godhead, as did also Mary by washing his feet. But what doth the pope that holds forth his feet to be kissed? Is not this he that sits as God in the temple of God? Is not this *Dominus Deus noster Papa?* Learned he not this abominable insolency of Dioclesian, that bloody persecutor? who as he was the first Roman emperor that would be worshipped as God, so he was the first that wore shoes embellished with precious stones, and held forth his feet to be kissed of his prostrate suitors. (Eutropius.)

Ver. 17. Whose fan] viz. The preaching of the gospel.

Ver. 18. And many other things preached he] Being *concionator admirabilis* (as Keckerman saith of Jeremy), an admirable preacher, full of pregnant instructions and admonitions, he did no miracle indeed, but he uttered many sweet oracles, which St Luke here passeth over, that he may hasten to speak of Christ, his main design.

Ver. 19. For Herodias his brother Philip's wife] Whom it was not lawful for Herod to have, though Philip were dead, as Josephus saith he was. This was the case so much controverted here and beyond seas in Henry VIII.'s time, touching his marriage with his brother Arthur's widow, by Papal dispensation. The king had first a scruple cast into his mind about it by the bishop of Baion, the French ambassador, who came to him to consult of a marriage between the Lady Mary and the Duke of Orleans, whether Mary were legitimate, &c. This gave occasion to the casting the pope's authority out of England. Mary was forced, for fear of death, to renounce the bishop of Rome, and to acknow-

ledge her mother's marriage to have been incestuous and unjust, &c. Though afterwards she set up the pope here again, and it was her policy so to get and keep the crown upon her head.

And for all the evils which Herod, &c.] John reproved him with the same liberty that Herod committed them. So did John Chrysostom the great ones of his time. *Ita quidem ut etiam Ducum, Eutropii et Gainæ, imo ipsius Imperatoris errata reprehenderet:* he spared not dukes, princes, nay, not the Emperor himself. (Osiand. Hist. Eccles. Cent. 5.)

Ver. 20. Added yet this] There is no stint in sin; but as one wedge makes way for another, so here. As after Jonathan and his armour-bearer, came the whole host, so.

Ver. 21. And praying, the heaven was opened] Prayer is the key of God's kingdom, and must be used, as at other times, so especially when we or ours receive the sacraments; though the most, if urged hereto, must say, if they say truly, as 1 Sam. xvii. 39, I cannot go with these accoutrements, for I am not accustomed to them.

Ver. 22.] See the note on Matt. iii. 16, 17.

Ver. 23. Being, as was supposed] But falsely: for Joseph was no more than his *Pater politicus*, as Postellus calleth him, his foster-father, reputed father.

Which was the son of Eli] That is, his son-in-law. For Eli was Mary's natural father; and it is Mary's genealogy that is here described; but put upon Joseph, because the Hebrews reckon not their genealogies by women, but by men only. (So Ruth i. 11—13.)

Ver. 24, 25, &c.] St Luke reckoneth from the last of Christ's progenitors to the first. And first he mentioneth private men, not read of in the Scriptures. 2. Captains after the Babylonish captivity. 3. Kings and men of great name in and before the captivity. 4. Private persons again before David up to the patriarchs. 5. Lastly, the patriarchs themselves up to Adam the protoplast, the first and common parent.

Ver. 27. Which was the son of Neri] Salathiel was naturally the son of Neri, but legally, and by succession, the son of Jechoniah, Matt. iv. 12, for he succeeded him in the kingdom. Neri, which signifieth my candle, seemeth to have been so named from the candle which the Lord reserved for David and his house, 2 Chron. xxi. 7.

Ver. 30. Which was the son of Simeon] Our Saviour's genealogy is here the more accurately described, because there were that would have substituted and put false Christs upon the Church, Ezra ii. 62. The priests that could not produce their genealogies were outed.

Ver. 34, 35. Which was the son of Thara] So there are reckoned ten generations from Abraham to Noah. And again, ten from Noah to Adam.

Ver. 36. Which was the son of Cainan] This name crept, by some means, into the Greek copies after Jerome's time, say Beza and Paræus.

Others say that St Luke herein followed the Septuagint's translation, out of wisdom and charity to the Hellenists or Greek-Jews that had received it, and read it. 2. That writing for heathens, he followed the heathen's Bible in his quotations. 3. That in his genealogies he was to be a copier, not a corrector.

Ver. 38. *Which was the Son of God*] Not by generation, but creation. Therefore the Syriac translator hath it *Demen Elaha, A Deo*, of God, not *Bar Elaha*, the Son of God.

CHAPTER IV.

Ver. 1. *Returned from Jordan, and was led*] No sooner out of the water of baptism, but in the fire of temptation. After greatest feelings, we are to expect sharpest assaults; neither can we better quench the devil's fiery darts, than with the water of baptism. We read, saith Luther, of a certain holy virgin, who, whensoever solicited to sin, would stop the tempter's mouth with this one answer, *Christiana sum*, I am a Christian. *Intellexit enim hostis statim virtutem baptismi et fidei—et fugit ab ea.* Satan could not abide the mention of baptism, but fled from her presently.

Ver. 2. *Being forty days*] During which time he was set upon all sorts of temptations. These three here recorded were likely the very worst, *in quibus diabolus omnes astus et fraudis suæ sacculos deplevit* (as one saith), wherein the devil did his utmost.

Ver. 3. *Command this stone*] "Bread of deceit is sweet to a man; but afterwards his mouth shall be filled with gravel," Prov. xx. 17. Compare this verse with verse 9, and see how the devil usually tempteth by extremes, to make men offend either in defect or excess. Thus he tempted master Knox upon his death-bed, if not to despair, then to presume that heaven should be his, for his zeal in the Scottish Reformation. (Perkins.)

Ver. 4.] See Matt. iv. 4.

Ver. 5. *Showed unto him all the kingdoms*] In a visible landscape of his own making, presented to the eye.

Ver. 6. *To whomsoever I will I give it*] The pope, as heir to the devil, takes upon him to be *Dominus regnorum mundi*. Boniface VIII. wrote to Philip, king of France, that he was Lord of all, both temporals and spirituals, in all countries. *Os papæ et culeus diaboli in eodem sunt prædicamento*, saith one. But, *Cui volo do illa* is God's only to say, Dan. iv. 22.

Ver. 7. *If thou wilt worship*] *Papa dulia adorandus*, say the Canonists.

Ver. 8. *Get thee behind me*] See the note on Matt. iv. 10.

Ver. 9—12.] See notes on Matt. iv. 9—11.

Ver. 13. *He departed from him for a season*] We must look for the other bout, and in a calm prepare for a storm. The tempter is restless and impudent; so that a man is to expect, if he live out his days, to be urged to all sins, to the breach of every branch of the ten commandments, and to be put to it in respect of every article of the Creed.

Ver. 14. *In the power of the Spirit*] Without which the word is preached to no purpose. *Cathedram in cælo habet, qui corda docet*, saith Augustine. It is with the word and spirit, as with the veins and arteries; as the veins carry the blood, so the arteries carry the spirits to quicken the blood.

Ver. 15. *Glorified of all*] Envy itself was throttled, which yet usually waits upon virtue. Every Zopyrus hath his Zoilus. Lipsius complaineth (*an Justus ipse viderit*) that now-a-days men have left off, not only to do things praiseworthy, but also to praise those that do so.

Ver. 16. *Where he had been brought up*] The Jews were to be kind to the Egyptians, and to pray for the prosperity of Babylon, where they had been bred and fed. "Be ye thankful," Colos. iii. 15, viz. to your friends and benefactors.

And stood up for to read] In honour of the word that he read. So Neh. viii. 5, a commendable custom.

Ver. 17. *He found the place*] Whether he looked for it, or it so fell out by a providence, it is uncertain. Origen, after his fall, lighting on that text, Psal. l., "What hast thou to do to take my words," &c., fell into a passion of weeping, and came out of the pulpit, as not able to speak to the people. Augustine hearing from heaven, *Tolle, lege*, and happening upon that place, Rom. xiii. 14, "Put ye on the Lord Jesus Christ," &c., was presently converted thereby. So was Cyprian, by reading the prophecy of Jonah.

Ver. 18. *He hath anointed me to preach*] Therefore the gospel is a sure saying, and worthy of all acceptation, sith it is an effect of the Holy Spirit: doubt not of its excellency, authority, certainty, sufficiency. See my "True Treasure."

Ver. 19. *The acceptable year of the Lord*] A joyful jubilee. Let us not stand out the time, lest we be bored in the ear by the devil.

Ver. 20. *Were fastened on him*] A good help against distractions. Our hearts are fickle and fugitive, if not hard held to it.

Ver. 21. *This day is this scripture, &c.*] This the sum of his sermon, as were also the prophecies we read, the heads only and short notes of the prophets' larger discourses. Brevity breeds obscurity.

Ver. 22. *Is not this Joseph's son?*] And what of that? But it is still the course of our hearers, to look round about us, if possibly they may find any hole in our coat, through which to slight and slip the cords of our doctrine, though they cannot but admire it.

Ver. 23. *Physician, heal thyself*] That is, thy country. So that for a man to cure his country, is to cure himself.

Ver. 24. *No prophet is accepted*] See the note on Matt. xiii. 57.

Ver. 25. *Many widows were in Israel*] q. d. God hath mercy on whom he will have mercy,

&c. He is a free agent, and may do with his own as he pleaseth. If the prophets, by the Spirit's direction, healed and helped foreigners sooner than Israelites, what so great wonder that Christ did not that for his own country that he did for others?

Ver. 26. *That was a widow*] A calamitous name, 2 Sam. xiv. 5. The Hebrews call her Almanah, a dumb woman, because either she dare not or may not speak for herself: but God professeth himself the patron of such; and he can speak for them in the hearts of their greatest adversaries. Happy they in such an advocate.

Ver. 27. *Naaman the Syrian*] Nor he neither so long as he looked upon God's Jordan with Syrian eyes.

Ver. 28. *And all they in the synagogue*] Though but plain rustics, yet they soon understood this saying of preaching to the Gentiles: which put them into an anger, and our Saviour into a danger.

Ver. 29. *Thrust him out of the city*] As unworthy to tread on their pavement. And so mad they were, that they could neither stay till the business were brought to a judicial trial, nor forbear execution till the sabbath were over.

Ver. 30. *But he passing, &c.*] Like a second Samson; his own arm saved him. This might have convinced his adversaries, but that they were mad with malice.

Ver. 31. *And came down to Capernaum*] Contempt drives away Christ. And woe be unto you if I forsake you, Hos. ix. 12. Contend earnestly for the faith, sith it is but once delivered to the saints, Jude 3. You must never expect another edition of it.

Ver. 32. *For his word was with power*] He preached not *frigide et trepide*, as the scribes: but uttered oracles, and did miracles.

Ver. 33. *And in the synagogue*] See notes on Mark i. 23.

Ver. 34. *The Holy One of God*] The pope will needs be called "Most Holy;" and so lifts up himself above Christ.

Ver. 34—37, &c.] See notes on Mark i. 23, 24, and on Matt. viii. 14—16, &c.

CHAPTER V.

Ver. 1. *As the people pressed upon him*] THIS was both an argument of the truth of his humanity (that he was thronged and thrust together by the unmannerly multitude) and a part of his passion.

Ver. 2. *Were washing their nets*] Though they laboured last night, and had taken nothing. *Ferendum et sperandum.* Hope beguiles calamity, as good company doth the way.

Ver. 3. *He prayed him*] Gr. He gently asked him, ἠρώτησεν, will you be pleased to thrust out a little? See Phil. ii. 8, 9. *Posse et nolle, nobile est.*

Taught the people out of the ship] Any place served him for a pulpit. So if men be desirous to hear, they will make a mat a seat, a pair of legs a seat.

Ver. 4. *Let down your nets*] This is the fare he pays them, for the use of their ship. No man loseth by Christ.

Ver. 5. *We have toiled all night, &c.*] *Omnia feci, et nihil expedit,* said Severus the emperor. (Spartian.) See Hab. ii. 13; Hag. ii. 6. If God stop not that hole in the bottom of the bag, all will run through.

And have taken nothing] If ministers be put so to complain, it is to be feared that Satan caught the fish ere they came at their net.

Ver. 6. *And their net brake*] Yet the fishes got not out, which some note for another miracle.

Ver. 7. *Filled both the ships*] Here the dumb fishes do clearly preach Christ to be the Son of God.

Ver. 8. *For I am a sinful man*] Gr. A man a sinner, ἀνὴρ ἁμαρτωλὸς, a very mixture and compound of dirt and sin. See the like phrase, Numb. xxxii. 14.

Ver. 9. *And he was astonished*] Gr. Fear seized upon him, and surrounded him, περίεσχεν, as Tacitus saith, *Induere pavores.*

Ver. 10. *Thou shalt catch men*] See the note on Matt. iv. 19.

Ver. 11. *They forsook all, and followed him*] They had given their names to him before, John i. 43; but now they see by this miracle his power to provide for them, they leave all to live with him. We love to see how we shall subsist.

Ver. 12. *If thou wilt, thou canst*] It is a ready way to speed, to found our prayers upon the power of God.

Ver. 13. *I will, be thou clean*] So ready is Christ to gratify his suppliants, yea, to be commanded by them, Isa. xlv. 11.

Ver. 14. *For a testimony unto them*] For a Bill of Indictment against them. Reprobates shall give a heavy account to God of all the means and offers of grace.

Ver. 15. *But so much the more*] Fame follows them that fly from it, and the contrary: as the crocodile doth.

Ver. 16. *And he withdrew*] Pray, if you mean to prosper.

Ver. 17. *And the power of the Lord*] So it is, when any ordinance is afoot.

Ver. 18. *And, behold, men brought*] See the notes on Matt. viii. 2, 3, &c., and on Mark ii. 3, &c.

Ver. 19. *They went upon the house-top*] Which (according to the custom of building in those Eastern countries) was flat laid, and surrounded with battlements, Deut. xxii. 8.

Ver. 20. *Thy sins are forgiven thee*] Let our sicknesses mind us of our sins, that we soon seek pardon.

Ver. 23. *Whether is easier*] q. d. Neither of either: for both are equally hard, and feasible to God alone.

Ver. 24, 25, &c.] See Matt. ix. 2, &c.; Mark ii. 3, &c.

Ver. 26. *Strange things*] Gr. παράδοξα, paradoxes, things that we never thought to have seen; and above belief, had we not seen them.

Ver. 29. And Levi made him a great feast] *Epulum splendidum*, a sumptuous feast; so St Luke's word δοχὴν here signifieth. But when St Matthew himself speaks of it, he saith only that Christ came home and eat bread with him: to teach us, saith one, that another man's mouth should praise us, and not our own, Prov. xxvii. 2. See the note.

Ver. 33, 34, &c.] See Matt. ix. 14; Mark ii. 18.

Ver. 35. And then shall they fast] This is fulfilled, saith Bellarmine, in our Lent fasts. But this was fulfilled, say we, when Christ was crucified, and the apostles mourned. Papists set fasts are mere mock fasts.

Ver. 39. The old is better] That is, milder, and so pleasanter. *Vetustate enim vina mitescunt, quia vetustas igneum calorem, acerbitatem, et fæces e vino tollit.* (Piscator.) Age clarifies wine, and ripens it.

CHAPTER VI.

Ver. 1. On the second sabbath after the first] Jerome saith that he asked Nazianzen what this second sabbath after the first was. Nazianzen answered, I'll tell you that when I come next into the pulpit, for there you cannot contradict me. *Ita per jocum dixit* (saith Melancthon) *quod hodie serio multi imitantur.* See the note on Matt. xii. 1.

Ver. 2. That which is not lawful] Our Saviour grants that it had not been lawful indeed, but in case of hard hunger.

Ver. 3. Have ye not read] Yes, over and over, but either understood not, or, through malice, dissembled it. *Quilibet nostrum de lege interrogatus facilius quam nomini suo respondet*, saith Josephus. The Jews were all very well versed in the Scriptures.

Ver. 4, 5.] See Matt. xii. 3, 4; Mark ii. 24.

Ver. 6. And it came to pass] See the notes on Matt. xii. 9—11, &c.

Ver. 11. They were filled with madness] That is, with extreme rage and anger, which is a short madness—*Et rectam tollit de cardine mentem.*

Ver. 12. He went out into a mountain to pray] He premiseth prayer, being to make choice of the twelve. If Eliezer prayed when to seek a wife for Isaac, Gen. xxiv.; if Solomon prayed for wisdom, ere he set upon the temple work; if Ezra fasted and prayed ere he committed the golden and silver vessels to them that kept them, Ezra viii. 21, 30; should there not prayer be made for ministers ere they be set over God's house and people?

Ver. 13. And of them he chose] See notes on Matt. x. 1.

Ver. 14—16.] See notes on Matt. x. 12, &c.; Mark iii. 14; vi. 7.

Ver. 17. And stood in the plain] And yet he delivered the same sermon (in effect) that he delivered at another time, sitting on the mount, Matt. v. 2, δὶς καὶ τρὶς τὰ καλὰ.

Ver. 18. And they that were vexed] This was more uncomfortable and incurable than other natural diseases. *Sed omnipotenti medico nullus insanabilis occurrit morbus*, saith Isidore; to an Almighty physician no disease can be incurable.

Ver. 20. Blessed be ye poor] Here we have a repetition of that famous sermon on the mount, Matt. v. 6, 7. See the notes there.

Ver. 21. See Matt. v. 4, 6.

Ver. 22. And cast out your name] *Ubicunque invenitur nomen Calvini, deleatur,* saith the Index Expurgatorius. Persecutors proscribe true professors, *tanquam nequissimos et lucis hujus usurâ indignos.* After John Huss was burnt, his adversaries got his heart, which was left untouched by the fire, and beat it with their staves. A friar preaching to the people at Antwerp, wished that Luther were there, that he might bite out his throat with his teeth, as Erasmus testifieth. (Ep. xvi. *ad obtrectat.*)

Ver. 23.] See Matt. v. 12.

Ver. 24. But woe unto you that are rich] sc. In this world only, and not to God-ward. See notes on James v. 1—3. Every grain of riches hath a vermin of pride and ambition in it.

Ver. 25. Woe unto you that laugh now] Worldlings' jollity is but as a book fairly bound, which, when it is opened, is full of nothing but tragedies.

Ver. 26. When all men shall speak well] What evil have I done, said Aristides, when one told him he had every man's good word. *Male de me loquuntur, sed mali*, saith Seneca. *Malis displicere, laudari est.* When Doeg blasted David, he thinks the better of himself, Psal. lii. 8. Latimer says he was glad when any objected indiscretion against him in his sermons; for by that he knew the matter was good, else they would soon have condemned that.

Ver. 27, 28.] See Matt. v. 44; Rom. xii. 20.

Ver. 29. That smiteth thee on the one cheek] Socrates, when one gave him a box on the ear in the market-place, said, *Quam molestum est nescire homines quando prodire debeant cum galea?* What an odd thing it is to go abroad without a head-piece.

Ver. 30. Give to every man, &c.] General Norrice never thought he had that that he gave not away. It is not lack, but love of money, that maketh men churls. Men believe not that of Martial,

Extra fortunam est quicquid donatur egenis;
Quas dederis solas semper habebis opes.

Ask them not again] Or if thou take the benefit of the law to recover them, do it without hate or heat; as tilters break their spears on each other's breasts, yet without wrath or intention of hurt.

Ver. 31. And as ye would that men, &c.] The most part of the Turk's civil justice is grounded upon this rule, as is above noted.

Ver. 32.] See Matt. v. 46.

Ver. 34.] See Matt. v. 42.

Ver. 35. *Lend, hoping for nothing*] No, not the principal, in case thy brother be not able to repay it. Thomas Tomkins, martyr, a weaver, dwelling in Shoreditch, whensoever any had come to borrow money of him, would show them such money as he had in his purse, and bid them take it; and when they came to repay it again, so far was he from usury, that he would bid them keep it longer till they were better able. (Acts and Mon.) The usurer breeding money of money to the third and fourth generation, prove like the butler's box (saith one), which at length draws all the counters to it. Our Saviour, in the former verse, maketh him worse than other sinners, who lend to receive the like; but he lends to receive the more.

To the unthankful and to the evil] An unthankful man is a naughty man; nay, he is an ugly man, Psal. cxlvii. 1.

Ver. 36.] See the note on Matt. v. 48.

Ver. 37.] See Matt. vii. 1.

Ver. 38. *Into your bosom*] The Jews wore large and loose garments so that they could bear away much in their bosoms. Hence this expression.

Ver. 39.] See Matt. xv. 14.

Ver. 40.] See Matt. x. 24.

Ver. 41.] See Matt. vii. 3.

Ver. 43.] See Matt. vii. 16.

Ver. 44, 45.] See Matt. xii. 33—35.

Ver. 46.] See Matt. vii. 21; Mal. i. 6.

Ver. 47.] See Matt. vii. 24.

Ver. 48. *When the flood arose*] Every man is that in truth, that he is in a temptation.

Ver. 49. *And immediately it fell*] Want of due humiliation, at first conversion, is the ground of apostasy; unless there be care to do it better afterwards, and to make up that which is yet wanting; to cast up the loose earth, *ut in solido extruat*, as Vitruvius adviseth his builder. (Architect. i. 5.)

CHAPTER VII.

Ver. 1.] See Matt. viii. 5.

Ver. 2. *And a certain centurion's servant*] Piscator thinks that this history is not the same with that Matt. viii. 5. His reasons may be read in his Scholia on that place.

Ver. 3. *He sent unto him*] St Matthew saith, he went unto him, *sc.* by his messengers.

Ver. 4. *That he was worthy*] So they held him: but he held himself unworthy, ver. 6. God in like manner saith that Jerusalem had received double for her sins, Isa. xl. 2. But Jerusalem herself saith, Our God hath punished us less than our sins, Ezra ix. 13. Too much, saith God; Too little, saith she; and yet how sweetly and beautifully doth this kind of contradiction become both?

Ver. 5. *Built us a synagogue*] Antiochus had burnt up the synagogues in sundry places. This man, now converted, is content to be at cost for God and his people. So the Israelites, received to favour again after their foul fall in setting up the golden calf, brought enough and to spare toward the work of the tabernacle.

Ver. 6. *For I am not worthy*] So saith Jacob of himself, Gen. xxxii. 10; so Paul, 1 Cor. xv.; so the Baptist, Matt. iii.; so Augustine, *Non sum dignus quem tu diligas, Domine*, I am not worthy of thy love, Lord.

Ver. 7. *But say in a word*] Send thy Mandamus, as Psal. xliv. 4.

Ver. 8. *For I also*] See the note on Matt. viii. 9.

Ver. 9. *He marvelled*] See the note on Matt. viii. 10.

Ver. 10.] See Matt. viii. 13.

Ver. 11. *A city called Nain*] A fair town not far from Tiberias, and watered by that ancient river, the river Kishon, Judges v. 21, as saith Jerome.

Ver. 12. *There was a dead man*] Though a young man. Our decrepit age both expects death and solicits it, but vigorous youth looks strangely upon that grim sergeant of God. *Senibus mors in januis, adolescentibus in insidiis*, (Bern.) Death seizeth on old men, and lays wait for the youngest.

Carried out] *sc.* Out of the city, for without the gates were the burying-places of old, for fear of annoyance by ill air. Hence harlots were called *mœchæ bustuariæ*, because they were thrust out of the city to play their pranks, where the dead were buried, as being dead while they lived. (Turneb. *Adversar.*)

Ver. 13. *He had compassion on her*] Of his own free accord, and unrequested, he raised him. Christ had a most tender heart. How shall he not pity and provide for his praying people?

Ver. 14. *Young man, I say unto thee, Arise*] Had he said as much to all the dead (as once he shall, *Surgite mortui, venite in judicium*) they had certainly all risen immediately.

Ver. 15. *Delivered him to his mother*] To be a Scipio to her; the staff and stay of her old age.

Ver. 16. *And there came a fear upon all*] This was *timor amicalis*, a fear of reverence, for it produced thankfulness.

Ver. 17. *And this rumour*] Here the Sun of righteousness, that hath healing in his wings, shone forth in his strength, and drew all eyes to him.

Ver. 18. *And the disciples of John*] Having a zeal for their master, but not according to knowledge, see Matt. xi. 2.

Ver. 19. *Art thou he that should come*] The soul resteth not till it pitch upon Christ. See the notes on Matt. xi. 2, &c.

Ver. 20—22, &c.] See notes on Matt. xi. 2.

Ver. 23. *And blessed is he*] This is check to them for their preposterous zeal for John, their master. Therefore, also, our Saviour commends not John till they were departed.

Ver. 28. *But he that is least*] This is no small comfort to the ministers of the gospel, against the contempts cast upon them by the world. They are somebodies in heaven, whatever men make of them.

Ver. 29. *Justified God*] i. e. They glorified his word, Acts xiii. 48, and acknowledged his righteousness, repenting of their sins, and believing John's and Christ's testimony, which the Pharisees so pertinaciously rejected, and so deservedly perished. For as wine, a strong remedy against hemlock, yet mingled with it doubleth the force of the poison; so it is with the word when mingled with unbelief, and cast away with contempt.

Ver. 30. *Rejected the counsel of God*] Being *ingrati gratiæ Dei*, as Ambrose speaketh, and so much the further off, for that they saw the people so forward.

Ver. 31.] See Matt. xi. 16, 17, &c.

Ver. 33. *Neither eating bread*] But locusts and wild honey.

Ver. 35. *Of all her children*] That is, her disciples, Psal. xxxiv. 11.

Ver. 36. *Sat down to meat*] It was fit he should feast sometimes, that fared so hard mostly.

Ver. 37. *A woman*] Not that woman, say some, mentioned Matt. xxvi. 6, and John xi. 2, but some other.

A sinner] A strumpet, a she-sinner, as their mates call such.

Ver. 38. *To wash his feet*] They that make their eyes a fountain to wash Christ's feet in, shall have his side for a fountain to wash their souls in.

Kissed his feet] But how many now refuse those kisses of his mouth, Cant. i. 2, by despising the word preached, that sweet pledge of his love!

Ver. 39. *This man, if he were a prophet*] See the picture of a hypocrite, slighting and censuring his betters.

What manner of woman this is] Syr. What an ill name she hath, for a light hussy.

Ver. 40. *I have somewhat to say to thee*] He that receives a courtesy, we say, sells his liberty. But so did not Christ at Simon's, at Martha's, &c., table. His mouth was not stopped with good cheer. He entertains the Pharisees with as many menaces as they do him with messes of meat.

Ver. 41. *There was a certain creditor*] Christ tells the supercilious and self-conceited Pharisee by this parable, that himself was a sinner also as well as the woman, and as a debtor to God's judgment, had as much need of his grace in Christ for remission of sin and removal of wrath.

Ver. 42. *And when they had nothing to pay*] We are all non-solvents, stark beggars, and bankrupts, having nothing of our own but sin and hell; nothing to say for ourselves why we should not to prison, but that of Augustine, *Ego admisi, Domine, unde tu damnare potes me, sed non amisisti, unde tu salvare potes me;* Lord, I have done enough to undo me for ever, but thou hast yet enough to make me happy for ever. I acknowledge the debt, that is all I can do. Oh cross the book, and draw the red lines of Christ's blood over the black lines of my sins.

Ver. 43. *Thou hast rightly judged*] See here

and imitate our Saviour's candour: *cui virtuti per se pulcherrimæ grande pretium raritas addidit, nostro quidem ævo*, saith one, this is a rare and rich virtue.

Ver. 44. *She hath washed my feet with tears*] Her heart was a sacred limbeck, out of which those tears were distilled. Never did any man read his pardon with dry eyes.

Washed my feet with tears, &c.] We read not that the Virgin Mary ever did as this greater sinner did. Repentance is the fair child of that foul mother, sin, as the Romans said of Pompey, Εχθροῦ πατρὸς φίλτατον τέκνον. And it is question whether more glorifies God, innocence or penitence?

Ver. 45. *Thou gavest me no kiss*] Which yet was their usual way of salutation, 1 Pet. v. 14.

Ver. 46. *Mine head with oil*] Which yet was ordinary at solemn feasts. But Simon was too short, as not understanding the worth of his present guest.

Ver. 47. *For she loved much*] Nam, notificativum est, non impulsivum. Her love was an argument (not a cause) that her sins were forgiven her.

Ver. 48. *Thy sins are forgiven thee*] Melancthon makes mention of a godly woman, who having upon her death-bed been much conflicted, and afterwards much comforted, brake out into these words, Now, and not till now, I understand the meaning of those words, Thy sins are forgiven. It is storied of another, that courting a courtesan, and understanding that her name was Mary; he remembered Mary Magdalen, and forbearing to commit that act of filthiness that he intended, became a sound convert.

Ver. 49. *Who is this that forgiveth sins also?*] Ignorance of Christ and his office bred this offence, as it doth many others. It is easy to stumble in the dark.

Ver. 50. *Go in peace*] Faith hath *virtutem pacativam*, Rom. v. 1. It lodgeth a blessed calm in the conscience, and fortifies the heart against all discouragements. Men may mutter, as here they did, but the answer, or rather demand of faith is, Who shall condemn? it is Christ that justifieth, Rom. viii. 34. Better be envied then pitied.

CHAPTER VIII.

Ver. 1. *He went through every city*] To teach us unweariableness in God's work. He went about doing good: so should we, waiting all opportunities.

Ver. 2. *Which had been healed*] Exod. xxxi. After sickness they were to offer to God the ransom of their lives. Hezekiah testified his thankfulness for recovery by a song; these good women, by following Christ; when they might have staid at home with more ease to themselves, and more thank of their friends. Nay, very heathens, after a fit of sickness, would consecrate something to their gods.

Mary, called Magdalen, out of whom went seven devils] Which some interpret of seven deadly sins.

Ver. 3. *Joanna the wife of Chuza, Herod's steward*] Or treasurer, as the Arabic calleth him, his vicar-general, or protetrarch. This court-lady followeth Christ: so did Serena the empress, who was therefore martyred by her husband Dioclesian. So Elizabeth, Queen of Denmark ; of whom Luther testifieth (in Epist. ad Jo. Agricol.) that she died a faithful professor of the reformed religion ; and addeth, *Scilicet Christus etiam aliquando voluit Reginam in cœlum vehere.* Christ would once save a queen: which he doth not often.

Ver. 4. *And when much people, &c.*] See the notes on Matt. xiii. 2, 3, &c.

Ver. 11.] See Matt. xiii. 18.

Ver. 12. *Taketh away the word*] Lest, if it should lie long upon their hard hearts, it should break through them with its weight, as being able to save their souls, Jam. i. 21.

Ver. 13. *With joy*] Which yet was but a flash.

Ver. 14. *Go forth, &c.*] viz. About their worldly businesses ; which, as the lean kine in Pharaoh's dream, devour the fat, and it is nothing seen by them. After awhile they remember no more than the man in the moon doth, what they had heard delivered.

Ver. 15. *In an honest*] Referred to the end and intent in the action.

And good heart] In respect of inward renewed qualities.

Having heard the word, keep it.] As food or physic, which if not kept, profiteth not. They incorporate it into their souls, so as it becomes an ingrafted word ; they are transformed into the same image, conformed to the heavenly pattern.

With patience] Or, with tarriance for the fit season, ἐν ὑπομονῇ. Not as that rath-ripe fruit, ver. 13, and Psal. cxxix.

Ver. 16. *No man, when he hath lighted, &c.*] *q. d.* Though to you it is given to know mysteries, &c., as verse 10, yet not for your own use only, but that your light may shine before men.

Ver. 17.] See Matt. xvi. 26 ; Mark iv. 22 ; Luke xii. 2.

Ver. 18. *Take heed therefore how ye hear*] For else ye shall neither bear good fruits, nor be borne with for your barrenness. All shall out, and you shall smart for it.

Even that which he seemeth to have] There is a great deal of seemingness abroad ; and every grace hath its counterfeit. *Simia quam similis, turpissima bestia, nobis,* saith Ennius. But God strips men of common gifts ; and counterfeit complexion will not long hold.

Ver. 19—21.] See Matt. xii. 46 ; Mark iii. 31.

Ver. 22, 23, &c.] See Matt. viii. 23 ; Mark iv. 36.

Ver. 25. *Where is your faith ?*] It is not the having faith, but the living by it, the actuating of it, that helps us in an exigence.

Ver. 26.] See Matt. viii. 28 ; Mark v. 2.

Ver. 27. *A certain man which had devils*] All Pharaoh's cruelty exercised over the Israelites, was nothing to this. Oh then the inexpressible torments of the damned ! *Utinam ubique de Gehenna dissereretur !* saith a Father (Chrysostom). I could wish men would discourse much and oft of hell.

Ver. 29. *And was driven of the devil*] As a horse is by his rider (so the word ἠλαύνετο signifieth) or a ship with oars. All wicked men are acted and agitated by the devil, Eph. ii. 2, persecutors especially. *Quod si videris aliquando persecutorem tuum nimis sævientem, scito quia ab ascensore suo diabolo perurgetur.* If persecutors sometimes be more moderate, it is because the devil spurs not so hard. (Bernard.)

Ver. 30. *And he said, Legion*] We must be ready and well-appointed to resist ; for the devil sets upon us not without military discipline and singular skill. *Cataphractus incedit Satan,* saith Luther. The devil marcheth well armed and in good array.

Ver. 31. *To go out into the deep.*] *i. e.* Hell, that bottomless deep, Rev. xx. 3 ; 2 Pet. ii. 4, where they could do no more hurt: which would be another hell unto them. Augustus, consulting Apollo's oracle, was told, that a Hebrew child had stopped his mouth, and sent him with a mittimus to hell, &c. (Pucer *de Orac.*)

Ver. 33. *And the herd ran violently*] So would the possessed man soon have done, but that God preserved him.

Ver. 35. *Sitting at the feet of Jesus*] As fearing lest, if he departed, he should be repossessed. So we see it is an old error and weakness for men to be too strongly conceited of Christ's corporeal presence.

Ver. 36, 37.] See Matt. viii. 33, 34.

Ver. 38. *Sent him away*] Christ would not have him depend upon his bodily presence, but upon his Almighty power.

Ver. 39. *Show how great things*] This was all the fee Christ called for for all his cures. He is content that we have the benefit, so he may have the glory of what he does for us.

Ver. 40. *When Jesus was returned.*] viz. Into Galilee, where he was highly honoured.

Ver. 41, 42, &c.] See Matt. ix. 18 ; Mark v. 22.

CHAPTER IX.

Ver. 1, 2, &c.] See Matt. x. 1 ; Mark iii. 13 ; vi. 7.

Ver. 3. *Take nothing for your journey*] But preach the gospel, and depend upon divine providence. Look you to your work, and God will take care for your wages. This the disciples might do, but this was no warrant to those *male-feriati* amongst us, who (if fame belie them not) pretending to an immediate call from God to go and preach the gospel in Galilee, sold their estates, set forward for that place, taking neither scrip nor scrap with them ; resolving to trust God for their necessary sustentation. Is not this the efficacy of error? Are not these *a diabolo dementatis,* besotted by the devil?

Ver. 5.] See Matt. x. 14; Mark vi. 11; Luke x. 11; Acts xiii. 51.

Ver. 6. *And healing everywhere*] Those miracles of healing ascribed to Vespasian by heathen historians (Dio *et alii*), but falsely, do belong properly and alone to Christ's disciples.

Ver. 7. *And he was perplexed*] *Pendebat, animi dubius.* He stood amused and amazed : he stuck in the mud, as it were, and could find no way out. This is the import of the Greek word διηπόρει. Thus the wicked in the fulness of his sufficiency is in straits, as Zophar hath it, Job xv. 22.

Ver. 8.] See Matt. xiv. 1, 2.

Ver. 9. *And he desired to see him*] With a faint and fruitless desire : for he never stirred out of doors to see Christ, though he believed that God had raised him from the dead. So true is that of Abraham, Luke xvi. 31. Perhaps he desired to see whether it were John or not.

Ver. 10.] See Matt. xiv. 13; Mark vi. 30, 32.

Ver. 11. *And he received them*] Weary though he were, yet never weary of well-doing.

Ver. 12.] See Matt. xiv. 15; Mark vi. 35; John vi. 5.

Ver. 13. *Except we should go, &c.*] Which is a thing not only improbable, but impossible. They held it an absurd notion.

Ver. 14—17.] *Vide ubi supra.*

Ver. 18.] *As he was alone praying*] *Examinationi preces præmittendæ.* All our sacrifices should be salted with this salt.

Ver. 19. *But some say Elias*] This Pythagorean transanimation is held by the Jews to this day, viz. (*ut singuli tertio renascantur*) against so many clear testimonies of Scripture to the contrary.

Ver. 20.] See Matt. xvi. 13, 14; Mark viii. 28.

Ver. 22.] See Matt. xvii. 22.

Ver. 23, 24.] See Matt. x. 38; Mark xvi. 24; Luke xiv. 27; xvii. 33.

Ver. 25.] See Matt. xvi. 26; Mark viii. 36.

Ver. 26.] See Matt. x. 33; Mark viii. 38; Luke xii. 9; 2 Tim. ii. 12.

Ver. 27.] See Matt. xvi. 28; Mark ix. 1.

Ver. 28. *About eight days*] Putting the two utmost days also into the reckoning. See the notes on Matt. xvii. 1, &c.

Ver. 29. *And as he prayed*] *Dum ipsius mens tota Deo se immergeret,* saith one (Luc. Burgens.). Christians, whilst they are praying, are ofttimes carried out and beyond themselves. See Matt. xvii. 2, 3, and the notes there.

Ver. 31. *And spake of his decease*] Gr. of his exodus ; in reference to that expedition or departure of Israel out of Egypt (τὴν ἔξοδον). It signifieth a translating from a condition and state of hardship ; and is also used by St Peter, 2 Pet. i. 15. Death to the saints is but an out-going to heaven, Phil. i. 21, a loosing from the shore of life, and launching out into the main of immortality.

Ver. 34. *There came a cloud*] See the note on Matt. xvii. 5.

Ver. 37.] See Matt. xvii. 14 ; Mark ix. 17, &c.

Ver. 39. *And bruising him*] As in the falling sickness, it falls out.

Ver. 44. *Let these sayings sink, &c.*] *Ponite, reponite,* lay up (θέσθε) the sayings of my sufferings, notwithstanding this people's vain applauses. The best balm cast into water sinks to the bottom ; the baser sort floats on the top.

Ver. 45. *They understood not this saying*] So besotted they were with that carnal conceit of an earthly kingdom, still retained by the Jews to this day.

Ver. 46.] See Matt. xviii. 1; Mark ix. 34.

Ver. 49.] See Mark ix. 38.

Ver. 51. *That he should be received up.*] The word ἀναλήψεως (Poly. Lyser.) implies a metaphor from fathers owning and acknowledging their children after long absence.

He set his face] He steeled his forehead against all discouragements, ἐστήριξε.

Ver. 53. *And they did not receive him*] Such is the hatred that idolaters bear against all God's true worshippers. *Illam domum in qua inventus fuerit hæreticus diruendam decernimus* : It was a decree of the Council of Toulouse against the Albigenses.

Ver. 54. *And when his disciples*] These two brethren, sons of thunder, how soon was their choler up! they had quick and hot spirits.

Wilt thou that we command] It were to be wished that we would first consult with Christ in his word, ere we stir hand or foot to revenge.

Ver. 55. *But he turned and rebuked them*] He did it not slightly, and by-the-by, but seriously, and on set purpose ; so must we rebuke and rebate our vindictive spirits, our unruly lusts, when like kine in a strait they rush and ride one upon the back of another.

Ye know not what manner of spirits ye are of] Not of Elias's spirit, as ye imagine ; this wildfire was never kindled on God's hearth, as his zeal was ; you are men of another mould than Elias. He was a minister of indignation, you of consolation ; his actions fit not you, because your persons are not like his. It is a rare thing to be of an heroical spirit, saith the moralist, Σπάνιον τὸ Θεῖον ἀνδρὰ εἶναι. (Aristot.) Every man cannot be an Elias or a Phineas, Num. xxv. 8. To that height of heat, ordinary men's tempers are not raised.

Ver. 57.] See Matt. viii. 19.

Ver. 58. *And Jesus said unto him*] Christ had felt his pulse and found his temper, that he looked after outward things only ; and therefore he lets him know what to trust unto.

But the Son of man] Ezekiel with the Septuagint is, υἱος ἀνθρώπου, the son of man, but Christ is ὁ υἱος τοῦ ἀνθρώπου, that is, the son of that man, of that first man Adam. He was the next and only other common person.

Ver. 59.] See Matt. viii. 21.

Ver. 62. *No man having put his hand*] Christ here happily alludeth to that which Elisha did, 1 Kings xix. 19. Ploughmen that look back, cannot but make baulks.

CHAPTER X.

Ver. 1. *Other seventy also*] As his heralds, to foreshow his coming to Jerusalem, and to proclaim the true Jubilee.

Ver. 2.] See Matt. ix. 37.

Ver. 3. *Go your ways*] Christ had no sooner bidden them pray, but he answers their prayers. When we bid our children ask us for this or that, it is because we mean to give it them.

As lambs among wolves] *Sed sollicitudo pastoris boni effici ut lupi in agnos audere nil possint*, saith Ambrose. The care of the good shepherd is the safety of the flock.

Ver. 4. *Salute no man*] For that your task is long, your time is little.

Ver. 5—7.] See Matt. x. 11, &c.

Ver. 8. *Such things as they set before you*] Not seeking after dainties. It becomes not a servant of the Highest, to be a slave to his palate. *Epicurei, dum palato prospiciunt, cœli palatium non suspiciunt*, saith the heathen. (Cicero.)

Ver. 9.] See Matt. iii. 2; iv. 17.

Ver. 10.] See Matt. x. 14; Acts xxxviii. 51.

Ver. 11. *That the kingdom of God*] There is in unbelief an odious unthankfulness; such judge themselves unworthy of eternal life, Acts xiii. 44; they are condemned already, John iii. 18.

Ver. 12.] See Matt. xi. 24.

Ver. 13.] See Matt. xi. 21.

Ver. 16. *He that despiseth you*] Julius Pflugius, complaining to the emperor of wrong done to him by the Duke of Saxony, received this answer from him, *Tua causa erit mea causa;* so saith Christ to all his servants. *Causa ut sit magna, magnus est actor et author ejus; neque enim nostra est*, saith Luther to Melancthon.

Ver. 17. *And the seventy returned again with joy*] We are all naturally ambitious, and desirous of vain-glory. A small wind blows up a bubble. Pray down this vanity.

Ver. 18. *Fall from heaven*] That is, from men's hearts, which he accounts his heaven; but is cast out by the mighty gospel.

Ver. 19. *To tread on serpents*] See the note on Mark xvi. 18. Good ministers tread so hard on the old serpent's head, that it is no wonder he turns again, and nibbleth at their heels.

Ver. 20. *That your names are written*] That you are enrolled burgesses of the new Jerusalem. Paul by his privilege of being a Roman escaped whipping; we by this escape damnation. The sinner engrosseth his name in the book of perdition.

Ver. 21. *I thank thee, O Father,* &c.] With this prayer the Anabaptists of Germany usually began their sermons, thinking thereby to excuse their lack of learning. (Scultet. Annal.) And

then protested that they would deliver nothing but what was revealed to them from above.

Ver. 22.] See Matt. xxviii. 18; and John iii. 15.

Ver. 23. *Blessed are the eyes,* &c.] How blessed, then, are they that hear this arch-prophet in heaven. Moses and Elias, conversing with Christ on the mount, could much better discourse of his decease, and other divine doctrines, than ever they could whilst here upon earth. An infant of one day there is much beyond the deepest doctor here.

Ver. 24. *Many prophets and kings*] Many righteous, saith Matthew, xiii. 17. Righteous persons are kings.

Ver. 25.] See Matt. xxii. 35.

Ver. 27. *With all thy heart, and,* &c.] *Serviendum Deo toto corde; id est, amore summo, more vero, ore fideli re omni: Hoc non sit verbis. Marce, ut ameris, ama.* (Martial.)

Here some weak Christians are troubled, as conceiting that they love their children, friends, &c., better than God. But it is answered, 1. When two streams run in one channel (as here nature and grace do) they run stronger than one stream doth. When a man loves God and the things of God, grace is alone; nature yields nothing to that. 2. We must not judge by an indeliberate passion. (D. Sibbs on 1 Cor. ii. 9.) The love of God is a constant stream; not a torrent, but a current, that runs all our life-time, but runs still, and without noise, as the waters of Shiloh and of Nilus, *nullas confessus murmure vires*, that runs smoothly. (Claudian.)

With all thy strength] That is, saith a divine, in our particular places. A magistrate must execute justice for God's sake, &c.

Ver. 28.] See Matt. xix. 17.

Ver. 29. *Who is my neighbour?*] They counted no man their neighbour but their near friends.

Ver. 30. *And Jesus answering*] Gr. ὑπολαβὼν. Taking the tale out of his mouth, being ready with his answer. For he is that *Palmoni Hammedabber*, in Dan. viii. 13, that prime prolocutor.

Ver. 31. *And by chance*] Indeed by the providence of God overruling the matter, as it doth in things that to us are merely casual and contingent.

Ver. 32. *Passed by on the other side*] Αντιπαρῆλθεν. For fear of legal pollution. But two duties never meet so as to cross one another; the one of them yields, and the execution of the yielding duty for the present hath reason of an offence. This Levite's legal strictness was here a vice; he should rather have showed mercy to his brother in misery. So that the rule, negatives always bind, intends not that they are of an indispensable nature; but that every particular instant of time is to be observed for their obedience, while and where they stand of force. (Huet. of Cons.)

Ver. 33. *A certain Samaritan*] *Turnebus dictos putat Parabolanos, quasi æmulos Samaritani. Hoc autem nomine vocabantur, qui curandis de-*

bilium corporibus deputabantur. Those that looked to sick people were hence called Parabolanes, or Samaritans. This Samaritan is Christ. So they called him, John viii. 48, but in a worse sense. See the note there.

Ver. 34. *Pouring in oil and wine*] Wine to search, and oil to supple. Wine signifies the sharpness of the law (saith Melancthon), oil the sweetness of the gospel. Now, so great is the natural sympathy and harmony between the vine and the olive; that the olive being grafted into the vine, brings forth both grapes and olives.

Ver. 35. *Two pence*] The Old and New Testament, say Optatus and Ambrose.

Ver. 36. See the note on ver. 29. God delights to make men their own judges, that they may be self-condemned, αὐτοκατάκριτοι.

Ver. 37. *Go, and do thou likewise*] Help him that hath need of thee, though he be a stranger; yea, or an enemy.

Ver. 38. *A certain village*] viz. Bethany, John xi. 1. See the note there.

Ver. 39. *Sat at Jesus' feet*] As his disciples, Acts xxii. 3. So the children of the prophets of old, whence that expression, "Knowest thou that the Lord will take away thy master from thy head to-day?" 2 Kings ii. 3.

Ver. 40. *Martha was cumbered*] Diversely distracted, περιεσπᾶτο. In multitude of worldly business, the soul is like a mill, where one cannot hear another, the noise is such as taketh away all intercourse. We should look at the world but only out at the eye's end, as it were.

Ver. 41. *Thou art careful*] Christ prefers attention before attendance. To hearken is better than the fat of rams, 1 Sam. xv. 22.

Ver. 42. *But one thing is necessary*] That *bonum hominis*, Mic. vi. 8, that *totum hominis*, Eccles. xii. 13; the happiness, the whole of a man, viz. to hear the word of God and keep it. The original hath it thus, there is need of one thing; that is, say some, of one dish only: but the other sense is the better.

That good part] *Non tu malam, sed illa meliorem*, saith Augustine. Thou hast done well, but she better.

CHAPTER XI.

Ver. 1. *When he ceased*] Or, rested, ὡς ἐπαύσατο; for he had been tugging hard with God in prayer, and labouring even to lassitude.

Ver. 2—4.] See Matt. vi. 9, &c.

Ver. 3. *Our daily bread*] Our super-substantial bread, τὸν ἐπιούσιον : so Erasmus rendereth it, and interpreteth it of Christ; for he thought that in so heavenly a prayer there should have been no mention of earthly things; wherein he was greatly deceived. For temporals also must be prayed for.

Day by day] That we may from day to day depend upon thy providence for provisions, and, as a grave man of God once said, whereas many

others have and eat their bread stale, let us receive it and eat it daily new from thine hand.

Ver. 4. *For we also forgive*] So that our forgiving of others seemeth, for God's promise' sake, to be as it were the intervenient cause, or the *sine qua non*, of God's forgiving us, saith learned Beza.

And lead us not, &c.] One argument that we shall persevere, is, the prayers of the whole church, offering up this daily sacrifice, lead us not, &c.

Ver. 5. *Three loaves*] He asketh no more, but receiveth as many as he needeth. So do all God's suitors. His ears are not only open to their prayers; but his eyes also are upon their necessities, to give them more than they ask or think.

Ver. 6. *For a friend*] See Prov. xvii. 17, with the note there.

Ver. 7. *Trouble me not*] The carnally secure, cast into Jezebel's bed, unworthily answer Christ on this sort, when he stands at the door and knocks by the hammer of his word and the motions of his Spirit, which they slight and withstand.

Ver. 8. *Because of his importunity*] Gr. His impudency, ἀναίδειαν; a metaphor from beggars, that will not be said nay, but are impudently importunate.

Ver. 9. *Ask and it shall be given*] Ask, seek, knock. It is not a simple repetition of the same thing, but an emphatical gradation, and shows *instantissimam necessitatem*, saith Augustine. *Nec dicitur quid dabitur*, saith he, to show that the gift is a thing *supra omne nomen*, above all name.

Ver. 10.] See Matt. vii. 7.

Ver. 11. *For every one*, &c.] Sozomen saith of Apollonius, that he never asked anything of God that he obtained not. *Hic homo potuit apud Deum quod voluit*, said one concerning Luther; he could have what he would of God.

Ver. 12, 13.] See Matt. vii. 9—11.

Ver. 14. *And it was dumb*] So it was a double miracle. God's favours seldom come single; there is a series, a concatenation of them, and every former draws on a future.

Ver. 15.] See Matt. ix. 34; xii. 24.

Ver. 16—19, &c.] See Matt. xii. 38; xvi. 1; Mark iii. 24.

Ver. 21. *When a strong man armed*] *Qui se dedebant, arma tradebant.* (Cæsar de Bell. Gall. lib. 3.) They that yielded threw down their arms.

Ver. 24. *Seeking rest*] His only rest is to molest and mischief men.

Ver. 25. *Swept and garnished*] By a little formal repentance, and a few faint resolutions of reformation.

Ver. 26. *Seven other spirits*] As the jailor lays a load of iron on him that had escaped. None are worse than those that have been good, and are naught; and might be good, but will be naught.

Ver. 27. *Blessed is the womb that bare thee*]
So the heathen poet,

> ——*qui te genuêre beati,*
> *Et mater fælix, et quæ dedit ubera nutrix.*
> (Ovid, Metam. lib. 4.)

Ver. 28. *Yea, rather, blessed*] His disciples
were more blessed in hearing Christ, than his
mother in bearing him.

Ver. 29. *Were gathered thick together*] All
on a heap, ἐπαθροιζομένων, either to see a sign, or
to hear what he would say to the motion.

Ver. 30. *So also shall the Son of man be*] sc.
A sign, not of confirmation, but of condemnation.

Ver. 31, 32.] See Matt. xii. 41, 42.

Ver. 33. *No man, when he hath lighted, &c.*]
Our Saviour here warneth those that had given
some good hope of their repentance, that they
cherish their light, and walk by it.

Ver. 34. *When thine eye is single*] A single
eye is that that looks on God singly, abstracted
from all other things.

Ver. 35, 36.] See Matt. vi. 22, 23.

Ver. 36. *Having no part dark*] The regenerate man is *totus diaphanus*, like a crystal glass,
with a lamp in the midst.

Ver. 37. *Sat down to meat*] And yet, at their
own tables, he sets the Pharisees forth in their
colours, and entertaineth them with as many
menaces as they do him with messes of meat.

Ver. 38. *That he had not washed*] This the
Pharisees deemed as great a sin as to commit
fornication. (Godw. Antiq. Heb. 49.)

Ver. 39.] See Matt. xxiii. 25.

Ver. 40. *Did not he that made, &c.*] Ought he
not, therefore, to be served with both? It is the
hidden man of the heart that he most regardeth;
the law of the mind that he would have chiefly
observed.

Ver. 41. *But rather give alms*] So Daniel
counsels Nebuchadnezzar, Dan. iv. 27. Ralph,
Bishop of Chichester, A. D. 1070, drawing towards his end, delivered unto the poor with his
own hands whatsoever he had in the world (I
inquire not with what intention), leaving himself scarce clothes to cover him. Alexander V.,
Bishop of Rome, was liberal to the poor (saith
the historian), that he left nothing to himself,
so that he would merrily say that he was a rich
bishop, a poor cardinal, and a beggarly pope.

Of such things as ye have] Gr. As are within,
τὰ ἔνοντα, either within the platter (send morsels
to the hungry) or within your hearts; for riches
get within their owners many times, and do
more possess them than are possessed by them;

> ——*difficile est opibus non tradere mentem.*

Ver. 42. *But woe unto you*] Notwithstanding
your tithing of pot-herbs, wherein you think
you take course that all things may be clean to
you, ver. 41. Or woe unto you, for that through
covetousness you exact the utmost of your
tithes, &c. So some sense this text.

Ver. 43.] See Matt. xxiii. 6.

Ver. 44. *For ye are as graves*] As the deep
grave keeps the stinking carcase from offending
any one's smell, so doth the dissembling hypocrite so cleanly carry the matter that hardly
the sharpest nose, &c.

Ver. 45. *Thou reproachest us also*] Who
meddled with them, but that their own consciences accused them? It is a rule of Jerome,
*Ubi generalis de vitiis disputatio est, ibi nullius
personæ est injuria; neque carbone notatur quisquam, quasi malus sit, sed omnes admonentur ne
sint mali.* Where the discourse is of all, there
is no personal intimation of any.

Ver. 46.] See Matt. xxiii. 4.

Ver. 47.] See Matt. xxiii. 29.

Ver. 48. *And ye build their sepulchres*] And
so ye set up the trophies of your fathers' cruelty.

Ver. 49. *Therefore also said the wisdom of
God*] That is, Christ himself, the essential
wisdom of his Father, Matt. xxiii. 34.

Ver. 50, 51.] See Matt. xxiii. 35.

Ver. 52. *Woe unto you, lawyers*] I see well,
said father Latimer, that whosoever will be busy
with *Væ vobis*, he shall shortly after come *coram
nobis*, as Christ did. (Acts and Mon.)

For ye have taken away the key of knowledge]
By taking away the Scriptures, and all good
means of knowledge; as do also the Jesuits at
this day. At Dole, a university in Burgundy,
they have not only debarred the people of the
Protestant books, but especially also forbid them
to talk of God, either in good sort or bad. In
Italy they not only prohibit the books of the
reformed writers, but also hide their own treatises,
in which the tenet of the Protestants is recited,
only to be confuted; so that you shall seldom
there meet with Bellarmine's works, or any of
the like nature, to be sold.

Ver. 53. *To urge him vehemently*] ἐνέχειν. Out
of deep displeasure to bear an aching tooth towards him (as Herodias did toward the Baptist,
Mark vi. 19), waiting him a shrewd turn.

And to provoke him to speak] ἀποστοματίζειν.
Not to stop his mouth about many things, as
the Rhemists falsely render it. They asked him
captious questions to make him an offender for
a word, Isa. xxix. 21.

Ver. 54. *Seeking to catch something*] But there
was no guile or gall found in his mouth, saith
St Peter, intimating that they sought it.

CHAPTER XII.

Ver. 1. *Beware of the leaven*] WHICH our
eyes cannot discern from dough by the colour,
but only our palate, by the taste. Such is hypocrisy, which also, as leaven, is: 1. spreading;
2. swelling; 3. souring the meal; 4. impuring
and defiling the house where it is, though it
be but as much as a man's fist.

Ver. 2—5, &c.] See notes on Matt. x. 26—
29, &c.

Ver. 8. *Whosoever shall confess me*] Cyprian,
reproving the rashness of those Christians that
would go on their own accord to the heathen

magistrates, professing themselves Christians, whereby they were put to death. Hath a good and elegant speech: *Confiteri nos magis voluit, quam profiteri.* Christ would have us confess him; he saith not profess him. Now he confesseth that doth it being asked, as he professeth that doth it of his own free accord.

Ver. 10.] See Matt. xii. 31, 32; Mark iii. 28.

Ver. 11. *Take ye no thought*] See the note on Matt. x. 19, and Mark xiii. 11. Alice Driver, martyr, at her examination, put all the doctors to silence, so that they had not a word to say, but one looked upon another. Then she said, Have ye no more to say? God be honoured; you be not able to resist the Spirit of God in me, a poor woman. I was an honest poor man's daughter, never brought up in the university as you have been. But I have driven the plough many a time before my father, I thank God; yet notwithstanding in the defence of God's truth, and in the cause of my Master, Christ, by his grace I will set my foot against the foot of any of you all, in the maintenance and defence of the same. And if I had a thousand lives it should go for payment thereof. So the chancellor condemned her, and she returned to the prison as joyful as the bird of the day. (Acts and Mon.)

Ver. 13. *Master, speak to my brother*] While Christ was busily discoursing about the best things, this importunate fellow interrupts him with this unpleasing, and, therefore, unreasonable request, τὸ ἄκαιρον πανταχοῦ λυπηρὸν (Isoc.). But our Saviour soon rejects it, as out of the compass of his calling, and so cuts off from his adversaries all occasion of cavilling at him as a usurper of the magistrate's office.

Ver. 14. *A judge or a divider over you*] It is work enough for a minister rightly to judge of the estate of his flock, and to divide the word of God unto them daily and duly. "What is that to thee?" said Christ to Peter when he meddled with that which belonged not to him, John xxi. 21. *Age quod tui muneris est,* said Valentinian to Ambrose. Do thine own business. And *Verbi minister es, hoc age,* was Mr Perkins' motto. *Clericus in foro est piscis in arido.*

Ver. 15. *Take heed, and beware of covetousness*] This our Saviour adds after "who made me a judge?" to teach us not to go to law with a covetous mind; but as Charles the French king made war with our Henry VII., more desiring peace than victory.

For a man's life consisteth not, &c.] He can neither live upon them nor lengthen his life by them. Queen Elizabeth once wished herself a milk-maid; Bajazet envied the happiness of a poor shepherd that sat on a hill-side merrily reposing himself with his homely pipe. Therein showing, saith the historian, that worldly bliss consisteth not so much in possessing of much, subject to danger, as enjoying in a little contentment, void of fear. Covetous men by gaping after more lose the pleasure of that they possess, as a dog at his master's table swalloweth the whole meat he casteth him without any pleasure, gaping still for the next morsel.

Ver. 16. *The ground of a certain rich man*] Gr. ἡ χωρὰ. The country; for he had laid field to field till he was the only landholder thereabouts, and had a country of corn, Isa. lviii.

Ver. 17. *And he thought within himself*] He was up with the more and down with the less; he cast up his reckonings, as covetous men's manner is, and after long debate to and fro, concluded what to do.

He talked to himself, &c.] διελογίζετο. A marvellous proper word for the purpose.

Ver. 18. *My barns*] So *my* fruits, and *my* goods, all was his; God came not into this epicure's thoughts. *Hic Deus nihil fecit,* as one wittily twitted Pope Adrian, talking after the same rate.

Ver. 19. *Eat and drink, and be merry*] A right epicure, one that had made his gut his god; another Sardanapalus, that did eat that in earth that he digested in hell, as Augustine hath it. How many, alas, are there, that having one foot in the grave and the other in hell, do yet put far away thoughts of either! These, when they should be building their tombs, are building their tabernacles, *Donec mors vitæ studium prævertat, longa conantes opprimat.* (Sen. Consol. ad Marc. xi.)

Ver. 20. *Thou fool, this night, &c.*] This rich fool, when, like a jay, he was pruning himself in the boughs, came tumbling down with the arrow in his side; his glass was run, when he thought it to be but new turned. He chopt into the earth before he was aware: like as one that, walking in a field covered with snow, falleth into a pit suddenly. He was shot as a bird with a bolt, whilst he gazed at the bow. And this may be any man's case. Which made Austin say he would not for the gain of a world be an atheist for one half hour; because he knew not but God might in that time call him.

Then whose shall those things be? &c.] As thy friends are scrambling for thy goods, worms for thy body, so devils for thy soul. We read of Henry Beaufort, that rich and wretched cardinal, bishop of Winchester, and chancellor of England in the reign of King Henry VI., that perceiving he must needs die, he murmured that his riches could not reprieve him. Fie, quoth he, will not death be hired? will money do nothing? No; it is righteousness only that delivereth from death. (Fox, Martyrol.)

Ver. 21. *Rich to God*] That is, rich in faith, Jam. ii. 5; rich in good works, 1 Tim. vi. 18.

Ver. 22—25.] See Matt. vi. 25, 26, &c.

Ver. 26. *For the rest*] For superfluities, when ye cannot provide yourselves of necessaries.

Ver. 27, 28. *Consider the lilies, &c.*] Women and children use herbs and flowers to look on and smell to; apothecaries and others use them for food and physic; divines and all good people, for information and instruction in the best things; this being the chief use and end of all the creatures, *ut scalæ nobis, et alæ fiant*, that they help us on towards heaven.

Ver. 29. *Neither be ye of doubtful mind*] μή μετεωρίζεσθε. Hang not in suspense, as meteors do in the air, not certain whether to hang or fall to the ground. *Meteora dicta volunt quod animos hominum suspensos, dubios, et quasi fluctuantes faciant.* Aristotle himself confesseth, that of some meteors he knew not what to say, though of some other he could say somewhat. One interpreter renders this word, "make not discourses in the air," as the covetous man doth, when his head is tossed with the cares of getting or fears of losing commodity ; or it may note his endless framing of projects for the compassing of his desires. The Syriac rendereth it, "Let not your thoughts be distracted about these things." Surely as a clock can never stand still, so long as the plummets hang thereat ; so neither can a worldling's heart, for cares and anxieties. These suffer him not to rest night nor day ; being herein like unto the flies of Egypt, or those tyrants, Isa. xvi. 10.

Ver. 32. *Fear not, little flock*] Gr. little, little flock. There is in the original a double diminutive. If we divide the known parts of the world into three equal parts, the Christians' part is but as five, the Mahometans' as six, and the idolaters' as nineteen. Among the best Churches, the most are the worst, as Philip. iii. 18. Chrysostom could not find a hundred in Antioch that he could be well persuaded of that they should be saved.

Ver. 33. *A treasure in the heavens*] As a merchant being to travel into a far country, doth deliver his money here upon the exchange, that so he may be sure to receive it again at his arrival in that country ; so let us that are passing into another country lay up something that may stand us in stead in that day.

Ver. 34. *There will your heart be*] Your inwardest affection, your chief joy and trust.

Ver. 35. *Let your loins be girded*] It implies, 1. readiness ; 2. nimbleness, handiness, and handsomeness. A loose, discinct, and diffluent mind is unfit to serve God. Here it is, ungirt, unblest.

Ver. 36. *And knocketh*] sc. By the hammer of his word and Spirit, or by the hand of death, summoning you thereto by some sickness, death's harbinger.

Ver. 37. *Blessed are those servants*] So ver. 38 and 43. They are three times said to be blessed that watch. *Terque quaterque beati : Fœlices ter et amplius.* Horat.

Ver. 38. *In the second watch*] For *serius aut citius*, death will be upon us ; neither is it sure that he will knock or give warning. Watch, therefore ; sith at the next puff of breath thou mayest blow away thy life. *Fabius Senator, poto in lactis haustu uno pilo, strangulatus est*, saith Pliny. Fabius was choked with a hair in a draught of milk.

Ver. 39.] See Matt. xxiv. 43.

Ver. 40. *Be ye therefore ready*] Matt. xxiv. 45 ; see the note there.

Ver. 41. *Lord, speakest thou*, &c.] The disciples ever dreamt of some singular happiness, some immunity and privilege, that they should have above others. Hence this question, that gave occasion to the ensuing parables.

Ver. 42—46.] See Matt. xxiv. 46, 47, &c.

Ver. 47. *Which knew his Lord's will*] None are so filled with God's wrath as knowing men. *Sapientes sapienter descendunt in infernum*, saith Bernard. The devil is too hard for them.

Ver. 48. *Much is given*] To know our Master's will is the great talent of all other. There is a "much" in that. There is a special *depositum*, as the word here used importeth. (παρέθεντο. Hinc παρακαταθήκη, 1 Tim. i. 18 ; vi. 20.)

Ver. 49. *To send fire on the earth*] That is, that persecution that is *evangelii genius*, as Calvin wrote to the French king, and dogs at the heels the preaching of the truth.

And what will I if it be already kindled?] As if he should say, Let it kindle as soon as it will, I am contented ; I know much good will come of it.

Ver. 50. *And how am I straitened*] This painful preconceit of his passion was a part of our Saviour's passion. This made him spend many a night in prayer, bewailing our sins, and imploring God's grace, and he was heard in that which he requested, Heb. v.

Ver. 51—53.] See Matt. x. 34.

Ver 54.] See Matt. xvi. 2.

Ver. 57. *Yea, and why even of yourselves*] By consulting with your own consciences, which would, if rightly dealt with, tell you, that I am that Messiah you have so long looked for.

Ver. 58. *Give diligence*] δὸς ἐργασίαν, *Purus Putus Latinismus*, saith Drusius. *Da operam ; Id est, festina, et labora, omnesque modos cogita quomodo ab eo libereris*, as Theophylact expounds it. Be at utmost pains to get freed from him.

Ver. 59. *Till thou hast paid the very last mite*] It is good to compound quickly with the Lord, and to take up the suit before it come to execution and judgment, lest we be forced to pay, not only the main debt, but the arrearages too, that is, the time of God's long-suffering and patience, here and hereafter.

CHAPTER XIII.

Ver. 1. *Told him of the Galileans*] So called from Judas Gaulonites, or Galilæus, their captain ; to whose faction also belonged those four thousand murderers, Acts xxi. 38. For Pilate had not authority over the Galileans properly so called. See Josephus, xviii. 2.

Ver. 2. *Because they suffered such things*] None out of hell ever suffered more than those worthies, Heb. xi. Shall any therefore condemn that generation of God's children? Psal. lxxiii. 15. See Lam. iv. 6 ; Dan. ix. 12.

Ver. 3. *Except ye repent*] *Aut pœnitendum, aut pereundum.* Men must either turn from sin or burn in hell.

Ver. 4. The tower of Siloam] A tower, belike, upon the wall of Jerusalem, which stood by the fish-pool of Siloam, mentioned John ix. 17.

Ver. 5. But except ye repent] Except the best of you all repent more and more when ye see the examples of God's wrath, &c. God would not have the wounds of godly sorrow so healed up in his own children, but that they should bleed afresh upon every good occasion. *De aliorum plagis faciamus medicamenta vulneribus nostris.* Make best use of others' miseries.

Ver. 6. A vineyard] So the Church is frequently called. See the note on Matt. xxi. 33.

Ver. 7. Cut it down] Trees that are not for fruit are for the fire. God will lay down his basket and take up his axe. He will not always serve men for a sinning-stock.

Ver. 8. Lord, let it alone this year] Happy that people that have praying vine-dressers to intercede for them! God will yield somewhat to prayer, when he is bitterly bent against a people or person.

Till I shall dig, &c.] *Donec eam ablaqueavero et stercoravero.* (Beza.) Ministers must try their utmost to fulfil their ministry that they have received of the Lord, Col. iv. 17.

Ver. 9. Then after that thou shalt cut it down] The fig-tree, they say, if it bear not the fourth year after it is planted, will never bear at all. If good be not done at first coming of the gospel to any place, seldom is any good ever done there.

Ver. 10. On the sabbath] The soul's market-day, on which the Lord Christ sells to his people "gold tried in the fire, white raiment, eye-salve," &c., Rev. iii. 18.

Ver. 11. And was bowed together, and could in no wise lift up herself] This infirmity might proceed from the gonorrhœa; but, besides that, the devil had a hand in it, for she was bound by Satan, verse 16. *Novi quandam mulierem* (saith Dr Garenceires) *quæ adhuc in vivis est—quæ cum tribus abhinc annis gonorrhœa simplici laboraret, ea neglecta, tantam seminis jacturam intra annum passa est, ut quæ prius erectæ et firmæ staturæ fuerat, luxatis vertebris non solum gibbosa facta est, verum etiam in tantam κύβωσιν incidit, ut mentum umbilico* (stupendum dictu) *ferme insideat: vicinis interea illud pro miraculo habentibus.* (De Tabe Anglicana.)

Ver. 12. Thou art loosed] For she had been bound by Satan, verse 16. All wicked worldlings are worse bound, and go grovelling, but feel it not, look not out for help, look not up to heaven, till laid upon their backs by death, as swine ready to be stuck.

Ver. 13. And he laid his hands upon her] Both to show his charity, and to signify that his quickening flesh is that ordinary instrument whereby he maketh us partakers of his saving grace.

Ver. 14. Answered with indignation] He that will be angry and not sin must be angry at nothing but at sin.

Ver. 15. Thou hypocrite] The Syriac rendereth it *Assumens vultum*, thou that settest a good face upon it, thou that personatest a better man than thou art; thou picture of piety, &c.

Ver. 16. Whom Satan hath bound] So he held Job in captivity, chap. xlii. 10, by afflicting his body, buffeting his soul for a year together, say the Hebrews; for seven years, saith Suidas.

Ver. 17. For all the glorious things] Which yet his adversaries sought to deprave and denigrate, as if done by I know not what superstitious abuse of the name Jehovah.

Ver. 18.] See Mark iv. 30, 31.

Ver. 19.] See Matt. xiii. 31.

Ver. 20.] See Matt. xiii. 33.

Ver. 21.] See Matt. xiii. 33.

Ver. 22.] See Matt. ix. 35; Mark vi. 6.

Ver. 23. Are there few, &c.] Few received Christ in the flesh, John i. 12: he wondered at one good Nathaniel. They are *Methe mispar* that look towards heaven. *Apparent rari nantes in gurgite vasto.* The most rest on that old popish rule, To follow the drove.

Are there few?] A curious question, and therefore not vouchsafed an answer: whereas otherwhere, in things needful to be known, the Scripture oft answers the questions and objections of men's hearts only. "Jesus knowing their thoughts," &c.

Ver. 24. Strive to enter] Strive even to an agony; or as they did for the garland in the Olympic games, to the which the word ἀγωνίζεσθε, here used, seemeth to allude. All would come to heaven, but all like not the way; they would not *per angusta ad augusta pervenire*: they like well of Abraham's bosom, but not of Dives' door. But let none think to live in Delilah's lap, and then to rest in Abraham's bosom; to dance with the devil all day, and then to sup with Christ at night; to fly to heaven with pleasant wings, to pass *à deliciis ad delicias, è cœno ad cœlum*, &c., to go to heaven in a feather-bed.

Ver. 25. And hath shut to] God is not always with men in the opportunities of grace. He hath his season, his harvest for judgment, Matt. xiii. 30, when troops of those that forget God are turned into hell, Psal. ix. 17.

Ver. 26. We have eaten and drunk, &c.] These pretenders to Christ perish by catching at their own catch, hanging on their own fancy, making a bridge of their own shadow, &c.; they verily believe that Christ is their sweet Saviour, &c., when it is no such matter; they trust to Christ, as the apricot tree that leans against the wall, but is fast rooted in the earth: so are these in the world, &c.

We have eaten and drunk in thy presence] Even at thy table, but it became a snare to them.

Ver. 27.] See Matt. vii. 23, and xxv. 40, with the notes.

Ver. 28.] See Matt. viii. 12; xiii. 42; xxiv. 51.

Ver. 29. And shall sit down] As at a sumptuous supper. When, therefore, we are invited to a full feast, think of heaven: as Fulgentius beholding at Rome the majesty of the emperor, the glory of the senate, the lustre of the nobility, cried out, How beautiful is Jerusalem the celestial, sith Rome the terrestrial appeareth with such splendour. So Master Esty, when he sat and heard a sweet concert of music, seemed upon this occasion carried up for the time beforehand to the place of his rest, saying very passionately, What music may we think there is in heaven? (Dr Hall's Art of Divine Meditation.)

Ver. 30.] See Matt. xix. 30; xx. 16; Mark x. 31.

Ver. 31. *For Herod will kill thee*]

Tu vero Herodes sanguinolente time. (Beza, Ep.)

If Herod or these Pharisees had been as wise as Pilate's wife, they would never have meddled with that just man.

Ver. 32. *To-day and to-morrow*] *i. e.* As long as I list, without his leave. Faith makes a man walk about the world as a conqueror.

I shall be perfected] Or, I shall be sacrificed, as Pareus rendereth it, τελειοῦμαι, *In sacrificium offerar.*

Ver. 33. *Out of Jerusalem*] That slaughter-house of the saints, that bloody city, Isa. i. 21; Ezek. xxiv. 6.

Ver. 34, 35.] See Matt. xxiii. 37.

CHAPTER XIV.

Ver. 1. *They watched him*] Gr. παρατηροῦμενοι, They superstitiously and maliciously observed him. (Aristot. lib. ii. Rhet.) *Accipit pro eo quod est ulciscendi tempus captare.* They watched as intently as a dog doth for a bone; they pried as narrowly into his actions as Laban did into Jacob's stuff.

Ver. 2. *A certain man before him*] A fit object, and that was sufficient to move him to mercy, who himself, by sympathy, took our infirmities and bare our sicknesses.

Ver. 3. *And Jesus answering*] viz. Their thoughts, which were naked and open; naked (for the outside) and dissected, quartered, and, as it were, cleft through the back-bone (for the inside), before him with whom they had to deal, Heb. iv. 13.

Ver. 4. *And he took him*] Good must be done, however it be taken.

Ver. 5. *Pull him out on the sabbath-day*] The Jew of Tewkesbury, that would not be pulled out of the jakes whereinto he fell on their sabbath-day, perished deservedly.

Ver. 6. *And they could not answer*] Yet ran away with the bit in their mouths.

Ver. 7. *When he marked*] Ministers, though they may not be time-servers, yet they must be time-observers, and sharply reprove what they meet with amiss in their people.

Ver. 8. *When thou art bidden of any man to a wedding*] When should a man rather feast than at the recovery of his lost rib?

Ver. 9. *Thou begin with shame*] As passing for a proud fool: a style good enough for a self-exalter.

Ver. 10. *Then shalt thou have worship*] *Honor est in honorante,* therefore to be the less esteemed, because without us, and mostly but a puff of stinking breath, not once to be valued.

Ver. 11. *For whosoever*] See the note on Matt. xxiii. 12.

Ver. 12. *Nor thy rich neighbours*] *Laudent te esurientium viscera, non ructantium opulenta convivia,* saith Jerome. Bishop Hooper had his board of beggars, who were daily served by four at a mess, with wholesome meats, before himself sat down to dinner. (Acts and Mon.)

Ver. 13. *Call the poor*] Christ prefers charity before courtesy.

Ver. 14. *At the resurrection of the just*] Called theirs, because they only shall have joy of that day. It were well for the wicked if they might never rise to judgment, or trot directly to hell, and not be brought before the Lamb to be sentenced.

Ver. 15. *Blessed is he,* &c.] This man seems to have "tasted of the good word of God, and of the powers of the world to come," Heb. vi. 5. Happy he, if he fed heartily thereon. This, saith Luther, is *sancta crapula.*

Ver. 16. *Made a great supper*] Δεῖπνον, παρὰ τὸ δεῖν πονεῖν. They are happy that get to heaven; they rest from their labours. The ancients dined frugally, supped liberally. Be of good cheer, said that martyr to her husband that suffered with her; for though we have but an ill dinner, we shall sup with Christ.

Ver. 17.] See Matt. xxii. 3.

Ver. 18. *I have bought,* &c.] *Licitis perimus omnes.* More die by meat than by poison. *Cavete, latet anguis in herba.* What more lawful than a farm? what more honourable of all pleasures than marriage? But these men had not so much bought their farms, &c., as were sold to them: not so much married wives, as were married to them. *Uxori nubere nolo meæ,* Martial.

Ver. 19. *I have bought five yoke of oxen*] This answers those that plead their necessities, and that they seek not superfluities (as farm upon farm, &c.), but only, a sufficiency. What could be more necessary than oxen, sith without them he could not follow his husbandry? Worldliness is a great hindrance to heaven, though a man cannot be charged with any great covetousness. These all excused themselves out of heaven, by bringing apologies why they could not go to heaven. Never yet any came to hell but had some pretence for their coming thither. Our vile hearts will persuade us that there is some sense in sinning, and some reason to be mad.

Ver. 20. *And therefore I cannot come*] Note that the voluptuary is peremptory, and saith flatly he "cannot come." Sensual hearts are void of the Spirit, Jude 18, 19. Miry places could not be healed by the sanctuary waters, Ezek. xlvii. 11; fleshly lusts fight against the soul, 1 Pet. ii. 11. Those that dance to the timbrel and harp, say, " Depart from us," Job xxi. 11. Better be preserved in brine than rot in honey.

Ver. 21. *Then the master of the house being angry*] And good reason he had : for, *Non modo pluris putare quod utile videatur, quam quod honestum, sed hæc etiam inter se comparare et in his addubitare, turpissimum est,* saith the honest heathen (Cicero *de Officiis*). Surely as Pharaoh said of the Israelites, " They are entangled in the land, the wilderness hath shut them in," Exod. xiv. 3, so may we say of many, They are entangled in the creature, the world hath shut them in, they cannot come to Christ : they are shut up in a cave, as those five kings, Joshua x. ; and have hardness of heart, as a great stone, rolled to the mouth, and honours, riches, and pleasures as so many keepers, &c.

Ver. 22.] See Matt. xxii. 9, 10.

Ver. 23. *Compel them*] This may be meant (saith Mr Perkins) of the Christian magistrate : for that is the magistrate's duty in respect of the outward profession.

Ver. 24. *None of those men*] Sith they thus judge themselves " unworthy of eternal life," Acts xiii. 46, and are miserable by their own election, Jonah ii. 8.

Ver. 25. *And there went great multitudes with him*] Expecting great things from him, and gaping after an earthly felicity. These he strives to undeceive in the following verses.

Ver. 26. *And hate not his father*, &c.]¹ Much more his farm and his oxen. It was not these, but the inordinate love of these, that detained them, as Christ here intimateth. Your house, home, and goods, yea, life, and all that ever ye have (saith that martyr), God hath given you as love tokens, to admonish you of his love, to win your love to him again. Now will he try your love, whether ye set more by him or by his tokens.

Ver. 27.] See Matt. x. 38, and xvi. 24.

Ver. 28. *Intending to build a tower*] Rodulphus Gualther being in Oxford, and beholding Christchurch College, said, *Egregium opus : Cardinalis iste instituit collegium, et absolvit popinam.* A pretty business ! a college begun and a kitchen finished.

Counteth the cost] Let him that intendeth to build the tower of godliness sit down first and cast up the cost, lest, &c.

Ver. 29, 30. *Begin to mock him, saying*, &c.] Of all things, men love not to be jeered ; for there is none but thinks himself worthy of some regard, and is therefore impatient of reproaches. If neither fear of God nor shame of men prevail with us, *actum est.*

Ver. 31. *Sitteth not down first*] To consult, and so with good advice to make war. *Romani sedendo vincunt,* saith Varro. Thou shalt succour us out of the city, 2 Sam. xviii. 3.

Ver. 32. *He sendeth an ambassage*] *Mittamus preces et lachrymas cordis legatos,* saith Cy-

¹ μισεῖ, *ex* מאס *ex odio reprobavit, respuit.*

prian. *Currat pænitentia, ne præcurrat sententia,* saith Chrysologus. Repent, ere it be too late.

Ver. 33. *That forsaketh not*] Gr. ἀποταξάμενος, that bids not farewell to all.

Ver. 34. *Salt is good*] This was a sentence much in our Saviour's mouth, Matt. v. 13 ; Mark ix. 50 ; and is here used to set forth the desperate condition of apostates.

Ver. 35. *He that hath ears to hear*] This is usually added by our Saviour in matters of greatest consequence and nearest concernment. See the note on Matt. xiii. 9, 43.

CHAPTER XV.

Ver. 1. *All the publicans and sinners*] Christ familiarized himself with these despised persons, and thereby much won upon them. Affability easily allureth, austerity discourageth ; as it did that honest citizen, which having in himself a certain conflict of conscience, came to Master Hooper the martyr's door for counsel ; but being abashed at his austere behaviour, durst not come in, but departed, seeking remedy of his troubled mind at other men's hands.

Ver. 2. *But the scribes and Pharisees*] Being sick of the devil's disease, and doing his lusts, John viii. 44.

Ver. 3—6.] See Matt. xviii. 12.

Ver. 7. *Joy shall be in heaven*] Would we then put harps into the angels' hands, ditties into their mouths ? repent.

Ver. 8. *If she lose one piece*] One Testor. *Drachma enim valebat septem denarios cum dimidio.* (Breerwood *de Num.*) Jude 1. See the margin of our new translation.

And sweep the house] σαροῖ, *everrit,* not *evertit,* as the vulgar hath it corruptly : and Gregory with others were deceived by it in their descants and glosses, nothing to the purpose.

Ver. 9. *Rejoice with me*] What greater joy than to have had a hand in the conversion of a sinner from the error of his way ?

Ver. 10.] See ver. 7. The tears of sinners are the wine of angels, saith Bernard : who himself, for a certain time after his conversion, remained as it were deprived of his senses, by the excessive consolations he had from God.

Ver. 11. *And he said*] A third parable to the same purpose : and all to persuade us of God's readiness to receive returning sinners. This is not so easily believed, indeed, as most men imagine.

Ver. 12. *He divided unto them his living*] Gr. τὸν βίον, his life. Our life is called the " life of our hands," Isa. lvii. 10, because it is upheld by the labour of our hands.

Ver. 13. *Gathered all together*] *Convasatis veluti omnibus.*

With riotous living] Ασώτως.² Not caring to save any part, *sibi nihil reservans, imo seipsum non servans,* being such as safety itself could not

² ἄσωτος quasi ἄσωστος, unsaveable.

save; whence the Latins call such a man *perditum*, an undone person. Such were those of whom Seneca saith, that *singulis auribus bina aut terna dependent patrimonia*, hanged two or three good lordships at their ears. And such are those amongst us that turn lands into laces, great rents into great ruffs, &c. The expenses of Apicus' kitchen amounted to more than two millions of gold.[1] He having eaten up his estate, and finding by his account that he had no more than 200,000 crowns remaining, thought himself poor, and that this sufficed not to maintain his luxury; whereupon he drank down a glass of poison.

Ver. 14. *And when he had spent all*] And left himself nothing at all, *præter cœlum et cœnum*, but air to breathe in and earth to tread on, as that Roman prodigal boasted; who had made his own hands his executors, and his own eyes his overseers, drawing much of his patrimony through his throat, and spending the rest upon harlots, who left him as bare as crows do a dead carcase. Ruin follows riot at the heels.

Ver. 15. *To feed swine*] Which to a Jew, that held swine an abomination, must needs be grievous.

Ver. 16. *And he would fain have filled his belly*] The stomach of man is a monster (saith one), which, being contained in so little a bulk as his body, is able to consume and devour all things.

And no man gave him] A swinish life he had led, and now would have been glad of swine's meat.

Ver. 17. *And when he came to himself*] For till then he had been beside himself, and not his own worthy. *Nebulo* (saith one) cometh of Nabal; fool of φαῦλος: ἄνοια et ἀνομία are of near affinity. Evil is Hebrew for a fool, &c. Wickedness is called the "foolishness of madness," Eccles. vii. 25.

Ver. 18. *Against heaven, and before thee*] That is, I have not only thee, but the whole heaven for a swift witness against me of mine offences and out-bursts. "The heaven doth declare mine iniquity, and the earth riseth up against me," Job xx. 27.

Ver. 19. *I am not worthy*] So Austin, *Domine, non sum dignus quem tu diligas*. So another, *Non sum dignus, Domine, sed sum indigens*. Sense of misery must precede sense of mercy. Let God but hear such words as these fall from his Ephraims, and he will soon melt over them, Jer. xxxi. 19, 20; Hos. xi. 8. Henry the son of our Henry II., crowned by his father, and rebelling against him, died before his father at Martel in Normandy, where his father lay at siege. His father refusing to visit him (as fearing his own life), but sending his ring in sign of forgiveness, the dying prince most humbly with floods of tears kissing the same, made a most sorrowful confession of his sins: and feeling death approach, would needs be drawn (as an unworthy sinner) out of his own bed, and laid upon another strewed with ashes, where he died; which being

[1] *H. S. millies in culinam congessit.* Sen.

related, the old king fell upon the earth, and weeping bitterly (like another David for his Absalom) mourned very sore. (Speed, 522.)

Ver. 20. *When he was yet a great way off*] *Tantum velis et Deus tibi præoccurret*, saith a father. The prodigal was but conceiving a purpose to return, and God met him, Isa. lxv. 24.

And kissed him] One would have thought he should have kicked him, or have killed him rather, but God is *Pater miserationum*, he is all bowels. The prodigal came, the father ran; God is slow to anger, swift to show mercy.

Ver. 21. *Father, I have sinned*] Confess, and the mends is made. *Homo agnoscit, Deus ignoscit.* Acknowledge but the debt, and he will cross the book.

And am no more worthy, &c.] *Infernus sum, Domine*, said that holy martyr, Mr Hooper, at his death. Lord, I am hell, but thou art heaven; I am soil, and a sink of sin, but thou a gracious God.

Ver. 22. *The best robe*] That white raiment of Christ's righteousness, Rev. iii. 18; that rich and royal array, Psal. xlv. 14, the righteousness (δικαιώματα) of the saints, Rev. xix. 8.

Ver. 23. *And bring hither the fatted calf*] Christ is that fatted calf, saith Mr Tindal, martyr, slain to make penitent sinners good cheer withal, and his righteousness is the goodly raiment to cover the naked deformities of their sins.

Ver. 24. *For this my son was dead, &c.*] So fareth it with every faithful Christian. He was dead, but now lives, and cannot be insensible or ignorant of such a change.

Ver. 25. *His elder son*] The self-justiciary, that is good in his own eyes, and needs no repentance.

Ver. 26. *What these things meant*] Hypocrites understand not the just man's joys, nor the sweet intercourse that is betwixt God and his people.

Ver. 27. *Safe*] Gr. ὑγιαίνοντα, in health. *Quod sanitas in corpore, id sanctitas in corde.* The sanctified man is the only sound man.

Ver. 28. *And he was angry*] *Christi consilium est ostendere, iniquum esse qui fratri in gratiam recepto obtrectat, etiamsi sanctitate Angelis non cedat.* Calvin.

Ver. 29. *And yet thou never gavest me a kid*] Much less a calf. Hypocrites hold God to be in their debt, and through discontent weigh not his favours, as being never without some ailment.

Ver. 30. *But as soon as this thy son*] He saith not, this my brother; he would not once own him, because in poverty.

Which hath devoured thy living] *q. d.* which you were so hasty to give unto him before your death (which you need not have done), and now he hath made a fair hand of it.

Ver. 31. *All that I have is thine*] In thy conceit at least. Thou holdest thyself happy howsoever, and seemest to have one foot already in the porch of paradise. Self-deceivers will needlessly set up their counter for a thousand pounds, and will not believe but their penny is very good silver. They lay claim to all, as the madman of

Athens did to all the ships that came into that harbour, as his.

Ver. 32. *Was lost, and is found*] Of himself he left his father; yet is he called the lost son.

CHAPTER XVI.

Ver. 1. *A certain rich man which had a steward*] MASTERS had need look well, 1. To the choosing of their servants. Solomon saw Jeroboam, that he was industrious, and therefore, without any respect at all to his religion, he made him ruler over all the charge of the house of Joseph, but to his singular disadvantage. Comp. 1 Kings xi. 28, with chap. xii. 3. 2. To the using of them; most men make no other use of their servants than they do of their beasts; while they may have their bodies to do their service, they care not if their souls serve the devil. Hence they so oft prove false and perfidious.

Ver. 2. *Give an account of thy stewardship*] *Villicus rationem cum Domino suo crebro putet*, said Cato. Stewards should often account with their masters.

Ver. 3. *I cannot dig, &c.*] They that will get wisdom must both dig and beg, Prov. ii. 3, 4.

Ver. 4. *They may receive me*] This is that wit he showed for himself, and for the which he is here commended: teaching us by all lawful means (not by any unlawful, as he) to provide for ourselves, and to preserve our reputation.

Ver. 5. *How much owest thou?*] Some are ever owing; and may say of debt, as the strumpet Quartilla did of her virginity, *Junonem meam iratam habeam, si unquam me meminerim virginem fuisse*. Petron.

Ver. 6. *Take thy bill*] The scope of this parable is, *ut profusionem charitate erga pauperes compensemus*, saith Beza, that we expiate, as it were, our prodigality, by showing mercy to the poor, Dan. iv. 27.

Ver. 7.] See ver. 5.

Ver. 8. *And the Lord commended*] Gr. ὁ κύριος, that Lord, viz. the steward's Lord, not the Lord Christ who relateth this parable. Or if we understand it of Christ (as the Syriac here doth), yet he herein no more approveth of this steward's false-dealing than he doth of the usurer's trade, Matt. v. 27; or the thieves, 1 Thess. v. 2; or the dancers, Matt. xi. 17; or the Olympic games, 1 Cor. ix. 24.

Because he had done wisely] The worldling's wisdom serves him (as the ostrich's wings) to make him out-run others upon earth, and in earthly things; but helps him never a wit toward heaven.

Are in their generation wiser] A swine that wanders can make better shift to get home to the trough than a sheep can to the fold. We have not received the spirit of this world, 1 Cor. ii. 12, we cannot shift and plot as they can; but we have received a better thing. The fox is wise in his generation, the serpent subtle, so is the devil too. When he was but young, he outwitted our first parents, 2 Cor. xi. 3.

Than the children of light] As the angels are called angels of light, 2 Cor. xi. 14. God's children are the only earthly angels, have a Goshen in their bosoms, can lay their hands on their hearts with dying Œcolampadius, and say, *Hic sat lucis.* (Melch. Adam.)

Ver. 9. *Make unto yourselves friends*] *Quibus officia præstita fidem defuncti apud Deum testificentur, illa comprobantem, et gratis coronantem.* (Beza.) Testify your faith by your works, that God of his free grace may commend and crown you.

Of the mammon of unrighteousness] The next odious name to the devil himself. This mammon of iniquity, this wages of wickedness, is not gain, but loss.

They may receive you] That is, that either the angels, or thy riches, or the poor, may let you into heaven.

Ver. 10. *He that is faithful*] Mr Diodati's note here is, " The right use of riches in believers is a trial of their loyal use of their spiritual graces and gifts. And, on the contrary, the abuse of the one showeth the abuse of the other. God likewise taketh away his spiritual graces from them, who do not use the temporal ones well."

Ver. 11. *In the unrighteous mammon*] Or the uncertain, vain, deceitful wealth of this world, which yet most rich men trust in, as if simply the better or safer for their abundance. Hence Drusius derives mammon from *aman*, which signifieth to trust.

Ver. 12. *In that which is another man's*] Riches are not properly ours, but God's, who hath entrusted us, and who doth usually assign them to the wicked, those men of his hand, for their portion, Psal. xvii. 14, for all the heaven that they are ever to look for. Better things abide the saints, who are here but foreigners, and must do as they may.

Who shall give you that which is your own?] *Quod nec eripi nec surripi potest.* Aristotle relateth a law like this made by Theodectes, that he that used not another man's horse well should forfeit his own.

Ver. 13.] See Matt. vi. 24.

Ver. 14. *And they derided him*] Gr. ἐξεμυκτήριζον, they blew their noses at him in scorn and derision. They fleered and jeered, when they should have feared, and fled from the wrath to come. *Naso suspendere adunco.* Horat.

Ver. 15. *For that which is highly esteemed, &c.*] A thing that I see in the night may shine, and that shining proceed from nothing but rottenness. There may be *malum opus in bona materia*, as in Jehu's zeal. Two things make a good Christian, good actions and good aims. And though a good aim doth not make a bad action good (as in Uzzah), yet a bad aim makes a good action bad (as in Jehu, Hos. i. 4, whose justice was approved, but his policy punished).

Ver. 16.] See Matt. xi. 11.

Ver. 17.] See Matt. v. 18.

Ver. 18.] See Matt. v. 32; xix. 9; Mark x. 5.

Ver. 19. There was a certain rich man] Not once named, as Lazarus was, though never so little esteemed of men. God knew him by name, as he did Moses; when the rich man's name is written in the earth, rots above-ground, is left for a reproach.

Which was clothed in purple, &c.] Gr. ἐνεδιδύσκετο, was commonly so clothed. It was his every day's wear, as the word implieth. (*Verbum est quasi frequentativum.* Pasor.)

Ver. 20. A certain beggar named Lazarus] Or Eleazar (as Tertullian and Prudentius call him), who having been Abraham's faithful servant, now resteth in his bosom.

Ver. 21. And desiring to be fed with the crumbs] Many poor folk have but prisoners' pittances, which will neither keep them alive nor suffer them to die.

The dogs came and licked his sores] When Sabinus was put to death for whispering against Sejanus, his dog lay down by his dead body, brought to his mouth the bread that was cast to him; and when Sabinus was thrown into the river Tiber, the dog leapt after him, endeavouring to keep him up, that he might not sink into the bottom. Pliny.

Ver. 22. Into Abraham's bosom] A metaphor from feasts, say some; from fathers, say others, who imbosom and hug their children when wearied with long running about, or have met with a knock, and come crying unto them.

And was carried by the angels] Through the air, the devil's region, do the angels conduct the saints at death; who may therefore call death, as Jacob did the place where he met the angels, Mahanaim, Gen. xxxii. 2. For like as the palsy-man was let down with his bed through the tiling before Jesus, Luke v. 18, so is every good soul taken up in a heavenly couch through the roof of his house, and carried into Christ's presence by these heavenly courtiers; who as in life they are our supporters, Psal. xci., so after death our porters, as here, by the angels; as if they had striven which should have a part.

And was buried] Possibly with as much noisome stench and hurry in the air, as at Cardinal Wolsey's burial. A terrible example there is in the Book of Martyrs of one Christopher Landsdale, an unmerciful courtier, who suffering a poor lazar to die in a ditch by him, did afterwards perish himself in a ditch.

The rich man also died] Perhaps he was choked, as Hardicanutus (noted for epicurism, A.D. 1041) was at a marriage at Lambeth, most men rejoicing to be rid of him; in memory whereof Hocktide (a feast of scorning) was a long time after continued in this kingdom, saith our chronicler.

Ver. 23. Being in torments] Having punishment without pity, misery without mercy, sorrow without succour, crying without compassion, mischief without measure, torments without end and past imagination.

And Lazarus in his bosom] Which more vexed him than his own torments, saith Chrysostom.

He lifted up his eyes] So oft lifted up (saith one) in a false devotion.

Ver. 24. And cool my tongue] In his tongue he was most tortured, *quia plus lingua peccaverat*, saith Cyprian. So Nestorius the heretic had his tongue eaten up with worms.[1] So Thomas Arundel, Archbishop of Canterbury, and Stephen Gardiner, Bishop of Winchester (two notorious persecutors), died with their tongues thrust out, big swollen, and black with inflammation of their bodies. A spectacle worthy to be noted of all such bloody burning persecutors.

Ver. 25. Son, remember, &c.] Son he calls him, with respect either *ad procreationem carnis, aut ad ætatem*, saith Piscator. But as it was but cold comfort to Dives in flames that Abraham called him son, so those that have no more to shroud themselves under than a general profession, shall find that an empty title yields but an empty comfort at last.

That thou in thy lifetime] Gregory the Great could never read these words without horror: lest himself, having such honours here, should be shut out of heaven. Jam. v. 5, "Ye have lived in pleasure upon earth;" which is a purgatory, not a paradise.

Receivedst thy good things] Wicked men then have not only a civil title, but a right before God to earthly things. It is their portion, Psal. xvii. 14. And what Ananias had was his own, Acts v., while he had it. God gave Egypt to Nebuchadnezzar for his pains at Tyre. It is hard to say they are usurpers. They shall not (saith one) be called to an account at the last day for possessing what they had, but for abusing that possession. As when the king gives a traitor his life, he gives him meat and drink that may maintain his life. So here God deals, not as that cruel d'Alva did, who starved some prisoners after he had given them quarter, saying, Though I promised you your lives, I promised not to find you meat. (Grimst. Hist. of Netherl).

Ver. 26. There is a great gulf fixed] viz. By the unmovable and immutable decree of God, called mountains of brass, Zech. vi. 1, from between which all effects and actions come forth as so many chariots. ἐστήρικται. *Firmissimum Dei statutum.* Jansen.

Ver. 27. I pray thee therefore] Are not the Popish doctors hard driven, when they allege this text to prove that the dead do take care of the living, and pray for them?

Ver. 28. Lest they also come into this place] This he wisheth, not for their good, but for his own. For he knew that if they were damned, he should be double damned, because they were brought thither partly by his lewd and loose example.

Ver. 29. Let them hear them] Hell is to be escaped by hearing the word read and preached, John v. 25; Isa. lv. 3.

Ver. 30. They will repent] Bellarmine is of opinion that one glimpse of hell were enough to

[1] *Nestorii lingua vermibus excisa.* Evang.

make a man not only turn Christian and sober, but anchorite and monk; to live after the strictest rule that might be. Such a sight or report might work much upon the judgment, but it is the gospel only that works upon the affections, and produceth repentance never to be repented of.

Ver. 31. *Though one rose from the dead*] As Lazarus did, and yet they listened as little to him as to Christ, John xii. 10; but sought to kill him also.

CHAPTER XVII.

Ver. 1, 2.] See the notes on Matt. xviii. 6, 7.
Ver. 3.] See Matt. xviii. 15.
Ver. 4.] See Matt. xviii. 21.
Ver. 5. *Lord, increase our faith*] A most necessary request in this case. For the more any man believeth that God for Christ's sake hath pardoned him, the readier he will be to pardon others.

Ver. 6. *If ye had faith as a grain of mustard seed*] Faith as a grain of mustard seed is *parva, humilis, sed et acris, fervida*, small and low, but withal sharp and lively; it must have acrimony and vivacity, and then it may remove mountains.

Ye might say unto this sycamine tree, &c.] That was a senseless slander of the Jews, that Christ stole the true name of God out of the holy of holies, by which means he wrought all his miracles; and that, lest he should lose it, he cut a hole in his thigh, and sewed it therein. Get we but the true faith of God closed up in our hearts (that most holy faith, as St Jude (20) calleth it), and you may work wonders. See the note on Matt. xvii. 20.

Ver. 7. *But which of you*, &c.] Whereas the disciples, having begged increase of faith, might presume to obtain it as having deserved it; Christ shows here that God is debtor to none; and that they must do their utmost in duty, and expect God's leisure and pleasure for the reward. It is a mercy in God (so David accounteth it) "to render to a man according to his works," Psal. lxii. 12.

Ver. 8. *Gird thyself and serve me*] It implies, first, readiness; secondly, nimbleness, handiness, and handsomeness. A loose, discinct, and diffluent mind is unfit to serve God. The deacons cried of old in the Church meetings, *Oremus, attendamus*, Let us pray, let us attend to prayer, &c.

Ver. 9. *Doth he thank that servant*] God owes us no thank; and yet of his grace he even thanks us, and thinks himself beholden to us. See 1 Pet. ii. 19, with the note there. See also Luke vi. 34. This is *dignatio stupenda*, a wonderful condescension.

Ver. 10. *We have done that was our duty*] Or, our debt; and it is no matter of merit to pay debts. This made William Wickam, founder of New College, &c., profess he trusted in Jesus Christ alone for salvation: Charles V. did the

like, when he came to die.[1] And in times of Popery, the ordinary instruction appointed to be given to men upon their death-beds, was, that they should look to come to glory, not by their own merits, but by the virtue and merit of Christ's passion; that they should place their whole confidence in his death only, and in no other thing; and that they should interpose his death betwixt God and their sins, betwixt them and God's anger. (Dr Usheir in a sermon on Eph. iv. 13.)

Ver. 11. *He passed through Samaria and Galilee*] Albeit he had forbidden his apostles to pass into those parts till after his death; yet he manifested by many arguments that the gospel belonged, and should shortly be preached, to those poor paynims, that as yet sat in darkness and in the shadow of death.

Ver. 12. *Stood afar off*] For so they were charged, Levit. xiii. 45, 46, as also to cover their lips, for fear of infecting others.

Ver. 13. *And they lifted up their voices*] These sought themselves only in their prayers, as do hypocrites; and nought esteemed the love of Christ. So did those that fasted to themselves, Zech. vii. 6; more to get off their chains than their sins. Ephraim "is an empty vine, he beareth fruit to himself," Hos. x. 1. The Church keeps her fruit for her Beloved.

Ver. 14. *Go show yourselves unto the priests*] As if ye were already cleansed. They did so, though they saw no sense for it; and before they came to the priests they were cleansed indeed. Make your "requests known to God with thanksgiving," Phil. iv. 6. As who should say, Make account to speed, and be ready with your thanks, as if you had what you ask of God.

Ver. 15. *And one of them*] It is ten to one if any return to give thanks. Men make prayer their refuge, but not their recompense. Hezekiah returned not according to his receipts.

And with a loud voice] He was as earnest in praises as he had been in prayers. Our thanks should be larger and louder than our requests, because God prevents us with many mercies, and denies nothing; we have it either in money or money's worth.

Ver. 16. *Giving him thanks*] A thankful man is worth his weight in gold. *Sed perraro grati homines reperiuntur*, saith Cicero (*pro Planc.*). *Plerique ut accipiant importuni, donec acceperint, inquieti; ubi acceperint, ingrati*, saith the father. Most pray, but pay not.

Ver. 17. *Were there not ten cleansed?*] Christ keeps count how many favours men receive from him, and will call them to a particular account thereof. He is an austere man this way.

But where are the nine?] Erasmus tells of a Popish dolt, that thought he could prove that there were ten worlds from those words of Christ, *Nonne decem facti sunt mundi?* Another presently disproved him with the words following, *Sed ubi sunt novem?* But where are the nine?

Ver. 18. *There are not found*] The Syriac

[1] Cade of the Church, Parei Medul. 883.

and some others read these words question-wise, and so it is more emphatical. Are there not found that returned? &c. *q. d.* That is admirable, that is abominable.

Ver. 19. *Thy faith hath made thee whole*] Whole on both sides. Thus gratitude ingratiates with Christ, and gets more grace.

Ver. 20. *When the kingdom of God, &c.*] This they asked in scorn: *q. d.* You tell us oft of the kingdom of God, and that it is at hand; but when comes it once? All things continue as they did, &c.

Cometh not with observation] That is, with outward pomp or superstitious seeking after.

Ver. 21. *The kingdom of God is within you*] It is spiritual, Rom. xiv. 17. Or, it is among you, but that you cannot see wood for trees. You seek me as absent, whom you reject present.

Ver. 22. *And he said unto his disciples*] *q. d.* This doctrine concerns you also, as well as the perverse Pharisees. You shall be ere long at a great loss for me; look to it therefore, and bestir you.

Ver. 23.] See Matt. xxiv. 23; Mark xiii. 21.

Ver. 24. *For as the lightning*] *q. d.* From mine ascension, and so forwards, you are not to look for me again till I come to judgment; and then I come on a sudden. Many devices there are in the minds of some, to think that Jesus Christ shall come from heaven again, and reign here upon earth a thousand years. But they are, saith a good divine, but the mistakes of some high expressions in Scripture, which describe the judgments poured out upon God's enemies, in making a way to the Jews' conversion, by the pattern of the last judgment. (Mr Cotton upon the Seven Vials.)

Ver. 25. *But first must he suffer*] He must, because God would have it so. *Voluntas Dei, necessitas rei.*

Ver. 26.] See the notes on Matt. xxiv. 37; 1 Peter iii. 20.

Ver. 27. *They did eat, they drank*] An elegant asyndeton. For the reason whereof, see the note on Matt. xxiv. 38.

Ver. 28. *They did eat, they drank*] It is not said here, as ver. 27, they married wives; they affected rather those odious *concubitus, qui non utrinque resolvunt* (Ovid). The Turkish pashas have their catamites, which are their serious loves; for their wives are used but to dress their meat, to laundress, and for reputation, saith one that had been amongst them. Sodomy (saith he) in the Levant is not held a vice. (Blount's Voyage.)

Ver. 29. *But the same day*] A fair sunshine morning had a foul dismal evening. *Nescis quid serus vesper vehat.* Thou knowest not what a great-bellied day may bring forth. *Omnem crede diem tibi diluxisse supremum.* Think every day thy last day. (Horat.)

Ver. 30. *Even thus shall it be*] Security ushereth in destruction. The Judge standeth before the door, as is easy to foresee: watch, therefore, Jam. v. 9.

Ver. 31. *He which shall be on the housetop*] An hyperbolical expression, usual among the Jews, to denote matter of haste.

Ver. 32. *Remember Lot's wife*] Who either out of curiosity or covetousness turned her back, and she was turned. We are as hardly drawn off the world as a dog from a fat morsel.[1] Those that set forth of Italy with Galeacius, Marquis of Vicum (who left all for the liberty of conscience at Geneva), many of them when they came to the borders of Italy, and considering what they forsook, first looked back, afterward went back again, and were taken by the Spanish Inquisition, and made publicly to abjure the Christian religion. Remember the horrible history of Julian of old, and the lamentable case of Spira a-late, said the Lady Jane Grey, prisoner, to Harding, the apostate. *Lege historiam* (saith one), *ne fias historia; lege judicia, ne fias exemplum judicii.*

Ver. 33.] See the notes on Matt. xvi. 25, and x. 39.

Ver. 34, &c.] See Matt. xxiv. 40, 41, with the notes.

Ver. 37. *Where, Lord?*] Or, whither, Lord, viz. shall they be taken of whom thou speakest? To heaven, saith he. See the notes on Matt. xxiv. 28.

Ver. 38. *There the eagles*] Those vulturine eagles that are said to fly two or three days before to the place where armies are to meet and carcases shall be.

CHAPTER XVIII.

Ver. 1. *Always to pray and not to faint*] Gr. ἐκκακεῖν, not shrink back, as sluggards in work or cowards in war. Prayer should be redoubled and reinforced, as those arrows of deliverance, 2 Kings xiii. 19. The woman of Canaan prays on when denied; and Jacob holds with his hands when his thigh is lamed. He wrestled with slight and might, he raised dust, as the word signifies, and would not away without a blessing.[2] James, surnamed the Just (Christ's kinsman), had his knees made as hard as camel's knees with much praying, as Eusebius witnesseth. Father Latimer, during his imprisonment, was so constant and instant in prayer, that ofttimes he was not able to rise off his knees without help. Yea, Paulus Æmilius, being to fight with Perses, king of Macedonia, would not give over sacrificing to his god Hercules, till he saw certain arguments of a victory. As loathing of meat (saith a divine) and painfulness of speaking are two symptoms of a sick body, so irksomeness of praying and carelessness of hearing, of a sick soul.

Ver. 2. *Which feared not God, nor regarded man*] These two, fear of God and shame of the world, God hath given to men as curbs to re-

---

[1] *Ut canis ab uncto corio.*

[2] *Etiam post naufragium tentantur maria.*

strain them from outrage. But sin hath loaded such an impudency in some men's faces that they dare do anything.

Ver. 3. *Avenge me of mine adversary*] A downright request, without either logic or rhetoric to set it forth or enforce it; to teach us that though our prayers be but blunt or broken language, if importunate, they shall prevail nevertheless.

Ver. 4. *And he would not for awhile*] There is a passive injustice. *Non faciendo nocens, sed patiendo fuit*, saith Ausonius of Claudius. Not to do justice is injustice.

Ver. 5. *She weary me*] Gr. ὑπωπιάζη, she buffet me, or club me down. God must be pressed in prayer till we put him (as you would say) to the blush, or leave a blot in his face, unless we may be masters of our requests. *Vota fundimus, cœlos tundimus, Deum tangimus, misericordiam extorquemus.* (Tertul. Apol.)

Ver. 6, 7. *Hear what the unjust judge saith*] *Hic paria non inter se conferuntur, sed minus cum majore*, saith Beza.

Ver. 7. *Though he bear long with them*] When they are at the utmost under. When their enemies are above fear, and they below hope; when there is not faith in earth to believe, then are there bowels in heaven to relieve and restore them.

Ver. 8. *Shall he find faith upon earth?*] God oft stays so long till the saints have done looking for him, when they have forgot their prayers, and he comes, as it were, out of an engine.

Ver. 9. *That they were righteous, and despised others*] Pray to be preserved from this perilous pinnacle of self-exaltation.

Ver. 10. *The one a Pharisee*] A Doeg may set his foot as far and farther within the sanctuary as a David. The Pharisee and publican went both of them up to private prayer.

Ver. 11. *God, I thank thee*] *Non vulnera, sed munera ostendit*, he shows not his want, but his worth, and stands not only upon his comparisons, but upon his disparisons,—I am not as this publican. No, for thou art worse; yea, for this, because thou thinkest thee better. But of Pharisees it might be said, as Arnobius did of the Gentiles, *Apud vos optimi censentur, quos comparatio pessimorum sic facit.* They are very good that are not very bad. Ἀντιπρόσωπος βλέπων τῷ Θεῷ διελέγετο. (Basil.) *Velut dignus qui cum Deo colloqueretur.* (Erasm.)

I am not as other men are] Pride wears a triple crown with this motto, *Transcendo, Non obedio, Perturbo.* This Pharisee held himself the whole piece, and all others a remnant only, as Basil of Seleucia hath it; he takes his poor counter and sets it down for a thousand pounds; he priceth himself above the market.

Ver. 12. *I fast twice a week*] Cardinal Bellarmine did more, for he fasted thrice a week, saith he that writes his life. John, Archbishop of Constantinople, he who first affected the style of Universal Bishop, was surnamed Nesteutes, from his frequent fasting. Monday and Thursday were the

Pharisees' fasting days, because Moses went up to the mount on a Thursday, and came down on a Monday, saith Drusius. The Manichees fasted on the sabbath, from whence the whole week here taketh its denomination in the original.

I give tithes] He braggingly made a gift of that which he was bound to pay.

Ver. 13. *Smote upon his breast.*] In token of indignation, and that he would have smitten his sin so hard if he could have come at it.

God, be merciful, &c.] Here was much in few. The Publican prayed much though he spake little. As a body without a soul, much wood without fire, a bullet in a gun without powder, so are words in prayer without spirit. *Oratio brevis penetrat cœlum.* The hottest springs send forth their waters by ebullitions. Prayer is called a charm, Isa. xxvi. 16. Now, in a charm or enchantment, in three or four words there is much efficacy.

To me, a sinner] This prayer was oft in Mr Bradford's mouth, and likewise in Mr Samuel Crook's. See his Life, page 32.

Ver. 14. *Justified rather than the other*] The Pharisee was not at all justified; neither is there more or less in justification. But our Saviour here useth a popular kind of expression.

Ver. 15—17] See the notes on Matt. xix. 13; Mark x. 13.

Ver. 18. *And a certain ruler*] St Mark, x. 17, saith that this ruler came running, which argues his earnestness, and in a man of quality was unusual, for such walk softly for most part, and in state, *Gressu grallatorio.*

Ver. 19—21, &c.] See Matt. xix. 16, 17, &c.

Ver. 22. *Yet lackest thou one thing*] Yea, all things. But our Saviour speaketh thus by a holy irony.

Ver. 23, 24] See Matt. xix. 23, 24, &c.

Ver. 25. *It is easier for a camel*] *Caveant ergo divites* (saith an interpreter) *et solicite; mane, vesperi, interdiu, noctu, secum de periculosa vitæ suæ ratione commententur.* Let rich men therefore weigh their danger, and beware.

Ver. 26, 27, &c.] See Matt. xix. 26, 27, &c.

Ver. 31—33] See Matt. xx. 17; Mark x. 32.

Ver. 34. *And they understood none, &c.*] Prejudicate opinions of Christ's earthly kingdom hung as so many bullets at their eye-lids, that they could not perceive so plain a truth.

Ver. 35, 36, &c.] See Matt. xx. 29; Mark x. 46.

CHAPTER XIX.

Ver. 1. *And passed through Jericho*] "An accursed city," John vi. 26, with 1 Kings xvi. 34; and yet Christ hath here a plentiful harvest, poor blind men, rich Zaccheus; to show the truth of what he had affirmed in the former chapter, that a rich man also might possibly enter into the kingdom of heaven.

Ver. 2. *And behold*] This "behold" one compareth to a hand in the margin of a book, pointing to some notable matter. Another, to the sounding of a trumpet before some proclamation.

There was a man named Zaccheus] He should by his name have been a puritan (in the best sense), but he was an arch-publican, a public sinner, not simple, but subtle, a griping extortioner, a rich but wretched sycophant.

Ver. 3. *Because he was little of stature*] τυτθὸς ἀνὴρ. Homer. St Paul was but a little man (say some, and thence had his name) but of a notable spirit. *Deus maximus est in minimis*, saith one, *et sæpe compensat defectus corporis ingenii dotibus.* God is much seen in small things ; and he many times recompenseth defects in the body with gifts of the mind. Hence that of the poet,

———*In parvo regnat corpore virtus.*

Ver. 4. *And he ran before*] Forgetful of his rank and quality. Rich men and rulers use not to run, much less to climb trees, as boys do for birds' nests. But his earnest desire to see his Saviour, and especially a gracious impulse of the Holy Spirit, made him thus seemingly immodest, and unmindful of keeping a decorum.

Ver. 5. *Zaccheus, make haste*] Christ is that good shepherd that knoweth all his sheep, and calleth them by name.

Make haste, and come down] Heaven is a matter of greatest haste : we must not adjourn, as he did once, *In crastinum seria*, more weighty businesses till to-morrow.

To-day I must abide at thy house] Christ not only invites but even obtrudes himself as it were upon Zaccheus : it is happy having such guests. He doth the same to us, when he sends unto us his poor servants to press upon our charity. Unworthy we are surely to give an alms to poor Christ, &c.

Ver. 6. *And he made haste and came down*] Gilbert Foliot, Bishop of London, A. D. 1161, misliking much Archbishop Becket's pride and obstinacy, would often exhort him to humility in these words, *Ad Zacchæum non divertisset Dominus, nisi de sycomoro jam descendisset*, i. e. Christ had never dined with Zaccheus, had he not first yielded to come down from the sycamore tree.

Ver. 7. *They all murmured*] So corrupt was their judgment concerning the offices and condition of the Messiah ; so ill-set were their affections, that themselves neglecting the grace of God that was offered, they take it ill that any other should partake of it.

By false accusation] After the manner of sycophants, ἐσυκοφάντησα. It seems it was his practice, that if any had spoke aught against him, he accused them as wrongers of the law, and that he did nothing to them but what he had law for.

Ver. 8. *The half of my goods*] See the like in Tyrus converted, Isa. xxiii. 17, 18.

I restore him four-fold] Which was the law for things stolen. Fraud is no better than theft. Restitution is necessary to remission of sin. God hates *holocaustum ex rapina*, as Sultan Selymus could tell his counsellor Pyrrhus, who persuaded

him to bestow the great wealth he had taken from the Persian merchants, upon some notable hospital for relief of the poor. The dying Turk commanded it rather to be restored to the right owners, which was done accordingly ; to the great shame of many Christians, who mind nothing less than restitution, &c. When Henry III. of England had sent the friar Minors a load of frieze to clothe them, they returned the same with this message, that he ought not to give alms of what he had rent from the poor, neither would they accept of that abominable gift. Master Latimer saith, " If ye make no restitution of goods detained, ye shall cough in hell, and the devils will laugh at you." Henry VII. in his last will and testament, after the disposition of his soul and body, he devised and willed restitution should be made of all such monies as had unjustly been levied by his officers. Queen Mary restored again all ecclesiastical livings assumed to the Crown, saying, that she set more by the salvation of her own soul than she did by 10 kingdoms. A bull came also from the pope at the same time, that all others should do the like, but none did. Latimer tells us that the first day that he preached about restitution, one came and gave him 20 *lib.* to restore. The next day another brought him 30 *lib.* Another time another gave him 200 *lib.* Mr Bradford hearing Latimer on that subject was struck in the heart for one dash of a pen which he had made without the knowledge of his master, and could never be quiet till, by the advice of Mr Latimer, restitution was made, for which he did willingly forego all the private and certain patrimony which he had on earth. I myself (saith Mr Burroughs) knew one man that had wronged another but of five shillings, and fifty years after could not be quiet till he had restored it.

Ver. 9. *He also is a son of Abraham*] That is, freely elected, Rom. ix. 1, a follower of Abraham's faith, Rom. iv. 12, and a doer of his works, John viii. 39. Who then can say but he is his son, and shall rest in his bosom ?

Ver. 10.] See Matt. xviii. 11.

Ver. 11. *That the kingdom of God*] A temporal earthly kingdom, such as they expected by the Messiah. And it should seem that hearing our Saviour say he came " to seek and to save that which was lost," they mistook him so far as to think that he meant the Jewish kingdom, the public liberty, &c. This misconceit he confuteth in the following parable.

Ver. 14. *Sent a message*] Instead of sending a lamb to this ruler of the earth, Isa. xvi. 1, of the covering his altar with the calves of their lips, Hos. xiv. 3. Such masterless monsters are rife everywhere, such dust-heaps are found in every corner.

Ver. 15. *And when he was returned*] He went at his ascension, and returns at the general resurrection. At what time he will first reckon with his servants, and then with his enemies. Judgment shall then also begin at God's own house.

Ver. 16. *Thy pound hath gained*] Not my pains, but thy pound hath done it. " By the grace of God I am that I am," saith Paul, that *constantissimus gratiæ prædicator*, as Austin calleth him.

Ver. 17—19, &c.] See Matt. xxv. 21, 22, &c.

Ver. 23. *Into the bank*] Gr. Unto the table, or (according to some copies) " unto the usurers," τοῖς τραπεζίταις, whom Beza here rightly calleth *humani certe generis perniciosissimas pestes*, the most pernicious pests of mankind.

Ver. 27. *Slay them before me*] Howbeit " the beast and the false prophet," that is, the pope and his janizaries, shall not have the favour to be slain as the common sort of Christ's enemies are, but shall be " cast alive into the burning lake," tormented more exquisitely, Rev. xix. 20, 21.

Ver. 28. *He went before*] To meet death in the face. This was true magnanimity. Herein he showed himself the Captain of our salvation, though perfected by sufferings.

Ver. 29. *Bethphage and Bethany*] Bethphage was one mile out of Jerusalem, Bethany two.

Ver. 30. *Go ye into the village*] Into Bethphage, that was in their view as they went from Bethany.

Ver. 31, 32, &c.] See notes on Matt. xxi. 1—3, &c.

Ver. 41. *He beheld the city*] That common slaughter-house of the prophets. Our Lord is said to have been slain at Rome, Rev. xi. 8, because crucified at Jerusalem by the Roman authority.

And wept over it] Shall not we weep over the ruins of so many fair and flourishing churches, that now lie in the dirt? Christ wept in this day of his solemn inauguration. It shall be in our last triumph only that all tears shall be wiped from our eyes; till then our passions must be mixed, according to the occasions.

Ver. 42. *Oh, if thou hadst known*] They had *cognitionem historicam non mysticam, speculativam non affectivam, apprehensionis non approbationis, discursivam non experimentalem.*

At least in this thy day] The time of grace is fitly called a day in regard of, 1. Revelation; 2. Adornation; 3. Consolation; 4. Distinction; 5. Speedy preterition. Amend before the drawbridge be taken up. No man can say he shall have 12 hours to his day.

But now they are hid from thine eyes] Yet they lived under the ministry long after, and no outward change to be discerned. As Plutarch writes of Hannibal, that when he could have taken Rome, he would not; when he would, he could not: so the procrastinators.

Ver. 43. *For the days shall come*] God hath his days for vengeance, as man hath his day for repentance. There is a prime of every man's life and of every man's ministry. The Levite lingered so long that he lost his concubine, she came short home; so doth many a man's soul for like reason.

Shall cast a trench about thee] Because, like the wild ass, thou wouldest not otherwise be tamed and kept within compass of God's commandments.

Ver. 44. *One stone*] See Matt. xxiv. 2; Mark xiii. 2.

Because thou knewest not the time of thy visitation] Though thou be called the valley of vision, and the notation of thy name be the vision of peace, yet thou neither knowest the things of thy peace nor the time of thy visitation, as being blinded with malice and obstinacy.

Ver. 45, 46.] See Matt. xxi. 12, 13, &c.; John ii. 14; with notes.

Ver. 47. *He taught daily*] The nearer he drew to his end the more intent he was upon the work, that he might say, as afterwards he did in that heavenly prayer of his, " I have finished the work which thou gavest me to do," John xvii. 4.

But the chief priests] Wild beasts cannot endure fire; no more can wicked men away with zeal. Tigers are enraged with sweet odours; beat up a drum to them and they will tear themselves for anger.

Ver. 48. *Were very attentive to hear him*] Gr. ἐξεκρέματο, hanged on him, as the bee doth on the flower, the babe on the breast, or the little bird on the bill of her dam. Christ drew the people after him, as it were, by the golden chain of his heavenly eloquence.

CHAPTER XX.

Ver. 1. *The chief priests and scribes came*] Gr. ἐπέστησαν, " came suddenly upon him." As an expected storm; the devil drove them.

Ver. 2, 3, &c.] See notes on Matt. xxi. 23; Mark xi. 27.

Ver. 4. *The baptism of John*, &c.] *q. d.* If John were sent by God to testify, as he did, there is no colour of cause why ye should question mine authority.

Ver. 8. *Neither tell I you*, &c.] God's servants should be ready with their answer upon sudden assaults, and not to seek of such arguments as may stop the mouth of an adversary. When a nimble Jesuit asked, Where was your religion before Luther? answer was presently returned, In the Bible, where your religion never was.

Ver. 9.] See Matt. xxi. 33; Mark xii. 1.

Ver. 16. *God forbid*] viz. that they should ever kill the Son of God sent unto them. We cannot get men to believe that their hearts are half so bad or their ways so dangerous as the preacher makes of them.

Ver. 17. *What is this then that is written*, &c.] *q. d.* If it be not so as I say, that you shall kill the Messiah, how is it that the Scripture saith as much? Press men with Scripture testimonies; that is the readiest way of sound conviction. It was a good speech of Augustine to Manichæus, contesting with him for audience: Hear me, hear me, said the heretic. Nay, saith Augustine, *Nec ego te, nec tu me, sed ambo audiamus aposto-*

lum dicentem, peccatum non cognovi, &c. It is not what I say, or what thou sayest, but what the Scripture saith, that we must stand to.

Ver. 19. *They perceived*] Conscience, their domestical chaplain, told them so much. God hath a witness to his truth in every man's bosom.

Ver. 20. *They sent forth spies*] Gr. ἐγκαθέτους, fishers, that with net and bait catch the silly fish and feed on them; such were these emissaries, these catch-poles.

Which should feign themselves just men] Hypocrites only act religion, play devotion; as stageplayers they act a sultan, when they are but so many sowters; as ferrymen they look one way and row another; they have holiness written upon their outsides, as Vorstius' book had *De Deo* in the front and blasphemy in the text. They cry out *Templum Domini*, the temple of the Lord, but care not for the Lord of the temple. But religion, as it is the best armour, so it is the worst cloak; and will serve hypocrites as the disguise Ahab put on and perished, or as Absalom's mule served her master, &c.

Ver. 21.] See Matt. xxii. 16; Mark xii. 14.

Ver. 27, 28, &c.] See Matt. xxii. 23, &c.; Mark xii. 18.

Ver. 35. *Nor are given in marriage*] Hence some collect, that the difference of sexes shall continue after the resurrection: wherefore else should our Saviour say, that they shall then neither marry nor be given in marriage? *Sed hic ἐπέχω.* Haymo is over-confident, I suppose, in that gloss he gives here, *Quod viri in suo sexu resurgent, fœminæ in sexu muliebri. Erunt habentes membra genitalia, non autem voluntatem coeundi.*

Ver. 36. *Die any more*] That there should be any further use of matrimony, for the propagation of mankind.

Ver. 38. *For all live to him*] Even in their bodies also, which he now by rotting refineth; and shall as certainly raise, as if they were already raised, sith all things are present with him.

Ver. 39. *Thou hast well said*] Because he had set down the Sadducees, who were their counter-factionists.

Ver. 41.] See Matt. xxii. 42; Mark xii. 35.

Ver. 45.] See Matt. xxiii. 1—5; Mark xii. 38; Luke xi. 43.

Ver. 47. *Greater damnation*] Shall be double damned, because dissembled sanctity is double iniquity.

CHAPTER XXI.

Ver. 1.] See the notes on Mark xii. 41.

Ver. 2. *Casting in thither two mites*] That is, two eighth parts of an half-penny, saith the Syriac. See the notes on Mark xii. 41, 42, &c.

Ver. 5, 6, &c.] See notes on Matt. xxiv. 1, 2, &c.

Ver. 7—9, &c.] See Matt. xxiv. 3, 4, &c.

Ver. 12.] See Matt. xxiv. 9; Mark xiii. 9.

Ver. 13. *And it shall turn to you*, &c.] Whilst the valour of the martyrs and the savageness of the persecutors strove together, till both, exceeding nature and belief, bred wonder and astonishment in beholders and hearers.

Ver. 14.] See Matt. x. 19; Mark xiii. 11; with notes.

Ver. 18.] See Matt. x. 30; with notes. See also for explication, 1 Sam. xiv. 25; 2 Sam. xiv. 11; Acts xxvii. 34.

Ver. 19. *In your patience possess*] That is, enjoy yourselves, however the world goes with you. He that cannot have patience had need make up his pack and get out of the world, for here is no being for him. Burleigh, lord treasurer, was wont to say that he overcame envy more by patience than pertinacy.

Ver. 20. *Jerusalem compassed with armies*] By Cestius Gallus, a little before that fatal siege by Titus. So God gave his people this sign, to take best course for their own safety.

Ver. 21.] See Matt. xxiv. 16; Mark xiii. 14.

Ver. 22, 23.] See Matt. xxiv. 15—17.

Ver. 24. *Until the times of the Gentiles*] The Gentiles then shall not always tread down Jerusalem. Those kings of the East, the Jews, may, likely, have their way prepared to it, through Euphrates, Rev. xvi. 12, and Jerusalem be again inhabited by them, even in Jerusalem, Zech. xii. 6. But this will be not long before the last day, ver. 25.

Ver. 25.] See Matt. xxiv. 29; Mark xiii. 24; 2 Peter iii. 10.

Ver. 26. *Men's hearts failing them*] What marvel though wicked men be dispirited, and even ring their bells backwards, when they shall see all on a light fire? Moses himself may tremble at the terror of the mount, and Abraham show some trepidation in such a fright.

Ver. 27. *Coming in a cloud*] As on a chariot. See Rev. i. 7.

Ver. 28. *Look up*] You that shall then be found alive shall soon be caught up, 1 Thess. iv., and fully freed from all evils and enemies.

Ver. 29.] See Matt. xxiv. 32; Mark xiii. 38.

Ver. 33.] See Matt. v. 18.

Ver. 34. *Take heed that your hearts*] The disciples themselves had in them the common poison of nature, and so were obnoxious even to the most reproachful evils. That πανσπερμία, if watered with the temptation of Satan, what sin may it not produce in the best, unless God prevent? Let the best take heed that they be not *irregulares gulares*, making the corpse a cloak-bag, the gut a gulf, &c. A full belly makes a foul heart: the rankest weeds grow out of the fattest soil.

Ver. 35. *As a snare*] See Eccles. ix. 12, with the note there.

Ver. 36. *That ye may be accounted worthy*] Great is the emphasis of this word, καταξιωθῆτε (saith learned Beza), for it gives us to understand that we owe all to the free election of God, who loved us first, and so accepted us for worthy, Rev. iii. 4.

Ver. 37. *And in the day*] So he divided his

time between preaching and praying; as did also his apostles, Acts vi. 4. See the note there.

Ver. 38. *Came early in the morning*] *Manicabat*, saith the Vulgar, imitating the Greek, ὤρθριζε. Let our people look upon their forwardliness, and be ashamed of their long-lying, tardy coming to hear the word.

CHAPTER XXII.

Ver. 1. *Now the feast of unleavened bread, &c.*] IT is good to bring Bibles to church. Socrates relates of one Sabbatius a Novatian bishop, that, reading this text, added such things of his own as carried away many simple people from the faith.

Ver. 2. *How they might kill him*] Not put him to death as judges, but kill him as cutthroats, ἀνέλωσι. So Acts ii. 23.

Ver. 3. *Then entered Satan*] He stood but at the door till now, that the business was concluded on.

Ver. 4. *And communed with the chief priests*] *Suopte ingenio, ut reprobi angeli*, saith an interpreter.

Ver. 5. *And covenanted*] Judas sold his salvation, and they bought their damnation, saith one. He made a match with mischief, and soon had enough of it.

Ver. 6. *And he promised*] ἐξωμολόγησε, by mutual stipulation (saith Beza), wherein the one asketh, Dost thou promise to do such a thing? the other answereth, I do promise. Like as of old it was, *Credis? Credo. Abrenuncias? Abrenuncio.* Believest thou? I do believe. Forsakest thou? I do forsake.

Ver. 7. *The day of unleavened bread, when, &c.*] It must be our care to cast out all filthiness of flesh and spirit (that old leaven) before we communicate, 1 Cor. v. 7. First throw the baggage into the brook Kidron (the town-ditch) and then "kill the Passover," 2 Chron. xxx. 14.

Ver. 8—10, &c.] See Matt. xxvi. 17, 18, &c.; Mark xiv. 12.

Ver. 15. *With desire have I desired*] How much more should we come with strong affections and lusty appetites to this holy supper! It is a virtue here to be a holy glutton, and to drink hearty draughts; that we may go from the table, as Christ from Jordan, full of the Holy Ghost. For this end consider what is before thee, as Prov. xxiii. 1, not to restrain appetite, but to provoke it. And the rather because Christ thus earnestly thirsted after our salvation, though he knew it should cost him so dear. See Luke xii. 50.

Ver. 16. *Until it be fulfilled*] Until the old passover be abolished, and the new brought in place, by my death and resurrection.

Ver. 17. *And he took the cup*] The cup of the common supper, John xiii. 2, 3.

Ver. 18.] See Matt. xxvi. 29; Mark xiv. 25.

Ver. 19.] See Matt. xxvi. 26; Mark xiv. 22.

Ver. 23. *And they began to inquire*] Therefore the Lord had not perfectly pointed out the traitor to them; or if he did, they either heard not, or heeded not.

Ver. 24. *There was also a strife*] This was so much the worse in them, because immediately after the sacrament, and before the passion, which our Saviour had told them should fall out within two days after. Neither was this the first time that they had thus faulted, and were reproved for it.

Ver. 25. *The kings of the Gentiles, &c.*] In striving for precedency, the disciples showed themselves but Gentiles, who stand upon their birth and privileges.

Exercise lordship over them] As he did with a witness (of whom Melancthon writeth) that wrung money from his miserable subjects, by knocking out their teeth, one by one, till he had what he would. (Joh. Manlii, *loc. com.*)

Are called benefactors] *Nedibim*, bountiful princes, Psal. xlvii. 10, and lxxxiii. 12. Such an one was Titus son of Vespasian, who never sent away any suitor sorrowful; and was the author of this brave speech, *Hodie non regnavimus, quia neminem affecimus beneficio*: We seem not to have reigned this day, because we have done no man a good turn to-day.

Ver. 26.] See Matt. xx. 25; Mark x. 42.

Ver. 27. *I am among you as he that serveth*] *i. e.* Not as a master, but rather as your fellow-disciple. The prophets had their scholars to wait upon them, and to minister to them. God's Levite had one man to ride with him, Judges xix. 11; Balaam had two, Numb. xxii. 22.

Ver. 28. *Ye are they which have continued, &c.*] Agrippa having suffered imprisonment for wishing Caius emperor, the first thing Caius did after he came to the empire, was to prefer Agrippa to a kingdom. He gave him also a chain of gold as heavy as the chain of iron that was upon him in prison. And shall not Christ richly reward all those his suffering servants?

Ver. 29. *And I appoint*] Gr. διατίθεμαι, I bequeath as by my last will and testament. See Heb. ix. 17.

Ver. 30. *That ye may eat and drink, &c.*] As Mephibosheth and Chimham at David's table, which was a high favour.

Ver. 31. *Simon, Simon*] *q. d. Mi charissime* Simon. Piscat.

Satan hath desired, &c.] As a challenger desireth to have one of the other side to combat with, as Goliath did. He cannot harm us without leave. So he desired to have Job, and had him.

That he may sift you] *Cribratione Satanæ non perditur, sed purgatur frumentum*, saith Zanchy. See the note on Matt. iii. 12.

Ver. 32. *But I have prayed*] So the plaster is ready made before the wound be given; for else the patient might perish, as those do that are stung with scorpions, if not presently anointed with oil of scorpions.

That thy faith fail not] It is our faith that

Satan chiefly assaulteth: he knows that *nihil retinet qui fidem perdidit.* (Seneca.)

Strengthen thy brethren] So he doth notably, in both his Epistles, dooming apostates most severely, 2 Pet. ii.

Ver. 33. *Lord, I am ready*] Thus Peter overweened his own abilities; being *melius semper animatus quam armatus*, better affected than appointed.

Ver. 34.] See Matt. xxvi. 34; Mark xiv. 30; John xiii. 38.

Ver. 35.] See Matt. x. 9; Luke x. 4.

Ver. 36. *But now he that hath,* &c.] Here the Captain of our salvation cries, Arm, arm; and under the name and notion of corporal weapons he intends all manner of spiritual preparations.

Ver. 37. *For the things concerning me*] *i. e.* Concerning my state of humiliation.

Ver. 38. *It is enough*] *q. d.* You speak absurdly: I mean not such kind of swords; let me hear no more of them.

Ver. 39.] See Matt. xxvi. 36; Mark xiv. 32; John xiv. 4.

Ver. 40.] See Matt xxvi. 41; Mark xiv. 38.

Ver. 41. *And he was withdrawn*] For privacy' sake to pray, though loth to leave their company, through extreme perplexity, which made him return so oft to them, calling upon them to watch with him.

Ver. 42. *If thou be willing*] He was so astonished with the greatness of his present pressures, that he seems for a time to suffer some kind of forgetfulness of his office.

Ver. 43. *And there appeared*] To show that he had made himself lower than the angels, Heb. ii. 7, he received comfort from an angel that was his servant. So in his agony he was glad of his apostles' company, and the help of their poor prayers.

Ver. 44. *And being in an agony*] Μὴ διὰ τοῦτο ἄτιμος, ὅτι διὰ σὲ ταπεινός. saith a Greek father. Alphonsus is honoured in histories for this, that he abased himself so far as to help one of his subjects out of a ditch. Shall not Christ much more be honoured that helped all his out of the ditch of damnation?

He prayed more earnestly] ἐκτενέστερον, he bent, as it were, all his nerves, he intended the utmost activity of his spirit and of his speech; to make atonement for our dull and drowsy devotions.

Great drops of blood] Clotty blood (θρομβοὺς αἵματος) issuing through flesh and skin in great abundance. Œcolampadius tells of a certain poor man, who being kept hanging in the truss of the cord (which is a certain hanging by the hands behind, having a weighty stone fastened at their feet) the space of six hours, the sweat that dropped from his body for very pain and anguish, was almost blood. But here was no "almost" in our Saviour's bloody sweat: while without any external violence, merely by the force of his own saddest thoughts working upon him, *sanguinem congelatum quasi extruserit.* (Bucholcer.) So great was Scanderbeg's ardour in battle, that the

blood burst out of his lips. But from our Champion's, not lips only, but whole body burst out a bloody sweat. Not his eyes only were fountains of tears, or his head waters, as Jeremiah wished, chap. ix. 1, but his whole body was turned, as it were, into rivers of blood: a sweet comfort to such as are cast down for that, that their sorrow for sin is not so deep and soaking as they could desire.

Falling down to the ground] Through clothes and all, in a cold night; so great was the pressure of his passion here begun. He wept with his members; a strange kind of watering of a garden, as one saith.

Ver. 45. *He found them sleeping*] Who should have waked, and wiped off his sweat (as the angel did Theodorus the martyr's), but they rather added to it by their security. (Socrates, Theodoret.)

Ver. 46, 47.] See Matt. xxvi. 47; Mark xiv. 43; John xviii. 3.

Ver. 48. *Judas, betrayest thou,* &c.] *Sic Judæi, sub prætextu pietatis maxime delinquebant; et Deo osculum sine amore præbebant.* (Bucholcer.) Julian the Apostate was no friend to Basil, though he wrote to him, φίλος φίλῳ καὶ ἀδελφὸς ἀδελφῷ. Nor was Libanius the more to be believed for saying (in Epist. ad Basilium), Βασιλείου μὲ ἐπαινήσαντος κατὰ πάντων ἔχω τὰ νικητήρια. If Basil commend me, I despise other men's worse censures.

Ver. 49. *Lord, shall we smite?*] But before he could answer, Peter smote, which might easily have cost him his life. *Quod dubites, ne feceris,* is a safe rule.

Ver. 50.] See Matt. xxvi. 51; Mark xiv. 47; John xviii. 10.

Ver. 51. *And he touched his ear,* &c.] After he had laid them flat on the ground. So he tried them both ways; but nothing would do.

Ver. 52. *Captain of the temple*] See the note on Acts iv. 1.

Ver. 53. *And the power of darkness*] The "dark places of the earth are full of the habitations of cruelty," Psal. lxxiv. 20. Creatures kept in the dark are fierce and furious. Had they known, they would never have crucified the Lord of glory, 1 Cor. ii. 8. "I did it ignorantly," saith Paul concerning his persecuting the saints, 1 Tim. i. 13.

Ver. 54.] See Matt. xxvi. 57.

Ver. 55.] See Matt. xxvi. 69; John xviii. 25.

Ver. 56, 57, &c.] *Vide ibidem cum notis.*

Ver. 61. *And looked upon Peter*] A stroke from guilt broke Judas' heart into despair: but a look from Christ broke Peter's heart into tears.

Ver. 62.] See Matt. xxvi. 75. *Titubatio Petri, omnium petra.*

Ver. 63.] See Matt. xxvi. 27; Mark xiv. 65; John xviii. 22. See Isa. l. 6. They scoffed him, not so much with their tongues as hands; plucking his beard, and pulling away hair and skin too, as the word δέρειν importeth.

Ver. 65. *And many other things*] Shooting

their sharpest arrows at him, even bearded arrows, which being once got into the flesh, cannot easily be pulled out but by tearing the flesh round about : and far worse than those shot by the Turks at the crucifix, when they sacked Constantinople, railing also, and spitting at it, and calling it the God of the Christians.

Ver. 66.] See Matt. xxvii. 1.

Ver. 67.] Here the president of the council examineth him, as ver. 70 the assessors.

Ver. 68, 69.] Christ's answer is partly reprehensory, partly concessory and comminatory ; for it is a confession of the truth mixed with menaces of condign punishment.

Ver. 70. *Ye say that I am*] Or, as Mark hath it more plainly, "I am," Mark xiv. 62. Christ here useth a vulgar kind of speech, to consent to what another saith.

Ver. 71.] See Matt. xxvi. 65.

CHAPTER XXIII.

Ver. 1.] See Matt. xxvii. 2 ; John xviii. 28.

Ver. 2. *Perverting the people*] Gr. διαστρέφοντα, turning them upside down, wreathing them from their right minds. So ver. 5. He "stirreth up the people," Gr. ἀνασείει, he maketh an earthquake in them ; *rectum tollit de cardine mentem*, he throws them off the hinges.

Ver. 3.] See Matt. xxvii. 11 ; Mark xv. 2 ; John xviii. 33.

Ver. 4.] See John xviii. 38.

Ver. 5. *He stirreth up the people*] In the present tense, *q. d.* He doth nothing else ; he maketh it his whole trade and constant practice, *Mendacium putidum.*

Ver. 6. *He asked*] As desirous to rid his hands of him.

Ver. 7. *He sent him*] So seeking to ingratiate with Herod.

Ver. 8. *He was exceeding glad*] As if he had got some juggler or enchanter, that would show him some pleasant sight.

Ver. 9. *But he answered him nothing*] Princes use to correct the indecencies of ambassadors by denying them audience, as if silence were the way royal to revenge a wrong. Christ spoke not a word to Herod (saith one), because Herod had taken away his voice by beheading the Baptist, who was *vox clamantis.*

Ver. 10. *Vehemently accused him*] Gr. εὐτόνως, with great intention of spirit, and contention of speech. *Clamant, ut Stentora vincant.*

Ver. 11. *Set him at nought*] Gr. ἐξουθενήσας, made nobody of him.

Arrayed him in a gorgeous robe] Or a white robe, as the old interpreter hath it, λαμπρὰν. Pilate's soldiers clad our Saviour in purple (a colour more affected by the Romans), Herod in white, as more affected by the Jewish nobility.

Mocked him] Gr. ἐμπαίξας, handled him like a boy, or made a baby of him, made sport with him.

Ver. 12. *Pilate and Herod were made friends*]

Two dogs that are fighting can easily agree to pursue the hare that passeth by them. Martial brings in the hare thus complaining :

In me omnis terræque aviumque, marisque rapina est :
   Forsitan et cœli, si canis astra tenet.

In littore Siculo cum lepus canum venaticorum vim evasisset, à cane marino captus dicitur : est enim voracissima maris bellua, saith Bodin. The wicked can easily unite against the saints.

Ver. 13, 14.] See Matt. xxvii. 23 ; John xviii. 38.

Ver. 15. *No, nor yet Herod*] Nor any man alive, though he had the devil to help him. The poets bring in Momus, finding fault with the creaking of Venus' pantofle. But Christ was ἀμνὸς ἄμωμὸς, as St Peter calleth him, 1 Pet. i. 19, the spotless Lamb of God, in whom Momus himself could find nothing amiss, after long seeking. See John xiv. 30.

Ver. 16. *I will therefore chastise him*] And so he did, purposely to move pity, John xix. 1, but all in vain : yea, though he afterwards presented him a pitiful spectacle, with "Behold the man."

Ver. 17. *For of necessity*] *Tyrannus ille trium literarum Mos*, would needs have it so. See John xviii. 29 ; Matt. xxvii. 15.

Ver. 18. *Release unto us*] What marvel though murderers desire a murderer ? *Similis similem sibi quærit.*

Ver. 19.] See John xviii. 40, with the note.

Ver. 20. *Pilate therefore, willing, &c.*] I read of one that did verily think that Pilate was an honest man, because he was so unwilling to crucify Christ. But this arose only from the restraint of natural conscience against so foul a fact.

Ver. 21. *Crucify him, crucify him*] As if they should say, Do it twice over, rather than fail. The modern Jews, as mad as their forefathers, say that rather than we Gentiles should have benefit by their expected Messiah, they would crucify him an hundred times over.

Ver. 22. *The third time*] It is well observed here, that Peter for fear denied Christ three times, and yet repented ; Pilate three times justified Christ, and yet for popular favour condemned him. It may teach us neither to despair if we repent, nor presume because we have begun well.

Ver. 23. *And they were instant with loud voices*] It is said of Nestorius the heretic, that he was *homo superbus, et indoctus, sed audax, et magnæ loquentiæ ; quâ unicâ fretus, nihil non audebat ; et quidem sæpenumero fæliciter, quod volebat, obtinebat ;* a proud dunce, but bold and loud-spoken, whereby he had what he would many times. (Zanchius.)

Ver. 24.] See Matt. xxvii. 26 ; Mark xv. 15.

Ver. 25. *Him that for sedition*] The Jews, before they were banished out of this kingdom, threw bags of poison into the wells and fountains that the people were to drink of ; and so endeavoured to poison them all. So deal those that sow sedition ; these are the pests, the botches of human society.

Ver. 26.] See Matt. xxvii. 32 ; Mark xv. 21.

Ver. 27. *Which also bewailed*] This was all they could do, and it was much they durst do it in so evil a time. In the reign of Tiberius, one Vitia was punished with death for that she had lamented Geminus her son, executed as friend to Sejanus. And because they could not accuse women for attempting against the State, their tears were criminal, saith Tacitus.

Ver. 28. *Weep not for me*] We are not so much to lament Christ's dolorous sufferings (as Papists use to do in their histrionical descriptions of his passion) as to lay to heart and lament our sins, the cause of all. When a Papist came to Master Hooper at the stake, and said, " Sir, I am sorry to see you thus," " Be sorry for thyself, man," said hearty Hooper, " and lament thine own wickedness, for I am well, I thank God, and death to me for Christ's sake is welcome." (Acts and Mon.)

Ver. 29. *Blessed are the barren*] Better be so than bring forth children to the murderer. Hence Hosea prays for barrenness as a blessing on his people, Hos. ix. 14.

Ver. 30.] See Rev. vi. 16, with the note.

Ver. 31. *What shall be done in the dry ?*] Lo, little sucklings also are here called dry trees, sere-wood, such as God's wrath will soon kindle upon.

Ver. 32.] See Matt. xxvii. 38.

Ver. 33. *Which is called Calvary*] As sad a sight to our Saviour, as the bodies of his slain wife and children were to Mauricius the emperor, who was soon after to be slain also by the command of the traitor Phocas. Let us learn to consider the tyranny and deformity of sin as oft as we pass through churchyards and charnel-houses. Historians tell us that the way whereby Christ went bearing his cross to Calvary is at this day called The Dolorous Way.

There they crucified him] Christ's cross, with his naked and bloody body, being lift up on high, was let fall with violence into a mortise, that his joints were dissolved, said Origen to Alexander Severus the emperor.

Ver. 34. *Father, forgive them*] See the sweet mercy of Christ, mindful and careful of his enemies when the pains of hell had taken hold of him, and they, like so many breathing devils, were tormenting him. *Pendebat et tamen petebat,* saith Augustine. He was slain by them, and yet he begged for them.

Ver. 35. *Derided him*] Gr. ἐξεμυκτήριζον, blew their noses at him.

Ver. 36. *Offered him vinegar*] Instead of wine, which kings drink much of.

Ver. 37.] See Matt. xxvii. 42.

Ver. 38. *Greek, Latin, and Hebrew*] This venerable eulogy and epitaph, set upon our Saviour's cross, proclaimed him King of all religion, having reference to the Hebrews ; of all wisdom, to the Greeks ; of all power, to the Latins.

Ver. 39. *Which were hanged, railed, &c.*] Sic

plectimur à Deo, nec flectimur tamen (saith Salvian), *corripimur, sed non corrigimur.* There are many, *quos multo facilius fregeris, quam flexeris,* saith Buchanan. *Monoceros interimi potest capi non potest.* The wicked are the worse for that they suffer, and will sooner break than bend.

Ver. 40. *But the other answering*] Silent he was for a while, and therefore seemed to consent ; till hearing Christ's prayers and the enemies' outrages, he brake out into this brave confession, worthy to be written in letters of gold.

Ver. 41.] See Matt. xxvii. 38. This good thief, like the olive-tree, bore fruit late, but great store of that which was excellent.

Ver. 42. *Lord, remember me*] By this penitent prayer he made his cross a Jacob's ladder, whereby the angels descended to fetch up his soul. So did Leonard Cæsar, burnt at Rappa in Bavaria, whose last words were these, " Lord Jesu, suffer with me, support me, give me strength : I am thine, save me," &c. (Scultet. Annal.) See the note on Matt. xxvii. 38.

Ver. 43. *Verily I say unto thee*] See the infinite love of Christ to penitent sinners, in that when he hung upon the tree, and was paying dear for man's sin, he rejected not this malefactor's petition. Shall he not hear us now that all is paid and finished ?

To-day shalt thou be with me] This is not every man's happiness. A pardon is sometimes given to one upon the gallows ; but whoso trusts to that, the rope may be his hire. It is not good to put it upon the psalm of Miserere and the neck-verse (saith one), for sometimes he proves no clerk. Most deal with repentance as country people do with physicians,—love not to have to do with them till they fear they are gasping the last breath. The mole begins not to see till he be at point of death : *Oculos incipit aperire moriendo, quos clausos habuit vivendo,* saith Pliny. The serpent stretcheth not himself out straight till he hath received his death's wound. But what if God should say to such lingerers, as the crab in the fable did to the dying serpent, *At oportuit sic vixisse,* " It is too late now, you should have lived so ? "

Ver. 44.] See Matt. xxvii. 25 : Mark xv. 33.

Ver. 45.] See Matt. xxvii. 51 ; Mark xv. 38.

Ver. 46.] See Matt. xxvii. 50.

Ver. 47. *Certainly this was a righteous man*] Bennet the martyr, in King Henry VIII.'s days, being brought to execution, the most part of the people (he exhorted them with such gravity and sobriety), as also the scribe who wrote the sentence of condemnation against him, did pronounce and confess that he was God's servant, and a good man. So when Wiseheart and March the martyrs went toward the stake, they were justified by the beholders, as innocent and godly persons. (Acts and Mon.)

Ver. 48, 49.] See Matt. xxvii. 54.

Ver. 50.] See Matt. xxvii. 57 ; Mark xv. 43 ; John xix. 38.

Ver. 51. *The same had not consented*] This proved him to be a good man and a just, as Psal. i. 1. Sir John Cheek was drawn in for fear of death to be present at the condemnation of some of the martyrs. The remorse whereof so mightily wrought upon his heart, that not long after he left this mortal life; whose fall, though it was full of infirmity, yet his rising again by repentance was great, and his end comfortable, saith Master Fox. So by the malice and subtilty of Stephen Gardiner, Cromwell was commanded by King Henry VIII. to read the sentence of condemnation against Mr Lambert the martyr, for the which Cromwell afterwards asked him forgiveness.

Waited for the kingdom of God] Gr. προσεδέχετο, entertained and embraced it.

Ver. 52, 53.] See Matt. xxvii. 58—60.

Ver. 54, 55.] See Matt. xxvii. 61.

Ver. 56. *And rested the sabbath day*] From all servile work, yea, that (otherwise most honourable) work of embalming Christ's dead body.

CHAPTER XXIV.

Ver. 1. *Very early in the morning*] About which time, probably, our Saviour rose.

Ver. 2.] See Matt. xxvii. 60, 66.

Ver. 3. *Found not the body*] But the graveclothes only, John xx. 6. As Samson, shut up in Gaza, took the gates on his shoulders, and went his way in despite of his enemies; so did Christ here. These women came first, by a wonderful providence, before the apostles, to confute that impudent lie made by the priests, that the disciples had stolen away the body.

Ver. 4. *Two men stood*] Two angels in the habit of men.

Ver. 5, 6.] See Matt. xxviii. 5, 6.

Ver. 7.] See Matt. xvii. 23; Mark ix. 31; Luke ix. 22.

Ver. 8. *And they remembered his words*] Which at first hearing they understood not, heeded not. So the new birth of some is like the birth of the elephant, fourteen years after the seed injected into the womb.

Ver. 9. *And told all these things*] *Per os mulieris mors ante processerat, per os mulieris vita reparatur*, saith Ambrose. So, chap. i., an angel of light communeth with a woman about man's salvation, as an angel of darkness had done (Gen. iii.) about his fall and destruction.

Ver. 9. *And told all these things*] For it was a day of good tidings, as those lepers said in another case, 2 Kings vii. 9, the sum of all the good news in the world.

Ver. 10. *And other women*] Who were to be *Apostolorum Apostolæ*, as the ancients speak.

Ver. 11. *As idle tales*] Set on with great earnestness, λῆρος *a* λά, *particula intensiva, et* ἐρῶ, *valde dico*.

Ver. 12. *And stooping down*] *Obstipo capite et propenso collo.* We need not doubt therefore of the certainty of this history of Christ's resurrection.

Ver. 13. *About threescore furlongs*] About six miles.

Ver. 14. *And they talked together*] So did Elias and Elisha, when the heavenly chariot came to sunder them. Christ is still with two or three met for such an holy purpose.

Ver. 15. *Jesus himself*] He made the third amongst them, as Dionysius, the king of Sicily, wished that he might be admitted into fellowship of friendship with those two fast friends, Damon and Pythias. (Cic. *de Offic.*) Christ still delights to be one among those that meet to confer about the things of his kingdom.

Ver. 16. *But their eyes were held*] *Ut ulcus suum discipuli detegerent, ac pharmacum susciperent*, saith Theophylact. That they may tell their own disease and receive healing.

Ver. 17. *That ye have one to another*] Gr. that ye toss one to another, as a ball is tossed betwixt two or more. ἀντιβάλλετε, *tu cum duo pilâ lusitant.*

And are sad] Christ loves not to see his saints sad; he questions them as Joseph did his prisoners, "Wherefore look ye so sadly to-day?" Gen. xl. 7, and as the king did Nehemiah, chap. ii. 2.

Ver. 18. *And one of them, whose name was Cleophas*] They that hold the other of these two to have been St Luke, are refuted by the preface he hath set before the Acts, saith Beza.

Art thou only a stranger, &c.] Tragedies have no prologues, as comedies have, because it is supposed that all men take knowledge of public calamities. (Natal. Comes.)

Ver. 19. *Which was a prophet*] Yea, and more than a prophet. But the disciples were wondrous ignorant, till the Spirit came down upon them, Acts ii.

Ver. 20. *Delivered him*] viz. to the Roman governor. Hence he is said to have been crucified at Rome, Rev. xi. 8.

Ver. 21. *But we trusted*] *q. d.* Indeed now we cannot tell what to say to it. Here their hope hangs the wing extremely, their buckler is much battered, and needs beating out again. *Ferendum et sperandum*, said the philosopher. (οἰστέον καὶ ἐλπιστέον. Epictet.) And good men find it more easy to bear evil than to wait for good, Heb. x. 36.

Ver. 22. *Made us astonished*] When they should rather have believed without sciscitation; but that their hearts were yet still stupefied.

Ver. 23. *Saying that they had seen a vision*] But you (wisely) thought that they had dreamt a dream rather, that they had doted and dreamt waking, ver. 11.

Ver. 24. *Certain of them*] viz. Peter and John. See John xx. 6, with the notes there.

Ver. 25. *O fools*, &c.] Those in a lethargy must have double the quantity of physic that others have. Some slow-bellies must be sharply rebuked, that they may be sound in the faith, Tit. i. 12, 13.

Ver. 26. *Ought not Christ*] *Ne Jesum quidem audias gloriosum, nisi videris crucifixum*, saith Luther in an epistle to Melancthon. *Agentem fortiter oportet aliquid pati*, said a Theban soldier, out of Pindarus, to Alexander, when he had received a wound in battle. For the which sentence he liberally rewarded him. τὸν δρῶντα δεινὰ καὶ παθεῖν δεῖ.

Ver. 27. *The things concerning himself*] Christ is author, object, matter, and mark of Old and New Testament: the babe of Bethlehem is bound up (as I may so say) in these swathing-bands. Turn we the eyes of our minds to him, as the cherubims did their faces toward the mercy-seat. The angels do, 1 Pet. i. 12.

Ver. 28. *And he made as though he would, &c.*] So did the angels to Lot, Gen. xix. 2. See the like, Josh. viii. 5, 6; 1 Kings iii. 24. If Solomon might make as though he would do an act that was unlawful, we may surely do the like in things indifferent. Yet this was never done, as is well observed, but, 1. By those that had authority over others; 2. For some singular good to them with whom they thus dealt.

Ver. 29. *But they constrained him*] Though they had been sharply rebuked by him, whom they knew to be no other than a mere stranger to them.

For it is toward evening] Cry we, now if ever, ere it be too late,

Vespera jam venit, nobiscum Christe maneto.
Extingui lucem nec patiare tuam.

Ver. 30. *And blessed it*] It is thought they knew him by his ordinary form of giving thanks before meat.

Ver. 31. *Their eyes were opened*] The free and entire use of their inward and outward senses was restored unto them.

Ver. 32. *Did not our hearts burn*] By that spirit of burning (Isa. iv. 4) that kindleth the fire of God (Cant. viii. 6) on the hearth of his people's hearts, while the mystery of Christ is laid open unto them. *Ego vero illius oratione sic incendebar*, saith Senarclæus, concerning Darius the martyr, *ut cum eum disserentem audirem, Spiritus Sancti verba me audire existimarem.* Methought when I heard him, I heard the Holy Ghost himself speaking to me.

While he opened] Preaching then is the key of the Scripture.

Ver. 33. *The same hour*] Late though it were, and they weary, yet they return the same 'night, not sparing themselves to do good to others.

Ver. 34. *Appeared to Simon*] 1 Cor. xv. 5. To Peter Christ appeared severally; because as he offended more heinously than the rest of the disciples, so he was more grievously troubled.

Ver. 35.] See the notes on verse 30. *Ex benedictionis forma solemni ipsi Christo antequam panem frangeret*, saith Calvin here.

Ver. 36.] See Mark xvi. 14; John xx. 19.

Ver. 37. *But they were terrified and affrighted*] *Tam meticulosa est incredulitas. Ut etiam tutissi-*

ma *et maxime tranquilla timeat*, saith Brentius here.

Ver. 38. *Why do thoughts arise*] How easily can the Lord trouble us, by turning our own thoughts loose upon us.

Ver. 39. *Behold my hands, &c.*] With those stamps of dishonour that the Jews did me with wicked hands. These he retained even after his resurrection, as for the confirmation of his apostles, so for our instruction, not to think much to suffer loss of honour for our brethren's good and comfort.

Ver. 40. *He showed them his hands, &c.*] For their better assurance and settlement; that they might both remember his resurrection (2 Tim. ii. 8), and with greater power give witness to it, Acts iv. 33.

Ver. 41. *Believed not for joy*] This was partly the joy of faith; and yet through mixture of the flesh, it became some hindrance to their faith. So Abraham laughed, and yet said in his heart, "Shall a child be born to him that is an hundred years old?" &c., Gen. xvii. 17. Strong affections, though from good principles, may possibly miscarry us. Watch therefore.

Ver. 42. *Broiled fish*] Left of last night's supper, *prandium quasi perendium*.

Ver. 43. *And did eat*] Not out of any natural necessity or desire after meat, as once before his passion; but for confirmation of their faith.

Ver. 44. *And in the Psalms*] When a book is set forth, verses of commendation are oft set before it. Christ by this one sentence hath more honoured and authorized the Book of Psalms, than all men could have done by their prefaces and eulogies prefixed thereunto. The Turks disclaim both Testaments, yet swear as solemnly by the Psalms of David as by the Alcoran of Mahomet.

Ver. 45. *Then opened he their understanding*] He enlightened both organ and object, as Acts xvi. 14.

Ver. 46. *Thus it is written, &c.*] All things done and suffered by our Saviour were punctually and exactly foretold and forshowed by Moses and the prophets; and especially by Isaiah, who writes more like an evangelist than a prophet; and is therefore called the Evangelical Prophet. (Jerome.)

Ver. 47. *And that repentance, &c.*] Blessed be God, saith one, that after our shipwreck by Adam, there is such a plank as repentance for a poor sinner to swim to heaven upon. It is a mourning for sin, as it is *offensivum Dei, et aversivum à Deo*. It is *commissa plangere, et plangenda non committere*, as Ambrose hath it; to bewail what is done amiss, and to do so no more.

Ver. 48. *And ye are witnesses*] Therefore prepare to preach the Gospel to every creature. And take it for a singular seal of my love, that notwithstanding your late shameful defection and deserting of me, I shall yet employ you as my witnesses, and make use of your ministry.

Ver. 49. *Until ye be endued*] Gr. ἐνδύσησθε, clothed. Carnal men are naked men; when the saints are arrayed with that fine white linen and shining, Rev. xix. 8.

Ver. 50. *As far as to Bethany*] Where his three dear friends dwelt, Lazarus, Martha, and Mary. From hence he went to his cross, and from hence he would go to his crown.

He lift up his hands] As a good householder, or rather as the high priest of the New Testament: *benedixit, id est, valedixit*, he blessed them, and so bade them farewell.

Ver. 51. *And it came to pass*] See Mark xvi. 19; Acts i. 9.

Ver. 52. *With great joy*] Yet could they not hear of his ascending to the Father without great sorrow, John xiv. and xvi. We grieve for that sometimes that we have great cause to take comfort in; such is our weakness and waywardness.

Ver. 53. *Praising and blessing God*] *Inter laudum devotiones, promissum Spiritus Sancti adventum, promptis per omnia paratisque cordibus exspectant.* (Beda.) So putting themselves into a fit posture to receive the comfort that Christ had promised them.

A

COMMENTARY OR EXPOSITION

UPON

THE GOSPEL ACCORDING TO ST JOHN,

WHEREIN THE TEXT IS EXPLAINED, SOME CONTROVERSIES ARE BRIEFLY DISCUSSED, DIVERS COMMONPLACES HANDLED, AND MANY REMARKABLE MATTERS HINTED, THAT HAD BEEN BY FORMER INTERPRETERS PRETERMITTED.

CHAPTER I.

Ver. 1. *In the beginning*] HERE this heavenly eagle, John the Divine, soars at first out of sight (ὁ Θεόλογος κατ᾽ ἐξοχὴν). Here doth God *detonare ab alto*, thunder from on high, saith Calvin. St Austin stands amazed at the mystical divinity here delivered. This barbarian (said the philosopher, concerning our evangelist) hath comprised more stupendous stuff in three lines than we have done in all our voluminous discourses.[1] Happy had it been for him if he had been made, by this first chapter, of an atheist, a true Christian, as learned Junius was.[2] But he only admired it, and so left it where he found it; as too many do the Word at this day.

Was the Word] Personal, and enunciative. Isaiah, vi. 1, saw him on the throne, and heard him speaking; Daniel, viii. 13, calleth him *Palmoni hammedabber*, "that excellent speaker," and asketh him of the vision; the Syriac interpreter here calleth him *Meltha*, "the Word uttered;" and the Chaldee, *Pithgam Adonai*, "the Lord, the Word."

And the Word was with God] Which sweetly sets forth his co-eternity and co-existency with the Father (τὸ συναΐδιον καὶ ἐνυπόστατον), saith Chrysostom. Moscopulus renders it, *secundum Deum*, as being the express image of the Father. Others, *ad Deum;* as importing a deliberation and conference of the Father and the Son.

And the Word was God] Θεὸς, without an article: hence the Arians cavil that the Son is not God co-equal, but a secondary God, inferior to the Father. See Gal. i. 3. The Father is also called Θεὸς, without an article: therefore this follows not. This whole Gospel is a continuate demonstration of Christ's Deity, which began to be denied, while this evangelist lived, by Ebion, Cerinthus, and other odious antichrists.

Ver. 2. *The same was in the beginning*] In the instant of creation, as Gen. i. 1, therefore also before the creation, therefore from eternity, Eph. i. 4; 1 Pet. i. 10; Prov. viii. 22, 23.[3] "The Lord possessed me" (saith Christ, the essential Wisdom of God there) "in the beginning of his way." Arius corrupted the Greek text, reading it thus,[4] "The Lord created me in the beginning," &c.; and therehence blasphemously inferred that Christ was no more than a creature. But he was "set up from everlasting, from the beginning, or ever the earth was,"

---

[1] Amel. Platonic. ap. Clem. Alex.
[2] Funccius in Vita Sua, Operib. præfix.

[3] *Hinc Johannes augustum illud et magnificum Evangelii sui initium assumpsit.* Mercer. *in loc.*
[4] *Pro* ἔκτησε *substituit* ἔκτισε.

ver. 23.[1] Hence he is called the "Ancient of days," Dan. vii. 9. And Thales, one of the seven Sages of Greece, styleth him, "The most ancient of anything that hath being." πρεσβύτατον τῶν ὄντων.

With God] Being *alius* from his Father, not *aliud;* a distinct person, yet co-essential and co-eternal; for he was with him in the beginning of "the creature which God created," as himself speaketh, Mark xiii. 19.

Ver. 3. *All things were made by him*] So he was not idle with the Father (though he were his darling, sporting always before him, Prov. viii. 30), but by him, as by a principal efficient and co-agent with the Father and the Holy Ghost, all things were made; as some shadow and obscure representation of his wisdom, power, goodness, &c., seen in the creature, as the sun is seen in water, or as letters refracted in a pair of spectacles are beheld by a dim eye. We can see but God's back-parts, and live; we need see no more, that we may live, Exod. xxxiii. 23.

And without him was nothing made] This is added for the more certainty: it being usual with the Hebrews, thus by negation to confirm what they have before affirmed, where they would assure that the thing is so indeed; as Psal. xcii. 15; John vii. 18.

Ver. 4. *In him was life*] As he created, so he quickeneth and conserveth all, being the Prince and principle of life, Acts iii. 15; both of natural life, Acts xvii. 28 (the heathen could say as much[2]), and of spiritual, 1 John v. 12. Hence his members are called "heirs of the grace of life," 1 Pet. iii. 7, and all others are said to be "dead in trespasses and sins," Eph. ii. 1, living carcases, walking sepulchres of themselves. In most families (as in Egypt, Exod. xii. 40) there is not one, but many dead corpses, as being "alienated from the life of God, through the ignorance that is in them," Eph. iv. 18.

Ver. 5. *And the light shineth*] The light both of nature and of Scripture. The former is but a dim half-light, a rush candle, that will light a man but into utter darkness. The latter is a clear thorough-light: the commandment is a lamp, *et lex, lux*, and the law is light, Prov. vi. 23. As for the gospel, it is set up as a beacon on a hill, Tit. ii. 11, ἐπεφάνη, or as the sun in the firmament, Luke i. 78, 79, bringing "life and immortality to light," 2 Tim. i. 10; where God by his Holy Spirit enlighteneth organ and object, Acts xxvi. 18, and shineth on the heart, in the face of Jesus Christ, 2 Cor. iv. 6.

And the darkness comprehendeth it not] Nor will be comprehended by it, Phil. iii. 12, but repels it, rebels against it, Job xxiv. 13; imprisons it, as those wizards did, Rom. i. 18; spurns at it (as Balaam the devil's spelman did, Numb. xxiv. 1, 2, when he set his face toward the wilderness, and resolved to curse howsoever); execrates it, as the Ethiopians do the rising sun.

(Herodot.) The morning is to such as the shadow of death, Job xxiv. 17; for being born in hell, they seek no other heaven.

Ver. 6. *There was a man sent from God*] As he ran not, till sent, Jer. xxiii. 32. St Paul holds it not only for incredible, but for impossible, that men should preach that are not sent, Rom. x. 15. So he declined not his ambassage, as did Jonah, ἀπαιτούμενος τὴν ἀποστολὴν; who was therefore met with by another messenger of God, and sent into the whale's belly to make his sermon for Nineveh; and in his prayer before, to acknowledge out of sad experience that they that hunt "after lying vanities" (as he had done) "forsake their own mercies," Jonah ii. 8.

Ver. 7. *The same came for a witness*] This he performed with a witness, *verbis non solum disertis, sed et exertis.* He witnessed plainly and plentifully, with a clear and punctual pronunciation, profession, indigitation, ver. 26, 29, 32, 36.

That all men through him might believe] Our Saviour expected that men should have come as far to hear his forerunner and him as the Queen of Sheba came to hear Solomon, Matt. xii. 42. But the one thing necessary lies, alas, neglected. Men will run to hell as fast as they can: and if God cannot catch them (saith Mr Shephard) they care not, they will not come to Christ that they might live, John v. 40.

Ver. 8. *He was not that light*] As some sinisterly conceited, which therefore occasioned that most necessary digression, ver. 6—10, and drew afterwards, from the Baptist himself, that most vehement profession, ver. 20, "He confessed and denied not, but confessed," &c. He knew well the danger of detracting in the least degree from God's glory. To look upon it only, and lust after it, is to commit spiritual fornication with it in our hearts; for it is God's beloved spouse, and he being jealous, cannot bear a co-rival. Look upon it therefore but with a single eye, Matt. vi. 22, and in all addresses to God, give the honour to him; take humility to thyself, as Austin well adviseth.[3] Let that be thy motto that was his, *Propter te, Domine, propter te.* Study God's ends, and we may have anything of him, as Moses, Exod. xxxii.

Ver. 9. *Which lighteth every man,* &c.] Or, that coming into the world, lighteth every man; all, with the light of reason, Job xxxv. 11; his own, with a supernal and supernatural light (to know heavenly things is to ascend into heaven, Prov. xxx. 3, 4), an affecting, transforming light, 2 Cor. iii. 18, such as maketh a man to be a child of light, Eph. v. 8, "partaker of the inheritance of the saints in light," Colos. i. 2. Any created understanding at most is but (as Æschylus saith of fire stolen by Prometheus) παντέχνου πυρὸς σελὰς, a beam of that light essential.

Ver. 10. *He was in the world*] Here the evangelist goes on where he left: resumes, and proceeds in his former argument, ver. 5.

---

[1] *Uncta sum in reginam et dominatricem oleo lætitiæ.* Psal. xlv. 7.

[2] *Est Deus in nobis, agitante calescimus illo.*

[3] *Illi da claritatem, tibi humilitatem.* Aug. ad Bonifac., ep. 205.

And the world was made by him] This is the second time here set forth, and reinforced, that we may the better observe and improve it. See the like, Rev. iv. 11, "For thou hast created all things, and by thee they are and were created," without help, tool, or tiresomeness, Isa. xl. 28. That one word of his, *fiat*, made all : shall we not admire his architecture ?

And the world knew him not] Man is here called "the world," and Mark xvi. 15, he is called "every creature." This little world knew not Christ, for God had hid him under the carpenter's son ; his glory was inward, his kingdom came not by observation. And because the world knew not him, therefore it knoweth not us, 1 John iii. 1. Princes, the saints, are in all lands, Psal. xlv. 16, but they lie obscured, as did Melchizedek. The moon (say astronomers) hath at all times as much light as in the full ; but oft, a great part of the bright side is turned to heaven, and a lesser part to the earth. So it is with the Church.

Ver. 11. *He came unto his own*] His peculiar picked people ; as "touching the election, beloved for the Father's sake," Rom. xi. 28 (ownness makes love), though the more he loved the less he was beloved. This may be the best man's case, 2 Cor. xii. 15. Learn we to deserve well of the most undeserving. God shines upon the unthankful also, Luke vi. 35. Christ came to the "stiff-necked and uncircumcised in heart and ears," Acts vii. 51. His comfort was (and may be ours), "Though Israel be not gathered, yet I shall be glorious," &c., Isa. xlix. 5.

And his own received him not] Nay, they peremptorily and pertinaciously "denied the holy One and the just ; and desired a murderer to be given unto them," Acts iii. 14. For the which their inexpiable guilt, they are, as it were, cast out of the world by a common consent of nations, being a dejected and despised people. Howbeit, we long and look daily for their conversion, their resurrection, as St Paul calleth it, Rom. xi. 15. And Augustine argueth out of the words, Abba, Father, that there shall one day be a consent of Jews and Gentiles in the worship of one true God. There are that say out of Dan. xii. 11, that this will fall out A. D. 1650. *Fiat, fiat.*

Ver. 12. *To them he gave power*] Or, privilege, preferment, prerogative royal, heavenly honour, οὐρανίαν τιμὴν, as Nonnus here rendereth it, and fitly. For if sons, then heirs, Rom. viii. 17. Hence that *Ecce admirantis*, 1 John iii. 1, and that "Who am I ?" 2 Sam. vii. 18, with xiv. Kings can make their first-born only heirs, as Jehoshaphat, 2 Chron. xxi. 3 ; but here all are heirs of God and co-heirs with Christ.

Even to them that believe in his name] Though with never so weak a faith, such as may seem to be rather unbelief than faith, Mark ix. 24. The least bud draws sap from the root, as well as the greatest branch. The weakest hand may receive

a ring. *Credo languida fide, sed tamen fide*, said Dr Cruciger on his death-bed. A weak faith is a joint possessor, though no faith can be a joint purchaser of this precious privilege here specified. (Selneccer. pædag. Christ.)

Ver. 13. *But of God*] Whose sons therefore they are, and so "higher than the kings of the earth," Psal. lxxxix. 27, as those that prolong the days of Christ upon earth, being begotten by the travail of his soul, Isa. liii. 10, 11. Hence faith is said to adopt us, ver. 12, in like sort as it justifies us, viz. by virtue of its object, Christ.[1] Hence, Psal. lxxii. 17, there is said to be a succession of Christ's name ; it is begotten, as one generation is begotten of another. This is true nobility, where God is the top of the kin, religion the root. Beatus Ludovicus would be called *Ludovicus de pissiaco*, rather than take greater titles, because there he became a Christian. He thought no birth equal to a new birth in Christ, no parentage to that of God to his Father.

Ver. 14. *And the Word was made flesh*] Put himself into a lousy, leprosy suit of ours, to expiate our pride and robbery, in reaching after the Deity, and to heal us of our spiritual leprosy ; for ἀκατάληπτον ἀθεράπευτον, if he had not assumed our flesh he had not saved us. (Nazianzen.) *Induit ergo sordes nostras*, saith one. He therefore condescended to our rags ; and so

Dwelt amongst us] Dwelt as in a tent or booth, ἐσκήνωσεν. He alludes to soldiers pitching their tents ; or rather to the feast of tabernacles, in or near the time of which celebrated, by consent of many authors of best note, our Saviour was born.

Ver. 15. *John cried, saying*] He entered upon his calling in the year of Jubilee, which was wont to be published by the voice of a crier, with the sound of a trumpet. And hitherto allude the prophets and evangelists, that say he cried, and call him, "the voice of a crier."

Ver. 16. *Of his fulness*] Which is both repletive and diffusive ; not only of plenty, but of bounty ; not a fulness of abundance only, but of redundance too. In Christians is *plenitudo vasis ;* but in Christ, *fontis :* these differ (say the schoolmen) *ut ignis, et ignita.* Take a drop from the ocean, and it is so much the less ; but the fulness of the fire is such, that light a thousand torches at it, it is not diminished.

And grace for grace] That is (say some) the grace of the New Testament for the grace of the Old. And so in the next verse, "grace" shall answer to the moral law, "truth" to the ceremonial. Or (as others) "grace for grace ;" that is, a latitude answerable to all the commands, a perfection answerable to Christ's own perfection. As the father gives his child limb for limb, part for part, &c., so doth this "Father of Eternity," Isa. ix. 6. There are that render it "grace against grace," as in a glass is face against face. See 2 Cor. iii. 18. Or "grace

---

[1] Γεγενημένον ἐκ Διὸς ἔρνος. Homer.

Filiabitur nomine ejus. Trem.

upon grace," that is, one grace after another, a daily increase of graces. *Gratiam novâ gratiâ cumulatam.* Pasor.

Ver. 17. *For the law, &c.*] *Lex jubet, gratia juvat. Petamus ut det, quod ut habeamus jubet,* saith Augustine. We have his promise ever going along with his precept. The covenant of grace turns precepts into promises, and the Spirit of grace turns both into prayers.

Ver. 18. *The only begotten Son*] In the year of grace 1520, Michael Servetus, a Spaniard, taught that there is no real generation or distinction in God, and was therefore worthily burnt at Geneva, in the year 1555. He would not recant; and yet feeling the fire, could not with patience endure it, but kept an hideous roaring till his life was exhausted, crying out to the beholders to dispatch him with a sword. (Bellarm. i.; de Christo, i.; Calvin Opusc.)

He hath declared him] ἐξηγήσατο. In a divine and extraordinary manner, as the word here used imports.

Ver. 19. *Jews sent priests*] Whose proper office it was to inquire into new doctrines, and by preserving, to present knowledge to the people, who were to "seek the law at the priest's mouth," Mal. ii. 7. Cicero complains of his Roman priests, that they were good honest men, but not very skilful. *Bonos illos quidem viros, sed certe non pereruditos.* (Cic. xx. de Fin.) And Varro upbraids them with their ignorance of much about their own gods and religions. (Aug. C. D. iv. 1.)

Ver. 20. *He confessed and denied not, but confessed*] Sincerely and studiously; he put away that honour with both hands earnestly, as knowing the danger of wronging the jealous God in his glory, that is, as his wife. All the fat was to be sacrificed to God. It is well observed, that 19 times doth John use this kind of double affirmation. First, to strengthen our belief. Secondly, to show how sparing he was of an oath. Thirdly, for the greater certainty of the thing.

Ver. 21. *Art thou Elias? And he saith, I am not*] sc. That Elias that you imagine, Elias the Tishbite, by a transanimation (μετεμψύχωσις Pythagorica). As neither was he an angel, as some in Chrysostom's time would gather out of Mal. iii. 1. They that wrest the Scriptures are blinded, as Papists, and other brain-sick heretics.

Ver. 22. *Who art thou? that we may give answer*] They would not be soon said or satisfied. How much more should God's messengers go through-stitch with their errand and ambassage; binding men's sins upon their consciences if they be stubborn or stupid; and having in a "readiness to revenge all disobedience?" 2 Cor. x. 6. When the Æqui and Volsci (a certain people in Italy) bade the Roman ambassador in scorn *ad quercum dicere, se interim alia acturos,* tell their tale to the oak that stood by, they had somewhat else to do than to hear him. He presently replied, *Et hæc sacrata quercus audiat, fœdus à vobis esse violatum:* Let this consecrated oak

hear and bear witness that you have broke your covenant, and shall dearly answer it. (Livy.)

Ver. 23. [*I am the voice of one crying*] Christ spake not a word to Herod, saith one; because Herod had taken away this voice of his in beheading the Baptist. See the note on Mark i. 3. The Reverend Sam. Crook was wont to say to his friends rejoicing with him, and blessing God for him, "I am nothing but a voice."

In the wilderness] Not in the temple; to show that the legal shadows were now to vanish. Chrysologus calls John Baptist, *fibulam legis et gratiæ.*

Ver. 24. *Were of the Pharisees*] Men of renown in the congregation, for more authority' sake: and such as by their office were to inquire into new doctrines and their authors.

Ver. 25. *Why baptizest thou then?*] Why dost thou innovate anything in the rites of religion? A change they looked for under the Messiah, and had learned it out of Jer. xxxi. But this testimony brought by John Baptist out of Isaiah, to prove his own calling, either they did not or would not understand; nor yet do they seek to be better informed by him.

Ver. 26. *I baptize with water*] The Baptist here meaneth the same that St Paul doth, 1 Cor. iii. 6, 7. See the note on Matt. iii. 11. Christ rains down righteousness upon all his baptized; to whom it is not only a sign, but also a seal, as circumcision is called, not only by St Paul, Rom. iv., but also by a Jew doctor, more ancient than their Talmud. Of Wilfride, first Bishop of Chichester, A. D. 700, it is storied that he converted to the faith many pagans in those parts. And a day being appointed for their baptism, they had no sooner received the same, but immediately it rained plentifully, the want whereof had caused a dearth the space of three years before; so that many died daily for hunger, and divers joining hand-in-hand (forty or fifty in a company) threw themselves headlong into the sea.

Ver. 27. *I am not worthy*] Yet Christ held him worthy to lay his hand upon his head in baptism. And there is one that tells us (but who told him?) that for his humility on earth, he is preferred to that place in heaven from which proud Lucifer fell.

Ver. 28. *In Bethabara*] That is, by interpretation, the place of passage, or *trajectum,* where Israel passed over Jordan. So the acts of Joshua and Jesus begin both at a place. Baptism also is first administered where it was of old fore-shadowed. Christ is the true Bethabara, Ephes. ii. 18; we sail to heaven on his bottom.

Ver. 29. *Taketh away*] Or, that is taking away, ὁ αἴρων, by a perpetual act, as the sun doth shine, as the spring doth run, Zech. xiii. 1. This should be as a perpetual picture in our hearts. As we multiply sins, he multiplieth pardons, Isa. lv. 7.

Ver. 30. *Preferred before me, for he was before me*] Much ado the Baptist had to persuade this, the vulgar did so admire him for his strict and holy life; for John did no miracle, John x. 41. Holiness hath reverence. Of God himself it is said, "Holy and" therefore "reverend is his name."

Ver. 31. *And I knew him not*] By face not at all; lest the people should think that this was done and said by consent or compact aforehand betwixt them. Nor did John ever know Christ so fully till now: his former knowledge was but ignorance, in comparison; none are too good to learn. The very angels know not so much of Christ, but they would know more, Ephes. iii. 10, and therefore look intently into the mystery of Christ, as the cherubims did into the ark, 1 Pet. i. 12.

But that he should be manifested] Ministers must hold up the tapestry, as it were, and show men Christ. They are the mouth of the Holy Ghost, whose office it is to take of Christ's excellencies, and hold them out to the world, John xvi. 14.

Ver. 32.] See the note on Matt. iii. 16; Mark i. 10.

Ver. 33. *And I knew him not*] i. e. Not so perfectly till I heard that testimony from heaven. Christ is not known all at once: but as by steps and stairs men went up to Solomon's temple; and as the trumpet in the mount sounded lower at first, and then louder and louder, till at last it was heard all the camp over; so is it here. "The path of the just is as the shining light, that shineth more and more unto the perfect day," Prov. iv. 18.

Ver. 34. *And I saw and bare record*] They that would persuade others, must be strongly persuaded themselves ("We believed, therefore have we spoken," 2 Cor. iv. 13; and "knowing therefore the terror of the Lord, we persuade men," 2 Cor. v. 11); or at least they must seem so to be, as those odious apostates, Judas, Demas, Ecebolus, Speiser, Pendleton, Harding (Bishop Jewel's adversary), who was one while a thundering preacher, wishing he could cry out against Popery as loud as the bells of Osney; and exhorting the people after this sort (as Mr Fox testifieth) a little before King Edward VI. died,— that if trouble come, they should never shrink from the true doctrine of the gospel which they had received; but take it rather for a trial sent of God, to prove them, whether they would abide by it or no. All which to be true (saith mine author) they can testify that heard him, and be yet alive; who also foreseeing the plague to come, were then much confirmed by his words. (Acts and Mon.)

Ver. 35. *John stood*] Ready pressed to preach Christ, as Paul did at Athens in the market, to every one that met with him, Acts xvii. 17. Christ must be preached in season, out of season, *volentibus, nolentibus*. If the Cynics thought it their duty to admonish all they met, and if men would not listen they counted it an easy loss to cast away a few words upon them; how should Christians (and especially ministers) much more do so.

Ver. 36. *Behold the Lamb of God*] *Eximius ille aqnus et singularis*, that notable Lamb, typed out by the paschal lamb, and by that lamb that was the daily morning and evening sacrifice in the temple; that Lamb without blemish of original corruption, and without spot of actual transgression, 1 Pet. i. 19. A lamb in his passion, but a lion in his resurrection, Rev. v. 5, to whom every man is bound to send a lamb (in token of homage) as unto "the Ruler of the whole earth," Isa. xvi. 1.

Ver. 37. *And they followed Jesus*] So powerful is a word or two (many times) touching Christ and his cross to change the heart. Paul showeth that the very report of his bonds did a great deal of good in Cæsar's court, Phil. i. 13. Bilney's confession converted Latimer. Galeacius Caracciolus (that Italian marquis) was wrought upon by a similitude used by Peter Martyr, reading on the 1st Epist. to the Corinthians. So were Earl Martinengus and Hieronymus Zanchius (both of them *Canonici Lateranenses*) by some seasonable truth falling from the same mouth. Luther having heard Staupicius say that that is kind repentance which begins from the love of God, ever after that time the practice of repentance was sweeter to him. Also this speech of his took well with Luther, "The doctrine of predestination begins at the wounds of Christ." (Melch. Adam. in Vita Luther.)

Ver. 38. *What seek ye*] He saith still in effect as much as all this to all his suitors; and infinitely scorns that it should be said that any one seeketh him in vain, Isa. xlv. 19. He is found of them that sought him not, and saith, "Behold me" to every passenger, Isa. lxv. 1. Here he offers himself to these two disciples, and speaks first. He of his own accord (without any monitor) is wont to aid us. "His eyes are upon the righteous, as well as his ears are open to their prayers," Psal. xxxiv. 15. Should he not see as well as hear, and prevent as well as follow us with his favours, we should want many things, and it would go full ill with us.

Ver. 39. *Come and see*] A most gracious invitation. That self-seeking scribe, Matt. viii. 19, met with far other entertainment. Let men bring to Jesus Christ but lawful petitions and honest aims, and they may have what they will of him.

Ver. 40. *One of the two*] See here how mean and slender the Catholic Church was at first. Two poor men only follow Christ, who yet had the promise of the "heathen for his inheritance, and the uttermost parts of the earth for his possession," Psal. ii. 8. "Despise not therefore the day of small things," Zech. iv. 10. The cloud of an hand-breadth may shortly muffle the whole heaven: the little stone cut out without hands may bring down the huge image, and break it to pieces, Dan. ii. 45: the dry root of Jesse prove a tree so tall, that, like that of Nebuchadnezzar, the height thereof shall reach unto heaven, and the sight thereof to the end of all the earth, Dan. iv. 11. *Nec minor ab exordio nec major in-*

crementis ulla, said he of Rome, say we of the Church. (Eutrop. Hist. lib. 1.)

Ver. 41. *He first findeth*] Yet afterwards Peter outstript Andrew in faith and forwardness for Christ; as likewise Luther did Staupicius, &c. So the first become last, and the last first. But charity is no churl; Andrew calleth Simon, and Philip, Nathaniel, &c.; as a loadstone draws to itself one iron ring, and that another, and a third, so, &c.

We have found the Messiah] Little it was that he could say of Christ's person, office, value, virtue, &c., but brings him to Christ. So let us do ours to the public ordinances. Do the office of the sermon-bell at least, we know not what God may there do for them. Bring them as they did, the palsy man upon his bed, and lay them before the Lord for healing.

Ver. 42. *Cephas, which is by interpretation a stone*] Not a head, as some Popish buzzards would needs have it (not knowing a difference between Cephas and κεφαλὴ), and all to prove Peter head of the Church. Some of them have said that the damnation of us Protestants is so plainly set down in our own Bibles, that there needs no more for convincing us thereof, but that we have our eyes in our heads (when we open the book) and be able to read it. But he that first interpreted Cephas a head (against this clear text calling it a stone) either had not his eyes in his head, or else must needs be as perfect a stranger to the Bible as that Bishop of Dunkelden, in Scotland, that thanked God he knew neither the Old Testament nor the New. Or as that other Dutch bishop, Albertus Vindelicorum Episcopus, of whom Luther writeth, that lighting upon a Bible, and being asked (after that he had read awhile in it) what book it was; "I know not," said he, "what book it is; but this I know, that there is nothing in it that I can find to make for our religion."

Ver. 43. *Follow me*] Together with Christ's word there went out a power. His words are operative and efficacious. This Porphyry the atheist, and Julian the Apostate, understood not; and therefore lighting upon this and the like places of the gospel, they blasphemously affirmed that either the evangelists were liars or the apostles fools, that with one word only of our Saviour would be drawn to follow him. So the Papists blaspheme assurance, which they have not, as if it bred security and looseness. They may as well say the sea burns or fire cools.

Ver. 44. *Now Philip was of Bethsaida*] So was Andrew and Peter, who would not be wanting to preach to this town, and pray for it. But all in vain; whence that, "Woe unto thee Bethsaida," Matt. xi. 21. Christ would not suffer so much as the blind man he had cured to go thither, Mark ix. 27.

Thou art the Son of God] For else thou couldst never have known me so thoroughly at so great a distance. The Samaritess, John iv., believed on the same ground ("Come see a man

that told me all that ever I did"), but not so soon; *Discrimen est à Deo, non natura*. God and not nature made the difference. That message that God had accepted a ransom, had a present effect upon that distressed man, Job xxxiii. 24, in reviving his spirit. Not so upon David, though it were delivered to him by the mouth of Nathan, 2 Sam. xii. 13, with Psal. li. 8. God is a free agent, and gives grace and peace at his own pleasure.

Ver. 45. *Philip findeth Nathaniel*] Whom some make to be the same with Bartholomew. I affirm nothing.

We have found] The Greek word imports the sudden and unexpected finding of such a community as he looked not for. See Isa. lxv. 1. ἐυρήκαμεν. ἔυρημα, *lucrum insperatum, et repente oblatum*.

Ver. 46. *Can there any good, &c.*] When men take a toy in their heads against a place or person, they are ready to reason in this manner. Good Nathaniel was in the common error, as was likewise Philip, in the former verse, with his Jesus of Nazareth, the son of Joseph. Four words only, and scarce ever a true one. Epidemical diseases are soon caught.

Ver. 47. *Behold an Israelite, &c.*] Here Christ wondereth at his own work of renovation, as wonderful, doubtless, as that of creation. Or the upright person hath here an *ecce* for imitation, as the hypocrite for detestation, Psal. lii. 7.

Ver. 48. *Before that Philip, &c.*] Christ thinks of us when we little think of him. See Rom. v. 10.

Ver. 50. *Thou shalt see greater things*] Strange sights, marvellous light, matchless mysteries, multifarious wisdom, even the wisdom of God in a mystery: heaven opened, and angels of God ascending and descending, ver. 51, and curiously prying (1 Pet. i. 12) into that great mystery of godliness, God manifested in the flesh, &c.

Ver. 52. *Upon the Son of man*] The Jacob's ladder, the bridge that joineth heaven and earth together, γεφυρώσας, as Gregory hath it.

CHAPTER II.

Ver. 1. *There was a marriage*] Whether St John's marriage, I have not to say. Some will have it so.

Ver. 2. *Jesus was called*] That was the way to have all sanctified, 1 Tim. iv. 3, and disorders prevented. *Cave, spectat Cato*, was the old watch-word.

Ver. 3. *And when they wanted wine*] Wine then may be wanting, though Christ be at the wedding; yea, bread, though Christ be at the board. But the hidden manna is ever ready; and anon in our Father's house will be bread enough, and wine, God's plenty.[1] What though we beg our bread here, heaven will make up all; *in eo quod pascimur pane cum angelis ? &c.* Luther.

---

[1] *Mendicato pane hic vivamus, annon hoc pulchre sarcitur,*

and it is but winking, and we are there presently, said that martyr.

The mother of Jesus saith unto him] To show her authority belike over him. Howsoever, she was too hasty with him, and is taken up for halting. It is not for us to set the sun by our dial.

Ver. 4. *What have I to do with thee ? &c.*] Is it fit to prescribe to the only wise God? to send for the king by a post ? The Chinese whip their gods if they come not at a call.

Ver. 5. *His mother saith to the servants*] Not a word to her Son, though he had publicly reproved her. " Once I have spoken, but I will not answer," saith Job, xl. 5. Jonah, reprehended by God, shuts up his prophecy in silence, in token of his true repentance. David was dumb because it was God's doing, Psal. xxxix. 9. Bring God into the heart, and all will be hushed.

Ver. 6. *After the manner of the purifying, &c.*] But who required these things at their hands ? Men are apt to over-do in externals. The devil strove to bring this superstition into the Christian Church by the heretic Ebion, and hath done it by the pseudo-Catholics, with their lustral water and sprinkling of sepulchres, for the rise whereof Baronius refers us, not to the Jews, but to Juvenal's sixth satire.

Containing two or three firkins] For ostentation' sake. Superstition is pompous and ambitious.

Ver. 7. *Up to the brim*] God permits his people an honest affluence. Christ supplies them here with great store of wine, to the quantity of a thousand and eight hundred pounds, as Beza computes.[1] No small gifts fall from so great a hand, Jam. i. 5.

Ver. 8. *The governor of the feast*] The Jews had a sort of officers at their feasts, called *præfecti morum*, οἰνόπται, ὄφθαλμοι, the eyes and overseers of the feast, that took care that none should drink too much. The Latins called them dictators; the Greeks, symposiarchs. Howbeit, among the Greeks, those officers' power extended no farther than to see that at feasts or banquets men drank small draughts only at first, which by degrees they increased till they came to their height of intemperancy; at which point, when they were arrived, they kept no rule nor order: whereas, before, to drink out of one's turn, or beyond his allowance, was counted incivility.[2]

Ver. 9. *The water that was made wine*] Doth not Christ daily turn water into wine, when of water falling upon the vine, and concocted by the heat of the sun, he produceth the grape, whence wine is expressed? His love (that is better than wine, Cant. i. 2) turned brown bread and water into manchet and wine, to the martyrs in prison.

Ver. 10. *Every man at the beginning*] *Ingenium hominum adumbrat, natura fallax et sophisticum.*

Sic Satan nos ad se allicere solet, Pantheris in morem : Christus contra. His work is worst at first ; the best is behind ; the sweetest of honey lies in the bottom.

Ver. 11. *This beginning, &c.*] For as for his miraculous disputation with the doctors, and fasting forty days, these were rather miracles wrought upon Christ than by him. He works his first miracle for confirmation of God the Father's first ordinance.

His disciples believed on him] So they did before, but now more. So 1 John v. 13. The apostle writes to " them that believed on the name of the Son of God, that they might believe on the name of the Son of God," *i. e.* that they might be confirmed, continued, and increased in it. Faith is not like Jonah's gourd that grew up in a night; or like a bullet in a mould, that is made in a moment. But as the sound of the trumpet grew louder and louder; and as they went up to Solomon's throne by steps and stairs ; so men proceed from faith to faith, till they come to full assurance.

Ver. 12. *To Capernaum*] Where he had hired him a house; for the foxes had holes, &c., but the Son of man had not a house of his own to put his head in, Matt. viii. 20.

Ver. 13. *And Jesus went up to Jerusalem*] In obedience to the law, and to preach the gospel in the great congregation.

Ver. 14. *And found in the temple*] The Talmudists tell us that it was grown to a custom to set up tables in the temple, and money-changers at them, that those that ought to offer half a shekel might have those at hand that might change their bigger money, or take to pledge what else they brought. Here also they might buy oxen, sheep, doves, for sacrifice, which the covetous priests oft received, and then sold them again to others.

Sitting] The Jews at this day being great usurers, and through much sitting and not stirring about, are thought to stink, so as they are said to do: sedentary lives are subject to diseases. *Plerique omnes mensarii sunt, fœneratoriam exercentes, ideo fœtent.* (Beza, Annot.)

Ver. 15. *And when he had made a scourge*] Here he put forth a beam of his Deity ; whiles, as another Samson, he lays heaps upon heaps (yet without bloodshed) with the jaw-bone of an ass. Zeal is attended by revenge, 2 Cor. vii. 11.

The changers' money] Gr. small money, Κέρμα παρὰ τὸ κείρειν, *in minuta frusta concidere.*

Ver. 16. *And said to the dove-sellers*] These (belike, as more tractable, and not so gross offenders) he deals more gently with, but bids them be packing. I expect not (saith Rev. Rolloc) a plenary and perfect reformation of the Church, after so horrible an apostasy under antichrist, till Christ come again to judgment.[3] And yet that Church of Scotland is said to have this rare privilege above many others ; that since the Reform-

---

[1] *Nimirum ad libras mille octingentas : quod pertinet ad miraculi magnitudinem.*
[2] *Hinc pergræcari :* and as merry as a Greek.

[3] *Non expecto plenam perfectamque reformationem Ecclesiæ, &c.*

ation there wrought, they have, without heresy, or so much as a schism, retained unity, with purity of doctrine.[1]

An house of merchandise] So he calls it, for all their goodly pretexts of good intentions. So the churchwarden of Ipswich was much trounced and troubled in the High-commission, for writing over the place where the spiritual court was kept, "My house shall be called an house of prayer, but ye have made it a den of thieves," Nov. 6, 1635.

Ver. 17. *The zeal of thine house*] Apostates, on the other side, eat up their zeal of God's house. But as in falling forward is nothing so much danger as backward; so the zealot, though not so discreet, is better than the apostate: howbeit, zeal should eat us up (saith Mr Vines), but not eat up our wisdom, nor should pride eat up our zeal. Mr Greenham had this saying of David oft in his mouth, and well he might. He also usually prayed that he might keep up his young zeal with his old discretion.

Ver. 18. *What sign*] They might have seen sign enough, in his so powerful ejecting of those money-merchants. But Church reformations are commonly thus diversely entertained. The disciples call it zeal, the Jews rashness.

Ver. 19. *Destroy this temple*] This was the same in effect with that sign of the prophet Jonah, Matt. xii. 39, 40. His resurrection was a plain demonstration of his Deity, *Superas evadere ad auras, hic labor, hoc opus est*, befitting a God, Rom. i. 4.

Ver. 20. *Forty and six years*] All, save what lacks; for it was six years' work only, but they reckon the interim of interruption, Ezra iii.— vii., to aggravate the matter. So they are not only blinded, but hardened.

Ver. 21. *The temple of his body*] Wherein the "Godhead dwelt bodily," Col. ii. 9, that is, personally, as he dwelt in the material temple sacramentally, and doth dwell in the hearts of his people spiritually. This tabernacle of Christ's body was not made with hands, nor built by the power of nature, Heb. ix. 2.

Ver. 22. *His disciples remembered*] In the mean time they murmured not, much less opposed. "We can do nothing against the truth," when at worst, "but for the truth," 2 Cor. xiii. 8. They laid up what they understood not; and as the water casts up her dead, so did their memories that which seemed dead therein, by the help of the Holy Ghost.

Ver. 23. *Many believed*] *Fides fuit minime fida, quippe historica, ex miraculis nata.* These thought they had laid hold on Christ, but they did but as children that think they catch the shadow on the wall. There is a great deal of this false faith abroad. The sorcerers seemed to do as much as Moses.

Ver. 24. *Did not commit himself unto them*] Who yet would needs obtrude upon him. None are so impudent as hypocrites; they deceive themselves, they would do others; God, too. I read not (saith one) in Scripture of a hypocrite's conversion; and what wonder? for whereas, after sin, conversion is left as a means to cure all other sinners; what means to recover him, who hath converted conversion itself into sin?

Ver. 25. *For he knew what was in man*] Artificers know the nature and properties of their works, and shall not Christ of the heart? He searcheth men's hearts, and trieth the reins, which of all their inwards are the most inward;[2] besides that they are the seats and springs of all our thoughts and lusts. *Deus intimior nobis intimo nostro*, saith one, God is nearer to us than we are to ourselves, and knows our thoughts long before, as a gardener knows what flowers he shall have at spring, because he knows the roots.

CHAPTER III.

Ver. 1. *A ruler of the Jews*] EITHER a chieftain of the Pharisees, as he was, Luke xiv. 1; or one of the Sanhedrim, one of the 70 seniors, whose learning hung in their light, 1 Cor. ii. 8. Yet was neither learned Nathaniel, nor Nicodemus, a master of Israel, excluded from Christ's discipline (saith Joan. de Turrecremata), lest if he had admitted simple men only, it might have been thought they were deceived through their simplicity.[3]

Ver. 2. *We know*] But will not know. Hence they became sinners against the Holy Ghost, Matt. xii. 23, &c. The devil that commits this sin every day, is full of objective knowledge, and thence hath his name.[4]

No man can do these miracles] Those jugglers of Egypt, Jannes and Jambres, did but cast a mist, and beguile the sight of Pharaoh and his followers. How Tindal hindered the juggler of Antwerp, that he could not do his feats, see Acts and Monuments, fol. 985.

Ver. 3. *Except a man be born again*] *E supernis*, Erasm. Except a man be first un-made (as St Peter expounds our Saviour) and new-made up again, ταῖς ἁμαρτίαις ἀπογενόμενοι, 1 Pet. ii. 24; except the whole frame of the old conversation be dissolved, and a better erected, there is no heaven to be had. Heaven is too hot to hold unregenerate persons; no such dirty dog ever trampled on that golden pavement, it is an undefiled inheritance, 2 Pet. i. 3.

Ver. 4. *How can a man*, &c.] He understands no more of the doctrine of regeneration (though he could not but have often read of it in Ezekiel, and elsewhere) than a common cow-herd both the darkest precepts of astronomy, 1 Cor. ii. 14. All

---

[1] *Est Ecclesiæ, Scoticanæ, privilegium rarum, præ multis, quod sine schismate, nedum hæresi, unitatem cum puritate doctrinæ retinuerit. Sic in Elog. præfator. de Confess. in princip.* Syntag. Confess. p. 6, edit. Geneva.

[2] *Nihil corde ac renibus magis intimum; adeo ut per mul-*

tos meatus atque incurvos anfractus deferri elaborati cibi debeant, antequam eo possint perduci.

[3] *Ne si solos simplices vocasset, credi possit quod jussent ex simplicitate decepti.*

[4] Δαίμων *quasi* Δαήμων. Plato. *Miracula a didolo edita sunt præstigiæ, imposturæ, phantasmata, ludibria.* Bucholcer.

this is gibberish to him. Water ariseth no higher than the spring whence it came; so the natural man can ascend no higher than nature.

Ver. 5. *Be born of water, and the Holy Ghost*] That is, of the Holy Ghost working like water, cooling, cleansing, &c. In allusion, belike, to that first washing of a new-born babe from his blood, Ezek. xvi. 4. Or else to those Levitical washings, and not without some reference to Nicodemus and his fellow-Pharisees, who placed a great part of their piety in external washings, as do also the Mahometans at this day. Every time they ease nature (saith one that had been amongst them) they wash those parts, little regarding who stands by. If a dog chance to touch their hands, they wash presently; before prayer they wash both face and hands, sometimes the head and privities, &c.

Ver. 6. *That which is born of the flesh, &c.*] Whole man is in evil, and whole evil in man. Quintilian saw not this, and therefore said, that it is more marvel that one man sinneth than that all men should live honestly; sin is so much against man's nature. Many also of the most dangerous opinions of Popery (as justification by works, state of perfection, merit, supererogation, &c.) spring from hence; that they have slight conceits of concupiscence, as a condition of nature. Yet some of them (as Michael Bains, professor at Lovain, &c.) are sound in this point.

Ver. 7. *Marvel not, &c.*] viz. Through unbelief, for otherwise it is a just wonder, far beyond that of natural birth, which, but that it is so ordinary, would surely seem a miracle; *Miracula assiduitate vilescunt.*

Ver. 8. *The wind bloweth, &c.*] *Libero et vago impetu.* Watch, therefore, the gales of grace; we cannot purchase this wind (as sailors in Norway are said to do) for any money. This hawk, when flown, will not easily be brought to hand again.

Ver. 9. *How can these things be?*] Christ had told him that the manner of the Spirit's working is incomprehensible, and yet he is at it, How can these things be? *Sed scribo hæc frustra* (saith Luther in a certain letter of his to Melancthon) *quia tu secundum philosophiam vestram, has res ratione regere, hoc est, ut ille ait, cum ratione insanire pergis.*

Ver. 10. *Art thou a master, &c.*] The Pharisees and philosophers, for their learning, are called "princes of this world," 1 Cor. ii. 8. And yet, had they known, they would never have crucified the Lord of glory. *Indocti rapiunt cœlum, &c.* The poor are gospelized (εὐαγγελίζονται, Matt. xi. 5), not only receive it, but are changed by it. But Bellarmine cannot find in all the Bible where remission of sin is promised to such as confess their sins to God; *Promissio de remittendis peccatis eis qui confitentur Deo non videtur ulla extare in divinis literis.* (Bell. de Justif. i. 21.)

And knowest not these things] Carolostadius was eight years doctor when he began to read

the Scriptures, whereof he had very little understanding; and yet at the taking of his degree he had been pronounced *sufficientissimus.*

Ver. 11. *Ye receive not our witness*] Our Saviour joins himself with the prophets (whose writings Nicodemus had read so negligently), and takes it for a dishonour that he should have written for men the great things of his law, and they continue strangers thereto, Hos. viii. 12.

Ver. 12. *If I have told you earthly things*] That is, spiritual things under earthly gross similitudes, of wind, water, &c. In the mystery of Christ, the best of us are *acute obtusi.* But for the natural man, that cannot tell the nature of the wind, or enter into the depth of the flower or the grass, &c., how should he possibly have the wit to enter into the deep things of God, especially if darkly delivered?

Ver. 13. *And no man hath ascended, &c.*] Objection. Therefore all but Christ are shut out of heaven. Solution. The Church and Jesus make but one Christ, *caput et corpus unus Christus,* 1 Cor. xii. 12. He counts not himself full without his members, who are called the "fulness of him that filleth all," Ephes. i. 23.

Ver. 14. *And as Moses lifted up the serpent*] There it was, *Vide et vive;* here, *Crede et vive.* And as there, he that beheld the serpent, though but with a weak squint-eye, yea, but with half an eye, was cured. So here, if we look upon Christ with the eye, though but of a weak faith, we shall be saved. Doctor Cruciger, when he lay a dying, cried out, *Credo languidâ fide, sed tamen fide,* I believe with a weak faith, but with a faith, such as it is. (Selneccer. in pædag. Christ. p. 321.)

Ver. 15. *That whosoever believeth*] Faith is the soul's hand (*fidei mendica manus,* saith Luther); foot, whereby we come to Christ; mouth (*hic credere est edere,* saith Austin); wing, whereby we soar up and fetch Christ into the heart, John vi. 35, 36.

Ver. 16. *God so loved the world*] This is a *sic* without a *sicut,* there being nothing in nature wherewith to parallel it. The world, that is, all mankind fallen in Adam. This the apostle fitly calleth God's philanthropy, Tit. iii. 4, it being a sweet favour to the whole kind of us that any are saved by Christ.

Ver. 17. *Not to condemn the world*] Unless it be by accident, because they will not be saved; they will not have heaven upon Christ's terms, they will not part with their fat and sweet (with the vine in Jotham's parable, Judg. ix. 13), no, not for a kingdom; they will not be constrained to live happily, reign eternally.[1]

Ver. 18. *Is condemned already*] The sentence is passed, the halter about his neck; there wants no more than to turn him off the ladder of life, and he is gone for ever. In the mean while he hangs but by one rotten-twined thread over hell-fire.

Because he hath not believed] He saith not, because he hath committed adultery, murder. *Cogi posse negat.* Hor. Epist. 2.

---

[1] *At Paris ut vivat regnetque beatus*

There is no righteousness now but of faith ; no sin (saith one) but from unbelief; for thy sins against the law are not imputed unto thee, if thou do but believe the gospel. It is unbelief that shuts a man up close prisoner in the law's dark dungeon, whence faith only can fetch us out, συγκεκλεισμένοι, Gal. iii. 23.

Ver. 19. *This is the condemnation*] This is hell above-ground and aforehand. Affected ignorance is the leprosy in the head, which makes a man undoubtedly unclean and utterly to be excluded, Lev. xiii. 44.

Ver. 20. *For every one that doeth evil*] As the Ethiopians are said to curse the sun for its bright and hot shining. (Herodot.) Christ came a light into the world; his gospel hath appeared as a beacon on a hill, or as the sun in heaven (ἐπεφάνη, Tit. ii. 12), his saints shine as lamps, &c. Now when men hate these, as thieves do a torch in the night, and fly against the lights as bats do, this is condemnation.

Ver. 21. *But he that doeth truth*] *Tenebriones Papistæ male sibi conscii, æternum atri, et tetri sunto, et habentor, qui non tam cute, quam corde Æthiopici, solem quo magis luceat, eo magis execrentur.* But our hearts (as our climate) have more light than heat. Sir Philip Sydney used to say of Chaucer, that he wondered how in those misty times he could see so clearly ; and how we in these clearer times go on so stumblingly. "If any be ignorant, let him be ignorant," saith Paul, 1 Cor. xiv. 38. And so much any one knows, as he does of God's will, as the apostle intimates, when he tells us that "Christ knew no sin," that is, he did none, 2 Cor. v. 21.

Wrought in God] Right. 1. *Quoad fontem,* a pure heart. 2. *Quoad finem,* the glory of God. Else they are but *splendida peccata,* sins in a silken suit. (Aug.)

Ver. 22. *And baptized*] Wherever we are we must be doing. If Moses may not do justice in Egypt, he will do it in Midian, Exod. ii. 14—17. I had rather be sick, said Seneca, than out of employment, *Malim mihi male esse quam molliter.*

Ver. 23. *And John also was baptizing*] Here ministers may learn not to be wanting to their duties, though God stir up others about them of greater parts and better success to obscure them. *Verbi minister es, hoc age,* was Mr Perkins' motto. *Summum culmen affectantes, satis honeste vel in secundo fastigio conspiciemur,* saith Columella. And, *prima sequentem, honestum est in secundis, tertiisve consistere,* saith Cicero. Every man cannot excel, nor is it expected.

Ver. 24. *Cast into prison*] The primitive bishops were found more frequently in prisons than palaces. Bocardo became a college of Quondams, as the Marian martyrs merrily called it. If Petronius could tell Cæsar that he had rather be with Cato in the prison-house than with him in the senate-house ; why should it grieve any to suffer bonds with and for Christ ? Chrysostom had rather be Paul a prisoner of

Jesus Christ than Paul rapt up into the third heaven. (Homil. in Eph. iii. 1.) Μετὰ Κάτωνος ἐν οἰκήματι, μᾶλλον ἤ μετὰ σοῦ ἐνταῦθα εἶναι βούλομαι. (Dio Cass.)

Ver. 25. *And the Jews*] Who joined themselves to John's disciples, craftily and maliciously, that they might both set against Christ; like as the Jesuits at this day will cunningly comply with the Lutherans, and seem to side with them, that they may both set against the Calvinists.

About purifying] That is, baptism, called elsewhere the laver of regeneration, Tit. iv. 5, and by a Father, ᾿Αλεξιτήριον καθάρτικον, a purging preservative. "Not the putting away of the filth of the flesh," saith Peter, but a better thing, 1 Pet. iii. 21.

Ver. 26. *Rabbi, he that was with thee*] They envied for John's sake, as Joshua did for Moses, and with as little thank. John would have been glad they had gone after Christ, as Andrew did. Howsoever, it was good news to John that Jesus was so frequented and busied.

Ver. 27. *A man can receive nothing*] There is much in this word "man," as Beza thinks, to set forth the most miserable indigency of all mankind by nature.[1] The Greeks, when they set forth one miserable indeed, they call him τρισάνθρωπον, thrice a man.

Ver. 28. *Ye yourselves bear me witness*] I should rather choose the just commendation of one good man (saith Rolloc upon this text) than the foolish admiration of a whole multitude. *Equidem pluris fecerim justam commendationem,* &c. Demetrius hath good report of the truth itself, that is enough for him, 3 John 12.

Ver. 29. *The friend of the bridegroom*] Such is every faithful minister, 2 Cor. xi. 2, whose office is to woo for Christ, and not (as some) to speak one word for him and two for himself. This is foul play.

Ver. 30. *He must increase, but,* &c.] And this was John's great joy. That man hath true light that can be content to be outshined by others ; and nothing will more try a man's grace than questions of emulation. Ezekiel can commend Daniel his contemporary, matching him with Noah and Job for his power in prayer, Ezek. xiv. 14. And Peter highly praiseth Paul's epistles, though he had been publicly reproved by him at Antioch, 2 Pet. iii. 15 ; Gal. ii. 11. Yea, Plato called Aristotle ἀναγνώστην et νοῦν, the intelligent reader. And Aristotle is said to have set up an altar in honour of Plato, with this inscription,—

Nulla ferent talem secla futura virum.

But Luther showed himself so much discontent at the reformation wrought at Wittenberg in his absence, by Carolostadius, because it was done without him, that he doubted not to approve those things, that till then he had disapproved, and to disapprove what before he had approved of. So hard it is for a man willingly and gladly to see his equals lifted over his head *magnum habere momentum.*

[1] *Videtur hominis appellatio*

in worth and opinion. Self-love makes men unreasonable, and ever teacheth them to turn the glass to see themselves bigger, others lesser, than they are.

Ver. 31. *He that cometh, &c.*] Hitherto Christ hath been compared with John. In the rest of the chapter he stands compared, first, with all men; secondly, with the faithful, and infinitely preferred before them all. "He is the chief of ten thousand," Cant. v. 10; or the standard-bearer, which ever are the goodliest.

Is earthy] *Terra est,* so Augustine renders it, in the same sense as "he is flesh," ver. 6. God will smite this "earth with the rod of his mouth," Isa. xi. 6.

Speaketh of the earth] As ducklings have always their bills in the mud, as swine are ever rooting in the mire; like that fish in the Gospel, either dumb, or nothing but gold in their mouths.

Ver. 32. *No man receiveth*] i. e. None to speak of; comparatively none. *Rari quippe boni,* saith Juvenal. *Rari sunt qui philosophantur,* saith Ulpian the lawyer. *Perraro grati reperiuntur,* saith Cicero the orator. All men have not faith, saith the apostle, 2 Thess. iii. 2; no, not of those that profess the faith. Though a gun be discharged at a whole flight of birds, there are but a few killed. Though the net be spread over the whole pond, but a few fishes are taken; many thrust their heads into the mud, and the net passeth over them; so most hearers do busy their heads with their own sensual or worldly thoughts, and so escape the power of the word.

Ver. 33. *Hath set to his seal, &c.*] Hath given God a testimonial, such as is that, Deut. xxxii. 4. After which, God also sets his seal (*quasi in redhostimentum*) to the believer, Ephes. i. 13.

Ver. 34. *Speaketh the words of God*] This the true believer is convinced of; and therefore sets to his seal, as to an undoubted truth. He is fully persuaded, as St Luke was, i. 1.

Ver. 35. *The Father loveth the Son*] Therefore faith may have firm footing. God hath laid help upon one that is mighty, Psal. lxxxix. 19, that our faith and hope may be in God, 1 Pet. i. 21.

Ver. 36. *Hath eternal life*] 1. *In promisso.* 2. *In pretio.* 3. *In primitiis.* He stands already on the battlements of heaven, he hath one foot in the porch of paradise.

He that believeth not] There is a two-fold unbelief, one in the understanding, and is opposed to faith, ἀπιστία; the other in the will and lives, and is opposed to obedience, ἀπείθεια, Heb. viii. 10. For cure of both, God hath promised to write his laws both in the minds of his people and in their hearts too.

The wrath of God abides upon him] μένει, as in its mansion-place, as upon its basis, *tanquam trabali clavo fixa,* saith one; there it nestles, settles, and never will away. The unbeliever can neither avoid it nor abide it.

CHAPTER IV.

Ver. 1. *Baptized more disciples*] Baptizing was used by the Jews before John or Christ took it up, from which custom, though brought in without commandment, our Saviour authorizeth a seal of entering into his rest; using the Jews' weakness as an allurement thither.

Ver. 2. *Jesus himself baptized not*] A sweet comfort, that Christ is said not to baptize those whom the disciples baptized. The sacraments administered by ministers are no less effectual than if we had received the same from Christ's own hands.

Ver. 3. *He left Judea*] God must be trusted, not tempted.

Ver. 4. *He must needs go*] Happy for them that they lay in our Saviour's way, to be looked upon; his feet drop fatness. Luther had rather be with Christ in hell than in heaven without him, *Malim præsente Christo esse in inferno, quam absente eo in cœlo.* Luther in Gen. xxx.

Ver. 5. *Jacob gave to his son Joseph*] Having first won it with "his sword and his bow," Gen. xlviii. 22; that is, with his prayer and supplication (saith the Chaldee paraphrast); which, as Saul's sword and Jonathan's bow, never return empty, 2 Sam. i. 22.

Ver. 6. *Jesus therefore, being wearied*] And in that he himself had suffered, he was the more able and apt to help this poor Samaritess. So the apostle bids us pity those in adversity, as being ourselves in the body, i. e. in the body of flesh and frailty, subject to such misery.[1] He that hath had the tooth-ache, will pity those that have it. *Non ignara mali, &c.* We are orphans all (said Queen Elizabeth, in her speech to the children of Christ's Hospital), let me enjoy your prayers, and ye shall be sure of mine assistance.

Ver. 7. *A woman of Samaria*] A poor tankard-bearer, such as Festus calls *Canalicolas, quod circa canalem fori consisterent,* because they were much about the conduits. (Becman. de Originib.)

Ver. 8. *To buy meat*] For our Saviour lived not upon alms; but although he became poor to make us rich, 2 Cor. viii. 9, yet had he a bag, and that so big as that it required a bearer, John xii. 6, his friends and followers supplying him with money for his necessary uses and for relief of the poor.

Ver. 9. *Askest drink of me?*] The Samaritans knew that they were slighted of the Jews, and took it ill, *Gens hæc* (saith Giraldus Cambrensis, of the Irish) *sicut et natio quævis barbara, quanquam honorem nesciant, honorari tamen supra modum affectant.* No man would be slighted, how mean soever.

For the Jews have no dealings, &c.] Josephus writeth, that at Samaria was a sanctuary opened by Sanballat for all renegade Jews, &c. The Jews therefore hated the presence, the fire, the fashion, the books of a Samaritan. Neither was there any hatred lost on the Samaritan's part; *condolere,* Heb. v. 2; xiii. 3.

---

[1] μετριοπαθεῖν, *Proportionate ad miseriam*

for if he had but touched a Jew, he would have thrown himself into the next water, clothes and all; both of them equally sick of a *noli me tangere*. (Epiphanius.)

The gift of God] That is, Christ himself, called by St Paul the benefit, εὐεργεσία, 1 Tim. vi. 2. Let him not be to us as Jether's sword to him, which he drew not, used not; but as Goliath's sword to David, none to that. None but Christ, none but Christ, said that martyr.

Ver. 11. *Sir, thou hast no bucket*] See how witty we are naturally, with our armed dilemmas, to reject grace offered, and with both hands, as it were, to thrust away from us eternal life, ἀπωθεῖσθε, Acts xiii. 46.

Ver. 12. *Our father Jacob*] Josephus tells us that these Samaritans, whiles the Jews prospered, would needs be their dear cousins; but when they were in adversity (as under Antiochus) they would utterly disown and disavow them. They wrote to Antiochus, because he tormented the Jews, to excuse themselves as none such; and they styled Antiochus, the mighty God. Oh, baseness!

Ver. 13. *Shall thirst again*] So shall all they, *quibus avaritiæ aut ambitionis salsugo bibulam animam possidet.* He that seeks to satisfy his lusts goes about an endless business. Give, give, is the horse-leech's language. The wordling hath enough to sink him, not to satisfy him.

Ver. 14. *Shall never thirst*] His lips water not after homely provision, that hath lately tasted of delicate sustenance.

Clitorio quicunque sitim de fonte levarit,
Vina fugit, gaudetque meris abstemius undis.
(Ovid, Metam. xv.)

Ver. 15. *Sir, give me this water*] We would all have immortality, but here on earth. Some think she jeers our Saviour here; who therefore in the next words arouseth her conscience.

Ver. 16. *Go, call thy husband*] It was a great favour in Christ to receive that sinful woman that washed his feet with her tears and wiped them with her hair, and not to kick her out of his presence, as the Pharisees expected. How much greater is this, to fetch in an idolatrous harlotry that fled from him, to entertain her that had rejected him? &c. Well might St Paul say, that the "grace of our Lord is exceeding abundant," or doth abound to flowing over, as the sea easily overfloweth mole-hills. ὑπερεπλεόνασε, 1 Tim. i. 14.

Ver. 17. *I have no husband*] *Lucretius ait, quasdam mulieres effugere unius viri torum, ut omnium fiant torus.* (Sphinx Philos.)

Jesuitæ etiam sunt
Connubisanctifugæ, clammeretricitegæ.

Ver. 18. *He whom thou now hast, &c.*] Here he comes home to her conscience; so must all that will do good on it, striving not so much to please as to profit. Bees are killed with honey but quickened with vinegar. The eagle, though she love her young ones dearly, yet she pricketh and beateth them out of the nest: so must preachers drive men out of the nest of pleasure. John Speiser, preacher at Augsburg in Germany, did his work so well at first, that the common strumpets left the brothel-houses (then tolerated) and betook themselves to a better course, A.D. 1523. Yet afterwards he revolted to the Papists and miserably perished. (Scultet. Annal. 118.)

Ver. 19. *Sir, I perceive that thou art a prophet*] To the "hidden man of the heart," 1 Pet. iii. 4, the plain song ever makes the best music. The Corinthian idiot, convinced of all, and having the secrets of his heart ript up by the two-edged sword, "falls down upon his face worshipping God," and reporteth that "God is in the ministers of a truth," 1 Cor. xiv. 24, 25.

Ver. 20. *Our fathers, &c.*] No sooner doth she acknowledge him a prophet, but she seeks to be satisfied in a case of conscience. *Proh stuporem nostrum!* Woe to our dulness.

Ver. 21. *Ye shall neither in this mountain, &c.*] Herod's temple at Jerusalem was so set on fire by Titus's soldiers, that it could not be quenched by the industry of man. And at the same time Apollo's temple at Delphi was utterly overthrown by earthquakes and thunderbolts, and neither of them could ever since be repaired. The concurrence of which two miracles (saith mine author) evidently showeth that the time was then come when God would put an end both to Jewish ceremonies and heathenish idolatry, that the kingdom of his Son might be the better established. (Godw. Antiq. Heb.)

Ver. 22. *We know what we worship*] Christ also, as man, worshippeth, being less than himself as God. Christ is worshipped by angels as God, being greater than himself as man.

Ye worship ye know not what] And yet these Samaritans thought themselves the only right worshippers. As Turks hold themselves the only Mussulmans, that is, true believers; as Hermotimus, the Stoic in Lucian, thought his sect the best of all other, as being ignorant of any other himself.

Ver. 23. *The Father seeketh such*] Oh how should this fire up our hearts to spiritual worship! that God seeks for such, with, "Let me see thy face, hear thy voice," Cant. ii. 14. He soliciteth suitors.

Ver. 24. *God is a Spirit*] *Omnes nominis Jehovæ literæ sunt spirituales ut denotetur Deum esse spiritum.* (Alsted.) Though, to speak properly, God is not a spirit. For, first, spirit signifies breath, which indeed is a body, but because it is the finest body, the most subtle and most invisible, therefore immaterial substances, which we are not able to conceive, are represented unto us under this name. Secondly, God is above all notion, all name. *Afri dicunt Deum ignotum Anon*, i. e. *Heus tu, quis es?* One being asked what God is, answered, *Si scirem, Deus essem.*[1] That which Augustine saith concerning time (the measure of all our motions) may much more be said concerning God, in whose hands are all our times and motions; *Si nemo ex me quærat, scio:*

[1] Plut. lib. de Isid. et Osiride.

si quærenti explicare velim, nescio. When I am not asked, methinks I know somewhat of him; but let me go about to say what he is, and I find I know nothing at all. Confess. xi. 14.

In spirit and truth] As opposed to formality and hypocrisy.

Ver. 25. *I know that Messias, &c.*] As who should say, we are not altogether so ignorant as you would make us, ver. 23. A dead woman must have four men to carry her out, as the proverb is: we are apt to think our penny good silver.

Ver. 26. *I that speak unto thee, &c.*] No sooner do we think of Christ with any the least true desire after him, but he is presently with us. He invited himself to Zaccheus's table, &c. *Tantum velis, et Deus tibi præoccurret,* said a father.

Ver. 27. *That he talked with the woman*] *Solum cum sola.* (Beza.) He might do that we must beware of, lest concupiscence kindle. Abraham may see Sodom burning, Lot may not.

Yet no man said] All ill thoughts and sinister surmises, of superiors especially, are to be presently suppressed and strangled in the birth.

Ver. 28. *Left her water-pot*] She had now greater things in hand, better things to look after. As Alexander, hearing of the riches of the Indies, divided his kingdom among his captains.

Ver. 29. *Come, see a man, &c.*] Weak means may, by God's blessing, work great matters. He can make the words of Naaman's servant greater in operation than the words of great Elisha, and by a poor captive girl bring him to the prophet.

Ver. 30. *Then they went out*] More to see the news than else; as Moses' curiosity led him nearer the bush, wherehence he was called. It is good to come to the ordinances, though but for novelty; absence is without hope. What a deal lost Thomas by being out of the way but once.

Ver. 31. *Master, eat*] *Animantis cujusque vita in fuga est,* and must be repaired by nutrition, in a natural course. Only we must eat to live, and not live to eat only, as belly-gods.

Ver. 32. *I have meat to eat, &c.*] Abraham's servant would not eat till he had despatched his errand, Gen. xxiv. 33. When we are to woo for Christ, we should forget our own interests and occasions. *Quærite primum, &c.*

Ver. 33. *Hath any man brought, &c.*] "Are not these yet carnal, and talk as men?" 1 Cor. iii. 3. How dull and thick-brained are the best, till God rend the veil, and enlighten both organ and object!

Ver. 34. *My meat is to do the will*] Job, xxiii. 12, preferred it before his necessary food, that should keep him alive. So did Christ, when disappointed of a breakfast at the barren fig-tree, and coming hungry into the city, he went not into a victualling-house but into the temple, where he taught the people most part of that day, Matt. xxi. 17, 23.

Ver. 35. *Say ye not, there are yet three months*]

As who should say, ye so long for the time, that ye count how many months, weeks, days it is to harvest; should ye not be much more solicitous of such a heavenly harvest? These Samaritans do but hang for mowing, &c.

Ver. 36. *That he that soweth, &c.*] That is, that both the prophets that sowed and the apostles that reaped, &c., for the people were prepared by the writings of the prophets to be wrought upon by the apostles. The Samaritans also had the Bible, agreeing, for most part, with that we have from the Jews. The copy of this Samaritan Bible was first brought from Damascus into Christendom by one Petrus de Valle, A. D. 1626.

Ver. 37. *That saying true, &c.*] Camerdrius recites the Senary at large.

Ἄλλοι μὲν σπείρουσ', ἄλλοι δ' αὖ ἀμήσονται.

Ver. 38. *Other men have laboured*] Laboured even to lassitude, as the word κεκοπιάκασι signifies (κοπιάω, κόπτω). The ministry is not then an easy trade, an idle man's occupation. Luther was wont to say, *Sudor œconomicus est magnus, Politicus major, Ecclesiasticus maximus,* The householder hath somewhat to do, the magistrate more, but the minister most of all.

Ver. 39. *For the saying of the woman*] An unlikely means to effect so great a matter. But what is that to the Almighty? So Junius professeth, that the very first thing that turned him from atheism was conference with a countryman of his, not far from Florence. The next was, the majesty of the Scriptures, which he observed in John i. So for our forefathers in times of Popery, Mr Fox observeth, that by the reading of Chaucer's books some were brought to the knowledge of the truth. And in that rarity of books and want of teachers, this one thing I greatly marvel at (saith he), to note in the registers, and consider how the word of God did multiply so exceedingly as it did amongst them. For I find that one neighbour resorting to and conferring with another, eftsoons, with a few words of their first or second talk, did win and turn their minds to that wherein they desire to persuade them touching the truth of God's word and sacraments.

Ver. 40. *Were come unto him*] We no sooner believe, but we would fain see, and be brought *a spe ad speciem.*

Ver. 41. *Because of his own word*] This is it alone that is the foundation of faith, and converts the soul, Psal. xix. 7. That of good wives winning their husbands, 1 Pet. iii. 1, is meant by way of preparation only in general. And that of winning a soul by private admonition, Jam. v. ult., is meant of persuading them to some good duty, or to receive some truth, or to forsake some one evil or error.

Ver. 42. *Not because of thy saying*] Properly, because of thy prittle-prattle, Διὰ τὴν σὴν λαλίαν, *propter loquacitatem tuam.* So perhaps it seemed to some of them at first, who believed indeed when they heard him. Plato gives a good rule, Consider not so much τìς as τì, who saith, as *what* is said. Prejudicate opinion bars up the understanding; muddy water in a vessel causeth the best liquor to run over. *Intus existens prohibet alienum.*

Ver. 43. *After two days he departed*] Though never so much made of, we must away when there is something elsewhere to be done for God.

Ver. 44. *Jesus himself testified*] Had testified, when he was cast out at Nazareth; therefore he came no more there. A minister that can do no good once in the place where he lives, is bound to remove, though the fault be not in him, but the people, saith an interpreter here; otherwise (if for self-respects he there abide) it is to be feared that he will lose his gifts, and either fall into errors and heresies, or prove but a dull and dry doctor. *Metuendum est ne donum quod acceperis, omittas vel degeneres in errores, vel hæreses, vel si retineas puritatem doctrinæ, evadas tamen frigidus et aridus doctor.* (Rolloc. *in loc.*)

Ver. 45. *The Galileans received him*] Though those of Nazareth would not, others did. He that is sent and gifted by God shall have one where or other to exercise his gifts, as the English exiles at Geneva, Zurich, &c.; as Zanchius, when he could not rest at Argentina, was received at Clavenna.

Having seen all the things he did, &c.] Christ's miracles were as the sermon-bell, that called them together. These the men of Nazareth also had seen, but with prejudice, and therefore to no profit.

Ver. 46. *A certain nobleman*] One that belonged to the king, βασιλικὸς, a royalist; for so the vulgar flatteringly styled Herod the tetrarch. Few noblemen came to Christ; this, not till he was driven to him by his son's sickness. "Not many noble are called," 1 Cor. i. 20; if any, they are as black swans, and thinly scattered in the firmament of a state, even like stars of the first magnitude.

Ver. 47. *Besought him that he would, &c.*] Even Darius, king of Persia, can give order for prayers to be made at Jerusalem for the "king's life and his sons," Ezra vi. 10, when he had seen divers of his children die before him, as Ctesias relateth.

Ver. 48. *Except ye see signs, &c.*] Our Saviour first chides him, and upon his well-bearing of that, accommodates him. He saw the courtier's unbelief more dangerous to his soul than the disease could be to his son's body.

Ver. 49. *Sir, come down*] He fumes not at reproof (as many great ones would have done, *Tange montes, et fumigabunt*), but "suffers the word of exhortation," Heb. xiii. 22, being subdued thereunto by affliction.

Ver. 50. *Thy son liveth*] Is in very good health; for *non est vivere, sed valere, vita* (Martial). So God is better to us oft-times than our prayers, than our hopes.

Ver. 51. *Thy son liveth*] So the son was restored by his father's faith. It is a benefit to be born of good parents. Personal goodness is profitable to posterity.

Ver. 52. *Then inquired he, &c.*] By a sweet providence, that God might be the more glorified and the man's faith confirmed. "All things co-operate," &c., Rom. viii. 28. So at the same time wherein the states of Germany (after long debate) concluded for the truth of the gospel, Luther came leaping out of his closet where he had been praying (though many miles distant) with *vicimus, vicimus* in his mouth. So Musselborough field was won by the English the selfsame day and hour wherein those Balaam's blocks (idolatrous images) were burnt at London by order of Parliament.

Ver. 53. *And he himself believed*] With a justifying faith, introduced at first by a common faith.

Ver. 54. *This is again the second miracle*] God keeps count of what he doth for us, and will call us to a reckoning. Should not we keep a register? write up the noble acts of the Lord? make a catalogue of them, such an one as was that Judg. x. 11, 12? "Did not I deliver you from the Egyptians, and from the Amorites, and from the children of Ammon, and from the Philistines? The Zidonians also, and the Amalekites, and the Maonites did oppress you, and ye cried unto me, and I delivered you out of their hand." According to this form, and many the like in sacred Scripture, we should polish and garnish, embroider and embellish, the *magnalia Dei*, great works of God; for else we undervalue them, which he will not bear with.

CHAPTER V.

Ver. 1. *A feast of the Jews*] THIS was the feast of Pentecost. Others say the Passover, which came but once a year. The true Christians (for whom the true Passover was sacrificed, 1 Cor. v. 9) keep a continual feast or holy-day, ἑορτάζωμεν, with the unleavened bread of sincerity aud truth, ver. 8. Diogenes could say, that a good man keeps holy-days, and hath gaudies all the year about.[1] "Let my people go, that they may hold a feast unto me," Exod. v. 1. In other messages it is, "that they may serve me."

Ver. 2. *Having five porches*] Built, belike, by some well-affected persons, at the motion of God's ministers, for the use of such impotent folk as here lay looking and languishing at Hope's Hospital. Like as King Edward VI. was moved by a sermon of Bishop Ridley's, touching works of charity, to grant his two houses in London, Bridewell and the Savoy, for such like good uses; together with lands and monies for their maintenance.

Ver. 3. *Of impotent folk*] That had tried all other ways, and could not otherwise be cured, *Omnipotenti medico, nullus insanabilis occurrit morbus.* (Isidore.)

Ver. 4. *For an angel went down*] The miracle of this pool was granted to the Jews, partly to strengthen them in the true worship of God

[1] πᾶσαν ἡμέραν ἑορτὴν ἡγεῖται. Laert.

under the persecution of Antiochus, in the fail of prophecy; partly to retain them in their religious course of sacrificing to the true God, against the scoffs of the Romans (that were now their lords). Such a virtue being given to that water, wherein their sacrifices were wont to be washed. See a more sovereign bath than this, Zech. xiii. 1; an ever-flowing and over-flowing fountain, not for one at once, as here, but for all that come, they may wash and be clean, wash and be whole.

At a certain season] Once a year only, *Semel quotannis*, saith Tertullian. Others (more probably) at all their great feasts, when the people met out of all parts at Jerusalem, taking κατὰ distributively, as Matt. xxvii. 15.

Troubled the water] Not in a visible shape, likely; but as it appeared by a visible troubling of the waters and a miraculous healing of the diseased. But that troubled waters should do cures was the greater wonder: sith holy wells (as they call them) and waters that heal are commonly most calm and clear. It was a witty allusion hereunto of him that said, Angels trouble the clear stream of justice at certain times.

Ver. 5. Thirty and eight years] A long while to be in misery: but what is this to eternity of extremity! We need have something to mind us of God, to bring us to Christ. King Alured prayed God always to send him some sickness, whereby his body might be tamed, and he the better disposed and affectioned to God-ward.

Ver. 6. And knew that he had been, &c.] Christ's eye affected his heart, Lam. iii. 51, he could not but sympathize, and succour this poor cripple, out of his mere philanthropy, which moveth him still, μετριοπαθεῖν, to show mercy according to the measure of our misery, whereof he bears a part, Heb. v. 2.

Ver. 7. I have no man, &c.] He looked that Christ should have done him that good office; and could not think of any other way of cure. How easy is it with us to measure God by our model, to cast him into our mould, to think he must needs go our way to work!

Ver. 8. Rise, take up thy bed, &c.] A servile work upon the sabbath-day. This our Saviour here commends, not as a servile work, but for confirmation of the truth of a miracle greatly tending to God's glory; like as, another time, he bade them give meat to the damsel he had raised, not for any necessity, but to ensure the cure.

Ver. 9. And immediately the man] Christ's words are operative (together with his commands there goes forth a power, as Luke v. 17). So they were in the creation, Gen. i. So they are still in regeneration, Isa. lix. 21. *Dei dicere, est efficere.*

Ver. 10. It is the sabbath, it is not lawful, &c.] *Vere, sed non sincere.* It more troubled them that Christ had healed him than that the sabbath had been broken by him. The poorer Swedes always break the sabbath, saying that it is only for gentlemen to keep that day.

Ver. 11. He that made me whole, &c.] So, it

seems, Christ had healed him, in part, on the inside also; and given him a ready heart to obey, though it were *contra gentes*, as they say.

Ver. 12. What man is he] Not that made thee whole, but that bade thee take up thy bed, &c. They dissembled the former, and insisted only upon the latter, which shows the naughtiness of their hearts.

Ver. 13. Had conveyed himself away] Lest by his presence that work should be hindered. True goodness is public-spirited, though to private disadvantage, and works for most part unobserved, as the engine that doth all in great businesses is oft inward, hidden, not taken notice of.

Ver. 14. Findeth him in the temple] Praising God, likely, for his unexpected recovery. So Hezekiah, the first work he did when off his sick bed, Isa. xxxviii. 22.

Behold, thou art made whole, &c.] Here is, 1. *Commemoratio beneficii.* 2. *Commonitio officii.* 3. *Comminatio supplicii. Ingentia beneficia, ingentia flagitia, ingentia supplicia.*[1]

Ver. 15. Told the Jews] Of a good intent, surely, to honour Christ, however it were taken by the spiteful Jews, *Probi ex suâ naturâ cæteros fingunt.* The disciples could not imagine so ill of Judas as it proved. Mary Magdalene thought the gardener (whoever he were) should have known as much and loved Jesus as well as she did.

Ver. 16. Therefore did the Jews persecute Jesus] This he foreknew would follow, and yet he forbore not. In the discharge of our consciences (rightly informed and regulated) we must not stand to cast perils; but do our duties zealously, whatever come of it. This courage in Christians, heathens counted obstinacy, but they knew not the power of the Spirit, nor the privy armour of proof that saints have about their hearts.

Ver. 17. My Father worketh] Yet without labour or lassitude, in conserving the whole creature. This he doth every day, and yet breaketh not the sabbath; *Ergo nec ego.*

Ver. 18. The Jews sought the more] Persecution is (as Calvin wrote to the French king) *Evangelii genus*, the bad genius, the devil that dogs the gospel. *Ecclesia hæres crucis* (saith Luther). Truth breeds hatred, saith the heathen, as the fair nymphs did the ill-favoured fauns and satyrs. *Veritas odium parit.* Ter.

Ver. 19. The Son can do nothing, &c.] He denies not himself to be the Son though they quarrelled him: but sweetly sets forth the doctrine of his Deity, which they so much stomached and stumbled at.

Ver. 20. For the Father loveth the Son] This noteth that eternal power of doing miracles that is in Christ. As that which follows, "He will show him greater works," &c., is to be referred to the declaration of that his power.

That ye may wonder] Though ye believe not; for such was the hardness of their hearts grown;

---

[1] Magdeburgens præf. ad cent. 5.

as neither ministry, misery, miracle, nor mercy could possibly mollify. "Behold, ye despisers, and wonder, and perish," Acts xiii. 41.

Ver. 21. *Raiseth up the dead*] Bringing them from the jaws of death to the joys of life; which none can do but God alone.

Ver. 22. *The Father judgeth no man*] viz. The Father alone, but by the Son, to whom all judicatory power is committed.

Ver. 23. *He that honoureth not the Son*] As Jews and Turks do not. Nor Papists, that (upon the matter) despoil him of his threefold office, and so deny the Lord that bought them.

Ver. 24. *He that heareth my word*] As death came into the world by the door of the ear, so doth life eternal, Isa. lv. 3. God was in the still voice, and the oracle bade, " Hear ye him," Matt. xvii.

Ver. 25. *The dead shall hear the voice*] The dead in sins shall believe the promises, and shall live the life of grace here and of glory in heaven.

Ver. 26. *So hath he given to the Son*] What wonder, then, if faith, apprehending the infinite fountain of life, derive thence some rivulet of life, and apply the same to us for spiritual quickening?

Ver 27. *Because he is the Son of man*] Or, as he is the Son of man.[1] By virtue of the hypostatical union, his manhood came as near to God as could be. He had the best natural parts both of mind, Isa. xi. 2, 3, and body, Psal. xlv. 2 ; and the best supernatural, whereby he found favour also with God, Luke ii. 52, for he had more near familiarity with the Godhead than ever had any creature, together with a partner-agency with his Godhead, in the works of mediation, 1 Tim. ii. 5. In the state of exaltation, the manhood hath, 1. Excess of glory. 2. The grace of adoration together with the Godhead. 3. Judiciary power, as here and Acts xvii. 30.

Ver. 28. *Marvel not at this*] And yet who can but marvel at this great mystery of godliness, whereat angels stand amazed? yea, whereat he himself wonders; and therefore calls his own name Wonderful, Isa. ix. 6. It is truly affirmed of Christ, that he is created and uncreated, without beginning, and yet began in time, a Jew according to the flesh, and yet God blessed for ever, &c. The manner hereof is to be believed, not discussed ; admired, not pried into, &c. *Mirari decet non rimari.*

His voice] Put forth by the ministry of mighty angels, and called by the apostle κέλευσμα, 1 Thess. iv. 16 ; a metaphor from water-men, who call upon one another, and strike oars together, as it were with one consent.

Ver. 29. *They that have done good*] In die judicii plus valebit conscientia pura quam marsupia plena. Bern., Dan. xii. 1, 2. Though other things be darkly delivered, yet when the Jews were to lose land and life, the resurrection is plainly described. So Heb. xi. 35.

Unto the resurrection of damnation] As Pharaoh's baker came forth to be hanged when the butler was exalted. Good therefore is the counsel given us by the heathen orator, *Ita vivamus, ut rationem nobis reddendam arbitremur.* The wicked shall come forth of their graves like filthy toads, against that terrible storm, Psal. ix. The elements shall melt like scalding lead upon them, &c., 2 Pet. iii.

Ver. 30. *I can of mine own self do nothing*] But by the power communicated unto me, in that eternal generation.

As I hear] So ver. 19, " as I see," which Beza understandeth to be spoken in respect of his human nature, as it is hypostatically united to the divine.

Ver. 31. *My witness is not true*] That is, fit, firm, valid, *foro humano. Concessio rhetorica.* Beza.

Ver. 32. *There is another that beareth witness*] God the Father, by this miracle wrought upon the impotent man. Give we real testimony to our profession by our practice. *Mallem obedire quam miracula facere*, said Luther. Profligate professors do put religion to an open shame.[2]

Ver. 33. *Ye sent unto John*] As unto an oracle: but when his answer pleased you not, you rejected it, of mere obstinacy and malice to my person and office. There is an odious unthankfulness in unbelief: for it rebelleth against the light, rejecteth the medicine, refuseth to be reformed, hateth to be healed. Wine is a strong remedy against hemlock ; yet mingled with it, doubleth the force of the poison. So it is with the Word of life when mingled with unbelief.

Ver. 34. *That ye might be saved*] This was that he sought in all his oracles and miracles. Salvation properly notes the privative part of our happiness ; because it is easier to tell from what we are saved than to what.

Ver. 35. *He was a burning, &c.*] Burning in himself, and shining to others ; or as it was said of Basil, thundering in his doctrine and lightning in his life. (Nazianzen.) And of Rogers and Bradford, that it was hard to say whether there were more force of eloquence and utterance in preaching, or more holiness of life and conversation, to be found in them. Like Aaron, they had pomegranates for savour, as well as bells for sound.

For a season to rejoice][3] But he soon grew stale to them ; so that they made no more reckoning of him than of " a reed shaken with the wind," Matt. xi. 7. *Principes favebant Luthero, sed jam iterum videtis ingratitudinem mundi erga ministros*, &c., said good Melancthon, in the year of grace 1559.

Ver. 36. *The works which the Father hath given me*] Lo, Christ accounts his work a gift. So John xvii. 4.

The works that I do, bear witness] Let our works likewise speak for us, Matt. v. 16, as they

---

[1] ὅτι, id est καθότι. Beza.
[2] *Virtutis stragulam pudefacis*, said Diogenes to Antipater ; who, being vicious, wore a white cloak.

[3] ἀγαλλιασθῆναι, to dance a galliard. It was a formal joy, or jollity rather. John Manl.

did for the primitive Christians; of whom Athenagoras (their ambassador to the emperor) boldly saith, Οὐδεῖς χριστιανὸς πονηρὸς εἰ μὴ ὑποκρίνηται τὸν λόγον. No Christian is evil-mannered unless it be such as dissemble themselves to be Christians. And Justin Martyr confesseth of himself, that beholding the piety of Christians' life and constancy in death, he gathered that it was the true religion that they professed. *Non aliunde noscibiles quam de emendatione vitiorum*, saith Tertullian of the Christians of his time. And Chrysostom speaketh of some in his days, whose lives were angelical, they so walked up to their principles.

Ver. 37. *Hath borne witness of me*] By the voice from heaven, and the descending of the Holy Ghost in the shape of a dove, Matt. iii. 16; yet ye have neither heard his voice, nor seen his shape. Who so blind as he that will not see? Isa. xlii. 19.

Ver. 38. *And you have not his word abiding in you*] As an "engraffed word," Jam. i. 21: ye have heard it, but with your bodily ears only, with those gristles that grow upon your heads: ye have not drawn up the ears of your minds to the ears of your bodies, that one sound piercing both, ye might believe; ye have not mixed the word with faith in your hearts, as in a vessel, &c.

Ver. 39. *Search the Scriptures*] *Audite sæculares, comparate vobis Biblia, animæ pharmaca*, saith Chrysostom. But Bibles lie (like old almanacs) moulding in corners, while play-books (the devil's catechisms) are even worn out with over-diligent perusal. It is a sad complaint which Reverend Moulin makes of his country-men, the French Protestants; whiles they burned us, saith he, for reading the Scriptures, we burnt with zeal to be reading of them. Now with our liberty is bred also negligence and disesteem of God's word. Is it not so also with us?

They are they which testify of me] The babe of Bethlehem is bound up in these swathing-bands. He is both author and matter of the Scriptures, and is therefore called the Word. The dignity of the Scriptures (saith one) and the majesty of Christ mutually look on one another: as the sun doth on the stars, and the stars on the sun. For as the excellency of the sun appears by the glory of the stars, to whom it giveth light: so the majesty of Christ is manifest by the Scriptures, to whom he giveth credit. On the other side, as the glory of the star is magnified, because it is the light of the sun: so the credit of the Scripture is exalted, because they concern the Son of God.

Ver. 40. *Ye will not come to me*] Though clearly convinced by the Scriptures. See their obstinacy and malice. Amos, vi. 12, compareth such untameable, untractable, masterless monsters, to horses running upon a rock, where first they break their hoofs and then their necks.

Ver. 41. *I receive not honour from men*] q. d. I need you not, though I complain you come not

to me. It is for your sakes that I seek to you; Christ could be happy, though all men should miscarry: as the sun would shine, though all the world were blind. He seeks not ours, but us.

Ver. 42. *Ye have not the love of God*] Though ye pretend zeal for his glory, to your opposing of me, yet there is *aliud in titulo, aliud in pyxide.* Hypocrites are like Egyptian temples, beautiful without, but within, some cat or such like thing to be worshipped.

Ver. 43. *Him will ye receive*] As they did Barchochab; and that Pseudo-Moses (the devil he was) that cozened so many of them in Crete, A. D. 434, persuading them to cast themselves after him into the sea, which should part, and make them way into their own country again, whereby many of them perished.

Ver. 44. *Which receive honour one of another*] Faith empties a man of himself, purgeth upon ambition, and is an act of the will; else the seeking of praise with men could be no impediment to the act of believing. Surely, as Pharaoh said of the Israelites, "they are entangled in the land, the wilderness hath shut them in;" so may we say of many, they are entangled in the creature, the world hath shut them in, they cannot come to Christ. They are shut up in the cave of the world, as those five kings in a cave, Josh. x. 18; have hardness of heart, as a great stone rolled to the mouth, and honours, riches, and pleasures, are so many keepers, &c.

Ver. 45. *Do not think that I*] That is, that I only.

Even Moses] So your faithful ministers (whom men pretend to love and reverence, but obey not their doctrine), these shall judge you.

Ver. 46. *For he wrote of me*] Both clearly and mystically, in the many sacrifices and ceremonies of the law. Whence Theodoret calleth Moses, τὸν τῆς θεολογίας ὠκεανὸν, ἐξ οὗπερ πάντες πόταμοι καὶ πᾶσα θάλαττα, the main ocean of divinity, out of whom all the prophets and apostles have watered their several gardens. And Pareus closeth up his commentary upon Genesis, with these words, *Quicquid Scripturarum sacrarum dehinc sequitur, hujus est Commentarius.*

Ver. 47. *But if ye believe not his writings*] He that will not take God's word in one place will take it in no place.

CHAPTER VI.

Ver. 1. *After these things*] i. e. A good while after; Herod having beheaded the Baptist, and being perplexed at the fame of Jesus, whom therefore he desired to see, but for an evil purpose, Luke ix. 8, 9.

Ver. 2. *And a great multitude followed him*] Though he went privately into a desert place belonging to Bethsaida, Luke ix. 10. The Sun of righteousness could not be hid, for he had "healing in his wings," Mal. iv. 2.

Ver. 3. *And Jesus went up into a mount*] See

the note on Matt. v. 1. He would have been private till the passover and refreshed himself with his disciples; but seeing God had now put a new opportunity into his hands of benefiting many, he would not neglect it.

Ver. 4. *And the passover*] The third passover (likely) after his baptism. And this might occasion him to speak of the spiritual eating of himself, the true Paschal: for even "Christ our passover was sacrificed for us," 1 Cor. v. 7.

Ver. 5. *He saith unto Philip*] The people took no thought for food. Christ doth it for them. And surely if he so far provided for those, that out of a sudden motion, and no great good intention, came out after him, can we think he will be wanting to those that seek him constantly, and with full purpose of heart adhere unto him?

Ver. 6. *And this he said to prove him*] To discover him to himself: for that a man is in truth that he is in a temptation. See the note on Matt. xiv. 17.

Ver. 7. *Two hundred penny-worth*] And where will you have half the money? send them away therefore, rid your hands honestly of them, and let us rest and refresh ourselves, as we resolved to do when we first retired hither. Thus he.

Ver. 8. *One of his disciples*] He uttered the sense of all the twelve, Mark vi. 37, being no whit wiser than the rest, though the eldest disciple of them all, John i. 41.

Ver. 9. *Five barley loaves and two small fishes*] Was not Tyrabosco hardly driven, when from these five loaves and two fishes, he concluded seven sacraments? So in the second Council of Nice under Irene, John (one of the legates of the Eastern churches) proved the making of images lawful, because God had said, "Let us make man after our own image." A sound argument to overthrow one of God's commandments! and yet it prevailed.

Ver. 10. *Make the men sit down*] And they did so, though they saw no sense for it. This kind of blind obedience is very acceptable: *Clausis oculis Deum sequi debemus ducem.* We must wink and put ourselves into God's hand to be led whither he pleaseth.

Ver. 11. *He distributed to the disciples*] These five loaves (by a strange kind of arithmetic) were multiplied by division, and augmented by subtraction. The Macedonians found, that not getting, but giving, is the way to thrive, 2 Cor. ix. 8. *Ex fame quæstum captabat Josephus; et benignitate sua emit Egyptum: Nos etiam cœlum.* So in spiritual alms and good offices: God's gifts grow in the hands of them that employ them, to feed many. *Salienti aquarum fonti undas si tollas, nec exhauritur, nec extenuatur, sed dulcescit. Scientia, docendi officio, dulcedinem sentiat, non minutias.*

Ver. 12. *When they were filled*] See the note on Matt. xiv. 20.

Ver. 13. *Filled twelve baskets*] See 1 Kings xvii. 15, 16, and Matt. xiv. 20, with the note.

Ver. 14. *This is of a truth that prophet*] Yet anon they are at it, "What sign showest thou?"

that you may know them to be the Pharisees' disciples. Of whose sour leaven also that in the next verse savours; where they would needs take him by force to make him a king, ver. 30. They could not imagine a Messias that had not an earthly kingdom.

Ver. 15. *Take him by force*] Superstition will needs obtrude upon Christ will-worship, whether he will or no, and despite him with seeming honours, as the Lycaonians would needs have stolen a sacrifice upon Paul and Barnabas; and the savages of Nova Albion upon Sir Francis Drake and his company, at their parting with them. They had set it on fire ere we were aware, saith he; we laboured by all means to withhold or withdraw them, but could not prevail, till at length we fell to prayers and singing of psalms, whereby they were allured immediately to forget their folly, and leave their sacrifice unconsumed, suffering the fire to go out; and imitating us in all their actions, they fell a lifting up their hands and eyes to heaven as they saw us to do.

Ver. 16. *His disciples went down to the sea*] By Christ's own command, Matt. xiv. 22; Mark vi. 45, yet they met with a sore storm. So may the best with trouble, in their most lawful employments, Psal. xxxiv. 18. But these make them look to their tackling, patience; to their anchor, hope; to their helm, faith; to their card, the Word; to their Captain, Christ, who is ever at hand.

Ver. 17. *Jesus was not come to them*] This was worse to them than the storm. It was woeful with Saul when the Philistines were upon him, and God would not come at him, nor answer him, 1 Sam. xxviii. 15. So when danger or death is upon a man, and God is far from him. That doom, "I will not show you favour," Jer. xvi. 13, was worse than their captivity.

Ver. 18.] See the note on Matt. xiv. 24.

Ver. 19, 20. *They were afraid*] See Matt. xiv. 26, 27.

Ver. 21. *Immediately the ship was at land*] A dying saint hath no sooner taken death into his bosom, but he is immediately landed at the quay of Canaan, at the kingdom of heaven. *Fugiendum est ad clarissimam patriam: ibi pater, ibi omnia,* said Plotinus the Platonist. (Aug. C. D. ix. 17.)

Ver. 22. *On the other side of the sea*] The lake of Gennesareth: over the which those were said to pass, that passed some creeks or bays to go the nearer way.

Ver. 23. *After that the Lord had given thanks*] See the note on Matt. xiv. 19.

Ver. 24. *Seeking for Jesus*] But not for Jesus' sake. See ver. 25.

Ver. 25. *Rabbi, when camest thou hither?*] This question they moved, not so much to learn what they knew not, as to make show of what they knew before. But two things make a man truly virtuous,—good actions and good aims. *Finibus non officiis à vitiis discernuntur virtutes,* saith Augustine: The end maketh or marreth the act. *Christus opera nostra non tam actibus quam finibus pensat*, saith another. The glory of God should consume all sinister ends, as the sunlight puts out the fire, or as Moses' serpent swallowed up the sorcerers' serpents.

Ver. 26. *Because ye did eat of the loaves*] More than for love, *Vix diligitur Jesus propter Jesum.* (Aug.) But as the mixed multitude came out of Egypt with Israel for a better fortune, and as he, Matt. xx. 13, "agreed for a penny;" as the harlot looks to the love-tokens more than to the donor; so was it here. Worldlings, *Ubi non vident quæstum, rident Christum : Ubi datur ut edant, adduci possunt, ut credant :* they serve not the Lord Jesus Christ, but their own bellies.

Haud facile invenias multis e millibus unum
Virtutem pretium qui putet esse sui.

Ver. 27. *Labour not for the meat, &c.*] When Basil was tempted with money and preferment, he answers, *Pecuniam da quæ permaneat, ac continuo duret, gloriam quæ semper floreat.* The fashion of this world passeth away, as the water of a river that runs by a city, or as a fair picture drawn upon the ice that melts away with it. Men come to the world's felicities, as to a lottery, with heads full of hopes, but return with hearts full of blanks.

Labour for the meat that endureth] We may not dream of a delicacy in God's ways, or think that good things will drop out of the clouds to us, as towns were said to come into Timotheus' toils whilst he slept. We must be at pains for heaven. *Laborandum* was one of the emperor's mottoes, and may be every Christian's. Strive they must even to an agony (Αγωνίζεσθε, Luke xiii. 24), ere they can get into the strait gate : together with our stooping, there must be a certain stripping of ourselves.

Ver. 28. *That we might work*] We would still be working, weaving a web of righteousness of our own, spinning a thread of our own to climb up to heaven by, that we might say with the spider, *Nulli debeo ;* and with that Popish meritmonger, *Cœlum gratis non accipiam,* I will not have heaven of free cost. Men would have heaven as a purchase. I would swim through a sea of brimstone, said one, that I might come to heaven at last. But those that cry *hæc ego feci*, Luther wittily calls the devil's *fæces ;* as those that seek to be saved by their good works, he fitly calls the devil's martyrs ; because they suffer much and take much pains to go to hell. Let us all take heed of this piece of natural Popery ; and learn to be in duty in respect of performance, and yet out of duty in respect of dependance. We are all apt to do otherwise ; and like broken chapmen we would still be chaffering, if but for small matters ; and think to be saved for a company of poor beggarly businesses.

Ver. 29. *This is the work of God*] The τὸ ἔργον. It is an easy matter to believe (thinks the worldling), but he that goes about it shall find it as hard a work to believe the gospel, as to

keep the law.[1] For God must enable to both. *Non minus difficile est nobis velle credere* (saith Beza) *quam cadaveri volare.* We believe with much conflict, saith another.[2] The combat was not so great betwixt Michael and Satan about Moses' dead body, as between Satan and the believer concerning Christ's living body. Faith is fain to tug and wrestle for it, till it sweat again.

Ver. 30. *What sign showest thou ?*] sc. From heaven ; such as manna was (see the notes on Matt. xii. 38), for otherwise, they wanted for no signs. But Christ's doctrine discontented them : and hence these peevish questions, or cavils rather, all to slip collar. In the kingdom of Congo, in Africa, the Portuguese, at their first arrival, finding the people to be heathens and without God, did induce them to a profession of Christ, and to be baptized in great abundance, allowing of the principles of religion ; until such time as the priests pressed them to lead their lives according to their profession ; which the most part of them in no case enduring, they returned back again to their gentilism, forgetting also soon after the very names they received when they were baptized.

Ver. 31. *Our fathers did eat manna in the desert*] Here they bewray themselves, and confirm what our Saviour had said of them, ver. 26, viz. that they followed him only for provender. *Sic sorex suo perit indicio.* So the fish sepia is discovered and taken by the black colour that it casteth up purposely to conceal itself.

Ver. 32. *I am the true bread*] Whereof manna was but a type ; manna is said to have all sorts of good tastes in it : Christ hath so to his. Manna descended in the dew ; so doth Christ in his word preached. See Exod. xvi. 14, &c. ; Numb. xi. 7, &c., with the notes.

Ver. 33. *Which came down from heaven*] From the highest heaven (not out of the middle region of the air only, as manna), and is the true ambrosia.

Ver. 34. *Lord, evermore give us this bread*] This they speak jeeringly, as the woman of Samaria did in like case, John iv. 15.

Ver. 35. *I am that bread of life*] Christ, passing by that bitter scoff of theirs, proceeds to teach them. The servant of the Lord must "not strive, but be gentle unto all men, apt to teach, patient in meekness, instructing those that oppose themselves," &c., 2 Tim. ii. 24.

Shall never hunger] That is, shall never be painfully or despairingly hungry, utterly destitute of grace and glory ; but shall continually feed at the feast of a good conscience, and at length sit down with Abraham, Isaac, and Jacob, in the kingdom of heaven.

Ver. 36. *Ye have seen me*] But not savingly. Your understandings have been gilded over with a common kind of supernatural light, Heb. vi. 4, but not to a transmentation. You have seen me as a traveller seeth the pomp and splendour of a foreign court, or as men see far countries in maps, with an intuitive insight, &c.

[1] Rogers of Faith.

[2] Dike of the Deceitful Heart.

Ver. 37. *All that the Father giveth me*] Gr. πάντα, all things, that is, the whole community of Christians, all the elect, of which number you plainly show yourselves to be none by your want of the faith of God's elect, that distinctive character. Wisdom is justified of all her children.

I will in no wise cast out] Gr. οὐ μὴ ἐκβάλω ἔξω, I will not not, cast out out. A powerful speech, and a most comfortable consideration. Who would not come to Jesus Christ upon such sweetest encouragement? Surely as all that were in debt and distress came to David, and he became their captain; so should all afflicted spirits come to the Son of David, the Captain of our salvation. *Non autem pedibus itur ad Christum, sed affectibus*, &c., where this life-giving carcase is, thither let the eagles resort.

Ver. 38. *Not to do mine own will*] As man, he did his Father's will; as God, he hath the same will with the Father.

Ver. 39. *I should raise it up again*] By virtue of the union, a substance is preserved, and shall be raised up again to glory; yea, "the dead in Christ shall rise first," 1 Thess. iv. 16, by virtue derived from Christ's resurrection, and by the mighty influence thereof. For he was raised to be a root and fountain of all supernatural life, both of our souls and bodies.

Ver. 40. *Which seeth the Son and believeth*] This these Jews did not, ver. 36. Some slight knowledge of Christ they had; but it amounted not to a saving faith. See the note on ver. 36. Meteors hang awhile in the air, but are not of strength enough to ascend to the upper region; hence they soon vanish.

And I will raise him up] This is four several times repeated, that we may rest secure of it, and be comforted. *Fiducia Christianorum resurrectio mortuorum*, saith Tertullian.

Ver. 41. *The Jews therefore murmured*] They were as good at this as ever their fathers had been in the wilderness, and afterwards, Zech. vii. 12; Acts vii. 51.

Ver. 42. *The son of Joseph*] Who was *Christi pater putativus, politicus, secundum dici, non secundum esse.*

How is it then] Wretched men dare reprehend what they do not comprehend.

Ver. 43. *Murmur not among yourselves*] q. d. I give you no just cause so to do. You carry your galls in your ears, as some creatures are said to do, hence you are so embittered; your mouths are out of taste, and hence you so disrelish my doctrine.

Ver. 44. *No man can come to me, except*, &c.] Down then goes the Dagon of free will, with all that *vitreum acumen* of all the patrons thereof; whether Pagans or Papagans, Pelagians or Semipelagians. Let them say never so much *Ignavis opus est auxilio divino; Quod vivimus Deorum munus est; quod bene sancteque vivimus, nostrum.* (Sen.) A wiser than the wisest of them tells us here another tale; and elsewhere, John xv. 5, " Without me ye can do nothing." Where Austin observes that our Saviour saith not *perficere*, but

facere ; nor doth he say, Without me ye can do no hard thing, but nothing. And the same father noteth that *sub laudibus naturæ latent inimici gratiæ.* The friends of free will are enemies to free grace.

God the Father draw him] By a merciful violence, *ex nolentibus volentes facit.* See the note on Cant. i. 4. The Father draweth, and the man cometh; that notes the efficacy of grace, and this the sweetness of grace. Grace works strongly, and therefore God is said to draw; and it works sweetly too, and therefore man is said to come.

Ver. 45. *And they shall be all taught of God*] i. e. All the children of the Church, Jer. xxxi. 34, and why not the infants of believing parents also? sith they are disciples, Acts xv. 10, taught of God from the least to the greatest, Isa. liv. 13; dedicated in their baptism to the Father, Son, and Holy Ghost by their parents' promise, purpose, and prayer, and so put under God's teaching; whereof they are capable, as also of the operation of the Holy Ghost, even from their mother's womb, Luke i. 15. God also hath promised to pour his Spirit upon them, Joel ii. 28 ; Isa. lix. 21. And after our Saviour had here said " They shall be all taught of God," he presently subjoineth, " Every one that hath heard, and hath learned of the Father, cometh unto me." Where note, that he saith not, Whosoever hath heard and learned of the preacher, but of the Father, cometh unto me. Now, infants can come unto Christ, and none must forbid them. They have also the full sight of God's face in heaven ; they may therefore have a glimpse of it here ; they being his children, Ezek. xvi. 20, 21, his servants, Levit. xxv. 41, 42, in covenant with him, Deut. xxvi. 10—12.

Ver. 46. *He hath seen the Father*] And hath it in commission to manifest him to all his, by working faith (either actual, or, at least, virtual, as in infants) in their hearts, whereby they see him that is invisible, being well seen in Moses' optics.

Ver. 47. *Hath life eternal*] sc. In Christ's purchase, in God's promise, in the first-fruits of the Spirit, who resteth upon the elect as a Spirit of glory and of God, 1 Pet. iv. 14.

Ver. 48. *I am that bread of life*] That not only uphold and maintain spiritual life, but do also begin and beget it. And this our Saviour often inculcateth here, as most needful to be known and most comfortable to be considered.

Ver. 49. *Did eat manna*] They fed upon sacraments, and yet many of them perished eternally. A man may go to hell with font-water on his face, and be haled from the table to the tormentor, as he, Matt. xxii. 13.

Your fathers did eat, &c.] They sought only the satisfying of their bodily hunger, and they had it, but yet are dead. Manna could not immortalize them, as the poets feign their ambrosia did their dunghill deities. " Meats for the belly, and the belly for meats, but God will destroy both it and them." These mentioned in the text fed upon sacraments, and yet they died in God's displeasure, 1 Cor. x. 3, 5. The carcase of the sacrament cannot give life, but the soul of it, which is Christ; neither do the sacraments work as physic, whether men sleep or wake, by virtue inherent in them, *ex opere operato, sed ex opere operantis*, *i. e.* according to the disposition and qualification of the party that partaketh.

Ver. 50. *This is the bread*] Δεικτικῶς, pointing to himself. So David, "this poor man" (meaning himself) "cried, and the Lord heard him," &c., Psal. xxxiv. 6. So *Hic sat lucis*, said Œcolampadius on his death-bed, laying his hand on his breast.

Ver. 51. *If any man eat*, &c.] *Hic edere est credere*, saith Augustine; faith being the soul's hand, mouth, stomach, &c. The Fathers commonly expounded this part of our Saviour's sermon as spoken of the sacrament of the Lord's supper; and so fell into that error, that none but communicants could be saved; wherefore also they gave the sacrament to infants, and put it into the mouths of dead men, &c. We are not to think that either our Saviour spake here properly, and *ex professo*, of the sacramental eating of his flesh and drinking of his blood; or that this discourse pertains nothing at all thereunto. The Papists have expunged a great part of Origen's commentary upon this chapter, as directly making against their monster of transubstantiation. And Cardinal Campeius affirmed against Luther, that faith is not necessary to him that receiveth the sacrament. As for Bellarmine, although we believe, saith he, that all virtues are found in the Church, yet that any man may be absolutely said to be a member of the true Church, we do not think that any inward virtue is required, but only an external profession of the faith, and such communion of the sacraments, as is received by the outward man.[1] This mark very well agrees to the Church of Rome, wherein if any be truly virtuous, it is by mere accident, as Cicero wittily said of the epicures, that if any one of them were good, he was merely overcome by the goodness of his nature; for they taught a licentious looseness, *Si quando viri boni sint, vinci bonitate naturæ.*

Ver. 52. *Strove among themselves*] They tumultuously contradicted, murmured, mutinied, which was a sign of their obstinacy and contempt. For otherwise it is not only lawful, but needful, modestly to make inquiry how we may eat Christ spiritually.

Ver. 53. *Except ye eat the flesh*, &c.] Fulbert, Bishop of Chartres (who lived in the eleventh century), speaking upon the eucharist, hath these words, "Except ye eat the flesh of the Son of man," &c. *Facinus vel flagitium videtur jubere. Figura ergo est, præcipiens passioni Domini esse communicandum tantum, et suaviter et utiliter recondendum in memoria, quod pro nobis caro ejus crucifixa et vulnerata est.* Now in the year of Christ 1608, there was set out an edition of him in Paris, where we have interserted, after *Figura*

ergo est, these words, *Dicit Hæreticus*, to make what Fulbert spoke *assertivè* from Augustine, to speak *recitativè* of the heretic, as if the heretic should say, This is a figure, &c., which if admitted, then there is no transubstantiation. The words produced by Fulbert are indeed St Augustine's.[2] And the publisher of Fulbert being told hereof, that the words were Augustine's, that he had branded with heresy, he put afterwards his *Dicit Hæreticus* amongst his errata, as ye may read in Bishop Usher's answer to the Jesuit's challenge, page 15.

Except ye eat the flesh] That is, except ye spiritually apprehend Christ by faith, *Crede et manducasti*, saith Austin, Believe and thou hast eaten. By the actuation of our faith we even lean on Christ's bosom as that beloved disciple did; *Cruci hæremus, sanguinem fugimus, et intra ipsa Redemptoris nostri vulnera fugimus linguam*, saith Cyprian.

Ver. 54. *Whoso eateth my flesh*] Because this was a hard point to believe, therefore it is so oft repeated and inculcated. *Verba toties inculcata viva sunt, vera sunt, sana sunt, plana sunt.*

Ver. 55. *For my flesh is meat indeed*] That that will do the deed. It is neither painted meat nor enchanted, but real and substantial; yet not corporal but spiritual. Our Richard II. was starved at Pomfret Castle by being tantalized; for his diet being served in, and set before him in the wonted princely manner, he was not suffered either to taste or touch thereof. (Speed.) The great Caliph of Babylon was used in like manner by Haalon brother to Mango, great Khan of Tartary; saving that he had not meat set before him, but gold, silver, precious stones, whereof he was, by way of derision, willed to eat, and make no spare, &c. True believers meet with meat indeed, and by a *Crapula Sacra*, as Luther calleth it, feeding hard thereupon, they are nourished infallibly to eternal life.

Ver. 56. *He that eateth my flesh*, &c.] That is, that partaketh of my person, merits, passions, privileges; he that receiveth me in all mine offices and efficacies.

Ver. 57. *So he that eateth me, liveth by me*] All out of Christ then, though they seem to have the only life of it (as Nabal, 1 Sam. xxx. 6, "Thus shall ye say to him that liveth"), yet in true account they are no better than living carcases, walking sepulchres, of themselves. Christ is the only principle and Prince of life; and his people only are heirs together of the grace of life, 1 Pet. iii. 7.

Ver. 58. *This is that bread*] Here our Saviour returns to that comparison he had made before betwixt manna and his flesh; and so concludes as he began. A pattern for preachers.

Ver. 59. *These things said he in the synagogue*] In a set sermon, and yet to little purpose; for many made defection. *Vultures unguento fugantur, et scarabei rosâ*, say Pliny and Ælian. When we have spent all our wind on our people, their hearts will be still apt to be carried away

---

[1] Bell. iii. 2, de Eccles. milit.

[2] De Doct. Christ. ii. 16.

with every wind of contrary doctrine or satanical suggestion.

Ver. 60. *This is an hard saying*] The hardness was in themselves, not in the word; but that must bear the blame howsoever; as she in Seneca that was stricken with sudden blindness, and then cried out of the light. A hypocrite is not discovered, till upon some critical point. If it come to a matter of cost, he cries, "What needs this waste?" if of pains, "This is an hard saying."

Ver. 61. *When Jesus knew in himself*] For they had not yet discovered what pinched them; but only muttered it among themselves, *aversantium* v ore, in a discontented manner. They had done much better if they had opened their minds to Christ and sought satisfaction. But men will sooner talk against a preacher by "the walls and in the doors of their houses," Ezek. xxxiii. 30 (taking everything with the left hand, and by the left handle), than either candidly interpret, or let him be his own interpreter.

Ver. 62. *What and if ye shall see the Son of man ascend*] Then you shall not be scandalized (so some sense it); or then you shall much more be scandalized, so Maldonat, who saith he could like the other sense well enough, but that it is the Calvinists'. So George, Duke of Saxony, said, he could have thought well of a reformation, if Luther had not wrought it. (Grinæus in Hagg. præfat.)

Ver. 63. *It is the Spirit that quickeneth*] Had those carnal Capernaites but stayed out our Saviour's sermon, they might have been satisfied for the sense of his words, that they so stumbled at, and had not patience to hear him here expounding himself. *Quoniam Christiani* (*Pontificii*) *manducant Deum, quem adorant, sit anima mea cum philosophis*, said Averroes; who, had he consulted with sound divines, might have known more.

It is the Spirit that quickeneth] *i. e.* The Godhead united to the human nature conveyeth life to the believer. That being the fountain, this the conduit; and union being the ground of communion. Wicked men want the spirit and life of Christ, who though he took every man's flesh, yet that of itself profiteth them nothing. *A communione naturæ ad communicationem gratiæ non valet argumentum.*

Ver. 64. *But there are some of you that believe not*] And hence it is that you so grossly mistake me, and that you find no more benefit by me and my words. Unbelief rejects the remedy, frustrates the means, holds a man in universal pollution, Heb. iii. 12, and leaves him under a double condemnation; one from the law wherein Christ found him, and another from the gospel for refusing the remedy, that blessed bath of Christ's blood, Zech. xiii. 1, whereunto even the princes of Sodom are invited, Isa. i. 10, and for despising it, doomed, Ezek. xxiv. 13, as a malefactor dead in law, and yet rejecteth the offer of a pardon. In Ket's sedition, when King Edward VI.'s pardon was offered the rebels by a herald, a lewd boy turned toward him his naked posteriors, and used words suitable to that gesture.

One standing by discharged an arquebuse upon the boy, and struck him dead in the place.[1] How shall those escape that neglect so great salvation, which at first began to be spoken by the Lord? Heb. ii. 3.

Ver. 65. *Therefore said I unto you*] Here some may object, if faith be not in man's power, why doth he yet complain? and why are any destroyed for lack of faith? Hereunto I might answer with the apostle, "Nay, but, O man, who art thou that repliest, or chattest against God?" But for further satisfaction, know, 1. That faith was once in man's power. 2. That no unbeliever doth what he might do to believe. 3. That unbelief is in a man's power, who wittingly and willingly, and by his own election, forsaketh his own mercies, John ii. 8; Matt. xxiii. 37; there is an uncounsellable obstinacy in it.

Unless it be given him] That divine traction then, ver. 44, is a free gift: there is no *meritum ex congruo*. Our effectual conversion is *gratuita et inopinata*, Eph. i. 11. We cannot concur or contribute toward it. Nothing can prepare for grace but grace. Neither can we bring forth good things any otherwise than as Sarah's dead womb brought forth a child; it was not a child of nature, but of the mere promise.

Ver. 66. *Many of his disciples*] They stumbled at the word and fell backward. This is reckoned by St Peter a note of a reprobate, 1 Pet. ii. 8. And indeed few sins are more dangerous than that of picking quarrels at God's word, taking up weapons against it, and snuffing at it, Mal. i. 13; replying against it, Rom. ix. 19, 20; casting reproaches upon it, Jer. xx. 8, 9; enviously swelling at it, Acts xiii. 45; gathering odious consequences from it, Rom. iii. 8: such are in the ready road to apostasy, and so to perdition, Heb. x. ult.

Ver. 67. *Will ye also go away?*] *q. d.* This general defection of those temporaries may possibly tempt you to it. Evil men endanger good men, as weeds the corn, as bad humours the blood, or an infected house the neighbourhood. *Nemo errat sibi ipsi, sed dementiam spargit in proximos.* (Seneca.) No man falls single, but draws company along with him, as the dragon with his tail drew down the stars of heaven; as tall cedars bear down with them the shrubs that grow under them. As when Hymenæus and Philetus (two such eminent professors) fell away, the apostle, for the better settling of such as were shaken thereby, was fain to caution, "Nevertheless the foundation of God standeth sure," &c. And "in a great house" (such as God's is) "there are vessels of all sorts, some to honour, and some to dishonour," 2 Tim. ii. 19, 20.

Ver. 68. *Thou hast the words of eternal life*] In going from thee, therefore, we shall go out of God's blessing. Nay, we shall go upon our own death, upon hell-mouth. The Roman law was, *Transfugas, ubicunque inventi fuerint, quasi hostes interficere licet.* Runagates and renegadoes are

---

[1] Life of Edward VI., by Sir John Heywood.

sure to die for it; when those that live by those lively oracles of the gospel shall live for ever.

Ver. 69. *We believe and have known*] In matters of divinity we must first believe, and then know; not know, and then believe. In human sciences it is otherwise. Men are brought to assent and believe by experience, knowledge, and sense; as to believe that fire is hot, &c. But here, belief and assent go before experimental knowledge, sense, and use.

Ver. 70. *Have not I chosen you twelve, &c.*] q. d. If ye believe and will abide by it, look well to your footing; it will shortly be tried what stability is in you, when such an angel as Judas shall show himself to be a devil. Stand fast; for you are like to be shaken, as he in the history said, when he whipped the pillars and public statues before the earthquake, which he had, by a prophetical spirit, foretold. (Simeon Monach.)

Ver. 71. *He spake of Judas Iscariot*] Which some derive of the Syriac word signifying strangling, as if he were so named by an anticipation; like as our roaring boys will needs be so called now, by a woeful prolepsis, here for hereafter. But what a hard heart had Judas, and how fearfully was he satanized and transformed into a breathing devil, that could hear all this, and not be affected therewith! *Hypocritis nihil stupidius*, Nothing is more stupid or more stubborn than a hypocrite. David fitly compareth him to the deaf adder; which although by spitting out his poison he might renew his age; yet he stoppeth both his ears, lest he should hear the voice of the charmer.

CHAPTER VII.

Ver. 1. *For he would not walk in Jewry*] THE Roman rule in battle was, *Nec fugere, nec sequi*, Neither to fly dangers nor to follow them. The Christian's motto is, *Nec temere, nec timide*, Neither timorous, nor temerarious. As we must not basely desert the cause of Christ when called out to defend it, but ἢ τὰν ἢ ἐπὶ τὰν, as she said to her son (Plutarch), Either vanquish or die, as the Black Prince's father said to him, Either live with the gospel or die for it; so we may not rashly run ourselves upon unnecessary dangers, but decline them where we can with a good conscience. He that flieth may fight another time, said Demosthenes, ῥίψασπις. Christians also are permitted to fly, when they are sought for to the slaughter, so it be with the wings of a dove and not with the pinions of a dragon. It was a masculine resolution of that good woman celebrated by Jerome, *Non ideo negare volo, ne peream: sed ideo mentiri nolo, ne peccem.* I will rather die than lie.

Ver. 2. *The feast of tabernacles*] The Jews at this feast dwelt without doors, in booths and bowers, in remembrance of their wandering of old through the wilderness. This gave occasion to Plutarch, and other profane heathens, to devise and broach so many base lies of the Jews, as if they were worshippers of Bacchus. Florus calls the temple of Jerusalem, *impiæ gentis arcanum.* Another tells us that the Jews were forced to rest every seventh day, for an evil disease they had cleaving unto them.

Ver. 3. *Depart hence*] Saucily enough, and sarcastically too; pricked on by ambition, likely, which ever rideth without reins, and cares not whose ruins it buildeth upon.

Ver. 4. *For there is no man, &c.*] Here they proceed to charge Christ with folly; and presume to lesson him with their

Vile latens virtus: quid enim submersa latebris Proderit? Obscuro veluti sine remige puppis: Vel lyra quæ reticet, vel qui non tenditur arcus.
Claudian.

Ver. 5. *For neither did his brethren believe*] This the Jews at this day read with much wonderment; and take occasion from this text to slander our Saviour's miracles, as nothing so manifest as we conceive them, sith his own kindred believed not in him.

Ver. 6. *My time is not yet come*] sc. My time of journeying to Jerusalem; I must take my best opportunity, when I may go up with most safety. You may take your own time: you can hardly take amiss, sith the world loveth his own, John xv. 19; and huggeth them to death, as the ape doth her young.

Ver. 7. *But me it hateth, because I testify*] *Obsequium amicos, veritas odium parit*, Truth breeds hatred, as the fair nymphs are feigned to bring forth the ill-favoured fauns and satyrs. *An expectes ut Quintilianus ametur?* said he; Canst thou expect that I with my plain-dealing should be favoured? Quintilian saith of Vespasian the emperor, that he was *patientissimus viri*, one that could well endure to be told his own. And of Gerson (that great Chancellor of Paris) it is recorded that he rejoiced in nothing so much as in a round reprehension by some faithful friend. But few such to be found nowadays. *Prædicare jam nihil aliud est, quam totius orbis furorem in se derivare*, said Luther out of his own daily experience. They "hate him that reproveth in the gate." Preachers are called lights, which sore eyes cannot look upon without offence. Salt also they are called, which cast upon wounds, maketh them smart grievously. Hence the world's hatred, as Zech. i. 11; all the earth was at rest, and desired not to be disquieted by the sound of a trumpet.

Ver. 8. *I go not up yet*] q. d. I will ere long: lest haply they should think that he disliked the public services, and would not come at them, because of the manifold corruptions that were then crept into them. All which notwithstanding, Christ never separated, nor commanded others so to do, but the contrary: "Go show thyself to the priest," Matt. viii. 4; "The scribes and Pharisees sit in Moses' chair; hear them," Matt. xxiii. 2. It is noted as a great fault in Eli's time, that men "abhorred the offering of the Lord," though the sin of the priests was very great before the Lord, and all was out of order; yet in abhorring the sacrifice, they "transgressed, even to a cry," 1 Sam. ii. 17.

Ver. 9. *He abode still in Galilee*] Which he needed not to have done, could he but have complied with the world, as his kinsmen did. But that man purchaseth his peace at too dear a rate that payeth his honesty to get it.

Ver. 10. *Not openly, but as it were in secret*] To kindle the desire of seeing and hearing him so much the more; or to discover whether there were any numbers disposed by his first preaching to receive him, to the end he might not show himself in vain. He had lost most of his hearers, who thenceforth walked no more with him, John vi. 66; yet might haply afterwards have a better mind to him.

Ver. 11. *Where is he?*] Not, "where is Jesus?" They could not find in their hearts to call him by his name, they were so full of malice against him. So Joseph's brethren called him not Joseph, but the Dreamer: Saul asked not for David, but the son of Jesse. After Stephen Brune the martyr was put to death, his adversaries commanded it to be cried, That none should make any more mention of him, under pain of heresy. And *ubicunque invenitur nomen Calvini, deleatur*, saith the *Index expurgatorius*. But what saith our Saviour, " Blessed are ye, when men shall hate you, and cast out your name as evil, for the Son of man's sake," Luke vi. 22. The wise historian observed, that the statues of Brutus and Cassius, *Eo præfulgebant, quod non visebantur*. (Tacit. Annal.) And Cato said, he had rather men should question why he had no statue or monument erected to him than why he had.

Ver. 12. *For some said*] All men were not of a mind concerning Christ. Sooner shall the fingers of their hands be all of a length, than men will be all of a judgment in matters of religion. *Nullum bellum citius exardescit, nullum deflagrat tardius quam theologicum, ut sacramentarium.* (Bucholcer.)

Ver. 13. *For fear of the Jews*] Who had made an order (it seems) somewhat like that of the Jesuits' edict at Dola in the country of Burgundy, that for prevention of heresy, no man should speak of God, either in good sort or bad. This the Jews did, 1. To save themselves a labour of confuting our Saviour's doctrine. 2. To persuade the people that it was such horrible blasphemy as was not fit to be named. So the Papists debar the people all sound of the religion, in prohibiting the books of the reformed writers, and hiding their own treatises, wherein the tenet of the Protestants is recited only to be confuted: so that you shall seldom in all Italy meet with Bellarmine's works or any of the like nature to be sold.

Ver. 14. *About the midst of the feast*] That he might have the better audience.

Went up into the temple and taught] *Sacerdotum tunc fere muta officia, populi cæca obsequia, ut am apud Pontificios.*

Ver. 15. *And the Jews marvelled*] As well they might; but this marvel of theirs came to nothing. Look how a swine, finding a precious jewel, grunts only, and goes his way: so here.

Ver. 16. *My doctrine is not mine*] As if he had said, this should not be *scandalum, sed scala;* not a stumbling-block, but a ladder to lift you up to see the Divine handiwork, and to make you say, as Ezek. iii. 12, " Blessed be the glory of the Lord from his place:" sith I have my learning from above, and am (as Nicodemus acknowledged) " a teacher sent from God."

Ver. 17. *If any man will do his will*] Let knowledge and practice run parallel, and mutually transfuse vigour and vivacity, the one into the other. Keep open the passage between your heads and hearts, that every truth may go to the quick.

Ver. 18. *Seeketh his own glory*] All seducers are self-seekers, and drive on their own interests, how to set up themselves in the hearts of the people: they study their own share more than God's, and yet they would seem to do otherwise; as those proud boasters that cried out, " Let the Lord be glorified," Isa. lxvi. 5; and the Swenckfeldians (stenck-feldians Luther calleth them, from the ill-savour of their opinions) entitled themselves with that glorious name, " The confessors of the glory of Christ." Schlusserib.

Ver. 19. *Did not Moses give you the law*] q. d. You bear me still an old grudge, an aching tooth, for healing an impotent man upon the sabbath-day, chap. v. But *Quis tulerit Gracchos,* &c. (Juv.) Yourselves are greater sabbath-breakers a fair deal. P. Clodius (the most irreligious of all the Romans), *religionem in Ciceronis domo neglectam questus est,* complained of Cicero's family, for neglect of religion.[1] Who so forward to cry, Treason, treason, as Athaliah the arch-traitor alive? and who cry out so much, Persecution, persecution, as Papists and other fierce persecutors?

Ver. 20. *Thou hast a devil*] This he passeth by as a frontless slander, not worth refuting, but proceeds to maintain the lawfulness of that he had done on the sabbath-day. Sincerity throws off slanders, as Paul did the viper; yea, in a holy scorn, it laughs at them, as the wild ass doth at the horse and his rider. Wicellius and Cochleus say that we betrayed the Rhodes (saith Melancthon), and some other such foul businesses they lay to our charge. These are such gross lies, that we need not disprove them; let them tell as many such lies of us as they will, *dicant ipsi talia quoad velint,* our names are oiled, they will not stick.

Ver. 21. *And ye all marvel*] i. e. ye all murmur: but he speaks the best of them, as not willing to enrage them.

Ver. 22. *Moses therefore*] *Tam severus sabbati exactor,* As strict as he was for the observation of the sabbath, yet he was not against circumcision, and the healing again of the child's wound,

[1] Cicero de Harusp. Respons.

upon that day. And if any object that circumcision was a sacrament, and so a sabbath-day's work, it may be answered, 1. That this cure also was much to the glory of God. 2. That the man was cured on both sides, and received both *sanitatem in corpore, et sanctitatem in corde*.

Ye on the sabbath day circumcise] q. d. If you may wound a man on the sabbath day, may not I heal one? If you may heal on the sabbath one member of the circumcised, may not I make a man whole every whit? If you be at pains to cure such a one with your hand, may not I without pains cure a man with my word only? What if circumcision be a sacrament? so was this that I have done a special means of bringing much glory to God.

Ver. 23. *That the law of Moses should not be broken*] Gr. loosened, shattered. The law is one entire copulative; so that he that offendeth in any point is guilty of all, James ii. 10. Hence when the sabbath was broken, the Lord said to Moses, "How long refuse ye to keep my commandments and my laws?" Exod. xvi. 28.

Ver. 24. *Judge not according to the appearance*] Nothing is more ordinary with many than to precipitate a censure, to exercise their critics, and to reprehend that which they do not comprehend. *Arbitror*, saith Augustine (de Trin. i. 3), *nonnullos opinaturos me sensisse quod non sensi, aut non sensisse quod sensi*, I suppose that divers in reading some places in my books will think that I thought that which never came into my mind to think, and the contrary. This was his fear, and this befell him, as Baronius witnesseth. *Compertum est*, saith Erasmus. It is well known that many points are condemned as heretical in Luther's books, which in Augustine's and Bernard's books are read and received for good and orthodox.[1] Hill, in his Quartern of Reasons, saith, the Catholics follow the Bible, but the Protestants force the Bible to follow them. And the author of the Gag for the New Gospel assures his Catholics, that our condemnation is so expressly set down in our own Bibles, and is so clear to all the world, that nothing more needs hereto than that they know to read, and to have their eyes in their heads, at the opening of our Bible. This is their judgment of us. But what among themselves? He that tastes an egg, saith Erasmus, at an undue time, is cast into prison, and made to answer for his heresy; but he that spends all the Lord's day in drinking, drabbing, diceing, is called a good fellow, and passeth unpunished. *Qui totam diem Dominicam vacat temulentiæ scortis et aleæ, audit bellus homo, &c.*

Ver. 25. *Then said some of them of Jerusalem*] That knew more of the ruler's mind than the vulgar, who believed not that there was any such deadly designs, ver. 26. Howbeit these wits of Jerusalem take no notice at all of God's hand in Christ's deliverance, and his present boldness in so extreme a danger.

Ver. 26. *But lo, he speaketh boldly, and they*

[1] Erasm. epist. ad Cardinal. Maguntin.

say nothing to him] God restrained them, putting his bit in their jaws, his hook in their nostrils. In the year 1159, lived John, bishop of Salisbury, *qui et præsens præsentem Pontificem redarguit, et Polycraticon conscripsit, in quo clerum libere flagellat*, who reproved the pope to his face, and wrote his Polycraticon, wherein he freely scourgeth the clergy. (Jacob. Revius.) After this, Robert Grosthead, bishop of Lincoln, called the pope in a letter, Antichrist sitting in the chair of Pestilence, and next to Lucifer himself. As in battle they that stand it out do usually speed best; so here, many times.

Ver. 27. *No man knoweth whence he is*] This error might arise out of some texts of Scripture misunderstood, as Isa. liii. 8; Psal. cx. 4. We should, whenever we open the Bible, pray, "Lord, open mine eyes, that I may see the wondrous things of thy law," Psal. cxix. 18.

Ver. 28. *Ye both know me*] Either this is an irony, or else a heavy aggravation of their sin; a proof that they sinned that sin unto death, 1 John v. 16, for which there remains no more sacrifice, Heb. x. 26. Two sorts of men in our times are in danger of this sin: 1. Hypocritical professors. 2. Those they call the wits of the world, your most knowing men.

Ver. 29. *But I know him*] And am known of him. I will not therefore be baffled or beaten out of my confident boasting by any your frontless affronts or basest buffooneries.

Ver. 30. *Because his hour was not yet come*] i. e. God would not suffer them. Those that bandy and bend their forces against the Lord and his Anointed are bounded by him, in whose hands alone are the issues of death, with the manner and time.

Ver. 31. *Many of the people believed on him*] Some fruit followed his doctrine; these lesser fishes began to bite. They are said to believe that were not altogether averse, but began to be better affected. The very first stirrings in the womb of grace are accepted of God, Eph. ii. 1; he blesseth our buds, Isa. xliv. 5.

Ver. 32. *The Pharisees heard*] They had their scouts, and lay *perdu* to listen, and to keep down Christ. Like unto these are the Jesuits at this day, who give out that the devil stirred up Luther to trouble the Church; and God hath sent them forth to withstand and hinder him.

Ver. 33. *Yet a little while am I with you*] Christ is but a while with men in the opportunities of grace. There is a prime of man's life, yea, a prime of every man's ministry. Christ stands (not sits at the door) and knocks. Now, while one is standing, he is going.

Ver. 34. *Ye shall seek me, &c.*] Because ye shall die in your sins, which is worse than to die in a ditch.

Ver. 35. *Teach the Gentiles*] Which the Jews could not endure to think on. They profess at this day, that rather than the heathen bastards should have benefit by their Messias, they would crucify him over and over, Luke iv. 25. The rustics of Nazareth understood our Saviour of preaching to the Gentiles, which put them into an anger, and him into a danger.

Ver. 36. *What manner of saying is this?*] He would not tell the Jews what he meant by this dark saying. His disciples he told afterwards, chaps. xiii. and xvi. "The secret of the Lord is with them that fear him," Psal. xxv. 14: when the wicked shall be neither of his court nor council.

Ver. 37, 38. *In the last day*] In this eighth day (which the Jews called Hosanna Rabbah) they read the last section of the law, and likewise began the first; lest they might otherwise seem more joyful in ending their sections than willing to begin them. (Tremel. ex Talmud.) Upon this day also, by the institution (say they) of Haggai and Zechariah (but more likely by their own superstition), they did, with great solemnity and joy, bring great store of water from the river Shiloh to the temple; where it being delivered unto the priests, it was poured upon the altar, together with wine; and all the people sang that of the prophet, Isa. xii. 3, "With joy shall ye draw water out of the wells of salvation." Hereunto our Saviour is thought to allude, ver. 38, "Out of his belly shall flow rivers of water;" provided that he believe in me, so as the Scripture saith he should. For so (after Chrysostom) Heinsius, De Dieu, and others expound it.

He that believeth on me, as the Scripture hath said] sc. That men should believe on me, to such I make a promise, that out of his belly, that is (by a catachresis), out of the bosom and bottom of his soul "shall flow rivers," &c.: he shall not only have sufficient for himself, but wherewith to refresh others.

Ver. 39. *But this spake he of the Spirit*] Which is many times compared (as to fire, so) to water for its properties of cooling, cleansing, quenching thirst, fructifying, &c.

Should receive] Princes at their inauguration use to receive great gifts of their subjects. Christ also received gifts, not of his subjects, but of his Father, Psal. lxxvi. 19; and it was for men, and on men he bestowed them, Eph. iv. 8, as holding it a "more blessed thing to give than to receive," Acts xx. 35.

Because that Jesus was not yet glorified] As the sun, the nearer it runs to the earth, the weaker (as in winter); but the higher in heaven, the hotter and more effectual: so this Sun of righteousness.

Ver. 40. *Of a truth this is the prophet*] This was somewhat, but not enough; this was well, but not all. The bustard's wings serve him to get up a little from the earth, but not to bear him up far toward heaven.

Ver. 41. *Shall Christ come out of Galilee?*] Satan (that subtle sophister), though he confessed Christ to be the Holy One of God, Mark i. 24, yet he calleth him Jesus of Nazareth, to nourish the error of the multitude, that thought he was born there, and so not the Messias. Neither did his cunning deceive him, as here appeareth. *Satan etsi semel videatur verax, millies est mendax,*

et semper fallax, saith Bucholcerus. *Diabolus capite blanditur, ventre oblectat, et cauda ligat,* saith Rupertus.

Ver. 41. *Others said, This is the Christ*] Why, this was somewhat like; and if they held them to this, no man can say with the fiducial assent of his heart, "that Jesus is the Christ, but by the Holy Ghost," 1 Cor. xii. 3. He was Christ before he was Jesus, John vi. 27. Jesus is nothing else but *Christus protensus et effusus,* Cant. i. 5. Christ shows him to be a sealed Saviour, anointed and appointed by the Father to that blessed office.

Shall Christ come out of Galilee?] Galilee of the Gentiles, whose manners likely they had learned by so near neighbourhood. Some countries have an ill name. Can any good come out of Nazareth? Hesiod complains of Ascre where he was born, that it was good for nothing (Ασκρὴ χεῖμα κακὴ, θέρος ἀργαλεὴ, &c.) *In mea patria,* saith Jerome, *Deus est venter, et in diem venitur, et sanctior est ille qui ditior.* In my country they are neither temperate, nor provident, nor godly given. And Buchanan cries out that he was born, *nec cœlo, nec solo per sæculo erudito,* where learning was not in fashion. But as little Hippo was better known by great Austin, who was bishop of it, than he by Hippo; so was Galilee by Christ, than he by Galilee. And as hardly as it was thought of, he is not ashamed to call himself Jesus of Nazareth, Acts xxii. 8, which yet was commonly cast as a reproach upon him.

Ver. 42. *Hath not the Scripture said?*] See the note on Matt. ii. 5.

Ver. 43. *So there was a division*] And yet these were the visible Church and favourers of Christ. That is no just cause of offence then that some take at our dissensions. *Raro enim abit sine aliquibus dissensionibus etiam inter bonos et sanctos hæc vita* (Bucholcer), still Satan is thus busy, and Christians are thus improvident, that as if they wanted enemies, they deal blows among themselves, and fly in one another's faces. It was never well since the Church was "all of one heart, and one soul, neither was there any controversy at all amongst them," as one ancient Greek copy hath added to that text, Acts v. 32.

Ver. 44. *Some of them would have taken him*] *Semper crudelis est superstitio.* There can be no greater argument of an ill cause than a bloody persecution: whereas truth holds herself by mildness, and is promoted by patience.

Ver. 45. *Why have you not brought him?*] Out of the pride of their power they wonder what should hinder. But the Lord knoweth how to deliver his, 2 Pet. ii. 9; and wherein the enemies deal proudly, he is above them, Exod. xviii. 11.

Ver. 46. *Never man spake like this man*| It is good to come to the word, though with ill intent; they that come to see fashions only, as Moses came to the bush, may be called as he was. They that come but to sleep, may be taken napping, as Father Latimer saith. They that come to catch, may be caught, as these in the text. The serpent that comes forth to sting, may be charmed ere he go back. When Henry Zutphen was preacher at Breme, the holy Catholics could not be idle, but sent their chaplains to every sermon, to trap him in his words. But God (whose footpaths are in the midst of the flood) would have his marvellous power to be seen in them, for he converted many of them; insomuch, that the greater part of them that were sent to hearken, did openly witness his doctrine to be God's truth, against which no man could contend, and such as in all their life before they had not heard, persuading them likewise that they, forsaking all impiety, should follow the word of God, and believe the same, if they would be saved. But the chief priests, canons, and monks were so indurate and hardened, with Pharaoh, that they became the worse for these admonitions.

Ver. 46. *Never man spake*] For he spake with grace, Psal. xlv. 2, and with gravity, Matt. vii. 29. *E cujus ore nil temere excidit*, saith Scaliger, of Virgil, may we much more of Christ; they were all oracles that he uttered, honey-drops that fell from him. Of Christ it might better be said than ever it was of M. Crassus, the Roman orator, *Cæteros a Crasso semper omnes, illo autem die etiam ipsum a sese superatum.* Cic. de Orat. lib. i.

Ver. 47. *Are ye also deceived?*] As the rude rabble are? we looked that you should have stuck to us. How ill taken was England's defection from the pope's devotion! England was the first that took upon it the pope's yoke, and the first that shook it off again. What wondering was there at Luther, Vergerius, Caracciolus, and other stiff Papists, when they made escape out of Babylon! Apostates they were called for so doing, and Luther confesseth the action; but withal addeth, that they were holy apostates, and had made defection only from the devil, who therefore set up his bristles at them, and pursued them with so much spite. *Prorsus Satan est Lutherus*, saith he in a certain epistle, *sed Christus vivit et regnat, Amen.* (Ep. ad Spalat.)

Ver. 48. *Have any of the rulers,* &c.] *Argumentum stultum*, saith Theophylact. *Sapientes sapienter in infernum descendunt*, saith one. And *Potentes potenter torquebuntur*, saith another. None so deep in hell as knowing men; they are too wise to be saved by the foolishness of preaching. But Paul, the babbler, must be heard, ere heaven can be had.

Ver. 49. *But this people,* &c.] He howled and wept (said Dr. Story concerning Philpot) in the convocation-house, and made such ado as never man did, even as all the heretics do when they lack learning to answer. When as yet Mr Philpot disputing in the convocation-house against the sacrament of the altar, made this offer: If I shall not be able to maintain by God's word that I have said, and confound any six of you, let me be burned with as many fagots as be in London, before the court-gate: and this he ut-

tered with great vehemency of spirit, which the cankered doctor haply called howling and weeping.

Ver. 50. *Nicodemus saith unto them*] Good blood will not belie itself; love, as fire, will not long be hid. Crœsus's dumb son could not but speak to see his father ready to be slain.[1] Nicodemus, though hitherto a night-bird, now shows himself for Christ in a council. How far had Judas out-stripped Nicodemus till it came to the upshot! Nicodemus was only a night-professor, Judas in the sight of all. Nicodemus a slow scholar, Judas a forward preacher. Yet at last, when Judas betrayed Christ in the night, Nicodemus faithfully professed him in the day, &c.

Ver. 51. *Doth our law condemn any man*] This was no great matter to say, and yet it did the deed; so God would have it. Now, he is ever like himself; and whensoever he pleaseth, he both can and will dissipate all our enemies' endeavours, and that in the very nick of time. This we have had plain and plentiful experience of in this land a-late, when we were at such an under, that our enemies seemed to be above fear, and we below hope: when there was not faith in earth to believe, then were there bowels in heaven to turn our captivity like streams in the south.

Before it hear him, and know what he doth?] Humphrey, Duke of Gloucester, was condemned before heard; and murdered by the Popish bishop. So was the Lord Cromwell, whose enemies durst not bring him to his answer, nor try him by his peers, but procured an act of attainder, and so put him to death unheard.

Ver. 52. *Art thou also of Galilee?*] They thought to mock him out of his religion, as the devil doth many at this day. But Nicodemus was well resolved; and if we can bear reproach for Christ, it is an argument we mean to stick to him; as the servant in the law, that was brought to be bored in the ear. And Cajetan gives the reason, *Ut si non horreret servitutem, horreret saltem ignominiam publicam, ut multos habeat inspectores et testes.*

Ver. 53. *And every man went,* &c.] Nicodemus, with one word seasonably put in, dissolves the council; and keeps them, for this time, from attempting against Christ. See what one man may do against a mischievous multitude other whiles. *Ille regit dictis animos, et pectora mulcet.* (Virgil.) What a stickler was Nehemiah at Jerusalem, Paphnutius at the Nicene Council, Wickliffe, Huss, Luther, in their generations. It is good to be doing, though there be few or none to second us; and though we be asked, as that good Bishop Liberius was by the Arian emperor Constantius, *Quota pars es tu orbis terrarum?* (Theodoret, ii. 16.) It is said of Luther, *Quod unus homo solus totius orbis impetum sustinuerit.*

---

[1] ἄνθρωπε, μὴ κτεῖνε Κροῖσον. Herod.

CHAPTER VIII.

Ver. 1. *Jesus went unto the mount of Olives*] His usual oratory. There he prayed by night, and then early in the morning he came again into the temple to preach. Thus he divided his time betwixt praying and preaching. So did the ministers of the Old Testament, Deut. xxxiii. 10, and of the New, Acts vi. 2. So must all that will do good of it; sith Paul may plant, Apollos water, but God only gives increase, 1 Cor. iii. 6.

Ver. 2. *And taught them*] See the note on ver. 1.

Ver. 3. *And the scribes, &c.*] *Deest hæc historia apud quamplurimos interpretes.* (Beza.)

Ver. 4. *In the very act*] Gr. in the very theft; perhaps to intimate the great theft that is in adultery, whiles the child of a stranger carries away the goods or lands of the family; which therefore the adulteress is bound in conscience to confess, ἐπ' αὐτοφώρῳ. St Paul gives charge, that no man go beyond and defraud his brother in the matter; that is, in the matter of the marriage-bed; but that every one possess his vessel, that is, his wife, the weaker vessel, in sanctification and honour, as some interpret it.[1]

Ver. 5. *Such should be stoned*] Adultery was to be punished with death. Society and the purity of posterity could not otherwise continue amongst men; which is well observed by divines to be the reason why adultery is named, under it all uncleanness being forbidden, when yet other violations are more heinous, as sodomy and bestiality; nevertheless, other sins do not so directly fight against society, which the law mainly respects. (Huet of Cons.)

Ver. 6. *And with his finger wrote on the ground*] That he wrote downward (as the Syrians then did, and as the Chinese now do, and so their lines at the top do begin again) is very probable.[2] But what he wrote (whether those words, Jer. xxii. 29, or those Matt. vii. 3) nothing certain can be determined; the Scripture is silent; and where the Scripture hath not a tongue, we need not have ears; write he did (like himself we may be sure, as Quintilian saith of Julius Cæsar, *illum eodem animo scripsisse, quo bellavit*, that he wrote with the same spirit he sought), and perhaps he thus wrote on the ground to show that sin, which is written before God, Isa. lxv. 6, and graven as it were with a pen of iron, and with the point of a diamond, Jer. xvii. 1, is pardoned and blotted out by Christ as easily as a writing slightly made in the dust.

Ver. 7. *He that is without sin amongst you*] Not that is impeccable, and not subject to sin (as the Greek, ἀναμάρτητος, may here seem to sound), but that allows not himself, wallows not in some gross sin, yea, perhaps in this very sin, *Clodius accusat mœchum.* (Juvenal.) Thus our Saviour wrings those supercilious and censorious hypocrites, who hated *virum, non vitium;* as it is said

of Crassus the Roman, that he was very severe against covetousness in others, when there was not a more covetous person than himself. *Carere debet omni vitio qui in alterum paratus est dicere*, said a heathen. He had need be unblameable that blameth another. And therefore the apostle, after that he had said, "Have no fellowship with the unfruitful works of darkness, but reprove them rather;" he soon after addeth, "walk circumspectly, not as fools," &c., Eph. v. 11, 15.

Ver. 8. *And again he stooped down*] In sign of slighting, or that he might give them the more confidence of going out, see verse 6. Our Saviour dealt by this adulteress somewhat like as the Areopagites dealt by the dame of Smyrna, whom they appointed to appear some hundred years after, to show that they would neither condemn nor acquit her. (Rous, Arch. Att.)

Ver. 9. *Convicted by their own conscience*] Which is God's spy and man's overseer, *index, judex, vindex:* so that sinners are self-condemned, αὐτοκατάκριτοι, and oft betrayed by their own blushing and heart-beating, when yet the offence is secret. Yea, a man feels an inward shame in his own heart, disgracing and abusing him, though he make no outward show of it. For albeit an innocent person, upon the foulness of an aspersion, may conceive shame, as did David, Psal. xliv. 15, yet it is usually the effect of an ill conscience.

Ver. 10. *Where are those thine accusers?*] She might have answered as Tertullian in another case not unlike, *Facti sunt a corde suo fugitivi*, they are fled before their own consciences, which convicted them, as it were, by argument, ver. 9, ἐλεγχόμενοι.

Ver. 11. *Neither do I condemn thee*] Hence an Anabaptist will argue that adultery is not to be punished (as they did from that text, "whoremongers and adulterers God will judge," therefore men ought not to meddle with them).[3] But they may as well say that inheritances are not to be divided between brethren, because our Saviour refused to divide them, Luke xii. 14, it being without the lists of his calling, no proper employment of his.

Ver. 12. *I am the light of the world*] Αὐτόφως, ut Plato loquitur, quia Αὔταυτος, ut Scaliger.

The light of life] Light in good and bad men differs as the light of the sun (wherein is the influence of an enlivening power) and the light of torches.

Ver. 13. *Thy record is not true*] i. e. it is not sure and sufficient. There is the same Hebrew word for *veritas* and *firmitas*, truth and certainty.

Ver. 14. *Yet my record is true*] For I am "Amen, the faithful and true witness," Rev. iii. 14, yea, the God of Amen, Isa. lxv. 16, and so the only sufficient witness concerning myself.

Ver. 15. *I judge no man*] viz. after the flesh, as ye do. Christians are antipodes to the world; yea, they have their feet there where other men's heads are; they go not only another, but

---

[1] Defraud, i. e. *in re Venerea, in adulterio. Sic intelligunt.* Jerome, Chrysost., Heinsius.   [2] Masius in Gram. Syr.

[3] *Anabaptistæ scripserunt adulteria non esse punienda per homines*, &c. Joh. Manl.

an upper way to work, Prov. xv. 24. Like eagles, they delight in high flying.

Ver. 16. *For I am not alone*] But all one with the Father.

Ver. 17. *It is also written in your law*] He calleth it their law, because he was above law; and needed not (but for their weakness) to have confirmed thus his doctrine by Scripture; as being to be believed upon his bare word, *αὐτόπιστος*.

Ver. 18. *I am one that bear witness*, &c.] Christ is *alius* from his Father, not *aliud*; another person, not another thing. As in the person of Christ there is *aliud et aliud* (against Eutyches), not *alius et alius* (against Nestorius). In this text, the Divinity of Christ is plainly distinguished from his humanity; how else should he and the Father be two witnesses to himself?

Ver. 19. *If ye had known me*, &c.] For milk is not so like milk as Christ is like his Father.

Ver. 20. *For his hour was not yet come*] And they could neither hasten it nor prevent it. No man hath power over the life of another. "My times are in thine hand," saith David. See the note on chap. vii. 44.

Ver. 21. *Ye shall die in your sins*] A heavy doom, the very door to damnation. It is a sad thing to die in prison, to die in a ditch, but far worse to die in your sins. This is to be slain with death, according to that, Rev. ii. 21, "I will kill her children with death." All men die, but wicked men only are killed with death. As a godly man said, that he did *ægrotare vitaliter*, so do all the righteous, *mori vitaliter*, because they have hope in their death; which to them is as the valley of Achor, a door of hope to give entrance into Paradise. Whereas to the wicked it is as a trap-door to let them into hell; so that it is a just wonder, that foreseeing their danger they go not roaring and raving out of the world. Nothing should be done (we say) to trouble a dying person, no shrieking or crying out. Oh take heed and prevent the shriekings of conscience at that hour, &c. Take heed ye die not in your sin, in that your sin of unbelief, *ἐν τῇ ἁμαρτίᾳ*. *In hoc peccato* (as Beza here rendereth it), for unbelief shuts a man up close, prisoner in the law's dark dungeon, till death come with a writ of *Habeas corpus*, and hell with a writ of *Habeas animam*, &c.

Ver. 22. *Will he kill himself*] *q. d.* Then indeed we cannot, because we will not bear him company in so vile an act. A scurrilous jeer; so little did the heart-piercing sermons of our Saviour work upon them.

Ver. 23. *Ye are from beneath*] *Vos infernales estis, Ego Supernus.* (Beza.) So the wicked are called the inhabitants of the earth and of the sea, Rev. xii. 12, in opposition to the Church, which is said to be in heaven, and called "Jerusalem which is above," Gal. iv. 26.

Ver. 24. *For if ye believe not*, &c.] And yet Venator the Arminian saith, *Nego hanc propositionem, Nemo potest salvus fieri, qui Christo per veram fidem non est insitus.* Is not this to con-

tradict Christ to his face? what an *os durum* is this!

Ver. 25. *Even the same that I said*, &c.] To wit, "the way, the truth, and the life." Some render it thus: *Prorsus id quod loquor vobiscum,* I am the very same Word that I speak with you.

Ver. 26. *I have many things to say*] But I see I do but lose my sweet words upon you. I shall therefore turn you over to my Father with a *non-convertentur*, that he may take an order with you, and make you hear the rod, sith you would not the word, Mic. vi. 9. Those that tremble not in hearing, shall be ground to pieces in feeling, said blessed Bradford.

Ver. 27. *They understood not*] Though he cited them to God's dreadful tribunal, and threatened them with his judgment. The devil had strangely stupified them; like the smith's dog, whom neither the hammer above him nor the sparks of fire falling round about him can awake; like birds in a belfry or fishes in the sea, not affrighted at any ringing or roaring made there.

Ver. 28. *When ye have lifted up the Son*, &c.] 1. Upon the cross, as the brazen serpent was upon a pole. And, 2. By the cross to the crown, though they intended no such thing. If there be any way to heaven on horseback (said Bradford) it is by the cross.

Ver. 29. *And he that sent me is with me*] So that I shall not labour altogether in vain, but accomplish the work that he hath given me to do. So shall all God's faithful ministers (though they may think all their labour lost, and be ready to cry out, *Eheu quam pingui macer est mihi taurus in arvo*). Yet, if they strive to do always those things that please him, he will both protect and prosper them.

Ver. 30. *Many believed on him*] See the note on chap. vii. 31.

Abideth not in the house] Is not heir of the promises; though it be ordinary with such *præsumendo sperare, et sperando perire* (as one saith), to presume and perish.

Ver. 31. *If ye continue in my word*] *Non quæruntur in Christianis initia, sed finis*, said Jerome. And that which is but almost done, is not done, saith Basil.[1] It is the evening that crowns the day, and the last act that commends the whole scene. Temporary flashings are but like conduits running with wine at the coronation, that will not hold; or like a land-flood, that seems to be a great sea, but comes to nothing.

Ver. 32. *The truth shall make you free*] From the tyranny of sin and terror of hell. Paul's freedom saved him from whipping, Acts xxii. 29, this, from perishing.

Ver. 33. *Were never in bondage*] When yet they were scarce ever out of bondage to one enemy or another. At this time they were vassals to the Romans. But brag is a good dog. Pride will bud, Ezek. vii. 10. Spaniards are said

[1] *τὸ παρ᾽ ὀλίγον γεγονὸς, οὐ γέγονεν.*

to be impudent braggers and extremely proud, in the lowest ebb of fortune. There is not a more vain-glorious people this day under heaven than the Jews (saith Alsted). *Antiquum obtinent,* they are no changelings, they fill up the measure of their fathers' sins.

Ver. 34. *Is the servant of sin*] Hath as many lords as lusts : [1] that as Augustine said of Rome in her pride, she conquered countries, but was vanquished of vices ; [2] and as the Persian kings commanded the whole world, but were commanded by their wives and concubines ; so is it with sin's slaves. This slavery they may easily shake off, saith Seneca ; wherein the wise man was utterly out, heavenly-wide, as Sir Philip Sidney Englisheth *toto errat cœlo.*

Ver. 35. *But the Son abideth ever*] This is a part of that spiritual birth-right, John i. 12. God hath charged Christ to see to the safe-keeping of the body and soul of every true believer, John vi. 39, 40.

Ver. 36. *Free indeed*] Not seemingly so, or in conceit only, as those lost libertines, 2 Pet. ii. 1, 19. Ahaz thought himself helped or hurt by the gods of Syria ; but he only thought so, 2 Chron. xxviii. 23, and all such fond thoughts perish, Psal. cxlvi. 4.

Ver. 37. *I know that ye are Abraham's seed*] But that will not bear you out ; nay, you will fare the worse for it, Rom. ii. 9 ; the Jew is first in punishment, because first in privilege. It was cold comfort to Dives, in flames, that Abraham called him son ; to Judas, that Christ called him friend ; or to the rebellious Jews, that God calleth them his people ; sith they were the people of his wrath, and the people of his curse, and should speed no better than the children of the Ethiopians, Amos ix. 7.

Because my word hath no place] This was worse than the former, because the root of it ; even an evil heart of unbelief, which holds a man in an universal pollution, and maketh him a kill-Christ.

Ver. 38. *And ye do*] Or, do ye that which ye have seen with your father, and so show yourselves the devil's imps, brats of fathomless perdition : do so.

Ver. 39. *Abraham is our father*] But it ill appeareth by your practice. Degenerate plants ye are, and such as shame your father, as much as Augustus' three children did him, whom he usually called his *tres vomicas, tria carcinoniata,* three botches and carbuncles.

Ver. 40. *A man that hath told you the truth*] Yea, but you tell them not toothless truth, but such as breeds hatred. He that prizeth (preacheth) truth, shall never prosper by the possession or profession thereof, saith Sir Walter Raleigh. And, truth is a good mistress, saith another ; but he that followeth her too close at heels, may hap have his teeth struck out. The hearing of truth galls, as they write of some creatures, that they have *fel in aure. Prædicare, nihil aliud est,*

quam derivare in se furorem mundi, said Luther, who had the experience of it.

Ver. 41. *We have one Father, even God*] Yet God is not in their heads, Psal. x. 4, nor heart, Psal. xiv. 1, nor words, Psal. xii. 4, nor ways, Tit. i. 16. In such a posture of distance, nay, defiance, stand wicked men. And yet none so forward to call God Father, Jer. iii. 4, 5.

Ver. 42. *If God were your Father*] So that there is no true piety nor fear of God where Christ is rejected. *Frustra utitur, qui Christo non innititur,* saith Bernard. If the historian could say, *Ut quisque Sejano intimus, ita ad Cæsaris amicitiam validus : contra, quibus inoffensus esset, metu et sordibus conflictabantur.* (Tacitus.) No man could be inward with the emperor but by the favour of Sejanus ; and to be out with him, was to be utterly unhappy. How much more may we say the same of Christ, who is all in all with the Father ? If any will be Christless, they must be comfortless.

Ver. 43. *Why do ye not understand my speech ?*] Any more than if I spake to you in a strange language. So many of our hearers.

Ver. 44. *Ye are of your father the devil*] Who hath set his limbs in you, so that ye are as like him as if spit out of his mouth. Satan is called the god of this world, because as God at first did but speak the word, and it was done ; so if the devil do but hold up his finger, give the least hint, they obey him.

The lusts of your father ye will do] If the fruits of the flesh (said Bradford) grow out of the trees of your hearts, surely, surely, the devil is at inn with you. You are his birds, whom when he hath well fed, he will broach you and eat you, chaw you and champ you, world without end, in eternal woe and misery, &c.

And abode not in the truth] *Si Satan in conspectu Dei tantas res ausus est, quid apud nos non audebit ?* (Bucholcer.)

When he speaketh a lie, he speaketh of his own] And so when we do evil, we work *de nostro, et secundum hominem,* 1 Cor. iii. 3. It is as impossible for us naturally to do good as for a toad to spit cordials.

For he is a liar, and the father of it] The devil did only equivocate to our first parents, and yet is here called a liar, and 2 Cor. xi. 3, a cozener. A lie hath been always held hateful ; but equivocation is now set forth of a later impression. The Jesuits have called back this pest from hell, a-late, for the comfort of afflicted Catholics, as arch-priest Blackwell and provincial Garnet shamed not to profess. *Est autem Satanæ pectus semper fæcundissimum mendaciis,* saith Luther. He began his kingdom by a lie, and by lies he upholds it, as were easy to instance. See my notes on Genesis iii.

Ver. 45. *And because I tell you the truth*] See the note on ver. 40.

Ver. 46. *Which of you convinceth me of sin*] q. d. Have you anything against my life, that ye thus

---

[1] *Servitus gravissima est sibi ipsi servire.* Sen.

[2] *Victrix Gentium, captiva vitiorum.* Aug. *Captivarum suarum captiva.* Plutarch.

stiffly refuse to receive my doctrine? Do not (as every minister should do) *vivere concionibus, concionari moribus*, live sermons, as well preach them? Paul knew nothing by himself, 1 Cor. iv. 4. And Chrysostom saith that the souls and lives of ministers should be purer than the sunbeams.

Ver. 47. *He that is of God heareth God's word*] With attention of body, intention of mind, and retention of memory. And this is God's ear-mark.

Ye therefore hear not] But either refuse or rage at what you hear, as tigers do at the sound of a drum. And this is a sore sign of a reprobate goat.

Ver. 48. *That thou art a Samaritan*] And why a Samaritan, trow, but that they thought the worst word in their bellies good enough for him? Malice cares not what it saith, so it may kill or gall; and these dead dogs (as he calleth Shimei, 2 Sam. xvi. 9) will be barking. The primitive persecutors used to put Christians into bears' and dogs' skins, or other ugly creatures, and then bait them; so do the wicked put the saints into ugly conceits, and then speak against them.

Ver. 49. *I have not a devil*] This crime touched his doctrine (as the other his person only), therefore he makes answer to it; but no otherwise than by a simple denial, which in some cases is sufficient. *Didicit ille maledicere, et ego contemnere*, saith he in Tacitus. If a wise man speak evil of thee, endure him; if a fool, pardon him, saith another. If Genebrard rail upon Calvin, if Bolsecus or Baldwin call him twenty devils, he can slight or pity them. As, if Luther call me a devil, saith he, yet I will honour him as a servant of God. A reviler, as he affirmeth without reason, so he may be dismissed without refutation.

Ver. 50. *There is one that seeketh and judgeth*] The less a man strives for himself, the more is God his champion; those that honour him he will honour. Those that drown all self-respects in his glory, and study his share more than their own, shall be found to "praise, and honour, and glory," in that great amphitheatre at the last day, 1 Pet. i. 7.

Ver. 51. *Verily I say unto you*] This he speaketh for the comfort of the better sort among those refractory Jews whom he had so sharply handled. So Zuinglius, when in his sermons he had thundered out God's judgments against the wicked, he would commonly conclude with these words, *Probe vir, hoc nihil ad te :* this is not spoken to thee, thou good soul.

He shall never see death] That is, shall never taste of death, as the Jews interpret it, ver. 52. Chrysostom distinguisheth between seeing and tasting death. *Sed hallucinatur; eodem enim recidunt*, saith Drusius. But Chrysostom is out here, for they are the same. And our Saviour meaneth that such an one shall not die eternally; he shall *mori vitaliter*, as one saith, live though

he die. (See Mr Dugard's Death and the Grave.)

Ver. 52. *Now we know thou hast a devil*] Thus, whether Christ pipe or weep to these froward children, he prevails nothing. Neither promises nor menaces affect reprobates, *neque duci ad Christum, neque trahi possunt*, as Calvin here noteth, they will neither be led unto Christ nor drawn to him.

Ver. 53. *Art thou greater than our father Abraham which is dead?*] They rise no higher than to a natural life. "Our life is hid with Christ in God," Col. iii. 3, as the pearl is hid in the shell, as Christ was hid under the carpenter's son, so as that the buzzards of this world could see no beauty in him.

Ver. 54. *It is my Father that honoureth me*] According to that, "Them that honour me, I will honour," 1 Sam. ii. 30; this is a bargain of God's own making. Fame follows virtue, as the shadow the body; or if not, yet she is *proprio contenta theatro*, content with her own applause.

Ver. 55. *Yet ye have not known him*] There is a twofold knowledge of God. 1. Apprehensive; 2. Affective, or *cognoscitiva*, standing in speculation, and *directiva vitæ*.

Ver. 56. *Your father Abraham rejoiced to see*] He saw it afar off, and saluted it, ἀσπασάμενοι, Heb. xi. 13. His good old heart danced levaltos within him, as children use to dance about a bonfire (so the word ἠγαλλιάσατο signifies), with an exuberancy of joy, that joy of faith. The Fathers say that he saw Christ's birth at the valley of Mamre, Gen. xviii., and his passion in the mount Moriah, Gen. xxii.

Ver. 57. *Thou art not yet fifty*] No, nor much past thirty; and yet he had so spent himself in winning souls and weeping over the hardness of men's hearts, that he seemed to the Jews to be much older than he was, as some conceive. Sure it is that Mr John Fox, the martyrologue, by the infinite pains that he took in compiling that elaborate work (which he finished in eleven years without the help of any other man), grew so lean and withered that his friends knew him not.

Ver. 58. *Before Abraham was, I am*] "I am that I am," in regard of mine eternal generation. And as mediator, "I am Jesus Christ, yesterday, to-day, and for ever," Heb. xiii. 8.

Ver. 59. *Then took they up stones*] This is *merces mundi*, the world's wages. Let us look up with Stephen, and see heaven, as he did, through a shower of stones.

CHAPTER IX.

Ver. 1. *He saw a man which was blind*] THIS was enough to move Christ to mercy, the sight of a fit object. When God sets us up an altar be we ready with our sacrifice.

Ver. 2. *Who did sin, this man?*] How could he sin before he was born? But the disciples dreamt of a Pythagorical transanimation; hence this foolish question. *Imbuti erant Judei dogmate μετεμψυχώσεως.* Beza.

Ver. 3. *But that the works of God, &c.*] *Hinc Alexander Ales, Pœna, inquit, duplicem habet ordinationem, Unam ad culpam, quæ præcedit; alteram ad gloriam, quam præcedit.* God sometimes afflicts for his own glory, but sin is ever at the bottom. And though God does not always afflict his for sin, as Job, yet Job shall do well to consider that God "exacteth of him less than his iniquity deserveth," as Zophar telleth him, Job xi. 6.

Ver. 4. *While it is day*] As other men do, Psal. civ. 22. None can say he shall have twelve hours to his day. And night (death) is a time of receiving wages, not of doing work. On this moment depends eternity; on the weakest wire hangs the greatest weight.

Ver. 5. *I am the light of the world*] See chap. xii. 46. He is light essential, the Father of lights, the Sun of righteousness; who at his nativity was as a bridegroom coming out of his chamber, in his life rejoiced as a strong man to run his race, Psal. xix. 5; in his passion he was clouded, brake forth in his resurrection, darts out his beams of grace since his ascension, and shall finish all at his return to judgment.

Ver. 6. *Made [clay]*] As he did at first in making man (the poets tell us some such thing of their Prometheus), to show that this cure was done by that Almighty power that he put forth in the Creation.

Ver. 7. *He went his way and washed*] He obeyed Christ blindling. He looked not upon Siloam with Syrian eyes, as Naaman did upon Jordan; but, passing by the unlikelihood of a cure by such means, he believeth, and doth as he was bidden, without sciscitation.

Ver. 8. *Is not this he that sat and begged?*] As once blind Belisarius did with *Da obolum Belisario.*

Ver. 9. *I am he*] Thus their doubting (by divine disposition) made much for the manifestation of Christ's power in the fore-mentioned miracle.

Ver. 10. *How were thine eyes opened?*] It is good to ask Christ's illuminates such savoury questions, how they were called out of darkness into marvellous light? what discoveries of himself Christ had made unto them, &c. Austin (Confess. vi. 2) confesseth that before his conversion he was of this opinion, that it was impossible for him to find such comfort as now he did in a Christian life. Cyprian saith as much of himself to his friend Donatus, beginning his epistle thus, *Accipe quod sentitur, antequam dicitur.*

Ver. 11. *I went and washed, and received sight*] His blind obedience made him see. Let God be obeyed readily without reasoning or wrangling, and success shall not be wanting. God calleth for *Curristas non Quæristas.* Luther.

Ver. 12. *I know not*] For Christ disappeared, as John v. 13. See the note there.

Ver. 13. *They bring him to the Pharisees*] Who should have been moved with the miracle to think the better of him that wrought it; and have better informed those that brought the man to them, with what mind soever. But they had conceived such an incurable prejudice, such a deadly hatred against Christ, that what he did they presently condemn, as George Duke of Saxony did Luther's reformation, as the monks of Mentz did the reformation begun there by Hermanus their archbishop, professing that they would rather receive Mahometanism than submit to that new religion, as they called it; as Philip king of Spain would choose rather to have no subjects than Lutheran subjects; and out of a blind and bloody zeal, suffered his eldest son Charles to be murdered by the cruel Inquisition, because he seemed to favour the truth.

Ver. 14. *It was the sabbath day*] And our Saviour knew it would be as ill resented as that other miracle on the sabbath day done, John v., for which they sought to kill him. Men be they pleased or displeased, duty must be discharged. *Tenenda regula, cœcos ac duces cœcorum negligendos esse.*

Ver. 15. *How he had received his sight*] Gr. how he had recovered his sight. It may be that (to lessen the miracle) they would have had it, that the man had not been born blind, but only recovered that sight that once he had enjoyed. *Αναβλέπειν proprie est eorum qui videndi facultatem aliquando habuerunt.* Malevolence ever strives to deteriorate and deprave that good which it cannot for shame absolutely deny. "An ungodly man diggeth up evil," Prov. xvi. 27, and a froward fellow forgeth strife, ver. 28; he digs, and then sows the seed of sedition in every furrow where he can find footing.

Ver. 16. *This man is not of God*] True, if he had indeed made no conscience of keeping the sabbath. Sanctifying the Lord's day in the primitive times was a badge of Christianity. When the question was propounded, *Servasti Dominicum?* Hast thou kept the sabbath? the answer was returned, I am a Christian and may not do otherwise. *Christianus sum, intermittere non possum.* The enemies and hinderers of sanctifying the sabbath are called unbelievers, vagabonds, and wicked fellows, Acts xvii. 2, 5. That late great Antisabbatarian prelate (Bp White) so much cast off by the rest after he had served their turns, might well have cried out with Cardinal Wolsey, Surely, if I had been as careful to serve God as I was to please men, I had not been at this pass. *Semetipsum detestatus est, quod Regi potius quam Deo studuisset placere.* (Scultet.)

How can a man that is a sinner] Yes, that he may, by divine permission, or at least he may do something like a miracle; as the false prophets and Antichrist. Suetonius tells us that Vespasian cured a blind man by spitting upon his eyes. And Dio testifieth that he healed another that had a weak and withered hand, by treading upon it. And yet Vespasian lived and died a pagan.

This therefore was no convincing argument that the Jews here used.

Ver. 17. *He is a prophet*] The more the Pharisees opposed the truth, the more it appeared. *Veritas abscondi erubescit*, saith Tertullian. The Reformation was much furthered in Germany by the Papists' opposition. Among many others two kings wrote against Luther, viz. Henry VIII. of England and Ludovicus of Hungary. This kingly title being entered into the controversy, made men more curious. And as it happeneth in combats that the lookers-on are ready to favour the weaker and to extol his actions, though they be but mean; so here it stirred up a general inclination toward Luther, saith the author of the Hist. of the Council of Trent. Luther also in an epistle to the Elector of Saxony, triumpheth and derideth the foolish wisdom of the Papists in causing him and the other Protestant princes to rehearse the confession of their faith in a public assembly of the states of Germany, and in sending copies thereof to all the courts of Christendom for advice; whereby the Gospel was more propagated, and the cause of Christ more advanced, than if many preachers had been sent out and licensed.

Ver. 18. *But the Jews did not believe*] The Pharisees, who held themselves the only Jews, that is, true confessors; like as the Swenckfeldians entitled themselves the "confessors of the glory of Christ;" the Anabaptists style themselves the "meek of the earth;" the Antinomians will needs be called the "hearers of the gospel and of free grace," &c.

Ver. 19. *Is this your son?*] Here they try another trick to obscure the miracle; but it would not be. " God taketh the wise in their own craftiness." Again, "The Lord knoweth the thoughts of the wise, that they are vain," 1 Cor. iii. 19, 20.

Ver. 20. *We know that this is our son*] They answer obliquely and over-warily; but Christ had better deserved of them. Squirrels ever set their holes to the sunny side. Politic professors, neuter-passive Christians, will be sure to keep on the warmer side of the hedge; neither will they launch farther into the sea than they may be sure to return safe to the shore. Cyprian calleth such double-minded men, *palpatores temporum, in lenitate tantum constantes*, giddy-brains.

Ver. 21. *He is of age*] ἡλικίαν ἔχει. *Fœlix ab ἡλιξ ἡλικία*, say the etymologists, *ut fœlix sit homo floridæ et vegetæ ætatis, corpore et animo valens.* (Becman.)

Ver. 22. *Put out of the synagogue*] This was that kind of excommunication they called Niddui, or separation; and such were by the Greeks called Ἀποδεδοκιμασμένοι and Ἀμνημόνευτοι. There were two other more heavy kind of excommunications in use among the Jews, Cherem and Samatha or Maranatha, which they derive as low as from Enoch, Jude 14. The heathens also had their public execrations, not rashly to be used against any; *Est enim execratio res tristis, et mali Ominis*, saith Plutarch; who therefore highly

commends that Athenian priest, that being commanded by the people to curse Alcibiades, refused to do it. That archflamen of Rome, the pope, is like a wasp; no sooner angry but out comes a sting (an excommunication), which, being once out, is like a fool's dagger, rattling and snapping without an edge. *Cum Pontifex Rom. diras in Ludovic 12, Gall. Regem evomeret; Atqui (ait rex) Precandi ille, non imprecandi causa pontifex constitutus est.* (Firron. lib. 2. de Gestu. Gallor.) It was grown to a proverb among our forefathers, *In nomine Domini incipit omne malum.* John Cornford (one of the six last that were burnt in England for the true religion), when he heard himself and his fellows excommunicated, stirred with a vehement zeal of God, and proceeding in a more true excommunication against the Papists, in the name of them all, pronounced sentence against them in these words, In the name of our Lord Jesus Christ, and by the power of his Holy Spirit and the authority of his holy Catholic and Apostolic Church, we do give here into the hands of Satan to be destroyed, the bodies of all those blasphemers and heretics that do maintain any error against his most holy word, or do condemn his most holy truth for heresy, to the maintaining of any false church or feigned religion; so that by this thy just judgment, most mighty God, against thine adversaries, thy true religion may be known, to thy glory, and our comforts, and to the edifying of all our nation. Good Lord, so be it.

Ver. 23. *He is of age*] See ver. 21, 22.

Ver. 24. *Give God the glory*] It appears, Josh. vii. 19, and 1 Sam. vi. 5, that this was some solemn form, in use among that people when they required an oath of delinquents. This the hypocrites made use of, as when the devils adjured Christ by the living God not to cast them out. So their forefathers would persecute godly men, and molest them with Church censures, and then say, " Let the Lord be glorified," Isa. lxvi. 5. With like honesty, as the conspirators in King Richard II.'s time here in England indorsed all their letters, with " Glory be to God on high, on earth peace, good will towards men." This poor man might have answered as Robert Smith the martyr did, when Bonner began the sentence of death against him, *In Dei nomine*, Ye begin in a wrong name, said he.

Ver. 25. *Whether he be a sinner or no, &c.*] That is, a notorious impious man, as you affirm him. And this is an ironical speech; as if he should say, You may make of him what you will, and call him at your pleasure; he is as he is. And this one thing I know, and will testify, that whereas as I was blind, now I see; yea, and I see day at a little hole too. If this man were not of God, he could do nothing, ver. 33.

Ver. 26. *What did he to thee? how opened he thine eyes?*] How fain would envy here have fastened her fangs, and have found somewhat to say, whereby to cast a slur on the miracle. They are even question-sick, as those 1 Tim. vi. 4. *Et si non aliqua nocuissent, &c.* They feed upon their own hearts, because they cannot come at Christ's.

Ver. 27. *Will ye also be his disciples?*] A bold speech of so mean a man, so little enlightened, to the chief priests and Pharisees. Such was that of Dirick Carver, martyr, to Bonner, Your doctrine is poison and sorcery. If Christ were here, you would put him to a worse death than he was put to before. You say you can make God; you can make a pudding as soon, &c. And that of Henry Lawrence, who being to subscribe the bill of his examination, wrote, Ye are all antichrist, and him ye follow, &c. And that of Anthony Parsons; Thou callest us thieves, said the bishop of Salisbury. I say, quoth Anthony, ye are not only thieves, but murderers, ye are rather bitesheeps than true bishops. (Acts and Mon.)

Ver. 28. *Then they reviled him*] As an apostate from the law, a noveller, a Nazarite, a disciple of Christ, Thou art his disciple, say they, and therefore a dolt, a dunce; as at this day in Italy and at Rome, the most honourable name of Christian is usually abused to signify. (D. Fulke.) The primitive persecutors painted Christ with an ass's head and a book in his hand (as Tertullian saith), to signify that all his disciples, though they pretended learning, yet they were silly and ignorant people. *Est enim Satanæ pectus mendaciis fœcundissimum*, saith Luther. The basest can revile (as the abjects did David, Psal. xxxv. 15) and every black-mouth cast dirt upon Christ's disciples as the offscouring of all things, 1 Cor. iv. 13.

Ver. 29. *We know not whence he is*] i. e. Whence he had his mission and commission to act the part of a prophet. His parents they knew, but doubted of his authority, as Papists and sectaries do of ours. To whom we answer, that we received our ministry immediately from Jesus Christ, whose ambassadors we are: and that his inward call is the main, whether it be that of approbation, as of godly ministers, or the other of Providence as of evil, such as were Judas, Demas, Nicolas, those that preached Christ of envy, Phil. i. 15, &c.

Ver. 30. *And yet he hath opened mine eyes*] Which was a foretold sign of the Messiah, Isa. xxxv. 4, 5, and an office whereto Paul was sent of God, Acts xxvi. 18. And surely if God set such a seal to a man's ministry, as to make him instrumental to the conversion of others, it is a sweet and singular confirmation, Jer. xxiii. 22; 1 Cor. ix. 2, 3.

Ver. 31. *We know that God heareth not sinners*] Their incense smells of the hand that offers it: the leper's lips should be covered, according to the law: the wicked "compass God with lies," Hos. xi. 12, when they cry, "My Father, my Father," &c. This is one of those natural notions that the devil could never blot out of man's mind, that God heareth not sinners; he will never accept of a good motion from a bad mouth, as that state in story would not. *Hinc Achilles Homericus*, ὅς κε θεοῖς ἐπιπείθηται μαλὰ

τ' ἔκλυον αὐτοῦ. He silenced the devil acknowledging him: and of witches' good prayers one saith, *Si magicæ, Deus non vult tales: si piæ, non per tales.*

Ver. 32. *Since the world began was it not heard*] Those historians then that have ascribed such a power to Vespasian, as to cure men that were born blind, are in no wise to be believed. (Dio in Vespas.) Vopiscus (who himself was one of them) ingenuously confesseth (in Vita Aureliani), *neminem historicorum non aliquid esse mentitum*, that they are all liars more or less, especially in setting forth the lives and acts of their emperors.

Ver. 33. *If this man were not of God, he could do nothing*] i. e. Nothing of this nature, he could not work a true miracle. The devil's miracles, *ut plurimum, sunt præstigiæ, imposturæ, phantasmata, ludibria.* (Bucholcer.)

Ver. 34. *Thou wast altogether born in sins*] Because born blind: so they upbraid him with his misery, as if therefore a notorious offender. This is harsh and rash judgment.

And dost thou teach us?] Oh, take heed of that. But a mortified man will yield to learn of anybody: "a little child shall lead him," Isa. xi. 6. Learned Apollos was better instructed by a couple of poor tent-makers, Acts xviii. 26.

Ver. 35. *And when he had found him*] So when the pope had excommunicated Luther, and the emperor proscribed him, Christ Jesus was with him, and carried on the work. *Longe majora parturit mihi jam calamus*, saith he: *Nescio unde veniunt istæ meditationes.* And in his book of the Babylonish Captivity he professeth, *Se quotidie, velit, nolit, doctiorem fieri.* (Luth. Epist.)

Ver. 36. *Who is he, that I might believe on him?*] A man of God, he held Christ, verse 33. The Son of God he yet knew him not to be; but was willing to be further informed, as appeareth by this question. They that hold fast what they have already received till Christ come, shall have more light, Rev. ii. 25; and a little strength well improved, may have "a great door, and effectual, opened," Rev. iii. 8.

Ver. 37. *Thou hast both seen him*] This seems to have been but some part of the discourse that passed betwixt them, to make the man believe. Or if it were all, then we see as in a mirror the mighty power of Christ's word. Well might he say, chap. vi. 63, "The words that I speak unto you, they are spirit, and they are life." Well might Mr Fox say in his Acts and Monuments, speaking of the people of God here in England in the reign of Henry VIII., when they began to lift up their heads out of the puddle of Popery, "This one thing I greatly marvel and muse at, to note in the registers, and consider how the word of God did multiply so exceedingly as it did amongst them. For I find that one neighbour resorting and conferring with another, eftsoons with a few words of their first or second talk did win and turn their minds to that wherein they desired to persuade them, touching the truth of God's word and sacraments."

Ver. 38. *And he worshipped him*] sc. as the Son of God, with divine adoration. This our Saviour would not have suffered had he not been of God. And being so, and to us so good a God, we must not only *adorare Christum, sed et adulari*, as Tertullian hath it, do him all the honour we can devise.

Ver. 39. *For judgment I am come*] To judge, much otherwise than those unjust judges have done, that have cast out this poor servant of mine for a blasphemer. Bishop Bonner having a blind harper before him, said, that such blind abjects, that follow a sort of heretical preachers, when they come to the feeling of the fire, will be the first that will fly from it. To whom the blind man said, that if every joint of him were burnt, yet he trusted in the Lord not to fly. A blind boy, that had suffered imprisonment at Gloucester not long before, was brought to Bishop Hooper the day before his death. Mr Hooper, after he had examined him of his faith, and the cause of his imprisonment, beheld him stedfastly, and the water appearing in his eyes, said unto him: "A poor boy, God hath taken from thee thy outward sight, for what consideration he best knoweth, but hath given thee another sight much more precious: for he hath endued thy soul with the eye of knowledge, and faith," &c. It is a worthy speech of Mr Beza upon this text, *Prodeant omnes Pharisæorum nostri temporis Academiæ*. Let all our University-Pharisees come forth together: that blind and heretical church (as they call it) hath, by the blessing of God, children of seven years old that can before all the world confute and confound their erroneous doctrines, *Habet ecclesia illa cæca et heretica septennes pueros, qui teste universo mundo*, &c.: witness the children of Merindal and Chabriers, John Fetty's child of eight years old, that told Bonner's chaplain (who said Fetty was an heretic,) My father is no heretic, but you are a heretic, for you have Balaam's mark. This child they whipt to death. Alice Driver, martyr, nonplust all the doctors that examined her: and then said, God be honoured; you be not able to resist the Spirit of God in me a poor woman. I was never brought up in the University as ye have been: but I have driven the plough many a time before my father, and yet I will set my foot against the feet of any of you all, &c.

Ver. 40. *Are we blind also?*] Yes, none more: for who so blind as he that will not see? "Who is blind as he that is perfect, and blind as the Lord's servant?" Isa. xlii. 19. "Thou blind Pharisee," saith our Saviour, Matt. xxiii. 26; and again, "Ye blind guides," ver. 24; and "Ye fools and blind," oft in that chapter. And yet these passed in those days for the only wise men (1 Cor. i. 20, "Where is the wise? where is the scribe?"), and had as good a conceit of themselves (a sure argument of their spiritual blindness) as the Chinese have at this day,

when they usually say that all other nations of the world see but with one eye, they only with two. St Paul (who knew them, *intus et in cute*, as well as one man could know another) speaks out their conceits. "Thou art confident," saith he, "that thou thyself art a guide of the blind, a light to them that are in darkness, an instructor of the foolish," &c., Rom. ii. 19. And hence their swelth, their ruth, and their ruin. For as swelling is an ill symptom to the body, so is pride in the soul: and as the body may die of an inward bleeding, so may the soul of spiritual pride. And as none more often miscarry in the waters than your most skilful swimmers, so neither do any sooner fall into the condemnation of hell, or lie deeper therein, than the most knowing men, and those of greatest parts, which they usually overween, and are too well conceited of. *Raram facit scientia cum modestia mixturam.* Learning with modesty, as it is rare, so it is καλὸν καλῶς (saith one), most amiable and attractive. It is like the coupling of a muse and a grace,

—————*aut ubi flavo*
Argentum, Pariusve lapis circundatur auro.
                                                    Virg.

Ver. 41. *But now ye say, We see*] If, after conviction, men run away with the bit in their mouths, the sin is the greater: but their case is deplorable, *qui quod verum sit neque sciunt, neque sustinent dicere*, as Basil complains of the Western Church in his time.

CHAPTER X.

Ver. 1. *Verily, verily, I say unto you*] AMEN is in Holy Scripture either prefixed to a discourse, and then it is a particle of certain and earnest asseveration, when it is doubled especially, as here: or else affixed; and then it is either of assent or assurance, or both, as in the end of the Lord's prayer.

Ver. 2. *But he that entereth in by the door*] That is, called by Christ to the office of his under-shepherd. *In physicis aër non facit seipsum ignem, sed fit a superiori*, saith Aquinas.

Is the shepherd of the sheep] To the which is required, that he be both learned and loving. This note ariseth out of the notation of the word here used. (Ποιμὴν quasi οἰμὴν, of οἴς, a sheep, and μάω, to desire earnestly.)

Ver. 3. *To him the porter openeth*] That is, God approveth such, and usually seals to their ministry, Jer. xxiii. 22, giving them a testimonial, 2 Cor. iii. 2.

Ver. 4. *He goeth before them*] According to the custom of shepherds in that country, not to drive their sheep, but to lead them, as David shows in his divine Bucolicon, Psal. xxiii. 2.

Ver. 5. *A stranger will they not follow*] For they have senses exercised to discern good and evil, Heb. v. 14; "yea, they have a spirit of discerning," 1 Cor. xii. 10; "the mind of Christ,"

1 Cor. ii. 16; and though simple to evil, yet are wise in that which is good. They are sheep, but rational; their service a reasonable service, Rom. xii. 1; their obedience the obedience of faith, Rom. xvi. 26; they try before they trust, they look before they leap, and so grow to such a certainty in that truth they hold, such a plerophory of knowledge, Col. ii. 3; that it is impossible for them to be fully or finally deceived, Matt. xxiv. 24. False and heterodox doctrines they hate, Psal. cxix. 104; and all such impostors as seek to buzz doubts into their heads, Rom. xvi. 17.

Ver. 6. *But they understood not*] So thick-brained and incapable we are, till that vail be rent, Isa. xxv. 7. Those that have a blemish in their eye, the more wishly they look into any-thing the less they see of it, as Vives hath it. So it is here. *Lusciosi, si quando oculorum aciem intendunt, minus vident.* (Vives in Aug. C. D. lxxxi. 6.)

Ver. 7. *I am the door*] Heaven-door, so Christ is pleased to call himself, because "through him we have an access by one Spirit unto the Father," Eph. ii. 18; and, "in him we have boldness and access with confidence by the faith of him," Eph. iii. 12. Why our Saviour compares himself to these ordinary and obvious objects of our senses, see the note on chap. xv. 1.

Ver. 8. *All that ever came before me, &c.*] Manes (that mad heretic) made an argument from this text against Moses and the prophets, as going before Christ. But Austin answereth, Moses and the prophets came not before Christ, but with Christ. Intruders, whether before or since our Saviour's days, are these thieves and robbers. Ah, whoreson-thieves, rob God of his glory! said Dr Taylor, martyr, in a dream, of the scribes and Pharisees of his time.

Ver. 9. *And shall go in and out, &c.*] That is, shall live securely, and be fed daily and daintily, as David shows, Psal. xxiii., where he sweetly strikes upon the whole string through the whole hymn.

Ver. 10. *The thief cometh not but for to steal*] How slily soever heretics seek to insinuate with their pithanology and feigned humility, whereby they circumvent and beguile the simple, it is deadly dealing with them. Shun their society as a serpent in your way, as poison in your meat. Spondanus (the same that epitomized Baronius) gives his reader Popish poison to drink so slily, saith one, as if he were doing somewhat else, and meant no such matter. *Perniciosissimum Hildebrandinæ doctrinæ venenum lectoribus ebibendum, quasi aliud agens, propinat.* And learned Billius observes the like of Socrates, the ecclesiastical historian, a cunning Novatian. Swenckfeldius, who held many dangerous heresies, did yet deceive many by his pressing men to a holy life, praying frequently and fervently, &c., by his stately expressions, ever in his mouth, as of illumination, revelation, deification, the inward and spiritual man. (Scultet. Annal.) Some are so cunning in their cogging the die, as St Paul

phraseth it, ἐν τῇ κυβείᾳ, Eph. iv. 14; in the conveyance of their collusion, that, like serpents, they can sting without hissing; like cur-dogs, suck your blood only with licking; and in the end kill you and cut your throats without biting. Muzzle them therefore, saith St Paul, and give them no audience. ἐπιστόμιζε, Tit. i. 11; iii. 10. Placilla the empress, when Theodosius, senior, desired to confer with Eunomius the heretic, dissuaded her husband very earnestly; lest, being perverted by his speeches, he might fall into heresy. Anastasius II., Bishop of Rome, in the year 497, whilst he sought to reduce Acacius the heretic, was seduced by him. (Sozomen, vii. 1.) A little leaven soon soureth the whole lump. One spoonful of vinegar will quickly tart a great deal of sweet milk, but a great deal of milk will not so soon sweeten one spoonful of vinegar. Error (saith a noble writer) is like the Jerusalem-artichoke; plant it where you will, it over-runs the ground and chokes the heart.

Ver. 11. *I am the good shepherd*] So he is by an excellency, for he left his glory to seek out to himself a flock in the wilderness. "He feeds them among the lilies," Cant. ii. 16; gives them golden fleeces, and shepherds to keep them, after his own heart; watcheth over them night and day in his Migdal-Eder, or tower of the flock, Gen. xxxv. 21; seeks them up when lost, bears them in his bosom, and gently leads those that are with young, Isa. xl. 11; pulls them out of the power of the lion and the bear, punisheth such as either push with the horn or foul with the feet, Ezek. xxxiv. 19; washeth them in his own blood, and so maketh them kings and priests to God, Rev. i. 5, &c., so that they need not fear the spiritual Assyrian, Mic. v. 5.

Ver. 12. *The wolf scattereth*] To non-residents and other unconscionable ministers, Christ will say as once Eliab did to David, "With whom hast thou left those poor few sheep in the wilderness?" *Vare, redde legiones*, said Augustus, sighing. The like will this good shepherd say, judging; *Pan curet oves, oviumque magistros*, say many of our pluralists and idol shepherds. About Hildebrand's time, so great was the negligence and wickedness of the clergy, that some set forth letters, as dated from the devils of hell to them; wherein they give them many thanks for the souls they had sent to hell, in such abundance as never was known before.

Ver. 13. *The hireling fleeth*] Yet is not every one that fleeth to be judged an hireling presently. There is a lawful flight, as when the quarrel is personal, &c. Christ fled oft when persecuted; so may we. God hath made us not as butts to be perpetually shot at; but as the marks of rovers, moveable, as the wind and sun may best serve. *Fuge, fuge, Brenti, cito, citius, citissime:* so friendly did a senator of Hala advise Brentius. He embraced the advice, and saved his life by it. (Melch. Adam. in Vit. Brentii.)

Ver. 14. *And know my sheep*] With a knowledge of approbation and delight. *Verba no-*

titiæ apud Hebræos secum trahunt affectum, Psal. i. 6.

Ver. 15. *I lay down my life*] Yet as man he was ζῶον φιλόζωον. (Æsop, Fab.) *Quis vitam non vult?* saith Augustine ; and *Quis enim vult mori? prorsus nemo*, saith another. And, "skin after skin," or skin upon skin, " and all that a man hath will he give for his life," said that old deceiver, truly, Job ii. 4. Yet our Saviour held not his life dear for his sheep's safety. Because he saw we should fall sore (said that angel, John Bradford) therefore he would suffer sore. Yea, if his once suffering had not been enough, he would yet once more come again. God the Father, I am sure, saith he, if the death of his Son incarnate would not serve, would himself and the Holy Ghost also become incarnate, and die for us.

Ver. 16. *And other sheep I have*] viz. The elect Gentiles, whose conversion to Christ was, among other types, not obscurely fore-shadowed, Levit. xix. 23—25, as some divines think. The first three years in Canaan the Israelites were to cast away the fruits of the trees, as uncircumcised. So our Saviour planted the gospel in that land for the first three years of his public ministry. But the uncircumcisions are cast away ; that is, to the uncircumcised Gentiles the doctrine of Christ is not declared by general and public preaching. The fruit of the fourth year was consecrated to God : that is, Christ in the fourth year from his baptism laid down his life for his sheep, rose again, ascended, and sent his Holy Spirit ; whereby his apostles and others were consecrated as the first-fruits of the promised land. But in the fifth year, the fruit of the gospel planted by Christ began to be common, when the same doctrine was not shut up in the strait bounds of Judæa, or walls of the temple, but was made known (and shall be more and more) to all nations, for the obedience of faith, Rom. xvi. 26.

There shall be one fold] Of Jews and Gentiles. The full and final restoration of the Jews will fall out in the year 1650, as some have calculated out of Dan. xii. 11. I wait and wish it.

Ver. 17. *Therefore doth my Father love me, because*] This " because " is *nota consecutionis, non causæ*, saith Beza.

I lay down my life] I do it even now ; for he suffered many a little death all his life long, and at length the cursed death of the cross.

That I might take it again] For Christ's being life essential, swallows up death in victory, as the fire swallows up the fuel, as Moses' serpent swallowed up the sorcerers, serpents, &c.

Ver. 18. *I lay it down of myself*] A necessity there was of our Saviour's death, but it was a necessity of immutability (because God had decreed it, Acts ii. 23), not of coaction. He died willingly. Therefore, when he gave up the ghost, he cried with a loud voice, which shows that his life was not then spent ; he might have retained it longer if he would ; and thereupon the centurion concludes him to be the Son of God.

Ver. 19. *There was a division, therefore, &c.*] This our Saviour foresaw, and yet forbears not. God's truth must be spoken, however it be taken. Men, be they pleased or displeased, God must be obeyed, and his whole will declared. If men refuse to receive it, we must turn them over to God, with a *non convertentur*, and then let him alone with them.

Ver. 20. *He hath a devil, and is mad*] It was a wonder if the heavens did not sweat, the earth melt, and hell gape at the hearing of these horrid blasphemies. Tigers rage at the fragrancy of sweet spices ; so did these monsters at our Saviour's sweet sermons.

Ver. 21. *These are not the words, &c.*] Wisdom is ever justified of her children. They fitly argue from his oracles and miracles, both which this evangelist doth more largely relate, purposely to prove our Saviour's Divinity, and is therefore styled " John the Divine."

Ver. 21. *The feast of the dedication*] viz. Of the temple newly purged from the pollutions of Antiochus, that little antichrist. Ἐγκαίνια, *initialia, sive renovalia*. So when the Christian temple, the Church, was purged from the Popish abominations (called the tramplings of the Gentiles, Rev. xi. 2), by those two witnesses, that is, by Luther and other heroical reformers, there was great joy among God's people. And in the year 1617, as the pope proclaimed a jubilee for the peace of Italy and Austria, &c., so the reformed Churches in Germany did the same, for God's mercy in restoring to them the gospel, just a hundred years before : for in the year 1517, Luther began to decry the pope's indulgences. (Bucholcer.) In like sort, at the same time, when the Greeks were busy in their Olympic games, the prophet Isaiah saw that glorious vision of God in his majesty, Isa. vi. 1, 2 (as the divine chronologer observes it), singing with seraphims, that sweetest trisagion, " Holy, holy, holy, Lord God of hosts." The new Jerusalem, which signifies the state of the Church in this world (saith Rev. Dr Sibbs), when it shall be refined to the utmost, is all of fine gold and precious stones, &c., to show the excellency of reformation ; which golden times are yet to come, and will prove very festival.

Ver. 23. *And Jesus walked in the temple*] Taking the opportunity of that public meeting to do good, as the bee is abroad so soon as the sun ariseth. The Greeks were great walkers, as the Stoics in their porch, &c. But the Turks wonder to see a man walk to and fro, and usually ask him whether he be out of his way, or out of his wits ? (Biddulph.) Pliny said to his nephew, when he saw him walk out some hours without studying, *Poteras has horas non perdere.*

In Solomon's porch] So the Jews called that porch (for honour's sake) which they built again after the Captivity ; and which, together with the whole temple, was beautified by Herod the Great, to curry favour with the people, which yet would not be, for they hated him extremely. *Partim ambitione ductus, partim Judæorum benevolentiam captans.* (Bez. Annot. in John i. 20.)

Ver. 24. *How long dost thou make us to doubt ?*] They lay the blame upon him as if (Heraclitus-like) he were a dark doctor; when themselves were blind, and did shut the windows lest the light should come in unto them. God's ministers must look for the like measure. Howbeit God darkens their doctrine sometimes (as he dealt by Ezekiel) for the sins of the people.

Ver. 25. *I told you, and ye believed not*] q. d. Your malice lies in the way, that neither mine oracles nor miracles can work upon your hearts. Therefore also Christ chargeth them with a double unbelief: Ye believe not, saith he; and again, Ye believe not: this is the damning sin against the gospel; yea, this some will have to be that sin against the Holy Ghost, for which there is no pardon.

Ver. 26. *Ye believe not, because ye are not, &c.*] Reprobates cannot believe, yea, they cannot but resist the external offers of God's grace. The word, sacraments, and all God's common temporal favours, are, in respect of external participation, communicated to them by way of concomitancy only, because they are intermixed with the elect.

Ver. 27. *My sheep hear my voice*] Buxtorf in his "Tiberias" noteth, that the seventh verse of the one-and-twentieth of Jeremiah consisteth of two-and-forty words and of a hundred-and-sixty letters. I am not at leisure to count the words and letters of this and the following verses; but it is easy to observe in them those five links of that golden chain of God's grace in our salvation: "my sheep," there is election; "hear my voice," there is vocation; "and I know them," there is justification; "and they follow me," there is sanctification; "and I give unto them eternal life," there is glorification.

Ver. 28. *They shall never perish*] This is the good Shepherd's promise: is he now as good as his word, if he suffer his sheep to wander and perish, whom by promise he was tied so to keep, as that they should not wander, as they are naturally apt to do, to their destruction? *Pastor oves spondet se absolute servaturum, nunquid liberabit fidem?* Prideaux.

Ver. 29. *No man is able to pluck them*] Impostors seek to thrust us from God, Deut. xiii. 5, and to drag disciples after them, with such violence, as if they would pluck them limb-meal (as the word ἀποσπᾶν signifies, Acts xx. 30), so to deceive, if it were possible, the very elect, Matt. xxiv. 24. A thing is said to be possible, *vel respectu Dei, vel respectu rei.* True grace, in itself considered, is easily separable from him that hath it, who, left to himself also, would soon lose it. But with respect to God, by whose power the saints are kept (as in a strong guard or garrison, φρουρούμενοι, 1 Pet. i. 5), through faith unto salvation, it is impossible that any of his should finally miscarry.

Ver. 30. *I and my Father are one*] Both for nature or essence, and for one consent, both in

willing and working. Out of the harbour of Goodwin's sands the pilot cannot make forth, they say, without sinking in those sands, unless he so steer his ship, that he bring two steeples, which stand off, so even in his sight, that they may seem to be but one. So is it here.

Ver. 31. *Then the Jews took up stones*] This is the world's wages to faithful ministers. Many conceit discharge of their duty without persecution; they would pull a rose without pricks. *Non decet, ut sub capite spinis coronato vivant membra in deliciis.* (Zanchius.)

Ver. 32. *From my Father*] i. e. *Ejus authoritate fretus.* (Beza.) All our works must be done in God, and for God; then they are of the right stamp, and carry heaven in them, Heb. vi. 9. Besides that, they are unanswerable syllogisms, invincible demonstrations, to confute and convert even pagans, saith Chrysostom.

Ver. 33. *But for blasphemy*] These were holy persecutors, in pretence at least. So Maximinian thought the blood of Christians would be an acceptable sacrifice to his gods. *Christianum sanguinem Diis victimam esse gravissimam.* (Tertul.) So Francis II. of France and Philip II. of Spain held the same opinion of the Lutherans in their dominions. Zeal without knowledge is like mettle in a blind horse.

Ver. 34. *In your law*] So he calls it, to show that there was no necessity on his part to prove what he delivered by any Scripture, sith he was to be believed on his bare word, αὐτόπιστος; but for their sakes only he did it.

Ver. 35. *Unto whom the word of God came*] That have their authority from God, whose substitutes and vicegerents princes are, and of whom they have their patent. With what face then can the schoolmen defend Thomas Aquinas in that paradox, *Dominium et prælatio introducta sunt ex jure humano?*

Ver. 36. *Hath sanctified and sent*] Sanctified, that is, anointed, and that in both his natures, as whole Christ. For his anointing imported; 1. His consecration or ordination to the office of a Mediator, and so the Godhead also was anointed. 2. Qualification or effusion of fulness of graces; as the holy oil was compounded of divers spices, so the manhood, and that without measure, as far as a finite nature was capable of.

Ver. 37. *If I do not the works of my Father, believe me not*] Thus said Christ, but so saith not Christ's, vicar, as the pope will needlessly be called. His *placita* must be obeyed, not examined; and though by his evil example he draw thousands to hell, none must mute, or say so much as What doest thou?

Ver. 38. *But if I do, though ye, &c.*] q. d. Stumble not at the meanness of my person, condition, followers, &c. When it was sometimes disputed among the Romans in the council, using to deify great men, whether Christ, having done many wonderful works, should be received into the number of the gods? it was at length concluded (saith the historian) *quod non deberet recipi inter Deos, pro eo quod non haberet cultores, propter hoc quod paupertatem prædicaret et eligeret, quam mundus contemnit.*

Ver. 39. *Therefore they sought again to take him*] They could not answer his arguments, they turn them therefore to a course of violence, wherein they doubted not but to be too hard for him. Thus they dealt with Ridley and Latimer at Oxford; thus with other martyrs, who yet overcame them by the blood of the Lamb, yea, were more than conquerors, Rom. viii. A fagot will make you recant, saith the Bishop to Mr Hawks, martyr. No, no, said he, a point for your fagot; you shall do no more, and your master to help you, than God permits you. In the year 1166, the synod at Oxford burned in the foreheads, and afterwards banished out of the realm, thirty Dutch doctors that taught here the right use of wedlock and the sacraments. (Alsted. Chronol.)

Ver. 40. *And went again beyond Jordan*] The farther from Jerusalem the safer. Jerusalem was then as Rome is now, the saints' slaughter-house. *Roma radix omnium malorum.*

Into the place where John first baptized] As well for his own comfort (for there he had heard at first from heaven, "This is my beloved Son," &c.) as for the people's conversion and confirmation, who there called to mind John's testimony of Jesus, and believed.

Ver. 41. *John did no miracle*] Lest he should be mistaken for the Messias. But how got he then so much credit? By his mortified conversation especially. "Holy and reverend is God's name," saith the Psalmist; therefore reverend, because holy. Holiness hath honour in the consciences of the very worst.

But all things that John spake] The word works not sometimes, till many years after it hath been preached, as here; and as they say of the elephant, that she goes with young thirteen years after she hath conceived.

Ver. 42. *And many believed on him there*] Place is no prejudice to the powerful operation of the word, when by the Spirit it is made prolifical and generative.

CHAPTER XI.

Ver. 1. *Bethany, the town of Mary,* &c.] Not the tower (*castellum*) of Mary and Martha, as some monks have doted; *digni sane qui ad grammatices elementa remittantur,* saith an interpreter. Bethany was a small town or village nigh to Jerusalem, where dwelt these three, Lazarus and his two sisters, all in one house (though *fratrum concordia rara*), to whom our Saviour joins himself a fourth in their friendship. "Behold how good and how pleasant it is for brethren to dwell together in unity." Surely there the Lord "commands the blessing, even life for evermore," Psal. cxxxiii. 1, 3.

Ver. 2. *It was that Mary which anointed*] This makes her name "as an ointment poured forth," Cant. i. 3. And she spared for no cost, being

of her mind, it seems, that said, *Ego si bonam famam servasso, sat ero dives.* (Plaut.)

Ver. 3. *Behold, he whom thou lovest is sick*] This was enough to say to a loving Saviour. We need not be careful in anything, more than to make our wants known to God, Phil. iv. 6, and let him alone to help us, how and when he pleaseth. So, to mind and move Christ for the labouring Church, it shall suffice to say, She whom thou lovest is sick, is in ill case, &c. But St Augustine asketh, *Si amatur, quomodo infirmatur?* Oh, well enough: afflictions are Christ's love-tokens. "As many as I love," saith he, "I rebuke and chasten." God may give the dearly beloved of his soul into the hand of her enemies, Jer. xii. 7.

Ver. 4. *But for the glory of God*] Happy Lazarus, though sick and dead, to be an instrument of glory, to be given to God. St Paul stood a-tip-toes (ἀποκαραδοκία), as it were, to see which way Christ might be most magnified in his body, whether by life or by death, Phil. i. 20.

Ver. 5. *Jesus loved Martha*] The saints are all round about his throne, Rev. iv. 4, because he is alike near to them for solace and tuition. Howbeit, as man, living amongst men, he was affected to some more than some, as to these three, and the beloved disciple. These were his Jedediahs, his singularly affected, and this was a high prerogative. Plato commendeth his country of Athens for antiquity of the people, &c., but chiefly for this, that they were beloved of the gods, τό πρῶτον καὶ μέγιστον ἐστὶ ὅτι τυγχάνει οὖσα θεοφιλής. (Plato.)

Ver. 6. *He abode two days*] Waiting to be gracious, but as a God of judgment, he knows best when to deal forth his favours, Isa. xxx. 18. To prescribe to him is to set the sun by our dial. This Cæsar terms sauciness in his soldiers.

Ver. 7. *Then after that saith he,* &c.] When help is seasonable, his fingers itch, as the mother's breast aches when it is time the child had suck.

Ver. 8. *And goest thou thither again?*] Yea, with the hazard of his life, to the help of his friend. The ancients painted friendship, a fair young man bare-headed, in a poor garment, at the bottom whereof was written, Death and Life, in the upper part, Summer and Winter; his bosom was open, so that his heart might be seen, whereupon was written, *Longe, prope,* a friend at hand and afar off. (Wilkins' Com. in Muret. orat. 1. de laud. lit.)

Ver. 9. *Are there not twelve hours?*] q. d. Is there not an appointed time to man upon earth? Job vii. 1. Shall I not live out my stint? The Turks shun not the company of those that have the plague; but, pointing upon their foreheads, say, It was written there at their birth when they should die. (Blount's Voyage into Levant.) A priest, indeed, might enter without danger into a leprous house, because he had a calling from God so to do. A man may follow God dry-shod through the Red Sea. This our Saviour calls here "to walk in the day" by an excellent and elegant similitude. But he that keeps not within

God's precincts may not look for his protection. I commend the charity, but I question the discretion, of Mr Stafford, public professor of divinity in Cambridge, who, hearing that a certain priest, called Sir Henry Conjuror (in King Henry VIII.'s days), lay sore sick of the plague, was so moved with pity to the poor priest's soul, that he came to him, exhorted, and so laboured him, that he would not leave him before he had converted him, and saw his conjuring-books burnt before his face. Which being done, Mr Stafford went home, and immediately sickened, and shortly after most Christianly deceased. He might have, I confess, an extraordinary call to his work. But Zanchius somewhere maketh mention of a colleague of his in the ministry, that by the like means took his death, and much bewailed upon his death-bed that he had not yielded to Zanchius advising him to the contrary.

Ver. 10. *But if any man walk in the night*] As good Josiah did, in that rash expedition against Pharaoh-Necho ; either hoping to ingratiate with the Assyrian, or fearing to have an over-heavy neighbour of the Egyptian : he went up to battle, not so much as asking leave of the Lord, though he had Jeremiah at hand, and Zephaniah, and a whole college of seers besides. The best are sometimes miscarried by their passions to their cost.

Ver. 11. *Lazarus sleepeth*] The saints are said to die in Christ, to sleep in Jesus, Rev. xiv. 13 ; 1 Thess. iv. 14. The Greeks call their churchyards dormitories, sleeping-places (κοιμητήρια). The Germans call them God's Acre, because their bodies are sown there to be raised again. The Hebrews Beth-chajim, the house of the living.

Ver. 12. *If he sleep, he shall do well*] Sleep (saith one) is the nurse of nature, the sweet parenthesis of all thy griefs and cares.

Ver. 13. *Jesus spake of his death*] Which profane writers also do call a sleep, but only because the functions of the faculties are extinct by death ; therefore they call it an iron sleep, an eternal sleep, &c. Christians call death a sleep, because it is to them a sweet rest in their beds, warmed and perfumed for them by Christ's body laid in the grave ; with whom also they look to rise to life eternal. *Ut somnus mortis, sic lectus imago sepulchri.* "Thy dead men shall live, with my dead body shall they arise," Isa. xxvi. 19.

Ver. 14. *Then said Jesus unto them plainly*] Because they understood him not. Ministers must be "gentle to all men, apt to teach, patient, in meekness instructing the ignorant," yea, the insolent, 2 Tim. ii. 24, 25. Augustine confesseth he was glad to use some words, sometimes, to his hearers that were not Latin, to the end that they might understand him.

Ver. 15. *I am glad for your sakes*] If the confirmation and increase of faith in his be so great a joy to Christ, how acceptable must it needs be unto him, that we believe at first on his name ! we cannot do him a greater honour, a more pleasing service. None greater in the father's house than the prodigal returned. And what a high price did our Saviour set on the centurion's faith !

Ver. 16. *Let us also go that we may die with him*] A blunt speech, and (as some think) overbold. He would die with Christ, and so would Peter ; yet none so shamefully forsook him, when it came to the proof, as these two. Thomas was to seek, when he should have seen Christ risen : he had not yet recovered his fright at our Saviour's apprehension.

Ver. 17. *That he had lain in the grave four days*] So that he might seem now to come too late. The faith of the two sisters must needs be much shaken, to see their brother dead, though Christ had sent them word he should not die. Hold out, faith and patience, God will be seen in the mount ; he usually reserves his hand for a dead-lift, when our faith begins to flag and hang the wing, when our strength is gone, and we have given up all for lost. "Now will I arise," saith the Lord, "now will I be exalted, now will I lift up myself," Isa. xxxiii. 10.

Ver. 18. *About fifteen furlongs*] Not full two miles : a short walk, and hence so great a resort to the place ; not without a special providence of God, who ordereth all to his own glory. The Jews came only to comfort the sisters, and to condole with them (it is a mercy in misery to find such friends, *qui mœroris et funeris pondera luctuosa participabunt*, as Cyprian hath it, that will set to their shoulders, and bear a part), but God had a further end in that meeting, *ne obscura esset Lazari resurrectio*, that there might be many witnesses of Lazarus' resurrection ; who might also thereby be made partakers of the first resurrection, Rev. xx. 6.

Ver. 19. *To comfort them*] A pious office, and yet never thought of by the superstitious Papists, amidst all those vain fopperies they prescribe to be done about the dead. Only, what the ancients used for the comfort of the living is perverted by them to the pretended service and help of the dead.

Ver. 20. *But Mary sat still in the house*] So, while faith sits at the centre, love walks the round. *Dicit Fides, Parata sunt mihi omnia : Dicit Spes, Mihi ista servantur : Dicit Charitas, Ego curro ad illa*, saith Bernard.

Ver. 21. *Lord, if thou hadst been here, &c.*] Was she sure of that ? but why was he dead, if Christ would not, though he were not there ? We are all too much fastened to his bodily presence : howbeit, we never come to believe indeed till we are well persuaded of his omnipotency. But how fitly may many a poor soul say to the bloody non-resident, Sir, if thou hadst been here, my brother, child, husband, had not been dead in his sins ?

Ver. 22. *Whatsoever thou wilt ask*] This is our comfort, that our Advocate is all in all with his Father, and may have what he will of him. What need we any other "master of requests" than Christ ? If David will hear Joab for Absalom ; and Herod, Blastus for the Tyrians, Acts xii. 20 ; what may not we hope ?

Ver. 23. *Thy brother shall rise again*] Let this consideration comfort us in the decease of our dearest friends, they are not lost, but laid up with Christ, who will bring them back with him at his coming, 1 Thess. iv. 14. As the same divine hand that buried Moses, that locked up this treasure and kept the key of it, brought it forth afterwards glorious in the transfiguration. The body that was hid in the valley of Moab appeared again in the hill of Tabor.

Ver. 24. *In the resurrection*] The Syriac hath it *Benuchama*, in the consolation. So the resurrection was ever to the disconsolate believers of both Testaments, Dan. xii. 2 ; Heb. xi. 35. In the primitive Church, when they repeated that article of the creed, " I believe the resurrection of the flesh," they would point to their bodies, and say, *etiam hujus carnis*, even of this very flesh.

Ver. 25. *He that believeth in me, though, &c.*] Oh the wonderful force of faith ! Questionless (saith a reverend man, Mr S. Ward) justifying faith is not beneath miraculous in the sphere of its own activity, and where it hath warrant of God's word, &c.

Ver. 26. *Believest thou this ?*] He saith not, Understandest thou this ? For the mysteries of the Christian religion, saith Rupertus, are much better understood by believing than believed by understanding.

Ver. 27. *I believe that thou art the Christ*] What could Peter say more ? Matt. xvi. 16. Damaris may be as dear to God as Dionysius, a woman (of no note otherwise) as an Areopagite, Acts xvii. 34.

Ver. 28. *Called Mary her sister secretly*] By Christ's command ; and secretly, belike, she did it, lest any should tell the Pharisees, and Christ thereby be brought into danger. " Be wise as serpents."

Ver. 29. *She arose quickly*] Love is winged, and a ready heart makes riddance of God's work. His people are free-hearted, Psal. cx. 3. Where the carcase is, there will these eagles be ; they scour to his presence, as the doves to the columbary, they fly as the clouds, &c., Isa. lx. 8.

Ver. 30. *Was not yet come into the town*] To eat and refresh himself after his long journey ; he would do his work first, as Abraham's servant, Gen. xxiv. 33.

Ver. 31. *She goeth unto the grave*] That, Niobe-like, she might weep herself into a tombstone. *Ex eorum more qui luctus sui irritamenta quærunt.* Calvin. Such a heathenish custom it seems they had amongst them, and many other funeral rites, forbidden by the law. But what should dropsy-men do eating salt meats ?

Ver. 32. *She fell down at his feet*] Giving him divine honour, before all the Jews that were present. So did not Martha, that we read of. Mary had been more diligent in hearing and meditation of the word ; hence her greater love and respect to Christ.

Ver. 33. *When Jesus saw her weeping*] Tears are most effectual orators to Christ ; when he was going to the cross, he could find time to look back and comfort the weeping woman.

And was troubled] So as for the present he could not utter himself. Yet these passions in Christ were, as clear water in a crystal glass, without sin.

Ver. 34. *Where have ye laid him ?*] He could tell well enough ; but yet would be told by them. So, he knows our wants before we open them, and sometimes is pleased to prevent us with a supply ; but usually he will hear from us. Come he will to our relief and succour, but he will have his people's prayers lead him. " I came for thy words," saith the angel, Dan. x. 12 ; ix. 21. Whilst he was speaking in prayer, Gabriel came with " weariness of flight," and touched him " about the evening oblation," which was the hour of prayer.

Ver. 35. *Jesus wept*] He wept with those that weep. And the same tenderness he retains still toward his afflicted. As Aaron, though he might not lament his two sons slain by God's hand in the sanctuary, Levit. x. 3, yet he had still the bowels of a father within him ; so hath Christ now, in the heavenly sanctuary ; he hath lost nothing by heaven.

Ver. 36. *Behold how he loved him*] What ! for shedding some few tears for him ? Oh how then did he love us for whom he shed the dearest and warmest blood in all his heart ! *Ama amorem illius*, &c., saith Bernard.

Ver. 37. *And some of them said*] Thus our Saviour is diversely interpreted and censured ; and so it is still with his ministers. When we see our auditors before us, little do we know with what hearts they are there, nor what use they will make of their pretended devotion. Doeg may set his foot as far within the tabernacle as David. If some come to serve God, others come to observe their teachers and pick quarrels ; yea, if conscience might be judge, many a hearer would be found to have a Herod's heart toward his minister.

Ver. 38. *Groaning in himself*] To consider, belike, the woeful effects of sin that brought death into the world, even on the best ; and makes them a ghastly and loathsome spectacle, so that Abraham desires to bury his beloved Sarah out of his sight. Believe me who have made trial of it, saith Augustine, open a grave, and in the head of the dead man ye shall find toads leaping that are begotten of his brain ; serpents crawling on his loins, that are bred out of his kidneys ; worms creeping in his belly, that grow out of his bowels. *Mihi experto crede, quod apertis sepulchris in capitibus invenietis bufones saltantes generatos ex cerebro.* (Serm. 48.) *Ecce quid sumus, et quid jam erimus : Ecce in quod resolvimur : En peccati originem et fœditatem !* saith that father.

Ver. 39. *By this time he stinketh*] Ay, the better for that ; Christ's power will be the more manifested. As St Austin said of one that hit him in the teeth with the sins of his youth : The more desperate was the disease, the greater honour redounded to the physician that cured me. Beza's answer to one that did the like to him, was, *Hic homo invidet mihi gratiam Christi.*

Ver. 40. *Said I not unto thee, &c.*] A foul fault in her to be so incredulous ; and enough, without the greater mercy of Christ, to have marred all. For unbelief is so vile and venomous an evil, as that it transfuseth a kind of dead palsy into the hands of omnipotency, Mark vi. 5. Christ, that can do all things by his absolute power, can do little or nothing by his actual power, for unbelievers. He cannot, because he will not.

Ver. 41. *Father, I thank thee that, &c.*] Beginning to pray, he brings his thanks in his hand, as sure to speed. So must we, Phil. iv. 6. And therefore in the law, whatever request they had to God, they must be sure to come with their peace-offerings, in token of thankfulness : that they might sing with the Psalmist, " Praise waiteth for thee, O God, in Sion," Psal. lxv. 1. It is said of Tiberius the emperor, that he never denied his favourite Sejanus anything, and oftentimes prevented his request, so that he needed only to ask and give thanks. (Tacitus.) All God's people are his favourites, and may have anything that heart can wish or need require.

Ver. 42. *And I knew that thou hearest me always*] And he always liveth to make intercession for his ; who therefore may boldly believe, that they shall want nothing that is good for them, sith he is " All in all " with the Father, and may have what he will. In any strait go but to God, and cry as he did, *Conqueror tibi lachrymis Jesu Christi,* and doubt not of a gracious return of thy prayer.

Ver. 43. *Lazarus, come forth*] If this voice of Christ had been directed to all the dead, they had presently risen ; as sure as they shall rise when the Lord himself shall descend with a shout, with the voice of an archangel, crying, *Surgite mortui, venite in judicium.* Pliny reports of the lioness, that she brings forth her whelps dead, and so they remain for the space of three days, until the lion coming near to the place where they lie, lifts up his voice and roars so fiercely, that presently they are raised from death to life. The prophet Jeremiah tells us the like of this Lion of the tribe of Judah, Jer. xxv. 30, 31. See the place.

Ver. 44. *And he that was dead*] But where was his soul therewhile ? *In manu Dei,* not in purgatory, as Papists say, for that is against their own principles. They send none to purgatory but men of a middle make, betwixt just and unjust. Now Lazarus was surely a very good man, else had he not been so dear to Christ. But that purgatory is the pope's invention, as Tindal hath it : hear St Augustine, *Nemo se decipiat, fratres : duo enim loca sunt, et tertius non est visus. Qui cum Christo regnare non meruit, cum diabolo, absque dubitatione, peribit.*

Ver. 45. *Believed on him*] And so God had his

honour and Christ his end in this, according to ver. 4.

Ver. 46. *But some of them, &c.*] Lo, reprobates will not believe, though one rose from the dead to them.

Ver. 47. *Then gathered the chief priests*] Like unto this was the Council of Trent gathered on purpose to suppress Christ in his true worshippers, and carried by antichrist with such infinite guile and craft, without any sincerity, upright dealing and truth, as that themselves will even smile in the triumphs of their own wits (when they hear it but mentioned), as at a master-stratagem.

Ver. 48. *The Romans shall come, &c.*] And so they did ; the thing that they feared came upon them, for their inexpiable guilt in killing the Lord Jesus. Demades, when the emperor sent to his countrymen of Athens to give him divine honour, and they were loth to yield unto it, but consulted about it : Take heed, says he, you be not so busy about heavenly matters as to lose your earthly possessions. These refractory Jews lost both.

Ver. 49. *Ye know nothing at all*] Why no : you know all, Caiaphas, all the assessors are but asses to you. *Hoc est superbire, quasi super alios ire.* This fellow would have made a fine duke of Russia, by whom it is cautioned that there be no schools, lest there should be any scholars but himself. So the Gnostics bragged that they were the only knowing men. (Irenæus.) And the Jesuits at this day tell us that the empire of learning is confined to their territories. *Penes nos est imperium literarum.* (Eudæm.)

Ver. 50. *That one man should die for the people*] A brutish and bloody sentence ; as if evil might be done that good may come thereof. So, when Farellus, that worthy reformer, came first to Geneva, and was convented there by the bishop, as a disturber of the public peace, one of the Popish assessors cried out, Away with this pestilent Lutheran ; better he perish than the town be disquieted. To whom Farellus answered, *Noli Caiaphæ voces, sed Dei verba proferre,* Speak not in the language of Caiaphas, but in the word of God. (Scultet. Annal.)

Ver. 51. *This he spake, not of himself*] God spake through him, as through a trunk, or as the angel spake in Balaam's ass. Wholesome sugar may be found in a poisoned cane, a precious stone in a toad's head, a flaming torch in a blind man's hand.

Ver. 52. *Gather together in one*] In one spiritual body, though in place never so distant one from another, Ephes. iv. 4. " My dove is but one, the daughters saw her and blessed her," Cant. vi. 9. No such oneness, entireness, anywhere else. Other societies may cleave together as the toes of clay in Nebuchadnezzar's image, but not incorporate.

Ver. 53. *Then from that day forth*] So baneful is evil counsel, from the mouth of a man of mark especially, to set men agog upon mischief.

Ver. 54. *Into a city called Ephraim*] Not elsewhere mentioned; built, perhaps, in honour of their father Ephraim, by the posterity of those rash sons of his, that had brought grief to his heart, and to make amends for their miscarriage. See 1 Chron. vii. 21, 22.

Ver. 55. *Before the Passover, to purify themselves*] They had their Parasceve and Proparasceve, their preparation and fore-preparation. We must also purify ourselves before the sacrament from all filthiness of flesh and spirit, 1 Cor. vii. 1, cast all the baggage into the brook Kidron (that is, the town ditch), and then kill the Passover, 2 Chron. xxx. 14. The very heathens had their *cænam puram* before their sacrifices.

Ver. 56. *Then sought they for Jesus*] Whether these were his friends or enemies, the doctors are divided.

Ver. 57. *Had given a commandment*] So diligent were they, and earnest to execute that cruel decree of the council. This is check to our oscitancy in the best things. What a shame is it, that they should outwork the children of light in a thorough despatch of their deeds of darkness, and be at more pains to go to hell than we will be to go to heaven.

CHAPTER XII.

Ver. 1. *Came to Bethany*] To convert some, confirm others, and to refresh himself with his fast friends, ere he fell into the hands of his bloody enemies. So Cromwell, Earl of Essex, going to his death, first called for his breakfast, and cheerfully eating the same, and after that meeting the Lord Hungerford going likewise to his execution, and perceiving him to be all heavy and doleful, with cheerful countenance and comfortable words asking him why he was so heavy, he willed him to pluck up his heart, and to be of good comfort: For, said he, there is no cause for you to fear, for if you repent and be heartily sorry for that you have done, there is for you mercy with the Lord, who for Christ's sake will forgive you; therefore be not dismayed. And though the breakfast we are going to be sharp, yet, trusting to the mercy of the Lord, we shall have a joyful dinner. And so went they together to the place of execution, and took their death cheerfully.

Ver. 2. *That sat at table*] Being invited by Simon the leper at whose house this feast was kept, as some will have it.

Ver. 3. *Of spikenard, very costly*] Herodotus reckons an alabaster box of ointment (μύρου ἀλάβαστρον) among the precious gifts that Cambyses sent for a present to the king of Ethiopia. Mary thinks nothing too good for him, whom her soul loved. She will honour him with the best of her substance; she knew there was nothing lost; but though it took from the heap, yet it increased the heap; as it is said of tithes and offerings, Mal. iii. This made David so free and frolic, that he would not serve God of that which cost him nothing; and that he made such

plentiful preparation for the temple-work. It is both love and good husbandry to make our service to God costly: his retributions are bountiful. This ointment in the text was a costly confection, like that of the Church, "Spikenard and saffron, calamus and cinnamon," &c., Cant. iv. 14. Now Galen writes that in his time cinnamon was very rare, and hard to be found, except in the store-houses of princes. And Pliny reports that a pound of cinnamon was worth a thousand denarii, that is, 150 crowns of our money. This good woman held, as Tertullian afterwards did, that *Pietatis nomine sumptum facere, est lucrum facere*, to spend upon pious uses was the way to greatest gain.

Ver. 4. *Then said one of his disciples*] St Matthew tells us, that all the disciples said thus. Judas was of so great esteem and authority amongst them, that what he did they are all said to do. So cunningly he had carried his conspiracy, that they all suspected themselves rather than Judas; every one said, Is it I?

Ver. 5. *Sold for three hundred pence*] He, the thief, had quickly computed and cast it up. Pliny tells us that a pound of ordinary ointment might be had for ten pence; but the best was worth three hundred and ten pence. So that Judas was much about the good, as they say. And Mary spared for no cost; as neither did Justinian in his rich communion table, offered up by him in the temple of Sophia in Constantinople, that had in it, saith the author, all the riches of land and sea. Cedren. Hist.

Ver. 6. *He was a thief*] It is the conceit of Tertullian, that even Judas carried himself honestly and right, *usque ad loculorum officium*, till he bare the bag. When once he came to be master of the money he grew into such a devilish humour of covetousness, that rather than he would be out of taking, he would sell his very Saviour. And a fair match he made: for, as Austin saith, Judas sold his salvation, and the Pharisees bought their damnation.

And had the bag, and bare] Our Saviour then had a bag for store, and so big that it had need to have one specially deputed to bear it; this was Judas; who could be well content to bear the cross on his back, so he might bear the bag in his hand; which he thought (as all covetous men do) to be the best tongue a man can use for himself, as the Greek word γλωσσόκομον here used importeth. But what an odious piece of hypocrisy is that in the Capuchin friars, that none of them may take or touch silver! at the offer thereof they start back, as Moses from the serpent; yet have they ever a boy with a bag in their company, that takes and carries it, and never complains of either metal or measure.

Ver. 7. *Let her alone*] Christ crossed the traitor in his covetous desire of fingering such a sum. Hence his discontent put him upon that desperate design of contracting with the chief priests. He is resolved to have it, however he come by it; *Rem, rem, quocunque modo rem.* Horat. Take heed of discontent. It was the devil's sin that threw him out of heaven. Ever since which this restless spirit loves to fish in troubled waters, to dwell in a darkened soul : as in Saul, envious at David : and as some heretics, missing of preferment, have invented their heresies, *ut se consolarentur*, as Epiphanius observed.

Against the day] Being at a feast he speaketh of his funeral.

Ver. 8. *The poor ye have always with you*] To give to when you please ; and in gratifying whom, ye may glorify God and secure your substance ; for *Manus pauperum gazophylacium Christi*, saith an ancient.

But me have ye not always] And yet we have, in his poor members, the family of faith. Hence Salvian sticks not to say, that Christ is *maximus mendicorum*, the greatest of beggars ; and addeth, *Non eget miseriâ sed eget misericordiâ : non eget deitate pro se, sed eget pietate pro suis.* (Salv. ad Eccles. Cathol. iv.)

Ver. 9. *And they came, &c.*] Do the Pharisees what they could to the contrary. Truth may be opprest, not supprest. *Impii sunt piorum ἐργοδιῶκται.* This people (like those branches of palm-trees borne by them, ver. 13) spread and sprang up the more they were held under by the high priests. (βαία, παρὰ τὸ βαίνειν, a scandendo.)

But that they might see Lazarus] And fish somewhat out of him concerning the future estate of the dead. But here they lost their labour.

Ver. 10. *That they might put Lazarus also to death*] In malice is steeped the venom of all vices. What a giant-like madness was this, to take up arms against heaven itself! to seek to kill a man, only because God had made him alive ! was it not because they were even acted and agitated by the devil ? *Si videris aliquando persecutorem tuum nimis sævientem, scito quia ab accensore suo dæmone perurgetur*, saith Bernard. These Pharisees had sinned that sin to death ; which made another, in the same case, wish that his wife and children and all the world might be damned together with him. (Mr Burr, Moses' Choice.) Hacket at the gallows cried out, O heavenly God, show some miracle out of the cloud to convert these infidels and deliver me from mine enemies. But if not, I will set the heaven on fire, and with these hands pluck thee out of thy throne : and other speeches he used, more unspeakable. Camden's Elizabeth.

Ver. 11. *Because that by reason of him*] This was it that embittered the Pharisees, as it doth now their successors the Papists. Bellarmine bewrays his grief, and tells us that ever since we proclaimed the pope to be that Antichrist, his kingdom hath not only not increased, but daily more and more decreased. *Ab eo tempore quo per vos Papa Antichristus esse cœpit, non modo non crevit ejus imperium, &c.* (De Papa Rom. iii. 21.) And Erasmus being asked by the Elector of Saxony, why Luther was so hated by the Popish clergy ? For two great faults that he had com-

mitted, said he, for meddling with the pope's triple crown and the monks' fat paunches. (Scultet. Annal.)

Ver. 12. *On the next day much people*] The envious Pharisees feeding the while upon their own hearts. Israel never increased so fast as when Pharaoh most oppressed them. *Plures efficimur quoties metimur*, saith Tertullian.

Ver. 13. *Took branches of palm-trees*] Plutarch writeth that the Babylonians make 360 benefits of the palm-tree, and therefore do highly honour it. Pintus upon Daniel telleth us, that the palm-tree will not grow in a fat ground, but in a light and sandy ; and if the soil be strong and fertile, they must cast salt and ashes at the root, to qualify the strength of the ground. Sure it is, that if prosperity be not seasoned with the salt of grace it will be unfruitful and unprofitable.

Hosanna, Blessed is the King, &c.] This shows they were well seen in David's psalms, which are, saith Chrysostom, a rich storehouse of all good doctrines : πάντων ἀγαθῶν διδαγμάτων ταμεῖον. And they are so penned, saith Athanasius, that every man may think they speak *de se, in re sua*, of himself, and for his particular purpose ; which of other parts of Scripture cannot be affirmed.

Ver. 14. *When he had found a young ass*] To make religion dance attendance upon policy (saith one) is to set the ass upon Christ, and not Christ upon the ass. These three things, saith Luther, will be the ruin of religion, unthankfulness, security, and carnal policy. *Sapientia mundi, quæ vult omnia redigere in ordinem.* (Melch. Adam.)

Ver. 15. *Sitting upon an ass*] Not upon a stately palfrey, as an earthly potentate ; but upon a silly ass, without pomp, to comfort the poorest, and to teach us humility, tolerance, patience. An ass is a beast profitable (whence he hath his name in the original), but born to bear burdens.[1] *Oneramus asinum*, saith Bernard, *et non curat, quia asinus est.* But what notorious asses are those superstitious Papists, that show the ass's tail in Genoa in Italy, whereon our Saviour rode, for a relic, and give it divine worship. Are not these given up to the very efficacy of error ?

Ver. 16. *These things understood not, &c.*] They only beheld it as a pretty pageant. They had read it often, in the prophet, and now saw it acted ; yet were never the wiser, for present. Read, or hear, though thou understandest not ; God may drop in divine light when thou least lookest for it.

Ver. 17. *When he called Lazarus, &c.*] This notable miracle, the evangelist, as he had punctually described it, chap. xi., so he cannot but again and again recite it. We should set forth God's noble acts, and not be sated. David never tires talking of what God had done for his soul. Those in heaven have no rest (and yet no unrest neither) crying, " Holy, holy, holy," &c., Rev. iv. 8.

Ver. 18. *For this cause also the people met him*] To the Pharisees' extreme grief and regret ; to

---

[1] ὄνος, παρὰ τό ὀνήσαθαι. *Hinc Heraclidæ* *Sophistæ*, πόνου ἐγκώμιον, ὄνου *dixit* ἐγκώμιον.

show that there is neither "wisdom, nor understanding, nor counsel against the Lord," Prov. xxi. 30.

Ver. 19. *Perceive ye how ye prevail nothing?*] Thus they stir up one another to more madness, as if hitherto they had been over-mild, and used too much gentleness. So Stephen Gardiner, being charged of cruelty by Bradford, answered, I for my part have been challenged for being too gentle oftentimes. Which thing Bonner confirmed, and so did almost all the audience, that he had been ever too mild and moderate. So Bonner in open court to the Lord Mayor: They report me (said he) to seek blood, and call me bloody Bonner, whereas, God knows, I never sought any man's blood in all my life. But a certain unknown good woman, in a letter to Bonner, told him his own in these words: Indeed you are called the common cut-throat and general slaughter-slave to all the bishops of England. And therefore it is wisdom for me and all other simple sheep of the Lord to keep us out of your butcherly stall, as long as we can, especially since you have such store already, that you are not able to drink all their blood, lest you should break your belly: and therefore ye let them lie still and die for hunger, &c. Thus she to Bonner. As for Dr Story, who was hanged, drawn, and quartered, for his treason in Queen Elizabeth's reign; I see (said he in open Parliament) nothing to be ashamed of (though he had been a furious persecutor under Queen Mary), so less I see to be sorry for, but rather because I have done no more; wherein he said there was no default in him, but in them, whom he oft and earnestly had exhorted to the same; being not a little grieved, therefore, with them, for that they laboured only about the young and little sprigs and twigs, while they should have stricken at the root (the Lady Elizabeth he meant) and clean rooted it out. The Lord Paget in a certain consultation said, that King Philip should never have any quiet commonwealth in England unless the Lady Elizabeth's head were stricken from her shoulders. Whereunto the Spaniards answered, God forbid that their king and master should have such a mind, to consent to such a mischief. A writ came down, while she was in the Tower, subscribed with certain hands of the council, for her execution, Stephen Gardiner being the engineer. Mr Bridges, Lieutenant of the Tower, mistrusting false play, presently made haste to the queen, who renounced and reversed it. And yet of her, that was true that Josephus writeth of Alexandra, *Ipsa solum nomen regium ferebat, cæterum omnem regni potestatem Pharisæi possidebant.*

Ver. 20. *Greeks*] That is, proselytes or transmarine Jews, that read the Greek version, and were called Hellenists.

Ver. 21. *Sir, we would see Jesus*] That is, we would have private conference with him; for they had seen him, likely, as he came riding into the city. Our Saviour seems not to have yet admitted them, because the time appointed for their calling was not yet come. "Everything

is beautiful in its time," Eccles. iii. 11; but as fish and flesh, so other things too, are naught out of season.

Ver. 22. *Andrew and Philip tell Jesus*] Therefore we may desire the saints departed to mediate for us to Christ, say the Papists. A pitiful poor argument. *Illi sic garriant, nos aliter credamus.* (Augustine.)

Ver. 23. *That the Son of man should be glorified*] That is, crucified; but he looked through death, and saw heaven beyond it: so must we; then shall we say, "Surely the bitterness of death is past," 1 Sam. xv. 32. This made Simeon sing out his soul, *Egredere, o anima mea;* Hilarion chide it out; Taylor fetch a frisk, when he was come near the place where he was burned; Bradford put off his cap, and thank God, when the keeper's wife brought him word he was to be burned on the morrow; Roper stand in the fire with his arms stretched out like a rood; Hawks clap his hands over his head three times, when they were all on a light fire. (Acts and Mon.)

Ver. 24. *Except a corn of wheat, &c.*] The apostles thought Christ should have been presently glorified. He lets them here know that he must first suffer, before he enter into his glory; bear the cross, before he wear the crown; pass the stroke of death's flaming sword, before he come into paradise. *Ne Jesum quidem audias gloriosum, nisi videris prius crucifixum.* (Luth. epist. ad Melanct.)

Ver. 25. *He that loveth his life*] As Christ loved not his life to the death for us, so neither must we for him. If every hair of my head were a man, I would suffer death in the opinion and faith that I am now in, said John Ardley, martyr, to Bonner. God be praised, said Dr Taylor, since my condemnation, I was never afraid to die. God's will be done; if I shrink from God's truth, I am sure of another manner of death than had Judge Hales.

Ver. 26. *If any man serve me, let, &c.*] Art thou not glad to fare as Phocion? said he to one that was to die with him; οὐκ ἀγαπᾷς μετὰ Φωκίονος ἀποθανούμενος. (Plut.) How much more to die with and for Christ!

Ver. 27. *Now is my soul troubled*] *Christi perturbatio nos tranquillat, et infirmitas firmat,* saith Augustine.

Father, save me from this hour] As man, he naturally feared and deprecated death; such a dreadful death especially as he was to suffer. Δι' ἀγνώστων σοῦ παθημάτων, saith the Greek litany; by thine unknown sufferings, good Lord, deliver us. Howbeit, this was but with his sensitive will; for his rational will was ever the same with that of his Father.

Ver. 28. *Then came there a voice from heaven*] God sometimes gives a sensible answer to the prayers of his people, as they are praying, or immediately after, as Dan. ix. 21; Acts iv. 31. And Luther, praying for the good success of God's cause in Germany, came leaping out of his study, with *Vicimus, vicimus,* in his mouth.

Ver. 29. *That it thundered; others said, An*

angel, &c.] But the apostles and some few others understood that it was neither thunder nor an angel, but God that spake. *Fuerunt præter Apostolos etiam aliqui minus sinistri interpretes.* (Calvin.) In like sort now-a-days God speaks by his word, but few hear him in it. The word of God (saith Forbes on Rev. xiv.) hath three degrees of operation in the hearts of men. First, it falleth to men's ears, as the sound of many waters; a confused sound, which commonly bringeth neither terror nor joy, but yet a wondering and acknowledgment of a strange force, and more than human power, Mark i. 22, 29; Acts xiii. 41. The second effect is, the voice of thunder; which brings not only wonder, but fear: these two may be in the reprobate, as Felix, and the multitude in our text. The third effect, proper to the elect, is the sound of harping; whiles the word not only ravisheth with admiration, and striketh the conscience with terror, but also filleth it with sweet peace and joy.

Ver. 30. *But for your sakes*] That ye might believe; which if ye do not, how shall ye escape that neglect so great salvation, such a heavenly preacher? See then that ye refuse not, that ye shift not off, him that speaks from heaven; see that ye turn not from him, whose voice once shook the earth, but now heaven too, παραιτήσησθε, Heb. xii. 25, 26.

Ver. 31. *The prince of this world*] Gratian saith, the devil is called the prince of this world, as a king at chess, or as the cardinal of Ravenna, only by derision. The power he hath is merely usurped, and because the world will have it so, which even lieth down in that wicked one, as St John hath it, that is, under the power and vassalage of the devil, 1 John v. 10. It is wholly set upon wickedness, as Aaron saith of the people, Exod. xxxii. 22.

Ver. 32. *And if I be lifted up, &c.*] Pope Urban VI. said that these words, " Give unto Cæsar the things which are Cæsar's," were abolished when Christ was lifted up from the earth, and drew all things to him; that is (as he expounds it), when Christ ascended, he drew to the pope's empire all kings and their kingdoms, making him King of kings and Lord of lords. (Jacob. Rev. de vit. Pon.) Is not this a sweet interpreter?

I will draw all men unto me] As the wind called *Cæcias*, being a north-east wind, contrary to the nature of the north wind, drives not away clouds, but draws them to him.

Ver. 33. *Signifying what death, &c.*] Be lifted up betwixt heaven and earth, as Absalom was, *Absolon Marte furens pensilis arbore obit*, who therein, saith Gretser the Jesuit, became a lively figure of Christ crucified. *Sed o mirum et delirum figurativæ crucis fabrum!*

Ver. 34. *We have heard out of the law*] But had they never heard out of the law that Christ must first suffer, and then enter into his glory? Isa. liii. 2; Dan. ix. 26. There is none of us Jews, saith Josephus, but being asked of any point of the law, can answer to it more readily than tell his own name. *Quilibet nostrum de lege interrogatus, facilius quam nomini suo respondet.* Is it then ignorance or malice that they thus cavil and quarrel our Saviour?

Ver. 35. *Yet a little while is the light, &c.*] The day of grace, which is very clear and bright, is usually a short one. Therefore break off your sins by repentance; be abrupt in the work, for life is short, opportunities headlong, and once past, irrecoverable. He is the wise man that prefers opportunity before time, in laying hold upon eternal life; but fools are *semper victuri*, saith Seneca, they will, and they will, &c.; so they trifle, and by futuring, fool away their own salvation. Amend before the draw-bridge be taken up. Charles, king of Sicily and Jerusalem, was called Cunctator: not in the sense as Fabius, because he stayed till opportunity came, but because he stayed till opportunity was past. Too many such. Manna must be gathered in the morning, or not at all; and not kept till the morrow, lest it stink.

Ver. 36. *Whiles ye have the light*] God is but a while with men in the opportunities of grace; and this will be a bodkin one day at the hearts of unbelievers, that they "loved darkness rather than light:" viz. when they are cast into outer darkness.

Ver. 37. *But though he had done, &c.*] The evangelist being now by course of the history to pass on to the description of Christ's death and passion, thinks good first to remove this dead Amasa (the Jews' unbelief) out of the way (that none might stop or step aside for it), by assigning the true cause thereof, their own unmalleable obstinacy.

Ver. 38. *That the saying of the prophet*] These unbelievers were not such, because the prophet had so foretold it; but the prophet therefore foretold it, because they should be such. Like as Joseph's foretelling the famine was no cause of it, but an antecedent only.

Ver. 39. *Therefore they could not believe, &c.*] They could not, because they would not, saith Theophylact out of Chrysostom, who yet extolleth man's free will more than is meet. *Pelagianis nondum litigantibus, patres securius loquebantur*, saith Augustine, contra Julian. i. 2.

Ver. 40. *He hath hardened their hearts*] With a judiciary hardness. This is in some respect worse than hell; sith (besides that God inflicts it as a punishment of former obstinacy) it is one of the greatest sins, and so far greater an evil than any of the greatest punishments. Hence it was the saying of a reverend man, " If I must be put to my choice, I had rather be in hell with a sensible heart, than live on earth with a reprobate mind."

Ver. 41. *When he saw his glory*] His train only in the temple, Isa. vi. 1, where the seraphims are said to hide their faces with two wings, as with a double scarf, before God's glorious brightness, that would put out their eyes else; they clap their wings on their faces, as men do their hands when the lightning flasheth in their eyes.

Ver. 42. *Lest they should be put out*, &c.] Which would redound to their disgrace, and this these ambitionists could not away with. But what saith a reverend divine? " Bravely contemn all contumelies and contempts for thy conscience, taking them as crowns, and confirmations of thy conformity to Christ."

Ver. 43. *They loved the praise of men*] Which what is it else but a little stinking breath? These have their reward, *Mercedem suam, non Dei*, saith Jerome. How much better Luther! *Haud velim, Erasmi, gloriâ aut nomine vehi: Major est mihi timor in laudibus, gaudium vero in maledictis et blasphemiis.* (Epist. ad Nic. Hansm.)

Ver. 44. *Jesus cried*, &c.] As being now to cry his last to them, and is therefore so earnest in his contestation. This was the *Conclamatum est* to this perverse people, his farewell sermon, &c.

Ver. 45. *Seeth him that sent me*] For God was in Christ reconciling the world to himself, and in him the God-head dwelt bodily, Col. ii. 9. So that in all our addresses we must fix the eye of faith on the human nature of Christ, and there speak as to our God. Like as where I see the body of a man, there I know his soul is, and therefore I speak to his understanding, when and where I see his body, because they are not severed; so, viewing by faith Christ's manhood now glorified, I there see and speak to the great God, because I know he is there personally united.

Ver. 46. *I am come a light into the world*] Not by participation only (as the apostles were the lights of the world, Matt. v. 14) but by nature. How prodigiously blasphemous then was that bishop in the Council of Trent, that (in his oration there made) applied this text to the pope, who at that time was Paul the Third, an odious hypocrite. (Cornel. Episcop. Bipontin.)

That whosoever believeth in me, &c.] And he that this way seeks the kingdom of heaven, must, with him in Justin, look for this Sun of righteousness in the west; that is, dying upon the altar of his cross: so shall he become king of heaven. (Stratonis servus, ap. Justin.)

Ver. 47. *I judge him not*] viz. While I am here on earth. I sustain another person now, that men may come apace to me without fear. Some ancient heretics held, that God in the time of the law was a severe judge; and now, in the days of the gospel, he was all made of mercy and mildness. But the apostle saith somewhat otherwise, Heb. ii. 1—3. God is more peremptory in his judgments now than ever of old. And chap. xii. 29, he telleth us that even our God also, as well as the God of the Jews, " is a consuming fire."

Ver. 48. *The word that I have spoken*] If the word shall judge us, then ought it much more to be a judge of our doings now, said Mr Philpot, martyr. Therefore let it be president in all assemblies and judgments, saith Beza: as in the Nicene Council, Constantine caused the Bible to be set on a desk, as judge of all controversies.

Ver. 49, 50. *For I have not spoken of myself*] The divine authority of gospel doctrine is here, in the close of this last sermon *ad populum*, most gravely asserted by our Saviour; as that which is undoubtedly authentic, because it comes from the Father, *e cujus ore nil temere excidit*. David (saith one) sets the 119th Psalm as a poem of commendation before the book of God. The Son of David (say I) sets this text as his Imprimatur, his authoritative licence, at the end of the gospel. And as a friend once wrote to Ægidius, Abbot of Nuremberg, concerning the 119th Psalm, that they were, *verba vivenda, non legenda*, words not to be read, but lived; the same may I affirm of our Saviour's sermons, and I know that his commandment is life everlasting.

CHAPTER XIII.

Ver. 1. *That he should depart*, &c.] This definition of death, saith Calvin, pertains to the whole body of the Church. It is to the saints no more than a passage to the Father, an in-let to eternal life. Whether a Christian's death be a burnt-offering (of martyrdom), or a peace-offering (of a natural death), whether it be by a sudden change, as Elijah's, or a lingering sickness, as Elisha's, it is a sweet sacrifice ascending to God, as Manoah's angel ascending in the smoke. This made Basil, when the emperor's lieutenant threatened to kill him, cry out, εἴθε γένοιτο μοὶ, I would he would; for so should he soon send me to my heavenly Father, to whom I now live, and to whom I desire to hasten, πρὸς ὅν ἐπείγομαι πόρρωθεν. (Basil.) This made Velcurio, a Dutch divine, when he lay upon his death-bed, break out into these sweet words (Joh. Manli. *loc. com.*), *Pater est Amator, Filius Redemptor, Spiritus Sanctus Consolator; quomodo itaque tristitiâ affici possim?* The Father loves me, the Son redeemed me, the Holy Ghost comforts me; how then can I be cast down at the approach of death? And the like triumphant words were uttered to me by my late reverend good friend and father, Mr John Jackson, pastor of Binton, in Warwickshire, when he lay a-dying, and laid his last charge upon me, to preach Christ, who had swallowed up death in victory.

To the end he loved them] Such fast friends are hard to find. φίλος εὐμετάβλητον ζῶον, A friend is a very changeable creature, saith Plato; as soon on and as soon off again; as soon in and as soon out, as Joab's dagger was; clear at the top and muddy at the bottom, as ponds are; white at the waxing of the moon, and black at the waning of it, as the fish scolopidus in the river Araxis is said to be. Andronicus, the Greek emperor, whom but yesterday he had used most kindly, and enrolled among his best friends, upon them to-day he frowned and tyrannized most cruelly; so that you might have seen, saith the historian, the same man the same day (as is reported of Xerxes's admiral) to be crowned and beheaded, to be graced and disgraced. So of Tiberius and Mahomet, the first emperor of the Turks, it is said, that in their love there was no assurance; but their least displeasure was death. Christ, whom he loves once he loves ever, and though we break oft with him, yet he abides faithful, 2 Tim. ii. 13, and his foundation standeth steady, having this seal, "The Lord knoweth them that are his," ver. 19.

Ver. 2. *The devil having now put*] He is likely at one end of every temptation to sin; as the hand of Joab was in the tale of the woman of Tekoah. He rubs the fire-brand of evil concupiscence, and makes it send out sparkles.

Ver. 3. *Jesus knowing, &c.*] This is prefaced to the washing of his disciples' feet, to show that he did it not rashly, or out of baseness of spirit, as forgetting the dignity of his person and place, as Ahaz did, 2 Kings xvi. 7, and those, Isa. lvii. 9, and David also in the court of Achish. There is a τὸ πρέπον, a comeliness to be kept in every condition.

Ver. 4. *He riseth from supper*] So the rite of the Paschal supper required; as Beza showeth in his annotations upon Matt. xxvi. 20.

Ver. 5. *After that he poureth water, &c.*] So doth the pope once a year in an apish imitation of our Saviour. As likewise, when he is new elected, in his solemn Lateran procession, he takes copper out of his chamberlain's lap, and scatters it among the people, and (lie and all) saith, "Silver and gold have I none." (Dr Hall on Matt. v. 20.)

Ver. 6. *Then cometh he to Peter*] He came first to him (for the former verse sets forth his intent rather than his act of washing). And yet St Chrysostom tells of some that would needs have it, that he began with Judas. Like as the Papists say that our Saviour appeared first, after his resurrection, to the Virgin Mary; though the text be plain that he first showed himself to Mary Magdalene. These are like him in Aristotle, that thought that everywhere he saw his own shape and picture going before him.

Ver. 7. *But thou shalt know hereafter*] Different degrees of knowledge are bestowed at several times. Our hearts are like narrow-mouthed vessels; but then shall we know if we follow on to know the Lord, Hos. vi. 3, and take heed that we leak not, Heb. ii. 1.

Ver. 8. *Thou shalt never wash my feet*] This was an immoderate modesty, a proud humility; so is it in them that refuse gospel comforts, because they are unworthy, *Domine, non sum dignus, at sum indigens*, said Pomeran. *Tibi adest nimia humilitas*, Thou hast too much humility, said Luther to Staupicius. So the Baptist was as much to blame in refusing to wash Christ (Matt. iii. 14) as Peter here to be washed by him. Luther said of Melancthon's self-denying humility, *Soli Deo omnia deberi tam obstinate asserit, ut mihi plane videatur in hoc*

saltem errare, quod Christum ipse fingat longius abesse cordi suo quam sit revera: Certe nimis nullus in hoc est Philippus. Philip is worse conceited of himself than is fit.

Ver. 9. *Lord, not my feet only*] Here he seems to be as far out on the other side. How hard is it to hold a mean. *Medio tutissimus ibis.* (Ovid.) Virtue is placed between two extremes, as the planet Jupiter between cold Saturn and fiery Mars.

Ver. 10. *Needeth not, save to wash his feet*] For though bathed in that blessed fountain, Zech. xiii. 1, and fully justified, yea, and freed from the stain and reign of sin, yet not from the relics, to keep us humble; that when we look upon our feathers, we may withal look upon the feet still defiled, and so be still cleansing ourselves "from all filthiness of flesh and spirit," 2 Cor. vii. 1. The inwards and the feet in a sacrifice were to be washed above the rest; because the entrails contain the excrements; and the legs, because they tread in the dirt. Answerable whereunto, we are called upon to wash our hearts, Jer. iv. 14, and our feet, here. The comparison seems to be taken from those that are washed in baths; for though their whole bodies besides are washed; yet going forth, they touch the earth with their feet, and so are fain to wash again.

Ver. 11. *He knew who should betray him*] And yet he vouchsafed to wash his feet. This was *stupenda dignatio*, a wonderful condescension, an unparalleled patience.

Ver. 12. *Know ye what I have done to you?*] This was our Saviour's usual order, to catechise his disciples after he had said or done anything for their instruction. So did the apostles, Gal. vi. 6, 1 Cor. xiv. 19, and the primitive pastors; they had their *Credis? credo: Abrenuncias? abrenuncio*, as it were by an echo, as the word importeth. (Κατηχέω, *Sicut in eccho una vox his audiri debet, tam ex catechumeno, quam ex ipso catechista.* Pasor.)

Ver. 13. *Ye call me Master and Lord*] A little before our Saviour came in the flesh, the Jewish doctors had taken up divers titles in this order; Rabbi, Rabban, Rab, Rabba, Gaon, Moreh, Morenu, and Morehtsedeck. These they did arrogantly appropriate to themselves; but Christ was the true owner of them all.

Ver. 14. *Ye ought also to wash one another's feet*] What so great matter is it then to salute others, to seek reconciliation with them, &c.? Angels think not themselves too good to serve the saints; kings and queens shall bow down to them with their faces toward the earth, and lick up the dust of their feet, Isa. xlix. 23.

Ver. 15. *For I have given you an example*] ὑπόδειγμα. This St Peter calls ὑπόγραμμον, a copy for us to write after, 1 Pet. ii. 21. And in the same chapter saith that we should preach forth Christ's virtues, ἐξαγγείλητε, ver. 9; our lives should be as so many sermons upon Christ's life, whilst we strive to express him to the world in all his imitable graces. This is to walk in Christ,

Col. ii. 6, to walk as Christ walked, 1 John ii. 6. The meditation of Christ's meekness converted the eunuch, Acts viii. 32, 33, &c. And we read of an earl, called Eleazarus, that being given to immoderate anger, was cured of that disordered affection by studying of Christ, and of his patience. This meditation he never suffered to pass from him, before he found his heart transformed into the similitude of Jesus Christ. *Crux pendentis, cathedra docentis.* (*In vita ejus apud* Surentius.)

Ver. 16. *The servant is not greater, &c.*] This answers all our exceptions against brotherly offices: I am his elder, better, greater than he, &c. But which of us can say, I am a god? Christ washed his disciples' feet, though he knew that the Father had given all things into his hands, &c., as is expressly and for this very purpose noted here by the evangelist, ver. 3.

Ver. 17. *If ye know these things, &c.*] Knowledge without practice is but as rain in the middle region; or as a horn in the unicorn's head, which if it were in a wise man's hand, would be very useful and medicinable, but as now is hurtful.

Ver. 18. *I know whom I have chosen*] Judas he had not chosen, but to the apostleship only. All this Judas hears, and is not moved at it; such a stupifying sin is hypocrisy. The Germans have a proverb, *Quem Deus excæcaturus est, huic primum oculos claudit.* (Bucholcer.) And the Latins say, *Deus quem destruit, dementat,* God besots the man whom he means to destroy.

Ver. 19. *Ye may believe that I am he*] And that ye may not stumble or stagger, though ye see Judas play the traitor, 2 Tim. ii. 18, 19. The apostasy of Hymenæus and Philetus, a pair of eminent professors, was like to have shaken many; insomuch as the apostle was fain to make apology: "Nevertheless, the foundation of God remaineth sure," &c.

Ver. 20. *Verily, verily I say, &c.*] Here our Saviour seems to go on where he left, ver. 17, that between being a digression. Digressions, saith one, are not always and absolutely unlawful. (Bifield on the Coloss.) God's Spirit sometimes draws aside the doctrine to satisfy some soul, which the preacher knows not; and sparingly used, it quickeneth the attention. But God may force it, yet man may not frame it; and it is a most happy ability to speak punctually, directly to the point.

Ver. 21. *He was troubled in spirit*] The Stoics then were out, in holding that passions befall not a wise man; and Jesuited Gonzaga was not so much to be magnified, who would not permit any man to love him;[1] and when his father died, all the grief he took was no more than this; Now, said he, there is nothing hindereth me to say, "Our Father which art in heaven." Christ was thoroughly troubled here, that

any one so highly advanced by him (as in the former verse, "he that receiveth whomsoever I send, receiveth me," &c.) should be so ill-minded towards him as to betray him. *Ideo deteriores sumus, quia meliores esse debemus,* saith Salvian. We are therefore the worse, because we should be better. It was no small aggravation to Solomon's sin that he forsook that God that had appeared unto him twice, 1 Kings xi. 9. Our offences are increased by our obligations.

Ver. 22. *Looked one upon another doubting, &c.*] Our Saviour sifted them; and hereby put them upon the duty of self-examination; ever seasonable, but especially before the sacrament, as here, Let a man examine himself (and do it exactly, as the word signifies, δοκιμαζέτω, 2 Cor. xi. 28), though the heart hang off never so much. Men are as loth to review their actions and read the blurred writing of their hearts, as schoolboys are to parse their lessons and false Latins they have made. But this must be done, or they are undone for ever. And sparing a little pains at first, doubles it in the end; as he who will not cast up his books, his books will cast him up at length.

Ver. 23. *Now there was leaning on Jesus' bosom*] So must we do at the sacrament, by the actuation of our faith, ascending up into heaven, and fetching down Christ into the heart, that we may have intimate and entire communion with him.[2] By the force of our faith at the Lord's table, *cruci hæremus, sanguinem fugimus, et intra ipsa redemptoris nostri vulnera figimus linguam,* saith St Cyprian (de Cœna Dom.).

Ver. 24. *Simon Peter therefore beckoned*] Peter, that heretofore could not think his heart so unsound as to deny his Master, now feareth the ugly monster of fearless betraying. In man's heart, as in the sea, there is that Leviathan, therefore also creeping things innumerable, Psal. civ. 26.

Ver. 25. *He then lying on Jesus' breast*] *Ad pectus allapsus,* as laying his ear to our Saviour's mouth, that he might whisper him who it was;[3] for things were as yet secretly carried, and the traitor not discovered, save to John only, who knew Christ's soul-secrets, and afterward received his revelation.

Ver. 26. *He it is to whom I shall, &c.*] Here our Saviour not only feeds his hungry enemy, but shows him like courtesy as we do to one we drink to at table; yea, though he knew the traitor would make an ill use of it. Thus should a Christian punish his persecutors. No vengeance but this is heroical, and fit for Christ's followers. Thus Bradford saved Bourn, that helped to burn him. Saunders, sent to prison by Stephen Gardiner, gave God thanks that had given him at last a place of rest and quietness where he might pray for the bishop's conversion. It was grown to a proverb concerning Cranmer, Do my Lord of Canterbury a shrewd turn, and

---

[1] *Cæterum* στωιχότερος *videtur vester Gonzaga, &c.* Dr Prideaux contra Eudemon.

[2] *Calceis exuti, et pulvinis innixi, in lectulis semisupini ja-*

cebant. Calvin. in loc.

[3] *In accubitu mos ille ut accumberent uxores in sinu virorum.* Lips. ad Tacit. xi.

then you may be sure to have him your friend while he liveth. Henry VII., emperor of Germany, feeling himself poisoned in the sacramental bread by a monk, called him, and said unto him, *Domine, recedatis, &c.*, Begone, sir, for if my followers find you, you will die for it.[1]

Ver. 27. *Satan entered into him*] Gat more full possession of him. Let them that depart the public assemblies ere all be done, as Judas did, take heed they meet not the devil at the door. The fourth Council of Carthage excommunicated such, and so delivered them up to Satan, which is a grievous punishment; for then they lie open to all wickedness, as Ananias, whose heart Satan had filled from corner to corner. Luther when he had read certain letters sent to him from Vitus Theodorus, fetched a deep sigh, and said, *Heu quam furit Satan, et impellit securos homines ad horrenda flagitia, quæ corpus et animum perdunt!* Oh how the devil rageth and driveth on secure persons to horrible and damnable wickedness! That which moved Luther to say so, was a sad relation made in that letter, of a certain widow, who being with child by a young scholar, could not have her child baptized unless she would tell the priest who was the child's father; whereat she being grievously vexed, first killed her child and then hanged herself. Which when the scholar heard of, he likewise stabbed himself to death. The priest understanding what tragedies had followed upon his refusing to baptize the child, hanged himself also. Now, who can doubt but all this was done by the instigation of the devil? Men usually defy him and spit at his name; but they spit not low enough, they spit him out of their mouths, but not out of their hearts; there he plays *Rex*, and so long cares no more for their cursing of him than he doth for holy water.

That thou doest, do quickly] This is no command, but a prediction by way of detestation; like as when God said to Balaam, Go, for I know thou wilt go after the wages of wickedness. Some note here that, even to Judas, Christ saith, "That thou doest, do quickly," so odious is dulness unto him. (Ward's Serm.)

Ver. 28. *Now no man at the table knew, &c.*] For John had not told Peter the secret committed to him by Christ, though he were very desirous to have known it;

Si sapis, arcano vina reconde cado.

A friend that can both keep counsel and give counsel, is worth his weight in gold. When one desired to see Alexander's treasure, he bade one of his servants show him, not his talents of silver, but his trusty friends, οὐκ ἀργυρίου τάλαντα, ἀλλὰ τοὺς φίλους.

Ver. 29. *For some of them thought*] An example of Christian simplicity. As bad men muse as they use, so good men measure others by themselves; and so are often deceived, as here. " Charity thinketh no evil," 1 Cor. xiii. 5.

Or that he should give something to the poor]

Christ had not much, yet had somewhat for the poor; so must the poor day-labourer, Eph. iv. 28, the necessitous widow, Mark xii. 42.

Ver. 30. *He then having received the sop*] So many having received the Supper of the Lord, eat their bane and drink their poison; that they eat is sauced, and that they drink is spiced, with the bitter wrath of God, their hearts are woefully hardened, and their dispositions to sin seven times more inflamed than ever before.

Ver. 31. *Therefore when he was gone out*] The room being rid of the traitor, Christ deals more freely and familiarly with the rest, and arming them against the scandal of the cross, he calls his death his glory, esteems his crown of thorns more precious than Solomon's diadem; looks upon his wales as spangles, his blows on the face as ingots, his wounds as gems, his spittings on as sweet ointment, his cross as his throne. This is a paradox to flesh and blood; Jews and Gentiles jeer at it; as Lucian the atheist, who rails upon Christ blasphemously, calling him the crucified impostor; ἀνασκολοπισμένον σοφιστήν. (Luc. in Vita Peregr.) And as for Christians, they foolishly believe, saith he, that they shall enjoy immortality and live in bliss for ever; therefore they set light by life, yea, many of them offer themselves voluntarily to be slain for their superstition. *Persuaserunt sibi infælices se immortalitate fruituros.* Thus he. And another heathen proconsul, Actius Antoninus, *in Asia cum persequeretur Christianos* (Tertul.), when he had tired himself with killing Christians, and saw no end of it, but that they came thicker upon him crying out, "We are Christians," &c., he cursed them, and cried out, *O miseri, si libet perire, num vobis rupes aut restes desunt?* O wretches, can you find no other way to die, but I must be troubled with you?

Ver. 32. *And shall straightway*] Thus for the "joy that was set before him, he endured the cross, despising the shame, as being shortly to sit down at the right hand of the throne of God," Heb. xii. 2. Look we on him, and do likewise. There were in Greece certain fields called Palæstræ, where young men exercised themselves in wrestling. In these were set up statues of some valiant champions, that the young wrestlers might fix their eyes upon them, and so be encouraged. Can we choose a better champion than Christ to eye and imitate, should we be called to resist unto blood, striving against sin? He did not only *sanguinem suffundere, sed effundere.* And how did he support himself under the cross, but by the fore-thought of the crown?

Ver. 33. *Little children, yet a little while*] Here our Saviour useth the self-same words to his apostles, which before he had used to the Jews, with whom he was angry; so to cut off all hope from them of his corporeal presence. The fiction of the ubiquity began about the time of Berengarius; was fostered and furthered by Gerson, Chancellor of Paris, who first taught *et nostri devoti, morte moriemini.* Func.

[1] *Domine, recedatis; nam si percipiunt Teutonici,*

the real communication of properties, by means whereof the human nature of Christ received this prerogative, said he, that at his supper (and then only) it might be in many places at once, wheresoever the supper was celebrated. But in the year of Christ 1524 Jacobus Faber Staupulensis taught at Paris, that by the same reason Christ might be as well corporally present in all places at once, as he was at the supper. For which doctrine of the ubiquity he was opposed the year following by one Natalis Beda, and by the Sorbonists banished out of France. This is the nativity of that famous ubiquity, which being cast out of France, Luther brought back into the Churches of Germany; Brentius furbished it over, and Smidelinus obtruded it upon many places and persons, whether they would or no; whence he is surnamed, *Ubiquitatis Apostolus.* How much better that good woman in the Book of Martyrs, that being asked by the bishops, "Dost thou believe that the body of Christ is in the sacrament really and substantially?" "I believe," said she, "that that is a real lie, and a substantial lie." Domitius Calderinus, the Italian, who flourished in the year 1442, when he was called by his friends to go to mass, was wont to say (as Vives tells us), *Eamus ad communem errorem.*

Ver. 34. *A new commandment, &c.*] New, *ratione claritatis et facilitatis;* for now there is abundance of spirit given by Christ, who writes this affection in our hearts, as of old the law was written in stone. Besides that, he is become a new pattern and example of the rule; and so it is become a new commandment, not in respect of the matter of the duty, but of the form of observing it. For the old rule was, "Thou shalt love thy neighbour as thyself." But now that form ("as I have loved you") hath something in it that is more express; and, for the incomparable sufficiency of the precedent, is matchless, and more full of incitation to fire affection; there being far more incentives and motives to love, since Christ came and gave himself for us. And this is appointed here, for the disciples' and our solace in the want of Christ's bodily presence, as loving fellow-members to strive by all means to delight in the loving society one of another.

Ver. 35. *By this shall all men know*] Other men's disciples are known by their titles, habits, ceremonies, &c., as the pope's shavelings (which yet is grown so bald a business, that now they begin to be ashamed of it); but love is Christ's cognizance, acknowledged by very heathens, who could say, that no people in the world did love one another so as Christians did. *Vide ut invicem se ament Christiani! dixerunt Pagani, referente.* (Tertulliano in Apologet.) As the curtains of the tabernacle were joined by loops, so are true Christians by love. Philadelphia is blamed for nothing, Rev. iii. 18.

Ver. 36. *Whither goest thou?*] That deep conceit he had drunk in of an earthly kingdom, so hung in his light, that he could not see whither

Christ was ascending. A little saucer held close to the eyes hinders the sight of a huge hill.

But thou shalt follow me] Perhaps in the same kind of death; but to heaven, most certainly.

Ver. 37. *I will lay down, &c.*] Peter was *melius semper animatus quam armatus*, better affected than appointed. His heart deceived him, as did David's, Psal. xxxix. 1, 2. He said he would look to his ways, bridle his tongue, &c. But soon after he brake his word, "My heart was hot within me." *Petrus se Christo opposuit, se cæteris præposuit, sibi totum imposuit.* Chrysost.

Ver. 48. *The cock shall not crow*] Christ mentioneth the cock, *quia tam strenuum pugnatorem decebat tale præconium.* So, Rev. vi. 13, pastors revolt, as green figs fall off, with no ado. In the Palatinate they fell to Popery as fast as leaves fall in autumn.

CHAPTER XIV.

Ver. 1. *Let not your heart, &c.*] OUR Saviour sweetly proceeds in his swan-like song. Ælian tells us that he once heard a dying swan sing most heavenly and harmoniously, εὐφωνότατον καὶ ᾠδικώτατον. (Hist. Var. lib. i.) The poet shows the manner of it, when he saith

—longa canoros
Dat per colla modos—

Of the Syrens (on the contrary) it is reported that how sweetly soever they sang before, yet at death they make a horrid noise and unpleasant roaring. *Mortis articulo instante, et sanguine male affecto valde horride mugiunt Sirenes.* Semblably, good men utter their best usually at last, the wine of the spirit being then strongest and liveliest in them. Whereas wicked men are then usually at worst, and go out with a stench, as the devil is said to do. And as Melancthon said of Eccius's last wicked work, written of priests' marriage, *Non fuit cygnea cantio, sed ultimus crepitus: et sicut felis fugiens pedit, sic ille moriens hunc crepitum cecinit.* (Melch. Adam. in Vit. Calv.) So of Baldwin the apostate, one saith that *vivere simul et maledicere desiit*, he died cursing, as that wretch did swearing, who desperately also desired the standers-by to help him with oaths and to swear for him.

Ver. 2. *I would have told you*] And not have fed you with false hopes of an Utopian happiness, as the devil deals by his, whom he brings into a fool's paradise; as Mahomet by his, to whom he promises in paradise delicious fare, pleasant gardens, and other sensual delights eternally to be enjoyed, &c. Christ is no such impostor.

Ver. 3. *I will come again, &c.*] Oh look up and long for this "consolation of Israel;" say as Sisera's mother, "Why are his chariots" (those clouds) "so long in coming?"

Heu pietas ubi prisca? profana o tempora! Mundi Fax! Vesper! prope Nox! o mora! Christe veni.

There may ye be also] Christ counts not himself full till he have all his members about him: hence the Church is called "the fulness of him that filleth all things," Eph. i. 23.

Ver. 4. *And whither I go ye know*] Some little knowledge they had, such as Thomas in the next verse denies to be any at all; yet Christ acknowledgeth it. The tenor of the new covenant requires no set measures of grace. The first springings in the womb of grace are precious before God, Eph. ii. 1; he blesseth our buds, Isa. lxi. 11, and in our dunghill of ignorance can find out his own part of knowledge, as here.

Ver. 5. *Lord, we know not whither thou goest, &c.*] No, Thomas? what, are ye also ignorant? They knew, but knew not that they knew: their knowledge was yet but confused and indistinct; they saw men, but as it were walking like trees, till their eyes were better anointed with the eye-salve of the Spirit. A man (saith Gataker) may have grace, and yet yet know it not (as the embryo hath life, and yet knoweth it not), yea, he may think he hath it not, as we seek for keys that are in our pockets; or think we have lost a jewel, that we locked up in our chest: yea, as the butcher looketh for the candle that sticketh in his hat, by the light of that he seeketh.

Ver. 6. *I am the way, and the truth, &c.*] As if he should say, Thou hast no whither to go but to me, nor which way to go but by me, that thou mayest attain eternal life. Which made Bernard say, *Sequemur, Domine, te, per te, ad te: Te quia Veritas, per te quia Via, ad te quia Vita.* And this was one of those sweet sayings that old Beza had much in his mouth a little before his death. (Melch. Adam. in Vitis exter.)

No man cometh unto the Father, but by me] Christ hath paved us a new and living way to God, with his own meritorious blood: and his flesh stands as a screen betwixt us and those everlasting burnings, Isa. xxxiii. 14. Let Papists say of their saints, *Per hunc itur ad Deum, sed magis per hunc.* Let us say of all their he and she saints, as that heathen, *Contemno minutos istos Deos, modo Jovem (Jesum) propitium habeam.*

Ver. 7. *And from henceforth ye know him*] Or else the more shame for you, having had me (his express image) so long amongst you. Christians have a privilege above the Church of the Old Testament. The sea about the altar was brazen, 1 Kings vii. 23, and what eyes could pierce through it? Now, our sea about the throne is glassy, Rev. iv. 6, like the crystal, clearly conveying the light and sight of God in Christ to our eyes.

Ver. 8. *Lord, show us the Father*] They would have seen the Father face to face with their bodily eyes, as they saw the Son. But that no man can do and live, Exod. xxxiii. We cannot see the sun *in rota,* as the schools speak, in the circle wherein it runs, but only in the beams. So

neither can we see God in his essence; in his Son we may, who is the resplendency of his Father's glory, ἀπαύγασμα, Heb. i. 3.

Ver. 9. *Have I been so long, &c.*] May not Christ justly shame and shent us all for knowing no more of him all this while? Ignorance under means of knowledge is a blushful sin, 1 Cor. xv. 34.

Ver. 10. *The words that I speak*] Our Saviour allegeth for himself the Divinity both of his word and works. He was mighty, saith Peter, both in word and deed. Ministers also must, in their measure, be able to argue and approve themselves to be men of God, by sound doctrine and good life. And not be, as our Saviour saith the Pharisees were, and as Epictetus saith many philosophers were such, ἄνευ τοῦ πράττειν, μέχρι τοῦ λέγειν, that is, as far as a few words would go.

Ver. 11. *Believe me that I am, &c.*] Take my bare word without any further pawn or proof. This is an honour due to Christ only, that he is αὐτόπιστος, He is Amen, "the faithful and true witness," Rev. iii. 14.

Ver. 12. *And greater works than these*] Greater in regard of the matter, as converting 3000 souls at a sermon, reducing a great part of the world to the obedience of Christ, &c. But yet less than those Christ did, for the manner. For, 1. They did not them in their own name, but in his. 2. They preached not that they were gods, as he, but they preached Christ the only Lord, and themselves the Church's servants, for Jesus' sake. They were the white horses on which Christ rode abroad the world, "conquering and to conquer," Rev. vi. 2. In memory whereof, as it may seem, the Saxon princes, having borne a black horse till then in their military ensigns, did, after they had received the faith and were baptized, bear a white horse, and gave it for their arms. And Tertullian could say in his time, that *Britannorum inaccessa Romanis loca, Christo tamen subdita.*

Ver. 13. *That I will do*] An undoubted argument of Christ's Divinity, that he hears and grants prayers. When the people, in Ahab's time, saw God answering Elijah by fire from heaven, they cried out, "The Lord he is God, the Lord he is God," 1 Kings xviii. 39. "O thou that hearest prayers" is a description the Psalmist gives of God, Psal. lxv. 2.

Ver. 14. *If ye shall ask anything, &c.* This is not a vain repetition. *Nunquam satis dicitur, quod nunquam satis discitur.* (Seneca.) When God spake but once, David heard it twice. Oh that we would once hear and believe, what Christ for our comfort hath said over so often!

Ver. 15. *If ye love me, keep my commandments*] No better way to seal up love than by being obedient. "How canst thou love me," said she, "when thy heart is not with me?" Judg. xvi. 15. Hushai, to show his love to David, set upon that difficult and dangerous service for him, of insinuating into Absalom's counsels, and defeating them.

Ver. 16. *And he shall give you another Comforter*] Or, pleader, deprecator, advocate, παράκλητον. Properly it signifies such an one as we send for, when we are in any danger, to advise and counsel us. The devil is called the accuser, Κατήγορος, in full opposition to this name and title given here to the Holy Spirit; whose office it is (as this attribute here imports) to make intercession in our hearts to God for us; and upon our true repentance to make our apology, 1 Cor. vii. 11; to comfort us, by discovering our graces, 1 Cor. ii. 12, and by pleading our evidences, Rom. viii. 18, which they that refuse to read over and rest upon, they help Satan, the accuser, taking his part against themselves, and pleading his cause against the Spirit their Comforter.

That he may abide with you for ever] The Spirit (saith Dr Sibbs) is Christ's vicar-general, with whom he leaves us, and by whom he is with us to the end of the world.

Ver. 17. *For he dwelleth with you*] Next to the love of Christ in dwelling in our nature, we may wonder at the love of the Holy Ghost, that will dwell in the dark dog-hole of our defiled souls; and be there as those two golden pipes, Zech. iv., through which the two olive branches empty out of themselves the golden oils of all precious graces; which are, therehence, called "the fruits of the Spirit," Gal. v. 22, "yea, the Spirit," ver. 17. God also in giving us his Spirit, is said to give us all good things, Matt. vii. 11, with Luke xi. 13.

Ver. 18. *I will not leave you comfortless*] Orphans, or darkling, ὀρφάνους ab ὄρφνη, *tenebræ.* I your Lord am taken indeed from your head for a while, but you shall have the supply of my Spirit, Phil. i. 19. And I, even I, will come again to you ere long; yea, I am now upon the way; I come to fetch you, I come to meet you, I come, I come, ἔρχομαι, *Dedit me in viam.*

Ver. 19. *But ye see me*] The spiritual man hath "the mind of Christ," 1 Cor. ii. 16, and those things revealed unto him that natural eye never saw, carnal ear never heard, neither hath it entered into the heart of man the things which God hath prepared for them that love him; neither prepared only, but imparted to his aforehand, even in this life. For he reserves not all for the life to come, but gives a grape of Canaan in this wilderness, such as the world never tasted of.

Ver. 20. *That I am in my Father and you in me*] Oh happy union, the ground of communion! interest! the ground of influence! Hence we have communication of Christ's secrets, 1 Cor. ii. 6; the testimony of Jesus, 1 Cor. i. 5; consolation in all afflictions, 2 Cor. i. 5; sanctification of all occurrences, Phil. i. 21; participation of Christ's merit and Spirit, and what not?

Ver. 21. *And I will love him, and manifest, &c.*] Increase of the saving knowledge of Christ is promised as a singular reward of our love to him and fruit of his love to us, ἐμφανίσω, *tacite et clam indicabo.* (Eras.) *Imo palam et in media*

luce. Beza. This is, saith Agur, "to ascend into heaven," Prov. xxx. 3, 4. This is, saith our Saviour elsewhere, the great talent of all others. There is a "much" in it, Luke xii. 48. This is, saith St Paul, the Christian's riches, 1 Cor. i. 5; and David reckons of his wealth by it, Psal. cxix. 32.

Ver. 22. *How is it that thou wilt manifest, &c.*] Many a wise question the disciples ask him in this chapter; and yet our Saviour bears with their rudeness, and gently instructs them, preaching as they were able to hear, Mark iv. 33. So did Paul, 1 Cor. ix. 22. So must all ministers, 2 Tim. ii. 25, if they mean to do good on it.

Ver. 23. *Jesus answered and said unto him*] Our Saviour, passing by that frivolous question, proceedeth in his discourse. Some follies are best confuted by silence. One having made a long and idle discourse before Aristotle, concluded it thus: I doubt I have been too tedious unto you, Sir Philosopher, with my many words. In good sooth, said Aristotle, you have not been tedious to me, for I gave no heed to anything you said. (Plutarch, de Garrulitate.)

Ver. 24. *But the Father's*] Therefore to be obeyed, because of divine authority. God's impress makes authentic, and binds every good heart to obedience. *Veniat, veniat verbum Domini, et submittemus ei, sexcenta si nobis essent colla,* said Baldassar, a godly Dutch divine (in Epist. ad Œcolamp.).

Ver. 25. *These things have I spoken unto you*] And truly I may seem to have spoken to small purpose (*verba quid incassum non proficientia perdo ?*) by anything that you have yet profited. But cast not away your confidence that hath so great recompense of reward. For the Comforter shall be your remembrancer, and cause your memories (as the sea doth) to cast up your dead notions, &c., as ver. 26.

Ver. 26. *But the Comforter, &c.*] The Spirit teacheth only things consonant to Scripture, and is thereby discerned from a spirit of delusion. He is not *novarum revelationum architectus,* as Papists, Mahometans, Anabaptists, and Libertines would make him. The Jews also had many traditions and unwritten verities (as they called them) wherewith they believed their scribes and doctors were inspired, for the people's better direction in observing the law. These they called *Mashlamnuthoth, Completiones, Perfectiones,* because they thought that the written law was perfected and completed by them. (Buxtorff.) These were those our Saviour cried down, Matt. xv. 3. And the prophet tells us, that in vain shall we look to hear the voice behind us, where our "eyes see not our teachers," Isa. xxx. 20, 21.

Ver. 27. *Peace I leave with you*] As a farewell or legacy; *Sacrosancta εἰρήνη nobis committitur, non ἔρυννις, aut ἔρις*: Christ is the Prince of Peace, yea, he is our peace, saith the apostle, and brings true peace, which is a piece of his kingdom, Rom. xiv. 17. Of him it may be more truly said than it was of our Henry VII., that he came in, *Ut cum pacem exulantem exul, extorremque extorris concomitatus esset, reducem quoque redux apportaret.* (Twinus Comment. de rebus Britann.)

Not as the world, &c.] They cry peace when there is no peace, and make fair weather when such a storm of God's wrath is ready to burst out as shall never be blown over. They complement, and wish peace, when war is in their hearts: as the pope sent away Henry III., emperor, in peace, but it was, saith the historian, *Qualem scilicet pacem Judas simulavit, non qualem Christus reliquit*, i. e. such as Judas, counterfeit, not such as Jesus left his people. (Auth. Apolog. de unit. Eccles.)

Ver. 28. *My Father is greater than I*] To wit, as I have voluntarily submitted myself to the office of a mediator. Lo, here this Sun of righteousness is gone back ten degrees in the dial below his Father. "Thou hast made him little less than the angels," Psal. viii. 5; there (as man) he is gone back ten degrees below the angels. "I am a worm and no man," Psal. xxii. 6; there he is gone back ten degrees below men. "A living dog is better than a dead lion," Eccles. ix. 4; there he is gone back ten degrees below worms. For he was not so much as a living worm, but was laid in the grave as a dead lion, there to have been meat for worms, but that it was impossible for God's Holy One to see corruption. See how he emptied and humbled himself, ἐκένωσεν, that he might exalt and fill us with his fulness, ἱκάνωσεν.

Ver. 29. *And now I have told you before*] Which none beside God himself could do, but by divine revelation. The knowledge of future contingents is of God only, and of such as to whom he is pleased to communicate it; as he did to the prophets, who when they foretold things only as in their causes, they might fall out or not, as Isa. xxxviii. 1; Jonah iii. 4; and 1 Kings xxi. 20; but when they foretold things *ut futura in seipsis*, then they fell out infallibly. The devil also may come acquainted with such things, and be able to foretell them, if God reveal them to him, as he did Ahab's death; and as Trithemius the abbot and Cusanus the cardinal foretold a change of religion to fall out in the year 1517, which was the year wherein Luther began to stickle for Christ against the pope.[1]

Ver. 30. *Hereafter I will not, &c.*] Make we the best of our Christian friends while we have them; as we would do of a borrowed book or tool, that we know not how soon they may be sent for by the right owner.

The prince of this world cometh] In his limbs and instruments, those breathing devils that put Christ to death. Persecutors are set a-work by Satan; "the devil shall cast some of you into prison," Rev. ii. 10. Why? Is he become a justice of peace, to send men to prison? Yes, by his agents. But why would Christ be

so used by him and his? Hear the next words.

Ver. 31. *But that the world may know*] Not you only, but all must take notice of my ready obedience to the will of my heavenly Father, even to the suffering of death. Christ's passion must shine as a perpetual picture in our hearts; therefore it is so accurately described by all the four evangelists, whereas his birth is recorded but by two of them only.

CHAPTER XV.

Ver. 1. *I am the true vine, &c.*] OUR Saviour's way lying (as it is thought) by the vineyards, he takes that occasion of comparing himself to a vine, as he doth elsewhere to many other creatures, everywhere obvious; that therein, as in so many optic glasses, we may see him, and be put in mind of him. *Tam Christi meminisse opus est, quam respirare*, saith a Father. A bee can suck honey out of a flower that a fly cannot. Fire will be aspiring; so will true grace.

Ver. 2. *Every branch in me*] That thinks himself to be in me, and is so thought to be by others, but proves not to be so. These are said to "deny the Lord that bought them, to trample on the blood of the covenant, wherewith they were sanctified, to wallow in the mire from which they had been washed," 2 Pet. ii. 1, 22; Heb. x. 20. So here, to be branches in Christ, and yet unfruitful. Not that they ever were in Christ, but seemed to be so; as a pole fixed in the earth, but not rooted; as a rotten leg cleaves to the body, but is no part of it; or, as wens and ulcers, which are taken away without loss to it.

He purgeth it] Αἴρει, καθαίρει, *Amputat, putat.* Of all possessions, saith Cato, none requires more pains about it than that of vineyards. Corn comes up and grows without the husbandman's care, Mark iv. 27, he knows not how. But vines must be dressed, supported, sheltered, pruned every day almost; lopped they must be ever and anon, lest the juice be spent in leaves. And if it be painful to bleed, it is worse to wither. Better be pruned to grow than cut up to burn.

Ver. 3. *Through the word, &c.*] Which is the pruning knife, to lop off our luxuriances, rotten boughs, raw grapes, to pare off our gum of pride, moss of formality, *Vinitoris cultellus ad sordes purgandas.* (Col.) The word hid in the heart keeps from sin, as an amulet, Psal. cxix. 11, and keeps youth from uncleanness, ver. 9; mixt with faith, it purgeth upon corruption, Acts xv. 9, and will not suffer men to rest in sin.

Ver. 4. *As the branch cannot bear fruit, &c.*] All our sap and safety is from Christ. The bud of a good desire, the blossom of a good resolution, and the fruit of a good action, all come from him, *Gratia prævenit nos ut velimus, et subsequitur ne frustra velimus.* (Augustine.)

---

[1] Cusanus *obiit*, A. D. 1464. Trithem. *scripsit an.* 1508. *Genius vero qui Trithemio hæc dictavit, albus an ater*

fuerit, ego non facile dixerim. Bucholcer.

Ver. 5. *The same bringeth forth much fruit*] Christ is a generous vine, a plant of renown; and all his are "filled with the fruits of righteousness," Phil. i. 11, have hearts full of goodness, as those Rom. xv. 14, and lives full of good works, as Tabitha, Acts ix. 33. *In Bucholcero vivida omnia fuerunt; vivida vox, vividi oculi, vividæ manus, gestus omnes vividi.* (Melch. Ad. in Vita.) Nehemiah never rested doing good for his people; he was good all over. Like the Egyptian fig-tree, that bears fruit seven times a year, or the lemon-tree, which ever and anon sendeth forth new lemons, as soon as the former are fallen off; or the plain of Campania, now called *Terra de lavoro*, which is extolled for the most fruitful plat of earth that is in the universe.

For without me ye can do nothing] This is point blank against the doctrine of free-will. *Sub laudibus naturæ latent inimici gratiæ*, saith Augustine. These will needs hammer out their own happiness, like the spider, climbing by a thread of her own weaving, with motto accordingly, *Mihi soli debeo*. Whereas the apostle demandeth, Who made thee to differ? Grevinchovius the Arminian boldly answers, *Ego meipsum discerno*, I make myself to differ. This he had learned from heathens belike: That we live, is from God; but that we live well, is from ourselves, saith Seneca. And this is the judgment of all men, saith Cicero, that prosperity is to be sought of God, but wisdom is to be taken up from ourselves. St Augustine was of another judgment, and saith, *Ciceronem, ut faceret homines liberos, fecisse sacrilegos. Quod vivamus deorum munus est; quod bene vivamus, nostrum. Judicium hoc omnium mortalium est*, &c. (Cic. de Nat. Deor.; Aug. C. D. 5.)

Ver. 6. *Cast them into the fire, and they are burned*] So they must needs be, may some say; but his meaning is, that temporaries, of all others, make the fiercest, hottest fire, because they are trees most seared and fuel fully dry. Nahum tells us that such are but as stubble laid out in the sun a-drying, that it may burn the better, chap. i. 10; or like grapes, let to hang in the sunshine till they be ripe for the wine-press of God's wrath, Rev. xv. 16.

Ver. 7. *Ask what ye will, and it*, &c.] Either in money or money's worth. If ye ask and miss it is because ye ask amiss. One was wont to say of Luther that he could have of God what he would; *Vir iste potuit quod voluit*. And being one time very earnest with God for the recovery of a godly useful man, he cried out, *Fiat voluntas mea*, Let my will be done; and then he falls off sweetly, My will, Lord, because thy will; *Mea voluntas, Domine, quia tua.*

Ver. 8. *Herein is my Father glorified*, &c.] There is not (saith one) so much of the glory of God in all his works of creation and providence as in one gracious action that a Christian performs; how much more in a life full of good fruits! This makes others say, Surely God is in them. *Vere magnus est Deus Christianorum*, said one Calocenius a heathen. God also ac-counts that he receives a new being, as it were, by those inward conceptions of his glory, and by those outward honours that we do to him, especially when we study God's ends more than our own, and drown all self-respects in his glory. Surely, they that do thus may have what they will (saith one), and God even think himself beholden to them.

Ver. 9. *Continue ye in my love*] In the love wherewith I do dearly love you. As who should say, Suffer yourselves to be loved by me. Lo, the Lord Christ even makes love to the good soul, and woos entertainment.

Ver. 10. *Even as I have kept my Father's*] Christ's obedience must be our pattern of imitation. All his actions were either moral or mediatory. In both we are to imitate him. In the former by doing as he did, Matt. xi. 29; 1 Pet. ii. 23. In the latter, by similitude, translating that to our spiritual life which he did as mediator; as to die to sin, to rise to righteousness.

Ver. 11. *These things have I spoken, that*, &c.] Sound joy is wrought in the heart by the hearing of the word; "Make me to hear joy and gladness, that the bones which thou hast broken" (with the sense of sin and fear of wrath) "may rejoice," Psal. li. 8. And God creates the fruit of the lips to be peace, Isa. xlv.

That my joy may remain in you] The temporary's joy, as it is groundless, like weeds that grow on the top of the water, so it is but frothy and flashy, such as may wet the mouth, but not warm the heart, smooth the brow, but not fill the breast: like a slight dash of rain, or a handful of brushwood, &c., Eccles. vii. 6. The true Christian's joy is full and firm, solid and substantial, *Gaudium in re, gaudium in spe, gaudium de possessione, gaudium de promissione.* He hath still enough to make him everlastingly merry under whatsoever misery. He can turn into his counting-house, and find there sufficient to sustain him, as David did, 1 Sam. xxx. 6.

Ver. 12. *This is my commandment*] Love is the complement of the law and the supplement of the gospel.

Ver. 13. *Greater love than this*, &c.] Of any such love, but in Christ, we shall hardly read. David in a passion may wish, "Would God I had died for thee;" but in cold blood I doubt whether he would have done it. A certain citizen of Toledo, being condemned to die, his son ceased not by prayers and tears to entreat that he might die for his father; which accordingly he did. (B. Fulg. i.) But this is rare, for life is sweet, and love is cold in this case. Every man is his own next neighbour.

Ver. 14. *If ye do whatsoever*, &c.] In desire and endeavour lifting at the latch, though ye cannot open the door, and looking to both the *magnalia* and *minutula* of the law; *Boni Catholici sunt* (saith Augustine) *qui et fidem integram sequuntur, et bonos mores.* And they are written in the book of life (saith Bernard) that do what they can, though they cannot do what they should. *Qui quod possunt, faciunt, etsi quod debent, non possunt.*

Ver. 15. *I call you not servants*] And yet it was the top of David's titles, to be the servant of the Lord; and the height of his ambition, to be a door-keeper in his house. All his servants are sons, and all his sons heirs.

But I have called you friends] It was a high honour of old to be the king's friend. Such honour have all his saints: Christ doth freely unbosom himself unto them.

Ver. 16. *And ordained you, that you should go, &c.*] Not that ye should lord it over your brethren (as the pope ordained his caterpillars), and get up the best of the land for your private use and pleasure. The pope, when he maketh his cardinals, useth these words, *Estote confratres nostri, et principes mundi.* The archbishopric of Toledo is said to be worth a hundred thousand pounds a year: a greater revenue than some kings have.

That whatsoever ye shall ask, &c.] Bernard in his Meditations giveth divers rules of strictness, of purging the heart, of being faithful and fruitful, *et cum talis fueris* (saith he) *memento mei*, intimating, that then they might have what they would of God, for themselves or others, that were so qualified.

Ver. 17. *That ye love one another*] That ye hold together, because the world will hate you. A spirit of perversities made way for the ruin of Egypt, Isa. xix. 14, 16, 17. *Si collidimur frangimur*, if we clash we break. Of the ancient Britons, Tacitus tells us that nothing was so destructory to them as their dissensions, *Dum singuli pugnant universi vincuntur.* And of the Thracians, Herodotus saith, that if they had been all of one mind they had been invincible. Keep therefore the staff of binders unbroken, Zech. xi. 7, 14. "Keep the unity of the spirit in the bond of peace," Ephes. iv. 3. In the cause of religion every subdivision is a strong weapon in the hand of the enemy; as in the disagreement of Luther and Zuinglius. The Jesuits have a practice of running over to the Lutherans, pretending to be converts; but it is only to keep up that bitter contention that is between the Calvinists and Lutherans; the virulency whereof is much fomented by these renegade Jesuits.

Ver. 18. *If the world hate you, &c.*] As it will because it is condemned by your contrary practice, and is carried on by a contrary principle. Moab was irked because of Israel, or, did fret and vex at them, Numb. xxii. 3, 4. Bats fly against the light. Some barbarous nations curse the sun when it shines hot upon them, and shoot up their arrows against it.

Ye know that it hated me first] Shall we think to speed better than our betters? Elias is not better than his fathers. Luther was angry with those that set forth his sufferings, sith they were nothing to the sufferings of Christ. All our troubles are but as the slivers and chips of his cross.

Ver. 19. *If ye were of the world, &c.*] They jangle among themselves, and intertear one another as dogs fighting. For though there be not a disagreement in hell (being but the place of retribution, not of action), yet on earth there is no sound peace among the wicked. Howbeit let Ephraim be against Manasseh, and Manasseh against Ephraim, they will be soon against Judah; as if a hare ran by dogs that are fighting, they will agree to pursue the hare.

Therefore the world hateth you] As inhospitable savages do those that land on their coasts; as the Cyprians, for an old grudge, slay all Jews they meet with, though but cast upon their coasts by contrary winds. *Odio humani generis, et per flagitia invisi*, saith Tacitus of Christians. (xv.) *Tanti non est bonum, quanti est odium Christianorum.* David's adversaries sought not only his life, but his soul, his damnation too; as that monster of Milan, mentioned by Bodinus. Now we commit thy soul to the devil, said the persecutors to John Huss. And Jerome of Prague could hardly obtain a confessor, being, it seems, conscientious that way.

Ver. 20. *Remember the word, &c.*] Else all is lost, 1 Cor. xv. 2. Naturally the word runs through us, as water through a riven vessel: *Pleni rimarum sumus, huc atque illuc diffluimus.* Our memories are as sieves, that retain the chaff, let go the good corn; or as nets, that keep the pelf, let go the clean water; or as hour-glasses, that are no sooner full, but running out again. Beseech we God to put his finger upon the hole, and to make his word an engrafted word unto us, to settle it upon our souls, μήποτε παραρυῶμεν, Heb. ii. 1.

If they have kept my saying, &c.] But they will do neither. Holy Melancthon, being himself newly converted, thought it impossible for his hearers to withstand the evidence of the gospel; but after he had been a preacher awhile, it is said he complained that old Adam was too hard for young Melancthon.

Ver. 21. *Because they know not him, &c.*] For had they known, they would not have crucified the Lord of glory. St Paul thanks his ignorance for all his cruelties to Christians. Ignorance is a breeder, and great-bellied. Aristotle makes it the mother of all misrule and mischief. (Ethic. iii.)

Ver. 22. *If I had not come, &c.*] Here our Saviour shows that their ignorance was affected, as theirs is with us. *Qui ut liberius peccent, libenter ignorant*, they shut the windows lest the light should come in. (Bernard.) *Sic fit, ubi homines majorem vitæ partem in tenebris agunt, ut novissime solem quasi supervacuum fastidiant.* (Seneca, Epist.) This is the ignorance to which mercy is denied, Isa. xxvii. 11.

Ver. 23. *He that hateth me*] It is wonder how any should, yet we read of God-haters, Rom. i. 30, and all sin is a kind of God-slaughter, *Omne peccatum est Deicidium.* The wicked wish there were no God, when David cries out, *Vivat Deus*, Psal. xviii. 46.

Ver. 24. *Works which none other man did*]

More stupendous, because by my own power, and all to the people's profit. These were of use in the Church's infancy, and Papists boast of them still; but those are the devil's lying wonders, 2 Thess. ii. 9. As for our religion, *Pudet diabolum Lutheri doctrinam miraculis confirmare,* saith Gretser the Jesuit. But we answer with Augustine, He that now looks for a miracle is himself a great miracle: *Qui adhuc prodigia quærit magnum est ipse prodigium.* Christ was the only Thaumaturgus, or wonder-worker. This is attested by Josephus the Jew, and confessed by Mahomet.

Ver. 25. *They hated me without a cause*] So they dealt by David, so by Christ, and so still by his members. There is but the same pageant acted over again as of old. *In moribus compositi, et modesti sunt,* was the worst the persecutors could say of the Waldenses, those ancient Protestants. They are good in their lives, true in their speeches, hearty in their affections. (Bp Usher.) *Sed fides eorum est incorrigibilis et pessima,* saith the Dominican Inquisitor, concerning the Hussites. So the Bishop of Aliff, in the Trent Council, said that as the faith of the Catholics was better, so the heretics exceeded them in good life. *Hominis vita magno omnium consensu probatur,* said Erasmus of Luther, *Tanta est morum integritas, ut nec hostes reperiant quod calumnientur.* And yet a friar of Antwerp wished that Luther were there that he might bite out his throat with his teeth, as the same Erasmus testifieth.

Ver. 26. *Whom I will send unto you from, &c.*] Christ hath satisfied the wrath of the Father; and now the Father, and Christ both, as reconciled, send the Spirit, as the fruit of both their loves, and as an earnest, which is part of the whole sum.

Ver. 27. *And ye also shall bear witness*] Thus Word and Spirit go together, according to the promise, Isa. lix. 21. The manna of the Spirit comes down from heaven in the dews of the ministry of the gospel, Numb. xi. 2; 1 Pet. i. 22.

CHAPTER XVI.

Ver. 1. *That ye should not be offended*] As with a thing unexpected and intolerable. Darts foreseen are dintless. Crosses coming on the sudden find weak minds secure, make them miserable, leave them desperate.

Ver. 2. *Whosoever killeth you, &c.*] Maximinian, the persecutor, thought that the blood of Christians would be a well-pleasing sacrifice to his gods: *Christianorum sanguinem Diis gratissimam esse victimam.* (Tertul.) Budæus thinks that the apostle, 1 Cor. iv. 13, alludes to those heathenish expiations, wherein certain condemned persons were brought forth yearly with garlands upon their heads, and offered up as sacrifices to their gods, in time of any contagious infection especially; and these they termed καθάρματα and περιψήματα. At Colen certain divines preached, that the death of certain heretics (as they called them) should pacify the wrath of God which then plagued Germany grievously with a strange kind of sweating sickness. (Budæus in Pandect.) In the sixth Council of Toledo, it was enacted that the king of Spain should suffer none to live in his dominions that professed not the Roman Catholic religion. King Philip, accordingly, having hardly escaped shipwreck, as he returned from the Low Countries, said he was delivered by the singular providence of God to root out Lutheranism, which he presently began to do, professing that he had rather have no subjects than such. Another Catholic king said that if he thought his shirt were infected with that heresy, he would tear it from his own back, and rather go woolward; nay, if any member of his body had caught the contagion, he would cut it off, that it might creep no further. *O sancta simplicitas!* said John Huss, when at the stake he observed a plain country fellow busier than the rest in fetching fagots.

Ver. 3. *Because they have not known*] Through blind zeal. "The dark corners of the earth are full of cruelty," saith the Psalmist. And "they shall not destroy in all mine holy mountain;" "for knowledge shall cover the earth, as the waters do the sea," Psal. lxxiv. 20; Isa. xi. 9. See the notes on chap. xv. 21.

Ver. 4. *Ye may remember, &c.*] And act, what I have foretold and taught you. The difference between divinity and other sciences is, that it is not enough to know, but you must do it; as lessons of music must be practised, and a copy not read only, but written after. *Non est hæc umbratilis philosophia, sed quæ ad usum et praxin aptanda.* (Calvin.)

Ver. 5. *None of you asketh me, &c.*] This they had asked him, but not as well a-paid of his going; this he would have of them, and of us, when we part with friends that die in the Lord, say as he, *Tulisti liberos quos ipse dederas; non contristor, quod recepisti; ago gratias, quod dedisti.* (Jerome ad Julian.)

Ver. 6. *Sorrow hath filled your hearts*] So that you are, for the time, not more uncomfortable than uncounsellable. Thus also it fared with those Israelites in Egypt; their ears were so full of gall, that meek Moses even lost his sweet words upon them, Exod. vi. 9. Passions are headstrong, and can hear no counsel:

Fertur equis auriga, nec audit currus habenas.

Ver. 7. *I will send him unto you*] This our Saviour oft repeats, that they might once take notice of it, as an inestimable favour, that God should pour forth his Spirit upon all flesh, Joel ii. 28. What so precious as spirit? what so vile as flesh? It is received among the Turks, that when Christ said that though he departed, he would send them a Comforter, it was added in the text, And that shall be Mahomet; but that the Christians in malice toward them have razed out those words. Is not this the efficacy of error?

Ver. 8. *And when he is come, &c.*] This text had been easy, had not commentators made it so knotty.

He will reprove] Or undeceive the world, by refuting those odd conceits and erroneous opinions, that men had before drunk in, and were possest of, ἐλέγξει. *Ita ut nihil habeat, quod prætexat.* He shall clearly convince them of the hatefulness of sin, of the necessity of getting righteousness, both imputed and imparted; both that of justification inherent in Christ, imputed to us, and that of sanctification also, imparted by Christ, inherent in us; this latter is here called judgment, as it is likewise Matt. xii. 20. Till he bring forth (ἐκβάλῃ) judgment to victory; that is, weak grace (called before a broken reed, smoking wick) to perfect conquest over corruption. *Cum vi quadam, frustra obsistente Satana.* Compare with this text that of the apostle, 1 Cor. vi. 11: Such were some of you (*scilicet, mundus immundus*), but ye are (in general) washed from your sins, of the hatefulness whereof ye are now clearly convinced; and (in particular) ye are sanctified by the Spirit of our God, and ye are justified in the name, that is, by the merit, of the Lord Jesus the righteous, who is the propitiation for our sins.

Ver. 9. *Of sin, because they believe not in me*] Our Saviour instanceth in the greatest of sins, unbelief; which was the first sin, and is still the root of all the rest, Heb. iii. 12. It is a sin against the gospel, and rejects the remedy, that bath of Christ's blood, to the which even the princes of Sodom are invited, Isa. i. 10. It gives God the lie, and subjects a man to the rigour, coaction, and curse of the law.

Ver. 10. *Of righteousness, because, &c.*] What strength is there in that reason? This: Christ took upon him to be our surety, and he must acquit us of all our sins ere he can go to his Father.

Ver. 11. *Of judgment, because the prince, &c.*] Satan is, by the mighty work of the Holy Ghost, cast out of his trenches, forts, cages, castles, heaven of men's hearts, ὀχυρώματα, 2 Cor. x. 4; corruption is dejected, though not utterly ejected, Luke x. 18. "The Spirit lusteth against the flesh." So that as we cannot do what good we would, because of the flesh; so neither what evil we would, because of the spirit.

Ver. 12. *But ye cannot bear them now*] Because your spirits are dulled with worldly sorrow. But the Spirit shall be unto you a powerful *removens, prohibens.*

Ver. 13. *He will guide you into all truth*] Many are the benefits that we receive by the Spirit. "The fruit of the Spirit is in all goodness, and righteousness, and truth," Eph. v. 9. This our Saviour delivers to his disciples at several times, and by degrees, as they could bear it. Here he represents him as a guide to godliness. Simeon was brought into the temple by the instinct of the Spirit. Paul would have gone to a certain place, but the Spirit would not suffer him. Lo, such is the working of the Holy Ghost still in men's hearts, "The steps of a good man are ordered by the Lord, and he delighteth in his way," Psal. xxxvii. 23. Kings suffer their children to ride with them, but yet set tutors and governors to overrule them. So here. And because *Delicata res est Spiritus Dei,* therefore we must observe and obey his motions, which are the sound of his goings, the footsteps of his anointed, Psal. lxxxix. 51. We should lay ourselves (as instruments) open to the Spirit's touch, submit to his discipline, as Paul did, Gal. ii. 20. And this requires a great deal of self-denial.

Ver. 14. *He shall glorify me, &c.*] And if the Holy Ghost could not use any better means to glorify Christ, than to take of his excellencies, and hold them out to the world, what should ministers, the mouth of the Holy Ghost, do rather?

Ver. 15. *All things that the Father hath, &c.*] So that if we can but marry the heir, we have all. The Father saith unto him, as he did to his eldest son, Luke xv. 31, "Son, thou art ever with me, and all that I have is thine;" therefore we may go boldly to him for all things needful for life and godliness. When Joseph sent to Jacob, that Pharaoh had put all into his hands, he was not a little comforted that one so near to him in nature was so able to accommodate him. Let us also come boldly to the throne of grace, sith our flesh and blood hath all power to do us good. Christ, as mediator, is able to make all grace abound toward us, that we "always, having all sufficiency in all things, may abound to every good work," 2 Cor. viii. 8. Well might Ignatius say, *Ignis, crux, et diaboli tormenta in me veniant, tantummodo ut Jesum nanciscar.*

Ver. 16. *A little while, and ye shall not see me*] This "little" seemed a long while to them, so that they began to doubt (though it were but the third day after his death) whether or no it were he that should redeem Israel, Luke xxiv. 21. (*Dubito, a duo et ito,* Becman. *Sic* Διστασις.) God's help seems long, because we are short. A short walk is a long journey to feeble knees. It is but for a moment in his anger that God hides his face from his, though it should be during life; he hath an eternity of time to reveal his kindness in. And to say that God hath cast you off, because he hath hid his face from you, Isa. liv. 7, 8, is (saith Mr T. Goodwin) a fallacy fetched out of the devil's topics. When the sun is eclipsed, foolish people think it will never recover light, but wise men know it will; and at such a time, though the earth want the light of the sun, yet not the influence thereof; so neither are the saints at any time without the power, heat, and vigorous influence of God's grace, when the light and comfort of it is intercluded.

Ver. 18. *We cannot tell what he saith*] We know here but in part; the greatest part of our knowledge is the least part of our ignorance, saith one. Man's heart, saith another, may be compared to a vessel, the means to a pipe; the Spirit of God to the wheel that beats the water into the pipe; the minister is the servant that opens the cock. (August.) And then the reason why we know but in part is, either the cock always runs not, or not always in the same measure; and sometimes our vessels are filled with other things (as the apostles here were with worldly grief and the conceit of an earthly kingdom), and so they run over; and usually our vessels run over, and lose what we received by the means.

Ver. 19. *Now Jesus knew that they were, &c.*] He graciously prevents their requests, so he doth ours often; and usually in Scripture the answer is given, the question concealed. God thereby providing for men's infirmity, who are ready to ask such odd questions, as the disciples here do, to the discovery of their own dullness.

Ver. 20. *Ye shall weep and lament*] So long as ye abide in this valley of tears, as the Septuagint render that, Psal. lxxxvi. 6; εἰς τὴν κοιλάδα τοῦ κλαυθμῶνος. *In hoc exilio, in hoc ergastulo, in hac peregrinatione, in hac valle lachrymarum,* as Bernard hath it. "My tears have been my meat," saith David, Psal. xlii. 3, alluding to the hart, which, being pursued, sheds tears. These, instead of gems, were the ornaments of David's bed, saith Chrysostom. The Church's eyes are as the pools of Heshbon, ever glazed with the tears of compunction or compassion, Cant. vii. 5. Tertullian speaketh of himself, that he was born to nothing else but sorrow and mourning. Athanasius, by his tears, as by the bleeding of a chafed vine, cured the leprosy of that tainted age. Jerome, writing of his own life, saith that there were furrows in his face and icicles from his lips with continual weeping.

But the world shall rejoice] The merry Greeks of the world laugh themselves fat, and are so afraid of sorrow that they can never find time to be serious; counting it no sport unless they may have the devil their playfellow; no mirth but madness; no venison sweet but that which is stolen. These are forbidden to rejoice in anything, Hos. x. 1. *Etiam si læta tibi obveniant omnia, non est tamen quod læteris.* (Ribera.) But if they do, there is a snare or cord in the sin of the wicked, to strangle their joy with; "but the righteous sing and rejoice," Prov. xxix. 6. Woe be to mirthmongers, that fleer when they should fear, Luke vi. 25.

But your sorrow shall be turned into joy] God shall soon give you beauty for ashes, the oil of gladness for the spirit of heaviness, &c.; he shall turn all your sighing into singing, all your laments into laughter, your sackcloth into silks, your ashes into ointments, your fasts into feasts, your wringing of hands into applauses, &c.

Ver. 21. *A woman when she is in travail*] The sorrow of a saint is oft compared to that of a travailing woman, Isa. xxvi. 17; Jer. vi. 24, &c. 1. In bitterness and sharpness; which made Medea say, that she had rather a thousand times be slain in battle than once bring forth a child. *Millies in bello perire mallem, quam semel parere.* 2. In utility; it tends to a birth. 3. In hope and expectation, not only of an end, but also of fruit.

4. In that there is a certain set time for both. And *Finis edulcat media.* (Keckermann.)

Ver. 22. *And ye now therefore have sorrow*] No sorrow like to that, when we see not Christ in his favour. He hides his love oft, as Joseph did, out of increasement of love; and then we cannot see him for crying; as Mary Magdalene could not, she was so bleared. But when he seemeth farthest from us, his heart is with us; and he must needs look through the chinks, as in the Canticles, to see how we do, as that martyr expresseth it. (Saunders, in a letter to his wife and friends.) There is a presence of Christ that is secret, when he seems to draw us one way, and to drive us another, Cant. v. 6.

Ver. 23. *And in that day ye shall, &c.*] q. d. Ye shall be so exact and so expert, that you shall not need to ask such childish questions as hitherto ye have done. This is like that of the prophet, "They shall not each man teach his neighbour, saying, Know the Lord! for they shall all know me, from the least to the greatest," Jer. xxxi. 34. "They shall be all taught of God." *Cathedrum in cœlo habet qui corda docet,* saith Augustine. And *Quando Christus docet, quam cito discitur quo docetur?* So St Ambrose, *Nescit tarda molimina spiritus sancti gratia.* When the Spirit undertakes to teach a man, he shall not be long a-learning. Now all God's people have "the unction that teacheth them all things," 1 John ii. 20. And as in pipes, though of different sounds, yet there is the same breath in them; so is there the same spirit in Christians of all sizes.

Ver. 24. *Hitherto ye have asked nothing*] To what ye should have asked, and might have obtained. Prayer, as those arrows of deliverance, should be multiplied, 1 Kings xiii. 19; the oftener we come to God the better welcome; neither can we anger him worse than to be soon said or sated. It was more troublesome to Severus the emperor to be asked nothing than to give much. *Molestius erat ei nihil peti, quam dare.* When any of his courtiers had not made bold with him he would call him, and say, *Quid est cur nihil petis?* &c., What meanest thou to ask me nothing? So Christ here.

Ask, that your joy may be full] Pray, that ye may joy. Draw water with joy out of this well of salvation. David was excellent at this. His heart was oft more out of tune than his harp. He prays, and then cries, "Return to thy rest, O my soul." In many of his Psalms the beginnings are full of trouble, as Psal. vi., xxii., li.; but by that time he prayed a while, the ends are full of joy and assurance, so that one would imagine, saith Peter Moulin, that those Psalms had been composed by two men of a contrary humour. Hudson the martyr, deserted at the stake, went from under the chain; and having prayed earnestly, was comforted immediately, and suffered valiantly.

Ver. 25. *These things have I spoken, &c.*] He spake plain enough, but they were so slow of heart and dull of hearing, that they thought he spake to them in riddles and parables. *Legum obscuritates non assignemus culpæ scribentium, sed inscitiæ non assequentium.* (Sex. Cecil. apud Gell.) So though the prophet dealt with the people as with little ones newly weaned, mincing and masticating their meat for them, laying before them " precept upon precept, line upon line," &c., yet was he to them (through their singular stupidity) as one that lisped half words, or spake in a strange tongue, Isa. xxviii. 10—12. *Ac si blæsis esset labiis.*

Ver. 26. *At that day ye shall ask,* &c.] Christ had promised them further light, but yet expects they should pray for it. Prayer is a putting the promises in suit; we must pray them over ere we get the performance, Ezek. xxxvi. 37. Christ himself was to ask of his Father the world for his inheritance, &c., Psal. ii.

Ver. 27. *For the Father himself loveth you*] We say majesty and love cannot dwell together. *Non benè conveniunt, nec in una sede morantur majestas et amor :* because love is the abasing of the soul to all services. But it is otherwise in God ; majesty and love meet in his heart ; so that of his own free accord he will give us anything we ask, and as it were prevent a mediator, crowning his own graces in us.

Ver. 28. *Again, I leave the world,* &c.] So Plotinus the philosopher, when he died, said, τὸ ἐν ἐμοὶ θεῖον ἀνάγω ἐπι τὸ πρωτογόνον θεῖον. (*Sponte etiam non rogante me. Ut apud* Hom. σπείδοντα καὶ αὐτὸν ὀτρύνειν.) Nay, Julian the apostate (if Marcellinus may be credited) went out of the world with these words in his mouth, *Vitam reposcenti naturæ, tanquam debitor bonæ fidei, redditurus exulto.*

Ver. 29. *His disciples said unto him*] How apt are we to overween our little nothing of knowledge or holiness, to swell with big conceits of our own sufficiency ! and, when we see never so little, to say presently, with her in the poet, *Consilii satis est in me mihi ?* (Arachne ap. Ovid ;) to think we understand (as St Paul hath it) " all mysteries, and all knowledge ! " 1 Cor. xiii. 1. How truly may it now be said of many, as Quintilian saith of some in his time, that they might have proved excellent scholars, if they had not been so persuaded of themselves already ? " Conceitedness cuts off all hope of proficiency," ἡ οἴησις ἐστὶ τῆς προκοπῆς ἐγκοπὴ.

Ver. 30. *Now we are sure,* &c.] What ! not till now ? Nicodemus was before you then, John iii. 2. But better late than never : *Nunquam sero, si serto.*

Ver. 31. *Do ye now believe ?*] I know, ere trouble comes, you are jolly fellows. But it is easy to swim in a warm bath : and every bird can sing in a sun-shine day. We shall see shortly what you can do. " If ye faint in the day of adversity, your strength is small," Prov. xxiv. 10. Hard weather tries what health ; hot service, what courage.

Ver. 32. *Behold, the hour cometh,* &c.] So bladder-like is the soul, that filled with earthly vanities, though but wind, it grows great and swells in pride ; but if pricked with the least pin of piercing grief, it shriveleth to nothing.

Ver. 33. *These things have I spoken*] This sermon of our Saviour then would be read in time of trouble. It hath *virtutem pacativam,* if mixt with faith.

That in me ye might have peace] Though surcharged with outward troubles. Josiah died in peace, according to the promise, though slain in war. True grace, like true gold, comforts the heart ; alchemy gold doth not.

In the world ye shall have tribulation] There is no avoiding of it ; it is not a paradise, but a purgatory to the saints. It may be compared to the Straits of Magellan, which is said to be a place of that nature, that which way soever a man bend his course, he shall be sure to have the wind against him. (Heyl. Geog.)

I have overcome the world] Therefore we are more than conquerors, because sure to overcome aforehand, Rom. viii. 37. We are triumphers, 2 Cor. ii. 14. We need do no more, then, as those in Joshua, but set our feet on the necks of our enemies, already subdued unto us by our Jesus.

CHAPTER XVII.

Ver. 1. *And lift up his eyes to heaven*] This and the like outward gestures in prayer, as they issue from the fervency of the good heart, so they reflect upon the soul, whose invisible affections by these visible actions, in the saints, are the more inflamed. Howbeit, hypocrites, though they have their hands elbow deep in the earth, will seem to pierce heaven with their eyes lift up in prayer. *Videntur torvo aspectu cœlum ad se attrahere,* saith Calvin somewhere ; they so fix their eyes in public prayer, as if they would leave them on the roof of the church ; when all is but histrionical, theatrical, counterfeit, πρὸς τὸ θεαθῆναι, to be seen of men, Matt. vi. 1. The eagle, when she soareth highest, have ever an eye to the prey below ; so hath the hypocrite to profit, credit.

The hour is come] q. d. I ask not before the time is come, I am ripe and ready for thy kingdom. Some would be in heaven ere they have done their work upon earth. But what said that ancient ? *Domine, si tibi sim necessarius, non recuso vivere :* Lord, if thou hast any further service for me to do, I am willing to live longer. When we come to heaven, the reward will be so large, that we shall repent us (if it were possible there to repent for anything) that we have done no more work. It is not lawful, saith Capel, to wish for death simply, neither to be set free from the troubles, fears, and cares of sin, nor that we would not conflict, nor wrestle any longer (for this were to serve ourselves, and seek our own ease and ends) but in hatred to sin, as it is sin.

Ver. 2. *That he should give eternal life*] And what more free than gift ? Note this against our merit-mongers, who not only cry with Novatus, *Non habeo, Domine, quod mihi ignoscas ;* I have done nothing that thou shouldest forgive me ; but with Vega, *Vitam æternam gratis non accipiam.*

I will not have heaven for nothing. How much better St Augustine, *Homo agnoscat*, saith he, *ut Deus ignoscat*. And William Wickam, founder of New College, who though he did many good works, yet he professed that he trusted to Jesus Christ alone for salvation.

Ver. 3. *That they may know thee*] To know God in the face of Christ, is heaven aforehand; *Qui non habet Christum in horoscopo, non habet Deum in medio cœli.* (Bucholcer.) "By his knowledge shall my righteous servant justify many," saith God concerning Christ, Isa. liii. 11, that is, by faith; which enfolds assent of the judgment, consent of the will, and affiance or assurance of the heart. Papists place faith in the will only, and exclude knowledge. Nay, Bellarmine affirmeth that faith may be better defined by ignorance (that mother of devotion) than by knowledge. They dig out men's eyes (as they dealt by Samson) and then make sport with them; they confine faith to the will, that they may do what they will with the understanding and the heart; as the friars send men on pilgrimage, that they may lie with their wives the while.

Ver. 4. *That thou gavest me to do.*] Our Saviour counts his work a gift; so should we take it for a favour, that he employs us, that we may have any office about him, that we may magnify him with our bodies, "whether by life or death," Phil. i. 19. As a heretic I am condemned, said Mr Bradford, and shall be burned, whereof I ask God heartily mercy that I do no more rejoice than I do, having so great cause as to be an instrument, wherein it may please my dear Lord God and Saviour to suffer. And the greatest promotion, said Latimer, that God giveth in this world, is, to be such Philippians to whom it is given, not only to believe, but also to suffer. Ignatius professed he had rather be a martyr than a monarch. John Noyes took up a fagot at the fire, and kissed it, saying, Blessed be the time that ever I was born to come to this. The apostles rejoiced that they were graced so as to be disgraced for Christ, Acts v. 41.

Ver. 5. *With the glory which I had, &c.*] Our Saviour then is no upstart God, and of a later standing, as the Arians and Mahometans would make of him. Mahomet speaks very honourably of Christ, except only in two things. First, he denied that he was crucified, but that some other was crucified for him. Secondly, he took up the opinion of the Arians, to deny his Divinity. Arius at Constantinople, sitting upon the close stool, purged out his guts. Mahometism is now there in that place, as it were the excrements of Arius.

Ver. 8. *I have manifested thy name*] The Jews seek to detract from the glory of our Saviour's miracles, by giving out, that he did them by I know not what superstitious or magical use of the name Jehovah. (Bernard.) But that name of God that he is here said to manifest, is that *nomen majestativum*, that holy and reverend name of God, set down Exod. xxxiv. 6, 7, a name that would fill our hearts with heaven, and answer all our doubts, had we but skill to spell out all the letters in it.

Ver. 7. *Now they have known, &c.*] That the gospel is a plot of God's own contriving, and no device of man, as that *Evangelium regni* was, set out by the family of love; and those fanatics mentioned by Irenæus, that were besotted with an opinion of themselves, that they accounted their own writings to be gospels. In the year 1220, certain monks at Paris set out a gospel full of all filthiness and blasphemy, naming it *Evangelium æternum*. And in the book called Conformitates S. Francisci, made in the year 1389, it is written, that the same book is better than the gospel, and St Francis set in Lucifer's chair above angels. The Council of Constance comes in with a *non obstante* against Christ's institution, withholding the cup from the laity. And when the pope sets forth any bulls, commonly he concludes thus; *Non obstantibus constitutionibus et ordinationibus Apostolicis, cæterisque contrariis quibuscunque*, and the pope's interpretation of Scripture, be it what it will, seem it never so contrary to the Scripture, is *ipsissimum Dei verbum*, the very word of God, saith Hosius.

Ver. 8. *For I have given unto them*] A sweet and precious gift. It was the Jews' primary privilege that unto them were committed the oracles of God. There is a "chiefly" set upon it, Rom. iii. 2, πρῶτον, *Primarium quiddam et res magni momenti*.

Ver. 9. *I pray for them*] Christ hath left us this prayer here recorded, as a pattern of that intercession he incessantly maketh for us at the right hand of his heavenly Father. Joab was heard for Absalom: shall not Christ for us? Solomon denied his mother's request, 1 Kings ii. 22; God will not deny Christ's. The prodigal came without a mediator to his father, and was embraced; much more shall we, presented by Christ.

Ver. 10. *And I am glorified in them*] It will be a singular prop to our prayers, if we so carry ourselves, that Christ in his daily intercession may give this testimony of us to the Father. He undertakes for us as it were, and gives his word, that we, being mindful of our reconciliation by him, shall shun sin by his grace, and not provoke him as before. This should cause us to live so as Christ may have credit by us, and we may have courage to come to God by Christ.

Ver. 11. *Keep through thine own name*] "The name of the Lord is a strong tower," Prov. xviii. 10; "A munition of rocks," Isa. xxxiii. 18. Hither the saints run for the securing of their comforts and safe-guarding of their persons, as conies do to their burrows, all creatures to their refuges, as the Shechemites fled to their tower, when their city was beaten down to the ground, Judg. ix. 51. The lame and blind, the most shiftless creatures, when they had gotten the stronghold of Sion over their heads, thought then they might securely scorn David and his host, and yet their hold failed them, 2 Sam. v.

6, 7. So doth not God, those that fly to his name. Pray to be kept by it.

Ver. 12. *But the son of perdition*] This exception shows that Judas was never of Christ's body, for can he be a Saviour of a son of perdition? But why is he then excepted? First, by reason of his office he seemed to be of his body. Secondly, our Saviour speaketh here in particular of the twelve; and to be an apostle was in itself but an outward calling.

Ver. 13. *And these things I speak in the world*] Not for his own or his Father's sake, but for the comfort of his disciples; to cure them of their anxiety and anguish, when they heard him praying and providing such things for them. For this also it was, that he prayed thus in their presence (when at other times he went apart), for their consolation doubtless and instruction. Mr Bradford, martyr, when he shifted himself in a clean shirt made for his burning, he made such a prayer of the wedding-garment, that some of those that were present were in such great admiration, that their eyes were as truly occupied in looking on him as their ears gave place to hear his prayer.

Ver. 14. *I have given them thy word, &c.*] I have put my word into their mouth, therefore the world hateth them; Persecution being the black angel (as Calvin said) that dogs the gospel. When our Saviour preached at Nazareth, so long as he was opening his text, they admired him; but when he came to apply it close to their consciences, they pulled him out of the pulpit, and would have broken his neck down the hill, Luke iv. 29. The book that the angel gave John to eat "was sweet in his mouth, but bitter in his belly," Rev. x. 9; to note that the knowledge of divine truths is pleasant, but the publishing of them, whereby the fruit thereof might come to the rest of the members (like the concoction and distribution of meat digested in the stomach), is full of trouble.

Ver. 15. *That thou take them out of the world*] Many godly men, weary of the world's ill usages, are found oft sitting under Elijah's juniper, and wishing to die; for what are they better than their fathers? "Oh that I might have my request!" saith Job, "and that God would grant me the thing that I long for." And what was that, trow you? "Even that it would please God to destroy me; that he would let loose his hand, and cut me off," Job vi. 8, 9. But was that well prayed, Job? Or was that wisely done, Jonah? to fret one while at God's goodness to the Ninevites? to faint another while at the loss of the gourd? and both times to wish to die, saying, "It is better for me to die than to live"? Jonah iv. 3, 8. Were it not better to serve out your time, with David, Acts xiii. 36; to finish your course, with Paul, 2 Tim. iv. 7; to wait till your change shall come, Job xiv. 14; well assured that that "wicked one shall not touch you," as St John hath it, 1 John v. 18; that is, *tactu qualitativo* (as Cajetan senseth it), with a deadly touch?

Ver. 16. *They are not of the world, &c.*] Here indeed they have their commoration, but their conversation is in heaven, πολίτευμα, Phil. ii. 21: they are clothed with the Sun of righteousness, and have the moon (all earthly things) under their feet, Rev. xii. 1. Pearls, though they grow in the sea, yet they have affinity with the heaven, the beauty and brightness whereof they resemble: so here. It is Chrysostom's comparison.

Ver. 17. *Sanctify them by thy truth*] Affect their hearts therewith, that they may the better affect others; speaking *a corde ad cor*, which is the life of preaching. *Quod jussit et gessit*, saith Bernard of one; καὶ ἔδειξε, καὶ ἐδίδαξε, saith Basil of another. A minister had need to pray, as Elisha did, for a doubled and trebled spirit, that he may out of the good treasure of his heart bring forth good things, new and old, for the people's use.

Ver. 18. *Even so have I sent them, &c.*] Therefore they have need that there be put upon them of my Spirit, that they may be fit for the work. This boon none are to expect, but they that are sent of Christ, and such are sure to be gifted.

Ver. 19. *And for their sakes do I sanctify*] As both priest, altar, and sacrifice; and this Christ did from the womb to the tomb; at his death especially, when this Paschal Lamb was roasted in the fire of his Father's wrath, that his people might be made partakers of his holiness, Heb. x. 10. Here also it is worth the noting, that these petitions in our Saviour's prayer do so sweetly depend one upon another, that if you take away one, you deface the other. Phavorinus in Gellius, comparing between the style of Lysias and Plato, observes this difference; *Quod si ex Platonis oratione aliquid demas mutesque de elegantia tantum detraxeris; si ex Lysiæ, de sententia.*

Ver. 20. *Neither pray I for these alone*] Lo here a sure and sweet haven for all believers to have recourse to, where they may sit and sing away care of miscarrying; for here Christ doth as much as if he should solemnly swear to secure and set them safe from danger, sith the Father denies him nothing, John xi. 42.

Ver. 21. *That they all may be one*] Though not by the same kind of union whereby the Father and the Son are one, yet by a union every way as real and indissoluble; such as whereby the world may be convinced that Christ is the very Messiah, and the faithful the true Church. So it was acknowledged in the primitive times, Acts iv. 32. But what a sad thing was it, that a heathen should soon after have cause to say, *Nullæ infestæ hominibus bestiæ, ut sunt sibi ferales plerique Christiani;* No beasts are so mischievous to men, as Christians are one to another. (Am. Marcellinus, ii. 2.) *Tristissima illa persecutio sub Diocletiano, potissime orta est a petulantia, superbia et rixis sacerdotum.* (Euseb.) They had not so learned Christ. Love and humility are his cognizances. Why then should the Turk have occasion to say, that he should sooner see his fingers all of a length, than Christian princes all of a mind? Why should the Jew stumble at our dissensions, which is one of the main scandals they take from Protestants?

Ver. 22. *And the glory which thou, &c.*] That is, the grace, which is glory begun, as glory is grace perfected; we are here " transformed into the same image from glory to glory," 2 Cor. iii. 18; "and set together in heavenly places in Christ Jesus," Eph. ii. 6. "Such honour have all his saints." Such things are found in them as do accompany or comprehend salvation, Heb. vi. 9, ἐχόμενα, τοῦτ᾽ ἐστὶ κατεχόμενα. Scholiast.

Ver. 23. *I in them, and thou in me*] Christ was the only fit mediator; as being God for the business with God; and man for the business with man. He is the bridge that joineth heaven and earth together, saith Gregory. He is that ladder of ascension to God; faith first lays hold upon Christ as man, and by it, as by a mean, makes way to God; and in it embraceth the Godhead, which is of itself fire consuming. We may safely sail through Christ's blood into the bosom of the Father.

Ver. 24. *Father, I will, &c.*] Every word is full of life and joy. I would not (saith Mr Baxter) for all the world that one verse had been left out of the Bible. And again the same author elsewhere saith, there is more worth in those four chapters, John xiv.—xvii., than in all the books in the world besides. (Saint's Everlasting Rest.)

Ver. 24. *Be with me, where I am*] It is part of Christ's joy that we shall be where he is. He will not therefore be long without us. David is sent by God to Hebron to be crowned: he will not go up alone, but takes with him all his men, with all their households. They shall take such part as himself, notwithstanding their late mutiny at Ziklag. So dealeth the Lord Christ with all his, and this should digest all their sorrows. Christ will not be happy alone; as a tender father, he can enjoy nothing if his children may not have part with him.

Ver. 25. *O righteous Father*] God's righteousness is either, 1. Of equity, to punish offences. Or, 2. Of fidelity, to make good his promises. In which respect it is no arrogancy nor presumption (said Master Glover, martyr) to burthen God, as it were, with his promises; and of duty to claim his aid, help, and assistance.

Ver. 26. *That the love, &c.*] *Claritas in intellectu parit ardorem in affectu. Ignoti nulla cupido.*

CHAPTER XVIII.

Ver. 1. *Over the brook Cedron*] THIS was the town ditch, 2 Chron. xxx. 14, and had its name from its darkness or muddiness; for it received the baggage, as a common sink. Not far from hence was the valley of Hinnom, wherein there was kept a continual fire for the burning of dead carcases and other garbage, as Kimchi notes upon Psal. xxvii. Hence hell is called Gehenna.

Ver. 2. *And Judas also which betrayed him*] No such danger to Christ's Church by any as by apostates and false brethren, Gal. ii. 4. Julian of a forward professor became a furious persecutor, and drew more from the faith by fraud and craft than all the heathen emperors before him had done by their force and cruelty. He persecuted by his persuasions, as Nazianzen witnesseth, and called back the bishops that were banished by Constantine, that, by their mutual wranglings amongst themselves they might embroil and overthrow the Church. *Eo tantum fine ut ipsi ob mutuam inter se contentionem bello intestino oppugnarent ecclesiam.* (Sozom.) About the year of grace 1240, one Robert, a Bulgarian, fell off from the Waldenses, and, turning to be a Dominican, he proved to be a sore enemy to the Church of Christ, in Flanders especially. Bishop Bonner was at first advanced by Cromwell, and seemed much to dislike Stephen Gardiner for his Popery. His words to Grafton at Paris when he was newly made bishop of London, were these, Before God, the greatest fault that I ever found in Stokesly (who was his predecessor) was for vexing and troubling of poor men for their religion, as Lobly the bookbinder, and others, for having the Scripture in English; and (God willing) he did not so much hinder it, but I will as much further it, &c. Baldwin the renegado and Bolsecus (that was hired by the Papists to write Calvin's life) were desperate enemies to the truth they had formerly professed. Harding, that had conference with Jewell, was once a zealous Protestant, and chaplain to Lady Jane Grey. Champian of St John's college in Oxford, proctor of the University, 1568, dissembled the Protestant religion, which he afterwards opposed to his utmost. So did Parsons, who was of Baliol college, till he was for his dishonesty expelled with disgrace, and fled to the Papists. Christ's greatest enemies are usually those of his own house. He was of the society of Jesus that betrayed him.

Ver. 3. *Judas having then received a band*] These are the enemies' best arguments, and those they fly to when all is done. So the Jesuits, those sworn sword-men of Satan, give out that their weapons are only *preces et lachrymæ*, prayers and tears; and that it is unlawful for them to use any other, even then when they are about their most bloody designs. (Camd. Eliz. Epist. to Reader.) A late king of France (after his revolt to Popery) being persuaded by a great duke about him not to readmit the Jesuits, which had been justly banished the realm, he answered suddenly, "Give me then security for my life." He therefore admitted them, even into his bosom, giving them his house for a college; and in a public speech, saying, That they were Timothies in the house, Chrysostoms in the chair, Augustines in the schools, &c. But what came of it? One of the pope's slaughter-slaves, by the instigation of the Jesuits, stabbed him to the heart: these Timothies proved Judases; these Chrysostoms, Catalines; these Augustines, assassins. (Vita David Parei, Operib. præfix.)

Cometh thither with lanterns, &c.] Hypocrites may be compared (saith one) to those soldiers in the Gospel which came to seek Christ with lights and lanterns, as if they meant not to miss of him; yea, they brought clubs and staves, as if they would fight for him: yet, when he saith, Here I am, take you up my cross, they stumble at the cross, and fall backwards. (Essays Divine and Moral.)

Ver. 4. *Went forth and said unto them*] Met his enemy in the face, after he had prayed; whereas, till then, he feared. See the power of prayer. So Esther, when she had fasted and prayed, found her heart fortified against the fear of man; and putting her life in her hand, went boldly to the king. So Hudson the martyr, of whom afore.

Ver. 5. *Jesus of Nazareth. Jesus saith, I am he*] They called him Jesus of Nazareth by way of reproach. He takes it upon him, and wears it for a crown. And should not we do likewise?

And Judas also, &c.] With what face could the traitor stand there? But being full of the devil he was past grace, and could blush no more than a sackbut. *Effrænis et effrons.*

Ver. 6. *As soon then as he had said, &c.*] Here our Saviour let out a little beam of the majesty of his Deity, and 500 men fell before him. *Quid autem judicaturus faciet, qui judicandus hoc fecit?* saith Augustine. "The wicked shall not stand in judgment," saith David, Psal. i. 7. Christ shall "smite the earth with the rod of his mouth," saith Isaiah; and with "the breath of his lips shall he slay the wicked," Isa. xi. 4. Godly men (who have but a drop of Christ's ocean, a spark of his flame) have a daunting presence. When Valens the persecuting emperor came to St Basil, while he was in holy exercises, it struck such a terror into him, that he reeled, and had fallen, had he not been upheld by those that were with him. And another time, when he should have subscribed an order for St Basil's banishment, such a sudden trembling took his right hand, that he could write never a good letter, whereupon he tore the order for anger, and there was an end of the business. When an officer was sent to apprehend a godly deacon at Miltenberg (a town in the territory of Mentz), the deacon, embracing him, said, *Salve, frater, frater enim vero meus es, en adsum, transfode me, suffoca me*, Here I am, brother, stab me, hang me, do what you will with me. The officer, as if changed from heaven, answered, Sir, you shall receive no hurt from me. *Domine, a me quidem nihil mali expectes.* (Scultet. Annal.) And when the boars ran in to kill the deacon, he delivered him, and set him safe out of danger. Judas dealt not so by Jesus, but as he fell with the rest, so rose with the rest, who desperately went on with their devilish design, nothing daunted by their late disaster.

Ver. 7. *Then asked he them again*] Though struck to the earth they desist not: so the Sodomites, smitten with blindness, grope for the door. Pharaoh, in that palpable darkness, rageth against God, and menaceth Moses. *Monoceros interimi potest, capi non potest:* stubborn men will sooner break than bend. Man, saith Polybius, is held the wisest, but to me he seemeth the most foolish of all creatures; for they, where they have miscarried once, will not easily be driven thither again. *Solus homo ab ævo ad ævum peccat fere in iisdem:* only man will not be warned, though he have soundly smarted. (Solinus.) We load an ass (saith Bernard) and he cares not, because he is an ass and born to bear burdens; but if you would drive him into a ditch, or thrust him into the fire, he shuns it as well as he can, because he loves life and fears death: *Cavet quantum potest, quia vitam amat, et mortem timet.* Yet silly man fears not his eternal bane.

Ver. 8. *Let these go their way*] This seems to indent with the Jews ere he yielded himself their prisoner. As a good shepherd, he interposeth between the wolf and the flock: as a heavenly eagle, he hath ever an eye to his nest, when he flieth highest from it.

Ver. 9. *That the saying might be fulfilled, &c.*] Christ spake it of their souls, it is here applied to their bodies. God hath a fatherly care of both, and will not lay more upon the outward man than the inward shall be enabled to undergo. Hence that of the prophet, "Behold, I have tried thee, but not as silver," Isa. xlviii. 10. Why so? because God's weak children having far more dross in them than good ore, would never be able to abide a strict trial.

Ver. 10. *The servant's name was Malchus*] A busy fellow belike in surprising our Saviour. But it was a sad omen (saith a noble and renowned writer, Lord Brook) that Peter's sword should cut off the ear of Malchus, which signifies a king or kingly authority. How the pope hath lifted up himself, ἐπὶ πᾶν σέβασμα, above all that is called Augustus, or emperor, is better known than that it need be here related. And if bishops forbear (saith he) to touch the sceptre (which they strive to sway), it is but as once Mercury spared Jupiter's thunderbolts, which he durst not steal, lest they should roar too loud, or at least burn his fingers.

Ver. 11. *Put up thy sword*] Our Saviour checks him for his inordinate zeal; wherein to be over-carried, is easy and ordinary. The memorable story of William Gardiner, martyr in Portugal, who in the very presence of the king and his nobles could not forbear, but fell upon the cardinal, as he was acting a mass. See Acts and Monuments, fol. 1242. So William Flower, upon an Easter-day at Westminster, seeing a priest ministering the sacrament of the altar to the people, struck and wounded him upon the head, and also upon his arm and hand, with a wood-knife. In the which so doing, as indeed he did not well, nor evangelically; so being afterwards examined by Bishop Bonner, he did no less confess his not well-doing in the same, submitting therefore himself willingly to punishment, when it should come. Howbeit, touching his belief in the sacrament and popish ministration, he neither did nor would submit himself. But when he was tempted to turn, and also threatened, he answered, Do what ye will, I am at a point; for the heavens shall as soon fall, as I will forsake mine opinion, &c. At his execution, first his hand being held up against the stake, was stricken off. At the which, some that were present affirmed, that he shrunk not, but once a little stirred his shoulders. (Acts and Mon.)

Ver. 12. *Took Jesus and bound him*] This was done τοῦ λόγου ἡσυχάζοντος, as Irenæus hath it, while the Deity rested; for he could as easily have delivered himself as he did his disciples, but this sacrifice was to be bound with cords to the altar; he was pinioned and manacled, as a malefactor. So was not Abner; "his hands were not bound, nor his feet put into the fetters," 2 Sam. iii. 34. But Christ was bound for our transgressions, he was "bruised for our iniquities." Paul, by his privilege, was freed from whipping; but we by Christ's bondage, from those chains of darkness, 2 Pet. ii. 4, σειραῖς ζόφου ταρταρώσας, from those scourges and scorpions in hell.

Ver. 13. *And led him away to Annas first*] Who would not go to bed (late though it were) till he had seen Christ brought bound before him, and then cried out, likely, as Hannibal did, when he saw a pit full of man's blood, *O formosum spectaculum!* So Stephen Gardiner would not sit down to dinner till the news came of the good bishops burnt at Oxford. Then he came out rejoicing, and saying to the Duke of Norfolk, Now let us go to dinner; but it was the last that ever he eat for it. "Shall they escape by iniquity?" No, "in anger cast them down, O God," Psal. lvi. 7.

Ver. 14. *Now Caiaphas was he,* &c.] So Balaam, the devil's spelman, spake excellently of the star of Jacob. See the notes on chap. xi. 51, 52.

Ver. 15. *That disciple was known to the high priest*] Perhaps for that he and his father Zebedee were wont to serve the fat priests with the best and daintiest fish (for this other disciple was John, who had first fled with the rest, and now came sculking in to see what would become of his Master). Of the ass-fish Aristotle affirmeth (De Nat. Animal.) that he of all other creatures hath his heart in his belly; such a thing was this priest.

Ver. 16. *But Peter stood at the door*] Better he had kept him further off. He that will not fall into the ditch, must not walk too near the brim. Peter might better have bestowed himself somewhere else. *Longe utilius fuisset, gemere, et precari in obscuro aliquo angulo,* saith Musculus. It had been better for him to have been praying in a corner than thus to put himself upon a danger, unless he had known himself the stronger. Luther comforted the men of Miltenberg by an epistle; and because they were forbidden to meet and talk together about matters of religion, upon pain of death, he adviseth those of them that were strong in the spirit to do their duty, notwithstanding the danger. But for the weaker sort, he exhorteth them to rejoice secretly in the Lord, and to pray to him for further strength, that they may be able to make a bold and wise profession of his truth. *Qui infirmiores sunt, tacite in Domino gaudeant, Deumque rogent, ut se quoque animet ad publicam veritatis professionem.*

Ver. 17. *He saith, I am not*] False dissimulation is true denial. A silly wench is too hard for this stout stickler, who was alway *Melius animatus quam armatus,* as one observeth of him; *Sic Elias fulminator ad Jesebelis minas trepidat, factus seipso imbecillior.* "Thou also standest by faith: be not high-minded, but fear," Rom. xi. 20.

Ver. 18. *And warmed himself*] But whiles he warmed without, he cooled within. Evil company is a great quench-coal, an ill air for zeal to breathe in, it casts a damp. "For the abundance of iniquity, the love of many waxeth cold," Matt. xxiv. 12. Peter's evil example was a compulsion to other good people, Gal. ii. 14. What marvel then if the swearing, cursing soldiers compelled him to do the like? They were the trunks through which the devil delivered himself, jeering at and railing upon Christ, no doubt, &c.

Ver. 19. *Asked Jesus of his disciples*] Questioned him in the spiritual court first, as an heretic; as afterwards in the temporal court, for a seditious person. So the Papists condemned married priests for Nicolaitanes, in the Synod of Milan, A. D. 1067. Virgilius, a German bishop, and a great mathematician, they condemned for an heretic, for affirming that there were antipodes. Paulus II., pope, pronounced them heretics that did but name the name Academy, either in jest or in earnest. Innocent II. condemned Arnoldus Brixius of heresy, for saying that the clergy should have their temporalities taken away, and be tied to their spirituals only. Bonner objected to Philpot the martyr, that he found written in his book, *In me Joanne Philpotto ubi abundavit peccatum, superabundavit et gratia.* And when the bishop of Worcester exhorted Philpot, before he began to speak, to pray to God for grace: Nay, my lord of Worcester, said Bonner, you do not well to exhort him to make any prayer; for this is the thing these heretics have a singular pride in, that they can often make their vain prayers, in the which they glory much: for in this point they are like to certain arrant heretics, of whom Pliny makes mention, that they sing *Antelucanos hymnos,* &c. Was not this well aimed? Those he spoke of were the primitive Christians, whom Pliny excuseth to Trajan the persecutor. But it is easy for malice to make heresy what it pleaseth, when it is armed with power, and can make havoc at pleasure.

Ver. 20. *I spake openly to the world*] Truth is bold and barefaced; when heresy hides itself, and loathes the light, *Veritas abscondi erubescit.* What said John Frith, martyr, to the archbishop's men, that would have let him go and shift for himself? If you should both leave me here, and go to Croydon, declaring to the bishops that you had lost Frith, I would surely follow as fast after as I might, and bring them news that I had found and brought Frith again. Do ye think that I am afraid to declare my opinion to the bishops of England in a manifest truth?

Ver. 21. *Why askest thou me?*] We are to be ready always to give an answer to those that ask us a reason of our hope, so they do it to learn of us, and not to ensnare us. Thus I kept the ban-dogs at staves' end (said Nicholas Shetterden, martyr), not as thinking to escape them, but that I would see the foxes leap above-ground for my blood, if they can reach it (so it be the will of God), yet we shall then gape and leap for it. Mr Hawks, martyr, asked a parson that examined him, what kin he was to the weather-cock of Paul's? And told one Miles Huggard, a hosier in Pudding Lane, who began to question him, that he could better skill to eat a pudding and make an hose, than in Scripture either to answer or oppose.

Ver. 22. *One of the officers*] Because our Saviour gave not the high priest his usual titles, but dealt freely with him, this officer, to curry favour, *Veluti pontificii honoris vindex*, beats our Saviour with his hand or stick, and is the better thought of. Like master, like man. So the bishop of Geneva's servant discharged his pistol at Farellus (that faithful man of God) when he was convented before his Lord; but by God's good providence, missed him. *Disploso sclopeto a Vicarii famulo, sed frustra impetitur.* (Scultet.) Great men's vices go as seldom unattended, as their persons; they shall be sure of such about them as will lick up their spittle, and load the mouse with the lion's praises. *Ne leonum laudibus murem obruas.*

Ver. 23. *If I have spoken evil*] Christ bears with the officer's insolency, but forbears not to clear his own innocence. We must, when aspersed, labour as the eclipsed moon, by keeping our motion, to wade out of the shadow and recover our former splendour.

Ver. 24. *Bound to Caiaphas the high priest*] Who should have done our Saviour better justice than to have suffered him, bound and uncondemned, to be injuriously beaten before his face. But the times were then lawless and licentious for the sins of the people. *Tales sunt principum mores, quales subditorum humores, ut malo nodo non desit malus cuneus.*

Ver. 25. *He denied it, and said, I am not*] Take heed by this example, *Patres nos instruunt tum docentes, tum labentes*, saith Augustine. Seest thou such as Peter to make shipwreck? Look well to thy tackling. They that will not profess Christ (unless they repent with Peter, which Stephen Gardiner said at his death that he could not) shall be sorted with such in participation of plagues, as through excess of pain and defect of patience, gnaw their own tongues, Rev. xvi. 10.

Ver. 26. *Whose ear Peter cut off*] A great mercy it was that Peter had not then been hewed in a hundred pieces, by the ruffianly soldiers. But God had designed him to a further service. "My times are in thy hand," saith David. They were deceived, that swore to kill Paul by such an hour, Acts xxiii. 12.

Ver. 27. *Peter then denied again*] He that is fallen down one round of hell's ladder, knows not where he shall stop or stay, till he come to the bottom. Sin is of an encroaching nature, modest and maidenly at first; but yield to it once, and there is no ho with it.

The cock crew] And withal Christ looked back upon him, as a piece of his suffering, with καὶ σὺ τέκνον Πέτρε, What thou, my friend, Peter? Scipio had rather Hannibal should eat his heart with salt than Lælius give him a cross word.

Ver. 28. *Lest they should be defiled*] Putid hypocrisy! they stand upon legal defilements, and care not to defile their consciences with innocent blood. What is this, but to strain at a gnat and swallow a camel? τὸν ἀνδρίαντα γαργαλίζειν. So Saul seemed to make an heinous matter of eating the flesh with the blood, 1 Sam. xiv. 33, when it was nothing with him to spill the blood of innocent Jonathan. Nay, he was so scrupulous, that he would not so much as name a guilty man or sinner, but, in casting of lots, instead of saying, Show the innocent or guilty, he said, Show the innocent or upright person, as Tremellius reads it; yet at the same time (as is well observed) he made no conscience of bloody oaths. So Doeg was detained before the Lord, either because it was the sabbath, or his vow was not finished, &c. But when he went thence, he became death's-man to the Lord's priests.

Ver. 29. *Pilate then went out unto them*] It was much he would gratify them so far in their "Stand further off, for I am holier than thou;" that he would yield to their superstition, which he could not but contemn. But the very Turk, so the Christians pay him his yearly tribute (which is one fourth part of their increase, and a Sultan for every poll), permitteth them the liberty of their religion.

Ver. 30. *If he were not a malefactor*] Why? what evil had he done them? Might he not have said to them, as Themistocles to his Athenians, Are ye weary of receiving so many benefits by one man?

Ver. 31. *It is not lawful for us*] That is, upon this or any such like day, upon an holy-day, or holy-day eve. For otherwise they had power, or at least took it at their pleasure, as when they stoned Stephen, Acts vii., and would have killed Paul, Acts xxiv. But note, that they would seem to do all according to law by any means, so would their successors, the Catholics. Which, if it be so (saith Mr Fox), how did they then to Anne Askew, whom they first condemned to death, and then set her on the rack? By what law did they call up Master Hooper, and imprison him for the Queen's debt (when the Queen in very deed did owe him four-score pounds), and kept him a year and a half in prison, and gave him never a penny? By what law did Bishop Bonner condemn and burn Richard Mekins, a lad of fifteen years, when the first jury had quit him, and at the stake he revoked all heresy, and praised the said Bonner to be a good man; and also having him in prison, would not suffer his father and mother to come to him, to comfort their own child? What law had they to put Mr Rogers, our proto-martyr, in prison, when he did neither preach nor read lectures after the time of the Queen's inhibition? And when they had kept him in his own house half a year, being not deprived of any living, yet would not let him have one halfpenny of his own means to relieve him, his wife and eleven children? By what law was Thomas Tompkins' hand burned, and after his body consumed to ashes? What good law or honesty was there to burn the three poor women at Guernsey, with the infant child falling out of the mother's womb, whenas they all before recanted their words and opinions, and were never abjured before. So, what right or order of law did Stephen Gardiner follow, in troubling and imprisoning Judge Hales, when he had done nothing either against God's law or man's, proceeding in order of law against certain presumptuous persons, which, both before the law and against the law then in force, took upon them to say their mass?

Ver. 32. *Signifying what death he should die*] This shows that the Jews had power to put to death, but by a providence he was brought to Pilate, that according to the manner of the Romans he might be crucified; that kind of death being not, otherwise, in use among the Jews. Hence our Lord is said to have been crucified at Rome, Rev. xi. 8.

Ver. 33. *Entered into the judgment hall again*] For without, among the people, there was nothing but clamour and confusion; much like to that *regnum Cyclopum, ubi οὐδεὶς οὐδὲν οὐδένος ἀκούει*. Pilate therefore retires himself into the palace, that he might more sedately set himself to sift the business.

Ver. 34. *Sayest thou this of thyself*] As who should say, If thou dost this of thyself, what reason is it that thou shouldest be both judge and witness? if others have done it, why are not mine accusers brought face to face? If to be accused be enough to make a man guilty, none shall be innocent. Judges are to proceed *secundum allegata et probata*.

Ver. 35. *Am I a Jew?*] This he asketh in scorn of that nation; hateful among the heathens for their difference from them in religion. Caius the emperor cast them out with their orator Philo, who came to make apology for them against Appion of Alexandria, their adversary and accuser. Strabo, of mere spite, saith that Judea is a dry and barren country, when the Scripture calleth it a land flowing with milk and honey, plenty and dainty; and Tacitus cannot but grant as much. (Aug. C. D.) Florus calleth the temple at Jerusalem, *impiæ gentis arcanum*, a sanctuary for rogues, as the Papists say of Geneva. Seneca jeers them for casting away the seventh part of their time upon a weekly sabbath. Juvenal plays upon their circumcision.

Plutarch tells a long story of their feast of tabernacles, which, saith he, they keep in honour of Bacchus (σύμπος). Tacitus saith, they were called *Asinarii*, because they worshipped the golden head of an ass. (Annal. xxi.) No wonder though profane Pilate disdain to be held a Jew, when they were thus traduced!

Ver. 36. *My kingdom is not of this world*] Christ could not be received as a God into the Pantheon at Rome, for that he wanted worshippers, preached poverty, and chose mean men for his disciples. Domitian the emperor, after he had banished John into Patmos, and Domicillia Flavia, his own sister's daughter, with many more, into Pontus, and put divers to death for that they were Christians, he commanded all such Jews as he could find to be put to death, that were of the stock of David. Amongst whom, meeting with some Christians also, that were allied to Christ, and understanding that they were poor harmless people, he dismissed them, and by proclamation forbade any more to be martyred. (Euseb. iii. 20.)

Ver. 37. *That I should bear witness of the truth*] Our Saviour speaketh religiously to a profane person; so doth Jacob to Esau, Gen. xxxiii. 5. Each countryman is known by his language. God will turn to all his people a pure lip, Zeph. iii. 9. They are none of his that can shift their sails to the setting of every wind, tune their fiddles to other men's bass, and as the planet Mercury, be good in conjunction with good, and bad with bad.

Ver. 38. *What is truth?*] In a scornful, profane manner. As indeed profane spirits cannot bear savoury words, but they turn them off with a scorn. What is truth? *Fastidientis atque irridentis vox, non interrogantis*, saith Beza. Some think it is *vox admirantis;* as if Pilate wondered at Christ, that when his life was in question he should talk of truth, *q. d.* Your life is in danger, and talk you of truth? Politicians think religion niceness. However it was, or with what mind soever, out he goes, and stays not an answer; as Saul bade the priest bring to him the ark, but, ere that could be done, draws forth his army, 1 Sam. xiv.

Ver. 39. *But ye have a custom*] An ungain, ungodly custom it was, Prov. xvii. 15, whatever were the ground of it. *In ista consuetudine turpe et crassum fuit vitium.* (Calv.) Some think it was in memory of Jonathan, rescued from his father by the people. Others, that the feast might be celebrated with the greater joy and gladness. Others, more probably, in remembrance of their deliverance from the Egyptian bondage. But why should any Barabbas escape by it? "A bloody man shall flee to the pit, and no man may stay him," Prov. xxviii. 17.

Ver. 40. *Now Barabbas was a robber*] And a murderer too, Acts iii. 14, yet preferred before Christ, who was also crucified in the midst of two thieves, as the worst of the three. Thus he was *peccatorum maximus*, both by imputation, for he bore our sins, which were all made to meet upon him, Isa. liii. 6, and by reputation, for he was "numbered with the transgressors," ver. 12, and made "his grave with the wicked," ver. 9.

CHAPTER XIX.

Ver. 1. *Took Jesus and scourged him*] So God scourgeth every son whom he receiveth, Heb. xii. 6. One Son he had that was *sine corruptione et flagitio*, but none that was *sine corruptione et flagello*. In him therefore that rule held not, *Flagitium et flagellum, sicut acus et filum*, Punishment follows sin, as the thread follows the needle.

Ver. 2. *And the soldiers platted a crown of thorns*] Prickly and sharp as the point of a sword (so the word signifieth). Ἀκανθὴ *videtur ortum a voce* ἀκὴ, *cuspis, acies, mucro*. (Pasor.) And our Saviour being of the finest constitution, must needs be extreme sensible. The soldiers did this (it is thought) by the command of Pilate, to give content to the Jews, and to move them thereby (if it might be) either to condemn him or commiserate him. But nothing would do but his death; these blood-hounds would not otherways be satisfied. Godfrey of Boulogne, first king of Jerusalem, refused to be crowned with a crown of gold, saying that it became not a Christian there to wear a crown of gold, where Christ for our salvation had sometime worn a crown of thorns. Some report that he would not be otherwise crowned than with a crown of thorns, as he kneeled at our Saviour's sepulchre; to testify (perhaps) that he did dedicate his head and life to Christ crucified, and despised not for his sake a crown of thorns here so he might wear a crown of glory with him in heaven. *Tradunt coronam spineam ei esse impositam flexis genibus ad sepulchrum Dominicum procumbenti.* (Bucholcer.) Canutus, for like purpose, set his crown upon the crucifix. It is not fit, sith the head was crowned with thorns, that the members should be crowned with rose-buds, saith Zanchius.

Ver. 3. *And said, Hail, King of the Jews*] They scoff at him, as a ridiculous and stage-play king, whom therefore they clothed with purple, which was a colour affected by the emperors and nobility of Rome; as Herod, for like cause, clothed him in white, ἐν ἐσθῆτι λαμπρᾷ, a colour much worn by the nobility of the Jews, Jam. ii. 2.

And they smote him with their hands] So do hypocrites still by their unchristian practice, when they bend the knee to Christ with ludibrious devotion. They have the voice of Jacob, but the hands of Esau. Their words are God's, their deeds the devil's, as John Capocius told Pope Innocent III., preaching peace and sowing discord. *Verba tua Dei plane sunt, facta vero diaboli videntur.*

Ver. 4. *That ye may know that I find no fault*] But why did he not then deliver him out of their hands? Pusillanimity and popularity would not suffer him; but howsoever he shall give testimony to his innocency. So when Dr Weston was gone from Mr Bradford, martyr (with whom he had had conference), the keeper told Bradford that the doctor spake openly that he saw no cause why they should burn him. This Weston being prolocutor in the divinity schools at Oxford, when Cranmer was brought forth to dispute, thus began the disputation, *Convenistis hodie, fratres, profligaturi detestandam illam hæresin de veritate corporis Christi in Sacramento,* &c. At which divers learned men burst out into a great laughter, as though even in the entrance of the disputation he had bewrayed himself and his religion. God will have such words fall sometimes from the mouths of persecutors, either wittingly, or by mistake, as shall one day rise up in judgment, and out of their own mouths condemn them.

Ver. 5. *Pilate saith, Behold the man*] q. d. If ye be men, take pity upon a man so miserably misused; and if ye be good men, let him go that is innocent. But these monsters, like those beasts at Ephesus, had put off manhood; and for good men amongst them, it fared with Pilate, pleading for Christ, as it did with him at Nola in the story, who when he was commanded by the Roman censor to go and call the good men of the city to appear before him, went to the churchyards, and there called at the graves of the dead, "O ye good men of Nola, come away, for the Roman censor calls for your appearance," for he knew not where to call for a good man alive.

Ver. 6. *Crucify him, crucify him*] So afterwards the primitive persecutors cried out, *Ad bestias, ad bestias, Christianos ad leones*, imputing the cause of all public calamities to them, as Tertullian testifieth. So they cried out at Geneva against Farellus, when the bishop first convented him, *In Rhodanum, in Rhodanum*, as the Papists still cry out against the professors of the truth, *Ad ignem, ad ignem*, to the fire with them, to the fire with them. *Tollantur sacrilegi, tollantur.* Indeed in the form and style of their own sentence condemnatory, they pretend a petition to the secular power, *In visceribus Jesu Christi ut rigor juris mitigetur, atque ut parcatur vita;* so they will seem outwardly to be lambs, but inwardly they are ravening wolves. Witness that chancellor of Salisbury, Dr Jeffery, who was not only contented to give sentence against certain martyrs, but also hunted after the high sheriff, not suffering him to spare them, though he would. So Harpsfield, archdeacon of Canterbury, being at London when Queen Mary lay a-dying, made all post-haste home to despatch those six whom he had then in his cruel custody; and those were the last that suffered for religion in Queen Mary's reign.

I find no fault in him] No wonder! For he was (as Peter saith) "A lamb without blemish" (of original sin), "and without spot" (of actual sin), 1 Pet. i. 18. Neither was it without a sweet providence of God that he should be so often absolved from the desert of death, that thereby we might escape the manifold deaths that we had so well deserved.

Ver. 7. *The Jews answered him, &c.*] When they saw that the treason they laid to his charge would not do the deed, they accused him of blasphemy another while, that by some means or other they might take away his life. Thou, and such as thou (said Bonner to Thomas Brown, martyr), report I seek your blood; to whom he answered, Yea, my lord, indeed ye be a bloodsucker; and I would I had as much blood as is water in the sea for you to suck. Another unknown good woman told this bishop in a letter, that he had such store of Christ's lambs already in his butcher's stall, that he was not able to drink all their blood, lest he should break his belly, and therefore he let them lie still and die for hunger. My lord (said Mr Saunders to Bonner), you seek my blood, and you shall have it; I pray God you may be so baptized in it, that you may hereafter loathe blood-sucking, and become a better man.

Ver. 8. *He was the more afraid*] Christ's innocence did before triumph in Pilate's conscience. But now, that he hears that he made himself the Son of God, he was in a mighty maze, "he was afraid," saith the text, of lifting up his hand against God. The greatest men, if not utterly debauched and satanized, cannot but quake at the apprehension of God: and as the worms, when it thunders, wriggle into the corners of the earth; Caligula (that dared his Jove to a duel with that hemistich in Homer, ἤ μ' ἀνάειρ' ἤ ἐγώ σε, Either kill me, or I will kill thee), when it thundered, covered his eyes with his cap, running under the bed or any bench-hole. (Sueton. in Calig.)

Ver. 9. *Whence art thou?*] He questioneth not Christ of his country, but of his condition, *q. d.* Art thou a man or a God? Such a dunghill deity, he meant, as the heathens worshipped. And therefore our Saviour would not once answer him. Especially since if he should have asserted his Deity, Pilate likely would have acquitted and dismissed him; whereas Christ knew that he was now and here to be condemned. There are that think that Pilate's wife's dream was from the devil, who sought thereby to have hindered the work of our redemption, which could not be wrought but by the death of Christ.

Ver. 10. *Speakest thou not unto me*] No, and yet St Paul saith, he "witnessed a good confession before Pontius Pilate," 1 Tim. vi. 13; because he had said sufficient before, and was now ready to seal up the truth with his blood. But to be delivered he would not once open his mouth to Pilate. So Mr Saunders had so wholly devoted himself to the defence of Christ's cause, that he forbade his wife to sue for his delivery; and when other of his friends had by suit almost obtained it, he discouraged them, so that they did not follow their suit. I pray you let me make labour for you, said one Cresswell to Master Bradford. You may do what you will, said Bradford. But tell me what suit I shall make

for you, quoth Cresswell. Forsooth, said the other, that you will do, do it not at my request; for I desire nothing at your hands. If the Queen will give me life, I will thank her; if she will banish me, I will thank her; if she will burn me, I will thank her; if she will condemn me to perpetual imprisonment, I will thank her. Life in God's displeasure is worse than death; and death in his true fear is true life.

I have power to crucify thee] To crucify an innocent man? Who gave him that power? But profane persons bear themselves over-bold upon their power, as if they were little gods within themselves. So Cæsar told Metellus he could as easily destroy him as bid it to be done. So Caligula speaking to the consuls, I laugh, said he, to think that I can kill you with a nod of my head, and that this fair throat of my wife's shall be presently cut if I but speak the word. *Rideo quod uno nutu meo jugulare vos possim, et uxori tam bona cervix, simul ac jussero, demetur.*

Ver. 11. *Except it were given thee from above*] Therefore be good in thine office, lest thou give a dear account to him that is higher than the highest, as Solomon hath it; who therefore calls the judgment-seat "the holy place," Eccl. viii. 10. Pilate was afterwards kicked off the bench by Caius, for his perverting of justice, and, for grief and shame, became his own death's-man.

Ver. 12. *But the Jews cried out, saying, &c.*] They return again to their former accusation, and enforced it. One way or other they are bent to have his blood. In King Edward VI.'s days, when the Duke of Somerset was cleared of the treason laid to his charge, yet he must suffer (so his potent enemies would have it) for I know not what slight suspicions of felony. At which time also, Sir Thomas Arundel was, among others, with some difficulty condemned. Unhappy man (saith the historian) who found the doing of anything, or of nothing, dangerous alike.

Ver. 13. *When Pilate therefore heard that saying*] That saying, and the base fear of being shent by Cæsar, makes him warp and go against his conscience. But should not judges be men of courage? Should not the standard be of steel? the chief posts in the house be heart of oak? Solomon's tribunal was underpropt with lions, to show what metal a magistrate should be made of. It is a mercy to have judges, *modo audeant quæ sentiunt,* saith the orator, so they dare do their consciences. (Cic. pro Milone.)

Ver. 14. *Behold your King*] *q. d.* A likely matter that this poor man should affect the kingdom; and not rather that he is like to lose his life, by forged cavillation. Christ himself was misreported and falsely accused, saith Father Latimer, both as touching his words and meaning also. Korah and his complices object to the meekest of men with one breath, pride, ambition, usurpation of authority, *Invenies apud Tacitum frequentatas accusationes majestatis: unicum crimen eorum qui crimine vacabant.* (Lips. in Tacit.)

Ver. 15. *We have no king but Cæsar*] Why but, Is there no king in Sion? is her counsellor perished? saith the prophet, Micah iv. 9. Did not these men look for a Messiah? Or if not, will they reject the Lord from being their King? Oh, how blind is malice, how desperately set upon its ends and enterprises! But in Christ's kingdom this is wonderful, saith Zanchius, that this King willeth and causeth that the kingdoms of the world be subject to his kingdom; and again he willeth and causeth that his kingdom be also subject to the kingdoms of the world. *In regno Christi hoc mirabile est, quod iste rex vult et efficit.* (Zanch. Miscel.)

Ver. 16. *Then delivered he him, &c.*] Overcome by their importunity, and over-awed by the fear of Cæsar to condemn the innocent. It was Cato's complaint, that private men's thieves are laid by the heels, and in cold irons; but these public thieves that wrong and rob the common-wealth sit in scarlet, with gold chains about their necks. Sinisterity is an enemy to sincerity.[1] All self-respects and corrupt ends must be laid aside by men in authority and justice, as Moses speaks, that is, pure justice without mud must run down, Deut. xvi. 20. *Durescite, durescite*, said the smith to the duke, that durst not do justice.

Ver. 17. *And he, bearing his cross, &c.*] This was the Roman fashion (as Plutarch relates it), that every condemned person should bear that cross that anon should bear him.[2] Hence grew that expression of our Saviour, "He that will be my disciple must take up his cross," and so "fill up that which is behind," Col. i. 24.

Into a place called the place of a skull] Where his tender heart was pierced with grief, no doubt, at the sad sight of such a slaughter of men made by sin; like as it could not but be a sore cut and corrosive to Mauritius, to see his wife and children slain before him, when himself was also to be next stewed in his own broth. St John is exact in setting down our Saviour's sufferings, and this for one.

Ver. 18. *Where they crucified him*] An ignominious, accursed, and dolorous death; for he was nailed to the tree in the hands and feet, which are the most sensible parts, as fullest of sinews; and therefore (in so fine a body as his especially) of most exquisite sense. Look wistly upon sin in this glass, and love it if thou canst. For our sins were the nails and ourselves the traitors that fastened him to the tree. Pilate and his soldiers, Judas and the Jews, were all set a-work by us. Learn to lay the blame on thyself, and say, It was my gluttony that reached a cup of gall and vinegar to his mouth; mine incontinency that provided stripes for his back; mine arrogancy that platted a crown of thorns upon his head; mine inconstancy that put a reed into his hand; my treachery that nailed his

hands and feet; my vanity that grieved his soul to the death; my self-love that thrust a spear into his side, &c. *Adsum ego qui feci.* (Virgil.)

Ver. 19. *Jesus of Nazareth, &c.*] To persuade the people to bow superstitiously at the name of Jesus, Papists commonly (but ridiculously) teach in their pulpits, that Christ himself on the cross bowed his head on the right side, to reverence his own name, which was written over it; as Sir Edwin Sands relates from his own experience.

Ver. 20. *In Hebrew, Greek, and Latin*] In Hebrew, for the Jews who gloried in the law; in Greek, for the Grecians who gloried in wisdom; in Latin, for the Romans who most gloried in dominion and power. As if Pilate should have said, This is the King of all religion, having reference to the Hebrews; of all wisdom, to the Greeks; of all power, to the Romans. The Holy Ghost would also hereby commend unto us the dignity and study of these three languages, to be retained for ever in the Church of Christ.

Ver. 21. *Write not, The King of the Jews*] They would needs be mending *Magnificat*, as they say; and this of pure spite, that the disgrace might rest only upon Christ, and not at all reflect upon their nation. Whereas, in truth, nothing so ennobleth, as any the least relation to Christ. Bethlehem, where he was born, is, though the least, yet therefore "not the least among the cities of Judah," Matt. ii. 69; Mic. v. 2. Among those that were marked, Rev. vii. 5, Judah is reckoned first, of all the tribes by Leah's side, because our Lord sprang out of Judah; and Naphthali is named first among those that came by Rachel's side, because at Capernaum (in that tribe) Christ dwelt; which therefore also is said to be lifted up to heaven, Matt. xi. 23. *Ut utrobique superemineat Christi prærogativa.*

Ver. 22. *What I have written, I have written*] i. e. I am unchangeably resolved it shall stand. So God saith, I am that I am; that is, I am yesterday, and to-day, and the same for ever. Learn we may of Pilate to be constant to a good cause.[3] Marcellus the pope would not change his name, according to the custom, to show his immutability, that he was no changeling.

Ver. 23. *Took his garments*] Christ, as Elias, being now to ascend into heaven, did willingly let go his garments; and the rather that he might clothe us with his righteousness. Let us suffer with joy by the spoiling of our goods, as knowing in ourselves (not only by books or relation of others) that we have in heaven a better and more enduring substance, Heb. x. 32. But what a wise fool was Sir Thomas More, who being brought to the Tower, a malefactor, and one of the officers demanding his upper garment for a fee, meaning his gown, he said he should have it; and took him his cap, saying, it was the

---

[1] *Privatorum fures in nervo et compedibus vitam agunt; publici in auro et purpura visuntur.* Cato ap. Gel. xi. 18.

[2] τῷ σώματι τῶν κολαζομένων ἕκαστος ἐκφέρει τὸν ἑαυτοῦ σταυρόν. Plut.

[3] *Non retractat homo profanus, quod, vere licet, sine mento et consilio de Christo scripsit.* Cal.

uppermost garment that he had. So, when he was to be beheaded, he said to the hangman, I pray you let me lay my beard over the block, lest you should cut it. He thought it no glory, unless he might die with a mock in his mouth. These be the world's wizards.

Now the coat was without seam] *Christi tunica est unica :* they that rent it by schisms, are worse than the rude soldiers. There can be no greater sin committed, saith Cyprian, than to break the unity of the Church : yea, though one should suffer martyrdom, yet cannot he expiate his thereby sin of discord. This, saith Chrysostom, is a bold, but a true speech of Cyprian.[1] And like to this, is that of Œcolampadius to the Lutherans in Switzerland ; Our error may be pardoned, so that Christ by faith be apprehended, *Discordiam, neque si sanguinem fundamus, expiabimus,* but the blot of our discord we cannot wash off with our heart-blood. (Œcol. ad fratres in Suevia.)

Ver. 24. *That the Scripture might be fulfilled*] So exactly is the Old Testament fulfilled in the New. The testimonies whereof are cited not only by way of accommodation, but because they are the proper meaning of the places. The soldiers could not cast the dice upon our Saviour's garments, but it was foretold. This shows that our redemption by Christ is no imposture, but a plot of God's own contriving. Let this settle us against all doubtings.

Ver. 25. *Now there stood by the cross, &c.*] The men were fled, the women stood to it. Souls have no sexes. Manoah's wife was the more manly of the two. Priscilla is sometimes set before Aquila. When St Paul came first to Philippi, he had none that would hear him, but a few women, Acts xviii. 18 ; Rom. xvi. 3 ; 2 Tim. iv. 19 ; Acts xvi. 13.

Ver. 26. *When Jesus therefore saw his mother*] In the midst of his miseries he thinks of his mother, and takes care for her well-doing after his decease. Doctor Taylor, the martyr, among other things he said to his son at his death, laid this charge upon him : When thy mother is waxed old, forsake her not, but provide for her to thy power, and that she lack nothing ; for so will God bless thee, and give thee long life upon earth and prosperity. The Athenians punished such with death as nourished not their aged parents. And St Paul saith, that to requite parents is good and acceptable before God, 1 Tim. v. 4. καλὸν, *sc. coram hominibus.* (Scult.)

Ver. 27. *The disciple took her, &c.*] A precious *depositum ;* the house was the better she abode in ; yet dare we not deify her, as the Papists ; as neither will we vilify her, as the author of the Female Glory basely slanders some of us, that we rudely call her Moll, God's maid. *Os durum !* Our parents, saith the heathen, are our household gods, Θεοὶ ἐφέστιοι. (Hierocles.) Honour them we must both in word and deed. That

our Saviour here calls her woman, and not mother, was either because he would not add to her grief, who was now pierced to the soul with that sword Simeon spake of, Luke ii. 35 ; or, lest he should create her further trouble, if she had been known to be his mother ; or, for that, being now in his last work, and ready way to heaven, he knew none after the flesh. Thomas Watt, martyr, spake thus at his death to his wife and six children : Wife and my good children, I must now depart from you ; therefore henceforth know I you no more, &c. But whereas Christ commends the care of his mother to his beloved disciple, with, Behold thy mother, the Samians used the like speech, when to the richer of the citizens, the mothers of those who died in the wars were given to be maintained by them, Σοὶ ταύτην δίδωμι τὴν μητέρα.

Ver. 28. *That the Scripture might be fulfilled*] It is a high point of heavenly wisdom to do our ordinary business in obedience to God's command, and with an aim at his glory ; to go about our earthly affairs with heavenly minds, and in serving men to serve God ; to taste God in the creature, and whether we eat or drink, or whatever else we do, to set up God, 1 Cor. x. 31. Every action is a step either to heaven or hell. The poor servant in being faithful to his master, " serves the Lord Christ," Col. iii. 24, who was more careful here of fulfilling the Scripture and working out our salvation, than of satisfying his own most vehement thirst.

Ver. 29. *Now there was set a vessel full of vinegar*] Cold comfort : they used to give others wine to comfort them, according to Prov. xxxi. 6, and mingled myrrh with the wine (*granum thuris in calice vini*), that might attenuate their blood, and so help to despatch them ; as also to cause a giddiness in them, that they might be the less sensible of their pain. But they dealt much worse with our Saviour, mingling for him, in mockery, vinegar and gall, to add to his other misery. This he drank, that we might drink of the heavenly *nepenthes,* that torrent of pleasure, Psal. xvi. 11.

Ver. 30. *It is finished*] Christ would not off the cross till all were done that was here to be done ; that which remained being rather a play than a work to him. The consideration whereof should cast us into a real ecstasy of joy and admiration ; nothing like that counterfeit ecstasy whereinto Rondeletius saw a priest at Rome to feign himself to fall whenever he heard those words of Christ, *Consummatum est,* It is finished. But the physician observing this counterfeit careful in his fall to lay his head in a soft place, he suspected the dissimulation, and by the threats of a cudgel quickly recovered him.

Ver. 31. *Because it was the preparation*] Their preparation to the sabbath began at three of the clock in the afternoon.[2] The best and wealthiest

---

[1] *Inexpiabilis discordiæ macula martyrii sanguine ablui et passione purgari non potest.* Cypr. de Unit. Eccles. Chrysost. Hom. xi. ad Ephes.

[2] They might go no farther on the preparation-day than three *parsæ, i. e.* twelve miles, lest coming home too late they might not have leisure to prepare. Buxt. Synagog. Judaica. In Meth. Curandi, cap. de Catal. p. 98.

of them, even those that had many servants, did with their own hands further the preparation; so that sometimes the masters themselves would chop herbs, sweep the house, cleave wood, kindle the fire. Our ancestors also were wont to give over work on the Saturday, when it rang to even-song. And usually as men measure to God in preparation, he re-measureth to them in bless-ing. King Edgar ordained that Sunday should be solemnized in this land from Saturday, nine of the clock, till Monday morning. The Jews, be-fore their preparation, had their fore-preparation; and before their sabbath, their fore-sabbath, their *sabbatulum ante sabbatum.*[1] Those of Tiberias began the sabbath sooner than others; those at Tsepphore continued it longer, adding *De profano ad sacrum.* We are now so far from this, that we trench upon the holy time, and say, "When will the sabbath be over?" yea, in too many places God's sacred sabbath is made the voider and dung-hill for all refuse businesses; as by others, it is made as Bacchus' orgies, with ales, May-games, &c. So that it should be named according to these men's observing of it, *Dæmoniacus potius quam Dominicus,* as Alsted hath it. (Encyclo-pædia.)

Ver. 32. *Brake the legs of the first*] The good thief also had his legs broke and his life taken away; though by his repentance he made his cross a Jacob's ladder, whereby angels descended to fetch up his soul.

Ver. 33. *And saw that he was dead already*] He took his own time to die; and therefore, ver. 31, it is said, "that he bowed his head, and gave up the ghost;" whereas other men bow not the head till they have given up the ghost. He also cried with a loud voice and died, which shows that he wanted not strength of nature to have lived longer if he had listed.

Ver. 34. *But one of the soldiers with a spear*] What an odd conceit is that of the Papists, that from the Greek word λόγχη, have made this sol-dier's name Longinus![2] and to make up the tale, they tell the people, that whereas before he had been blind, by the anointing of his eyes with the watery blood that came out of Christ's side, he received his sight, became a Christian, a mar-tyr, a canonized saint, and that his relics were afterwards worshipped. The lance and nails that tormented Christ were graced with a holy-day by Pope Innocent VI., and this eulogy, *Ave ferrum triumphale, intrans pectus tu vitale cœli pandis ostia, &c.*[3]

There came out blood and water] The *pericar-dium* being pierced, which nature hath filled with water to cool the heat of the heart. Hereto St John alludes, when he saith, 1 John v. 6, that "Christ came by water and blood," to teach us, that he justifieth none by his merit but when he sanctifieth by his Spirit. *Possumus etiam hinc*

asseverare ex latere Christi fluxisse nostra sacra-menta, saith Calvin, We may safely say that our sacraments issued out of Christ's side.

Ver. 35. *And he that saw it, &c.*] Nothing so sure as sight. One eye-witness is more than ten ear-witnesses.[4] It is probable that the apostles that were so conversant with our Saviour had their day-books, wherein they recorded his daily oracles, and other occurrences, and out of which they compiled the Gospels.

His record is true] The gospel is called the testimony, Isa. viii. 20, because it beareth wit-ness to itself. The law is called light (*lex, lux*), because by itself it is seen to be of God, as the sun is seen by its own light.

Ver. 36. *Not a bone of him was broken*] So he appeared to be the true Paschal Lamb, that was roasted whole in the fire of his Father's wrath, to deliver us from the wrath to come. The sol-diers could not break his legs, because God had otherwise ordered it. *Voluntas Dei, necessitas rei.*

Ver. 37. *They shall look upon him*] This is not a threat, but a promise, Zech. xii. 10, fulfilled, Acts ii. 37, when Peter's hearers felt the nails, wherewith they had crucified Christ, sticking fast in their own hearts, and piercing them with hor-ror, κατενύγησαν.

Ver. 38. *A disciple of Jesus, but secretly for fear*] A disciple he was, though a dastard. In-firmities, if disclaimed, discard us not. Uzziah ceased not to be a king, when he began to be a leper. Joshua the high priest, though ill-clothed, yet stood before the angel, Zech. iii. 2; Christ did not abhor his presence, nor reject his service. The Church calleth herself black, Cant. i. 5, but Christ calls her fair, &c. In peace-offer-ings they might offer leavened bread, to show that God will bear with his people's infirmities.

Ver. 39. *And there came also Nicodemus*] An-other night-bird, a chieftain in the ecclesiastical state, as Joseph of Arimathea (or Ramath, Sam-uel's country) was in the civil. The faith of these two now breaks out, though it had long lain hid, as the sun under a cloud, as seed under a clod: now they manifest their love to Christ, so cruelly handled, as the true mother did hers to her child, when it was to be cut in two.

Ver. 40. *With the spices, as the manner of the Jews*] To testify their hope of a resurrection. In an apish imitation of whom, the Gentiles also, though they had no such hope, kept a great stir, and made much ado about the decent burial of their dead. *Habent et vespæ favos, et simiæ imi-tantur homines,* saith Cyprian.

Ver. 41. *A new sepulchre*] Fit for him that was the "first-born from the dead, the first-fruits of them that sleep." Besides else it might have been said, that some other had risen, and not he (saith Theodoret), as Mahomet saith that Christ was not crucified, but another for him. ἵνα μὴ

---

[1] προπαρασκευή, Matt. xxvii. 62. προσάββατον, Mark xv. 42. *Ante-sabbatum Vetus ecclesia vigiliam vocabat.* Bux-torf.

[2] *Notetur turpis pontificiorum lapsus in Longino, et inscitia Græcæ linguæ.* Cartw.

[3] *In Deorum numerum relatus ut de* Francis. Bembus. Hist. Ven.

[4] *Plus valet oculatus testis unus quam auriti decem. Ex quibus postea Historia Evangelica est contexta.* Scult. Annal.

συκοφαντισθῇ ἡ ἀνάστασις, ὡς ἄλλου ἀναστάντος.

Ver. 42. *Because of the Jews*] That they might not do servile work on the sabbath, though it were to inter Christ's body. See Luke xxiii. 56.

CHAPTER XX.

Ver. 1. *The first day of the week*] Now the Christian sabbath, in honour of Christ's resurrection, and therefore called "the Lord's day," Rev. i. 10; as the holy supper is called "the Lord's supper," 1 Cor. x.; as the saints are called κυριακὴ, kirk, church. The title of the 24th Psalm is, "A Psalm of David." To this the Greek addeth, "Of the first day of the week," meaning that this psalm was wont to be sung in the temple every first day of the week, which now is the Christian's sabbath; and of Christ, his Church and kingdom, and the entertaining of his gospel, doth this psalm intreat. Let every one of us keep sabbath, saith Ignatius, in a spiritual manner, rejoicing in the meditation of the law, not in the rest of the body. ἕκαστος ἡμῶν σαββατιζέτω πνευματικῶς. (Ignat. ep. iii. ad Magnes.) And in those primitive times when the question was asked, *Servasti Dominicum?* Hast thou kept the Lord's day? the answer was returned, *Christianus sum, intermittere non possum:* I am a Christian, and may not do otherwise. The Jews gave that honour to their sabbath, that they named from it all the other days of the week, as the first, second, third day, &c., of the sabbath, which we from the heathens (a worse pattern) name Monday, Tuesday, Wednesday, &c. *Ex instituto Mercurii Trismegisti.*

Ver. 2. *Then she runneth*] *Amor addidit alas,* love is impatient of delays. Christ cometh leaping over the "mountains of Bether," Cant. ii. 17; all manner lets and impediments. And the Church, as impatient as he, bids him "Make haste, my beloved, and be like to a roe," Cant. viii. 4, or to a fawn of the harts, which when it fleeth, looketh behind it, saith the Chaldee paraphrast there. She affects not only a union, but a unity with him.

Ver. 3. *Peter therefore went forth*] He despaired not though he had grievously fallen. The saints cannot fall so far, but that God's supporting hand is ever under them. They may be doused over head and ears in the waters of iniquity, yea, sink twice to the bottom, yet shall rise again and recover; for the Lord puts under his hand; yea, as he that stumbleth, and yet falleth not, gets ground by his stumbling, so it is here.

Ver. 4. *So they ran both together*] But the swifter of foot they were, the slower in faith; for "he that believeth maketh not haste," Isa. xxviii. 6. They believed not fully the resurrection; when they heard the news of it, and from the angels too, they stirred not, but rejected it as a fable. Now that they hear (though but by a woman only) that the Lord's body was removed to another sepulchre (though that were but a

rash report, and nothing so) they run amain. Oh the dullness that is found in the best!

Ver. 5. *Yet went he not in*] He durst not; so some fearful are afraid of every step, saying, as Cæsar at Rubicon, Yet we may go back; and as the king of Navarre told Beza, that he would launch no further into the sea, than he might be sure to return safe to the haven. *Pelago se non ita commissurus esset quin, quando liberet, pedem referre posset.*

Ver. 6. *Following him and went in*] John came first; Peter entered first: "soft and fair goes far:" soft fire makes sweet malt: leap Christians are not much to be liked; such as quickly step out of profaneness into profession. Hot at hand seldom holds out. The stony ground immediately received the seed with joy, and started up suddenly, εὐθέως; but the good ground brings forth fruit with patience or tarriance, ἐν ὑπομονῇ, Luke viii. 15. Walk deliberately, and ponder the paths of thy feet, as Solomon bids, Prov. iv. 26. A Christian's progress is as the sun, which shines more and more to the perfect day, Prov. iv. 18; and as the trumpet in Mount Sion, Exod. xx. 18, which sounded louder and louder till it was heard all the country over.

Ver. 7. *And the napkin that was about his head*] These grave-clothes were evidences of our Saviour's resurrection, and are therefore mentioned by the evangelist. But what shift made Paleottus, Archbishop of Bonony, for matter, who wrote a great book of the shadow of Christ's dead body in the sindon or linen-cloth, wherein it was wrapped! This book was also commented upon by the professor of divinity there. Had not these men little to do? Did they not, as one saith,

Magno conatu magnas nugas agere?
Tenet insanabile multos—Scribendi Cacoethes.

Ver. 8. *And he saw and believed*] i. e. He believed his own eyes, that the Lord's body was not in the sepulchre; but, as Mary Magdalene had told them, so they mis-believed, that it was taken away to some other place, further from Calvary, for honour's sake, that he might not lie buried with the wicked. Hence it is that in the next verse it is added, that "as yet they knew not the Scripture."

Ver. 9. *For as yet they knew not the Scripture*] Which yet was clear enough in this point, Psal. xvi. 10; cx. 1; Isa. liii. 10, 11. The resurrection of our Saviour was not obscurely shadowed out in Adam waking out of sleep, Isaac received after a sort from the dead, Joseph drawn out of prison to be Lord of Egypt, Samson bearing away the gates of Gaza, David advanced to the kingdom, where there was but a step betwixt him and death; Jonah preserved in the whale's belly, &c.

Ver. 10. *Went again to their own home*] Waiting till God should further enlighten both organ and object, as Mary also did, Luke ii. 19, 51.

Ver. 11. *Mary stood at the sepulchre, weeping*] Some think it was because she conceived that the Jews had gotten away our Saviour's dead body to dishonour it; as the popish persecutors digged up Bucer's and many other good men's bones to burn them. She wept where she had no such cause; so do too many, women especially, who should do well to keep their tears for better uses, and not wash foul rooms with sweet waters. Needless tears must be unwept again.

Ver. 12. *And seeth two angels*] Sent for her sake, and the rest, to certify them of the resurrection. It is their office (and they are glad of it) to comfort and counsel the saints still, as it were by speaking and doing after a spiritual manner, though we see them not, as she here did. The philosopher told his friends when they came into his little and low cottage, "The gods are here with me," ἐντεῦθεν οὐκ ἄπεισι Θεοί: sure it is that God and his angels are ever with his people, when they are weeping especially.

Ver. 13. *Woman, why weepest thou?*] Angels pity human frailty still, and secretly suggest comfort. But Mary had no such cause to cry, if she had known all, but to rejoice rather; so hath a Christian, in what condition soever, all things reckoned. Had Elizabeth known she should have been queen, she would not have wished herself a milk-maid. Saints are "heirs of the kingdom," saith James, ii. 5, heads destinated to the diadem, saith Tertullian; what mean they then to be at any time in their dumps?

Ver. 14. *She turned herself back*] As not able to abide the brightness of those glorious angels any longer. To the gardener therefore she addresseth herself for further direction. See what a happiness it is to be taught by the ministry of men, like ourselves, and to have angels about us, but invisible.

Ver. 15. *Woman, why weepest thou? whom seekest thou?*] Where the angels left, the Lord begins. God hath for our sakes taken the preaching of the gospel from the angels, and given it to ministers, who have thenceforth also changed names; for ministers are called angels, Rev. ii. 1, and angels ministers, Heb. i. 14.

Ver. 16. *Jesus saith unto her, Mary*] Christ is nearest to such as, with Mary, cannot see him for their tears, if with her in humility they seek after him. He calls her but by her name, and she acknowledgeth him. The ear, we say, is first up in a morning; and nothing so soon awakes us as to be called by our names. How easily can Christ call up our drowsy hearts, when he pleaseth; and (when we are even turned away from him, as Mary here was) make us reciprocate and cry Rabboni? Mary! saith Christ; Master! saith Mary; and presently she clasps about his feet, having her heart as near to his heart, as her hands were to his feet. What a meeting of love (saith a divine hereupon) will there be between the new glorified saint and the glorious Redeemer?

Ver. 17. *Touch me not, &c.*] She had caught him by the feet (as the Shunammite did Elisha, as the Shulamite did her spouse), and there she would have held him longer, out of inconsiderate zeal, Matt. xxviii. 2; Cant. iii. 4; but that he takes her off this corporal conceit, that she may learn to live by faith, and not by sense; to be drawn after him to heaven, whither he was now ascending, and to go tell his brethren what she had seen and heard, *Ne morere, sed ad perturbatos discipulos accurre et quod vidisti renuncia.* (Pet. Martyr.)

Ver. 18. *Mary Magdalene came and told*] She had told them and troubled them before with a conceit that they had (but to what end, or whither, she knew not) removed the Lord's body; fitly therefore is she sent to assure them of the resurrection. And though loth to depart, yet she bridles her affections, though never so impetuous, and brings them to be wholly at Christ's beck and check.

Ver. 19. *When the doors, &c., for fear of the Jews*] The sheep had been scattered, but now were by the great Shepherd re-collected (according to the promise, Zech. xiii. 7, "I will turn my hand upon the little ones"); yet, sensible of their late fright, they show some trepidation. Afterwards, when the Spirit came down upon them, they not only set open the doors, but preached Christ boldly in the temple without dread of danger. So did Basil; when the emperor threatened him with bonds, banishment, &c., he wished him to affright babies with such bugbears; his life might be taken away, but not his faith; his head, but not his crown.[1] So Luther, at first so fearful and faint-hearted, that in the year 1518, he wrote thus to the Pope Leo X.: *Vivifica, occide, voca, revoca, approba, reproba, vocem tuam vocem Christi in te præsidentis et loquentis agnoscam.* I lay myself prostrate at your holiness' feet, together with all that I am and have; quicken me, kill me, call me, recall me, approve me, reprove me, I shall acknowledge your voice to be the very voice of Christ, ruling and speaking in you. Yet afterwards he took more courage; witness, among many other things, that brave answer of his to one that told him that both the pope and the emperor had threatened his ruin, *Contemptus est a me Romanus et favor et furor.* And when Spalatinus had sent unto him to inquire whether he would go to Worms, and appear in the gospel's cause, if Cæsar summoned him? Go, said he, I am resolved to go, though I were sure to encounter so many devils there as are tiles upon the houses. *Omnia de me præsumas præter fugam et palinodiam. Fugere nolo, multo minus recantare.* (Luth. Epist.)

Ver. 20. *He showed unto them his hands, &c.*] For their further confirmation; so he doth unto us every time we come to his table. But oh, how should our hearts long to look for ever upon the human nature of Christ, clothed with an exuberancy of glory, at the right hand of his heavenly Father! and to consider that every vein in that blessed body bled, to bring us to heaven! Augustine was wont to wish that he might have the happiness to see these three things, *Romam in flore, Paulum in ore, et Christum in corpore.* But I should take venerable Bede's part rather, and say with him, *Anima*

---

[1] *Pueris illa terriculamenta proponenda.*

mea desiderat Christum regem meum videre in decore suo : Let me see my King Christ in his heavenly beauty.

Ver. 21. *Then said Jesus to them again, Peace*] The common salutation amongst the Jews (the Turks at this day salute in like sort, *Salaum aleek ;* the reply is, *Aleek salaum,* that is, Peace be unto you). This our Saviour purposely redoubleth, to persuade them of pardon for their late shameful defection from him, and their backwardness to believe his resurrection. Sin is soon committed, but not so easily remitted ; or, if in heaven, yet not in our own consciences, till which there is little comfort. Christ, to confirm them, is pleased again to employ them, and to count them faithful, putting them again into the ministry, 1 Tim. i. 13. A calling not more honourable than comfortable ; the very trust that God commits to a man therein, seals up love and favour to him.

Ver. 22. *He breathed on them, and saith, &c.*] Otherwise, who had been sufficient for these things ? The ministry is a burden to be trembled at by the angels themselves, saith Chrysostom.[1] Father Latimer, when at the coming in of the six articles, he, to keep a good conscience, resigned up his bishopric, putting off his rochet, he suddenly gave a skip in the floor for joy, feeling his shoulders so light, and being discharged, as he said, of such a heavy burden. Now the Spirit where he is bestowed by Christ, heaves at one end (as St Paul's word imports) and takes off the brunt of the business from us. He oils our wheels, and makes us drive merrily. He helps our infirmities (Rom. viii. 26 ; *ἀντιλαμβάνεσθαι, Est manus proprium, ut ait Galenus*), edgeth our spirits, steeleth our faces, filleth us with matter, furnisheth us with words, doth all our work for us. When I first came into this city (said Calvin, upon his death-bed, in his speech to his fellow-ministers) I found all out of frame, and met with many malicious opposites. But our Lord Christ so settled and strengthened me, who by nature (to speak truth) am easily daunted, *ut nullis illorum conatibus cesserim,* that I stoutly withstood them.

Ver. 23. *Whose soever sins ye remit, &c.*] Remission of sin is the chief benefit of the gospel : and for the creed (which is the sum of the gospel) all the former articles are perfected in that of " remission of sins ; " and all the following articles are effects of it. Now none can remit sins, but God ; to speak properly. Papists tell us of one that could remove mountains, but to remit sins is peculiar to God alone. Man may remit the trespass, but God only the transgression. Howbeit ministers may, and in some cases must, " declare unto man his righteousness," Job xxxiii. 23 ; pronounce, in Christ's name, the truly penitent righteous in God's sight, by Christ's righteousness freely imputed and given unto them. They must also retain, by the same authority, and bind upon impenitent

sinners (so continuing) their sins to destruction, " Having in a readiness to revenge all disobedience," 2 Cor. x. 6. This we may do, as ministers, and more we claim not.

Ver. 24. *But Thomas, one of the twelve*] A man cannot be wilfully absent from the public assemblies but once, without great danger and damage. Thomas was absent perhaps about some weighty cause. It may be he lurked and lay close for fear of the Jews ; or it may be he was providing, and settling his own private affairs, now his Master was slain ; but whatever the cause was, the effect was grievous ; he was woefully hardened.

Ver. 25. *I will not believe*] Ah, wilful Thomas (quoth Mr Bradford, martyr) ; I will not, saith he : so adding to his incredulity, obstinacy. But yet Christ appeared unto him, and would not lose him, &c.

Ver. 26. *The doors being shut*] Although it be said, that when Christ came to his disciples the doors were shut, yet have I as much to prove that the doors opened at his coming, as ye to prove that he came through the door, said Robert Smith, martyr, to the doctor that disputed with him.

Ver. 27. *Then saith he to Thomas*] Who was not excommunicated by the rest, but gently borne with, till Christ should cure him. Neither did he forsake their meetings, though he believed not their relation. It is good to stand in Christ's way, to be found at the foddering place, Cant. i. 8. But some, like spiritual vagabonds, as Cain, excommunicate themselves from God's presence, in the use of the means ; we may write, Lord, have mercy upon such, as utterly deplored.

Ver. 28. *My Lord and my God*] This is true faith indeed, that individuates God, and appropriates him to itself.[2] Were it not for this possessive " mine," the devil might say the creed to as good purpose as we. He believes there is a God and a Christ ; but that which torments him is, he can say " my " to never an article of the faith.

Ver. 29. *Blessed are they that have not seen*] We see Christ in the flesh by the eyes of the apostles ; like as the Israelites saw Canaan by the eyes of the spies ; and this is sufficient unto faith, as the evangelist showeth in the next verses.

Ver. 30. *And many other signs, &c.*] If Cicero could say of Socrates (whose words Plato had recorded), and could request the like of his readers, concerning Lucius Crassus, that they would imagine much more good of them than they found written ; how much more might St John do the same concerning Christ !

Ver. 31. *These things are written*] He speaks this of the writ of the other three evangelists also. Matthew wrote his Gospel eight years after Christ, Mark 10, Luke 15, and John 42, in the days of Trajan. He died in the 101st year of his own age.

[1] *Onus ipsis etiam Angelis tremendum.*

[2] *ἡ πίστις ἰδιοποιεῖται τὸν Θεόν.* Chrysost.

CHAPTER XXI.

Ver. 1. *After these things Jesus showed himself*] Some have been of opinion that this chapter was not written by John (because he concluded his history in the end of the last chapter), but added by some other, as the last chapter of Deuteronomy was to Moses' writings. These should have observed, that in the former chapter those arguments only are set down by the evangelist that fell out at Jerusalem for the manifestation of Christ's resurrection; as in this chapter, those whereby he approved the truth of his resurrection in Galilee also, according to his promise, Matt. xxvi. 32; that they might believe and remember that Jesus Christ of the seed of David was verily raised from the dead according to the gospel, 2 Tim. ii. 8: this being a doctrine of greatest consequence and comfort, 1 Cor. xv. 5. Peter thought himself sufficiently assured of it, and therefore said, I go a fishing; but he was deceived, and needed further confirmation.

Ver. 2. *There were met together Simon, &c.*] When good and godly men meet, when chaste and honest people assemble together, it is not to be called a faction, but a court rather, saith Tertullian.[1] Those are a faction, that conspire against good men. The society of such is like the slime and filth that is congealed, where many toads and other vermin join together. God dwells in the assembly of saints; shall we, like stoics, sty up ourselves, and not daily run into their company? He that comes when ointments and sweet spices are stirring, doth carry away some of the sweet savour, though he think not of it: so here. See Prov. xiii. 10.

Ver. 3. *I go a fishing, &c.*] Being not yet employed in the public ministry, he would not be idle, and that he might not be chargeable to the Church. This life is in Isaiah called, "The life of our hands," because it is to be maintained by the labour of our hands. We are to earn ere we eat, 2 Thess. iii. 8. *Res age tutus eris.* Ovid.

And that night they caught nothing] Labour we never so hard, unless God bless it, and stop that hole in the bottom of the bag, Hag. i. 1, those secret issues and drains of expense, at which men's estates run out, we shall be forced to say with Severus the emperor, *Omnia feci et nihil profuit.* (Spartian.)

Ver. 4. *But when the morning*] Mourning lasteth but till morning, Psal. xxx. 5. *Flebile principium melior fortuna sequetur,* said Queen Elizabeth, when she was to be sent to the Tower.

Ver. 5. *Children, have ye any meat?*] This he saith as seeming to be some housekeeper, who passing by fishermen, calls to them, as willing to buy their fish for the use of his family. Galeacius Caracciolus, that noble marquis of Vico (that

left all for Christ, preferring the blessing of God before the world's warm sun), would go into the market at Geneva and cater for his household; grieving for nothing more than that he had not wherewithal to keep a better house for the relief of the poor. And in that respect only he wished himself as great a man at Geneva as he was in Italy. (His Life by Crashaw.)

Ver. 6. *Cast the net on the right side, &c.*] This counsel he gives as a stranger, who haply might see a confluence of fish there, being on the shore, which they in the ship saw not. They obey him therefore, as content to lose one labour more, if it must be so; they knew not what another draught might produce. It is good to be doing in God's way: sooner or later success will ensue. Bind not the Lord to a day; wake not my beloved till he please; he will pay us for all our pains and patience. Consider but our, 1. distance, 2. dependence, and we will wait.

Ver. 7. *Therefore that disciple, &c.*] Now they see the cause why, till then, they caught nothing was, that they might the better know him to be the Lord. God will one day let us see that he in very faithfulness afflicts us; and that however yet it seems so for a season, it is not in vain to have sought his face. John knew not our Saviour by sight here, but by the multitude of fishes that came to hand by his direction. The Rochellers might easily see as much, when they were miraculously relieved by that shoal of shell-fish cast upon their shore in a strait siege, whereby their city was miraculously preserved.

Ver. 8. *And the other disciples came, &c.*] They came all to Christ, but Peter sooner; he cast away all care of his fish, having the Lord to go to. It is best to be first and forwardest in a good matter; not only to make a shift to get to heaven, but to have an abundant entrance thereinto, to come bravely into the haven, by adding one grace to another, as Peter hath it, 2 Pet. i. 2, 11. It is a low and unworthy strain in some (saith one) to labour after no more grace than will keep life and soul together, that is, soul and hell asunder. But that man for heaven, and heaven for him, that sets up for his mark, "the resurrection of the dead," Phil. iii. 11, that is, by a metonymy of the subject for the adjunct, that perfection of holiness that accompanieth the state of the resurrection. Paul was *Insatiabilis Dei cultor,* saith Chrysostom.

Ver. 9. *And fish laid thereon and bread*] A feast of Christ's own providing; to assure them that they should never want necessaries; superfluities they may want without prejudice. Nature is content with a little, grace with less. Luther dined oft with a herring, Junius with an egg; as knowing, that they were not to live to eat, but eat to live. Ill doth it become a servant of the Highest to be a slave to his palate. *Epicurus dum palato quid sit optimum judicat, cæli palatium non suspexit,* saith Ennius.

Ver. 10. *Which ye have now caught*] He saith

---

[1] *Cum boni, cum probi coeunt, cum pii, cum casti congregantur, non est factio dicenda sed curia, et e contrario illis nomen factionis accommodandum. Tert. Apol. adver. Gent. 39.*

not, Which I have caused you to catch. God is pleased to say, for our encouragement, that we do such and such good works, when it is he that doth all our works, in us and for us. *Certum est nos facere quod facimus, sed ille facit ut faciamus.* (Aug.) The bowls of the candlestick had no oil but that which dropped from the olive-branches.

Ver. 11. *Yet was not the net broke*] When God will bless a man, all second causes shall co-operate and contribute their help. As when he will cross us, the strongest sinew in the arms of flesh shall crack, our likeliest projects miscarry; he will curse our blessings, blast our proceedings, as King John confessed, "ever since I was assoiled, and subject to the see of Rome, I never prospered."[1] Oto, one of the pope's *muscipulatores*, mice-catchers, as the story calls them, sent hither by Gregory IX., after three years' raking together of money by most detestable arts, at last departing hence, he left not so much money in the kingdom as he either carried with him or sent to Rome before him. Such notable fishers are Peter's pretended successors; all is fish with them that comes to net.

Ver. 12. *None of the disciples durst ask him*] They were ashamed to move further question in that which was to them all so evident. Neither yet may we imagine that they sat silent all dinner while in their Master's presence, as monks and Turks use to do;[2] but that, although they were abashed to ask him who he was, yet they both asked and answered many other more profitable questions. Our Saviour never came to any man's table, but he besprinkled the dishes with the salt of savoury discourse; so should we, but so (alas) we do not. Plato and Xenophon thought it fit and profitable that men's speeches at meals should be written. And if Christians should so do, what kind of books would they be?

Ver. 13. *Taketh bread and giveth them*] As his manner was before his death, and with his usual form of grace before meat, by the which those two that had his company to Emmaus knew him, Luke xxiv. 35. Those that receive not the creatures with thanksgiving are worse than heathens, 1 Tim. iv. 4. The Greek word for a dinner comes of another word that signifieth prayers, which they usually premised to their repasts.[3] Hesiod gives this precept, Eat not of a dish that hath not first been offered in sacrifice.[4] An elegant and pious precept, saith Melancthon, drawn no doubt from the holy patriarchs. The people would not taste of their good cheer till Samuel had blessed it, 1 Sam. ix. 13. And Moses bade them eat and drink before the Lord. Mine oxen and fatlings are prepared, saith that king, Matt. xxii. 4. It is in the original, are sacrificed, τεθυμένα. So was Nebuchadnezzar's good cheer, which therefore Daniel would not taste of.

Ver. 14. *This is now the third time, &c.*] Adam died, and we hear no more of him; not so the second Adam. "If a man die, shall he live again?" Job xiv. 14. Not till the general resurrection surely. Many devices there are in the minds of some, that there shall be a first resurrection of the martyrs only, and that they shall reign on earth a thousand years. Alsted saith, this thousand years shall begin in the year 1694. But these, saith a divine, are but the mistakes of some high expressions in Scripture; which describe the judgments poured out upon God's enemies in making a way to the Jews' conversion by the pattern of the last judgment. (Cotton upon the Seven Vials.)

Ver. 15. *Lovest thou me more than these?*] As thou hast not spared to profess and promise (for when the rest said nothing, Peter said he would lay down his life for him), and as thou now pretendest, by casting thyself into the sea, to come first to me.

Thou knowest that I love thee] Being asked of the measure, he only answereth of the truth, *q. d.* for the quantity I can say little, but for the truth I dare affirm. The upright are perfect in God's account. And Peter had now turned his crowing into crying.

Feed my lambs] These were his first care. The Syriac addeth, ܠܝ *li, mihi*, feed them for me. And Drusius reckons this amongst the eastern apothegms, *Quicquid agas, propter Deum agas.* Whatsoever thou doest, do it for God's sake. *Propter te Domine, propter te*, was a godly man's motto; it should be every minister's especially.

Ver. 16. *Feed my sheep*] That is, *Supremum in Ecclesia Dominium tibi assere.* Lord it over the Church, saith Baronius. *Regio more impera,* reign as a king, saith Bellarmine. Christ, on the contrary, saith, The kings of nations exercise dominion over them, but ye shall not do so. And Peter himself saith to his fellow-elders, Feed the flock of God, not as lording it over God's heritage, 1 Pet. v. 2, 3. Indeed ποιμαίνω, here used, sometimes signifies to govern (usually to feed), but βόσκω, the other word twice used here in this text, always signifies to feed. But they catch at government, let go feeding. It is as rare a thing to hear a bishop preach amongst them, said Dr Bassinet, as to see an ass fly. *Fisco potius apud multos consulitur quam Christo; attonsioni potius gregis quam attentioni.*

Ver. 17. *Jesus saith unto him the third time*] To confirm him doubtless against the consciousness of his three-fold denial, and to re-authorize him in his apostleship.

Lovest thou me?] A minister had need have his heart inflamed with a most ardent affection to Christ; for else he will never suffer that hardship, devour those difficulties, and get over all those impediments that he is sure to be encumbered with. The ministry, believe it, is not an idle man's occupation, he must preach the word, be

[1] *Postquam Deo reconciliatus me ac mea regna (proh dolor) Rom. subjeci ecclesiæ, nulla mihi prospera, sed omnia contraria advenerunt.* John Rex.

[2] *Turcæ perpetuum silentium ternent, ut muti.* Cusp. de Cæsario.

[3] ἄριστον, ἀπὸ τῶν ἀρῶν, *a precibus quas præmittebant.*

[4] Μηδ'ἀπὸ χυτροπόδων ἀνεπιρρέκτων ἀνέλοντα ἔσθειν.

instant in season, out of season, &c., cry in the throat (*Clamare ut Stentora vincat*), lift up his voice like a trumpet, speak till he spit forth his lungs, and yet to no more purpose many times than Beda did when he preached to a heap of stones. Now this he will never do, unless the love of Christ constrain him, 2 Cor. v. 14, with 1 Cor. xvi. 22.

Peter was grieved] Either in remembrance of his former false play; or else, as thinking our Saviour somewhat distrusted his fidelity; or else, surely, he was as much to blame to be grieved, as David was to be angry, when God had made a breach upon Uzzah, 2 Sam. vi. 8.

Feed my sheep] My sheep with golden fleeces, with precious souls; every soul being more worth than a world, as our Saviour reckons it, who only went to the price of it, Matt. xvi. 26. Can that be wholesome meat then that is sauced with the blood of souls? Will it not be bitterness in the end?

Ver. 18. *Another shall gird thee*] That is, cord thee, manacle and pinion thee, carry thee prisoner whither thou wouldst not. Peter would, and he would not suffer. Every new man is two men, hath two contrary principles in him, flesh and spirit. The spirit is willing, the flesh weak and wayward. This made the martyrs many of them chide themselves, and crave prayers of others. Bishop Ridley said to the smith, as he was knocking in the staple, Good fellow, knock it in hard, for the flesh will have its course. So Rawlins White, martyr, going to the stake, and meeting with his wife and children, the sudden sight of them so pierced his heart, that the very tears trickled down his cheeks. But he soon after, as though he had misliked this infirmity of his flesh, began to be as it were angry with himself, insomuch that in striking his breast with his hand, he used these words, Ah flesh, stayest thou me so? wouldst thou fain prevail? well, I tell thee, do what thou canst, thou shalt not, by God's grace, have the victory. So Latimer in a letter to Bishop Ridley, Pray for me, I say; pray for me, I say; for I am sometimes so fearful that I would creep into a mouse-hole; sometimes God doth visit me again with his comforts; so he cometh and goeth, to teach me to feel and know my infirmity.

Ver. 19. *By what death he should glorify God*] Martyrdom is the lowest subjection that can be to God, but the highest honour. *Vere magnus est Deus Christianorum*. The God of the Christians is a great God indeed, said one Calocerius, a heathen, beholding the patient sufferings of the primitive martyrs. Justin Martyr confesseth of himself, that seeing the piety of Christians in their lives and their patience in death, he gathered that that was the truth that they so constantly professed and sealed up with their blood. And of one Adrianus it is reported, that seeing the martyrs suffer such grievous things, he asked the cause; one of them named that text, " Eye hath not seen, nor ear heard," &c. The naming of which words and seeing of such sufferings, so

converted him, that afterwards he became a martyr. To account Christ precious as a tree of life, though we be fastened to him as to a stake to be burned at, this is the greatest honour we can do him upon earth. This is to magnify Christ, as Paul did, Phil. i. 20; to follow Christ close at heels, as Peter did here, who also had the manner of his death foretold him, 2 Pet. i. 14. As had likewise Bishop Hooper, when he had given him for his arms, a lamb in a fiery bush, and the sunbeams from heaven descending down upon the lamb, rightly purporting by what death he should glorify God.

Ver. 20. *Then Peter turning about*] Peter, though restored and resettled in his apostleship, is not without his infirmities. They that are cured of a phrensy are not without their mad tricks sometimes.[1] No pomegranate so sound but hath one rotten kernel in it. No book so well printed but hath some errata. David saw so many in himself, that he cries out, " Who can understand the errors of his life? oh purge me," &c., Psal. xix. 12. They that dream of perfections here suffer a merry madness.

Ver. 21. *And what shall this man do*] When Peter considered that John was dearly beloved and yet not alike forewarned of suffering death, as himself was, he began to doubt whether Christ spake this of love to him or not. Nothing is more ordinary with us than to question God's affection when we are in affliction; to conceive hard things of God and heavy things of ourselves, as if no children, because chastised. Whereas we should learn to look through the anger of God's corrections, to the sweetness of his loving countenance, as by a rainbow we see the beautiful image of the sun's light in the midst of a dark and waterish cloud. (See my " Love-Tokens," Doct. 2, Use 1.)

Ver. 22. *If I will that he tarry*] *Si eum volo manere*. This the Vulgar corruptly reads, *Sic eum volo manere*. Ambrose, Austin, Bede, Lyra, Rupert, &c., retain this reading. Trapezuntius defends it, Bessarion opposeth it, the Greek text refutes it. Yet is the Vulgar translation so extolled and idolized by the Papists, that if the originals differ from it anywhere, they must be corrected by it, and not it by the originals. *Sed Hebræi bibunt fontes, Græci rivos, Latini paludes*, saith Reuchlin.

Ver. 23. *Among the brethren*] So are all Christians. *Sanctior est copula cordis quam corporis.*

That that disciple should not die] Some to this day deny that he is dead. Beza tells us of a certain impostor in his remembrance, that gave out at Paris that he was John the Evangelist, and was afterward burnt at Toulouse. Some have fabled, that after he had commanded his grave to be made, and had laid himself down in it, the next day it was found empty, and he rapt up alive into Paradise, whence he shall come together with Enoch and Elias at the last day to confound Antichrist. *O quantum est in rebus inane!* It is not for us to " follow cunningly

[1] *Quisque aliquid fatuitatis habet adjunctum.* Melanct.

devised fables," 2 Pet. i. 16, but to attend to that sure word of truth, as unto a light shining, &c., ver. 19, accounting every particle of it precious, sith the change of one letter may breed so much error and cause so much contention.

Ver. 24. *This is the disciple*] Not the doctor, the master, as *Magistri nostri Parisienses*. So the Sorbonists will needs be styled. The school-men have their *Doctor Angelicus*, *Doctor Seraphicus*, *Doctor resolutissimus*. So Bacon the Carmelite was called, because he would endure no guessing or maybes. The Italian friars, as they increase in their supposed holiness, so they proceed in their titles, from *Padre Benedicto* to *Padre Angelo*, then *Archangelo*, *Cherubino*, and lastly, *Cerephino*, which is the top of perfection. Our evangelist delights not in any of these swelling titles. He doth not so much as name himself in all this work of his, takes no other style than the beloved disciple, makes no more of himself than a witness to the truth, a recorder of what he had heard and seen. The proud person speaks "great swelling words of vanity," 2 Pet. ii. 18; he loves uppermost rooms, and to be called Rabbi, Rabbi, to be cried up and pointed at for a nonesuch, Matt. xxiii. 6. I hear, saith Tertullian (speaking of the pope, who then began to peep out), that there is a decree published in peremptory terms, *Pontifex scilicet Maximus*, *Episcopus episcoporum*, &c. I ever hated the pride of that Roman Church, saith Basil.[1] Ambition, like the crocodile, groweth while it liveth; like the ivy, which rising at the feet, will over-peer the highest wall; or, like the mary-gold (a flower of no good smell), which opens and shuts with the sun. Humility, on the contrary, is like the lily, saith Bernard, or violet, which grows low to the ground, hangs the head downward, and hides itself with its own leaves. It prefers the *Euge* of conscience before the *Hic*

est of the world: and were it not that its fragrant smell betrays it to the observation of others, would choose to live and die in its well-contenting secrecy.

Ver. 25. *I suppose that even the world itself*, &c.] *Nec Christus, nec cælum patitur hyperbolen*, saith one. In speaking of Christ or his kingdom, a man can hardly hyperbolize. Much had St John said of our Saviour, yet nothing to what he might have said. All that ever he did was divine, and deserved to be chronicled. That commendation that Velleius Paterculus falsely gives to Scipio, that *Nihil in vita nisi laudandum aut fecit, aut dixit, aut sensit*, He never in all his life did, spoke, or thought anything but what was praiseworthy, is true only of Christ. That which the Ecclesiastical History relates of Bennus, that he was never seen or heard by any to swear, lie, or be rashly angry, to speak or do anything that beseemed not God's servant, is a praise proper to Christ, even as he was man. (Sozom. vi. 28.) But, consider him as God, and then that of Gratian the emperor is true, in his Epistle to St Ambrose, *Loquimur de Deo, non quantum debemus, sed quantum possumus*. We speak of God, not so much as we ought, but so much as we can. *Nemo sapientiam Dei immensam in omnem eternitatem exhauriet*. He is indeed like the pool Polycritus writes of, which in compass, at the first, scarce seemed to exceed the breadth of a shield; but if any went in it to wash, it extended itself more and more. *Tantum recedit, quantum capitur*, saith Nazianzen. When therefore the apostle saith, "That the world itself could not contain the books that should be written," *Hoc non vult*, saith Augustine, *de mole librorum, nec de locali capacitate, sed quod Spiritus Sanctus nostri habuerit rationem, et ea selegerit conscribenda, quæ in hac infirmitate credentes capere possint*.

[1] *Odi fastum illius ecclesiæ. Hunc ὀφρὺν δυτικὴν appellare solitus est.*

A

COMMENTARY OR EXPOSITION

UPON

THE ACTS OF THE APOSTLES,

WHEREIN THE TEXT IS EXPLAINED, SOME CONTROVERSIES ARE BRIEFLY DISCUSSED, DIVERS COMMONPLACES
HANDLED, AND MANY REMARKABLE MATTERS HINTED, THAT HAD BEEN BY FORMER
INTERPRETERS PRETERMITTED.

CHAPTER I.

Ver. 1. *Of all that Jesus began, &c.*] IF Hen. Stephanus could say of Laertius, that he wrote the lives of the philosophers *aureo libello illo* in that golden book of his; and (as another hath it) *opere utilissimo, et auro contra non charo*;[1] how much better may the same be said of the holy evangelists setting forth the oracles and miracles of Christ and his apostles! If Julius Scaliger thought twelve verses in Lucan better than the whole German empire, what high thoughts ought we to have of these divine records! In the monastery at Ratisbon is a New Testament written all in letters of gold, saith Melancthon, who saw it. (Joh. Manl. loc. com.) Gold was not good enough for such a purpose.

Ver. 2. *Had given commandments*] As the Church's Lawgiver, Isa. xxxiii. 22; 1 Cor. xi. 23.

Ver. 3. *Speaking of the things*] Those that are leaving the world should leave wholesome counsel to those that survive them.

Ver. 4. *Wait for the promise*] And put it in suit by their daily prayers, Luke xi. 13.

Ver. 5. *Shall be baptized*] See Matt. iii. 11.

Ver. 6. *Restore again*] They dreamt of a distribution of honours and offices here on earth as in the days of David and Solomon.

Ver. 7. *It is not for you*] This key God carries under his own girdle.

Ver. 8. *After that the Holy Ghost is come upon you*] Montanus the heresiarch wickedly affirmed that, next unto the apostles, this Scripture was fulfilled upon him and his courtesan Philumena. (Beza in loc). Prodigious blasphemy! And *ejusdem farinæ*, a loaf of the same leaven it is, that the Turks believe that when Christ said that "although he departed, he would send the Comforter," it was added in the text, "And that shall be Mahomet;" but that the Christians in malice toward them have razed it out. (Abbot's Geog.)

[1] *Vos. de Hist. Græc.* ii. 13.
[2] Νικατώριον ὄρος. Strabo.

Ver. 9. *And a cloud*] Look not therefore for revelations from heaven (saith Aretius), but search the Scriptures, for those are they that testify of Christ.

Ver. 10. *Looked stedfastly*] Or intently, ἀτενίζοντες: wistly, as taken with that sweet sight. See the note on Matt. xxviii. 7.

Ver. 11. *Shall so come*] *De tempore ne quære*, not a word of the time when, in answer to that over-curious question, ver. 6. Solomon's temple was finished in the year of the world 3000; whether Christ's shall be consummated in 3000 more, I have not to say.

Ver. 12. *From the mount*] Near unto which he had been apprehended, viz. at Bethany, and from whence he had thus triumphantly ascended up on high, leading captivity captive, &c., Eph. iv. 8, and making an open show of his conquered enemies as a public spectacle of scorn and derision, ἐδειγμάτισεν, Col. ii. 15. In which respect, how well might this mount Olivet have received that name of Nicatorium,[2] which Alexander the Great gave to a certain Mountain not far from Arbela, as a constant trophy of that famous victory that he there gat over Darius, with whom he fought for the empire of the world.

Ver. 13. *They went into an upper room*][3] As most remote from company, and so fittest for God's service. In Madrid it is a custom, that except some composition be made, all the upper rooms of their dwellings belong to the king. (Heyl. Geog.) Let the spirits of our minds be reserved for God.

With the women] Who might make masculine prayers, having eyes like the pools in Heshbon, Cant. vii. 4.

Ver. 15. *The number of names*] Nominum, *id est, hominum*, or of the chieftains that were fit to act in the election.

Ver. 16. *Brethren*] Not underlings, as Popish bishops, who must say *Placet* to that which in the pope's name is proposed to them.

Ver. 18. *And all his bowels gushed out*] Be-

[3] ὑπερῷον *superior pars domus Spartanorum lingua.* Eustath.

cause he had no bowels of compassion toward his Master, be burst in the midst with a huge crack (as the word ἐλάκησε signifieth), by a singular judgment of God. So Foxford, chancellor to the bishop of London, a cruel persecutor in Henry VIII.'s time, died suddenly in his chair; his belly being burst and his guts falling out before him. So Arius voiding out his bowels, sent his soul as an harbinger to the devil to provide room for his body. Papias (that ancient millenary, scholar to St John) tells us (*In Traditionibus quas vocant Apostolicis*), that Judas having hanged himself, the rope broke, and he lived some time after, and was crushed to death by the fall of a cart that was to pass by him; but this is a mere fiction of his, and it gives us cause to credit Eusebius, who saith that this Papias, though much reverenced for opinion of his holiness and learning, yet was *homo ingenii pertenuis*, a slender-witted man.

Ver. 19. *In their proper tongue*] i. e. In the Syriac tongue; for the Jews in the Babylonish captivity lost their language.

Ver. 20. *In the book of Psalms*] That common magazine of wholesome lessons, as Basil hath it.[1]

Ver. 21. *Wherefore of these*] To make up the breach again; like as the crowned saints fill up the room in heaven of the apostate angels.

Ver. 22. *Must one be ordained*] To answer the ancient types.

Ver. 23. *Joseph called Barsabas*] The centurists think that this Joseph Barsabas was the same with that Joses called Barnabas afterwards by the apostles, Acts iv. 36. This Joseph, seeing it was God's mind not to make choice of him now to succeed Judas in the apostleship, was content with a lower condition; therefore afterwards God called him to that high and honourable office of an apostle.

Ver. 24. *Which knowest the hearts*] *Thales Milesius, qui sapientissimus inter septem fuisse creditur, interrogatus num lateret Deos injuste agens? respondit, Ne cogitans quidem.* Thales being asked whether evil deeds are hidden from God? answered, No, nor evil thoughts neither.

Ver. 25. *Go to his own place*] A place of his own providing; and that he had purchased with that wages of wickedness, ver. 18. Bellarmine tells us of a desperate advocate in the court of Rome, who being exhorted on his death-bed to make his peace with God, made this speech to him; Lord, I have a word to say to thee, not for myself, but for my wife and children, *Ego enim propero ad inferos, neque est ut aliquid pro me agas;* for I am hasting to hell, neither is there anything that I would beg of thee in my own behalf. And this he spake, saith Bellarmine (who was by the while), as boldly and without fear, as if he had been but to take his journey only to some near neighbouring village.

Ver. 26. *They gave forth their lot*] Either into the bosom, Prov. xvi. 23, or lap, or pot, or some other vessel in use for that purpose.

CHAPTER II.

Ver. 1. *And when the day of Pentecost*] This feast was instituted in remembrance of the law delivered to Moses in the mount, 50 days after their departure out of Egypt. Answerably whereunto the Holy Ghost (and God's love thereby, Rom. v. 5) is sent out and shed abroad the 50th day after that Christ our Passover was sacrificed for us, 1 Cor. v. 7.

Ver. 2. *As of a rushing mighty wind*] *Nescit tarda molimina gratia Spiritus Sancti*, saith Ambrose. "The Spirit of God is a spirit of power," 2 Tim. i. 7.

Ver. 3. *Cloven tongues*] Teaching them both ὀρθοτομεῖν, to divide the word aright, and also ὀρθοποδεῖν, as some will have it; their tongues being cloven, as their feet were into toes, teaching them too to foot it aright. Diodorus Siculus tells us of a certain island beyond Arabia, the inhabitants whereof have cloven tongues so that therewith they can alter their speech at their pleasure, imitate the tunes of divers birds, and (which is more strange) they can perfectly speak to two persons and to two purposes at once; to one with one part of their tongue and to another with the other part; *Sed fides sit penes Authorem*, believe it who will.

Ver. 4. *As the Spirit gave them utterance*] ἀποφθέγγεσθαι, to utter divine apothegms, grave and gracious sentences, or rather oracles; those *Magnalia Dei*, ver. 11; *Mirabilia legis*, Psal. cxix. 18 (see 2 Pet. i. 21). *Cedro digna et Cerite cerâ.* Horat.

And they were all filled with the Holy Ghost] And so gifted for their offices and employments in the Church. The heathens tell us that Hesiod, being filled with a sudden inspiration by the Muses, became of a sordid neatherd a most skilful poet. And Tully saith, no man ever grew famous *sine aliquo afflatu divino*, without some inbreathing from on high.

Ver. 5. *And there were dwelling, &c.*] Even in Jerusalem (for their ancient idolatries and latter unthankfulness) there be not to be found at this time a hundred households of the Jews. (Breerwood's Inquiries.)

Ver. 6. *Were confounded*] Or troubled, transported, amazed, and amused, συνεχύθη, as ver. 7.

Ver. 7. *Galileans*] ——— *crassoque sub aere nati.* (Martial.)

Ver. 8. *Every man in our own tongue*] Cleopatra was so skilful in the Eastern tongues that she could readily answer the Ethiopian, Hebrew, Arabian, Syrian, Median, Parthian ambassadors that came unto her; turning and tuning her tongue with ease (as an instrument of many strings,[2] saith Plutarch) to what dialect soever she listed.

Ver. 9. *Parthians and Medes, &c.*] Those strangers of the dispersion, 1 Pet. i. 1.

---

[1] κοῖνον ταμεῖον ἀγαθῶν διδαγμάτων.

[2] ὥσπερ ὄργανον τι πολύχορδον.

Ver. 10. *Proselytes*] Jethro was the first proselyte to the Jewish Church that we read of in Scripture.

Ver. 12. *The wonderful works*] The magnifical, majestical things of God; they praised him according to his excellent greatness, Psal. cl. 2.

What meaneth this?] Gr. "What will this be, or come to?"[1] And here began their conversion. Let none "despise the day of small things," Zech. iv. 10: God put little thoughts into Ahasuerus's head, but for great purposes, Esth. vi. 1. The word falls oft upon men's ears, "as the sound of many waters" at first, working wonder only. Next "as the voice of thunder," working fear also, as it did on these here, ver. 37. Lastly, as the harmony of harpers, filling the heart with peace and joy through believing, as one observeth from Revelation xiv.

Ver. 13. *Others mocking, said, These men, &c.*] χλευάζοντες, contumeliously cavilling, as those epicures at Athens did, Acts xvii. 32. And that mocker, Doctor Morgan, who being set to examine Mr Philpot, martyr, asked him, How know you that you have the Spirit of God? Philpot answered, By the faith of Christ which is in me. Ah, by faith, do you so? (quoth Morgan). I ween it be the spirit of the buttery, which your fellows have had that have been burned before you, who were drunk before they went to their death, and I ween went drunk unto it. Philpot replied: It appeareth by your communication that you are better acquainted with the spirit of buttery than with the Spirit of God. Thou hast the spirit of illusion and sophistry, which is not able to countervail the Spirit of truth. And God, I tell thee, shall rain fire and brimstone upon such scorners of his word and blasphemers of his people as thou art, &c.

Ver. 14. *But Peter standing up*] (σταθεὶς, consistens.) Buckling close to them, and not suffering them to carry it away so; *Constantem et præsentem Petri animum declarat.* Beza.

Ver. 15. *Seeing it is but the third hour*] This was then an argument more than probable. Now men are grown such husbands, as that by that time they will return their stocks, and have their brains crowing before day.

Ver. 16. *But this is that*] Thus the Old Testament is fulfilled in the New.

Ver. 17. *In the last days*] God keeps his best till last. Not so the devil.

I will pour out of my Spirit upon all flesh] The best thing upon the basest. Oh wonderful goodness!

Ver. 18. *And on mine handmaids*] Souls have no sexes, Gal. iii. 28.

Ver. 19. *Wonders in heaven*] See Joel iii. 15; Matt. xxiv. 29; Mark xiii. 24; Luke xxi. 25.

Ver. 20. *The sun shall be turned*] He seems to set forth the great troubles of the world under the gospel.

Ver. 21. *Shall be saved*] Therefore to be able

to pray is better than to be able to prophesy, Matt. vii. 22.

Ver. 22. *A man*] From Adam, but not by Adam.

Ver. 23. *And by wicked hands, &c.*] *Facinus vincire civem Romanum*, saith the orator. It was much (may we say) for the Son of God to be bound, more to be beaten, most of all to be slain. *Quid dicam in crucem tolli?* (Cicero in Ver.)

Ver. 24. *It was not possible*] For he was life essential, and therefore "swallowed up death in victory," 1 Cor. xv. 54.

Him being delivered by the determinate counsel of God] *Quod dum devitatur impletur*, saith Gregory. The wicked's intense rage carries on God's decree against their wills; for while they sit backward to his command, they row forward to his decree; *dum sua cuique Deus fit dira libido.*

Ver. 25. *Be moved*] Tossed as a ship by tempest.

Ver. 26. *My tongue*] Heb. "my glory." With the tongue bless we God, James iii. 9, which is the best way of ennobling it.

Ver. 27. *My soul in hell*] That is, my body in the grave. So Rev. xx. 13. Death and hell, *i. e.* the grave, are cast into the burning lake. To the three degrees of our Saviour's humiliation, are answerable the three degrees of his exaltation: to his death, his resurrection; to his burial, his ascension; to his abode a while in the grave, his sitting at the right hand of his heavenly Father.

Ver. 28. *Thou hast made known*] *i. e.* Thou givest me experience, or thou hast made me partaker of.

Ver. 29. *His sepulchre is with us*] Repaired, likely, when the city was rebuilt. See Matt. xxiii. 29.

Ver. 30. *Out of the fruit of his loins*] That is, out of the Virgin Mary; the son of whose secundines Christ was, being hewn without hands out of that mountain, Dan. ii. 45.

Ver. 31. *Neither his flesh*] It was a pious error in those good women that embalmed his body to preserve it from corruption.

Ver. 32. *Hath God raised up*] Adam died, and we hear no more of him; but the second Adam rose and reigneth for ever.

Ver. 33. *Exalted*] See the note in ver. 27.

Ver. 34. *Is not ascended*] viz. Bodily, and to sit at God's right hand as King of the Church: that is Christ's royalty.

Ver. 35. *Thy footstool*] They that will not bend shall break; Christ will fetch in his rebels, and set his feet of fine brass on the necks of them, Rev. i. 15.

Ver. 36. *Lord and Christ*] Messiah the Prince, Dan. ix. 25.

Ver. 37. *They were pricked*] Punctually pricked and pierced (κατενύγησαν). They felt the nails wherewith they had crucified Christ sticking fast in their own hearts, as so many sharp daggers or stings of scorpions, 2 Cor. xii. 7.

[1] τὶ ἂν θέλοι τοῦτο εἶναι.

Sin is set forth by a word that signifieth the head of a bearded arrow sticking in the flesh (σκόλοψ). After that Socrates was put to death at Athens, Aristophanes rehearsed a tragedy of his concerning Palamedes, who had been executed by the Grecians long before, at the siege of Troy. In this tragedy were these verses,[1]

Ye have slain, ye have slain of Greeks the very best,
(Ah me) that never any did infest.

The people at the hearing of these lines were so moved that they presently fell upon the authors of Socrates' death, and drew them forth to punishment. Oh that we could be as nimble to apprehend and be avenged upon our sins, the cause of Christ's death.

Ver. 38. *Peter said unto them, Repent*] μετανοήσατε. Belike then they had not yet repented, for all they were pricked at heart. Nay, Peter prescribes it for a remedy, which taxeth their folly that take the disease for the remedy, and are over-forward to minister comfort or e'er men have sorrowed after God, and to a transmentation. The English are not sick soon enough, saith one, and they are well again too soon. It is true of their minds, as well as of their bodies, *Currat ergo pœnitentia, ne præcurrat sententia;* and let our fasts be according to an old canon, which defines their continuance *usque dum stellæ in cœlo appareant*, till stars be seen in the sky. It is not for men to scarf up their wounds till they are thoroughly searched, not to get out of the furnace of mortification till their hearts melt, as Josiah's did, and fall asunder in their bosoms, like drops of water. Penitency and pain are words of one derivation, and very near of kin. Never was any wound cured without sensible pain: never any sin healed without soaking sorrow. Let none dream of a delicacy in the ways of God; nor hope for sound comfort, till they have thoroughly repented. The Hebrews, as they express sin and punishment by the same word, so do they repentance and comfort, נחם.

Ver. 39. *Even as many*] The devil sweeps all (of maturity) that are not called, as out of the covenant.

Ver. 40. *With many words did he testify*] διεμαρτύρετο, in God's name, for his sake, and by his authority, as Paul charged Timothy, 2 Tim. ii. 14, and as Bradford bespake his friend: I beseech you, I pray you, I desire you, I crave at your hands with all my very heart. I ask of you with hand, pen, tongue, and mind; in Christ, through Christ, for Christ; for his name, blood, mercy, power, and truth's sake, that you admit no doubting of God's final mercies toward you, howsoever you feel yourself.

Ver. 41. *Were baptized*] They gave up their names to Christ, and took his mark upon them.

Ver. 42. *Doctrine and fellowship*] So the Philippians, chap. i. 5. See the note.

Ver. 43. *Fear came upon*] The enemies were overawed, and durst not moot or attempt against the Church.

Ver. 44. *Were together*] There is a special tie to constancy in the communion of saints and community of supplies.

And had all things common] This was voluntary, not necessary. *Non fuit præceptum, sed susceptum,* saith Piscator.

Ver. 45. *And sold*] So Tyrus when once converted, Isa. xxiii. 17, 18.

Ver. 46. *Breaking bread*] Friendly feeding together, and (after their love-feasts) celebrating the Lord's Supper every Lord's day at least: whence it was anciently called *Panis Hebdomadarius*.[2] That of George Tankerfield, a martyr in Queen Mary's days, was singular and extraordinary. For when the hour drew on that he should suffer, he called for a pint of Malmsey and a loaf, that he might eat and drink that in remembrance of Christ's death and passion, because he could not have it ministered unto him by others, in such manner as Christ commanded. And then he kneeled down, making his confession to the Lord, with all which were in the chamber with him. And after that he had prayed to the Lord, and had read the institution of the holy Supper by the Lord Jesus, out of the evangelists, and out of St Paul, he said: O Lord, thou knowest I do not this to derogate authority from any man, or in contempt of those which are thy ministers; but only because I cannot have it ministered according to thy word. And when he had so spoken, he received it with thanksgiving.

Ver. 47. *Such as should be saved*] Heirs of the kingdom, Jam. ii. 5. Heads destined to the diadem, saith Tertullian.

CHAPTER III.

Ver. 1. *At the hour of prayer*] THE Jews had their *stata precibus tempora*, set hours of prayer. See Psal. lv. 17; Dan. vi. 10; Acts x. 3, 30.

Ver. 2. *To ask alms*] This ought not to have been suffered, Deut. xv. There might not be a beggar in Israel. But all was out of order, as it useth to be among a people nigh to destruction.

Ver. 3. *Asked an alms*] The Dutch beggars ask not, but look pitifully.

Ver. 4. *Look on us*] Together with this word there went forth a power, as Luke v. 17.

Ver. 5. *Expecting*] God was better to him than his expectation. God presseth kindness upon his suitors, and heapeth it upon them, as Naaman upon Gehazi, 2 Kings v.

Ver. 6. *Silver and gold have I none*] The new-elected pope, in his solemn Lateran procession, must take copper out of his chamberlain's lap, and scatter it among the people, saying, Gold and silver have I none. Whenas Petrarch writeth that when Pope John XXII. died, his heirs

---

[1] Εκτάνετε, ἐκτάνετε ἄριστον τῶν Ἑλλήνων, τὸν ἀηδίαν μηδένα βλάψαντα.

[2] *Moris erat convesci et convivari et celebrare cœnam Dom.* Tertul.

found in his treasury 250 tons of gold. And when Pope Boniface VIII. was taken and plundered by Philip the Fair, king of France, there was more store of treasure carried out of his palace than all the kings of the earth could show again, saith the historian. Every pope hath the sign of the cross on his pantofle shining gloriously with pearls and precious stones, *ut plenis faucibus crucem Christi derideat*, saith mine author in derision of Christ's cross. (Heidelfield.)

Ver. 7. *His feet and ancle bones*] "The Lord raiseth them that are crooked," but (as a further favour, and far better than that former) "he loveth the righteous," Psal. cxlvi. 8, as he did this cripple, whom he healed on the inside also.

Ver. 8. *Into the temple*] There to hang up his crutches, as it were.

Walking and leaping] Weak Christians are commonly most affectionate, as this cripple when first cured leaped for joy.

Ver. 9. *Praising God*] Not the apostles. We may pay the messenger, but return thanks chiefly to the sender.

Ver. 10. *And they knew*] There could be therefore no collusion.

Ver. 11. *Held Peter and John*] Fearing perhaps lest, if he should lose them, he should lose his limbs again. So that demoniac, Mark v. 18.

Ver. 12. *Why look ye*] We are ready to pay our rent to a wrong landlord.

Ver. 13. *Denied him*] Crying out, We have no king but Cæsar, John xix.

Ver. 14. *But ye denied*] This he again beats upon, and drives home to the head.

Ver. 15. *And killed*] Wherein they were but our workmen, Zech. xii. 10.

Ver. 16. *And his name*] That is, Christ himself, as God's name is oft put for God's self.

Ver. 17. *I wot that through ignorance*] Peter excuseth not their fact, but thus far forth mitigateth it, that it was not the sin against the Holy Ghost, which can never be forgiven. This must be carefully cautioned, and the weak informed that they despair not. This irremissible sin is wilful blaspheming of God, and the work of his Spirit, out of revenge, Heb. x. 29; a will to crucify Christ again.

Ver. 18. *By the mouth of all his prophets*] All the prophets spake but with one mouth; such a sweet consent and happy harmony there is in all their writings, as if done by one only.

Ver. 19. *Repent and be converted*] The first word comprehendeth contrition and confession. The second, faith and reformation. The first, repentance *for* sin; the second, repentance *from* sin. *Da pœnitentiam, et postea indulgentiam*, said dying Fulgentius.

Ver. 20. *Preached unto you*] Or handed to you, or put into your hands, προκεχειρισμένον.

Ver. 21. *Whom the heavens must receive until*, &c.] Note this against the Ubiquitaries, whose error was first broached by Gerson, about the time of the Council of Constance. Afterwards, defended at Paris by Jacobus Faber Stapulensis, A. D. 1524, who was therefore banished the next year out of France. (Scultet. Annal.) But Luther brought it into Germany, Brentius stickled for it, and Smidelinus obtruded it upon many, even against their wills; and was therefore called the apostle of the Ubiquity. The author of the Practice of Piety thus distinguisheth: *Secundum esse naturale Christus non est ubique, secundum esse personale Christus est ubique*, even the body of Christ. It was objected as a heresy against Thomas Man, martyr, that he had affirmed, That the Father of heaven was the altar, and the second person the sacrament: and that upon the Ascension-day, the sacrament ascended upon the altar, and there abideth still. But what an audacious heretic is he that writes of the "mortality of the soul," to interpret this place thus, "The heavens must contain him," that is, he "must be in the sun;" for he holds that there is no heaven till the resurrection.

Until the times of restitution] This Plato hammered at in his great revolution; when, after many thousands of years, all things shall be again *statu quo prius*, as they were at first.

Ver. 22. *Like unto me*] 1. A man, as I am. 2. A prophet, and more than a prophet, the archprophet, to whom Moses must vail bonnet.

Ver. 23. *Shall be destroyed*] As it justly befell the refractory Jews; wrath came upon them to the utmost, 1 Thess. ii. 16.

Ver. 24. *All the prophets*] The prophet Isaiah especially, who speaks more like an evangelist than a prophet, and is therefore called the "evangelical prophet" (Jerome).

Ver. 25. *Ye are the children*] Here he comforts them, being now cast down.

Ver. 26. *To bless you*] Eph. i. 3.

CHAPTER IV.

Ver. 1. *The captain of the temple*] THE Jews had a band of garrison-soldiers deputed for the service and safety of the temple, Matt. xxvii. 65. These forces had many officers, Luke xxii. 4, and one chieftain, here called their captain, στράτηγος; as in their wars with the Romans afterwards, Eleazar the son of Ananias the high priest was in this office, a bold and proud youth, as Josephus describeth him.

Ver. 2. *Being grieved*] Being sick of the devil's disease, as Moab was, Numb. xxii. 3, 4, "fretting and vexing" at God's Israel, and eating up their own hearts, because they could not tear out theirs.

Ver. 3. *Put them in hold*] In the sergeant's ward, τήρησις, not in the gaol or dungeon. God doth by degrees inure his to suffer hardship. *Pauciores* (saith Cajuto in an epistle to the brethren of Basilea) *vobiscum perimuntur, quod ita Domino visum est, ut stabiliantur seu lenibus pluviis, et sementis mollioribus plantulæ in arbores maximas prodituræ.* God tempteth not his above what they are able, 1 Cor. x. 13.

Ver. 4. *And the number*] A goodly increase.

The lily is said to be increased by its own juice that flows from it. (Pliny.) So the Church.

Ver. 5. *On the morrow*] Malice is restless. Stephen Gardiner would not sit down to dinner till he had heard of the bishops burnt at Oxford.

Ver. 6. *And Annas*] The same old man, still no changeling, ἡ παλαι γύνη, as it was said of Helena.

Ver. 7. *By what power*] God's, or the devil's? in God's name, or by the black art?

Ver. 8. *Filled with the Holy Ghost*] i. e. with wisdom and fortitude, according to Christ's promise, Matt. x. 19, 20; Luke xxi. 15. See the notes there.

Ver. 9. *If we this day be examined of the good deed*] q. d. Evil times we must needs say they are, when good deeds and evil are dangerous alike; when to cure or to kill is equally criminal. "Should I not visit for these things, saith the Lord?" &c. Bede said of the ancient Britons, immediately before their destruction by the Saxons, that they were come to that height of wickedness, as to cast an odium upon pious and profitable persons, *tanquam in adversarios*, as if they had been public enemies, not fit to be endured.

Ver. 10. *Be it known unto you all*] Here was spiritual mettle, steeling the soul against whatsoever opposition. When a man's strength would fall loose, the spirit hems him about, comprehends and keeps him together, Acts xx. 22, and makes him more than a man: as it did the apostles here, and afterwards Athanasius, Luther, and others, *qui totius orbis impetum sustinuerunt*, who stood out against a world of adversaries. (Tertul.)

Ver. 11. *You builders*] Such you should be, and profess to be, *sed ædificatis in Gehennam*, ye build backward.

Ver. 12. *For there is no other name*] We have no co-saviour, we need no other master of requests in heaven, but Christ. Say we of popish saints and mediators, as that heathen did, *Contemno minutulos istos deos modo Jovem propitium habeam*. William Tracy, Esq., in Henry VIII.'s time, made it in his will, That he would have no funeral pomp at his burial, that he passed not upon a mass, that he trusted in God only, and hoped by him to be saved, and not by any saint, &c. Hereupon his body was taken up and burnt as a heretic, A. D. 1532. Some schoolmen (saith Acosta) promise salvation without the knowledge of Christ. And Sleidan telleth us, that at the Council of Trent, the salvation of heathens, by the sole strength of nature without Christ, was much talked of. And Venator, the Arminian, saith, I deny this proposition, no man can be saved that is not set into Christ by a lively faith. The divines of Collen set forth a book *De Salute Aristotelis*. And Erasmus [1] (whether in jest or earnest I know not) useth this litany, *Vix possum me continere quin dicam Sancte Socrates ora pro nobis*. But if any do seriously fancy any other way to salvation besides Christ, that pro-

[1] Erasm. in Præf. ad Tusc. Cic. Quæstiones.

verb mentioned by Aristotle in his Meteorology, is verified of him, viz. κακὰ ἐφ' ἑαυτὸν ἕλκει, ὡς τὸ κακίας νέφος, he is a wicked and wretched miscreant.

Ver. 13. *Unlearned and ignorant men*] *Indoctos elegit Christus et idiotas, sed oculavit in prudentes: simulque dona dedit et ministeria.* The primitive persecutors slighted the Christians for a company of hard illiterate fellows; and therefore they used to paint the God of the Christians with an ass's head, and a book in his hand, saith Tertullian, to signify, That though they pretended learning, yet they were silly and ignorant people. Bishop Jewel, in his sermon upon Luke xi. 15, cites this out of Tertullian, and applies it to his times. Do not our adversaries the like, saith he, against all that profess the gospel? Oh, say they, Who are those that favour this way? None but shoemakers, tailors, weavers, and such as never were at the University. These are the bishop's own words. Bishop White said in open court, some few years since, That the Puritans were all a company of blockheads. The Jesuits say the same of all the Protestants; and that the empire of learning is within their dominion only.[2] But have they not picked up the best of their crumbs under our tables? and have not our English fugitives exceeded all their fellow-Jesuits in show of wit and learning?

Ver. 14. *They could say nothing*] The Arabian interpreter adds, *Ut authoritate uterentur in eos*, That they might punish them. They were clearly convinced, and yet ran away with the bit between their teeth; they would hold their own, howsoever, lest they should be taxed of lightness.

Ver. 15. *They conferred*] *Sic festucam quærentes unde oculos sibi eruant*, as Bernard hath it. They sought straws to put out their own eyes withal.

Ver. 16. *A notable miracle*] A signal sign that all the country rang of.

Ver. 17. *That they speak henceforth to none*] They must cut out their tongues then, for, as new wine, they must vent or burst. When Valens the Arian emperor threatened Basil with banishment, torment, death, &c.; Let him fright babies, said he, with such bugbears, and not me. He may take away my life, but not my love to the truth.

Ver. 18. *Command them not to speak at all*] So in the year of grace 494, Anastasius the emperor persecuted those that would not obey an edict of his, That no man should commend or condemn the Council of Chalcedon. (Alsted. Chron.) So Heraclius commanded that none should say, That there was either one or two wills in our Saviour Christ. So, the Jesuits not long since set forth an edict at Dola, that none should speak of God, either in good sort or in bad.

Ver. 19. *Whether it be right*, &c.] This was a principle held very fast by the heathens. Antigona in Sophocles saith, *Magis obtemperandum est Diis apud quos diutius manendum erit, quam*

[2] *Penes se esse literarum imperium.* Eudæm. in Casaub.

hominibus, quibuscum admodum brevi tempore vivendum est. Better obey God with whom we must ever live, than men with whom we have but a while to continue. And Euripides saith well (in Phœnissis), "Should we not obey the commands of princes?" *Non, si impia, injusta, et male imperata sint:* No, if they command evil things. And in Iphigenia, *Obediemus, inquit, Atridis honesta mandantibus; sin vero inhonesta mandabunt, non obediemus.*

Ver. 20. *For we cannot but speak*] As Crœsus' dumb son did for his father.[1] Strong affections if they find no vent, the heart will cleave; as the waters undermine when they cannot overflow.

Ver. 21. *Finding nothing how*] With what face they could do anything against them, though their fingers even itched to be doing something. Bucer so carried himself here in England, that neither his friends could sufficiently praise, nor his foes find any fault with him. And for Luther, *Non leve præjudicium est,* said Erasmus, *tantam esse morum integritatem, ut nec hostes reperiant quod calumnientur.* His life is so unblameable that his greatest enemies cannot blemish him.

Because of the people] Those that are most terrible to others are not without their terrors. Dionysius the tyrant durst not be barbed but by his own daughters. Masinissa, king of Numidia, committed the guard of his body to dogs; which he could sooner trust than men, whom he had by his cruelty displeased and provoked.

Ver. 22. *Above forty years old*] An old cripple, therefore the greater miracle; so it is to convert an old sinner (that is habituated and long accustomed to evil courses) from the error of his way; sith it is true of many others as well as of Flemings, that *quo magis senescunt, eo magis stultescunt,* they grow crooked and aged with good opinions of themselves without cause; and can seldom or never be set straight again.

Ver. 23. *And being let go*] For there was no hope of altering them. The heavens shall sooner fall than I will renounce my religion, said one martyr. And if I had as many lives to lay down as I have hairs upon my head, I would lose them every one rather than change my mind, said another. This courage in Christians the persecutors counted obstinacy; but they knew not the power of the Spirit, nor the *æs triplex circa pectus,* the privy armour of proof that the saints have about their hearts.

Ver. 24. *Lord*] Master, controller, Δέσποτα. Thou that madest and managest all things. Pitch upon fit attributes of God in prayer.

Ver. 25. *The heathen rage*] Or make a stir. The devil being cast out of heaven makes ado, so do unruly spirits led by him.

Ver. 26. *Gathered together*] Heb. Took counsel together. They plot and plough mischief to the Church, but all in vain, Psal. xxxvii. 12; Job iv. 8.

Ver. 27. *Both Herod and Pontius Pilate, &c.*] So of old, Psal. ii. 1, 2, &c., and Psal. lxxxiii. 5—

[1] ἄνθρωπε, μὴ κτεῖνε τὸν Κροῖσον.

7. So a-late against Luther, the emperor, the pope, the kings of Spain, France, England, Hungary, which two last wrote against him, as did also Eckius, Roffensis, Cajetan, Sir Thomas More, Johannes Faber, Cochlæus, Catharinus, Pighius, *summo conatu acerrimo desiderio, non vulgari doctrina* (as Pareus saith), with all eager desire, utmost endeavour, and extraordinary learning. But what said he to all this? *Agant quicquid possunt Henrici, Episcopi, atque adeo Turca, et ipse Satan; nos filii sumus regni,* &c. Let the Henries, the bishops, the Turk, and the devil himself, do what they can, we are the children of the kingdom, worshipping and waiting for that Saviour, whom they and such as they spit upon and crucify. *Præter vitam hanc misellam, Satanas et mundus eripere nobis nihil potest. At vivit et in sempiternum regnat Christus,* &c.; with many like golden sentences, which a man would fetch upon his knees (saith Mr Samuel Clark) from Rome or Jerusalem.

Ver. 28. *For to do whatsoever, &c.*] *Divinum consilium dum devitatur, impletur. Humana sapientia dum reluctatur, comprehenditur.* (Greg.)

Ver. 29. *Behold their threatenings*] The Church fares the better for the menaces and blasphemies of their enemies. *Quo magis illi furunt, eo amplius procedo,* saith Luther.

Ver. 30. *And that signs and wonders*] *Etiamsi rumpantur adversarii, et toti inferi in rabiem ebulliant,* saith Calvin here; though earth and hell both burst with envy.

Ver. 31. *The place was shaken*] So God testifieth to his Church that he shook them, as men do young trees, to settle them, Hag. ii. 7. God shaketh all nations, not to ruin, but to refine them; as by rotting he refineth our dead bodies, Phil. iii. 21.

Ver. 32. *Were of one heart*] *In primitiva Ecclesia,* saith Tertullian, *Christiani animo animaque inter se miscebantur, et omnia præter uxores, indiscreta habebant. Sed fraternitas omnis hodie extincta est, et unanimitas primitiva non tantum diminuta (de quo Cyprianus suis temporibus queritur) sed e medio penitus sublata esse videtur.* One ancient Greek copy hath these words added to the ordinary reading, "Neither was there any controversy at all amongst them." (Patric. Jun. in Not. ad Clem.)

Ver. 33. *Great grace was upon them all*] Dropped down, as it were, upon them from heaven. God it is that fashioneth men's opinions, and maketh them think well of us. He gave Solomon honour as well as wisdom. And of him it was, that whatsoever David did, pleased the people. Paul goes to God for acceptance of his service, which yet was the bringing of alms. And such are usually very welcome.

Ver. 34. *Neither was there any*] This got them so much favour among all. Heathens acknowledged that there was no such love as among Christians.

Ver. 35. *According as he had need*] The distribution was done with discretion. See Psal. cxii. 5. King Edward VI., moved thereto by a sermon of Bishop Ridley's, gave Christ's Hospital, the Savoy, and Bridewell for the use of the poor, 1. by impotency; 2. by casualty; 3. by ill husbandry; with singular discretion. Doctor Taylor, martyr, took the ablest of his parishioners once a fortnight to the almshouse, and among other poor men, that had many children or were sick, to see what they lacked in meat, drink, bedding, or any other necessaries, and procured a supply for them.

Ver. 36. *Surnamed Barnabas*] See the note on chap. i. 23, with Philem. 7.

Ver. 37. *At the apostles' feet*] As the fittest place. Do we tread upon the minerals, and cannot we contemn them?

CHAPTER V.

Ver. 1. *With Sapphira his wife*] HER name signifieth beautiful, or spacious. She might be so on the outside, as those apples of Sodom, the Egyptian temples, or Jewish sepulchres; but her heart was rotten, and not right with God. Hypocrites are called vipers, Matt. iii. 7, which are outwardly specious, inwardly poisonous. The swan is white in feathers, but of a black skin; and was therefore reputed unclean, and unmeet for sacrifice.

Ver. 2. *And kept back part*] Interverted, ἐνοσφίσατο, purloined, nimmed it away. Here was a concurrence of hypocrisy, sacrilege, diffidence, and ambition; for he would be thought as good as the best, and therefore laid that he brought at the apostles' feet, &c. Hypocrites shall be uncased; no goat in a sheepskin shall steal on Christ's right hand at the last day.

Ver. 3. *Why hath Satan*] The first motion of selling his possession was of the Holy Ghost; but Beelzebub had soon fly-blown and corrupted it.

Ver. 4. *Was it not thine own*] Wicked men have a right to earthly things as their portion, Psal. xvii. 14. God gave Tyrus to Nebuchadnezzar.

Ver. 5. *Fell down, and gave up*] So did Nightingal, parson of Crondal by Canterbury; who, on a Shrove Sunday, reading to the people the pope's bull of pardon sent into England by Cardinal Pool, fell suddenly down dead out of the pulpit, and never stirred hand nor foot: witnessed by all the country round about. Philbert Hamlin, martyr, had instructed in the truth a certain priest his host, who afterwards revolted. Hamlin prophesied to him that nevertheless he should die before him. He had no sooner spoke the word, but the priest going out of the prison was slain by two gentlemen who had a quarrel to him. Whereof when Hamlin heard, he affirmed he knew of no such thing; but only spake as God guided his tongue. Whereupon immediately he made an exhortation of the providence of God, which, by the occasion thereof, moved the hearts of many, and converted them to God.

Patrick Hamilton, a Scotch martyr, being in the fire, cited and appealed the black-friar called Campbell that accused him, to appear before the High God as general Judge of all men, to answer to the innocency of his death betwixt that and a certain day of the next month, which he there named. The friar died immediately before the day came without remorse of conscience, &c. The Judge of the earth keepeth his petty sessions now, letting the law pass upon some few, reserving the rest till the great assizes, 1 Tim. v. 24. Some flagitious persons he punisheth here, lest his providence, but not all, lest his patience and promise of a general judgment, should be called in question. (Aug. in Psal. xxx.) Very remarkable was God's hand upon Mistress Hutchinson (that Jezebel of New England) and her family, all slain (some say burnt) by the Indians. One of her disciples falling into a lie, God smote him in the very act, that he sunk down into a deep swoon. And being by hot waters recovered, and coming to himself, he said, Oh God, thou mightest have struck me dead, as Ananias and Sapphira, for I have maintained a lie.[1]

And great fear came on all] God takes some malefactors, and hangs them up in gibbets as it were; that others, warned thereby, may hear, and fear, and do no more so. *Alterius perditio tua sit cautio. Cavebis autem si pavebis.* Seest thou another suffer shipwreck? look well to thy tackling.

Ver. 6. *And the young men arose*] Decent burial this hypocrite had, though he deserved it not. Temporaries enjoy many outward privileges *per consortium.*

Ver. 7. *Not knowing what was done*] And thinking to find her husband in highest honour among the apostles. "But the eyes of the wicked shall fail, and their hope shall be as the giving up of the ghost," Job xi. 20.

Ver. 8. *Yea, for so much*] Sin had woaded an impudency in her face. How much better that brave woman in St Jerome, who being upon the rack said, *Non ideo negare volo, ne peream; sed ideo mentiri nolo, ne peccem,* I will rather die than lie.

Ver. 9. *To tempt the Spirit*] That is, to make trial of him whether he be omniscient and able to detect and punish your hypocrisy. No man is a gross hypocrite, but he is first an atheist.

Ver. 10. *Then fell she down*] Melancthon makes mention of a cursing woman, that had her neck writhed by the devil, as her mouth was full of cursing and bitterness, A. D. 1551.

Ver. 11. *And great fear*] See the notes on ver. 5. *Laudo Venetos, apud quos unicum publicæ pecuniæ intervertisse denarium, non infame solum est, sed et capitale.* Among the Venetians, it is death to diminish a penny of the public stock.[2]

Ver. 12. *Were many signs and wonders*] Which were as so many sermon bells to bring men to the Church; and as so many wings to carry the gospel abroad the world.

Ver. 13. *Durst no man join himself*] None of

[1] Mr Weld's Preface to his Story.

[2] Zenecat. in Observat Politic. i.

the powerful enemies of the Church durst insinuate (for fear of the danger) as Sanballat and Tobiah would have done in Nehemiah's days; and as the Jesuits now-a-days have a practice of running over to the Lutheran Church, pretending to be converted, and to build with them; but it is only to keep up that bitter contention between the Calvinists and Lutherans.

Ver. 14. *And believers were the more added*] So little lost the Church by that dreadful doom that befell Ananias and Sapphira, Isa. xxvi. 9. Hypocrites are but the wens, or rather botches, of the Church. When God's judgments are upon them, the inhabitants of the earth will learn righteousness; they will wash their feet in the blood of the wicked, Psal. lii. 6. Let the Lord but kill Jezebel's children with death, and then all the Churches will take knowledge that it is He that searcheth the reins and heart, and that giveth unto every man according to his works, Rev. ii. 23.

Ver. 15. *The shadow of Peter passing by*] Upon these stupendous miracles, as upon so many eagles' (or rather angels') wings, was the gospel carried abroad the world then. And the establishing of the Reformation begun a-late by Luther, &c., to be done by so weak and simple means, yea, by casual and cross means, against the force of so potent and politic an adversary as the pope, is that miracle which we are in these times to look for.

Ver. 16. *And they were healed every one*] Christ is Jehovah the Physician, Exod. xv. 26. He hath a most happy hand, and was never foiled by any disease, Psal. ciii. 3. *Omnipotenti medico nullus insanabilis occurris morbus;* to an Almighty Physician no disease can be incurable. (Isidore.)

Ver. 17. *With indignation*] Gr. With zeal: but it was that bitter zeal, Jam. iii. 14, that grows not but in Satan's gardens.

Ver. 18. *Put them in the common prison*] Bocardo (when the good bishops were there in Queen Mary's days) was called a college of quondams: and almost all other prisons in England were become right Christian schools and Churches, saith Mr Fox.

Ver. 19. *But the angel of the Lord*] There was one Laremoth, chaplain to the Lady Anne of Cleves, a Scotchman, to whom, being in prison in Queen Mary's days, it was said, as he thought, once, twice, thrice, Arise and go thy ways. Whereupon he arising from prayer, a piece of the prison wall fell down, and he escaped beyond sea.

Ver. 20. *Stand and speak*] Stand close to the work, stir not a foot, start not a hair's-breadth.

Ver. 21. *They entered into the temple early, &c.*] True obedience is prompt and present, ready and speedy, without delays and consults, Psal. cxix. 60; Mark i. 18. Zech. v. 9, they had wings, and wind in their wings, to note, as Junius observes, their ready obedience.

Ver. 22. *But when the officers came*] As at a lottery, they came with heads full of hopes, but returned with hearts full of blanks.

Ver. 23. *We found no man within*] This might well have made them to desist. But what said the prophet long before? "Lord, when thy hand is lifted up, they will not see;" howbeit, "they shall see, and be ashamed for their envy at thy people," &c., Isa. xxvi. 11.

Ver. 24. *They doubted of them*] *Conturbabantur, et ad angustias inexplicabiles detrusi hæsitabant,* they were at their wit's end, διηπόρουν, and could not tell what in the world to do with them. Herod was troubled in like sort, Luke ix. 7. So was Diocletian, who therefore laid down the empire, because he could not conquer the Christians, merely out of discontent; so did Charles V.

Ver. 25. *Behold, the men whom ye put in prison*] Surely there is neither wisdom, nor understanding, nor counsel against the Lord, Prov. xxi. 30. God's mind is fulfilled by them that have least mind to it; human wisdom, whilst it strives for masteries, is shamefully foiled and over-mastered.

Ver. 26. *And brought them without violence*] The apostles made no resistance, but showed themselves patient and peaceable, blameless amidst a perverse generation, and harmless as doves, that neither provoke the hawk nor project revenge; but when pursued, they save themselves if they can, by flight, and not by fight.

Ver. 27. *They set them before the council*] Where the high priest might well have done, as the prolocutor here in the convocation held at London, A. D. 1553, did; he confessed that those dejected ministers before them had the word on their side; but the prelates in place had the possession of the sword.

Ver. 28. *And intend to bring this man's blood upon us*] They pretend the doctrine, but this was the thing that most troubled them; they should be counted kill-Christs. It is but just that οἱ πράξοντες τὰ μὴ καλὰ, τλήσωσι τὰ μὴ φιλὰ: they that do things not honest, should both hear and bear things not delightful. (Eurip.) But wicked men love not to be told their own; neither accept they of the punishment of their iniquity, Deut. xxvi. 41. They report me to suck blood (said Bonner in open court) and call me Bloody Bonner! whereas, God knows, I never sought any man's blood in all my life. The very same day wherein he had burned good Mr Philpot, being drunk with blood, and not well knowing what he did, he delivered Richard Woodman with four more (whom but two days before he had threatened to condemn, and the very morrow after he sought for again, yea, and that earnestly), requiring of them but to be honest men, members of the Church Catholic (which they promised), and to speak good of him; and no doubt (saith Woodman) he was worthy to be praised, because he had done the devil his master such doubty service. A certain unknown good woman in a letter to him did him right. Indeed, said she, you are called the common cut-throat, and general slaughter-slave to all the bishops of England, &c.

Ver. 29. *We ought to obey God rather than men*] This is a principle granted and grafted in us by nature. I love and embrace you, O Athenians (said Socrates, in his Apology), but yet I will obey God rather than you. See more in the note on chap. iv. ver. 19; Matt. xxii. 21. The article is twice repeated when our Saviour speaks of God, more than when of Cæsar; to show that our special care should be to give God his due.

Ver. 30. *Ye slew and hanged on a tree*] Constantine the Great, in honour of our Saviour, took away by a law that custom of crucifying men, in use, till then, among the Romans: a lingering and cruel kind of death; as was likewise that of impaling, very usual, saith Illyricus, among the ancients. The malefactors had a stake or pale (σκόλοψ) thrust in at their fundament, and it came out again at their shoulders; so that if the stake did not pierce their hearts or vitals, as it was thrust up, they lived sometimes two or three days in exquisite pain and torment. And to this kind of cruel death, saith he, St Paul seemeth to allude, 2 Cor. xii. 7.

Ver. 31. *To be a Prince and a Saviour*] Σωτῆρα. *Hoc vero quantum est?* saith Cicero (In Ver.) *Ita magnum, ut Latino uno verbo exprimi non possit. Is nimirum soter est qui salutem dedit.* The Greek word for "Saviour" is so emphatical, that other tongues can hardly find a fit word to express it. Antigonus Σωτὴρ ἐκρίθη, Antigonus (for liberty restored to the Lacedemonians) was counted and called a "Saviour;" so was the Roman Fabricius at Athens, Hunniades in Hungary, &c. Before them all, Joseph was called by Pharaoh Taphnath-Paaneath, that is (as Jerome interpreteth it), the "Saviour of the world." Several kings of Syria, who had the name Antiochus common to them, were distinguished by glorious epithets. One was called Antiochus ὁ Μέγας, the Great; another, Antiochus Ἐπιφανὴς, or Illustrious; a third, Antiochus Θεὸς, which signifies God; a fourth, Antiochus Σωτὴρ, that is, Saviour; a fifth, Antiochus Εὐπάτωρ, a most indulgent father. Christ is all these more truly and by an excellency. A great God above all gods, an illustrious Prince and Saviour (as the apostle here styleth him), a most tender-hearted Father, who could not only wish, with David, to die for his Absaloms, but did it in very deed, and all to purchase repentance, and thereby remission of sins; according to that holy petition of an ancient, First give repentance, and then pardon. (Hilar.)

Ver. 32. *To them that obey him*] πειθαρχοῦσιν. The Syriac and Arabic have it, To them that believe in him, πιστεύουσιν. It comes all to one pass; for neither is faith without obedience, nor obedience without faith; and both are from the Spirit.

Ver. 33. *They were cut to the heart*] They were so vexed as if they had been cut with a saw, διεπρίοντο; or the gnashing of their teeth sounded as the reciprocation of a saw.

Ver. 34. *Named Gamaliel*] Who was, say the Jews, the son of Simeon, Luke ii. 25, the son of Hillel. See chap. xxii. 3.

Ver. 35. *Take heed to yourselves*] Anger is an evil counsellor; do nothing rashly. Alexan-

der slew those in his heat whom afterwards he would have revived with his heart-blood. Ambrose, absolving Theodosius the emperor, enjoined him to stay the execution of whatsoever statute, till thirty days were over.

Ver. 36. *Rose up Theudas*] See Joseph. Antiq. xviii. 20; xvii. 12.

Ver. 37. *Rose up Judas of Galilee*] Or Judas Gaulonites. It was the blood of his followers that Pilate mingled with their sacrifices, Luke xiii. 1. To his faction belonged those hacksters or murderers, Acts xxi. 38, who might very well be of the sect of the Essenes, called by some Hashom, that is, rebels; because, under pretence of asserting the public liberty, they taught the Jews not to acknowledge the Roman Empire; choosing rather to endure the most exquisite torments than to call any man living Lord. (Joseph. xviii. 2.)

Ver. 38. *Let them alone, for if, &c.*] Perilous counsel, but profitable to the Church; God so ordering it, as he doth all, for the best to his.

Ver. 39. *Ye cannot overthrow it*] Neither you, nor kings and tyrants to help you; so one ancient Greek copy readeth it. Diocletian laid down the empire in great discontent, because he could not, by any persecution, suppress the true Christian religion. (Beza.) So did Charles V., a politic prince, and a sore enemy to the Church. He, when he had in his hand Luther dead, and Melancthon, Pomeran, and other preachers of the gospel, alive; he not only determined not anything extremely against them, or violated their graves, but also entreating them gently, sent them away; not so much as once forbidding them to publish openly the doctrine that they professed. For it is the nature of Christ's Church, that the more that tyrants spurn against it, the more it flourisheth and increaseth.

Ver. 40. *And to him they agreed*] So did the enraged people to the elders, alleging the example of Micah the Morasthite, Jer. xxvi. 18. See the use and efficacy of history, which hath its name, say some, παρὰ τὸ ἱστάναι τὸν ῥοῦν, of stopping the tream of violence.

Ver. 41. *Worthy to suffer shame*] That they were graced so to be disgraced for Christ, *Elegantissimum oxymorum*, saith Casaubon. So Phil. i. 29, "To you it is given (as an honorary) to suffer." Which (saith Father Latimer) is the greatest promotion that God gives in this world. *Martyr etiam in catena gaudet*, saith Augustine. Master Glover, martyr, wept for joy of his imprisonment. And God forgive me, said Master Bradford, my unthankfulness for this exceeding great mercy, that among so many thousands he chooseth me to be one in whom he will suffer, &c. The martyrs in Severus the emperor's days, released for a season, seemed to come, *e myrotheca non ergastulo*, saith Eusebius (v. 2), out of a perfuming-house rather than a prison-house; merry they were and much cheered, that were so much honoured as to suffer for Christ.

Ver. 42. *They ceased not*] *Crescit igitur animus*

cum adversis. The more outrageous the one the more courageous the other party.

CHAPTER VI.

Ver. 1. *Of the Grecians*] Ἑλληνισταὶ, *Græcists;* such (say some) as were by birth and religion Hebrews, but dispersed among the Gentiles; those to whom James and Peter wrote their Epistles. Others think they were Greek proselytes, that were circumcised, and read the Septuagint.

Ver. 2. *It is not reason*] ἀρεστὸν, an arrest or order, saith Erasmus; a plea, judgment, or sentence, saith Budæus.

Serve tables] And do other such offices for the relief of the poor. Bishop Hooper is famous for his board of beggars, who till they were served every day with whole and wholesome meats, he would not himself sit down to dinner. *Laudent te esurientium viscera, non ructantium opulenta convivia,* said Jerome to Demetrius, "Charity is better than courtesy."

Ver. 3. *Full of the Holy Ghost and wisdom*] i. e. Civil wisdom to manage the public stock, and to put all to the best for the relief of the necessitous saints. "I wisdom dwell with prudence, and find out knowledge of witty inventions," Prov. viii. 12.

Ver. 4. *To prayer, and to the ministry*] Between these two they divided their time. An argument of their integrity in the ministry. If we were to preach only, saith the apostle, we could then wait upon tables; but the one half of our time is to be taken up in prayer, the other in preaching. So the priests of old: "They shall teach Jacob thy judgments," saith Moses, "they shall also put incense before thee," Deut. xxxiii. 10. So Paul begins, continues, and endeth his epistles with prayer. So Luther professeth that he profited more in the knowledge of the Scriptures by prayer in a short space, than by study in a longer; as John by weeping got the sealed book opened.

Ver. 5. *Prochorus, Nicanor, and Timon*] *Hi tres celebrantur seduli in lectitandis sacris.* (Malcolm.) These three (as David's first three worthies) are famous for their unweariableness in God's work.

Ver. 6. *They laid their hands*] So putting the blessing upon them. A very ancient rite, borrowed from the Church of the Old Testament.

Ver. 7. *A great company of the priests*] Despair not therefore of the worst; God hath his time to call them. Wicliffe was a great enemy to the swarms of begging friars, with whom it was harder to make war than with the pope himself; whom he pronounced Antichrist, and made him lose in England his tenths and Peter-pence. Howbeit, sundry of the friars fell to him, and embraced his opinions; amongst whom, one that was the pope's chaplain, professing that he came out of his order and out of the devil's nest. (Speed.)

Ver. 8. *And Stephen, full of faith*] He "using the office of a deacon well, did purchase to himself a good degree, and great boldness in the faith which is in Christ Jesus," 1 Tim. iii. 13. A diligent man stays not long in a low place.

Ver. 9. *Certain of the synagogue*] There were colleges at Jerusalem, as now at our Universities, whither foreigners came for learning-sake. These withstood Stephen; like as in the beginning of the Reformation, Eckius, Roffensis, More, Cajetan, Faber, Cochlæus, Catharinus, Pighius, all these wrote against Luther (besides the two kings of England and Hungary), *summo conatu, acerrimo desiderio, non vulgari doctrina,* as one saith.[1] In like sort Rochester, Rastal, More, set at once against John Frith, martyr; whereof the one by the help of the doctors, the other by wresting the Scriptures, and the third by the help of natural philosophy, had conspired against him. But he, as another Hercules, fighting with all three at once, did so overthrow and confound them, that he converted Rastal to his part.

Ver. 10. *By which he spake*] "Because he convinced them with great boldness, neither could they withstand the truth." These words are found in one very ancient copy, as Beza witnesseth.

Ver. 11. *Then they suborned*] This they had learned of that old man-slayer, John viii. 44.

Ver. 12. *Caught him, and brought him*] *Sic vi geritur res,* the adversaries' best arguments. In the conclusion of the disputation at Oxford with Cranmer, Ridley, and Latimer, Weston the prolocutor triumphed with *Vicit veritas;* he should rather have said, *Vicit potestas.* Not right, but might hath carried it.

Ver. 13. *Blasphemous words*] So was Athanasius accused.

Ver. 14. *Shall destroy this place*] sc. Unless they repent.

And shall change the rites] But shall change them for the better. This they cunningly concealed, and made the worst of things, therefore they are counted false witnesses; like as Doeg's tongue was a false tongue (though he spake but the truth), Psal. cxx. 3, and deceitful, Psal. lii. 4, condemned to be broiled on coals of juniper, which burn very fiercely, and are a great while ere they go out. A report or testimony may be false, either by denying, disguising, lessening, concealing, misconstruing things of good report; or else by forging, increasing, aggravating, or uncharitably spreading things of evil report; which though they be true, yet if I know them not to be so; or knowing them to be true, if I divulge them not for any love to the truth, nor for respect to justice, nor for the bettering of the hearer or the delinquent, but only to disgrace the one and incense the other; I cannot avoid the imputation of a slanderer and false witness.

Ver. 15. *As it had been the face of an angel*] Such was the purity of his conscience, the goodness of his cause, and the greatness of his courage. There is a history of a Dutch martyr, who

---

[1] Pareus in Medul. Hist.

calling to the judge that had sentenced him to the fire, desired him to lay his hand upon his heart; and then asked him whose heart did most beat, his or the judge's? Many of the martyrs went with as good cheer to die as to dine. Cromwell going to his death, eat a hearty breakfast. Ridley called it his wedding-day. And another, clipping the stake he was burnt at, said, "Welcome, mine own sweet wife, welcome the cross of Christ."

CHAPTER VII.

Ver. 1. *Are these things so?*] A FAIR hearing Stephen should have, but his death was aforehand resolved on.

Ver. 2. *The God of glory*] Before whom seraphims (those heavenly salamanders) clap their two wings, as a double scarf, on their faces, as not able to bear his brightness, Isa. vi. 2; or as men are wont to clap their hands on their eyes, in a sudden flash of lightning. *Sol reliqua sidera occultat, quibus et lumen suum fœnerat*, saith Pliny, ii. 6.

Ver. 3. *Get thee out, &c.*] Both Abraham's great temptations began thus. See the note on Gen. xii. 1, 2, &c.

Ver. 5. *No, not so much as*] A holy proverb: Deut. ii. 5, "Even to the treading of the sole of the foot." The first purchase that Abraham made was for a burial-place.

Ver. 6. *Four hundred years*] Beginning at the birth of Isaac.

Ver. 7. *And serve me in this place*] *Servati sumus ut serviamus*, Luke i. 74. The redeemed (among the Romans) was to be at the service of the redeemer all his days.

Ver. 8—18.] See my notes on Gen. xvii. 11; xxxvii. 28; xli. 37; xlii. 1; xlv. 4, 16; xlvi. 27.

Ver. 19. *Dealt subtilly*] "Let us deal wisely," saith he, Exod. i. 10; "subtilly" saith this text, κατασοφισάμενος. The world's wisdom is but subtilty, sophistry, fallacy. And God took this wizard in his own craftiness, 1 Cor. iii. 19; for your labouring men have the lustiest children.

Ver. 20. *Exceeding fair*] Passing pretty, a proper child, as the apostle hath it, Heb. xi. 23. Justin maketh mention of his beautiful personage; and by this, as by an instrument, God moved his parents first, and then the princess, to pity and preserve him. The Greek word ἀστεῖος, here rendered fair, signifies fine, trim, elegant, so as citizens are when trimmed up in their bravery upon days of festivity.

Ver. 21.] See notes on Exod. ii. 5.

Ver. 22. *And Moses was learned*] See my Common-place of Arts. Lactantius saith of Tertullian, that he was *in omni genere doctrinæ peritus*, skilful in all kinds of learning. Jerome saith of him, that his works contained *cunctam seculi doctrinam*, all the learning of the world; better may this be said of Moses and his writings.

Ver. 23.] See Heb. xi. 24, with the note.

It came into his heart] sc. By an impulse of the Holy Spirit; for till then it seems he had slighted them; but now he began to be sick of the affliction of Joseph, whereby he was even broken to shivers, as the Hebrew word *Shevarim* signifies, Amos vi. 6.

Ver. 24. *And avenged him*] Wherein haply he was too hasty to do justice before his time; which might cost him, and cause him forty years' exile in Midian.

Ver. 25. *But they understood not*] For by this time they through long and hard oppression (which makes even a wise man mad, Eccles. vii. 7) had well-nigh forgotten the promise of deliverance out of Egypt; and having been born in hell (as the proverb is) they knew no other heaven.

Ver. 26. *Sirs, ye are brethren*] In this Egypt of the world, all unkind strifes should easily be composed, did we but remember that we are brethren.

Ver. 27. *He that did the wrong*] None so ready to except and exclaim, as the wrong-doer; the patient replies not.

Ver. 28. *Wilt thou kill me, &c.*] If this Hebrew had been well pleased, Moses had not heard of his slaughter; now in choler all will out. If this man's tongue had not thus cast him in the teeth with blood, he had been surprised by Pharaoh, ere he could have known the fact was known; now he grows jealous, flies and escapes. No friend is so commodious in some cases as an adversary.

Ver. 29. *Then fled Moses*] And by being banished, was the better fitted to be king in Jeshurun.

Ver. 30.] See Exod. iii. 2.

Ver. 31. *He wondered at the sight*] How many come to the ordinances to see and to be seen! they may hear that, with Moses here, that may do them good for ever.

Ver. 32.] See Exod. iii. 6.

Ver. 33. *Put off thy shoes*] Thy fleshly affections, and be wholly at my disposal, in the business whereabout I shall send thee.

Ver. 34. *I have seen, I have seen*] To my grief and regret. God is said to suffer in the sufferings of his people. The Father, Isa. lxiii. 9, the Son, Acts ix. 4, the Holy Ghost, 1 Pet. iv. 14.

Ver. 35. *By the hands*] That is, by the authority and conduct. Hands are not here taken for service, but ruledom; and Christ is set above Moses, as Heb. iii. 5.

Ver. 36. *And in the wilderness*] Where their garments were no whit the worse for wearing. Why then should we question the incorruptibility of our bodies at the resurrection?

Ver. 37. *Like unto me*] See the note on Acts iii. 22.

Ver. 38. *Lively oracles*] That is, life-giving oracles. The law is said to be the "strength of sin," 1 Cor. xv. 56. But this is by accident, through our corruption.

Ver. 39. *Thrust him from them*] The present government is alway grievous, Ἀεὶ τὸ παρὸν βαρὺ, as Thucydides observeth. *Alleva jugum, Alleva jugum*, said those in Rehoboam's days, that were all for a relaxation.

Ver. 40. *Make us gods*] That is, an image, or representation of God. This was not to keep their promise, Exod. xix. 8.

Ver. 41. *And offered sacrifice to the idol*] That is, to the devil, Psal. cvi. 37, who is εἰδωλο-χαρὴς, as Synesius calls him. Howbeit the idolaters pretended herein to worship Jehovah, Exod. xxxii. 4, 5. Their mawmet, if it would not make a god, would make an excellent devil; as the mayor of Doncaster told the wise men of Cockram concerning their ill-shaped rood.

Ver. 42. *Of the prophets*] The twelve small prophets were in one volume.

Ver. 43. *Of your god Remphan*] Amos v. 26, called Chiun. These are but divers names of the same idol; the Hebrews calling it by one name, the Egyptians by another. See Selden de Diis Syris.

Ver. 44. *Our fathers had the tabernacle*] He had made answer to their first accusation touching blasphemous words against the law. Now for the tabernacle and temple, he takes off that too: and showeth that God's worship is not now to be tied to any one place more than another.

Ver. 45. *Brought in*] This argued and aggravated their *levitatem plus quam desultoriam*, monstrous giddiness in running after strange gods, having the true God so near them as never any people had. (Beza.) It might be said of them as it was once of Baldwin the apostate, that he had *religionem Ephemeram*, for each day a new religion: or as Lactantius writeth of some idolaters in his time, that they feigned what they pleased, and then feared what they feigned.

Ver. 46. *Who found favour*] This he made more account of than of his crown and sceptre, Psal. iv. 6. Like as when he gave Ziba the lands of Mephibosheth, Ziba begged a further and better boon; " I humbly beseech thee that I may find grace in thy sight, my lord, O king," 2 Sam. xvi. 4. What is air without light? or daily bread without pardon of sin? God's favour sugars all comforts.

Ver. 47. *But Solomon built him a house*] A stately house indeed, one of the seven wonders of the world (how basely soever Florus writeth of it, out of his deep and desperate hatred of that nation and their religion): far beyond that Ephesian temple of Diana, built all of cedar, in an apish imitation of it; or the Turks' mosques, which yet are very magnificent; the Great Turk also never comes into them but (for reverence' sake to his God) he lays aside all his state and attendance.

Ver. 48. *Howbeit, the Most High dwelleth not*] This he subjoineth, because the Jews bore themselves so bold upon the temple, and made such ado about it, as if God were tied to it (as the Chinese chain their gods, that they may be sure of them), crying, " The temple of the Lord, the temple of the Lord," when they little respected the Lord of the temple. The disciples also were taxed with this error, Matt. xxiv., and thought

that the temple and the world must needs end together; *quasi absque stationibus non staret mundus*. But our Saviour undeceiveth them there.

Ver. 49. *Heaven is my throne, and earth my footstool*] And accordingly there are *Bona throni* and *bona scabelli*, as the schools distinguish. God and his graces are the good things of his throne: earth and outward comforts are the good things of his footstool. These we may have, but not love (God hath put all things under our feet, Psal. viii. 6). Those we must covet and aspire unto. But with most men now-a-days the word and the world may seem altered and inverted; earth is their throne, and heaven is their footstool; so little they look after this, and so much that. The Duke of Alva said, he had so much to do on earth, that he had no time to look after heaven.

Ver. 50. *Hath not mine hand made all these things?*] Therefore I need not your handiwork, though I am pleased to accept of it; which you are to look upon as a wonderful condescension. " God humbleth himself to behold the things that are in heaven and in earth," Psal. cxiii. 6. If he look out of himself upon the saints and angels (how much more upon us!) it is a condescension.

Ver. 51. *Ye stiff-necked, &c.*] Henry Lawrence, martyr, being required to put his hand in subscribing to his answers, he wrote these words under the bill of their examination, Ye are all Antichrist, and him ye follow, and here his hand was staid, and sentence read against him:

And uncircumcised in heart] Ye that to your sinews of iron have added brows of brass; to your natural hardness, that which is habitual: being more tough than timber that hath long lain soaking in the water, having brawny breasts and horny heartstrings.

Ver. 52. *Of whom ye have been now the betrayers, &c.*] This was to deal plainly and freely with them; this was *Mordaci radere vero*, to tell them the naked truth, whatever it cost him. Let those tigers tear him with their teeth which now they were whetting; he hath but a life to lose, and lose it he cannot in a better cause, &c.

Ver. 53. *And have not kept it*] The Jews were so far from being a law to themselves, αὐτόνομοι (as the Thracians are said to be), that (more like the Athenians) whereas they had excellent laws, but naughty natures, *Moribus suis quam legibus uti mallent*, they lived not by their laws, but by their lusts rather. (Val. Max.)

Ver. 54. *They were cut to the heart*] But that I believe that God and all his saints will take revengement everlasting on thee, I would surely, with these nails of mine, be thy death, said friar Brusierd in a conference with Mr Bilney, martyr. Another friar of Antwerp, preaching to the people, wished that Luther were there, that he might bite out his throat with his teeth.[1] Plutarch relateth of the tigers, that if any one do but strike up a drum in their hearing, they grow stark mad, insomuch as at length they tear their own flesh. So, many savage people are extremely disquieted

[1] Erasm. Epist. xvi.

at the hearing of the word, and that merely through their own corruption; like as it is not the tossing in a ship, but the stomach that causeth sickness; the choler within, and not the waves without.

Ver. 55. *And Jesus standing*] As ready to revenge the injuries done to his proto-martyr. *Christus stat ut Vindex, sedet ut Judex.*

Ver. 56. *Behold, I see, &c.*] Christ as man could see as far into heaven as Stephen now did, who could not therefore but stand stoutly to it. Creatures of an inferior nature will be courageous in the eye of their masters. A believer by the eye of his faith, through the perspective of the promises, may also see into heaven. But what a tale is that which the monkish writers tell of Mulfin, Bishop of Salisbury, whom (because he displaced secular priests and put in monks) they make to be a very holy man; and report of him that when he lay a dying, he cried out suddenly, "I see the heavens open, and Jesus Christ standing at the right hand of God," and so died. (Speed. 335.)

Standing on the right hand] Showing by that posture how ready he is to appear for his people. And surely if it could be said of Scipio, that Rome could not fall while Scipio stood, neither would he live to see Rome fall; how much more truly may it be said of Christ, that neither shall the Church fall while Christ standeth at the right hand of his Father, neither can Christ stand there, his Church falling.

On the right hand of God] As Christ is at the right hand of the Father, so is the Church at the right hand of Christ, Psal. xlv.

Ver. 57. *Ran upon him*] Being acted and agitated by the devil, who had now wholly possessed them; so that they were even satanized, and transformed into so many breathing devils.

Ver. 58. *And stoned him*] As a blasphemer. Our proto-martyr in Queen Mary's days was Mr Rogers; as in Germany Henry and John, two Augustine monks, were the first that were burnt for Lutheranism. (Scultet. Annal.) They suffered at Brussels, A. D. 1523, and sang in the flames. He was a bold Israelite that first set foot into the Red Sea, saith one. These proto-martyrs shall be renowned to all posterity.

Ver. 59. *And they stoned Stephen*] Bembus wrote a dainty poem concerning Stephen, and therein hath this verse, much admired by Melancthon.

Ibat ovans animis, et spe sua damna levabat.

He saw heaven through that shower of stones. Becket's friends advised him to have a mass in honour of St Stephen, to keep him from the hands of his enemies. He had so, but it profited him not.

Lord Jesus, receive, &c.] Luther's last prayer was this, "My heavenly Father, thou hast manifested unto me thy dear Son Jesus Christ. I have taught him, I have known him; I love him as my life, my health, and my redemption, whom

the wicked have persecuted, maligned, and with injury affected: draw my soul to thee." After this he said, "I commend my spirit into thy hands, thou hast redeemed me, O God of truth," &c.

Lord, lay not this sin, &c.] *Ne statuas.* Set it not upon their score, or account. St Augustine is of opinion that this prayer of St Stephen's was of avail for St Paul's conversion. He stood when he prayed for himself, he kneeled when he prayed for his enemies; to show (saith one) the greatness of his piety, and of their impiety, not so easily forgiven. He was more sorry for their riot than for his own ruin.

CHAPTER VIII.

Ver. 1. *And Saul, &c.*] IT is all one to hold the sack and to fill it, to do evil or to consent to it.

And Saul was consenting to his death] Gr. ἀναιρέσει, "to his murder;" for it was no better, Acts xii. 2; v. 33. *Damnari, dissecari, suspendi, decollari, piis cum impiis sunt communia. Varia sunt hominum judicia: ille fœlix qui judice Deo absolvitur,* saith Erasmus concerning Berquin, the martyr, burnt in Germany. Dorotheus witnesseth, that when Stephen was stoned, there were 2000 other believers put to death the same day. Certain it is, that after Mr Rogers had broken the ice here under Queen Mary, there suffered in like sort, one archbishop, four bishops, 21 divines, eight gentlemen, 84 artificers, 100 husbandmen, servants, and labourers, 26 wives, 20 widows, nine virgins, two boys, and two infants; in all 277. Some say a great many more.

And they were all scattered] To the Church's great advantage, which, like the sea, what ground it loseth in one place, it getteth in another. So at Melda in France (10 miles from Paris), Brissonet, the bishop thereof, desirous of a reformation, put away the monks and called in the help of divers godly ministers. But being persecuted by the Sorbonists, he soon fell off from the profession of the truth; and those good ministers (Faber, Farellus, Ruffus, and others) were driven into divers other places of France, where they planted several churches; the destruction of one being the edification of many.[1] Farellus, one of those fore-mentioned ministers, was God's instrument of gaining the inhabitants of Geneva, Lausanne, Novocoma, &c.

Ver. 2. *Carried Stephen*] συνεκόμισαν, On their shoulders, lamenting, with knocking their breasts, &c., as the word κοπετὸν imports: no whit afraid of those mad murderers. So the primitive Christians would not be kept from visiting the confessors in prison, *Tamet si multis terroribus, minis, et periculis interdictum erat,* as Chrysostom witnesseth in his oration of the two martyrs. So certain good people took up and buried the bodies of Ursula and Mary, two noble virgins, burnt at Delden in Lower Germany, which the executioner could in no wise consume with fire, *rum fuit ædificatio.* Scultet. Annal.

---

[1] *Unius Ecclesiæ destructio multa-*

but left them lying on the ground. And the like is reported touching the hearts of Zuinglius and Cranmer.

Ver. 3. *Made havoc of the church*] Being (as some think) that ravening wolf of the tribe of Benjamin, prophesied of by Jacob, Gen. xlix. 27.

Ver. 4.] See the notes on ver. 1. *Trucidabantur et multiplicabantur*, saith Austin. They were never the fewer for being slain. *Plures efficimur quoties metimur*, saith Tertullian. *Ecclesia totum mundum sanguine et oratione convertit*, saith Luther; the Church converts the whole world by her sufferings and prayers.

Ver. 5. *Then Philip*] Not Philip the apostle (for they all abode at Jerusalem, ver. 1), but Philip the deacon. He that is faithful in a little shall be made master of more.

Ver. 6. *And the people, &c.*] A corrupt place, and bewitched by the sorceries of Simon Magus; yet even there God had a people. Justin Martyr was of this city.

Ver. 7. *Crying with a loud voice*] To show that they went out perforce, and with a very ill will.

Ver. 8. *And there was great joy*] So there was at Berne; for when the reformation was first received they pardoned (for joy) two condemned persons and called home all their banished. So there was at Geneva; the inhabitants whereof, upon the like occasion, stamped new money with this inscription, *Post tenebras lux*. So also there was among the Helvetians, who caused the day and year when reformation began amongst them to be engraved in a pillar, in letters of gold, for a perpetual memory to all posterity, A. D. 1528.

Ver. 9. *Which before time, &c.*] Or, which was master of the magicians, προυπῆρχεν. *Sed quæ traduntur de modo disceptationis Petri cum Simone Mago* δραματικὰ *potius quam* ἰστορικὰ *esse videntur.*

Bewitched the people] Gr. ἐξιστῶν. Carried them out of themselves, as in an ecstasy, so that they were more his than their own.

Some great thing] Such a blab the devil had blown up there, as a small wind may blow up a bubble.

Ver. 10. *This man is the great power of God*] Epiphanius saith that this varlet called himself God the Father and the Son, and his harlot Helena (an horrible thing to be spoken) the Holy Ghost. Justin Martyr witnesseth, that he had near unto Rome a statue erected, with this inscription, *Simoni Deo sancto*, To Simon the holy God. Prodigious boldness and baseness!

Ver. 11. *He had bewitched them with sorcery*] It fell out in the year of grace 434, that a certain seducer, who called himself Moses, persuaded the Jews in Crete that he was sent from heaven with commission to repossess them of the Promised Land. Him therefore they gladly followed (a great sort of them) with their wives and children to the sea-side; where he bade them to cast themselves after him from a steep rock into the sea. This they did, and there perished many

of them; and many more had done, but that (by a providence) sundry were caught up by Christian fishermen there present at that time, and carried safe to land. These, after they were recovered, carried notice to their fellows, how fearfully they had been deluded by the devil, who had personated Moses; and divers of them, moved by their late calamity, became Christians. In the year 759, certain Persian magicians persuaded themselves and many others, that if they sold all they had and cast themselves naked from the town wall, they should fly up to heaven immediately; *perierunt hac insaniâ permulti*, saith the historian. Many perished by believing this senseless lie. (Funccius in Chronol.)

Ver. 12. *They were baptized both men and women*] Who were admitted to baptism on this condition, that their infants also and their whole families should be consecrated to God; for so runs the covenant, Gen. xvii. 7. If any ask why Christ and the apostles did not set down plainly, that infants were or might be baptized? it is answered that none (then) questioned the lawfulness of it, because it was generally done. Again, if when infants were brought to be baptized (as they were brought to Christ to be blessed) the apostles had rejected them, the believing Jews (and others) would have excepted, and demanded why they might not as well be baptized, as once they were circumcised? and the apostles would have given them an answer. St Peter, speaking of baptism, limiteth it thus: "Baptism saveth, not the putting away of the filth of the flesh, but," &c., 1 Pet. iii. 21. Would not the evangelist here as well have said, men and women were baptized, only infants were not? If it be further objected, that it is in vain to give the sacrament to infants that understand not what is done to them, we answer, that the same may be said touching the sacrament of circumcision, which yet was done to infants, by God's appointment. Thus to object therefore, is to "charge God foolishly," Job i. 22. Again, were Christ's parables uttered in vain, because not presently understood? Or was it to no purpose that he laid his hands upon infants and blessed them? is it in vain to give physic to children, fools, or mad-men, that know not what we do to them?

Ver. 13. *Simon himself believed*] As the devils also believe, with an historical faith, a mere flash, which therefore soon came to nothing.

And when he was baptized] Pity that that fair water was spilt upon so foul a face. But circumcision avails nothing without faith that works by love. Unregenerate Israel is to God as Ethiopia, Amos ix. 7. Baptism to such is not God's mark, but the devil's brand.

Ver. 14. *They sent Peter and John*] Those pillars, Gal. iii.; ii. 9, to confirm Philip's doctrine, and found a church by their apostolic authority.

Ver. 15. *The Holy Ghost*] That is, those extraordinary gifts of tongues, healing, &c.

Ver. 16. *For as yet he was fallen upon none of*

them] *sc.* In those extraordinary gifts of tongues and miracles.

Ver. 17. *Then laid they their hands on them*] After the manner of the priests, who laid their hands on the beast that was to be sacrificed, and so consecrated them to God.

Ver. 18. *He offered them money*] As Simoniacs still do their corrupt patrons, so crucifying Christ afresh between two thieves. Benefices are now bestowed, saith one, *non ubi optime, sed ubi quæstuosissime.* As if a man should bestow so much bread on his horse, because he is to ride on him, &c.

Ver. 19. *Give me also this power*] Base spirits have low conceits of the high things of God. The stream riseth not above the spring. *Omnia Romæ venalia;* all things at Rome are soluble and saleable.

Ver. 20. *But Peter said unto him*] Philip took him for a right honest man, and baptized him; but Peter soon smelt a fox, and drew him out of his den into the open light. Hypocrites shall be sooner or later detected; their name must rot.

Thy money perish with thee] So said that noble Italian marquis, Caracciolus, to the Jesuit that tempted him to revolt for money.[1] Let their money perish with them, said he, that esteem all the gold in the world worth one day's society with Jesus Christ and his Holy Spirit; and cursed be that religion for ever that goes that way to work.

Ver. 21. *Thou hast neither part nor lot*] *Neque pars, neque sors,* no manner of interest in this faith, much less in this sacred office of preaching, and laying hands upon others. (*Dictio proverbialis.*) The Jews boast, that in Portugal and Spain they have millions of their race to whom they give complete dispensation to counterfeit Christianity, even to the degree of priesthood; and that none are discovered but some hot spirits, whose zeal cannot temporize. Are not these perfect Simoniacs?

Ver. 22. *Repent therefore*] Repentance is *post naufragium tabula,* it is the fair daughter of a foul mother, i. e. sin, which (if not repented of) will soon work our ruth and ruin.[2]

If perhaps the thought] Επίνοια to be cured by μετάνοια. Thought is not free; but if evil, must be reversed by repentance, or will undo us for ever, Jer. iv. 14.

Ver. 23. *Thou art in the gall,* &c.] The apostle alludeth to Deut. xxix. 18. Sin is a bitter potion, a deadly poison, which therefore we must quickly cast up again by confession, ere it get to the vitals. Simon Magus is here convinced by the very show of godliness, under which he hoped to have lurked; as the fish sepia is bewrayed by the black colour which she casteth out to cover her.

Ver. 24. *Pray for me*] Some from these words conclude his effectual conversion. He trembleth at God's justice, and imploreth his mercy. *Hæc*

certe non minima sunt pœnitentiæ signa, saith judicious Calvin; these were no small signs of sound repentance.

Ver. 25. *When they had testified*] That is, with great gravity and liberty declared. (διαμαρτυρόμενοι.)

In many villages of the Samaritans] Accounting with Luther, that *vilissimus pagus est palatium eburneum in quo est pastor et credentes aliqui;* the meanest village may become an ivory palace, by having in it a faithful pastor and some few believers.

Ver. 26. *Which is desert*] Which way is desert, that is, less frequented, because up-hill and down-hill. So is the way to heaven, and therefore little travelled.

Ver. 27. *Candace*] This, saith Pliny, was a common name to the Ethiopian queens, as Cæsar was to the Roman emperors. Her country might haply be that large region of Nubia, which had from the apostles' time (as it is thought) professed the Christian faith; but hath again above a hundred years since forsaken it, and embraced instead of it, partly Mahometanism, and partly idolatry; and that by the most miserable occasion that might befall, namely, famine of the word of God through lack of ministers.

Ver. 28. *Sitting in his chariot, read*] Time is to be redeemed for holy uses. Pliny seeing his nephew walking for his pleasure, called to him, and said, *Poteras hasce horas non perdidisse;* You might have better bestowed your time than so. *Nullus mihi per otium dies exit,* saith Seneca. And Jerome exhorted some godly women, to whom he wrote, not to lay the Bible out of their hands, until being overcome with sleep, they bowed down their heads, as it were to salute the leaves below them with a kiss.

Ver. 29. *Then the Spirit said*] *sc.* By revelation, or secret inspiration.

Ver. 30. *And heard him read*] He read as he rode. Pliny was always reading or writing, or doing something, *quo ad vitam communem aliquem fructum ferre posset,* whereby he might benefit himself or others. Mr Bradford the martyr held that hour of his life lost, wherein he had not done some good with his hand, tongue, or pen. Seneca saith, I have no time to spare or spend idly; I see men do not so much want time as waste it.[3] This they would not do, if they considered that upon this little point of time hangs the crown of eternity. Oh, make much of time, said Thomas Aquinas, especially in that weighty matter of salvation. Oh how much would he that now lies frying in hell rejoice, if he might have again but the least moment of time, wherein to make his peace with God!

Ver. 31. *How can I, except some man*] The mathematics are so called, because they cannot be learned without a teacher. No man is αὐτοδίδακτος, in heavenly literature. He that here is scholar to himself, hath a fool to his master.

Ver. 32. *The place of the Scripture*] The

---

[1] His Life by Crashaw.
[2] ἐχθροῦ πατρὸς φίλτατον τέκνον. De Pompeio Romani.

[3] *Non parum habemus temporis, sed multum perdimus.*

parcel, saith the Syriac, פמוקא; the partition or section, say the Hebrews, הפטרה. Amongst us, Stephen Langton, Archbishop of Canterbury, first divided the Bible into chapters in such sort as we now account them; Robert Stephens into verses, *imperitissime plerunque textum dissecans*, saith Scultetus, not doing so well as he might.

Ver. 33. *His judgment was taken away*] That is, he was set safe from his enemies, that judged and executed him. He rose, and reigneth in despite of them.

And who shall declare his generation ?] *Sæculum ejus*. (Beza.) Or can tell how long his kingdom shall last? for being raised from the dead, he dieth no more. He may as well die at the right hand of his Father as in the hearts of his children.

Ver. 34. *I pray thee of whom*] Incredible gain is to be got by conference in all arts; so here. All Christ's scholars are ζητητικοὶ, questionists, though not question-sick, as those triflers in Timothy, 1 Tim. vi. 4.

Ver. 35. *And preached unto him*] Of preaching we may say in comparison of other ordinances, for the getting of knowledge, as David did of Goliath's sword, there is none to that.

Ver. 36. *What doth hinder*] He stood not upon the reproach of Christian religion, what the courtiers at home would censure of him. He would hardly suffer death for Christ that cannot suffer little breath for him.

Ver. 37. *Is the Son of God*] Both by eternal generation, Prov. viii. 22—30, and by hypostatical union, Matt. iii. 17.

Ver. 38. *And he baptized him*] Set Christ's mark upon him, that seal of the new covenant. The Jacobites (a kind of mongrel Christians in Asia) sign their children, many in the face, some in the arm, with the sign of the cross, imprinted with a hot burning iron, at or before baptism; but we have not so learned Christ.

Ver. 39. *Went on his way rejoicing*] Bernard, for a certain time after his conversion, remained, as it were, deprived of his senses, by the excessive consolations he had from God. Cyprian confesseth to Donatus, his friend, that before his conversion he thought it was impossible for him to change his manners, and to find such comfort as now he did in a Christian life. He beginneth thus, *Accipe quod sentitur antequam discitur*. Augustine saith the same of himself (Confess. vi. 12).

Ver. 40. *At Azotus*] A city of Palestine, called anciently Ashdod, whence the Anakims could not be driven out, Josh. xi. 22.

CHAPTER IX.

Ver. 1. *And Saul yet breathing*] As a tired wolf, that wearied with worrying the flock, lies panting for breath. See the note on chap. viii. 3.

Ver. 2. *Letters to Damascus*] The high priest. it seems, then had power at Damascus, and else-where out of Judea, to bind and beat his Jews, for misdemeanour in point of their religion. See Acts xviii. 15.

Ver. 3. *And as he journeyed*] So Petrus Paulus Vergerius, the pope's nuncio, *dum confutationem Evangelicorum meditatur, fit Evangelicus;* moved, perhaps, by the fearful example also of Francis Spira, whereof he had been an eye-witness.

Ver. 4. *Fell to the earth*] Christ unhorsed him, but did not destroy him. He is not such a monarch as loves to get authority by sternness, as Rehoboam, but by gentleness. And though gone to heaven, yet hath he not changed his nature with change of honour; but together with beams of glory, there are still in him the same bowels of pity that he had here upon earth.

Why persecutest thou me ?] As unskilful hunters, shooting at wild beasts, may kill a man; so those that shoot at the saints, hit Christ. Their sufferings are held his, Col. i. 24; their reproach his, Heb. xiii. 13. God is more provoked than Nehemiah, Neh. iv. 3, 5. Christ retaineth still compassion, though free from personal passion; and, though freed from feeling, he hath still yet a fellow-feeling.[1] Let such amongst us take heed what they do, who, whiles they pronounce our Church antichristian, &c., strike at the beast, but wound the Lamb.

Ver. 5. *To kick against the pricks*] A metaphor from oxen pushing back upon the goad, when they are pricked therewith, as Beza showeth out of Æschilus.

Ver. 6. *It shall be told thee*] Christ teacheth him not immediately, but sendeth him to a preacher; so to grace his own ordinance.

Ver. 7. *Hearing a voice*] Not Christ's voice, but Saul's only, chap. xxii. 9.

Ver. 8. *He saw no man*] This bodily blindness was a means to open the eyes of his mind, as Gehazi's leprosy cured his soul.

Ver. 9. *And he was three days*] In this three days' darkness, some gather by computation of time, that he was now rapt up into the third heaven, and heard those wordless words, ῥήματα ἄῤῥητα, 2 Cor. xii. 4, after that he had been thoroughly humbled. Luther likewise lay (after his conversion) three days in desperation, as Mr Perkins remembereth in his book of Spiritual Desertion. His temptations were so violent, *ut nec calor, nec sanguis, nec sensus, nec vox superesset*, as Justus Jonas reporteth of Luther, that was by and saw it. (Epist. ad Melancthon.) The like is recorded concerning Mr Bolton, by Mr Bagshaw in his Life.

Ver. 10. *And there was a certain*] See here the necessity and use of the ministry: "If there be a messenger with a man, an interpreter, one among a thousand, to show unto man his uprightness," &c., Job xxxiii. 23. *Unus e millibus*. The Vulgar translation corruptly hath it, *unus e similibus*.

Ver. 11. *The street called Straight*] God's people are so dear to him, that their walls are

---

[1] *Manet compassio etiam cum impassibilitate.* Bernard.

ever before him, Isa. xlix. 16; he loveth the streets the better they dwell in, the air the better they breathe in, Psal. lxxxvii. 5, 6.

For behold he prayeth] He never prayed till now, though a strict Pharisee. So Dan. ix. 13. The captives in Babylon prayed not in those 70 years; because they fasted to themselves, and prayed more to get off their chains than their sins, Zech. vii. 5, 6. Prayer is the breath of the spirit, Rom. viii. 26; Jude 20. And prayer without the spirit is but an empty ring, a tinkling cymbal.

Ver. 12. *And hath seen in a vision*] It is not certain whether these be Christ's own words, or St Luke's; neither is it much material.

Ver. 13. *Then Ananias answered*] The best have their unnecessary fears, and think they have reason on their side; but convinced, they soon subscribe to God. *Veniat, veniat verbum Domini*, said one, *et submittemus ei sexcenta si nobis essent colla.*

How much evil he hath done] And is therefore not lightly to be trusted. It is a rule in the Civil Law, *Semel malus semper præsumitur esse malus:* but God can soon alter a man's mind and manners, as he did Saul's.

Ver. 14. *And here he hath authority*] Therefore he was more than 20 years old (as Ambrose and Theodoret make him to be) at his first conversion. For here he hath authority committed unto him, not incident to so very a youth.

Ver. 15. *A chosen vessel to bear*] In matters of holiness we are rather patients than agents, that we may ascribe all to God's grace; therefore he compares us not to active instruments, as tools in the hand of a workman, but to passive instruments, such as dishes or vessels (as here) that bear and carry treasure, meat, or such-like, 2 Cor. iv. 7. Acts xiii. 15, "Ye men and brethren, if there be in you" (as in so many vessels of honour) "any word of exhortation, say on." But what a mouth of blasphemy opened Quintinus the libertine, who scoffing at every of the apostles, *Paulum vocabat vas fractum* (as Calvin testifieth),[1] called Paul a broken vessel: so in the year 1519, *Scioli quidam Tiguris jactabant hæc tria, scilicet, &c. Quis tandem Paulus? nonne homo est? Apostolus est sed suburbanus tantum, &c. Ego tam cuivis Thomæ vel Scoto credo quam Paulo.* Some, no wiser than they should be, cast out slighting speeches to this purpose: What was Paul more than another man? an apostle, indeed, but of an inferior order; none of the twelve that conversed with Christ; neither made he any one of the articles of the Creed. I would as soon believe Thomas or Scotus, as Paul, &c. I tremble to relate how basely some Jesuits have spoken of St Paul, as savouring of heresy in some places; and better perhaps he had never written.

Before the Gentiles and kings, &c.] Μεγίστη τοῦ κηρύγματος σάλπιγξ ὁ Παῦλος, saith a Greek father. Paul was God's chief herald, the gospel's loudest trumpet.

Ver. 16. *How great things he must suffer*] Op-

position is (as Calvin wrote to the French king) *Evangelii genius*, the evil angel that dogs the gospel. And *prædicare*, said Luther, *nihil aliud est quam derivare in se furorem totius mundi:* To preach, is to get the evil will of the world.

Ver. 17. *Putting his hands*] Partly so to consecrate him to the Lord's work, and partly to obtain for him the gifts of the Holy Ghost.

Ver. 18. *There fell from his eyes*] God also at the same time tore the covering, rent the veil that was spread over the eyes of his understanding, Isa. xxiv. 7. See "The Blind Eye Opened" in a discourse on Eph. v. 8, by my entire friend Mr Dugard.

Ver. 19. *With the disciples*] For as he desired to cleave perpetually to the head, so to join himself to his members, to incorporate with the Church.

Ver. 20. *And straightway he preached*] He conferred not with flesh and blood, Gal. i. 16, but fell presently to work, and followed it close, as afraid to be taken with his task undone. Chrysostom saith of Paul, that he was *insatiabilis Dei cultor*, an insatiable server of God.

Ver. 21. *Is not this he?*] It is, and it is not: it is not *Ille ego qui quondam*, but *ego non sum ego*. He is another man than he was, and this the whole Church shall soon hear of: like as a bell cannot be turned from one side to another, but it will make a sound, and report its own motion.

Ver. 22. *Proving that this, &c.*] Συμβιβάζων. Proving it by comparing Scripture with Scripture, by laying one place to another, as joiners fit all the parts of their work together, that each part may perfectly agree with the other, Neh. viii. 8. The Levites read the law, and gave the sense, causing the people to understand the reading, *dabant intelligentiam per Scripturam ipsam:* so Tremellius rendereth it. Parallel texts, like glasses, set one against another, cast a mutual light. The lapidary brightens his hard diamond with the dust shaved from itself; so must we clear hard Scriptures.

Ver. 23. *And after many days*][2] sc. After three years. So long he had to settle, ere God called him forth to suffer. The skilful armourer trieth not an ordinary piece with musket-shot. The wise lapidary brings not his softer stones to the stithy: the good husbandman turns not the wheel upon his cummin, nor his flail upon his vetches, Isa. xxviii. 25.

Ver. 24. *But their laying await*] Some friend likely had advertised him, as a senator of Hala did Brentius, when some had conspired his death, *Fuge, fuge, Brenti, cito, citius, citissime.* Flee speedily, away for thy life. (Melch. Adam.)

Ver. 25. *Let him down, &c.*] It is not unlawful then to fly in some cases. Tertullian was too rigid in condemning all kind of flight, in time of persecution; God hath not set us as standing marks, or butts, to be shot at.

Ver. 26. *They were all afraid of him*] Openheartedness is an argument of folly, *Fide, diffide.* Our Saviour would not lightly commit himself to

---

[1] Instruct. adv. Libert., ix.

[2] ἡμέραι ἱκαναὶ *diebus sufficientibus.*

any, John ii. 24. Try whom you mean to trust. Paul was somewhile a probationer ere he could be admitted.

Ver. 27. *And how he had preached boldly*] See the notes on verses 21 and 29.

Ver. 28. *And he was with them*] *sc.* With Peter and James, Gal. i. 18, 19. For the other apostles were then absent, about their Lord's business.

Ver. 29. *And he spake boldly*] The soul, by the witness of the Spirit, finds increase of spiritual mettle, and is steeled against opposition.

Disputed against the Grecians] These had been St Stephen's greatest adversaries, Acts vi. 1, 9, and then Saul was very forward to join with them. Now that he was turned Christian, they sought his death, having first given out (as Epiphanius testifieth) that he turned merely out of discontent, because he could not obtain to wife the high priest's daughter. Truth (saith one) hath always a scratched face. The devil was first a liar, and then a murderer. Those that kill a dog (saith the French proverb) make the world believe he was mad first. The credit of the Church must first be taken away, and then she is wounded, Cant. v. 6. Before the French massacre, it was given out that the Huguenots in their night-meetings committed most abominable uncleannesses.

Ver. 30. *To Tarsus*] His own country, that he might there break the bread of life where he first drew the breath of life, as Bishop Jewel desired to do. Physician, heal thyself, that is, thine own native country, said they to our Saviour, Luke iv. 23.

Ver. 31. *Then had the churches rest*] As when Paul was converted, the Churches rested; so, much more, when sin and Satan shall be destroyed, shall the state of the saints be most restful and blissful in heaven.

Ver. 32. *As Peter passed through all quarters*] Being notably active for Christ, according as it was charged upon him, Luke xxii. 32, "When thou art converted, strengthen thy brethren." The most that the saints can do for Christ is not the one half of that they could beteem him.

Ver. 33. *Had kept his bed eight years*] A long while surely; but what was this to an eternity of extremity in hell? Oh, take heed, and be forewarned to flee from that wrath to come. And meanwhile, every man that seeth another stricken with such chronical diseases as the palsy, and himself spared, is bound to keep a passover.

Ver. 34. *And Peter said*] After he had prayed for him, likely. It is the prayer of faith that healeth the sick. Thus Epaphroditus was given in as an answer to St Paul's prayer, and Miconius to Luther's, after he had been almost spent with a consumption.[1]

Ver. 35. *And Saron*] Alias Assaron, the same perhaps with Acheron or Ekron, counted by the very heathens the devil's house; for there Beelzebub, the prince of devils, was worshipped, 2 Kings i. 3.[2]

Ver. 36. *Full of good works and alms-deeds*] For there are other good works besides alms-deeds, though many Papists, and some as silly, have shrunk up charity to an hand-breadth, to giving of alms. Let our works be done in God, John iii. 21, and for God, 1 Cor. x. 31. Let there be good actions and good aims; and then they shall be the works of God, John vi. 28.

Ver. 37. *When they had washed*] This they did to show their hope of a joyful resurrection. The heathens also, though their lives and hopes ended together, yet they washed their dead in an apish imitation of this Church custom. *Faciunt et vespæ faves; simiæ imitantur homines.*

Ver. 38. *They sent unto him*] As loth to lose so useful a member, so dearly missed among them. Some when they die are no more missed than the sweepings of a house or the parings of the nails. But when good people die, there is a general loss and lamentation.

Ver. 39. *They brought him*] Love is officious, and thinks not too much of any labour.

And showing him the coats and garments] A worthy employment for a wealthy woman. The like is reported of Queen Anne Boleyn. And I knew a very gracious matron (one mistress Alice Smith of Stratford-upon-Avon) that found herself thus usually busied; being one of those few that both lived and died with honour.

Ver. 40. *Put them all forth*] That he might pray with more privacy and freedom. For he knew well that the prayer of faith could not heal the sick only, as Æneas, ver. 34, but raise the dead too, Heb. xi. 35.

Ver. 41. *Presented her alive*] To her own loss for a little while; but so God might be glorified and the Church gratified, she was well contented.

Ver. 42. *And many believed*] So when Lazarus was raised, John xi. 45. See the note there.

Ver. 43. *With one Simon a tanner*] Of mean rank and despicable, but religious and hospitable. Of such, and not of great ones, consisted this Church of Christ at Joppa. The poor are gospellized, εὐαγγελίζονται, Matt. xi. 5. The lesser fishes bite soonest. *Grandior solet esse Deus in parvulis, quam in magnis.* See the note on chap. x. 6.

CHAPTER X.

Ver. 1. *A centurion of the band*] He might well have been a commander in the thundering legion, *qui plus precando quam prœliando potuerunt,* κεραυνοβόλος. *Preces sunt bombardæ et instrumenta bellica Christianorum,* said Luther, who also spared not to tell the Elector of Saxony, his protector and patron, that he by his prayers would secure his Highness's soul, body, and estate engaged in the gospel's cause. *Sive id credat Celsitudo vestra, sive non credat. Imo Judico,* saith he, *C. V. plus a me præsidii et tutelæ habiturum esse quam mihi præstare, &c.* Yea, I am

---

[1] Melch. Adam in Vit. Luth.

[2] *Flectere si nequeo superos, Acheronta movebo.* Virg.

of the mind that your Highness hath more safety from me than I have from you.

Ver. 2. *A devout man, &c.*] εὐσεβής. Not of the king's religion, whatever it be, as those Melchites in Nicephorus. And as Tertullian tells us in his Apology, that the people were bound to worship those gods only that the Senate decreed should be worshipped. Cornelius was a right worshipper.

With all his house] A man is really that he is relatively. David would show his sincerity by being good at home, Psal. ci. 2.

Ver. 3. *About the ninth hour*] Which was the time of the evening sacrifice, when the joint prayers of the Church were ascending as incense.

Ver. 4. *Thy prayers and thine alms*] Dr Powel relateth this saying of Leotinus Prince of Wales, that when he was moved by some to make war upon our Henry III., *Ego, inquit, formido ejus eleemosynas magis certe multo quam ejus copias.* And the queen-mother of Scotland was heard to say, that she more feared the fastings and prayers of John Knox and his disciples than an army of twenty thousand men.

For a memorial before God] How did the angel know this? Angels have a threefold knowledge: 1. Natural; 2. Revealed, as Dan. ix., and here; 3. Experimental, Ephes. iii. 10.

Ver. 5. *Call for one Simon*] Though an angel certifies Cornelius's prayers were accepted, yet he reads not to him the doctrine of redemption, but refers him to Peter. The office of preaching the gospel is taken from the angels (who first preached it to the shepherds) and given to the ministers.

Ver. 6. *With one Simon a tanner*] God knoweth all his by name, and condition of life.

Ver. 7. *A devout soldier*] Cornelius had either found him, or made him so. Nero complained that he could never find a faithful servant; and no wonder, for those that were good, cared not to come about him: and those that were bad, he cared not to make better, as being himself desperately wicked. *Qualis herus, talis servus.* The master's faults go as little unattended as their persons.

Of them that waited on him] The Syriac hath it, of them whom he esteemed highly. Good servants are rare and precious.

Ver. 8. *And when he had declared*] He knew well the worth of a faithful messenger, Prov. xxv. 13. Howbeit the more to affect their hearts, and the better to effect his design, he sets God before them, and shows them the whole matter. God's commands carry a divine authority, and soon prevail with the religious. *Dicto citius dicta peragunt.* They say with him in the poet (Lucan),

Jussa sequi, tam velle mihi, quam posse, necesse est.

Ver. 9. *Upon the housetop to pray*] He got upon the leads, as well to avoid distraction as to excite devotion by a full view of heaven above.

Ver. 10. *He fell into a trance*] His soul was

sundered, as it were, for a season, from his body, whilst he talked with God. So our Saviour was transfigured as he was praying. John was in the spirit on the Lord's day, when he received his revelation; Paul was rapt up into the third heaven. Giles of Bruxelles (a Dutch martyr), in his prayers was so ardent, kneeling by himself in some secret place, whiles he was a prisoner, that he seemed to forget himself. Being called many times to meat, he neither heard nor saw those that stood by him, till he was lift up by the arms, and then gently he would speak unto them, as one awaked out of a sweet sleep.

Ver. 11. *And saw heaven opened*] sc. The visible heaven, the air; for, as for the third heaven, it openeth not without a miracle, as some think.

Ver. 12. *Were all manner of fourfooted*] Gr. πάντα. All, that is, some of all sorts; so, *omne animal*, every living creature, is said to be in Noah's ark; and in the like sense, Christ is said to die for all.

Ver. 13. *Kill and eat*] Peter was hereby taught not to kill and slay in battle, as many of his warlike pretended successors have done, but to kill that corruption that he found in the Gentiles, by the sword of the Spirit, &c. Julius II. can turn him either way, to Peter's keys or Paul's sword.[1]

Ver. 14. *Common or unclean*] By commonness there is contracted an uncleanness. It is hard to deal in the world, and not be defiled with the corruption that is in the world through lust.

Ver. 15. *That call not thou common*] Or profane thou not, σὺ μὴ κοίνου. See the note on ver. 14.

Ver. 16. *Received up again into heaven*] The Church's original is from heaven, Apoc. xxi., and thither she shall be taken up again. As in the mean space, our commoration is on earth, our conversation in heaven, Phil. iii. 19.

Ver. 17. *Stood before the gate*] They pressed not in till licensed; they knew that Jews would not easily converse with them being Gentiles. This was their modesty, not oft seen in soldiers.

Ver. 18. *And called and asked*] Whether death will use so much manners as these did, viz. to call and ask for us, or e'er he seizeth us, it is uncertain. *Senibus mors in januis, adolescentibus in insidiis*, saith Bernard. The young man hath death at his back, the old man before his eyes, saith Aquinas. And that is the more dangerous enemy that pursueth thee, than that which marcheth up toward thy face. Be sober, be vigilant: of domesday there are signs affirmative and negative, not so of death; and yet every man's death's day is his domesday.

Ver. 19. *While Peter thought on*] διενθυμουμένου, Gr. thought in his mind; *cogitabat quasi coagitabat.* He was busily plodding, and the Spirit came in to help him. Divine meditation is a studious act of the mind, searching the knowledge of a hidden truth, by the discourse of reason. Or, it is a stedfast and earnest bending of the mind upon some heavenly matter, for the settling of

---

[1] *Cum Petri nihil efficiant ad prælia claves auxilio Pauli forsitan ensis erit.*

our judgments and bettering of our heart and lives.

Ver. 20. *Doubting nothing*] Or, not arguing the case, μηδὲν διακρινόμενος, but readily yielding the obedience of faith.

Ver. 21. *Peter went down*] He sent not for them up, much less made he them to wait three days at the gate (as that pope did Henry the emperor) before they could have a hearing.

Ver. 22. *That feareth God*] Not with a base fear, as those mongrels, 1 Kings xvii. 32, that feared the Lord for his lions sent amongst them (like as some Indians at this day fear the devil because he beats them), but with an amicable, filial, reverential fear, which gat him a good report among all the nation of the Jews; such as St Paul thus bespeaketh, "Men of Israel, and ye that fear God," Acts xiii. 16.[1]

Ver. 23. *Certain brethren from Joppa*] Who were well paid for their courteous pains, when (for confirmation of their faith) they beheld the kingdom of Christ propagated and preached to the Gentiles also.

Ver. 24. *Cornelius waited for them*] So the people waited for Zacharias, Luke i. It is fit the people should wait for the minister, not the minister for the people, Zech. viii. 21.

Ver. 25. *Worshipped him*] Not as God, with divine worship; yet with too much humility, which Peter correcteth. The word must be glorified, the ministers not over-admired.

Ver. 26. *But Peter took him up*] *Longe aliter papa*, the pope (Diocletian-like) holds forth his toe to be kissed, and suffers his parasites to deify him.

Tu vere in terris diceris esse Deus.

I myself also am a man] We must glorify the word, not the preacher, Acts xiii. 48.

Ver. 27. *He found many that were come together*] With good and honest hearts, hungering and thirsting after righteousness, resolved to be ruled by God, and to pass into the likeness of the heavenly pattern. Lord, saith Nazianzen, I am an instrument for thee to touch. I am only thy clay and wax, said another.

Ver. 28. *Not call any man unclean*] *Scilicet, quoad communem vitæ usum; Nam alioqui omnes naturâ impuri; i. e.* in regard of civil conversation. By nature (it is true) we are all unclean.

Ver. 29. *Without gainsaying, as soon as sent for*] *Hoc est sanctum fidei silentium*, saith Calvin, this was the holy silence of faith; this was to preach Christ the Lord; and himself the Church's servant, for Jesus' sake. A servant is not αὐτόματος, one that moveth absolutely of himself; he is ὑπηρέτης and ὄργανον, saith Aristotle, the master's instrument, and wholly his, ὅλως ἐκείνου, 1 Cor. iv. 5. Peter's pretended successor styleth himself the "servant of God's servants;" but is nothing less.

For what intent] This he desireth to know of them, that he might not shoot at rovers, run at uncertainty; but be able to conclude his dis-

course, as he did, *Det Deus, ut sermo meus adeo commodus sit, quam sit accommodus*, God grant my speech may be as profitable as it is seasonable.

Ver. 30. *I was fasting until, &c.*] Fulness breeds forgetfulness; but fasting maketh a man capable of heavenly visions of divine glory. The three great fasters, Christ, Moses, and Elias, met gloriously in Mount Tabor.

Ver. 31. *Cornelius, thy prayer is heard*] This was a singular happiness, and a sure seal of his good estate to Godward, Psal. lxvi. 18, 19; John ix. 31. Every access to God with success, every gracious return of prayer, sealeth up this comfort to the soul, that sith He that hath the keys of David hath once opened unto us not only a door of utterance, but a door of entrance to the throne of grace, it shall never be shut again any more.

Ver. 32. *He is lodged, &c.*] God takes notice of every circumstance of his people's affairs; their very walls are ever before him, Isa. xlix. 16. He thinks the better of the houses they lodge in, and looks upon all that favour them with special content; "I will bless them that bless thee," Gen. xii. 3. See the note there.

Ver. 33. *Now therefore we are all, &c.*] All of a mind to serve the Lord with one shoulder, Zeph. iii. 9; as Hezekiah's servants joined together in that laudable work of copying out those proverbs of Solomon for the Church's use, Prov. xxv. 1.

Present before God] Whom we look full in the face, ἐνώπιον, seeing him by faith who is invisible, and setting ourselves to receive the law at his mouth, to hear the word, not of a mortal man, but of the ever-living God.

To hear all things] sc. With due reverence and diligence; not to jeer at anything that is commanded thee of God, that hath the stamp and impress of God upon it, that comes *cum privilegio*, and appears to be *cor et anima Dei* (as Gregory calleth the word), the counsel and mind of God. Lo, these were right hearers. Oh for such nowadays! Ours (alas) have *corpora in sacellis, animos in sacculis*, as Ezekiel's had, chap. xxxiii. 31, and as serpents have their bodies in the water, but their heads out.

Ver. 34. *No respecter of persons*] That is, of their outward state and condition, as country, sex, wealth, wisdom, &c. Outward things neither help nor hurt, please nor displease God, but as they are in a good or bad man; as a cipher by itself is nothing, but a figure being set before it, it increaseth the sum.

Ver. 35. *He that feareth him and worketh righteousness*] This is the whole duty of man, as Eccles. xii. 13. *His duobus membris comprehenditur totius vitæ integritas.* (Calvin.)

Ver. 36. *Preaching peace*] For God speaks peace to his people; he creates the fruit of the lips to be peace; he, by his promises powerfully applied, lodgeth a blessed calm in the conscience, and saith to the distempered affections, Peace, and Be still, hushing all; for he is Lord of all.

Ver. 37. *After the baptism*] See how orderly

[1] *Duo sint timores, servilis et amicalis.* Beda.

Peter preacheth (like as Luke writeth, καθεξῆς, *sigillatim*), giving his hearers a distinct and punctual narrative of the life and death of Jesus Christ, of his offices and efficacies. To speak clearly and coherently, to cast his matter into a good mould and method, as it is not every man's happiness, so it is no small commendation to him that can skill of it; and must be endeavoured by all that would win upon their people's affections, and draw them to duty, as the Athenian orators, who were there-hence called Δημάγωγοι, people-leaders.

Ver. 38. *Oppressed of the devil*] The devil complained in the days of Diocletian that he could not give right oracles, because of the Christians. (Euseb. ii.) And those that conspired against Athanasius, cried out, that by his prayers he hindered their proceedings. (Ruffin. i. 33.) The soldiers that went against the Angrognians, told their captain that the ministers of that place, with their prayers, so conjured and bewitched them, that they could not fight.

Ver. 39. *And we are witnesses*] Eye-witnesses (which are far better than ear-witnesses) and ancient witnesses, such as of whom Aristotle saith, πιστότατοι οἱ παλαιοὶ ἀδιάφθοροι γὰρ; the more ancient the more credible. *Plus valet oculatus testis unus quam auriti decem.* (Plaut.)

Ver. 40. *Him God raised*] Christ's death he despatcheth in a word, as a thing well known. His resurrection (because more questioned, and of greater moment to beget faith) he more largely discourseth.

Ver. 41. *Eat and drink with him*] *In nihilum abiit cibus post resurrectionem sumptus.*

Ver. 42. *Ordained of God*] Gr. ὡρισμένος, determined, and by definitive sentence concluded.

Ver. 43. *Shall receive remission of sins*] Together with all the purchase of his passion. But this is instanced as a principal piece thereof, and worthily. David had a crown of pure gold upon his head, Psal. xxi., but he blesseth God for a better crown, Psal. ciii. 3, 4, viz. pardon of sin.

Ver. 44. *While Peter spake, &c.*] As manna descended in the dew, so doth the Holy Ghost in and by the preaching of the word, Gal. iii. 2; Isa. xxx. 20, 21.

Ver. 45.] See the note on verse 23 of this chapter.

Ver. 46. *Speak with tongues*] This diversity of tongues, laid at first on mankind as a curse, Gen. xi., God turned into a blessing to his Church, which yet some of the Christian Corinthians abused to pomp and ostentation, 1 Cor. xiv.; which, as copperas, will turn milk into ink; or as leaven, which turns a very passover into pollution.

Ver. 47. *Can forbid water*] Plain water, without oil, salt, spittle, cream, or other popish additaments.

Ver. 48. *To be baptized*] The use of the sacraments is to seal up adoption in infants, and faith in those of riper years.

Ver. 48. *And he commanded them to be bap-*

tized] And so to be incorporated into Christ's body the Church: that they might be saved by the " washing of regeneration, and the renewing of the Holy Ghost," Tit. iii. 5. It is a noble question in divinity, seeing regeneration is attributed both to the word and to baptism, how the one worketh it differently from the other? Or, if both work it, why is not one superfluous?

CHAPTER XI.

Ver. 1. *Had also received the word*] NOT only informed, but reformed: yea, so transformed the Churches were into the same image of the word from glory to glory, that they became at length conformed to Christ in holiness and righteousness.

Ver. 2. *Contended with him*] They should rather have commended him: so hard it is to part with a rooted error: so ordinary it is for faithful ministers to meet with such as will dare to reprehend what they do not comprehend, and precipitate a censure.

Ver. 3. *Saying, Thou wentest in, &c.*] This was now no fault, but in their conceit only. Ignorance is the mother of many mistakes, and miscarriages thereupon. How exceedingly was Job mis-censured by his friends; Gideon and Jephthah by the Ephraimites, Judg. viii. 1, and xii. 1; the two tribes and half by their brethren, Josh. xxii. Athanasius passed for a sacrilegious person, a profane wretch, a bloody persecutor, a blasphemer of God, &c. Cyril and Theodoret excommunicated one another for heresy, *Postea comperti idem sentire*, upon a mere mistake. Basil complains that he was hardly dealt with by brethren that were of the same judgment with himself, but understood him not. Augustine had suffered so long in this kind, that at length he thus resolves, *Non curo illos censores qui vel non intelligendo reprehendunt, vel reprehendendo non intelligunt:* I care not for those blind censurers that speak evil of that they know not, and of those they understand not.[1] Charity would teach them to take everything the best way; and not, as logicians do, *sequi partem deteriorem*, to pick out the worst.

Ver. 4. *But Peter rehearsed*] With singular modesty he seeks to satisfy them (if reason will do it), and to quench their wild-fire by casting milk upon it. Zuinglius and Œcolampadius endeavoured to do the like by Luther and his disciples, but could never effect it. In the year 1533, he wrote a very bitter epistle to the Senate of Frankfort, *Qua Zuinglianos Archi-diabolos appellat, è suggestu repellendos, ditione ejiciendos*, wherein he calleth the Zuinglians arch-devils; and judgeth that they ought to be kept out of the pulpit, driven out of the country.[2] In the year 1567, at Antwerp the Lutherans joined themselves to the Papists against the Calvinists.[3] Still Satan is thus busy, and Christians are thus malicious, that, as if they wanted enemies, they

[1] Cont. Faust. xxii. 34.

[2] Scultet. Annal.   [3] Bucholcer, Chronol.

fly in one another's faces; yea, cut one another's throats: as the English and Scots do at this day, to the inconceivable grief of all the godly on both sides. *Deus meliora.*

Ver. 5, 6, &c.] See the notes on that part of the former chapter whereof this is but a repetition.

Ver. 16. *Then remembered I*] Very seasonably; the Holy Spirit suggesting, as a remembrancer; like as the evil spirit did to those cankered kill-Christs, Matt. xxvii. 63.

Ver. 17. *What was I that I could withstand God?*] Whose power is irresistible, whose will is a law, yea, *Voluntas Dei, necessitas rei:* and God hath put a secret instinct (as into the bee, the stork, and other creatures to do their kind, so) into all his children to submit to his will, to say Amen to God's Amen, and to put their *fiat* and *placet* to his, Acts xxi. 14.

Ver. 18. *They held their peace*] And by their silence showed they were satisfied: as did Jonah, by shutting up his prophecy in silence, and giving God the last. It is easier to deal with 20 men's reasons than with one man's will. Convince an humble man of his error or passion, and he will yield presently; whereas a proud opinionist stands as a stake in the midst of a stream; lets all the good reason you can allege pass by him, but he stands where he was. "Nay, but we will have a king," &c. "The word that thou speakest unto us in the name of the Lord, we will not hear."

Ver. 19. *Now they which were scattered abroad*] See the note on Acts viii. 1.

Ver. 20. *Spake unto the Grecians*] Not the Grecizing Jews (as chap. vi. 1), but the Grecians which were Gentiles, to whom the light now began to break forth, and the partition-wall to be broken down.

Ver. 21. *And a great number believed*] God sealing his approval of that they did, by an extraordinary success. He hath a mighty hand and can fetch in multitudes at his pleasure. We hope he is doing some such great work in New-England. He can make a law to bring forth in one day, a "nation to be born at once," Isa. lxvi. 8.

Ver. 22. *And they sent forth Barnabas*] A very fit man; for he was a "son of consolation," and would handle those young plants with all tenderness. Wring not men's consciences, saith Dr Sibbs, you may hap to break the wards of them if you do.

Ver. 23. *That with purpose of heart*] As it is recorded of Caleb, that he "fulfilled after God," Numb. xiv. 24. *Caleb implevit post me.* It stands men upon to see that their work, though it be but mean, yet it may be clean; though not fine, yet not foul, soiled and slubbered with the slur of a rotten heart. Let them consent to take whole Christ in all his offices and efficacies, and that *pro termino interminabili*, never to part more.

Ver. 24. *For he was a good man*] Few such now-a-days.

Rari quippe boni—
Jam nec Brutus erit, Bruti nec avunculus usquam.
(Juvenal.)

Anthony de Guevara tells a merry story of the host at Nola, who when he was commanded by the Roman censor to go and call the good men of the city to appear before him, went to the churchyard, and there called at the graves of the dead, Oh ye good men of Nola, come away, for the Roman censor calleth for your appearance: for he knew not where to call for a good man alive. The Scripture complains that there is none that doeth good, that is, none in comparison, none to the mad multitude, that, like Jeremiah's figs, are naught, stark naught. Phocion was surnamed Bonus; but the excellency of a godly man is (Barnabas-like) to be full of the Holy Ghost and of faith, to follow God fully as Caleb, Numb. xiv. 24; to have a heart full of goodness, as those Romans; a life full of good works, as Tabitha; shining full fair, as a right orient and illustrious star with a singularity of heavenly light, as good Noah did in his generation; and as holy Joseph, whose life, saith Bucholcer, was a constellation, yea, a very heaven bespangled with brightest stars of glorious graces.

Ver. 25. *Then departed Barnabas to Tarsus for to seek Saul*] Not fearing to be outshined by him, who was now grown an admirable preacher, and an insatiable worshipper of Christ,[1] but seeking the setting-up of Christ's kingdom by all means possible. To rejoice in and to improve the good parts of others for a public benefit (though it eclipseth thy light), and that from the heart, this is indeed to get above others; this is more than to excel others in any excellency, if this be wanting.

Ver. 26. *Called Christians*] Called so by divine direction, as the word χρηματίσαι signifieth. There were, saith a learned antiquary, certain heretics who (as the Samaritans joined Jewish ceremonies with heathenish rites, so they) joined Christ and Moses, law and gospel, baptism and circumcision. (Godwin's Antiq. Heb.) Of their beginning read Acts xv. 2. These were called Nazarites; either of malice by the Jews, to bring the greater disgrace upon Christian religion, or else because at first they were true though weak Nazarites, that is, Christians misled by Peter's Judaizing at Antioch, Gal. ii. 11. Hence it is thought that the Church at Antioch, in detestation of this new-bred heresy, fastened upon them by the name of Nazarites, forsook that name, and called themselves Christians. But what a shameful thing is it, that the most honourable name of Christian is at this day in Italy and at Rome a name of reproach, and usually abused to signify a fool or a dolt. (Fulke Not. on Rhem. Test.)

First in Antioch] Which had been the residence and bare the name of Antiochus, that bloody persecutor. Here then that prophecy

[1] *Insatiabilis Dei cultor.* Chrysost.

was most sweetly fulfilled, Isa. lx. 14, "The sons of the afflicters shall come bending to thee," &c. And so it was, somewhat above a hundred years since, at Spira in Germany, where those of the reformed religion were first called Protestants. (Parei. Medul.) Howbeit some have observed that this name is not so new, but of an ancient standing; for they fetch it from 2 Chron. xxiv. 19, "Yet he sent prophets to them to bring them again unto the Lord, and they testified against them; but they would not give ear:" which latter clause the Vulgar interpreter (and the Douay doctors in their English translation of the Old Testament follow him) rendereth thus: *Quos Protestantes illi audire nolebant.* Dr Poyns also (a Popish writer) tells us, that it was foretold in the Old Testament that the Protestants were a malignant Church, and he allegeth for proof this place in the Chronicles, though little to his purpose. A better divine tells us Englishmen, that we were never Protestants indeed till we took the late protestation, that brought us into the band of the covenant, and is to us as circumcision once to the Israelites, a Gilgal, the rolling away of our reproach; there being nothing, as some could hit us in the teeth (but untruly and uncharitably), that made us differ from Rome but a bare proclamation.

Ver. 27. *From Jerusalem unto Antioch*] The Church whereof was now grown so famous by the pious labours of Paul and Barnabas, that many holy and learned men resorted thither, as to a common school or academy.[1] So did divers, in our forefathers' days, to Zurich, Basil, Geneva, but especially to Wittenberg, where Luther and Melancthon laboured in the Lord's work, to the good of many:

Divisæ his operæ, sed mens fuit unica; pavit
Ore Lutherus oves, flore Melancthon apes.

Ver. 28. *And there stood up one*] So Bishop Hooper prophesied, long before, of his own death. For, taking Mr Bullinger by the hand, at his return from Zurich, There, said he, where I take most pains you shall hear of me to be burnt to ashes. And being made bishop, he took for his arms a lamb in a fiery bush, and the sunbeams descending down upon the lamb; rightly denoting, as it seemeth, the order of his suffering, which afterward followed. So father Latimer ever affirmed of himself, that the preaching of the gospel would cost him his life; to the which he no less cheerfully prepared himself, than certainly was persuaded that Winchester was kept in the Tower (in King Edward VI.'s days) for the same purpose; and it proved so. In November, 1572, appeared a new star in Cassiopeia, and continued sixteen months. Theodore Beza wittily applied it to that star at Christ's birth, and to the infanticide then, and warned Charles IX., author of the French massacre, to beware, in this verse:

Tu vero Herodes sanguinolente time.

The fifth month after the vanishing of this star,

[1] κοινὸν παιδευτήριον πάντων

the said Charles, after long and grievous pains, died of exceeding bleeding. Spotswood, Archbishop of St Andrews, a deep and subtle dissembler, who had discouraged, and by degrees extirpated, most of the faithful ministers of Scotland, thought it seasonable (A. D. 1639) to repair into England, where he died a martyr, to the design of bringing in Popery and slavery. And so was the prediction of Mr Walsh, a famous Scotch minister, fulfilled upon him, who in a letter to the bishop, written 1604, told him he should die an outcast.

Great dearth throughout the world] Suetonius and Josephus make mention of this famine. It went hard when this voice was uttered in the market-place at Rome, *Pone pretium humanæ carni.* At Antioch in Syria, many of the Christians engaged in the holy war (as they called it) were glad, through famine, to eat the dead bodies of their late slain enemies. This was that Antioch here mentioned in the text.

In the days of Claudius Cæsar] Who was an arrant slowbelly, counted for a fool by his own mother Antonia, judged unworthy of the empire by his own sister Livilla, poisoned at length by his own wife Agrippina, and her son Nero, *qui dixit boletos* Θεῶν βρῶμα εἶναι, *quod Claudius boleto in numerum Deorum relatus esset.* The times were then so bad when he ruled the empire, *ut nihil amplius virtus esse putaretur quam* τὸ γενναίως ἐπιθανεῖν, saith the historian. (Dio.) What marvel, then, though God scourged the world with extreme famine; wherein the Church also was inwrapped, but graciously provided for, as ever she is in a common calamity.

Ver. 29. *Every man according*] For to stretch beyond the staple is to mar all. A good man showeth mercy, but yet ordereth his affairs with discretion, Psal. cxii. 5.

Ver. 30. *Which also they did*] *Nos non eloquimur magna, sed vivimus*, said the primitive Christians. This age aboundeth with mouth-mercy (Go, and be fed, warmed, &c., Jam. ii.), which is good cheap. But a little handful were better than a great many such mouthfuls.

By the hands of Barnabas and Saul] Paul prays hard that their service might be accepted of the saints, Rom. xv. 31, though one would think they should be very welcome, coming on such an errand.

CHAPTER XII.

Ver. 1. *Now about that time*] THAT the famine lay sore upon the Church. Afflictions seldom come single. The saints usually fall into divers temptations at once, Jam. i. 2. *Fluctus fluctum trudit.* Job's messengers tread one upon the heels of another.

Herod the king] Nephew to Herod the Great, brother to Herodias, and father to that Agrippa, Acts xxv. and xxvi.

Ver. 2. *And he killed James, the brother*] So ἀνθρώπων. *Sic de Athenis.* Thucyd.

styled to distinguish him from the other James, called James the Less, kinsman to Christ, and bishop of Jerusalem, as the ancients style him. (Chrysost. Hom. xxxiii. in Act.) It was wonder that Herod killed no more, seeing this took so well with the people, whose favour he coveted. When Stephen the protomartyr of the Church was stoned, Dorotheus testifieth that two thousand other believers were put to death the same day; but God hath set bounds to that sea of malice that is in persecutors' hearts, which they cannot go beyond: Psal. lxxvi. 10, "The remainder of wrath shalt thou restrain."

Ver. 3. *And because he saw, &c.*] *Sejanus ferox scelerum, quia prima provenerunt*, saith Tacitus. It is an old trick of tyrants to curry favour with the wicked, by shedding the blood of the godly.

Ver. 4. *To bring him forth to the people*] But God had otherwise determined. *Sciat Cels. Vestra*, saith Luther in a letter to the Elector of Saxony, *et nihil dubitet longe aliter in cœlo quam Norimbergæ de hoc negotio conclusum esse*, i. e. God in heaven hath decreed otherwise of this business than the emperor hath at Nuremberg; and the will of the Lord must be done, when all is done. "Yet have I set my King," &c., Psal. ii. 6.

Ver. 5. *Earnest prayer was made*] *Oratio sine malis, est ut avis sine alis.* These good souls strained and stretched out themselves in prayer, ἐκτενὴς, as men do that are running in a race. *Puriores cœlo afflictione facti*, as Chrysostom saith of them.

Ver. 6. *Peter was sleeping*] As having cast himself into God's everlasting arms. So did David, Psal. iii. So did Mr Rogers, our protomartyr in Queen Mary's days, when he was warned suddenly to prepare for the fire, he then being found asleep, scarce with much shogging could be awaked; at length, being raised and bid to make haste, then (said he) if it be so, I need not to tie my points.

Ver. 7. *And a light shined in the prison*] Gr. ἐν τῷ οἰκήματι, in the habitacle or conclave. So Solon first called the prison at Athens. So Petronius told Cæsar he had rather be with Cato ἐν οἰκήματι, in the prison-house, than with him in the senate-house.

And he smote Peter on the side, &c.] Cuthbert Simson, a martyr in Queen Mary's days, about midnight, being in prison (whether in a slumber or awake, I cannot tell, saith Mr Fox), heard one coming in, first opening the outward door, then the second, afterward the third, and so looking in to the said Cuthbert, having no candle or torch that he could see, but giving a brightness or light most comfortable to his heart, saying Ha unto him, and departed again. Who it was he could not tell, nor I dare define. This that he saw he declared oft to many; at the sight whereof he received such joyful comfort, that he also expressed no little solace in telling and declaring the same.

His chains fell off from his hands] Prisoners were bound with one or two chains to one or two soldiers, who (as keepers) were also bound with the same chains.

Ver. 8. *And follow me*] See here how by degrees (and not all at once) God oftentimes sendeth forth his prisoners (his afflicted ones) out of the pit wherein is no water, Zech. ix. 11. He is a "God of judgment," and waits a fit time to deal forth his favours, Isa. xxx. 18; he crumbles his mercies, as the cloud dissolves drop-meal upon the earth; we have his blessings by retail, to maintain commerce and communion between him and us. Have patience therefore, and wait for full deliverance. We know not what we lose by making haste, and not holding up our hands, as Moses did, to the going down of the sun. If God have begun to enlarge us, he will in due time do it to the full. If we should not be in straits sometimes, God should have "no tribute from us;" as those malignants suggested against those returned captives, Ezra iv. 13.

Ver. 9. *And wist not that it was true*] So Psal. cxxvi. 1. God is oft better to his than their hopes, and doth exceeding abundantly for them above all that they can ask or think, Eph. iii. 20. He will do so much more when they come to heaven; for then, oh, the unutterable ecstasies! At first sight, surely

Claudicat ingenium, delirat linguaque, mensque.
                                              Lucret.

Ver. 10. *When they were passed*] God could have delivered him all at once; but he knew that *cito data cito vilescunt*, Lightly come by is lightly set by. He would have us also to weigh well the several passages and circumstances of our deliverance, that he may have the honour of all. Hence those catalogues in Scripture, with an enumeration of particulars. See the note on verse 8.

Ver. 11. *Now I know of a surety*] Faith cannot be idle, or ungrateful for benefits received. If Peter have none else to tell it to, he will tell himself what God had done for him by his angel; and what great cause he had to be really and substantially thankful. So doth David, Psal. ciii. 1—4, &c. A good man can never be alone; for, in defect of other company, he can fruitfully converse with himself, and commune with his own conscience, and thereupon lift up many an humble, joyful, and thankful heart to God.

Ver. 12. *Where many were gathered together praying*] Great is the force of joint prayer, when Christians set upon God *quasi manu facta*, as in Tertullian's time, they sacked and ransacked heaven by their prayers. *Preces fundimus, cœlum tundimus, misericordiam extorquemus*, saith he. We beseech not God only, but we besiege him too; we beg not barely, but bounce at heaven-gates.

Ver. 13. *To hearken*] Before she opened, lest some pursuivant or such like evil angel at that time of the night should have haunted them. Opposition is *Evangelii genius*, saith Calvin. Piety is no target against persecution.

Ver. 14. *She opened not the door for gladness*]

For "fear and great joy," as those other good women, Matt. xxviii. 8, who had their passions; which stoics allow not in their wiseman, nor popish padres in their wretched novices.

Ver. 15. *It is his angel*] Or, it is his messenger, or one come from him. See a like place, Luke vii. 24. Angels use not to stand at door and knock, and wait for an opening. Fernelius (holding that each saint hath his angel-guardian) tells us out of the rabbins, that Adam's angel was called Raziel, Abraham's Zachiel, Isaac's Raphael, Jacob's Peniel, and Moses' Metraton. But this may as well pass for a Jewish fable.

Ver. 16. *But Peter continued knocking*] He flung not away in displeasure, because not at first knock admitted. We must also continue instant in prayer. The hand of faith never knocked in vain at the gate of grace; but then, it "maketh not haste," it can willingly wait in hope of a good use and issue of all; yea, it can be content to want that particular blessing it would have; as knowing that God's people shall reap if they faint not; they shall certainly have their prayers out, either in money or money's worth.

Ver. 17. *And he departed and went*] *Cedendum quidem interdum furori, sed ita ut nihilo negligentius fiat opus Domini,* saith Beza here; who also proves that he went not now to Rome, as the Papists would have it; though Bellarmine holds it not *de fide,* that he was ever there.

Ver. 18. *There was no small stir*] Huddle or hubbub, τάραχος, with fear and care how they should answer it; but this was but part of their punishment, and the least part too; there was a worse matter followed, ver. 19. Lo, so it fareth with all graceless persons. They are not without their crosses here, but the worst is behind. What they feel here is but a typical hell, a foretaste of eternal torment. All their present sufferings are but as drops of wrath forerunning the great storm, a crack foregoing the ruin of the whole house. The leaves only of the tree fall upon them here; the tree itself will shortly fall upon them, and crush them to pieces.

Ver. 19. *That they should be put to death*] This was just in God, but unjust in Herod. He is safest that hath least to do with tyrants.

Ver. 20. *Because their country, &c.*] Should not God's manifold mercies move us to make peace with him? Will he not else curse our blessings, and destroy us "after that he hath done us good?" Josh. xxiv. 20.

Ver. 21. *And upon a set day*] When there were solemn shows and plays acted in honour of Cæsar. God picks out his time to be avenged on his enemies, then when it may be most for his glory and their utter confusion.

Herod arrayed in royal apparel] In cloth of silver, saith Josephus, which being beaten upon by the sun-beams, dazzled the people's eyes, and drew from them that blasphemous acclamation, *Hunc homines decorant, quem vestimenta decorant,* εἵματα ἀνήρ. The most (as it is said

of the Bohemian cur) fawn upon a good suit. It was a fault of old, James ii. 3.

Ver. 22. *It is the voice of a god*] ἥδιστον ἄκουσμα ἔπαινος, saith Xenophon. Men naturally hear nothing with more delight than their own commendation; fair words make fools vain, put them into their paradise. How much better Charles V., who coming to Paris, and entertained with a speech by one of the king's counsellors, that tended much to his commendation; answered, *Ideo sibi gratam esse orationem quod eum commonefecisset quod talis esse deberet, i. e.* That the orator rather taught him what he ought to be than told him what he had been.

Ver. 23. *Because he gave not glory*] Joseph is trusted with all Potiphar's goods, not with his wife: Glory is God's beloved Spouse; in the enjoying whereof he is a jealous God, admitting no co-rival, in heaven or earth, Isa. xlii. 8; to look upon it, and lust after it, is to commit spiritual adultery with it in our hearts.

And he was eaten of worms] σκωληκόβρωτος. Or with lice, as his grandfather Herod had been before him; as the tyrant Maximinus (who had set forth his proclamation engraven in brass, for the utter abolishing of Christ and his religion) was after him.[1] So was Philip II., king of Spain, who swore he had rather have no subjects than Lutheran subjects. And when he had very narrowly escaped drowning in a shipwreck, he said he was delivered by the singular providence of God to root out Lutheranism; which he presently began to do, &c. But God was even with him soon after. See Scriban. de Institut. Princip. xx. An evil end also befell Diagoras the atheist; who when he had made a famous oration against a deity, the people came applauding him, and said he had almost persuaded them, but only they thought that if any were God, he was for his eloquence' sake; whereupon this wretch, like Herod, was content to be thought a god; which soon wrought his ruin. Good therefore is the counsel of the apostle, "Let us not be desirous of vain-glory," of popular applause; which what is it else but a blast of stinking breath, a meteor that liveth in the air, a *Magnum nihil,* a glorious fancy, Gal. v. 26; and if derogatory to God's honour, as here, it proves pernicious and destructive.

And gave up the ghost] His death was *precationis opus potius quam morbi,* as it was said of Arius the heretic, who was brought to confusion by the prayers of Alexander the good bishop of Constantinople. (Socrat. lib. i. cap. 15.) Josephus saith, Herod at his death much complained of the people's vanity in deifying him. But no man is flattered by another that hath not first flattered himself.

Ver. 24. *But the word of God*] The Church is invincible; and truth may be oppressed a while, but not utterly suppressed. The Israelites never increased so as when Pharaoh kept them under. Fish thrive best in salt waters. The ground that is most harrowed is most fruitful. Camomile,

---

[1] *Sic et Sylla pediculari morbo periit.* Plutarch.

the more you tread it the more you spread it, and the palm-tree's posy is, *Nec premor nec perimor*. All the power of the empire could not prevail against Luther.

CHAPTER XIII.

Ver. 1. *Now there were, &c.*] BISHOP RIDLEY expounded the Acts and Paul's Epistles every morning in his family, giving to every man a New Testament, hiring them besides with money to learn by heart certain principal chapters, but especially this thirteenth chapter of the Acts.

Herod's foster-brother] *Puer collactaneus*, σύντροφος, one that had sucked of the same milk with Herod Antipas, who beheaded the Baptist. The love of foster-brothers in Ireland (saith Camden) far surpasseth all the loves of all men. But Manaen hated all for Christ.

Ver. 2. *As they ministered*] λειτουργούντων. The Greek Scholiast hath it, κηρυττόντων, "as they preached," which is the chief office of a minister, and his highest honour. Others interpret it, "as they prayed," so the Syriac and Arabic. The Papists only, "as they sacrificed," to countenance their abominable idol of the mass.

Ver. 3. *Laid their hands on them*] So separating and consecrating them to the work, as they did of old the beast for sacrifice, by laying their hands thereon.

Ver. 4. *Sailed to Cyprus*] This island was anciently for its wealth called Macaria, that is, The Blessed. The people therein generally lived so at ease and pleasure, that thereof the island was dedicated to Venus, who was at Paphos especially worshipped, and much filthiness committed; yet thither are these apostles directed by the Holy Ghost, and a great man (with many others) converted to the faith. The Romans were invited by the wealth of the place to over-run it, *Ita ut jus ejus insulæ avarius magis quam justius simus assequuti*, saith Sextus Rufus. But Christ (of his free grace) without any such motive, seized upon it by his gospel, and gathered a Church in it.

Ver. 5. *At Salamis*] A city of Cyprus, at the east side of it, over against Syria.

Ver. 6. *Whose name was Barjesus*] The son of Jesus; so he had called himself, as if of nearest alliance to our Saviour. The Syriac hath it Barshuma, the son of name or renown.

Ver. 7. *Which was with the deputy*] The greater opposites to the truth have been ever the greatest courtiers. The Arians in their age. And of them the Jesuits learned it, and of them the Arminians, as Utenbogardus in the Low Countries, and Canterbury here.

Ver. 8. *But Elymas*] Elymais is a part of Persia, the proper country of the magicians given to devilish arts. The devil daily commits the sin against the Holy Ghost, by opposing the known truth.

Ver. 9. *Who also is called Paul*] Here Saul is first called Paul, for memory (it is probable) of the first spoils he brought into the Church, not the head, but the heart of this Sergius

Paulus. The popes likewise change their names at their enthronization, to show, saith the Gloss *ad permutationem nominis, factam mutationem hominis*. But if they change at all, it is for the worse, as *Pius Secundus, Sextus Quintus*, &c. Pope Marcellus would needs retain his old name, to show his constancy, and that in his private estate he had thoughts worthy of the popedom.

Set his eyes on him] As if he would have looked through him. After which lightning followed that terrible thunder-crack, ver. 10. Bajazet, of his fiery looks, was surnamed Gilderun, or lightning. In Tamerlane's eyes sat such a rare majesty, as a man could hardly endure to behold them without closing of his own; and many with talking with him, and often beholding of them, became dumb. The like is reported of Augustus. And of St Basil it is reported that when Valens the Arian emperor came unto him, while he was in his holy exercises, it struck such a terror into the emperor, that he reeled and had fallen had he not been upheld by those that were near him.[1] Godly men have a daunting presence.

Ver. 10. *O full of all subtilty and all mischief*] Gr. ῥαδιουργία, maleficiency, thou that by long dealing hast gotten a dexterity in evil doing. This was plain dealing, such as Master Philpot, martyr, used to Morgan, and other popelings that set upon him; such as Maris, the blind bishop of Bithynia, used to Julian the Apostate. For when Julian had said to him, Behold thou art blind; thinkest thou that the Galilean thy God careth for thee? Maris replied, *O tu impie Apostata! gratias ago Deo meo, qui me cæcum reddidit, ne vultum tuum videam ita ad impietatem prolapsum*. O thou wicked apostate! I bless my Lord Christ who hath made me blind, that I might not see thy cursed countenance. When Servetus condemned Zuinglius for his harsh handling of him, he answers, *In aliis mansuetus ero, in blasphemiis in Christum non ita*, In other things I will use mildness, but not in dealing with those that blaspheme Christ.[2] *Mihi sane Auxentius erit diabolus quamdiu Arianus*, said Hilary, I shall think Auxentius to be no better than a devil so long as he continues an Arian.

Enemy of all righteousness] The adulterer is an enemy to chastity, the drunkard to sobriety, &c., but he that hindereth others from heaven is an enemy to all righteousness.

To pervert the right ways] To dig them up, to ditch them over (διαστρέφων), so as they are not passable. The conversion of great men is of great consequence. Hence Paul was so loth to lose the proconsul.

Ver. 11. *Not seeing the sun*] A philosopher being asked whether it were not a pleasant thing to see the sun? answered, that is τυφλοῦ τὸ ἐρώτημα, a blind man's question. Life without light is a lifeless life.

Ver. 12. *Being astonished, &c.*] The word worketh not kindly till it be received with admiration.

Ver. 13. *John departing from*] Being weary of the work, he showed them a slippery trick.

[1] Greg. Orat. de Laudib. Basilii.   [2] Epist. in Servet.

Many will do something for God that will suffer little or nothing for him. The king of Navarre told Beza he would launch no further into the sea than he would be sure to return safe to the haven.[1] Though he showed some countenance to religion, yet he would be sure to save himself.

Ver. 14. *They sat down*] Bullinger's note here is very good. *Non importune nec impudenter se ingerunt Paulus et Barnabas, nec more Anabaptistarum clamitant, Audite verbum Domini, pœnitentiam agite ; sed silentes expectant dicendi occasionem.* Paul and Barnabas do not importunately and impudently thrust themselves into the pulpit, nor do they cry out (after the manner of the Anabaptists), Hear the word of the Lord, repent of your sins, &c., but they wait in silence for a fit opportunity, and till they are called to speak.

Ver. 15. *And after the reading*] In the synagogues the Scripture was first read, and then opened and applied ; so it ought to be in the Christian churches.

If ye have any word of exhortation] See the note on Acts ix. 15.

Ver. 16. *And ye that fear God*] This is the proper character of an Israelite indeed.

Ver. 17. *Chose our fathers*] Separating them by a wonderful separation, as the Hebrew word signifieth, Exod. xxxiii. 16.

Ver. 18. *Suffered he their manners*] ἐτροποφόρησεν, As a mother bears with her child's frowardness ; or as a husband bears with his wife's crossness, which yet he liketh not. *Uxoris vitium, aut tollendum aut tolerandum*, saith Varro in Agellius.

Ver. 19. *And when he had destroyed seven nations*] Who had "filled the land from one end to another with their uncleanness," Ezra ix. 11 ; so that God was forced to sweep it with the besom of destruction ; like as, before that, the face of the old world was grown so foul that God was fain to wash it with a flood.

Ver. 20. *About the space, &c.*] It was not all out so long ; therefore he saith, "about the space," ὡσεὶ ; thereby teaching us in doubtful things to deliver ourselves doubtfully, and not to be overconfident. See John iv. 6.

Ver. 21. *By the space of forty years*] Taking into the account the days of Samuel's government.

Ver. 22. *Fulfil all my will*] Gr. Θελήματα, "all my wills," to note the universality and sincerity of his obedience. We should therefore strive to do all the wills of God, because we have done heretofore all the wills of the flesh, Ephes. ii. 2.

Ver. 23. *A Saviour, Jesus*] The Greek word here rendered Saviour is so emphatical, that other tongues can hardly find a fit word to express it, as Cicero noteth. *Sotera inscriptum vidi Syracusis. Hoc quantum est ? Ita magnum ut Latino uno verbo exprimi non possit.*

Ver. 24. *The baptism of repentance*] See the note on Luke iii. 3.

Ver. 25. *John fulfilled his course*] From this word (δρόμον) rendered "course," the dromedary

hath his name, who is marvellous swift, and will run a hundred miles a day. But the Germans call a dull and slow man a dromedary, *per antiphrasin.* (Minshew.)

Ver. 26. *The word of this salvation*] Salvation is potentially in the word, as the harvest is in the seed.

Ver. 27. *Read every sabbath*] Many live in places of great knowledge, and yet remain grossly ignorant, understand no more what they read or hear than a cowherd doth the most abstruse precepts of astronomy.

Ver. 28.] See the note on Matt. xxvii. 22.

Ver. 29. *And when they had fulfilled*] Though no thank to them, no excuse to their wickedness. *Divinum consilium dum devitatur, impletur.* But whereas all is fulfilled that was foretold, that plainly proves that Jesus was the Christ, and that our redemption by Christ was a plot of God's own laying.

Ver. 30.] See the note on Matt. xxviii. 6.

Ver. 31. *Who are his witnesses to the people*] Of our Saviour's resurrection there were many witnesses, both living (as the angels, the women, the soldiers, the apostles, those 500 brethren at once, 1 Cor. xv. 6) and dead (such as were the earthquake, the empty grave, the stone rolled away, the clothes wrapt up together, &c.), and all little enough. But " why should it be thought a thing incredible that God should raise the dead ? " Acts xxvi. 8. See the note there.

Ver. 32. *And we declare unto you glad tidings*] Even the sum of all the good news in the world, and that which should swallow up all discontents. The old Church had ἐπαγγελίαν, the promise only ; but we now have εὐαγγελίαν, the joyful tidings, good news from heaven.

Ver. 33. *In the second Psalm*] Erasmus testifieth, that some ancient copies here have it, " in the first Psalm ; " either because the first and second were of old but one Psalm, or because the first is not properly a Psalm, but a preface to the Psalms ; like as the 119th Psalm is set (saith one) as a poem of commendation before the book of God, mentioning it in every verse, testimonies, laws, statutes, word, &c.

This day have I begotten thee] That is, I have this day of thy manifestation in the flesh made known that thou art my Son, as well by my testimony of thee as by thine assumption of human nature.

Ver. 34. *To return to corruption*] That is, to the grave, that house of corruption ; which yet the Hebrews call Beth chajim, the house of the living, because of the promise " thy dead men shall live," &c. The Germans call the place of burial God's Acre, because the dead body, though sown there in corruption, yet riseth again in incorruption.

Ver. 35.] See the note on Acts ii. 31.

Ver. 36. *After he had served*] *Martinus decumbens, Domine, dixit, si adhuc populo tuo sum necessarius, non recuso laborem.* Lord, serve thyself upon me, and then let me depart in peace. (Sever. Epist. iii.)

---

[1] *Pelago non ita commissurus esset, quin quando liberet, pedem referre posset.*

Ver. 37. *Saw no corruption*] No consumption of the flesh, much less of the bones too, καταφθορὰν; only he saw φθορὰν, a separation of soul and body for a season, διαφθορὰν; though neither soul nor body was at all by death sundered from the Deity. But as a man that draws a knife, and holds still the knife in one hand and the sheath in the other, the knife and sheath are separated the one from the other, but neither of them is sundered from him that holdeth them, so here.

Ver. 38. *Be it known unto you therefore*] q. d. It is a shame for any not to take knowledge of this which is so fundamental. Of other things a man may be ignorant without danger of damnation; but not of this. This is a principal piece of *Quicunque vult*.

Ver. 39. *And by him all that believe are justified*] This saying of St Paul is the more to be heeded, saith an interpreter, because it is the very basis, foundation, and state of Christian religion, whereby it is distinguished from all other religions whatsoever. Jews, Turks, Pagans, and Papists explode an imputed righteousness; as if we could not be justified by the righteousness of Christ apprehended by faith. The Papists (as Saul) forbid us to eat of this honey, this precious comfort in Christ (viz. justification by faith alone), as if hereby we should be hindered in our pursuit against sin; whereas indeed it is the only strength and help against it. Hold fast therefore the faithful word; and transmit this doctrine safe and sound to posterity. It was Luther's great fear, that when he was dead it would be lost again out of the world.

Ver. 40. *Beware therefore lest*] Ministers must mix law and gospel together in their discourses. Sour and sweet make the best sauce.

Ver. 41. *Behold, ye despisers*] These the Scripture makes to be the worst sort of men; those that jeer when they should fear, and despise what they should give greatest regard unto; hell even gapes for such, though they will not be persuaded so, till it be all too late; as Pliny saith of moles, that they begin not to see till pangs of death are upon them. He that despiseth his way shall perish, saith Solomon.

Ver. 42. *The Gentiles besought*] Where a powerful ministry is settled, there some souls are to be converted. A master that sets up a light hath some work to be done thereby.

Be preached to them the next sabbath] Or in the interim betwixt the two sabbaths. A warrant for week-day lectures, *Intra proxime sequens sabbatum, interjectum tempus significatur*, saith Beza.

Ver. 43. *To continue in the grace*] The end is better than the beginning, saith Solomon. *Non quæruntur in Christianis initia sed finis*, saith Jerome.

Ver. 44. *And the next sabbath day*] The apostles had been busy with them on the foregoing week days, the better to prepare them to hear with profit on the sabbath, that queen of days, as the Hebrews call it.

Ver. 45. *Contradicting and blaspheming*] In-temperate tongues cause God many times to take away the word.

Ver. 46. *But seeing ye put it from you*] Gr. ἀπωθεῖσθε. Ye shove and thrust it from you, as it were with sides and shoulders; noting their desperate incredulity and obstinacy. And this was the very period of that day of grace spoken of by our Saviour, Luke xix. 42, "Oh, if thou hadst known, at the least in thy day," &c. Now that the offer was made so fully and clearly, how could they escape that neglected so great salvation?

Ver. 47. *I have set thee*] This, spoken at first to Christ, is here applied to his messengers and ministers, who are labourers together with Christ, 1 Cor. iii. 9, and are in Scripture called both lights and saviours, Matt. v. 14; Obad. 21; 1 Tim. iv. 16.

Ver. 48. *Glorified in the word*] That is, received it into their hearts (as some copies read this text, ἐδέξαντο), suffering it to indwell richly in them (as becometh such a guest), Col. iii. 16; yea, to rule and bear sway, yielding thereunto the obedience of faith, which is the greatest honour that can be done to the word; as the contrary is, to despise prophesying, 1 Thess. v. 19, to cast God's word behind our backs, Psal. l. 17, to trample on it; which the very Jews and Turks are so far from, that they carefully take up any paper that lieth on the ground, lest it should be any part of the Scripture, or have the name of God written in it. (Paræus, Proleg. in Gen.)

As many as were ordained, &c.] Election therefore is the fountain, whence faith floweth; men are not elected of faith foreseen, and because they believe, as the Arminians would have it.

Ver. 49. *And the word of the Lord*] It ran and was glorified, as the apostle hath it. So fitly is it compared to leaven, for its spreading property, Matt. xiii. 33. See the note there.

Ver. 50. *The devout and honourable women*] *Satan per costam tanquam per scalam ad cor ascendit.* (Gregory.) The devil breaketh many a man's head with his own rib. When the hen is suffered to crow, much evil ensueth. Satan makes use of women still to hinder men from heaven.

But the Jews] Stirred up by Satan, who cannot brook the dilatation of Christ's curtains.

Ver. 51.] See the note on Matt. x. 14.

Ver. 52. *With joy, and with the Holy Ghost*] There must needs be music in the Spirit's temple, and at that continual feast: the sweet-meats whereof is the assurance of heaven, as Father Latimer phraseth it. 2 Thess. iii. 1; Prov. xv. 15.

CHAPTER XIV.

Ver. 1. *And it came to pass in Iconium*] See the note on Acts viii. 1.

Ver. 2. *Made their minds evil affected*]

Envenomed (ἐκάκωσαν) their minds with rage against the brethren, but God made peace, as the ancient copies add here, Beza *ex* Beda. His peace that passeth all understanding guarded their hearts and minds in Christ Jesus.

Ver. 3. *Which gave testimony to the word*] It is usual with St Luke to oppose the good success of the gospel to the malicious actings of the mad world against it; that God's people might not be discouraged.

Ver. 4. *But the multitude was divided*] ἐσχίσθη, *Scinditur incertum studia in contraria vulgus.* Christ came not to send peace, but a sword. Yet is not he the cause of division, but the occasion only, and that by accident. (So sin is the occasion, not the cause, that grace aboundeth.) They that quarrel at God's ordinances for this may as well quarrel at the Lord's supper; which though a sacrament of love, a communion, yet hath occasioned much dissension: witness that *bellum Sacramentarium*, than the which never any kindled sooner is quenched slower.

Ver. 5. *And to stone them*] Stephen had the maidenhead of this kind of death: as that martyr, who was threatened with whipping, wished that he might have the maidenhead of that kind of suffering (for he had not heard of any that had been so served): and as Basil, threatened by Valens with death, cried out, εἴθε γένοιτο μοὶ, I would it might be so.

Ver. 6. *Fled unto Lystra*] They had their Lord's good leave to do so, Matt. x. 23. He had made them, not as butts, to be perpetually shot at; but as the marks of rovers, moveable, as the wind and sun may best serve.

Ver. 7. *And there they preached the gospel*] Which shows that their flying proceeded from prudence, and not from inconstancy, lightness, or cowardice.

Ver. 8. *And there sat a certain man*] This was (likely) one of those many miracles done at Lystra; a signal one, and therefore instanced.

Ver. 9. *Perceiving that he had faith*] Not by any skill he had in physiognomy, but by special revelation; without the which, strong confidence one may have of another man's true grace, but no certainty either of sense or of science.

Ver. 10. *And he leaped and walked*] Together with Paul's word there went forth a power: so there doth in all holy ordinances; Psal. cxlvi. 8, "The Lord giveth sight to the blind, he raiseth up the crooked, he loveth the righteous." This cripple might be very well one of those righteous, whom God out of his special love restored to the use of his limbs. A favour that he granteth sometimes to the wicked, whom yet he loveth not.

Ver. 11. *The gods are come down*] See the force of an evil custom, and of a vain conversation, received by tradition from the fathers, 1 Pet. i. 18: these Lycaonians had heard out of the fables of their poets that Jupiter and Mercury came down of old to visit Lycaon their progenitor, and that for the discourtesy he offered them, they transformed him into a wolf.

Hereupon they used to offer sacrifice to those dunghill-deities, and now they suppose they have them in human shape amongst them.

Ver. 12. *He was the chief speaker*] Gr. ἡγούμενος τοῦ λόγου, a master of speech. Paul was another Pericles, who thundered and lightened in his orations; [1] another Phocion, who was εἰπεῖν δεινότατος, saith Plutarch, a most powerful speaker; another Cyneas, who conquered more cities by his eloquence than his master Pyrrhus did by his puissance. In Rogers and Bradford, martyrs, it was hard to say whether there were more force of eloquence and utterance in preaching (saith Mr Fox) or more holiness of life and conversation. Paul was eminent in both.

Ver. 13. *And would have done sacrifice*] So the savages of Nova Albion, as they were very much taken with our singing of Psalms and other holy exercises (saith Sir Francis Drake) while we were among them; so when they could not prevail with us to stay longer there, they stole upon us a sacrifice, and set it on fire ere we were aware. We laboured by all means to withhold or withdraw them, but could not prevail; till at last we fell to prayers and singing of Psalms, whereby they were allured immediately to forget their folly, and leave their sacrifice unconsumed (for they supposed us to be gods indeed): suffering the fire to go out, and imitating us in all our actions, they fell a lifting up their hands and eyes to heaven, as they saw us to do.

Ver. 14. *They rent off their clothes*] In token of their holy indignation and utter detestation; they knew the Lord's jealousy would soon smoke against any that shall but cast a lustful look at his glory (which is as his wife, and which he will "by no means give unto another," Isa. xlii. 8). By this act of theirs therefore they show how they abhorred the motion or mention of any such matter.

Ver. 15. *Of like passions, &c.*] Passions are here put for whatsoever differenceth man from the Divine nature.

Ver. 16. *Suffered all nations, &c.*] That we walk not as other Gentiles, in our own ways, but know and serve the true God, is of his singular grace and favour. The ancient inhabitants of this land were as barbarous and brutish as any under heaven. Cicero (*De Nat. Deorum*) parallels the Britons and Scythians. Jerome ever sets them in opposition to some other nation that is most tamed and civilized. *Sed Britannorum inaccessa Romanis loca Christo tamen subdita,* saith Tertullian. Christ subdued those whom the Romans could never come at to conquer.

Ver. 17. *He left not himself*] Here they might object, that God in suffering men so to wander, showed not himself so kind and bountiful. The apostle answers, that God had sufficiently sealed up his general love and goodness, in doing good, giving rain from heaven, &c. Stars are the storehouses of God's good treasure, which he openeth to our profit, Deut. xxviii. 12. By their influence they make a scat-

---

[1] *Intonabat, fulgurabat, totam Græciam permiscebat.* Cic.

ter of riches upon the earth, which good men gather, bad men scramble for. Every of the heavenly bodies is a purse of gold, out of which God throws down riches and plenty upon the earth.

And fruitful seasons] If St Paul had thought well of the Sibyl's oracles (saith learned Beza) it was wonder he had not here mentioned them. Casaubon and Obsopæus reckon them for no better than officious lies.

Ver. 18. *Scarce restrained they the people*] See ver. 13. Man's nature is marvellous prone to idolatry, and the devil helps after; for he is εἰδωλοχαρὴς, saith Synesius : for he knows that creature-worship is devil-worship, Psal. cvi. 37 ; Rev. ix. 20.

Ver. 19. *And there came thither*] The devil, when he is driven to his last shift, stirs up his instruments to use violence, which yet prevaileth not.

And having stoned Paul] At Athens, if the comedians pleased not the people, they were overwhelmed with stones. This was hard measure; yet such as ministers many times meet with. But what a strange change was here on a sudden! was there no mean betwixt deifying and stoning? How soon turns the wind into a contrary corner. *Varium et mutabile vulgus. Neutrum modo ; mas modo vulgus.*

Ver. 20. *He rose up*] He starts up when stoned with a *sic, sic oportet intrare ;* so heaven is gotten by pains, by patience, by violence, persecution being our inseparable companion. *Sic petitur cœlum.*

Ver. 21. *They returned again to Lystra*] The love of Christ constrained them to imperil themselves for his glory; for the promoting whereof they loved not their lives unto the death, Rev. xii. 11. The loadstone, we know, draweth iron; yea, sendeth forth his attractive virtue to the absent needle, through the box of wood, wherein it is inclosed; and pierceth through the table to the iron under it. Let our love to Jesus Christ break through all.

Ver. 22. *We must through much tribulation*] *Plana via ad patriam cœlestem est crux,* saith Malcolm. If there be any way on horseback to heaven, surely this is the way, said another martyr (Bradford). If any think to go to heaven without tribulation, he must (as the emperor Constantine told the heretic Acesias) *Erigito scalam et solus ascendito,* erect a ladder, and go up alone. Some there are that take up a delicate profession; they would divide betwixt Christ and his cross, but they are fairly mistaken. Some think to go to heaven in a whirlwind, or as the passengers at sea, be brought to the haven sleeping. But what saith Zanchy, *Non decet ut sub capite spinis coronato vivant membra in deliciis. Neque frumenta in horreum reponuntur, nisi flabellis bene à paleis, aristis, et glumis repurgata. Neque lapides in templo Solomonis collocantur, nisi scalpellis et*

malleis bene cæsi. If the head were crowned with thorns, the members must not dream of a delicacy. The stones were not set into Solomon's temple till hewn, neither is the corn brought into the garner till winnowed.

Ver. 23. *Ordained them elders*] Giving their votes by lifting up their hands, after the fashion of the Greeks, χειροτονήσαντες ; whence that of Tully, *porrexerunt manus, psephisma natum est.* Or else laying on their hands, as the apostles used to do in ordaining of ministers. Stephanus saith, that this word when it governeth an accusative case (as here it doth) signifies not to "give suffrage," but to "create, ordain, elect."

Ver. 24. *And after they had passed through Pisidia*] At Antioch in this country they had planted a Church before. (See chap. xiii. 14, 15, &c.) Now being to return to the other Antioch in Syria (whence they had been sent out at first), they pass through Pamphylia, a country that lay toward the mountain Taurus.

Ver. 26. *Recommended to the grace of God*] This shows that they set not upon the work in their own strength, but wholly depended upon the free grace of God, *qua nolentem prævenit ut velit, volentem subsequitur, ne frustra velit,* saith holy Augustine, who was a great advancer of grace, and abaser of nature; as being wholly of St Paul's spirit, for which the Papists sharply censure him. (Stapleton, Sixt. Senens.)

Ver. 27. *Preached the word in Perga*] A city of Pamphylia, much addicted to the worship of Diana, who was therehence called Pergea. *Gratia nullo modo est gratia, quæ non est gratuita,* saith Augustine. Note this against the doctrine of merits foreseen, and free-will.

And how he had opened the door of faith] Indeed of heaven, by the preaching of the doctrine of faith : there being no other ordinary way of attaining salvation either for Jews or Gentiles, as St Paul proves in his Epistle to the Romans ; [1] as in that to the Colossians, he determineth, that the soul is spoiled by philosophy, if it be not after Christ, Col. ii. 8. Those school-divines, therefore, *qui salutem spondet absque Christi cognitione* (as Acosta hath it), who open a door to heaven without faith in Christ, were much mistaken. And so were those Collen divines too, that wrote a book of the salvation of Aristotle ; whom they make to be Christ's forerunner in naturals, like as John Baptist was in supernaturals.

Ver. 28. *There they abode*] As in a receptacle of rest, a place of free profession; such as Geneva hath been for many years to the persecuted Protestants, which makes the wicked Papists give out, that it is a professed sanctuary of all manner of roguery ; that the people there are blasphemers of God and all his saints, yea, that they are grown barbarous, and eat young children, &c. And this the common people are taught to believe as gospel.

---

[1] Cant. viii. 9. "If she be a door," *i. e.* if she have faithful ministers, which, as a door, open the way to Christ.

CHAPTER XV.

Ver. 1. And certain men, &c.] CERINTHUS, the heretic, with his complices, saith Epiphanius. These are said to "subvert the gospel," Gal. i. 7. A little thing untowardly mingled, mars all, saith Chrysostom.

Ver. 2. No small dissension] We must earnestly contend for the faith of the gospel, accounting every parcel of truth precious, Jude 3. How zealous was Paul in this case, Gal. ii. 5 ; i. 7; v. 12. He wisheth them not only circumcised, but served as the Turks do their eunuchs, whom they deprive of all their genitals, so that they are forced to supply the uses of nature with a silver quill.[1]

Ver. 3. By the Church] That is, by the community of God's people, who therefore (as it may seem) sided with Paul and Barnabas, against those disturbers.

They passed through Phenice and Samaria] They took a long journey for a public good. Calvin was wont to say, that he would gladly sail over ten seas [2] to settle a general peace and good agreement in the reformed Churches. Terentius (that noble general under Valens the emperor), when he was bidden ask what he would, and it should be done, asked nothing but that the Church might be freed from Arians. And when the emperor tore his petition, he said that he would never ask anything for himself, if he might not prevail for the Church: this that he might, he would undertake any pains, undergo any peril by sea or land. (Theodoret, iv. 32.)

Ver. 4. They were received of the Church] i. e. By the body of the people ; for the apostles and elders have a peculiar place assigned them.

Ver. 5. But there rose up] These are not Luke's words, but the apostles continuing their speech : they declared all things that God had done with them, and how they had been opposed by certain of the Pharisees' sect, &c.

Ver. 6. And the apostles and elders, &c.] This was the first Christian council. The four following general councils,[3] Gregory the Great held of equal authority almost with the four Gospels. *In posterioribus conciliis* (saith Luther) *nunquam de fide, sed semper de opinionibus et quæstionibus fuit disputatum : ut mihi conciliorum nomen pene tam suspectum et invisum sit quam nomen liberi arbitrii.* He fitly compareth the late Popish councils to the meeting of foxes, which, going about to sweep a room with their tails, raise dust, but rid none

Ver. 7. And when there had been much disputing] Each part striving for victory, till the apostles stood up and determined. It was no matter between Austin and Jerome, in their disputations, who gained the day ; they would both win, by understanding their errors. But Basil in his latter time grew to a great dislike of councils and

conferences,; because men usually met in their own strength there, and strove not so much for verity as victory, for truth as for triumph.

Ver. 9. Purifying their hearts by faith] Faith (as a neat house-wife) sweeps clean, and suffers never a slut's corner in the soul. It is ever purging upon corruption, and lets out the life-blood of it ; for it shows a man a better project than to lie sucking at the botches of carnal pleasures, or to be basely affixed to earthly profits. Every true believer beareth a brush at his back, as we say of a trim man. His faith consecrateth his heart, and maketh it, of the devil's thoroughfare, God's enclosure.

Ver. 10. Now, therefore, why tempt ye God] Or (as Jerome in a certain epistle to Augustine reads this text, and so it runs more smoothly), "Why attempt ye to put a yoke upon the neck of the disciples," &c. Ceremonies were abolished by Christ, and had no use after his death, but by accident ; as he who buildeth a vault, letteth the centrals stand till he put in the key-stone, and then pulleth them away : so here.

Ver. 11. That through the grace] We sail to heaven all upon one bottom ; we climb up all by one ladder. If any conceit another way, he must erect a ladder and go up alone : he shall (as Aristotle somewhere saith) κακὰ ἐφ' ἑαυτον ἕλκειν ὡς τὸ κακίας νέφος, plunge himself into remediless misery.

Ver. 12. Then all the multitude kept silence] See here the picture of a lawful council, guided by the word and Spirit of God. It was not a Cyclopical assembly, *ubi οὐδεὶς οὐδὲν οὐδενὸς ἀκούει*, nor as in Alcibiades' army, where all would be leaders, no learners, &c. Or, as the Jews at this day in their Jeshiboth, or academies, meet to dispute, but talk all together confusedly : the rabbins with their scholars, &c.

Ver. 13. James answered] Who seemed to be a pillar, Gal. ii. 9, and was so, both of the college of apostles and of the Church at Jerusalem.

Ver. 14. Simeon hath declared, &c.] q. d. He hath done it very well, only he hath not alleged any text of Scripture for confirmation ; which therefore I will add. In Popish councils the Holy Scripture is in a manner set aside ; and the decrees of fathers, schoolmen, and former councils brought in place thereof. At the Council of Basil, when the Hussites refused to admit of any doctrine that could not be proved by Scripture, Cardinal Cusan made answer, that the Scriptures pertained not to the being of the Church, but to the well-being only, and that they were to be expounded according to the current rite of the Church, *qua mutante sententiam, mutetur et Dei judicium.* (Jac. Rev. de Vit. Pont.)

Ver. 15. And to this agree, &c.] The Scriptures must over-rule ; as Cyril saith in a synod at Ephesus, upon a high throne in the temple there lay *sanctum Evangelium*, the holy gospel.

Ver. 16. Which is fallen down] Christ came when all seemed to be lost and laid on heaps.

[1] *Non circumcidantur modo, sed et abscindantur.* Chrys.
[2] *Ne decem quidem maria, &c.* Beza.
[3] *Nicen., Constantinopol., Ephesinum, et Chalcedonense.*

He still reserveth his holy hand for a dead-lift, and delighteth to help those that are forsaken of their hopes. This Branch grew out of the roots of Jesse; when that goodly family was sunk so low, as from David the king to Joseph the carpenter, Isa. xi. 1.

Ver. 17. *May seek the Lord*] All saints are seekers in this sense, Psal. xxiv. 6. They seek not his omnipresence, but his gracious presence, Psal. cv. 4.

Ver. 18. *Known unto God, &c.*] And consequently the calling of the Gentiles is foreknown and fore-appointed by him, as a thing to be done in due time, though they be never circumcised.

Ver. 19. *That we trouble not*] Gr. παρενοχλεῖν. Trouble them more than needs; they will meet with trouble enough otherwise in the way to heaven. "I would they were even cut off" that thus trouble their consciences, Gal. v. 12.

Ver. 20. *And from fornication*] Which is here reckoned among things indifferent, κατὰ δόξαν, οὐ κατὰ θέσιν, because the Gentiles esteemed it (falsely) a thing indifferent. *Non est flagitium (mihi crede) adolescentulum scortari, potare, fores effringere*, said he in Terence. So in the Turk's Alcoran, the angel being demanded concerning venery, is brought in answering, that God did not give men such appetites to have them frustrate, but enjoyed, as made for the gust of man, not for his torment, wherein his Creator delights not. But what saith the Scripture? "Whoremongers and adulterers God will judge."

Ver. 21. *For Moses of old time, &c.*] This is alleged as a reason why they should as yet abstain from those indifferents, because the Jews, having been accustomed to Moses's writings, could not quickly be drawn to let go the legal ceremonies, which were now to have an honourable burial, by degrees to be abolished. The ceremonies before Christ's passion were neither deadly nor dead; after his passion they were not deadly for a time (whiles the temple stood), though dead after a sort. But from that time forward they were both dead and deadly, saith Aquinas.

Ver. 22. *Chief men among the brethren*] For authority' sake; and that the false apostles might not say that those letters were counterfeit or surreptitiously gotten.

Ver. 23. *And wrote letters by them*] For the better confirmation of the weak and confutation of the wilful, to be as a standing monument.

Ver. 24. *Subverting your souls*] ἀνασκευάζοντες. Pulling down that which had been set up, ravelling out that which had been well knit before. The word signifies unvesselling them, unpacking them (as wares packed up in a vat to be sent beyond sea), scattering them, and bringing all into a confusion.

Ver. 25. *To send chosen men with our beloved*] *Delectos cum dilectis.* See ver. 22 and 27.

Ver. 26. *Men that hazarded their lives, &c.*] One ancient copy adds εἰς πάντα πειρασμὸν, to all sorts of trials and tribulations. Love, as it is a passion, so it is tried rather by passions than actions.

Ver. 27. *We have sent Judas and Silas*] Men skilful in comforting consciences and resolving cases, as ver. 32. Conscience is a diamond, and will be wrought on by nothing but dust of diamond, such as contrition hath ground it to. How like the motion of a puppet, the language of a parrot, is the best discourse, in this subject of conscience, of the not interested man! He is one of a thousand that can declare unto man his righteousness, Job xxxiii. 23. Those that would have oil for their lamps, comfort for their consciences, must repair to them that sell it, Matt. xxv. 9.

Ver. 28. *For it seemed good to the Holy Ghost*] That is only a lawful synod wherein the Holy Ghost is present and president. Nothing was resolved by the Trent fathers, but all in Rome; so that a blasphemous proverb was generally used, which I forbear to relate; let him that list read it in the Hist. of Council of Trent, fol. 497. See also fol. 822.

Then these necessary things] Not always and every way necessary (except that of fornication to be avoided), but necessary for preserving the peace of the Church as then it was, by bearing with the weaker Christians. Things inconvenient, even in matters of religion, may be done in some cases to redeem a far worse inconvenience. These burthens are here called necessary things, and they are said to do well, if they observed them, ver. 29. See the note on chap. xvi. 3.

Ver. 29. *And from fornication*] Some Greek copies add, " and whatsoever ye would not should be done to you, that ye do not the same to others;" which is a general rule, and a foundation of the former. As for fornication, it is here reckoned among things indifferent, because the Gentiles held it so; as the Papists now account it a very small sin; but so did not the council. See 1 Cor. x. 8, and Heb. xiii. 4, with the notes. A learned man telleth us, that that impostor Mahomet hath (in an apish imitation of this decree of the holy synod) forbidden his followers the self-same things, saving that he nameth swine's flesh in the place of fornication. See the note on ver. 20.

Ver. 30. *And when they had gathered the multitude*] This was fair dealing indeed. Among Papists, the people are held in gross ignorance; and taught to believe as the Church believes; which what it is, they must neither understand nor inquire after. One of their bishops boasted that if Luther had not started up when he did, and stood in their way, they could have persuaded the common people to eat grass as horses, or do anything else they had enjoined them. (Scultet. Annal.)

Ver. 31. *They rejoiced for the consolation*] How should we rejoice in Christ our Saviour, who bare our sins, &c., and freed us from the burden and brunt of both crime and curse!

Ver. 32.] See the note on ver. 27.

Ver. 33. *They were let go in peace*] *i. e.* Judas was, but not Silas, upon second thoughts, ver. 34. After their office put upon them by the synod was faithfully discharged, they did not give over the Lord's work and take their ease; but set themselves to do further service. The Roman generals, after they had once triumphed over their enemies, did no more service to the state. But Cato (of whom Lucan witnesseth that he did *toti natum se credere mundo*) is worthily commended, for that after the honour of a triumph he was no less sedulous and solicitous of a weal public than before: we must never think we have done enough for God.

Ver. 34. *To abide there still*] Upon second thoughts, after he had leave to depart, he stayed there a while longer. This Silas is thought to be the same with Sylvanus, as Joshua is the same with Jehoshua, Hag. ii. 2; Zech. iii.

Notwithstanding it pleased Silas] *sc.* Upon better deliberation and more probability of being there serviceable to God and useful to his Church. *Martinus decumbens, Domine, dixit, si adhuc populo tuo sum necessarius, non recuso laborem.* (Sever. Epist. 3.) Choice spirits are all for God; they still study his ends more than their own.

Ver. 35. *Teaching and preaching*] *i. e.* Being instant and earnest, *non frigidi docent, sed instant et urgent*, saith Calvin here; they lay their bones to the Lord's work, they set their sides and their shoulders to it, as those that would do the deed.

With many others also] In the primitive times, saith Mr Baxter (Pref. to Saint's Everlasting Rest), every church had many ministers, whereof the ablest speakers did preach most in public; and the rest did the more of the less public work. But now sacrilege and covetousness will scarce leave maintenance for one in a church, &c.

Ver. 36. *And see how they do*] Whether that wicked one (or troubler, ὁ πονηρός, Matt. xiii. 39) hath not cast his club amongst them, or corrupted their minds from the simplicity that is in Christ, 2 Cor. xi. 3. How soon were the Galatians unsettled by seducers and sect-makers, chap. i. 6. What ill work made those deceitful workers at Corinth, in St Paul's absence; and the heretics in the primitive Church, and the Anabaptists in Germany, &c. While Moses was but a while in the mount, the people had gotten them a golden calf. When Calvin was cast out of Geneva but for a short space, Sadoletus wrote a very smooth and subtle epistle to the inhabitants, to persuade them to return back to Popery. We ministers seldom find our work as we left it, we had need therefore visit often, and handle our sheep, &c., to see how they do, and whether (as Gaiuses) their souls as well as bodies be in health and prosper, 3 John 2.

Ver. 37. *To take with them John*] Who was Barnabas's sister's son, Colos. iv. 10. Hence Barnabas might be so desirous to promote him. Paul was also afterwards better conceited of him, as may be seen Colos. iv. 10.

Ver. 38. *Who departed from them*] Providing for his own ease; for they were then to take a tedious and dangerous journey over the high hill Taurus. This John liked not, but left them, and went his ways.

Ver. 39. *And the contention, &c.*] The paroxysm (παροξυσμος) or fit of a fever, so great was the commotion, the perturbation. St Luke being a physician, saith Brentius, useth here a physical expression. Heed must be taken that we overshoot not in the best causes, lest if we be overshot, God's wrath be kindled against us. There is a most sad story of the dissension between Luther and Carolostadius, both good men. And another as sad of those that fled to Frankfort hence in Queen Mary's days; yet among them there were such grievous breaches that they sought the lives one of another, picking out some words against the emperor, in a sermon that Master Knox had preached in England long before, and now accusing him for them to the magistrates of Frankfort, upon which divers of them were fain to fly.

That they departed asunder] And we read not that they joined any more together after this. Barnabas we find halting together with Peter, Gal. ii. 13, rather than he would walk uprightly together with his old associate Paul, ver. 14, for the which Paul reproved Peter, who yet maketh honourable mention of Paul, 2 Pet. iii. 15, which was his holy ingenuity. But much to be commended were Basil and Eusebius, who perceiving the Arians to improve a difference betwixt them to the prejudice of the orthodox, were soon reconciled, and united their forces against the common enemy.

Ver. 40. *Being recommended by the brethren*] Whereby it appeareth that the Church took Paul's part, and God blessed his labours wherever he came; whereas Barnabas lies buried, as it were, and little more is henceforth recorded of him, unless it be that his temporizing with Peter, Gal. ii. So Lot is no more heard of after his incest, Gen. xix. 36. If we commit such things we deserve but a short story. (Babington *in locum*.)

Ver. 41. *And he went*] Being incessant and unsatisfiable in his master Christ's service.

CHAPTER XVI.

Ver. 1. *But his father was a Greek*] Both by nation and religion. This was an unlawful marriage, Exod. xxxiv., Deut. vii., and might be a means to humble the good woman, when once she came to a sight of her sin. David had his best children by Bathsheba, as Solomon, Nathan, of whom came Christ, &c. God can turn our sins to our good and comfort, as the skilful apothecary can make of a poisonful viper a wholesome triacle.

Ver. 2. *Which was well reported of by the brethren*] This is part of the reward of virtue, and follows it, as the shadow doth the body. See the note on Eccles. vii. 1, and on 3 John 12.

Ver. 3. *Took and circumcised him*] Paul circumcised Timothy, as a Gentile; in that, for a Jew to be circumcised was no yieldance. And those words, "they all knew his father to be a Greek," demonstrate, he went in estimation for a Gentile. Calvin refusing to administer the communion in Geneva, and to use therein unleavened bread or wafer-cakes, was compelled to depart the city; and was not received thither again until he had allowed of the same kind of bread. *De quo postea restitutus, nunquam contendendum putavit ; minime tamen dissimulans quid alioqui magis esset probaturus.*[1] See the note on chap. xv. 28.

Ver. 4. *They delivered them the decrees*] Which were agreeable to the Scriptures. And if Gregory thought that the decrees of the four first general councils were to be received with like reverence and respect as the four holy Gospels, how much more these! But what a tyrant is the pope to obtrude his decretals, and the decrees of his councils (though directly opposite to the revealed will of God), upon the consciences of the misled multitude, to be observed, with a *Non-obstante?* The Council of Constance (for instance) comes in with a *Non-obstante* against Christ's institution, withholding the cup from the sacrament; so for prayers in an unknown tongue, singing of psalms, ministers' marriage.[2] When the pope sets forth any bulls, commonly he concludes thus, *Non obstantibus et ordinationibus Apostolicis, cæterisque contrariis quibuscunque.*

Ver. 5. *Established in the faith, and increased in number*] Some were converted by their ministry, others confirmed. This is still the fruit of faithful preaching, which is far more effectual hereunto than other ordinances; like as the rain from heaven hath a fatness with it, and a special influence, more than other standing waters, and as milk from the breast is most nourishing.

Ver. 6. *And were forbidden*, &c.] This was a heavier judgment upon those coasts than to be denied a harvest, or the light of the sun. Prize the preaching of the gospel as a singular privilege. They that are without a teaching priest are without God, 2 Chron. xv. 3. There were ambassadors sent out of Nubia in Africa to the king of Habassia, to entreat him for a supply of ministers to instruct their nation, and repair Christianity gone to ruin among them; but they were rejected.[3] Amos's famine of the word is far more deplorable than Samaria's famine of bread in that strait siege.

Ver. 7. *But the Spirit suffered them not*] The Spirit still lusteth against the flesh, and the flesh against the Spirit, in the hearts of the regenerate, so that they cannot do what they would, Gal. v. 17. As they cannot do what good they would in regard of the flesh, so neither what evil they would in regard of the Spirit.

Ver. 8. *Came down to Troas*] The relics of old

Troy, called also Antigonia and Alexandria, as Pliny testifieth.

Ver. 9. *Into Macedonia and help us*] The ministers are those by whom God helpeth his perishing people, and pulleth them out of the devil's danger. Hence they are called saviours, Obad. 21; 1 Tim. iv. 16; redeemers, Job xxxiii. 24, 28; co-workers with Christ, 2 Cor. vi. 1.

Ver. 10. *Assuredly gathering*] It was not therefore a bare vision, but set on upon their spirits by the testimony of the Holy Spirit, as all visions are that come from God. We read in the Roman history of a vision that Brutus had the night before that unhappy fight at Philippi, calling him into Macedonia too, but for his utter ruin. This was a vision from the devil, doubtless, that old man-slayer. Cuthbert Simpson's vision, and afterwards Mr Laremouth's (who was chaplain to Queen Ann of Cleve), whereby they were comforted in and delivered out of prison, we may read of in the Book of Martyrs. Cardinal Cusan foretold, by some vision that he had, a reformation of religion that should fall out A. D. 1507, which was above fifty years after his death. John Trithemius foretold the same A. D. 1508. *Genius vero qui Trithemio hæc dictavit, albus an ater fuerit, ego non facile dixerim. Merito suspectum est piis, &c.,* saith Bucholcerus. Who told him so much I cannot tell; but it was the devil in all likelihood. But what a strange conference was that which Luther had with the devil, by his own confession; whereby he was admonished of many abuses of the mass, which thereupon he wrote against. Is Satan divided against himself? Comes any good out of such a Nazareth? Need we not to prove the spirits, whether they be of God? How many have we now-a-days (our modern enthusiasts) that dream their Midianitish dreams, and then tell it for gospel to their neighbours as wise as themselves! that lead men into the lion's mouth (that roaring lion, I mean), under pretence of a revelation; as that old impostor did the young prophet, 1 Kings xiii.

Ver. 11. *We came with a straight course*] Or with a speedy course. The straight way is the next way :[4] "How long wilt thou go about, O backsliding daughter?" Jer. xxxi. 22. *Impii ambulant in circuitu,* saith the Psalmist, the wicked walk the round; so doth the devil, that great peripatetic, seeking to circumvent, Job i. 7. But the righteous look straight before them, Prov. iv. 25, and make straight paths for their feet, Heb. xii. 13; so that they soon finish their course with joy, and live long in a little time.

To Samothracia] An island over-against Thracia; wherefore see Pliny, iv. 11.

Neapolis] A city near Philippi, in the borders between Thracia and Macedonia.

Ver. 13. *And on the sabbath*] A day that God had sanctified to be a means to convey sanctity into the hearts of his hidden ones, as here of

[1] Beza in Vita Calvini.   [2] Caranza Sum. Concil. sess. 13.
[3] Alvarez Hist. Æthiop. c. 137.

[4] εὐθυδρομής, *Utrumque significat, et recte et cito currentes.* Lorin.

Lydia the purpuris, Ezek. xx. 12. It is his ex-chequer-day, his market-day.

Where prayer was wont to be made] Or where was a public oratory. So the synagogues are called by Philo in his ambassage to Caius the emperor, *minus invidioso nomine.*

Unto the women which resorted] St Paul (it may seem) at first had no other hearers but a few women at Philippi. But afterwards they became a flourishing Church. *Nec minor ab exordio, nec major incrementis ulla*, saith Eutropius concerning Rome; so may we say concerning the Church of Christ.

Ver. 14. *Whose heart the Lord opened*] Man's heart is naturally locked up and barricaded against God, till he, by his mighty Spirit, make forcible entrance, beating the devil out of his trenches, 2 Cor. x. 4.

Ver. 15. *If ye have judged me to be faithful*] Not else, upon no other condition doth she desire it; for hypocrites are the botches of society; as Augustus was wont to term his three untoward children, *tres vomicas, tria carcinomata*, three mattery imposthumes or ulcerous sores. (Sueton. in Aug.)

Ver. 16. *Possessed with a spirit*, &c.] These the seventy seniors usually call ἐγγαστριμύθους, because the devil spake out of their bellies. For which cause also the Hebrews called them Oboth, or bottles; because the bellies of those women that were thus made use of by the devil were swelled as big as bottles. (Beza in loc.) In the year of grace 1536, a certain damsel at Frankfort in Germany, being possessed with a devil, and stark mad, swallowed down pieces of money with much gnashing of her teeth; which monies were presently wrung out of her hands and kept by divers, &c. This is a true story, reported by Andrew Ebert the minister of the place, who wrote the same to Luther, requesting his advice; which was, to pray hard for her, &c. (Bucholc. Chr.)

Ver. 17. *These men are the servants*] Satan *etsi semel videatur verax, millies est mendax et semper fallax.* Mark i. 25; John viii. 47.

Ver. 18. *Paul being grieved*] Paul took no joy in such a testimony. High words become not a fool. To be praised by a praiseless person is no praise at all.

Ver. 19. *Their gains were gone*] ἐξῆλθεν, was gone forth together with the devil. They that count all fish that comes to net, will in the end catch the devil and all. You are his birds, saith Bradford to such, whom when the devil hath well fed, he will broach you and eat you, chaw you and champ you, world without end, in eternal woe and misery.

Ver. 20. *Trouble our city*] Faithful preachers have ever been by the wicked accounted trouble-towns; these covetous caitiffs had not so much ingenuity as the devil himself, ver. 17.

Ver. 21. *Neither to observe*, &c.] An ordinary thing to oppose the placits and devices of men to the truth of God.

Ver. 22. *Rent off their clothes*] i. e. the apostles' clothes.

And commanded to beat them] What? before they had examined the matter? This was preposterous justice; like that of those that in the morning hang the offender, and sit upon him in the afternoon; or those spoken of by Æneas Sylvius (cap. 20, Europ.), that hang up such as are suspected of theft, and three days after judge of the suspicion. Whereas, on the contrary, a judge is to retain the decency and gravity of the law, which is never angry with any man. *Lex non irascitur, sed constituit.* Alexander in his anger slew those friends of his, whom afterwards he would have revived again with his own heart-blood.

Ver. 23. *Laid many stripes*] These were those marks of the Lord Jesus which the apostles so gloried of, as an old soldier doth of his scars and wounds received in battle. *Hæ sunt gemmæ et pretiosa ornamenta Dei*, saith Munster, concerning his ulcers whereof he died. So might Paul and Silas well say of their stripes, Τὰ δεσμὰ περιφέρω τοὺς πνευματικοὺς μαργαρίτας, saith Ignatius in his Epistle to the Ephesians: I bear my bonds as so many spiritual pearls of price. It was with sweet-briar, in some sense, that these apostles were whipt.

Ver. 24. *Fast in the stocks*] The word τὸ ξύλον signifieth such a pair of stocks, as wherein they used to make fast feet and neck too, saith Beza out of Nonius. Divers of our martyrs were thus stocked in the bishop of London's coal-house; as Mr Philpot, and that martyr that rejoiced that she might have her foot in the hole of the stocks in which Master Philpot had been before her.

Ver. 25. *Sang praises unto God*] His presence turns a prison into a palace, into a paradise. "From the delectable orchard of the Leonine prison;" so the Italian martyr Algerius dated his letter to a friend. "I was carried to the coal-house," saith Mr Philpot, "where I with my fellows do rouse together in the straw as cheerfully, we thank God, as others do in their beds of down." Philip, Landgrave of Hesse, being a long time prisoner under Charles V., was demanded what upheld him at that time? He answered, that he felt the divine consolations of the martyrs.

Ver. 26. *There was a great earthquake*] See the great power of prayer. It shaketh heaven and earth, Luther saith; there is a kind of omnipotency in it.

Ver. 27. *And the keeper of the prison*] In whom the earthquake had wrought a heart-quake, as it had also (though not to so good purpose) in the magistrates, ver. 35. Read the note thereon. We read that the people of Antioch, though many of them gave their hands for Chrysostom's banishment, yet, terrified by an earthquake, immediately they sent for him again.

Ver. 28. *But Paul cried with a loud voice*, &c.] We should likewise cry *Cave miser*, when we see a man busily cutting the throat of his own poor soul, by wilful wickedness, or pitching headlong into hell through despair of God's mercy. "Of some have compassion, making a difference,"

Jude 21; and others save with fear, pulling them out of the fire of hell, as the angel pulled Lot out of Sodom, and as God pulled Joshua the high-priest as "a brand out of the fire," Zech. iii. This Jerome calleth *Sanctam violentiam, optabilem rapinam*, a holy violence, a desirable ravage; and the law of God requireth not only our observation, but our preservation; to cause others to keep it, as well as ourselves.

Ver. 29. *And sprang in*] As John the Evangelist with like speed sprang out of the bath, when Cerinthus the heretic came into it, lest some evil, for his sake, should befall him from heaven. (ἐξήλατο τοῦ βαλανείου, Eus.)

Ver. 30. *What must I do to be saved?*] A reverend divine said once to a poor soul, that told him he was troubled about his salvation; I tell thee, said he, it is able to trouble the whole world.

Ver. 31. *Believe on the Lord Jesus*] This is the condition on our part required; or rather a stipulation that God hath promised to work in us and for us.

Ver. 32. *And they spake unto him*] So Master Tindal, during the time of his imprisonment, converted his keeper, together with the keeper's daughter, and others of his household. Also the rest that were with him in the prison, said, That if Tindal were not a good Christian man, they could not tell whom to trust. The word of God is not bound, saith Paul the prisoner, Phil. i. 13. His bonds were manifest in all Cæsar's court, and to all others. In the Book of Martyrs we read also of one Bowler, a perverse Papist, converted by Doctor Sands and Master Bradford, whose keeper he was for above twenty weeks; and afterwards became their son, begotten in their bonds.

Ver. 33. *He and all his straightway*] God's work is of great importance, and must be presently done, whatever else is left undone. "If ye will inquire, inquire, return, come," Isa. xxi. 12.

Ver. 34. *And rejoiced, believing*] A prick with a pin may and doth many times let out corruption as well as lancing. Some suffer more throes in the new birth, some less. But many meet with greatest trials and terrors after conversion. When men take little fines, they mean to take the more rent.

Ver. 35. *The magistrates sent*] In one ancient Greek copy there is this addition, "And when it was day, the magistrates met together in the market-place; and calling to mind the earthquake that had been that night, they feared, and sent the sergeants, saying, Let these men go." See ver. 27.

Ver. 36. *And the keeper of the prison*] As glad to be the messenger of such good tidings; for he knew well the misery of captivity; by which term therefore, all that Job suffered is summarily set forth, chap. xlii. 10.

Ver. 37. *They have beaten us*] A Roman, by the Valerian law, might not be bound; by the Porcian law, he might not be beaten or put to death, but by the Romans themselves, with the

consent of the people. This privilege Paul pleads, and well he might; for the name of a Roman citizen was terrible to other nations. Though we may not return evil for evil, yet we may use all lawful means to right and secure ourselves.

And now do they thrust us out?] Doctor Fuller the chancellor came to William Wolsey the martyr, whom he had imprisoned, and said, Thou dost much trouble my conscience; wherefore I pray thee depart, and rule thy tongue, so that I hear no more complaint of thee; and come to church when thou wilt, and if thou be complained of, so far as I may, I promise thee I will not hear of it. "Master Doctor," quoth he, "I was brought hither by a law, and by a law I will be delivered," &c.

Ver. 38. *And they feared when they heard, &c.*] Their sin troubled them not, but their danger; for *Irasci populo Rom. nemo sapienter potest.* It was not safe dashing against the rock of Rome's power. Tully tells us, that *Hæc vox, Civis Romanus sum, sæpe in ultimis terris*, &c. This one word, "I am a Roman," relieved and rescued many in the utmost parts of the earth, and among barbarians.

Ver. 39. *And they came and besought them*] The matter is well amended since yesterday. How suddenly crest-fallen are these grandees of Philippi, how bladder-like do they shrivel to nothing, that erst swelled with the wind of pride and passion! So did the king of Sodom, Manasseh, Saul, &c.

Ver. 40. *And departed*] Yet so, as that St Paul soon after visited them with that golden Epistle to the Philippians.

CHAPTER XVII.

Ver. 1. *Where was a synagogue of the Jews*] Who did much hurt there by their crossness, neither pleasing God nor profiting men, 1 Thess. ii. 15.

Ver. 2. *Out of the Scriptures*] Wherein they were wondrous expert. *Quilibet nostrum de lege interrogatus facilius quam nomen suum recitat*, saith Josephus. We have the Scriptures at our fingers' ends.

Ver. 3. *Alleging*] Or laying it so plain before their eyes (παρατιθέμενος), that they could not but see it, unless they were of those *qui festucam quærunt unde oculos sibi eruant*, as Bernard hath it, who seek straws to put out their own eyes withal.

Ver. 4. *Consorted with Paul*] Were knit unto them in the straitest bonds, as man and wife, brother and sister: *Sanctior est copula cordis quam corporis.* No such bond as religion, προσεκληρώθησαν.

Ver. 5. *Of the baser sort*] *Viles et venales*, saith one, *Vagi, otiosique*, saith another, such as had little to do but to walk the streets and run on errands, the rascality and sink of the city.

Set all the city on an uproar] *Quia perturbato statu melius consequi valent quod volunt.* The devil loves to fish in troubled waters. When he hath set all on a hurry, as in Saul, then he can the sooner enter and play his pranks. So can his instruments.

Ver. 6. *Turned the world, &c.*] ἀναστατοῦντες. So Elias was called the troubler of Israel, Luther the trumpet of rebellion. It is not the gospel, but men's corruption, that breeds the trouble; as it is not the sea, but the foulness of men's stomachs, that makes them sea-sick.

Ver. 7. *Whom Jason hath received*] ὑποδέδεκται. *Clanculum excepit*, so Erasmus well rendereth it, hath closely and covertly entertained them, as Obadiah did the Lord's prophets.

Contrary to the decrees of Cæsar] *Unicum crimen eorum, qui crimine vacabant.* Tacit.

Ver. 8. *And they troubled the people and the rulers*] The devil and his agents, as they are of turbulent spirits, like Ishmael, Pope Urban (who was therefore called Turban, from his trouble-someness), and the Jesuits; so they love to fish in troubled waters, and to set all on a hurry by incensing rulers against the people of God, and seeking to persuade them that they are anti-magistratical. Hence the devil eftsoons casteth some of them into prison, Rev. ii. 10; *sc.* by his imps and instruments armed with authority.

Ver. 9. *When they had taken security*] It was happy that security would be taken, till the heat was over. For,

Ut fragilis glacies frangitur ira mora. Ovid.

Ver. 10. *Went into the synagogue*] As he had done before at Thessalonica, and had sped so ill. Heroic spirits are no wit dismayed with diffi-culties; but rather whetted on thereby to more diligence in duty. And the servant of the Lord must not despond or desist, but be apt to teach, "patient, in meekness instructing those that op-pose themselves, if peradventure God will at any time give them repentance," &c., 2 Tim. ii. 24, 25.

Ver. 11. *These were more noble*] Better gentle-men (εὐγενέστεροι). Virtue is instead of a thou-sand escutcheons. "Since thou hast been preci-ous in my sight, thou hast been honourable," Isa. xliii. 4. The nobles of Israel made their staves (the ensigns, haply, of their honour) instruments of the common good, Numb. xxi. 18; when the nobles of Tekoah are blemished in their blood for this, that they "put not their necks to the work of their Lord," Neh. iii. 5. The Biscanies vaunt of themselves among the Spaniards, that they are the right Hidalgoes, that is, gentlemen, as the Welshmen do here. But Christian nobility is the best and truest where God himself is the top of the kin, and religion the root; in regard whereof all other things are but shadows and shapes of nobleness. The Jews of Berea were more noble, or of better descent, *Non per civilem dignitatem, sed per spiritualem dignationem*, as one saith: Not by civil descent, but by spiritual ad-vancement.

Ver. 12. *Therefore many of them believed*] There are certain abilities and actions we have,

and may perform without special grace; in the employment whereof we are to expect the effect-ual work of the Spirit. See it in these noble Bereans; they brought their bodies to the assem-bly, took the heads of Paul's sermons very truly, repeated and examined the notes they had taken, and yet were unconverted, as appears by this verse. Now if any of us do hide the like talent, we are not to expect the Spirit of sanctification. As our liberty in external acts (as to come to church to hear, &c.) is still some, so must our endeavours be answerable.

Ver. 13. *They came thither also*] Thus they pleased not God and were contrary to all men; wherefore "wrath is come upon them to the ut-most," 1 Thess. ii. 15, 16.

Ver. 14. *To go as it were to the sea*] This was a high point of wisdom, not to send Paul the next way to Athens, but about by the sea for avoiding of danger.

Ver. 15. *Brought him unto Athens*] The eye of Greece, but woefully now bemisted with the fog of superstition, as our universities also have been of late. Athens was a pleasant and ancient city. Cecrops is said to have been king of it in Moses's time. It was anciently called κόσμος κόσμου, "the ornament or glory of the world." But Gregory Nazianzen reports of it that it was the plaguiest place in the world for superstition; and he acknowledgeth it a great mercy that he and Basil were preserved from those infections.

Ver. 16. *His spirit was stirred*] The word παρωξύνετο signifies, he was almost beside him-self (such was his zeal) to see the idolatry of the Athenians. So was William Gardiner, an Eng-lish merchant and martyr in Portugal, who, when the cardinal, in a mass before the king, began to take the ceremonial host, to toss it to and fro round about the chalice, making certain circles and semicircles, he not being able to suffer any longer, went to the cardinal, and in the presence of the king and all his nobles and citizens, with the one hand he snatched the cake from the priest, and trod it under his feet, and with the other hand overthrew the chalice, &c. See the like history of William Flower, who wounded the mass-priest at Westminster, &c. (Acts and Mon. fol. 1430.) There are that tell us that this book of the Acts is discerned to be written by Luke, by his physician's language here, παρωξύνετο, he "was in a fever fit," and chap. xv. 39, ἐγένετο οὖν παροξυσμός, "the contention was so sharp betwixt them." The word signifies such a sharpness as is in vinegar; and it is used by physicians to denote the sharpness of the feverish humour when it is acting in a fit. It troubled St Paul, that the fountain was so troubled, the eye of Greece so darkened,[1] the "ornament of the world" so slurred with "abominable idolatries," as St Peter expresseth it, 1 Pet. iv. 3.

Wholly given to idolatry] Pausanias reckons up more idols almost in Athens than in all Greece besides. And Xenophon saith that the Athenians kept double the holy-days and festi-

---

[1] Τῆς Ἑλλάδος ὀφθαλμός. Diod.

vals to what others did. "Ephraim is joined to idols, let him alone," *q. d.* there is no hope of him, Hos. iv. 16. They that make them are like unto them, so are all they that worship them, as blockish as those Balaami-blocks they worship. No Church could be founded at Athens; they for their idolatry were given up to strong delusions, vile affections, just damnation. They were too wise to be saved by the foolishness of preaching.

Ver. 17. *With them that met with him*] If anybody would but lend him a little audience, he would preach to them, such was his zeal. The word must be preached in season, out of season, &c., *volentibus, nolentibus.*

Ver. 18. *Certain philosophers, &c.*] The deep theorems of philosophy (said King James) make one learned, but seldom better, and oftentimes worse, mere atheists. There is an Arabic proverb, *Cum errat eruditus, errat errore erudito.* And *Indocti rapiunt cœlum,* saith Aug. *Melior est humilis rusticus qui Deo servit, quam superbus Philosophus, &c.,* saith a devout Dominican. (Erpen. Cent. 2. Prov. xxviii. 6.)

What will this babbler say?] Seminilega, σπερμο- λόγος, by a metaphor from little birds, that yield neither good meat nor good music, but only pick up grain, and live by other men's labours. Master Rogers (our late proto-martyr) interpreteth it a prater, trifler, news-carrier, that tells whatsoever men will have him for gain; that will for a piece of bread say what you will have him.

A setter forth of strange gods] Rogers renders it, a preacher of new devils.

Jesus and the resurrection] Anastasis, or the resurrection, they took for some new goddess, saith Œcumenius.

Ver. 19. *Brought him unto Areopagus*] A cruel court where Socrates lost his life for the very same crime that St Paul is here charged with; viz. an endeavour to introduce new deities. (Laertius.) That the apostle came off not only with safety, but some success (for Dionysius, one of the judges, was converted), see a sweet providence. Paul wanted a place to preach in; they brought him to Areopagus as a delinquent, where he hath an opportunity of doing God a great deal of good service. So Charles V., emperor, sent the confession of the Protestant Churches to divers princes of Europe to ask their opinions; hereby the gospel was exceedingly spread and propagated; which gave occasion to Luther to deride *Pontificiorum stultam sapientiam,* the foolish wisdom of the Papists, in a certain epistle to the elector of Saxony. (Scultet. Annal. 274.)

Ver. 20. *For thou bringest certain strange things*] Or, new, never heard of, ξενίζοντα. Yet not so new neither as they thought for; see Rom. xi. 2—4; xvi. 25, 26. Papists upbraid us with the novelty of our religion, and ask us where it was till Luther's time? We answer (as one once did), "In the Bible, where their religion never was." See Catalog. Test. verit., and Mr Bernard's Look beyond Luther, Dr Featlie's Conference with Fisher, &c. They boast much of antiquity, as once the Gibeonites did of old shoes and mouldy bread. We refer them to Alex. Cook's Abatement of Popish Brags, and Guild's Popish Boasting of Antiquity; besides abundance of other good authors.

Ver. 21. *For all the Athenians, &c.*] The selfsame truth is testified by Demosthenes, in an answer to Philip's letter. ἡμεῖς οὐδὲν ποιοῦντες ἐν- θάδε καθήμεθα πυνθανόμενοι εἴ τι λέγεται νεώτερον. We (saith he to his countrymen of Athens) to speak truth, sit here, doing nothing but trifling out our time, and listening what news abroad. This their national itch after novelties, made them the more willing to hear Paul speak. It is not amiss to hearken how it goeth with the Church, that we may rejoice with those that rejoice, and weep with those that weep; *Cum singulis pectus meum copulo,* saith Cyprian. Eli sat to hear what became of the ark; which when it was taken, it is hard to say whether was first broke, his heart or his neck.

Ver. 22. *You are too superstitious*] You are fearers of evil spirits; so one renders it; and Paul elsewhere tells the Corinthians that what they sacrificed to idols they sacrificed to devils, 1 Cor. x. 20.

Beza renders ὡς δεισιδαιμονεστέρους, *quasi religiosiores* (as if the apostle had used a euphemismus), somewhat superstitious, or rather religious; the better to insinuate, for the Athenians had tender ears, and loved to hear toothless truths; which made Demosthenes call upon get their ears healed. (*Orat. de Ord. Civ.*)

Ver. 23. *I found an altar*] A high-altar, βωμός, seems to come from במה a high place. St Paul, as he preached without a pulpit, ver. 17, so he takes his text off one of their altars. Anything serves turn, so he may do good.

To the unknown God] That uncertainty that attends idolatry caused those mariners to call every man to his God, Jonah i. 5. And lest they might all mistake the true God, they awaken Jonas also to call upon his God. Hence these Athenians worship an unknown God; and hence, the heathens generally closed their petitions with *Diique Deæque omnes.* (Serv. *in Georg.* i.)

Pausanias (in Attic.) mentioneth this altar, To the unknown God. Lucian saith the neighbour countries would swear by him unknown at Athens. The cause of erecting this altar some affirm to have been a fearful vision appearing to Philippides (sent ambassador to the Lacedæmonians concerning aid against the Persians), and complaining that he (that is, the great god Pan) was neglected and other gods worshipped, promising likewise his help. They therefore being victorious, and fearing the like event, built a temple and altar to the unknown God. Others say, that the plague being hot at Athens, and no help to be had from their gods, they surmising some other power to have sent and set on the disease, set up this altar, on which was written, To the gods of Asia, Europe, and Africa, to the unknown and strange God. (Justin Martyr. Œcumen. Θεοῖς Ἀσίας καὶ Εὐρώπης καὶ Λιβύης, Θεῷ ἀγνώστῳ καὶ ξένῳ.

Ver. 24. *Dwelleth not in temples*] See the note on Acts vii. 48.

Ver. 25. *Neither is worshipped*] *Colitur vel delinitur*, collogued with, or complimented. *Colendi verbum ἀπὸ τοῦ κολακεύειν, dictum volunt eo quod plerunque Dei hominumque cultus cum adulatione et hypocrisi est conjunctus. Sic a* λατρεύειν, *Gallicum flatter.* Some derive the word here used, θεραπεύω, of the Hebrew Taraph or Teraphim, idols or images, Gen. xxxi. 30, Judg. xvii. 5. God is not so worshipped. (Stuchius *de Sacrif. Gentil.*; Avenarius; Ainsworth.

Ver. 26. *And hath made of one blood*] This our brainsick diggers do much beat upon, and would therefore lay all level, and have all things common. One of their progenitors came to the Emperor Sigismund, and calling him brother, asked him for means; because he was his brother, and one of the same blood. He gave him a testor, and told him, if all his brethren would do the like for him, he should soon become a rich man.

Ver. 27. *They might feel after him*] Grope after him, as blind men, ψηλαφήσειαν. The apostle dealing here with philosophers, disputes philosophically, showing them, most learnedly and divinely, the true use of natural philosophy, which they were utterly ignorant of. Crucifer oft contemplated the footsteps of God in the creature, saying with Paul, that God was so near unto us that he might be almost felt with hands.

Though he be not far] Not so far as the bark is from the tree, the skin from the flesh, or the flesh from the bones. *Deus intimior nobis intimo nostro.* He is nearer to us than we are to ourselves, though we see him not. (Bugentag.) Like as if one hear a preacher by night, though he see him not, yet he knows he is there present; so in this case.

Ver. 28. *For in him we live*, &c.] The heathen could say,

Est Deus in nobis, agitante calescimus illo.

We move] Understand it as well of the motions of the mind as of the body.

And have our being] As the beams have their being in the sun, and an accident in the subject. *Scholastici dependentiam creatorum a Creatore partim luci, quæ in aere remoto Sole extinguitur, partim vasculo aquam contentam circumscribenti, partim sigillo in aqua impresso comparant.*

As certain also of your own poets] Note that the apostle nameth not Aratus, whom he citeth, though he were his own countryman, a Cilician; notwithstanding the piety of that poet's beginning, Εκ Διὸς ἀρχώμεσθα, or the divineness of his subject, the heavens, a more sublime and pure matter than useth to be in the wanton pages of other poets. Some sentences of heathenish authors are found in Scripture, as the Egyptian spoils furnished the Israelites, and David helped himself with Goliath's sword: so the Holy Ghost strikes the heathens with their own weapons, *Propriis pennis configimur*, as Julian the Apostate complained, and therefore forbade the Christians

to send their children to the heathen schools, lest they should be wounded with their own weapons.

Ver. 29. *That the Godhead is like*] *Qui primi deorum simulachra induxerunt, errorem auxerunt, metum dempserunt*, saith Varro, as Calvin cites his words. Plutarch saith it is sacrilege to worship by images. They were atheists by night that worshipped the sun and atheists by day that worshipped the moon, as Cyril wittily speaketh.

Ver. 30. *God winked at*] Regarded not. God accounted the times of paganism before Christ (for all their knowledge), even times of ignorance, and looked over or beyond them (as the word ὑπεριδὼν here signifieth), having respect only to the times of Christianity.

Ver. 31. *Because he hath appointed a day*] Knowing therefore the terror of the Lord, and the dreadfulness of that great day, "what manner of men ought we to be in all holy conversation and godliness," 2 Pet. iii. 11; breaking off our sins by repentance, and being abrupt in the work, sith the very next moment thou mayest hear that summons that Pope Julius II. did, and was found dead the next day, *Veni miser in judicium*, Come, thou wretch, receive thy judgment. (Jac. Renig.) Hence Austin professed that he would not, for the gain of the world, be an atheist for half an hour; because he knew not how suddenly Christ might come to judge him. *Aut pœnitendum aut pereundum.*

Ver. 32. *Some mocked*] Three sorts of hearers, some derided, others doubted, a few believed, as Dennis and Damaris, but no Church here founded. They were too wise to go to heaven. Not a scholar in Oxford would look upon the good Bishops Ridley and Cranmer, prisoners in Bocardo, that college of quondams, as it was then called.

Ver. 33. *So Paul departed*] They said they would hear him again at better leisure (εἰς αὔριον τὰ σπουδαῖα, as that trifler said), but they never had another opportunity: procrastinators seldom speed better; it fareth with them as Plutarch writes of Hannibal, that when he could have taken Rome he would not, when he would he could not. See Jer. xiv. 19.

Ver. 34. *Dionysius the Areopagite*] Not the astrologer, as some have made him, nor the author of the Heavenly Hierarchy made by some superstitious monk; but a senator or judge in that court of Mars' Hill in Athens, crowned with martyrdom for the Christian religion, in the year of grace 96, as Trithemius writeth.

And a woman named Damaris] Damaris as well as Dennis. Souls have no sexes. In Christ "there is neither male nor female, bond nor free," Gal. iii. 28. It is easy to observe, saith a grave divine, that the New Testament affords more store of good women than the Old. In the preceding chapter, when Paul came first to Philippi, he had none that would hear him, but a company of good women, Acts xvi. 13.

CHAPTER XVIII.

Ver. 1. *And came to Corinth*] A city very rich, but very loose and luxurious. *Magna cognatio ut rei sic nominis, divitiis et vitiis.* The Corinthians had within their city the temple of Isis, and without it the temple of Venus, to whom there were well-nigh a thousand courtesans consecrated. They held fornication to be no sin; hence the apostle is so earnest against it, 1 Cor. v.

Ver. 2. *Had commanded all Jews, &c.*] Wicked men are sick of the saints, and long to be rid of them, not considering that they bear up the pillars of the earth, and that God gratifies his children with the preservation of the wicked, as he did Paul with the lives of those infidels that were in the ship with him, Acts xxvii. 24. Howbeit they are frequently as foolish as this Claudius who banished God's true servants; or, as the stag in the emblem, which by biting the boughs off the trees under which she lay hid from the hounds and hunters, bewrayed and betrayed herself into their hands.

Ver. 3.] *He abode with them and wrought*] Being no less busy in his shop among his tents than in his study among his books and parchments, 2 Tim. iv. 13. So Musculus, persecuted and driven out of his place, was forced for a poor living to dig and weave. (Melch. Adam.) And another late martyr, though he were one of the greatest scholars in Christendom, yet in banishment or flight for conscience served the mason.

Ver. 4. *Persuaded the Jews*] Men may speak persuasively, but God only can persuade. Gen. ix. 27, Japheth's children were to be won by persuasion. Therefore Christ sent forth to them not soldiers, but fishers, who might work upon them *docendo non ducendo, monendo non minando*, by informing them, not by enforcing them.

Ver. 5. *And when Silas and Timothy*] Good people one kindle another. Paul was much heated with the zeal of God by the company of these two good men. Two flints, though both cold, yet yield fire when smitten together. Billets one kindle another. Iron sharpeneth iron, so doth the face of a man his friend.

Ver. 6. *And when they opposed*] Gr. Αντιτασσομένων, And when they bade him battle. A military term.

Your blood be upon your own heads] Answerable to their wish, Matt. xxvii. 25, and according to their manner of putting their sins upon the head of the sacrificed creature, Lev. i. 4; iii. 2.

Ver. 7. *Whose house joined hard to the synagogue*] *Quo magis pungeret Judæos;* for this Justus was (likely) a Gentile. But they were *toties puncti et repuncti, minime tamen ad resipiscentiam compuncti*, like those bears in Pliny, they could not be awakened with the sharpest prickles; such a dead lethargy had the devil cast them into.

Ver. 8. *And many of the Corinthians*] When

Crispus the chief ruler of the synagogue believed, many of the Corinthians believed also. Great men are the looking-glasses of the country, according to which most men dress themselves. Alexander the Great naturally held his head aside, his courtiers did the like. When Francis the French king was polled for the better healing of a wound in his head, all about him, and many others, cut off their long hair, &c.

Ver. 9. *But speak, and hold not thy peace*] i. e. Speak out the whole truth plainly and plentifully, be not for any self-respects found guilty of a sinful silence. *Inveniar sane superbus, &c., modo impii silentii non arguar, dum Dominus patitur,* saith Luther (Epist. ad Staupic.). Let me be counted proud, passionate, impudent, anything, so that I betray not the Lord's cause by a cowardly silence.

Ver. 10. *For I am with thee*] As to behold thy behaviour (*Cave, spectat Deus*), so to support, defend, and deliver thee. If a child be in the dark, yet, having his father by the hand, he fears nothing. David feared not the "vale of the shadow of death," that is, death in its most horrid and hideous representations, and all because God was with him, Psal. xxiii. 4.

Ver. 11. *And he continued there*] Gr. ἐκάθισε, He sat down there a great while, though he met with many discouragements and little love, with loss of love, 2 Cor. xii. 15, and unworthy usage, being forced to labour with his hands for a poor living. Howbeit, inasmuch as God had much people there, he, as a good soldier of Jesus Christ, suffered hardship, and sacrificed himself to the service of their faith (Isidore); not seeking theirs by them, and "catching them by craft," 2 Cor. xii. 16, as the fox doth the fowls that fall upon him when he feigns himself a dead carcase.

Ver. 12. *And when Gallio was*] This Gallio was brother to Seneca, who being a great courtier, obtained for him of Claudius the emperor to be made deputy of Achaia, as Tacitus testifieth.

Ver. 13. *Contrary to the law*] That is, contrary to our law. For the Romans had granted liberty to the Jews to worship God as their own law prescribed.

Ver. 14. *Or wicked lewdness*] The Greek word, ῥαδιούργημα, doth elegantly set forth the disposition of a lewd man; which is to be easily drawn to any wicked way. If the devil do but hold up his finger, he may have him at his beck and obedience; he is the devil's clay and wax, and may be wrought to anything with a wet finger.

Ver. 15. *A question of words or names*] Gallio esteemed no better of divine doctrine than vain words, and airy discourses. His brother Seneca jeereth the Jews for casting away a seventh part of their time upon a weekly sabbath. Profane persons hold it a madness to be so conscientious. *Philosophandum, sed paucis. Religiosum esse oportet, sed non religantem.*[1] A little religion serves turn well enough.

Ver. 16. *And he drave them from the tribunal*] As so many *Vitilitigatores, qui de lana sæpe caprina*

[1] Aug. de Civ. Dei.

rixantur, that contended for trifles, and such as deserved the whipping-post, which is the punishment that the Turks put such among them to as are litigious.[1]

Ver. 17. *Took Sosthenes*] A beloved brother of St Paul's, 1 Cor. i.

Ver. 18. *In Cenchrea*] A haven of the Corinthians. Here he was shorn, as a Nazarite, for the sake of some weak Jews, whom herein he gratified and gained to the faith. The popish shaving is so bald a ceremony, that some priests in France are ashamed of the mark, and few of them have it that can handsomely avoid it.

Ver. 19. *And reasoned with the Jews*] Whose salvation he dearly desired, Rom. ix. 3, and therefore never gave them over, though he had small thanks for his labour. His love to them was like the ivy, which if it cleaves to a stone or an old wall, will rather die than forsake it.

Ver. 20. *He consented not*] Though lovingly invited, and otherwise easy to be entreated. There was therefore something in it more than ordinary. Θεῷ ἕπου, follow God whithersoever he leadeth thee, was a maxim amongst heathens. (Boeth. Consol.) *Magnus est animus qui se Deo tradidit,* saith Seneca (Epist. cvii.); that is a brave spirit that hath given up itself to God; and that is a base degenerate spirit which stands off; *et Deum mavult emendare, quam se,* and had rather find fault with God than with himself.

Ver. 21. *Keep this feast*] As waiting an occasion, by that solemn meeting, of winning many to Christ. Paul was *insatiabilis Dei cultor,* as Chrysostom truly saith of him. George Eagles the martyr, for his great pains in travelling from place to place to confirm the brethren, was surnamed Trudgeover the World.

Ver. 22. *And gone up*] *sc.* To Jerusalem, which stood on high in respect of Cœle Syria and the sea-coasts.

Ver. 23. *Strengthening all the disciples*] For as natural life needs nourishing, and young plants watering; so do the saints need confirmation, and Christ hath provided it for them, Luke xxii. 32; Eph. iv. 11, 12.

Ver. 24. *An eloquent man*] *Et eruditum sonat et prudentem,* saith Erasmus. It imports, 1. skill in the words; he could expound well: 2. good locution; he could well express his exposition. Matter in form, as they do all in nature, so also in art. Good matter well habited is more acceptable.

Ver. 25. *Taught diligently*] According to that skill he had. Of Lactantius, Jerome passeth• this judgment: *Lactantius quasi quidam fluvius Tullianæ eloquentiæ utinam tam nostra potuisset confirmare, quam facile aliena destruxit.* So Tully (*De Nat. Deor.*) wished that he could as easily find out the true God as he could disprove the false gods.

Ver. 26. *And expounded unto him*] A humble man will be glad to learn of the meanest that is. " A little child shall lead him," Isa. xi. 6. One man may, for counsel, be a God to another, as Moses was to Aaron.

Ver. 27. *Helped them much, who had believed through grace*] For faith is a fruit of free grace. We can glory in nothing, saith Austin, because no good thing is ours; we bring forth faith and the fruits thereof, as Sarah's dead womb brought forth a child; it was not a child of nature, but of the mere promise; so are all our graces. Others read it thus: " He helped them through grace, who had believed :" that is, he freely communicated to the brethren that grace that he had received, as a good steward; and helped them what he could toward heaven. True grace is diffusive; and is therefore compared to fire, water, wind, light, to spices and aromatic trees, that sweat out their precious and sovereign oils for the good of others. Apollos was not of those that desire rather *proficere* than *prodesse,* to inform themselves than to instruct others; to know than to teach, to be seraphims, for illumination, than to be angels, for ministry: account, he knew, was to be given of his time and of his talents to an austere master, &c.

Ver. 28. *Convinced the Jews*] Who might have been convinced out of their own Cabala, that Christ was come: but that seeing they saw, but perceived not.

CHAPTER XIX.

Ver. 1. *While Apollos was at Corinth*] A mercy of God to the Church, that in Paul's absence they should be so well provided of a preacher.

Ver. 2. *Have ye received the Holy Ghost*] That is, the extraordinary gifts of the Holy Ghost in prophecy, tongues, &c., as ver. 6.

Ver. 3. *Unto John's baptism*] That is, unto John's doctrine sealed by baptism. This Paul shows to be nothing so, ver. 4. Whence Piscator collecteth that they were baptized by some of John's disciples into John's name, as if he had been the Christ. For that John had some such zealots about him, appears by John iii. 26, &c.

Ver. 4. *John verily baptized with the baptism of repentance*] That is, he taught the doctrine of repentance: see the next note on ver. 5. It is not to be thought that those were by Paul re-baptized who were formerly baptized by John; for if that had been necessary, Christ would have baptized his disciples again: but he baptized none himself, John iv.; and they baptized not themselves.

Ver. 5. *They were baptized*] That is, say some, they were re-baptized, because baptized before in a wrong name. Therefore Paul first catechiseth them, ver. 4. Others say that it was rather their renewing to their baptism than their baptism to them; and not that they took any other than that of John, but that they now began to entertain and apply it to the right intent. (Mr Lightfoot, Harm.)

[1] *Temere litigantes publice flagellis cæduntur.*

Ver. 6. *And prophesied*] By a divine and evident inspiration they expounded the writings of the prophets, and also foretold future events.

Ver. 7. *And all the men were about twelve*] These twelve, being the first-fruits of this Church, were endued with extraordinary gifts to be for elders and rulers there: for these gifts were not common to all believers, as Beza well noteth.

Ver. 8. *The things concerning the kingdom of God*] The subject matter of his discourse were faith, righteousness, life eternal. Of these things he disputed, and so informed their judgments: and these things he persuaded, and so reduced all to practice. Lo, this is preaching. Every sound is not music; neither is every pulpit discourse, preaching.

Ver. 9. *But when divers were hardened*] Hardness of heart is either natural or habitual: and this again is increased either by doing (that is, by resisting the word of God), or by suffering it to pass by us without amendment of life.

He departed from them and separated] So did Zuinglius and Luther separate from the Papists for like reason. It was laid to Luther's charge that he was an apostate. *Confitetur se esse apostatam, sed beatum et sanctum, qui fidem diabolo datam non servavit.* An apostate he confessed himself: but one that had fallen off from the devil only.

In the school of one Tyrannus] In one ancient copy it is added, "From the fifth hour to the tenth hour;" so indefatigable a preacher was Paul, a very χαλκέντερος, or iron-sides. He had a golden wit in an iron body, as one saith of Jul. Scaliger.

Ver. 10. *So that all they that dwelt in Asia*] Which now (according to the notation of its name) became אֶשׁיָּה *Esh-jah*, the fire of God; not from the fire which at first they worshipped as God; but from the fire of grace kindled upon the hearth of their hearts, and making them shine as lamps in their lives. Father Latimer, when he was demanded the reason why so much preaching and little practice? answered, *Deest ignis*, the fire of God is wanting, there is not a coal to warm at; it was otherwise now at Ephesus; all was on a light fire, which opened to St Paul that great door and effectual, 1 Cor. xvi. 9, so that all they that dwelt in Asia were fired up to a holy contention in godliness.

Ver. 11. *And God wrought special miracles*] *Virtutes non vulgares*, yet ordinary in the infancy of the Church, but now not to be expected. Manna ceased when they came to Canaan; as if it would say, Ye need no miracles now you have means. So here.

Ver. 12. *Handkerchiefs or aprons*] Which having been touched by Paul's body, became sovereign (by a miracle) to cure diseases and cast out devils.

Ver. 13. *Exorcists*] But of these (having no call from God, but unwarrantably emulating Paul, and yet using good words) we may say, as one doth of witches with their good prayers (as they call them), *Si magicæ, Deus non vult tales; si piæ, non per tales.* If magical, God will none of them; as if good prayers, yet because out of an evil mouth, he rejects them.

Ver. 14. *Seven sons of one Sceva*] All fathers, but especially ministers, should use all utmost care that their children be well educated and instructed; and not think it sufficient to say of them as Pope Paul III. did of his dissolute son Farnesius, *Hæc vitia me non commonstratore didicit*, He never learned it of his father.

Ver. 15. *Jesus I know, and Paul*] Jesus had destroyed his works, and Paul had felt his fingers, 2 Cor. xii. 7, and yet thrown him out of his trenches, 2 Cor. x. 4.

Ver. 16. *So that they fled out, &c.*] *Non omnia possumus omnes.* Albeit the eagle in the fable did bear away a lamb in her talons with full flight, yet a raven endeavouring to do the like was held entangled, and fettered in the fleece. Every exorcist must not think to do as Paul did, nor every preacher as Latimer did. He had my fiddle and my stick, said he of one that preached his sermons, but wanted my resin.

Ver. 17. *And fear fell on them all*] See the note on Acts v. 5.

Ver. 18. *Confessed and showed their deeds*] With detestation, being moved thereto by the fear of God's judgments. This they did publicly, not in the priest's ear, as Papists, nor out of a brain-sick humour, as the Anabaptists at Sangall (*Cæperunt plurimi enormia sua delicta profiteri, alius furta, alius adulteria, alius alia, non sine admiratione audientium, non sine stomacho conjugum maritis talibus nihil non imprecantium*, saith Scultetus); but with discretion and detestation. Oftentimes the very opening of men's grievances easeth the conscience, as the very opening of a vein cools the blood. Howbeit it is neither wisdom nor mercy to put men upon the rack of confession, further than they can have no ease any other way. (Dr Sibbes.)

Ver. 19. *Which used curious arts*] The Ephesians were much addicted to the black art. Whence that ancient proverb, Εφέσια γράμματα, Ephesian learning for necromancy. Cornelius Agrippa's dog had a devil tied to his collar, as some write. And Paracelsus (or else Erastus belies him) had one confined to his sword pommel.

Ver. 20. *So mightily grew the word of God and prevailed*] Happy it is for a people or person, when the word falls upon their spirits in the power of it, and subdues them; when the peace of God ruleth in their hearts (βραβενέτω, Col. iii. 15), and every high thought is so captivated to the obedience of Christ, that they can say, as Judg. viii. 22, "Rule thou over us," &c. "For thou hast delivered us from the hand of Midian."

Ver. 21. *Purposed in the spirit*] i. e. By the instinct of the Holy Spirit, his counsellor and conduct, by whom all his actions were moderated. So he went bound in the spirit, Acts xx. 22. So Simeon came by the spirit into the temple, Luke ii. 27. And so still, the steps of every good man are ordered by the Lord, Psal. xxxvii. 23.

Ver. 22. In Asia] i. e. At Ephesus, the chief city of Asia the Less. See the note on ver. 10.

Ver. 23. No small stir] Covetousness, as itself is idolatry, so it upholds idolatry (as here) under a pretext of piety. *Deos quisque sibi utiles cudit*, saith Epictetus. *Ubi utilitas, ibi pietas*, saith another. The Papists are sound in those points that touch not upon their profit, as in the doctrine of the Trinity, &c. Luther was therefore so much set against (as Erasmus told the Elector of Saxony) because he meddled with the pope's triple crown and the monks' fat paunches. (Scultet. Annal.)

Ver. 24. Which made silver shrines] Gr. temples, *Templa portatilia*, small portable temples, resembling that greater temple of Diana; as now the *Agnus Dei* among the Papists. (Beza.) Some say they were little houses or caskets to put the idols in. (Casaubon.) Others, small coins stamped with the image of that famous temple. (Piscator.) Idolatrous trinkets they were, such as brought no small gain to the craftsmen, to whom gain was godliness.

Ver. 25. By this craft we have our wealth] And wealth is the wordling's god, which he prizeth, as Micah did his mawmet; and can as hardly forego it. What a cursing made Micah's mother in the loss of her eleven hundred shekels of silver, Judg. xvii. 2, and what a hubbub raised Micah all the country over, when the Danites had despoiled him of his dunghill-deity, Judg. xviii. So did the silversmiths here, and they thought they had reason to be thus mad when their trade was taken away.

Ver. 26. They be no gods] The town-clerk then told a loud lie, ver. 7. Politicians think they may lawfully lie for peace' sake. Howbeit Paul decried Diana's temple and worship with better discretion than Abdias the bishop burnt down the temple of the fire (which the Persians worship) at Persepolis. Whereupon not only he himself was slain, but all the temples of the Christians throughout Persia were overthrown, and many Christians put to death; the Persian priests being their chief persecutors, A. D. 413. (Funccius.)

Ver. 27. This our craft] Whereof they had the patent, the monopoly, τὸ μέρος. *Dictio est mercimoniorum et negotiorum, in genere significans illud quod in divisione obvenit*, saith Lorinus. *Istud quod nobis est peculiare.* So Beza renders it.

To be set at nought] Gr. εἰς ἀπελεγμὸν ἐλθεῖν. To be refuted, disgraced, decried, and we greatly damnified. *Nobis refutatum intercidat.* (Beza.) This was the Diana they strove for, and about which they raised all this uproar. So the poor Waldenses were persecuted, not for detestation of their tenets, but out of a jealousy lest these men's plain-dealing should discover their drifts and mar their markets.

And her magnificence should be destroyed] Her majesty, μεγαλειότητα. *Utinam æque saltem reverenter de Dei nomine hodie homines loquerentur*, saith Malcolm. I would men would but use like reverence in speaking of the true God.

Ver. 28. They were full of wrath] The Greek word θυμός signifieth the heating or heaving of the blood by the apprehension of the injury offered; hot and fiery anger, such as was that of Nebuchadnezzar, seven-fold hotter than his fiery furnace, Dan. ii.

Great is Diana] Papists boast and write much of the Romish greatness, as Lipsius and others. We grant them to be that great whore in the Revelation, chap. xvii. 18.

Ver. 29. And the whole city was filled with confusion] See the note on chap. xvii. 1.

Ver. 30. The disciples suffered him not] i. e. They persuaded him otherwise, and prevailed. It is best, if a man can so order his affairs, as not to need the counsel of others. And the next best is to rest in good counsel, and to be ruled by it. But he that is uncounsellable is ripe for ruin, and that without remedy, Prov. xxix. 1.

Ver. 31. Certain of the chief of Asia] Not rulers, but priests, saith Beza, whose office was to set forth stage-players in honour of the gods. These, though bad enough, had some good affection to the Christian religion, and cautioned Paul not to come into the theatre. Christ finds some friends amongst the worst of men.

Ver. 32. Knew not wherefore, &c.] No more do the most of our common hearers. They follow the drove, and believe as the Church believeth. They will say, they come to Church to serve God; but who that God is, how to be served, wherein, and in whom to be served, they know not. *Si ventri bene sit, si lateri*, as Epicurus in Horace, if the belly may be filled, the back fitted, it sufficeth them.

Ver. 33. And they drew Alexander] The coppersmith, who was here near to martyrdom, yet afterwards made shipwreck of the faith, 1 Tim. i. 19, 20, and did the apostle much evil, and greatly withstood not his person only, but his preachings, 2 Tim. iv. 15, 16, which was a sin of a high and heinous nature.

Would have made his defence] He would have excused his countrymen the Jews (who therefore put him forward), and have turned all the rage of the people upon the apostles. But by a sweet providence of God he could not have audience.

Ver. 34. That he was a Jew] The Jews were generally hated of the Gentiles, and especially after their return from the Babylonish captivity, because they cried down all gods and religions but their own, and would never be drawn again to worship other gods, for which sin they had so exceedingly smarted. At this day the Jews for their inexpiable guilt in crucifying Christ, and their implacable hatred to his people, are by a common consent of nations banished out of the world, as it were. The very Turks themselves so hate the Jews for their crucifying Christ, that they used to say in detestation of a thing, *Judæus sim, si mentiar*, I would I might die a Jew then. Neither will they permit a Jew to turn Turk, unless he be first baptized.

All with one voice cried out, &c.] So the Papists

cry up, *ad ravim usque*, their Lady of Loretto, of Sichem, of Walsingham, &c., and have nothing in their mouths so much as the Church, the Church; wherein, like oyster-wives, they do easily out-cry us.

Ver. 35. *Great goddess Diana*] Who yet as great as she was, being busy at Alexander's birth (as he said), could not be at leisure to save her temple at Ephesus from burning. Like as Baal was so hot in the pursuit of his enemies, that he could not be at hand to help his friends, 1 Kings xviii. 27.

And of the image that fell] A very ancient image made by Canetias a certain artificer, and for the antiquity of it, said by the covetous priests to have fallen down from Jupiter, that it might be the more venerable. By a like craft the Popish priests now show some shivers of the cross whereon our Saviour suffered, yea, some shreds of the tail of that ass whereupon he rode to Jerusalem.

Ver. 36. *Ye ought to be quiet*] Or, sedate, composed, kept within compass, "to do nothing rashly or headlonly:" *Temeritas enim comitem τὴν μετάνοιαν ἔχει.*

Ver. 37. *Blasphemers of your goddess*] This was false: but this politician held it lawful to redeem peace with a lie. Not so St Paul, who knew that after his departure from Ephesus grievous wolves would enter in, Acts xx. 29. And yet because he could not stay to preach unless he would have restored some Pharisaical observations, and unless, for peace' sake, he would have yielded to the rites and image of Diana, he left the place, because he must not do the greatest good by any evil means.

Ver. 38, 39, &c.] As the town-clerk here quieted the tumultuating people, so ought we to compose unruly passions. Say to them, 1. Ye ought to do nothing rashly. 2. The law is open; so is God's ear, to whom vengeance belongeth. 3. We are in danger of this day's uproar, &c.

Ver. 39. *In a lawful assembly*] Such as this could not be. *Cum boni, cum probi coeunt, non est factio dicenda sed curia: ut e contrario, illis nomen factionis accommodandum est, qui in odium bonorum et proborum conspirant.* (Tertul. Apol., xxxix.)

Ver. 40. *For we are in danger*] Danger we all desire to decline, whether it be of life, limb, estate, &c., but venture our souls daily to the danger of damnation: this is practical atheism, rank folly.

Ver. 41. *Dismissed the assembly*] And so Demetrius was cozened. See here the power of civil prudence and flexanimous eloquence. (*Videsis* Cic. de Oratore, i.)

CHAPTER XX.

Ver. 1. *Into Macedonia*] GREAT Alexander's country, called at this day Albany, and is subject to the Turk.

Ver. 2. *Into Greece*] sc. To Corinth, whence he wrote the Epistle to the Romans.

Ver. 3. *And there abode three*] Gr. ποιήσας, "Was doing there," he was in continual action. Life consists in action; so doth spiritual life, Isa. xxxviii. 16. And by this reason one may live more in a month than another in many years. In this sense Seneca saith (Epist. lxvii.), *Quamvis vitæ paucos fecerimus dies.* See the same word used thus, Matt. xx. 12.

Ver. 4. *Sopater of Berea, Aristarchus and Secundus, &c.*] These all were the very "glory of Jesus Christ," 2 Cor. viii. 23, and yet counted the off-scouring of all things (περίψημα, 1 Cor. iv. 13): these precious sons of Zion, comparable to fine gold, were esteemed as earthen pitchers, Lam. iv. 2. These worthies of whom the world was not worthy, Heb. xi. 38, were cast out of the world as it were by an ostracism. These jewels of Jesus Christ, these "excellent ones of the earth," these earthly angels, were shamefully slighted, and trampled upon by the fat bulls of Bashan with the feet of insolency and cruelty. Howbeit as stars (though we see them sometimes in a puddle, though they reflect there, yet) have they their situation in heaven; so God's saints, though in a low condition, yet they are fixed in the region of happiness. Content they are to pass to heaven (as Christ their head did) as concealed men, and would not change estates with the earth's mightier monarchs.

Ver. 5. *Tarried for us at Troas*] See the note on chap. xvi. 8.

Ver. 6. *In five days*] Let them that please read here Ptolemy's first table of Asia, where they shall have this whole voyage of St Paul daintily described.

Ver. 7. *Continued his speech till midnight*] *Media nocte vigilabant, ut eos condemnent qui media die dormiunt*, saith Chrysostom. Jacob, fearing his brother, slept not all that night. If Samuel thought it had been God that spake to him, he would not have slept. Whilst Ishbosheth slept, Baanah and Rechab took off his head. After the disciples slept, being bidden watch, they fled from Christ and forswore him, Matt. xxvi. 40.

Ver. 8. *And there were many lights*] Night-meetings are lawful, and, in some cases, needful; though carnal men will calumniate, and muse as they use. Caligula thought there was not a chaste man upon earth, because himself was most detestably unchaste.

Ver. 9. *Being fallen into a deep sleep*] Woe to many now-a-days, when God shall once send out summonses for sleepers.

Ver. 10. *His life is in him*] After that Paul prayed for him, life returned; or else because he knew it should return, he speaks of it as a done thing.

Ver. 11. *And eaten*] After the celebration of the Lord's supper, followed the use of daily food. *Animantis cujusque vita est in fuga*, saith the philosopher; so that were it not for the repair of nutrition, natural life would be soon extinguished. So would spiritual life also.

Ver. 12. *And were not a little comforted*] Not so much for the young man's recovery, as for the love of God sealed up unto them therein: this was the kernel, the other but the shell.

Ver. 13. *Assos*] A chief city of Mysia, called also Apollonia, on the Asiatic shore.

To go a-foot] Haply for his health's sake, or for more conveniency of visiting the brethren, whose edification he minded more than his own ease.

Ver. 14, 15. *Mytilene*] An island of the Cyclades, now called Metelino. See what great difficulties these good men devoured for the glory of God and good of his people. The love of Christ constrained them (*amor addidit alas*) and the recompense of reward in heaven quickened them; *Quis enim non patiatur, ut potiatur?* Who would not suffer for such a felicity?

Ver. 16. *To be at Jerusalem*] Not so much to observe the legal rites, which he knew to be then abrogated (only *sepelienda erat synagoga cum honore*), as to edify the Church, by declaring to the faithful there how Christ's kingdom was propagated abroad, and by confuting the slanderous aspersions cast upon him by evil-minded men.

Ver. 17. *From Miletus*] A city of Asia, lower than Ephesus.

Ver. 18. *Ye know*] This the apostle speaketh, not out of vain-glory or desire of popular applause, but partly for their imitation (all things in a minister should be eximious and exemplary), and partly to procure credit to his doctrine by setting forth the holiness of his life; sith *quod jussit, et gessit*, as Bernard, *nec verbis solum prædicavit, sed et exemplis*, as Eusebius saith of Origen, he did what he taught; and his life was nothing else but a transcript of his sermons. This would be a real apology for him against the false apostles.

Ver. 19. *Serving the Lord, &c.*] Here is a mirror for ministers.

Ver. 20. *With many tears*] He went weeping from house to house, beseeching them to be reconciled to God, persuading them, as knowing the terror of the Lord, 2 Cor. v. 10.

Ver. 21. *Testifying*] Not barely preaching, but vehemently pressing (as matters of greatest importance).

Repentance towards God] Not a desperate repentance (as was that of Judas), that drives men from God, but such as draws them towards him, and brings them before him, submitting to his justice, and imploring his mercy, as at the meet at Mizpeh, 1 Sam. vii. 5.

Faith towards Jesus Christ] Repentance is put first, because initial repentance is a preparation to effectual faith. See Mark i. 15, with the note.

Ver. 22. *I go bound in the spirit*] Paul's spirit did not hang loose, but it was girt up in a resolution to go through with the work, whatsoever came of it. The Spirit hems us about, comprehends and keeps us, when a man's own strength would fall loose. It is not so with every ungirt gospeller, that hath a loose, discinct, and diffluent mind, and no supernatural strength to support him.

Ver. 23. *Bonds and afflictions abide me*] Let no faithful minister dream of a delicacy, or think by any discretion to prevent affliction, but be ready, as a good soldier of Jesus Christ, to suffer hardship. To preach is nothing else but to derive upon himself the hate and rage of graceless men, saith Luther.

Ver. 24. *Neither count I my life dear*] *Singula prope verba spirant martyrium*, as one saith of Cyprian's writings. When one said to Julius Palmer the martyr, Take heed, it is a hard matter to burn; Indeed, said he, it is for him that hath his soul linked to his body, as a thief's foot in a pair of fetters. Amongst all the vain mockeries of this world (said the Duke of Somerset at his death in King Edward VI.'s time) I repent me of nothing more than of esteeming life more dear than I should.

Ver. 25. *Shall see my face no more*] viz. In the flesh, and upon earth. But in heaven we shall see and say, ἰδοὺ ὁ Παῦλος καὶ ὁ Πέτρος (as Chrysostom thinks), Lo, that is Paul, and the other is Peter. In the transfiguration, Peter knew Moses and Elias, as if he had been long acquainted with them. And yet that was but a glimpse of heaven.

Ver. 26. *I take you to record*] Happy is that man that can be acquitted by himself private, in public by others, in both by God.

I am pure from the blood of all men] The apostle hath an eye here (doubtless) to that flaming place of Ezek. iii. 18, "His blood will I require at thine hands;" which words are *fulmina, non verba*, saith Erasmus, not words, but light-bolts.

Ver. 27. *All the counsel of God*] sc. that concerneth you to know, to your eternal salvation by Christ alone. See Luke vii. 30, with the note.

Ver. 28. *Hath made you overseers*] ἐπισκόπους. But many are *Aposcopi* rather than *Episcopi*, saith Espensæus; by-seers rather than overseers.

Which he hath purchased with his blood] The Church is to Christ a bloody spouse, an Aceldama, or field of blood; for she could not be redeemed with silver and gold, but with the blood of God; so it is called by a communication of properties, to set forth the incomparable value and virtue thereof.

Ver. 29. *Shall grievous wolves enter*] Or fat wolves: for βαρὺς in Greek comes of בְּרִיא in Hebrew, which signifies fat, as some etymologists have observed; a fit epithet for seducers, which fat themselves with the blood of souls. Now it is well observed that heretical seducers are fitly compared to wolves in divers respects. First, wolves are dull-sighted by day, but quick-sighted in the night;[1] so are pernicious seducers sharp-witted for error, but dull to apprehend the truth of sound divinity. Secondly, as the wolf deals gently with the sheep at first, carrying it away unhurt upon his back till he have brought it to the place where he means to strangle it:

---

[1] *Lupus interdiu oltusius, nocte clarius videt.* Gesner.

even so deal seducers; they first draw their proselytes into lighter errors, and then into blasphemous and damnable heresies. And thus *homo homini lupus est*, one man becomes a wolf to another. Thirdly, as a wolf begets a wolf, so doth a deceiver a deceived.[1] Fourthly, as the wolf is said to strike a man dumb, if he spy the man before the man spy him;[2] so when seducers prevail, they strike men dumb in respect of savoury communication or Christian profession. Fifthly, as the wool of a wolf, if it be made into a garment, will prove but an odious garment, breeding vermin upon him that shall wear it, as Plutarch speaks; so the good which poor seduced souls think they receive by impostors, it will prove corruption in the end. Lastly, as wolves are of a ravenous disposition and insatiable, so seducers hunger after gain, Rom. xvi. 18, and thirst after blood of souls, as those Matt. xxiii. 6.

Ver. 30. *To draw away disciples*] ἀποσπᾶν, to tear them limb-meal by a violent avulsion and distraction, compelling them by their persuasions to embrace those distorted doctrines, διεστραμμένα, that produce convulsions of conscience, Deut. xiii. 5. Such are said to thrust men out of God's ways.

Ver. 31. *Night and day with tears*] Good men weep easily, saith the Greek poet;[3] and the better any is, the more inclined to weeping; as David than Jonathan, 1 Sam. xx. Some (as they say of witches) cannot weep for sin. But they that weep not here, where there are wiping handkerchiefs in the hands of Christ, shall have their eyes whipt out in hell.

Ver. 32. *Able to build*] As being God's arm, and mighty instruments of his power, 1 Cor. i. 18; Rom. i. 16.

Ver. 33. *I have coveted no man's, &c.*] *Non opes, non gloriam, non voluptates quæsivi, &c. Hanc conscientiam aufero quocunque discedo*, said Melancthon. (Melch. Adam.)

Ver. 34. *These hands have ministered*] More shame for them to suffer it. *Sed rara ingeniorum præmia, rara item et merces*, saith one; and *Nescio quomodo bonæ mentis soror est paupertas*, saith Petronius; and, *Paupertas est philosophiæ vernacula*, saith Apuleius. Let God's servants keep them honest, the world will keep them poor enough.

Ver. 35. *It is more blessed*] Epicurus could say, τοῦ εὖ πάσχειν τό εὖ ποιεῖν καλλίον καὶ ἥδιον, that to do good was not only better, but sweeter also than to receive good. Julius Cæsar counted nothing his own that he bestowed not upon others. And it better pleased Cyrus to give than to possess any good thing that he had. Διδοὺς μᾶλλον ἢ κτώμενος ἥδεται. (Xenoph.)

Ver. 36. *And prayed with them all*] *O verum valedicendi morem Christianis dignum*, saith one. Now it's no parting without potting and healthing. *Quæ turpissima* κυκλοποσία, *Principum derisio, à parasitis traxit originem*, saith Pasor.

Which cursed custom had its beginning from court-parasites.

Ver. 37. *And they all wept sore*] *Expletur lachrymis egeriturque dolor*. It was noted and noticed by the very heathens that there were no people under heaven so loving one to another as the primitive Christians: *animo animaque inter se miscebantur*, saith Tertullian of them: it should seem so indeed by this mutual melting-heartedness. Well might the heathen beholders say, *Vide ut invicem se ament Christiani*, See how these Christians love one another; like as the Jews when they saw Jesus weep over Lazarus, said, "Behold how he loved him," John xi.

Ver. 38. *Sorrowing most*] They are out, then, *qui ferream et immanem constantiam exigunt a fidelibus*, who exact of Christians a stoical apathy or insensibleness to crosses and sorrowful occurrences. (Calvin.) Religion doth not root out natural passions, but regulate them. The parting with dear friends (which are as a man's own soul, Deut. xiii. 6) is so grievous that death itself is called a "departure."

CHAPTER XXI.

Ver. 1. *We came with a straight course*] εὐθυδρομήσαντες. So shall all those that make "straight paths for their feet," Heb. xii. 13, whose eye-lids look straight before them, Prov. iv. 25, who ponder their paths by the weights of the word, ver. 26.

Ver. 2. *Phœnicia*] A region of Syria: the woman of Canaan was a Syrophœnician.

Ver. 3. *Now when we had discovered Cyprus*] *Vox nautica*, a mariner's term; so is συνεσταλμένος, 1 Cor. vii. 29. St Paul was a great trader of Christ both by land and sea; and had terms ready for both. See the note there.

Ver. 4. *And finding disciples*] Such as Isaiah had long since foretold should leave hoarding and heaping wealth, and find another manner of employment for it, to feed and clothe God's saints, Isa. xxiii. 18.

That he should not go up, &c.] They understanding by his divine revelation, what danger Paul was in, out of charity, and not by any special command of the Spirit, forewarned him, and desired him not to go up.

Ver. 5. *And prayed*] See the note on chap. xx. 36.

Ver. 6. *We took ship*] Leaving them on shore: we shall one day meet, and never more be separated. *O dieculam illam, &c. Euge, Deo sit laus et gloria, quod jam instet horula illa gratissima.*[4] O that day! O that joy! *Castigemus mores et moras*. (Bernard.) Let us ripen apace, and hasten to that heavenly home, that glorious panegyris, Heb. xii. 23.

Ver. 7. *And abode with them one day*] *Suavis hora, sed parva mora*, short and sweet abode.

Ver. 8. *Philip the Evangelist*] He was at first

---

[1] *Omne simile generat sibi simile.* Plin. viii. 22.
[2] *Lupi me videre priores.* Virg.

[3] ἀγαθοὶ δ᾽ ἀριδάκρυες ἄνδρες.
[4] *Greserus moribundus.* Melch. Adam.

but a deacon ; but having well used that lower office, he was advanced to this. A fruitful man shall not sit long in a low place : God will call him forth to a higher employment, and make him master of much, that was so " faithful in a little," Luke xvi.

Ver. 9. *Did prophesy*] That is, they had the gift of foretelling future things by divine inspiration. This was every way extraordinary.

Ver. 10. *A certain prophet*] So called *a procul fando*, as some will have it. These New Testament prophets were next to the apostles in office ; and are mentioned together with them in laying the foundation of Christianity, Eph. iii. 5, ii. 20.

Ver. 11. *So shall the Jews*] Who were ever most bitter enemies to Christians, and so they continue. Among the Turks every vizier and pasha of state useth to keep a Jew of his private council ; whose malice, wit, and experience of Christendom, with their continual intelligence, is thought to advise most of that mischief which the Turk puts in execution against us. Are those then well-advised that desire that the Jews may have free commerce amongst us, as they have in Poland ? where they not only curse all Christians publicly in their daily prayers, but boldly print against our religion whatsoever they please ? (Buxtorf. Synag. Jud.)

Ver. 13. *What mean you to weep ?*] Ecclesiastical history mentioneth one Phileas, a nobleman and a martyr, who going to execution, seemed as one deaf at the persuasions and blind at the tears of his friends ; *Nam quomodo potest terrenis lachrymis flecti cujus oculi cœlestem gloriam contuentur ?* said one Philoramus defending him, and was therefore beheaded with him.

I am ready, not to be bound] This was a brave Roman resolution. *Necesse est ut eam, non ut vivam*, said Pompey. The Lacedæmonians were wont to say, It is a shame for any man to fly in time of danger ; but for a Lacedæmonian, it is a shame for him to deliberate. How much more for a Christian, when called by God to suffer ! Go (said Luther), I will surely go (sith I am sent for) in the name of our Lord Jesus Christ, yea, though I knew there were so many devils to resist me as there are tiles to cover the houses in Worms. Spalatinus had sent to Luther, to inquire whether or no he would go to Worms, and appear in the gospel's cause, if Cæsar summoned him ; *Omnia de me præsumas* (said he) *præter fugam, et palinodiam. Fugere nolo, multo minus recantare. Ita me confortet Dominus.* Socrates would not hearken to his friend Criton, persuading him to shift for himself by a dishonourable flight. And when some friends dealt with Dr Taylor, martyr, not to appear before Stephen Winchester, but to fly ; Fly you (said he), and do as your conscience leads you ; I am fully determined, with God's grace, to go to the bishop, and to his beard to tell him that he doth naught. True zeal is of a most masculine, dis-

engaged, courageous nature, and ready to say, Shall I change mine opinion, because *Hoc Ithacus velit ?* remit of my diligence for fear of death ? Oh that I might enjoy those wild beasts prepared for my torments, said blessed Ignatius.[1] And oh that it might be so with me, said Basil, threatened with death by Valens the Arian emperor.[2] So we read of another holy bishop, who when his hand was threatened to be cut off, cried out, *Seca ambas*, nay, cut off both.

Ver. 14. *The will of the Lord be done*] *Vox vere Christianorum*, saith one, *Voluntas Dei, necessitas rei.* A godly man says Amen to God's Amen ; and puts his *Fiat* and *Placet* to God's. One said, he could have what he would of God. Why ? how was that ? Because whatsoever was God's will, that was his. It is said that I shall be burned in Smithfield (said blessed Bradford), and that very shortly, *Fiat voluntas Domini : Ecce ego, mitte me.* Mr Beza's last text was the third petition of the Lord's prayer, " Thy will be done," &c. *In qua deficere potius quam desinere visus est*, saith he that writeth his life. (Melch. Adam.)

Ver. 15. *We took up our carriages*] A military term ; we trussed up our fardels, made up our packs, our bag and baggage, ἐπισκευασάμενοι, *instructi et comparati ad quævis nimirum pericula subeunda*, said Beza, being ready prest and prepared to whatsoever hazard.

Ver. 16. *An old disciple*] A gray-headed experienced Christian, a father, 1 John ii. 13. Such as those mentioned Psal. xcii. 12—14. A Christian hath his degrees of growth. Ye have his conception, Gal. iv. 19 ; birth, 1 Pet. i. 13 ; childhood, 1 Cor. iii. 1, 2 ; youth or well-grown age, when he is past the spoon, 1 John ii. 13 ; his full-grown age, Eph. iv. 13 ; old age, as 1 John ii. 13, and here. An "old disciple," and yet a disciple still not too old to learn. Solon said, I wax old ever learning somewhat.[3] Julianus, the lawyer, said, that when he had one foot in the grave, yet he would have the other in the school. Chytreus, when he lay a dying, lift up himself to hear the discourse of some friends that visited him ; and said, that he should die with so much the better cheer if he might better his knowledge by what they were speaking of. (Melch. Adam.)

With whom he should lodge] viz. When we came to Jerusalem. This Mnason was another Gaius, the host of the Church. The Waldenses were so spread in Germany that they could travel from Colen to Milan in Italy, and every night lodge with hosts of their own profession, which was a great comfort to them. (Cade of the Church.)

Ver. 17. *Received us gladly*] Gr. ἀσμένως, smilingly. *Dat bene, dat multum, qui dat cum munere vultum.* When we come to the new Jerusalem, the whole court of heaven shall meet us, and greet us with great joy.

Ver. 18. *Unto James*] The son of Alpheus,

---

[1] Ὀναίμην τῶν θηρίων τῶν ἐμοὶ ἡτοιμασμένων.
[2] Εἴθε γένοιτο μοί.

[3] Γηράσκω αἴει πολλὰ διδασκόμενος.

called by St Mark, "James the less," and by some of the ancients, Bishop of Jerusalem.

Ver. 19. *He declared particularly*] Gr. καθ' ἓν ἕκαστον, "one by one." So Moses tells Jethro all things one by one what God had done for Israel, Exod. xviii. 8. We must not relate God's loving-kindness in the lump or by wholesale, but be punctual and particular.

Ver. 20. *Many thousands*] Therefore not to be slighted.

Ver. 21. *To forsake Moses*] An odious and false imputation. All that St Paul taught was, that the legal rites and customs were only shadows of things to come, but the body is of Christ, Col. ii. 17; and that Christians should know and use their freedom in wisdom and charity, Gal. ii. 3; 1 Cor. viii. 13.

Ver. 22. *The multitude must needs come together*] And be satisfied, for else that sinister opinion which they have conceived of thee will be increased, and they will take all for granted that is alleged against thee. Now a heathen sage could say (and there is much truth in it), *Negligere quid de se quisque sentiat, non solum arrogantis est, sed et dissoluti*: It is a sign of a proud lewd person not to care what people think of him.

Ver. 23. *A vow on them*] A voluntary vow of Nazariteship, which yet is agreeable to the law's præscript.

Ver. 24. *And all may know*] There is a real confutation of calumnies.

Ver. 25. *And from fornication*] See the note on Acts xv. 20.

Ver. 26. *Purifying himself*] See Augustine's Epistles 11 and 19.

Ver. 27. *The Jews which were of Asia*] St Paul's good intent had but evil success; but his conscience was his comfort, as 2 Cor. i. 9, 12. So was holy Melancthon's; when but coarsely dealt with, and threatened with banishment,[1] this he could say for himself, I have not sought for myself wealth, honour, pleasure, or victory over mine adversaries. This conscience I take with me, whithersoever they shall drive me.

Ver. 28. *Crying, Men of Israel, help, this is the man*, &c.] An admirable and graphical description of this tumult; every circumstance set forth to the life as it were. No poet could have done it with more skill and artifice. There is as good rhetoric in the Bible as in any heathen orator whatsoever. It was therefore a foolish and profane fear of Politian, Longolius, Bonamicus, and other Logodædali, that if they should read the Scriptures, they should mar the purity of their style. "This is the man that teacheth," &c. There is not a true word in all this outcry. So Elias was called a troubler, Luther a trumpeter of rebellion, Melancthon a blasphemer of God and his saints, Calvin a Mahometan, Zanchius an Anabaptist, a Swenckfeldian, Novatian, and what not? Arminius paved his way first by aspersing and sugillating the fame and authority of

Calvin, Zuinglius, Beza, Martyr, and other champions of the truth. The Papists reported the Waldenses (those ancient Protestants) to be Manichees, Arians, Catharists, &c., as they do us to be libertines, enthusiasts, atheists, &c. *Contra sycophantæ morsum non est remedium*. They set their mouths against heaven, and their tongue walketh through the earth, Psal. lxxiii. 9. But God will cut out such false tongues, Psal. xii. 3, and broil them upon coals of juniper, Psal. cxx. 4.

Ver. 29. *Whom they supposed*] But was that sufficient ground to make such a coil, to raise such an uproar? Passions are head-long and head-strong; like heavy bodies down steep hills, once in motion, they move themselves, and know no ground but the bottom.

Ver. 30. *The doors were shut*] That he might not there take sanctuary.

Ver. 31. *And as they went about to kill him*] The devil was first a liar and then a murderer. The persecutors ever first belied the Church, and then did their worst against her. Slander is a kind of murder, and makes way for it, Ezek. xxii. 9, as in the massacre of Paris. The monks had given out before that the Protestants met for no other purpose but to feast their carcases, and then (the lights being put out) to satisfy their unlawful lusts promiscuously. Thus they prepared and provoked the people to that bloody butchery, and so slew the innocent Huguenots twice; like as it is said of Humphrey, Duke of Gloucester, that he was thought by the people of England to be doubly murdered, viz. by detraction and deadly practice.

Ver. 32. *Who immediately took soldiers*] An admirable example of God's good providence, who delighteth to reserve his hand for a dead-lift, to save those that are forsaken of their hopes. He cometh unlooked for, as it were out of an engine, ἀπὸ μηχανῆς.

They left beating of Paul] Who could better bear it, because he had felt worse fingers than theirs, when that messenger of Satan buffeted him, 2 Cor. xii. And surely if the philosopher (when brayed in a mortar by his cruel Scythians) could bear it patiently, saying, Beat on Anacharsis' wind-bang, meaning his body,[2] much more could the apostle by the force of his faith. Especially, since his suffering reached only to his flesh, his soul was untouched thereby, Col. i. 24.

Ver. 33. *To be bound with two chains*] As if he would have presently punished him. This he did to satisfy the mad multitude.

Ver. 34. *For the tumult*] All was on a hurry, as it was chap. xix. at Ephesus, *vel ut in regno Cyclopico*.

Into the castle] Called Antonia, near the temple, where the soldiers kept garrison.

Ver. 35. *He was borne of the soldiers*] Who considered as little what a precious pack they now had upon their backs, as once the Midianitish merchants did, what a price they had in their

---

[1] *Dixerunt adversarii se mihi non relicturos esse vestigium pedis in Germ.*

[2] *Tundite Anach. folliculum.*

hands, viz. Joseph, the jewel of the world and lord of Egypt.

Ver. 36. *Away with him*] Yea, but stay, Paul's time was in God's hand, who had told him that after he had been at Jerusalem he must see Rome too. In the mean time it might be some comfort to Paul to hear the same words (and perhaps by the same men) used of him, as had been before of his Master Christ, Away with him, &c. It is sufficient for the servant to be as his Lord. Art thou not glad to fare as Phocion? said he to one that was to suffer with him.[1] Holy Ignatius took great comfort in this, that though he suffered death for Christ, yet in the day when God should make up his jewels, he should reckon not only from the blood of righteous Abel to the blood of Zacharias son of Barachias, but from the blood of Zacharias to the blood of mean Ignatius. We have mentioned before that martyr that rejoiced that she might have her foot in the hole of the stocks in which Mr Philpot had been before her. When Luther thought he should die of an apoplexy, it comforted him that the apostle John had died of that disease. How much more should it do us, that we "fill up that only which is behind of the afflictions of Christ in our flesh," Col. i. 24, and that suffering together, we shall also reign together!

Ver. 37. *Canst thou speak Greek*] Ay, no man better, whensoever he pleased; witness his gallant apology to Tertullus, chap. xxiv., and again his most accurate apology to Agrippa, chap. xxvi., wherein (Pericles-like) *fulgurabat, intonabat*, &c., he lightened one while, thundered another, did what he would with his audience, became master of their affections, being as potent in his divine rhetoric as Cicero in his human; who, as it is said, while he pleaded for Ligarius, disarmed the angry emperor and got pardon for the poor suppliant.

Ver. 38. *Art not thou that Egyptian?*] Of whom read Joseph. ii. 10, de Bello Jud., and Antiq. xx.

That were murderers] Assassins, cut-throats. These were of the faction of Judas Gaulonites or Galileus. See Luke xiii. 1. (Godw. Heb. Antiq.)

Ver. 39. *Of no mean city*] And yet more ennobled by Paul than Paul was by it; like as Hippo was better known by Austin than Austin was by Hippo, whereof he was bishop; the Island Co by Hippocrates than Hippocrates by Co; King Archelaus by his friend Euripides than Euripides by Archelaus.

Ver. 40. *In the Hebrew tongue*] i. e. In the Syriac, a daughter of the Hebrew, and the mother tongue of them who were called Hebrews.

CHAPTER XXII.

Ver. 1. *Men, brethren, and fathers*] THEY that spake for themselves before the Areopagites in Athens, were required to do it ἄνευ παθῶν καὶ

προοιμίων, without passions or prefaces, not so here.

Ver. 2. *In the Hebrew tongue*] See the note on chap. xxi. 41.

Ver. 3. *At the feet of Gamaliel*] Among the Jews, the Rabbi sat, termed וישב or the sitter: the scholar was called מהאבק or one that lies along in the dust, a token of the scholar's humility, subjecting himself even to the feet of his teacher, as here, and Luke x. 39, and 2 Kings ii. 5. Knowest thou not that the Lord will take thy master from thine head? A phrase taken from their manner of sitting in the schools. This same custom (saith one) it is thought St Paul laboured to bring into the Christian Church, 1 Cor. xiv. 6. (Godw. Antiq. Heb.)

And was zealous toward God] With a blind zeal, which is no better than mettle in a blind horse, than fire on the chimney-top, than the devil in the demoniac, which threw him into the fire sometimes, and sometimes into the water.

Ver. 4—6, &c.] See the notes on chap. ix. 1, 2, &c.

Ver. 8. *I am Jesus of Nazareth*] Why saith our Saviour, Jesus of Nazareth? Doth any good come out of Nazareth? Why saith he not rather, I am Jesus the Son of God, the heir of the world? &c. Nazareth was a reproach cast upon Christ; and he glories in it: should not we prefer the reproach of Christ before the highest honour the world can do us?

Ver. 9. *But they heard not*] See the note on Acts ix. 7.

Ver. 10—13.] See Acts ix. 16, 17, &c.

Ver. 14. *Hath chosen thee*] Gr. προεχειρίσατο, hath handled thee beforehand. Beza, "hath designed thee." Erasmus, "hath prepared thee," viz. by unhorsing and blinding thee. *Schola Crucis, schola lucis.*

Ver. 15. *Of what thou hast seen*] sc. When rapt into the third heaven, 2 Cor. xii. 2, which might very well be in that three days' darkness. See the note on Acts ix. 9.

Ver. 16. *Wash away thy sins*] By being inwardly baptized in the blood of Christ, by his merit and spirit. For there is *baptismus flaminis, et baptismus fluminis*, Matt. iii. 11; hence we read of baptisms, Heb. vi. 2, and of the washing of regeneration, and renewing of the Holy Ghost, Tit. iii. 5. See Acts ii. 38, with the note.

Ver. 17. *Even while I prayed*] Then especially God's people are rapt and ravished. See the note on chap. x. 10.

Ver. 18. *They will not receive*] And I have ordained thee for a better purpose than to lie idle. He therefore that heareth, let him hear, and he that forbeareth, let him forbear. God will not always be with men in the opportunities of grace, but make them know the worth by the want, Ezek. iii. 27.

Ver. 19. *Lord, they know that I imprisoned*] Therefore no wonder though they of Jerusalem reject my testimony, as a light giddy-headed fellow,

---

[1] οὐκ ἀγαπᾶς μετὰ Φωκίωνος ἀποθανούμενος. Plut. Apoph.

who now teach that religion that I lately persecuted; *sed præstat herbam dare quam turpiter pugnare.* Luther was counted and called an apostate, he confessed the action; but blessed God that had given him grace to fall off from the devil. Bugenhagius having read some few leaves of Luther's book *de Captivitate Babylonica,* rashly pronounced Luther the most pestilent heretic that ever troubled the Church. But shortly after, reading the book through, and wisely weighing the arguments therein used and urged, he recanted his former censure, and publicly averred and maintained that all the Christian world was out, and Luther only in the right; *Hic vir unus et solus verum videt,* said he to his collegioners; many of whom he convinced and converted to the truth. (Scult. Annal.) It is judged by many that the fear of disgrace began to work upon Paul here (as it had done upon Jonah, iv. 2), *q. d.* I shall be counted a moon-calf; a *Retraxit* shall be entered against me, as is against a plaintiff that will not proceed in his suit.

Ver. 20. *When the blood of thy martyr*] An honour not afforded to any angel in heaven, said Father Latimer. God forgive me mine unthankfulness, said Bradford, for this, that I must die a martyr, that Christ will be magnified in my mortal body, whether it be by life or by death. Stephen, Christ's proto-martyr! Antipas, my faithful martyr! what an high style is this! Ignatius professed that he had rather be a martyr than a monarch. He called his bonds his spiritual pearls, and triumphed in his voyage to Rome to suffer, to think that his blood should be found among the mighty worthies, such as Abel, Stephen, Antipas, &c.[1]

Ver. 21. *And he said unto me, Depart*] Which good Paul was full loth to do; having (with the vine-dresser in the Gospel, Luke xiii. 8) both digged and begged for his unworthy countrymen, till there was no remedy, 2 Chron. xxxvi. 16, till the very last period of their day of grace, Acts xiii. 46. See the note there.

Ver. 22. *And they gave him audience*] The Jews to this day will not hear of the Gentiles having any interest in their Messiah, they call us bastard Gentiles, and curse us Christians in their daily prayers, with a *Maledic Domine Nazaræis.* They stick not to say that rather than we should have any benefit by their Messiah, they would crucify him a hundred times over. Thus to this present they please not God, and are contrary to all men, 1 Thess. ii. 15. We must pity them and pray for them, as Psal. xiv. 7. Lopez the traitor, at Tyburn, affirmed that he loved Queen Elizabeth as he loved Jesus Christ; which from a Jew was heard not without laughter. (Camd. Eliz.)

Ver. 23. *And as they cried*] A graphical description of their unreasonable rage and rout. Well might our Saviour say, Beware of men acted and agitated by the devil, Matt. x. 17; and St Paul pray to be delivered from absurd and wicked men, 2 Thess. iii. 2, as bad as those

beasts that he encountered at Ephesus, 1 Cor. xv. 32. Let a bear robbed of her whelps meet a man rather than a fry of furious fools in their folly, Prov. xvii. 12.

Ver. 24. *Examined by scourgings*] Politicians consider not oft what is just, but what is of use for the present purpose, be it right or wrong. Paul is here commanded to be scourged, and then examined. This is *hysteron proteron,* justice turned topsy-turvy.

Ver. 25. *A man that is a Roman*] A citizen of Rome might neither be bound nor beaten. See the note on Acts xvi. 37. Paul by this freedom escaped whipping; we by that which Christ hath purchased us, not for gold or silver, but his own blood, 1 Pet. i. 19, escape the pain of eternal torment.

Ver. 26. *This man is a Roman*] The centurion might believe St Paul upon his bare word, because if any claimed that privilege and could not prove it, he was to die for so doing.

Ver. 27. *He said, Yea*] And withal he made it out (likely) by sufficient proof to be so; he produced some convincing evidence, though it be not here recorded. All God's people are fellow-citizens with the saints, burgesses of the new Jerusalem, free denizens of heaven, Ephes. ii. 19; Heb. xii. 23; where their names are enrolled long since, as the manner was at Rome, and likewise at Jerusalem, Psal. xlviii. 3. But they must look up their evidences, and be able to prove their interest by irrefragable arguments, when Satan shall roar upon them and shake his chain at them. It should be our care and study to find out that which Luke calls the certainty, chap. i. 4, and not be led by conjectural suppositions, but be fully persuaded, ver. 1, and get such a victorious faith as the gates of hell may not prevail against. God is no way wanting to us herein, as having made heaven ours both by covenant and his testament. His covenant he hath written not only in his word, but also in our hearts; and we have witnesses thereof, three in heaven, and three on earth; his seals also and oath to confirm it. And lest we should think that covenant may break, he hath likewise given us heaven by testament, confirmed by the death of the Testator. A certainty therefore may be had of our interest in heaven, of our names written there; and that is an ignorant distinction among Papists, that men may have a certainty of hope, but not of faith in matters of salvation.

Ver. 28. *With a great sum*] Or, with long service. This privilege was first sold at a dear rate to foreigners, but afterwards for a small matter. (Dio in Claudio.)

But I was freeborn] Tarsus, Paul's country, was a Roman colony, and made free of Rome by M. Antonius.

Ver. 29. *Then straightway they departed from him*] Thus wonderfully and opportunely doth the Lord free his people, sometimes, from evils and enemies, when in human apprehension there is no way of escape.

[1] τὰ δεσμὰ περιφέρω τοὺς πνευματικοὺς μαργαρίτας. Ep. ad Ephes.

Ver. 30. *And brought Paul down*] sc. From the castle, or from the rock Antonia. See chap. xxi. 34.

CHAPTER XXIII.

Ver. 1. *In all good conscience*] GOOD, both with the goodness of integrity and of tranquillity. *A recta conscientia transversum unguem non oportet quenquam in omni sua vita discedere*, saith Cicero (Ep. ad Attic.). Let a man keep his conscience clear. Better offend all the world than conscience.

Ver. 2. *To smite him on the mouth*] So when Henry Zutphen, martyr, was bound hard to a ladder and cast into the fire, he no sooner began to pray and to repeat his creed, but one struck him upon the face with his fist, saying, Thou shalt first be burned, and afterwards pray and prate as much as thou wilt. (Acts and Mon.)

Ver. 3. *God shall smite thee*] He was afterwards cruelly slain by Manaimus, a captain of the Jews in the beginning of the Jewish wars. As Master Bradford went towards the stake, he was met by a brother-in-law of his, called Roger Beswick, which as soon as he had taken Bradford by the hand, Woodroof, sheriff of London, came with his staff and brake the said Roger's head, that the blood ran about his shoulders. But within half a year after, God so struck Woodroof on the right side with a palsy, or whatever it was, that for eight years' space, to his dying day, he was not able to turn himself in his bed, &c.

Thou whited wall] That is, thou hypocrite, Matt. xxiii. 27. So Master Philpot, martyr, to Doctor Morgan that scoffed him, I must now tell thee (said he), thou painted wall and hypocrite, that God shall rain fire and brimstone upon such scorners of his word and blasphemers of his people as thou art. What an arrogant fool is this (said Bonner to Philpot), I will handle thee like an heretic and that shortly. I fear nothing (answered Philpot) that you can do to me; but God shall destroy such as thou art; and that shortly, as I trust. So when Shaxton, Bishop of Salisbury, said to William Wolsey, martyr, and some others with him, Good brethren, remember yourselves and become new men; for I myself was in this fond opinion that you are now in, but I am become a new man; Wolsey replied, Ah, you are become a new man! Woe be to thee, thou wicked new man; for God shall justly judge thee, &c.

Ver. 4. *Revilest thou God's high priest?*] Some think it was not the high priest himself, but his surrogate, such as Dic of Dover was to the Archbishop of Canterbury, active against the martyrs in Queen Mary's days, and known by that name.

Ver. 5. *I wist not, brethren*] Whether he spake seriously or ironically it is doubtful. He might not know him, as having been long absent from Jerusalem. Or his present heat might so darken his judgment, that he might not for present acknowledge the high priest's authority. It was certainly some disadvantage to Paul, that (although provoked and unjustly smitten) he called the high priest whited wall; he was glad to excuse it by his ignorance. We may not be too bold or too forward to speak in a good matter, lest we overshoot. Luther confessed before the emperor at Worms, that in his books against private and singular persons he had been more vehement than his religion and profession required. And he cried our Henry VIII. mercy for his uncivil handling of him.

Ver. 6. *But when Paul perceived*] Paul wanted not human prudence; wise as serpents we should be to improve all advantages that we may with the safety of our consciences. Religion doth not call us to a weak simplicity; but allows us as much of the serpent as of the dove. The dove without the serpent is easily caught; the serpent without the dove stings deadly. Their match makes themselves secure, and many happy.

Of the hope and resurrection] For *fiducia Christianorum est resurrectio mortuorum*, saith Tertullian. Christians look for great things at that great day, and in that other world, which the Hebrews call *sæculum mercedis*, the world of wages.

Ver. 7. *A dissension betwixt the Pharisees*] So among Papists, the priests disparage the Jesuits, the Jesuits the priests, the priests again the monks, the monks the friars, and the Jesuits all.

Ver. 8. *Sadducees say there is no resurrection*] The occasion of this heresy is said to be this: when Antigonus taught that we must not serve God, as servants do their masters, for hope of reward, his scholars Sadoc and Baithus understood him as if he had utterly denied all future rewards or recompense attending a godly life; and thence framed their heresy, denying the resurrection, world to come, &c.

Ver. 9. *We find no evil in this man*] God, when he pleaseth, can find patrons of his cause amongst his very enemies. (Beza.)

But if a spirit or an angel, &c.] It is well observed by a reverend man from this Scripture, that men will grant truths or not, as their passions lead them. Before Paul discovered himself to be a Pharisee, they all with one consent cried out, "This man is not worthy to live." But now that he shows himself to be on their side, "I am a Pharisee, and the son of a Pharisee," oh how finely do they mince the matter. "Perhaps an angel hath revealed it to him;" he was an honest man then. So men either judge, or not judge, as their passions and affections carry them.

Ver. 10. *To take him by force*] This the soldiers did, for none other end than to prevent sedition and man-slaughter; but God had a further end in it, viz. to preserve his servant for further noble employment; *ideoque cœcas manus illuc dirigit*, saith Calvin, and therefore he directeth their blind hands thereunto. The truth is, every creature walks blindfold. Only he that dwells in light sees whither they go.

Ver. 11. *The Lord stood by him*] Turned his prison into a palace, as likewise he did to Algerius, Christ's prisoner, and Master Philpot, who writes thus to his friends, Though I tell you that I am in hell in the judgment of this world, yet assuredly I feel in the same the consolation of heaven, I praise God; and this loathsome and horrible prison is as pleasant to me as the walk in the garden of the King's Bench.

Ver. 12. *Bound themselves, &c.*] The constable of France, when he covenanted with God, that if he had the victory at St Quentin's he would set upon Geneva, thought no doubt that he had made a great good bargain with God. Much like to Julian the emperor, who going against the Persians, made his vow that if he sped well, he would offer the blood of Christians. But what did God? Came not both their vows to like effect? " My times are in thy hand," saith David. Pilate could do nothing against Christ were it not given him from above. Commit we therefore ourselves to God in well-doing, as to a faithful Creator.

Ver. 13. *And they were more than forty*] The assassins are a kind of most desperate men among the Mahometans, who, strongly deluded with the blind zeal of their superstition, and accounting it meritorious by any means to kill any great enemy of their religion, for the performance thereof, as men prodigal of their lives, they desperately adventure themselves into all kinds of dangers. Such also are the Spahyels among the Turks, a kind of voluntary horsemen in mere devotion to gain paradise by dying for the Mahometan's cause. (Blount's Voyage.)

Ver. 14. *And they came to the chief priests and elders*] With whom they knew they should hereby ingratiate. Rulers' vices as seldom go unattended as their persons. If Herod mock Christ, his men of war will do so too, Luke xxiii. 11. " If a ruler hearken to lies, all his servants are wicked," Prov. xxix. 12.

Ver. 15. *As though he would inquire*] Craft and cruelty are combined in the Church's enemies; neither of them wanteth his mate, as the Scripture speaketh of those birds of prey and desolation, Isa. xxxiv. 16, and as the asp is said never to wander alone without his companion with him.

Ver. 16. *And when Paul's sister's son*] A sweet providence that this boy should be by, to detect and defeat their wicked counsel. God will be seen in the Mount; he suffereth oft his enemies to go to the utmost of their tether, and then pulls them back with shame to their task. He delights to make fools of them. He lets them have the ball on their foot till they come to the very goal, and yet makes them miss the game.

Ver. 17. *And said*] i. e. prayed, ver. 18. The poor man speaks supplications, Prov. xviii. 23, puts his mouth in the dust, speaks as out of the ground in a low language, in a submissive manner, when a suitor especially; for in that case the answer commonly cuts off half the petition, as the echo doth the voice.

Ver. 18. *Paul the prisoner*] But therein happier than any potentate (Psal. lxxxix. 27), with all his chains of gold. Τιμὴ ἁλύσεις, δεσμα μαργαρίται, said Ignatius; my chain is my honour, my links pearls. One hour changed Joseph's fetters into gold chains, his stocks into a chariot, his gaol into a palace, Potiphar's captive to his master's Lord, the noise of his gyves into *abrech*. So and much more than so shall it be with all Christ's prisoners at his coming; besides their prison-comforts in the mean while; those divine consolations that Philip Landgrave of Hesse, prisoner to Charles V., for defence of the truth, said that he sensibly felt in the time of his sad captivity, *Divinas Martyrum consolationes se sensisse dixit*. This made Chrysostom say that he had rather be Paul the prisoner of Jesus Christ than Paul rapt up into the third heaven. (Homil. in Ephes. iii. 1.)

Ver. 19. *Took him by the hand*] Courtesy and affability in high degree is very attractive; it easily allureth men's minds, as do fair flowers in the spring the passenger's eyes.

Ver. 20. *As though they would*] See ver. 15.

Ver. 21. *Which have bound themselves*] Gr. ἀνεθεμάτισαν, wished themselves dead, or given up to the devil, except they brought their purpose to pass; and likely enough they had their wish, for they missed of their purpose. Cursing men are cursed men. See ver. 17.

Ver. 22. *See thou tell no man*] Taciturnity is reckoned among the virtues. *Detexit facinus fatuus, et non implevit*, saith Tacitus (that best historian) of a fool that could not keep his own counsel, and so marred the design.

Ver. 23. *At the third hour of the night*] A well-chosen season is the greatest advantage of any action, which, as it is seldom found in haste, so it is often lost in delay.

Ver. 24. *That they may bring him safe*] The vulgar Latin adds, For he feared lest the Jews would take him away by violence and kill him, and so he should suffer blame, as if he had been hired to permit it. But this the Greek hath not.

Ver. 25. *And he wrote a letter*] Gr. an epistle, *cujus ornamentum est ornamentis carere*, saith Politian.

Ver. 26. *Unto the most excellent*] Felix was (as likewise Haman) of base birth, but highly advanced in court by means of his brother Pallas, a great favourite of Nero's, insomuch as he became husband to three queens successively, as Suetonius writeth. He cruelly killed Jonathan the Jewish priest, and committed many other outrages in this province; so that being complained of at Rome, he had been put to death, but for the greatness of his brother, who begged his pardon. (Josephus.)

Ver. 27. *Understood that he was a Roman*] He saith nothing of binding him to have been scourged against the law. Nature needs not be taught to tell her own tale. Every man strives to make his own penny as good silver as he can.

Ver. 28. *I brought him forth into their council*] As being himself ignorant of their religion; and haply having as evil an opinion of it as Cicero had, who disdained at the Jews for their slighting the Roman superstition, and censured their religion as false, because they and their religion were in subjection to the Romans.[1]

Ver. 29. *Questions of their law*] Which these profane heathens held to be mere trifles and niceties, *quæ nec ignoranti nocent, nec scientem juvant*, as Seneca saith. See Acts xviii. 15, with the note there.

Ver. 30. *And gave commandment to his accusers*] For no man is bound to accuse himself; and, *De secretis non judicat lex*. In the courts of men it is safest to plead *Non feci*, saith Quintilian (though in God's court it is otherwise).

Ver. 31. *To Antipatris*] So called by Herod (who had repaired it) in honour of his father Antipater. Christ, the everlasting Father, Isa. ix. 6, hath his name far better propagated and perpetuated by his sons and daughters, Psal. lxxii. 17, his name shall endure for ever (*filiabitur nomine ejus*) by a continual succession of spiritual children (so the Hebrew word signifieth), who shall build his house, and keep up his name, much better than Rachel and Leah did the house of Israel, Ruth iv. 11.

Ver. 32. *And returned to the castle*] Whereof see chap. xxi. 34.

Ver. 33. *Presented Paul also before him*] And so was fulfilled in him that of our Saviour, Matt. x. 18. See the note there. Neither was he more afraid of Felix, than Moses and Micaiah were to stand before Pharaoh and Ahab, when once they had seen God in his majesty. *Animo magno nihil magnum*. (Seneca.)

Ver. 34. *Of what province he was*] So the Romans called the countries by them subdued; looking upon themselves as lords of the world, Luke ii. 1. See the note.

Ver. 35. *I will hear thee*] *Pergam te audire, et auditionem absolvam* (so Beza rendereth the Greek, διακούσομαι), I will hear thee out, when thine accusers are come. In the mean while I will keep, οὖς ἀδιάβλητον, mine ear free.[2] I will not be prepossessed; nor hear one tale till I may hear both. This was well done of Felix, and judge like; *qui*

Si statuat aliquid, parte inaudita altera,
Æquum licet statuerit, haud æquus fuerit.

At Rome, the accuser had six hours allotted him to accuse; the guilty or defendant had nine hours to make his answer. This Felix knew full well.

CHAPTER XXIV.

Ver. 1. *With a certain orator*] ONE of those *sordida poscinummia* (as Plautus phraseth it), those *leguleiorum fæces decem-drachmariæ*, as another styleth these mercenary orators, *qui linguas habent venales*. It is reported of Nevessan (a better lawyer than an honest man) that he should say,

he that will not venture his body shall never be valiant: he that will not venture his soul, never rich.

Ver. 2. *Tertullus began to accuse him*] *Prosperior Afro Oratori eloquentia quam morum fama*, saith Tacitus. (Tacit. Annal.) *Ciceronis linguam omnes fere mirantur, pectus non ita*, saith Augustine (Confess. iv. 3). The Duke of Buckingham, speaking to the Londoners for Richard III., gained the commendation, that no man could deliver so much bad matter in so good words and quaint phrases. Such another was Tertullus, wittily wicked, *et malo publico facundus*, eloquent for mischief to other men. There is a story of a poor man who complained to his king that a man (naming a lawyer) had taken away his cow from him. I will hear, said the king, what he will say to the matter. Nay, saith the poor man, if you hear him speak, then have I surely lost my cow indeed.

Ver. 3. *We accept it always*] So they say, the sooner to ingratiate; when in truth they worthily hated Felix for his oppression and cruelty. *Nota hypocrisin cum assentatione*, saith Beza. "In his estate shall stand up a vile person," Dan. xi. 21, that, is Antiochus Epiphanes. And yet Josephus reports that the Samaritans writing to him, because he tormented the Jews, to excuse themselves that they were no Jews, styled him, by flattery, Antiochus the mighty God. *Romani, propter omnia quæ a Nerone fiebant etiam scelera, quasi gratias agentes, sacra faciebant:* such was their baseness, and such were these Jews.

Ver. 4. *That I be not further tedious unto thee*] Gr. ἵνα μὴ ἐπὶ πλεῖον σε ἐγκόπτω, that I hinder thee not in thine haste to other businesses; that I put not a stop to thy praise-worthy proceedings, by a troublesome prolixity, &c. Thus he cunningly insinuateth into the judge's affections; which is one of the rhetorical precepts: and another is (Tertullus likely had learned it out of Tully), *Non ad veritatem solum, sed etiam ad opinionem eorum qui audiunt, accommodanda est oratio*. An orator may make a little bold with the truth to give his hearers content. Socrates in his apology, "My lords" (said he to his judges), "I know not how you have been affected with mine accusers' eloquence while you heard them speak; for my own part, I assure you that I, whom it toucheth most, was almost drawn to believe that all they said, though against myself, was true: when they scarcely uttered one word of truth."

Ver. 5. *A pestilent fellow*] Gr. λοιμόν, a botch, *sicut Scelus pro scelerato: Tubulus quidam, paulo supra Ciceronem, Prætor fuit, homo tam Projecte improbus, ut ejus nomen non hominis sed vitii esse videretur*. (Lips. Antiq. Lect.) Now if so precious a man as Paul (than whom, saith Chrysostom, the earth never bare a better since it bore Christ) were counted and called a pest, let not us think much to be so esteemed.

And a mover of sedition] So Elias was held,

---

[1] *Gens illa quam chara Diis immortalibus esset docuit, quod est victa quod elocata, quod servata.* Cic. pro L. Flacco.

[2] καθαρὸν οὖς φυλάττω καὶ ἀδιάβλητον, said Alexander.

and called the "troubler of Israel;" *Luther Tuba rebellionis.* So it was said to one Singleton, sometime chaplain to the Lady Ann Boleyn, that he was the murderer of Packington, and afterwards that he was a stirrer-up of sedition and commotion, who also suffered as a traitor for the same; where in very deed the true cause was nothing else but for preaching the gospel, saith Master Fox. And he might as safely say as Mr Latimer did in his third sermon before King Edward VI., "As for sedition, for aught that I know, methinks I should not need Christ, if I might so say." (Acts and Mon.)

Of the sect of the Nazarenes] Who stirred up the people to stand up for their liberty against the Romans, saith an interpreter.

Ver. 6. *To profane the temple*] A loud lie: but innocency is no target against calumny.

Ver. 7. *Took him out of our hands*] Wherein he did well, though he hear ill; as public persons must look to do.

Ver. 8. *By examining of whom*] By this outfacing boldness, and these specious pretences, they hoped to have swayed the governor to deliver up the prisoner to their pleasure without any more ado, and to have condemned him unheard. But God had otherwise ordered it.

Ver. 9. *And the Jews assented*] With what face could they do it, but that their faces were hatched with impudence; and they had taken an order with their consciences not to trouble them: "Trouble me not, for I am in bed," as he in the Gospel said to his neighbour.

Ver. 10. *Forasmuch as I know, &c.*] Paul was a stately orator when he listed, as here. Porphyry said it was pity that such a man as Paul should be bestowed upon our religion. How bravely doth he here unstarch the orator's speech, and make his own defence.

Ver. 11. *There are yet but twelve days*] And therefore in so short a time I could surely do no such great matters as they charge me with.

Ver. 12. *And they neither found me in the temple*] As he had argued from the circumstance of time, ver. 11 (to disprove their empty allegations), so here of place. It fared with the apostle as the historian saith it did with Cuthbert Tunstal, bishop of Durham, who was sent to the Tower for concealment of (I know not what) treason written to him (I know not by whom), and not discovered until (what shall I call) the party did reveal it. False accusers, as they affirm without reason, so they may be dismissed without refutation: unless we will answer them with a downright denial, as here. It falls out often, that plain-dealing puts craft out of countenance.

Ver. 13. *Neither can they prove the things*] And if to be barely accused be sufficient to make a man guilty, no man shall be innocent. It is happy if we can write (as the Lady Elizabeth did in Woodstock windows),

"Much alleged against me:
Nothing proved can be."

Ver. 14. *Which they call heresy*] Hæresis est vox Ecclesiæ peculiaris. Antiquitus enim dicebatur, In hac hæresi sum, id est in hac sum sententia vel sic sentio. (Tull. Paradox.) Ecclesiastical writers take it for an error in religion, for an opinion repugnant to the word of God. There must be in it, *Error in ratione, et pertinacia in voluntate.* Fevardentius, that fiery friar, feigns 1400 errors and heresies, all which he fathers and fastens on the Calvinists. Genebrard imputes to Calvin as an error, that he taught Christ to be αὐτόθεος, God of himself. It is not so long since, whosoever amongst us was not an Arminian, was *eo nomine* a doctrinal Puritan, as he was then termed; and now, he that was the old English Puritan, cried out upon as the worst of men, and greatest Heteroclite.[1]

Ver. 15. *And have hope toward God, which themselves also allow*] The Jews generally believed no article of the faith more than this, John xii. 24; Acts xxiii. 8. The primitive times yielded some that denied it, 1 Cor. xv.; so do these unhappy times of ours: we must all look to our standing, and get our hearts ballasted with grace (as the bee, when she is to fly against the wind, ballasteth her body with some little stone carried betwixt her feet), that we be not whirled about with every wind of doctrine. A man is to expect, if he live out his days, to be urged to the breach of every branch of the Decalogue, and to be put to it in respect of every article of the creed. Provide for a storm: shipmen in a calm, or at a haven, look to their tacklings: see the ship be well ballasted, victualled, watered, &c.

Ver. 16. *And herein*] Or, meanwhile (ἐν τούτῳ, i. e. χρόνῳ, ἀσκῶ), for this cause do I exercise myself: or, I use diligence, skill, and conscience; I lay my policy, or bend my wit, I discipline and inure myself.

Ver. 17. *To bring alms to my nation*] And therefore should have been better welcomed; a present makes room for a man, Prov. xviii. 16. But it is God alone that fashioneth men's opinions and affections: and therefore, Rom. xv., St Paul prayeth that this service of his might be accepted of the saints themselves. The Jews at this day send their alms yearly from all parts to Jerusalem for the maintenance of the praying poor that live there.

Ver. 18. *Purified in the temple*] Therefore surely not profaning of it: unless they will say of me, as Diogenes did of Antipater (who being vicious, wore a white cloak, the ensign of innocency), that he did *virtutis stragulam pudefacere*, put honesty to an open shame: or unless they will concur in opinion with their utter enemy Florus, who calleth the temple at Jerusalem *impiæ gentis arcanum, libidinum sacrarium,* &c. Virgil.

Ver. 19. *Who ought to have been here before thee*] For those that are here to accuse me, speak but by hearsay, which is *tam ficti pravique tenax quam nuntia veri,* a loud liar, for most part.

[1] —— *pudet hæc opprobria nobis et dici potuisse et non potuisse refelli.*

Ver. 20. Or else let these same here say] This is the best defence, that is thus fetched from the accusers themselves, who are apt to make the worst of everything and to aggravate faults beyond truth. This is no small prejudice to Luther's adversaries, said Erasmus, that they cannot but say he lives honestly. And the like is recorded of Bucer, Bradford, others; the Papists could not find fault with their lives, only they taxed them for heresy; but so they could not Paul, unless they would conclude themselves also heretics, ver. 21.

Ver. 21. Except [it be, &c.] And if this be a fault in true account, why are not all the whole nation of the Pharisees faulted, that hold the same thing? Is that Nævus in me that is Venus in them? Or is that a vice in Caius that is a virtue in Titus? Are they not apparently partial in themselves, and become judges of evil thoughts? Jam. ii. 4. If Dioscorus the heretic could cry out in the Council of Chalcedon, I am cast out with the Fathers, I defend the doctrine of the Fathers, I transgress them not in any part; may not I more truly lay the like claim to the Pharisees, those fathers of our nation?

Ver. 22. He deferred them, and said] Truly and timely spake the orator, *De vita hominis nulla satis diuturna cunctatio esse possit* (see Deut. xvii. 3). In a case of life and death there cannot be too much caution and cunctation.

Ver. 23. And to let him have liberty] This shows that Felix himself found that it was malice, more than matter, that moved the Jews to prosecute. And the same perhaps is hinted in the former verse, " having more perfect knowledge of that way ; " that is, as some sense it, being well acquainted with their courses, and knowing it to be their common practice to accuse innocent men of mere spite. But why then did not Felix punish those malicious men, and let Paul go? why is he still a prisoner, though a free prisoner, under a keeper, or with some chain on him? Oh, it is a mercy to have judges *modo velint quæ possint, modo audeant quæ sentiant,* so they be willing to do what they may, and dare do what they judge fit to be done. (Cic. pro Milone.)

Ver. 24. With his wife Drusilla] The sister of King Agrippa, and wife of Abidus, king of Emesenes, whom she had basely forsaken, and came and joined herself to this Felix (Joseph. Antiq. 20), worthy therefore to have been hanged, as Joan queen of Naples, was at a window for like treachery by Lewis, king of Hungary. (Heyl. Geog. 167.)

Ver. 25. Of righteousness, temperance, &c.] Whereas Felix did many things there tyrannously and had greater regard to gain than to justice; and whereas Drusilla, a Jewess, was not only married to an uncircumcised man, but also a filthy adulteress,—Paul in a certain kind of grave wisdom, which yet had joined with it great liberty of speech, reasoneth and disputeth of things that he knew principally wanting in his hearers.

Felix trembled] See the force of conscience, which, like Samson's wife, conceals not the riddle, Judg. xvi. 17 ; like Fulvia a courtesan, who de-clared all the secrets of her foolish lover Cneius, a noble Roman, bewrays and betrays those that harbour her. She is a watch and will at length give warning. (Sallust. Bell. Cat.)

Go thy way for this time, &c.] The president of St Julian's being sent to Angrogne would have forced a poor man to re-baptize his child. He, after he had prayed, required of the president that he would write and sign the same with his own hand, that he would discharge him before God of the danger of that offence, and that he would take the peril upon him and his. The president hereat was so confounded, that he spake not one word a good while after. Then said he, " Away, thou villain, out of my sight." After that he was never called more. (Acts and Mon.)

Ver. 26. He hoped also, &c.] *Fuit Felix inexplebilis gurges,* as Tacitus testifieth. He trembled, and yet gaped after money. A man may as soon find a harvest in a hedge as the least goodness in a covetous heart. *Privatorum fures in nervo et compedibus ætatem agunt ; publica in auro et purpura visuntur.* (Cato apud Gell. lib. xi. 18.) Public thieves are gallant fellows. And covetousness is a dry-drunkenness. Justice is oft made a hackney by them to be backed for money ; and a golden spur brings her to the desired journey's end of injury and wrong. Whereas a judge, as he should have nothing to lose, so he should have nothing to get, he should be above all price or sale ; and justice justice, as Moses speaketh, that is, pure justice without mud should run down amain, Deut. xvi. 26.

Ver. 27. Willing to show the Jews, &c.] Politicians care not to gratify others and serve their own turns, with the loss of right and good conscience. In the reign of Henry II. of France, A. D. 1554, many were there burnt for religion, not without the indignation of honest men, who knew that the diligence used against these poor people was not for piety or religion, but to satiate the covetousness of Diana Valentina, the king's mistress, to whom he had given all the confiscation of goods made in the kingdom for cause of heresy. (Hist. of Council of Trent.)

CHAPTER XXV.

Ver. 1. Now when Festus] WHO succeeded Felix in the government, as after Festus came Albinus, and after him Florus, under whom Jerusalem was sacked and ruined. That heavy curse was executed upon this wretched people, Lev. xxvi. 17, " If ye still trespass against me, I will set princes over you that shall hate you," mischievous, odious princes ; odious to God, oppressive to the people. After the revolt of the ten tribes, they had not one good king. And a Popish writer complains, that for many successions the see of Rome *non merita est regi nisi à reprobis,* had deserved to be ruled by none but reprobates. When Phocas had slain Mauricius, there was an honest poor man (saith Cedrenus) who was wonderful importunate at the throne of grace, to know a reason why that wicked man prospered so in his design; he was answered again by a voice, that there could not be a worse man found, and that the sins of Christians did require it.

Ver. 2. Informed him against Paul] ἐνεφάνισαν, they gave him private intelligence (so the word signifies, saith Erasmus), they buzzed false reports into his ears: an old practice of persecutors. *Proprie significat tacite et clam indicare.* Truth seldom goes without a scratched face. The Arminians endeavoured to persuade the States of Holland that the orthodox pastors sought to diminish the authority of the civil magistrates, and to affect and arrogate to themselves a power collateral or equal to their power.[1]

Ver. 3. Desired favour] Or a good turn, χάριν: such was their impudency.

Ver. 4. That Paul should be kept, &c.] How easily can God defeat the most cunning contrivances of his Church's enemies! He sees and smiles, he looks and laughs. Commit we therefore ourselves to him in well-doing, as unto a faithful Creator, 1 Pet. iv. 19.

Ver. 5. That are able] Or well appointed, well provided of moneys and other necessaries for such an enterprise. He that prosecutes another need be well underlaid.

Ver. 6. Commanded Paul to be brought] This is now the third time: and what if it had been the thirtieth? Cato (the very best of the Romans) as he was two-and-thirty times accused, so he was two-and-thirty times cleared and absolved.

Ver. 7. Laid many and grievous complaints against Paul] Whereby to take away his precious life: which because they could not, they had little comfort of their own. Some of their own Talmudists have observed that the devil was as much wounded with that restraint that he should not take away Job's life, as Job was with all those wounds that the devil inflicted on his body.

Ver. 8. Neither against the law of the Jews] *Quam multa quam paucis!* said Tully of Brutus' laconical epistle: and the same may I say of this defence, How much in a little! See the note on Acts xxiv. 12.

Ver. 9. Wilt thou go up to Jerusalem?] Irreligious persons that are not acted by the Spirit of God, we see how flexible and inclinable they are to corrupt counsels and courses. Before, he would not yield to the Jews' motion; now he would. "A double-minded man is unstable in all his ways," ἄστατος, Jam. i. 6.

Et tantum constans in levitate sua.

But should not the chief posts in a building be heart of oak? should not the standard be made of metal of proof? Fabricius is famous for his well-knit resolution; sooner might a man turn the sun out of his course than draw him to do anything that was not just and equal. As, on the other side, those Athenian judges shall be infamous to all posterity, who when they had determined to condemn Phryne (that stinking

[1] *Act. Synod. Dordrecht. præfatione.*

strumpet), were yet drawn to acquit her, after that they beheld her beautiful bosom, which Hyperides (her advocate) had purposely laid open (pulling her clothes aside) to move them to show her mercy. (Plut. in Hyperid.)

Ver. 10. I stand at Cæsar's judgment-seat] We may safely make our just defence when falsely accused, and take the benefit of the law. Ambrose would be judged at Milan, where he was known; and Athanasius refused to be censured by corrupt councils.

Ver. 11. I appeal to Cæsar] Who though a lion, 2 Tim. iv. 17, yet I hope to be *tutus sub umbra leonis*, against a manifest violence of a corrupt judge, notoriously forestalled and preoccupied. *Judex, locusta civitatis est, malus.* (Scaliger.)

Ver. 12. Hast thou appealed, &c.] *Elegans loquendi forma*, saith Piscator: such as are those, 1 Cor. vii. 18, 21, 27; Rom. xiii. 3. A cutted kind of speech, say others, savouring of discontent.

Ver. 13. King Agrippa and Bernice] Son and daughter to that Herod mentioned Acts xii. They were known, saith Josephus, to live in detestable incest. It pleased God that his faithful servant Paul should plead for his life before these two filthy beasts; which he did freely and modestly.

Ver. 14. A certain man left in bonds] Wherein he glorieth more than others in their gold chains, Ephes. iii. 1; Philem. 1. *Non ita beatum Paulum puto*, saith Chrysostom, Ephes. iii. 1, *quod in cœlum raptus, quam quod in carcerem conjectus:* I hold not Paul so happy in his rapture as in his captivity.

Ver. 15. To have judgment against him] *Damnationem*, saith Beza. This was the favour they craved of Festus, ver. 3. So a writ came down while the Lady Elizabeth was in the Tower, subscribed with certain hands of the council for her execution, Stephen Gardiner being the chief engineer; but God prevented them. The Lord Paget in a certain consultation said that King Philip should never have any quiet commonwealth in England unless Lady Elizabeth's head were stricken from her shoulders. The Spaniards thereto answered, God forbid that their king and master should have such a mind to consent to such a mischief. (Acts and Mon.)

Ver. 16. Have the accusers face to face] Here was no oath *ex officio* to force a man to accuse himself. Among the Romans the accusers sat in those seats that were at the left hand of the judge; the accused and his advocate at the right hand. The accuser had three hours allotted him, the defendant six. And if he were cast, yet was he not given up to his adversaries to be punished at their pleasure (as these Jews would have had it) but as the judge appointed it.

Ver. 17. Without delay] This was well; judges should dismiss timely those whom they cannot presently despatch, as Jethro advised, Exod. xviii. It is recorded of Sir Thomas More, to his eternal commendation, that when he was Lord Chancellor, and sat in the Court of Chancery, he called for the next cause, and there was none remaining. But what meaneth Festus here to crack so much of his diligence in doing justice?

Cur ego, si nequeo, ignoroque, Poeta salutor.
                                             Horat.

What is the honour of this world, or the applause of men (though well deserved), but a puff of stinking breath? and what advantageth it a man to have the world's *Euge*, and God's *Apage*?

Ver. 18. *Of such things as I supposed*] They accused Paul of sedition; but because they failed in the proof, he makes it nothing. This is said by the historian (Tacitus) to be the *commune crimen eorum qui crimine vacabant*, the innocent man's crime.

Ver. 19. *But had certain questions*] See how basely this profane fellow speaketh of God's true service. These cocks on the dunghill know not the price of that pearl, and do therefore avile it. They took occasion also from the contentions of the Church's doctors, to condemn their doctrine. It was therefore a devilish device of Julian the Apostate, to call home those heterodox and heretical bishops that had been banished by Constantine, that they might embroil and darken the Church by their mutual discords amongst themselves, and so bring the Christian religion into disgrace.

Ver. 20. *And because*] He tells not Agrippa, that to gratify the Jews (who in all likelihood had bribed him) he asked, whether he would go up to Jerusalem; but pretends another matter. Nature need not be taught to tell her own tale, or to make the best of her own case, bad though it be. And this is incident to the very best, as to do what we can to hide our bodily deformities, so our moral defects and frailties. What dost thou here, Elias? saith God. I have been very zealous for the Lord of hosts, saith he. He had rather say so, than, I was fearful of Jezebel, and here I hide me from her malicious pursuit. But were it not better to speak out, and to acknowledge all with aggravation of circumstances? sith such only find mercy as in confession show the Lord the iniquity of their sin, the filthiness of their lewdness, the abomination of their provocations.

Ver. 21. *Send him to Cæsar*] That is, to Nero. But for memory of their two first emperors, Cæsar and Augustus, all their successors bore these two names. Many other swelling titles they had; but all or most of them, till Constantine, died unnatural deaths, and got nothing by their adoption or designation, *nisi ut citius interficerentur*, but to be sent out of the world the sooner.

Ver. 22. *I would also hear the man*] More for his mind's sake, and to see what he would say for himself, than out of any desire to learn of him. So Herod desired to see Christ, as a man would see some juggler act his feats, and make him sport.

Ver. 23. *With great pomp*] Gr. μετὰ πολλῆς φαντασίας, with great phantasy, or vain show. For no better is all worldly pomp and state. Of Cardinal Wolsey's twenty great mules passing through London, laden with roasted eggs, and rotten shoes, and other like treasure, as was discovered by the fall of one mule that cast his burden, read Acts and Monuments, fol. 899. My Lord Cardinal, said Bayfield, the martyr, is no good man; for Christ never taught him to follow riches, promotions, worldly pomp, as he doth; to wear shoes of silver and gilt, set with pearls and precious stones. Christ had never two crosses of silver, two axes, nor pillars of silver and gilt, &c.

Ver. 24. *That he ought not to live any longer*] All malice is bloody, and is therefore called murder; because it wisheth him out of the world whom it maligneth. See the note on ver. 7.

Ver. 25. *Nothing worthy of death*] What an honour and comfort was this to the apostle! Lysias acquits him, so doth Felix, and now Festus; neither doth Agrippa dissent. See the note on ver. 6.

Ver. 26. *To write unto my lord*] Κύριος signifieth one that hath rule or dominion, being a word of relation.[1] This title was first affected by tyrants; but afterwards the good princes suffered it to be given unto them, as appeareth by Pliny's Epistle to Trajan. The emperors disclaimed only the name of king, to avoid the hatred of the people, and yet sought the full right of kings, and to destroy the liberty of the people. But God calls them kings, 1 Pet. ii. 13, 17. God hateth hypocrisy in whomsoever; and will unmask even kings, if they dissemble.

Ver. 27. *For it seems to me unreasonable*] And should not God's people be as careful to perform unto him a reasonable service, Rom. xii. 1, such as whereof they can render a sound and intelligible reason out of the word of God? Should they not prove what that good, and holy, and acceptable will of God is, ver. 21, by taking warrant from his word, and doing all to his glory? Is not this to do the works of God, John vi. 28, and to do them in God, John iii. 22, and for God, according to that, *Quicquid agas propter Deum agas?* καλὸν καλῶς. And is not the contrary will-worship, Col. ii. 22; spiritual fornication, Psal. cvi. 39; idol-worship, Numb. xv. 32; devil-worship, 1 Cor. x. 20, with Acts xvii. 23; Apoc. ix. 20?

CHAPTER XXVI.

Ver. 1. *And answered for himself*] This the apostle doth most artificially and effectually. *Raptare eum judices credas*, as one saith concerning Cicero, *involvere, præcipitem agere, nec incendere auditorem, sed ipsum putes ardere: animorum denique quendam credas Deum.*

Ver. 2. *I think myself happy*] *Est quædam putativa felicitas*, saith an interpreter here, *si concedatur nobis causam nostram aperte agere. Bea-*

---

[1] *Deducitur a* κύρος, *authoritas.*

titudo autem vera in peccatorum remissione, &c., Psal. xxxii. 1, 2. It is a kind of happiness to have fair hearing before men ; but the true happiness is to find favour with God.

Ver. 3. *To be expert in all customs and questions*] As being a Jew, and conversant among the Jews (for he was Herod's son), and therefore a more competent judge.

Ver. 4. *My manner of life from my youth*] And although with some, *Principium fervet, medium tepet, exitus alget*, their best is at first, as Nero (who now reigned at Rome) for his first five years was very hopeful; yet that is not ordinary. A good beginning hath for most part a good ending, and a young saint proves an old angel.

Ver. 5. *After the most straitest sect*] There were three several sects among the Jews, Pharisees, Sadducees, and Essenes ; which last lived a monastic kind of life, and besides the Bible, studied physic : whence also they had their name of Asa, to heal. The Pharisees were most in request, professing extraordinary strictness, as those *districtissimi Monachi*, those puritan monks among the Papists (as one calleth them) that carried wooden crosses at their backs continually, and pretended for it Matt. x. 38.

Ver. 6. *For the hope of the promise*] The goodness of his cause made much for his comfort. It is one thing to suffer as a martyr, and another thing to suffer as a malefactor. *Ibi erat Christus, ubi latrones : similis pœna, dissimilis causa.* Christ and the thieves were in the like condemnation, but their cause was not alike. (Augustin.) Samson died with the Philistines, by the fall of the same house ; *simili quidem pœna, sed dissimili culpa, et diverso fine ac fato*, but for another end, and by a different destiny. (Bucholcer.) Together with the Lord Cromwell, was beheaded the Lord Hungerford ; neither so Christianly suffering, nor so courageously dying for his offence committed against nature. (Speed.) Blessed are they that suffer "for righteousness' sake," Matt. v. 10 ; and, "for thy sake are we slain all the day long," Psal. xliv. 22. And, *O beata Apocalypsis, quam bene mecum agitur qui comburar tecum?* said a certain martyr when he saw the Revelation cast into the fire with him. (Fox.) So might St Paul say by that hope of the promise made of God unto the fathers, for the which he now stood and was judged.

Ver. 7. *Instantly serving God*] And yet finding enough to do, when they have done their utmost, to get to heaven. The time is short, the task long ; *Castigemus ergo mores et moras.*

> *Præcipita tempus, mors atra impendet agenti.*
>   Silius.

Ver. 8. *Why should it be thought a thing incredible?*] Philosophy indeed is against it. *A privatione ad habitum*, &c. *Et redit in nihilum, quod fuit ante nihil*, as the epicure in Ecclesiastes concludeth. But first, many heathens believed a resurrection ; as Zoroaster, Theopompus, and Plato. And the Stoic's opinion was, that the world should be dissolved by fire or water ; and all things brought to a better state, or to the first golden age again.[1] Secondly, no article of the faith was more generally believed among the Jews than this, John xii. 24 ; Acts xxiii. 8. Hence they called their burying-places *Domus viventium*, the houses of the living, בֵּית חַיִּים : the Greeks called them *dormitories*, or sleeping-houses, κοιμητήρια, as holding that their dead should once awake again, and be filled with God's image, Psal. xvii. ult. The Germans call the churchyard God's Acre ; because the bodies are sown there to be raised again. What if those profane popes (sons of perdition), Leo X. and Julius II., jeer at the resurrection, as if anything were impossible with God? cannot he that made man at first of nothing make him up again of that substance of the body that is preserved after death, though never so dispersed ? God knows where every part and parcel of it is, and can easily bring it together again. In the transfiguration, that body of Moses which was hid in the valley of Moab, appeared glorious in the hill of Tabor ; that we may know that these bodies of ours are not lost, but laid up, and shall as sure be raised in glory as they are laid down in corruption. Do we not see a resurrection of the creatures every spring ? and the corn we sow, doth it not first rot and then revive ? See we not men of ashes to make glass ? and cannot a skilful gardener discern his several seeds when mixed together, and gather every one of them to their own kind ? Have we not observed how those little balls of quicksilver dispersed, will not mix with any of another kind ; but if any man gather them, they run together of their own accord into one mass ? why then should it be thought a thing incredible with any, that God should raise the dead ? *Consentaneum est Phœnicem*, saith Nyssen. It is probable enough, that that Phœnix that was found in the reign of Nero (and perhaps at this very time when St Paul was thus pleading for the resurrection) might signify the resurrection of Christ, and of all believers by him ; according to that of the prophet, "Thy dead men shall live, together with my dead body shall they arise : awake and sing, ye that dwell in the dust ; for thy dew is as the dew of herbs, and the earth shall cast out the dead," Isa. xxvi. 19.

Ver. 9. *Contrary to the name*, &c.] Tertullian testifieth, that in the primitive Christians, *nomen damnabatur, non crimen aut scelus : solum nomen innocuum, hominibus innocuis esse pro crimine, &c.* And Tacitus to the same purpose, that when Nero had set the city on fire for his pleasure, and then fathered it upon the Christians, a great company of them were presently slaughtered, *haud perinde in crimine incendii, quam odio humani generis, convicti:* Not for any fault whereof they could be convicted, but out of a general hatred of their persons and religion.

Ver. 10. *I gave my voice*] So did Gerson to

[1] Sen. Nat. Quæst. iii. 26, 27.

the condemnation of John Huss and Jerome of Prague at the Council of Constance, against his conscience doubtless. (Joh. Manl.) So did the Lord Cromwell to the condemnation of Lambert the martyr; for the which he afterwards cried him mercy. And so did Sir John Cheek, in Queen Mary's days, out of a base fear of the bishops; he was, saith Mr Fox, through the crafty handling of the Catholics, allured first to dine and company with them; at length drawn unawares to sit in place where the poor martyrs were brought before Bonner and other bishops, to be condemned; and so to give his voice, or seem to do so by his presence there. The remorse whereof so mightily wrought in his heart, that not long after he left this mortal life; whose fall though it was full of infirmity, yet his rising again by repentance was great, and his end comfortable.

Ver. 11. *Compelled them to blaspheme*] So the ancient persecutors compelled many not only to renounce their religion, but to curse Christ. (Plin. Epist. ad Trajan.) When the Emperor Heraclius sent ambassadors to Chosroes, king of Persia, to desire peace of him, he received this threatening answer: I will not spare you, till I have made you curse your crucified God, and adore the sun. He was afterwards (like another Sennacherib) deposed and murdered by his son Siroes.

And being exceedingly mad, I persecuted] He was not then so mad in persecuting, but when God turned the stream, he was judged by some as mad in preaching, 2 Cor. v. 13, and pressing toward the high prize which he persecuted (that is, his word, διώκω, Phil. iii. 14) with as much eagerness as ever he had done God's poor saints and servants.

Ver. 12, 13.] See Acts ix. 2, with the notes.

Ver. 14. *I heard a voice*] I not only saw a sign. So in the transfiguration, a voice came forth to them from the excellent glory. *Signo verbum est conjungendum.* God in the sacraments, for the furtherance of our faith, affects both our learned senses, as Aristotle calleth our sight and hearing; giving us his word both audible and visible.

Ver. 15.] See Acts ix. 5.

Ver. 16. *But rise and stand upon thy feet*] Thus,

Dejicit ut relevet; premit ut solatia præstet:
Enecat, ut possit vivificare, Deus.

Ver. 17. *Delivering thee from*] For though thou art sent to them for their greatest good, viz. "To open their eyes," &c., ver. 18, yet they shall fly at thine eyes, as frantic people fly in the faces of their physicians; they shall fly against the light that thou shalt set up amongst them, as bats do, because their works are evil; they shall kick and wince, as horse and mule at those that come to cure them, Psal. xxxii. 9. But I will deliver thee, fear not.

Ver. 18. *To open their eyes, &c.*] An excellent description of St Paul's commission to preach,

by the five ends or effects of it, viz. conversion, faith, remission of sins, sanctification, salvation.

Ver. 19. *I was not disobedient*] As I should have been if I had taken flesh and blood into counsel, Gal. i. 16 (see the note there); but silencing my reason, I exalted my faith, and putting myself into God's hands, said,

Te duce, vera sequor : te duce, falsa nego.

Ver. 20. *Works meet for repentance*] Gr. "worthy of repentance," that weigh just as much as repentance doth. The Syriac hath it, works equal and even with repentance. See my note on Matt. iii. 8.

Ver. 21. *Went about to kill me*] Gr. διαχειρίσασθαι, to tear me in pieces, or pull me limb-meal with their own hands, as the senators did Romulus, and afterward Cæsar. The Italians that served the French king, having taken the town of Barre, did out of hatred of religion rip up a living child, and taking out his liver, being as yet red-hot, they did eat it as meat. Many children there at the same time had their hearts pulled out, which in rage those cannibal Papists gnawed with their teeth. (Acts and Mon.)

Ver. 22. *Saying none other thing*] Truth is one and the same in all ages; it is also ancient, and ever at agreement with itself. As on the other side, error is new, manifold, dissonant, and contradictory to itself, and much more to the truth. Paul delivered no new truths, but stood in the good old way of Moses and the prophets, and followed them, κατὰ πόδα. Those that stumble from the ancient ways, to walk in "new paths, in a way not cast up," they are people that "forget God," Jer. xviii. 15, to sacrifice to new gods, that came newly up, Deut. xxxii. 17; they are none of God's ancient people, Isa. xliv. 7, but an upstart generation, that knew not Joseph.

Ver. 23. *That Christ should suffer*] This verse may be fitly called a little Bible, a short gospel, a model of the mystery of godliness. The Greek runs thus, "Whether Christ should be a sufferer;" εἰ παθητὸς ὁ Χριστὸς, &c., "whether he should be the first that should rise from the dead." As if St Paul should hold forth these questions, and offer to prove them out of the prophets and Moses: and hence (haply) that way of expounding the Scriptures, by propounding doubts and questions. Abulensis hath his eightscore questions (and more than a good many sometimes) upon the shortest chapter in the Bible. The schoolmen were great questionists; and they had it from the Artemonites, a sort of heretics, A. D. 220, that, out of Aristotle and Theophrastus, corrupted the Scripture, by turning all into questions. In detestation of whose vain jangling and doting about questions (Jac. Revius, 1 Tim. vi. 4), Luther saith, *Prope est ut jurem:* I durst swear, almost, that there was not one school-divine that rightly understood one chapter of the Gospel. So that we may say of their expositions as one did once, when being asked whether he should read such a comment upon Aristotle? he answered, Yes, when Aristotle is understood, then read the comment.

Ver. 24. *Much learning hath made thee mad*] *Cere diminuit bovem*, as Ennius hath it. Paul was indeed a man of much learning; for besides the Bible, and the Jewish records, he had read the poets (whom also he citeth) and Plato, from whom he borrowed that excellent word ἀναζωπυρεῖν, 2 Tim. i. 6, "Stir up thy gift," &c. But if Paul were so great a scholar, why did not Festus show him more favour, or at least do him better justice? Æneas Sylvius was wont to say of learning, that popular men should esteem it as silver, noblemen as gold, princes prize it as pearls. Festus might possibly have heard or read of Antonius Triumvir, that when Varro (his very enemy, and of a contrary faction) was listed for death, he thus gallantly superscribed his name, *Vivat Varro vir doctissimus*: Let Varro have his life for his learning' sake. And if Antipater (saith Sir Walter Raleigh, Hist. of the World) upon his conquest had carried all other actions never so mildly, yet for killing Demosthenes, all that read his eloquent orations do condemn him for a bloody tyrant to this day.

Ver. 25. *I am not mad*] Paul rather pitieth his ignorance than blameth his blasphemy, and allegeth his own words for a proof of his no-madness; like as Sophocles produced a tragedy he had lately made, that was full of art and wit, when his sons would have begged him for a dotard. These real apologies are most powerful; when thus managed, especially, with "meekness of wisdom."

Ver. 26. *For this thing was not done in a corner*] Neither Christ's passion, nor Paul's conversion. Rome rang of the former, and it was seriously debated in the senate-house, whether Christ should not be received into the number of the gods? Tiberius would have had it so; but it was carried against him, because of the poverty of Christ's life and the infamy of his death. And as for Paul's conversion, it was far and near talked of. For as a bell cannot be turned from one side to another, but it will make a sound and report its own motion; so will the turning of a sinner from evil to good; such a sinner especially: his conversion was *toto notissima cælo*: like the trumpet of God in Mount Sinai, it filled the whole country.

Ver. 27. *I know thou believest*] sc. The truth of what the prophets spoke concerning Christ, and that are accordingly fulfilled in him. Faith hath for its general object the whole Holy Scripture; but for its special object the promises, or rather Christ revealed in the promises. All the Israelites beheld the wilderness and the whole hemisphere; but such only as were stung, looked up to the brazen serpent, and were healed. Devils and reprobates may believe the truth of the Scriptures, and see far into the mystery of Christ by a common illumination, but true believers only can close up themselves in the wounds of Christ, and by a particular faith receive healing by his stripes.

Ver. 28. *Almost thou persuadest me*] Here

he was nigh God's kingdom, who yet (for aught we find) never came there. Almost he could be content to be, but altogether may chance bring a chain with it. Jehu will not part with his calves, lest he venture his kingdom. Policy is ever entering caveats against piety. It is thought of Cardinal Pole, that toward his latter end, a little before his coming from Rome to England, he began somewhat to favour the doctrine of Luther, and was no less suspected at Rome, and therefore put by the popedom; notwithstanding the pomp and glory of the world did afterwards carry him away to play the Papist. Such as these Philo calleth *semperfectæ virtutis homines*, cakes half-baked, Hos. vii. 8. See the note there.

To be a Christian] The profane philosophers called the Christians *credentes*, that is, believers, by way of reproach, because they did not argue by reason, but take things upon trust. "We believe and know" (not, we know and believe) "that thou art the Son of the living God," John vi. 69. *Illi garriant, nos credamus*, saith Austin. Let them jeer us for our faith, let us believe nevertheless; and our faith shall be one day found "to praise, honour, and glory," 1 Pet. i. 7. If Agrippa had been right, he would have esteemed it the highest honour to be able to say, Christian is my name, and Catholic my surname. Those that might well have been his masters and makers, viz. Constantinus, Valentinianus, and Theodosius (three emperors), called themselves *Vasallos Christi*, not Christians only, but the vassals of Christ, as Socrates reporteth: and Justinian the emperor styled himself, *Ultimum servorum Christi*, the meanest of Christ's servants.

Ver. 29. *I would that all*] Charity is no churl; there is no envy in spiritual things, because they may be divided *in solidum*: one may have as much as another, and all alike. Self-love writes, as that emperor did, τὰ εἰς ἐμαυτὸν, For mine own use only. It makes men like those envious Athenians, who sacrificed for none but themselves and their neighbours of Chios. But true Christian love wisheth well to the community. "I would to God" (said Mr Dod) "I were the worst minister in England" (and England had but a few better), not wishing himself worse than he was, but other men better.

Ver. 30. *The king rose up and the governor*] A little of such sad discourse served their turn: they were soon sated, and ready to say as Antipater king of Macedonia did, when one presented him a book treating of happiness, he answered, οὐ σχολάζω, I have somewhat else to do than to learn or listen to such businesses; when perhaps they might never have the like opportunity of hearing such a persuasive preacher while they breathed again, as Paul was.

Ver. 31. *This man doth nothing worthy*] Here Festus, consenting with the rest, condemneth himself. See chap. xxv. 25.

Ver. 32. *If he had not appealed*] Which if he had not, this free-man of Rome had been "free among the dead," Psal. lxxxviii. 5, free of that company ere this time of day. There was a necessity of his appeal, for the saving of his life. And he is the better contented with his present condition, because he had been told in a vision that he must go to Rome also, Acts xxiii. 11 ; while it was in store, and not yet come to that—*tota est jam Roma lupanar*, Rome is no better than a great brothel-house. That once " faithful city is now become a harlot ; it was full of judgment ; right-eousness lodged in it, but now murderers," Isa. i. 21.

CHAPTER XXVII.

Ver. 1. *It was determined*] FIRST by God, chap. xxiii., and then by the ordinary magistrate guided by God.

Ver. 2. *One Aristarchus, &c.*] St Paul's fellow-traveller first, and then fellow-prisoner too, yea, fellow-worker unto the kingdom of God, and a great comfort to him, Col. iv. 10, 11 ; Acts xix. 29 ; xx. 4, *Optimum solatium, sodalitium.* There-fore David so bewails the loss of Jonathan. St Paul counts it a singular mercy to him that Epaphroditus recovered, Phil. ii. 27. And St John found himself furthered and quickened by the graces of the elect lady, 2 John 12.

Ver. 3. *Liberty to go to his friend*] A great favour : there is no small comfort in the com-munion of saints. This heathen persecutors knew, and therefore banished and confined the Christians to isles and mines, where they could not have access one to another. (Cyprian.)

Ver. 4. *Because the winds, &c.*] The Straits of Magellan is such a place, that which way so-ever a man bendeth his course (saith one) he shall be sure to have the wind against him.

Ver. 5. *And when we had sailed*] These things are therefore particularly set down, that we may see Paul's perils by sea no less than by land ; and say with Solomon, " No man knoweth either love or hatred " by all that befalleth him, Eccles. ix. 1. See the note there.

Ver. 6. *Sailing into Italy*] To show that they had a terrible tempestuous time of it all along, from Sidon to Malta. So have the saints of God here, for most part, *ab utero ad urnam*, from the womb to the tomb, from the birth to the burial. This made Solomon prefer his coffin be-fore his cradle, Eccles. vii. 1, yea, before his crown ; as Queen Elizabeth also did ; for indeed, this life is pestered with so many miseries and molestations, satanical and secular, that it were to be accounted little better than hell were it not for the hopes of heaven, that sweetest harbour and haven of happiness. (Bernard.)

Ver. 7. *Salmone*] A high cliff of Crete. See Strabo, lib. ii., and the use of geography and other sciences, to the better understanding of the Scriptures.

Ver. 8. *Called The fair havens*] Which name it retains also at this day, Calos Limenas : for better cause, I believe, than the sea called Paci-fic, or calm, which Sir Francis Drake ever found rough and troublous above measure.

Ver. 9. *Now when much time was spent*] Not spilt ; for that Paul was not idle all that while, see Tit. i. 5, and Beza's annotations thereupon. *Nolite tempus in nugis conterere*, saith one. Time is a precious commodity. Of all other possessions a man may have two at once ; but two moments of time together no man could ever have. There-fore Cato held, that a wise man should be able *tam otii quam negotii rationem reddere*, to give an account of his leisure as well as of his labour. (Cic. de Senectute.) *Nullus mihi per otium dies exit*, saith Seneca, I spend no day idly. And Pliny said to his nephew when he saw him walk out some hours without studying, *Poteras has horas non perdere*, You might have better bestowed your time. The common complaint is, we want time ; but the truth is, we do not so much want it as waste it ; *Non parum habemus temporis, sed multum perdimus.* (Sen.)

Because the fast was now past] The Jews' yearly fast, Levit. xxiii. 27, which fell out in the seventh month, that answereth to our October, when navigation is dangerous. This yearly fast (or feast of expiation, as it is called) was insti-tuted, that they that had committed heinous of-fences worthy of death, and could not by offering up particular sacrifices for them, and confessing them, but hazard the loss of their lives, might have this day of expiation for all their sins what-soever ; God of his goodness so providing for the worst of his people.

Ver. 10. *But also of our lives*] Which every creature, from the highest angel to the lowest worm, maketh much of. Why is living man sor-rowful ? Lam. iii. 39. As if the prophet should say, He hath cause to rejoice that he is yet alive amidst all his sorrows. A living dog is better than a dead lion. " Joseph is yet alive." This was more worth to Jacob than all Joseph's hon-our. It is the Lord's mercy that we are not con-sumed. Skin for skin, &c. It should not be grievous to any man to sacrifice his estate to the service of his life.

Ver. 11. *Nevertheless the centurion*] Profane persons, trusting more to their own carnal wisdom than to God's word, cast themselves wilfully into the greatest dangers. Believe the prophets, and ye shall prosper. The wicked pass on and are punished, Prov. xxii. 3. We cannot get men to believe, till they feel, as Pharaoh.

Ver. 12. *And lieth toward the south-west*] It is a just complaint that a modern writer maketh of many men's spirits amongst us now-a-days ; that they lie like this haven, toward the south-west and north-west, two opposite points. (Mr Burroughs. Heart Div.) Methinks it should lie heavy upon those men's spirits that first divided us, by pub-lishing and pressing their new-fangled fancies.

Ver. 13. *Supposing that they had, &c.*] God maketh many times the strongest sinew of the arm of flesh to crack.

Fallitur augurio spes bona sæpe suo.

Ver. 14. *Called Euroclydon*] A stormy blast coming from the east,

Una Eurusque Notusque ruunt, creberque procellis
Africus, et vastos volvunt ad littora fluctus.

(Virg. Æneid. ii. 28.) This wind is by Pliny called *Navigantium pestis*, the mariner's misery. How happy is the Church, to whom, what wind soever bloweth, blows good and comfort, Cant. iv. 16. As for others, like as here, after a soft south wind arose Euroclydon; so to them after a false peace will be a sad storm, *Tranquillitas ista tempestas erit.*

Ver. 15. *Could not bear up*] Or direct the eye against the wind, could not look it in the face. There is an elegancy in the original, because part of the foreward of the ship is by mariners called the "ship's eye," ἀντοφθαλμεῖν. (*Verbum Polybianum.* Hist. iv.)

Ver. 16. *To come by the boat*] i. e. To recover, take up, and save the boat, that the waves should not break it.

Ver. 17. *Undergirding the ship*] With trusses or strong ropes, for fear lest she should split.

Ver. 18. *And being exceedingly tossed*] Seneca speaking of such as have lived long to little purpose, not improving their time and their talents, he saith that their lives are like ships in a storm, *multum jactati sunt, non navigarunt,* tossed much, but have sailed nothing; or like a millstone, that is ever moving, but removes not at all; or as when men make imperfect dashes, they are said to scribble, but do not write.

Ver. 19. *The tackling of the ship*] *eth hacchelim,* Jonah i. 15, which is almost our word "tackling."

Ver. 20. *All hope that we, &c.*] God delights to help those that are forsaken of their hopes: he reserveth his hand for a dead-lift. Good therefore and worthy all acceptation is the prophet's counsel, Isa. l. 10, 11. A child of light walking in darkness must do as these here, when neither sun nor star appeared for many days, cast the anchor of hope within the veil of heaven, pray and wait till the day dawn, and the day-star appear in his heart.

Ver. 21. *Gained this harm*] i. e. Prevented it. Prevision is the best way of prevention, but for want of prudent forecast "men pass on and are punished." *Leo cassibus irretitus dixit, si præscivissem.* Men might by wisdom redeem many miseries.

Ver. 22. *Be of good cheer*] So Bishop Ridley being once tossed by a sad tempest, Be of good cheer, said he to the boatmen, and ply your oars; for this boat carrieth a bishop that must be burned, not drowned. So Cæsar said to the ferryman in a storm, *Noli timere; Cæsarem fers, et fortunam Cæsaris:* Never fear; Cæsar is of better fortune, than to die by drowning. That was a memorable speech of a philosopher, who being in danger of shipwreck in a light starry night, said, "Surely I shall not perish, there are so many eyes of providence over me." Much more may a saint say so.

Ver. 23. *Whose I am, and whom I serve*] Lo, how holily he speaks, and like a Christian, among a company of profane and rude soldiers and seamen; so doth Jacob in his intercourse with Esau: these, saith he, are the children whom God of his grace hath given me, Gen. xxxiii. 5. Ubiquity is a sure sign of sincerity. An upright man is the same in all companies and in all conditions; as a pearl is a pearl, though cast into a puddle; as gold will glister whether cast into the fire or the water. Good blood will not belie itself; neither will a good spiritual constitution show itself otherwise than by suitable both communication and conversation.

Ver. 24. *God hath given thee all*] It is for the godly's sake that the wicked are spared and favoured. To the wicked, God saith concerning his servants, as the prophet once said to Jehoram, "Surely were it not that I regard the presence of Jehoshaphat king of Judah, I would not look toward thee, nor see thee," 2 Kings iii. 14.

Ver. 25. *For I believe God*] The believer walks about the world as a conqueror. Faith drinks to him in a cup of nepenthes, and bids him sing away sorrow; "But if ye will not believe, surely ye shall not be established," Isa. vii. 9.

Ver. 26. *We must be cast*] Where our ship being broke, we shall be brought safe to land by an all-powerful hand of God, who delights to help at a dead-lift. And this is here foretold, that it may not be thought to fall out by hap-hazard.

Ver. 27. *In Adria*] That is, in the Adriatic Sea.

Ver. 28. *Fifteen fathoms*] A sign they were nearer shore than before.

Ver. 29. *Wished for the day*] Wish we as much for the day of redemption, when after much tossing on this glassy sea, we shall safely land at the haven of happiness, at the quay of Canaan, the kingdom of heaven.

Discupio solvi, tecumque, o Christe, manere;
Portio fac regni sim quotacunque tui.

Ver. 30. *And as the shipmen*] So to shift for themselves, not caring what became of the passengers. A private-spirited man is *totus in se,* like the snail, still within-doors, at home; and though he may look abroad sometimes, and seem well affected to others, yet he seeks himself; as the snail creeping abroad out of the walls and hedges, yet still keeps within its own house.

Ver. 31. *Ye cannot be saved*] God must be trusted, but not tempted, by wilful neglect of due means. He is not tied to them, but yet doth usually work by them. See my note on Matt. iv. 4.

Ver. 32. *Then the soldiers*] According to St Paul's counsel, who was now somebody with them. Indeed he was grown, by much exercise and experience, *harum rerum callentissimus, et vir in omnibus rebus excellentissimus,* as one saith of him, a most gallant man, and every way accomplished.

Ver. 33. *Having taken nothing*] i. e. Having made no set meal but by snatches and catches. When life is in danger, all is laid aside till that be secured. Oh that we were likewise wise for our souls; surely if we knew our danger, we should neither eat nor drink till we had made our peace with God. For is it nothing to lose an immortal soul? to purchase an ever-living death?

Ver. 34. *Not an hair*] A proverbial speech, Luke xxi. 18. See Matt. x. 30, with the note.

Ver. 35. *In presence of them all*] He was not ashamed of God's service before those heathens. No more was Abraham, who built an altar to his God wherever he came. That was the first work he did, not fearing the idolatrous Canaanites. A bold and wise profession is required of every Christian. It is no gold that glitters not.

Ver. 36. *Then were they all of good cheer*] By Paul's good example. For as one bad man may hinder much good, Eccles. ix. 18, so on the contrary.

Ver. 37. *We were all two hundred, &c.*] And that not one of this "all" should miscarry, was a miracle of God's mercy; sith all of them could not swim (likely), and being so low brought with fear and fasting, how could they so bestir themselves, as in that case was requisite? Or being so many on a cluster, how did they not one hinder another? But God was in the shipwreck; and if he command deliverance, it shall be done with ease and expedition. In case their skill or strength fail, "he shall spread forth his hands in the midst of them, as he that swimmeth spreadeth forth his hands to swim," Isa. xxv. 11, with great facility he shall do it: the motion in swimming is easy, and with a slight; strong, violent strokes in the water, would rather sink than support.

Ver. 38. *Cast out the wheat*] *Fastidientes divinum verbum, et damnum et dedecus pati oportet.* "Behold! they have rejected the word of the Lord, and what wisdom is in them?" Jer. viii. 9.

Ver. 39. *They discovered a creek*] Then chiefly are we to look for tempests when we draw nighest to the shore, to the haven. Our last encounter at death is like to be the sharpest. The Israelites never met with such opposition as when they were to take possession of the land. Then all the kings of Canaan combined against them.

Ver. 40. *Hoised up the mainsail*] Which before they had struck, by reason of the violence of the storm. If God afflict, we must carry our sail accordingly, Ruth i. 20.

Ver. 41. *Where two seas met*] The men of Malta show a certain place at this day which they call *lascala di San Paulo*, Saint Paul's arrival.

Ver. 42. *To kill the prisoners*] An ill requital of Paul's kindness. But soldiers make but a sport of killing men. "Let the young men arise and play before us," said Abner.

Ver. 43. *Willing to save Paul*] By whom he had been hitherto saved; and in whom he saw that goodness that could not but attract all hearts not congealed into steel and adamant. I read of a monster, who that night that his prince pardoned and released him, got out and slew him; this was Michael Balbus. (Zonaras in Annal.) Such another was bloody Bonner, act-

ive in bringing the Lord Cromwell (who had been his great patron) to an untimely death. In like sort dealt Bishop Watson by Mr Rough, and Bishop Bourn by Mr Bradford, who had saved their lives with the hazard of their own. William Parry was for burglary condemned to die, but saved by Queen Elizabeth's pardon; this ungrateful man afterwards sought to requite her, by vowing her death, A. D. 1584, and was therefore worthily executed as a traitor; and indeed hanging was too good for him. (Speed.) The senate of Basil first tortured, and then burnt to ashes, a villain called Paulus Sutor, that murdered an old man that had done him many fatherlike courtesies, A. D. 1565, as judging, that to render evil for evil is brutish, but to render evil for good is devilish. (Lonicer.) Lycurgus the Lacedæmonian law-giver would make no law against such, *quod prodigiosa res esset beneficium non rependere,* because it could not be imagined that any would be so unworthy as not to recompense one kindness with another. If this centurion should have done otherwise than he did in saving Paul, by whose prayers and for whose sake he and his company had escaped, no time would have worn out his utter disgrace and infamy.

Ver. 44.] *Hominum malitiam vincit Dei bonitas,* saith Beza here. God's goodness overcometh man's badness.

CHAPTER XXVIII.

Ver. 1. *And when they were escaped*] SOME of them escaped perhaps as narrowly as did Sir Thomas Challoner, who when he was young, served under Charles V. in the expedition of Algiers; where being shipwrecked, after he had swam till his strength and his arms failed him, at the length catching hold of a cable with his teeth, he escaped, not without the loss of some of his teeth. He was afterwards knighted for his valour at Mussleborough field, and died A. D. 1566. (Camd. Britan.)

Ver. 2. *And the barbarous people*] So the Grecians (and afterwards the Romans) called all other nations besides themselves. But now the Grecians, having lost their ancient liberty and glory, by means of the Turkish oppression, are become no less barbarous than those rude nations whom they before scorned. Which misery, with a thousand more, they may justly impute to their own ambition and discord.

Ver. 3. *And fastened on his hand*] Thus, many are the troubles of the righteous; but out of them all the Lord delivereth them. No country hath more venomous creatures than Egypt, none more antidotes; so godliness hath many troubles, and as many helps against trouble. The devil's design here was to have destroyed Paul, but he was deceived. So he desired to have Peter, Luke xxii. 31, *sc.* to hell, but that was more than he could do.

Ver. 4. *Yet vengeance suffereth not, &c.*] *Nemo*

scelus gerit in pectore, qui non idem habet Nemesin in tergo. The fall of Blackfriars slew well-nigh a hundred, whereof two were priests; a third having taken water, together with many others that had escaped, purposing to go into Flanders, were drowned at London-bridge shortly after, the boat being overturned.

Ver. 5. *And he shook off the beast*] So should we do false and slanderous reports; or rather make a good use of them; as the skilful apothecary of the flesh of this poisonful beast makes a wholesome theriacle (θηριακὰ), or treacle, as we call it.

And felt no harm] No more did Queen Elizabeth, when Squier, the traitor, sent by Walpool the Jesuit, had poisoned the pummel of her saddle. The vigour of the poison (said the Jesuit) is such, as neither continuance of times nor subtilty of air could check or unvirtuate. And yet, albeit the season were hot, and the veins open to receive any malign tainture, her body thereupon felt no distemperature, nor her hand felt no more hurt (saith Speed) than Paul's did when he shook off the viper into the fire.

Ver. 6. *That he should have swollen*] Or, have been inflamed, πίμπρασθαι, viz. with the viper's venom. The devil's darts are called fiery for the dolour and distemper they work, Eph. vi. 16; in allusion likely to the poisoned darts that the Scythians of old and other nations now use in war, dipped in the blood and gall of vipers, the venomous heat of which, like a fire in their flesh, killed the wounded with torments; the likest hell of any other, saith one. These fiery darts sting the wicked, as the fiery serpents did the Israelites. The saints shake them off without hurt, though not always without smart.

Ver. 7. *Who received us, and lodged us three days courteously*] Gr. φιλοφρόνως, of a friendly mind. As he is the best Christian that is most humble, so is he the truest gentleman that is most courteous. And as fair flowers in the spring draw passengers' eyes, so doth courtesy in high degrees win men's affections.

Ver. 8. *Sick of a fever*] Which hath its name both in Greek and Latin from the fire that is in it, πυρετὸς. *Febris a fervore.* The difference is not so great whether a man broil in the bed, or at a stake by frying a faggot: fear it not.

Ver. 9. *Came and were healed*] On both sides (likely), and hence their forwardness and free-heartedness, ver. 10.

Ver. 10. *Who also honoured us*] *Perraro grati reperiuntur*, saith Cicero. A thankful man is worth his weight in gold, saith Mr Ward. The Italian hath a proverb, *Seiapato il morbo, fraudato il santo;* when the disease is departed, the saint is defrauded, viz. of the honour that was vowed to be done to him. Not so here.

Ver. 11. *Whose sign was Castor and Pollux*] Seamen say that if these two stars arise not together, it is a sign of an ensuing tempest. Dissension is a forerunner of destruction.

Ver. 12. *Syracuse*] The metropolis of Sicily, where lived and died that famous mathematician, Archimedes; who by his art so long held out the city against Marcellus the Roman general, that beleaguered it. (Plut.)

Ver. 13. *Came to Rhegium*] Which hath its name of breaking, *a ῥήγνυμι, rumpo;* because, say some, there the sea broke off Sicily from Italy, which was before but one continent. The like they report concerning France and England.

Ver. 14. *Seven days*] For mutual enjoyment of one another; there being no such comfort upon earth, next to communion with God, as the communion of saints, 2 John 12, that our joy may be full. This, heathens knew, and therefore relegated Christians and confined them to isles and mines, where they could not have access one to another. (Cyprian, Epist.)

Ver. 15. *They came to meet us*] So Paul entered Rome as a long-looked-for triumpher.

Ver. 16. *Paul was suffered to dwell*] So Bradford, prisoner in the King's Bench, was in so good credit with his keeper, that he had license to go all about the city without a keeper, &c. Yea, to ride into Oxfordshire to a merchant's house of his acquaintance, &c.

Ver. 17. *After three days*] Ministers should free themselves as much and as soon as may be from sinister suspicions. For they must never think to do good on those that have conceived an incurable prejudice against them.

Ver. 18. *Because there was no cause*] See chap. xxv. 25.

Ver. 19. *To accuse my nation of*] But to defend Christ's cause and mine own innocency, with as little reflex on the Jews as may be. It is an ill business to defame a whole nation (one's own especially), as Scaliger, that proud hypercritic, who gave this base and unmannerly character, *Gothi belluæ, Scoti non minus, Angli perfidi, inflati, feri, contemptores, stolidi, amentes, inertes, inhospitales, immanes.* The Goths are beasts, so are the Scots. As for the English, they are perfidious, proud, fierce, scornful, fools, madmen, sluggards, inhospitable, cruel.

Ver. 20. *For the hope of Israel*] That is, for the resurrection of the dead and that eternal life that Israel hopes and looks for. *Hallucinantur philosophi, qui sapientem non metu solum sed et spe vacare vellent. Spes in terrenis incerti nomen boni, spes in divinis nomen est certissimi,* Heb. xi. 1. Hope in God, saith every David to himself, Psal. xliii. ult.

I am bound with this chain] At Rome, such prisoners as had liberty to go abroad, had a long chain, the one end whereof was fastened to their right hand, and the other end was tied to a soldier's left hand, who was to be his keeper. Thus was St Paul bound, likely.

Ver. 21. *We neither received letters*] Not because the priests and elders were now grown better-minded toward Paul than they were wont to be (for malice is like the crocodile, that groweth as long as it liveth; and, as we use to say of runnet, the older it is, the stronger), but that they could not so well deal with him at such a distance; and besides, being so far off them, he could be no such eye-sore to them.

Ver. 22. *Everywhere it is spoken against*] *Nomen in Christianis damnabatur, non crimen*, saith Tertullian. When Attalus the martyr was put to death at Lyons, a table was set up over his head with this inscription, *Hic est Attalus Christianus*, This is Attalus the Christian; that was all they had to charge him with. So when Polycarp was martyred, all the crime objected against him was, that he confessed himself to be a Christian. Nero made this cruel edict, Whosoever confessed himself to be a Christian, let him be presently put to death without any more ado, as a convicted enemy of mankind.[1]

Ver. 23. *There came into his lodging*] Tertullian telleth us that it was forbidden the primitive Christians by a public statute, to have temples or places of public meetings. It is yet better with us, blessed be God. We have, as Joseph provided them in Egypt, a granary or store-house in every city, and village for most part.

Ver. 24. *And some believed not*] The word, as Moses, slays the Egyptian, saves the Israelite. It is to some the savour of life, to others of death, as Obed-edom was blessed for the ark, the Philistines cursed.

Ver. 25. *And when they agreed not*] They jarred. It is a metaphor from musical instruments that make no harmony, ἀσύμφωνοι.

Had spoken one word] A terrible stinging word, that would stick in their souls and flesh, as the envenomed arrows of the Almighty, throughout all eternity.

Ver. 26. *Hearing, ye shall hear*, &c.] A heavy ear is a singular judgment. *Antagoras, cum Thebaidos librum apud Bœotos recitaret, nec quisquam recitanti applauderet, complicato volumine, Merito, inquit, Bœoti vocamini, quia boum habetis aures.* (Erasm. Chiliad.) The Greeks have a proverb, *Asino quispiam narrabat fabulam, ac ille movebat aures.*

Seeing, ye shall see] Speculatively. *And not*

[1] *Sine ulteriore sui defensione capite plectitur.*

perceive] *i. e.* Practically, as given over for their wilfulness to spiritual blindness.

Ver. 27. *Is waxed gross*] "Their heart is as fat as grease; but I delight in thy law," saith David, Psal. cxix. 70. Naturalists tell us that fat-hearted men are dull-witted. Γαστὴρ παχεῖα λεπτὸν οὐ τίκτει νόον. It is a heavy case when men have got a kind of hoof over their hearts, *callum obductum, corneas fibras*, brawny breasts, horny heart-strings.

Their eyes have they closed] Gr. ἐκάμμυσαν. They have winked, they shut the windows, lest the light should come in. *Ut liberius peccent, libenter ignorant*, saith Bernard. *Sponte quidem reluctantur veritati, non tamen fortuito*, saith Beza.

Ver. 28. *That the salvation of God*] *i. e.* The gospel, that "grace of God that bringeth salvation," Tit. ii. 11, and is the power of God to salvation to as many as believe, Rom. i. 16; therefore called the word of this life, that is able to save souls; and hath heaven in it, potentially, as the kernel hath the tree, or the seed the harvest.

Ver. 29. *Had great reasoning*, &c.] It is not the gospel, but the contempt of the gospel, that breedeth questions and quarrellings.

Ver. 30. *And received all that came in unto him*] Being a genuine child of the Church, set forth by that πανδοχεῖον, Luke x. 34, that inn that receives and succours all sin-sick passengers. Christ himself (saith one) was therefore born in an inn, to signify that in the Church there is lodging for all. Let our houses be little churches and receptacles for the righteous, as Paul's was, Col. ii. 5; so that a stranger coming thither, may behold our holy order, and say, as Jacob did of Bethel, "This is the house of God, this is the gate of heaven," Gen. xxviii. 17.

Ver. 31. *Preaching the kingdom*, &c.] Mr Bradford, during the time of his imprisonment, preached twice a day continually, unless sickness hindered him; where also the sacrament was often ministered. And through his means (the keeper so well did bear with him) such resort of good people was daily at his lecture, and ministration of the sacrament, that commonly his chamber was well nigh filled.

Deus dedit his quoque finem.

A
COMMENTARY OR EXPOSITION

UPON THE

EPISTLE OF ST PAUL TO THE ROMANS.

CHAPTER I.

Ver. 1. *Paul*] A LITTLE man, it should seem by his name (such as was James the Less, Mark xv. 40) : but as the Church of Philadelphia (discommended for nothing), though she had but a little strength, yet had a great door set open ; and as Bethlehem was the least, and yet not the least among the princes of Judah ; so was this apostle the last, 1 Cor. xv. 8 (and perhaps the least in stature), as one born out of due time.[1] But God (who loves to be *maximus in minimis*) had designed him to great services, and gifted him accordingly, so that he was no whit behind the very chiefest of the apostles, 2 Cor. xii. 5 ; and for pains-taking, he laboured more abundantly than they all, 1 Cor. xv. 10. Hence Chrysostom calleth him *insatiabilem Dei cultorem*, an insatiable servant of Christ. And himself seems as insatiable an encomiast of this apostle (the apostle he commonly nameth him "by an excellency"), for he hath written eight homilies in his commendation. And if any think he hath said too much, it is because either they have not read him, or cannot judge of his worth. *Qui tricubitalis cœlos transcendit* (as the same father saith), little though he were, yet he got above the heavens.[2]

A servant of Jesus Christ] This is a higher title than monarch of the world, as Numa, second king of Rome, could say.[3] Constantinus, Valentinus, and Theodosius, three emperors, called themselves *Vasallos Christi*, the vassals of Christ, as Socrates reporteth.

Ver. 2. *Promised*] Fore-showed and fore-shadowed in the types of the ceremonial law (which was their gospel, it was Christ in figure), and in the writings of the prophets ; only by degrees and piece-meal, πολυμερῶς. God spake of old to our fathers, by his servants the prophets, Heb. i. 1. All was in riddles to what it is now ;

and that saying took place, *Et latet, et lucet.* It is close, and yet clear.

Ver. 3. *Concerning his Son*] Here is a lofty and lively description of Christ's sacred person. The whole Epistle being the confession of our Churches, as Melancthon calleth it, who therefore went over it ten several times in his ordinary lectures (Scultet. Annal.) : the Epistle being such, as never can any man possibly think, speak, or write sufficiently of its worth and excellency. Mr Perkins adviseth, in reading the Scripture, first to begin with the Gospel of John, and this Epistle to the Romans, as being the keys of the New Testament. And for this Epistle to the Romans, Cardinal Pole adviseth to begin at the twelfth chapter, and read to the end ; and practise the precepts of repentance and mortification, and then set upon the former part of the Epistle, where justification and predestination are handled.

According to the flesh] i. e. Either his body or his human nature, called a swift cloud (as some will have it), Isa. xix. 1, " Behold, the Lord rideth upon a swift cloud, and shall come into Egypt." And, the habitable part of God's earth, Prov. viii. 31. For the Word dwelt amongst us, John i. 14. And here was *habitatio Dei cum carne*, God dwelling with flesh, which the magicians held impossible, Dan. ii. 11. It was much for God to " pour out his Spirit upon all flesh," the best thing upon the basest, Joel ii. 28. But it was more, for the fulness of the Godhead bodily to inhabit it, Col. ii. 9. See the note on 1 Cor. i. 2. St Paul seems to have learned of the holy angels, thus to salute, Luke ii. 14. See the note there.

Ver. 4. *Declared to be, &c.*] Gr. ὁρισθέντος, defined ; for definitions explain obscurities.

With power] For, *Superas evadere ad auras, Hic labor, hoc opus est*—a work befitting a God. See Eph. i. 20, with the note there.

---

[1] See the note on Acts xiii. 9 ; Rev. iii. 9 ; Matt. ii. 6, with Mic. v. 2 ; 1 Cor. xv. 8.

[2] *Grandior solet esse Deus in parvulis quam in magnis. In formicis major anima quam in elephantis, in nanis quam in gigantibus. Aut illum non audiĕrunt, aut judicare non possunt, ut olim de Crasso et Antonio dixit.* Cicero de Orat.

[3] τοῦ Θεοῦ ὑπηρεσίαν βασιλεύειν ἐνόμιζεν. Plut.

The Spirit of holiness] The divine essence of Christ, 2 Cor. xiii. 4, which sanctifieth the human nature assumed by him.

Ver. 5. *For obedience to the faith*] That is, to the gospel (that doctrine of faith), or to Christ, who is oft put for faith (whereof he is the proper object) in this Epistle. " Kiss the Son," &c. " Hear him." Psal. ii. 12 ; Matt. xvii. 5.

Ver. 6. *Ye are the called*] With a high and heavenly calling, Heb. iii. 1.   See the note there.

Ver. 7. *Called to be saints*] Those then that are called, are saints whilst alive, and not only those that are canonized by the pope after they are dead *in numerum Deorum ab Ecclesia Romana relati,* as Bembus profanely speaketh of their St Francis, a sorry man, of whom (as once of Becket 48 years after his death) it may well be disputed whether he were damned or saved. Pope Callistus III. sainted some such in his time, as of whom Cardinal Bessarion, knowing them for naught, said, These new saints make me doubt much of the old.

Grace be to you, and peace]   See the note on 1 Cor. i. 2.

Ver. 8. *Your faith is spoken of*]   See chap. xvi., and Juvenal, Tacitus, and other profane writers, who bitterly exagitate the doctrines and practices of those Roman Christians.   Now that must needs be good that such men speak evil of: and as Jerome writeth to Austin, *Quod signum majoris gloriæ est, Omnes hæretici me detestantur:* the heretics hate me ; and that is no small grace to me.

Ver. 9. *Whom I serve in my spirit*] That is, with all the faculties of my soul concentred and co-united.

Ver. 10. *I might have a prosperous journey*] This he prayed, and this he had by such a way as he little dreamt of.   Little thought Paul, that when he was bound at Jerusalem, and posted from one prison to another, that God was now sending him to Rome ; yet he sent him, and very safe with a great convoy.   God goes oft another way to work for our good than we could imagine.

Ver. 11. *That I may impart*] There is no envy in spiritual things, because they may be divided *in solidum;* one may have as much as another, and all alike. *Scientiarum (sic et gratiarum) ea vis est natura ut quo plus doceas, et alteri de tuo largiare, eo ditior ac doctior fias,* saith Bodina. Such is the nature and property of sciences and graces, that the more you communicate them, the more you increase them.

Ver. 12. *That I may be comforted*] Or, exhorted. *Ad communem exhortationem percipiendam,* saith Beza out of Bucer, and others. The meanest of Christ's members may contribute somewhat to the edifying even of an apostle, 2 John 12. That favourite of Christ would be furthered and quickened by the graces of a woman. Now when such grandees in grace have benefit by communion of saints, how much more may they whose measures are less !   The very angels

know not so much but they would know more, Eph. iii. 10 ; 1 Pet. i. 12.

Ver. 13. *But was let hitherto*] Either by Satan, 1 Thess. ii. 18; or by the Holy Spirit otherwise disposing of him, as Acts xix. 6, 7 ; or by some intervenient but important occasion, as chap. xv. 20, 21.

Ver. 14. *I am debtor*] Because entrusted with talents for that purpose, 1 Cor. ix. 16.   See the note there.   It might more truly be said of Paul than it was of Cato, that he did—*toti natum se credere mundo,* believe himself born for a common good (Lucan) ; or, than it was said to Bucer by his physicians, *Non sibi se, sed multorun utilitati esse natum,* that he was born for the benefit of many. (Melch. Adam.)

Ver. 15. *So as much*] *Quicquid in me situm est, promptum est.*   A notable expression.

Ver. 16. *For I am not ashamed*] As men are apt to be ; whence that fatherly charge, 2 Tim. i. 8.   Do ye think (said John Frith, martyr, to the archbishop's men that would have let him go) that I am afraid to declare mine opinion unto the bishops of England in a manifest truth ? If you should both leave me here, and go tell the bishops that you had lost Frith, I would surely follow as fast after as I might, and bring them news that I had found and brought Frith again.

For it is the power, &c.] Eternal life is potentially in the word preached, as the harvest is potentially in the seed.

Ver. 17. *The just shall live by faith*] Hab. ii. 4, that is, they shall enjoy themselves by their faith, in greatest disasters or dangers, when others are at their wit's ends.   That is the prophet's sense ; and the apostle not unfitly applieth it to prove justification by faith alone, for if a man live by faith he is just by faith.

Ver. 18. *Who hold the truth*] Hold the light of their consciences (which is as a prophet from God) prisoner.   The natural man, that he may sin the more securely, imprisons the truth, which he acknowledgeth, and lays hold on all the principles in his head, that might any way disturb his course in sin, locking them up in restraint.   Hence it appears that no man is righteous in himself, or by his own righteousness, which was the τὸ κρινόμενον. Those of the philosophers that knew most, as Socrates, Aristotle, Plato, &c., are belied if they were not vicious in their practice, *et de virtute locuti, Clunem agitant.* (Juvenal.) Plato had the knowledge of one God ; but durst not say so publicly.   It is neither easy (saith he) to find out the Creator of all, nor safe to communicate the knowledge of him to the vulgar.   So Seneca wrote a book (now lost) against superstitions ; but saith Austin, *Libertas affuit scribenti, non viventi : colebat quod reprehendebat, agebat quod arguebat, quod culpabat adorabat :* He lived not after his own writings, but worshipped what he reproved ; he did what he decried, he bowed before that he blamed ; saying (as Domitius Calderinus when he went to mass) *Eamus ad communem errorem,* Let us go for company to that which we cannot but condemn for a common error. (Bucholcer.)

Ver. 19. *Because that which may*] Heathens might know God the Creator, *per species creaturarum* (as they speak), either in way of negation, or causality, or eminence: not so God the Redeemer.

Ver. 20. *Are clearly seen*] *Pervidentur.* As in a mirror, or as on a theatre. *Ut solem in aquis, sic Deum in operibus contemplamur.* God (saith one) is best seen in his works, as the sun in the west.[1]

Ver. 21. *Neither were thankful*] How then shall we answer to God our hateful unthankfulness, which is (saith one) "a monster in nature, a solecism in manners, a paradox in divinity, a parching wind to dam up the fountain of divine favours. Woe be to our Solifugæ that abuse gospel-light; these put not light "under a bushel" (as the poor Paynims did) but under a dung-hill; *Gravis est lux conscientiæ,* saith Seneca; but *gravior est lux Evangelii,* say we. A heavy account will they give that abuse the light of nature; but much heavier they that "receive the grace of God in vain."

But became vain in their imaginations] Gr. διαλογισμοῖς, in their reasonings, disputations, discourses upon serious deliberation. They stood not to their own principles (as, that there is one God only, that this God is to be worshipped, &c.), but were atheists by night that worshipped the sun, and atheists by day that worshipped the moon, as Cyril saith wittily.

Ver. 22. *Professing themselves to be wise*] Aristotle, nature's chief secretary, writeth many things most absurdly concerning God; as, that he is a living creature, that he worketh not freely, but by a kind of servile necessity; and that therefore he deserveth no praise or thanks from men for his many benefits, sith he doth but what he must needs do. These are Aristotle's absurd assertions. And yet at Stuckard in Germany was found a doctor of divinity that preached to the people, that the Church might be sufficiently well taught and governed by Aristotle's ethics, though we had no Bible. And the Collen divines set forth a book, concerning Aristotle's salvation, and called him Christ's fore-runner in naturals, as John Baptist had been in supernaturals. But what saith St Paul, 1 Cor. ii. 14, "The natural man receiveth not," &c. Gr. ψυχικὸς, the souly-man, that doth *excolere animam,* such as Aristotle, Tully, &c., who the wiser they were, the vainer they were, and the further from God and his kingdom; their learning hung in their light, and served but to light them into utter darkness.[2]

Ver. 23. *Made like to corruptible man*] God made man in his own image; and man (to be even with him, as it were) will needs make God after his image.

And four-footed beasts] God therefore justly

gave them up to sodomy, which did abase them below the beasts; that there might be an analogy between the sin and the punishment. This is called a "meet recompense," ver. 27. They dishonoured God, they dishonoured therefore themselves. They would not know nor honour him, they shall not therefore know nor spare one another, &c.; so severely will God punish the contempt of and rebellion against the light.

And creeping things] In Lapland the people worship that all day for a god, whatsoever they see first in the morning, be it a bird or worm.

Ver. 24. *Gave them up to uncleanness*] Aristotle confesseth the disability of moral knowledge to rectify the intemperance of nature; and made it good in his practice; for he used a common strumpet to satisfy his lust. Socrates is said to have had his catamite *inter Socraticos,* &c. (Juvenal.)

Ver. 25. *Who changed*] They tare out their natural principles and turned atheists, as Diagoras, who yet was an atheist more with his tongue than with his heart; for having cried down a deity in a famous oration, he yet suffered himself to be deified by the people for his eloquence. *Qua ornari ab eo Diabolus quærebat,* as Austin writeth to a learned but lewd person of his times. See my Common-place of Atheism. *Epicurus verbis reliquit Deos re sustulit,* saith Cicero (De Nat. Deor.).

Ver. 26. *Into that which is against nature*] So against nature, that children (nature's end) and posterity is utterly lost by it. Paul seems to point here at Messalina (that shame of her sex), the wife of Claudius the emperor.

Ver. 27. *Leaving the natural*] As at this day in the Levant, sodomy is held no sin. The Turkish pashas have many wives, but more catamites, which are their serious loves. (Blount's Voyage.)

Burned in their lust] Gr. ἐξεκαύθησαν, "were scalded." Some men put off all manhood, become dogs, worse than dogs. Hence Deut. xxiii. 18, "The price of a dog," that is, of a buggerer, as Junius and Deodatus expound it.

Ver. 28. *To a reprobate mind*] Or, an injudicious mind; or, a mind rejected, disallowed, abhorred of God; or a mind that none hath cause to glory in, but rather to be much ashamed of.

Ver. 29. *With all unrighteousness*] The mother of all the ensuing misrule.

Wickedness] The Syrian saith, "bitterness." See Jer. ii. 19. The word πονηρία may be rendered troublesomeness, as the devil is called ὁ πονηρὸς, the troublesome one, the molester of God's people; restless in himself and disquieting others.

Envy, murder] Three such agnominations are found in this black beadroll.[3] The apostle seems delighted with them, as was likewise the prophet Isaiah. Of which noble two, I may well say as one doth of Demosthenes and Cicero, *Demos-*

---

[1] *Sæculum est speculum, quo Deum intueamur.*
[2] *Quanto doctiores tanto nequiores, ut Syri venales apud Ciceronem.* Athenæus brings Plato bewailing his fond love

to a filthy harlot.
[3] πορνεία, πονηρία. φθόνου, φόνου. ἀσυνέτους, ἀσυνθέτους. κακοήθεια, κακία.

thenes Ciceroni præripuit ne esset primus orator, Cicero Demostheni, ne solus.

Malignity] Or, morosity, crossness, ill conditions ; or an evil disposition, that taketh everything the worst way ; whenas a better disposition would make a better exposition, and take things by the right handle.

Whisperers] These are worse than backbiters, because they work under-ground, like as the wind that creeps in the chinks and crevices in a wall, or the cracks in a window, prove commonly more dangerous than a storm that meets a man in the face upon the champaign. *A vento percolato, et ab inimico reconciliato libera nos.*

Ver. 30. *Haters of God*] And so God-murderers, 1 John iii. 15. See the note there.

Ver. 31. *Implacable*] That will not hear of a truce, much less of a peace. *Nihil se libentius facere dictitabat Cæsar, quam supplicibus ignoscere.* (Cæsar. Comment.) And surely, as any one is more manly, he is more merciful, as David, 2 Sam. i. 12. And, on the contrary, the basest natures are most vindictive ; neither will they ever be heartily reconciled. Their reconciliations are *vulpinæ amicitiæ*, fox-like friendships.

Ver. 32. *Have pleasure*] Or they patronize, applaud, and approve, συνευδοκοῦσι· this is set last, as worst of all ; it comprehends all kinds of consent. (Theop.) To hold the bag is as bad as to fill it. The law of God requires not only our observation but our preservation, to cause others to keep it, as well as ourselves ; and to rebuke, at least by a cast of our countenance (as God doth, Psal. lxxx. 16), those that violate it. There is little difference, *faveasne sceleri, an illud facias,* whether thou commit sin or consent to it.

CHAPTER II.

Verse 1. *Therefore thou art inexcusable*] Though thou have no pleasure in them that do evil, as chap. i. 32, but dost superciliously censure them, being thyself otherwise as bad. Cato is said to have exercised usury, to have prostituted his wife, to have slain himself. God oft sets a *Noverint universi* upon the world's wizards, for the foulest fools.

Ver. 2. *Which commit such*] As Cato, ver. 1, whom yet Velleius affirmeth to have been *hominem virtuti simillimum.* But God judgeth not as man.

Ver. 3. *Thinkest thou*] This is preaching to the conscience, to the quick. Our exhortations should be as forked arrows to stick in men's hearts ; and not wound only, as other arrows. A poor hermit came to our Richard I., A. D. 1195, and preaching to him the words of eternal life, bade him be mindful of the subversion of Sodom, and to abstain from things unlawful : otherwise, said he, the deserved vengeance of God will come upon thee. The hermit being gone, the king neglected his words. But afterwards falling sick, he more seriously bethought himself, and

waxing sound in soul as well as in body, he grew more devout, and charitable to the poor. (Hoveden. Speed.)

Ver. 4. *The goodness of God*] Gr. τὸ χρηστὸν, his native goodness, ready to be employed to the behoof and benefit of the creature, Tit. iii. 4. Now as the beam of the sun shining on fire doth discourage the burning of that ; so the shining of God's mercies on us should dishearten and extinguish lust in us. This is so equal and needful a duty, that Peter picks this flower out of Paul's garden, as one of the choicest, and urgeth it upon those to whom he writes, 2 Pet. iii. 15.

Ver. 5. *Treasurest up unto thyself*] *Sicut mittentes pecuniam in gazophylacium, quod, ubi jam impletur, confringitur,* saith Stella upon Luke. In treasuring, there is, 1. Laying in ; 2. Lying hid ; 3. Bringing out again, as there is occasion. Wicked persons, while by following their lusts they think they do somewhat to their happiness, shall in the end find, *pro thesauro carbones,* those burning coals, Psal. cxl. 10.

Ver. 6. *Who shall render*] The Papists hence infer merit of works. But it is well observed that the Church in the Canticles is nowhere described by the beauty of her hands, or fingers. Christ concealeth the mention of her hands, that is, of her works (Cotton on Canticles) : 1. Because he had rather his Church should abound in good works in silence than boast of them (especially when they are wanting), as Rome doth. 2. Because it is he above that worketh all our works for us, Isa. xxvi. 12 ; Hos. xiv. 4 ; John xv. 5. *Certum est nos facere quod facimus ; sed ille facit, ut faciamus.* (Augustine.) We do what we do ; but it is He that causeth us so to do. See the note on Matt. xvi. 27.

Ver. 7. *Who by patient continuance*] Or, by suffering persecution for righteousness' sake. Gordus the martyr said, "It is to my loss, if you bate me anything in my sufferings." *Majora certamina, majora sequuntur præmia, ὅπου πλείων κόπος, πολὺ κερδὸς,* saith Ignatius. Much pains hath much gains.

Ver. 8. *But unto them that are contentious*] That wrangle and thwartle against clearest truths, searching the devil's skull for carnal arguments, as those Athenians, Acts xvii. ; being refractory as Pharaoh, who would not sit down under the miracle, but sent for the magicians. And though the word doth eat up all they say, as Moses's rod did, yet harden they their hearts, as Pharaoh, and resolve to curse, as Balaam, whatever come of it. These are those contentious ones, ἐξ ἐριθείας.

Ver. 9. *Of the Jew first*] *Qui ideo deteriores sunt, quia meliores esse deberent.* Who are therefore worse, because they should be better. Salvian.

Ver. 10. *Peace*] Safety here and salvation hereafter.

To every man that worketh good] Yet not for his work's sake, because no proportion between the work and the wages ; no more than between a crown and a nutshell. That wretched monk therefore died blasphemously, who said, *Redde mihi æternam vitam quam debes,* Pay me eternal life, that thou owest me. And how dare Bellarmine say, that good works are *mercatura regni cælestis,* the price we pay for heaven? or that other Papist, God forbid, that we should enjoy heaven as of mere alms to us: no, we have it by conquest. Strange impudence!

Ver. 11. *For*] See the note on Acts x. 34.

Ver. 12. *Perish without law*] Or, though they had no written law, as that of Moses.

Ver. 13. *But the doers of the law*] The Scriptures are *verba vivenda non legenda,* as Egidius, Abbot of Nuremberg, said of the 119th Psalm. *Boni Catholici sunt qui et fidem integram sequuntur, et bonos mores.* (Aug.) Lessons of music must be practised, and a copy not read only but acted. Divinity must be done as well as known.

Ver. 14. *Do by nature, &c.*] Velleius saith that Cato was *Homo virtuti simillimus, cui id ¦solum visum est rationem habere, quod haberet justitiam, omnibus humanis vitiis immunis, &c.* Aristides, Phocion, and Socrates were famous for their integrity. (Plin. vii. 31.)

Are a law to themselves] The Thracians gloried that they were αὐτόνομοι, living laws, walking statutes.

Ver. 15. *Their thoughts meanwhile*] Or, betwixt whiles: or in every interim of this life, μεταξὺ. Other faculties may rest; an obscene dream by night shall not escape conscience's record; it is *index, judex, vindex,* God's spy and man's over-seer; and it is better to have it sore than seared.

Ver. 16. *According to my gospel*] Which promiseth heaven to believers. This is comfort to those that are faithful in weakness, though but weak in faith. The sentence of the last day shall be but a more manifest declaration of that judgment that the Lord in this life, most an end, hath passed upon men. Heathens shall be judged by the law of nature; profligate professors by the law written, and the word preached; believers by the gospel, which saith, "If there be a willing mind, God accepteth," &c.

Ver. 17. *Restest in the law*] So spending thy time in a still dream, but thou shalt have sick waking, then when God shall send out summons for such sleepers. Men dream their Midianitish dreams, and tell them for law or gospel to their neighbours, Judg. vii. 13.

Ver. 18. *Being instructed out of the law*] Gr. κατηχούμενος, Being well catechised and principled, thou art able to discern the doctrines, and choose the best. Luther somewhere professeth himself to be *discipulum catechismi,* a scholar to the catechism; and those that are not well seen in the principles, can make no good progress in religion.

Ver. 19. *Of the blind*] The Chinese say that all other nations see but with one eye, they with two. The Pharisees were called *Pekachin aperti,* open-eyed: because they only saw. One of them

was called *Or hagnolam,* "The light of the world." In Scripture, wise men only are termed Seers, *Pekakim,* Exod. xxiii. 8. " Are we also blind ?" say they to our Saviour, *q. d.* No, we scorn it : and yet how oft hear we in that one chapter, Matt. xxiii., " Thou blind Pharisee, ye fools and blind."

Ver. 20. *Which hast the form of knowledge*] A platform of wholesome words, a system, a method artificially moulded, μόρφωσις, such as tutors and professors of arts and sciences have, and do read over again and again to their auditors.

Ver. 21. *Teachest thou not thyself?*] He that knows well and does worse is but as a whiffler which carrieth a torch in his hand to show others his own deformities. I have read of a woman, who living in professed doubt of the Godhead, after better illumination and repentance, did often protest that the vicious life of a great scholar in that town did conjure up those damnable doubts in her soul. *Neronis illud (quantus artifex pereo?) quadrabit in te peritum et periturum.* That is the best sermon that is digged out of a man's own breast. Origen's teaching and living were said to be both one. Eusebius said that he preached not by his words only, but by his practice; and that thereby he had almost persuaded Alexander Severus the emperor to be a Christian; his mother Mammæa he fully persuaded. But Ferdinand I., emperor, complained of some divines that they were *in sua ipsorum vitia facundi satis,* bitter against those vices in others which they too much favoured in themselves.[1]

Ver. 22. *Thou that sayest*] Hypocrites can talk of religion, as if their tongues did run upon pattens, they are fair professors, but foul sinners; as was that carnal cardinal Cremensis, the popes' legate, sent hither, A. D. 1114, to interdict priests' marriages, and being taken in the act with a common strumpet, he excused it by saying he was no priest himself, but a corrector of them.

Dost thou commit sacrilege?] The chronicler noteth of Queen Mary, that she restored again all ecclesiastical livings assumed to the crown, saying that she set more by the salvation of her own soul than she did by ten kingdoms. Shall not she that abhorred not idols rise up and condemn those that do, and yet commit sacrilege? (Speed's Chron.)

Ver. 23. *Through breaking*] By shooting short, or beyond, or wide of the mark, by omission, commission, or failing in the manner.

Ver. 24. *For the name of God, &c.*] Heretics and hypocrites do still with Judas deliver up the Lord Christ to the scoffs and buffetings of his enemies. Augustine (De Civ. Dei, i. 52) complains of the ancient heretics, that in them many evil-minded men found matter of blaspheming the name of Christ because they also pretended to the Christian religion. Epiphanius addeth, that for the looseness of such men's lives, and the baseness of their tenets, many of the heathens shunned the company of Christians, and would not be drawn to hear their sermons. Origen

---

[1] *Non verbis solum sed exemplis Grammatici de* *Ulisis erroribus disserentes suos non vident.* Bern.

before them both cries out, *Nunc male audiunt, castiganturque vulgo Christiani, quod aliter quam sapientibus convenit vivant, et vitia sub obtentu nominis celent,* &c. There is an ill report goes of Christians for their unchristian conversation, &c. Ammianus Marcellinus, a heathen historian, deeply taxeth the pride, luxury, contentions, covetousness of the bishops in his time, and the deadly hatreds of common Christians. *Nullæ infestæ hominibus bestiæ sunt, ut sibi ferales plerique Christiani,* saith he. A sad thing that a heathen should see and detest such hellish miscarriages among Christians. Bellarmine telleth us of certain heretics anciently called *Christianocategori,* that is, accusers of Christians, because for their sakes Christians were accused as worshippers of idols.[1] Papists give the same offence to Jews, who call scandal *Chillul Hesham,* a profaning of God's name, which they hold the greatest of sins.

Ver. 25. *If thou keep the law*] Which thou art thereby bound to do, either by thyself, or by thy surety Christ Jesus.

Thy circumcision is made uncircumcision] Thou art no whit privileged by it. Unregenerate Israel is to God as Ethiopia, Amos ix. 7.

Ver. 26. *If the uncircumcision*] Which it can never do. But admit it could, &c.

Ver. 27. *Judge thee*] Men's guilt is increased by their obligations, as was Solomon's in departing from God, who had appeared unto him twice, 1 Kings xi. 9.

Ver. 28. *Neither is that circumcision*] See Col. ii. 11, with the note there. Inward circumcision is (as Origen describeth it) *Purgatio animæ et abjectio vitiorum,* or (as St Paul in the place above named) the putting off old Adam with his actions, by the circumcision of Christ, by his merit and Spirit.

Ver. 29. *Which is one inwardly*] An Israelite indeed, John i., that hath put away the foreskin of his heart, Jer. iv. 4. That worshippeth God in spirit, rejoiceth in Christ Jesus, and hath no confidence in the flesh, Phil. iii. 3.

Whose praise is not] He seeks not the applause of men, but God's approbation ; and holds the *Euge* of conscience far better than the world's *Hic est.* The holy virgin was so far from affecting the vain praises of men, that she was troubled when truly praised of an angel.

CHAPTER III.

Ver. 1. *What advantage*] Gr. τὸ περισσον, what odds, singular thing, prerogative ?

Ver. 2. *Chiefly, because that,* &c.] This was their prime privilege, that they were God's library-keepers, that this heavenly treasure was concredited unto them. Other nations are said to have been without God, because without those lively oracles, 2 Chron. xv. 3; Eph. ii. 12. Prize we this privilege, and improve it. You must never expect another edition of the faith once received, Jude 3, once for all.

[1] De Eccles. Triumph. lib. ii. 11.

Ver. 3. *The faith of God*] That is, his faithful promises, opposed to man's perfidy. *Fides quia fit quod dictum est.* God is faithful, saith the apostle oft.

Ver. 4. *Every man a liar*] viz. By nature. But, Isa. lxiii. 8, God's people are "children that will not lie," they will die rather. *Non ideo negare volo, ne peream, sed ideo mentiri nolo ne peccem,* saith she upon the rack, of whom St Jerome writeth. The officers of Merindol answered the bishop that moved them to abjure, that they marvelled much that he would persuade them to lie to God and the world. And albeit that all men by nature are liars, yet they had learned by the word of God that they ought diligently to take heed of lying in any matter, be it never so small, &c.

Every man a liar] So he is either by imposture, and so in purpose, or by impotency, and so in the event, deceiving those that rely upon him, Psal. lxii. 9.

That thou mayest be justified in thy sayings] David speaketh of the truth of Nathan's reprehension ; Paul applies it to the truth of God in his promises also. Let us give him a testimonial, John iii. 33; such as is that Deut. xxxii. 4, "A God of truth and without iniquity, just and right is he."

And mightest overcome] Mayest be pure, saith David, Psal. li. 4. *Zacah* in the Syriac is used for overcoming. *Vincit veritas, et dare non dignis res mage digna Deo est.*

Ver. 5. *Is God unrighteous*] Such heart-boilings there were in the rejected Jews. And Job said little less, till God, over-hearing him, steps, as it were, from behind the hangings, and takes him up for it, Job xxxviii. 2. "Who is this," saith he, that talketh thus ? How now ?

Ver. 6. *I speak as a man*] q. d. Is there not such language heard in some men's hearts ?

For then how shall God judge the world] How shall every transgression and disobedience receive a just recompence of reward ? Heb. ii. 2. God's will is the absolute rule of right, *nec tantum recta, sed regula.* (Bonav.)

Ver. 7. *For if the truth of God*] Here the former objection is repeated, explicated, and more fully answered, that every mouth might be stopped. *Ferunt ranas lampade supra lacum, in quo tumultuantur, appensa, illius fulgore repercussas conticescere.* (Lomelius.) So gainsayers are silenced, when the truth is thoroughly cleared.

Ver. 8. *As we be slanderously reported*] So are the reformed Churches by the black-mouthed Papists. See the Abatement of Popish Brags, by Alex. Cook, the Preface ; Eudæmon Joannes against Casaubon, and Calvino-Turcismum, &c.

Whose damnation is just] In the year of grace 1552, a monk of Berlin in Germany, who in the pulpit charged St Paul with a lie, was suddenly smitten with an apoplexy, whiles the word was yet in his mouth, and fell down dead in the place on St Stephen's day, as they call it. (Scultet. Annal.)

Ver. 9. *That they are all under sin*] Whole

evil is in man, and whole man in evil. *Homo est inversus decalogus.* Man by nature is no better than a filthy dunghill of all abominable vices. His heart is the devil's storehouse, throne, nest. His eyes great thoroughfares of lust, pride, vanity, &c. His life a long chain of sinful actions, a web of wickedness spun out and made up by the hands of the devil and the flesh, an evil spinner, and a worse weaver. (Mr Whately's New Birth.)

Ver. 10. *As it is written*] What the prophets had said of some particular people or person is here applied to the whole race of mankind, because by nature there is never a better of us. Κακοὶ μὲν θρίπες, κακοὶ δὲ καὶ ἶπες. (Eras. Adag.)

Ver. 11. *None that seeketh*] That seeketh and fetcheth him out of his retiring-room, as she did, Mark vii. 24, 25.

Ver. 12. *Become unprofitable*] Or rotten, nasty, stinking, as the Hebrew hath it, Psal. xiv. 3. The old world was grown so foul, that God was forced to wash it with a deluge.

Ver. 13. *The poison of the asps*] Of that sort of asps that spit their venom far from them upon the by-standers. (πτυάδες.) There is a great deal of such vermin and venom in that new-found world of wickedness, the tongue, James iii. It is easy to observe that St Paul here, making the anatomy of a natural man, stands more on the organs of speaking than all other members, and showeth how his tongue is tipped with fraud, his lips tainted with venom, his mouth full of gall, his throat a gaping grave, his tongue as a rapier to run men through with, and his throat as a sepulchre to bury them in. As for the asp, they write of her, That whereas her poison is so deadly, that the part infected cannot be cured but by cutting off, *succurrit periclitantibus benignior natura, et noxiosissimo animali caliginosos obtutus dedit.* (Jo. Wover.) *Aspidi* (saith Pliny, viii. 23) *hebetes oculi dati, eosque non in fronte, sed in temporibus habet.*

Ver. 14. *Full*] Γέμει, As a ship that hath its full freight and lading.

Ver. 15. *Swift to shed blood*] As Paul, till God stopped him in his cursed career.

Ver. 16. *They mind nothing but mischief.*]

Ver. 17. *They are restless and troublesome.*]

Ver. 18. *There is no fear of God*] This is set last, as the source of all the former evils.

Ver. 19. *Guilty*] Culpable, and such as cannot plead their own cause without an advocate. (Chrysos.)

Ver. 20. *Therefore by the deeds of the law*] This is directly against Popish justification by works, merits, &c. Those misled and muzzled souls did worse than lose their labour that built religious houses, *Pro remissione et redemptione peccatorum, pro remedio et liberatione animæ, in eleemosynam animæ, pro salute et requie animarum patrum et matrum, fratrum et sororum, &c.* These were the ends that they aimed at, as appears in stories. And here observe how the once faithful city of Rome is now become a harlot, Isa. i. 21, 22; her silver is become dross, her wine mixed

with water, yet with blood, now since the Council of Trent, Rev. xvi. 3, 5; and this Epistle of Paul to the Romans is now 'become the Epistle of Paul against the Romans; like as *Roma* is become *Amor inversus.*

Ver. 21. *But now*] Since Christ came.

Ver. 22. *Upon all*] So that none shall hinder their happiness.

Ver. 23. *All have sinned*] The first man defiled the nature, and ever since the nature defileth the man. Adam was a parent, a public person, a parliament man, as it were; the whole country of mankind was in him, and fell with him.

Short of the glory of God] i. e. Of his image now obliterated, or of his kingdom, upon the golden pavement whereof no dirty dog must ever trample. It is an inheritance undefiled, 1 Pet. i. 4.

Ver. 24. *Being justified freely*] Because the apostle's word δωρέα is expounded by Varinus to be χαρίτος ἀλλαγὴ, therefore Thammerus will needs conclude from this text that God by justifying us, doth but pay for our pains, give us what we have earned. *Cœlum gratis non accipiam*, saith Vega. *Opera bona sunt cœli mercatura*, saith another. Heaven is the purchase of good works.

By the redemption] i. e. By faith applying this redemption, wrapping herself in the golden fleece of that Lamb of God.

Ver. 25. *To be a propitiation*] Or a covering, in allusion to the law; where the ark covering the two tables within it, the mercy-seat covering the ark, and the cherubims covering the mercy-seat and one another, showed Christ covering the curses of the law, in whom is the ground of all mercy; which things the angels desire to pry into, as into the pattern of God's deep wisdom.

For the remission of sins] Gr. πάρεσιν, for the relaxation or releasement of sins, as of bonds or fetters.

Ver. 26. *To declare*] Gr. ἔνδειξις, for a clear demonstration or pointing out with the finger.

Ver. 27. *Where is boasting then, &c.*] A certain sophister would hence prove the authority of the Church. He read the words thus, by a mistake of their short-hand writing, *Ubi est gloriatio? Ecclesia est*, for *exclusa est.*

Ver. 28. *A man is justified by faith*] Here St Paul shows himself a pure Lutheran, and is therefore sharply and blasphemously censured by some Jesuits for a hot-headed person, who was so transported with the pangs of zeal and eagerness beyond all compass in most of his disputes, that there was no great reckoning to be made of his assertions. (Speculum Europæ.) Yea, he was dangerous to read, as savouring of heresy in some places, and better perhaps he had never written. Four years before the Council of Trent, Cardinal Contarenus asserted the doctrine of justification by faith alone, in a just tractate, and was therefore soon after poisoned. Cardinal Pole is thought to have been sound in this point. Bellarmine reproves Pighius for consenting to Luther herein, whom he undertook to confute, and yet Bellarmine himself with his *tutissimum est,* doth as much upon the matter. *Magna est veritas, et valebit,* Great is the truth, and shall prevail.

Ver. 29. *Is he the God of the Jews only*] That is, Doth he justify the Jews only? For he is their God only whom he justifieth. Now men are said to be justified effectively by God, apprehensively by faith, declaratively by good works. The schoolmen are very unsound in this capital article of justification, and are therefore the less to be regarded. *Nam quæ de gratia Dei justificante scholastici scribunt, commentitia universa existimo,* saith Cardinal Pighius, who is therefore much condemned by Bellarmine, but without cause.

Ver. 30. *And uncircumcision*] All by one way, lest he should seem not to be one, but *alius et alius.*

Ver. 31. *We establish the law*] Which yet the Antinomians cry down, calling repentance a legal grace, humiliation a back-door to heaven; grieving that they have grieved so much for their sins, &c., that they have prayed so oft, and done other holy duties. Islebius Agricola (the first Antinomian that ever was) and his followers held these unsound opinions; That the law and works belong only to the court of Rome; that so soon as a man begins to think how to live godlily and modestly, he presently wandereth from the gospel; that a man was never truly mortified till he had put out all sense of conscience for sin; that if his conscience troubled him, that was his imperfection, he was not mortified enough; that St Peter understood not Christian liberty when he wrote those words, "Make your calling and election sure;" that good works were *perniciosa ad salutatem,* destructive to men's souls; with a deal of such trash. All which, this Islebius afterwards condemned and recanted in a public auditory, and printed his revocation. Yet when Luther was dead, he relapsed into the same error, and hath at this day amongst us too many disciples. We have need, therefore, to take St Paul's part, to stablish the law, to settle it, now that it is falling (as the Greek word, ἱστῶμεν, signifies), to make it valid, ἱκανῶμεν (as some copies have it), sufficient and effectual to those ends for which it was given, viz. to discover transgression and to restrain it, Gal. iii. 19; to humble men for sin, Rom. iii. 19, 20; to be a schoolmaster to Christ, and a rule of life, that, according to his royal law, James ii. 8, we may live royally above the rank of men, in obedience; whilst by the gospel, we obtain grace in some measure to fulfil the law; having a counterpart of it in our hearts, and a disposition answerable to it in all things, Heb. viii. 8—10 with 2 Cor. iii. 2, 3; as the lead answers to the mould, as tally answers tally, indenture indenture. That was a good saying of Luther's, Walk in the heaven of the promise, but in the earth of the law; that in respect of believing, this of obeying. Another of his sayings was, That in the justification of a sinner, Christ and faith were alone *tanquam sponsus cum sponsa in thalamo,* as the bridegroom and bride in the bed; howbeit it is such a faith as works by love. A third golden saying of his was, He that can

rightly distinguish betwixt law and gospel, let him praise God for his skill, and know himself to be a good divine.

CHAPTER IV.

Ver. 1. *As pertaining to the flesh*] THAT is, As touching his works, ver. 2, called also the letter, chap. ii. 27, and the law a carnal commandment, Heb. vii. 16.

Ver. 2. *But not before God*] Who when he begins to search our sacks, as the steward did Benjamin's, can find out those our thieveries that we thought not of; bring to mind and light those sins that we had forgot, or not observed. When he comes to turn the bottom of the bag upwards it will be bitter with us. Abimelech's excuse was accepted, and yet his sin was chastised, Gen. xx. 6. *Væ hominum vitæ quantumvis laudabili, si remota misericordia judicetur.* The best lamb should abide the slaughter, except the rams were sacrificed, that Isaac might be saved.

Ver. 3. *Abraham believed God*] Latomus of Louvain was not ashamed to write that there was no other faith in Abraham than what was in Cicero. And yet our Saviour saith, Abraham saw my day and rejoiced; so did Cicero never. Another wrote an apology for Cicero, and would needs prove him to have been a pious and penitent person, because in one place he hath these words, *Reprehendo peccata mea, quod Pompeio confisus, ejusque partes secutus fuerim.* A poor proof: *Hoc argumentum tam facile diluitur, quam vulpes comest pyrum.* (Joh. Manl.)

Ver. 4. *Now to him that worketh*] Yet it is an act of mercy in God to render to a man according to his works, Psal. lxii. 12; Exod. xx. 6. God's kingdom is not *partum,* but *paratum,* Matt. xxv. 34, not acquired, but prepared.

But of debt] Not so indeed, Rom. xi. 31, but according to the opinion of the merit-monger, who saith as Vega, *Cœlum gratis non accipiam.*

Ver. 5. *His faith*] Yet not as a work, not in a proper sense, as Arminius and Bertius held, but as an act of receiving Christ.

That justifieth the ungodly] i. e. Him that was ungodly; but being justified is made godly also; or the ungodly, that is, him that is not perfectly godly; for Abraham is here made the ungodly person.

Ver. 6. *Unto whom God imputeth*] Ten times the apostle mentioneth this grace of imputed righteousness in this chapter. Yet the Papists jeer it, calling it putative righteousness, so speaking evil of the things they know not. Stories tell us of a Popish bishop that lighting by chance upon this chapter, threw away the book in great displeasure, and said, *O Paule, an tu quoque Lutheranus factus es?* Art thou also a Lutheran, Paul? But if the faith of another may be profitable to infants at their baptism, as Bellarmine holdeth, why should it seem so absurd a thing, that Christ's righteousness imputed should profit those that believe on him?

The Jews indeed at this day being asked, Whether they believe to be saved by Christ's righteousness? They answer, That every fox must pay his own skin to the slayer. Thus they reject the righteousness of God, Rom. x. 3. As their fathers did, so do they, Acts vii. 51. The Lord open their eyes, that they may convert and be saved.

Ver. 7. *Are covered*] Sic velantur ut in judicio non revelentur; so covered as that he never see them again, but as the Israelites saw the Egyptians dead on the shore.

Ver. 8. *Imputeth not*] Chargeth it not, setteth it not upon his score, 2 Cor. v. 19.

Ver. 9. *Cometh this blessedness*] This is the third time that the apostle avoucheth the universality of the subject of justification. For this he had done once before, chap. iii. 23, and again, chap. iii. 29—31. The Scripture doth not use, saith one, to kill flies with beetles, to cleave straws with wedges of iron, to spend many words where there is no need.

Ver. 10. *In circumcision*] As the Jew would have it. No such matter.

Ver. 11. *A seal of the righteousness*] Circumcision is called a sign and a seal by a doctor of the Jews more ancient than their Talmud Zohar, Gen. xvii.

That righteousness might be imputed] How foolish is that inference of Thammerus, that because the word here used to signify imputed comes of a word that signifies reason, therefore the righteousness of faith must be such as a man may understand and comprehend by reason (λογισθῆναι, λόγος).

Ver. 12. *Walk in the steps*] That herein personate and express him to the life, as Constantine's children, saith Eusebius, did their father.

Ver. 13. *Heir of the world*] That is, of heaven, say some; of Canaan, say others, the pleasant land, more esteemed of God than all the world besides, because it was the seat of the Church. A man is called every creature, Mark xvi. 5; the Church is called all things, Col. i. So Canaan is called the world, and Tabor and Hermon put for the east and west of the whole world, Psal. lxxxix. 12.

Ver. 14. *Faith is made void*] See the note on Gal. iii. 12, and v. 2. That Epistle to the Galatians is an epitome of this to the Romans, and lends light to it. It is *compendium, sed non dispendium.*

Ver. 15. *No transgression*] sc. Is imputed by men where there is no law written. See chap. v. 13.

The law worketh wrath] That is, manifesteth it, and so seemeth to work it, as likewise affliction doth corruption in God's children; stir the puddle with a stick, and the mud will soon be on the top of the water. Rub the brand, and sparkles will fly abroad.

Ver. 16. *It is of faith*] Fidei mendica manu.

That it might be by grace] Paul was a great advancer of the grace of God, and abaser of man. For he knew that as wax and water cannot meet together, so neither can Christ and anything else, in the work of man's salvation.

Ver. 17. *Who quickeneth the dead*] As he doth when he maketh a man a believer, Ephes. i. 19; he fetcheth heart of oak out of a hollow tree, and a spiritual man out of a wild-ass colt. See both these metaphors, Job xi. 12.

Ver. 18. *Who against hope, &c.*] Elegans Antanaclasis propter speciem contradictionis, saith Piscator. Spes in terrenis, incerti nomen boni; spes in divinis, nomen est certissimi, saith another.

Believed in hope] It is the nature of faith to believe God upon his bare word; and that against sense in things invisible, against reason in things incredible: sense corrects imagination, reason corrects sense, but faith corrects both. It will not be, saith sense; it cannot be, saith reason; it both can and will be, saith faith, for I have a promise for it.

Ver. 19. *He considered not*] Gr. οὐ κατενόησε, He cared not for all his own body, &c.; he never thought of that.

When he was about a hundred years old] This the Scripture makes a great matter; whereas Terah was a hundred and thirty when he begat Abraham; but because Abraham had his child by faith, therefore was it a great matter. And so, saith a divine, in all other things that we have, do, or suffer, if they be by faith, they are great things.

Ver. 20. *Giving glory to God*] Confessing and exalting God, as Luke xvii. 18, giving him a testimonial, as it were, John iii. 33, with Deut. xxxii. 4.

Ver. 21. *Being fully persuaded*] Gr. πληροφορηθείς, being carried on with full sail, and going gallantly towards heaven.

Ver. 22.] See the note on ver. 5, 6. God, by reason of his faith, held him to be as sufficiently disposed to obtain the accomplishment of his promises, as if he had had all the righteousness required by the law to receive God's benefits. (Diodat.)

Ver. 23. *For his sake alone*] But for our instruction and encouragement, Rom. xv. 4. See the note there.

Ver. 24. *That raised up Jesus*] And with him all believers, Col. iii. 1; Rom. vi. 4.

Ver. 25. *Who was delivered, &c.*] Not that his death had no hand in our justifying, but because our justification begun in his death, was perfected by his resurrection. Redemption we have by Christ's abasement, application of it by his advancement. This one verse is an abridgment of the whole gospel, the sum of all the good news in the world, the grand inquest of all the ancient prophets, 1 Pet. i. 11. Adore we the fulness of the Holy Scriptures.

CHAPTER V.

Ver. 1. *Being justified by faith*] As he had said, chap. iv. 24.

We have peace with God] A blessed calm lodged in our consciences; like as when Jonah was cast overboard, there followed a tranquillity. This is that continual feast, a very heaven beforehand, an anticipation of glory, οὐρανὸς πρὸ οὐρανοῦ.

Ver. 2. *We have access*] προσαγωγὴν, Christ leading us by the hand, and presenting us to the Father, with, "Behold, here am I, and the children whom thou hast given me." Ephes. ii. 18.

Wherein we stand] ἑστήκαμεν, not stirring a foot, for any temptation or persecution. A metaphor from soldiers keeping their station in the battle.

Ver. 3. *We glory in tribulations*] As an old soldier doth in his scars of honour. See Gal. vi. 17; 2 Cor. vii. 4. *Feri Domine, feri; nam a peccatis absolutus sum*, saith Luther: Strike, Lord, and spare not, sith I am acquitted by thee from my sins. *Seca ambas*, cried out that good bishop, when his hand was threatened to be cut off. A man that hath got his pardon is not troubled though he lose his glove or handkerchief, nor though it should prove a rainy day.

Ver. 4. *And experience, hope*] Without hope patience is cold almost in the fourth degree, and that is but a little from poison.

Ver. 5. *Hope maketh not ashamed*] As among men, many lie languishing at hope's hospital, as he did at the pool of Bethesda, John v., and return as they did from the brooks of Tema, Job vi. 17. Or, as men go to a lottery with heads full of hopes, but return with hearts full of blanks. The Dutch have a proverb to this purpose, *Sperare et expectare, multos reddit stultos*. And we say, He that hopes for dead men's shoes, may hap go barefoot. Bad men's hopes may hop headless, they may perish in the height of their expectancies. Not so those that hope in God; they shall yet praise him who is the help of their countenance, and their God, Psal. xliii. ult. *Nunquam confusi, Deo confisi.*

Ver. 6. *Christ died for*] A sufficient evidence of God's dearest and deepest love shed abroad in our hearts, as a most sweet ointment.

Ver. 7. *Yet peradventure for a good man*] For a public person. Lilloe stepped between the murderer and King Edwin his master to intercept the deadly thrust. (Speed's Chron.) A common soldier lost his life at Musselborough field to save the Earl of Huntly's life; so did Nicolas Ribische to rescue Prince Maurice at the siege of Pista.

Ver. 8. *God commendeth*, &c.] Herein God lays naked to us the tenderest bowels of his fatherly compassions, as in an anatomy. A young student in history (saith Polybius) should have the whole history of the world under his view; and should reduce all into one body.[1] God, by giving his Son for us, showed us all his love at once, as it were embodied. All other spiritual blessings meet in this, as the lines in the centre, as the streams in the fountain. If the centurion were held worthy of respect because he loved our nation (said they) and built

[1] ὑπὸ μίαν σύνοψιν ἄγειν καὶ σωματοποιεῖν.

us a synagogue, what shall we say of Almighty God, who so loved our souls that he gave his only begotten Son, &c.

Christ died for us] "Behold how he loved him," said those Jews, when they saw Christ weep for him, John xi. 37. What shall we say of this love of his beyond compare, in bleeding for us? *Ama amorem illius*, &c. Oh love that love of his, and never leave meditating on it, *donec totus fixus in corde, qui totus fixus in cruce*, till he be wholly fixed in your hearts, who was wholly fastened to the tree for your sakes. (Bernard.)

Ver. 9. *Much more then*] It is a greater work of God to bring men to grace, than being in the state of grace, to bring them to glory; because sin is far more distant from grace than grace is from glory.

Ver. 10. *We shall be saved*] Here the apostle reasoneth from regeneration to eternal life, as the lesser.

Ver. 11. *Not only so*] Not in tribulation only do we glory (as ver. 3), but in the whole course of our lives. Yet not without some damps and dumps, whilst here. Whilst I live (saith Rollec), I never look to see perfect reformation in the Church, or feel perfect ravishing joys in mine heart. Here Christ comes to his Spouse as a wooer only, and gives her no more than the prelibations and foretastes of his love, as a bunch of the grapes of Canaan.

Ver. 12. *As by one man*] Yet Anabaptists deny original sin, as did also the Pelagians of old, confuted by Augustine. Egranus, a German preacher, said (as Melancthon reporteth) that original sin is a mere fiction of Augustine and other divines; and that, because there was no such word found in the Scriptures. (Joh. Manl.) Papists say that original sin is the smallest of all sins, not deserving any more of God's wrath, than only a want of his beatifical presence; and that, too, without any pain or sorrow of mind from the apprehension of so great a loss. There have been amongst us that have said, that original sin is not forbidden by the law. Directly, indeed, and immediately it is not; but forbidden it is, because cursed and condemned by the law. In original sin is a tacit consent (eminently) to all actual sin. And some understand this text of all sin, both original and actual.

And so death passed upon all men] As a sentence of death on a condemned malefactor; or, as those diseases that are called by physicians *corruptio totius substantiæ*; or as the rot overrunneth the whole flock, διῆλθεν.

Ver. 13. *Sin is not imputed*] In men's esteem, as chap. iv. 15.

Ver. 14. *Death reigned*] From the reign of death, he concludes the reign of sin. Infants are no innocents; the first sheet or blanket wherein they are covered is woven of sin, shame, blood, and filth, Ezek. xvi. 46.

Ver. 15. *Many be dead*] Many is here put for all, as all for many, 1 Tim. ii. 3.

Ver. 16. *Of many offences*] *i. e.* Of all, whether imputed to us, inherent in us, or issuing from us.

Ver. 17. *Abundance*] That is, abundant grace.

Ver. 18. *By the offence of one*] We were all in Adam, as the whole country in a parliament-man. And although we chose not, God chose for us.

Ver. 19. *Many*] That is, all except Christ, sinners, tainted with sins, guilt, and filth.

Ver. 20. *But where sin abounded*] But then it is where sin that abounded in the life, abounds in the conscience in grief and detestation of it, as the greatest evil. Bonner objected to Mr Philpot, martyr, that he found written in his book, *In me Joanne Philpotto ubi abundavit peccatum, superabundavit et gratia.* This he said was an arrogant speech. *Novum crimen, C. Cæsar.* (Acts and Mon.)

That the offence might abound] Either by accident, through man's corruption, and not of God's intention, Rom. vii. 13. Or if ἵνα be taken causally, it must be interpreted by Gal. iii. 19. God gave the law after the promise, to advance the promise. The law was added because of transgression, *sc.* that hereby guilt and danger being discovered, we might acknowledge the riches of free grace and mercy.

Ver. 21. *That as sin hath reigned*] That is, the wrath of God by sin.

Through righteousness] Imputed and imparted.

By Jesus Christ] See how sweetly the end answers the beginning of the chapter, and how Christ is both author and finisher, &c.

CHAPTER VI.

Ver. 1. *Shall we continue*] *Quasi dicat*, that were most unreasonable, and to an ingenuous nature, impossible. To argue from mercy to liberty, is the devil's logic. Should we not after deliverance yield obedience? said holy Ezra, chap. ix. 13, 14. A man may as truly say, the sea burns, or fire cools, as that certainty of salvation breeds security and looseness.

Ver. 2. *Live any longer therein*] Fall into it we may and shall; but it is not the falling into the water that drowns, but lying in it; so it is not falling into sin that damns, but living in it.

Ver. 3. *Baptized into his death*] *Hoc est baptizari pro mortuis*, saith Beza, to be buried with Christ in baptism, Col. ii. 12, in putting off the body of the sins of the flesh, ver. 11.

Ver. 4. *We are buried*] Burial is a continuing under death, so is mortification a continuate dying to sin, *Mors quædam perpetuata;* sin is by degrees abated, and at length abolished, when once our earthly tabernacles are dissolved.

Walk in newness of life] *Resurrectione Domini configuratur vita, quæ hic geritur.* Walk as Christ walked after his resurrection.

Ver. 5. *For if we have been planted*] Burying is a kind of planting. The Dutch call the burial-place God's Acre.

Ver. 6. *The body of sin*] For whole evil is in man, and whole man in evil.

Is crucified] Which is a lingering but a sure death.

Should not serve sin] As those do that commit it, John viii. 34; not only act it, but are acted by it, having as many lords as lusts, victors as vices. Tit. iii. 3.

Ver. 7. *Is freed from sin*] Anacreon saith the like, ὁ θανὼν οὐκ ἐπιθυμεῖ; death is the accomplishment of mortification. It doth at once what death doth by degrees. Herbs and flowers breed worms, which yet at last kill the herbs and flowers. So sin bred death, but at last death will kill sin. A mud-wall, whiles it standeth, harboureth much vermin, which when it falleth fly away; so doth corruption, when once these cottages of clay fall to ruin.

Ver. 8. *We shall also live*] Then we are said properly to live, when our regeneration is perfected in heaven. To live here, is but to lie a dying.

Ver. 9. *Death hath no more, &c.*] Christ, being the life essential, swallowed up death in victory, as the fire swalloweth up the fuel, and as Moses' serpent swallowed up the sorcerers' serpents.

Ver. 10. *He died unto sin*] That is, to abolish sin, as chap. viii. 2.

Ver. 11. *Reckon ye also*] By faith, reason and reckon yourselves wholly dead in and through Christ, who once died perfectly to sin, as a common person.

Ver. 12. *Let not sin therefore*] As if the apostle should say, we preach purity and not liberty, as the adversary suggesteth, ver. 1 of this chap. with chap. iii. 8. Let not sin reign; rebel it will; but do not actively obey and embrace the commands of sin, as subjects to your king. Let sin be dejected from its regency, though not utterly ejected from its residency. Give it such a deadly wound that it may be sure to die within a year and a day. Sprunt it may, and flutter as a bird when the neck is broken, but live it must not.

Ver. 13. *Unto sin*] As Satan's general, who hath his trenches, 2 Cor. x. 4; his commanders, as here, and his fighting soldiers, 1 Pet. ii. 11; his weapons, as here.

Ver. 14. *Sin shall not have dominion*] Rebel it may, but reign it shall not in any saint. It fareth with sin in the regenerate, as with those beasts, Dan. vii. 12; they had their dominion taken away, yet their lives were prolonged for a season and a time.

Ye are not under the law] *i. e.* Under the rigour, irritation, curse of the law, *Quatenus est virtus peccati.* Or, "ye are not under the law," *sc.* of sin, as Rom. vii. 23, 25.

Ver. 15. *Shall we sin, because, &c.*] Some Antinomian libertines would persuade men that God is never displeased with his people, though they fall into adultery, or the like sin, no, not with a fatherly displeasure; that God never chastiseth his people for any sin, no, not with a fatherly chastisement; that God seeth no sin in his elect; that the very being of their sin is abolished out of God's sight; that they cannot sin, or if they do, it is not they but "sin that dwelleth in them," &c. What is this but to "turn the grace of God into wantonness," which there-hence becometh the savour of death to death unto them; like as Moses' rod, cast on the ground, turned to a serpent; or as dead men's bodies, when the marrow melteth, do bring forth serpents? *Corruptio optimi pessima.*

Ver. 16. *His servants ye are*] Sinners, though not drunk, yet are not their own men, but at Satan's beck and check, whom they seem to defy, but indeed deify.

Ver. 17. *That form of doctrine*] Gr. "That type or mould;" the doctrine is the mould, hearers the metal, which takes impression from it in one part as well as another. And as the metal hath been sufficiently in the furnace, when it is not only purged from the dross, but willingly receiveth the form and figure of that which it is cast and poured into, so here.

Ver. 18.] *Versus est planus,* saith Pareus.

Ver. 19. *After the manner of men*] That is vulgarly, *Crassius et rudius loquor,* by a similitude drawn from human affairs of easy and ordinary observation.

To uncleanness, and to iniquity] Mark the opposition, there are three tos in the expression of the service to sin; but in the service of God only two. Wicked men take great pains for hell; would they but take the same for heaven, they could not likely miss of it.

Ver. 20. *Free from righteousness*] That is, utterly void of grace, and did therefore sin lustily and horribly, earnestly opposing with crest and breast whatsoever stood in the way of their sins and lusts.

Ver. 21. *Whereof ye are ashamed*] Where sin is in the saddle, shame is on the crupper. Men would have the sweet, but not the shame of sin; and the credit of religion, but not go to the cost of it.

Ver. 22. *Become servants to God*] *Phrasis vulgatissima est, Deum colere. Non secus atque agri fertiles inprimis et optimi, sic Dei cultus, fructus fert ad vitam æternam uberrimos.*

Ye have your fruit unto holiness] Every good work increaseth our holiness, and so hability for obedience.

Ver. 23. *For the wages of sin*] The best largesse or congiary (ὀψώνιον) that sin gives to his soldiers is death of all sorts. This is the just hire of the least sin.[1] The Jesuits would persuade us, that some sins against which the law thundereth and lighteneth, are so light in their own nature, *Ut factores nec sordidos, nec malos, nec impios, nec Deo exosos reddere possint.* (Chemnit. de Theol. Jesuitar.) But as there is the same roundness in a little ball as in a great one; so the same disobedience in a small sin as in a greater. Indeed there is no sin little, because no little God to sin against. Every sin hales hell at the very heels of it.

[1] ἁμαρτία ψυχὴ θανάτου, και

CHAPTER VII.

Ver. 1. *Know ye not, brethren*] BELLARMINE saith of his Romans (more true perhaps of these), *Romani sicut non acumina, ita nec imposturas habent,* As they are not very knowing, so not cunning to deceive.

Ver. 2. *She is loosed, &c.*] And so at liberty to marry again, though Jerome compare such to the unclean beasts in the ark, and to vessels of dishonour in a house, yea, to dogs that return to their vomit; which was his error. *Patres legendi cum venia,* saith one.

Ver. 3. *So then if*] The sectaries then are out that say now-a-days, that if they have husbands and wives that will not turn saints, that is, sectaries, they may leave them, and marry others.

Ver. 4. *That we should bring forth fruit*] The ministry of the word, saith one, is the bridal-bed; wherein God by his Spirit doth communicate with our souls his sweetest favours, and maketh them be conceived with the fruits of righteousness to everlasting life.

Ver. 5. *In the flesh*] In our pure naturals.

The motions of sin] Those maladies of the soul (παθήματα).

By the law] By the irritation of the law.

Did work] Gr. did inwardly work (ἐνηργεῖτο).

Ver. 6. *Not in the oldness of the letter*] That is, not in that old kind of life that we lived under subjection to the law, to the irritation, co-action, and curse of it.

Ver. 7. *I had not known lust*] Involuntary evil motions. The apostle calleth concupiscence sin, saith Possevine the Jesuit, but we may not say so. Most of the most dangerous opinions of Popery spring from hence, that they have slight conceits of concupiscence, as a condition of nature. But inward bleeding will kill a man, so will concupiscence, if not bewailed. The Council of Trent saith, that it is not truly and properly a sin, albeit it be so called, because it proceeds from sin, and inclines a man to sin. Neither want there amongst us that say, that original sin is not forbidden by the law; directly indeed, and immediately, it is not; but forbidden it is, because cursed and condemned by the law.

I had not known sin] The law of nature discovers not original sin with its evil lusts. True it is that a philosopher could say (Timon apud Laertium),

πάντων μὲν πρώτιστα κακῶν ἐπιθυμία ἐστιν,

Concupiscence is the root of all evil; but whether he understood what himself said, I greatly question. *Erras, si tecum vitia nasci putas,* saith Seneca; *supervenerunt, ingesta sunt:* Thou mistakest if thou thinkest that thy vices were born with thee, they came in since, they were brought into thee. *Tam sine vitio quam sine virtute nascimur,* saith another; We were born θάνατος ψυχῆς. Nazianzen.

as well without vice as without virtue. Quintilian saith it is more marvel that one man sinneth, than that all men should live honestly; sin is so against the nature of man.

Thou shalt not covet] The word *concupisco* is inceptive: to show (saith one) that the very first motion is sin, though no consent be yielded.

Ver. 8. *By the commandment*] Not commandments. Papists abolishing, or at least destroying, the sense of the second commandment, by making it a member of the first, that they may retain the number of ten words (so loth are heretics to have their asses' ears seen) they divide this last; which yet Paul here calls the commandment; and sure he knew better than they the analysis of the law.

Wrought in me all manner of concupiscence] The more the law would dam up the torrent of sinful lusts, the higher did they swell. (*Nitimur in vetitum.*) Corruption doth increase and begin by the law. The more God forbids sin, the more we bid for it: as if we did sin on purpose to provoke God; as if God had need deal with us as he did in the story, who was wont to command the contrary when he would have anything done, because he knew they would cross him. Howbeit, although sin thus take occasion by the law, yet this is *per accidens*, as in the dropsy, it is not the drink that is to be blamed for increasing the disease, but the ill distemper of the body.

Ver. 9. *For I was alive*] As being without sense of sin, and conscience of duty.

Sin revived] sc. In sense and appearance.

And I died] sc. In pride and self-justice.

Ver. 10. *Ordained to life*] By life and death understand peace and perturbation.

Ver. 11. *Deceived me*] Irritated my corrupt nature, and made me sin the more, *per accidens*, as Pharaoh was the worse for a message of dismission.

Ver. 12. *The commandment*] *Vis legis in mandando et præcipiendo.* The word (ἐντολή) properly signifieth an affirmative precept.

Ver. 13. *Exceeding sinful*] Sin is so evil that it cannot have a worse epithet given it. Paul can call it no worse than by its own name, "sinful sin."

Ver. 14. *Sold under sin*] But yet ill a-paid of my slavery, and lusting after liberty.

Ver. 15. *I allow not*] Gr. οὐ γινώσκω, I know not, as being preoccupated, Gal. vi. 1, wherried and whirled away by sin before I am aware or have time to consider.

Ver. 16. *I consent unto the law*] I vote with it, and for it, as the rule of right; I wish also well to the observance of it, as David did, Psal. cxix. 45.

Ver. 17. *It is no more I*] Mr Bradford, martyr, in a certain letter thus comforteth his friend: At this present, my dear heart in the Lord, you are in a blessed estate, although it seem otherwise to you, or rather to your old Adam; the which I dare now be bold to discern from you, because you would have it not only discerned, but also

[1] *Domine, libera me a malo homine, meipso.*

utterly destroyed. God (saith another reverend man) puts a difference between us and sin in us, as betwixt poison and the box that holds it.

Sin that dwelleth in me] An ill inmate that will not out, till the house falleth on the head of it; as the fretting leprosy in the walls of a house would not out till the house itself were demolished. Sin, as Hagar, will dwell with grace, as Sarah, till death beat it out of doors.

Ver. 18. *Dwelleth no good thing*] *Horreo quicquid de meo est, ut sim meus*, saith Bernard. It was no ill wish of him that desired God to free him from an ill man, himself.[1] For, though engrafted into Christ, yet we carry about us a relish of the old stock still. Corruption is, though dejected from its regency, yet not ejected from its inherency; it intermingleth with our best works.

How to perform] Gr. κατεργάζεσθαι, to do it thoroughly; though I am doing at it, as I can.

Ver. 19. *For the good, &c.*] Nature, like Eve and Job's wife, is always drawing us from God. As the ferryman plies the oar, and eyes the shore homeward, where he would be, yet there comes a gust of wind that carries him back again; so it is with a Christian. Corruption, egged with a temptation, gets as it were the hill, and the wind, and, upon such advantages, too oft prevaileth.

Ver. 20. *It is no more I*] Every new man is two men. See the note above on ver. 17.

But sin that dwelleth in me] A scripture ill applied by that female Antinomian; who when her mistress charged her for stealing her linens and other things which she found in her chest or trunk, she denied that she stole them; and when she was asked how they came to be laid and locked up there? Did not you do this? No, said she, "it was not I, but sin that dwelleth in me." See the note on chap. vi. 15, and vii. 17.

Ver. 21. *When I would do good*] Something lay at the fountain-head, as it were, and stopped him when he would do his duty. But God valueth a man by his desires.[2] There oft cometh a prohibition from Chancery to stay proceedings at common law, so here; when we would pray, meditate, confer, &c., we are hindered and interrupted. But God considereth it; and as the service of a sick child is doubly accepted, so here.

Evil is present] We can stay no more from sinning than the heart can from panting and the pulse from beating. Our lives are fuller of sins than the firmament of stars or the furnace of sparks. Erasmus was utterly out, that said with Origen, *Paulum hoc sermone balbutire; quam ipse potius ineptiat*, saith learned Beza. So Joannes Sylvius Ægranus, a learned but a profane person, reprehended Paul for want of learning, and said, *Quod usus sit declamatoriis verbis, non congruentibus ad rem, &c. Nominabat sophisma, quod diceremus homines non posse implere legem.* (Joh. Manl.)

Ver. 22. *I delight*] Germanicus reigned in the Romans' hearts, but Tiberius in the provinces. So here.

[2] *Tota vita boni Christiani sanctum desiderium est.* Aug.

Ver. 23. *A law in my members*] Called the deeds of the body, Rom. viii. 13, because corruption acteth and uttereth itself by the members of the body.[1] The πανσπερμία (*vox Empedoclea*) is within, but easily and often budgeth and breaketh out.

Warring against the law] The regenerate part. *Plato in Cratylo pulchre ait ; Ut mentem appellamus νόον, ita legem dicimus νόμον, quasi μένοντα νόον, alioqui mens hominum vagatur.*

And bringing me into captivity] The sins of the saints (those of daily incursion) are either of precipitancy, as Gal. vi. 1, or of infirmity ; when a man wrestles, and hath some time to fight it out, but for want of breath and strength, falls, and is in some captivity to the law of sin ; this is the worse.

Ver. 24. *O wretched man*] We must discontentedly be contented to be exercised with sin while we are here. It is so bred in the bone, that till our bones, as Joseph's, be carried out of the Egypt of this world, it will not out. The Romans so conquered Chosroes the Persian, that he made a law, that never any king of Persia should now war against the Romans. (Evagrius.) But let us do what we can to subdue sin, it will be a Jebusite, a false borderer, yea, a rank traitor, rebelling against the Spirit. Only this we may take for a comfortable sign of future victory, when we are discontent with our present ill estate, grace will get the upper hand ; as nature doth, when the humours are disturbed, and after many fit. And as till then there is no rest to the body, so neither is there to the soul. The conflict between flesh and spirit is as when two opposite things meet together (cold salt-petre and hot brimstone), they make a great noise. So doth Paul here, Miserable me, &c. Basil fitly compareth him to a man thrown off his horse, and dragged after him crying out for help. Another, to one that is troubled with a disease called the *mare*, or *Ephialtes ;* which (in his slumber) maketh him think that he feels a thing as big as a mountain lying on his breast, which he can no way remove, but would fain be rid of.

Who shall deliver me] Nothing cleaves more pertinaciously, or is more inexpugnable, than a strong lust.

From this body of death] Or, this dead body, by a Hebraism, this carcase of sin to which I am tied and long held, as noisome every whit to my soul as a dead body to my senses ; and as burdensome as a withered arm or mortified limb, which hangs on a man as a lump of lead. Some remnants of sin God hath left in us, to clear to us his justifying grace by Christ's righteousness. This the apostle falls admiring, Rom. viii. 1, "Now then there is no condemnation," &c. ; as I might well have expected, being carried captive to the law of sin. Herein also Christ deals as some conquerors, who had taken their enemies prisoners, but yet killed them not immediately, till the day of triumph came. This will keep the saints nothing in their own eyes, even when they are

ἐπιθυμίαν Plato πολυκέφαλον *appellat.*

filled brimfull with grace and glory in another world.

Ver. 25. *I thank God, &c.*] The Grecians being delivered but from bodily servitude by Flaminius the Roman general, called him their saviour ; and so rang out, Saviour, saviour, that the fowls in the air fell down dead with the cry. How much greater cause have we to magnify the grace of Christ, &c.

So then, with the mind, &c.] The stars by their proper motion are carried from the west to the east ; and yet by the motion of obedience unto the first mover, they pass along from the east unto the west. The waters by their natural course follow the centre of the earth, yet yielding to the moon, they are subject to her motions ; so are saints to God's holy will, though corrupt nature repine and resist. Grace is the prince in the regenerate soul. The will may sometimes be drawn away from the king and fly to the enemy, as David fled to Achish for fear ; yet when he went abroad to fight, he killed the Philistines in the south country, and he carried still a loyal heart to his king ; so in this case. A ravished woman *vexari potest, violari non potest*, may be vexed, but not violated. We read of one that (when she could not otherwise help herself) thrust her shears into the belly of an unclean bishop that would have forced her.

CHAPTER VIII.

Ver. 1. *There is therefore now*] Now, after such bloody wounds and gashes, chronicled chap. vii. Though carried captive, and sold under sin, yet not condemned, as might well have been expected. This the apostle doth here worthily admire.

No condemnation] *Non una condemnatio ;* οὐδὲν κατάκριμα, not one condemnation. There is none in heaven, God doth not condemn them : none on earth, their own heart and conscience doth not condemn them : no word, no commandment, no threatening. An unbeliever shall have a double condemnation ; one from the law which he hath transgressed, and another from the gospel, which he hath despised : as a malefactor, that being condemned and dead in law, rejecteth his prince's pardon. But it is otherwise with those that are in Christ Jesus. The law cannot condemn them, because they have appealed : the gospel cannot, because they have believed. God will "cast out condemnation for ever," as one renders that place, Matt. xii. 10, ἕως ἂν ἐκβάλῃ εἰς νῖκος τὴν κρίσιν. (Lud. de Dieu.)

Ver. 2. *For the law of the Spirit*] That is, Christ revived and risen hath justified me. See the note on chap. iv. 25.

Ver. 3. *It was weak through the flesh*] Which was irritated by the law, and took occasion thereby.

In the likeness of sinful flesh] Christ condescended to our rags, *sordes nostras induit*, took our passions and infirmities natural, but not sinful. He was in all things like unto us, but in sin: as the brazen serpent was like the fiery serpents, but only it had no sting.

Ver. 4. *Might be fulfilled*] In us *applicative*, in Christ *inhæsive*.

Ver. 5. *Do mind the things*] For want of a better principle. The stream riseth not above the spring.

Ver. 6. *To be carnally*] The quintessence of the flesh's wittiness, or rather wickedness, φρόνημα.

Ver. 7. *Because the carnal mind*] The best of a bad man is not only averse, but utterly adverse to all goodness. *Homo est inversus decalogus*, Job xi. 12, an ass's foal for rudeness, a wild ass's for unruliness.

Neither indeed can be] Spiritual arguments to a carnal heart are but warm clothes to a dead man. He hath brought a miserable necessity of sinning upon himself: his soul and all the powers thereof being but the shop of sin; his body and all the parts thereof tools of sin; his life and all his actions of both soul and body a trade of sin.

Ver. 8. *Cannot please God*] Their best works are but dead works, saith the author to the Hebrews; but silken sins, saith Augustine. Lombard citeth that Father, saying thus, *Omnis vita infidelium peccatum est: et nihil bonum sine summo bono*. The whole life of unbelievers is sin: neither is there anything good without the chiefest good. Ambrose Spiera, a Popish postiller, censureth this for a bloody sentence, *Crudelis est illa sententia*, saith he.

Ver. 9. *He is none of his*] As the merchant sets his seal upon his goods, so doth God his Spirit upon all his people, Ephes. i. 13.

Ver. 10. *The body is dead*] Death to the saints is neither total, but of the body only, nor perpetual, but for a season only, ver. 11.

Ver. 11. *Your mortal bodies*] As he hath already quickened your souls.

Ver. 12. *Not to the flesh*] We owe the flesh nothing but stripes, nothing but the blue eye that St Paul gave it. It must be mastered and mortified. Drive this Hagar out of doors, when once it grows haughty.

Ver. 13. *If we live after the flesh*] We must not think to pass *E cœno ad Cœlum*, to dance with the devil all day, and sup with Christ at night, to fly to heaven with pleasant wings. Beetles love dunghills better than ointments; and swine love mud better than a garden; so do swinish people their lusts, better than the lives of their souls. *At Paris ut vivat regnetque beatus, Cogi posse negat.* (Horat.) That carnal cardinal said, that he would not part with his part in Paris for Paradise.

But if ye mortify the deeds, &c.] Either a man must kill here, or be killed, *Aut fer, aut feri*, as Queen Elizabeth often sighed and said to herself concerning the Queen of Scots. Valentinian the emperor dying, gloried of one victory above the rest, and that was his victory over the flesh. *Inimicorum nequissimum devici, carnem meam*, said he. Be always an enemy to the devil and the world, but specially to your own flesh, said Robert Smith, martyr, in a letter to his wife. Surely, as the Prince of Orange said to his soldiers at the battle of Newport when they had the sea on the one side and the Spaniards on the other; If, saith he, you will live, you must either eat up these Spaniards, or drink up this sea; so must men either eat up their fleshly lusts, or drink of the burning lake: Fire and brimstone shall be else the portion of their cup, Psal. xi. 6.

Ver. 14. *For as many as are led*] As great men suffer their sons to go along with them, but set tutors to overlook and order them; so dealeth God by his; the Spirit leadeth them into all goodness, righteousness, and truth, Eph. v. 9, and fetcheth them again in their out-strays.

Ver. 15. *The spirit of bondage*] Δουλείας, as 2 Tim. i. 7, Δειλείας. The law will convince the judgment; but it is the gospel that convinceth the lust and the affection, and so sendeth us to treat with God as a Father, by fervent prayer. The Spirit is here called a "spirit of bondage;" because by the law he enlighteneth a man to see his bondage and slavery to sin and Satan, and his subjection to God's wrath and vengeance.

Ver. 16. *Beareth witness*] What an honour is this to the saints, that the Holy Ghost should bear witness at the bar of their consciences.

Ver. 17. *And if sons, then heirs*] All God's sons are heirs; not so the sons of earthly princes. Jehoshaphat gave his younger sons great gifts of silver, of gold, and of precious things, with fenced cities in Judah; but the kingdom gave he to Jehoram, because he was the firstborn, 2 Chron. xxi. 3. God's children are all higher than the kings of the earth, Psal. lxxxix. 27.

Ver. 18. *Are not worthy to be*, &c.] Heaven will pay for all; hold out therefore, faith and patience. When Saul had the kingdom, some despised him, but he held his peace, though a man afterwards froward enough. What is a drop of vinegar put into an ocean of wine? What is it for one to have a rainy day, who is going to take possession of a kingdom? *Pericula non respicit Martyr, coronas respicit*, saith Basil. A Dutch martyr feeling the flame to come to his beard, Ah, said he, what a small pain is this to be compared to the glory to come! Luther said he would not take all the world for one leaf of the Bible. What then would he take for the glory that it revealeth? St Paul useth a word here that signifieth (upon a good account justly cast up, and the matter well weighed) to conclude, resolve, and determine, as Rom. iii. 28; vi. 11, λογίζομαι. The globe of the earth is, as mathematicians compute, 21,000 miles in compass, and above: yet compared to the greatness of the starry sky, it is but as a centre or little prick to the circle, to which it beareth no proportion; much less do our afflictions to heaven's happiness.

Ver. 19. *For the earnest expectation*] Gr. "The intent expectation of the creature expecteth:" a Hebrew pleonasm, and withal a metaphor either from birds that thrust a long neck out of a cage, as labouring for liberty; or else from those that earnestly look and long for some special friends coming, as Sisera's mother, who looked out at a window, and cried through the lattice, "Why is his chariot so long in coming?" Judges v. 28.

Ver. 20. *Subject to vanity*] The creature is defiled by man's sin, and must therefore be purged by the fire of the last day; as the vessels that held the sin-offering were purged by the fire of the sanctuary.

Ver. 21. *Because the creature itself*] See Mr Wilcox's discourse upon these words, printed, together with his Exposition of the Psalms, Proverbs, &c., in folio. The creature is said to be subject to vanity and bondage of corruption, 1. As corruptible. 2. As teachers of men, and they will not learn; so that they lose their labour. 3. As they are instruments of man's punishment. 4. As they are forced to serve wicked men's turns and uses, who have no peace with the creature, and should have no service from them.

Ver. 22. *The whole creation groaneth*] Even the very heavens are not without their feebleness and the manifest effects of fainting old age. It is observed that since the days of Ptolemy, the sun runs nearer the earth by 9976 German miles, and therefore the heavens have not kept their first perfection.

And travaileth] How Mr Bradshaw pitied the poor beast he rode on, and said, that men take too much liberty in killing and misusing some contemptible creatures, see in his Life by Mr Clark, p. 139.

Ver. 23. *The first-fruits*] Which the creatures have not, and yet they groan: how much more we!

The redemption] Our full and final deliverance.

Ver. 24. *For we are saved by hope*] Hope is the daughter of faith, but such as is a staff to her aged mother.

Ver. 25. *Then do we with patience*] Religious men find it more easy to bear evil than to wait till the promised good be enjoyed, Heb. x. 36. The spoiling of their goods required patience; but this more than ordinary.

Ver. 26. *Helpeth our infirmities*] Lifts with us and before us in our prayers. Or helpeth us as the nurse helpeth her little child, upholding it by the sleeve. ($\sigma \nu \nu \alpha \nu \tau \iota \lambda \alpha \mu \beta \acute{\alpha} \nu \epsilon \tau \alpha \iota$. Beza.)

For we know not what, &c.] The flesh with her murmurings maketh such a din that we can hardly hear the voice of the Spirit, mixing with the flesh's roarings and repinings, his praying, sighs, and sobbings.

But the Spirit itself] Prayer is the breath of the Spirit, who doth super-expostulate for us, $\upsilon \pi \epsilon \rho \epsilon \nu \tau \upsilon \gamma \chi \acute{\alpha} \nu \epsilon \iota$, inditing our prayers. We cannot so much as *suspirare*, unless he do first *inspirare*, breathe out a sigh for sin, if he breathe it not into us.

With groanings that cannot be uttered] He that would have unspeakable joy, 1 Pet. i. 8, must by the Spirit stir up unutterable groanings.

Ver. 27. *Knoweth the mind, &c.*] *Quomodo enim non exauditur spiritus a patre, qui exaudit cum patre?* (Augustine.)

Ver. 28. *All things work together*] Not affliction only (as some would here restrain it), but sin, Satan, all. *Venenum aliquando pro remedio fuit*, saith Seneca. *Medici pedes et alas cantharidis, cum sit ipsa mortifera, prodesse dicunt.* The drinking of that wine wherein a viper hath been drowned, cureth the leprosy. The scorpion healeth his own wounds, and the viper (the head and tail being cut off) beaten and applied, cureth her own biting. God changeth our grisly wounds into spangles of beauty, and maketh the horrible sting of Satan to be like a pearl pin, to pin upon us the long white robe of Christ, and to dress us with the garment of gladness.

Ver. 29. *Conformed to the image*] In holiness, say some; in glory, say others; in affliction, is the apostle's meaning. Art not thou glad to fare as Phocion? said he to one that was to die with him. (Plut. in Apophtheg.) May not Christ better say so to his co-sufferers?

Ver. 30. *Them also he called, &c.*] If ye feel not faith (said that holy martyr), then know that predestination is too high a matter for you to be disputers of, until you have been better scholars in the school-house of repentance and justification, which is the grammar-school wherein we must be conversant and learned, before we go to the university of God's most holy predestination and providence.

Them he also justified] Vocation precedeth justification. *Deus justificat fide jam donatos, sicut damnat prius induratos.* (Cameron.)

Them he also glorified] That is, he keepeth them glorious by his glorious Spirit, even in this life, from impenitent sin, and maketh them stable and constant in godliness.

Ver. 31. *What shall we say then?*] q. d. Predestination, vocation, justification, glorification? What things be these? We cannot tell what to say to these things, so much we are amazed at the greatness of God's love in them. A brave conclusion of the whole disputation concerning justification by faith alone.

If God be for us, &c.] Maximilian the emperor so admired this sentence, that he caused it to be set in chequer-work upon a table, at which he used to dine and sup, that having it so often in his eye, he might always have it in mind also.

Ver. 32. *He that spared not*] *Qui misit unigenitum, immisit spiritum, promisit vultum, quid tandem tibi negaturus est?* saith Bernard. *Nihil unquam ei negasse credendum est, quem ad vituli hortatur esum*, saith Jerome.

Ver. 33. *Who shall lay anything*] This is that confident interrogatory of a good conscience, $\epsilon \pi \epsilon \rho \acute{\omega} \tau \eta \mu \alpha$, 1 Pet. iii. 21.

It is God that justifieth] Some read it questionwise thus, Shall God that justifieth? No such matter. And if the judge acquit a prisoner, he cares not though the jailor or fellow-prisoners condemn him; so here.

Ver. 34. *Who is he that condemneth?*] To the sentence of death he opposeth Christ's death.

Who is even at the right hand] And as Christ is at the right hand of his Father, so is the

Church at the right hand of Christ, Psal. xlv. 10, a place of dignity and safety.

Ver. 35. *Who shall separate us*] Who shall separate me ? saith the Syriac.

Ver. 36. *We are killed all the day*] In Diocletian's days 17,000 Christians are said to have been slain in the space of a month. In the Parisian massacre 30,000 in as little space, and within the year 300,000.

As sheep to the slaughter] That lamentable story of the Christians of Calabria that suffered persecution, A. D. 1560, comes home to this text. For being all thrust up in one house together, as in a sheep-fold, the executioner comes in, and among them takes one, and blindfolds him with a muffler about his eyes, and so leadeth him forth to a larger place, where he commandeth him to kneel down. Which being done, he cutteth his throat, and so leaveth him half dead ; and taking his butcher's knife and muffler all of gore blood, he cometh again to the rest, and so leading them one after another, he despatcheth them, to the number of 88, no otherwise than doth a butcher kill his calves and sheep.

Ver. 37. *We are more than conquerors*] What is that ? Triumphers, 2 Cor. ii. 14. We do over-overcome ; because through faith in Christ we overcome before we fight, and are secure of victory.[1] And again, "we are more than conquerors," because we gather strength by our opposition (as that giant that fought with Hercules is fabled to do, by his falling to the earth), we conquer in being conquered. The tormentors were tired in torturing Blandina : and, We are ashamed O emperor ; the Christians laugh at your cruelty and grow the more resolute, said one of Julian's nobles to him.

Ver. 38. *For I am persuaded*] Or, I am sure by what I have heard out of God's word.[2] He that hath this full assurance of faith, goes gallantly to heaven. What (saith the world) should a rich man ail ? The Irish ask such, What they mean to die ? But I wonder more at such as have the riches of full assurance, yea, that have but the assurance of adherence, though not of evidence, what they mean to walk heavily. Mr Latimer says that the assurance of heaven is the sweetmeats of the feast of a good conscience. There are other dainty dishes in this feast, but this is the banquet.

Ver. 39. *For the love of God*] viz. Wherewith he loved us. For he loveth his own to the end, and in the end, John xiii. 1. See the note there. The wife of Camerarius heard Sarcerius interpreting this text and ver. 35 thus, and was much comforted after a sore conflict. (Joh. Manlii, loc. com.)

CHAPTER IX.

Ver. 1. *I say the truth, &c.*] As any one is more assured of his own salvation, the more he desireth the salvation of others. Charity is no churl ; as we see here in Paul.

Ver. 2. *Continual sorrow*] Such as a woman in travail hath, ὀδύνη. So Gal. iv. 19.

Ver. 3. *Were accursed*] Devoted to destruction, ἀνάθεμα, as those malefactors among the heathens were, that in time of common calamity were sacrificed to their infernal gods, for pacifying their displeasure, that the plague might cease. Out of greatest zeal to God and love to his countrymen, the apostle wisheth himself anathema, that is, not to be separated from the Spirit and grace of Christ (for so he should have sinned), but from the comforts of Christ, the happiness that comes in by Christ, as one well interpreteth it. *Charitas exuberans optat etiam impossibilia*, saith Luther ; his over-abounding charity wisheth impossibilities ; but his wish was *voluntas conditionata*, saith one. His love to the Church was like the ivy, which if it cleave to a stone or an old wall, will rather die than forsake it. Somewhat like to this holy wish was that of Ambrose, that the fire of contentions kindled in the Churches might (if it were the will of God) be quenched with his blood. And that of Nazianzen, that (Jonah-like) he might be cast into the sea, so by it all might be calm in the public.

Ver. 4. *The adoption*] For Israel was God's first-born, and " so higher than the kings of the earth," Psal. lxxxix. 27.

And the glory] The ark of the covenant, 1 Sam. iv. 21, whence Judea is called " the glorious land," Dan. xi. 41. As for the ark, it is elsewhere called God's face, Psal. cv. 4. Yea, God himself, Psal. cxxxii. 5.

The covenants] The moral law in two tables.

The giving of the law] The judicial law.

The service] The ceremonial law.

The promises] Of the gospel made to Abraham, and his seed for ever. These promises are a precious book, every leaf whereof drops myrrh and mercy.

Ver. 5. *Of whom is Christ*] This is as great an honour to all mankind (how much more to the Jews!) as if the king should marry into some poor family of his subjects.

Ver. 6. *Not as though the word*] That word of promise, ver. 4, which is sure-hold, " Yea and Amen."

For they are not all Israel] *Multi sacerdotes, et pauci sacerdotes*, saith Chrysostom, *multi in nomine, et pauci in opere.* So here.

Ver. 7. *Neither because they are*] This profiteth them no more than it did Dives that Abraham called him son.

Ver. 8. *The children of the promise*] Abraham by believing God's promise, begat, after a sort, all believers, yea, Christ himself, the head of his seed, his Son according to the flesh, but more according to the faith.

Ver. 9. *At this time*] See the note on Gen. xviii. 10.

Ver. 10. *But when Rebecca*] She, and not

---

[1] ὑπερνικῶμεν. *Super superamus. Super vincimus.*

[2] πέπεισμαι, scil. *Ex verbi prædicatione efficaci ut indicat tacite hoc verbo.* Beza.

Isaac, is named, because she received the oracle, whether from the mouth of Melchisedec or some other way, I have not to determine.

Ver. 11. *For the children, &c.*] Here the apostle wadeth into that *profundum sine fundo*, predestination.

Being not yet born] Sapores son of Misdates, king of Persia, began his reign before his life. For his father dying, left his mother with child, and the Persian nobility set the crown on his mother's belly, acknowledging thereby her issue for their prince, before she as yet had felt herself quick. God elects not of foreseen faith or works, but of free grace.

Ver. 12. *Shall serve*] Servitude came in with a curse, and figureth reprobation, Gen. ix. 25; John viii. 34, 35; Gal. iv. 30.

Ver. 13. *Esau have I hated*] i. e. I have not loved him, but passed him by; and this preterition is properly opposed to election.

As it is written] Malachi is alleged to explain Moses. It was rightly observed by Pareus (in the close of his Comment upon Genesis) that all the following Scriptures are but expositions of that first book.[1]

Ver. 14. *Is there*] Carnal reason dares reprehend what it does not comprehend. (Para.)

Ver. 15. *I will have mercy, &c.*] *Dei voluntas est ratio rationum, nec tantum recta, sed regula.*

Ver. 16. *So then it is not, &c.*] *Nec volentis, nec volantis* (as a nobleman gave it for his motto), though a man could run as fast as a bird can fly.

Ver. 17. *Raised thee up*] For a vessel of wrath, and an instance of my justice.

Ver. 18. *Therefore*] God being a free agent, cannot be unjust; he is bound to none.

Whom he will, he hardeneth] There is a threefold hardness of the heart: 1. Natural and hereditary, whereby all men are by nature not only averse from, but also adverse to, the motions of grace; this is called a neck possessed with an iron sinew, Isa. xlviii. 4. 2. Actual, adventitious, voluntary; which is, when, by often choking good motions, a man hath quit his heart of them; being arrived at that dead and dedolent disposition, Ephes. iv. 18, past feeling, and ripe for destruction. This is called a brow of brass in the above-named text, Isa. xlviii. 4. 3. Judiciary, penal hardness; which is when God, for a punishment of the former, withholds his graces, and delivers a man up to Satan to be further hardened, and to his own heart's lusts, which is worse. The incestuous person was delivered up to Satan, and yet repented; but he that is delivered up to his own heart, to a reprobate mind, cannot be renewed by repentance; but is in the ready road to that unpardonable sin. And this last is here meant.

Ver. 19. *Why doth he yet find fault*] *Queritur*, saith the Vulgar; which interpretation cozened Aquinas, as if it had been written *Quæritur*. So Luke xv. 8. Gregory the Great and others, for

Everrit, read *Evertit;* which mistake produced many groundless glosses.

Ver. 20. *That repliest against God*] Gr. Αντα-ποκρινόμενος, chattest and wordest it with him?

Ver. 21. *Of the same lump*] The apostle alludeth to man's creation, and therehence ascendeth to God's eternal decree of predestination.

Ver. 22. *Fitted to destruction*] *Non dicit Deum eos aptasse ad interitum, ne videretur dicere Deum eis indidisse peccatum, quo ad exitum præparentur.* (Molinæus.)

Ver. 23. *And that he might*] He rejected some, that his mercy might the more appear in the election of others.

The riches of his glory] That is, of his mercy wherein he principally glorieth, and for the which he is most of all glorified.

Ver. 24. *Even us*] Not me Paul only hath he assured of vocation, and so consequently of election to eternal life.

Ver. 25. *And her beloved*] Jer. xii. 7. God calls the Church the beloved of his soul, or (as the Septuagint and Vulgar read it) his beloved soul, τὴν ψυχὴν τὴν ἠγαπημένην.

Ver. 26. *The children, &c.*] This is such a royalty, John i. 12, as the apostle worthily wondereth at, and sets an *Ecce* upon it.

Ver. 27. *A remnant*] Reserved for royal use. *Diaconos paucitas honorabiles fecit*, saith Jerome. *Sic et sanctos*, say I.

Ver. 28. *A short work*] When once he sets to work to cut off hypocrites.

Ver. 29. *Except the Lord of Sabaoth*] That is, of hosts. God is commander-in-chief of all creatures. The Rabbins well observe that he hath *Magnleh Cheloth*, and *Matteh Cheloth*, two general troops, as his horse and foot, the upper and lower troops ready prest. (Kimchi.)

Ver. 30. *Which is of faith*] Faith wraps itself in the righteousness of Christ, and so justifieth us.

Ver. 31. *The law of righteousness*] That is, the righteousness of the law.

Ver. 32. *For they stumbled*] So they do to this day. So do Papists and carnal Protestants. *Non frustra Lutherus in libris toties vaticinatus videtur, sese vereri dictitans, ne se extincto vera illa justificationis disciplina prorsus apud Christianos exolescat.*[2]

Ver. 33.] See the note on 1 Pet. ii. 6.

Shall not be ashamed] That is, shall be confirmed, comforted, established. The Scripture loves to speak with the least in promising good to God's people: or else by way of exclamation, " Oh how great is thy goodness which thou hast laid up for them that fear thee!" *q. d.* it is unutterable; fitter to be believed than possible to be discoursed, Psal. xxxi. 19.

CHAPTER X.

Ver. 1. *My heart's desire*] So it should be ours. See my True Treasure, chap. vii. sect. 2.

---

[1] *Quicquid dehinc scripturarum est, hujus est commentarius.*

[2] John Fox, Christus Triumphans, Epist.

Ver. 2. *They have a zeal of God*] So had those two Rabbins, David Rubenita and Shelomoh Molchu, that set upon the Emperor Charles V. to persuade him to Judaism, and were therefore put to a cruel death, A. D. 1530. (Alsted. Chron.) So had Latimer before his conversion: I was as obstinate a Papist, saith he, as any was in England: insomuch that when I should be made Bachelor in Divinity, my whole oration went against Philip Melancthon and his opinions, &c. Being a priest, and using to say mass, he thought he had never sufficiently mingled his massing wine with water: and moreover that he should never be damned, if he were once a professed friar; with divers such superstitious phantasies. (Acts and Mon.) Zeal without knowledge is as wild-fire in a fool's hand; it is like the devil in the demoniac, that casts him sometimes into the fire and sometimes into the water.

Ver. 3. *For they being ignorant*] The soul that is without knowledge is not good, and he that (without knowledge) hasteth with his feet, sinneth, Prov. xix. 2; the faster he goeth, the farther he is out.

Ver. 4. *For Christ is the end, &c.*] q. d. Ay, and for Christ's sake, is the righteousness of God. But the Jews submit not to Christ, therefore not to the righteousness of God. Christ, saith Austin, is *Legis finis interficiens, et perficiens.* The ceremonial law he hath slain and taken out of the way: the moral law he hath fulfilled for us, and we by him, *sc.* by faith in his name, which maketh his obedience to become ours.

Ver. 5. *Shall live by them*] This do and live; that is, saith Luther, *morere*, die out of hand: for there is no man lives and sins not. We can as little cease to sin as the pulse to beat, heart to pant, &c.

Ver. 6. *Say not in thine heart*] The law preacheth faith in Christ, as well as the gospel.

Ver. 7. *Into the deep*] Those deeps of the earth, Psal. lxxi. 20.

Ver. 8. *The word is nigh thee*] Moses meant it of the law, but it more fitly agreeth to the gospel. The babe of Bethlehem is swathed up in the bands of both Testaments: he is author, object, matter, and mark of both. Therefore if we will profit in hearing, teaching, reading, we must have the eye of our minds turned toward Christ, as the faces of the cherubims were toward the mercy-seat.

Ver. 9. *That if thou shalt confess*] That is, if thou shalt call upon the name of the Lord, as it is expounded, ver. 13.

Ver. 10. *For with the heart, &c.*] Plutarch tells us that of all plants in Egypt, that they call Persica is consecrated to their goddess Isis, and that for this reason, because the fruit of it is like a heart, the leaf like a tongue.

Ver. 11. *Shall not be ashamed*] Maketh not haste, saith the prophet. Shame and confusion follow haste and precipitancy: *Sed Deo confisi nunquam confusi.*

Ver. 12. *Is rich unto all, &c.*] He cannot therefore be poor that can pray; for he shall have out his prayer, either in money or money's worth.

Ver. 13. *Shall be saved*] Though he miss of that particular mercy he asketh, he is certainly sealed up to salvation.

Ver. 14. *How shall they hear, &c.*] The word read is of divine use and efficacy; but of preaching we may say as David did of Goliath's sword, " There is none to that." Milk warmed is fitter for nourishment; and the rain from heaven hath a fatness with it, and a special influence, more than standing waters; so there is not that life, operation, and blessing in the word read as preached.

And how shall they preach unless they be sent] Here you have that *scala cœli*, ladder of heaven, as a good old martyr called it; and we must not presume to alter the rounds of this ladder. The apostle holds it for impossible that any should preach that are not sent. Let such look to it, as run before they are sent, press into the pulpit without a call thereunto. Let them remember Nadab and Abihu with their strange fire, Core and his complices with their dismal usurpations, Uzzah and Uzziah with their exemplary punishments, &c. God hanged these up in gibbets, as it were to warn others.

Ver. 15. *How beautiful are the feet*] How much more their faces! " Surely I have seen thy face as the face of God," said Jacob to Esau, Gen. xxxiii. 10, that is, honourable and comfortable. We know how Cornelius received Peter; and the Galatians, Paul, till they were bewitched from him, Gal. iv. 14. But it must be remembered that we " glorify the word," not the preacher, Acts xiii. 48.

Ver. 16. *Who hath believed our report?*] Gr. ἀκοὴν, our hearing, passively taken. So Cæsar and Cicero use *auditio* for report and rumour. Some sit before a preacher as senseless as the seats they sit on, pillars they lean to, dead bodies they tread on. Others rage, *Tange montes et fumigabunt, &c.*

Ver. 17. *By the word of God*] That is, by the word of God's command, sending out preachers gifted for the purpose, and saying to them, " Go preach," &c.

Ver. 18. *Yes verily; their sound, &c.*] *Sonus tonus*, ὁ φθόγγος. David saith only, " their line," Psal. xix. 2. That accurate and artificial frame of the heaven preacheth, as it were, the infinite wisdom and power of the Creator. All God's works are his *Regii professores*, his Catholic preachers, or real postilles (as one calleth them) of his divinity. The world (saith Clem. Alex.) is *Dei Scriptura*, God's great Bible with three great leaves—heaven, earth, and hell. David's words are here very fitly applied to the sound of the gospel; the circle whereof is like that of the sun, universal to the whole world; and the motion not unlike: for it arose in the east of Judea, went thence to the south of Greece, and then to the west of Italy and the Latins ; from whence it is come to these northern parts of the world (the very utmost angle of the universe), where that it may continue, let us pray,

Vespera nunc venit, nobiscum Christe maneto :
Extingui lucem nec patiare tuam.

" All that I fear," saith Mr Baxter, " is, lest Mr Herbert be a true prophet, and the gospel be in its solar motion travelling for the American parts, and is quitting its present place of residence and unworthy professors and possessors : and then farewell England." Contempt drove Christ from Nazareth, his own country, which he came purposely to heal. Confer Jer. li. 9, Ezek. xxiv. 13.

Ver. 19. *Did not Israel know*] *sc.* That the Gentiles were to be called ? they were oft told of it.

Ver. 20. *Is very bold*] So that for his boldness he was sawn asunder, saith Jerome.

Ver. 21. *Stretched*] A metaphor from a mother.

CHAPTER XI.

Ver. 1. *I say then, Hath God, &c.*] ´As I may seem to have said, chap. x. Ministers must do their utmost to prevent mistakes. Zuinglius, when in his sermons he had terrified the wicked, was wont to shut up with *Bone vir, hoc nihil ad te,* Thou good man, I mean not thee.

Ver. 2. *Saith of Elias*] A man of such transcendent zeal, that to heighten the expression thereof some have legended of him, that when he drew his mother's breasts, he was seen to suck in fire.

Ver. 3. *And I am left alone*] To withstand and reform the common corruptions. Some have commended it to our consideration, that from the first service in the temple when it was built, and the time of Elijah's reformation, was about a hundred years. And from the reformation in King Edward VI.'s days until now is about the same proportion of time.

Ver. 4. *The image of Baal*] Τῇ Βάαλ, to that lady, as our modern idolaters also call the Virgin Mary, whom they despight with seeming honours. They would persuade the world, that Christ by dying obeyed not his Father only, but his mother too, that she is the complement of the Trinity, that she entreateth not, but commandeth her Son, is the most imperious mother of our Judge, with many like horrid blasphemies, which I tremble to relate.[1]

Ver. 5. *According to the election of grace*] St Paul was *Constantissimus gratiæ prædicator,* as Austin calleth him, a most constant preacher of God's free grace.

Ver. 6. *Then is it no more of works*] Whatsoever conferrumination of grace and works Papists dream of. They think that as he that standeth

[1] Salazar Jesuita in Prov. viii. 19, 23, 29.

on two firm branches of a tree is surer than he that standeth upon one only ; so he that trusteth to Christ and works too is in the safest condition. But, 1. They are fallen from Christ that trust to works, Gal. v. 4. 2. He that hath one foot on a firm branch, and another on a rotten one, stands not so sure, as if he stood wholly on that which is sound. But let them be Moses' disciples, let us be Christ's. Set not up a candle to this Sun of righteousness ; mix not thy puddle with his purple blood, thy rags with his raiment, thy pigeon's plumes with his eagle's feathers. He can and will save his to the utmost, Heb. vii. 25. Detest all mock stays ; and account accursed for ever that blasphemous direction of the Papists to dying people, *Conjunge, Domine, obsequium meum cum omnibus quæ Christus passus est pro me.* Join, Lord, mine obedience with all that Christ hath suffered for me.

Ver. 7. *Israel*] *i. e.* The carnal Israelite.

He seeketh for] viz. Righteousness and salvation by works.

Hardened] By a judiciary hardness.

Ver. 8. *The spirit of slumber*] So that with those bears in Pliny they cannot be awakened with the sharpest prickles ; and with those asses in Etruria, that feeding upon henbane they lie for dead, and awake not till half-hilded. Such a dead lethargy is now befallen Papists.

Ver. 9. *Be made a snare*] As the bait is to the birds.

Ver. 10. *Bow down*] *i. e.* Bring them down into bondage and misery. Compare Lev. xxvi. 13.

Ver. 11. *Have they stumbled*] He that stumbleth and comes not down, gets ground.

Ver. 12. *How much more their fulness*] O *dieculam illam ! dexter mihi præ lætitias alit oculus.* How long, Lord, holy and true ?

Ver. 13. *I magnify mine office*] I make the utmost of it by gaining souls to Christ.

Ver. 14. *And might save some*] Ministers must turn themselves as it were into all shapes and fashions, both of spirit and speech, to win people to God.

Ver. 15. *Be the reconciling*] Not as a cause, but as an occasion.

Life from the dead] That is, *Res summe bona,* saith Phocius, a special good thing.

Ver. 16. *If the first-fruit be holy*] Not with a natural, but a federal holiness, as 1 Cor. vii. 14.

Ver. 17. *Were grafted in*] Gr. ἐνεκεντρίσθης, pricked into the middle, the centre of the olive.

Ver. 18. *Boast not*] Gr., throw not up thy neck, in a scornful insulting way, but rather pity and pray for them. (Isidor. Solil.)

Ver. 19. *Thou wilt say*] Carnal reason will have ever somewhat to say, and is not easily set down. (Greg. Moral.)

Ver. 20. *Be not high-minded, but fear*] *Alterius perditio tua sit cautio,* saith one. *Ruina majorum sit cautela minorum,* saith another. Seest thou thy brother shipwrecked ? look well to thy tackling.

Ver. 21. *Take heed lest*] Cavebis autem si pavebis.

Ver. 22. *Severity*] Gr. Ἀποτομίαν, Resection or cutting off, as a chirurgeon cutteth off proud and dead flesh. The dispersion of the Jews for this sixteen hundred years and upward is such, as that one of their own Rabbins concludeth from thence that their Messias must needs be come; and they must needs suffer so much for killing him. Epiphanius testifieth, that after the destruction of Jerusalem, the Jews of Tiberias had this custom, when any of their friends or kindred were at the point of death, they would secretly whisper them in the ear to this purpose: Believe in Jesus of Nazareth, whom our rulers crucified; for he shall come again to judge thee at the last day. Fincelius also (Lib. iii. *de miraculis*) tells of a certain converted Jew of Ratisbon, who being demanded (amongst other questions put to him by the Christians) why the Jews did so exceedingly desire the blood of Christians, answered that that was a great secret amongst them, known to none but their chiefest Rabbis; but this was their custom, to anoint their dying friends with the blood of Christians, and to use words to this effect: If he that was promised in the law and prophets hath already appeared, and that Jesus who was crucified were the true Messias, let this blood of an innocent man, who died in the faith of Jesus, cleanse thee from thy sins, and be a means to further thine eternal happiness. Oh the severity of God! and oh the obstinacy and misery of this hard-hearted people!

Ver. 23. *God is able*] He can fetch heart of oak out of a hollow tree, and of carnal make a people created again, Psal. cii. 18; Eph. ii. 10.

Ver. 24. *Contrary*] Therefore nature contributes nothing toward the work of conversion.

Ver. 25. *That blindness in part*] It is neither total nor perpetual. Lyra was a famous English Jew. Tremellius was also a Jew born; they are but *methe mispar*, a very few that are yet converted. They pretend (but maliciously) that those few that turn Christians in Italy are none other than poor Christians hired from other cities to personate their part. But when God shall have united those two sticks, Ezek. xxxvii. 19, and made way for those three kings of the East, Rev. xvi. 12, then it shall be said of Jacob and Israel, "What hath God wrought?" Numb. xxiii. 23. Jachiades (a Jew doctor) upon those words, Dan. xii. 4, would have us believe that God sealed up the time of the coming of the Messiah; that for their sins, which are many, it is deferred, &c., but concludeth his animadversions there with this truth, *Verum enimvero Deus nos dignabitur clarissima visione; cum Deus reducet Zionem, tunc intelligemus res ipsas, prout sunt, i. e.* God shall vouchsafe us a most clear vision at that time when he shall bring back the captivity of Zion, and then we shall understand things even as they are.

Ver. 26. *Shall turn away ungodliness*] That is, He shall pardon their sin. The prophet Isaiah

hath it, Unto them that turn from transgression in Jacob, &c. They whose persons are justified, have their lusts mortified.

Ver. 27. *When I shall take*] By the spirit of judgment and of burning, Isa. iv. 4, with xxvii. 9.

Ver. 28. *They are enemies*] *i. e.* Hated of God, as appears by the opposition; and banished, as it were, by a common consent of nations, out of human society. See 1 Thess. ii. 15, 16.

Ver. 29. *Are without repentance*] When God is said to repent, it is *Mutatio rei non Dei, effectus non affectus, facti non consilii*, a change, not of his will, but of his work. Repentance with man is the change of his will; repentance with God is the willing of a change. But what a sweet comfort is this, that God's favour is so constant that what he hath written he hath written, that there is no blotting out of the book of life (*Nulla litura in decretis sapientum*, say the Stoics), that is, I have blessed him, and he shall be blessed; and that his blessing is (as Thucydides saith of a well-composed history), κτῆμα εἰς ἀεὶ ξυγκείμενον, an everlasting possession.

Ver. 30. *Through their*] By occasion of their unbelief. *Pungit Judæos et humiliat Gentes,* saith one.

Ver. 31. *That they also*] It noteth not the cause, but the event, as 1 Cor. xi. 19.

Ver. 32. *For God hath concluded*] Or locked them all up in the law's dark dungeon, συνέκλεισε, Gal. iii. 22. Unbelief breaks all the law at an instant by rejecting Christ, as the first act of faith obeys all the law at an instant in Christ.

That he might have mercy upon all] Luther in a very great conflict was relieved and comforted by the often repeating of this sweet sentence.

Ver. 33. *O the depth of the riches*] The Romans dedicated a certain lake, the depth whereof they knew not, to Victory, so should we admire the unsearchable counsels of God, being subdued to that which we cannot subdue to our understandings. God, saith one, is like the pool Polycritus writeth of, which in compass at first scarce seemed to exceed the breadth of a shield, but if any went into it to wash, it extended itself more and more. (Aristot. de Mirab. Auscult.) And Chrysostom speaking of the love of God in Christ, Oh, saith he, I am like a man digging in a deep spring; I stand here, and the water riseth up upon me; and I stand there, and still the water riseth upon me. Oh, dive we not into this deep; for here (as in the salt waters), the deeper, the sweeter.

Past finding out] It is with us here as with hounds at a loss, having neither footsteps nor scent left of the game they pursue (ἀνεξιχνίαστοι). Let it satisfy us for present, that at the last day of judgment we shall see a harmony in this discord of things; and that the reason of God's ways, now hid, shall then be made manifest. In the mean space know, that *Arcana dei, Arca Dei* (Augustine), pry not into it, lest ye perish; but hold this for certain, God's judgments are sometimes secret, always just.

Ver. 34. *Who hath been his counsellor*] Alphonso the wise (the fool rather) was heard blasphemously to say, that if he had been of God's counsel at the creation, he could have advised and ordered many things much better than now they are. This Alphonso, the tenth of that name, king of Spain, who by a just hand of God upon him deprived of his kingdom, and died in public hatred and infamy.

Ver. 35. *Who hath first given to him*] Do we not owe him all that we have and are? And can a man merit by paying his debts?

Ver. 36. *For of him*] As the efficient cause, and "through him" as the administering cause, and "to him" as the final cause, are all things. A wise philosopher could say, that man is the end of all in a semicircle; that is, all things in the world are made for him, and he is made for God.

To whom be glory for ever] God, saith one, counts the works and fruits that come from us to be ours, because the judgment and resolution of will whereby we do them is ours. This he doth to encourage us. But because the grace whereby we judge and will aright comes from God, ascribe we all to him. So shall he lose no praise, we no encouragement.

CHAPTER XII.

Ver. 1. *I beseech*] *Volumus et jubemus* became the pope's style, A. D. 606.

By the mercies of God] His manifold mercies, διὰ τῶν οἰκτιρμῶν. *Per miserationes amplificationis causa.* (Beza.) We that have received so many mercies, must not only *servire Deo, sed et adulari*, saith Tertullian. Mercy calls for duty; deliverance commands obedience, and there is so much disingenuity in the contrary, that holy Ezra thinks heaven and earth would be ashamed of it, Ezra ix. 13, 14. The cords of kindness are called "the cords of a man," Hos. xi. 4; rational motives befitting the nature of a man. So that to sin against mercy is to sin against humanity; it is bestial, and fits a man for destruction, Rom. ix. 22; like as when physic which should remove the disease, doth co-operate with it, then death comes with the more pain and speed. No surfeit more dangerous than that of bread: no judgment more terrible than that of mercy despised and abused. Abused mercy turns into fury. *Patientia læsa fit furor.*

That ye present] As they of old did their sacrifices at the altar. With the burnt-offering, which signified the sacrificing of the flesh, was joined the sin-offering, that is, Christ. Faith applies Christ to the believer, and the believer to Christ.

Your bodies] That is, your whole person. *Cainistæ sunt*, saith Luther, *offerentes non personam, sed opus personæ.* They are Cainists that offer to God the work done, but do not offer themselves to God.

A living sacrifice] In the old law they had many kinds of sacrifices killed and offered. Now,

saith Origen, instead of a ram we kill our ireful passions; instead of a goat our unclean affections; instead of flying fowls our idle thoughts, &c.

Ver. 2. *To this world*] To the corrupt customs and courses of wicked worldlings. See them set forth, Rom. xiii. 13; Eph. iv. 18—20; 1 Pet. iv. 3, and shun them. Erasmus rendereth it, *Ne accommodetis vos ad figuram*, Accommodate not yourselves to the figure and fashion of the world; do not personate and act the part of such; as a player doth, when he playeth the drunkard or wanton on the scaffold or stage (so μὴ συσχηματίζεσθε signifies). St Paul writeth to his Corinthians, not to company with fornicators of this world, or with the covetous, or with extortioners, or idolaters, lest they should conform to them, 1 Cor. v. 9, 10. For as the creatures living in the several elements are commonly of the temperature of the element they live in (as the fishes, cold and moist like the water; the worms, cold and dry as the earth, &c.), so are we apt to conform to the company we converse with. It is both hard and happy not to do as the rest do; but to be like fishes, that retain their sweetness in the salt sea; like salamanders, that remain unscorched in the fire; like pearls, that growing in the sea, have the colour and brightness of heaven; like oil, that will easily overtop all other liquors, and not commingle; ever holding constant a countermotion to the course of the world and corruptions of the times; that amidst all, a good conscience may be kept, that richest treasure and dearest jewel that ever the heart of man was acquainted with.

But be ye transformed] Gr. metamorphosed, the old frame being dissolved, and a new form acquired.

That ye may prove] sc. By your practice.

Ver. 3. *But to think soberly*] Gr. φρονεῖν εἰς τὸ σωφρονεῖν, to be wise to sobriety. Socrates made no distinction between wisdom and sobriety, σοφίαν καὶ σωφροσύνην non distinguebat. (Xenoph.) We shall be sober, if we take not that upon us that we have not, nor brag of that which we have. There is an elegancy in the original that cannot be rendered.

Ver. 4. *For as we have*, &c.] See 1 Cor. xii. 12, which is a commentary on this text.

Ver. 5. *One body in Christ*] See the note on 1 Cor. xii. 12, 13.

And every one members] Try thy membership, if, 1. Sociable with Christ and Christians. 2. Useful and serviceable to the body. 3. Compassionate, as Paul; "Who is afflicted," saith he, "and I burn not?" I feel twinges when others are hurt; and I hold myself a debtor (as a member) to Greeks and barbarians, to the wise and unwise, be they but of the body, Rom. xi. 4.

Ver. 6. *According to the proportion*] That form of sound words, 2 Tim. i. 13, those principles of the doctrine of Christ, Heb. vi. 1, with which all interpretations of Scripture must bear due proportion.

Ver. 7. *Or ministry*] Take it either largely for the whole ministry, as 1 Cor. xii. 5; Acts i.

17 ; or more strictly for the office of a deacon, as Acts vi.

Ver. 8. Or he that exhorteth] The pastor properly so called. See the note on Eph. iv. 11.

Ver. 9. Abhor that which is evil] Hate it as hell itself, ἀποστυγοῦντες, so the word signifies ; *Mihi certe Auxentius nunquam aliud quam diabolus erit, quia Arianus*, saith Hilary, I shall look upon Auxentius no otherwise than as upon a devil, so long as he is an Arian.

Ver. 10. Be kindly affectioned] As natural brethren and more. *Arctior est copula cordis quam corporis.* We are brethren in Adam according to the flesh, in and by Christ according to the Spirit.

Ver. 11. Not slothful] Or, not driving off till it be too late (ὀκνηρός, *cunctator*). Charles, the son of Charles Duke of Anjou, who was king of Sicily and Jerusalem, was called Carolus Cunctator, not in the sense as Fabius, because he stayed till opportunity came, but because he stayed till opportunity was lost.

Fervent in spirit] Gr. ζέοντες, seething hot. God, who is himself a pure act, loveth activeness in men ; the very rest of heavenly bodies is in motion in their proper places.

Ver. 12. Rejoicing in hope] Hope makes absent joys present, wants, plenitudes, and beguiles calamity as good company doth the time. But without hope, patience is cold almost in the fourth degree, and that is but a little from poison. It was a dotage of the Stoics, that a wise man should be free, as from fear, so from hope too. How much better the Elpistici, another sort of philosophers, who held hope to be the only stay and staff of man's life, without which to live were but to lie a-dying ! This life would be little better than hell, saith Bernard, were it not for the hopes of heaven. *Sed superest sperare salutem*, and this holds head above water, this keeps the heart aloft all floods of afflictions, as the cork doth the line, as bladders do the body in swimming. *Ibat ovans animis et spe sua damna levabat*, saith Bembus concerning St Stephen going to his death. (*Vivere spe vidi qui moriturus erat.* Ovid.) He that seeth visions of glory, and hath sure hopes of heaven, will not matter a shower of stones ; he that is to take possession of a kingdom will not stand upon a foul day. Hope unfailable is grounded upon faith unfeigned, which is seldom without its joy unspeakable and full of glory, 1 Pet. i. 8.

Patient in tribulation] Bearing up under pressures, as among many other martyrs Nicholas Burton, who by the way to the stake, and in the flame, was so patient and cheerful, that the tormentors said, the devil had his soul before he came to the fire, and therefore his senses of feeling were past. (Acts and Mon.)

Continuing instant in prayer] Constant and instant, προσκαρτεροῦντες. A metaphor from hunting dogs, that give not over the game till they have got it. Nazianzen saith of his sister Gorgonia, that she was so given to prayer, that her knees seemed to grow to the very ground. Of Trasilla, it is reported, that being dead she was found to have her elbows as hard as horn, by leaning to a desk at which she used to pray. St James is said to have had knees as hard as camel's knees, by his continual kneeling in prayer. And Paul the Eremite was found dead kneeling upon his knees, holding up his hands, lifting up his eyes ; so that the very dead corpse seemed yet to live and to pray to God. (Jerome.)

Ver. 13. To the necessity] Gr. χρείαις, to the uses of the saints, not staying till they be in necessity.

Ver. 14. Bless them] See the note on Matt. v. 44.

Ver. 15. Weep with them that weep] St Cyprian's compassion is remarkable, *Cum singulis pectus meum copulo, mœroris et funeris pondera luctuosa participo : cum plangentibus plango, cum deflentibus defleo, &c.* I partake in every man's grief, and am as much affected and afflicted as if it were mine own case.

Ver. 16. Be of the same] This verse had been easy had not interpreters obscured it, as Origen observeth.

Ver. 17. Recompense to no man] In reason, revenge is but justice ; Aristotle commends it, the world calls it manhood ; it is doghood rather. The manlier any man is, the milder and more merciful, as David, 2 Sam. i. 12, and Julius Cæsar, who wept over Pompey's head presented to him, and said, *Non mihi placet vindicta, sed victoria*, I seek not revenge, but victory.

Ver. 18. As much as lieth in you] Let it not stick on your part. Give not offence carelessly, take not offence causelessly. See the note on Matt. v. 9. It is the first office of justice, saith Tully, to hurt nobody, unless first provoked by injury. But how true and trim a sentence, saith Lactantius, hath Tully here marred by adding the last, "unless ! " Mahomet's laws run thus : Avenge yourselves of your enemies ; rather do wrong than take wrong ; kill the infidels, &c. Profess love to thine enemy, saith Machiavel ; and if he fall into the water up to the knees, give him thine hand to help him out ; if up to the waist, help him likewise ; but if up to the chin, then lay thine hand upon his head and duck him under the water, and never suffer him to rise again. But we " have not so learned Christ." Seneca could say, *Immane verbum est ultio*, Revenge is a bloody word ; and *Qui ulciscitur excusatius peccat*, He is somewhat excused (but not altogether) from doing evil, that seeketh revenge.

Ver. 19. Avenge not yourselves] Some take the sword into their own hands ; and, lest they should seem Anabaptists in taking two blows for one, will give two blows for one.

Give place to wrath] sc. To the wrath and vengeance of God, which he seemeth to prevent that seeks revenge. Or, "give place to wrath." Do nothing in thine heat, but walk into the garden, as Ahasuerus did, when kindled against Haman, Esth. vii. 7. Theodosius was advised by Ambrose to say over the Lord's prayer ; Augustus by Athenodorus, to repeat the Greek alphabet, before they determined anything in their anger.

Or, give place to wrath] *Currenti cede furori*, set not thy wit to his (for anger is a short madness), but bear with his weakness that wrongeth thee.

Ver. 20. *Thou shalt heap*] Thou shalt melt him, and make him thy friend for ever.

Ver. 21. *Be not overcome*] *In rixa is inferior est, qui victor est*, saith Basil. In revenge of injuries, he is the loser that gets the better. Hence the apostle disgraceth it, by a word that signifieth disgrace or loss of victory, ἥττημα, 1 Cor. vi. 7. When any one provokes us, we use to say, We will be even with him. There is a way whereby we may be, not even with him, but above him; that is, forgive him, feed him with the best morsels, feed him indulgently (so the apostle's word ψώμιζε in the former verse signifies), feast him, as Elisha did his persecutors; providing a table for them, who had provided a grave for him. "Set bread and water before them," saith he, and mark what followed; "The bands of Syria came no more after that time," by way of ambush or inroad, "into the bounds of Israel," 2 Kings vi. 22, 23. In doing some good to our enemies (saith a grave divine hereupon) we do most to ourselves: God cannot but love in us that imitation of his mercy, who bids his sun to shine on the wicked and unthankful also; and his love is never fruitless. It is not like the winter sun that gives little heat, but like the sun in his strength, that warms and works effectually upon the rest of the creatures.

But overcome evil] This is the most noble victory. Thus David overcame Saul, and Henry VII., emperor of Germany, overcame the priest that poisoned him at the sacrament; for he pardoned him, and bade him be packing. (Func. Chron.) So did not Jacup the Persian king, who perceiving himself poisoned by his adulterous wife, enforced her to drink of the same cup; and because he would be sure she should not escape, with his own hand he struck off her head. (Turkish Hist.) But this (to say truth) was not revenge, but justice. Henry IV. of France was wont to say, that he made all the days of those golden, who had most offended him; that so, the lead of their wickedness might be darkened by the gold of his goodness.

CHAPTER XIII.

Ver. 1. *Let every soul be subject*] IN things lawful only; for else we must answer as those apostles did, Acts iii. 29, and as Polycarp, who being commanded to blaspheme Christ, and to swear by the fortune of Cæsar, peremptorily refused, and said, We are taught to give honour to princes and potentates, but such honour as is not contrary to God's religion.

Ordained of God] In regard of its institution, though for the manner of its constitution it is of man.

Ver. 2. *Resisteth the power*] His authoritative commands, not his personal.

Receive to themselves damnation] κρῖμα, 1 Cor. xi. 31, 32. *Pœnam sibi auferent*, saith Piscator, they shall receive punishment, to wit, from the magistrate; as Aretine deserved to do, who by longer custom of libellous and contumelious speaking against princes, had got such a habit, that at last he came to diminish and disesteem God himself.

Ver. 3. *For rulers are not, &c.*] They should not be. But Jeroboam set a net on Mizpeh, and spread a snare upon Tabor, to watch who would go from him to Judah to worship, Hos. v. 1.

A terror to good works, but to the evil] The sword of justice (saith one) must be furbished with the oil of mercy; yet there are cases wherein severity ought to cast the scale. *Duresce, Duresce, o infœlix Lantgravie*, said the poor smith to the Landgrave of Thuring, more mild than was for his people's good. *Bonis nocet, qui malis parcit*. Edward the Confessor was held a bad prince, not by doing, but enduring ill.

Ver. 4. *For he is the minister*] It was written upon the sword of Charles the Great, *Decem præceptorum custos Carolus*, Charles is Lord Keeper of the Decalogue.

For he beareth not the sword in vain] Like St Paul in a glass window, or St George (as they call him) on a sign-post.

A revenger to execute wrath] But now we see how every man almost will be a pope in his own cause, depose the magistrate, at least appeal from him to himself.

Upon him that doeth evil] Whether the evil be civil or religious; *Non distinguendum, ubi scriptura non distinguit*. (See Mr Burroughs' Heart-divisions.) Note this against those that hold that magistrates have nothing to do in matters of religion. See Deut. xiii. 6; Ezra vii. 26; Dan. iii. 29; 1 Pet. ii. 13, 14. Their laws bind the conscience *per concomitantiam*, by way of concomitancy; because they depend upon the law of God, and are agreeable to it; which primarily and *per se* bindeth. As the soul is said to be in a place *per concomitantiam*, because it is in the body; so here.

Ver. 5. *But also for conscience' sake*] Good rulers we must obey as God; bad, for God. διὰ τὸν Θεὸν. (Basil.)

Ver. 6. *Attending continually*] As born for the benefit of many. The Parliament in the 25 Edward III. is known to posterity by the name of *Benedictum Parliamentum*. So shall this present Parliament (A. D. 1646) for their continual attendance upon the Lord's work, bending themselves to the business (as the word προσκαρτεροῦντες signifies) and holding out therein with unparalleled patience.

Ver. 7. *Render therefore to all their dues*] He saith not their unjust exactions. Melancthon makes mention of a cruel prince, that to get money of his subjects, would knock out their teeth, first one tooth and then another, unless they would bring him in such sums of money as he required.[1]

Fear to whom, &c.] *i. e.* Reverential observance, far beyond that which Q. Fabius Maximus yielded to his son, when he became consul. (Liv. Decad. iii. lib. 4.)

Ver. 8. *Owe no man, &c.*] The Persians reckoned these two for very great sins: 1. To be in debt. 2. To tell a lie; the latter being oft the fruit of the former. (Xenophon, Gell. xii. 1.) By the 12 tables of Rome, he that owed much, and could not pay, was to be cut in pieces, and every creditor was to have a piece of him according to the debt. (Acts and Mon.) When Archbishop Cranmer discerned the storm which afterwards fell upon him in Queen Mary's days, he took express order for the payment of all his debts; which when it was done, a most joyful man was he; that having set his affairs in order with men, he might consecrate himself more freely to God. (Mr Wilkins' Debt-book.) Let us therefore (saith a reverend man) be thus far indulgent to ourselves, as to shake off the deadly yoke of bills and obligations, which mancipate the most free and ingenuous spirit, and dry up the very fountains of liberality. Yea, they so put a man out of aim that he cannot set his state in order, but lives and dies entangled and puzzled with cares and snares; and after a tedious and laborious life passed in a circle of fretting thoughts, he leaves at last, instead of better patrimony, a world of intricate troubles to his posterity and to his sureties; which cannot be managed by those who understand them not, but to great disadvantage. We read of a certain Italian gentleman, who being asked how old he was? answered, that he was in health; and to another that asked how rich he was? answered, that he was not in debt: *q. d.* He is young enough that is in health, and rich enough that is not in debt.

But to love one another] This is that desperate debt that a man cannot discharge himself of, but must ever be paying, and yet ever owing. As we say of thanks, *Gratiæ habendæ et agendæ*, thanks must be given, and yet held as still due; so must this debt of love.

Ver. 9. *Briefly comprehended*] Capitulated, fulfilled, saith the Syriac, summed up, ἀνακεφαλαιοῦται. St Bartholomew is quoted by Dionysius to have said of divinity, Καὶ πολλὴν καὶ ἐλαχίστην, *Et magnam esse et minimam*, that it was large and yet little, as containing much matter in few words.

Ver. 10. *The fulfilling of the law*] The filling up of the law in this, that it closeth the duties of the law with the glory of a due manner, and seateth them upon their due subjects, with the unwearied labours of a constant well-doing.

Ver. 11. *To awake out of sleep*] Whiles the crocodile sleepeth with open mouth, the Indian rat gets into his stomach, and eateth through his entrails. Whiles Ishbosheth slept upon his bed

at noon, Baanah and Rechab took away his head. Security ushereth in destruction. Go forth and shake yourselves, as Samson did when the Philistines were upon him; lest Satan serve you, at least for your souls, as Captain Drake did the Spaniard at Taurapasa in the West Indies, for his treasure; he found him sleeping securely on the shore, and by him 13 bars of silver to the value of 40,000 ducats, which he commanded to be carried away, not so much as once waking the man. (Camden's Elisa.) Or lest Christ himself deal by us, as Epaminondas did by the watchman, whom he found asleep; he thrust him through with his sword, and being blamed for so severe a fact, he replied, *Talem eum reliqui, qualem inveni*, I left him as I found him.

For now is our salvation nearer] Stir up yourselves therefore, and strain toward the mark. There is a Greek word (νύσσα) signifying the end of a race, which is derived of a word that signifieth to spur or prick forward(νύσσω). Surely, as they that run their horses for a wager, spur hardest at the race's end; so, sith our salvation is nearer now than ever it was, therefore we should run faster now than ever we did. When a cart is in a quagmire, if the horses feel it coming, they'll pull the harder; so must we, now that full deliverance is hard at hand. Rivers run more speedily and forcibly when they come near the sea, than they did at the spring; the sun shineth most amiably towards the going down. *Tempus jam est* (said old Zanchius to his friend Sturmius, who was elder than he) *ut ad Christum et cœlum stelliferum a terra properemus*, &c. It is even high time for you and me to hasten to heaven; as knowing that we shall shortly be with Christ, which is "far far the better," Phil. i. 23.

Ver. 12. *The night*] Here it is taken for all unregeneracy, which (as the night) is full of error, terror, &c. *Nox pudore vacat.* This night with the saints is far spent, or already past, *Transivit, Præteriit*, as Cyprian and Jerome here render it.

Ver. 13. *Let us walk honestly*] Handsomely, fashionably, mannerly, with a holy shamefacedness (εὐσχημόνως).

Not in chambering] Properly, lying a-bed or long-lying (κοίταις).

Ver. 14. *But put ye on*] Augustine confesseth that he was converted by reading and pondering this text.

And make not provision] Make not projects, cater not for the flesh.

CHAPTER XIV.

Ver. 1. *Him that is weak, &c.*] THAT is, not thoroughly persuaded of all things pertaining to Christian liberty about things indifferent.

Receive] *Affectu charitatis*, put him into your bosoms, bear with his weaknesses, &c. Bucer rejected none, though different in some opinions, in whom he found *aliquid Christi*, anything of

---

[1] *Primo unum dentem evellebat minitans.*

Christ, whose weaklings are to be handled with all tenderness. (Haymo.)

But not to doubtful] Make him not question-sick, 1 Tim. vi. 4. Wring not men's consciences, you may hap to break the wards if you do.

Ver. 2. *Eateth herbs*] Rather than meats forbidden by the law, Dan. i. 11. The ancient Latins were as well apaid of herbs to eat, as if they had had all manner of dainties. Green herbs were both food and physic to them. *Holus ab ὅλου.*

Ver. 3. *For God hath received him*] viz. For his household servant, which David counted a greater dignity than to be king of Israel. And Justinian the emperor styled himself *Ultimum servorum Dei*, the meanest of God's servants.

Ver. 4. *Who art thou, &c.*] The wisdom from above is without censuring, without hypocrisy, saith St James, iii. 17. Intimating, that the greatest censurers are mostly the greatest hypocrites. And as any one is more wise, he is more sparing of his censures.

Ver. 5. *Let every man be fully persuaded*] It is a safe rule, *Quod dubites ne feceris*, In doubtful cases be sure to take the surer side. (Plin. Epist.)

Ver. 6. *For he giveth God thanks*] A custom used by the very heathens to their gods, as is to be read in Homer and Virgil, but grown clean out of use among the Catholics in France and Italy. (Sir Ed. Sands, Spec. Europæ.) But if they that give thanks at meat do eat to God, to whom do they eat that give none?

Ver. 7. *For none of us liveth to himself*] St Paul stood, as it were, on tiptoes, ἀποκαραδοκία. Phil. i. 20, to see which way he might best glorify God, by life or by death.

Ver. 8. *We are the Lord's*] Death divides us not from Christ, but brings us home to him, 2 Cor. v. 6. It is but winking (as that martyr said), and thou shalt be in heaven presently.

Ver. 9. *That he might be Lord*] He won his crown before he wore it; he fought for it, and having vanquished all enemies, he accomplished and proclaimed the victory in his glorious resurrection, triumphed in his wonderful ascension, leading captivity captive, &c., Eph. iv. 7.

Ver. 10. *But why dost thou, &c.*] Three things are not subject to our judgment: 1. The councils of God. 2. The Holy Scriptures. 3. The persons of men. Be not therefore rash in rejecting, or sour in censuring your fellow-servant; but let your moderation herein be known to all men; and the rather, because the Lord is at hand, Phil. iv. 5.

The judgment-seat of Christ] Who gives the Lamb in his escutcheon; and wilt thou give the lion?

Ver. 11. *As I live, saith the Lord*] As true as I live, is an oath, as appears here, and Numb. xiv. 21, with Psal. xcv. 11. Forbear it, therefore.

Ver. 12. *So then every one, &c.*] It was excellent counsel that the orator gave his hearers, *Ita vivamus ut rationem nobis reddendam arbitre-*

mur. (Cic. IV. in Ver.) Let us so live as those that must give an account of all at last.

Ver. 13. *Any more*] As they formerly had done; being over-sour and supercilious.

A stumbling-block, or an, &c.] A lighter or greater offence to make him go halting to heaven.

Ver. 14. *I know and am persuaded*] Many, on the contrary, are persuaded before they know; and such will not be persuaded to know. The Valentinian heretics had a trick to persuade before they taught, as saith Tertullian. The old sectaries had their pithanology, insinuative and persuasive language; so have the modern; and hence so many dissonant opinions amongst us. If ye speak with several tongues (so hold several opinions) will not he that comes in think ye are mad? 1 Cor. xiv. *Dii boni, quomodo hic vivunt gentes!* How strangely do people live here, said a stranger, observing our divisions in Henry VIII.'s time, which (alas) were nothing comparable to these of our days, and all because simple men and silly women are soon persuaded to that they understand not. The silly-simple believeth everything: weak as water on a table, which with a wet finger may be led any way. (*Pethi,* Prov. xiv. 15.)

By the Lord Jesus] Who hath pulled down the partition-wall, and purchased our Christian liberty.

Ver. 15. *But if thy brother be grieved*] It is his weakness to be grieved thereat, but gratify him howsoever. What one speaks of a plain place of Scripture, this verse, saith he, had been easy, had not commentators made it knotty; the like saith another of a Christian's condition, it is gracious, happy, clear, sure, sweet, did not erroneous judgments vex and unsettle them.

Ver. 16. *Let not then your good*] That is, your Christian liberty purchased by Christ.

Be evil spoken of] Gr. be blasphemed. Contumely cast upon the people of God is blasphemy in the second table. God, for the honour that he beareth to his people, counts and calls it so.

Ver. 17. *For the kingdom of God, &c.*] That was a swinish saying of Epicurus, that eternal life should be nothing else but a continual eating of the fat and drinking of the sweet, even unto an incessant surfeiting and drunkenness, κραιπάλην καὶ μέθην αἰώνιον. The Turks at this day promise Paradise to such as die in war for the Mahometan faith, where they shall have delicious fare, pleasant gardens, all sensual delights, eternally to be enjoyed, notwithstanding any former sins. Fit lettuce for such lips.

Ver. 18. *Is acceptable to God*] And he is a happy man that can be acquitted by himself in private, in public by others, in both by God.

Ver. 19. *Wherewith one may edify another*] Discords among good people do *edificare in gehennam*, as Tertullian phraseth it, build backwards. One of the main scandals the Jews take from Protestants is their dissension.

Ver. 20. *The work of God*] That work of faith, 1 Thess. i. 3, wrought by the mighty power of

God, Ephes. i. 19, who puts not forth great power but for great purposes.

Ver. 21. *It is good neither to eat,* &c.] It will be no grief of heart (as Abigail once told David in another case, 1 Sam. xxv. 31) to have forborn in case of scandal. A great grief it would be if by some rash word we should betray a brother, or smite out the eye of our dearest child; should we then destroy the life of grace in another by our unadvised walking?

Ver. 22. *Hast thou faith*] *Posse, et nolle, nobile est.* Forbear for fear of offence, unless it be in point of necessary duty: for then we may not do evil, that good may come, Rom. iii. 8.

Ver. 23. *Is damned*] Both of his doubting conscience, which soundeth heavily, as a shaulm; and of God, who is greater than his conscience.

CHAPTER XV.

Ver. 1. *Ought to bear*] As porters do their burdens, as pillars do the poise of the house, or rather as parents have their babes in their arms. Βαστάζειν.

And not to please ourselves] *Bis desipit, qui sibi sapit,* Prov. iii. 7.

Ver. 2. *Please his neighbour*] Though he cross himself: this is true Christian love, and driven almost out of the world by sinful self-love, which causeth men to dislike those things in others that they favour and flatter in themselves.

Ver. 3. *For even Christ*] And we should express him to the world, preach abroad his virtues by our practice, 1 Pet. ii. 9. Our lives should be as so many sermons upon the life of Christ. This is to walk in Christ, Col. ii. 6, as Christ, 1 John iii. 6.

Ver. 4. *For whatsoever things,* &c.] Here the apostle meets with an objection. For some man might say, that that saying of the Psalms pertains to David, how therefore is it applied to Christ? He answers, Whatsoever things, &c. *q. d.* We must learn to see Christ in David; David in the history, Christ in the mystery; David as the type, Christ the truth.

That we through patience] Hence the Scriptures are called, The word of Christ's patience, Rev. iii. 10, because they patient the heart under God's holy hand; and are better called physic for the soul (ἡ τῆς ψυχῆς ἰατρεία) than ever was the library of Alexandria.

And comfort of the Scriptures] As the blood and spirits are conveyed by the veins and arteries, so is the Spirit by the promises, helping the soul to lay itself upon Christ by faith, which is a grace of union, and so of establishment.

Ver. 5. *Now the God of patience*] The soul is then only in good plight when the heaven answers the earth, Hos. ii. 21; when Christ the Sun of righteousness shines into it.

Ver. 6. *With one mind and one mouth*] It is recorded to the high commendation of the Church of Scotland, that for this 90 years and upwards they have kept unity with purity without schism, much less heresy. (Syntag. Confession, Prefat.)

Ver. 7. *To the glory of God*] That is, of heaven, the joys whereof it is as impossible to comprehend as it is to compass the heaven with a span, or contain the ocean in a nut-shell. Such comfort there is in the presence of Christ (though but in the womb), as it made John to spring. What then shall it be in heaven?

Ver. 8. *Now I say that Jesus*] Paul proveth particularly in this and the following verses that Christ hath taken both Jews and Gentiles to his glory.

Ver. 9. *And that the Gentiles*] Though they had no such promises, might glorify God's free grace in the day of their visitation.

Ver. 10. *Rejoice*] That your names are also written in heaven, and that ye are enrolled in the records of the new Jerusalem.

Ver. 11. *All ye Gentiles*] As being received into the glory of God, ver. 7.

Ver. 12. *In him shall the Gentiles trust*] Isaiah hath it, "To him shall the Gentiles seek:" to seek to God then argues trust in God. He that hopes not, praises not, or but faintly.

Ver. 13. *Fill you with all joy,* &c.] Note here that joy and peace are the means whereby faith worketh hope.

Ver. 14. *Full of goodness*] The excellency of a godly man is to follow God fully, as Caleb, Numb. xiv. 24; to have a heart full of goodness, as these Romans, a life full of good works, as Tabitha, Acts ix. 33. These shall receive a full reward, 2 John viii.

Ver. 15.] Chrysostom truly saith of St Paul, that he was *insatiabilis Dei cultor,* one that thought he could never do God or his Church service enough.

Ver. 16. *Ministering the gospel*] Serving about holy things or doing sacred offices, as the priests under the law, to whom the apostle all along this verse alludes in an elegant allegory, ἱερουργοῦντα λείτουργον; the ministry is a divine and heavenly function. All other callings are for the world, and draw to the world; but this, both in the preparation and execution, draweth to God, keepeth us with God, and to be ever mindful of the things of God.

Ver. 17. *I have therefore,* &c.] So have all God's faithful ministers at this day against the contempts and contumelies cast upon them by the mad world, ever beside itself in point of salvation. There is a pamphlet lately published that sticks not to make that sacred and tremendous function of the ministry to be as mere an imposture, as verya mystery of iniquity, as arrant a juggle, as the Papacy itself. (The Compas. Samaritan.)

Ver. 18. *To make the Gentiles,* &c.] Christ by his gospel subdued the Britons, whom the Romans with all their force could never subdue, as Tertullian observed.[1]

Ver. 19. *So that from Jerusalem*] Chrysos- loca Christo tamen subdita.

[1] *Britannorum inaccessa Romanis*

tom observeth, that Plato came three times to Sicily to convert Dionysius the tyrant to moral philosophy, and could not. But Paul fetched a great compass, converted many souls, planted many Churches; and why? Christ sat upon him as upon one of his white horses, and went forth conquering and to conquer, Rev. vi. 2.

Ver. 20. *Lest I should build*] Lest I should seem to do anything unbeseeming the office of an apostle: there is a decorum to be kept in every calling.

Ver. 21. *But as it is written*] In obedience to this divine oracle, the apostle preached to those that had not heard, yet neglected not those that had.

Ver. 22. *For which cause*] By planting Churches and preaching where was more need.

Ver. 23. *These many years*] The Romans were converted to the faith betimes. Some of them were "in Christ before Paul," Rom. xvi. 7. Christ made haste also to convert England, whose religion before was *tristissimum superstitionum chaos* (as Camden hath it), a most sad chaos of superstitions. Sabellicus testifieth that Brittany was the first of all the provinces that publicly professéd Christ. And as we were the first that took upon us the yoke of Papal tyranny (so that England was called the Pope's Ass), so were we the first that shook it off again.

Ver. 24. *For I trust to see you*] *Ipse aspectus viri boni delectat*, saith Seneca. There is a great deal of sweetness in the society of saints, and much good to be gotten thereby. Sometimes (saith a grave divine) though we know that which we ask of others as well as they do, yet good speeches will draw us to know it better, by giving occasion to speak more of it; wherewith the Spirit works more effectually, and imprints it deeper, so that it shall be a more rooted knowledge than before. For that doth good that is graciously known, and that is graciously known that the Spirit seals upon our souls.

Ver. 25. *To minister unto the saints*] The highest angel in heaven may not hold himself too good to serve the saints.

Ver. 26. *It hath pleased them*] It hath not been squeezed out of them, as verjuice is out of a crab, but freely and cheerfully they have contributed, ευδόκησαν.

For the poor saints which are at Jerusalem] The Jews do at this day send their alms yearly from all parts to Jerusalem for the maintenance of the poor that live there, and spend their time praying for the welfare of the whole nation.

Ver. 27. *Their debtors they are*] And so are we to pity and pray for them. See my "True Treasure," sect. 2, chap. 7.

Ver. 28. *When I have sealed*] That is, safely delivered, as if it were under seal.

This fruit] This sweet ripe fruit of their faith and love, their alms.

Ver. 29. *In the fulness of the blessing*] Christ may use one of less grace to do more good than one of more (for there are diversities of operations, as well as of gifts, 2 Cor. xii. 6), but usually

he delights to honour those of most sincerity, with most success, 1 Cor. xv. 10.

Ver. 30. *For the Lord Jesus Christ's sake*] This is one of those passages in St Paul, than the which there can nothing possibly be imagined more grave, divine, excellent, saith Beza.

That ye strive together] Even to an agony, as the word συναγωνίσασθαι imports. Spiritual beggary is the hardest and richest of all trades, as one said. Learn of this great apostle to beg prayers with all earnestness. Pray for me, I say, pray for me, I say, quoth father Latimer. Pray for me, pray for me, for God's sake pray for me, said blessed Bradford.

Ver. 31. *That my service which*, &c.] One would have thought that the apostle coming with alms to them, should easily have been well accepted; but he saw cause to seek God for such a mercy, sith it is he alone that fashions men's opinions, and gives favour and kind acceptance. Besides wisdom, he gave Solomon honour.

Ver. 32. *Be refreshed*] See the note on Rom. i. 12; 2 John 12.

Ver. 33. *Now the God of peace*] A fit attribute for the present purpose. It is a commendable policy in Christians, when they pray, to propound God to their mind in such notions, and under such titles, as whereby they may see in God the things they desire of God.

CHAPTER XVI.

Ver. 1. *Servant of the Church*] A *diaconess* to minister to the sick, as 1 Tim. v. 9, not a *prædicantisse*, to preach or have Peter's keys at their girdle. (Dr Bastwick against Independency.)

Ver. 2. *As becometh saints*] Who are great princes, states, in all lands, Psal. xlv., and to be observed accordingly, even worthy of God, 3 John 6.

Ver. 3. *Salute Priscilla*] She is first mentioned, haply as more forward than her husband in the best things. So was Manoah's wife and Nazianzen's mother.

Ver. 4. *Who have for my life*] A rare example. Fast friends are in this age for the most part gone on pilgrimage (said one once), and their return is uncertain.

Ver. 5. *The church that is in their house*] The house of George Prince of Anhalt, for the good orders therein observed, is said to have been Ecclesia, Academia, Curia.

The first fruits of Achaia] The first that received the gospel there. A singular commendation, a sweet happiness. God's soul hath desired such first ripe fruits, Mic. vii. 1, such primroses.

Ver. 6. *Greet Mary*, &c.] It is profitable that men of great parts and place should preserve their memory with others, though it be but in a salutation; for it may be a means to fire up affection to godliness in such whom they so remember.

Ver. 7. *Who are of note*] Επίσημοι, noble, notable Christians, old, experienced, gray-headed disciples. Christianity finds or makes us honourable.

Ver. 8. *Greet Amplias*] Piety is no enemy to courtesy: it doth not remove, but rectify it.

Ver. 9. *Our helper in Christ*] A sweet sign to him, that his name was written in the book of life, Phil. iv. 3.

Ver. 10. *Approved in Christ*] A high style, far beyond that of the Great Turk, with all his big-swollen titles.

Ver. 11. *My kinsman*] In the flesh, but more in the faith, that surest tie.

Ver. 12. *Who labour in the Lord*] Though not so much as Persis did, yet doth he not defraud them of their due commendation; *Prima sequentem honestum est in secundis tertiisque consistere.* (Cic. De Orator.) Every man must not look to excel; let him be doing, as he is able.

Ver. 13. *His mother and mine*] His by nature, mine by affection. The apostles parted with parents and friends at home, found them abroad.

Ver. 14. *Salute Asyncritus, &c.*] Nothing is said of these; for haste perhaps, or else because they were (as one saith of Jesse, the father of David) *Viri, probi et honesti, minus tamen clari,* Good honest men, but not much noted. Or, lastly, for that the apostle had no very good opinion of them, as he seems not to have had of Demas, Col. iv. 14, who yet would needs be one in the apostle's register there; a place he will have, though it be the last place. Hermas here mentioned was reputed by some of the ancients to be the author of that Apocryphal Book called "Pastor;" wherein he dealt not so fairly and faithfully in relating what he had received from the apostles, being *sublatæ fidei author.*

Ver. 15. *And Olympas*] *Viri nomen, non mulieris.* The name not of a woman, but of a man, saith Beza.

Ver. 16. *With a holy kiss*] The Independents at Arnheim in Holland propounded this kiss of love to be practised amongst them. So for anointing the sick with oil, singing of hymns by one man, all the rest being silent, σκοπεῖτε.

Ver. 17. *Mark them which*] Set a watchful and a jealous eye upon them, as upon pests and enemies. And here, let not our *episcopi* (whose office it is chiefly) be *aposcopi,* over-seers be by-seers, but look well to the flock, lest these wolves worry them, Acts xx. 29.

And avoid them] Gr. ἐκκλίνατε. Decline them studiously, as ye would do a serpent in your way, or poison in your meats.

Ver. 18. *But their own bellies*] They pretend the service of Christ to their worldly and wicked respects, by a dissembled sanctity, which is double iniquity. The Duke of Bavaria is even eaten up with those Popish flesh-flies, friars and Jesuits. It was an honest complaint of a Popish writer, We, saith he, handle the Scriptures, *tantum ut nos pascat et vestiat,* only for a livelihood; we serve God for gain: as children will not say their prayers unless they be promised

their breakfasts. Cajetan writing on Matt. v. 13, "Ye are the salt of the earth," confesseth ingenuously of himself and his fellow-prelates, that whereas by their places they should have been the salt of the earth, they had lost their savour, and were good for little else but looking after the rites and revenues of the Church.[1] And such were many of our English prelates grown, before their late extirpation. If you put not into the mouths of these Cerberuses, they would even prepare war against you. Therefore their "sun went down, and the day grew dark over them," Mic. iii. 5, 6. All seducers are self-seekers: "they teach things that they ought not, for filthy lucre's sake," Tit. i. 11. They are like eagles that soar aloft towards heaven, not for any love of heaven, but that they may spy their prey the sooner, seize upon it the better: or like those ravens in Arabia, that, full-gorged, have a tunable sweet record; but empty, they screech horribly. In *parabola oves capras suas quærunt,* as the ferryman looks one way, rows another.

And by good words, &c.] Those locusts in the Revelation have faces like women, insinuative and flattering. The Valentinian heretics had an art to persuade before they taught, whereas the truth persuadeth by teaching, it doth not teach by persuading. (Tertullian.)

They deceive] As cheaters do, by the cogging of a dye, ἐν τῇ κυβείᾳ, Eph. iv. 14. *Fallax artificium, vel potius artifex fallacia,* saith Erasmus on that text, a cunning kind of cozenage.

Ver. 19. *For your obedience, &c.*] Whereas the Romans might object, Are we also of those simple ones? Your obedience, saith he, is famous all the world over. Howbeit I would have you wise to that which is good, but simple concerning evil. This simplicity is no disparagement, to be unskilled in the devil's depths, Rev. ii. 24.

Ver. 20. *Shall bruise Satan*] Sincerity of a little grace shall be rewarded with abundance of greater graces. Christ our champion hath already won the field, and will shortly set our feet upon the necks of our spiritual enemies. The broken horns of Satan shall be the trumpets of our triumph, and the cornets of our joy.

Ver. 21. *Timotheus my work-fellow*] Of Timothy, read Acts xvi. 1, 2. Of Lucius, Acts xiii. 1. Of Jason, Acts xvii. 5. Of Sopater, Acts xx. 4.

Ver. 22. *I Tertius who wrote, &c.*] Either from the apostle's mouth, or rather out of his foul papers.

Ver. 23. *Gaius mine host*] Baptized by Paul, for whom therefore, and for other good men, he thought he could never do enough, 1 Cor. i. 14. Such another was Phœbe, ver. 2, who had been a succourer, or an hostess, to many, and to myself, saith Paul, *Multis hospitium præbuit.*

Ver. 24. *The grace of our Lord*] This is the seal of all St Paul's Epistles, 2 Thess. iii. 17.

Ver. 25. *Which was kept secret*] Even from

---

[1] *Evanuimus ac ad nihilum utiles, nisi ad externas ceremonias, externaque bona.*

the very angels, 1 Pet. i. 12, who do daily profit in the knowledge of this secret, Eph. iii. 10.

Ver. 26. According to the commandment] The writings of the prophets concerning the mystery of Christ were not made known to the world by hap-hazard, but by a special command of God.

For the obedience of faith] Though God purposed good to his people before all worlds, yet that is concealed till such time as they yield this obedience of faith: like as water that runs under-ground, is hid a long time till it break out suddenly, and then we discover that there was a stream ran under-ground; as Arethusa and other rivers do.

Ver. 27. To God only wise, &c.] So say I for these few notes thus finished. All that I shall now add is this distich,—

Pars superat cœpti, pars est exacta laboris :
Hic teneat nostras anchora jacta rates.

A

COMMENTARY OR EXPOSITION

UPON THE

FIRST EPISTLE OF ST PAUL TO THE CORINTHIANS.

CHAPTER I.

Ver. 1. Through the will of God] NOT the faculty in God, whereby he willeth, but his act, the thing that he willeth. This will of God is either secret or revealed, Deut. xxii. 29. And this revealed will is either of his pleasure, *Placiti*, or of his good pleasure, *Beneplaciti*. The former is also in things where the effect is evil; and so God willeth in respect of the end, but not of the means to the end; as in sin, and some miseries. The latter is in those things only where the effect is good, as here, and Rom. xii. 2. It was for the very great good of the Church that God would have Paul to be a chosen vessel, to bear his name before the Gentiles, &c., Acts ix. 15. So that *Cor Pauli est cor Christi*, as Chrysostom hath it; for, " We have the mind of Christ," 1 Cor. ii. 16.

Sosthenes our brother] And companion in the kingdom and patience of Christ, Rev. i. 9; Acts xviii. 17. There he was despitefully entreated, here highly honoured. Christ is a liberal pay-master: never any did or suffered aught for his sake that complained of a hard bargain. It is to my loss (said that martyr) if thou bate me anything in my sufferings. *Majora certamina, majora sequuntur præmia*, saith Tertullian.

Ver. 2. Called to be saints] i. e. Either such as are sanctified by habitual infusion, or such as are sanctified by baptismal profession only, that are in covenant with God by sacrifice, Psal. l. 6, and are in Christ, though they bear no fruit, John xv. 2. These two sorts of saints make up a true visible Church.

With all that in every place] The apostles then wrote not their Epistles for the particular uses of those times only, as the Jesuits will have it.

Ver. 3. Grace be to you and peace] All peace that flows not from the sense of God's love and favour, is as that of the Romans with the Samnites, unsound and uncertain. *Pax infida, pax incerta.* (Livius.) See the note on Rom. i. 7.

Ver. 4. I thank my God] Thus he begins most of his Epistles. *Deo gratias* was ever in Austin's mouth, who had Paul's spirit. Every gracious man is a grateful man. The same Greek word. (χάρις) signifieth grace and thanks. Only that part of Abraham's seed that is as the stars of heaven, can in their courses sing a song of praise to God. True it is, that " all his works praise him ;" that is, they give matter and occasion so to do; but his saints only bless him, in manner as Paul here doth, Psal. cxlv. 10, and bring actual glory to him, Ephes. i. 11, 12. Wicked men cannot say, I thank my God, for they have no true notion of God, but as of an enemy ; and therefore all their verbal thanks are but as music at funerals, or as the trumpet before a judge, no comfort to the mourning wife or guilty prisoner.

For the grace of God] Intending to chide them, he first commends them, that he may preserve in their hearts an opinion of his love, whilst he rebuked them sharply, that they might be sound in the faith.

Ver. 5. Ye are enriched] See here what is the Christian's riches. And so David reckons of his wealth, Psal. cxix. 32. He cannot be poor in whom the word of God dwells richly, Colos. iii.

16, especially if he be free of discourse, able and willing to communicate. A dumb Christian is to be blamed, as well as a dumb minister.

Ver. 6. *The testimony of Christ*] The gospel, called also the testimony, Isa. viii. 20. To the law, and to the testimony.

Ver. 7. *So that ye come behind, &c.*] Yet were babes and carnal, chap. iii. 2, 3, and fell short in many graces. We must distinguish between gifts and graces, and covet these rather than those, 1 Cor. xiii. 1.

Ver. 8. *In the day of our Lord Jesus*] Eleven times in these first ten verses (as Chrysostom well observeth) the apostle mentioneth the Lord Jesus Christ, who was to him, and should be to us, *mel in ore, melos in aure, jubilum in corde*, honey in the mouth, music in the ear, joy in the heart. (Bernard.) The Jews used to cast to the ground the Book of Esther, before they read it, because the name of God is not in it. This is ill done of them. But that is recorded to the commendation of Augustine, that he cast by Cicero's writings (though otherwise very delightful to him) because he found not in them that mellifluous name of Jesus.

Ver. 9. *Unto the fellowship*] Union being the ground of communion: so that all is in him is for us. I give my goods to the saints, saith David, in the person of Christ.

Ver. 10. *That there be no divisions*] To break unity in the Church is to cut asunder the very veins and sinews of the mystical body of Christ.

By the name of our Lord] Which is like to suffer by your dissensions, and whereof you ought to be as tender as of treading upon your parents that begat you.

Perfectly joined] Schisms disjoint men; yea, shake them out of their senses, and fright them out of their wits, 2 Thess. ii. 2. See the note there.

Ver. 11. *Of the house of Chloe*] A godly matron she was no doubt, and a good office herein she did her neighbours: though, likely, she had little thank for her labour; as likewise Joseph had for bringing his brethren's evil report to their father, Gen. xxxvii. 2.

That there are contentions] These oft breed schisms; as did the contention between Luther and Carolostadius; and many of the ancient heresies sprang from private grudges and discontents, *in sui solatium*, for a sorry comfort to those that broached them.

Ver. 12. *And I of Christ*] *q. d.* I care neither for Paul nor Apollo, &c. As some say nowadays, they are neither Papists nor Protestants, but Christians, that is, just nothing, flat atheists. Heraclius the emperor being imprudently carried away by some bishops into the opinion of the Monothelites, when that heresy was afterwards condemned by the Council of Jerusalem, the emperor, being ashamed to recant, became a mere neutralist, and held neither one way nor other. And have we not some like-minded amongst us, who are yet to choose their religion; resolving to resolve on nothing, because (forsooth) there are so many sects and controversies, and such differences in opinion and contradictions of preachers, therefore they will suspend, serve God (as they call it), and not trouble themselves to know whether side hath the better? But these might know, 1. That truth is but one and the same; *Christi tunica est unica*, Christ's coat is seamless, his truth single, and at good agreement with itself. 2. That we have a most sure word, 2 Pet. i. 19, sure, and sufficient to perfect the man of God; and that *Non est litigiosa juris scientia sed ignorantia*, as the lawyers used to say, it is not the too much knowledge, but the ignorance of the Scriptures that begets strife. 3. That God's elect have a promise to be taught of God, to be kept from being finally deceived; to be brought to a certainty and full assurance of what they should hold, so evidently and clearly will God by his Spirit speak to their consciences, that they shall hold fast the faithful word, though they cannot answer every cavil and be unmoveable as the centre, as Mount Zion that cannot be stirred. Matt. xxiv. 24; John x. 4, 5; Job xxii. 21; 1 Thess. i. 5; John vii. 17; 1 John ii. 20; Psal. xix. 7; Prov. i. 4; Isa. lii. 6; John vi. 45.

Ver. 13. *Baptized in the name*] Gr. "Into the name," so as to be called by my name. Those then that will needs be called Franciscans, Lutherans, &c., do after a sort disclaim their baptism, and become runaways from Christ.

Ver. 14. *I thank God*] He noteth and noticeth herein a sweet providence, beyond all that he then imagined, when he was at Corinth. God is to be seen in every special occurrence.

Ver. 15. *Lest any should say*] *q. d.* God hath so disposed of it, that none can with any colour or cause, or show of sense, say such a thing.

Ver. 16. *Whether I baptized any*] His colleagues belike did it (whiles he was otherwise busied), with a particular examination and instruction in those principles, Heb. vi. 2.

Ver. 17. *Not to baptize*] As my chief work (so Jer. vii. 22), but to preach and plant Churches, wherein he had a very happy hand; as had likewise Farellus among our late reformers, *Qui Mompelgardenses, Aquileienses, Lausannenses, Genevenses, Novocomenses Christo lucrifecit*, he gained five cities with their territories to Christ. (Melch. Adam. in Vit. xi.)

Not with wisdom of words] Which yet St Paul could have done as well as another; witness his artificial unstarching of the orator's speech, Acts xxvi. But he liked not to put the sword of the Spirit into a velvet scabbard, that it could not pierce, to speak *floride plus quam solide*, as those self-seekers at Corinth did, that sought more to tickle the ear than to affect the heart. It repented Augustine (and well it might) that when he was young he had preached more *ut placeret, quam ut doceret*, to please than to profit. And Luther was wont to say, he is the best preacher that preacheth *vulgariter, trivialiter, maximeque ad populi captum*. Not but that there is a lawful use of rhetoric in sermons, so it be free from ostentation. See the Preface to my God's Love-tokens.

Ver. 18. *To them that perish, foolishness*] As it is to the Jews at this day, who rail against Christ's person, calling him the hanged God, the woof and the warp, Lev. xiii. 52, because these two make the figure of the cross. And being asked whether they believe to be saved by Christ's righteousness, they answer, That every fox must pay his own skin to the flayer. The pagans also jeered at Christ and his people, as did Julian, Lucian, Porphyry, &c.

Ver. 19. *For it is written*] Thus the Old Testament is fulfilled in the New, whiles the world's wizards are dazzled, dulled, and disannulled, ἀθετήσω.

Ver. 20. *Where is the wise?*] The teacher of traditions; the Jews had a proverb, οἱ σοφοὶ ἡμῶν δευτερῶσι.

Where is the scribe?] Or the text-men, those that proceed according to the literal interpretation.

Where is the disputer?] The teachers of allegories and mysteries, 1 Tim. i. 4.

Ver. 21. *The world by wisdom*] Not the Jews by their deep doctors, nor the Gentiles by their wits and wizards (*qui tanquam noctuæ ad solem caligabant*), could grope out God, Acts xvii. 27, ψηλαφήσειαν.

By the foolishness of preaching] An ironical concession; so the mad world esteemeth it, who shall rue for ever the contempt of it, crying out, *Nos insensati*, &c.

Ver. 22. *For the Jews require,* &c.] The reason of their rejecting the gospel is, they are prepossessed against it; they look for that that it affordeth not. A prejudicate opinion bars up the understanding. *Intus existens prohibet alienum*, like muddy water in a vessel, that causeth the most precious liquor to run over.

And the Greeks seek after wisdom] Which yet they attained not. For *Sapiens est cui res sapiunt prout sunt*, saith Bernard, he is a wise man who conceiveth of things as they are: and all the wisdom of man is only in this, that he rightly know and worship God, saith Lactantius. But this these Greeks could never skill of; no, not these Corinthians (till called and sanctified), who yet were famous for their wisdom (Periander, one of the seven wise men, was a Corinthian), and their city be called by the orator (Cicero) *lumen Græciæ*, the light of Greece. But whereto tended their light but to light them into utter darkness? And what was all their wisdom without Christ, but earthly, sensual, devilish? Jam. iii. 15. Earthly, managing the lusts of the eyes unto the ends of gain; sensual, managing the lusts of the flesh unto ends of pleasure; and devilish, managing the pride of life unto ends of power.

Ver. 23. *But we preach Christ*] We not only preach of him, but we preach him, we give what we preach. It is the special office of the ministry to lay Christ open, to hold up the tapestry, to unfold the hidden mysteries of Christ. The Holy Ghost in them taketh of that which is Christ's, and showeth to men, John xvi. 15.

Unto the Jews a stumbling-block] These Philistines cannot conceive how out of the eater should come meat, and out of the strong, sweet.

Unto the Greeks] These jeered at Jesus and the resurrection, as at a couple of strange gods, Acts xvii. 18. Cato profanely saith, *Stultitia est morte alterius sperare salutem*. It is a folly to expect safety by the death of another. The gospel was to the Jews a stumbling-block, and to the Greeks a laughing-stock. They both stumbled on the bridge, and so fell into the ditch of destruction.

Ver. 24. *Christ the power of God*] Opposite to the power of miracles required by the Jews.

And the wisdom of God] Opposite to the Grecian's worldly wisdom.

Ver. 25. *Because the foolishness*] The wisest man compared to God, *Simia videbitur, non sapiens*, said Heraclitus, as Plato relateth it, he will appear to be an ape rather than a wise man. But what meant that malicious fool Genebrard, to call Reverend Beza, Theomorus for Theodorus? Was it not of God, so to direct the tongue of this Caiaphas the second, that in Beza and himself might this Scripture be fulfilled, τὸ μωρὸν τοῦ Θεοῦ σοφώτερον τῶν ἀνθρώπων, &c., " The foolishness of God," &c.

Ver. 26. *Not many mighty*] The eagle and lion were not offered in sacrifice, as the lamb and the dove were. It is hard for great ones to deny themselves. Hence it grew to a proverb in times of Popery, that hell was paved with priests' shaven crowns and great men's head-pieces. *Rasis sacrificulorum verticibus et magnatum galeis*. (Jerome.) Indeed if men might pass *de deliciis ad delicias, e cœno ad cœlum*, as Jerome hath it; if they could dance with the devil all day, and sup with Christ at night; if they might live all their lives long in Delilah's lap, and then go to Abraham's bosom when they die, they would have a fine time of it. But that cannot be, and hence so many mighties miscarry.

Not many noble] Blessed be God that any; as Galeacius Caracciolus an Italian marquis, and nephew to Pope Paul V., was converted by Peter Martyr reading upon this First Epistle to the Corinthians; George Prince of Anhalt, a pious preaching prince, converted by Melancthon; Ulysses Martinengus, earl of Baccha, another Italian convert, and some few more that might be instanced. But good nobles are black swans (saith one) and thinly scattered in the firmament of a state, even like stars of the first magnitude. We may say of such, as Luther (in Epist. ad John Agricol.) doth of Elizabeth Queen of Denmark, a pious princess, *Scilicet Christus etiam aliquando voluit reginam in cœlum vehere.*

Ver. 27. *But God hath chosen*] In our Church assemblies the meaner usually, like little fishes, bite more than the greater. The poor are gospelized, Matt. xi. 5.

Ver. 28. *Things which are not*] i. e. That are

nought set by, 1 Sam. xxv. 6. Thus shall ye say to him that liveth, that is, to him that is rich; for poor men are reputed as dead men. They have but prisoners' pittances, which will keep them alive, and that is all. Arrian upon Epictetus hath observed, that in a tragedy there is no place for a poor man, but only to dance.

Ver. 29. *That no flesh*] Proud flesh will soon swell, if it have but anything to fasten on. The devil will also easily blow up such a blab.

Ver. 30. *But of him are ye*] q. d. Albeit ye have nothing of your own, yet in Christ you have all; for in him is all fulness both repletive and diffusive, both of abundance and of redundance too, both of plenty and of bounty.

Is made unto us wisdom] This notes out Christ's prophetical office.

Righteousness and sanctification] By his priestly office.

Redemption] By his kingly office, having fully delivered his from sin, death, and hell; all which is not fully done till after death. And that is the reason why redemption is here set last. See Rom. viii. 23; Luke xxi. 28.

Ver. 31. *Glory in the Lord*] Acquiesce and exult in him, which is the end why God hath done all this for us in Christ.

CHAPTER II.

Ver. 1. *Not with excellency*] St Paul's speech was *neque lecta, neque neglecta*, neither curious nor careless. Politian could say, that it is an ornament to an epistle to be without ornaments. And yet he had so little grace as to prefer Pindar's Odes before David's Psalms. Hosius also, the cardinal, thought David's Psalms unlearned, applying that, *Scribimus indocti doctique poemata passim. Os durum!* The Holy Scriptures have a grave eloquence, but want those pompous and painted words that carnal rhetoricians hunt after. There is difference between a pedantic style and a majestic. *Non Oratorum filii sumus sed, Piscatorum*, said that great divine to Libanius the rhetorician, that tickled his hearers with tinkling terms, and delighted to wit-wanton it with lascivious phrases of oratory.

Ver. 2. *To know anything*] To profess or teach any other skill. All the wisdom of a man is in this one thing, saith Lactantius, *Ut Christum cognoscat et colat*, that he know and worship Christ. *Hoc nostrum dogma, hæc sententia est*, &c.

Ver. 3. *In weakness*] In misery, and in a mean condition, labouring with his hands, &c., Acts xviii. 3.

And in fear] Of adversaries, or through care of discharging my duty amongst you.

Ver. 4. *With enticing words*] Religion is not a matter of parts, words, or wit. The devil cares not for the sons of Sceva's adjurations. Abana and Pharphar may scour, but Jordan only can cure. God's holy things must be handled, *Sancte magis quam scite*, with fear and reverence, rather than with wit and dalliance. Let ministers set out the work of God as skilfully and adornedly as they can, but still aim at the winning of souls. Let not the window be so painted as to keep out the light. (The Saint's Everlast. Rest.) Some frothy discourses are like children's babies, that when you have taken away the dressing, you have taken away all; or like beautiful pictures, which have much cost bestowed on them to make them comely and desirable to the eye; but life, heat, and motion there is none. *O pulchrum caput! sed sensus non inest*, said the ape in the fable. *Prudentibus viris non placent phalerata, sed fortia*, said Bishop Jewel, who ever loved a manlike eloquence, but not that which is effeminate. No more did Reverend Mr Samuel Crook, but ever shunned those more gay and lighter flourishes of a luxuriant wit, wherewith the emptiest cells affect to be most fraught, as they who for want of wares in their shops set up painted blocks to fill up vacant shelves. (Clark's Lives; Life of Master Crook, by W. G.)

In demonstration of the Spirit] With demonstrations fetched out of the very marrow of the Scriptures. It must be an elaborate speech that shall work upon the conscience. A man must enlighten with his own other men's understandings, and heat by his own other men's affections. *Si vis me flere*, &c. (Horat.) Bonaventure's words in preaching were *non inflantia sed inflammantia*, not high-swelling, but inflaming his hearers. (Mr Clark's Life of Bonav.)

Ver. 5. *That your faith*, &c.] A human testimony can breed but a human faith. Aaron's bells were of pure gold; our whole preaching must be Scripture-proof, or it will burn, and none be the better for it. *Ut drachmam auri sine imagine principis, sic verba hortantis sine authoritate Dei contemnunt homines*, saith Lipsius.

In the power of God] In the gospel that lodgeth a certainty in the soul.

Ver. 6. *Wisdom among the perfect*] Or those that are grown to maturity. Some think the apostle borroweth this term from the pagans' superstition, who admitted none to their most secret ceremonies, but only persons well prepared and purified for many years.

Yet not the wisdom, &c.] Which is like the labour of moles, that dig dexterously underground, but are blind above-ground, and never open their eyes, saith Pliny, till pangs of death are upon them. Cry we after Christ, as the blind man in the gospel did, who when he was asked, What wouldest thou have? "Lord," saith he, "that mine eyes may be opened." Philosophers observe, that *lumen est vehiculum influentiæ;* light begets the flower in the field, the pearl in the sea, the precious stone in the earth; so the foundation of all renovation is illumination. O cry aloud to the Father of lights, to give the light of the knowledge of the glory of God in the face of Jesus Christ, 2 Cor. iv. 6. This will hold out, when the wisdom of this world and the *philosophorum facile principes* "come to nought."

That come to nought] That are tumbled into

hell with all their learning (*nos cum doctrinis nostris, &c.* Aug.), which doth but light them into utter darkness.

Ver. 7. *Wisdom of God in a mystery*] Whiles God did not divide himself into a merciful Father and a just Judge (as Valerius speaketh of Zaleucus), but declared himself to be both a perfectly merciful Father, and withal a perfectly just Judge; which was such an act of wisdom as the world never heard of. This is that great mystery of godliness, 1 Tim. iii. 16.

Ver. 8. *Which none of the princes*] He calleth the Pharisees and philosophers princes, for their learning, as being himself a scholar. Only he might well have said of them, as Tully of others in another case, *Mihi quidem nulli satis eruditi videntur, quibus nostra sunt ignota*, I cannot take them for scholars that partake not of our learning. (Cic. de Poetis Latinis.)

None of the princes of this world knew] Because their learning hung in their light. So it fared with Ulpian the chief lawyer, Galen the chief physician, Porphyry the chiefest Aristotelian, and Plotinus the chief Platonist, who were profest enemies to Christ and his truth. So were Libanius and Lucian, the chief scholars of their time. None miscarry oftener than men of greatest parts. None are so deep in hell as those that are most knowing. They see no more into the mystery of Christ than illiterate men do into the profound points of astronomy. As a man may look on a trade and never see the mystery of it; or he may look on the letter, and never understand the sense; so here.

For had they known it, &c.] It was ignorance then that crucified Christ, Acts iii. 17. And St Paul thanks his ignorance for his persecuting and blaspheming, 1 Tim. i. 15. "The dark places of the earth are full of the habitations of cruelty," Psal. lxxiv. 20. And they proceed from evil to evil, because they know not me, saith the Lord, Jer. ix. 3. Surely as toads and serpents grow in dark and dirty cellars, so doth all sin and wickedness in an ignorant and blind soul. The Platonists held, that men sin only by ignorance. And *Omnis peccans est ignorans*, saith Aristotle. In blind alehouses is abundance of disorder, &c.

Ver. 9. *Eye hath not seen*, &c.] It is reported of one Adrianus, that seeing the martyrs suffer such grievous things, he asked the cause; one of them answered, "Eye hath not seen, nor ear heard, neither have entered into the heart of man, the things that God hath prepared for them that love him." The naming of which text so wrought upon him that afterward he became a martyr.

The things which God hath prepared] As he prepared Paradise for Adam, so heaven for all his. Yet he reserves not all for the life to come, but gives a few grapes of Canaan in this wilderness. And so this text is to be understood of gospel joy and those present comforts that the saints have here, that *præmium ante præmium;* for not only after, but in the doing of God's will there is great reward, Psal. xix. 11, such as natural eye hath not seen nor ear heard: the stranger meddleth not with this joy; it is the sparkle of that white stone, it is that new name known to none but those that have it; it is a comfort confined to the communion of saints.

Ver. 10. *But God hath revealed*] The Chinese use to say of themselves, that all other nations of the world see but with one eye, they only with two. This is most true of the natural man compared to the spiritual.

Ver. 11. *Save the Spirit*, &c.] Man knows his inward thoughts, purposes, and desires, but the frame and disposition of his own heart he knows not, Jer. xvii. 9.

Knoweth no man] How can he that cannot tell the form and quintessence of things, that cannot enter into the depths of the flowers, or the grass he treads on, have the wit to enter into the deep things of God, hid from angels till the discovery, and since that they are students in it?

But the Spirit of God] With this heifer of his, therefore, we must plough, if we will ever understand his riddles.

Ver. 12. *Not the spirit of the world*] The world lieth down in that unclean one, and is under the power and vassalage of that spirit that worketh in the children of disobedience, as a smith in his forge, 1 John v. 19; Eph. ii. 2. It is wholly "set upon wickedness," as Aaron saith of the people, Exod. xxxii. 22.

That we might know] A sweet mercy; the cormorants of the world will not let their heirs know what they will do for them till they die. But God assures his of heaven aforehand. Thus we have not received of the spirit of this world; we cannot shift and plot as they can; but we have received a better thing, and have no reason to repine.

Ver. 13. *But which the Holy Ghost teacheth*] So that not the matter only, but words also of Holy Scripture are dictated by the Spirit, and are therefore to be had in higher estimation, 2 Pet. i. 21.

Comparing] Or co-apting (συγκρίνοντες), fitting spiritual words to spiritual matters, that all may savour of the Spirit.

Ver. 14. *But the natural man*] This mere animal (ψυχικὸς), that hath no more than a reasonable soul and natural abilities, Jude 19. Such was that sapless fellow, נבל Psal. xiv. 1, that may have a disciplinary knowledge, that is, by hearsay, as a blind man hath of colours, but not an intuitive *per speciem propriam*. The water riseth no higher than the spring from whence it came; so natural men can ascend no higher than nature. If the unreasonable creatures could draw a picture of God, said Xenophanes, they would certainly paint him like themselves, *quia scilicet nihil animal animali superius cogitare potest*, because they can think of nothing above themselves.

Neither can he know them] They that are blear-eyed and weak-sighted, if at any time they set themselves to see better into a thing, they see the worse (Vives in Aug. de Civ. Dei, xxii. 6), so here; nay more, in our nature there is an antipathy to divine truth. We love the law better than the gospel, and any truth better than the law.

Because they are spiritually] Ambrose reads, Because he is spiritually judged, being delivered up to a reprobate sense. But the other reading is better.

Ver. 15. *Judgeth all things*] By his spirit of discerning, 1 Cor. xiv., his spiritual senses exercised to discern good and evil, Heb. v. 14, his undoubted persuasion of that truth he professeth, Colos. ii. 3, and whereof he hath felt the sweetness, Colos. i. 9. Papists will needs have this spiritual man that judgeth all things, yet he himself is judged of none, to be the pope. But when this Epistle was written, there was no such thing as a pope; no such doctrine, as that the pope is infallible; that he must not be contradicted though he speak blasphemy or heresy; no, though he should draw thousands of souls after him to hell, say the Canonists, those abominable slow-backs. St Paul, who had the mind of Christ, was never of this mind.

Is judged of no man] Of no natural man, who can judge no more of divine truths than a blind man can do of colours, or a sick man of meats. And herein the poorest idiot (saith one), being a sound Christian, goeth beyond the profoundest clerks that are not sanctified, that he hath his own heart instead of a commentary, to help to understand even the most needful points of the Scripture.

Ver. 16. *But we have the mind of Christ*] This is a privilege confined to the communion of saints, to have communication of Christ's secrets, to be as it were of his court and council. One saith of Dr Sibbs, that he was a man spiritually rational, and rationally spiritual, one that seemed to see the insides of nature and grace, and the world and heaven, by those perfect anatomies he had made of them all.

CHAPTER III.

Ver. 1. *Could not speak unto you*] UNLESS I would beat the air, and lose my sweet words: *q. d.* You quarrel me for a shallow trivial teacher, when yourselves are in fault, as not yet capable of more mysterious matter. Our Saviour preached (not as he could have preached, but) " as the people were able to hear," Mark iv. 33. So the author to the Hebrews, chap. v. 11. Some impute not their profiting to the minister, as he in Seneca, that having a thorn in his foot complained of the roughness of the way as the cause of his limping. Or as she in the same author, that being struck with a sudden blindness, bade open the windows, when as it was not want of light, but want of sight that troubled her.

As unto carnal, even as unto babes] Or, at least as unto babes, not yet past the spoon, and that must have their meats masticated for them by their nurses.

Ver. 2. *I have fed you with milk*] Ministers must condescend to their hearers' capacities, though they be slighted for so doing, as Paul was; or jeered, as Isaiah, chap. xxviii. 9, 10, for his " line upon line, precept upon precept," *Kau lekau*, and *Zau lezau;* the sound of the words carries a taunt, as scornful people by the tone of their voice and rhyming words, scorn at such as they despise.

Ver. 3. *For ye are yet carnal*] It is a shame for Christians to be like other men, as Samson was after he had lost his hair. It ill becomes those excellent ones of the earth, princes in all lands, to contend and quarrel, as those *terrigenæ fratres* used to do. By the laws of England, noblemen have this privilege, that none of them can be bound to the peace; because it is supposed that the peace is always bound to them, and that of their own accord they will be careful to preserve it.

Envying and strife, &c.] These overflowings of the gall and spleen came from a fulness of bad humours.

And walk as men] Christians should be as Saul was, higher than the people by head and shoulders. Something singular is expected from them, Matt. v. 47; they should have their feet where other men's heads are, Prov. xv. 24. When we do evil, we work *de nostro et secundum hominem,* we do our kind, as the devil when he speaks lies, speaks *de suo,* of his own, John viii. 44.

Ver. 4. *For when one saith, &c.*] So those that will needs be called Lutherans, *Jurantque in verba magistri.* Did not Luther play the man, when he and other Dutch divines advised Philip Landgrave of Hesse, a pious prince, to marry a second wife, that is, an adulteress, whiles his lawful wife was yet alive? And might he not deceive and be deceived in other things as well as in that? (Zanch. Miscel. Epist. Dedicat.)

Are ye not carnal?] Nay, will not the world think ye are mad? as the apostle speaks in a like case, 1 Cor. xiv. 23. Will they not think worse? See John xvii. 21, 23. If Christians unite not, if they fall out and wrangle, the world will think " thou never sentest me," saith our Saviour.

Ver. 5. *But ministers*] Not masters, as *Magistri nostri Parisienses.* (Præfat. in 1 Sentent.) So the Sorbonists will needs be called, contrary to James iii. 1. Bacon the Carmelite was called Doctor *resolutissimus,* because he would endure no May-bes.

Ver. 6. *But God gave the increase*] The harp yields no sound till it be touched by the hand of the musician. The heart is never made good till the heavens answer the earth, Hos. ii. 21, till God strikes the stroke. Holy Melancthon being newly converted, thought it impossible for his hearers to withstand the evidence of the gospel. But soon after he complained that old Adam was too hard for young Melancthon. No man can run the point aright, except God give wind to his sails; as, if he speak the word, our words shall be not only like Peter's angle, which took a fish, but like Peter's net, which enclosed a multitude of fishes.

Ver. 7. *So then neither is he, &c.*] This made Cyril to conclude his preface to his catechism, with *Meum est docere, vestrum auscultare, Dei perficere.* I may teach, and you hear, but God must do the deed when all is done. Else we may preach and pray to the wearing of our tongues to the stumps (as Bradford said), and to no more purpose than Bede did when he preached to a heap of stones.

Ver. 8. *And he that watereth are one*] Why then are not you at one? Should ye not follow your leaders, press their footsteps? Surely you would, did you not more mind party than peace. *Maxima pars studiorum, est studium partium;* a hateful kind of study.

Shall receive his own reward] Those ambitious doctors that draw disciples after them, hunting after popular applause (that empty blast of stinking breath), shall have that for their reward; let them make them merry with it. When faithful ministers shall shine as stars, Dan. xii. 3.

Ver. 9. *For we are labourers, &c.*] Let ministers hence learn their, 1. Dignity; 2. Duty. *Fructus honos oneris, Fructus honoris onus.* Who would not work hard with such sweet company?

Ver. 10. *As a wise master-builder*] Artificers also have their wisdom, as Aristotle yieldeth. "For his God doth instruct him to discretion, and doth teach him," Isa. xxviii. 26. As he did Bezaleel and Aholiab.

Ver. 11. *Which is Jesus Christ*] The doctrine of his person and offices is the foundation of Christian religion, and must therefore be kept pure and entire by all means possible. Arius's ὁμοιούσιος, would not be yielded; nor Nestorius' Θεοδόχος, for Θεοτόκος. So religious were the old bishops, that they would not alter or exchange a letter or a syllable in these fundamentals. Every particle of truth is precious, and not to be parted with.

Ver. 12. *Wood, hay, stubble*] Rhetorical strains, philosophical fancies, that tend not to edification. There are that together with the gold, silver, and ivory of sound and savoury truths, have, as Solomon's ships had, store of apes and peacocks, conceits and crotchets. Now if he that imbaseth the king's coin, deserve punishment; what do they that instead of the tried silver of divine truths, stamp the name and character of God upon Nehushtan, their own base brazen stuff?

Ver. 13. *For the day shall declare it*] That is, the light of the truth, or time, the father of truth, or the day of death, when many recognize and recant their errors, shall show them their sin.

Ver. 14. *If any man's work abide*] Error as glass is bright, but brittle, and cannot endure the hammer or fire, as gold can, which, though rubbed or melted, remains firm and orient.

Ver. 15. *He shall suffer loss*] Of his work (his laborious loss of time) and of some part of his wages.

Yet so as by fire] Not of purgatory (a Popish fiction) but of the Holy Ghost. Or (as one interprets it) like unto them who save themselves naked out of the fire without carrying away any of their goods; so his person shall be saved, but he shall not have the reward of a well qualified minister.

Ver. 16. *Ye are the temple of God*] Not God's building only, as ver. 9, but his temple. A mud wall may be made up of anything, not so the walls of a temple or palace, that must have other materials.

And that the Spirit of God, &c.] Next to the love of Christ indwelling in our nature, we may wonder at the love of the Holy Ghost, that will dwell in our defiled souls. (Dr Sibbs on Eph. iv. 30.) Let our care be to wash the pavement of this temple with our tears, to sweep it by repentance, to beautify it with holiness, to perfume it with prayers, to deck it with humility, to hang it with sincerity. *Delicata res est Spiritus Dei;* the Holy Ghost will dwell in a poor, so it be a pure house. Religion loves to lie clean, as was a grave speech of an ancient saint.

Ver. 17. *Which temple ye are*] Man is God's temple; God man's altar. Demosthenes (contra Aristog.) could say, that man's heart was God's best and most stately temple, *Justitia, verecundia, et observantia legum communitum.*

Ver. 18. *Let no man deceive himself*] *Bis desipit, qui sibi sapit. Consilii satis est in me mihi,* said she in the poet. (Arachne ap. Ovid, Metam.) Nothing so easy as to over-ween.

Let him become a fool] Let him come to the well with an empty pitcher. *Intus existens prohibet alienum.* Agur (if a man may believe him) is more brutish than any man, Prov. xxx. 2, 3. See there how he vilifies, yea, nullifies himself before God. So did blessed Bradford, as appears by the subscriptions of many of his letters.

Ver. 19. *He taketh the wise*] ὁ δρασσόμενος, those natural brute beasts, made to be taken and destroyed, 2 Pet. ii. 12; God takes them and makes fools of them.

In their own craftiness] When they have eviscerated themselves like spiders, tried all conclusions, beaten their brains, searched the devil's skull for new devices, done all that may be done (as the word πανουργία imports) to effect their designs. *Versutia veteratoria.* God lets them carry the ball on the foot till they are almost at the goal, go to the utmost of their tether, and then pulls them back with shame enough to their task. Thus he dealt by Sennacherib, Haman, Herod, others.

Ver. 20. *Of the wise*] Such as excel in natural gifts, that are the choicest and most picked men. The Psalmist saith only of men, Psal. xciv. 12.

Ver. 21. *Let no man glory in men*] That is, that they are such as one's scholars or followers, seeing the Church is not made for them, but they for the Church.

For all things are yours, &c.] *Hæc est magnæ nostræ Chartulæ Epitome,* saith Sam. Ward. This is an epitome of the Church's grand grant or charter. A Christian hath interest in, and right to, all these things, 1. Entirely, Eph. i. 23, and ii. 10; Col. iii. 11.　2. Refinedly, the curse is removed, Gal. iii. 13; Prov. x. 22.　3. Really, 1 Cor. vii. 31; Eph. i. ult.　4. Safely, Prov. i. 33.　5. Serviceably, Rom. viii. 28.　6. Satisfyingly, Psal. xxii. 26. So that the poor Christian, saith one, is like the usurer, who goes meanly and fares hard, but hath thousands out at use.

Ver. 22. *All are yours*] Though not in possession, yet in use, or by way of reduction, as we say, the worst things are God's children, and in reversion those best things above.

Ver. 23. *And ye are Christ's*] We hold all we have *in capite* tenure in Christ. From Christ therefore let us take our denomination. The name of Jesuits savoureth of blasphemous arrogance.

CHAPTER IV.

Ver. 1. *Let a man so account*] Quasi dicat, though we are yours, as chap. iii. 22, devoted to the service of your faith, yet are we not to be slighted, but respected as Christ's high stewards.

Ministers of Christ] Gr. ὑπηρέτας, "under-rowers" to Christ the master-pilot, helping forward the ship of the Church toward the haven of heaven.

Stewards of the mysteries] Dispensing all out of God's goods, and not of our own; setting bread and salt upon the table (that is, preaching Christ crucified) whatever else there is.

Ver. 2. *That a man be found faithful*] Giving every man his due proportion of fit food, Matt. xxiv. 45, not as he in the emblem, that gave straw to the dog, and a bone to the ass.

Ver. 3. *But with me it is, &c.*] A good minister reviled, may reply, as once a steward did to his passionate lord, when he called him knave, &c., Your honour may speak as you please, but I believe not a word that you say; for I know myself an honest man. *Non curo illos censores, qui vel non intelligendo reprehendunt, vel reprehendendo non intelligunt*, saith Augustine. Augustus did but laugh at the satires and buffooneries which they had published against him. Severus the emperor was careful of what was to be done by him, but careless what was said of him. ἐμμελὴς τῶν πρακτέων, ἀμελὴς δὲ τῶν περὶ αὐτοῦ λογοποιουμένων. (Dio.) Do well and bear ill is written upon heaven's gates, said Mr Bradford the martyr. Thou art an heretic, said Woodroof the sheriff, to Mr Rogers the protomartyr, in Queen Mary's days. That shall be known, quoth he, at the day of judgment. Some men flatter me, saith Politian, some others slander me, I think neither the better nor the worse of myself for that; no more than I think myself taller or lower for that my shadow is longer in the morning, and shorter at noon. A Spanish Jesuit, saith Beza (Epist. ad Calvin), disputing with us about the Eucharist, called us foxes, apes, serpents, &c. My answer was, that we believed it no more than we believed transubstantiation.

Ver. 4. *Yet am I not, &c.*] Paul a chosen vessel, but yet an earthen vessel, knew well that he had his cracks and his flaws, which God could easily find out.

Ver. 5. *Until the Lord come*] Tot argumenta quot verba, saith Paraeus, every word here hath its weight. There shall be a resurrection one day of names as well as of bodies. Let that stay us when belied or misreported.

And then shall every man have praise of God] His faith (now haply hid, or not noticed) shall then be "found to praise, honour, and glory," 1 Pet. i. 7,—praise from the mouth of the Judge, honour in the hearts of saints and angels, glory in the kingdom of heaven after the judgment ended. Christ shall then be not only his compurgator, but his encomiast.

Ver. 6. *I have in a figure, &c.*] i. e. I have represented and reprehended your partialities under our names, when I brought you in saying, "I am of Paul, and I of Apollos," &c., 1 Cor. i. 12. For the heads of your factions were your own ambitious doctors, whose names I yet spared, and took the business upon myself and Apollos, for your sakes.

Ver. 7. *For who maketh thee*] He directeth his speech to those *Theologi gloriae*, as Luther usually calleth such, those vain-glorious, self-ascribing pastors at Corinth, that sought to bear away the bell from Paul, and would not stick to answer this demand of his, *Quis te discernit?* As that insolent Arminian did, *Ego meipsum discerno*, I make myself to differ. (Greuinchovius.)

And what hast thou, &c.] There are that would hammer out their own happiness, like the spider, climbing by the thread of her own weaving, with motto accordingly, *Mihi soli debeo*.

Why dost thou glory] As great a folly as for the groom to be proud of his master's horse, the stage-player of his borrowed robes, or the mud wall of the sunshine. Of all the good that is in us, we may well say as the young man did of his hatchet, Alas, master, it was but borrowed.

Ver. 8. *Now ye are rich*] Crescit oratio, saith Piscator here. The apostle riseth in his expressions, and that all along by an ironical reprehension. These Corinthians had riches, and gifts, and learning; and carried aloft by these waxen wings, they domineered and despised others.

Ver. 9. *As it were men appointed to death*] As when he fought with beasts at Ephesus. The heathens in their public calamities would commonly call out, *Christianos ad leones*, To the lions with these Christians, as if they had been the cause. (Tertul. Apol. cap. xl.) Ignatius suffered in this sort.

A spectacle to the world] As those that were first led in triumph, and then had back again to the prison, there to be strangled. (Piscator.)

Ver. 10. *We are fools, &c.*] Not to the world only, but in your account too. For these Corinthians undervalued and depressed Paul under their silly shallow-headed verbalists, not worthy to carry his books after him for sound and substantial learning.

Ver. 11. *Even to this present*] Thus he complaineth, not out of impatience (for he was active in his sufferings), but to stain their pride, that permitted it so to be, when it was in their power to have relieved him.

Ver. 12. *And labour, working, &c.*] Whereas they might object, Are you hungry, thirsty, naked ? It is because you are idle. No, saith he, " we labour, working with our hands " (a shame for you to suffer it), and yet can hardly sweat out a poor living. This one example of Paul is much pleaded in these times by men of perverse minds to dispute God out of his own. One apostle works with his hands, or two, now and then at pleasure; all the rest live upon the Church (for could those fishermen catch fish in the forests, deserts, or streets ?), yet one Paul is set against all the rest of the apostles ; yea, set together by the ears with himself; anything to save their purses.

Ver. 13. *Being defamed, we entreat*] Though Luther call me devil, said Calvin, yet I will honour him as a servant of God.

We are made as the filth of the world] q. d. The filth of filth ; for the whole world lies in wickedness, as a foul sloven in a slough, or as a carrion in the slime of it. The word περικαθάρματα signifies, the sweepings of the world, or the dirt scraped off the pavement thereof.

And the off-scouring of all things] Detersorium, sordes, purgamenta, rejectamenta. Piaculares et abominabiles, saith Paræus. The word signifies the dung-cart, saith Mr Burroughs, that goes through the city, into which every one brings and casts his filth. Every one had some filth to cast upon Paul and the apostles. Constantine, a citizen of Rhoan, with three others, being for defence of the gospel condemned to be burned, were put into a dung-cart, who thereat rejoicing, said that they were reputed here the excrements of the world, but yet their death was a sweet odour unto God. Budæus is of opinion that the apostle here alludeth to those expiations in use among the heathen, performed in this manner. Certain condemned persons were brought forth with garlands upon their heads in manner of sacrifices ; these they would tumble from some steep places into the sea, offering them up to Neptune with this form of words, περίψημα ἡμῶν γένου, " Be thou a propitiation for us." (Bud. Pandec.) So for the removal of the pestilence they sacrificed certain men to their gods : these they called καθάρματα, filth, loading them with revilings and cursings. (Suidas in περίψημι.)

Ver. 14. *To shame you*] An innocent person sometimes, upon the fulness of an aspersion, may conceive shame, as David did, Psal. xliv. 15, yet usually shame is the effect of an evil conscience, and may prove, by God's blessing, a means of repentance, 2 Thess. iii. 14.

Ver. 15. *Ten thousand instructors*] Gr. pedagogues, who oft prove orbiliusses, sharp and severe above measure, *Verberibus pluunt, co-*

laphis grandinant. So did these Corinthian school-masters, 2 Cor. xi. 20. They were also too well skilled in the Doric dialect, crying, Give, give ; and taught little more than elegant elocution.

I have begotten you through the gospel] For together with the word there goeth forth a regenerating power, Jam. i. 18. The exhortations thereof are operative means of sanctification, and practical ; as when God said, " Let there be light," or Christ said, " Lazarus, come forth." The Spirit maketh the seed of the word prolifical and generative ; and hence ministers are made fathers, as Moses was father to Aaron's children, Numb. iii. 1, who are therefore there called " his generation." And as *propriissimum opus viventis est, generare sibi simile,* as saith the philosopher, it is the most proper work of every living thing to beget its like ; so here.

Ver. 16. *Be ye followers of me*] As dear children. *A bove majori discit arare minor.* (Ovid.) Constantine's children resembled their father exactly, they put him wholly on, saith Eusebius, and were, as it were, very he, ὅλον ἐνεδύσαντο τὸν Κωνσταντῖνον.

Ver. 17. *For this cause*] That ye may be followers of me, and know what I do.

Of my ways which be in Christ] It is of excellent use to know what good men, especially ministers, do, as well as what they say. Ministers' lives should be a transcript of their sermons, or as so many sermons on the life of Christ.

Ver. 18. *Now some are puffed up*] Swelling in the body is an ill symptom. So it is in the soul. A swelling wall will shortly fall.

Ver. 19. *Not the speech of them which are puffed up*] Dicta factis deficientibus, erubescunt. Malo autem miserandum quam erubescendum, saith Tertullian, either add practice, or leave profession for shame.

Ver. 20. *The kingdom of God*] i. e. The administration of his ordinances and government of the Church.

Ver. 21. *With a rod, or in love ?*] Both ; but (as children) we think not so. *Sed sinite virgam corripientem, ne sentiatis malleum conterentem,* saith one father. (Bern.) *Non erudit pater nisi quem amat, nec corripit nisi quem diligit,* saith another. (Jerome.)

CHAPTER V.

Ver. 1. *As is not so much as named*] To wit, without detestation. The apostle seems to allude to Antiochus Soter, who married his stepmother Stratonice, being first like to die for love of her, as Erasistratus the physician told his father. (Ælian.) Of this incestuous marriage came Antiochus Theos, or Antiochus the god, so called of the Milesians, because he did put down their tyrant Timarchus. This god was poisoned by his wife Laodice.

Among the Gentiles] In Mexico and those parts, whoredom, sodomy, and incest (those

Spanish virtues, as one calleth them) are common without reproof; the pope's pardons being more rife in those parts than in any part of Europe for these abominable filthinesses, whereout he sucketh no small advantage. (Sir Fra. Drake.) Notwithstanding, the Indians abhor this most loathsome living; showing themselves in respect of the Spaniards, as the Scythians did in respect of the Grecians, whom they so far excelled in life and behaviour as they were short of them in learning and knowledge. Who hath not heard of the abhorred incest of the house of Austria? King Philip II. could call Archduke Albert both brother, cousin, nephew, and son. (Spec. Europ.) For all this was he to him either by blood or affinity; being uncle to himself, cousin-german to his father, husband to his sister, and father to his wife; and all this by papal dispensation. The Papists themselves write with detestation, that in Rome a Jewish maid might not be admitted into the stews of whoredom, unless she would be first baptized. (Espenc. de Continen. iii. 4.)

That one should have his father's wife] Ethelbald, king of West Saxons, with great infamy marrying his father's widow Judith, enjoyed his kingdom but two years and a half. (Daniel's Hist. of Eng.)

Ver. 2. *And ye are puffed up*] And yet ye are puffed up (so Piscator reads it), viz. with your spiritual gifts, and your brave teachers; whereas you have more cause to be cast down for your other men's sins now made yours, because unlamented by you. There were great divisions among them at this time; and when this incest fell out, the other faction thought they had an advantage against the whole party, and this puffed them up,—Nay, do ye not see what one of them hath done, &c.?

And have not rather mourned] That any of you should incur the censure of excommunication; at which time they did anciently fast and lament.

Ver. 3. *Have judged already, &c.*] *q. d.* I by mine apostolical authority do excommunicate him. And yet how fiercely doth learned Erastus contend with Calvin and Beza about excommunication, denying the Church any such power. The Jews had their three sorts of excommunication. The heathen also had theirs; among the old Gauls, if any one did not obey the decrees of their Druids or priests, he was forbidden their sacrifices; and therehence shunned by all as a wicked man, he had no benefit of their laws, nor any respect given him, &c.

Ver. 4. *With the power of our Lord*] Promised, Matt. xviii. 18—20. This makes it to be a heavy case to be rightly excommunicated. Indeed it may fall out that Jonah shall be cast out of the ship, when Ham shall be reserved in the ark. "Your brethren that hated you, that cast you out for my name's sake, said (for a pretence), Let the Lord be glorified; but he shall appear to your joy, and they shall be ashamed," Isa. lxvi. 5. When the sentence of excommuni-

tion began with, *In nomine Domini*, to be read against a certain martyr, he cried out, as well he might, You begin in a wrong name. And another of them, together with his five fellow-sufferers, did formally excommunicate their persecutors. It grew to a common proverb, by the abuse of this ordinance in those corrupt times, *In nomine Domini incipit omne malum.*

Ver. 5. *To deliver such an one to Satan*] That he may learn not to blaspheme, that is, not to cause others to blaspheme or speak evil of the good way of God, for his flagitious courses.

Ver. 6. *Your glorying is not good*] It is the height of wickedness to glory in wickedness, as Lamech, Gen. iv., and Alexander Pheræus, who consecrated the javelin wherewith he had slain Polyphron. Protagoras boasted that he had spent forty years in corrupting of youth. (Plato.) Mark Antony vomited out a book concerning his own ability to eat and drink much. Joannes à Casa, dean of the pope's chamber, wrote a poem in commendation of his own beastly sin of sodomy. And Stokesly, Bishop of London in King Henry VIII's. time, lying at point of death, rejoiced, boasting that in his life-time he had burned fifty heretics, that is, good Christians. (Acts and Mon.)

A little leaven leaveneth, &c.] One spoonful of vinegar will soon tart a great deal of sweet milk; but a great deal of milk will not so soon sweeten one spoonful of vinegar. One sinner may destroy much good, saith Solomon, Eccles. ix. ult. He may be a common mischief, if tolerated, by spreading the infection of his wickedness, which is more catching than the plague.

Ver. 7. *As ye are unleavened*] viz. In part sanctified. Every new man is two men. Many a one that is merry in company hath a shrew at home; so have the best their inward troubles. The comfort is, that God overlooks our involuntary infirmities, and accounts us unleavened, when yet there is much still to be purged out. The leper, when his leprosy began but to heal, was pronounced clean, because then he went on still to heal, and his leprosy to shale off.

Ver. 8. *Let us keep the feast*] The benefits we receive by Christ should crown the calendar of our lives with continual festivals; yea, make us everlastingly merry at our *convivium juge* of a good conscience. Diogenes could say, that a good man keeps every day holy-day. (Plut.) And the Jews were bound to rejoice at all their feasts. "Eat therefore thy meat with joy, and drink thy wine with gladness, sith God now accepteth thy works," Eccles. ix. 7.

Ver. 9. *Not to company with fornicators*] Dion Chrysostom saith, that Corinth was the most luxurious and lascivious city in the world. πόλιν ἐπαφροδιτάτην. Strabo saith, that Venus had a most stately temple there, that was kept by above a thousand beautiful courtesans. Another saith, that it was the brothel-house of Greece, and a most filthy mart-town of abominable lusts. (Molin.) Tully indeed calleth it *lumen Græciæ*, the light or eye of Greece. It might be so in some respects. But surely this sin was no small snuff in this light, but a blemish in this eye.

Ver. 10. *Yet not altogether, &c.*] Here he lets them know that in that former epistle (not extant now) he meant not that they should wholly sever themselves from those wicked that are yet without the Church (for that they cannot do), but from profligate professors, discinct Christians, that they may be ashamed.

Ver. 11. *Not to keep company*] Gr. συναναμί-γνυσθαι, not to be mingled with them. The rivers of Peru, after they have run into the main sea, yea, some write twenty or thirty miles, they keep themselves unmixed with the salt water; so that a very great way within the sea men may take up as fresh water as if they were near the land. So at Belgrade in Hungary, where the Danube and Sava (two great rivers) meet, their waters mingle no more than water and oil, &c. We must so converse with the wicked, as that we commingle not, by holding any needless society with such, no, not with him that is called a brother, but belies his profession. Yet still must we perform to such, though excommunicated, offices of charity, natural and civil duties, as those of parents toward their children, of children toward their parents, and the like. But come not near such stinking stuff, except ye have the wind of it.

Ver. 12. *Them also that are without*] These come not under the verge of Church censures, Rev. xxii. 15.

Ver. 13. *Therefore put away*] Gr. ἐξαρεῖτε, Ye will put away, *q. d.* I hope ye will, though hitherto ye have not. Soft words and hard arguments do soonest prevail, especially when we reprove or admonish not in our own, but in God's words, as here the apostle doth out of Deut. xiii. Some warmth must be in a reproof, but it must not be scalding hot. *Ægros, quos potus fortis non curavit, ad salutem pristinam aqua tepens revocavit*, saith Gregory. They that could not be cured with strong potions, have been recovered with warm water. Gentle showers, and dews that distil leisureably, do comfort the earth, when dashing storms drown the seed.

CHAPTER VI.

Ver. 1. *Go to law before the unjust*] ALL unbelievers are, 1. Void of Christ's righteousness imputed; 2. Of true civil righteousness, as being self-seekers in all. 3. They oppress the saints, and draw them before the judgment-seats, James ii. 6, where they are so ill dealt with ofttimes, that they come to be of Themistocles' mind, who professed, that if two ways were showed him, one to hell, and the other to the bar, he would choose that which went to hell, and forsake the other.

And not before the saints] Christians first brought their causes before the bishops to be judged. And hence grew their power (as Paræus noteth), which the Christian emperors first would

not, and afterwards could not, take away from them. This raised papacy and prelacy to such a height, they would be princes as well as bishops.

Ver. 2. *Shall judge the world*] That is, the wicked, called the inhabitants of the earth, and of the sea, Rev. xii. 12, in opposition to the burgesses of the New Jerusalem, Phil. iii. 20. And let this comfort us under the perverse censures of worldly men, mad and beside themselves in point of salvation. The Lord seeth that their day is coming, Psal. xxxvii. 13.

Ver. 3. *Things that pertain to this, &c.*] That serve to and satisfy the body only, being *nec vera, nec vestra*, Luke xvi. 11, 12.

Ver. 4. *If then ye have judgments*] As the Corinthians, being many of them merchants, had many lawsuits. But if men's hearts were not bigger than their suits, there would not be half so many.

Who are least esteemed] Rather than go to law before heathen judges. The lowest, if of any judgment, are high enough for such a purpose. Why should those *sordida poscinummia, qui latrocinia intra mœnia exercent*, as Columella hath it, those *Crumenimulgæ*, the unconscionable lawyers, make a spoil of us; and then when they die, build hospitals for fools, as one of them did, saying, Of fools I got my estate, and to fools I will leave it. Of those that go to law, we may well say, as Charondas once did of those that go to sea, *Se non mirari qui semel mare ingressus sit, sed qui iterum*, that he marvelled not at those that went once, but at those that would go again.

Ver. 5. *No, not one that shall be able*] Our late judge Dier, if there came any controversies of poor men to be tried before him, would usually say, that either the parties are wilful, or their neighbours uncharitable, because their suits were not quietly ended at home. (The Practice of Quietness.)

Ver. 6. *But brother goeth to law*] Once it was counted ominous to commence actions, and follow suits. Of common barreters, we may say as the historian doth of mathematicians, *Genus hominum quod in nostra repub. et vetabitur semper, et retinebitur.* (Tacit.)

But brother] Still Satan is thus busy, and Christians are thus malicious; that, as if they wanted enemies, they fly in one another's faces, as did Epiphanius and Chrysostom, Luther and Zuinglius, Hooper and Ridley, Taylor and Lambert, those English exiles at Frankfort in Queen Mary's days, and Knox, &c.

Ver. 7. *There is utterly a fault*] Gr. ἥττημα, a disgrace, a loss of victory: *q. d.* By your litigious lawing one another, you betray a great deal of weakness and impotency of affection. These be ignoble quarrels, *Ubi et vincere inglorium est, et atteri sordidum.* See the note on Rom. xii. 21.

Because ye go to law] Lightly for every small offence (which if Mahometans do, they are publicly punished), and with spiteful vindictive spirits; whereas in going to law, men should not be transported with hate or heat, but as tilters break their spears on each other's breasts, yet without wrath or intention of hurt, so, &c. The French are said to be very litigious, and full of law-suits.

Ver. 8. *Nay, you do wrong*] In person and name.

And defraud] Of goods and estate.

And that your brethren] Which very name should charm and allay all discords, as betwixt Abraham and Lot, Gen. xiii. 8. Aristotle could say, It is better to suffer wrong than to do it. And, I know how to bear injuries, Εγὼ μὲν ἐπίσταμαι ἀδικεῖσθαι, said Chilo to his brother, who took it ill that he was not chosen to be one of the judges.

Ver. 9. *Shall not inherit*] It is an undefiled inheritance, 1 Pet. i. 4 ; no dirty dog ever trampled on that golden pavement, Rev. xxii. 15. Heaven spewed out the angels ; shall it lick up the unrighteous ? The serpent could screw himself into Paradise, but no wicked could ever get into heaven. There is no happiness to be had without holiness. Let none think to break God's chain, as Balaam, Numb. xxiii. 10.

Ver. 10. *Nor thieves, nor covetous*] These two be fitly set together, as near akin ; so are drunkards and railers.

Nor extortioners] Whose sin is properly immoderate getting, as that of the covetous consists in pinching and saving. So 1 Tim. iii. 3.

Ver. 11. *Such were some of you*] Oh the infinite goodness of God, that would once look upon such walking dunghills, such monstrous miscreants !

But ye are washed] In general ; as in particular, 1. *Ye are sanctified*] And that by the Spirit of our God. 2. *Ye are justified*] And that in the name, or by the righteousness, of our Lord Jesus Christ. His blood cleanseth us from sins, both guiltiness and filthiness. It is like to those sovereign mundifying waters, which so wash off the corruption of the ulcer, that they cool the heat and stay the spread of the infection, and by degrees heal the same. See the note on Rom. xi. 26, and on Rev. xix. 8. God never pays our debts, but he gives us a stock of grace.

Ver. 12. *All things are lawful*] viz. All indifferent things, amongst which the Corinthians reckoned not only meats and drinks, but also fornication (their national sin). The devil perhaps had persuaded them, as he hath done the Turks at this day, that God did not give men such appetites to have them frustrate, but enjoyed, as made for the gust of man, not for his torment, wherein his Creator delights not. Now the apostle grants, that for meats all things are lawful (yet in case of offence or intemperance, they may become inexpedient, and so unlawful). But for fornication, it was utterly unlawful, as he proves by many powerful arguments.

But I would not be brought] As those swinish surfeiters, that wearing their brains in their bellies (with the ass fish), their guts in their heads, do dig their graves with their own teeth ; being

like the mule, which cannot travel, they say, without a bottle of hay hanging at his nose.

Ver. 13. *God shall destroy*] The belly shall be destroyed in the other world, not for the substance of it, but for the use of it. And the same may be said for the difference of sexes ; the parts shall remain, the use cease. Cato said well, that he was an ill commonwealth's man, *qui inter guttur et inguen, cuncta sub ventris ditione posuisset*, that was a slave to his sensual appetite.

Ver. 14. *And will also raise us up*] He will make our vile bodies to be like unto his glorious body, the standard. Shall we then defile them with the kitchen-stuff of uncleanness ?

Ver. 15. *Shall I then take*] Scipio, when a harlot was offered him, said, *Vellem, si non essem imperator*, I would, if I were not a general. Say thou, if I were not a Christian.

And make them the members of a harlot] A saint cannot indeed be made the member of a harlot (saith a reverend man), because not κολλώμενος, glued or knit to any sin. Though a member of Christ and sin may fall one upon another, and touch each other ; yet they are of a mouldering nature, and will not cleave together. Water and oil violently shaken together may seem to mingle, but will not continue so long ; there is no coalition, because they are of diverse natures ; the one remaineth water still, and the other oil.

Ver. 16. *Is one body*] By a most strict but vicious and infamous bond (saith an interpreter), which is sufficient to untie or break any other bond, though lawful and holy, either corporal or spiritual.

Ver. 17. *Is one spirit*] That is, one spiritual body : while Christ lays hold on us by his Spirit, we lay hold on him by faith. Hence the Church is called Christ, 1 Cor. xii. 12, and the fulness of Christ, Eph. i. 23. We have the honour of making Christ perfect, as the members do the body.

Ver. 18. *Flee fornication*] φεύγετε. With post-haste flee it.

Læta venire Venus, tristis abire solet.

Be not of those men that are called *Borboritæ* of their miry filthiness, whom Epiphanius and Œcumenius speak of.

Ver. 19. *That your body is the temple*] Shall we make the temple of God the stews of Satan ? See chap. iii. 16. Antiochus and Pompey never prospered after that they defiled the temple.

Ver. 20. *Ye are bought*] Shall I drink the blood of these men ? saith David. So, shall I abuse my body, the price of Christ's blood, abandon it to venery ? &c.

Glorify God in your body] The very Manichees that denied God to be the author of the body, fasted on sabbath days, and in fasting exercised a humiliation of the body. *Pone in pectore dextram.* (Pers.) Let God have heart and hand, mind and mouth, faith and feet, spirit, soul, and body, 1 Thess. v. 23, all which are his by a manifold right.

CHAPTER VII.

Ver. 1. *Whereof ye wrote unto me*] Certain cases of conscience they had propounded, which here he answers. This he could do excellently, and so could Luther, as having had experience, and been much beaten and exercised with spiritual conflicts. Conscience is a diamond, and will be wrought on by nothing but dust of diamond, such as contrition hath ground it to.

It is good for a man] Now since the fall, it is good, *i. e.* convenient for the many troubles of the married state. It is not evil to marry, but good to be wary, else *conjugium* may prove *conjurgium*, marriage a mar-age.

Ver. 2. *To avoid fornication*] Gr. πορνείας, fornications, comprehending all lustful burnings, self-pollutions, and all other impurities of a single life. How many are there that enter into God's ordinance (marriage) through the devil's portal (fornication), that take such liberty before, that after marriage they rue it all the days of their lives.

Let every man have his own wife] Not many wives. Turks may have as many as they can keep. And some sensualists plead now for polygamy. See Mal. ii. 15. *Scotorum natio uxores proprias non habet*, saith Jerome of the old Scots. And too many amongst us are sick of a pleurisy.

Ver. 3. *Let the husband, &c.*] Let them be chaste between themselves, and beware both of excess and defect. Chastity is a man's honour, 1 Thess. iv. 5. And modesty is the best preserver of nuptial chastity. Marriage as well as meats must be sanctified by the word and prayer. God must be sent for to bless this physic to the soul. Raging lust is a great enemy to conjugal love.

Ver. 4. *The wife hath no power, &c.*] The husband's body is servant to the wife, and the wife's to the husband : they have passed themselves one to another by mutual covenant, and God keeps the bonds, Prov. ii. 17; Mal. ii. 14.

Ver. 5. *To fasting and prayer*] *Preces nobis jejuniis alendum et quasi saginandum.* Fastingdays are soul-fatting days : prayer is edged and winged thereby.

That Satan tempt you not] The temptation is strong to fornication, stronger to adultery. Watch therefore. Our nature is catching this way ; and once in, it is not so easy to come off. This is a searing sin, Hos. iv. 11 ; Eph. iv. 19.

Ver. 6. *And not of commandment*] Among the Jews marriage was not held a thing indifferent, or at their own liberty to choose or refuse, but a binding command. (Targum on Gen. i. 28.) Hereto Paul seems in this verse to allude. At this day every Jew is bound to marry about 18 years of age, or before 20 ; else he is accounted as one that liveth in sin.

Ver. 7. *For I would that all, &c.*] He had a peculiar gift, that he was so eminently chaste ; such as might be in reprobates. So Moses' meekness was partly from his natural temper. And Luther's not being tempted to covetousness was much helped by the freeness and generousness of his spirit.

Ver. 8. *I say therefore to the unmarried*] Yet doth not the apostle simply prefer virginity or viduity before marriage as better. The Saturnalian heretics said that marriage was of the devil. And the blemish will never be wiped off some of the ancient fathers, who, to establish their own idol of I know not what virginity, which they themselves had not, have written most wickedly and basely of marriage. If the same God had not been the author of virginity and marriage, he had never countenanced virginity by marriage, as he did in the blessed Virgin.

Ver. 9. *Let them marry*] There is no lust so hot and violent, but God's medicines rightly applied will cool and heal. Only remember that it is not the having, but the loving of a wife that keepeth a man chaste and clean. And that God doth use to correct excess and dalliance betwixt married couples, with strong temptations after strange flesh.

Better to marry than burn] As an oven heated by the baker, Hos. vii. 4. As those pagans were scalded, Rom. i. 27, and these papagans still are, that are forbidden to marry, and yet cannot contain.

Ver. 10. *Yet not I*] By prudential advice only.

But the Lord] Not in so many words, but by just consequence drawn from Matt. xix. 6.

Ver. 11. *Or let her be reconciled*] *Ut quæ modo pugnarant jungant sua rostra columbæ.* (Ovid.) Why should married couples be as glass, that being once broke can never be pieced again ? The Lord hates putting away, Mal. ii. 16.

Ver. 12. *Let him not put her away*] For to the pure all things are pure. *Uxoris vitium aut tollendum, aut tolerandum est*, saith Varro in Gellius. Mend a bad wife, if thou canst ; bear with her, if thou canst not.

Ver. 13. *If he be pleased, &c.*] If he blaspheme not Christ, force her not to deny the faith, &c., as that king of Denmark that would have compelled his wife to go to mass, who was therefore forced to fly for her life to her brother the elector of Brandenburg (as Luther relateth), where she died Christianly.

Ver. 14. *But now they are holy*] With a federal holiness, and are therefore to be baptized, as being partakers of the covenant of grace. The Habassines (a kind of mongrel Christians in Africa) have an odd conceit, that the souls of infants departing before baptism, are saved by virtue of the eucharist received by the mother after conception, which sanctifies the child in the womb. Anabaptists play the devil's part (saith a late writer) in accusing their own children, and disputing them out of the Church and covenant of Christ ; affirming them to be no disciples, no servants of God, not holy, as separated to him, when God saith the contrary, Lev. xxv. 41, 42; Deut. xxix. 10—12, &c.; Acts xv. 10, and here.

Ver. 15. *But God hath called us to peace*] To domestical peace, which they that want, *Plus quam dimidiæ beatitudinis suæ parte privati sunt,* saith Aristotle; They have lost the greater half of the happiness of their lives. This was verified in Phoroneus the lawgiver, and Sylla the Roman general. (Bruson.)

Ver. 16. *Whether thou shalt save*] And to have any hand in saving a soul is the highest honour.

Ver. 17. *But God hath distributed*] In case you should not save your yoke-fellow, yet keep your station, be content with your condition, and adorn it, 1 Pet. iii. 1, 2. It is the duty of a Christian (said Luther) to believe things invisible, to hope for things deferred, and to love God when he shows himself contrary to us.

Ver. 18. *Let him not become uncircumcised*] Some Jews, for fear of Antiochus, made themselves uncircumcised, 1 Maccab. i. 16. Others for shame after they were gained to the knowledge of Christ, as here. This was done by drawing up the fore-skin with a chirurgeon's instrument. And of this wicked invention Esau is said to be the first author and practiser. (Godw. Antiq. Hebr.)

Ver. 19. *But the keeping of the commandment*] This is that *bonum hominis,* Mic. vi. 8, that *totum hominis,* Eccles. xii. 23, that one thing necessary, that is better than sacrifice, 1 Sam. xv. 22. *Mallem obedire, quam miracula facere,* saith Luther; I had rather obey than be able to do miracles.

Ver. 20. *Abide in the same calling*] And therein learn to "maintain good works," or to be their crafts-masters, to excel in their profession, *honestis functionibus præesse,* as some render the apostle there, Tit. iii. 8, 14. Αἰὲν ἀριστεύειν καὶ ὑπείροχον ἔμμεναι ἄλλων. These things are good and profitable unto men.

Ver. 21. *Use it rather*] Liberty is that we lost by sin, and affect by nature. *Servus est nomen officii.* A servant is not αὐτόματος, one that moveth absolutely of himself, he is the master's instrument, and ὅλως ἐκείνου, wholly his, saith Aristotle. Oh that we could be God's servants in that sort!

Ver. 22. *For he that is called*] See a parallel place to this, Jam. i. 9, 10. Our preferment in Christ should make us hold up our heads, but not too high, and be cheerful, but not withal scornful. *Læti simus in Domino, sed caveamus a recidivo.* Bern.

Ver. 23. *Ye are bought with a price*] The redeemed among the Romans were to addict themselves to the service of their redeemers, and to observe them as their parents all days of their lives.

Be not ye the servants of men] When they command you things forbidden by Christ, or when they would tyrannize over your consciences, as the Jesuits, that require blind obedience. Cardinal Tolet saith, The people may merit at God's hand in believing a heresy, if their teacher propound it; for their obedience is meritorious. (Cases of Conscience.) If a priest teach it (saith Stapleton), be it true, and be it false, take it as God's oracle. If the Church should approve and authorize Arianism or Pelagianism, saith Erasmus (Epist. ad Firkeimer), I would do so too. But so would no wise man.

Ver. 24. *Let every man wherein,* &c.] This is the same with ver. 20. The apostle inculcateth it, as we not only anoint our benumbed limbs with ointments, but also rub and chafe them in.

Ver. 25. *I give my judgment*] The Rhemists (after Erasmus) render it counsel, and thereupon ground a distinction between Divine commands and counsels. But the word γνώμην betokens *viri boni rectum et verum judicium,* saith Magirus, the right and sound judgment of some good man. (In Arist. Ethic.) And surely if the apostle had no express command from Christ, neither had he any counsel from him concerning this business.

Ver. 26. *I suppose therefore*] This is his judgment, his vote or verdict: the first part thereof we have here; the second, ver. 28; the third, ver. 35.

Ver. 27. *Art thou bound to a wife?*] A manifest metaphor from oxen. Hence we call them yoke-fellows:

Quam male inæquales veniunt ad aratra juvenci;
Tam premitur magno, &c. (Ovid. Epist.)

Dare not to yoke thyself with any untamed heifer that bears not Christ's yoke.

Ver. 28. *Thou hast not sinned*] If any man call lawful marriage a sinful defilement, he hath the apostate dragon dwelling in him, saith Ignatius. (Epist. ad Philadelph.) And yet the Papists teach that it is a far greater sin for a priest to have a wife than to keep many harlots.

Such shall have trouble in the flesh] Mark that he saith, "in the flesh;" the delights of wedlock will be alloyed with troubles, to avoid surfeit. Before marriage people promise themselves much happiness in that estate, and think they could live together with all delight; but after, they see they are deceived, and therefore need to go to school to learn how to behave themselves one toward another.

But I spare you] q. d. No more of that; and yet I'll show you a way how you may 'scape, or at least mitigate those troubles in the flesh. Thus this First Epistle of Paul to the Corinthians, though in weight of argument it be far inferior to the preceding Epistle to the Romans, yet in variety of things it ought to be judged equal, and in order of time before the other. *Thesaurus sane est, imo vere mundus rerum cognitu dignissimarum,* as Erasmus saith of Pliny's Natural History: surely it is a treasure, yea, a very world of things, most worthy to be understood.

Ver. 29. *This then I say, brethren*] The best counsel I can give you, is, that you hang loose to all these outward comforts, as having yourselves but a while to be here. You have a long task, and but a little time. God hath hanged the heaviest weights upon the weakest wires; for upon this moment depends eternity. *Castigemus igitur mores et moras nostras.* Up, therefore, and be doing.

The time is short] Gr. συνεσταλμένος, contracted and rolled up, as sails used to be by the mariners, when the ship draws nigh to the harbour. Others say, it is a metaphor from a piece of cloth rolled up, only a little left at the end. So hath God rolled up all his works, only he hath left a little at the end, and then all his glory shall appear. The time is short, saith the apostle, and you have business enough another way; therefore let other things (as wiving and buying, &c.) pass, and mind the main. There is water little enough to run in the right channel, therefore let none run beside. Some that have lain a dying would have given a world for time: as I have heard (saith a reverend man) one crying day and night, Call time again. And I also have known the like of a great lady of this land. Let us therefore use all speed and diligence, lest (so as children have usually torn their books) we have ended our lives before we have learned our lessons; or (as Themistocles) we begin but to be wise when we come to die.

They that have wives, &c.] Not be uxorious, sith they know not how soon God may take from them, as he did from Ezekiel, the delight of their eyes, their dearest spouses. The Jews at this day have a custom, when a couple are married, to break the glass wherein the bridegroom and bride drank; thereby to admonish them of their dying condition, and that there must be a parting again ere long. (Sphinx. Philos.)

Ver. 30. *And they that weep*] viz. In the loss of wife or children: let them moderate their grief, as Abraham did in the loss of Sarah, Gen. xxiii. 2. "He came to weep for her;" where the Hebrew hath one little letter extraordinary, to note, that Abraham wept but a little for her; and this, not because she was old and over-worn (as the Rabbins give the reason), but because he had hope of a happy resurrection, 1 Thess. iv. 14, and because she was his still, though dead; therefore he so oft in that chapter calleth her "my dead," ver. 4, 11, 13, 15.

And they that rejoice] In the marrying of wives, or birth of children. The marriage-day is called the day of "the rejoicing of a man's heart," Cant. iii. 11: and when should men be merry rather than at the recovering of the lost rib? But he was to blame that said, he had married a wife, and therefore he could not come. And he was a wiser man that said, *Uxori nubere nolo meæ.* (Martial.)

As if they possessed not] Mind earthly things we must, as if we minded them not: as a man may hear a tale, and have his mind elsewhere; or as a man that baits at an inn, his mind is somewhere else. A right believer (saith Mr Ward) goes through the world as a man whose mind is in a deep study; or as one that hath special haste of some weighty business. *Rebus non me trado, sed commodo,* saith Seneca. Be not wholly dulled

or drowned in the world; look at it out of the eyes' end only, lest, as the serpent Scytale, it bewitch us with its beautiful colours, and sting us to death.

Ver. 31. *As not abusing it*] Not shooting our affections over-far into it. David was as a weaned child, Paul as a crucified man. If Job's heart had not been weaned from the world, when as yet he wallowed in worldly wealth, he could not have borne so bravely the ruin of so rich a state without repining. The devil hath no way to entangle us, but to say, as he did to Christ, *Mitte te deortum,* Cast thyself down, pitch upon the bait, eat and devour hook and all. We have no safer way to escape him, than by minding the main, and looking upon all things here below as by-businesses. The Fathers make this observation here; that the joys of this world are but *quasi,* as if they were joys, not joys indeed, but shadows or figures, as Isa. xxix. 8, like the commotions of the affections in a dream.

For the fashion of this world] The word σχῆμα signifies a mathematical figure, which is a mere notion, and nothing in substance. So Psal. xxxix. 6, "Surely every man walketh in a vain shadow," he leadeth an imaginary life, rather than a life itself. The pomp of this world is but a fantasy, Acts xxv. 23. (See the note there.) The glory of it, an opinion. The word here used intimateth that there is nothing of any firmness or solid consistency in the creature. It is but a surface, outside, empty promise; all the beauty of it is but skin-deep. The word here used signifies, say some, such a fashion as is in a comedy or stage-play, where all things are but for a while, to please the eye.

Passeth away] Temporals are as transitory as a hasty headlong torrent. The posting sun of all worldly pleasure, after a short gleam of vain glistering, sets in the ocean of endless sorrow. In the pope's enthronization, before he is set in his chair, and puts on his triple crown, a piece of tow or wad of straw is set on fire before him, and one appointed to say, *Sic transit gloria mundi,* The glory of this world is but a blaze. It is indeed an *ignis fatuus,* a walking fire that leadeth men into brakes and ditches. And so some render this text. The fashion or hue of this world deceiveth, misleadeth, carrieth men another way, out of their way, παράγει. *Fallit, transversum agit.* (Bud.) For of the world we may say as Plutarch saith of Herodotus, Both the words and shows of it are full of fraud. Δολερὰ μὲν τὰ σχήματα, δολερὰ δε τὰ ῥήματα. *Nec tantum fallacia sunt quia dubia* (saith Lactantius), *sed et insidiosa, quia dulcia.*

Ver. 32. *Without carefulness*] That unavoidably attendeth the marriage-state, Gen. xxx. 30; 1 Tim. v. 8.

Ver. 33. *Careth how he may please*] He taketh extraordinary care to please, and so doth she, ver. 34. The word μεριμνᾷ implies a dividing of the mind into divers thoughts, casting this way and that way, and every way, how to give best content. That is a happy study.

Ver. 34. *Careth for the things*] *Expeditius vacat.*

Holy both in body and spirit] For contemplative wickedness and mental uncleanness also greatly displeaseth God. *Incesta est, et sine stupro, quæ stuprum cupit,* saith Seneca (In Declam.) ; and, *Quæ quia non licuit non facit, illa facit,* saith Ovid. The very desire to do evil is to do evil. The Romans punished one of their Vestal Virgins for uttering this verse only :

Fælices nuptæ ! moriar ni nubere dulce est.

Oh! 'tis a brave thing to be married.

How she may please her husband] As Sarah did Abraham, calling him lord; as Rebecca did Isaac, by providing him the meat that he loved; as Livia did Augustus, by observing his disposition, and drawing evenly with him, being a piece so just cut for him, as answered him rightly in every joint.

Ver. 35. *That you may attend, &c.*] Gr. εὐπρό-σεδρον. That you may sit close to him, as Mary did, Luke x. 40, whilst Martha was distracted about much service. Let every man bend himself to banish and beat away distractions,

Nam neque chorda sonum reddit, quem vult manus et mens
Poscentique gravem persæpe remittit acutum.

Hor. de Art. Poet.

Ver. 36. *If she pass the flower*] Childhood is counted the flower of age : so long the apostle would have marriage forborne. While the flower of the plant sprouteth, the seed is green, unfit to be sown.

Ver. 37. *And hath so decreed*] Reserving still a liberty of doing otherwise, if need require : which Popish votaries do not.

Ver. 38. *Doth better*] 1. For the better waiting upon God's work without distraction. 2. For the better bearing of persecution.

Ver. 39. *She is at liberty*] The Montanists therefore (and with them Tertullian in his old age) were in an error that condemned second marriage, and said it was no better than fornication. *Secundas nuptias pro fornicationibus habent.* (Aug.) Howbeit that of Jerome is not to be disliked. Think daily of death; and that will be enough to forbid the bans of second marriage.

Ver. 40. *But she is happier*] *i. e.* She shall live more at ease, and have less to care for. And we should contract our cares into as narrow a compass as we can, in hard times especially.

CHAPTER VIII.

Ver. 1. *Now as touching things*] ANOTHER case that they had propounded to him in their letter, chap. vii. 1.

We know] So all pretend. *Sed nummos habuerunt Athenienses ad numerandum, et scientiam ad sciendum.*

That we all have knowledge] But that is not sufficient, unless we have love too. There be many things concur to the making up of a good work, a lawful action.

Knowledge puffeth up] A metaphor from a pair of bellows, blown up and filled with wind. The French fitly call fools *Fols, a follibus, qui nihil continent nisi aerem,* from bellows. Such are all proud fools.

Knowledge puffeth up] Swelling us above measure, unless humility, laid on as a weight, keep us down, and charity regulate our knowledge for the good of others. Knowledge without love is as rain in the middle region. But how foolish were they of whom Austin maketh mention, that neglected the means of knowledge, because knowledge puffeth up, and so would be ignorant, that they might be humble, and want knowledge, that they might want pride. This was to be like Democritus, who plucked out his eyes, to avoid the danger of uncleanness. Or that silly friar, to whom Sir Thomas More wrote this distich ;

Tu bene cavisti, ne te ulla occidere possit
Littera : nam nota est littera nulla tibi.

Thou takest good care the letter kill thee not :
Thy skill is such, thou knowest not B from Bot.

Ver. 2. *If any man think*] This one thing I know, that I know nothing, said Socrates. Neither know I this yet, that I know nothing, saith another. Though I know myself ignorant of many things (saith a third), yet I dare boldly profess with Origen, *Ignorantiam meam non ignoro,* I am not ignorant that I am ignorant. The greatest part of our knowledge is but the least part of our ignorance. And yet how apt are we to think we know all that is knowable : as in Alcibiades' army all would be leaders, none learners. Epicurus said, that he was the first man that ever discovered truth, and yet in many things he was more blind than a beetle. (Aug. de Civ. Dei, 16.) Aratus the astrologer vaunted, that he had counted the stars and written of them all. *Hoc ego primus vidi,* said Zabarel. And Laurentius Valla boasted, that there was no logic worthy to be read but his, which therefore he called, *Logicam Laurentinam.* Joseph Scaliger is for his human learning called by one *Dæmonium et miraculum hominis naturæ,* a matchless man. But surely it had been happy for him to have been ignorant of this one thing, that he knew so much. He might, by his skill in languages, have much advanced the literary republic, had he not so much admired himself, and more seriously affected to seem witty than ponderous. Wine is good, when it goes to the heart to cheer it; but when it fumes all up into the head, it maketh it giddy : so doth knowledge. Nestorius the heretic bragged that he alone understood the Scriptures; and that, till his time, all the world was benighted. He afterwards fell into horrid blasphemy, and died in banishment.

Ver. 3. *But if any man love God*] And his

neighbour for God's sake; his friends in God, his foes for God.

The same is known of him] That is, knows him savingly, Gal. iv. 9, is taught of God, 1 Thess. iv. 9, who only gives true wisdom, James i. 5.

Ver. 4. *Is nothing in the world*] A mere fiction it is, that the idol representeth a brat of man's brain. We may well say of it, as one doth of Scaliger's doctrine *De emendatione temporum*, that it is in a manner wholly fictitious, and founded upon the confines of nothing. Nothing the idol is, in respect of the divinity ascribed unto it, as the following words show. Or nothing, that is, of no virtue or value. " Shall I bow down to yonder jackanapes ? " said that martyr (Julius Palmer), pointing to the rood in Paul's.

None other God but one] This the wiser heathen also acknowledged, and for opposing the multitude of gods Socrates suffered. Cicero in his books of the Nature of the Gods, takes pains to show the vanity of heathen deities. And after all, wisheth that he were as well able to find out the true God as to discover the false.

Ver. 5. *That are called gods*] Hesiod reckons up 30,000 of them that were in his time, Τρίς γὰρ μύριοι εἰσὶν ἐπὶ χθονὶ πουλυβοτείρῃ ἀθάνατοι. What an army may we think there were of them in after-ages !

As there be gods many] The serpent's grammar first taught *Deum pluraliter declinare*, " Ye shall be as gods," Gen. iii., saith Damianus.

And lords many] Demi-gods, heroes, whose images were worshipped. Ninus was the first that made an image for his father Belus, and all that came to see it were pardoned for all their offences; whence in time that image came to be worshipped. But they did a very ill office that first brought in images, saith Varro (as Calvin citeth his words), " for they increased error and took away fear." And Plutarch saith, It is sacrilege to worship by images.

Ver. 6. *But to us there is but one God*] Be the gods of the heathen good-fellows (saith one), the true God is a jealous God, and will not share his glory with another.

Of whom are all things, and we for him] So that God is the first cause and the last end of all: which two are the properties of the chief good.

Ver. 7. *Unto this hour*] Though they have been better taught and clearly convinced, yet they stiffly retain, at least, some tincture of their old odd superstitious conceits. No man's speech, whether he be learned or unlearned (saith Cicero), shall ever persuade me from that opinion which I have taken up from mine ancestors concerning the worship of the immortal gods. (De Nat. Deor. iii.)

Their conscience being weak] That is, not rightly informed of the true nature of things indifferent.

Is defiled] By doing what they doubt of.

Ver. 8. *But meat commendeth us not*] This is another objection : meat is indifferent. The apostle answers,

Ver. 9. True, it is indifferent, so it prove not a stumbling-block to the unresolved. For in such a case thou must suspend thy liberty, and forbear to exercise it.

Ver. 10. *Be emboldened*] This is, *Proficere in pejus, ædificare in gehennam*, as Tertullian hath it. Whiles men look upon parti-coloured objects, they bring forth spotted fruits, as Laban's sheep did.

Ver. 11. *Thy weak brother perish*] Revolt to paganism, or at least pollute his conscience with mortal sin, which shall be set upon thy score. And hast thou not sins enough of thine own to answer for ?

Ver. 12. *And wound their weak consciences*] Gr. τύπτοντες, beat upon it to make it sound heavily, as a shaulm. Sin is as a stroke upon the heart, 2 Sam. xxiv. 10.

Ye sin against Christ] Who holds himself highly concerned in the misusages of his servants. It is an idle misprision to sever the sense of an injury done to any of the members, from the head. Joab had slain Abner and Amasa. David appropriates it; " Thou knowest " (saith he to Solomon) " what Joab did to me." The arraignment of mean malefactors runs in the style of wrong to the king's crown and dignity. So here.

Ver. 13. *While the world standeth*] We must stand unchangeably resolved, neither to give offence carelessly, nor to take offence causelessly.

CHAPTER IX.

Ver. 1. *Am I not an apostle, &c.*] THAT is to say, Do I require you to do anything more than I myself do daily, in parting with my proper rights ? All things in a minister should be exemplary, and for imitation; Tit. ii. 7, " In all things show thyself a pattern of good works." The word τύπος, there used, signifies a thing that makes the stamp on the coin, or the mould whereinto the vessel is cast and shaped.

Have I not seen the Lord ?] viz. In visions and ecstasies. The false apostles reported him no apostle because he had not conversed with Christ in the flesh. It is ordinary with seducers to detract from the truth's champions, that they may be the better esteemed of. Thus Bellarmine rejecteth the fathers and others that make not for him as heretics. To Irenæus, Tertullian, Eusebius, and Luther (said he) I answer, *Omnes manifesti hæretici sunt*, they are all manifest heretics. So Arminius's course was to detract from the authority and fame of Calvin, Zanchi, Beza, Martyr, &c., that he might build himself upon better men's ruins. (Synod. Dordec. Præfat.) The Jesuits speak most basely of St Paul, as making much against many of their tenets; and stick not to teach in their pulpits, that he was not secure of his preaching but by conference with St Peter; nor that he durst publish his Epistles till St Peter had allowed them. Zuinglius mentioneth some bold fellows in his time, A. D. 1519, that spake very contemptuously of this great apostle : *Quis tandem Paulus, &c.* Calvin telleth us that Quintinus the Libertine called him *Vas fractum*, a broken vessel. And Leo Judæ, in his preface to Bullinger's book against the Catabaptists, noteth, that albeit there were sundry sorts of those sectaries, and all at odds amongst themselves, yet they all concurred in this, that they vexed and disparaged the godly preachers of the truth. And do they not still *antiquum obtinere,* hold to their old wont ?

Ver. 2. *The seal of mine apostleship*] See the like, Jer. xxiii. 22, and Matt. xxi. 28, where our Saviour proveth John Baptist's ministry to be from heaven, by the success.

Ver. 3. *Mine answer to them, &c.*] Or, this is mine apology to those that cavil and quarrel my calling, viz. that I have converted you and others ; a real proof, an ocular demonstration. So 2 Cor. xiii. 3—5.

Ver. 4. *To eat and to drink*] At the Church's charge ; so that we do it moderately without excess, as Josiah did, and it went well with him, Jer. xxii. 15.

Ver. 5. *To lead about a sister*] At the Church's charge likewise. The Papists that deny the lawfulness of minister's marriage, are condemned and cursed by their own canon-law (Distinct 29 and 31.) See Acts and Monuments, fol. 1008. Paphnutius opposed this proposition in the Nicene Council, and prevailed.

Ver. 6. *To forbear working*] At our trade ? Yes, or else I should easily be of Melancthon's mind, who when one had said of the ministry, that it was the art of arts, and the science of sciences ; if he had added (said Melancthon) that it is the misery of miseries, he had hit the nail on the head. (Joh. Manl. loc. com. 471.)

Ver. 7. *Who goeth a warfare, &c.*] Ministers, as they should be valiant as soldiers, diligent as husbandmen, vigilant as shepherds (*Pastor, arator, eques, &c.*), so should they live of their labour, as every tinker and tapster doth. It is a sign of gasping devotion, when men are so close-handed to their ministers whose very cold water goes not unrewarded.

Ver. 8. *Or saith not the law*] Not of nations only, as ver. 7, but of God expressly, *Verbis non solum disertis, sed et exertis ?*

Ver. 9. *Doth God take care for oxen ?*] He doth, doubtless, John iv. 11 ; he preserveth man and beast ; he heareth the young ravens that cry to him only by implication. Doth he not then much more take care for men, for ministers ? The Hebrews have a proverb, *Bos debet edere ex tritura sua,* The ox should eat of the corn he treadeth out. But now-a-days, by slight or might, they so muzzle the poor labouring ox that they make an ass of him, saith one. In many places they allow him nothing but straw, for treading out the corn ; and so much straw as themselves please, saith another. Do they not now go about to deal by Christ's faithfulest servants, as those Grecians did, that put an engine about their

servants' neck (called πανσικοπὴ) which reached down to their hands, that they might not so much as lick of the meal, when they were sifting it ? (Dr Stoughton.) It was long since complained of, that many dealt by their ministers as carriers do by their horses, they laid heavy burdens upon them, and then hung bells about their necks : hard work and good words they shall have ; but easy commons and slight wages ; as if they were of the chameleon kind, and could live by air, &c. The statute of mortmain provided that men should give no more to the Church, but now *tempora mutantur.*

Ver. 10. *Should plough in hope*] Of maintaining his life by his labour, which is therefore called "the life of our hands," because it is upheld by the labour of our hands : *Ludit, qui sterili semina mandat humo.* (Propert.)

Ver. 11. *Is it a great thing, &c.*] Do not we give you gold for brass ? Cast we not pearls before you ? Alexander the Great gave Aristotle for his book *de Natura Animalium*, 800 talents, which is 800,000 crowns at least. Theodorus Gaza translated that book into Latin, and dedicated it to Pope Sixtus. The pope asked him how much the rich outside of the book stood him in ; Gaza answered, forty crowns. Those forty crowns he commanded to be repaid him, and so sent him away without any reward for so precious a piece of work. *Interrogavit asinus papa quanti ornatus constaret ?* (John Manl. loc. com.) How well might the poor old Grecian sit and sing,

Heu male nunc artes miseras hæc sæcula tractant, Spes nulla ulterior. (Juven. Satir. 7.)

Ver. 12. *If others be partakers*] If your ordinary pastors, &c., for the false apostles preached gratis (as some gather out of 2 Cor. xi. 12), partly to draw more disciples, and partly to bring an odium upon the apostle, if he should not do the like.

Ver. 13. *Live of the things of, &c.*] Yea, they lived plentifully and richly, as appears by the liberal gifts of those Levites for Passover-offerings, 2 Chron. xxxv. 9.

Ver. 14. *Even so hath the Lord*] Note that "so," saith one ; "that is, as they of old lived at the altar by tithes, so ministers now. How else will men satisfy their consciences in the particular quantity they must bestow upon the ministers ? The Scripture speaks only of the tenth part."

Ver. 15. *Better for me to die*] To be hunger-starved than to do anything to the prejudice of the gospel. Affliction is to be chosen rather than sin, Job xxxvi. 21. *Quas non oportet mortes præeligere*, saith Zuinglius, Epist. 3. What death should not a man choose, nay, what hell, rather than to sin against his conscience ? Daniel chose rather to be cast into the lions' den than to bear about that lion in his own bosom. The primitive Christians thought it far better to be thrown to lions without, than to be left to lusts within. *Ad leonem magis quam lenonem.* (Tertul.) *Potius in ardentem rogum insiluero, quam ullum peccatum in Deum commisero*, said a good man once. I will rather leap into a bonfire, than wilfully commit any wickedness. The mouse of Armenia will rather die than be defiled with any filth. If her hole be besmeared with dirt, she will rather choose to perish with hunger than be polluted. Such was Paul here, and such we ought all to be.

Ver. 16. *I have nothing to glory of*] My glorying is, that I preach it gratis, and thereby stop an open mouth, 2 Cor. xii. 16—18, give them the lie that falsely accuse me that I make a prize of you.

Yea, woe is unto me] It was death for the high-priest to enter the tabernacle without his bells. Preach, man, preach; thou wilt be damned else, said one to his friend. Be instant, or stand over the work in season, out of season, ἐπίστηθι. See Jacob's diligence, Gen. xxxi. 40. And Paul's, Acts xx. 20—28, &c., which one rightly calleth St Paul's trumpet, the voice whereof may be to every minister, like that trumpet in Mount Sinai, that hath both *clangorem et horrorem:* or as Samuel's message, making Eli's two ears to tingle and his heart to tremble. (Barlow.) Let him give good heed to it, and then say with the civilian (Ulpian), *Perquam durum est: sed ita lex scripta est.* Hard or not hard it must be done, or I am utterly undone. Preach I must, or perish.

Ver. 17. *I have a reward*] Yet not earned, but of free grace, God crowning his own works in us. He was a proud Papist that said, *Cœlum gratis non accipiam*, I will not have heaven for nought. (Vega.) And he another, that said, *Opera bona mercatura regni cœlestis*, Good works are the price of heaven. (Bellarm.) God will cast all such merit-merchants out of his temple.

But if against my will] *Virtus nolentium, nulla est.* God will strain upon no man. All his servants are a free people, Psal. cx. 3. All his soldiers volunteers. They fly to their colours as the doves to their windows, Isa. lx. 8.

Ver. 18. *What is my reward then?*] My *merces mundi*, all that I have here.

That I abuse not] *i. e.* That I make no indiscreet use of it. *Non opes, non gloriam, non voluptates quæsivi* (said holy Melancthon). *Hanc conscientiam aufero quocunque discedo.* I never sought wealth, honour, or pleasure. This my conscience tells me, whatever becomes of me.

Ver. 19. *That I may gain the more*] The Greek word for gain signifieth withal the joy and delight of the heart in gaining. It signifies also craft or guile, such as is that of the fox; which when he is very hungry after prey, and can find none, he lieth down and feigneth himself to be a dead carcase, and so the fowls fall upon him, and then he catcheth them. So must a minister deny himself to gain his hearers. κέρδος quod κέαρ ἥδει.

Ver. 20. *And unto the Jews*, &c.] Not in conforming to their impieties; but, 1. In the use of things indifferent; 2. In merciful compassion toward them.

To them that are under the law] Though not Jews born, yet proselytes, as the Ethiopian eunuch, Cornelius, &c.

Ver. 21. *That I might gain them*] A metaphor from merchants, *Qui κερδαίνοντες οὐ κοπιῶσι*, who are never weary of taking money. (Naz.) St Paul harps much upon this string, out of a strong desire of winning souls to God. Ministers must turn themselves into all shapes and fashions both of spirit and speech to gain souls to God. Christ useth every engine of wisdom (πάσῃ σοφίας μηχανῇ, saith Clemens Alexand.) that he may convert some. Ministers should labour to be masters of their people's affections, δημαγωγοί, as the Athenian orators were called, *i. e.* people-leaders.

Ver. 22. *To the weak*] Not pressing upon them the austerities of religion, but condescending and complying with them, as far as I could with a good conscience.

That I might save some] This is the highest honour in the world, to have any hand in the saving of souls. Let all of an ability put forth themselves hereunto; and if they have not fine manchet, yet give the poor people barley bread, or whatsoever else the Lord hath committed unto them, as Bucer bade Bradford. (Acts and Mon.)

Ver. 23. *That I might be partaker*] *i. e.* That I might be saved together with you. For the bell may call men to the Church, though itself never enter. The field may be well sowed with a dirty hand; the well yield excellent water, though it have much mud. Noah's builders were drowned: and the sign that telleth the passenger there is wholesome diet or warm lodging within, may itself remain in the storms without. See 1 Tim. iv. 16. *Nihil turpius est Peripatetico claudo.* Oh how many heavenly doctrines are in some people's ears, that never were in the preacher's heart. So true is that of Hilary, *Sanctiores sunt aures plebis, quam corda sacerdotum.*

Ver. 24. *Know ye not*] The apostle argueth from their profane sports, yet approveth them not; as neither doth the Lord patronize usury, Matt. xxv. 27; injustice, Luke xvi. 1; theft, 1 Thess. v. 2; dancing, Matt. xi. 17.

So run that ye may obtain] Here is the race, but above the crown, saith Ignatius to Polycarp. (ὧδε μὲν ἐστὶ τὸ στάδιον, ἐκεῖ δὲ οἱ στέφανοι.) Run to get the race, said Mr Bradford to his fellow-sufferers, you are almost at your journey's end. I doubt not but our Father will with us send to you also, as he did to Elias, a fiery chariot to convey us into his kingdom. Let us therefore not be dismayed to leave our cloak behind us, that is, our bodies to ashes. (Acts and Mon.)

Ver. 25. *Is temperate in all things*] These luxurious Corinthians were much addicted to their belly; he calls them therefore to temperance. Ill doth it become a servant of the Highest to be a slave to his palate, to have *animum in patinis et calicibus*, as the Sybarites. A man may eat that on earth that he must digest in hell. (Aug.)

Ver. 26. *Not as uncertainly*] For, 1. I forget those things that are behind, all worldly things, I set those by. 2. I have *oculum ad metam* (which was Ludovicus Vives' motto), an eye upon the mark. 3. I strain and stretch toward it. See all these Phil. iii. 13, 14. Duties are not to be done in a lazy, formal, customary strain, like the pace the Spaniard rides; but with utmost diligence and expedition.

That beats the air] As young fencers use to do, but I beat mine adversary.

Ver. 27. *My body*] My body of sin in the whole man, not mine outward man only. If we find the devil practising upon the flesh, the way is not to revile the devil, but to beat the flesh. Give it a blue eye, leave a blot in the face of it, as the word ὑπωπιάζω signifieth; batter it as those were wont, that tried masteries with plummets of lead; we owe it nothing but stripes, Rom. viii. 12. It is of a slavish nature, and must be held hard under, δουλαγωγῶ; as slaves thrust into a mill, or bound to an oar.

A castaway] Cast out of heaven, as they were out of the fencing schools, that were either cross or cowardly; or that could offend, but not defend. An orator (how much more a preacher!) should be *vir bonus dicendi peritus*, a good man able to discourse. (Quintilian.) Diogenes blamed those orators that studied *bene dicere, non bene facere*, to speak well, but not to do accordingly. And Chrysostom saith, *Nihil frigidius est doctore verbis solummodo philosophante. Hoc non est doctoris sed histrionis.* A wordy doctor is an unworthy creature, and more fit to make a stage-player than a preacher.

CHAPTER X.

Ver. 1. *I would not that ye should*] *Historiæ fidæ monitrices*, saith Bucholcer. There is very good use to be made of other men's examples. *Historia* hath its name, saith Plato, of stopping the flux of errors and evil manners. (παρὰ τὸ ἱστάναι τὸν ῥοῦν, in Crat.) For *mutato nomine de te fabula narratur.* What bitter effects sin hath produced in some men, it may in any man. *Lege igitur historiam, ne fias historia.*

Ver. 2. *And were all baptized*] And yet were rooted out and rejected. Baptism saveth; not the putting away of the filth of the flesh, but, &c., 1 Pet. iii. 21. By this text it appears that infants also were baptized unto Moses, who was a typical mediator; therefore they ought to be into Christ, the true. It is here objected that those infants did also eat manna and drink of the rock; therefore by a like reason, they should also now receive the Lord's supper. For answer, 1. How doth it appear that they did eat manna, &c.? 2. Though they did, yet they may not communicate at the Lord's table, because they cannot "examine themselves, nor discern the Lord's body," and are therefore flatly forbidden to come there, chap. xi. 28, 29.

Ver. 3. *And did all eat*] They fed upon sacra-

ments, and yet died in God's displeasure. The carcase of the sacrament cannot give life, but the soul of it, which is the thing represented. It is well observed that sacraments do not work as physic, whether men sleep or wake, *ex opere operato*, by virtue inherent in them; but *ex opere operantis*, according to the disposition and qualification of the party that partaketh.

Ver. 4. *The same spiritual drink*] Here was no dry communion.

That spiritual rock that followed them] The waters of the rock, the virtue and benefit, went along with them. See Psal. cv. 41; Deut. ix. 21. So should the efficacy of the Lord's supper with us. We should walk in the strength of it, as Elijah did of his cake.

Ver. 5. *They were overthrown*] They died with the sacramental meat in their mouths. Our privileges excuse us not, but aggravate our enormities.

Ver. 6. *Were our examples*] Worthily are they made examples, that will not take them. *Alterius perditio tua sit cautio.* The destruction of others should be a terror to us, that we may wash our feet in the blood of the wicked, Psal. lii. 6. It is a just presage and desert of ruin, not to be warned.

As they also lusted] As at Kibroth Hattaavah, where by a hasty testament they bequeathed a new name to the place of their burial.

Ver. 7. *And rose up to play*] Now if they were so cheered and strengthened by these murdering morsels, should not we be made active and abundant in God's word by the dainties of God's table?

Ver. 8. *And fell in one day*] The apostle, instead of the cloak of heat of youth, puts upon fornication a bloody cloak, bathed in the blood of twenty-three thousand. (Knewstub. on Com. 7.)

Three and twenty thousand] Moses mentions 24,000, whereof one thousand were the chief princes, the others inferiors, provoked to sin by their example. But why doth the apostle insist in the special punishment of the people? To show (saith learned Junius) how frigid and insufficient their excuse is, that pretend for their sins the examples of their superiors.

Ver. 9. *Neither let us tempt*] By provoking him to jealousy, as ver. 22, especially by idolatry, that land-desolating sin.

Ver. 10. *As some of them also*] viz. Numb. xiv. And God said Amen to it, ver. 28. May he not justly say the same to our detestable God-damn-me's? "As truly as I live, saith the Lord, as ye have spoken in mine ears, so will I do to you."

Ver. 11. *For our admonition*] God hangs up some, as it were, in gibbets, for public example. See ver. 6. Let us therefore set a memorandum upon God's punishments; and mark his spits with our stars. Let us be wise by other men's woes; take a pearl out of the serpent, a good stone out of the toad's head, suck sweet honey out of bitterest weeds, &c.

Upon whom the ends, &c.] These then are the last and worst days, the very lees and dregs of time. Now the worse the times are, the better we should be; and the rather, because an end of all things is at hand.

Ver. 12. *That thinks he' stands*] If he do but think so, if he be no more than a seemer, he will fall at length into hell-mouth. A man may live by a form, but he cannot die by a form. Therefore rather seek to be good than seem to be so.

Ver. 13. *But such as is common*] Such as is human, πᾶν προσδοκᾶν δεῖ ἄνθρωπον ὄντα. (Xenophon.) Either such as is incident to men as men, Job v. 6; or such as men may well bear without buckling under it; or such as come from men, not from devils; "Ye wrestle against flesh and blood," &c. Or you are yet only allured to idolatry, not forced by persecution. You gratify your idolatrous acquaintance with your presence at their idol-feasts; you are tempted and soon taken.

But God is faithful] When Mr Latimer stood at the stake, and the tormentors about to set fire to him and Ridley, he lifted up his eyes toward heaven with an amiable and comfortable countenance, saying these words, *Fidelis est Deus,* &c. Ridley also at the stake, with a wondrous cheerful look, ran to Latimer, embraced and kissed, and, as they that stood near reported, comforted him, saying, Be of good heart, brother, God will either assuage the fury of the flame, or else will strengthen us to abide it. (Acts and Mon.)

But will with the temptation] He proportioneth the burden to the back, and the stroke to the strength of him that beareth it. I thank God, said Mr Bradford, my common disease (which was a rheum, with a feebleness of stomach) doth less trouble me than when I was out of prison, which doth teach me the merciful providence of God toward me.

Ver. 14. *Flee from idolatry*] He calleth their sitting at the idol's feasts, though without intent of honouring the idol, by the name of idolatry; because, 1. Hereby they yielded a tacit consent to that sin. 2. Petty matters pave a causey for the greater.

Ver. 15. *I speak as to wise men*] i. e. Well skilled in the doctrine of the sacraments, from one of which I am about to argue. Piscator, after he had read some of the Fathers, gave over for this reason, because scarce any of them did rightly understand the use and efficacy of baptism.

Judge ye what I say] Jovianus the emperor was wont to wish that he might govern wise men, and that wise men might govern him.

Ver. 16. *The cup of blessing*] Not the chalice, but the common cup. Calvin chose rather to leave Geneva than to use unleavened bread or wafer-cakes at the Lord's supper. (*Diest. de ratione studii Theol.*) We may not symbolize with idolaters.

Is it not the communion] Doth it not signify

and set forth, yea, as an instrument, effect and exhibit this communion?

Ver. 17. *And one body*] By the force of faith and love. Cant. vi. 9, "My dove is but one; the daughters saw her, and blessed her." No such oneness, entireness anywhere as among the saints. Other societies are but as the clay in the toes of Nebuchadnezzar's image, they may cleave together, but not incorporate one into another.

Ver. 18. *Are not they which eat, &c.*] See Levit. vii. 15; hence he infers that these Corinthians also eating of the idol's sacrifices, were defiled with idolatry; *a pari.*

Ver. 19. *What say I then*] He prevents a mistake. See chap. viii. 4. Ministers must in their discourses meet with all objections as much as may be.

Ver. 20. *They sacrifice to devils*] A good intention then excuseth not. The Gentiles thought they had sacrificed to God. So do the Papists, who yet worship devils, whiles they worship idols of gold, and silver, and brass, and stone, Rev. ix. 20. The devil is εἰδωλοχαρὴς, saith Synesius, an idol-lover.

Ver. 21. *Partakers of the Lord's table*] Name and thing. The Popish opinion of mass was, that it might not be celebrated but upon an altar, or at least upon a *superaltare*, which must have its prints and carects, or else the thing was not thought to be lawfully done. Our communion table they call an oyster-board. (Acts and Mon.)

And the table of devils] Redwald, king of East Saxons, had in the same church one altar for Christian religion, and another for sacrifice to devils. (Camden.)

Ver. 22. *Do we provoke the Lord*] As Caligula that dared his Jove to a duel; as the raging Turk at the last assault of Scodra most horribly blaspheming God. But who knoweth the power of his anger? Psal. xc. 11. It is such as none can avert or avoid, avoid or abide. To such therefore as will needs provoke the Lord, we may well say, as Ulysses' companions said to him, when he would needs provoke Polydamas;

Σχέτλιε τίπτ' ἐθέλεις ἐρεθίζεμεν ἄγριον ἀνδρὰ.
What mean'st thou, wretch, to enrage this
    cruel man?

Ver. 23. *All things are not expedient*] *An liceat, an deceat, an expediat,* are three most needful questions. (Bernard.) Things lawful in themselves may be unseemly for our state and calling; unbehoveful also to the benefit of others. Think unlawful for thee whatsoever implies either inexpediency or indecency.

Ver. 24. *Let no man seek his own*] Self miscarries us all, and makes us eccentric in our motions, nothing more.

Ver. 25. *Whatsoever is sold, &c.*] A portion of the consecrated flesh was usually sold by the priests, who make their markets of it, as Augustine upon the Romans testifieth.

Ver. 26. *For the earth is the Lord's*] God,

of his bounty, spreads a table for all; make no scruple therefore, eat freely.

Ver. 27. *And ye be disposed to go*] Our Saviour, when he saw that John's austerity was censured, took his liberty in the use of creatures, and convenient company-keeping, Luke vii. 33, 34. I do not find where ever he was bidden to any table and refused. Not for a pleasure of the dishes, but for the benefit of so winning a conversation.

Ver. 28. *The earth is the Lord's*] Therefore in case of scandal abstain. Why shouldest thou use this creature, as if there were no more but this? suspend thy liberty; hast not thou all the world before thee?

Ver. 29. *Why is my liberty judged*] As a profane licence. We should be shy of the very shows and shadows of sin, *Quicquid fuerit male coloratum*, as Bernard hath it; if a thing look but ill-favoured, abstain from it.

Ver. 30. *For if I by grace*] Or, by thanksgiving. The same Greek word, χαρὶς, signifies both; to teach us, that a grateful man is a gracious man. The unthankful and the evil are set together as the same, Luke vi. 35. God is "kind to the unthankful, and to the evil."

Ver. 31. *Whether therefore ye eat, &c.*] Of a reverend Scotch divine it is said, that "he did even eat and drink and sleep eternal life." These common actions also are steps in our Christian walking, despise them not, therefore, but refer them to that supreme scope. Socrates, even in his recreations, profited his companions no less than if he had been reading lectures to them. παίζων οὐδὲν ἧττον ἐλυσιτέλει τοῖς συνδιατρίβουσιν αὐτῶ. (Xenoph.) Plato and Xenophon thought it fit and profitable that men's speeches at meals should be written. *Quicquid agas propter Deum agas*, saith one. *Propter te Domine, propter te*, saith another. (Drus. Apophth.) The glory of God ought to eat up all other ends, as Moses' serpent did the sorcerers' serpents; or as the sun puts out the light of the fire. Jovinian the emperor's motto was, *Scopus vitæ Christus*.

Ver. 32. *Give none offence*] This is another end we should aim at, the edification of others. *Finibus non officiis, a vitiis discernuntur virtutes.* (Augustine.) Two things make a good Christian: good actions and good aims.

Ver. 33. *Not seeking mine own profit*] This, saith Chrysostom, is the most perfect canon of Christianity, the top-gallant of true religion.

CHAPTER XI.

Ver. 1. *Be ye followers of me*] THIS verse properly belongs to the former chapter. The distinguishing of the books of Scripture into chapters is not very ancient. But that of verses was devised and done by Robert Stephens, *Pio quidem at tumultuario studio*, as Scultetus saith well, with a good intent, but with no great skill, as appears here and in divers other places. The apostle, chap. x. 33, had showed his own practice:

here he calls upon them to do accordingly. As the ox follows the herd, so will I follow good men. *Etiamsi errant*, saith Cicero, although they do amiss. *Sicut bos armenta, sic ego bonos viros.* (Cic. ad Attic.) This was more than St Paul desires. Be ye followers of me, saith he; but only so far as I am of Christ, not an inch further. Christians are not bound, as Latimer saith, to be the saints' apes; labouring to be like them in everything. It is Christ's peculiar honour to be imitated in all morals absolutely.

Ver. 2. *And keep the ordinances*] Gr. the traditions or doctrines by word of mouth. These are, 1. Dogmatical, concerning faith and practice, 2 Thess. ii. 15. 2. Ritual; and these again are, 1. Perpetual, as that of the manner of administering the two sacraments; 2. Temporary, as that of abstaining from certain meats, Acts xv. 28, 29. And those other pertaining to the observing of external order and decency in Church assemblies. And of these the apostle here speaketh. (Sclater.)

Ver. 3. *The head of the woman is man*] Were it not an ill sight to see the shoulders above the head, the woman usurp authority over the man? αὐθεντεῖν, 1 Tim. ii. 12. A prudent wife commands her husband by obeying, as did Livia.

Ver. 4. *Dishonoureth his head*] As they accounted it then and there. In other places it is otherwise. The French preach covered. The Turks neither kneel nor uncover the head at public prayer, as holding those postures unmanly. Several countries have their several customs. Basiliades, duke of Muscovy, showed himself a tyrant in nailing an ambassador's hat to his head, for not uncovering it before him.

Ver. 5. *Praying or prophesying*] That is, joining with the man that prayeth or prophesieth, and going along with him in her heart. Thus the king and all Israel with him offered sacrifice before the Lord, 1 Kings viii. 62. And thus the unlearned say Amen, 1 Cor. xiv. 16. See the note on Rom. xvi. 1.

Ver. 6. *For a woman to be shorn*] Our *Hicmuliers* hold it now no shame. If Henry VI. had seen such creatures, he would have cried out, as once he did at the sight of naked breasts, Fie, fie, ladies, in sooth you are to blame. (Daniel's Hist.)

Ver. 7. *He is the image and glory of God*] Even as an image in the glass doth look toward us, from whom it is reflected. So, saith one, doth God's image in us make the eyes of our minds view him the author of it in us. (Bayn's Letters.) And as the eye becometh one with that which it seeth, and is after a sort in that light it beholdeth; so are we by the vision of God, which is begun in us, one with him and in him.

The woman is the glory of the man] Either because he may glory in her, if she be good; or because she is to honour him, and give glory to him.

Ver. 8. *But the woman of the man*] Of a bone she was made, and but one bone, *Ne esset ossea,* saith a divine (Vitis Palatina); a bone of the side it was, not of the head (she is not to be his mistress), not of the foot (she is not to be his handmaid), but of the side, to show that she is a companion to her husband. A bone from under the arm, to mind the man of protection and defence to the woman. A bone not far from his heart, to mind him of dilection and love to the woman. A bone from the left side, to put the woman in mind that, by reason of her frailty and infirmity, she stands in need of both the one and the other from her husband.

Ver. 9. *For the woman*] sc. To serve her, unless it be some women (as Artemisia, Zenobia, Blandina), specially called to and qualified for government. Amongst whom Queen Elizabeth, that female glory, is famous, of whom a great French duchess said, that she was *Gloriosissima, et omnium quæ unquam sceptrum gesserunt fœlicissima fæmina*. Besides her sex, there was nothing in her woman-like or weak.

Ver. 10. *To have power*] That is a veil, called in Hebrew Radid, of Radad, to bear rule. And indeed what was this subjection to the husband, but a kind of power and protection derived to the wife, in respect of her former estate?

Because of the angels] Present in the assemblies of the saints. This was set forth of old by the hangings of the tabernacle wrought with cherubims within and without. Others understand this text of ministers, frequently called angels, Hag. i. 12, 13; Rev. ii. and iii.; Judg. ii. 1 (that angel is thought to be Phineas); Eccles. v. 6. "Neither say thou before the angel" (i. e. before the Lord's priest) "it was an error." (Vorstius.) Some think the apostle argues from the example of the angels; we should imitate their modesty, who were wont to cover their faces, to testify their subjection toward God.

Ver. 11. *Nevertheless neither is*] This is added for the woman's comfort. There must be all mutual respects and melting-heartedness betwixt married couples, which being preserved fresh and fruitful, will infinitely sweeten and beautify the marriage state. Love is a coin that must be exchanged betwixt them, and returned in kind. "Husbands, love your wives," Colos. iii. 16. He saith not, Rule over your wives, as he had said, Wives, submit yourselves to your husbands, but Love your wives; yea, let all your things be done in love: for neither is the man without the woman; he is not complete without her, he wants a piece of himself; neither is the woman without the man, she cannot subsist without him, as the vine cannot without a supporter. The rib can challenge no more of her than the earth can of him, &c.

Ver. 12. *But all things of God*] God consulted not with man to make him happy, saith one. As he was ignorant while himself was made, so he did not know while a second self was made out of him. Both that the comfort might be greater than was expected; as also that he might not upbraid his wife with any great de-

pendence or obligation, he neither willing the work, nor suffering any pain to have it done.

Ver. 13. *Judge in yourselves*] All Christ's sheep are rational, able to discern of things that differ, having their senses thereunto exercised, Heb. v. 14. But some sins are condemned by common sense, as here; and religion is founded upon so good reason, that though God had not commanded it, yet it had been our wisest way to have chosen it. But lust doth oft so blear the understanding, that a man shall think he hath reason to be mad, and that there is great sense in sinning.

Ver. 14. *That if a man hath long hair*] Bushes of vanity, which they will never part with, said Marbury, until the devil put a candle into the bush. But our gallants object, that the apostle here intendeth such hair as is as long as women's hair. Whereunto we answer, That Homer calleth the Greeks hair-nourishing men (καρηκομοῶντας Αχαίους, Homer), who yet did not wear their hair long as women. How Cromwell handled the shag-haired ruffian, see Acts and Monuments of the Church, fol. 1083. How God hath punished this unnatural sin by that loathsome and horrible disease in the hair, called *Plica Polonica*, see Hercules de Saxonia; and out of him Mr Bolton in his Four Last Things, page 40. It begun first, saith he, not many years ago in Poland; it is now entered into many parts of Germany. And methinks our monstrous fashionists, both male and female, the one for nourishing their horrid bushes of vanity, the other for their most unnatural and cursed cutting their hair, should every hour fear and tremble, lest they should bring it upon their own heads, and amongst us in this kingdom. Our Henry I. repressed the wearing of long hair, which though it were a gaiety of no charge, yet for the indecency thereof, he reformed it, and all other dissoluteness. (Daniel's Hist.) See Mr Prins' Unloveliness of Love-locks. See also a book entitled *Diatriba Theologica de capillis, constans disputatione Textuali, ad* 1 Cor. xi. 14, 15.

Ver. 15. *Her hair is given her*] Now it is a vile thing to go against nature. Cyprian and Austin say that garish apparel is worse than whoredom; because whoredom only corrupts chastity, but this corrupts nature.

Ver. 16. *Seem to be contentious*] *A doctore glorioso, et pastore contentioso, et inutilibus questionibus, liberet Ecclesiam suam Dominus*, said Luther. From a vain-glorious doctor, from a contentious pastor, and from endless and needless controversies, the good Lord deliver his Church. The word rendered "seem," signifieth, "is pleased to be, desires and hath a will to be, yea, boasts and prides himself in it," δοκεῖ δοκησίσοφος. This is a foul fault in any, but especially in ministers; who must see (saith Luther) that those three dogs follow them not into the pulpit, pride, covetousness, and contentiousness. A quarrelsome person is like a cock of the kind, ever bloody with the blood of others and himself;

and divisions are Satan's powder-plot to blow up religion.

We have no such custom] viz. To strive about trifles, but to submit to our teachers, Heb. xiii. 17. It is a vile thing, saith Bifield (on 1 Pet. iii.), to vex our ministers by our obstinacy; yea, though they were not able to make so full demonstration, yet when they reprove such things, out of a spiritual jealousy and fear that they corrupt the people's hearts, they are to be heard and obeyed.

Ver. 17. *I praise you not*] q. d. I discommend and dispraise you. The Corinthians were in many things faulty and blame-worthy. St Paul deals plainly and freely with them, and would not therefore take their offered kindness, 2 Cor. xii., lest he should be engaged to them, and by receiving a courtesy, sell his liberty.

Ver. 18. *There be divisions*] Gr. σχίσματα, schisms, rents, yea, and that about the sacrament of the Lord's supper (that bond of love), through Satan's malice. Now there can be no greater sin committed, saith Chrysostom, than to break the peace of the Church. Cyprian saith, It is an inexpiable blemish, such as cannot be washed off with the blood of martyrdom.[1] The error of it may be pardoned (saith Œcolampadius in his epistle to the Lutherans of Suevia) so there be faith in Christ Jesus; but the discord we cannot expiate though we should lay down our lives to do it.

Ver. 19. *There must be heresies*] Therefore much more schisms, which also, for most part, do degenerate into heresies; as an old serpent into a dragon. In the time of Pope Clement V., Frederic, king of Sicily, was so offended at the evil government of the Church, that he began to question the truth of the Christian religion. But Arnoldus de Villanova confirmed and settled him by this and such like places of Scripture, "Offences must come, there must be heresies," &c., God having so decreed and foretold it. It behoves that there be heresies in the Church; as it is necessary there should be poison and venomous creatures in the world, because out of them God will work medicine s

May be made manifest] As they are now, if ever, in these shedding and discriminating times. So in the Palatinate they fell to Popery, as fast as leaves in autumn.

Ver. 20. *This is not to eat*, &c.] When the Lord's supper therefore is not rightly administered, it is no longer his; especially if the substantials thereof be omitted. As in those sacrifices, Hos. ix. 4, "Their bread for their soul shall not come into the house of the Lord;" that is, the bread for their natural sustenance. He speaks of that meat-offering, Levit. ii. 5, appointed for a spiritual use, yet called the "bread for their life or livelihood;" because God esteemed it no other than common meat. So Jer. vii. 21, in scorn he calls their sacrifice, flesh, &c.

Ver. 21. *Every one taketh*] Eateth and communicateth with those of his own sect and fac-

[1] Hom. 11. ad Ephes.

tion only, not staying for others. Such among the Philippians were those of "the concision," chap. iii. 2, that made divisions, and cut the Church into little pieces and sucking congregations, making separation.

Ver. 22. *What, have ye not houses?*] Here he abolished their love-feasts, for the disorder that fell out therein. The Greek Church nevertheless retained them; but the Roman Church laid them down, as Justin Martyr witnesseth.

Ver. 23. *For I have received*] *Rectum est regula sui et obliqui.* The apostle seems to rectify them, by reducing them to the first institution; and by letting them know that he had his authority from heaven; he received what he delivered, and delivered what he received, keeping nothing back, Acts xx. 27.

The same night, &c.] It was his last bequeath to his Church, for a καθαρτήριον ἀλεξίκακον, as Ignatius hath it, a sovereign both purgative and preservative.

This is my body] *En præclaram illam consecrationem*, Behold that goodly consecration (saith Beza) for the which the shavelings say that they are more holy than the very Virgin Mary; for that Mary only conceived Christ, but they create him. Whereunto the Virgin might well reply, that she carefully nourished Christ, whom they cruelly devour. Dost thou believe (said the doctor to the martyr) that Christ's body and blood is in the eucharist really and substantially? I believe, saith he, that that is a real lie, and a substantial lie. When Cranmer was brought forth to dispute in Oxford, Dr Weston, Prolocutor, thus began the disputation, *Convenistis hodie, fratres, profligaturi detestandam illam hæresin de veritate corporis Christi in Sacramento, &c.* At which mistake, divers learned men burst out into a great laughter.

Ver. 25. *He took the cup*] See the note on Matt. xxvi. 27.

Ver. 26. *Ye do show*] We need no other crucifix to mind us of Christ's passion. Hence this sacrament was by some ancients termed a sacrifice, viz. representative and commemorative, but not properly, as the Papists make it.

Till he come] There shall be a Church then, and the pure worship of God, till the world's end, maugre the malice of tyrants and heretics.

Ver. 27. *Shall be guilty*] Because they profane the holy symbols and pledges of Christ's blessed body and blood. These are in some sense as guilty as those that spit upon Christ's face, or that spilt his blood. As the Donatists, that cast the holy elements to dogs; or as that wretched Booth, a Bachelor of Arts in St John's College in Cambridge, who being popishly affected, at the time of the communion took the consecrated bread, and forbearing to eat it, conveyed and kept it closely for a time, and afterwards threw it over the college wall. Not long after this, he threw himself headlong over the battlements of the chapel and so ended his life. (Bishop Morton, Instit. of the Sac.)

Ver. 28. *Let a man examine*] A metaphor

from metallaries or lapidists, as they try their metals or precious stones, and do it exactly, that they be not cozened; so here, men must make an exact scrutiny.

And so let him eat] After preparation, participation. The heathens had their *cœna pura*, the night before their sacrifices. The Russians receive children after seven years old to the communion, saying, that at that age they begin to sin against God. But can they say, that at that age they can examine themselves and receive preparedly? Chrysostom calleth the Lord's table, that "dreadful table" (φρικώδης), and the ancients call the sacraments "dreadful mysteries" (τὰ φρικτὰ μυστήρια).

Ver. 29. *For he that eateth and drinketh unworthily*] He saith not unworthy (for so we are all) but unworthily, that is, unpreparedly, for a good work may be spoiled in the doing, as many a good tale is marred in the telling, and many a good garment in the making.

Eateth and drinketh damnation] He that came in without a wedding-garment on his back, went not away without fetters on his feet. He was taken from the table to the tormentors. God's table becomes a snare to unworthy receivers; they eat their bane, they drink their poison. Henry VII., emperor of Germany, was poisoned in the sacramental bread by a monk; Pope Victor II. by his sub-deacon in the chalice; and one of our bishops of York by poison put into the wine at sacrament. God will deal with ill communicants as Job xx. 23. They will speed no better than Amnon did at Absalom's feast; or than Haman did at Esther's. Sin brought to the sacrament, picks out that time to petition against them, as Esther did against Haman at the banquet of wine, Esther vii. 2, 6. So that they shall cry out as that emperor aforementioned did, *Calix vitæ calix mortis*, The cup of life is to us a cup of poison.

Ver. 30. *Many are weak*] The mortality at Corinth began at God's house, and that for unworthy communicating. God will be sanctified of all that draw near to him. He loves to be acquainted with men in the walks of their obedience, and yet he takes state upon him in his ordinances, and will be served like himself, or we shall hear from him. What manner of men therefore ought we to be that come so near to God in this holy ordinance? Nadab and Abihu can tell you that the flames of jealousy are hottest about the altar. Uzza and the Bethshemites, though dead, do yet tell you that justice as well as mercy is most active about the ark. Judgment begins at God's own house, 1 Pet. iv. 17; and the destroying angel begins at the sanctuary, Ezek. ix. 5.

Ver. 31. *We should not be judged*] God should be prevented, and the devil put out of office, as having nothing to say against us, but what we have said before. Let us therefore up and be doing at this most needful but much neglected work of self-judging, that God may acquit us. First search and try our ways, as ex-

aminers, Lam. iii. 40. Next, make a bill of indictment, and confess against ourselves, as informers; aggravating all by the circumstances. Thirdly, step from the bar to the bench, and pass sentence upon ourselves, as so many judges: when we are to come to the Lord's supper especially. Otherwise blind Popery shall rise up in judgment against us and condemn us. We read of William de Raley, bishop of Winchester, A. D. 1243, that being near death, he had the sacrament brought unto him. And perceiving the priest to enter his chamber with it, he cried out, "Stay, good friend, let the Lord come no nearer to me: it is more fit that I be drawn to him like a traitor, that in many things have been a traitor unto him." (Godwin's Catalogue.) His servants therefore, by his commandment, drew him out of his bed unto the place where the priest was, and there with tears he received the sacrament; and spending much time in prayer afterwards, he so ended his life. The like is reported of William Langespe, base son of King Henry II., and Earl of Salisbury; that lying very sick, the bishop brought the sacrament. He understanding of the bishop's coming, met him at the door half naked, with a halter about his neck, threw himself down prostrate at his feet, and would not be taken up until, having made confession of his sins with tears and other signs of sincere repentance, he had received the sacrament in most devout manner.

Ver. 32. *That we should not, &c.*] *Ferre minora volo, ne graviora feram.*

Ver. 33. *Wherefore, my brethren*] He that reproveth and adviseth not, doth as it were snuff the lamp and not pour in oil.

CHAPTER XII.

Ver. 1. *I would not have you ignorant*] To wit, of the only author and true end of them, "lest ye be vainly puffed up by your fleshly mind," Col. ii. 18. Ignorance breeds pride, Rev. iii. 17.

Ver. 2. *Even as ye were led*] It is the misery of a natural man that hath not his heart established with grace, to be carried away as he is led, to be wherried about with every wind of doctrine, to have no mould but what the next seducer casteth him into; being blown like a glass into this or that shape, at the pleasure of his breath.

Ver. 3. *Calleth Jesus accursed*] As the wicked Jews do at this day in their daily prayers and abbreviature; and as the Gentiles did of old, and these Corinthians among the rest. But now they would rather die than do so; as Pliny writes to Trajan the emperor, that he could never force any that were Christians indeed, either to invocate the gods, or to do sacrifice before the emperor's image, or to curse Christ, *Quorum nihil cogi posse dicuntur qui sunt revera Christiani.* (Plin. Epist.)

And that no man can say, &c.] That is, no man can, with the fiducial assent of his heart, acknowledge Christ to be the only Lord, whom he is to worship by the same impulsions, by which another curses and blasphemes him, but by such peculiar motives as are suggested and revealed unto him by the Holy Ghost.

Ver. 4. *But the same Spirit*] As the divers smell of flowers come from the same influence, and the divers sounds in the organ from the same breath.

Ver. 5. *Differences of administrations*] i. e. Ecclesiastical functions, all of them the *dona honoraria* of the Lord Christ, Eph. iv. 8—11.

Ver. 6. *Diversities of operations*] The Holy Ghost may use one of less grace to do more good than one of more; though he delights to honour those of most sincerity with most success, as 1 Cor. xv. 10.

Ver. 7. *To profit withal*] We are neither born nor born again for ourselves. If we be not fit to serve the body, neither are we fit to be of the body; he is not a saint that seeketh not communion of saints. *Pudeat illos, qui ita in studiis se abdiderunt, ut ad vitam communem nullum fructum ferre possint*, saith Cicero. They may well be ashamed that employ not their talents for a public good.[1] The Greek word τὸ συμφέρον importeth such a kind of profit, as redounds to community. It seemeth to be a metaphor from bees, that bring all the honey they can get to the common hive.

Ver. 8. *The word of wisdom*] "The tongue of the learned," to time a word, Isa. l. 4, to set it upon its circumferences, Prov. xxv. 11, to declare unto man his righteousness, when not one of a thousand can do it like him, Job xxxiii. 23.

The word of knowledge] This, say some, is the doctor's office, as the former word of wisdom is the pastor's (Mr Edwards). But the essential difference betwixt pastors and doctors in each congregation is much denied by many learned and good divines. Others by "the word of wisdom" will have understood knowledge infused by divine revelation; as by "the word of knowledge," that knowledge that is acquired by study and industry. (Barlow. Taylor upon Titus.)

Ver. 9. *To another faith*] The faith of miracles, which a man may have, and yet miscarry, 1 Cor. xiii. 2. So doth not any one that hath the faith of God's elect; that fails not, Luke xxii. Some say the apostle here meaneth historical faith; and this seems the more probable, because he speaketh of the working of miracles, ver. 10.

Ver. 10. *Discerning of spirits*] They discerned not men's hearts of themselves (for to God only), but by a special work of God's Spirit discovering them to their eyes, as Peter discerned Ananias, and afterwards Simon Magus, whom Philip mistook and baptized. (Rolloc. de Vocatione.)

Ver. 11. *One and the self-same Spirit*] Who yet is called the seven spirits of God, Rev. i. 4, for his manifold and sundry operations.

Dividing to every man severally, as he will]

It is reported that in Luther's house was found written, *Res et verba Philippus. Res sine verbis Lutherus. Verba sine re Erasmus.* Every one hath his own share; all are not alike gifted; yet by "one and the self-same Spirit," that one and that self-same Spirit, as the Greek text runs, repeating the article, very elegantly and emphatically, τὸ ἕν καὶ τὸ αὐτὸ πνεῦμα.

Ver. 12. *So also is Christ*] Mystical Christ, the Church. Christ the Saviour of his body (Ephes. v. 23) accounts not himself complete without his Church, Eph. i. *ult.* So God is called Jacob, Psal. xxiv. 6.

Ver. 13. *For by one Spirit, &c.*] By the testimony of the two sacraments, whereof we all partake, the apostle proveth that we are all but one body, and should therefore as bees bring all our honey to the common hive.

Are we all baptized] The apostles received all into the Church that believed and were baptized, without particular probation for some days, weeks, months, or years, and entering into a private solemn covenant.

And have been all made to drink] *Potionati sumus*, saith Piscator, and so prove ourselves to be of the corporation and company of believers. But what was the meaning of that passage in the old Church catechism, "There are but two sacraments only, as generally necessary," &c. Are there any more than two, though not absolutely and generally necessary to all men in all times, states, and conditions whatsoever? The Papists themselves say, that five of their sacraments at least are not generally necessary.

Ver. 14. *Not one member, but many*] As man's body curiously wrought, and as it were by the book, Psal. cxxxix. 16. Had God left out an eye or hand in his commonplace-book (saith one) thou hadst wanted it.

Ver. 15. *If the foot should say, &c.*] Inferiors must not envy those above them, but be content, sith it is God that cutteth us out several conditions; and a scavenger may honour God in his place, as well as a minister in his.

Ver. 16. *If the ear*] A man had better be blind, lame, dumb, than deaf; because by the ear life enters into the soul, Isa. lv. 3.

Ver. 17. *If the whole body, &c.*] It is proper to God to be πανοφθαλμὸς, all eye; *Sic spectat universos quasi singulos, sic singulos quasi solos.*

Ver. 18. *God hath set, &c.*] And he, as only wise, doth all in number, weight, and measure. Shall we not rest in what he hath done as best? "What can the man do that cometh after the king?" Eccles. ii. 12.

Ver. 19. *Where were the body?*] So the body politic consisteth not of a physician and a physician (saith Aristotle), but of a physician and a husbandman, &c.

Ver. 20. *But now are they many members, &c.*] 1. Use. 2. Necessity. 3. Honour. 4. Comeliness. 5. Mutual consent commend these things. Let every man try his membership (1. If sociable with Christ and his people; 2. If useful and serviceable to the body; 3. If sensible and

[1] *Paulum sepultæ distat inertiæ celata virtus.* Hor.

compassionate, &c., being himself also in the body), as was before advised.

Ver. 21. *The eye cannot say, &c.*] Superiors may not slight their inferiors, sith they cannot be without them, as one time or other they will be forced to acknowledge. It was a saying of General Vere to the king of Denmark, that kings cared not for soldiers until such time as their crowns hung on the one side of their heads.

Ver. 22. *Which seem to be, &c.*] As the organs of nourishment, not so noble, but more necessary than those of the senses.

Ver. 23. *And those members*] As the organs of excretion and generation, called less honourable and uncomely, *non per se, sed comparate,* comparatively in respect of those parts that are singularly comely.

Our uncomely parts, &c.] It was at the abomination of Baal-peor, or Priapus, that his worshippers said, *Nos, pudore pulso, stamus sub Jove, cœlis apertis,* &c. God taught our first parents to make coverings to hide their nakedness, and the contrary is oft threatened as a curse, Isa. iii. 17.

Ver. 24. *For our comely parts*] A fair face needs no dress, is its own testimonial, a bait without a hook, said Socrates, δελεὰρ ἄνευ ἀγκίστρου.

Ver. 25. *Should have the same care*] As if the heel do but ache, the whole condoleth and cureth, and careth; and yet without dividing care, that there might be no schism in the body.

Ver. 26. *And whether one man suffer*] This spiritual sympathy, *mirum est quam frigide tractetur inter Christianos hodie,* saith Aretius on this text. See the note on ver. 20 and 27. Luther in a certain epistle of his to Lampertus Thorn, a prisoner for Christ, thus writeth, *Consolabor me quod vestra vincula mea sunt, vestri carceres et ignes mei sunt; sunt vero, dum ea confiteor et prædico, vobisque simul compatior, et congratulor,* that is, I doubt (and it is a grief to me) that I shall never have the honour of martyrdom as you have. But herein I can comfort myself, that your bonds are my bonds, your imprisonment and burning at a stake mine; for so they are so long as I confess and extol them; so long as I both suffer with you and rejoice with you. (Tom. ii. Epist.)

Ver. 27. *Now ye are, &c.*] St Cyprian's sympathy is remarkable, *Cum singulis pectus meum copulo, mœroris et funeris pondera luctuosa participo; Cum plangentibus plango, cum deflentibus defleo.* Hereby he showed himself a living member.

Ver. 28. *Diversities of tongues*] This comes in last, either to bid check to their pride, who gloried so much in their many languages; or because he meant to say more to it in the words following.

Ver. 29. *Are all teachers?*] Yes, some would have it so, as in Alcibiades' army all were leaders, no learners.

Ver. 31. *Covet earnestly, &c.*] Ζηλοῦτε, ambite. This is the best ambition. Christians should strive to excel, and be the best at what they undertake. Melancthon saith that Frederick the elector of Saxony had cropped off the tops of all virtues.

A more excellent way] What was that? Charity to God and men, chap. xiii. 1. Graces are better than gifts. A shopful of barrels enrich not, unless full of commodities. Gifts as to heaven are but the lumber of a Christian; it is grace maketh him rich toward God; and is therefore chiefly to be coveted. Care also is to be taken that we get not the spiritual rickets; grow big in the head (in gifts), decay in the vitals, i. e. in grace and the exercise of it.

CHAPTER XIII.

Ver. 1. *Though I speak with the tongues*] The Corinthians gloried much in this gift of tongues; but this a man may have, and yet perish, as Mithridates, who is said to have spoken two and twenty languages. And Cleopatra was a great linguist, she could give answers to Ethiopian, Hebrew, Arabic, Syrian, Median, and Parthian ambassadors, saith Plutarch; yea, she could turn and tune her tongue as an instrument of many strings to what dialect she pleased. τὴν γλῶτταν ὥσπερ ὄργανον τὶ πολύχορδον εὐπετῶς τρέπουσα.

And of angels] Not that angels have tongues; as neither have they wings, though they are said to fly, and even unto weariness of flight, Dan. ix. 21. A certain friar undertook to show to the people a feather of the angel Gabriel's wing, and so verified the old proverb, "a friar, a liar." But the apostle here useth a high kind of expression, such as is used Acts vi. 15; Psal. lxxviii. 25. Unless, perhaps, saith Chrysostom here, the angels have *suo modo sua colloquia.* The schoolmen have great disputes about it, and tell us that when an angel hath a conceit in his mind of anything, with a desire that another should understand it, it is enough, it is done immediately. But are not these they that intrude into those things that they have not seen? Colos. ii. 18, understanding neither what they say nor whereof they affirm, 1 Tim. i. 7. Like unto these are our new millenaries, that upon a mistake of some high expressions in Scripture, which describe the judgments poured out upon God's enemies in making a way to the Jews' conversion by the pattern of the last judgment, think that Jesus Christ shall come from heaven again, and reign here upon earth a thousand years. (See Mr Cotton's Sixth Vial.)

Or a tinkling cymbal] Sounding only for pleasure, but signifying nothing. Tiberius the emperor was wont to call Apion the grammarian *cymbalum orbis,* the cymbal of the world, for his much prattle. (Sueton.) And Jerome inveighs against some in his time, *qui verbis tinnulis et emendicatis utebantur,* that used only tinkling and tickling words, without weight or worth.

Ver. 2. *And have not charity*] If I knew and

did all for ostentation, not for edification; as Stephen Gardiner, who blew up his gifts to the view of others, as butchers blow up their flesh. Chrysostom saith that to show mercy is a more glorious work than to raise from the dead. Removing of mountains is instanced, because noted by our Saviour as a master-miracle, Matt. xvii. 20; Luke xvii. 6. A man may cast out devils, and yet be cast to the devil.

And have not charity, it profiteth me nothing] The same is true of all other parts of obedience, whether active or passive. If we were as constant frequenters of the Church as Anna the prophetess was of the temple, Luke ii., *si aures nostræ ad portam Ecclesiæ fixæ essent*, saith one, if our ears were nailed to the church doors, if our knees were grown as hard as camel's knees with much kneeling before the Lord, if our faces were furrowed with continual weeping, as Peter's is said to have been, yet if we wanted charity, all were nothing.

Ver. 3. *Though I bestow all my goods*] Unless I draw out my soul as well as my sheaf to the hungry, Isa. lviii. 10. Many shrink up charity to an handbreadth, to giving of alms.

And though I give my body, &c.] As Servetus the heretic did at Geneva, A. D. 1555. So Mauzius the Anabaptist gave his body to be drowned at Tigure, A. D. 1527. (Scultet. Annal.) Fisher, Bishop of Rochester, to be beheaded for holding the pope's supremacy. Friar Forest, to be hanged for the same cause. And how many of our popish martyrs (malefactors or traitors, I should say) have worn the Tyburn tippet, as Father Latimer phraseth it! And more of them must, for they be some of them knaves all, as the L. Audley chancellor of England once said to the thirteen Calais prisoners for religion, whom he discharged; and like bells they will never be well tuned till well hanged. For why? they are *flabella et flagella Reip.*, &c.

Ver. 4. *And is kind*] χρηστεύεται, or, is easy to be made use of, ready to any good office. Charity is no churl.

Vaunteth not itself] With the scorn of others. Arrianus saith, that he is πέρπερος, that blameth others and is restless in himself. Such a one was Timon of old and Laurentius Valla of late.

Is not puffed up] Hence charity is portrayed as a naked child with a merry countenance, covered in a cloud, with a bloody heart in the right hand, giving honey to a bee without wings.

Ver. 5. *Behave itself unseemly*] αἰσχημονεῖ, or, doth not disgrace any one.

Is not easily provoked] παροξύνεται, falls not into any sharp fit, as they did, Acts xv. 39, so as that her teeth are set on edge, or that she should show her anger by the trembling of the body.

Thinketh no evil] Is not suspicious, or doth not meditate revenge.

Ver. 6. *Rejoiceth with the truth*] *Nulla est igitur inter malos charitas, sed conjuratio potius*, saith a grave expositor. It is not charity, but conspiracy, that is found in wicked men. (Dr Sclater.)

Ver. 7. *Beareth all things*] στέγει, *tegit*. Covereth faults with her large mantle, dissembleth injuries, swalloweth down whole many pills that would prove very bitter in the chewing. The Greek word is *metaphora a tignis*, say some, and signifies, that charity "beareth all things," as the cross main beam in a house supporteth the whole building. (Pareus a Lapide.)

Believeth all things] Is candid and ingenuous, yet not blind and blockish. No man may ravish me out of my wits, saith one; to conclude as Walter Mapes did of his Church of Rome, after he had related the gross simony of the pope, *Sit tamen Domina materque nostra Roma baculus in aqua fractus, et absit credere quæ vidimus*. If a Papist see one of their priests kissing a woman, he is by their canon law bid to believe that the priest is giving her counsel only. Their rule to their novices is, *Tu et Asinus unum estote*.

Endureth all things] Love, as it is a passion, so it is tried rather by passions than actions.

Ver. 8. *Prophecies, they shall fail*] The archprophet shall teach us immediately, as he had done Moses and Elias, who appearing to Christ in the transfiguration, knew and could say far more to our Saviour for his comfort and confirmation against the bitterness of his death than ever they could whilst here living upon earth, Luke ix. 31.

Whether there be knowledge] Got by study, and communicated to others. For *Lilmod lelammed*, say the rabbins, we therefore learn that we may teach.

Ver. 9. *We prophesy in part*] We therefore know but imperfectly, because we are taught but imperfectly. My greatest knowledge, said Chytræus, is to know that I know nothing. (Melch. Adam.) And not only in most other things am I ignorant, said Augustine (Epist. cxix. chap. xxi.), but even in the Scriptures (my chief study and trade of life) *multo plura nescio quam scio*. The rabbins in their comments upon Scripture, when they meet with hard knots that they cannot explicate, they solve all with this, *Elia cum venerit, solvet omnia*, Elias, when he comes, shall assoil all our doubts. Erastus at point of death said, that he therefore held it a happiness to die, because now he should fully understand an answer to all those harder questions wherein here he could have no satisfaction. (Melch. Adam, in Vita Erasti.)

Ver. 10. *Then that which is in part*] As the old slough falls off when the new skin comes on. As a man returns no more to the free-school that hath proceeded in the university.

Ver. 11. *When I was a child*] Adrian VI., before he became pope, taxed the Church of Rome for many errors: but afterwards, being desired to reform them, he wickedly abused these words for an answer, "When I was a child, I spake as a child, &c., but now being a man," &c.

Ver. 12. *In a glass*, &c.] See Numb. xii. 8.

But then face to face] i. e. Distinctly, clearly,

immediately, beatifically. And surely, if Lipsius thought when he did but read Seneca that he was even upon Olympus' top, above mortality and human things; what a case shall we be in, when we shall behold Christ in his glory, and consider that every vein in that blessed body bled to bring us to bliss! If the mathematics alone are so delectable, that men think it sweet to live and die in those studies; what shall we think of heaven's happiness, which we shall one day clearly apprehend, but not fully comprehend?

Now I know in part] The present tense in grammar is accompanied with the imperfect; the perfect with the *plusquam perfectum*. And such is the condition of our present and future happiness.

Even as I am known] We shall know the creatures by knowing God; as God now knows all his works by knowing himself.

Ver. 13. *The greatest of these*] Because longest lasting. Gifts that suppose imperfection in us, as faith and hope, or misery in others, as pity, &c., shall be put away. Secondly, because it is diffusive of itself to the use of others; whereas faith and hope are private goods; they are confined to the person of the believer. That was a memorable saying of Elizabeth Folks, martyr, at the stake, " Farewell all the world, farewell faith, farewell hope;" and so taking the stake in her hand, she said, " Welcome love."

CHAPTER XIV.

Ver. 1. *Follow after charity*] Διώκετε, follow it hot-foot, as they say; pursue and practise it. It is more than to desire or to be zealous of a thing, as it follows in the next words, Ζηλοῦτε, " Be zealous of spiritual gifts." Follow charity close, as the hunter doth his prey, or as the persecutor doth the martyr, that will hide or escape if he can. Charity may be fitly compared to the precious stone Pantarb, spoken of by Philostratus; a stone of great beauty and of strange property; so bright it is and radiant, that it gives light in the darkest midnight; and that light is of that admirable virtue, that it brings together the stones that it reacheth into heaps, as if they were so many hives of bees; but nature, lest so precious a gift should be undervalued, hath not only hid this stone in the secret bowels of the earth, but hath also put into it a property of slipping out of the hands of those that hold it, *Nisi provida ratione teneatur*, unless they hold it fast indeed.

Ver. 2. *In an unknown tongue*] So they that preach in a kind of a Roman English, and not in a low language to the people's capacity.

But unto God] *Canit sibi et Musis*, as the proverb is; and as good he may hold his tongue, for God needs him not.

Ver. 3. *To edification, to exhortation*] These three ends every preacher ought to propound to himself: 1. Edification in knowledge and holiness. 2. Exhortation, that is, reprehension and

admonition. 3. Consolation, lest that which is lame be turned out of the way, Heb. xii. 13.

Ver. 4. *Edifieth the Church*] Therefore prophecy is the more worthy, because profitable. *Prodesse melius quam præesse.*

Ver. 5. *I would that ye all spake with tongues*] Gr. " I will." He here prefers prophesying (which was most edifying) before speaking with tongues, which they most affected, because it served most *ad pompam*, for applause and admiration.

Ver. 6. *If I come unto you, &c.*] This you would not like in me. And is that *Venus in Caio* that is *Nævus in Titio?* a blemish in one that is a beauty in another?

By revelation, or by knowledge, or, &c.] Piscator reads it by revelation or by knowledge; that is, either by prophesying or by doctrine. The apostle expounding himself.

Ver. 7. *Except they give a distinction*] *Unisono nihil auribus molestius.* Discords in music make the best harmony. Through all Turkey there runs one tune, nor can every man play that; yet scarce any but hath a fiddle with two strings.

Ver. 8. *For if the trumpet*] Similies are excellent for illustration, and must be fetched from things familiar.

Ver. 9. *Ye shall speak into the air*] You shall lose your labour, and may as well keep your breath to cool your broth.

Ver. 10. *So many kinds of voices*] Seventy-two material languages, they say.

Ver. 11. *A barbarian*] So the Grecians called all nations that spoke not their language. It is reported that nowhere at this day is spoken more barbarous language than at Athens, once the Greece of Greece. (Neand. Chron.)

Ver. 12. *To the edifying of the Church*] Clouds when full pour down, and the presses overflow, and the aromatical trees sweat out their precious and sovereign oils; and every learned scribe must bring out his treasure for the Church's behoof and benefit.

Ver. 13. *Pray that he may interpret*] Pope Innocent III. never prayed thus; for he said, that the Church decreed the service in an unknown tongue, *Ne sacrosancta verba vilescerent*, lest the holy words should be under-prized. But public prayers in an unknown tongue, saith Erasmus, must be attributed to the change of time itself in Italy, France, and Spain, for there a long time the Latin was understood of all. But when afterwards their speeches degenerated into those vulgar tongues now there used, then the language, not of the service, but of the people, was altered.

Ver. 14. *Is unfruitful*] In regard of others' edification. It were a great grace, said Lambert the martyr, if we might have the word of God diligently and often spoken and sung unto us in such wise, that the people might understand it; then should it come to pass that craftsmen should sing spiritual psalms sitting at their work, and the husbandman at his plough, as wisheth St Jerome. Pavier, town-clerk of London in Henry VIII.'s time, was a man that in no case could abide to hear that the gospel should be in English; insomuch that he once swore a great oath, that if he thought that the king's Highness would set forth the Scripture in English, and let it be read of the people by his authority, rather than he would so long live, he would cut his own throat. But he broke promise, for shortly after he hanged himself.

Ver. 15. *I will pray with understanding*] To an effectual prayer there must concur *intentio et affectus*, the intention of the mind and the affection of the heart; else it is not praying, but parroting. I have read of a parrot in Rome, that could distinctly say over the whole Creed. (Sphinx. Philos.)

Ver. 16. *Say Amen*] This the apostle reckons for a great loss. The poor misled and muzzled Papists are enjoined not to join so far with a Protestant in any holy action, as to say Amen. But in that there is no so great loss. (Specul. Europ.)

Ver. 17. *But the other is not edified*] This we should all labour, viz. to edify others. Synesius speaks of some, who having a treasure of tongues and other abilities in them, would as soon part with their hearts as their meditations; the canker of whose great skill shall be a witness against them.

Ver. 18. *I thank my God, &c.*] Skill in tongues is, as now, a great blessing. Indeed at first when men began θεομαχεῖν, to fight against God, they were compelled λογομαχεῖν, to babble in divers languages, 72, as Epiphanius affirmeth. But God hath turned this curse into a blessing unto his people, Acts ii., and as in the first plantation of the gospel, so in the late reformation; God sent it before, as his munition to batter the forts of Antichrist, who had banished arts and languages, overspreading all with barbarism and atheism. *Græce nosse suspectum erat. Hebraice fere hæreticum.*

Ver. 19. *In an unknown tongue*] A Parisian doctor tells us that though the apostle would have God's service to be celebrated in a known tongue, yet the Church for divers weighty reasons hath otherwise ordered and appointed it. (Benedict.) The Mahometans read their Alcoran (which they supposed were profaned if it were translated into vulgar tongues) and perform their public devotions in the Arabic tongue, which is their learned language. (Montan. in 1 Cor. xiv.)

Ver. 20. *Be not children*] *Mentibus scilicet, sed moribus*, Matt. xviii. 3. See the note there.

In malice be ye children] In innocency and ignoscency.

In understanding be men] Is it not a shame to have no more understanding at 80 than at eight years of age?

Ver. 21. *With men of other tongues*] God threatened the Jews, that sith they would not hearken to their own prophets, they should hear foreign enemies, Isa. xxviii. 11; Jer. v. 15. So those that will not obey the sweet command of Christ, "Come unto me," shall have one day no

command to obey, but that dreadful *discedite*, "Depart from me," &c.

Ver. 22. *But for them which believe*] To confirm and comfort believers; this is the chief end of preaching. Let this comfort those that cannot say they have converted any by their ministry.

Ver. 23. *Will they not say ye are mad?*] And may they not say as much if we jangle and dissent in opinion, one holding this, and another that. Ammianus Marcellinus taxed the ancient bishops of his time for their hateful miscarriage in this kind.

Ver. 24. *He is convinced of all*] God smiteth the earth with the rod of his mouth, and with the breath of his lips doth he slay the wicked, Isa. xi. 4. By his word he telleth a man (as he did the Samaritaness, John iv.) all that ever he did.

Ver. 25. *The secrets of his heart*] God's word is a curious critic, Heb. iv. 12, "a discerner of the thoughts," &c. It finds and ferrets out secret sins.

Ver. 26. *Let all things, &c.*] There is edifying even in appointing of fit Psalms.

Ver. 27. *Or at the most by three*] Lest the hearers be tired out. Our infirmity will not suffer any long intention, either of body or mind. Long services can hardly maintain their vigour, as in tall bodies the spirits are diffused. Erasmus hath observed that Origen never preached above an hour, oft but half an hour: *Consultius judicabat crebro docere, quam diu*, saith he. He held it better to preach oft, than long. (Eras. Præfat. ad Orig. Opera.)

Ver. 28. *Let him keep silence*] Such as stuff their sermons with Greek and Latin are here silenced, further than they interpret the same. If thou canst help my hearers to Greek and Latin ears (saith a reverend preacher) they shall have Greek and Latin enough.

Ver. 29. *Let the other judge*] But is not this a disparagement to the prophets? may some say: no, but an honour. 1 Thess. v. 20, 21, after "despise not prophesying," he subjoineth, "try all things."

Ver. 30. *That sitteth by*] And is extraordinarily inspired and qualified; a little otherwise than our enthusiasts, that brag of their *lumen propheticum*.

Ver. 31. *That all may learn*] The most learned may learn something by the discourses of others less learned than themselves. Apollos, a learned teacher, may yet be taught by a tent-maker. The Jewish rabbins acknowledge that they came to understand Isa. xiv. 23, by hearing an Arabian woman mention a besom in her language to her maid, אטאטא (R. David in Radic.)

Ver. 32. *Are subject to the prophets*] To be scanned and examined: which they should not be, unless they took their turns in course to prophesy. *Eloquere*, said one, *ut quid sis videam*: Speak, that I may see what is in thee.

Ver. 33. *Not the author of confusion*] *Nec author, nec fautor.* Unquiet spirits are of the devil, who keeps ado, and fills the Church with confusion by his turbulent agents and emissaries, sowing sedition and spreading schisms.

Ver. 34. *Let your women, &c.*] See the note on Rom. xvi. 1.

Ver. 35. *Ask their husbands*] Who therefore must dwell with them according to knowledge, 1 Pet. iii. 7, and be manly guides unto them in the way to heaven. The master's breast must be the household's treasury.

For it is a shame for women, &c.] She was a singular example that taught the Greek and Latin tongues at Heidelberg, A. D. 1554; her name was Olympia Fulvia Morata, an Italian, of the city of Ferrara. Ancient histories indeed make mention of one Aratha, who read openly in the schools at Athens 25 years, made 40 books, and a hundred philosophers to her scholars. Leoptia likewise wrote against Theophrastus; Corinna oft contended with Pindarus in versifying.

Ver. 36. *What? came the word, &c.*] As if he should say (and he saith it with some displeasure), Are ye the first, or the only Christians? are ye too good to be admonished? take heed lest your arrogancy and high-spiritedness lay you low enough, even in that slimy valley, Job xxi. 31, 32.

Ver. 37. *The commandment*] And therefore to be obeyed by the best of you. *Aut faciendum, aut patiendum: Aut pœnitendum, aut pereundum.* Either do it, or die for it.

Ver. 38. *But if any man be ignorant, &c.*] If stubbornly ignorant and uncounsellable, let him take his own course. I have cleared the truth in things now controverted, and there I rest me. Who so blind as he that will not see? such put not light under a bushel, but under a dunghill, and shall give a heavy account of it to God. When I hear men (saith Lord Kemp) under all the means that we enjoy, yet think that their ignorance shall excuse them, it makes me think of the answer of the agent of Charles V., emperor to the ambassador of Sienna. The Siennois having rebelled against the emperor, sent their ambassador to excuse it; who when he could find no other excuse, thought in a jest to put it off thus: What, saith he, shall not we of Sienna be excused, seeing we are known to be all fools? the agent replied, Even that shall excuse you, but upon the condition which is fit for fools, which is, to be kept bound and enchained.

Ver. 39. *Wherefore, brethren*] This he adds as a corollary, to prevent mistakes, as if that he were an enemy either to prophecy or tongues, so soberly and orderly used. *Arbitror nonnullos in quibusdam locis librorum meorum, opinaturos me sensisse quod non sensi, aut non sensisse quod sensi,* saith Augustine (lib. iii. de Trin. c. 3): I foresee that some will construe many passages of my writings far otherwise than I intend them: and it fell out accordingly, as Baronius testifieth. (Annal. tom. 6, A. D. 450, n. 17.)

Ver. 40. *Let all things, &c.*] A general rule of great moment. In things both real and ritual

decency and order must be observed in Church-meetings. For this the Colossians are much commended, chap. ii. 5. Our Saviour caused the people whom he had fed to keep order in their sitting on the grass; they sat down rank by rank, as rows or borders of beds in a garden; so the Greek imports.[1] Whereupon an expositor noteth, *Ordinatim res in Ecclesia facienda,* order must be observed in the Church.

CHAPTER XV.

Ver. 1. *And wherein ye stand*] ἑστήκατε, a military term, as Martyr noteth. Satan overthroweth the faith of some, 2 Tim. ii. 18, and by this very engine wherewith he assaulted these Corinthians, *ibid.* So that the apostle was fain to make apology, ver. 19, to make a barricado.

Ver. 2. *By which also ye are saved*] Eternal life is potentially in the word, as the harvest is potentially in the seed, or as the tree is in the kernel or scion, Jam. i. 21.

If ye keep in memory] He limiteth the promise of salvation to the condition of keeping in memory what they had heard. *Tantum didicimus, quantum meminimus,* said Socrates; many have memories like nets, that let go the fair water, retain the filth only; or like sieves, that keep the chaff, let go the corn. If God come to search them with a candle, what shall he find but old songs, old wrongs, &c.? not a promise of any word of God hid there: for things of that nature they are like Sabinus in Seneca, that never in all his life could remember those three names of Homer, Ulysses, and Achilles. But the soul should be as a holy ark, the memory like the pot of manna, preserving holy truths.

Ver. 3. *First of all*] Christ is to be preached with the first, as being the *prora et puppis* of man's happiness, John xvi. 14. It is the office of the Holy Ghost to take of Christ's excellencies, and hold them out to the world. What then should ministers, the mouth of the Holy Ghost, do rather?

Ver. 4. *According to the Scriptures*] Which both foreshowed and foreshadowed it in Adam's waking, Isaac's reviving, as it were from the dead, Joseph's abasement and advancement, Samson's breaking the bars and bearing away the gates of Gaza, David's being drawn out of the deep, Daniel's out of the den, Jeremiah's out of the dungeon, Jonah's out of the belly of hell, Matt. xii. 39, &c.

Ver. 5. *Seen of Cephas*] Adam died, and we hear no more of him. But Christ showed himself after death in six several apparitions for our confirmation.

Then of the twelve] So they are called for the rotundity of the number, *utcunque unus vel alter vel deesset vel abesset.* Judas had made one long letter of himself, *Longam literam fecit.*

Ver. 6. *Above five hundred*] The number of believers were then greater than some would viii. 14. Cartwright.

---

[1] πρασιαὶ πρασιαὶ, *Hebraisc. ut* Exod.

gather out of Acts i. 15. Those 120 may seem to have been chieftains, such as that any one of them might have been thought meet to succeed Judas in his apostleship.

Ver. 7. *Seen of James*] This is not mentioned in the Gospel, as neither that of Peter, ver. 5.

Ver. 8. *One born out of due time*] *Quasi malo astro abortus, et adversante natura coactus.* One that deserved to be rejected, as that forlorn infant, Ezek. xvi. 4, 5.

Ver. 9. *I am the least of the apostles*] Not come to my just bigness, as one born out of due time, and not without violence. *Paulus quasi Paululus,* saith one, because he was least in his own eyes, "less than the least of all saints," Eph. iii. 8. Melancthon was of a like self-denying spirit, insomuch as Luther thought he went too far this way ; *Certe nimis nullus in hoc est Philippus,* Philip is too low-conceited.

Not meet to be called] True humility, as true balm, ever sinks to the bottom of the water, when pride, like oil, ever swims on the top.

Ver. 10. *I laboured more abundantly*] See 2 Cor. xii. 23 ; Rom. xv. 19. George Eagles, martyr in Queen Mary's days, for his great pains in travelling from place to place to confirm the brethren, was surnamed, Trudge over the world. Might not St Paul have been fitly so surnamed ?

Not I, but the grace of God] So those good servants, Luke xix. 16, Not we, but thy talents have gained other five, and other two, &c. Let God have the entire praise of all our good. We should boast and glory of nothing, because nothing is ours, saith holy Austin, who (being wholly of St Paul's spirit) was a great advancer of the grace of God, and abaser of man against all those patrons of nature with their *vitreum acumen,* bright but brittle sharpness of wit, as he styleth it.

Which was with me] Present with me, not which did work with me, as the Synergists would have it.

Ver. 11. *So we preach, and so ye believed*] A happy compliance, when the hearers' affections and endeavours do answer the affections and endeavours of the preacher, as here, and at Ephesus, Acts xx. 31—37 ; when people deliver themselves up to the form of doctrine, and are cast into the mould of the word, Rom. vi. 17.

Ver. 12. *No resurrection*] More than that of regeneration, Matt. xix. 28, that estate of the gospel called a new heaven and a new earth, 2 Pet. iii. 13, the world to come, Heb. ii. 5, that resurrection already past, 2 Tim. ii. 18, that first resurrection, Rev. xx. 5.

Ver. 13. *Then is not Christ risen*] But of Christ's resurrection there were many both living and dead witnesses, as the earthquake, empty grave, stone rolled away, clothes wrapt up, &c.

Ver. 14. *Then is our preaching vain*] Never was there any imposture put upon the world as Christianity, if Christ be yet in the grave.

Ver. 15. *False witnesses of God*] For they might safely say with Jeremiah, Lord, if we be deceived, thou hast deceived us.

Ver. 16. *Then is not Christ raised*] And so God's decree is cassated, Acts xiii. 33, with Psal. i. 7.

Ver. 17. *Ye are yet in your sins*] Rom. iv. 25. If he had not been let out of prison, our debt had remained upon us. But God sent his angel to roll away the stone, as the judge sends an officer to fetch one out of prison, and to release him. And this is the strength of our Saviour's reason, John xvi. 10, The Spirit shall convince the world of righteousness (that I am Jehovah their righteousness), because I go to the Father, which I could not have done, unless you were acquitted of all your sins.

Ver. 18. *Asleep in Christ*] The Germans call the churchyard God's Acre, because the bodies are sowed therein, to be raised again. The Greeks call them κοιμητήρια, sleeping-houses. The Hebrews call the grave Bechajim, the house of the living, Job calls it the congregation-house of all living, Job xxx. 23. As the apostle calls heaven the congregation-house of the first-born, Heb. xii. 23.

Ver. 19. *Most miserable*] Because none out of hell ever suffered more than the saints have done.

Ver. 20. *The first-fruits, &c.*] As in the first-fruits offered to God, the Jews were assured of God's blessing on the whole harvest ; so by the resurrection of Christ, our resurrection is insured.

Christ is risen] This was wont to be the form of salutation among Christians of old, *Christus resurrexit,* Christ is risen from the dead.

Ver. 21. *By man came also, &c.*] God's justice would be satisfied in the same nature that had sinned.

Ver. 22. *Shall all be made alive*] The saints shall be raised by virtue of the union with Christ to glory, the wicked shall be dragged to his tribunal by his Almighty power as a judge, to be tumbled thence into hell-torment.

Ver. 23. *At his coming*] As in the mean time their very dust is precious ; the dead bodies consumed are not so destroyed, but that there is a substance preserved by a secret influence proceeding from Christ as a head. Hence they are said to be dead in Christ, who by rotting refineth them.

Ver. 24. *Delivered up the kingdom*] Not his essential kingdom, as God, but his economical, as Mediator.

Ver. 25. *Till he hath put*] And after too, but, 1. Without adversaries ; 2. Without any outward means and ordinances.

Ver. 26. *That shall be destroyed*] It is already to the saints swallowed up in victory, so that they may say to it, as Jacob did to Esau, "Surely I have seen thy face as the face of God." This Esau, death, meets a member of Christ with kisses instead of frowns, and guards him home, as he did Jacob to his father's house.

Ver. 27. *All things under his feet*] This, Psal. viii. 7, 8, spoken of man in general, is properly applied to the man Christ Jesus ; in whom also t extendeth to the saints, who are therefore more glorious than heaven, earth, or any creature, and shall have power over all, Rev. ii. 26. (Cameron. de Eccles.)

Ver. 28. *That God may be all in all*] Till sin and death be abolished we have no access to God but by Christ. But after that all enemies be trod under foot, then shall we have an immediate union with God; yet so, as that this shall be the proper and everlasting praise of Christ, as he is the procurer of that union.

Ver. 29. *Which are baptized*] The several senses that are set upon this text, see in Beza, Piscator, but especially our new annotations upon the Bible.

Ver. 30. *In jeopardy every hour*] Carrying our lives in our hands, as both the Hebrews and Greeks phrase it, ἐν τῇ χειρὶ τὴν ψυχὴν ἔχειν. (Athenæus.)

Ver. 31. *By our rejoicing*] i. e. By our infirmities, afflictions, wherein he so much glorieth, 2 Cor. xi. and xii., as an old soldier doth of his scars. As if the apostle should say, I appeal to all those miseries that I have suffered amongst you for a testimony.

Ver. 32. *If after the manner, &c.*] Paul fought with beasts at Ephesus after the manner of men, that is, say some, the men of Ephesus fought with him after the manner of beasts. (Beza, Sclater.) Others more probably understand it literally; If after the manner of men, that is, as men use to do, to show their valour (he meaneth those *Bestiarii* among the Romans), I have been cast to the beasts, and have either overcome them, as Lysimachus did the lion, or have been spared by them, as *corpora sanctorum martyrum tangere multoties refugiebant bestiæ*, saith the historian, what advantageth it me, &c. And this latter sense is a stronger argument of the resurrection. (Chrysost. Ambros.)

Let us eat and drink] An ill inference of men of corrupt minds, and destitute of the truth. Chrysostom saith, There were a sort of such in his time, as said δός μοὶ τὴν σήμερον καὶ λάβε τὴν αὔριον, Give me to-day, and take thou to-morrow (τὴν αὔριον τὶς οἶδεν. Anacreon.) And have not we those that say, Let us be merry while we may, we shall never be younger, *Ede, bibe, lude, post mortem nulla voluptas*. It was wisely done of the Romans to banish Alæcus and Philiscus, a couple of swinish epicures, lest they should by their evil communication and conversation corrupt others. St Paul, though he allegeth this saying out of Isa. xxii. 13, yet he alludeth (likely) to Sardanapalus's epitaph at Tarsus, a city built by this Sardanapalus, Εσθιε, πίνε, παῖζε, ὡς τῆς ἀλλὰ τούτου οὐκ ἄξια, *Ede, bibe, lude; nam cætera omnia nec hujus sunt;* Eat, drink, sport; for all other things are not worth a fillip: for so his statue was carved as if his hands had given a fillip, and his mouth had spoken these words. (Greg. Posthum.)

Ver. 33. *Evil communication*] Evil words are not wind, as most imagine, but the devil's drivel, that leaves a foul stain upon the speaker, and oft sets the like upon the hearer. Shun obscene borborology (saith one) and unsavoury speeches thou losest so much of thine honesty and piety as thou admittest evil into thy tongue.

Ver. 34. *Awake to righteousness*] Go forth and shake yourselves (as Samson did) out of that dead lethargy whereinto sin hath cast you; your enemies are upon you, and you fast asleep the while.

I speak this to your shame] Ignorance is a blushful sin. Are ye also ignorant? said Christ to his apostles; q. d. that is an arrant shame, indeed. The Scripture sets such below the ox and the ass.

Ver. 35. *But some man will say*] Some epicure will object, and say, How can these things be? *A privatione ad habitum non datur regressus.* See the note on Acts xvii. 18.

Ver. 36. *Thou fool*] A hard knot must have a hard wedge, a dead heart a rousing reproof. He confutes atheists from the course of nature, which they ascribe so much unto.

Ver. 37. *And that which thou sowest*] This is an answer to the epicure's second demand, ver. 35, with what body do they come? with a dead, diseased, rotten body, &c.? No, no, saith the apostle. Sin is only rotted with its concomitancies, infirmities; but the rotting of the body is but as the rotting of corn under the clod, that it may arise incorruptible. Or as the melting of an old piece of plate in the fire, to bring it out of a better fashion. Christ was buried in a garden, to note that death doth not destroy our bodies, but only sow them: the dew of herbs will revive them again. See the note on ver. 18.

Ver. 38. *But God giveth it a body*] *Deus naturæ vires et vices ita moderatur*, &c., saith one. God so orders all, that nothing is done without him. The same Hebrew word מלילה that signifieth an ear of corn, doth also signify a word; because every field of corn is a book of God's praise, every land a sheaf, every sheaf a verse, every ear a word, every corn of wheat a letter to express the power and goodness of God.

Ver. 39. *All flesh is not the same*] This is another answer to the epicure, who might haply reply, and say, If man's flesh, when rotted, shall revive, why not likewise the flesh of other creatures? The apostle answereth, "All flesh is not the same," &c. Man's flesh only is informed by a reasonable and immortal soul, not so the flesh of other creatures: and hence the difference.

Ver. 40. *There are also celestial*] Stars and spirits (the inhabitants of that other heaven) I find, saith a divine, like one another. Meteors and fowls in as many varieties as there are several creatures. Why? Is it because man, for whose sake they were made, delights in variety, God in constancy? Or is it because that in these God may show his own skill and their imperfection?

The glory of the terrestrial] The glory of our terrestrial bodies shall at the resurrection be celestial; they shall be more like spirits than bodies, so clear and transparent, saith Aquinas, that all the veins, humours, nerves, and bowels shall be seen, as in a glass: they shall be conformed to the glorified body of Christ, as to the standard.

Ver. 41. *One star differeth, &c.*] The morning star is said to cast a shadow with its shine. " Canst thou bind the sweet influences of the seven stars ? " Job xxxviii. 31, whose work is to bring the spring, and which, like seven sisters or lovers (as the word signifies), are joined together in one fair constellation. Or " loose the bands of Orion ? " the star that brings winter, and binds the earth with frost and cold. " Canst thou bring forth Mazzaroth," the southern constellations ? " Or canst thou guide Arcturus with his sons," that is, the northern stars, those storehouses of God's good treasure, which he openeth to our profit ? Deut. xxviii. 12.

Ver. 42. *So also is the resurrection*] Whether there are degrees of glory, as it seems probable, so we shall certainly know, when we come to heaven. Three glimpses of the body's glory were seen, in Moses' face, in Christ's transfiguration, and in Stephen's countenance.

Ver. 43. *It is raised in power*] The resurrection will cure all infirmities. At Stratford-le-Bow were burned in Queen Mary's days, at one stake, a lame man and a blind man. The lame man after he was chained, casting away his crutch, bade the blind man be of good comfort, for death would heal them both ; and so they patiently suffered.

Ver. 44. *A spiritual body*] Luther saith the body shall move up and down like thought. Augustine saith, they shall move to any place they will, as soon as they will. As birds (saith Zanchius) being hatched, do fly lightly up into the skies, which being eggs, were a heavy and slimy matter ; so man being hatched by the resurrection, is made pure and nimble, and able to mount up into the heavens.

Ver. 45. *A quickening spirit*] Christ is called a spirit from his Deity, as Heb. ix. 14, and a quickening spirit, because he is the principle of life to all believers.

Ver. 46. *And afterward, that is spiritual*] Nature, art, grace, proceed from less perfect or more perfect. Let us advance forward, and ripen apace, that we " may be accounted worthy to obtain that world and the resurrection from the dead," Luke xx. 35.

Ver. 47. *Of the earth, earthy*] Gr. dusty, slimy, *ex terra friabili.* Let this pull down proud flesh. Let us throw this proud Jezebel out of the windows of our hearts, and lay her honour in the dust, by remembering that we are but earth and dust. Adam of Adamah, red earth ; *homo ab humo.* Humility comes from the same root, because it lays a man flat on the ground ; and because, like the earth, it is the most weighty of all virtues.

The Lord from heaven] Not for the matter of his body, for he was " made of a woman ; " but for the original and dignity of his person, whereof see a lively and lofty description, Heb. i. 2, 3.

Ver. 48. *They that are earthy*] κέραμος ὁ ἄν-θρωπος, *Vulgus fictilis.* Man is but an earthen pot, Isa. lxiv. 8.

Ver. 49. *The image of the heavenly*] See Phil. iii. 21. Our bodies shall be fashioned like to Christ's glorious body in beauty, brightness, incorruption, immortality, grace, favour, agility, strength, and other unspeakable qualities and excellencies. Whether they shall have that power as to toss the greatest mountains like a ball, yea, to shake the whole earth at their pleasure, as Anselm and Luther think, I have not to say.

Ver. 50. *Flesh and blood*] The body as it is corruptible, cannot enter heaven, but must be changed ; we shall appear with him in glory. The vile body of Moses, that was hid in the valley of Moab, was brought forth glorious in the hill of Tabor, Matt. xvii. 3.

Ver. 51. *I show you a mystery*] Not known till now to any man living. This, likely, was one of those wordless words, ῥήματα ἄῤῥητα, that Paul heard in his rapture, 2 Cor. xii. 4.

Ver. 52. *The trumpet shall sound*] As at the giving of the law it did, Exod. xix. 16. If the law were thus given (saith a divine), how shall it be required ? If such were the proclamation of God's statutes, what shall the sessions be ? I see and tremble at the resemblance ; the trumpet of the angel called to the one ; the trumpet of the archangel shall summon us to the other. In the one the mount only was on a flame ; all the world shall be so in the other. To the one Moses says, God came with ten thousands of his saints ; in the other thousand thousands shall minister to him, and ten thousand thousands shall stand before him.

Ver. 53. *For this corruptible*] Pointing to his body, he speaketh, as Psal. xxxiv. 6, " This poor man cried, the Lord heard him." So the old believers, when they rehearsed the creed, and came to that article, I believe the resurrection of the flesh, they were wont to add, *Etiam hujus carnis,* even of this self-same flesh. So Job xix. 27.

Ver. 54. *Death is swallowed up*] As the fuel is swallowed up by the fire ; as the sorcerers' serpents were swallowed up by Moses' serpent.

Ver. 55. *Death, where is thy sting ?*] This is the sharpest and the shrillest note, the boldest and the bravest challenge, that ever man rang in the ears of death. *Sarcasmo constat et hostili derisione, qua mors ridenda propinatur,* saith one. Death is here out-braved, called craven to his face, and bidden do his worst (*Tollitur mors, non ne fiat, sed ne obsit.* Aug.). So Simeon sings out his soul, Hilarion chides it out, Ambrose is bold to say, I am neither ashamed to live, nor afraid to die. Anne Askew, the martyr, thus subscribeth her own confession : Written by me, Anne Askew, that neither wisheth for death, nor feareth his might ; and as merry as one that is bound towards heaven. Mr Bradford being told he should be burned the next day, put off his cap, and lifting up his eyes, praised God for it.

Ver. 56. *The sting of death is sin*] Christ having unstinged death, and as it were disarmed it, we may safely now put it into our bosoms, as we may a snake whose sting is pulled out. If it shoot forth now a sting at us, it is but an enchanted sting, as was that of the sorcerers' serpents. Buzz it may about our ears, as a drone bee; but sting us it cannot. Christ, as he hath taken away not sin itself, but the guilt of sin; so not death itself, but the sting of death.

Ver. 57. *But thanks be to God, &c.*] Here St Paul, Christ's chief herald, proclaims his victory with a world of solemnity and triumph.

Ver. 58. *Always abounding, &c.*] This will strengthen faith, as the oft knocking upon a stake fastens it. When faith bears fruit upward, it will take root downward.

Forasmuch as ye know] Bestir you therefore. It troubled a martyr at the stake that he should then go to a place where he should ever be receiving wages and do no more work. It will repent us (if it were possible to repent in heaven) that we began no sooner, wrought no harder.

CHAPTER XVI.

Ver. 1. *Collection for the saints*] THE poor believers at Jerusalem, Rom. xv. 26, who had suffered hard things of their own countrymen, 1 Thess. ii. 14, and taken joyfully the spoiling of their goods, Heb. xi. 34, and were therefore relieved by the Churches of the Gentiles at Paul's motions, Gal. ii. 10. The word here used for saints signifieth such as are taken off from the earth.[1] The saints, though their commoration be upon earth, their conversation is in heaven.

Ver. 2. *Upon the first day*] The Christian sabbath, the Lord's day, as the Greek scholiast well renders it; which to sanctify was in the primitive times a badge of Christianity. When the question was propounded, *Servasti Dominicum?* Hast thou kept the Lord's day? The answer was returned, *Christianus sum; intermittere non possum,* I am a Christian, I can do no less than keep the Lord's day. But the world is now grown perfectly profane (saith Dr King, on Jonah, Lect. 7), and can play on the Lord's day without book; the sabbath of the Lord, the sanctified day of his rest, is shamelessly troubled and disquieted.

Lay by him in store] Gr. as a treasure, 1 Tim. vi. 18. *Manus pauperum gazophylacium Christi,* The poor man's box is Christ's treasury.

As God hath prospered him] Gr. εὐοδῶται, Given him a good arrival at the end of his voyage, and enabled him; for we may not stretch beyond the staple, and so spoil all.

Ver. 3. *Your liberality*] Gr. your grace; that which having received of God's free grace you do as freely part with to his poor people.

Ver. 4. *That I go also*] And go he did, Rom. xv. 25; Acts xxiv. 17. The very angels hold not themselves too good to serve the saints.

Ver. 5. *When I shall come, &c.*] He was not

[1] *Non ὅσιοι, sed ἅγιοι, ab a et γῆ.*

then yet come into Macedonia, neither was this Epistle written at Philippi (as the subscription saith), a chief city of Macedonia.

Ver. 6. *Yea, and winter with you*] They had ill deserved such a favour of him; for the more he loved them the less he was beloved of them, 2 Cor. xii. 15; but sought he not theirs, but them. Discourtesies must not discourage us from God's work. Calvin, though but coarsely used at his first coming to Geneva, brake through all.

Ver. 7. *If the Lord permit*] The Lord ordereth a good man's goings, Psal. xxxvii. See Acts xvi., with James iv. 13. It was rather rashness than valour in our Richard I., who being told (as he sat at supper) that the French king had besieged his town of Vernoil in Normandy, protested that he would not turn his back until he had confronted the French. And thereupon he caused the wall of his palace that was before him to be broken down toward the south, and posted to the sea-coast immediately into Normandy.

Ver. 8. *But I will tarry at Ephesus*] From thence then he wrote this Epistle, and not at Philippi, as the subscription hath it. See ver. 5.

Ver. 9. *And effectual*] ἐνεργής, or, busy, that requires great painstaking. The ministry is not an idle man's occupation, as some fools think it.

And many adversaries] Truth never wants an opposite. In the beginning of the late Reformation, Eckius, Roffensis, Cajetan, More, Faber, Cochlæus, Catharinus, Pighius, all these wrote against Luther, *Summo conatu, acerrimo desiderio, non vulgari doctrina,* as one saith, with utmost desire and endeavour.

Ver. 10. *For he worketh, &c.*] So doth every faithful minister, though of meaner parts: the vine is the weakest of trees, but full of fruit. A little hand may thread a needle. A little boat may do best in a low river. Philadelphia had but a little strength, Rev. iii. 8, and yet it served turn, and did the deed.

Ver. 11. *Let no man despise him*] For his youth; for he hath lived much in a little time (as it is said of our Edward VI.), and is an old young man, μειρακιογέρων, as was Macarius the Egyptian.

Ver. 12. *I greatly desired him*] Paul did not compel or command him as the pope takes upon him to do, even to princes and potentates. Oh that all kings would answer him in this case, as Philip the Fair of France did Pope Boniface, claiming a power there to bestow prebends and benefices: *Sciat tua maxima fatuitas.* (Alsted. Chron.)

Ver. 13. *Watch ye, &c.*] Solomon's wisdom, Lot's integrity, and Noah's sobriety felt the smart of the serpent's sting. The first was seduced, the second stumbled, the third fell, whiles the eye of watchfulness was fallen asleep.

Ver. 14. *Let all your things, &c.*] Love is the saint's livery, John xiii. 35. Heathens acknowledged that no people in the world did love one another so as Christians did. In the primitive times, *Animo animaque inter se miscebantur,* as Tertullian speaketh. But now, alas, it is far otherwise, love began to grow cold among these Corinthians. Hence this sweet and savoury counsel. Charity in Christ's days was much decayed, in Basil's time, dried up. Latimer saw such a lack of it, that he thought the last day would have been just then. It were to be wished that this apostolical precept were well practised; and that we were all (in a sober sense) of the family of love.

Ver. 15. *To the ministry of saints*] To serve them in collecting and distributing alms to the necessitous.

Ver. 16. *That ye submit*] Giving them due honour, doing them all good offices.

Ver. 17. *They have supplied*] viz. Your absence; for in them I take a short view of you all.

Ver. 18. *They have refreshed*] *Ipse aspectus viri boni delectat.* It is some comfort to see a good man's face.

Ver. 19. *Aquila and Priscilla*] Paul's fast friends and constant companions, worth their weight in gold.

Ver. 20. *With a holy kiss*] Not hollow, as Joab and Judas; not carnal, as that harlot, Prov. vii. 13. See Rom. xvi. 16.

Ver. 21. *With mine own hand*] Well known to the Corinthians, to prevent imposture.

Ver. 22. *If any man love not*] That is, desperately hate. A sin so execrable, that the apostle would not once name it. So the Jews would not name leaven at the Passover, nor a sow at any time, but called it *dabar achar*, another thing.

Anathema, Maranatha] Accurst upon accurst, put over to God to punish. This is a dreadful curse. (Elias Thisbit.) See a gracious promise, Ephes. vi. 24. God may suffer such as love the Lord Jesus Christ in sincerity, to be *Anathema secundum dici* (as Bucholcer said), but not *secundum esse*. See an instance, Isa. lxvi. 5, and say with David, "Let them curse, but do thou bless, Lord."

Ver. 23. *My love, &c.*] Though I have sharply rebuked you, &c., Tit. i. 13.

THE SECOND EPISTLE OF ST PAUL TO THE CORINTHIANS.

CHAPTER I.

Ver. 1. *Our brother*] In the faith, not in the flesh. *Sanctior est copula cordis quam corporis*, Prov. xviii. 24.

Ver. 2. *From God the Father*] The Father is the fountain, the Son the conduit, whereby all good things are derived to us.

Ver. 3. *The Father of mercies*] Only it must be remembered that as he is *Pater miserationum*, so he is *Deus ultionum*, Psal. xciv. 1. As he hath *ubera*, so he hath *verbera*. Christ is girt about the paps with a golden girdle, to show his love, but yet he hath eyes like flaming fire, and feet like burning brass, Rev. i., to look through and keep under his enemies.

The God of all comfort] It is he that shines through the creature, which else is but as the air without light. It is he that comforteth by the means. It is not the word alone, for that is but as the veins and arteries that convey the blood and spirits. So the Spirit being conveyed by the promises, helpeth the soul to lay itself upon Christ by faith, and so it is comforted. Sometimes comfort comes not by the use of the means till afterwards, that he may have the whole glory: Cant. iii., the Church found not him whom her soul loved, till she was a little past the watchmen. The soul is apt to hang her comforts on every hedge, to shift and shirk in every by-corner for comfort. But as air lights not without the sun, and as fuel heats not without fire; so neither can anything soundly comfort us without God.

Una est in trepida mihi re medicina, Jehovæ
  Cor patrium, os verax, omnipotensque manus.
                              Nath. Chytræus.

Ver. 4. *By the comfort wherewith*] How forcible are right words, especially when uttered more from the bowels than the brain, and from our own experience; which made even Christ himself a more compassionate High Priest, and Luther such a heart-affecting preacher, because from his tender years he was much beaten and exercised with spiritual conflicts, as Melancthon testifieth (in Vita). He was also wont to say, that three things make a preacher, reading, prayer, and temptation. Reading maketh a full man, prayer a holy man, temptation an experienced man.

Wherewith we ourselves are comforted] Goodness is communicative. Mr Knox, a little before his death, rose out of his bed; and being asked wherefore, being so sick, he would offer to rise? He answered, that he had had sweet meditations of the resurrection of Jesus Christ that night, and now he would go into the pulpit, and impart to others the comforts that he felt in his soul. (Melch. Adam.)

Ver. 5. *As the sufferings of Christ*] So called, either because the saints suffer for Christ, or because they have him suffering with them, Acts ix. 4. God is more provoked than Nehemiah, Nehem. iv. 3, 5.

So our consolation] As the lower the ebb, the higher the tide, ὅπου πλέων κόπος, πολὺ κέρδος, saith Ignatius. The more pain, the more gain. It is to my loss if you bate me anything in my sufferings. As the hotter the day, the greater the dew at night; so the hotter the time of trouble, the greater the dews of refreshing from God.

Ver. 6. *And whether we be afflicted*] Let the wind sit in what corner soever it will, it blows good to the saints, Cant. iii. 16. Though north and south be of contrary qualities, yet they make the Church's spices to flow and give forth their scent.

Ver. 7. *So shall ye be also, &c.*] Our troubles therefore are compared to the throes of a travailing woman, that tend to a birth, and end in comfort, John xvi. 21.

Ver. 8. *For we would not, &c.*] It is of great use to know the sufferings that others have sustained before us. The primitive Christians kept catalogues of their martyrs. Dr Taylor the martyr at his death gave his son Thomas a Latin book, containing the sayings and sufferings of the old martyrs, collected by himself. In the English seminaries beyond seas, they have at dinner time their martyrology read, that is, the legend of our English traitors.

We despaired even of life] God is oft better to us than our hopes; he reserves usually his holy hand for a dead-lift, he comes in the nick of time, and our extremity is his opportunity. See the note on Luke xviii. 8.

Ver. 9. *But we had the sentence*] Gr. Ἀπόκριμα, the answer or denunciation of death. Here we must distinguish between answers of trial and direct answers. This was of the former sort, for Paul died not at that time. When Leyden was so long and so strictly besieged by the Duke of Alva, that they were forced for their sustenance to search and scrape dunghills, &c., and the duke, in the language of blasphemy, threatened the defendants with cruel death, that very night the winds turned, the tide swelled, and the waters came in, and forced him to raise the siege.

That we should not trust] Hope is never higher elevated than when our state in all men's eyes is at lowest.

Ver. 10. *In whom we trust*] Experience breeds confidence. Thou hast, thou shalt, is an ordinary medium made use of by the Psalmist.

Ver. 11. *You also helping together*] The best may have benefit by the prayers of the meanest. Melancthon was much cheered and confirmed by the prayers of certain women and children, whom he found tugging with God in a corner for the settling of the reformation in Germany. (Selneccer, Pædagog. Christian.)

Ver. 12. *For this is our rejoicing, &c.*] He was merry under his load, because his heart was upright. The sincere will well stand under great pressures, because they are sound. Whereas if a bone be broke, or but the skin rubbed up and raw, the lightest load will be grievous.

And godly sincerity] A fine word he here useth, εἰλικρινεία; and it is a metaphor either from the eagle that trieth her young by holding them forth against the full sight of the sun (so should we the motions of our minds to the word of God); or else from a wise and wary chapman, that holds up the cloth he buys betwixt his eye and the sun. (Arist. Plin.)

Ver. 13. *Than what ye read, &c.*] Or, than what you can both recognize and approve of; for you have known me through and through.

Ver. 14. *You have acknowledged in part*] q. d. You ought to have done it more fully; but you have been carried away, as ye were led by the false apostles.

Ver. 15. *A second benefit*] Gr. "grace," not converting only, but confirming also. All is but enough.

Ver. 16. *And to pass by you*] So indefatigable and unsatisfiable was he in doing God service. Calvin said, *Ne decem quidem maria*, &c., that it would not grieve him to sail over 10 seas, about a uniform draught for religion.

Ver. 17. *Did I use lightness*] So the false apostles suggested against him. Ministers must carefully clear themselves of suspicions and aspersions cast upon them, either by a verbal or real apology.

Ver. 18. *Our word toward you, &c.*] God's children are all such as will not lie, say and unsay, blow hot and cold with a blast, Isa. lxiii. 8. *Christianus est, non mentietur*, He is a Christian, he will not lie, was an old proverb. Sophronius testifieth of Chrysostom, *nunquam eum mentitum fuisse*, that he was never taken in a lie.

Ver. 19. *For the Son of God*] What is that to the purpose? Thus: if the gospel that Paul preached be not yea and nay, then neither are Paul's promises yea and nay. This is his intendment, else his inference is nothing. And by that which follows, it reacheth all Christians; q. d. Look what a Christian doth promise, he is bound by the earnest-penny of God's Spirit to perform. He dares no more alter his words to the discredit of his profession than the Spirit of God can lie. (Mr Cotton on the Seven Vials.)

Ver. 20. *In him are yea and amen*] That is, truth and assurance. They will eat their way over all Alps of opposition, as one speaketh.

Ver. 21. *Hath anointed us*] i. e. Consecrated and qualified us.

Ver. 22. *Sealed us*] As the merchant sets his seal upon his goods.

The earnest of the Spirit] Whereof God should undergo the loss, if he should not give the inheritance, as Chrysostom noteth. The Greeks bought usually *repræsentata pecunia*, for ready money; and this was to buy *Græca fide*; howbeit sometimes they gave earnest: and this ἀῤῥαβών, or earnest, was (usually) the hundredth part of the whole bargain. See the note on Eph. i. 14.

Ver. 23. *I call God to record*] He purgeth himself by oath. So those, Joshua xxii. 22.

Ver. 24. *Dominion over your faith*] As masters of your consciences ; such as the bridge-maker of Rome (Pontifex Romanus) will needs be, Rev. xvii. 1. The purple whore sitteth upon the nations, *i. e.* she useth them vilely and basely, sitting upon their consciences. Stephen, king of Polonia, was wont to say that these three things God had reserved to himself : 1. To make something of nothing. 2. To know future events. 3. To have dominion over men's consciences.

CHAPTER II.

Ver. 1. *That I would not come again*] *Ille dolet quoties cogitur esse ferox.* It goes as much against the heart of a good minister as against the hair with his people, if he say or do anything to their grief. It is no pleasure to him to fling daggers, to speak millstones, to preach damnation, &c. But there is a cruel lenity, as was that of Eli to his sons ; and evil men must be sharply rebuked, that they may be sound in the faith, Tit. i. 13.

Ver. 2. *But the same which is made, &c.*] Nothing can cure a faithful minister of his *cordolium*, of his heart's grief, but his people's amendment. "Now we live if ye stand fast in the Lord," 1 Thess. iii. 8, else we are all amort, and you kill the very hearts of us.

Ver. 3. *Of whom I ought to rejoice*] Nothing sticks a man more than the unkindness of a friend, than expectation of love dashed and disappointed. All evils, as elements, are most troublesome, when out of their proper place, as impiety in professors ; injustice in judges ; unkindness or untowardness in a people toward their pastor, &c.

Ver. 4. *With many tears*] *Non tam atramento, quam lachrymis chartas illevit,* saith Lorinus (in Acts xxii. 19). St Paul's Epistles were written rather with tears than with ink.

Ver. 5. *Have caused grief*] Wicked livers are Hazaels to the godly, and draw many sighs and tears from them. Lot's righteous soul was set upon the rack by the filthy Sodomites. Jeremiah weeps in secret for Judah's sins. Paul cannot speak of those belly-gods with dry eyes, Phil. iii. 18.

Ver. 6. *Sufficient to such a man*] The Novatians therefore were out, that refused to receive in those that repented of their former faults and follies. The Papists burnt some that recanted at the stake, saying, that they would send them out of the world while they were in a good mind.

Ver. 7. *Should be swallowed up*] It was a saying of Mr Philpot, martyr, Satan goes about to mix the detestable darnel of desperation with the godly sorrow of a pure penitent heart.

With overmuch grief] Some holy men (as Master Leaver) have desired to see their sin in the most ugly colours, and God hath heard them ; but yet his hand was so heavy upon them therein, that they went always mourning to their graves ; and thought it fitter to leave it to God's wisdom to mingle the portion of sorrow, than to be their own choosers. (Dr Sibbs, on Psal. xlii. 5.) It is a saying of Austin, Let a man grieve for his sin, and then joy for his grief. Sorrow for sin, if it so far exceed, as that thereby we are disabled for the discharge of our duties, it is a sinful sorrow, yea, though it be for sin.

Ver. 8. *Confirm your love, &c.*] Gr. κυρῶσαι, ratify it, and declare it authentic, as it were in open court, and by public sentence (as Gal. iii. 15), and that at mine instance, as an advocate, παρακαλῶ.

Ver. 9. *Whether ye be obedient*] First to the Lord, and then to us by the will of God, 2 Cor. viii. 5. Confer Heb. xiii. 17 ; Isa. l. 10.

Ver. 10. *To whom ye forgive*] Or, gratify. Mercy is that we must mutually lend and borrow one of another. Let the rigid read Gal. vi. 1.

Ver. 11. *Lest Satan*] That wily merchant, that greedy blood-sucker, that devoureth not widows' houses, but most men's souls, see ver. 7. πλεονεκτηθῶμεν.

For we are not ignorant] He is but a titular Christian that hath not personal experience of Satan's stratagems, νοήματα, his set and composed machinations, his artificially-moulded methods, his plots, darts, depths, whereby he outwitted our first parents, and fits us a pennyworth still, as he sees reason.

Ver. 12. *A door was opened*] An opportunity offered. Where the master sets up a light, there is some work to be done ; where he sends forth his labourers, there is some harvest to be gotten in.

Ver. 13. *I had no rest, &c.*] Gr. ἄνεσιν, no relaxation, viz. from my former cares and anxieties about you, because he was not yet returned to tell me how it was with you, 2 Cor. vii. 6. God's comforts are either rational, fetched from grounds which faith ministereth ; or real, from the presence of comfortable persons or things.

Ver. 14. *Now thanks be to God*] *Deo gratias* was ever in Paul's mouth, ever in Austin's ; and a thankful man is ever ready with his present, as Joseph's brethren were, Gen. xliii. 26.

Causeth us to triumph] Maketh us more than conquerors, even triumphers ; whiles he rides upon us as upon his white horses, all the world over, "conquering and to conquer," Rev. vi. 2.

Ver. 15. *A sweet savour*] The Church is the mortar, preaching the pestle, the promises are the sweet spices, which being beaten, yield a heavenly and supernatural smell in the souls of the godly hearers. (Bifield on 1 Pet. ii.)

Ver. 16. *The savour of death*] Aristotle writeth, that vultures are killed with oil of roses. Swine (saith Pliny) cannot live in some parts of Arabia, by reason of the sweet scent of aromatical trees there growing in every wood. Tigers are enraged with perfumes. *Vipera interficitur palmis,* saith Pausanias. Moses killed the Egyptian, saved the Israelite. Obed-Edom was blessed for the ark, the Philistines were cursed. The sun of the gospel shining upon one that is ordained to eternal life reviveth and quickeneth him ; but lighting upon a child of death it causeth him to stink more abominably. Gregory in his Morals saith that "this word is like the planet Venus, which unto some is Lucifer, a bright morning star arising in their hearts, whereby they are roused up, and stirred from iniquity; but to the other is Hesperus, an evening star, whereby they are brought to bed, and laid asleep in impiety." Œcumenius tells us, that the fragrancy of precious ointment is wholesome for doves, but kills the beetle, *columbam vegetat, scarabæum necat*, &c.

And who is sufficient] And yet now who is it almost that thinks not himself sufficient for that sacred and tremendous function of the ministry? "Who am I?" saith Moses; "Who am I not?" saith our upstart. Bradford was hardly persuaded to become a preacher. Latimer leaped when he laid down his bishopric, being discharged, as he said, of such a heavy burthen. Luther was wont to say, that if he were again to choose his calling, he would dig, or do anything rather than take upon him the office of a minister; so said reverend Mr Whately of Banbury once in my hearing.

Ver. 17. Which corrupt the word] Gr. καπη-λεύοντες, which huckster it, by handling it craftily and covetously, not serving the Lord Jesus Christ, but their own bellies; as those popish trencher flies and our court parasites, who served for false glasses, to make bad faces look fair, and doubted not to adulterate the milk of the word, to the hurt of men's souls.

In the sight of God] It is impossible to speak as in God's presence, and not sincerely; such as do so are not acquainted with that "holy hypocrisy" commended in Dominic the founder of the Dominican friars (Vincent. Belnac. Episc. in hist. Sancti Dom.), whom he was wont to admonish, to feign themselves more virtuous than indeed they were, when they came in company with the laity, that they might get the more respect to themselves and to their doctrine. This was one of the "devil's depths," τὰ βάθη τοῦ Σατανᾶ, Rev. ii. 24; whereunto God's faithful ministers are perfect strangers.

CHAPTER III.

Ver. 1. Do we begin again, &c.] As we had done before, chap. i. 12.

To commend ourselves] *Quod magnificum referente alio fuisset, ipso qui gesserat recensente vanescit.* (Plin.) "Let another man praise thee, and not thine own mouth," Prov. xxvii. 2. *Laus proprio sordescit in ore.* But the apostle was necessitated to it.

As some others, letters of commendation] As the false apostles, who carried it by testimonial; in giving whereof, many good people are much to blame. Beauty needs no letters of commendation, saith Aristotle; much less doth virtue, where it is known. If moral virtue could be seen with mortal eyes, saith Plato, it would soon draw all hearts to itself.

Ver. 2. You are our epistle] The fruitfulness of the people is the preacher's testimonial; as the profiting of the scholar is the teacher's commendation.

Written in our hearts] Or rather in your hearts, as tables; the Spirit writing thereon, by his ministers as pens, that form of doctrine, Rom. vi. 17, that law of their minds, Rom. vii. 23, Heb. viii. 10, to be known and read of all men.

Ver. 3. Ministered by us] Who are devoted to the service of your faith, and are the Lord Christ's secretaries.

But in fleshy tables] In the softened heart God writes his law, puts an inward aptness, answering the law of God without, as lead answers the mould, as tally answers tally, as indenture answers indenture.

Ver. 4. Such trust have we] i. e. Such boldness of holy boasting. If Tully could say, Two things I have to bear me bold upon, the knowledge of good arts and the glory of great acts; how much more might Paul!

Ver. 5. Not that we are sufficient] Lest they should think him arrogant. Cyrus had this written upon his tomb, "I could do all things," πάντα ποιεῖν ἐδυνάμην, as Arrianus reports. So could Paul too; but it was through Christ which strengthened him, Phil. iv. 13.

All our sufficiency is of God] Had not ministers then need to pray? *Bene orasse est bene studuisse*, saith Luther. And whether a minister shall do no more good to others by his prayers or preaching, I will not determine (saith a reverend writer), but he shall certainly by his prayers reap more comfort to himself; whereto I add, that unless he pray for his hearers as well as preach to them, he may preach to as little purpose as Bede did, when he preached to a heap of stones; and that if people pray not for their ministers, they may prove *ministrorum opprobria*, like Laban's lambs, or Pharaoh's kine; they may thank themselves for their minister's insufficiency and their own non-proficiency.

Ver. 6. Not of the letter] To wit, of the law, which requireth perfect obedience, presupposing holiness in us, and cursing the disobedient; but the gospel (called here the Spirit) presupposeth unholiness, and, as an instrument, maketh us holy, John xvii. 17; Acts x. 32. For we preach Christ, 1 Cor. i. 23. We give what we preach. The Spirit is received by the preaching of faith, Gal. iii. 2. This manna is rained down in the sweet dews of the ministry of the gospel, 1 Pet. i. 22.

For the letter killeth] Many popish priests, that hardly ever had seen, much less read, St Paul's writings, having gotten this sentence by the end, "The letter killeth," took care of being killed, by not meddling with good literature. Hence that of Sir Thomas More to one of them,

Tu bene cavisti, ne te ulla occidere possit
Littera: nam nulla est littera nota tibi.

Ver. 7. The ministration of death] That is, the law. David was the voice of the law awarding death to sin, "He shall surely die." Nathan was the voice of the gospel awarding life to repentance for sin, "Thou shalt not die."

For the glory of his countenance] Which yet reflected not upon his own eyes. He shone bright and knew not of it : he saw God's face glorious, he did not think others had so seen his. How many have excellent graces and perceive them not !

Ver. 8. *Be rather glorious*] Let this comfort the ministers of the gospel under the contempts cast upon them by the mad world, ever beside itself in point of salvation. See Isa. xlix. 5.

Ver. 9. *Exceed in glory*] A throne was set in heaven, Rev. iv. 2 ; not in the mount, as Exod. xxv. 9. The pattern of our Church is showed in the heavens themselves, because of that more abundant glory of the gospel above the law. And therefore also John describeth the city far greater and larger than Ezekiel, Rev. xxi. ; because Ezekiel was a minister of the law, John of the gospel. (Brightman in loc.)

Ver. 10. *Had no glory*] To speak of, and in comparison. The light of the law was obscured and overcast by the light of the gospel. The sea about the altar was brazen, 1 Kings vii. 23, and what eyes could pierce through it ? Now our sea about the throne is glassy, Rev. iv. 6, like to crystal, clearly conveying the light and sight of God in Christ to our eyes.

Ver. 11. *Much more that*, &c.] As the sun outshineth Lucifer his herald.

Ver. 12. *Plainness of speech*] Or, much evidence, as John x. 24 ; xi. 14 ; xvi. 29 ; with much perspicuity and authority we deliver ourselves ; we speak with open face, not fearing colours.

Ver. 13. *Could not stedfastly*, &c.] Could not clearly see Christ the end of the law, Rom. x. 4 ; Gal. iii. 14.

Ver. 14. *But their minds*] Unless God give sight as well as light, and enlighten both organ and object, we can see nothing.

Which vail is done away] See Isa. xxv. 7. Faith freeth from blindness ; we no sooner taste of that stately feast by faith, but the vail of ignorance, which naturally covereth all flesh, is torn and rent.

Ver. 15. *The vail is upon their hearts*] By a malicious and voluntary hardening, they curse Christ and his worshippers in their daily devotions, and call *Evangelium Avengillaion* the gospel a volume of vanity or iniquity. (Elias in Thisb.)

Ver. 16. *When it shall turn*] Of the Jews' conversion, and what hinders it, see the note on Rom. xi. 7, 8, 25.

Ver. 17. *The Lord is that Spirit*] Christ only can give the Jews that noble spirit, as David calleth him, Psal. l. 12, that freeth a man from the invisible chains of the kingdom of darkness.

Ver. 18. *Are changed*] As the pearl by the often beating of the sunbeams upon it becomes radiant.

From glory to glory] That is, from grace to grace. Fulness of grace is the best thing in glory. Other things, as peace and joy, are but the shinings forth of this fulness of grace in glory.

CHAPTER IV.

Ver. 1. *As we have received mercy*] Sith we have so freely been called to the ministry of mere mercy, we show forth therein all sedulity and sincerity. When I was born, said that French king, thousand others were born besides myself. Now what have I done to God more than they, that I should be a king, and not they ? Tamerlane having overcome Bajazet, asked him whether ever he had given God thanks for making him so great an emperor ; who confessed ingenuously he never thought of it. To whom Tamerlane replied, that it was no wonder so ungrateful a man should be made a spectacle of misery. For you, saith he, being blind of one eye, and I lame of a leg, was there any worth in us why God should set us over two such great empires of Turks and Tartars ? (Leunclav. Annal. Turc.) So may ministers say, What are we that God should call us to so high an office ? &c.

We faint not] We droop not, we flag not, οὐκ ἐκκακοῦμεν, we hang not the wing, though hardly handled. For, *Prædicare nihil aliud est quam derivare in se furorem totius mundi*, as Luther said.

Ver. 2. *The hidden things of dishonesty*] All legerdemain and under-hand dealing. They that do evil hate the light, love to lurk. But sin hath woaded an impudency in some men's faces, that they dare do anything.

To every man's conscience] A pure conscience hath a witness in every man's bosom. See 1 Cor. xiv. 24. St Paul did so preach and live, that every man's conscience could not choose but say, Certainly Paul preacheth the truth, and liveth right ; and we must live as he speaketh and doeth. One desired a misliving preacher to point him out a nearer way to heaven than that he had taught in his sermons ; for he went not that way himself. Of such an one it was once said, That when he was out of the pulpit, it was pity he should ever go into it ; and when he was in the pulpit, it was pity he should ever come out of it. St Paul was none such, as all knew.

Ver. 3. *To them that are lost*] It is a sign of a reprobate goat, John viii. 43, 47. "Sensual, having not the Spirit," Jude 19. The devil holds his black hand before their eyes, that they may fall blindling into hell. Herein he dealeth as the eagle, which setting on the hart, saith Pliny, lights upon his horns, and there flutters up and down, filling his eyes with dust borne in her feathers, that at last he may cast himself from a rock.

Ver. 4. *The god of this world*] The devil usurps such a power, and wicked men will have it so. They set him up for God : if he do but hold up his finger, give the least hint, they are at his obedience, as God at first did but speak the word, and it was done. All their buildings, ploughings, plantings, sailings, are for the devil. And if we could rip up their hearts, we should find written therein, The god of this present world.

Ver. 5. We preach not ourselves] We are Christ's paranymphs or spokesmen, and must woo for him. Now if we should speak one word for him and two for ourselves, as all self-seekers do, how can we answer it?

Ver. 6. Hath shined] The first work of the Spirit in man's heart is to beat out new windows there, and to let in light, Acts xxvi. 18. And then, *Semper in sole sita est Rhodos, qui et calorem et colorem nobis impertit.* (Æneas Sylv.)

Ver. 7. In earthen vessels] Gr. ἐν ὀστρακίνοις, in oyster-shells, as the ill-favoured oyster hath in it a bright pearl. *Vilis sæpe cadus nobile nectar habet.* In a leathern purse may be a precious pearl.

Ver. 8. We are troubled on every side] This is the world's wages to God's ministers. *Veritas odium parit.* Opposition is *Evangelii genius,* said Calvin. Truth goes ever with a scratched face.

We are perplexed] Pray for me, I say, pray for me, saith Latimer; for I am sometimes so fearful, that I could creep into a mouse-hole; sometimes God doth visit me again with comfort, &c. There is an elegancy here in the original that cannot well be rendered (ἀπορούμενοι, ἀλλ᾽ οὐκ ἐξαπορούμενοι). Tertullian hammers at it in his *Indigemus, sed non perindigemus.* Beza hath it *Hæsitamus at non prorsus hæremus.* Mr Dike "staggering," but not wholly sticking.

Ver. 9. Persecuted, but not forsaken] The Church may be shaken, not shivered; persecuted, not conquered. (*Concuti, non excuti.*) *Roma cladibus animosior,* said one; it is more true of the Church. She gets by her losses, and, as the oak, she taketh heart to grace from the maims and wounds given her. *Duris ut ilex tonsa bipennibus.*

Niteris incassum Christi submergere navem :
Fluctuat, at nunquam mergitur illa ratis :

as the pope wrote once to the Great Turk.

Cast down, but not destroyed] *Impellere possunt,* said Luther of his enemies, *sed totum prosternere non possunt : crudeliter me tractare possunt, sed non extirpare : dentes nudare, sed non devorare : occidere me possunt, sed in totum me perdere non possunt.* They may thrust me, but not throw me; show their teeth, but not devour me; kill me, but not hurt me.

Ver. 10. The dying of the Lord] A condition obnoxious to daily deaths and dangers.

Might be made manifest] As it was in Paul, when being stoned, he started up with a *Sic, sic oportet intrare,* Thus, thus must heaven be had, and no otherwise.

Ver. 11. For we which live, &c.] Good men only are heirs of the grace of life, 1 Pet. iii. 7. Others are living ghosts and walking sepulchres of themselves.

Ver. 12. Death worketh in us] It hath already seized upon us, but yet we are not killed with death, as those were, Rev. ii. 23. As a godly man said, that he did *ægrotare vitaliter;* so the saints do *mori vitaliter,* die to live for ever.

But life in you] q. d. You have the happiness to be exempted, while we are *tantum non interempti,* little less than done to death.

Ver. 13. The same spirit] That you have, and shall be heirs together of heaven with you, though here we meet with more miseries.

I believed, and therefore, &c.] The spirit of faith is no indweller where the door of the lips open not in holy confession and communication.

Ver. 14. Shall present us with you] Shall bring us from the jaws of death to the joys of eternal life.

Ver. 15. That the abundant grace] This is one end wherefore God suffers his ministers to be subject to so many miseries, that the people might be put upon prayer and praise for their deliverance.

Ver. 16. Yet the inward man] Peter Martyr dying, said, "My body is weak, my mind is well, well for the present, and it will be better hereafter." This is the godly man's motto.

Ver. 17. For our light affliction] Here we have an elegant antithesis, and a double hyperbole, beyond Englishing. For affliction, here is glory; for light affliction, a weight of glory; for momentary affliction, eternal glory.

Which is but for a moment] For a short braid only, as that martyr said. Mourning lasteth but till morning. It is but winking, and thou shalt be in heaven presently, quoth another martyr.

Worketh unto us] As a *causa sine qua non,* as the law worketh wrath, Rom. iv. 15. If our dear Lord did not put these thorns into our bed, we should sleep out our lives and lose our glory : affliction calls to us as the angel to Elijah, Up, thou hast a great way to go.

A far more exceeding] An exceeding excessive eternal weight. Or, a far most excellent eternal weight. *Nec Christus nec cælum patitur hyperbolen,* saith one. Here it is hard to hyperbolize. Words are too weak to express heaven's happiness. The apostle heard wordless words, ῥήματα ἄρρητα, 2 Cor. xii. 4, when he was there, and in speaking of it commonly useth a transcendent super-superlative kind of language. The Vulgar interpreter's *supra modum in sublimitate,* Erasmus' *mire supra modum,* Beza's *excellenter excellens,* falls a far deal short of St Paul's emphatical Grecism here. Διπλασιάζει, saith Chrysostom. He could not comprise it in one single word, he doubleth it therefore, and yet attaineth not to what he aimeth at.

Weight of glory] The apostle alludeth to the Hebrew and Chaldee words which signify both weight and glory, כבוד יקד. Glory is such a weight, as if the body were not upheld by the power of God, it were impossible it should bear it. Joy so great, as that we must enter into it; it is too big to enter into us. "Enter into thy

Master's joy," Matt. xxv. Here we find that when there is great joy, the body is not able to bear it, our spirits are ready to expire; what shall it then be in heaven?

Ver. 18. *Whiles we look not*] Gr. σκοπούντων, whiles we make them not our scope, our mark to aim at. Heaven we may make our mark, our aim, though not our highest aim.

At the things that are seen] Whiles we eye things present only, it will be with us as with a house without pillars, tottering with every blast, or a ship without anchor, tossed with every wave.

But at the things which are not seen] *Pericula non respicit martyr, coronas respicit; plagas non horret, præmium numerat; non videt lictores inferne flagellantes, sed angelos superne acclamantes*, saith Basil; who also tells us how the martyrs that were cast out naked in a winter's night being to be burned the next day, comforted themselves and one another with these words, Sharp is the cold, but sweet is Paradise; troublesome is the way, but pleasant shall be the end of our journey; let us endure cold a little, and the patriarch's bosom shall soon warm us; let our foot burn awhile, that we may dance for ever with angels; let our hand fall into the fire, that it may lay hold upon eternal life. Δριμὺς ὁ χείμων, &c., Basil. εἰς τοὺς μαρτ.

But the things which, &c.] The Latins call prosperous things *res secundas*, because they are to be had hereafter; they are not the first things, these are past, Rev. xxi.

CHAPTER V.

Ver. 1. *For we know*] Not we think, or hope only; this is the top-gallant of faith, the triumph of trust; this is, as Latimer calls it, the sweetmeats of the feast of a good conscience. There are other dainty dishes in this feast, but this is the banquet. The cock on the dunghill knows not the worth of this jewel.

Our earthly house] In the wonderful frame of man's body the bones are the timberwork, the head the upper-lodging, the eyes as windows, the eyelids as casements, the brows as penthouses, the ears as watch-towers, the mouth as a door to take in that which shall uphold the building, and keep it in reparations; the stomach as a kitchen to dress that which is conveyed into it; the guts and baser parts as sinks belonging to the house, &c., as one wittily descants.

Our earthly house of this tabernacle] Our clay cottage. Man is but *terra friabilis*, a piece of earth neatly made up. The first man is of the earth earthy; and his earthly house is ever mouldering over him, ready to fall upon his head, 1 Cor. xv. 47. Hence it is called "the life of his hands," because hardly held up with the labour of his hands, Isa. lvii. 10. Paul, a tentmaker, elegantly compares man's body to a tent. Plato also in his dialogue of death, calleth the body a tabernacle, τὸ σκῆνος. A house the body is called, as for the singular artifice showed in the framing of it (the woman's body is, by a specialty, called God's building, Gen. ii. 22, because her frame consisteth of rarer room; of a more exact composition, say some, than man's doth), so, secondly, because the soul dwells in it; the reason whereof (besides God's will, and for the order of the universe) Lombard gives this, that hereby man might learn and believe a possibility of the union of man with God in glory, notwithstanding the vast distance of nature and excellence.

We have a building of God] The ark, transportative till then, was settled in Solomon's temple; so shall the soul be in heaven. As when one skin falls off, another comes on; so when our earthly tabernacle shall be dissolved or taken down, we shall have a heavenly house. The soul wears the body as a garment, which when it is worn out, we shall be clothed with a better suit, we shall change our rags for robes, &c. *Itaque non plangimus, sed plaudimus, quando vitam claudimus, quia dies iste non tam fatalis quam natalis est.*

Ver. 2. *For in this*] That is, in this tabernacle of the body. How willingly do soldiers burn their huts, when the siege is ended; being glad that their work is done, and that they may go home and dwell in houses.

We groan earnestly] As that *avis Paradisi*, which being once caught and engaged, never leaves sighing, they say, till set at liberty. (Macrob.) The Greeks call the body δέμας, the soul's bond, and σῶμα, *quasi* σῆμα, the soul's sepulchre.

To be clothed upon] By a sudden change, and not to die at all, as 1 Thess. iv. 17; 1 Cor. xv. 51, 52. *Quis enim vult mori? prorsus nemo.* Death when it comes will have a bout with the best, as it had with Hezekiah, David, Jonah, others. For nature abhors it, and every new man is two men. But when a Christian considers that *non nisi per angusta ad angusta perveniatur*, that there is no passing into Paradise but under the flaming sword of this angel death that standeth at the porch; that there is no coming to the city of God, but through his strait and heavy lane; no wiping all tears from his eyes, but with his winding-sheet, he yields, and is not only content, but full glad of his departure; as in the mean while he accepts of life rather than affects it, he endures it rather than desires it, Phil. i. 23.

Ver. 3. *If so be that, &c.*] q. d. Howbeit, I know not whether we shall be so clothed upon, that is, whether we that are now alive shall be found alive at Christ's coming to judgment, whether we shall then be found clothed with our bodies, or naked, that is, stript of our bodies.

Ver. 4. *Do groan, being burdened*] viz. With sin and misery, whereof we have here our backburdens. And surely great shame it were (as that martyr, Mr Bradford, said) that all the whole creatures of God should desire, yea, groan in their kind for our liberty, and we ourselves to loathe it, as doubtless we do, if for the cross, yea, for death itself, we with joy swallow not up all sorrow that might let us from following the

Lord's call and obeying the Lord's providence, &c.

Might be swallowed up of life] Not as a gulf or fire swallows up that that is cast into it, but as perfection swallows up imperfection, as the perfecting of a picture swallows up the rude draught, as perfect skill swallows up bungling, or manhood childhood, not extinguishing, but drowning it that it is not seen. (Dr Preston.)

Ver. 5. *He that hath wrought us*] Curiously wrought us in the lowermost parts of the earth, that is, in the womb, as curious workmen perfect their choice pieces in private, and then set them forth to public view, Psal. cxxxix. 15, with Eph. iv. 9. Others expound it by Rom. ix. 23.

The earnest of the Spirit] He saith not the pawn, but the earnest. A pawn is to be returned again, but an earnest is part of the whole bargain.

Ver. 6. *Therefore we are confident*] Not hesitant, or halting, as Adrian the emperor was, and as he that cried out on his death-bed, *Anxius vixi, dubius morior, nescio quo vado*, I have lived carefully, I die doubtfully, I go I know not whither. Socrates also, that wisest of philosophers, could not with all his skill resolve his friends whether it were better for a man to die or live longer. Cicero, comforting himself as well as he could by the help of philosophy against the fear of death, cries out and complains at length, that the medicine was too weak for the disease, *nescio quomodo, imbecillior est medicina quam morbus;* it is the true Christian only that can be confident that his end shall be happy, though his beginning and middle haply may be troublesome, Psal. xxxvii. 37.

Whilst we are at home] Or stay for a night as in an inn, ἐνδημοῦντες. A man that comes into an inn, if he can get a better room, he will; if not, he can be content with it; for, saith he, it is but for a night. So it should be with us.

Ver. 7. *For we walk by faith*] Which puts our heads into heaven, sets us on the top of Pisgah with Moses, and therehence descries and describes unto us the promised land, gives us to set one foot aforehand in the porch of Paradise, to see as Stephen did Christ holding out a crown, with this inscription, *Vincenti dabo.*

Not by sight] Sense corrects imagination, reason sense, but faith corrects both, thrusting Hagar out of doors, when haughty and haunty grown. But as Nabash, so the devil labours to put out the right eye of faith, and to leave us only the left eye of reason.

Ver. 8. *And willing rather*] Death is not to be desired as a punishment of sin, but as a period of sin; not as a postern gate to let out our temporal, but as a street door to let in eternal life.

To be present with the Lord] This Bernard calleth *Repatriasse.* Plotinus the philosopher could say when he died, that which is divine in me I carry back, ἐπὶ τὸ πρωτόγονον θεῖον, to the original divine, that is, to God. (Synes. ep. 139.) But whether this man believed himself or not, I greatly doubt.

Ver. 9. *Wherefore we labour*] Our hope of heaven maketh us active and abundant in God's service. The doctrine of assurance is not a doctrine of liberty, but the contrary, 1 John iii. 3. We make it our ambition, φιλοτιμούμεθα, saith the apostle here, to get acceptance in heaven, waiting till our Father shall call us home, and passing the time of our sojourning here in fear, 1 Pet. i. 17. The saints have their commoration upon earth, ἐνδημοῦντες, their conversation in heaven.

Ver. 10. *For we must all, &c.*] This great assize will not be such an assembly as that of Ahasuerus, of his nobles, princes, and captains only; nor such as the biddings of rich men to their feasts, of their rich neighbours only; but like the invitation of that householder that sent his servants to compel all to come in, Luke xiv. 12. On that day Adam shall see all his nephews together.

Appear before, &c.] Be laid open, and have all ript up, φανερωθῆναι. Our sins that are now written as it were with the juice of lemons, shall then by the fire of the last day be made legible. And as in April both wholesome roots and poisonable discover themselves, which in the winter were not seen, so at the day of judgment good and evil actions. (Mac. Hom. 12.)

The things done in his body] That is, the just reward of those things; *In die judicii plus valebit conscientia pura, quam marsupia plena.* (Bernard.) Then shall a good conscience be more worth than all the world's good. And this was that that made Paul so sincere a preacher and so insatiable a server of God, as Chrysostom calleth him.

Whether it be good or bad] Wicked men shall give an account, 1. *De bonis commissis,* of goods committed to them. 2. *De bonis dimissis,* of good neglected by them. 3. *De malis commissis,* of evils committed. 4. *De malis permissis,* of evils done by others, suffered by them. *Itaque vivamus,* saith the orator. (Cic. iv. in Ver.) Let us so live as those that must render an account of all.

Ver. 11. *Knowing therefore the terror, &c.*] What a terrible time it will be with the wicked, who shall in vain tire the deaf mountains with their hideous outcries to fall upon them, &c.

We persuade men] To flee from the wrath to come; to repent and be converted, that their sins may be blotted out, when the times of refreshing shall come, Acts iii. 19. We speak persuasively to this purpose, but it is God only that persuades.

Ver. 12. *Which glory in appearance*] Gr. ἐν προσώπῳ, in the face. Hypocrites, as they repent in the face, Matt. vi. 16, so they rejoice in the face, not in the heart. Their joy is but skin deep, it is but the hypocrisy of mirth; they do not laugh, but grin; their hearts ache many times when their faces counterfeit a smile; their mirth is frothy and flashy, such as smooths the brow but fills not the breast, such as wets the mouth but warms not the heart.

Ver. 13. *It is to God*] i. e. When to the world we seem mad of pride and vain-glory, yet then we respect only God's glory.

It is for your sakes] *i. e.* For your learning, that we are more modest and sparing in commending our apostleship. It is a good rule, *Quicquid agas, propter Deum agas*, do all for God's sake.

Ver. 14. *The love of Christ, &c.*] As reward hath an attractive, and punishment an impulsive, so love hath a compulsive faculty. This love of Christ had so closed in St Paul, so hemmed him in, and begirt him round, that his adversaries reported him a mad-man, as ver. 13 ; he erred in love toward his sweet Saviour, and even exhaled his blessed soul in continual sallies, as it were, and expressions of his dear affection to the Lord Jesus. The word συνέχει he here useth, imports that he was even shut up by his love to his dear Lord, as in a pound or pinfold, so that he could not get out. He had meditated so much upon Christ's love, *donec totus fixus in corde, qui totus fixus in cruce*, that his heart was turned into a lump of love.

Then were all dead] All the body suffered in and with Christ the head, and so are freed by his death, Heb. ii. 9, as if themselves in person had died.

Ver. 15. *Should not henceforth*] *Servati sumus ut serviamus.* The redeemed among the Romans were to observe and honour those that ransomed them as parents, all their days.

Ver. 16. *No man after the flesh*] *i. e.* We esteem no man simply the better or worse for his wealth, poverty, honour, ignominy, or anything outward. See Jam. i. 9—11. Thomas Watts, martyr, spake thus at his death to his wife and children : Wife, and my good children, I must now depart from you, therefore henceforth know I you no more ; but as the Lord hath given you to me, so I give you again to him, whom I charge you see that ye obey. (Acts and Mon.)

Though we have known Christ] As possibly Paul might have known Christ in the flesh ; for Jesus of Nazareth was a prophet mighty in deed and word before God and all the people, Luke xxiv. 19. Austin wished that he might have seen three things : Rome flourishing, Paul preaching, Christ conversing with men upon earth. Bede comes after, and correcting this last wish, saith, Yea, but let me see the King in his beauty, Christ in his heavenly kingdom. Paul was so spiritualized that he took knowledge of nothing here below ; he passed through the world as a man in a deep muse, or that so looks for a lost jewel, that he overlooks all besides it.

Ver. 17. *Is a new creature*] Either a new man or no man in Christ. Get into him therefore with all speed ; for till this be done, though thou shouldest spend thy time in gathering up pearls and jewels, thou art an undone creature.

All things are become new] The substance of the soul is the same, the qualities and operations altered. In regeneration our natures are translated, not destroyed, no, not our constitution and complexion. As the melancholy man doth not cease to be so after conversion, only the humour

is sanctified to a fitness for godly sorrow, holy meditation, &c., so of other humours.

Ver. 18. *And all things are of God*] He is both author and finisher of our faith, the God of all grace, the Father of all lights, &c.

And hath given us the ministry] He hath taken this office from the angels, those first preachers of peace, Luke ii. 10, 14. The angel told Cornelius his prayers were heard in heaven ; but for the doctrine of reconciliation he refers him to Peter, Acts x. 36.

Ver. 19. *That God was in Christ, &c.*] As the salt-waters of the sea, when they are strained through the earth, they are sweet in the rivers ; so (saith one) the waters of majesty and justice in God, though terrible, yet being strained and derived through Christ, they are sweet and delightful.

Reconciling the world] What the apostle meaneth by this, see his own exposition, Rom. xi. 15.

Ver. 20. *Ambassadors for Christ*] And therefore sacred persons, not to be violated on pain of God's heavy displeasure : " Do my prophets no harm." They that would annihilate the ministry, go to pull the stars out of Christ's hand ; and they will find it a work not feasible.

As though God did beseech you] God's grace even kneels to us. *En flexanimam suadæ medullam ;* who can turn his back upon such blessed and bleeding embracements ?

Ver. 21. *To be sin for us*] That is, a sin offering, or an exceeding sinner, as Exod. xxix. 14. So Christ was, 1. By imputation, for our sins were " made to meet upon him," as that evangelical prophet hath it, Isa. liii. 6. 2. By reputation, for he was reckoned among malefactors, ibid. And yet one Augustinus de Roma, archbishop of Nazareth, was censured in the Council of Basil for affirming that Christ was *peccatorum maximus*, the greatest of sinners. See Aug. Enchirid. xli. Christ so loved us, saith one, that he endured that which he most hated, to become sin for us (he was made sin passive in himself to satisfy for sin active in us), and the want of that which was more worth than a world to him, the sense of God's favour for a time. *Ama amorem illius, &c.,* saith Bernard. There are two things in guilt, saith a late reverend writer (Dr Sibbs) : 1. The merit and desert of it ; this Christ took not. 2. The obligation to punishment ; this he took, and so he " became sin," that is, bound to the punishment of sin. The son of a traitor loseth his father's lands, not by any communion of fault, but by communion of nature, because he is part of his father. The son is no traitor ; but by his nearness to his father is wrapped in the same punishment ; so here. In a city that is obnoxious to the king's displeasure, perhaps there are some that are not guilty of the offence ; yet being all citizens, they are all punished by reason of their communion. So Christ, by communion with our natures, took upon him whatsoever was penal that belonged to sin, though he took not, nor could take, the demerit of sin.

Who knew no sin] That is, with a practical knowledge; with an intellectual he did, else he could not have reproved it. We know no more than we practise. Christ is said to "know no sin," because he did none.

That we might be made, &c.] As Christ became sin, not by sin inherent in him, but by our sin imputed to him; so are we made the righteousness of God, by Christ's righteousness imputed and given unto us. This the Papists jeeringly call "putative righteousness."

CHAPTER VI.

Ver. 1. *As workers together*] Not as coadjutors, but as instruments, such as God is pleased to make use of. See the note on 1 Cor. iii. 9.

The grace of God in vain] That ambassage of grace, chap. v. 20; or that unspeakable gift of Christ, ver. 21, which many use as homely as Rachel did her father's gods,—she hid them in the litter and sat on them; or as that lewd boy in Kett's conspiracy, who when the king's pardon was offered the rebels by a herald, he turned toward him his naked posteriors, and used words suitable to that gesture. One standing by discharged a harquebuss upon the body. (Life of K. Edward VI., by Sir John Hay.)

Ver. 2. *Now is the accepted time*] He purposely beats upon the τὸ νῦν, because opportunity is headlong, and, if once past, irrecoverable. Some are *semper victuri*, as Seneca saith, they stand trifling out their time, and so fool away their salvation. God will not always serve men for a sinning-stock. *Patientia læsa fit furor.* Do we therefore as millers and mariners, who take the gale when it cometh, and make use of it, because they have not the wind in a bottle.

Now is the day of salvation] And God will not suffer men twice to neglect it. If once past, it will never dawn again. Catch therefore at opportunities, as the echo catcheth the voice, Psal. xxvii., take the nick of time. God is more peremptory now than ever, Heb. ii. 2, 3.

Ver. 3. *Giving no offence*] A minister should be as Absalom was, without blemish from head to foot. His fruit should be, as that of Paradise, fair to the eye and sweet to the taste. A small fault is soon seen in him, and easily either imitated or upbraided. God appointed both the weights and measures of the sanctuary to be twice as large as those of the commonwealth.

Ver. 4. *In much patience*] Or tolerance, suffering hardship, as good soldiers of Jesus Christ.

In afflictions] Out of which there is little or no use of patience; at least she cannot have her perfect work, James i. 4.

In necessities] Want of necessaries.

In distresses] Such straits as that we are at a stand, and have not whither to turn us, στενοχωρίαις; we are in a little ease as it were.

Ver. 5. *In imprisonments*] Chrysostom saith, he had rather be Paul cast into a prison than Paul rapt up into Paradise.

Ver. 6. *By pureness*] By lamb-like simplicity or sincerity. Religion loves to lie clean, said one. Godliness must run through our whole lives as the woof doth through the web. See Isa. xxxiii. 14. No gold or precious stone is so pure as the prudent mind of a pious man, said divine Plato. οὔτε χρυσὸς, οὔτε ἄδαμας οὕτως ἀστράπτει ὥσπερ ἀγαθῶν ἀνδρῶν νόος συμφράδμων.

Ver. 7. *On the right hand, &c.*] Against the world's both *irritamenta* and *terriculamenta*, both allurements and affrightments. *Contemptus est a me Romanus et favor et furor*, saith Luther, when the pope one while enticed him and another while threatened him. When he was offered to be cardinal if he would be quiet, he replied, No, not if I might be pope. When he was told that he should find no favour; *Quid vero facere poterunt?* (said he) *occident? Nunquid resuscitabunt, ut iterum occidant?* What will they do? will they kill me? But can they raise me to life again that they may kill me again? Can they kill me the second time? (Epist. ad Spal.)

Ver. 8. *By honour and dishonour, &c.*] It is written on heaven doors (said that martyr), "Do well and hear ill." A bad report is the ordinary reward of very well doing; which made Luther wax proud even of his reproach. *Superbus fio*, said he, *quod video nomen pessimum mihi crescere.* Jerome also writeth to Augustine, *Quod signum majoris gloriæ est, omnes hæretici me detestantur*, This is my glory, that none of the heretics can give me a good word or look. It was a divine saying of Seneca, No man sets better rate upon virtue than he that loseth a good name to keep a good conscience. *Qui boni viri famam perdidit ne conscientiam perderet.*

As deceivers] Aspersed for such, as Christ was, Matt. xxvii. 63. And Lucian blasphemously termeth him ἐσκολοπισμένον σοφίστην, the crucified cozener.

Ver. 9. *As unknown*] To the world, 1 John iii. 1, 2. A prince in a strange land is little set by, as not known. Unkent, unkist, as the northern proverb hath it.

Well known] To them that have spiritual judgment, and can prize a person to his worth, which the world's wizards cannot do, Isa. liii. 2, 3.

And not killed] God will have a care of that; he corrects in measure, he smites his not at the root, but in the branches, Isa. xxvii. 8. As it is a rule in physic still to maintain nature, &c., so doth God still keep up the spirits of his people by cordials, Isa. lvii. 16.

Ver. 10. *As sorrowful, yet, &c.*] God's works are usually done *in oppositis mediis*, as Luther said. Out of the eater he brings meat, &c. This riddle the world understands not. The Fathers observe here, that the apostle brings in the saints' sorrow with a *quasi*, as if it were a sorrow in show or conceit only; but when he speaks of their joy, there is no such *quasi*.

Yet possessing all things] Godliness hath an αὐτάρκεια, a self-sufficiency, 1 Tim. vi. 6. *Cui cum paupertate bene convenit, pauper non est*, saith Seneca. A contented man cannot be a poor man;

especially if a godly man; for why? the Father (that Ancient of days) filleth his memory; the Son (the wisdom of the Father) filleth his understanding; the Holy Ghost the Comforter filleth his will; and so he must needs have all that thus hath the haver of all.

Ver. 11. *Our mouth is open unto you*] We speak thus freely unto you, out of our deep affection towards you; we even carve you a piece of our heart, we pour forth ourselves in this flood of speech, that thereby ye may take a scantling of our over-abundant love to your souls. κεχηνότες, open-mouthed men, are put for fools oftentimes in Lucian and Aristophanes; but in another sense than the apostle here useth it. A large heart maketh a man full in the mouth, as if it sought that way to get out to the thing affected.

Ver. 12. *Ye are not straitened in us*] *Non habitatis angustè in nobis;* so Piscator renders it.

But ye are straitened] Ye are bankrupts in love, ye comply not, ye do not reciprocate. Plain things will join every point one with another; not so round and rugged things.

Ver. 13. *I speak as unto my children*] Here are soft words, hard arguments. This is the way to win; and that was a sad complant, 2 Cor. xii. 15. Love lost is a bitter affliction.

Ver. 14. *Be not unequally yoked*] Dare not, saith Mr Ward, to yoke thyself with any untamed heifer that bears not Christ's yoke. *Quam male inœquales veniunt ad aratra juvenci?* (Ovid. Epist.) An ox and an ass might not be coupled together in the law; and hereunto the apostle seems to allude. The doctors of Douay upon Lev. xix. 19: Here all participation, say they, with heretics and schismatics is forbidden. Philip king of Spain said, He had rather have no subjects than subjects of divers religions. And out of a bloody zeal, suffered his eldest son Charles to be murdered by the bloody Inquisition, because he seemed to favour our profession.

Ver. 15. *What concord hath Christ*] Those moderators that plead for a correspondency with Popery, would make a pretty show if there were no Bible. But if these reconcilers (as Franciscus de Sancta Clara, and his fautors) were the wisest men under heaven, and should live to the world's end, they would be brought to their wits' end before they could accomplish this work's end, to make a reconciliation betwixt Christ and Antichrist, betwixt Rome and us. What harmony or concord, saith our apostle, can be betwixt such? they can never fall in, or make music together in one choir.

Ver. 16. *I will dwell in them*] Gr. ἐνοικήσω ἐν αὐτοῖς, I will indwell in them. This notes God's nearest communion with them. He setteth them before his face continually, Psal. xli. 12, as loving to look upon them. The philosopher told his friends, when they came into his little low cottage, The gods are here with me: ἐντεῦθεν οὐκ ἄπεισι Θέοι. God and angels are with his saints.

And walk in them] As they did in Solomon's porch, and other walks and galleries about the temple. And hereunto the prophet alludes,

Zech. iii. 7. The Turks wonder to see a man walk to and fro, and usually ask such whether they be out of their way or out of their wits. (Biddulph.)

Ver. 17. *And be ye separate*] For gross idolatry and for fundamental errors only must we separate. Corruptions grew so great in the Church of Rome, that it justly occasioned first the separation of the Greek Churches from the Latin, and then of the reformed Churches from the Roman. Machiavel observed, that after the thousandth year of Christ, there was nowhere less piety than in those that dwell nearest to Rome. (Disp. de Rep.) And Bellarmine bewails it, That ever since we cried up the pope for antichrist, his kingdom hath not only not increased, but hath greatly decreased. (Lib. iii. de Papa Rom. c. 21.)

And I will receive you] So you shall be no losers, I will put you into my bosom. God imparteth his sweetest comforts to his in the wilderness, Hos. ii. 14.

Ver. 18. *I will be a Father*] The fundamental, meritorious, impulsive, and final causes of this precious privilege, see set forth, Eph. i. 5, 6.

Saith the Lord Almighty] This is added by our apostle to Jer. xxxi. 9. And not without cause; as for authority' sake, so to intimate that our adoption is a work of God's almighty power. See that sixfold gradation used by the apostle to set forth this truth, Eph. i. 19, having prayed before that their eyes might be enlightened to see the power that wrought in them.

CHAPTER VII.

Ver. 1. *Having therefore, &c.*] FAITH in the promises purifieth the heart, Acts xv. 9, and argueth notably from mercy to duty, melting the hardness of it by the consideration of the promises. Let a cart loaded go over a frozen river, the cart breaks the ice, but it remains ice still. But let the sun shine upon the river, and it dissolveth it. The apostle saith not, Having these menaces, but, Having these promises.

From all filthiness] Sin defileth a man worse than any jakes or leprosy. It is the devil's excrement, it is the corruption of a dead soul. Seldom or never is there a birth of saving grace, but there follows it a flux of mortification.

Of flesh and spirit] i. e. Both of the outward and inward man. Or of flesh, that is, worldly lusts, and gross evils, as uncleanness, earthly-mindedness, &c. And of spirit, that is, more spiritual lusts, as pride, presumption, self-flattery, &c. These lie more up in the heart of the country, as it were; those other in the frontiers and skirts of it.

Perfecting holiness] Propounding to ourselves the highest pitch and the best patterns. And having for our motto that of Charles V., *Plus ultra*, further yet. And here let faith and obedience make a perfect pair of compasses. Faith as the one foot must be pitched upon the centre,

God, while obedience (as the other) walks about in a perfect circle of all good duties. He will not crush but cherish that worm Jacob. "He will not break the bruised reed," &c.

In the fear of God] Which is the fountain whence holiness flows. See Prov. viii. 13.

Ver. 2. Receive us] Gr. χωρήσατε, *Locum date.* Make room for us in your hearts and houses. Set wide open the everlasting doors that the King of glory may come in triumphantly, riding upon us, his white horses, Rev. vi. 2.

We have wronged no man] Ministers must so live that they may, if need be, glory of their innocency and integrity, as did Moses, Samuel, Paul, Melancthon.

We have corrupted no man] viz. As the false apostles had done with their leaven of false doctrine, which eateth as a canker, 2 Tim. ii. 17, or a gangrene, which presently overruns the parts, and takes the brain. Protagoras in Plato boasted that of those sixty years that he had lived, he had spent forty in corrupting of youth.

We have defrauded no man] We have cunningly made sale of no man, as those old impostors that made prize of their prisoners, 2 Pet. ii. 3. And as those Popish *Muscipulatores*, or mice-catchers, as the story calleth them, that raked together their Peter-pence and other monies here in England by most detestable arts. Polydore Virgil was one of these ill officers, that left not so much money in the whole kingdom sometimes as they either carried with them or sent to Rome before them.

Ver. 3. I speak not this, &c.] Though cause enough he had to condemn them for their shameful tenacity toward him, whom they basely suffered to labour for his living and to preach gratis, against all right and reason.

To die and to live with you] Such faithful friends are in this age all for the most part gone on pilgrimage, and their return is uncertain, as once the Duke of Buckingham said to Bishop Morton in Richard III.'s time. Jonathan and David, Pylades and Orestes, Polistratus and Hippoclides, are famous for their love one to another. These two last, being philosophers of Epicurus' sect, are said to have been born the same day, to have lived together all their days, and to have died in the same moment of time, being well stricken in years. (Valer. Max.) But the love of Irish foster-brothers is said far to surpass all the loves of all men. (Camd. Elizab.)

Ver. 4. I am exceeding joyful] Gr. ὑπερπερισσεύομαι, I do over-abound exceedingly with joy. Others may revel, the godly only rejoice: they have an exuberancy of joy, such as no good can match, no evil over-match. Witness the martyrs, ancient and modern. Oh how my heart leapeth for joy, said one of them, that I am so near the apprehension of eternal bliss! God forgive me mine unthankfulness and unworthiness of so great glory. In all the days of my life I was never so merry as now I am in this dark dungeon. Believe me there is no such joy

in the world as the people of Christ have under the cross. Thus and much more Mr Philpot, martyr. (Acts and Mon.)

Ver. 5. Our flesh had no rest] Our spirit had no unrest. The outward man suffers much sometimes, when the inward remains unmolested. Philip, Landgrave of Hesse, being asked how he could so well bear his seven years' imprisonment, answered, *Se divinas martyrum consolationes sensisse*, that he felt the divine consolations of the martyrs, which as bladders bore him aloft all waters.

Ver. 6. God that comforteth] This is a most sweet attribute of God, such as we may profitably plead and produce in prayer. He loves to comfort those that are forsaken of their hopes. He will not crush but cherish that worm Jacob. "He will not break the bruised reed," &c.

By the coming of Titus] Who came very opportunely, even while Paul was writing this Epistle, 2 Cor. ii. 12, 13. God's comforts are therefore sweet because seasonable. He never comes too soon, nor stays too long. He waits to be gracious, as being a God of judgment, Isa. xxx. 18. Were we but ripe, he is ready, and will lift us up in due time, 1 Pet. v. 6.

Ver. 7. Your earnest desire] Of seeing me, or rather of satisfying me.

Your fervent mind] Gr. your zeal, both against the incestuous person and the false apostles, St Paul's adversaries.

Ver. 8. Though it were but for a season] Gr. for an hour. In sin, the pleasure passeth, the sorrow remaineth; but in repentance, the sorrow passeth, the pleasure abideth for ever. God soon poureth the oil of gladness into broken hearts.

Ver. 9. That ye sorrowed to repentance] Gr. εἰς μετάνοιαν, to a transmentation, to a thorough change both of the mind and manners. *Optima et aptissima pœnitentia est nova vita*, saith Luther. Which saying (though condemned by Pope Leo X.) is certainly an excellent saying. Repentance for sin is nothing worth without repentance from sin. If thou repent with a contradiction (saith Tertullian) God will pardon thee with a contradiction. Thou repentest, and yet continuest in thy sin. God will pardon thee, and yet send thee to hell. There is a pardon with a contradiction.

Sorry after a godly manner] Gr. ἡ κατὰ Θεὸν λύπη, according to God. This is a sorrowing for sin, as it is *offensium Dei, aversivum a Deo.* This both comes from God and drives a man to God, as it did the Church in the Canticles, and the prodigal.

Ver. 10. Godly sorrow worketh] Sin bred sorrow, and sorrow, being right, destroyeth sin; as the worm that breeds in the wood, eats into it and devours it. (Chrysost.) So that of this sorrow according to God we may say as the Romans did of Pompey the Great, that it is the fair and happy daughter of an ugly and odious mother. (Εχθροῦ πατρὸς φίλτατον τέκνον. Plutarch.) It may fitly be compared to Faustus, son of Vortigern king of Britain (incestuously begotten of his own daughter) who wept himself blind (saith the chronicler) for the abominations of his parents.

Repentance never to be repented of] That is, saith one, never to fall back again, for a man in falling back, seemeth to repent him of his repentance (ἀμεταμέλητον). Others interpret it, such a repentance as a man shall never have cause to repent of. (Marbury on Repentance.) Job cursed the day of his birth ; but no man was ever heard to curse the day of his new birth. For it is repentance to salvation, it hath heaven ; it is that rainbow, which if God see shining in our hearts, he will never drown our souls.

But the sorrow of the world] That which carnal men conceive either for the want or loss of good, or for the sense or fear of evil.

Worketh death] As it did in Queen Mary, who died (as some supposed by her much sighing before her death) of thought and sorrow either for the departure of King Philip, or the loss of Calais, or both. There are that interpret death in this place, of spiritual death, because it is opposed here to life and salvation. (Dike on the Heart.)

Ver. 11. *What carefulness*] Gr. what study, which (saith Tully) is an earnest and serious bending and applying of the mind to something with a great deal of delight. σπουδὴ. *Vehemens ad aliquam rem magna cum voluptate applicatio.* It is rendered here carefulness, not that of diffidence, but that of diligence, putting a man upon those wholesome thoughts, What have I done ? what shall I do ? &c.

Yea, what clearing] Gr. apology or defence. The old interpreter renders it satisfaction. It may be (saith Mr Bradford) he meant a new life, to make amends thereby to the congregation offended. As the devil is called the accuser, so the Spirit is called the Comforter or pleader for us ; because as he maketh intercession in our hearts to God, so upon true repentance he helpeth us to make apology for ourselves ; not by denying our sins or defending them, but by confessing and disclaiming them, as a child to his father.

Yea, what indignation] Or stomach, as Ephraim, Jer. xxxi. 19. The publican who smote himself upon the breast, he would have knocked his corruptions, if he could have come at them, as those, Isa. xxx. 22, that polluted the idols that they had perfumed, and said unto them, Get you hence, be packing. "What have I to do any more with idols ?" Hos. xiv. 8. Out of doors with this Tamar, here is no room for her. So foolish was I, and so very a beast, saith David, Psal. lxxiii. How angry and hot was he against himself, 2 Sam. xxiv. 10.

Yea, what fear] Of God's heavy displeasure, and of doing any more so. The burnt child dreads the fire. He that hath been stung, hates a snake.

Yea, what vehement desire] As that of Rachel after children, as that of David after the water of the well of Bethlehem, as that of the hunted hind after the water-brooks, Psal. xlii. 1. David panted and fainted after God. That martyr cried out, None but Christ, none but Christ.

Yea, what zeal] Which is an extreme heat of all the affections for and toward God. David's zeal ate him up. Paul was just as mad for Christ as ever he had been against him, 2 Cor. v. 13, with Acts xxvi. 11.

Yea, what revenge] Out of the deepest self-abhorrency, buffeting the flesh, and giving it the blue-eye, as St Paul (that crucifix of mortification) once did. Thus the women parted with their looking-glasses, Exod. xxxv. 22. Mary Magdalen wiped Christ's feet with her hair, wherewith she had formerly made nets to catch fools in. Cranmer burnt his right hand first, wherewith he had subscribed, and oftentimes repeated in the flames, This unworthy right hand, so long as his voice would suffer him. The true penitentiary amerceth himself, and abridgeth his flesh of some lawful comforts, as having forfeited all. These seven signs of godly sorrow are to be seen in the repenting Church, Cant. v., as in a worthy example or emblem. " I sleep," there is indignation, " but my heart waketh," there is apology. " I arose to open," &c., there is study or care and diligence. " My soul failed," there is her zeal. " I sought him, I called on him," there is her vehement desire. " The watchmen found me, they smote me," &c., there is her revenge, while she shrank not for any danger, but followed Christ through thick and thin in the night among the watch. And all this shows her fear of being again overtaken with drowsiness.

To be clear in this matter] Because they had heartily repented of it. *Quem pœnitet peccasse, pene est innocens.* Repentance is almost equivalent to innocence. (Sen. in Agam.) *Imo plus est propemodum a vitiis se revocasse, quam vitia ipsa nescivisse,* saith Ambrose.

Ver. 12. *Not for his cause*] That is, not so much for his cause.

That suffered the wrong] viz. The father of the incestuous person. Compare Gen. xlix. 4.

But that our care for you] That the Church might not suffer, as allowing such foul facts. How the primitive Christians were slandered by the heathens in this kind, who knows not ? Cenalis, bishop of Auranches, wrote against the Church at Paris, defending impudently that their assemblies were to maintain whoredom. Such reports also they cast abroad a little before the massacre. They tell the people in Italy that Geneva is a professed sanctuary of all roguery, that in England the people are grown barbarous, and eat young children, &c.

Ver. 13. *His spirit was refreshed*] After his long and tedious toil and travel to come to you, he never thought much of his labour. Calvin said that it would not grieve him to sail over ten seas, *Ne decem quidem maria,* about a uniform draught for religion.

Ver. 14. *I am not ashamed*] As I should have been, had it proved otherwise. Lying is a blushful sin, and therefore the liar denies his own lie, because he is ashamed to be taken with it ; and our ruffians revenge it with a stab.

Ver. 15. *Whiles he remembereth*] Deep affections make deep impressions.

Ver. 16. *I rejoice therefore*] Thus by praising them, he further winneth upon them, whom before he had more sharply handled. Sour and sweet make the best sauce.

CHAPTER VIII.

Ver. 1. *Of the grace of God*] It is a favour, yea, an honour to us, that we may relieve poor Christ in his necessitous members, Psal. xvi. 2. When therefore he sets us up an altar, be we ready with this sacrifice, Heb. xiii. 16.

Ver. 2. *In a great trial of affliction*] For affliction tries what metal we are made of. Alchemy gold will not endure the seventh fire as true gold will. Affliction (the trial of our faith) is more precious than gold, 1 Pet. i. 7. What then is faith itself so tried ? Rev. iii. 18.

The abundance of their joy] Whilst the spirit of glory and of God rested upon them, 1 Pet. iv. 14. Well may grace be called the divine nature ; for, as God brings light out of darkness, riches out of poverty, &c., so doth grace : it turns dirt into gold, &c. The world wonders (said that martyr) how we can be so merry in such extreme misery. But our God is omnipotent, which turneth misery into felicity. See the note on 2 Cor. vii. 4.

Their deep poverty] Gr. ἡ κατὰ βάθους πτωχεία, their poverty being now at the very bottom, and having little left beside hope ; they were even exhausted, and yet gave liberally. Giles of Brussels, martyr, gave to the poor whatsoever he had, that necessity could spare, and only lived by his science, which was of a cutler. Some he refreshed with his meat, some with his clothes, some with his household stuff. One poor woman there was brought to bed, and had no bed to lie in ; to whom he brought his own bed, himself content to lie in the straw.

Unto the riches of their liberality] Gr. ἁπλότης, of their simplicity, in opposition to that crafty and witty willingness of the covetous to defend themselves from the danger of liberality ; wherein also they are utterly mistaken ; for not getting, but giving is the way to thrive. See the note on Matt. vi. 4.

Ver. 3. *Yea, and beyond their power*] One such poor Macedonian might well shame a hundred rich Corinthian curmudgeons. They knew that *Manus pauperum est gazophylacium Christi*, and might haply have heard of their once King Alexander the Great, how that when he had undertaken the conquest of the Persian empire, he gave away his treasure ; and being asked where it was, he pointed to the poor, and said, *In scriniis*, in my chests ; and when he was further asked what he kept for himself, he answered, *Spem majorum et meliorum*, The hope of greater and better things.

They were willing] Gr. Αὐθαίρετοι, they were volunteers, full of cheerful charity. So were Aidanus, and after him Mr Fox, who gave his horse to a poor beggar that answered him discreetly. Mr Greenham also gave more than he could spare ; so that he usually wanted money to get in his harvest.

Ver. 4. *Receive the gift*] Gr. χάριν, the grace, *i. e.* the alms ; it being of God's free grace that we have, 1. What to give ; 2. Hearts to give it. For naturally we are all like children, which though they have their bosoms, mouths, and both hands full, yet are loth to part with any.

Ver. 5. *Not as we hoped*] God is usually better to us than our hopes.

First gave their own selves to the Lord] Ay, this is the right way of giving alms ; and this is done by faith, the work whereof is to be an empty hand, *Mendica manus* (as Luther calleth it), a beggar's hand to receive it ; but when it hath received, it gives back again itself and all, and thinks all too little, as Mary Magdalen did her precious ointment.

And unto us by the will] The good soul delivers up itself to Christ's faithful ministers, and saith in effect to them, as Luther, before he was better informed, wrote to Pope Leo X., A. D. 1518, *Prostratum pedibus me tibi offero, cum omnibus quæ sum et habeo : — Vocem tuam vocem Christi in te præsidentis et loquentis agnoscam :* I humbly prostrate myself with all that I have and am at thy feet. (Scult. Annal.)

Ver. 6. *So he would finish*] *Finis opus coronat.* "The end is better than the beginning," saith Solomon. Charles V.'s emblem was *Ulterius.* Titus was here desired to take up the whole alms, and not to faint till he had finished, Gal. vi. 9.

Ver. 7. *As ye abound in faith*] He purposely commendeth them, that he may the better insinuate into them. Ministers may profitably praise their people in some cases, that they may the sooner win them to duty ; for there is no so sweet hearing (saith Xenophon) as a man's own commendation, ἥδιστον ἄκουσμα ἔπαινος.

Ver. 8. *To prove the sincerity*] Gr. τὸ γνήσιον, the germanity, the naturalness, legitimateness opposed to bastardliness. This age aboundeth with mouth-mercy, which is good cheap, and therefore like refuse fruit is found growing in every hedge. But a little handful were worth a great many such mouthfuls, Isa. lviii. 18. Complaint is made that there is not any one that taketh Sion by the hand. St James tells of some in his time that would feed their poor brethren with good words and good wishes, James ii. 15, 16, as if they had been of the chameleon kind, to live with Ephraim upon wind, Hos. xii. 1. But what said the poor man to the cardinal who denied him a penny which he begged, and offered him his blessing, which he begged not ? If thy blessing had been worth a penny, I should not have had it : keep it therefore to thyself. (Carle.)

Ver. 9. *He became poor*] Not having where to lay his head, nor wherewith to pay tribute, till he had sent to sea for it. Lo, he that was heir of all things, Heb. i. 2, was scarce owner of anything, but disenriched and disrobed himself of all, that through his poverty he might crown us with the inestimable riches of heavenly glory; this is such a motive to mercifulness as may melt the most flinty heart that is. Riches imply two things: 1. Plenty of that which is precious. 2. Propriety; they must be good things that are our own; and so, those only are rich that have interest in Christ's purchase.

Ver. 10. *But also to be forward*] Gr. to be willing. This the apostle makes to be more than to do, that is, than to do with an ill will, or for by-respects. *Virtus nolentium nulla est.* Christ will enjoy his spouse's love by a willing contract, not by a ravishment; the title of all converts is a willing people, Psal. cx. 3.

Ver. 11. *Now therefore perform*] Unless our willing of good be seconded with endeavour, it is nothing worth. Balaam wished well to heaven; so did he that came kneeling to our Saviour with Good master, &c.; but they stuck at the hardship of holiness, without which there is no heaven to be had; they would not come off here, and therefore gat nothing by their short-winded wishes. Solomon compares such sluggards to the door that turns on the hinges, but yet hangs still upon them, it comes not off for all the turnings. Their purposes without performances are like a cloud without rain; and not unlike Hercules' club in the tragedy, of a great bulk, but stuft with moss and rubbish. *Virtutem expotant contabescuntque relicta.* (Peri.)

Ver. 12. *It is accepted*] *Sic minimo capitur thuris honore Deus.* Noah's sacrifice could not be great, yet was greatly accepted. Jacob had his sons take a little of every good thing, and carry for a present to the lord of Egypt. Saul and his servant present Samuel with the fourth part of a shekel, to the value of about our fivepence. Thankfulness (they had learned) was not measured by God and by good men by the weight, but by the will of the retributor. God calls for that which a man's heart inclines him to do, be it more, be it less; so low doth his highness stoop to our meanness, preferring the willingness of the mind before the worthiness of the work. That poor widow's mite was beyond the rich man's magnificence, because it came out of a richer mind.

Ver. 13. *And you burdened*] Gr. θλίψις, pinched or pressed, viz. with poverty.

Ver. 14. *Your abundance*] That your cup may overflow into their lesser dishes, that your superfluities both in respect of the necessity of nature and exigency of estate (as the schoolmen speak) may supply the wants of God's poor afflicted.

A supply for your want] Those that lend mercy may have need to borrow. The Shunammite that refused once to be spoken for to the king by the prophet, little thought she should afterwards have craved that courtesy of his man Gehazi. Those that stand fastest upon earth have but slippery footing. No man can say that he shall not need friends. Pythias was so wealthy a man, that he was able to entertain Xerxes' whole army, consisting of a million of men; yet afterwards he became so poor that he wanted bread.

Ver. 15. *He that had gathered much*] He that was so nimble as to gather more than his neighbour was to supply his neighbour, that every man might have his omer. Now the equity of this law being common and perpetual, the apostle draweth his argument from it. Riches, saith one, are but as manna; those that gathered more of it had but enough to serve their turn (or if they gathered more, it was but a trouble and annoyance to them), and they that gathered less had no want. Let the rich account themselves the poor man's stewards. "Withhold not good from the owners thereof (the poor) when it is in the power of thy hand to do it," Prov. iii. 37. See the note there.

Ver. 16. *But thanks be to God*] Deo gratias was ever in Paul's mouth, and in Austin's, and should be in ours.

Ver. 17. *But being more forward*] A good heart is ready to every good work, waiting the occasions thereof, Tit. iii. 1; as the bee, so soon as ever the sun breaks forth, flies abroad to gather honey and wax.

Ver. 18. *Whose praise is in the Gospel*] St Luke, likely, who first wrote the Gospel, as some gather out of Luke i. 1, and whom Ambrose highly commendeth for the most clear and distinct gospel-writer.

Ver. 19. *Chosen of the Churches*] This compared with Acts xiii. 1, 2, it may seem the apostle meaneth not Luke, but Barnabas; though others think Timothy. (Danæ in 1 Tim. vi. 12.)

Ver. 20. *Avoiding this*] As shipmen avoid a rock or shelf, στελλόμενοι; for it is a seafaring term, and shows how shy we should be of doing aught that may render our honesty suspected. *Ego si bonam famam servasso, sat dives ero*, said he in the Comedy.

Ver. 21. *Providing*] Projecting, procuring, προνοούμενοι. A good name is a great blessing, and therefore the same word in Hebrew signifieth both, Prov. xxviii. 20, בְּרָכָה.

Ver. 22. *Whom we have oft*] Some are of opinion that Luke is here deciphered rather than ver. 19. Whoever it was, it is much for his honour, that Apelles-like he was approved in Christ, and active for the Church, Rom. xvi. 10.

Ver. 23. *Messengers*] Gr. apostles, *emandati*, ambassadors of special and high employment.

The glory of Christ] So the Church is called "the glory," Isa. iv. 5; God's glory, Isa. xlvi. 13; a crown of glory, and a royal diadem in the hand of Jehovah, Isa. lxii. 3; the throne of God, Exod. xvii. 6; the throne of glory, Jer. iv. 21; the ornament of God, yea, the beauty of his ornament, set in majesty, Ezek. vii. 20. There is not so much of the glory of God (saith one) in all his works of creation and providence, as in one gracious action that a Christian performs.

Ver. 24. *Wherefore show ye*] As by an ocular

demonstration, or as by pointing the finger, *ἐνδείξασθε*.

Before the Churches] In the face of the Churches, *εἰς πρόσωπον*, whose eyes are now full set upon you, to see what entertainment ye will give to their messengers. A Christian is like a crystal glass with a lamp in the midst.

CHAPTER IX.

Ver. 1. *The ministering to the saints*]. OR the service that ye owe the saints in ministering to their necessities, *διακονία*. Amadeus, duke of Savoy, Stephanus, king of Hungary, Hooper, bishop of Gloucester, and Doctor Taylor, martyr, are famous for their labour of love in ministering to the saints.

Ver. 2. *Was ready*] To wit, in their resolutions; for the collection was not yet made.

And your zeal] i. e. Your liberal contribution out of deep affection, and a holy emulation to exceed others in bounty.

Ver. 4. *In this same confident boasting*] Gr. "in this confidence of glorying." A metaphor from hunters, who confidently expect the beast, and valiantly set upon him. *Sic Latini dicunt, subsistere aprum.*

Ver. 5. *Not of covetousness*] *Non ut extortum aliquid*, saith Piscator, *vel ut illiberale aliquid.* Not as wrung out of you, squeezed out, as verjuice is out of a crab. Covetous persons part with their penny as with blood out of their hearts. *Citius aquam ex pumice, clavam ex manu Herculis extorqueas.* God will set off all hearts from such misers, in their misery, that are so unreasonably merciless. Bounty or blessing (for so the Greek word *εὐλογία* signifies) is here fitly opposed to covetousness; and St Paul concludes, that when church-contributions are not free and liberal, covetousness is the cause.

Ver. 6. *Which soweth bountifully*] Gr. "that soweth in blessings," *ἐν εὐλογίαις*; alluding to Ezek. xxxiv. 26; Eccl. xi. 1, "Cast thy bread upon the water," that is, upon fat and fertile places, *loca irrigua.* A metaphor from seedsmen, who eat not all, sell not all, but sow some; so should we sow that we have upon the backs and bellies of the poor; sow more of this seed in God's blessed bosom, the fruit whereof we are sure to reap in our greatest need.

Ver. 7. *According as he purposeth*] God straineth upon none. See Levit. v. 6, 12, and xiv. 10, 21, 30. Liberality implieth liberty.

God loveth a cheerful giver] *Dat bene, dat multum, qui dat cum munere vultum.* One may give with his hand, and pull it back with his looks.

Ver. 8. *And God is able*] Fear not therefore lest yourselves should want hereafter, if you should give liberally now. Is not mercy as sure a grain as vanity? Is God like to break?

Having all sufficiency] He saith not, "superfluity." Enough we shall be sure of, and an honest affluence, if fit for it, and can make us friends with it. *Bonus Deus Constantinum*

magnum tantis terrenis implevit muneribus, quanta optare nullus auderet, saith Austin (De Civit. Dei). God gave Constantine more wealth than heart could wish, and he was no niggard of it to poor Christians.

In all things] The apostle useth many "alls," on purpose to cross and confute our covetousness, who are apt to think we have never enough.

Ver. 9. *He hath dispersed abroad*] General Norice was like that bishop of Lincoln, that never thought he had that thing that he did not give. Of Mr Wiseheart, the Scottish martyr, it is reported, that his charity had never end, night, day, nor noon. He forbare one meal in three, one day in four for the most part to bestow it on the poor. He never changed his sheets but he gave them away.

His righteousness endureth for ever] Never did a charitable act go away without the retribution of a blessing. See the note on Matt. x. 42.

Ver. 10. *And multiply your seed sown*] He that soweth seemeth to cast away his seed, but he knows he shall receive it with usury. Isaac had a hundred-fold increase. In Egypt, so far as the river Nile watereth, the ground is so fruitful, that they do but throw in the seed, and have four rich harvests in less than four months. *Temporalia Dei servis impensa non pereunt, sed parturiunt. Si dedisses tres aureos, accepisses trecentos*, said that bishop of Milan to his servant, that had not given so much to the poor as he had appointed him. (John Manlii, loc. com.) If we never sow we shall never reap, said that good poor minister that bade his wife give three pence (his whole stock) to a poor brother. Another good man having nothing left, and his wife desiring to know how he and his family should live, he answered, he would now put his bond in suit, pray over the promises, and not doubt of the performance. (Rogers.)

Ver. 11. *Which causeth through us*] Whilst we not only relieve them, but instruct them, as Bishop Hooper did his board of beggars, as Dr Taylor the martyr did the alms-people of Hadleigh, and other poor of his parish. As Giles of Brussels did, ministering wholesome exhortation of sound doctrine to them he relieved, and so eliciting from them many thanksgivings unto God.

Ver. 13. *For your professed subjection*] Whilst you testify your faith by your works, as they produced the coats that Dorcas made, to prove her a devout woman; and as, Numb. xiii. 13, it appeared by the fruits it was a good land. Heathens acknowledged that no people in the world did love one another so as Christians did.

Ver. 14. *And by their prayer for you*] A poor Christian's prayers cannot be bought too dear. "I will restore comfort to him, and to his mourners," Isa. lvii. 18. Such can do much with God. *Et cum talis fueris, memento mei*, saith Bernard to his poor, but pure friend. How heartily prayeth Paul for Onesiphorus, 2 Tim. i. 18.

Ver. 15. *For his unspeakable gift*] That is, for Christ (saith Theophylact, whom Piscator followeth), who is called the gift, by an excellency, John iv. 10, and the benefit, 2 Tim. vi. 2.

CHAPTER X.

Ver. 1. *By the meekness and gentleness*] Whom in those sweet virtues I desire to imitate. The praise of Christ's meekness recorded by the prophet, and explained by Philip, converted the eunuch, Acts viii.

Who in presence am base] i. e. Despicable, because I take not upon me, and bear a port, as the false apostles do. Meekness of spirit commonly draws on injuries. A crow will stand upon a sheep's back pulling off wool from her sides.

Am bold toward you] So mine adversaries report me, as if I were over bold and busy by my letters.

Ver. 2. *That I may not be bold*] That you necessitate me not. *Non nisi coactus hoc facio*, said that emperor that subscribed a warrant to put one to death.

With that confidence] It was but confidence, but they made the worst of it, and called it boldness, *Quam vitio verterunt*. Evil-will never speaks well.

Ver. 3. *We do not war, &c.*] The ministry is a kind of militia, 1 Tim. i. 18. Christ rideth on ministers, as his white horses, conquering and to conquer, Rev. vi. 2.

Ver. 4. *Are not carnal*] i. e. Weak, opposed here to mighty. The flesh is weak as water, therefore called the old man, old leaven, &c. These weak weapons of the false apostles (here intimated and taxed) are human eloquence, artificial composures, &c., of those verbalists, *Qui exceptis verbis tinnulis et emendicatis, nihil loquuntur*, as Jerome hath it.

But mighty through God] Note here the apostle's modesty. Not we, saith he, but our weapons are mighty; and not through us that wield them, but through God that works by and with them. See the note on 1 Cor. xv. 10.

To the pulling down of strong-holds] Forts, munitions, trenches, cages of foul spirits inhabiting men's hearts.

Ver. 5. *Casting down imaginations*] As the spittle that comes out of a man's mouth slayeth serpents, so doth that which proceedeth out of the mouths of God's faithful ministers quell and kill evil imaginations, carnal reasonings, which are that legion of domestic devils, that hold near intelligence with the old serpent. *Nemo sibi de suo palpet : quisque sibi Satan est*. Corrupt reason, like Eve and Job's wife, is always drawing us from God. Out of doors with this Hagar.

And bringing into captivity] See here the process of St Paul's ministry. He overthrows, captivates, subdues to the obedience of the Lord Christ. See the like, Jer. i. 10. Chosroes, king of Parthia, was so subdued by the Romans, that he made a law that none of his successors should ever wage war with them again. So here.

Ver. 6. *And having in a readiness*] Vengeance is every whit as ready in God's hand, as in the minister's mouth. See Matt. xvi. 19; xviii. 18. Elisha hath his sword as well as Jehu and Hazael, 1 Kings xix. 17. God hews men by his prophets and slays them by the words of his mouth, Hos. vi. 5. By preaching, Christ many times smites the earth, Isa. xi. 4; his word lays hold on them, Zech. i. 6, and that which they have counted wind, hath become fire to devour them, Jer. v. 13, 14.

Ver. 7. *Do ye look on things*] q. d. Are ye so weak as to be cozened by an outside, to be carried away with shows and shadows of true worth ? Do not many things glister besides gold ? Every bird that hath a seemly feather, hath not the sweetest flesh ; nor doth every tree that beareth a goodly leaf, bring good fruit. Glass giveth a clearer sound than silver, &c.

Even so are we Christ's] The Rogation heretics would have made the world believe that they were the only Catholics. The Arians called the true Christians Ambrosians, Athanasians, Homousians, &c. The Donatists made themselves the only true Church, &c.

Ver. 8. *And not for destruction*] If it prove so, it is by accident, and not as we intend it. See the note on 2 Cor. ii. 16.

Ver. 9. *Terrify you by letters*] As the false apostles object against me. Aspersions must be carefully cleared, when the fruit of a man's ministry is thereby impeached and impeded.

Ver. 10. *Weighty and powerful*] As often as I read Paul's Epistles, *Non verba, sed tonitrua audire mihi videor*, saith Jerome, Methinks I hear not words, but thunder-claps. But that his bodily presence was not weak, nor his speech contemptible, see Acts xiii. 10, together with the note thereon.

Ver. 11. *Such will we be, &c.*] That we have not hitherto been so, was because we spared you. *Posse et nolle nobile*, saith Chrysostom. Kindness is godliness, Isa. xl. 6, חֶסֶד.

Ver. 12. *For we dare not*] This he speaks by an irony, whereof he is full in this Epistle ; and may therefore be called as Socrates was, ὁ εἴρων.

But they measuring themselves, &c.] Turning the other end of the perspective, they see themselves bigger and others lesser than they are. So bladder-like is the soul, that filled with earthly vanities, though but wind, it grows great and swells in pride. Oh pray to be preserved from this perilous pinnacle of self-exaltation. Look into the perfect law of liberty, and draw nigh to God. The nearer we come to God, the more rottenness we find in our bones. The more any man looks into the body of the sun, the less he seeth when he looks down again.

Ver. 13. *But we will not boast, &c.*] As any man is more worthful, he is more modest : full vessels yield no such sound as empty casks do. A vessel cast into the sea, the more it fills the deeper it sinks ; the loaden scale goes downward ;

the most precious balm sinks to the bottom. The good ear of corn, the fuller it is, the lower it hangs the head.

Ver. 14. For we stretch not, &c.] ὑπερεκτείνομεν, we tenter not ourselves beyond our scantling.

Ver. 15. Not boasting of things] Ammianus Marcellinus tells of one Lampadius, a great person in Rome, who through all parts of the city, where other men had bestowed cost in building, he would set up his own name, not as a repairer of the work, but as the chief builder. Of the same fault Trajan the emperor is said to have been guilty; whence he was commonly called *Herba parietina*, or Wall-wort.

Ver. 16. In the regions beyond you] This was a piece of the braggadocio false apostles' vain boasting, as it is now of the Jesuits, those *Circulatores* and *Agyrtæ*, that compass sea and land, crack of what conversions they have wrought in India and Africa, and, Lampadius-like, take it ill at any man's hand that commend them not every time they spit upon the ground. (Amm. Marcell.) Caius the emperor was ready to destroy the whole senate, because they did not deify him for marching with his whole army to the ocean, and fetching thence a few oyster-shells, *Quibus spoliis acceptis magnifice gloriabatur, quasi oceano subacto.* (Dio, in Vita Caligulæ.)

Ver. 17. Glory in the Lord] See the note on 1 Cor. i. 31.

Ver. 18. Whom the Lord commendeth] As he did his servant Job, chap. i. 8. And as he did his handmaid Sarah, for calling her husband lord, though there was never a good word besides in the whole sentence, 1 Pet. iii. 6 with Gen. xviii. 22. Neither was Job so patient, but that he had his out-bursts. All which notwithstanding "ye have heard of the patience of Job," &c., James v. 11. He is not challenged at all for his impatience, but crowned and chronicled for his patience. See here the wonderful goodness of God toward his; and take comfort in his white stone, against the black coals of ill-affected persons.

Is approved] δόκιμος, or, will pass for current coin in heaven. When slips are abroad, men will take heed what money they take.

CHAPTER XI.

Ver. 1. In my folly] How foolish were the Pharisees, John vii. 49, and after them the Gnostics, the Illuminates, and now the Jesuits, that boast themselves to be the only knowing men! Palemon the Grammarian, that bragged that all learning was born with him, and would die when he died! Epicurus, that he first found out the truth! (Sueton.) Richardus de S. Victore, that gave out that he knew more in divinity than any prophet or apostle of them all! These were fools to purpose; the apostle was put upon a necessity of commending himself, so to vindicate his ministry from the contempt cast upon him by the Corinthians.

Ver. 2. For I am jealous] q. d. My dear love to you puts me upon thus praising myself.

With a godly jealousy] Gr. with a zeal of God, called the flame of God, Cant. viii. 6, such as was that of Job over his children, for fear they should sin against God; not such as was that of the Pharisees over the Galatians, the hypocrisy of jealousy, Gal. iv. 17.

For I have espoused you] Gr. I have fitted you, as things that are pieced together are glued or soldered. ἡρμοσάμην, *Velut ea quæ glutino aut ferrumine committuntur.* (Erasm.)

To one husband] Here the cedar taketh the thistle to wife (*tantus tantillos*), and doth all the offices of a husband to her, 2 Kings xiv. 9; Ezek. xvi. 8. 1. He first loveth his Church, and then purifieth her, Ephes. v. 25, 26. (Ahasuerus had the virgins first purified and perfumed before he took them to his bed.) 2. He puts upon her his own comeliness, as Eleazar put the jewels upon Rebecca (hence she is called Callah of the perfection of her attire, ornaments, and beauty, Jer. ii. 32). 3. He maketh love to her by his paranymphs, his ministers, who woo for him, and present her to Christ as a chaste virgin. 4. He cohabits with her; Cant. vii. 5, "The king is tied in the rafters." 5. He rejoiceth over her, Isa. lxii. 4, 5. 6. He doth the marriage duty to her, and maketh her the mother of us all, Gal. iv. 26; Rom. vii. 1. 7. He nourisheth and cherisheth her, Ephes. v. 29. 8. He hateth putting away, Mal. ii. 16, and provideth for her eternal welfare, Ephes. i. 27; Col. i. 21, 22.

Ver. 3. But I fear] Jealousy is made up of love, fear, and anger.

By his subtilty] He mustered all his forces, or rather all his frauds, together to cheat her. That old serpent, when he was young, outwitted our first parents; now that he is old, and we young, Ephes. iv. 14, what will he not do, if we watch not? Bellarmine saith of his Romanists, *Romani sicut non acumina, ita nec imposturas habent*, that they are neither sharp nor subtle. The devil is both, and so are they; witness their crafty cruel both positions and dispositions; this old serpent having lent them both his seven heads to plot and his ten horns to push.

So your minds should be corrupted] Satan hath his νοήματα, set and composed machination, 2 Cor. ii. 11, whereby he adulterateth our νοήματα, our judgments.

From the simplicity, &c.] Of all graces Satan would beguile us of this simplicity; the world calls it silliness, sheepishness.

Ver. 4. But if he that cometh] Giddy hearers, whirred about with every novelty, have no mould but what the next teacher casts them into; being blown like glasses into this or that shape at the pleasure of his breath. See John v. 43.

Ver. 5. The very chiefest apostles] Either he meaneth those pillars, Peter, James, John, &c., Gal. ii. 6; or the false apostles, whom he styleth chiefest by an irony, because they sought to bear away the bell, and be counted prime preachers.

Ver. 6. But though I be rude in speech] Gr.
an idiot, a plain, downright, home-spun, homely-
spoken person.   The ancients busied themselves
(saith Cyril), οὐκ ἐν εὑρεσιλογίᾳ, not about coin and
new-coined language, but ἐν ἀποδείξει τῶν θείων
γραφῶν, about solid demonstrations drawn out of
the Holy Scriptures.   Jerome reports of Didymus
that he was an apostolic writer, as you might
easily gather by his style, *Tam sensuum nomine
quam simplicitate verborum.*   His matter was as
lofty as his language low and ordinary.   Jerome
himself is much commended by learned men,
Quod ubique non sit æque Latinus, that he is not
always so curious and choice of his words.   But
what reason he had, I see not, to censure St Paul
so sharply as he doth, *Ob sensus involutos, elo-
quium implicatum, et artis Grammaticæ imperi-
tiam,* for his intricate sense, dark elocution, and
unskilfulness in grammar learning.   True it is,
he was a plain preacher, as he here acknowledgeth; and why he affected plainness, he telleth us,
1 Cor. i. 17, as stooping to vulgar capacities.
But that he could play the orator if he pleased,
appears Acts xvii. 22, &c., and Acts xxvi. 2; insomuch as the Lycaonians called him Mercury,
because he was "a master of speech," Acts xiv. 12.
And as for his Epistles, there is as good rhetoric
found in them as in any heathen orator whatsoever.   Demosthenes is but dull to him; and
Austin's wish was to have seen *Paulum in ore,*
Paul preaching, which he would have esteemed
a high happiness.

Ver. 7. I have preached to you freely] Because
he gat his living with his hands, that he might
preach gratis, they despised him as a mean me-
chanic.   This is *merces mundi,* the world's wages.
Nil habet infœlix paupertas, &c.   Ministers must
have an honourable maintenance (and not be
forced to weave for a living, as Musculus was,
or to serve the mason, as another great scholar),
or else they will be shamefully slighted.

Ver. 8. I robbed other churches] *Grandis metaphora,* saith Piscator, I took maintenance from
them (as the apostle presently expounds himself), I made a prey and prize of them, ἐσύλησα.

Ver. 9. And wanted] Gr. and was behind-hand.

I was chargeable to no man] I was none of
those drones that chill the charity of well-disposed
people, as the cramp-fish benumbeth those that
touch or come near it. (κατενάρκησα, νάρκη, *Tor-
pedo.*)

Ver. 10. As the truth of Christ is in me] He
confirms it with an oath, that he will not take
a penny of them whiles he preacheth in those
parts.   A minister should be careful of whom he
receives a kindness.   Note further from this
text, that lawful things, when they prove inexpedient and gravaminous, may be forborne by the
bond of a covenant.

Ver. 11. Because I love you not?] It should
be a minister's care to preserve in the hearts of
his people an opinion of his love to them.   For
if they once conceive an incurable prejudice
against him, that he hates them, or the like,
there is no good will be done.

Ver. 12. That I may cut off occasion] There
were those that waited for it, as earnestly as a
dog doth for a bone, as we say.   *Habuerunt suos
cucullos omnes docti et heroici quolibet tempore,*
saith Melancthon.   Every Zopyrus hath his
Zoilus.

That wherein they glory] They, likely, had
feathered their nests, and so might well afford
to preach gratis.   Paul, though not so well
underlaid, would not come behind them in that
neither.   He would not be less busy (though he
laboured hard for it) in building staircases to
heaven, than they were in digging descents
down to hell.

Ver. 13. Deceitful workers] They seemed to
labour, but indeed they loitered, or worse; seeking to set up themselves in the hearts of God's
people.

Transforming themselves, &c.] The Manichees
derived their name of manna, because they held
that whatsoever they taught was to be received
as food from heaven.   Montanus said he was
the Comforter, &c.   Novatus called himself
Moses, and a brother that he had, Aaron.   The
family of love set out their *Evangelium regni.*
The Swenckfeldians (Stinckfeldians Luther called
them, from the ill savour of their opinions) entitled themselves with that glorious name, The
confessors of the glory of Christ. (Schlussenburg.)

Ver. 14. Satan himself is, &c.] Satan, saith
one, doth not always appear in one and the same
fashion, but hath as many several changes as
Proteus among the poets.   At Lystra he appears
like a comedian, as if a scene of Plautus were to
be presented on the stage.   At Antioch like a
Jesuit, with traditions in his mouth.   At Athens
he sallies out like a philosopher; at Ephesus
like an artificer; and her eat Corinth he is transformed into an angel of light.   Fiery serpents
full of deadly poison are called seraphims, Numb.
xxi. 6; Isa. xxx. 6.

Ver. 15. As the ministers of righteousness] *Cavete a Melampygo.*   Try before you trust; sectaries
and seducers are very subtle and insinuative; the
locusts have faces like women; know them and
avoid them.   When one commended the pope's
legate at the Council of Basil, Sigismund the
emperor answered, *Tamen Romanus est,* Yet he is
a Roman.   So, let Satan or his agents come never
so much commended to us in his sugared allurements, let us answer, Yet he is a devil.   Sin
draws the devil's picture in a man; envy is the
devil's eye, falsehood his tongue, oppression his
hand, hypocrisy his cloven foot, &c.

Ver. 16. Let no man think me] There was
never man, nor action, but was subject to variety
of censures and misconstructions, foolish men
daring to reprehend that which they do not comprehend.   I like St Augustine's resolution in
this case.   *Non curo illos censores, qui vel non
intelligendo reprehendunt, vel reprehendendo non
intelligunt.*

Ver. 17. I speak it not after the Lord] Neither
by his command nor example, but permission
only.

Ver. 18. *Glory after the flesh*] Or in the flesh, Gal. vi. 13, or have confidence in the flesh, Phil. iii. 4.

Ver. 19. *For ye suffer fools*] *Inter indoctos etiam Corydus sonat.* (Quintilian.) Wise men hold them for fools whom fools admire for wise men. As one saith of attorneys, *Quod inter opiliones se jactitent jurisperitos, inter jurisperitos ne opilionum quidem æstimatione habeantur.* (Rex Platonicus.)

Ver. 20. *For ye suffer, if, &c.*] As the Popish penitentiaries, those miserably misled and muzzled creatures. They write of our King Henry II., that going to Canterbury to visit the sepulchre of his own martyr, Thomas Beckett, coming within the sight of the church, he alighted, and went three miles on his bare feet, which with the hard stones were forced to yield bloody tokens of his devotion on the way. (Daniel's Hist.) Clemens V., pope, caused Dandalus, the Venetian ambassador, to come before him tied in chains, and to wallow under his table with dogs, whilst his Holiness sat at supper. The pope lashed Henry IV. of France (in the person of his ambassador at Rome) after the singing of every verse of Miserere, until the whole Psalm was sung out. *Sed exorto jam evangelii jubare, sagaciores (ut spero) principes ad nutum Romani Orbilii non solvent subligacula,* saith a great divine. (Gab. Powell on Tolerat.)

If a man take of you] By way of gratuity, but not of wages; or by their followers, and not by themselves. No capuchin among the Papists may take or touch silver. This metal is as very anathema to these, as the wedge of gold to Achan; at the offer whereof he starts back, as Moses from the serpent. Yet he carries a boy with him that takes and carries it, and never complains of either metal or measure.

Ver. 21. *As though we had been weak*] i. e. Worthless and spiritless. But mistake not yourselves; I am another manner of man than you imagine me. It is said of Athanasius, that he was *Magnes et Adamas;* a loadstone in his sweet, gentle, drawing nature, and yet an adamant in his resolute, stout carriage against heretics and evil-doers. (Nazianzen.)

Ver. 22. *Are they Israelites*] God's select, peculiar. "Happy art thou, O Israel; who is like unto thee, O people!" Deut. xxxiii. 29. The Jews say that those seventy souls that went with Jacob into Egypt were as much as all the seventy nations of the world. Tabor and Hermon, the east and west of Judea, are put for the east and west of the world, Psal. lxxxix. 12.

Ver. 23. *In labours more abundant*] Chrysostom calleth Paul, *Insatiabilem Dei cultorem,* an unweariable servant of God.

Ver. 24. *Forty stripes save one*] That they might be sure not to exceed the set number of stripes, limited by the law, Deut. xxv. 3.

Ver. 25. *Thrice was I beaten, &c.*] By the Roman magistrates, as also the martyrs were by the Romish bishops. Thomas Hinshaw was beaten with rods by Bonner, and abode his

fury so long as the fat-paunched bishop could endure with breath, and till for weariness he was fain to cease. So also he dealt by John Willis, and by Mr Bartlet Green, who greatly rejoiced in the same.

I have been in the deep] *Sine nave in mari fui,* so the Syriac renders it. For 24 hours together I have been floating in the sea.

Ver. 26. *By mine own countrymen*] *A Gentilibus meis, et a Gentibus.*

Ver. 27. *In weariness and painfulness*] Here is dainty rhetoric. Tully calleth Aristotle's Politics, *Aureum flumen orationis,* a golden flood of eloquence in respect of the purity of the style and the excellency of the matter. May it not be more truly said of this great apostle's writings?

Ver. 28. *That which cometh, &c.*] *Quasi agmine facto, et repetitis vicibus.* His care came upon him, as an armed man, and gave him no rest or respite. The Greek word ἐπισύστασις holds out the cumber; he had as it were all care numbered, and mustered together, and that with anxiety, μέριμνα, with the same solicitude that a man hath about business of his own: yet held he out his whole race without cessation or respiration.

The care of all the Churches] Calvin was no otherwise affected toward the Churches though far remote, than if he had borne them upon his shoulders, saith Beza. He often sighed out, *Usquequo Domine,* over the poor afflicted Churches of Christ, with the miseries whereof he was much more affected than with any of his own private miseries. I could not but love the man (said Theodosius of Ambrose) for that, whilst he lived, and when he died, he took more care for the Church than for himself, *Magis de ecclesiarum statu, quam de suis periculis angebatur.*

Ver. 29. *Who is weak*] By passion.

And I am not weak] By compassion.

And I burn not] πυροῦμαι, i. e. am exceedingly grieved. Compare Psal. x. 2; vii. 14. He hotly pursueth the poor. The apostle was even scorched and scalded with sorrow and holy indignation, he felt twinges when others were hurt.

Ver. 30. *I will glory of the things*] As a conqueror of his spoil, or as an old soldier of his scars. The apostle glorieth in those things that his adversaries condemned as infirm in him. The afflictions also of the best may fitly be called their infirmities; because they are apt to bewray weakness in them. Like as when fire comes to green wood, there issueth out abundance of watery stuff, that was not discerned before; and as, when the pond is empty, the mud, filth, and toads appear.

Ver. 31. *Which is blessed for ever*] And therefore to be blessed, as he that is the Father of our Lord Jesus Christ. This is a praise that he much stands upon, Rom. xv. 6. And surely if all generations shall call the Virgin blessed, for that she was the mother of Christ, Luke i. 48, how much more, &c.

Ver. 32. *In Damascus*] The chief city of

Syria, built (say some) in the place where the blood of Abel was spilt, and thence called Damesek, *i. e.* a bag of blood. Thither Paul marched with a bloody mind, but was miraculously converted, and so powerfully confounded his countrymen there, that they incensed the governor against him, to his great peril. That is the guise of godless persecutors, to attempt that against the truth by arms that they cannot effect by arguments. See Acts ix. 23, 24.

Ver. 33. *And through a window, &c.*] An honest shift, though against the Roman law of leaping over the walls. *Quia leges semper ad æquitatem flectendæ sunt,* saith Cicero. The sense of the law [is the law, and not always the letter. *Apices juris non sunt jus.*

And escaped his hands] Of the lawfulness of flight in some cases, see the note on Matt. x. 23; Acts ix. 24.

CHAPTER XII.

Ver. 1. *It is not expedient for me*] Because it carries a show at least of pride and folly; and Christians must be shy of the very shows and shadows of sin, ministers especially, whose practice easily passeth into an example. Howbeit for the Corinthians it was expedient, because they thought more meanly of Paul than was meet.

To visions and revelations] The false apostles, haply, boasted of such as some seducers do now-a-days, who dream Midianitish dreams, and then tell the same to their neighbours for gospel. But take heed, the old prophet may bring men into the lion's mouth, by telling them of an angel that spake to him.

Ver. 2. *I knew a man in Christ*] *i. e.* A Christian and approved, 2 Cor. xiii. 5.

Above fourteen years ago] See the note on Acts ix. 9. All this while till now, he had held his tongue. Taciturnity (in some cases) is a Christian virtue. Either be silent, or say somewhat that is better than silence, was an old moral precept, ἢ σιγᾷν, ἢ κρείττονα σιγῆς λέγειν.

Ver. 3. *Whether in the body, &c.*] So far did he forget and neglect his own body, which is so dear and near a thing, in comparison of that incomparable delight he then took in the Lord. "Oh that joy! O my God, when shall I be with thee!" These were the dying words of the last Lord Harrington, that was in heaven aforehand. "O the joys, the joys, the unspeakable joys that I feel in my soul!" said another that was even entering into heaven, and had a foretaste of eternal life. Peter in the transfiguration was so transported, that he never thought of a tabernacle for himself, Matt. xvii.; he cared not to lie without doors, so he might longer enjoy that glimpse of heaven's glory.

Ver. 4. *How that he was caught •up*] Not locally (likely) but in spirit, as Acts vii. 56; Ezek. viii. 3.

Into Paradise] Heaven, whereof that earthly paradise was but a dark shadow. Jerome comforting a young hermit, bade him look up to heaven, *Et Paradisum mente deambulare,* to take a few turns in Paradise by his meditations, assuring him that so long as he had Paradise in his mind and heaven in his thought, *tamdiu in eremo non eris,* he should not be sensible of his solitariness.

Unspeakable words] ῥήματα ἄρρητα, wordless words, such as words are too weak to utter. *Nec Christus nec cœlum patitur hyperbolen.* A man cannot hyperbolize in speaking of Christ and heaven, but must entreat his hearers, as Tully doth his readers, concerning the worth of L. Crassus, *Ut majus quiddam de iis quam quæ scripta sunt suspicarentur,* that they would conceive much more than he was able to express. It is as easy to compass the heaven with a span or contain the sea in a nut-shell, as to relate heaven's happiness.

Ver. 5. *Yet of myself I will not glory*] *Non nisi coactus, ut supra.* Paul was a model of modesty, a very crucifix of mortification, as one calleth him.

But in mine infirmities] *i. e.* My troubles, so called, either because under them we seem infirm and contemptible; or else, for that afflictions oft show our infirmities, our impatience, &c., they make us sick of the fret, &c.

Ver. 6. *Lest any man should think of me*] Let no man, saith Gregory, desire to seem more than he is, that so he may be more than he seems. It pleaseth me not, saith Augustine, that by many I am thought to be that which I am not. For truly they love not me, but another for me, *si non quod sum, sed quod non sum diligunt,* if they love not that I am, but that I am not.

Ver. 7. *And lest I should be exalted*] So lest Ezekiel should be lifted up with his many rare visions he is frequently called "son of man," to put him in mind of his mortal, miserable condition.

A thorn in the flesh] A corruption edged with a temptation. Satan sent some Delilah to lull Paul asleep in her lap, and bind him with withes of green delights; but his watchful soul, displeased deeply with that flesh-pleasing force, complained thereof, shaked himself, and so found ease.

To buffet me] Perhaps in a proper sense Paul might feel the devil's fingers; take it metaphorically for temptations, and then they are fitly called buffetings, because they come so thick upon a man's spirit that he can hardly take breath. He dogs good hearts with foulest lusts sometimes, as of atheism, idolatry, blasphemy, murder. In all or any of which, if the soul be merely passive (as the word buffeting here implies) they are Satan's sins and our crosses only.

Lest I should be exalted] If Paul had not been buffeted, who knows whither he would have swelled? He might have been carried higher in conceit than before he was in his ecstasy. This "thorn in his flesh" was a means to let out the imposthumated matter of pride out of his heart.

Ver. 8. *I besought the Lord thrice*] i. e. Frequently and fervently. God respecteth not the arithmetic of our prayers, how many they are; nor the rhetoric of our prayers, how neat they are; nor the geometry of our prayers, how long they are; nor the music of our prayers, how melodious they are; nor the logic of our prayers, how methodical they are; but the divinity of our prayers, how heart-sprung they are. Not gifts, but graces prevail in prayer.

Ver. 9. *My grace is sufficient for thee*] God sometimes gives pardoning grace where yet he denies prevailing grace. He roots not out all our Canaanites at once, but leaves some to try and exercise us. "I thank God in Christ, sustentation I have, but suavities spiritual I taste not any," saith Mr Bain, describing the temper of his own spirit. He also went out of the world with far less comfort than some weaker Christians enjoy, God letting Satan loose upon him. (Bain's Life by Mr Clark.)

For my strength is made perfect] It is an act of as great power in God to keep our spark of grace alive amidst so many corruptions, as to keep a fire alive upon the face of the sea. The angels are kept with much less care, charge, and power, than we; because they have no bias, no weight of sin hung upon them.

Ver. 10. *Therefore I take pleasure*] εὐδοκῶ, I am well a-paid of them, I reckon them among God's love-tokens, pledges of his love, and badges of my sonship.

For when I am weak, then, &c.] This is a seeming contradiction. God, saith Luther, doth most of his works *in mediis contrariis*, by contraries. Διὰ τῶν ἐναντίων ἐναντία οἰκονομεῖται. He hath a way by himself, saith Nazianzen, that he may be the more admired.

Ver. 11. *For in nothing am I behind*] And yet there were a sort of silly souls (that thought themselves jolly fellows) in the days of Zuinglius, A.D. 1519, that talked thus at Zurich: *Quis tandem Paulus? nonne homo est? Apostolus est, sed suburbanus tantum, non ex* 12 *viris, non cum Christo est conversatus, articulum fidei non composuit.* What was Paul? but a man. An apostle he was, but of an inferior rank; he was not of the twelve; he conversed not with Christ; he composed not any of the 12 articles of the Creed. We would as soon believe Thomas or Scotus, as Paul, &c. "I am as much an apostle as they, who are more than much apostles," saith St Paul here (for so the Greek runs); but (*contra sycophantæ morsum non est remedium*) he cannot be heard.

Ver. 12. *In all patience*] A grace to be gloried in; Job is crowned and chronicled for it.

Ver. 13. *Forgive me this wrong*] A pleasant irony, such as whereof this Epistle is full. It is said of a wise man, *Quod objecta probra ut visus nocturnos, et vanas somniorum imagines digno supplicio puniat, festivo scilicet contemptu et oblivione, vel si tanti est, misericordia elevet.* (John Wover in Polymath.)

Ver. 14. *For I seek not yours*] Not the fleece, but the flock. He had not those instruments of a foolish shepherd, *forcipes et mulctram*, the shears and milk-pail, &c. The whole senate can witness, saith Beza, that whereas Calvin had a very small stipend, yet was he so far from being discontent therewith, that a more ample allowance being freely offered him, he obstinately refused it. All the goods that he left behind him when he died, his library also being sold very dear, came scarce to 300 French crowns. *Non opes, non gloriam, non voluptates quæsivi*, said Melancthon, I never sought riches, pleasures, or preferments; this conscience I carry with me, whithersoever I go. (Melch. Adam.) I do ingenuously profess, saith Mr Rollock, that of all my stipends I have not laid up two pence, for I never cared for the things of this world. Luther never found himself once tempted to covetousness. And herein I could wish we were all Lutherans.

But the parents for the children] We use to say, that one father will better provide for nine children than nine children will for one father. Howbeit, our spiritual fathers (though they seek us, and not ours, yet) they should find both "us" and "ours;" "us," in our obedience; "ours," in our recompence.

Ver. 15. *Spend and be spent*] If like clouds we do sweat ourselves to death, so souls may be brought home to God, it is a blessed way of dying. Mr Samuel Cook's motto was *Impendam et expendar*, I will spend and be spent; this he cheerfully verified.

The less I be loved] This is many a good man's grief, but his reward is nevertheless with God. The nurse looks not for her wages from the child, but from the parent.

Ver. 16. *Being crafty I caught*] A blessed craft, a high point of heavenly wisdom, Dan. xii. 3. It is written of the fox, that when he is very hungry after prey, and can find none, he lieth down and feigneth himself to be a dead carcase, and so the fowls fall upon him, and then he catcheth them. St Paul hungering after the souls' health of his Corinthians, denies himself to gain them.

Ver. 17. *Whom I sent unto you*] It is said of the pope, that he can never lack money so long as he can hold a pen in his hand; he can command it and have it. But St Paul could not skill of those arts.

Ver. 18. *In the same spirit*] Who worketh with his own tools only, and is ever like himself in all the saints; through whose whole course godliness runs, as the woof doth through the web, as the spirit doth through the body.

In the same steps] With an upright foot, Gal. ii. 14, in Christ, Col. ii. 6, as Christ, 1 John ii. 6.

Ver. 19. *That we excuse ourselves*] And so yield a fault.

I speak before God] The witness of my innocency, Job xvi. 19; Gen. xx. 6.

For your edifying] Whilst ye conceive no ill opinion of us, which, like muddy water in a vessel, might cause the most precious liquor of our doctrine to run over.

Ver. 20. *And that I shall be found*] *Crudelem medicum intemperans æger facit.* (Mimus.) We delight not to fling daggers at men's faces; but if men be not told their own, and that with some sharpness, they will on in sin to their utter ruin. Sharp waters clear the eyesight; and bitter potions bring on sweet health. A weak dose doth but stir bad humours and anger them, not purge them out; so it fareth with sins.

Lest there be debates, envyings, &c.] King Edward IV., the night before his death, said to his kinsmen and friends, I remember it to my grief, that there hath been discord amongst you a great time, not always for great causes, but poor mistakings.[1] Some, like salamanders, live always in the fire; like trouts, they love to swim against stream; like Phocion, they think it a goodly thing to dissent from others.

Whisperings] See the note on Rom. i. 29.

Swellings] That is, taking things unkindly, so that the heart even riseth against another, and we cannot away with him, would have nothing to do with him. Now, as the swelling of the spleen is very dangerous for health; and of the sails, for the overbearing of a little vessel; so is this swelling of the heart by passion, especially if it break out at the lips by tumults, that is, by telling this body, running to that, filling the town with it. *Cœlum mugitibus implet.*

Ver. 21. *That have not repented*] Impenitence maketh sin mortal, saith St John, 1 Epist. v. 16, or rather immortal, as saith St Paul, Rom. ii. 5. It is not the falling into the water that drowns, but lying in it. God's people may sink once and again to the bottom, but the third time they rise and recover by repentance.

CHAPTER XIII.

Ver. 1. *Of two or three witnesses*] So he calleth his threefold admonition. God's word neglected will one day be a swift witness against the contemners. Moses shall accuse men, John v. 46. God's word lay hold on them, Zech. i. 6, and stick in their hearts and flesh, as fire, throughout all eternity, Jer. v. 14.

Ver. 2. *I told you before*] *Sed surdo fabulam,* no telling would serve turn. Many are so wedded and wedged to their sins, that nothing will sunder them but an extraordinary touch from the hand of heaven.

Ver. 3. *A proof of Christ speaking in me*] The Church is *Christi docentis auditorium,* saith Bernard, the place wherein he ordinarily teacheth, who hath his school on earth, though his chair in heaven. *Scholam habet in terris, Cathedram in cælis.*

Ver. 4. *Crucified through weakness*] i. e. *Ex afflicto ejus statu,* as Gal. iv. 14 (Aug.), as having voluntarily subjected himself to all sorts of sufferings for our sakes.

[1] Daniel's Hist. of England.

Ver. 5. *Examine yourselves*] The final trial of our eternal estate doth immediately and solely appertain to the court of heaven. Indeed the disquisitive part belongs to us, the decisive to God.

Prove your own selves] Redouble your diligence in this most needful but much neglected duty of self-examination; an error here is easy and dangerous; hence the precept is doubled; so Zeph. ii. 1. *Excutite vos, iterumque excutite,* as Tremellius renders it, Fan yourselves, yea, fan yourselves. He doubleth his phrase, as it were his files. Men are as loth to review their actions, and read the blurred writing of their hearts, as school-boys are to parse their lessons, and false Latins they have made; the eyes also of their minds are as ill set as those of their bodies, so that they see nothing inwards, though these windows of the soul should be like the windows of Solomon's temple, broad inward, 1 Kings vi. 4: and men should try themselves thoroughly, for God will; as, though scholars will not scan their verses, their master will. " Let every man therefore prove his own work," Gal. vi. 4; so shall he save God a labour, and put the devil out of office. Whereas, sparing a little pains at first doubleth it in the end, as he that will not cast up his books, his books will cast up him at length.

Know ye not your own selves?] *Nosce teipsum,* Know thyself, say the heathens, came down from heaven; sure it is none can ascend to heaven unless he know himself.

Except ye be reprobates?] Gr. counterfeits, adulterine. Every soul is either the spouse of Christ, or the devil's strumpet.

Ver. 6. *But I trust that ye shall know*] Whereas they were ready to retort that they were no reprobates, he should well know, let him see that himself were not one. I trust ye shall know, saith he, that we are no reprobates, counterfeits, or unapprovable, opposed to approved, ver. 7.

Ver. 7. *Though we be as reprobates*] viz. In your esteem. The good heart is content to vilify, yea, nullify itself, so God may be glorified and his people edified; let him be a footstool, or what ye will, to help Christ into his throne. *Prorsus Satan est Lutherus, sed Christus vivit, et regnat. Amen,* saith Luther. Let me be called a devil, or anything, so Christ may be exalted. (Epist. ad Spalat.)

Ver. 8. *For we can do nothing*] A temporary may so fall away, as to persecute the truth that he once professed, and the ministry that he once admired. Never falls a saint so far in his greatest relapses. Bishop Latimer tells of one, who fell away from the known truth, to mocking and scorning it; yet was afterwards touched in conscience for it. Beware of this sin, saith he; for I have known no more than this that repented. It is a very dangerous precipice. (Lat. Serm. afore K. Edw.)

Ver. 9. *Even your perfection*] Or, your restoration, or joining again, κατάρτισιν. His meaning is, saith Beza, that whereas the members of this Church were all, as it were, dislocated and out of joint, they should now again be joined together in love, and they should endeavour to amend what was amiss amongst them, either in faith or manners.

Ver. 10. *And not to destruction*] Unless by accident; or, if to the destruction of the flesh, it is that the spirit might be saved in the day of the Lord Jesus, 1 Cor. v. 5. See the note there and on 2 Cor. x. 8.

Ver. 11. *Finally*] Gr. λοιπὸν, that which yet remains to say more, and then an end.

Be perfect] Or, piece again.

Be of one mind] For matter of opinion.

Live in peace] For matter of affection.

The God of love] The author and fautor.

Ver. 12. *With a holy kiss*] A custom proper to those times. See the note on Rom. xvi. 16, and on 1 Cor. xvi. 20.

Ver. 13. *All the saints salute you*] Sanctity is no enemy to courtesy; it doth not remove but rectify it.

Ver. 14. *The grace of our Lord*] A friendly valediction or fatherly benediction.

A

COMMENTARY OR EXPOSITION

UPON THE

EPISTLE OF ST PAUL TO THE GALATIANS.

CHAPTER I.

Ver. 1. *Who raised him from the dead*] And by the same almighty power causeth dead souls to hear the voice of the Son of God in his ministers and live, John v. 25; Eph. i. 19.

Ver. 2. *The Churches of Galatia*] They are not dischurched though much corrupted. Uzziah ceased not to be a king when he began to be a leper; the disease of his forehead did not remove his crown.

Ver. 3. *Grace be, &c.*] See the note on Rom. i. 7. This Epistle to the Galatians is an epitome of that to the Romans. Peter Martyr observeth that Paul deals more mildly in that Epistle to the Romans than in this to the Galatians; because the Galatians were at first well instructed in the matter of justification, but afterwards did mix other things with Christ; therefore he so sharps them up, yea, thundereth against them.

Ver. 4. *From this present evil world*] Bewitched wherewith the Galatians were relapsed from Christ. A subtle and sly enemy it is surely, and hath cast down many wounded; yea, many strong men have been slain by it, as by Solomon's harlot, Prov. vii. 26.

Ver. 5. *To whom be glory*] The benefit of our redemption should make us lift up many a humble, joyful, and thankful heart to God.

Ver. 6. *That ye are so soon*] Giddy-headed hearers have *religionem ephemeram*, are whirred about with every wind of doctrine, being con-

stant only in their inconstancy, as Ecebolus, Balduinus, and our modern sectaries. The bishops and doctors of England (said that martyr) in their book against the pope's supremacy, spoke as much as Luther or any Lutheran ever did or could. If they dissembled, who could ever so deeply, speaking so pithily? if not, who could ever turn head to tail so suddenly and so shortly as these did?

Removed from him, &c.] From Christ and me his apostle. Luther often in his books testifieth that he was much afraid, lest when he was dead, that sound doctrine of justification by faith alone would die also. It proved so in sundry places of Germany. Men fell to Popery as fast as leaves fall in autumn. The word here rendered removed, signifieth properly transported or transplanted. He alludes (saith Jerome) to the word *Galal*, to roll, as if he should say, You are Galatians, that is, rolling and changing, falling from the gospel of Christ to the law of Moses.

Ver. 7. *There be some*] That would fain have blended Pharisaism and Christianity, Acts xv. 5.

That trouble you] ταράσσοντες. As camels with their feet trouble the waters they should drink of.

And would pervert the gospel] They pretended only to bring in a Jewish rite or two, and yet are said to pervert the gospel, μεταστρέψαι. *Ea quæ post tergum sunt, in faciem convertere*, as Jerome hath it, to turn that before that should be behind; to speak distorted things, διεστραμμένα, such as produce convulsions of conscience, Acts xx. 30. A little thing untowardly mingled mars all. The monstrous heresy of Nestorius lay but in one letter, θεοδόχος, and of Arius, but in one syllable, ὁμοιούσιος.

Ver. 8. *Or an angel*] Not an evil angel (as Ambrose understands it), but a good angel, *per impossibile*, as John viii. 55.

Than that which we, &c.] Or besides that which we have preached. He saith not, contrary to that, but besides that; for indeed that which is directly besides, is indirectly against the gospel.

Ver. 9. *Than that ye have*] Of the camel it is said, that he will never carry any more weight than what at first is laid upon him; nor go one foot beyond his ordinary journey. Conscience will not budge nor yield a hair for an angel's authority. Stand fast in the good old way, and find rest, Jer. vi. 16.

Ver. 10. *For do I now persuade men*] That is, men's doctrines and devices.

Or do I seek to please men] Ut κοινοφιλὴς, *qui ab omnibus gratiam inire cupit, quem quidam per jocum Placentam vocat.* Men-pleasers, that curry favour with all, and covet to be counted no meddlers. These lose a friend of God. Neither do they long hold in with those whom for present they do so much please. Constantine checked a preacher, *qui ausus est imperatorem in os beatum dicere*, that was so bold as to call him a blessed man to his face, thinking thereby to ingratiate. (Euseb. de Vit. Const.) Theodoric, an Arian king, did exceedingly affect a certain deacon, although an orthodox. The deacon thinking to please him better and get preferment, became an Arian; which when the king understood, he changed his love into hatred, and caused his head to be struck from his shoulders. Erasmus, by seeking to please both sides, was neither owned by the Papists nor honoured by the Protestants, *Pusillanimitas et ἀνθρωπαρέσκεια in præclaro hoc Dei organo præpotuere.* Dastardliness and manpleasance prevailed too much with him, who otherwise did the Church of God singular good service. (Amama.) How much better had he done if passing by Placenza he had held a straight course to Verona! but he durst not (as Luther) meddle either with the pope's triple crown, or with the monks' fat paunches, lest for his *Væ vobis* he should have been brought *coram nobis*, as father Latimer said. He held it best policy to keep his finger out of the sore: and either to say no more than Eli did to his sons, " Why do ye such things," &c., or than Jehoshaphat did to Ahab, " Let not the king say so." *As pruriginosa istorum hominum scabies aspetiori certe strigili fricanda fuerat*, saith Amama. But those men's mangy hides deserved a sharper currycomb.

For if I yet pleased men] As once I did while I was a Pharisee.

I should not be, &c.] That rule holds good in rhetoric, but not in divinity, *Non ad veritatem solum, sed etiam ad opinionem eorum qui audiunt, accommodanda est oratio.* (Cic. in Partib.)

Ver. 11. *Is not after man*] This he often inculcateth, because the false apostles had buzzed such a thing into their ears to disparage his ministry.

Ver. 12. *Received it of man*] i. e. Of mere man. Jesus Christ is more than a man.

Ver. 13. *And wasted it*] ἐπόρθουν. As an enemy's country with fire and sword. Mars is styled πτολίπορθος. (Homer.)

Ver. 14. *Above many mine equals*] Porphyry said it was great pity such a man as Paul was ever cast away upon the Christian religion. The monarch of Morocco told the English ambassador in King John's time, that he had lately read Paul's Epistles, which he liked so well, that were he now to choose his religion, he would, before any other, embrace Christianity; but every one, saith he, ought to die in his own religion; and the leaving of the faith wherein he was born was the only thing that he disliked in that apostle.

Ver. 15. *Who separated me from,* &c.] How knew he this, but by the event? Whosoever is lawfully called to the ministry may conceive that he also was sanctified thereunto from the womb, and should therefore do his utmost in the work. *Verbi minister es, hoc age*, was Mr Perkins' motto.

Ver. 16. *To reveal his Son in me*] Not only as in an object (wherein the power and grace of Christ might shine and appear), but as by an instrument of revealing and preaching Christ to many.

I conferred not with flesh] i. e. With carnal reason, an evil counsellor for the soul, Rom. viii. 7. Indeed in human governments, where reason is shut out, there tyranny is thrust in; but where God commandeth, there to ask a reason is presumption, to oppose reason is flat rebellion.

Ver. 17. *But I went into Arabia*] Of this journey Luke maketh no mention in the Acts. Into these tents of Kedar came St Paul, and made them, by his preaching, comely as the curtains of Solomon, Cant. i. 5. Rude they were, but rich; black, but comely, when they had this precious man amongst them especially, who became a blessing to all places wheresoever he came. Contrary to that which is said of the Great Turk, that wherever he sets his foot he leaves desolation behind him. Arabia was Felix indeed when St Paul was there.

Ver. 18. *To see Peter*] Not by way of idle visit, but thoroughly to observe the history of his Christian practice for godly imitation.[1] *Historiæ sunt fidæ monitrices.*

Ver. 19. *But other of the apostles*] These were busily attending upon their particular charges and offices, according to Rom. xii. 7.

Ver. 20. *Behold, before God, I lie not*] This he solemnly sweareth for their satisfaction. An oath may be lawfully taken to help the truth in necessity, and not otherwise. Hence the Hebrew word Nishbang is a passive, and signifieth " to be sworn," rather than to swear.

---

[1] ἱστορῆσαι, *videndo observare.*

Ver. 21. *Afterwards I came*] He kept, belike, a diary of his travels, and was able to give a good account of his daily courses. It is not to be doubted, but that our Saviour's disciples kept a register of his holy oracles and miracles, out of which the history of the gospel was afterwards compiled and composed. Father Latimer did the like, as appeareth by his discourses. Mr Bradford also had a journal or day-book, wherein he used to set down all such notable things as either he did see or hear, each day that passed.

Ver. 22. *And was unknown*] So far was Paul from learning aught of them.

Ver. 23. *Now preacheth the faith*] A marvellous conversion. I was a obstinate Papist (saith Latimer of himself) as any was in England. Insomuch that when I should be made bachelor of divinity, my whole oration went against Philip Melancthon and his opinions.

Ver. 24. *And they glorified God*] " Whoso offereth praise, he glorifieth me," Psal. l. 23. God accounts himself as it were to receive a new being, by those inward conceptions of his glory, and by those outward honours that we do to him.

CHAPTER II.

Ver. 1. *I went up*] To that first Christian council, Acts xv.

With Barnabas] His constant companion, till that bitter bickering, Acts xv. 39. See the note there.

Ver. 2. *By revelation*] i. e. By God's special direction; for he ordereth a good man's goings, Psal. xxxvii. 23.

I communicated unto them] ἀνεθέμην, I laid open the matter freely and familiarly, as unto bosom-friends.

But privately] For all good men are not fit to be trusted with secrets, but only such as can both keep counsel and give counsel.

Or had run in vain] Lest, if it should be thought that I had not held good correspondence with those other apostles, I might lose the fruit of my ministry.

Ver. 3. *Was compelled to be circumcised*] i. e. I would not yield he should be; lest I should seem to countenance them that held circumcision necessary to salvation. In the year of grace 1549, the ministers of Magdeburg did stoutly oppose them of Wittenberg and Leipsic, and set forth many books against them, because they dealt deceitfully, and by their Adiaphora, or things indifferent, as they called them, they paved a way to Popery. (Alsted. Chron.) And this was our case till this late blessed Reformation. It was not without cause that Peter Martyr commended it to the care of Queen Elizabeth, that church-governors endeavour not to carry the ark of the gospel into England upon the cart of needless ceremonies.

Ver. 4. *Unawares brought in*] παρείσακτοι, or privily slipt in, pretending piety to their worldly or wicked respects. With such ill instruments the Church hath ever been pestered, 2 Pet. ii. 1. These hell-scouts are skulking in every corner.

To spy out our liberty] viz. Of circumcising or not circumcising Titus, that they might pick a quarrel with us.

That they might bring us into bondage] sc. To the ceremonial law. Carolostadius attempted some such thing in Luther's days, and by him was opposed. (Bucholcer.)

Ver. 5. *To whom we gave place*] We must stick close to the truth, and stickle hard for it, accounting each parcel thereof precious, and not to be parted with for any good. How religious were the apostles and ancients this way! They would not yield for an hour, or exchange one letter or syllable of that holy faith, wherewith Christ had betrusted them.

Ver. 6. *Seemed to be somewhat*] Opinion sets the price; when gold is raised from 20s. to 22s., the gold is the same, estimation only raiseth it.

In conference added nothing to me] They could tell him nothing which he knew not before; when they came to talk together, he found that they did not only hold and teach the same things, but *in iisdem verbis, in iisdem syllabis*, in the self-same words and syllables as he did, as Melancthon wisheth all men would.

Whatsoever they were] Augustine being oppressed with the authority of the Fathers, saith he regardeth not *quis, sed quid*, the worth of the man, but the weight of his reasons.

Ver. 7. *As the gospel of, &c.*] He equalizeth himself to Peter in office and dignity; though pseudo-apostles and pseudo-catholics deny him that honour. St Peter, Jesuits commend for a worthy spirit, when they censure St Paul for a hot-headed person, &c. And because James is named before Peter, ver. 9, Bellarmine saith that this text is corrupted (*Latini quidem Petrum præponunt non sine falsi crimine*); but what will he say to 1 Cor. ix. 5; John i. 44; Acts xv. 13; xxi. 18, where it appeareth that not Peter but James was president of the council, because he spake the last, and concluded all?

Ver. 8. *For he that wrought, &c.*] He argues from the success of his and Peter's ministry to the lawfulness of their calling to the work. So he doth 1 Cor. ix. 1—3; 2 Cor. xiii. 4, 5. See the notes there. He also ascribeth the glory of all to God, when he saith "was mighty in me." A phrase not unlike that other, 1 Cor. xv. 10, " Not I, but the grace of God." And again, not we, " but the weapons of our warfare are mighty through God," &c., 2 Cor. x. 4.

Ver. 9. *Who seemed to be pillars*] Of the Church, or of the college of apostles. The apostle seems to intimate that even then men began to attribute more than was meet to those holy apostles. This degenerated afterwards into gross superstition, διασυρτικῶς, dictum. (Cam.)

And they unto the circumcision] Yet were they not so tied up by this agreement, but that they might preach upon fit occasion to the Gentiles too, as might Paul and Barnabas to the Jews; but the Gentiles were their chief charge, and among them they had greatest success.

Ver. 10. *Remember the poor*] Those Jews that embraced Christianity in Palestine were therefore turned out of all by their unkind countrymen, Heb. x. 34. Hence this care of the apostles, and this forwardness in St Paul. About the beginning of the Reformation in France, the Duke of Lorrain had proscribed some thousands of his Lutheran subjects, who were forced to feed upon haws and acorns, &c. The divines of Strasburgh in Germany, moved with pity towards these poor brethren, ceased not till by their discourses they had prevailed with the senate there to take those miserable exiles into their city, and to provide for them, till they might be conveniently conveyed to other places. (Scultet. Annal.)

Ver. 11. *But when Peter*, &c.] I would gladly learn (said that martyr) why the seat of the primacy (to grant that) should be rather at Rome than[1] elsewhere? They answer, because Peter's chair was at Rome. This is even like to this, because Moses the greatest prophet, and Aaron the first priest, exercised their office until their death in the desert, therefore the principallest place of the Jews' Church shall be in the wilderness. But grant them their reason that it is good, what should Antioch claim? For Peter's chair was there also, when Paul gave him a check, which was unseemly and unmannerly done of Paul, that would not give place to his president and better. Thus far Mr Bradford. Cardinal Baronius withstands Paul as much as ever he did Peter, and blasphemously affirmeth that Peter was not to be blamed, but Paul a great deal more. Bellarmine saith, It was not Peter but Cephas, one of the seventy. A sorry shift, so loth are heretics to have their ass's ears seen. Jerome affirmeth (Epist. 89 ad Augustin.) that Paul reproved Peter *simulate non serio, nec sensisse quod scripsit*, seemingly and not seriously, and that he wrote otherwise than he thought, in saying that Peter walked not uprightly according to the truth of the gospel. But Augustine refuteth this as an error in Jerome, in his 19th epistle to him, and Aquinas also disliketh it; because, ver. 12, Paul sets down a weighty and urgent cause of his reproof. Nevertheless, he doth not call Peter a hypocrite, as Julian the Apostate said he did; for every one that falleth of infirmity is not presently a hypocrite; though he may, in some particular, act the part of a hypocrite. (Cyril ix. in Julian.)

Ver. 12. *For before that certain*] This history pertains to Acts xv. 30—35, but is not there recorded, that we might search the Scriptures, and compare place with place. So God hath scattered the duties of husbands and wives up and down the Scriptures, that men learning to be good husbands, they may learn also to be good men.

Fearing them of the circumcision] It was not danger that he feared, but offence, wherein he

had not done amiss, but that in avoiding a less scandal he fell into a far greater.

Ver. 13. *And the other Jews dissembled*] The sins of teachers are the teachers of sins; and great men's faults go as seldom unaccompanied as their persons.

Barnabas also] Adhering to Peter rather than to Paul, his old companion, not without a tincture perhaps of the old bitter bickering. "Try all things;" good men may seduce us, as here Peter did Barnabas, and as those would have done Paul, Acts xxi. 12. How many learned able men hath the authority of Luther misled in the point of consubstantiation! Ursin was carried away with it awhile; till he was turned from it by the reading of Luther's own arguments; they were such plain paralogisms. (Melch. Adam.)

Ver. 14. *That they walked not*] Ministers must both ὀρθοτομεῖν and ὀρθοποδεῖν, divide the word rightly and foot it uprightly.

I said to Peter before them all] The fault was public, reproof must be according, 1 Tim. v. 20. In the year 1159 lived Joannes Sarisburiensis, who both reproved the pope to his face and also wrote his Polycraticon, wherein he freely scourgeth the popish clergy.[1] As long before that, in the year 705, Adelin, elect bishop of Sherborn (or Salisbury), while he stayed at Rome for the pope's approbation, the same pope (his name was Sergius) was charged with adultery; for which foul fault this bishop was bold to reprehend his Holiness sharply. (Godw. Catal.)

Why compellest thou, &c.] Peter's example was a compulsion. The company we keep compel us to do as they do.

Ver. 15. *We who are Jews*] The apostle proceedeth in his speech to the Jews at Antioch.

And not sinners of the Gentiles] Because under the covenant of grace; their sins and iniquities will I remember no more. As for the Gentiles, they wanting the rule of God's law, ran headlong into every sin, without restraint or control, Eph. iv. 19.

Ver. 16. *Knowing*] Here is more than an implicit faith or a conjectural confidence.

Ver. 17. *But if whiles we seek*] This is the same in sense with Rom. iii. 31. If we should argue from mercy to liberty, from free justification to lewd and loose conversation, would not all the world cry shame on us? I read of a monster who that night that his prince pardoned and released him, got out and slew him. This was Michael Balbus, who slew the emperor Leo Armenius. Is it possible that any should offer to do so to Christ?

Ver. 18. *For if I build again*] As I should, if I should license any man to sin, because justified by faith. Christ came by water as well as by blood; he justifies none but whom he also sanctifies.

Ver. 19. *Am I dead to the law*] *i. e.* Am freed from the curse, rigour, and irritation of the law. Or, am freed from sin, as Rom. vi. 7.

Ver. 20. *Christ liveth in me*] Luther's motto *redarguit*. Revius in hist. Pont.

[1] *Præsens præsentem pontificem*

was *Vivit Christus*, Christ liveth ; and if he were not alive, I would not wish to live one hour longer. Let the Lord live, saith David, Psal. xviii. 46. Yea, let him live in me, saith Paul. Let him act me, let him think in me, desire, pray, do all in me. Lord, saith Nazianzen, I am an instrument for thee to touch. Christ dwells in that heart most largely that hath emptied itself of itself. The Israelites felt not the sweetness of manna, till they had spent the flesh-pots and other provisions of Egypt.

And gave himself for me] True faith individuateth Christ, and appropriateth him to a man's self. This is the pith and power of particular faith. Mistress Lewis the martyr, being set upon by Satan a little before she suffered, was much comforted and helped by this text.

Ver. 21. *I do not frustrate*] viz. By seeking to be justified by the law. Ambrose renders it, *Non sum ingratus gratiæ Dei*, I am not ungrateful to the grace of God ; I do not repudiate, cassate, nullify it.

Dead in vain] Because he attains not his end in dying, which was not only to leave us a pattern of patience, as Anabaptists hold ; but to merit for us remission of sins, and imputation of his righteousness for our justification.

CHAPTER III.

Ver. 1. *O foolish Galatians*] THOSE that are sick of a lethargy must have double the quantity of physic given them that other men have in other diseases. These Galatians were in a spiritual lethargy, and are therefore thus sharply rebuked, that they might be sound in the faith.

Who hath bewitched you] Or, bemisted you, and dazzled your eyes, Tit. i. 13. The word properly signifies to overlook, as they call it, or to kill with the eyes, by casting out venomous beams as the basilisk, and as witches are said to do. ἐβάσκανε αρὰ τὸ φάεσι καίνειν. (Plin. vii. 2.)

Hath been evidently set forth] As a remedy, by looking whereon ye might have been cured or kept from that bewitching by the eye, like as the stung Israelites were healed by looking on the brazen serpent.

Crucified amongst you] In the evidence of the doctrine of Christ crucified, and in the administration of the Lord's Supper, that lively picture of Christ on the cross. The Greek word προεγράφη signifieth to paint forth a thing, Rom. xv. 4, by a theological painting, not artificial, as the Papists would have it to warrant crucifixes.

Ver. 2. *Or by the hearing of faith*] The manna of the Spirit comes down from heaven in the dews of the ministry of the gospel, Numb. xi. 9 ; 1 Pet. i. 21. If our eyes see not our teachers, we cannot expect to hear the voice behind us, Isa. xxx. 20, 21.

Ver. 3. *Are ye so foolish ?*] Those then that have the Spirit may play fools in some particulars. Those that are recovered of a frenzy, have yet some mad fits sometimes.

Made perfect by the flesh] As Nebuchadnezzar's image, whose golden head ended in dirty feet.

Ver. 4. *If it be in vain*] q. d. It is not in vain. God keepeth the feet of the saints, that they cannot altogether lose the things they have wrought, they cannot fall below his supporting grace ; the Lord puts under his hand, Psal. xxxvii. Yet it cannot be denied that a hypocrite may suffer, and all in vain, 1 Cor. xiii. 3, as did Alexander the coppersmith, who was near unto martyrdom, Acts xix. 34. See the note on 1 Cor. xiii. 3.

Ver. 5. *Or by the hearing of faith*] Faith (and so life) is let into the soul by the sense of hearing, Isa. lv., to cross the devil, who by the same door brought death into the world.

Ver. 6. *It was accounted to him*] This the Papists jeeringly call a putative righteousness. The Jews also deride it, and say, that every fox shall yield his own skin to the flayer. See Rom. iv. 9, 11, 12.

Ver. 7. *The same are children, &c.*] And heirs together with him of the world, Rom. iv., which is theirs in right, though detained a while from them by the Amorites, till their sins be full.

Ver. 8. *And the Scripture foreseeing*] Scripture therefore is not a brute dead thing, as the Jesuits blaspheme. Excellently spake he, who called the Scripture, *Cor et animam Dei*, The heart and soul of God. (Greg. in Reg. 3.)

Preached the gospel] There is gospel therefore in the Old Testament.

In thee shall all nations] See my note on Gen. xii. 3. " All nations shall be blessed," *i. e.* justified by faith.

Ver. 9. *Are blessed, &c.*] For they only are blessed whose sins are remitted, Psal. xxxii. 1. Oh, the blessedness of that man, saith the Psalmist.

Ver. 10. *Are under the curse*] *Aut faciendum, aut patiendum*, He that will not have the direction of the law, must have the correction.

That continueth not in all] Deut. xxvii. 26. Heb. Shall stand firm, as a four-square stone, יקום, τετράγωνος.

In the book of the law to do them] Done they must be exactly, upon pain of God's curse. For a groat too short in payment of some dues required, our William the Conqueror forced the monks of Ely to lay down a thousand marks, saith the chronicler. The law is no less strict with those that are not freed by Christ.

Ver. 11. *Shall live by faith*] As being justified by faith. See the note on Rom. i. 17.

Ver. 12. *And the law is not of faith*] Because it promiseth not life to those that will be justified by faith, but requireth works.

Ver. 13. *Christ hath redeemed us*] As man he bought us, as God he redeemed us, saith Jerome. For to redeem is properly to buy some things back that were mortgaged. *Qui redimit, emit quod suum fuit, et suum esse desiit.*

Cursed is every one that hangeth] The tree whereon a man was hanged, the stone wherewith he was stoned, the sword wherewith he was beheaded, and the napkin wherewith he was strangled, they were all buried, that there might be no evil memorial of such an one, to say, This was the tree, sword, stone, napkin, wherewith such an one was executed.[1] Constantine abolished this kind of death out of the empire. But what an odd custom was that of the Tiberenes to hang their best friends in courtesy, *Longasque ex iis literas facere quos charos habebant?* The death on the tree (saith one) was accursed above all kinds of death; as the serpent was accursed above all beasts of the field. Both for the first transgression, whereof the serpent was the instrument, the tree the occasion. (Sphinx Philos.)

Ver. 14. *The promise of the Spirit*] That is, the spiritual promise made to Abraham and his spiritual posterity.

Ver. 15. *I speak after the manner*] I set the matter forth to you by a familiar comparison.

Though it be but a man's testament] William Tracy, Esq., of Gloucestershire, made in his will, that he would have no funeral pomp at his burying, neither passed he upon a mass. And he further said, that he trusted in God only, and hoped by him to be saved, and not by any saint. This gentleman died, and his son as executor brought the will to the bishop of Canterbury to be proved, which he showed to the Convocation; and there most cruelly they judged that he should be taken out of the ground and be burnt as a heretic, A. D. 1532. Dr Parker, chancellor of Worcester, executed the sentence, and was afterwards sent for by King Henry VIII., who laid high offence to his charge, &c. It cost him £300 to have his pardon. (Acts and Mon.)

Ver. 16. *Which is Christ*] Mystical Christ, that is, whole Christ; for he accounts not himself complete without his members, who are therefore called his fulness, Eph. i. 23. *Caput et corpus, unus est Christus*, saith Augustine, the head and members make but one Christ.

Ver. 17. *Four hundred and thirty, &c.*] This space of time betwixt the promise and the law, the Divine providence cast into two equal portions, of 215 before the people's going down into Egypt, and 215 after their being there. (Lightfoot's Har. Prolegom.)

Ver. 18. *Gave it to Abraham*] Gr. κεχάρισται, freely gave it. What more free than gift? And what better freehold than the divine promise?

Ver. 19. *Because of transgressions*] Which are discovered by the law. Sight of misery must go before sense of mercy. *Lex, lux*, the law is a light (saith Solomon), which lays all open, as 1 Cor. xiv. 25, and threateneth destruction to transgressors.

And it was ordained, &c.] Therefore it is not to be disrespected, though we cannot attain eternal life by it.

In the hand of a mediator] That is, of Moses, who was a mediator of that communication of the law to the people, Exod. xx. 19. Christ is the only Mediator of expiation. And of Christ alone some take this text.

Ver. 20. *Is not a mediator of one*] q. d. God and men were at odds, else what use of a mediator? Sin is the makebate, as being a transgression of the law.

But God is one] One and the same now as of old in taking vengeance on the law's transgressors. Or, God is one party disagreeing or displeased.

Ver. 21. *Have given life*] That is, have justified a sinner. But herein lay the law's weakness through the flesh, Rom. viii. 3.

Ver. 22. *But the Scripture*] The law and the prophets.

Hath concluded all] Gr. Hath clapt them up close prisoners. All in the neuter gender (both men and women), to prevent cavils. συνέκλεισεν πάντα.

That the promise, &c.] That he might have mercy upon all, Rom. xi. 32. See the note there.

Ver. 23. *But before faith came, &c.*] i. e. Before Christ came; faith is put for the object of faith.

We were kept under the law] φρουρούμεθα, as in a prison or garrison, being circled with a compassing strength. The sinner, having transgressed, is kept by the law, as with a guard or garrison, that he cannot escape unless he be delivered by Christ. Some learned men make this expression of the apostle here, "Kept under the law," to denote the duty of a schoolmaster; as one who is to give an account of such as are committed to his charge.

Ver. 24. *The law was our schoolmaster*] Such an one as that Livy and Florus speak of in Italy, who brought forth his scholars to Hannibal; and if he had not been more merciful than otherwise, they had all perished.

Ver. 25. *But after that faith*] That is, the gospel, or Christ the author and matter of the gospel. See ver. 23.

Ver. 26. *The children of God*] Gr. The sons of God, grown up at man's estate; *Qui manum ferulæ subduximus*, who are no longer under a schoolmaster. How we are the children of God by faith, see the note on John i. 12.

Ver. 27. *Baptized into Christ*] And so have had your adoption sealed up unto you, like as in the civil adoption there were certain rites and ceremonies usually performed.

Have put on Christ] To justification and sanctification. See the note on Rom. xiii. 14. This is to be clothed with the sun, Rev. xii. 2. Some think the apostle alludeth here to a custom they had in the primitive times, that those that were to be baptized should come to the church on Whit-Sunday (called therefore *Dominica in albis*) and put upon them white clothing.

Ver. 28. *Ye are all one in Christ*] Souls have no sexes, and Christ is no respecter of persons. The servant paid the half-shekel, as well as the master, Exod. xxx.

Ver. 29. *Heirs according*] Heirs are kept short in their nonage, and sometimes forced to borrow of servants; but when once at years, they have all. So shall the saints in heaven, though here hard put to it.

---

[1] Casaub. ex Maimonide.

CHAPTER IV.

Ver. 1. *Differeth nothing from a servant*] In allusion whereunto there is written upon the prince's arms, *Ich dien*, that is, I serve. Henry the Second, king of England, crowned his eldest son Henry whilst he was yet alive; which made his ambition quite turn off his obedience. Ambition ever rides without reins. That king, at his son's coronation, renounced the name of king for that day, and as sewer, served at the table; for which he was thus requited, My father, said he, is not dishonoured by attending on me, for I am both a king and a queen's son, and so is not he. After this he bore arms against his father, and died in open rebellion.

Ver. 2. *But is under tutors*] Those under the law were but alphabetaries in comparison of those under the gospel.[1] The sea about the altar was brazen, 1 Kings vii. 23, and what eyes could pierce through it? Now our sea about the throne is glassy, Rev. iv. 6, like to crystal, clearly conveying the light and sight of God to our eyes.

Ver. 3. *When we were children*] Gr. νήπιοι, infants, babies, that must be pleased with rattles; so the old Church with carnal ceremonies.

Ver. 4. *But when the fulness of the time*] This answers to that time appointed of the Father, ver. 2. Plato said that God doth always γεωμετρεῖν, he doth all things in number, weight, and measure; he never comes too soon, neither stays he too long.

God sent forth his Son] Out of his own bosom. May not we say as they did, John xi. 36, Lo! how he loved us. This was an hyperbole of love. Should we not say again, as they did, Judg. viii. 22, "Rule thou over us, &c., for thou hast delivered us from the hand of Midian."

Made of a woman] Of the sanctified substance of the holy Virgin. Note this against Marcionites and Anabaptists.

Made under the law] Circumcised the eighth day, and so made a debtor to do the whole law; which he perfectly fulfilled, and yet (for us) suffered the curse.

Ver. 5. *To redeem them, &c.*] To buy them off, who were in worse case than the Turkish galley-slaves chained to an oar.

That we might receive the adoption] That is, the possession of our adoption, the full enjoyment of our inheritance.

Ver. 6. *Crying, Abba, Father*] God hath no still-born children. Paul was no sooner converted, but behold he prayed, Acts ix. 11. The spirit of grace is a spirit of supplication, Zech. xii. 10. And when God sends this spirit of prayer into our hearts, it is a sure sign that he means to answer our desires; like as when we bid our children say, I pray you, father, give me this, we do it not, but when we mean to give them that which we teach them to ask. The gemination,

"Abba, Father," noteth fiducial, filial, vehement affection; and it is made the first word we can speak, when we are made sons, to cry "Abba, Father."

Ver. 7. *And if a son, &c.*] See the note on Rom. viii. 17.

Ver. 8. *Ye did service*] Here all religious service done to any but God is manifestly condemned as impious, whether in pagans or papagans.

Ver. 9. *Or rather are known of God*] Whose gracious fore-knowing and fore-appointing of us to eternal life is the ground and foundation of our illumination and conversion, our love to him a reflex of his love to us.

Ver. 10. *Ye observe days*] The Christian Church knows no holy-days, besides that honourable Lord's day, Isa. lvii. 14, Rev. i. 10, and such holy feasts, as upon special occasions the Church shall see fit to celebrate, as Novemb. 5, &c.

Ver. 11. *Lest I have bestowed labour*] Gr. κοκοπίακα, even to lassitude, as a day-labourer. Other work-folks find their work as they left it; but a minister hath all marred many times between sabbath and sabbath, or if but awhile absent, as Moses was in the mount.

Ver. 12. *Be as I am*] No longer a legalist, as once, Phil. iii. 5, 8.

Ye have not injured me at all] He was above their buffooneries and indignities. When an inconsiderate fellow had stricken Cato in the bath, and afterwards cried him mercy, he replied, I remember not that thou didst strike me. (Seneca.) *Tu linguæ, ego aurium dominus*, said one to another that railed on him. I cannot be master of thy tongue, but I will be master of mine own ears. (Tacit.) One having made a long and idle discourse before Aristotle concluded it thus, I doubt I have been too tedious to you, sir philosopher, with my many words. In good sooth, said Aristotle, you have not been tedious to me, for I gave no heed to anything you said.[2] Momus in Lucian tells Jupiter, It is in thy power whether any one shall vex or wrong thee. St Paul here shakes off the affronts and injuries offered unto him with as much ease as once he did the viper, Acts xxviii. 5. Some would have swelled, and almost died at the sight of such a thing; he only shook it off, and there was no hurt done.

Ver. 13. *Through infirmity of the flesh*] That is, though much broken with many miseries, yet I spared not to take pains amongst you. Zachariah, though he ceased to speak, yet he ceased not to minister; he took not his dumbness for a dismission, but stayed out the eight days of his course, Luke i.

Ver. 14. *And my temptation*] That is, mine afflictions, whereby the Lord tempts his, feels which way their pulses beat, and how they stand affected toward him.

Which was in my flesh] My spirit being haply untouched. For oft the body is weak, the soul

---

[1] ὁ μηδὲ τὸν Αἴσωπον πεπατηκώς. Aristophanes.

[2] Plutar. de Garrulit. οὐδὲν πάσχεις κακόν, ἂν μὴ προσποιῇς.

well. Afflictions may reach but to the outward man. Job never complained till he was wet through, till the waters went over his soul.

Nor rejected] Gr. ἐξετύσατε, ye spit not on, as they did that spat in Christ's face.

Even as Christ Jesus] Who hath said, "He that receiveth you, receiveth me." It was a common saying at Constantinople, Better the sun should not shine than that Chrysostom should not preach.

Ver. 15. *Where is then the blessedness*] *q. d.* Time was when ye held yourselves happy in me, and blessed the time that ever ye saw and heard me.[1] Is the change now in me or in yourselves? Thus the Jews rejoiced in John for a season, but he soon grew stale to them, John v. 35. See the note there. *Neutrum modo, mas modo vulgus.*

Ver. 16. *Am I therefore become, &c.*] Truth breeds hatred, as the fair nymphs did the ugly fauns and satyrs. The hearing of truth galls, as they write of some creatures, that they have *fel in aure,* gall in their ears. It was not for nothing therefore that the orator called upon his countrymen to get their ears healed before they came any more to hear him. To preach, saith Luther, is nothing else but to derive upon a man's self the rage of all the country. And therefore when one defined the ministerial function to be *Artem artium et scientiam scientiarum,* the art of arts and science of sciences, Melancthon said, If he had defined it to be *miseriam miseriarum,* the misery of miseries, he had hit it.

Because I tell you the truth?] He that prizeth truth (saith Sir Walter Raleigh) shall never prosper by the possession or profession thereof. *An expectas, ut Quintilianus ametur?* When we seek to fetch men out of their sins, they are apt to fret and snarl; as when men are wakened out of their sleep, they are unquiet, ready to brawl with their best friend.

Ver. 17. *They zealously affect you*] *Depereunt vos;* as jealous woers they would have you whole to themselves without a co-rival, ἔρως et ἔρις, *cognata sunt.*

They would exclude us] As standing in their way. This is the guise of all sectaries and seducers, they denigrate the true teachers that they may be the only men.

That you might affect them] Our Antinomians call upon their hearers to mark, it may be they shall hear that which they have not heard before, when the thing is either false, or if true, no more than ordinarily is taught by others.

Quid dignum tanto ferat hic promissor hiatu?
Hor. de Art. Poet.

Ver. 18. *To be zealously affected in a good thing*] In a good cause, for a good end, and in a good manner. There is a counterfeit zeal, as is that of the Popish martyrs, or traitors rather, of whom Campian in his epistle to the honourable counsellors of Queen Elizabeth, *Quamdiu vel unus quispiam e nobis supererit qui Tiburno vestro fruatur, &c.* As long as there shall be left any

[1] μακαρισμὸς, *Beatitudinis prædicatio.* Beza.

one of us to wear a Tyburn tippet, we will not cease our suit.

And not only when I am present] Sith even absent I teach and tell you the truth of God by letters.

Ver. 19. *Till Christ be formed*] That you may seek for salvation by him alone. Together with the word there goes forth a regenerating power, James i. 18. It is not a dead letter and empty sound, as some have blasphemed. Only let us not, as Hosea's unwise son, stay in the place of breaking forth of children, proceed no further than to conviction; much less stifle those inward workings for sin, as harlots destroy their conceptions, that they may not bear the pain of childbirth.

Ver. 20. *And to change my voice*] To speak to your necessity; for now being absent I shoot at rovers, and am at some uncertainty (ἀπορούμαι) how to frame my discourse to you.

Ver. 21. *Ye that desire, &c.*] That are ambitious of slavery, of beggary, ver. 9. How many have we at this day that rejoice in their bondage and dance to hell in their bolts!

Ver. 22. *For it is written*] It was enough of old to say, "It is written;" there was no need to quote chapter and verse, as now. Men were so ready in the Scriptures, they could tell where to turn to anything at first hearing.

Ver. 23. *Was born after the flesh*] In an ordinary way, as all others are; for Hagar was young, and Abraham not old.

Was by promise] *i. e.* By a supernatural power, by a divine miracle.

Ver. 24. *Which things are an allegory*] That is, they signify or import an allegory, Ἀλληγορούμενα; or they, being the things that they were, represented and typed out the things that they were not. So did the brazen serpent, the deluge, the Red Sea, &c. As for those allegories of Origen, and other wanton wits, luxuriant this way, what are they else but *Scripturarum spuma,* as one calleth them, Scripture froth?

Ver. 25. *For this Agar is mount*] The Arabians call Mount Sinai, Agar. Twice Hagar fled thither, Gen. xvi., xxi., it being in her way home to Egypt. From her the Arabians are called Hagarenes, and since (for more honour' sake) Saracens, of Sarah, Hagar's mistress.

Answereth to Jerusalem] That is, to the Jewish synagogue, born to bondage, as Tiberius said of the Romans, that they were *homines ad servitutem parati.*

Ver. 26. *But Jerusalem which is above*] That is, the Christian Church, the heavenly Jerusalem, the panegyris and congregation of the first-born, whose names are enrolled in heaven, Heb. xii. 23. The Hebrew word for Jerusalem is of the dual number; to show, say the Cabalists, that there is a heavenly as well as an earthly Jerusalem, and that the taking away of the earthly was intimated by the taking away of the letter *jod* out of Jerusalem, 2 Sam. v. 13. (Amama in Coronide.) Let us upon the sight of any famous city lift up our hearts with holy Fulgentius and say, *Si talis est Roma terrestris, qualis est Roma cœlestis?* If there be such stateliness and sweetness here, what is there in that "City of the great King?"

Ver. 27. *For it is written*] When these testimonies of the Old Testament are thus cited in the New, it is not only by way of accommodation, but because they are the proper meaning of the places.

Ver. 28. *Now we, brethren, as Isaac*] This the Jews to this day will not hear of, but call us Mamzer Goi, bastardly Gentiles.

Ver. 29. *Persecuted him*] By cruel mockings and real injuries, challenging the birthright and deriding the covenant, &c. Moses's word, מצחק Gen. xxi. 9, holds forth, that Ishmael did not only himself mock Isaac, but made others also to mock him, exposing him to their jeers. The Papists made way for their great project of perdition in 88, by dividing the people here under the terms of Protestant and Puritan, and provoking them thereby to real and mutual both hate and contempt. (George Abbot's Answer.)

Even so it is now] And so also it is now, may we say at this day. For what do Papists persecute us for else, but because we reject their justification by works? They poisoned their own Cardinal Contarenus, for that he declared himself sound in this point, by a book that he set forth some four years before the Council of Trent.

Ver. 30. *Shall not be heir*] No justiciary can be saved. A Papist cannot go beyond a reprobate. *Purus putus Papista non potest servari.* Rev. xix. 21.

Ver. 31. *We are not children, &c.*] q. d. We are in a far better condition than legalists. "I have blessed Ishmael," saith God; "twelve princes shall he beget; but my covenant will I establish with Isaac," Gen. xvii. 20, 21. And such honour have all his saints.

CHAPTER V.

Ver. 1. *Be not again entangled*] ἐνέχεσθε. As oxen tied to the yoke. Those that followed Judas Galileus, Acts v. 37, chose rather to undergo any death than to be in subjection to any mortal. (Joseph. xviii. 2.) If civil servitude be so grievous, what ought spiritual to be? Those poor misled and muzzled souls that are held captive in the pope's dark dungeon, have an ill time of it. Ever since, being reconciled to the Roman Church, I subjected myself and my kingdoms (said King John of England) to the pope's authority, never anything went well with me, but all against me, *Nulla mihi prospera, sed omnia adversa evenerunt.*

Ver. 2. *Behold, I Paul*] q. d. As true as I am Paul, and do write these things.

Christ shall profit you nothing] For he profits none but those that are found in him, not having their "own righteousness, which is of the law, but that which is through the faith of Christ, the righteousness which is of God through faith," Phil. iii. 9. As Pharaoh said of the Israelites, "they are entangled in the land, the wilderness hath

shut them in," Exod. xiv. 3; so may it be said of Pharisaical and Popish justiciaries, they are entangled in the fond conceits of their own righteousness, they cannot come to Christ. A man will never truly desire Christ till soundly shaken, Hag. ii. 7.

Ver. 3. *That he is a debtor*] viz. If he be circumcised with an opinion of meriting thereby. Christ will be our sole Saviour, or none; he will not mingle his precious blood with our puddlestuff. Those that will look unto him must look off all things else, as the apostle's word ἀφορῶντες importeth, Heb. xii. 2.

Ver. 4. *Christ is become of none effect*] Woe then to popish merit-mongers. William Wickham, founder of New College, though he did many good works, yet he professed he trusted to Jesus Christ alone for salvation. So did Charles V., emperor of Germany. So did many of our forefathers in times of Popery. (Parei Hist. Profan. medul. Dr Usher on Eph. iv. 13.)

Ye are fallen from grace] It cannot hence be concluded that the apostle speaks conditionally, and it may be understood of the true doctrine of God's free grace.

Ver. 5. *For we through the Spirit*] We apostles hope for righteousness by faith. If you will go to heaven any other way, you must erect a ladder, and go up alone, as Constantine said to Acesius the Novatian heretic, *Erigito scalam, Acesi, et solus ascendito.*

Ver. 6. *Neither circumcision*] Unregenerate Israel is as Ethiopia, Amos ix. 7.

But faith that worketh] *Justificamur tribus modis. Effective a Deo, apprehensive a fide, declarative ab operibus.* Faith justifies the man, and works justify faith. To be a mother in Israel, is having Rachel's eye and Leah's womb.

Ver. 7. *Ye did run well*] Why do ye now stop or step back? *Tutius recurrere quam male currere,* was the Emperor Philip's symbol. (Reusner Symb.) Better run back than run amiss; for in this case, "He that hasteth with his feet, sinneth," Prov. xix. 2. But to run well till a man sweats, and then to sit down and take cold, may cause a consumption.

Who did let you?] Gr. "Threw a block in your way," ἐγκόπτειν, *transversum aliquid struere.*

Ver. 8. *This persuasion*] Sectaries and seducers have a strange art in persuading, πιθανολογία, Col. ii. 4. And although we think ourselves able enough to answer and withstand their arguments, yet it is dangerous dealing with them. The Valentinian heretics had a trick to persuade before they taught. (Tertullian.) Arius could cog a dice, and cozen the simple and heedless hearer.

Ver. 9. *A little leaven*] viz. Of false doctrine, Matt. xvi. 6. See the note there.

Ver. 10. *But he that troubleth you*] That heresiarch, or ring-leader of the faction. The beast and the false prophet are taken and cast alive into a lake, &c., when the common sort seduced by them had an easier judgment, Rev. xix. 20, 21.

Ver. 11. *Why do I yet suffer persecution*] From

the Jews zealous of the law. It is well observed that the nearer any are unto a conjunction in matters of religion, and yet some difference retained, the deeper is the hatred.[1] A Jew hates a Christian worse than he doth a Turk or Pagan. A Papist hates a Protestant worse than he doth a Jew, &c.

Ver. 12. *I would they were even cut*] Not circumcised only, cut round, but cut off, *Non circumcidantur modo, sed et abscindantur.* (Chrys.)

That trouble you] That turn you upside down, or that turn you out of house and home.

Ver. 13. *Only use not your liberty*] *In maxima libertate, minima licentia.* Therefore ἀναστατοῦν-τες, are men the worse, because they should be better. Christ came to call sinners, not to licentiousness, but to repentance, Mark ii. 17, to take his yoke upon them, Matt. xi. 29, to hire out their members servants to righteousness, Rom. vi. 16. Hence it is, that as St Paul's Epistles largely prove free election and justification by Christ; so the Epistles of James, Peter, and John, press to love and new obedience, lest any should argue from mercy to liberty. *Nemo sit liber in fraudem fisci,* saith the civil law. (Valer. Max. ii. 1.) It was enacted among the Athenians, that whosoever, having been a bondman, was convicted of ingratitude for his manumission, should lose his liberty : the Romans made such slaves again ; which punishment they term *Maximam capitis diminutionem.* (Justin Instit. i. 16.)

Ver. 14. *For all the law*] *i. e.* All the second table. The Scripture oft appropriateth the law to the second table, as Rom. xiii. 8 ; Ephes. vi. 2, &c. A man must exercise the first table in the second, the duties of his general calling in his particular calling. In the first commandment, saith Luther, the keeping of all the laws is enjoined, *Primo præcepto reliquorum omnium observantia præcipitur.* Neither can any one love his neighbour as himself, but he that loves God above all.

Ver. 15. *But if ye bite,* &c.] *Si collidimur, frangimur,* If we clash, we break. Dissolution is the daughter of dissension, said Nazianzen. The Turks pray to God to keep the Christians at variance. Israelites in Egypt vexed one another ; and Christians, as if they wanted enemies, fly in one another's faces. This is a sad foretoken of a deadly consumption.[2] When the Eastern Churches were all to pieces among themselves, in came the Goths and Vandals, and afterward the Turks and Tartars.[3] When the French Churches began to jangle and jar about discipline, God suffered the Parisian massacre. Our present hideous dissensions (like those civil wars of Rome—*nullos habitura triumphos,* Lucan), do as plainly foretell the removing of our candlestick, in case we repent not, as if we had received letters from heaven to that purpose. We read in our chronicles, that those who were born in England in the year after the great mor-

tality, A. D. 1349, wanted some of their cheek-teeth. Men seem to have more now than usual ; there was never such biting and snarling. England is a mighty animal (saith a great politician), which can never die except it kill itself. And to the same purpose the Lord Rich in a speech to the justices in King Edward VI.'s days, " Never foreign power (saith he) could yet hurt, or in any part prevail in this realm, but by disobedience and misorder among themselves. That is the way wherewith God will plague us if he mind to punish us. And so long as we do agree amongst ourselves, we may be sure that God is with us, and that foreign power shall not prevail against us."

Ver. 16. *This I say then*] For an antidote against abuse of Christian liberty. Set the Spirit, as Pharaoh did Joseph, upon the chief chariot of your hearts, and let all be at his beck and check.

Ver. 17. *For the flesh lusteth*] Every new man is two men. What can a man see in the Shulamite, but as the appearance of two armies, Cant. vi. 13 ? These maintain civil broils within her, as the two babes did in Rebecca's womb. All was jolly quiet at Ephesus, till Paul came thither ; but then there arose no small stir about that way, Acts xix. 23. So is there in the good soul.

So that ye cannot do the things, &c.] As ye cannot do the good that ye would, because of the flesh (Rom. vii. 21, something lay at the fountain-head, and stopt it), so neither can ye do the evil that ye would, because of the Spirit. In which respect, setting the ingratitude aside, the sins of godly men are less than others, because the flesh cannot carry it without some counterbuffs.

Ver. 18. *Ye are not under the law*] For where the Spirit is, there is liberty from the rigour, irritation, and malediction of the law.

Ver. 19. *Now the works of the flesh*] Sinners are sore labourers ; wicked men great workmen. Would they take but half that pains for heaven that they do for hell, they could not, likely, miss of it. The Hebrew and Greek words for sin import labour (Gnamal, πονηρία).

Are manifest] φανερὰ, they lie above-ground, and are condemned by the light of nature. Wicked men also hang out their sins to the sight of the sun, Isa. iii. 9, that they must needs be manifest even to a natural conscience ; not so the fruits of the Spirit.

Ver. 20. *Idolatry*] This is fitly set after those fleshly sins, as commonly accompanied with them, 1 Cor. x. 7, 8. Sir Walter Raleigh knew what he said, that were he to choose a religion for licentious liberty and lasciviousness, he would choose the Popish religion.

Ver. 21. *Murders, drunkenness*] This is oft the mother of murder. Domitius, the father of Nero, slew Liberius, an honest man, because he refused to drink so much as he commanded him.

---

[1] Dr Day upon 1 Cor. xvi. 9.
[2] Camer. Med. Hist. cent. 2.

[3] Melch. Adam. in Vita Bulling.

(Sueton.) Alexander killed many of his dear friends in his drunkenness, whom he would have revived again (but could not) with his own heart-blood. Once he invited a company to supper, and provided a crown of 180 pounds to be given to those that drank most. One and forty killed themselves with drinking to get that crown. Mr Samuel Ward in his Woe to Drunkards maketh mention of many brought by this swinish sin to untimely shameful ends in a brutish and bestial manner; among the rest, one of Aylesham in Norfolk, a notorious drunkard, drowned in a shallow brook of water with his horse by him. The like whereunto is fallen out in the place where I now live, this instant November 14th, A. D. 1650. At a blind clandestine alehouse, a company of odious drunkards having drunk all the three outs (that is, ale out of the pot, money out of the purse, and wit out of the head), one of them, making homeward, was drowned in a shallow ditch, his body not yet buried : upon his soul I pass no definitive sentence; but what hope can we comfortably conceive of such? Another of the same crew (rebuked by his father at the same time for his ill husbandry) swore he would hang himself; which also he did presently, and had perished by his own hands, had not his father come seasonably and cut the halter. O these alehouses! the pest-houses of our nation, the very sinks and sources of all villany.

Ver. 22. *The fruit of the Spirit*] The spirit of grace are those two golden pipes, Zech. iv., through which the two olive-branches empty out of themselves the golden oils of all precious graces into the candlestick, the Church. Hence grace is here and elsewhere called the fruits of the Spirit, pleasant fruits, Cant. iv. 16; vi. 2; John xv. 16.

Long-suffering] It hath been questioned by Aquinas whether a man can be long-suffering, *sine auxilio gratiæ*, without the help of grace. But that which is right is a fruit of the Spirit.

Gentleness] Gr. χρηστότης. Usefulness, sweetness.

Faith] That is, faithfulness, as Matt. xxiii. 23; 1 Tim. v. 12; Tit. ii. 10.

Ver. 23. *Meekness, temperance*] Queen Elizabeth was famous for these two virtues. King Edward VI. called her by no other name than his sweet sister Temperance. (Camd. Elizab.) She did seldom eat but one sort of meat, rose ever with an appetite, and lived about 70 years. Next to the Holy Scripture she preferred (as the best piece) Seneca's book of Clemency. When she said, that book had done her much good; yea, said one, but it hath done your subjects much hurt. (Sir W. Vaughan, Mr Heyrick's Three Sermons.)

Against such there is no law] 1 Tim. i. 9. As for the works of the flesh, there is no gospel. The righteous need no law to compel them, therefore they shall have none to condemn them. The law confineth them to live in that element where they would live; as if one should be con-

fined to Paradise, where he would be, though there be no such law.

Ver. 24. *And they that are Christ's*] When Christ came in the flesh, we crucified him; when he comes into our hearts, he crucifies us.

Have crucified the flesh] To crucify is not absolutely and out-right to kill; crucifixion is a lingering death, no member being free from pain. If then we so repent of sin (as that which crucified Christ), we so pierce the old man, that we are sure he will die of it, though he be not presently dead, this is mortification. Those beasts, Dan. vii. 12, had their dominion taken away, and yet their lives were prolonged for a season.

With the affections] Sinful sudden passions.

And lusts] More deeply rooted in our natures, and so not so easily overcome.

Ver. 25. *If we live in the Spirit*] Spiritual men only are heirs of life, 1 Pet. iii. 7, all others are dead in trespasses.

Let us walk] Walk orderly, by line and by rule, march in rank, στοιχῶμεν. Life consists in action. Life, saith the philosopher, is such a faculty as whereby creatures move themselves in their own places. The godly esteem of life by that stirring they find in their souls; as else they lament as over a dead soul, Isa. xxxviii. 15, 16.

Ver. 26. *Let us not be desirous of vain-glory*] *Ingens dulcedo gloriæ* (saith Æneas Sylvius) *facilius contemnenda dicitur, quam contemnitur.* It was this vice that raised so much trouble in Germany betwixt Luther and Carolostadius, and that bred the sacramentary war that is not yet ended. It was a saying of Luther, From a vain-glorious doctor, from a contentious pastor, and from unprofitable questions, the good Lord deliver his Church.

Provoking one another, envying one another] And so discovering your weakness, as the vain-glorious peacock doth his filthy parts behind, while he delighteth to be seen and to behold his own tail.

CHAPTER VI.

Ver. 1. *If a man be overtaken*] Gr. προληφθῇ, be taken before he is aware, before he hath time to consider, or bethink himself of better. It is of incogitancy that the saints sin; put them in mind, and they mend all. It is of passion, and passions last not long. "There is no way of wickedness in them; they stand not in the way of sinners, they sit not down in the seat of scorners," Psal. i. 1; cxxxix. 24.

Restore such a one] Gr. καταρτίζετε, set him in joint again. A metaphor from chirurgeons and bone-setters who handle their patients tenderly. Or from such as take a mote out of one's eye gently and warily.

Lest thou also be tempted] I have known a good old man, saith Bernard, who when he had heard of any that had committed some notorious offence, was wont to say with himself, *Ille hodie, et ego cras*, He fell to-day, so may I to-morrow. Mr Bradford set down in his day-book what good he saw in any man, bewailing the want of it in himself, and praying for more grace; as if he saw or heard of any evil in another, he noted it, as in danger to do so himself; and still added, Lord, have mercy upon me. (Pref. to his Serm. of Rep.)

Ver. 2. *Bear ye one another's burdens*] When after reprehension sin is become a burden, set to your shoulder, and help to lift it off. "Support the weak, be patient toward all," 1 Thess. v. 14. Nature hath taught the deer to help one another in swimming, the cranes one another in flying; one stone bears up another in buildings contrived by art, &c.

Ver. 3. *Think himself to be something*] The self-deceiver takes his counter, and sets it up for a thousand pound, as the Pharisees and Laodiceans. Of such it may be said, as Quintilian somewhere of some overweeners of themselves, that they might have proved excellent scholars if they had not been so persuaded already.

Ver. 4. *But let every man prove*] This is an excellent remedy against self-deceit, and a means to make one fit to reprove others with mercy and meekness.

And then shall he have rejoicing] *Ut testimonium perhibeat conscientia propria, non lingua aliena*, saith Augustine, that thine own conscience and not another man's tongue may testify for thee. *Omnis Sarmatarum virtus extra ipsos*, saith Tacitus. All the self-deceiver's goodness is shored up by popularity or other base respects.

Ver. 5. *For every man shall bear*] Be thorough therefore in the work of self-examination. Sparing a little pains at first, doubles it in the end; as he who will not cast up his books, his books will cast up him at length. The misery of most men is, that their minds are as ill set as their eyes, neither of them look inwards. How few are there that turn short again upon themselves so as to say, What have I done? Woe to all such when God shall send out summons for sleepers, when he comes to search Jerusalem with candles, and punish the men that are settled on their lees, &c., Zeph. i. 12.

Ver. 6. *Communicate unto him*] Not contribute as an alms, but communicate as a right; see Philem. 17; as wages for his work, Mark vi.; as pay for his pains, 1 Cor. ix. 14. See the note there.

Ver. 7. *Be not deceived*] Think not all well saved that is withheld from the minister. It is a saying in the civil law, *Clericis Laici sunt oppido infensi*; many think it neither sin nor pity to beguile the preacher. But God is not mocked, neither will he be robbed by any, but they shall hear, Ye are cursed with a curse, Mal. iii. 8, 9, even with Shallum's curse, Jer. xxii. 11—13, that used his neighbour's service without wages, and would sacrilegiously take in a piece of God's windows into his wide house, ver. 14.

God is not mocked] They that would mock God, *imposturam faciunt, et patientur* (as the emperor said of him that sold glass for pearls), they mock themselves much more.

Ver. 8. *For he that soweth to his flesh*] He that neglecting his poor soul, cares only to feather his nest and to heap up riches. *Si ventri bene, si lateri*, as Epicurus in Horace; if the belly may be filled, the back fitted, let the soul sink or swim, he takes no thought.

Ver. 9. *And let us not be weary*] Let us not give in as tired jades, ἐκκακῶμεν; hot at hand seldom holds out. Let us not slack our pace in religion, let not our tears begin to freeze; for this, if it doth not lose, yet it may lessen and lighten our crown. Ambrose noteth of the fig-tree, that whereas other trees first blossom and then bring forth fruit, in the fig-tree it is otherwise, *Poma decidunt ut folia succedant*, the figs fall off, that, leaves may come in their place. So many that begin in fruits, end in leaves, such are they that weary of well-doing, lose the things that they have wrought, 2 John 8. See the note.

For in due season we shall reap] We must not look to sow and reap in a day; as he saith of the Hyperborean people, far north, that they sow shortly after the sun rising with them, and reap before the sun set; that is, because the whole half-year is one continual day with them. (Heresbach de Re Rustica.)

If we faint not] *Quærendi defatigatio turpis est cum id quod quæritur, sit pulcherrimum*, It is a shame to faint in the search of that, which being found will more than pay for the pains of searching. Caleb was not discouraged by the giants, therefore he had Hebron the place of the giants, so those that faint not in the way to heaven shall inherit heaven.

Ver. 10. *As we have therefore opportunity*] Catch at it, as the echo catcheth the voice. Joseph took the nick of time to gain Egypt to the king, by feeding the hungry; so may we to get heaven. I read of a Roman emperor who when he heard of a neighbour dead, he asked, And what did I for him before he died? Let us ask ourselves the same and the like questions.

Who are of the household] Of the family of faith, God's household servants. That was a desperate resolve of Aigoland, king of Arragon, who coming to the French court to be baptized, and asking who those lazars and poor people were that waited for alms from the Emperor Charlemagne's table? When one answered him that they were the messengers and servants of God; I will never serve that God, said he, that can keep his servants no better. (Turpine.)

Ver. 11. *How large a letter*] Gr. with what good great text letters. I have written unto you with mine own hand (no fair hand; the greatest clerks are not always the best scribes), and not by any Tertius, or other amanuensis, Rom. xvi. 22, to show his love, and prevent imposture, 2 Thess. ii. 2. (Chrysost. Theophylact.)

Ver. 12. *To make a fair show*] Gr. εὐπροσωπῆσαι,

to set a good face on it, before the Jews especially, and to ingratiate with them.

For the cross of Christ] That is, for the doctrine of the cross, or of justification by the death of Christ crucified.

Ver. 13. *Keep the law*] Rom. ii. 23. Jerome doubteth not to pronounce that man accursed, that saith it is impossible to keep the law. *Sed quid visum sit Hieronymo, nihil moramur ; nos quid verum sit inquirimus*, saith Calvin. But let Jerome hold as he will, we know there is no such thing.

That they may glory in your flesh] That they may pride themselves in the multitude of their followers, and curry favour with the Jews by gaining many proselytes.

Ver. 14. *But God forbid, &c.*] The saints keep a constant counter-motion, and are antipodes to the wicked. They thus and thus, but I otherwise.

Whereby the world is crucified] I look upon the world as a dead thing, as a great dunghill, &c. That harlot was deceived in St Paul, in thinking to allure him by laying out those her two fair breasts of profit and pleasure ; he had no mind to be sucking at those botches ; he was a very crucifix of mortification. And in his face (as one said of Doctor Raynolds) a man might have seen *veram mortificati hominis idæam*, the true portraiture of a mortified man.

And I to the world] q. d. The world and I are well agreed. The world cares not a pin for me, and I (to cry quittance with it) care as little for the world.

Ver. 15. *For in Christ Jesus*] That is, in the kingdom of Christ.

But a new creature] Either a new man, or no man.

Ver. 16. *According to this rule*] viz. Of the new creature. Or the doctrine of this Epistle.

Peace be on them] Not only in them, or with them, but " on them," maugre the malice of earth and hell.

Ver. 17. *From henceforth let no man*] Here he takes upon him as an apostle, and speaks with authority, Σεμνῶς καὶ δεινῶς.

I bear in my body the marks] As scars of honour. Paul had been whipped, stocked,

stoned, &c. The marks of these he could better boast of than those false apostles of their circumcision. And hereby it appeared that he refused not, as they did, to suffer persecution for the cross of Christ. In the year 1166, the Synod held at Oxford in the reign of Henry II., banished out of England 30 Dutch doctors (which taught the right use of marriage, and of the sacraments), after they had first stigmatized or branded them with hot irons. (Alsted Chron.) John Clerk of Melden, in France, being for Christ's sake whipped three several days, and afterwards having a mark set in his forehead, as a note of infamy, his mother beholding it (though his father was an adversary) encouraged her son, crying with a loud voice, *Vivat Christus ejusque insignia*, " Blessed be Christ, and welcome be these prints and marks of Christ." The next year after, *sc.* A. D. 1524, he brake the images without the city, which his superstitious countrymen were to worship the next day. For the which he was apprehended, and had his right hand cut off, his nose pulled off with pincers, both his arms and both his breasts torn with the same instrument; and after all he was burned at a stake. In his greatest torments he pronounced that of the Psalmist, " Their idols are silver and gold, the works of men's hands," &c. (Scultet. Annal.) I conclude this discourse with that saying of Pericles, " It is not gold, precious stones, statues, that adorns a soldier, but a torn buckler, a cracked helmet, a blunt sword, a scarred face." Of these Biron, the French marshal, boasted at his death. And Sceva is renowned for this, that at the siege of Dyrrachium, he so long alone resisted Pompey's army, that he had 220 darts sticking in his shield, and lost one of his eyes, and yet gave not over till Cæsar came to his rescue.[1] Mr Prinne's Stigmata Laudis are better known than that they need here to be related.

Ver. 18. *Be with your spirit*] Spirituals are specially to be desired for ourselves and ours. *Cætera aut aderunt, aut non oberunt.* Other things we shall either have, or not want, but be as well without them.

---

[1] *Densamque ferens in pectore sylvam.* Lucan.

A

COMMENTARY OR EXPOSITION

UPON THE

EPISTLE OF ST PAUL TO THE EPHESIANS.

CHAPTER I.

Ver. 1. *To the saints—to the faithful*] FITLY; for it is by faith that we become saints, Acts xv. 9.

Ver. 2. *Grace be to you, and peace*] These go fitly together; because we must seek our peace in the free grace and favour of God. The ark and mercy-seat were never sundered.

Ver. 3. *Blessed be God*] *Gratiæ cessat decursus, ubi gratiarum recursus.* A thankful man shall abound with blessings.

With all spiritual blessings] ἐν πάσῃ εὐλογίᾳ πνευματικῇ, wisdom, prudence, &c., ver. 8, a Benjamin's portion, a goodly heritage; called here spiritual blessing in the singular. All, and yet but one blessing; to note that spiritual blessings are so knit together, that they all make up but one blessing; and where God gives one, he gives all.

Ver. 4. *He hath chosen us in him*] Christ was mediator therefore from eternity, viz. by virtue of that human nature which he should assume.

That we should be holy] God elected us as well to the means as to the end. Note this against libertines. For as they (Acts xxvii. 31) could not come safe to land that left the ship; so neither can men come to heaven but by holiness. Cyrus was moved to restore the captivity by finding himself fore-appointed to this glorious service 170 years before he was born, Isa. xliv. 28. Should not we likewise be excited to good works by this that we were elected to them?

Without blame] Or blot, Eph. v. 27. *Absque querela*, Luke i. 6.

Before him] *i. e.* In purity of heart, 2 Kings xx. 3.

In love] In sanctity of life.

Ver. 5. *Having predestinated us*] Interpreters have observed that this word that signifies to predestinate is but six times to be found in the New Testament (never in the Old), being referred but twice to things, Acts iv. 28 and 1 Cor. ii. 7, four times to persons, Rom. viii. 29,

30, Eph. i. 5, 11, and never applied to reprobates, but to elect persons only. Howbeit divines under predestination do usually consider the decree both of election and reprobation. The doctrine hereof men should not adventure to teach till they have well learned and digested it. In the year 1586, Jacobus Andreas, the Lutheran, and Theodore Beza, conferred and disputed for eight days' space at Montpelier: the issue of which conference was unhappy, for from that time forward the doctrine of predestination was much misused and exagitated. (Alsted. Chron.)

Ver. 6. *To the praise of the glory*] This is the end whereunto it is destined; and hence it is called predestination. Note here, that all the causes of predestination are merely without us. The efficient, God; the material, Christ; the formal, the good pleasure of his will; the final, the praise of God's glorious grace.

Wherein he hath made us accepted] Gr. ἐχαρίτωσεν, He hath ingratiated us, he hath justified us, made us gracious in his beloved Son our Mediator, *gratificavit.* And although there be an inequality of expressions in duty, *quoad nos*, in us, yet there is a constancy of worth and intercession by Christ, *propter nos*, for us. Pareus rendereth these words thus, *Nos sibi gratis effecit gratos*, He hath freely made us well thought of.

Ver. 7. *In whom we have redemption*] As captives ransomed at a price. What this price was, see 1 Pet. i. 19. Should not Christ therefore reap the travails of his soul? Isa. liii.

The forgiveness of our sins] This David counted his crown, and prized it above his imperial diadem, Psal. ciii. 3, 4.

Ver. 8. *In all wisdom and prudence*] That properly respecteth contemplation, this action. Socrates made no distinction betwixt them. For, said he, who so knoweth good to practise it, and evil to avoid it, he is a man truly wise and prudent.

Ver. 9. *The mystery of his will*] That is, the gospel, a mystery both to men, 1 Cor. ii. 8, and angels, Eph. iii. 10.

Ver. 10. *That in the dispensation*] God is the best economic; his house is exactly ordered for matter of good husbandry, οἰκονομία. "Dispensation of the fulness of time" is (by a metonomy of the adjunct) put for "fulness of times," wisely dispensed. (Bain.)

Gather together in one] Gr. ἀνακεφαλαιώσασθαι, recapitulate, reduce all to a head, re-collect, to restore all things, and bring them to their primitive perfection.

Both which are in heaven] The crowned saints, and perhaps the glorious angels, who (according to some divines) being in themselves changeable creatures (and therefore called Shinan, that is, mutable, Psal. lxviii. 17), receive confirmation by Christ, so that they cannot leave their first station, as did the apostate angels. Others think that the angels stand not by means of Christ's mediation, but of God's eternal election, and are therefore called the elect angels.

Ver. 11. *We have obtained inheritance*] Or we are taken into the Church, as magistrates were by lot into their office. Or we are made God's inheritance, as Deut. xxxii. 9. It imports our free and unexpected vocation. *In sortem adsciti sumus*, ἐκληρώθημεν; we were sorted out, singled out for a picked peculiar people.

After the counsel of his own will] God doth all by counsel, and ever hath a reason of his will, which though we see not for present, we shall at last day. Meanwhile submit.

Ver. 12. *Who first trusted*] It is a singular honour to be first in so good a matter. Hope is here put for faith, whereof it is both the daughter and the nurse.

Ver. 13. *After that ye believed*] They, 1. Heard. 2. Believed. 3. Were sealed, *i. e.* full assured. Assurance is God's seal; faith is our seal. God honours our sealing to his truth by his sealing by his Spirit. We yield first the consent and assent of faith, and then God puts his seal to the contract. There must be the bargain before the earnest.

Ver. 14. *Which is the earnest*] Not the pawn, but the earnest, *Quia pignus redditur, arrha retinetur*, saith Jerome. A pawn is to be returned again, but an earnest is part of the whole sum, and assures it. We here have eternal life, 1. *In pretio*; 2. *In promisso*; 3. *In primitiis.*

Ver. 15. *Your faith in the Lord Jesus*] Love is the fruit of faith, therefore the apostles pray for increase of faith, that they might be able seven times a day to forgive an offending brother, Luke xvii. 5. See the note there.

Ver. 16. *Making mention of you*] Whether a minister shall do more good to others by his prayers or preaching, I will not determine (saith a grave divine), but he shall certainly by his prayers reap more comfort to himself.

Ver. 17. *The Father of glory*] That is, the glorious Father, Acts vii. 2. Chrysostom expounds it the Father of Christ, as chap. i. 3.

The Spirit of wisdom and revelation] So called, because he revealeth unto us God's depths, and reads us his riddles, 1 Cor. ii. He enlightens both the organ and object; he anoints the eyes with eye-salve, and gives both sight and light. (Saint's Progress, by Dr Taylor.)

Ver. 18. *The glory of his inheritance*] The glory of heaven is inconceivable, Rev. xxi., search is made through all the bowels of the earth for something to shadow it by. No natural knowledge can be had of the third heaven, nor any help by human arts, as Aristotle acknowledgeth. The glory thereof is fitter to be believed than possible to be discoursed.

Ver. 19. *And what is the exceeding*] Here is a most emphatical heap of most divine and significant words to express that which can never sufficiently be conceived or uttered. A sixfold gradation the apostle useth to show what a power God puts forth in working the grace of faith. Indeed this power is secret, and like that of the heavens upon our bodies; which (saith one) is as strong as that of physic, &c., yet so sweet, and so secretly insinuating itself with the principles of nature, that as for the conveyance of it, it is insensible, and hardly differenced from that of the principles of nature in us; therefore the apostle prayeth for these Ephesians here, that their eyes may be enlightened to see the power that wrought in them, &c.

Ver. 20. *Which he wrought in Christ*] God puts forth the same almighty power in quickening the heart by faith, that he did in raising up his Son Christ from the dead; it must needs then be more than a moral suasion that he useth. Christ wrought the centurion's faith, as God; he wondered at it, as man. God wrought, and man marvelled; he did both, to teach us where to bestow our wonder.

Ver. 21. *Far above all principality*] *Quantum inter stellas luna minores.* Oh do but think with thyself (saith one), though it far pass the reach of any mortal thought, what an infinite, inexplicable happiness it will be to look for ever upon the glorious body of Jesus Christ, shining with incomprehensible beauty; and to consider that even every vein of that blessed body bled to bring thee to heaven; and that it being with such excess of glory hypostatically united to the second person in Trinity, hath honoured and advanced thy nature above the brightest cherub.

To be the head over all things] That is, all persons, all the elect, as Gal. iii. 22. Christ is head over angels too, but in another sense than over the Church: viz. 1. As God, he giveth them whatsoever they are or have. 2. As Mediator also, he maketh use of their service for the safety and salvation of the Church. The holy angels are great friends to the Church, but not members of it; "For Christ took not on him the nature of angels, but the seed of Abraham," Heb. ii. 16. Besides, "he sanctified his Church, and washed it with his blood," Ephes. v. 26. But this he did not for the angels, &c. See the note on ver. 10.

Ver. 23. *The fulness of him*] That is, of Christ, who having voluntarily subjected himself to be our Head, accounts not himself complete without his members. In which respect we have the honour of making Christ perfect as the members do the body.

That filleth all in all] Not only all the saints, but all of the saints ; all their capacities, all their powers, parts, desires, endeavours. Thus he filleth, πάντα, ἐν πᾶσι, all, and in all ordinances, occurrences, providences, relations, comforts, &c.

CHAPTER II.

Ver. 1. *Who were dead*] Natural men are living carcases, walking sepulchres of themselves. In most families it is, as once it was in Egypt, Exod. xii. 30, no house wherein there is not one, nay, many dead corpses. Howbeit, the natural man, though he be theologically dead, yet is ethically alive, being to be wrought upon by arguments, hence, Hos. xi. 4, "I drew them by the cords of a man," that is, by reason and motives of love, befitting the nature of a man. So the Spirit and Word work upon us still as men, by rational motives, setting before us life and good, death and evil.

Ver. 2. *Wherein ye walked*] Hence Acts xiv. 16. Sin is called a way, but it leads to the chambers of death.

According to the course of this world] The mundaneity or worldliness of the world (as the Syriac rendereth it), which is wholly set upon wickedness (as Aaron saith of his worldlings, Exod. xxxii. 22), and takes no care for the world to come.

According to the prince, &c.] The devil by whom wicked men are acted and agitated. Gratian was out in saying that Satan is called prince of the world, as a king of chess, or as the cardinal of Ravenna, only by derision. Evil men set him up for their sovereign, and are wholly at his beck and obedience.

The spirit that now worketh] As a smith worketh in his forge, an artificer in his shop. A natural man, as he is the heir of original and father of actual sin, so his soul and all the powers thereof are but Satan's shop of sins ; his body and all the parts thereof, tools of sin ; his life, and all his actions of both soul and body, a trade of sin, by the same reason.

Ver. 3. *Among whom also we all, &c.*] Let the best look back oft on what they were before calling, that they may thankfully cry out with Iphicrates, ἐξ οἵων εἰς οἷα, from what misery to what dignity are we advanced !

Fulfilling the desires] Gr. the wills of the flesh. Now therefore we must as diligently fulfil not the will, but the wills of God, as David did, Acts xiii. 22.

The children of wrath] De ires. Gregory the Great said of the English boys that were presented to him, *Angli quasi Angeli*. And demanding further what province they were of in this island, it was returned, that they were called *De ires ;* which caused him again to repeat the word, and to say, that it were great pity but

that by being taught the gospel, they should be saved *de ira Dei*, from the wrath of God. (Abbot's Geog.) Whereunto we are subject, even as in nature a child is to the commands and restraints of his father ; being *damnati priusquam nati*, as Augustine hath it, damned ere born into the world.

Ver. 4. *But God who is rich in mercy*] Such a mercy as rejoiceth against judgment, as a man against his adversary which he hath subdued, James ii. 13.

Ver. 5. *Hath quickened, &c.*] The very first stirrings in the womb of grace are precious to God ; he blesseth our very buds, Isa. xliv. 3, according to the Geneva translation.

Even when we were dead] This is again repeated, because hardly believed. We are apt to conceit better of ourselves than there is cause for, and can hardly be persuaded that we are dead in sins and trespasses, and lie rotting and stinking in the graves of corruption, much worse than Lazarus did after he had lain four days in his sepulchre. We would be sorry but our penny should be as good silver as another's, and are ready, with the Pharisee, to set up our counter for a thousand pound. In fine, a dead woman we say must have four to carry her forth. A man shall have much ado to persuade the merry Greeks of this world, but that they have the only life of it, and that others are dead in comparison of them. Hence this iteration of the blow upon the natural man, to knock him down dead, as it were, to bring him to Paul's pass, Rom. vii. 9.

Ver. 6. *And made us sit together*] We have taken up our rooms aforehand in heaven, whereunto we have just right upon earth by virtue of the union, the ground of communion, 1 John v. 12. He that hath the Son hath life ; he hath possession of it, as by turf and twig.

Ver. 7. *In his kindness toward us*] We come not to the knowledge of God but by his works. And even this way of knowing him we naturally abuse to idolatry.

Ver. 8. *For by grace ye are saved*] So ver. 5, and everywhere almost St Paul is a most constant preacher of the grace of God, as Chrysostom styleth him. *Sub laudibus naturæ latent inimici gratiæ*, saith Augustine. The patrons of man's free will are enemies to God's free grace.

Ver. 9. *Lest any man should boast*] As that fool did that said, *Cœlum gratis non accipiam*, I will not have heaven but at a rate. (Vega.) *Non sic Deos coluimus, aut sic vivimus, ut ille nos vinceret*, said the emperor Antoninus Philosophus. We have not so lived and deserved of God that the enemy should vanquish us.

Ver. 10. *For we are his workmanship*] ποίημα, his artificial facture, or creature, that wherein he hath showed singular skill, by erecting the glorious fabric of the new man.

Created — to good works] In the year 1559 there was published a paradox, that good works are pernicious to salvation of men's souls.

David George, the broacher of this heresy, was digged up and burnt at Basil.

God hath before ordained] *i. e.* By his eternal decree. Our vivification then is not a work of yesterday; but such as God hath with singular complacency contemplated from all eternity, rejoicing in that habitable part of his earth, Prov. viii. 31.

Ver. 11. *Who are called uncircumcision*] In great scorn and reproach, as 1 Sam. xvii. 26. Howbeit unregenerate Israel was to God as Ethiopia, Amos ix. 7. And Jether, by nature an Ishmaelite, 1 Chron. vii. 17, was for his faith and religion called an Israelite, 2 Sam. xvii. 25.

Ver. 12. *Strangers from the covenant*] The saints only are heirs to the promises; but the devil sweeps all the wicked, as being out of the covenant. They stuff themselves with promises, till they have made them a pillow for sin, Deut. xxix. 19. *Sed præsumendo sperant, et sperando pereunt.*

Having no hope] But such as will one day hop headless; such as will serve them as Absalom's mule served her master, when she left him hanging by the head betwixt heaven and earth, as rejected of both.

Without God in the world] Because without a teaching priest, and without law, 2 Chron. xv. 3. As it is said of the poor Brazilians at this day, that they are *sine fide, sine rege, sine lege.* This was the case of our pagan predecessors.

Ver. 13. *Are made nigh by the blood*] Christ hath paved us a new and living way to the throne of God's grace by his own most precious blood. Oh happy *lapidi-pavium!* Oh Golgotha become our Gabbatha! John xix. 13, 17.

Ver. 14. *For he is our peace*] That is, our peace-maker and peace-matter.[1] When he was born, there was among all nations a general *aut pax, aut pactio*, as Florus observeth. When he took his name, he would not have it either entirely Hebrew, as Jesus, or entirely Greek, as Christ, but both Jesus and Christ, to show (saith one) that he is our peace that hath reconciled two into one, &c.

Ver. 15. *Having abolished in his flesh*] That is, by his death in the flesh, Col. i. 22. At which time the veil rent, and the ceremonies died, only they were to be honourably buried.

For to make in himself] Gr. "to create;" *sc.* by regeneration, Gal. vi. 15. So by conjoining he new-created them, and by new-creating he conjoined them.

Ver. 16. *In one body*] *Ubi igitur Separatistæ?* saith one. All other sins destroy the Church consequentially; but division and separation demolish it directly.

Having slain the enmity] Not the ceremonies only, as ver. 15, but sin, that great makebate, that sets God at odds with his own creature.

Ver. 17. *To them that were nigh*] That is, "the children of Israel, a people near unto him," Psal. cxlviii. 14.

Ver. 18. *We both have an access*] With good

assurance of success. The Persian kings held it a piece of their silly glory to hold off their best friends, who might not come near them but upon special licence, Esth. i. Not so our King. "Oh come, for the Master calleth thee!"

Ver. 19. *Fellow-citizens with the saints*] Paul, as a citizen of Rome, escaped whipping, Acts xxii. 6; we, as citizens with the saints, escape hell tortures and torments.

Ver. 20. *Upon the foundation*] Foundation is taken either for Christ, 1 Cor. iii. 11; Matt. xvi. 16, or the doctrine of the Scriptures which teach salvation only by Jesus Christ, as here and Rev. xxi. 14.

Ver. 21. *Fitly framed together*] Or, perfectly joined together by the cement of the Holy Spirit, working in the saints faith in Christ and love one toward another, which the apostle calleth the bond of perfection.

Ver. 22. *For a habitation of God*, &c.] The Father makes choice of this house, the Son purchaseth it, the Holy Ghost taketh possession of it. This happiness he best understandeth that most feeleth. The cock on the dunghill knows it not.

CHAPTER III.

Ver. 1. *For this cause*] To wit, that you may be a habitation of God, through the Spirit.

I Paul, the prisoner] I hold not St Paul so happy for his rapture into Paradise (saith Chrysostom upon this text) as for his imprisonment for Christ.

Ver. 2. *Of the dispensation*] Gr. economy. The Church is God's house, 1 Tim. iii. 15. Paul was faithful therein as a steward, Matt. xxiv. 45.

Ver. 3. *As I wrote before in few*] *sc.* chap. i. 9 and ii. 3, &c. Fulness of matter in fewness of words. This is the Scripture's precellency above all human writings.

Ver. 4. *My knowledge in the mystery*] The highest point of heavenly learning; and hereby he proveth his calling to the ministry. The priest's lips should both preserve knowledge and present it to the people, to give them the knowledge of salvation by the remission of their sins, Mal. ii. 77; Luke i. 7. An ass might not be coupled with an ox in ploughing. No ignorant doltish ass may plough in God's field, the Church; such as was that silly soul, who coming to be ordained, and being asked by the bishop, *Esne dignus?* answered, No, my lord, I shall dine anon with your men.

Ver. 5. *Was not made known*] *sc.* So clearly and particularly. Peter himself could hardly be persuaded to it, Acts x. 14; xxxiv. 35.

Ver. 6. *Gentiles should be fellow-heirs*] Coheirs, concorporate, and consorts; three sweet societies, the former founded upon the two latter.

Ver. 7. *By the effectual working*, &c.] Enabling me to accept and improve that gift of

---

[1] εἰρήνη παρὰ τὸ εἰς ἓν εἴρειν.

God's grace; whereunto I should otherwise turn not the palm, but the backside of the hand.

Ver. 8. Less than the least] Great Paul is least of saints, last of apostles, greatest of sinners. The best balsams sink to the bottom, the godliest buildings have lowest foundations; the heaviest ears of corn hang downward; so do the boughs of trees that are best laden.[1] Ignatius in his epistles saith, I salute you who am *ultimus*, the last and least of all others. So in another epistle, *Tantillitas nostra*, our meanness.

The unsearchable riches] Gr. ἀνεξιχνίαστον. Not to be traced out. Should not ministers be made welcome that come to men on such golden messages? In Christ are riches of justification, Tit. ii. 14; sanctification, Phil. iv. 12, 13; consolation, 2 Cor. xii. 9; glorification, 1 Pet. i. 5.

Ver. 9. And to make all men see] Gr. to illighten them, far more than the preaching of the prophets could, 2 Pet. i. 19. To us now is a great light sprung up, Matt. iv. 16.

The fellowship] οἰκονομία. Or (as some copies have it) the dispensation.

Who created all things] i. e. Restored, repaired. Hence gospel days are called the world to come, Heb. ii. 5.

Ver. 10. Might be known by the Church] As by a glass or theatre.

The manifold wisdom, &c.] Gr. πολυποίκιλος, that hath abundance of curious variety in it, such as is seen in the best pictures or textures. This the very angels look intently into (as the cherubims in the tabernacle did into the mercyseat), and are much amused and amazed thereat. They see then man's salvation by Christ is a plot of God's own devising. Their experimental knowledge is much increased by their observation of God's daily dealing with his people.

Ver. 11. According to the eternal purpose] Of calling and saving the Gentiles by Christ; a secret that the angels themselves could not understand till the fore-appointed time came.

Ver. 12. Boldness and access] True peace draws men to God, false drives them from God. Uprightness hath boldness, serenity hath security. The word προσαγωγὴ, rendered access, signifies such an access as is by manuduction. As Isaac took Rebecca, or as Joseph took his two sons Manasseh and Ephraim by the hand, and presented them to Jacob; so doth Christ take his people and lead them into his Father's presence.

Ver. 13. Wherefore I desire] αἰτοῦμαι, *mendico*. Or, I beg of God, as one would do an alms, Acts iii. 2, humbly, heartily. And here the apostle returns to his former discourse, after a long digression, ver. 2 to ver. 13.

At my tribulations for you] For your sakes am I maliced and molested by the Jews; by whose means also I am now a prisoner.

Ver. 14. For this cause] sc. That ye faint not, but gather strength.

I bow my knees] A most seemly and suitable gesture, usual among all nations but Turks, who

[1] *Opulentissima metalla, quorum in alto latent venæ.* Sen.

kneel not, nor uncover the head at prayer, as holding those postures unmanly. And yet they pray five times every day (saith Mr Terry), what occasion soever they have either by profit or pleasure to divert them.

Ver. 15. Of whom the whole family] Or, paternity; πατριὰ, *parentela*. God is the only Father, to speak properly, Matt. xxiii. 9. The Father of all the fatherhood in heaven and earth.

Ver. 16. According to the riches of his glory] That is, of his grace; so 2 Cor. iii. 18. See the note there.

Ver. 17. That Christ may dwell] As the sun dwells in the house by his beams. Faith fetcheth Christ into the heart, as into his habitation; and if he dwell there, he is bound to all reparations.

Ver. 18. The breadth and length, &c.] God's mercy hath all the dimensions. "Thy mercy, O God, reacheth to the heavens," Psal. xxxvi. 5. There is the height of it. "Great is thy mercy toward me, and thou hast delivered my soul from the lowest hell," Psal. lxxxvi. 13. There is the depth of his mercy. "The earth is full of thy goodness." There is the breadth of it. "All the ends of the earth have seen thy salvation." There is the length of it. The apostle sets out Christ's love with the four dimensions of the cross; to put us in mind (say the ancient writers) that upon the extent of the tree was the most exact love with all the dimensions in this kind represented, that ever was.

Ver. 19. With all the fulness of God] That is, of Christ's diffusive fulness, in whom the Godhead dwelt bodily, and in whom we are complete, Col. ii. 9, 10.

And to know the love of Christ which passeth knowledge] Chrysostom speaking of this love of God in Christ, Oh, saith he, I am like a man digging in a deep spring; I stand here, and the water riseth upon me; I stand there, and still the water riseth upon me. But though we cannot ever know it all, yet we may and must grow in the knowledge of this love of Christ, in the searching of this sea that hath neither bank nor bottom; and where, as in the salt waters, "the deeper the sweeter."

Ver. 20. Exceeding abundantly] Gr. ὑπὲρ ἐκ περισσοῦ, more than exceedingly or excessively. God hath not only a fulness of abundance, but of redundancy; of plenty, but of bounty. He is oft better to us than our prayers.

According to the power] The apostle begins his prayer with mention of God's fatherly mercy; he shuts it up with a description of his power. These two, God's might and God's mercy, are the Jachin and Boaz, the two main pillars of a Christian's faith, whereon it rests in prayer.

Ver. 21. Glory in the church of Christ] Who is the refulgency of his Father's glory, Heb. i. 3.

CHAPTER IV.

Ver. 1. Worthy of the vocation] There is a τὸ πρεπὸν, a seemliness appertaining to each caliing; so here. We must walk nobly and comfortably, as becometh the heirs of God and co-heirs of Christ. Scipio, when a harlot was offered him, answered, *Vellem, si non essem Imperator;* I would if I were not general of the army. Antigonus being invited to a place where a notable harlot was to be present, asked counsel of Menedemus, what he should do? He bade him only remember that he was a king's son. So let men remember their high and heavenly calling, and do nothing unworthy of it. Luther counsels men to answer all temptations of Satan with this only, *Christianus sum,* I am a Christian. They were wont to say of cowards in Rome, There is nothing Roman in them: of many Christians we may say, There is nothing Christian in them. It is not amiss before we be serviceable for the world, to put Alexander's questions to his followers, that persuaded him to run at the Olympic games, Do kings use to run at the Olympics? Every believer is God's first-born; and so higher than the kings of the earth, Psal. lxxxix. 27. He must therefore carry himself accordingly, and not stain his high blood.

Ver. 2. *With all lowliness and meekness*] These are *virtutes collectaneœ,* as Bernard calleth them, a pair of twin-sisters, never asunder.

Ver. 3. *The unity of the Spirit*] That is, unanimity; this keeps all together which else will shatter and fall asunder. The daughter of dissension is dissolution, saith Nazianzen.

Endeavouring] σπουδάζοντες, Or using all possible carefulness: this imports, 1. The necessity; 2. Difficulty of the duty. Satan will endeavour, by making division, to get dominion.

Ver. 4. *In one hope of your calling*] That is, unto one inheritance, which we all hope for. Fall not out therefore by the way, as Joseph charged his brethren.

Ver. 5. *One baptism*] The author to the Hebrews speaketh of baptisms, chap. vi. 2. But either he puts the plural for the singular; or else he meaneth it of the outward and inward washing, which the schools call *baptismum fluminis et flaminis.* See the note on Matt. iii. 11.

Ver. 6. *One God and Father of all*] Have we not all one Father? saith Malachi (ii. 10). Why then dissent and jar we? How is it that these many ones here instanced unite us not? "My dove, mine undefiled is but one," Cant. vi. 9.

Ver. 7. *According to the measure*] And may not Christ do with his own as he listeth? Those of greater gifts are put upon hotter service, στέργε παρόντα.

Ver. 8. *He led captivity captive, &c.*] As in the Roman triumphs, the victor ascended up to the Capitol in a chariot of state, the prisoners following on foot with their hands bound behind, and they threw certain pieces of coin abroad, to be picked up by the common people; so Christ in the day of his solemn inauguration into his heavenly kingdom, triumphed over sin, death, and hell, Col. ii. 15, and gave gifts to men.

And gave gifts unto men] The Hebrew hath it, Psal. lxxvi. 19, "Thou receivest gifts for men." Christ received them that he might give them, and said, "It is a more blessed thing to give than to receive." The Psalmist adds, "Even for the rebellious." To them also Christ gives common gifts, for the behoof of his people. Augustus in his solemn feast gave gifts; to some gold, to others trifles. So God in his ordinances, to some saving grace, to others common grace, and with this they rest content.

Ver. 9. *Into the lower parts*] That is, into his mother's womb; according to Psal. cxxxix. 15, "I was curiously wrought in the lowest parts of the earth," *i. e.* in the womb, where God formed and featured me: like as curious workmen, when they have some choice piece in hand, they perfect it in private, and then bring it forth to light for men to gaze at.

Ver. 10. *Far above all heavens*] That is, above all visible heavens, into the third heaven; not in the Utopia of the Ubiquitaries.

That he might fill all things] viz. With the gifts of his Holy Spirit; for the further he is from us in his flesh, the nearer by his Spirit; he is more efficacious absent than present.

Ver. 11. *Some pastors and teachers*] Distinct officers, Rom. xii. 7, 8, yet one man may be both, 1 Cor. xii. 28, 29. The essential differences between pastors and teachers in each congregation is much denied by many learned and godly divines.

Ver. 12. *For the perfecting of the saints*] καταρτισμὸν, for the jointing of them whom the devil hath dislocated.

Ver. 13. *Unto the measure of the stature*] Or age; that age wherein Christ filleth all in all, as chap. iii. 19. The saints (say some) shall rise again in that vigour of age that a perfect man is at about 33 years old, each in their proper sex; whereunto they think the apostle here alludeth. In heaven (say others) we shall all have an equal grace, though not an equal glory.

Ver. 14. *Be no more children*] But young men, 1 John ii. 14, strong men. Many men's heads now-a-days are so big (like children that have the rickets) that all the body fareth the worse for it.

Tossed to and fro] As a feather or froth upon the waves, whirred about with every wind of doctrine; unstable souls, as St Peter calls them; simple, that believe everything, as Solomon hath it; giddy hearers, that have no mould but what the next teacher casteth them into, being blown like glasses into this or that shape at the pleasure of his breath.

By the sleight of men] Gr. ἐν τῇ κυβείᾳ, by men's cogging of a die, the usual trade of cheaters and false gamesters.

Whereby they lie in wait to deceive] Gr. Unto a method of deceiving. The devil and his disciples are notable method-mongers, so as to deceive, if it were possible, the very elect; but that they cannot do fundamentally, finally, Matt. xxiv. 24. See the note there.

Ver. 15. *But speaking the truth*] Or, doing

the truth, as the Vulgar hath it, ἀληθεύοντες.
Truthifying, or following the truth, as one rendereth it.   St John bids, love in truth, 1 John iii.
18. St Paul, speak or do the truth in love.
And again, let all your things be done in love.

Ver. 16. Compacted by that, &c.] The saints
are knit unto Christ by his Spirit, as fast as the
sinews of his blessed body to the bones, the flesh
to the sinews, the skin to the flesh. The erroneo-
ous are like a bone out of joint; it will cost
many a hearty groan before they be reduced to
their right place.

Unto the edifying of itself in love] Our souls
thrive and are edified as love is continued and
increased. Nothing more furthereth growth in
grace and power of godliness in any place or person, observe it where and when you will.

Ver. 17. This I say therefore] Matters of
great importance must be urged and pressed with
greatest vehemence.

As other Gentiles walk] Singular things are
expected from saints; who are therefore worse
than others, because they should be better.

Ver. 18. Having the understanding darkened]
By the devil's black hand held before their eyes,
2 Cor. iv. 4. See the note there.

Alienated from the life of God] That is, from
a godly life, which none can live but those that
partake of the divine nature, 2 Pet. i. 4.

Because of the blindness] Gr. πώρωσιν, callum
obductum. Hardness, brawniness, a hoof upon
their hearts, *corneas fibras,* brawny breasts, horny
heart-strings. The Greek word imports a metaphor from the hard hand of hardest labourers.
They say in philosophy, that the foundation of
natural life is feeling; no feeling, no life: and
that the more quick and nimble the sense of
feeling is in a man, the better is his constitution.
Think the same we may of life spiritual.

Ver. 19. Who being past feeling] Under a
dead and dedolent disposition, being desperately
sinful. Some there are of cauterized consciences,
that, like devils, will have nothing to do with God,
because loth to be tormented before their time.
They feeling such horrible hard hearts, and privy
to such notorious sins, they cast away souls and
all for lust, and so perish woefully, because they
lived wickedly; having through custom in evil
contracted such a hardness, as neither ministry,
nor misery, nor miracle, nor mercy could possibly
mollify. As ducklings dive at any little thing
thrown by a man at them, yet shrink not at the
heaven's great thunder; so is it with these, till
at length they become like the smith's dog,
whom neither the hammers above him nor the
sparks of fire falling round about him can
awake.

Have given themselves over] They make it
their felicity to pass their time lasciviously, as
though they were born (as Boccas saith of himself) *per l'amore dalle dame,* for the love of
women.

Ver. 20. But ye have not so learned Christ.]
Caracalla never minded any good, *quia id non
didicerat* (saith Dio), *quod ipse fatebatur,* because

he had never learned it, as himself confessed.
One main cause of Julian's apostasy were his
two heathenish tutors, Libanius and Jamblichus,
from whom he drank in great profaneness. Christians cannot say but they have had the best
teacher; they must therefore walk up to their
principles lest they shame their profession, discredit their Master, who seemeth to say to them,
as Samson once did to his brethren, Do not you
bind me; the Philistines I care not for. Do not
you dishonour me, &c.

Ver. 21. Ye have heard him, &c.] When
Christ speaks once, we must hear him twice, as
David did, Psal. lxii. 11, to wit, by an after
deliberate meditation; for otherwise we learn
nothing.

Ver. 22. That ye put off, &c.] As the beggar
puts off his rags, as the master puts off his bad
servant, as the porter puts off his burden, as the
husband puts off his lewd wife, as the serpent
his slough, or as the captive maid, when she was
to be married, put off the garments of her captivity, Deut. xxi. 13.

The old man which is corrupt] Sin is said to
be the old man, because it lives in man so as sin
seems to be alive and the man dead; and because God will take notice of nothing in the sinner but his sin.

According to the deceitful lusts] Sin, though
at first it fawn upon a man, yet in the end (with
Cain's dog lying at the door) it will pluck out
the very throat of his soul, if not repented of.
Like the serpent, together with the embrace, it
stings mortally. Hence the ruler's meat is called
deceivable, Prov. xxiii. 3. There being a deceitfulness in sin, Heb. iii. 13, a lie in vanity, Jonah
ii. 8. Lust hath a deceit in it, as here.

Ver. 23. In the spirit of your mind] That is,
in the most inward and subtle parts of the soul,
the bosom and bottom, the *vis vivifica,* and very
quintessence of it. This he calls elsewhere the
wisdom of the flesh, Rom. viii. 7, that carnal
reason, that, like an old beldam, is the mother
and nurse of those fleshly lusts that fight against
the soul.

Ver. 24. Which after God is created] The
new man is nothing else but the happy cluster
of heavenly graces.

And true holiness] Or, holiness of truth. Opposite to that deceitfulness of lusts, ver. 22.

Ver. 25. Wherefore putting away lying] A
base tinkerly sin, as Plutarch calls it, shameful
and hateful: therefore the liar denies his own
lie, as ashamed to be taken with it. Tully
indeed alloweth his orator the liberty of a merry
lie sometimes; but Vives utterly disliketh it
in him at any time.[1] And the apostle, Gal. i.
10, shows that we must not speak truth to
please men, much less lie; no, though we could
win a soul by it, Rom. iii. 7. Where then will
the Jesuits appear with their *piæ fraudes,* as
they call them? and Jacobus de Voragine, that
loud liar, with his golden legend? It were much
to be wished that that golden age would return,

[1] Lib. 2, de Oratore. Lib. 4, de trad. discip.

that the argument might proceed, *Sacerdos est, non fallet. Christianus est, non mentietur.*

For we are members] Of the same holy society. Shall we not be true one to another? shall we not abhor sleights and slipperiness in contracts and covenants?

Ver. 26. *Be angry and sin not*] The easiest charge under the hardest condition that can be. Anger is a tender virtue, and must be warily managed. He that will be angry and not sin, let him be angry at nothing but sin.

Let not the sun go down] If ye have overshot in passion, let it not rest or roost in you, lest it become malice. Plutarch writeth that it was the custom of Pythagoras' scholars, however they had been at odds, jarring and jangling in their disputations, yet before the sun set to kiss and shake hands as they departed out of the school.[1] How many are there that professing themselves the scholars of Christ, do yet nevertheless not only let the sun go down, but go round his whole course, and can find no time from one end of the year to the other to compose and lay aside their discords! How should this fire be raked up when the curfew-bell rings! William the Conqueror commanded that cover-few bell. It were well that some were admonished every night to cover the fire of their passions, that their wrath might not be *memor ira*, as Virgil hath it, and ἀἐιμνηστος, as that of the Athenians, who hated all barbarians, for the Persians' sake, and forbade them their sacrifices, as they used to do murderers. (Rous's Arch. Attic.) Leontius Patritius was one day extremely and unreasonably angry with John, Patriarch of Alexandria: at evening, the patriarch sent a servant to him with this message; "Sir, the sun is set;" upon which Patritius reflecting, and the grace of God making the impression deep, he threw away his anger, and became wholly subject to the counsel of the patriarch. (Taylor's Life and Death of Christ.)

Ver. 27. *Neither give place, &c.*] Vindictive spirits let the devil into their hearts; and though they defy him, and spit at him, yet they spit not low enough; for he is still at inn with them, as Mr Bradford speaketh. As the master of the pit oft sets two cocks to fight together, to the death of both, and then, after mutual conquest, suppeth with both their bodies; so, saith Gregory, dealeth the devil with angry and revengeful men.

Ver. 28. *Let him labour, working, &c.*] This is the best remedy against poverty, which oft prompts a man to theft, Prov. xxx. 9. See the note there. The Grand Turk himself must be of some trade (Peacham); and Seneca said he had rather be sick in his bed than idle. How much more should "all ours learn to maintain good works for necessary uses, that they be not unfruitful!" Tit. iii. 14.

That he may have to give] Day-labourers then must do somewhat for the poor. And indeed, alms should not be given until it "sweat in a

[1] Plut. lib. περὶ φιλαδελφ.

man's hand," saith he, in the Book of Martyrs. Giles of Brussels gave away to the poor whatsoever he had that necessity could spare, and only lived by his science, which was that of a cutler. (Acts and Mon.)

Ver. 29. *Let no corrupt communication*] Gr. σαπρὸς. Rotten, putrid speech. A metaphor from rotten trees, or stinking flesh, or stinking breath. Shun obscene borborology and filthy speeches.

Ver. 30. *And grieve not, &c.*] As men in heaviness cannot despatch their work as they were wont; so neither doth the Spirit. If we grieve the Holy Ghost, how should we expect that he should comfort us? It is a foul fault to grieve a father; what then the Spirit? *Delicata res est spiritus Dei*, saith Tertullian, God's Spirit is a delicate thing, and must not be vexed. "It is a holy thing, that Spirit of that God" (so the original hath it, τὸ πνεῦμα τὸ ἅγιον τοῦ Θεοῦ), "whereby we are sealed," and so are declared to be the excellent ones of the earth; for whatsoever is sealed, that is excellent in its own kind, as Isa. xxviii. 25, *hordeum signatum*, sealed barley, &c.

Ver. 31. *Let all bitterness, &c.*] If the godly man suddenly fall into bitter words, it maketh the Holy Ghost stir within him.

And clamour and evil speaking] These are as smoke to the eyes, and make the spirit ready to loathe and leave his lodging.

Be put away from you] When any lust ariseth, pray it down presently (saith one); for otherwise we are endangered by yielding to grieve, by grieving to resist, by resisting to quench, by quenching, maliciously to oppose the Spirit. Sin hath no bounds, but those which the Spirit puts, whom therefore we should not grieve.

Ver. 32. *And be ye kind*] χρηστοὶ. Sweet-natured, facile, and fair-conditioned; as Cranmer, whose gentleness in pardoning wrongs was such, as it grew to a common proverb, Do my Lord of Canterbury a displeasure, and then you may be sure to have him your friend while he liveth. He never raged so far with any of his household servants, as once to call the meanest of them varlet or knave in anger, much less to reprove a stranger with any reproachful word. *Homo Φιλόξενος, nec minus Φιλόλογος*, saith Tremelius of him, and much more in praise of his courtesy and piety.

CHAPTER V.

Ver. 1. *Be ye therefore followers*] IN forgiving one another.

As dear children] God hath but a few such children. See the notes on Matt. v. 45, 48.

Ver. 2. *Hath loved us, and hath given*] When Christ wept for Lazarus, "Lo, how he loved him," said the Jews, John xi. 35, 36. When he poured forth his soul for a drink-offering for us, was not this a surer seal of his endeared love?

An offering and a sacrifice] By this to expiate our sins, by that to mediate and make request for us; and so to show himself a perfect High Priest.

Ver. 3. *But fornication and all uncleanness*] As standing in full opposition to that sweet-smelling savour, ver. 2, being no better than the corruption of a dead soul, the devil's excrement. That people fitly punished this filthy sin, who put the offenders' heads into the paunch of a beast where all the filth lieth, and so stifled them to death.

Let it not be once named] Much less acted as in stage-plays. *Ludi præbent semina nequitiæ.* (Ovid. Trist.) How Alipius was corrupted by them, St Austin tells us. How the youth of Athens, Plato complaineth. One of our countrymen professeth in print, that he found theatres to be the very hatchers of all wickedness, the brothels of baudery, the black blasphemy of the gospel, the devil's chair, the plague of piety, the canker of the commonwealth, &c. He instanceth on his knowledge, citizens' wives confessing on their death-beds that they were so impoisoned at stage-plays, that they brought much dishonour to God, wrong to their marriage-beds, weakness to their wretched bodies, and woe to their undone souls. (Spec. Belli Sacri.) It was therefore great wisdom in the Lacedæmonians to forbid the acting of comedies or tragedies in their commonwealth, and that for this reason, lest either in jest or earnest anything should be said or done contrary to the laws in force amongst them. (Plutarch.) What a sad complaint was that of the apostle, 1 Cor. v. 1, that that which was not so much as named amongst heathens was done by a Christian; whereas the rule of piety here is, that those sins should not be so much as named amongst Christians which are done by the Gentiles.

Ver. 4. *Neither filthiness*] Borborology, ribaldry, the language of hell. Some men as ducks have their noses always guzzling in the gutter of obscene talk. Of Eckius' last book concerning priests' marriages, Melancthon saith, *Non fuit Cygnea cantio, sed ultimus crepitus : Et sicut felis fugiens pedit, sic ille moriens hunc crepitum cecinit. Legi librum, subinde accipiens partem ad cloacam ; alioqui non legissem.* These filthy speakers make *podicem ex ore,* as one phraseth it.

Nor jesting] Salt jests, scurrility, jocularity, dicacity, to the just grief or offence of another. This consists not with piety and Christian gravity. Aristotle useth the word εὐτραπελία, here found in a good sense, for urbanity, facility, and facetiousness of speech, in a harmless way. But Jason in Pindarus saith, that he lived twenty years with his tutor Chiron, and never in all that time heard him speaking or acting οὐτ᾽ ἔργον οὐτ᾽ ἔπος εὐτράπελον, anything scurrilous or abusive to another. On the contrary, our Sir Thomas More never thought anything to be well spoken, except he had ministered some mock in the communication, saith Edward Hall the chronicler, who therefore seemeth to doubt whether to call him a foolish wise man or a wise foolish man. *Quid nobis cum fabulis, cum risu ? non solum profulos, sed etiam omnes jocos arbitror declinandos,* saith Bernard. What have we to do with tales and jests? Tertullian saith he was *Nulli rei natus nisi pœnitentiæ,* born for nothing else but for repentance. *Crede mihi, res severa est gaudium verum,* saith Seneca, True mirth is a severe business.

Which are not convenient] τὰ μὴ ἀνήκοντα. As not conducing to the main end of our lives.

But rather giving of thanks] A special preservative against the former evils, the filth and power of those base vices. And the word rather imports an extraordinary earnestness to be used in giving thanks to God.

Ver. 5. *Who is an idolater*] Dancing about his golden calf, and saying to his wedge of silver, "Thou art my confidence," Job xxx. 24; which yet shall prove but as Achan's wedge to cleave his soul in sunder, and as that Babylonish garment to be his winding-sheet.

Ver. 6. *Let no man deceive you*] So as to make you think there is no such danger in fornication, covetousness, &c. There wanted not such proctors for hell in the primitive times, as may be gathered out of 2 Pet. ii. and the Epistle of Jude. Against these he here cautioneth.

Ver. 7. *Be not ye therefore partakers*] Lest by infection of their sin ye come under infliction of their punishment. We are accountable as well for sins of communion as of commission; and he knew what he said, that prayed, From mine other-men's sins, good Lord, deliver me. Evil men endanger good men as weeds the corn, as bad humours the blood, or an infected house the neighbourhood. And when an overflowing storm sweeps away the wicked, the tail of it may dash their best neighbours, Zech. ix. 3. Hamath lay nigh to Damascus in place, and therefore partook with it in punishment.

Ver. 8. *For ye were sometimes darkness*] Which hath in it (as Mr Dugard well noteth) : 1. Error. 2. Terror. 3. Inconsistency with light. 4. Impossibility of reducing itself to light.

But now are ye light] *Semper in sole sita est Rhodos,* saith Sylvius. The saints are always in the sunshine.

Walk as children of light] A godly man should be like a crystal glass with a light in the midst, which appeareth through every part thereof. He is in the light, and shall be more.

Ver. 9. *For the fruit of the Spirit*] Why grace is called fruit, see the note on Gal. v. 22.

Ver. 10. *Proving what is acceptable*] By the practice of what you know. Let your knowledge and obedience run parallel, mutually transfusing life and vigour one into another.

Ver. 11. *Have no fellowship*] No needless society for fear of infection; get the wind of those stinking carcases; "hate the garment spotted by the flesh," that is, avoid ill company (saith Perkins), as Lev. xv. 4. The Lacedæmonians would not suffer a stranger to be with them above three days; and shall we associate ourselves with such as are strangers to God?

Works of darkness] Work done in the dark must be undone again, or else we are sure to be thrust into outer darkness, where we shall never see light again till we see all the world on a light fire.

But rather reprove them] At least by your contrary courses, as Noah condemned the old world, by being righteous in his generation, Rev. xiv., those that stood with the Lamb, had his Father's name on their foreheads, led convincing lives: so did Luther, Bucer, Bradford, &c.

Ver. 12. *For it is a shame*] *Sit honos auribus.* Joannes à Casa so far forgot both honesty and nature, that he boasted openly of his beastly sodomy; yea, most impudently commended that odious sin in an Italian poem, set forth in print. Faber of Vienna, another filthy Papist, published such a stinking book that Erasmus thus wrote to him,

> *Mente cares, si res agitur tibi seria : rursus*
> *Fronte cares, si sic ludis amice Faber.*

Which are done of them in secret] Sin secretly committed shall be strangely discovered, either by the sinner himself, as Judas, or by his companions in evil. When the solder is once melted, this glass will fall in pieces, and all will out.

Ver. 13. *But all things that are, &c.*] Or, But all these things, viz. these unfruitful works of darkness, whilst they are reproved or discovered by the light (viz. of the word, as 1 Cor. xiv. 24; Heb. iv. 12) are made manifest; so that thereby they grow abashed and abased before God and men.

Ver. 14. *Wherefore he saith*] Or, the Scripture saith. See the like, James iv. 6. But he giveth (or the Scripture giveth) more grace. It convinceth not only, but converteth; it discovereth not only, but cureth corrupt hearts. These waters of the sanctuary are healing, Isa. ix. 2; xxvi. 19; lx. 1. Some there are that interpret this "he" of our Saviour Christ, and take this saying for a sentence of his; such as was that, Acts xx. 35. Others read, Therefore the light saith, &c.

Awake, thou that sleepest] *Lex jubet, gratia juvat : præcipit Deus quod ipse præstat,* God giveth us to do what he biddeth us to do.

Ver. 15. *See then that ye walk circumspectly*] Precisely, exactly, accurately, by line and by rule, and as it were in a frame, striving to get up to the top of godliness, as the word importeth; to keep God's commandments to the utmost, to go to the extremity of it, ἀκριβῶς εἰς ἄκρον βαίνειν. Hereunto if we stand straightly, one may say safely, Lord, if I be deceived, thou and thy word have deceived me.

Not as fools] Christians must excel others, standing as standard-bearers.

But as wise] Great need we have to fly to Christ, who dwells with prudence, Prov. viii., to stand upon our watch. (Σοφὸς ab Heb. Tsopheh. Speculator.) And when we walk, to tread gingerly, step warily; sith as those *funambulones,* rope-walkers (it is Tertullian's comparison), if we tread but one step awry, we are utterly gone.

Ver. 16. *Redeeming the time*] As wise merchants, trading for the most precious commodity, and taking their best opportunity. The common complaint is, We want time; but the truth is, we do not so much want it, as waste it. *Non parum habemus temporis, sed multum perdimus.* (Sen.) The men of Issachar were in great account with David, because they had understanding of the times, to know what Israel ought to do, 1 Chron. xii. 32. So are they in great account with God that regard and use the season of well-doing. It is reported of holy Ignatius, that when he heard a clock strike, he would say, here is one hour more now past that I have to answer for. And of Mr Hooper the martyr, that he was spare of diet, sparer of words, and sparest of time; for he well knew that whereas of all other possessions a man might have two at once, he cannot have two moments of time at once, for any money.

Because the days are evil] Corrupted by the devil, who hath engrossed our time, and out of whose hands we must redeem time for holy uses and pious purposes.

Ver. 17. *But understanding what*] Drawing your knowledge into practice, as ver. 10. For "the fear of the Lord, that is wisdom, and to depart from evil is understanding," Job xxviii. 28 : where wisdom (proper to the understanding) is ascribed to the will, because practice should be joined to knowledge. Hence also, Eccles. x. 2, "A wise man's heart is at his right hand," because his heart teacheth his hand to put things in practice.

Ver. 18. *And be not drunk with wine*] Nothing so opposite to an accurate life as drunkenness; which therefore is not specially prohibited in any one of the Ten Commandments (saith a divine) because it is not the single breach of any one, but in effect the violation of all and every one; it is no one, but all sins, the inlet and sluice to all other sins, and by them to the devil. Behemoth lieth in the fens, Job xl. 21, he finds no rest in dry places, sober souls, Luke xi. Oh that our carousers were persuaded (as Mahomet told his followers) that in every grape there dwelt a devil.

Wherein is excess] Excessive drinking then is drunkenness; when as swine do their bellies, so men break their heads with filthy quaffing; and are besotted in their very parts, as a snuff of a candle in the socket, drowned in the tallow; a stench, but little or no light remains. Such a deep drunkard was Diotimus, surnamed Tundish, and young Cicero, surnamed Tricongius; and such are not a few at this day amongst us, to the great shame of our nation.

But be filled with the Spirit] Call for flagons of this holy wine, Cant. ii. 5, that goeth down sweetly, causing the lips of those that are asleep to speak, Cant. vii. 9. This is called by Luther, *Crapula sacra,* a spiritual surquedry or surfeit.

Ver. 19. *Speaking to yourselves, &c.*] As drunkards sing and halloo over their cups in their good-fellow meetings; so in a sober sense, do you express your spiritual jollity in psalms, &c.

Melody in your hearts unto the Lord] This is the best tune to any psalm. Spiritual songs they are called, both because they are indited by the Spirit, and because they spiritualize us in the use of them.

Ver. 20. *Giving thanks always*] In our deepest miseries let us sing cheerfully, as Paul and Silas in the dungeon, as Philpot and his fellows in the coal-house, as many martyrs in the flames, as Luther did in a great conflict with the devil: *Venite*, said he to his company, *in contemptum diaboli Psalmum de profundis quatuor vocibus cantemus:* Let us sing the 130th Psalm in despite of the devil. (John Manli. loc. com.) Happy was that tongue in the primitive times that could sound out *aliquid Davidicum*, anything of David's doing.

Ver. 21. *Submitting yourselves*] This is a general admonition to all inferiors, whose duties are afterwards described. Thus in the second table of the law, the fifth commandment for order and obedience is fitly premised to the following precepts.

In the fear of God] This frameth the heart to a ready and regular submission. Hence that saying of Luther, *Primo præcepto reliquorum omnium observantia præcipitur*, The first commandment includes the other nine.

Ver. 22. *Wives, submit, &c.*] This includes reverence, obedience, &c. God hath scattered the duties of husbands and wives up and down the Scriptures, that they may search, and by learning to be good husbands and wives, they may learn also to be good men and women.

As unto the Lord] Who taketh himself dishonoured by wives' disobedience. And though husbands may remit the offence done to them, yet they cannot remit God's offence, but there must be special repentance.

Ver. 23. *For the husband is the head*] And would it not be ill-favoured to see the shoulders above the head?

Ver. 24. *Therefore as the Church*] Denying herself to please Christ, making his will her law.

In everything] In all her husband's lawful commands and restraints. A wife should have no will of her own, but submit to her husband's; albeit there are that merrily say that when man lost free-will, woman took it up.

Ver. 25. *Husbands, love your wives*] He saith not, rule over them (in answer to submit, ver. 22), for this they can readily do without bidding; but love your wives, and so make their yoke as easy as may be. *Columbæ trahunt currum Veneris.*

Ver. 26. *That he might sanctify*] The maids were first purified and perfumed before Ahasuerus chose one. But here it is otherwise. Sanctification is a fruit of justification. The Lord will not have a sluttish Church, and therefore he came not by blood only, but by water also, that clean water of his Spirit, whereby he washeth away the swinish nature of his saints, so that they desire no more to wallow in the mire.

Ver. 27. *That he might present*] As Isaac did

his Rebecca, adorned with his jewels. See Ezek. xvi. 14. *Tales nos amat Deus, quales futuri sumus ipsius dono, non quales sumus nostro merito*, saith an ancient Council.

Ver. 28. *As their own bodies*] No man may hide himself from his own flesh at large, Isa. lviii. 7, that is, from his neighbour of the same stock; much less from a wife, which is such another as himself, Gen. ii. 18, nay, his very self, as here.

Ver. 29. *For no man ever hated*] No man but a monk, who whips himself, or a mad-man, Mark v. 5, who cuts himself. It was the saying of the Emperor Aurelius, a wife is to be oft admonished, sometimes reproved, but never beaten. And yet of the Russian women it is reported, that they love that husband best that beats them most, and that they think themselves else not regarded, unless two or three times a day well-favouredly swadled. Chrysostom saith, It is the greatest reproach in the world for a man to beat his wife.

But nourisheth it, and cherisheth it] Θάλπει. As the hen doth her chickens, or as the cock-pigeon doth the eggs.[1] Contrariwise the pie hunts away his mate about autumn, lest he should be forced to keep her all the winter; and so becometh the hieroglyphic of an unkind husband.

Even as the Lord, the Church] Lo, this is the pattern of all true love, whether to ourselves or others.

Ver. 30. *Of his flesh, and of his bones*] Whilst he that is joined to the Lord is one spirit, 1 Cor. vi. 17. This union is neither natural, nor corporal, nor political, nor personal, but mystical and spiritual; and yet it is no less true and real than that of God the Father and God the Son, John xvii. 21, 22. For as the Holy Ghost did unite in the Virgin's womb the Divine and human natures of Christ, and made them one person; by reason whereof Christ is of our flesh and of our bones; so the Spirit unites that person of Christ, his whole person, God-man, with our persons, by reason whereof we are of his flesh and of his bones.

Ver. 31. *For this cause, &c.*] See the note on Matt. xix. 5, and on Gen. ii. 24.

Shall be one flesh] By virtue of that covenant of God betwixt married couples, Prov. ii. 17, for he keepeth the bonds of wedlock.

Ver. 32. *This is a great mystery*] To wit, this mystical marriage with Christ. It passeth the capacity of man to understand it in the perfection of it. Preachers can make it known but in part, and hearers can but in part conceive it. Let us therefore wait for perfect understanding of it, till all things be perfected in Christ.

Ver. 33. *Nevertheless*] *q. d.* But that I may return to my former discourse, from the which I have somewhat digressed for your satisfaction.

See that she reverence] 1. In heart, as Sarah did Abraham, and she is crowned and chronicled for it, 1 Pet. iii. 6. 2. In her speeches both to him, and of him, as the spouse in the Canticles. 3. In all her gestures and deportments; for she

[1] *Columbarum masculus ipse ovis incubat.*

may scold with her looks, &c. *Vulta sæpe læditur pietas.* God hath a barren womb for mocking Michal.

CHAPTER VI.

Ver. 1. *Children, obey your parents*] As Isaac did Abraham in submitting to be sacrificed; as Christ became obedient even to the death of the cross.

For this is right] Good and acceptable before God and men, 1 Tim. v. 4. See the note on Matt. xv. 4.

Ver. 2. *First commandment with promise*] To wit, with special promise of long life. See more in the note on Matt. xv. 4.

Ver. 3. *And thou mayest live long*] Good children help to lengthen their parents' days, as Joseph did Jacob's. God therefore lengthens theirs in *redhostimentum*, as it were. Or if he take from them this long lease, he gives them a freehold of better value.

Ver. 4. *Provoke not, &c.*] God forbids bitterness and austerity in husbands, Col. iii. 19; masters, Col. iv. 1; parents here, and Col. iii. 21. Superiors must so carry themselves as to be at once loved and feared.

But bring them up in the nurture, &c.] Or, nourish them and nurture them. The latter is as needful as the former. They that nourish their children only, what do they more than the unreasonable creatures? The blessing upon posterity is entailed to piety in the second commandment. If I may see grace in my wife and children, said reverend Claviger, *Satis habeo, satisque mihi, meæ uxori, filiis et filiabus prospexi*, I shall account them sufficiently cared for. (Selneccer.) Let parents labour to mend that by education that they have marred by propagation; for else they are *Peremptores potius quam parentes*, parricides rather than parents, and shall dearly answer for their poor children, which like Moses in the flag-bed, are ready to perish if they have not help. Nurture is a great help to nature; and some sons honour not their fathers, because, as Eli, they honoured their sons, that is, they corrected not, but cockered them, 1 Sam. ii. 29; 1 Kings i. 5, 6.

Ver. 5. *Servants, be obedient*] The centurion was happy in his servants: and no marvel, for he was a loving master. See the note on Matt. viii. 6. And observe here that inferior duties are first described; because, 1. They are less willing to subject themselves. 2. They should be readier to perform duty than to expect it. 3. Hereby they shall win upon their superiors, who will lie the heavier upon them if there be strife who shall begin. (Bernard.)

Ver. 6. *Not with eye-service*] And yet it were well if we would do God, our great Master, but eye-service. For his eye is ever upon us, and pierceth into the inward parts. So that they much deceive themselves, who think all is well because no man can say to them, Black is thine eye.

Ver. 7. *As to the Lord*] In obedience to his will, and with reference to his glory,

Ver. 8. *Whether he be bond or free*] The centurion did but complain of the sickness of his servant, and Christ, unasked, says, I will come and heal him. He that came in the shape of a servant, would go down to the sick servant's pallet, would not go to the bed of the rich ruler's son.

Ver. 9. *Do the same things*] That is, Do your parts and duties by them; and use them as men, not as beasts. *Eadem dicit, non opere et officio, sed modo et proportione*, saith Estius.

Forbearing threatening] Those blusters and terrible thunder-cracks of fierce and furious language found in the mouths of many masters, if never so little crossed. *Severitas nec sit tetra, nec tetrica:* Servants should be chidden with good words, with God's words, and not reviled. (Sidon. Epist.)

Ver. 10. *Be strong in the Lord*] For by his own strength shall no man prevail, 1 Sam. ii. 9. Get God's arm, wherewith to wield his armour, and then you may do anything.

Ver. 11. *Put on the whole armour*] Or else never think to do the fore-mentioned duties; we have a busy adversary to deal with. The Turks bear no weapons but in travel; then some of them seem like a walking armoury; so must a Christian be. Coriolanus had so used his weapons of a child-little, that they seemed as if they had been born with him, or grown into his hands.[1] Seneca reports of Cæsar that he quickly sheathed his sword, but never laid it off. No more must we.

The wiles of the devil] Gr. The methods or way-layings of that old subtile serpent, who like Dan's adder in the path, biteth the heels of passengers, and thereby transfuseth his venom to the head and heart, Gen. xlix. 17. Julian by his craft drew more from the faith than all his persecuting predecessors could do by their cruelty. So doth Satan more hurt in his sheepskin than by roaring like a lion.

Ver. 12. *Not against flesh and blood*] Hereby the apostle meaneth not so much the corruption as the weakness of our natures, *q. d.* We have not only to conflict with weak, frail men, but with puissant devils. Look to it therefore, and lie open at no place; but get on every piece of this spiritual armour, whether those of defence (as the girdle of truth, breast-plate of righteousness, the shoes of peace and patience, the helmet of hope), or those of offence, as the sword of the Spirit and the darts of prayer. Fetch all these out of the Holy Scriptures, which are like Solomon's tower, where hang a thousand shields and all the weapons of strong men. The apostle here soundeth the alarm, crying, Arm, arm, &c.

But against principalities] So wicked men make the devils, by being at their beck and obedience. Observe here, saith an interpreter, in the Holy Ghost a wonderful pattern of candour: he praiseth what is praiseworthy in very enemies. How then shall not the saints be accepted and

---

[1] ἐγγενῆ καὶ ἔμφυτά. Plutarch.

acknowledged, sith they sin not of malicious wickedness, as devils do?

Against spiritual wickedness] Gr. πνευματικὰ τῆς πονηρίας, The spirituals of wickedness, those hellish plots and satanical suggestions, black and blasphemous temptations, horrid and hideous injections, &c. Whereby he seeks to dispirit and defeat us, by setting before us the difficulties of Christian warfare; like as some inhospitable savages make fearful delusions by sorcery upon their shore, to fright strangers from landing.

In high places] ἐν τοῖς ἐπουρανίοις, or, about our interest in those heavenly privileges, which the devil would wring from us, and rob us of. He strove with the angel about the body of Moses; but with us about our precious souls. And herein he hath the advantage, that he is above us, and doth out of the air assault us, being upon the upper ground, as it were.

Ver. 13. *That ye may be able to withstand*] Not seeking to resist Satan's craft with craft, fraud with fraud, *sed per apertum martem*, but by open defiance. He shoots, saith Greenham, with Satan in his own bow, who thinks by disputing and reasoning to put him off. To argue the case with him is but, as the proverb hath it, to light a candle to the devil. Button up his mouth therefore, as our Saviour did, Mark i. 25, and buckle close to him and he will fly, James iv. 7, for he is but a coward.

Est Leo si fugias; si stas, quasi musca recedit.

And having done all to stand] Charles V. while he was putting on his armour looked pale, and seemed fearful; but when once armed, he was bold as a lion, and feared no colours.

Ver. 14. *Stand therefore*] στῆτε, a military expression. A man may well say to the Christian soldier, as Simon in the ecclesiastical history did to the pillars, which he whipped before the earthquake, Stand fast, for ye shall be shaken.

Your loins girt about] Here, if ever, "ungirt, unblest." He is a loose man that wants this girdle of sincerity.

The breast-plate of righteousness] Inherent righteousness, 1 John iii. 7, that insureth election, 2 Peter i. 10. The use of a breast-plate is to keep the vital parts from being mortally wounded, that a man be not stricken down without recovery; so doth righteousness the soul. "Treasures of wickedness profit nothing; but righteousness delivereth from death," Prov. x. 2. This is that *æs triplex circa pectus*, that privy armour of proof, that the saints have about their hearts, so that that "wicked one toucheth them not" with any deadly touch, 1 John v. 18. It is well observed by some, that in all this panoply there is no mention of a back-plate (as there is of a breast-plate), because the Christian soldier should never fly, but be like Androclid, whom when one derided, because being lame he went to the wars, he answered merrily, he came to fight, and not to run away.

Ver. 15. *And your feet shod*] As one that is well booted or buskined can walk unhurt amidst briars and brambles, so may he amidst Satan's snares, whereof all places are full, that is, fortified with gospel comforts, whereby God creates peace.

Ver. 16. *Above all*] ἐπὶ πᾶσιν, Or, over and upon all. For the word here rendered a shield, cometh from another word that signifieth a door, θυρεὸς, θύρα; to note, that as a door or gate doth the body, so the shield of faith covereth the whole soul. Let us be therefore (as Epaminondas), *Non de vita, sed de scuto solliciti.* Sceva at the siege of Dyrrachium so long alone resisted Pompey's army, that he had 220 darts sticking in his shield, and lost one of his eyes, and yet gave not over till Cæsar came to his rescue.

To quench all the fiery darts] Pointed and poisoned with the venom of serpents, which set the heart on fire from one lust to another; or fiery for the dolour and distemper that they work: in allusion to the Scythian darts, dipped in the gall of asps and vipers; the venomous heat of which, like a fire in their flesh, killed the wounded with torments the likest hell of any other. The apostle here might allude to the custom of soldiers in those times, who, to prevent the mischief of those impoisoned darts, had shields made of raw neats' leather, and when the fiery darts lighted upon them they were presently quenched thereby. (Polyb. Vegetius.)

Ver. 17. *The helmet of salvation*] Hope which holds head above water, and maketh the soul with stretched-out neck expect deliverance, Rom. viii. 19, crying out not only, *Dum spiro, spero*, but *Dum expiro, spero.*

And the sword of the Spirit] Wherewith our Saviour beat the devil on his own dunghill, the wilderness, fetching all out of that one book of Deuteronomy, Matt. iv. See the notes there.

Ver. 18. *Praying always*] Prayer is not only a part of the armour, but enables to use all the rest. It is not only a charm for that crooked serpent, Leviathan, Isa. xxvi. 16, to enchant him, but a whip (*Flagellum Diaboli*) to torment him, and put him into another hell, saith Chrysostom. It fetcheth Christ into the battle, and so is sure of victory. It obtaineth fresh supplies of the Spirit, Phil. i. 19, and so maketh us more than conquerors, even triumphers. It driveth the devil out of the field, and maketh him fly from us. *Tanquam si leones ignem expuentes essemus*, saith Chrysostom. Especially if we go not to the battle δορπόν ἑλόντες, with our breakfast, as Nestor in Homer, but "fasting and praying." For some kind of devils are not cast out but by fasting and prayer.

And watching thereunto] That we be not surprised at unawares. The bird Onocratalus is so well practised to expect the hawk to grapple with her, that even when she shutteth her eyes, she sleepeth with her beak exalted, as if she would contend with her adversary. Let us likewise stand continually upon our guard. The devil watcheth and walketh the round, 1 Pet. v. 8. Watch therefore.

Ver. 19. *And for me*] Ministers must be especially prayed for, that they may have a door not only of utterance, but of entrance to men's hearts, and so be able to save themselves and those that hear them. In praying for such, we pray for ourselves.

Ver. 20. *I am an ambassador*] Venerable for mine age and authority, as the word πρεσβεύω signifieth. The ancient and the honourable are usually employed as ambassadors. *Cognata sunt* γῆρας and γέρας. Old age and honour are akin in the Greek tongue.

In bonds] Gr. In a chain; instead of a chain of gold (worn commonly by ambassadors), and far more glorious, I bear about my bonds (saith Ignatius in his Epistle likewise to the Ephesians), as so many spiritual jewels or ensigns of honour.[1] Oh, said Alice Driver, here is a goodly necker-chief, blessed be God for it, when the chain was put about her neck.

That therein I may speak boldly] He saith not that I may be freed from my chain, but that I may do my office well in my chain. Let God serve himself upon us, and then no matter what becomes of us. *Martinus decumbens, Domine, dixit, si adhuc populo tuo sum necessarius, non recuso laborem.* (Sever. Epist. iii.)

Ver. 21. *But that ye may know*] It is of good use to the Church to know the lives and affairs of men eminent in goodness and of exemplary holiness, that others may express them; as Poly-carp did John the Evangelist, as Irenæus did Polycarp, as Cyprian did Tertullian, Paræus did Ursin, &c.

Ver. 22. *Comfort your hearts*] It is God that comforts by the creatures, as by conduit-pipes. The air yields light as an instrument; the water may heat, but not of itself. When a potion is given in beer, the beer of itself doth not work, but the potion by the beer. So in this case.

Ver. 23. *Peace be to the brethren*] These only be the children of peace, Luke x. 10. The wicked are like the troubled sea, Isa. lvii. 20, which may seem sometimes still, but is never so, no more are they. The peace of prosperity they may have, but not of tranquillity. *Sinceritas serenitatis mater.* Hence it followeth,

Ver. 24. *In sincerity*] ἐν ἀφθαρσίᾳ. Or, "im-mortality," opposite to that Anathema Mara-natha, 1 Cor. xvi. 23.

A
COMMENTARY OR EXPOSITION
UPON THE
EPISTLE OF ST PAUL TO THE PHILIPPIANS.

CHAPTER I.

Ver. 1. *With the bishops and deacons*] THE word priest is never used at all for a minister of the gospel by the apostles, no, nor by the more ancient Fathers, as Bellarmine himself con-fesseth.[2] And yet how eager were our late factors for Rome to have priested us all, but that God better provided for us!

Ver. 2. *Grace be to you*] See the note on 1 Cor. i. 2, and on Ephes. i. 2.

Ver. 3. *Upon every remembrance*] And no wonder; for these were those famous Mace-donians, that first gave themselves to the Lord, and then to their faithful ministers by the will of God, 2 Cor. viii. 5. See the note there, and compare Isa. 1. 10.

Ver. 4. *Making request with joy*] Those that grieve their faithful ministers, and quench the Spirit in them, do it to their own singular dis-advantage.

Ver. 5. *For your fellowship*] A good man can-not tell how to go to heaven alone. No sooner had the Philippians received the gospel, but they were in fellowship to a day. The communion of saints was with them a point of practice as well as an article of belief. The apostles' creed was anciently briefer than now. The mention of the Father's being "maker of heaven and earth," the Son's death and descending into hell, and the communion of saints, being wholly omitted; haply as implied sufficiently in other articles. But surely if the creed were called *Symbolum*, as a sign or badge to difference Christians from infidels and wicked people, there was little

[1] τὰ δεσμὰ περιφέρω τοὺς πνευματικοὺς μαργαρίτας.

[2] De Cultu Sanct. lib. iii. cap. 4.

reason to leave out the communion of saints, this being a main distinctive character; there being no such fellowship as among the saints, Cant. vi. 9.

Ver. 6. *That he which hath begun a good work*] Gr. ἐναρξάμενος, "That he which hath in-begun a good work in you;" for the work is wholly inward and spiritual, saith an interpreter. So God is said to indwell in his people, 2 Cor. vi. 16, as if he could never have enough communion with them.

Will perform it] Or perfect it. God doth not use to do his work by the halves, but goes through-stitch with it, 1 Thess. v. 24; Psal. cxxxviii. 8. Only we must pray as Luther was wont to do, "Confirm, O Lord, in us what thou hast wrought, and perfect the work that thou hast begun in us to thy glory. So be it." And as Queen Elizabeth prayed, "Look upon the wounds of thy hands, and despise not the work of thy hands. Thou hast written me down in thy book of preservation with thine own hand; oh read thine own hand-writing, and save me," &c.

Ver. 7. *Partakers of my grace*] That is, ye communicate with me in my sufferings, which he here calleth his " grace ; " and tells them, ver. 29, "to you it is given," as an honorary, "to suffer for Christ's sake." *Crudelitas vestra gloria nostra*, said those primitive martyrs. (Tertull.) I had rather be a martyr than a monarch, saith Ignatius. It is to my loss, if you bate me anything in my sufferings, saith Gordius to his tormentors. *Gaudebat Crispina cum tenebatur, cum audiebatur, cum damnabatur, eum ducebatur*, saith Augustine (in Psal. cxxxvii.) : Crispina rejoiced when she was apprehended, convented, condemned, executed.

Ver. 8. *I long after you all*] Here the apostle practised his own precept of fatherly affection, φιλόστοργοι, Rom. xii. 10. Pray for me, mine own heart-root in the Lord, *quem in intimis visceribus habeo ad convivendum et commoriendum*, saith Bradford in a letter to his fellow-martyr, Laurence Saunders.

Ver. 9. *And in all judgment*] Or, sense. The soul also hath her senses as well as the body. And these must be exercised to discern good and evil, Heb. v. 14, those two learned senses especially (as Aristotle calleth them), the eye and the ear, Job xxxiv. 3 ; Jer. ii. 31. Further, observe here, that knowledge and sense or judgment, are two things. Young trees are more sappy, but old trees are more solid.

Ver. 10. *Approve the things*] Or, try the things that differ, that ye be not cheated, and so undone, as many a man is by purchasing a counterfeit commodity at an unreasonable rate. A Bristol stone looks like a diamond, and many things glister besides gold.

Ver. 11. *Being filled with the fruits*] The excellency of a Christian is to follow God fully, as Caleb, Numb. xiv. 24; to have a heart full of goodness, as those, Rom. xv. 14 ; a life full of good works, as Tabitha, Acts ix. 33. See the note on Gal. v. 22.

Ver. 12. *Rather unto the furtherance*] So were Luther's troubles. *Quo magis illi furunt*, saith he, *eo amplius procedo*. The more they rage, the more the gospel spreadeth. It was a pleasant sight (saith one) to have beheld Christ and Antichrist striving for masteries. (Scultet. Annal.) For whatsoever the pope and the emperor attempted against the gospel, Christ turned it all to the furtherance of the gospel. The pope's bull, the emperor's thunderbolt, amazed not men, but animated them to embrace the truth ; weakened them not, but wakened them rather.

Ver. 13. *In all the palace*] So in the Diet held at Augsburgh in Germany, A. D. 1530. Cæsar reading the Protestants' confession, and sending it abroad to other Christian princes, as desiring their advice about it, dispersed and spread it more in all parts than all the Lutheran preachers could have done. For which cause Luther laughs agood at the foolish wisdom of the Papists, in a certain epistle of his to the elector of Saxony. When Bonner allowed William Hunter, martyr, no more than an half-penny a day in prison, he confessed that he lacked nothing, but had meat and clothing enough, yea, even out of the court, both money, meat, clothes, wood and coals, and all things necessary. What friends John Wicliff found, both in the court of England and in the court of Bohemia, is famously known ; and yet the proverb is,

Exeat aula qui velit esse pius—

Ver. 14. *Are much more bold*] This is the fruit of the saints' sufferings. *Ecclesia totum mundum sanguine et oratione convertit*, saith Luther. As the lily is increased by its own juice that flows from it, so is the Church by its sufferings. This caused Julian to spare some Christians whom he could have wished out of the world. I thank our Lord God (said Bp Ridley, in a letter of his to Bradford) that since I heard of our dear brother Rogers' departing, and stout confessing of Christ and his truth even unto death, my heart, blessed be God, rejoiced of it; neither ever since that time I have felt any lumpish heaviness, as I grant I have felt sometimes before. So Bradford in a letter to Cranmer, Latimer, and Ridley, prisoners at Oxford : Our dear brother Rogers hath broken the ice valiantly. As this day I think hearty Hooper, trusty Taylor, and sincere Saunders end their course and receive their crown. The next am I, which hourly look for the porter to open me the gates after them to enter into the desired rest. God forgive me mine unthankfulness for this exceeding great mercy.

Ver. 15. *Some indeed preach Christ*] Such self-seekers there are now-a-days not a few. Two things make a good Christian, good actions and good aims. Though a good aim doth not make a bad action good, as we see in Uzzah, yet a bad aim makes a good action bad, as in these preachers. They preached Christ, so did the devil, who yet was silenced by Christ, Mark i. 24, 25.

Ver. 16. Preach Christ of contention] Striving to bear away the bell from me, as the better preachers. And with such ambitionists the Church of Christ hath ever been pestered. This made Luther pray, *A doctore glorioso, et a pastore contentioso, liberet ecclesiam suam Dominus,* From vain-glorious and contentious preachers, the good Lord deliver his Church. This made Strigelius when he was on his death-bed bless God that now he should be freed *ab immanibus et implacabilibus odiis theologorum,* from the cruel and implacable hatreds of dissenting divines. (Melch. Ad. in Vit. Strig.) This drew that counsel from Luther to preachers, that they should see that those three dogs did not follow them into the pulpit,—Pride, covetousness, and envy.

Supposing to add affliction to my bonds] As immane cruelty, such as Job and David oft complain of, Job vi. 14; Psal. lxix. 26. Queen Elizabeth hated no less than did Mithridates, such as maliciously persecuted virtue forsaken of fortune, saith Camden.

Ver. 17. Knowing that I am set] κεῖμαι, or, laid by the heels. They of love help out at a dead-lift, and do my office abroad; as Marulla, a maid of Lemnos, seeing her father slain in the gate, took up his weapons, and not only revenged his death, but helped to keep out the Turks, who hoped to have surprised the city on the sudden.

Ver. 18. Christ is preached, &c.] *Prorsus Satan est Lutherus, sed Christus vivit, et regnat, Amen,* saith Luther in an epistle of his to Spalatinus : Luther is called a devil; but be it so, so long as Christ is magnified, I am well apaid. All private respects should be drowned in the glory of God. But he is a base-spirited man that is *totus in se,* like the snail, still within-doors, and at home. I would to God (saith Mr Dod) I were the worst minister in England; not wishing himself worse than he was, but other men better. Yea, Pedaretus, a heathen, a Lacedæmonian, when he was not chosen into the number of the three hundred counsellors of state, I thank thee, O God (said he), that thou hast given to this city so many men that are better than I am, and fitter to bear office.

Ver. 19. This shall turn to my salvation] God maketh all to co-operate, and turneth all about to the best; as the skilful apothecary maketh of a poisonful viper a wholesome triacle. See the note on Rom. viii. 28, and on Gen. l. 20.

And the supply of the Spirit] ἐπιχορηγία. Fresh supply of subsequent grace, as of the latter rain to the corn, and as the influence of the heavens to fruit-trees, without which they cannot bear, though they be fitted to bear fruit.

Ver. 20. According to my earnest] ἀποκαραδοκία, St Paul stood as it were on tiptoes to see which way he might best glorify God by life or by death.

Ver. 21. And to die is gain] Because death to a good man is the day-break of eternal bright-

ness, *janua vitæ, porta cœli,* as Bernard hath it, a valley of Achor, a door of hope to give entrance into Paradise, to bring them *malorum omnium ademptionem, bonorum omnium adeptionem.*

Ver. 22. What I shall choose, I wot not] As a loving wife sent for by her husband far from home, and yet loth to leave her children, is in a muse and doubt what to do, so was the apostle. He had *mortem in desiderio, et vitam in patientia* (as Fulgentius hath it), he rather endured life than desired it, he accepted it rather than affected it.

Ver. 23. For I am in a strait] Plato in the eighth of his laws hath a like speech, The communion of the soul with the body, κοινωνία ψυχῇ καὶ σώματι διαλύσεως οὐκ ἐστι κρείττων, is not better than the dissolution, as I would say if I were to speak in earnest. But whether Plato believed himself so saying, I have reason to make question, when I consider that his master Socrates, when he came to die, doubted whether it were better with the dead or with the living, as both Plato and Cicero testify.

Having a desire to depart] ἀναλῦσαι, to loose from the shore of life, and launch out into the main of immortality. Or it may be rendered, to return home, or to change rooms. A believer when he dieth, doth but *repatriasse* (as Bernard phraseth it), return home; he doth but change his place, and not his company, as dying Dr Preston said. He is ready to chide out his soul with *Quid hic facio?* as Monica, Austin's mother, did, What make I here so far from mine own country? or with an *Egredere o anima mea,* as Hilarion did, Go forth, O my soul, to Jesus thy bridegroom; haste, haste, haste to thine happy home. *Euge, Deo sit laus et gloria, quod jam mea instet liberatio, et horula gratissima,* said Graserus, when death was upon him : O blessed be God for this blessed hour. O what a happy change shall I now make from night to day, from darkness to light, from death to life, from sorrow to solace, from a factious world to a happy being! as Mr John Holland, a Lancashire minister, said, when he was even ready to depart. Oh wish heartily to die the death of these righteous; and let that be the unfeigned sense of thy soul, which Camerarius left in his will, should be written on his tombstone (Melch. Ad.) :

Vita mihi mors est, mors mihi vita nova est.

Life is to me a death, death's a new life.

Or that emortual of George Fabritius (Bucholcer Index Chronol.),

Σοὶ χάριν οἶδα Θεῷ εὐσπλάγχνῳ ὅς μ' ἐδίδαξας
Ἐν βιοτῇ τε θανεῖν, ἐν θανάτῳ δὲ βιοῦν.

Thanks to my gracious God, who doth me give, In life to die, and in death's hand to live.

And to be with Christ] This was all his song ever since he had been in the third heaven. So Mr Bolton, lying on his death-bed, said, I am by the wonderful mercies of God as full of comfort as my heart can hold, and feel nothing in my soul but Christ, with whom I heartily desire to be. (His Life by Mr Bagshaw.)

Which is far better] πολλῷ μᾶλλον κρεῖσσον, Far, far the better. A transcendent expression, such as is that 2 Cor. iv. 17. See the note there.

Ver. 24. *Is more needful for you*] Mr Bolton dying, and desiring to be dissolved, being told that it was indeed better for him to be with Christ, but the Church of God could not miss him, nor the benefit of his ministry, he thus replied with David, 2 Sam. xv. 25, 26, "If I shall find favour in the eyes of the Lord, he will bring me again, and show me both it and his habitation. But if otherwise, lo, here I am, let him do what seemeth good in his eyes." No man is born, much less born again, for himself, but for the benefit of many, as Bucer's physicians said to him, *Non sibi se, sed multorum utilitati esse natum,* that he was not born for himself, but for the good of God's Church; the welfare whereof he had zealously promoted. Dr John Reynolds being persuaded by his friends to give over his incessant pains in the Lord's work for his health's sake, finely answered out of Juvenal,

Et propter vitam vivendi perdere finem :

Nor yet, for love of life, lose that dare I
That is the main, care of community.

Ver. 25. *And joy of faith*] That is, for your full assurance, which is that highest degree of faith, whereby a believer having gotten victory over his doubtings, triumpheth with a large measure of joy.

Ver. 26. *That your rejoicing*] Gr. Your glorying or exulting in this, that God hath given me in, as an answer to your prayers. It is surely a sweet thing to hear from heaven. David often boasts of it, Psal. vi. and lxvi.

Ver. 27. *Only let your conversation*] *q. d.* If you would that God should hear you, and deliver me, be ready prepared for the receipt of such a mercy. The fountain of divine grace will not be laden at with foul hands, Psal. lxvi. 17. The leper's lips should be covered, according to the law.

Let your conversation] πολιτεύεσθε, your civil conversation, your common commerce, and interdealings with men also. Hippocrates took an oath of his followers to keep their profession unstained, and their lives unblameable.[1] When our life is contrary to our profession, it is a slander to the gospel; and it may be said of us, as a low countryman said to a gentleman that commended the Spaniards for their devotion and their often blessing and crossing themselves : No doubt, quoth he, they are holy men; crosses without, and the devil within.

Striving together for the faith] As the barons of Polonia professed to do, by their starting up at the reading of the Gospel, and drawing out their swords half way, in testimony that they would stick and stand to the defence of that truth to the very death. (A.D. 965, Jo. Funccius.) Help

the truth in necessity, strive with it, and for it. Say of it, as she did of the shield she gave her son going to the battle, ἢ τὰν ἢ ἐπὶ τὰν (Plutarch), Either bring this back, or be brought back upon it. Or, as the Black Prince's resolution in fight was, either to vanquish or perish. The serpent, they say, if he be so environed that he must of necessity pass through one of them, will sooner adventure upon the fire or flame than upon the shadow of the poplar tree. The mouse of Armenia will rather die than be defiled with any filth ; insomuch, as if her hole be besmeared with dirt, she will rather choose to be taken than to be polluted. Let us resolve either to live with the faith of the gospel, or to die for it. The Athenians bound their citizens by oath, to fight for defence of their religion both alone and with others. ἀμυνῶ δὲ καὶ ὑπὲρ ἱερῶν καὶ ὑπὲρ ὁσίων καὶ μόνος καὶ μετὰ πολλῶν.

Ver. 28. *And in nothing terrified*] πτυρόμενοι. A metaphor from horses, when they tremble and are sore affrighted. He that feareth God need fear none else, Psal. iii. But with the horse in Job xxxix. 22, he mocketh at fear, and is not affrighted ; neither turneth he back from the sword.

Ver. 29. *For unto you it is given*] As a high honour not only to believe (though that is a great matter ; for he that believeth hath set to his seal that God is true, hath given God a testimonial, such as is that Deut. xxxii. 4), but also (as a further favour) to suffer for his sake : this is the lowest subjection that can be to God, but the highest honour both to him and us. This made Latimer, after the sentence pronounced on him, cry out, "I thank God most heartily for this honour." Saunders said, "I am the unmeetest man for this high office that ever was appointed to it." "Such an honour it is," said Careless, martyr, "as the greatest angel in heaven is not permitted to have. God forgive me mine unthankfulness."

Ver. 30. *Which ye saw in me*] Acts xvi. 19, 23, 24, &c. See the notes there.

CHAPTER II.

Ver. 1. *If there be [therefore]* A most passionate obtestation, importing his most vehement desire of their good agreement ; whereunto he conjures them, as it were, by all the bonds of love betwixt him and them. Matters of importance must be pressed with utmost vehemence, Col. iii. 14. Love is charged upon us above all those excellent things there reckoned up.

If any comfort of love] As there is very much, making the saints to enjoy one another's society with spiritual delight, Psal. xvi. 3, and to communicate with gladness and singleness of heart, Acts ii. 46. The Lord doth usually and graciously water the holy fellowship of his people with the dews of many sweet and glorious re-

[1] ἅγιως καὶ ὁσίως τηρήσω καὶ τὸν βίον καὶ τὴν τέχνην ἐμὴν.

freshings; so that they have a very heaven upon earth, for kind the same with that above, and differing only in degrees.

If any bowels and mercies] *Ipsa suada, credo, si loqui posset, non potuisset, ἐμφατικοτέρως, ubi quot verba, tot tela*, &c., saith Dr Morton; that is, persuasion itself could not speak more persuasively, here are so many words, so many weapons, able to pierce and work upon any heart not possest with an iron sinew.

Ver. 2. *Being of one accord, of one mind*] Hereunto those many " ones " should move us mentioned by our apostle, Eph. iv. 4, 5. See the notes there, and on Acts iv. 32; they were of one heart. *Animo animaque inter se miscebantur*, saith Tertullian of those primitive Christians; yea, they were *una anima*, one soul (so Tremellius rendereth this text out of the Syriac), all informed with one and the same soul; all as one man, in the matters of God's worship.

Ver. 3. *Let nothing be done through strife*] These are those hell-hags that set the Church on fire, φιλονεικεία and φιλαρχία: if these men could be cast out of men's hearts, great hopes there were, πάντας εἰς τὸ θεῖον κήρυγμα ὁμοφώνως καὶ ὀρθοδόξως συνδραμεῖν, as Isidore hath it, that all men would soon consent in one and the same truth, and be at peace among themselves.

Let each esteem other better than themselves] *Non minus vere, quam humiliter*, as Bernard glosseth; because in some gift or other, at least in the measure or use, another may be better than us.

Ver. 4. *Look not every man*, &c.] Self is a great stickler, but must be excluded where love shall be maintained. He that is wholly shut up within himself is an odious person; and the place he lives in longs for a vomit to spew him out. It is his pleasure, his profit, and his preferment (saith one) that is the natural man's trinity; and his carnal self that is these in unity. Indeed it is that flesh that is the principal idol; the others are deified in the relation to ourselves.

Ver. 5. *Let this mind be in you*] We should strive to express Christ to the world, not as a picture doth a man in outward lineaments only, but as a child doth his father in affections and actions. Our lives should be as so many sermons upon Christ's life, 1 Pet. ii. 9.

Ver. 6. *To be equal with God*] Gr. Equals, that is, every way equal; not a secondary inferior God, as the Arians would have him. See the notes on John i. 1, 2, 3, 4. Hold fast this truth; it is of the foundation, it is the rock whereon the Church is built, Matt. xvi. 18; and all the devils in hell shall not wrest this place from me, for a clear proof of the Divinity of Christ, saith learned Calvin.

Ver. 7. *But made himself*, &c.] Gr. ἐκένωσεν, "emptied himself," suspended and laid aside his glory and majesty, and became a sinner both by imputation (for God made the iniquity of us all to meet upon him, Isa. liii. 6) and by reputation, for he was reckoned not only among

men, but among malefactors, ver. 9. Hence he is said to be sent in the likeness of sinful flesh, Rom. viii. 3.

And took upon him the form of a servant] Yea, of an evil servant, that was to be beaten.

In the likeness of men] Yea, he was a worm and no man, *nullificamen populi*, as Tertullian hath it. Christ vilified, nullified himself to the utmost, *ex omni seipsum ad nihil redegit*, as Beza expounds the former part of this verse, of everything he became nothing.

Ver. 8. *He humbled himself*] The Sun of righteousness went 10 degrees back in the dial of his Father, that he might come to us with health in his wings, that is, in his beams.

Became obedient unto death] That is, to his dying day, saith Beza. He went through many a little death all his life long, and at length underwent that cursed and painful death of the cross, his soul also being heavy to the death, Matt. xxvi., he suffered the insufferable wrath of God for a season. *Ne perderet obedientiam, perdidit vitam*, saith Bernard.

Ver. 9. *Wherefore God also*, &c.] "Wherefore" denoteth not the cause, but the order of Christ's exaltation, as a consequent of his sufferings, as some conceive.

Ver. 10. *That at the name*] Gr. In the name. The Papists stiffly defend the ceremony of bowing at the name of Jesus, to countenance the adoration of their deified images, altars, and their host; teaching in their pulpits, that Christ himself on the cross bowed his head on the right side, to reverence his own name, which was written over it.[1] But name is here put for person, bowing of the knee for inward subjection. It is taken out of Isa. xlv. 33.

Ver. 11. *And that every tongue*] The heathens were wont to say, *Mutus sit oportet qui non laudarit Herculem*. Let that tongue be tied up for ever that cries not out with David, *Vivat Dominus*, and with Luther, *Vivat et regnet Christus, Amen*.

Ver. 12. *Work out your salvation*] κατεργάζεσθε. The reason that men still tremble, and are still troubled with this doubt, and that fear, is, because their salvation is not wrought out, something is left undone and their conscience tells them so.

With fear and trembling] Opposed to carnal security. Those venturous bold spirits that dare live in any evil, so it stare not in their faces, and have not a heart fearful of the least evil, aspire not to immortality.

Ver. 13. *For it is God which worketh*] Therefore work out, &c. As *acti agentes, moti moventes*, as the inferior orbs move, as acted by the superior. When God hath turned, and doth touch us, we must move; and whilst the Spirit imbreathes us, we must turn about like the mill.

To will and to do] *Sub laudibus naturæ latent inimici gratiæ*, saith Augustine; who stood so much for grace, that the schoolmen say he yielded too little to free-will. That we live is

---

[1] Sir Edwin Sands in Spec. Europ.

the gift of the gods (saith Seneca) ; that we live well, is of ourselves. A base speech ! So Cicero (De Nat. Deor.), *Judicium hoc omnium mortalium est fortunam a Deo petendam, a seipso sumendam sapientiam.* For which impious sentence Augustine saith of him, *Eum, ut faceret homines liberos, fecisse sacrilegos.* (De Civ. Dei, 5.)

Ver. 14. *Without murmurings*] Gr. ὀργῆς, wrath and rancour, or discontent, which makes men's lips like rusty hinges seldom to move without murmuring and complaining.

And disputings] Or wranglings about trifles, niceties or novelties, things whereof we can have neither proof nor profit. Zanchy thus distinguisheth these two ; murmurings are secret complaints one of another, like to the grunting of hogs ; disputings are open contentions and quarrels.

Ver. 15. *Blameless and harmless*] Gr. ἀκέραιοι, hornless, or sincere, without mixture of deceit or guile, Israelites indeed.

The sons of God] Dignity enforceth duty. Remember that thou art a king's son, said he to Antigonus, and thou canst not do amiss.

Without rebuke] Ἀμώμητα, such as envy itself cannot justly tax, or fasten her fangs on. *Si Luthero faverem ut viro bono, quod fatentur et hostes,* &c., saith Erasmus, who yet loved him not. Luther is a good man, as his very enemies cannot but acknowledge. So Bucer, Bradford, Melancthon. Christians should excel others, standing as standard-bearers, higher than others, as Saul was by the head and shoulders ; being without blemish from head to foot, as Absalom ; fair to the eye and good to the taste, as the tree of knowledge, Gen. iii. 6.

In the midst of a crooked] As Noah was righteous in his generation ; as Joshua would serve Jehovah, though alone ; as David therefore loved God's testimonies, because other men kept not his law ; as Elijah amidst the Baalites cries, *Zelando zelavi ;* the worse they were, the better was he. Baruch kindled himself (*accendit seipsum,* Trem.) from other men's coldness, and quickened himself from other men's dulness, Neh. iii. 20.

As lights in the world] φωτῆρες, luminaries, great lights, such are the sun and moon, that give light to others. Some wicked have greater common gifts than the godly ; as many metals are brighter and more orient than the heavens : yet as those metals are not fit to convey the light of the sun, nay indeed they would stop it ; so neither are the wicked fit to shine the true light into us ; but Christ and Christians, those lights of the world. Such as Chrysostom was, whom Theodore styleth *eximium orbis terrarum luminare,* a famous light of the Church ; and others said, that the sunlight might better be spared than Chrysostom's preaching.

Ver. 16. *Holding forth the word*] ἐπέχοντες, as an ensign, or rather as the hand doth the torch, or the watch-tower the light, and so the haven to weather-beaten mariners.

Ver. 17. *Yea, and if I be offered*] Or, be poured out as a drink-offering upon the sacrifice, &c., to seal up my doctrine, whereby I have brought you to the obedience of faith. Bishop Ridley in a letter to Bishop Brooks of Gloucester, writeth thus : " As for the doctrine which I have taught, my conscience assureth me that it was sound and according to God's word, to his glory be it spoken ; the which doctrine, the Lord being my help, I will maintain, so long as my tongue shall wag, and breath is within my body, and in confirmation thereof seal the same with my blood."

Ver. 18. *For the same cause also,* &c.] The hearers' affections and endeavours should exactly answer to the affections and endeavours of the preacher, as the elders of Ephesus did, Acts xx. 31, 37 ; and as those religious Romans did, chap. vi. 17, and these Philippians, 2 Cor. viii. 5.

Ver. 19. *That I also may be of good comfort*] ἐμψυχῶ, that I may be inspirited. For when Silas and Timotheus were come from these Macedonians, Paul was pressed in spirit, and set vigorously upon the Lord's work, Acts xviii. 5.

Ver. 20. *Like-minded*] ἰσόψυχον, an *alter ego* to me. True friendship transformeth us into the condition of those we love, as Eusebius into his friend Pamphilus the martyr, whence he was called Eusebius Pamphili. *Amicitia sit tantum inter binos qui sunt veri, et bonos qui sunt pauci.* (Jerome.)

Ver. 21. *For all seek their own*] If it were so then, what wonder if now, as was so long since foretold, 2 Tim. iii. 2. Self must be shouldered out, and Christ's share studied more than our own ; all private interests let fall, and all self-respects drowned in the glory of God and the public good ; or else we want that pious ingenuity that becometh saints. It is said of Cato, that he did — *toti genitum se credere mundo,* That the care of the community lay upon him. (Lucan.) Timothy was of a choice and excellent spirit that naturally cared for the Churches' welfare ; few such now-a-days. See the note on ver. 3.

Ver. 22. *As a son with the father*] Happy son in such a father, 1 Tim. i. 2. If Jason the Thessalian held himself so happy in his tutor Chiron (Pindar. lib. 4, Pyth.), Alexander in his Aristotle, Paul in his Gamaliel, how much more was Timothy in Paul the aged, Philem. ver. 9, whose not only doctrine but manner of life he knew fully and followed faithfully, 2 Tim. iii. 10, as a diligent disciple !

Ver. 23. *So soon as I shall see*] For his life was now in suspense by reason of that roaring lion Nero, whom Tertullian wittily calleth *Dedicatorem damnationis Christianorum, quippe qui orientem fidem primus Romæ cruentavit.*

Ver. 24. *Shall come shortly*] Whether ever he did come or no we know not. *Fallitur augurio spes bona sæpe suo.* Good hopes are often frustrated. Howbeit the word here signifieth an " assured confidence ; " and is seldom or never used, but when the thing followeth, which thus is trusted.

Ver. 25. *Necessary to send to you*] It is not

meet that a pastor be long absent from his people. Moses was away but 40 days, and before he came again Israel had made them a golden calf. A godly minister when he is abroad is like a fish in the air; whereinto if it leap for recreation or necessity, yet it soon returns to his own element.

Ver. 26. For he longed after you] ἐπιποθῶν. The word signifieth such a vehement desire, as is impatient of delays. His heart was where his calling was.

And was full of heaviness] Gr. ἀδημονῶν, he was out of the world, as it were, and could not take comfort in any company.

Ver. 27. For indeed he was sick] Which should not have been, if St Paul could have cured him, as he did others. This shows that the apostles cured the sick, and did miracles, not by their own power, or at their own pleasure, &c.

But God had mercy on him] A great mercy it is to recover health, and highly to be prized. After sickness, offer to God the ransom of thy life, as they did, Exod. xxxi. Bless Jehovah thy physician, so he is called, Exod. xv. 26. Thus did David, Psal. ciii. 3. Thus Hezekiah, Isa. xxxvi. 9. Thus the very heathens, whose custom was after a fit of sickness to consecrate something to their gods.

But on me also] For it is a very sore affliction to lose a dear friend, which is as a man's own soul, Deut. xiii. 6, and is there set after brother, son, daughter, wife of a man's bosom, as dearer than all of them.

Lest I should have sorrow] God's care is that we suffer in measure, Isa. xxvii. 8; and according as we can, 1 Cor. x. 13. See the note there.

Ver. 28. That when ye see him] And receive him as risen from the dead. God knows how to commend his mercies to us, by threatening us with the loss of them; for *Bona a tergo formosissima*. We know best the worth of mercies by the want of them.

Ver. 29. Hold such in reputation] Or set a just price, a due estimate upon them. Horrible is the contempt that is now cast upon the ministry, by our novellers, as if they had learned of Campian to say, *Ministris eorum nihil vilius.*

Ver. 30. Not regarding his life] Gr. Ill providing for his life, casting away all inordinate care of it, as if he had put on that Roman resolution, *Necesse est ut eam, non ut vivam*, Needsly I must go, not needsly live.

CHAPTER III.

Ver. 1. Rejoice] Or farewell in the Lord. *Salutem in sospitatore.*

To write the same things to you] So 1 Cor. v. 9; John xv. 1—5. Some gather out of Matt. v. 1, with Luke vi. 20, that our Saviour preached the same sermon twice over. Men are dull to conceive, hard to believe, apt to forget, and slow to practise heavenly truths, and had therefore great need to have them much pressed, and often

inculcated. Neither let any cry out, *Occidit miseros crambe repetita magistros.* Surfeit not of God's manna, say not it is a light meat, because lightly come by, or the same again. Austin persuades the preacher so long to pursue and stand upon the beating and repeating of one and the same point, till by the gesture and countenance of the hearers he perceives that they understand and relish it. It was Melancthon's wish, that men did not only teach the same things, but *in iisdem verbis, in iisdem syllabis*, in the same words, in the same syllables. He himself went over the Epistle to the Romans 10 several times in his ordinary lectures. (Scultet. Annal.) Hippias liked not to have ἀεὶ ταὐτὰ, ever the same things; but Socrates desired to have οὐ μόνον ἀεὶ ταὐτὰ, ἀλλὰ καὶ περὶ τῶν αὐτῶν, not only always the same words, but about the very same matters; sith a good thing cannot be heard too often.

Ver. 2. Beware of dogs] That is, seducers and sectaries, who though dead dogs, yet will be barking at godly ministers. And though the dogs of Egypt would not move their tongues against Israel, Exod. xi. 7, yet these greedy dogs, Isa. vi., can both bark and bite better men than themselves, being set on by the devil. *Homines perfrictæ frontis*, impudent as dogs. Ravenous also when they get among the flocks, Ezek. xxii. 25. Further, they are crouching, colloguing creatures, 2 Tim. iii. 4: but believe them not; receive them not; for like dirty dogs they will but bemire you with fawning; yea, like cur-dogs, they will suck your blood with licking, and in the end kill you, and cut your throats without biting. Beware of them, therefore, beware, saith the apostle here.

Beware of evil workers] Deceitful workers, 2 Cor. xi. 13, that seem to build staircases for heaven, when indeed they dig descents down to hell, taking great pains to very evil purpose.

Beware of the concision] For circumcision; as Diogenes called Zeno's διατριβὴν κατατριβήν and Euclid's σχολὴν χολήν. (Laert.) The Holy Scriptures have many such elegant and pleasant passages, as Prov. xxv. 27; Hos. iv. 15; Gal. v. 12; Isa. v. 7, &c. There is one that senseth it thus, Beware of the concision, that is, of those that make divisions and cut the Church into little pieces, and sacking congregations, making separation. So Piscator, *Qui conantur vos ab ecclesia Dei rescindere*, who seek to sunder you from the Church. The Donatists affirmed that there were no true Churches but theirs, and were also divided among themselves, *in minutula frustula*, as Austin saith.

Ver. 3. For we are the circumcision] Such as have our luxuriancies lopped off, our unruly passions mortified, Col. ii. 11, casting them away as a wretched foreskin.

Ver. 4. Confidence in the flesh] That is, in external privileges, which yet profit not those that rest in them. An empty title yields but an empty comfort at last. God cares for no retainers, that only wear his livery but serve themselves. A man may go to hell with baptismal water on his face; yea, the sooner for his abused privileges.

Ver. 5. *A Hebrew of the Hebrews*] That is, by both father's and mother's side. Some think that hereby he argueth the ancientness of his stock and lineage, as being continued from Abraham, called the Hebrew; or from Eber. (Dr Airay.) *Sed genus et proavos, &c.* Of some ancient families it may be said as of some books, that they are *adorandæ rubiginis*, of more antiquity than authority or respect.

Ver. 6. *Concerning zeal*] A blind misguided zeal. See the note on Rom. x. 2. If zeal be not qualified with knowledge all will be on fire, as the *primum mobile*, they say, would be with its swift turning about, but for the countermotion of the lower spheres.

Ver. 7. *Loss for Christ*] Christ is to be sought and bought at any hand, at any rate. This is to play the wise merchant, Matt. xiii. 44—46. See the notes there. Esteem we Christ, as the people did David, 2 Sam. xviii. 3, more worth than ten thousand; as Naomi did Ruth, better than seven sons, Ruth iv. 15; as Pharaoh did Joseph, There is none so wise and worthy as thou, said he, Gen. xli. 39. Let burning, hanging, all the torments of hell befall me, *tantummodo ut Jesum nansciscar*, so that I may get my Jesus, said Ignatius. None but Christ, none but Christ, said Lambert, lifting up such hands as he had, and his fingers' ends flaming. We cannot buy this gold too dear. Paul is well content to part with a sky full of stars for one Sun of righteousness. Nazianzen put this price upon his Athenian learning (wherein he was very famous), that he had something of value to part with for Christ. So did Galeacius Caracciolus abandon all to enjoy the pure ordinances of Christ at Geneva. See that famous epistle written to him by Mr Calvin, prefixed before his Commentary on the First Epistle to the Corinthians.

Ver. 8. *And do count them but dung*] Dog's dung (as some interpret the word σκύβαλα, *quasi* κυσίβαλα), or dog's meat, coarse and contemptible. Paul's sublime spirit counts all dung, yet is content, for Christ, to be counted the off-scouring of all things.

Ver. 9. *And be found in him*] Out of whom all are lost in the wilderness of worldly lusts, and woefully wander; yet not so wide, as to miss of hell. Paul's desire is therefore to be found in Christ, at such time as he is sought for by the justice of God, to be brought to condign punishment.

Ver. 10. *And may know him*] Not notionally only (for so a man may do out of every catechism) but practically; not apprehensively only, but affectively; not with that knowledge that is *cognoscitiva*, only standing in speculation, but that is *directiva vitæ*, as the apostle here expounds himself. A natural man may have a disciplinary knowledge of Christ, that is, by hear-say, as a blind man hath of colour, not an intuitive, *i. e. per speciem propriam, &c.*

Ver. 11. *I might attain to the resurrection*]

That is (by a metonymy of the subject for the adjunct), that perfection of holiness that accompanieth the estate of the resurrection. True grace never aims at a pitch, but aspireth to perfection. It is a low and unworthy strain in some to labour after no more grace than will keep life and soul together, that is, soul and hell asunder (as one speaketh). But that man for heaven, and heaven for him, that sets up for his mark the resurrection of the dead, that would be as perfect now as the glorified saints shall be at the day of judgment.

Ver. 12. *But I follow after*] Gr. Διώκω, I persecute, I follow hot-foot with utmost eagerness. By this then he signifieth how greedily and incessantly he pursued after the perfect knowledge of Christ, having it as it were in chase, and resolved not to rest till he had attained unto it. (Airay.) Well might Chrysostom call St Paul an insatiable, greedy, devouring worshipper of God.

Ver. 13. *I count not myself*] *Si dixisti satis est, periisti.* Satiety is a dangerous disease, and the next step to a declension. The eagle's emblem is *sublimius;* the sun's *celerius*, Psal. xix. 3; the wheat's *perfectius*, Mark iv. 28; Ezekiel's *profundius*, chap. xlvii. 4; Christ's *superius*, Luke xiv. 10; and Paul's *ulterius*.

Reaching forth] ἐπεκτεινόμενος, straining and stretching out head and hands and whole body to lay hold on the mark or prize proposed. A manifest metaphor from runners in a race, *qui caput, totumque corpus, et vires exerunt, ac præcipites ad scopum ruunt*, who throw themselves forward like a dart, and stretch out their arms to take hold of the mark. *Prono et quasi præcipiti corpore ferri ad scopum.* (Beza a Lapide.)

Ver. 14. *I press toward, &c.*] The ark of the covenant was but a cubit and a half high; so were likewise the wheels of the caldron. Now we know that a cubit and a half is but an imperfect measure, which shows (saith one) that no man in this life is perfectly perfect. Let us strive to perfection, as Paul did; and then, *Summum culmen affectantes, satis honesti vel in secundo fastigio conspiciemur.* A man may fully fall in with the forwardest followers of Jesus Christ, and yet fall short of perfection. It is with Christians (saith Columel well) as with Jonathan's signal arrows, two fell short, and but one beyond the mark; so where one shoots home to the mark of the high calling in Christ, many fail of it.

Ver. 15. *As many as be perfect*] Comparatively, or conceitedly so.

God shall reveal] Several measures of knowledge and holiness are given to the saints at several times. We are narrow-mouthed vessels, and cannot receive all at once. "Whither I go thou canst not follow me now; but thou shalt follow me afterwards," John xiii. 36. See the notes there.

Ver. 16. *Let us walk by the same rule*] To wit, of the word; and then you may say, Lord, if I be deceived, thou hast deceived me. Or it may be rendered thus, Let us proceed by one rule; for the word στοιχῶμεν is military, and signifies to go on in order, according to the general's commands; who else may justly punish our prosperous disobediences, our disorderly successes.

Ver. 17. *Be followers together of me*] *Longum iter per præcepta, brevius per exempla.* Everything in a minister should be exemplary, τύπος. We must propound to ourselves the highest pitch and the best patterns of perfection; even those of most raised parts and graces, of unwearied industry in services, and undaunted magnanimity in suffering; follow the forwardest Christians with a desire to overtake them; dwell upon their exemplary lives till ye be changed into the same image.

Ver. 18. *And now tell you weeping*] *Non tam atramento quam lachrymis chartas inficiebat Paulus.*[1] Paul was a man of many tears, and might well say here, as Master Fox concludes the story of Lady Jane Grey, *Tu quibus illa legas incertum est, Lector ocellis; Ipse quidem siccis scribere non potui.*

Ver. 19. *Whose god is their belly*] A scavenger, whose living is to empty, is to be preferred before him that liveth but to fill privies; as they do that make their gut their god, that dunghill deity. Such a one was that Pamphagus, Nabal, Dives, and others, that digested in hell what they ate on earth. They say the locust is all belly, which is joined to his mouth and endeth at his tail. The spider also is little else than belly. The dolphin hath his mouth almost in his very belly; the ass-fish hath his heart in his belly. (Solinus. Aristot.) *In mea patria Deus venter est, et in diem vivitur.* In my country (saith Jerome) their belly is their god, they live from hand to mouth, &c. Epicurus said, that eternal life was nothing else but an eternal eating and drinking; ὥστε πάντα χρόνον διάγειν μεθύοντας. See my Common-place of Abstinence.

Who mind earthly things] As they have their hands elbow-deep in the world, so their minds are shut in their chests, as dead bodies are buried in coffins; they are interred in the Golgotha of this world, as moles in their hillocks.

Ver. 20. *For our conversation*] Our civil conversation, or our burgess-ship, while we live by heaven's laws, and go about our earthly businesses with heavenly minds; this a carnal man cannot skill of.[2] A fly cannot make that of a flower that a bee can do. There is a generation whose names are written in the earth, Jer. xvii. 13; these make earth their throne, heaven their footstool, Isa. lxvi. 1, and are loth to die, because they have treasures in the field. But the saints, though their commoration be on earth, yet their conversation is in heaven; as the pearl grows in the sea, but shines in the sky; as stars, though seen sometimes in a puddle, yet have their situation in heaven; as a wise man may sport with children, but that is not his main business. *Corpore am-*

bulamus in terra corde habitamus in cœlo, saith Austin. Our bodies are on earth, our hearts in heaven (as his was that did even eat and drink and sleep eternal life). We live by the same laws as saints and angels in heaven do. If Satan offer us outward things in a temptation (as he did Luther a cardinalship), we send them away from whence they came, as Pelican sent back the silver bowl (which the bishop had sent him for a token) with this answer, *Astricti sunt quotquot Tiguri cives et inquilini, bis singulis annis, solenni juramento, &c.* We, the citizens and inhabitants of Zurich, are twice a year solemnly sworn to receive no gift from any foreign prince; so we, the citizens of heaven, are bound by solemn and sacred covenants not to accept of Satan's cut-throat kindnesses. *Serpens ille capite blanditur, ventre oblectat, cauda ligat.* (Rupert.)

—*Timeo Danaos et dona ferentes.*

We like not the devil's donatives.

Ver. 21. *Like unto his glorious body*] Which is the standard. See the notes on 1 Cor. xv. Now we may say to our souls as he did to his, *O anima, quam deforme hospitium nacta es?* Poor soul, what an ill lodging-room hast thou got! But at the resurrection all shall be mended. Then these vile bodies shall shine as the sun, and be so clear and transparent, that all the veins, humours, nerves, and bowels shall be seen as in a glass, saith Aquinas, that the soul may sally out at every part, and sparkle through the body as the wine through the glass, saith another author. Three glimpses of glory were seen, 1. In Moses' face; 2. In Christ's transfiguration; 3. In Stephen's countenance.

CHAPTER IV.

Ver. 1. *Dearly beloved and longed for*] WHAT heart-melting language is here! Ministers must woo hard for Christ, and speak fair, if they will speak to purpose: "though I might be much bold in Christ to enjoin thee, yet for love's sake I rather beseech thee," Philem. 8, 9. How oft are men fain to sue for that which is their own; and how heart-glad if by fair entreaties they can gather up their debts!

Ver. 2. *I beseech Euodias*] A couple of disagreeing sisters, whom the apostle seeketh to reconcile, and it was a wonder if they could resist his rhetoric. O that I could but once find you together one (said Austin of the differences between Jerome and Ruffinus); I would fall down at your feet with much love and many tears; I would beseech you for yourselves, and one another, and for weak Christians' sake who are offended thereat, you would not suffer those dissensions to spread, &c. *Hei mihi qui vos alicubi reperire non possum, &c.*

Ver. 3. *And I entreat thee also*] All men should contribute their help to the composing of differ-

---

[1] Lotin in Acts xxii. 19.

[2] πολίτευμα. *Ut municipes cœlorum nos gerimus. Sic reddit Piscator.*

ences, and bring their buckets, as it were, to quench this unnatural fire, when once kindled.

True yoke-fellow] Not Paul's wife (for he had none, 1 Cor. vii. 7), but either the husband of one of the fore-mentioned women, or some special and principal pastor at Philippi.

Which laboured with me in the gospel] Not by preaching, but by partaking of the combats and difficulties that I there underwent, with masculine spirits. *Significatur certamen, quale est athletarum*, saith Estius. In these good women, besides their sex, there was nothing woman-like or weak.

Ver. 4. *Rejoice in the Lord*] That is the true and only joy (said Mr Philpot the martyr), which is conceived not of the creature, but of the Creator; to this all other joys being compared are but mournings, all delights sorrows, all beauty filth, &c. Other joy besides this may wet the mouth, but not warm the heart; smooth the brow, but not fill the breast.

And again I say, Rejoice] No duty almost more pressed in both Testaments than this of rejoicing in the Lord. It is no less a sin not to rejoice than not to repent.

Ver. 5. *Let your moderation*] Or equality, such as was that of David, Psal. xxvi. 12. The scales of his mind hung equal, giving him liberty in all occurrences to enjoy himself. All immoderations are enemies to health; so they are also to the quietness of the mind. (Hippocrates.) Against these (as against poisons) there be two kinds of antidotes, prayer and patience, the one hot, the other cold, the one quenching, the other quickening. The word τὸ ἐπιεικὲς, here used by the apostle, properly signifieth moderation in law businesses, or in laying claim to a man's own right, the preferring of equity before extremity (Arist. Ethic. v. 10), as holding utmost right to be utmost wrong. *Summum jus summa injuria.* Austin tells us that it was grown to a proverb among his countrymen, *Ut habeas quietum tempus, perde aliquid.* For a quiet life, part with some part of thy right, as Abraham did, Gen. xiii. 9.

The Lord is at hand] To right you and recompense you, to pay you for all your pains and patience. *Judex pro foribus*, saith St James, chap. v. 9.

Ver. 6. *In nothing be careful*] Or care for nothing, viz. with a care of diffidence and distrust. See the note on Matt. vi. 25, 26, &c.

But in everything by prayer] This is the best cure of care. "Cast thy burden" (or thy request) "upon the Lord," saith David, Psal. lv. 22, "and he shall sustain thee." Remove thy trouble from thyself to God by virtue of that writ or warrant, and then all shall be well. "They looked unto God, and were lightened," Psal. xxxiv. 5. Luther in a certain epistle of his to Melancthon complaineth thus: *Ego certe oro pro te, et doleo te pertinacissimam curarum hirudinem meas preces sic irritas facere:* I pray for thee, but to no purpose so long as thou givest so much way to carking cares.

Supplication with thanksgiving] We should come to pray with our thanks in our hands, standing ready with it, as Joseph's brethren stood with their present, Gen. xliii. 25. In the old law, what special request soever they had to make, or what sacrifice soever to offer, they were commanded still to come with their peace-offerings. Prayer goes up without incense when without thankfulness. The Church ascends daily to her beloved Christ in these pillars of smoke, Cant. iii. 6, for she knows that unthankfulness hindereth much the restful success of prayer. And the apostle seemeth here to hint that God taketh no notice of their prayers that do not withal give thanks.

Ver. 7. *And the peace of God*] Prayer hath *virtutem pacativam.* "Acquaint thyself with God and be at peace," Job xxii. 21. Pray, "that your joy may be full," John xvi. 24. David prays down his distempers, Psal. vi. and cxvi., and then cries out, "Return to thy rest, O my soul;" he rocks himself asleep in this sort; and sets all to rights oft-times, even then when his heart was more out of tune than his harp. Would you then have that peace of God, that most precious jewel that ever the heart of man was acquainted with? do as you are here advised: 1. Pray for that you want, and give thanks for that you have: (a sacrifice of praise is called a "pay-offering," or a "peace-offering," because peace ensues upon it.) 2. Be always doing something that is good, as ver. 8, 9, for as every flower hath its sweetness, so every good union hath its comfort. This is so true, that very heathens (upon the discharge of a good conscience) have found comfort and peace answerably. How boldly did Abimelech bear himself upon his integrity; and what a blessed composedness had holy Noah, who was righteous in his generation, and therefore *sat mediis tranquillus in undis.*

Shall keep your hearts] φρουρήσει, keep as with a guard, or as in a garrison. Solomon's bed was not so well guarded with his threescore valiant men, all holding swords, Cant. iii. 7, 8, as each good Christian is by the power of God without him and the peace of God within him. This peace, like David's harp, drives away the evil spirit of cares and fears; it soon husheth all. God can soon raise up in his an army of powerful thoughts and meditations, so as their very inward tranquillity arising from the testimony of a good conscience (called here, their minds), and the sweet sabbath of spirit, the composedness of their affections (called here, their hearts), can make and keep them secure and sound, yea, bring aid when they are close besieged by sin and Satan.

Ver. 8. *Whatsoever things are true*] This is that little Bible, as the eleventh to the Hebrews is by one fitly called a little Book of Martyrs. In this one verse is comprised that *Totum hominis*, Eccles. xii. 13; that *Bonum hominis*, Micah vi. 8. For if ye do these things here enjoined, ye shall never fall, but go gallantly into heaven, as St Peter hath it, 2 Pet. i. 10, 11.

Ver. 9. *And heard, and seen in me*] *Est aliquid quod ex magno viro vel tacente proficias.* The very sight, nay thought, of a good man oft doth good. Whereas the tongue or heart of a wicked man "is little worth," Prov. x. 20. If their thoughts and discourses were distilled, they are so frothy they would hardly yield one drop of true comfort.

And the God of peace] "Not only the peace of God," as ver. 7. Austin somewhere fisheth a mystery out of the word *pax*, which consisteth of three letters, saith he, to note the Trinity, from whom is all true peace. Others have observed that all the letters in Jehovah are *quiescent*, letters to teach the same truth.

Ver. 10. *Hath reflourished*] Ανεθάλετο. It had deflourished then for a season, and withered, as an oak in winter, Isa. vi. 13, and as a teil-tree whose sap is in the root. The best tree may have a fit of barrenness. So may the best men suffer some decays for a season; the spiritual life may run all to the heart, as a people conquered in the field runs to the castle. Howbeit, as Eutychus's life was in him still, and he revived, though he seemed to be dead, and as trees in the spring grow green again, so do the relapsed saints.

Ver. 11. *In respect of want*] The wicked in the fulness of his sufficiency is in straits, Job xx. 22. Contrariwise, the godly man in the midst of his straits is in a sufficiency. "He hath all things," as having the haver of all things.

For I have learned] In Christ's school, for nature teacheth no such lesson.

Optat ephippia bos piger, optat arare caballus.
Horat.

The labourers were not content with their penny, Matt. xx. 13. They that have enough to sink them, yet have not enough to satisfy them, as a ship may be over-laden with gold and silver, even unto sinking, and yet have compass and sides enough to hold ten times more. It is God only that fills the heart, and maketh a man say truly with Jacob, and not feignedly, as Esau, I have enough, my brother. Esau had a deal, but Jacob had all, because he had the God of all (*Rabb-li, Col-li*, Gen. xxxiii. 9, 11).

Ver. 12. *I know both how, &c.*] Sound bodies can bear sudden alternations of heat and cold: so cannot distempered bodies.

Both how to be abased] So Chilo (one of the seven wise men of Greece) said to his brother, who took it ill that he was not chosen to be one of the judges, I know how to be injuriously dealt with; but I hardly believe him.[1] Socrates also could tell Archelaus, that offered him large revenues, My mind and mine estate are matches.[2] But flesh and blood could never carry him so far, for all his saying so. It is God alone that fashioneth a man's heart to his estate, Psal. xxxiii. 15, as a suit of clothes is fitted to the body.

I am instructed] μεμύημαι, I am initiated; I am a young scholar, newly entered in this high point of heavenly learning of Christian practice. I have entered into religion, as it were, I have consecrated myself (the word is wondrous significant) and am religiously taught it; I see it is a mystery, but I have got the mastery of it.

To suffer want] Either patiently to wait for what I desire, or contentedly to want what God denieth.

Ver. 13. *I can do all things*] A Christian walks about the world like a conqueror, having power given him over all, Rev. ii. 26, 27. It was a vain brag of that heathen prince that caused it to be engraven upon his tombstone, πάντα ποιεῖν ἐδυνάμην, I could do all things. (Cyrus Major. Arrian.) None can say so but the man in Christ, without whom also he himself can do nothing, John xv. 5. Suffer nothing, as the word ἰσχύω here used properly signifieth.

Ver. 14. *Ye have well done*] For hereby as you have sealed up your love to me, and engaged me to pray for you (as for Onisephorus, 2 Tim. i. 18), so you have gotten a good testimony to yourselves that ye are members of Christ's mystical body. The tongue is far enough from the toe, the heel from the head, yet when the toe or heel is hurt, the rest of the members sympathize and seek help for it. So here.

Ver. 15. *But ye only*] One poor Philippian shamed a hundred close-fisted Corinthians. Araunah gave like a king, 2 Sam. xxiv. 23, and is therefore crowned and chronicled: Zech. ix. 7, "Ekron shall be as the Jebusite," that is, as this famous Jebusite Araunah, that parted with his freehold for pious uses. (Tremel.)

Ver. 16. *Ye sent once and again*] Charity's fountain runs fresh, *More perennis aquæ*, and is never dried up. "The liberal man deviseth liberal things," and holdeth that only his own that he hath given to others. *Hoc habeo quodcunque dedi*, saith Seneca (De Ben. vi. 3).

Ver. 17. *Not because I desire a gift*] As those cormorants that "with shame do love, Give ye," Hos. iv. 18, as if they could speak no other but the Doric dialect, the horse-leech's language. St Paul was none of these.

That may abound to your account] For God keeps an exact account of every penny laid out upon him and his, that he may require it; and his retributions are more than bountiful.

Ver. 18. *I have all*] viz. That you sent, and I give you an acquittance, which the Greeks, from the word ἀπέχω here used, call Αποχή. Compare Prov. iii. 37.

I abound, I am full] As a bird with a little eye, and the advantage of a wing to soar with, may see far wider than an ox with a greater; so the righteous with a little estate, joined with faith and devotion, may feel more comfort and see more of God's bounty than one of vast possessions, whose heart cannot lift itself above the earth. They say, it is not the great cage that maketh the bird sing. Sure we are, it is not the great estate that brings always the inward joy, the cordial contentment. A staff may help a travel-

---

[1] Εγὼ μεν ἐπίσταμαι ἀδικεῖσθαι. Laert.

[2] Arrian. *apud Stobæum*.

ler, but a bundle of staves may be a burthen to him. The greatest thing in the least compass, saith one, is a contented mind in a man's body; which if a man have, *deliciosius vivit etiam is qui teruntium non habet, quam si in unum hominem confles sexcentos Sardanapalos*, he hath all things, though he want everything.

Ver. 19. *But my God*] Whom I serve as an ambassador in bonds, Ephes. vi. 20, and therefore surely he will repay you the sums you have sent me.

Shall supply] Gr. πληρώσει, shall fill up, as he did the widow's vessels: Shut the doors upon thee, saith the prophet, 2 Kings iv. 4. It was time to shut the doors, when one little vessel must overflow and fill up many greater.

According to his riches in glory] All God's supplies to his come tipped and gilt with a glory upon them, saith one. Providences below, graces within, heaven above; as they have a lovely scarlet blush of Christ's blood upon them; so they are rayed upon with a beam of divine love to them that are in Christ.

Ver. 20. *Now unto God*] Paul cannot mention God's bounty without a doxology.

Ver. 21. *Every saint*] A great encouragement to the meaner to be so respected.

Ver. 22. *All the saints salute you*] Christianity is no enemy to courtesy. God's scholars are taught better manners than to neglect so much as salutations.

They that are of Cæsar's household] When Cæsar himself lived and died an unconverted caitiff and a cast-away. So did Seneca, for aught we can find by his writings, though some would have him to be here designed among the rest. See the note on Rom. i. 18.

Ver. 23. *The grace of our Lord*] With this wish of grace, grace to them, he both begins and ends. Wisdom is the principal thing, Prov. iv. 7.

THE EPISTLE OF ST PAUL TO THE COLOSSIANS.

CHAPTER I.

Ver. 1. *Paul an apostle, &c.*] THIS golden Epistle is an epitome, as it were, of that other to the Ephesians; like as that he writeth to the Galatians is an abstract of that other to the Romans.

Ver. 2. *Which are at Colosse*] A city in Phrygia, swallowed up by an earthquake not long after this Epistle was written. God's judgments are sometimes secret, but ever just. It may be that these Colossians, being led away with the error of those false teachers (who sought to entangle them with many pharisaical observations and philosophical speculations, chap. ii.), had fallen from their own stedfastness, 2 Pet. ii. 17, had suffered a heart-quake, being shaken in mind, 2 Thess. ii. 2, and were sucked in by the whirlpool of divers and strange doctrines, μὴ περιφέρεσθε, Heb. xiii. 9. I affirm nothing, but God sometimes speaks from heaven against heretics: as he did against Arius, Nestorius, Stephen Langton, Stephen Gardner, Arminius (who craftily revived the Pelagian heresy), all which died miserably; that I speak not of those two monsters in New England brought forth by Mistress Hutchinson and Mistress Dyer, and the fearful end that the former of these two women came to, being burnt with her family by the savages of that country. *Aliorum perditio tua sit cautio.* Christ will have all the Churches know, Rev. ii. 23, that he is jealous of his glory, and will revenge the quarrel of his covenant. Those primitive Churches sinned away their light, and are therefore now given up to darkness. *Infatuati seducebantur, et seducti judicabantur*, saith Austin; that is, being infatuated, they were seduced; and being seduced, they were justly punished. (Melancth.) They were first overspread with Arianism, and therefore now with Mahometism, which is nothing else but *Arii stercus*, the odour of Arius, as one rightly calleth it.

Ver. 3. *We give thanks—praying, &c.*] Prayer and thanks (saith one) are like the double motion of the lungs; the air that is sucked in by prayer is breathed out again by thanks.

Ver. 4. *And of the love, &c.*] Faith in Christ Jesus maketh love to all the saints. Therefore they go commonly coupled in Paul's Epistles. And therefore when the disciples heard how oft they must forgive an offending brother, "Lord, increase our faith," say they, Luke xvii. 5. See the note there.

Ver. 5. *For the hope*] It is hope (saith an interpreter here) that plucks up the heart of a man to a constant desire of union by faith with God and of communion by love with man. But by "hope" is here meant the "object of hope."

Ver. 6. *As it is in all the world*] Eusebius saith that the gospel spread at first through the world like a sun-beam, Ἀθρόως οἶα τὶς ἡλίου βολὴ. The reformation begun by Luther in Germany went on abroad Christendom, as if had been carried upon angels' wings. That of the Church of England is such as former ages despaired of, the present admireth, and the future shall stand amazed at. It is that miracle, saith one, which we are in these times to look for. (Spec. Europ.)

Ver. 7. *Who is for you a faithful minister*]

Epaphras was their city-preacher; whom therefore the apostle here so highly commendeth. Luther is much blamed by his best friends for opposing and disparaging Carolostadius among his own charge at Orlamund, A.D. 1524. (Scultet. Annal.) A faithful minister should have all good respect, before his own people especially.

Ver. 8. *Who also declared unto us*] His heart was over-joyed with his people's forwardness, and he could not but impart it to the apostle. It was a pride in Montanus to over-ween his Pepuza and Tymium, two pelting parishes not far from Colosse, and to call them Jerusalem, as if they had been the only churches in the world. But this was a commendable practice of Epaphras to relate to St Paul the good he found in his people, that he by an Epistle might further encourage and quicken them.

Ver. 9. *In all wisdom and spiritual*] See the note on Ephes. i. 8, where you have the same expression. And indeed this Epistle hath many passages common with that, and seemeth to have been written soon after that, *cum adhuc quæ ad Ephesios scripserat, in animo hærerent*, while the things that he had written to the Ephesians were yet fresh in his mind and memory. (Grotius.)

Ver. 10. *That ye might walk worthy*] By walking before God, with God, after God, according to God, as it is phrased in several Scriptures, all to one purpose. See the note on Ephes. iv. 1.

Unto all pleasing] As Enoch walked with God, and thereby got this testimony, that he "pleased God," Heb. xi. 5. So David did all his wills, and was therefore a "man after his heart," Acts xiii. 22. The many alls here used in the 9th, 10th, and 11th verses show that he that will please God must be a "throughout Christian." Now he, and only he, is such, whose whole nature is elevated by the spirit of grace; and all whose principles, practices, and aims are divine and supernatural.

Ver. 11. *And long-suffering with joyfulness*] The joy of the Lord is the strength of the soul, Nehem. viii. 10, as true gold comforts and strengthens the heart, that alchemy doth not. At the death of Francis Gamba, a Lombard, that suffered martyrdom, the friars brought in their hands a cross for him to behold, to keep him from desperation at the feeling of the fire. But his mind, he said, was so replenished with joy and comfort in Christ, that he needed neither their cross nor them.

Ver. 12. *Of the saints in light*] So that though cast into a dark dungeon, the saints may clap their hands upon their bosoms, as Œcolampadius upon his death-bed did, and say, *Hic sat lucis*, Here within is plenty of divine light.

Ver. 13. *And hath translated us*] A word taken from those that plant colonies, and cause the people to translate their dwellings into another country, μετέστησεν. (Bishop Davenant.)

From the power of darkness] Every natural man is under the power of darkness, nay, of the devil, Acts xxvi. 18, as the malefactor that goes bound and pinioned up the ladder is under the power of the executioner. Imagine (saith one) a man driven out of the light by devils; where he should see nothing but his tormentors, and that he were made to stand upon snares and gins with iron teeth ready to strike up and grind him to pieces, and that he had gall poured down to his belly, and an instrument raking in his bowels, and the pains of a travailing woman upon him, and a hideous noise of horror in his ears, and a great giant with a spear running upon his neck, and a flame burning upon him round about. Alas, alas, this is the state of every one that is out of Christ, as these places show, whence these comparisons are taken, Job xviii. 7, 8; xx. 24, 15; xv. 20, 21, 26, 30.

Ver. 14. *Even the forgiveness, &c.*] See the note on Matt. i. 21. Sin is the greatest evil; as that which sets us farthest from God the chiefest good; and as that which procureth and embittereth all other evils that befall us. Christ therefore redeemeth his "Israel from their iniquities," Psal. cxxx. 8; he crosseth out of God's debt-book the black lines of their sins with the red lines of his own blood, and so "redeemeth his Israel out of all their troubles," Psal. xxv. 22.

Ver. 15. *Who is the image*] The express image of his person, Heb. i. 2. Milk is not so like milk as this Son is like the Father. By whom also God (otherwise invisible) is manifested to us. And here, he that would see God must set the eyes of faith upon the manhood of Christ; for he "that seeth the Son, seeth the Father." When a man looketh into a crystal-glass, it casteth no reflex to him; but put steel upon the back of it, it will cast a reflex. So put the humanity (as a back of steel) to the glass of the God-head, and it casteth a comfortable reflex to us. As without this, if we look upon God, we see indeed some small sparks of his glory to terrify and amaze us; but in Christ (God and man) we behold the lively and express face of God; not any more as a fearful and terrible Judge, but a most gracious and loving Father to comfort and refresh us.

The first-born of every creature] As being begotten of the substance of the Father, after a wonderful manner, before all beginnings, and as being the heir of all his Father's goods. And so this text is parallel to that Heb. i. 2.

Ver. 16. *For by him were all things*] This is a high praise to Christ, Rev. iv. 11. See the note on John i. 3.

Whether they be thrones or dominions] *i. e.* angels with their several degrees or dignities. But what difference there is between these four words, let them tell us that are able (saith Austin), so they prove what they tell us; for my part, I confess I know it not.

Ver. 17. *By him all things consist*] They would soon fall asunder, had not Christ undertaken to uphold the shattered condition thereof, by the word of his power.

Ver. 18. *And he is the head*] See the note on Eph. i. 22. Angels are under Christ as a head of government, of influence, of confirmation, not of redemption, as we. (Elton.)

The first-born from the dead] *sc.* of those that rise to eternal life. Others rose, but to die again, and by virtue of his resurrection; as the first-born among the Jews communicated his good things to his brethren.

Ver. 19. *In him should all fulness*] In a vessel or treasury an emptiness may follow a fulness: not so here. See the note on John i. 14.

Ver. 20. *To reconcile all things*] That is, all the saints, who are worth all, better than all, more worth than a world of wicked men, Heb. xi. 38. The Jews have a saying, that those seventy souls that went with Jacob into Egypt, were as much as all the seventy nations in the world. What account God maketh of them in comparison of others, see Isa. xliii. 3, 4.

Ver. 21. *Enemies in your mind*] Haters of God, Rom. i. 30, and so, God-slayers, 1 John iii. 15. *Omne peccatum est Deicidium.*

Ver. 22. *To present you holy and unblameable*] By his righteousness imputed and imparted; though most interpreters expound this text of sanctification, and not of justification or future perfection.

Ver. 23. *If ye continue in the faith*] All the promises are made to perseverance in grace. He that continueth to the end shall be saved. Be faithful to the death, and thou shalt have a crown of life. Matt. xxiv. 13; Rev. ii. 10. But *fugitivo nulla corona;* if any withdraw he falleth into hell-mouth, Heb. x. 39.

Grounded and settled] When faith bears fruit upward, it will take root downward, and make a man as a tree by the river's side, and not as the chaff in the fan, Psal. i. 3, 4, or as the boat without ballast.

Preached to every creature] That is, to every reasonable creature, Mark xvi. 15. Though to many we preach to no more purpose than Bede did when he preached to a heap of stones: these are unreasonable creatures, 2 Thess. iii. 2.

Ver. 24. *And fill up that which is behind*] Christ suffered much for Paul; it is but meet therefore that Paul should suffer somewhat for Christ. All our troubles are but the slivers and chips, as it were, of his cross.[1] When the Jews offered our Saviour gall and vinegar, he tasted it, but would not drink. He left the rest for his Church, and they must pledge him, not to expiate sin, but for their trial and exercise.

Of the afflictions of Christ] That is (say some), of the Church; the afflictions whereof are said to be the afflictions of Christ, by reason of the sympathy between the head and the members, Acts ix. 4; 2 Cor. i. 5; Heb. xi. 26.

For his body's sake] For the confirmation of men's minds in the truth of the gospel.

Ver. 25. *According to the dispensation*] What a horrid blasphemy therefore is that of the Jesuits, who stick not to tell the people in their pulpits that St Paul was not secure of his preaching, but by conference with St Peter, nor that he durst publish his Epistles till St Peter had allowed them! (Spec. Europ.)

[1] ὑστερήματα, *non* προτερήματα

Ver. 26. *But now is made manifest*] God hath now opened his whole heart to his saints, Rev. xi. 3. See the note on Rom. vi. 25, and on Matt. iv. 16.

Ver. 27. *The hope of glory*] All the saints are said to worship in the altar, because they place all their hope of life in Christ's death alone.

Ver. 28. *Whom we preach*] Ministers do not only preach of Christ, but preach Christ, that is, they give what they speak of. As the manna came down in the dew, so doth the Spirit in the ministry of the gospel.

Ver. 29. *I also labour, striving*] Labour to lassitude, strive even to an agony. Good ministers are great pains-takers; and God that helped the Levites to bear the ark, 1 Chron. xv. 26, will help his servants by his Spirit, working in them with power.

CHAPTER II.

Ver. 1. *For I would that ye knew*] Little do most men know what incessant care and pains their faithful ministers take for their souls' health. But we would they should know it, and know those that labour among them, and are over them in the Lord, and to "esteem them very highly in love for their work's sake," 1 Thess. v. 12, 13.

Ver. 2. *That their hearts may be comforted*] Ministers are "sons of consolation," whiles by them God maketh the heart to hear of joy and gladness, Psal. li. 8, and createth the fruit of their lips peace, peace, &c., Isa. lvii. 19.

Being knit together] No such comfort upon the earth, as in the communion of saints; it differeth from the happiness of heaven but in degrees only.

Of the full assurance of understanding] Such as was that of St Luke, chap. i. 3. See the note there.

Ver. 3. *In whom are hid*] What so great a matter is it then if we be obscured, and our good parts not so noticed? *Usque adeone scire tuum nihil est?* (Pers.) Christ was content his treasures should be hid. *In maxima sui mole se minimum ostendunt stellæ.*

All the treasures of wisdom] Out of Christ then there is no true wisdom or solid comfort to be found. "The depth saith, It is not in me, and the sea saith, It is not with me," Job xxviii. 14. The world's wizards cannot help us to it, Jer. viii. 9. *Nescio quomodo imbecillior est medicina quam morbus,* saith Cicero concerning all philosophical comforts: The medicine is too weak for the disease. And as for wisdom, that of the flesh serves the worldling (as the ostrich's wings) to make him out-run others upon earth and in earthly things, but helps him never a whit toward heaven. Since the fall, every man hath *principium læsum,* his brain-pin cracked (as to heavenly things), neither can he recover but by getting into Christ.

Ver. 4. *With enticing words*] With probable ἀνταναπλήσω. *Vicissim rursum impleo.*

and persuasible speeches, πιθανολογία. It is not safe for simple men to hear heretics; for though they may think themselves able enough to answer them, yet they have a notable faculty of persuading the credulous and less cautelous. The Valentinian heretics had an art to persuade before they taught. (Tertull.) The locusts have faces like women. In the year 497, Pope Anastasius II., seeking to reduce the heretic Acacius, was seduced by him.

Ver. 5. Your order, and the stedfastness] Faith and order, that is, doctrine and discipline, saith one. These two make the Church "fair as the moon, clear as the sun, and terrible as an army with banners," Cant. vi. 10.

The stedfastness of your faith] Gr. στερέωμα. The firmament of your faith. As in the first creation, so in the new creature, there is first the light of knowledge; secondly, the firmament of faith; thirdly, repentant tears and worthy fruits, as seas and trees, &c.

Ver. 6. So walk ye in him] Continue well-affected, as ye were at your first conversion; fall not from your own stedfastness, 2 Pet. iii. 17. Happy is he that can say in a spiritual sense (as it was said of Moses), that after long profession of religion his sight is not waxed dim nor his natural strength abated.

Ver. 7. Abounding therein with thanksgiving] Thankfulness for smaller measures of grace gets more. *Efficacissimum genus est rogandi, gratias agere.* (Plin. Panegyr.)

Ver. 8. Lest any man spoil you] A metaphor either from sheep-stealers or plunderers, συλαγωγῶν. Seducers plunder men of their precious souls. They take them prisoners, 2 Tim. iii. 6. They make merchandise of them, 2 Pet. ii. 3; or bring them into bondage, smiting them on the face, 2 Cor. xi. 20. Constantius the emperor suspecting Julian's proneness to paganism, sent him to be carefully grounded in Christianity to Nicomedia; but he frequented by stealth the company of Libanus and Jamblichus the philosophers, who warped him fully to their bent; which brake out afterwards.

Through philosophy] In the year of Christ 220, the Artemonites, a certain kind of heretics, corrupted Scripture out of Aristotle and Theophrastus, turning all into questions, as afterwards the schoolmen also did, that evil generation of dunghill divines, as one calleth them. Tertullian not unfitly saith, that the philosophers were the patriarchs of the heretics. Not but that there is an excellent and necessary use of philosophy, truly so called; but the apostle meaneth it of their idle speculations and vain deceits, those airy nothings, as the apostle expounds himself. See the note on Rom. i. 21, 22.

And not after Christ] The Gentiles then could not be saved by their philosophy without Christ. And yet not only the divines of Cullen set forth a book concerning the salvation of Aristotle, whom they called Christ's forerunner in naturals, as John Baptist was in supernaturals; but also some of the school doctors, grave men (saith

Acosta), do promise men salvation without the knowledge of Christ. (Agrippa, Balæus.)

Ver. 9. All the fulness of the Godhead bodily] That is, essentially, not in clouds and ceremonies, as once between the cherubims, which the Jews called Shechinah; whereunto the apostle here alludeth.

Ver. 10. And ye are complete] Ye have that true happiness of a man, which philosophers hunted after in the thicket of earthly vanities, and lost themselves in the chase. Varro makes report of 288 several opinions that they had about this subject, and were out in all, whilst they caught at the shadow of fruits in a hedge of thorns, but could not come at the Tree of Life, Christ Jesus, in whom we are complete.

Ver. 11. Made without hands] Oh how honourable (saith an interpreter) is the work of mortification, even as to make those huge heavens, &c.

By the circumcision of Christ] Which circumciseth our hearts, pulling off that wretched foreskin.

Ver. 12. Buried with him in baptism] Which succeedeth in the place of circumcision, and is also to us a seal of the righteousness of faith, Rom. iv. 11. There were (saith one) many ceremonies in baptism used in the primitive Church, viz. putting off old clothes, drenching in water, so as to seem to be buried in it, putting on new clothes at their coming out; to which Paul alludeth in these two verses.

Of the operation of God] In the work of faith God putteth forth the same Almighty power that he did in raising Christ from the dead, Ephes. i. 19, 20. See the note on that text.

Ver. 13. And you being dead] See the note on Ephes. ii. 1.

Hath he quickened] The first springing in the womb of grace is precious before God.

Ver. 14. Blotting out the hand-writing] Crossing out the black lines of our sins with the red lines of his Son's blood.

Ver. 15. He made a show of them] A plain allusion to the Roman triumphs. See the note on Ephes. iv. 8. Christ made the devils a public spectacle of scorn and derision, as Tamerlane did Bajazet the Great Turk, whom he shut up in an iron cage made like a grate, in such sort, as that he might on every side be seen; and so carried him up and down, as he passed through Asia, to be of his own people scorned and derided.

Ver. 16. Let no man therefore judge you] That is, set not up any such for a judge over your consciences; or, if any usurp such an authority, slight him, according to that, Gal. v. 1. *Periculosum est in divinis rebus ut quis cedat jure suo,* saith Cyprian. In things of God we should be tender of our liberty.

Ver. 17. Which are a shadow] And so a sign of Christ, obscurely and imperfectly representing him to the old Church, and now abolished by his coming in the flesh. In the twelfth year of our Saviour's age (the same year wherein he taught in the Temple, Luke ii.) the sanctuary was polluted by the casting about the bones of dead men through every part and porch thereof, at the very feast of the Passover, in the night time. This Josephus saith was done by the Samaritans, out of hatred to the Jewish services. But God had surely a special hand in it, to show that people that those shadows were to vanish, now that Christ the body was come and showed himself.

Ver. 18. *Let no man beguile you*] Gr. βραβενέτω, brave it over you. Confer Exod. viii. 9, " Glory over me," *Gloriam assume supra me*, as thou hast done over thy sorcerers ; I give thee this liberty. See also Judges vii. 2 ; Isa. x. 15.

In a voluntary humility] A proud humility. They would not dare to worship God, but angels, &c., yet were vainly puffed up by their fleshly minds. And something like this was that of the Baptist in refusing to wash Christ, and of Peter in refusing to be washed by him, John xiii. 8.

And worshipping of angels] Setting them up, as Papists do, for mediators of intercession. Let not us acknowledge any other master of requests in heaven but Christ alone, 1 John ii. 1. But what a piece of knavery is that in Surius and Caranza, who rendering that passage of the Laodicean Council, chap. xxxv., οὐ δεῖ χριστιανοὺς ἀγγέλους ὀνομάζειν, Christians may not pray to angels ; they make the words to be, *Non oportet Christianos ad angulos congregationes facere*, Christians may not be corner-creepers ; and the title they make, *De iis qui angulos colunt*, of those that worship (not angels, but) corners ; against all sense. What ! will they put out the eyes of God's people ? as he said, Numb. xvi. 14. Or do they not rather, *Festucam quærere unde oculos sibi eruant*, as Bernard hath it, seek straws to put out their own eyes withal ?

Intruding into those things] ἐμβατεύων, or invading those things, blind and bold, busy about such matters, as whereof there is neither proof nor profit. Of this sort of seducers was that daring Dionysius, that writeth so confidently of the heavenly hierarchy ; the schoolmen also with their curious speculations and new niceties, as Scotellus and others.

Vainly puffed up by his fleshly mind] Corruption is the mother of pride, as the devil the father. " He is the king of all the children of pride," Job xli. 34.

Ver. 19. *And not holding the head*] This is worse than all the former, that they despoiled Christ of his dignity ; as if he alone were not sufficient to cherish and increase his Church.

With the increase of God] That proceeds from God, that is, from the Spirit of Christ the head ; to which growth is opposed that vain puffing up, ver. 18, whereby men do not increase, but swell ; grow bigger indeed, but weaker, as a gouty hand.

Ver. 20. *Are ye subject to ordinances*] Why do ye dogmatize ; or be burdened with rites or traditions, as they now are in the Papacy ? John Aunt, a Roman Catholic, in his humble appeal to King James, in the sixth chapter of that pamphlet, thus blasphemeth God,—The God of the

Protestants (whom he knows to be the Father, Son, and Holy Ghost) is the most uncivil and evil-mannered God of all those who have borne the names of God upon earth ; yea, worse than Pan, god of the clowns, which can endure no ceremonies nor good manners at all.

Ver. 21. *Touch not, taste not, &c.*] The words of those impostors, which are here mimetically, or by way of imitation, related. See the like Eccles. x. 14, where the wise man graphically describeth the fool's tautologies, " A man cannot tell what shall be, and what shall be, who can tell ? " As for the sense, an excellent textman gives it thus : " Touch not," viz. a woman, 1 Cor. vii. 1. " Taste not ; " viz. meat. " Handle not ; " viz. money, meddle not with secular contracts. (Dr Sclater.) This was that holy hypocrisy practised by these ancient seducers, and still commended by the Popish padres to their novices, and that with much eagerness, "touch not, taste not, handle not," without a copulative. The Capuchin friars at this day may not take or touch silver. This metal is as very anathema to these, as the wedge of gold to Achan, at the offer whereof they start back, as Moses from the serpent ; yet they have ever a boy with them, that takes and carries it, and never complains of either metal or measure. In the year of grace 1453, John Capistranus, a Minorite, was sent by Pope Nicholas into Germany, and other countries, to preach and persuade obedience to the see of Rome ; and that he might win authority to his doctrine, he strictly forbade feasting and sporting, and other civil exercises, lawful to be used ; by which holy hypocrisy (as they call it) he gained the reputation of a very pious man, when he was nothing less. (Funccius.) But these things have a show of wisdom in neglecting the body, &c., and silly souls are much taken with such shows, as children are with gaudies and gewgaws.

Ver. 22. *Which all are to perish*] The very daily perishing of food and raiment are types of thy perishing also, saith a divine.

Ver. 23. *And neglecting of the body*] Gr. ἀφειδεία. Not sparing of it, as the old and new Baalites, those Flagellantes; and those also amongst us (good otherwise), that pinch their bodies too much with penury or excessive fasting, are blameworthy. The body is the soul's servant, and that it may be *Par negotio*, neither *supra* nor *infra negotium*, it must have due honour and nourishment.

CHAPTER III.

Ver. 1. *If ye then be risen with Christ*] As ye profess to be, chap. ii. 12.

Seek those things, &c.] As Christ risen spake and did only the things pertaining to the kingdom of God, Acts i. 3, and waited alway for his exaltation into heaven ; there should be continual ascensions in our hearts. The Church is compared to pillars of smoke, *elationibus fumi*, Cant. iii. 6, as having her affections, thoughts, desires upward, heaven-ward. (Tremel.)

Ver. 2. *Set your affections on things*] Things above out-last the days of heaven, and run parallel with the life of God and line of eternity. Things on earth are mutable and momentary, subject to vanity and violence; when we grasp them most greedily we embrace nothing but smoke, which wrings tears from our eyes, and vanisheth into nothing. Here then the wise man's question takes place, "Wilt thou set thine eyes upon that that is not?" Prov. xxiii. 5. Wilt thou rejoice in a thing of nought? Amos vi. 13. Most people are nailed to the earth, as Sisera was by Jael: they go bowed downward, as that woman in the Gospel that had a spirit of infirmity, and was bound by Satan; they strive (with the toad) who shall die with most earth in their mouths. Surely the saying of that Roman general to the soldier that kept the tents, when he should have been fighting in the field, *Non amo nimium diligentes*, I like not those that are thus over-busy, will be used of God, if when he calls us to seek after and set our affections upon the things above, we are wholly taken up about things of an inferior alloy. *Cor camera omnipotentis regis*, the heart of man is an inverted Pyramis, narrow below, almost sharpened to a point, that it might touch the earth no more than needs must; and broad above, to receive the influence of heaven. But surely, as we used to say of a top, the keen point of it is toward the earth, but it is flat and dull enough toward heaven; so are most men's affections. "My brethren, these things ought not so to be," as St James speaketh in another case. Our souls should be like a ship, which is made little and narrow downward, but more wide and broad upward.

And not on things on earth] Set not thy heart upon the asses, said Samuel to Saul, sith the desire of all Israel is to thee; so, set not your affections on outward things, sith better things abide you. It is not for you to be fishing for gudgeons, but for towns, forts, and castles, said Cleopatra to Mark Antony. So neither is it for such as hope for heaven to be taken up about trifles; as Domitian spent his time in catching flies, and Artaxerxes in making hafts for knives. There is a generation of *Terrigenæ fratres*, whose names are written in the earth, Jer. xvii. 13, called the inhabitants of the earth, Rev. xii. 12, in opposition to the saints and heirs of heaven. These may with the Athenians give for their badge the grasshopper, which is bred, liveth, and dieth in the same ground, and though she hath wings, yet flieth not; sometimes she hoppeth upwards a little, but falleth to the ground again. So here. Or at best, they are but like the eagle, which soars aloft not for any love of heaven; her eye is all the while upon the prey, which by this means she spies sooner and seizeth upon better.

Ver. 3. *For ye are dead*] Crucified to the world, as Paul, Gal. vi. 14, weaned as a child from the breasts, or rather botches of the world, as David, Psal. cxxxi. 1. Dead also in regard of daily miseries, Isa. xxvi. 19; 1 Cor. xv. 31.

And your life is hid] As the pearl is hid, till the shell be broken; or as the life of flowers in winter is hid in the root; or as God hid Christ under the carpenter's son.

Ver. 4. *Then shall we appear*] What then do we loading ourselves with thick clay, or moiling ourselves here as muck-worms?

Ver. 5. *Mortify therefore*] Sin hath a strong heart, and will not be done to death but with much ado. *Peccata sæpe raduntur, sed non eradicantur.* Something is done about sins, little against them; as artificial jugglers seem to wound themselves, but do not; or as players seem to thrust themselves through their bodies, but the sword passeth only through their clothes. Some part with sin, as Jacob did with Benjamin, because otherwise he should starve; or as Phaltiel did with Michal, lest he should lose his head; but to cast it away because it is *offensivum Dei, et aversivum a Deo*, an offence against God, and a breach of his law, this is mortification; this is more than to have seraphical knowledge and cherubinical affections in any duty. This (saith a Father) is the hardest text in all the Bible, and the hardest task in all Christianity that we can go about; but hard or not hard, it must be done, or we are undone, and check must be given to our corruptions, though full mate we cannot give.

Covetousness, which is idolatry] For it robs God of his flower, his trust, and draws a man away from all the commandments, Psal. cxix. 36. See the note on Ephes. v. 5.

Ver. 6. *On the children of disobedience*] Unpersuadable, uncounsellable persons, that regard not good courses or discourses.

Ver. 7. *When ye lived in them*] Man's life is a walk, and each action a step either to heaven or hell.

Ver. 8. *Filthy communication*] The devil's drivel. See the note on Ephes. v. 4.

Ver. 9. *Lie not one to another*] No, not in jest, lest ye go to hell in earnest. See the note on Ephes. iv. 25.

Ye have put off the old man] As the serpent doth his slough, the eagle his bill, the lizard his skin in spring and autumn. (Arist. Hist. Animal. viii.)

Ver. 10. *After the image*] If moral virtue could be beheld with mortal eyes, saith the philosopher, it would stir up wonderful loves of itself. How much more would the image of God in the hearts of his people! See the note on Ephes. iv. 24.

Of him that created him] Adam and Eve were not then created simple and stupid, and without the use of reason; else they would not have been so deceived; as the Rabbins, and, after them, the Socinians have dreamed.

Ver. 11. *Christ is all, and in all*] Not only in the hearts of men, but in all things else, ἐν πᾶσι, in the neuter gender. This second Adam hath filled all things again; neither is there anything else required to justification and salvation.

Ver. 12. *As the elect of God, holy and beloved*] Therefore holy, because elect, and therefore beloved, because holy; as God's name is holy, and therefore reverend, Psal. cxi. 9. God chose his for his love, and now loves them for his choice.

Bowels of mercies] Draw out thy soul as well as thy sheaf to the hungry, Isa. lviii. 10. Steep thy thoughts in the mercies of God, saith one, and they will dye thine, as the dye-vat doth the cloth.

Humbleness of mind] Even to be content to "be trampled upon," as the word signifieth;[1] or to be laid low as earth, as Paul, Phil. iv. 12; to have a low mind in a high conversation, as Athanasius (ὑψηλου βίας ταπεινὸν φρόνημα). Humility is the veil of a Christian, that maketh the bride look most lovely.

Ver. 13. *If a man have a quarrel*] Occasions will be given, and offences will fall out. Now it is the glory of a man to pass over a transgression, Prov. xix. 11; see 1 Sam. x. 27; and to forgive where there is just cause of complaint. If no quarrel, no thank.

Ver. 14. *Above all these*] "Put on love," as the upper garment, the "parti-coloured coat," whereby all God's children are known (as Joseph, and Tamar, David's daughter, were), the cognizance of every true Christian, John xiii. 35. See the note there.

The bond of perfectness] Or the couple, the juncture, the tie, σύνδεσμος. As the curtains of the tabernacle were joined by loops, so are all true Christians by love.

Ver. 15. *And let the peace of God rule*] βραβευέτω, *Sit certaminis moderator*: let it rule after the manner of a moderator or an umpire. Let it over-see and over-rule in all your personal discords. Or (as others sense it) let it carry away the prize, or distribute the garlands.

And be ye thankful] sc. To those that are courteous and beneficial to you.[2] *Ingratum dixeris, omnia dixeris.* Lycurgus would make no law against unthankfulness, because he could not think there could be any such evil committed. If there be any sin in the world against the Holy Ghost, said Queen Elizabeth in a letter to Henry IV. of France, it is ingratitude. This, saith one, is a monster in nature, a solecism in good manners, a paradox in divinity, a parching wind to dam up the fountain of divine and human favours. (Camden.) *Ventus urens et exsiccans.*

Ver. 16. *Dwell in you richly*] ἐνοικείτω πλουσίως, indwell in you, as an ingraffed word, incorporated into your souls; so concocted and digested by you, as that you turn it *in succum et sanguinem*, into a part of yourselves. This is your riches; and thus David reckons of his wealth, Psal. cxix. 32.

Teaching and admonishing one another] It is rightly observed by a late reverend writer,[3] that although we know that which we ask of others as well as they do, yet good speeches will draw us to know it better, by giving occasion to speak more of it, wherewith the Spirit works more

effectually, and imprints it deeper, so that it shall be a more rooted knowledge than before. For that doth good that is graciously known; and that is graciously known that the Spirit seals upon our souls.

In psalms and hymns] Papists forbid people to sing psalms, and permit only choristers to sing, lest the music should be marred. (Binnius.) But the apostle biddeth every saint to sing. And Nicephorus writeth that the Christians of his time, even as they travelled and journeyed, were wont to sing psalms. Tatianus also saith, That every age and order among the Christians were Christian philosophers, yea, that the very virgins and maids, as they sat at their work in wool, were wont to speak of God's word. (Hist. Eccl. iii. 37.)

With grace in your heart] This is the best tune to any Psalm.

Ver. 17. *Do all in the name*] By the warrant of his word, and with an aim to his glory. For his sake and service; and to God's acceptance, through Christ's assistance.

Ver. 18. *Wives, submit yourselves*] Inferiors are ordered before superiors to teach them to do duty before they expect it. Love descendeth, duty ascendeth. Submit is a short word, but of large extent. It comprehendeth, 1. Reverence; "Let the wife see that she reverence her husband," Eph. v. 33, as Sarah did, and is chronicled for it, 1 Pet. iii. 6. But God hath a barren womb for mocking Michal. 2. Obedience to all his lawful commands and restraints, as the Shunammite, 2 Kings iv. 22, and the Shulamite, who lives by Christ's laws, and yields to his will, direction, and discretion.

As it is fit] *Ut decet*, as it is comely; and women love comeliness, delight to be neat. Hereby wives shall appear comely, first, to God, 1 Pet. iii. 4. Next, to men in the gate, Prov. xxxi. 23, 31. Thirdly, to their husbands and children, Prov. xxxi. 28. Fourthly, to all, even opposites, as being an ornament to sincerity and holiness, Titus ii. 3.

In the Lord] Though the husband's will be crooked (so it be not wicked), the wife's will is not straight in God's sight, if not pliable to his. *Sed liberum arbitrium, pro quo tantopere contenditur, viri amiserunt, uxores arripuerunt*, saith an author.

Ver. 19. *Husbands, love your wives*] He saith not, Rule over them, subdue them if they will not submit, but love them, and so win them to your will; make their yoke as easy as may be, for they stand on even ground with you, as yokefellows, though they draw on the left side. "Yet is she thy companion, and the wife of thy covenant," Mal. ii. 14. He therefore that is free may frame his choice to his mind; but he that hath chosen must frame his heart to his choice.

Uxorem vir amato, marito pareat uxor :
Conjugis illa sui cor, caput ille suæ.

---

[1] ταπεινὸς, *quasi* πατεινὸς, *vel* ἰδαφεινὸς.
[2] *Arbor honoretur cujus nos umbra tuetur.*
[3] Dr Sibbs on Cant. v.

And be not bitter against them] Nothing akin to Nabal, to those Chaldeans, a bitter and furious nation, or to that star, Rev. viii. 11, called wormwood, that embittered the third part of the waters. The heathen, when they sacrificed at their marriage-feasts, used to cast the gall of the beasts sacrificed out of doors; to signify that married couples should be as doves without gall. (Plut. *præc. conjug.*) *Vipera virus ob venerationem nuptiarum evomit*, saith Basil. The viper, going to copulate, vomiteth up her venom; and wilt not thou, for the honour of marriage, lay aside thy bitterness and boisterous behaviour?

Ver. 20. *In all things*] *Vultu sæpe læditur pietas.* See the note on Eph. vi. 1.

Ver. 21. *Provoke not your children*] See the note on Eph. vi. 4.

Lest they be discouraged] ἀθυμῶσιν, dispirited, and through despondency grow desperate in their resolutions.

Ver. 22. *Not with eye service*] See the note on Eph. vi. 5, 6. It is in the original, " Not with eye-services," in the plural, μὴ ἐν ὀφθαλμοδουλείαις; to show that do they never so much service, yet if not in sincerity, all is lost.

Fearing God] That hath power to cast body and soul to hell. Fear him more than you do your masters, that have power over the flesh only.

Ver. 23. *Do it heartily, as to the Lord*] This is to make a virtue of necessity, whiles in serving men we serve the Lord Christ, going about our earthly businesses with heavenly minds, with not only an habitual, but an actual intention, as much as may be, of glorifying God in all.

Ver. 24. *The reward of inheritance*] And so be made of servants sons, whose it is to inherit.

For ye serve the Lord Christ] Whiles godliness runneth through your whole lives, as the woof doth through the web, and you seek to approve yourselves to Christ in all your actions and employments.

Ver. 25. *But he that doth wrong*] Be it but by not doing right to poor servants, which in those days were bond-slaves. Note here, saith an interpreter, the apostle's candour; he was not of the humour of lawyers, that seldom speak much but for great men, or when they may have great gifts.

CHAPTER IV.

Ver. 1. *That which is just and equal*] See they must both to the well choosing and the well using of their servants.

Ye also have a master] Eccl. v. 8, " There be higher than they;" and wherein they deal proudly, God is above them, Exod. xviii. 11.

Ver. 2. *Continue in prayer*] Constant and instant in it, wait upon it, lay all aside for it (as the word προσκαρτερεῖτε signifieth, Acts vi. 2); while prayer stands still, the trade of godliness stands still.

And watch in the same] Against dulness of spirit, drowsiness of body, Satanical suggestions, secular distractions, &c.

With thanksgiving] Have your thanks ready, for you are sure to speed.

Ver. 3. *Withal, praying also for us*] See the note on Eph. vi. 19. By the word a door is opened into heaven.

Ver. 4. *As I ought to speak*] As every sound is not music, so neither is every pulpit discourse a sermon.

Ver. 5. *Walk in wisdom*] Neither giving offence carelessly, nor taking offence causelessly.

Redeeming the time] Opportunities are headlong, and must be timously laid hold on, or all is lost. See the note on Ephes. v. 16. It is said of Hooper the martyr, that he was spare of diet, sparer of words, and sparest of time. Latimer rose usually at two of the clock in a morning to his study. Bradford slept not commonly above four hours in the night, and in his bed, till sleep came, his book went not out of his hand. He counted that hour not well spent wherein he did not some good, either with his pen, tongue, or study. These worthies well weighed what a modern writer hath well observed, that they that lose time are the greatest losers and wastefullest prodigals. For of all other possessions two may be had together, but two moments of time (much less two opportunities of time) cannot be possest together.

Ver. 6. *Seasoned with salt*] Of mortification and discretion : even our common communication must be so seasoned; as we powder most those meats that be most apt to putrefy, and as upon our uncomely parts we put the more comeliness.

Ver. 7. *All my state shall Tychicus*] See the note on Ephes. vi. 21.

Ver. 8. *And comfort your hearts*] See the note on Ephes. vi. 22.

Ver. 9. *With Onesimus a faithful*] Once unprofitable, but now profitable, faithful, and beloved. Plato went thrice to Sicily to convert Dionysius, and lost his labour. Polemo of a drunkard, by hearing Xenocrates, became a philosopher. But Ambrose saith well of him, *si resipuit a vino, fuit semper tamen temulentus sacrilegio*, if he repented of his drunkenness, yet he continued drunk with superstition. *Philosophia non abscindit vitia, sed abscondit.* Paul's convert proved better, a faithful preacher and a beloved brother.

Ver. 10. *Marcus, sister's son to Barnabas*] Hence Barnabas stood so stiff for him against Paul his faithful fellow-traveller, Acts xv. 37. See the note there. Natural affection sways overmuch with some good men, as it did with Eli, and perhaps with Samuel, 1 Sam. viii. 1, 3.

If he come unto you, receive him] St Paul had now a better opinion of him than once, when he brake with Barnabas about him. He was not of the Novatian opinion, never to think well again of those that had fallen through infirmity, albeit they repented. They are not to be liked, that say, I never liked him since, &c.

Ver. 11. *These only are my fellow-workers*] St

Paul complains of fickle and false friends, that forsook him in his distress, as Demas, 2 Tim. iv. 10, 16, that like Job's friends proved miserable comforters, and as the brooks of Tema, which in a moisture swell, in a drought fail; or as the river Novanus in Lombardy, that at every midsummer solstice swelleth and runneth over the banks, but in mid-winter is clean dry. Howbeit Marcus, Aristarchus, Onesimus, Onesiphorus, and some few others, stuck to him. A great mercy: *Optimum solatium, sodalitium.*

Ver. 12. Epaphras, who is one of you] See chap. i. 7, and the note there. This Epaphras is thought to be the same with Epaphroditus; as Sylvanus is called Silas, and Jehoshuah Joshua, by an abbreviature.

Always labouring fervently] Constant and instant in prayer, according to that ver. 2.

Complete in all the will of God] Gr. πεπληρωμένοι, carried on end by it, with full career; as a ship is by a full gale.

That ye may stand perfect] In his absence especially, for then the devil is most busy, as he was with the people when Moses was but a while in the mount, Exod. xxxii.

Ver. 13. And them that are in Laodicea] A minister must be like the sun, that shineth not only within its own orb, but illighteneth all round about it and within the reach of it.

Ver. 14. And Demas] He will needs be one, and is, but without any title of honour, as the rest. He began to be suspected; and he afterwards proved an utter apostate, and (as Dorotheus saith) an idol-priest at Thessalonica.

Ver. 15. Salute the brethren] Christianity is no enemy to courtesy. It removes not, but rectifies it.

The brethren which are in Laodicea] There God had his remnant, there Christ was Amen, the faithful and true witness, and there there were such as by a new creation of God were begotten again, even among so careless a multitude, Rev. iii. 14. There remain in Constantinople at this day above 20 churches of Christians; and in Thessalonica above 30, besides very many churches abroad in the province, &c. The whole country of Asia the Less, wherein stood Colosse, Laodicea, and Hierapolis, is now under the power and superstition of the Turk; yet no doubt God hath his remnant there. (*Chytræ de statu Ecclesiar.*)

Ver. 16. Read the Epistle from Laodicea] Other good books then must be read as well as the Scriptures; yet not idle pamphlets and love toys. These should be burnt, as those curious books were, Acts xix.

Ver. 17. And say to Archippus] Archippus was a pastor of the Laodicean Church; so that before St John's time in Patmos they began to cool.

Take heed to the ministry] Gr. see to it, that is, to thyself, and to all the flock, Acts xx. 28, as Ezek. xxxi. 39, to strengthen the weak, to heal the infected, to splint the sprained, to reduce the wandering, to seek the lost, to cherish the strong: work enough. *Age ergo quod tui muneris est,* as Valentinian said to Ambrose. *Clericus in oppido, piscis in arido,* saith another. "What is that to thee?" John xxi. 22. The Church is thy proper element, the pulpit thy right *ubi;* the sanctuary should be the centre of all thy circumference. It is a good hearing that the Levite makes haste home, Judges xix. An honest man's heart is where his calling is. And this charge, by how much the more sacred it is, so much the more attendance it expects. Even a day breaks square with the conscionable.

That thou fulfil it] By preaching the word in season, out of season, &c., and so doing the work of an evangelist, fulfilling his ministry, 2 Tim. iv. 2—5. This to do the people were to excite their pastor; yet with all due respect and reverence to his office, 1 Tim. v. 1, μηὲπιπλήξης. An elder must not be lashed or jerked with the scourge of the tongue as a puny, but entreated as a father.

Ver. 18. Remember my bonds] To pray for me, and minister to me, &c. This he here inserteth as his last charge, that they may the better remember and practise it. Something we should leave with those we love that may stick by them, and stand them instead when we are gone or have done with them.

THE FIRST EPISTLE OF ST PAUL TO THE THESSALONIANS.

CHAPTER I.

Ver. 1. Paul and Sylvanus] OTHERWISE called Silas, Acts xv. 40, as Jehoshuah the high-priest is called Joshua, Ezra iii. 2, and v. 2. It is not therefore unlawful to abbreviate names.

Unto the church of the Thessalonians] Thessalonica, the chief city of Macedonia, is now known by the name of Salonicks, and is under the Turk. For the plantation of a Church here, see Acts xvii. 1—3, &c., together with the notes. There are 30 churches of Christians in it at this day, and but three of Mahometans.

Ver. 2. We give thanks to God] Thus he beginneth most of his Epistles with thanksgiving; this being held to be the first that ever he wrote to any of the Churches, the beginning of his strength, as Reuben (Jacob's first-born), and the excellency of dignity, Gen. xlix. 3.

Ver. 3. Remembering without ceasing] A good memory is required to assiduity in prayer. All the faculties are exercised, and the whole man hard wrought.

Your work of faith] We believe not without much conflict. When faith goes about to lay hold on Christ, the devil raps her on the fingers, and would beat her off. Hence the believer hath such ado to believe.

And labour of love] Every man's love is as his labour is, Heb. vi. 10. Therefore also love and labour are of one root in Latin, because love is diligent and laborious.

And patience of hope] To wait the accomplishment of God's promises. Thus every Christian virtue hath its proper distinctive character, to difference it from that which is counterfeit.

In the sight of God] True grace will stand to God's trial, which false grace cannot abide; as alchemy gold cannot pass the seventh fire; nor doth it comfort the heart as true gold doth.

Ver. 4. Knowing, brethren beloved of God] Knowing it by the judgment of charity, not of infallibility. He that believeth hath the witness in himself, 1 John v. 10. But the white stone, the new name, and the hidden man of the heart are not certainly known to any, but to such as have them. Howbeit, holy men in some degree are known one to another, to make the communion of saints the sweeter. Strong confidence one may have of another's salvation; but no certainty either of sense or of science, much less of faith, or immediate revelation.

Ver. 5. For our gospel came not] Hence he collects their election, according to Acts xiii. 48.

The ministry sent to a place is an argument of some elect there. A husbandman would not send his servant with his sickle to reap thistles and nettles only.

As ye know what manner] The Church is endued with the spirit of discerning; and ministers should approve themselves spiritual in word and conversation, 2 Cor. xii. 10.

Ver. 6. Followers of us and of the Lord] The apostles walked in Christ, Col. ii. 6; as Christ, 1 John ii. 6; their lives were a commentary upon his life, 1 Pet. ii. 9.

Received the word in much affliction] Opposition is (as Calvin wrote to the French king) *Evangelii genius*, the black angel that dogs the gospel at the heels. To preach (saith Luther) is nothing else but to get the ill-will of the world.

With joy of the Holy Ghost] Which bore them up above all persecutions, as blown bladders bear a man up aloft all waters.

Ver. 7. So that ye were ensamples] Gr. τύποι, types, moulds, patterns of piety, to those that were in Christ long before them. A brave commendation, and not every man's happiness. Affliction to some is like a growing ague, or as a warm rain to garden-herbs, that maketh them shoot up sensibly in one night.

Ver. 8. For from you sounded out] *A vobis diffamatus est sermo.* Remigius, commenting upon this place, telleth us that the apostle here speaketh somewhat improperly, by saying *diffamatus* for *divulgatus*. This man knew not (belike) that St Paul wrote in Greek and not in Latin; so great was the ignorance of that ninth age. The Greek word importeth that from the Thessalonians the word of the Lord sounded out as a trumpet, and resounded as an echo, ἐξήχηται. *A vobis ebuccinatus est sermo Domini;* so Vatablus rendereth it.

So that we need not to speak] A good people may ease their pastor of a great deal of pains.

Ver. 9. What manner of entering in, &c.] The pastor hath his part and share in the people's commendation. If they grow famous, he cannot lie obscured.

Ye turned to God from idols] They gave not the half turn only from east to south, but the whole turn, from the east to west, from idols to God, Hos. vi. 4. Ephraim shall say, " What have I to do any more with idols?" Hos. xiv. 8; those Balaam blocks, those mawmets and monuments of idolatry, those images of jealousy? Ephraim is now no longer as a cake half-baked, as a speckled bird, Jer. xii. 9. Better be a Papist than an atheist, a gross idolater than a profligate professor, a carnal gospeller.

Ver. 10. *And to wait for his Son*] This is pinned as a badge to the sleeve of every true believer, that he looketh and longeth for Christ's coming to judgment. The old character of God's people was, they waited for the consolation of Israel, Christ's first coming; so is it now, the earnest expectation of his second coming.

Which delivered us from the wrath to come] This is the Etymon, the notation of his name Jesus, a Saviour. Salvation properly betokeneth the privative part of man's happiness, but includeth the positive too. King Alphonsus, when he saw a poor man pulling of his beast out of a ditch, he put to his hand to help him. Is it not more that Christ should stoop so low as to help us (who were in worse condition than the beasts that perish) out of the ditch of destruction? The devil is said to be λέων ὠρυόμενος, a roaring lion, but our comfort is, that the Lion of the tribe of Judah is ὁ ῥυόμενος he that delivereth us from the wrath to come. The Sun of righteousness (as Pelbartus saith, allegorizing God's covenant signified by a rainbow) falling into a cloud of passion, is our security against a deluge of damnation.

The wrath to come] There is a present wrath that men suffer; and who knoweth the power of this wrath? Even according to a man's fear, so is God's wrath, Psal. xc. 11. Let a man fear never so much, he shall be sure to feel more, when God's wrath falls upon him. A timorous man can fancy vast and terrible fears; fire, sword, racks, scalding lead, boiling pitch, running bell-metal. Yet all this is but as a painted fire to the wrath to come, that eternity of extremity, which graceless persons shall never be able to avoid or to abide.

CHAPTER II.

Ver. 1. *Our entrance in unto you*] THE word preached in any place doth usually work best at first. After a while men become like unto birds in a belfry, that can well enough bear the noise of the bells and not be frighted.

Ver. 2. *But even after that, &c.*] From this to the 13th verse, ministers may as in a mirror see how they ought to behave themselves in the house of God.

We were bold in our God] The Church, as the palm-tree, spreadeth and springeth up the more it is oppressed; as the bottle or bladder that may be dipt, not drowned; as the oak that sprouts out the thicker from the maims and wounds it receiveth.[1] This daunted Diocletian, and made him lay down the empire in discontent. This caused Julian the Apostate to leave off force, and use fraud to draw men from the truth.

Ver. 3. *Was not of deceit, nor, &c.*] Neither for profit, pleasure, nor preferment (the worldling's trinity). A minister, as he should have

[1] *Duris ut ilex tonsa bipennibus.*

nothing to lose, so he should have nothing to get, but should be above all price or sale. He hath too impotent a spirit, whose services, like the dial, must be set only by the sun of self-respects. True grace is of a most masculine, disengaged, noble nature, and remits nothing of its diligence either for fear of a frown or hope of a reward.

Ver. 4. *But as we were allowed*] Enabled and counted faithful, 1 Tim. i. 12.

Not as pleasing men] See the note on Gal. i. 10. Men be they pleased or displeased, God must not be displeased.

But God] Who looketh upon displeasing service as a double dishonour.

Which trieth our hearts] And so knoweth our aims, *Quicquid igitur agas, propter Deum agas. Propter te, Domine, propter te*, as he cried. It stands me upon, saith one, to see, that though my work be but mean, yet it may be clean; though not fine, yet not foul, soiled and slubbered with the slur of a rotten heart, sith it is God I have to deal with. (Drus. Apophth.)

Ver. 5. *For neither at any time*] Sinisterity of ends is here opposed to sincerity in God's works. And flattery, covetousness, ambition, declared to be the fountains of insincerity.

Nor a cloak of covetousness] This sin goes usually cloaked with the name and pretence of good husbandry. The ordinary language of the world is, " He is a man somewhat with the hardest, a little with the nearest, a little too much for the world, but yet a marvellous honest, a wondrous good man." Covetousness is seldom without feigned words, 2 Pet. ii. 3, to hide it from others without, or subtle thoughts and evasions to blind-fold the conscience within. Alcibiades embroidered a curtain with lions and eagles to cover his pictures of owls and apes; so all sin hath its vizard; neither is there any wool so coarse but will take some colour.

God is witness] That he flattered not; he reports himself to them, that he coveted not; he appeals to God, who is not mocked with masks or specious pretences, but will pull off the vizard, wash off the covetous man's varnish with rivers of brimstone. Religion, as it is the best armour, so it is the worst cloak: and will serve self-seekers, as the disguise Ahab put on and perished, 1 Kings xxii. The covetousness of the court of Rome was anciently muttered forth in that saying, *Curia Romana non petit ovem sine lana;* and again, *In parabola ovis, capras suas quærunt.* This the poor people were ever sensible of; but durst say little. There is a story of Walter Mapes (sometime archdeacon of Oxford), who relating the gross simony of the pope for confirming the election of Reinold, bastard son to Jocelin, bishop of Sarum, into the see of Bath, concludeth his narration thus, *Sit Domina tamen materque nostra Roma baculus in aqua fractus; et absit credere quæ vidimus*, i. e. Nevertheless let our lady and mother of Rome be as a staff in the water, that seems only to be broken; and far be it from us to believe our own eyes. They durst not see, or at least say what they saw; but now all is laid open, and shall be much more at the last day, when (as at a great fair) all fardels shall be uncorded, and all packs opened.

Ver. 6. *Nor of men sought we glory*] *Theologus gloriæ dicit malum bonum, et bonum malum* (saith Luther), *Theologus crucis dicit id quod res est :* A vain-glorious preacher calleth good evil, and evil good, &c.

Ver. 7. *But we were gentle*] This is the way to win; for man is a curst, crabbed creature, and may be led, but not easily dragged to duty. Soft words and hard arguments soonest prevail with him.

Ver. 8. *So being affectionately desirous*] Honing and hankering after you. The Greek word signifieth the most swaying heart-passion, the most effectual affection. (ἱμειρόμενοι. *Cupidine rapti.*)

But also our own souls] Greater love than this hath no man; and such a love ought there to be in every pastor toward his people. Love is liberal, charity is no churl.

Ver. 9. *Our labour*] Even to lassitude, yea, to solicitude.

And travail] So, to spare them, he spared not himself.

Ver. 10. *Ye are witnesses, and God also*] Happy is that man that can be acquitted by himself in private, in public by others, in both by God : standers-by may see more.

How holily, and justly, and unblameably] Here he practised his own precept, Tit. ii. 12. And herein lies the difference between divinity and other sciences, that it is not enough to prescribe it, but you must practise it, as lessons of music, and as a copy must not be read only, but acted also.

Ver. 11. *As a father*] Before, as a mother, ver. 7, a nurse not mercenary, but natural, with greatest tenderness and indulgence. Here he tempers his mother-like meekness with the gravity and authority of a father. Ministers must turn themselves, as it were, into all shapes and fashions, both of speech and spirit, to win people to God.

Ver. 12. *Walk worthy of God*] Whose livery we wear, whose image we bear, whose kingdom we are called unto, &c. Those that stood with the Lamb, Rev. xiv., had his Father's name on their foreheads. Our out-strays reflect upon God, who will require and requite.

Ver. 13. *Not as the word of men*] Whom yet he maketh use of to cast down Satan's strong-holds, as he made use of little David against Goliath, and of the frogs and flies against Pharaoh, and of the ram's horns against Jericho. This treasure, these pearls, he giveth us in vile oyster-shells, 2 Cor. iv. 7.

As the word of God] With reverence and diligence, with all good affection and attention. When Samuel knew it was God that called him (and not Eli) he had no more mind to sleep. " We are all here present before God," saith Cornelius, Acts x. 33. And " God is in you of a

truth," saith the Corinthian convert, 1 Cor. xiv. 25.

Ver. 14. *Of your own countrymen*] Malice against the truth breaks all bonds of nature or amity. Moab was irked because of Israel, or vexed at them, Numb. xxii. 3, 4, though they were allied to Israel, who passed by them peaceably, and by the slaughter of the Amorites, freed them from evil neighbours, which had taken away part of their country, &c. The English Papists in four years sacrificed 800 of their innocent countrymen in Queen Mary's days. In the holy war (as they called it) against the Waldenses (those ancient Protestants) in France, the pope's great army took one great populous city, and put to the sword 60,000, among whom were many of their own Catholics. For, Arnoldus the Cistercian abbot (being the pope's legate in this great war) commanded the captains and soldiers, saying, *Cædite eos, novit enim Dominus qui sunt ejus,* i. e. Down with them all, for God knoweth which of them are his. (Cæsarius Heisterbach. Hist. v. 21.) And the issue of this was, *ut potius cæsi, fugati, bonis ac dignitatibus ubique spoliati sint, quam ut erroris convicti resipuerint,* i. e. that they were rather slain, scattered, spoiled of their goods and dignities, than brought by a sight of any error to sound repentance, saith Thuanus, an ingenuous Papist.

Ver. 15. *Who both killed the Lord*] And are therefore banished out of the world, as it were, by a common consent of nations, for their inexpiable guilt. Even in Jerusalem there be hardly to be found a hundred households of them. (Breerwood Inquir.) In Cyprus it is present death for any Jew to set his foot upon the island. (Dio. Cass.) In Thessalonica and Constantinople there are divers thousands of them, but at every Easter they are in danger of death, if they but stir out of doors, because at that time they crucified our Saviour. (Biddulph.) The Turks themselves so hate the Jews for crucifying Christ, that they use to say in detestation of a thing, " I would I might die a Jew." Neither will they permit a Jew to turn Turk, unless he be first baptized. The Romans permitted other nations to call themselves Romans after they had conquered them; but so they would not 'suffer the Jews to do, though they complied never so much, and were their servants (as August. in Psal. lviii. witnesseth), lest there should some blot stick to the glory of the Romans, by that odious and sordid people. *O Marcomanni, O Quadi!* said one emperor.

And their own prophets] Whose slaughter (though long since done) is in recent remembrance with God, and is reckoned and registered together with the death of Christ himself.

And have persecuted us] They still curse the Christians in their daily prayers, which they close up with a *Maledic, Domine, Nazaræis.* Lopez at Tyburn affirmed, that he had loved Queen Elizabeth as he loved Jesus Christ. Which from a Jew was heard not without laughter. (Camden's Elizabeth.)

And they please not God] Yet they challenged the title of God's Church, as the Papists will needs be the only Catholics. They cried, *ad ravim usque*, The temple of the Lord, when they nothing regarded the Lord of the temple.

And are contrary to all men] Being herein rather Ishmaelites than Israelites, Gen. xvi. 12. The trout delights to swim against stream. The herb alexander will agree with no other herb but itself. Such antipodes are our Jesuits, so insufferably ambitious and impudent, that neither their doctrine nor their conversation pleaseth those of their own religion.

Ver. 16. *Forbidding us to speak to the Gentiles*] Bale out of Capgrave reporteth, that St Asaph (as they called him) had this saying oft in his mouth, *Quicunque verbo Dei adversantur, saluti hominum invident*, Those that are against the preaching of the word, do envy the salvation of men. Such were Stephen Gardiner, and before him Archbishop Arundel, who died of a grievous swelling in their tongues, and that deservedly; *quod verbum Dei alligassent, ne suo tempore prædicaretur*, saith the historian, because they had hindered the preaching of the word.

To fill up their sin alway] Bounds are set to sin by the Divine decree, Zech. v. 7. Wickedness is compared to a woman pressed in an ephah; when the measure is full, the business is finished. See the note on Matt. xxiii. 32. The bottle of wickedness, when once filled with those bitter waters, sinketh to the bottom.

Wrath is come upon them to the uttermost] Or, until the end: wrath is come upon them finally (εἰς τέλος), so as it shall never be removed; cloud, which at length covered the whole heaven; so some interpret it. God's wrath is like Elijah's, or as thunder, which you hear at first a little roaring noise afar off; but stay awhile, it is a dreadful crack. "Who knoweth the power of thy wrath?" saith Moses, Psal. xci. The Jews are to this day a people of God's wrath and curse.

Ver. 17. *For a short time*] Or, In a short time, suddenly. See Acts xvii. 9, 10.

Being taken away] Or separated, as orphans are from their dear parents, or parents from their deceased children, ἀπορφανισθέντες. The separation of friends is so grievous, that death itself is styled no other than a departure.

Ver. 18. *But Satan hindered us*] He still doth his utmost to hinder the communion of saints, and to keep them asunder. He knows two are better than one; and therefore he stirred up the primitive persecutors to banish the Christians, and to confine them to isles and mines, where they could not have access one to another: whether Satan hindered Paul by sickness, or by imprisonments, or tempests at sea, who can resolve? saith one. (Cyprian. Epist.) He hindered him, by casting a necessity upon him of disputing often with the Stoics and Epicures which were at Athens, saith another interpreter.

Ver. 19. *For what is our hope, &c.*] A very lively and lofty expression, such as the apostle ordinarily useth in speaking of heavenly glory. *Nec Christus, nec cœlum patitur hyperbolen*, A man can hardly hyperbolize in speaking of heaven.

Ver. 20. *For ye are our glory and joy*] Let no no man therefore envy us these temporary good things, a competent maintenance: there are better things abide us above.

CHAPTER III.

Ver. 1. *No longer forbear*] στέγοντες, or, stand under our burden of vehement desire after you. See a like expression, Isa. xlii. 14. As a travailing woman bites in her pain as long as she is able, and at length cries out aloud; so God is patient till he can hold no longer, &c.

We thought it good] *Publica privatis anteferenda bonis*, A public spirit is a precious spirit. And that is a golden saying of divine Plato, ἡ δὲ δικαιοσύνη ἀλλότριον μὲν ἀγαθόν, οἰκεία δὲ ζημία. (De Rep. lib. 3.) Goodness is all for the good of others, though to its own disadvantage; like as nature will venture its own particular good for the general. As heavy things will ascend to keep out vacuity, and to preserve the universe.

Ver. 2. *To establish you*] Who haply are somewhat unsettled by the troubles that befell me amongst you. But as young trees shaken, root the better, so should you. Capito in an epistle to the brethren at Basil, writeth thus, *Pauciores vobiscum perimuntur, quod ita Domino visum est ut stabiliantur seu lenibus pluviis, ac sementis mollioribus, plantulæ in arbores maximas prodituræ.*

Ver. 3. *That no man should be moved*] Gr. σαίνεσθαι, flattered, as a dog flattereth, by moving his tail, *q. d.* The devil, by flattering you, with promise of more ease by a contrary course, will but do as a dirty dog, defile you with fawning.

That we are appointed thereunto] viz. By God's decree, whereunto if damned ghosts must subscribe, Rom. ix. 19, 20, how much more should God's elect! 1 Pet. i. 6. It is but a delicacy to dream of heaven to be had without much hardship. Many would fain pull a rose without pricks, feed on manchet, pass *a deliciis ad delicias*: they would sit in the seat of honour with Zebedee's children, but not drink the cup of affliction. This will not be. Elijah must to heaven, but in a whirlwind. Daniel must be brought through lions and leopards to the meek Lamb of God, Messiah the Prince. John shall hear the harmony of harpers, but first the noise of thunder. The Israelites had five days of sorrow before their feast of joy, Lev. xxiii. 27, 34. The first handsel God gave them in their voyage to the promised Canaan, was bitterness and thirst. It was by Marah that they came to Elim; neither could they taste of the sweet waters of Siloam, till they had crossed the swift streams of Jordan. We cannot sing the song of Moses, of God's servants, and of the Lamb, but we must first swim through a sea of burning glass, Rev. xv. 2, 3. *Non nisi per angusta, ad augusta.*

Ver. 4. *We told you before*] Darts foreseen are dintless: pre-monition is the best pre-munition. Troubles foretold come never a whit the sooner, but far the easier; whereas coming unexpected, they find weak minds secure, make them miserable, leave them desperate.

Ver. 5. *To know your faith*] That is, your perseverance and increase in faith. That which the devil mainly endeavoureth, is, to hinder and unsettle our faith, as he dealt by Eve and Peter, Luke xxii. 31, 32, to batter this buckler, Ephes. vi. 16, for then he knows he may do what he will with us. *Omnia perdidit, qui fidem amisit.* (Seneca.)

Lest by some means the tempter] Who feels our pulses, and fits his assaults accordingly. See the note on Matt. iv. 3.

And our labour be in vain] So it proves many times by Satan's malice. Other labourers can find their work as they left it, not so ministers; the devil cometh and marreth all.

Ver. 6. *And brought us good tidings*] Here the devil was disappointed. He had been nibbling, but could not fasten: this matter was not malleable. God stints him, and staves him off, when he would worry his poor lambs, turning all to their eternal good.

Ver. 7. *We were comforted*] Nothing so cheereth up the heart of a godly minister as his people's tractableness. If this be wanting, his very heart is broke, though they be otherwise never so kind and courteous to him.

Ver. 8. *For now we live*] A joyless life is a lifeless life. An unsuccessful pastor hath little or no joy of his life. "Thus shall ye say to him that liveth," 1 Sam. xxv. 6, that is, that liveth at heart's ease. "All the days of the afflicted are evil," Prov. xv. 15. As good be out of the world (say they) as have no joy of the world. Now, "I have no greater joy," saith St John, "than to hear that my children walk in the truth," 3 John 4. This revived his good old heart, and made it dance levaltos in his bosom.

Ver. 9. *For what thanks*, &c.] q. d. No sufficient thanks. Spiritual joy vents itself by an infinite desire of praising God, whereby it seeks to fill up the distance betwixt God and the good soul. In our thanksgivings let there be *modus sine modo*, as Bernard hath it. Let us still deliberate what more to do, as David, Psal. cxvi. 12.

Ver. 10. *Night and day praying exceedingly*] Prayer must be constant and instant, with utmost assiduity and intention of affection, Luke xviii. 1. See the note there.

And might perfect that which is lacking in your faith] Faith is not as Jonah's gourd, that grew up in a night; or as a bullet in a mould, that is made in a moment, but is perfected by degrees; and so made even (as the word καταρτίσαι signifies here in the original) and complete.

Ver. 11. *Now God himself*, &c.] At the very mentioning of prayer, he falls a praying. Good affections soon kindle in a gracious heart.

Direct our way unto you] "A man's heart deviseth his way, but the Lord directeth his steps,"

Prov. xvi. 9. Let God be our pilot, if we mean to make a good voyage of it. Let our hand be on the stern, our eye on the star; let our course, as the mariner's, be guided by the heavens.

Ver. 12. *To increase and abound*] By doubling his word, he signifieth a double portion of God's grace, which he wisheth unto them; we are sure to receive as much good from God by prayer as we can bring faith to bear away. "Hitherto ye have asked me nothing." Ask, saith Christ, ask enough, open your mouth wide, &c.

Ver. 13. *To the end he may stablish*] Love is of a ferruminating, stablishing property. That grace will not hang together, nor hold out, that is severed from charity.

CHAPTER IV.

Ver. 1. *How ye ought to walk*] EVERY good man is a great peripatetic, walks much. Christ also walks; so doth the devil, apostates, heretics, worldlings; but with this difference: Christ walketh in the middle, Rev. i. 13, ii. 1; the devil to and fro, up and down, Job i. 7, his motion is circular, and therefore fraudulent, 1 Pet. v. 8. Apostates run retrograde, they stumble at the cross, and fall backward. Heretics run out on the right hand, worldlings on the left, James i. 14. Hypocrites turn aside unto their crooked ways, Psal. cxxv. 5. They follow Christ, as Samson did his parents, till he came by the carcase; or as a dog doth his master, till he meeteth with a carrion. The true Christian only walks so as to please God; his eyes look right on, his eyelids look straight before him, Prov. iv. 25. He goes not back, with Hezekiah's sun, nor stands at a stay, as Joshua's, but rejoiceth as a strong man to run his race, as David's sun, Psal. xix. 5. Yea, he "shineth more and more unto the perfect day," as Solomon's, Prov. iv. 18.

Ver. 2. *For ye know what*, &c.] It is expected therefore that ye do them; else the more heinous will be your sin, and the more heavy your reckoning, Isa. lix. 11, 12. What brought such roarings and trouble on them, and that when salvation was looked for? Our iniquities testify to our faces, and we know them.

Ver. 3. *For this is the will of God*] This is his prescribing will, which we must obey; as we must submit to his disposing will, the will of his providence, and grow acquainted with his approving will, the will of his gracious acceptance, Matt. xviii. 14; John i. 23.

Ver. 4. *To possess his vessel*] That is, his body, wherein the soul is, *Tota in toto, et tota in quolibet parte.* If any ask, why so glorious a soul should be in this corruptible body? Besides God's will, and for the order of the universe, Lombard gives this reason, that by the conjunction of the soul with the body (so far its inferior) man might learn a possibility of the union of man with God in glory, notwithstanding the vast distance of nature and excellence, the infiniteness of both in God, the finiteness of both in man.

In sanctification and honour] Chastity is a man's honour; incontinency sets on an indelible blot, Prov. vi. 33. *Castus, quasi καστὸς, ornatus. Sic ἄγνος ab ἄγος, veneratio.*

Ver. 5. *Not in the lust of concupiscence*] Or, in the disease of lust, that dishonourable disease, Rom. i. 26, that wasteth not only the substance of the body, but the honesty and the honour of it.

Ver. 6. *That no man go beyond or defraud*] Or, oppress or cheat. Theft by unjust getting is either ἐπιβολὴ or ἐπιβουλὴ, by violence or cunning contrivance. What else is this but *crimen stellionatus*, the very sin of cozenage?

The Lord is the avenger] Though haply they lie out of the walk of human justice, as not coming under man's cognizance.

Ver. 7. *For God hath not called us*] See the note on Eph. iv. 1. It is a sure rule given by the ancients, *Confusiones libidinum sunt signa cujuslibet sectæ.* Simon Magus had his Helena, Carpocrates his Marcellina, Apelles his Philumena, Montanus his Priscilla and Maximilla, &c.

Ver. 8. *He therefore that despiseth*] That thinks it a trick of youth to fornicate, and a trick of wit to over-reach or oppress; that holds it a matter of nothing to set light by the former lessons; he shall find that he hath to deal with God and not man in this business; and that it is by the Spirit of God that we have spoken unto him, who will punish their contempt of his counsels.

Ver. 9. *Ye need not that I write*] Sith the divine nature, whereof ye are partakers, prompteth you to it, as common nature doth brethren to love one another. The very name of a brother is potent enough to draw affections.

Are taught of God] Therefore have no such need to be taught by men, as those that are yet strangers to the life of God. *Quando Christus magister, quam cito discitur quod docetur?* saith Augustine. *Nescit tarda molimina gratia Spiritus sancti*, saith Ambrose. All Christ's scholars are nimble and notable proficients.

To love one another] The affections are such things as the Lord only can meddle with; therefore the apostle saith, you " are taught of God to love one another."

Ver. 10. *Towards all the brethren*] This universality of their love showed the sincerity of it, and that it was for the truth's sake, 2 John 2. One or more good men may be favoured of those that love no good man, as Jeremiah was of Nebuzaradan, because he foretold the victory.

Ver. 11. *Study to be quiet*] Gr. Be ambitious of peace; as earnest and eager after it, as the ambitionist is after honour. Who commonly rides without reins, rides over other men's heads to compass his desire. The original is, φιλοτιμεῖσθαι, love the honour to be quiet, or to rest and live in silence and not to be noted or noticed, *ut qui vivens moriensque fefellit*, affecting rather quietness from the world than any great acquaintance with it.

And to do your own business] Not oaring in other men's boats, not meddling in other men's

bishoprics, 1 Pet. iv. 15. *Tu fuge ceu pestem, τὴν πολυπραγμοσύνην.* Choler in the gall is useful to the body; but if it overflow, the body grows distempered. Let every man keep to his place, and affect to be no meddler, not to suffer as a busy-body. *Intra pelliculam tuam te contine*, keep within your circle; eccentric motions cannot be right.

With your own hands] Or else with your own brains, as students, which is by far the harder labour.

Ver. 12. *Lack of nothing*] He becometh poor that dealeth with a slack hand, but the hand of the diligent maketh rich, Prov. x. 4. Jabal that dwelt in tents and tended herds had Jubal to his brother, the father of music. Jabal and Jubal, industry and plenty, not without sweet content, dwell together.

Ver. 13. *But I would not have, &c.*] Ignorance is the mother of mistake, and of causeless trouble, of error and terror; as the Roman soldiers were once much affrighted at the sight of the moon's eclipse, till the general had undeceived them by a discourse of the natural cause thereof.

That ye sorrow not] *Non est lugendus qui moritur, sed desiderandus*, saith Tertullian. Abraham mourned moderately for his deceased wife, Gen. xxiii. 2, as is imported by a small *caph* in the word *libcothah*, to weep. So did David for the child born in adultery, though for Absalom he exceeded. It is one of the dues of the dead to be lamented at their funerals.[1] But Christians must know a measure, and so water their plants, as that they drown them not.

Even as others, which have no hope] *Lugeatur mortuus, sed ille quem Gehenna suscipit, quem Tartarus devorat, &c.* Let that dead man be lamented whom hell harboureth, whom the devil devoureth, &c. But let us (whose departed souls angels accompany, Christ embosometh, and all the court of heaven comes forth to welcome) account mortality a mercy; and be grieved that we are so long detained here from the company of our Christ, saith Jerome.

Ver. 14. *Sleep in Jesus*] Dead in Christ. The union then is not dissolved by death. But as by sleep the body is refreshed; so by death it is refined. Let our care be to cleave close to Christ in the instant of death; so shall he be to us, both in life and death, advantage.

Ver. 15. *By the word of the Lord*] Or, in the word, &c., in the self-same words that the Lord used to me, probably, when I was rapt up, 2 Cor. xii. 2, 4, and heard wordless words.

Shall not prevent them] They shall rise ere we shall be rapt, and as they have been before us in death, so shall they be in glory; now priority is a privilege.

Ver. 16. *With a shout*] *Ingenti angelorum jubilo, et acclamatione*, saith Aretius. With a huge applause and acclamation of angels, ἐν κελεύσματι, such as is that of mariners, when near the haven—*Italiam Italiam læto clamore salutant*

---

[1] Νομιζόμενα. *Justa defunctorum.*

(Virg. Æneid), or that of soldiers, when to join battle with the enemy.

And with the trump of God] To require the law, in manner as it was given. Mount Sinai only was then on a flame, but now the whole world, &c. Then God came with ten thousand of his saints; but now thousand thousands shall minister to him, and ten thousand thousands shall stand before him.

Ver. 17. *Then we which are alive*] He speaketh thus of himself as alive at Christ's coming, because we should daily expect it, and even hasten to it.

Shall be caught up together] This is that mystery mentioned 1 Cor. xv. 51, and not till now made known to the world. See the note there.

In the clouds] As Christ also ascended, Acts i. 9. These be the waggons and chariots that Christ will send for us, as Joseph sent his father's family down to Egypt.

And so shall we ever be, &c.] Oh blessed hour! oh thrice happy union! Nothing ever came so near it as the meeting of Jacob and Joseph, or of those two cousins, Mary and Elizabeth, Luke i.

Ver. 18. *Wherefore comfort, &c.*] Scripture comforts come home to the heart, so do not philosophical. *Nescio quomodo* (saith Cicero of such *medicina*) *morbo est imbecillior*. And albeit it is marvellous sweet to meditate (as Mr Knox found it on his death-bed, so that he would have risen and gone into the pulpit to tell others what he had felt in his soul, Melch. Adam. in Vit.), yet there is a special force of strong consolation in Christian communication, which the Lord usually watereth with the dews of divine blessing.

CHAPTER V.

Ver. 1. *But of the times and the seasons*] When Christ shall come to judgment, this is to be reckoned *inter arcana imperii*. See the note on Matt. xxiv. 36. The times and the seasons God hath put in his own power, Acts i. 7. This is a key that he keepeth under his own girdle. Let it suffice us to know that "this is the last hour," that "the ends of the world are come upon us, and that the Lord is at hand." "The time is short" (saith our apostle, 1 Cor. vii. 29), or rolled up, as a piece of cloth, only a little left at the end. Moses brake the tables 1582 years before the birth of Christ. *Non existimo, &c.*, I do not think (saith holy Melancthon) that the time since the end of the Jewish polity shall be much longer than that was before the end thereof. Watch, therefore, and " be diligent that ye may be found of him in peace, without spot, and blameless," 2 Pet. iii. 14.

Ver. 2. *The day of the Lord*] That day, by a speciality, Luke xxi. 34, that great day, Rev. vi. 17, that day of the declaration of God's just judgment, Rom. ii. 5, 16, that day of Christ, 2 Thess. ii. 2, of God, 2 Pet. iii. 12, wherein he will show himself to be God of gods and Lord of lords.

As a thief in the night] Who giveth no warning, Matt. xxiv. 43. See the note there.

Ver. 3. *For when they shall say*] Security is the certain usher of destruction, as in Benhadad's army, and Pompey's before the Pharsalian field. Some of them contended for the priesthood, which was Cæsar's office, others disposed of the consulships and offices in Rome, as if all were already their own; Pompey himself being so wretchedly reckless, that he never considered into what place he were best to retire if he lost the day.

Then shall sudden destruction] As philosophers say, that before a snow the weather will be warmish; when the wind lies, the great rain falls; and the air is most quiet when suddenly there will be an earthquake.

As travail upon a woman] 1. Certainly; 2. Suddenly; 3. Irresistibly, inevitably.

Ver. 4. *Should overtake you as a thief*] Though it come upon you as a thief in a time uncertain. Free you are from the destruction of that day, though not altogether free from the distraction of it, till somewhat re-collected you remember that now your redemption draweth nigh. Hence the saints love Christ's appearing, 2 Tim. iv. 8; look for it with stretched-out necks, and long after it, Rev. xxii. 20.

Ver. 5. *We are not of the night, &c.*] Alexander willed that the Grecians and barbarians should no longer be distinguished by their garments, but by their manners (Qu. Curtius); so should the children of light and of darkness.

Ver. 6. *As do others*] What wonder that the Grecians live loosely? saith Chrysostom; but that Christians do so, this is worse, yea, intolerable.

But let us watch and be sober] We must not be like Agrippa's dormouse that would not awake till cast into boiling lead, or Matthiolus's asses fed with hemlock, that lie for dead, and are half hilded ere they can be aroused. (Comment. in Dioscor.) But rather we should resemble Aristotle and others, who were wont to sleep with brazen balls in their hands, which falling on vessels purposely set on their beds' sides, the noise did dissuade immoderate sleep.

Ver. 7. *Are drunk in the night*] But now, alas, drunkenness is become a noon-day devil. Once Peter's argument (saith Mr Harris) was more than probable, " These men are not drunk, for it is but the third hour of the day." Now men are grown such husbands as that by that time they will return their stocks, and have their brains crowing before day.

Ver. 8. *Be sober*] Drunkenness misbeseemeth any man, but especially a saint; for it robs him of himself, and lays a beast in his room.

Putting on the breastplate of faith and love] Faith is the forepart of this breastplate, whereby we embrace Christ, and love the hinder part thereof, whereby we embosom the saints.

Ver. 9. *God hath not appointed us*] As he hath all drunken beasts, 1 Cor. vi. 10. Yea, all those dry drunkards, Isa. xxviii. 1, that will not awake (though never so much warned) out of the snare of the devil, &c., 2 Tim. ii. 25.

Ver. 10. *Whether we wake or sleep*] That is, live or die, our souls cannot miscarry; because God will have out the full price of his Son's death. See Rom. xiv. 8, with the note there.

Ver. 11. *Comfort yourselves together*] This he subjoins as a singular help to the practice of the former points of duty. Social charity whets on to love and good works, as iron whets iron, as one billet kindleth another, &c.

Ver. 12. *And we beseech you, brethren*] Do not so exhort and edify one another as to think that now the public ministry is no further useful or needful. Let your pastors have all due respect, be your gifts never so eminent.

Ver. 13. *Very highly*] Gr. ὑπὲρ ἐκ περισσοῦ, more than exceeding.[1] Turks and Papists shall else condemn us, who honour every hedge-priest of theirs, and have them in singular esteem, above their merits. The Grecians gave great respect to their philosophers above their orators, because these taught them how to speak, but those how to live well.

For their work's sake] Which is high and honourable, divine and heavenly, a worthy work, 1 Tim. iii. 1. Such as both in the preparation to it and execution of it draweth them to God, keepeth them with God, and to be ever mindful of God, and no less active for God, Ephes. iv. 12, by gathering together the saints and building up the body of Christ.

And be at peace among yourselves] So shall your pastor have the better life, and follow his work with more content and comfort.

Ver. 14. *Warn them that are unruly*] Cry *Cave miser*, stop them in their cursed career, tell them that hell gapes for them, and is but a little before them; snatch them out of the fire, saving them with fear, Jude 23. Neglect of private admonition, how it stings the consciences of the best at death, see Mr Hiron's Life prefixed to the second part of his worthy works. See also Mr Baxter's Saint's Everlasting Rest, p. 497.

Comfort the feeble-minded] The dispirited, faint-hearted, sick, and sinking under the sense of sin and fear of wrath. A Christian should have feeding lips and a healing tongue. The contrary whereunto is deeply detested, Ezek. xxxiv. 4.

Support the weak] Set to your shoulder and shore them up, ἀντέχεσθε. Deal not as the herd of deer do with the wounded deer, forsake and push it away from them. Christ gathereth his lambs with his arm, and bears them in his bosom, Isa. xl. 11. He had a great care of his weaker tribes when they marched through the wilderness, for in their several brigades he put a strong tribe to two weak tribes, as Judah to Issachar and Zabulon, &c. The Greek word here rendered support, signifieth *sublevare alioqui ruituros*, saith Beza, to keep up those that would else go to the ground.

Ver. 15. *See that none render*] Nothing is so natural to us; and Aristotle commends revenge as a piece of manhood, when indeed it is doghood rather. Excellently Lactantius, *Non est minus mali referre injuriam, quam inferre.* It is as bad to recompense wrong as to do wrong. See the notes on Matt. v. 44 and Rom. xii. 17.

But ever follow that which is good] Not to do good is to do evil; not to save a man when we can, is to destroy him, Mark iii. 4. See the note there.

Ver. 16. *Rejoice evermore*] A duty much pressed in both Testaments, but little practised by many of God's whinnels, who are ever puling and putting finger in the eye, through one discontent or another. The wicked may not rejoice, Hos. ix. 1; the saints must, Psal. xxxii. 11 and xxxiii. 1, and that continually, striving to an habitual cheerfulness, which is when faith heals the conscience, and grace husheth the affections, and composeth all within; what should ail such a man, not to be perpetually merry?

Ver. 17. *Pray without ceasing*] While prayer standeth still, the trade of godliness stands still. All good comes into the soul by this door, all true treasure by this merchant's ship. Paul beginneth, continueth, and concludeth his Epistles with prayer. Nehemiah sends up ejaculations ever and anon. Of Carolus Magnus it was spoken, *Carolus plus cum Deo quam cum hominibus loquitur*, that he spake more with God than with men. Our hearts should be evermore in a praying temper; and our set times of prayer should not be neglected, though we be not always alike prepared and disposed thereunto. Disuse breeds lothness to do it another time. Mahometans, what occasion soever they have, either by profit or pleasure, to divert them, will pray five times every day.[2] *Oratio est quantitas discreta*, saith the philosopher. *Oratio debet esse quantitas continua*, saith our apostle. A Christian must ever be praying habitually, and vitally too; for, *semper orat qui bene semper agit.* He hath manifold occasions of calling actually upon God, as, 1. His daily morning and evening sacrifice, the neglect or non-performance whereof the Jews counted and called an "abomination of desolation." 2. The sanctification of creatures, calling, and relations. 3. New mercies. 4. New infirmities. 5. Variety of crosses. 6. Faintness of faith, spiritual desertions, temptations of Satan. 7. Sweetness of meditation. 8. Forethought of his last account, &c. Neither let any say we cannot awhile; for, 1. "A whet is no let;" a bait by the way is no hinderance to the journey; time spent in prayer hindereth not our business; for though it take so much from the heap, yet it increaseth the heap, as it is said of tithes and offerings, Mal. iii. Blind Popery could say, Mass and meat hindereth no man's thrift. 2. The greater the business, the more need there is of prayer to speed it; to be as oil to the wheel, as wings to the bird. Jacob, after he had seen

---

[1] *Apud Græcos majori in honore habebantur philosophi quam oratores. Illi enim recte vivendi, &c.* Lactantius.

[2] Lawless Liberty, in a sermon by Mr Terry.

God at Bethel, lift up his feet, and went lustily on his journey, Gen. xxix. 1. 3. How much idle time spend we, either in doing nothing, or worse, that might better be bestowed in this holy duty! Only take heed that frequency breed not formality, that we pray not in a lazy, customary, bedulling strain, like the pace the Spaniard rides, but rousing up ourselves, and wrestling with God, set we sides and shoulders to the work, lift up hearts and hands to heaven, lean upon Christ's bosom as the beloved disciple did, lie hard upon him, as she did upon Samson, to learn out his riddle; press him as they did the prophet, till he was even ashamed to say them nay, 2 Kings ii. 17, till you put him to the blush, and leave "a blot in his face," ὑπωπιάζη, as the importunate widow dealt by the unjust judge, Luke xviii. 5. So this is prayer; and thus we are to "continue instantly in prayer," to wait upon it (as the word προσκαρτερεῖν signifieth), and to persevere in it, as David did, Psal. xxvii. 4, and cxix. 81, 82.

Ver. 18. *In everything give thanks*] If God give prosperity, praise him, and it shall be increased, saith Augustine. If adversity, praise him, and it shall be removed, or at least sanctified. Job blessed God as well for taking as giving, Job i. He knew that God afflicted him, *non ad exitium, sed ad exercitium*, to refine him, not to ruin him. But this is *Christianorum propria virtus*, saith Jerome, a practice proper to Christians, to be heartily thankful for crosses. Basil spends all his sermon upon this text in this theme. Every bird can sing in a summer's day, and it is easy to swim in a warm bath; but in deep affliction to cover God's altar, not with our tears, as Mal. ii. 13, but with the calves of our lips, Hos. xiv. 2, this none can do but the truly religious.

Ver. 19. *Quench not the Spirit*] In his motions or graces. See the canon for the fire on the altar, and observe it, Lev. vi. 12, 13. Confess here as Hezekiah did, 2 Chron. xxix. 6, 7. And take the apostle's counsel, 2 Tim. i. 6. Stir up this fire on the hearth of our hearts; let the priest's lips blow it up into a flame; despise not prophesying, &c. It may be quenched either by the withdrawing of fuel (neglect of ordinances) or by casting on water (falling into foul courses).

Ver. 20. *Despise not*] i. e. Highly honour, and preciously esteem, as an honorary given by Christ to his Church at his wonderful ascension, Psal. li. 17; Eph. iv. 8, 11.

Prophesying] That is, preaching, 1 Cor. xiv. 3, so called because they took their texts out of some of the prophets.

Ver. 21. *Prove all things*] Take nothing that you hear upon trust (Νῆφε καὶ μέμνησο ἀπιστεῖν, Epicharm.), but bring all to the test, Isa. viii. 20. To the law, *i. e.* the Old Testament, and to the testimony, *i. e.* the New, which is by St John often called the testimony. Mercer observes that of the Hebrew word *ozen* for an ear,

cometh *Moznaiim* for a pair of balances; to note that we must weigh what we hear; our two ears must be as balances for that purpose.

Hold fast that which is good] Orthodox, current, agreeable to, and approvable by, the Scriptures, especially that which God hath made good and sweet to your own souls. Hold fast that thou hast, &c. Hast thou found honey? eat it, Prov. xxv. 16. Go on to heaven eating of it, as Samson did of his honey-comb.

Ver. 22. *Abstain from all, &c.*] Whatsoever is heterodox, unsound, and unsavoury, shun it, as you would do a serpent in your way or poison in your meats. Theodosius tare the Arian's arguments presented to him in writing, because he found them repugnant to the Scriptures. And Austin retracteth even ironies only, because they had the appearance of lying. God commanded the Jews to abstain from swine's flesh; they would not so much as name it, but in their common talk would call a sow *dabbar Achar*, another thing. (Elias Thisbit.)

Ver. 23. *That your whole spirit, soul, body*] The temple consisted of three parts, so doth man; the body is as the outer court, the soul as the holy place, the spirit as the most holy. So the world is three stories high, the earth, the visible heaven, and the third heaven.

Ver. 24. *Faithful is he, &c.*] Prayer must be founded upon the faithfulness of God in fulfilling his promises. Hereby faith will be strengthened, and affection excited. Prayer is a putting the promises in suit.

Ver. 25. *Brethren, pray for us*] The best may need the prayers of the meanest. God will have us beholden herein one to another, 1 Cor. xii. 21, 22. How earnest is that great apostle in begging prayers, Rom. xv. 30. Pray for me, I say, pray for me, I say (quoth father Latimer), for I am sometimes so fearful that I could creep into a mouse-hole; sometimes God doth visit me again with his comfort. (Acts and Mon.)

Ver. 26. *With an holy kiss*] Our very civilities should savour of sanctity, and our common conversation relish of religion, Zech. xiv. 20, 21.

Ver. 27. *That this epistle be read*] It is a matter of greatest necessity and importance that the Holy Scriptures be daily and duly read by all. A sad complaint it is, which Reverend Moulin makes of his countrymen the French Protestants: Whiles they burned us, saith he, for reading the Scriptures, we burnt with zeal to be reading of them. Now, with our liberty is bred also negligence and disesteem of God's word. (Moulin's Theophilus.) And is it not so with us at this day? Our ancestors in Henry VIII.'s time would sit up all night in reading and hearing, and were at great charges. Some gave five marks for a Bible, that we may have for five shillings.

Ver. 28. *Amen*] Amen is, 1. Assenting; 2. Assevering; 3. Assuring.

THE SECOND EPISTLE OF ST PAUL TO THE THESSALONIANS.

CHAPTER I.

Ver. 1. *In God our Father, and the Lord, &c.*] As God is in his people of a truth, 1 Cor. xiv. 25, so are they in God; and as Christ is at God's right hand, so is the Church at Christ's right hand, Psal. xlv. 9. Yea, they are in him, and part of him, &c.

Ver. 2. *Grace be to you, &c.*] See the note on 1 Cor. i. 2.

And the Lord Jesus Christ] Who is both the fountain, John i. 16, and the conduit, John i. 17; for of his fulness we have all received grace for grace. Grace, that is, God's favour and reconciliation; for grace, that is, for the favour and love that God the Father bare unto his Son, Eph. i. 6.

Ver. 3. *We are bound to thank God*] Duty is a debt, and a good heart is not well till it have discharged it. As he that hath somewhat lying on his stomach cannot be at ease till he hath got it up, so neither must we, till disburdened in sounding forth God's praises for the good he hath bestowed on us, or on others for our use. This, saith Luther, is *sancta crapula;* and it can be no hurt to have our hearts thus overcharged.

Because that your faith groweth exceedingly] As corn or plants do after a binding drought. They were under persecution, ver. 4, and gat by it. Storms of persecution beat God's people into their harbour; make them look to their tackling, patience; to their anchor, hope; to their helm, faith; to their card, the word of God; to their captain, Christ; whereas security, like a calm, maketh us forget both our danger and deliverer. Adversity hath whipt many a soul to heaven, saith one, which otherwise prosperity had coached to hell. We are like to children's tops, saith another, that will go but little longer than they are whipt. How oft are we sitting down on earth, as if we were loth to go any further, till affliction call to us, as the angel to Elijah, " Up, thou hast a great way to go," and then we trigg.

Ver. 4. *For your patience and faith*] Faith patienteth the heart, by putting the head into heaven before-hand, and giving a man a glimpse of future glory. Faith drinks to a suffering saint in a cup of Nepenthes, and saith, " Be of good courage, and of good carriage under the cross." *Flebile principium melior fortuna sequetur.* The right hand of the Lord can mend all. Faith wraps itself in the promises, lays the soul upon Christ, and maketh it of weak to become

strong, Heb. xi. 34. Whatsoever cross cometh upon it, faith is either as a wreath betwixt the shoulder and the burden, that it wring not, or else a remover of it from the soul to God, by virtue of that writ or warrant, Psal. lv. 22, " Cast thy burden," &c.

Ver. 5. *Which is a manifest token*] ἔνδειγμα, *indigitatio.* The saints' sufferings here are an ocular demonstration of a future judgment, wherein all their wrongs shall be righted, all their labour of love recompensed. This held Job's head above water, when else he had been overwhelmed with the floods of affliction, Job xix. 25. So Dan. xii. 1, 2. Though things be otherwise darkly delivered, yet when the Jews were to lose land and life, then plainly the general judgment is mentioned : so Heb. xi. 35.

Ver. 6. *To recompense tribulation*] To trouble these troublers of Israel, and that throughout all eternity, because they would be always troubling God's people if they might; as it is said of the scorpion, that there is not one minute wherein it doth not put forth the sting. (Pliny.)

Ver. 7. *Rest with us*] As Noah's ark, after much tossing, rested upon the mountains of Ararat ; as the ark of the covenant, formerly transportative, was at length settled in Solomon's temple. The word ἄνεσιν here used properly signifieth remission and relaxation from hard labour, Apoc. xiv. 13, " they rest from their labours." And as the sleep of a labouring man is sweet, so here.

With his mighty angels] Oh what a glorious day must that needs be, when so many glorious suns shall shine at once; the Lord Christ outshining them all, *velut inter ignes luna minores!* he will not leave one angel in heaven behind him, Mark viii. 38.

Ver. 8. *In flaming fire*] Natural fire, 2 Pet. iii. 6, 7, whereby the elements shall melt like scalding lead upon the wicked, whiles they give account with all the world on a flaming fire about their ears. Of this last dreadful fire the very heathen had some blind notions. *Esse quoque in fatis meminit,* &c. (Ovid, Metam. lib. i.) Lucretius and Tully (De Nat. Deor.) say somewhat to it, but little to the purpose.

And that obey not the gospel] This is the grand sin of this age, John iii. 19. No sin will gripe so in hell as this. This will be a bodkin at the heart one day, I might have been delivered, but I have wilfully cut the throat of my poor soul by refusing those rich offers of mercy made me in the gospel.

Ver. 9. *Who shall be punished*] Here is the pain of sense, of eternity, of extremity.

From the presence] Here is the pain of loss, which is of the two the greater.

And from the glory of his power] God will set himself to inflict upon the damned such a measure of misery as his power can extend unto.

Ver. 10. *To be glorified*] This is the chief end of his coming, like as he reprobateth some that his mercy in electing others may the more appear.

To be admired] When they shall be seen to shine as the firmament, nay, as the stars, Dan. xii. 3, nay, as the sun, Matt. xiii. 14, nay, as Christ himself, that Sun of righteousness, to the great admiration of all men. Admiration is the overplus of expectation; Christ admired at his own work in the Centurion's faith, in Nathaniel's integrity (" Behold an Israelite indeed "), in his spouse's beauty, Cant. iv. How much more shall others admire it at that day, when grace shall become glory, when there shall be no spot, wrinkle, or other deformity! when the saints shall set the crown upon Christ's head, Cant. iii. 11, and cast down their crowns at his feet, Rev. iv. 10, 11, saying, " Thou art worthy," &c.

Ver. 11. *The work of faith with power*] Without which power neither the goodness of God, nor the good pleasure of his goodness, that is, his decree of glorifying us, nor the work of faith, could be effected.

Ver. 12. *That the name of our Lord*] It is much for the honour of the saints that Christ shall account himself glorified in their glory. Neither is it for their honour only, but for their advantage; for this glory of Christ shall redound unto them; therefore it is added by the apostle, " And ye in him."

CHAPTER II.

Ver. 1. *Now we beseech you, brethren*] CHRIST's spokesmen must be fair-spoken, so wooing for him that they may win upon men's hearts, leading by the hand those that are willing, and drawing after a sort those that are less willing, that they may present them as a chaste virgin to Christ, 2 Cor. xi. 2. This earnest obtestation imports that it is both easy and dangerous to be carried away by seducers; for the Scripture doth not use to " cleave straws with beetles," to be so serious in a slight matter. " We beseech you," of all loves, ἐρωτῶμεν (ab ἔρως, love). Brethren, womb-brethren, as near in nature as is possible.[1] " By the coming of our Lord Jesus," whom you love, look and long for; "and by your gathering together," ἐπισυναγωγὴ, as ever you desire and hope to hover under his wings, as the chickens under the hen's, that the infernal kites catch you not at that day.

By the coming of our Lord] He draweth an argument from the matter underhand wherewith their hearts were now heated beforehand. It must

be an elaborate speech that shall work upon the heart.

And by our gathering together unto him] In that last and great day, when all the eagles shall be gathered to that once dead, but now all-quickening carcase, Matt. xxiv. 28; when the sign of the Son of man shall be lifted up as an ensign, and all the saints shall repair to it, as the soldiers do to their colours, Ephes. i. 10.

Ver. 2. *That ye be not soon shaken*] Σαλευ-.θῆναι (a nomine σάλος, salum). As seamen are tossed by a tempest, and even brought to their wits' ends, Psal. cvii. 27. That ye be not shaken out of your wits, and put beside yourselves; so the words may be rendered. And indeed errors and heresies *sanam tollunt de cardine mentem*, drive men out of their little wits; as we see by woeful experience at this day.

Or be troubled] Or, terrified, θροεῖσθαι, as with a sudden hubbub, alarm, tumult, uproar. It imports such perturbation as ariseth from rumour, Mark xiii., or relation of something troublesome.

Neither by spirit] Pretended revelations, such as was that whereby the old impostor cozened that young prophet into a lion's mouth.

Nor by word] Traditions, unwritten verities, &c.

Nor by letter] Counterfeited, supposititious, spurious, such as were those Gospels that went under the names of St Thomas, St Bartholomew, &c. Or by wresting and writhing that passage of his former letter, 1 Thess. iv. 17, to another meaning than ever the apostle intended it. So St Austin was served, and he foresaw it: I believe, saith he, that some of my readers will imagine *me sensisse quod non sensi, aut non sensisse quod sensi*, that I was in many things of another mind, than ever I was indeed. And it fell out accordingly; for as Baronius witnesseth, after St Austin's death there arose up divers, *Qui ex ejus scriptis male perceptis complures invexerunt errores*, who by mistaking of what he had written, brought in many pernicious errors, and vouched him for their author. (Baron. Annal. tom. 6.)

As that the day of Christ] Peter's scoffers asked, " Where is the promise of his coming ? " as if Christ would never come. These were afraid he would come too soon, and take them with their task undone. The devil usually tempteth by extremes, as he did our Saviour, Matt. iv., and as he did Mr Knox upon his deathbed, first to despair, by setting his sins before him; and then to presumption, by reminding him of his reformations.

Is at hand] Just now, this present year, for so the Greek ἐνέστηκεν signifieth. This fear racked and almost wrecked their minds, as a storm forceth a ship riding in the road to cut cable.

Ver. 3. *Except there come a falling*] Gr. ἀποστασία, an apostasy, viz. of people from the truth, when the whole world went a wondering and a wandering after the beast, Rev. xiii. 3. To the fathers these prophecies of Antichrist were riddles. The prophecy is sealed to the end, Dan. xii., till unsealed by event. Austin saith ingenu-

---

[1] Ἀδελφὸς ab ἀ et δελφὺς, *uterus : fratres uterini.*

ously, he understood not this text. And herein he did better than those other of the Latin Fathers that interpreted it of the falling away of sundry nations from the Roman empire. Daniel set forth Antichrist typically in that little Antichrist, Antiochus; Paul topically, in this chapter. John writeth the mystery of Antichrist in his Revelation; Paul sets a commentary upon him, and graphically describeth him, calling him apostasy in the abstract here, as some will have it; and in the next verse, "that man of sin," that is, *merum scelus*, as Beza hath it.

And that man of sin] That breathing devil, so portentously, so peerlessly vicious, *Ut ejus nomen non hominis, sed vitii esse videatur* (as Lipsius saith of one Tubulus, a Roman prætor), that sin itself can hardly be more sinful.

The son of perdition] Destined to destruction, even to be cast alive into the "lake of fire burning with brimstone," Rev. xix. 20. Well might Pope Marcellus II. strike his hand upon the table, and say, *Non video quomodo qui locum hunc altissimum tenent, salvari possunt*, I see not how any pope can be saved. (Onuph. in Vita.) When I was first in orders (said Pope Pius Quintus) I had some good hopes of salvation; when I was made a cardinal, I doubted; but now that I am pope, I do almost despair. (Cornel. a Lapide in Numb. xi. 11.)

Ver. 4. *Who opposeth himself*] ἀντικείμενος, who standeth in full opposition to Christ, as a counter-christ. The enemy and adversary is this wicked Haman, Esth. vii. 6, so this "man of sin," that Antichrist of Rome. When the pope sets forth any bulls, commonly he thus concludes, *Non obstantibus constitutionibus Apostolicis, cæterisque contrariis quibuscunque*, The constitutions and ordinances of the apostles, and all things else to the contrary notwithstanding. The pope's interpretation of Scripture, though it never so much cross the text, yet it is ito be esteemed the very word of God, saith Hosus: *Tamen est ipsissimum Dei verbum.*

And exalteth himself] *Perfrica frontem*, said Calvus to Vatinius, *et digniorem te dic qui Prætor fieres quam Catonem*. Pope Boniface III. set a good face upon it, and arrogated the title of Universal Bishop. The ancient Romans painted Pride with three crowns on her head. On the first was inscribed *Transcendo*, on the second, *Non obedio*, on the third, *Perturbo*. The modern Romans see all this daily acted by their bishop.

Above all that is called god] In the year 1540 Pope Paul III. suffered himself to be thus blasphemously flattered, *Paulo tertio optimo maximo in terris Deo*. In the year 1610, books were printed at Bonony and at Naples, with this inscription, *Paulo V. vice-deo, Christianæ reipublicæ monarchæ invictissimo, Pontificiæ omnipotentiæ conservatori acerrimo*: To Paul V., vice-god, most invincible monarch of Christendom, most stout defender of the papal omnipotency. The pope can do all that Christ can do, and is more than God, saith Hostiens:s the canonist, and after him Zabarel:

Of wrong he can make right, of vice virtue, of nothing something, saith Bellarmine. (Lib. i. de Pontif. Rom.) He is lifted above the angels, so that he can excommunicate them; he can dispense against not only the law of nature, but against all the evangelists, prophets, and apostles, saith Pope John XXIII. *in extrav.*; one of his parasites clawed him thus,

Oraclis vocis mundi moderaris habenas :
Et merito in terris diceris esse Deus.

Or that is worshipped] σέβασμα. Or, that is august, above princes and potentates. He is cried up for "Lord of lords and King of kings," one that hath both the swords throughout the world, and an illimited empire over all reasonable creatures, *Dulia adorandus*, &c. How he trod upon the emperor of Germany, and how he lashed Henry II. of England, and Henry IV. of France till the blood followed, is better known than that I need here to relate. *Sed exorto Evangelii jubare sagaciores (ut spero) principes ad nutum Romani Orbilii non solvent subligacula*, saith one. Our Richard I., going for the Holy Land, had conference with one Joachim, a Cistercian abbot, being then in Calabria, near Sicily; whom, at his coming, he heard preaching and expounding the Apocalypse touching the afflictions of the Church, and concerning Antichrist, which (said he) was then born and in the city of Rome, and shall be advanced to the see apostolic; of whom the apostle said, "He shall extol himself above all that is called God;" and that the seven crowns were the kings and princes of the earth, that obeyed him. (Hoveden.) Much about the same time, Pope Celestine crowned the emperor Henry and his empress Constantia at Rome with his feet, and kicked off the same crown again. (Speed.)

Sitteth in the temple of God] Sitting is a style proper to the pope; who is said not to reign, but to sit so many years or months; and his place of dominion is called his "see," or "seat." Robert Grossetête, bishop of Lincoln, called him in a letter, "heretic, Antichrist sitting in the chair of pestilence, and next to Lucifer himself." Benedictus the Sorbonist affirmeth that the ass in the history of Balaam signifieth the Church. *An quia Pontifex Balaam est qui ei insidet?* saith Dr Raynolds, *i. e.* Doth he not mean by it, that the pope is Balaam that sitteth upon that ass? (De Idolol. Rom.) England was once called the "pope's ass," for bearing his burdens, and obeying his mandates. But beside the present Reformation (which is such in ages past despaired of, the present admire, and the future shall stand amazed at), in the year 1245 (lo, so long since) the pope was denied entrance into England; it being said that he was but like a "mouse in a satchel," or a snake in one's bosom, who did but ill repay their hosts for their lodging. (Scultet. Annal.)

Ver. 5. *Remember ye not*] Satan usually hides from us that which should help us. But as the soul should be as it were an holy ark; so should the memory be as the pot of manna, preserving holy truth for constant use.

Ver. 6. *What withholdeth, &c.*] viz. The Roman empire, which had its rise, reign, and ruin, whereupon the popedom was founded, and grew to that excessive greatness, that it laboured with nothing more than with the weightiness of itself.

Ver. 7. *For the mystery of iniquity*] Policy palliated with the name of piety ; dissembled sanctity, which is double iniquity. The Council of Trent (where Popery was established by a law in all parts of it, and a divorce sued out from Christ) was carried by the pope and his complices with such infinite guile and craft, as that themselves will even smile in the triumphs of their own wits (when they hear it but mentioned) as at a master-stratagem, a very mystery of iniquity. (Spec. Europ.)

Doth already work] In those ancient apostates and antichrists St John complaineth of. Tertullian condemneth the bishop's sprouting ambition in these words, I hear that there is a peremptory edict set forth alate, *Pontifex scilicet maximus. Episcopus episcoporum dicit*, &c. Thus saith the chief priest, the bishop of bishops, &c. *Odi fastum illius Ecclesiæ*, saith Basil, I hate the pride of that Western Church.[1] Ammianus Marcellinus (a heathen historian) sharply taxeth the Roman bishops of his time for their pride and prodigality. How stiffly did Gregory the Great oppose John of Constantinople for affecting the title of universal bishop ; and yet how basely did the same Gregory collogue with Phocas the emperor, that himself might be so styled. This Phocas, a wild, drunken, bloody, adulterous tyrant, advanced the bishop of Rome (Gregory's successor) to the primacy, and was therefore slaughtered by Heraclius, who cut off his wicked hands and feet, and then his genitals by piece-meal. (Zonaras.)

Until he be taken out of the way] That is, the Roman emperor have removed his seat to Constantinople, that Rome may become the nest of Antichrist. Joannes de Columna writeth, that Otho, emperor of Germany, thought to have seated himself at Rome (as former emperors had done), and began to build him there a stately palace. But at the earnest importunity of the Romans he gave over that design. The like had been attempted 300 years before by Constans, nephew to Heraclius, but could never be effected. This was a singular providence of God (saith Genebrard, a Popish chronologer) that the kingdom of the Church prophesied of by Daniel might have its seat at Rome. If he had said, that the kingdom of Antichrist, prophesied of by St Paul and St John, might have its seat in that city seated upon seven hills, he had said the very truth, he had hit the nail on the head.

Ver. 8. *And then shall that wicked*] Gr. ἄνομος, that lawless, yokeless, masterless monster, to whom in the Council of Lateran, 1516 (one year only before Luther stood up to reform), there was granted plenary power over the whole

Church ; which was never settled upon him in any former Council. Pope Nicholas I. said, that he was above law, because Constantine had styled the pope God. But the very gloss derides him for this inference.

With the spirit of his mouth] *i. e.* With the evidence of his word in the mouths of his faithful ministers. *Vide catalogum testium veritatis.* Bellarmine confesseth to his great grief, that ever since the Lutherans have declared the pope to be Antichrist, his kingdom hath not only not increased, but every day more and more decreased and decayed. (Lib. iii. de Papa Rom. cap. 21.) What long hath been the opinion and fear of some not unconsiderable divines, that Antichrist, before his abolition, shall once again overflow the whole face of the west, and suppress the true Protestant Churches, I pray God to avert.

With the brightness of his coming] At the last day. The holy city shall they tread under-foot forty and two months, Rev. xi. 2, that is (as some compute it) till the year of grace 1866. But that is but a conjecture. No more is that other, that Solomon's temple was finished in the year of the world 3000 ; and was destroyed, together with the city, by the Romans, in the year of the world exactly 4000, therefore the spiritual temple shall be consummated in 3000, or perhaps in 4000 more. (Lightfoot's Harm. 206.)

Ver. 9. *After the working of Satan*] Who (as God's ape) works effectually in his and by his agents upon others. By corrupt teachers Satan catcheth men, as a cunning fisher by one fish catcheth another, that he may feed upon both.

And lying wonders] The devil is ashamed (saith the Jesuit Gretser) to confirm Luther's doctrine by miracles. But he that now requireth miracles to make him to believe, is himself a great miracle, saith Austin.

Ver. 10. *And with all deceiveableness*] Popery is nothing else but a great lie, a grand imposture, a farrago of falsities and heresies. It is not without cause that the centurists say, "That all the old heretics fled, and hid themselves in the popish clergy." (Cent. x. c. 11.)

Because they received not the love] This is the great gospel-sin, punished by God with strong delusions, vile affections, just damnation. *Infatuati seducentur, seducti judicabuntur.* Given up by God, they shall be seduced, and being seduced they shall be condemned. It is Austin's note upon this text.

Ver. 11. *Strong delusion*] Gr. the efficacy of error. As in those at Genoa, that show the ass's tail whereupon our Saviour rode, for a holy relic, and perform divine worship to it. (Wolph. Mem. Lect.) And in those that wear out the marble crosses graven in the pavements of their churches, with their often kissing them. (Spec. Europ.) The crucifix which is in the city of Burgos, the priests show to great personages, as if it were Christ himself ; telling them that his hair and nails do grow miraculously, which they cut and pare monthly, and give to noblemen, *cumspecte vestiti, epulas curantes profusas*, &c.

[1] This he called ὀφρὺν δυτικήν. *Vehiculis insidentes cir-*

as holy relics. The Jesuits confess that the legend of miracles of their saints is for most part false; but it was made for good intention: and herein, that it is lawful and meritorious to lie, and write such things, to the end the common people might with greater zeal serve God and his saints; and especially to draw the women to good order, being by nature facile and credulous, addicted to novelties and miracles. (Spanish Pilgr.)

Ver. 12. *That they all might be damned*] Heresy is the leprosy in the head, Levit. iii. 29, which is utterly incurable, and destroys the soul. See Rev. xix. 21.

Had pleasure in unrighteousness] These are delivered up to that dead and dedolent disposition, Eph. iv. 19, losing at length all passive power also of awakening out of the snare of the devil, who taketh them alive at his pleasure, 2 Tim. ii. 26.

Ver. 13. *But we are bound*, &c.] Lest they should be discouraged with the former discourse, the apostle tells them, that being elect they cannot be finally deceived. So the author to the Hebrews, chap. vi. 9. Zuinglius, after that he had terrified the wicked, was wont to come in with *Bone vir, hoc nihil ad te*: This is nothing to thee, thou faithful Christian. We cannot beat the dogs, but the children will cry, and must therefore be stilled and cheered up.

And belief of the truth] That is, of Christ the object, in the glass of the gospel.

Ver. 14. *To the obtaining of the glory*] This is the end of faith, as faith is of effectual calling.

Ver. 15. *Stand fast*] Though never so many fall from the faith. Falling stars were never but meteors. God also will have the tree of his Church to be shaken sometimes, that rotten fruit may fall off; and that there may be a shedding of the good from temporaries.

Hold the traditions] Hold fast by these, that ye may stand the faster.

Ver. 16. *And good hope*] The fruit of everlasting consolation, Rom. xv. 4. And well called good, because it hath for its object the greatest good, and that which is of greatest certainty, Heb. xi. 1.

Ver. 17. *Stablish you*] Taking you by the hand, and laying hold on you, like as ye lay hold upon his word, ver. 15.

CHAPTER III.

Ver. 1. *Finally, brethren*, &c.] *Quod superest*, τὸ λοιπὸν, That which yet remains, brethren. Ministers have never done, but have somewhat more to say (*Redit labor actus in orbem*) when they have said their utmost.

Pray for us] As he had done for them, chap. ii. 16, 17. See the like, 1 Thess. v. 23, 25, with the notes. Oh, pray (said a dying Dutch divine) that God would preserve the gospel: *Pontifex enim Rom. et Concilium Tridentinum mira moliun-*

tur, For the pope and his Trent conventicle are plotting strange businesses.

May have free course] Gr. τρέχη, may run its race, as the sun doth, Psal. xix. Eusebius saith that the gospel spread at first through the world like a sun-beam. (Hist. ii. 3.)

And be glorified] As it was, Acts xiii. 48. The word never worketh till it be received with admiration.

Ver. 2. *From unreasonable*] ἀτόπων, men compact of mere incongruities, solecising in opinion, speeches, actions.

For all men have not faith] And are therefore unreasonable; nothing is more irrational than irreligion. An unbeliever is no better (but in some respects worse) than a beast; a brutish person skilful to destroy, Ezek. xxi. 31.

Ver. 3. *But God is faithful*] Though men be faithless; and though they be evil, as verse 2, yet he shall keep you from evil, from whatsoever adverse power either of men or devils. Thus the saints may find and fetch comfort from God under whatsoever disasters. They go always under a double guard, the peace of God within them, Phil. iv. 7, φρουρήσει, and the power of God without them, 1 Pet. i. 5, φρουρούμενοι. How then can they possibly miscarry?

Ver. 4. *That ye both do and will do*] *Qui monet ut facias quod jam facis, ille monendo laudat*, &c. Here the apostle, orator-like, entereth their bosoms; and by praising their present obedience, artificially wresteth from them a redoubled diligence; *Virtus laudata crescit*. Thus being crafty, he catcheth them with guile, as he did those Corinthians, 2nd Epist. xiii. 16. It must be an elaborate discourse that shall work upon the heart.

Ver. 5. *And the Lord direct*] Or rectify your crooked hearts and distorted affections, that stand across to all good, till God set them to rights, κατευθύναι. Men's persuasions are but as a key to a lock that is out of order, unless God cooperate.

Ver. 6. *Now we command you*] To show how hardly we are divided from evil company, as loth to depart as Lot's wife out of Sodom, *Velut canis famelicus ab uncto corio*.

That ye withdraw yourselves] That ye shun them as studiously as the seaman doth a rock or shelf, στέλλεσθαι, *Nautarum proprium*.

From every brother that walketh disorderly] From every profligate professor, and carnal gospeller, that walketh *contra gnomonem et Canonem Decalogi, cuique vita est incomposita, et pessime morata* (as an interpreter speaketh), contrary to God, and to every good work reprobate.

And not after the tradition] sc. That men should sweat out their living, and earn it before they eat it. Sin brought in sweat, Gen. iii. 19. And now, not to sweat, increaseth sin.

Ver. 7. *For yourselves know*] You idle addleheads, ver. 11. For to these he here directs his speech, that by doing nothing, had learned at length to do naughtily. *Nihil agendo male agere discimus.*

We behaved not ourselves disorderly] Gr. ἠτακτή-σαμεν, We brake not our ranks, as unruly soldiers.

Ver. 8. *Any man's bread for nought*] But earned it before we eat it. Bread should not be eaten, till it sweat in a man's hand, or head.

Ver. 9. *Not because we have not power*] Posse et nolle nobile est. (Chrysost.) See the notes on 1 Cor. ix. 4—11.

But to make ourselves an example] Those therefore that have enough to live on, must yet be doing something whereby the world may be the better; and not think to come hither merely as rats and mice, only to devour victuals, and to run squeaking up and down. These are ciphers, or rather excrements in human society. By the law of Mahomet, the Great Turk himself is bound to exercise some manual trade or occupation (for none must be idle), as Solyman the Magnificent, that so threatened Vienna, his trade was making of arrow-heads; Achmat the Last, horn rings for archers. (Peacham.)

Ver. 10. *That if any would not work*] In the sweat of thy nose shalt thou eat thy bread, was the old sanction, Gen. iii. 19; yea, Paradise, that was man's storehouse, was also his workhouse. They bury themselves alive, that, as body-lice, live on other men's labours; and it is a sin to succour them. Seneca professed, that he had rather be sick in his bed than out of employment.

Ver. 11. *Working not at all*] But making religion a mask for idleness; whose whole life is to eat, and drink, and sleep, and sport, and sit, and talk and laugh themselves fat. These are an odious sort of Christians; a kind of vagrant people that, having little to do, are set a-work by the devil; for idleness is the hour of temptation. Standing pools are full of vermin. Behemoth lieth in the fens, Job xl. 21.

But are busy-bodies] Nihil agentes, sed curiose satagentes: Not working at home, but over-working abroad, though to no purpose or profit.

Ver. 12. *That with quietness*] Being no meddler in other men's matters, but minding his own.

Res tuas age. The pragmatical person is an odious person, and the place where he lives longs for a vomit to spew him out. See the note on 1 Thess. iv. 11.

Ver. 13. *Be not weary in well-doing*] No, not to those disorderly (and therefore less worthy) walkers, if in extreme necessity, or if thereby ye may win them from the error of their way. As if any prove refractory and irreformable.

Note that man] σημειοῦσθε, or, notice him, as infamous; brand him, beware of him; let him see a strangeness in you toward him.

That he may be ashamed] Gr. ἵνα ἐντραπῇ. Ut quærat ubi se possit præ pudore occultare. (Cameron.) That he may turn into himself, or turn short again upon himself; recognize his disorders, and return to a better course. The repenting prodigal is said to come to himself, Luke xv. 17, and those relenting Israelites to bethink themselves, or to bring back to their hearts, 1 Kings viii. 47. The Greek here signifies that he may hide his head for shame; *Sed illum ego periisse dico, cui periit pudor.* (Curtius.) He is past grace that is past shame.

Ver. 15. *Yet count him not, &c.*] If there be but *aliquid Christi*, anything of Christ to be discerned in him.

But admonish him as a brother] Conscience is a nice and sullen dame; man a cross, crabbed creature, and will hardly be wrought upon by a stoical sourness, or an imperious boisterousness; but must be gently handled, and fairly admonished. Gentle showers comfort the earth, when dashing storms drown the seed.

Ver. 16. *Now the Lord, &c.*] He begins, continues, and concludes with fervent prayer. All our sacrifices should be salted with salt, perfumed with this incense of prayer, Col. iii. 17.

The Lord be with you all] Thus he poureth out his affection, by prayer upon prayer for them. A sweet closing up!

Ver. 17, 18. *So I write, The grace, &c.*] This is that St Paul would have every of his Epistles stamped with his own hand, viz. prayer for all his people.

THE FIRST EPISTLE OF ST PAUL TO TIMOTHY.

CHAPTER I.

Ver. 1. *By the commandment of God*] FOR how should he have preached except he had been sent? This he mentioneth, Rom. x. 15, as a thing impossible.

Of God our Saviour] So the Father also is here called. *Hoc autem quantum est?* (saith Tully), *Is nimirum Soter est, qui salutem dedit.* The Greek word here used is so emphatical, that other tongues can hardly express it.

Our hope] So Christ is called, because the perfection of our life is hid with Christ in God. Something we have in possession, but more in reversion.

Ver. 2. *Mine own son*] This the apostle speaketh ἀπὸ πολλῆς φιλοστοργίας, "out of deep affection," as Chrysostom observeth.

Grace, mercy, and peace] Not only grace and peace, as to others. When we pray for ministers, we must be more than ordinarily earnest for them with God. These three are joined together only in the Epistles of Timothy and Titus; as Theophylact out of Chrysostom hath observed.

Ver. 3. *That they teach no other doctrine*] Either for matter or manner, for substance or circumstance. What hideous heresies are now-a-days broached and preached amongst us in city and country. See Mr Edwards' Gangrena, the first and second part.

Ver. 4. *Endless genealogies*] It is but laborious loss of time to search into those things, whereof we can neither have proof nor profit; the gains will not pay for the pains, the task is not worthy the toil. Toilsome toys they are, hard to come by, but of no use or worth; like an olive or date-stone, hard to crack the one, or cleave the other; but nothing, or nothing worth aught, when crackt or cloven, within either. The shell-fish among the Jews was counted unclean, because it had but a little meat, and a great deal of labour to get it.

Ver. 5. *Now the end of the commandment*] Or, of the charge, to wit, of that charge, to teach no other doctrine, &c., ver. 3, 4. As if the apostle had said, This is that that a teacher should aim at, to beget such a love in his hearers' hearts, as may speak them true believers and good livers. *Boni Catholici sunt* (saith Augustine) *qui et fidem integram sequuntur, et bonos mores.* Those are good Catholics that believe well and live well.

Ver. 6. *Some having swerved*] ἀστοχήσαντες.

"Having missed the mark," as unskilful shooters, being "heavenly-wide," as Sir Philip Sidney Englisheth that proverb, *Toto errant cœlo.*

Having turned aside unto vain jangling] Ignoble quarrels, *ubi vincere inglorium est, atteri sordidum,* wherein a man cannot quit himself so as to come off with credit or comfort. (Mr Burroughs.) Mr Dod never loved to meddle with controversies of the times; he gave that reason, he found his heart the worse when he did. Grinæus, provoked by Pistorius to dispute, sent back the letters (not so much as opening the seal) with this answer out of Chrysostom, *Inhonestum est, honestam matronam cum meretrice litigare,* It is no honour for an honest matron to scold with a harlot. (Melch. Adam.) See the note on ver. 4.

Ver. 7. *Understanding neither what*] *Non curo illos,* saith Augustine, *qui vel non intelligendo reprehendunt, vel reprehendendo non intelligunt.* I pass not for the censures of such as dare to reprehend what they do not comprehend.

Nor whereof they affirm] And are therefore to be slighted. Galatinus (saith Mr Sarson), as he affirmeth without reason, so he may be dismissed without refutation.

Ver. 8. *If a man use it lawfully*] For discovery of sin, for manuduction to Christ, and for a rule of life. *Lex, lux,* Prov. vi. 23. Xenophon telleth us, that this was the drift of the Persian laws, to keep men from acting, yea, from coveting, anything evil or idle, κεῖται.

Ver. 9. *Is not made for a righteous*] For he is freed by Christ from the coaction, malediction, and irritation of the law. The law lieth not upon the righteous (so the Greek soundeth), it urgeth not upon them, as it doth upon the wicked. To these it is as chains and shackles, to the righteous as girdles and garters, which gird up his loins and expedite his course the better. It confineth him (saith Rev. Dr Preston) to live in that element where he would live; as if one should be confined to Paradise, where he would be, though there were no such law. The wicked (on the contrary) it confineth to the place where he would not be, and to the actions that he would not do; as Shimei confined, leapeth over the pale after profit and pleasure, and dieth for it.

But for the lawless, &c.] Those masterless monsters, that send messages after Christ, saying, "We will not have this man to reign over us." But shall they thus escape by iniquity? "In thine anger thou wilt cast down these people, O God," Psal. lvi. 7. *Aut faciendum, aut patiendum.* They that will not bend shall break; they that will not be Christ's subjects, shall be his footstool: his arrows are sharp in the hearts of the king's enemies, whereby the people (that fall not down before him) fall under him, Psal. xlv. 5.

Ver. 10. *For men-stealers*] That steal away other men's children; so those that steal other men's books and writings, and set them out in their own name; as one dealt by Diagoras, who thereupon, out of discontent (because he that had done it was not presently stricken with a thunderbolt) became an atheist. (Diod. Sic.) So Fabricius stole Tremellius' Syriac translation, Villa Vincentius stole Hyperius' Treatise *De ratione studii Theologici*, and Possevinus lately translated Dr James's *Cyprianus redivivus* into his *Apparatus Theologicus*, and made it his own doing. *Sic vos non vobis.*

And if there be any other thing] For the apostle took no delight to mention more of this cursed crew; but leaves them to the law to handle and hamper them, as unruly beasts, dogs, lions, leopards, are chained and caged up that they may not do mischief.

Ver. 11. *Of the blessed God*] Blessed in himself, and to be everlastingly blessed of all creatures. Hence he is called, " The blessed," Mark xiv. 61. And frequently in the Commentaries of the Hebrew Doctors he is set forth by this title, *Baruch hu*, " he [that is blessed."

Ver. 12. *Who hath enabled me*] Christ sends none but whom he gifts. *Asinos elegit Christus et idiotas, sed oculavit in prudentes, simulque dona dedit et ministeria.*

Ver. 13. *Who was before a blasphemer*] Chrysostom observes it of Paul, as his greatest honour, that although he had obtained pardon of God for his sins, yet he is not ashamed to reckon them up to the world. So David does penance in a white sheet, as it were, Psal. li. title. So Augustine writeth books of confessions. And I was as obstinate a Papist, saith Latimer, as any was in England, and so servile an observer of the Popish decrees, that I thought I had never sufficiently mingled my massing-wine with water, and that I should never be damned if I were once a professed friar. Also when I should be made Bachelor of Divinity, my whole oration went against Philip Melancthon and his opinions. And standing in the schools when Mr Stafford (a godly orthodox divine) read, Latimer bade the scholars not to hear him, exhorted the people not to believe him. And yet the said Latimer confessed himself, that he gave thanks to God that he asked him forgiveness before he departed.

Ver. 14. *Was exceeding abundant*] Hath abounded to flowing over, ὑπερεπλεόνασε, as the sea doth above mole-hills. " I will scatter your sins as a mist," saith God, " and they shall be cast into the midst of the sea." Note these two metaphors, and despair, if thou canst. Paul was a blasphemer (and so sinned against the first table), he was also a persecutor (and sinned against the second table), he was injurious (and so came near

unto the unpardonable sin), and yet he obtained mercy; albeit his ignorance was not invincible, but of a brave disposition. Cheer up therefore and despond not. There is a pleonasm of free grace for thee in other Scriptures, as Ephes. ii. 7; Rom. v. 20, but here is a superpleonasm.

Ver. 15. *This is a faithful saying*] Worthy to be credited and embraced, as it was by Bilney the martyr, who by this promise was much comforted in a great conflict. So was Ursine by John x. 29. Another by Isaiah lvii. 15. And another by Isaiah xxvi. 3, saying that God hath graciously made it fully good to his soul.

Of whom I am chief] *Primus, quo nullus prior*, as Gerson expounds it; *Imo quo nullus pejor*, as Augustine, worser than the worst. The true penitentiary doth not elevate but aggravate his sins against himself, is ever full in the mouth this way, as Dan. ix. 5. Paul veils all his top-sails, we see, and sits down in the dust; vilifying and nullifying himself to the utmost.

Ver. 16. *Might show forth*] By full demonstration and sufficient evidence, ἐνδείξηται, so that all might see and say, There is mercy with Christ that he may be feared, yea, mercy rejoicing against judgment, that he may be everlastingly admired and adored.

For a pattern to them, &c.] Therefore the apostle was assured of remission in an ordinary way, and not by any special revelation.

Ver. 17. *Invisible*] God is too subtle for sinew or sight to bear upon. We can but see his back parts and live; we need see no more, that we may live.

Now unto the King immortal] Paul cannot mention the great work of our redemption without a thankful acclamation. The Grecians being restored to liberty by the Roman general Q. Flaminius, he was entertained by them with such applauses and acclamations, while they roared out Saviour, Saviour, that the very birds that flew over them, astonished with the noise, fell to the ground. When Hunniades had overthrown Mosites, the Turk's general, at his return from the camp, some called him the father, some the defender of his country; the soldiers, their invincible general; the captives, their deliverer; the women, their protector.

The only wise God] The temple of Sophia in Constantinople is now the Turk's chief mosque, and by them still called Sophia, because they hold, even as we do, that the wisdom of God is incomprehensible.

Ver. 18. *Son Timothy*] This is Timothy's task, whom the apostle fitly calleth son, according to the custom both of those and these times. *Patres eos dicimus qui nos catechesi instituerunt*, saith Clement: We call them fathers that instruct and catechise us. Hence Numb. iii. 1, those there mentioned were Aaron's sons by nature, and they are called Moses's sons, because he taught and instructed them.

Ver. 19. *Holding faith and a good conscience*] A good conscience, saith one, is as it were a chest wherein the doctrine of faith is to be kept safe, which will quickly be lost if this chest be once broken. For God will give over to errors and heresies such as cast away conscience of walking after God's word. What a blind buzzard then was that Popish inquisitor, who said of the Waldenses, You may know the heretics by their words and manners: *Sunt enim in moribus compositi et modesti; superbiam in vestibus non habent:* They are neither immodest in their carriage, nor proud in their apparel. (Dr Usher de Christ. Eccles. success.) Like unto this was the speech of the bishop of Aliff in a sermon preached at the Council of Trent; that as the faith of the Catholics was better, so the heretics exceeded them in good life. (Hist. of Council of Trent.) But can they live well if heretics? how can the treasure be safe, if the ship wherein it is laid be split and broken? Surely a corrupt opinion will soon corrupt a man's life, as rheum falling from the head doth putrify the lungs and other vital parts.

Ver. 20. *That ye may learn*] *Ut castigati discant;* that being buffeted and bodily tormented by Satan, as Acts xiii. 2 (for as yet there were no Christian magistrates), they may learn, παιδευθῶσι.

Not to blaspheme] That is, not to hold erroneously, and to live scandously, to the reproach of the gospel. Confer Prov. xxx. 9.

CHAPTER II.

Ver. 1. *Supplications*] OR, deprecations indited by that Spirit of supplication, or of deprecation, as some render it, Zech. xi. 10.

Prayers] Strictly taken for petitions or requests of good at God's hands, which go commonly accompanied with vows of better obedience, as Gen. xxviii. 21, 22; Psal. li. 14. Hence they have their name, προσευχαὶ.

Intercessions] Interparlings with God, either for ourselves (whilst we stand upon interrogatories with him, 1 Pet. iii. 21, as Paul doth, Rom. viii. 33—35, and expostulate as David often, but especially when Satan, sin, and conscience accuse us), or for others, while we complain to God against such as wrong them, and withal set ourselves seriously to implore his aid for their relief and rescue, ἐντεύξεις, ἐπερώτημα.

For all men] i. e. For all sorts of men, as the word "all" is used Luke xi. 42.

Ver. 2. *For kings, &c.*] Though persecutors, if they have not yet sinned against the Holy Ghost, as Julian had. *Voluit scilicet Christus etiam aliquando Reginam in cœlum vehere,* saith Luther of Elizabeth, Queen of Denmark, who lived and died in the truth of the gospel. God hath his, even among great ones too.

A quiet and peaceable life] Quiet, from inbred tumults and commotions; and peaceable, from foreign invasions and incursions of the enemy. See Jer. xxix. 7.

In all godliness and honesty] And not come to eat the bread of our souls with the peril of our lives, as they do in divers places of this land at this day. *Det meliora Deus.* He will do it.

Ver. 3. *For this is good, &c.*] viz. This praying for all men. And should we not frame to that that God accepts without questioning or quarreling? Let us not dispute, but despatch our Master's will.

Ver. 4. *Who will have all men, &c.*] God willeth, to wit, with a will whereby he inviteth, and putteth no bar; not with a will whereby he effecteth it, taking away all impediments.

That all men] Not distributively taken, but collectively, as thrice in one verse, Col. i. 28.

Should be saved] viz. If they do what he commandeth: God doth not tie himself to cause them to do what he commandeth, that they may be saved.

And to come to the knowledge] The only way to salvation. Pray therefore that their eyes may be opened, Acts xxvi. 18.

Ver. 5. *For there is one God*] sc. Both of kings and subjects, both of heathens and Christians. Go boldly to him therefore, for yourselves and others. "Have we not all one Father?" Mal. ii. 10. "Art not thou our Father?" Isa. lxiii. 16. "O Lord" (saith the Church in Habakkuk), "art not thou from everlasting my God, mine Holy One?" It was a bold question, but God approves it, and assents to it in a gracious answer ere they went further: "We shall not die," say they abruptly; by a cast of God's countenance they could tell so much. So true is that of Jamblichus a heathen (but herein he speaks more like a Christian), *Supplicatio familiares et Deorum domesticos facit eos, qui ea utuntur.* Prayer gives a humble boldness and a holy familiarity with God unto those that use it; and again, prayer, saith he, is like a key whereby we may open God's treasury, and take out of it plentiful mercy for ourselves and others.

Between God and men] Gr. of God and men; he is God for the business with God; and man, for the business with man.

One Mediator] Not of redemption only (as the Papists grant), but of intercession too. We need no other master of requests in heaven, but the man Christ Jesus, who being so near us in the matter of his incarnation, will never be strange to us in the business of intercession. But what horrible blasphemy is that of the Papists, who in their devotions say thus, By the blood of Thomas Becket, which he did spend, make us, Christ, to climb where Thomas did ascend! (Acts and Mon.)

Ver. 6. *A ransom*] Gr. ἀντίλυτρον, a counterprice; such as we could never have paid, but must have remained, and even rotted in prison, but for our all-sufficient surety and Saviour.

Ver. 7. *A teacher of the Gentiles*] His Epistles therefore should be highly prized by us Gentiles, and diligently studied. St Peter admires them, 2 Pet. iii. 15, and commends them to the Church's reading. And because there are some things in them hard to be understood, and easy to be wrested from their right meaning, ver. 16, it was therefore grave advice that one gives young Christians, that they should begin at the latter end of St Paul's Epistles, which treateth of points of practice. Sith a corrupt life can never have a sound judgment.

Ver. 8. Pray everywhere] Any place now (be it but a chimney) may make a goodly oratory, John iv. 21.

Lifting up holy hands] Better washed than Pilate's were, rinsed in that blessed fountain of Christ's blood, Zech. xiii. 1. Else, God utterly abhors them, Isa. i. 15, 16. The priests had their laver to wash in, before they sacrificed. The Turks at this day before prayer wash both face and hands, sometimes their head, and other parts of the body. But what saith St James, chap. iv. 8, and the prophet Jeremiah, chap. iv. 14 ? The fountain of goodness will not be laden at with foul hearts and hands.

Without wrath] Or, rancour, Matt. v. 24. God will not be served till men be reconciled. When Abraham and Lot were agreed, then God appeared.

Or doubting] Heb. xi. 6 ; James i. 6 ; without disceptation or reasoning with carnal reason.

Ver. 9. In like manner also] Men have had their lessons. Now for women they are taught modesty in their attire (such as may neither argue wantonness nor wastefulness), silence in the Church, subjection in the family.

Or costly array] Which yet great ones may wear ; but they may not buy it with extortion, and line it with pride ; sith clothes are the ensigns of our shame, our fineness is our filthiness, and our neatness our nastiness. See Isaiah iii., where the prophet inveighs, as if he had viewed the ladies' wardrobes in Jerusalem.

Ver. 10. But which becometh] Our common conversation should be as becometh the gospel of Christ, πολιτεύεσθε, Phil. i. 27. And it is a sure sign of a base mind, to think that one can make himself great with anything that is less than himself ; or that he can win more credit by his garments than by his graces. The worst apparel, saith one, is nature's garment ; the best, but folly's garnish.

Ver. 11. Let the woman learn] Not to teach, to wit, in the public assemblies, be she never so learned or godly. See the note on Rom. xvi. 1.

Ver. 12. Nor to usurp authority] As they will easily do if suffered to preach, αὐθεντεῖν, to have what she will. Preachers are rulers, guides, captains, Heb. xiii. 7, 17. If the hen be suffered to crow once, &c. A prudent wife commands her husband by obeying him, as Sarah, Livia.

But to be in silence] *Video, taceo,* I see and say nothing, was Queen Elizabeth's motto. Where should the tongue be but in the head ?

Ver. 13. For Adam was first formed] ἐπλάσθη. As the vessel is formed by the potter out of the clay. See Gen. ii. 7. The common opinion is, that the very same day ἐπλάσθη καὶ ἐξηλάσθη, he was formed and driven out ; that he lodged not one night in Paradise ; so sudden was the ser-

pent's seducing, his wife's consenting, his yielding, God's execution.

Then Eve] For Adam's use and help, therefore she must not take upon her. Howbeit the Jews are out, that hold women to be of a lower creation, made only for the propagation and pleasure of man ; also that they have not so divine a soul as men, and therefore they suffer them not to enter into the synagogue, but appoint them a gallery without. Their Rabbins (who have as many foolish dreams about the Old Testament as the Friars have about the New) conceive both Adam and Eve to be created without the use of reason ; and that the tree of knowledge was to accelerate it. Socinians also say (but falsely) that they were as simple and weak as little children ; otherwise they would not have so sinned. *Cujus contrarium verum est.*

Ver. 14. And Adam was not deceived] *i. e.* He was not deceived so much by his judgment (though also by that too) as by his affection to his wife, which at length blinded his judgment. Look we well to our affections ; for by these maids Satan still wooeth the mistress.

Being deceived, was in the transgression] *Uxor mea tota in fermento est,* said he in Plautus. See my notes on Gen. iii. 6. Yet Adam sinned more than Eve, because he had more wisdom and strength. He could set his affections as the artificer doth his clock, to make it strike when and what he will.

Ver. 15. Saved in child-bearing] διὰ *pro* ἐν, *ut* Rom. xi. 28. Not by it, as by a cause ; but notwithstanding the cross laid upon all child-bearing women, Gen. iii. 16, they shall have free entrance into heaven, if they continue in faith and charity, &c.

CHAPTER III.

Ver. 1. If a man desire] As no woman, so neither may every man desire the office of a minister, but such only as are gifted and fitted for such a service.

He desireth a good work] But a hard work. The ministry is not an idle man's occupation, but a sore labour ; *Onus ipsis etiam angelis tremendum,* saith Chrysostom, a burden too heavy for an angel's shoulders ; a pains nothing short of that of a travailing woman, saith Melancthon after Paul, Gal. iv. 19. There were that read this text thus, *Quicunque desiderat episcopatum bonum, opes desiderat.* But this was a foul mistake at best. That is a good observation of Estius, that the former word, ὀρέγεται, rendered desire, importeth a more earnest desire (such as is that after meat when one is hungry) than the other following, ἐπιθυμεῖ. "He desireth a good work," *quod eadem res nomine Episcopatus desideretur ardentius, quam nomine operis et officii,* because the same thing by the name of episcopacy is more ardently desired than by the name of work and duty. That hypocrisy of the

Canonists is very ridiculous, not admitting any to personal government in the Church, unless he either seem to refuse it, or unwillingly to undertake it, though he had never so much laboured it. The Bishop of Metis answered cunningly, when being demanded whether he desired a bishopric, he replied, *Nolens volo, et volens nolo*, I do, and I do not. One reporteth of a priest that used to have a net spread upon his table where he dined, that he might mind St Peter, that fisher of men. But when by his diligent preaching he had gotten a bishopric, he did take away the net, for he had got what he fished for.

Ver. 2. A bishop then must be blameless] That is, every faithful pastor must be such as against whom no just exception can be laid, no gross fault objected. Involuntary failings and unavoidable infirmities have a pardon, of course, both with God and all good men.

The husband of one wife] *sc.* At once. The Egyptian priests were forbidden also polygamy.

Vigilant] νηφάλιον, pale and wan with watching, οὐ χρὴ παννύχιον εὕδειν βουλήφορον ἄνδρα (Homer) : a public person should not sleep a whole night together.

Sober] σώφρονα, that can contain his passions and keep a mean.

Of good behaviour] κόσμιον.[1] *Compositus, modestus.* Neat and handsome in his outward habit, venerable in all his behaviour.

Given to hospitality] *Quicquid habent clerici, pauperum est :* the minister's chest is the poor man's box.

Apt to teach] Not able only, as Dr Taylor, martyr, who preached not only every Lord's day and holy day, but whensoever else he could get the people together. (Acts and Mon.) *Prædicationis officium suscipit, quisquis ad sacerdotium accedit,* saith Gregory. (Greg. Pastor.) He is no minister that is no preacher.

Ver. 3. Not given to wine] No ale-stake, tavern-haunter, that sits close at it, till the wine inflame him.

No striker] Either with tongue or hand. Such as were Timotheus Herulus, A. D. 467 ; Pope Julius III., who cast away his keys, and girt on his sword ; Bishop Bonner, who usually buffeted the poor martyrs brought before him, pulling off their beards, &c. *Cognata vitia sunt vinolentia et violentia, sicut et magna cognatio est, ut rei, sit nominis, divitiis et vitiis.*

Not greedy of filthy lucre] So as to get by unjust arts and sinful practices, as the pope by allowing the stews in Rome, and elsewhere. See Fiscus Papalis by Crashaw.

But patient] ἐπιεικῆ, Easily parting with his own right for peace' sake, as Abraham did, as no covetous man will do.

No brawler] Or wrangler, quarrelsome, like a cock of the game, that is still bloody with the blood of others and of himself.

Not covetous] ἀφιλάργυρον. Not a lover of silver ; and that (Euclio-like) sits abrood upon his heaps of evil-gotten goods, and will part with nothing.

Ver. 4. One that ruleth well] προϊστάμενον. A good priest in his own family, which he daily perfumes with evangelical sacrifices, till his house, as the house of David, be as God, as the angel of the Lord before them, Zech. xii. 8.

Having his children in subjection] Yet Pope Pelagius forbids a bishop to have either wife or children ; whereof this wise reason is given, because children are *argumentum ambulans super terram*, A walking argument of their father's incontinency. *Os durum !* His successor Paul III. had no wife indeed, but children he had. One of whom, named Petro Alvigi Farnesis, having first forced and then poisoned Cosmus Chærius, bishop of Fanum, received no other check or chastisement of his father the pope but this, *Hæc vitia me non commonstratore didicit*, He never learned those vices of his father.

Ver. 5. For if a man know not how] A very cogent argument from the less to the greater ; used also by our Saviour, Luke xvi. 11, 12. Eli was justly taxed and Augustus heavily upbraided with their domestical disorders, as therefore unfit for government.

Ver. 6. Not a novice] νεόφυτος. Rude and proud, a young scholar or newly converted, but well experimented, and sufficiently commended by men of worth. He that offered to run a race was led about by the crier, to see what any one present could object against him, ere he was suffered to run, as Chrysostom reporteth.[2] So it should be here. Was he not a fit man to be a doctor of divinity, and a teacher in Israel, who being asked something touching the Decalogue, denied that he had ever any such book as that in his study ? Another[3] (and he a bishop) taking up a Bible, and reading in it awhile, when one asked him what book he had there, he answered, What book it is I know not ; but this I know, that it speaketh altogether against our religion. An ass might not be coupled with an ox in ploughing. No ignorant doltish ass may plough in God's field the Church. *Asinos elegit Christus et idiotas*, saith Dr Beddingfield, *sed oculavit in prudentes ; simulque dona dedit et ministeria.* Christ chose illiterate men, but made them learned and teachers of others.

He fall into the condemnation of the devil] διάβολος. That is, be condemned as the devil is, for his pride. Or, lest he come under the censure of calumniating persons, who have one common name (in Greek) with the devil. See 1 Tim. iii. 11 ; 2 Tim. iii. 3 ; Tit. ii. 3.

Ver. 7. A good report of them, &c.] For a workman that needeth not to be ashamed ; such a one as may muzzle the black mouth of any Campian, that shall say, as he doth of our Church, *Ministris eorum nihil vilius ;* this is most true of Popish greasy hedge-priests. See the note on ver. 6.

Of the devil] Or, of the slanderer, who by

---

[1] *Bene moratum.* Hieron. ad Damasum.
[2] Chrysost. Hom. xxii. ad Pop. Antioch.
[3] Amama, Antibarb. præfat. Luther. Chytræus.

carrying tales and finding faults, do the devil's work. See the note on ver. 6.

Ver. 8. *Not double-tongued*] διλόγους. That can turn their tales, and tune their fiddles to the base of the times, saying as the company says, being as the planet Mercury, good in conjunction with good, and bad with bad. *Lingua in vitulis marinis duplex est,*[1] Sea-calves are double-tongued. Ministers must neither be sea-calves nor moon-calves; doubled-tongued, nor unstable, or double-minded, James i. 8. See the note on Acts ii. 3.

Ver. 9. *Holding the mystery*] See the note on 1 Tim. i. 19.

Ver. 10. *Being found blameless*] The world will look round about them, and expect (though unjustly) an angelical perfection.

Let them use the office of a deacon] *Diaconus* is said to come of κονὶς, which signifieth dust, to show that such should be "dustily diligent."

Ver. 11. *Must their wives be grave*] As themselves must, ver. 6. Gravity is such an elixir, as by contaction (if there be any disposition of goodness in the same metal) it will render it of the property. So that deacons' wives cannot be otherwise than grave and gracious, having such husbands as is above described.

Ver. 12. *Husbands of one wife, &c.*] See the notes on ver. 2 and 4.

Ver. 13. *A good degree*] Or a fair step to a higher order, *i. e.* to a bishopric or presbytership.

And great boldness in the faith] The peace of a good conscience and the plerophory of faith. This those that are faithful in the ministry shall be sure of; the former preferment they may possibly fail of. Like as when the twins strove in Rebecca's womb, the worst came forth first, and had the best place, Gen. xxv. 25; so the unworthiest are oft exalted, Psal. xii. ult., but the best have that which is better.

Ver. 14. *Hoping to come unto thee*] And to be an eye-witness of thy diligence, whereof I doubt not, joying in the mean while, "and beholding your order, and the stedfastness of your faith in Christ, Col. ii. 5.

Ver. 15. *In the house of God*] See here the dignity of the Church, and the duty of ministers, which is to be faithful as stewards in all God's house. But what mean the Papists so to cry up the Church even above the Scriptures (as the Council of Basil did by their Cardinal Cusanus in answer to the Hussites), nay, above Christ himself, as Hosius and others. Can they mean honestly (quoth that martyr) that make so much of the wife and so little of the husband? Bastard children are all for their mother, and are called by her name, &c.

Ver. 16. *And without controversy*] Learned Cameron beginneth this verse at those words before, "The pillar and ground of truth, and confessedly great is that mystery of godliness, God manifested in the flesh," &c. It being a usual form of speech among the Jews (as he proveth

out of Maimonides) to preface these very words, "The pillar and ground of truth," to any special doctrine touching religion. The word here rendered "without controversy," signifieth "confessedly," *q. d.* It is so under the broad seal of public confession.

Great is the mystery of godliness] A mystery, because above natural capacity. And a "mystery of godliness" the gospel is called, because, being believed, it transformeth men into the same image, and stirs up in them admirable affections of piety.

God manifested] Out of the bosom of his Father, out of the womb of his mother, out of the types of the law, &c.

In the flesh] Christ condescended to our rags, he put on a lousy suit of ours, *induit sordes nostras,* he took our flesh, when it was tainted with treason; our base nature, after it was fallen; which was a wonderful fruit of love: as if one should wear a man's colours or livery after he is proclaimed traitor, it is a great grace to such a man; so here. (Dr Sibbs.)

Justified in the Spirit] Or, "by the Spirit," that is, by the divine nature, Rom. i. 4, and by the Holy Ghost too; the second person raised up itself, but yet it was by the Holy Ghost too; which he used, not as an instrument, but as a common principle with himself, of equal dignity, only differing in order of persons. We shall also be justified and cleared of all false imputations at the resurrection, which shall be of names as well as of bodies. The sun shall scatter all the clouds, &c.

CHAPTER IV.

Ver. 1. *Speaketh expressly*] *Verbis non disertis solum, sed et exertis.* Abroad and aloud, that it may be heard all the Church over, ῥητῶς.

Some shall depart from the faith] As did the ancient heretics the Papists (in whom all the old heretics seem to have fled and hid themselves), and the present prodigious sectaries with their *opinionum portenta,* our modern Antitrinitarians, Arians, Anti-scripturists, Anabaptists, &c.

Doctrine of devils] Vented by Satan's emissaries and instruments. About the time of Pope Hildebrand, letters were dispersed up and down, that were said to be sent from hell; wherein the devil gives great thanks to the Popish clergy for the great multitudes of souls that by their seductions came thronging to hell more than ever in any age before. (Mat. Paris, Hist. A. D. 1072.) Nicolas Orum, an Oxford doctor, is said to have written those letters. He preached also at Rome, before the pope and his cardinals; discovering and condemning their errors, and foretelling their destruction.

Ver. 2. *Speaking lies in hypocrisy*] It was grown to a common proverb, "A friar, a liar." One of them undertook to show a feather of the wing of the angel Gabriel. The pope, to honour and encourage Tyrone the rebel, sent him (but who will

---

[1] *Tyriosque bilingues.* Virg. Bartholin. in Anatom.

believe it?) a plume of Phœnix' feathers. The poor people are persuaded to believe that the thunder of the pope's excommunication hath so blasted the English heretics, that their faces are grown all black and ugly as devils; their eyes and looks ghastly, their breaths noisome and pestilent, that they are grown barbarous, and eat children, blaspheme God and all his saints.

Having their consciences seared] There is more hope of a sore, than of a seared, conscience, a dead and dedolent disposition, Eph. iv., a heart that hath contracted a kind of hoof.

Ver. 3. *Forbidding to marry*] Papists forbid some to marry at any time, as the clergy; all, at some times, and that not as a precept of conveniency, but necessity and holiness. In Anselm's time, cursed sodomitry and adultery passed free without punishment, where godly matrimony could find no mercy. The cardinal of Cremona, after his stout replying in the Council of London against the married estate of priests, was shamefully taken the night following with a notable harlot. They hold that it is far better for a priest to keep many whores than to have a wife. This, say they, is the heresy of the Nicolaitans.

To abstain from meats] As the Papists superstitiously do upon certain days, when to eat an egg is punished with imprisonment. (Schol. in Epist. ad Episc. Basil.) *Qui autem totam diem Dominicam vacat temulentiæ, scortis et aleæ, audit bellus homo*, saith Erasmus: But he that spends the whole Lord's day in drinking, dicing, and drabbing, is let go for a good fellow.

Which God hath created] He made the grass before he made the beasts, and the beasts before man, that all might have food convenient for them.

Ver. 4. *If it be received with thanksgiving*] Whilst we taste the sweetness of the Creator in the creature, and are stirred up thereby to praise his name. Doves at every grain they pick look upwards, as giving thanks. The elephant is said to turn up towards heaven the first sprig or branch that he feedeth on, &c. Birds chirp and sing to their Maker.

Ver. 5. *By the word*] Of permission, Acts x. 15, and of promise, a new right purchased by Christ, &c.

And prayer] For his leave and blessing, that "staff of bread," &c. This is to eat to the Lord, Rom. xiv. 6; to imitate Christ, Matt. xiv.; Paul, Acts xxvii. 35; Samuel, 1 Sam. ix. 13.

Ver. 6. *Nourished up in the words*] Such are fittest to be made ministers as have been well bred, and inured to the reading of the Scriptures; as have sucked in holy learning together with their mother's milk. Quintilian adviseth that the child that is intended for an orator, should from two or three years old be accustomed to hear and babble out good language, the best words and best pronounced. *Quanto id in Theologo futuro expetendum curandumque magis*, &c.? saith Amama; how much more needeth such care and pains be taken with the child that is dedicated to the ministry, that he may become (as Quintilian saith an orator should be) *vir bonus dicendi peritus*, a good man and well able to deliver himself in good terms. I have known some (saith Peach) for their judgment in arts and tongues very sufficient; yet to have heard their discourse (so defective were they in their own tongue) you would have thought you had heard Loy talking to his pigs, or Johannes de Indagine declaiming in the praise of wild geese. Of Matthew Doringus, a Popish commentator, Steuchus (a Papist too) saith truly, that he is not worthy to be named *ob universam V. T. scripturam fœdissima barbarie conspurcatam*, for defiling all the Old Testament with his base barbarisms, as the harpies did the good meat they seized on.

Ver. 7. *But refuse*] Gr. παραιτοῦ, make a fair excuse. Shift them off, set them by, say thou art not at leisure to attend to them, hast no time to lose upon them. *Poteras has horas non perdidisse*, said Pliny to his nephew, You might have found you somewhat else to do.

Exercise thyself] Lay aside thine upper garments, as runners and wrestlers use to do, and bestir thee lustily, γύμναζε, *Te nudum exerce*. See Heb. xii. 1.

Ver. 8. *For bodily exercise profiteth little*] Somewhat it doth (if rightly used) toward the strengthening of the body, preserving of the health, subduing of the flesh.

But godliness is profitable to all things] The Babylonians are said to make 360 several commodities of the palm-tree (Plutarch); but there is a μυριομακαριότης, a thousand benefits to be got by godliness. Godly persons are said in Latin, *Deum colere*, because they are sure by sowing to the Spirit to "reap of the Spirit life everlasting," Gal. vi. 8. Besides that, in this world they "shall obtain joy and gladness" (outward and inward comforts), but "sorrow and sighing shall flee away," Isa. xxxv. 10.

Ver. 9. *This is a faithful saying*] And yet who hath believed our report? The promises are good freehold, and yet little looked after. Godliness hath but cold entertainment, because she lives much upon reversions.

Ver. 10. *For therefore*] Because godliness hath so much happiness laid up in the promises, ver. 8, and there is so much certainty of the performance of those promises, therefore we both do and suffer, 1 Cor. xv. 58. *Finis edulcat media.*

Who is the Saviour of all men] Not of eternal preservation, but of temporal reservation. For every man should die the same day he is born, the wages of death should be paid him presently; but Christ begs wicked men's lives for a season, saith one. Sin hath hurled confusion over the world, brought a vanity on the creature. And had not Christ undertaken the shattered condition of the world to uphold it, it had fallen about Adam's ears, saith another divine.

Specially of those that believe] Who therefore

are in a special manner bound to observe and obey him. Among the Romans they that were saved were wont to crown him that saved them, and to honour him as a father all their days. Σέβεται δὲ τοῦτον ὡς πατέρα, Polyb. vi. We must also set the crown upon Christ's head, Cant. iii. 11, and obey this everlasting Father, Isa. ix. 6.

Ver. 11. *These things command and teach*] Teach the tractable, command the obstinate, lay God's charge upon all.

Ver. 12. *Let no man despise, &c.*] But how should I help it? might he say; the apostle answereth, " Be thou an example to the believers, a pattern of piety;" for holiness hath honour, wisdom maketh the face to shine; natural conscience cannot but stoop to the image of God, wherever and in whomsoever it discerneth it: οὐ γὰρ τὸ νέον εὐκαταφρόνητον ὅταν Θεῷ ἀνακείμενον ᾖ, saith Ignatius (Epist. ad. Magnes.) Youth seasoned with the fear of God is not easily despised.

But be thou an example] Gr. τύος, such a thing as maketh the stamp upon the coin. *Exemplis sciola hac ætate magis ædificant ministri quam concionibus.* Reason indeed should rule, and is therefore placed in the head. But when reason cannot prevail, example will.

Ver. 13. *Give attendance to reading*] First to reading, and then to exhortation; bringing as a good scribe, out of a good treasure, new and old. Father Latimer notwithstanding both his years and constant pains in preaching, was at his book most diligently about two of the clock every morning. A rare example.

Ver. 14. *Neglect not the gift*] God's gifts groan under our disuse or misuse; and God hearing gives them the wings of an eagle; so that such may say as once Zedekiah did, " When went the Spirit of the Lord from me to thee?" God dries up the arm and darkens the eye of idle and idol shepherds, Zech. xi. 17.

With the laying on of the hands] A custom that came from the Church of the Old Testament, Gen. viii. 14; Lev. i. 4 and iii. 2, is laudably used to this day in the ordination of ministers, but foolishly and sinfully abused by the upstart sectaries.

Ver. 15. *Meditate upon these things*] And so digest them, turn them *in succum et sanguinem.* Let your heart study a good matter, that your pen may be as the tongue of a ready writer, Psal. xlv. 1, and not present crude and rude stuff. When it was objected to Demosthenes that he was no sudden speaker, but came ever to the court after premeditation, he answered, *Se si fieri posset, dicturum non tantum scripta sed etiam sculpta;* that he would not only write but engrave, if he could, what he was about to utter in public. The same Demosthenes also would have such an one branded for a pernicious man to the commonwealth, who durst propose anything publicly which he had not beforehand seriously pondered. What impudency then is it in a preacher so to do. It was a wise speech of Aristides, who being required by the emperor to speak something propounded *ex tempore*, answered, Propound to-day, and I will answer to-morrow; for we are not of those that spit or vomit things, but of those that elaborate them, οὐ γὰρ ἐσμέν τῶν ἐμούντων, ἀλλὰ τῶν ἀκριβούντων. Melancthon answered Eccius in like manner, who hit him in the teeth with his slowness in answering arguments. So did Augustine deal by Vincentius Victor, a rash young man, who boldly censured him for his unresolvedness concerning the original of a reasonable soul, and vaunted that he could do it without demurs or delays.

That thy profiting may appear to all] *i. e.* That it may appear thy gifts increase daily, by thy good husbandry.

Give thyself wholly to them] Gr. ἐν τούτοις ἴσθι, Be thou in them: *totus in hoc sis.* It was Mr Perkins' motto, *Verbi minister es, hoc age,* Thou art a minister of the word, make it thy whole business.

Ver. 16. *Thou shalt both save*] What a high honour is this to faithful ministers, that they should be styled saviours in a sense? So Job xxxiii. 24; Obad. 21; James v. 21. Only it must be their care to save themselves as well as their hearers; and that it be not said of them, as once it was of Laertes, the father of Ulysses, that he ordered all things well, but neglected himself. One desired a bad-living preacher to point him out a nearer way to heaven than that he had taught in his sermons; for he went not that way himself.

CHAPTER V.

Ver. 1. *Rebuke not an elder*] Lash him not with the scourge of the tongue, as a puny boy, μὴ ἐπιλήξῃς. *Ne plagam inflixeris.* Jerk him not as the pope did Henry IV. of France in the person of his ambassador, or as the bishops and their shavelings did Henry II. of England till the blood followed. This is not civil usage for an elder.

Ver. 2. *With all purity*] Not with some only, but " with all purity," for fear of the worst, ἐν πάσῃ ἀγνείᾳ: and lest any impure motion therewhile creep into the heart unawares. The souls of ministers should be purer than the sunbeams, saith Chrysostom. They are by their office the lights of the world: let no snuff abide in them, they are *fullones animarum,* fullers of men's souls, to make and keep them white; let them take heed of a smutch. *Turpe est doctori, &c. Nihil turpius est Peripatetico claudo.* It is a shame for a teacher to be found faulty.

Ver. 3. *Honour widows indeed*] That is, such as are widows not by divorce, but by the death of their husbands, and loss of their children; such as was Naomi. Honour them, that is, take them into the college of widows, to be maintained at the Church's charge. In this sense ministers are to have double honour (see ver. 17), which is therefore so termed, because they testified thereby the virtues of those so sustained.

Ver. 4. *Let them learn first to show*] Such any one is in truth, as he is at home, Psal. ci. 2. The hypocrite's virtues (as that of the Sarmatians) run all outward. Something he seems abroad, but follow him home, and you shall soon see what he is: follow stage-players into their attiring-house where they disrobe themselves, and then it will appear they are vile varlets. Like unto this apostolic precept, was that of Chilo, one of the wise men of Greece, τῆς αὐτοῦ οἰκίας καλῶς προστατεῖν, to govern honestly a man's own family. (Laert. in Vita.)

And to requite their parents] See the note on Matt. xv. 4. The storks feed their dams when old; though the young kites expel their dams, and with their bills and wings beat them out of their nest. Boughs bend toward their root, &c.

Ver. 5. *Trusteth in God*] Whereas while she had a husband and children, she trusted overmuch in them. The αἱμαρροοῦσα sought not to our Saviour till all her money was gone. Zeph. iii. 12, they are an afflicted poor people, therefore they trust in the name of the Lord. When the apostle saith of the widow indeed, that she is desolate, he seemeth to allude to the Greek word for a widow, which comes of a verb that signifies to be desolate and deprived, χῆρα a χήρω, *desolor, destituo*. So the Latin *vidua a viduando*, and the Hebrew *almanah* of *alam*, to be dumb; because death having cut off her head, she hath none to speak for her.

And continueth in supplications, &c.] As Anna the prophetess did, Luke ii. A noble woman of Savoy, mother to John Galeaz, duke of Milan, after her husband's decease, caused a coin to be made, upon the one side whereof she drew these words, *Sola facta, solum Deum sequor*, Being left alone, I follow God alone.

Ver. 6. *Is dead while she liveth*] *Cum careat pura mente, cadaver agit.* Pamphilius in Terence saith the like of a light housewife. *Sane hercle homo voluptati obsequens fuit dum vixit.* St Paul's Greek cannot well be rendered but by Terence's Latin, and Terence's Latin cannot well be put into other Greek.

But she that liveth in pleasure] Gr. σπαταλῶσα. The delicate dame, such as were those wanton daughters of Sion, those mincing minions mentioned Isa. iii., as also those of Tyre and Sidon, those of Phœnicia, so called from the Syriac *phinneck*, delicate: the Greeks call them τρυφεροὶ, such as lie melting in sensual delights and sinful pleasures, in the froth whereof groweth that worm that never dieth, James v. 5. I have read of a gallant addicted to uncleanness, who at last meeting with a beautiful dame, and having enjoyed his fleshly desires of her, found her in the morning to be the dead body of one that he had formerly sinned with, which had been acted by the devil all night, and left dead again in the morning. Sure he had but ψυχρὸν παραγκάλισμα, a cold armful of her at length (as Lycophron saith of an evil wife), and if God had given grace, it might have brought him to better courses; but where that is wanting, no warning will serve

turn. Jeroboam had as great a miracle wrought before him in the drying up of his hand, as St Paul at his conversion, yet was he not wrought upon, because the Spirit did not set it on. Besides, grace is seated in the powers of nature. Now carnal sins disable nature, and so set men in a greater distance from grace, as taking away the heart, Hos. iv. 11.

Ver. 7. *And these things give in charge*] Often inculcate and set on with a great deal of vehemency, that religion suffer not.

Ver. 8. *But if any provide not*] That they may have Gaius's prosperity, *Mentem sanam in corpore sano*: though the apostle's meaning here is chiefly as touching bodily nourishment and outward accommodations.

Specially for those of his own house] Socrates, an infidel, took care of the welfare of his family and allies, as Lipanius testifieth, τῶν οἰκείων ἐπεμέλησε καὶ τῶν ἐκ τοῦ γένους ἐφρόντησε. Bishop Ridley was very kind and natural to his kinsfolk. And the Lord Cromwell, before the time of his apprehension, took such order for his servants, that many of them, especially the younger brethren, which had little else to trust unto, had honestly left for them in their friend's hands to relieve them, whatsoever should befall him.

Ver. 9. *The wife of one man*] As Anna, Luke i. 36. Such are held to be more modest, to whom the thought of death hath been enough to forbid the bans of second marriage.

Ver. 10. *Well reported of, &c.*] "A good name is better than precious ointment," Eccles. vii. 1; and "rather to be chosen than great riches," Prov. xxii. 1. Provident we must be to preserve it, learning of the unjust steward by lawful, though he did it by unlawful, means; for our Saviour noted this defect, when he said, "The children of this world are wiser in their generation than the children of light," Luke xvi. 8.

Ver. 11. *To wax wanton*] To run away (as pampered palfreys) with the bit betwixt their teeth, and to play the jades, καταστρηνιάζειν.

Ver. 12. *Having damnation*] Or public reproach, as ver. 14, for their desultory lightness and inconsiderate rashness.

Cast off their first faith] Not that of their baptism (as divers of the Indians do that have been baptized by the Spaniards), but their vidual promised chastity and service to the saints.

Ver. 13. *They learn to be idle*] It is an art soon learned, by doing nothing to do naughtily. *Nihil agendo male agere discunt*, Idleness is the hour of temptation, and an idle person is the devil's tennis-ball, tossed by him at his pleasure.

Wandering about from house to house] As vagrants, or as pedlars opening their packs, and dropping here a tale and there a tale. A practice flatly forbidden by God, Levit. ix. 16, "Thou shalt not go up and down as a talebearer." The Hebrew word signifieth a pedlar, רָגַל whence רֶגֶל for a foot. And another Hebrew word used for defaming or slandering, Psal. xv. 3, properly noteth a footing or trotting it up and down, prying and spying and carrying tales and rumours, 2 Sam. xix. 27. The Greek word also ἀργέω, and the Latin word *arguo*, first signifies to be idle, and next to reprehend others. (Beckman de Origin. ling. Lat.) Because they that have little to do at home, will be over-busy abroad, in censuring and slandering others.

And not only idle] The first-born of idleness is, to do nothing; the next issue that she hath is, to do evil. *Otium negotium*, Idleness is a kind of business.

But tattlers also] Gr. φλύαροι, triflers; *Magno conatu magnas nugas agunt.* The Rabbins have a proverb, "That ten kabs of speech descended into the world, and the women took away nine of them."

And busy-bodies] For " every fool will be meddling," Prov. xx. 3.

Speaking things, &c.] It is a very hard thing well to manage many words: ἐν πολυλογίᾳ πολυμωρία, *In multiloquio stultiloquium.*

Ver. 14. *Give none occasion to the adversary*] The devil or his instruments, whose mouths he oft borrows to blaspheme and rail with, who also watch as diligently for an occasion to speak evil of profession as a dog doth for a bone; they pry more narrowly into every miscarriage than Laban did into Jacob's stuff.

Ver. 15. *Turned aside after Satan*] Revolted from Christian religion, going out of God's blessing into the world's warm sun. These could not choose unto themselves a worse condition.

Ver. 16. *Have widows*] That are widows indeed, that have neither children nor nephews to relieve them, ver. 3, of whom by the law of nature they may require θρεπτήρια, aliment and succour.

And let not the church be charged] How then will Church-robbers answer it, if Church-chargers be in fault? let them give us a just commentary upon Prov. xx. 25, and remember Cardinal Wolsey, and his sacrilegious instruments; five of whom came to fearful ends, as Scultetus recordeth, and concludeth with this wish, *Utinam his et similibus exemplis edocti discant homines res semel Deo consecratas timide attrectare*, I would that men would be warned by these examples, and better advise how they meddle with Church-maintenance, thereby to enrich themselves. (Scultet. Annal.)

Ver. 17. *Worthy of double honour*] viz. Countenance and maintenance; that they may give themselves continually and cheerfully to preaching and prayer, Acts vi. 4. Let them have reverence and recompence.

They who labour] οἱ κοπιῶντες, even to lassitude, as he doth that cleaveth wood, or that toileth in harvest, or that goeth on warfare, 2 Tim. ii. 3, 4. Preaching is a painful work and enfeebleth a man exceedingly, whence the prophet cries out, " My leanness, my leanness." And our Saviour, at little past 30, was reckoned by the Jews to be toward 50, John viii. 57. It is supposed by divines that he had so spent himself in preaching, that he seemed to the Jews to be much older than he was.

Ver. 18. *Thou shalt not muzzle, &c.*] See the note on 1 Cor. ix. 9.

Worthy of his hire] Of his meat, Matt. x. 10; of his wages, as here. Hardest labourers have meat and drink and double wages. Among the Athenians, tragedians and comedians were said to labour in teaching the people, εἰς διδαχὴν ἐργαζόμενοι, and therefore highly honoured; for this it was also that the ancients laid out so much money upon their theatres. But what was their pains to ours? and are we yet begrudged a livelihood.

Ver. 19. *Receive not an accusation*] If to be accused were sufficient to make a man guilty, no good minister should be innocent. *Prædicare nihil aliud est quam derivare in se furorem totius mundi*, saith Luther. Truth hath always a scratcht face. Men hate him that reproveth in the gate. Every fool hath a bolt to shoot at a faithful preacher.

Ver. 20. *Them that sin*] i. e. Those presbyters that sin publicly, scandalously, as did Peter, Gal. ii. 14, and those who were convicted by two or three witnesses, as ver. 19. Rebuke before all, yet not as if they were whipping boys. See the note on ver. 1 of this chapter. But if the fault be not known abroad, that rule of our Saviour takes place, Matt. xviii. 15, 16. Constantine the Great was heard to say, " That if he should take a presbyter in the act of adultery, he would cover the matter with his imperial robe, rather than it should come abroad to the scandal of the weak and scorn of the wicked."

Ver. 21. *Without preferring one*] Or, without precipitation or prejudice. χωρὶς προκρίματος. *Omne judicium a se aufert, qui ad causam præjudicium affert.* A judge must not sit to hear persons, but causes; therefore justice is drawn blindfold.

Doing nothing by partiality] κατὰ πρόσκλισιν, by tilting the balance on the one side, as the word signifies. An even hand must be carried betwixt party and party. The contrary whereunto is called by the Greeks ἑτερομέρεια, siding.

Ver. 22. *Lay hands suddenly on no man*] The best that can come of rashness is repentance. Scipio would not yield that a wise man should ever come in with " had I wist," οὐκ ᾤμην. (Plutarch.) In ordination of ministers all possible care and caution is to be used. Chrysostom thinks that earnestness used by the apostle in the former verse, belongs chiefly to this. Some also make the two last verses a reason of this.

Neither be partaker of other men's sins] Whom thou shalt rashly ordain, and so thrust upon the people to their and thine infinite disadvantage. " From mine other men's sins (saith one), good Lord, deliver me." The Athenians had their δοκιμασία, which was a solemn examination of the magistrates, whether fit to govern or no; and of the orators, whether not incontinent, prodigal, unkind to parents, &c.; for if so, they were dis-privileged, and not suffered to plead or speak publicly. (Rous's Archæol. Attic.)

Keep thyself pure] See ver. 2, and know that

sin is a filthy thing, and defileth the soul worse than any jakes can do the body; as our Saviour shows, Matt. vii. 23.

Ver. 23. *Drink no longer water*] Timothy, living among the luxurious Ephesians, was so abstemious that the apostle is fain to prescribe him physic. Hypocrites will be chaste only in the mountains where are no women, and sober in Scythia where are no vines; but Lot was chaste in the midst of Sodom, and Anacharsis temperate among the debauched Athenians. The faithful in the world are like a pearl in a puddle; they lose nothing of their virtue, though amidst the vicious; like heavenly salamanders, they remain unscorched in the fire; like fishes, they retain their freshness in the salt waters.

But use a little wine] *Modice, hoc est medice, pro remedio parcius, non pro deliciis redundantius*, saith Ambrose; who also somewhere relateth of one Theotimus (a good name but a bad man) that he was so far from taking St Paul's advice, that having a disease upon his body, and told by the physician that unless he drank less wine he was like to lose his eyes, *Vale lumen amicum*, " Farewell, sweet eye-sight," said he, choosing rather to lose his sight than his sin; so will many their souls; being like affected to their base lusts, as the panther is said to be to man's dung, which it exceedingly desireth and maketh after.

Ver. 24. *Some men's sins*] The Judge of the earth keepeth his petty-sessions now, letting the law pass upon some few, reserving the rest till the great assizes. Some wicked God punisheth here, lest his providence, but not all, lest his patience and promise of judgment, should be called into question, as Augustine hath observed.

Ver. 25. *Cannot be hid*] As putrid hypocrisy shall be detected (for the name of the wicked must rot), so wronged innocency shall be cleared, as the eclipsed moon wades out of the shadow, and recovers her splendour.

CHAPTER VI.

Ver. 1. *Count their own masters*] AND not under a pretence of Christian liberty, and because in Christ Jesus there is neither bond nor free, seek to shake off the yoke of obedience that God hath hung upon their necks. See 1 Pet. ii. 28.

That the name of God and his doctrine, &c.] Be traduced as a doctrine of liberty. Heathens lay at the catch, 1 Pet. ii. 12, spying and prying (as the word ἐποπτεύσαντες there signifies), and imputing all public judgments to Christian miscarriages. *Nunc male audiunt castiganturque vulgo Christiani* (saith Lactantius, de opif. Dei ad Demet.) *quod aliter quam sapientibus convenit, vivant, et vitia sub obtentu nominis celent.* Christians are very hardly spoken of at this very day, because their conversation is not as becometh the gospel of Christ, but they think to cover their faults with the fig-leaves of profession.

Ver. 2. *Partakers of the benefit*] i. e. Of Christ,

who is here called the benefit, as John iv. 10, the gift of God.

Ver. 3. *If any man teach otherwise*] ἑτεροδιδασκαλεῖ, discover himself heterodox out of affectation of singularity, &c., as divers do in this licentious age; broaching things different from the received doctrine, as holding it, with Phocion, a goodly thing to dissent from others.

Consent not to wholesome words] Words that have a healing property in them. The Scripture (as that library of Alexandria) may be properly said to be the soul's physic, ἡ τῆς ψυχῆς ἰατρεία. By the reading of Livy, Curtius, Aventinus, and other historians, many are said to have been recovered of divers desperate diseases. *O facile et beatum curationis genus*, saith John Bodin (de Utilit Historiæ). But the reading of the Holy Scriptures doth a far greater cure than this upon the soul. King Alphonsus, cured of a fever by reading Q. Curtius, cried out, *Valeat Avicenna, vivat Curtius*, Farewell physic, well fare history. May not we better say so of these wholesome words, this doctrine according to godliness, purposely composed for the promoting of piety in the world?

Ver. 4. *He is proud*] Gr. τετύφωται, he is blown up, big-swollen. Swelling is a dangerous symptom in the body; but much more in the soul. Pride and self-conceit is a bastard (saith one) begot betwixt a learned head and an unsanctified heart; which being once conceived in the soul, causeth it to swell till it burst asunder with unthankfulness to God for the bestowing, with envy, scorn, and disdain of men in the imparting of such gifts as may be to them beneficial. Some think that the apostle alludeth here to the wind Typhon, which the ancients held hurtful to men's wits and senses; so that those that were blasted with it ran mad.

Knowing nothing] sc. Aright, and as they ought to know, 1 Cor. viii. 2. See the note there. The Gnostics boasted that they knew all things knowable. Irenæus saith, that they were so besotted with an opinion of themselves, that they accounted their own writings to be gospel. Such self-admirers also were the Illuminates (as they called themselves), the Manichees, the Novatians. And such are now the Jesuits, the sectaries, &c.; and other *maleferiati fanatici*, who lest they should not be reputed to know something unknown to others, profess skill beyond the circumference of possible knowledge.

Doting about questions] Gr. Question-sick. As the schoolmen, and our new questionists. But God loveth *curristas non quæristas*, saith Luther.

And strifes of words] λογομαχίας, frivolous questions and quarrels. The wit of heretics and schismatics will better serve them to devise a thousand shifts to elude the truth than their pride will suffer them once to yield and acknowledge it.

Ver. 5. *Perverse disputings*] παραδιατριβαὶ, endless and needless discourses and exercises, opposite to those above, chap. iv. 13—15. The

Greek word signifieth galling one another with disputes, or rubbing one against another, as scabbed sheep will, and so spreading the infection.

Of men of corrupt minds] That want not time but waste it, *aliud agendo.* As Lactantius saith of some brain-sick idolaters in his time, they feigned what they pleased, and then feared what they feigned; so many conceit what they like, and then think themselves bound to justify their wild conceivings.

From such withdraw thyself] G.r ἀφίστασο, stand off, keep at a distance, as you would from one that hath a plague sore; say of them to yourselves and others, as Austin doth of certain heretics, *Illi garriant, nos credamus.* Let them prate as they please, let us hold fast the faithful word.

Ver. 6. *But godliness with contentment*] True piety hath true plenty, and is never without a well-contenting sufficiency, a full self-sufficiency. The wicked in the fulness of his sufficiency is in straits, Job xx. 22. Contrariwise the godly in the fulness of their straits are in an all-sufficiency.

Ver. 7. *We can carry nothing out*] But a winding-sheet, as Saladin's shirt, which he commanded to be hung up at his burial, a bare priest going before the bier, and proclaiming, Saladin the mighty monarch of the East is gone, and hath taken no more with him than what you see. (Carlon. Chron.) Indeed I read of one that being ready to die, clapped a twenty-shilling piece of gold into his mouth, and said, Some wiser than some; if I must leave all the rest, yet this I will take with me. (Mr Rogers' Treatise of Love.) But this was none of the wisest men, you will say; as that great caliph of Babylon was none of the happiest, that was starved to death by the great Cham of Cataia, amidst the infinite treasures of gold, silver, and precious stones that he and his predecessors had most covetously heaped together, whereof he willed him to eat, and make no spare. It is with us in the world (saith one) as it was in the Jewish fields and orchards; pluck and eat, they might, while there; not pocket, or put up. Or as boys that rob an orchard and meet with the owner at the door.

> ——*modo quem fortuna fovendo*
> *Congestis opibus donisque refersit opimis,*
> *Nudum tartarea portarit navita cymba.*
>   De Annibale, Silius Ital.

Ver. 8. *And having food and raiment*] Houses are not named: for that then they were to stand ready to run from place to place, and to leave house and all behind them. Food and raiment, τροφὴν οὐ τρυφὴν, σκεπάσματα οὐ κοσμήματα, as Isidore here elegantly observeth, Food not junkets, raiment not ornament; garments *quasi* guardments to guard us from the cold air. Nature is content with a little, grace with less; as, not to starve, not to thirst, μὴ ῥιγᾶν, μὴ διψᾶν, saith Galen; *Cibus et potus sunt divitiæ Christianorum,* saith Jerome. Bread and water with the gospel are

good cheer, saith another. Epicurus could say, that he would think himself as happy as might be, *si aquam haberet et offa m,* if he could get but a morsel of meat and a mouthful of water. (Ælian.) This was strange from Epicurus. But *Epicurei mihi videntur melius facere quam dicere,* saith Tully. Epicurus and his followers practised better than they held. (Cic. de Fin. ii.) A little of the creature will serve turn to carry a man through his pilgrimage. *Insaniæ igitur damnandi sunt* (saith Vives), *qui tam multa tam anxie congerunt, quum sit tam paucis opus.* He is little better than mad that heaps up such a deal, when far less will do the deed.

Let us be content] Gr. ἀρκεσθησόμεθα. Let us have enough, let us count it enough, if we have necessaries (to maintain our state, and live like ourselves); though we have not superfluities, let it seem sufficient.

Ver. 9. *But they that will be rich*] That are resolved to have it, howsoever—*rem, rem, quocunque modo rem.*[1] "He that hasteth to be rich shall not be innocent," Prov. xxviii. 20.

And a snare] As the panther, which so loveth man's dung, that if it be hanged a height from it, it will leap, and never leave it till it have burst itself in pieces to get it.

Drown men in destruction and perdition] *Ita demergunt ut in aquæ summitate rursus non ebulliant,* So as they never show themselves above water any more.[2] We read of the inhabitants of Oenoe, a dry island beside Athens, that they bestowed much labour to draw into it a river to water it, and make it more fruitful. But when all the passages were opened, and the receptacles prepared, the water came in so plentifully, that it overflowed all; and at the first tide drowned the island and all the people. So fareth it with many covetous caitiffs, who seem to be of Nevessan the lawyer's mind, "He that will not venture his body shall never be valiant; he that will not venture his soul shall never be rich." Hubertus, an English cormorant, made this will: I yield my goods to the king, my body to the grave, my soul to the devil. How much better Aristippus and Crates the Theban, with their *Hinc abite malæ divitiæ: satius enim est a me vos demergi,* &c.: they threw their riches into the sea, saying, Hence, hence, base trash! better we drown you in the sea than that you should drown us in perdition and destruction. Plutarch reports of one Philoxenus, that finding his heart too fast affected to his wealth, he made away with it; and said, nay swore, that he would part with it rather than be undone for ever by it.[3] Christians have a better way to dispose of their riches than to throw them away, Psal. xvi. 3; Luke xvi. 9. But many rich wretches do as Heliogabalus did, who provided silken halters to hang himself withal, ponds of sweet water to drown himself with, gilded poisons to poison himself with, rather than to fall into the hands of his enemies. So do these strangle, drown, poison their precious souls with profits,

---

[1] *Divis qui fieri vult, et cito vult fieri.* Juv.
[2] βυθίζουσι, such a drowning as is desperate.

[3] μὰ τοὺς θεοὺς ἐμὲ, ταῦτα, τὰ ἀγαθὰ οὐκ ἀπολεῖ, ἀλλ᾽ ἐγὼ ταῦτα. Plut.

pleasures, and preferments, &c., and many times meet with perdition and destruction, that is, with a double destruction, temporal and eternal, as some expound it.

Ver. 10. *For the love of money*] Phocylides saith the same, ἡ φιλοχρημοσύνη μητὴρ κακότητος ἀπάσης. Covetousness is the mother of all mischief. Bion called it the metropolis of misdemeanor. Timon, the proper element of evils. There are that draw it through all the commandments, and demonstrate it to be a breach of all.

The root of all evil] As there is life in the root when there is no sap in the branches; so covetousness oft liveth when other vices die and decay, as in old men, who because they are likely to leave the world, spit on their hands and take better hold.

They have erred from the faith] Selling themselves to the devil, as Judas, Ahab, that pope for seven years' enjoyment of the popedom.

And pierced themselves through] *Undique transfixerunt*, They have galled and gored themselves. The covetous man hath his name in Hebrew of a word that signifieth sometimes to pierce or wound, Psal. x. 3, with Joel ii. 8. He that will be rich takes no more rest than one upon a rack or bed of thorns; when he graspeth earthly things most greedily, he embraceth nothing but smoke, which wringeth tears from his eyes, and vanisheth into nothing. Three vultures he hath always feeding upon his heart, care in getting, fear in keeping, grief in spending and parting with that he hath; so that he is in hell beforehand.

Ver. 11. *But thou, O man of God*] If Timothy were that angel of the Church of Ephesus, Rev. ii. 1, that left his first love (as some think he was), this counsel was but needful. Christ cautions his disciples to beware of worldliness, Luke xxi. 34.

Flee these things] *Remis velisque*, with all thy might, that thou be not tacked with them, taxed for them.

Follow after righteousness] These be notable counterpoisons against covetousness. Paul shows him a better project; points him a sovereign amulet or antidote made up of these precious ingredients: 1. Righteousness, which gives every man his own. 2. Godliness, which gives God likewise his own (this the covetous man cannot awhile to do). 3. Faith, which feareth no famine, quelleth and killeth distrust. 4. Love, a professed enemy to sinful self-love, that nurse of covetousness. 5. Patience, to wait upon God, and not to make haste to be rich. 6. Meekness, in case of cross accidents; when the covetous, troubled by others, troubleth his own house, and meditateth revenge.

Ver. 12. *Fight the good fight*] Not only follow after the former graces, but fight for them, rather than fail of them.

Lay hold on eternal life] While others lay hold on wealth, honours, &c. Catch at the crown, which is hanged up on high, as it were, and provided for conquerors only, that so fight

as to finish, 2 Tim. iv. 7, 8. *Tempus est nos de illa perpetua jam, non de hac exigua vita cogitare*, could the heathen orator say (Cic. ad Attic. x.). It is high time now we should think of heaven. Catch at the opportunity, as the echo catcheth the voice.

Ver. 13. *Who before Pontius Pilate*] Not dissembling the truth, though jeered by Pilate, who scornfully asked him, "What is truth?" *q. d.* Do you stand upon your life, and yet talk of truth? John xviii. 38. Julian and his heathen instruments had set out certain foolish and false relations under Pilate's name, purposely to cast dirt upon Christ, which are refuted by Augustine and Cyril.

Ver. 14. *Without spot*] Of foul sins, Deut. xxxii. 5.

Unrebukeable] So as no just exception can be laid against thee for allowance of lesser evils.

Until the appearing] ἐπιφάνειαν. *Illustrem illum adventum*, as Beza renders it; the bright, clear, or radiant appearing. St Paul would have Timothy so carry himself as if Christ should then come, and to remit nothing of his zeal, though he should live till that time.

Ver. 15. *Which in his times he shall show*] Let no man therefore ask, Where is the promise of his coming? Though he be slow, yet he is sure; and his time is the best time; wait, James v. 7.

The blessed and only potentate] A lively and lofty description of God, whom yet none can possibly describe. One being asked, what God was, answered, *Si scirem, Deus essem*.

Ver. 16. *Dwelling in the light*] So that the seraphims in their addresses to him, clap their wings on their faces, Isa. vi. 2, as men are wont to do their hands when the lightning flasheth in their eyes.

Nor can see] We can see but God's back parts and live: we need see no more that we may live for ever.

Ver. 17. *That they be not high-minded*] The devil will easily blow up his blab, if we watch not. Should the ant think herself some great business, because gotten upon her hillock? or the sumpter-horse, because laden with treasure? Should the Egyptian ass think himself worshipful for bearing the golden Isis upon his back? And yet so it falls out in common experience. Many men's good and their blood rise together; their hearts are lifted up with their estates, as a boat that riseth with the rising of the water. Every grain of riches hath a vermin of pride and ambition in it. *Magna cognatio ut rei, sic et nominis, divitiis et vitiis.*

In uncertain riches] Riches were never true to any that trusted to them. *Vitrea est fortuna: cum splendet, frangitur.* Riches, as glass, are bright but brittle. (Mimus.) Some render it the unevidence of riches (ἀδηλότης); and indeed they do not evidence God's special love; they are blessings of his left-hand, of his footstool, *bona scabelli.* "Not many rich," &c.

Who giveth us all things richly to enjoy] Thus

riches cannot do for us. The covetous enjoys nothing, nor the sick, nor the discontented, nor any else, unless with riches God gives us himself. Our God should therefore be trusted, because he is, 1. A living God. 2. A giving God. The Athenians made their gods standing with their hands upwards, as if they were more willing to receive than to give. (Archæol. Attic. xlvi.) But our God openeth his hand, and lets fall his blessing upon everything living, and holds it a more blessed thing "to give than to receive," Acts xx. 35.

Ver. 18. *That they do good*] Not the richer the harder; as the sun moveth slowest when it is at the highest in the zodiac, or as the moon when it is fullest of light gets farthest off from the sun.

Rich in good works] This is to be rich in God, Luke xii. 21, when our works are good, *Quoad fontem et quoad finem.*

Ready to distribute] A virtue much commended in the kings of Egypt (Diod. Sic. i.); practised by the Pythagoreans, Essenes, but especially by those primitive Christians, Acts iv. See my Common-place of Alms, and to those many examples there set forth of Christian

bounty, add that of Mr Fox, who never denied any that asked him aught for Jesus' sake. And being once so asked by a poor man, he questioned him whether he knew Jesus Christ? And finding signs that the man was a believer, he gave him his horse, when he had no money. I commend not his discretion, but his zeal and charity were admirable. The like is reported of Aidanus, as hath been said before. Queen Anne Boleyn gave in alms fourteen or fifteen thousand pounds in three-quarters of a year, as Mr Fox reporteth; accounting that she had nothing of her own but what she had given away. *Hoc habeo quodcunque dedi.* (Seneca.)

Ver. 19. *Laying up in store*] As wise merchants, happy usurers, parting with that which they cannot keep, that they may gain that which they cannot lose.

On eternal life] Or as some copies have it, "Of life indeed," τῆς ὄντως ζωῆς. *Æterna vita, vera vita.* (Augustine.)

Ver. 20. *That which is, &c.*] viz. The treasure of true doctrine, esteeming every particle of it precious, as the filings of gold.

Ver. 21. *Which some professing*] Gr. Promising, as the Gnostics and other heretics.

THE SECOND EPISTLE OF ST PAUL TO TIMOTHY.

CHAPTER I.

Ver. 1. *Paul, an apostle, &c.*] THE preface of this Epistle seems to be an abridgment of that of the Epistle to the Romans. See the notes there.

Which is in Christ Jesus] All out of Christ are living carcases, walking sepulchres of themselves.

Ver. 2. *Grace, mercy, and peace*] See the note on 1 Tim. i. 2.

Ver. 3. *Whom I serve from my forefathers*] Those twelve tribes, that served God instantly, day and night, Acts xxvi. 7. That was a desperate resolution of the heathen orator (Tul. de Nat. Deor. p. iii.), *Me ex ea opinione, quam a majoribus accepi de cultu Deorum immortalium, nullius unquam oratio, aut docti, aut indocti movebit.* I will never stir an inch from the religion of my forefathers, for any man's persuasion. Paul forsook his Phariseeism and forefathers to serve God, as Abraham, Isaac, and Jacob had done with a pure conscience.

Ver. 4. *Being mindful of thy tears*] Timothy was a man of many tears, so was David, Paul, Luther, Bradford, of whom it is said, that he did seldom eat but he bedewed his trencher with tears, and that few days passed him without

plenty of tears shed before he went to bed: —Αγαθοὶ δ' ἀριδάκρυες ἄνδρες.

Ver. 5. *In thy grandmother Lois, and mother*] A sweet happiness to any child to have a good mother and grandmother. For these have great opportunity of dropping good things into their little Lemuels, as being much about them. The mothers of the kings of Judah are constantly mentioned; and as they were good or evil, so were their children. *Partus sequitur ventrem,* The birth follows the belly. The grandmothers also, as they oft love their nephews better than their own immediate children (for love descendeth), so if they be religious (*expertus loquor*) they have a strong influence upon them, and are a means of much good unto them, as was Naomi, no doubt, to Obed, Ruth iv. 16, though she were but his grandmother-in-law.

Ver. 6. *Stir up the gift*] Blow up thy smaller spark into a flame. Grace in us is like a dull seacoal fire, saith one, which if not now and then blown and stirred up, though there be no want of fuel, yet will of itself at length die and go out. The word ἀναζωπυρεῖν, here used by the apostle, is Plato's word. The apostle seems to have been well read in Plato's writings. Though I grant the word is also found in the Greek text, Gen. xlv. 27, and the apostle here might very well allude to the fire of the altar that came from heaven, and was day and night kept in by the priests. See the canon for that fire, Levit. vi. 12, 13, Hezekiah's confession, 2 Chron. xxix. 6, 7, the good housewife's candle, Prov. xxxi. 18, the wise virgins' lamps, Matt. xxv. 8, our Saviour's charge, Luke xii. 35, and do accordingly.

Ver. 7. *The spirit of fear*] δειλείας, called elsewhere the spirit of bondage, δουλείας, Rom. viii. 15. The law will convince the judgment; but it is the gospel that convinceth the lust and the affection.

Of power and of a sound mind] These two fitly stand together. Sin unrepented of, lies rotting at the heart, and by rotting weakeneth it, as a rotten rag hath no strength.

Ver. 8. *Afflictions of the gospel*] Affliction is *Evangelii genius*, saith Calvin; hence it is called "the word of Christ's patience," Rev. ii.

According to the power of God] For unless he supports us by his power, we shall never bear up in affliction.

Ver. 9. *With a holy calling*] All that follows (to those words in the end of ver. 10, "through the gospel") comes in by a parenthesis, and is so to be read.

Ver. 10. *By the appearing*] By his coming in the flesh; of which also the Psalmist speaketh, Psal. xcvi. 13.

Brought life and immortality to light] As he drew light out of darkness at the creation. And as he then made light on the first day of the week, so on the same day he abolished death, &c., by his resurrection from the dead; by virtue also whereof

Et sensus scopulis, et sylvis addidit aures;
Et Diti lachrymas, et Morti denique vitam.
De Orpheo Manilius.

Ver. 11. *A teacher of the Gentiles*] His writings therefore should be the more highly prized and studied by us Gentiles, as being properly ours; like as Psal. cxxvii. was a song made (specially) for Solomon.

Ver. 12. *I know whom I have trusted*] Here was not a faint hope, or a conjectural confidence, but a plerophory of faith. The reason whereof is rendered by a Father, *Quia in charitate nimia adoptavit me, quia verax in promissione, et potens in exhibitione*, Because God, who of his free grace hath adopted me, is both able and faithful to fulfil his promises. (Bernard.) That was a notable speech of Luther (apud Jo. Manlium), *Ipse viderit ubi anima mea mansura sit, qui pro ea sic sollicitus fuit, ut vitam pro ea posuerit.* Let him that died for my soul, see to the salvation of it.

That which I have committed] A child that hath any precious thing given him cannot better secure it than by putting it into his father's hands to keep; so neither can we better provide for our souls' safety than by committing them to God. *Tutiores autem vivimus, si totum Deo damus, non autem nos illi ex parte et nobis ex parte committimus:* We shall be sure to be safest, if we commit ourselves wholly to God, and seek not to part stakes with him therein. (Aug. de Bono

Persev. cap. 6.) The ship that is part in the water and part in the mud is soon beaten in pieces.

Ver. 13. *Hold fast the form*] The catechistical principles, that method, system, short sum of divinity, that St Paul had compiled for Timothy's use; called here not only a form, τυπὸς ὑποτύπωσις, as Rom. vi. 17, but a short form or brief method, such as hath both perspicuity and brevity, a platform, draught, or delineation, according to which Timothy was to steer, as by a compass.

Of wholesome words] That have a property in them, and wherein there is nothing froward or perverse, Prov. viii. 8, nothing that may hurt or hinder thy soul's health; such as were the writings of Rabbins and philosophers, wherein (to say the best of them)

Sunt bona mista malis, sunt mala mista bonis;

together with the gold, silver, and ivory of some sound truths, they have store of apes and peacocks, toys and trifles; yea, some snakes and serpents, that may destroy the precious soul.

In faith and love] The sum of all sound doctrine and Christian duty.

Ver. 14. *That good thing that was,* &c.] Thy crown of recompense, Rev. iii. 11. Or thy converts, thy crown of rejoicing, 1 Thess. ii. 19. Or the purity of thy doctrine, 1 Tim. vi. 20. The gospel is Christ's *depositum* with us, committed to our keeping; as our souls are our *depositum* with him, committed to his. (Theophyl.) Let us therefore strive together for this faith of the gospel, Phil. i. 27, resolving either to live with it or die for it. Let us earnestly contend for this faith "once (only) delivered," Jude 3. Once for all; another edition of it is never to be expected. "Hold fast the faithful word," as with both hands, Tit. i. 9. O pray, pray, said a Dutch divine, upon his death-bed, *pontifex enim Romanus, et Concilium Tridentinum mira moliuntur*, for the pope and his complices are doing their utmost to bereave us of our present enjoyments. And are there not still such factors for the devil, such pioneers hard at work amongst us? Let us carefully countermine them.

Ver. 15. *All they which are in Asia*] All the ministers there. These stars fell from heaven, Rev. vi. 13, as fast as the fig-tree makes abort, with any never so light and gentle a wind. (Plin.)

Phygellus and Hermogenes] Famous only for their recidivation and apostasy. Hermogenes took after Hermogenes the retrograde rhetorician; who at 22 years of age was an excellent orator, but by 24, *mente lapsus est*, forgat all his skill, and became a very dunce, *nulla evidente causa*, saith mine author (C. Rhodigin).

Ver. 16. *He oft refreshed me*] Gr. ἀνέψυξε, poured cold water upon me, as that angel did upon the racked limbs of Theodorus the martyr, mentioned by Socrates and Ruffinus in the days of Julian the Apostate.

Ver. 17. *He sought me out very diligently*] σπουδαιότερον, with vehement desire and intention of affection, not as a coward seeks after his enemy, whom he hopes he shall never find, but as Saul sought David, or as the wise men the babe of Bethlehem, &c.

Ver. 18. *The Lord*] That is, God the Father "grant he may find mercy of the Lord," that is, of God the Son, as "Jehovah from Jehovah," Gen. xix. 24.

That he may find] For his care in finding out me, ver. 17.

CHAPTER II.

Ver. 1. *Be strong*] TOGETHER with the word there goes forth a power, as Luke v. 17. Exhortations are God's means to make us such as he requireth us to be.

In the grace that is in Christ Jesus] Weak grace may evidence pardon of sin; but it is strong grace that can overcome the temptations of Satan, 1 John ii. 12, 14, and bear up the heart in strong consolation.[1] The blessing upon man in the first creation was, "Increase and multiply;" in the second, "Grow in grace, be strong," &c.

Ver. 2. *Commit them to faithful men*] No talent is given us for private and proper use, but that we be trading and transmitting it also to others. Synesius speaks of some, who having a treasure of abilities in them, yet would as soon part with their hearts as with their meditations, &c., the canker of whose great skill shall be a witness against them.

Ver. 3. *Endure hardship*] Never dream of a delicacy; think not to find God in the gardens of Egypt, whom Moses found not but in the burning-bush. Many love Canaan, but loathe the wilderness; commend the country, but look upon the conquest as impossible; would sit in the seat of honour with Zebedee's children, but not drink the cup of affliction. These deceive themselves.

As a good soldier, &c.] Christ saith to us (as the Black Prince's father sent to him, fighting as it were in blood to the knees, and in a great distress), Either vanquish or die; as the Prince of Orange said to his soldiers at the battle of Newport, when they had the sea on the one side, and the Spaniards on the other, If you will live, you must either eat up these Spaniards or drink up this sea.

Ver. 4. *With the affairs*] Or, gainful negotiations with marriage matters, say the Papists here, but without all show of sense. The Council of Chalcedon strictly forbiddeth ministers to meddle in worldly matters: *Clericus in oppido, piscis in arido.* (Canon 31.) The apostle seemeth to allude to the Roman soldiers, who might not be tutors to other men's persons, proctors of other men's causes; they might not meddle with husbandry, merchandise, &c.

Ver. 5. *Except he strive lawfully*] *Tam circa ciborum quam continentiæ ac honestatis rationem,*

saith Cassianus, except for matter and manner he observe the laws of wrestling, both for preparation and execution. Aristotle saith, Not he that had a strong body, but he that ran well had the crown in the Olympic games; it was not he that had an athletical ability, but he that wrestled best, that gat the garland.

Ver. 6. *The husbandman labouring first*] *Spes alit agricolas. Næ illi falsi sunt* (saith Sallust, in Jugur.) *qui diversissimas res expectant, ignaviæ voluptatem, et præmia virtutis.* They are utterly out, that think to have the pleasure of sloth and the guerdon of goodness.

Ver. 7. *Consider what I say*] Apply to thyself these forementioned similes, and so buckle close to thy business.

And the Lord give thee] Unless God open Hagar's eyes, she cannot see the fountain that is hard by. Rebecca cooks the venison, but Isaac only blesseth.

Ver. 8. *Remember that Jesus*] Remember it for thine encouragement; that Christ, for a reward of his sufferings, was both raised and exalted, Phil. ii. 9.

Ver. 9. *But the word of God is not bound*] It runs and is glorified, 2 Thess. iii. 1, being free and not fettered. I preach, though a prisoner, saith Paul; so did Bradford and other martyrs. Within a few days of Queen Mary's reign, almost all the prisons in England were become right Christian schools and churches (saith Mr Fox), so that there was no greater comfort for Christian hearts than to come to the prisons to behold their virtuous conversation, and to hear their prayers, preachings, &c. The Earl of Derby's accusation in the Parliament house against Mr Bradford was, that he did more hurt (so he called good evil) by letters and conferences in prison, than ever he did when he was abroad by preaching.

Ver. 10. *That they may also obtain*] viz. By my pains in preaching, though bound, and by example of my patience in suffering bonds, &c.

Ver. 11. *It is a faithful saying*] A sound and a sure assertion, Rom. viii. 17. Afflictions are the *præludia triumphi.*

If we be dead] As Christ, ver. 8. Or, for Christ, if we be in deaths often, and at length lose our lives for his name's sake.

Ver. 12. *If we suffer*] No wearing the crown but by bearing the cross first. *Ne Jesum quidem audias gloriosum, nisi videris prius crucifixum,* saith Luther (Epist. ad Melancthon). Christ himself was not glorified till first crucified. Queen Elizabeth is said to have swam to her crown through a sea of sorrow; so must we.

If we deny him] See the note on Matt. x. 33. God usually retaliates, pays men home in their own coin, proportions jealousy to jealousy, provocation to provocation, Deut. xxii. 21; Isa. lxvi. 3, 4.

Ver. 13. *If we believe not*] See the note on Rom. iii. 3. Some sense it thus: though we prove perfidious, yet he is no loser by us, as having all within himself. Howbeit hereby we

---

[1] Θᾶττον ἂν εἰδῇς τὴν καρδίαν ἢ τὰ ἐν τῇ καρδίᾳ.

show that we have no interest in Christ; for he cannot deny himself, though we can deny him.

Ver. 14. *Strive not about words*] Either out of novelty or niceness. As Longolius, who would not use the word *Ecclesia*, but instead thereof, *Respublica Christiana*. Another Italian bishop for *Episcopus* took up the heathenish word *Flamen;* so Castalio for *Angelus* hath *Genius.* (Joh. Manl. loc. com.) And Pomponius Lætus was full of such like fooleries, airy contestations, and empty strifes. (Lud. Vives.) Or, strive not with words, bandying contumelious speeches (which is but to wash off dirt with dirt). Bishop Montague could not name any one, that did never so little dissent from him, without a reproach, as Rivet noteth of him. *Arbitror te veritate convictum, ad maledicta converti,* saith Jerome to Helvidius, I suppose thou hast nothing to say against the truth, and dost therefore fall a railing at me that defend it. Or, think not to carry it by big and boasting words without better proof, but stone thine adversaries with arguments, as Athanasius adviseth; burn heretics with the fire of charity, as Luther teacheth.

Ver. 15. *Study to show thyself*] There are crept into God's sanctuary such Levites to divide the word, that are not worthy the place of Gibeonites to cleave wood; like those unlearned logicians in Plato, *Lacerant doctrinas, sicut caniculi panniculos,* saith he; they tear up a text, and torment it, they wrest the Scriptures and wrong them, set them upon the rack, and make them speak what they never meant. These should be driven from the work, as those bastard Levites were by the Tirshatha, Ezra ii. 63.

Rightly dividing the word of God] The Syriac renders it, "Rightly preaching the word." Æschines saith, an orator's oration and the law (so a preacher's sermon and the word) must be unisons.[1] And if Galen could say, that in anatomizing man's brain, physicians must carry themselves as men do in the temple, how much more must divines do so, in dividing God's Holy Word! The metaphor seems to be taken either from the priests of the law, who were to cut up the sacrifices accurately, and to lay them upon the altar orderly; or else from householders, that cut and carve to every one at table their share of meat. So must ministers, and not do as he in the emblem, that gave straw to the dog and a bone to the ass, but see that every one have their proper portion: this is workmanlike, such as need not be ashamed.

Ver. 16. *But shun*] Gr. περίστασο, go round about them, viz. to suppress them on every side. St Peter calls them bubbles of words, full of wind, 2 Pet. ii. 18.

For they will increase] The Greek word προκόψουσι signifies, to "cut a thing before," to make a passage for other things: as in some countries they cut a passage for their sheep because of the ice. Sure it is that error is of an encroaching nature. Let the serpent but wind in his head, and he will quickly bring in

his whole body. He that saith yea to the devil in a little, shall not say nay when he pleases; he that tumbleth down the hill of error, will never leave tumbling till he comes to the bottom. The popish superstition at first grew secretly, the tares were hid under the corn; but now they overtop and choke it. How many (now-a-days) first turn Separatists, then Antinomians, then Anabaptists, then Arminians, then Socinians, Anti-scripturists, Anti-trinitarians, Stark-atheists. The London ministers in their late vindication complain of this wretched defection of many of their formerly forward hearers, and not without cause. It were far easier to write a book of apostates in this age than a book of martyrs.

Ver. 17. *Eat as doth a gangrene*] Which presently overruns the parts, and takes the brain, pierceth into the very bones, and if not suddenly cured by cutting off the part infected, kills the patient. Lo, such is heresy and error, which made Placilla the empress earnestly beseech her husband Theodosius senior, not to confer with Eunomius the heretic, lest he should be perverted by his speeches. (Sozom. vii. c. 7.) Anasius II., bishop of Rome, A. D. 497, while he sought to win Acacius the heretic, was seduced by him. (Jac. Revius, de Vit. Pont.) Error is exceeding infectious, and for most part mortal, as the leprosy in the head was held to be. Jealousy, frenzy, and heresy can hardly be cured, saith the Italian proverb.

Ver. 18. *Have erred*] Gr. ἠστόχησαν, have missed the mark, as unskilful archers, or as inconsiderate mariners, by misreckoning of a point, they have missed the haven and run upon the rocks.

That the resurrection is past] These were (likely) the progenitors of Marcion, who taught that there was no resurrection of the body to be believed, but of the soul only from sin. (Epiph. Hæres. 43.) This heresy is now revived amongst us, and raked again out of the grave; as many other also are and will be, by this lawless liberty.

And overthrow the faith of some] Not the grace, but the profession of faith; and this they are ever doing at (the word ἀνατρέπουσι is in the present tense), that they may undo their disciples; by digging at the foundation thus, that they may demolish the whole fabric.

Ver. 19. *Nevertheless the foundation*] viz. Of God's election, which is here compared to a sealed book: on the one side of the seal is written, "The Lord knoweth them that are his." On the other side, "And let every one that nameth," &c. This the apostle setteth forth, for the better settling of such as were shaken by the fall of Hymenæus and Philetus, two such forward professors.

Standeth sure] As on a rock. Our English word "sure" seems to come from the Hebrew *tzur*, a rock.

Having this seal] A seal is for two ends, safety and secrecy. The Jews use to write on the back of their sealed packets, *Nun, Cheth, Shin,* that

[1] χρὴ τὸ αὐτὸ φθέγγεσθαι τὸν ῥήτορα καὶ τὸν νόμον. Æsch.

is, *Niddui, Cherem*, and *Shammatha*, all sorts of excommunication to him that shall offer to break up sealed businesses. God's hidden ones are in a safe hand, and out of danger of utter apostasy, though he eftsoons suffereth the tree of his Church to be shaken, that rotten fruit may fall off.

The Lord knoweth them, &c.] In respect of the freeness of his election and immobility of his affection. Howbeit this knowledge that God hath of his, is carried secret, as a river underground, till he calls and separates us from the rest.

That nameth the name of Christ] He may have an infallible seal of salvation, that but nameth Christ's name in prayer, that can say no more than Abba, Father, desiring and resolving to depart from iniquity.

Ver. 20. *There are not only*, &c.] Wonder not therefore, murmur not that there are a mixture of good and bad in God's house. He knows how to serve himself of both, Rom. ix. 20—22. Neither be offended that some of great note fall away, as did Hymenæus and Philetus. God hath his vessels of all sorts.

Ver. 21. *Purge himself from these*] From these seducers or arch-heretics, those vessels of dishonour, whose doctrine defileth worse than any kitchen-stuff or leprosy.

He shall be a vessel, &c.] You know (said John Careless, the martyr, in a letter to Mr Philpot) that the vessel before it be made bright is soiled with oil and many other things, that it may scour the better. Oh happy be you that you be now in this scouring-house; for shortly you shall be set upon the celestial shelf as bright as angels, &c.

Ver. 22. *Fly also youthful lusts*] φεῦγε, Fly them he must with post-haste, though such a chaste and chastened piece as he was. Youth is a slippery age, slippery as glass, easily contracting dust and filth, as the word used by David importeth, Psal. cxix. 9, and should therefore cleanse its ways by cleaving to the word. Youth is a hot age, as the Greek word signifies;[1] a black dark age, as the Hebrew word noteth, Eccl. xi. 10. Therefore put away evil from thy flesh, saith the wise man there, out of his own experience. St Paul repeats and inculcates this precept upon his son Timothy, as men do not only anoint their flesh, but rub in the ointment. He knew that all was but enough. *Summopere cavendum divino præconi, ne dicta factis deficientibus erubescant. Nihil turpius Peripatetico claudo*, saith one.

But follow righteousness, faith, &c.] Let not the devil find thee idle, but do what thou canst to be out of the way when the temptation cometh. Keep close to God in other matters, Eccl. vii. 26; Prov. xxii. 14; exercise thyself in duties of piety with an upright heart, Prov. xxiii. 26, 27; vi. 23, 24; ii. 10, 11, 16; Rom. i. 28.

Ver. 23. *But foolish and unlearned*, &c.]

παραιτοῦ. *Vitiligatorum nænias devita.* Shift them off, set them by as seeds of sedition. Shake off vain questionists as great triflers. Such were the schoolmen, in detestation of whose vain jangling and doting about questions Luther saith, *Prope est ut jurem nullum esse Theologum Scholasticum qui unum caput Evangelii intelligat;* I could almost swear that there is not a schoolman that understands one chapter of the New Testament. One of their doctors said, that he had publicly expounded the Book of Job; but by that time he came to the 10th and 11th chapters, he did verily believe that Job was more vexed and tortured by his interpretations than ever he had been by his botches and ulcers. (Joh. Manl. loc. com.)

Ver. 24. *Must not strive*] μάχεσθαι, scold, wrangle, *Ne rixando amittatur veritas, ut fere fit,* lest by striving about the truth we utterly lose it. *Facta est fides Evangeliorum, fides temporum, et cum fides una esse debeat, eo pene ventum est ut nulla sit.* A sad complaint of Hilary. Erasmus observeth, that in the primitive times there were so many sects and heresies, and so much pretending to the truth by them all, that it was a witty thing to be a right believer. A late writer complaineth, that a Christian now is not the same thing as formerly. Our heads are so big (like children that have the rickets) that all the body fares the worse for it.

Patient] Or, tolerant of evil, both persons and occurrences; he shall have his back-burden of both, and must both bear and forbear:[2] *Taceo, Fero, Spero*, must be his motto, as it was Hyperius'.

Ver. 25. *Those that oppose themselves*] Though they should deal as absurdly with us as those that deny the snow to be white, &c. Aristotle forbids to dispute with such.[3] But Christ commands not only by force of argument to convince them, Jude 22, but also to handle them gently, and in meekness to instruct them.

If God will give them, &c.] Repentance is God's gift: neither is it in the power of any to repent at pleasure. Some vainly conceit that these five words, Lord, have mercy upon me, are as efficacious to send them to heaven, as the Papists that their five words of consecration are to transubstantiate the bread. But as many are undone (saith a divine) by buying a counterfeit jewel; so many are in hell by mistake of their repentance.

Ver. 26. *Recover themselves*] ἀνανήψωσι. Put away their spiritual drunkenness, 1 Sam. i. 14, and go forth and shake themselves, as Samson, out of sin's lethargy. "Out of the snare of the devil," *i. e.* heretical doctrines or sensual pleasures; both which do intoxicate men's brains and make them dead drunk.

Taken alive] But to be destroyed, 2 Pet. ii. 12, without repentance unto life, Acts xi. 18. Ἐζωγρημένοι, taken alive, and in hunting.

---

[1] ἤθεος, of αἴθω, *uro*; ἀΐζεος, of ζέω, *ferveo*.

[2] ἀνεξίκακον. ἀνέχου καὶ ἀπέχου. *Sustine, abstine.*

[3] ἐλέγχετε διακρινόμενοι. *Arguite disputatos; sic* Lorinus *vertit.*

CHAPTER III.

Ver. 1. *Perilous times*] Gr. καιροὶ χαλεποί, hard times. Hard hearts make hard times. *Ejusmodi tempora descripsit* (saith Casaubon of Tacitus, and the same may we say of St Paul) *quibus nulla unquam aut virtutum steriliora, aut virtutibus inimiciora;* he describeth these last and loosest times of the world, barren of virtues, but abounding with vices. There was never any but Noah, that with two faces saw both before and behind. But that Ancient of days, to whom all things are present, hath here told us that the last shall be the worst.

Ver. 2. *Lovers of their own selves*] This sinful self-love is the root of all the rest that follow in this black bead-roll.

Boasters] Or, arrogant, as that Pyrgopolynices, Isa. x. 8—11, Thrasonical Lamech, Gen. iv. 23, where he brags and goes on to out-dare God himself. Spaniards are said to be impudent braggers, and extremely proud in the lowest ebb of fortune.

Ver. 3. *Without natural affection, &c.*] True Christians live soberly, as touching themselves, righteously toward men, and godly towards their God, Tit. ii. 12. But these antipodes are, as touching themselves, self-lovers, silver-lovers, pleasure-mongers, incontinent, boasters, proud, heady, high-minded. As for their carriage towards others, they are blasphemers, disobedient to parents, without natural affection, truce-breakers, or irreconcileable, ἄσπονδοι, false accusers, or devils, fierce or savage, despisers of those that are good, traitors, &c. And as to God, they are not lovers of God, but unthankful, unholy. And such dust-heaps as these a man may find in every corner of the Church.

Ver. 4. *Heady*] Head-long and head-strong. rash and inconsiderate, *Qui non vident* πρόσσω καὶ ὀπίσσω, that look not well about them, but make desperate adventures. The Greek word προπετεῖς signifieth such as fly before they are fledged.

Lovers of pleasure] Not considering that the pleasure passeth, but the pain that attends it is perpetual, φιλήδονοι. (Chrysost.) *Momentaneum est quod delectat, æternum quod cruciat.* Let not men take pleasure in pleasure. It was not simply a sin in Esau to go a hunting; but yet the more he used it, the more profane he waxed, and came at length to contemn his birth-right. Who are void of the Spirit but sensual ones? Jude 18, 19. Who say to God, Depart from us, but those that dance? Job xxi. 10, 11. Better be preserved in brine than rot in honey. These pleasure-mongers are at last as the worst of all. Such a one was Catullus, who wished all his body were nose, that he might spend all his time in sweet smells. Such was Philoxenus, who likewise wished that his neck were as long as a crane's, that he might take more delight in meats and drinks. Such was Boccas the poet,

who said that he was born *por lamore delle donne*, for the love of women. But in the kingdom of pleasure virtue cannot consist. These voluptuaries (as one saith of them) are, *Magis solliciti de mero quam de vero: Magisque amantes mundi delicias quam Christi divitias:* as those recusant guests; the worst of all whom, and least excusable, was that epicure, who had married a wife, and therefore could not come.

Ver. 5. *Having a form of godliness*] Hollow professors are as hollow trees in an old wood; tall, but pithless, sapless, unsound. Their formality is fitly compared to a bulrush, whereof the colour is fresh, the skin smooth; he is very exact that can find a knot in a bulrush, Isa. lviii. 5. But peel it, and what shall you find within but a kind of spongeous unsubstantial substance? &c. These, as if religion were a comedy, do in voice and gesture act divine duties, in heart renounce them. Hypocrites only act religion, play devotion; like they are to the ostrich, saith Hugo, *qui alas habet sed non volat*, which hath wings but flies not. God is in their mouths, but not in their reins, as the prophet Jeremy complaineth; and all they do is an effect rather of art and parts, than of the heart and grace; shells not kernels, shadows and pageants of piety, not heart-workings. The swan in the law was rejected for sacrifice, because of her black skin under white feathers. Art may take a man more than nature; but with God the more art, the less acceptance: he loveth truth in the inwards, Psal. li. 6.

Ver. 6. *Creep into houses*] Gr. ἐνδύνοντες, shoot themselves into the inner rooms of houses, *qui sese immergunt*, by their pithanology and counterfeit humility, as the Jesuits and many of our modern sectaries.[1] That creep like ferrets or weasels, as the Syriac here hath it.

Lead captive silly women] Gr. αἰχμαλωτίζοντες, take them prisoners, and then make price of them, 2 Pet. ii. 3. *Egregiam vero laudem, et spolia ampla refertis.* (Virgil.) But *omnes hæreses ex gynæciis.* It is the guise of heretics to abuse the help of women, to spread their poisonful opinions. They get an Eudoxia, Justina, Constantia on their side; and so work upon Adam by Eve. Of women they have ever made their profit, that have attempted any innovation in religion.

Ver. 7. *Ever learning, and never able*] Because resolved not to lose their lusts. *Intus existens prohibebat alienum;* there was that within that kept out holy learning. It was therefore an excellent prayer of holy Zuinglius before his public lectures, Father of lights, enlighten our minds and open our hearts, so as that we may both understand thine oracles and be transformed into them. (Scultet. Annal.)

Ver. 8. *Now as Jannes and Jambres*] Numenius the Pythagorean calleth him Mambres. These were those Egyptian sorcerers: their names St Paul had either by tradition, or out of some Jewish records. Apuleius in his second apology

---

[1] *Mulierculas Jesuitæ pio studio semper complecti solent.*

mentioneth one Joannes among the chief magicians. The Babylonian Talmud also maketh mention of these two by name, as chief of the sorcerers of Egypt. (Tract. Menachoth, cap. ix.)

Resist the truth] Not so much us as the truth. So Alexander the copper-smith did greatly withstand Paul's preachings, chap. iv. 15; this was far worse than to withstand his person.

Ver. 9. *As theirs also was*] Exod. viii. 19. When they were set, and could not with all their skill make a louse, but by further resistance manifested their folly unto all men. So did that juggler of Antwerp, all whose enchantments were made void by Mr Tindal the martyr, present at that supper, where and when he should, but could not, play his feats, and show his cunning.

Ver. 10. *But thou hast fully known*] παρηκολού-θηκας. Or, thou hast exactly trod in my track, followed my footsteps; as Irenæus did Polycarp's, as Paræus did Ursin's; whence Paulus Melissus,

——— *Sacra docente Pareo,*
Vividus Ursini spiritus ora movet.

Ver. 11. *What persecutions I endured*] Gr. οἴους, what manner of persecutions. A Christian may without sin be sensible of injuries and indignities. Only it must be the mourning of doves, and not the roaring of bears. A sheep may be as sensible of the biting of a dog as a swine is, though he raise not such a dust, make not such a din.

Ver. 12. *Yea, and all that will live*] Carry they the matter never so discreetly, they must suffer. Many dream of a delicacy, they conceit a godly life without persecution. These would pull a rose without pricks. *Armat spina rosas, mella tegunt apes.* (Boetius.) Thucydides complains of his countrymen, that none of them would ταλαιπωρεῖν διὰ τὸ καλὸν, suffer aught for goodness' sake. Too few there are that now-a-day's will do so.

Ver. 13. *Shall wax worse and worse*] *In deterius proficient*, a sorry kind of profiting, *quando Andabatarum more res procedat.* Thus the Illuminates (as they called themselves), a pestilent sect in Arragon, professing and affecting in themselves a kind of angelical purity, fell suddenly to the very counterpoint of justifying bestiality. (Spec. Europ.) And though these men and their light are quenched some while since, yet under pretence of new lights have not our church-forsakers wheeled and wheeled about so long to the right-hand, that they are perfectly come round to the left? See the note on chap. ii.

Ver. 14. *But continue thou, &c.*] Gr. μένε. Abide, keep thy station. Thou shalt surely be put to it, as that prophetical man in the ecclesiastical history went to the pillars a little before an earthquake, and bade them stand fast, for they should shortly be shaken.

Ver. 15. *And that from a child*] Gr. ἀπὸ βρέφους, from a suckling. As all children, so those especially that are dedicated to the work of the ministry, should be betimes inured to

Scripture-learning. See the note on 1 Tim. iv. 6. The story of Mistress Elizabeth Wheatenhall, daughter of Mr Anthony Wheatenhall, of Tenterden in Kent, late deceased, is very memorable. She being brought up by her aunt, the Lady Wheatenhall, before she was nine years old (not much above eight), could say all the New Testament by heart; yea, being asked where any words thereof were, she would presently name book, chapter, and verse. Timothy was so sweet a child, that if that had not been his name, it might have been his surname, as Vopiscus saith of Probus the emperor. (David's Love to God's Word, by Mr Stoughton. Epist. to Reader.)

To make thee wise] Gr. σὲ σοφίσαι, to wise thee, that thou mayest wise others, as Dan. xii. 3. The same Hebrew word שׂכל signifieth, 1. To understand; 2. To instruct others; 3. To prosper.

To salvation] He is the wise man that provides for eternity. And when all the world's wizards shall very wisely cry out in hell, *Nos insensati*, We fools counted their lives madness; they shall shine as the brightness of the firmament, Dan. xii. 3. *Sapientes sapienter descendunt in infernum.*

Ver. 16. *All Scripture is given*] Gr. Θεόπνευστος, breathed by God, both for matter and words. What frontless heretics then are our upstart anti-scripturists, that dare affirm that the Scriptures are not divine, but human invention, and that the penmen wrote as themselves conceived; they were the actions of their own spirit, &c. Also that the Scriptures are insufficient and uncertain, &c. Papists likewise speak and write basely of the Holy Scriptures, as Bishop Bonner's chaplain, who called it "his little pretty God's-book." Gifford and Raynolds say, the Bible contains something profane and apocryphal. A certain Italian bishop told Espencœus that his countrymen were charged not to read the Scriptures, *ne sic fierent hæretici*, lest they should thereby be made heretics. (Expenc. in Tit. i.) But Gregory calls the Bible *Cor et animam Dei*, the heart and soul of God; Augustine, a fortress against errors; Tertullian calleth it *Nostra digesta*, Our digests, from the lawyers; and others, Our pandects, from them also. *Classicus hic locus est*, saith Gerhard upon the text. This is a classical place to prove the perfection of the Scriptures against Papists, and whatsoever adversaries, who argue it of insufficiency, accounting traditions or revelations to be the touchstone of doctrine and foundation of faith. If the Scriptures be profitable for all these purposes, and able to make a minister perfect, &c., who can say less of it than that it is the soul's food, ψυχῆς τροφὴ, as Athanasius calleth it; the invariable rule of truth, κάνων τῆς ἀληθείας ἀκλινὴς, as Irenæus: the touchstone of errors, the aphorisms of Christ, the library of the Holy Ghost, the circle of all divine arts, the wisdom of the cross, the cubit of the sanctuary.

And is profitable for instruction] See my True Treasure, p. 40. And hereunto add, for consolation, according to Rom. xv. 4, though this also is here comprehended in doctrine and instruction for righteousness. The same Greek word, παρακαλέω signifieth to exhort and to comfort.

Ver. 17. *That the man of God*] The minister, and so consequently the people too, for whose use the minister hath all. This is observed of them, that still the scholar goes one step farther than the teacher.

May be perfect] ἄρτιος (*omnibus numeris absolutus*), with a perfection of parts, able and apt to make use of the Holy Scriptures to all the former purposes, for the behoof or benefit of his hearers. The authority of the Fathers, saith a grave and learned divine, I never urge for necessity of proof (the Scripture is thereto all-sufficient and super-abundant), but only either in some singular points to show consent; or, 2. In our controversies against anti-christians, anti-nomists, Neo-pelagians; or, 3. When some honest passage of sanctification or seasonable opposition to the corruption of the times is falsely charged with novelty, singularity, and too much preciseness. (Mr Bolton's Four Last Things.)

CHAPTER IV.

Ver. 1. *I charge thee therefore*] Matters of greatest importance must be pressed with greatest vehemence. As God putteth not forth great power but for great purpose, Eph. i. 18, 19, so neither must we use great earnestness but in affairs of great moment. It is a weakness to be hot in a cold matter, but worse to be cold in a hot matter. Farellus persuading Calvin (then a young student, and bound for Italy) to stay and help in the Lord's work at Geneva, pronounced God's curse upon his studies (which Calvin pretended) in case he staid not. Whereupon, *Non ausus fuit Calvinus ad Farelli tonitrua plus quam Periclea*, saith mine author, *jugum vocationis, quod sibi a Domino imponi videbat, detrectare.* Calvin durst not stir after such a charge, but staid it out there to his dying-day. (Melch. Adam. in Vita Calv.)

Ver. 2. *Be instant*] Gr. ἐπίστηθι, stand over it, stand close to it. Chrysostom, at Antioch, having preached many sermons against swearing, was at length asked when he would preach upon another subject? He answered, When you leave swearing, I will leave preaching against swearing.

In season, out of season] On the Lord's day, on the week-day, *Volentibus nolentibus dic importunus, Tu vis errare, tu vis perire, ego nolo*, saith Augustine. Let men know whether they will or no, that for lack of preaching they shall not perish. The show-bread stood all the week before the Lord; to show, that preaching is not out of season on any day. The friars of Basil held that it was *Lutheranum diebus profanis prædicare*, heretical to preach on working days.

(Melch. Adam.) But Anthony Person, martyr, told his persecutors that they were bite-sheeps and not bishops for neglecting to preach. It being as great a wonder at Rome to hear a bishop preach as to see an ass fly, said Dr Bassinet. But Bishop Ridley preached usually every sabbath-day and holy-day; so did Bishop Jewel, Dr Taylor, martyr, Mr Bradford, even during his imprisonment; preaching, reading, and praying was all his whole life. He did sharply reprove sin, pithily improve errors, sweetly preach Christ crucified, earnestly persuade to a godly life.

With all long-suffering, &c.] *Si decimus quisque, si unus persuasus fuerit, ad consolationem abunde sufficit*, saith Chrysostom. If you gain but the tithe of your hearers, or less, it is well.

Ver. 3. *Sound doctrine*] Which, as honey, *vulnera purgat, ulcera mordet*, purgeth green wounds, but causeth pain to exulcerate parts. (Alex. Aphtod. problem.) Children, though they love and lick in honey, yet will not endure to have it come near their lips when they have sore mouths. There are that are mad against the medicine, and fly in the faces of their spiritual physicians that come to cure them: they are sick of a *Noli me tangere*, and had rather perish in their sins than part with them. These must be pitied as people out of their right minds, and pulled out of the devil's paws; this, saith Jerome, is *sancta violentia, optabilis rapina*, a holy violence, a desirable rapine; they will thank us, if ever they recover; as if not, yet our reward is with the Lord. The physician is paid, whether the patient live or die. A minister must exhort "with all long-suffering," and oft sigh out with good old Jacob (troubled at his children's untowardness), "Lord, I have waited for thy salvation," Gen. xlix. 18.

Having itching ears] Which must have clawing preachers; such as will never *auriculas mordaci radere vero* (Horat.), deal plainly and faithfully with their souls.

Ver. 4. *Turn their ears from the truth*] Aristotle writeth (De Mirabil. Auscult.) that vultures are killed with oil of roses. Sweet smells enrage tigers. Swine cannot live in some parts of Arabia, saith Pliny, by reason of the pleasant scent of aromatical trees there growing in every wood.

Ver. 5. *Endure afflictions, do the work*] *Honor ministerii est in onere, dignitas in diligentia, corona in contemptu.*

Make full proof] πληροφόρησον, or, accomplish thy ministry. So executing every part of it, as to make it thy whole business. *Verbi minister es, hoc age*, was Mr Perkins' motto. Thou art a minister, look to it.

Ver. 6. *Ready to be offered*] To be poured out as a drink-offering upon God's altar.[1] Thus the apostle expresseth himself emphatically, pathetically, elegantly, setting forth by what death he should glorify God, viz. by being beheaded. Whether my death be a burnt-offering, a drink-offering (by fire or sword), or a peace-offering

---

[1] σπένδομαι. He speaks of it as done already.

(that I die in my bed), I desire it may be a free-will offering, a sweet sacrifice to the Lord.

The time of my departure] He makes nothing of death. It was no more betwixt God and Moses but "Go up and die." So betwixt Christ and Paul, but launch out, and land immediately at the fair haven of heaven.

Ver. 7. *I have fought a good fight*] The nearer anything is to the centre, the more strongly and swiftly it moveth. The wine of the Spirit is strongest in the saints, when they are drawing to an end. His motions are quickest when natural motions are slowest, most sensible when the body begins to be senseless, most lively when the saints are a-dying. See this in Moses' swan-like song; David's last discourse to his son Solomon and his nobles; our Saviour's farewell to the world in that last sweet sermon and prayer of his, John xiii. 14—17, wherein there is more worth, saith Mr Baxter, than in all the books in the world besides. When excellent Bucholcer was near his end, he wrote his book *de Consolatione Decumbentium*, Of the Comfort of Sick People. Then it was that Tossanus wrote his *Vade mecum;* Dr Preston, his Attributes of God; Mr Bolton, his Joys of Heaven; and before them all, Savonarola, the Italian martyr, his Meditations upon the 51st Psalm, *Verbis vivis, animatis sententiis, et spiritus fervore flagrantissimis,* in most lively expressions, and with most heavenly affections. (Sixtus Senens.) Indeed, the saints are most heavenly when nearest to heaven; like as rivers, the nearer they grow to the sea, the sooner they are met by the tide.

Ver. 8. *There is laid up a crown*] Beyond a crown the wishes of mortal men extend not. Alexander, inviting many to supper, provided a crown of 180 pounds to be given to those that drank most. One and forty killed themselves with drinking to get that crown. Shall these do more for a trifle than we will do for heaven?

A crown of righteousness] So salvation is called; not for that it is of right due to us, but because it is purchased for us by the righteousness of Christ, and shall be freely given to those that are justified by faith.

Ver. 9. *Do thy diligence, &c.*] We want much of our comfort in the want of a friend, Eccl. iv. 9. *Optimum solatium sodalitium.* How doth David bemoan the loss of Jonathan! How did Dr Taylor prize the company of his fellow-prisoner, that angel of God, as he called him, John Bradford! What a mercy did St Paul count it that sick Epaphroditus recovered! Phil. ii. 27.

Ver. 10. *Demas hath forsaken me*] Blazing comets, as long as they keep aloft, shine bright; but when they begin to decline from their pitch, they fall to the earth. Jonathan followed the chase well, and with greedy pursuit, till he met with the honey; so doth many a Demas.

Having loved this present world] Or, embraced it, ἀγαπήσας: that withered harlot had taken him with her eye-lids; that old Circe had bewitched him, that shall one day be burnt up by

fire, for her enticing men. Divorce the flesh from the world, and then the devil can do us no harm. He hath no way to entangle us but to say, as he did to our Saviour, *Mitte te deorsum,* Cast thyself down, embrace this present world, follow after these lying vanities.

And is departed unto Thessalonica] Where he became an idol-priest, as saith Dorotheus. So Harding (Bishop Jewel's adversary) was one while a thundering preacher, wishing he could cry out against Popery as loud as the bells of Oseney; yet afterwards proved a filthy apostate, and an utter adversary to the truth: and yet the world favoured him not; for the most he could get of his Holiness for all the good service he did him was but a prebend of Gaunt, or to speak more properly, saith Dr Featly, a gaunt prebend. Stapleton (another turn-coat) was made professor of a petty university, scarce so good as one of our free-schools in England. Saunders was starved. Allin was commonly called the starveling cardinal. If any of the world's darlings speed better, let them take that counsel that was given by one to John III., king of Portugal, viz. to meditate every day a quarter of an hour on that divine sentence, "What shall it profit a man to win the whole world, and lose his own soul?"

Ver. 11. *For he is profitable*] Once unprofitable (Acts xv. 38, see the note there), but now profitable, Philem. 11.

Ver. 12. *Tychicus have I sent*] For what end, see Eph. vi. 22, with the note there.

Ver. 13. *The cloak that I left*] O *supellectilem Apostolicam!* (Eras. *in loc.*) Oh what a small deal of household stuff had this great apostle, saith Erasmus; a cloak to keep off the rain, and a few books and writings. *Tota etiam supellex mea est chartacea,* saith he in another place: All my stock is in books. (Eras. in Farrag. Epistol.) And of judicious Calvin it is reported, that all the goods that he left behind him, his library being sold very dear, came scarce to 300 florins, that is, about £90 of our money. "Seekest thou great things for thyself?" Jer. xlv. 5.

But especially the parchments] Note-books of his own making or collecting: these are highly prized by students. Julius Cæsar, being forced to swim for his life, held his Commentaries in one hand above water, and swam to land with the other.[1] And what a sweet providence of God was that, that when Heidelberg was sacked and ransacked by the Spaniards, Ursin's Catechism, enlarged by Pareus, but not yet published, was taken among other books for pillage, and by him dropped in the streets, but taken up by a young student, and afterwards printed by Philip Pareus, to the great benefit of all good people!

Ver. 14. *Alexander the coppersmith*] Who was once *martyrio propinquus,* saith Calvin, near unto martyrdom in Paul's cause, Acts xix. 33. A glorious professor may become a furious persecutor. "Let him that stands take heed lest he fall."

[1] *Major fuit cura Cæsari libellorum quam purpuræ.*

The Lord reward him] This is neither a curse nor a railing speech, saith an ancient, but a prediction well beseeming an apostle, that avenged not himself, but rather gave place to wrath, Rom. xii. 19. (Author quæst. apud Just. Mar.)

Ver. 15. *He hath greatly resisted our words*] Or, our preachings, not our persons only. This was a foul fault. See 1 Thess. iv. 8; Exod. xvi. 8.

Ver. 16. *No man stood with me*] So that Paul might have said as Socrates did, φιλοὶ, οὐδεὶς φιλὸς, My friends, I have never a friend. And as Plato, A friend is a very mutable creature, εὐμετάβλητον ζῶον. Or, as he in Plautus, *Ut cuique homini res parata est, firmi amici sunt. Si res lassæ labant, itidem amici collabascunt.*

Ver. 17. *The Lord stood*] God is never so sweet and so seasonable to his saints as in the day of their deepest distress. He loves to help those that are forsaken of their hopes.

The preaching might be fully known] Or, soundly proved to be a divine ordinance, by my constancy and contempt of death.

Out of the mouth of the lion] Nero, who first *orientem fidem Romæ cruentavit*, as Tertullian speaketh, put Christians to death, and made a bloody decree, that whosoever confessed himself a Christian should, without any more ado, be put to death as a convicted enemy of mankind. Tertullian calleth him *Dedicator damnationis Christianorum*, The dedicator of the condemnation of Christians.

Ver. 18. *And the Lord shall deliver*] Experience breeds confidence. St Paul got an opportunity after this from Rome to make an excursion to plant and confirm Churches, returned again to Rome, and was there martyred by bloody Nero, as it is storied.

Unto his heavenly kingdom] So David argues from temporals to eternals, Psal. xxiii. 5, 6.

Ver. 19. *Salute Prisca*, &c.] See the note on Rom. xvi. 3.

Ver. 20. *At Miletum sick*] See the note on Phil. ii. 27.

Ver. 21. *Do thy diligence*, &c.] The apostle quickeneth Timothy, as Tully did his friend, *Quamobrem si me amas, &c., si dormis expergiscere, si stas ingredere, si ingrederis curre, si curris advola. Credibile non est quantum ego in amore et fide tua ponam.* Make all possible haste hither, for I rely much upon thy love and loyalty.

And Claudia] An English (or rather British) woman, who went to Rome, was converted by Paul, married a Roman gentleman called Pudens (as here) for his parts, but before called Rufus. It is thought she sent the gospel first into England. (See Antiq. Britan. Camden in Britan., Matth. Parker, Bale, Godwin's Catalogue, Speed's Chron., &c.) This is no article of our faith.

Ver. 22. *Grace be with you*] God's blessing be with you always, Amen. Even now toward the offering of a burnt sacrifice, said that martyr (Lau. Saunders) in a letter to certain friends.

THE EPISTLE OF ST PAUL TO TITUS.

CHAPTER I.

Ver. 1. *The faith of God's elect*] NOT the election of God's faithful ones, as the Arminians make it.

And the knowledge of the truth] It is usual with St Paul in the beginning of his Epistles, to utter much in few, and to set down the sum of the whole gospel, as here he doth justification, sanctification, and the hope of salvation, and all by the acknowledging of the truth. This Epistle is called the abridgment of all St Paul's Epistles; but especially of those two to Timothy, whom he more largely instructeth in point of Church-government, because a younger man than Titus, and not so well exercised in ecclesiastical affairs. (Estius.)

Ver. 2. *God that cannot lie*] The word of promise binds God; therefore it seems, saith one, that it is stronger than God; for he can as soon deny himself as his promise.

Promised] That is, purposed, as 2 Tim. i. 9, or decreed to promise, or promised to Christ, or

promised to our first parents from the beginning of ages, *ante multa sæcula*, so some sense it.

Ver. 3. *Manifested his word*] As when he said plainly, "He that believeth in the Son hath eternal life."

Ver. 4. *Common faith*] Common to the communion of saints, ver. 1, and to them proper and peculiar; for all men have not faith, 2 Thess. iii. 2. Or common, that is, *Symbolo Apostolico comprehensum*, saith one, contained in the Apostle's Creed.

Ver. 5. *Set in order*] Gr. ἐπιδιορθώσῃ, *conficias*, set straight, or make up the things that I left unfinished. Straighten the things that grow crooked in the Church.

In every city] Crete had a hundred cities, and was therefore called ἑκατόμπολις; as Thebes had a hundred gates, and was therefore called ἑκατόμπυλος.

Ver. 6. *The husband of one wife*] Here the apostle canonizeth, saith Scultetus, the marriage of ministers.

Ver. 7. *A bishop must be blameless*] As was Moses, Samuel, Paul, Bradford, Bucer, &c., who led convincing lives; so that their foes could not in anything stain them, nor their friends sufficiently commend them. It is better, saith one, to live so as thine enemies may be amazed at thy virtues than that thy friends should have cause to excuse thy vices.

Not soon angry] ὀργίλος, *biliosus et bellicosus*, testy and tetchy, easily blown up into rage, that will not be laid down without revenge.

Ver. 8. *Temperate*] ἐγκρατής. No slave to his fleshly appetite, but one that can master himself and give laws to his lusts. See my Commonplace of Abstinence.

Ver. 9. *Holding fast, &c.*] ἀντεχόμενον. As with tooth and nail, against those gainsayers that would snatch it from us.

Ver. 10. *For there are many unruly*] Lawless, yokeless, masterless men, untractable, untameable, that refuse to be reformed, hate to be healed. God will hamper these Belialists, 2 Sam. xxiii. 6.

Ver. 11. *Whose mouths must be stopped*] Gr. ἐπιστομίζειν, muzzled, as bandogs are. Frogs, they say, will leave croaking if but a light be hanged over the lake wherein they are. Let but the truth come clearly in place, and heretics will be soon silenced. But if they will not, another course must be taken with them.

Ver. 12. *Even a prophet of their own*] Epimenides, the poet, who by his countrymen the Cretians was counted a prophet, and had divine honours done to him after his death. This uncircumcised poet Paul brings here into the temple, as before he had done Aratus, Acts xvii. 28, and Menander, 1 Cor. xv. 33.

The Cretians are always liars] So were the Carthaginians, *Tyriique bilingues.*[1] The French had so often deceived the English that such as they mean to deceive they call by a common byword, *Les Anglois*, The English. The Cretians were loud liars, even to a proverb. Of Dolon, Homer saith, that he had an art in lying. But Eudæmon Joannes (that Cretian demoniac) wins the whetstone from all his countrymen, whiles he blusheth not to tell the world in print that these are the doctrines and practices of the Protestants, to worship no God, to frame our religion to the times, to pretend the public cause to our private lusts, to break our words as we see good for our purpose, to cover deadly hatred under fair flatteries, to confirm tyranny by shedding the blood of innocents. (Eudæmon Joannes contra Casaub.) Evil beasts, cruel as well as crafty. These two are seldom separated; as some write of the asp, that he never wanders alone without his companion; and as the Scripture speaks of those birds of prey and desolation, Isa. xxxiv. 16, "None of them wanteth his mate."

Slow bellies] That is, given to sloth and idleness, and luxurious gluttons.

Ver. 13. *Rebuke them sharply*] Gr. ἀποτόμως, cuttingly, precisely, rigidly, severely, and to the quick. A metaphor from chirurgeons, who

must not be melch-hearted, saith Celsus,[2] but pare away the dead flesh, *Ne pars sincera trahatur.* Howbeit, that is a good rule given by a godly divine, that although there must be some warmth in a reproof, yet it must not be scalding hot. Words of reviling and disgrace, they scald, as it were. But words that tend to stir up the conscience to a due consideration of the error or evil reproved, they be duly warm, and tend to make the physic work more kindly. *Evangelizatum non maledictum missus es*, said Œcolampadius to Farellus: *laudo zelum, modo non desideretur mansuetudo. Vinum et oleum in tempore suo infundendum. Evangelistam non tyrannicum legislatorem præstes.* Thou art sent to preach, not to rail. Thy zeal I commend, so it be mingled with meekness. Wine must be poured into men's wounds one while and oil another. Thou must show thyself a peaceable preacher, not a tyrannical law-giver. (Œcolamp. Ep. ad Gul. Farel.) Rebuke, exhort, with all long-suffering, saith Paul to Timothy, 2 Epist. iv. 2. Timothy, they say, was somewhat sharp and tart in his reproofs; and is therefore exhorted to patience and meekness. Titus was gentle, and of a mild disposition; and is therefore thus spurred on to sharpness and severity. The Cretians also were (possibly) a worse people than the Ephesians, and were therefore to be more hardly handled. Let it ever be remembered that matters of moment must be wisely but yet seriously dealt with. To tell wicked men of their sins so softly as Eli did his sons, or reprove them so gently as Jehoshaphat did Ahab ("Let not the king say so"), doth usually as much harm as good; like a weak dose in physic, it stirreth the humours, but purgeth them not.

Ver. 14. *Not giving heed to Jewish fables*] Wherewith their Talmud is full farced, which whiles they hug over-hard, as Cleopatra did the snakes that sucked her blood, they perish.

Of men that turn from the truth] ἀποστρεφόμενοι, with utter aversation and detestation, as a man turns his body from a loathsome object. These are those that will not endure sound doctrine, 2 Tim. iv. 3.

Ver. 15. *Unto the pure all things, &c.*] This Piscator (in Mark xiv. 3) holds a sufficient warrant for us to use, *Ne forte*, and other heathen expressions; like as the apostles used χρηματίζεσθαι χρηματισμος, &c., abused by the Greeks to signify their wicked and devilish oracles. But Pasor is utterly against it. (Prefat. ad Lexic.)

Is nothing pure] Their own table is a snare to them, yea, God's table. The saints are kept at hard commons, but have their keeping of freecost: the wicked have larger cates, but pay sweetly.

Conscience is defiled] To wit, with sins, and so can no more judge of it than a man can discern of colours in a foul and soiled glass.

Ver. 16. *They profess that they know*] *Aliud in titulo, aliud in pyxide.* Outside Christians

---

[1] *Fides Punica.* Virgil. *Cres semper mendax, mala bellua, et helluo deses. Cretizare cum Cretensib. vide* Erasm.

[2] *Chirurgos misericordes esse non oportet.*

Adag. ἴσκε ψεύδεα πολλὰ λέγειν ἐτύμοισιν ὁμοῖα. Hom.

who perform, as Ephraim, dough-baked duties, are almost persuaded, as Agrippa, come near God's kingdom with that young Pharisee; faint chapmen that go without the bargain, as he did that came kneeling to our Saviour, and saying, "What shall I do to inherit eternal life?" These do *virtutis stragulam pudefacere*, put honesty to an open shame, as Diogenes said to Antipater, who being vicious, wore a white cloak, the ensign of innocency.

Being abominable] Gr. βδελυκτοὶ (a βδέω, pedo), such as stink above ground, and are of an offensive savour.

To every good work reprobate] ἀδόκιμοι, or injudicious; such as cannot make a right judgment of any good works, so as to approve and relish them, to see a beauty in them, as good, &c.

But in works they deny him] Which is, as if a man should confess his faith in English and deny it again in Latin. These are no better than devils wrapt up in Samuel's mantle; hot meteors, shooting and showing like stars.

CHAPTER II.

Ver. 1. *But speak thou, &c.*] *Quasi dicat*, the worse others are, the better thou must be; keeping a constant counter-motion to the corrupt courses that are in the world through lust. A pearl in a puddle retains its preciousness; and fish in the salt waters retain their freshness.

Ver. 2. *That the old men be sober, &c.*] Not as it is said of the Flemings, that *quo magis senescunt eo magis stultescunt*, the elder the foolisher. (Erasm. in Moriæ Encom.) Solomon and Asa were so. And the heathen sages wisely warn us, that old age is to be feared, as that which comes not alone, but brings with it many diseases both of body and mind. *Sæpe fit ut Satan, quem juvenem capere non potuit, annosum fallat et capiat*, saith Bucholcerus. Many that have held out well in youth, have failed and been shamefully foiled in old age.

Ver. 3. *In behaviour*] ἐν καταστήματι, or, in habit, apparel, gait, gesture.

Teachers of good things] As was Bathsheba, Prov. xxxi. 1, 2; Lois, 2 Tim. i. 5; Monica, &c.

Ver. 4. *To be sober*] Or wise, teaching them as schoolmasters do their disciples; so the word σωφρονίζωσι signifies. He was a foolish man that said, Μισῶ σοφὴν γυναῖκα,'I love not to have a woman wise. (Eurip.) "A prudent wife is of the Lord." Such an one was Abigail, and Aspasia, Milesia, the wife of Cyrus, who was said to be Καλὴ καὶ σοφὴ, fair and wise withal. (Ælian. xii. 1.) To love their husbands, though old and less lovely, as that famous Valadaura in Ludovicus Vives.

To love their children] And to seal up their love, not by hugging them to death, as apes do their young; but by educating them in the fear and admonition of the Lord, as Bathsheba, Prov. xxxi. Plutarch speaks of a Spartan woman, that

when her neighbours were showing their apparel and jewels, she brought out her children, virtuous and well-taught, and said, These are my ornaments and jewels. Mothers must learn to love their children's souls, 1 Pet. iii. 4.

Ver. 5. *To be discreet, chaste, &c.*] *Conjugium humanæ divina Academia vitæ.* Much good may be learned by wedlock.

Keepers at home] Carrying her house on her back, as the snail doth. Sarah was found in the tent, so was Jael the wife of Heber. The Egyptian women ware no shoes, that they might the better keep home.

Ver. 6. *Young men likewise exhort*] See the note on 2 Tim. ii. 22.

Ver. 7. *A pattern of good*] Gr. τυπὸς, a stamp. Digging thy sermons out of thine own breast, and living them, when thou hast done.

Ver. 8. *May be ashamed, having, &c.*] Oh it is a brave thing to stop an open mouth, to throttle envy, to cut off all occasion of evil-speaking.

Ver. 9. *Not answering again*] Not chatting or thwarting. *Servus sit monosyllabus Domino*, saith one. Apelles painted a servant with his hands full of tools, to signify his diligence; with broad shoulders to bear wrongs; with hind's feet to run swiftly about his business; with the ears of an ass, and his mouth shut with two locks, to signify that he should be swift to hear and slow to speak.

Ver. 10. *Not purloining*] Interverting, embezzling their master's estates, ordinary among the Romans, which made them call servants and thieves by one name,[1] ordinary among the Hebrews; whence that saying of R. Gamaliel, *Marbe gnabadim, marbe gezel*, He that multiplieth servants, multiplieth thieves. (Pirke-aboth, chap. i.) Ordinary also amongst us, whence that proverb, "He that will be rich must ask his servant's leave."

Ver. 11. *For the grace of God, &c.*] This is rendered as a reason why servants should be faithful, because to them also belongeth the promise of salvation, yea, the reward of inheritance, as if they were sons, and to them the gospel is preached as well as to others.

Hath appeared] ἐπεφάνη. As the sun in heaven, or as a beacon on a hill.

Ver. 12. *Denying ungodliness*] Every gospeltruth strikes at some sin, and thereby may be discerned.

Soberly, righteously, and godly] This is the Christian man's motto, his symbol, and the sum of his whole duty.

Hæc tria perpetuo meditare adverbia Pauli:
Hæc tria sint vitæ regula sancta tuæ.

The Egyptians when they praised their deceased friends, were wont to commend them for these three things, their godliness, righteousness, and temperance. (Diod. Sicul.)

Ver. 13. *Looking for*] As with necks stretcht out, or head put forth, ἀποκαραδοκία, Rom. viii.

---

[1] *Audent cum talia fures.* Virgil.

19 ; as Sisera's mother looked out of her lattice for her son's happy return, Judg. v. 28.

Ver. 14. *That he might redeem us*] God will have the price of Christ's blood out; he will thoroughly purge us.

A peculiar people] Gr. A people that comprehend all that God sets any store by, that contain all his gettings; called elsewhere the people of acquisition, περιούσιος, 1 Pet. ii. 9. The word here used Jerome saith he sought for among human authors, and could not find it. Therefore some think the Septuagint feigned this, and ἐπιούσιον, used also in the Lord's prayer. Theophylact saith it signifieth such a people as are conversant about their master's business, procuring of wealth and riches for him.

Zealous of good works] Give God thine affections, else thine actions are still-born, and have no life in them. Now zeal is the extreme heat of all the affections, when they are seething or hissing hot, as the apostle's word is, Rom. xii. 12, when we love God and his people out of a pure heart fervently, ζέοντες. *Non amat qui non zelat*, saith Austin, he loveth not at all in God's account, whose love is not ardent, desires eager, delights ravishing, hopes longing, hatred deadly, anger fierce, grief deep, fear terrible, voice, eyes, hands, gestures, actions, all lively, as in holy Bucholcer, Luther, Laurentius, Athanasius, Ignatius, Paul, Baruch, Neh. iii. 20, he earnestly fortified, *seipsum accendit;* he burst out into a holy heat, he wrought with a kind of anger against himself and others, because the work went on no faster. He was not of his temper that said, *Deum colo, uti par est*, I go as far for God as in discretion it is fit. *Religiosum oportet esse, sed non religantem;* such and such are more precise than wise. The reserved professor never shows himself but at halt-light; he follows Christ but afar off, as Peter, or as the people followed Saul (they tremble after him, 1 Sam. xiii. 7); he is afraid of every new step, saying as Cæsar at Rubicon, Yet we may go back. Carnal discretion controls his fervency, cools his courage, keeps him that he cannot be zealous of good works, which he doth at the best in a loose, lazy, perfunctory strain, like the pace the Spaniard rides, like Adonikam, that was the last that set foot forward toward the return of the captives, and therefore had his lot below his brethren, Ezra viii. 13. Where is now our ancient zeal, heating and whetting (saith a reverend zealot)? Oh how cold and careless, how dissolute, and dilute are we! May it not be said of most of our hearts and houses, as Isa. xlvii. 14, there is not a coal to warm at? May not the old complaint be well renewed, " There is none that calleth upon thy name, that stirreth up himself to take hold of thee?" Isa. lxiv. 7. Let God's love in the work of our redemption be duly pondered (as here), and it will fire us up to a holy contention in godliness.

These things speak and exhort] Lest men

should think we should only preach of Christ and grace, preach thou obedience and zeal, saith the apostle.

Ver. 15. *Let no man despise thee*] περιφρονείτω, *Nemo te plus sapere ausit.* Or have occasion to think himself wiser than thee. He saith not, as 1 Tim. iv. 12, " Let no man despise thy youth," for Titus was (likely) elder than Timothy. Mr Calvin thinketh that these words are spoken to the people; they are, for most part, of delicate ears, and cannot abide plain words of mortification.

CHAPTER III.

Ver. 1. *To be ready to every*] As the bee, so soon as ever the sun breaks forth, flies abroad to gather honey and wax. A ready heart makes riddance of religious duties.

Ver. 2. *To speak evil of no man*] Unless it be in an ordinance, for the reformation of the unruly; pleasing all in that which is good to edify.

Ver. 3. *For we ourselves also*] I Paul, and thou Titus, were as bad as others; let us therefore show all mercy and meekness to others. *Aut sumus, aut fuimus, aut possumus esse quod hic est.*

Serving divers lusts] As the Persian kings were lords of the world, but slaves to their concubines.[1] The Assyrians led away the Egyptians naked and barefoot, Isa. xxix. 2, so doth Satan sinners. Hence, though never so great, they are called vile persons, as Antiochus, Dan. xi. 21, because they have as many lords as lusts. Felix, at that very time that he trembled before Paul, could not but covet and expect a bribe from him.

Hateful] Gr. στυγητοί, of στύξ. Horrible, as hell itself, or justly odious to others.

Ver. 4. *Kindness and love*] His native goodness, and his communicated goodness to us, not yet existing, nay, resisting.

Ver. 5. *Which we have done*] We that are bankrupts in Adam, would yet fain be doing, and think to be saved for a company of poor beggarly duties; as bankrupts will be trading again, though but for pins, &c.

But according to his mercy] God is no merchant; his kingdom is not *partum*, but *paratum.* He that said, *Cœlum gratis non accipiam*, I will not have heaven on free cost, went without it. (Vega.)

He saved us by the washing of regeneration] So baptism saveth us, 1 Pet. iii. 21. It sacramentally saveth, by sealing up salvation to the believer : hence it is called the laver of regeneration. It is a noble question in divinity (saith Mr Burgess, Vindic. Legis.), seeing regeneration is attributed both to the word and to baptism, how one worketh it differently from the other. Or if both work it, why is not one superfluous?

Ver. 6. *Which he shed*] Gr. ἐξέχεεν, Poured out (as it were by pail-fulls) his Spirit (the best

---

[1] *Captivarum suarum captivi.* Plutarch. *Roma victrix gentium, captiva vitiorum. O rem miseram ! Dominum ferre non potuimus, conservo servimus.* Cic. Epist.

thing) upon all flesh (the basest thing), Joel ii. 28.

Ver. 7. *Be made heirs*] Not purchasers; all is of free grace. *Horreo quicquid de meo est, ut sim meus.* Paul was a most constant preacher of grace. (Bernard. Augustine.)

Ver. 8. *That thou affirm constantly*] Be well settled in it thyself, and avouch and aver it confidently to others; being ready to make it good, if questioned, Διαβεβαιοῦσθαι.

Be careful] Bend their wits, and beat their brains, φροντίζωσι.

To maintain good works] To exceed and excel others in their honest functions and faculties; to be their crafts-masters, to bear away the bell from all that are of the same trade or profession. This was Tully's study, to be best at anything he ever undertook: should it not then be a believer's? Αἰὲν ἀριστεύειν καὶ ὑπείροχον ἔμμεναι ἄλλων, παντων κράτιστον. (Plutarch.)

Ver. 9. *But foolish questions*] Such as is that of the Papists, whether an ass drinking at the font do drink the water of baptism, and so may be said to be baptized? *Est questio digna asinis,* saith Melancthon. Such questionists are (as Stapleton saith of Bodin) *magni nugatores,* great triflers.

Ver. 10. *A man that is a heretic*] All heresies are found to flow (saith Chemnitius) either from the supercilious pride of Samosatenus, or from the sophistry of Arius, or from the ignorance of Ætius. (Loc. Com., i. 2.) These men's wits will better serve them to devise a thousand shifts to elude the truth, than their pride will suffer them once to yield and acknowledge it. And here this rule of St Paul takes place. Nestorius was an unlearned and proud man, but very bold and well-spoken; insomuch as thereby he oft carried it, and so seduced the emperor Theodosius, as that Cyril, a very good bishop, was thrown out of his place. Howbeit he was afterwards restored again with honour, when the emperor had better bethought himself, and the heretic Nestorius was condemned and cast out. (Zanch. Misc. Epist. Dedicat.)

After the first and second admonition reject] Or, avoid, *devita,* which some Popish dolts interpreted *de vita tolle,* kill them (as Erasmus reporteth), so to justify their bloody practice of putting Protestants to death. But what saith the same Erasmus speaking of Berquin the martyr, burnt by them for religion; *Damnari, dissecari, suspendi, exuri;* To be condemned, hanged, quartered, burned, beheaded, are things common to good and bad people. (Scultet. Annal.) To condemn, hang, quarter, burn, behead, is a thing common to righteous judges with pirates and tyrants. The judgments of men are various; happy is he that is absolved by God the Judge of all. And this was as much as he durst say against their proceedings, who for saying so much as he did, hardly escaped with this reproach, that for Erasmus they named him Erat-mus; because he so truly but bitterly biteth their ulcers.

Ver. 11. *Is subverted*] Gr. ἐξέστραπται, Is turned topsy-turvy, as a tumbler that hath his heels in the air and his head on the earth; as a ship turns up her keel, or as a man "wipeth a dish and turneth it upside down," 2 Kings xxi. 13; some render it thus, He hath the fairest side outward, and make it a metaphor from foul linen, the foul side turned inward; as if he should have said, such a man, whatsoever shows he maketh, is a naughty man. (Mr Cranford on 2 Tim. ii. 17.)

Ver. 11. *Condemned of himself*] Sith, as a headstrong horse, he gets the bit between his teeth, and runs away. Thus did the Pharisees, *Toties puncti, et repuncti, minime tamen ad resipiscentiam compuncti,* as one saith; they shut the windows lest the light should come in, and so were condemned, by their own consciences. Or, "he is condemned of himself" by excommunicating himself from the holy assemblies (as our church-forsakers do), which other sinners are condemned to by the Church. The fornicator, the adulterer, the murderer, &c., are cast out of the Church by the Church officers. But heretics condemn themselves by a wilful departure from the Church; *quæ recessio propriæ conscientiæ videtur esse damnatio,* and this seems to be the sense of the apostle's self-condemned, saith Jerome upon this text.

Ver. 12. *Come unto me to Nicopolis*] The inhabitants of this city are said so to have hated the braying of an ass, that they would not endure to hear the sound of a trumpet. So some pretend such a hatred of hypocrisy, that they will not abide the profession of piety.

Ver. 13. *That nothing be wanting*] Those that labour in the Lord's work must have all necessary accommodations and encouragements. They must be set forth and brought forward on their journey and in their negotiations worthy of God, 3 John 6. *Deductione honorifica,* Acts xv. 3; xx. 38; xxi. 5. A Balaam will not deal hardly with his ass, if once he perceive the Lord to be in him and to speak by him; shall we deal unworthily with God's ministers, in whom God is of a truth, 1 Cor. xiv. 25, and hath given unto them the ministry of reconciliation? 2 Cor. v. 8.

Ver. 14. *To maintain good works*] See the note on ver. 8 of this chapter.

That they be not unfruitful] As drone-bees or body-lice, living upon others' labours, and so opening the mouths of heathens who will be ready to say, as he once did, *Odi homines ignava opera, philosopha sententia,* I hate those that can give fair words, but that is all they are good for. See we not how every creature in its kind is fruitful? The sun, moon, and stars in their courses restlessly move to impart their light, heat, and influence to the inferior creatures. The clouds fly up and down emptying themselves, to enrich the earth, from which notwithstanding they reap no harvest. The earth is cut and wounded with shares and coulters, yet is patient, and yields her riches and strength to the tiller; yea, what herb, plant, or tree grows upon the earth which is not in its kind fruitful, spending itself and the principal parts of its sap and moisture in bringing forth some pleasant berry or such-like fruit? (Plin.) And shall only man remain unfruitful, and not serve God and man with cheerfulness in the abundance of all things? Shall he be like the cypress tree, which the more it is watered, the more it is withered? Or like cyparet, whose neither fruit, nor leaves, nor berry, nor shadow is useful, but rather hurtful? Hear what Cicero saith, *Pudeat illos qui ita vixerunt, tu ad vitam communem nullum fructum afferre possint.* Let them learn to be ashamed of their sloth that have so lived, as to have been altogether useless and unfruitful.

Ver. 15. *That love us in the faith*] That best ligament of love. The Church is the only daughter of her mother, and is called Ecclesia, of calling all hers together. Religion hath its name of binding, because it binds men all in a bundle, and makes them be of one heart and of one soul, Acts iv. 32, to serve the Lord with one shoulder, Zeph. iii. 9, to glorify God with " one mind and with one mouth," Rom. xv. 6, there being no such oneness in the world as among true believers.

THE EPISTLE OF ST PAUL TO PHILEMON.

Ver. 1. *Paul a prisoner, &c.*] This is a notable Epistle, and full of worth; each word having its weight, each syllable its substance. From an abject subject, the receiving of a runaway servant, St Paul soars like a heavenly eagle, and flies a high pitch of heavenly discourse. *Elocutione tota gravis et brevis, densus sententiis, sanus judiciis,* &c., as Lipsius saith of Thucydides, may we say of our apostle, *Plena roboris et lacertorum est tota epistola.* (Lips.)

Our dearly beloved] ἀγαπητῷ, *diligibili.* Or our lovely one, as Jerome renders it.

And fellow-labourer] This shows, say some, that Philemon was a minister of the gospel. That he was a master of a family, is out of question; and his name, which signifies a lover, suits well with his condition; as doth likewise his servant Onesimus, which signifieth profitable. They are not complete Christians that are not good at home as well as abroad; they walk not in a perfect way, that look not to do domestical duties, Psal. ci. 2, by the careful performance whereof we are fitter to serve God or converse with men; as may appear by the situation of the fifth commandment, which stands between the two tables, and hath an influence upon both.

Ver. 2. *And to our beloved Apphia*] For Appia, but this was the manner of pronunciation at Tarsus, St Paul's country. This Apphia was (saith Theodoret) Philemon's wife; whose good-will might make much to the furtherance of St Paul's suit.

And Archippus our fellow-soldier] Who seems to have sojourned with Philemon. See the note on Col. iv. 17.

And to the church in thy house] Every Christian family is a church. But Philemon's house was (belike) a public meeting-house, and so continued for many years after, as Theodoret witnesseth.

Ver. 3. *Grace to you, &c.*] See the note on 1 Cor. i. 3, and on 2 Cor. i. 2.

Ver. 4. *I thank my God*] Thus the apostle begins most of his Epistles. As any man is more or less gracious, so is he thankful. The same Greek word for grace signifieth thankfulness, χαρὶς. Neither is there anything that seals up more comfort to the soul than for a man to be able from the bottom of his heart to praise God. Self-love may make a hypocrite pray from the bottom of his heart, &c.

Ver. 5. *Hearing of thy love and faith*] Love is first mentioned, as more noticed. But faith is the mother-grace, the womb wherein love and all the rest of that heavenly offspring are conceived.

Ver. 6. *That the communication, &c.*] This is that which St Paul prayed for Philemon, ver. 4. For the fifth verse comes in by a parenthesis.

Ver. 7. *The bowels of the saints are refreshed*] Gr. ἀναπέπαυνται. Rested, as it were after much toil and travel, which made their hearts ache.

Ver. 8. *That which is convenient*] τὸ ἀνῆκον, or, that which is thy duty. *Officium autem est jus actionis ad quemcunque statum pertinens,* saith Jul. Scaliger.

Ver. 9. *Yet for love's sake, &c.*] Here is brave oratory, such as might well mollify the hardest heart; *Petendo movet, et movendo petit.*

Paul the aged] And therefore venerable. *Cognata sunt.* Old age and honour are in the Greek tongue very near akin; γῆρας et γέρας. It is a crown (saith Solomon), and that of glory, when found in the way of righteousness, Prov. xvi. 31. These bear a resemblance of the Ancient of days, Dan. vii. These are like flowers which have their roots perfect when themselves are withering; these, like roses, keep a sweet savour though they lose their colour. These give greatest glimpse at their going down. *Magna fuit semper capitis reverentia cani,* Acts xxi. 16.

Ver. 10. *My son Onesimus*] Ignatius, in his Epistle to the Ephesians, maketh mention of Onesimus, as pastor of Ephesus, next after Timothy. The Roman Martyrologue saith, that he was stoned to death at Rome, under Trajan the emperor. Paul calleth him his son because his convert. See 1 Cor. iv. 15; so Cyprian calleth Cæcilius (who converted him) *novæ vitæ parentem*, the instrument of his life; and Latimer saith the like of his blessed St Bilney, as he calleth him.

Ver. 11. *But now profitable*] So is every true convert; there is little cause that men should boast they are no changelings, sith whosoever is in Christ is a new creature. Sir Anthony Kingstone came to Mr Hooper the martyr a little before his death, and said, I thank God that ever I knew you; for God did appoint you to call me, being a lost child. For by your good instructions, whereas I was before both an adulterer and fornicator, God hath brought me to forsake and detest the same. Savoy, for the strait passages infested with thieves, was once called Malvoy, or ill-way; till a worthy adventurer cleared the coasts, and then it was called Savoy or Salvoy, the safe way. Such a change there is in every good soul.

Ver. 12. *That is mine own bowels*] Pray for me, mine own heart-root in the Lord (said Mr Bradford in a letter to Mr Saunders), *Quem in intimis visceribus habeo ad convivendum et commoriendum.*

Ver. 13. *In the bonds of the gospel*] Which is bound after a sort, when the preachers thereof are imprisoned.

Ver. 14. *Would I do nothing*] *Posse et nolle nobile est.* He that goes to the utmost of his chain may possibly break a link. *Concedamus de jure ut careamus lite.* Part with somewhat for peace' sake. (Augustine.)

Ver. 15. *For perhaps he therefore*] God hath a hand in ordering our disorders to his own glory and our good. He teacheth us by our temptations. This made Mr Fox say that his graces did him most hurt, and his sins most good.

He departed for a season] Here the apostle makes the best of an ill matter. Converts are to be gently handled, and their former evil practices not to be aggravated.

Ver. 16. *Both in the flesh*] Perhaps Onesimus was Philemon's kinsman.

And in the Lord] *Sanctior est copula cordis quam corporis.* "He that is joined to the Lord is one spirit," 1 Cor. vi. 17.

Ver. 17. *A partner*] κοινωνὸν. One in common with thee. *Amicorum omnia communia.*

Receive him] προσλαβοῦ. Take him to thee, put him in thy bosom, make much of him. How effectually doth this great apostle plead the cause of this poor fugitive, now happily brought home to Christ. He deals as one that had himself received mercy, 1 Cor. vii. 25. Steep thy thoughts (saith one) in the mercies of God, and they will dye thine, as the dye-vat doth the cloth, Col. iii. 12.

Ver. 18. *If he hath wronged thee*] His shameful escape the apostle sweetly mitigateth by the name of wrong; his theft, of debt. See ver. 15, and compare herewith Gen. xlv. 5.

Put that on mine account] To the like effect speaks the Lord Christ on our behalf to his heavenly Father, in his daily intercession.

Ver. 19. *Thou owest unto me, &c.*] If Cleanthes gave himself to his master Socrates; if Alexander could say that he owed more to Aristotle that taught him than to Philip that begat him; if another could say that he could never discharge his debt to God, to his parents, and to his schoolmaster; how deeply then do men stand obliged to their spiritual fathers and teachers 'in Christ!

I will repay it] Philemon, though rich, is suspected to be somewhat too covetous, from this expression.

O quam difficile est opibus non tradere mores;
Et cum tot Cræsos viceris, esse Numam!

Howbeit in both the Testaments we shall scarce read of any godly man tainted with covetousness. Luther saith of himself, that though he otherwise had his flaws and frailties, yet the infection of covetousness never laid hold on him. *Heu Germana illa bestia non curat aurum*, said one of his adversaries, wiser than the rest, that would have stopped his mouth with money. But Seneca was naturally covetous, which he shrouds covertly in that sentence of his in his book de Tranquillitate, *Nec ægroto nec valeo*, I am neither sick nor well. It had been well for him if he could have said with that dying saint, My body is weak, my soul is well. As for those Epistles pretended to be written to him by St Paul, they are bastard and counterfeit, they savour not of his apostolical gravity and majesty, which shineth even in this to Philemon, being the least of all his Epistles. In those forged Epistles far higher matters are spoken of; but, alas, how coldly, how dryly and poorly! yet here behold a poor petty matter is set forth with that pithiness and powerfulness of speech, as is admirable. (Dyke.)

Ver. 20. *Yea, brother, let me have joy*] ὀναίμην, or benefit by thee; an elegant allusion it is in the original to the name of Onesimus; and it is as if the apostle embracing Philemon, and hanging about his neck, should say, I prythee now let me be so far beholden to thee.

Ver. 21. *Knowing that thou wilt, &c.*] Who could ever have the heart to resist such rhetoric? Is not here the very marrow of most powerful persuasion (*Suadæ medulla*), a golden flood of eloquence? as Tully saith of Aristotle's Politics.

Ver. 22. *But withal, prepare, &c.*] Thus he despatcheth his own private business in one word, as it were; his main care was, that Onesimus might do well: a fair mirror for ministers.

Ver. 23. *Epaphras my fellow-prisoner*] Clapped up, belike, for visiting and countenancing St Paul, to whom he was sent by the Colossians with relief, whiles he was prisoner at Rome. The ecclesiastical history telleth us of one Phileas a martyr, who going to execution, seemed as one deaf at the persuasions and blind at the tears of his friends, moving him to spare himself. And when one Philoramus defending him said, *Quomodo potest terrenis lachrymis flecti, cujus oculi cœlestem gloriam contuentur?* How can he be moved with earthly tears, who hath his eyes full fed with heavenly glory ? he also was taken in, and both presently beheaded.

Ver. 24. *Marcus, Aristarchus, Demas*] Here Demas was in good credit with the apostle, but soon after ¦fell away ; like as glass, and some baser metals, shine brightest in the fire when nearest of all to melting, or as the candle giveth a great blaze when going out with a stench. Hypocrites have their *non-ultra* when the godly man's motto is (as was Charles V.'s) *Ulterius*, Further yet, on, on.

Ver. 25. *The grace of our Lord*] Say the world what it will, a grain of grace is worth a world of wealth. The blessings that come out of Sion are better than any that come out of heaven and earth, Psal. cxxxiv. 3 ; for they outlast the days of heaven, and run parallel with the life of God and line of eternity. Pray for them therefore in the behalf of ourselves and others, as Paul constantly doth for grace, not with graceless Nero, but with the Lord Jesus Christ, one good cast of whose pleased countenance was better to David than his crown and sceptre, Psal. iv. 7, 8.

THE EPISTLE OF ST PAUL TO THE HEBREWS.

CHAPTER I.

Ver. 1. *God who at sundry times, &c.*] See my True Treasure.

God who in times past, &c.] The Hebrews had generally a lighter esteem (though without cause) of the prophets than of the law ; and of such of the books of Holy Scripture as had not the names of God or Lord in them (as Esther, Canticles, &c.) than of those that had. Our apostle, for more authority' sake, begins his Epistle with that *nomen majestativum* (Tertul.), that holy and reverend name of God, so precious and pleasant to Hebrew ears ; and wades at first into that *Profundum sine fundo*, that bottomless depth of divinity : prefixing Θεὸς, Θεὸς (as Pausanias testifieth that the ancients even among the heathens were wont to do, in all their sacred writings), the name of God, for a preface, *captandi gratia ominis boni*, in token and hope of better speed and success.

Ver. 2. *Hath in these last days*] God doth his best works last (our last also should be our best, as Thyatira's, Rev. ii. 19) ; the sweetest of honey lies in the bottom. Contrarily, Satan (Laban-like) shows himself at parting ; and (as the panther doth the wild beasts) inveigleth silly souls (into sin), and then devoureth them, James i. 14, 15 ; 1 Pet. v. 8.

Heir of all things] Be married to this heir, and have all. *Ubi tu Caius, ego Caia*, may the Shulamite say to her husband, as the Roman ladies said to theirs.

By whom also he made the worlds] Visible and invisible, Col. i. 16 ; or the ages under the Old and New Testament ; which last (chap. ii. 5) he calleth the world to come.

Ver. 3. *Who being the brightness of his glory, &c.*] A beam of that sun, and the express image of his person, a stamp of that seal. This is somewhat, but who can declare his generation ? Some glimpses we may have by such similitudes ; the full understanding of this inconceivable mystery we must wait for till we come to heaven. The word ἀπαύγασμα signifieth the glittering refulgency.

Upholding all things] Both in respect of being excellencies and operations. Seneca, rendering the reason why Jupiter was by the ancient Romans surnamed Stator, saith it was *quia ejus beneficio stant omnia*, because all things are upheld by him. How much better may this be said of Christ ! Sin had hurled confusion over the world, which would have fallen about Adam's ears (saith one) had not Christ undertaken the shattered condition thereof, to uphold it. He keeps the world together, as the hoops do the barrel. He also keeps all in order ; *disponens etiam membra culicis et pulicis*, disposing of everything even to the least and lightest circumstance. (Aug.) Hence that of our Saviour, " The Father worketh hitherunto, and I also work," John v. 17 ; hence that of the orator, *Curiosus est et plenus negotii Deus*, God taketh care of all, and is full of business. (Cic. lib. 1 de Nat. Deor.)

Purged our sins] By his merit and spirit.

Ver. 4. *Better than the angels*] Therefore is his doctrine, the gospel, with more heed to be heard, than the law ordained by angels in the hand of a mediator, that is, Moses, Gal. iii. 19.

Ver. 5. *This day*] Either the day of eternity, and so it is meant of Christ's eternal generation ; or else the fulness of time, wherein God brought his first-begotten into the world, and mightily declared him to be the Son of God by the resurrection from the dead, Acts xiii. 33 ; Rom. i. 4.

I will be to him a Father, and he shall be to me a Son] αὐτόθεος. The second person is of himself, as God ; of his Father, as a Son ; because the Father communicateth to him his own nature, and that by generation ; whence he is called " his begotten Son ; " and his " only begotten ; " because by generation God hath no more sons but him ; he is called the " Father of spirits," Heb. xii. 9 ; of all men, Mal. ii. 10, as he is Creator and conserver of all ; and of " all good men," by the grace of adoption and regeneration, 2 Cor. vi. 18 ; John i. 12.

Ver. 6. When he bringeth in the first-begotten] He is the "only begotten," and yet is called the first-begotten ; because he hath the right of first-born over his brethren, and was begotten before the world was.

And let all the angels of God] The manhood of itself could not be thus adored (because it is a creature), but as it is received into unity of person with the Deity, and hath a partner agency therewith, according to its measure, in the work of redemption and mediation, Phil. ii. 9.

Ver. 7. A flame of fire] Hence they are called seraphims, because they flame, like heavenly salamanders, in the fire of pure and perfect love to God and his people ; and cherubims, from their winged swiftness ; swift they are as the wind ; which may seem to be the sense of this text, compared with Psal. civ. 4, 5.

Ver. 8. Thy throne, O God, is for ever] Christ is God, then, as is here set forth by many arguments. God hath laid " help on one that is mighty." " I and the Father am one."

Ver. 9. Hath anointed thee] This imports two things : 1. Ordination to his office, and so the Godhead also of Christ was anointed. 2. Qualification for it, and so the manhood only. And as the holy oil was compounded of divers spices, so was Christ filled with all gifts and graces, Acts x. 38 ; but especially with wisdom as a Prophet, holiness as a Priest, and power as a King.

Above thy fellows] i. e. Above all kings and potentates, Psal. lxxxix. 28. Or above all Christians, who partake of thine anointing, John i. 20, and are made kings and priests, Rev. v. 10. It may also be rendered *pro consortibus tuis*, for thy fellows, as importing a fulness in Christ for us, John i. 16.

Ver. 10. The works of thy hands] Psal. viii. 3, they are called the works of God's fingers, artificially elaborated ; that heaven of heavens especially, whose artificer and workman is God, Heb. xi. 10, τεχνίτης. The apostle there intimates that it is curiously and cunningly contrived.

Ver. 11. They shall perish] The visible heavens are defiled with man's sin, and shall therefore be purged by the last fire, as the vessels that held the sin-offering were to pass the fire.

They shall all wax old] See the note on Rom. viii. 22.

Ver. 12. But thou art the same] As in essence, so in will and counsel. Repentance with man is the changing of his will ; repentance with God is the willing of a change ; *Mutatio rei, non Dei, effectus non affectus, facti non consilii.*

Ver. 13. Sit on my right hand] As mine equal in honour and power. It seems to be a metaphor from some king, who, having an only begotten, lets him in the throne as heir and successor to reign with him, and use right of dominion over all as partner in the empire. Thus David dealt by Solomon, Vespasian by Titus, and our Henry II. by his eldest son Henry, whom he crowned

while he was yet alive ; though afterwards he suffered him not to be what himself had made him.

Until I make thine enemies, &c.] Till the mystery of man's redemption be finished, death the last enemy destroyed, 1 Cor. xv. 26, the saints perfected and placed at his right hand, Matt. xxv. 33 ; Rev. iii. 21 ; Psal. xlv.

Ver. 14. Are they not] See my Common-place of Angels.

Sent forth to minister, &c.] The saints are the spouse, the bride, yea, the members of Christ ; and so in nearer union than angels or any creature. This the devil envied, and fell from his station.

CHAPTER II.

Ver. 1. We should let them slip] Or, run out, παραρρυῶμεν, as water runs through a riven vessel. The word mingled with faith in the heart, as Acts xvi. 14, must be carefully kept, and it will safely keep us, Prov. vi. 20—22. Some render it, *Nequando præter fluamus*, lest we pass by the things we have heard, as a river swiftly passeth by the side of a city, as the fashion of this world passeth away, as a picture drawn upon the ice soon vanisheth, &c. The Arabic rendereth it, " lest we fall," the Syriac, " lest we perish." They must needs fall and never rise again, perish without remedy, that reject the remedy, that hate to be healed, that spurn at the grace of the gospel, which is *post naufragium tabula*, the power of God to salvation. This is as if a condemned prisoner should reject a pardon.

Ver. 2. For if the word, &c.] Moses' law, Gal. iii. 19.

Was stedfast] Ratified with this sanction, *Aut faciendum, aut patiendum*, either do it, or die.

And every transgression and disobedience] That is, every commission and omission.

Ver. 3. If we neglect] He saith not, if we reject, renounce, persecute ; but if we neglect, let slip, shift off, as the word παραιτήσησθε is, Heb. xii. 25, and as those recusant guests did, Matt. xxii. Say we rather with Samuel, " Speak, Lord, for thy servant heareth." And with that Dutch divine, *Veniat, veniat verbum Domini, et submittemus illi, sexcenta si nobis essent colla.* Let the Lord utter his mind, and he shall have ready obedience, whatever come of it.

So great salvation] The doctrine of the gospel, that " grace of God that bringeth salvation," Tit. ii. 11. I am fully persuaded (saith a late learned light of our Church, Dr Preston) that in these days of grace the Lord is much more quick and peremptory in rejecting men ; the time is shorter, he will not wait so long as his was wont to do. The ground is, " How shall we escape if we neglect, &c. ? which at the first began to be spoken by the Lord, and was confirmed," &c. This is somewhat like St Luke's preface to his Gospel, chap. i. ver. 2. Hence some have thought that he also was the author of this Epistle.

Ver. 4. *And with divers miracles*] Whereby, as by the wings of the wind, the doctrine of the gospel was divulged at first. But he that now requireth a miracle, is himself a miracle. The establishing of the present reformation is and will be that miracle which we are in these times to look for. It is that which the former age had despaired of, the present admireth, and the future shall stand amazed at.

Ver. 5. *For unto the angels, &c.*] The Jews, as they had embraced the Pythagorean transanimation, Matt. xvi. 14, so the Platonic opinion of angels moving the heavens, and ordering the world; whom therefore they worshipped, intruding into those things whereof there was no sound either proof or profit, Col. ii. 18. The angels (say Proculus the Platonist and Plutarch) are messengers that carry God's mind to men and men's requests to God.[1] But who told them all this? *Egregie dicis, sed quomodo probas?* said Aristotle of Moses, may we better say of these bold affirmers.

Ver. 6. *But one in a certain place*] The full sense is, but he hath subjected it to Christ, as David testified, Psal. viii. 4, 5; where whatsoever is spoken to man is here applied to the man Christ Jesus; and so is proper to the saints by virtue of their union with Christ. In which respect they are more glorious than heaven, angels, or any creature.[2]

Ver. 7. *A little lower*] Or, for a little while, *Paulisper*, viz. *Ab utero ad urnam*, from the womb to the tomb, from his birth to his burial, from his abasement to his advancement.

And didst set him over the works] Lions hate apes, but fear men; whereof no other probable reason can be given, but this here in the text; insomuch as the most timorous men dare kick and beat the hugest elephants.

Ver. 8. *Under his feet*] It is not said, under his hands, but under his feet: 1. That he may trample upon them with his feet, and not dote upon them with his heart. 2. That by them, as by a step or stirrup, he may raise his heart to things above. A sanctified fancy can make every creature a ladder to heaven.

He left nothing] No, not angels.

Not yet all things put under him] The creature rebelleth against man, because he rebelleth against God.[3] If the Master be set upon, the servants will draw, and fight for him.

Ver. 9. *But we see Jesus*] The saints hold all *in capite* tenure in Christ. Now in him all things are already subjected unto us, and made serviceable to our salvation.

For the suffering of death] Or that he might be in a condition to suffer death, this Sun of righteousness went ten degrees backward, not only below his Father, John xiv. 28, but below the angels; for man (as man) is inferior to the angels.

Taste death for every man] i. e. For every

such man as must be led unto glory, ver. 10; as is of Christ's brethren, 11; as is given of God to Christ, 13; and for none other.

Ver. 10. *For it became him*] That is, God, whose perfect wisdom, justice, &c., shineth most clearly in that great work of our redemption; than the which God could not have done anything more beseeming himself; whatever the world's wizards conceit to the contrary, 1 Cor. i. 23.

For whom are all things] See the note on Rom. ii. 36.

To make the captain, &c.] He that is captain of the Lord's hosts, Josh. v. 14, is also " Captain of our salvation." This is comfort.

To make perfect] Or, consecrate, τελειῶσαι. The priests were first consecrated with oil, then with blood; so was Christ first by the Spirit, and then by his own blood.

Ver. 11. *Are all of one*] viz. of Adam; only with this difference; that we are of Adam, and by Adam, but Christ was of Adam, not by Adam, for he was not begotten, but made, and so original sin was avoided.

He is not ashamed] Christ was not ashamed of us, when we had never a rag to our backs; should we be ashamed of him and his service?

Ver. 12. *I will declare, &c.*] Psal. xxii. 22. A psalm of Christ's sufferings, entitled upon Ajaleth Shachar, that is, "the morning-stag," such a one as the huntsmen singleth out to hunt for that day. Christ thus hunted, and praying for deliverance, promiseth to praise God's name amidst his brethren, that is, "his faithful servants."

Ver. 13. *I will put my trust in him*] Which he needed not, had he not been a man subject to misery.

And the children, &c.] Christ is the everlasting Father, Isa. ix. 6, and the saints are the travail of his soul, that prolong his days upon earth, Isa. liii. 10, 11; *Filiabitur nomine ejus*, Psal. lxxii. 17. There shall be a succession of Christ's name, till he present all his to his heavenly Father at the last day, with, "Behold, I, and the children whom thou hast given me."

Ver. 14. *Children are partakers*] παιδία, little children. Christ also became a little child, the babe of Bethlehem, Isa. ix. 6. Catch him up, as old Simeon did; kiss him, lest he be angry, Psal. ii. Stumble not at his weakness, but gather assurance of his love, and grow up unto the measure of the stature of the fulness of Christ, Ephes. iv. 13.

Took part of the same] Whence they are called Christ's partners or consorts, Heb. i. 9; and they may better say to him than Ruth did to Boaz, "Spread thy skirt over thy handmaid; for thou art a near kinsman, one that hath right to redeem," Ruth iii. 9.

Him that had the power of death] As the hangman hath the power of the gallows, " to kill men with death," Rev. ii. 23. He hath not

---

[1] πορθμεύοντες τὰ τῶν Θεῶν πρὸς ἀνθρώπους.

[2] *Accommodatio est facilis ad personam Christi, si interpretes non vellent esse nimis ingeniosi.* Ames. in Psal. viii. 5.

[3] *Rebellis facta est, quia homo numini, creatura homini.* Aug.

imperium principis, but *carnificis,* saith a Lapide. And that power of his also, as to the saints, is cassated, nullified, made void and of none effect, as the word καταργήσῃ signifieth. He may roar upon them, and shake his chain at them; not ruinate them, or once set his fangs in them.

Ver. 15. *And deliver them*] So that to those that are in Christ, death is but the day-break of eternal brightness; not the punishment of sin, but the period of sin. It is but a sturdy porter, opening the door of eternity; a rougher passage toᵗ eternal pleasure. What need they fear to pass the waters of Jordan to take possession of the land, that have the ark of God's covenant in their eye? *Tollitur mors, non ne sit, sed ne obsit.* As Christ took away, not sin, but the guilt of it, so neither death, but the sting of it.

Who through fear of death] The king of terrors, as Job calleth death, that terrible of all terribles, as Aristotle. Nature will have a bout with the best when they come to die. But I wonder (saith a grave divine) how the souls of wicked men go not out of their bodies, as the devils did out of the demoniacs, rending, raging, tearing, foaming. I wonder how any can die in their wits, that die not in the faith of Jesus Christ. Appius Claudius loved not the Greek *zeta,* because when it is pronounced, it representeth the gnashing teeth of a dying man. Sigismund the emperor, being ready to die, commanded his servants not to name death in his hearing, &c. The like is reported of Lewis XI., king of France, who to put by death when it came, sent for Aaron's rod and other holy relics (as they reputed them) from Rheims; but all would not do. Cardinal Beaufort, perceiving that death was come for him, murmured that his great riches could not reprieve him. *Stat sua cuique dies.* Now, death is nature's slaughterman, God's curse, and hell's purveyor; and must needsly therefore be terrible to those whose lives and hopes end together, and who say as one dying man did, *Spes et fortuna valete.*

Ver. 16. *For verily he took not*] ἐπιλαμβάνεται. Or, for nowhere took he, *q. d.* We find not anywhere, either in the Scriptures or in any Church record.

But he took] He assumed, apprehended, caught, laid hold on, as the angel did on Lot, Gen. xix. 16, as Christ did on Peter, Matt. xiv. 31, as men use to do upon a thing they are glad they have got and are loth to let go again. It is a main pillar of our comfort, that Christ took our flesh, for if he took not our flesh, we are not saved by him. But he not only took it, but overtook it by running after it, as the shepherd doth the sheep that is run away. A shepherd with a sheep upon his shoulder, engraved upon the communion cup, in the primitive times of the gospel, imported the same notion that here seems implied.

Ver. 17. *In all things*] Except in sin; as the brazen serpent was like the fiery serpent, but had no sting, ἀκατάληπτον, ἀθεράπευτον.

To make reconciliation] To expiate our sins, and to appease God's wrath, ἱλάσκεσθαι.

Ver. 18. *He is able to succour*] And no less apt than able; as he that hath been poor, or troubled with toothache, will pity those that are so. Queen Elizabeth said in her speech to the children of Christ's hospital, as she rode through Fleet Street, We are orphans all; let me enjoy your prayers, and ye shall be sure of mine assistance.

Non ignara mali, miseris succurrere disco.

CHAPTER III.

Ver. 1. *Holy brethren*] HOLY, because partakers of a calling that is heavenly. 1. *Ratione fontis,* Phil. iii. 14, 15. 2. *Ratione finis,* to the fruition of heavenly privileges in Christ.

Consider] Gr. κατανοήσατε. Bend your minds with utmost diligence upon him.

The apostle and high priest] Those two chief offices of both Testaments, *ut ubique superemineat Christus.*

Ver. 2. *As also Moses was faithful*] And yet how unworthily handled by the author of the Marrow of Modern Divinity, that sly Antinomian, in divers passages of his book, as might easily be instanced. How much better (herein at least) Bellarmine! *Moses vir Deo longe acceptissimus,* saith he, *quo nihil habuit antiqua aetas mitius, sapientius, sanctius:* Moses a man highly accepted in heaven for his meekness, wisdom, holiness.

Ver. 3. *Worthy of more glory than Moses*] In whom these Hebrews trusted, John v. 45. And the Jews at this day hold that the law of nature shall bring to heaven those that observe it, but the Hebrews (unto whom the law of Moses was peculiarly given) by keeping it shall have a prerogative of glory. Poor seduced souls!

Ver. 4. *He that built all things*] Moses and all.

Is God] That is, Christ, whom he had proved to be God by many arguments, chap. i. Messias therefore is to be preferred before Moses.

Ver. 5. *As a servant*] *Famulus ingenuus,* a servant of the better sort, a man of worship, as the word seemeth to import (θεράπων, *ex verbo* θεραπεύειν); though it be honour enough to be Christ's servant, of the meanest in his family. Constantinus, Valentinianus, and Theodosius, three emperors, called themselves *Vassallos Christi,* the vassals of Christ, as Socrates testifieth.

Ver. 6. *Whose house are we*] And he is bound (by his own promise) to repair. He also is our dwelling-house, Psal. xc. 1, and by the civil law, *De domo sua nemo extrahi debet, aut in jus vocari.* A man's house is his castle.

If we hold fast] See here a just description of the invisible Church of Christ.

Ver. 7. *Wherefore as the Holy Ghost*] It is well observed by Calvin, that the words after "wherefore," to ver. 12., should be enclosed with a parenthesis, and then the sense is clear. If Jerome and Egranus had observed so much in this and other places, they would not so sharply have censured St Paul for his obscurities and incongruities, and lame senses and sentences. (Jerome Epist. ad Algesiam. Joh. Egran. apud Jo. Manl. loc. com.)

Ver. 8. *Harden not your hearts*] Some hearts are so hard that neither ministry, nor misery, nor miracle, nor mercy can possibly mollify them. Such a heart is in some respects worse than hell. And if God broke David's bones for his adultery, and the angels' backs for their pride, the Lord, if ever he save any, will break his heart too. As when he marks out a man for eternal misery, he denies him his grace; and then the sinner hardens his own heart by his own inward pravity. Like as when an owner denies to prop up or repair a ruinous reeling house, the house falls by its own ponderousness.

Ver. 9. *Tempted me*] God must be trusted, but not tempted, as he is, when men, 1. Question and awake his power; 2. Limit the Holy One of Israel, and presume to prescribe to him, set him a time, &c; 3. Neglect the use of means, and serve not his providence.

Ver. 10. *I was grieved*] The Hebrew text hath it, I was nauseated, and ready to rid my stomach at them, to spew them out of my mouth.

They do alway err] They must needs err that know not God's ways. Yet cannot they wander so wide as to miss of hell.

Ver. 11. *They shall not enter*] This the apostle propounds to unbelievers of his time, that they may beware. *Alterius perditio tua sit cautio.* Seest thou another suffer shipwreck? look well to thy tackling.

Ver. 12. *In departing from*] ἀπιστία parit ἀποστασίαν. Infidelity is the mother of apostasy; as in Cranmer: but worse in John Dudley, Duke of Northumberland, in Queen Mary's days, who being brought to the scaffold on Tower-hill, and having promise of life if he would recant his profession, dastard-like forsook his Master, and exhorted the people to the Romish religion. Which his death-sermon afterwards came forth in print by authority. (Speed's Chron.)

Ver. 13. *But exhort one another*] A special preservative from apostasy. See my Commonplace of Admonition, and my treatise on Mal. iii. 17.

Lest any of you be hardened] Continuance in sin hardeneth the heart, and gradually indisposeth it to the work of repentance. *Qui non est hodie,* &c. There is a deceitfulness in sin, a lie in vanity, Jonah ii. 8. Doctor Preston relateth of one in Cambridge, that had committed a great sin, and had this temptation upon him, Do the act again, and your conscience will trouble you no more. He did it again, and then he grew a very sot indeed and went on in his wickedness.

Ver. 14. *For we are made partakers*] Christ's consorts, co-heirs with him, Rom. viii. 17. This we are in present, if we persevere to the end.

The beginning of our confidence] Gr. ὑποστάσεως, of our subsistence, or substance, that is, of our faith, Heb. xi. 1, whereby we subsist, and become sons of God, as Ambrose expounds it. The Greek signifieth the very first act of faith, whereby we began to subsist in Christ.

Ver. 15. *While it is said*] sc. To you now, as it was said to them of old, ver. 7. We must see our own names written on every precept, promise, example, &c., Hosea xii. 4. There God spake with us.

To-day if ye will hear, &c.] The negligent spirit cries, *Cras Domine,* To-morrow, Lord. *In crastinum seria.* But who can tell what a great-bellied day may bring forth? Either space or grace may be denied. God may leave men under his ordinances, as rocks in the midst of rivers, as blind at noon-day.

Ver. 16. *Howbeit not all*] Yet all fell in the wilderness save Joshua and Caleb. Good men are oft wrapt up in a common calamity. The righteous perisheth, Isa. lvii. 1, so the world thinketh; "But whether they live, they live unto the Lord, or whether they die, they die unto the Lord," Rom. xiv. 8. The good corn is cut down together with the tares, but to another, and to a better purpose.

Ver. 17. *Whose carcases fell*] Gr. κῶλα. Whose members, joints, limbs. *Cadavera a cadendo.* Oh that we could make that use of their disaster, that Waldus the French merchant (father and founder of the Waldenses) did of that sad sight that befell him. For walking in the streets, and seeing one fall suddenly dead, he went home and repented of his Popish errors and profane courses.

Ver. 18. *To them that believe not*] Or, that will not be persuaded, uncounsellable persons, that acquiesce not in wholesome advice.

Ver. 19. *Because of unbelief*] A bloody sin, John iii. 19. No sin will gripe so in hell as this. The devil will keep holy-day there, in respect of unbelievers.

CHAPTER IV.

Ver. 1. *Let us fear*] WITH a fear not of diffidence, but of diligence. See the note on Phil. ii. 12, and on 1 Cor. x. 12.

Lest a promise] Some render it thus, Lest we should seem to fall short of the promise that is left us, &c. But where is that promise left us, may some say? It is closely couched in the former commination, chap. iii. 18. God sware that unbelievers should not enter, and therefore intimates a promise that believers shall enter. A bee can suck sweet honey out of bitter thyme, so cannot a fly do.

To come short of it] To come lag and late, ὑστερηκέναι, when the gate is shut, the drawbridge taken up, as those foolish virgins, or as lazy race-runners, or as those that come a day after the fair, an hour after the feast, and so are frustrated.

Ver. 2. *The word preached*] Gr. ὁ λόγος τῆς ἀκοῆς, the word of hearing, *i. e.* the promise that fell from the preacher's lips into their ears. *Nescio quid divinum in auscultatione est*, saith one ; I know not what divine business there is in hearing ; but sure I am that what we hear doth more deeply affect us, and more firmly abide with us, and stick by us, than what we read.

In them that heard it] In their hearts, as in so many vessels. Faith and the promise meeting make a happy mixture, a precious confection.

Ver. 3. *For we which have believed*] Believers (and they only) have heaven beforehand *in pretio, in promisso, in primitiis*, in the price that was paid for it, in the promise of it (which is sure-hold), and in the first-fruits, the graces of the Spirit, which are as those grapes in the land of Canaan.

Ver. 4. *And God did rest*] Here the apostle showeth what that rest of believers is. Not that seventh-day's rest, ver. 5, nor that other rest, Psal. xcv., meant of the land of Canaan, but another and better, typified in both those, viz. a spiritual resting from our own works of sins, so as God resteth in his love to us, Zeph. iii. 17, and we sweetly acquiesce in our interest in him, Psal. cxvi. 7.

Ver. 5. *If they shall enter*] q. d. Then never trust me more. Yet Ambrose here taketh the words for a forcible affirmation, q. d. *Si introibunt, bene habebunt.*

Ver. 6. *Seeing therefore it remaineth*] This is a deduction from the former text of the Psalmist. Such as is that of our Saviour, Matt. xxii. 32, from Exod. iii. 6. And such inferences rightly drawn are the very word of God, 1 Cor. vii. 10.

Ver. 7. *After so long a time*] Four hundred years almost passed between Joshua's and David's days. David's to-day was not Joshua's to-day.

To-day if ye will hear] That day of salvation, wherein the Lord doth offer us mercy in the ministry of his word, showing us our misery, and exciting us to use the remedy.

Ver. 8. *For if Jesus, &c.*] That is, Joshua, who had his name changed when he was sent as a spy into Canaan, Numb. xiii. 16, from Oshea to Joshua, from Let God save, to God shall save. Under the law (which brings us, as it were, into a briery wilderness) we may desire, wish, and pray, that there were a Saviour, but under the gospel we are sure of salvation. Our Jesus is Jehovah our Righteousness.

Ver. 9. *A rest to the people of God*] Gr. A sabbatism, an eternal rest, a sabbath that hath neither evening, Gen. ii. 2, nor labour, Rev. xiv. 13. But they shall enter into peace, rest in their beds, Isa. lvii. 2 ; be ravisht in spirit, receive the full import and purport of the weekly sabbath, rest from travail and trouble, Apoc. i. 10. 2. Of the seventh-year sabbath : for the creature, the ground shall rest from its vanity and slavery, Rom. viii. 20, 21. 3. Of the seventh

seven-year sabbath, the Jubilean sabbath ; for their debts shall be all discharged, their mortgages released, their persons set at liberty from sin and Satan's slavery.

Ver. 10. *From his own works*] From the servile works of sin, Psal. xviii. 23. These are our own works. As a lie is the devil's own, John viii. 44, "When he speaketh a lie, he speaketh of his own ;" so when we do evil, we work *de nostro et secundum hominem*, 1 Cor. iii. 3. It is as impossible for us naturally to do good as for a toad to spit cordials.

Ver. 11. *Let us labour*] Here he resumes and re-inforces his former exhortations ; that his words may be as nails and goads fastened by the masters of the assemblies. The judgment is first to be illightened by doctrine, and then the affections to be inflamed by exhortation ; like as, in the law, first the lamps were lighted, and then the incense burned.

Fall after the same example] God hangs up some malefactors, as it were in gibbets, for a warning to others.[1] Jethro grew wise by the plagues that befell his neighbour-prince Pharaoh, as Rabbi Solomon observeth. And Belshazzar is destroyed for not profiting by his father's calamities ; Dan. v. 22, "Thou hast not humbled thy heart, though thou knewest all this."

Ver. 12. *Quick and powerful*] Gr. Lively and energetical ; *sc.* in hearts that can tremble at God's judgments, as David did, Psal. cxix. 120. As for hypocrites, the word will ransack them, and give them a very glimpse of the judgment to come, as it did Felix, Herod, &c. God smiteth the earth with this rod of his mouth, Isa. xi. 4, he dasheth them in the teeth, and maketh them spit blood, as it were ; hewing them by his prophets, and slaying them by the words of his mouth, Hos. vi. 5 ; Rev. xi. 5.

Soul and spirit] See the note on 1 Thess. v. 23. It affecteth not only the lower parts of the soul, which are less pure, but the purest also, and most supreme ; even the spirit of the mind, the bosom as well as the bottom of the soul.

And of the joints and marrow] The *minima* and *intima*, the least things and the most secret.

And is a discerner] Gr. A curious critic judging exactly, and telling tales of the hearers, disclosing the words that they speak in their very bed-chambers, as 2 Kings vi. 12.

Ver. 13. *Neither is there any creature*] No, not the creature of the heart, the most secret thoughts and intentions.

That is not manifest in his sight] Or in the sight of it, that is, of the word preached ; but every the least fibre, the smallest string in the heart, that would escape the sight of the most exact anatomist, is hereby cut up. See 1 Cor. xiv. 24.

But all things are naked and open] Naked, for the outside, and opened, dissected, quartered, cleft in the back-bone (as the word τετραχηλισμένα here signifieth), for the inside. Erasmus rendereth it, *resupinata*, making it a metaphor

---

[1] *Exemplo alterius qui sapit, ille sapit.*

from those that lie with their faces upwards, that all passengers may see who they are. Theodoret readeth it, Hath the throat cut. So opened (say some others) as the entrails of a man that is anatomized, or of a beast that is cut up and quartered; and not only naked, as when the skin is pulled off. He useth a metaphor (saith an interpreter) taken from a sheep whose skin is taken off, and he hanged up by the neck with his back toward the wall, and all his entrails laid bare, and exposed to open view.

Unto the eyes of him] Or rather, of it, of the word, wherewith we have to do. The word, like a sacrificing sword, slits open, and as it were unridgeth the conscience.

Ver. 14. *We have a great high priest*] Who by a new and living way will bring us into the rest above mentioned. A great high priest Christ is, because, 1. Real, not typical; 2. Eternal, and needed not succession, as Aaron; 3. Entering (not into the holy places made with hands, but) into heaven itself, Heb. ix. 23.

Ver. 15. *Which cannot be touched*] Christ retaineth still compassion, though freed from personal passion. And though freed from feeling, hath still yet a fellow-feeling, Acts ix. 5; Matt. xxv. 35.[1] Trajan the emperor being blamed by his friends for being too gentle toward all, answered that being an emperor he would now be such toward private men as he once, when he was a private man, wished that the emperor should be towards him. Christ hath lost nothing of his wonted pity by his exaltation in heaven.

Tempted] Or, pierced through, πεπειραμένον. Luther was a piercing preacher, and met with every man's temptations; and being once demanded how he could do so? Mine own manifold temptations (said he) and experiences are the cause thereof; for from his tender years he was much beaten and exercised with spiritual conflicts.

Yet without sin] Tempted Christ was to sin, but not into sin.

Ver. 16. *Let us therefore come boldly*] In the sense of sin to wrap ourselves in Christ's righteousness, and so go boldly to the throne of grace; this (saith a reverend man) is an honour to Christ our high priest. Luther prayed reverently to God, and yet boldly, as to his friend.

Throne of grace] The altar of incense stood against the mercy-seat, but yet there was a veil between them. We when we pray, must act our faith upon the throne of grace, though we see it not.

CHAPTER V.

Ver. 1. *Both gifts*] Of things without life.

And sacrifices] Of living creatures.

For sins] Christ, as God, was the priest and altar to offer up and to sanctify the sacrifice; and, as God-man, he was the sacrifice; for the Church was purchased by the blood of God, Acts

[1] *Manet compassio etiam cum impassibilitate.*

xx. 28. A bloody Spouse she was unto him, as in a sense it may be said.

Ver. 2. *Who can have compassion*] μετριοπαθεῖν. Or, bear anything with reason, and not be easily angry, but show as much mercy as is meet for his, whether they have ignorantly offended, or upon deliberation. They cannot commit more than he can remit.

He is compassed with infirmity] Christ was compassed with that which we call miserable, not that we call sinful infirmity.

Ver. 3. *He ought as for the people*] A priest is a person by God's appointment taken from amongst men, and for men to offer gifts and sacrifices for sin in their and his own behalf.

Ver. 4. *And no man taketh, &c.*] Or if he do, he shall smoke and smart for it, as did Nadab and Abihu, Uzzah and Uzziah, &c. *In physicis aer non facit seipsum ignem, sed fit a superiori,* as Aquinas noteth upon this text. No man might come uncalled to the king of Persia upon pain of death. What then shall become of such as come without a call to the King of heaven? Christ would not let the devil preach him, Mark i., *quia extra vocationem,* as one well noteth, because he had no calling to such an office.

Ver. 5. *Glorified not himself*] As the pope doth, who will needs be styled *Pontifex maximus,* the greatest high priest (whereas Christ is called only the great, and not greatest high priest, Heb. iv. 14). Pope Hildebrand especially, whom when no man would advance to Peter's chair, he gat up himself. *Quis enim melius de me judicare potest quam ego?* said he, Who can better judge of me than myself? (Heidfeld.)

But he that said unto him] He glorified him, or made him high priest.

To-day have I begotten thee] Add the words following, "Ask of me," &c., and the sense is full. For to ask of God those things that pertain to the people's safety and salvation, is the proper office of a high priest. Christ as he expiated his people's sins by his own blood, so he made intercession for them, 1. A little before his attachment, John xvii. 1, 2, &c; 2. In the very time when the sacrifice was hanged up, Luke xxiii. 34; 3. In the heavenly sanctuary, Heb. ix. 24.

Ver. 6. *Thou art a high priest, &c.*] The former proof was not so evident; but this puts the matter out of all question. A minister should use sound speech that cannot be contradicted; that he that is of the contrary part may be ashamed, having nothing reasonably to oppose, Tit. ii. 8. The Jew would object that Christ was not of the tribe of Levi, therefore no priest. The apostle answers; Yes, a priest, but after another order, and proves it. This is συμβιβάζειν, *collatis testimoniis demonstrare,* as Paul did, Acts ix. 22, to confirm and assert.

Ver. 7. *Prayers and supplications*] Gr. ἱκετηρίας, deprecations, and most ardent requests, uttered with deep sighs, hands lifted up, and manifold moans, in a most submissive manner.

With strong crying and tears] Be our hearts so hard (saith one) that we cannot pray for ourselves or others? cry *Conqueror tibi lachrymis Jesu Christi*, I cry to thee with Christ's tears.

Unto him that was able to save him, &c.] Neither let any here object that many martyrs suffered with less ado, nay, with great joy and triumph. For, 1. What were all their sufferings to his? 2. He therefore suffered the worst, that they might the better suffer. 3. They were lifted up with the sense of God's love, which he for present felt not. 4. Their bodily pains were miraculously mitigated; as Rose Allen, being asked by a friend how she could abide the painful burning of her hand held over a candle, so long till the very sinews cracked asunder? She said, at the first it was some grief to her; but afterward, the longer she burned the less she felt, or well near none at all. Sabina, a Roman martyr, crying out in her travail, and being asked by her keeper how she would endure the fire next day; Oh, well enough, said she, for now I suffer in child-birth for my sins, Genesis iii., but then Christ shall suffer in me and support me.

And was heard in that he feared] ἀπὸ τῆς εὐλαβείας, or, He was heard (that is, delivered) from his fear. For no sooner had he prayed, but he met his enemies in the face, and asked them, "Whom seek ye?" I am he.

Ver. 8. *Yet learned he obedience*] He came to know by experience what a hard matter it was thus to obey God. *Schola crucis, schola lucis.* Gideon, by threshing the men of Succoth, taught them, Judg. viii. 7—16. God's chastisements are our advertisements, παθήματα μαθήματα. *Nocumenta documenta.* See my Treatise on Rev. iii., p. 145.

Ver. 9. *And being made perfect*] τελειωθείς. Or, being offered up in sacrifice; or, being completed by this experimental knowledge of passive obedience also.

The author] And finisher too, chap. xii. 2. Gr. αἴτιος, The cause, viz. by his merit and efficacy.

Ver. 10. *Called*] Gr. προσαγορευθείς, spoken unto, called by name, or entitled an high priest, &c.; therefore he is truly so. For persons and things are as God calleth them.

Ver. 11. *Of whom we have, &c.*] The digression here begun holds on to the end of the next chapter.

Hard to be uttered] Gr. Hard to be expounded. But difficulty doth not dishearten, but rather whet on heroic spirits to a more serious search: it doth not weaken, but waken their earnestness; not amate, but animate them.

Seeing ye are dull] Gr. Slow-paced and heavy-handed, νωθροὶ, *ex* νε *et* θέω, *curro*. Our minds are like narrow-mouthed vessels. Our Saviour therefore spake as the people could hear, Mark iv. 33, like as Jacob drave as the little ones could go.

Ver. 12. *Ye have need that one*] But people plead their rotten charters of age and marriage against catechism.

Ver. 13. *In the word of righteousness*] That is, in the more solid doctrine of the gospel concerning Christ, who is our righteousness.

Ver. 14. *To them that are of full age*] Or that are perfect, τελείων, comparatively perfect, not only past the spoon, but full grown.

Who by reason of use] Gr. By reason of habit, got by continual custom and long practice, as in an expert artist.

Have their senses exercised] αἰσθητήρια, their inward senses, for the soul also hath her senses, as the body hath. Instead of seeing, faith; of hearing, obedience; of smelling, hope; of tasting, charity; of touching, humility. These are exercised in the saints with such an exercise as wrestlers use, or such as contend for victory, put forth to the utmost, as that which they have been trained up to, and can therefore very well skill of.

To discern good and evil] "Doth not the ear try words? and the mouth taste his meat?" Job xii. 11. "Eye hath not seen," &c., 1 Cor. ii. 9. Where the carcase is the eagles will be. Saints have a spiritual sagacity, and they lay hold on eternal life.

CHAPTER VI.

Ver. 1. *Let us go on unto perfection*] Gr. φερώμεθα, let us be carried on, as with a force, Acts ii. 2, breaking through all impediments, aiming at the highest pitch, and eyeing the best patterns. It is a low and unworthy strain in some to labour after no more grace than will keep life and soul together, that is, hell and soul asunder.

Repentance from dead works] These are the six principles of Christian religion, that must be laid as a foundation. *Certa semper sunt in paucis,* saith Tertullian. Fundamentals are but few; few they are in number, but many in virtue; in sight small, but great in weight; like gold, which being solid, is contracted into a narrow room, but may be drawn into so large an extent, that one angel may cover an acre of ground, as the naturalists have observed. The Apostles' Creed (anciently called *Symbolum*, a sign or badge to distinguish Christians from infidels and wicked people) was heretofore briefer than now. The mention of the Father's being maker of heaven and earth, the Son's burial and descending into hell, and the communion of saints, being wholly omitted, haply are not necessary for all men to know, as Suarez saith, or sufficiently implied in other articles, or known by the light of reason; and so not making difference between Christians and heathens. (Dr Ussier.) The Papists have lately coined twelve new articles by the authority of Pope Pius IV., A. D. 1564, raised out of the Council of Trent, and added to the Nicene Creed, to be received with oath, as the true catholic faith, to be believed by as many as shall be saved. Those that list to see them, may read the epistle before Bishop Jewel's works, and Sir Humphrey Land's *Via Tuta*. Whereunto if they will add the Jesuit's new ten commandments, let them read the Spanish Pilgrim.

Ver. 2. *Doctrine of baptisms*] Inward and

outward. *Flaminis et fluminis,* of water and of the Spirit, that "washing of regeneration and renewing of the Holy Ghost," Tit. iii. 5. Calvin thinks the apostle meaneth the solemn rites or set days of baptizing. Others, the doctrine of both the sacraments; one being figuratively put for both, and the mention of the Lord's supper omitted, because the doctrine thereof was not anciently propounded to the *catechumeni,* or young Christians; neither were they suffered to see it administered.

And of laying on of hands] Hereby is meant the whole ministry and order of Church government, as prescribed by the word. The Scripture is to be taken in the largest sense, if nothing hinder, neither matter, phrase, nor scope. (Wilson's Theol. Rules.)

Ver. 3. *If God permit*] If God give me life and ability, and you capacity and stability; for many fall away, whose damnation sleepeth not.

Ver. 4. *Who were once enlightened*] φωτισθέν-τες, as with a flash of lightning. Knowing persons, and those they call the wits of the world, are in the greatest danger of the unpardonable sin; which begins in apostasy, holds on in persecution, ends in blasphemy.

And have tasted] As cooks do their sauces with the tip of their finger only; or as the Israelites tasted the fruits of the land, and yet perished in the wilderness. Men may taste that which they spit out again, as physicians oft do.

The heavenly gift] Gr. Supercelestial gift, *i. e.* Christ, who is called the gift, John iv. 10, and the benefit, 1 Tim. vi. 2.

Partakers of the Holy Ghost] Of his common and inferior gifts and operations. These a man may lose, and have his dispositions to sin seven times more inflamed than before, Matt. xii. 44.

Ver. 5. *And have tasted the good word*] Catching at the promises, as children do at sweetmeats, rejoicing therein, as the stony-ground hearers did, conceiving a rolling opinion, as Haman did, that they are the men whom the King of heaven will honour.

And the powers of the world to come] *i. e.* The wonderful works of the world to come, as glorification, resurrection, last judgment, whereinto a hypocrite may see far, and have a glimpse of heaven, or a flash of hell upon his conscience, as Balaam, Spira.

Ver. 6. *If they shall fall away*] Totally and finally, as Judas and Julian did, and as Mr John Glover thought he had done, and did therefore eat his meat against his appetite, only defer the time of his damnation, which, by mistake of this text, he thought he could not possibly avoid. But God, who comforteth those that are cast down, did not only at last rid him out of all his fears, but also framed him to such mortification of life, as the like lightly hath not been seen, saith Mr Fox, who knew it.

And put him to an open shame] As if they had not found him the same that they took him for. In those that have wilfully resisted divine truths made known to them, and after taste, despised

them, a persuasion that God hath forsaken them (set on strongly by Satan) stirs up a hellish hatred against God; carrying them to a revengeful desire of opposing whatsoever is God's, though not always openly (for then they should lose the advantage of doing hurt), yet secretly and subtlely, and under pretence of the contrary, as one well observeth.

Ver. 7. *And bringeth forth herbs*] So the fruitful Christian (that, watered with the word and Spirit, bringeth forth a harvest of holiness) shall receive the blessing of increase, John xv. 2. Such trees as brought forth fruit fit for meat were not to be destroyed, Deut. xx. 19; but trees that were not for fruit were for the fire, Matt. iii. 10. The earth thankfully returns her burden to the painful tiller. Let earth teach earth: *terram quam terimus, terram quam gerimus,* the earth we tear, the earth we bear.

Ver. 8. *Is rejected, and is nigh to cursing*] The sin against the Holy Ghost is therefore unpardonable, because God (not suffering himself to be derided, or his Spirit of truth to be found a liar) smiteth these sinners against their own souls, with blindness and reprobacy of mind. Whence follows, 1. An impossibility of repentance, sith it is the work of that Spirit whom they have despited, and will not suffer any saving operation of his to fasten on their souls. 2. Such a desperate fury invadeth them, that they resist and repudiate the matter of remission, the blood of Christ, whereby if they might have mercy, yet they would not; but continue raving and raging against both the physic and the physician, to their endless ruth and ruin.

Ver. 9. *But, beloved, we are persuaded*] He would not be mistaken. Zuinglius, when he had inveighed against vice, would usually close up his discourse with *Probe vir, hæc nihil ad te.* All this is nothing to thee, thou honest man. (Scult. Annal.) We can hardly beat the dogs out of doors but the children will cry.

Things that accompany salvation] Gr. ἐχόμενα, *i. e.* κατεχόμενα, that have salvation, that comprehend it, are contiguous to it, and touch upon it. Grace and glory differ not but in degree.

Ver. 10. *For God is not unrighteous*] That is, unfaithful, 1 John i. 9. There is a justice of fidelity as well as of equity.

To forget your work] The butler may forget Joseph, and Joseph forget his father's house; but forgetfulness befalls not God, to whom all things are present, and before whom there is written a book of remembrance for them that fear the Lord, and think upon his name, Mal. iii. 17.

Ver. 11. *Do show the same diligence*] A man may as truly say the sea burns, or fire cools, as that certainty of salvation breeds security and looseness.

To the full assurance] All duties tend to assurance, or spring from it. Strive we must to the riches of full assurance, Col. ii. 2. But in case our assurance be not so fair, yield not to temptations and carnal reasonings. Coins that have little of the stamp left, yet are current.

Ver. 12. *That ye be not slothful*] A ready heart makes riddance of God's work. Shake off sloth. *Spontaneæ lassitudines morbos loquuntur,* saith Hippocrates. Sure I am that dulness and luskishness argue a diseased soul.

But followers of them] It was a good law that the Ephesians made, that men should propound to themselves the best patterns, and ever bear in mind some eminent man, αἰὲν ὑπομιμνήσκεσθαί τινος τῶν τῇ ἀρετῇ χρωμένων.

Ver. 13. *For when God made promise*] Of those many that by faith and patience had inherited the promises, the apostle instanceth in Abraham, famous both for his faith in God's promise, ver. 13, and for his patience, ver. 15.

Ver. 14. *Blessing I will bless thee*] Now he whom God blesseth shall be blessed, as Isaac said of Jacob, Gen. xxvii. 33.

Ver. 15. *After he had patiently endured*] Waited many years for an Isaac, and yet longer for eternal life. " I have waited for thy salvation, O Lord," saith dying Jacob, Gen. xlix. 18.

Ver. 16. *Swear by the greater*] So do not they that swear by sundry creatures and qualities, God can hardly spare such, Jer. v. 7. That passage, " As thy soul liveth," is not an oath, but an asseveration, or obtestation only, conjoined with the oath.

And end of all strife] The end of an oath is to help the truth in necessity, and to clear men's innocency, Exod. xxii. 11.

Ver. 17. *God willing more abundantly*] His word is sufficient, yet tendering our infirmity he hath bound it with an oath, and set to his seal. His word cannot be made more true, but yet more credible. Now two things make a thing more credible: 1. The quality of the person speaking; 2. The manner of the speech. If God do not simply speak, but solemnly swear, and seal to us remission of sins, and adoption of sons by the broad seal of the sacraments, and by the privy seal of his Spirit, should we not rest assured?

Ver. 18. *We might have strong*] Such as swalloweth up all worldly griefs, as Moses' serpent did the sorcerers' serpents, or as the fire doth the fuel. The sacraments are God's visible oaths unto us; he taketh, as it were, the body and blood of his Son into his hand, and solemnly sweareth to bestow upon us all the purchase of Christ's passion. Should not therefore the joy of the Lord be our strength? Neh. viii. 10. The comforts of philosophy are λέσχαι καὶ φλύαραι (as Plato hath it, as Socrates found it when he was to die), that is, toys and trifles. *Nescio quomodo imbecillior est medecina quam morbus,* saith Cicero, the disease is too hard for the medicine. But the consolations of God are strong in themselves, and should not be small with us, Job xv. 11.

To lay hold upon the hope, &c.] Gr. κρατῆσαι, to lay hold by main force, and so to hold as not to lose our hold, when the devil would pull it from us. It is our faith that he fights against, our hope that he would shred us off. Look to it.

Ver. 19. *Both sure and stedfast*] *Spes in terrenis, incerti nomen boni: Spes in divinis, nomen est certissimi.*

And which entereth into that] This anchor is cast upward, and fastened not in the depth of the sea, but in the height of heaven, whereof it gets firm hold and sure possession. Now that ship (saith one) may be tossed, not shipwrecked, whereof Christ is the pilot, the Scripture the compass, the promises the tacklings, hope the anchor, faith the cable, the Holy Ghost the winds, and holy affection the sails, which are filled with the graces of the Spirit.

Ver. 20. *Whither the fore-runner*] Like as the high priest once a year entered into the holy of holies to pray for the people.

CHAPTER VII.

Ver. 1. *For this Melchisedec*] SOME make him the same with Shem; others say it was the Holy Ghost; others say it was Christ himself under the habit of a king and priest. It is most probable that he was a mortal man, and a Canaanite, but yet a most righteous man, and a priest of the most high God by special dispensation; and that Chedorlaomer and the other kings that over-ran the country, and spoiled it, forbare, out of reverence to the man and his office, to meddle with Melchisedec's territories.

Ver. 2. *Gave a tenth part of all*] So to set forth his thankfulness to God for the victory. The Lord is the man of war, Exod. xv. 3; the Lord and victor of wars, as the Chaldee there expresseth it. Conquerors should send to him, as Joab to David, to take the honour of the day, 2 Sam. xii. 28. The very heathens, after a victory, would consecrate something to their gods. The Romans had a custom, when they had received any great victory, the conqueror in his triumphant chariot rode to the capitol, where in all humility he did present a palm to Jupiter, and offer in sacrifice a white bullock; so acknowledging it was his power whereby the conquest was achieved.[1]

Ver. 3. *Without father*] viz. That we find mentioned in the Holy Scripture. Hence the Melchisedechian heretics held that he was the Holy Ghost; or at least some created angel. See Cunæus de Rep. Heb. iii. 3. Without father and mother he was not in respect of generation, but in respect of commemoration; his parents are not mentioned: no more are Job's, or the three children's.

Like unto the Son of God] As having neither fellow nor successor. And being a lively type of Christ, who is the true Trismegist, in regard of his three offices. The heathens called their Mercury (haply the same with Melchisedec)

---

[1] ——*laurumque superbam in gremio Jovis abscissis depo-nere Pœnis. Et taurum album Jovi mactabant.* Livy.

Trismegist, or thrice-great; because he was the greatest philosopher, the greatest priest, and the greatest king. (Marcil. Ficin. in arg. ad Tris. Pimandr.)

Ver. 4. *How great this man was*] It is goodness that renders a man great, and the grace of God that ennobleth, Isa. xliii. 4; Heb. xi. 2. Keep close to God, and then ye shall be some of God's Rabbins, as Daniel calls them, chap. ix. 27. See Job xxxii. 9. Great men indeed, not with a belluine, but with a genuine, greatness.

The tenth of the spoils] Gr. ἀκροθίνια, the top of the heap.

Ver. 5. *To take tithes of the people*] If tithes be Jewish, saith M. Harris, and yet ministers must have a maintenance, how will men satisfy their consciences in the particular quantity they must bestow upon them? the Scripture speaks only of the tenth part. Can any show us where the old apportion is reversed, and which is that *quota pars* now that conscience must rest in?

Ver. 6. *Received tithes of Abraham*] Gr. δεδεκάτωκε, tithed or tenthed Abraham, by the same divine right whereby he blessed him. Melchisedec did not take only that which Abraham was pleased to give him, but he tithed him, saith the text, he took the tenths as his due.

Ver. 7. *The less is blessed, &c.*] The pastor therefore blessing his people according to his office, is greater than his people in that respect.

Ver. 8. *That he liveth*] Tithes then are due to the ministers of Christ that liveth, because due to Melchisedec, to whom Abraham paid them as a priest and tithe-taker, and type of Christ. Who therefore should receive them for him, but those that are in his stead? 2 Cor. v. 20.

Ver. 9. *Levi also paid tithes*] If any shall object, so did Christ also, sith he was in the loins of Abraham too; it may be answered, that though Christ was of Abraham, yet he was not by Abraham. But Levi was both.

Ver. 10. *In the loins of his father*] So we were all in the loins of Adam when he fell (as all the county is in a parliament-man), and fell with him.

Ver. 11. *If therefore perfection*] i. e. Justification, sanctification, salvation.

Ver. 12. *A change also of the law*] "For we are not under the law, but under grace." The gospel is *post naufragium tabula*, a plank after shipwreck, and hath its remuneration, Heb. xi. 6, viz. of grace and mercy. By law here some understood only the law of priesthood.

Ver. 13. *Pertaineth to another tribe*] That of Judah, ver. 14, which therefore is first reckoned, Rev. vii., among those that were sealed; as of those that came by Rachel, Nepthalim hath the first place; because in that tribe Christ dwelt, viz. at Capernaum; *Ut utrobique superemineat Christi prærogativa.*

Ver. 14. *Nothing concerning priesthood*] For when Reuben, by defiling Bilhah, lost his birthright, the birthright was given to Joseph, the kingdom to Judah, and the priesthood to Levi. But God translated the priesthood, and settled

it upon his son Christ, who sprang out of Judah, in a time when it was commonly bought and sold to the vilest of men, and all was out of order.

Ver. 15. *After the similitude of Melchisedec*] i. e. After an order distinct and different from that of Aaron.

Ver. 16. *Of a carnal command*] i. e. External and ceremonial.

But after the power] Both of God the Father, who made him a priest, and of God the Son, who is the Father of eternity, Isa. ix. 6, and a Priest for ever; which word "for ever" the apostle expoundeth and improveth in the last clause of this verse, "the power of an endless life."

Ver. 17. *For he testifieth*] Thus the author still argueth out of Scripture, as knowing that *quicquid non habet authoritatem ex Scripturis, eadem facilitate contemnitur qua approbatur*, whatsoever is not grounded upon Scripture authority is as easily rejected as received. (Jerome.)

Ver. 18. *For there is verily a disannulling*] Gr. ἀθέτησις, an outing, cassating, expunging.

Of the commandment] See the note on ver. 12 and 16.

For the weakness and unprofitableness] sc. To justify, sanctify, save, Rom. viii. 2; though as a schoolmaster to Christ, and a rule of life, it is of singular use still.

Ver. 19. *But the bringing in*] The law is a superintroduction to Christ our hope, who is the end of the law to every believer, Rom. x. 4.

We draw nigh to God] Having boldness and access with confidence, Ephes. iii. 11, by the faith of Christ our High Priest; who leads us by the hand, and presents us to his Heavenly Father, as Joseph did his two sons to Jacob, that he might bless them.

Ver. 20. *Not without an oath*] A singular confirmation: what a monstrous sin then is unbelief!

Ver. 21. *And will not repent*] Will not change his mind upon pretence that second thoughts are better. Those that can play with oaths, and can slip them as easily as monkeys do their collars, have nothing of God in them.

Ver. 22. *Jesus was made a surety*] As he was our surety to God for the discharge of our debt (the surety and debtor in law are reputed as one person), so he is God's surety to us, for the performance of his promises. Christ was the surety of the first covenant (saith one), to pay the debt; of the second covenant, to perform the duty.

Ver. 23. *By reason of death*] Neither their holiness nor learning could privilege them from death's impartial stroke. *Non te tua plurima Pantheu, labentem texit pietas.* All our learning also is soon refuted with one black *theta*, which understanding us not, snappeth us unrespectively without distinction, and putteth at once a period to our reading and to our being.

Ver. 24. *He continueth ever*] What need then is there of a vicar, as the pope will needs be styled?

An unchangeable] Gr. ἀπαράβατον, impassable. He needeth no successor.

Ver. 25. *To the uttermost*] Perpetually and

perfectly, so as none shall need to come after him to finish what he hath begun. He is a thorough Saviour, a Saviour *in solidum*, and doth not his work to the halves. How blasphemous then is that direction of the Papists to dying men, *Conjunge, Domine, obsequium meum cum omnibus quæ Christus passus est pro me*: Join, Lord, mine obedience with all those things that Christ hath suffered for me.

Ver. 26. *Who is holy*] As the high priest of old, Lev. xxi. 18; Exod. xxviii.

Harmless] Without any birth-blot.

Undefiled] Free from actual pollution, without original blemish or actual blot, 1 Pet. i. 19.

Higher than the heavens] That is, than the angels, those heavenly courtiers, Dan. x. 13.

Ver. 27. *Who needeth not daily*] καθ᾽ ἡμέραν. Or, on a certain day of the year, *sc.* at the feast of the expiations, Levit. xvi. 29; see Heb. x. 1.

First for his own sins] Else how could he stand before God for others? the priests therefore had their laver wherein to wash, before they offered any man's sacrifice. The brazen altar stood without, the incense altar of gold within the sanctuary; to signify that our own lusts must be sacrificed ere we take upon us to pray for ourselves or others. David observeth this method, Psal. xxv. and Psal. li. He first gets pardon for himself, and then makes request for Sion.

Ver. 28. *For the law maketh*] As if the apostle should say, Shall I sum up and shut up all in a word? the law maketh men high priests which have infirmity, &c. Dull scholars must have it over and over. *Nunquam satis dicitur, quod nunquam satis discitur.* (Seneca.)

CHAPTER VIII.

Ver. 1. *Who is set on the right hand*] AND is therefore a King, as well as a Priest, as was Melchisedec.

Ver. 2. *A minister of the sanctuary*] λειτουργὸς. Or, a public officer, an agent for the saints, about holy things.

Which the Lord pitched] Christ's body was conceived in the virgin's womb, not by human generation, but by divine operation. See chap. ix. 11; John i. 14. He was the stone cut out of the mountain without hands, Dan. ii.; the rose of Sharon that grows without man's care, Cant. ii. 1.

Ver. 3. *Somewhat also to offer*] To wit, his own body, "an offering and a sacrifice to God for a sweet-smelling savour," Ephes. v. 2. By Mount Olivet stood the garden of Gethsemane, where Christ was taken and led into the city through the sheep-gate to be offered up like an innocent sheep, on the altar of his cross, for the sins of his people.

Ver. 4. *He should not be a priest*] Because not of the tribe of Levi, whose priesthood lasted so long as Christ lived on earth, and was done away by his death.

Ver. 5. *Of heavenly things*] So he calleth the mystery of Christ, showed hereby to Moses in the mount, and shadowed out to the people by the services of the tabernacle. All which were Christ in figure; the ceremonial law was their gospel; indeed then all was in riddles, Moses was veiled, and that saying was verified, *Et latet et lucet.*

Ver. 6. *Of a better covenant*] Or rather testament (διαθήκη and not συνθήκη), heaven being conveyed to the elect by legacy. It is part of God's testament to write his laws in our hearts, &c. All that he requires of us, is to take hold of his covenant, to receive his gift of righteousness, to take all Christ, &c., and this also he hath promised to cause us to do, ver. 10. Isa. lvi. 6; Rom. v. 17.

Ver. 7. *Had been faultless*] Such as had not been weak and unprofitable, chap. vii. 18; see the note there. If the people could have performed it, and have been perfected by it. If it could have conveyed grace, as ver. 10. The law may chain up the wolf, the gospel only changeth him; the one stops the stream, the other heals the fountain; the one restrains the practice, the other renews the principles. God therefore gave the law after the promise, Gal. iii. 19, to advance the promise.

Ver. 8. *For finding fault with them*] Or, finding fault with it, that is, with the covenant; he saith to them, "Behold, the days," &c. So Junius readeth and senseth it.

Ver. 9. *The covenant that I made*] He meaneth not here the covenant of grace made with Abraham, but circumcision, the legal ceremonies and services, that burden which neither they nor their fathers could bear.

When I took them by the hand] Teaching them to go, taking them by the arms, Hos. xi. 3, keeping their feet, 1 Sam. ii. 9, and leading them through the deep, as a horse in the wilderness, that they should not stumble, Isa. lxiii. 13.

And I regarded them not] Heb. Although I was an husband unto them, *q. d.* Yet nevertheless they forsook the guide of their youth, and forgat the covenant of their God, Jer. xxxi. 32; Prov. ii. 17. Therefore God regarded them not, or cared not for them, as the Greek hath it, ἠμέλησα. "If you forsake him, he will forsake you," 2 Chron. xv. 2.

Ver. 10. *I will put my laws*, &c.] God's covenant is to write his laws and promises "in his people's minds," so that they shall have the knowledge of them; "and in their hearts," so that they shall have the comfort, feeling, and fruition of them.

Ver. 11. *And they shall not teach*] The full performance of this promise is reserved to the life to come; when we shall need no ordinances, but shall be all taught of God.

For all shall know me] Not apprehensively only, but effectively, and with a knowledge of acquaintance, as the Church thought she should know him amidst all his austerities, Isa. lxiii. 16. "Art not thou our father?"

Ver. 12. *I will be merciful*] I will be propitious through Christ, the propitiation for our sins, 1 John ii. 2.

To their unrighteousness, and their sins and iniquities] All kinds and degrees of sins, Exod. xxxiv. 5; Micah vii. 17. All sins and blasphemies shall be forgiven to the sons of men, Matt. xii. 31. I was a blasphemer, saith Paul (that was a grievous sin against the first table), I was a persecutor (that was a great sin against the second table), yet I obtained mercy; why then should any one despair?

Will I remember no more] *Nihil oblivisci solet præter injurias*, saith Cicero of Cæsar. He was wont to forget nothing but shrewd turns. And of our Henry VI. it is storied that he was of that happy memory that he never forgat anything but injury. (Daniel Contin. by Trussel.) Let us but remember our sins with grief, and God will forget them. Let us see them to confession, and we shall never see them to our confusion. He is a forgiving God, Neh. ix. 31. None like him for that, Micah vii. 18. He doth it naturally, Exod. iv. 36; abundantly, Isa. lv. 7; constantly, Psal. cxxx. 4; John i. 27; Mal. iii. 6.

Ver. 13. *He hath made the first old*] He hath antiquated and abolished it. This the apostle often inculcates, because the Jews went about to establish their own righteousness, and it is a piece of Popery natural to us all, to think to go to heaven by our good meanings and good doings.

Is ready to vanish away] So is the old man in God's people; that is their comfort.

CHAPTER IX.

Ver. 1. *Then verily the first covenant*] HERE the apostle proveth what he had propounded, chap. viii. ver. 5, that this assertion might be sound, such as cannot be condemned, Tit. ii. 8.

Ordinances] Gr. δικαιώματα, justifications, viz. ceremonial, ritual, typical.

A worldly sanctuary] *i. e.* Terrene and shadowy, opposed to true and heavenly.

Ver. 2. *The first wherein was*, &c.] He speaks nothing of the outer court, as not pertinent to his present purpose. But there was both in the tabernacle and temple, the holy of holies, the sanctuary, and the court of the people: answerable whereunto are in man, "The spirit, soul, and body," 1 Thess. iii. 23. And as the cloud, 1 Kings viii. 10, 11, filled first the most holy place, and then the holy, and then the outer court, so doth the Holy Ghost renew the spirit of our minds, and then our wills and affections, and then the outward man.

Ver. 3. *And after the second veil*] This was not of any hard debarring matter, but easily penetrable then, and now also rent by Christ, to show our easy access to God with confidence "by the faith of him," Eph. iii. 11.

Ver. 4. *The golden censer*] Or the altar of incense, which though it belonged to the most holy place, yet was placed without the veil, Exod. xxx. 6, &c., that it might be of daily use, the sweet incense offered thereon easily piercing through the veil, and filling the most holy with its savour.

Wherein was the golden pot, &c.] In or near to the ark of the covenant was this golden pot of manna, and Aaron's rod, and the tables of the Testament, and the propitiatory or covering, and a crown of gold round about it. To insinuate thus much, saith one, that we must be like the ark of the covenant, being builded and reared up still toward the mark; not only when the Lord feedeth us with the sweet manna of his mercy, but also when he afflicteth us with the sharp rod of his correction, and always keep the tables of the Testament, which are the commandments, that by faith in Christ, who is the propitiation for our sins, we may obtain the golden crown of eternal life.

And the table of the covenant] It may here be objected, that, 1 Kings viii. 9, and 2 Chron. v. 10, it is said there was nothing in the ark save the two tables of stone. For answer, ἐν ᾖ, "in which," relates not to ark, but tabernacle; so Junius observeth and reconcileth. Calvin and Pareus give other answers. *Videsis*, their conceit is not to be misliked, that say the ark is the Church, the tables the word, the manna the sacraments, and the rod the discipline.

Ver. 5. *And over it the cherubims*] The ark covering the law within it, the mercy-seat upon it, and over them two cherubims covering one another; all these set forth Christ covering the curses of the law, in whom is the ground of all mercy, which things the angels desire to pry into, as into the pattern of God's unsearchable wisdom and goodness.

Ver. 6. *Were thus ordained*] Gr. κατεσκευασμένα, prepared, fitted, finished by the hand of the artificer, and therefore called worldly in a good sense, ver. 1.

Ver. 7. *For the errors*] Gr. ἀγνοήματα, The not knowings of the people; those errors that they could not help, and yet must else have answered for. *Ignorat sane improbus omnis*, saith Aristotle. Ignorance is the source of all sin, the very well-spring from which all wickedness doth ooze and issue. What will not an ignorant man do, who knows not but he may do anything? "The dark places of the earth are full of the habitations of cruelty," Psal. lxxiv. 20. Christ therefore expiated the ignorances of his people.

Ver. 8. *The way into the holiest*] That is, into heaven, typified thereby.

Was not yet made manifest] In regard of performance, and that evidence of faith and doctrine that is held forth under the gospel. The mystery of Christ was manifested piece-meal and parcel-wise, Heb. i. 1.

Ver. 9. *Which was a figure*] Gr. παραβολὴ, a parable, that is, such a form of service as intimated some greater matter than to the sense appeared; and called upon the people to look through the type to the truth of things, through the history to the mystery.

Ver. 10. *And carnal ordinances*] Such as carnal men might easily perform, and as were very suitable to the disposition of a carnal heart. Hence, Ezek. xx. 25, they are called "commandments that were not good," because they commanded neither virtue nor vices in themselves; and ill people rested in the outward acts.

Till the time of reformation] Gr. Of direction or correction, that is, evangelical and spiritual worship, that shall take place in the Church, till the times of the restitution of all things shall come at the last day, Acts iii. 21.

Ver. 11. *Of good things to come*] *i. e.* Of spirituals that were expected as things to come, when Christ came with a cornucopia, a horn of salvation in his hand. The Latins call prosperous things *Res secundas*, things to come.

A more perfect tabernacle] *i. e.* His human nature, not made with hands, nor of this building, that is, not by the power of nature, by the ordinary course of generation.

Ver. 12. *Neither by the blood of calves*] As the Levitical high priest did, ver. 7.

Having obtained] Gr. εὑρόμενος, having found. See Rom. iv. 1. The Latins also use *invenire* or *acquirere*, to find, for to obtain. See also Matt. xvi. 25. Christ overcame by suffering, and by his own blood purchased his Church, as an Aceldama, or field of blood.

Ver. 13. *The ashes of a heifer*] Gr. Ashes and cinders mixt together, as a monument of Christ's most base and utmost afflictions, and of our justification and sanctification through faith in his name. σποδὸς. *Sordidus cinis, et cum carbones extincti permisti sunt.*

Sprinkling the unclean] With a hyssop-bunch; to note that none can have comfort either by the merit or Spirit of Christ, without true mortification.

Ver. 14. *By the eternal Spirit*] That is, by his Deity, called the Spirit of holiness, Rom. i. 4, and the Spirit, 1 Tim. iii. 16, that gave both value and virtue to his death, both to satisfy and to sanctify.

Purge your conscience] This is that eternal redemption, ver. 12.

From dead works] The most specious performances of unregenerate persons are but dead works, because they proceed not from a principle of life, and have death for their wages, Rom. vi. A will written with a dead man's hand can hold no law. God will be served like himself.

Ver. 15. *For the redemption*] Here he showeth the reasons why it was needful that Christ should enter by his own blood, ver. 2, *sc.* to expiate our sins, and to possess us of heaven.

Ver. 16. *For where a testament is*] See the note on chap. viii. 6. Here the testator is Christ, heirs the saints, legacies the gifts of the Spirit, executor the Holy Ghost, witnesses apostles, martyrs, &c.

Ver. 17. *While the testator liveth*] For it is in his power to alter it at his pleasure, as reason requireth. Our Henry II. first crowned, and then cast off his eldest son Henry, not suffering him to be what himself had made him.

Ver. 18. *Was dedicated*] Or initiated to holy use, Levit. xvi. 15, 16, ἐγκεκαίνισται.

Ver. 19. *He took the blood*] See Exod. xxiv. 8.

And sprinkled both the book] Which, as it seemeth, was laid on the altar to be sanctified thereby. The very book of God is sprinkled with the blood of Christ, that it may be opened and of use to the faithful.

Ver. 20. *Saying, This is the blood,* &c.] A tropical and sacramental expression, whereunto our Saviour seemeth to allude in those words of his, "This cup is the new testament in my blood," &c. The sacraments of the Old Testament had a resemblance unto the New; but that was for works of the law, this is for remission of sins.

Ver. 21. *He sprinkled with blood*] This sprinkling had a fore-shadowing of the sprinkling of the blood of Jesus Christ, 1 Pet. i. 2, Isa. lii. 15; by his finger, that is, by his Spirit, Luke xi. 20, with Matt. xii. 28.

Ver. 22. *Purged with blood*] Which yet of itself impureth and fouleth.

Ver. 23. *But the heavenly things*] Those spiritual good things set forth by the types of the law; or the Church under the gospel, called Jerusalem that is above, &c.

Ver. 24. *To appear in the presence*] As a lawyer appears for his client, opens the cause, pleads the cause, and it is carried, ἐμφανισθῆναι.

Ver. 25. *Not that he should offer*] As Popish mass-mongers will have it. *Eamus ad communem errorem* (said Domitius Calderinus to his friends, when they persuaded him to go to mass, A. D. 1442), Let us go to the common error.

Ver. 26. *To put away sin*] To abrogate it, Heb. i. 18, to bind it in a bundle, seal it up in a bag, Dan. ix. 24, cast it behind him as cancelled obligations, Mic. vii., blot out the black handwriting with the red lines of his blood drawn over it.

Ver. 27. *It is appointed*] Gr. ἀπόκειται, it lieth as a man's lot. *Stat sua cuique dies.* Our last day stands, the rest run. The Jews at this day pray (such is their blindness) for the dead, that that bodily death may serve as an expiation of all his sins. (Leo Moden. Rites of Jews.)

But after this the judgment] Every man's death's day is his doomsday. Many of the Fathers held that men's souls were not judged till the last day. Which opinion is as contrary to purgatory (for which Bellarmine allegeth it) as the truth.

Ver. 28. *The second time without sin*] Imputed to him, as Isa. liii. 6; 2 Cor. v. 21. See the note there.

CHAPTER X.

Ver. 1. *A shadow of good things,* &c.] THAT is, of Christ, saith one. When the sun is behind, the shadow is before; when the sun is before, the shadow is behind. So was it in Christ to them of old. This Sun was behind, and therefore the law or shadow was before; to us under grace the Sun is before, and so now the ceremonies of the law, these shadows, are behind, yea, vanished away.

Ver. 2. *No more conscience of sin*] Christ, though he took not away death, yet he did the sting of death, so though he took not away sin, yet he did the guilt of sin.

Ver. 3. *Made of sins every year*] A solemn confession of them, and what great need they had of a Saviour to expiate them, laying their hands on the head of the sacrifice, in token that they had in like sort deserved to be destroyed.

Ver. 4. *Should take away sins*] And so pacify conscience; for sin is to the conscience as a mote to the eye, as a dagger to the heart, 2 Sam. xxiv. 10, as an adder's sting to the flesh, Prov. xxiii. 32.

Ver. 5. *But a body hast thou prepared*] A metaphor from mechanics, who do artificially fit one part of their work to another, and so finish the whole, κατηρτίσω. God fitted his Son's body to be joined with the Deity, and to be an expiatory sacrifice for sin.

Ver. 6. *Thou hast had no pleasure*] viz. As in the principal service and satisfaction for sin.

Ver. 7. *Lo, I come*] As an obedient servant bored through the ear, Exod. xxi., with Psal. xl. 6, 7, wise and willing to be obsequious. *Servus est nomen officii*, a servant is the master's instrument, and ὅλως ἐκείνου, saith Aristotle, wholly at his beck and obedience.

It is written of me] Christ is author, object, matter, and mark of Old and New Testament. Therefore if we will profit thereby, we must have the eyes of our minds turned toward Christ, as the faces of the cherubims were toward the mercy-seat.

Ver. 8. *Which are offered by the law*] To the great cost and charge of the offerers. This we are freed from, and are required no more than to cover God's altar with the calves of our lips.

Ver. 9. *Lo, I come*] True obedience is prompt and present, ready and speedy, without shucking and hucking, without delays and consults, Psal. cxix. 60.

He taketh away the first] Clear consequences drawn from Scripture, are sound doctrine, Matt. xxii. 32. See the note there.

Ver. 10. *By the which will*] That is, by the execution of which will, by the obedience of Christ to his heavenly Father.

Ver. 11. *Take away sin*] *Separando auferre*, sunder it from the soul, strike a parting blow betwixt them, περιελεῖν. *Undique tollere.*

Ver. 12. *But this man*] Opposed to the plurality of Levitical priests. One sacrifice, and once for ever, not many and often, as they. And he sat down, when as they stood daily offering oftentimes. Note the antithesis, and Christ's precellency.

On the right hand of God] Which he could

not have done if he had not expiated our sins. John xvi. 10, " Of righteousness, because I go to my Father." He could not have gone to his Father if he had not first fulfilled all righteousness, and fully acquitted us of all our iniquities.

Ver. 13. *Expecting till his enemies*] Admire and imitate his patience. The God of peace shall tread Satan and the rest under our feet shortly, Rom. xvi. 20.

Ver. 14. *He hath perfected*] He would not off the cross till all was finished.

Ver. 15. *The Holy Ghost also witnesseth*] viz. By inspiring the penmen, 2 Tim. iii. 16, acting and carrying them into all truth, 2 Tim. i. 21, as it were by a holy violence, φερόμενοι.

Ver. 16. *I will put my laws*] See the note on Heb. viii. 10.

Ver. 17. *Will I remember no more*] Therefore there needs not any repetition of a sacrifice for sin in the New Testament.

Ver. 18. *Where remission of sin is*] viz. An impletory remission, as now in the New Testament, not a promissory, as under the Old.

Ver. 19. *To enter into the holiest*] viz. By our prayers, which pierce heaven and prevail with God.

Ver. 20. *By a new*] Fresh, and as effectual at all times as if Christ were but newly sacrificed for us. *Tam recens mihi nunc Christus est, ac si hac hora fudisset sanguinem*, saith Luther. Christ is even now as fresh to me as if this very hour he had shed his precious blood. πρόσφατον, *Recens mactatus.*

Which he hath consecrated, or new made for us] Paradise had a way out, but none that ever we could find in again. Heaven hath now a way in (*sc.* this new and living, or life-giving, way, a milky way to us, a bloody way to Christ), but no way out again.

Through the veil, that is, his flesh] Whereby we come to God, dwelling bodily therein. Like as where I see the body of a man, there I know his soul is also, because they are not severed; so is it here. The veil or curtain in the sanctuary did hide the glory of the holy of holies; and withal ministered an entrance into it for the high priest.

Ver. 21. *Over the house of God*] As Jehoiadah was over the temple, presided and commanded there, 2 Kings ii. 5. All power is given to Christ both in heaven and earth, for our behoof and benefit.

Ver. 22. *Let us draw near*] Come, for the Master calleth, Mark x. 49.

With a true heart] That is, with a heart truly and entirely given up to God, uprightly propounding God's service in prayer, and that out of a filial affection, delighting to do his will, and therefore well content to wait, or, if God see good, to want what it wisheth, desirous rather that God's will be done than our own, and that he may be glorified though we be not gratified; acknowledging the kingdom, power, and glory to be his alone. This is a true heart.

In full assurance of faith] πληροφορία. Not with a quarter or half wind, but with full assurance, such a gale of faith as fills the sails of the soul, and makes it set up its top-gallant, as it were.

Having our hearts sprinkled, &c.] Faith ever purgeth from sin, and worketh repentance from dead works.

Ver. 23. *Without wavering*] Gr. ἀκλινῆ, without tilting or tossing to one side or other. This amounts to more than that conjectural confidence of the Popish *dubitanei*, and that common faith that holds men in suspense, and hangs between heaven and earth as a meteor.

Ver. 24. *And let us consider*] Christians must study one another's cases, the causes and cure of their spiritual distempers, solicitous of their welfare.

To provoke unto love] To whet on, as Deut. vi. 7, to sharpen and extimulate, as Prov. xxvii. 17, to rouse and raise up their dull spirits, as 2 Pet. ii. 13, to set an edge on one another, as boars whet their tusks one against another, saith Nazianzen, ὡς ὕων ὀδόντες ἀλλήλους θήξαντες.

Ver. 25. *Not forsaking*] Schism is the very cutting asunder of the very veins and arteries of the mystical body of Christ. We may not separate, but in case of intolerable persecution, heresy, idolatry, and Antichristianism.

The assembling of ourselves together] ἐπισυναγωγὴ, in Church assemblies and Christian meetings, as ever we look for comfort at the coming of our Lord Jesus Christ, and our gathering together (the same word as here) unto him, 2 Thess. ii. 1; the day whereof approacheth, as in this text. Christ will come shortly to see what work we make in this kind.

As the manner of some is] It was then, it was afterwards, and is still in these siding and separating times. The Donatists made a horrible rent for the life of Cæcilian. So did divers others for the pride and profaneness of Paulus Samosatenus. But never was there any schism so causeless and senseless as that of our modern sectaries.

Ver. 26. *For if we sin wilfully*] Against the grace of the gospel, despising and despiting it, as those that fall into the unpardonable sin. Some good souls by mistakes of this text have been much afflicted, as Master John Glover. Other odious apostates have utterly despaired. Others of the ancients have unworthily cashiered this Epistle out of the canon, because of this passage.

There remaineth no more sacrifice] For sins against the law, though against knowledge, there was an atonement, Lev. vi. 1, though it were for perjury; but for this sin against the gospel, that repudiates the remedy, there is no sacrifice; abused mercy turns into fury.

Ver. 27. *Fearful looking for*] Though judgment be not speedily executed, yet it is certainly to be expected. Winter never rots in the air, or dies in the dam's belly, as they say. Could but men foresee what an evil and a bitter thing sin is, they durst not but be innocent.

Ver. 28. *He that despised*] i. e. He that with a high hand violated it, or fell into any capital crime, and it came to light, died without mercy.

As for those heinous offences, that not being discovered, and sufficiently proved, came not under the Judge's cognizance, the Lord, for the easing of men's consciences, and for the saving of their lives, appointed the yearly feast of expiations, Levit. xvi. 29.

Ver. 29. *Who hath trodden under foot*] Respecting him no more than the vilest and filthiest dirt in the street, or the most abject thing in the world, as Ambrose expounds it; he disdains to receive benefit by Christ's propitiatory and expiatory sacrifice, he would not if he might, he is so Satanized. King Henry VI., going against Richard Duke of York (that ambitious rebel), offered them a general pardon. (Speed. 898.) This was rejected them, and called " A staff of reed," or "glass-buckler." In Ket's conspiracy, when King Edward VI.'s pardon was offered to the rebels by a herald, a lewd boy turned toward him his naked posteriors, and used words suitable to that gesture. (Sir John Hayward.) Desperate apostates deal as coarsely with Christ; they hold him for a scorn, as an offender that is carted, Heb. vi. 6.

The blood of the covenant] That is, the blood of Christ, whereby the covenant is sealed, the Church purchased, the atonement procured, and heaven opened for our more happy entrance.

Wherewith he was sanctified] By external profession, and by participation of the sacraments.

An unholy thing] Gr. A common profane thing, as if it were the blood of a common thief, or unhallowed person, yea, or of a dead dog. In the Passover they sprinkled the door and lintel with blood, but not the threshold, to teach them that they must not tread upon the blood of Jesus, as they do in a high degree that sin against the Holy Ghost.

And hath done despite, &c.] Spitting at him their hellish venom, persecuting and blaspheming his immediate effect, work, and office; and this out of desperate malice and desire of revenge, without any colour of cause or measure of dislike. One that had committed this sin, wished that his wife and children and all the world might be damned together with him.

Ver. 30. *I will recompense*] And if God will avenge his elect, Luke xviii. 7, how much more his Son and his Spirit!

Ver. 31. *It is a fearful thing*] For who knoweth the power of his anger? even according to thy fear is thy wrath, Psal. xc. 11. A melancholy man can fancy vast and terrible fears, fire, sword, racks, strappadoes, scalding lead, boiling pitch, running bell-metal, and this to all eternity; yet all these are nothing to that wrath of God which none can either avoid or abide.

Ver. 32. *But call to remembrance*] q. d. You cannot utterly fall away, as those above mentioned; forasmuch as you have given good proof already of the reality of your graces.

After ye were illuminated] Till they had a sight of heaven they could not suffer; but no sooner out of the water of baptism, but they were presently in the fire of persecution.

Ver. 33. Made a gazing-stock] Gr. θεατρι-ζόμενοι, set upon a theatre; take it either properly, or metaphorically, both befell Christians. See 1 Cor. iv. 9.

Ye became companions of them] Sympathy hath a strange force; as we see in the strings of an instrument; which being played upon (as they say), the strings of another instrument are also moved with it. (Dr Sibbs.) After love hath once kindled love, then the heart being melted is fit to receive any impression. Two spirits warmed with the same heat, will easily solder together.

Ver. 34. For ye had compassion] Gr. Ye sympathized. See the note on ver. 33.

And took joyfully] The joy of the Lord was their strength, as it was theirs, Acts v. 41, who took it for a grace to be disgraced for Christ.

The spoiling of their goods] If a heathen could say when he saw a sudden shipwreck of all his wealth, Well, Fortune, I see thou wouldest not have me to be a philosopher; should not we, when called to quit our moveables, say, Well, I see that God would have me to lay up treasure in heaven, that is subject neither to vanity nor violence?

Knowing in yourselves] Not in others, in books, &c., but in your own experience and apprehension, in the workings of your own hearts.

That ye have in heaven] When we lose anything for God, he seals us a bill of exchange of better things, or a double return. He will recompense our losses, as the king of Poland did his noble servant Zelislaus; having lost his hand in his wars, he sent him a golden hand. These Hebrews had lost their goods, but not their God. Here is the dry rod blossoming.

Ver. 35. Cast not away your confidence] Sith it is your shield and buckler, Eph. vi. 16; but if battered with temptations, beat it out again. Demosthenes was branded with the name of Ριψασπις, one that had lost his buckler.

Ver. 36. For ye have need of patience] Whereas they might object, But where is this recompense you tell us of? Oh, saith he, you have need of patience to wait God's time of recompense. Good men find it oft more easy to bear evil than to wait till the promised good be enjoyed. The spoiling of their goods required patience, but this more than ordinary.

That after ye have done the will of God] viz. By suffering it, and long-suffering, till he reward it.

Ver. 37. For yet a little while] Tantillum, tantillum, adhuc pusillum. A little, little, little while, ἔτι γὰρ μικρὸν ὅσον, ὅσον. God's help seems long, because we are short. Were we but ripe, he is full ready. Hence this ingemination, " he that shall come, will come," &c., q. d. he will, he will, his mind is always upon it, he is still a coming to deliver. With this sweet promise Rev. Mr Whatley comforted himself a little before his death. And Bishop Jewel, persuading many to patience, oft said, hæc non durabunt ætatem, this is but for awhile. (Mr Leigh's Annotat.)

Ver. 38. Now the just shall live by faith] In the want of feeling; he shall rest upon God in the fail of outward comforts, as the believing Jews were to do in the Babylonish captivity, Hab. ii. 4, quoted here by the apostle, though with some variation of words.

But if any man draw back] Gr. ὑποστείληται. Steal from his colours, run from his captain, revolt from Christ, turn renegado, relinquishing his religion, as did Julian, Lucian, and other odious apostates.

My soul shall have no pleasure] Christ hath no delights in dastards, turn-coats, run-a-ways, he will not employ them so far as to break a pitcher, or bear a torch, Judg. vii. 7. Baldwin the French lawyer, that had religionem ephemeram, as Beza said of him, for every day a new religion, being constant to none, became Deo hominibusque quos toties fefellerat invisus, hated of God and men, whom he had so oft mocked. Theodoric, an Arian king, did exceedingly affect a certain deacon, although an orthodox. This deacon thinking to ingratiate, and get preferment, became an Arian. Which when the king understood, he changed his love into hatred, and caused the head to be struck from him, affirming that if he kept not his faith to God, what duty could any one expect from him? (Melch. Adam.)

Ver. 39. Who draw back unto] Apostates have martial law, they run away but into hell-mouth. A worse condition they cannot likely choose unto themselves; for they are miserable by their own election, Jonah ii. 8, and are wholly destined to utter destruction. Transfugas arboribus suspendunt, saith Tacitus of the old Germans; they hang up run-a-ways. And transfugas, ubicunque inventi fuerint, quasi hostes interficere licet, saith the civil law. Run-a-ways are to be received as enemies, and to be killed wherever they be found.

To the saving of the soul] Gr. εἰς περιποίησιν ψυχῆς, to the giving of the soul. A metaphor from merchants, who either get more or lose what they have; or else haply from gamesters, who keep a stake in store, however the world go with them.

CHAPTER XI.

Ver. 1. Now faith is the substance] HAVING mentioned the life of faith, chap. x. 38, and the end of faith (or the reward of it, 1 Pet. i. 9), the salvation of the soul, ver. 39, he now descends to the description of this glorious grace, James ii. 1, and saith that it is the substance or subsistence or basis and foundation of things hoped for. It is the same that our author had called confidence, chap. x. 35. Polybius, speaking of Horatius' keeping the field against the enemy's forces, saith, that the enemies more feared his ὑπόστασις (the word here used), his confident binding upon the victory, than his strength. Faith is the vital artery of the soul (saith one), Hab. ii. 4, and by the eye of it, through the perspective glass of the promises, a Christian may see into heaven. Faith doth antedate glory; it doth substantiate things not seen. Faith altereth the tenses, and putteth the future into the present tense, Psal. lx. 6. It is reported of the crystal that the very touching of it quickeneth other stones and puts a lustre and beauty upon them. (Gul. Parisiens.) This is true of faith; it makes evil things present, far off; and good things far off, present.

The evidence of things, &c.] The index, ἔλεγχος, or the clear conviction by disputation, or by making syllogisms from the word. Indeed it is the word (to speak properly) that is the convincing evidence of things not seen; but because the word profiteth not further than it is mingled with faith in the heart, therefore that which is due to the word is here ascribed to faith.

Ver. 2. *The elders obtained*, &c.] Gr. ἐμαρτυρήθησαν, were attested unto; and are here eternalized in this notable chapter, this little book of martyrs, as one fitly calleth it. Faith honoureth God, and gives him a testimonial, John iii. 33, such as is that Deut. xxxii. 4. God therefore honoureth faith, according to 1 Sam. ii. 30, and gives it his testimonial, as here in this truly-named golden legend.

Ver. 3. *Through faith we understand*] It is the nature of faith to believe God upon his bare word, and that against sense in things invisible, and against reason in things incredible. Sense corrects imagination, reason corrects sense, but faith corrects both. *Aufer argumenta ubi fides quæritur. Verba philosophorum excludit simplex veritas Piscatorum*, saith Ambrose. I believe, and that is enough, though I cannot prove principles and fundamentals of faith.

That the worlds were framed] Gr. κατηρτίσθαι, *affabre facta*, "were neatly made up."

By the word of God] By that one word of his, *Fiat*, Let it be so and so. By the way, take notice, that faith here described is taken in a large sense, as it hath not the promises only, but the whole word of God for its object. Look how the Israelites with the same eyes and visive faculty wherewith they beheld the sands and mountains, did look upon the brazen serpent also, but were cured by fastening upon that alone; so by the same faith whereby we are justified, we understand that the worlds were framed by the word of God, and believe all other truths revealed; and yet faith as it justifieth looks upon Christ alone, not knowing anything here but Christ and him crucified, as is well observed by a learned divine.

Were not made of things, &c.] Of any pre-existent matter, as Plato held. See my notes on Gen. i. 1.

Ver. 4. *A more excellent sacrifice*] Good actions and good aims make a man good in the sight of God. Cain may offer as well as Abel. Doeg may set his foot as far within the sanctuary

as David, the Pharisee as the publican, but with different success.

God testifying of his gifts] By fire from heaven, or some other visible expression of his gracious acceptation, whereby Abel's faith was confirmed touching life and salvation in Christ. Paulus Phagius tells us out of the Rabbins, that a face of a lion was seen in the heavenly fire inflaming the sacrifice. (Annot. in Chal. Paraphr.) Which (if it be true) did probably shadow out the "Lion of the tribe of Judah," of whom all the sacrifices were types.

Being dead yet speaketh] λαλεῖται, or, is yet spoken of, being registered for the first martyr in the Old Testament, as Stephen was in the New, and as Mr Rogers was here in the Marian persecution.

Ver. 5. *By faith Enoch was translated*] μετετέθη, or carried from one place to another. He changed his place, but not his company, for he still walked with God, as in earth, so in heaven.

That he should not see death] The Arabic version addeth, he was translated into paradise, where a plentiful amends was made him for that which he wanted of the days of the years of the lives of his fathers, in the days of their pilgrimage, Gen. xlvii. 9.

And was not found] And yet the Lord killed him not, as the Chaldee hath, Gen. v. 24, but took him up in a whirlwind, say the Hebrew doctors, as Elijah was. He was changed as those shall be that are found alive at Christ's second coming, 1 Cor. xv. 51, the soul and body being separated, and in a moment reunited. *Subitus erit transitus a natura corruptibili in beatam immortalitatem*, saith Calvin there.

That he pleased God] εὐηρεστηκέναι, he walked with God in all well-pleasing, being fruitful in every good work, Col. i. 10. Hence that testimony given him by his own conscience, that he gave God good content.

Ver. 6. *But without faith*] That is, without Christ, in whom the Father is well-pleased, John xiv. 6.

For he that cometh to God] sc. *Forma pauperis*, that cometh a begging to him in the sense of his own utter indigence, as Jacob's sons came to Joseph, and as the Egyptians hard bestead came to him, saying, "We will not hide it from my lord, how that our money is spent," &c., Gen. xlvii.

Must believe that he is] Zaleucus, law-giver of the Locrians, speaketh thus in the proem to his laws, *Hoc inculcatum sit, esse Deos*, let this be well settled in men's minds that there is a Deity, and that this Deity will reward the devout. But what an odd conceit was that of the Cretians, to paint their Jupiter without either eyes or ears! And what an uncertainty was she at that prayed, *O Deus quisquis es, vel in cælo, vel in terra*, O God, whoever thou art, for whether thou art, and who thou art, I know not. (Medea.) This uncertainty attending idolatry caused the heathens to close up their petitions with that general *Diique*

Deæque omnes, Hear, all ye gods and goddesses. (Servius in Geor. lib. 1.) And those mariners, Jonah i. 5, every man to call upon his God; and lest they might all mistake the true God, they awaken Jonah to call upon his God. Christian petitioners must settle this, that their God is *Optimus, Maximus*, such in himself, and such toward them, as he stands described in his holy word.

Ver. 7. *Moved with fear*] Opposed to the security of the old world, who would know nothing till the very day that the flood came, Matt. xxiv. Noah trembled at God's judgments, whilst they hanged in the threatenings; and was no less affected than if himself had been endangered. See the like in Habakkuk, after that he threatened the Chaldeans, chap. iii. 16, and in Daniel, chap. iv. 19. Noah took things foretold him by God by the right handle, as the word εὐλαβηθεὶς properly signifieth.

By the which he condemned the world] Of deep and desperate security, that dead lethargy whereinto sin and Satan had cast them. Their heathen posterity in scorn termed him Prometheus; and feigned him to be chained to Caucasus with a vulture feeding upon his entrails, in regard of his foretelling the flood, and providing an ark to escape it, near the mountain Caucasus.

And became heir] Heir-apparent; he was hereby evidently declared to be such.

Ver. 8. *When he was called*] A man may follow God dryshod through the Red Sea. He is to be obeyed without sciscitation, with a blind obedience. Abraham winked, as it were, and put his hand into God's, to be led whithersoever he pleased. *Magnus est animus, qui se Deo tradidit; pusillus et degener qui obluctatur.* (Seneca.) That is a brave man indeed that can wholly resign himself up to God—*Quo fata trahunt, retrahuntque, sequamur.* (Virgil.)

Ver. 9. *He sojourned in the land*] There he had his commoration, but in heaven his conversation, content to dwell in tents till he should fix his station above.

With Isaac and Jacob] Perhaps together, as near neighbours. When Abraham parted with Lot, he would part with him no further than the right hand is from the left, Gen. xiii. 9. There is singular comfort in the society of saints.

Ver. 10. *Which hath foundations*] Heaven hath a foundation, earth hath none; but is hanged upon nothing, as Job speaketh. Hence things are said to be *on* earth, but *in* heaven.

Whose builder and maker] Gr. Whose cunning artificer and public workman. God hath bestowed a great deal of skill and workmanship upon the third heaven.

Ver. 11. *Because she judged him*, &c.] At first she laughed, through unbelief, at the unlikelihood; but afterward she bethought herself, and believed. This latter is recorded, the former pardoned. So Gen. xviii. 12, "Sarah laughed within herself, saying, After I have waxen old shall I have pleasure, my lord being old also?" Here was never a good word but one, viz. that

she called her husband lord, and this is recorded to her eternal commendation, 1 Pet. iii. 6. Isaac then was not a child of nature, but of the mere promise; so are all our graces. We bring forth good things, as Sarah's dead womb brought forth a child.

Ver. 12. *As the stars*, &c.] The seed of Abraham (saith one) are of two sorts. Some are visible members of a Church, yet have earthly hearts, dry and barren as the sand. Others as the stars of heaven, of spiritual hearts, minding things above.

Ver. 13. *And embraced them*] Gr. Saluted them, kissing Christ in the promises, and interchangeably kissed of him, Cant. i. 1, being drawn together (as the word signifies) by mutual dear affection. ἀσπασάμενοι *ab à simul et* σπάω, *traho.*

Ver. 14. *That they seek a country*] *Fugiendum est ad clarissimam patriam; ibi pater, ibi omnia.* Away, home to our country, saith one, there is our Father, there is our all, saith Plotin. (ap. Aug. de Civ. Dei). To die, is, in Bernard's language no more than *repatriasse*, to go home again.

Ver. 15. *If they had been mindful*] But to that they had no mind at all, because there idolatry too much prevailed, Joshua xxiv. 2; Gen. xxxi. 19, yet not so much as among the Canaanites, Deut. xii. 31.

Ver. 16. *God is not ashamed*] But honoureth them as his confederates, because for his cause they renounced the world. No man ever did or suffered anything for God that complained of a hard bargain.

Ver. 17. *Abraham when he was tried*] Of ten trials which Abraham passed, this last was the sorest. No son of Abraham can look to escape temptations when he seeth that bosom in which he desireth to rest so assaulted with difficulties.

Offered up his son Isaac] Ready he was so to have done, and therefore it is reputed and reckoned as done indeed, 2 Cor. viii. 12. See the note there.

Ver. 18. *Of whom it was said*] This was one of those many promises that Abraham might think were all lost in the loss of his Isaac. Never was gold tried in so hot a fire.

Ver. 19. *That God was able*] He founded his faith upon God's fidelity and omnipotency. These are the Jachin and the Boaz, the two main pillars whereupon faith resteth.

Ver. 20. *By faith Isaac blessed*] Patriarchal benedictions were prophetical; the blessing of godly parents is still very available for the good of their children; and justifying faith is not beneath miraculous in the sphere of its own activity and where it hath warrant of God's word.

Ver. 21. *When he was a dying*] The Spirit's motions are then many times quickest when natural motions are slowest; most sensible when the body begins to be senseless; most lively when the saints lie a-dying. The sun shines most amiably toward the descent. The rivers, the nearer they run to the sea, the sooner they are met by the tide. So here.

Ver. 22. *Gave commandment concerning*] He

died upon the promise, and held possession by his bones, to testify his firm hold of heaven.

Ver. 23. Hid three months of his parents] That they hid him no longer argued weakness of their faith, which yet is both commended and rewarded.

He was a proper child] ἀστεῖον, fair to God, Acts vii. 20, having a divine beauty and comeliness. Special endowments are a foretoken of special employment. The very heathen in choosing their kings had a special eye to bodily beauty. See 1 Sam. x. 23; xvi. 19; xvii. 42.

Not afraid of the king's commandment] Because unjust and impious. See the note on Acts iv. 19.

Ver. 24. When he was come to years] Gr. μέγας γενόμενος, grown a great one, and so knew what he did, understood himself sufficiently.

Refused to be called the son of Pharaoh's] And so to succeed in the kingdom (for we read not of any son that Pharaoh had), yea, in the kingdom of Ethiopia too; for being sent on his foster-father's quarrel against the king of Ethiopia, histories tell us that he afterwards married that king's daughter; for the which he was checked of his brother and sister, Numb. xii. 1. But he could have told them, that for denying the title of son of Pharaoh's daughter, he was soon after called Pharaoh's god, Exod. vii. 1; and what he lost in Ethiopia, was sufficiently made up to him when he became king in Jeshurun. Howsoever, *gratius ei fuit nomen pietatis quam potestatis*, as Tertullian saith of Augustus, he more prized piety than power.

Ver. 25. Choosing rather to suffer] The happiest choice that ever the good man made. It was a heavy charge that Elihu laid upon Job, that he had chosen iniquity rather than affliction, Job xxxvi. 21. The Church is said to come from the wilderness (of troubles and miseries), leaning on her beloved, Cant. viii. 5. The good soul will not break the hedge of any commandment to avoid any piece of foul way. *Quas non oportet mortes præeligere?* saith Zuinglius. What deaths had we not better choose, what punishment undergo, yea, what hell not suffer, rather than go against our consciences rightly informed by the good word of God?

The pleasures of sin for a season] Job fitly calleth sparks the sons of fire, being ingendered by it upon fuel, as pleasures are by our lusts upon the object. But they are not long-lived, they are but as sparks, they die as soon as begotten, they perish with the use, Col. ii. 22. Good God, said Lysimachus, for how short pleasure how great a kingdom have I lost! May not the voluptuous epicure say so much better? Oh what madmen are they that bereave themselves of a room in that city of pearl for a few carnal pleasures in this land of Cabul, or of dirt, as Hiram called the cities that Solomon had given him, 1 Kings ix. 13.

Ver. 26. Esteeming the reproach, &c.] Reproach is here reckoned as the heaviest part of Christ's cross. And if we can bear reproach for him, it is an argument we mean to stick to him, as the

servant in the law that was content to be bored in the ear would stick to his master.

Than the treasures in Egypt] Egypt for its power and pride is called Rahab, Psal. lxxxvii.: famous it was for its learning, 1 Kings iv. 30; Acts vii. 23; and is still for its fruitfulness; so that where the Nile overfloweth, they do but throw in the seed, and have four rich harvests in less than four months. Thence Solomon had his chief horses, 2 Chron. ix., and the harlot her fine linen, Prov. vii. 16, and yet Moses upon mature deliberation esteemed the reproach of Christ, &c. So did Origen choose rather to be a poor catechist in Alexandria than, denying the faith, to be with his fellow-pupil Plotinus in great authority and favour. To profess the truth whiles we may live upon it, this argues no truth; but to profess it when it must live upon us, upon our honours, profits, pleasures, this is praiseworthy, and argues not only truth, but strength of grace, 1 Sam. xiv. 26. It argued there was much power in that oath when none dared to touch one drop of that honey; so, to resist strong temptations, argues strong grace.

For he had respect, &c.] We may safely make any of God's arguments our encouragements; look through the cross, and see the crown beyond it, and take heart, *Quis non patiatur, ut potiatur?* Moses cast an eye (when he was on his journey) to cheer him in his way, ἀπέβλεπε, he stole a look from glory; he goes to his cordial, and renews his strength, gets fresh encouragement. Columbus, when his men were weary, and resolved to come back, besought them to go on but three days longer. They did so, and discovered America. Heaven is but a little before us. Hold out, faith and patience.

Ver. 27. As seeing him who is invisible] An elegant kind of contradiction. Let us study Moses' optics, get a patriarch's eye, see God, and set him at our right hand, Psal. xvi. This will support our courage, as it did Micaiah's, who, having seen God, feared not to see two great kings in their majesty.

Ver. 28. Through faith he kept the passover] It is the work of faith rightly to celebrate a sacrament. Speak therefore to thy faith at the Lord's supper, as Deborah did to herself, "Awake, awake, Deborah, awake, awake, utter a song."

Ver. 29. They passed through the Red Sea] Which threatened to swallow them, but yet preserved them. Faith will eat its way through the Alps of seemingly insuperable difficulties, and find unexpected out-gates.

As by dry land] Israel saw no way to escape here, unless they could have gone up to heaven, which because they could not, saith one, heaven comes down to them, and paves them a way through the Red Sea.

Assaying to do were drowned] Here that holy proverb was exemplified, "The righteous is delivered out of trouble, and the wicked cometh in his stead," Prov. xi. 8. See Isa. xliii. 3. God usually infatuateth those whom he intendeth to destroy, as these.

Ver. 30. *By faith the walls of Jericho*] So do daily the strongholds of hell, 2 Cor. x. 4. See the note there. Wherein, albeit the Lord requite our continual endeavours for the subduing of our corruptions during the six days of this life, yet we shall never find it perfectly effected till the very evening of our last day.

Ver. 31. *With them that believed not*] To wit, that gave not credit to those common reports of God and his great works, but despised them as light news, and refused to be at the pains of further inquiry.

When she had received the spies] Whom to secure she told a lie, which was ill done. The apostle commends her faith in God, but not her deceit toward her neighbour, as Hugo well observeth.

Ver. 32. *Of Gideon, of Barak, &c.*] Here the names only of sundry worthies of old time *per prœteritionem conglobantur*, are artificially wound up together for brevity' sake. All these were not alike eminent, and some of them such as, but that we find them here enrolled, we should scarce have taken them for honest men; yet by faith, &c. Christ carries all his, of what size or sort soever, to the haven of heaven, upon his own bottom, as a ship doth all the passengers that are therein to the desired shore.

Ver. 33. *Wrought righteousness*] Civil and military, spiritualized by faith and heightened to its full worth. The Scripture maketh it a great matter, that Abraham should have a child when he was a hundred years old, whereas Terah his father was 130 when he begat Abraham. But because Abraham had his child by faith, therefore it was a great matter. And so in all things whatsoever that we have, do, or suffer, if they be by faith, they are great things indeed.

Obtained promises] Faith winds itself into the promises, and makes benefit thereof. A bee can suck honey out of a flower, so cannot a fly do. Faith will extract abundance of comfort in most desperate distresses out of the precious promises, and gather one contrary out of another, honey out of the rock, &c., Deut. xxxii. 36.

Ver. 34. *Escaped the edge of the sword*] As David by the force of his faith escaped Saul's sword, Eliajah Ahab's, Elisha the Syrians', 2 Kings vi. &c., and divers of God's hidden ones at this day have escaped by a strange providence, when studiously sought after as sheep to the slaughter. See the Prefatory Epistle to Mr Shaw's Sermon.

Out of weakness were made strong] And here their strength was to sit still, as theirs was, Isa. xxx. 7. They thought their strength had been in the help of Egypt; but the prophet tells them, whatsoever strength they expect from Egypt they shall have it here. Your Egypt "is to sit still" (so the words may be read); by sitting still you shall have an Egypt; whatsoever succour you might think to have that way, you shall have it this way.

Ver. 35. *Women received*] As the Sareptan Shunammite, widow of Nain, &c. No such mid-wife as faith; it hath delivered even graves of their dead.

Others were tortured] Gr. ἐτυμπανίσθησαν, they were tympanized, distended, stretched upon the rack, as a sheep's-pelt is upon a drum-head. Others render it, "They were bastonaded or beaten with bars or cudgels to death," as if it were with drum-sticks.

Not accepting deliverance] On base terms; they scorned to fly away for the enjoyment of any rest, except it were with the wings of a dove, covered with silver innocency. As willing were many of the martyrs to die as to dine. The tormentors were tired in torturing Blandina. And, We are ashamed, O emperor! The Christians laugh at your cruelty, and grow the more resolute, said one of Julian's nobles. *Illud humiliter sublime et sublimiter humile, nisi in Christi Martyribus non videmus*, saith Cyprian. This the heathens counted obstinacy (Tertul. in Apolog.); but they knew not the power of the Spirit, nor the privy armour of proof that the saints have about their hearts.

That they might obtain a better resurrection] The resurrection they knew would recruit and rectify them. This held life and soul together. So Dan. xii. 3. These miserable caitiffs, saith Lucian (the atheist of the Christians of this time), have vainly persuaded themselves of a glorious resurrection, and hence their fool-hardy forwardness to die. Other of the heathens jeered the Christians, and told them they needed not to care for their lives, since they should rise again. Will you, said they, *rediturœ parcere vitœ*, spare your carcases that shall rise?

Ver. 36. *Of cruel mockings*] As Jeremiah, Amos, Elisha, "Go up, bald-pate, go up," &c. "To heaven, as they say" (but who will believe it?) "that your master Elijah did." So they mewed at David, mocked at Isaiah, chap. xxviii. 10 (the sound of the words, as they are in the original, carries a taunt), jeered our Saviour, Luke xvi. 14. See these Hebrews upon the stage, as mocking-stocks, chap. x. 33.

Ver. 37. *Were tempted*] ἐπειράσθησαν, or (as others read the words) They were burned. One saith that it was almost as great a miracle that Joseph did not burn when his mistress tempted him, as it was for the three children not to burn in the Babylonish fire. Luther was oft tempted to be quiet, with great sums of money and highest preferments. Julian by this means drew many from the faith.

In sheep-skins and goat-skins] That might have rustled in silks and velvets, if they would have yielded. *Sœpe sub attrita latitat sapientia veste.*

Afflicted, tormented] None out of hell were ever more afflicted than the saints, to the wonder and astonishment of the beholders.

Ver. 38. *Of whom the world*] They were fitter to be set as stars in heaven, and be before the Lord in his glory. The world was not worthy of their presence, and yet they were not thought worthy to live in the world.

Ver. 39. *Received not the promise*] viz. Of Christ's incarnation.

Ver. 40. *Some better thing*] i. e. Christ, that great mystery, as 1 Tim. iii. 16; that chief of ten thousand, &c.; that gift, John iv. 10; that benefit, 1 Tim. vi. 2.

CHAPTER XII.

Ver. 1. *With so great a cloud*] Or, cluster of witnesses, whose depositions we should hearken to, and rest in. Justin Martyr confesseth of himself, that seeing the pious lives and patient sufferings of the saints, he concluded that this was the truth they professed, and sealed with their blood. These, in things imitable, are as the cloud that led Israel; but in things unwarrantable (for in many things we fail all) as the black of the cloud, which whoso followeth with the Egyptians, is like to be drowned as they.

Let us lay aside every weight] ὄγκος, or burden, or swelth. He that runs in a race will not have a burden upon his back, or shut up himself in a strait-bodied suit.

The sin which doth so easily beset us] εὐπερίστατος, or that sticks so close to us, or that troubles and puzzles us, or that curbs and girds us in, that we cannot run at liberty. Inordinate passions (saith one) come like foul weather, before we send for them; they often prevent all action of the will; but good affections are so overlaid with sin (which compasseth us about), that if we gather not wind under their wing (so ponderous the flesh is) they cannot mount up to purpose.

Let us run with patience] This seems to be a contradiction (as one observeth), for running is active, patience passive; but he that here runs without patience never gets to the end of the race; for in the race of God's commandments, men have foul play; one rails, another stops him, &c.

The race] Gr. ἀγῶνα, the strife-race, for we must run and fight as we run, strive also to outstrip our fellow-racers.

Ver. 2. *Looking unto Jesus*] Gr. ἀφορῶντες, looking off those things that may either divert or discourage, and looking unto Jesus with loving and longing looks. A Persian lady being at the marriage of Cyrus, and asked how she liked the bridegroom? How? said she; I know not. I saw nobody but mine own husband. Saints have a single eye, an eye of adamant, which will turn only to one point, to Christ alone.

The author and finisher] The Alpha and Omega, the beginner and ender. In all other things and arts, *non est ejusdem invenire et perficere*, the same man cannot begin and finish. But Christ doth both, Phil. i. 5.

Endured the cross] Ran with courage, though he ran with the cross upon his back all the way.

Despising the shame] Whereof man's nature is most impatient. Christ shamed shame (saith an interpreter), as unworthy to be taken notice of,

in comparison of his design. So, according to his measure, did that nobleman, who when he came into jeering company of great ones, would begin and own himself for one of those they called Puritans. This was much better than that scholar in Queen's college, mentioned by Mr Burroughs, who professed he had rather suffer the torments of hell than endure the contempt and scorn of the Puritans.

Ver. 3. *For consider him*] Gr. ἀναλογίσασθε, *comparationem instituite*. Make the comparison betwixt Christ and yourselves, betwixt his sufferings and yours, and then you will see a difference. Our troubles are but as the slivers and chips of his cross. I am heartily angry (saith Luther) with those that speak of my sufferings, which if compared with that which Christ suffered for me, are not once to be mentioned in the same day.

Lest ye be wearied and faint] Gr. ἐκλυόμενοι, loosened, as the nerves are in a swoon or palsy; or, let go, as water spilt upon the ground. This to prevent keep your eye upon your Captain and that cloud before mentioned. There were in Greece certain fields called Palæstræ, where young men exercised themselves in wrestling, running, &c. In these were set up statues of sundry valiant champions, that the young men that ran or wrestled, might fix their eye upon them, and be encouraged. When Jerome had read the life and death of Hilarion, he folded up the book, and said, Well, Hilarion shall be the champion that I will follow.

Ver. 4. *Ye have not yet resisted*] q. d. You may do, and must look to do. And if you cannot endure words for Christ, how will you endure wounds? If you have run with the footmen, and they have tired you, how can ye contend with horses? Jer. xii. 5.

Striving against sin] That is, against sinners that persecute you, or the sin that doth so easily beset you, and solicit you to spare yourself, and rather to yield a little than to suffer so much. The tabernacle was covered over with red (and the purple-fathers tell us they take that habit for the same intent), to note that we must defend the truth even to the effusion of blood. If we cannot endure martyrdom (if called thereunto) and sweat a bloody sweat for Christ's sake, we cannot be comfortably assured that we are of his body. *Christo submittemus* (said that Dutch martyr) *sexcenta si nobis essent colla:* We will submit to Christ, though we should suffer never so many deaths for his sake. John Leaf, a young man burnt with Mr Bradford, hearing his own confession, taken before the bishop, read unto him, instead of a pen took a pin, and so pricking his hand, sprinkled the blood upon the said bill of his confession, willing the messenger to show the bishop that he had sealed the same bill with his blood already. See the story of William Pikes, Acts and Mon., p. 1853.

Ver. 5. *And ye have forgot the exhortation*] Or, have ye forgot the consolation?[1] Are the consolations of God small unto you? Job xv. 11.

---

[1] *Legenda hæc sunt cum interrogatione.* Pisc.

Do ye, instead of wrestling with God, wrangle with him, refusing to be comforted (as Rachel), out of the pettishness of your spirits, as he, Psal. lxxvii. 2? Will ye not, as children, eat your milk, because you have it not in the golden dish? Will ye be like the hedgehog, of which Pliny reporteth, that being laden with nuts and fruits, if the least filbert fall off, will fling down all the rest in a pettish humour, and beat the ground with her bristles.

Despise not thou the chastening] See my Love Tokens, p. 37. Count it not a light matter, a common occurrence, such as must be borne by head and shoulders, and when things are at worst, they will mend again. This is not patience but pertinacy, strength but stupidity, "the strength of stone, and flesh of brass," Job vi. 12. When Gallienus the emperor had lost the kingdom of Egypt, What? said he, *Sine lino Egyptio esse non possumus?* cannot we be without the hemp of Egypt? but shortly after he was slain with the sword. When the Turks had taken two castles in Chersonesus, and so first got footing in Europe, the proud Greeks said that there was but a hog-sty lost, alluding to the name of the castle. But that foolish laughter was turned within a while into most bitter tears. When Calais was lost under Queen Mary, those of the faction strove to allay the Queen's grief, saying that it was only a refuge for runagate heretics, and that no Roman Catholic ought to deplore, but rather rejoice at the damage :

> *At regina gravi jamdudum saucia cura,*
> *Vulnus alit venis—*

Nor faint when thou art rebuked] If we faint in the day of adversity, our strength is small, saith Solomon, Prov. xxiv. 10; and it is, *Non quia dura, sed quia molles patimur,* saith Seneca; not for that we suffer hard things, but because we are over-soft that suffer them. As is the man, so is his strength, said they to Gideon, Judg. viii. 21. Joseph's bow abode in strength, even when the iron entered into his soul, Gen. xlix. 24; and Job's stroke was heavier than his groaning, Job xxiii. 2. *Invalidum omne natura querulum,* saith Seneca : It is a weakness to be ever puling. See my Love Tokens.

Ver. 6. *For whom the Lord loves*] Whom he entirely loveth and cockereth above the rest of his children. That son in whom he is well pleased, saith Mercer on Prov. iii. 12, whom he makes his white boy, saith Theophylact here. See my Love Tokens.

And scourgeth every son] Lays upon them hard and heavy strokes. When Ignatius came to the wild beasts, Now, saith he, I begin to be a Christian. *Omnis Christianus crucianus,* saith Luther. And he hath not yet learned his A B C in Christianity, saith Bradford, that hath not learned the lesson of the cross. When Munster lay sick, and his friends asked him how he did, and how he felt himself, he pointed to his sores and ulcers (whereof he was full), and said, *Hæ*

sunt gemmæ et pretiosa ornamenta Dei, &c., These are God's gems and jewels wherewith he decketh his best friends, and to me they are more precious than all the gold and silver in the world. (Joh. Manl. loc. com.)

Ver. 7. *God dealeth with you,* &c.] Corrections are pledges of our adoption and badges of our sonship. One Son God hath without sin, but none without sorrow. As God corrects none but his own, so all that are his shall be sure to have it; and they shall take it for a favour too, 1 Cor. xi. 32.

Ver. 8. *Then are ye bastards*] *Qui excipitur a numero flagellatorum, excipitur a numero filiorum,* saith one. He that escapes affliction may well suspect his adoption. I have no stronger argument against the pope's kingdom, saith Luther, than this, *quod sine cruce regnat,* that he reigns without the cross. They have no changes, surely they fear not God.

Ver. 9. *And we gave them reverence*] *Pater est, si pater non esses,* &c., It is my father, &c. This cooled the boiling rage of the young man in Terence. Nicolas of Jenvile, a young French martyr, when he was condemned and set in the cart, his father coming with a staff would have beaten him; but the officers, not suffering it, would have struck the old man. The son crying to the officers, desired them to let his father alone, saying he had power over him to do what he would.

And live] For corrections of instruction (and God never chastiseth, but withal he teacheth, Psal. xciv. 12) are the way of life, Prov. vi. 23, and xv. 31. See my Love Tokens.

Ver. 10. *After their own pleasure*] To ease their stomachs, vent their choler, discharge themselves of that displeasure they have (and perhaps without cause) conceived against us. Not so the Lord; "Fury is not in me," saith he, Isa. xxvii. 4. Though God may do with his own as he pleaseth, yet he doth never over-do. For it goes as much against the heart with him, as against the hair with us; it is even a pain to him to be punishing, Lam. iii. 33.

That we might be partakers] Thus bitter pills bring sweet health, and sharp winter kills worms and weeds, and mellows the earth for better bearing of fruits and flowers. The lily is sowed in its own tears, and God's vines bear the better for bleeding. The walnut tree is most fruitful when most beaten, and camomile the more you tread it, the more you spread it. Aloes kill worms, and stained clothes are whitened by frosting.

Ver. 11. *The peaceable fruit of righteousness*] That crown of righteousness wrought out unto us by afflictions, 2 Cor. iv. 17. These are the preludes of our triumph, yea, a part of our salvation. Look therefore through the anger of God's corrections, saith one, to the sweetness of his love therein, as by a rainbow we see the beautiful image of the sun's light in the midst of the dark and waterish cloud. And look upon these afflictions as on so many wayward and touchy guests, which while they stay, watch every officer, but when they depart, they pay freely.

Unto them which are exercised thereby] Gr. exercised naked in the fencing-school, as invincible champions. By suffering they are made more able to suffer as well-beaten soldiers, or porters to the cross. Thus David was better able to bear with Shimei, because he was under that great affliction of Absalom's rebellion.

Ver. 12. *Lift up the hands*] Pluck up your good hearts, and buckle close to your business; how else will you run the race that is set before you? ver. 1. Gird up the loins of your minds; a drooping spirit makes no riddance of the way. Set all to rights, as the word ἀνορθώσατε signifieth.

Ver. 13. *Make straight paths*] Seek not by-ways (those highways to hell), leap not over the hedge of any commandment, so to escape any piece of foul way; but as those kine of the Philistines held straight on their way to Bethshemesh, 1 Sam. vi. 12, though they had calves at home; so let us to heaven, though we have divers things to divert us. "Let thine eyes look right on; and let thine eyelids look straight before thee," Prov. iv. 25.

Ver. 14. *Follow peace*] Gr. pursue it, though it flee from you. I am for peace (saith David), but when I speak of it, they are for war, Psal. cxx. 7.

And holiness] Or chastity, 1 Thess. iv. 4; such a holiness as is opposed to fornication and profaneness, ver. 16.

Without which] The article may be neuter; and then the sense is, without which following peace and holiness, or a holy peaceableness, none shall see God to their comfort.

Ver. 15. *Lest any man fail*] Or, fall short, as chap. iv. 1; see the note there. Short shooting loseth many a game; he that in a race lieth down ere he come to the goal, gets not the garland. Perseverance crowns all our virtues. But it is an easy thing to fall a napping with the foolish virgins (yea, the wise also slumbered), which will prove to our cost when God shall send forth summons for sleepers.

Lest any root of bitterness] Any scandalous sin to the corrupting of others and the corroding of our own consciences, and out of which we recover not without much ado, till we have felt what an evil and bitter thing sin is, as David did, Psal. li.

Ver. 16. *Fornicator or profane*] He instanceth in some roots of bitterness. Esau's profaneness appeared in these particulars: 1. In that he was no sooner asked for the birthright but he yielded. 2. That he parted with it for a trifle, a little red, red, as he called it in his haste and hunger. 3. That he did this, being, as he thought, at point of death. 4. That he went his way when he had done, as if he had done no such thing, he showed no sign of remorse or regret. Hence he is four or five several times branded with, "This is Edom." This is he that had a low esteem of spiritual privileges, that judged a jewel of greatest price worth forty pence.

Who for one morsel, &c.] Many such Edomites now-a-days that prefer earth before heaven; a swine-sty before a sanctuary, as the Gadarenes; their part in Paris before their part in Paradise, as that carnal cardinal. *Vale lumen amicum*, said Theotimus; Farewell eyes, if I may not drink and do worse, ye are no eyes for me. (Ambrose.) He would rather lose his sight than his sin; so will many rather part with heaven than with their lusts. Oh what madmen are these that bereave themselves of a room in that city of pearl for a few carnal pleasures, &c. Pope Sixtus V. sold his soul to the devil to enjoy the popedom for seven years.

Ver. 17. *For ye know how that afterward*] *Sero inquit Nero.*

Ad prærepta venit possessaque gaudia sero.

(Sueton. Ner. c. 49. Ovid. Epis. Hel.) Esau came too short because too late. Think of the uncertainty of the gales of grace, and be nimble.

He was rejected] ἀπεδοκιμάσθη, or, repulsed. For Isaac, when he saw that he had done unwilling justice in blessing Jacob, he durst not reverse the blessing, for he feared an exceeding great fear, Gen. xxvii. 33. Neither natural affection nor Esau's importunity could make him repent and repeal what he had done.

Though he sought it carefully with tears] Tears they were of discontent, for he cries and at same time threatens his brother Jacob. Some weep for sin, some for misery, some for joy, some for compassion, some for revenge and in hypocrisy, as Esau here, who rued his deed, but repented not his sin.

Ver. 18. *For ye are not come, &c.*] q. d. You are not under the law, but under grace, beware therefore of profaneness and licentiousness. For think you that God hath hired you to be wicked? are you delivered to do all these abominations? Jer. vii. 10. Ought you not to walk gospel-high? Phil. i. 27. Will not the angel (Christ) that goeth along with you, destroy you after that he hath done you good, if ye turn not and repent according to the rules of the law, the gospel? Exod. xxxiii. 2—4.

Ver. 19. *And the sound of a trumpet*] Showing the nature of God's law, to manifest God's will, men's sins, and to warn them of the wrath deserved; likewise to summon them to appear before the Judge.

The voice of words] That is, the delivery of the decalogue, called the words of the covenant, Exod. xxxiii. 28, the ten words.

Ver. 20. *For they could not endure*] This shows the nature and use of the law, contrary to that of the gospel. It is a killing letter, written in blood, holding forth justice only, and no mercy.

Ver. 21. *Moses said, I exceedingly*] This Paul might have by tradition, or rather by revelation, unless he gathered it from Exod. xix. 19, compared with Dan. x. 8, 16, 17, 19.

Ver. 22. *But ye are come to Mount*] And the

blessings that come out of Sion (grace and peace that come by Jesus Christ) are better than all other blessings of heaven and earth, Ps. cxxxiv. 3.

The heavenly Jerusalem] As Jerusalem was distinguished into two cities, the superior and the inferior; so is the Church into triumphant and militant; yet both make up but one city of the living God.

To an innumerable company] Gr. To myriads, or many ten thousands of angels. Some have said that they are 99 to one, in comparison of the saints; grounding their conceit upon the parable of the lost sheep, Luke xv.

Ver. 23. *To the general assembly*] Or public meeting of a whole country, as at a great assize, or some solemn celebrity. The Roman emperors raised up ample amphitheatres in a circular form, that the people sitting round about, might have a commodious sight of such pleasant spectacles as were set before them. That which Pompey erected was of such extent, that it was able to receive 40,000 men, as Pliny witnesseth. But oh what a glorious amphitheatre is that of heaven! What a stately congregation-house! *O præclarum diem cum ad illud animorum concilium cœtumque proficiscar, et cum ex hac turba et colluvione discedam!* (Cic. de Senectute.) Surely, if Cicero or some other heathen could say so, how much more may we exult and say, Oh that dear day when we shall go out of this wretched world, and wicked company, to that general assembly of holy and happy souls! And how should we in the mean while turn every solemnity into a school of divinity; as when Fulgentius saw the nobility of Rome sit mounted in their bravery, it mounted his meditation to the heavenly Jerusalem. And another, when he sat and heard a sweet concert of music, seemed upon this occasion carried up for the time beforehand to the place of his rest, saying very passionately, What music may we think there is in heaven! (Mr Esty, Art of Meditat., by Dr Hall.)

Which are written in heaven] In Jerusalem records were kept of the names of all the citizens, Psal. xlviii. 3; so in heaven. And as the citizens of Rome might not accept of freedom in any other city; so neither should we seek things on earth, as those whose names are written in the earth, Jer. xvii.

Ver. 24. *That speaketh better things*] Every drop whereof had a tongue to cry for vengeance; whence it is called bloods, in the plural, Gen. iv. 10. But the blood of sprinkling (so Christ's blood is here called, either in allusion to the blood of the paschal lamb sprinkled on the door-posts, Exod. xii. 7, or else to the sprinkling of that blood of the covenant described Exod. xxiv. 8, with Heb. ix. 18) speaketh reconciliation, peace, and eternal life.

Ver. 25. *See that ye refuse not,* &c.] Gr. παραιτήσησθε, that ye shift him not off by frivolous pretences and excuses, as those recusant guests did, Matt. xxii. It is as much as your souls are worth. Look to it therefore.

That speaketh from heaven] By his blood, word, sacraments, motions of his Spirit, mercies, &c. If we turn our backs upon such bleeding embracements, and so kick against his naked bowels, what will become of us? And mark, that he speaketh of himself, as one.

Ver. 26. *Whose voice then shook,* &c.] viz. When he gave the law; what shall he do when he comes to judgment?

Not the earth only, &c.] Not men only, but angels, who stand amazed at the mystery of Christ. As for men, they will never truly desire Christ till they are shaken, Hag. ii. 7. God's shaking ends in settling; it is not to ruin, but to refine us.

Ver. 27. *And this word, yet once more*] The apostle commenteth upon the prophet whom he citeth, and from that word of his, Yet once, concludeth the dissolution of the present frame of the world by the last fire, and the establishing of that new heaven and new earth, wherein dwelleth righteousness, 2 Pet. iii. 12, 13. The force of Scripture words is then well to be weighed by those that will draw therehence right consequences. And they have done singular good service to God and his Church that have employed their time and their talents for the finding out the sense of the text, by fishing out the full import and signification of the original words. In which kind learned Mr Leigh, by his Critica Sacra upon both Testaments, hath merited much commendation. And now much more on his late elaborate Annotations upon the New Testament, whereby I confess I have received much help in this review.

Ver. 28. *A kingdom which cannot be moved*] As the mighty monarchies of the world could; for those had their times and their turns, their ruin as well as their rise, so that now they live but by fame only. Not so the kingdom of heaven. You may write upon it the Venetian motto, *Nec fluctu, nec flatu movetur;* Neither winds nor waves can stir it. We must so endeavour after grace, as if it were to be gotten by labour, and not bestowed by favour; yet must we acknowledge it to be free, as if we had not laboured at all.

With reverence] Gr. With bashfulness, as in God's holy presence. See Deut. xxiii. 13.

Ver. 29. *A consuming fire*] viz. To profligate professors, ungirt Christians, Isa. xxxiii. 14. And whereas the apostle saith Our God, he means the God of Christians also (as well as of Jews) is a consuming fire, see Exod. xxiii. 20, with the note. As he is *Pater miserationum*, a Father of mercies to the penitent, so he is *Deus ultionum*, a God of vengeance to the rebellious. And as there is a legal and evangelical repentance, so also faith, to be exercised of all his people. There is an evangelical faith, which is in applying of Christ in the promises. There is also a legal faith, which consists in believing the threatenings and the terrors of the Lord. And if any would dwell safely with this devouring fire, let him read and practise that in Isa. xxxiii. 14, 15. Hypocrites shall be afraid, and as women's paint falls off when they come near the fire, so shall theirs.

CHAPTER XIII.

Ver. 1. *Let brotherly love continue*] It shall continue in heaven ; pity therefore but it should on earth. No such heaven upon earth, next unto communion with God, as the communion of saints.

Ver. 2. *Have entertained angels*] As Abraham and Lot, who pursued hospitality, as the apostle speaketh, Rom. xii. 13, and had such guests as they hoped not for. The Galatians received St Paul as an angel ; so did Cornelius entertain Peter. Every child of God is an earthly angel ; and by entertaining them, angels also (which are their guardians) are entertained. The philosopher told his friends when they came into his little low cottage, ἐντεῦθεν οὐκ ἄπεισι Θεοὶ, the gods are here with me. God and his angels are where the saints are.

Ver. 3. *Remember them that, &c.*] Learn hence, saith one, that it is no new thing for the world to put bonds on them, who seek to bring them out of bondage. It is very probable that Micaiah was that disguised prophet, who brought to Ahab the fearful message of displeasure and death for dismissing Benhadad, for which he ever after hated him, and held him in prison.

As being yourselves also in the body] Not the body of Christ, or the Church, as Calvin senseth it, but in the body of flesh and frailty, subject to like afflictions ; so Erasmus, Beza, Pareus, and others. Now such as these must be remembered, so ver. 7 and 16. Hence this chapter is called by a divine, the Chapter of Remembrances, or the Remembrancer's Chapter.

Ver. 4. *Marriage is honourable*] And yet say the Rhemists, upon 1 Cor. vii. 9, marriage of priests is the worst sort of incontinency. Is not this to play the Antichrist ?

And the bed undefiled] *Admonemus in ipso etiam matrimonio quandam esse scortationis speciem, siquis puro Dei dono pure et sancte non utatur, ad eum finem cujus causa est institutum,* saith Beza. The marriage-bed, though lawful, may be defiled by excess, &c., and a man may be an adulterer of his own wife.

God will judge] The Anabaptists of Germany inferred from hence that therefore men ought not to punish adulterers ; for God reserved them to his own judgment. (Joh. Manl. loc. com.) Two of them, Monetarius and Hetserus, were notorious whoremongers ; being a pair of such preachers, as Zedekiah and Ahab were, whom the king of Babylon roasted in the fire, because they committed adultery with their neighbours' wives and spake lies in God's name, &c., Jer. xxix. 22, 23. But what a bold man was Latimer, bishop of Worcester, who presented to Henry VIII., for a new-year's gift, a New Testament with a napkin, having this posie about it, " Whoremongers and adulterers God will judge."

Ver. 5. *Let your conversation*] Gr. τρόπος, your turnings and windings in the world for a livelihood. Do your business not out of a desire to get silver, ἀφιλάργυρος, but to humble yourselves by just labour.

Be content with such things] Not to be content, is to be covetous. If men cannot bring their means to their mind, let them bring their mind to their means. (Clem. Alex.) A little will serve to bear our charges till we come home to heaven. *Bonus paucis indiget.* See the note on 1 Tim. vi. 6—8. The contented man sits and sings,

*Hoc alii cupiant : liceat mihi, paupere cultu
　Securo, chara conjuge posse frui.*

For he hath said] Five times in Scripture is this precious promise renewed ; that we may press and oppress it, till we have expressed the sweetness out of it, Isa. lxvi. 11.

I will not forsake thee] Gr. οὐδὲ οὐ μὴ, I will not not not forsake thee. Leave us God may to our thinking, but forsake us he will not. Only we must put this and other promises in suit, by praying them over. God loves to be bound by his own words, to be sued by his own bond. Now all this is nothing to the wicked who are strangers to the promises. These God will bring into the briers, and there leave them, Ezek. xxii. 20, and xxix. 5. His own he will never leave nor forsake ; or if he do, as sometimes he seems, yet he will not forsake them utterly, Psal. cxix. 8 ; no, that he will not. The Greek here hath five negatives, and may thus be rendered, " I will not not leave thee ; neither will I not not forsake thee." God may desert his people, but not disinherit them ; forsake them in regard of vision, not of union ; change his dispensation, not his disposition.

Ver. 6. *So that we may boldly say*] Having such a promise to build and found our faith upon, we may well proceed to this holy gloriation against all opposition.

Ver. 7. *Them which have the rule*] Gr. ἡγούμενοι, your captains, your guides (so ministers are called), your chieftains and champions, that bear the brunt of the battle, the heat of the day, and upon whom, as upon his white horses, the Lord Christ rideth about conquering and to conquer, Rev. vi. 2.

Considering the end] Gr. ἀναθεωροῦντες, reconsidering, perusing it over and over, and passing into the likeness of so holy a pattern.

Ver. 8. *Jesus Christ, the same*] This was the sum of their sermons, and is the substance of their and your faith ; which therefore you must stick to, standing fast in the street which is called Straight, Acts ix. 11, and not whirred about with divers and strange doctrines.

Ver. 9. *Be not carried about*] περιφερόμενοι. Error is a precipice, a vortex, or whirl-pool, which first turns men round, and then sucks them in. Islebius Agricola, that first Antinomian, did many times promise amendment ; and yet afterwards not only fell to his error again, but turned Papist, fell into the other extreme. So hard a thing it is to get poison out when once swallowed down. See the note on Eph. iv. 14.

With divers and strange doctrines] That agree neither with themselves nor with the truth.

That the heart be established] Ballasted as a ship, balanced as the bee with a little stone taken up by her, when she hath far to fly in a high wind, *Ne leve alarum remigium praecipitent flabra ventorum*, as Ambrose observeth, lest the bigger blast should dash her to the ground.

Not with meats] As if they were holy, or helpful to salvation. By meats understand all the legal ceremonies, opposed here to the gospel, that doctrine of grace.

Ver. 10. *We have an altar*] That is, a sacrifice, even Christ our passover, whose flesh is meat indeed, John vi., but to believers only, not to those that pertinaciously plead for ceremonies and services of the law, Gal. v. 4. *Hic edere, est credere.*

Ver. 11. *Are burnt without the camp*] And so the priests had no part of the sin-offering; to show that they have no part in Christ that adhere to the Levitical services. See Lev. xvi. 27.

Ver. 12. *Without the gate*] See how punctually the Old Testament is fulfilled in the New. Hardly could those before Christ divine what this meant, till he had suffered it, and the apostle had opened it. Event is the best key to types and prophecies.

Ver. 13. *Bearing his reproach*] The reproach of saints is the reproach of Christ, and their sufferings his, Col. i. 24, and Nehem. iv. 3—5. God is more provoked than Nehemiah. He that saith, " Vengeance is mine, I will repay," repays ofttimes, when we have forgiven, when we have forgotten; and calls to reckoning after our discharges.

Ver. 14. *For here we have none*] Improve this argument for the working our hearts off from the things of this world; the beauty of all which is but as a fair picture drawn upon the ice, that melts away with it.

But we seek one to come] And here we must all turn seekers. " Seek ye first the kingdom of God," &c., Matt. v. 33. See the note there.

Ver. 15. *The fruit of our lips*] Covering God's altar with the calves of our lips, Hos. xiv. 3. This shall please the Lord better than an ox or bullock, that hath horns and hoofs, Psal. lxix. 31. This also is the seeker's sacrifice, ver. 32.

Ver. 16. *Forget not*] We very easily forget what we care not to remember. The richer, the harder usually.

For with such sacrifices] How improvident are we that will not offer a sacrifice of alms when God sets up an altar before us.

Ver. 17. *That have the rule over you*] Gr. That are your leaders or captains. But now, as once in Alcibiades' army, most will be leaders, few learners. See the note on ver. 7.

And submit yourselves] Obey their doctrine, submit to their discipline.

As they that must give an account] These are *fulmina, non verba*, as Erasmus saith of a like place, Ezek. iii. 18; not words, but thunderbolts. Chrysostom (though he usually preached every day, and so excellently that it grew to a proverb, Better the sun shine not than that Chrysostom preach not, yet he) was exceedingly affected and affrighted with this dreadful passage; being ready to say with Job, " What shall I do, when God riseth up? and when he calleth to reckoning, what shall I answer?" Job xxxi. 14.

Ver. 18. *Willing to live honestly*] *Tantum velis, et Deus tibi praeoccurret.* David could wish well to the keeping of God's commandments, Psal. cxix. 4, 5, and affect that which yet he could not effect.

Ver. 19. *That I may be restored*] Prayer reigns over all impediments. See this excellently set forth by Mr Harris in his Peter's Enlargement.

Ver. 20. *Now the God of peace*] He that would reap prayers must sow them. What could the Hebrews do less than pray for him that prayed so heartily for them?

Our Lord Jesus] Here is his kingly office. God hath made him both Lord and Christ, Acts ii. 36.

That great Shepherd] That feedeth his people daily and daintily with divine doctrine. Here is his prophetical office.

Through the blood] Here is his priestly office. And here we must begin, if we will reckon them right.

Ver. 21. *In every good work, &c.*] Works materially good may never prove so formally and eventually; as when they are but external, partial, coactive, inconstant, &c.

Ver. 22. *Suffer the word*] Sharp though it be, and to the flesh tiresome, yet suffer it. Better it is that the vine should bleed than die. But many are like the nettle, touch it never so gently, it will sting you. *Tange montes et fumigabunt.* Offer to wake men out of their sleep, and they will brawl in that case with their best friends; yea, though it be with them here, as once it was with those that had the sweating sickness, if they slept they died. Few are now-a-days of Vespasian's mind, of whom Quintilian reporteth that he was *patientissimus veri*, very patient of truth, though never so tart. Or of Gerson's temper, who delighted in nothing more than a friendly reproof. This is now become as stronger physic, not fit for every complexion and state, &c.

Ver. 23. *Know ye that our brother*] Good news should be spread abroad, and are a fit matter for Christian epistles, as one well observeth from these words.

Ver. 24. *Salute all them*] This Epistle then was first read to the people, who are required to deliver the apostle's comments to their ministers. The Papists debar the people, not of the Scriptures only, but of all books of the reformed religion; and for a terror not to retain such books prohibited, I have seen (saith Sir Edwin Sands) in their printed instructions for confession, the hearing or reading of books forbidden set in rank amongst the sins against the first commandment.

They of Italy salute you] Few saints there now; the Italians hold integrity for little better than silliness; they blaspheme oftener than swear, they murder more than revile or slander.

And yet even in Italy there are full four thousand professed Protestants. But their paucity and obscurity (saith mine author) shall enclose them in a cipher.

Ver. 25. *Grace be with you*] See the note on Philem. 25.

THE EPISTLE GENERAL OF ST JAMES.

CHAPTER I.

Ver. 1. *To the twelve tribes*] Once very devout, Acts xxvi. 7; still the most nimble and mercurial wits in the world, but light, aerial, and fanatical, apt to work themselves into the fool's paradise of a sublime dotage.

Which are scattered abroad] Banished from Rome by the Emperor Claudius, Acts xviii. 1 (Sueton. xxv.), and called by St Peter, "strangers of the dispersion," 1 Pet. i. 1. The Jews at this day are a disjected and despised people, according to Deut. xxviii. 64, having neither country nor resting-place; even in Jerusalem there be not to be found at this day a hundred households of them. (Breerwood's Inq.)

Ver. 2. *Count it all joy*] The world wondereth (saith Mr Philpot the martyr) how we can be so merry in such extreme misery. But our God is omnipotent, who turneth misery into felicity. Believe me, there is no such joy in the world as the people of Christ have under the cross; I speak it by experience, &c. He counted it so upon mature deliberation, as the apostle here adviseth.

All joy] That is, full joy (by a Hebraism), complete and perfect; such as is the joy of merchants when they see their ships come laden in.

When ye fall into] Not go in step by step, but are precipitated, plunged. Or when ye fall among, as he that went down towards Jericho fell among thieves, Luke x. 30. When ye are so surrounded that there is no escaping them, being distressed, as David was, Psal. cxvi. 3.

Into divers temptations] Crosses seldom come single (*Catenata piorum crux*), as neither do mercies, but trooping and treading one upon the heels of another.[1] After rain cometh clouds, Eccl. xii. 2. As in April, no sooner is one shower unburdened, but another is brewed. And when the apostle calleth them temptations, he meaneth such afflictions as will put us hard to it, and show what metal we are made of; pressing and piercing crosses.

Ver. 3. *The trial of your faith*] Yea, such a well-knit patience, as maketh a man suffer after he hath suffered, as David did from Shimei, but first from Absalom. Tile-stones till baked are not useful; but well burnt and hardened they stand out all storms and ill-weather. See my Love Tokens, p. 170.

Knowing this] And therefore rejoicing, if not in the sense, yet in the use of your afflictions. See the note on Heb. xii. 10, 11.

Ver. 4. *Let patience have her perfect work*] Patience must not be an inch shorter than the affliction. If the bridge reach but half-way over the brook, we shall have but ill-favoured passage. It is the devil's desire to set us on a hurry; he knows his temptations will then work best.

Ver. 5. *If any of you lack wisdom*] That is, patience to bear afflictions as he ought, cheerfully, thankfully, fruitfully, so as to be able to say, "Well for the present, and it will be better hereafter," which is the patient man's motto, *Qui placide sortem ferre scit, ille sapit.* I thank thee, O Lord, for all my pain (said Francis of Assisi, in all his extremity), and I beseech thee, if thou think good, to add to it a hundred-fold more. *Feri Domine, feri,* said Luther; *a peccatis enim absolutus sum:* Smite, Lord, smite on, my sins are pardoned; all shall be for the best. Mr William Perkins, when he lay in his last and killing torment of the stone, hearing the by-standers pray for a mitigation of his pain, willed them not to pray for an ease of his complaint, but for an increase of his patience. (Dr Hall, Rem. of Profaneness.)

Let him ask it of God] It hath been questioned by some whether a man can have patience, *sine auxilio gratiæ*, without the help of God's grace. (Aquinas.) But Christians know they cannot. It is not patience but pertinacy in godless men, that call not upon God; it is stupidity of sense, not a solidity of faith; a reckless desperation, not a confident resolution: such was that patience put forth by Mithridates of old, and by Baltasar Gerardus the Burgundian, that slew the Prince of Orange, 1584, and for the same endured very grievous torments. True patience

---

[1] *Aliud ex alio malum.* Teren.

is the fruit of prayer; this wisdom from above is one of those perfect gifts that cometh down from the "Father of lights," who is therefore called the "God of patience and consolation." God, as he is skilful *in dirigendo*, pitiful *in corrigendo*, so will he be bountiful *in porrigendo*.

That giveth to all men liberally] Not scantily, sparingly, or with an ill will. He is no penny-father (as they say), but rich in mercy to all that call upon him. Ἀξιωματικώτατος μὲν ἐστίν ὁ βασιλεὺς ἡμῶν, saith Basil. (Consil. Mon. i.) Our king gives like himself, and according to his state; he is angry with those that ask him small matters. He doth not shift off his suitors as Antigonus did the philosopher; who first asked him a groat; he answered, that was too little for a king to give; he requested the king then to give him a talent; who replied, that that was too much for a beggar to crave.[1] God solicits suitors, John iv. 23, and complains (as the Emperor Severus once did of his courtiers), "Hitherto ye have asked me nothing." He gives also according to his excellent greatness; as Alexander the Great gave a poor man a city; and when he modestly refused it as too great for him, Alexander answered, *Non quæro quid te accipere deceat, sed quid me dare*, The business is not what thou art fit to receive, but what it becometh me to give. (Sen. de Benef. ii. 16.)

And upbraideth not] Neither with present failings, nor former infirmities. *Qui exprobrat, reposcit.* (Tacit.) So doth not God; unless in case of unthankfulness. For then he will take his own, and be gone, Hos. ii. 8, 9.

Ver. 6. *But let him ask in faith*] See the note on Heb. xi. 6.

Nothing wavering] We are too ready in temptation to doubt, yea, to hold it a duty to doubt. This (saith one) is to light a candle before the devil, as we use to speak.

Ver. 7. *That he shall receive*] Unless he strive against his doubting, and wade out of it, as the moon doth out of the cloud. *Qui timide rogat, negare docet;* He that prayeth doubtingly, shuts heaven-gates against his own prayers.

Ver. 8. *Unstable in all his ways*] As he is that stands on one leg, or as a bowl on a smooth table. Contrariwise, a believer is as a square stone set into the building, 1 Pet. ii. 7; shaken he may be, but he is rooted as a tree; wag he may up and down as a ship at anchor, but yet he removes not.

Ver. 9. *Rejoice in that he is exalted*] Gr. ἐν τῷ ὕψει αὐτοῦ, in his sublimity, in that high honour of his, John i. 12. This should make him hold up his head, but not too high; be cheerful, but not withal scornful. *Læti simus, sed non securi, gaudentes in Domino, sed caventes a recidivo.* (Bern.)

Ver. 10. *In that he is made low*] Drawn from that high esteem of outward excellencies. He is now made a greater man, because he seems too big for them; or low, that is, lowly.

Ver. 11. *Shall the rich man fade*] Perish

eternally, if he trust in uncertain riches, and not in the living God. See James v. 1. Thus that sapless fellow Nabal faded, when his heart died within him, nor could his riches any more relieve him than they did that rich and wretched cardinal, Henry Beaufort, Chancellor of England in the reign of Henry VI., who murmured at death, that his riches could not reprieve him till a further time. Fie (quoth he), will not death be hired? Will money do nothing? No; money here bears no mastery. (Acts and Mon.)

Ver. 12. *Blessed is the man*] Provided that God teach him, as well as chastise him, Psal. xciv. 12, instruct him as well as correct him. See my Love Tokens, par. 2.

He shall receive the crown] A man can be content to have his head broken with a bag of gold, so he may have it, when it is done. Eternal life is called "a crown:" 1. For the perpetuity of it; for a crown hath neither beginning nor ending. 2. For the plenty; because as the crown compasseth on every side, so there is nothing wanting in this life. 3. The dignity; eternal life is a coronation-day. (Bishop Lake.) Tertullian wrote his book *De corona militis* upon occasion of a certain Christian soldier's refusing to be crowned, and saying, *Non decet Christianum in hac vita coronari;* A Christian is to be crowned when he cometh to heaven.

Ver. 13. *I am tempted of God*] The inclination of man's heart to good, is of itself and properly of God, as light is of the sun. His inclination to evil is by accident only of God, like as darkness is of the sun-set by accident, being properly not of the sun, but of the earth.

Ver. 14. *Drawn away of his lust*] Δελεαζόμενος, Satan hath only a persuading sleight, not an enforcing might. Our own concupiscence carries the greatest stroke.

And enticed] As the silly fish is by the bait covering the hook, being first drawn aside into the clear water.[2] Or as the unwary younker, drawn to folly by some subtle she-sinner; who thereupon conceiveth, and bringeth forth a bastardly-brood.

Ver. 15. *When lust hath conceived*] As the plot of all diseases lies in the humours of the body; so of all sin, in the lust of the soul. There is in it a πανσπερμία, a tacit consent, a seed-plot of all sin.[3] The Papists say (but falsely) that it is the smallest of all sins, not deserving any more of God's wrath than only a want of his beatifical presence, and that too without any pain or sorrow of mind from the apprehension of so great a loss. There are also of ours that say, That it is not forbidden by the law; but sure we are, it is cursed and condemned (and therefore forbidden) by the law.

Ver. 16. *Do not err*] Wander not, as wandering stars, to whom is reserved the blackness of darkness for ever, Jude 13, by seeking to father your faults upon God, as Adam did, Gen. iii. 12.

---

[1] οὐ βασιλικὸν τὸ δόμα. οὐ κυνικὸν τὸ λῆμμα.

[2] Δελεὰρ, *quasi* δυλεὰρ, a δόλος.

[3] *Empedoclis vocabulum apud Aristot.*

Ver. 17. *Every good gift, &c.*] A hexameter verse in the Greek; as little intended perhaps by the apostle as the first line in Tacitus, which yet may be scanned a long verse.

And perfect giving] Not temporals only (which are good gifts), but spirituals also, those perfect givings. The greatest excellencies in us do as much depend upon God as the effigies in the glass doth upon the face that causeth it; or as the light doth upon the sun, that father of all the light in the lower world.

With whom is no variableness] παραλλαγὴ, no parallax, as there is with the sun, when he declines and leaves us darkling. This word notes the sun's motion from east to west, as the following word τροπὴ, turning, notes his motion every year from north to south. That which the apostle would here assert is, that God tempts no man to evil, because he is unchangeably good, and can be no other.

Ver. 18. *Of his own will begat he us*] Gr. ἀπεκύησε, brought he us forth, as a special instance of his free grace and fatherly goodness, Eph. i. 4, 5. The word properly signifies, He did the office of a mother to us, the bringing us into the light of life. The Hebrew word ילד also signifieth *genuit, peperit, parturiit; et est proprium fœminarum: quamvis eleganter de viro etiam et aliis rebus dicatur*, to bring forth. (Marenus in Arca Noæ.)

Ver. 19. *Swift to hear*] Reaching after that word of truth, the gospel, ver. 18, and drinking it in as the dry earth doth the dew of heaven. Life doth now enter into the soul at the ear, as at first death did, Gen. iii.

Slow to speak] We read oft, "He that hath an ear to hear, let him hear;" but never, he that hath a tongue to speak, let him speak; for this we can do fast enough, without bidding. But hath not Nature taught us the same that the apostle here doth, by giving us two ears, and those open; and but one tongue, and that hedged in with teeth and lips? It is also tied and bound fast by the root, and hath for guides and counsellors the brain above and the heart beneath it. Hence your wisest men are most silent; for they know that as some gravel and mud passeth away with much water, so in many words there wanteth not sin.

Slow to wrath] Slow to snuff at those that reprove you. See the note on Heb. xiii. 22. Rage not when touched, though to the quick.

Ver. 20. *For the wrath of man*] Unless it be as Moses' and Christ's anger was, pure and free from guile and gall, prompting us to pity and pray for the party, Exod. xxxii. 32; Mark iii. 5.

Ver. 21. *All filthiness*] Gr. ῥυπαρίαν, the stinking filth of a pestilent ulcer. Sin is the devil's vomit, the soul's excrement, the superfluity or garbage of naughtiness, περισσείαν, as it is here called by an allusion to the garbage of the sacrifices cast into the brook Kedron, that is, into the town-ditch. *Retentio excrementorum est parens morborum.* Out with it, therefore. Some say that the word rendered filthiness, properly signifies "the filth under the nails and armholes;" but translated to the mind, it signifies covetousness, as *sordes* in Latin; but here any kind of sin, especially inward, as superfluity may note outward evils, that do *superfluere*, float at top.

Receive with meekness] It is ill sowing in a storm: so a stormy spirit will not suffer the word to take place.

The engraffed word] ἔμφυτος, engraffed upon the heart, as the scion upon the stock, or sowed in the soul, and mingled with faith, that it may bring forth fruit to God.

Ver. 22. *And not hearers only*] The Panotii in Scythia are said to have such large ears, as that therewith they cover their whole bodies. (Isidore.) Such are our hearers only.

Deceiving your own souls] Either as by false reckoning or false reasoning; Gr. παραλογιζόμενοι, putting paralogisms and fallacies upon yourselves. For hypocrites may easily deceive not others only, but themselves too; as a drunken stage-player, that in his drunkenness acting a king's part, thinks himself a king indeed.

Ver. 23. *His natural face*] Gr. the face of his nativity, that wherewith he was born into the world. Pythagoras wished his scholars oft to view themselves in a glass, that if they were well-favoured, they might likewise be well-conditioned; as if otherwise, they might make it up in virtue.

Si mihi difficilis formam natura negavit,
Ingenio formæ damna rependo meæ.
                                    Ovid. Epist.

The law is a crystal glass, wherein a man may soon see his spiritual deformities, and be advertised of his duty. See the note on ver. 25.

Ver. 24. *Straightway forgetteth*] Naturalists make mention of a certain creature called *cervarius*, that though he be feeding never so hard and hungerly, if he cast but back his head, he forgets immediately the meat he was eating, and runs to look after new: the lynx is very sharp-sighted, but withal very forgetful; out of sight, out of mind straight.

Ver. 25. *Whoso looketh into, &c.*] παρακύψας, as into a glass, wishly and intently with the body bowed down. Get thee God's law as a glass to toot in, saith Mr Bradford (Ser. of Repent.); so shalt thou see thy face foul arrayed, and so shamefully saucy, mangy, pocky, and scabbed, that thou canst not but be sorry at the contemplation thereof. It is said of the basilisk, that if he look into a glass, he presently dieth: sin doth. Physicians in some kind of unseemly convulsions wish the patient to view himself in a glass, which will help him to strive the more when he shall see his own deformity; so reflect, &c.

The perfect law of liberty] The moral law, in opposition to the ceremonial, or so called because never is a man free indeed till out of a principle of love he keep God's law.

Not a forgetful hearer] Some are as hour-glasses, no sooner turned up but running out immediately. Their souls are like filthy ponds, wherein fish die soon and frogs live long; profane jests are remembered, pious passages forgotten.

Ver. 26. *Seem to be religious*] There is a great deal of this seemingness now abroad: *Aliud in titulo, aliud in pyxide. Verba tua Dei plane sunt, facta vero Diaboli*, as one told Pope Innocent III.: You speak like a God, but do like a devil; a fair professor, but a foul sinner. The form of religion is *honos;* the power *onus.* Many do but act it, play it: they do no more than assume it, as the angels did the dead bodies without a soul to animate them, or as Jeroboam's wife put on her demure apparel when she was to go to the prophet. The mere seemer is a juggler, Job xiii. 16, *imposturam facit et patitur: fumum vendidit, fumo peribit.* He is like the painted grapes that deceived the living birds, saith one, or the golden apples with this motto, " No further than colour;" touch them and they vanish.

But deceiveth] The heart first deceiveth us with colours, and when we are once a doting after sin, then we join and deceive our hearts by fallacious reasonings.

Ver. 27. *And widows*] A vine whose root is uncovered thrives not; a widow whose covering of eyes is taken away, joys not.

CHAPTER II.

Ver. 1. *The Lord of glory*] Or, " Have not the glorious faith of our Lord Jesus Christ," &c. Faith is a glorious grace indeed.

With respect of persons] i. e. Of their outward quality or conditions, as rich or poor, of this side or that, &c. Zanchy relates of a certain Frenchman, a friend of his, and a constant hearer of Calvin at Geneva, that being solicited by him to hear Viret, an excellent preacher, who preached at the same time that Calvin did, he answered, If St Paul himself should preach here at the same hour with Calvin, *Ego, relicto Paulo, audirem Calvinum*, I would not leave Calvin to hear Paul. This is not only partiality, but anthropolatry or man-worship, saith he. Grynæus reports a speech of George, duke of Saxony : Although I am not ignorant, saith he, that there are divers errors and abuses crept into the Church, *Nolo tamen amplecti Evangelium quod Lutherus annunciat*, yet I will none of that gospel-reformation that Luther preacheth. (Lect. in Hag.) *Compertum est*, it is for certain, saith Erasmus, that many things are condemned as heretical in Luther's writings, that in Austin's and Bernard's books are approved for sound and pious passages. (Erasm. Epist. ad Card. Mogunt.)

Ver. 2. *For if there come, &c.*] It is probable, saith an interpreter here, that the primitive Christians, the better to ingratiate with the richer pagans, gave them very great respect, contrary to that, Psal. xv. 4. But I rather think the apostle speaketh in this text of wealthier Christians, unworthily preferred before better but poorer persons.

Ver. 3. *That weareth the gay cloth*] As Hospinian tells us of the dogs that kept Vulcan's temple, and as others say of the Bohemian curs, that they will fawn upon a good suit, but fly upon one that is in ragged apparel. So is it with many; *Vestis virum.*

Ver. 4. *Are ye not then partial*] οὐ διακρίθητε, or, " Are ye not for so doing condemned in your own consciences? " Or, " Neither have ye so much as once doubted or questioned the matter within yourselves, whether in so doing you have not done amiss? "

Ver. 5. *Chosen the poor*] This the world wonders and stumbles at. The heathen Romans would not receive Christ (though they heard of his miracles and mighty works) into the number of their gods, because he preached poverty and made use of poor persons. Aigoland, king of Saragossa in Arragon, refused to be baptized because he saw many lazars and poor people expecting alms from Charlemagne's table; and asking what they were, was answered, That they were the messengers and servants of God. And can he keep his servants no better? said he. I will be none of his servants. (Turpine.) But what saith Christ? " I know thy poverty ; but (that is nothing) thou art rich," Rev. ii. 9. And the poor are gospellized, not only receive it, but are changed by it, Matt. xi. 5. We usually call a poor man a poor soul: a poor soul may be a rich Christian, and a rich man may have a poor soul; as he in the Gospel that had *animam triticeam*, a wheaten soul, Luke xii., and as those other rich fools in David's days, whose hearts were as fat as grease; they delighted not in God's law, Psal. cxix. 70.

Heirs of the kingdom] Heads destinated to the diadem, saith Tertullian.

Ver. 6. *Ye have despised the poor*] *Pauper ubique jacet.* Zeph. iii. 12, afflicted and poor are joined together; because poverty is an affliction, and makes a man trodden upon. Men go over the hedge where it is lowest. Therefore St Paul joins them together, " I have learned to want, and to be abased; " they that want shall be abased: Luke xv. 30, " This thy son." He saith not, This my brother, because in poverty; which is therefore to be deprecated and prayed against, as Prov. xxx. 8. 1. *Propter inediam*, as Gen. xxxvii. 25. 2. *Propter injuriam*, Psal. x. 9. 3. *Propter infamiam*, as here. Our Saviour calls that good beggar Lazarus, that is, God help me, Luke xvi. 29; as proper a name for a beggar as could be given.

Oppress you] καταδυναστεύουσιν, subjugate you, and bring your heads under their girdles; trample upon you with the feet of pride and cruelty; yea, devour you, as the greater fish do the lesser. *Feræ parcunt, aves vascunt, homines sæviunt*, saith Cyprian. The wild beasts spare Daniel, the ravenous ravens feed Elias; only men rage and ravage, they tyrannically oppress God's poor people (as the word here imports), acting therein the devil's part. See Acts x. 38 (where the same word is used) ; there is neither equity nor mercy to be had at their hands. Hence they are called men-eaters, cannibals, Psal. xiv. 4, and charged with beating God's people to pieces, and grinding the faces of the poor, Isa. iii. 15, with eating their very flesh and flaying their skins from off them, and breaking of their bones, and chopping them in pieces as for the pot, and as flesh within the caldron, Mic. iii. 3. This is a sin against race, grace, and place.

Draw you before the judgment-seats] Vex you with law-suits, and by might rob you of your right. *Cedit viribus æquum.*

Ver. 7. *Do not they blaspheme*] That is, cause to be blasphemed, as Rom. ii. 24 ; 1 Tim. i. 20. Marcellinus, a heathen historian, taxeth the Christians of his times for their dissensions, biting and devouring one another, till they were even consumed one of another. (Am. Mar. ii. 2.) A sad thing that a heathen should see such hellish miscarriages among Christ's followers.

Ver. 8. *If ye fulfil the royal law*] Acknowledging God's sovereignty, and sending a lamb to the ruler of the earth, Isa. xvi. 1, seeking the help of that free or noble spirit of his, Psal. li. 13, that royal, ruling spirit, as the Greek version there hath it.

Ver. 9. *Ye commit sin*] That is flat ; though ye have thought otherwise. See the note on ver. 4.

And are convinced of the law as transgressors] This they held either no sin or a small one, a peccadillo. The Civilian indeed saith, *De minutis non curat lex*, the law makes no matter of small matters. But God's law condemneth small faults : as the sunshine showeth us atoms, moths.

Ver. 10. *He is guilty of all*] The whole law is but one copulative, Exod. xvi. 18 ; Ezek. xviii. 10—13. He that breaketh one commandment habitually breaketh all ; not so actually. The godly keep those commandments that actually they break ; but a dispensatory conscience keeps not any commandment. *Deus non vult cum exceptione coli*, God will not be served with an exception, saith a learned interpreter here. He that repents with a contradiction (saith Tertullian) God will pardon him with contradiction. A man must not be *funambulus virtutum* (saith the same author), going in a narrow track of obedience ; but must do everything as well as anything, or all is lost ; his obedience must be universal, extending to the compass of the whole law.

Ver. 11. *For he that said*] "God spake all those words, and said ; " there is the same divine authority for one commandment as another, Exod. xx. 1. The Pharisees had their *minutula legis*, but Christ cries them down, Matt. v. The Jews at this day senselessly argue, " Cursed is he that abides not in all things," therefore he is not cursed that abides in some things only.

Thou art become a transgressor of the law] Now, every transgression and disobedience receiveth a just recompense of reward, Heb. ii. 2.

Ver. 12. *As they that shall be judged*] Or, as they that should judge by the law of liberty ; which is so called, because it doth freely and fully discover unto every man, without respect of persons, the errors and evils of his life. And we should walk as patterns of the rule. See the note on Matt. xi. 19. It is also called a law of liberty, because it is freely and willingly kept of the regenerate, to whom it is no burden or bondage.

Ver. 13. *For he shall have mercy*] See the note on Matt. v. 7.

And mercy rejoiceth against judgment] καταυχᾶται,[1] that is, the merciful man glorieth, as one that hath received mercy, and shall not come into condemnation ; for God's mercy rejoiceth against such a man's sins, as against an adversary which he hath subdued and trampled on.

Ver. 14. *Though a man say he hath faith*] Saying serves not the turn. Livy telleth us of the Athenians (Dec. iv.) that they waged word-war against Philip, king of Macedon ; *Quibus solis valebant*, and that was all they could do. Men may word it with God and yet miscarry, Isa. lviii. 2, 3 ; he is too wise to be put off with words ; he turns up our leaves, and looks what fruit ; whereof if he miss, he lays down his basket, and takes up his axe, Luke xiii. 7. Christianity is not a talking, but a walking with God ; and at the last day it shall be required of men, *non quid legerint, sed quid egerint, non quid dixerint, sed quomodo vixerint*, not what they have said, but how they have acted.

Can faith save him ?] That is, an ineffectual faith, that worketh not by love, such as is the faith of the Solifidians, a faith in profession only ; if a man say he hath faith, and no more, as good he might say nothing. *Quid verba quæro, &c. ?* That faith is easily wrought, which teacheth men to believe well of themselves, though their lives be evil.

Ver. 15. *If a brother or a sister*] As it may befall the best to be, and they are not of the chameleon kind, to live (with Ephraim) upon wind, Hos. xii. 1, to be fed with fair words, or to be clothed with a suit of compliments. Sion should be taken by the hand, Isa. li. 18. And Tyrus converted, leaves hoarding and heaping up wealth, and falls to feeding and clothing God's poor people, Isa. xxiii. 18.

Ver. 16. *And one of you say*] This age aboundeth with mouth-mercy, which is good cheap. But a little handful were better than a great many such mouthfuls.

Be ye warmed] But with what ? with a fire of words. Be filled ; but with what ? with a mess of words. Away with those airy courtesies. How many have we now-a-days that will be but as friends at a sneeze ! the most you can get of these benefactors is, " God bless you, Christ help you."

Ver. 17. *If dead, being alone*] That is, being workless ; for life discovers itself by action ; so

---

[1] *ab αὐχὴν, cervus :* treadeth on the neck of judgment.

doth true faith by trust in God, and love to men. A tree that is not for fruit, is for the fire.

Ver. 18. *My faith by my works*] It appeared by the fruits it was a good land, Numb. xiii. 23. It appeared that Dorcas was a true believer by the coats she had made ; so here.

Ver. 19. *Believe and tremble*] Gr. φρίσσουσι, roar as the sea, and shriek horribly, Acts xix. 29 ; Mark vi. 49. Their hearts ache and quake within them ; and shall any man mock at God's menaces ? Shall not the devils keep holiday in hell, in respect of such atheists ?

Ver. 20. *But wilt thou know*] *Interrogatio docturientis*, saith Piscator. A question made by one that is desirous to teach.

Thou vain man] Gr. Thou empty man ; for works without faith are nothing else but a nutshell without a kernel, grapes without juice, chaff without corn, saith Mercer in Jonah iii. 8.

Ver. 21. *Justified by works*] sc. *Declarative et in foro humano*, but not before God, Rom. iii. 2. It is faith that justifieth the man ; but they are works that justify faith to be right and real, saving and justifying.

Ver. 22. *Wrought with his works*] Or, was a help to his works, and was her own midwife to bring them forth of herself into the open light, Heb. xi. 17.

Was faith made perfect] That is, declared to be operative and effectual.

Ver. 23. *And it was imputed*] See the note on Gen. xv. 6, on Rom. iv. 3, and on Gal. iii. 6.

The friend of God] A very high style. If Eusebius held it such an honour to be the friend of Pamphilus, and Sir Fulk Greville, Lord Brook, to be friend to Sir Philip Sidney, causing it to be so engraven upon his tomb ; what is it to be the friend of God ? And yet such honour have all the saints.

Ver. 24. *By works a man is justified*] Declaratively, as by faith apprehensively, by God effectively.

Ver. 25. *The messengers*] Gr. The angels, so Luke vii. 24 ; Acts xii. 15. See the notes there.

Ver. 26. *As the body, &c.*] Yet is not charity the soul of faith, but the vital spirit only.

CHAPTER III.

Ver. 1. *Be not many masters*] Masters of opinions, that boldly obtrude upon others their own *placits*, and will not have them disputed or debated. Such are the Sorbonists, who rejoice to be called *Magistri nostri Parisienses*, our Masters of Paris. Bacon, the Carmelite, was called *Doctor resolutissimus*, because he would endure no guessing or may-bes. (Præfat. in 1 Sent.) The pope's parasites persuade the people, that what interpretation soever he gives of Scripture, be it right or wrong, it is without further trial to be received as the very word of God. *Est ipsissimum Dei verbum.* (Hosius.)

Knowing that we shall receive the greater condemnation] sc. If either we become heresiarchs

and sect-masters, Rev. xix. 20, or supercilious censurers of others, Matt. vii. 1 ; Rom. ii. 1.

Ver. 2. *For in many things, &c.*] This is *triste mortalitatis privilegium*, the sad privilege of mankind, as one phraseth it, to have leave to offend sometimes. Every pomegranate hath at least one rotten grain within it, saith Crates. And it is the honour of God alone to be perfect, saith Plato (Euphormio). Jerome pronounceth a curse upon him that shall say, that the fulfilling of the whole law is impossible to any. But *patres legendi cum venia;* Jerome was out in this, and too to blame, μόνου θεοῦ γέρας ἐστὶ εἶναι τετράγωνον. St James, a far better man than Jerome (for he was worthily called James the Just), affirmeth here of himself and other sanctified persons, We offend or stumble all, πταίομεν, *impingimus omnes.*

A perfect man] That is, a prudent man, Psal. xxxvii. 30, 31.

Ver. 4. *That they may obey us*] Horses, asses, camels, elephants, God in great wisdom, for the use of man, hath made without galls, that they might with the more ease be made tame and serviceable.

Whithersoever the governor] *Peterent cœlum Belgæ si navibus peti posset*, saith one. (Johnston, de Nat. Constant.)

Ver. 5. *Boasteth great things*] Gr. μεγαλαυχεῖ, It doth magnifically lift up itself, as an untamed horse doth his head. It exalts itself and exults of great things. It walketh through the earth, and faceth the very heavens, Psal. lxxiii. 9. It can run all the world over, and bite at everybody ; being as a sharp razor, that doth deceit, that instead of shaving the hair cutteth the throat, Psal. lii. 2. It is made in the shape of a sword ; and David felt it as a sword in his bones, Psal. xlii. 10. It is thin, broad, and long, as an instrument most fit to empty both the speaker's and the hearer's heart. It is of a flame-colour, as apt to set on fire the whole wheel of nature, ver. 6.

Behold how great a matter] Or wood. Camerarius tells a story of two brethren walking out in a star-light night. Saith one of the brethren, Would I had a pasture as large as this element ; and saith the other, Would I had as many oxen as there be stars. Saith the other again, Where would you feed those oxen ? In your pasture, replied he. What ? whether I would or no ? Yea, said he, whether you will or no. What, in spite of me ? Yes, said he. And thus it went on from words, till at length each sheathed his sword in the other's bowels.

Ver. 6. *A world of iniquity*] A new-found world. Not a city or country only, but " a world of iniquity," a sink, a sea of sin, wherein there is not only that Leviathan, but creeping things innumerable, Psal. civ. 26.

So is the tongue amongst our members] For better purpose it was there set, sc. in the midst betwixt the brain and the heart, that it might take the advice of both ; and that we might *verba prius ad limam revocare, quam ad linguam.*

That it defileth the whole body] Leaving a stain upon the speaker, and setting a stain upon the hearer; even the guilt and filth of sin.

The course of nature] Gr. The wheel of our nativity. Their breath, as fire devoureth, Isa. xxxiii. 10. "The poison of asps is under their lips," Rom. iii. 13. The venomous heat of which deadly poison, like a fire in the flesh, killeth the wounded with torments, the likeliest hell of any other. In the holy tongue *dabher* signifieth a word, *debher* a pest; to show (saith one) that an evil tongue hath the pestilence in it.

And is set on fire of hell] That is, of the devil (called elsewhere the gates of hell), as the Holy Ghost (on the other side) set on fire the apostles' tongues with zeal, that flame of God, Cant. viii. 6; Acts ii. 3. Evil speech is the devil's drivel; a slanderer carries the devil's pack. He hath his name in Hebrew from footing it, trotting and tracing up and down to sow strife: *Ragal*, to defame or slander; *regel*, a foot. In Greek the same word signifieth a devil and a slanderer. The tale-bearer carrieth the devil in his tongue (saith one), the tale-hearer in his ear.

Ver. 7. *For every kind of beasts, &c.*] See the note on Heb. ii. 7. Some creatures indeed may be taken, but not tamed, as the tiger, panther, monoceros, of which last it is testified, *quod interimi potest, capi non potest;* Slain he may be, but not taken. Such unruly talkers and deceivers the Church is pestered with, Tit. i. 10; 1 Thess. v. 14; sons of Belial, untamable, untractable, untouchable, unteachable, 2 Sam. xxiii. 6, 7; 1 Sam. xxv. 17.

Ver. 8. *But the tongue, &c.*] Where then are our justiciaries with their pretended perfection? David's heart deceived him: Psal. xxxix. 1, "I said I will look to my ways, I will bridle my tongue." But presently after, he shows how soon he brake his word. "My heart was hot," &c., and "I spake with my tongue." Pambus, in the ecclesiastical history, could never take out that one lesson read him out of Psal. xxxix. 1. There is one Bennus celebrated in the same ecclesiastical history for this (but I can hardly believe it), that he was never seen of any man to be angry, never heard to swear, or lie, or utter a vain word. (Sozomen, vi. 28.)

An unruly evil] There be but five virtues of the tongue reckoned by philosophers. But there are 24 several sins of the tongue, as Peraldus recounteth them. The Arabians have a proverb, *Cave ne feriat lingua tua collum tuum;* Take heed thy tongue cut not thy throat. An open mouth is oft a purgatory to the master. See note on ver. 6.

Full of deadly poison] Such as poisoneth itself, and poisoneth at a distance, which no other poison doth. Some poisons are not poisonful to some creatures; storks feed upon serpents, ducks upon toads, &c. But the tongue is a universal poison, &c.

Ver. 9. *Therewith bless we God*] And so make our tongues our glory.

Therewith curse we men] Yea, the best of men; as Core and his complices fear not to object to Moses the meek, with one breath, pride, ambition, and usurpation of authority. So Shimei cursed David, the pope curseth the Reformed Churches. But cursing men are cursed men; those detestable God-damn-mes especially, with their fearful self-damning imprecations, and innominate soul-damning oaths, God justly may, and doubtlessly doth, take many of them at their words, as he did those who wished they might die in the wilderness, Numb. xiv. 28.

Ver. 10. *Out of the same mouth*] As it did once out of the mouth of Pope Julius II., who in the battle of Ravenna on Easter-day, between him and the French, as he sat by the fire reading of his prayers, and having news of the defeat, he flung away his book, saying, *Sit ergo Gallus in nomine diabolorum*, The devil take the French. (Annal. Gallic.) Is not this that mouth that speaketh great things and blasphemies? Rev. xiii. 5. A loaf of the same bran was that foul-mouthed cardinal, who entering the city of Paris, and being met by the people who begged his blessing, blessed them at first; but when they came thicker upon him, and hindered his passage, he cursed them as fast; using these words, *Quandoquidem hic populus vult decipi, decipiatur in nomine diaboli, i. e.* Sith this people will needs be deceived, let them be deceived in the devil's name. *Os sceleratum et profanum!* (Dr Prideaux, Lect.) Plutarch in Dion tells of a land about Athens, that brings forth the best honey and worst poison. *In Polypidis capite bonum inest et malum.* Lo, such is the tongue.

Ver. 11. *Doth a fountain send forth*] The fountain, or rather the botch, of sensual and sinful pleasures doth. Sin is a bitter-sweet, γλυκύπικρον, the poison of asps, which first tickleth, and then killeth. All creature-comforts are *dulcis acerbitas*, saith one. *Amarissima voluptas*, saith another. (Tertul.)

Principium dulce est, at finis amoris amarus;
Læta venire Venus, tristis abire solet.

Ver. 12. *Both yield salt water and fresh*] That is strange that is reported of the rivers of Peru, that after they have run into the main sea, yea, some write 20 or 30 miles, they keep themselves unmixed with the salt water; so that a very great way within the sea men may take up as fresh water as if they were near the land. (Abbot's Geog.) But that is as sure as strange, that an eye-witness reporteth of the Danube and Sava (two great rivers in Hungary), that their waters meeting mingle no more than water and oil; so that near the middle of the river I have gone in a boat (saith mine author) and tasted of the Danube, as clear and pure as a well; then putting my hand not an inch farther, I have taken of the Sava as troubled as a street channel, tasting the gravel in my teeth. Thus they run 60 miles together. (Blount's Voyage.)

Ver. 13. *Who is a wise man*] Not he that words it most; for *multiloquio stultiloquium;* and as any one is more wise, he is more sparing of his censures; but every fool will be meddling. *Sapiens is est, cui res sapiunt prout sunt*, saith Bernard (lib. iii. cap. 30). He is a wise man that judgeth aright of everything. And all the wisdom of a man is in this one thing, saith Lactantius, *ut Deum cognoscat et colat*, that he know and worship God.

With meekness of wisdom] As it is said of Athanasius, that he was high in worth and humble in heart; a loadstone in his sweet, gentle, drawing nature, and yet an adamant in his wise and stout deportment towards those that were evil. (Nazianzen in encom. Athan.) Jerome and Austin in their disputations, it was no matter who gained the day; they would both win by understanding their errors. What a sweet resolution was that of Calvin, Though Luther call me devil, yet I will honour him as a servant of God.

Ver. 14. *Bitter envying*] Properly so called; for it flows from the gall; it shows that the man is in the gall of bitterness, and of kin to the star called wormwood, Rev. viii. 11. It is also an evil wherein is steeped the venom of all other vices. It is the observation of a late reverend divine, that Gen. xxxviii. 29. Pharez was the son of Tamar, division, of a palm-tree, which hath its name *ab amaritudine*, from bitterness, saith Pagnine. Division comes from bitterness, and envy drinks up the most part of its own venom. It infecteth also others with her venomous breath; as that maid mentioned by Avicen, who fed upon poison.

Glory not] viz. Of your wisdom.

Lie not against the truth] As if ye were true Christians, when in truth you are not so; Jesuits you may be (those great boutefeaus of the world), but Christians ye are none; ye have not so learned Christ.

Ver. 15. *Earthly, sensual*] Here is a true character of carnal wisdom; the world is a pearl in its eyes, it cannot see God. Earthly it is called, as managing the lusts of the eyes unto the ends of gain; sensual, managing the lusts of the flesh unto the ends of pleasure; and devilish, managing the pride of life unto the ends of power.

Ver. 16. *For where envying and strife is, &c.*] The number of two hath been therefore accounted accursed, because it was the first that departed from unity. Divisions (saith one) are like the torrid zone, nothing prospers under it. (Dr Rayner.) When the dogstar ariseth, no plants thrive as at other times. When a fire is kindled in a town, the bells ring backwards; when fires of contentions are kindled in places, all things go awry. (Mr Burr's Heart Divisions.)

Ver. 17. *Easy to be entreated*] Tractable, docile, not as horse and mule that must be ruled with rigour, not with reason, Psal. xxxii. 9. Without partiality (or, without judging), without hypocrisy. These two stand fitly together; to note, that the greatest censurers are usually the greatest hypocrites; and as any one is more wise, he is more sparing of his censures.

Ver. 18. *Is sown in peace*] Only we must not think to sow and reap all in a day. By the fruit of righteousness may be meant the crown of righteousness, 2 Tim. iv. 8, which Christ (the Prince of peace) shall put upon all the sons of peace, Luke x. 6; as, in the mean time, they shall be called the sons of God, Matt. v. 9, have not only the comfort, but the credit, the name and note of such.

CHAPTER IV.

Ver. 1. *From whence come wars*] THAT is, word-wars, needless and endless strifes and contentions. The Greek word πολεμοὶ properly signifies quarrels, that cause much bloodshed.

Among you] Being, 1. Brethren; and that one consideration should quash all quarrels; and should be like the angel that stayed Abraham's hand when the blow was coming. 2. Scattered brethren, James i. 1; and should not misery breed unity? Is it not enough, that blows great store are dealt you by the common adversary, but your own must add to the violence? Surely all unkind and unchristian strifes would easily be composed, did we not forget that we are brethren and fellow-sufferers.

Even of your lusts] Gr. ἡδονῶν, of your pleasures, for wicked men take pleasure in unrighteousness, it is their meat and drink, Prov. iv. 17, they cannot sleep, nay, live without it, ver. 16. Look how Tartarians feed upon carrion with as great delight as we do upon venison; as the Turkish galley-slaves eat opium as it were bread, and as the maid in Pliny fed on spiders, and digested them into nourishment; so do sensualists feed upon sin's murdering morsels, and swallow them down with delight.

Ver. 2. *Ye lust and have not*] viz. To the satisfying of your lusts; for that is an endless piece of work. Lust still cries Give, give; and is ever sick of a spiritual dropsy; the barren womb, the horseleech's daughter, the grave, is nothing to this gulf, to this curse of unsatisfiableness.

Because ye ask not] He must be of a sedate spirit that prays to purpose. How shall we think God will hear us when we hardly hear ourselves? Married couples must agree, that their prayers be not hindred, 1 Pet. iii. 7. There is no sowing in a storm; no taking physic in a hot fit, as aforesaid.

Ver. 3. *Ye ask and receive not*] Ye ask and miss, because ye ask amiss. It is the manner that makes or mars an action.

Ver. 4. *Ye adulterers and adulteresses*] You that have your hearts full of harlotry, that go a whoring from God after the creature, that mind only earthly things, Phil. iii. 19, and woo this *Mundus immundus*, this *Propudium*, this vile strumpet the world, that lays forth her two breasts of profit and pleasure, and ensnareth many; for the which she must be burnt, as a whore, by the fire of the last day.

Know ye not] Worldlings care not to know anything more than how to get, &c., their wits serve them not for better things; they cannot skill of these Scripture matters; they are brutishly ignorant of God and his will, of themselves and their duties.

Is enmity with God] That such both hate God, and, interchangeably, are hated of God.

Ver. 5. *That the Scripture saith in vain*] No, it doth not only say, but do; not only convince us that an evil and an envious spirit possesseth us (such a spirit as lusteth to have other men's abilities eclipsed, that so our candle might shine alone), but also it giveth more grace; it not only convinceth, but converteth the soul, Psal. xix. 7. It causeth a man to rejoice heartily in the good parts of others; and this is more than to excel others in any excellency if this be wanting.

Ver. 6. *But he giveth*] Or, "it," that is, the Scripture "giveth," &c., transforming us into the same image, and conforming us to the heavenly pattern by the Spirit that breatheth in it.

God resisteth the proud] Gr. ἀντιτάσσεται, " setteth himself in battle-array against such," above all other sorts of sinners, as invaders of his territories, and foragers or plunderers of his chief treasures. Pray therefore to be preserved from the perilous pinnacle of self-exaltation. God defieth such as deify themselves; he knoweth them afar off, Psal. cxxxviii. 6, he cannot abide the sight of them. Neither need we wonder, sith (as Boetius well observeth) whereas all other vices fly from God, pride lets fly at him; yea, flies in his face, and seeks to dethrone him; as we see in that proud prince of Tyre, Ezek. xxviii., who thought himself first wiser than Daniel, ver. 3; then, that he exceeded the high priest in all his ornaments, ver. 13; then, he thought himself to be above Adam, ver. 13; then above the cherubims, 14; and lastly, he said he was God himself, and sat in the seat of God. So the pope, 2 Thess. ii. 4.

But giveth grace to the humble] Humility is both a grace, and a vessel to receive grace. God poureth the oil of his grace into broken vessels, contrite spirits.

Ver. 7. *Submit yourselves therefore to God*] Gr. ὑποτάγητε, set yourselves under him, not above him; as the proud person doth, ver. 6. Sit at his feet to receive his law, as scholars sat at the feet of their teachers (see Deut. xxxiii. 3, with the note), obey him as your superior in all things; say to him, *Jussa sequi tam velle mihi quam posse necesse est.*

Resist the devil] i.e. Worldly and fleshly lusts stirred up by the devil, Eph. iv. 26. Lust resisted is sin materially, not formally; for the guilt is done away, in that we do not allow it, but abhor it, as some are of opinion. (Mr Capell on Tempt.)

And he will flee from you] He is but a coward therefore; for like the crocodile, if you follow him he fleeth, if you flee from him he followeth you. In all other fights, the first encounter is sharpest, but here, easiest; for the old serpent having his head bruised and crushed, cannot now so easily thrust in his mortal sting, unless we dally with him, and so lay ourselves open. *Est Leo si fugias: si stas, quasi musca recedit.*

Ver. 8. *Draw nigh to God*] viz. In duty, and he will draw nigh to you in mercy. Sanctify him, Lev. x. 3, and he will satisfy you, Psal. xci. 16. The very Turks are remorseless to those that bear up, but they receive humiliation with much sweetness.

Cleanse your hands] For there is no coming near God, Josh. xxiv. 19. The very heathens knew this; and had therefore their *cœna pura* before their solemn sacrifices; and the sacrificers were appointed to purify themselves some days before. (Godw. Antiq. Demosth.) We wash our hands every day; but, when to dine with some great man, we scour them with balls. God will be sanctified in all them that draw nigh to him, Lev. x. 3, he will be served like himself, he will be no loser by us.

Ye double-minded] Ye that have your hearts divided betwixt two, and as it were cloven asunder. Out with the corruption that cleaveth to your hearts; and then there will be a constancy and an evenness in your mouths and manners.

Ver. 9. *Be afflicted*] ταλαιπωρήσατε, or, Be miserable; ye are so, but see yourselves to be so. Or, afflict yourselves, viz. with voluntary sorrows for your sins. See that ye be active here.

And mourn] Savourly and soakingly, with a deep and downright sorrow, so as a man would do in the death of his dearest friend. The Greek word, πενθήσατε, imports a funeral-grief.

And weep] In judgment at least, and then, dry sorrow may go as far as wet, where tears will not come. But if it be possible, look not upon sin with dry eyes; point every sin with a tear.

Let your laughter be turned] Turn all the streams into this one channel, that may drive the mill, that may grind the heart. Meal was offered of old, and not whole corn.

And your joy to heaviness] κατήφεια,[1] such as makes a man hang down his head, and go heavily through grief and shame.

Ver. 10. *Humble yourselves*] He beats oft upon this most needful but much-neglected duty of humiliation, and all is little enough; there being nothing that more goes against the heart and the hair with us, than to go downward; and yet it must be done, or we are undone.

And he shall lift you up] The Lion of Judah rends not the prostrate prey. But as William the Conqueror ever held submission satisfactory for the greatest offences, and often received rebels into grace (Daniel's Chron.), so doth Christ much more. The sun in the morning gathereth clouds, but then it soon scattereth them again; so doth the Sun of righteousness cast men down, that he may raise them up again.

---

[1] *Tristitia cum vultus demissione.* Budæus.

Dejicit ut relevet, premit ut solatia præstet,
  Enecat ut possit vivificare Deus.

Ver. 11. *Speak not evil, &c.*] As Ezekiel's
hearers did of him " by the walls, and in the doors
of the houses," chap. xxxiii. 30, and as too many of
ours do ; for the which they will be full dearly accountable. The tale-bearer hath the devil in his
tongue, the tale-hearer in his ear.

Speaketh evil of the law] Which flatly forbiddeth detraction. And as the strokes given
upon the left side are felt upon the right, so it
is here. The law is evil spoken of when a
brother is evil spoken of.

And judgeth the law] As not severe enough, or
as over-strait. Plato commendeth that law of
the Lydians, that punisheth detractors like as
they did murderers. There is a murder of the
tongue also, Ezek. xxii. 9.

Ver. 12. *There is one law-giver*] What dost
thou then do perking into his place, by censuring
and defaming another; is not this to be a pope
in thine own cause, exalting thyself above God,
2 Thess. ii. 4, or at least appealing from him to
thyself ?

Ver. 13. *We will go into such, &c.*] As if they
were petty gods within themselves, and needed
not to call God into counsel, or to take his leave
along with them. But such confident exchange
language became not the mouths of scattered
exiles. And yet it is the common sin of dispersed Jews in all places to this day. And I
would it were their sin only ; and that this rude
and rash peremptoriness were not in use amongst
us also.

Ver. 14. *Ye know not what, &c.*] God delights
to cross such vain boasters, and to confute their
confidences, that speak and live as if their lives
were riveted upon eternity. They might easily
observe that many things fall out betwixt the
cup and the lip, betwixt the chin and the chalice.
Ne glorietur igitur accinctus quasi discinctus.
Sell not the hide before ye have taken the beast.
Who knows what a great-bellied day may bring
forth ? Prov. xxvii. 1. Whiles a woman is yet
with child, none can tell what kind of birth it
will be, Luke xii. 16, 17.

It is even a vapour] Thy breath is in thy
nostrils, ever ready to puff out; at the next puff
of breath thou mayest blow away thy life.
Petrarch relates of a certain holy man, that being
invited to a feast on the morrow, he answered,
I have not had a morrow-day to dispose of this
many a year ; if you would anything of me now,
I am ready (lib. iii. Memor.). Mere man is but
the dream of a dream, but the generation of a
fancy, but a poor feeble, unable, dying flash, but
the curious picture of nothing. Can a picture
continue that is drawn upon the ice ? What is
man, saith Nazianzen, but soul and soil, breath
and body (νοῦς καὶ χοῦς, *ex* Gen. ii. 7) ; a puff
of wind the one, a pile of dust the other, no
solidity in either ? Surely every man in his
best estate, when he is best underlaid, and settled
upon his best bottom, is altogether vanity, Psal.

xxxix. 5. Two fits of an ague could shake great
Tamerlane to death, in the midst of his great
hopes and greatest power, when he was preparing for the utter rooting out of the Othoman
family, and the conquest of the Greek empire.
(Turk. Hist.) What is man's body but a bubble ?
the soul the wind that filleth it ? the bubble
riseth higher and higher till at last it breaketh ;
so doth the body from infancy to youth, and
thence to age. So that it is improper to ask
when we shall die ? but rather when we shall
make an end of dying (said a divine), for first the
infancy dieth, then the childhood, then the youth,
then age, and then we make an end of dying.
Should we then live and trade as if our lives were
rivetted upon eternity ? To blame were those
Agrigentines who did eat, build, &c., as though
they should never die.

Ver. 15. *If the Lord will, &c.*] ἐὰν Θεὸς ἐθέλῃ.
So Socrates taught Alcibiades to say, " If God
will," &c. And another could say,

Nullius est felix conatus et utilis unquam,
  Consilium si non detque juvetque Deus.

Ver. 16. *In your boastings*] Of long life and
suitable success. God will shoot an arrow at
such suddenly, Psal. lxiv. 9, as he did at the rich
fool, Nebuchadnezzar, Haman, Herod, Sennacherib, and other braggadocios.

Ver. 17. *To him that knoweth*] Lest they
should reply, we know all this, that except we
live and God list, we can do nothing. Do ye
know to do well, saith he, and do it not ? this
increaseth your guilt. Sin against knowledge is
sin with an accent, wickedness with a witness,
such as is not to be excused by any plea or colour.
See John ix. 41, with the note.

CHAPTER V.

Ver. 1. *Go to now, ye rich men*] THOSE rich
wretches mentioned chap. ii. 6, 7, that blasphemed God and oppressed men. *Magna cognatio ut rei sic nominis, divitiis et vitiis.*

Weep and howl] Better weep here, where there
are wiping handkerchiefs in the hand of Christ,
than to have your eyes whipped out in hell.
Better howl with men than yell with devils.

That shall come upon you] Gr. ἐπερχομέναις,
that are even now stealing upon you.

Ver. 2. *Your riches are corrupted*] Being subject to vanity and violence, Matt. vi. 19. See
the note there. Provide yourselves therefore
bags that wax not old ; treasure that faileth
not, &c., Luke xii. 33.

Ver. 3. *And shall eat your flesh*] *i. e.* With
hell-fire, which shall consume your flesh, nay,
your souls, with eternal torments. Some strong
poison is made of the rust of metals ; none worse
than that of money.

For the last days] Wrath for the day of wrath ;
or store for old age, it being the old man's care,
as Plutarch observes, ὅτι οὐκ ἕξει θάψοντας καὶ
θρέψοντας, that he shall not have what to keep

him while alive, and what to bury him honestly when dead.

Ver. 4. Kept back by fraud crieth] Bloodshed, Gen. iv. 10, unnatural lust, Gen. xviii. 21, and oppression (whether by force or fraud), cry to God, and he will hear, for "he is gracious," Exod. xxii. 27. Oppression is a bony sin, Amos v. 12, 13.

Clamitat in cœlum vox sanguinis, et Sodomorum, Vox oppressorum, et merces detenta laborum.

Lord of Sabaoth] Who hath all power in his hand, and can easily reach you.

Ver. 5. Ye have lived in pleasure] Ye have lain melting in sensual delights, which have drawn out your spirits, and dissolved them, τρυφῇ, of θρύπτω.

Upon earth] No place of pleasure to good men, but of purgatory, banishment, and bondage. A place of that nature, that (as it is reported of the straits of Magellan) which way soever a man bend his course (if homeward) he is sure to have the wind against him. It was a heavy charge laid upon Dives, "Son, remember that thou in thy life time receivedst thy good things," Luke xvi. 25.

And been wanton] Fulness breeds forgetfulness, Deut. xxxii. 15. The word ἐσπαταλήσατε properly signifies, Ye have petulantly skipped up and down, like young kids; ye are so wanton that ye know not whether to go on your heads or on your feet. This was the guise of these rich rioters.

As in a day of slaughter] For sacrifice; when they used to have good cheer, Prov. vii. 14. And hereunto the wise man alludeth, Prov. xvii. 1. The apostle here seemeth to intimate that these rich sensualists lived upon the cream of sinning, and had such plenty that they picked out none but the sweetest bits to nourish their hearts withal.

Ver. 6. Ye have condemned and killed] Take it either properly, or metaphorically of usurers and extortioners, that not only rob, but ravish the poor that are fallen into their nets, Psal. x. 9, that is, their bonds, debts, mortgages, as Chrysostom interpreteth it; there is neither equity nor mercy to be had at their hands; hence they are called men-eaters, cannibals, &c. One saith there is more justice to be found in hell than here among men; for in hell no innocent person is oppressed.

And he doth not resist you] Meekness of spirit commonly draws on injuries and indignities from unreasonable men. A crow will stand upon a sheep's back, pulling off wool from her side, she durst not do so to a wolf or a mastiff. *Veterem ferendo injuriam invitas novam.*

Ver. 7. Be patient therefore] *q. d.* You poor oppressed ones, hold out faith and patience. You shall shortly have help. As the mother's breasts ache to be suckling, so doth God's heart yearn to be helping.

Unto the coming of the Lord] sc. By particular deliverance; and not only by the general judgment. Let patience have line and rope.

Waiteth for the precious fruit] Being *in novum annum semper dives*, as the proverb is, ever rich against the next year. *Spes alit agricolas*, Hope holds up the husbandman's heart.

And hath long patience] He looks not to sow and reap in a day, as the Hyperboreans are said to do, that sow shortly after the sun-rising with them, and reap before the sun set; because the whole half year is one continuate day with them. (Heresbach de re Rustic.)

Ver. 8. For the coming] See ver. 7. And he when he comes shall set all to rights. We shall see so much reason in his proceedings, which now we comprehend not, that we shall yield him the "only wise God."

Ver. 9. Grudge not, &c.] μὴ στενάζετε, groan not, grumble not, grow not sour and sullen one to another.

Lest ye be condemned] As Sarah had been, if the Lord had come, as she desired him, to judge betwixt her and her husband. The most guilty are commonly most querulous and complaintful.

The judge standeth before the door] If the magistrate be present we may not offend another to defend ourselves. *Ecce judex pro foribus;* therefore, Hold a blow, as we say.

Ver. 10. For an example of suffering] Examples very much affect us, as they did many of the martyrs. See the note on Matt. v. 12.

A bove majori discit arare minor.

Ver. 11. We count them happy] If they suffer as they should do, not else. Mithridates showed long patience, such as it was, forced and feigned. He was in a kind of fever called epialis, wherein men be cold without, but hot as fire within. This fever he quenched with his vital blood, shed with his own hand.

Ye have heard of the patience of Job] His impatience is not once mentioned against him; but he is crowned and chronicled here for his patience. God passeth by infirmities, where the heart is upright.

And have seen the end of the Lord] That is, how well it was with Job at the last. Or (as others will have it) what a sweet end the Lord Christ made; whereunto you were some of you eye-witnesses, and should be herein his followers.

And of tender mercy] Having for his motto that of the Emperor Rupert, *Miseria res digna misericordia*, Misery calleth for mercy.

Ver. 12. But above all things] Swear not in jest, lest ye go to hell in earnest. See the note on Matt. v. 34, 35, and on Matt. xxiii. 16, 18. Swear not in your passion (the apostle is here exhorting them to patience), as the Jews did ordinarily, and, so it were by the creature, held it no great sin, Matt. v. 33, and xxiii. 16. The swearer rends and tears God's name as a draper rasheth out a piece of cloth to the buyer. He makes his tongue a grenado to shoot out oaths and blasphemies against heaven. He shall one day smart for it in his tongue as Dives did, and be worse punished than the French were in the days of Louis XI., who punished swearing by searing the lips of the swearer with a hot iron.

Ver. 13. *Is any among you afflicted?*] Any one may, for grace is no target against affliction.

Let him pray] Not only because prayer is suitable to a sad disposition, but because it is the conduit of comfort, and hath *virtutem pacativam*, a settling efficacy. Besides, there is no time for hearing of prayers like the time of affliction. Then the saints may have anything of God with reason, for then his heart is turned within him, his repentings are kindled together, Hos. xi. 8. See Zech. xiii. 9; Psal. xci. 15. Then it was that Lot had Zoar given him; David, the lives of his enemies; Paul, all the souls in the ship, &c. See the promise, Psal. l. 15.

Is any man merry?] Gr. εὐθυμεῖ, is he right set, well hung on, as we say? All true mirth is from the rectitude of the mind, from a right frame of soul that sets and shows itself in a cheerful countenance.

Let him sing psalms] So that in all estates we must be doing somewhat for God. *Tam Dei meminisse opus est, quam respirare.* A Christian's whole life is divided into praying and praising, as David's Psalms are. If he begin with petition, he commonly concludes with thanksgiving. Thus, by a holy craft, he insinuates into God's favour, driving a trade betwixt earth and heaven, receiving and returning, importing one commodity and transporting another.

Ver. 14. *Is any man sick?*] "Behold, he whom thou lovest is sick," said Martha to our Saviour, John xi. *Si amatur, quomodo infirmatur,* saith Augustine. If Christ's friend, how comes he to be sick? Well enough; it is no new thing for Christ's best-beloved to be much afflicted.

Let him send for the elders] This help God hath provided for such as are by sickness disabled to pray for themselves. Sick Abimelech was sent to Abraham (a prophet) for prayers.

Anointing him with oil] As an extraordinary sign of an extraordinary cure. From mistake of this text, the Church instead of pastors had ointers and painters in times of Popery, who did not only *ungere*, but *emungere*, anneal men, but beguile them of their monies, and of their souls. Neither want there at this day, that hold this anointing the sick as a standing ordinance for Church members amongst us; and they tell of strange cures too effected thereby. I hope they aim better than Pflugius and Sidonius, authors of that wicked piece called the Interim, did; for they defended the Popish chrism and extreme unction, *ut ipsi discederent unctiores* (as one saith), that they might get fat bishoprics thereby. The Popish ointment differeth much from St James's oil, used as an outward symbol and sign till miracles ceased. See Mark xvi. 17; Acts iii. 16. Proculus, a Christian, healed Seve-

rus the emperor on this wise, as Tertullian testifieth. (Advers. Scapulam.)

Ver. 15. *And the prayer of faith*] The Greek word for prayer hath its denomination from well pouring out the heart, or from well cleaving to God.[1] Afflictions (saith one) cause us to seek out God's promise, the promise to seek faith, faith to seek prayer, and prayer to find God.

They shall be forgiven him] And so he shall be cured on both sides. He shall be sure to have his prayer out, either in money or money's worth, his labour shall not be in vain in the Lord.

Ver. 16. *Confess your faults*] To any such godly friend, as can both keep counsel and give counsel. Oftentimes the very opening of men's grievances easeth, the very opening of a vein cools the blood. Howbeit, it is neither wisdom nor mercy (saith a good divine) to put men upon the rack of confession, further than they can have no ease any way else. For by this means we raise a jealousy in them towards us, and oft without cause; which weakeneth and tainteth that love that should unite hearts in one.

The effectual fervent prayer] Gr. ἐνεργουμένη, the working prayer, that sets the whole man a-work to do it as it should be done, and so works wonders in heaven and earth, being after a sort omnipotent, as Luther said. The word rendered "effectual fervent," is by one rendered a thorough-wrought prayer. An allusion he maketh it to cloth, for such like, which we use to say is thoroughly well wrought, or but slightly wrought.

Availeth much] Jamblicus a profane writer hath such a commendation of prayer, as might well beseem a better man. He calleth it *clavem qua Dei penetralia aperiuntur, rerum divinarum ducem et lucem.* (Lib. v. c. 27.) The key of God's treasury, the guide to God. In the island called Taprobane, they sail not by any observation of the stars, they cannot see the north pole, but they carry birds along with them which they often let go, and so bend their course the same way, for the birds will make toward land. Let us oft send up prayers to heaven, and let our hearts go along with them, and they will certainly speed. God will come, but he will have his people's prayers lead him, Dan. x. 12. I came for thy word. He will help, but then we must work in prayer; and as when a cart is in a quagmire, if the horses feel it coming, they will pull the harder, so must we, when we find deliverance is coming, and that God is upon his way. Fervent prayer may fitly be resembled to the precious stone Pyrites, which if rubbed grows hot, and burneth the fingers; as, on the other side, dull prayers do little good, but are as the precious stone Diacletes, which having many virtues in it, loseth them all if put into a dead man's mouth, as naturalists tell us.

Ver. 17. *Subject to like passions*] For he fled at the threats of Jezebel, *Factus seipso imbecillior,*

---

[1] εὐχὴ παρὰ τὸ εὖ χέειν, vel   παρὰ τὸ εὖ ἔχεσθαι τοῦ θείου.

saith one; and he would have died, when under the juniper, discontented.

Ver. 18. And the earth brought forth] When the roots and fruits seemed all dried up, and the land past recovery. But prayer never comes too late, because God never doth.

Ver. 19. If any do err from, &c.] Err about fundamentals, fall into deadly heresy, damnable, Peter calleth it, 2 Epist. ii. 1.

Ver. 20. Shall save a soul] A high honour to have any hand in such a work.

Cover a multitude] *i. e.* He shall be a means that God shall cover them.

THE FIRST EPISTLE GENERAL OF ST PETER.

CHAPTER I.

Ver. 1. To the strangers] THAT is, to the provincial Jew. See the note on James i. 1. These strangers were (probably) those that came up to Jerusalem at Pentecost, and were converted by St Peter, Acts ii., to whom therefore he here writes, as to new-born babes, chap. ii. 2, and such as met with manifold afflictions for Christ's sake, chap. iii. 14, &c. He exhorts them therefore to stedfastness in the faith and constancy in trial. Christ's young plants need watering.

Ver. 2. Through sanctification unto obedience] To the means as well as to the end, to sanctification as well as to salvation. Some there be (saith Mr Philpot in an epistle of his to the congregation) that for an extreme refuge in their evil doings, run to God's election, saying, If I be elected I shall be saved, whatever I do. But such be great tempters of God, and abominable blasphemers of his holy election; these cast themselves down from the pinnacle of the temple in presumption, that God may preserve them by his angels through predestination. God's election ought to be with a simple eye considered, to make us more warily walk according to his word, and not set cock in the hoop, and put all on God's back, to do wickedly at large. Thus he.

Grace unto you, and peace be multiplied] πληθυνθείη, or, enlarged to the utmost, filled up and accomplished. He prays for further measures, that they might be past the spoon and get to a well-grown, full-grown age in Christ, Eph. iv. 13, until they came to be fathers, gray-headed, experienced Christians, such as the Psalmist speaketh of, Psal. xc. 12—14.

Ver. 3. Blessed be the God] A stately proem, and such as can hardly be matched again, unless it be that of St Paul to the Ephesians, chap. i. 3.

Unto a lively hope] Sure and solid, clearing the conscience, and cheering the spirit. *Vivere spe vidi qui moriturus erat.* If it were not for hope, the heart would break; as they do whose lives and hopes end together. True hope lives when the man dies. It hath for its motto, *Dum expiro, spero.* The righteous hath hope in his death, as St Stephen had; who

Ibat ovans animis, et spe sua damna levabat,

Went with good cheer to take his end. (Bembus.) And many of the holy martyrs went as willingly to die as ever they did to dine; they called it their wedding-day. They knew it was but winking only, and they should be in heaven immediately; hence their invincible courage at the hour of death. The ungodly are not so; their hopes are dying hopes, they are no better than as the giving up of the ghost, Job xi. 20.

Ver. 4. Undefiled, and that fadeth not] The two Greek words here used are also Latin; Amiantus is a precious stone (saith Doctor Playfere out of Isidore), which though it be never so much soiled, yet it cannot be blemished. And Amaranthus is the name of a flower, which being a long time hung up in the house, yet still is fresh and green, as Clemens writeth (Pædagog. p. 8). To both these possibly the apostle might here allude: and it is as if he should say, The crown that you shall receive shall be studded with the stone Amiantus, which cannot be defiled; and it is garnished with the flower Amaranthus, which is fresh and green, &c.

Ver. 5. Who are kept] φρουρούμενοι, as with a guard, or as in a garrison, that is, well fenced with walls and works, and so is made impregnable.

By the power of God] Much seen in the saints' perseverance. "My Father is stronger than all; none therefore can take you out of my hands, sith I and the Father are one," John x. 29 .30.

Ver. 6. Wherein ye greatly rejoice] Gr. ἀγαλλιᾶσθε, ye dance for joy, ye dance a galliard, or as children do about a bonfire; ye cannot but express your inward joy in your countenance, voice, and gesture.

If need be, ye are in heaviness] When our hearts grow a grain too light, God seeth it but needful to make us heavy through manifold temptations. When our water (as it were) looks but a little too high, our heavenly Father, a physician no less cunning than loving (saith

Bayn), doth discern it, and quickly fits us, whom he most tendereth, with that which will reduce all to the healthsome temper of a broken spirit.

Ver. 7. *That the trial of your faith*] If affliction (which is the trial of our faith) be so exceeding precious, what is faith then, and the promises whereon faith lays hold? There are that by the trial of faith understand here a well-tried faith, which is called "gold tried in the fire," Rev. iii. 18.

Ver. 8. *Whom having not seen*] They had not been, belike, at the feast of the Passover (at which time our Saviour suffered), but came up to the feast of Pentecost, and were converted, Acts ii.

And full of glory] Gr. δεδοξασμένη, glorified already; a piece of God's kingdom and heaven's happiness aforehand. Oh the joy! the joy! the inexpressible joy that I find in my soul! said a dying saint.

Ver. 9. *The end of your faith*] The period and perfection, the reward and meed of it, in all fulness. See Psal. xix. 12; Prov. xxii. 4. Some grapes of Canaan God gave them beforehand, to sustain them, not to satisfy them.

Ver. 10. *The prophets have inquired*] This highly sets forth the weight and worth of it, sith such men took such pains upon it. Base spirits are busied about light matters; as Domitian spent his time in catching flies, Artaxerxes in making knife-hafts; not so Caleb, "who had another spirit, and followed God wholly," Numb. xiv. 24. So did the ancient prophets, as Isaiah: whiles the merry Greeks were taken up at their Olympic games in the year 1540 from the Flood, the prophet Isaiah seeth that heavenly vision of Christ sitting on his throne, and heareth that thrice happy Trisagion, Isaiah vi. 1—3. (Buchol. Chron.) And in this disquisition and scrutiny, the prophets with singular desire and industry exercised themselves, as the two compound Greek words, ἐκζητεῖν ἐξερευνᾶν, used in the next verse do import.

Ver. 11. *Searching what, &c.*] ἐρευνῶντες, with greatest sagacity and industry, as hunters seek for game, and as men seek for gold in the very mines of the earth.

The sufferings of Christ, &c.] Macarius was utterly out in saying that the prophets knew that Christ should be born for man's redemption, but that they knew nothing of his death and sufferings. Isaiah writes of them more like an evangelist than a prophet, and is therefore called the "evangelical prophet."

Ver. 12. *Not unto themselves*] In regard of the accomplishment of those oracles that they uttered; and yet to themselves, in regard of their right and interest therein.

They did minister] None must hold themselves too good to serve the saints.

The angels desire to look into] To look wishly and intently, as the cherubims of old looked into the mercy-seat, Exod. xxv. 18, 19. παρακύψαι, *Prono capite et propenso collo accurate introspicere.*

Ver. 13. *Wherefore gird up, &c.*] We are seldom comforted, but we have need to be exhorted. So apt are our hearts to security, and so apt is Satan to interrupt our joys with his base injections. How soon did Hezekiah fondly overshoot himself to the Babylonish ambassadors, after his sweet intercourse with God in holy duties! And how shamefully did Jonah forget himself and break out into a brawl with God, after his embassage faithfully discharged to the Ninevites, and the sweet comforts that came in to his soul thereupon!

Gird up the loins of your mind, &c.] Gird yourselves and serve God, Luke xvii. 8. A loose, discinct, and diffluent mind is unfit for God's service. Girding implies, 1. Readiness; 2. Nimbleness, handiness, and handsomeness. The main strength of the body is in the loins. Therefore some say, the strong purposes and resolutions of the mind are here meant.

Hope to the end] Gr. τελείως, hope perfectly or entirely; *q. d.* do it not by halves; let there not be any odd reckonings between God and you, but work out your salvation, Phil. ii. 12. See the note there.

For the grace] That is, for the glory.

That is to be brought unto you] It must be brought unto us (such is our dulness), we will scarce go seek it, hardly be persuaded to live happily, reign everlastingly.

Ver. 14. *Not fashioning yourselves*] συσχηματιζό-μενοι. As a player is fashioned to the obscene speeches and carriages of him whom he personateth.

In your ignorance] Men may remain grossly ignorant amidst abundance of means, as these Jews did. "Who is blind but my servant? or deaf as my messenger?" &c., Isa. xlii. 19, 20.

Ver. 15. *In all manner of conversation*] Our very civilities must savour of sanctity, and our common conversation relish of religion. St Paul's civil conversation, πολίτευμα, was in heaven, Phil. iii. 20. Holiness must be written upon our bridles when we war; upon our cups when we drink, Zech. xiv. 20, 21. It is said of a certain Scotch divine, that he did even eat, and drink, and sleep eternal life.

Ver. 16. *Be ye holy*] *i. e.* Separate from sin, and dedicated to God, in conformity to whom stands our happiness. See the note on Matt. v. 48.

Ver. 17. *Of your sojourning*] παροικία, inchoatus, commoratio. Having your commoration on earth, but your conversation in heaven. *Fugiamus ad cœlestem patriam, &c.*, could a heathen say.

In fear] Those that fear, of all others, are most likely to hold out, Jer. xxxii. 40. It is a reverential, filial fear of God, as of a father, that is here required; causing us, 1. to have high and honourable conceptions of God in our hearts; "Sanctify the Lord God in your hearts, and let him be your dread, and fear ye him." 2. Making all honourable mention of him with our mouths, whether we speak to him, or of him, Eccles. v. 1; Deut. xxviii. 58. Presume not in a sudden unmannerliness to blurt out the dreadful name of God; much less to blaspheme it, and bore it through with hideous oaths and imprecations. To speak evil of one's father was death by Plato's law as well as by God's law; and Suidas testifieth of the same Plato and other heathens, that when they would swear by their Jupiter, out of the mere dread and reverence of his name, they forbear to mention him; breaking off their oath with a Mὰ τὸν, as those that only dared to owe the rest to their thoughts. 3. Walking before him in our whole course with a holy bashfulness, being evermore in the sense of his presence and light of his countenance, in the "fear of the Lord, and in the comfort of the Holy Ghost," as those ancient Christians, Acts ix. 31.

Ver. 18. Ye were not redeemed with silver and gold] These are poor things to purchase a soul with (more likely they are to drown it in perdition and destruction, 1 Tim. vi. 9). Our Saviour, who only ever went to the price of souls, tells us that one soul is more worth than a world, Matt. xvi. 26.

Received by tradition] Children are very apt to follow their parents' example, whether of good or evil. *Me ex ea opinione quam a majoribus accepi de cultu Deorum, nullius unquam movebit oratio,* saith Tully, I will never forsake that way of divine service that I have received from my forefathers.

Ver. 19. Without blemish] Of original pollution.

And without spot] Of actual sin: or thus, without blemish, that is, sound within; and without spot, right in the outward parts. A lamb may be fair without, that is rotten within. Christ was none such, but a complete sacrifice for sin.

Ver. 20. Who verily, &c.] So careful was God to make all sure concerning our redemption in Christ, saith one here.

Ver. 21. Might be in God] And so in a safer hand than our own; he hath laid help upon one that is mighty.

Ver. 22. Ye have purified] *Animabus vestris castificatis.* A metaphor from the legal purifications.

Ver. 23. Born again] A man shall never have occasion to curse the day of his new birth.

By the word of God] Made prolifical and generative by the Spirit, 1 John iii. 9. It is the Father that regenerateth us originally, Tit. iii. 5, the Son meritoriously and effectively, John xiv. 19; Ephes. v. 26; the Holy Ghost consummately and applicatorily, through faith wrought and increased in us by the word and sacraments, James i. 18. Acts xxii. 16, "Be baptized, and wash away thy sins," *i. e.* be renewed.

Ver. 24. All flesh is grass] To live is but to lie a-dying. Can a picture continue that is drawn upon the ice? *Fœnea quadam fœlicitate temporaliter florent,* saith Austin, after David, Psal. xxxvii. 2. The wicked flourish as grass, but they shall be cut down in their flourish.

Ver. 25. The word of the Lord, &c.] This sentence is the motto of the Dukes of Saxony. (Manlii, loc. com.) See Psal. cxix. 89. By the word of the Lord understand that which is written *in cordibus, non in codicibus;* in the heart, not in the book.

CHAPTER II.

Ver. 1. All malice and all guile] Out with this leaven utterly, 1 Cor. v. 7. Howsoever we otherwise fail, let us not in these be found faulty at all. These are not the spots of God's children, Deut. xxxii. 5. They are without gall, without guile, children that will not lie: they do not wallow or allow themselves in any kind of these evils; which are therefore plurally expressed.

Ver. 2. Desire the sincere] ἄδολον, as in children all speak and work at once, hands, feet, mouth. See David's desire, Psal. xlii. 1; cxix. 20, 40, 131. The Greek word ἐπιποθήσατε signifieth vehemently to desire. See Rom. i. 11; 2 Cor. v. 2; Phil. i. 8; ii. 16.

The sincere] Gr. Guileless, unmixed milk, not sugared or sophisticated with strains of wit, excellency of speech, &c., 1 Cor. ii. 1.

That ye may grow thereby] After generation, 1 Pet. i. 23, augmentation. That word which breeds us, feeds us; as the same blood of which the babe is bred and fed in the womb, strikes up into the mother's breasts, and there, by a further concoction, becometh white, and nourisheth it. And as milk from the breasts is more effectually taken than when it hath stood a while, and the spirits are gone out of it; so the word preached rather than read, furthereth the soul's growth. Let it be our care that we receive not the grace of God in vain; that we be not like the changeling Luther mentioneth, ever sucking, never batling; lest God repent him of his love and dry up the breasts; or send in the Assyrian to drink up our milk, Ezek. xxv. 4; that we be not always learning, and never to know the truth, 2 Tim. iii. 6, as ants run to and fro about a mole-hill, but grow not greater. A Christian should go from the word, as Moses did from the mount, as Naaman did out of Jordan, or as the woman of Samaria came to the well *peccatrix,* went away *prædicatrix,* saith Ambrose.

Ver. 3. If so be ye have tasted] As babes taste the milk they take down, Isa. lxvi. 11. We are bid to suck and be satisfied with the breasts of consolation, to press and oppress the promises, till we have expressed, and even wrung the sweetness out of them. This will make us even sick of love; our sleep will be pleasant unto us, and our hearts filled with gladness. The saints taste how good the Lord is, and thence they so long after him. *Optima demonstratio est a sensibus,* as he that feels fire hot, and that tastes honey sweet, can best say it is so.

Ver. 4. As unto a living stone] Living and all-quickening, as Acts vii. 38. Lively, that is, life-giving oracles. He that hath the Son hath life, 1 John v. 12.

Disallowed indeed of men] For the cock on the dunghill knoweth not the price of this jewel.

And precious] Far beyond that most orient and excellent stone Pantarbe, celebrated by Philostratus (in Vita Apol.) ; or that precious adamant of Charles Duke of Burgundy, sold for 20,000 ducats and set in the pope's triple crown. (Alsted Chron.)

Ver. 5. *Ye also as lively stones*] God's house is built of growing stones, of green timber, Cant. i.

To offer up spiritual sacrifices] Such as are prayers, Psal. cxli. 2 ; praises, Heb. xiii. 5 ; alms, Heb. xiii. 16 ; ourselves, Rom. xii. 1 ; our Saviour, whom we present as a propitiation for our sins, 1 John ii. 1, laying our hands on his head, seeing him bleed to death and consumed in the fire of his Father's wrath for our sins.

Ver. 6. *Wherefore it is contained*] The Jews were so well versed in Scripture, that in quoting of texts there was need to say no more to them than, It is written, It is contained, περιέχει, they could tell where to turn to the place presently ; and this was a great furtherance to the conversion of many of them, by the preaching of the apostles. Many amongst us are better seen in Sir Philip than in St Peter : in Monsieur Balzack's letters than in St Paul's Epistles ; like that bishop of Dunkelden in Scotland, they know little or nothing either of the Old or New Testament ; and therefore one may preach riffraff, popery, or any error unto them, and they know not how to disprove it.

Shall not be confounded] The Hebrew text hath it, "shall not make haste," Isa. xxviii. 16. Haste makes waste, as we say, and oft brings confusion. Children pull apples before they are ripe, and have worms bred of them.

Ver. 7. *He is precious*] Gr. τιμή, he is a price, or an honour. If you had not found all worth in him, you would never have sold all for him.

Ver. 8. *And a rock of offence*] Like that rock, Judg. vi. 21, out of which comes fire to consume the reprobate.

Which stumble at the word] An ill sign, and yet an ordinary sin. A bridge is made to give us a safe passage over a dangerous river ; but he who stumbleth on the bridge is in danger to fall into the river. The word is given as a means to carry us over hell into heaven ; but he who stumbles and quarrels at this means, shall fall in thither, from whence otherwise he had been delivered by it. Few sins are more dangerous than that of picking quarrels at God's word, and taking up the bucklers against it, snuffing at it, Mal. i. 13 ; chatting against it, Rom. ix. 19, 20 ; enviously swelling against it, Acts xiii. 45 ; casting reproaches upon it, Jer. xx. 8, 9 ; gathering odious consequences from it. Surely of such a man may say, as one doth of a hypocrite ; I read not in Scripture, saith he, of a hypocrite's conversion ; and what wonder ? for whereas after sin, conversion is left as a means to cure all

other sinners ; what means to recover him who hath converted conversion itself into sin ? so here ; what hope that he shall be saved who stumbleth at the only ordinary means of his salvation ?

Ver. 9. *But ye are a chosen generation*] A picked people, the dearly beloved of God's soul ; such as he first chose for his love, and then loves for his choice.

A royal priesthood] Or as Moses hath it, Exod. xx. 6, a kingdom of priests. Priests God's people are in respect of God, kings in respect of men. The righteous are kings : "many righteous men have desired," &c., saith Matthew, chap. xiii. 17 ; "many kings," saith Luke, chap. x. 24. Indeed they are somewhat obscure kings here, as was Melchisedec in the land of Canaan ; but princes they are in all lands, Psal. xlv. 16, and more excellent than their neighbours, let them dwell where they will, Prov. xii. 26.

A peculiar people] Gr. λαὸς εἰς περιποίησιν, a people of purchase : such as comprehend, as it were, all God's gettings, his whole stock that he makes any great reckoning of.

Show forth the praises] Gr. ἐξαγγείλητε, preach forth the virtues by our suitable practice. The picture of a dear friend should be hung up in a conspicuous place of the house ; so should God's holy image and grace in our hearts.

Vile latens virtus ; quid enim submersa tenebris
    Proderit ? (Claud.)

Jerome said that he did *diligere Christum habitantem in Augustino*, love Christ dwelling in Austin. So ought we to walk, that others may see and love Christ dwelling in us. He is *totus desiderabilis*, saith the spouse in the Canticles, v. 16, all over desirable ; and there is in him that which may well attract all hearts unto him.

Ver. 10. *Which in time past were not*] If Plato thought it such a mercy to him that he was a man and not a woman, a Grecian and not a barbarian, a scholar to Socrates and not to any other philosopher, what exceeding great cause have we to praise God that we are born Christians, not Pagans, Protestants, not Papists, in these blessed days of reformation, &c.

Ver. 11. *As pilgrims and strangers*] Excellently doth Justin Martyr describe the Christians of his time : they inhabit their own countries, saith he, but as strangers ; they partake of all as citizens, and yet suffer all as foreigners ; every strange land is a country to them, and every country a strange land. (Epist. ad Diog.)

And strangers, abstain] Thoughts of death will be a death to our lusts, Lam. i. 9. Her filthiness is in her skirts, and all because she remembereth not her last end. As the stroking of a dead hand on the belly cureth a tympany, and as the ashes of a viper applied to the part that is stung draws the venom out of it ; so the thought of death is a death to sin.

From fleshly lusts] Those parts in our bodies that are the chiefest and nearest both subjects and objects of lust and concupiscence, are like unto the dung-gate, 1 Chron. xxvi. 16, whereby all the filth was cast out of the temple. God hath placed them in our bodies, like snakes creeping out of the bottom of a dunghill, and abased them in our eyes, that we might make a base account and estimation of the desires thereof, as one well observeth.

Which war against the soul] Only man is in love with his own bane (beasts are not so), and fights for those lusts that fight against the soul. And whereas some might say that other lusts fight against the soul, as well as fleshly lusts, it is answered that other lusts fight against the graces, but these more against the peace of the soul. (Capell on Temptation.) Take we up therefore that motto of Otho II., *Pacem cum hominibus cum vitiis bellum ;* Let us quarrel with our faults and not with our friends.

Ver. 12. *Having your conversation honest*] Leading convincing lives, the best arguments against an atheist adversary.

They speak evil of you] See the note on Matt. v. 11.

Which they shall behold] Whiles they pry and spy into your courses (as the Greek word ἐποπτεύοντες imports) to see what evil they can find out and fasten on.

In the day of visitation] When God shall effectually call and convert them. See the note on Matt. v. 16.

Ver. 13. *Submit to every ordinance*] That is, although the ordinance or government in the manner of its constitution be from man, yet because of the necessity of its institution it is from God ; submit to it, though of man, for the Lord's sake. (Fuller's Answer to Dr Fern.) For although it is called here man's creature or ordinance, either in respect of man the subject, by whom it is exercised, or man the object, about whom it is conversant, or of man the end, to whose emolument it tendeth ; yet it is still the gift and institution of God, the primary author and provident ordainer. *A Deo sane est sive jubente, sive sinente,* Of God it is surely, either so commanding or so suffering it to be, saith Augustine (contra Faust. Man. xxii. 7).

Ver. 14. *Or unto governors*] In the kingdom of Christ, this is wonderful, saith Zanchy, that he wills and commands all princes and potentates to be subject to his kingdom, and yet he wills and commands likewise that his kingdom be subject to the kingdoms of the world.

Ver. 15. *Ye may put to silence*] Gr. φιμοῦν, muzzle, or halter up, button up their mouths, as we say. See the note on Matt. xxii. 34. It is an old fetch of the devil to persuade the world that faithful people are antimagistratical ; these must be powerfully confuted by our contrary practice.

Ver. 16. *As free*] See the note on Gal. v. 13.

As free, and not using, &c.] Free in respect of our consciences, exempted from human powers, and yet, as servants of God, bound in conscience

to obey him in obeying them, so far forth as he doth command us to obey them. (Downame.)

For a cloak] Or cover. This were to put light not under a bushel, but under a dunghill. Beza thinks the apostle here alludes to that old custom at Rome, that those that were manumitted or set free should go with their heads covered, who before used to go bareheaded. Religion is an ill cloak of maliciousness ; and will surely serve hypocritical libertines, as the disguise Ahab put on, and perished.

Ver. 17. *Honour all men*] As made in the image of God, as capable of heaven, and as having some special talent to trade with.

Honour the king] *i. e.* the Roman emperor, who disclaimed the name of a king to avoid the hatred of the people, and yet sought the full right of kings, and so to destroy the liberty of the people. But kings that will be honoured must be just, "ruling in the fear of God," 2 Sam. xxiii. 3.

Ver. 18. *To the froward*] Cross, crooked, frample, foolish. *Tortuosis, curvis.* The Greek word σκολιὸς comes of a Hebrew word סכל that signifies a fool.

Ver. 19. *This is thank-worthy*] τοῦτο γὰρ χάρις ἐστί. God accounts himself hereby gratified, as it were, and even beholden to such sufferers, this being the lowest subjection and the highest honour men can yield unto their Maker. God will thank such, which is *condescensio stupenda,* a wonderful condescension.

Ver. 20. *For what glory is it*] In peace-offerings there might be oil mixt, not so in sin-offerings. In our sufferings for Christ there is joy ; not so when we suffer for our faults.

Ver. 21. *Leaving us an example*] Gr. ὑπογραμμὸν, a copy or pattern. Christ's actions were either moral, or mediatory. In both we must imitate him. In the former, by doing as he did. In the latter, by similitude, translating that to our spiritual life, which he did as mediator ; as to die to sin, to rise to righteousness, &c., and this not only by example (as Petrus Abesardus held of old, and the Socinians at this day), but by virtue of Christ's death and resurrection working effectually in all his people ; not as an exemplary cause only, or as a moral cause by way of meditation, but as having force obtained by it, and issuing out of it, even the Spirit that kills sin, and quickens the soul to all holy practice. There is a story of an earl called Eleazar, a passionate prince, that was cured of that disordered affection by studying of Christ and his patience. *Crux pendentis cathedra docentis,* Christ upon the cross is a doctor in his chair, where he reads unto us all a lecture of patience. The eunuch, Acts viii. 32, was converted by this praise in Christ. It is said of Jerome, that having read the godly life and Christian death of Hilarion, he folded up the book, and said, Well, Hilarion shall be the champion whom I will follow. (In Vita ejus apud Surium.) Should we not much more say so of Christ ?

Ver. 22. *Who did no sin*] St Paul saith, "He

knew no sin," 2 Cor. v. 21, to wit, with a practical knowledge (we know no more than we practise) ; with an intellectual he did, for else he could not have reproved it.

Neither was guile found in his mouth] Which imports that they sought it. The wicked seek occasion against the godly.

Ver. 23. *But committed himself*] Or, the whole matter. We also shall do ourselves no disservice, by making God our chancellor, when no law else will relieve us. And indeed the less a man strives for himself, the more is God his champion. He that said, I seek not mine own glory, adds, But there is one that seeketh it, and judgeth. God takes his part ever that fights not for himself.

Ver. 24. *Who his own self*] Without any to help or uphold him, Isa. lxiii. 5 ; he had not so much as the benefit of the sun-light, when in that three hours' darkness he was set upon by all the powers of darkness.

Bare our sins] Gr. ἀνήνεγκεν, bare them aloft, viz. when he climbed up his cross, and nailed them thereunto. "Surely he hath borne our griefs, and carried our sorrows," Isa. liii. 4. He "taketh away the sins of the world," John i. 29.

That we being dead to sins] ἀπογενόμενοι, or, separated from sin, or unmade to it, cut off from it, the old frame being utterly dissolved.

By whose stripes] Or, weals. This he mentioneth to comfort poor servants, whipt and abused by their froward masters. *Sanguis medici factus est medicina phrenetici*, The physician's blood became the sick man's salve. We can hardly believe the power of sword-salve. But here is a mystery that only Christian religion can assure us of, that the wounding of one should be the cure of another.

Ver. 25. *As sheep*] Than the which no creature is more apt to stray, less apt and able to return. The ox knoweth his owner, &c.

CHAPTER III.

Ver. 1. *Be in subjection to your husbands*] Yet with a limitation : subject the wife must be to her husband's lawful commands and restraints. It is too much that Plutarch lays as a law of wedlock on the wife, to acknowledge and worship the same gods, and none else, but those whom her husband doth. Serena the empress suffered martyrdom under her cruel husband Diocletian ; and Elizabeth, wife of Joachimus, the Prince Elector of Brandenburg, was forced to fly to the court of Saxony, A. D. 1527, from the perpetual imprisonment provided for her by her popish husband (for receiving the sacrament of the Lord's supper in both kinds), and died in banishment. (Luther in Epistol.)

Be won by the conversation] κερδηθήσονται, *i. e.* Be prepared for conversion, as Austin's father and himself were, by the piety of his mother Monica. The Greek word for won signifieth gained, ἐποπτεύοντες ; and seems to allude to those

good servants, Matt. xxv., who traded their talents, and doubled them with their good husbandry.

Ver. 2. *Whiles they behold*] Curiously pry into. Carnal men watch the carriages of professors, and spend many thoughts about them.

Your chaste conversation] When Livia the empress was asked how had she got such a power over her husband that she could do anything with him ? She answered, *Multa modestia*, By my much modesty. (Dio in Aug.) A prudent wife commands her husband by obeying.

Coupled with fear] Not slavish fear of blows, but reverent fear : 1. Of offending God, by using unlawful means to get their husband's love, as by plaiting of the hair, &c. 2. Of offending their husbands by immodesty or frowardness.

Ver. 3. *Whose adorning*] *Mundus muliebris.* See Isa. iii. 18. Where the prophet as punctually inveighs against this noble vanity, as if he had viewed the ladies' wardrobes in Jerusalem.

Let it not be that outward] *Vestium curiositas, deformitatis mentium et morum indicium est*, saith Bernard. Excessive neatness is a sign of inward nastiness. It was a true saying of wise Cato, *Cultus magna cura, magna est virtutis injuria*, They are never good that strive to be over-fine. Superfluous apparel, saith Cyprian, is worse than whoredom. Lysander would not suffer his daughters to wear gorgeous attire ; saying it would not make them so comely as common.

Ver. 4. *But let it be the hidden*] *Vestite vos serico pietatis, byssino sanctitatis, purpura pudicitiæ. Taliter pigmentatæ Deum habebitis amatorem.* It is Tertullian's counsel to young women, Clothe yourselves, saith he, with the silk of piety, with the satin of sanctity, with the purple of modesty ; so shall you have God himself to be your suitor. (Lib. de Cult. Fœm.) Plutarch speaks of a Spartan woman that when her neighbours were showing their apparel and jewels, she brought out her children, virtuous and well taught, and said, These are my ornaments and jewels. (See Tit. ii. 4.)

In that which is not corruptible] Or, In the incorruption of a meek and quiet spirit, &c., a garment that will never be the worse for wearing, but the better. Some wives may seem to have been molten out of that salt pillar into which Lot's wife was transformed ; these, as they please not God, so they are contrary to all men.

Of great price] God makes great reckoning of a quiet mind, because it is like himself. He promiseth earth to the meek, and heaven to the incorrupt or sincere, and pure in heart.

Ver. 5. *Who trusted in God*] And therefore would not by unlawful means seek to get or keep their husband's love and favour ; but trusted God for that. So Hezekiah trusted in God, and pulled down the brazen serpent, 2 Kings xviii. 4, 5, opposing his presence to all peril.

Ver. 6. *Calling him lord*] See here, how in a great heap of sin, God can find out his own, and accept of it. There was no good word in all the whole sentence, but this, that she called her husband lord. God is pleased to single out this, and set it as a precious diamond in a gold ring to Sarah's eternal commendation. So Heb. xi. 31, mention is made of Rahab's entertaining the spies, and not of the lie she told : God lays the finger of mercy on the scars of our sins, as that limner in the story.

And are not afraid, &c.] Fear they must, ver. 2, and yet they must not. Fear God, but not their husband's undeserved checks or threats for obeying God. One fear must expel another, as one fire drives out another.

Ver. 7. *Likewise ye*] *Officium ascendit, amor descendit.*

According to knowledge] Where should wisdom be but in the head? This must be showed *Uxoris vitium aut tollendo, aut tolerando*, said Varro, either by curing or at least covering his wife's weaknesses.

As unto the weaker vessel] Glasses are to be tenderly handled ; a small knock soon breaks them. So here. *Vipera virus ob venerationem nuptiarum evomit*, saith Basil, The viper, for the honour of coupling with his mate, casts up his poison ; *et tu duritiem animi, tu feritatem, tu crudelitatem ob unionis reverentiam non deponis?* and wilt not thou for the honour of marriage cast away thy harshness, roughness, cruelty to a consort?

As being heirs] Souls have no sexes, Gal. iii. 28.

That your prayers be not hindered] Isaac prayed in the presence of his wife. This course of praying together, apart from others, being taken up by married couples, will much increase and spiritualize their affection one to another. But jarring will make them leave praying, or praying leave jarring.

Ver. 8. *Be courteous*] Gr. φιλόφρονες, friendly-minded, ready to any good office. Christianity is no enemy to courtesy, but includes it. See the practice of it in Abraham and the Hittites, Boaz and his reapers, the angels' and apostles' salutations, the primitive Christians' holy kiss, in use in Irenæus's time, and Tertullian's, till taken away for the abuse it grew into ; as likewise their love-feasts.

Ver. 9. *Railing for railing*] *Convitium convitio regerere, quid aliud est quam lutum luto purgare?* saith one. To render railing for railing, is to think to wash off dirt with dirt.

That ye should inherit a blessing] Blessings by words, properly, εὐλογίαν. They that will speak good words to men, shall hear good words from God ; they shall have his good word for them in all places, and in the hearts of their greatest enemies, as Jacob and Job had.

Ver. 10. *Love life*] Man is ζῶον φιλόζωον, a creature that loves life, saith Aristotle. Who is the man that willeth life? saith David, Psal. xxxiv. 12. And hereunto every man will be ready to answer, *Ego*, I do, as Austin observeth. But when the condition shall be added, *Cohibe linguam*, &c., Refrain thy tongue, &c., then, saith he, scarce any will appear, or accept the motion.

And see good days] That is, prosperous and

peaceable days ; for all the days of the afflicted are evil, Prov. xv. 15, a joyless life is no life. Rebecca was weary of her life, and so was Elijah when he sat under the juniper. *Multi etiam magni viri sub Eliæ junipero sedent.* It is many a good man's case.

Ver. 11. *Seek peace, and ensue it*] A contentious man never wants woe. *Ut habeas quietum tempus, perde aliquid*, was a proverb at Carthage, as Austin relates it ; *Et concedamus de jure ut careamus lite.* For a quiet life let a man part with his right sometimes.

Ver. 12. *For the eyes of the Lord*] Should not God see as well as hear, his children should want many things. We apprehend not all our own wants, and so cannot pray for relief of all. He, of his own accord, without any monitor, is wont to aid us.

His ears are open unto, &c.] Gr. His ears are unto their prayers ; *q. d.* though their prayers are so faint that they cannot come up to God, God will come down to them. He can feel breath, when no voice can be heard, Lam. iii. 56. *Fletu sæpe agitur non affatu.*

Ver. 13. *And who is he that will, &c.*] Natural conscience cannot but do homage to the image of God stamped upon the natures and works of the godly ; as we see in the carriage of Nebuchadnezzar and Darius toward Daniel. I have known some (saith Mr Bolton) the first occasion of whose conversion was the observation of their stoutness under wrongs and oppressions, whom they have purposely persecuted with extremest hate and malice.

Ver. 14. *But and if ye suffer*] *q. d.* Say you meet with such unreasonable men, made up of mere incongruities and absurdities, that will harm you for well-doing, yet you shall be no losers, 2 Thess. iii. 3.

Ver. 15. *Sanctify the Lord God*] Consider and conceive of him, as he stands described in the Scriptures, and as related to his people, resting upon his power and love, for safety here, and salvation hereafter.

Ready always to give an answer] Gr. To make apology, a bold and wise profession of the truth, with due observation of just circumstances. To dissemble is ever a fault ; but not to profess is then only a fault, when a man is silent, *Intempestive et loco minime idoneo*, at an unfit time and place. Let me be counted and called proud, or anything, *Modo impii silentii non arguar*, said Luther, so I be not guilty of a sinful silence.

To every man that asketh] Christians should in this case stay till they are asked. Cyprian reproveth the rashness of those in his time, that would go of their own accord to the heathen magistrates, professing themselves Christians ; whereby they were put to death. This made one of the persecutors cry out, *O miseri, si libet perire num vobis rupes aut restes desunt?* O wretches, can ye find no way else to despatch yourselves, but that I must be thus troubled with you? Christ, saith Cyprian, would have us rather confess than profess our religion. Now, he confesseth, that doth it being asked ; as he professeth, that doth it of his own free accord.

A reason of the hope] Not every trifling question or malicious cavil. Christ answered the governor not a word to some things, and yet he witnessed a good confession before Pontius Pilate, 1 Tim. vi. 13.

With meekness and fear] Lest you should dishonour a good cause by an ill carriage. Austin professeth this was it that heartened him, and made him to triumph in his former Manichism, that he met with feeble opponents, and such as his nimble wit was easily able to overturn. Carolostadius also had the right on his side, but was not able to make it out and maintain it against Luther.

Ver. 16. *Having a good conscience*] Which you cannot have if you deny or but dissemble the truth. George Marsh, martyr, being examined before the Earl of Derby, kept himself close in the point of the sacrament. But after his departure, thus he writes : I departed much more troubled in my spirit than before, because I had not with more boldness confessed Christ, but in such sort as mine adversaries thereby thought they should prevail against me ; whereat I was much grieved, for hitherto I went about, as much as in me lay, to rid myself out of their hands, if by any means, without open denying of Christ and his word, that could be done. (Acts and Mon.)

As of evil-doers] Malefactors, not martyrs.

They may be ashamed that falsely accuse] This is an excellent way of stopping an open mouth. Oh, these real apologies are very powerful. Thus did the primitive Christians plead for themselves, *Non aliunde noscibiles quam de emendatione vitiorum pristinorum*, saith Tertullian (ad Scapulam), known from all others by their reformed lives. Thus did those old Protestants the Waldenses ; *In moribus sunt compositi et modesti*, &c., said that popish inquisitor their professed adversary. Their doctrine, said he, is naught, but their lives are unblameable. The man's life (saith Erasmus concerning Luther) is approved of all men ; his veriest adversaries cannot accuse him for anything in point of practice. Louis king of France, having received certain complaints against the Protestants of Merindol and Chabriers, sent certain to inquire into the business, and hearing what they related to him, he swore a great oath that they were better men than either himself was, or any other of his subjects. (A. D. 1513.)

That falsely accuse your good conversation] We should so carry ourselves, saith Jerome, *ut nemo de nobis male loqui absque mendacio possit*, that no man might speak evil of us without a manifest lie. *Nec hostes reperiant quod calumnientur.*

Ver. 17. *That ye suffer for well-doing*] The cause, and not the pain, makes the martyr. Together with the Lord Cromwell was beheaded (in Henry VIII.'s time) the Lord Hungerford, neither so Christianly suffering, nor so quietly dying for his offence committed against nature. (Speed's Chron.) What a sad thing was that re-

lated by Eusebius, that the cruel persecution under Diocletian was occasioned chiefly by the petulancy, pride, and contentions of the pastors and bishops ! which gave occasion to the tyrant to think that Christian religion was no better than a wretched device of wicked men. Lactantius to the like purpose crieth out, *Nunc male audiunt castiganturque vulgo Christiani, quod aliter quam sapientibus convenit vivant, et vitia sub obtentu nominis celent :* Christians are hardly spoken of, and deeply censured by the vulgar, because they live not as becometh wise men ; but cover their vices under pretence of their religion. (De Opific. Dei, Procem.)

Ver. 18. *That he might bring us*] To reconcile and bring men again to God was the main end of Christ's coming and suffering. This is the wonderment of angels, torment of devils, &c.

The just for the unjust] Oh the vile dulness of our hearts, that cannot be duly affected herewith ! Behold, here was piety scourged for the impious man's sake, wisdom derided for the fool's sake, truth denied for the liar's sake, justice condemned for the unjust man's sake, mercy afflicted for the cruel man's sake ; life dies for the dead man's sake. What a suffering was that, when the Just suffered for the unjust, with the unjust, upon unjust causes, under unjust judges, and by unjust punishments, &c. Euripides saith it is but righteous that they that do things not good should suffer things not pleasant ; but what had that innocent " Lamb of God " done ?

Ver. 19. *He went and preached*] Righteousness, *i. e.* repentance, 1 Pet. ii. 5, and the faith of the gospel, 2 Pet. iv. 6, whereby some of those many that perished in the waters arrived at heaven, *Nunquam sero, si serio.* Christ went to them as an ambassador sent by his Father, and spake to their hearts.

Ver. 20. *Which sometimes were disobedient*] Gr. unpersuadable, uncounsellable. They jeered where they should have feared, and thought Noah no wiser than the prior of St Bartholomew's in London, who upon a vain prediction of an idle astrologer, went and built him a house at Harrow on the Hill, to secure himself from a supposed flood, foretold by that astrologer. (Holinshed.)

Ver. 21. *Baptism doth also now save*] It is of permanent use, and effectual to seal up salvation whensoever a man believes and repents. Hence we are once baptized for all. See Ephes. v. 26 ; Tit. iii. 5. The pope's decree says, that confirmation is of more value than baptism, and gives the Holy Ghost more plentifully and effectually. How fitly might the gloss have set upon this decree *Palea*, or *Hoc non credo*, as they use to do, when anything in the decrees pleaseth them not !

Not the putting away] That none bear himself bold upon his Christendom. Unregenerate Israel is to God as Ethiopia, Amos ix. 7. A man may go to hell with baptismal water on his face.

But the answer] ἐπερώτημα, the stipulation, or confident interrogation, such as is that of the apostle, Rom. viii. 33—35, and of Jeremiah pleading with God, chap. xii. 1, and reasoning the case with him. David from his circumcision promised himself victory over that uncircumcised Philistine; so may we from our baptism, against all spiritual wickednesses; bring but this confident answer of a good conscience, and the devil will never be able to abide by it. Luther maketh mention of a certain holy virgin, who usually quenched the devil's fiery darts with the water of baptism. For whensoever he tempted her to evil, she confidently answered *Christiana sum*, I am a Christian, I have been baptized, and therein promised to renounce the devil and all his works.[1] For to that custom of asking the party to be baptized, and taking his answer (*Credis? credo; abrenuncias? abrenuncio*), the apostle seemeth here to allude; or, as others are of opinion, to the manner of John's baptism, wherein people confessed (renounced) their sins, and asked him what they should do, Luke iii. 10.

Ver. 22. *Angels and authorities*] Psal. lxviii. 17. The word rendered angels signifieth seconds, as being second to Christ, or next to him. See Dan. x. 13.

CHAPTER IV.

Ver. 1. *Christ hath suffered*] As chap. iii. 18.

In the flesh] In human nature; so must we suffer in sinful nature, subduing it to God, and ceasing from sin, hailing it and nailing it to the cross of Christ. First have sin to the Cross of Christ; force it before the tree on which he suffered: it is such a sight as sin cannot abide. It will begin to die within us upon the first sight of Christ upon the cross. For the cross of Christ accuseth sin, shameth it, and by a secret virtue feedeth upon the very heart of it. 2. Use sin as Christ was used when he was made sin for us; lift it up, and make it naked by confession to God. And then pierce, 1. The hands of it, in respect of operation, that it may work no more. 2. The feet of it, in respect of progression, that it go no further. 3. The heart, in respect of affection, that it may be loved no longer.

Ver. 2. *That he no longer, &c.*] To spend the span of his transitory life after the ways of one's own heart is to perish for ever.

Ver. 3. *For the time past of our life may suffice us*] We may every one say with Austin, *Nimis sero te amavi Domine*. It should be a burden to our souls that we begin no sooner to love God.

In lasciviousness, lusts, &c.] The true picture of a pagan conversation, which yet is too common among those that call themselves Christians. The world is now grown perfectly profane, and can play on the Lord's day without book; making it as Bacchus' orgies, rather than God's holy day, with piping, dancing, drinking, drabbing, &c. We may say as once Alsted of his Germans, that if the Sabbath-day should be named according to their observing of it, *Dæmoniacus potius quam Do-*

[1] *Intellexit hostis statim virtutem*

minicus diceretur, it should be called not God's day, but the devil's.

Excess of wine] οἰνοφλυγίαις, or, red and rich faces, as they call them.

Revellings] κώμοις, stinks, saith the Syriac; drunkards are stinkards; as Luther called the Swenck-feldians, stink-feldians, from the ill savour of their opinions. Tacitus tells us that among the old Germans, it was no disgrace counted to continue drinking and spewing night and day, *Diem noctemque continuare potando.*

Banquetings] Gr. πότοις, compotations, or good-fellow meetings; some render it bibbings, sippings, tipplings, sitting long at it, though not to an alienation of the mind. How much more when they leave not till they have drank the three "outs" first; viz. Wit out of the head, money out of the purse, and ale out of the pot!

And abominable idolatries] Some idolatries then, say the Papists, are not abominable. A sweet inference. That all Papists are idolaters, Dr Reynolds hath plainly and plentifully proved in his learned work *De idololatria Romana*, never yet answered. Weston writeth that his head ached in reading it. But what a poor shift is that of Vasquez, expressly to maintain that the second commandment belonged to the Jews only; as holding it impossible to answer our arguments against their image-worship? Other popish writers utterly disannul the second commandment, making it a member of the first; and so, retaining the words, they destroy the sense and interpretation.

Ver. 4. *They think it strange*] Gr. ξενίζονται. That they think it a new world, marvelling what is come to you alate. It is I, said the harlot; but it is not I, said the convert, *At ego non sum.*

Into the same excess] Gr. ἀνάχυσιν, bubbling or boiling, as the raging sea foaming out its own filth.

Ver. 5. *Who shall give account*] Of their ungodly deeds and hard speeches, Jude 15. Angels did their first execution in the world upon luxurious Sodomites; they will be very active doubtless against such at the last day. See 2 Pet. ii. 10, and mark that word, chiefly.

Ver. 6. *For for this cause*] See the note on 1 Pet. iii. 19.

That they might be judged] Either by God chastising them, 1 Cor. xi. 32, or by themselves, ver. 31. The gospel melts the hearts of God's elect with voluntary grief for sin, it makes them condemn themselves in the flesh.

But live according to God] The Father of spirits, with whom the spirits of just men departed are made perfect, Heb. xii. 23. Eusebius and Austin make mention of certain Arabians, who said that the soul dies with the body, and revives not again till the resurrection of the body. This old heresy is now, among many others, digged out of the grave, and held by certain sectaries amongst us.

Ver. 7. *Be ye therefore sober, &c.*] To be sober in prayer (saith one) is to pray with due respect *baptismi, &c., et fugit ab ea.* Luther.

to God's majesty, without trifling or vain babbling; to let our words be few, Eccles. v. 3. Also it is to keep God's counsel, not to be proud or boast of success, or speak of the secret sweetness of God's love without calling; it is to conceal the familiarity of God in secret. Or, it is to submit our will to the will of God; being well pleased that He is in any way glorified, though we be not every way gratified.

And watch unto prayer] Against dulness of body, drowsiness of spirit, Satanical suggestions, distractive motions, which else will muster and swarm in the heart like the flies of Egypt.

Ver. 8. *Charity shall cover*] This is meant of mutual love, whereby we forgive offences one to another, and not that which should justify us before God in a Popish sense, as appears by the precedent words, and by Prov. x. 12.

Ver. 9. *Without grudgings*] Without shucking and hucking. See 2 Cor. viii. 12, with the note there.

Ver. 10. *Even so minister*] Clouds when full, pour down, and the spouts run, and the eaves shed, and the presses overflow, and the aromatical trees sweat out their precious and sovereign oils; and every learned scribe brings out his rich treasure, &c. "The manifestation of the Spirit is given to every man to profit withal," 1 Cor. xii. 7. There are some that make it their chief work *proficere potius quam prodesse*, to inform themselves, rather than to instruct others; to know, than to teach. Synesius inveighs against a sort of such in his times, as having a treasure of rare abilities in them, would as soon part with their hearts as with their conceptions, the canker of whose great skill shall be a swift witness against them. Cardan speaketh of one that had a receipt that would suddenly and certainly dissolve the stone in the bladder; and concludes of him that he was undoubtedly damned, because he never revealed it before he died, to any one.[1] Let men be ready to communicate the good they have, as the moon doth her borrowed light, as the stars are still in motion for the good of others; as the heart receiving spirits from the liver, ministereth them to the brain, and the brain to the other parts of the body.

Ver. 11. *If any man speak*] i. e. Preach. Every sound is not music, so neither is every pulpit discourse preaching.

As the oracles of God] Those lively and life-giving oracles, the Holy Scriptures. These he must expound with all gravity and sincerity, not seeking himself, nor setting forth his own wit and eloquence, so putting the sword of the Spirit into a velvet scabbard, that it cannot prick and pierce the heart. *Loquamur verba Scripturæ* (saith Ramus) *utamur sermone Spiritus sancti; denique divinam sapientiam et linguam nostra infantia et sophistica ne corrigamus: i. e.* Let us speak the very words of the Scripture, let us use the speech of the Holy Spirit; and not think to correct the divine wisdom and eloquence with our babbling and sophistry. It is not for us to wit-

[1] *Non dubito quin iste sit apud inferos.*

wanton it with God; his holy things must be handled *sancte magis quam scite* (as he once told the wanton vestal), that is, with fear and reverence rather than with wit and dalliance.

Which God giveth] χορηγεῖ, liberally and magnificently.

Ver. 12. *Think it not strange*] *Ne tanquam hospites percellamini.* Stand not wondering, and as if struck into a maze. Fain would this flesh make strange of that which the spirit doth embrace, saith Mr Saunders, martyr, in a letter to his wife. O Lord, how loth is this loitering sluggard to pass forth in God's path. It fantasieth forsooth much fear of fay-bugs. And were it not for the force of faith which pulleth it forward by the rein of God's most sweet promise, and of hope which pricks on behind, great adventures there were of fainting by the way. But blessed and everlastingly blessed be our heavenly Father, &c.

Concerning the fiery trial] John Brown of Ashford, through the cruel handling of Archbishop Warham, and Fisher, bishop of Rochester, was so piteously intreated (saith Mr Fox) that his bare feet were set upon the hot burning coals, to make him deny his faith; which notwithstanding he would not do, but patiently abiding the pain, continued in the Lord's quarrel unremoveable. See the like of Rose Allen, Acts and Mon. 1820.

As though some strange thing] Forecast afflictions, which being foreseen come no whit the sooner, but far the easier, it is a labour well lost, if they come not, well spent if they do; whereas coming upon the sudden, they find weak minds secure, make them miserable, leave them desperate. Bishop Latimer ever affirmed, that the preaching of the gospel would cost him his life, to the which he no less cheerfully prepared himself, than certainly was persuaded that Winchester was kept in the Tower for the same purpose; and the event did too truly prove the same. Being sent for to London by a pursuivant, and coming through Smithfield, he merrily said, "That Smithfield had long groaned for him." To the lieutenant of the Tower he said, "You look, I think, that I should burn; but except you let me have some fire, I am like to deceive your expectation; for I am like here to starve for cold."

Ver. 13. *But rejoice*] As the apostles did, Acts v. 41. See the note there.

Inasmuch as ye are partakers of Christ's sufferings] So they are called: 1. Because they are for his sake. 2. Because he suffereth with us; though not with a sense of pain, yet with a sense of pity; for in all our afflictions he is afflicted. 3. We fill up that which is behind of the sufferings of Christ, &c., Col. i. 24. See the note there.

With exceeding joy] Gr. ἀγαλλιώμενοι, dancing a galliard, leaping levaltos, lifting up your heads, because your redemption draweth nigh. Vincentius, laughing at his tormentors, said that death and tortures were to Christians *jocularia et ludicra*, matters of sport and pastime; and walking upon hot burning coals, he boasted that he walked upon roses. Other martyrs said that they felt no more pain in the fire than if they lay upon a bed of down. Constantine embraced Paphnu tiu, and kissed his lost eye; so will Christ deal at the last day by his suffering servants.

Ver. 14. *Happy are ye*] μακάριοι. See the note on Matt. v. 11, 12. The word signifies, ye are out of harm's way; out of the reach of danger.

Resteth upon you] ἀναπέπαυται, with great delight and content. How strangely were the holy martyrs spiritualized and elevated, carried out of themselves and beyond themselves, as were easy to instance. We read of some godly men so overwhelmed with joy, that they have cried out, Hold, Lord; stay thine hand, I can bear no more! like weak eyes that cannot bear too great a light. "The Spirit of glory and of God" is by the Syriac interpreter rendered "the glorious Spirit of God."

Resteth upon you] sc. by divine abode or dwelling, which the Hebrews call Shechinah. The heart of a believer reproached for the name of Christ is no private place; but a place where God taketh pleasure. It is the house of God; and over-against it is the gate of heaven. He seems here to allude to Isa. iv. 5.

Ver. 15. *As a busy-body*] Gr. A bishop in another man's diocese, a pragmatical person that meddleth with other men's matters without call or commendation.

Ver. 16. *Suffer as a Christian*] Under the Emperor Antoninus the philosopher, there fell out a very bitter storm of persecution in France, which swallowed up sundry martyrs, as Maturus, Pothenus, Attalus, and Blandina; which good woman, in the midst of all her sufferings, oft cried out, *Christiana sum*, I am a Christian. By which word she gathered new strength, and became more than a conqueress. (Bucholcer.) So Sabina, another glorious Roman martyr, crying out when she was in prison, and being asked by the jailor how she would endure the fire next day, that made now so much ado in her travail? "Very well," said she, "I doubt not: for now I suffer as a sinner, but then I shall suffer as Christian." (John Manl.) They were wont to say of cowards in Rome, that there was nothing Roman in them. I would we had not cause to say of many Christians, that there is nothing Christian in them. He and he only is a right Christian, and can quit himself accordingly both in doing and dying for Christ (if called thereunto), whose person is united to Christ by the ligament of a lively faith, and whose nature is elevated by the Spirit of regeneration; and whose principles, practices, and aims are divine and supernatural.

Let him not be ashamed] He need not; Christ is not a Master that a man need be ashamed of. He was not ashamed of us, when we had never a rag to our backs, nay, when we were "in our blood, in our blood, in our blood," and no eye pitied us, Ezek. xvi. 5, 6.

Let him glorify God] viz. for his great preferment, Phil. i. 28. See the note there.

Ver. 17. *Judgment must begin*] The mortality

at Corinth began at the believers, 1 Cor. xi. 30. Infidels escaped scot-free.[1] God's cup is first sent to Jerusalem. There was bread in Moab, when there was none in Israel, Ruth i. 1. The stormy shower lighteth first on the high hills, and having washed them, settleth with all the filth in the valleys.

Ver. 18. *Scarcely be saved*] Hard and scarce; not at all from outward miseries (whereof he is sure to have his back-burden), and not without somewhat ado from hell-torments. The wise virgins had no oil to spare; the twelve tribes served God instantly and constantly day and night, and all little enough, Acts xxvi. 7.

Where shall the ungodly, &c.] Surely nowhere: not before saints and angels, for holiness is their trade. Not before God, for he is of "more pure eyes," &c. Not before Christ, for he shall come in flaming fire rendering vengeance. Not in heaven, for it is an undefiled inheritance, &c.

Ver. 19. *Commit the keeping*] As a precious depositum. So did our Saviour both in his life-time, 1 Pet. ii. 23, and at his death, Luke xxiii. 46. So did Stephen and all the holy martyrs after him. Archbishop Cranmer oft repeated these words in the flame, "Lord Jesus, receive my spirit." A certain Spanish monk that stood by and heard him, ran to a nobleman there present, and cried out that Cranmer died in great desperation, *ratus desperationis fuisse voces*, as conceiving those to be words of despair.

As unto a faithful] Who will rather unmake all than we shall miscarry. And doth still manage all occurrences to the glory of his name and the good of those that trust in him, Psal. cxxiv. 8.

CHAPTER V.

Ver. 1. *Who am also an elder*] Gr. A fellow-elder, not a commander, a lord paramount, a compeer and consort to the blessed Trinity, as Pope Leo I.[1] and Nicolas III. blasphemously said he was.

Ver. 2. *Feed the flock*] Being both learned and loving. The Greek word for a shepherd (ποιμὴν, quasi οἰμὴν, ab ὄϊς, ovis, et μάω) signifieth one that earnestly desireth after his sheep.

Feed the flock] That is, rule them, say the pope's janizaries. True it is the word signifieth sometimes to govern; usually to feed; but they catch at government, led go feeding.

Not by constraint, but willingly] It is with the pastors of Germany for most part, saith Melancthon, as with him in Plautus, that said, *Ego non servio libenter : herus meus me non habet, libenter tamen utitur me ut lippis oculis.* I serve of no good will, my master also hath as little good will to use my service; and yet he makes such use of me as he doth of some eyes, which we must have or none.

Not for filthy lucre] As your church-choppers and money-changers, that take up the ministry

---

[1] *Leo I. Petrum in consortium individuæ Trinitatis assumptum jactavit.*

only as a trade to pick a living out of it. We preach the gospel amongst us, saith a Popish writer, *tantum ut nos pascat et vestiat*, merely for food and raiment. Christ's faithful under-shepherds, though as men they have natural necessities and relations, and as labourers in the word and doctrine, they have need of "communicating with others by way of giving and receiving" of this world's good, yet they have higher aims, which of ready mind they duly prosecute, &c. There is a worm called *clerus*, that destroyeth honeycombs; so doth the Popish clergy the Lord's inheritance. But *Clerus Angliæ* was wont to be *stupor mundi*, the world's wonder for height of holiness and depth of learning.

Ver. 3. Neither as being lords] About the year 1620 the clergy and laity of England set themselves against the pope's exactions; and when the legate alleged that all churches were the pope's, Magister Leonardus made answer, *Tuitione non fruitione, defensione non dissipatione.* (Jac. Revius in Vit. Pontif.)

Ver. 4. Ye shall receive a crown] A crown imports perpetuity, plenty, dignity, the height of human ambition. *Quarta perennis erit* was Sir Thomas Bodly's posy. *Manet ultima cœlo* was Henry III.'s of France, who was first crowned king of Poland. See the note on James i. 12.

Ver. 5. Yea, all of you be subject] In regard of love and modesty, not of change and confusion of offices.

Be clothed with humility] The Greek word ἐγκομβώσασθε imports that humility is the riband or string that ties together all those precious pearls, the rest of the graces; if this string break, they are all scattered. Humility, as charity, is the band of perfection; yea, the word κόμβος here used signifies not only *alligare*, but *innodare*, say some; to tie knots as delicate and curious women used to do of ribands to adorn their heads or bodies, as if humility were the knot of every virtue and the grace of every grace. Contrariwise, how ugly and unseemly is pride on the back of honour and head of learning, face of beauty, &c. Chrysostom calleth humility the root, mother, nurse, foundation, and band of all virtues. Basil, the storehouse, treasury of all good, θησαυροφυλάκιον.

God resisteth] See the note on James iv. 6. As pride resisteth God in a special manner, so God in a special manner resisteth it.

And giveth grace] i. e. Honour and respect; as appears by the opposition, and by Prov. iii. 34, 35.

Ver. 6. Under the mighty hand of God] If God can blow us to destruction, Job iv. 9, nod us to destruction, Psal. xviii. 16, what is the weight of that mighty hand of his that spans the heavens and holds the earth in the hollow of them?

That he may exalt you] The lower the ebb, the higher is the tide. A deluge of sorrows may assault us, but they shall exalt us. And the lower the foundation of virtue is laid, the higher shall the roof of glory be over-laid.

In due time] In the opportunity of time, in a fit season. The very Turks, though remorseless to those that bear up, yet receive humiliation with much sweetness.

Ver. 7. Casting all your care] Your carking care, your care of diffidence. I will now with you sing away care, said John Careless, martyr, in a letter to Mr Philpot, for now my soul is turned to her old rest again, and hath taken a sweet nap in Christ's lap. I have cast my care upon the Lord which careth for me, and will be careless, according to my name. It is our work, saith another, to cast care; it is God's work to take care. Let us not, by our soul-dividing thoughts, take his work out of his hand.

Ver. 8. Your adversary the devil] Satan envies our condition that we should enjoy that paradise that he left, the comforts he once had. Hence he disturbs us, and is restless out of his infinite hatred of God and goodness; as the scorpion still puts forth his sting, and as the leopard bears such a natural hatred against men, that if he see but a man's picture, he flies upon it, and tears it. Hannibal, whether he conquered, or was conquered, never rested. Satan is over-overcome, and yet he walks up and down seeking to devour: he commits the sin against the Holy Ghost every day, and shall lie lowest in hell; every soul that he drew thither by his temptation shall lie upon him, and press him down as a millstone under the unsupportable wrath of God. The word ἀντίδικος, here rendered an adversary, properly signifies an adversary at law. Against whom we have an advocate, Jesus Christ, the just one, 1 John ii. 2, who appears for us, Heb. ix. 24, to non-suit all accusations, and to plead our cause. The devil, the accuser, oft makes that to be treason in the saints that is but petty-larceny. In prosperity he makes us lay our hearts too near it; in adversity, to lay it too near our hearts. He is ever assaulting us, and is therefore called ὁ πειράζων, the tempter, in the present tense; not lazy at his business, but ever in motion for some mischief to us. *Si per anticam ejicias, per posticam denuo solet irrepere*, If you throw him out at the street-door, he will creep in again at the back-door. Watch him therefore. *Non enim unquam dormitat vigil ille Synagogæ suæ Episcopus*, as Amama calleth him. *Ut teipsum serves non expergiscere?* (Horat.)

Whom he may devour] Gr. καταπίῃ, whom he may drink up at one draught.

Ver. 9. Stedfast in the faith] Gr. στερεοὶ, stiff, solid, settled.

That the same afflictions] Art not thou glad to fare as Phocion? said he to one that was to die with him. (Plutarch.) Ignatius, going to suffer, triumphed in this, that his blood should be found among the mighty worthies, and that when the Lord maketh inquisition for blood, he will recount from the blood of righteous Abel, not only to the blood of Zacharias, son of Barachias, but also to the blood of mean Ignatius.

Ver. 10. But the God of all grace] Thus the apostle divides his time betwixt preaching and prayer, according to his own advice, Acts vi. 4, and the practice of those ancient ministers, Deut. xxxiii. 10.

Ver. 11. *To him be glory, &c.*] *Non loquendum de Deo sine lumine*, said the heathen; we may not mention God but with praise to his name, say we.

Ver. 12. *I have written briefly*] Gr. In few. The Holy Scripture hath fulness of matter in fewness of words, the whole counsel of God shut up in a narrow compass. The Lord knows that much reading is a weariness of the flesh, Eccl. xii. 12, and hath therefore provided for our infirmity.

Ver. 13. *The Church that is at Babylon*] At Rome, say the Papists, that they may prove Peter to have been bishop of Rome. But though this be far-fetched, yet here they grant us that mystical Babylon mentioned in the Revelation. It is probable that St Peter meant no other Babylon than the metropolis of Chaldæa, where he, being the apostle of the circumcision, preached to those dispersed Jews, and other Gentiles that he had converted.

Ver. 14. *With a kiss of charity*] So called, because their love to one another was by this symbol or ceremony both evidenced and increased.

THE SECOND EPISTLE GENERAL OF ST PETER.

CHAPTER I.

Ver. 1. *A servant*] THE pope, who will needs title himself, A servant of servants, is herein the successor not of Peter, but of cursed Ham. He stamps in his coin, that nation and country that will not serve thee shall be rooted out, and so bewrays his putid hypocrisy.

Like precious faith] Precious as gold tried in the fire; that maketh rich, Rev. iii. 18. And like precious (though of different degrees) in regard of, 1. The Author, God. 2. The object, Christ. 3. The means of working it, the Spirit and Word. 4. The end of it, salvation. 5. The essential property of it, of handfasting us to Christ. A child may hold a ring in his hand, as well though not as fast as a man. Let it be our care to be faithful in weakness, though weak in faith: let that faith we have be right, be of price, though not of so great price, though not like precious to such and such eminent believers. Suppose a simple man should get a stone and strike fire with it, and thence conclude it a precious stone; why, every flint or ordinary stone will do that. So to think one hath precious faith because he can be sober, just, chaste, liberal, &c.; why, ordinary heathens can do this: a man may be undone by buying a false commodity at an unreasonable rate.

Through the righteousness of God] i. e. of Christ; and it is so called, not because it is the righteousness of the Godhead, but of him that is God.

Ver. 2. *Through the knowledge*] There is not a new notion, or a further enlargement of saving knowledge, but it brings some grace and peace with it. All the grace that a man hath, it passeth through the understanding; and the difference of stature in Christianity grows from different degrees of knowledge. "Grace and truth came by Jesus Christ," John i. 17.

Ver. 3. *To glory and virtue*] To glory as the end, to virtue as the means. The very heathens made their passage to the temple of honour through the temple of virtue. Do worthily, and be famous, Ruth iv. 11.

Ver. 4. *Exceeding great and precious*] Every precious stone hath an egregious virtue in it; so hath every promise. The promises, saith Cardan, are a precious book, every leaf drops myrrh and mercy. The weak Christian cannot open, read, apply it; Christ can, and will for him.

That by these ye might be partakers] As the sun when it applies its beams to a filthy disposed matter, and stays upon it, begins to beget life and motion, and makes a living creature; so do the promises applied to the heart make a new creature. See 2 Cor. iii. 6.

Of the divine nature] That is, of those divine qualities, called elsewhere "the image of God, the life of God," &c., whereby we resemble God, not only as a picture doth a man in outward lineaments, but as the child doth his father in countenance and conditions. It was no absurd speech of him that said, That the high parts that are seen in heroical persons, do plainly show that here is a God. Neither can I here but insert the saying of another, Well may grace be called the divine nature; for as God brings light out of darkness, comfort out of sorrow, riches out of poverty, and glory out of shame; so doth grace turn the dirt of disgrace into gold. As Moses' hand, it turns a serpent into a rod. In fine, to be made partaker of the divine nature, noteth two things, saith a reverend man: 1. A fellowship with God in his holiness; the purity which is eminently and infinitely in God's most holy nature, is formally of *secundum modum creaturæ*, fashioned in us. 2. A fellowship with God in his blessedness, viz. in the beatifical vision and brightness of glory. (Dr Reynolds.)

Ver. 5. *And besides this*] q. d. As God hath given you all things pertaining to life and godliness, and hath granted you exceeding great and precious promises, so must you reciprocate, by giving all diligence, or making all haste, that ye be not taken with your task undone. *Acti agamus.*

Add to your faith] Faith is the foundation of the following graces; indeed they are all in faith radically. Every grace is but faith exercised. To faith must be added virtue, *i. e.* holy conversation; lest we be counted and called Solifidians. It was the counsel of Francis Spira to those about him, Learn all of me, to take heed of severing faith and obedience. I taught justification by faith, but neglected obedience; therefore is this befallen me.

And to virtue, knowledge] For the regulating of our obedience, that we go not blindling to work, that we may perform a reasonable or intelligible service. "For without knowledge the mind is not good; and he that (not understanding his way) hasteth with his feet, sinneth," Prov. xix. 2; the faster he runs, the further he is out. The Samaritans' service was rejected, because they worshipped they knew not what. The Romans were full of goodness, because full of knowledge, Rom. xv. 14.

Add] Gr. ἐπιχορηγήσατε, Link them hand in hand, as virgins in a dance. Or, provide yourselves of this rich furniture; one grace strengtheneth another, as stones do in an arch.

Ver. 6. *And to knowledge, temperance*] That ye be wise to sobriety, not curiously searching into those things whereof ye can neither have proof nor profit. Some are as wise as Galilæus, who used perspective glasses to descry mountains in the moon; and lest they should not be reputed to know something unknown to others, they profess skill beyond the periphery of possible knowledge.

And to temperance, patience] Those that will be temperate as aforesaid, and not pass the bounds of sobriety in searching after curiosities, shall be looked upon by the wits of the world as dull fellows (Mr Perkins was esteemed by Mr Bolton before his conversion, a dry preacher, &c.), and therefore they have need of patience. Only they must add to their

Patience, godliness] In the power of it; not suffering themselves to be mocked out of their religion. Moderation in this case is but mopishness. And though in our own cause we must show all long-sufferance, yet when God's glory is concerned, it is our duty to be blessedly blown up with zeal for his name, as Moses was at the sight of the golden calf; and as Zuinglius told Servetus, taxing him for his sharp invectives against him: In other things, saith he, I can bear as much as another; but in case of God's dishonour, I have no patience.

Ver. 7. *And to godliness, brotherly kindness*] Zeal for God should eat us up, but not eat up our love to God's people. Fire purgeth gold, but burneth it not; the fire of zeal may be warming, comforting, not scalding or scorching. Moses was angry with the people, but prayed for them.

Christ was angry with the Pharisees, but grieved withal for the hardness of their hearts, Mark iii. 5.

And to brotherly kindness, &c.] Love we must all men, but especially the family of faith; as our Saviour loved the young man, but not so as he did Lazarus, Mark x. 21; John xi. 3.

Ver. 8. *If these things be in you*] What God doth for us, he doth by grace in us. And it is the growing Christian that is the assured Christian. Whilst we are yet adding to every heap, we shall be both *actuosi et fructuosi;* and so get more abundant entrance, and further into the kingdom of Christ.

Ver. 9. *But he that lacketh these*] Those that add not to their stock of grace, shall have no comfort either from the time past, for they shall forget they were purged from their sins, or from thoughts of the time to come, for they shall not be able to see things far off, to ken their interests to the kingdom of heaven.

Cannot see far off] μυωπάζοντες, Being purblind, blinking. *Lusciosi, qui siquando oculorum aciem intendunt ut certius aliquid cernant, minus vident quam ante,* saith Vives. If weak-sighted men look wistly upon a thing, they see it no whit the better, but much the worse.

And hath forgotten] As if he had been dipt in the lake of Lethe, and not in the laver of baptism. Divers of the Spanish converts in America forget not only their vow, but their very names that they received when they were baptized.

Ver. 10. *Give diligence*] Say not here as Antipater king of Macedon did, when one presented him a book treating of happiness, οὐ σχολάζω, I am not at leisure. But do this one thing necessary, with all expedition. Do it also with all thy might, with utmost intention of affection and contention of action; so to show thy seriousness in a point of so great importance. Thy bed is very soft, or thy heart very hard, if thou canst sleep soundly in an uncertain condition; I mean till thy salvation be secured and settled to thee: till that "entrance be ministered unto thee abundantly into Christ's everlasting kingdom," ver. 11, that thou mayest go to heaven *alacri animo, ac plena fiducia* (as Luther speaketh), with a cheerful mind and full assurance; not of hope only (as the Papists ignorantly distinguish) but of faith too; of hope unfailable, and of faith unfeigned; the highest degree whereof is *plerophoria,* or full assurance.

Your calling and election] We must not go (saith one) to the university of election, before we have been at the grammar-school of vocation; first, we are to begin below at our sanctification, before we can climb to the top of God's counsel, to know our election. This must be calculated by that.

Sure] Some copies have it, sure by good works; and indeed these settle the soul, 1 Cor. xv. 58; as a stake, the more it is stuck into the ground, the faster it sticks.

Ye shall never fall] Stumble ye may; but he that stumbles and falls not, gets ground.

Ver. 11. *Ministered unto you abundantly*] Ye shall go gallantly into heaven, not get thither as many do, with hard shift and much ado. A ship may make a shift to get into the harbour, but with anchors lost, cables rent, sails torn, mast broken; another comes in with sails and flags up, with trumpets sounding, and comes bravely into the haven: so do fruitful and active Christians into Christ's kingdom.

Into the everlasting kingdom] Not so into this world, which is like a candlestick, where ye may see orchards and gardens curiously drawn, but ye cannot enter into them.

Ver. 12. *I will not be negligent*] Ministers must carefully watch and catch at all opportunities of benefiting the people. Dr Taylor, the martyr, preached at Hadleigh his charge on any day, as oft as he could get the people together; and once a fortnight at least went to the almshouse, and there exercised his charity both spiritual and corporal.

Ver. 13. *To stir you up*] Gr. διεγείρειν, to rouse you and raise you, *ex veterno torporis, teporis et oblivionis.* Grace in the best is like a dull sea-coal fire; which, if not stirred up, though it want no fuel, will yet easily go out of itself.

Ver. 14. *I must put off*] See the note on 2 Cor. v. 1. What is this life, but a spot of time betwixt two eternities? Our tents shall be taken down.

Ver. 15. *After my decease*] Gr. ἔξοδον, mine out-going, or passage to heaven. The apostle in this expression hath respect doubtless to that, Luke ix. 31; Dan. vi. 15, refers to Psal. ii. 1.

To have these things always, &c.] *Dilexi virum* (said Theodosius concerniug Ambrose) I could not but love the man exceedingly for this, that when he died he was more solicitous of the Churches than of his own dangers. And I am in no less care (saith Cicero) what the commonwealth will do when I am dead, than while I am yet alive. Luther in many places of his books tells us, he was much afraid that the true doctrine of justification by faith alone would be, after his death, much defaced if not utterly lost out of the Church. And it fell out accordingly in part, by the pestilent opinions and endeavours of Flacius, Osiander, and other busy-broachers of errors, about that fundamental point. While Luther lived, they forbore to vent themselves. But when his head was laid, Osiander was heard to boast *Leonem mortuum esse; vulpes a se flocci pendi,* that the lion was dead: and for the foxes (meaning Melancthon and the rest), he cared not for them. (Melch. in Vit. Osiand.)

Ver. 16. *Cunningly devised fables*] σεσοφισμένοις. Artificially composed and compiled, not without a show of wisdom and truth, to deceive silly people. The Jesuits confess that the legend of miracles of their saints is for most part false; but it was made, say they, for good intention, that the common people (the females especially) might be drawn with greater zeal to serve God and his saints. And what shall we think of their Dominic's holy hypocrisy which he com-

mended to his novices; and for the which he is so highly commended by Vincentius Episcopus Beluacensis in his life?

Ver. 17. *This is my beloved Son*] See the notes on Matt. iii. 17, and xvii. 5.

Ver. 18. *When we were with him*] Witnesses of his glory, and the same were shortly after witnesses of his agony. Envy not the gifts or honours of others, sith they have them upon no other terms than to undergo the sorer trials.

In the holy mount] Holy for the while, as are our churches, during the public assemblies, viz. with a relative, not an inherent holiness.

Ver. 19. *A more sure word*] The authority of the Scriptures is greater than of an angel's voice, of equal command to God's audible and immediate voice, and of greater perspicuity and certainty to us; for besides inspiration, it is both written and sealed.

As unto a light] As the governor of a ship hath his hand on the stern, his eye on the polestar; so should we on Christ the day-star, Rev. ii. 28; xxii. 12.

Until the day dawn] Till there be a more full gospel-light.

And the day-star] Christ the star of Jacob, the bright morning-star, Rev. iii., the Sun of righteousness, Mal. iv.

Ver. 20. *Of any private interpretation*] That is, of human interpretation: private is not here opposed to public, but to divine, or to the Holy Ghost. The old prophet may bring a man into the lion's mouth, by telling him of an angel that spake to him. How many have we in these days that dream their Midianitish dreams, and then tell it for gospel to their neighbours?

Ver. 21. *As they were moved*] φερόμενοι. Forcibly moved, acted, carried out of themselves to say and do what God would have them.

CHAPTER II.

Ver. 1. *Who privily shall bring in*] παρεισάξουσιν, or, fraudulently foist in false doctrines under the title of truth, and pretext of piety. Some truths shall teach, the better to persuade to their falsehoods. Together with the gold, silver, and ivory orthodox tenets, they have store of apes and peacocks, as Solomon's ships had. *Sunt mala mista bonis, sunt bona mista malis.*

Denying the Lord that bought them] Or, freed them, viz. from their former idolatries and enormities, *ut verbum* ἀγοράζειν *frequentius significat,* saith one. Or that bought them, as they conceited, and others charitably imagined; but it proved otherwise, as appeared by their apostasy. Christ is said to buy reprobates, in the same sense wherein it is said that the gods of Damascus smote or plagued Ahaz, 2 Chron. xxviii. 23, that is, in his opinion they did so: for an idol is nothing in the world, and can do neither good nor evil, Jer. x. 5; 1 Cor. viii. 4. Or, that bought them, viz. in laying down a sufficient price for all sinners, in taking upon him the common nature of all men, and in preaching to them in the gospel that he died for sinners indefinitely, offering salvation, and beseeching them to receive it.

Ver. 2. *The way of truth shall be, &c.*] The ancient Christians were generally hated and hooted at by the heathens for the heretics' sake, who were also a kind of Christians, as Augustine complaineth (De Civ. Dei). And Epiphanius addeth that many Pagans refused to come near the Christians to join with them in any good exercise, *Improbis scelestorum illorum factis consternati*, as being offended at the unclean conversation of divers heretics, the Priscillianists especially, whose doctrine was,

Jura, perjura, secretum prodere noli.

Ver. 3. *With feigned words*] Covetousness is never without a cloak and flattering words (1 Thess. ii. 5) for a colour; as, what wool is so coarse, but will take some or other colour? Seducers pretend the glory of God and good of souls to their worldly and wicked practices, Phil. iii. 18, 19. And hereunto they want not fine set words, forms of speech, whereby they first carry captive silly souls, and then make price or merchandise of them; driving a trade with hell, and being factors for the devil, who will thank them well one day for their diligence; like as in the days of Hildebrand letters of thanks were said to be sent from hell to the Popish clergy for those great numbers of souls every day sent thither by their means. (Mat. Paris, A. D. 1072.)

Ver. 4. *If God spared not the angels*] Though but for one sin only, and that in thought only. It sprang from the admiration of their own gifts, it was confirmed by pride and ambition, it was perfected by envy, stirred by the decree of exalting man's nature above angels in and by Christ. Some say it was a transgression of some commandment in particular (not expressed), as Adam was.

Ver. 5. *Bringing in the flood*] And so burying them all in one universal grave of waters. In this universal deluge God swept away all: as if he had blotted that out of his title, Exod. xxxiv. 6, and now took up that emperor's motto, *Fiat justitia et pereat mundus*, Let justice be done, though the whole world be undone.

Ver. 6. *And turning the cities*] Burying them likewise in the Dead Sea, after that he had rained down hell from heaven upon them. See my notes on Gen. xix. 24, 25.

Making them an ensample] Hanging them up in gibbets, as it were, that others might hear and fear.

Ver. 7. *Vexed*] Gr. καταπονουμενοι, labouring under it, as under a heavy burden, and as much tortured as if he had been set upon a rack, as it is ver. 8.

Ver. 8. *In seeing and hearing*] Every sinful Sodomite was a Hazael to his eyes, a Hadadrimmon to his heart.

Vexed his righteous soul] Guilt or grief is all that the good soul gets by conversing with the wicked.

Ver. 9. *The Lord knoweth how*] He hath ways of his own, and commonly goeth a way by himself, such as we think not of; helping them that are forsaken of their hopes. Peter (if any man) might well say, "The Lord knoweth how to deliver his;" for he had been strangely delivered, Acts xii.

Ver. 10. *But chiefly*] See the note on Heb. xiii. 4.

That walk after the flesh] That is, the harlot; as filthy dogs follow after a salt-bitch: so the harlot is called, Deut. xxiii. 18. The Helvetians had an old custom in their towns and villages, that when they received any new priest into their churches, they used to premonish him before, to take his concubine, lest he should attempt any misuse of their wives and daughters.

To speak evil of dignities] Here we have a lively picture of the Popish clergy. Aretius, by a longer custom of libellous and contumelious speaking against princes, had got such a habit, that at last he came to diminish and disesteem God himself. How boldly and basely doth Baronius bellow against the king of Spain his sovereign! and he defends himself against another cardinal, reprehending his fierceness, thus, An imperious (impetuous he should have said) zeal hath no power to spare God himself.

Ver. 11. *Which are greater in power*] viz. Than the mightiest monarch, Dan. x. 20, and are therefore called principalities and powers, 1 Pet. iii. 22. Mighty ones, Isa. x. 34. See 2 Thess. i. 7; Exod. xii. 23—27; 2 Sam. xxiv. 15; 2 Kings xix. 35. This is all for our comfort, they being our guardians. See my Common-place of Angels.

Ver. 12. *As natural brute beasts*] Some men put off all manhood, fall beneath the stirrup of reason, and are bestialized, yea, satanized. Such a one was that man mentioned by Luther, who was so possessed with an unclean spirit, a vehement *impetus*, a spirit of whoredom (as the prophet calleth it), that he was not ashamed to spew out of his foulest mouth these filthiest words, If I might be sure that this life would always last with me, I would wish no other heaven but to be carried from one brothel-house to another, from one harlot to another, *Væ dementiæ, et impietati*. (Horndorf. Theatr.)

Speak evil of the things] Dare to reprehend what they do not comprehend, dispraise sound doctrine; yea, the Holy Scriptures, blaspheming them and their priests, as Sanctius doth the prophet Ezekiel; calling the description of the temple made by him, chap. xlviii. 41—43, &c., *insulsam descriptionem*, a senseless description. See his argument upon chap. xl.

Ver. 13. *To riot in the day-time*] See the note on 1 Thess. v. 7. The word here rendered riot, comes of a root that signifies to break, for there is nothing that doth so break and emasculate the minds of men as rioting and revelling;

luxury draws out a man's spirits, and dissolves him. (τρυφὴ, a θρύπτω, *frango*.) Hence Venus is called λυσιμελὴς by the ancients, and harlots are called *cruces*, crosses, by the young man in Terence. Solomon's prodigal found them no better, Prov. v. 11, after he had paid for his learning.

Spots they are] σπίλοι, blots of goodness, botches of Christian society. Such are the Jesuits, who tell us they can dally with the fairest women and yet not lust after them. Such was that profligate priest, who persuaded many maids and matrons to lie with him under a pretence of religion; *asserens impietatis et hypocriseos plenam esse fiduciam, qua castitate et pudicitia sua potius quam Christi gratia niterentur*, telling them that that faith of theirs was naught and counterfeit, whereby they were drawn to rest more upon their chastity and modesty than upon Christ's grace and merits. (Theatr. Histor. Horndorf.) I much doubt we have many such merchants, such *marcidi bibauldi*, rascal ribalds (as Math. Paris calls them), now abroad amongst us, in these last and loosest times.

Ver. 14. *Having eyes full of adultery*] Gr. Of the adulteress, as if she were seen sitting in the eyes of the adulterer. The wanton Greek was said to have in his eyes οὐ κόρας ἄλλα πόρνας, *non virgines sed meretrices*, not maids but minions.[1] Archilaus the philosopher told a young wanton, *Nihil interest quibus membris cinædi sitis, posterioribus an prioribus*. The leper was to shave his eyebrows, to teach us to take away the lust of the eyes, Levit. xiv. 9. These, like Jacob's sheep, too firmly fixed on beautiful objects, make the affections bring forth spotted fruit. And it is as easy to quench the fire of Etna as the thought fixed by lust.

And that cannot cease to sin] Though they have made many covenants with God, promises to men. So Prov. xix. 19. They break all, as easily as Samson did the new ropes.

Exercised with covetous practices] Which they constantly follow, as the artificer doth his trade.

Ver. 15. *The wages of unrighteousness*] The mammon of unrighteousness, wages of wickedness.

Lucra injusta putes justis æqualia damnis.
Dum peritura paras, per male parta peris.

Ver. 16. *The dumb ass speaking*] The angel (some think) spake in the ass, as the devil had done in the serpent. Who now can complain of his own inability and rudeness to reply in a good cause, when the dumb ass is enabled by God to convince his master? There is no mouth into which God cannot put words; and how oft doth he choose the weak and unwise to confound the learned and mighty! (Dr Hall's Contempl.) Benedictus the Sorbonist affirmeth, that the ass in Balaam's history signifieth their Church, *An quia Pontifex Balaam est qui ei insidet?* saith Dr Reynolds. Meaneth the man that the pope is that Balaam that rideth on the ass?

Ver. 17. *These are wells*, &c.] Not fitted

nor filled with wholesome doctrine, but as the brooks of Tema, Job vi. 17, in a moisture they swell, in a drought they fail. The river Novanus in Lombardy at every midsummer solstice swelleth, and runneth over the banks; but in midwinter is clean dry. So these.

Ver. 18. *Great swelling words*] Gr. ὑπέρογκα, bubbles of words, full of wind, big-swollen fancies, *sesquipedalia verba*. Swenckfeldius the heretic bewitched many with those big words (ever in his mouth) of illumination, revelation, deification, the inward and spiritual man, &c. Faith, he said, was nothing else but God himself indwelling in us. And have we not those now that tell their disciples they shall be Christed, Godded, &c.?

Through much wantonness] As Hetserus and Monetarius the Anabaptists, who corrupted many matrons whom they had drawn to their side. (Joh. Manl. loc. com.) David George, a ringleader amongst them, was so far from accounting adulteries, fornications, incest, &c., to be sins, that he did recommend them to his most perfect scholars, as acts of grace and mortification. This man (or monster rather) was confident that the whole world would in time submit to him, and be of his mind. And are not our Ranters (as they call themselves) come up to him, and gone beyond him in their most prodigious opinions and practices?

Ver. 19. *Promise them liberty*] As Mahometism, and Popery, which is an alluring, tempting, bewitching religion. Sir Walter Raleigh knew what he said, that were he to choose a religion for licentious liberty and lasciviousness, he would choose the Popish religion. No sin past, but the pope can pardon; no sin to come, but he can dispense for it. No matter how long men have lived in any sin (though it be the sin against the Holy Ghost), extreme unction at last will salve all.

Ver. 20. *Again entangled*] As a bird in a gin, as a beast in a snare. *Sæpe familiaritas implicavit, sæpe occasio peccandi voluntatem fecit.* (Isidor. solil. ii.)

The latter end is worse] They fall *ab equis ad asinos*, from high hopes of heaven into hellmouth, where they shall have a deeper damnation, because they disgrace God's housekeeping, as if they did not find that they looked for in religion.

Ver. 21. *It had been better*] *Nocuit sane Judæ fuisse apostolum, et Juliano Christianum.* To begin well and not to proceed is but to aspire to a higher pitch, that the fall may be the more desperate. *Non quæruntur in Christianis initia, sed finis*, saith Jerome. Bp. Bonner seemed at first to be a good man, and a favourer of Luther's doctrines. Harding was once a powerful preacher against Popery, afterwards a cruel persecutor of the truth. Dr Shaxton, bishop of Salisbury, said to William Wolsey, martyr, and to others brought before him, Good brethren, remember yourselves and become new men. For I myself was in this fond opinion that you are now in, *Vitiis nobis in animum per oculos est via*. Quintil.

---

[1] Plutarch. Κόρη *puellam et pupillam oculi significat.*

but I am now become a new man. Ah, said Wolsey, are you become a new man? woe be to thee, thou wicked new man! for God shall justly judge thee for an apostate.[1] Islebius Agricola, that first Antinomian, condemned his error, publicly recanted it, and printed his revocation. Yet, when Luther was dead, he relapsed into that error.

Ver. 22. *The dog is turned*] *Proverbia hæc sunt Canonica, quæ Christiano nauseam commoverent.* God will spew out apostates for ever, teaching them how they should have spewed out their sin.

CHAPTER III.

Ver. 1. *This second epistle*] So must ministers with one sermon peg in another, and never cease beating and repeating the same point, saith St Augustine (de Doct. Christian.), till they perceive by the gesture and countenance of the hearers, that they understand it and are affected with it.

I stir up] Gr. διεγείρω, I rouse you, who perhaps are nodding with the wise virgins, Matt. xxv. 5.

Your pure minds] Gr. Pure as the sun. Chrysostom saith of some in his time that they were *ipso cœlo puriores*, more pure than the visible heavens; and that they were more like angels than mortals. Hom. lv. in Matt.

Ver. 2. *Mindful of the words*] See the note on 1 Cor. xv. 2. Run to this armoury of the Scriptures for weapons against seducers and epicures.

Ver. 3. *Scoffers*] Those worst kind of sinners, Psal. i. 1; those abjects of the people, Psal. xxxv. 15; those pests (λοιμός), as the Septuagint render them, Psal. i. 1; those atheists that jeer when they should fear, and put far away the evil day, that make no more matter of God's direful and dreadful menaces than Leviathan doth of a sword; he laugheth at the shaking of a spear, Job xli. 29. They make children's play of them, as the word here used importeth, ἐμπαῖκται.

Ver. 4. *Where is the promise, &c.*] The sleeping of vengeance causeth the overflow of sin (the sinner thinks himself hail-fellow with God, Psal. l. 21), and the overflow of sin causeth the awakening of vengeance.

Ver. 5. *Willingly ignorant of*] A carnal heart is not willing to know what it should do, lest it should do what it would not, Acts xxviii. 27. *Ut liberius peccent, libenter ignorant,* saith Bernard of such: That they may sin the more freely, they are willingly ignorant. They wink wilfully that they may not see, when some unsavoury potion is ministered to them, as Justin Martyr expresseth it.

That by the word of God] And that by the same word again they may as soon be dissolved, yea, reduced to their first original, nothing. A learned man propoundeth this question, How did the Lord employ himself before the world? And his answer is this: A thousand years to him are but as one day, and one day as a thousand years. Again, Who knoweth (saith he) what the Lord hath done? Indeed, he made but one world to our knowledge; but who knoweth what he did before, and what he will do after? Thus he. (Dr Preston of God's Attrib.)

And the earth standing, &c.] God hath founded the earth upon the seas, and established it upon the floods, Psal. xxiv. 2. This Aristotle reckons among the wonders in nature, and well he may. (Lib. de Mirab.) God hath set the solid earth upon the liquid waters for our conveniency, Psal. civ. 6, 7. This, if wicked atheists would well weigh, it would make them tremble, Jer. v. 22. But they have either so much to do, or so little to do, that they think not at all on these standing miracles. Or, if they do, yet for want of grace all their thoughts of this nature soon vanish; they are but like prints made on the water; as soon as the finger is off, all is out.

Ver. 6. *Being overflowed with water*] Therefore that is not altogether true, that all things continue as they were at first, as the scoffers affirmed, ver. 4.

Ver. 7. *Reserved unto fire*] The old world was destroyed with water, *propter ardorem libidinis,* for the heat of their lust, saith Ludolphus; the world that is now shall be destroyed with fire, *propter teporem charitatis,* for their want of love. This latter age of the world is so filthy (saith another) that it cannot be washed with water, and shall therefore be wasted with fire.

Ver. 8. *One day is with the Lord, &c.*] *Nullum tempus occurrit regi;* how much less to the Ancient of days! In God there is no motion or flux; therefore a thousand years to him are but as one day.

Ver. 9. *Not willing that any one should perish*] See the note on 1 Tim. ii. 4. Not willing that any of his should perish.

But that all should come to repentance] Gr. χωρῆσαι, withdraw, go aside, retire into some private place for the purpose of repentance. It is a great work and requires privacy. He that will make verses or do anything serious that requires study, will get alone, sequester himself from company. He that would commune with his own heart, pour forth his soul, and make his peace with God, must get into a corner. "He sitteth alone, and keepeth silence," Lam. iii. 28; he summons the sobriety of his senses before his own judgment, and thinking seriously on his evil ways, "he turneth his feet to God's testimonies," Psal. cxix. 59.

Ver. 10. *The heavens shall pass, &c.*] The very visible heavens are defiled with men's sins, Rev. xviii. 5, and must therefore be purged by fire; as the vessel that held the sin-offering was in the time of the law.

With a great noise] ῥοιζηδὸν, such a noise as the sea makes in a great storm, or like the hiss-

[1] Q. Ann Boleyn procured Latimer and Shaxton to be made bishops, for the good opinion she had of them both.   Acts and Mon. 1558.

ing of parchment shrivelled up with heat, as others make the comparison.

Shall be burnt up] This the very heathens knew in part, as appears by the writings of Lucretius, Cicero de Natura Deorum, Ovid's Metam. lib. i.

Ver. 11. *What manner of men*] ποταπούς, even to admiration, *quales et quanti*, as the word signifies, Mark xiii. 1. How accurate, and how elevated above the ordinary strain!

In all holy conversation and godliness] Gr. ἐν ἁγίαις ἀναστροφαῖς καὶ εὐσεβείαις, in holy conversations and godlinesses, in the plural; to show that godliness should run through our whole conversation, as the warp runs through the woof.

Ver. 12. *Looking for*] As Sisera's mother looked out at a window, and expecting the return of her son, said, " Why are his chariots so long in coming ?" so should we look up and long for Christ coming in the clouds, those chariots that carried him up, and shall bring him back again.

And hasting unto] *Votis accelerantes*, speeding and accelerating. True it is that God hath set the day wherein he will judge the world in righteousness, Acts xvii. 31, and we cannot alter it; yet we may be said to hasten it by our preparations and prayers. *O mora ! Christe veni*, " Come, Lord Jesus, come quickly."

The heavens being on fire, &c.] A far greater fire than that at Constantinople, where 7000 houses are said to have been on fire at once, A.D. 1633. (Blount's Voyage.)

And the elements shall melt] And fall like scalding lead or burning bell-metal on the heads of the wicked, who shall give a terrible account with the world all on fire about their ears. Whether this shall fall out in the year 1657 (as some conjecture, because in the year of the world 1657 the old world was drowned, and because the numeral letters in *MUnDI ConfLagratIo*, make up the same number), I have nothing to affirm. (Alsted. Chron.) Sure it is, the saints shall take no hurt at all by this last fire, but a great deal of benefit. Methodius writeth that Pyragnus (a certain plant so called) grows green and flourishes in the midst of the flames of burning Olympus, as much as if it grew by the banks of a pleasant river. And of this he saith that himself was an eye-witness. *Præclarum sane novissimi diei indicium et documentum.*

Ver. 13. *According to his promise*] Which is good sure-hold. For he pays not his promises with fair words, as Sertorius did, but with real performances.

Ver. 14. *That ye may be found of him*] Watching, working, well-doing. See the note on Matt. xxiv. 42, 44.

Ver. 15. *That the long-suffering*, &c.] Rom. ii. 4, which sentence Peter picks out of Paul's Epistles, as one of the choicest, and urgeth it here.

Even as our beloved brother, &c.] *Ingenium est profiteri per quos profeceris*, saith Pliny. St Peter makes honourable mention of St Paul; so Ezekiel of his contemporary Daniel.

Ver. 16. *Hard to be understood*] See my True Treasure. In things necessary the Scripture is plain and easy; and the very entrance thereinto giveth light, saith David, Psal. cxix. 30; yea, subtilty and sagacity, saith Solomon, Prov. i. 4. And for the more dark and difficult places, *Legum obscuritates non assignemus culpæ scribentium, sed inscitiæ non assequentium*, saith he in Gellius, the fault is not to be laid upon the Scriptures, but upon our unskilfulness and inability to understand them.

Which they that are unlearned and unstable] That for want of sacred learning are unsettled, ill-bottomed; and do therefore, like Peter on the water, walk one step and sink another. Our fore-fathers (saith Speed out of Walsingham) did not without great reason distinguish the people into learned and lewd; because such are commonly lewd who are not learned. Sure we are out of this text, that they are unstable that are unlearned; and that men therefore err because they know not the Scriptures in the right sense of them, Matt. ii. 2; they err in heart because they know not God's ways, and become a prey to seducers, because "ever learning, but never come to the knowledge of the truth," 2 Tim. iii. 7. "The simple believeth every word," saith Solomon, Prov. xiv. 1. The blind man swalloweth many a fly, saith our English proverb. The god of this world blinds the minds of his vassals, keeps them ignorant, and then doth what he will with them, as the Philistines did with Samson when they had digged out his eyes. He useth the same method ordinarily to carry on his designs, that he took in the *Parlamentum indoctum*, the lack-learning Parliament, held here A. D. 1404, in the reign of Henry IV. (Speed, 775) ; or as in the Council of Ariminum. The Arians have procured the exile of the orthodox learned bishops, and perceiving the company that was left, though they were very unlearned, yet they would not be persuaded directly to disannul anything that had been before concluded in the Council of Nice, did abuse their ignorance in proposing the matter, and drawing them to their side. For they demanded of them whether they would worship ὁμοούσιον, or Christ ? These not understanding the Greek word, rejected it with execration, being, as they thought, opposed unto Christ. (Ruffin. Eccles. Hist. lib. x.)

Wrest, as they do, &c.] When we strive to give unto the Scriptures, and not to receive from it the sense, when we factiously contend to fasten our conceits on God, like the harlot, take our dead and putrified fancies, and lay them in the bosom of the Scriptures, as of a mother, when we compel them to go two miles which of themselves would go but one, when we put words into the mouths of these oracles by mis-inferences or mis-applications, then are we guilty of this sin of wresting the Scriptures. Tertullian speaketh of some that murder the Scriptures to serve their own purposes. And the same author fitly calleth Marcion, the heretic, *Murem Ponticum*, the rat of Pontus, because of his gnawing and tawing the Scripture to make it serviceable to his errors (*Cædem Scripturarum faciunt*); this is a very dangerous sin, when men shall writhe the Scripture, and set it on the tenters to fit it to their fancies, as Scyron and Procrustes are said to have fitted their guests to the bed of brass which they had framed to their own bigness.

Ver. 17. Beware lest] *Cavebis autem si pavebis.* Let him that stands take heed lest he fall. Be not high-minded, but fear. Fear a snake under every flower, a snare under every new truth. Try the spirits whether they be of God or not, because many false prophets are abroad, who deceive the hearts of the simple, and make them fall from their own stedfastness. Try therefore before ye trust; look before ye leap. *Alioqui saliens antequam videas, casurus es antequam debeas, i. e.* If ye look not before ye leap, ye will fall before ye would. (Bernard.) Therefore walk circumspectly, tread gingerly, step warily, lift not up one foot till ye have found sure footing for the other, as those, Psal. xxxv.

6. Take the apostle's counsel here: never more need than now-a-days, *quando facta est fides Evangeliorum fides temporum. Nam aut scribuntur fides ut volumus; aut, ut volumus intelliguntur,* as Hilary complains of those better times.[1] It is grown a witty thing now amongst such variety of opinions to hold the truth, and to be a sound believer, as Erasmus once said. Beware therefore (every man for himself) lest ye also, swimming down the stream of the times, "and led away with the error of the wicked, fall from your own stedfastness." And (for a sovereign preservative) "grow in grace, and in the knowledge," &c.: grow downward howsoever; grow in humility, and God will both teach and "save the humble person," Psal. xxv.; Job xxii. 2.

Fall] As leaves fall from the trees in autumn.

Ver. 18. *But grow*] In firmness at least, as an apple doth in mellowness; as oaks grow more slowly than willows and bulrushes, yet more solidly, and in the end to a greater bulk and bigness.

THE FIRST EPISTLE GENERAL OF ST JOHN.

CHAPTER I.

Ver. 1. *That which was from the beginning*] CHRIST, the eternal God. See the note on John i. 2.

Which we have heard, &c.] The man Christ Jesus, the arch-prophet.

Which we have seen] And what so sure as sight? See Luke i. 2. αὐτόπτης, this was denied to many kings and prophets, Luke x. 24. To have seen Christ in the flesh was one of the three things that Austin wished, which yet St Paul set no such high price upon, in comparison of a spiritual sight of him, 2 Cor. v. 16. See the note there.

Which we have looked upon] ἐθεασάμεθα, diligently and with delight. How sweet shall be the sight of him in heaven! With what inconceivable attention and admiration shall we contemplate his glorified body outshining the brightest cherub!

And our hands have handled] *i. e.* With whom we have most familiarly conversed, sitting with him at the same table, and eating some bushels of salt with him, as the Greek word, Acts i. 4, seems to import, συναλιζόμ. ab ἅλς, *sal.* Christ's faithful ministers that have the honour to handle his law (as the phrase is, Jer. ii. 8) come nearest to the apostles in this glorious privilege.

Ver. 2. *For the life was manifested*] Christ, who is "life essential," swallowed up death in

victory, and "brought life and immortality to light by the gospel," 2 Tim. i. 10.

Ver. 3. *Declare we unto you*] That (Theophilus-like) ye may be at a certainty, fully persuaded, Luke i. 1, having a plerophory or "full assurance of understanding, to the acknowledgment of the mystery of Christ," Col. ii. 2. See the note there.

And truly our fellowship] If any should object, Is that such a preferment to have fellowship with you? What are you? &c. He answereth, As mean as we are, we have "fellowship with the Father and Son." Union being the ground of communion, all that is theirs is ours. This made Moses cry out, "Happy art thou, O Israel!" or, "Oh the happiness of thee, O Israel!" the "heaped-up happiness. Who is like unto thee?" Deut. xxxiii. 29. The saints, how mean soever, are (in true account) the world's paragons, the only earthly angels, because in "fellowship with the Father and the Son," that is, with the Father by the Son.

Ver. 4. *And these things write we*] Out of the Scriptures, those wells of salvation, draw we waters with joy, Isa. xii. 4, suck these breasts of consolation, and be satisfied, Isa. lxvi. 11. *Nusquam inveni requiem nisi in libro et claustro,* saith one. Chrysostom brings in a man laden with inward troubles, coming into the church; where, when he heard this passage read, "Why art thou cast down, my soul, &c., hope in God," &c., he presently recovered comfort. (Hom. in Genes.) There is a singular efficacy in the promises to comfort

[1] Hil. ad Constant. *in libro, quem illi exhibuit.*

those that are cast down, Rom. xv. 4. See the note there.

Ver. 5. *That God is light*] He is αὐτόφως, light essential, and they that walk with him must be as so many crystal glasses with a light in the midst; for can two walk together, and they not be agreed? Amos iii. 3. That was a devilish sarcasm of the Manichees, that God (till he had created light) dwelt in darkness, as if God were not eternal light, and dwelt in light unapproachable, 1 Tim. vi. 16. But what madmen were the Carpocratian heretics, who taught (even in St John's days, as Epiphanius testifieth) that men must sin, and do the will of the devils; otherwise they could not enter into heaven! These might well be some of those Antichrists he complaineth of chap. iv., and of those libertines and liars he here argueth against.

Ver. 6. *If we say that, &c.*] As they do that profess to know God, but in works do deny him, Tit. i. 16. See the note there.

And walk in darkness] There is a child of light that walks in darkness, Isa. l. 10, but that is in another sense. The wicked also that are here said to walk in darkness have their sparkles of light that they have kindled, Isa. l. 11, but it is as a light smitten out of a flint, which neither warms nor guides them, but dazzleth their eyes, and goes out, so that they lie down in sorrow.

Ver. 7. *We have fellowship one, &c.*] That is, God and we; inasmuch as we are made partakers of the divine nature, and are pure as God is pure, 1 John iii. 3, in quality though not in an equality. We have fellowship with God : 1. In his holiness. 2. In his happiness.

And the blood of Jesus] That whereas God's pure eye can soon find many a foul flaw in the best of us (our righteousness being mixed, as light and darkness, dimness at least, in a painted glass, dyed with some obscure and dim colour, it is transparent and giveth good, but not clear and pure light), lo, here is a ready remedy, a sweet support, " the blood of Jesus Christ his Son cleanseth us from all sin." And God beholding us in the face of his Son, seeth nothing amiss in us; no more than David did in lame Mephibosheth, when he beheld in him the features of his friend Jonathan.

Ver. 8. *If we say that we have*] If any should be so saucy, or rather silly, as to say with Donatus, *Non habeo, Domine, quod ignoscas*, I have no sin for Christ to cleanse me from, he is a loud liar, and may very well have the whetstone. St James for his innocent conversation was surnamed Justus; and yet, putting himself into the number, he saith, " For in many things we offend all," James iii. 2.

Ver. 9. *If we confess*] *Homo agnoscit, Deus ignoscit.* And *Confessio peccati est vomitus sordium animæ.* (Aug.) Judah (his name signifies confession) got the kingdom from Reuben. No man was ever kept out of God's kingdom for his confessed badness; many are for their supposed goodness; as those justitiaries in the former verse, whose hearts are big-swollen with high conceit of themselves; and whose lips are held close by the devil; who knows well there is no way to purge the sick soul but upwards.

He is faithful] And yet Bellarmine saith that he cannot find in all the book of God any promise made to confession of sin to God. (De Justific. 1. 21.) He might have seen (besides other places not a few) Prov. xxviii. 13; Psal. xxxii. 5, &c., that this very text is a most heavenly promise of mercy to those that confess heartily, and not hollowly. The word faithful also refers to God's promises, as just doth to the blood of Christ (the ransom received) whereby the saints are cleansed, and it stands not with God's justice to demand the same debt twice, viz. of the surety and of the debtor.

From all unrighteousness] All without exception; why then should we put in conditions, and as it were interline God's covenant? He is a sin-pardoning God, Neh. ix. 31; no God like him for that in heaven and earth, Mic. vii. 17; he multiplieth pardon, as we multiply sin, Isa. lv. 7; he doth it freely, for his own sake, naturally, Exod. xxxiv. 6; constantly, Psal. cxxx. 4, and here. The blood of Jesus Christ cleanseth (not, he hath cleansed or will cleanse, but he doth it) daily and duly, constantly and continually. This should be as a perpetual picture in our hearts.

Ver. 10. *We make him a liar*] For the Scripture hath concluded all under sin, Rom. xi. 32. See the note there.

CHAPTER II.

Ver. 1. *That ye sin not*] Presuming upon an easy and speedy pardon. The worser sort of Papists will say, When we have sinned, we must confess; and when we have confessed, we must sin again, that we may confess again; so making account of confessing, as drunkards do of vomiting. But we have not so learned Christ. If his word dwell richly in us, it will teach us to deny ungodliness, &c.; to forsake as well as confess sin, and not after confession, to turn again to folly, or (as those that are dog-sick) to their former vomit. With confession of sin must be joined confusion of sin, Prov. xxviii. 13. We may not do as those Philistines, that confessed their error and yet sent away the ark of God, 1 Sam. vi. 3. Nor as Saul, " I have sinned, yet honour me before the people," 1 Sam. xv. 30. Nor yet as those perverse Israelites, " We have sinned, we will go up;" though God had flatly forbidden them at that time to go up against the Amorites; and for their presumptuous attempt brought them back by weeping cross, Deut. i. 41—43, &c. Sin confessed must be, 1. Disallowed in our judgments. 2. Disavowed and declined in our wills and affections. 3. Cast out of our practice; Ephraim shall say, " What have I to do any more with idols?" Hos. xiv. 8. He shall pollute the images that he had once perfumed: he shall angrily say unto them, Get you hence, Isa. xxx. 22.

And if any man sin] Being taken before he is aware, Gal. vi. 1. See the note there.

We have an advocate] Who appears for us in heaven, and pleads our cause effectually. See Heb. ix. 24.

Jesus Christ the righteous] Or else he could not go to the Father for us. See the note on John xvi. 10.

Ver. 2. *He is the propitiation*] Heb. *Copher*; he coffers up, as it were, and covers our sins, Psal. lxxviii. 38. See the note on Rom. iii. 25. The Hebrew word כֹּפֶר used for covering and propitiating of sin, is (Gen. vi.) used of the pitch or plaster whereby the wood of the ark was so fastened that no water could get in.

But also for the sins of the whole world] That is, of all the faithful, both of Jews and Gentiles, that *mundus ex mundo*, that world of whom the world is not worthy, Heb. xi.

Ver. 3. *We know that we know him*] By a reflex act of the soul; hence the assurance of faith, the fruit of fruitfulness, 1 Cor. xv. 58.

That we know him] With a knowledge not apprehensive only, but affective too.

If we keep his commandments] *Si facimus præcepta, etiamsi non perficiamus;* If we think upon his commandments to do them, Psal. ciii. 8, aim at them, as at a mark, Psal. cxix. 6.

Non semper feriet quodcunque minabitur arcus.

Wish well to an exact obedience which yet we cannot attain to, Psal. cxix. 4, 5; be doing at it as we can, following after righteousness, Prov. xv. 9, as a poor 'prentice follows his trade, though he be nothing less than his craft-master; and lastly, be humbled for our daily aberrations, resolving and striving to do better: this is that evangelical keeping of God's commandments, which God (measuring the deed by the desire, and the desire by the sincerity thereof) will accept and crown, through Christ our propitiation.

Ver. 4. *He that saith, I know him*] Here he disputeth against Verbalists and Solifidians. See James ii. 14, with the note there.

Is a liar] *i.e.* A hypocrite; his spot is not the spot of God's children, Deut. xxxii. 5, for they are children that will not lie, Isa. lxiii. 8. They all deserve that title of honour that was given of old to Arrianus the historian, viz. φιλαλήθης, A lover of truth. They know that the God whom they serve, desireth "truth in the inward parts," Psal. li. 6, and that *dicta factis deficientibus erubescant* (as Tertullian hath it), words without deeds will not bear a man out in the end. It is a question whether the desire of being, or dislike of seeming, sincere, be greater in the good heart. Not so every loose and ungirt Christian, every profligate professor, that denieth that in deed that he affirmeth in word.

Ver. 5. *In him verily is the love of God perfected*] St John was a mere compound of sweetest love. As iron put into the fire, seemeth to be nothing but fire, so he (the beloved disciple) was turned into a lump of love. Hence he so presseth love, perfect love, to God and his peo-

ple. And Jerome tells us, that living to a very great age at Ephesus, he would get up into the pulpit; and when through weakness of body he could say no more, he would say, "Little children, love one another;" *Si hoc solum fiat, sufficit*, If this be well done, all is done. (Jerome in cap. vi. ad Gal.)

That we are in him] In communion with him, and in conformity to him.

Ver. 6. *To walk even as he walked*] This is the same with that Col. ii. 6, to walk in Christ; and with that, 1 Pet. ii. 21, to follow his steps. See the note there.

Ver. 7. *I write no new commandment*] The apostle studiously declineth the suspicion of novelty. We should ever set a jealous eye upon that which is new, and stand in the old way, Jer. vi. 16, in the ancient paths, Jer. xviii. 15. God's people are called the ancient people, Isa. xliv. 7. And idolaters are said to sacrifice to new gods, that came newly up, Deut. xxxii. 17. Truth, as wine, is better with age, Luke v. 39. And of witnesses, Aristotle well saith, the older they are, the more credible, because less corrupted, πιστό-τατοι οἱ παλαιοί, ἀδιάφθοροι γάρ (Rhet. i.). As we prefer the newest philosophy, so the ancientest divinity; and we may justly suspect them of falsehood and delusions, who arrogate to themselves to utter oracles, to bring to light new truths, &c.

Ver. 8. *A new commandment*] See the note on John xiii. 34. "A new commandment" it is called, saith a late learned interpreter, 1. Because it was renewed by the Lord after it had been as it were antiquated, and almost extinguished. 2. Because it was commanded to such men as were new or renewed. 3. Because it was an excellent commandment.

Ver. 9. *And hateth his brother*] As Paul presseth faith, and Peter hope, so John love, those three cardinal virtues, 1 Cor. xiii. 13. See the note on ver. 5.

Is in darkness] Yea, in the prince of darkness, who acteth and agitateth him, as he did Cain. Holy Greenham oft prayed, that he might keep up his young zeal with his old discretion.

Ver. 10. *None occasion, &c.*] Gr. σκάνδαλον, No scandal, *i. e.* no occasion of spiritual falling, whereby a man is made any manner of way worse, and backwarder in goodness. *Quod fieri potest vel dicto, vel facto, sive exemplo in moribus*, saith learned Lyserus, which may be done by word, deed, or evil example.

Ver. 11. *He that hateth, &c.*] There is a passion of hatred (saith a famous divine). This is a kind of averseness and rising of the heart against a man, when one sees him so that he cannot away with him, nor speak to nor look courteously or peaceably upon him, &c. 2. A habit of hatred, when the heart is so settled in this alienation and estrangement, that it grows to wish and seek his hurt. This is man-slaughter, 1 John iii. 5.

Ver. 12. *I write unto you, little children*] A Christian hath his degrees of growth; childhood,

1 Cor. iii. 1, 2 ; youth or well-grown age, when he is past the spoon, as here ; old age, Acts xxi. 16.

Because your sins are forgiven you] Though perhaps you as yet know it not, through weakness of faith and strength of corruption.

Ver. 13. *Him that is from the beginning*] The Ancient of days. Old men love to speak of ancient things. These are ancient things, 1 Chron. iv. 22. You know him with a knowledge of acquaintance ; you have had much familiarity and intercourse with him, you are not far from knowing even as also you are known, 1 Cor. xiii. 12. To this pitch of perfection all God's people must aspire, as all men do follow after old age.

Because ye have overcome the wicked one] "The glory of young men is their strength," Prov. xx. 29. The Hebrew word there rendered young men, signifieth choice men, *sc.* for military employments ; neither can they better show their valour than by resisting the devil, that he may fly from them. Weak grace may evidence pardon of sin ; but it is strong grace that can overcome the temptations of Satan.

Because ye have known the Father] We say, He is a wise child that knows his father (and the Greeks have a proverb to the same purpose, Hom. Od.) ; but God hath no child so young that more or less knoweth him not. The bastardly brood of Rome are all for their mother.

Ver. 14. *Because ye have known him*] The same again as ver. 13, which to a carnal heart may seem superfluous. *Et certe si humano ingenio conscripti essent libri illi, quos pro sacris (ita ut verissime sunt) agnoscimus et veneramur, bonum alicubi dormitasse Homerum disceremus,* said one. But far be it from us to reprehend what we cannot comprehend.

Ver. 15. *Love not the world*] You fathers, and you young and strong men, let me caution you (before I speak again to the little children, ver. 18), to beware of worldliness. A man may be very mortified, and yet very apt to dote on the world.

If any man love the world] Have it he may, and use it too, as the traveller useth his staff (which either he keeps or casts away, as it furthers or hinders his journey), but love it he must not, unless he will renounce the love of God. See the note on Matt. vi. 24 ; Col. iii. 2. Aristotle in his Politics teacheth, by the example of Thales, that philosophers may be rich ; but he excellently addeth ἄλλα οὐ τοῦτο ἐστὶ περὶ οὗ σπουδάζουσι, howbeit this is not their chief study ; it is but a by-business with them. (Polit. i., cap. ult.)

The love of the Father is not in him] The sunbeams extinguish the fire ; so doth the love of the world the love of God. But some not so much as roving at God, make the world their standing mark.

Ver. 16. *The lust of the flesh, the lust of, &c.*] That is, pleasure, profit, preferment ; the worldling's trinity, as one saith. Compare herewith Christ's three-fold temptation, Luke iv. 3—9, and St James's character of worldly wisdom, James

iii. 15, with the note there. It is his pleasure, his profit, and his honour (saith a divine) that is the natural man's trinity, and his carnal self that is these in unity. And to the same purpose the Christian poet,

> *Ambitiosus honos, et opes, et fœda voluptas,*
> *Hæc tria pro trino numine mundus habet.*

But is of the world] Base and bootless. *Nec verum, nec vestrum.* To know the vanity of the world (as of a mist) you must go a little from it.

Ver. 17. *And the world passeth away*] As the stream of a swift river passeth by the side of a city. *Animantis cujusque vita in fuga est,* Life itself wears out in the wearing, as a garment ; all things below are mutable and momentary. Wilt thou set thy heart upon that is not ? saith Solomon.

And the lust thereof] So that although thou wert sure to hold all these things of the world, yet they may be suddenly lost to thee, because thou canst not make thine heart delight in the same things still. Not the world only, but the lust thereof, passeth away ; there is a curse of unsatisfiableness lies upon the creature, ἁπάντων ἡ πλησμονὴ, saith the orator ; There is a satiety of all things. The world's comforts are sweeter in the ambition than in the fruition ; for after a little while we loathe what we lusted after, as Amnon did Tamar. Men first itch, and then scratch, and then smart. *Dolor est etiam ipsa voluptas.* Cruciger used oft to say,

> *Omnia prætereunt, præter amare Deum.*

Ver. 18. *Little children*] Children may easily be cozened, and made to take a sheep-counter for an angel, because broader and brighter ; so young Christians are soon seduced ; hence they are cautioned. See the note on chap. i. 5.

Ver. 19. *But they were not of us*] No more were our Anti-trinitarians, Arians, Anti-scripturists, ever of our Church, otherwise than as wens and botches, whatever our adversaries aver and cavil. So of old, because the Waldenses and Manichees lived in the same places, and were both held heretics, the Papists maliciously gave out that the Waldenses (those ancient Protestants) were defiled with the errors of the Manichees and Catharists, which yet they ever abhorred.

Ver. 20. *But ye have an unction*] That oil of gladness, the Holy Ghost. In derision thereof, Domitian, the tyrant, cast St John into a caldron of boiling oil, but he by a miracle came forth unhurt.

Ye know all things] Not all things knowable, but all things needful to be known.

Ver. 21. *Because ye know not, &c.*] Because ye are utterly ignorant ; for God hath no blind children, but they all know him from the least to the greatest. Howbeit, the angels know not so much, but they would know more, Ephes. iii. 10. Should not we ?

Ver. 22. *That denieth that Jesus*] Papists deny him as a King, in setting up the pope ; as a

Priest, in setting up the mass; as a Prophet, in piecing their human traditions to the Holy Scriptures.

Ver. 23. *The same hath not the Father*] See the note on John v. 23. Mahomet speaks very honourably of Christ, but denies his Divinity, and that he was crucified. He acknowledged that he was the word and power of God, and that all that believe in him shall be saved, &c.

Ver. 24. *Let that therefore abide*] Persevere and hold fast the faith of the gospel without wavering in it, Ephes. iv. 14, or starting from it, 2 Pet. ii. 20. Be as the centre, or as Mount Sion, stedfast and unmoveable. Stand fast; for ye are sure to be shaken: the tree must be shaken, that rotten fruit may fall off.

Ver. 25. *Even eternal life*] Hold therefore the doctrine of faith sound and entire by the hand of faith, that ye may receive the end of your faith, the salvation of your souls.

Ver. 26. *That seduce you*] That carry you into by-ways, highways to hell.

Ver. 27. *But the anointing*] See ver. 20. It was an aggravation of the fall of Saul, 2 Sam. i. 21, as "though he had not been anointed;" so for the saints to fall from their own stedfastness.

Ver. 28. *Little children, abide in him*] q. d. Your enemies are many and crafty; therefore keep home, keep home; this shall be no grief unto you, nor offence of heart, as she said, 1 Sam. xxv. 31.

Ver. 29. *Is born of him*] And exactly resembles him, as a child doth his father. See 1 Pet. i. 17, and the note on Matt. v. 9.

CHAPTER III.

Ver. 1. *Behold what manner*] Qualem et quantum, as 2 Pet. iii. 11. See the note on John i. 12. If Jacob was at such pains and patience to become son-in-law to Laban, if David held it a great matter to be son-in-law to the king, what is it then to be sons and daughters to the Lord Almighty? 2 Cor. vi. 18.

The world knoweth us not] Princes unknown are unrespected; unkent, unkist, as the Northern proverb hath it. After the sentence was pronounced upon Mr Bainham, the martyr, he was counselled by Mr Nicholas Wilson to conform himself to the Church; to whom he answered, I trust I am the very child of God, which ye blind asses, said he, do not perceive. The "king's daughter is all glorious within," her beauty is inward, Psal. xlv. 13; she is black, but comely as the tents of Kedar, Cant. i. 5; rough, but rich; as the tabernacle in the wilderness, covered with goat's hair, but within costly and curious; as Brutus's staff in the story, *cujus intus solidum aurum corneo velabatur cortice.* (Plut.) All righteous men are kings, as may appear by comparing Matt. xiii. 17 with Luke x. 24; they are kings in righteousness as Melchisedec, but somewhat obscure ones as he; they must be content to pass to heaven as Christ their head did, as concealed men. Their glorious faith, James ii. 1, now not notified or regarded, shall one day be "found to praise, honour, and glory," 1 Pet. i. 7.

Ver. 2. *What we shall be*] Great things we have in hand, but greater in hope; much in possession, but more in reversion. Let this comfort us against the contempts cast upon us by the world, blind and besides itself in point of salvation.

For we shall see him as he is] Now we see as in a glass obscurely, 1 Cor. xiii. 11, as an old man through spectacles, as a weak eye looks upon the sun; but in heaven we shall see him as he is, so far as a creature is capable of that blissful vision.

Ver. 3. *Purifieth himself*] That is true hope that runs out into holiness. Faith and hope purge, and work a suitableness in the soul to the things believed and hoped for.

Even as he is pure] In quality, though not in an equality. There shall be *comparatio*, though not *æquiparatio*.

Ver. 4. *Sin is the transgression*] As there is the same roundness in a little ball as in a bigger, so the same disobedience in a small sin as in a great. Papists tell us that concupiscence is not truly and properly a sin (Concil. Trident.); but St Paul saith otherwise, Rom. vii. There are amongst us, that say, that original sin is not forbidden by the law; but sure we are it is cursed and condemned by the law, as that which hath in it a tacit consent to all sin. *Peccatum est dictum, factum, concupitum contra æternam legem,* saith Austin (contra Faust. xxii. 27). Any want of conformity to the eternal law is sin.

Ver. 5. *To take away our sins*] Shall sin live that killed Christ? Shall I drink the blood of these men? said David of those that but ventured their lives for him. Oh that each Christian would turn Jew to himself, and kill the red cow, &c.; present himself a whole burnt sacrifice to God; not going about to frustrate the end of Christ's incarnation and passion, by retaining that sin that he came to take away, lest that doleful sentence be passed upon him, that was once upon the stubborn Jews, "Ye shall die in your sins," John vii.

Ver. 6. *Sinneth not*] Sin may rebel, it cannot reign in a saint. He sinneth not sinningly; there is no way of wickedness in him, Psal. cxxxix., he loves not sin, he lies not in it, but riseth again by repentance, and is restless till that be done, and done to purpose.

Ver. 7. *Let no man deceive you*] As if you might pass *e cœno in cœlum;* fly to heaven with dragon's wings; dance with the devil all day, and sup with Christ at night; live all your lives long in Delilah's lap, and then go to Abraham's bosom when you die. These are the devil's dirt-daubers that teach such doctrine, his upholsterers that sew such pillows, Ezek. xiii. 18.

He that doth righteousness is righteous] Provided that he do it from a right principle. For otherwise men may naturally perform the outward act of righteousness, and yet not be right-eous persons; as Ahab humbled himself. Alexander the Great, when he had killed Clitus, was troubled in conscience, and sent to all kinds of philosophers (as it were to so many ministers) to know what he might do to appease his conscience and satisfy for that sin. Uriah, that brought in the altar of Damascus, is called "a faithful witness," Isa. viii. 2, true of his word; yet no man looketh upon him as righteous. It is not, saith a reverend man, in divinity as in moral philosophy, where *justa et juste agendo simus justi*, by doing righteous things and right-eously we are made righteous; but we have the *esse* first, and then the *operari*, &c., the habit, and then the act.

Ver. 8. *He that committeth sin*] ποιῶν, that makes a trade of it, and can art it (as the word properly signifieth), not act it only.

Is of the devil] Bears his image, wears his livery; is as like him as if spit out of his mouth.

For the devil sinneth] Or is a sinning; he never ceaseth to sin, he commits the sin against the Holy Ghost every moment.

That he might destroy the works] The devil then hath his works in the very hearts of the elect, for whose cause Christ came into the world, that he might unravel the devil's work, break his head, Gen. iii. 15. The Son of the woman, our Saviour (not the Virgin Mary, as Papists blasphemously affirm, *illa conteret tibi caput*) breaks the serpent's head, that first of the devil's works against mankind: trampled upon him and triumphed over him on the cross, and will tread him under our feet also shortly. But what a bold conceit is that of Josephus, that God, when he said "He shall bruise thy head," meant no more but this, Every son of Eve, when-soever he meeteth with a serpent, shall strike it upon the head, which containeth in it somewhat hurtful to mankind. (Antiq. Judaic. i. 2.)

Ver. 9. *For his seed*] The new nature, which causeth that sin cannot carry it away without some counter-buffs. The Spirit quickens the word: as there is a spirit in the natural seed that maketh it prolifical; so here.

He cannot sin] i. e. Sinningly, so as to be transformed into sin's image: cannot do wicked-ly with both hands earnestly, Mic. vii. He sin-neth not totally and finally, he cannot so fall as apostates; for the seed of God ever abideth in him. Bellarmine is forced to confess that this is the hardest place in all the Bible, urged for proof of perseverance in grace.

Ver. 10. *In this the children of God*] As David's daughters were known by their garments of divers colours, 2 Sam. xiii. 18; so are God's children by their piety and charity.

Ver. 11. *That we should love, &c.*] This beloved disciple was all for love. See the note on chap. ii. 9, and on chap. ii. 5.

Ver. 12. *Who was of that wicked one*] Tertullian calleth Cain the devil's patriarch. Cain is dead, saith another, but I could wish that he did not still live in his heirs and executors, *Qui cla-vam ejus sanguine Abelis rubentem, ut rem sacram circumferunt, adorant et venerantur*, who bear about and make use of Cain's club, to knock on the head God's righteous Abels. (Bucholcer.)

And slew his brother] Gr. ἔσφαξε, cut his throat. *Acerbissima sunt odia* (*ut ita nominem*) *Theologica*, saith one. These divinity hatreds are most deadly. Such fratricides were Alphonsus Diazius, and Charles, king of France, stirred up by Pope Urban to kill his brother Manford, king of Sicily.

Because his own works, &c.] The old enmity, Gen. iii. 15. So Numb. xxii. 3, 4. Moab was irked because of Israel, or did fret and vex at them, as Exod. i. 12, yet they were allied, and passed by them in peace, and, by the slaughter of the Amorites, freed them from evil neighbours which had taken away part of their land, and might do more, as one hath well observed.

Ver. 13. *Marvel not, my brethren*] Sith it was so from the beginning, and the very first man that died, died for religion; so early came martyrdom into the world.

Ver. 14. *We know that we have passed*] Not we think, we hope, &c. If we would not have with the merchant an estate hanging upon ropes, *fortunam rudentibus aptam*, and depending upon uncertain winds, let us make sure work for our souls. This is a jewel that the cock on the dung-hill meddles not with. *Sensum electionis ad gloriam in hac vita nullum agnosco*, saith Greevinchovius the Arminian, I know no such thing as assurance of heaven in this life. Papists allow us nothing beyond a conjectural confidence, un-less by special revelation. Miserable comforters! They tell us that to taste though but with the tip of a rod (Jonathan-like) of this honey will hinder us in the chase of our lusts; but believe them not; for the joy of the Lord is our strength, Neh. viii. 10.

Because we love the brethren] This is to be seen in the natives of New England. The first appearance of grace in them is, their love and respect to those that are truly gracious.

Ver. 15. *Whosoever hateth his brother*] Not to love then is to hate, as not to save a man is to kill him, Mark iii. 4.

Is a murderer] Because he wisheth him out of the world, as Caracalla did his brother Geta, of whom he said, *Divus sit, modo non sit vivus*, I would he were in heaven or anywhere, so that I were rid of him. By like reason we may say that sin is God-murder; forasmuch as sinners are God-haters, Rom. i. 30, and could wish there were no God, that they might never come to judgment. The godly man, on the contrary, cries out with David, *Vivat Deus*, "Let the Lord live, and blessed be the God of my salvation," &c., Psal. xviii. 46.

Ver. 16. *Because he laid down*] See the note on John xv. 13; Rom. v. 8.

We ought also to lay down our lives] If Pylades can offer to die for Orestes merely for a name, or out of carnal affection at the best; should not Christians lay down their own necks one for

another, as Aquila and Priscilla did for Paul?
Rom. xvi. 4.

Ver. 17. *This world's goods*] Gr. τὸν βίον, livelihood, which is all that the world looks after.

And shutteth up his bowels, &c.] Not drawing
out unto him both his sheaf and his soul, Isa.
lviii. 9. But locking up as with a key (so the
Greek κλείσῃ here signifies) both his barn and his
bowels; not considering his brother's necessity
and his own ability.

Ver. 18. *Let us not love in word*] Words are
light-cheap; and there is a great deal of mouth
mercy abroad. Julian the Apostate is not presently a friend to Basil, though he write unto him,
φίλος φίλῳ, καὶ ἄδελφος ἀδέλφῳ, Thou art my friend
and beloved brother. The Roman legions loved
Otho the emperor, saith Dio the historian, and
gave him all respect, οὐκ ἀπὸ τῆς γλώττης, ἀλλὰ
καὶ ἀπὸ τῆς ψυχῆς, not from the teeth outward,
but from the heart-root. See the notes on Jam.
ii. 14—16.

Ver. 19. *And shall assure our hearts*] This,
saith father Latimer, is the sweetmeats of the
feast of a good conscience. There are other
dainty dishes in this feast, but this is the banquet.

Ver. 20. *If our heart condemn us*] Conscience
is God's spy and man's overseer, *Domesticus index,
judex, carnifex;* God's deputy judge, holding
court in the whole soul, bearing witness of all
a man's doings and desires, and accordingly excusing or accusing, absolving or condemning,
comforting or tormenting. *Quid tibi prodest non
habere conscium, habenti conscientiam?* saith one;
and another, *Turpe quid acturus, te sine teste
time. Inprimis reverere te ipsum.* Look to
conscience.

*Conscia mens ut cuique sua est, ita concipit intra,
Pectora pro facto spemque metumque suo.* (Ovid.)

Ver. 21. *Then have we confidence*] Sincerity is
the mother of serenity, *Sine qua, tranquillitas
omnis tempestas est,* saith Isidore. Uprightness
hath boldness. It is not a peace, but a truce,
that the wicked have; such a storm will befall
them as shall never be blown over. Israel is the
heir of peace, Gal. vi. 16; Isa. xxxii. 17.

Ver. 22. *And whatsoever we ask*] sc. According
to his will. *Fiat voluntas mea, quia tua,* said
Luther. I can have what I will of God, said
one; for my will shall be concentric with his will.

Because we keep] The obedience of faith em-
boldens us; yet may no man say as the prodigal,
" Give me the portion that belongeth to me." It
was a proud speech of that emperor (Antonin.
Philo.) that said, *Non sic Deum coluimus, aut sic
viximus, ut ille nos vinceret,* We have not so served
God, that the enemy should overcome us. It
was much worse in that arrogant Papist that said,
God forbid that we should enjoy heaven as of
alms to us; no, we have it by purchase or conquest.

Ver. 23. *And this is his commandment*] This is
the sum and substance of the gospel, that we believe and love; and the more we believe God's

love to us, the more love shall we bear one to
another; for our love is but a reflex of his.

*And love one another, as he gave us command-
ment*] Lo, love is a commandment; we should
therefore not only submit, but embrace it joyfully as a gift.

Ver. 24. *By the Spirit*] Christ hath satisfied
the wrath of the Father; and now the Father and
Christ both, as reconciled, send the Spirit, as the
fruit of both their loves, to inherit our hearts.
And truly, next unto the love of Christ indwelling in our nature, we may well wonder at the
love of the Holy Ghost that will dwell in our
defiled souls.

CHAPTER IV.

Ver. 1. *But try the spirits*] As lapidaries do
their stones, as goldsmiths do their metals. A
Bristol stone may look as well as an Indian diamond; and many things glitter besides gold. Try
therefore before you trust that which is doctrin-
ally delivered unto you; being neither over
credulous, the fool believeth everything; nor
rashly censorious, as those were that said of our
Saviour, " This man blasphemeth." See the note
on 1 Thess. v. 21.

Because many false prophets] Both the old
Church, Deut. xiii. 1, and the new, Acts xx. 30,
were ever pestered with them.

Ver. 2. *Hereby know ye the spirit*] Bring it to
this test. Gold may be rubbed or melted, it
remains orient; so doth truth. Whereas error,
as glass (bright, but brittle), cannot endure the
hammer of fire.

That confesseth] That preacheth Christ crucified.

Ver. 3. *Is not of God*] And yet he is not
called an Atheist, or an Antitheist, but Antichrist, that is, an opposite to Christ; as if his
opposing should not be so much to Christ's
nature or person, as to his unction and function.

Ver. 4. *And have overcome*] viz. In your Head,
Christ, and by the help of his Holy Spirit, your
sweet inhabitant, whereby ye are more than
conquerors, because sure to overcome and triumph.

Ver. 5. *They are of the world*] i. e. The seducers; fit lettuce for such lips; *Dignum patella
operculum. Vos infernates estis,* " Ye are from
beneath, I am from above," saith Christ, John
viii. 23.

Therefore speak they of the world] The water
riseth not (unless forced) above the fountain.
Out of the warehouse, the shop is furnished.
Carnal teachers gratify their hearers with pleasing positions. The Papists in their petition to
King James for a toleration, plead this as an
argument, That their religion is agreeable to
men's nature: and indeed it is an alluring, tempting, bewitching religion, giving way to all licentiousness and lasciviousness. So Mahomet in his
Alcoran tells his followers concerning venery,
That God did not give men such appetites to

have them frustrate, but enjoyed, as made for the gust of man, not for his torment; and a great deal more of such paltry stuff.

Ver. 6. *Heareth us*] Christ's sheep are rational; they can discern his voice from that of a stranger, and will hear it not with that gristle only that grows upon their heads, but with the ear of their soul, which trieth doctrines as the mouth doth meat, Job xxxiv. 3, and knoweth the spirit of truth and the spirit of error.

Ver. 7. *Beloved, let us love one another*] This beloved disciple breathes nothing but love; as if he had been born with love in his mouth, as they say.

Ver. 8. *Knoweth not God*] If moral virtue could be seen with mortal eyes, saith Plato, it would draw all hearts unto it. If God were well known, he could not but be best beloved, and all that are his, for his sake.

For God is love] Not formally, but causally, say schoolmen; he is the fountain of love, and draws all hearts that have any knowledge of him. See ver. 16. Cant. i. 3, with the note.

Ver. 9. *In this was manifested*] The very naked bowels of his tenderest compassions are herein laid open unto us, as in an anatomy. God so loved his Son that he gave him the world for his possession, Psal. ii. 7; but he so loved the world that he gave Son and all for its redemption.

Ver. 10. *Not that we loved, &c.*] *Deus prior nos amavit, tantus, tantum, et gratis, tantillos et tales.* God, though so great, loved us first and freely, though such and so worthless. "He loved us, because he loved us," saith Moses, Deut. vii. 7, 8, the ground of his love being wholly in himself. He works for his own name's sake, Ezek. xx. 9, 14, 22, 44, four several times, notwithstanding his word and oath, 13, 15, 23.

Ver. 11. *If God so loved us*] His one example easily answereth all our objections, taketh off all our excuses; as that our brother is our inferior, our adversary, of whom we have better deserved, &c.

Ver. 12. *No man hath seen God*] If we read that any hath seen him, we must understand it, that indeed they did see *Mercavah, velo harocheb*, the chariot in which God rode, but not the rider in it, as that Rabbi speaketh. (Rab. Maim. More Nevochim, iii. 7.)

His love is perfected in us] i. e. Either actively; our love is demonstrated in the excellency of it. Or else passively; the love that God beareth to us is abundantly declared perfect, in that he worketh such a gracious inclination in us. And in this latter sense understand the apostle, ver. 17, touching love made perfect.

Ver. 13. *He hath given us of his Spirit*] That is, of the fruits of his Spirit, his holy motions and graces. For through the two golden pipes the two olive-branches empty out of themselves the golden oils of all precious graces, into the candlestick, the Church.

Ver. 14. *And we have seen*] sc. By special privilege (that which natural eye never saw, ver. 12), the back-parts of Jehovah, his wisdom, justice, mercy, &c.; we can see no more and live, we need see no more that we may live.

Ver. 15. *Whosoever shall confess*] See the note on 1 Cor. xii. 3.

Ver. 16. *And we have known and believed*] That is, we know by believing. See the note on John vi. 69.

God is love] Pellican tells of some in his time that used to read this piece of Scripture to their friends at their feasts. A pious practice surely, and well beseeming those that feast before the Lord. The primitive Christians had at such times their kiss of love, 1 Pet. v. 14. And St Austin had these two verses written on his table,

Quisquis amat dictis absentum rodere famam,
Hanc mensam vetitam noverit esse sibi.

Ver. 17. *In the day of judgment*] Those that bear his image shall hear his *euge;* he will own them and honour them, and their faith that worketh by love, "shall be found unto praise, honour, and glory at the appearing of Jesus Christ," 1 Pet. i. 7. He that was so willingly judged for them, shall give no hard sentence against them.

Ver. 18. *There is no fear in love*] But complacence and acquiescence in the person beloved.

Perfect love casteth out fear] *Timorem scilicet servilem illum, non amicalem.* (Beda in Prov. i.)

Because fear hath torment] *Quem metuunt, oderunt,* Whomsoever men fear, they hate, saith the proverb. And *odium timorem spirat,* saith Tertullian. Hatred hath fear, which sets the soul on a rack, as it were, and renders it restless.

Ver. 19. *Because he first loved us*] See the note on ver. 10. Mary answers not Rabboni till Christ first said unto her, Mary. Our love is but the reflex of his. And as the reflected beams of the sun are weaker than the direct, so are our affections weaker than God's. That is a memorable saying of a modern writer, as a great brightness of the air at midnight argueth the shining of the moon, and that presumeth an illumination of the sun, because these depend one upon another; so the diffusing of our charity on our neighbours proveth our love to God; and our love to God presumeth his love to us first, for the inseparable dependance they have on each other.

Ver. 20. *If a man say, I love God*] If he did so, he would hardly say so in a vaunting way howsoever. "Charity vaunteth not itself; is not puffed up," 1 Cor. xiii. 4. Christ loves secret service, Cant. ii. 14. They that bear him greatest love make least show thereof before others. Master Bartlet Green, when he had been beaten and scourged with rods by Bishop Bonner, and he greatly rejoiced in the same (saith Master Fox), yet his shamefaced modesty was such that he would never express any mention thereof (lest he should seem to glory too much in himself), save that only he opened the same to one Mr Cotton of the Temple (a friend of his) a little before he suffered martyrdom. (Acts and Mon.

1684.) *Vasa quæ magis continent, minus sonant.* (Seneca.)   But empty casks sound loudest: and baser metals ring shrillest.

Whom he hath seen] Sight usually maketh love. Juvenal greatly wondereth at one, *Qui nunquam visæ flagrabat amore puellæ,* who loved a party whom he had never seen.

How can he love God] That is, saith Dr Rainolds, He that cannot endure to look on that little glimpse and ray of holiness which is in his brother, in one of the same infirmities and corruptions with himself, will much less be able to abide the light of the Sun of righteousness, and the most orient, spotless, and vast holiness that is in him.

Ver. 21. *And this commandment we have from him*] Lo, here a singular evidence of God's great love to us, that he commandeth us also the love of our neighbour as well as of himself: *quasi non tam de se amando fuerit sollicitus, quam de proximo nostro diligendo,* saith Aretius. Our Saviour therefore, summing up the law, joineth those two precepts, "Thou shalt love the Lord thy God with all," &c., and "Thou shalt love thy neighbour as thyself." Yea, God prefers mercy before sacrifice; and is content that his own immediate service should be intermitted, rather than offices of love to our brother omitted. "Leave there thy gift, and go thy way; first be reconciled," Matt. v. 24.

Love his brother also] If he be a good man, love him in God; if bad, for God.

CHAPTER V.

Ver. 1. *Whosoever believeth*] viz. FIRMLY and fiducially with assent of mind, and consent of will. See the note on 1 Cor. xii. 3, and on John i. 12.

Loveth him also that is begotten] His love, as Aaron's ointment, floweth down from the head to the meanest member. God's image, wheresoever it appeareth, is very lovely.

Ver. 2. *That we love the children of God*] Really, aright, and not for self or sinister respects. Godliness begins in the right knowledge of ourselves, and ends in the right knowledge of God. A Christian begins with loving God for himself, but he ends in loving himself and others in and for Christ.

Ver. 3. *For this is,* &c.] See the note on John xiv. 15.

His commandments are not] See the note on Matt. xi. 30.

Ver. 4. *Even our faith*] Which shows a man a better project, puts his head into heaven beforehand, gives him to taste of the hidden manna. Now his mouth will not water after homely provisions, that hath lately tasted of delicate sustenance. Are we afraid of men? saith one. Faith sets hell before us. Are we allured by the world? Faith sets heaven before us. It was by the force of his faith, that Luther brake out into those words, *Contemptus est a me Romanus et favor et furor,* I care neither for Rome's fawnings nor frownings.

Ver. 5. *But he that believeth*] A believer walketh about the world as a conqueror. He saith of these things here below, as Socrates did when he came into a fair, and saw there sundry commodities to be sold, *Quam multis ego non egeo? Nec habeo, nec careo, nec curo,* as another said, I neither have these things, nor need them, nor care for them. He hath his feet where other men's heads are, Prov. xv. 24; Rev. xii. 1. He sets not his desire upon the asses, sith he is assured of the kingdom. He looks upon the world as Hiram did on the cities Solomon had given him, which he called Cabul, that is, the land of dirt. His eye is upon Uranople, the new Jerusalem, the crowns and palms of that golden country. Children admire gawds and gewgaws; but let a nobleman (that hath been used to the pomp and bravery of the court) pass by a whole stall of such toys and trifles, he never casts his eye towards them.

Ver. 6. *That came by water and blood*] So to fulfil and answer the legal washings and sacrifices; so to signify that he justifieth none by his merit but whom he sanctifieth by his Spirit; and so to set forth the two sacraments of the New Testament. See the note on John xix. 34.

Ver. 7. *Three that bear record*] viz. That Jesus Christ is the Son of God. These three heavenly witnesses have given testimony hereof in earth. See the note on John v. 32 and viii. 18.

These three are one] In essence and will. As if three lamps were lighted in one chamber, albeit the lamps be divers, yet the lights cannot be severed; so in the God-head, as there is a distinction of persons, so a simplicity of nature.

Ver. 8. *The Spirit and the water*] The Spirit of sanctification testified by saving graces and new divine gifts, the water of repentance, and the blood of Christ applied by faith. These be the three witnesses of a man's happiness here. When the waters of sanctification are troubled and muddy, let us run to the witness of blood.

Ver. 9. *If we receive,* &c.] If two or three witnesses establish a truth with men, shall we deny that honour to God's testimony?

Ver. 10. *Hath the witness in himself*] Carries in his heart the counterpane of all the promises.

Hath made him a liar] As one may deny God in deed as well as in word, so he may give him the lie too in like manner, sc. by going away, and not heeding all the grace that he offereth by Christ; for such a one saith in effect, Tush, there is no such thing as Christ; or at least no such benefit to be reaped by his passion as they would persuade us, &c.

Ver. 11. *That God hath given to us,* &c.] How plain is the Holy Scriptures in things needful to salvation! These God hath written for us, as it were, with the beam of the sun, that none may plead difficulty. But we are, most of us, of the Athenian strain, of whom Tully says the proverb went, *Athenienses scire quæ recta sunt, sed facere nolle*, that they knew what was right, but had no mind to make use of it. (Cic. de Senect.)

Ver. 12. *Hath life*] For he is the prince and principle of life; and all out of him are dead while they live. *Non ille diu vixit, sed diu fuit*, saith Seneca of one; *non multum navigavit, sed multum jactatus est*, of another at sea; he was long, but lived little; he was much tossed, but not much furthered; he moved much, but removed not at all, as a horse in a mill, as a dog in a wheel, &c. See the note on John i. 4.

And he that hath not the Son hath not life] *Negatio contrarii auget vim affirmationis.* 1 Kings xx. 1; Deut. xxxiii. 6; Prov. xxx. 11; 1 Sam. i. 11. See the note on John i. 20.

Ver. 13. *That ye may know that ye have eternal life*] sc. In the pledges and first-fruits of it, in the true graces of the Spirit, whereof there are many marks and evidences laid down in this Epistle, that we might be at a certainty; not a certainty of hope only (as Papists foolishly distinguish), but of faith too; even a full assurance.

That ye may believe] That ye may be confirmed, continued, and increased in it.

Ver. 14. *According unto his will*] One said he could have what he would of God; and, *Fiat voluntas mea*, said Luther in a certain prayer, but then he finely falls off with *mea voluntas, Domine, quia tua;* let my will be done, Lord, but so far forth as it is thy will. This was when he prayed for the life of Miconius (who was fallen into a deep consumption) and prevailed with God for it.

Ver. 15. *We know that we have*] *Iste vir potuit quod voluit*, That man could do what he would with God, said one concerning Luther. See the note on John xv. 16.

We have the petitions that we desired of him] If we can perceive and discern that God listeneth, the thing is done. Now the former we may find, first, by a cast of God's countenance, by a smile of his face, Psal. xxii. 24; xxxiv. 15, for a godly man is admitted to see as well as speak; like a good angel, he is ever looking on the face of God; and can gather by that how he shall speed in his suit. The upright shall dwell in his presence, Psal. cxl. 13, when the hypocrite shall not come before him, Job xiii. 16. Secondly, By the answer of a man's own conscience, 1 John iii. 20. God answers us by this, as he did the high priest by Urim and Thummim, and as he answered Elijah by fire from heaven that consumed his sacrifice. This faithful petitioners seldom fail of, Psal. xxxv. 13; vi. 8, 9; Phil. iv. 6, 7.

Ver. 16. *A sin which is not unto death*] When John Frith and Andrew Hewet were at the stake, Dr Cook openly admonished all the people that they should in no wise pray for them, no more than they would do for a dog; at which words Frith, smiling, desired the Lord to forgive him. (Acts and Mon. fol. 946.) In its own nature all sin is mortal; but in a saint,

being tempered with faith and repentance, it is as quicksilver tempered with ointment and killed.

There is a sin unto death] That unpardonable sin of doing despite to the Spirit of grace. Rockwood, a chief persecutor at Calais in the days of Henry VIII., to his last breath, staring and raging, cried, He was utterly damned; and being willed to ask God mercy, he brayed and cried out, "All too late! for I have sought maliciously the deaths of a number of the honestest men in the town, whom I knew to be so; all too late, therefore, all too late." Another that had committed this sin to death, wished that his wife and children and all the world might be damned together with him. (Mr Burroughs' Mos. Choice.)

Ver. 17. *There is a sin not unto death*] All sins and blasphemies shall be forgiven unto men, but the blasphemy against the Holy Ghost, &c. See the note on Matt. xii. 31, 32. Every sin (in the desert considered) hales hell at the heels of it. *Flagitium et flagellum ut acus et filum.* There is no venial sin in itself. But the unpardonable sin is here distinguished from all other sins; 1. By the nature of it; it is not any one sin against the law, nor yet is it the direct breach of the whole law, Heb. x. 28; but it is a sin against the gospel, a wilful and malicious refusing of pardon upon such terms as the gospel offereth it, scorning to be beholden to God for any such free favour. 2. By the effect, it is a sin unto death, it is infallibly damning, there is no expiation, but a certain fearful expectation of fiery indignation to devour these adversaries, Heb. x. 27. God not suffering himself to be derided, nor his Spirit to be despited, smites them with an incurable blindness and reprobacy of mind; whereupon follows, 1. An impossibility of repentance, Heb. vi. 6. 2. A desperate fury whereby they continue raving and raging both against the physic and the physician, to their own endless ruth and ruin.

Ver. 18. *Sinneth not*] sc. That sin to death, ver. 16, nor other sins, as other men do. See the note on chap. iii. 9.

And that wicked one toucheth him not] viz. *Tactu qualitativo*, as Cajetan expoundeth it, with a deadly touch; he thrusts not in his sting so far as to infuse the venom of that sin that is properly his sin, John viii. 44, and with which he toucheth their spirits that become the serpent's seed. He toucheth them not so as the needle is touched by the loadstone; so as to partake of his devilish spirit, and to be wholly carried after him.

Ver. 19. *Lieth in wickedness*] As a lubber in a lake, as a carcase in its slime. *In fermento tota jacet uxor*, saith he in Plautus. "This people is wholly set upon wickedness," said Aaron, Exod. xxxii. 22, is under the power and vassalage of the devil; *Nil mundum in mundo. Nihil aliud est totus mundus ante conversionem, nisi aut hara porcorum, aut colluvies rabidorum canum*, saith

Austin. The whole world, before conversion, is no better than a filthy hog-sty, or a kennel of mad dogs.

Ver. 20. *And we know*] This he brings in here for a corollary and conclusion of all.

Ver. 21. *Keep yourselves from idols*] Negatively at least (as those 7000 in Israel, that had not bowed their knees to Baal), if not positively, by open declaration of your utter dislike, as did Daniel and his associates. Irenæus reproveth the heretics called Gnostici, for that they carried about the image of Christ in Pilate's time, after his own proportion; using also for declaration of their affection towards it, to set garlands upon the head of it; so soon crept this cursed sin into the primitive Church. Soon after the Council of Nice, arose a sharp contention between Irene the empress and her son Constantine VI., who destroyed images; for the which she unnaturally put out his eyes. About which time, as Eutropius writeth, the sun was darkened most terribly for 17 days together; God showing by that, how much he misliked those proceedings. Letters were sent by Queen Mary and her council, to examine Mr Flower why he wore about his neck written, *Deum time, idolum fuge ;* and to stir up Bishop Bonner to proceed against all that did the like. Arguments and authorities alleged by Bishop Ridley against images in churches may be read, Acts and Mon. fol. 1928, &c. Martin was much grieved that this sentence of St John was set in our churches, in the place where the rood-loft formerly stood.

THE SECOND EPISTLE OF ST JOHN.

Ver. 1. *The elder to the elect lady*] SALMERON the Jesuit saith (but very absurdly) that Seneca's letters to St Paul, and St Paul's to Seneca (as they are called), are for matter not much unlike this of St John to the Elect Lady, and to Gaius, and that of St Paul to Philemon. *Judicium sit penes lectorem.* Methinks they are not more like than harp and harrow. See the note on Philemon, ver. 19. That censure passed on him by Erasmus is very right; *Si legas,* &c. : If thou read Seneca as a pagan, he wrote Christianly; but if as a Christian, he wrote paganishly.

Ver. 2. *For the truth's sake*] This is the love that will hold again, and is a sure sign of love unfeigned, when it is thus well founded. Sinisterity is opposite to sincerity. Some love the saints as Isaac loved Esau, for the venison that he brought him, &c.

Ver. 3. *Grace be with you,* &c.] This blessing belongs not only to the lady and her children, but to all that rightly read and hear the words of this Epistle, Rev. i. 13.

Ver. 4. *I rejoiced greatly*] This cheered up his good old heart more than any outward respects or courtesies whatsoever. See 1 Thess. iii. 8.

I found] εὕρηκα, I found by long and diligent observation, that which was worth finding; εὕρημα.

Of thy children] Not all, but some of them. It is seldom seen that all a whole family are right for religion. Noah had a Ham, Abraham an Ishmael, Isaac an Esau, &c.

As we have received a commandment] The gospel also commands obedience and holy conversation. Of unruly Christians, profligate professors, we may say, There's nothing Christian in them ; as of cowards they were wont to say at Rome, There was nothing Roman in them. Truly, either this is not gospel (said learned Linaker, when he had read our Saviour's sermon in the mount) or we are not gospellers. A young man told the senators of Rome that he came for to see Rome, and found it not ; for, said he, either ye be not Romans of Rome, or else this is not Rome of the Romans. We may even marvel as much as Constantius the emperor did, and say with him, I wonder how it comes to pass that many of my people are worse now than before they became Christians.

Walking in the truth] Not taking a step or two, not breaking or leaping over the hedge to avoid a piece of foul way, but persisting in a Christian course, &c., not starting aside to the right hand or the left.

Ver. 5. *Not as though I wrote a new commandment*] A new commandment our Saviour calleth it, John xiii. 34. *Quia exuto veteri induit nos novum hominem,* as Austin gives the reason; because the old man being put off, it puts on us the new man. Or, as others, because that when the scribes and Pharisees by false glosses and corrupt interpretations had put it out of date, Christ restored it by a true interpretation, Matt. v. 43—45, &c., and revived and illustrated it by his own practice and example, as Paul also observeth, Eph. v. 2; Phil. i. 9.

That we love, &c.] God lays no other commands upon us than what we may perform by love, that lighteneth and sweeteneth all. His subjects and soldiers are all volunteers, Psal. cx. 3.

Ver. 6. *As ye have heard*] He studiously declines the suspicion of novelty. Τὰ καινὰ κενὰ. See the note on 1 John ii. 7.

Ver. 7. *For many deceivers*] Gr. πλάνοι, cheaters, cozeners, such as can cog a die to deceive the unskilful, Eph. iv. 14, cast a mist to delude even the quick-sighted.

Are entered into the world] Where the Church also sojourneth, as the unclean beasts were together with the clean in Noah's ark ; or as Esau was in the same womb and afterwards in the same family with Jacob ; or as thieves lodge in the same inn with true men, who should therefore be sober and watch. *Mundus Medœa est Jasonis, hoc est Satanœ sponsa.* (Aretius.) The world is the spouse of Satan, and yet the godly must lie as it were in the lap of this Delilah. Let Samson look to his locks.

Ver. 8. *That we lose not, &c.*] The godly, when they fall into foul courses, or grow remiss and leave their first love, may lose what they have wrought, 1. In respect of the praise of men ; 2. In respect of their own former feelings of God's favour ; 3. In respect of the fulness of their reward in heaven. The Nazarite that broke his vow was to begin all anew, Numb. vi.

Ver. 9. *Hath not God*] And so consequently hath nothing. *Habet omnia qui habet habentem omnia*, He hath all that hath the haver of all. (Aug.) But *sine Deo omnis copia est egestas*, Plenty without God becomes penury. (Bern.) The wicked, for want of God, in the fulness of his sufficiency is in straits, Job xx. 22 ; as he that hath God for his portion, in the fulness of his straits is in a sufficiency.

Ver. 10. *And bring not this doctrine*] If he hold not the foundation, but be found heterodox and heretical.

Receive him not, &c.] *Illam domum in qua fuerit inventus hœreticus diruendam decernimus,* Down with that house that harbours a heretic, said the Council of Tholouse in their constitution against the Albigenses, whom they mistook for heretics.

Neither bid him God speed] Show not love where you owe nothing but hatred. "I hate every false way," saith David. And I shall look upon Auxentius as upon a devil, so long as he is an Arian, said Hilarius. St John sprang out of the bath wherein Cerinthus the heretic was washing, and said, Let us be gone, lest the house fall on our heads.

Ver. 11. *Is partaker of his evil*] 1. By his sinful silence and dissimulation. 2. Next, by confirming the sinner in his evil way. 3. Lastly, by offence given to others.

Ver. 12. *That our joy may be full*] See, saith one, an apostle furthered and quickened by the graces of a woman. When such grandees in grace have benefit by communion of saints, how much more they whose measures are less !

Ver. 13. *The children of thine elect*] Who probably sojourned with St John for education-sake. The lady might say to the apostle, as he in Virgil did to Æneas,

——— *sub te tolerare magistro*
Militiam ——— tua cernere facta
Assuescant, primis et te mirentur ab annis.

THE THIRD EPISTLE OF ST JOHN.

Ver. 1. *Unto the well-beloved Gaius*] A RICH Corinthian, rich in this world and rich in good works ; a rare bird, at Corinth especially, where St Paul found them the richer the harder, and far behind the poor Macedonians in works of charity, Rom. xvi. 23 ; 1 Cor. i. 14.

Ver. 2. *That thou mayest prosper*] Gr. εὐοδοῦσ-θαι, that thou mayest make a good voyage of it, and come safe and sound to thy journey's end.

Even as thy soul prospereth] By the blessing of him that dwelt in the bush, Deut. xxxiii. 16. Now the soul prospereth when it hath close communion with God, and enjoys the light of his loving countenance, preferring his favour before the world's warm sun.

Ver. 3. *Testified of the truth*] This was their ingenuity, thus, at least, to requite their host by giving testimony of his liberality, and this his liberality proved the truth of his faith, and his good estate to God-ward, as did Dorcas's garments made for the poor. *Lipsius conqueritur*

desiisse homines non modo laudanda facere, sed laudare. (l. ii. Epis. 70.)

Ver. 4. *I have no greater joy*] See the note on 2 John 4.

Walk in truth] Not walk to the alehouse, walk about with tales to shed blood, walk after the flesh, as too many of our hearers do, to our singular heart-break.

Ver. 5. *Thou dost faithfully*] That is, out of faith, and as beseemeth a faithful Christian. They that give alms, &c., and not out of faith, they do worse than lose their labour, for they commit sin.

And to strangers] Though they be not yet converted to the faith, and made brethren, thy liberality may work upon them, and win them, as Alban.

Ver. 6. *After a godly sort*] Gr. ἀξίως τοῦ Θεοῦ, worthy of God, as seeing God in them, and as beseemeth his servants, who are princes in all lands, Psal. xlv.

Ver. 7. *They went forth*] To preach and gain souls to God. And this they did gratis, as Paul, because the false apostles did so at Corinth, seeking occasion against the true teachers, 2 Cor. xi. 12.

Ver. 8. *That we might be fellow-helpers*] And so receive a prophet's reward. See the note on Matt. x. 41.

Ver. 9. *I wrote unto the church*] *sc.* Of Corinth, where Paul baptized Gaius, and where Diotrephes seems to have been a great sect-master, and chief of those deceitful workers that there so much disparaged Paul.

Diotrephes, who loveth, &c.] Ambition is like the crocodile, which groweth as long as it liveth. What stirs made proud Paulus Samosatenus in the primitive Church! What continual quarrelings were there between the bishops of Constantinople and of Rome for the primacy, and between the archbishops of Canterbury and of York for precedency! What a deal suffered learned Zanchy at Argentina from his ambitious colleagues; and divers of our English divines and others, from the lordly prelates! Pareus was wont to say that the chief cause of all the Church's troubles was the churchmen's affectation of dominion. This trouble-town if we could cast out of the Church, said he, great hopes there were that we should all εἰς τὸ θεῖον κήρυγμα ὁμοφρόνως καὶ ὀρθοδόξως συνδραμεῖν, concur and consent in one and the same truth. (Isidor. Pelus. iv. ep. 54.)

Ver. 10. *Prating against us*] One would wonder what he could prate against St John, and yet he did, and that maliciously. True it is, he did but trifle and play the fool (as the Greek word φλυαρῶν signifies) in that he prated; but he showed his malice nevertheless. So do the Jesuits, as in many other their practices, so in this, that in their writings against us they confirm that with glorious words and arguments which we stick not at; to make the world believe that we deny all that which they so busily and so bravely prove, and so to make us odious; whereas they leave the main matter in controversy utterly unproved, thinking to carry it away with outfacing and great words. The word signifieth *pompose sed nugaciter loqui*, to talk big bubbles of words, saith Aretius; who also telleth us that it is a metaphor taken from over-seething pots,

that send forth a foam; or (as as others will have it) from overcharged stomachs, that must needs belch.

Forbiddeth them that would] Such as Gaius was; that himself only might have the prick and the praise. This is the property of envy, as we see in Saul, in the Pharisees, in Tiberius Cæsar, who, tiger-like, laid hold with his teeth on all the excellent spirits of his times. *Nero etiam omnium erat æmulus, &c.* He forbad Lucan the poet to make verses, only because he could do it very excellently.

Ver. 11. *Follow not*] Make not such a man as Diotrephes your pattern for imitation; though he ruffle it amongst you, and will needs be the only man.

Hath not seen God] *sc.* With the eyes of his mind, whatever he may boast of visions of revelations; believe him not.

Ver. 12. *Of all men*] Of all good men; for God reckons of men according to their goodness. As a good name only is a name, Eccl. vii. 1, and a good wife only a wife, Prov. viii. 22.

And of the truth itself] That is enough. Doth the truth report well of a man? then he needs not care what the world can say.

And ye know that our record is true] This is one of John the Evangelist's praises, John xxi. 24, and may confirm that he was the author of this and the two former Epistles. For his truth, we may better say of him than Sophronius doth of John Chrysostom, *Nunquam eum mentitum fuisse*, that he never told lie; and that he was *eximium orbis terrarum luminare*, as Theodoret styles him.

Yea, and we also] Which we do not use to do without special caution. It is a fault to be too forward to testify of any.

Ver. 13. *I will not with ink*] In vain is the word written in books, unless it be also written in our hearts, Jer. xxxi.

With paper] Which was of old made of a certain plant of Nilus called Papyrus, but now it is made of rags, *miro ingenio, et utili rebus mortalium*, to the great benefit of mankind. (Aretius.)

Ver. 14. *But I trust*] He could promise nothing peremptorily, but submits to God. See the note on James iv. 15.

Face to face] As iron whets iron, so doth the face of a man his friend.

THE EPISTLE GENERAL OF ST JUDE.

Ver. 1. *Jude the servant*] To distinguish him from Judas the traitor, lest he should suffer by mistake, as Nicholas the deacon is thought to do, as if he were the author of the sect of the Nicolaitans, which Christ hated. This Jude or Judas, was also surnamed Lebbæus, that is, hearty; as Hooper the martyr was called hearty Hooper. He was indeed a hearty friend to the truth, earnestly contending for the faith once delivered unto the saints; and (*hæreticorum malleus*) a hammer against heretics, whom he describeth here to the life, and opposeth them to his utmost.

To them that are sanctified] Or to them that are beloved, as other copies have it.

Preserved] "Kept by the power of God through faith unto salvation," 1 Pet. i. 5.

Ver. 2. *Mercy unto you*, &c.] Mercy from the Father, peace from the Son, and love from the Holy Ghost.

Ver. 3. *Of the common salvation*] That wherein all saints have a share.

For the faith] That faith of the gospel, Phil. i. 27, the doctrine of faith.

Once delivered] Once for all, not only as but one only rule, but as but once sent to a nation. So that if lost, or any way corrupted, it will not be given again; another edition of it is not to be expected. Contend earnestly for it, therefore, conflict one after another, as the word ἐπαγωνίζεσθαι signifies. Hold fast the faithful word, as with both hands, Tit. i. 9. See the note. Resolve either to live with the gospel, or to die for it. Be zealous in the defence of it, and strive your utmost. When Carolostadius opposed Luther's consubstantiation, but weakly, faintly, and insufficiently, Zuinglius said he was sorry that so good a cause wanted shoulder. *Non satis humerorum haberet.* In the conference at Possiacum in France, Beza (speaker for the Protestants), entering into the matter of the Eucharist, spake with such heat, that he gave but ill satisfaction to those of his own party (saith the author of the History of the Council of Trent), so that he was commanded to conclude. How true this is I know not; sure it is, that in falling forward is nothing so much danger as in falling backward; so he that contendeth earnestly for the truth, though he may carry some things indiscreetly, yet he is far better than a faint chapman or a feeble champion. Austin was much heartened and hardened in his Manichism, because he met with weak opponents, such as his nimble wit could easily overturn.

Ver. 4. *For there are certain men*] Not worthy to be named, as that rich glutton, Luke xvi.

Crept in unawares] παρεισέδυσαν, stealing their passage, and making as if they minded nothing less. Thus Socrates (the writer of the Ecclesiastical History) was a close Novatian, as the learned Jacobus Billius observeth; he favoureth that heresy all along his history, *sed ita oblique, ut minus perspicaci Lectori non tam dolori suo atque iræ obsequi quam veritatis rationem habere videatur,* but he doth it so cunningly, that a man would think he did it out of pure regard to the truth. (Observat. Sacrar. i. 26.) So Spondanus, the epitomizer of Baronius, drinks to his readers the pernicious poison of Hildebrand's heresies, *quasi aliud agens,* as if he intended no such matter.

Ordained to this] Gr. προγεγραμμένοι, written down, enrolled, set down in the black bill.

Turning the grace of our God] Gr. μετατιθέμενοι, translating it from its proper end, perverting it, by arguing from mercy to liberty, which is the devil's logic. *Corruptio optimi est pessima.* Learned men have conceived, saith Plutarch, that as of oxen, being dead and rotten, there breed bees, of horses wasps, of asses beetles; so men's bodies, when the marrow melteth and gathereth together, do bring forth serpents. The grace of God, if turned into wantonness, becometh the "savour of death unto death."

Ver. 5. *Afterward destroyed*] Their preservation was but a reservation, as was Sennacherib's, Pharaoh's, and theirs whom God threatened to destroy, after that he had done them good, Josh. xxiv. 20.

Ver. 6. *Kept not their first estate*] Their original integrity or principality. Of this sin of the angels, the cause was the will of the angels, good in itself (but mutable and free), not by working neither, but by not working, saith a divine.

But left their own habitation] Being driven thence and hurried into hell.

He hath reserved in everlasting chains, &c.] There are two sorts of chains, saith Mr Leigh. First, those which torment the devil, God's wrath, and his own conscience. Secondly, those which restrain him, his own finiteness, and God's providence.

Ver. 7. *Giving themselves over*] *In scortationem effusæ,* wearying and wearing themselves out with that beastly sin, ἐκπορνεύσασαι ἐκ ἐπίτασιν habet; as did Proculus, Messalina, and Lais, who died in the act of uncleanness. (ἀπέθανε βινουμένη, Athen. xiii.) The word here used signifies, saith

Aretius, *Scortationi immori, et contabescere illius desiderio,* To waste and consume with that cursed concupiscence. Such a one was that filthy lecher mentioned by Luther, who desired no other heaven than to live always here, and be carried from one stews to another. He died betwixt a couple of notorious strumpets.

And going after strange flesh] See the note on Gen. xix. 5.

Are set forth] Gr. πρόκεινται, are thrown forth.

For an example] Herodotus saith the like of the destruction of Troy, that the ruins and rubbish thereof are set forth for an example of this rule, τῶν μεγάλων ἀδικημάτων μεγάλαι εἰσι καὶ αἱ τιμωρίαι παρὰ τοῦ Θεοῦ, that God greatly punisheth great offences.

Ver. 8. *Likewise also*] Or, yet nevertheless; albeit these dreadful executions are set before them for an example.

These filthy dreamers] Or, these sound sleepers, these whom the devil hath cast into a dead lethargy of damned security. (Sopiti. Beza.) Or, these Nebelamites, that pretend dreams and divine inspirations. See Jer. xxix. 24, 31.

Defile the flesh] By nocturnal pollutions, which we must pray against. The devil can fasten that filth upon the soul when we sleep, that he cannot do at another time.

Despise dominion] Gr. ἀθετοῦσι, set it at nought. See the note on 2 Pet. ii. 10. Under pretence of Christian liberty, they "set it aside," they "put it from its place" with scorn and contempt.

And speak evil of dignities] Gr. blaspheme glories: so the Papists do familiarly those princes they count heretics, as Henry IV. of France, whom they called Huguenot-dog, &c. Our Edward VI., bastard. Of Queen Elizabeth they reported in print some years after her death, that she died without sense or feeling of God's mercies. Sanders calleth her the English wolf; Rhiston, the English lioness, far surpassing in cruelty all the Athaliahs, Maacahs, Jezebels, Herodiases, that ever were. *Os durum!* (Rivetti Jesuita vapulans, 263.)

Ver. 9. *About the body of Moses*] As desirous thereby to set up himself in the hearts of the living. There is a strange strife still, not of earthly, but of spiritual powers, about the possession of man's heart. If Satan can get that, he is safe. And so Satan's vicar. It was a watchword in Gregory XIII.'s time in Queen Elizabeth's days, "My son, give me thy heart." Be in heart a Papist, and go where you will, and do what you will.

Durst not bring against him a railing accusation, but said, The Lord rebuke thee] Let us also answer the devil in like sort: or as Grynæus (out of Chrysostom) when he sent back Pistorius's railing letters, not so much as opening the seal, *Inhonestum est honestam matronam cum meretrice litigare,* It is not seemly for an honest matron to scold with a base harlot.

Ver. 10. *Of those things which they*] So do the Papists in railing against imputed righteousness,

assurance of salvation, the testimony of God's Spirit witnessing with our spirits, &c.

In those things they corrupt themselves] As in eating, drinking, carnal copulation, &c., holding neither mean nor measure, as he in Aristophanes (in Ranis), ὅστις γε πίνειν οἶδε καὶ βινεῖν μόνον, who was good for nothing else but to epicurize.

Ver. 11. *In the way of Cain*] The devil's patriarch, the first apostate; this was fulfilled literally in Alphonsus Diazius, who slew his brother John, because he was a Protestant; and mystically, in all that are guilty of spiritual parricide.

And ran greedily] Gr. ἐξεχύθησαν, were poured out, as water out of a bottle; they ran headlong after the wages of wickedness, not caring which way they came by it, so they had it. *Instar aquæ diffluentis projecta est eorum intemperies,* saith Calvin, their lust-like water illimited, ran all abroad, &c.

Ver. 12. *These are spots*] Or rocks, or muddy holes, that harpy-like not only devour, but defile all that they touch, σπιλάδες, παρὰ τὸ σπᾷν τὴν ἔλην, a trahendo lutum.

In your feasts of charity] See these described by Tertullian (Advers. Gentes, c. 39).

When they feast with you] Thrusting themselves into your company, whether invited or not; sin having woaded an impudency in their faces.

Feeding themselves] As fatted cattle fitted for the slaughter.

Without fear] Of being ensnared by the creatures, Prov. xxiii. 2.

Clouds they are] Light, and constant only in their inconstancy. The philosopher saith, *Insalubre admodum cœlum est quod pluviam promittit non demittit,* That is an unwholesome air that promiseth rain, but performs it not. It is ill conversing with these waterless clouds.

Twice dead] Killed with death, Rev. ii. 23. Such as for whom hell gapeth.

Plucked up by the root] Trees that are not for fruit are for the fire.

Ver. 13. *Raging waves of the sea*] Unsettled, turbulent, and arrogant spirits; boldly belching out their abominable opinions and detestable doctrines.

Wandering stars] That were never better than meteors. Sir Francis Drake in his Travels reporteth that in a certain island to the southward of Celebes, among the trees night by night did show themselves an infinite swarm of fiery-seeming worms flying in the air, whose bodies, no bigger than an ordinary fly, did make a show, and give such light as if every twig on every tree had been a lighted candle, or as if that place had been the starry sphere. Lo, such were these impostors.

Ver. 14. *And Enoch also*] Enoch foretold the day of judgment before Noah the deluge. That day is longer before it comes, but shall be more terrible when it is come.

Behold] One calleth this word a starry note; another compares it to a hand in the margin of a book pointing to some notable thing; another compares it to the sounding of a trumpet before some proclamation, to procure attention; and it is no more than need, so heedless we are of our soul's health. Hence the heathen's *hoc agite*, in their sacred services. And the deacons in Chrysostom's time were appointed to call oft upon the people in these words, *Oremus, attendamus*, Let us pray, let us mark. I am afraid, saith a divine, most of us do believe the predictions of Scripture but as we believe the predictions of an almanac, which tells you that such a day will be rain, and such a day will be wind; you think it may come to pass, and it may not. So here; such a threatening may be fulfilled, and it may not; let us venture it; it may be "the Lord will deal" with us not according to his present menaces, but "according to all his wondrous works," as those rebellious Jews suggested to Jeremiah, chap. xxi. 2.

The Lord cometh] Syr. *Maranatha*. Hence the Jews say that the great excommunication Maranatha was instituted by Enoch.

With ten thousand of his saints] Or, with his holy myriads; *sc.* of saints and angels; he shall not leave one of them behind him in heaven, Matt. xxv. 31. And whereas it is said, The Lord cometh, it shows that he is already on his way, and will be with us shortly. Where St Jude had this prophecy of Enoch it much matters not. The Jews have yet at this day some relics of it in their writings. And Tertullian tells us (de Habitu Mulierum), (but who told him I know not), that the book of Enoch's prophecies were preserved by Noah in the ark, and that they continued and were read until the times of the apostles. But because they contained many famous testimonies concerning Jesus Christ, the Jews out of malice suppressed and abolished the whole book.

Ver. 15. *To convince all*] To set them down, to leave them excuseless, speechless, self-condemned, ἐλέγξαι.

Of all their hard speeches] Their rude, crude, crooked, cross speeches, uttered with perverse lips; so Solomon calls them, Prov. iv. 24, as if the upper lip stood where the nether lip should.

Ver. 16. *These are murmurers*] *Ut porci saginati*, saith Aretius, as boars in a frank, they grunt against God's ways and worshippers, like so many *Caii Grunnii Corocottæ*.

Complainers] *Invalidum omne natura querulum*, saith Seneca. Weak ones are never without their ailments.

After their own lusts] So many lusts, so many lords.

Great swelling words] Bubbles of words. See the note on 2 Pet. ii. 18. The Syriac renders it, stupendous stuff. They amaze their hearers with sesquipedalian words, and sublime businesses, big-swollen fancies, &c.; they tell them they shall hear that which they never heard before, and therefore call upon them to mark; whenas the thing is either false, or if true, no more than ordinarily is taught by others: with as much confidence as ignorance they counsel the simple by portentous words and phrases abhorrent from Christian religion, truth, and sobriety; and which wise men lament whiles fools applaud and admire.

Having men's persons] Licking up their spittle, as it were, and loading the mouse with the elephant's praises. *Ungunt pariter et emungunt*.

Ver. 17. *Of the apostles*] Paul and Peter, from whom St Jude borroweth much of this his Epistle. See my Preface to God's Love Tokens.

Ver. 18. *Mockers*] Who fleer when they should fear. See the note on 2 Pet. iii. 3.

Who should walk after their ungodly lusts] Gr. the lusts of ungodliness, whereby the heart is turned away from God and godliness.

Ver. 19. *Who separate*] From Church assemblies, upon pretence of newer lights, greater holiness. The Arabic renders it, intermitters, *sc.* of Church-worship. Such as upon pretence of a more than ordinary holiness, and I know not what imaginary perfection, thought they might give over hearing of the word, as having immediate teaching; and separated from holy duties, as the words following show.

Sensual] Gr. ψυχικοὶ, animal; such as have no more than a reasonable soul, and are yet in their pure naturals, 1 Cor. ii. 14, and by their profane practices *animas etiam incarnaverunt*, have turned their very spirits into a lump of flesh.

Having not the Spirit] Unless it be the spirit of delusion, as Muncer the Anabaptist had, who wrote a book against Luther, dedicated it "To the most illustrious Prince Christ" (as his words are), upbraideth Luther with want of the Spirit, and calleth him a carnal man, a silly soul. (Scultet. Annal. 338.)

Ver. 20. *Building up*] By holy conference, a singular help, a most needful but too much neglected duty.

Praying in the Holy Ghost] Whose creature fervent prayer is.

Ver. 21. *Keep yourselves*] Remit nothing of your former fervour. But keep afoot and alive that twofold love of God: 1. That of desire, and earnest delight and intense longing after him, as our chiefest good. 2. Of delight and complacency, whereby we hug and embrace him, solacing ourselves in the fruition of him.

Ver. 22. *And of some*] Or (according to other copies), "Refell their false reasonings," and dispute them out of their errors. ἐλεεῖτε, alias ἐλέγχετε.

Ver. 23. *Out of the fire*] viz. of hell; as the angel pulled Lot out of Sodom, as ye would save a drowning man, though ye pulled off some of his hair to save him.[1] *Hic est depingendus Satan et Tartarus, et carcer atrocissimus et luctuosus, in quo vere sit stridor dentium et fletus*, saith Aretius. Those that are obstinate, and receive not reproofs, are to be terrified and told of the horror of hell, those seas of vengeance, that worm that never dieth, torments without end and past imagination.

Even the garment spotted] As Nero's was,

[1] *Hæc est sancta violentia, optabilis rapina.* Jerome.

when he rode in the same horse-litter with his own mother. (Sueton.) The phrase is thought to be taken either from legal impurities of leprous garments, by touching of which men were defiled, Levit. xv; or else from the profuse drunkenness and filthiness of the Gnostics, which sometimes defiled their garments.

Ver. 24. *That is able*] q. d. I can only counsel you, it is God must keep you.

Ver. 25. See the note on 1 Tim. i. 17.

THE REVELATION OF ST JOHN THE DIVINE.

CHAPTER I.

Ver. 1. *The Revelation*] OR manifestation of many divine mysteries by the Mediator (who came out of his Father's bosom) to John, who had the mind of Christ, and that purposely for the behoof and benefit of the family of faith, who are all of his cabinet-council, John i. 18; 1 Cor. ii. 16; Gal. vi. 10; Psal. xxv. 14.

Things which must shortly] That is, sooner or later in their proper season. God's time seems long, because we are short. *Nullum tempus occurrit regi*, saith the lawyer. The Ancient of days is not to be limited.

Ver. 2. *Who bare record of the word*] This John the divine, then, was John the Evangelist, whatever Dennis of Alexandria dispute to the contrary. It was Moses's honour (saith one), who was God's peculiar favourite, to be penman of the first book of the Old Testament; and it was John's honour, Christ's peculiar favourite, to be the penman of the last book of the New Testament.

Ver. 3. *Blessed is he that readeth*] sc. With attention, affection, application, and practice; as knowing that this book hath *tot sacramenta, quot verba*, so many words, so many mysteries (Jerome epist. ad Paulin.); and that these words are *vivenda non legenda*, not more to be read than to be lived, as one said once of the 119th Psalm. (Ægid. Abbas Norimberg.) Neither must we only live up to the words of this prophecy, but die for it also, and be content to be burned with it, if called thereto; as that holy martyr, who when he saw the Revelation cast into the fire with him, cried out, *O beata Apocalypsis, quam bene mecum agitur qui tecum comburar!* O blessed Revelation, how happy am I to be burned in thy company!

Ver. 4. *From him which is*] An august description of the Father by a manifest allusion to Exod. iii. 14. Some critic reading the words ἀπὸ ὁ ὢν καὶ ὁ ἦν as they lie in the original, would be apt to complain of an incongruity, and to say, *Nove et duriter dictum.* But God, methinks, should have leave given him by these Logodædali, to pronounce his own name undeclined, and by an outrule, who himself is undeclined, and comes not under any rule. *Non debent verba cœlestis oraculi subesse regulis Donati.* (Greg.)

And from the seven spirits] So the Holy Ghost is here called, for his manifold gifts and operations in the hearts of those seven, and all other Churches. In like sort he is called the seven golden pipes through which the two olive branches do empty out of themselves the golden oils of all precious graces into the golden candlestick the Church, Zech. iv. 2, 3. So some interpret those seven eyes upon one stone, Zech. iii, 9, concerning the Spirit in his several operations upon Christ, according to Isa. xi. 2. There is a prophetical perfection of this number of seven, with which the Spirit of God is much delighted in this prophecy; seven Churches, seven stars, seven candlesticks, seven lamps, seven seals, &c.

Ver. 5. *And from Jesus Christ*] Who is here set last of the three persons, because more is to be said of him; both as touching his threefold office, and a threefold benefit therehence redounding unto us.

That hath loved us] See Ezek. xvi. 6—9. Christ, that heavenly pelican, revived his dead young ones with his own heart-blood. (Pierii Hieroglyph.) He saw the wrath of God burning about them, and cast himself into the midst thereof, that he might quench it. Judah offered to be bound that Benjamin might go free. Jonathan perilled his life and quitted his kingdom for love of David. Arsinoe interposed her own body betwixt the murderer's weapons and her children. But what was all this to this incomparable love of the Lord Jesus? When the Jews saw him weeping for Lazarus, "Behold," they say, "how he loved him." When we see him weeping, bleeding, dying for us, shall not we much more say so?

Ver. 6. *And hath made us kings*] To rule in righteousness, to lord it over our lusts, to triumph over and trample on all our spiritual adversaries, being more than conquerors through him that loved us, and laid down his life for us, that we might reign in life by one Jesus Christ, Rom. v. 17. And surely if (as Peter Martyr once wrote to Queen Elizabeth) kings are doubly bound to serve God, both as men and kings; what are we, for this spiritual kingdom?

And priests unto God] To offer up to him the

personal sacrifice of ourselves, Rom. xii. 1, the verbal of praise, and real of alms, Heb. xiii. 15, 16. See the note on 1 Pet. ii. 9.

Ver. 7. *Behold, he cometh*] He is already upon the way, and will be with us shortly. Let us hasten his coming, and say as Sisera's mother, Why are his chariots (his clouds) so long in coming? Why tarry the wheels of his chariots? Judges v. 28.

Shall wail] Gr. κόψονται, shall smite their breasts or thighs; the elect as repenting, the reprobate as despairing. *Iisdem quibus videmus, oculis, flemus;* so here, ὄψονται καὶ κόψονται, they shall look and lament.

Ver. 8. *Which is, and which was*] The Father is called "He that is," Exod. iii. 13. The Son "He that was," John i. 1. The Holy Ghost, "He that cometh," John xvi. 8—13, as Aretius observeth. Or, by this periphrasis may be understood the indeterminable eternity of the Son of God. Much like whereunto both in sound and sense is that which the heathens ascribed to their Jupiter in that solemn hymn of theirs. (Pausan.)

Ζεὺς ἦν, Ζεὺς ἐστὶ, Ζεὺς ἔσσεται, ὦ μέγαλε Ζεῦ.

God was, and God is, God shall be for ever a great God.

Ver. 9. *In the kingdom and patience*] Christ hath a twofold kingdom; 1. Of power; 2. Of patience. *Nec nisi per angusta ad augusta,* &c. I have no stronger argument against the pope's kingdom, saith Luther, *quam quod sine cruce regnat,* than this, that he reigns without the cross. The glory of Christ's Church (said George Marsh, martyr) stands not in outward shows, in the harmonious sound of bells and organs, nor yet in the glistering of mitres and copes, &c., but in continual labours and daily afflictions for his name's sake. (Acts and Mon. fol. 1423.)

Was in the isle Patmos] He tells us not how he came thither, he boasteth not of his banishment. *Virtus proprio contenta theatro,* Virtue is no braggart. Eusebius telleth us that he was banished thither by Domitian; and that there he wrote his Revelation. In allusion whereunto, Luther called the place Patmos where he lay hid by the elector of Saxony, when the emperor had proscribed him, and promised a great reward to any one that should bring him alive or dead to the court. Here it was that Luther translated the New Testament into Dutch, and wrote divers useful treatises, viz. at Wartburg, his Patmos. (Scultet. Annal.)

Ver. 10. *I was in the Spirit*] Acted by him, and carried out of himself, as the demoniac is said to be in the unclean spirit, as being acted and agitated by him. See the note on 2 Pet. i. 21.

On the Lord's day] The first day of the week, the Christian sabbath, Matt. xxiv. 20, called the Lord's day, from Christ the author of it; as is likewise the Lord's supper, and the Lord's Church, kirk, κυριακὴ, the very word here used. To sanctify this sabbath was in the primitives a badge of a Christian. For when the question was asked, *Servasti Dominicum?* Keepest thou the sabbath? The answer was returned, *Christianus sum, intermittere non possum,* I am a Christian, I must keep the Lord's day. This day was also called anciently *dies lucis,* the day of light (as Junius observeth), partly because baptism (which the ancients called φωτισμὸν), was administered on that day; but principally, because by the duties of this day rightly performed, the minds of men are illuminated, and they translated out of darkness into Christ's marvellous light.

And heard behind me] Not before me; implying that the Spirit calleth upon us, being secure, passing by, and not regarding those things it calls for.

As of a trumpet] To teach us that the things here delivered to the Church must be ever sounding in our ears and hearts, indwelling richly in us, Col. iii. 16. I confess the matter is very mysterious and obscure. Hence Cajetan's *exponat cui Deus concesserit,* Let him expound it that can; I can say little to it. Hence Calvin (as Bodine reports him, Method. Hist. vii.) being asked his opinion about the Revelation, ingenuously confessed, *se penitus ignorare quid velit tam obscurus scriptor,* &c., That he, for his part, knew not what to make of it. Hence also Graserus, *Mihi inquit, tota Apocalypsis valde obscura videtur; et talis cujus explicatio citra periculum vix queat tentari;* Methinks, saith he, the whole book of the Revelation is wondrous dark, and indeed such as without danger of doing amiss, a man can hardly take in hand to interpret. I confess that I have hitherto profited less by the reading of no part of the Bible than by this so very dark a prophecy: thus he. Howbeit difficulty doth but whet on heroic spirits; and obscurity should not weaken but waken our diligence. God would have us to inquire into these things, though they be far above us; what else meaneth this trumpet, and that blessing so solemnly proclaimed with the sound of a trumpet, to him that readeth, and those that hear the words of this prophecy? ver. 3. All cannot read, but all must hear. And let him that readeth or heareth, understand, Matt. xxiv. 15. What if there be a veil laid over this Revelation, will it not be rarified by reading, and by degrees wholly worn away? Especially, if when we open the book we pray with David, "Lord, open mine eyes, that I may see the wondrous things of thy word:" and not pray only, but weep, as St John did, till this sealed book were opened.

Ver. 11. *Send it to the seven*] As all Holy Scripture, so this piece especially, may well be called, The Epistle of Almighty God to his creature. (Greg. Mag.) It is directed to these seven Churches, because then the most famous and flourishing. There also this evangelist had long time taught; and, as some say, was president over them.

Which are in Asia] *sc.* in Asia the Less, which therefore haply bears the name of the whole, because it was the Asia of Asia, like as Athens was called the Greece of Greece.

Ver. 12. And being turned I saw] It is well observed here by a learned interpreter (Mr Brightman), that every godly endeavour doth receive some fruit greater than a man can hope for; John turned himself to behold the man, and behold (over and besides) seven candlesticks, which he had not the least suspicion of.

Seven golden candlesticks] Candlesticks the Churches are called, for the light they have and give; golden, for their worth and price; as much above other men as gold is above other metals. As God is the gold of his people ("the Almighty shall be thy gold," saith Eliphaz, Job xxii. 25), so they are his; yea, his peculiar treasure: they comprehend all his gettings, Tit. ii. 14, they are the people of his acquisition, 1 Pet. ii. 9.

Ver. 13. And in the midst] Christ is in the holy assemblies, in the beauties of holiness; he walketh in his garden, Cant. vi. 1, he comes in to see his guests, Matt. xxii. 11. The face of God is seen in Sion, Psal. lxxxiv. 7.

A garment down to the feet] As a counsellor, Isa. ix. 6.

And girt] It implies readiness, nimbleness, handiness, and handsomeness. We also must gird ourselves, and serve the Lord Christ, Luke xvii. 8.

About the paps] This implies his entire love, seated in the heart.

Ver. 14. White like wool] Noting his antiquity, or rather his eternity and unspeakable purity. Thales, one of the heathen sages, called God πρεσβύτατον τῶν ὄντων, the most ancient of beings. (Diog. Laert.)

As a flame of fire] Sharp and terrible, such as pierce into the inward parts, Heb. iv. 13. See the note there. The school of nature teacheth, that the fiery eye needeth not outward light; that seeth *extra mittendo*, by sending out a ray, &c.

Ver. 15. And his feet] He stood firm then when he was cast into the fire of his Father's wrath. He trod the wine-press alone, and set his feet on the necks of all his and our enemies. He lost no ground, when he grappled with the devil on his own dunghill, Matt. iv. "He will also bruise Satan under our feet shortly," Rom. xvi. 20.

As the sound of many waters] Audible, terrible, forcible. Some Catadupes are deafened by the fall of this Nilus. (Som. Scip.) But the spouse cries out, "O thou that dwellest in the gardens, the companions hearken to thy voice; cause me to hear it," Cant. viii. 13.

Ver. 16. And he had in his right hand] See here the dignity and safety of a faithful minister. Whiles a child hath his father by the hand, though he walk in the dark, he fears nothing. Godly ministers not only have Christ by the hand (who as he will not cast away a perfect man, so neither will he take the ungodly by the hand, saith Bildad, Job viii. 20), but are held fast in Christ's right hand, "that teacheth him terrible things," Psal. xlv. 4, against such as seek to pull them

thence. It is well observed by a worthy writer, that about the time of the silencing of ministers, many churches in England were torn at once (within our remembrance) with terrible lightning; and almost no place else but churches were touched, especially in the lower parts of Devonshire, where many were scorched, maimed, and many had their brains struck out, as they sat in churches; as at the church of Anthony in Cornwall, near Plymouth, on Whit-sunday, 1640. (See the relation in print.)

A sharp two-edged sword] The word, like a sacrificing sword, slits open, and, as it were, unridgeth the conscience.

Ver. 17. I fell at his feet as dead] The nearer any one comes to Christ, the more rottenness entereth into his bones.

And he laid his right hand] The same right hand wherein he held the seven stars, ver. 16. *Christus sic omnibus attentus, ut nulli detentus; sic curat universos quasi singulos, sic singulos, quasi solos.* Every godly minister is Christ's particular care.

Fear not] Till rid of fear we are not fit to hear.

Ver. 18. That liveth and was dead] So can every regenerate man say, Luke xvi. 32; Eph. ii. 1. See the note there. All saints are "heirs of the grace of life," 1 Pet. iii. 7.

And have the keys] The pope, therefore, is not key-keeper, as he falsely boasteth, tellingus, that God hath put under his feet the beasts of the field, the fowls of the air, and the fish of the sea; that is (as he interprets it), all the souls in earth, heaven, and purgatory. Christ, as a conqueror, hath the keys of hell and death delivered unto him.

Ver. 19. Write the things which thou hast seen] That is, the gospel, the history of Christ (as some think), which he wrote at Ephesus after his return from Patmos, above forty years after our Saviour's death.

Ver. 20. The mystery] In this whole book there are so many words, so many mysteries, which made Cajetan forbear to comment upon it; [1] though many monks (far less able than he) thought it a goodly thing to be meddling in these mysteries, which they as little understood as he that derived *Apocalypsis* of Aπò, re, et clipsor, quod est velo, quoth Faber the Augustinian monk.

Are the angels] Ministers are fitly called stars, which affect these inferior things by motion, light, and influence.

Are the seven churches] Lighted by Christ the High Priest morning and evening continually; and thereby as much differenced from the rest of the world, as Goshen was from Egypt in that palpable darkness. But now (alas) they have sinned away the light, and are fearfully darkened. Let us take heed how we put our light, not under a bushel but under a dunghill, as do our libertines, so that we may well cry out with Polycarp, *Deus, ad quæ nos tempora reservasti?* Lord, what times are these?

---

[1] *Apocalypsim fateor me nescire exponere juxta sensum literalem: exponat cui Deus concesserit.*

CHAPTER II.

Ver. 1. *Unto the angel*] This was Timothy, as some think; who not stirring up the gift of God that was in him, had remitted somewhat of his former fervour. By the style here given him ("angel") he is monished not more of his dignity than of his duty. That angel at Bochim, Judg. ii. 1, is thought to have been Phineas. And some interpret that of Solomon, "Neither say thou before the angel, that it was an error of the priest," Eccles. v. 6. It is good counsel to ministers that one gives, *Angelorum induistis nomen, induite et naturam, ne sit (ut dixit nonnemo) nomen inane, crimen immane :* Ye have put on the name, put on also the nature of angels; lest an empty name fill up the measure of your sins.

Of the church of Ephesus] ἔφεσις vel ἄφεσις. Languishing Ephesus hath not her name for nought; for she was so named of remissness or slackening her hold, wherewith she is here upbraided, *Conveniunt rebus nomina sæpe suis.*

Ver. 2. *I know thy works and thy labour*] Not thy works only, but thy labour in doing them, and what ends thou puttest upon them. How accurately did our Saviour cast up and count how long the multitude had been with him, how little they had to eat, how ill it would fare with them if sent away fasting, &c., Matt. xv. 32.

And how thou canst not bear] Moved with a zeal of God, and having a stomach for him. *Mihi sane Auxentius nunquam aliud quam diabolus erit, quia Arianus,* saith Hilary: I shall look upon Auxentius as upon a devil, so long as he is an Arian.

Ver. 3. *And hast borne*] Bear the false apostles thou couldst not; but hast borne much from them. *Morientium nempe ferarum violentiores sunt morsus.* Beasts bite hardest when to bite their last.

Ver. 4. *Thou hast left thy first love*] Those first-ripe fruits that Christ's soul desireth, Micah vii. 1, that kindness of youth, that spousal-love, that God so well remembereth, Jer. ii. 2. This Ephesus had left, and so became Aphesis, remiss and reckless, possest with a spirit of sloth and indevotion. And surely he is a rare and happy man that can say in a spiritual sense (as it was said of Moses), that after long profession of zeal, his sight is not waxed dim, his holy heat not abated, that runs not retrograde, as did Solomon, Asa, others, with whom the end was worse than the beginning.

Ver. 5. *From whence thou art fallen*]   viz. From thy former feelings and present fitness for God's kingdom, Luke ix. 62.

And repent] See the practice of this second repentance in the relapsed spouse returning to her old husband, Cant. v. See the note on 2 Cor. vii. 11. See an excellent letter of the Lady Jane to that apostate Harding, sometime her chaplain, Acts and Mon. fol. 1292, and what sweet counsel Bradford afterwards gave the same Hard-ing, Ib. fol. 1564, besides the example of Mr Bartlet Green, martyr, fol. 1680.

And do the first works] Begin the world again (as the Nazarite was to do that had broken his vow, Numb. vi.), and, to set thee up afresh, make a gathering of prayers, and see that thy works be better at last than at first.

And remove thy candlestick] Sins are the snuffs that dim our candlestick and threaten the removal of it. And surely if we repent not, a removal thereof may be as certainly foreseen and foretold as if visions and letters were sent us from heaven, as to these seven Churches. There is a prophecy in Thelesphorus, reported, that Antichrist shall never overcome Venice, nor Paris, nor London; but we have a more sure word of prophecy here. This nation is sick of a spiritual pleurisy; we begin to surfeit on the bread of life. When God sees his mercies lying under table, it is just with him to call to the enemy to take away.

Except thou repent]   *Minatur Deus ut non puniat.* God therefore menaceth, that men may be warned. As a bee stings not till provoked; so neither doth God punish till there be no remedy, 2 Chron. xxxvi. 16. *Currat ergo pœnitentia, ne præcurrat sententia,* saith one; *mittamus preces et lacrymas cordis legatos,* saith another. Haste, haste, haste, to meet the Lord with entreaties of peace; lest we be laid waste as Sodom and desolate as the people of Gomorrah, Isa. i. 9.

Ver. 6. *But this thou hast*] That they might not say, when called upon to repent, Nay, but there is no hope, Jer. ii. 25; xviii. 12. Christ picks out that which is praiseworthy in them, and commends it. Despair carries men to hell, as the devils did the swine into the sea; cast not away therefore your confidence, &c.

The works of the Nicolaitans] Who taught a community of wives, and that it was but a thing indifferent to commit adultery. (Irenæus, Theod.)

Ver. 7. *Let him hear*] Not with that gristle only that grows upon his head, but with the ear of his heart. Let him draw up the ear of his heart to the ear on his head, that one sound may pierce both. Or, Let him hear, &c., that is, Let him hear for himself, hear and know that (each member for his own good) that was delivered to the whole Church.

To eat of the tree of life] This tree is Christ. The devil also (as he loves to be God's ape) hath prompted Mahomet to promise to such as die in war for the Mahometan faith, delicious fare in Paradise, pleasant walks, and other sensual delights eternally to be enjoyed, notwithstanding any former sins.

Ver. 8. *Of the church in Smyrna*] Sweet-smelling Smyrna, the poorest but purest of the seven.

Ver. 9. *I know thy works and tribulations*] Mark (saith one) the conjunction, "works and tribulations." Active stirring Christians are like to suffer much. Of Sardis and Laodicea only, we read not of any troubles they had.

And poverty, but thou art rich] Poverty discommends not any to Christ; money bears no mastery in his kingdom. Thou art poor, saith he here; but that is neither here nor there; it is a matter of nothing, that, stumble not therefore at the Church's poverty. She is ever rich: 1. In reversion, and hath heaven and happiness; she is ever rich in bills and bonds. 2. In an apparent pledge that is worth all the world besides; that is, in Christ. If he have given us his Son, &c. All is yours who are Christ's, &c.

That say they are Jews] That is, right-worshippers, as the Turks at this day style themselves Mussulmans, that is, the only true believers; Papists, the only Catholics. *Faciunt et vespæ favos, et simiæ imitantur homines.* Cyprian.

Ver. 10. *Fear none of those things*] Quit thy heart of that cowardly passion, and die rather than deny the truth. Put on that resolution, *Necesse esse ut eam, non ut vivam,* Duty must be done, though I die for it.

Behold, the devil] viz. By his imps and instruments whom he acts and agitates, Eph. ii. 2. But he and his are over-ruled and limited; for he shall cast some of you, not all of you, into prison, not into hell, that ye may be tried, not destroyed; and this for ten days only, not for any long continuance.

Be thou faithful unto death] Say as one martyr did, "The heavens shall sooner fall than I will deny my dear Lord;" and as another martyr, "Though you may pluck my heart out of my bowels, yet shall you never pluck the truth out of my heart."

A crown of life] A crown without cares, co-rivals, envy, end. Kings' crowns are so weighty with cares, that oft they make their heads ache. Not so this crown; the joys whereof are without measure or mixture.

Ver. 11. *Shall not be hurt of the second death*] Shall not be killed with death, as ver. 23. Death shall not be to him (as it is to the wicked) a trap-door to hell, but *janua vitæ, porta cœli,* an inlet into life eternal. (Bern.)

Ver. 12. *And to the angel*] See the note on ver. 1, and on chap. i. 16.

Ver. 13. *Even where Satan's seat is*] There was the court of King Attalus (*discedat ab aula Qui velit esse pius;* "flee thee away, O thou seer, for this is the king's court," Amos vii. 13), and there was afterwards the seat of the Roman persecuting proconsuls, *Qui ab ascensore suo Satana perurgebantur,* as Bernard hath it. Such a seat of Satan is both old and new Rome. At Constantinople (which was called new Rome) Arius, that arch-heretic, *sedens in latrina effudit intestina,* voided his entrails at the stool, and left Mahometism there behind him as his excrement. Yet, as at Pergamos also God had a Church, so hath he still even at Constantinople; the patriarch whereof, Cyril, hath lately set forth a confession of the faith of those Eastern Churches, agreeable in all points almost to the Protestant religion, but diametrically opposite to Popery.

Thou holdest fast] κρατεῖς, as with tooth and nail, or by main strength.

Who was slain] An honour not granted to the angels of heaven, as Latimer was wont to say.

Ver. 14. *I have a few things*] More he might have had, but the Lord is not extreme to mark what is amiss in his weak but willing people. The high places were not removed; nevertheless (though that was his fault) the heart of Asa was perfect all his days, 2 Chron. xv. 17.

And to commit fornication] Nothing hath so enriched hell (saith one) as fair faces. These were those Balaam's-blocks that Israel so stumbled at.

Ver. 15. *The doctrine of the Nicolaitans*] See the note on ver. 6. In the year 1067, the popish synod of Milan made laws against simony and the heresy of the Nicolaitans; by which latter they meant priest's-marriage. *Brutum fulmen, novum crimen.*

Ver. 16. *Or else I will come unto thee*] He was in the midst of the seven golden candlesticks before. But when he comes to correct, he comes out of his place, Isa. xxvi. 21, and it is a motion that he hath no such mind to, Lam. iii. 33, it is to do his work, his strange work, Isa. xxviii. 21.

With the sword of my mouth] With fearful threatenings, terrible executions, having vengeance in readiness for the disobedient, 1 Cor. x. 6. Elisha had his sword as well as Jehu and Hazael theirs, 1 Kings xix. 17. See Hosea vi. 5; Jer. i. 10; Isa. xi. 4.

Ver. 17. *Of the hidden manna*] That is, of Christ, whom none of the princes of this world knew; but God hath revealed him to his hidden ones by the Spirit, 1 Cor. ii. 8, 10, with Psal. lxxxiii. 3, and given them to taste of that heavenly gift.

A white stone] In token of absolution. With this white stone may the saints comfort themselves against all the black coals wherewith the world seeks to besmear them. If Libanius could say, βασιλείου μὲ ἐπαινέσαντος κατὰ πάντων ἔχω τὰ νικητήρια (In epist. ad Basil.), Let Basil praise me, and I shall sing away all care, whoever reproacheth me; may not we much more say so of Christ? "It is he that justifieth us; who shall condemn us?" Rom. viii. 34.

A new name] Better than that of sons and daughters, Isa. lvi. 5. The assurance whereof is (saith Father Latimer) the sweetmeats of the feast of a good conscience, which is inconceivable and full of glory.

Ver. 18. *Who hath his eyes, &c.*] See the note on chap. i. 14, 15.

Ver. 19. *The last to be more*] This is not every man's happiness. See the note on ver. 4. It is a disputable question (saith one) whether any Christian (except he die soon after his conversion) do go on from strength without some sensible decay of the inward power of that grace wherewith he is endued.

Ver. 20. *Thou sufferest that woman Jezebel*] It

is a fault, then, not only to be active in evil, but to be passive of evil. *Non faciendo malus, sed patiendo fuit*, said the poet concerning the Emperor Claudius. The kings of the earth are taxed, Rev. viii., for not rooting out the Romish religion and setting up the truth.

Ver. 21. *And I gave her space to repent*] "In space comes grace" proves not always a true proverb. They that defer the work, and say that men may repent hereafter, say truly, but not safely. The branch that bears not timely fruit is cut off, John xv. 2. The ground that yields not a seasonable and suitable return is nigh unto cursing, Heb. vi. 8. The chick that comes not at the clucking of the hen becomes a prey to the kite, &c.

Ver. 22. *Behold, I will cast her into a bed*] A bed of affliction for that bed of security upon which she had stretched herself, Amos vi. 4. God hath his season, his harvest for judgment, Matt. xiii. 30. Men may expect a time of healing when they shall find nothing else but a time of trouble, Jer. xiv. 19. One may defer a sore till it be incurable. See Ezek. xxiv. 13.

Ver. 23. *And I will kill her children with death*] All men die (saith a divine, descanting upon this text), but all are not killed with death. As a godly man said, that he did *ægrotare vitaliter*, so godly men do *mori vitaliter*. He that can so die, is fit to die; and the contrary. Oh, it is a woeful thing to be killed with death.

Ver. 24. *But unto you I say*] Here Christ comes with his fan, shedding and shoaling out his own from others, that they might not be disheartened, when worse men were menaced.

The depths of Satan] That science falsely so called, 1 Tim. vi. 20. Those profound points, which the impostors professed and pretended to: as the Gnostics, who would needs be held the only knowing men; the Illuminates, and other seducers, who had taken up a trick to qualify their devilish doctrines with the name of depths or profundities. Depths they are granted to be, but depths of the devil; the whisperings and hissing of that old serpent, not the inspirations of God's Spirit.

Ver. 25. *Hold fast*] κρατήσατε, hold by strong hand, tug for it, with those that would take it from you.

Ver. 26. *And keepeth my works*] In opposition to Jezebel's works, *q. d.* that keepeth himself unspotted of the world, that foul lust that lieth in that wicked one, 1 John v. 19.

Ver. 27. *And he shall rule them*] *q. d.* I will communicate myself wholly to him. See Psal. cxxxix. 6—9; Matt. xix. 28; 1 Cor. vi. 2, 3.

Ver. 28. *I will give him the morning star*] *i. e.* I will clear his wronged innocency, Psal. xxxvii. 6, and grant him a glorious resurrection, Dan. xii. 3.

Ver. 29. *He that hath an ear*] See the note on ver. 7.

CHAPTER III.

Ver. 1. *I know thy work*] *Sapiens nummularius Deus est ; nummum fictum non recipiet.* (Bernard.) Though men may be deceived, God is not mocked. He knows that many cry, "The temple of the Lord," that yet nothing care for the Lord of the temple. *Deifica professio et diabolica actio.* (Ambrose.) God likes not such creaking and cracking.

And that thou hast a name] Many content themselves with a name of Christians; as if many a ship hath not been called Safe-guard or Good-speed which yet hath fallen into the hands of pirates.

And art dead] All thy specious works therefore are but dead works; thou canst not serve the living God.

Ver. 2. *Be watchful*] Rouse up thyself, and wrestle with God, shake thee out of sin's lethargy, as Samson went out and shook him when the Philistines were upon him.

That are ready to die] Because tainted with the infection of hypocrisy, that pernicious mangood.

Perfect before God] Gr. full, without halting or halving. *Omnis Sarmatarum virtus extra ipsos.* (Tacitus.) All the hypocrite's goodness runs outward; it is shored up by popularity, or other base respects.

Ver. 3. *And thou shalt not know*] Calamity the more sudden, the more terrible; for, 1. It amates and exanimates a man, as an unexpected storm doth a mariner, and as Satan intended Job's messengers should do him. 2. It can as little be prevented as Eglon could prevent Ehud's deadly thrust.

Ver. 4. *Thou hast a few names*] Though no thanks to the pastor, who was a mercenary eye-servant. Here the people's praise is the pastor's shame. These good souls were but few, their names (as one said of the good emperors) might have been written within the compass of a ring. *Rari quippe boni* (Juvenal, Sat. 13) ; *Diaconos paucitas honorabiles fecit*, saith Jerome. Christ's flock is little. Few received him in the flesh, John i. 12; he wondered at one good Nathaniel. At his coming shall he find faith upon the earth? Yes, sure, saith one; now he may find many faiths, such as they be; so many men, so many faiths; but few that hold faith and a good conscience together, 1 Tim. i. 19, whereby they have put on Christ, Gal. iii. 27; Ephes. iv. 24; Rev. xvi. 15.

They shall walk with me in white] That is, they shall be glorified with perfect righteousness, purity, charity, dignity, and festivity.

For they are worthy] In Christ's account and acceptation. Like as those were not worthy that came not when called to the participation of his benefits, Matt. xxii. 8.

They are worthy] *Non dignitate sua, sed dignatione divina.* Or, They are worthy, not absolutely, but in comparison of those before mentioned.

Ver. 5. Clothed in white] See the note on ver. 4.

The book of life] Wherein the just that live by faith are written.

But I will confess his' name] His well-tried faith shall be found to praise, honour, and glory, at the appearing of Jesus Christ, 1 Pet. i. 7. See the note there.

Ver. 6.] See the note on chap. ii. 7.

Ver. 7. That is holy] And therefore to be "sanctified in righteousness," Isa. v. 16.

True] And therefore to be trusted.

That hath the key of David] And is therefore to be sought unto for a door both of utterance and of entrance, Col. iv. 13 ; 2 Cor. ii. 12 ; Acts xvi. 14.

Ver. 8. An open door] A fair opportunity of doing thyself good; which those that go about to deprive thee of shall be sure to lose *oleum et operam*, their toil and tallow.

A little strength] A little grace well improved may do great matters, and set heaven open to a soul. The vine is the weakest of trees, but the most fruitful. Philadelphia with her little strength is discommended for nothing, she made all best use of it.

Ver. 9. I will make them] The conversion of the Jews shall be the wonder of the Gentiles.

Which say they are Jews, and are not] The perverse Jews at this day pretend (but maliciously) that those few Jews that turn Christians are not of them, but poor Christians hired from other places to personate their part. (Blount's Voyage, p. 112.)

That I have loved thee] The Church is τὴν ψυχὴν τὴν ἠγαπημένην, the "dearly beloved of God's soul," Jer. xii. 7, or (as the Septuagint render it) his beloved soul.

Ver. 10. The word of my patience] So called, 1. Because we must suffer for the truth of it. 2. Because, hid in the heart, it worketh patience.

I will keep thee] From the hurt, if not from the smart of it ; from the common distraction, if not from the common destruction.

Which shall come upon all the world] So the Romans in their pride called their empire.

To try them that dwell] sc. By that sharp and sore persecution under Trajan the emperor.

Ver. 11. That no man take thy crown] Not that crown of eternal life (for that is unloseable), but that honour that God hath put upon thee, ver. 9. A Christian may, by falling into reproachful courses, "lose what he hath wrought," 2 John 8. 1. In respect of the praise of men. 2. In respect of inward comfort. 3. In respect of the degrees of glory in heaven ; he may miss of being a pillar in the temple of God, as ver. 1.

Ver. 12. Will I make a pillar] Pillars are both the firmament and ornament of temples. Understand it of that fulness and constancy both of grace and of glory in heaven.

Which is new Jerusalem] It was a pride in Montanus to overween his Peruza and Tymium

(two pelting parishes in Phrygia) and to call them Jerusalem, as if they had been the only churches. (Euseb. v. 15.) And surely, it is nothing else but pride in the Brownists to avow that their churches are nothing less than the new Jerusalem coming down from heaven : that the very crown, sceptre, and throne of Christ's kingdom consists in them. (See Mr Bailey's Dissuasive, p. 17.)

My new name] viz. That which he received from his Father in his exaltation, Ephes. i. 20 ; Phil. ii. 9.

Ver. 14. And unto the angel] Archippus, it may be ; for he was a pastor here, and began to cool long before this, Col. iv. 17.

These things saith the Amen] The God of Amen, as Isaiah calleth him, faithful in performing his promises to the remnant that he reserved in this lukewarm Church, among so careless a multitude. To these Christ became a beginning of the creation of God ; so the new birth is here called, as being of no less fame and wonder than the making of the world.

Ver. 15. That thou art neither cold] Such are our civil justiciaries, politic professors, neuter-passive Christians ; a fair day mends them not, and a foul day pairs them not ; peremptory never to be more precise ; resolved to keep on the warm side of the hedge, to sleep in a whole skin, suffer nothing, do nothing, that may interfere with their hopes or prejudice their preferments.

I would thou wert] Better be a zealous Papist than a lukewarm Protestant. A zealous Papist (saith one) dare tell us to our heads that our religion is error, ourselves heretics, our end destruction ; that one heaven cannot hold us hereafter, one church now ; that our damnation is so clearly set down in our own Bibles, that there needs no more to assure us thereof than to open our eyes and read it ; that if we be not damned, he will be damned for us, &c. This is better than forlorn recklessness in right religion, and that detestable indifferency above specified. (Campian, Rat. 10 ; Bristow, Mot. 36 ; Coster ad Osiand.)

Ver. 16. I will spue thee out] I will please myself in thy just punishment. Ah (saith God, as one ridding his stomach), "I will ease me of mine adversaries, I will avenge me of mine enemies," Isa. i. 24. Now the basest places are good enough to cast up our gorge in. The hypocrites' punishment must needs be heavy. Laodicea is commonly looked upon as a type of England. And surely that *facies hypocritica* of our nation is *facies hippocratica*, a mortal complexion, a sad prognostic.

Ver. 17. Because thou sayest] *Si dixisti, satis est, periisti*, saith Augustine. He that thinks he knows anything, knows nothing yet as he ought to know, 1 Cor. viii. 2.

And knowest not] Whatever thou deemest and dreamest of thyself, as setting up thy counter for £1000, and working thyself into the fool's paradise of a sublime dotage.

That thou art wretched and miserable, &c.]

Semper inops, misera, infelix, rerum omnium egena, as Favolius saith of Athens, and her inhabitants at this day under the Turk.

Ver. 18. *I counsel thee*] Having first convinced thee, ver. 17, who before wert uncounselable; the Gibeonites sent not for Joshua till besieged; the Gileadites sought not after Jephthah till distressed; nor will men hearken after Christ till driven out of themselves.

To buy of me] " Buy the truth and sell it not." Make a thorough sale of sin and all (with the wise merchant) to purchase Christ the pearl of price, for whom St Paul (that great trader both by sea and land, 2 Cor. xi. 23, 25, 26) counted all but dung and dog's meat, Phil. iii. 7, 8. Diogenes taxed the folly of the men of his times (may not we the men of ours?) *quod res pretiosas minimo emerent, venderentque vilissimas plurimo,* that they undervalued the best things, but overvalued the worst.

Gold tried in the fire] Precious faith, 1 Pet. i. 7.

White raiment] The righteousnesses of the saints, that of justification, and the other of sanctification.

And that the shame of thy nakedness] But be covered as the priest's nakedness was by his linen-breeches. Nature teacheth us to cover our nakedness; therefore when a man hath committed a sin, he blusheth; the blood as it were would cover the sin. Aaron by making the golden calf had made the people naked unto their shame among their enemies, Exod. xxxii. 5. Maximilian the emperor, when he yielded up the ghost, gave charge that none should see his dead body naked. *Erat enim omnium mortalium verecundissimus,* saith mine author. Buy we this white raiment of Christ; so shall our sins never shame us.

Eye-salve] That unction, 1 John ii. 20. Light and sight, the saving knowledge of heavenly mysteries.

Ver. 19. *As many as I love*] q. d. Think not that I hate you, because I thus chide you. He that escapes reprehension may suspect his adoption. God had one Son without corruption, but none without correction. We must look through the anger of his correction to the sweetness of his loving countenance; as by a rainbow we see the beautiful image of the sun's light in the midst of a dark and waterish cloud. See more in my Treatise upon this verse, the second edition.

And repent] So they did in likelihood; for Eusebius commends this Church as greatly flourishing in his time. Oh the divine rhetoric and omnipotent efficacy of repentance, saith a divine. This is the rainbow, which if God seeth shining in our hearts, he will never drown our souls.

Ver. 20. *Behold, I stand*] Christ stands, he doth not sit; now whilst a man is standing he is going. Christ is but a while with men in the opportunities of grace; he will not always wait their leisure. The Church sought him (when once gone) with many a heavy heart, Cant. iii.

And knock] By the hammer of my word and hand of my Spirit.

And open the door, &c.] sc. By teachableness and obedience. This is not spoken of the first act of conversion (*quæ gratuita est et inopinata*), but of the consequences of it; in which man, who being dead hath been made alive, ought to co-operate with God's grace.

Ver. 21. *To sit with me in my throne*] The thrones of those eastern kings were large and capacious, after the manner of a couch, set on high and covered with tapestry, so that besides the king's own room, others whom the king would honour might sit by him in the same throne. (Lud. de Dieu. in loc.) And hereunto our Saviour seemeth here to allude. This honour he promiseth to him that overcometh, as Alexander the Great by his last will left his dominions τῷ κρατίστῳ, to the worthiest of his princes, to him that should best deserve it.

And he with me] Christ is no niggardly or beggarly guest. His reward is with him, he brings better commodities than Abraham's servant did, or the Queen of Sheba, gold, raiment, eye-salve, &c.

Even as I also] That is, because I also overcame, by virtue of my victory, ὡς for ὅτι. See the like John xvii. 2; Luke iv. 36. It is by Christ that we do over-overcome, Rom. viii. 37.

CHAPTER IV.

Ver. 1. *A door was opened in heaven*] That is, preparation was made for the manifestation of more heavenly mysteries.

Was as it were of a trumpet] To rouse and raise up his attention. For it might fare with him as with a drowsy person, who though awaked, and set to work, is ready to sleep at it. Compare Zech. iv. 1.

Come up hither] Not by local motion, but by mental illumination.

I will show thee] That thou mayest show the Church, that they have a most glorious and almighty deliverer.

Ver. 2. *I was in the spirit*] See chap. i. 10. That is, I was ravished into a spiritual ecstasy.

And behold a throne] So Isaiah was prepared for his prophecy by such a sight, chap. vi. 1, And Ezekiel (besides that stupendous vision, chap. i.) heard behind him a voice of great rushing, saying, " Blessed be the glory of the Lord from his place," chap. ii. 12.

Sat on the throne] As judge of heaven and earth, Gen. xviii. 25.

Ver. 3. *Like a jasper and a sardine*] God is here resembled (saith Mr Cotton) by three precious stones, holding forth the three persons in Trinity. A jasper having (as they say) a white circle round about it, representing the eternity of the Father. A sardine stone of a fleshy colour representing Jesus Christ, who took our flesh upon him. An emerald, being of a green colour, refreshing the eyes of them that look upon it, representing the Spirit, who is (as the rainbow) a token of fair weather, and is a comfortable refresher, wheresoever he cometh.

And there was a rainbow] Which is *signum gratiæ et fœderis*, a sign of grace and of the covenant of mercy, which is always fresh and green about Christ's throne of grace.

Ver. 4. *And round about*] The saints are round about God, Psal. lxxvi. 11, a people near unto him, Psal. cxlviii. 14.

Four and twenty elders] A full senate, a stately amphitheatre of the first-born, whose names are written in heaven, clothed as priests, crowned as kings and conquerors.

Ver. 5. *Lightnings and thunderings*] Is not destruction to the wicked? and a strange punishment to persecutors? Job xxxi. 3. Who ever hardened himself against God's Church and prospered? Job ix. 4. Have these workers of iniquity no knowledge, who eat up God's people as they eat bread? Psal. xiv. 4. Surely, if they had but so much wit for themselves as Pilate's wife had in a dream, they would take heed of having anything to do with just men. If any man will hurt God's witnesses, fire proceedeth out of their mouth and devoureth their enemies, Rev. xi. 5. It was therefore no ill counsel that a martyr gave his persecutors, If thou wilt not spare us, yet spare thyself. It is a fearful thing to fall into the punishing hands of the living God.

The seven spirits] See chap. i. 4.

Ver. 6. *A sea of glass*] The word, say some; the world, others. The word is to us a crystal glass, giving us a clear sight of God and of ourselves, 2 Cor. iii. 18; Jam. i. 23. The world is to God a sea of glass, *corpus diaphanum*, a clear transparent body, he sees through it.

Four beasts] ζῶα, or living wights, not angels, but ministers, those earthly angels, who are set forth, 1. Full of eyes for their perspicacity and vigilancy. 2. Furnished with six wings apiece for their pernicity and promptitude to scour about for the people's benefit. 3. Qualified with all necessary endowments, for the discharge of their duties, being bold as lions, painful as oxen, prudent as men, delighted in high flying, as eagles.

Ver. 8. *Full of eyes within*] To look to themselves also as well as to the flock, Acts xx. 28, lest while they preach to others, &c., 1 Cor. ix. 27.

They rest not] Gr. They have no rest, and yet they have no unrest neither, the sweet content they take in their continual employment is fitter to be believed than possible to be discoursed.

Holy, holy] This they double, treble, and warble upon, nine times over.

Ver. 9. *And when those beasts*] When the preachers are performing their office, as heralds of God's praises.

Ver. 10. *The four and twenty elders*] The people yield their assent, and say, Amen; the want whereof St Paul accounts no small loss, 1 Cor. xiv. 16.

And cast their crowns] Canute, king of England, set his crown upon the crucifix, and proclaimed, saying, Let all the inhabitants of the world know that there is no mortal man worthy the name of a king, but he to whose beck heaven, earth, and sea, by his laws eternal are obedient. (Hen. Huntington.) When the Great Turk cometh into his temple, he lays by all his state, and hath none to attend him all the while. Solomon's mother set the crown upon his head (so doth the Church upon Christ's head) in the day of his espousals, Cant. iii. 11.

Ver. 11. *Thou art worthy*] If we would have our souls set as a pearl in that fair ring of heavenly courtiers that compass the Lamb's throne, let us praise God as they do.

For thou hast created] Our service must not be rash but reasonable, Rom. xii. 1, such as whereof we can render a reason. God hates a blind sacrifice, a Samaritan's service, when men worship they know not what nor why, John iv. 22.

And were created] God's power put forth in the creation and administration of the world is twice here mentioned; as that which can never be sufficiently admired and adored. See my notes on Gen. i.

CHAPTER V.

Ver. 1. *In the right hand*] GR. On, or at the right hand. There it lay ready, but none could make aught of it, till the Lamb took it, not only at, but out of the Father's right hand, and opened it, ver. 7.

A book written] This book of the Revelation, which till the Son of man had received of his heavenly Father to show unto his servants, neither they nor he (as Son of man) knew (so much at least) of that day and hour of his second coming.

And on the back side] As wanting room within. Like that of the poet,

> *Scriptus et in tergo, necdum finitus Orestes.*
> (Juven. Sat. 1.)

Sealed with seven seals] To note the great secrecy and gradual discovery of the divine counsels.

Ver. 2. *And I saw a strong angel*] Angels are very desirous to know the mystery of Christ, 1 Pet. i. 11, and to profit daily in that knowledge, Eph. iii. 10.

Ver. 3. *Nor under the earth*] That is, in the sea, as Exod. xx. 4.

Neither to look thereon] Or, therein, because sealed up.

Ver. 4. *And I wept*] Out of a deep desire of knowing the contents of this book. And as our Saviour going toward his cross, turned again to the weeping women, and comforted them, so he soon satisfied the desire of this his dejected disciple. Tears are effectual orators. Luther got much of his insight into God's matters by this means. So did Melancthon when he wept on those words, *Quos fugiamus habemus (pontificios) quos sequamur non intelligimus.* It is said of Sir Philip Sidney, that when he met with anything that he well understood not, he would break out into

tears, —— *faciles motus mens generosa capit.*
The spouse, seeking him whom her soul loved,
had eyes like the pools of Heshbon glazed with
tears, Cant. vii. 4. And Daniel had greatest
revelations after three weeks of heaviness, chap.
x. 2.

Ver. 5. *And one of the elders*] A common
Christian points the divine to the arch-prophet,
whom for present he thought not on. An eloquent Apollos may be better informed by a tent-
maker, and a great apostle be comforted by an
ordinary Roman, Acts viii. 26; Rom. i. 12.
This elder in the text seems to be the patriarch
Jacob (saith one), because from his prophecy the
name of lion is given to Christ, Gen. xlix. 9.

Behold, the Lion of the tribe of Juda] So Moses
sets forth our Saviour. And fitly, 1. For the
excellency of his strength. 2. For his heroical
spirit. 3. For his principality; the lion is the
king of beasts. 4. For his vigilancy; the lion
sleepeth with open eyes. (Gerhard.)

The Root of David] So the prophets. "They
have Moses and the prophets," saith Abraham,
Luke xvi. 29. "To the law and to the testimony," Isa. viii. 29. If any speak not according
to this word, it is because there is no light in
them, nor to be gotten from them.

Hath prevailed] Gr. ἐνίκησεν, hath overcome,
or surpassed, *sc.* all creatures in worth, to do
this great work.

Ver. 6. *In the midst of the throne*] As a fit
mediator betwixt God and men, even the man
Christ Jesus, who gave a ransom, 1 Tim. ii. 5, 6.

A Lamb as it had been slain] This form of
speech is put (saith an interpreter) to show the
continual recent virtue of Christ's death eternally
effectual before God, as whereby once for all he
hath purchased eternal redemption. Some think
that he still retains in heaven the prints and
scars of those wounds that he received on earth
in his hands, feet, and side. His glorified body
(saith one) is that golden censer, which through
the wounds that are in it, as through chinks or
holes, fumeth forth always a pleasant and sweet
savour in the nostrils of his Father. It is also
the note of a learned interpreter here, that the
benefit of knowing the prophecies concerning the
Church, Christ, before he was slain, had it not
so as he had after his death. It was the purchase of the blood of Christ to have those things
opened.

Having seven horns] Plenty of power. Antichrist hath but two horns, chap. xiii. 11.

And seven eyes] No want of wisdom, no need
of a visible head to the Church or any other vicar-
general to Christ, than the Holy Ghost, called here
"the seven spirits of God sent forth into all the
earth."

Ver. 7. *And he came and took*] As Mediator
he took it, as God he gave it. All things are
delivered unto him of the Father; and no man
knoweth the Father but the Son, and he to whom
the Son revealeth him, Matt. xi. 27. See the
note there.

Ver. 8. *Fell down before the Lamb*] As they
had done before the throne, chap. iv. See John
v. 23. Divine adoration is an honour due to the
manhood of Christ also, as it is taken into union
with the Godhead.

Golden vials, &c.] Vessels narrow beneath
and wide upwards; so is the heart of a believer,
narrow below, almost sharpened to a point, that
it might touch the earth no more than needs
must; and wide above, to receive the influence
of heaven. Gold is pure and precious; so are
the prayers of a pure heart.

Full of odours] Therefore sweet to God, because Christ pours into them of his odours, Rev.
viii. 3.

Which are the prayers of saints] That is, their
own prayers and praises, recorded ver. 9. And
this is added as an exposition to let us know
what is meant by odours. See the like, John u.
21, and vii. 39; Rev. i. 20.

Ver. 9. *And they sung*] A general joy in
heaven and earth. Surely, it is a pleasant thing
to see the light; how much more to see the light
of the knowledge of God in the face of Jesus
Christ! 2 Cor. iv. 6. What a deal of triumph
and exaltation is here all the Church over upon
the opening of this book upon the receipt of this
revelation! Should not this excite and kindle in
our hearts a more earnest desire of understanding these mysteries? "Oh I could find in my
heart to fall afresh upon the study of the Revelation, had I strength to do it," said my reverend
old master unto me, a little before his death; Mr
John Ballam, I mean, minister of the word for
many years at Evesham, where I heard him (in
my childhood) preaching many a sweet sermon
upon the second and third chapters of this book.

A new song] For the new work of redemption,
besides that old song, chap. iv., for that of creation.

Out of every kindred] Let this be noted
against the doctrine of universal redemption that is
now again so violently cried up amongst us.

Ver. 10. *And we shall reign on the earth*]
Reign over our lusts; reign with and in Christ
over all our enemies by a spiritual, not secular
sceptre; and at last judge the world, 1 Cor. vi. 2.

Ver. 11. *Round about the throne and the beasts*]
That is, round about the beasts and the elders.
Angels encamp about the saints, as ministering
spirits, and are glad of the office, that their God
manifested in the flesh may be seen of them, 1
Tim. iii. 16, and the multifarious wisdom of God
in man's redemption be displayed unto them,
Ephes. iii. 10.

Ver. 12. *With a loud voice*] Betokening their
earnest affection; which also is here notably expressed by the many particulars they ascribe to
Christ, as if they could never give enough to him.
Now if angels, who have nothing so much benefit
by him, do thus magnify him, how much more
should we! Our hearts should be enlarged, our
mouths opened, and we not a little vexed at our
own vile dulness in being no more affected with
these indelible ravishments.

Ver. 13. *And every creature*] The whole creation groaneth under vanity, and rejoiceth as it were in the forethought of that liberty of the sons of God at the last day, whereof it shall partake, Rom. viii. 21. See the note there.

Ver. 14. *And the four beasts*] The saints were the precentors in this blessed choir, and now they are the succentors also, Rev. xiv. 3. They began the song, and so conclude it, as having far greater benefit by Christ than all other creatures, and God expects a proportion, that our returns be somewhat answerable to our receipts. (Sarson.) The saints upon earth sing a new (that is, an excellent) song in the honour of Christ, ver. 9, 10. Heaven answers as by an echo, the music upon earth in the mean time continuing, ver. 11, 12 (where note that this song of angels putteth Christ in the third person; he took not upon him the nature of angels, he is nearer to us); all creatures come in as the chorus, ver. 13, and as man began, so he ends the anthem, ver. 14.

CHAPTER VI.

Ver. 1. *One of the seals*] THAT is, the first of the seals, as Gen. i. 4; Mark xvi. 2. Under these seven seals falls Rome pagan (saith Mr Cotton), as under the seven trumpets Rome Christian, under the seven vials Rome antichristian. So all the judgments in the Revelation are still upon Rome. Hence Mr Dent calls his exposition upon the Revelation, The Ruin of Rome.

The noise of thunder] This beast was like a lion, chap. iv. 7, whose roaring is as thunder.

Ver. 2. *And behold a white horse*] The apostles and apostolic preachers of the primitive times, white for their purity of doctrine, discipline, and conversation; horses for their nimble and swift spreading the gospel, which ran ἀθρόως οἷα τὶς ἠλίου βολὴ, through the world like a sunbeam (as Eusebius hath it), and was carried as on eagles' or on angels' wings. A horse hath his name in Hebrew from devouring the ground by his swiftness, and was therefore by the heathens dedicated to the sun, whose "going forth is from the end of the heaven, and his circuit unto the ends of it," Psal. xix. 6. Cranzius tells us that the Saxon princes, before they became Christians, gave a black horse for their arms; but being once baptized, a white horse; with reference haply to this text.

He that sat on him] Christ, chap. xix. 11, Psal. lxv. 5. The conquerors entered into Rome carried on a white horse.

Had a bow] The doctrine of the gospel, whereby the people fall under him, Psal. xlv. 4.

Conquering, and to conquer] *Britannorum inaccessa Romanis loca, Christo tamen patuerunt*, saith Tertullian (Advers. Jud. vii.). Christ came and conquered this kingdom, which the Romans with all their power could not do. *A Christo vinci, summa victoria est; vinciri, summa libertas*, saith another. There is no such conquest as to be conquered by Christ; no such liberty as to be bound by him.

Ver. 3. *Come and see*] John's better attention is called for. How dull and drowsy are the best in perceiving and receiving heavenly mysteries! A sea-coal fire, if not stirred up, will die of itself, so will our spark and spunk of light. Christ calls upon those that had come far to hear him, saying, "Let him that hath an ear hear," Matt. xiii. See Zech. iv. 1.

Ver. 4. *That was red*] Portending troubles and tragedies, bloody wars and terrible persecutions. Those ten first were so cruel, that St Jerome writes in one of his epistles that for every day in the year were murdered 5000, except the first day of January.

To him that sat thereon] Christ, Matt. x. 34; Zech. i. 8. He stands over his Church as the Agonothetes. So he did at St Stephen's martyrdom, Acts vii.: he moderates and overrules the enemy's cruelty.

And that they should kill one another] viz. The persecutors should rise up and destroy one another, as the Romans did the Jews, and the Jews the Romans in divers provinces. And as the emperors, who got nothing (most of them) by their adoption or designation to the empire, *nisi ut citius interficerentur*, but to be cut off the sooner. (Tacit.) All or most of the persecuting Cæsars died unnatural deaths.

A great sword] That of the gospel, Ephes. vi. 17, which takes away peace, by accident, Matt. xxiv. 6. Christ threateneth the contempt of the gospel with wars and rumours of wars. Our late Edgehill battle was fought in the vale of Red-horse; as if God had meant to say, "I have now sent you the red horse, to avenge the quarrel of the white."

Ver. 5. *A black horse*] Famine discolours and denigrates, Lam. iv. 7, 8. It accompanies war for the most part, and in sieges is very extreme, as at Samaria, where an ass's head was worth four pounds; at Rome, where this proclamation was made in the market, *Pone pretium humanæ carni;* at Scodra, where horses were dainty meat, yea, they were glad to eat dogs, cats, rats, &c. At Antioch in Syria, where many Christians (in the holy war, as they called it) were glad to eat the dead bodies of their late slain enemies. (Turk. Hist.)

Had a pair of balances] Gr. ζυγὸν, the beam of scales. To show that bread should be delivered out by measure, as is threatened, Ezek. iv. 6; Deut. xxvi., and men should be stinted and pittanced.

Ver. 6. *In the midst*] The voice of the Lamb, chap. v. 6, who appoints and orders all; he cuts us out our several conditions, cautioning for the wine and oil, when other food faileth.

A measure of wheat] χοῖνιξ, a quart, say some, a pottle others, an allowance for a day. Among the Greeks, saith Suidas, *Chœnix dietim dabatur.* And that the Israelites in the wilderness (according to Rabanus) had each of them three chœnices of manna by the day, that was to be ascribed to the divine bounty, as Junius noteth.

Ver. 7.] See the note on ver. 3.

Ver. 8. *A pale horse*] Fit for pestilence and pale death to ride on.

And hell followed] *sc.* To them that were killed with death, Rev. ii. 23 (see the note there), that died in their sins, which is far worse than to die in a ditch.

Over the fourth part of the earth] That is, of the Roman empire. This fell out in the days of Decius; Orosius bearing witness that the pestilence which then raged did extend no further *quam ad profligandas ecclesias edicta Decii cucurrerunt*, that is, than the proclamations of Decius came for the overthrow of the Churches.

And with death] *i. e.* The pestilence, that harbinger and purveyor of death : this is somewhere called " God's evil angel ;" and by ecclesiastical writers mortality. Hippocrates calleth it τὸ θεῖον, the divine stroke, because God hath a special hand in it.

Ver. 9. *Under the altar*] *i. e.* Under Christ, Heb. xiii. 10, under his custody and safeguard, or, under the altar, that is, lying at the bottom of the altar, as beasts newly slain for sacrifice. See Phil. ii. 17 and 2 Tim. iv. 6. The ten persecutions and (after them) the eruptions of the Goths, Vandals, Huns, and Herula, heaped on massacres of martyrs.

Which they had] Gr. εἶχον, which they had, and would not be drawn by any terrors or tortures to part with. They may take away my life, said one, but not my faith ; my head, but not my crown.

Ver. 10. *And they cried*] When God intends deliverance to his people, he poureth out upon them " the spirit of grace and supplication," Zech. xiii. 9, 10.

How long, O Lord] Calvin had this speech always in his mouth, breathing out his holy desires in the behalf of the afflicted Churches, with whose sufferings he was more affected than with anything that befell himself. (Beza in Vita.)

Dost thou not judge and avenge] The glorified souls cannot be properly said to desire revenge ; but the cry which they make must be understood to be the provocation of God to vengeance which their sufferings produce in the same sort as Abel's blood is said to cry. (Thorndike.)

That dwell on the earth] In opposition to the inhabitants of heaven. As names written in heaven stand opposed to those that are written in the earth, Luke x. 20 ; Jer. xvii. 13.

Ver. 11. *And white robes*] Their innocency was cleared, and their persecutors convinced. God would speak for them in the hearts of their greatest enemies.

Until their fellow-servants also] We doubt not, saith a learned interpreter here (Mr Forbes), but that the crowned saints do in general know the afflicted condition of the Church militant, and do wish them deliverance ; but our special necessities and occurrences of particular persons they cannot know. Brother Bradford, said

Bishop Ridley, a little before he was offered up, so long as I shall understand that thou art in thy journey, by God's grace I shall call upon our heavenly Father to set thee safely home ; and then, good brother, speak you for the remnant that are to suffer for Christ's sake, according to that thou then shalt know more clearly. (Acts and Mon.) But this is to be taken with a grain of salt.

That should be killed] Under Licinius, Julian the Apostate, and the Arian emperors.

Ver. 12. *There was a great earthquake*] Understand hereby those horrible commotions and confusions that fell out in the Roman empire upon those ten bloody persecutions, and the earnest supplications of the saints which can work wonders in heaven and earth. The death and destruction of the persecutors was (as it was said of the death of Arius) *precationis opus non morbi*, the effect of faithful prayers calling for full and final vengeance. (Socrates i. 15.)

The sun became black] It is ordinary in Scripture to set forth horrible commotions of commonwealths by such figurative expressions as these, Jer. iv. 23, &c. ; Joel ii. 10, &c. ; Isa. xiii. 10.

Ver. 13. *And the stars*] Rome's dunghill deities, together with their chemarims or chimney-chaplains, the priests. Confer Isa. xxxiv. 4 ; Dan. viii. 10 ; Exod. xii. 12 ; Num. xxxiii. 4.

Ver. 14. *And every mountain*] See the note on ver. 12. *Cinis quidam noxius e Visuvio emissus, Romam venit (inquit Dio) ita ut incolæ putare cœperunt omnia sursum deorsum ferri, solemque in terram cadere, ac terram in cœlum conscendere.* I myself saw, saith Bellarmine, a huge hill removed by an earthquake, and brought down to a town, which was wholly covered by it, and as it were buried under it. Perhaps he meant Pleurs in Rhetia, which was overcovered suddenly with a mountain, so that 1500 persons were buried there alive.

Ver. 15. *And the kings of the earth*] Who came in to help their gods against the mighty, against Constantine, Theodosius, &c., that threw out their priests, and pulled down their temples. These kings and grandees were Maximianus, Maximinus, Maxentius, Galerius, Licinius, Julianus, &c., and their complices, who were routed, ruined, and driven into holes and corners by the Christian emperors, and afterwards so pursued by divine justice, that they came to shameful ends. Diocletian poisoned himself, Maximinian hanged himself ; Maximinus likewise and Maxentius became their own death's-men ; Galerius died of a loathsome disease ; Julian had his death-wound from heaven, and died raving and blaspheming. (Euseb. Hist., Item de Vita Const.)

Ver. 16. *And said to the mountains*] Which yet was but a poor shelter ; for mountains melted and rocks rent at his presence. So that if wicked men cry to the hills, Help us, they will give an echo, Help us. For God's wrath is upon the creature for man's sin.

Ver. 17. *Who shall be able to stand*] They could not stand before their own misgiving hearts and soul-condemning consciences; how much less before God that was greater than their hearts! God sent his hornet, which drove out these Canaanites, Exod. xxiii. 28. *Facti sunt a corde suo fugitivi*, as Tertullian hath it.

CHAPTER VII.

Ver. 1. *And after these things*] THIS whole chapter is purposely interlaced between the opening of the sixth and seventh seal, for the support of the poor suffering saints, that they sink not under their many pressures.

Four angels] Ministers of indignation, whether good or evil angels the doctors are divided.

Holding the four winds] Those besoms of the air, as Rupertus calls them, and Scripture emblems of spiritual influence, John iii. 8; Cant. iv. ult.; Ezek. xxxvii. 9. The holding of the winds may peradventure intimate here that peace and ease in which God suffereth worldly men to live, and be overtaken, even upon the point of his great judgments, 1 Thess. v. 3. He made fair weather before Pharaoh till he had him in the heart of the Red Sea.

Nor on any tree] The philosopher compares men (the Scripture good men oft) to trees, which by benign winds are filled with fruits.

Ver. 2. *Another angel*] Whether Christ, or Constantine acted by Christ, it much matters not.

Having the seal] Whereof Christ is the great Lord-keeper.

With a loud voice] Out of his great care of his elect. As Crœsus' dumb son burst out into loud speech to save his father, ἄνθρωπε, μὴ κτεῖνε τὸν Κροῖσον. (Herod.)

To the four angels] Who are at Christ's beck and check.

Ver. 3. *Hurt not*] Reprobates oft fare the better for those few righteous that are amongst them; they are therefore singularly foolish for seeking to rid them, and root them out, as the heathen emperors did. These resemble the stag in the emblem, that fed upon the leaves which hid him from the hunter; and Samson-like, by pulling down the pillars, they bring the house upon their own heads.

In their foreheads] Not in their hands only, as the vassals of Antichrist (ch. xiii. 16), who have free liberty to dissemble, deny their religion, do anything, so the Catholic cause be thereby advanced. My son, give me thy heart, said Gregory XIII. to our English Papists, let who will have thy tongue and outward man.

Ver. 4. *A hundred forty and four thousand*] A competent company. Not so many as the locusts, chap. xiii., and yet more than most thought they had been.

Ver. 5. *Twelve thousand*] Out of each tribe so many, God inclines towards all the elect with an equal good-will; neither shall any one complain justly that others have been more regarded than he, as one well observeth here.

Ver. 6. *Of the tribe of Naphthali*] Who is first reckoned among those by Rachel's side, because at Capernaum in this tribe Christ inhabited. Any relation to him ennobleth. Bethlehem, though it be the least, is yet not the least among the princes of Judah, for that out of her came the governor of Israel, Matt. ii. 6, with Mic. iii. 6.

Ver. 7. *Of the tribe of Levi*] Levi is taken in, Dan cut out of the roll for his shameful recidivation and revolt from the true religion, Judges xviii. This, Jacob foresaw and bewailed in that holy ejaculation on his death-bed, Gen. xlix. 18. There is no reckoning made or account given of this tribe (as there is of the rest), 1 Chron. vii. The fable of Antichrist to come of Dan, is so thin a device, that Bellarmine could not but see through it, and disclaim it (Lib. iii. de Pont. Rom. cap. xii.).

Ver. 8. *Of Joseph*] That is, of Ephraim, who, though Joseph's younger son, yet had the first birthright. Ephraim is not named (though tacitly intended here) because joined to idols; let him alone therefore, saith God, Hos. iv. 17.

Ver. 9. *A great multitude*] All the faithful from the apostles to the end of the world. In all ages there were some that sought righteousness; neither was it ever so hard with the Church as the host at Nola (in the story) made it; who when he was commanded by the Roman censor to go and call the good men of the city to appear before him, went to the church-yards, and there called at the graves of the dead, O ye good men of Nola, come away, for the Roman censor calls for your appearance; for he knew not where to call for a good man alive. In the very midst of Popery there were many faithful witnesses, and more of such as (like those two hundred that went out of Jerusalem after Absalom) went on in the simplicity of their hearts, and knew not anything, 2 Sam. xv. 11. (Anton. di Guevara.)

Clothed with white robes] See the note on chap. iii. 4.

And palms in their hands] In token of victory over all spiritual enemies. This was hinted at by those palms engraved in Solomon's and Ezekiel's temple.

Ver. 10. *Salvation to our God*] Not to this or that popish saint or mediator; of all whom these triumphers might say, as that heathen once, *Contemno minutos istos deos, modo Jovem (Jesum) propitium habeam*, I care not for all those small gods, so I may have Jesus on my side.

Ver. 11. *And all the angels*] See the note on chap. v. 11.

Ver. 12. *Amen; Blessing and glory, &c.*] The angels assent to what the saints had said, and add much more, according to their greater measure of knowledge and love to God: write we after this fairer copy.

Ver. 13. *And one of the elders*] See the note on chap. v. 5.

Ver. 14. *Which came out of great tribulation*] It is but a delicacy that men dream of to divide Christ and his cross. The bishop of London, when he had degraded Richard Bayfield, martyr, kneeling upon the highest step of the altar, he smote him so hard on the breast with his crosier-staff, that he threw him down backward, and brake his head so that he swooned; and when he came to himself again, he thanked God that he was delivered from the malignant Church of Antichrist, and that he was come into the true Church of Christ militant, and I hope shall be anon with him in the Church triumphant. (Acts and Mon.)

And made them white] Other blood stains what is washed in it; this blood of the spotless Lamb whitens and purifies.

Ver. 15. *Therefore are they*] Not for the whiteness of their robes, but because they are washed in the meritorious blood of the Lamb.

Before the throne of God] A good man is like a good angel, always standing before the face of God.

Shall dwell among them] Gr. σκηνώσει, shall pitch his tent, or shall keep the feast of tabernacles amongst them, or shall hover and cover over them, as the cloud did over Israel in the wilderness; so that under his shadow they shall safely and sweetly repose themselves.

Ver. 16. *They shall hunger no more*] They shall be as it were in heaven beforehand, having, *Malorum ademptionem, bonorum adeptionem*, freedom from evil, and fruition of good, here in part, hereafter in all fulness.

Ver. 17. *Shall feed them and lead them*] An allusion to Psal. xxiii. 2, where David seems to resemble powerful and flourishing doctrine to green pastures, and the secret and sweet comforts of the sacraments to the still waters.

And God shall wipe away] A metaphor from a nurse, which not only suckleth her dear child crying for hunger, but also wipes off the tears.

CHAPTER VIII.

Ver. 1. *The seventh seal*] THE business or parts whereof are the seven trumpets, that sound a dreadful alarm against the Roman empire, ready now to be ruined for the innocent blood, and upon the instant suit of the martyrs, chap. vi. 10.

There was silence in heaven] That is, in the Church on earth, often called the kingdom of heaven. This half-hour's silence was either for horror and admiration, or for ardent expectation, or (as some will have it) for religious awe and devotion. Christ the high priest, being now about to offer incense (those prayers of the martyrs, chap. vi. 10), there was in the Church (as used to be in the temple at such times, Luke i. 10) a deep silence. So among the Romans, the people in time of worship were enjoined *favere linguis*, to spare their tongues. And in the Greek Church one stood up and cried, Σίγα λαὸς, ἄφεσις, λαὸς, Peace, people, leave off your discourse. Among the heathen Athenians in the time of divine rights, the priests craved silence of the people in these words, Εὐφημεῖτε, σίγα, πᾶς ἔστω λεώς,

Be whist, all ye people, good words or nothing. *Male ominatis parcite verbis.* (Archæol. Attic. 55. Horat.)

Ver. 2. *Which stood before God*] In a waiting posture, ready pressed to do his pleasure.

Seven trumpets] To be sounded several times, to show that God suffereth not his whole wrath to arise at once against his creatures, but piece-meal and by degrees; proving if peradventure they will repent and recover out of the snare of the devil, who are taken captive by him at his will.

Ver. 3. *And another angel*] An angel after another manner; not by nature, but by office. Christ, the Angel of the covenant. For I cannot be of his mind (Mr Brightman) who makes this angel to be Constantine; the odours given him, to be the power of calling the council; the golden altar, Christ in the midst of this holy assembly; the thick cloud of odours, the whole matter brought most happily to effect; which yet is a pious interpretation.

Much incense] The merit of his own precious passion, Heb. ix. 24, and xiii. 5.

Upon the golden altar] viz. Himself, as chap. vi. 9.

Ver. 4. *The smoke of the incense*] The saints' prayers perfumed with Christ's odours ascended, that is, were highly accepted in heaven, Acts x. 4; Exod. iii. 9, as well appeared by the answer they had here in the next verse. The Church is said to ascend out of the wilderness of this world with pillars of smoke, Cant. iii. 6. *Elationibus fumi*, with raised affections, and with strong supplications, wherein how many sweet spices are burned together by the fire of faith, as humility, love, &c. All which would stink worse in God's nostrils than the onions and garlic of Egypt, did not Christ perfume and present them.

Ver. 5. *And filled it with the fire of the altar*] Fire, in token of fierce indignation, and from the altar; for Christ came to send fire on the earth, Luke xii. 49; fire and sword, Matt. xii. 34; through men's singular corruption and obstinacy in not stooping to the sceptre of this kingdom. Hence fire and brimstone, storm and tempest, a fearful looking for of judgment and fiery indignation, which shall devour the adversaries, Heb. x. 27. From the same altar, Christ, prayers go up, vengeance comes down.

Ver. 6. *Prepared themselves*] Having got sign, as it were, by that which Christ did in the former verse, they set to in order to sound their trumpets.

Ver. 7. *Hail and fire mingled with blood*] Instead of the fire of love (saith Mr Forbes) mixed with the sweet rain of healthsome doctrine and spirit of Christian lenity, the fire of contention and frosty hailstones of destruction ruled all. Yea, so far herein were the bishops carried one against another, as it is monstrous what malice, falsehood, and cruelty they practised, especially in the time of Constans, Constantius, and Valens, the Arian emperors.

And the third part of trees] Men of mark.

And all green grass] Meaner men.

Were burnt up] Were tainted with errors and heresies, whereof this age was so fertile and full that (as Jerome speaketh) it was a witty thing to be a right believer.

Ver. 8. *A great mountain*] Some notable heresiarch, possibly Pelagius, a monk of Bangor, Morgan by name, that is, in the Welsh tongue, a seaman. This Morgan travelling beyond sea to spread his heresy, called himself Pelagius, by a Greek word of the same signification; because it sounded better in the ears of foreign nations. Hence Augustine, *Quid eo pelago* (saith he) *vult mergi Pelagius, unde per petram liberatus est Petrus?* (Lib. i. de Grat. Christ. advers. Pelag.)

Ver. 9. *And the third part*] Heresy as a gangrene spreads and kills; as the leprosy in the head, it renders a man utterly unclean, Levit. xiii. 44. So cunning are some seducers, and so close in the conveyance of their collusion, that if possible the very elect may be deceived.

And the third part of the ships were destroyed] That is, of the Churches, even those that were planted by the apostles themselves, those principal pilots. Howbeit not all the Churches, but a third part only: when the Church was in the wilderness, when Antichrist most reigned and raged, God did preserve some ships, some fundamental doctrines, and the essence of baptism, and the essence of a true ministry dispensing them; and they, that is, her pastors, fed her there, Rev. xii. 6—14.

Niteris incassum Christi submergere navem;
Fluctuat, at nunquam mergitur illa ratis.

Ver. 10. *There fell a great star*] Falling stars were never but meteors. That grand apostate of Rome may well be meant by this blazing, burning comet. He was in falling by degrees from the time of Constantine till Phocas, who sat upon the chair of pestilence.

Burning as it were a lamp] He seems to allude to that kind of comet that is called Lampadias. (Mede.)

The third part of the rivers] i. e. Corrupted true doctrine, and perverted the Scriptures with his false glosses.

Ver. 11. *Was called Wormwood*] Because himself was in the gall of bitterness, and did embitter others. See Jer. xxiii. 15, and Deut xxix. 18, with Junius's note there.

Ver. 12. *And the third part of the sun*] The prelates and patriarchs.

And the third part of the moon] The inferior church officers.

And the third part of the stars] The community of Christians. All began to be spread over with gross ignorance, not only of heavenly truths, but of human sciences, which are here called the night in comparison of gospel light. Gregory the Great (thought to be that angel mentioned in the next verse), though better than any who succeeded him in the Popedom, calling himself the servant of God's servants, and carrying himself modestly in the days of Mauritius the emperor, yet when Mauritius was slain by the traitor Phocas, how

basely did he claw the traitor, and collogue with him; commending to his care the Church of Rome, and often minding him of Peter's primacy, and of that speech of our Saviour, "Thou art Peter," &c., for no other end but that he might enlarge his jurisdiction over all Churches, by the favour of that parricide?

And the day shone not] It was a gloomy and dismal day with the purer Church of Christ.

Ver. 13. *And I beheld and heard an angel*] ἀγγέλου ἀετοῦ, or, an eagle, as some copies read it. See the note on ver. 12. Gregory the Great seems to be pointed at, who is said to be the worst of all the popes that went before him, and the best of those that came after him. Hence he is brought in flying betwixt heaven and earth. And that he cried with a loud voice; pointing at and painting out that to be Antichrist that should challenge to himself the title of universal bishop, and had a host of priests ready to follow him. *Hic prope est, et in foribus*, said he, and he said right; for his immediate successor, Boniface III., fulfilled the same that he had foretold.

CHAPTER IX.

Ver. 1. *A star fall from heaven*] Gr. πεπτωκότα, That had fallen from heaven, viz. when the third angel sounded, chap. viii. 10, then the bishop of Rome began to fall; but here, in Boniface III. and his successors, "He is fallen, he is fallen" from his primitive integrity into the deepest gulf of impiety. The Jesuits (to blind the matter) tell us that by this star is meant Luther, whom Satan sent out to disturb the Church, and God sent them to withstand him. (Scultet. Annal.) Bugenbagius also, a Dutch divine, when he first read Luther's book of the Babylonish Captivity, rashly pronounced him the most pestilent heretic that ever the Church was pestered with. But a few days after, having thoroughly read and weighed the contents of that book, he recanted, and affirmed that all the world was deceived, and Luther only was in right; and so not only himself became a Lutheran, but many others also persuaded by him.

The key of the bottomless pit] Whereinto he lets souls innumerable; so that in the days of Hildebrand letters were set forth as sent from hell, wherein the devil and his angels give the Popish clergy many thanks for sending them in so many souls as they never had in any age before. (Mat. Paris, A. D. 1072.) This key of the bottomless pit is (saith Whitaker) *facultas expromendi et docendi diabolicas doctrinas*, his faculty of broaching and teaching doctrines of devils.

Ver. 2. *And there arose a smoke*] Of heretical opinions and flagitious practices. All the old heretics fled and hid themselves in the Popish clergy. Those dark corners also of the earth are full of the habitations of cruelty. Take heed (said the Lord Audely, chancellor of England) how you deal with Popish priests; for (you may believe me) some of them be knaves all. (Acts and Mon., fol. 1117.) Petrus de Aliaco long since wrote, *Ad hunc statum venit Romana Ecclesia, ut non esset digna regi nisi per reprobos*, The Church of Rome hath for a long season been ruled by a rabble of reprobates. (De Reform. Eccl.)

The sun and the air were darkened] That is, saith Carthusian, the prelates and the people.

Ver. 3. *Locusts upon the earth*] So the monks, friars, Jesuits, &c., are fitly called for their numerosity and voracity. The Jesuits have sometimes maintained 200,000 scholars. The duke of Bavaria's house is so pestered with them (saith one), that notwithstanding his great revenues, he is very poor, as spending all his estate upon those Popish flesh-flies. Think the same of other princes and places where they are received.

As the scorpions of the earth] They are the sorest soul-sting (saith an interpreter) that ever the world had. Pliny testifieth of the scorpion, that there is not one minute wherein it doth not put forth a most venomous sting to do mischief. It creeps on crookedly, and so it strikes the more at unawares. Its sting is not so much felt at first, but soon proves incurable. It is of a very angry nature (saith one interpreter), and there is a word in the Greek tongue taken from a scorpion, signifying to exasperate and to provoke like a scorpion.

Ver. 4. *And as it was commanded*] As David charged his captains to handle the young man Absalom gently, so and much more solicitous is the Lord of his servants' safety.

The grass of the earth, nor any green thing] I say that under the Papacy was true Christianity, saith Luther (Contra Anabap.), yea, the very kernel of Christianity.

Which have not the seal of God, &c.] Profession, that outward mark of a Christian; and of such there were in the worst of times, even in the darkest midnight of damned Popery, a considerable company. As at this day there are said to be even in Italy 4000 professed Protestants: as in Seville itself, a chief city of Spain, there are thought to be no fewer than 20,000 Protestants. (Spec. Europ.)

Ver. 5. *And to them it was given*] This is oft repeated in this book, to show that though Antichrist and his actuaries bandy and bend all their forces to destroy souls, yet they are bounded by God, and can do no more than is given them from above.

Five months] Locusts used to live no longer. See Pliny, lib. xi. cap. 29. There are that interpret these five months of those 500 years, wherein the pope stood in his full pride and power. For, *ab eo tempore quo per vos Papa Antichristus esse cœpit* (saith Bellarmine) *non modo non crevit ejus imperium, sed semper magis ac magis decrevit*, Since you first began to call the pope Antichrist, he hath lost a great part of his command and commodity. (De Pap. Rom., lib. iii. cap. 21.)

As the torment of a scorpion] Pliny testifieth that of all creeping things that are poisonful, the sting of a scorpion is most cruel and grievous.

Ver. 6. *Shall men seek death*] Being brought

through anguish of conscience, and fear of wrath, to that pitiful plight that Roger bishop of Salisbury was, in King Stephen's time, through long and strait imprisonment. He was so hardly bestead (saith the historian) *ut vivere noluerit, mori nescierit*, that live he would not, die he could not. Popish pardons, pilgrimages, dirges, &c., would not quiet or cure distempered consciences, or shake out the envenomed arrows of the Almighty, that stuck fast in them, *hæret lateri lethalis arundo*. A broken leg is not eased by a silken stocking. *Nescio quomodo imbecillior est medicina quam morbus*, said Tully of his philosophical consolations; so may these well say of their Popish paltry applications, The medicine is too weak for the malady. The Papists say, that the reformed religion is a doctrine of desperation. This we are sure is true of theirs, as were easy to instance in Stephen Gardiner, Dr Pendleton, Francis Spira, Guarlacus, Bomelius, Latomus, Crescentius.

Ver. 7. *Like unto horses*] Fed and fierce, to run and rush into the battle, as being driven by the devil. *Si videris persecutorem tuum nimis sævientem, scito quia ab ascensore suo dæmone perurgetur*. (Bernard.)

Were as it were crowns] Triple crowns, mitres, head-tires, shaven crowns; which last is a ceremony so bald, that some priests in France are now ashamed of the mark, and few of them have it that can handsomely avoid it. (Spec. Europ.)

As the faces of men] "But beware of men," Matt. x. 17. See the note there. Yea, beware of those that are looked upon as good men, who yet may act for Satan and not discern it, Matt. xvi. 23. The temptation lies in this, when angels from heaven, men of singular parts and piety, preach other doctrines, Gal. i. 6; 2 Cor. xi. 15.

Ver. 8. *As the hair of women*] Insinuative, and inductive to sin.

As the teeth of lions] Joel i. 6. Catching and carrying to their dens all they can come by, as Tecelius did out of Germany, as Otto sent by Gregory IX. did out of England, where he left not so much money as he either carried with him or sent to Rome before him.

Ver. 9. *And they had breast-plates*] Their pretended donations, privileges and exemptions from the secular power; shaking their tippets at kings, whom they have trampled on, and forced to go barefoot on the hard stones, till they bled again. Thus dealt they by our Henry II.; yea, they lashed him with rods upon the bare, and said, *Domine, noli minari; nos enim nullas minas timemus, qui de tali curia sumus quæ consuevit imperare regibus et imperatoribus:* Sir, never threaten us; for we care not for your threats, as being of that court that commands kings and emperors. (Jac. Revius de Vit. Pontif. p. 149.)

And the sound of their wings] They are loud and bold-spoken, make a great noise, raise a great dust, and thereby think to carry it. Herein they are like the heretic Nestorius, who is said to have been *homo indoctus, superbus, contemptor Patrum, sed audax et magne loquentiæ*, a proud ass, but bold

saith Luther; To preach is to get the ill-will of the world.

Ver. 11. *Thou must prophesy*] For all the sorrow, thou and thy successors must set close to the Lord's work, for the regaining of those peoples, nations, &c., whom Antichrist hath enslaved. Or thus: Thou must prophesy, that is, before the time of fulfilling of all things, this book of the Revelation shall be made as clear as if John were come to prophesy again before men, and to give us a revelation of his Revelation, according to Isa. xxx. 26. (Mr Burr, on Hosea.)

CHAPTER XI.

Ver. 1. *A reed*] That is, the word of God, that little book that he had newly eaten. This is the only rule of faith and discipline whereby all in the Church must be made and meted.

Like unto a rod] Or, sceptre. The word is that rod of Christ's strength, whereby he rules in the midst of his enemies, Psal. cx. 2. It is that right sceptre, Psal. xlv. 6, which he sways and whereby he sovereigns. The Proverbs of Solomon are called in Hebrew *Mishle*, or master-sentences, Prov. i. 1 (a *Mashal, dominari*). And the Scriptures bear the title of Chieftains, Prov. viii. 6, and of lords of collections, as some render it, Eccles. xii. 11.

Measure the temple of God] The Church, that had been so woefully wasted and oppressed by Antichrist, that it stood in need of new measuring and repairing.

That worship therein] In the temple, as being all spiritual priests; and in the altar, as placing all their confidence in Christ's death alone.

Ver. 2. *But the court*] The antichristian rout, cast out as reprobate silver, as refuse stuff, not worth the measuring.

Given unto the Gentiles] Antichrist and his adherents. Papagans are no better than Pagans. " Are ye not the children of the Ethiopians unto me, O children of Israel ? saith the Lord," Amos ix. 7.

The holy city] The true Church. See Dan. vii. 21; Eph. ii. 19.

Forty and two months] This number is one and the same with 1260 days. The allusion is unto Dan. vii. 25.

Ver. 3. *And I will give unto my two, &c.*] *sc.* Power to purge the Church, and to stand for the truth, all the while it was trodden under foot. *Videsis Catalogum Testium veritatis ab Illyrico editum.* Zuinglius recordeth that Luther and he (both at one time, the one not knowing nor hearing of the other) began to write against the pope's indulgences. And of Luther and Melancthon one writes thus,

Divisæ his operæ, sed mens fuit unica ; pavit
Ore Lutherus oves, flore Melancthon apes.

Unto my two witnesses] The whole succession of faithful preachers, under the tyranny and rage of Antichrist. These are said to be two, that is,

few; or two, that is, enough, Deut. xvii. 6; or two, in reference to those noble twos, Moses and Aaron, Elijah and Elisha, Zerubbabel and Joshua, in allusion to whom these witnesses are here described.

Clothed in sackcloth] As calling men to repentance; or as bewailing their blindness; or as wanting better clothing.

Ver. 4. *These are the two olive trees*] See Zech. iv. 3, 11, 14. In this book of the Revelation the Holy Ghost borrows all the elegancies and flowers in the story of the Old Testament, thereby to set out the story of the New in succeeding ages.

Ver. 5. *Fire proceedeth out of their mouths*] So that a man were better anger all the witches in the world than God's faithful witnesses; for they have ever vengeance in a readiness for the disobedient, 2 Cor. x. 6. God inflicting what they either denounce or desire of him against their adversaries.

Ver. 6. *That it rain not*] That the influence of divine grace be withheld from those that despise the gospel; so that they become as those mountains of Gilboa, 2 Sam. i. 21, or that accursed earth, Heb. vi. 8.

Ver. 7. *And when they shall have finished*] Like as Christ, that faithful and true witness (as he is called, Rev. iii. 14), when he had preached much about the same time as here, was slain by a Roman governor, raised with an earthquake, and received up into heaven in a cloud; so these. And, οὐκ ἀγαπᾷς μετὰ φωκίωνος ἀποθανούμενος. (Plut.) Art thou not glad to fare as Phocion? said he to one that was to suffer with him. These two witnesses could not be killed while they were doing, but when they had done their work. No malice of man can antedate my end a minute (saith one hereupon) while my Master hath work for me to do.

Shall overcome them] By arms, not by arguments.

And kill them] This killing, whether it be already past, or yet to come, it is hard to say. But if to come, some think it shall be but a civil death, that is, of them as witnesses only, not a natural death as men; and so the same persons shall rise again, and enjoy the fruits of their former labours and ascend into a greater glory. (Mr Thos. Goodwin.)

Ver. 8. *And their dead bodies*] This shows it cannot be meant of a natural death; for how should their bodies lie dead (in that sense) for three years and a half, or (say as it were) for a shorter time ?

Of the great city] Rome, of whose greatness Lipsius and Stapleton have written. See chap. xvii. 18, and xviii. 2—6. Hence she is called the great whore, and great Babylon, not without reference unto the old Babylon; which was so great a city, that when it was taken by Cyrus, some part of it knew not what condition they were in till three days after. (Herodot. Arist. Pol.)

Where also our Lord was crucified] For he was put to death by a Roman judge, by a Roman authority, by a kind of death proper to the Romans, &c. He is also crucified in Rome in his members, word, spirit, and worship.

Ver. 9. *Three days and a half*] i. e. For a short time, till out of their ashes others should arise to stickle for Christ. The pope never rested, but had one or other faithful witness to oppose him; either to his face (as Joannes Sarisburiensis, *Qui præsens præsentem Pontificem redarguit;* and Mancinellus, who reproved Alexander VI. in a sermon at Rome, and had therefore his hands cut off, and his tongue cut out, whereof he died), or else in some more remote part of his dominion, as Savonarola (whom Guicciardin and Mirandula highly commend), Petrarch, who writeth thus, *Babylon altera, nempe propinquior, atque recentior, adhuc stat, cito itidem casura, si essetis viri;* Babylon would soon down, would you but play the men; besides a cloud of other witnesses, that might here be called in. (Jac. Rev.)

Not suffer their dead bodies] So fulfilling that, Psal. lxxix. 2. Some they would not suffer to be buried; others they digged up again after burial, as (besides many of our martyrs) they unburied and burned the bones of Hermannus Ferrariensis after they had sainted him, because he was said to have followed the doctrine of the Waldenses, those ancient Protestants. (Jac. Rev.) Cardinal Pole had a purpose, if he had lived, to have taken up King Henry VIII.th's body, and to have burned it. It was generally observed, that as Winchester and Bonner did always thirst after the blood of the living, so was Cardinal Pole's lightning (for the most part) kindled against the dead; and he reserved this charge only to himself.

Ver. 10. *Shall rejoice over them*] As they did at the Council of Constance, when they had burnt John Huss and Jerome of Prague. So upon the news of the bishop burnt at Oxford, Gardiner came out rejoicing to the Duke of Norfolk; Now, said he, let us be merry and go to dinner. But it was the last he did eat, and he went to hell to digest it too.[1] So upon the news of the French massacre, a jubilee was proclaimed at Rome; the Cardinal of Lorrain gave a thousand crowns to the messenger; the pope caused the massacre to be painted in his palace. Those of Ireland he will surely portray in his chapel or oratory. (Thuanus.)

These two prophets tormented them] As Elias did Ahab, Jeremiah and Amos their flagitious countrymen, and as the martyrs here did their persecutors. Dr Fuller came to William Woolsey his prisoner, and said, Thou dost much trouble my conscience; wherefore I pray thee depart and rule thy tongue, so that I hear no more complaint of thee, and come to church when thou wilt, &c. The end of carnal joy is sorrow (saith Mr Bradford, martyr, in a certain letter). Now let the whoremonger joy with the drunkard, swearer, covetous, malicious, blind-buzzard, St John. For the mass will not bite them, nor make them to blush as preaching will. Now may they do what

they will; come devils to the church, and go devils home; for no man must find fault; and they are glad of this. Now have they their heart's desire, as the Sodomites had when Lot was gone, &c.

Ver. 11. *And they stood upon their feet*] That is, they set themselves stoutly and vigorously to fight against Antichrist. As William Ockam, who being excommunicated by the pope for writing some things against him, fled to Ludovicus the emperor, who was likewise excommunicated, and said unto him, *Tu me gladio defende a Papæ injuriis, et ego te verbis ac scriptis defendam,* Defend thou me with arms, and I will defend thee with arguments. The bishops also of those times that sided with the emperor, though they were none of the best, yet they resolved and avowed never to yield to the pope, *Sed si excommunicaturus veniret, excommunicaturus abiret, cum aliter se habeat antiquorum canonum authoritas.*

Ver. 12. *To heaven in a cloud*] As Christ did. See the note on ver. 7.

And their enemies beheld] Not without rage and regret to see how they were crossed, and the truth more and more propagated. *Trucidabantur et multiplicabantur,* saith one. The Church as the lily is increased by its own juice; *Totum mundum sanguine et oratione convertit,* saith Luther; She converts all the world by her sufferings and supplications.

Ver. 13. *A great earthquake*] Since the Reformation, what stirs and broils have there been all over Christendom! God's sword hath ridden circuit, Ezek. xiv. 17, and is not yet sheathed, nor can it, Jer. xlvii. 6, 7, as being still in commission.

And the tenth part, &c.] *Ruit alto a culmine Roma.* Louis XII., king of France, threatened that he would destroy Rome, and coined money with an inscription to that purpose, *Se perditurum Babylonem cui cum hac inscriptione monetæ, minatus est.* George Fransperg (a general under Charles Bourbon), that sacked the city of Rome, caused a halter to be carried near his colours, saying that with that he would hang the pope; encouraging his soldiers (who were most of them Lutherans) with the great opportunity they had to get spoils. (Hist. of the Council of Trent.) But the sins of that city are not yet full.

Gave glory to the God of heaven] Confessed their sins, as Achan, and changed their minds, as those Mal. iii. 18. It is said of the Burgundians, that being afflicted and oppressed by the Huns, they applied themselves to Christ the God of the Christians, whom, after a long debate, they concluded to be the Almighty God. (Alsted. Chron.)

Ver. 14. *The second woe is past*] Visionally past, not eventually.

The third woe] Woe to the wicked, but joy to the saints. At once the sun rises upon Zoar, and the fire falls down upon Sodom. Abraham stands upon the hill, and sees the cities burning.

Ver. 15. *Great voices in heaven*] i. e. Great joy and triumph in the Church militant.

Are become the kingdoms] They have re-

---

[1] *In terris manducant quod apud inferos degerunt.*

nounced Popery, given up their names to the gospel, and received the Reformation.

For ever and ever] Not for a thousand years only, as the millenaries hold.

Ver. 16. *And the four and twenty elders*] See the note on chap. iv. 9.

Ver. 17. *Because thou hast taken*] Thou hast slain and subdued those thine enemies, that sent messengers after thee, saying, " We will not have this man to rule over us."

Ver. 18. *Were angry*] *Sed vanæ sine viribus iræ;* the wrath of these men turned to the glory of God.

That they should be judged] According to their prayer, and thy promise, chap. vi. 10, 11.

And shouldest destroy them] God usually retaliates and proportions jealousy to jealousy, provocation to provocation, Deut. xxxii. 21; frowardness to frowardness, Psal. xviii. 26; contrariety to contrariety, Lev. xxvi. 18, 21; destruction to destruction, as here. He pays them home in their own coin.

Ver. 19. *And the temple of God*] Abundance of light shall be diffused in the Church, and heavenly mysteries more clearly revealed and more commonly understood.

The ark of his testament] That is, the secret mysteries of God. The ark was in a secret place; and seen by none but the high priest once a year.

And there were lightnings] Utter destruction to the wicked, as there was to Jericho, at the sound of the seventh trumpet, Josh. vi. 16.

CHAPTER XII.

Ver. 1. *And there appeared*] THIS and the two next following chapters are an exposition of the former vision.

A great wonder] As shadowing out and showing great wonders.

In heaven] That is, in the Church, or (according to some) in the visible heaven, where sun, moon, and stars are.

A woman] *Alma mater Ecclesia.* The Church is called a woman, for her, 1. Weakness; 2. Fruitfulness; 3. Lovingness, 2 Sam. i. 26.

Clothed with the sun] With Christ's own comeliness, Ezek. xvi. 14. She is also conspicuous, Matt. v. 14, and scorched with persecution, Cant. i. 6. All which notwithstanding she is comely. *Uxor fulget radiis mariti,* saith the Civilian.

And the moon under her feet] She treads upon the world's trash, bears patiently all changes and chances; and though the curs of the world bark at her, she shines still :

En peragit cursus surda Diana suos.

A crown of twelve stars] A crown in token of victory.

Twelve stars] Those white horses, chap. vi. 2, the twelve apostles and their successors, in and by whom mystical Christ goeth forth conquering and to conquer.

Ver. 2. *And she being with child*] And so soon smelt out by the bears of the world. *Ursa prægnantem mulierem non solum uteri gravitate notam, sed eam etiam quæ pridie conceperit, solam ex omni turba consectatur.* (Bodin. Theatr. Nat.)

Cried travailing] Being hard beset with cruel persecutors, she longs to be delivered of a Christian emperor, that might put her out of her pain and misery.

She cried] viz. In her prayers to God and apologies to men.

Ver. 3. *Another wonder in heaven*] That is, in the Church, which is called heaven ; for, 1. Its original is from heaven, John i. 13. 2. Its tendency to heaven, Heb. xi. 14. 3. Its conversation in heaven, Phil. iii. 20. 4. Its dependence upon heaven, James i. 17.

A great red dragon] A dragon the devil is called for his sharp-sightedness (the dragon hath a very quick eye, and is said to sleep with open eyes, Mr Arrowsmith), as also for his mischievousness to mankind ; and lastly for his serpentine subtilty, Gen. iii.[1] The comfort is, that as the devil is a lion, so is Christ; there is courage for courage. And as the devil is a serpent, so Christ compares himself to the brazen serpent ; there is wisdom for wisdom. A great dragon the devil is, as being god of the world ; and red all over with the blood of souls, which he hath swallowed down, as St Peter hath it, 1 Pet. v. 8. It noteth him also to be a fiery dragon, fiery red, full of wrath and rancour.

Seven heads] To plot, and ten horns to push men into the pit of hell.

Seven crowns upon his head] Pretended authority for what he did against the Church. It passed in France in manner of a proverb, that the modern Council (of Trent) had more authority than that of the apostles, because their own pleasure was a sufficient ground for the decrees, without admitting the Holy Ghost. That popish council was carried with such infinite guile and craft, that the Papists themselves will even smile in the triumphs of their own wits (when they hear it but mentioned) as at a masterstratagem. By these seven crowns some understand the supremacy of the Roman empire, prevailing against the Church.

Ver. 4. *And his tail drew*] A monstrous tail for length and strength. One interprets it of his dog-like flattering tail, whence the proverb grew, *Cauda blandiri,* κέρκῳ σαίνειν. Julian the Apostate drew many from the faith by flatteries and fair promises. Luther was offered a cardinalship to be quiet. (Bp. Carlton's Thankf. Remem.) The pope offered Queen Elizabeth to confirm the English Liturgy by his authority, granting also the use of the sacraments under both kinds, so that she would join herself to the Roman Church. And how the pope clawed our king when he was in Spain, A. D. 1623, is better known than that I need here to relate. (Jac. Revius, vit. Pontif.)

And the dragon stood before the woman] This

[1] δ ράκων παρὰ τὸ δέρκειν. παρὰ τὸ ἐρᾶν ἄχος. Scalig.

implieth, 1. His readiness and nearness ; 2. His instance and diligence.

For to devour her child] As that dragon Pharaoh (so he is called, Isa. li. 9) sought to make away the new-born babes of Israel, Exod. i. Thus the dragon Maximinus devoured Alexander the son of Mammæa ; and thus Decius devoured the two Philips, because they seemed somewhat to favour the Christians. Thus Philip, king of Spain, suffered his eldest son Charles to be murdered by the cruel Inquisition, because he was any whit inclinable to the reformed religion. Constantine the Great had liked to have lost his life for the like cause, but that God strangely preserved him for a better purpose.

Ver. 5. And she brought forth a man-child] Constantine, the Christian Church's first and chief champion.

Who was to rule all nations] The whole Roman empire, but especially to overrule and subdue the Church's many and mighty enemies, as Constantine did most notably.

Caught up to God and to his throne] To rule in the Church next under God himself. And to this height of honour he was caught when the empire was cast upon him, not once thinking of it. *Bonus Deus Constantinum magnum tantis terrenis implevit muneribus, quanta optare nullus auderet,* saith Augustine. (De Civ. Dei, v. 25.)

Ver. 6. And the woman fled] viz. After the battle mentioned in the next verse was fought and finished. See ver. 13, 14.

Into the wilderness] This notes her afflicted and desolate condition, forced now to live in poverty and exile.

Where she hath a place] To wit, that temple that was so exactly measured, chap. xi. 12, called here a wilderness, as was that of Judea, Matt. iii., because but thinly inhabited. The elect are but a handful to a houseful of Atheists and Papists. Or else in allusion to the wilderness of Arabia, through which the Israelites fled from that dragon Pharaoh.

That they should feed her there] Those two prophets, chap. i. 1, were appointed to feed these hidden ones, Psal. lxxxiii. 3, with the hidden manna, Rev. ii. Their time and hers agree.

Ver. 7. And there was war] viz. Whilst the woman was bringing forth ; and after that her son was advanced to the empire.

Michael and his angels] Constantine and his armies.

Against the dragon] Maximinus, Maxentius, Licinius, and other tyrants, acted and agitated by the devil.

Ver. 8. And prevailed not] They were so totally routed and ruined, that they could never rally or rage any more. *Jucundum Christiano homini spectaculum est, quasi coram cernere certantem Christum cum Antichristo,* saith one, concerning Luther's reformation. (Scultet. Annal.) It was a pleasant sight to see Christ and Antichrist striving for the better. For whatsoever the pope with his bulls, or the emperor with his light-bolts, did to hinder it, still the gospel ran and was glorified ; and as then, so ever since, maugre the malice of Rome and of hell. Their late utmost endeavours, and some successes for a season, were but as the last spruntings or bitter bites of dying beasts.

Ver. 9. Was cast out] Full sore against his will. If the enemies had but as much power as malice, the Church should never rest. But they shall be utterly routed and outed, as at this day they are here to our great comfort.

That old serpent] When he was young he outwitted our first parents, 2 Cor. xi. 3, then when their reason was not depraved. Now that he is old, and we but children, Eph. iv. 14, had we not need look to him, and not be ignorant of his wiles ?

Which deceiveth the whole world] Having for that purpose his set and composed machinations, 2 Cor. ii. 11, his methods artificially moulded, Ephes. vi. 11, his depths, sleights, coggings of a dice, &c. And herein he is incessantly exercised, as the participle of the present tense noteth, ὁ πλανῶν.

Ver. 10. And I heard a loud voice] Great joy was throughout the Churches of Christ, as great cause there was, when Constantine came to the empire. That was very remarkable, that Constantine being now a conqueror, should cause a table to be hanged up on high before the doors of his palace, wherein was painted a dragon that lay thrust through with a dart under his own and his subjects' feet. (Euseb. in Vita Constan.)

For the accuser of our brethren] So the devil is called, saith one, in direct and full opposition to that special name and office of the Holy Ghost, the Comforter, or pleader for us, παράκλητὸς. The Russians are so malicious one towards another, that you shall have a man hide some of his own goods in the house of him whom he hateth, and then accuse him for the stealth of them ; just so deals the devil many times by God's dearest servants. The word κατήγορος, here rendered the accuser, signifieth not any kind of accuser, saith a learned divine, but such a one as accuseth before a king.

Which accuseth them] And upon some such articles too as he is able to prove against them. Hence he is said to stand at Joshua's right hand, at the upper hand, because his accusation was as true as vehement, Zech. iii. 3. But here is the comfort, Christ appears in heaven for us (as a lawyer appears for his client), to nonsuit all the devil's accusations, Heb. ix. 24. The Spirit also (as an advocate, παρακλητὸς) makes request in our hearts to God for us, and helpeth us to make apologies for ourselves, 2 Cor. vii. 11. But may not the saints say to Satan (first drawing them to sin, and then accusing them) as he did to Joab ? 2 Sam. xviii. 12, 13.

Ver. 11. By the blood of the Lamb] By his merit and spirit, Christ's blood (as Pliny saith of Polium) is a preservative against serpents.

And they loved not their lives] When one said to a certain martyr, Take heed, it is a hard matter to burn ; Indeed, said he, it is for him that hath his soul linked to his body, as a thief's foot is in a pair of fetters. (Acts and Mon.) In the days of that bloody persecutor Diocletian, *Certatim gloriosa in certamina ruebatur*, saith Sulpitius, *multoque avidius tum martyria gloriosis mortibus quærebantur, quam nunc Episcopatus pravis ambitionibus appetuntur.* Those ancient Christians showed as glorious power in the faith of martyrdom, as in the faith of miracles; the valour of the patients and the savageness of the persecutors striving together, till both, exceeding nature and belief, bred wonder and astonishment in beholders and readers.[1] One martyr said, Can I die but once for Christ? Another, Had I as many lives as I have hairs upon mine head, they should all go. *Hanc animam in flammis offero Christe tibi*, saith Jerome of Prague.

Ver. 12. Rejoice, ye heavens] Ye that have your conversation in heaven, and shall shortly remove your tents thither.

Woe to the inhabiters of the earth] Earthworms that load themselves with thick clay, and strive with the toads, who shall die with most earth in their mouths.

And of the sea] Seamen are, for most part, very profane and godless. See Jude 13; Isa. lvii. 20. Mr Brightman by these inhabitants of the sea understandeth the clergymen, as they call them, who set abroach gross, troubled, brackish, and sourish doctrine, which doth rather bring barrenness of godliness to their hearers, and doth gnaw their entrails, than quench their thirst, or yield any other good fruit.

For the devil is come down] Indeed he was cast down; but that the devil dissembles, and makes as if he came for his pleasure-sake, and so makes the best of an ill matter.

Having great wrath] Indignation, commotion of mind, perturbation of spirit, inflammation or heaving of the blood, by apprehension of an injury, θυμὸν. Satan's malevolence was a motive to his diligence. Natural motion is more swift and violent toward the end of it.

Because he knoweth] By the signs of the last judgment, which cannot be far off, and by conjectures, wherein he hath a singular sagacity.

That he hath but a short time] He therefore makes all haste he can to outwork the children of light, in a quick despatch of deeds of darkness. Certain hawks in colder countries are most eager and earnest to take their prey when the day-light there is of least continuance.

Ver. 13. He persecuted the woman] As the matter of his calamity. The devil infinitely hates Christ, and sins that sin against the Holy Ghost every moment. His instruments also, carried with hellish malice, cease not to malign and molest the Church, to their own utter ruin: for Christ must reign when all is done.

Ver. 14. Two wings of a great eagle] That is, sufficient means of safety and protection from peril, Exod. xix. 4. By this great eagle, some mighty personage seems to be designed, Ezek. xvii. 3—7. And this may very well be Constan-

tine, whose peculiar surname was Great: but yet so (saith Mr Forbes) as that the great honour and riches, wherewith, as with wings, he upon good intention endowed the Church, is an occasion to make her flee to the wilderness, all true and sincere religion by degrees decaying in the visible Church.

Where she is nourished for a time] See the note on chap. viii. 9.

A time, times, and a half time] That is, a year, two years, and half a year, even three years and a half, as chap. xi. 9.

Ver. 15. Cast out of his mouth water] Those barbarous nations, Goths, Huns, Vandals, Lombards, others, stirred up by the devil to over-run the empire, and afflict the Church. Or else it may mean those pestilent and poisonful heresies, Arianism, and the rest, wherewith the Church was infested, according to that of Solomon, "The mouth of the wicked belcheth out evil things," Prov. xiv. 28.

Ver. 16. And the earth helped the woman] That is, the multitude of Christians meeting in the general councils, those four first especially held at Nice against Arius, at Constantinople against Macedonius and Eunomius, at Ephesus against Nestorius, and at Chalcedon against Eutyches. These helped the Church exceedingly against inundations of heresies; and were therefore by Gregory the Great received and embraced as the four Gospels.

And the earth opened her mouth] An allusion to Num. xvi. 22. Look how the earth swallowed up those malcontents, so did God root out pernicious heresies with their authors and abettors, by the power of the Scripture and the zeal of the orthodox doctors, so that they suddenly vanished out of sight, after a marvellous manner.

Ver. 17. Was wroth with the woman] Who yet had done him no wrong; but he and his are mad with malice (when their designs miscarry especially), and are ready to sue the Church, as he in Tully did another, *quod totum telum corpore non recepisset*, because he had not taken into his body the whole dagger wherewith he had stabbed him. (Orat. pro C. Rab. Posth.)

To make war] That war which is mentioned chap. xiii. 7.

With the remnant of her seed] As a little seed corn is reserved out of a great heap for store, which is nothing to the whole crop; so is the small number of true believers reserved by grace, nothing to the whole field and crop of the world.

Which keep the commandments] A just description of a godly Christian. *Boni catholici sunt qui et fidem integram sequuntur et bonos mores.* To be sound in faith and holy in life, this is the kernel of Christianity. (Aug.)

CHAPTER XIII.

Ver. 1. And I stood] WHERE I might best see the beast that came out of the sea.

[1] *Non majori unquam triumpho vicimus quam cum decem annorum stragibus vinci non potuimus.* Sulp.

I saw a beast] The Church, flying into the wilderness from the dragon, falls upon this beast, which is nothing better than the dragon under a better shape. *Sic aliud ex alio malum.* This beast is that Antichrist of Rome.

Rise up] Not all at once, but by degrees.

Out of the sea] Out of the bottomless pit, chap. xi. 7 ; 2 Thess. ii. 9.

Having seven heads] To plot.

And ten horns] To push. Craft and cruelty go always together in the Church's enemies. The asp never wanders alone ; and those birds of prey go not without their mates, Isa. xxxiv. 16.

And upon his horns] The kings that are the pope's vassals. See Rev. xvii. 11. These are the props of his power.

The name of blasphemy] This is his true name ; his pretensed name is mystery.

Ver. 2. *Like unto a leopard*] Which is the female among the panthers, the property whereof is, as Pliny telleth us, with her sweet smell to allure the beasts unto her, hiding her terrible head, till she hath them within her reach, and then teareth them in pieces. Just so dealeth Rome with her unhappy proselytes. The Papacy is an alluring, tempting, bewitching religion. No sin past, but the pope can pardon it ; none to come, but he can dispense with it, *Etiamsi per impossibile, matrem Dei quis vitiasset*, said Tecelius.

As the feet of a bear] Which stands firm on her hinder feet, and fights with her fore feet ; so doth the Papacy with its canons, decrees, traditions, &c.

As the mouth of a lion] Wide, ravenous, roaring, and insatiable.

And the dragon gave him his power] This bargain was offered to Christ, Matt. iv., but he would none of it. The bramble in Jotham's parable thought it a goodly thing to reign ; so did not the vine and fig-tree.

Ver. 3. *One of his heads as it were wounded*] Either by the invasion of the Goths ; or by that fatal schism in the Church of Rome, A. D. 1378, when there sat three popes at once for 40 years together : or by the falling away of the Protestants from the Popedom, from the days of Wicliff, John Huss, the Waldenses, Luther, to this present. Bellarmine bewails the business, that ever since we began to count and call the pope Antichrist, his kingdom hath greatly decreased. (Lib. iii. de Papa Rom. cap. 21.) And Cotton the Jesuit confesses, that the authority of the pope is incomparably less than it was ; and that now the Christian Church is but adminutive.

And his deadly wound was healed] By that false prophet, ver. 11, that is, by the Sorbonists, Jesuits, Trent-fathers, and other Popish chirurgeons. The Jesuits give out that the devil sent out Luther, and God raised up them to resist him ; but great is the truth, and will prevail, when all falsehood shall fall to the ground. It is but a palliate cure we here read of.

And all the world] *sc.* Of Roman Catholics.

Wondered] Or had wondered till the beast was wounded.

Ver. 4. *And they worshipped*] Admiration bred adoration. Idolatrous Papists are worshippers of the devil ; whom though in word they defy, yet indeed they deify.

Who is like unto the beast ?] *Papa potest omnia, quæ Christus potest*, saith Hostiensis ; The pope can do whatsoever Christ can do ; yea, and more too, it should seem by these wise wonderers : for who is like unto the beast ? say they. *Papa est plus quam Deus*, saith Francis Zabarel ; The pope is more than a God. And why ? for of wrong he can make right, of vice, virtue, of nothing, something, saith Bellarmine. (De Pap. Rom. lib. iv.) Mosconius cannot be content to derive *papa* from *papæ*, the interjection of admiring, because he is *stupor mundi*, the world's wonderment (that ye may know him to be the beast here mentioned), but he must style him the King of kings and Lord of lords, having ruledom over all rational creatures, *Dulia adorandus*. (De Majestat. Militant. Eccles. i. 1.)

Ver. 5. *And there was given unto him*] As once was to Antiochus, that little antichrist, Dan. vii. 25. What cracks the pope makes of his illimited power and prerogatives, who knows not ? what blasphemies he belcheth out of the fable of Christ, of eating his pork, *Al despito di Dio*, in despite of God ; of suffering himself to be styled "the Lamb of God that taketh away the sins of the world," as Pope Martin IV. did ; of drinking a health to the devil, as another of them did, who hath not heard ? Baronius, at the year 964, reckoning up certain of the popes, calleth them monsters, an abomination of desolation in God's temple, &c. Cardinal Benno saith of Pope Hildebrand, that he was a blasphemer, a murderer, a whoremaster, a necromancer, a heretic, and all that is naught. The Church of Rome (saith another of their own writers) had deserved now for a long time no better of God than to be ruled by reprobates. Marcellus II., pope of Rome, said, that he could not see how any pope could be saved. (Jac. Revius, p. 275.)

Forty and two months] Here Mr 'Brightman calculates and pitches the ruin of Antichrist upon the year 1686, or thereabouts.

Ver. 6. *In blasphemy against God*] As when Pope Leo I. and (after him) Nicholas III. affirmed, that Peter their predecessor was taken into fellowship with the blessed Trinity, as one with them. See ver. 5.

And his tabernacle] Christ's humanity (John i. 14, and ii. 19), this he blasphemeth, by transubstantiating a crust into Christ. Or, the Church of Christ, which he counteth and calleth the synagogue of Satan.

And them that dwelt in heaven] The glorified saints, whom either he despiteth with obtruded honours, such as they acknowledge not ; or else barks and rails at incessantly as arch-devils, detestable heretics, common pests, &c., as Luther, Melancthon, Calvin, whose very name he hath commanded to be razed out of all books, where-soever any man meets with it, *Ubicunque invenitur nomen Calvini, deleatur.* (Ind. Expur.)

Ver. 7. *To make war with the saints*] As he did with the Albigenses, publishing his Crusades against them, as if they had been Saracens, and destroying ten hundred thousand of them in France only, if Perionias may be believed. Not to speak of the many thousands since slain in battle by the pope's champions in Germany, France, Ireland, and now also in England; besides those many more that have died for religion by the bloody Inquisition, by the hands of the hangman, 3600 in the Low Countries by the command of the Duke of Alva, 800 here in Queen Mary's days, &c. The beast hath even made himself drunk with the blood of the saints.

And to overcome them] So it seemed, but so it was not. See Rev. xii. 21. The saints never more prevail and triumph than when it seems otherwise. Of them the enemies may say, as the Persians did once of the Athenians at the field of Marathon (Stobæus),

Βάλλομεν, οὐ πίπτουσι, τιτρώσκομεν, οὐ φοβέονται.

We fell them, yet they fall not; thrust them
through,
They feel no mischief, but are well enough.

Over all kindreds and tongues] Here the Holy Ghost points to the Popish Catholicism. The Jesuits will still needsly have the Roman Church to be the Catholic Church, though so many kindreds, tongues, and nations have utterly disclaimed it. Herein they are like that mad fellow Thrasilaus in Horace, who laid claim to all the ships that came into the harbour at Athens, though he had no right to the least boat there.

Ver. 8. *Whose names are not written*] He then that lives and dies a Papist cannot be saved.

Slain from the foundation] sc. 1. In God's purpose; 2. In his promise; 3. In the faith of his people; 4. In the sacrifices; 5. In the martyrs; the first that ever died, died for religion. Christ undertook to pay our debt in the fulness of time; and hence we were enlarged. A man may let a prisoner loose, upon a promise to pay the debt a year after.

Ver. 9. *If any man have an ear*] q. d. Let all that have souls to save, beware of this beast; for is it nothing to lose an immortal soul? to purchase an ever-living death? *Purus putus Papista non potest servari.* Confer Rev. xix. 21. It is confessed of all, that a learned English apostate Papist cannot be saved.

Ver. 10. *He that leadeth into captivity*] q. d. Be of good cheer; Antichrist shall one day meet with his match, drink as he brewed, be paid in his own coin, filled with his own ways, have blood again to drink, for he is worthy. See Isa. xxxiii. 1, and 2 Thess. i. 6.

Here is the patience] q. d. Here is matter for the trial exercise and increase of the saints' graces. Hard weather tries what health. The walnut-tree is most fruitful when most beaten. Or, here

is support for the saints, and that which may well make them to hold out faith and patience.

Ver. 11. *And I beheld another beast*] Another in shape, but the same in substance with the former. For here Antichrist appears not as an emperor, but as an impostor. That these two are both one, see Rev. xvii. 11, and xix. 20.

Coming up out of the earth] Set up by earthly men and earthly means, of base beginning, *Gigas quasi νηγενὴς. Ego supernas, vos infernates estis,* saith our Saviour to the Jews, "I am from above, ye are from beneath; "ye are earth-sprung, as so many mushrooms, John viii. 23.

And he had two horns] Two horns in his mitre, two keys in his hand, two swords borne before him, a two-fold pretended power, secular and sacred, as king and priest, in the Lamb's stead, whose ape he is.

Spake as a dragon] That is, saith Diodatus, he used an absolute command over consciences, raised himself through devilish pride and execrable boasting, Rev. xviii. 7. Or thus; though he hath two horns like the Lamb, that is, professeth the meekness and innocency of Christ, yet he speaks like the dragon, which is to be understood partly of his blasphemies, partly of his diabolical doctrines, partly of hellish courses thundered out against true professors, and partly of his great promises to those that adore him. (Downh. of Antich.)

Ver. 12. *And he exerciseth*] The power of speaking blasphemies, of waging wars, of ruling over kindreds, tongues, and nations, &c., notwithstanding his wounded head, which is after a sort cured by the sedulity and subtilty of the Jesuits, and other the pope's emissaries. The first beast, saith Forbes, is the kingdom of Rome under the Pontificality; the second beast is the Pontificality wonderfully quickening the wounded beast to that estate; both are one and the same, except in consideration, as I have said.

Ver. 13. *And he doth great wonders*] By his art of juggling; for true miracles he can do none, nor his master the dragon to help him. Hence they are called lying wonders, 2 Thess. ii. 9, 10, sorceries, Rev. xviii. 23, and impostures here, ver. 14.

So that he maketh fire] As another Elias. This the pope doth daily by his excommunications, casting fire-brands, as it were, from on high at those that slight him; and moreover he telleth us of some, that for withstanding his edicts were thunder-struck to death. (Aventin. Annal.)

Ver. 14. *That they should make an image*] An emperor, saith Aretius, an image of him at least, chosen indeed by the seven electors of Germany, but confirmed by the pope; who therefore is said to give life to the image of the beast, whereby he both speaketh and acteth, ver. 15. For if the pope confirm not the new elect, he is no emperor.

Ver. 15. *Should be killed*] What slaughters Charles V. made at Magdeburg and elsewhere by the pope's appointment, and what bloody work hath been done in Germany now for this eight and twenty years, or thereabouts, by the now emperor and his father, against the Protestant party, I need not here to relate.

Ver. 16. *All both small and great*] Emperor and else. The pope having by his nephew persuaded the king of Bohemia, Maximilian (afterwards emperor), to be a good Catholic, with many promises of honours and profits, intimating the succession of the empire, which else he should hardly obtain, was answered by the king, that he thanked his Holiness, but that his soul's health was more dear to him than all the things in the world. Which answer they said in Rome was a Lutheran form of speech, and signified an alienation from that Sea; and they began to discourse what would happen after the old emperor's death. (Hist. of the Coun. Trent, p. 418.)

To receive a mark] The Popish clergy say, that in their ordination they receive an indelible character. They may choose whether they will have it in their foreheads (where it cannot be hid) or in their right hands, where they may either hide it or show it as they think good. See the note on Rev. vii. 3. The mark common to all the Popish rabble is, St Peter's keys branching out itself in every antichristian doctrine and idolatrous practice. I can never sufficiently admire (saith Mr Heyrick) the speech of blessed Luther, who though he was very earnest to have the communion administered in both kinds contrary to the doctrine and custom of Rome, yet he professeth, If the pope, as pope, commanded him to receive in both kinds, he would but receive in one kind. It is a general rule among the best, that what the pope commands, as pope, though it be good or indifferent, as to pray, read, lift up an eye, hand, to wear black or white, &c., it is a receiving of the mark of the beast, &c. (Mr Heyrick's Serm., p. 108.)

Ver. 17. *Might buy or sell*] As at Rome, oaths, laws, vows, are soluble, and all things else are saleable. *Romæ omnia venalia.*

Vendit Alexander cruces, altaria, Christum :
  Vendere jure potest : emerat ille prius.

The pope sells crosses, altars, Christ, and all:
Well he may sell, for he bought them at the stall.

Also it is well known that the pope flatly forbids trade and traffic with all whom he hath excommunicated, as he did with the Albigenses in the Lateran Council, and as he did with one Tooly in Queen Mary's days, who being hanged for felony, and defying the pope, was (after his death) suspended and excommunicated, that no man should eat or drink, buy or sell with him, bid him good morrow. (Acts and Mon.)

Or the name of the beast] To be called a Roman Catholic, which is better esteemed among Papists than the name of a Christian. It is notoriously known, saith Dr Fulke, that the most honourable name of Christian is in Italy and at Rome a name of reproach, and usually abused to signify a fool or a dolt. (Annot. in Acts xi. sec. 4.)

Or the number of his name] That keep some-

what more aloof, and yet privily comply with Papists, and drive the same design with them, though more slyly and covertly, and to themselves perhaps unperceivedly. What is the reason the pope will not dispense in Spain or Italy, if a Papist marry a Protestant, yet here he will; but because such Protestants receive the number of his name, and will soon be drawn to him?

Ver. 18. *Here is wisdom*] That is, work for wisdom, as ver. 10. Here is "the patience and faith of saints."

It is the number of a man] Such as a man, by search, may find out, if he have his wits about him, as we say. Others sense it thus, the whole number of the beast, whatsoever is numbered to belong unto him, is but the number of a man; human inventions and will-wisdom. Men will have it so, and this is the sum of all Popish religion. Or it is called the "number of a man," because men do number. (Mr Cotton.) The philosopher affirms that man is therefore the wisest of creatures, because he alone can number, *Bruta non numerant.* This is an essential difference.

Six hundred threescore and six] Amongst the many conjectures, that of λατεῖνος seems to me most probable, as most ancient and authentic. The year of Rome's ruin is by some held to be 1666. It is plain, saith one, Satan shall be tied up 1000 years; 666 is the number of the beast; Antichrist shall so long reign; these two together make the just number.[1] Luther observeth, that about the year 666, the pope assumed to be ἀνεπεύθυνος, uncontrollable. Others observe, that Phocas (that adulterous assassin), Boniface the purchaser of supremacy, and Mahomet the grand impostor, brake forth together about the same time, to the great devastation and hazarding of all Christendom.

CHAPTER XIV.

Ver. 1. *A Lamb*] In opposition to that counterfeit lamb, chap. xiii. 12. A lion he can show himself at pleasure.

Stood] Ready pressed for action, as at the stoning of Stephen, or he stood sentinel for such as he here reserved to himself under the reign and rage of Antichrist.

A hundred forty and four thousand] The same that were sealed, chap. vii., all the holy martyrs, confessors, believers.

Having his Father's name] His Father and their Father, his God and their God; this was written on their foreheads, as "holiness to the Lord" was upon the high priest's, Exod. xxviii. 36. For the constancy of their confession; they were not "ashamed of the gospel of Christ," Rom. i. 16, nor "afraid with any amazement," 1 Pet. iii. 6.

Ver. 2. *As the voice of many waters*] The word of God (called here a voice from heaven) hath, saith Mr Forbes, three degrees of operation in the hearts of men. 1. It works wondering (as the

---

[1] *Bernardus asseverat Antichristum futurum meridianum dæmonem quia a meridie erit, et ibi sedebit.* In Cant. ser. 33.

sound of many waters) and acknowledging of a strange force and more than human power, Mark xii. 23; Luke iv. 32; John vii. 46. 2. It works not only wonder but fear, as thunder doth ; thus it wrought in Felix, and may do in any reprobate. 3. It works in the elect peace and joy ; it makes music in the soul, far sweeter than that of harpers, 1 Pet. i. 8.

Ver. 3. A new song] See the note on chap. v. 9.

But the hundred, &c.] To whom alone it was given to understand the mysteries of God's kingdom. Others could not skill of it.

From the earth] *i. e.* From the Antichristian rout and rabble. These dunghill cocks meddle not with that jewel, the joy of faith, but speak evil of that they know not.

Ver. 4. Which were not defiled with women] Which have not moiled themselves with fornication corporal or spiritual, as those Israelites, Numb. xxiv., by Balaam's counsel, and as Papists at this day, seduced by those effeminate locusts, chap. ix. 8. As for their shavelings that plead this text to prove marriage a defilement, let them hear the apostle, Heb. xiii. 4, and another almost as ancient: *Si quis coinquinationem vocet commixtionem legitimam, habet inhabitatorem draconem apostatam ;* If any call lawful marriage a defilement, that man hath a devil dwelling in him. (Ignatius.)

These are they which follow the Lamb] · As the seaman's needle doth the north pole ; or as the hop, in its growing, winding about the pole, follows the course of the sun from east to west, and can by no means be drawn to the contrary, choosing rather to break than yield.

These were redeemed] For royal use. See ver. 3.

Being the first-fruits] Separated and sanctified unto him from the rest of the world.

Ver. 5. And in their mouth] Children they are that will not lie, Isa. lxiii. 8, neither is a deceitful tongue found in their mouth, Zeph. iii. 13. They will rather die than lie. The officers of Merindol answered the bishop that moved them to abjure, that they marvelled much that he would go about to persuade them to lie to God and the world ; affirming that they punished their children very sharply when they took them with a lie, even as if they had committed a robbery, for the devil is a liar. (Acts and Mon. fol. 866.)

For they are without fault] 1. By imputation ; 2. By inchoation.

Ver. 6. And I saw another angel] This is held to be John Wicliff, who wrote more than two hundred volumes against the pope, and was a means of much good to many. The Lady Ann, wife to King Richard II., sister to Wenceslaus, king of Bohemia, by living here was made acquainted with the gospel ; whence also many Bohemians coming hither, conveyed Wicliff's books into Bohemia, whereby a good foundation was laid for the following reformation.

In the midst of heaven] Not *in fastigio cœli*, in the height of heaven, as some render it ; but allow

rather, and as it were in the mid-heaven, because of the imperfection of his doctrine when it was first divulged.

Having the everlasting gospel] The ancient truth, no new doctrine. A gentleman being asked by a Papist, Where was your religion before Luther ? answered, In the Bible, where yours never was. It is called the eternal gospel (saith Brightman), as if the Holy Ghost would on purpose meet with the offence of those times, when the truth (that was restored) should commonly be condemned of novelty.

Ver. 7. Fear God] Let one fear drive out another (as one fire doth another) ; the fear of God, the fear of your fellow-creatures, who draw you to idolatry. For this it is that the second commandment is the first with punishment.

Give glory to him] By confessing your sins and amending your ways. See Josh. vii. 19 ; Jer. xiii. 16.

For the hour of his judgment is come] The judgment that he will exercise upon idolaters and their mawmets, as once in Egypt. See John xii. 31 ; Acts xvii. 30, 31 ; Acts xiv. 15.

And the fountains of waters] *Quantum miraculi sit in admiranda illa fluminum perennitate, nemo, credo, philosophorum satis explicare hactenus potuit*, saith Bucholcer.

Ver. 8. And there followed another angel] Martin Luther with his book De Captivitate Babylonia, which when Bugenhagius first read, he rashly censured for the most pestilent book that ever was written ; but upon better deliberation he retracted his former sentence, and became a means to convert many others.

Of the wine of the wrath] Of the intoxicating enraging wine, that sets men a madding after her :

Nam Venus in vinis, ignis in igne furit.

There is a story of Walter Mapes, sometime Archdeacon of Oxford, who relating the pope's gross simony, concludes his narration thus, *Sit tamen Domina materque nostra Roma baculus in aqua fractus : et absit credere quæ vidimus.* Rome had ravished this man out of his wits.

Ver. 9. And the third angel] Understand by this third angel, all the reformers and preachers of the gospel after Luther, to the end of the world.

If any man worship] See Mr Perkins's Treatise. A Papist cannot go beyond a reprobate.

And receive his mark] He saith not this of those that have the name or the number of the beast. For we doubt not but many were carried away by him, as those 200 were by Absalom in the simplicity of their hearts, 2 Sam. xv. 11, knowing nothing of his treason.

Ver. 10. Of the wine of the wrath of God] Wine for wine. God delights to retaliate and proportion ; as he that said, *Fumos vendidit, fumo pereat*, He sold smoke, and by smoke let him perish. *Imposturam faciunt et patientur*, as the emperor said of them that sold glass for pearls : They cozened others, themselves shall be cozened much more.

Without mixture] viz. Of mercy, with which God usually moderateth the cup of believers' afflictions. See James ii. 13. They only sip off the top of God's cup, *Illud tantum quod suavius est et limpidius :* Reprobates drink the dregs. They shall have an evil, an only evil without mixture of mercy, Ezek. vii. 5. Judgment without mercy, darkness without light. Philosophers say that in this world *non dantur puræ tenebræ,* there is no mere darkness; but reprobates, that here preferred darkness before light, shall be cast into utter darkness without the least glimpse of light. *Non surget hic afflictio.* God will make an utter end; " Affliction shall not rise up the second time," Nahum i. 9. The wicked shall be totally and finally consumed at once.

In the presence of the holy angels] Who shall be not spectators only, but executioners also, as once at Sodom.

In the presence of the Lamb] Notwithstanding their *Agnus Dei's,* and other superstitious trumperies.

Ver. 11. *And the smoke of their torment*] *Utinam de gehenna ubique dissereretur,* saith Chrysostom. Would to God men would everywhere think and talk more of hell, and of that eternity of extremity that they shall never else be able to avoid or to abide. Surely one good means to escape hell is to take a turn or two in hell by our daily meditations.

Ver. 12. *Here is the patience*] See chap. xiii. 10. The beast, being thus declared and declaimed against, will rage above measure ; hold out therefore, faith and patience.

Ver. 13. *A voice from heaven*] That voice of Christ, John v. 24 ; viii. 51.

Write, Blessed are the dead] Though by the pope accursed and pronounced damned heretics.

Which die in the Lord] Especially if for the Lord ; which is (saith Father Latimer) the greatest promotion in the world, such as is not granted to any angel in heaven.

From henceforth] As well as heretofore in those primitive persecutions. Or, from henceforth, that is, presently from the very time of their death, ἄπαρτι, *evestigio, a modo, ab ipso mortis tempore.* This puts out the very fire of purgatory ; for if all believers die in Christ, and are blessed, and that presently, then none are to be purged.

Rest from their labours] The sleep of these labourers, oh how sweet is it ! *Quale sopor fessis in gramine*—they get the goal, they enter the haven :

> *Italiam socii læto clamore salutant.*

A Christian here is like quicksilver (which hath in itself a principle of motion, but not of rest), never quiet ; but as the ball upon the racket, ship upon the waves, &c. Death brings him to his rest, Isa. lvii. 2.

And their works follow them] They die not with them, as Hortensius's Orations did. *Mors privare potest opibus, non operibus,* Death may deprive a man of his wealth, but not of his works.

Ver. 14. *A sharp sickle*] An instrument to cut down corn, Deut. xvi. 9, and the bunches and branches of the grapes, Isa. xviii. 5. It betokens sharp and sudden vengeance. What more beautiful to behold than the field before harvest, than the vineyard before the vintage, &c. ? This is spoken for the consolation of the persecuted people of God.

Ver. 15. *Thrust in thy sickle*] This is not a command, but a request of the faithful, which is soon fulfilled. It is like that of the Church, Psal. cii. 3, " Arise, O Lord, and have mercy upon Zion ; for the time to favour her, yea, the set time, is come."

Ver. 16. *And he that sat on the cloud*] That is, Christ, who soon condescendeth to the suits of his servants. *Iste vir potuit quod voluit,* said one concerning Luther. The death of Arius was *precationis opus, non morbi,* the fruit of prayer, rather than the effect of his disease, saith another. He was brought to confusion by the prayers of Alexander, the good bishop of Constantinople.

Ver. 17. *And another angel*] The community of faithful Christians that combine against Antichrist, to pull him out of his throne and cut his comb.

Ver. 18. *And another angel*] A type of true pastors, saith Mr Forbes ; by whose plain and powerful preaching the other are informed and stirred up to consecrate their hands to the Lord. Such an angel was Zuinglius, who died in battle ; such was Beza in that battle that was fought *in campis Druidensibus ;* such were the Angrognian ministers, and such were sundry of our late army preachers, Mr Marshal, Mr Ash, my dear brother Mr Thomas Jackson, now of Gloucester, &c.

Which had power over fire] Not *Christum et Evangelium flammeum prædicans,* as a popish varlet slandered Beza at the forementioned sight, but as the pacifying the fire of contention amongst brethren, and setting them all together against the common enemy.

Thrust in thy sharp sickle] Fall on, quit you like men, be valiant for the Lord of hosts ; " Cursed is he that doth the Lord's work negligently. Cursed is he that withholdeth his sword from blood." Thus the faithful ministers strengthened the hands and hearts of the soldiers to battle, and made them stick close to their colours and commanders.

Are fully ripe] Ripe for vengeance, as the Amorites were, when they had filled the land from one end to another with their uncleanness, Ezra ix. 11. About the year of grace 1414, Theodoricus Urias, an Augustinian in Germany, complained, that the Church of Rome was then become, *ex aurea argenteam, ex argentea ferream, ex ferrea terream, superesse ut in stercus abiret ;* of gold silver, of silver iron, of iron earth, which would shortly turn to muck. (Jac. Revius.)

Ver. 19. *And the angel thrust in*] Down go the Antichristians immediately, by the power and prowess of the Christian armies, thus edged and eneagered by their preachers. This we have seen fulfilled in our late wars to our great comfort, at Edge-hill and Nazeby fight especially.

Into the great wine-press] *Lacus iste locus cædis.* This wine-press is called Armageddon, chap. xvi. 16.

Ver. 20. *And the wine-press was trodden*] viz. By Christ the King, with his heavenly horsemen, chap. xix. 13, 14.

Without the city] i. e. Without the Church, haply in Judea, whither the pope being driven from Rome, shall fly and sit, till Christ shall unroost him with the brightness of his coming, 2 Thess. ii. 8.

Even unto the horse-bridles] To confute the pride and cruelty of those bloody Papists that threatened to ride their horses up to the saddle-skirts in the blood of the Lutherans. (Flac. Illyr.) So Farnesius, Minerius, Felix of Wurtemburg, Sir Charles Ellerker, Charles IX. of France, that cruel Queen, who when she saw some of her Protestant subjects lying dead, and stripped upon the earth, cried out, The goodliest tapestry that ever she beheld. These and the like shall be one day glutted with blood, which they have so barbarously thirsted after. *Satia te sanguine, quem sitiisti,* &c., as she said of Cyrus. (Justin, lib. i.)

CHAPTER XV.

Ver. 1. *And I saw another sign*] DISTINCT from the former, and describing the utter overthrow of Antichrist in this and the following chapters.

Great and marvellous] A just wonder it was indeed, the miracle that we in these last times are to look for, that the kingdom of Antichrist should be so easily and suddenly overturned by the preaching of the gospel, as once the walls of Jericho were by the blowing of rams' horns.

Seven angels] i. e. Certain chieftains of the reformed Churches.

Having the seven last plagues] Being the several parts of the seventh trumpet, and said to be the last that shall in this life be inflicted; though far worse follow in hell, whereof all these are but typical. Here the leaves only (as it were) fall upon reprobates, but hereafter the whole trees. Here they pay but the use-money only, but there the whole principal.

Ver. 2. *As it were a sea of glass*] The word of God mingled with the virtue of the Holy Ghost, say some. The world full of affliction, say others.

Having the harps of God] Hearts full of heaven.

Ver. 3. *And they sing*] There cannot but be music in the temple of the Holy Ghost.

The song of Moses] As being delivered out of spiritual Egypt.

And the song of the Lamb] That mentioned chap. xiv. 3, and the same in effect with that of St Paul, 1 Tim. i. 15, 17.

Ver. 4. *Who shall not fear thee*] q. d. How mad are the enemies, how sottish is the world that fear not thee who art the proper object of fear! Psal. lxxvi. 11. The Greeks call him Θεὸς, quasi Δεὸς, fear; the Chaldee *Dechilah* for the same reason; and Jacob styled him "The fear of his father Isaac."

For thou only art holy] Before it had been said of his Holiness, Who is like unto the beast? Now, Who shall not fear thee, O Lord? for thou only art holy.

For all nations shall come] As being deeply affected with thy heaviest plagues upon Antichrist; they shall better bethink themselves, "They shall return and discern betwixt the righteous and the wicked," Mal. iii. ult.

Are made manifest] i. e. Are begun to be, and more and more shall be, if our sins hinder not.

Ver. 5. *The temple of the tabernacle*] These words are all one with those chap. xi. 19, to the consideration whereof we are here recalled, after so long an interruption.

Ver. 6. *Clothed in pure*] Habited as holy priests.

With golden girdles] Here an interpreter gives this note, that they which are lewd and vicious, though never so wise, politic, rich, and valiant, shall not be God's instruments to plague Antichrist and his kingdom. (Mr Bernard.) This their priestly apparel showeth also how that these angels come forth in the Church's cause, and for her sake, without any by and sinister respect. They are all of them sincere professors of the truth of Christ, their breasts girded with the golden girdles of truth.

Ver. 7. *And one of the four beasts*] The faithful pastors, by their divine discourses of the pure worship of God, the intolerable tyranny of Antichrist, &c., stir up the spirits of God's servants to set themselves against that man of sin, and to execute upon him the judgment written. "This honour have all his saints," Psal. cxlix. ult.

Seven golden vials] Vessels of large content, but narrow mouths; they pour out slowly, but drench deeply, and distil effectually the wrath of God, which may be let out in minims, and yet do great matters; as there may be much poison in little drops. These vials are said to be golden, to show that this anger is holy.

Full of the wrath of God] Filled out of the cup of his wrath, mentioned in the former chapter.

Ver. 8. *And the temple was filled*] This shows that God graciously approves and miraculously protects the reformed Churches. See Exod. xl. 34, 35; 1 Kings viii. 10. So he did the Hussites in Bohemia. All Germany was up in arms against them. *Actum jam de Hussitis videbatur. Verum Germani, nondum viso hoste, Panico terrore perculsi, diffugerunt,* saith the historian. And when things seemed to be in a desperate condition, the Germans, smitten with a panic terror, fled all away before they had looked the enemy in the face. How wonderfully is Geneva preserved in the midst of many mighty enemies! What should I speak of Rochelle relieved, and Leyden rescued, both from heaven! We of this nation have lately seen as much of God's glory and power in our temple as ever did any.

Till the seven plagues] No Antichristian could understand the end of the seven plagues, till beaten into a better mind. *Vexatio dat intellectum.*

CHAPTER XVI.

Ver. 1. *Go your ways*] A PROOF of the divine calling of the ministers of the gospel. This commission came out of the temple, as obtained by the prayers of the saints.

Pour out the vials] See the note on chap. xv. 7.

Upon the earth] Upon Antichrist and his adherents. *Roma facta est ex aurea ferrea, ex ferrea terrea*, said one of her own favourites. It is said, chap. xii. 16, that the earth helped the woman; and yet here that the vials of God's wrath were poured out upon the earth; to teach us, saith one, that men may be useful for the public, and yet not freed from God's wrath. But that by the by only.

Ver. 2. *And the first went*] They went not all at once. Note the patience of God, waiting men's return unto him.

Upon the earth] Antichrist's footstool, his branded slaves.

A noisome and grievous sore] The French disease, say some; the devil's disease, say others, viz. spite and envy at the Reformation wrought in Bohemia, Germany, England, &c., upon the discovery of the Papists' hypocrisy and filthiness.

Ver. 3. *Upon the sea*] The popish council (called a sea, from the concourse thereunto from all parts), that of Trent especially, with their deadly decrees, making the traditions of the Church the rule of faith, &c. And these deadly decrees were written with the blood of heretics.

Died in the sea] As the fishes of Jordan do as soon as they fall into the *Mare mortuum*, and as the fishes in the river Nile did, when the waters thereof were turned into blood.

Ver. 4. *Upon the rivers, &c.*] The persecutors and impostors, the Jesuits especially, who have lately added twelve new articles (by the authority of Pope Pius IV.) raised out of the Council of Trent, and added to the Nicene Creed, to be received with others as the true catholic faith, to be believed by as many as shall be saved. And those that receive them not, are not suffered to live amongst them. This is worse than the six articles in Henry VIII.'s time, that whip with six cords, as they called it. See these twelve articles in the Epist. prefixed to Bishop Jewel's works.

Ver. 5. *The angel of the waters*] The same that poured forth his vial upon the waters, ver. 4.

Thou art righteous] God's judgments are sometimes secret, always just, and so to be

acknowledged. We shall one day see the reason of all, and say as Jehu did, 2 Kings ix. 36.

Ver. 6. *For they have shed*] As Minerius that monster, the cruel Duke of Alva, bloody Bonner, the Guises, and other of the pope's champions. Duke d'Alva boasted of it, that he had put 36,000 Protestants to death; but they were rescued by the goodness of God and by the prowess of Queen Elizabeth, and now they are got from under the altar, as ver. 7. (Acts and Mon.; Camden.)[1]

Thou hast given them blood to drink] As Tomyris dealt by Cyrus, the Parthians by Crassus, the Romans by those Jews that cried out, "His blood be upon us," &c., as our laws do by the priests and Jesuits, and those that receive them, proceeding against such as traitors to the state. The putting out of the French king's eyes, who promised before with his eyes to see one of God's true servants burned; the death of Charles IX. of France, author of the Parisian massacre, by exceeding bleeding at sundry parts of his body; who seeth not to be the just hand of God upon them? This Charles beholding the bloody bodies of the butchered Protestants, in that execrable massacre, and feeding his eye upon that woeful spectacle, breathed out this bloody speech, *Quam bonus est odor hostis mortui!* How sweet is the smell of a slain enemy! and shortly after breathed out his accursed soul, *Inter horribilium blasphemiarum diras*, saith the historian, *tantam sanguinis vim projiciens*, &c., after that Beza had forewarned him (but in vain) by that verse,

Tu vero Herodes sanguinolente time.

So Julian, Attila, Felix of Wurtemburg, Henry III. of France, stabbed in the same chamber wherein he, then being Duke of Anjou, had contrived the French massacre. So let thine enemies perish, O Lord.

Talia quisque luat, qualia quisque facit!

Ver. 7. *And I heard another*] That in the mouth of two witnesses this truth might be established. Let God be justified, and every mouth stopped.

Out of the altar] Under which lie the souls of those that were slain for the testimony of Jesus, chap. vi. See the note above on ver. 6.

Ver. 8. *Upon the sun*] The pope's supremacy, say some, the Scriptures, say others, by the light whereof they are laid open to the world (dancing naked in a net, and yet not seeing their own nakedness, as Mr Philpot, martyr, told Chadsey), and by the dint whereof, " God smites the earth," Isa. xi. 4, that is, the consciences of those popelings, glued to the earth. He even " hews them by his prophets, and slays them by the words of his mouth," Hos. vi. 5. But this interpretation touching the Scriptures some hold to be dangerous; because upon what subject soever these vials fell, the wrath of God fell together with

---

[1] See the Mirror or Looking-glass both for Saints and Sinners, set forth by my most loving and highly honoured friend, Mr Sam. Clarke, pastor and preacher of the word at Bennett Fink, London; unto whom not only I give thanks for his help in this publication, but also all the Churches that shall get good thereby.

them upon the same, ver. 1; they understand therefore by sun the house of Austria, or the highest authority that holds on Rome.

Ver. 9. *And men were scorched*] Or parched, scalded, roasted, ἐκαυματίσθησαν. This is by accident in regard of the Scriptures; for the Lord speaketh peace to his people; and his word is good to those that are good, Micah ii. 7. But as Origen saith of devils, so may we say of Papists; there is no greater torment to them than the word of God. *In hoc eorum omnis flamma est, in hoc uruntur incendio.* Hence they burn up Bibles, *tanquam doctrinam peregrinam*, as strange doctrine. (Spec. Europ.) Hence they censure St Paul as savouring of heresy, and could find in their hearts to purge his Epistles. Eckius is not afraid to say, that Christ did never command his disciples to write, but to preach only. (Enchirid. loc. com. cap. Eccles.) Bellarmine saith, the Bible is no more than *commonitorium*, a kind of storehouse for advice. Hosius saith that the pope's interpretation, though it seem never so repugnant to the Scripture, is nevertheless *ipsissimum Dei verbum*, the very word of God. The Council of Basil answered the Hussites (requiring Scripture proofs for such doctrines as were thrust upon them), that the Scriptures were not of the being of the Church, but of the well-being only; that traditions were the touchstone of doctrine and foundation of faith.

And blasphemed the name of God] The truth of God contained in the Scriptures. What a devil made thee to meddle with the Scripture? said Stephen Gardiner to Marbeck. They tell us of divers that have been possest by that means; and assure us that our condemnation is so expressly set down in our own Bibles, and is so clear to all the world, that nothing more needs hereto than that we know to read, and to have our eyes in our heads at the opening thereof. (Alex. Cook.)

Ver. 10. *Upon the seat of the beast*] This city of Rome, which was never yet besieged (since it became the seat of Antichrist) but it was taken, and shall be again shortly to purpose. Rather, say some, by seat is meant his kingdom, the pope's singular sole authority and monarchical frame of church government.

And his kingdom was full of darkness] ἐσκοτωμένη. It appeared to be so (as motes appear in the sunshine) by the clear light of truth shining upon it. A Scottish mist is here already fallen upon a piece of his kingdom, and what further service God hath for their and our armies to do against the pope in Ireland, or elsewhere, we expect and pray God grant us good agreement among ourselves, and then much may be done abroad.

And they gnawed their tongues] Being as mad with malice, as Boniface VIII. was of discontent, who being suddenly taken prisoner at his father's house by Sara Columnus his mortal enemy, and brought to Rome, laid up in the castle of St Angelo, within thirty-five days after most miser-

ably died in his madness, rending himself with his teeth, and devouring his own fingers. (Turk. Hist. i. 26.)

Ver. 11. *And blasphemed the God of heaven*] As they did in '88, when the Spaniards gave out that Christ was turned Lutheran; and as Faux the gunpowder traitor did, when he told those that took him, that not God, but the devil, had brought to light and to nought that desperate design. (Lonicer. Theatr. Histor.) Thus they set their mouths against heaven, and their tongue walketh through the earth; as if Augustus Cæsar were dealing with some god Neptune; or the three sons, trying their archery at their father's heart, to see who can shoot nighest. What an execrable blasphemy is that of John Hunt, a Roman Catholic, in his humble appeal to King James in the 6th chapter of that Pamphlet: "The God of the Protestants is the most uncivil and evil-mannered God of all those who have borne the names of gods upon the earth, yea, worse than Pan, god of the clowns, which can endure no ceremonies nor good manners at all." See Dr Sheldon's Mark of the Beast.

And repented not] This leopard (chap. xiii. 2) can never change his spots, because they are not in the skin, but in the flesh and bones, in the sinews and most inward parts. Tigers rage and tear themselves at the sound of a drum, and at the smell of sweet spices; so do these savage Papists, when called to repent.

Ver. 12. *Upon the great river Euphrates*] i.e. Upon whatsoever yet hindereth the destruction of spiritual Babylon and the coming in of the Jews, as the Turkish empire.

That the way of the kings] Christians, say some, who are kings in righteousness, and come from the East, or from Christ, "That dayspring from on high," Luke i. 78. Others understand this text of the Jews, who are most of them in the East, dispersed through Turkey, Tartary (the ten tribes especially), and China.[1] Junius saith, that which is called the "land of Sinim," Isa. xlix. 12, may probably be meant of China; which if it be the meaning, there may be many of the Jews, whose conversion we daily expect and pray for. See Isa. xi. 15, 16; Zech. x. 10, 11.

Ver. 13. *Three unclean spirits*] Spiritual fathers, as the Papists call their Jesuits, who seek to subject all to the pope, and the pope to themselves, being *ultimus diaboli crepitus*, as one speaketh, the last attempt of a daring devil. These are the pope's janizaries, bloodhounds, vultures, whose nest (as Aristotle saith) cannot be found, yet they will leave all game to follow an army, because they delight to feed on carrion.

Like frogs] For their filthiness, impudency, loquacity, with their continual brekekekex coax coax. (Aristoph.)

Come out of the mouth] That is, by the counsel and command, by virtue of that vow of mission, whereby the Jesuits are bound to the pope, to go whither he shall send them, about whatso-

[1] Tartars of Tothar, a remnant or residue.

ever attempt he shall enjoin them. Yea, if their governors command them a voyage to China or Peru, without dispute or delay they presently set forward. Hence haply they are called spirits.

Ver. 14. The spirits of devils] Or breathing devils.

Working miracles] Lying wonders, 2 Thess. ii. 9.

Unto the kings of the earth] The pope's nuncios, legates *a latere*, and other emissaries, stir up the spirits of princes to embroil the world with wars, for the upholding of his tottering greatness; but all in vain. The greatest impostors have ever been the greatest courtiers. The Arians in their age, and of them the Jesuits learned it. As Pharaoh's frogs, they get into kings' bedchambers.

And of the whole world] Papists shall call in the help of foreign princes out of Asia, Africa, America, to suppress the heretics, as they call them. But with evil success; for they shall associate themselves only to be broken in pieces, Isa. viii. 9. *Exorientur, sed exurentur*, Rev. xix. 18. The mountain of the Lord shall be lifted up above all mountains. These auxiliaries shall speed no better than those subsidiary Syrians, 2 Sam. x. 18, 19.

Ver. 15. I come as a thief] Who gives no warning. See the note on Matt. xxiv. 44. I come suddenly, secretly, yea, and also violently and terribly. See chap. iii. 3; Luke xii. 34; 1 Thess. v. 2.

Blessed is he that watcheth] The prophecy is here interrupted (as Gen. xlix. 18) to fore-warn and fore-arm the saints; Luke xii. 37, 38, 43, they are three times said to be blessed that watch.

And keepeth his garments] Keepeth himself unspotted of the world, undefiled in the way.

Lest he walk naked, &c.] See chap. iii. 18.

Ver. 16. And he gathered] God hath an overruling hand in that which the frogs of Rome do at the courts of kings, and ordereth the disorders of the world to his own glory.

Called in the Hebrew Armageddon] That is, they shall receive such a famous foil, such as Sisera did at the waters of Megiddo, Judges v. 19.

Ver. 17. Into the air] The popish air, the kingdom of Satan, Ephes. ii. 2.

Saying, It is done] What is done? The mystery of iniquity is abolished, and the mystery of God is fulfilled. So Cicero when he had slain those of Catiline's conspiracy, he came to the people, and said, *vixerunt*, they were alive, but now the world is well rid of them.

Ver. 18. And there were voices] A description of the last judgment, when heaven and earth shall conspire together for the punishment of the wicked. See Matt. xxiv., 2 Pet. iii., and 2 Thess. i. 8.

Ver. 19. And the great city] The whole Antichristian state.

Divided into three parts] By the earthquake

disjected and dissipated. Or, divided into three parts, that is, into three factions, 1. Stiff Papists; 2. Converts; 3. Neuters.

And the cities of the nations] That came to aid Antichrist.

And great Babylon] Augustine and other ancients do call Rome the Western Babylon; and do so compare them, as that Abraham was born in the flourish of the first Babylon, Christ of the second. The Jesuits here, though they grant Rome to be Babylon, yet they would have it to be Rome heathen under the emperors, and not Rome Christian under the popes. But it must be Rome Christian, as it appears by a double departure: 1. Of Babylon from the Church, Rev. xvii. 3. Babylon is called a whore. 2. Of the Church from Babylon, Rev. xviii. 3. The temple of God is the seat of Antichrist, saith Paul, 2 Thess. ii.

The cup of wine] That wherein God delights, as a man would do to drink a cup of generous wine.

Ver. 20. Fled away] Either swallowed up by the water or consumed by the fire.

Ver. 21. A great hail] Bigger than that which brained the kings of Canaan, Josh. x.; perhaps this shall be fulfilled according to the letter. Howsoever, the elements shall melt like scalding lead upon Antichristians and other atheists; and they shall answer for all with flames about their ears.

CHAPTER XVII.

Ver. 1. And there came] This and the following chapters are set for the explanation of the dark and difficult passages in the former, in the three last vials especially.

One of the seven] Probably the seventh.

And talked with me] ἐλάλησε, λαλία, familiarly as the Samaritess with her countrymen, John iv. 42, or as the master with his scholar.

I will show unto thee] Thou shalt not only be an ear but an eye witness.

Segnius irritant animum demissa per aures,
Quam quæ sunt oculis commissa fidelibus.
                                        Horat.

The judgment] The damnation of her; the destruction is reserved to the next chapter.

Of the great whore] The whore of Babylon, more infamous and notorious than any Thais, Lais, Phryne, Messalina, Orestilla (*cujus præter formam nihil unquam bonus laudavit*, Sallust), or Pope Joan, of whom Funccius the chronologer speaketh thus; *Ego Funccius non dubito quin divinitus ita sit permissum ut fœmina fieret Pontifex eadem meretrix, &c.*; I doubt not but that God therefore permitted a notorious harlot to be advanced to the popedom (and this about the very time when the popes were most busy in subjecting the kings of the earth, and making them their vassals), that he might point out to men this whore here mentioned, with whom the kings of the earth committed fornication.

Ver. 2. *With whom the kings*] As submitting their sceptres to his keys; and becoming his feudatories.

And the inhabiters of the earth] So that she is not a noble whore only, but a common strumpet, prostituting herself to the meanest for their money, as in the pardon office.

Have been made drunk] Hence it is so difficult to convert idolaters: there is no dealing with a man that is drunk. "Whoredom and wine take away the heart," Hos. iv.

Of her fornication] Both spiritual and corporal. *Sixtus Quintus lupanar utriusque Veneris Romæ condidit* (saith Agrippa) *et decessit tabidus voluptate.*

Ver. 3. *Into the wilderness*] Whither the true Church fled, chap. xii., of which they must be (saith one) that can learn to know the Romish Church to be a whore, condemned of God.

I saw a woman] See the note on ver. 1.

Sit upon] Not going a-foot, as Christ and the apostles did, but magnificently mounted, as the pope is ever, either upon a stately palfrey (emperors holding his stirrup) or upon men's shoulders. England was once called the pope's ass, for bearing his intolerable exactions. This ass he held by the ears instead of a bridle.

Upon a scarlet-coloured beast] The proper colour of the Court of Rome; and it well serves to set forth their pomp and their hypocrisy. Innocent IV. gave a red hat to his cardinals, to show them (as he said) that they should be ready to shed their blood for the truth. But that painter was nearer the point, who being blamed by a cardinal for colouring the visages of Peter and Paul too red, tartly replied, that he painted them so as blushing at the stateliness and sinfulness of his successors.

Full of names of blasphemy] His head only before was busked with the blasphemy, chap. xiii. 1, now his whole body. Thus evil men and seducers grow worse and worse, deceiving and being deceived, 2 Tim. iii. 13.

Ver. 4. *In purple and scarlet*] Clothing for kings and nobles, over whom this whore domineers much more than the concubines did over the kings of Persia.

And decked with gold] Gr. κεχρυσωμένη, gilded with gold, to note her hypocrisy and outsideness, gold without, copper within. The pope styles himself the servant of God's servants, but yet stamps in his coin, "The nation and country that will not serve thee shall be rooted out." At the absolution of King John of England, 8000 marks of silver were presently delivered to Pandolfus the pope's legate, who trampled it under his feet as contemning that base matter, but yet received it and sent it away to Rome. (Daniel's Hist.)

And precious stones and pearls] Besides the rich stones that are in the pope's triple crown of inestimable price and value, he carries in his pantofle (which he holds out to be kissed) the picture of the cross, set in pearls and precious stones, *Ut plenis faucibus crucem Christi derideat,*

saith Hiedfeld. Pope Sixtus *quintus* was wont to give to Tiresa his harlot, pantofles covered with pearls. He spent two hundred and three-score thousand crowns upon a conduit, which he built for his pleasure; and yet he brought in fifty hundred thousand crowns into the new treasury built by himself in the castle of St Angelo. At the coronation of Pope Leo X., a thousand thousand crowns are said to have been spent in one day. Pope Paul II. was wont to sleep all day, and spend whole nights in weighing monies and beholding jewels and precious pictures, *uno eo die* 1,000,000 *aureorum expendit.* (Jac. Rev. 261.)

A golden cup full of abominations] Gold, if it be right, they say discovers and expels poison. Put poison into a cup of gold, and it will hiss and send up certain circles like rainbows. Hereby is signified (saith an author) that God threateneth judgment and fire to those that pour poison into divine doctrine, as the pope doth with his mad mixtures. He that argued from the letters of Papa, *P. Poculum, A. Aureum, P. Plenum, A. Abominationum,* argued no less wittily than that other, who of Roma made *Radix omnium malorum.*

Ver. 5. *Mystery*] This word mystery is in the pope's mitre, saith Brocard the Venetian, and many more who have been at Rome, and profess to have seen it. (Dr James of the Corr. of Script. Preface.) The whole antichristian state is a mystery of iniquity, 2 Thess. ii. 7, and is much conversant about mysteries, sacraments, ceremonies, pompous rites, &c.: murders, treasons, thefts, &c., they easily dispense with, but none of their ceremonies. Let God, say they, see to the breach of his own law; we will look to ours. Rome was raised in a mystery: she grew to her greatness insensibly and cunningly. Her bishop is both an Æmulus and an opposite to Christ; one that would seem like him, a vice-Christ, ἀντίχριστος, and yet is his chiefest adversary; this is the mystery of iniquity. See 2 Thess. ii. 7, with the note there.

Babylon the great] Rome, resembling the Assyrian Babylon in pride, idolatry, filthiness, but especially in cruelty toward the Church. See the Babylonian cruelty graphically described, Jer. li. 34, and make the comparison.

The mother of harlots] The Church of Rome to this day delights to be styled Holy Mother Church. Holy she is in the sense that the Hebrews call harlots. And such a mother, as bastards have for their mother, by whose name they are called; the father is seldom mentioned by them.

Ver. 6. *Drunken with the blood, &c.*] Bishop Bonner delivered Richard Woodman, with four more, requiring of them to be but honest men, members of the Church Catholic, and to speak good of him. And no doubt (saith Woodman) he was worthy to be praised, because he had been so faithful an aid in the devil his master's business, for he had burned good Mr Philpot the same morning. In whose blood his heart was so drunk as I suppose he could not tell what he did, as it appeared to us both before and after. For but two days before, he promised us we should be condemned that same day that we were delivered; yea, and the morrow after he sought for some of us again, yea, and that earnestly. He waxed dry after his great drunkenness; wherefore he is like to have blood to drink in hell, as he is worthy, if he repent not, &c. It is wisdom (said a certain unknown good woman in a letter to Bonner), it is wisdom for me and all other simple sheep of the Lord, to keep us out of your butcherly stall as long as we can; especially seeing you have such store already, that you are not able to drink all their blood, lest you should break your belly, and therefore let them lie still and die for hunger, &c. Thus I kept the bandogs at staves' end (said Shetterden the martyr), not as thinking to escape them, but that I would see the foxes leap aboveground for my blood, if they can reach it.

I wondered with great admiration] All things are portentous in the popedom; what monsters were Pope John XII., and Hildebrand, as Luitprandus (Lib. 6, de Reb. Gest. in Europ. in Vita Hildeb.) describes the one, and Cardinal Benno the other, both of their own side. *Tertia classis continet Papas vel potius πώπους,* saith Alstedius. After the thousandth year of Christ, there was nowhere less piety than in those that dwelt nearest to Rome, as Machiavel observeth.

Ver. 7. *Wherefore didst thou marvel?*] *Nil admirari prope res est una, Numici.* We wonder at things out of ignorance of the causes of them. *Hinc admiratio peperit philosophiam.*

Ver. 8. *Was and is not*] Was before the time of this revelation in the Roman government, which was afterwards usurped by the pope. A thing that the first bishops of Rome dreamt not of. And yet Tertullian (Lib. de Pudicitia) taxeth the rising ambition of the popes in his time, thus : I hear, saith he, that there is an edict set forth, and that very peremptory, in these terms, *Pontifex, scilicet maximus, Episcopus Episcoporum dicit,* Thus saith the high priest, the bishop of bishops. (Baron. Annal. tom. 4.) *Odi fastum illius Ecclesiæ,* I hate the pride of the Church of Rome, saith Basil.

Go into perdition] Go, not run; by degrees, not all at once. He now takes long strides toward the bottomless pit; which is but a little before him, and even gapes for him. There stands a cold sweat on all his limbs already.

Shall wonder] Admiration bred superstition; and illumination draws men off it. Julius Palmer, martyr, was a most obstinate Papist all King Edward's days; and yet afterwards, in Queen Mary's time, suffered most cruel death at the Papists' hands at Newbury, for the most ready and zealous profession of the truth. His words to one Bullingham, walking in Paul's after his conversion, were these; Oh that God had revealed these matters unto me in time past! I would have bequeathed this Romish religion, or rather irreligion, to the devil of hell, from whence it came. Believe them not, Bullingham, I will rather have these knees pared off than I will

kneel to yonder jackanapes (meaning the rood).

And yet is] In regard of that imperial power then extant, which the pope should afterwards take to himself.

Ver. 9. *Here is the mind*] q. d. Here is work for wise men to busy their brains about. *Sapientia est vel codicibus vel cordibus.*

Seven mountains] The Jesuits cannot deny but that Rome is here pointed at, as being set upon seven hills, ἑπταλόφος. So the ancient Rome was, whereof the present Rome is but a carcase, retaining nothing of the old but her ruins, and the cause of them her sins.

Ver. 10. *And there are seven kings*] That is, kinds of government.

Five are fallen] Kings, consuls, dictators, decemvirs, tribunes.

One is] i. e. The heathen emperor.

And the other is not yet come] sc. The Christian emperors.

A short space] sc. At Rome; for Constantine soon translated the seat of the empire to Byzantium, calling it Constantinople, and left Rome to be the pope's nest. (Zonaras.) The Emperor Constans, nephew to Heraclius, and after him, Otho, had some thoughts to set up again at Rome, but could not; that so the kingdom of the Church foretold by Daniel might there be seated, saith Genebrard : if he had said the kingdom of Antichrist foretold by John the divine, he had hit it.

Ver. 11. *He is the eighth*] viz. The Pontificality.

And is of the seven] i. e. Shall exercise that monarchical power that was before in the seven heads.

Ver. 12. *Are ten kings*] Of ten several kingdoms, Naples, Spain, Portugal, France, Polony, Bohemia, Hungary, Denmark, Sweden, and this of England, which as it was the first of the ten that submitted to the pope's yoke, so was it the first that shook it off again in Henry VIII.'s time.

Ver. 13. *These have one mind*] This is the unity or rather conspiracy of the Church of Rome. The Spouse only is but one, Cant. vi. 9. Other societies are but as the clay in the toes of Nebuchadnezzar's image, they may cleave together but not incorporate one into another. There is a great deal of seeming unity under Antichrist. The Turks also have as little dissension in their religion as any. But well may that garment have no seam that hath no shape. Bellarmine notes a providence, that in the ninth age there sprang up no new heresy. But how could there, when little religion was on foot besides superstition and heresies?

Ver. 14. *The Lamb shall overcome them*] 1. With a spiritual victory, by a sweet subjection, at least by a conviction of their consciences. 2. With an external victory, as the Imperialists in Germany, the Papists here.

Ver. 15. *Are peoples*] Fitly called waters for their instability and impetuosity.

Ver. 16. *These shall hate*] As base fellows

use to hate their harlots when they find them false.

And shall make her desolate] Shall deny to defend her.

And naked] By denying her maintenance, and laying her open to the world by their remonstrances. King Henry VIII. and the French king, some half a year before their death, were at a point to have utterly rooted the bishop of Rome out of their realms, and to exhort the emperor to do the same, or else to break off from him. The realm of France was ready (upon the pope's refusal to re-bless King Henry IV. upon conversion to them) to withdraw utterly from the obedience of his Sea, and to erect a new patriarch over all the French Church. The then archbishop of Burges was ready to accept it; and but that the pope, in fear thereof, did hasten his benediction, it had been effected, to his utter disgrace and decay. (Spec. Europ.)

And shall eat her flesh] Be so bitterly bent against her, that they could find in their hearts to tear her with their teeth. See Job xix. 22. We read of two notable thieves in the kingdom of Naples (the one called himself Pater noster, and the other Ave Maria) that had slain 116 men at several times and in several places. These two were at length taken and tormented to death by the command of the magistrate, with hot burning pincers, &c., and made to die piecemeal. It were but reason that Christian princes should use like zeal and severity against that grand soul-murderer the pope.

And burn her with fire] For an old bawd. It is reported that in Meroe, the priests of Jupiter had so bewitched the people with their superstition, that they would sometimes send to the king of Ethiopia for his head; which was never denied them, till it came to King Erganes, who upon so insolent a demand slew them all, and took away their priesthood. Why is not the same now done to the bridge-maker of Rome?

Ver. 17. *For God hath put*] As he sent Nebuchadnezzar against Tyre, Alexander against Asia, and Attila against Rome, who surnamed himself the World's Scourge; so he will one day send these kings against Rome. It had been burnt when Charles V. took it, but that the soldiers were kept in by a kind of violence. God's time was not yet come for that purpose.

Ver. 18. *Is that great city*] Rome, that *radix omnium malorum.* This is confessed by Bellarmine, Ribera, Alcasar, and other Jesuits. The Rhemists are so straited, that they know not which way to turn them, or how to deny so clear a truth, which yet they are not willing to acknowledge. The wit of heretics will better serve them to devise a thousand shifts to elude the truth, than their pride will suffer them once to yield and acknowledge it.

CHAPTER XVIII.

Ver. 1. *I saw another angel*] SOME excellent and worthy man (saith Mr Brightman), such a one as should come suddenly before he be looked for, as those things do that slip down from heaven.

Having great power] ἐξουσίαν, or authority; as having in hand a great business, viz. the denouncing of Rome's utter ruin.

And the earth was lighted] He delivered himself clearly and expressly, so as that all men may well understand his meaning. Ribera the Jesuit gives this note upon this text, that the judgment of Rome's desolation shall be (not kept secret, but) made manifest to all men.

Ver. 2. *And he cried mightily*] So to awaken Babylon, that slept no less securely than that old Babylon, whose king Shesach was feasting and carousing in the bowls of the sanctuary, when the city was taken the same night. The people also did so little fear it, that it was three days after the city was taken by Cyrus ere some of them heard what was befallen them. (Herodot. Arist. Pol.)

Is fallen, is fallen] Certo, cito, penitus, or, with a double fall. They have fallen culpably, and shall fall penally. This was also long since foretold by Sibylla in the eighth book of her oracles:

Καὶ σὺ θρίαμβος ἔσῃ κόσμῳ, καὶ ἄοιδος ἀπάντων.
Tota eris in cineres quasi nunquam Roma fuisses.

Rome (during the Roman felicity) was never taken but by the Gauls; but since it became pontifical, it hath been made a prey to all barbarous nations, and never besieged by any that took it not. There yet stands, near at hand, a second Babylon (saith Petrarch), *cito itidem casura, si essetis viri.* This would soon be down, if you would but stand up as men.

The habitation of devils] Which, by a sweet providence of God, for the good of mankind, are banished (as likewise fierce and wild beasts are) to deserts and dispeopled places. See Matt. xii. 43. (It is an allusion to Isa. xiii. 20; and xiv. 23; Jer. l. 39.) Yet not so, but that, by Divine permission, they haunt and pester the greatest throngs of people, yea, the holiest assemblies. Some take the words in another sense, thus, it is become an habitation of devils, that is, of idols; and this hath wrought her ruin. In the year 610, Boniface IV. instituted the feast of All Saints, after that he had begged of the emperor the Pantheon of Rome, which he consecrated to the honour of All Saints, and set up the Virgin Mary in the place of Cybele, the mother of the gods. (Alsted. Chron.)

Ver. 3. *For all nations*] All Roman Catholics.

The merchants of the earth] καπηλεύειν. The popish emissaries that huckster the word and make merchandise of men's souls, 2 Pet. ii. 3, after they have taken them prisoners, and made prizes of them, 2 Tim. iii. 6, αἰχμαλωτίζοντες.

Through the abundance of her delicacies]

στρήνους, or, of her insolencies. *Proh pudor!
hæc res est toto notissima cælo,* sang Petrarch 200
years since, speaking of the luxury and insolency
of the Court of Rome.

Ver. 4. *Another voice*] This was Christ's voice,
whether mediate or immediate it appears not.
See Jer. li. 45.

My people] A people Christ had, and still
hath, where Antichrist most prevaileth. There
are thought to be no less than 20,000 Protestants in Seville itself, a chief city of Spain. Even
in Italy there are full 4000 professed Protestants;
but their paucity and obscurity (saith Sir Edw.
Sands) shall enclose them in a cipher.

Partakers of her sins] *Esto procul Roma qui
cupis esse pius. Roma, vale, vidi, satis est vidisse,
&c.* John Knox refused the bishopric offered
him by King Edward VI., as having *aliquid commune cum Antichristo.* Adam Damlip, martyr,
had been a great Papist, and chaplain to Fisher,
bishop of Rochester; after whose death he
travelled to Rome, where he thought to have
found all godliness and sincere religion. In the
end he found there, as he said, such blaspheming
of God, contempt of true religion, looseness of
life, and abundance of all abominations, that he
abhorred any longer there to abide; although he
was greatly requested by Cardinal Pole there to
continue, and to read three lectures a week in
his house; for the which he offered him great
entertainment. (Acts and Mon.) The like is
recorded of Mr Rough, martyr, that being before
Bonner, he affirmed that he had been twice at
Rome, and there had seen plainly with his eyes
that the pope was the very Antichrist; for there
he saw him carried on men's shoulders, and the
false-named sacrament borne before him; yet was
there more reverence given to him than to that
which they counted their God. Mr Ascham
(schoolmaster to Queen Elizabeth) was wont to
thank God that he was but nine days in Italy,
wherein he saw in that one city of Venice more
liberty to sin, than in London he ever heard of
in nine years. (Mr Fuller's Holy State, f. 159.)

And that ye receive not of her plagues] *Mus-
culi ruinis imminentibus præmigrant, et aranei
cum telis primi cadunt,* saith Pliny: Mice will
haste out of a house that is ready to drop on
their heads, and spiders with their webs will
fall before the house falleth. Cerinthus the
heretic coming into the bath where St John was
washing, the apostle ἐξήλατο τοῦ βαλανείου,
sprang or leapt out of the bath, saith Eusebius
(lib. iv. 14); as fearing, lest being found in his
company he should partake of his plagues. It
is dangerous conversing with wicked men, 1. For
infection of sin; 2. For infliction of punishment.
Ambrose, closing up the story of Ahab and
Jezebel's fearful end, fitly saith thus: *Fuge ergo,
dives, hujusmodi exitum, sed fugies hujusmodi
exitum, si fugeris hujusmodi flagitium:* Fly therefore, O rich man, such an end as Ahab had, by
shunning such evils as Ahab did. (Amb. de
Nab. Jezreel, c. xi.)

Ver. 5. *For her sins have reached*] Gr. ἠκολού-
θησαν, have followed thick or been thwacked
one upon another, thick and threefold, as they
say: there hath been a concatenation, or a continued series of them, ἐκολλήθησαν. Others read,
Her sins are glued and soldered together; or
they cleave and are glued to heaven. Matthew
Paris speaking of the court of Rome, saith, *Hujus fœtor usque ad nubes fumum teterrimum exhalabat:* Her filthiness hath sent up a most noisome stench to the very clouds of heaven, as
Sodom's did; therefore shall Babel (the glory of
kingdoms) be as the destruction of God in Sodom
and Gomorrha, Isa. xiii. 19.

Ver. 6. *Double unto her double*] This is spoken
to the good kings that shall sack Rome, that they
do the Lord's work thoroughly, not sparing Agag,
as Saul did to the loss of his kingdom, nor dismissing Benhadad, as Ahab did to the loss of his
own life.

Ver. 7. *She hath glorified herself*] As mother
of Churches, queen of nations. Steuchus (one
of her parasites) saith, That kings have but the
use and administration of their kingdoms; the
right and property belongs to her. Pope Boniface wrote thus to Philip the Fair, king of France:
*Volumus te scire te in temporali et spirituali nobis
subjacere, &c. Contra sentientes pro insanis hæbe-
mus:* We would ye should know, that ye are to
be subject unto us both in temporals and spirituals; and that none that are in their right
minds can be otherwise minded. The king thus
answered him again, *Sciat tua maxima fatuitas,
&c.,* I would your singular foolishness should
know that I acknowledge no such subjection, &c.
(Alsted. Chron.) It was tartly and trimly replied by one Leonard to Rustandus the pope's
legate, claiming all the churches here in England
to be the pope's, *Omnes Ecclesias Papæ esse, tuitione non fruitione, defensione non dissipatione;*
That if the pope had such right to all the
churches, it was to defend them, not to devour
them. (Jac. Rev. de Vit. Pontif., p. 178.)

So much torment, &c.] Thus the sinner's cup
of honey endeth in the dregs of gall; as Herodotus writeth of the river Hypanis, that the first
day's journey from the fountain and head of it
the water is sweet and wholesome; but after that,
exceeding bitter. Pleasure and pain are tied together with chains of adamant. Oh how short
is the wicked man's Hilary-term!

Ver. 8. *Therefore shall her plagues*] Security
ushereth in destruction. God shall shoot at such
with an arrow suddenly, and fetch them off, as he
did the rich fool, Luke xii.

Come in one day] To confute their fond conceit
of an eternal empire. See the like, Isa. xlviii.
9. When the war began in Germany, A. D. 1619,
it was reported, that a great brass image of the
Apostle Peter (that had *Tu es Petrus, &c.,* Thou
art Peter, and upon this rock will I build my
Church, engraven about it) standing in St Peter's
church at Rome, there was a great and massy
stone fell down upon it, and so shattered it to
pieces, that not a letter of that sentence was left
legible, save these words, *Ædificabo Ecclesiam*

meam, I will build my Church. This was ominous to that tottering title of Rome, and might have taught the popelings, that God is about to build his Church upon the ruins of their worm-eaten title. The Lord thereby seemed to say the same unto them, that once he did to Israel by Ezekiel, "An end is come, the end is come, it watcheth for this, behold it is come," Ezek. vii. 6. *Sed surdis fabulam.* This hath been long and loud rung in their ears, but they will not be warned.

Death] That is, war, that deadly evil, called an evil, κατ' ἀντονομασίαν, Isa. xlv. 7, " I make peace, and create evil," that is, war : a woeful evil that hews its way through a wood of men, in a minute of time, from the mouth of a murdering-piece, and causeth thousands to exhale their breath without so much as " Lord, have mercy upon us." Hence the poet:

Omega nostrorum mors est, Mars Alpha malorum.

And mourning] πενθος. For the loss of dead friends.

And famine] The usual concomitant of war, in sieges especially. See the note on Rev. vi. 5.

For strong is the Lord] Full able to effect it, seem it to Babel's brats never so improbable or impossible.

Ver. 9. *Shall bewail her and lament*] κόψουσι, As with the " voice of doves, tabering upon their breasts," Nahum ii. 7. The chief of these mourners shall be the Spaniard likely; who yet hath no such great cause, if he look well about him; for he is yearly excommunicated by the pope, for detaining him from the kingdom of Sicily, as Baronius witnesseth. (In Respon. Apol. ad Card. Colum.) It were to be wished that he would imitate his predecessor Charles V., who upon a displeasure conceived against Pope Clement VIII., abolished the pope's authority throughout all Spain, *Exemplo ab Hispanis ipsis posteritati relicto, posse Ecclesiasticam disciplinam citra nominis Pontificii authoritatem conservari*, saith mine author, *i. e.* The Spaniards themselves setting forth to the world that the Church may be governed without the pope's authority. (Scultet. Annal. Decad. ii. p. 2.) But this Charles did in a passion only, and not from a settled resolution. For after this, when Pope Clement and his cardinals were imprisoned by the duke of Bourbon's men in St Angelo, Cæsar in Spain forbade all interludes to be played; and pageants prepared for the joy of the birth of his son Prince Philip to be pulled down. In France, by the court of Parliament, the duke of Bourbon was condemned of treason, his name and memorial accursed, his arms pulled down, his lands and goods confiscated. Neither would King Henry of England answer the emperor's letters, whereby he excused himself from having any hand in the action. (Speed, 1012.)

Ver. 10. *Standing afar off*] As fearing their own safety, they will not venture themselves for an old withered harlot, that is now (Lais-like) ready to be extinct in the last act of her uncleanness, Λαΐς τελευτῶσ' ἀπέθανε βινουμένη. (Athenæus, xiii.)

For in one hour] God will make short work of it when once he begins, Rom. ix. 28. This should be an encouragement to Christian princes and states, to set upon the service. The pirates' war was *incredibili celeritate et temporis brevitate confectum*, saith Austin, soon despatched ; so shall this. Papists vaunt now of their temporal felicity, as a note of their Church, and make catalogues of the strange victories that the Catholics have had. Bellarmine brags, that *vix unquam fuerunt hæretici superiores quando justo prælio dimicatum est* (tom. ii. lib. 4, cap. 14), the heretics scarce ever had the day when it came to be tried in a just battle. But if all this had been true (as it is not), yet at last, in one hour shall their judgment come. See chap. xix. 20, 22, with the notes.

Ver. 11. *And the merchants of the earth*] The pope's indulgencers, and other officers of his exchequer. What huge sums of money did Tecelius and his companions rake together out of Germany. The pope had yearly out of England above nine tons of gold ; Polydore Virgil was his collector of the Peter-pence here. Otto (one of the pope's *muscipulatores*, mice-catchers, as the story calls him) departing hence, left not so much money in the whole kingdom as he either carried with him or sent to Rome before him. (Joh. Manl., loc. com., p. 492.) It was truly and trimly said by Pope Innocent IV., *Vere enim hortus deliciarum Papis fuit tum Anglia, et puteus inexhaustus*, England was then a gallant garden to the pope, and a well-spring of wealth that could not be drawn dry. (Speed, 1027.) Cardinal Wolsey emptied the land of twelve-score thousand pounds, to relieve and ransom Pope Clement VII., imprisoned by the Duke of Bourbon. And being himself sent ambassador beyond sea for the pope's release, and coming through Canterbury toward Dover, he was seen to weep tenderly at mass for the pope's calamity.

For no man buyeth their merchandise] Men shall see further into their fopperies and knaveries than to endure to be any longer gulled and cheated. William of Malmesbury began to groan long since under the grievance. *Romani hodie* (saith he) *auro trutinant justitiam, pretio venditant canonum regulam :* The Romans now-a-days sell justice, sacraments, masses, dispensations, benefices, all. Mantuan comes after, and cries out,

——— *venalia nobis*
Templa, sacerdotes, altaria, sacra, coronæ,
Ignis, thura, preces, cœlum est venale, Deusque.

Temples, priests, altars, rites (I tell no tale),
Crowns, sacrifices, heaven, and God, are set to sale.

The leaguers here for the liberty of the kingdom in the days of King John, drove Martin, the pope's publican, out of the land; the king also cursed him grievously at parting, with *Diabolus te ad inferos ducat et perducat.* (Jac. Revius, lib.

iii., de Pont. Rom., cap. xxi.) But now much more than ever these merchants want chapmen, as Bellarmine sadly complains ; their markets are well fallen, their Euphrates much dried up.

Ver. 12. *The merchandise of gold*] All this is taken out of Ezekiel xxvii. All countries have catered and purveyed for the pope, who hath had it either in money or other commodity ; but money answered all things.

Thyine wood] A wild kind of cedar, very sweet and sound ; for it will not easily rot.

Ver. 13. *And cinnamon*] Galen writes that in his time cinnamon was very rare, and hard to be found, except in the storehouses of great princes. And Pliny reports, that a pound of cinnamon was worth 1000 *denarii*, that is, 150 crowns of our money.

And chariots] Or sedans, as we call them.

And slaves] Gr. σώματα, bodies, so slaves are called, because their master's commands reach only to their bodies, and not to their souls.

And the souls of men] Tecelius, the pope's pardon-monger, persuaded the people in Germany, that whosoever would give ten shillings should at his pleasure deliver one soul out of the pains of purgatory ; and as soon as the money rang in the bason, that soul was set at liberty. But if it were one jot less than ten shillings, it would profit them nothing. This gainful gullery Luther cried down with all his might, and so marred the market. This gave occasion to that saying of Erasmus, whom when the Elector of Saxony asked, why Luther was so generally hated ? He answered, For two faults especially ; he hath been too busy with the pope's crown and the monks' paunches. (Scultet. Annal. dec. i.)

Ver. 14. *And the fruits*] Those first ripe fruits, Micah vii. 1, greedily desired and bought up at any rate by the richer and daintier sort of people.

Which were dainty and goodly] Gr. λιπαρὰ καὶ λαμπρὰ, fat and fair-liking, pleasant to the eye as well as to the taste, confections, suckets, sweetmeats, second and third services.

Ver. 15. *Which were made rich by her*] By their fat benefices, commendams, golden prebendaries, some one yielding ten or twenty thousand by the year. The archbishopric of Toledo is worth a hundred thousand pounds a year ; which is a greater revenue than some kings have had. (Spec. Europ.) What a vast estate had Wolsey gotten. So that rich and wretched Cardinal Henry Beaufort, bishop of Winchester, and Chancellor of England in the reign of Henry VI., who asked, Wherefore should I die being so rich ? (Acts and Mon.)

Ver. 16. *With gold and precious stones*] All these avail not in the day of wrath. Neither need we envy wicked men their plenty ; it is their portion, all they are like to have. The whole Turkish empire is nothing else, saith Luther, *nisi panis mica, quam dives paterfamilias projicit canibus*, a crust cast to the dogs, by God the great householder. I have no stronger

argument (said the same Luther) against the pope's kingdom, *quam quod sine cruce regnat*, than this, that he suffered nothing. Surely there is the more behind, there will be bitterness in the end, no doubt.

Ver. 17. *So great riches come to nought*] Gr. ἠρημώθη, is desolated, or become a wilderness. Petrarch writeth, that in the treasury of Pope John XXII. were found by his heirs two hundred and fifty tons of gold. And of Boniface VIII. it is recorded that he was able to show more money than all the kings in Christendom.

And every shipmaster] *i. e.* Cardinal, patriarch, archbishop, though but titular and imaginary, without jurisdiction, as are the patriarchs of Constantinople, Antioch, Jerusalem, and Alexandria, which the pope successively consecrates, ever since the Holy Land and the provinces about it were in the hands of Christian princes, A. D. 1100, so loth is the pope to lose the remembrance of any superiority or title that he hath once compassed. (Spec. Europ.)

And all the company] The cardinals and archbishop's train and retinue, those in office especially. What a pompous family kept Wolsey, consisting of one earl, nine barons, very many knights and esquires, and others, to the number of four hundred. (Rex Platon., p. 26.)

And sailors] Bishops, abbots, priors, &c. In a parliament holden here at Leicester, A. D. 1413, in the reign of Henry V., a complaint was exhibited against the Popish clergy's excess. This bill (saith E. Hall the chronicler) made the fat abbots to sweat, the proud priors to frown, the poor friars to curse, the silly nuns to weep, and all her merchants to fear that Babel would then down. But God's time was not yet.

And as many as trade by the sea] All the clergy, the Jesuits especially, without whose lusty help (saith Mr Brightman) St Peter's fish-boat had stuck in the sand, and had rushed against the rocks long since.

Ver. 18. *What city is like unto this*] q. d. Who would have ever thought we should ever have seen this dismal day of Rome's destruction ? It was wont to be said, *Roma cladibus animosior*, Rome is unconquerable. The pope wrote once to the Turk that threatened him,

Niteris incassum Petri submergere navem ;
Fluctuat, at nunquam mergitur illa ratis.

Ver. 19. *And they cast dust*] As men willing to be as far under-ground as now they were above-ground. Having lost their livelihood, they had little joy of their lives.

All that had ships in the sea] All churchmen, *i. e.* all, for the most part ; some of them have little enough. Sanders was starved. Stapleton was made a professor of a petty university, scarce so good as one of our free-schools. On Harding his Holiness bestowed a prebend of Gaunt, or (to speak more properly) a Gaunt prebend. Allin was commonly called the starveling cardinal.

Ver. 20. *Thou heaven*] *i. e.* The Church on earth.

And ye holy apostles, &c.] *i. e.* Ye pastors and teachers, who as ye have been most shot at by her, so now you are especially called to triumph over her, Psal. lviii. 11.

Ver. 21. *And a mighty angel*] For further assurance a sign is added, and an allusion made to Jer. li. 63. And here it is easy to observe a notable gradation, an angel, a strong angel taketh a stone, and a great stone, even a millstone, which he letteth not barely fall, but casteth, and with impetuous force thrusteth into the bottom of the sea, whence it cannot be buoyed up. Thus is set forth to the eye also the irreparable ruin of Rome.

Ver. 22. *And the voice of harpers, &c.*] Thine organs and sackbuts, thy chanting and church-music, shall cease.

And the sound of a millstone] Anciently they used hand-mills, which did make a great noise in the cities, as Diodate here noteth.

Ver. 23. *And the light of a candle*] The candle of the wicked shall be put out, they that here love darkness better than light shall hereafter be thrust into σκότος ἐξώτερον, outer darkness, where they shall never see the light again till they see all the world on a light fire.

For thy merchants were the great men] The pope creates his cardinals by these words, *Estote fratres nostri et principes mundi*, Be ye brethren to us, and princes of the world. They hold themselves kings' compeers.

Ver. 24. *And in her was found*] Rome hath ever been the slaughter-house of the saints, as Jerusalem was before her, Matt. xxiii.

And of all that were slain] For she hath a hand in all the wars of Europe, besides all the Christian blood shed by her instigation, in those holy wars, as they called them, for the recovery of the land of Canaan.

CHAPTER XIX.

Ver. 1. *I heard a great voice*] In obedience to that exhortation, chap. xviii. 20, Rejoice over her, thou heaven, &c.

Saying, Alleluia] *i. e.* Praise the Lord. Was not he a wise man that gave this derivation of the word *Al altissimus, le levatus est, lu lugebant apostoli ja jam resurrexit? Acutum sane decompositum.* This word is in the Old Testament first used, Psal. civ. 35, where consuming of sinners is mentioned, as in the New Testament here, where the destruction of Antichrist is foretold. Praise is therefore here given to God in the Hebrew tongue, saith Mr Bulkly, because the Hebrews or Jews shall acknowledge the Lord Jesus with us.

Unto the Lord] Gr. Is the Lord's, as Psal. iii. 8. He is the true proprietary.

Ver. 2. *Which did corrupt the earth*] I read of one, who journeying to Rome, as soon as he came within the city shut his eyes, and so kept them; as resolving to see nothing in that city (which he knew to be very corrupt, and a cor-rupter of others) but only the Church of St Peter. (Sphinx Philos. p. 753.) See the note on chap. xviii. 4.

Ver. 3. *And again they said, Alleluia*] As unsatisfiable in performing so divine a duty. Some think that the Hebrew word is retained to import that after Rome is ruinated, the Churches of the Gentiles shall by their incessant praises provoke the Jews to join with them, and con-celebrate the mercy; like as the Spouse, by praising her Beloved, stirred up those dull daughters of Jerusalem to seek him with her, Cant. v. 9, 10, with chap. vi. 1.

And her smoke rose up] Like that of Sodom. Yet wretched Romanists will not be warned, whose judgment therefore is here revealed after that of the sitting of Rome.

Ver. 4. *And the four and twenty elders*] The former Alleluiah was more private; every good heart being lifted up with joy and thankfulness, when first they hear the good news of Antichrist's overthrow. Now is this the joint Alleluiah of the public congregation, praising and magnifying God. This may be a further means to move the Jews to come in.

Ver. 5. *And a voice came out*] This is the Lamb's voice, his all-quickening voice, which shall rouse and raise the dead and dedolent Jews; powerfully pulling the veil from their hard hearts, which yet were somewhat moved and mollified by the former Alleluiahs, so that now all the serv-ants of God, small and great, Jew and Gentile, shall praise him with one consent.

Ver. 6. *And I heard as it were the voice*] See how morigerous the saints are, and ready-hearted to obey God. No sooner are they bidden to praise God, but they are at it, *dicto citius.* See the like Psal. xxvii. 8.

Saying, Alleluia] This was the Hosanna Rabba, as the Jews call it; the *victoria Hallelujatica*, as the old Britons called their victory over the Saxons. The story is this. Under the conduct of Germanus (here in Britain), who came over from France to subdue the Pelagian heresy (which then prevailed amongst us), against a mighty army of Saxons and Picts, the Britons prevailed only by the three times pronouncing the word Hallelujah; which voice echoing and redoubling from the acclamation of his followers among the mountains, nigh to which the enemy had encamped, frighted them and won the conquest, upon which it was called *victoria Hallelujatica.* (Dr Ussier, de Brit. Eccles. Primord. p. 332.)

Reigneth] *i. e.* He now maketh it appear that he reigneth, which Averroes and some other of the world's wizards doubted of, yea, denied; be-cause they saw bad men prosper, good men suffer.

Ver. 7. *Hath made herself ready*] Being first made ready by the grace of Christ. *Certum est nos facere quod facimus; sed ille facit ut faciamus.* (Aug.) The bowls of the candlestick had no oil but that which dropped from the olive-branches, Zech. iv.

Ver. 8. *And to her was granted*] It is here

clear (saith Bernard) that there shall be as great difference between the state of God's Church now, and that which is to come after Rome's ruin, as between the time of honourable persons only betrothed, and the high, joyful, and glorious day of their public marrying; as between the time of a king coming on to his kingdom, and his actual and powerful reigning as king indeed.

That she should be arrayed] This also is given her, as well as her rich raiment; which she can no more put on by herself than she can purchase it.

Clean and white] Or, pure and bright. Pure, saith one, because imputed righteousness is pure indeed, and hath no spot in it; but not bright; you can see no great matter in it; it maketh no great show before men (as inherent righteousness doth, Matt. v. 16), but before God. A man may be very much defiled and subject to many scandals, and yet be clothed with the garment of imputed righteousness.

The righteousness of saints] Gr. righteousnesses, that twofold righteousness, imputed and imparted.

Ver. 9. *Write*] To wit, this ensuing sentence, for the use of posterity, worthy to be written in letters of gold.

Blessed are they that are called] So they have hearts to come at Christ's call, and not show themselves unworthy to taste of his supper by framing excuses, as those recusant guests did, Luke xiv.

These are the true sayings of God] q. d. This foregoing sentence is "a faithful saying, and worthy of all acceptation," 1 Tim. i. 15.

And I fell at his feet] So taken he was with the joyful tidings of his countrymen's (the Jews') conversion, that he fell down as Abraham did upon the good news of Isaac's birth, Gen. xvii. 17. And it may be he took this angel for Christ, the Angel of the covenant; but that was his error. *Triste mortalitatis privilegium est, licere aliquando peccare.* (Euphor.)

See thou do it not] ὅραμὴ, an elliptic and concise kind of speech in the Greek, betokening haste and displeasure at that was done. Papists will needs despite the angels with seeming courtesies and respects; and whereas the Council of Laodicea (cap. 35) saith, it behoveth Christians, ἀγγέλους μὴ ὀνομάζειν, not to pray to angels, Surius and Caranza make the words to be, *Non oportet Christianos ad angulos congregationes facere;* and the title they make *De iis qui angulos colunt*, in a clean contrary sense to the Council's intention.

Ver. 11. *And I saw heaven opened*] i. e. He saw things done before his eyes, as it were; so do not we, but are left to conjectures. Here is showed, saith one, the foil of the beast, bearer up of the whore, and no question but now highly chafed with her fall. This is the last and noblest act of Christ's riding, for the dragon and his vicars' utter destruction. Thus he. Here is showed, saith another interpreter, in what state the Church shall be in, upon the ruin of Rome, even as people standing in arms under their General Christ Jesus for a time, till the last battle be fought, and the enemies destroyed.

Behold, a white horse] Christ riding as an Emperor triumphing, and as a righteous Judge, Psal. ix. 8, and xcvi. 10, 13.

Ver. 12. *His eyes were as a flame of fire*] A quick-sighted Judge, an intelligent warrior. "Counsel and strength are for the war," 2 Kings xviii. 20.

And on his head were many crowns] Let the triple-crowned pope look to himself; Christ outcrowns him by far.

And he had a name written] His holy and reverend name Jehovah, importing his Godhead; for he is "Jehovah, our righteousness," Jer. xxiii. 6. And as thus, no man knows the Son but the Father, Matt. xi. 26; for as God he is incomprehensible, Judg. xiii. 18. "What is his name, or what is his Son's name, if thou canst tell?" Prov. xxx. 4. "Who shall declare his generation?" Isa. liii. 8. Or by this unknown name may be meant his dignity of being Head of his Church; which is incommunicable to any other, Phil. ii. 9.

Ver. 13. *Dipt in blood*] In the blood of his enemies, as a victor returning from a huge slaughter. Cæsar is said to have taken prisoner one million of men, and to have slain as many; Mahomet I. (emperor of the Turks), to have been the death of 800,000 men; Scanderbeg, to have slain 800 Turks with his own hand. But our Conqueror shall outdo all these; when he shall tread them in his anger, and trample them in his fury; and their blood shall be sprinkled upon his garments, and he will stain all his raiment, Isa. lxiii. 3.

The word of God] John i. 1, and v. 7. Hereby it appears that this was John the Evangelist that wrote this book. *Idiotismus Joannis.* (Pareus.)

Ver. 14. *And the armies which were in heaven*] The heavenly-minded heroes that fight his battles, are all in his livery, horsed and habited as he, in whom they are more than conquerors, because they are sure to conquer before they fight.

Ver. 15. *A sharp sword*] The word, Ephes. vi. 17; the rod wherewith he smiteth the earth, Isa. xi. 4; the breath of his mouth, whereby Antichrist shall be overthrown, as by force of arms, so also of arguments.

The nations] The paganish papagans. See the book entitled Paganopapismus; wherein is proved that papism is flat paganism, and that the Papists do resemble the very pagans in above seven-score several things.

And he treadeth the wine-press] At Armageddon, chap. xvi. 16.

Ver. 16. *And on his thigh*] Where his sword hangs, Psal. xlv. 3, to show that he will keep what he hath gained (*Vincere scis Hannibal, victoria uti nescis*, said one),[1] or "on his thigh," *qui filiabitur nomine ejus*, Psal. lxxii. 17, the name of

---

[1] *Non minor est virtus quam quærere, parta tueri.*

Christ shall endure for ever; it shall be begotten, as one generation is begotten of another; there shall be a succession of Christ's name; "he shall see his seed, he shall prolong his days, and the pleasure of the Lord shall prosper in his hands," Isa. liii. 10. Confer Gen. xlvi. 26. Or, "on his thigh," that is, on his lower parts, his people. Christ "will make the place of his feet glorious," Isa. lx. 13, that is, the Church in their lowest condition.

Lord of lords] This title the pope usurps; but what said Miconius in a letter to Calvin upon the view of the Church's enemies? *Gaudeo quod Christus Dominus est; alioqui totus desperassem,* I am glad that Christ is Lord of lords, for else I should have been utterly out of hope.

Ver. 17. *Standing in the sun*] Where he might best be heard, as a herald. And he well types out such, as by clear light of truth shall make known the certain destruction of the enemies, before the battle be fought.

Unto the supper of the great God] They that would not come to the supper of the Lamb shall be made a supper to the fowls of heaven.

Ver. 18. *That ye may eat*] He alludes to Ezek. xxxix. 4, 17. Gog and Magog were a type of Antichrist: "Behold, I am against thee, O Gog, the chief prince of Meshech and Tubal, saith the Lord," Ezek. xxxviii. 3; where, if Gog be the Great Turk, and Meshech Cappadocia, where he first settled himself, why should he be called "prince of Tubal" also, that is, of Spain, France, and Italy, as Jerome and Josephus interpret it (neither do Bellarmine and Gretser dissent)? Is it not to show that, after the fall of Babylon, the Antichristians shall call in the Turk and other pagan princes to invade and distress the Church, that they may all perish together, and feed the fowls with their dead carcases?

Ver. 19. *And I saw the beast*] The Church's enemies are even ambitious of destruction. Judgments need not go to find them out; they run to meet their bane.

Ver. 20. *And the beast was taken*] Taken suddenly, or as he was flying, and so thinking to escape.[1] Dio maketh mention of a notable thief that did much mischief in Italy (afterwards the pope's seat) in the days of Severus. This emperor used all the means he could to catch him, but could not do it, *Quippe qui visus non videbatur, non inveniebatur inventus, deprehensus non capiebatur,* saith the historian. But this subtle beast meeteth with his match and more; for he is caught and cast into the lake, &c. Christ is a conqueror so soon as ever he comes into the field, *Venit, vidit, vicit.* When the enemies are tumultuating, he comes upon them as out of an engine, and hurls them headlong into hell.

And with him the false prophet] This is the same with the beast; only the pope is called the beast in respect of his civil power, and the false prophet in respect of his spiritual. See the note on chap. xiii. 12. I remember, saith Aretius here, that many learned men in the year 1546

interpreted these words of the war that then was, and were confident that the emperor was the beast here mentioned, that should be overcome, and taken in battle by the Protestants; and together with him some false prophet of his (perhaps the pope), but it proved much otherwise, and the event showed that this application of the text was false.

Fallitur augurio spes bona sæpe suo.

These both were cast alive] Death shall not end their misery, but they shall suffer most exquisite torments. *Potentes potenter torquebuntur.*

Ver. 21. *Slain with the sword*] Not so deeply damned, and yet so slain as to be made a prey to the infernal vultures; and then the fattest carcase shall be the finest prey, the greatest sinners the sorest sufferers.

CHAPTER XX.

Ver. 1. *And I saw an angel*] CONSTANTINE the Great, the Church's male child, chap. xii.

Having the key] Not that key, chap. ix. 1, but another.

A great chain] The succession of Christian emperors.

Ver. 2. *And he laid hold on the dragon*] Chap. xii. 7, 9. He took him in a field fight, and since then till now we have heard little of him, more than that he substituted the beast, chap. xiii., whose destruction being declared, the prophecy returns to show the judgment of the dragon.

And bound him] From the open slaughtering of the saints, as he had done by the heathen emperors; for, from molesting and mischiefing of God's people, otherwise he is not bound one hour, Job i.; 1 Pet. v. 8. And how his vicegerent the beast hath bestirred him during the thousand years, who knows not?

A thousand years] *Hos explicare fateor trepide me aggredi,* saith Pareus. He begins the thousand at the destruction of the temple, A. D. 73, and so it ends in Pope Hildebrand, who stepped into that chair of pestilence, A. D. 1073. Others begin it at the birth of Christ, and end in Sylvester II. Others at Christ's passion, and end in Benedict IX. But they do best, in my opinion, that begin at Constantine and end in Boniface VIII., who is of his own said to have entered like a fox, reigned as a lion, and died as a dog. He excommunicated the French king, and published this decree, that the Bishop of Rome ought to be judged of none, although he should carry innumerable souls with him to hell.

Ver. 3. *And cast him into the bottomless pit*] That is, into the earth, chap. xii. 9, 12, chap. xiii. 11; the earth is the bottomless pit, out of which the beast was raised by the dragon.

Deceive the nations] The Gentiles, by defending Gentilism, and hindering the course of the gospel amongst them.

And after that he must be loosed] He must, be-

---

[1] ἱπιάσθη, *proprie dicitur de iis quos fugientes arripimus.* Beza.

cause God hath so decreed it, for the glory of his own name in the defence of his people, but destruction of his enemies. As also that the devil may show his malice, which God can restrain at his pleasure. Roger Holland, martyr, said to Bonner, This I dare be bold in God to speak, which by his Spirit I am moved to say: that God will shorten your hand of cruelty, that for a time you shall not molest his Church. And after this day in this place shall there not any be by him put to the fire and fagot. And it proved so; for none after that suffered in Smithfield for the testimony of the gospel. (Acts and Mon. fol. 1852.)

Ver. 4. *And they sat upon them*] Resting from former persecutions, and reigning in righteousness even here upon earth.

And judgment was given unto them] That is, say some, the spirit of discerning between Christianity and Antichristianism, or the clearing of their innocency, and doing them right, say others. Or, they had their chairs, seats, and consistories, wherein they did both preach the word and execute the Church censures, as some sense it.

And I saw the souls] This makes against the millenaries. Souls reign not but in heaven, there are " the spirits of just men made perfect," Heb. xii. True it is, as Mr Cotton well observeth, that there are many devices in the minds of some, to think that Jesus Christ shall come from heaven again, and reign here with his saints upon earth a thousand years. But they are, saith he, but the mistakes of some high expressions in Scripture, which describe the judgments poured out upon God's enemies in making way to the Jews' conversion, by the pattern of the last judgment. Thus he. The souls here mentioned are the same, I conceive, that were seen under the altar, Rev. vi. 9, and do cry, "How long, Lord?" These are not capable of a bodily resurrection, nor of an earthly reign.

And they lived and reigned with Christ] They, that is, those that sat on the thrones (not they that were beheaded), "lived and reigned," as spiritual kings (after the same manner as they are priests, ver. 6), for else there should be more kings than subjects.

With Christ] It is not said "with Christ upon earth;" this is an addition to the text; or if the words did import a reigning upon earth, yet this would not infer an earthly reign for a thousand years, in great worldly delights, begetting many children, eating and drinking, and enjoying all lawful pleasures, as some dream now-a-days. The conceit, I confess, is as ancient as Cerinthus, the heretic, and Papias (scholar to St John), a man much reverenced for opinion of his holiness, but yet *homo ingenii pertenuis*, saith Eusebius, not oppressed with wit. Jerome and Augustine explode it as a Jewish fable, and declare it to be a great error, if not a heresy; so do all the ὀρθογνώμονες at this day. The patrons of Christ's personal reign upon the earth are Mr Archer, and Mr Burroughes (Moses' Choice), who tells us that if the opinion of some concerning Christ's

coming to reign here in the world before the day of judgment be not a truth, he cannot make anything of many places of Scripture, as this place for one. But if he cannot, yet others can. See an answer to his and Mr Archer's chief arguments in Mr Bayly's Dissuasive from the Errors of the Times, chap. xxi. p. 238.

Ver. 5. *But the rest of the dead*] Dead in Baalworship, as Ephraim, Hos. xiii. 1; dead in sins, as Sardis, Rev. iii. 1.

Lived not again] By repentance from dead works, or they recovered not the life and immortality that is brought to light by the gospel.

Until the thousand years] Until, being taught better by God's faithful witnesses, they abjured Popery.

This is the first resurrection] From Romish superstitions. Mr Fox tells us that by the reading of Chaucer's books, some were brought to the knowledge of the truth. (Acts and Mon.) But here it must be remembered that a Papist must have two resurrections or conversions ere he can come to heaven. First, of a Papist he must become in judgment a true Protestant. 2. Of a Protestant at large, he must become a zealous practitioner of the truth he professeth. Like as corn must be first thrashed out of the straw, and then winnowed out of the chaff.

Ver. 6. *Blessed and happy is he*] The holy only have part in this resurrection, and are therefore happy, or out of harm's way, as the word μακάριοι signifies.

The second death hath no power] For they are brought from the jaws of death to the joys of eternal life, where is mirth without mourning, riches without rust, &c.

But they shall be priests] See the note on chap. i. 6.

They shall reign] The righteous are kings, Matt. xiii. 17, compared with Luke x. 24. "Many righteous" is the same with "many kings." See the note on ver. 4.

A thousand years] These thousand years begin (saith Mr Brightman) where the former ended, that is, in the year 1300, whereby continuance thereof is promised for a thousand years forward, among some of the Gentiles; and how long it shall reign afterwards among the Jews, He only knows that knows all. The most interpreters by a thousand years here understand not any definite time, as ver. 2 of this chapter, but an indefinite time, that is, for ever, as Psal. lxxxiv. 10. This thousand years they take for eternity, and a further degree of glory for such as are called forth to suffer. See Ezek. xxxvii.; Isa. xxvi. 19.

Ver. 7. *Satan shall be loosed*] i. e. Suffered to rise up in open rage against the open professors of the truth, and to make havoc of them, as he did of the Waldenses, Hussites, Huguenots, professors in Germany, Netherlands, Ireland, England, &c. He hath laid about him lately to purpose; besides those seas of Christian blood shed by the Turk, since the thousand years expired.

Ver. 8. *Gog and Magog*] That is, pope and Turk, saith Aretius; the pope a covert enemy to Christ; the Turk an overt, or open enemy; as Gog and Magog signify, Ezek. xxxviii. and xxxix. These are set forth by Ezekiel as the last enemies of God's people before Shiloh come; and presently after their utter overthrow, the state of the city and temple is notably described. So, after the pope and Turk in that last great battle at Armageddon routed and foiled, the New Jerusalem is in the following chapters excellently portrayed and depainted; that being a special type of this.

Ver. 9. *And they went up*] As a flood, Ezek. viii. 9, 16.

And compassed] As resolved that none should escape them, Psal. cxviii. 11, 12; 2 Kings vi. 14, 15, and xxv. 1.

The camp of the saints] The Church militant.

And the beloved city] The New Jerusalem, chap. xxi. 2. "The dearly beloved of God's soul," Jer. xii. 7; or, "God's dearly beloved soul," τὴν ψυχὴν τὴν ἠγαπημένην, as the Septuagint render it. (Spec. Europ.) For present the Turk is the bridle that holds in the pope with all his followers from any universal proceeding against the Protestants; who herein are greatly advantaged above them, in that their opposites lie between them and the Turk; or in that their countries, coasting so much as they do toward the north (as Denmark, Switzerland, &c.), are out of his way, and no part of his present aim. Italy is the mark he shoots at. And when once he shall rise against the true Church, fire from heaven shall devour him.

Ver. 10. *And the devil*] This Mr Brightman interprets of the Turk, called here the devil, because instigated and set awork by the devil. Albeit another learned expositor is of opinion, that by the fall of the beast and conversion of the Jews, the Turks and other states of the East shall be brought to embrace the gospel, being first taught thereto by some notable foil. What to think of this I know not; but cannot but like well of Diodate's note upon the fourth verse of this chapter; that in all this prophecy it is better and more sure to expect and stay for the explication by the event than to give it without any certain ground.

And shall be tormented] Gr. βασανισθήσονται, racked. The devil and the damned have punishment without pity, misery without mercy, sorrow without succour, crying without comfort, mischief without measure, torments without end and past imagination.

For ever and ever] This is as another hell in the midst of hell, and forceth them to cry, οὐαὶ, οὐαὶ, "woe, woe," as if they should say, οὐκ ἄει, οὐκ ἄει, "not ever, not ever, Lord." Whereto conscience answereth as an echo, ἄει, ἄει, "ever, ever." Hence that doleful οὐαι, "woe and alas" for evermore.

Ver. 11. *And I saw a great white throne*] A lively description of the last judgment, to show that henceforth, since the last great battle, the New Jerusalem should have no disturbance till Christ comes to judgment. His throne is said to be white, for like reason as he is said to sit upon a white cloud and a white horse, chap. xiv. and xix. He shall give most just and uncorrupt judgment.

From whose face the earth, &c.] To show either his terribleness or their renovation, 2 Pet. iii. 12; Rom. viii. 21.

Ver. 12. *Small and great*] It is the common opinion that men shall rise again in that tall and goodly stature of body wherein Adam was created; or at least in that vigour of age that a perfect man is at about 33 years old, each in their proper sex. And hereunto some think the apostle alludeth, Ephes. iv. 13. But Mr Brightman holds, that in the resurrection every one shall appear in that stature in which he departed out of this life, and that the contrary opinion doth manifestly contradict this Scripture.

And the books were opened] The books of conscience, saith Origen; of the Scriptures, saith Augustine; of both, say I; for according to law written shall the Judge pass sentence, the conscience either accusing or excusing.

Another book] That is, that of God's decree of free grace; the book that hath our names in it, and our pardon.

The book of life] That God's elect may be seen and known. God neither needeth nor useth books to judge by; but this is spoken after the manner of men. Mordecai's name was registered in the Chronicles of Persia. Tamerlane had always by him a catalogue of his best servants, and their good deserts, which he daily perused.

Ver. 13. *And the sea*] Those that perish in the waters, and those whose ashes were scattered upon the waters, as John Huss's; whom after they had burnt, they beat his heart with their staves, and cast his ashes into the river. But there is a substance of the saints' bodies preserved, by a secret influence from Christ their Head; and their dust is precious.

Ver. 14. *And death and hell*] There shall be an utter end of all evils and enemies, nothing left to disquiet the Church. She shall see them afar off, as Lazarus did the rich man, and be able to say of them, as she did of her accusers, John viii., "they are all gone."

Ver. 15. *And whosoever*] As those priests were cashiered that could not prove their pedigree, Ezra ii. 62, 63.

CHAPTER XXI.

Ver. 1. *And I saw a new heaven*] NEW for form and state, but the same as before for matter and substance; as an old garment translated is called a new one; and as whoso is in Christ is a new creature.

Passed away] *i. e.* Were purged from their vanity and defilements.

And there was no more sea] *i. e.* Trouble and tumult. The sea is of itself restless, and oft tossed with storms and tempests, Isa. lvii. 20. As for the element of water, it shall remain, probably, as earth, air, and fire do. Andreas thinks there shall be no more sea.

Ver. 2. The holy city] The Church in glory, saith Diodate. The Church wayfaring and warfaring, saith Brightman, whose interpretation of this text, *Nitur conjectura optabili magis quam opinabili,* saith Pareus, is more to be wished than imagined. The glory of Christ's bride is fitter to be believed than possible to be discoursed, saith Prosper. The Italians have this proverb amongst them, He that hath not seen Venice, believes not the bravery of it; and he that hath not lived some-while there, understandeth it not. This is much more true of Uranople, the New Jerusalem. St John's New Jerusalem, and Ezekiel's city and temple, from chap. xl. to the end, are contemporary (say some), and signify one and the same thing. (Haffen refferus.)

As a bride adorned, &c.] Bishop Ridley, the night before he suffered, invited his hostess and the rest at table to his marriage; for, said he, to-morrow I must be married. Some other martyrs went as merrily to die as ever they did to dine.

Ver. 3. And I heard a great voice] To confirm the vision, lest it should be thought a delusion.

Behold, the tabernacle] His special presence both of grace and glory is with his elect. See Ezek. xxxvii. 7, 28.

He will dwell with them] He will indwell in them, 2 Cor. vi. 16. See the note there. The enjoyment of God is heaven itself, therefore God is called heaven; "I have sinned against heaven."

Ver. 4. And God shall wipe away] As mothers do their children's tears. "Sorrow and sighing shall flee away." Baca shall be turned into Berachah, sighing into singing, misery into majesty; as Queen Elizabeth was exalted from a prisoner to a princess; and as our Henry IV. was crowned the very same day that, the year before, he had been banished the realm. (Daniel.)

No more death] For mortality shall be swallowed up of life.

Neither sorrow] πένθος. Properly for loss of friends; for we shall inseparably and everlastingly enjoy them. We shall sit down with Abraham, Isaac, and Jacob, have communion with them; not only as godly men, but as such and such godly men. And if with them, why not with others whom we have known and loved in the body?

Nor crying] κραυγὴ. *Qualis est in tragœdiis,* saith Aretius.

Nor any more pain] πόνος, Or, hard labour for a livelihood, to be gotten with the sweat either of brow or brain.

For the former things, &c.] The Latins call prosperous things *Res secundas,* because they are to be had hereafter; they are not the first things.

Ver. 5. Write; for these words are faithful] Though few men will believe them; for if they did, what would they not do or forego to get heaven? Cleombrotus reading Plato's book of the immortality of the soul, was so ravished with the con-

ceit thereof, that he cast himself headlong into the sea. But how many reading this better book of heaven's happiness, are no whit wrought upon thereby, or in the least measure moved to affect those things above, that run parallel with the life of God and line of eternity!

Ver. 6. It is done] As the punishment of the wicked, chap. xvi. 17 (see the note there), so the reward of the righteous is performed and accomplished.

I will give unto him] Whereas some good soul might say, I would it were once done. Have patience (saith God), I will shortly give unto him that is athirst to drink of that torrent of pleasure, that runs at my right hand, without any either let or loathing.

Clitorio quicunque sitim de fonte levarit,
Vina fugit, gaudetque meris abstemius undis.
                                                        Ovid. Metam.

Of the water of life, freely] But merit-mongers will not have it freely; therefore they shall go without it. *Cœlum gratis non accipiam,* saith Vega.

Ver. 7. He that overcometh] Gr. "He that is overcoming," or not yielding, though he hath not yet overcome; if he be but doing at it, and do not yield up the bucklers, ὁ νικῶν, *quasi* μὴ εἴκων.

Shall inherit all things] *Tanquam hæres ex asse.* All God's servants are sons, and every son an heir.

Ver. 8. But the fearful] Cowardly recreants, white-livered milk-sops, that pull in their horns for every pile of grass that toucheth them, that are afraid of every new step, saying as Cæsar at Rubicon, "Yet we may go back;" that follow Christ afar off, as Peter; that tremble after him, as the people did after Saul, 1 Sam. xiii. 7, and the next news is, "They were scattered from him," ver. 11. These lead the ring-dance of this rout of reprobates; and are so hated of Christ, that he will not employ them so far as to break a pitcher, or to bear a torch, Judges vii.

And unbelieving] Therefore fearful, because unbelieving, for faith fears no fay-bugs; but why do ye fear, ye small-faiths? saith our Saviour.

Ver. 9. One of the seven angels] The same, likely, that, chap. xvii. 1, had showed him the damnation of the whore. So studious and officious are the angels to serve the saints, Heb. i. 14.

The bride, the Lamb's wife] *Uxor fulget radiis mariti,* saith the civilian; so is it here.

Ver. 10. To a great and high mountain] As Moses was carried up into Mount Nebo that from thence he might view the promised land. He that would contemplate heaven, must soar aloft, fly a high pitch, &c. Take a turn with Christ in Mount Tabor, and be transfigured.

Ver. 11. Having the glory of God] Who putteth upon her his own comeliness, Ezek. xvi., as Rachel was decked with Isaac's jewels.

Even like a jasper] And so, like God himself, who is set out by a jasper, chap. iv. 3.

Clear as crystal] There is no such jasper in nature as is thus clear; but such a one must here be imagined. *Nec Christus, nec cœlum patitur hyperbolen.* In speaking of Christ or heaven it is hard to hyperbolize. Christ's blood (the true Pactolus) ῥεῖ τὸν πλοῦτον, floweth with riches. Uranople (the New Jerusalem) hath its foundation garnished with all manner of precious stones, to signify as well the durableness as the excellency of it. See ver. 19, 20.

Ver. 12. *And had a wall*] Far better than that of Babylon. Indeed this celestial China needs no wall to divide it from the Tartars; this is Arabia Felix, the people whereof live in security, and fear no enemy. They are in a far happier condition than the people of Tombutum in Africa, which are said to spend their whole time in singing and dancing.

And had twelve gates] Thebes had a hundred gates, and was therefore called ἑκατόμπυλος, but nothing so well set and so commodious for passengers as this city with twelve gates.

Twelve angels] As porters to let in, not as swordsmen to keep out, as the angel that stood sentinel at the porch of Paradise, Gen. iii.

Ver. 13. *On the east three gates*] The Church is collected and heaven filled from all quarters of the earth. Hence it is by one compared to the Samaritan's inn (πανδοχεῖον), because it receiveth and lodgeth all strangers that come. In the synagogue there was not lodging for all; the Ammonites and the Moabites were excluded the congregation of Israel. But Christ was born in an inn, to signify that in his kingdom all may be entertained. He is called the second Adam; the Greek letters of which name (as Cyprian noteth) do severally signify all the quarters of the earth.[1] His garments were divided into four parts, because out of what coast or part soever we come (saith a divine) Christ hath garments to clothe us, and room to receive us. There are that have observed that the name of God in all the chief languages consisteth of four letters (as יהוה Θεὸς, *Deus, Dieu, Gott,* &c.), to intimate that he hath his people in all the four quarters of the earth, out of all countries, nations, and languages.

Ver. 14. *And the wall*] A wall the Church hath about it, and a well within it, ver. 6. "A garden enclosed is my sister, my spouse, a spring shut up, a fountain sealed," Cant. iv. 12. This wall of the Church hath twelve foundations, that is, Christ the only foundation, 1 Cor. iii. 11, laid by the twelve apostles; in whose names also the sum of Christian faith is made up in those twelve articles of the creed. *Discessuri ab invicem Apostoli normam prædicationis in commune constituunt,* saith Cyprian. (De Symbol. Apostol.) The apostles being to be severed into several countries to preach the gospel, agreed upon this as the sum and substance of their sermons. It was called Symbolum, a sign or badge, to distinguish Christians from unbelievers.

Had twelve foundations] Foundation is taken either for Christ, 1 Cor. iii. 11; Matt. xvi. 16, or for the doctrine of the apostles teaching salvation only by Jesus Christ, as Ephes. ii. 20, and here.

[1] Α ἀνατολὴ, Δ δύσις, Α ἄρκτος, Μ μεσημβρία.

The Papists have lately added twelve new articles raised out of the Council of Trent, to be believed by as many as shall be saved; as above hath been noted.

Ver. 15. *Had a golden reed*] Not those twelve Trent articles, or any human invention, but the word, as chap. xi. 1, wherewith is measured not the temple only, as there, but the city, gates, and wall, as Ezek. xl.

Ver. 16. *And the city lieth four square*] So was Babylon of old (as Herodotus describeth it), which yet was taken by Cyrus, Alexander, and sundry other enemies. Heaven also is taken, but by another kind of violence than by force of arms. The solid square whereby it is here set forth commends it to us; 1. For stable and unshaken, Heb. xii. 28. *Immota manet,* as it is said of Venice, which yet stands in the sea, and hath but one street that is not daily overflowed (the Venetian motto is, *Nec fluctu nec flatu movetur*). 2. For such as looketh every way to the four corners of the earth, as Constantinople did; which is therefore said to be a city fatally founded to command.

Twelve thousand furlongs] About 300 Dutch miles. Nineveh was nothing to this city for bigness; no more is Alcair, Scanderoon or Cambalu, which yet is said to be 28 miles in circuit, being the imperial seat of the great Cham of Tartary. Quinsay, in the same kingdom, is said to be of all cities in the world the greatest; in circuit a hundred miles about, as Paulus Venetus writeth, who himself dwelt therein about the year 1260. But our New Jerusalem is far larger; 12,000 furlongs (according to some) make 1500 miles; and yet he that shall imagine heaven to be no larger than so, shall be more worthy to be blamed than the workmen were that built Westminster Hall; which King William II., the founder, found great fault with, for being too little; saying it was fitter for a chamber than for a hall of a king of England; and therefore took a plot for one far more spacious to be added unto it. (Dan. Chron.)

Ver. 17. *An hundred and twenty four cubits*] A cubit is six handfuls.

That is, of the angel] That appeared as a man, but bigger and higher than ordinary; now because this holy city is thus measured, and that with the measure of a man, some think it to be of the Church militant. But some other passages in this and the following chapters cannot be otherwise taken according to the letter, than of the state of full perfection. They do best, in my opinion, that take in both.

Ver. 18. *Was of jasper*] A stone of great worth and glory, the beauty whereof, saith one, it is easier to admire than to declare. It hath a variety of sweetness in it; such as none of the most cunning wits and sharpest eyes are able to distinguish. Heaven (we are sure) is such as eye hath not seen, ear hath not heard, &c. *Sermo non valet exprimere, experimento opus est.* Words are too weak to utter its happiness; get to it once, and you will say so. (Chrysost.)

Pure gold] A metal that shineth in the fire

wasteth not in the use, rusteth not with long lying, rotteth not though cast into brine or vinegar (as Pliny noteth), to show that this city is incorruptible, invincible.

Like unto clear glass] Glittering gold, such as this world affords not. No, not those two islands in India called Chryse and Arger, for the abundance of gold and silver there found, as Soline telleth us.

Ver. 19. *And the foundations*] The apostles and their faithful successors, who were *puriores cælo*, saith Chrysostom, clearer than the sky, the very stars of the world and flowers of the Churches, as Basil calleth them. The twelve patriarchs have, Exod. xxviii., each of them his precious stone inscribed with his name in the breastplate of judgment: a symbol of the Church under the law. Levi hath the chalcedony, Judah the smaragd. But here in the foundation of the New Jerusalem, the Church under the gospel, Levi hath the smaragd, and Judah the chalcedony (the tribes have their stones in Aaron's breastplate, according to their birth). Our Saviour's chalcedony in Levi's place tells us (saith Mr Sarson) that he hath put an end to legal sacrifices, and that he is both king and priest of his Churches.

Ver. 20. *The fifth, sardonyx*] Search is here made through all the bowels of the earth for something of worth to shadow out the saints' happiness; which if it could be fully known (as it cannot) it would be no strange thing or thankworthy for the most horrible Belialist to become presently the holiest saint, or the world's greatest minion the most mortified man. He that desires to know the natures and virtues of these precious stones, may read Epiphanius, Philo, Franciscus, Rurus, and others, *De gemmis;* Josephus also in the third book of his Jewish Antiquities. That was an odd conceit, and scarce worth relating, held by Anaxagoras, *Cœlum ex lapidibus constare, et aliquando collapsurum,* that heaven was made up of stones, and would one day fall upon men's heads. That other saying of his is much more memorable, when being asked, Wherefore he was born? He answered, *Ut cœlum contemplar,* that I might busy my thoughts about heaven.

Ver. 21. *And the twelve gates*] i. e. Gatekeepers, preachers of the righteousness that is by faith.

Were twelve pearls] All which do receive their lustre and worth from Christ, that pearl of price, Matt. xiii., like as the pearl by being oft beaten upon by the sunbeams, becometh radiant as the sun.

Was pure gold] Which no dirty dog may ever trample upon.

Ver. 22. *No temple*] No need of external worships and ordinances; for they are all taught of God; they see his face and hear his voice. Now we see but in part, because we prophesy but in part, 1 Cor. xiii. They that understand it of the Church on earth, say, there is no temple in opposition to the Jewish temple, but a gospel temple. But, ver. 25, "There shall be no night there,"

as here no temple. Now we shall not be above ordinances till above sin; which will not be in this world.

Ver. 23. *And the city had no need*] He saith not there shall be no sun or moon, but there shall be no such need of them as is now; for the Lamb shall outshine them, shine they never so gloriously, as they shall in that new heaven, Isa. xxx. 26.

Ver. 24. *And the nations*] See Isa. lx. 3; and that he speaketh of the life to come, see ver. 11, 18, 19, 21.

Do bring their glory] Despise and cast away all for heaven. Canutus set his crown upon the crucifix; which, according to the course of those times, was held greatest devotion. King Edward VI. assured the Popish rebels of Devonshire, that he would rather lose his crown than not maintain the cause of God he had taken in hand to defend. Nazianzen rejoiced that he had something of value (viz. his Athenian learning) to part with for Christ, &c.

Ver. 25. *For there shall be no night there*] And so no need to fear a sudden surprise by the enemy watching his opportunity. Their day above is ἀνέσπερος ἡμέρα, a nightless day, as a Father calls it.

Ver. 26. *And they*] i. e. The kings, as ver. 24.

Ver. 27. *And there shall in no wise*] Though the serpent could wind himself into paradise, yet no unclean person can come into this holy city. Tertullian called Pompey's theatre (which was the greatest ornament of old Rome) *arcem omnium turpitudinum,* the sty of all uncleanness. Heaven is none such.

CHAPTER XXII.

Ver. 1. *A pure river*] Not muddy as Nile, but clear as Calirrho. The allusion seems to be to that earthly paradise so well watered, Gen. ii., or else to Ezek. xlvii. This river is Christ, John iv. 14, and so is that tree of life, ver. 2. The second Adam is a quickening spirit. Apollonius telleth us (lib. 3, Argonaut.) that in the court of Æta, king of Colchis, were three fountains, which flowed, one with milk, another with wine, and a third with honey. In heaven there is all this and more.

Ver. 2. *In the midst of the street of it*] *In medio foro ejus,* where all may easily come by it; not kept with a strong guard, as the apples of Alcinous, Hesperides, &c.

Twelve manner of fruits] Heaven's happinesses are so many that they cannot be numbered, so great that they cannot be measured, so copious that they cannot be defined, so precious that they cannot be valued.

Every month] Like the lemon tree, which ever and anon sendeth forth new lemons as soon as the former are fallen down with ripeness.

And the leaves] No want of anything either for food or physic. *Ita balbutit nobiscum Deus.*

Ver. 3. *And there shall be no more curse*] No

casting out by excommunication; no cause of any such thing.

Of God and of the Lamb] He and the Father are one, John x. 30. See the note there.

Ver. 4. *And they shall see his face*] How we shall see God, whether with our minds only, or with bodily eyes we shall behold his invisible Majesty in the glorious face of Jesus Christ, there can be nothing determined.

And his name shall be] As servants of old had their master's name branded in their foreheads.

Ver. 5. *And there shall be no night*] See the note on chap. xxi. 25.

For the Lord God] He that is Αὐτόφως, light essential.

And they shall reign] Reign together with Christ; a part of whose joy it is that we shall be where he is, John xvii. 20: he will not be long without us.

Ver. 6. *And he said unto me*] This is the conclusion of the whole prophecy; and it is very august and majestical.

These sayings are faithful and true] Thus (among other evidences of its divinity) the Scripture testifies of itself; and we know that its testimony is true. Vapiscus saith of the ancient historians that there is none of them that hath not told many lies. Tertullian saith of Tacitus, that he was *mendaciorum loquacissimus*, a very loud and lewd liar. Baronius doth not compose annals, but coin them, saith one. But none of all this can be said of God's word of truth, void of all insincerity or falsehood.

The Lord God of the holy prophets] Some copies have it, The Lord God of the spirits of the prophets. He is the God of the spirits of all flesh, but of the spirits of prophets in a special manner; for those holy men spake no otherwise than as they were acted or imbreathed by the Holy Ghost, 2 Pet. i. 21. See the note there.

Sent his angel] As chap. i. 1. The authority therefore of this book is unquestionable, whatever some have surmised from chap. xx. 4, that it was the work of Cerinthus or some other millenary.

Ver. 7. *Blessed is he that keepeth*] In memory and manners, chap. i. Those were pronounced happy that read and hear, but so as they retain in mind and practise the contents of this book.

Ver. 8. *Saw these things and heard them*] So that there is no colour of cause why any one should doubt or distrust such a witness.

I fell down to worship] This is the second time. It is hard to say how oft a saint may fall into the same sin; howbeit they sin of incogitancy; put them in mind, and they mend all. They sin of passion, and passions last not long. There is no way of wickedness in them, they make not a trade of it, Psal. cxxxix. 24.

Ver. 9. *See thou do it not*] See the note on chap. xix. 10. This was a flat prohibition, not a merry repulse; as Lorinus and Veigas the Jesuits would have it.

For I am thy fellow-servant] Wicliff disal-

lowed the invocation of saints and angels, whom he called servants, not gods. For the word knave which he used, signified in those days a servant, not as it doth in our days a wicked varlet, as his enemies maliciously interpret it; Bellarmine for one, a man utterly ignorant of the English tongue.

Ver. 10. *Seal not*] Keep them not up for thine own proper use (as he did that wrote upon his writings, τὰ εἰς ἐμαυτὸν, things for myself), but freely impart them, and in such sort as that others may conceive and improve them.

For the time is at hand] And every day's events shall explain the prophecy.

Ver. 11. *He that is unjust, &c.*] q. d. Let things be foretold never so plainly, and fall out never so accordingly, yet wicked men will be uncounsellable, incorrigible, Isa. xxvi. 10. "But if any man be ignorant, let him be ignorant," 1 Cor. xiv. 38. He falls with open eyes, let him fall at his own peril: who so blind as he that will not see? "Ephraim is joined to idols, let him alone," Hos. iv. 14. He hath made a match with mischief, he shall have his belly full of it.

And he that is filthy, let him be filthy still] This is the last judgment we read of (befalling in this life) in all the New Testament. As that judgment of pining away in their iniquity (as if nothing could awaken them) is the last that God mentioneth, Lev. xxvi. 39, after those dismal ones there threatened to befall the people. It is contiguous, and as it were bordering upon hell itself.

Let him be righteous still] Let him persevere and proceed.

Ver. 12. *Behold, I come quickly*] Therefore quicken your pace, bestir yourselves lustily; your time is short, your task is long, your wages inconceivable.

Ver. 13. *I am Alpha and Omega*] And am therefore worthy to be believed in my predictions of future events, which I can easily bring about and effect, sith to me all things are present.

Ver. 14. *That they may have right*] That they may be assured of their interest in Christ and his kingdom. Plutarch tells of Eudoxus, that he would be willing to be burnt up by the sun presently, so he might be admitted to come so near it as to learn the nature of it. What then should not we be content to do or suffer for the enjoyment of Christ and heaven?

Ver. 15. *For without are dogs*] In outer darkness. The Irish air will sooner brook a toad or snake to live therein, than heaven will brook a sinner. It was not permitted to a dog to enter into the Acropolis or tower at Athens, διὰ τοῦ ἀκολάστου καὶ δυσώδους, for his heat in venery and ill savour, saith Plutarch. Goats, likewise, saith Varro, come not there (unless for necessary sacrifice once a year) lest they should hurt the olive. No filthy dogs or nasty goats get into heaven's tower, &c. The panther smells well among beasts (whom thereby she draweth about her), not so among men. God and the saints loathe what the wicked love and delight in, as the panther doth in man's excrements.

And whosoever loveth] Though he maketh it not. Some will not coin a false tale, that yet will spread it; these are equally guilty, and excluded God's kingdom, Psal. lii. 3.

Ver. 16. *Have sent mine angel*] With weariness of flight, as Dan. ix. 21.

I am the root] That bear up David by my Deity; but am born of him in regard of my humanity.

Ver. 17. *And the Spirit and the Bride*] *i. e.* The Bride sanctified and set a-work by the Spirit, Rom. viii. 26.

And let him that heareth say, Come] Abrupt sentences, full of holy affection; *q. d.* Let him pray daily, Thy kingdom come.

Heu pietas ubi prisca! profana o tempora! mundi
    Fæx! vesper! prope nox! o mora! Christe veni.

Mr Burroughs's last words were, I come, I come, I come! and so he gave up the ghost.

And let him that is athirst, come] *q. d.* If you think me long a-coming, come to me in mine or-dinances; there " I will stay you with apples, comfort you with flagons," Cant. ii. 5.

The water of life freely] See the note on chap. xxi. 6.

Ver. 18. *If any man shall add unto these things*] Either to this or to any of the foregoing books of Scripture, Deut. iv. 2; Prov. xxx. 6; Gal. iii. 15; 2 Tim. iii. 16, 17. All which notwithstanding, the Jews have added their *Deuteroseis*, the Turks their *Alfurta*, the Papists their unwritten verities, which they equalize (at least) to the Scriptures.

Ver. 19. *And if any man shall take away*] Sith every word of God is pure, precious, and profitable, Prov. xxx. 5; 2 Tim. iii. 16.

Ver. 20. *Even so; Come, Lord Jesus*] This is the common and constant vote of all good people; and is therefore pinned as a badge upon their sleeve, 1 Thess. i. 10. See the note there.

Ver. 21. *The grace of our Lord*] An epistolary conclusion. The Revelation is rather to be counted an epistle than a book. Read it as sent us from heaven, and ruminate what ye read.

Deo soli Gloria.